PHILIP'S

G000292546

STREE

London

st published 2000 by

ilip's, a division of
'opus Publishing Group Ltd
4 Heron Quays
ndon E14 4JP

cond edition 2003
st impression 2003

N 0 540 08465 4 paperback
N 0 540 08464 6 spiral

ted and bound in Spain
Cayfosa-Quebecor.

Contents

II **Key to map pages**
IV Administrative and Postcode boundaries
VI **Route planning**

X **Key to map symbols**
1 **Street maps**

228 **Keys to enlarged map pages and symbols**
229 **Enlarged street maps**

271 **Index**
395 **List of numbered locations**

407 Hospitals
408 Shopping, theatres, cinemas
410 Central London buses
412 Local rail and London Underground
414 Places of interest

Digital Data

The exceptionally high-quality mapping found in this atlas is available as digital data in TIFF format, which is easily convertible to other bitmapped (raster) image formats.

The index is also available in digital form as a standard database table. It contains all the details found in the printed index together with the National Grid reference for the map square in which each entry is named.

For further information and to discuss your requirements, please contact
Philip's on 020 7531 8438 or james.mann@philips-maps.co.uk

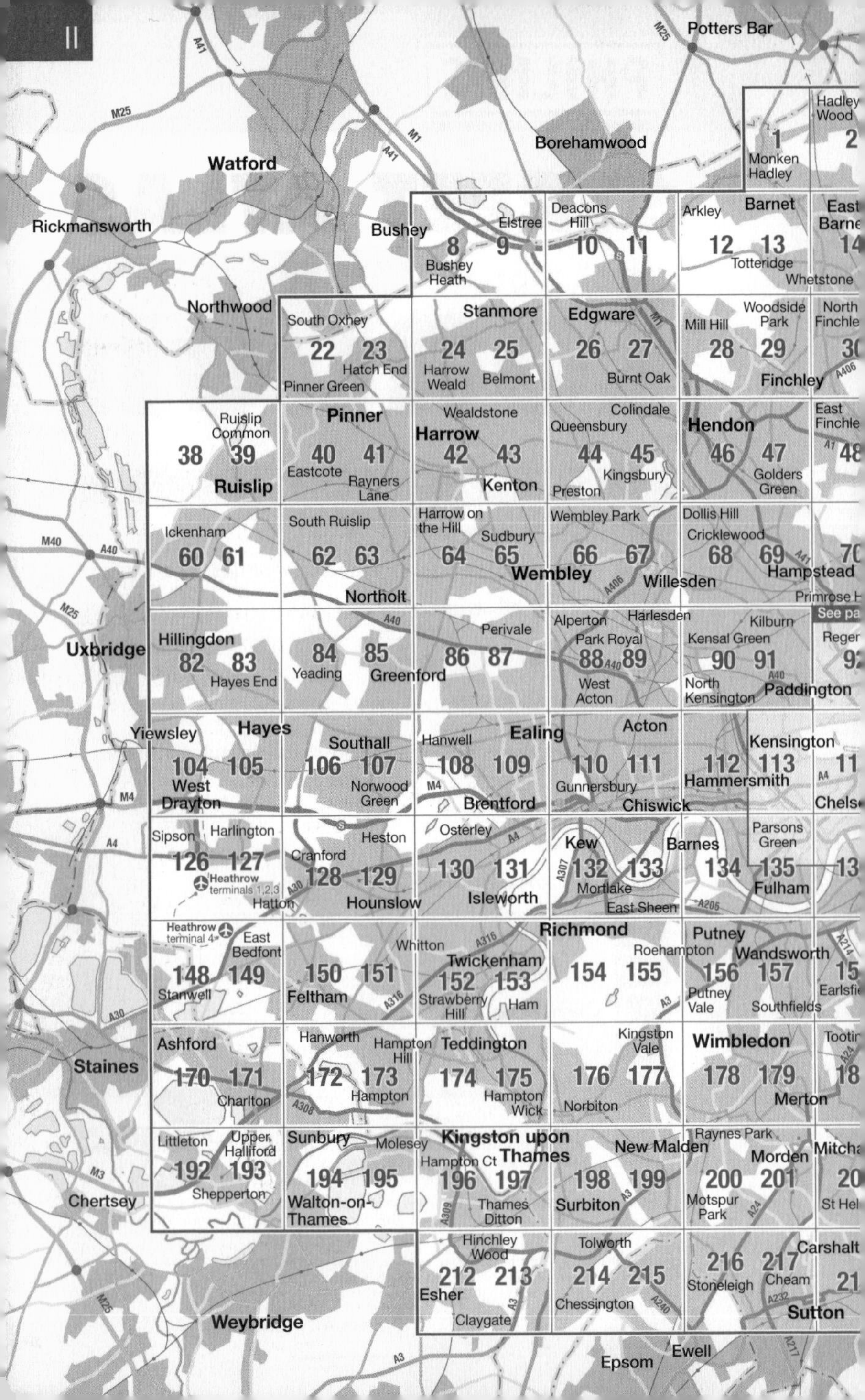

Potters Bar
M25
A41
M1
Hadley Wood
1
2
Monken Hadley
Watford
Borehamwood
Rickmansworth
Bushey
Elstree
Deacons Hill
Arkley
Barnet
East Barnet
8
9
10
11
12
13
14
Bushey Heath
Totteridge
Whetstone
Northwood
South Oxhey
Stanmore
Edgware
Mill Hill
Woodside Park
North Finchley
22
23
24
25
26
27
28
29
30
Hatch End
Harrow Weald
Belmont
Burnt Oak
Pinner Green
Finchley
A406
Ruislip Common
Pinner
Wealdstone
Colindale
Queensbury
Hendon
East Finchley
38
39
40
41
42
43
44
45
46
47
48
Harrow
Ruislip
Eastcote
Rayners Lane
Kenton
Kingsbury
Preston
Golders Green
A1
Ickenham
South Ruislip
Harrow on the Hill
Sudbury
Wembley Park
Dollis Hill
Cricklewood
M40
A40
60
61
62
63
64
65
66
67
68
69
70
Wembley
Willesden
Hampstead
Northolt
A406
Primrose Hill
M25
Alperton
Harlesden
Kilburn
See page
Regent
Perivale
Park Royal
Kensal Green
Uxbridge
Hillingdon
82
83
84
85
86
87
88
89
90
91
92
Yeading
Greenford
Hayes End
West Acton
North Kensington
Paddington
Yiewsley
Hayes
Southall
Hanwell
Ealing
Acton
Kensington
104
105
106
107
108
109
110
111
112
113
114
West Drayton
Norwood Green
M4
Brentford
Gunnersbury
Chiswick
Hammersmith
Chelsea
A4
Sipson
Harlington
Heston
Osterley
Kew
Barnes
Parsons Green
Cranford
126
127
128
129
130
131
132
133
134
135
136
Heathrow terminals 1,2,3
A30
Hatton
Hounslow
Isleworth
Mortlake
East Sheen
Fulham
A307
A205
Heathrow terminal 4
East Bedfont
Whitton
A316
Richmond
Putney
Roehampton
Wandsworth
A214
Twickenham
148
149
150
151
152
153
154
155
156
157
158
Stanwell
Feltham
Strawberry Hill
Ham
Putney Vale
Southfields
Earlsfield
A3
A30
Ashford
Hanworth
Hampton Hill
Teddington
Kingston Vale
Wimbledon
Tooting
Staines
170
171
172
173
174
175
176
177
178
179
180
Charlton
Hampton
Hampton Wick
Norbiton
Merton
A308
Littleton
Upper Halliford
Sunbury
Molesey
Kingston upon Thames
New Malden
Raynes Park
Morden
Mitcham
Hampton Ct
192
193
194
195
196
197
198
199
200
201
202
M3
Shepperton
Chertsey
Walton-on-Thames
Thames Ditton
Surbiton
Motspur Park
St Helier
A309
A24
Hinchley Wood
Tolworth
Carshalton
212
213
214
215
216
217
218
Stoneleigh
Cheam
Esher
Claygate
Chessington
A232
A240
Sutton
Weybridge
A217
Ewell
Epsom

Key to map pages

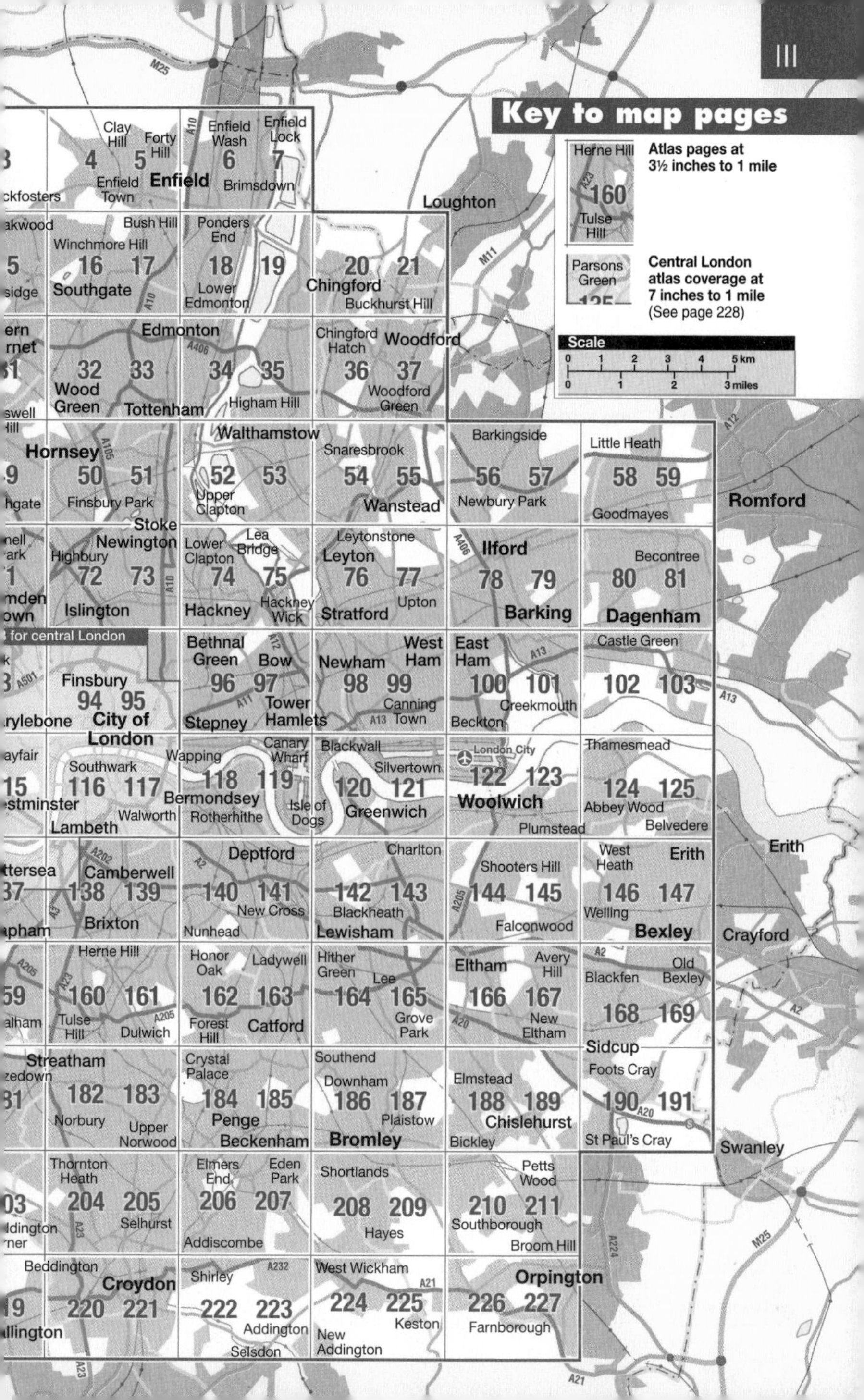

Herne Hill
A23
160
Tulse Hill
Atlas pages at 3½ inches to 1 mile
Parsons Green
Central London atlas coverage at 7 inches to 1 mile
(See page 228)
Scale
0 1 2 3 4 5 km
0 1 2 3 miles
M25
Loughton
M11
Clay Hill
Forty Hill
4 5
Enfield Town
Enfield
Enfield Wash
6
Enfield Lock
7
Brimsdown
A10
Winchmore Hill
Bush Hill
16 17
Southgate
Ponders End
18 19
Lower Edmonton
20 21
Chingford
Buckhurst Hill
Edmonton
A406
32 33
Wood Green
Tottenham
34 35
Higham Hill
Chingford Hatch
Woodford
36 37
Woodford Green
Hornsey
A105
50 51
Finsbury Park
Walthamstow
52 53
Upper Clapton
Snaresbrook
54 55
Wanstead
Barkingside
56 57
Newbury Park
Little Heath
58 59
Goodmayes
A12
Romford
Stoke Newington
Highbury
72 73
Islington
Lower Clapton
Lea Bridge
74 75
Hackney
Hackney Wick
Leytonstone
Leyton
76 77
Stratford
Upton
Ilford
78 79
Barking
Becontree
80 81
Dagenham
for central London
A501
Finsbury
94 95
City of London
Bethnal Green
Bow
96 97
Stepney
Tower Hamlets
A11
Newham
West Ham
98 99
Canning Town
A13
East Ham
100 101
Creekmouth
Beckton
Castle Green
102 103
Southwark
116 117
Walworth
Lambeth
Wapping
118 119
Bermondsey
Rotherhithe
Canary Wharf
Isle of Dogs
Blackwall
Silvertown
120 121
Greenwich
London City
122 123
Woolwich
Plumstead
Thamesmead
124 125
Abbey Wood
Belvedere
Erith
A202
Camberwell
138 139
Brixton
A3
Deptford
A2
140 141
New Cross
Nunhead
Charlton
142 143
Blackheath
Lewisham
Shooters Hill
A205
144 145
Falconwood
West Heath
Erith
146 147
Welling
Bexley
Crayford
Herne Hill
160 161
Tulse Hill
Dulwich
Honor Oak
Ladywell
162 163
Forest Hill
Catford
Hither Green
Lee
164 165
Grove Park
Eltham
Avery Hill
166 167
A20
New Eltham
Blackfen
Old Bexley
168 169
Sidcup
Streatham
182 183
Norbury
Upper Norwood
Crystal Palace
184 185
Penge
Beckenham
Southend
Downham
186 187
Plaistow
Bromley
Elmstead
188 189
Chislehurst
Bickley
Foots Cray
190 191
St Paul's Cray
Swanley
Thornton Heath
204 205
Selhurst
Elmers End
Eden Park
206 207
Addiscombe
Shortlands
208 209
Hayes
Petts Wood
210 211
Southborough
Broom Hill
A224
Beddington
Croydon
220 221
Shirley
A232
222 223
Addington
Selsdon
West Wickham
A21
224 225
Keston
New Addington
Orpington
226 227
Farnborough

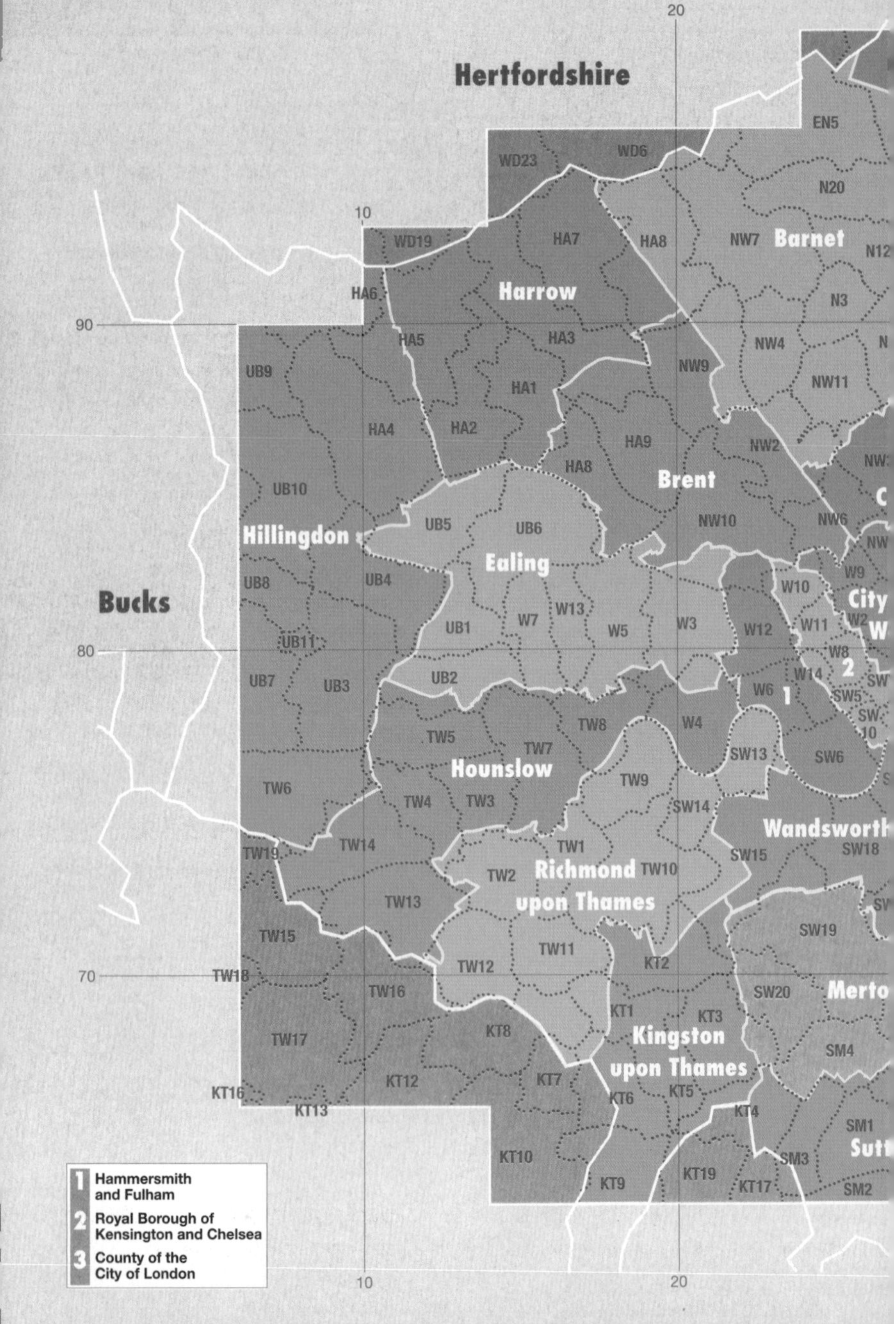
Hertfordshire
Bucks
Harrow
Barnet
Hillingdon
Brent
Ealing
Hounslow
Richmond upon Thames
Kingston upon Thames
Wandsworth
City
Merto
Sutt
EN5
WD6
WD23
WD19
N20
N12
N3
HA8
HA7
HA6
HA5
HA4
HA3
HA2
HA1
HA9
NW7
NW4
NW9
NW11
NW2
NW10
NW6
UB9
UB10
UB5
UB6
UB8
UB4
UB1
UB11
UB7
UB3
UB2
W7
W13
W5
W3
W12
W10
W11
W9
W2
W8
W14
W6
W4
SW13
SW6
SW5
SW14
SW15
SW18
SW19
SW20
SM4
SM1
SM2
SM3
TW5
TW7
TW8
TW6
TW4
TW3
TW9
TW1
TW2
TW10
TW14
TW19
TW13
TW15
TW11
TW12
TW18
TW16
TW17
KT2
KT1
KT3
KT8
KT7
KT12
KT16
KT13
KT6
KT5
KT4
KT10
KT9
KT19
KT17
1 Hammersmith and Fulham
2 Royal Borough of Kensington and Chelsea
3 County of the City of London
10
20
70
80
90

Major administrative and Postcode boundaries

County boundaries
London unitary authority boundaries
Postcode boundaries
Area covered by this atlas
Enfield
Haringey
Islington
Hackney
Waltham Forest
Redbridge
Tower Hamlets
Newham
Barking and Dagenham
Southwark
Lambeth
Lewisham
Greenwich
Bexley
Bromley
Croydon
Essex
Kent
EN2
EN3
EN1
N14
N21
N9
N13
N18
N22
N17
N8
N15
N4
N19
N16
N7
N5
N1
E4
E17
E10
E5
E8
E9
E2
E3
E1
E14
E15
E7
E12
E13
E6
E16
E11
E18
IG10
IG9
IG8
IG5
IG6
IG4
IG2
IG1
IG3
IG11
RM6
RM7
RM8
RM10
RM9
RM13
EC1
EC2
EC3
EC4
WC1
WC2
SE1
SE16
SE11
SE17
SE8
SE10
SE7
SE18
SE28
SE2
SE14
SE5
SE15
SE3
SE4
SE13
SE9
SE24
SE22
SE12
SE21
SE23
SE6
SE27
SE26
SE19
SE20
SE25
SW1
SW8
SW9
SW4
SW2
SW16
DA18
DA17
DA8
DA7
DA16
DA6
DA15
DA5
DA14
DA2
BR1
BR7
BR5
BR8
BR3
BR2
BR4
BR6
CR4
CR7
CR0
CR2
SM6
30
40
50
70
80
90
Scale
0
5
10 km
5 miles

Luton
Caddington
Slip End
Kensworth Common
Studham
Markyate
H
e
r
t
f
Jockey End
Flamstead
Trowley Bottom
Little Gaddesden
Great Gaddesden
TOLL
Water End
Nettleden
Potten End
Piccotts End
Gadebridge
Bourne End
Boxmoor
Hemel Hempstead
Whelpley Hill
Felden
Bovingdon
Bovingdon Green
Botley
Leyhill
Chipperfield
Flaunden
Latimer
Chenies
Sarratt
Little Chalfont
Chorleywood
Kings Langley
Primrosehill
Abbots Langley
Bedmond
Peter's Green
East Hyde
Kinsbourne Green
HARPENDEN
Hatching Green
Redbourn
Childwick Green
St. Albans
Townsend
St. Stephens
Chiswell Green
Bricket Wood
Radlett
Aldenham
Letchmore Heath
BOREHAMWOOD
Kimpton
Codicote
Blackmore End
Ayot St. Lawrence
Batford
Marshall's Heath
Wheathampstead
Ayot St. Peter
Sandridge
Jersey Farm
Marshalswick
Fleetville
The Camp
Sopwell
Colney Heath
London Colney
Colney Street
Shenleybury
Shenley
Green Street
Old Knebworth
Knebworth
Datchworth
Datchworth Green
Woolmer Green
Oaklands
Bull's Green
Burnham Green
Welwyn
Harmer Green
Digswell Park
Tewin
WELWYN GARDEN CITY
Panshanger
Woodhall
Hall Grove
Hatfield Hyde
Stanborough
Hatfield Garden Village
The Ryde
Hatfield
South Hatfield
Wildhill
Woodside
Bell Bar
Welham Green
Water End
Brookmans Park
South Mimms
SOUTH MIMMS SERVICES
POTTERS BAR
BARNET
Monken Hadley
Arkley
Elstree
East Barnet
Totteridge
LONDON GATEWAY SERVICES
Friern Barnet
Mill Hill
Finchley
Watford
Croxley Green
RICKMANSWORTH
Oxhey
Bushey
Bushey Heath
South Oxhey
Eastbury
Stanmore
Edgware
Maple Cross
Batchworth Heath
Chalfont Common
Chalfont St. Peter
Northwood
Hatch End
Harrow Weald
Harefield
Pinner
Wealdstone
Kingsbury
Ruislip Common
HARROW
Greenhill
Hendon
Gerrards Cross
DENHAM
Denham Green
Eastcote
Tatling End
Ruislip
Rayners Lane
G
r
e
Harrow on the Hill
Golders Green
Highgate
Hampstead
Denham
Fulmer
Ickenham
NORTHOLT
Wembley
Cricklewood
Stoke Poges
Uxbridge
Sudbury
Northolt
Willesden
Alperton
Iver Heath
Harlesden
Kilburn
Hillingdon
Perivale
NORTH CIRCULAR ROAD
Cowley
Yeading
Greenford
George Green
Iver
SLOUGH
Yiewsley
Hayes
Southall
EALING
Acton
Paddington
Kensington
West Drayton
Hanwell
Richings Park
Langley
Upton
HESTON SERVICES
Chiswick
Westminster
Harmondsworth
Harlington
Brentford
Hammersmith
Chelsea
Sipson
Cranford
Heston
Kew
Kew Br.
Datchet
Colnbrook
Longford
LONDON HEATHROW
Isleworth
Fulham
Poyle
HEATHROW AIRPORT
Mortlake
Putney
Horton
HOUNSLOW
Clapham
Stanwell
Stanwell Moor
Richmond
Wraysbury
West Bedfont
East Bedfont
Roehampton
Wandsworth
Hythe End
M1
M10
M25
M40
M4
A1(M)
A405
A414
A41
A40
A406
A4
A316
A30
A205
A214
A413
A1
A5
Lea
Ver
Colne
Res.
99

Scale
0 1 2 3 4 5 6 7 8 km
0 1 2 3 4 5 miles
Whempstead
Latchford
Much Hadham
Hadham Cross
Sacombe
Barwick
High Cross
Wadesmill
Tonwell
Thundridge
Baker's End
Perry Green
Allens Green
BISHOP'S STORTFORD
Thorley Street
Spellbrook
Gt. Hallingbury
Sawbridgeworth
High Wych
Wareside
Widford
Hunsdon
Ware
Hertford
Great Amwell
Stanstead Abbots
St. Margarets
Eastwick
Gilston
Hertford Heath
Hailey
Harlow
Netteswell
Churchgate Street
Potter Street
HODDESDON
Rye Park
Roydon
Gt. Parndon
Tye Green
Latton Bush
Brickendon
Roydon Hamlet
Broadley Common
Nazeing
Lower Nazeing
Broxbourne
Wormley
Turnford
Bumble's Green
Epping Green
Epping Upland
Thornwood Common
CHESHUNT
Coopersale Common
Epping
Ivy Chimneys
Fiddlers Hamlet
Waltham Cross
WALTHAM ABBEY
Upshire
Theydon Bois
Sheering
White Roding
Leaden Roding
Margaret Roding
Matching Tye
Matching
Abbess Roding
Matching Green
Foster Street
High Laver
Little Laver
Beauchamp Roding
Magdalen Laver
Hastingwood
Moreton
Fyfield
Willingale
Bovinger
Bobbingworth
Norton Mandeville
Shelley
North Weald Bassett
High Ongar
Toothill
Greensted
Chipping Ongar
Nine Ashes
Stanford Rivers
Little End
Stondon Massey
Stapleford Tawney
Kelvedon Hatch
Doddinghurst
Navestock Heath
Navestock Side
Pilgrims Hatch
BRENTWOOD
Forty Hill
High Beach
Enfield Wash
Sewardstone
Debden
ENFIELD
Sewardstonebury
Loughton
Abridge
STAPLEFORD
Epping Forest
Ponders End
Winchmore Hill
Chigwell
Stapleford Abbotts
Lambourne End
Chingford
Buckhurst Hill
Edmonton
Grange Hill
Chigwell Row
Havering-atte-Bower
Noak Hill
Harold Hill
Woodford Bri.
Hainault
Woodford
Collier Row
Tottenham
Barkingside
Gidea Park
Harold Wood
Great Warley
Little Warley
Walthamstow
Wanstead
Newbury Park
Romford
Cranham
Seven Kings
Leytonstone
Hornchurch
Stoke Newington
Leyton
Ilford
Becontree
Forest Gate
Manor Park
Rush Green
Elm Park
Upminster
Hackney
Barking
Dagenham
Hacton
Corbets Tey
North Ockendon
East Ham
South Hornchurch
Bethnal Green
Stratford
Shoreditch
West Ham
Beckton
Creekmouth
Rainham
South Ockenden
City
Poplar
Thames
Wennington
Aveley
North Stifford
LONDON CITY
Thamesmead
Woolwich Ferry
Blackwall Tunnel
North Woolwich
THURROCK SERVICES
Bermondsey
Belvedere
Erith
South Stifford
LAMBETH
Woolwich
Abbey Wood
Purfleet
Greenwich
Charlton
Plumstead
Dartford Crossing
West Thurrock
Grays
Peckham
Deptford
New Cross
Kidbrooke
Welling
Slade Green
Camberwell
TOLL
Lewisham
Bexleyheath
Crayford
Greenhithe
DARTFORD
Stone
Dulwich
Hither Green
Eltham
Swanscombe
SOUTH CIRCULAR ROAD
Catford
New Eltham
Bexley
Coldblow
Green
Street
GREEN SERVICES
Shelley Bowells
Norton Heath
Blackmore
Swallows Cross
Mountnessing
Shenfield
West Horndon
Little Thurrock
Essex
Hertford

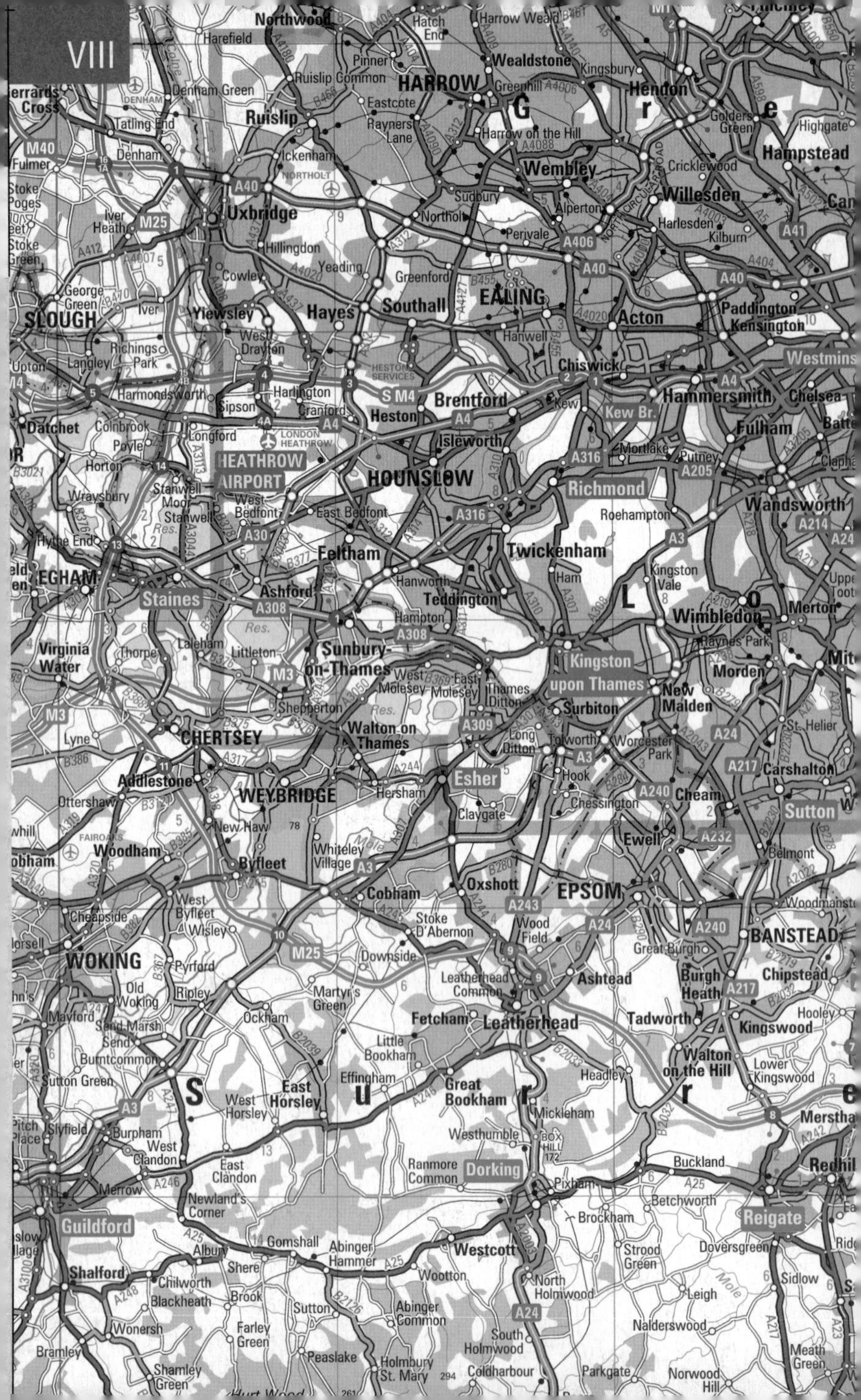
Northwood
Harefield
Hatch End
Harrow Weald
Wealdstone
Pinner
Ruislip Common
HARROW
Kingsbury
Hendon
Greenhill
Denham Green
Gerrards Cross
Eastcote
Ruislip
Rayners Lane
Harrow on the Hill
Golders Green
Highgate
Tatling End
Denham
Ickenham
Wembley
Cricklewood
Hampstead
M40
Fulmer
NORTHOLT
Willesden
Stoke Poges
A40
Uxbridge
Sudbury
Alperton
Northolt
Harlesden
Kilburn
Iver Heath
M25
Perivale
A406
A41
Hillingdon
Stoke Green
Cowley
Yeading
Greenford
A40
George Green
EALING
Iver
Yiewsley
Hayes
Southall
Acton
Paddington
Kensington
SLOUGH
West Drayton
Hanwell
Richings Park
Langley
Upton
Chiswick
Westminster
HESTON SERVICES
M4
Harmondsworth
Harlington
Brentford
Hammersmith
Chelsea
Sipson
Cranford
Heston
A4
Kew
Kew Br.
Datchet
Colnbrook
Fulham
Longford
LONDON HEATHROW
Poyle
Isleworth
Mortlake
Putney
HEATHROW AIRPORT
A316
Horton
HOUNSLOW
A205
Richmond
Wraysbury
Stanwell
Stanwell Moor
West Bedfont
East Bedfont
Wandsworth
A316
Roehampton
A214
Hythe End
A30
Res.
Feltham
Twickenham
A3
EGHAM
Kingston Vale
Ashford
Hanworth
Ham
Staines
Teddington
Wimbledon
Merton
A308
Hampton
Res.
A308
Raynes Park
Virginia Water
Thorpe
Laleham
Littleton
Sunbury-on-Thames
Kingston upon Thames
Morden
M3
West Molesey
East Molesey
Thames Ditton
New Malden
Shepperton
Res.
Surbiton
M3
Walton on Thames
A309
St. Helier
Lyne
CHERTSEY
Long Ditton
Tolworth
Worcester Park
A24
A3
A217
Carshalton
Addlestone
WEYBRIDGE
Esher
Hook
A240
Cheam
Hersham
Chessington
Sutton
Ottershaw
Claygate
New Haw
Ewell
A232
FAIROAKS
Woodham
Whiteley Village
Belmont
Byfleet
A3
Oxshott
EPSOM
Cobham
A243
West Byfleet
Woodmansterne
Cheapside
Wood Field
Wisley
Stoke D'Abernon
A24
A240
BANSTEAD
WOKING
M25
Downside
Great Burgh
Pyrford
Chipstead
Ashtead
Old Woking
Ripley
Leatherhead Common
Burgh Heath
A217
Martyr's Green
Hooley
Mayford
Ockham
Fetcham
Leatherhead
Tadworth
Kingswood
Send Marsh
Send
Little Bookham
Burntcommon
Walton on the Hill
Lower Kingswood
Sutton Green
Effingham
Headley
West Horsley
East Horsley
Great Bookham
Mickleham
Merstham
A3
Pitch Place
Slyfield
Burpham
West Clandon
Westhumble
BOX HILL
East Clandon
Ranmore Common
Dorking
Buckland
Redhill
Merrow
Pixham
Betchworth
Newland's Corner
Brockham
Guildford
Reigate
Gomshall
Abinger Hammer
Westcott
Strood Green
Doversgreen
Albury
Shere
Shalford
Wootton
Sidlow
Chilworth
North Holmwood
Leigh
Blackheath
Brook
Abinger Common
Sutton
A24
Wonersh
Farley Green
Nalderswood
South Holmwood
Bramley
Peaslake
Holmbury St. Mary
Coldharbour
Parkgate
Norwood Hill
Meath Green
Shamley Green
Hurt Wood
294
261

Tottenham
Woodford
Collier Row
Harold Wood
Gidea Park
Romford
Walthamstow
Barkingside
Wanstead
Newbury Park
Seven Kings
Cranham
West Horndon
Hornchurch
Leytonstone
Leyton
Ilford
Becontree
Rush Green
Upminster
Elm Park
Hackney
Forest Gate
Manor Park
Dagenham
Hacton
Corbets Tey
North Ockendon
Barking
East Ham
South Hornchurch
Bethnal Green
Stratford
Shoreditch
West Ham
South Ockenden
Rainham
Beckton
Creekmouth
Poplar
City
London City
Thames
Thamesmead
Wennington
Aveley
North Stifford
Blackwall Tunnel
North Woolwich
Woolwich Ferry
Belvedere
Little Thurrock
Bermondsey
Woolwich
Abbey Wood
Erith
Purfleet
South Stifford
Thurrock Services
Plumstead
Greenwich
Charlton
Deptford
Dartford Crossing
West Thurrock
Grays
Peckham
New Cross
Kidbrooke
Welling
Slade Green
Toll
Lewisham
Bexleyheath
Crayford
Dartford
Stone
Greenhithe
Dulwich
Hither Green
Eltham
Swanscombe
South Circular Road
Catford
New Eltham
Bexley
Coldblow
Grove Park
Mottingham
Sidcup
Wilmington
Bean
Betsham
Darenth
West Norwood
Sydenham
Chislehurst
Foots Cray
North Cray
Hawley
Sutton at Hone
Hextable
Swanley Village
Penge
Bromley
St. Paul's Cray
Swanley
Longfield
South Darenth
Beckenham
St. Mary Cray
Horton Kirby
Elmers End
Bickley
Petts Wood
Crockenhill
Hartley
Selhurst
Eden Park
Farningham
Addiscombe
West Wickham
Hayes
Bromley Common
Orpington
Fawkham Green
Shirley
Croydon
Eynsford
New Ash Green
Keston
Chelsfield
Addington
Farnborough
Well Hill
Maplescombe
Ash
South Croydon
New Addington
Green St. Green
West Kingsdown
Selsdon
Pratt's Bottom
Badger's Mount
Sanderstead
Leaves Green
Downe
Halstead
Shoreham
Fairseat
Stansted
Farleigh
Hamsey Green
Biggin Hill
Cudham
Knockholt Pound
Otford
Wrotham
Warlingham
Knockholt
Kemsing
Heaverham
Whyteleafe
South Street
Chevening
Dunton Green
Seal
Borough Green
Tatsfield
Chipstead
Riverhead
Ightham
Woldingham
Sevenoaks
Stone Street
Clacket Lane Services
Titsey
Brasted
Sundridge
Ivy Hatch
Plaxtol
Westerham
Brasted Chart
Cross Keys
Dunk's Green
Limpsfield
Limpsfield Chart
Whitley Row
Underriver
Godstone
Oxted
Ide Hill
Shipbourne
Church Town
Crockham Hill
Toy's Hill
Sevenoaks Weald
Oakhurst
Coldharbour
Bletchingley
Tandridge
Pittswood
Nutfield
Scale
0 1 2 3 4 5 6 7 8 km
0 1 2 3 4 5 miles
Hildenborough
Higham Wood
Crowhurst Lane End
Hilden Park
South Godstone
Crowhurst
Crouch House Green
Chiddingstone Causeway
Medway
How Green
Bough Beech
Leigh
Brook Street
Blindley Heath
Edenbridge
Outwood
Hever
Chiddingstone
Tonbridge
Tudeley
Horne
Eden
Marsh Green
Lingfield
Penshurst
Bidborough
Markbeech
M25
M26
M20
A2
A20
A21
A13
A12
A406
A102
A205
A232
A224
A282
A10
A127
A1400
A22
A25

Key to map symbols

Roads

- Motorway with junction number (22a)
- Primary route – single, dual carriageway
- A road – single, dual carriageway
- B road – single, dual carriageway
- Through-route – single, dual carriageway
- Minor road – single, dual carriageway
- Road under construction
- Rural track, private road or narrow road in urban area
- Path, bridleway, byway open to all traffic, road used as public path
- Tunnel, covered road
- Congestion Charge Zone boundary – Roads within the zone are outlined in red
- Gate or obstruction, car pound
- Parking, park and ride (P, P&R)
- Road junction name (Crooked Billet)
- Pedestrianised or restricted access area

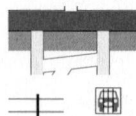

Public transport

- Railway station, private railway station
- London Underground station, Docklands Light Railway station
- Tramway or miniature railway with Tramlink station
- Bus, coach station

Scale

3½ inches to 1 mile 1:18103

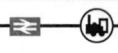

0 220yds 440yds 660yds ½ mile

0 250m 500m 750m 1km

Emergency services

- Ambulance, police, fire station
- Hospital, accident and emergen[cy] entrance

General features

- Market, public amenity site
- Information centre, post office (PO)
- Roman, non-Roman antiquity (VILLA, House)
- House number, spot height – me[tres] (100, .304)
- Christian place of worship
- Mosque, synagogue
- Other place of worship
- Houses, important buildings
- Woods, parkland/common
- Adjoining page number (123)

Leisure facilities

- Camp site, caravan site
- Golf course, picnic site, view po[int]

Boundaries

- Postcode boundaries (NW6)
- County and unitary authority boundaries (Westminster)

Water features

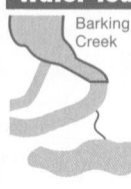

- Water name (Barking Creek)
- Tidal water
- River or canal – minor, major
- Stream
- Water

Abbreviations

Acad	Academy
Allot Gdns	Allotments
Bndstd	Bandstand
Btcl	Botanical
Bwg Gn	Bowling
Cemy	Cemetery
Ctr	Centre
C Ctr	Civic Centre
CH	Club House
Ctry Pk	Country Park
Coll	College
Ct	Court
Crem	Crematorium
Crkt	Cricket
Ent	Enterprise
Ex H	Exhibition Hall
Fball	Football
Gdns	Gardens
Glf C	Golf Course
Glf Crs	Golf Course
Drv Rng	Golf Driving Range
Gn	Green
Gd	Ground
Hort	Horticultural
Ind Est	Industrial Estate
Inst	Institute
Int	Interchange
Ct	Law Court
L Ctr	Leisure Centre
LC	Level Crossing
Liby	Library
Mkt	Market
Meml	Memorial
Mon	Monument
Mus	Museum
Nat Res	Nature Reserve
Obsy	Observatory
Pav	Pavilion
Pk	Park
Pl Fld	Playing Field
Pal	Royal Palace
PH	Public House
Recn Gd	Recreation Ground
Resr	Reservoir
Ret Pk	Retail Park
Sch	School
Sh Ctr	Shoppi[ng] Centre
Sp	Sports
Stad	Stadium
Sw Pool	Swimmi[ng] Pool
Tenn Cts	Tennis
TH	Town H[all]
Trad Est	Trading Estate
Univ	Universi[ty]
YH	Youth H[ostel]

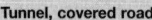

A1000 Potters Bar
VI
A
B
C
D
Wrotham Park
Wrotham Park
Home Farm
Cockshot Hill
Ganwick Farm
99
WAGON RD
6
A1000
Lower Kitt's End Farm
KITT'S END RD
BARNET RD
Kitt's End
Kitt's End Farm
Bartram's Quash
Hertfordshire Enfield
Pl Fld
Hadley Wood
5
PO
BARTRAMS
CRESCENT W
Great
GREENACRE CL
BEAUMONT PL
98
EN4
Barnet Enfield
HADLEY HIGHSTONE
Hertfordshire Barnet
Old Fold Manor
LANGLEY ROW
TAYLOR'S LA
OLD FOLD CL
OLD FOLD LA
MILL CNR
Tenn Cts
The Mount House (St Martha's Senior Sch)
Monken Hadley CE Prim Sch
CAMLET WAY
4
BROADGATES AVE
PAGITTS GR
PARKGATE AVE
PARKGATE CRES
2
EN5
BOUNDARY CL
Hadley Green
Convent
DURY RD
Allot Gdns
ST ALBANS RD
HADLEY GN W
HADLEY GREEN RD
Bournwell Hill
Monken Hadley
Monken Hadley Common
3
HADLEY GN
SUNSET VIEW
GLADSMUIR RD
Cemy
WROTHAM RD
HADLEY GR
FALKLAND RD
CHRIST CHURCH LA
LIVINGSTONE CT
FIRE STATION AL
HADLEY WOOD RD
Priddeon's Hill
BAKERS HILL
London Loop
THE CRESCENT
THE SPINNEY
The Tudor
97
High Barnet
TA Ctr
A1081
LUCAN RD
ALSTON RD
STRAFFORD RD
CARNARVON RD
P
Liby
CHIPPING CL
BRUCE RD
Barnet Mkt
GROVE CT
BELGRAVIA CL
HADLEY RIDGE
WYBURN AVE
EAST VIEW
BATH PL
LATIMER RD
LOWNDES LO
HADLEYVALE CT
CLIFFORD RD
Tudor Sp Gd
King George's Field
VINCENT CL
Allot Gdns
CH
Tenn Cts
TUDOR RD
JULIAN CL
HURST RISE
SLADE CT
2
SALISBURY RD
THE SPIRES
STAPLYTON RD
GREAT NORTH RD
HYDE CL
Hadley
SOUTH CL
NORFOLK RD
SANDFORD CT
Allot Gdns
GALDANA AVE
BOLEYN WAY
MORREL CL
WORTH CT
THE DRIVE
HART LO
MOON LA
MOXON ST
TAPSTER ST
BOSWORTH RD
WOODVILLE RD
HADLEY RD
Cromer Road Sch
THE AVENUE
THORNTON RD
LEATHERSELLERS CL
UNION ST
Sch
PO
Liby
Pl Fld
BURNSIDE CL
BARNET TRAD EST
VICTORS WAY
Tenn Cts
MEADWAY CL
ST MARK'S CL
PK
GILLINGS CT
HIGH ST
A411
PARK RD
QUEEN ELIZABETH CT
MEADWAY
MARTINS MOUNT
POTTER'S RD
SHERIDAN LO
Pl Flds
CROMER RD
SHAFTESBURY AVE
LEE CL
OOD ST
CATTLEY CL
Mus
MANOR CL
Barnet Coll
ELM
GORDON WAY
Queen Elizabeth's Sch
KINGSMEAD
HILLARY RISE
KING EDWARD RD
EN5
BARNARD LO
HEXHAM RD
PO
SUTHERLAND CL
Bwg Gns
ORCHARD RD
VICTORIA LA
P
High Barnet
SHELDON CT
HUGHENDON
HADRIAN CT
CHRISTOPHER CT
BULWER RD
BULWER GDNS
HASTINGS CL
ASEFIELD CT
PLANTAGENET RD
1
LEECROFT RD
MANORSIDE
PINECROFT CR
HILLSIDE GDNS
MANOR RD
WILLOW DR
Chipping Barnet
A1000
HILLSIDE MANS
BARNET HILL
St Catherine's Sch
POTTER'S LA
BRACKENWOOD LO
PROSPECT RD
WARWICK RD
AMBERLEY HO
VALE CT
GAINSBOROUGH CT
LEICESTER RD
DUNCAN CL
FALCON CT
THE RODINGS
Tenn Cts
FITZJOHN AVE
NEWLYN RD
NORMANDY AVE
BEDFORD AVE
MILTON AVE
WOODFALL AVE
VALE DR
P
RAVENSCROFT COTTS
ABBOTTS RD
THE HIGHLANDS
Highlands Gdns
WINDERMERE CT
BARNES CT
HANOVER HO
A110
96
COLGATE CT
HILLSIDE GDNS
HIGHWOOD CT
HIGHLANDS RD
HOMESTEAD CT
STATION RD
CHILTERN CT
COWBRAY
ASHLEY CT
BEAUFORT CT
SOMERSET RD
ELLESMERE GR
ELTON AVE
25
13
D
26
New Barnet
NORTH LO
THE WATSON HOMES
Allot
CEDAR LAWN
BARNET
UNDERHILL CT
POTTERIES
BROOK PL
WESTCOMBE DR
FAIRFIELD
A110
COLLINGWOOD CT
Lyonsdown Sch
RICHMOND

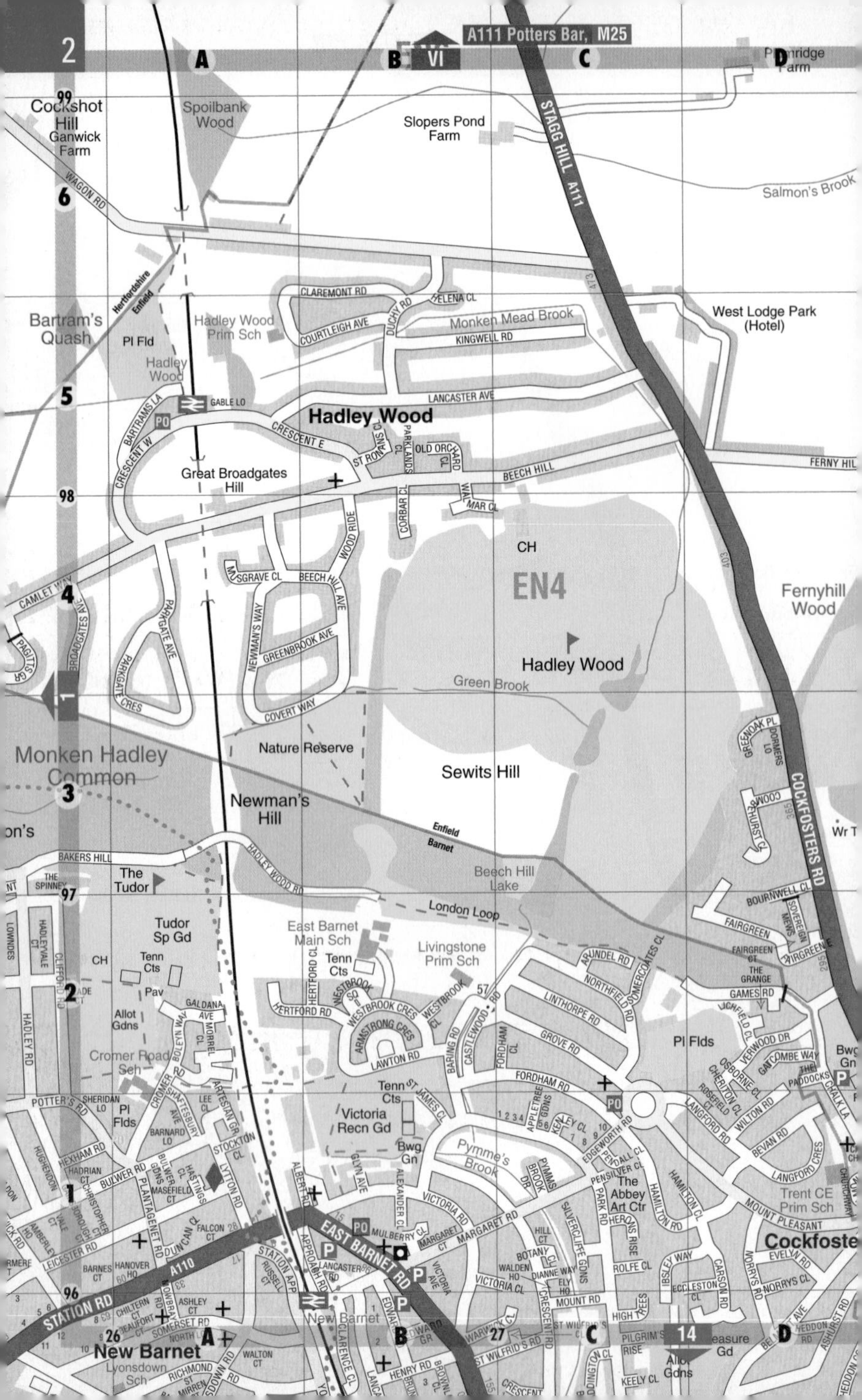
A111 Potters Bar, M25
VI
A
B
C
D
99
6
5
98
4
3
97
2
1
96
1
14
Cockshot Hill
Ganwick Farm
Spoilbank Wood
Slopers Pond Farm
Pimnridge Farm
STAGG HILL
A111
Salmon's Brook
WAGON RD
Hertfordshire
Enfield
Bartram's Quash
Pl Fld
Hadley Wood Prim Sch
Hadley Wood
CLAREMONT RD
DUCHY RD
HELENA CL
COURTLEIGH AVE
Monken Mead Brook
KINGWELL RD
West Lodge Park (Hotel)
473
LANCASTER AVE
GABLE LO
BARTRAMS LA
PO
Hadley Wood
CRESCENT W
CRESCENT E
ST ROMANS CL
PARKLANDS
OLD ORCHARD CL
FERNY HILL
Great Broadgates Hill
BEECH HILL
CORBAR CL
WALMAR CL
CH
EN4
WOOD RIDE
MUSGRAVE CL
BEECH HILL AVE
CAMLET WAY
BROADGATES AVE
PARKGATE AVE
NEWMAN'S WAY
GREENBROOK AVE
PAGITTS GR
PARKGATE CRES
COVERT WAY
Hadley Wood
Green Brook
403
Fernyhill Wood
Monken Hadley Common
Nature Reserve
Sewits Hill
Newman's Hill
GREENOAK PL
DORMERS LO
COOMBEHURST CL
365
COCKFOSTERS RD
Enfield
Barnet
Wr T
BAKERS HILL
HADLEY WOOD RD
THE SPINNEY
The Tudor
Beech Hill Lake
London Loop
BOURNWELL CL
SOVEREIGN MEWS
FAIRGREEN
FAIRGREEN CT
FAIRGREEN E
THE GRANGE
295
LOWNDES
HADLEYVALE CT
CLIFFORD RD
Tudor Sp Gd
CH
Tenn Cts
Pav
East Barnet Main Sch
Tenn Cts
Livingstone Prim Sch
HERTFORD CL
WESTBROOK SQ
WESTBROOK CL
WESTBROOK CRES
HERTFORD RD
ARMSTRONG CRES
57
CASTLEWOOD RD
ARUNDEL RD
NORTHFIELD RD
SOMERCOATES CL
LINTHORPE RD
GAMES RD
HADLEY RD
GALDANA AVE
MORREL CL
BOLEYN WAY
Allot Gdns
Cromer Road Sch
LAWTON RD
BARING RD
FORDHAM CL
GROVE RD
Pl Flds
VERWOOD DR
GATCOMBE WAY
THE PADDOCKS
CHALK LA
Bwg Gn
POTTER'S RD
SHERIDAN LO
Pl Flds
CROMER RD
SHAFTESBURY AVE
LEE CL
ARTESIAN GR
Tenn Cts
ST JAMES CL
Victoria Recn Gd
FORDHAM RD
APPLETREE GDNS
KELVEY CL
EDGEWORTH RD
OSBORNE CL
CHERITON CL
ROSEFIELD CT
WILTON RD
LANGFORD RD
BARNARD LO
STOCKTON CL
Pymme's Brook
PYMMS BROOK DR
PENDALL CL
BEVAN RD
HEXHAM RD
HADRIAN CT
BULWER RD
BULWER GDNS
HASTINGS CL
MASEFIELD CT
LYTTON RD
Bwg Gn
GLYN AVE
ALEXANDER CL
ALBERT RD
PENSILVER CL
The Abbey Art Ctr
HAMILTON CL
LANGFORD CRES
CHRISTOPHER CT
BOROUGH CT
PLANTAGENET RD
VICTORIA RD
PARK RD
SILVERCLIFFE GDNS
HAMILTON RD
Trent CE Prim Sch
AMBERLEY CT
VALE CT
DUNCAN CL
FALCON CT
28
PO
MULBERRY CL
MARGARET CT
MARGARET RD
HILL CT
HERONS RISE
MOUNT PLEASANT
LEICESTER RD
EAST BARNET RD
Cockfoste
BARNES CT
HANOVER HO
A110
STATION RD
STATION APP
RUSSELL CT
APPROACH RD
LANCASTER RD
VICTORIA AVE
BOTANY CL
WALDEN HO
DIANNE WAY
ELY HO
ROLFE CL
IBSLEY WAY
CARSON RD
EVELYN RD
NORRYS CL
MORRYS RD
VICTORIA CL
MOUNT RD
ECCLESTON CL
CRESCENT RD
HIGH TREES
CHILTERN CT
BEAUFORT CT
MOWBRAY RD
ASHLEY CT
SOMERSET RD
NORTH LO
New Barnet
EDWARD GR
WARWICK CL
27
ST WILFRID'S CL
ST WILFRID'S RD
PILGRIM'S RISE
Pleasure Gd
HEDDON RD
ASHURST RD
26
New Barnet
Lyonsdown Sch
WALTON CT
RICHMOND
CLARENCE CL
HENRY RD
BROWNING
DODDINGTON CL
KEELY CL
Allot Gdns
CRESCENT

A1005 Potters Bar, M25
A
B
C
D
VI
Wood
Little Beech
Wood
Roundhedge Hill
Botany Bay
Farm
A1005
THE RIDGEWAY
99
EN2
Salmon's Brook
6
Duncan's
Wood
Ash Wood
Cu
Park
Farm
5
FERNY HILL
Ferny Hill
Farm
Obelisk
Moat
Wood
P
Parkside
Farm
HADLEY RD
98
Ride
Wood
Leeging Beech
Rough Lot
EN4
Enfield Chase
4
Seedfield
Spinney
Icehouse
Wood
Williams
Wood
Trent
Country Park
Middlesex Univ
Trent Park
3
Oak
Wood
SHAWS
WOOD
COTTS
Shaws
Wood
ROOKERY COTTS
97
Pav
Sp Gd
Church
Wood
2
Merryhills Brook
Triangular
Wood
South Lodge
Farm
Cemy
Trent Park
Stables
EASTPOLE
COTTS
A110
P
Cockfosters
SNAKES LA
Trent Park
SOUTH
LODGE
CRES
LAKESIDE
SOUTH
LODGE
CRES
GREYSTOKE GDNS
LOWTHER
COCKFOSTERS RD
NORFOLK
CL
WEST
CL
EAST
CL
EASTPOLE
COTTS
LONSDALE DR
NETHERLANDS
CULGAITH
GDNS
1
N14
CH
MERRYHILLS DR
BRAYTON GDNS
CURTHWAITE GDNS
MOUNT CL
BRAEMORE
CT
HEDDON CT
STATION PAR
GLOUCESTER GDNS
KENT DR
WESTPOLE AVE
BRAMLEY RD
BELGRAVE GDNS
GROSVENOR GDNS
BRANTWOOD GDNS
CLIFTON GDNS
WOODEND
96
A111
Southgate
Sch
Pl Fld
B
15
29
C
Oakwood
D
30
BELGRAVE
CL
GERRARDS CL
MALCOLMS
WAY
HARPER CL
CARLTON
SOUTH LODGE DR
LONSDALE
FRESTON GDNS
LEYS GDNS
BALMORE CRES
SUSSEX WAY
MERRYHILLS
CT
STAFFORD
CL
ALEXANDRA
CT
THE
ORCHARD
PRINCE GEO
LOWER
KENWOOD AVE
BEVERIDGE CT
JENNER CT
ASHBURY CT

A
B
VII
C
D
King's Oak Plain
St John's CE Prim Sch
PARK RD
STRAYFIELD RD
ROSSENDALE CL
Nursery
THE RIDGEWAY
The Red House
Queenswood Farm
Rectory Farm
Turkey Brook
The Kings Oak (Private)
EN2
Cuckolds Hill
Hotel
KINGFISHER CT
OAK AVE
ROUND HEDGE WAY
MOUNT VIEW
HIGH OAKS
WILLIAM COVELL CL
SPRING COURT RD
ARAGON CL
Chase Farm
Allot Gdns
Cemy
Parkside Farm
HADLEY RD
RIDGE CREST
HAREFIELD CL
HUNTERS WAY
ALBUHERA CL
SHOOTERS RD
COMREDDY CL
LAVENDER HILL
LAVENDER GDNS
Leeging Beech Gutter
Vicarage Farm
FARORNA WLK
FARMLANDS
JAYCROFT
HARDY WAY
ACORN CL
HARRIS CL
LEE VIEW
HEDGE HILL
Gordon Hill
FAIRVIEW RD
HANSART WAY
DRAPERS RD
JOHN GOOCH DR
PADSTOW RD
HOLTWHITE'S HILL
BANKSIDE
WOODSIDE CT
Hog Hill
WOODRIDGE CL
Cts
Williams Wood
AMESBURY CT 1
CAPSTAN RIDE 2
KINGS CHACE VIEW 3
CROFTON WAY
LANSDOWNE HO
DUNRAVEN DR
AVALON CL
CHASEWOOD AVE
HEATHER DR
PERRY MEAD
SORBUS CT
MCADAM DR
WELLESLEY PARK MEWS
AUDLEY RD
VALLEY FIELDS CRES
CAVELL DR
BYCULLAH RD
ROWANTREE RD
COPPERWOOD LO
ROBSON CL
ROWANWOOD MEWS
North London Nuffield
THE GROVE
UPLANDS PARK RD
STOCKBRIDGE HO
CANFORD CL
HOLLY TREE LO
HERMITAGE CL
BYCULLAH AVE
ENGLEFIELD CL
CHASE RIDINGS
HAVENHURST RISE
VULCAN GATE
PARK WAY
WINDMILL GDNS
SLADES GDNS
THE GLADE
RIDGEMOUNT GDNS
CULLODEN RD
CEDARWOOD HO
FOSTER'S GN
BERKELEY LO
TEMPLE GR
PINEWOOD CT
TRENTWOOD SIDE
Allot Gdns
GRAFTON RD
ELMER CL
SLADES HILL
COLONELS WLK
FIONA CT
HIGH DENE
GLEBE AVE
THE OAKS
OAKDENE HO
TAUNTON DR
SLADES CL
SLADES RISE
HUNTING GATE CL
A1005
WINDMILL HILL
A110
ENFIELD RD
PO
LINKSIDE GDNS
LINKSIDE CL
LINKS SIDE
Liby
FOXMEAD CL
BINCOTE RD
COTSWOLD WAY
OLD PARK VIEW
MILLERS GREEN CL
HIGH ACRE
OLD PARK RD
CALSHOT WAY
WYNDCROFT CL
WAVERLEY RD
WINSMOOR CT 1
THORPE CT 2
WANSBECK CT 3
THE OLD SCHOOL HO 4
BARRYDENE CT 5
South Lodge Farm
EASTPOLE COTTS
A110
World's End
Merryhills Prim Sch
Salmon's Brook
CRESCENT RD
MOUNTFORD HO
THE HASELWOOD DR
CLAREMONT HTS
VERMONT CL
COPPICE
THE GLEN
OLD PARK RD S
CH
Enfield
COTSWOLD GN
GLENBROOK N
GLENBROOK S
CHILTERN DENE
SOUTH LODGE CRES
LAKESIDE
GREYSTOKE GDNS
LOWTHER DR
CORBY CRES
NETHERBY GDNS
CULGAITH GDNS
BEWCASTLE GDNS
LONSDALE DR N
Boxer's Lake
Highlands Sch
LONSDALE DR
MERRYHILLS DR
BRAYTON GDNS
CURTHWAITE GDNS
BRANTWOOD GDNS
CLIFTON GDNS
WOODEND GDNS
SILVERDALE
ROUNDHILL DR
RUSHEY HILL
LINDAL CRES
N21
Grange Park Prim Sch
CADWICK AVE
WORLDS END LA
TARNBANK
LATYMER
HANBURY DR
FLEMING DR
CORFIELD RD
SIMPSON CL
HANSEN DR
BUCHANAN CL
TRESILIAN AVE
MACLEOD RD
LONSDALE DR
BARNABAS CT
1 ADAM LO
2 ALTON
3 LISTON
4 PITMAN
5 SYDENHAM AVE
6 AVON HO
7 SYLVAN HO
8 ASPEN HO
16
UPLANDS WAY
Allot Gdns
ONSLOW
LANGHAM
CHEYNE
SOUTH LODGE DR
LOWER
KENWOOD AVE
BEVERIDGE CT 1
JENNER CT 2
ASHBURY CT 3
PENNINGTON DR
SEACOLE LO
TREVES CL
ANDERSON CL
DONOVAN PL
HIGHLANDS
99
98
97
96
30
31
6
5
4
3
2
1

Whitewebbs Park
Brook
VII
A
B
C
D
99
London Loop
Whitewebbs
Brayside Farm
CH
PH
Clay Hill
Hilly Fields Park
EN2
BRAMLEY HOUSE CT
ST JOHN'S TERR
CLAY HILL
PARK NOOK GDNS
ELM GDNS
HILLSIDE CRES
STRATTON AVE
KILVIN
TON DR
Allot Gdns
MALDEN'S BRIDGE
6
Forty Hall Farm
Forty Hill CE Prim Sch
P
Forty Hall
FORTY HILL
THE CLOCK HO
Nursery
FORTY HILL HO
Worcesters Prim Sch
OLD FORGE RD
PHIPPS HATCH LA
GLOUCESTER RD
CEDAR
PARK RD
BRODIE RD
GLENVILLE AVE
MERTON RD
STERLING RD
BURLINGTON RD
BRIGADIER HILL
BRIGADIER AVE
WOODLANDS RD
BROWNING RD
ST LUKE'S AVE
MORLEY HILL
WOODBINE GR
MYRTLE GR
VIOLET AVE
BIRKBECK RD
CONWAY GDNS
HENRY CL
KENSINGTON CT
PORTLAND DR
BURNHAM CL
PO
ROSSELL RD
ST GEORGE'S RD
GOAT LA
5
LIME TREE WLK
YORK TERR
CHANTRY CL
RIPLEY RD
WETHERBY RD
BLOSSOM LA
ST FAITH'S CL
WHITE HOUSE LA
RADCLIFFE AVE
St Michael's CE Prim Sch
LANCASTER RD
Lavender Prim Sch
Enfield Cty Sch
HAWTHORN GR
ACACIA RD
LAVENDER RD
ROSEMARY AVE
PRIMROSE AVE
RIDLER RD
MYDDELTON AVE
HALLSIDE RD
RUSSELL RD
BRIDGENHALL RD
LAYARD RD
IRKDALE AVE
MAHON CL
HOLBROOK CL
DOWLAND HO
GARNAULT RD
98
RADNOR GDNS
KENILWORTH CRES
INVERNESS AVE
BICKMOLLER RD
MYDDELTON CL
EASTBURY AVE
SINCLARE CL
ORCHARD CL
MELLING DR
LINDE
4
YOUNGMANS CL
GORDON HILL
BORROWDALE CT
BAILEY RD
BANK RD
LYNN ST
WALTON ST
DRAKE ST
LAUREL
LEA RD
ARMFIELD RD
PHILIP CT
KYNASTON RD
YORK HO
WEARDALE GDNS
LANCASTER HO
PRIORS MEAD
CANONBURY RD
ROCHESTER CL
Forty Hill Cemy
New River
CARISBROOK CL
TENNISWOOD RD
Sp Gd
BLACK FAN CL
TIPPETTS
WHITAKERS LO
St Michael's
GATER DR
JOHN KEATS LO
H
SHELLY LO
HEENE RD
FARR RD
THE DRIVE
BAKER ST
Chace Com Sch
IVINGHOE CL
BELL RD
COLLEGE GDNS
COLLEGE RD
WESTON RD
CHURCHBURY RD
BUCKINGHAM CL
SANDRINGHAM CL
Allot Gdns
Queen Elizabeth Stadium
Sp Ctr
HOLTWHITE AVE
GORDON RD
HALIFAX RD
BELLAMY RD
MANOR RD
St George's RC Prim Sch
CHEVIOTS HOSTEL
PILGRIMS CT
PEVENSEY AVE
BODIAM CL
COWDREY CL
ALDERSBROOK AVE
CHAILEY AVE
FILLEBROOK AVE
HERRONGATE CL
WILLOW RD
TRINITY ST
CHASE SIDE
NUNNS RD
CHEVIOT CL
CHEVIOT CT
Recn Gd
GRAEME RD
CONNAUGHT AVE
CARNARVON AVE
LAMBOURNE GDNS
LADYSMITH RD
3
Chase Side Prim Sch
CHASE SIDE AVE
MONASTERY GDNS
PARSONAGE LA
HEATH'S CL
RAVENS CL
St Andrew's Sch
CHURCHBURY LA
CHURCHBURY CL
CONNAUGHT CL
NEWBY CL
VICAR'S CL
MONKS CL
CHRISTCHURCH CL
LAMBS WLK
KINGS CLERE PL
CHASE SIDE PL
RIVERSIDE GDNS
PARSONAGE GDNS
CHASE GREEN AVE
WEST BANK
FLORENCE DR
CHASE COURT GDNS
CRICKETERS ARMS RD
HORSESHOE LA
DANBY CT
RIVER VIEW
Enfield Gram Sch
PORTCULLIS LODGE RD
FIR TREE WLK
RIVERSFIELD RD
EN1
97
Pl Fld
BUTTERFIELD ROW
CHASE GN
CHASE HILL
FLORENCE AVE
GENTLEMAN'S ROW
CHAPEL ST
HOLLY WLK
Enfield Cty Sch
Offices
C Ctr
SILVER ST
ORCHARD WAY
CALDER CL
GREENCROFT GDNS
THE VINERIES
PEARTREE RD
APPLE GR
Allot Gdns
KIMBERLEY GDNS
CRADDOCK RD
MAFEKING RD
George Spicer Prim Sch
COBHAM CL
Kingsmead Sch
2
Gram Sch
CHURCH LA
LITTLE PARK GDNS
BURLEIGH WAY
MARKET PL
ST ANDREW'S RD
FYFIELD RD
RIVER FRONT
WAVERLEY GDNS
GRESHAM CL
SHIRLEY RD
Ct
Liby
Enfield Chase
CHURCH ST
THE TOWN
A110
SAVOY PAR
SPICER CT
EATON RD
STANLEY RD
FOTHERINGHAM RD
SKETTY RD
CLYDACH RD
SOUTHBURY RD
BRYN-Y-MAWR RD
JULES THORN AVE
LC
SARNESFIELD RD
PALACE GDNS
SYDNEY RD
A105
GENOTIN RD
GENOTIN TERR
BOVRIL HO
RYLAND CL
Enfield Town Superstore
QUEEN'S RD
FELIX NEUBERGH CT
SEAFORD RD
BERESFORD GDNS
HALSTEAD RD
FALMER RD
CECIL AVE
Tenn Cts
TEMPSFORD
FIRBANK CL
OLD PARK AVE
CECIL RD
Enfield Town
Bwg Gn
Town Park
FROBISHER MEWS
RALEIGH RD
LONDON RD
ROSENEATH WLK
PARK AVE
CHALKWELL PARK AVE
Allot Gdns
LYNDHURST GDNS
CAMBERLEY AVE
BEVERLEY CL
BURLEIGH RD
WADDINGTON CL
CROSS RD
DOWNS RD
Recn Gd
PERCIVAL RD
BERTRAM RD
BERT WAY
CLIVE WAY
CLIVE RD
SOUTHBURY AVE
1
OLD PARK GR
ESSEX RD
TIPTREE DR
TIPTREE CT
LINCOLN CT
SALISBURY CT
PARK CRES
WALSINGHAM RD
POTTERSFIELD
ILLINGWORTH WAY
KINGSWOOD CL
LINCOLN CRES
HARMAN RD
JOHN ST
JAMES ST
AGRICOLA PL
HADRIAN'S RIDE
ROMANY WAY
LINCOLN RD
96
RIDINGS AVE
UVEDALE RD
WHITETHORN GDNS
17
33
34
ERMINE SIDE
Prim Sch
EAST CRES
WATERHEDGE MEWS
CHARLES ST
Liby
MAIN AVE
PRIVATE RD
Tenn Cts

6
Bulls Cross
A10 Hertford, M25
A1010 Waltham Cross, A10(A1055)
VII
Myddelton House
EN2
St Ignatius Coll
Forty Hill CE Prim Sch
Turkey Street
Crem
Enfield Wash
Albany Sch
Eastfield Prim Sch
Worcesters Prim Sch
Russet House Sch
Durants Sch
Coll
EN3
Carterhatch Jun & Inf Schs
Enfield Highway
Queen Elizabeth Stadium
Bishop Stopford's Sch
Suffolks Prim Sch
EN1
ENFIELD
GREAT CAMBRIDGE RD
HERTFORD RD
Enfield Coll
Durants Park
Brimsdown Jun & Inf Sch
George Spicer Prim Sch
Kingsmead Sch
Waverley Sch
SOUTHBURY RD
NAGS HEAD RD
St Mary's RC Prim Sch
Southbury Depot
Middlesex Univ
Ponders End
18
35
34
99
98
97
96

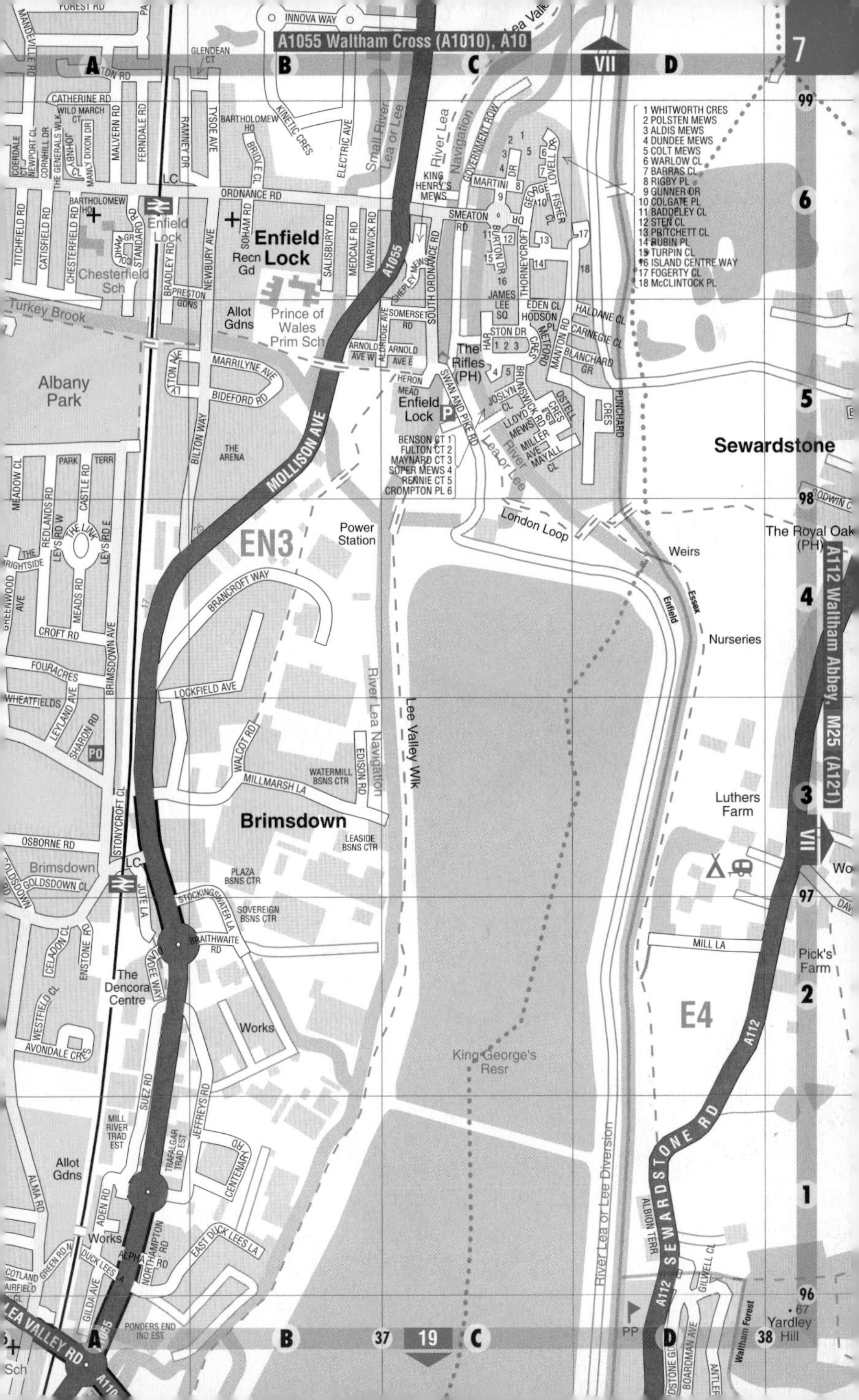
A1055 Waltham Cross (A1010), A10
A
B
C
VII
D
99
6
5
98
4
3
97
2
1
96
1 WHITWORTH CRES
2 POLSTEN MEWS
3 ALDIS MEWS
4 DUNDEE MEWS
5 COLT MEWS
6 WARLOW CL
7 BARRAS CL
8 RIGBY PL
9 GUNNER DR
10 COLGATE PL
11 BADDELEY CL
12 STEN CL
13 PRITCHETT CL
14 RUBIN PL
15 TURPIN CL
16 ISLAND CENTRE WAY
17 FOGERTY CL
18 McCLINTOCK PL
Enfield Lock
Recn Gd
Chesterfield Sch
Prince of Wales Prim Sch
Allot Gdns
Turkey Brook
Albany Park
The Rifles (PH)
BENSON CT 1
FULTON CT 2
MAYNARD CT 3
SOPER MEWS 4
RENNIE CT 5
CROMPTON PL 6
MOLLISON AVE
A1055
THE ARENA
EN3
Power Station
London Loop
Weirs
Sewardstone
The Royal Oak (PH)
Nurseries
Enfield
Essex
A112 Waltham Abbey, M25 (A121)
Luthers Farm
River Lea Navigation
Lee Valley Wlk
Brimsdown
WATERMILL BSNS CTR
LEASIDE BSNS CTR
PLAZA BSNS CTR
SOVEREIGN BSNS CTR
The Dencora Centre
Works
King George's Resr
MILL LA
Pick's Farm
E4
A112
SEWARDSTONE RD
River Lea or Lee Diversion
ALBION TERR
GILWELL CL
Waltham Forest
Yardley Hill
MILL RIVER TRAD EST
TRAFALGAR TRAD EST
PONDERS END IND EST
Allot Gdns
LEA VALLEY RD
A110
37
19
38
PP
Sch

M1 Luton, M25
A41 Watford (A4008), M1
Castle
A
B
C
VI
D
96
6
5
95
4
3
94
2
1
93
14
15
24
Tyler's Farm
Hilfield Park Resr
Ppg Sta
HILFIELD LA
TYLERS WAY
M1
A41
Pl Fld
Tenn Cts
Bushey Meads Sch
Meadow Wood Sch
Hart's Farm
ROSSWAY DR
WD23
Little Reddings JMI Sch
TURNER RD
SUTCLIFFE CL
FORD CL
GEDDES RD
GIRTIN RD
GULLAND CL
MOSTYN RD
MUNRO RD
HARCOURT RD
BARLEY CL
MEADOW RD
LEA CL
STOREY CT
MOAT CL
PO
EDRIDGE CL
REDDINGS AVE
RYDER CL
COOKS MEAD
COLDHARBOUR LA
GOODISON
WORTEN CL
THE BIRCHES
COTSWOLD AVE
CHEVIOT CL
PENTLAND RD
MENDIP RD
LITTLE BUSHEY LA
THE SQUIRRELS
CHILTERN CL
ASTON CL
KING GEORGE AVE
WENDOVER WAY
CHARTRIDGE CL
OUNDLE AVE
ROCKINGHAM GATE
DUNSMORE WAY
DUNSMORE CL
DUNSMORE
WAYSIDE AVE
CHILTERN AVE
PARKLANDS
P
Tenn Cts
Recn Gd
Bwg Gn
GREENSWARD
PERRY MEAD
ASHFIELD AVE
PASTURE CL
1 VALERIE CT
2 WINDSOR CT
COOMBE RD
IVINGHOE RD
LOWER TUB
THE FOUR TUBS
ALBANY CL
Caldecot Farm
HILFIELD LAS
CALDECOTE LA
A411
CLAYBURY
FAIR CL
A411 Watford
SOMERS WAY
CATSEY WOOD
KIMBLE CRES
GARRATTS RD
SHADY BUSH CL
RICHFIELD RD
RICHARDS CL
HARRIET WAY
WOODFIELD RISE
LITTLE POTTERS
ROSARY GDNS
CALDECOTE GDNS
TATE GDNS
Tenn Cts
Immanuel Coll
ELSTREE RD
WOODSTOCK RD
A409
MONTACUTE RD
ARDEN CL
HOWARD CL
MAGNAVILLE RD
PAYNESFIELD RD
CLARENCE CL
WARWICK CL
WILLOW DENE
OTWAY GDNS
WYATT CL
HOLLYGROVE
PRIORY VIEW
Bushey Heath
Allot Gdns
THE BRIARS
Allot Gdns
CLAY LA
HEATHBOURNE RD
Liby
HIGHLAND DR
CATSEY LA
VEGA RD
2 BURCHELL CT
BROOKE CL
UPTON CT
LODGE CL
PRIMROSE
SPARROWS HERNE
BROOKE WAY
CLARKS MEAD
HERNE CT
NIMMO DR
TITIAN AVE
EVERETT CL
Recn Gd
LANE GDNS
H
BUPA Bushey
Merry Hill Sch
LINNET CL
LANGHOLME
MERRY HILL RD
SWALLOW CL
ASH HILL CL
PARTRIDGE CL
GOLDCREST WAY
WREN CRES
SPARROWS WAY
LARKEN DR
LARKEN CL
PRIORY CT
COLES GN
A411
A4140
ST PETER'S CL
SPRINGFIELD
ORCHARD CL
THE PANTILES
LONGMEAD DR
Sch
GREENWOOD CL
WINDMILL ST
Allot Gdns
THE LAKE
THE COMYNS
ROSE LAWN
P
BELLE VUE LA
RUTLAND PL
THE RUTTS
POWIS CT
PICKETS CL
RUTHERFORD WAY
TRUNDLERS WAY
WINDMILL LA
THE CALLANDERS
MOUNT
WOODPECKER CL
WARREN RD
HOWTON PL
PO
P
HIGH RD
THORN AVE
DOWN WALONG
CLAIRE CT
ROBINSON CRES
STEVENS GN
SEQUOIA CL
BEAMISH DR
GIANT TREE HILL
CALIFORNIA LA
KNIGHTS CT
HEATH LO
LIME TREE WLK
Stanmore Common
ALLARD CRES
NICHOLSON DR
TREACY CL
FLORIDA CL
HARTSBOURNE PK
BENTLEY LO
THE LAURELS
ELDER CT
MAGPIE HALL RD
Sch
GILLAN GN
FINUCANE RISE
GLEED AVE
SHEPHERDS WLK
SHAW CL
FRANSHAMS
HIGHFIELD
HEATHBOURNE RD
Heathfield
PROWSE AVE
MUNGO-PARK CL
MCKELLAR CL
BUSHELL GN
HARTSWOOD GN
HARTSBOURNE RD
HIVE CL
BROADFIELDS
ALPINE WLK
LAURINO PL
LAKE DR
HARTSBOURNE AVE
GREENACRES
HIVE RD
HOLMBURY CT
BUSHEY
Hartsbourne Ctry Club
Hartsbourne Prim Sch
HARTSBOURNE CL
FAIRSEAT CL
THE COMMON
Tenn Cts
COMMON RD
TANGLEWOOD CL
Tenn Cts
A4140
PRIORY DR
PRIORY CL
Hertfordshire
Harrow
Harrow Weald Common
Bentley Priory
Tenn Cts
HA7
Levels Wood
A409
Harrow Weald Common
Grimsdyke Hotel
Deer Park
Heriot's

A5183 St Albans
Allot Gdns
VI
Home Farm
Aldenham Ctry Pk
Laboratory
DAGGER LA
ALDENHAM RD
Aldenham Resr
Sailing Club
Pav
Sp Gd
Tenn Cts
WD6
ELSTREE HILL N
B5378
ALLUM
THE BARTONS
St Nicholas CE Prim Sch
Elstree
LANDS' END
WATFORD RD
HIGH ST
A411
ELSTREE RD
PH
LISMIRRANE IND PK
SCHUBERT RD
BRITTEN CL
RODGERS CL
DELIUS CL
WEBBER CL
BEETHOVEN RD
SULLIVAN WAY
ELGAR CL
DYLAN CL
COATES RD
WEST VIEW GDNS
SUMMER GR
MAY GDNS
FORTUNE LA
Tenn Cts
Edgwarebury House Farm
NORTH WESTERN AVE (WATFORD BY-PASS)
CENTENNIAL AVE
CENTENNIAL PK
CENTENNIAL CT
ELSTREE HILL S
A5183
WD23
Hertfordshire
Harrow
Brockleyhill Farm
Barnet
M1
A5
4
Sp Gd
Brockley Grange
Tenn Cts
BROCKLEY HILL HO
Works
HA7
SIR HENRY FLOYD CT
Royal National Orthopaedic
Grove Farm
Pear Wood Cottages
Annandale
NUTT GR
A41 EDGWARE WAY (WATFORD BY-PASS)
BROCKLEY HILL
HA8
WARREN LA
Limes House
WOOD LA
Wood Farm
Pear Wood
Crkt Gd
Pav
Tenn Cts
Springbok House
Cloisters Wood
CH
Brockley Hill
Tenn Cts
SPRINGFIELD CL
HILLTOP WAY
LITTLE COMMON
A4140 STANMORE HILL
Stanmore Hall
FALLOWFIELD
AYLMER CL
AYLMER DR
HERIOTS CL
PINE CL
OLD FORGE CL
SPRING LAKE
HALL CL
DENNIS LA
GLANLEAM RD
REENGLASS RD
BERRY HILL
CHEVALIER CL
REES DR
PARTRIDGE CL
GRANTHAM CL
NEWLANDS CL
HAMLYN CL
PIPERS GREEN LA
St Johns
96
6
5
95
4
10
3
94
2
1
93
17
25
18

Elstree
WOODSIDE
BLATTNER CL
ALLUM LA
FIR TREE CT
HILL CREST LO
VI
DEACONS CL
Elstree
Furzehill Sch
CEDARS CL
OAKWAY
ELMWOOD AVE
A
B
C
D
Allot Gdns
Sch
96
A5183
B5378
ALLUM LA
KNOWL PK
KNOWL WAY
TAUBER CL
LODGE AVE
GRANGE RD
BISHOPS AVE
HARTFIELD AVE
DEACON'S HILL RD
CAVENDISH CRES
LAKESIDE
BERKELEY CL
ASCOT CL
HARTFIELD CL
HARTFIELD AVE
MELROSE AVE
TENNISON AVE
MILTON DR
BYRON AVE
VALE AVE
MASEFIELD AVE
LULLINGTON GARTH
CARRINGTON AVE
Cemy
6
ELSTREE HILL
THE RISE
WENTWORTH AVE
SHIREMEADE
SHERATON CL
LOWTHER CL
NICHOLAS RD
ALWYN CL
HADLEY CL
CLARE CL
BELMOR
SUMMER HILL
THE BARTONS
St Nicholas CE Prim Sch
ST NICHOLAS CL
NEW RD
OAK TREE CT
GEORGES MEAD
Elstree
5
PO
SUMMER GR
A411
FORTUNE LA
MAY GDNS
Abbotsbury
BARNET LA
DEACONS HTS
Deacons
WD6
Elstree Tunnel
Woodcock Hill
Tenn Cts
A411
Tenn Cts
95
Edgwarebury House Farm
The Leys
Penniwells Farm
4
Tenn Cts
Tenn Cts
Edgwarebury Ctry Club
Hertfordshire
Barnet
NW7
9
Hertfordshire
Barnet
M1
M1
3
Edgwarebury Farm
Bury Farm
Edgware Bury
EDGWAREBURY LA
94
A41
EDGWARE WAY (WATFORD BY-PASS)
Clay La
Cemy
Pav
Pl Fld
Broadfields Inf Sch
HARTLAND CL
Broadfields Jun Sch
MEADFIELD
MEADFIELD GN
WARRENS SHAWE CL
BURRELL CL
BUSHFIELD CL
BUSHFIELD CRES
PENTLAND AVE
RANNOCH CL
HAMONDE CL
CROMARTY RD
MORAY CL
KINGSLEY CT
2
HA8
HARTLAND DR
HA8
TAYSIDE DR
ALDRIDGE AVE
PARSONS RD
GLENDEVON CL
Sch
PO
PARSONS GR
GLENGALL RD
FRANCKLYN GDNS
HARROWES MEADE
BULLESCROFT RD
CH
Edgwarebury Park
WOLMER GDNS
CROSSGATE
BEULAH CL
CRANMER RD
ASHFORD CT
MARLBOROUGH AVE
NEWLANDS CL
GRANTHAM CL
HAMLYN CL
Barnet
Harrow
PIPERS GREEN LA
Tenn Cts
Pav
ROSENS WLK
WYRE GR
1
Edgwarebury
BROADFIELDS AVE
WINDSOR AVE
LYNFORD GDNS
BROCKLEY AVE
HA7
PARKSIDE DR
A41
BLACKWELL GDNS
HURSTMEAD CT
93
CHEVALIER CL
A5
SPUR RD
A410
GOLDSMITH CT
COLLINSON CT
POWIS
EATON CT
WOLMER CL
Sch
BROADHURST AVE
GRENVILLE CT
SPALDING CT
EDGWARE
18
BERRY HILL
ROCKLEYSIDE
REES DR
PARTRIDGE CL
A
CANONS CNR
1 WARE CT
2 WAKEMAN HO
3 ABINGDON CT
4 CHICHELLE HO
5 HAVILLAND CT
GARRICK CT
MARTYN CT
RAFFLES CT
B
STERLING AVE
19
26
C
RANELAGH CL
(WATFORD
BY-PASS)
D
A41
Pl Fld
WILLOW CT
Sch
PO
LONDON HO
STAMFORD
REENGLASS RD
A410
BROADFIELDS HTS
HAZEL GDNS
BALMORAL CT 1
SANDRINGHAM CT 2

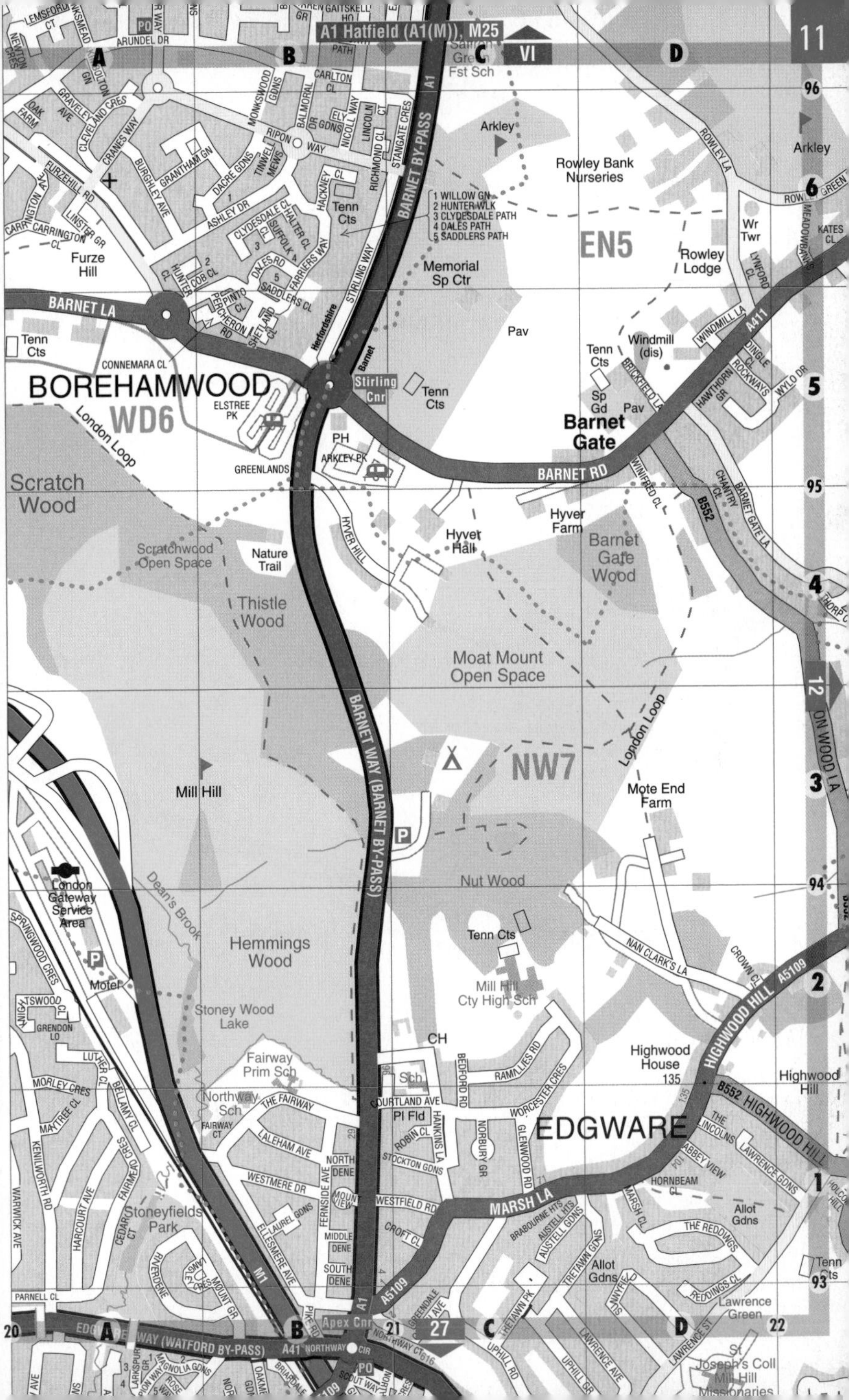
A1 Hatfield (A1(M)), M25
VI
A
B
C
D
96
6
5
95
4
3
94
2
1
93
20
21
22
27
12
Arkley
Rowley Bank Nurseries
ROWLEY LA
ROWLEY GREEN
MEADOWBANKS
KATES CL
Wr Twr
Rowley Lodge
LYNFORD CL
EN5
Memorial Sp Ctr
1 WILLOW GN
2 HUNTER WLK
3 CLYDESDALE PATH
4 DALES PATH
5 SADDLERS PATH
Tenn Cts
BARNET BY-PASS
A1
STIRLING WAY
RICHMOND CL
STANGATE CRES
LINCOLN CT
NICOLL WAY
ELY GDNS
BALMORAL DR
CARLTON CL
MONKSWOOD GDNS
RIPON WAY
TINWELL MEWS
HACKNEY CL
GRANTHAM GN
DACRE GDNS
ASHLEY DR
BURGHLEY AVE
CRANES WAY
CLEVELAND CRES
GRAVELEY AVE
OAK FARM
ARUNDEL DR
LEMSFORD CT
NEWTON CRES
PO
FURZEHILL RD
CARRINGTON AVE
CARRINGTON CL
LINSTER GR
Furze Hill
CLYDESDALE CL
HALTER CL
SUFFOLK
FARRIERS WAY
DALES RD
SADDLERS CL
COB CL
HUNTER CL
PINTO CL
PERCHERON RD
SHETLAND CL
BARNET LA
CONNEMARA CL
BOREHAMWOOD
WD6
ELSTREE PK
London Loop
Herfordshire
Barnet
Stirling Cnr
PH
ARKLEY PK
GREENLANDS
Pav
Windmill (dis)
WINDMILL LA
A411
DINGLE CL
ROCKWAYS
WYLO DR
HAWTHORN GR
BRICKFIELD LA
Sp Gd
Barnet Gate
BARNET RD
WINIFRED CL
B552
CHANTRY CL
BARNET GATE LA
Scratch Wood
Scratchwood Open Space
Nature Trail
HYVER HILL
Hyver Hall
Hyver Farm
Barnet Gate Wood
Thistle Wood
Moat Mount Open Space
BARNET WAY (BARNET BY-PASS)
NW7
Mote End Farm
Mill Hill
P
Nut Wood
London Gateway Service Area
Motel
Dean's Brook
Hemmings Wood
Stoney Wood Lake
Tenn Cts
Mill Hill Cty High Sch
NAN CLARK'S LA
CROWN CL
A5109
HIGHWOOD HILL
Highwood House
135
Highwood Hill
B552 HIGHWOOD HILL
CH
Sch
RAMILLIES RD
BEDFORD RD
WORCESTER CRES
COURTLAND AVE
Pl Fld
ROBIN CL
HANKINS LA
NORBURY GR
GLENWOOD RD
EDGWARE
THE LINCOLNS
LAWRENCE GDNS
ABBEY VIEW
HORNBEAM CL
MARSH LA
MARSH CL
Allot Gdns
THE REDDINGS
REDDINGS CL
Lawrence Green
LAWRENCE ST
St Joseph's Coll Mill Hill Missionaries
Fairway Prim Sch
Northway Sch
THE FAIRWAY
FAIRWAY CT
LALEHAM AVE
NORTH DENE
WESTMERE DR
FERNSIDE AVE
MOUNT VIEW
WESTFIELD RD
LAUREL GDNS
ELLESMERE AVE
MIDDLE DENE
SOUTH DENE
CROFT CL
STOCKTON GDNS
BRABOURNE HTS
AUSTELL HTS
AUSTELL GDNS
TRETAWN GDNS
TRETAWN PK
UPHILL RD
UPHILL GR
LAWRENCE AVE
SUNNYFIELD
GREENDALE
Apex Cnr
NORTHWAY CIR
NORTHWAY CT
EDGWARE WAY (WATFORD BY-PASS)
A41
M1
PIKE RD
Stoneyfields Park
CEDAR CT
RIVERDENE
LANSDOWNE
MOUNT GR
PARNELL CL
SPRINGWOOD CRES
GRENDON LO
LUTHER CL
BELLAMY CL
MORLEY CRES
MAYTREE CL
KENILWORTH RD
HARCOURT AVE
FAIRMEAD CRES
WARWICK AVE
LARKSPUR
MAGNOLIA GDNS
ROSE
SCOUT WAY

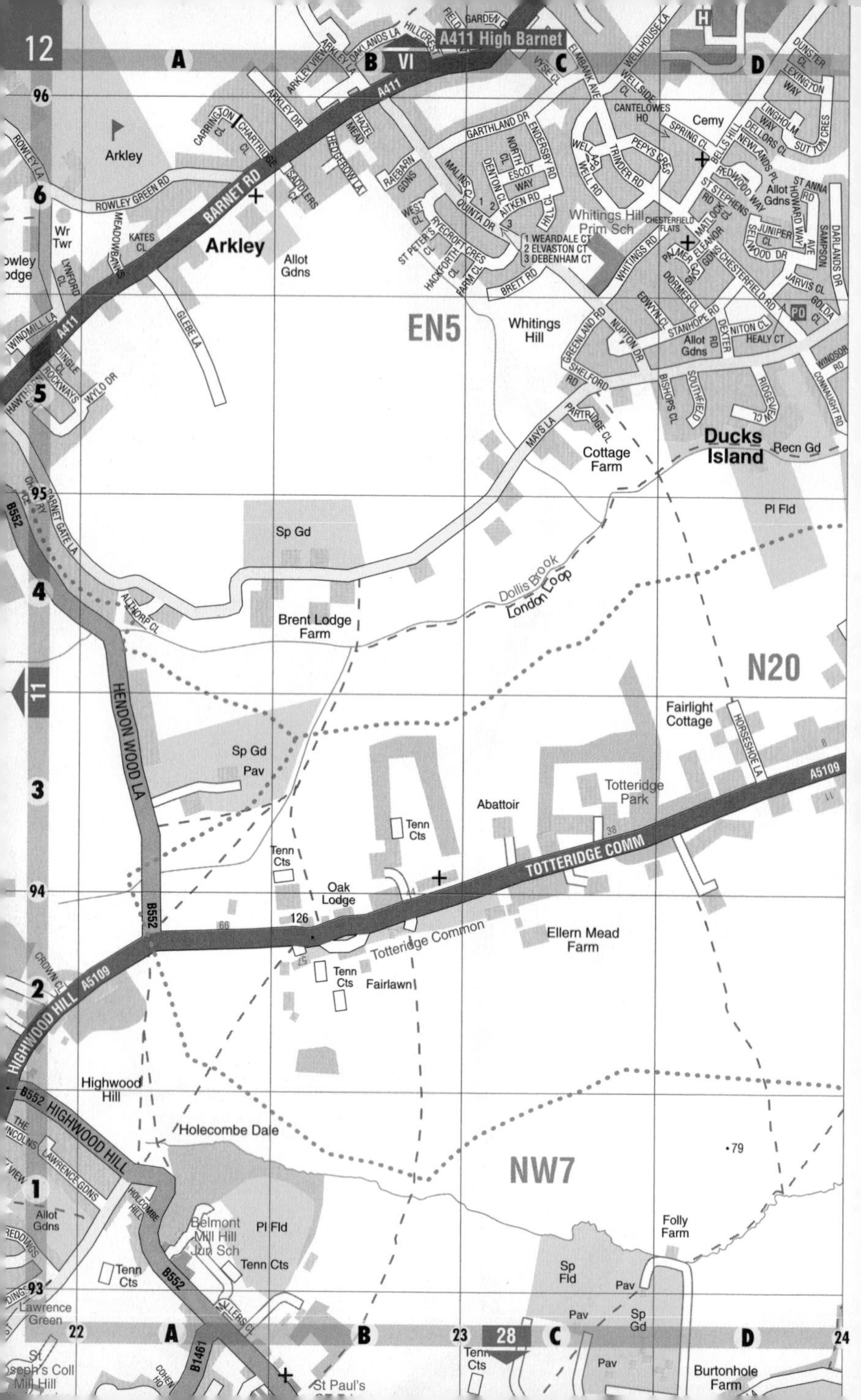
A411 High Barnet
A
B
C
D
VI
96
6
5
95
4
3
94
2
1
93
22
23
24
28
11
Arkley
Arkley
Allot Gdns
Wr Twr
Rowley Lodge
ROWLEY LA
ROWLEY GREEN RD
BARNET RD
A411
MEADOWBANKS
KATES CL
LYNFORD CL
WINDMILL LA
DINGLE CL
ROCKWAYS
HAWTHORN GDNS
WYLO DR
GLEBE LA
CARRINGTON CL
CHARTRIDGE CL
SADDLERS CL
HEDGEROW LA
HAZEL MEAD
ARKLEY DR
ARKLEY VIEW
ARKLEY LA
OAKLANDS LA
HILLCREST
FIELD
GARDEN CL
RAEBARN GDNS
WEST CL
ST PETER'S CL
RYECROFT CRES
HACKFORTH CL
FARM CL
MALINS CL
QUINTA DR
DENTON CL
NORTH CL
ESCOT WAY
AITKEN RD
HILL CL
ENDERSBY RD
GARTHLAND DR
VYSE CL
ELMBANK AVE
WELLHOUSE LA
WELLSIDE CL
CANTELOWES HO
SPRING CL
Cemy
PEPYS CRES
TRINDER RD
WELL RD
BELLS HILL
DELLORS CL
NEWLANDS PL
LINGHOLM WAY
SUTTON CRES
DUNSTER CL
LEXINGTON WAY
REDWOOD WAY
ST STEPHENS RD
Allot Gdns
ST ANNA RD
HOWARD WAY
JUNIPER CL
SELWOOD DR
AVE
SAMPSON
DARLANDS DR
1 WEARDALE CT
2 ELVASTON CT
3 DEBENHAM CT
Whitings Hill Prim Sch
CHESTERFIELD FLATS
WHITINGS RD
MATLOCK CL
ELEANOR GDNS
PALMER CL
DORMER CL
CHESTERFIELD RD
JARVIS CL
GOLDA CL
PO
BRETT RD
EN5
Whitings Hill
GREENLAND RD
NUPTON DR
EDWYN CL
STANHOPE RD
DEXTER RD
NITON CL
HEALY CT
Allot Gdns
WINDSOR RD
CONNAUGHT RD
SHELFORD RD
BISHOPS CL
SOUTHFIELD
RIDGEVIEW CL
PARTRIDGE CL
MAYS LA
Cottage Farm
Ducks Island
Recn Gd
Pl Fld
CHANTRY PCE
BARNET GATE LA
B552
Sp Gd
Dollis Brook
London Loop
ALTHORP CL
Brent Lodge Farm
N20
HENDON WOOD LA
Fairlight Cottage
HORSESHOE LA
Sp Gd
Pav
A5109
Totteridge Park
Abattoir
Tenn Cts
Tenn Cts
TOTTERIDGE COMM
Oak Lodge
126
66
Totteridge Common
Ellern Mead Farm
Tenn Cts
Fairlawn
CROWN CL
HIGHWOOD HILL
A5109
Highwood Hill
B552 HIGHWOOD HILL
THE LINCOLNS
LAWRENCE GDNS
Holecombe Dale
NW7
79
HOLCOMBE HILL
Allot Gdns
REDDINGS
Belmont Mill Hill Jun Sch
Pl Fld
Tenn Cts
Tenn Cts
Folly Farm
Sp Fld
Pav
B552
MILLERS CL
Lawrence Green
Pav
Sp Gd
B1461
COHEN HO
St Joseph's Coll Mill Hill
St Paul's
Tenn Cts
Pav
Burtonhole Farm

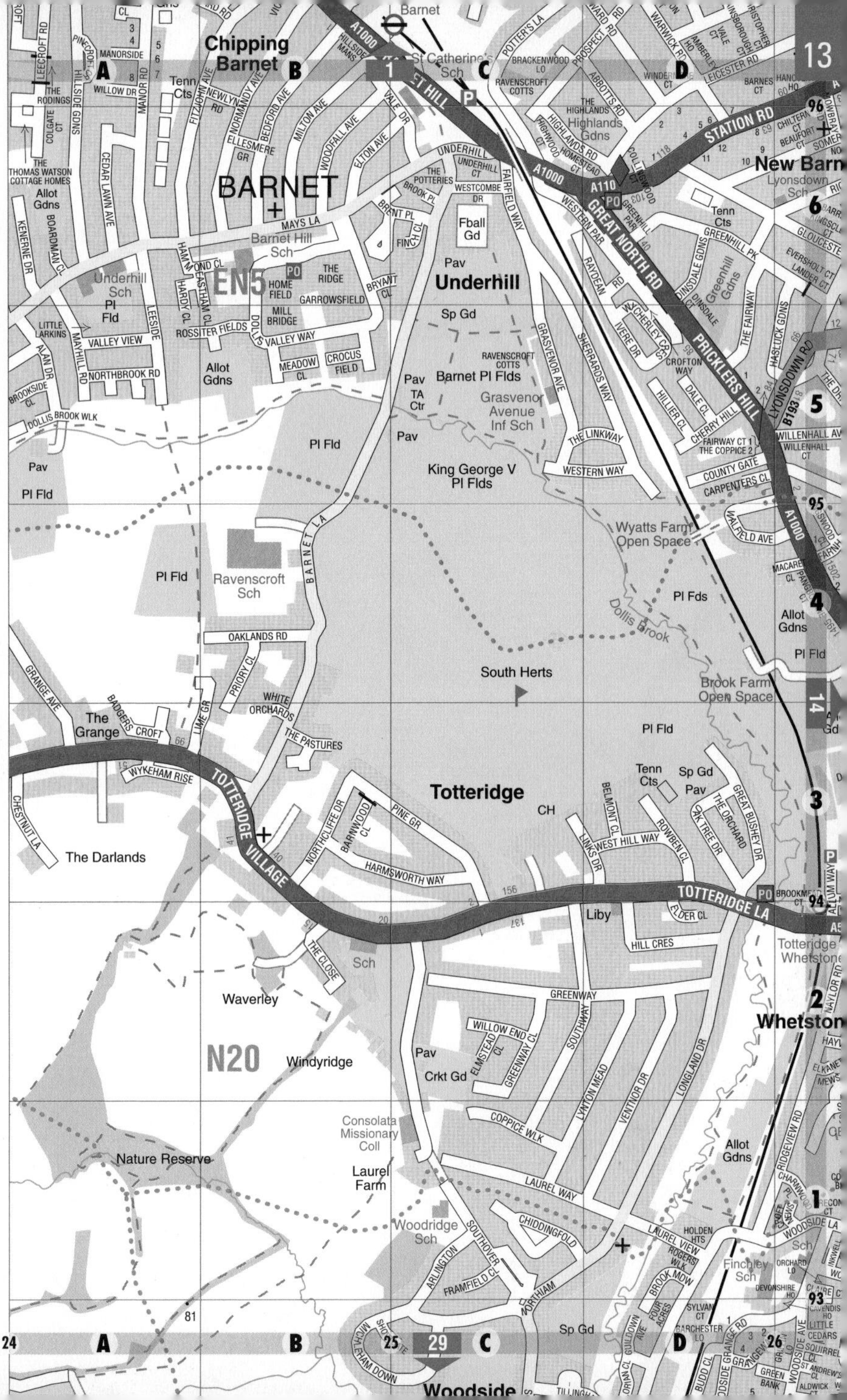
Chipping Barnet
BARNET
EN5
Underhill
Totteridge
N20
New Barnet
Whetstone
Woodside
A1000
A110
A5109
B193
GREAT NORTH RD
PRICKLERS HILL
STATION RD
LYONSDOWN RD
TOTTERIDGE VILLAGE
TOTTERIDGE LA
BARNET LA
MAYS LA
UNDERHILL
WESTCOMBE DR
FAIRFIELD WAY
GRASVENOR AVE
SHERRARDS WAY
THE LINKWAY
WESTERN WAY
LEECROFT RD
PINECROFT
MANORSIDE
WILLOW DR
HILLSIDE GDNS
MANOR RD
COLGATE CT
THE RODINGS
THE THOMAS WATSON COTTAGE HOMES
CEDAR LAWN AVE
FITZJOHN AVE
NEWLYN RD
NORMANDY AVE
BEDFORD AVE
ELLESMERE GR
MILTON AVE
WOODFALL AVE
ELTON AVE
VALE DR
KENERNE DR
BOARDMAN CL
HAMMOND CL
HARDY CL
EASTHAM CL
HOME FIELD
THE RIDGE
GARROWSFIELD
MILL BRIDGE
BRYANT CL
ROSSITER FIELDS
DOLLIS VALLEY WAY
VALLEY VIEW
LITTLE LARKINS
MAYHILL RD
NORTHBROOK RD
MEADOW CL
CROCUS FIELD
LEESIDE
ALAN DR
BROOKSIDE CL
DOLLIS BROOK WLK
Barnet Hill Sch
Underhill Sch
Allot Gdns
Pl Fld
Pav
Fball Gd
Sp Gd
Barnet Pl Flds
RAVENSCROFT COTTS
Grasvenor Avenue Inf Sch
TA Ctr
King George V Pl Flds
Ravenscroft Sch
OAKLANDS RD
PRIORY CL
WHITE ORCHARDS
THE PASTURES
GRANGE AVE
BADGERS CROFT
The Grange
LIME GR
WYKEHAM RISE
CHESTNUT LA
The Darlands
NORTHCLIFFE DR
BARNWOOD CL
PINE GR
HARMSWORTH WAY
South Herts
Wyatts Farm Open Space
Dollis Brook
Brook Farm Open Space
Pl Fds
Tenn Cts
CH
BELMONT CL
WEST HILL WAY
LINKS DR
ROWBEN CL
OAK TREE DR
THE ORCHARD
GREAT BUSHEY DR
Liby
ELDER CL
HILL CRES
Sch
THE CLOSE
Waverley
Windyridge
Nature Reserve
GREENWAY
SOUTHWAY
WILLOW END CL
ELMSTEAD CL
GREENWAY CL
Crkt Gd
COPPICE WLK
LYNTON MEAD
VENTNOR DR
LONGLAND DR
Consolata Missionary Coll
Laurel Farm
LAUREL WAY
Woodridge Sch
CHIDDINGFOLD
SOUTHOVER
ARLINGTON
FRAMFIELD CL
NORTHIAM
HOLDEN HTS
LAUREL VIEW
ROGERS WLK
BROOK MDW
FOUR ACRES
GUILDOWN AVE
SYLVAN CT
BARCHESTER LO
MICHLEHAM DOWN
Finchley Sch
Totteridge & Whetstone
RIDGEVIEW RD
WOODSIDE LA
WOODSIDE AVE
St Catherine's Sch
POTTER'S LA
BRACKENWOOD LO
RAVENSCROFT COTTS
PROSPECT RD
ABBOTTS RD
THE HIGHLANDS
Highlands Gdns
HIGHLANDS RD
HOMESTEAD
HIGHWOOD CT
COLLINGWOOD CT
WESTERN PAR
GREENHILL PAR
RAYDEAN RD
WYCHERLEY CRES
IVERE DR
DINSDALE GDNS
GREENHILL PK
Greenhill Gdns
THE FAIRWAY
HASLUCK GDNS
CROFTON WAY
HILLIER CL
DALE CL
CHERRY HILL
FAIRWAY CT
THE COPPICE
COUNTY GATE
CARPENTERS CL
WALFIELD AVE
WILLENHALL AV
Lyonsdown Sch
GLOUCESTER
EVERSHOLT CT
LANDER CT
Barnet
THE POTTERIES
BROOK PL
BRENT PL
FINCH CL
UNDERHILL CT
LEICESTER RD
WARWICK RD
BARNES CT
Woodside
24
25
26
29
A
B
C
D
1
2
3
4
5
6
93
94
95
96
14

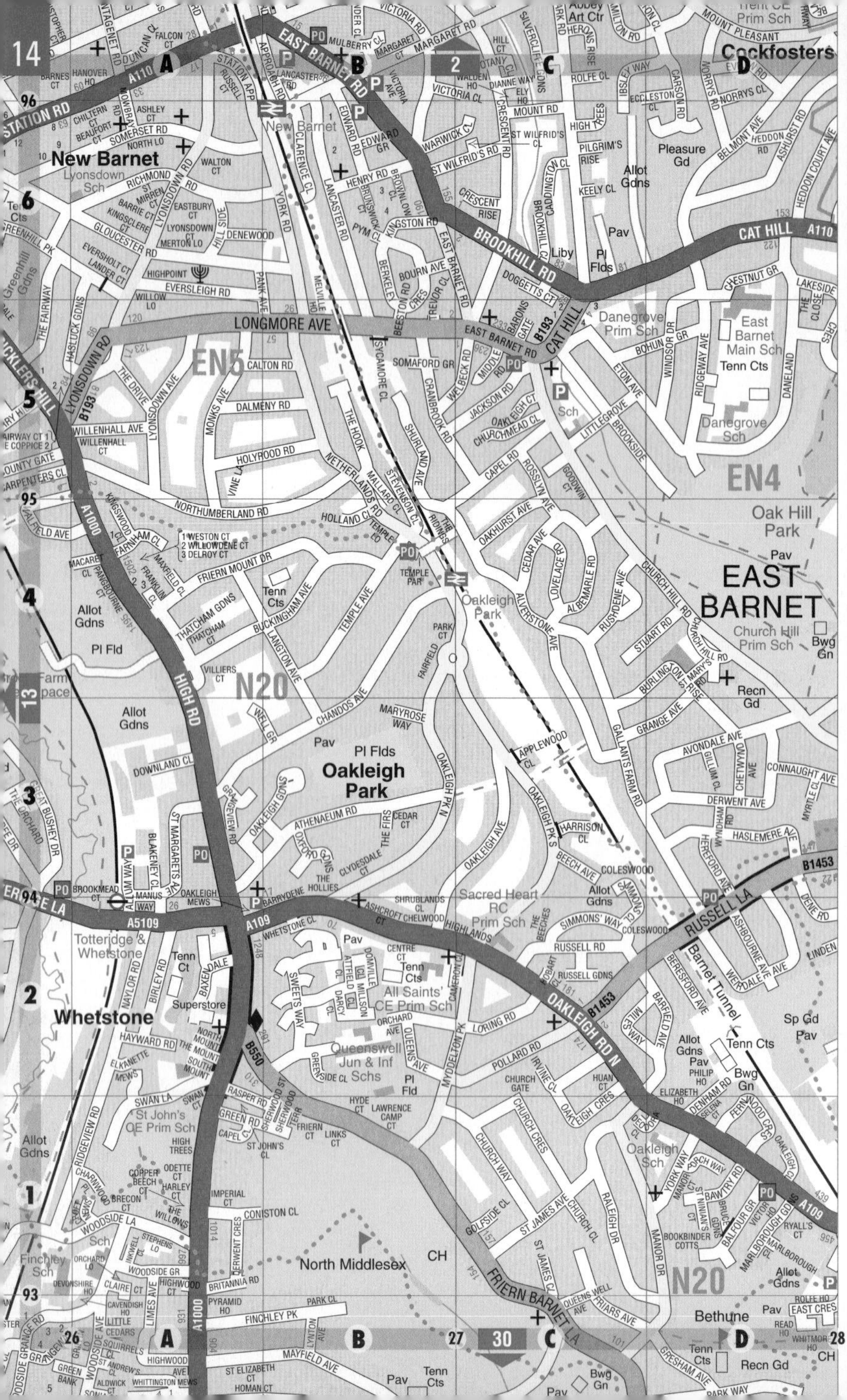
New Barnet
Cockfosters
EAST BARNET
Oakleigh Park
Whetstone
EN5
EN4
N20
STATION RD
EAST BARNET RD
BROOKHILL RD
CAT HILL
LONGMORE AVE
LYONSDOWN RD
HIGH RD
A1000
A110
A109
A5109
B193
B1453
B550
NORTHUMBERLAND RD
FRIERN MOUNT DR
CHURCH HILL RD
OAKLEIGH RD N
RUSSELL LA
FRIERN BARNET LA
ATHENAEUM RD
OAKLEIGH PK N
OAKLEIGH PK S
Totteridge & Whetstone
Oakleigh Park
New Barnet
Lyonsdown Sch
Danegrove Prim Sch
East Barnet Main Sch
Church Hill Prim Sch
Sacred Heart RC Prim Sch
All Saints' CE Prim Sch
Queenswell Jun & Inf Schs
St John's CE Prim Sch
Oakleigh Sch
Finchley Sch
Oak Hill Park
Pleasure Gd
Allot Gdns
Pl Flds
Recn Gd
Barnet Tunnel
North Middlesex
Bethune
Superstore
Greenhill Gdns
Abbey Art Ctr
Mount Pleasant
A
B
C
D
1
2
3
4
5
6
2
13
27
30
28
96
95
94
93

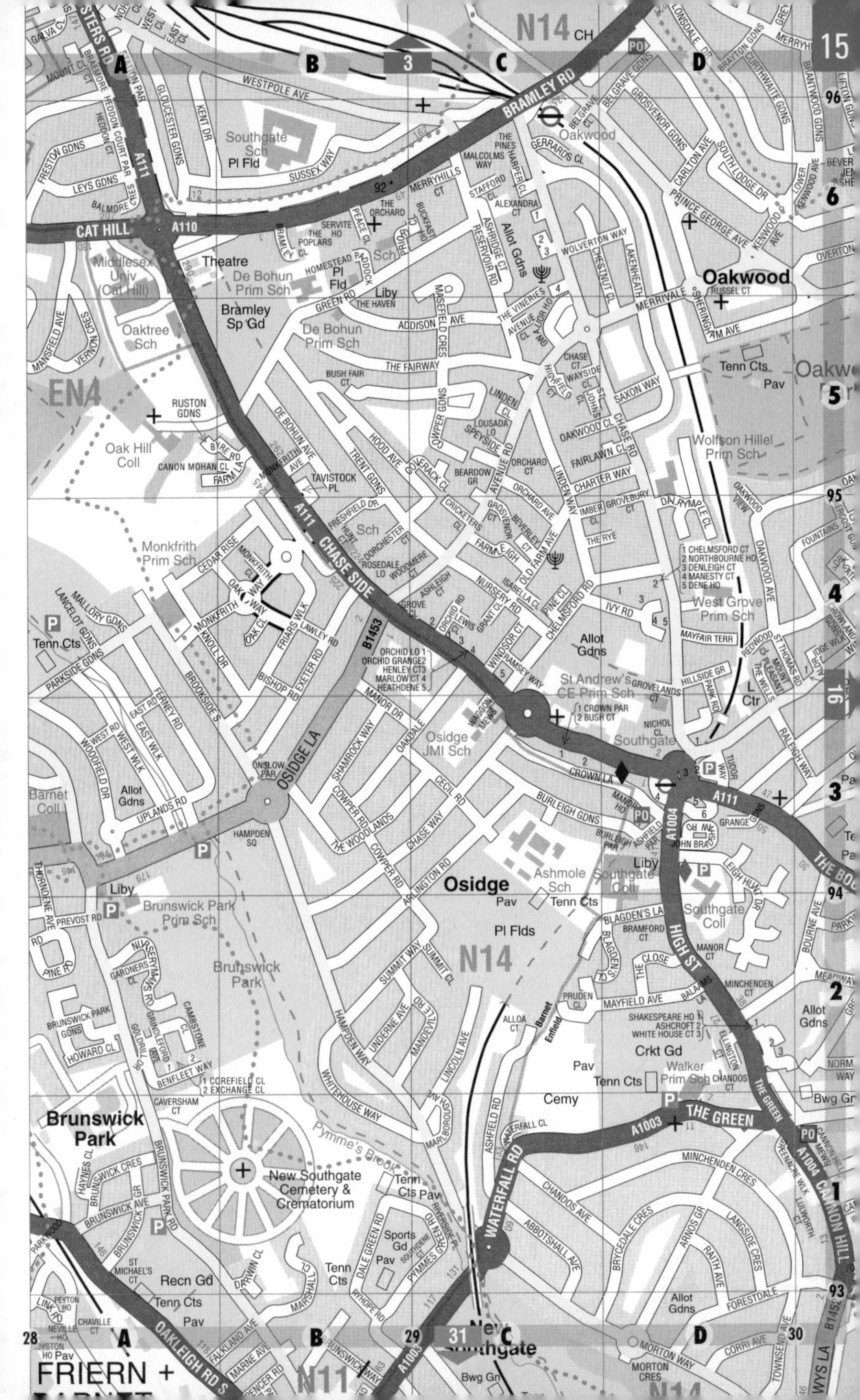

15
N14
A
B
C
D
3
BRAMLEY RD
WESTPOLE AVE
Southgate Sch
Pl Fld
SUSSEX WAY
GLOUCESTER GDNS
KENT DR
STATION PAR
HEDDON COURT PAR
HEDDON CL
BRAEMORE
MOUNT CL
FRESTON GDNS
LEYS GDNS
BALMORE CRES
A111
CAT HILL
A110
Middlesex Univ (Cat Hill)
Theatre
De Bohun Prim Sch
Bramley Sp Gd
Oaktree Sch
MANSFIELD AVE
VERNON CRES
EN4
RUSTON GDNS
Oak Hill Coll
CANON MOHAN CL
FARM LA
MERRYHILLS CT
THE ORCHARD
SERVITE HO
THE POPLARS
BRAMLEY CL
PEACE CL
PRIORY CT
BUCKFAST CT
HOMESTEAD PADDOCK
Pl Fld
Liby
THE HAVEN
GREEN RD
De Bohun Prim Sch
THE PINES
MALCOLMS WAY
STAFFORD CT
HARPER CL
ALEXANDRA CT
ASHRIDGE CT
RESERVOIR RD
Allot Gdns
MANSFIELD CRES
ADDISON AVE
THE FAIRWAY
BUSH FAIR CT
THE VINERIES
AVENUE CL
Oakwood
GERRARDS CL
BELGRAVE CL
BELGRAVE GDNS
GROSVENOR GDNS
CARLTON AVE
SOUTH LODGE DR
PRINCE GEORGE AVE
BRAYTON GDNS
CURTHWAITE GDNS
MERRYHILLS
LONSDALE DR
BRANTWOOD GDNS
LIFTON GDNS
KENWOOD AVE
LOWER KENWOOD AVE
OVERTON
WOLVERTON WAY
CHESTNUT CL
LAKENHEATH
MERRIVALE
SHERINGHAM AVE
RUSSEL CT
Oakwood
Tenn Cts
Pav
96
6
5
95
4
16
3
94
2
1
93
CHASE CT
WAYSIDE CT
HIGHFIELD CT
ST JOHNS CL
SAXON WAY
LINDEN CL
LOUSADA LO
SPEYSIDE
COWPER GDNS
HOOD AVE
TRENT GDNS
DE BOHUN AVE
MONKFRITH AVE
TAVISTOCK PL
COVERACK CL
AVENUE RD
ORCHARD CT
BEARDOW GR
OAKWOOD CL
FAIRLAWN CL
CHASE RD
CHARTER WAY
LINDEN WAY
Wolfson Hillel Prim Sch
DALRYMPLE CL
OAKWOOD VIEW
OAKWOOD AVE
FOUNTAINS
A111
CHASE SIDE
FRESHFIELD DR
HUNT CT
Sch
DORCHESTER CT
ROSEDALE LO
WOODMERE CT
CRICKETERS CL
GROSVENOR CT
ORCHARD AVE
BEVERLEY CT
FARMLEIGH
OLD FARM AVE
IMBER CL
GROVEBURY CT
THE RYE
1 CHELMSFORD CT
2 NORTHBOURNE HO
3 DENLEIGH CT
4 MANESTY CT
5 DENE HO
West Grove Prim Sch
Monkfrith Prim Sch
CEDAR RISE
MONKFRITH CL
OAK WAY
MONKFRITH WAY
KNOLL DR
OAK CL
FRIARS WLK
LAWLEY RD
ASHLEIGH CT
GROVE CL
ORCHID RD
LEWIS
GRANT CL
NURSERY RD
ISABELLA CL
PINE CL
CHELMSFORD RD
IVY RD
MAYFAIR TERR
REDWOOD CL
ST THOMAS RD
MOUNT PLEASANT
THE WELLS
HILLSIDE GR
PARK RD
L Ctr
Allot Gdns
MALLORY GDNS
LANCELOT GDNS
Tenn Cts
PARKSIDE GDNS
BROOKSIDE S
BISHOP RD
EXETER RD
B1453
ORCHID LO 1
ORCHID GRANGE 2
HENLEY CT 3
MARLOW CT 4
HEATHDENE 5
WINDSOR CT
RAMSEY WAY
St Andrew's CE Prim Sch
GROVELANDS CT
1 CROWN PAR
2 BUSH CT
NICHOL CL
Southgate
TUDOR WAY
RALEIGH WAY
FERNEY RD
EAST RD
EAST WLK
WEST RD
WEST WLK
WOODFIELD DR
Barnet Coll
Allot Gdns
UPLANDS RD
ONSLOW PAR
OSIDGE LA
MANOR DR
OAKDALE
SHAMROCK WAY
WAGGON MEWS
Osidge JMI Sch
CROWN LA
MANOR HO
BURLEIGH GDNS
A1004
A111
GRANGE GDNS
JOHN BRADSHAW RD
HAMPDEN SQ
CECIL RD
COWPER RD
THE WOODLANDS
CHASE WAY
BURLEIGH PAR
ASHFIELD PAR
Liby
LEIGH HUNT DR
THE BOURNE
THORNDENE AVE
PREVOST RD
Liby
Brunswick Park Prim Sch
ARLINGTON RD
COWPER RD
Osidge
Ashmole Sch
Southgate Coll
Pav
Tenn Cts
Pl Flds
BLAGDEN'S LA
BLAGDEN'S CL
BRAMFORD CT
HIGH ST
Southgate Coll
BOURNE AVE
PARK
PINE RD
GARDNERS CL
NURSERYMANS RD
Brunswick Park
N14
SUMMIT WAY
SUMMIT CL
THE CLOSE
MANOR CT
MINCHENDEN CT
MEADWAY
Allot Gdns
BRUNSWICK PARK GDNS
HOWARD CL
GOLDRILL DR
GRINDLEFORD AVE
CAMBSTONE CL
BENFLEET WAY
1 COREFIELD CL
2 EXCHANGE CL
HAMPDEN WAY
UNDERNE AVE
MANDEVILLE RD
LINCOLN AVE
ALLOA CT
Barnet
Enfield
PRUDEN CL
MAYFIELD AVE
BALAAMS LA
SHAKESPEARE HO 1
ASHCROFT 2
WHITE HOUSE CT 3
ELLINGTON CT
Crkt Gd
Pav
Tenn Cts
Walker Prim Sch
CHANDOS CT
NORMAN WAY
Bwg Gn
Cemy
WHITEHOUSE WAY
MARLBOROUGH AVE
GAVERSHAM CT
Brunswick Park
HAYNES CL
BRUNSWICK CRES
BRUNSWICK GR
BRUNSWICK AVE
BRUNSWICK PARK RD
New Southgate Cemetery & Crematorium
Pymme's Brook
Tenn Cts
Pav
ASHFIELD RD
WATERFALL CL
WATERFALL RD
A1003
THE GREEN
THE GREEN
CANNON HILL MEWS
GREENACRE WLK
A1004
CANNON HILL
MINCHENDEN CRES
CHANDOS AVE
ABBOTSHALL AVE
BRYCEDALE CRES
ARNOS GR
RAITH AVE
LANGSIDE CRES
LULWORTH
FORESTDALE
Allot Gdns
PARKWOOD
ST MICHAEL'S CT
Recn Gd
Tenn Cts
Pav
DARWIN CL
MARSHALL
Tenn Cts
DALE GREEN RD
Sports Gd
Pav
SOUTHDENE CT
PYMMES GREEN RD
RIVERSIDE PL
RYHOPE RD
LINK RD
PEYTON HO
NEVILLE HO
ROYSTON HO
CHAVILLE CT
OAKLEIGH RD S
FALKLAND AVE
MARNE AVE
SPENCER RD
BRUNSWICK WAY
28
A
B
29
31
New Southgate
C
D
30
MORTON WAY
MORTON CRES
CORRI AVE
TOWNSEND AVE
B1452
BOWES LA
N11
N14
Bwg Gn
FRIERN + BARNET

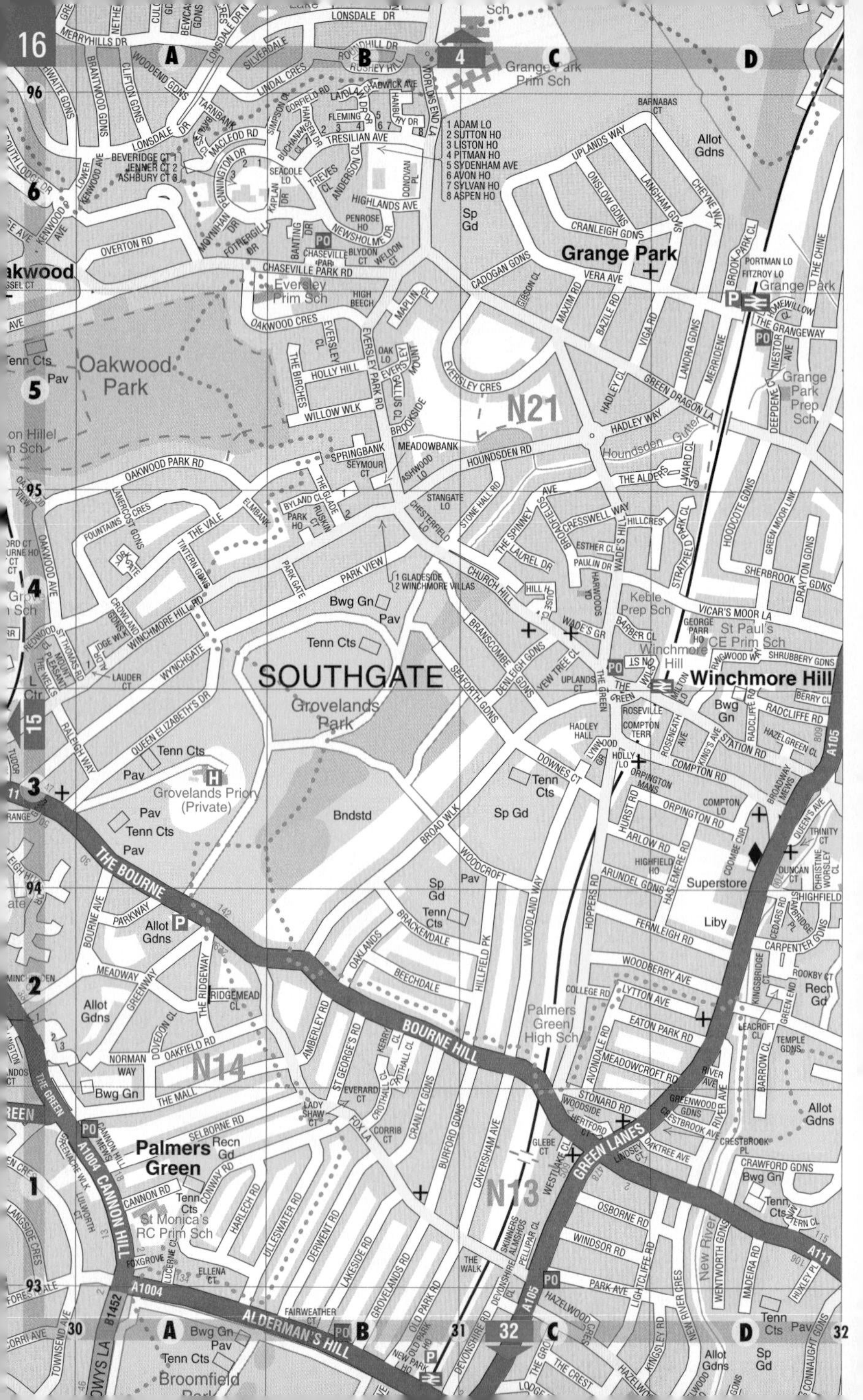
A
B
4
C
D
96
6
5
95
4
3
94
2
1
93
15
30
31
32
LONSDALE DR
MERRYHILLS DR
SILVERDALE
ROUNDHILL DR
RUSHEY HILL
WORLDS END LA
Grange Park Prim Sch
WOODEND GDNS
BRANTWOOD GDNS
CLIFTON GDNS
LINDAL CRES
TARNBANK
LONSDALE DR
MACLEOD RD
CORFIELD RD
LAIDLAW DR
CHADWICK AVE
HANBURY DR
FLEMING
TRESILIAN AVE
BUCHANAN CL
HANSEN DR
1 ADAM LO
2 SUTTON HO
3 LISTON HO
4 PITMAN HO
5 SYDENHAM AVE
6 AVON HO
7 SYLVAN HO
8 ASPEN HO
BARNABAS CT
UPLANDS WAY
Allot Gdns
BEVERIDGE CT
JENNER CT
ASHBURY CT
PENNINGTON DR
SEACOLE LO
TREVES CL
ANDERSON CL
DONOVAN PL
HIGHLANDS AVE
KENWOOD AVE
LOWER
ONSLOW GDNS
LANGHAM GDNS
CHEYNE WLK
CRANLEIGH GDNS
Sp Gd
OVERTON RD
MOYNIHAN DR
FOTHERGILL DR
KAPLAN DR
BANTING DR
PENROSE HO
NEWSHOLME DR
PO
CHASEVILLE PAR
BLYDON CT
WELDON CT
Grange Park
CADOGAN GDNS
CHASEVILLE PARK RD
Oakwood
Eversley Prim Sch
HIGH BEECH
MAPLIN CL
GIBSON CL
VERA AVE
MAXIM RD
BAZILE RD
BROOK PARK CL
PORTMAN LO
FITZROY LO
THE CHINE
HOMEWILLOW CL
THE GRANGEWAY
OAKWOOD CRES
EVERSLEY CL
EVERSLEY PARK RD
OAK LO
EVERSLEY MOUNT
VIGA RD
LANDRA GDNS
MERRIDENE
NESTOR AVE
Grange Park Prep Sch
Tenn Cts
Pav
Oakwood Park
THE BIRCHES
HOLLY HILL
GALLUS CL
BROOKSIDE
EVERSLEY CRES
N21
HADLEY CL
GREEN DRAGON LA
DEEPDENE CT
WILLOW WLK
HADLEY WAY
Houndsden Gutter
SPRINGBANK
MEADOWBANK
SEYMOUR CT
ASHWOOD LO
HOUNDSDEN RD
THE ALDERS
WARD CL
OAKWOOD PARK RD
LANERCOST GDNS
FOUNTAINS CRES
THE VALE
ELMBANK
BYLAND CL
THE GLADE
PARK HO
RUSKIN CT
STANGATE LO
STONE HALL RD
CHESTERFIELD LO
THE SPINNEY
BROADFIELDS AVE
CRESSWELL WAY
HILLCREST
STRATFIELD PARK CL
HOODCOTE GDNS
GREEN MOOR LINK
DRAYTON GDNS
OAKWOOD AVE
YORK GATE
TINTERN GDNS
PARK GATE
PARK VIEW
1 GLADESIDE
2 WINCHMORE VILLAS
CHURCH HILL
LAUREL DR
ESTHER CL
PAULIN DR
HARWOODS YD
WADE'S HILL
SHERBROOK GDNS
CROWLAND GDNS
WINCHMORE HILL RD
Bwg Gn
Pav
HILL HOUSE CL
Keble Prep Sch
VICAR'S MOOR LA
REDWOOD CL
ST THOMAS RD
MOUNT PLEASANT
THE WELLS
JUDGE WLK
ALDER CT
LAUDER CT
WYNCHGATE
Tenn Cts
BRANSCOMBE GDNS
WADE'S GR
BARBER CL
GEORGE PARR HO
St Paul's CE Prim Sch
Winchmore Hill
ELMWOOD
SHRUBBERY GDNS
SOUTHGATE
SEAFORTH GDNS
DENLEIGH GDNS
YEW TREE CL
UPLANDS CT
THE GREEN
WILSON ST
MILTON LO
Winchmore Hill
BERRY CL
L Ctr
Grovelands Park
RALEIGH WAY
QUEEN ELIZABETH'S DR
ROSEVILLE
COMPTON TERR
ROSENEATH AVE
KING'S AVE
STATION RD
RADCLIFFE RD
HAZELGREEN CL
HADLEY HALL
LYNWOOD
HOLLY LO
COMPTON RD
DOWNES CT
ORPINGTON MANS
BROADWAY MEWS
A105
TUDOR
Tenn Cts
Pav
H
Grovelands Priory (Private)
Bndstd
BROAD WLK
Sp Gd
HURST RD
COMPTON LO
ORPINGTON RD
QUEEN'S AVE
TRINITY CT
ARLOW RD
HIGHFIELD HO
ARUNDEL GDNS
CODDE CNR
DUNCAN CT
CHRISTINE WORSLEY CL
THE BOURNE
WOODCROFT
Sp Gd
Tenn Cts
HOPPERS RD
WOODLAND WAY
HASLEMERE RD
Superstore
CEDARS RD
STANBRIDGE RD
HIGHFIELD
BOURNE AVE
PARKWAY
Allot Gdns
P
BRACKENDALE
HILLFIELD PK
FERNLEIGH RD
Liby
CARPENTER GDNS
THE RIDGEWAY
GREENWAY
MEADWAY
OAKLANDS
BEECHDALE
WOODBERRY AVE
KINGSBRIDGE CT
ROOKBY CT
Recn Gd
GREEN END
RIDGEMEAD CL
COLLEGE RD
LYTTON AVE
EATON PARK RD
Palmers Green High Sch
LEACROFT CL
TEMPLE GDNS
Allot Gdns
DOVEDON CL
OAKFIELD RD
N14
AMBERLEY RD
BOURNE HILL
MEADOWCROFT RD
BARROW CL
NORMAN WAY
Bwg Gn
THE MALL
ST GEORGE'S RD
KERRY CT
CROTHALL CL
EVERARD CT
AVONDALE RD
STONARD RD
RIVER AVE
WOODSIDE
HERTFORD CT
GREENWOOD GDNS
CRESTBROOK AVE
THE GREEN
PO
CANNON HILL MEWS
SELBORNE RD
LADY SHAW CT
FOX LA
CORRIB CT
CRANLEY GDNS
BURFORD GDNS
CAVERSHAM AVE
GLEBE CT
WESTLAKE CL
GREEN LANES
LINDSEY CT
OAKTREE AVE
CRESTBROOK PL
CRAWFORD GDNS
Palmers Green
Recn Gd
CONWAY RD
HARLECH RD
ULLESWATER RD
DERWENT RD
N13
Bwg Gn
Tenn Cts
TERN CL
LANGSIDE CRES
LULWORTH CT
GREENACRE WLK
A1004
CANNON HILL
CANNON RD
Tenn Cts
St Monica's RC Prim Sch
LAKESIDE RD
OSBORNE RD
WINDSOR RD
A111
FOXGROVE
LUCERNE CT
ELLENA CT
THE WALK
SKINNERS ALMSHOS
PELLIPAR CL
DEVONSHIRE CL
LIGHTCLIFFE RD
New River
WENTWORTH GDNS
MADEIRA RD
HUXLEY PL
FORESTDALE
A1004
B1452
GROVELANDS RD
OLD PARK RD
PO
PARK AVE
HAZELWOOD CRES
NEW RIVER CRES
KINGSLEY RD
Tenn Cts
Pav
CONNAUGHT GDNS
FAIRWEATHER CT
ALDERMAN'S HILL
CORRI AVE
TOWNSEND AVE
Bwg Gn
Pav
Tenn Cts
Broomfield Park
OLD PARK HO
NEW PARK HO
DEVONSHIRE RD
THE CREST
HAZELWOOD
Allot Gdns
Sp Gd

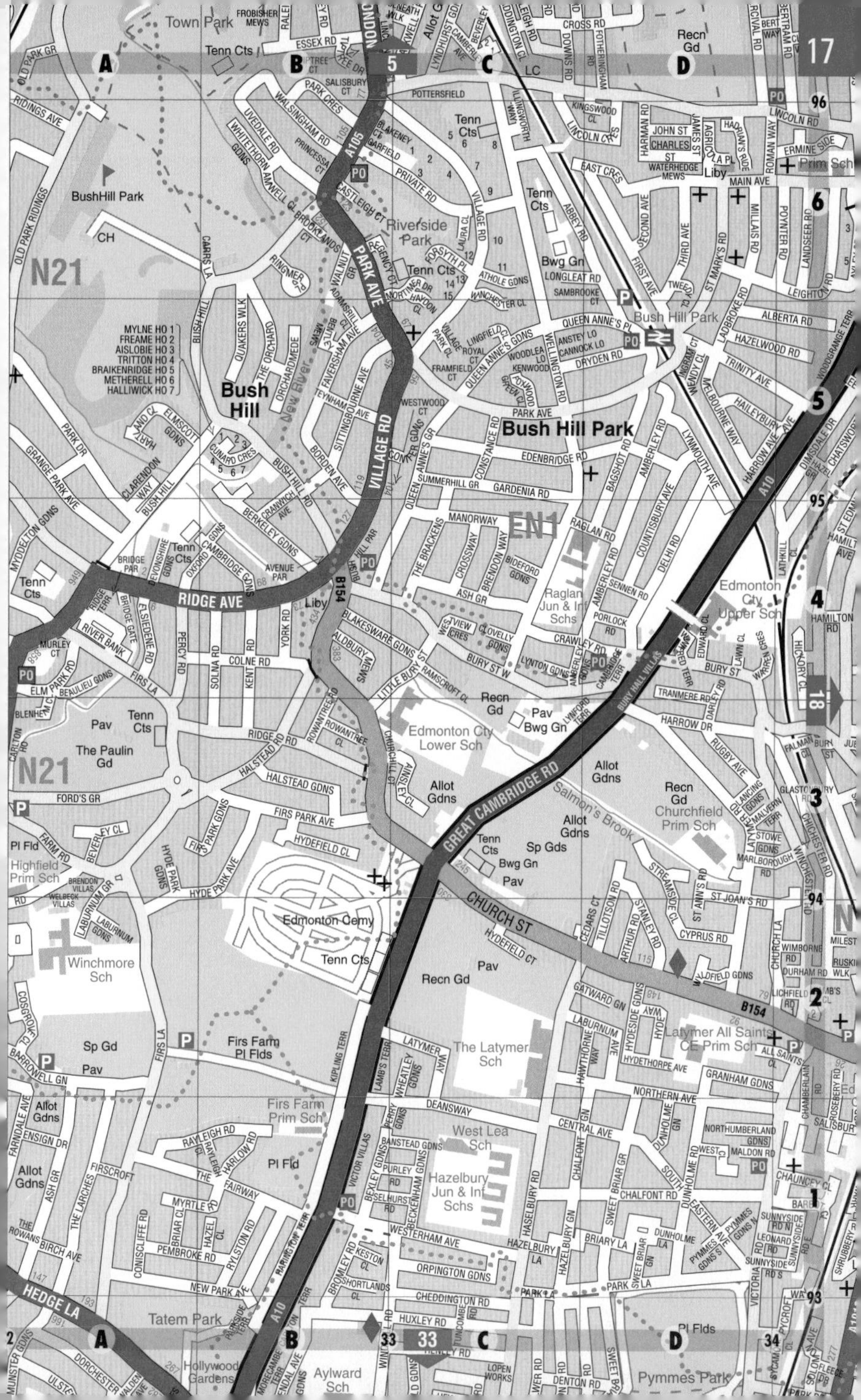

Town Park
FROBISHER MEWS
ESSEX RD
Tenn Cts
A
B
C
D
5
LC
Recn Gd
CROSS RD
DOWNS RD
FOTHERINGHAM
OLD PARK GR
RIDINGS AVE
OLD PARK RIDINGS
BushHill Park
CH
N21
SALISBURY CT
PARK CRES
POTTERSFIELD
WALSINGHAM RD
UVEDALE RD
WHITETHORN GDNS
BLAKENEY CT
GARFIELD
PRINCESSA CT
A105
PRIVATE RD
PO
ANNWELL CL
CASTLEIGH CT
BROOKLANDS CT
Riverside Park
REGENCY CT
PARK AVE
FORSYTH PL
Tenn Cts
VILLAGE RD
LAURA CL
ILLINGWORTH WAY
KINGSWOOD CL
LINCOLN CRES
JOHN ST
CHARLES ST
HARMAN RD
JAMES ST
AGRICOLA PL
HADRIAN'S RIDE
ROMAN WAY
LINCOLN RD
ERMINE SIDE
Prim Sch
96
EAST CRES
WATERHEDGE MEWS
Liby
MAIN AVE
6
SECOND AVE
FIRST AVE
THIRD AVE
ST MARK'S RD
MILLAIS RD
POYNTER RD
LANDSEER RD
LEIGHTON RD
ABBEY RD
Bwg Gn
LONGLEAT RD
SAMBROOKE CT
ATHOLE GDNS
WINCHESTER CL
MORTIMER DR
HAYDON CL
CARRS LA
RINGMER PL
WALNUT GR
ADAMSRILL CL
BENTLEY MEWS
FAVERSHAM AVE
LINGFIELD CL
VILLAGE PARK CL
ROYAL CT
FRAMFIELD CT
QUEEN ANNE'S GDNS
WOODLEA LO
KENWOOD
FOXWOOD GREEN CL
ANSTEY LO
CANNOCK LO
DRYDEN RD
WELLINGTON RD
QUEEN ANNE'S PL
Bush Hill Park
TWEEDY CL
LADBROKE RD
ALBERTA RD
HAZELWOOD RD
TRINITY AVE
HAILEYBURY AVE
WOODGRANGE TERR
5
INGRAM CT
WENDY CL
MELBOURNE WAY
LYNMOUTH AVE
HARROW AVE
A10
DIMSDALE DR
CHATSWORTH
95
BUSH HILL
QUAKERS WLK
THE ORCHARD
ORCHARDMEDE
New River
MYLNE HO 1
FREAME HO 2
AISLOBIE HO 3
TRITTON HO 4
BRAIKENRIDGE HO 5
METHERELL HO 6
HALLIWICK HO 7
Bush Hill
TEYNHAM AVE
SITTINGBOURNE AVE
WESTWOOD CT
PARK AVE
Bush Hill Park
EDENBRIDGE RD
AMBERLEY RD
BAGSHOT RD
HARTLAND CL
ELMSCOTT GDNS
CUNARD CRES
PARK DR
GRANGE PARK AVE
CLARENDON WAY
BUSH HILL
BUSH HILL RD
BORDEN AVE
VILLAGE RD
CONIFER GDNS
QUEEN ANNE'S GR
CONSTANCE RD
SUMMERHILL GR
GARDENIA RD
CRANWICH AVE
BERKELEY GDNS
MYDDELTON GDNS
BUSH HILL PAR
MANORWAY
THE BRACKENS
CROSSWAY
BRENDON WAY
EN1
RAGLAN RD
COUNTISBURY AVE
DELHI RD
BIDEFORD GDNS
Tenn Cts
Tenn Cts
BRIDGE PAR
DEVONSHIRE GDNS
OXFORD GDNS
CAMBRIDGE GDNS
AVENUE PAR
PO
B154
ASH GR
Raglan Jun & Inf Schs
SENNEN RD
Edmonton City Upper Sch
HAMILTON RD
4
RIDGE AVE
Liby
RIDGE TERR
BRIDGE GATE
ELSIEDENE RD
PERCY RD
YORK RD
BLAKESWARE GDNS
WESTVIEW CRES
CLOVELLY GDNS
PORLOCK RD
CRAWLEY RD
MURLEY CT
RIVER BANK
SOLNA RD
KENT RD
COLNE RD
ALDBURY MEWS
BURY ST W
LYNTON GDNS
CAMBRIDGE TERR
BURY HALL VILLAS
EDWARD CL
BURY ST
LAWN CL
WARREN CRES
HICKORY CL
ELM PARK RD
BEAULIEU GDNS
FIRS LA
LITTLE BURY ST
RAMSCROFT CL
Recn Gd
Pav
Bwg Gn
LYNFORD TERR
TRANMERE RD
DARLEY RD
18
BLENHEIM CL
CARLTON RD
Pav
Tenn Cts
The Paulin Gd
ROWANTREE RD
ROWANTREE CL
Edmonton City Lower Sch
HARROW DR
FALMAN CL
BURY ST
RUGBY AVE
N21
RIDGE RD
HALSTEAD RD
HALSTEAD GDNS
CHURCHILL CT
AINSLEY CL
Allot Gdns
GREAT CAMBRIDGE RD
Allot Gdns
Recn Gd
Churchfield Prim Sch
GLASTONBURY
3
FORD'S GR
P
FIRS PARK GDNS
FIRS PARK AVE
Salmon's Brook
Allot Gdns
LANCING GDNS
LATYMER RD
MALVERN TERR
STOWE GDNS
Pl Fld
FARM RD
BEVERLEY CL
HYDEFIELD CL
Tenn Cts
Sp Gds
Bwg Gn
MARLBOROUGH RD
WINCHESTER RD
CHICHESTER RD
Highfield Prim Sch
BRENDON VILLAS
WELBECK VILLAS
LABURNUM GR
HYDE PARK GDNS
HYDE PARK AVE
Pav
STREAMSIDE CL
ST ANN'S RD
ST JOAN'S RD
94
LABURNUM GDNS
Edmonton Cemy
CHURCH ST
CEDARS CT
TILLOTSON RD
ARTHUR RD
STANLEY RD
CYPRUS RD
CHURCH LA
MILEST
Winchmore Sch
HYDEFIELD CT
Tenn Cts
Pav
Recn Gd
WILDFIELD GDNS
WIMBORNE RD
DURHAM RD
RUSKIN WLK
GATWARD GN
LICHFIELD RD
LAMB'S CL
2
B154
COSGROVE CL
FIRS LA
P
Firs Farm Pl Flds
KIPLING TERR
LATYMER GDNS
LAMB'S TERR
WHEATLEY GDNS
The Latymer Sch
LABURNUM AVE
HAWTHORNE WAY
HYDESIDE GDNS
HYDE WAY
Latymer All Saints CE Prim Sch
ALL SAINTS CL
P
Sp Gd
BARROWELL GN
P
Pav
HYDETHORPE AVE
GRANHAM GDNS
CHAMBERLAIN
ROSEBERY RD
SALISBURY
FARNDALE AVE
Allot Gdns
ENSIGN DR
Firs Farm Prim Sch
DEANSWAY
PERRY GDNS
West Lea Sch
NORTHERN AVE
CENTRAL AVE
DUNHOLME GN
NORTHUMBERLAND GDNS
WEST CL
MALDON RD
PO
Allot Gdns
ASH GR
FIRSCROFT
RAYLEIGH RD
RAYLEIGH CL
HARLOW RD
Pl Fld
VICTOR VILLAS
BANSTEAD GDNS
BEXLEY GDNS
PURLEY RD
SELHURST RD
BECKENHAM GDNS
Hazelbury Jun & Inf Schs
HASELBURY RD
CHALFONT GN
SWEET BRIAR GR
DUNHOLME RD
SOUTH EASTERN AVE
CHALFONT RD
CHAUNCEY CL
BARB
1
THE LARCHES
THE FAIRWAY
MYRTLE RD
BRIAR CL
HAZEL CL
RYLSTON RD
CONISCLIFFE RD
PEMBROKE RD
PO
THE ROWANS
BIRCH AVE
WESTERHAM AVE
HAZELBURY LA
HAZELBURY GN
SWEET BRIAR GN
DUNHOLME LA
PYMMES GDNS N
PYMMES GDNS S
SUNNYSIDE RD N
LEONARD RD
SUNNYSIDE RD E
SUNNYSIDE RD S
VICTORIA RD
SHRUBBERY RD
BROMLEY RD
KESTON CL
ORPINGTON GDNS
SHORTLANDS CL
NEW PARK AVE
PARK LA
PARK LA
WAY
93
HEDGE LA
Tatem Park
PARKSIDE TERR
BARRINGTON TERR
A10
CHEDDINGTON RD
HUXLEY RD
TUNCOMBE RD
PYCROFT
Pl Flds
A
B
C
D
33
33
34
HENLEY RD
MUNSTER GDNS
DORCHESTER
ULSTER
Hollywood Gardens
MORECAMBE TERR
Aylward Sch
LOPEN WORKS
DENTON RD
SWEET BR
Pymmes Park
SOLONA
FLEECE DR

SOUTHBURY RD
Superstores
Southbury
Depot
Superstore
HERTFORD RD HIGH ST
NAGS HEAD
KAYS CT
DURANTS RD
St Mary's RC Prim Sch
A110
A10
A1010
A1055
B137
B154
6
A
B
C
D
DE MANDEVILLE GATE
MARTINBRIDGE TRAD EST
HAZLEMERE BSNS CTR
LINCOLN WAY
EMILIA CL
KINGSWAY
QUEENSWAY
PEERGLOW EST
Middlesex Univ
Liby
LOCKHART CL
DOVE CT
LORAINE CT
COLLEGE CT
GARFIELD RD
CARTONS CL
SWAN HO
EAGLE CL
WALTERS RD
CLYDESDALE
SEDCOTE RD
Ponders End
Recn Gd
Tenn Cts
STONEHORSE RD
SOUTH PL
CROMWELL CT
SCOTLAND GREEN RD
FREEMANTLE AVE
CURZON AVE
PERCY GDNS
KEATS CL
TENNYSON CL
Alma Sch
NAPIER RD
CURLEW HO
MERLIN HO
SOUTH ST
WADSWORTH CL
NAYLOR GR
St Matthew's CE Sch
LINCOLN RD
ALLENS RD
CLARENCE RD
RUTLAND CT
ORCHARD RD
NORTHFIELD RD
SOUTHFIELD RD
CHURCH RD
SUTHERLAND RD
NELSON RD
FALCON RD
FALCON CRES
GARDINER CL
ROBBINS HALL
CORMORANT HO
SILVER BIRCH CT
RYDAL WAY
KENNEDY AVE
WOODCOTE CL
Allot Gdns
REDBURN TRAD EST
WOODALL RD
DERBY RD
OSPREY MEWS
CONCORD RD
SUFFOLK RD
OXFORD RD
NORFOLK RD
GREAT CAMBRIDGE IND EST
1 BURLEIGH HO
2 BONINGTON HO
3 ROMNEY HO
4 CONSTABLE HO
5 REYNOLDS HO
6 GAINSBOROUGH HO
7 HOGARTH HO
BERTRAM RD
BERTRAM WAY
CLIVE RD
CLIVE WAY
SOUTHBURY AVE
LINCOLN RD
HADRIAN'S RIDE
ROMAN WAY
ERMINE SIDE
Prim Sch
AGRICOLA PL
MAIN AVE
MILLAIS RD
POYNTER RD
LANDSEER RD
AYLEY CROFT
LEIGHTON RD
ST MARK'S RD
PROGRESS WAY
Park
LADBROKE RD
ALBERTA RD
HAZELWOOD RD
TRINITY AVE
MELBOURNE WAY
HAILEYBURY AVE
HARROW AVE
WOODGRANGE TERR
ORCHARD TERR
WOODGRANGE AVE
WOODGRANGE GDNS
WOODSTOCK CRES
WOODPECKER CL
MAYFIELD CRES
CHESTER GDNS
ELMCROFT AVE
HILL RISE
GALLIARD CL
BEECH CL
MANSFIELD CL
CHATSWORTH DR
DIMSDALE DR
HAZEL GR
GALLIARD RD
SAVERNAKE RD
OAKLANDS AVE
ROSSDALE DR
BOUNDARY RD
SANDHURST RD
CLIFFORD RD
HERTFORD RD
Pl Fld
BEATRICE RD
DARTFORD AVE
NOTTINGHAM RD
CHELSFIELD GN
CHELSFIELD AVE
Recn Gd
Schs
ST EDMUNDS RD
Galliard Prim Sch
Tenn Cts
BEDFORD RD
HADLEIGH RD
LINGFIELD GDNS
KING EDWARD'S RD
ALEXANDRA RD
DAWSON TERR
CUCKOO HALL LA
SCARBOROUGH RD
ST ALPHEGE RD
CAUSEYWARE RD
TURIN RD
ST MICHAELS AVE
NIGHTINGALE RD
CORAN CL
WINTON CL
SHIRLEY GR
CHARLTON RD
HAMILTON AVE
LATHKILL CL
Edmonton City Upper Sch
Pav
Bwg Gn
Jubilee Park
CORNISH CT
BRIDLINGTON RD
RIPON RD
TRAMWAY AVE
ACWORTH CL
ELIZABETH RIDE
GRANARY CL
ST ANDREWS RD
EASTBROOK AVE
WELLSTEAD AVE
WARREN CL
CAMBOURNE AVE
HAMILTON RD
HICKORY CL
Houndsfield Prim Sch
DONCASTER RD
CLEVELAND RD
TUDOR RD
1 NATHAN CT
2 TOBY CT
3 HUTTON CT
Sch
EDWARD CL
LAWN CL
WARREN CRES
BURY ST
Pavs
Recn Gd
Stadium
HOUNDSFIELD RD
NORTH RD
BARRIE HO
ST JOSEPH'S RD
17
RUGBY AVE
FALMAN CL
BURY ST
JUBILEE CRES
RICHMOND CRES
HENDERSON RD
COLVILLE RD
WATER LA
DENNY RD
FOREST RD
EMSWORTH CL
ST MARY'S RD
PENFOLD RD
LOWDEN RD
SUTHERLAND RD
CRESCENT RD
SOUTH RD
BELMONT AVE
WOODLANDS RD
GLASTONBURY RD
GARFIELD RD
FINDON RD
CAROE CT
GROSVENOR RD
ST PETER'S RD
BRIERLEY AVE
DEVONSHIRE RD
CHAFFINCH CL
1 VERITY CT
2 HILARY CT
3 WREN CL
N9
LATYMER GDNS
MALVERN TERR
STOWE GDNS
MARLBOROUGH RD
CHICHESTER RD
SALMONS RD
JUNCTION RD
KENWOOD RD
BEAMISH RD
MILLBROOK RD
ROSEMARY AVE
KINGSMEAD
ELSTREE GDNS
WESTMINSTER RD
CHESTER RD
CUMBERLAND HO
ELDON RD
CONISTON GDNS
GRAHAM HO
GOODWIN HO
MARSH SIDE CL
WARLEY RD
HUNTINGDON RD
BUNTING CL
MARTIN CL
DUNNOCK CL
GOODWIN RD
DOMINION BSNS PK
PICKETT'S LOCK LA
ST ANN'S RD
WINCHESTER RD
CROYLAND RD
WRAMPLING PL
DICKENSON CL
CYPRUS RD
HENDON RD
CHURCH LA
WIMBORNE RD
DURHAM RD
MILESTONE CL
RUSKIN WLK
KINGSTON RD
BALHAM RD
CHISWICK RD
BOUNCES LA
BOUNCES RD
OXFORD RD
GORDON RD
CORNWALLIS RD
CORNWALLIS GR
CORNWALLIS AVE
BATH RD
WALLBROOK HO
WHITE HO
NASH RD
CLAVERINGS IND EST
NORTH WAY
CENTRE WAY
SOUTH WAY
DOVER RD
PENTLAND CL
BUXTON CL
WILDFIELD GDNS
LICHFIELD RD
LAMB'S CL
LION RD
ACTON CL
LACEY CL
NEWDALES CL
SAWYER CL
MONMOUTH RD
HENNESSY RD
STRIMON CL
LENA CRES
TIGRIS CL
HUDSON WAY
Sewage Works
Latymer All Saints CE Prim Sch
ALL SAINTS CL
THE GREEN
THE BROADWAY
NORTH SQ
THE NORTH MALL
Edmonton Green Sh Ctr
MARSDEN RD
WESTOE RD
HARTON RD
SEYMOUR RD
LOGAN RD
RANWORTH RD
EXETER RD
TOWN RD
DENSWORTH GR
ELLEN CT
NILE DR
VOLTA
PRESPA
GRANHAM GDNS
CHAMBERLAIN
ROSEBERY RD
Edmonton Green
ST JAMES RD
QUEEN'S RD
NELSON RD
SUMMER
SKILLE CL
WELLINGTON AVE
WESTBOURNE
EASTBOURNIA AVE
BRETT CT
ST MALO AVE
BOONE CT
GRANVILLE AVE
CHAD CRES
KARIBA CL
BADMA
MERIDIAN WAY
ARDRA RD
NORTHUMBERLAND GDNS
WEST
MALDON RD
SALISBURY
BRIDGE
THE MARKET SQ
THE SOUTH MALL
MENON DR
COLTHURST DR
ST GEORGE
KNIGHT'S LA
PLEVNA RD
EUSDON CL
HAYNES DR
Allot Gdns
BARROWFIELD CL
DUNHOLME RD
CHAUNCEY CL
BARBOT CL
PEEL CL
L Ctr
CLARKE MEWS
Lower Edmonton
EASTERN RD
PYMMES GDNS
SUNNYSIDE RD N
LEONARD RD
SUNNYSIDE RD S
VICTORIA RD
OSMAN RD
SHRUBBERY RD
BEACONSFIELD RD
FELIXSTOWE RD
FRASER RD
BROOKFIELD RD
Federation Cemy
DODSLEY PL
MONTAGU RD
Recn Gd
Liby
PEGAMOID RD
PRIDANE RD
BARNES RD
PRINCES RD
THORNTON RD
PYCROFT WAY
SEBASTOPOL RD
Fleecefield Prim Sch
BROOK CRES
Pl Flds
SYCAMORE
SOLOMON AVE
FLEECE
HOUSE MEWS
BRETTENHAM RD
BROOKSIDE RD
JEREMY'S GN
MONTAGU IND EST
34
35
93
94
95
96
1
2
3
4
5
6

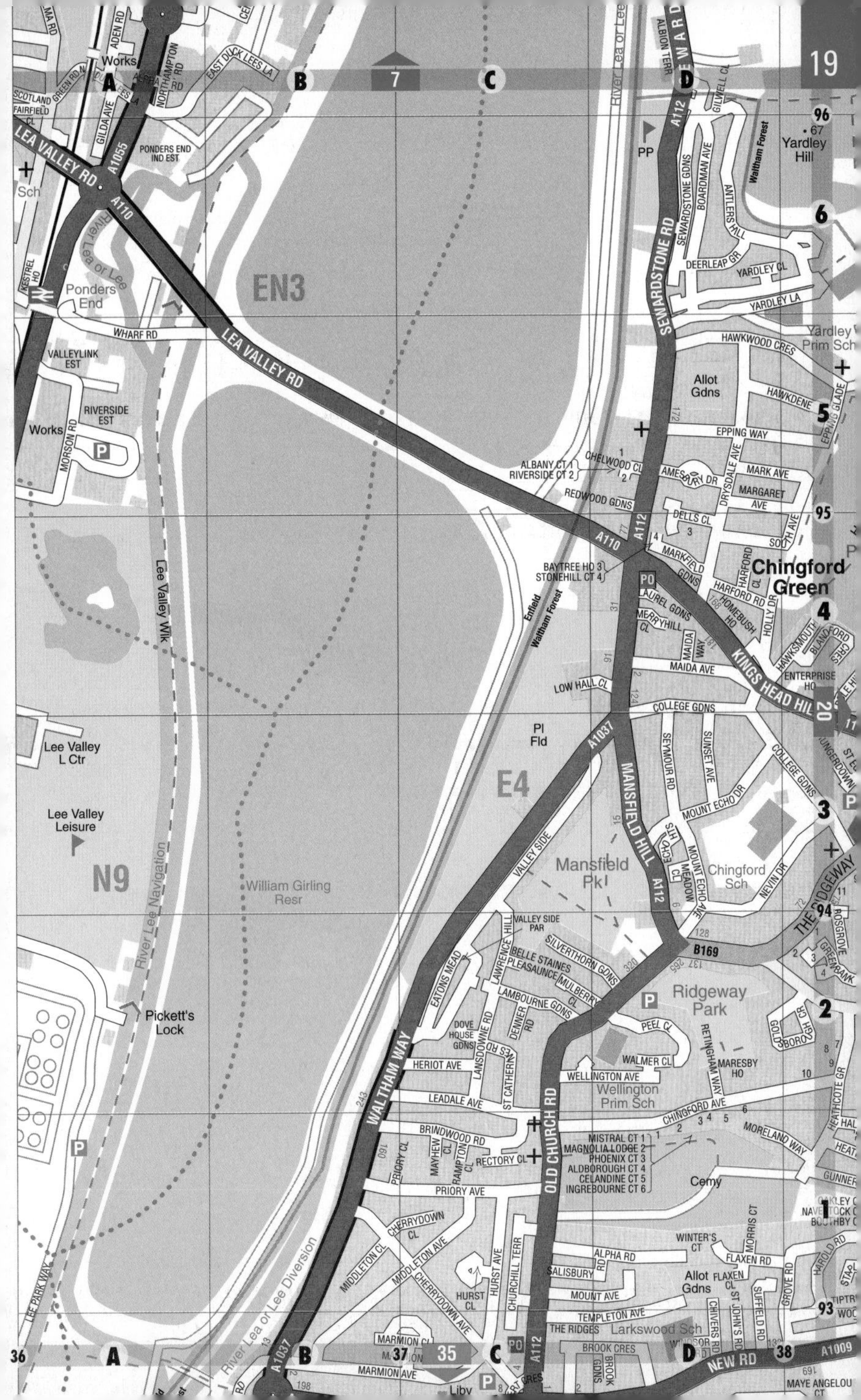
EN3
LEA VALLEY RD
A1055
A110
Ponders End
PONDERS END IND EST
WHARF RD
VALLEYLINK EST
RIVERSIDE EST
MORSON RD
Works
Sch
Lee Valley Wlk
River Lea or Lee
SEWARDSTONE RD
A112
SEWARDSTONE GDNS
BOARDMAN AVE
ANTLERS HILL
DEERLEAP GR
YARDLEY CL
YARDLEY LA
Yardley Hill
Yardley Prim Sch
Waltham Forest
HAWKWOOD CRES
HAWKDENE
EPPING WAY
EPPING GLADE
Allot Gdns
ALBANY CT 1
RIVERSIDE CT 2
CHELWOOD CL
AMESBURY DR
DRYSDALE AVE
MARK AVE
MARGARET AVE
SOUTH AVE
REDWOOD GDNS
DELLS CL
MARKFIELD GDNS
BAYTREE HO 3
STONEHILL CT 4
Chingford Green
HARFORD RD
HOMEBUSH HO
HOLLY DR
LAUREL GDNS
MERRYHILL CL
MAIDA WAY
MAIDA AVE
KINGS HEAD HILL
HAWKSMOUTH
BLANDFORD CRES
ENTERPRISE HO
LOW HALL CL
COLLEGE GDNS
SEYMOUR RD
SUNSET AVE
MOUNT ECHO DR
Enfield
Pl Fld
E4
A1037
MANSFIELD HILL
Mansfield Pk
VALLEY SIDE
ECHO HTS
MOUNT ECHO AVE
MEADOW CL
Chingford Sch
NEVIN DR
THE RIDGEWAY
B169
VALLEY SIDE PAR
SILVERTHORN GDNS
BELLE STAINES PLEASAUNCE
MULBERRY CL
LAMBOURNE GDNS
EATONS MEAD
LAWRENCE HILL
DENNER RD
DOVE HOUSE GDNS
LANSDOWNE RD
ST CATHERINES RD
Ridgeway Park
PEEL CL
RETINGHAM WAY
MARESBY HO
WALMER CL
WELLINGTON AVE
Wellington Prim Sch
HERIOT AVE
LEADALE AVE
WALTHAM WAY
CHINGFORD AVE
MORELAND WAY
BRINDWOOD RD
MAYHEW CL
RAMPTON CL
RECTORY CL
PRIORY CL
MISTRAL CT 1
MAGNOLIA LODGE 2
PHOENIX CT 3
ALDBOROUGH CT 4
CELANDINE CT 5
INGREBOURNE CT 6
OLD CHURCH RD
PRIORY AVE
Cemy
HEATHCOTE GR
GOLDSBOROUGH CR
CHERRYDOWN CL
MIDDLETON CL
MIDDLETON AVE
CHERRYDOWN AVE
HURST AVE
HURST CL
CHURCHILL TERR
ALPHA RD
SALISBURY RD
WINTER'S CT
MORRIS CT
FLAXEN RD
FLAXEN CL
Allot Gdns
MOUNT AVE
TEMPLETON AVE
THE RIDGES
Larkswood Sch
CHIVERS RD
ST JOHN'S RD
SUFFIELD RD
GROVE RD
HAROLD RD
BROOK CRES
BROOK GDNS
WINDSOR RD
NEW RD
A1009
MARMION CL
MARMION AVE
Lee Valley L Ctr
Lee Valley Leisure
N9
River Lee Navigation
William Girling Resr
Pickett's Lock
LEE PARK WAY
River Lea or Lee Diversion
Liby
MAYE ANGELOU
Ponders End

7
20
35

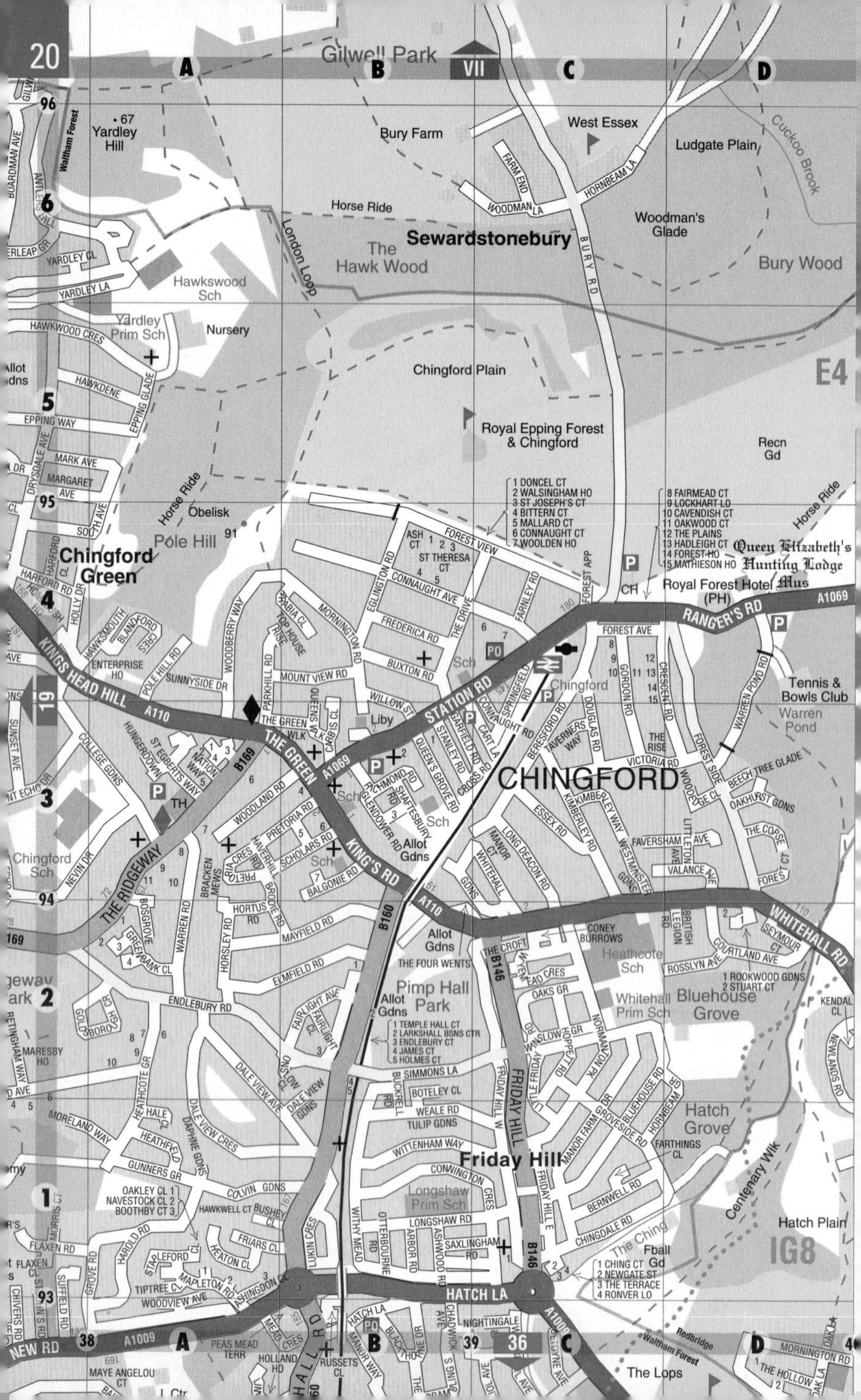
Gilwell Park
VII
A
B
C
D
Yardley Hill
Waltham Forest
Bury Farm
West Essex
Ludgate Plain
Cuckoo Brook
FARM END
HORNBEAM LA
WOODMAN LA
Horse Ride
Woodman's Glade
Sewardstonebury
London Loop
The Hawk Wood
BURY RD
Bury Wood
YARDLEY CL
YARDLEY LA
Hawkswood Sch
Yardley Prim Sch
Nursery
HAWKWOOD CRES
Chingford Plain
E4
HAWKDENE
EPPING GLADE
EPPING WAY
Royal Epping Forest & Chingford
Recn Gd
DRYSDALE AVE
MARK AVE
MARGARET AVE
SOUTH AVE
Horse Ride
Obelisk
Pole Hill
Chingford Green
HARFORD RD
HOLLY DR
1 DONCEL CT
2 WALSINGHAM HO
3 ST JOSEPH'S CT
4 BITTERN CT
5 MALLARD CT
6 CONNAUGHT CT
7 WOOLDEN HO
8 FAIRMEAD CT
9 LOCKHART LO
10 CAVENDISH CT
11 OAKWOOD CT
12 THE PLAINS
13 HADLEIGH CT
14 FOREST HO
15 MATHIESON HO
Queen Elizabeth's Hunting Lodge Mus
Royal Forest Hotel (PH)
FOREST VIEW
ASH CT
ST THERESA CT
CONNAUGHT AVE
EGLINTON RD
FARNLEY RD
FOREST APP
RANGER'S RD
A1069
FOREST AVE
KINGS HEAD HILL
A110
ENTERPRISE HO
HAWKSMOUTH
BLANDFORD CRES
POLE HILL RD
SUNNYSIDE DR
WOODBERRY WAY
ARABIA CL
TOP HOUSE RISE
MORNINGTON RD
FREDERICA RD
THE DRIVE
BUXTON RD
MOUNT VIEW RD
PARKHILL RD
WILLOW ST
STATION RD
Sch
PO
Chingford
SPRINGFIELD RD
GORDON RD
CRESCENT RD
DOUGLAS RD
WARREN POND RD
Tennis & Bowls Club
Warren Pond
19
SUNSET AVE
COLLEGE GDNS
HUNGERDOWN
ST EGBERTS WAY
NATION WAY
B169
THE GREEN
THE GREEN WLK
QUEENS WLK
CARBIS CL
Liby
Sch
STANLEY RD
GARFIELD RD
CART LA
CONNAUGHT RD
BERESFORD RD
TAVERNERS WAY
THE RISE
FOREST SIDE
VICTORIA RD
CHINGFORD
BEECH TREE GLADE
OAKHURST GDNS
THE COPSE
FOREST CT
WOODEDGE CL
TH
WOODLAND RD
RICHMOND RD
SHAFTESBURY RD
GLENDOWER RD
QUEEN'S GROVE RD
CROSS RD
ESSEX RD
KIMBERLEY RD
KIMBERLEY WAY
FAVERSHAM AVE
LITTLETON AVE
VALANCE AVE
WESTMINSTER GDNS
Chingford Sch
NEVIN DR
THE RIDGEWAY
PRETORIA RD
SCHOLARS RD
BALGONIE RD
HAVERHILL RD
BRODIE RD
PRETORIA CRES
BRACKEN MEWS
Allot Gdns
KING'S RD
MANOR CT
WHITEHALL GDNS
LONG DEACON RD
WHITEHALL RD
BRITISH LEGION RD
SEYMOUR CT
BOSGROVE
GREENBANK CL
WARREN RD
HORSLEY RD
HORTUS RD
MAYFIELD RD
B160
Allot Gdns
THE CROFT
CONEY BURROWS
Heathcote Sch
WYEMEAD CRES
OAKS GR
ROSSLYN AVE
COURTLAND AVE
1 ROOKWOOD GDNS
2 STUART CT
KENDAL CL
ELMFIELD RD
THE FOUR WENTS
Pimp Hall Park
B146
Whitehall Prim Sch
Bluehouse Grove
ENDLEBURY RD
FAIRLIGHT AVE
FAIRLIGHT CL
Allot Gdns
1 TEMPLE HALL CT
2 LARKSHALL BSNS CTR
3 ENDLEBURY CT
4 JAMES CT
5 HOLMES CT
WINSLOW GR
HOPPETT RD
NORMANTON PK
NEWLANDS RD
MARESBY HO
HEATHCOTE GR
DALE VIEW AVE
DALE VIEW GDNS
DALE VIEW CRES
SIMMONS LA
BUCKRELL RD
BOTELEY CL
WEALE RD
TULIP GDNS
FRIDAY HILL
FRIDAY HILL W
LITTLE FRIDAY RD
BLUEHOUSE RD
HORNBEAM RD
GROVESIDE RD
MANOR FARM DR
Hatch Grove
FARTHINGS CL
MORELAND WAY
HALE CL
HEATHFIELD
DAPHNE GDNS
WITTENHAM WAY
Friday Hill
CONNINGTON CRES
GUNNERS GR
COLVIN GDNS
Longshaw Prim Sch
BERNWELL RD
Centenary Wlk
OAKLEY CL 1
NAVESTOCK CL 2
BOOTHBY CT 3
HAWKWELL CT
BUSHEY CL
LONGSHAW RD
CHINGDALE RD
Hatch Plain
FRIARS CL
HEATON CL
WITHY MEAD
OTTERBOURNE RD
ARBOR RD
ASHWOOD RD
SAXLINGHAM RD
The Ching
FRIDAY HILL E
Fball Gd
IG8
FLAXEN RD
FLAXEN CL
GROVE RD
HAROLD RD
STAPLEFORD CL
MAPLETON RD
TIPTREE CL
ASHINGDON CL
WOODVIEW AVE
MORRIS CT
1 CHING CT
2 NEWGATE ST
3 THE TERRACE
4 RONVER LO
HATCH LA
CHIVERS RD
SUFFIELD RD
NEW RD
38
A1009
PEAS MEAD TERR
HOLLAND HO
MEAD CRES
HALL RD
RUSSETS CL
MANOR WAY
NIGHTINGALE CL
CHADWICK AVE
39
36
A1009
Redbridge
Waltham Forest
The Lops
MORNINGTON RD
THE HOLLOW
MAYE ANGELOU CT

A104 Epping (B1393), M25 (A121)
VII
A
B
C
D
A121 Loughton, M11 (A1168)
Long Hills
Centenary Wlk
Epping Forest
Palmer's Bridge
Mon
The Warren
Warren Hill
IG10
69 Warren Hill
Magpie Hill
Connaught Water
A1069
Ranger's Rd
Epping New Rd
A104
High Rd
A121
Manor Rd
Holmehurst
The Warren Wood (PH)
Trinity Terr
Powell's Forest
Oak Hall
The Ching
Waltham Forest
Epping Forest
Green Ride
LOUGHTON
Oaklands Sch
The Willows
Fair Meadside
Pollards Cl
Albion Hill
Albion Pk
High View Cl
Nursery Rd
Longfield
Westfield
Northfield
Little Dragons
High Silver
Connaught Ave
Ollard's Gr
Southernhay
Upper Pk
Cloverleys
Park Hill
High Gables
Hazelwood
Salcombe Pk
Grange Ct
Lower Park Rd
Waffenton Rise
Alghers Mead
Algers Rd
Algers Cl
Crescent View
The Crescent
Newham Ho
Newnham Cl
Summerfield Rd
Spring Gr
The Avenue
Hillcrest Rd
Station Rd
Old Station Rd
Pot Cotts
Tewkesb
The Sidings 1
Lukinstone Cl 2
Seymour Cl 3
Avenue Gate
North Farm
Swan La
View
Treetops
Kings Pl
Harvest La
Richmond Pk
Fallow Fields
The Chase
Mews
Woodcote
The Fountains
Regent's Pl
Pondfield End
The Stables
Tylers Cl
Felstead Rd
Kirby Cl
Thaxted Rd
Blackmore Rd
Guy's Retreat
The Drive
North End
Powell Rd
Roebuck La
Little Pluckett's Way
Ardmore La
Ardmore Pl
Hawsted
Greenhill
Luctons Ave
Sch
Queensbury
IG9
St John's CE Prim Sch
Forest Side
Waikato Lo
Ormonde Rise
Gladstone Rd
St John's Ct
Russell Rd
Amberley Rd
The Meadway
Stradbroke Gr
The Rise
Roding View
Loughton Way
River Rd
Rous Rd
Dene Rd
Hurst Rd
Fernside
Heron Cl
Starling Cl
Albany View
Elizabeth Ct
Fernbank
Church Rd
The Cedars
Whitehall Plain
Brook Rd
Chequers
Trent Rd
Hill's Rd
Osborne Rd
Westbury Rd
Scotland Rd
1 Rayburne Ct
2 The Laurels
3 Moblin Lo
4 Silvers
5 Makinen Ho
Palace Gdns
Dalefield
Boleyn Ct
St James Gate
The Green
Glenmead
Devon Cl
B170
Palmerston Rd
Roding La
Fairlands Ave
Forest Hts
Park Side
Westbury La
The Daiglen Sch
Langfords
Victoria Rd
Buckhurst Hill
Yew Cl
Beatrice Ct
Alfred Rd
Albert Terr
The Windsors
Tilney Dr 1
Tilney Rd 2
Tilney Ct 3
Hurstcombe 4
Stag La
Andrews Cl
Liby
Queen's Rd
Salisbury Gdns
King's Ave
Tuttlebee La
Oakland Pl
The Birkbeck
Chandos Cl
Beech Ave
Duchess Gr
The Drummonds
Wimborne Cl
Woodside
Princes Way
Princes Rd
Monarch Pl
Kings Pl
George Ct
Briar Cl
Lower Queen's Rd
Albert Rd
Mountbatten Ct
Elgar Cl
Cedar Cl
Allot Gdns
Buck City
Hempstead
Brancepeth Gdns
Whitehall La
Bancroft Ave
Almonds Ave
Birkbeck Gdns
Bentley Way
Redwood Cl
Lingrove Gdns
Beech La
Buckhurst Hill Ho
Knighton La
Holly House
Knighton Gn
High Road Buckhurst Hill
Lord's Bushes
Buckhurst Hill
Elm Cl
Lime Cl
Chestnut Cl
Cascade Rd
Cascade Cl
Maple Cl
Oak Rise
Hornbeam Cl
Birch Cl
Willow Cl
Holly Cl
Hornbeam Ho
Hornbeam Rd
Chestnut Ave
Buckhurst Way
Bourne Ho
Squirrel's La
Sp Gd
Reeds Forest
1 Hepworth Ho
2 Whitehall Lo
Hawthorns
Bancrofts Sch
Woodland Cl
Woodland Way
IG8
The Dell Cl
The Dell
Knighton Wood
Monkham's La
Essex
Redbridge
Forest Edge
Broadfield Way
Forest Rd
Belgrave Terr
Chiltern Way
A110
Woodford
Burlington Pl
The Glade
Forest Cl
Woodford Wells
Farm Cl
Farm Way
Walnut Way
Roding Valley
Station Way
1 Station App
2 Station Par
Trinity RC High Sch (Upper)
Woodside Rd
Forest Way
41
37
42
93
94
95
96
Montrose Cl
Mews Pl
St Antony's Sch
Aldeburgh Pl
Knighton Dr
Denehurst Gdns
Dale Gdns
Wells Sch
Belmont Cl
Barclay Oval
Monkham's La
Beresford Dr
Cherry Tree Rise
Sewa

A
B
C
D
VI
Young Hangings
Little Furze Prim Sch
Pl Fld
OTLEY WAY
ST ANDREWS RD
South Oxhey
Old Hangings
The Plantation
Pond Wood
Oxhey Wood Schs
Oxhey Woods
WD19
A4125 Watford
A4125
SANDY LA
Tenn Cts
Eastbury
Northwood HQ
Allot Gdns
Pl Fld
NORTHWICK RD
PRESTWICK RD
B4542
THE WOODS
PRETTY CNR
OXHEY RIDGE CL
OXHEY DR
Oxhey wood
Greenfields JMI Sch
ST ANDREWS TERR
Nanscot Wood
Hertfordshire
Harrow
Hillingdon
Pinnerwood House
Pinnerwood Farm
SEVEN ACRES
HA6
WATFORD RD
SOUTH VIEW RD
PARK VIEW RD
SHEFTON RISE
POTTER STREET HILL
PINNER HILL
NORTHWOOD
Pinner Hill
POTTERS HEIGHTS CL
HILLSIDE RD
Pinnerwood Park
Hillside Schs
Northwood & Pinner Com
A4125 Rickmansworth
A404 Rickmansworth, M25
A404
ALBURY DR
MARSWORTH AV
SOUTHACRE WAY
Pinner Wood Schs
ATHOL GDNS
LYNDHURST AVE
Northwood Comp Sch
NORTHWOOD HILLS CIR
Liby
PINNER RD
RICKMANSWORTH RD
UXBRIDGE ROAD (PINNER)
Recn Gd
Pinner Green
Tenn Cts
Pav
Northwood Recn Gd
Northwood
Fball Gd
JOEL ST
B472
Northwood Hills
PO
PINNER GN
B466
Allot Gdns
Harlyn Prim Sch
HAZELDENE DR
Little Common
THE CHEQUERS
Recn
40
93
92
91
90
10
11
6
5
4
3
2
1

A4008 Watford
Mutton Wood
VI
A
B
C
D
Levels Wood
93
LOWER TAIL
UPPER TAIL
HANGAR RUDING
BELLINGDON
Carpenders Park Cemy
COMPTON PL
ST GEORGE'S DR
HARROW WAY
ROMILLY DR
OULTON WAY
B4542
A4008
Valley View Farm
Harrow Weald Common
Grimsdyke Hotel
6
ASS HOUSE LA
Weald Wood
Woodhall Sch
127
LITTLE OXHEY LA
75
Burnt Oak Farm
OLD REDDING
Grims Dyke
HA3
WD19
Hertfordshire
Harrow
Oxheylane Farm
Stony Wood
CHERRY HILLS
Pl Fld
Sir James Altham Pool
OXHEY LA
5
WHITE CRAIG CL
ROYSTON PARK RD
SADDLERS CL
92
NEWLAND CL
Saddlers Mead
HIGHBANKS RD
MEADWAY CL
SYLVIA AVE
Pav
WEALDWOOD GDNS
LANGWORTHY
DERWENT AVE
LYNDON AVE
Grimsdyke Fst & Mid Sch
WITNEY CL
KENNEDY CL
OAKLEIGH RD
ROYSTON GR
CLONARD WAY
SEQUOIA PK
ROWLANDS AVE
4
THE AVENUE
THORNTON GR
ASHCROFT
Tenn Cts
OAKMEADE
HAZELCROFT
PINEWOOD CL
PINEWOOD AVE
OXHEY LA
COLBURN AVE
HILLVIEW CL
HILLVIEW RD
THORNDYKE CT
WALPOLE CL
CEDAR DR
Athletics Tk
HA5
RANDOLPH CT
LIMETREE CT
FURHAM FIELD
THE LAWNS
A4008
24
Pl Fld
Hatch End
P
BRAESIDE CL
MILNE FIELD
RIDGEWAY CT
SHERINGTON AVE
WESTFIELD PK
1
ELM
HATCH
2
STAPLEFIELD CL
FERNDOWN CL
BROADMEAD CL
GRIMSDYKE RD
168
106
A410
3
WESSEX DR
LANGLAND DR
ALBURY DR
HALLAM GDNS
WOODRIDINGS CL
LEEWAY
292
OAKDENE CL
UXBRIDGE ROAD (HATCH END)
DOVE PK
COVE PK
BEETON CL
Hatch End
Superstore
BONIFACE WLK
UFFORD RD
UFFORD CL
BONIFACE GDNS
TILLOTSON RD
CHICHELEY GDNS
LANGTON
WHITTLESEA CL
LYTTON RD
ALTHAM RD
FELDEN CL
LONSDALE CL
THE BROADWAY
PO
GABLE CL
ILDEA CL
Pl Flds
Pav
WINSTON CT
Hatch End High Sch
91
WHITTLESEA RD
WHITTLESEA PATH
COURTENAY AVE
HELSTON CL
ANSELM RD
AVON MEWS
DEVONSHIRE RD
CORNWALL RD
PARK VIEW
TOWERS RD
474
A410
LITTLECOTE PL
WELLINGTON RD
WELLINGTON AVE
WOODRIDINGS AVE
MULLION CL
WEST CHANTRY
CHANTRY RD
HEADSTONE LA
Shaftesbury Sch
St Teresa's Sch
ST BA
Pl Fld
Rugby Gd
Sp Gd
Pav
A404
SEYMOUR CL
NUGENT'S PK
CAVAN PL
NUGENTS CT
ST THOMAS' DR
OLD HALL DR
OLD HALL CL
LITTLE ORCHARD CL
HOLLY GR
River Pinn
JUXON CL
THEOBALD CRES
BANCROFT GDNS
AUGUSTINE RD
SECKER CRES
Headstone Lane
PARKFIELD HO
2
WOODHALL AVE
BARROW POINT LA
BURHILL GR
BARROWDENE CL
OAKHILL AVE
LITTLE MOSS LA
BRIANTS CL
GEORGE V AVE
RANDON CL
BROADFIELDS
FERNLEIGH CT
BARMOR CL
PARKFIELD AVE
Pav
MOSS LA
MOSS CL
Pinner Park Farm
Model Rly
HA2
Tenn Cts
Bwg Gn
Sp Gd
TEMSFORD CL
1
PARKFIELD CRES
FULBECK WAY
VERWOOD RD
ALMOND WAY
WILLOW CT
OAKHILL AVE
PAINE'S LA
BARROW POINT AVE
EAST END WAY
BLOOMSBURY CL
Pav
Allot Gdns
Pl Fld
Pinner Park Schs
90
PINNER PK
AVENUE RD
Cemy
13
41
A404
MELBOURNE AVE
GREYSTOKE AVE
14
HOLMWOOD
LEIGHTON AVE
CHISWICK CT
MANOR PARK DR
Open Air Theatre
Nower Hill
FASTGLADE
AINSDALE
BIRKDALE AVE
PARKFIELD
Tenn Cts
P

A
B
8
C
D
93
92
91
90
6
5
4
3
2
1
Bentley Priory
Levels Wood
Harrow Weald Common
Grimsdyke Hotel
Weald Wood
The Kiln
HA7
Deer Park
Heriot's Wood
Priory House
OLD REDDING
A409
PH
Harrow Weald Common
Tenn Cts
BROOKSHILL DR
Lower Priory Farm
Tenn Cts
Stony Wood
Copse Farm
Hillside
Bentley Wood High Sch
FLECKER CL
BROOKSHILL AVE
CLAMP HILL
BRIDGES RD
MASEFIELD AVE
BINYON CRES
SITWELL GR
HA3
BROOKSHILL
BROCKHURST CL
NEWBOLT RD
Harrow Coll (Harrow Weald Campus)
Allot Gdns
HARROW WEALD PK
ACACIA CL
KIPLING PL
Tenn Cts
Harrow Weald Cemy
WARBURTON CL
LAKELAND CL
FORTNUMS ACRE
CAIRN WAY
CHARTLEY AVE
WOODLANDS DR
ROWAN CL
COPPICE CL
HOLME WAY
HEATHER WAY
TEMPLARS DR
WEST DR
The Bannister Sp Ctr
Athletics Tk
BELLFIELD AVE
PARK DR
Pl Fld
LAVENDER GDNS
ALL SAINTS MEWS
THE COPPINS
CHARLWOOD CL
WINSTON CL
WEST DRIVE GDNS
CARRINGTON SQ
GILLIAN HO
CHERRY HILL
RICHMOND GDNS
KINGSTON PL
LAWRIE CT
GORDON AVE
BERWICK CL
BIRCH PK
ROSS CL
23
UXBRIDGE RD (HARROW WEALD)
FONTWELL CL
KELVIN CRES
STAMFORD CL
ELMS RD
WILSMERE DR
WYNCHGATE
WHITE GATE GDNS
DROMEY GDNS
TREVOR CL
HILL HO AVE
DAVENTRY DR
A410
HUTTON WLK
HUTTON GDNS
ARTILLERY PL
MEPHAM GDNS
MEPHAM CRES
HUTTON LA
BELSIZE RD
BOXTREE RD
WOOD KYNASTON
KYNASTON CL
MONRO GDNS
COLLEGE CL
KENTON LA
DRUMMOND DR
BONIFACE WLK
CHICHELEY GDNS
CHICHELEY RD
LANGTON RD
Whittlesea Sch
SILVER CL
Tenn Cts
Recn Gd
Bwg Gn
Pav
BELMONT LO
TWICKENHAM GDNS
LORRAINE PK
Weald Fst & Mid Schs
LAUREL PK
ALTON AVE
TILLOTSON RD
WHITTLESEA CL
STAFFORD RD
COLMER PL
BLACKWELL CL
HIGH VIEW CT
TALLACK CL
WHISPERWOOD CL
ROBIN HOOD DR
KINGFISHER CL
WOODPECKER CL
Hatch End High Sch
BOXTREE LA
MARICAS AVE
ELM TERR
ALMA ROW
Tenn Cts
BARNVIEW LO
COLLEGE HILL RD
CHESTNUT DR
WEALD RISE
Cedars Fst & Mid Schs
WHITTLESEA RD
WHITTLESEA PATH
HITHERWELL DR
Harrow Weald
HIGH RD
COLLEGE RD
PARK CL
HOLLYBUSH CL
THE AVENUE
RADNOR CT
HEADSTONE LA
Shaftesbury Sch
St Teresa's Sch
COURTENAY AVE
GREER RD
WEIGHTON RD
PARK CRES
WILLOW CT
JUNIPER CT
COLLEGE AVE
CHANTRY
ST BARNABAS CT
LONG ELMES
MEAD CL
BASLOW CL
ASTALL CL
HAREWOOD CT
COLLEGE HILL RD
BROADLAWNS CT
JUXON CL
THEOBALD CRES
BANCROFT GDNS
CARMELITE CL
STOX MEAD
STANHOPE AVE
PARK CRES
PARK RISE
MAISON ALFORT
THE MEADOW WAY
JOHN LAMB CT
THE BYE WAY
CHURCH LA
ADDERLEY RD
CONNAUGHT RD
AUGUSTINE RD
CARMELITE WLK
WINDSOR RD
CLEWER CRES
DERBY AVE
SEFTON AVE
ENDERLEY RD
DURRANT CT
RISINGHOLME CL
THE GREEN WAY
DRYDEN RD
Headstone Lane
SECKER CRES
BANCROFT RD
HAMPDEN RD
WEALD LA
BARCHESTER RD
FARMSTEAD RD
ENDERLEY CL
NEWTON RD
RISINGHOLME RD
ANNETTE CL
GREEN WAY GDNS
THE CROSS WAY
THE MIDDLE WAY
BISHOPS KEN RD
Allot Gdns
FISHER RD
HARKETT CT
FERNLEIGH CT
BROADFIELDS
BARMOR CL
COURTENAY GDNS
CARMELITE RD
CARMELITE WAY
CYPRESS RD
BRINSLEY RD
BENGARTH DR
NICOLA CL
WHITEFRIARS DR
Coll
Sch
SPENCER RD
THE BROADWAY
HIBBERT RD
Belmont Mid Sch
PARKFIELD AVE
Pav
HA2
TEMSFORD CL
FULBECK WAY
PARKFIELD CRES
SARITA CL
LEIGHTON RD
TOORACK RD
HARROW
HARKETT CL
BYRON RD
WARHAM RD
Sp Gd
VERWOOD RD
HARROW VIEW
WICKHAM RD
MARTHORNE CRES
ATHELSTONE RD
WHITEFRIARS AVE
MINSTREL CT
HIGH ST
CLAREMONT RD
BRUCE RD
ALMOND WAY
WILLOW CT
PINNER PARK AVE
PINNER PARK GDNS
TUDOR GDNS
TUDOR RD
LYNN CL
WHITEFRIARS TRAD EST
Sch
LADYSMITH RD
DOLPHIN CT
MONTROSE RD
ABERDEEN RD
LORNE RD
LOCKET RD
BYRON RD
TALBOT
Pinner Park Schs
HOLMWOOD
BARRATT WAY
Pl Fld
Coll
GRAHAM RD
CARDINAL WAY
STIRLING RD
THOMSON RD
ARCHERY
14
A
Sp Gd
B
15
42
C
D
PARKFIELD
TUDOR ENT PK
SHERATON
WOLSELEY RD
GRANT RD
AVONDALE
ST
STUART RD
Pav
Bwg Gns
Open Air Theatre
Tenn Cts
Tenn Cts
Headstone
HAVELOCK RD
Liby
LOMOND CT
GORDON RD
CECIL
HIGH ST
GEORGE
CANNING RD

A
B
9
C
D
93
6
5
92
4
26
3
91
2
1
90
18
17
43
STANMORE
Stanmore Hall
STANMORE HILL
A4140
ST JOHNS SCH
Sch
AYLMER DR
AYLWARDS RISE
FALLOWFIELD
ADELAIDE CL
EMBRY CL
EMBRY WAY
HERIOTS CL
PINE CL
OLD FORGE CL
SPRING LAKE
GREEN LANE COTTS
CULVER LANDS
STANMORE LO
GREEN LA
HILL CL
HALL FARM CL
DENNIS LA
EATON CL
HEWETT CL
Recn Gd
Bwg Gn
STANGATE GDNS
Pav
LABURNUM CT
COVERDALE CL
RAINSFORD CL
HALSBURY CL
THE WOODLANDS
BEN HALE CL
WOODSIDE CL
WINSCOMBE WAY
OLDFIELD CL
HOLLAND WLK
HOLLAND CL
OLD LODGE WAY
RIVERINE LO
BOWLS CL
LINDEN CL
DEARNE CL
THE CHANTRIES
T Cts
PYNNACLES CL
CHERCHEFELLE MEWS
CHURCH RD A410
THE BROADWAY
Liby
GREYFELL CL
DENNIS GDNS
OAK LODGE CL
UXBRIDGE RD
BENTLEY WAY
WHITE ORCHARDS
GRANVILLE MEWS
LADY AYLESFORD AVE
WOLSTENHOLME
RECTORY LA
RECTORY CL
TUDOR WELL CL
CHERRY TREE WAY
DOUGLAS CL
SHERBOURNE PL
ELLIOTT RD
BOYLE AVE
CAROLINE CT
EMBRY DR
DOWDING PL
CONWAY CL
THE CHASE
HOBB RD
TRENCHARD CL
SALMOND CL
Temple Pond
Tenn Cts
HA7
KENNETH GDNS
LEAVESDEN RD
CAPUCHIN CL
TEMPLE MEAD CL
GORDON AVE
SALISBURY HO
WEYMOUTH WLK
LINKS VIEW CL
SUNNINGDALE CL
WENTWORTH PL
GREENACRES DR
GLENEAGLES
GEORGIAN CL
MANOR HOUSE EST
Stanmore Coll
ELM PK
GLEBE CT
GLEBE RD
CLAIRE GDNS
HAIG RD
INGRAM CL
ALBEMARLE PK
BEAUCHAMP CT
MALCOLM CT
PARK CL
LEMARK CL
NELSON RD
BERNAYS CL
BEATTY RD
NARESBY FOLD
THE RIDGEWAY
WATER GDNS
SEPTEMBER WAY
ROSEDALE CL
LAURIMEL CL
LINDETH CL
SAVERNAKE CT
COLMAN CT
OLD CHURCH LA
WOLVERTON RD
CH
MEWS
COURTENAY
THE QUADRANGLE
GOLF CL
TRACY CT
ALGUIN CT
BARN CRES
LANSDOWNE RD
ABERCORN RD
CRANMER CL
Stanmore
Belmont
105
Sp Gd
Stanburn Schs
ACORN CL
OAK TREE CL
BELMONT LA
HONISTER GDNS
HONISTER CL
HONISTER PL
VERNON CT
BELLAMY CT
FLORISTON GDNS
FLORISTON CL
Allot Gdns
VERNON DR
ST EDMUNDS DR
HERMITAGE WAY
BEVERLEY GDNS
CURZON AVE
FELBRIDGE AVE
BELLAMY DR
WESTON DR
Belmont
BELMONT CIRC
MOUNTBEL RD
STATION PAR
YORK AVE
VENTNOR AVE
CLIFTON AVE
WETHERAL DR
KYNANCE GDNS
BRAITHWAITE GDNS
COLEDALE DR
ST ANDREWS DR
GYLES PK
HOMEMEAD
BROMEFIELD
WEMBOROUGH RD
HA3
DOBBIN CL
KENMORE AVE
ELGIN AVE
KINGSHILL DR
TENBY AVE
Kenton Lane Farm
GRANGE AVE
UPPINGHAM AVE
ROCKLANDS DR
JERSEY AVE
QUEENS CT
QUEENS AVE
IVANHOE DR
Pl Fld
Priestmead Schs
PEMBROKE AVE
IRVINE AVE
Recn Gd
BORROWDALE AVE
GRASMERE GDNS
CROSS RD
RADCLIFFE RD
ST ANDREWS CL
DERWENT CRES
HILIARY GDNS
ENNERDALE AVE
FORMBY AVE
MORLEY CRES W
MORLEY CRES E
Centenary Park
Park High Sch
Bwg Gn
Tenn Cts
CULVER GR
CHARMIAN AVE
CLYDESDALE AVE
PORTLAND CRES
BOOTHMAN HO
QUEENSBURY CIRC PAR
CARISBROOKE CL
FAIRWAYS
LANGLAND CRES
BROADCROFT AVE
COLLINS AVE
LAMORNA GR
LADYCROFT WLK
AMMERSH GR
PEARESWOOD GDNS
THISTLECROFT GDNS
BURNELL GDNS
CROWSHOTT AVE
PICKETT CROFT
LYON MEADE
BUSH GR
MAYCHURCH CL
Pav
Tenn Cts
Sp Gd
WIGTON GDNS
HA7
Works
DALSTON GDNS
HONEYPOT LA
A4140
PARR RD
HONEYPOT BSNS CTR
GARLAND RD
BRAMBLE CL
Liby
BRICK LA
B461
STATION PAR
WATERSFIELD WAY
BARTHOLOMEW CT
LONGCROFTE RD
CORNBURY RD
CLOYSTER WOOD
HOWBERRY CL
HOWBERRY RD
CHEYNEYS AVE
Whitchurch Schs
GREEN VERGES
WILDCROFT GDNS
WYCHWOOD AVE
WYCHWOOD CL
HA8
MARSH LA
VERSTON WAY
Allot Gdns
DU CROS DR
PETERS CL
TALMAN GR
ORFORD CT
ELIZABETH GDNS
MERRYFIELD GDNS
BEECH TREE CL
DENE GDNS
SANDYMOUNT AVE
CRAIGWEIL DR
CRAIGWEIL CL
CHARLBURY AVE
MERRION AVE
COPLEY RD
BELMONT
KERRY CT
KERRY AVE
OAKMEAD CT
VALENCIA RD
WARREN FIELDS
RUSPER CL
WHITE HOUSE DR
ARRAN DR
KNIGHTS RD
GLANLEAM RD
REENGLASS RD
LONDON RD
A410
Stanmore
MORECAMBE GDNS
WESTBERE DR
TINTAGEL DR
SNARESBROOK DR
COURT DR
BROCKLEY CL
PANGBOURNE DR
DOVERCOURT
HERONSLEA DR
Aylward Schs
DALKEITH GR
Tenn Cts
North London Collegiate
Tenn Cts
BERRY HILL
BROCKLEYSIDE
CHEVALIER CL
REES DR
PARTRIDGE CL
A5
DONNEFIELD AVE
CANONS PARK CL
Bwg Gn
Allot Gdns
Wood
House
LITTLE COMMON
HILLTOP WAY
SPRINGFIELD CL
PARK LA
Cts

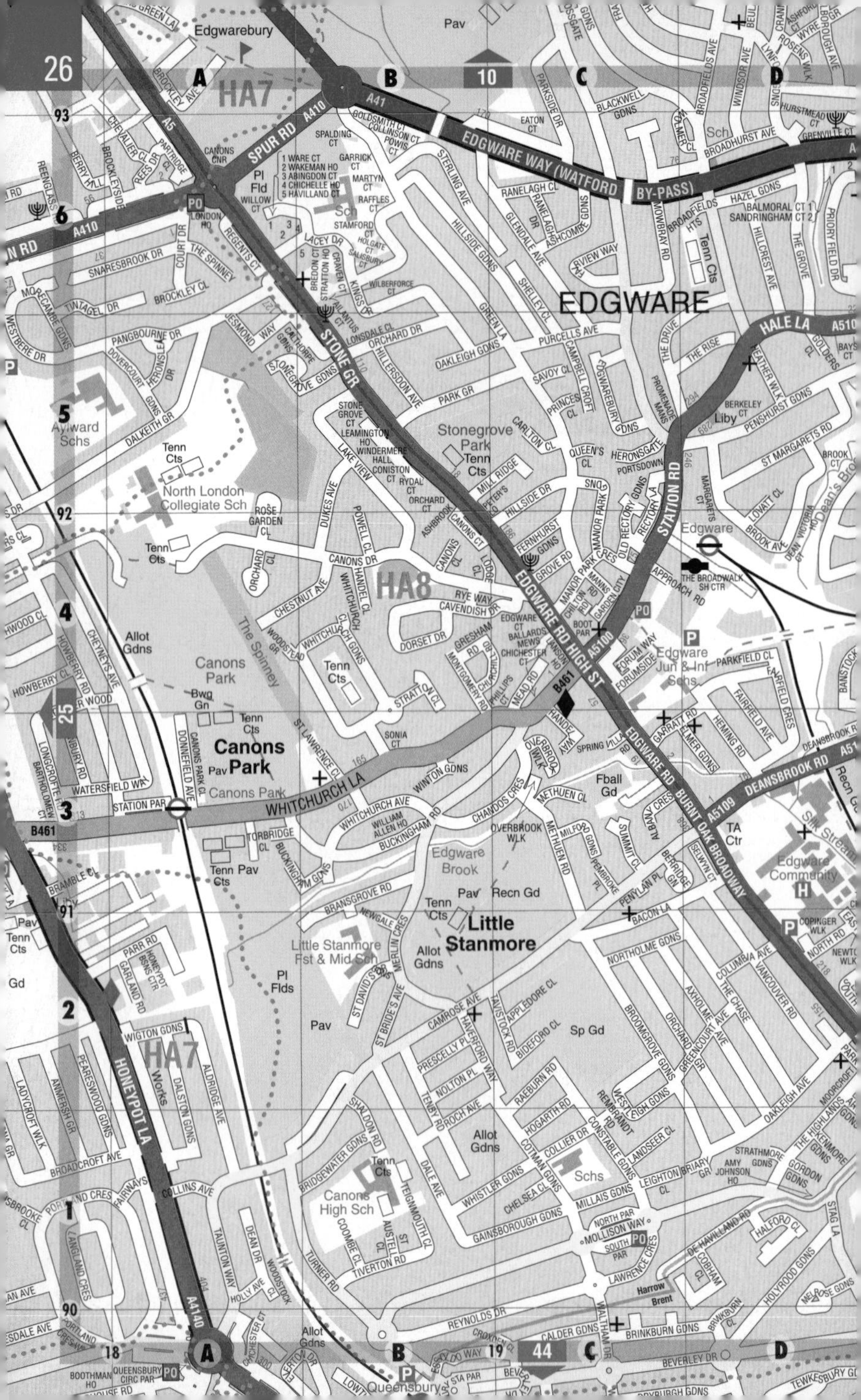
Edgwarebury
Pav
HA7
A
B
C
D
10
93
SPUR RD
A410
A41
A5
EDGWARE WAY (WATFORD BY-PASS)
CANONS CNR
PARTRIDGE CL
BROCKLEY AVE
BERRY HILL
BROCKLEYSIDE
CHEVALIER CL
REES DR
REENGLASS
GOLDSMITH CT
COLLINSON CT
POWIS CT
SPALDING CT
1 WARE CT
2 WAKEMAN HO
3 ABINGDON CT
4 CHICHELLE HO
5 HAVILLAND CT
GARRICK CT
MARTYN CT
RAFFLES CT
Pl Fld
WILLOW CT
Sch
STAMFORD CT
HOLGATE CT
SALISBURY CT
LACEY DR
EATON CT
PARKSIDE DR
BLACKWELL GDNS
BROADFIELDS AVE
WINDSOR AVE
HURSTMEAD CT
GRENVILLE CT
BROADHURST AVE
STERLING AVE
RANELAGH CL
RANELAGH DR
GLENDALE AVE
ASHCOMBE GDNS
MOWBRAY RD
BROADFIELDS HTS
Tenn Cts
HAZEL GDNS
BALMORAL CT
SANDRINGHAM CT
HILLCREST AVE
THE GROVE
PRIORY FIELD DR
6
PO
LONDON HO
REGENTS CT
THE SPINNEY
COURT DR
SNARESBROOK DR
BROCKLEY CL
TINTAGEL DR
MORECAMBE GDNS
WESTBERE DR
HILLSIDE GDNS
SHELLEY CL
FAIRVIEW WAY
EDGWARE
BREDON CT
STRATTON HO
CRAVEN CT
KINGS DR
WILBERFORCE CT
AILANTUS CT
LONSDALE CL
ORCHARD DR
GREEN LA
OAKLEIGH GDNS
PURCELLS AVE
CAMPBELL CROFT
SAVOY CL
PRINCES CL
EDGWAREBURY GDNS
THE DRIVE
THE RISE
PROMENADE MANS
HALE LA
A510
HEATHER WLK
GOLDERS CL
BERKELEY CT
PENSHURST GDNS
Liby
ST MARGARETS RD
PANGBOURNE DR
DOVERCOURT GDNS
HERONSLEA DR
JESMOND WAY
CALTHORPE GDNS
STONE GR
STONEGROVE GDNS
HILLERSDON AVE
PARK GR
5
Aylward Schs
DALKEITH GR
STONE GROVE CT
LEAMINGTON HO
WINDERMERE HALL
CONISTON CT
RYDAL CT
ORCHARD CT
LAKE VIEW
DUKES AVE
POWELL CL
Stonegrove Park
Tenn Cts
MILL RIDGE
PETER'S CL
CARLTON CL
QUEEN'S CL
HERONSGATE
PORTSDOWN
HILLSIDE DR
FERNHURST GDNS
MANOR PARK GDNS
OLD RECTORY GDNS
RECTORY LA
STATION RD
MARGARETS CT
BROOK CT
LOVATT CL
BROOK AVE
DEAN VICTORIA HO
Edgware
North London Collegiate Sch
ROSE GARDEN CL
92
Tenn Cts
ORCHARD CL
CANONS DR
WHITCHURCH CL
HANDEL CL
HA8
CANONS CL
CANONS CT
ASHBROOK
LODGE
GROVE RD
MANOR PARK CRES
MANNS RD
GARDEN CITY
CHILTON RD
THE BROADWALK SH CTR
APPROACH RD
EDGWARE RD HIGH ST
CHESTNUT AVE
RYE WAY
CAVENDISH DR
DORSET DR
4
Allot Gdns
The Spinney
Canons Park
CHEYNEYS AVE
HOWBERRY CL
HOWBERRY RD
WOODSTEAD GR
WHITCHURCH GDNS
Tenn Cts
GRESHAM RD
MONTGOMERY RD
CHURCHILL PL
EDGWARE CT
BALLARDS MEWS
CHICHESTER CT
PHILLIPS CT
MEAD RD
BOOT PAR
A5100
PO
FORUM WAY
FORUMSIDE
Edgware Jun & Inf Schs
P
PARKFIELD CL
FAIRFIELD AVE
FAIRFIELD CRES
HEMING RD
BANSTOCK
25
LONGCROFTE RD
BARTHOLOMEW CL
Bwg Gn
Tenn Cts
Canons Park
Pav
CANONS PARK CL
DONNEFIELD AVE
WATERSFIELD WAY
STATION PAR
Canons Park
ST LAWRENCE CL
STRATTON CL
SONIA CT
B461
HANDEL WAY
OVERBROOK WLK
SPRING VILLA RD
EDGWARE RD
GARRATT RD
ELMER GDNS
DEANSBROOK RD
A5109
BURNT OAK BROADWAY
Recn Gd
3
WHITCHURCH LA
WINTON GDNS
WHITCHURCH AVE
WILLIAM ALLEN HO
BUCKINGHAM RD
CHANDOS CRES
METHUEN CL
Fball Gd
ALBANY CRES
SUMMIT CL
TA Ctr
Silk Stream
Edgware Community
H
TORBRIDGE CL
BUCKINGHAM GDNS
Tenn Pav Cts
OVERBROOK WLK
Edgware Brook
METHUEN RD
MILFORD GDNS
PEMBROKE PL
BERRIDGE GN
SELWYN CT
PENYLAN PL
BRAMBLE CL
91
Pav
Tenn Cts
BRANSGROVE RD
NEWGALE
MERLIN CRES
Tenn Cts
Pav
Recn Gd
Little Stanmore
BACON LA
COPINGER WLK
P
NORTH RD
PARR RD
HONEYPOT BSNS CTR
GARLAND RD
Gd
Little Stanmore Fst & Mid Sch
Allot Gdns
NORTHOLME GDNS
COLUMBIA AVE
VANCOUVER RD
Pl Flds
ST DAVID'S DR
ST BRIDE'S AVE
APPLEDORE CL
AXHOLME AVE
THE CHASE
2
Pav
CAMROSE AVE
HAVERFORD WAY
TAVISTOCK RD
BIDEFORD CL
Sp Gd
BROOMGROVE GDNS
ORCHARD GR
GREENCOURT AVE
WIGTON GDNS
HA7
Works
HONEYPOT LA
ALDRIDGE AVE
DALSTON GDNS
PEARESWOOD GDNS
ANMERSH GR
LADYCROFT WLK
PRESCELLY PL
NOLTON PL
TENBY RD
ROCH AVE
RAEBURN RD
HOGARTH RD
REMBRANDT RD
CONSTABLE GDNS
WESTLEIGH GDNS
OAKLEIGH AVE
MOORCROFT
THE HIGHLANDS
BROADCROFT AVE
SHALDON RD
BRIDGEWATER GDNS
DALE AVE
Allot Gdns
COLLIER DR
COTMAN GDNS
LANDSEER CL
STRATHMORE GDNS
THE KENMORE GDNS
GORDON GDNS
Tenn Cts
Canons High Sch
TEIGNMOUTH CL
WHISTLER GDNS
CHELSEA CL
Schs
LEIGHTON CL
BRIARY GR
AMY JOHNSON HO
FAIRWAYS
COLLINS AVE
PORTLAND CRES
1
LANGLAND CRES
TAUNTON WAY
DEAN DR
COOMBE CL
AUSTELL CL
ST AUSTELL CL
GAINSBOROUGH GDNS
MILLAIS GDNS
NORTH PAR
MOLLISON WAY
SOUTH PAR
PO
LAWRENCE CRES
DE HAVILLAND RD
COBHAM CL
HALFORD CL
STAG LA
HOLYROOD GDNS
TIVERTON RD
TURNER RD
HOLLY AVE
WOODSTOCK CL
Harrow
Brent
MELROSE GDNS
90
A4140
REYNOLDS DR
CROYDEN CL
CALDER GDNS
BRINKBURN GDNS
BRINKBURN CL
WALTHAM DR
CHICHESTER CT
Allot Gdns
18
19
44
BEVERLEY DR
BOOTHMAN HO
QUEENSBURY CIRC PAR
PO
EVERTON DR
P
Queensbury
TEWKESBURY GDNS

Stoneyfields Park
A
B
C
D
11
M1
A1
A5109
MARSH LA
WESTFIELD RD
Allot Gdns
THE REDDINGS
REDDINGS CL
Lawrence Green
LAWRENCE ST
Tenn Cts
93
EDGWARE WAY (WATFORD BY-PASS)
A41
NORTHWAY CIR
Apex Cnr
PO
St Joseph's Coll Mill Hill Missionaries
6
DRAPER'S COTTAGE HOMES
SHAKESPEARE RD
MILTON RD
TAYLORSMEAD
TENNYSON RD
HAMMERS LA
NW7
TUDOR GABLES
Mill Hill Circus
1 WILTSHIRE CL
2 FRANCIS CT
VICTORIA RD
ALBERT RD
CONSORT HO
B1461
DAWS LA
5
SELVAGE LA
SUNBURY AVE
UPHILL RD
LAWRENCE AVE
FOXWOOD CL
RUSSELL GR
MILL WAY
WEYMOUTH AVE
UPHILL DR
NEWCOMBE PK
St Martin's Sch
GOODWYN AVE
THE BROADWAY A5100
Liby
HARTLEY AVE
A5100
HALE LA
DEAN'S LA
Dean's Brook
HALE GROVE GDNS
HALE DR
Schs
Sch
Univ of London Obsy
Bwg Gn
Pav
92
Tenn Cts
Mill Hill Park
HA8
Nature Reserve
Mill Hill Broadway
Lyndhurst Park
Allot Gdns
WOODLAND WAY
4
THE MEADS
DRYFIELD RD
GOLD LA
OLDBERRY RD
DEANSBROOK RD
HOMEFIELD RD
LYNDHURST AVE
WOODCROFT AVE
Woodcroft Park
WATFORD WAY (BARNET BY-PASS)
BUNN'S LA
THE RISE
28
FIVE WAYS RETAIL PK
FEATHERSTONE CT
BLOOMSBURY CL
3
ABBOTS RD
CARDINAL CT
Tenn Ct
Pav
Pl Fld
Sp Gd
SPALDING CL
WOLSEY GR
Watling Park
Burnt Oak
Tenn Cts
Sp Gd
FORTESCUE RD
WATLING AVE
Sch
Liby
Silk Stream
Burnt Oak
GRAHAME PARK WAY
Hendon Coll
91
2
Grahame Park
Grahame Park
St James's RC High Sch
EVERGLADE STRAND
BROADHEAD STRAND
GREAT STRAND
LITTLE STRAND
LOWER STRAND
Pl Fld
RAF Mus
1
AVION CRES
SILKSTREAM RD
Barnfield Prim Sch
Silkstream Park
PLAYFIELD RD
BURNT OAK BROADWAY
EDGWARE ROAD THE HYDE
A5
NW9
Pav
Pl Fld
Allot Gdns
BLACKCAP CT 1
BITTERN CT 2
BUNTING CT 3
LAPWING CT 4
RAVEN CL 5
LISTER CT 6
CURIE GDNS 7
FLEMING WLK 8
AEROVILLE
Tenn Cts
Colindale
Met Pol Cadet Training Sch
Battle of Britain Museum
Police HQ
90
HENDON
CHANCELLOR PL
AERODROME RD
CARLISLE RD
HOLMSTALL AVE
A
B
21
45
C
D
22
British Liby (Newspaper Liby)
Superstore
Peel Ctr

A
B
12
C
D
Belmont
Mill Hill
Jun Sch
Pl Fld
Tenn Cts
Folly
Farm
Sp
Fld
Pav
Sp
Gd
B552
93
Lawrence
Green
St
Joseph's Coll
Mill Hill
Missionaries
6
Tenn
Cts
B1461
COHEN
HO
DRAPER'S
COTTAGE HOMES
HAMMERS LA
St Paul's
CE Prim
Sch
Mill Hill
Sch
THE RIDGEWAY
Burtonhole
Farm
BURTONHOLE LA
HILLVIEW RD
ELEANOR CRES
Oakfields
SHAKESPEARE RD
TUDOR
GABLES
MILTON RD
TAYLORSMEAD
TENNYSON RD
BIRKBECK RD
BYRON RD
MARION RD
Goodwyn
Sch
Pl Flds
HIGH ST
HOLLIES END
119
St Vincent's
RC Sch
WENTWORTH
HALL
WINTERSTOKE GDNS
Allot
Gdns
WILLS GR
VINERIES BANK
Mount Sch
Drivers
Hill
PARTINGDALE
Mill Hill
Barracks
5
DAWS LA
P
Mill Hill
Arrandene
Open Space
School
Park
Univ of
London
Obsy
92
Bwg
Gn
Featherstone
Hill
NW7
MILESPIT HILL
WOODCOTE AVE
RUSHDEN GDNS
BITTACY PARK AVE
MAURICE BROWNE CL
Mill Hill
Park
4
MELDEX CL
Mill Hill
Cemy
ENGEL PK
SALCOMBE GDNS
BITTACY CL
BITTACY RISE
BITTACY HILL
WATFORD
WISE LA
PARKSIDE
HOLMDENE AVE
GLENMERE AVE
COPTHALL DR
THE RISE
27
SUNRISE VIEW
GRENFELL CT
MOORLANDS AVE
FEATHERSTONE RD
BROOKFIELD CRES
BROOKFIELD AVE
BROOKFIELD CL
Allot
Gdns
Copthall
Sch
MORETON CL
PO
Bittacy
Park
TUDOR CL
HOLLAND CT
RANDALL CT
HILLSIDE GR
PAGE MDW
PAGE CT
PURSLEY RD
SANDERS LA
GRANTS CL
WOODBERRY
TAVISTOCK AVE
SEATON SQ
FEATHERSTONE CT
BLOOMSBURY CL
FIVE WAYS
RETAIL PK
(BARNET BY-PASS)
CALDEW CT
MARDALE CT
SANDWICK CL
LADYSMITH CL
COLENSO DR
BAMPTON DR
PAGE ST
Chase Lodge
Pl Flds
Dollis
Jun & Inf Schs
65
3
FARM HOUSE CT
ROWLANDS CL
BRISTON MEWS
BRANCASTER DR
LONGFIELD AVE
FAKENHAM CL
AYLESHAM CL
BURNHAM CL
CH
ASHLEY WLK
ASHLEY LA
DEVONSHIRE CRES
DEVONSHIRE RD
ABERDARE GDNS
OAKHAMPTON RD
Copthall
Sch
Swimming
Pool
Pav
Pl Fld
91
TITHE WLK
A1
Hendon
Stadium
Hendon Cemy
& Crem
Hendon
Coll
GRAHAME PARK WAY
THE CL
CHADBURY CT
Hasmonean
High Sch (Girls)
Copthall
Sp Ctr
M1
2
Five Ways
Cnr
GILDA CT
Ashley La
St James's
RC High
Sch
Holders
Hill
AVION CRES
TITHE CT
HALL LA
Pl Flds
NW4
Pav
RAF
Mus
Pl
Fld
GREAT STRAND
WATFORD WAY
WESTSIDE
GREAT NORTH WAY (BARNET BY-PASS)
BARFORD CL
Putting
Gn
SUNNY
GARDENS
PAR
Allot
Gdns
ASHLEY CL
WOODTREE CL
TIMBERDEN
TURNBERRY CT
FERNSIDE
FAIRVIEW CT
LINKSWAY
MANOR HALL AVE
HOLDERS HILL RD
1
WHEATLEY CL
Tenn Cts
Pav
CHATSWORTH CL
CHATSWORTH AVE
MEADOW DR
SUNNINGFIELDS CRES
SUNNY HILL CT
SUNNY GARDENS RD
MANOR HALL DR
GARRICK DR
CLAYDON HO
RIDGE CL
HOLDERS HILL AVE
HOLDERS HILL CRES
Sch
Battle of
Britain
Museum
Police
HQ
Sunnyhill
Park
A41
ELWSLEY AVE
DOWNAGE
SHERWOOD RD
HENDON HALL CT
OCTOBER PL
90
HENDON
BUCKINGHAM CT
SOUTHFIELDS
CLARENDON GDNS
AERODROME RD
22
ST ANN'S CT
SUNNINGFIELDS RD
23
46
NURSERY CT
WESTCHESTER CT
GROVE HO
FARM CT
CANBERRA
HENDON LO
NURSERY WLK
H
The
Garden
EDINBURGH HO
MARKHAM CT
Peel Ctr

A
B
13
C
D
Woodridge Sch
CHIDDINGFOLD
LAUREL VIEW
HOLDEN HTS
Finchley Sch
ARLINGTON
SOUTHOVER
FRAMFIELD CL
NORTHAM
BROOKMDW
DEVONSHIRE HO
93
81
MICHLEHAM DOWN
SHORTGATE
Sp Gd
GUILDOWN AVE
FOUR ACRES
SYLVAN CT
BARCHESTER LO
WOODSIDE GRANGE RD
GRANGEWAY
BUDD CL
LORIAN CL
GREEN BANK
WOODSIDE AVE
LITTLE CEDARS
SQUIRRELS
HIGHWOOD
Gd
Woodside Park
Tenn Cts
Sp Gd
Bwg Gn
N12
BURTONHOLE LA
TILLINGHAM WAY
TWINEHAM GN
RIVERSIDE HO
HOLDEN RD
Woodside Park
STATION APP
Sch
THE OAKS
CLIVEDEN CL
6
ARDEN GRANGE
AVENUE RD
Folly Brook
PYCOMBE CNR
SCAYNES LINK
CHANCTONBURY WAY
Sp Gd
BROOKDENE
HOPTREE CL
HOLDEN AVE
WOODSIDE PARK RD
North Finchley
CISSBURY RING N
RODMELL SLOPE
SINGLETON SCARP
GARDEN CT
VICARAGE CT
THE GARTH
HOLMDENE
DOWNING CT
FINCHLEY LO
THE GABLES
CLARENDON HO
LODGE LA
Northside Prim Sch
LULLINGTON GARTH
OFFHAM SLOPE
WOLSTONBURY
WORCESTER CT
AVON CT
AVONDALE AVE
GAINSBOROUGH RD
PERCY RD
BARHAM CT
Allot Gdns
Frith Manor Sch
SUSSEX RING
ARGYLE RD
SPRINGFIELD CL
GAINSBOROUGH CT
NETHERFIELD RD
5
Sch
COLERIDGE RD
HUGHES
SADDLESCOMBE WAY
FOLKINGTON CNR
CISSBURY RING S
POYNINGS WAY
Tenn Ct
WESTBURY RD
NETHER ST
HOLMES AVE
APPROACH LA
ROSS AVE
GAWTHORNE AVE
ROBERTS RD
LIDBURY RD
KENNY RD
STEYNINGS WAY
WALMINGTON FOLD
COURT HOUSE RD
VIVIAN CT
QUEENSGATE CT
ALBANY
HUTTON GR
BIRKBECK RD
DALE GR
92
KELLY RD
PRICE CL
WARREN WAY
WILLIAMSON WAY
Inglis Barracks
DREW AVE
TWINN RD
WESTLINTON CL
LINKSIDE
Finchley
Allot Gdns
CHESTERFIELD RD
WESTBURY GR
NETHERCOURT AVE
FURSBY AVE
WESTLEIGH CT
HILLCOURT AVE
ALEXANDRA GR
MOSSBOROUGH CL
MOSS HALL CT
THYRA GR
GREENLAWNS
Superstore
NW7
FRITH LA
Tenn Cts
Pavs
BRENT WAY
MAPLE CL
WEST AVE
COURT HOUSE GDNS
THE LAURELS
MOSS HALL GR
PAMELA CT
THE LANTERNS
BURNBRAE CL
MOSS HALL CRES
4
CHRISTCHURCH
Moss Hall Schs
BLISSLAND CT
WOODBERRY WAY
Nether Court
HAMILTON WAY
SALIX CT
PENSTEMON CL
West Finchley
ESSEX PK
FINCHLEY CT
HARTLEY HO
Dollis Brook
FINCHLEY WAY
CEDAR CT
THE DRIVE
HOWCROFT CRES
WENTWORTH CL
BALLARDS LA
THE FOUNTAINS
30
GRANVILLE RD
BITTACY BSNS CTR
OAKDENE PK
LANSDOWNE RD
BROWNLOW RD
SEYMOUR RD
ROSSANNE HO
SOLAR CT
ETCHINGHAM CT
CHISLEHURST AVE
ROCKLANDS
GORDON RD
GROSVENOR RD
CRESTNUT ROW
NETHER CL
WENTWORTH AVE
WENTWORTH PK
GRUNEISEN RD
Bwg Gn
NIGEL CT
3
BITTACY CT
NEW RD
Allot Gdns
EVERSLEIGH RD
EVERSLEIGH CT
SELLERS HALL CL
FINCHLEY
HOLDENHURST AVE
NEYARD AVE
DOLLISCROFT
B552
ABERCORN CL
MALLOW MEAD
ABERCORN RD
ELM PARK RD
CORNWALL AVE
THE GROVE
GROVE AVE
FALKLAND AVE
ADAMS CL
CLAVERLEY VILLAS
ST PAUL'S WAY
WILLOW WAY
THE RIDGEWAY
Pavs
Tenn Cts
ETCHINGHAM PARK RD
PARK CRES
DOLLIS RD
LINKS VIEW
FRITH CT
BROOK CL
B1462
PO
Sch
CRESCENT RD
DOLLIS CT
NETHER ST
B1462
PARKSIDE
Victoria Park
91
QUEEN'S AVE
WOODLANDS AVE
THORNFIELD AVE
Pl Fld
Pav
Allot Gdns
BOSE CL
HOLDERS HILL PAR
DOLLIS PK
CRESCENT RISE
SHAKESPEARE RD
POPES DR
ALAN LO
ALBERT PL
REDBOURNE HO
PREMIER LO
REDBOURNE AVE
MILLERS YD
CLAVERLEY GR
PRINCES AVE
DORSET MEWS
DUKES AVE
VINES AVE
OAKFIELD CT
OAKFIELD RD
PARK VIEW RD
PARK AVE
Manorside Sch
2
LYNDHURST GDNS
BRUNSWICK HO
CLIFTON AVE
N3
DOLLIS MEWS
HERVEY CL
BERKELEY CT
CADOGAN GDNS
CLAIGMAR GDNS
STRATHMORE GDNS
LONG LA
SQUIRES LA
AVONDALE AVE
QUEEN'S AVE
HOLDERS HILL RD
HAWTHORN MEWS
CLAREMONT PK
Tenn Cts
GRASS PK
DOLLIS AVE
CHURCH CRES
VICTORIA AVE
PEWTERERS CT
Ct
Finchley Central
VINEYARD GR
MONTPELIER RD
CROMWELL RD
QUEENSWOOD PK
HENDON AVE
GRENVILLE CL
KINGSWOOD PK
PRIORY CL
RECTORY CL
Liby
RATHGAR CL
Schs
A5000
A598
COLLEGE
ARCADIA AVE
MOUTTON GR
STATION CL
STATION RD
DOUGLAS CT
ABINGDON
NURSERY AVE
VILLAGE RD
CYPRUS GDNS
ST MARY'S AVE
PRESTON PK
BLAKE LO
HENDON LA
GRAVEL HILL
REGENCY HO
SPENCER CL
THE AVENUE
GLENHILL CL
LICHFIELD GR
SYLVAN AVE
Pav
Allot Gdns
POINTALLS
1 COLERNE CT
2 CUMBERLAND GDNS
CYPRUS AVE
LABURNUM
Church End
Tenn Cts
Sp Gd
MANOR VIEW
DUDLEY RD
ROSEMARY AVE
CHARLES CT
1
Windsor Open Space
WINDSOR RD
WINDSOR CL
A504
ST MICHAEL'S
TEMPLE CL
BIBSWORTH RD
CYPRUS RD
EMBASSY LO
DERBY LO
ELLERTON LO
EAST END RD
Pav
Bwg Gn
MANOR COTTS
CRANMER CT
Coll
PAUL CT
WICKLIFFE AVE
GREENACRES
SALISBURY CT
ARUNDEL LO
NORTH CRES
A598 REGENT'S PARK RD
COLOSSEUM CT
STANHOPE CT
CAVENDISH AVE
TEMPLARS CRES
HOLMWOOD GDNS
WINDERMERE
PAVILION MEWS
SPRING PL
Akiva Sch
Sp Gd
Middlesex Cty Crkt Sch
BRIARFIELD AVE
TANGLE TREE CL
A406
BRIAR CL
RICHMOND
Pl Fld
90
SURREY CT
ELIZABETH HELEN CT
VOYSEY CL
SALISBURY AVE
ARDEN RD
MOUNTFIELD RD
LUKES CT
St Theresa's RC Prim Sch
EAST END RD
26
BENEDICT WAY
A
B
25
C
47
D
ERLEY GR
FITZALAN RD
STANHOPE AVE
MAYFLOWER LO
CHARD AVE
AMBERDEN
BASING WAY
NORTH CIRCULAR
REMEMBRANCE AVE
EAST END

14
48
29
A
B
C
D
N12
N20
N3
N2
N10
North Finchley
Colney Hatch
North Middlesex
Bethune
Recn Gd
Friary Park
Tenn Cts
Pav
Bwg Gn
Allot Gdns
St John's CE JMI Sch
Friern Barnet Sch
Christ Church CE Sec Sch
Pl Fld
Woodhouse Sixth Form Coll
Northside Prim Sch
Superstore
Summerside Prim Sch
The Compton Sch
Sp Ctr
Coppetts Wood
Nat Res
Coppetts Ctr
Fball Gd
Sp Gd
The Glebe Land Open Space
Sw Pool
Finchley Meml
Pl Flds
Our Lady of Lourdes RC Prim Sch
TA Ctr
Victoria Park
Manorside Sch
Tudor Prim Sch
St Pancras & Islington Cemetery
Greenfields Sch
Crem
Coldfall Wood
Coldfall Prim Sch
Fortismere Sch
Martin Prim Sch
Liby
FRIERN BARNET LA
WOODHOUSE RD
KINGSWAY
NORTH CIRCULAR RD
HIGH RD
BALLARDS LA
A1000
A1003
A598
A406
FRIERN PK
TORRINGTON PK
FRIARY RD
MAYFIELD AVE
FINCHLEY PK
FRIERN WATCH AVE
RAVENSDALE AVE
AVENUE RD
WOODSIDE PARK RD
LODGE LA
CHRISTCHURCH AVE
WOODBERRY WAY
FALLOW COURT AVE
ETON AVE
GRANVILLE RD
HOLDENHURST AVE
PARK CRES
WOODLANDS AVE
QUEEN'S AVE
CLIFTON RD
GLEBE RD
EAST END RD
ST PANCRAS CT
CHANDOS RD
CHURCH VALE
CREIGHTON AVE
OSIER CRES
MARRIOTT RD
EVERINGTON RD
HIGH VIEW RD
RALEIGH RD
COPPETTS CL
PARK WAY
THE RIDGEWAY
GRESHAM AVE
BETHUNE AVE
HOLLICKWOOD AVE
SUMMERS LA
BUXTED RD
WARNHAM RD
STANHOPE RD
CASTLE RD
ADDINGTON DR
KENVER AVE
SANDRINGHAM GDNS
WOODGRANGE AVE
GROVE RD
NETHER ST
HUTTON GR
ALEXANDRA GR
MOSS HALL CRES
ETCHINGHAM PARK RD
LONG LA
VINEYARD GR
NURSERY AVE
SQUIRES LA

Crematorium
BRUNSWICK AVE
BRUNSWICK PARK RD
A
B
C
D
15
Recn Gd
Tenn Cts
Pav
DARWIN CL
MARSHALL
DALE GREEN RD
GREEN RD
RIVERSIDE PL
WATER
ABBOTSHALL AVE
BRYCEDALE CRES
ARNOS GR
LANGSIDE CRES
SMITH AVE
LULWORTH
FORESTDALE
Allot Gdns
PEYTON HO
NEVILLE HO
CHAVILLE CT
ST MICHAEL'S CT
OAKLEIGH RD S
FALKLAND AVE
MARNE AVE
SPENCER RD
PARK VIEW CRES
BRUNSWICK WAY
THE HOMESTEAD
A1003
RHYPOE RD
RAVENSCRAIG RD
BROOKDALE
New Southgate
Bwg Gn
Pav
Tenn Cts
Arnos Park
N14
N11
MORTON WAY
MORTON CRES
CORRI AVE
TOWNSEND AVE
POWYS LA
B1452
A1004
93
6
FRIERN + BARNET
Allot Gdns
THE CRESCENT
COTSWOLD CT
BEACONSFIELD RD
COPPIES GR
CARLISLE AVENUE
THE PL
A109
HASLAM CT
BETSTYLE RD
MARCONI PL
CRANBROOK LA
A1110
Arnos Grove
WALKER CL
ARNOS RD
SEAFIELD RD
WILMER WAY
N13
DAWLISH AVE
ASHRIDGE GDNS
HOLLY PARK RD
BELLEVUE RD
PARKHURST RD
CARLTON RD
BELLVIEW MEWS
Sch
PO
BOWES RD
CROSS RD
OLD CHURCH CL
GROVE RD
BANK PAR
PEVERETT CL
WOODLAND RD
HIGH RD
BEAUFORT
THE LIMES AVE
LOMBARD
HOLDEN LO
SPRINGFIELD RD
PALMER'S RD
HIGHVIEW GDNS
SHAKESPEARE AVE
MILTON GR
CHAUCER CL
Liby
SUNNINGDALE
Bloomfield Sch
FRIERN BARNET RD
STANFORD CT
THE BROADWAY
Sp Gd
Pav
New Southgate
STATION APP
REGAL DR
WHITMORE CL
BROOK WAY
UPPER PARK RD
ADDERSWOOD WAY
A406
TELFORD RD (NORTH CIRCULAR RD)
BEXHILL RD
PEVENSEY AVE
HASTINGS RD
Bowes Prim Sch
BOWES RD (NORTH CIRCULAR RD)
5
Fld
POWYS CT
Tenn Ct
PRINCESS PARK MANOR
BARON CL
BALMORAL AVE
HIGHGROVE
DUCHESS CL
EARL CL
VISCOUNT CL
KENSINGTON
GRASSINGTON CL
STATION RD
LOWER PARK RD
CARADOC EVANS CL 1
ROBERTS HO 2
LORNE HO 3
SELLSBY CT 4
LOWER MAIDSTONE RD
STONEHAM RD
TOTNES VILLAS
EVESHAM RD
SHREWSBURY RD
OLLERTON RD
STANLEY RD
HIGHWORTH RD
UNION RD
WAKEFIELD RD
BOSWORTH RD
NATAL RD
92
B106
HARDWICKE RD
DEEPDALE CL
COVERDALE RD
KIRKBY CL
SWALEDALE
CATTERICK CL
KETTLEWELL
FRIERN BRIDGE RET PK
ARNCLIFFE CL
Superstore
TEWKESBURY TERR
MAIDSTONE RD
LANCASTER RD
WARWICK RD
YORK RD
HAYWOOD LO
DEANSWOOD
OAK LA
BROWNLOW RD
Bwg Gn
Tenn Cts
4
WESTBURY RD
GORING RD
PICKERING GDNS
MALHAM CL
SKIPTON CL
ILKLEY CL
OTLEY CL
SYCAMORE HILL
PEGASUS WAY
GARSDALE CL
HORNBEAMS RISE
ERBURN CL
WHARFDALE
ELM WAY
POPLAR GR
LABURNUM CL
GREENWAY
BOUNDS GREEN IND EST
NORTH WAY
SOUTH WAY
RING WAY
Middlesex Univ (Bounds Green)
MONRO DR
CLINE RD
TORRINGTON GDNS
THE DRIVE
Enfield
Haringey
BOUNDS GREEN RD
PARKDALE
EMBASSY CT
BOUNDS GREEN CT
ELEANOR
RICHMOND RD
SILVER BIRCH
ATLAS RD
NORTH CIRCULAR RD
PINKHAM WAY
LARCH CL
ORION RD
PERT CL
Hollickwood Park
HILLSIDE GDNS
CHURSTON GDNS
St Martin of Porres RC Prim Sch
Bwg Gn
Pav
BLAKE RD
LYNTON GDNS
WARWICK CT
PASSMORE GDNS
GORDON RD
RHYS AVE
A109
32
Schs
Colney Hatch
Pl Fld
HOPKINS CL
IRETON CL
FAIRFAX WAY
STRODE CL
CROMWELL RD
HALDANE CL
MELBOURNE CT
ALEXANDRA RD
NICOLL CT
PASSMORES 1
EDWARDS HO
EDWARDS DR 2
BADEN CT 3
Bounds Green
B106
ST GABLES CT
Fball Ctr
COLNEY HATCH LA
HAMPDEN RD
AUDLEY CL
PEMBROKE RD
STANLEY RD
JOSHUA CL
WADE CT
OAK AVE
Hollickwood Prim Sch
TUNNEL GDNS
WINTON AVE
WOODFIELD WAY
Wood Green Tunnel
WROXHAM GDNS
DURNSFORD RD
AMETHYST CL
PARK RD
PALACE RD
3
GEORGE CRES
Coppetts Wood Prim Sch
CROWN RD
ROMAN RD
BEDFORD RD
ALMA RD
SYDNEY RD
Muswell Hill
Allot Gdns
BIDWELL GDNS
Tenn Cts
PARK GR
PARK CT
EDITH RD
TREDEGAR RD
ANEURIN BEVAN HO
BAILEY CL
MAYA PL
91
CORBETT GR
IMPERIAL RD
PEMBROKE MEWS
ALMA CL
LOUIS MEWS
NEWTON AVE
Alexandra Park Sch
Bwg Gn
Pav
Recn Gd
CRESCENT RISE
BOLSTER GR
WOODRIDINGS CT
ALBERT CL
WHITEHEAD CT
THE VALE
ALBION AVE
CAMBRIDGE GDNS
MONKSWELL CT
HIGH RIDGE
Barnet
Haringey
CH
Rhodes Avenue Prim Sch
ALBERT RD
CRESCENT RD
DAGMAR RD
2
Recn Gd
Tenn Cts
HALLIWICK RD
WETHERILL RD
MAYFLOWER LO
BRIAN CT
RHODES AVE
GROSVENOR RD
Tenn Cts
YEWTREE CL
CLIFTON RD
HARCOURT RD
CLYDE RD
OUTRAM RD
PRINCES AVE
N22
Liby
N10
PO
SUTTON RD
GOODWYN'S VALE
WINDERMERE RD
GRASMERE RD
THIRLMERE RD
KENDALMERE CL
VICTORIA RD
ALEXANDRA AVE
BUCKINGHAM RD
WILTON RD
WILTON CT
BARNARD HILL
MUSWELL AVE
ALEXANDRA PARK RD
HAMPTON CT
TALBOT RD
ALEXANDRA PARK RD
PALACE GATES RD
VALLANCE RD
NORTH LO
ST SAVIOURS CT
ANDERTON CT
Alexandra Palace
BEDFORD RD
GREENHAM RD
THIRLESTONE CT
SEYMOUR CT
CHILTERN CT
PAGE'S CT
PAGE'S HILL
Allot Gdns
ST REGIS CL
ROSEBERY MEWS
AVENUE MANS
ELGIN RD
CECIL RD
CURZON RD
CONISTON RD
CRANBOURNE RD
ROSEBERY RD
GROVE AVE
THE AVENUE
The Lake
1
SOUTH TERR
NELSON MANDELA CL
ST MATTHEWS CT
Fld
Our Lady of Muswell RC Prim Sch
B106
LANSDOWNE RD
Alexandra Palace
Mast
DUKES AVE
PARKHAM WAY
B550
CAROLINE CL
THE CLOSE
Norfolk House Sch
MUSWELL RD
ROWAN
DONOVAN AVE
PALACE COURT GDNS
METHUEN PK
N8
90
EASTWOOD RD
TETHERDOWN
VICTORIA COTTS
PAGE'S LA
BURLINGTON RD
Muswell Hill
WHITEHALL LO
MUSWELL HILL BDWY
Fortismere Sch (South Wing)
A
B
29
49
C
D
30
Alexandra Park
The Grove
Pav
Bwg Gn
Tenn Cts
KINGS AVE
MEADOW DR
ELMS AVE
FIELD AVE
MUSWELL MEWS

A
B
C
D
16
50
30
31
93
92
91
90
6
5
4
3
2
1
St Monica's RC Prim Sch
CANNON RD
HARLECH RD
ULLESWATER RD
DERWENT RD
OSBORNE RD
WINDSOR RD
PARK AVE
WENTWORTH GDNS
MADEIRA RD
HUXLEY PL
New River
FOXGROVE
ELLENA CT
FORESDALE
A1004
ALDERMAN'S HILL
FAIRWEATHER CT
LAKESIDE
GROVELANDS RD
OLD PARK RD
NEW PARK HO
WALK
SKINNERS ALMSHOS
PELLIPAR CL
DEVONSHIRE RD
DEVONSHIRE CL
A105
HAZELWOOD CRES
LIGHTCLIFFE RD
KINGSLEY RD
NEW RIVER CRES
Tenn Cts
Pav
Sp Gd
Allot Gdns
CORRI AVE
TOWNSEND AVE
POWYS LA
B1452
Bwg Gn Pav
Tenn Cts
Broomfield Park
Bndstd
Sp Gd
BROOMFIELD AVE
PILGRIMS CL
Palmers Green
TRADE CL
St Annes Catholic High Sch for Girls (Upper)
THE GROVE
THE CREST
LODGE DR
THE RISEWAY
RIVERWAY
Hazelwood Jun & Inf Schs
HAZELWOOD LA
HAMILTON CRES
LYNBRIDGE GDNS
DOVERIDGE GDNS
CONNAUGHT GRANGE
LAWRENCE AVE
CALLARD AVE
WILMER WAY
DAWLISH AVE
ASHRIDGE GDNS
BROOMFIELD LA
ELMWOOD AVE
BELMONT AVE
BROOMFIELD AVE
BRIDGE DR
HAWTHORN AVE
DAVEY CL
SHAPLAND WAY
Liby
TH
CYRIL SMITH HO
OAKTHORPE RD
Sp Gd
Pav
CHIMES AVE
ARNOLD GDNS
CHERRY BLOSSOM CL
SUNNINGDALE
Broomfield Sch
CRANFORD AVE
BROOMFIELD COTTS 1
BROOMFIELD CT 2
WESTMINSTER DR
PALMERSTON CRES
ECCLESBOURNE GDNS
ECCLESBOURNE
N13
NORTH CIRCULAR RD
BIRCHWOOD CT
Pymme's Brook
Allot Gdns
Bowes Prim Sch
A406
BOWES RD (NORTH CIRCULAR RD)
Pl Fld
POWYS CT
LYNTON CT
PYMMES CL
ELMDALE RD
BROADWAY MEWS
REGENTS AVE
MILLSTREAM CL
HEREWARD GDNS
MELVILLE GDNS
PANTILES CL
BEALE CL
STANLEY RD
HIGHWORTH RD
WAKEFIELD RD
B106
HARDWICKE RD
LIVINGSTONE RD
MOFFAT RD
PYMMES RD
Allot Gdns
RIVERSIDE APARTMENTS
CLOCKHOUSE PAR
Clockhouse Junction
FAIRBROOK RD
FAIRBROOK CL
PRINCES AVE
UNION RD
BOSWORTH RD
NATAL RD
LANCASTER RD
YORK RD
HAYWOOD
BROWNLOW RD
ELVENDON RD
WISHAW WLK
Bwg Gn
Bowes Park
RUSSELL RD
PARKSIDE CT
COLLINGS CL
GRANVILLE
PALMERSTON RD
SIDNEY AVE
MELBOURNE AVE
KELVIN AVE
BELSIZE AVE
SPENCER AVE
Tottenhall Inf Sch
TOTTENHALL RD
GRENOBLE GDNS
St Michael-at-Bowes CE Jun Sch
ST CUTHBERTS RD
UPSDELL AVE
BERKSHIRE GDNS
WILDE PL
MEDESENGE WAY
WILLIAM HO
SANDCROFT CL
DEANS DR
COLET CL
GODOLPHIN
NORFOLK AVE
Enfield
Haringey
WARWICK
BEECH RD
WESTBURY RD
Tenn Cts
GORING RD
WHITTINGTON RD
WYNAUD CT
RIDGEON CT
OAK LA
PARKDALE
EMBASSY CT
BOUNDS GREEN CT
ELEANOR RD
RICHMOND RD
QUEEN'S RD
HERBERT RD
NORTHBROOK RD
MANOR RD
GRASMERE CT
LAWRENCE HO
MAXWELL HO
LIONEL HO
PALM CT
LASCOTT'S RD
CHESHIRE RD
PARKHURST RD
MARQUIS RD
LYNDHURST RD
MARYLAND RD
ARCADIAN GDNS
SYLVAN AVE
WOODSIDE RD
CROSS RD
WOLVES LA
THETFORD CL
Allot Gdns
New River Sp & Recn Ctr
GORDON RD
Bounds Green
A109
B106
QUEEN'S PAR
FLETTON RD
Schs
IRELAND PL
MYDDLETON MEWS
MYDDLETON RD
MARLBOROUGH RD
SHROPSHIRE RD
HAMPSHIRE RD
HIGH RD
GLENDALE AVE
ST GABLES
THOROLD RD
FERNWOOD
SIDNEY RD
Allot Gdns
Woodside Park
CROFTS LA
N22
Tenn Cts
PARK RD
PALACE RD
CLARENCE RD
ORCHARD CT
BARNES CT
OAK HO
KINGSLEY CT
REDRUTH CL
FALMOUTH
FULLERS COTTS
PORTREE CL
Pav
Bwg Gn
St Thomas More Sch
Tenn Cts
Pav
White Hart Lane Sch
Pav
THE CROSSWAY
PARK GR
TRINITY RD
TRURO RD
PORTERS AND WALTERS ALMSHOUSES
MOHR CT
1 ADAMS MEWS
2 THOMAS HARDY HO
Earlham Prim Sch
Pl Fld
Pl Fld
PARK VIEW GDNS
FIFE RD
PARK CT
EDITH RD
ANEURIN BEVAN CT
BAILEY CL
CORBETT GR
FIREMAN'S FLATS
IMPERIAL RD
ALESIA CL
NIGHTINGALE RD
EARLHAM GR
HIGHFIELD CL
CHAPMAN GN
Recn Gd
STIRLING RD
FORFAR RD
PERTH RD
PAISLEY RD
BOUNDS GREEN RD
FINSBURY HO
NEWBURY HO
PARTRIDGE WAY
ROSECROFT
FINSBURY RD
COMMERCE RD
MORANT PL
CANNING CRES
NEWNHAM RD
NEWNHAM
DOUGLAS RD
BERWICK RD
LEITH RD
SAXON RD
EASTERN RD
NORTHCOTT AVE
CORNWALL AVE
BASIL SPENCE HO
JOYCE BUTLER HO
TRINITY RD
NEVILLE PL
KINGS RD
RIVERSDALE GDNS
ELIZABETH BLACKWELL HO
ACACIA HO
CEDAR HO
DUNBAR RD
SOLWAY RD
MELROSE AVE
ELM RD
Tenn Ct
Bwg Gn
BRAEMAR AVE
Nightingale Gardens
WOOD GREEN
Sch
Ctr
COLAB CT
MOWBRAY CT
EWART GR
WILLIAMS GR
PROGRESS WAY
GEORGE LANSBURY HO
WINKFIELD RD
DAPHNE HO
ACACIA RD
ERICA HO
FIRS HO
KHALSA CT
Pav
GRANVILLE RD
DAGMAR RD
PRINCES AVE
OUTRAM RD
Allot Gdns
BUCKINGHAM RD
TERRICK RD
DORSET RD
ST MICHAEL'S TERR
PARK AVE
RANELAGH RD
SELBORNE RD
WOODLEIGH CT 1
GREENWOOD HO 2
LOUISE CT
PELLATT GR
ALBERT VICTORIA HO
MERLIN CT
CAMBRIDGE
ST ALBANS CRES
BRACKNELL CL
Crown Ct
LORDSHIP LA
COLDHAM CT
ANDRULA CT
ELLENBOROUGH
ALEXANDRA AVE
PALACE GATES RD
WOLSELEY RD
WARBERRY RD
RINGSLADE RD
WATSONS RD
CRANBROOK
BERNERS RD
HARDY PAS
GATHORNE RD
LYNDUM CT
TEMPLE TERR
COOMBE RD
ANDERTON CT
ALEXANDRA PARK RD
STATION RD
Avenue Gdns
Sch
BARRATT AVE
CUMBERLAND RD
RIVER PARK RD
VINCENT SQ
VINCENT RD
MOSELLE AVE
MORLEY AVE
SALISBURY RD
FARRANT AVE
GLADSTONE AVE
DARWIN RD
Alexandra Palace
BEDFORD RD
B138
STATION RD
BRADLEY RD
STATION RD
BRABANT RD
Wood Green
A109
WELLESLEY RD
BULLER RD
REDVERS RD
Noel Park Prim Sch
LYMINGTON AVE
HEWITT AVE
Wood Green Common
TOWER TERR
PARKLAND RD
JACK BARNETT WAY
CAXTON RD
THE BROADWAY
GLADSTONE AVE
PELHAM RD
NOEL PARK RD
ASHLEY CRES
RUSSELL AVE
Rec Gd
Noel Park
SOUTH TERR
Alexandra Prim Sch
WESTERN RD
CLARENDON RD
MAYES RD
Liby
GLADSTONE MEWS
BARBARA HUCKLESBURY CL
ALFRED FINDLEY HO
GARDNER CT
GLYNNE RD
MEADS RD
WILLINGDON RD
LAKEFIELD RD
WESTBURY AVE
N8
COBURG RD
SILSOE RD
BROOK RD
HORNSEY PARK RD
B138
A105
PAGE HIGH
BURY RD
WESTBEECH RD
THE SANDLINGS
COBHAM RD
A1080
SIRDAR RD
HAWKE PARK RD
1 KOBLENZ HO
2 WAT TYLER HO
3 NEWLAND HO
4 GOODWIN CT
5 GILLETT HO
6 MYDDELTON HO
7 CAMPSFIELD HO
Pl Fld
NEWLAND RD
Alexandra Park
PARK RIDINGS
MALVERN RD
COURCY RD
WHYMARK AVE
MANNOCK RD

A
B
C
D
17
51
34
93
92
91
90
6
5
4
3
2
1
HEDGE LA
PEMBROKE RD
NEW PARK AVE
Tatem Park
Hollywood Gardens
WESTERHAM AVE
ORPINGTON GDNS
CHEDDINGTON RD
HUXLEY RD
HENLEY RD
Aylward Sch
HEWISH RD
HINTON RD
OAKFIELD GDNS
LOPEN RD
HAZELBURY LA
BRIARY LA
PARK LA
Pl Flds
Pymmes Park
EDMONTON
Tenn Cts
Bwg Gn
Silver Street
SILVER ST
A406
A10
A111
Great Cambridge Junction
KENDAL PAR
WEST WAY
Liby
Millfield Theatre
FLORIN CT
Allot Gdns
STERLING WAY (NORTH CIRCULAR RD)
OSTLIFFE RD
Pl Fld
Oakthorpe Prim Sch
TILE KILN LA
LISTER GDNS
NEWTON WAY
PASTEUR GDNS
HALLSHAM TERR
WEIR HALL GDNS
DERWENT AVE
WINSFORD TERR
PENTYRE AVE
WATERMILL LA
PLOWMAN CL
GARMAN CL
WIGSTON CL
BULL LA
North Middlesex
H
BOLTON RD
SOMERSET RD
GLOUCESTER RD
BRIDPORT RD
WILBURY WAY
Recn Gd
Wilbury Prim Sch
LANSBURY AVE
TIVERTON RD
Pav
Sp Gd
Tenn Cts
Allot Gdns
AMERSHAM AVE
SHAFTESBURY RD
WEIR HALL AVE
Sp Gd
LANDMARK COMMERCIAL CTR
PRETORIA RD N
QUEENSLAND AVE
CANADA AVE
EMPIRE AVE
DEVONIA GDNS
Pl Flds
Enfield
Haringey
BARCLAY RD
Tenn Cts
DEVONSHIRE HILL LA
MAYFAIR GDNS
Pl Fld
Devonshire Hill Prim Sch
FRONTIER WORKS
DURBAN RD
Superstore
CONISTON RD
WHITE HART LA
CAMBRIDGE GDNS
OAK AVE
Middlesex Univ
Fball Gd
Recn Gd
COMPTON CRES
BARKHAM RD
BIGBURY CL
SOMERSET GDNS
SOMERSET HALL
CREIGHTON RD
PEACOCK EST
GIBSON BSNS CTR
WINGATE TRAD EST
Allot Gdns
White Hart Lane
The Moselle
WILLIAM ATKINSON HO
Tottenham Cemy
N17
RIVULET RD
COURTMAN RD
A1080
THE ROUNDWAY
WARKWORTH RD
PAXTON RD
Northumberland Pk Sp Ctr
Tottenham Hotspur Fball Club
CHURCH RD
Risley Avenue Jun & Inf Schs
Pl Fld
Bruce Castle Park
Bruce Castle Mus
MORTEYNE RD
RISLEY AVE
Tower Gardens
TOWER GARDENS RD
LORDSHIP LA
A109
HIGH RD
A1010
BRUCE GR
PEMBURY RD
SCOTLAND GN
TOTTENHAM
Pl Fld
Broadwater Farm Prim Sch
Moselle Sch
William C Harvey Sch
Lordship Recn Gd
Open Air Theatre
DOWNHILLS WAY
B155
WIMBORNE RD
THE AVENUE
SPERLING RD
Pav
Tenn Cts
Bruce Grove Prim Sch
Bruce Grove
A10
HOLCOMBE RD
MALVERN RD
SCALES RD
CHESNUT GR
HASTINGS RD
WILMOT RD
PENDENNIS RD

34
A
B
C
D
18
93
Pl Flds
6
5
4
3
2
1
92
91
90
EDMONTON
Upper Edmonton
TOTTENHAM
N18
N17
Federation Cemy
Recn Gd
Fleecefield Prim Sch
Angel Edmonton
ANGEL ROAD (NORTH CIRCULAR ROAD)
CONDUIT LA
Kenninghall
Cooks Ferry
A406
A1010
A1055
B137
A109
B179
A10
FORE ST
HIGH RD
MERIDIAN WAY
WATERMEAD WAY
BLACKHORSE LA
Angel Road
Raynham Prim Sch
Pl Fld
Tenn Cts
Bwg Gn
Montagu Ind Est
Eley's Est
Angel Rd Works
Superstore
Stonehill Bsns Pk
Lea Valley Trad Est
Kingsway Est
Edmonton Wharf
Chalk Bridge
Triumph Trad Est
Hotspur Ind Est
Royal London Est
Lake Bsns Ctr
Sp Gd
Bwg Gns
Nrthmbrlnd Park Ind Est
Leeside Trad Est
Leeside Works
Mowlem Trad Est
Leeside Ind Est
Unicorn Works
Northumberland Pk Sp Ctr
Tottenham Hotspur Fball Club
Northumberland Park
Coleraine Park Prim Sch
Rosebery Ind Pk
Allot Gdns
Tottenham Marshes
River Lee Navigation
River Lea or Lee Diversion
Lee Flood Relief Channel
Pymme's Brook
Lockwood Reservoir
Millmead Ind Ctr
Lockwood Ind Pk
Lea Valley Technopark
Down Lane Park
Bruce Grove
Uplands Bsns Pk
Forest Trad Est
35
52

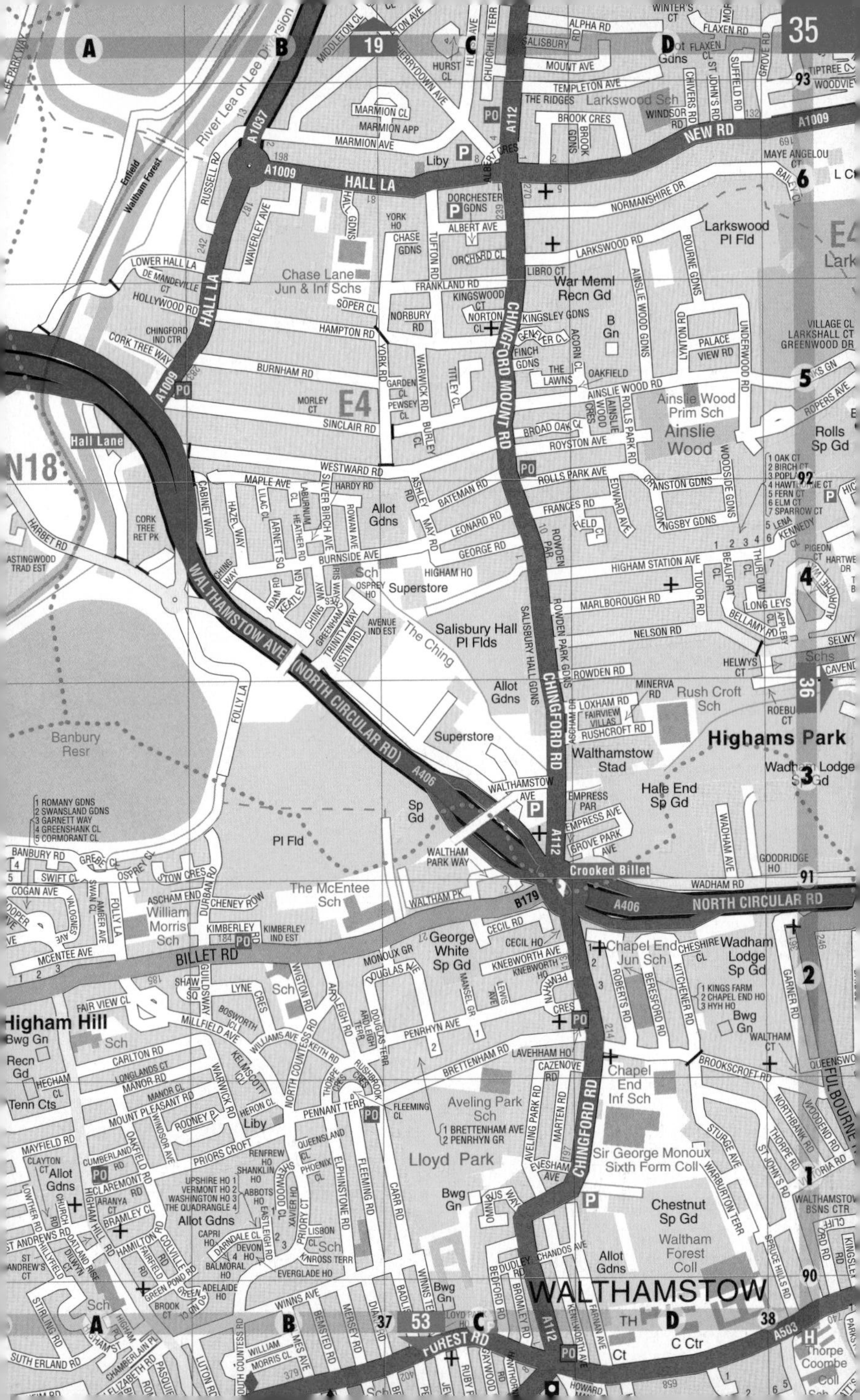
19
A
B
C
D
WINTER'S CT
ALPHA RD
SALISBURY RD
FLAXEN RD
FLAXEN CL
Pt Gdns
MIDDLETON CL
HERRYDOWN AVE
HURST CL
CHURCHILL TERR
MOUNT AVE
TEMPLETON AVE
THE RIDGES
Larkswood Sch
WINDSOR RD
CHIVERS RD
ST JOHN'S RD
SUFFIELD RD
GROVE RD
TIPTREE CL
WOODVIEW
93
MARMION CL
MARMION APP
MARMION AVE
BROOK CRES
BROOK GDNS
A1009
NEW RD
A1037
A112
River Lea or Lee Diversion
Enfield
Waltham Forest
RUSSELL RD
Liby
ALBERT CRES
MAYE ANGELOU CT
BAILEY CL
6
HALL LA
DORCHESTER GDNS
NORMANSHIRE DR
WAVERLEY AVE
HALL GDNS
YORK HO
CHASE GDNS
ALBERT AVE
Larkswood Pl Fld
TUFTON RD
ORCHARD CL
LARKSWOOD RD
BOURNE GDNS
E4
LOWER HALL LA
DE MANDEVILLE CT
HOLLYWOOD RD
Chase Lane Jun & Inf Schs
FRANKLAND RD
LIBRO CT
War Meml Recn Gd
AINSLIE WOOD GDNS
SOPER CL
KINGSWOOD CT
NORBURY RD
NORTON CL
KINGSLEY GDNS
B Gn
LAYTON RD
UNDERWOOD RD
PALACE VIEW RD
VILLAGE CL
LARKSHALL CT
GREENWOOD CT
CHINGFORD IND CTR
HAMPTON RD
GENEVER CL
FINCH GDNS
ACORN CL
CORK TREE WAY
YORK RD
WARWICK RD
TITLEY CL
CHINGFORD MOUNT RD
THE LAWNS
OAKFIELD
5
BURNHAM RD
GARDEN CL
PEWSEY CL
AINSLIE WOOD RD
Ainslie Wood Prim Sch
ROPERS AVE
MORLEY CT
SINCLAIR RD
BURLEY CL
WOOD CRES
AINSLIE CL
ROLLS PARK RD
Ainslie Wood
Rolls Sp Gd
PO
Hall Lane
BROAD OAK CL
ROYSTON AVE
N18
WESTWARD RD
1 OAK CT
2 BIRCH CT
3 POPLAR CT
4 HAWTHORNE CT
5 FERN CT
6 ELM CT
7 SPARROW CT
92
MAPLE AVE
HARDY RD
ASHLEY RD
BATEMAN RD
ROLLS PARK AVE
EDWARD AVE
CRANSTON GDNS
WOODSIDE GDNS
CABINET WAY
LILAC CL
LABURNUM CL
SILVER BIRCH AVE
Allot Gdns
FRANCES RD
FIELD CL
CONINGSBY GDNS
LENA KENNEDY CL
HAZEL WAY
ARNETT SQ
HEATHER RD
ROWAN AVE
MAY RD
LEONARD RD
ROWDEN PAR
PIGEON CT
HARTWELL DR
HARBET RD
CORK TREE RET PK
BURNSIDE AVE
GEORGE RD
HIGHAM STATION AVE
BEAUFORT CL
THURLOW CL
ASTINGWOOD TRAD EST
CHING WAY
Sch
HIGHAM HO
TUDOR RD
4
ADAM RD
KEATLEY GN
IRIS WAY
OSPREY HO
Superstore
ALDRIDGE WAY
MARLBOROUGH RD
LONG LEYS
CHING WAY
GREENHAM CL
TRINITY WAY
JUSTIN RD
AVENUE IND EST
Salisbury Hall Pl Flds
BELLAMY RD
APPLEBY CL
NELSON RD
SELWYN
WALTHAMSTOW AVE
(NORTH CIRCULAR RD)
The Ching
SALISBURY HALL GDNS
ROWDEN PARK GDNS
ROWDEN PARK GDNS
HELWYS CT
Schs
CAVENDISH
ROWDEN RD
36
Allot Gdns
MINERVA RD
Rush Croft Sch
ROEBUCK CT
FOLLY LA
LOXHAM RD
FAIRVIEW VILLAS
RUSHCROFT RD
ASCHAM DR
Banbury Resr
Superstore
CHINGFORD RD
Highams Park
Walthamstow Stad
Wadham Lodge Sp Gd
Hale End Sp Gd
3
A406
WALTHAMSTOW AVE
EMPRESS PAR
1 ROMANY GDNS
2 SWANSLAND GDNS
3 GARNETT WAY
4 GREENSHANK CL
5 CORMORANT CL
Sp Gd
EMPRESS AVE
WADHAM AVE
GROVE PARK AVE
Pl Fld
WALTHAM PARK WAY
GOODRIDGE HO
BANBURY RD
GREBE CL
OSPREY CL
Crooked Billet
SWIFT CL
STOW CRES
DURBAN RD
91
COGAN AVE
The McEntee Sch
WADHAM RD
SWAN CL
VALOGNES AVE
ASCHAM END
CHENEY ROW
WALTHAM PK
B179
NORTH CIRCULAR RD
AMBER AVE
William Morris Sch
KIMBERLEY RD
KIMBERLEY IND EST
George White Sp Gd
CECIL RD
CECIL HO
Chapel End Jun Sch
CHESHIRE CL
Wadham Lodge Sp Gd
MCENTEE AVE
BILLET RD
MONOUX GR
DOUGLAS AVE
KNEBWORTH AVE
KNEBWORTH HO
PENRHYN CRES
ROBERTS RD
BERESFORD RD
KITCHENER RD
GARNER RD
2
SHAW SQ
GUILDSWAY
LYNE CRES
Sch
WIGTON RD
ARDLEIGH RD
ARDLEIGH TERR
MANSEL GR
LEWIS AVE
1 KINGS FARM
2 CHAPEL END HO
3 HYH HO
FAIR VIEW CL
BOSWORTH CL
Higham Hill
Bwg Gn
MILLFIELD AVE
WILLIAMS AVE
PENRHYN AVE
Bwg Gn
WALTHAM CT
Sch
CARLTON RD
NORTH COUNTESS RD
KEITH RD
DOUGLAS TERR
BRETTENHAM RD
LAVEHHAM HO
CAZENOVE RD
Chapel End Inf Sch
BROOKSCROFT RD
QUEENSWOOD
Recn Gd
LONGLANDS CT
MANOR RD
KELMSCOTT CL
THORPE CRES
RUSHBROOK CRES
HEGHAM CL
MANOR CL
WARWICK RD
MOUNT PLEASANT RD
HERON CL
FLEEMING CL
Aveling Park Sch
NORTHBANK RD
WOODEND RD
FULBOURNE RD
Tenn Cts
RODNEY PL
PENNANT TERR
Liby
1 BRETTENHAM AVE
2 PENRHYN GR
AVELING PARK RD
MARTEN RD
STURGE AVE
THORPE RD
MAYFIELD RD
WINDSOR AVE
PRIORS CROFT
QUEENSLAND CL
Lloyd Park
Sir George Monoux Sixth Form Coll
VICTORIA RD
CLAYTON CT
Allot Gdns
CUMBERLAND RD
OAKFIELD RD
RENFREW HO
SHANKLIN HO
PHOENIX CL
ELPHINSTONE RD
FLEEMING RD
EVESHAM AVE
WARBURTON TERR
ST JOHN'S RD
1
CLAREMONT RD
UPSHIRE HO 1
VERMONT HO 2
WASHINGTON HO 3
THE QUADRANGLE 4
ABBOTS HO
SHERWOOD CL
CARR RD
Bwg Gn
OMNIBUS WAY
Chestnut Sp Gd
WALTHAMSTOW BSNS CTR
ARANYA CT
BRAMLEY CL
EASTLEIGH RD
XAVIER HO
PRIORY CT
LOWTHER RD
CHURCH RD
HIGHAM HILL RD
Allot Gdns
LISBON CL
ST ANDREWS RD
OATLAND RISE
HAMILTON RD
COLVILLE RD
CAPRI HO
DARNDALE CL
DEVON HO
Sch
KINROSS TERR
SPRUCE HILLS RD
Waltham Forest Coll
ST ANDREW'S CT
DILWYN CT
FAIRFIELD RD
BALMORAL HO
EVERGLADE HO
DUDLEY RD
CHANDOS AVE
Allot Gdns
90
GREEN POND RD
ADELAIDE HO
BROOK CT
WINNS TERR
Bwg Gn
BEDFORD RD
BROMLEY RD
WALTHAMSTOW
STIRLING RD
Sch
HIGHAM PL
WINNS AVE
DIANA RD
BADLIS RD
LLOYD PARK
A
B
C
D
37
53
38
HIGHAM ST
BEMSTED RD
MERSEY RD
A112
KENILWORTH AVE
FARNAN AVE
TH
A503
SUTHERLAND RD
CHAMBERLAIN PL
ELIZABETH RD
SOUTH COUNTESS RD
WILLIAM MORRIS CL
FOREST RD
PO
C Ctr
Ct
Thorpe Coombe
Coll
LUTON RD
HOWARD

A
B
C
D
20
HATCH LA
NEW RD
A1009
B146
The Ching
Fball Gd
1 CHING CT
2 NEWGATE ST
3 THE TERRACE
4 RONVER LO
Redbridge
Waltham Forest
The Lops
Woodford
MORNINGTON RD
THE HOLLOW
1 THE ALBANY
2 HATCHWOODS
3 HOBART CT
4 AURORA CT
MONTALT HO
CHINGFORD LA
VILLAGE HTS 1
MILL HO 2
PAYZES GDNS 3
Woodford Green Sch
FRIARS CL
HEATON CL
MAPLETON RD
TIPTREE CT
WOODVIEW AVE
ASHINGDON CL
PEAS MEAD TERR
HOLLAND HO
MAYE ANGELOU CT
L Ctr
BAILEY CL
LARKSHALL RD
B160
RUSSETS CL
Allot Gdns
Chingford Hatch
Larkswood Pl Fld
E4
Larks Wood
BOURNE GDNS
HATCH LA
MANOR WAY
NIGHTINGALE CL
WATERHALL AVE
GETOYNE AVE
BROOKHOUSE GDNS
Jubilee Sp Gd
LARKSWOOD CT
THE AVENUE
NIGHTINGALE AVE
FOREST GLADE
MONTALT RD
WOOD LA
KEYNSHAM AVE
LICHFIELD RD
MASON RD
MARION GR
VILLAGE CL 1
LARKSHALL CT 2
GREENWOOD DR 3
OAKDALE CT
OAKDALE GDNS
EAST VIEW
PALACE VIEW RD
UNDERWOOD RD
LYNTON RD
INKS GN
ROPERS AVE
AVRIL WAY
WARBOYS CRES
COOLGARDIE AVE
RICHMOND AVE
RICHMOND CRES
WRIGLEY CL
RODINGS CT
SUNNYDENE AVE
SHEREDAN RD
CLIVEDON RD
FALMOUTH AVE
The Highams Park
Boating Lake
COWELL LODGE
HENRY'S AVE
CREALOCK GR
BEECHWOOD DR
Ainslie Wood Prim Sch
Ainslie Wood
Bwg Gn
Rolls Sp Gd
MERRIAM CL
MARIEN CT
CASTLE AVE
BELMONT CL
SHELDON HO
TAMWORTH AVE
THE CHARTER RD
ELM GR
MILL LA
1 OAK CT
2 BIRCH CT
3 POPLAR CT
4 HAWTHORNE CT
5 FERN CT
6 ELM CT
7 SPARROW CT
HICKMAN AVE
JUBILEE AVE
Wks
Highams Park
CHURCH AVE
HANDSWORTH AVE
ST LEONARD'S AVE
GORDON AVE
Liby
MATHART CT
NESTA RD
Woodford Cty High Sch
CHURCHILL LO
LENA KENNEDY CL
PIGEON CT
HARTWELL DR
LC
BRIARVIEW CT
Schs
Allot Gdns
CONYERS CL
ARMSTRONG AVE
Rugby Fball Gd
IG8
TUDOR RD
THURLOW CL
ALDRICH WAY
THE BROADWAY 1
BROADWAY PAR 2
LAKEVIEW CT
JELLICOE CT
BEVERLEY RD
Sch
Hale End
SILVERDALE RD
LONG LEYS
APPLEBY CL
BELLAMY RD
SELWYN AVE
PRESTON AVE
VINCENT RD
BROOK MEADOW CL
BROOKFIELD PATH
ALDERS AV
CHURCHILL MEWS
HELWYS CT
CAVENDISH RD
HALDAN RD
NEWBURY RD
STUDLEY AVE
HOLLYWOOD WAY
THE OAKS
1 FUSCHIA CT
2 CAMELIA CT
3 AZALEA CT
4 PEONY CT
5 MATSON CT
HARMAN AVE
LODGE VILLAS
35
ROEBUCK CT
WICKHAM RD
BEECH HALL RD
BEECH HALL CRES
HOLLY CRES
THE BRIDLE PATH
Highams Park
Wadham Lodge Sp Gd
ALMA AVE
LYNDHURST RD
WINCHESTER RD
FORSTER CL
GALEBOROUGH AVE
OAK HILL CRES
OAK HILL CT
OAK HILL
MAPPERLEY DR
Hotel
THE ROSES
BUNCES LA
St Aubyn's Sch
HIGH ROAD WOODFORD GN
MALVERN AVE
SWANAGE RD
MORLEY AVE
THE HALE
FOREST MOUNT RD
FOREST DR
BENNINGTON RD
GASCOIGNE GDNS
WOODFORD NEW RD
EMPRESS AVE
WADHAM AVE
GOODRIDGE HO
EVANSTON AVE
THE CLOSE
HALE END RD
FRINTON DR
1 BEECH FARM COTTS
2 SWALLOW CT
3 LESTER HO
4 MONTSERRAT AVE
FULLER'S AVE
FULLER'S RD
WADHAM RD
NORTH CIRCULAR RD
SKY PEALS RD
OAK HILL GDNS
DERBY RD
DERBY CT
ARNOLD CT
CHELMSFORD RD
Wadham Lodge Sp Gd
CHESHIRE CL
KITCHENER RD
1 KINGS FARM
2 CHAPEL END HO
3 HYH HO
GARNER RD
THE HIGHAMS
FOREST VIEW RD
BRIDGE END
GUILDFORD RD
HEATHCROFT GDNS
LONGACRE RD
TREVOSE RD
COBHAM RD
RAILWAY TERR
PENTIRE RD
Thorpe Hall Prim Sch
CARNANTON RD
GRANTOCK RD
BEACONTREE AVE
SOUTHEND ROAD
PEEL RD
WALPOLE RD
CARNARVON RD
STANLEY RD
MALMESBURY RD
BUCKINGHAM RD
RECTORY
Bwg Gn
WALTHAM CT
BROOKSCROFT RD
QUEENSWOOD AVE
THORPE HALL RD
LANGDALE CL
Allot Gdns
GROVE RD
(NORTH CIRCULAR ROAD)
A406
NORTHBANK RD
WOODEND RD
THORPE RD
FULBOURNE RD
SPENCER RD
CHAUCER RD
MACDONALD RD
BELLE VUE RD
Waterworks Cnr
CRAIG GDNS
GROVE HILL
STURGE AVE
WARBURTON TERR
ST JOHN'S RD
VICTORIA RD
Wks
Whitefield Sch
WOODSTOCK RD
ULVERSTON RD
CASTLETON RD
HILLCREST RD
A503
A104
GROVE END
BRESSEY GR
WALTHAMSTOW BSNS CTR
CLIFFORD RD
KINGSLEY RD
E17
FOREST RD
Hyland House Sch
1 HEMPSTEAD RD
2 DENNIS CT
HIGH VIEW RD
BYRON AVE
RAYMOND AVE
WORDSWORTH AVE
GREENHEYS DR
SPRUCE HILLS RD
STOW
Liby
RADBOURNE CRES
WINSBEACH
TRISTRAM RD
Allot Gdns
Upper Walthamstow
39
54
CALVER CT
38
Woodside Schs
Thorpe Coombe
Coll
CORBETT RD
HAGGER CT
WOODLANDS RD
Tenn Cts
Bwg Gn
BEECH CT
MILLS HO
BISTERN AVE
AVONFIELD
Gilbert's Slade
BROADWALK
CHEYNE AVE
C Ctr

Knighton Wood
Woodford Wells
21
Woodford
Trinity RC High Sch (Upper)
St Antony's Sch
Wells Sch
Avon House Sch
Sp Gd
Trinity RC High Sch (Lower)
Roding Valley
IG9
IG8
Sp Gd
WOODFORD
River Roding
Ray Park
Ray Lodge Prim Sch
Fball Gd
Crkt Gd
Woodford Green Prep Sch
Liby
Woodford
Woodbridge High Sch
Woodford Green
Pl Fld
Allot Gdns
Allot Gdns
Sp Gd
Pl Fld & Sp Gd
Queen Mary & Westfield Coll (Halls of Residence)
Liby
Sch
Sch
Charlie Browns Rdbt
E18
South Woodford
Oakdale Jun Sch
WOODFORD TRAD EST
55
M11 Stansted Airport, M25
A113 Chigwell, M11 (A1168)
VII
A110
A104
HIGH ROAD WOODFORD GN
A1009
BROADMEAD RD
CHIGWELL RD
A113
M11
A406
A1400 SOUTHEND RD
HIGH RD
A1199
B168
GEORGE LA
THE VIADUCT
CHIGWELL RD
STATION WAY
CHERRY TREE RISE
1 STATION APP
2 STATION PAR
SNAKES LA E
SNAKES LA W
THE BROADWAY
WOODFORD GN
A B C D
93 92 91 90
6 5 4 3 2 1
41 42

A4180 Rickmansworth (A404
DUCKS HILL
Towers
Knightscote Farm
Dell
VI
A
B
C
D
Ashby Farm
90
Highbones
HA6
78
A4180
6
BREAKSPEAR MEWS
Bourne Farm
Youngwood Farm
Breakspear House
Nat Res
BREAKSPEAR RD N
Mad Bess' Wood
81
Warren Farm
North Riding Wood
5
P
89
Bayhurst Wood Countryside Park
South Harefield
Willow Tree Farm
4
Pl Fld
Lower Lodge
HA4
VI
48
FINE BUSH LA
Harefield Moor
UB9
St Leonard's Farm
43
BREAKSPEAR
3
65
WESTWOOD
41
Newyears Green
Pylon Farm
Elm Tree Farm
GREY
Highway Farm
NEWYEARS GREEN LA
High View Farm
Crows Nest Farm
PH
ALLONBY DR
EAMONT CL
GLOVERS GR
88
HARVIL RD
Braemar Farm
Old Clack Farm
2
72
Newyears Green Covert
TILE KILN LA
OLD PRIORY
GRAYS COTTS
Research Farm
Gatemead Farm
BREAKSPEAR RD S
River Pinn
1
67
UB10
Copthall Covert
Brackenbury Farm
87
PYNCHESTER CL
HOYLAKE CRES
Pl Fld
06
07
60
Uxbridge CH
THE MEAD
FIELD CL
Breakspear Jun & Inf Schs
BUSHEY CL
Copthall Farm
THALL

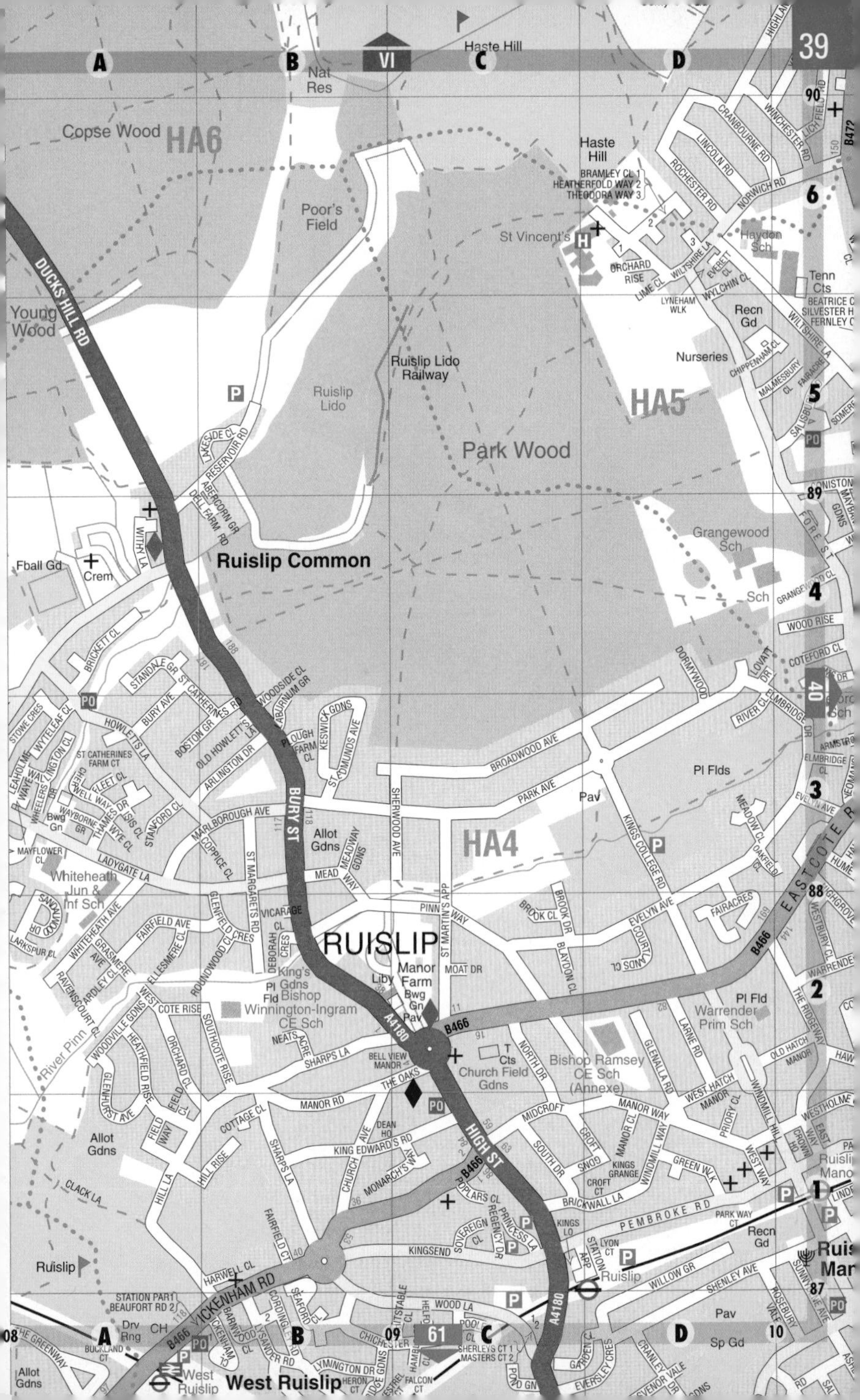
A
B
VI
C
Haste Hill
D
Nat Res
Copse Wood
HA6
Poor's Field
Haste Hill
BRAMLEY CL 1
HEATHERFOLD WAY 2
THEODORA WAY 3
St Vincent's
H
ORCHARD RISE
LIME CL
WILTSHIRE LA
EVERETT CL
WYLCHIN CL
LYNEHAM WLK
CRANBOURNE RD
LINCOLN RD
ROCHESTER RD
WINCHESTER RD
LICHFIELD RD
NORWICH RD
90
B472
6
Haydon Sch
Tenn Cts
BEATRICE CL
SILVESTER H
FERNLEY C
Recn Gd
Nurseries
CHIPPENHAM CL
MALMESBURY CL
FAIRACRE
SALISBURY
SOMERBY
5
PO
Young Wood
DUCKS HILL RD
P
Ruislip Lido Railway
Ruislip Lido
HA5
Park Wood
LAKESIDE CL
RESERVOIR RD
ABERCORN GR
DELL FARM RD
WITHY LA
CONISTON
89
MAYBANK GDNS
FORE ST
Grangewood Sch
Fball Gd
Crem
Ruislip Common
Sch
GRANGEWOOD CL
4
WOOD RISE
BRICKETT CL
188
STANDALE GR
ST CATHERINES RD
WOODSIDE CL
LABURNUM GR
DORMYWOOD
COTEFORD CL
LOVATT DR
RIVER CL
EMBRIDGE DR
40
PO
STOWE CRES
WYTELEAF CL
HOWLETTS LA
BURY AVE
BOSTON GR
OLD HOWLETT'S LA
PLOUGH FARM CL
KESWICK GDNS
ST EDMUNDS AVE
BROADWOOD AVE
ARMSTRONG
ELMBRIDGE CL
Pl Flds
LEAHOLME WAY
WELLINGTON CL
ST CATHERINES FARM CT
CHERWELL WAY
FLEET CL
WHEELERS DR
ARLINGTON DR
SHERWOOD AVE
PARK AVE
Pav
3
EVELYN AVE
Bwg Gn
WAYBORNE GR
THAMES DR
ISIS CL
WYE CL
STANFORD CL
MARLBOROUGH AVE
117
118
BURY ST
Allot Gdns
MEADWAY GDNS
HA4
KINGS COLLEGE RD
MEADOW CL
P
OAKFIELD CL
EASTCOTE RD
MAYFLOWER CL
LADYGATE LA
COPPICE CL
ST MARGARETS RD
MEAD WAY
Whiteheath Jun & Inf Sch
SANDWOOD DR
LARKSPUR CL
WHITEHEATH AVE
GRASMERE AVE
FAIRFIELD AVE
ELLESMERE CL
GLENFIELD CRES
ROUNDWOOD CL
VICARAGE CL
DEBORAH CRES
ST MARTIN'S APP
PINN WAY
BROOK CL
BROOK DR
BLAYDON CL
EVELYN AVE
COURTLANDS CL
FAIRACRES
169
B466
88
WESTBURY CL
HIGHGROVE
RUISLIP
King's Gdns
Manor Farm
Liby
MOAT DR
WARRENDER
RAVENSCOURT CL
ARDLEY CL
Pl Fld
Bishop Winnington-Ingram CE Sch
Bwg Gn
Pav
B466
Pl Fld
Warrender Prim Sch
2
THE RIDGEWAY
WEST GDNS
COTE RISE
SOUTHCOTE RISE
A4180
River Pinn
WOODVILLE GDNS
HEATHFIELD RISE
ORCHARD CL
NEATS ACRE
SHARPS LA
BELL VIEW MANOR
T Cts
Church Field Gdns
NORTH DR
Bishop Ramsey CE Sch (Annexe)
GLENALLA RD
LARNE RD
OLD HATCH MANOR
WEST HATCH MANOR
GLENHURST AVE
FIELD CL
THE OAKS
MANOR RD
PO
MIDCROFT
MANOR WAY
PRIORY CL
WINDMILL HILL
WESTHOLME
EAST WAY
CROWN RD
Allot Gdns
FIELD WAY
COTTAGE CL
HILL RISE
DEAN HO
KING EDWARD'S RD
CHURCH AVE
SHARPS LA
MONARCH'S WAY
HIGH ST
B466
SOUTH DR
CROFT GDNS
MANOR CL
KINGS GRANGE
WINDMILL WAY
GREEN WLK
WEST WAY
Ruislip Manor
CLACK LA
HILL LA
POPLARS CL
CROFT CT
BRICKWALL LA
1
P
PEMBROKE RD
PARK WAY CT
FAIRFIELD CT
KINGS LO
SOVEREIGN CL
REGENCY DR
PRINCESS LA
P
KINGSEND
LYON CT
P
Recn Gd
Ruislip
Ruislip Manor
HARWELL CL
STATION APP
Ruislip
WILLOW GR
SHENLEY AVE
ROSEBURY VALE
SUNNINGDALE AVE
87
PO
STATION PAR 1
BEAUFORT RD 2
TWICKENHAM RD
SEAFORD CL
CORDINGLEY RD
WHITSTABLE CL
HELFORD CL
WOOD LA
POOLE CL
P
A4180
Pav
D
10
08
THE GREENWAY
A
Drv Rng
CH
BUCKLAND CT
B466
PO
BARNWOOD CL
LYSANDER RD
B
09
CHICHESTER
61
C
SHERLEYS CT 1
MASTERS CT 2
GARDEN CL
EVERSLEY CRES
CRANLEY DR
GROSVENOR VALE
Sp Gd
Allot Gdns
P
West Ruislip
West Ruislip
LYMINGTON DR
HERON CT
FALCON CT
POND GN

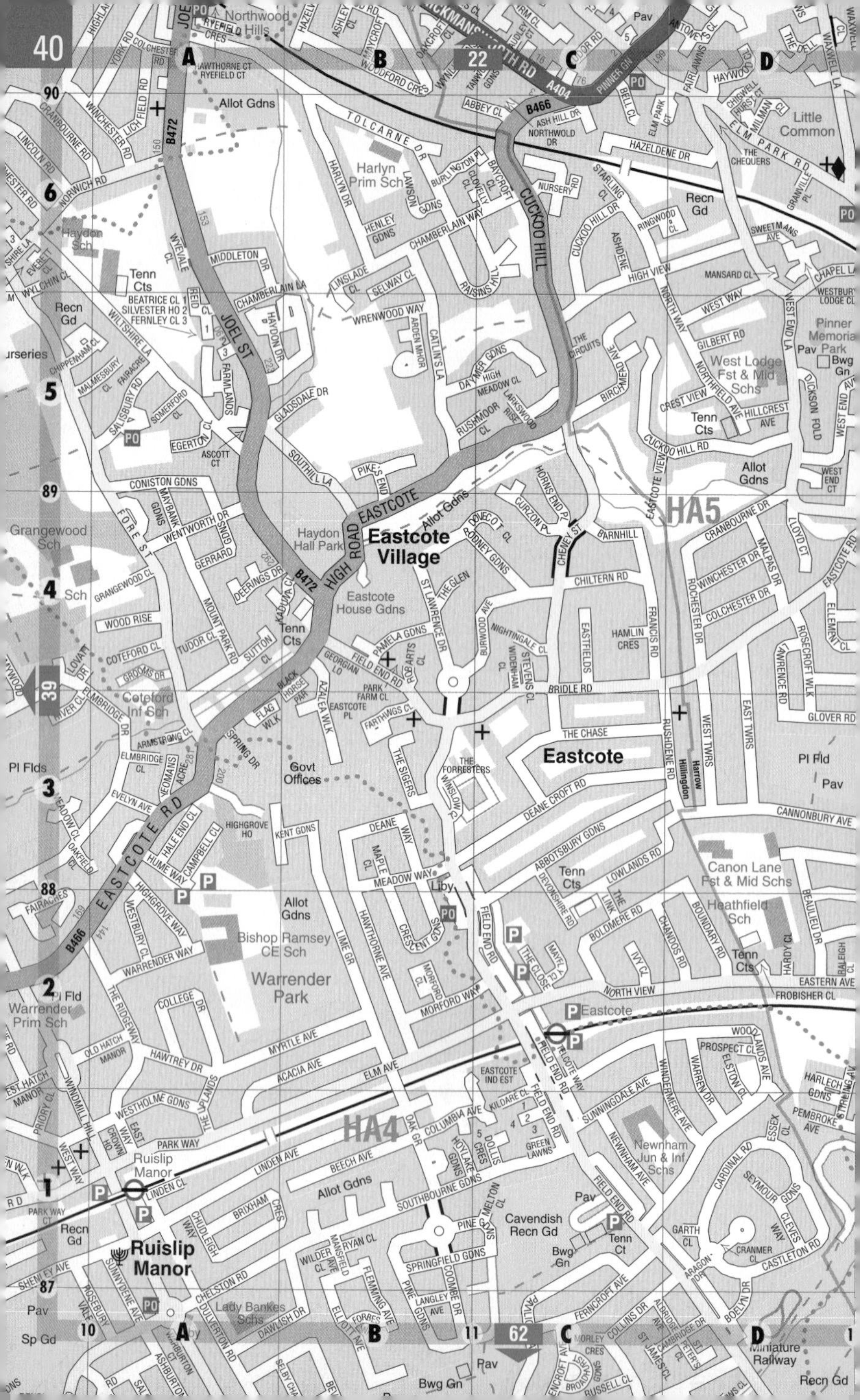
A
B
C
D
22
62
39
90
6
5
89
4
3
88
2
1
87
10
11
Northwood Hills
RYEFIELD CRES
COLCHESTER RD
YORK RD
HAWTHORNE CT
RYEFIELD CT
JOEL ST
B472
Allot Gdns
WINCHESTER RD
LICHFIELD RD
CRANBOURNE RD
LINCOLN RD
NORWICH RD
Haydon Sch
EVERETT CL
WYLCHIN CL
Tenn Cts
BEATRICE CL 1
SILVESTER HO 2
FERNLEY CL 3
Recn Gd
WILTSHIRE LA
CHIPPENHAM CL
MALMESBURY CL
FAIRACRE
SALISBURY RD
SOMERFORD CL
Nurseries
EGERTON CL
ASCOTT CT
WYEVALE CL
MIDDLETON DR
CHAMBERLAIN LA
REID CL
HAYDON DR
FARMLANDS
GLADSDALE DR
SOUTHILL LA
PIKE'S END
TOLCARNE DR
Harlyn Prim Sch
HARLYN DR
HENLEY GDNS
LAWSON GDNS
CHAMBERLAIN WAY
LINSLADE CL
SELWAY CL
WRENWOOD WAY
ARDEN MHOR
CATLIN'S LA
BURLINGTON PL
CLOVELLY CL
BAYCROFT CL
RAISINS HILL
DAYMER GDNS
HIGH MEADOW CL
RUSHMOOR CL
LARKSWOOD RISE
CUCKOO HILL
NURSERY RD
NORTHWOLD DR
ASH HILL DR
ABBEY CL
B466
A404
RICKMANSWORTH RD
PINNER GN
WOODFORD CRES
ASHLEY CL
MAYCROFT
OAKCROFT
BELL CL
ELM PARK CT
FAIRLAWNS CL
ANTONEYS CL
HAYWOOD CL
CHISWELL HURST CT
MILMAN CL
ELM PARK RD
Little Common
THE CHEQUERS
GRANVILLE PL
THE DELL
WAXWELL LA
Pav
PO
HAZELDENE DR
STARLING CL
CUCKOO HILL DR
ASHDENE
RINGWOOD CL
HIGH VIEW
NORTH WAY
MANSARD CL
SWEETMANS AVE
CHAPEL LA
WESTBURY LODGE CL
WEST WAY
WEST END LA
GILBERT RD
Pinner Memorial Park
Bwg Gn
West Lodge Fst & Mid Schs
NORTHFIELD AVE
CREST VIEW
HILLCREST AVE
DICKSON FOLD
WEST END AV
THE CIRCUITS
BIRCHMEAD AVE
CUCKOO HILL RD
EASTCOTE VIEW
Allot Gdns
WEST END CT
HA5
CRANBOURNE DR
LLOYD CT
EASTCOTE RD
WINCHESTER DR
MALPAS DR
ROCHESTER DR
COLCHESTER DR
ELLEMENT CL
ROSECROFT WLK
LAWRENCE RD
GLOVER RD
CONISTON GDNS
MAYBANK GDNS
WENTWORTH DR
FORE ST
GERRARD GDNS
Grangewood Sch
GRANGEWOOD CL
MOUNT PARK RD
WOOD RISE
TUDOR CL
SUTTON CL
COTEFORD CL
GROOMS DR
LOVATT DR
RIVER CL
ELMBRIDGE DR
Coteford Inf Sch
ARMSTRONG CL
ELMBRIDGE CL
YEOMANS ACRE
Pl Flds
EVELYN AVE
MEADOW CL
OAKFIELD CL
DEERINGS DR
KADUNA CL
Haydon Hall Park
HIGH ROAD EASTCOTE
Eastcote Village
Allot Gdns
Eastcote House Gdns
Tenn Cts
DOVECOT CL
RODNEY GDNS
CURZON PL
HORNS END PL
CHENEY ST
BARNHILL
CHILTERN RD
ST LAWRENCE DR
THE GLEN
BURWOOD AVE
NIGHTINGALE CL
WIDENHAM CL
STEVENS CL
EASTFIELDS
HAMLIN CRES
FRANCIS RD
PAMELA GDNS
ROBARTS CL
GEORGIAN LO
FIELD END RD
BLACK HORSE PAR
AZALEA WLK
PARK FARM CL
EASTCOTE PL
FLAG WLK
FARTHINGS CL
BRIDLE RD
THE CHASE
Eastcote
RUSHDENE RD
WEST TWRS
EAST TWRS
Harrow
Hillingdon
Pl Fld
Pav
SPRING DR
Govt Offices
THE SIGERS
THE FORRESTERS
WINSLOW CL
DEANE CROFT RD
CANNONBURY AVE
EASTCOTE RD
HIGHGROVE HO
HALE END CL
HUME WAY
CAMPBELL CL
KENT GDNS
DEANE WAY
MAPLE CL
MEADOW WAY
Liby
ABBOTSBURY GDNS
Tenn Cts
LOWLANDS RD
DEVONSHIRE RD
THE LINK
Canon Lane Fst & Mid Schs
Heathfield Sch
BEAULIEU DR
FAIRACRES
HIGHGROVE WAY
WESTBURY CL
WARRENDER WAY
Allot Gdns
Bishop Ramsey CE Sch
Warrender Park
LIME GR
HAWTHORNE AVE
CRESCENT GDNS
MORFORD CL
MORFORD WAY
THE CLOSE
MAYFLY CL
BOLDMERE RD
IVY CL
CHANDOS RD
BOUNDARY RD
Tenn Cts
HARDY CL
RALEIGH CL
EASTERN AVE
FROBISHER CL
NORTH VIEW
Warrender Prim Sch
THE RIDGEWAY
COLLEGE DR
OLD HATCH MANOR
HAWTREY DR
MYRTLE AVE
ACACIA AVE
ELM AVE
Eastcote
EASTCOTE WAY
EASTCOTE IND EST
WOODLANDS AVE
PROSPECT CL
WARREN DR
ELSTOW CL
WINDERMERE AVE
HARLECH GDNS
PEMBROKE AVE
STIRLING RD
WEST HATCH MANOR
PRIORY CL
WINDMILL HILL
WESTHOLME GDNS
THE UPLANDS
EAST WAY
CROWN HO
PARK WAY
COLUMBIA AVE
OAK GR
KILDARE CL
HA4
DOLLIS CRES
GREEN LAWNS
SUNNINGDALE AVE
NEWNHAM AVE
Newnham Jun & Inf Schs
ESSEX CL
CARDINAL RD
SEYMOUR GDNS
CLEVES WAY
Ruislip Manor
LINDEN CL
LINDEN AVE
BEECH AVE
HOYLAKE GDNS
Allot Gdns
SOUTHBOURNE GDNS
MELTON CL
Pav
Cavendish Recn Gd
Tenn Ct
Bwg Gn
GARTH CL
CRANMER CL
CASTLETON RD
ARAGON DR
PARK WAY CT
Recn Gd
CHUDLEIGH WAY
BRIXHAM CRES
WILDER CL
RYAN CL
MANSFIELD AVE
PINE GDNS
SPRINGFIELD GDNS
COOMBE DR
FLEMMING AVE
Ruislip Manor
SHENLEY AVE
ROSEBURY VALE
SUNNYDENE AVE
CHELSTON RD
DULVERTON RD
Lady Bankes Schs
DAWLISH DR
LANGLEY AVE
FORBES
ELLIOTT AVE
FERNCROFT AVE
COLLINS DR
ALDRIDGE AVE
ST JAMES CL
CAMBRIDGE DR
ST PETER'S
BOELYN DR
MORLEY CRES
BROADHURST
RUSSELL CL
Miniature Railway
Recn Gd
Sp Gd
Pav
ASHBURTON RD
Bwg Gn

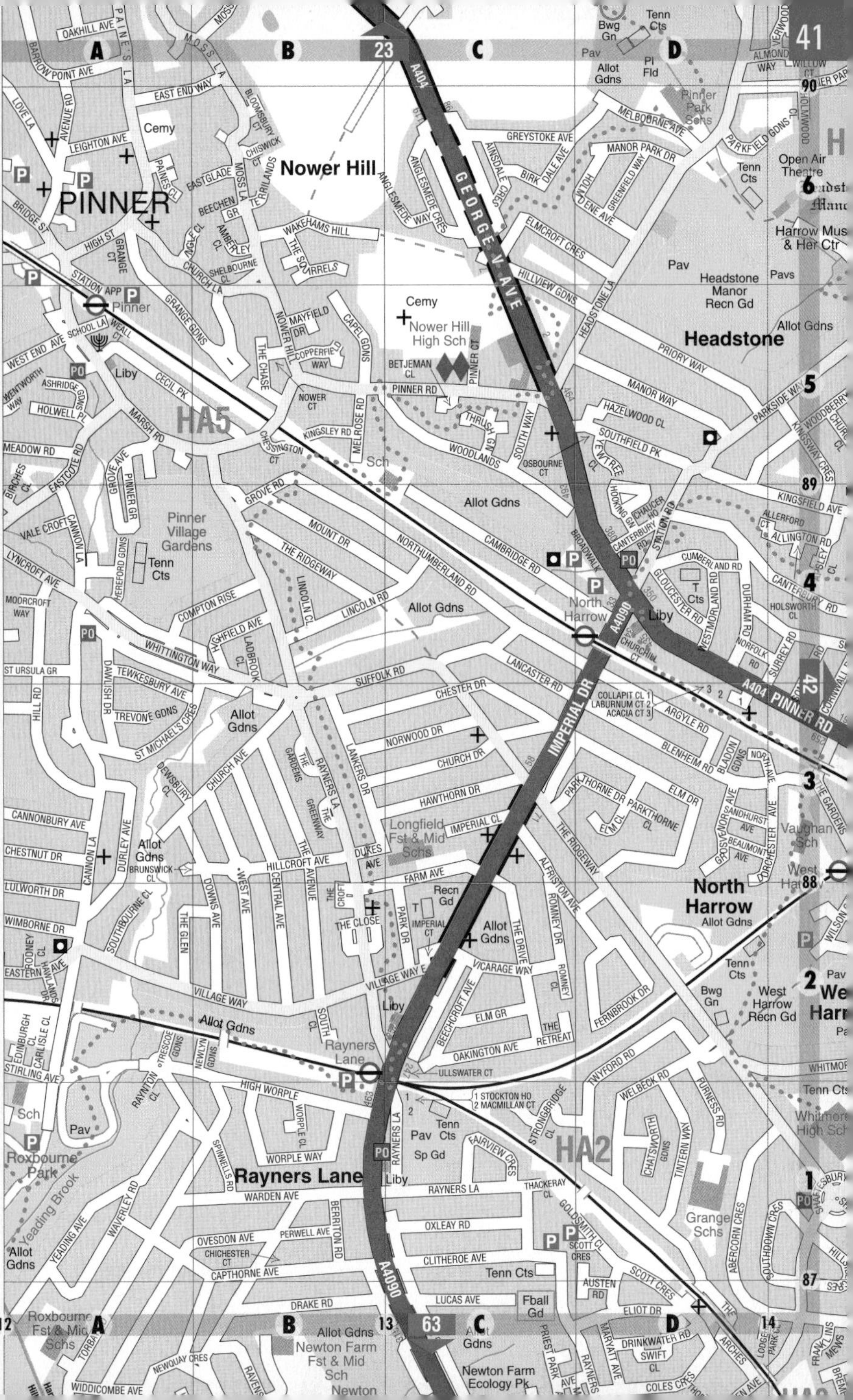
A
B
23
C
D
PINNER
Nower Hill
Headstone
North Harrow
Rayners Lane
HA5
HA2
A404
GEORGE V AVE
A4090
IMPERIAL DR
PINNER RD
Oakhill Ave
Paine's La
Moss La
Barrow Point Ave
East End Way
Love La
Avenue Rd
Leighton Ave
Cemy
Bloomsbury Ct
Chiswick Ct
Paines Cl
Eastglade
Beechen Gr
Terrilands
Anglesmede Cres
Anglesmede Way
Ainsdale Cres
Greystoke Ave
Birk Dale Ave
Melbourne Ave
Manor Park Dr
Greenfield Way
Holm Dene Ave
Pinner Park Schs
Parkfield Gdns
Open Air Theatre
Headstone Manor
Harrow Mus & Her Ctr
Bridge St
High St
Grange Ct
Angle Cl
Amber Cl
Shelbourne Cl
Church La
Wakehams Hill
The Squirrels
Elmcroft Cres
Hillview Gdns
Headstone La
Pav
Headstone Manor Recn Gd
Pavs
Allot Gdns
Station App
Pinner
School La
Weall Ct
West End Ave
Grange Gdns
Mayfield Dr
Capel Gdns
Nowerhill High Sch
Pinner Ct
Betjeman Cl
The Chase
Nower Hill
Copperfield Way
Nower Ct
Priory Way
Manor Way
Parkside Way
Woodberry
Liby
Cecil Pk
Wentworth Way
Ashridge Gdns
Holwell Pl
Marsh Rd
Chessington Ct
Kingsley Rd
Melrose Rd
Thrush Gn
South Way
Woodlands
Hazelwood Cl
Southfield Pk
Yewtree Cl
Osbourne Ct
Kingsway Cres
Meadow Rd
Birches Cl
Eastcote Rd
Grove Ave
Pinner Gr
Sch
Grove Rd
Hooking Gn
Chaucer Ho
Canterbury Ho
Station Rd
Kingsfield Ave
Allerford Ct
Allington Rd
Vale Croft
Cannon La
Pinner Village Gardens
Tenn Cts
Hereford Gdns
Mount Dr
The Ridgeway
Northumberland Rd
Cambridge Rd
Broadwalk
Cumberland Rd
Gloucester Rd
Westmorland Rd
Durham Rd
Canterbury Rd
Holsworth Cl
Lyncroft Ave
Moorcroft Way
Compton Rise
Lincoln Cl
Lincoln Rd
North Harrow
Churchill Ct
Norfolk Rd
Surrey Rd
Highfield Ave
Whittington Way
Ladbrook Cl
Lancaster Rd
St Ursula Gr
Hill Rd
Dawlish Dr
Tewkesbury Ave
Trevone Gdns
St Michael's Cres
Suffolk Rd
Chester Dr
Collapit Cl
Laburnum Ct
Acacia Ct
Argyle Rd
A404 PINNER RD
42
Norwood Dr
Church Dr
Blenheim Rd
Bladon Gdns
North Ave
Dewsbury Ct
Church Ave
The Gardens
Rayners La
The Greenway
Lankers Dr
Hawthorn Dr
Parkthorne Dr
Parkthorne Cl
Elm Dr
Elm Cl
Sandhurst Ave
Beaumont Ave
Dorchester Ave
Grosvenor Ave
Vaughan Sch
Cannonbury Ave
Chestnut Dr
Lulworth Dr
Wimborne Dr
Durley Ave
Brunswick Cl
Southbourne Cl
Downs Ave
West Ave
Central Ave
Hillcroft Ave
The Avenue
Dukes Ave
Longfield Fst & Mid Schs
Imperial Cl
Farm Ave
Recn Gd
Imperial Ct
The Croft
The Close
Park Dr
Alfriston Ave
Romney Dr
The Ridgeway
West Harrow
Rodney Ct
Hawlands Dr
Eastern Ave
The Glen
Village Way
Village Way E
Vicarage Way
The Drive
Romney Cl
Beechcroft Ave
Elm Gr
The Retreat
Fernbrook Dr
Bwg Gn
West Harrow Recn Gd
Wilson
Edinburgh Cl
Carlisle Cl
Stirling Ave
Trescoe Gdns
Newlyn Gdns
South Cl
Oakington Ave
Ullswater Ct
Twyford Rd
Welbeck Rd
Furness Rd
Whitmore
Tenn Cts
Whitmore High Sch
Raynton Cl
High Worple
Worple Cl
Stockton Ho
Macmillan Ct
Strongbridge Cl
Chatsworth Gdns
Tintern Way
Roxbourne Park
Spinnells Rd
Worple Way
Fairview Cres
Pav
Sp Gd
Yeading Brook
Warden Ave
Rayners La
Thackeray Cl
Goldsmith Cl
Grange Schs
Abercorn Cres
Southdown Cres
Shaftesbury
Yeading Ave
Waverley Rd
Ovesdon Ave
Perwell Ave
Berriton Rd
Oxleay Rd
Scott Cres
Chichester Ct
Capthorne Ave
Clitheroe Ave
Tenn Cts
Austen Rd
Drake Rd
Lucas Ave
Fball Gd
Roxbourne Fst & Mid Schs
Torbay
Allot Gdns
Newton Farm Fst & Mid Sch
63
Eliot Dr
Drinkwater Rd
Swift Cl
Priest Park Ave
Maryatt Ave
Rayners
The Arches
Lodge Park Cl
Franklins Mews
Newquay Cres
Widdicombe Ave
Newton Farm Ecology Pk
Coles Cres
Newton
Gdns
90
89
88
87
6
5
4
3
2
1
12
13
14

A
B
C
D
24
64
41
90
89
88
87
6
5
4
3
2
1
14
15
HA1
HA2
HA3
HARROW
Wealdstone
Headstone
Greenhill
West Harrow
North Harrow
Harrow on the Hill
Roxeth
Headstone Manor
Harrow Mus & Her Ctr
Open Air Theatre
Headstone Manor Recn Gd
Harrow & Wealdstone
Harrow-on-the-Hill
West Harrow
Harrow Sch
Harrow Coll
The Grove Open Space
St Anselm's RC Prim Sch
Whitmore High Sch
Vaughan Sch
Quainton Hall Sch
Norbury Sch
The John Lyon Sch
Grange Schs
West Harrow Recn Gd
Bowden House
PHOENIX IND EST
Running Tk
Pl Flds
A404 PINNER RD
A404
A4005
A409
A312
B458
A312 LOWER RD
BESSBOROUGH RD
GEORGE GANGE WAY
RAILWAY APP
STATION RD
SHEEPCOTE RD
GREENHILL WAY
COLLEGE RD
LOWLANDS RD
KENTON RD
TYBURN LA
PETERBOROUGH RD
HIGH ST
ROXETH HILL
PINNER VIEW
PINNER PARK AVE
PINNER PARK GDNS
HEADSTONE GDNS
HEADSTONE DR
KINGSFIELD AVE
CUNNINGHAM PK
CANTERBURY RD
SUSSEX RD
WHITMORE RD
PARKSIDE WAY
HARROW VIEW
WALTON RD
MARLBOROUGH HILL
HINDES RD
WELLESLEY RD
NEPTUNE RD
VAUGHAN RD
BUTLER AVE
SHAFTESBURY CIRC
MIDDLE RD
GRANGE FARM CL
WELLINGTON RD
HAVELOCK RD
GORDON RD
CECIL RD
PEEL RD
MASONS AVE
HERGA RD
FORWARD DR
CHRISTCHURCH AVE
WARRINGTON RD
BETHECAR RD
HEADSTONE RD
ROXBOROUGH RD
CHURCH HILL
GROVE HILL
FOOTBALL LA
RIFLE RANGE LA
HARROW PK

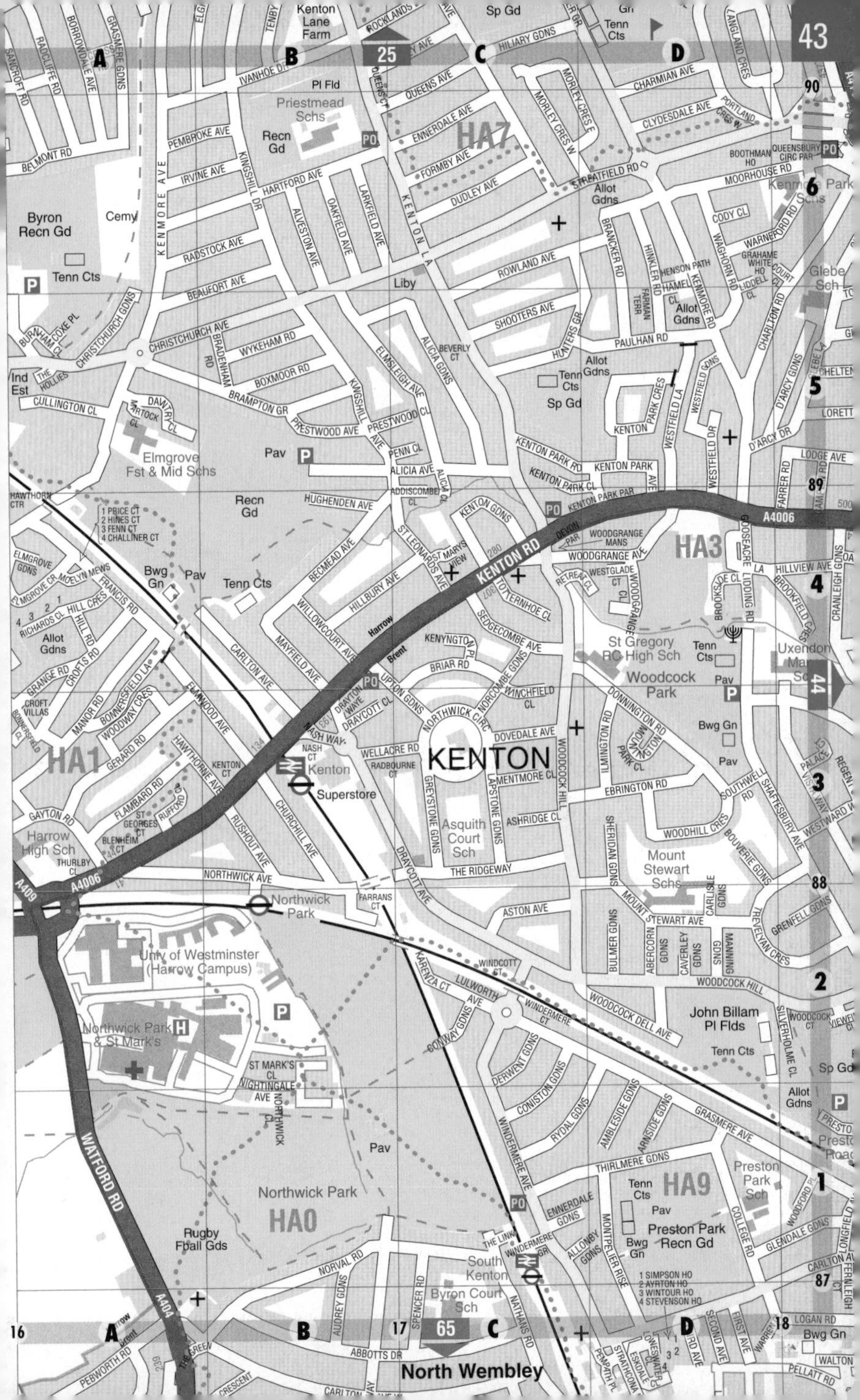
KENTON
Kenton Lane Farm
Sp Gd
Tenn Cts
25
A
B
C
D
RADCLIFFE RD
BORROWDALE AVE
GRASMERE GDNS
SANCROFT RD
IVANHOE DR
ROCKLANDS
HILIARY GDNS
LANGLAND CRES
Pl Fld
Priestmead Schs
Recn Gd
QUEENS AVE
QUEENS CT
ENNERDALE AVE
HA7
MORLEY CRES E
MORLEY CRES W
CHARMIAN AVE
CLYDESDALE AVE
PORTLAND CRES W
90
PEMBROKE AVE
KINGSHILL DR
FORMBY AVE
BOOTHMAN HO
QUEENSBURY CIRC PAR
BELMONT RD
IRVINE AVE
HARTFORD AVE
DUDLEY AVE
STREATFIELD RD
MOORHOUSE RD
Kenmore Park Schs
6
Byron Recn Gd
Cemy
KENMORE AVE
ALVESTON AVE
OAKFIELD AVE
LARKFIELD AVE
KENTON LA
Allot Gdns
CODY CL
WARNEFORD RD
RADSTOCK AVE
ROWLAND AVE
BRANCKER RD
HINKLER RD
HENSON PATH
HAMEL CL
KENMORE RD
WAGHORN RD
GRAHAME WHITE HO
LIDDELL CL
COURT CL
Glebe Sch
Tenn Cts
BEAUFORT AVE
Liby
SHOOTERS AVE
FARMAN TERR
CHARLTON RD
BURNHAM CL
COXE PL
CHRISTCHURCH GDNS
CHRISTCHURCH AVE
BRADENHAM RD
WYKEHAM RD
ELMSLEIGH AVE
ALICIA GDNS
BEVERLY CT
HUNTERS GR
PAULHAN RD
GLEBE LA
CHELTENHAM
Ind Est
THE HOLLIES
BOXMOOR RD
KINGSHILL AVE
Tenn Cts
Sp Gd
KENTON PARK CRES
WESTFIELD LA
WESTFIELD GDNS
D'ARCY GDNS
5
CULLINGTON CL
MARTOCK CL
DAWTRY CL
BRAMPTON GR
PRESTWOOD AVE
PRESTWOOD CL
KENTON
WESTFIELD DR
D'ARCY DR
LORETTO
Elmgrove Fst & Mid Schs
Pav
PENN CL
ALICIA AVE
ALICIA CL
KENTON PARK RD
KENTON PARK AVE
KENTON PARK CL
KENTON PARK PAR
LODGE AVE
FARRER RD
89
HAWTHORN CTR
1 PRICE CT
2 HINES CT
3 FENN CT
4 CHALLINER CT
Recn Gd
HUGHENDEN AVE
ADDISCOMBE CL
KENTON GDNS
DEVON PAR
WOODGRANGE MANS
A4006
GOOSEACRE
ELMGROVE GDNS
ELMGROVE CR
MOELYN MEWS
FRANCIS RD
ST LEONARDS AVE
BECMEAD AVE
ST MARYS VIEW
280
KENTON RD
WOODGRANGE AVE
WESTGLADE CT
HA3
LA
HILLVIEW AVE
CRANLEIGH GDNS
RICHARDS CL
HILL CRES
HILL RD
Bwg Gn
Pav
Tenn Cts
HILLBURY AVE
TOTTERNHOE CL
RETREAT CL
WOODGRANGE CL
BROOKSIDE CL
LIDDING RD
BROOKFIELD CRES
4
Allot Gdns
GRANGE RD
CROFTS RD
WILLOWCOURT AVE
MAYFIELD AVE
Harrow
Brent
SEDGECOMBE AVE
KENYNGTON PL
St Gregory RC High Sch
Tenn Cts
Uxendon Manor Sch
44
CROFT VILLAS
BONNERSFIELD LA
BONNERSFIELD CL
MANOR RD
WOODWAY CRES
CARLTON AVE
ELMWOOD AVE
BRIAR RD
NORCOMBE GDNS
WINCHFIELD CL
Woodcock Park
Pav
DONNINGTON RD
UPTON GDNS
DRAYTON WAYE
DRAYCOTT CL
NORTHWICK CIRC
DOVEDALE AVE
Bwg Gn
HA1
GERARD RD
HAWTHORNE AVE
NASH WAY
NASH CT
Kenton
WELLACRE RD
RADBOURNE CT
KENTON
WOODCOCK HILL
ILMINGTON RD
KENNINGTON PARK CL
PALACE VIEW
REGENT
3
KENTON CT
Superstore
LAPSTONE GDNS
MENTMORE CL
EBRINGTON RD
SOUTHWELL RD
SHAFTESBURY AVE
GAYTON RD
FLAMBARD RD
RUFFORD CL
ST GEORGES CT
GREYSTONE GDNS
Asquith Court Sch
ASHRIDGE CL
SHERIDAN GDNS
WOODHILL CRES
BOUVERIE GDNS
WESTWARD WAY
Harrow High Sch
BLENHEIM CT
THURLBY CL
RUSHOUT AVE
CHURCHILL AVE
DRAYCOTT AVE
THE RIDGEWAY
Mount Stewart Schs
88
A409
A4006
NORTHWICK AVE
Northwick Park
FARRANS CT
ASTON AVE
MOUNT STEWART AVE
CARLISLE GDNS
GRENFELL GDNS
TREVELYAN CRES
Univ of Westminster (Harrow Campus)
KARENZA CT
BULMER GDNS
ABERCORN GDNS
CAVERLEY GDNS
MANNING GDNS
WINDCOTT CT
LULWORTH AVE
WINDERMERE CT
WOODCOCK HILL
2
WOODCOCK DELL AVE
John Billam Pl Flds
SILVERHOLME CL
WOODCOCK CT
VIEWFIELD
Northwick Park & St Mark's
CONWAY GDNS
DERWENT GDNS
CONISTON GDNS
Tenn Cts
Sp Gd
ST MARK'S CL
NIGHTINGALE AVE
NORTHWICK CL
RYDAL GDNS
AMBLESIDE GDNS
ARNSIDE GDNS
GRASMERE AVE
Allot Gdns
PRESTON
Preston Road
WATFORD RD
Pav
WINDERMERE AVE
THIRLMERE GDNS
Preston Park Sch
Northwick Park
Tenn Cts
HA9
Pav
1
HA0
ENNERDALE GDNS
WOODFORD PL
Rugby Fball Gds
THE LINK
WINDERMERE GR
ALLONBY GDNS
MONTPELIER RISE
Bwg Gn
Preston Park Recn Gd
COLLEGE RD
GLENDALE GDNS
NORVAL RD
South Kenton
CARLTON AVE
LONGFIELD AVE
1 SIMPSON HO
2 AYRTON HO
3 WINTOUR HO
4 STEVENSON HO
FERNLEIGH CT
87
AUDREY GDNS
SPENCER RD
Byron Court Sch
NATHANS RD
SECOND AVE
FIRST AVE
WARREN
16
Harrow
Brent
A404
B
17
65
C
D
18
LOGAN RD
Bwg Gn
THE GREEN
ABBOTTS DR
LOWESWATER
ESKDALE
STRATHCONA
PEMPATH PL
WALTON
PEBWORTH RD
239
CRESCENT
North Wembley
PELLATT RD

A
B
C
D
26
66
43
90
89
88
87
18
19
20
6
5
4
3
2
1
A4140
A4006
HA8
HA3
NW9
Queensbury
Preston
TAUNTON WAY
DEAN DR
HOLLY AVE
WOODSTOCK
TURNER RD
TIVERTON RD
GAINSBOROUGH
MOLLISON WAY
SOUTH PAR
PO
LAWRENCE CRES
DE HAVILLAND
COBHAM CL
HALFORD CL
HOLYROOD GDNS
MELROSE GDNS
STAG LA
PORTLAND CRES
BOOTHMAN HO
QUEENSBURY CIRC PAR
CHICHESTER CT
ELLERTON DR
Allot Gdns
REYNOLDS DR
CROXDEN CL
CALDER GDNS
ESSOLDO WAY
WALTHAM DR
BRINKBURN GDNS
BRINKBURN CL
BEVERLEY DR
STA PAR
BEVERLEY DR
QUEENSBURY
TEWKESBURY GDNS
DRYBURGH GDNS
LOWTHER RD
P
MOORHOUSE RD
Kenmore Park Schs
CODY CL
WARNEFORD RD
GRAHAME WHITE HO
COURT
HODELL CL
WAGHORN RD
KENMORE RD
GLEBE AVE
GLEBE CRES
Superstore
HONEYPOT LA
CUMBERLAND RD
SANDHURST CL
SHERBORNE GDNS
WIMBORNE DR
WHITBY GDNS
NORTH WAY
TINTERN AVE
FAIRWAY AVE
PARK GDNS
GIRTON AVE
SANDHURST RD
WINCHESTER AVE
Eton Grove Open Space
Bwg Gn
Tenn Cts
ETON GR
BYRON AVE
RUGBY RD
Glebe Sch
TONBRIDGE CRES
MALVERN GDNS
WINCHESTER RD
ALEXANDER CT
RUTH CL
MARY CL
WESTMORELAND RD
GLENALMOND RD
CHARLTON RD
Recn Gd
St Bernadette's RC Fst & Mid Sch
PRINCES AVE
SHORTS CROFT
ROE LA
BACON LA
Roe Green Schs
Kingsbury High Sch
GROSVENOR CRES
WESTFIELD GDNS
GLEBE LA
CHELTENHAM PL
D'ARCY GDNS
LORETTO GDNS
SHREWSBURY AVE
Pav
HONEYPOT CL
COWBRIDGE RD
RUSKIN GDNS
ST PAUL'S AVE
ROSE BATES DR
PRINCES CL
D'ARCY DR
WESTFIELD DR
Tenn Cts
REPTON RD
LODGE AVE
FARRER RD
CAMPLIN RD
MORLAND RD
RADLEY GDNS
NEWNHAM WAY
CLIFTON RD
Allot Gdns
ELMCROFT GDNS
BERKELEY RD
BRAMPTON RD
MANOR CL
SUTHERLAND CT
Annexe
Roe Green Park
KENTON RD
PINECROFT
WINCKLEY CL
ORCHARD GR
LEYBOURNE RD
GOOSEACRE LA
HILLVIEW AVE
OAKDALE AVE
CRANLEIGH GDNS
CLAREMONT AVE
SALEHURST CL
KINROSS CL
TA Ctr
Kingsbury
KINGSBURY RD
WESTCROFT CT
OLD KENTON LA
BROOKSIDE
BROOKFIELD CRES
LIDDING RD
GREENWAY
CHAPMAN CRES
CHANTRY CL
MELBURY RD
MINTERNE RD
MOOT CT
GORE CT
CRUNDALE AVE
MERSHAM DR
SEDUM CL
LARKSPUR CL
Allot Gdns
Kingsbury Green Prim Sch
Tenn Cts
Uxendon Manor Sch
Claremont High Sch
FALCON WAY
VINE CT
LINDSAY DR
ORMESBY WAY
MELCOMBE GDNS
DORCHESTER WAY
PI Fd
JFS Sch
FRYENT CL
FIELDVIEW CT
WYNDALE AVE
VALLEY DR
WALTHAM AVE
Bwg Gn
BRANKSOME WAY
PRESTON HILL
THE GARTH
Sp Gd
Games Ct
PALACE CT
VISTA WAY
REGENT CL
REGAL WAY
HARGOOD CL
IMPERIAL WAY
THE LEYS
BUSH HILL RD
THE MALL
SANDY LA
SOUTHWELL RD
SHAFTESBURY AVE
WESTWARD WAY
TYLERS GATE
BELVEDERE WAY
CAMPION CL
ROBIN GR
Michael Sobell Sinai Sch
BROADVIEW
HAMPTON RISE
VANE CL
PAGE CL
EMERSON GDNS
SHAKESPEARE DR
BOUVERIE GDNS
CARLISLE GDNS
TREVELYAN CRES
GRENFELL GDNS
JOHN PERRIN PL
ARNOLD CL
TOOKEY CL
SHAKESPEARE CL
Sp Gd
FRYENT WAY
MANNING GDNS
PRESTON HILL
BELLAMY HO
KINCH GR
MAGNOLIA CT
WILSON CL
WILSON DR
LEDWAY DR
Fryent Country Park
WOODCOCK HILL
BRUCE HO
HILLSIDE GDNS
RYDAL CT
John Billam Pl Flds
SILVERHOLME CL
WOODCOCK CT
VIEWFIELD CL
JUBILEE CT
TOLEY AVE
OXENPARK AVE
RAVENSCROFT AVE
Tenn Cts
Pav
Sp Gd
UXENDON HILL
WENTWORTH HILL
ALVERSTONE RD
WYKEHAM HILL
Barn Hill Open Space
Barn Hill
• 86
Allot Gdns
PRESTON WAYE
GRASMERE AVE
Preston Road
UXENDON CRES
WEST HILL
BEVERLEY GDNS
Tenn Cts
SALTCROFT CL
SUMMERS CL
KINGSMERE CT
PADDOCKS GN
PILGRIMS WAY
Preston Park Sch
WOODFORD PL
LONGFIELD AVE
WEST CL
THE AVENUE
BRAMPTON GR
BARN HILL
COLLEGE RD
GLENDALE GDNS
Liby
CARLTON AVE E
FERNLEIGH CT
CARLTON PAR
PRINCESS AVE
CHARLTON RD
BASING HILL
EAST HILL
BARN WAY
MIDHOLM
BARN RISE
WICKLIFFE GDNS
SWINTON CL
SECOND AVE
FIRST AVE
WARREN
LOGAN RD
Bwg Gn
AYLANDS CL
ORCHID CT
WALTON GDNS
PELLATT RD
PRESTON
ELMSTEAD AVE
Tenn Cts
CENTURY HO 1
TAVERNERS CT 2
HILLVIEW CL
MAYFIELDS
LAWNS CT
CORRINGHAM
THE CROSSWAYS
EVERSLEY AVE
CAMEL CT
KINGS DR
GREENHILL WAY
THE PADDOCKS
ADAMS CL
GREENHILL

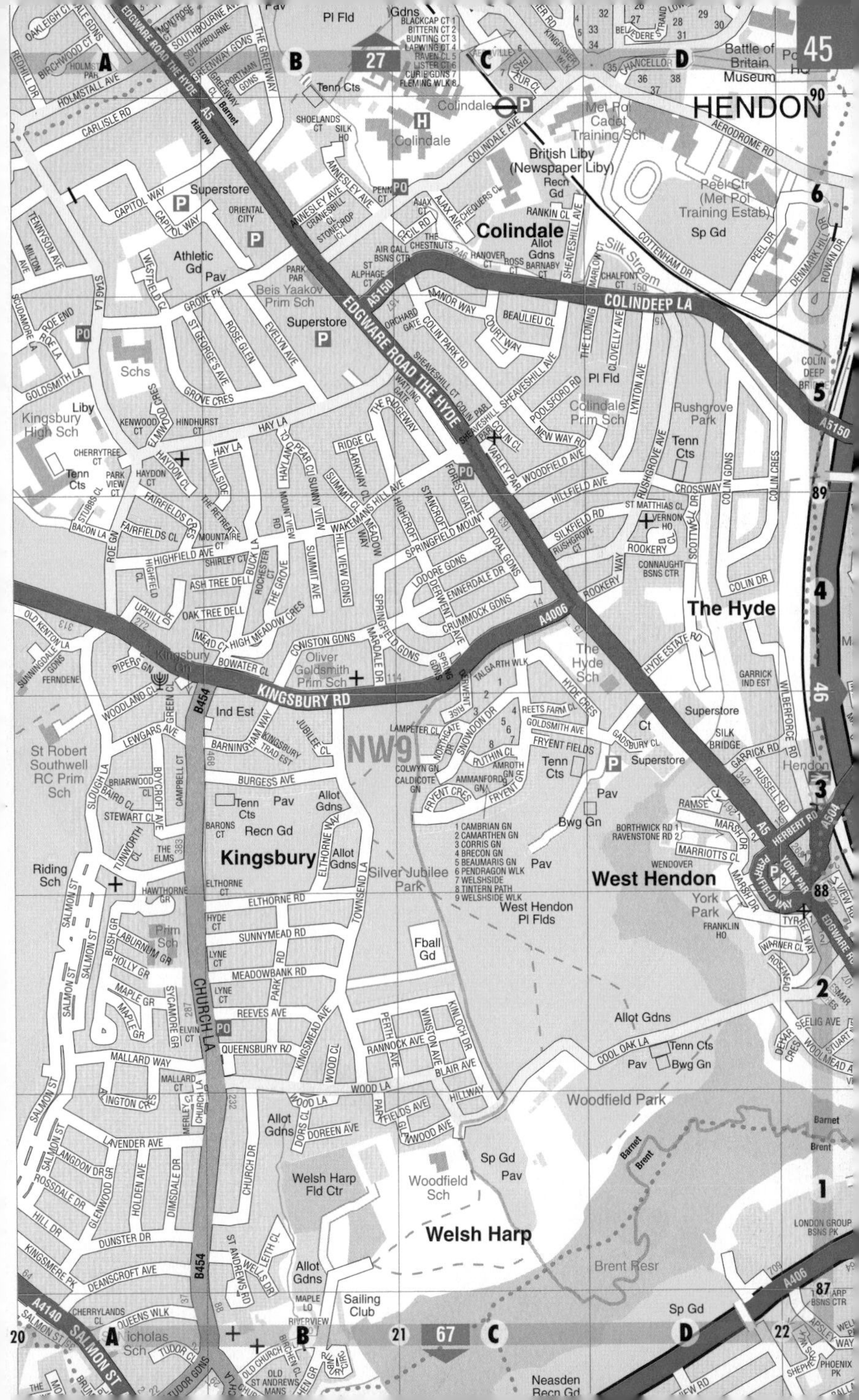
HENDON
Colindale
The Hyde
West Hendon
Kingsbury
Welsh Harp
NW9
EDGWARE ROAD THE HYDE
A5
A5150
COLINDEEP LA
KINGSBURY RD
A4006
CHURCH LA
B454
A4140
SALMON ST
A406
A504
AERODROME RD
COLINDALE AVE
Battle of Britain Museum
Met Pol Cadet Training Sch
British Liby (Newspaper Liby)
Peel Ctr (Met Pol Training Estab)
Colindale
Beis Yaakov Prim Sch
Superstore
Oriental City
Athletic Gd
Colindale Prim Sch
Rushgrove Park
Silk Stream
Kingsbury High Sch
Oliver Goldsmith Prim Sch
The Hyde Sch
St Robert Southwell RC Prim Sch
Riding Sch
Silver Jubilee Park
West Hendon Pl Flds
Allot Gdns
Woodfield Park
Woodfield Sch
Welsh Harp Fld Ctr
Sailing Club
Brent Resr
St Nicholas Sch
Neasden Recn Gd
London Group Bsns Pk
Garrick Ind Est
Connaught Bsns Ctr
Silk Bridge
York Park
Fball Gd
1 Cambrian Gn
2 Camarthen Gn
3 Corris Gn
4 Brecon Gn
5 Beaumaris Gn
6 Pendragon Wlk
7 Welshside
8 Tintern Path
9 Welshside Wlk
1 Blackcap Ct
2 Bittern Ct
3 Bunting Ct
4 Lapwing Ct
5 Raven Cl
6 Lister Ct
7 Curie Gdns
8 Fleming Wlk
Borthwick Rd 1
Ravenstone Rd 2
Barnet
Brent
Harrow
A B C D
27
67
90
89
88
87
46
20
21
22
1 2 3 4 5 6

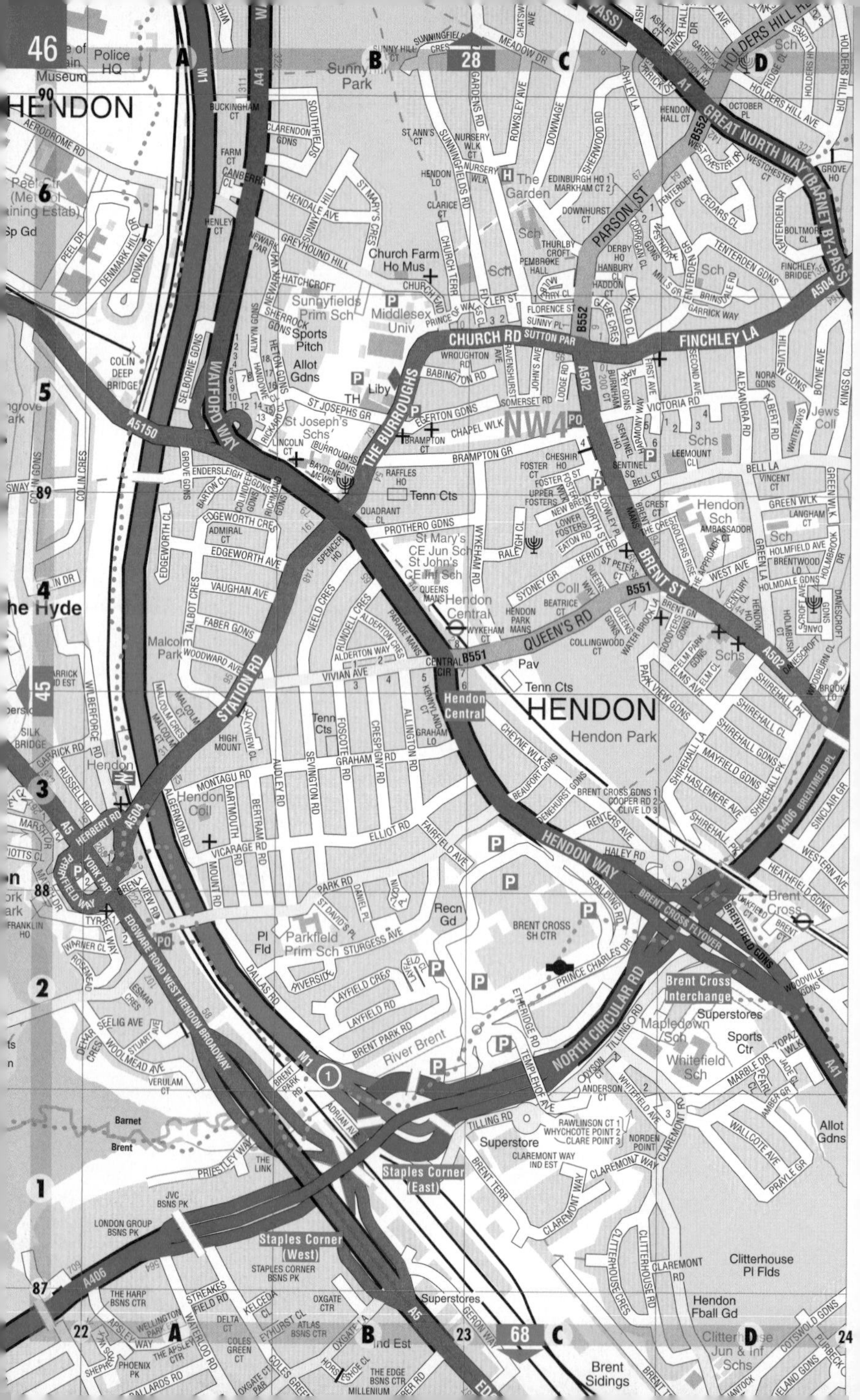
28
68
45
A
B
C
D
90
89
88
87
22
23
24
6
5
4
3
2
1
HENDON
Police HQ
Museum
Sunny Hill Park
AERODROME RD
Peel Ctr
Sp Gd
PEEL DR
DENMARK HILL DR
ROWAN DR
M1
A41
BUCKINGHAM CT
CLARENDON GDNS
SOUTHFIELDS
FARM CT
CANBERRA CL
HENLEY CT
HENDALE AVE
SUNNY HILL
ST MARY'S CRES
GREYHOUND HILL
NEWARK PAR
NEWARK WAY
HATCHCROFT
SHERROCK GDNS
Sunnyfields Prim Sch
Sports Pitch
Allot Gdns
Church Farm Ho Mus
CHURCH END
Middlesex Univ
Liby
TH
CHURCH TERR
CLARICE CT
HENDON LO
ST ANN'S CT
SUNNINGFIELDS RD
GARDENS RD
NURSERY WLK CT
NURSERY WLK
ROWSLEY AVE
DOWNAGE
SHERWOOD RD
ASHLEY LA
MEADOW DR
CHATSWORTH AVE
SUNNINGFIELDS CRES
SUNNY HILL CT
The Garden
Sch
EDINBURGH HO 1
MARKHAM CT 2
DOWNHURST CT
THURLBY CROFT
PEMBROKE HALL
DERBY HO
HANBURY CT
HADDON CT
FLORENCE ST
SUNNY PL
PRINCE OF WALES CL
FULLER ST
CHURCH RD
SUTTON PAR
FINCHLEY LA
B552
A502
PARSON ST
CORRIGAN CL
WESTHORPE
TENTERDEN GR
TENTERDEN CL
CEDARS CL
TENTERDEN GDNS
TENTERDEN DR
BOLTMORE CL
FINCHLEY BRIDGE
MILLS GR
BRINSDALE RD
GARRICK WAY
GREAT NORTH WAY (BARNET BY-PASS)
A1
A504
WESTCHESTER DR
WESTCHESTER CT
GROVE HO
OCTOBER PL
HOLDERS HILL AVE
HOLDERS HILL RD
HOLDERS HILL DR
HOLDERS HILL CRES
RIDGE CL
GARRICK PK
CLAYDON HO
HENDON HALL CT
ASHLEY CT
MANOR HALL DR
WROUGHTON RD
BABINGTON RD
RAVENSHURST AVE
JOHN'S AVE
LODGE RD
SOMERSET RD
BURNHAM CT
FIRST AVE
SECOND AVE
ALEXANDRA RD
ALBERT RD
HILLVIEW GDNS
BOYNE AVE
KINGS CL
NORA GDNS
WHITEWAYS
Jews Coll
VICTORIA RD
HARMONY WAY
NW4
PO
Schs
LEEMOUNT CL
BELL LA
VINCENT CT
GREEN WLK
LANGHAM CT
SENTINEL HO
SENTINEL SQ
BELL CT
CHESHIR HO
FOSTER CT
FOSTER ST
UPPER FOSTERS
NEW BRENT ST
LOWER FOSTERS
EATON RD
NORTH ST
COWLEY PL
RALEIGH CL
HERIOT RD
ST PETER'S CT
SYDNEY GR
QUEENS WAY
Coll
BEATRICE CT
HENDON PARK MANS
QUEEN'S RD
B551
COLLINGWOOD CT
WATER BROOK LA
BRENT GN
GOODYERS GDNS
ELM PARK GDNS
ELMS AVE
ELM CL
PARK VIEW GDNS
BRENT ST
CREST CT
THE CREST
GOLDERS RISE
THE APPROACH
Hendon Sch
AMBASSADOR CT
WEST AVE
CENTURY HO
HENDON CT
GREEN LA
HOLMFIELD AVE
BRENTWOOD LO
HOLMDALE GDNS
HOLMBROOK DR
DANESCROFT
CROFT AVE
DANE CT
HOLMBUSH CT
WOODBURN CL
BROOK LO
SHIREHALL PK
SHIREHALL CL
SHIREHALL GDNS
SHIREHALL LA
MAYFIELD GDNS
HASLEMERE AVE
A406
BRENTMEAD PL
SINCLAIR GR
WESTERN AVE
HEATHFIELD GDNS
Brent Cross
WATFORD WAY
A5150
ST JOSEPHS GR
St Joseph's Schs
THE BURROUGHS
EGERTON GDNS
CHAPEL WLK
BRAMPTON CT
BRAMPTON GR
BURROUGHS GDNS
BAYDENE MEWS
LINCOLN CT
RAFFLES HO
Tenn Cts
QUADRANT CL
PROTHERO GDNS
St Mary's CE Jun Sch
St John's CE Inf Sch
WYKEHAM RD
QUEENS MANS
Hendon Central
WYKEHAM CT
SPENCER HO
ALWYN GDNS
HETON GDNS
HANDOWE CL
RICKARD CL
SELBORNIE GDNS
COLIN DEEP BRIDGE
COLIN GDNS
COLIN CRES
ENDERSLEIGH GDNS
GROVE GDNS
BARTON CL
COLINDEEP GDNS
RICHMOND GDNS
EDGEWORTH CRES
ADMIRAL CT
EDGEWORTH AVE
EDGEWORTH CL
VAUGHAN AVE
TALBOT CRES
FABER GDNS
Malcolm Park
WOODWARD AVE
STATION RD
NEELD CRES
RUNDELL CRES
ALDERTON CRES
ALDERTON WAY
PARADE MANS
VIVIAN AVE
CENTRAL CIR
KENNYLAND CT
GRAHAM LO
ALLINGTON RD
CRESPIGNY RD
FOSCOTE RD
SEVINGTON RD
AUDLEY RD
GRAHAM RD
Tenn Cts
HIGH MOUNT
ELYVIEW CL
MALCOLM CT
MALCOLM CRES
MALCOLM PK
MONTAGU RD
DARTMOUTH RD
BERTRAM RD
ALGERNON RD
Hendon Coll
VICARAGE RD
MOUNT RD
ELLIOT RD
FAIRFIELD AVE
Pav
HENDON
Hendon Park
CHEYNE WLK
BEAUFORT GDNS
BRENT CROSS GDNS 1
COOPER RD 2
CLIVE LO 3
RENTERS AVE
HALEY RD
HENDON WAY
BRENT CROSS FLYOVER
BRENTFIELD GDNS
OAKFIELD CT
BRENT CT
WOODVILLE GDNS
Brent Cross Interchange
PARK RD
ST DAVID'S PL
DANIEL PL
NICOLL PL
Recn Gd
Pl Fld
Parkfield Prim Sch
STURGESS AVE
RIVERSIDE
LAYFIELD CRES
LAYFIELD CL
LAYFIELD RD
BRENT PARK RD
River Brent
DALLAS RD
BRENT CROSS SH CTR
SPALDING RD
PRINCE CHARLES DR
ETHERIDGE RD
TEMPLEHOF AVE
NORTH CIRCULAR RD
TILLING RD
Superstores
Mapledown Sch
Whitefield Sch
Sports Ctr
MARBLE DR
PEARL CL
TOPAZ WLK
JADE CL
AMBER GR
WALLCOTE AVE
PRAYLE GR
Allot Gdns
A41
DYSON CT
ANDERSON CT
WHITEFIELD AVE
CLAREMONT RD
RAWLINSON CT 1
WHYCHCOTE POINT 2
CLARE POINT 3
NORDEN POINT
Superstore
CLAREMONT WAY IND EST
CLAREMONT WAY
BRENT TERR
Staples Corner (East)
Staples Corner (West)
STAPLES CORNER BSNS PK
CLITTERHOUSE RD
CLITTERHOUSE CRES
CLAREMONT RD
Clitterhouse Pl Flds
Hendon Fball Gd
Clitterhouse Jun & Inf Schs
COTSWOLD GDNS
PURBECK DR
Brent Sidings
ADRIAN AVE
BRENT PARK RD
PRIESTLEY WAY
THE LINK
JVC BSNS PK
LONDON GROUP BSNS PK
THE HARP BSNS CTR
STREAKES FIELD RD
KELCEDA CL
OXGATE CTR
Superstores
GERON WAY
ATLAS BSNS CTR
EYHURST CL
DELTA CT
COLES GREEN CT
WELLINGTON PARK
APSLEY WAY
THE APSLEY CTR
PHOENIX PK
BALLARDS RD
WATERLOO RD
OXGATE CT PAR
COLES GREEN
HORSESHOE CL
THE EDGE BSNS CTR
MILLENIUM
Ind Est
A5
EDGWARE ROAD WEST HENDON BROADWAY
HERBERT RD
YORK PAR
PARKFIELD WAY
BRENT VIEW RD
TYREL WAY
FRANKLIN HO
WARNER CL
ROSEMEAD
ESMAR CRES
SEELIG AVE
DEKAR CRES
WOOLMEAD AVE
STUART AVE
VERULAM CT
Barnet
Brent
GARRICK RD
RUSSELL RD
WILBERFORCE RD
SILK BRIDGE
Hendon
GARRICK EST
MARSH DR
The Hyde
COLIN DR

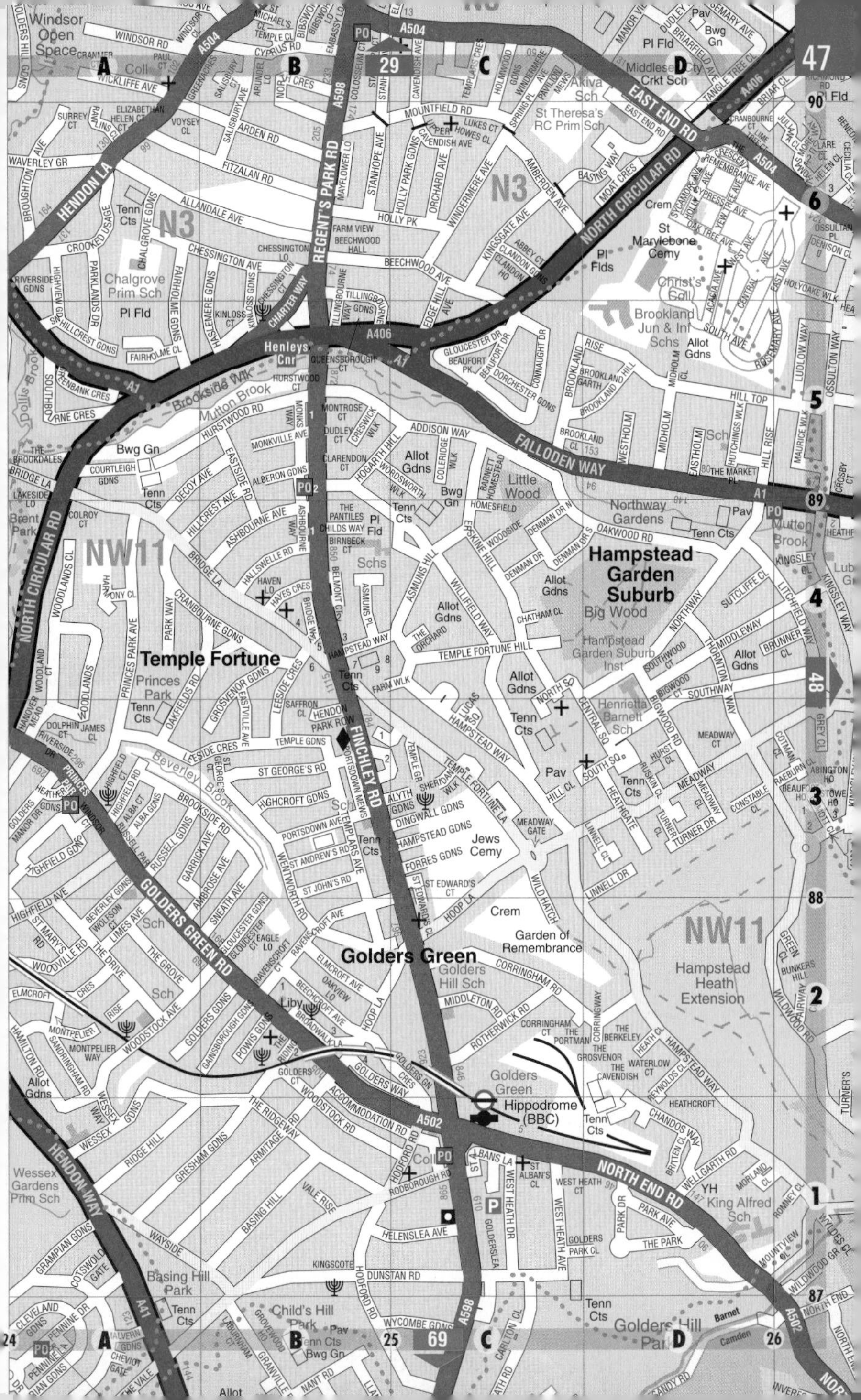
47
29
48
69
A
B
C
D
1
2
3
4
5
6
Windsor Open Space
Hampstead Garden Suburb
Temple Fortune
Golders Green
NW11
N3
Hampstead Heath Extension
Golders Hill Park
Big Wood
Little Wood
Northway Gardens
St Marylebone Cemy
Jews Cemy
Crem
Garden of Remembrance
Hippodrome (BBC)
Golders Green
Henleys Cnr
Chalgrove Prim Sch
Brookland Jun & Inf Schs
Akiva Sch
St Theresa's RC Prim Sch
Middlesex Cty Crkt Sch
Christ's Coll
Henrietta Barnett Sch
Hampstead Garden Suburb Inst
Golders Hill Sch
King Alfred Sch
Wessex Gardens Prim Sch
Basing Hill Park
Child's Hill Park
Brent Park
Princes Park
REGENT'S PARK RD
FINCHLEY RD
NORTH CIRCULAR RD
FALLODEN WAY
EAST END RD
HENDON LA
HENDON WAY
GOLDERS GREEN RD
NORTH END RD
HAMPSTEAD WAY
TEMPLE FORTUNE HILL
WILLIFIELD WAY
MEADWAY
SOUTHWAY
NORTHWAY
OAKWOOD RD
BRIDGE LA
HOOP LA
WEST HEATH DR
WEST HEATH AVE
A1
A41
A406
A502
A504
A598
Barnet
Camden
87
88
89
90
24
25
26

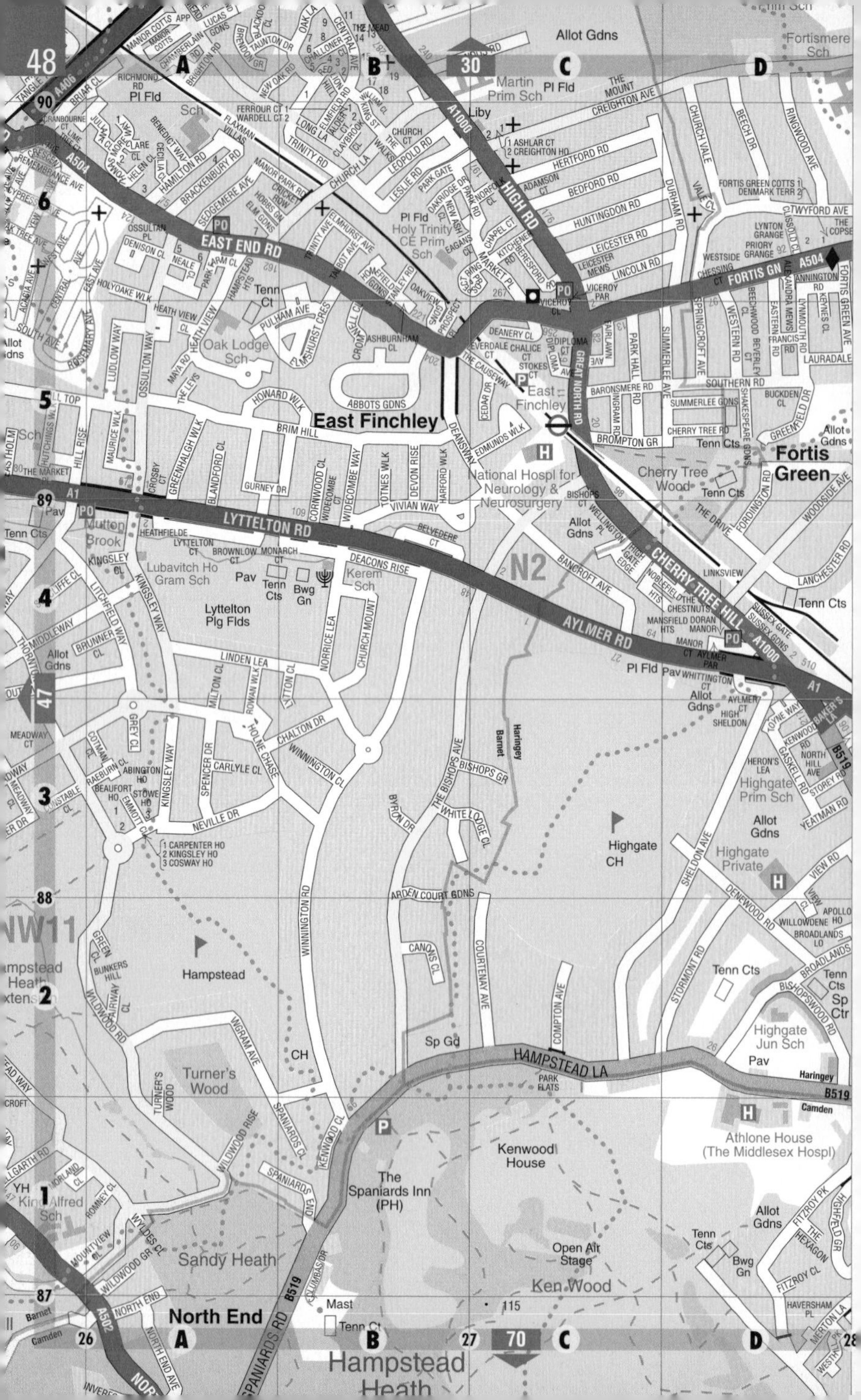
48
30
70
47
A
B
C
D
1
2
3
4
5
6
East Finchley
Fortis Green
N2
North End
Hampstead Heath
Hampstead
Highgate CH
Sandy Heath
Turner's Wood
Ken Wood
Kenwood House
The Spaniards Inn (PH)
Open Air Stage
Athlone House (The Middlesex Hospl)
National Hospl for Neurology & Neurosurgery
Cherry Tree Wood
Lyttelton Plg Flds
Lubavitch Ho Gram Sch
Kerem Sch
Oak Lodge Sch
Holy Trinity CE Prim Sch
Martin Prim Sch
Highgate Prim Sch
Highgate Private
Highgate Jun Sch
Fortismere Sch
King Alfred Sch
Allot Gdns
EAST END RD
HIGH RD
GREAT NORTH RD
LYTTELTON RD
AYLMER RD
CHERRY TREE HILL
FORTIS GN
HAMPSTEAD LA
SPANIARDS RD
NORTH END RD
WINNINGTON RD
THE BISHOPS AVE
COURTENAY AVE
SHELDON AVE
DENEWOOD RD
BISHOPSWOOD RD
KINGSLEY WAY
CHURCH LA
CREIGHTON AVE
HERTFORD RD
BEDFORD RD
HUNTINGDON RD
LEICESTER RD
LINCOLN RD
BRIM HILL
DEANSWAY
ABBOTS GDNS
A1
A1000
A504
A406
A502
B519
Barnet
Haringey
Camden

A
B
C
D
31
90
6
5
89
4
50
3
88
2
1
87
29
71
30
Muswell Hill
Our Lady of Muswell RC Prim Sch
Norfolk House Prep Sch
Alexandra Palace
N22
Alexandra Park
Mast
The Grove
Fortismere Sch
Fortismere Sch (South Wing)
Muswell Hill Prim Sch
HORNSEY
Queens Ave
A504
Muswell Hill Bdwy
Muswell Hill
B550
B106
Allot Gdns
Grove Lodge Garden
St Luke's Woodside
Tetherdown Prim Sch
Pl Fld
N10
Cranley Gardens
St James's CE Prim Sch
N8
Priory Rd
A1201
The Priory Park
Hornsey Central
Highgate Wood
Queen's Wood
Muswell Hill Rd
Pavs
Tenn Cts
Bwg Gn
Sp Gds
Highgate Wood Sch
Park Rd
Shepherds Hill Gdn
Crouch End
Highgate
Archway Rd
N6
Parkland Walk
YWCA Hostel
Coleridge Prim Sch
Crouch End Hill
A103
Hornsey Rise
B540
Hornsey La
N19
North Hill
Highgate Sch
St Michael's CE Prim Sch
B519
Highgate High St
Highgate Hill
Waterlow Park
St Joseph's RC Prim Sch
Highgate Cemy
Channing Sch
The Whittington
Archway
Upper Holloway

A
B
C
D
32
90
6
5
89
4
49
3
88
2
1
87
30
31
72
Noel Park
HORNSEY
Hornsey Vale
N8
Stroud Green
Harringay
N4
Finsbury Park
N19
Alexandra Prim Sch
MAYES RD
WESTERN RD
HORNSEY PARK RD
TURNPIKE LA
WESTBURY AVE
HIGH ST
PRIORY RD
CHURCH LA
TOTTENHAM LA
PARK RD
CROUCH END HILL
CROUCH HILL
HORNSEY RISE
STROUD GREEN RD
SEVEN SISTERS RD
GREEN LANES
WIGHTMAN RD
ENDYMION RD
Turnpike Lane
Ducketts Common
Hornsey
New River
Priory Park
Harringay Green Lanes
Crouch Hill
Parkland Wlk
Sp Arena
Manor House
Fball Practice Gds
A504
A105
A1080
A103
A1201
B138
B150
B152
A503
B540
1 KOBLENZ HO
2 WAT TYLER HO
3 NEWLAND HO
4 GOODWIN CT
5 GILLETT HO
6 MYDDELTON HO
7 CAMPSFIELD HO
1 TOPSFIELD PAR
2 BROADWAY PAR
1 NICHOLS CL
2 BRACKENBURY

TOTTENHAM
N17
N15
N4
N16
West Green
South Tottenham
Stamford Hill
STOKE
Bruce Grove
Seven Sisters
Downhills Park
Downhills Recn Gd
Chestnuts Recn Gd
Open Air Theatre
The Moselle
St Ann's General
East Resr
West Resr
Abney Park Cemy
Stoke Newington
Superstore
Allot Gdns
The Green Coll
TH
Sp Ctr
Arts Ctr
ARENA BSNS CTR
CRUSADER IND EST
THE GARDENS
SUMMIT EST
Haringey
Hackney
HIGH RD
STAMFORD HILL
WEST GREEN RD
ST ANN'S RD
PHILIP LA
BROAD LA
MONUMENT WAY
FOUNTAYNE RD
SEVEN SISTERS RD
AMHURST PK
MANOR RD
LORDSHIP PK
BELMONT RD
DOWNHILLS WAY
DOWNHILLS PARK RD
HIGHAM RD
CLYDE RD
SEAFORD RD
SUFFOLK RD
PLEVNA CRES
TOWN HALL APPROACH RD
TYNEMOUTH RD
SPRINGFIELD RD
CRAVEN PARK RD
CLAPTON COMM
PORTLAND AVE
DUNSMURE RD
HOLMLEIGH RD
LYNMOUTH RD
WOODBERRY DOWN
WOODBERRY GR
CHESNUT RD
HOLCOMBE RD
WELLINGTON AVE
CLIFTON GDNS
RAVENSDALE RD
OLINDA RD
EGERTON RD
A10
A1010
A503
A504
A107
A105
A1055
A1080
B152
B153
B155
B105
A
B
C
D
33
73
52
1
2
3
4
5
6
87
88
89
90

34
A
B
C
D
Lockwood Reservoir
Allot Gdns
Tottenham Hale
Down Lane Park
Tenn Cts
LEA VALLEY TECHNOPARK
MILLMEAD IND CTR
MILLMEAD BSNS CTR
LOCKWOOD IND PK
WATERMEAD WAY
MONUMENT WAY
HALE RD
FERRY LA
BROAD LA
FOUNTAYNE RD
Pymme's Brook
River Lee Navigation
River Lea or Lee Diversion
High Maynard Resr
Low Maynard Resr
Lee Flood Relief Channel
UPLANDS AVE
UPLANDS BSNS PK
BLACKHORSE LA
HIGHAMS LODGE BSNS CTR
FOREST TRAD EST
Willowfield Sec Sch
Blackhorse Road
N17
Sp Gd
TOTTENHAM HALE RET PK
FOUNTAYNE BSNS CTR
THE HIGH CROSS CTR
Resr No 1
Resr No 2
Resr No 3
Resr No 4
Resr No 5
Pl Flds
E17
Coppermill Prim Sch
Sp Ctr
RENSBURG VILLAS
COPPERMILL LA
Markfield Recn Gd
THE STONEBRIDGE CTR
Bwg Gn
Pav
N15
South Tottenham
51
Warwick Resr East
Warwick Resr West
Lee Valley Regional Park
Coppermill Stream
Water Works
N16
River Lea or Lee
Waltham Forest
Haringey
Hackney
Springfield Marina
Springfield Park
E5
Upper Clapton
Clapton Common
Walthamstow Marshes
Nature Reserve
E10
LEYTON IND VILLAGE
FOREST BSNS PK
DORMA TRAD PK
Lea Valley Riding Sch
Pl Fld
Leyton Marshes
Leeside Wharf
74
Lea Valley Ice Ctr
UPPER CLAPTON RD
MOUNT PLEASANT HILL
A107
A503
A1055
A1006
A104
B179
1
2
3
4
5
6
87
88
89
90
35

WALTHAMSTOW
E17
E10
35
54
75
A
B
C
D
1
2
3
4
5
6
FOREST RD
CHINGFORD RD
HOE ST
A112
A503
A104
A1006
B159
B161
HIGH RD
HIGH ROAD LEYTON
LEA BRIDGE RD
MARKHOUSE RD
BLACKHORSE RD
CHURCH RD
LEYTON GREEN RD
HIGH ST
ST JAMES'S ST
The Bell
Chestnut Sp Gd
Waltham Forest Coll
Allot Gdns
TH
C Ctr
Ct
Thorpe Coombe Coll Sch
The Holy Family Coll
Tenn Cts
Schs
Vestry Ho (Mus)
Liby
Walthamstow Central
Walthamstow Queens Road
Queens Road Cemy
South Grove Prim Sch
St James Street
Kelmscott L Ctr
Kelmscott Sch
St Saviour's CE Prim Sch
Barn Croft Sch
ROXWELL TRAD PK
CROMWELL EST
Sybourn Inf Sch Annexe
Fball Gd
The Lammas Sch
St Joseph's RC Inf Sch
Church Mead Jun Sch
George Mitchell Com Sch
Sp Gd
Leyton Midland Road
Dawlish Prim Sch
FAIRWAYS BSNS PK
Pl Flds
WINNS AVE
MILTON RD
CHURCH HILL
SELBORNE RD
ST MARY RD
GROSVENOR PARK RD
LIVINGSTONE RD
CLARENDON RD
MARKMANOR AVE
CAPWORTH ST
MANOR RD
GRANGE PARK RD
ESSEX RD
LYNMOUTH RD
HARTINGTON RD
CLACTON RD
BRUNEL RD
SOUTH ACCESS RD
OVERTON RD
BURWELL RD
SANDERSTEAD RD
LAMMAS RD

54
A
B
C
D
36
90
STOW
6
5
4
3
2
1
89
88
87
53
38
39
76
Whitefield Sch
WALTHAMSTOW BSNS CTR
FOREST RD
A503
Hyland House Sch
1 HEMPSTEAD RD
2 DENNIS CT
A104
BRESSEY GR
HIGH VIEW RD
BYRON AVE
RAYMOND AVE
WORDSWORTH AVE
GREENHEYS DR
SPRUCE HILLS RD
KINGSLEY RD
Liby
Woodside Schs
B160
Allot Gdns
Upper Walthamstow
CALVER CT
HILLSIDE GDNS
TRISTRAM CL
Tenn Cts
Bwg Gn
BEECH CT
MILLS HO
BISTERN AVE
PYRFIELD RD
Gilbert's Slade
BROADWALK
CHEYNE AVE
E18
Sp Gd
Snaresbrook
BUSHEY AVE
MALFORD GR
Thorpe Coombe
Coll Sch
PARKSTONE RD
ALBION RD
CORBETT RD
HAGGER CT
WOODLANDS RD
WAVERLEY RD
WAVERLEY AVE
CLAY CT
AVONFIELD CT
AVON RD
ATHLONE CT
MALLARD CT
HAVANT RD
TURNER RD
WYATT'S LA
BRANTWOOD RD
PROSPECT HILL
CHURCH HILL RD
UPPER WALTHAMSTOW RD
Nature Reserve
E17
DEAN GDNS
Wood Street
GREENWAY AVE
WOOD ST
FOREST RISE
ST PETER'S PATH
WOODLAND GDNS
WOODFORD NEW RD
OAKHURST CT
COLLEGE PL
Forest Sch
OAKHURST GDNS
THE FOREST
FOREST CT
BUXTON HO
BUXTON DR
RIVENHALL GDNS
BRADWELL CL
RAYNE CT
COPPICE WAY
LAUREL WAY
HERMITAGE WLK
HERMITAGE CL
Pav
WOODHAM CT
EAGLE LO
SNARESBROOK HO
ST AUBYNS
SNARESBROOK RD
Eagle Pond
MARLOWE RD
VALLENTIN RD
The Holy Family Coll
MONOUX ALMSHO
Tenn Cts
CHURCH LA
FAIRWAYS
BROWNING CL
GREENACRE GDNS
BROOKFIELD AVE
BARRETT RD
BURNS CL
ROSSLYN RD
EVELYN RD
GREVILLE RD
BROOKE RD
Warwick Sch for Boys
CHESTNUT AVE N
HOLMFIELD HO
Tenn Cts
Pav
Sp Gd
THE RISINGS
MORGAN AVE
FORESTERS DR
SALTERS RD
HAINAULT CT
LUCERNE GR
WOODSIDE PARK AVE
CLOCK HO
ROLAND RD
CHURCH END
SUMMIT RD
TRELAWNY CL
RAVENSWOOD RD
ADDISON RD
WILSON ST
Schs
OLIVER RD
CHESTNUT AVE S
FERNDALE AVE
A104
1 ST GEORGES CT
2 WHIPPS CROSS HO
3 BERTHAN GDNS
4 BEULEIGH CT
5 VINEWOOD CT
WHIPPS CROSS
Ct
Redbridge
Waltham Forest
A1199
ELLESMERE
VILLAGE CT
CHERRY CL
BEULAH RD
BRUNSWICK ST
ELLIS HO
MAYNARD RD
RAGLAN RD
TA Ctr
EASTERN RD
BARCLAY RD
SHERNHALL ST
ELM RD
WARWICK TERR
EATINGTON RD
FOREST VIEW
FULREADY RD
A114
Hollow Pond
CROMWELL RD
SALISBURY RD
BUTTERFIELDS
ST STEPHEN'S AVE
LEA BRIDGE RD
HALFORD RD
WEST END
STACEY CL
GROVE
FRASER RD
MERTON RD
COLLEGE RD
CARNARVON RD
LIVERPOOL RD
WHIPPS CROSS RD
E11
Centenary Walk
HOLLYBUSH HILL
GREG CL
THE BUNGALOWS
MATLOCK RD
PETERBOROUGH RD
Leyton Sixth Form Coll
Whipps Cross
Connaught Day
FOREST GLADE
KNOTTS GREEN MEWS
KNOTTS GREEN RD
LIVINGSTONE CT
LEYTON GREEN RD
NOTTINGHAM RD
ESSEX RD
Barclay Schs
ARROWHEAD CT
MAPLE RD
FLADGATE RD
HIGHSTONE CT 1
THE HERONS 2
KINGSLEY CT 3
AGINCOURT 4
POPLARS RD
A104
BELMONT PARK RD
ST HELIER'S RD
WHITEHOUSE EST
GRIGGS RD
E10
Leytonstone Sch
ST ANDREW'S RD
DYSON RD
PRESTON RD
WARDLEY LO
A112
HIGH RD
WILLIAM ST
MARKET PAR
CHELTENHAM RD
EPSOM RD
CHESTERFIELD RD
CANTERBURY RD
SANDRINGHAM RD
JAMES LA
CLARE RD
STANLEY HO
RIPLEY MEWS
COLWORTH RD
POPPLETON RD
CHADWICK RD
TEESDALE RD
FOREST LEA 1
WATERSHIP DOWN HO 2
BROMLEY
B159
ELY RD
COLCHESTER RD
CROMER RD
FOREST DR E
Gwyn Jones Sch
WADLEY RD
TEMPLE CL
ASHBRIDGE RD
HATFIELD HO
BEAUMONT RD
ABBOTTS PARK RD
BOSCOMBE AVE
ESSEX RD S
FOREST RD
CHERRYDEAL CT
MARGARET'S CT
WOODRIFFE RD
PERCY RD
SAMANTHA CT
LYTTON RD
ESTHER RD
CHESSINGTON MANS
A113
Green Man Int
Tenn Cts
Abbotts Park
LYNDHURST DR
FOREST DR W
INTEGER GDNS
HARLEY HO
REGINALD SORENSON CT
WALLWOOD RD
CORBETT CL
FILLEBROOK HALL
KINGSWOOD RD
LEMNA CT
JOHN DRINKWATER CL
A114
TILBURY RD
FLETCHER LA
LEIGH RD
WESLEY RD
GOODMAN RD
SERBIN CL
LAMBOURNE
CHILD CT
BRIAR CT
HAINAULT RD
EGERTON CT
HILLBORO CT
KING'S RD
QUEEN'S RD
QUEEN'S CT
CONNOR CL
GAINSBOROUGH RD
A106
KIRKDALE RD
LEMNA RD
BROWNING RD
FOREST VIEW
Allot Gdns
BEACONTREE RD
SKELTON'S LA
COOPER'S LA
FARMER RD
MIDLAND RD
Leyton Midland Road
MOYERS RD
THE PAVEMENT
THE SIDINGS
HAWBRIDGE RD
FAIRWOOD CT
CLARENDON RD
FAIRLOP RD
BLOOMSBURY CT
FAIRLOP CT
CHELMSFORD RD
AVONDALE CT
Leytonstone
CHURCH LA
Liby
AYLMER RD
GROVE RD
CARLTON RD
DACRE RD
BARFIELD RD
MORNINGTON RD
WOODVILLE RD
HARTLEY RD
Sch
BREWSTER RD
Bwg Gn
BOREHAM CL
CAVENDISH DR
BULWER CT
BULWER RD
DRAYTON RD
DRAYTON CT
BURGHLEY RD
HARVEY RD
LEYSPRING RD
George Mitchell Com Sch
Tenn Cts
HAINAULT BLDGS
Sp Gd
BELGRAVE RD
GROSVENOR RD
KING EDWARD RD
Norlington Sch for Boys
NORLINGTON RD
SCARBOROUGH RD
AVEBURY CT
SOUTHWEST RD
FILLEBROOK RD
HARRINGTON RD
BARCLAY RD
SILKS CT
ST AUGUSTINE'S CT
STANMORE RD
WOODBRIDGE HO
LEYBOURNE RD
CRAWLEY RD
A112
BRUNSWICK RD
LAWTON RD
B161
SCOTT'S RD
MORLEY RD
CLAUDE RD
PRETORIA RD
Sch
DYERS HALL RD
A12
CONNAUGHT RD
MICHAEL RD
VERNON RD
George Tomlinson Prim Sch
HAROLD RD
1 MOHMMAD KHAN
2 ST JOHN'S CT
3 HARVEY GDNS
4 ST MARY'S CT
LISTER RD
Leytonstone
JESSE RD
ALBERT RD
JERSEY RD
GUERNSEY RD
HAMPTON RD
MADEIRA RD
CRADOCK CT
BROCKWAY CL
DAVIES LA
Davies Lane Jun & Inf Sch
HIGH ROAD LEYTON
TENNYSON RD
Dawlish Prim Sch
DAWLISH RD
FRANCIS RD
Newport Schs
NEWPORT RD
ST ANNE'S RD
TWICKENHAM RD
CHERTSEY RD
RHODESIA RD
KIMBERLEY RD
SUMAL CT
DYERS HALL RD
JOSEPH RAY RD
Leytonstone High Road
A1006
GRANGE PARK RD
RYDER CT
BUCKLAND RD
EDGWICK RD
MURCHISON RD
Noor Ul Islam Prim Sch
RICHMOND RD
GREEN RD
NORMAN RD
SHORT RD
TRINITY CL
FERNDALE RD
MALVERN RD
Wanstead Flats

A
B
C
D
37
South Woodford
Oakdale
GLEBELANDS AVE
MALFORD CT
BEDFORD RD
DAISY RD
STATION PAS
GEORGE LA
B168
OAKDALE RD
COWSLIP RD
CHCROFT
ASHFORD
GRANVILLE RD
VICTORIA RD
A113
A11
M11
A406
WOODFORD TRAD EST
BOURNE CT
SOUTHEND RD
SOUTHEND RD
VIENNA CL
COBURG GDNS
90
NIGHTINGALES CT
PO
A1400
KINGSPARK CT
LANSDOWNE RD
CLEVELAND RD
MARLBOROUGH RD
PELHAM RD
CHIGWELL RD
OLD MILL CT
HAYSTOCKS
ANDERSON RD
CLAYBURY
IG8
E18
CLARENDON RD
ORFORD RD
PULTENEY RD
CADOGAN GDNS
ONSLOW GDNS
Hatton Sch
6
Pl Fld
THE DRIVE
WOODFORD RD
TAVISTOCK RD
TORRINGTON RD
ALEXANDRA RD
SHERWOOD AVE
SOUTHVIEW DR
MONMOUTH AVE
Roding Valley Park
Beal High Sch
BEECHWOOD PK
AVON WAY
BURTON RD
CHARNWOOD DR
ADMIRALS CL
HURSTWOOD AVE
Roding
WOODFORD BRIDGE RD
OSPREY CL
CRANBOURNE CT
LANCASTER AVE
BROXBOURNE AVE
CARSWELL CL
MEADOW WLK
Sch
FALCON WAY
HERMON HILL
CRANBOURNE AVE
ASHBOURNE AVE
Nightingale Prim Sch
Recn Gd
DEEPDENE CL
VICTORY RD
COLVIN GDNS
FOXGLOVE GDNS
MERINO CL
ROADING LA S
WHITNEY AVE
TORQUAY GDNS
5
EAGLE LA
CLOCK CT
TRAFALGAR PL
MAKEPEACE RD
ORCHARD CL
RODNEY RD
ELMCROFT CL
FLORENCE CT
LORNE GDNS
DEYNECOURT GDNS
Pl Fld
LAKESIDE AVE
LEIGH AVE
FALMOUTH GDNS
MALCOLM WAY
Wanstead
NELSON RD
ELMCROFT AVE
LIMES AVE
MERRIVALE AVE
SULTAN RD
WOODBURY CL
BURNHAM CRES
Allot Gdns
BRAINTREE AVE
SYLVAIN RD
WELLINGTON RD
HALSTEAD RD
ELDERFIELD WLK
CARLTON TERR
RUTLAND RD
EATON RISE
RANELAGH GDNS
Allot Gdns
PEAKETON AVE
89
BERGHOLT AVE
Snaresbrook
STATION APP
COWLEY RD
KEATS CL
NIGHTINGALE LA
EASTWAY
WARWICK RD
BUCKINGHAM RD
LAURA CL
IG4
MICHELL AVE
FOWEY AVE
Redbridge Jun & Inf Schs
THE RISE
HOLLYBUSH CL
WELLESLEY RD
STANSTEAD RD
HEREFORD RD
LEICESTER RD
GLOUCESTER RD
NORTH CIRCULAR RD
TRYFAN CL
COBBETTS AVE
4
FOREST CL
HOMESDALE CL
TRENT CT
HIGH ST
12
GROSVENOR RD
GROVE PK
NUTTER LA
PRESTON DR
VISTA DR
FAIRMEAD GDNS
EDWINA GDNS
SEWORTHY CL
BOURNE CL
CHURCH PATH
Sch
FITZGERALD RD
CLOCK HOUSE PAR
KENDON CL
THE AVENUE
Allot Gdns
Sp Gd
THE MEWS
ROSEMARY DR
FERNHALL DR
AVONDALE CRES
EAST ROW
WANSTEAD PL
11
REYDON AVE
ELM HALL GDNS
56
NEW WANSTEAD
Recn Gd
WESTMINSTER CT 1
SHERIDAN MEWS 2
GARDNER CL
Redbridge
Redbridge Rdbt
Redbridge
MARGARET WAY
VOLUNTARY PL
GREENSTONE MEWS
SPRATT HALL RD
CHAUCER RD
Liby
KINGFISHER AVE
HARRIER AVE
RECTORY CRES
CORBETT RD
RIVER CL
EASTERN AVE
A12
A12
WOODBINE PL
Wanstead
Liby
ELM CL
WIGRAM RD
RIVER CT
STUDLEY DR
EVANSTON GDNS
ADDISON RD
DRUMMOND RD
OAKHALL CT
REDBRIDGE LA W
ROYSTON CT 1
RODING LO 2
ROYSTON PAR 3
STUDLEY
STUDLEY CT
3
CASTLE
GORDON RD
DANGAN RD
A1008
CHESTER RD
L Ctr
CHESTNUT DR
THE GREEN
MANSFIELD RD
CAMDEN RD
SYDNEY RD
OAK HALL RD
Wanstead High Sch
ROYSTON GDNS
CARLISLE HO
Sch
Sch
CAMBRIDGE PK
E11
WANSTEAD
CARLISLE GDNS
HIGHSTONE AVE
EDGAR HO
DRAYCOT RD
ST MARY'S LO
ST MARY'S AVE
LANGLEY CRES
LANGLEY DR
WARREN RD
ROOK LO
WAKEFIELD GDNS
RIPON GDNS
88
CAMBRIDGE PARK RD
FELSTEAD RD
SEAGRY RD
COLEBROOKE DR
WELL COTTAGE CL
Lincoln Island
River Roding
Sp Gd
A406
ELSDON RD
NADIR CT
WOODCOTE RD
TENNYSON AVE
OVERTON DR
THE WARREN DR
RAYNES AVE
CH
B Gn
Rook I
2
Allot Gdns
NORTH
ENNERDALE CT 1
OAK LO 2
MALLARDS 3
HARLEY CT 4
A1008
BLAKE HALL RD
The Basin
Sp Gd
BUSH RD
OVERTON CT
Wanstead
Bush Wood
Wanstead Park
Reservoir Wood
Heronry Pond
1
Boat House
JACKSON CT 1
JOSEPH LISTER LODGE 2
Aldersbrook Prim Sch
WOODLANDS AVE
NORTHUMBERLAND AVE
E12
BLAKE HALL CRES
BELGRAVE RD
WINDSOR RD
ST GABRIEL'S CL
QUEENSWOOD GDNS
BRADING CRES
BURDEN WAY
INGATESTONE RD
ALBURY MEWS
HARPENDEN RD
MARGARETTING RD
CLAVERING RD
ARRAN DR
MARK WADE CL
WESTMORLAND CL
Allot Gdns
87
A116
A114
ALDERS CL
41
77
DOVER RD
SUNLAND WAY
Redbridge
Newham
42
RICHMOND WAY
LAKE HOUSE RD
HOOD LO 1
BUXTON LO 2
HERONGATE RD
ST MARGARET'S RD
WANSTEAD PARK
B Gn
HIGHFIELD CT

Clayhall
VII
A
B
C
D
6
5
4
3
2
1
90
89
88
87
42
43
78
55
IG1
IG2
IG4
IG5
A1400
A12
A123
A406
B192
WOODFORD AVE
EASTERN AVE
BEEHIVE LA
CRANBROOK RD
NORTH CIRCULAR RD
Clayhall Park
Gants Hill
Valentines Park
Valentines High Sch (Upper)
Cranbrook
The Lake
Redbridge
Redbridge Jun & Inf Schs
Beal High Sch
Hatton Sch
Highlands Prim Sch
River Roding
Pl Fld
Recn Gd
Sp Gd
Allot Gdns
Bwg Gn
Crkt Gd
Min Glf Crs
Cemy
Schs
Prep Sch
Liby
Coll
Ilford
Redbridge
Newham
WINNINGALES CT
CLAYBURY BROADWAY
BRINKWORTH RD
MARLBOROUGH DR
PEEL DR
STRADBROKE GR
MELLOWS RD
CHADACRE AVE
GAYFERE RD
MARLANDS RD
HEATHERLEY DR
STONELEIGH RD
STONELEIGH CT
HERENT DR
LORD AVE
ORIEL GDNS
LESSINGHAM AVE
RUSHDEN GDNS
TIVERTON AVE
DYMCHURCH CL
TIPTREE CRES
1 PUFFIN TERR
2 OYSTER CATCHER TERR
SANDPIPER TERR
BEAMINSTER GDNS
WINCANTON GDNS
MOSSFORD CT
HATFIELD CL 1
LOOE GDNS 2
CHERRY CT 3
LICHEN CT 4
LONGWOOD PAR
OAKLEAFE GDNS
MAPLEAFE GDNS
GREENLEAFE DR
GAYSHAM HALL
WERNETH HALL RD
ABBOTSWOOD GDNS
EARLSWOOD GDNS
MONKSWOOD GDNS
DELLWOOD GDNS
EVESHAM WAY
WRAY AVE
LONGWOOD GDNS
GLENTHORNE GDNS
WOODVILLE GDNS
HORPEDALE GDNS
BEATTYVILLE GDNS
ROSEDENE GDNS
QUEENBOROUGH GDNS
NORTHWOOD GDNS
GEORGEVILLE GDNS
EARIESVILLE GDNS
HAIGVILLE GDNS
SUNNYMEDE DR
SOUTHWOOD GDNS
LITTLE GEARIES
BRANDVILLE GDNS
WOODFORD BRIDGE RD
CARSWELL CL
BORROWDALE CL
LODGE HILL
WIDECOMBE GDNS
CONISTON GDNS
DERWENT GDNS
BABBACOMBE GDNS
KESWICK GDNS
AMBLESIDE GDNS
BRANTWOOD GDNS
GRASMERE GDNS
PARK VIEW GDNS
LORD GDNS
B Gn
1 HEDGELEY
2 QUEENS GATE
HIGHWOOD GDNS
WYCHWOOD GDNS
BEECHWOOD GDNS
HEDGEWOOD GDNS
COLLINWOOD GDNS
GLENWOOD GDNS
BRONTE CL
KENWOOD GDNS
GANTS HILL CRES
SHERE RD
WAREMEAD RD
ROLL GDNS
SEVEN WAYS PAR
GAYSHAM AVE
SWALLOW CT
BUTE RD
LOUDOUN AVE
HORE CL
PERSS
CHALFORD CT
JEFFERSON CL
ICKNIELD DR
GLENHAM DR
MARTLEY DR
PARHAM DR
HEADLEY APP
OTLEY DR
OTLEY APP
HEADLEY DR
TORQUAY GDNS
FALMOUTH GDNS
MERRIVALE AVE
BRAINTREE AVE
BERGHOLT AVE
MIGHELL AVE
FOWEY AVE
TRYFAN CL
RIDGEWAY GDNS
COLLEGE GDNS
GRANGEWAY GDNS
HIGHCLIFFE GDNS
FAIRMEAD GDNS
EDWINA GDNS
VISTA DR
FERNHALL DR
ROSEMARY DR
THE MEWS
AVON
REDBRIDGE LA E
WINDERMERE GDNS
DANEHURST GDNS
FLORENCE ROOT HO
INGLEHURST GDNS
SOMERSBY GDNS
GOSFORD GDNS
CROMBIE CL
RADNOR CRES
SUSSEX CL
LIMEWOOD CT
WYCOMBE RD
AVERY GDNS
ETHELBERT GDNS
WAYSIDE MEWS
MARGARET WAY
ELLESMERE GDNS
EVANSTON GDNS
STUDLEY DR
STUDLEY CT
CASTLE DR
CASTLE VIEW GDNS
DEVONPORT GDNS
HILL VIEW CRES
PRESTON GDNS
BEEHIVE CT
CLARENCE AVE
THE CRESCENT
PANFIELD MEWS
FRINTON MEWS
BRAMLEY CRES
BLENHEIM AVE
LONSDALE CRES
SOUTH VIEW CRES
LYNTON CRES
ALBEMARLE GDNS
ALBEMARLE APP
MIDDLETON GDNS
MIDDLEFIELD GDNS
BLOOMFIELD CRES
PERTH RD
CARLISLE HO
CARLISLE GDNS
STONEHALL AVE
WAKEFIELD GDNS
WANSTEAD LA
RIPON GDNS
WORCESTER GDNS
HEREFORD GDNS
ELY GDNS
WELLS GDNS
CANTERBURY AVE
GLOUCESTER GDNS
PETERBOROUGH GDNS
LINCOLN GDNS
1 GLOUCESTER CT
2 LINCOLN CT
3 PAVILION RD
ST HELEN'S RD
ST EDMUND'S RD
FAIRHOLME RD
MORNINGTON AVE
CRANBROOK RISE
1 BRAMLEY HO
2 CHARLOTTE CT
3 VI & JOHN RUBENS HO
ST GEORGE'S RD
MISTLEY THORN
ST ANDREW'S RD
WILSON RD
THE DRIVE
TRURO GDNS
CHELMSFORD GDNS
CHICHESTER GDNS
ROCHESTER GDNS
VAUGHAN GDNS
COWLEY RD
TILLOTSON RD
EMERSON RD
BETHELL AVE
THE SQUARE
HOLCOMBE RD
WHITFIELD CT
CLARENDON GDNS
EXETER GDNS
RANELAGH GDNS
ARLINGTON GDNS
REDCLIFFE GDNS
CAVENDISH GDNS
BEAUFORT GDNS
HIGHLANDS GDNS
LENNOX GDNS
STANHOPE GDNS
SACKVILLE GDNS
SEYMOUR GDNS
KENSINGTON GDNS
ENDSLEIGH GDNS
DE VERE GDNS
COURTLAND AVE
MAYFAIR AVE
EMPRESS AVE
BELGRAVE RD
WANSTEAD PARK RD
CH
WESTBURY RD
NORTHBROOK RD
ARGYLE RD
BEAL RD
MANSFIELD RD
GREENWAY CT
PARK AVE
Park Sch
VALENTINES RD
INGLEBY RD
GRANVILLE RD
MORLAND RD
BATHURST RD
AIRLIE GDNS
WARWICK GDNS
COVENTRY RD
MELBOURNE RD
WELLESLEY RD
ADELAIDE RD
BALFOUR RD
HERON CT
HAINAULT ST
ORLAND CL
HIGHLAND WAY
ANDERSON RD
COBURG GDNS
PEEL PL
PO
P

VII
Fairlop Waters Ctry Pk
Sch of Riding
Fairlop Waters
Ilford Jewish Prim Sch
Barkingside
IG6
Recn Gd
Fullwood Prim Sch
THE VILLAGE HOME
BARNARDO DR 1
SYCAMORE WLK 2
WALNUT CL 3
Fball Gd
Aldborough Hall Farm
Allot Gdns
Aldborough Hatch
IG2
Aldborough House Farm
HIGH ST
FREMANTLE RD
WAVERLEY GDNS
WESTMINSTER GDNS
HORACE RD
TRINITY RD
MOSSFORD GN
SANDRINGHAM GDNS
SANDRINGHAM CL
TANNERS LA
BARON GDNS
CRANBOURNE GDNS
TOLLESBURY GDNS
CRAVEN GDNS
HEYBRIDGE DR
COURT WAY
CARLTON DR
CARLTON CT
STATION RD
RACHEL CL
CROWN RD
DUKE GDNS
DUKE RD
CIVIC WAY
BARTON MEADOWS
ASTHALL GDNS
BURFORD CL
PRINCES RD
MULBERRY WAY
HATLEY AVE
HASTINGS AVE
CAMPBELL AVE
HAMILTON AVE
NORTH CROSS RD
SOUTH CROSS RD
POPLAR WAY
CORONATION CT
ALDWYCH AVE
WILLIAM CT
SHERWOOD RD
WARREN RD
HORNS RD
CHASE LA
NORTHDOWN GDNS
Pl Fld
1 NETLEY CT
2 SHIRLEY CT
3 KAREN TERR
4 VICTORIA COTTS
THE WHITINGS
HEATHSIDE CL
PERKINS RD
NETLEY RD
BIRKBECK RD
ABBEY RD
BUNTINGBRIDGE RD
PERRYMANS FARM RD
BUSH CL
DONINGTON AVE
ASHURST DR
EMMOTT AVE
ARDWELL AVE
SPRINGFIELD DR
BENTLEY DR
DENHAM DR
CANTLEY GDNS
YOXLEY DR
YOXLEY APP
UPPARK DR
YOUNGS RD
ARTILLERY CL
Sch
Newbury Park
KING GEORGE AVE
OAKS LA
SOUTHDOWN CRES
CHEVIOT WAY
LEYSWOOD DR
CAMBRIAN AVE
BRENDON GDNS
CHILTERN RD
MENDIP RD
HOMEFIELD AVE
STAPLEFORD AVE
Oaks Park High Sch
CROWFIELD AVE
AVENUE TERR
WHITES AVE
THE CLOSE
ACORN CT
William Torbitt Prim Sch
ST PETERS CL
OAKS LA
BURYSIDE CL
ROY GDNS
THE SHRUBBERIES
TORBITT WAY
ALDBOROUGH RD N
ALDBOROUGH RD
SPEARPOINT GDNS
RAMSGILL APP
RAMSGILL DR
APPLEGARTH DR
BAWDSEY AVE
SUNNINGHILL GDNS
SHENSTONE GDNS
A12
Seven Kings Water
GRENFELL GDNS
Bwg Gn
ALDBOROUGH CT
Sports Gd
SILVERDALE PAR
PARK AVE
SILVERDALE AVE
HOLLAND AVE
SELWYN AVE
58
Newbury Park
EASTERN AVE
CENTRAL PAR
HERTFORD RD
NEWBURY RD
NORTON CT
CHURCH RD
BUXTON RD
BROOK RD
SUFFOLK CT
SUFFOLK RD
WESSEX CL
CHEPSTOW CRES
Seven Kings Park
Bwg Gn
Farnham Prim Sch
MILTON CRES
EASTERNVILLE GDNS
CRANLEY RD
WESTERNVILLE GDNS
CRANLEY DR
BADGER CL
LYNDHURST GDNS
LANCING RD
CLIFTON RD
COTSWOLD GDNS
DELL CL
GLEBELANDS AVE
STAINFORTH RD
BRANCASTER RD
DEVONSHIRE RD
TRILLO CT
ST JOHNS RD
DOWNSHALL CT
DOWNSHALL AVE
LEICESTER GDNS
EPSOM RD
MERTON RD
BEDDINGTON RD
MORDON RD
MITCHAM RD
WALLINGTON RD
FARNHAM RD
REGENT GDNS
ROYAL CL
MEADS LA
QUEBEC RD
PARKLANDS CL
LYNN RD
NORMAN CT
WARDS RD
Sch
Westwood Rec Gd
Sp Gd
Seven Kings High Sch
RUSSELL GDNS
RAYMOND RD
MAFEKING AVE
LADYSMITH AVE
KIMBERLEY AVE
GLENCOE AVE
CHARTER AVE
Allot Gdns
ALDBOROUGH RD S
NORFOLK RD
ELGIN RD
CAMBRIDGE RD
LANSDOWNE RD
ST ALBANS RD
PEMBROKE RD
CHESTER RD
WESTWOOD RD
BLYTHSWOOD RD
KINGSWOOD RD
ATHOLL RD
Seven Kings
MONTREAL RD
AUCKLAND RD
COLOMBO RD
PERTH TERR
BRISBANE RD
TORONTO RD
WELLESLEY RD
DUNEDIN RD
LEY ST
BENTON RD
COLENSO RD
DURBAN RD
SPENCER RD
St Aidan's Sch
KINGS GDNS
MUNDON GDNS
FRIARS CL
LEEDS RD
BRADFORD RD
VICARAGE LA
IG3
Seven Kings
FARLEY DR
SIPPETTS CT
GODDARDS WAY
Christchurch Prim Sch
CHRISTCHURCH RD
BALFOUR RD
THOROLD RD
Canon Palmer RC Sch
SWINDON CL
CAMERON RD
A118
1 BALMORAL GDNS
2 ELECTRIC PAR
ASHGROVE RD
GRANTON RD
VERNON RD
FELBRIGGE RD
LOMBARD AVE
JAFFE RD
MEISTER CL
DRAYTON CL
CARRIAGE MEWS
HIGH RD
HIGHBURY GDNS
SALISBURY RD
SEVEN KINGS RD
HASLEMERE RD
GARTMORE RD
KENILWORTH GDNS
A1083
BARONS CT
REDBRIDGE ENT CTR
OAKLANDS PARK
FRANCIS
45
79
CLARK'S
Cemy
1 FRANCIS ST
2 FRANCIS RD
NORTH RD
CLAREMONT GDNS
NEW RD
LAMBOURNE RD
CLANDON RD
EYNSFORD RD
ELMSTEAD RD
TALBOT GDNS
WOODSTOCK GDNS
NUTFIELD GDNS
LYNFORD GDNS
46
A B C D
90 6 5 89 4 3 88 2 1 87

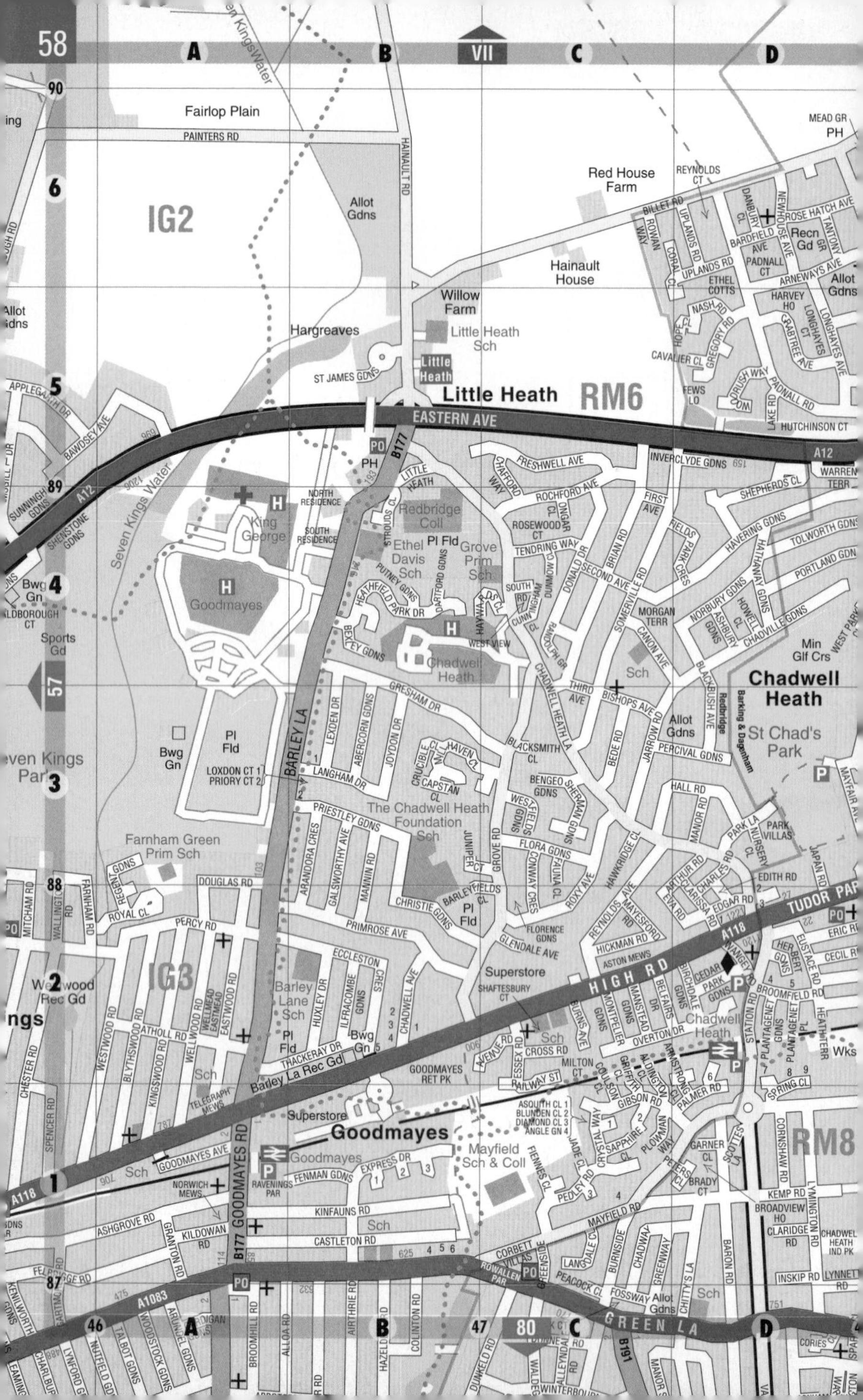
A
B
VII
C
D
Fairlop Plain
PAINTERS RD
HAINAULT RD
IG2
Allot Gdns
Red House Farm
REYNOLDS CT
BILLET RD
ROWAN WAY
UPLANDS RD
CORAL CL
DANBURY CL
NEWHOUSE AVE
ROSE HATCH AVE
Recn Gd
TANTONY GR
BARDFIELD AVE
PADNALL CT
ARNEWAYS AVE
MEAD GR
PH
Hainault House
ETHEL COTTS
HARVEY HO
LONGHAYES CT
LONGHAYES AVE
CRABTREE AVE
NASH RD
GREGORY RD
HOPE CL
CAVALIER CL
Willow Farm
Little Heath Sch
Hargreaves
ST JAMES GDNS
Little Heath
RM6
FEWS LO
DRUSH WAY
PADNALL RD
LAKE RD
HUTCHINSON CT
APPLEGARTH DR
BAWDSEY AVE
EASTERN AVE
A12
B177
PO
INVERCLYDE GDNS
WARREN TERR
SUNNINGHILL GDNS
SHENSTONE GDNS
Seven Kings Water
NORTH RESIDENCE
SOUTH RESIDENCE
King George
H
LITTLE HEATH
Redbridge Coll
FRESHWELL AVE
CHAFFORD WAY
ROCHFORD AVE
ONGAR CL
FIRST AVE
SHEPHERDS CL
ROSEWOOD CT
FIELDS PARK CRES
HAVERING GDNS
TOLWORTH GDNS
STROUDS CL
Ethel Davis Sch
Pl Fld
Grove Prim Sch
TENDRING WAY
DUNMOW CL
DONALD DR
BRIAN RD
SECOND AVE
PORTLAND GDNS
HATHAWAY GDNS
Bwg Gn
Goodmayes
ALDBOROUGH CT
Sports Gd
PUTNEY GDNS
HEATHFIELD PARK DR
DARTFORD GDNS
HAYWARDS CL
SOUTH RD
CUNNINGHAM CL
RANDOLPH GR
SOMERVILLE RD
MORGAN TERR
NORBURY GDNS
ASHBURY GDNS
HOWELL CL
CHADVILLE GDNS
Min Glf Crs
WEST PARK
BEXLEY GDNS
WEST VIEW
Chadwell Heath
CANON AVE
Sch
THIRD AVE
BISHOPS AVE
BLACKBUSH AVE
Redbridge
Barking & Dagenham
57
GRESHAM DR
CHADWELL HEATH LA
LEXDEN DR
ABERCORN GDNS
JOYDON DR
BARLEY LA
CRUCIBLE CL
MILL CL
HAVEN CL
BLACKSMITH CL
BEDE RD
JARROW RD
Allot Gdns
PERCIVAL GDNS
St Chad's Park
P
MAYFAIR AVE
Seven Kings Park
Pl Fld
LOXDON CT 1
PRIORY CT 2
LANGHAM DR
CAPSTAN CL
BENGEO GDNS
SHERMAN GDNS
HALL RD
MANOR RD
WESTFIELDS GDNS
PRIESTLEY GDNS
The Chadwell Heath Foundation Sch
JUNIPER CT
GROVE RD
HAWKRIDGE CL
PARK LA
NURSERY CL
PARK VILLAS
JAPAN RD
Farnham Green Prim Sch
ARANDORA CRES
GALSWORTHY AVE
MANNIN RD
FLORA GDNS
CONWAY CRES
FAUNA CL
ROXY AVE
ARTHUR RD
EVA RD
CLARISSA RD
CHARLES RD
EDITH RD
REGENT GDNS
DOUGLAS RD
MITCHAM RD
WALLINGTON RD
FARNHAM RD
CHRISTIE GDNS
BARLEYFIELDS CL
REYNOLDS AVE
MAYESFORD RD
EDGAR RD
TUDOR PAR
ROYAL CL
PERCY RD
PRIMROSE AVE
FLORENCE GDNS
HICKMAN RD
A118
ERIC RD
CECIL RD
GLENDALE AVE
ECCLESTON CRES
IG3
ASTON MEWS
CEDAR PARK GDNS
WANGEY RD
HERBERT GDNS
EUSTACE RD
Westwood Rec Gd
Barley Lane Sch
HUXLEY DR
ILFRACOMBE GDNS
CHADWELL AVE
Superstore
SHAFTESBURY CT
HIGH RD
BURNS AVE
MONTPELIER GDNS
MANSTEAD GDNS
BELFAIRS DR
BIRCHDALE GDNS
BROOMFIELD RD
WESTWOOD RD
BLYTHSWOOD RD
ATHOLL RD
KINGSWOOD RD
WELLWOOD RD
WELLMEAD EASTMEAD
EASTWOOD RD
THACKERAY DR
Bwg Gn
AVENUE RD
ESSEX RD
CROSS RD
OVERTON DR
Chadwell Heath
STATION RD
PLANTAGENET GDNS
PLANTAGENET PL
HEATH TERR
Wks
CHESTER RD
SPENCER RD
TELEGRAPH MEWS
Barley La Rec Gd
GOODMAYES RET PK
MILTON CT
RAILWAY ST
COULSON CL
GRIFFITH CL
ALDINGTON CL
ARMSTRONG CL
GIBSON RD
PALMER RD
SPRING CL
ASQUITH CL 1
BLUNDEN CL 2
DIAMOND CL 3
ANGLE GN 4
CRYSTAL WAY
SAPPHIRE CL
PLOWMAN WAY
GOODMAYES RD
GOODMAYES AVE
Goodmayes
EXPRESS DR
Mayfield Sch & Coll
JADE CL
PETERS CL
GARNER CL
SCOTTES LA
CORNSHAW RD
RM8
FENMAN GDNS
RAVENINGS PAR
FIENNES CL
PEDLEY RD
BRADY CT
KEMP RD
LYMINGTON RD
NORWICH MEWS
KINFAUNS RD
MAYFIELD RD
BROADVIEW HO
ASHGROVE RD
GRANTON RD
KILDOWAN RD
CASTLETON RD
CLARIDGE RD
CHADWELL HEATH IND PK
FELBRIDGE RD
CORBETT VILLAS
ROWALLEN PAR
GREENSIDE
LANGDALE CL
BURNSIDE
CHADWAY
GREENWAY
CHITTY'S LA
BARON RD
INSKIP RD
LYNNETT RD
PEACOCK CL
FOSSWAY
A1083
KENILWORTH GDNS
46
47
80
GREEN LA
B191
BROOMHILL RD
ALLOA RD
AIRTHRIE RD
COLINTON RD
HAZELDENE RD
TALBOT GDNS
WOODSTOCK GDNS
ARUNDEL GDNS
NUTFIELD GDNS
CHARLBURY GDNS
LYNFORD GDNS
DUNKELD RD
ALLEYNDALE RD
WINTERBOURNE RD
CORIES CL
90
89
88
87
6
5
4
3
2
1

A1112 Chigwell, M11 (A113, A1168)
ROMFORD
RM6
RM7
RM8
EASTERN AVE W
LONDON RD
WHALEBONE LA N
WHALEBONE LA S
RUSH GREEN RD
CROW LA
A12 Romford (A125), M25
A118 Romford, M25 (A12)
A124 Hornchurch
Crowlands Open Space
Central Park
Warren Comp Sch
Warren Jun Sch
St Edward's CE Comp Sch
Westlands Pl Fld
Crown Farm
Robert Clack Upper Sch
Robert Clack Lower Sch
All Saints RC Sch
Marks Gate Jun & Inf Schs
Boating Lake
Civic Ctr
Barking & Dagenham
Havering
1 HAWKWELL HO
2 BUTLER CT
3 LABURNUM HO
4 PEVEREL HO

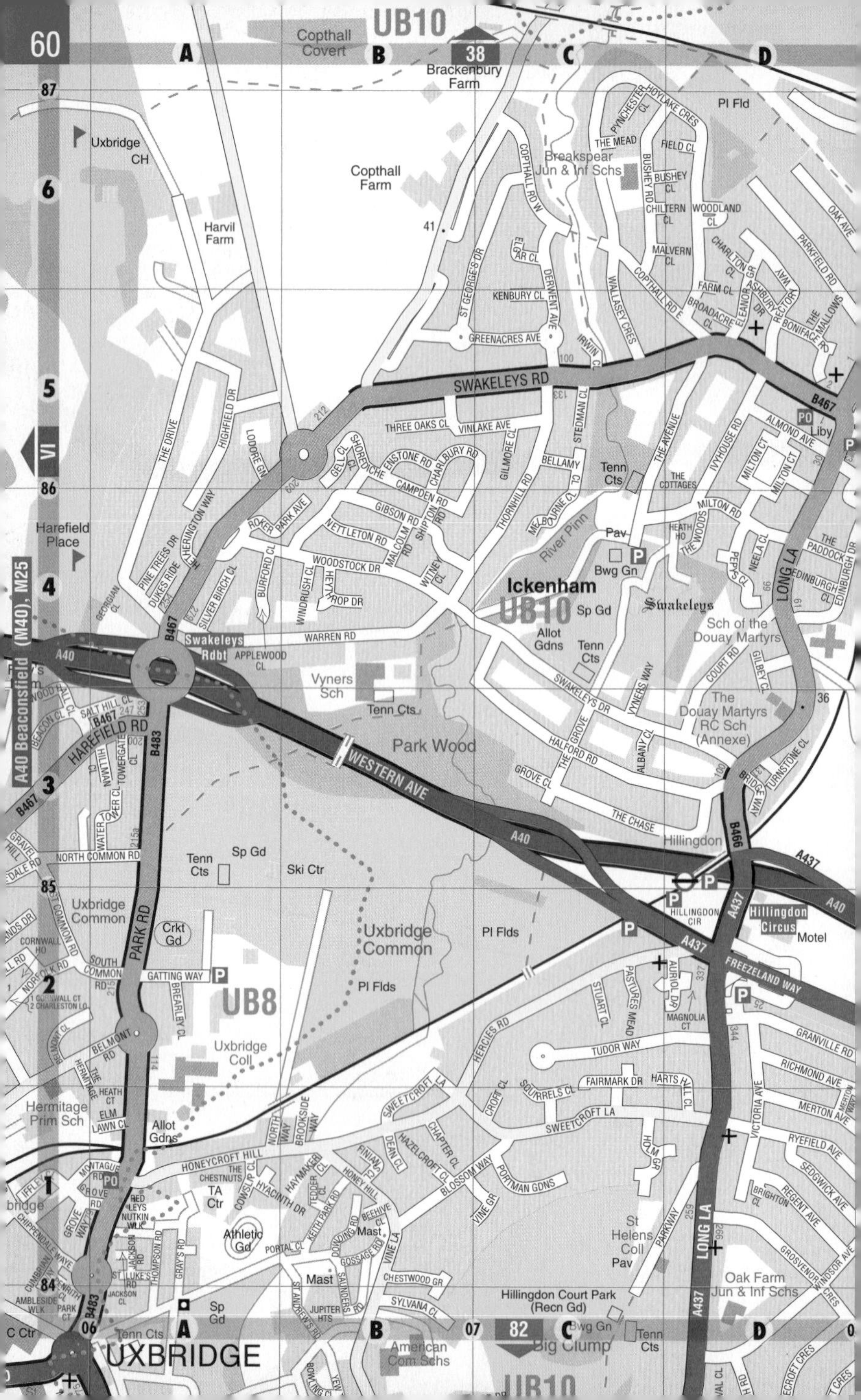
UB10
Copthall Covert
A
B
38
C
D
Brackenbury Farm
87
Uxbridge CH
Copthall Farm
6
Harvil Farm
41
Breakspear Jun & Inf Schs
Pl Fld
HOYLAKE CRES
PYNCHESTER CL
THE MEAD
FIELD CL
BUSHEY RD
BUSHEY CL
CHILTERN CL
WOODLAND CL
MALVERN CL
OAK AVE
PARKFIELD RD
CHARLTON CL
ASHBURY DR
RECTORY WAY
FARM CL
BROADACRE CL
ELEANOR GR
THE MALLOWS
BONIFACE RD
COPTHALL RD E
COPTHALL RD W
ELGAR CL
DERWENT AVE
ST GEORGE'S DR
KENBURY CL
WALLASEY CRES
GREENACRES AVE
IRWIN CL
100
5
SWAKELEYS RD
B467
212
133
STEDMAN CL
THE AVENUE
IVYHOUSE RD
ALMOND AVE
PO
Liby
THREE OAKS CL
VINLAKE AVE
GILMORE CL
BELLAMY CL
Tenn Cts
THE COTTAGES
MILTON CT
HIGHFIELD DR
LODORE GN
THE DRIVE
HETHERINGTON WAY
GELL CL
SHOREDITCH RD
ENSTONE RD
CHARLBURY RD
CAMPDEN RD
GIBSON RD
SHIPTON RD
THORNHILL RD
MELBOURNE CL
MILTON RD
HEATH HO
THE WOODS
NEELA CL
THE PADDOCK
VI
86
ROKER PARK AVE
NETTLETON RD
MALCOLM RD
WITNEY CL
River Pinn
Pav
Bwg Gn
P
PEPYS CL
EDINBURGH CL
LONG LA
Harefield Place
PINE TREES DR
DUKES RIDE
SILVER BIRCH CL
BURFORD CL
WOODSTOCK DR
WINDRUSH CL
HEYTHROP DR
Ickenham
UB10
Sp Gd
Swakeleys
Sch of the Douay Martyrs
4
GEORGIAN CL
A40 Beaconsfield (M40), M25
Swakeleys Rdbt
WARREN RD
APPLEWOOD CL
Allot Gdns
Tenn Cts
GILBEY CL
COURT RD
VYNERS WAY
A40
SALT HILL CL
BEACON CL
B467
HAREFIELD RD
HILLMAN CL
TOWERGATE CL
Vyners Sch
Tenn Cts
Park Wood
SWAKELEYS DR
The Douay Martyrs RC Sch (Annexe)
36
B483
3
WESTERN AVE
THE GROVE
HALFORD RD
ALBANY CL
GROVE CL
THE CHASE
TURNSTONE CL
BRIDGE WAY
WATER TOWER CL
NORTH COMMON RD
Tenn Cts
Sp Gd
Ski Ctr
A40
Hillingdon
B466
A437
85
Uxbridge Common
PARK RD
Crkt Gd
Uxbridge Common
Pl Flds
HILLINGDON CIR
Hillingdon Circus
Motel
A40
CORNWALL HO
SOUTH COMMON RD
NORFOLK RD
GATTING WAY
BREARLEY CL
UB8
Pl Flds
A437
FREEZELAND WAY
PASTURES MEAD
STUART CL
AURIOL DR
MAGNOLIA CT
2
1 CORNWALL CT
2 CHARLESTON LO
BELMONT CL
BELMONT RD
Uxbridge Coll
HERCIES RD
TUDOR WAY
GRANVILLE RD
RICHMOND AVE
MERTON AVE
THE HERMITAGE
HEATH CT
ELM LAWN CL
Hermitage Prim Sch
Allot Gdns
NORTH WAY
BROOKSIDE WAY
SWEETCROFT LA
CROFT CL
SQUIRRELS CL
FAIRMARK DR
HARTS HALL CL
SWEETCROFT LA
VICTORIA AVE
RYEFIELD AVE
1
MONTAGUE RD
PO
HONEYCROFT HILL
THE CHESTNUTS
HYACINTH DR
HAYMAKER CL
DEAN CL
HAZELCROFT CL
CHAPTER CL
FINIAN CL
HONEY HILL
BLOSSOM WAY
PORTMAN GDNS
VINE GR
HOLM GR
SEDGWICK AVE
REGENT AVE
BRIGHTON CL
GROVE RD
GROVE WAY
RED LEYS
NUTKIN WLK
TA Ctr
COWSLIP CL
TEDDER CL
KEITH PARK RD
BEEHIVE CL
DOWDING RD
Mast
VINE LA
St Helens Coll
Pav
PARKWAY
LONG LA
CHIPPENDALE WAYE
JACKSON RD
THOMPSON RD
GRAY'S RD
Athletic Gd
PORTAL CL
GOSSAGE RD
GROSVENOR CRES
WINDSOR AVE
84
CUMBRIAN WAY
PENRITH CL
AMBLESIDE WLK
PARK CT
ST LUKE'S RD
JACKSON CL
Mast
ST ANDREW'S RD
SAUNDERS RD
JUPITER HTS
CHESTWOOD GR
SYLVANA CL
Oak Farm Jun & Inf Schs
Hillingdon Court Park (Recn Gd)
Sp Gd
B483
06
Tenn Cts
A
B
07
82
C
Bwg Gn
Tenn Cts
D
C Ctr
UXBRIDGE
American Com Schs
Big Clump
UB10

Ruislip
A
B
39
C
D
PEMBROKE RD
PARK WAY CT
Recn Gd
KINGS LO
STATION APP
LYON CT
Ruislip
WILLOW GR
SHENLEY AVE
ROSEBURY VALE
Pav
Sp Gd
87
FAIRFIELD CT
SOVEREIGN CL
REGENCY DR
PRINCESS LA
HARWELL CL
ICKENHAM RD
B466
STATION PARK
BEAUFORT RD 2
Drv Rng
CH
BUCKLAND CT
THE GREENWAY
Allot Gdns
THE GREEN
HIGH TREES
HIGH ROAD, ICKENHAM
West Ruislip
SEAFORD CL
CORDINGLEY RD
LYSANDER RD
BARNWOOD CL
ICKENHAM CL
WHITSTABLE CL
HELFORD CL
WOOD LA
POOLE CL
CHICHESTER AVE
HAMBLE CL
LYMINGTON DR
HERON CT
BEMBRIDGE GDNS
KESTREL CT
FALCON CT
MERLIN CT
BLENHEIM CRES
SHERLEYS CT 1
MASTERS CT 2
POND GN
A4180
GARDEN CL
EVERSLEY CRES
CRANLEY DR
GROSVENOR VALE
COURTFIELD GDNS
DENBIGH CL
RUISLIP CT
RALEIGH CL
WILLOW GDNS
CORNWALL RD
HATHERLEIGH RD
KINGSWEAR RD
SALCOMBE WAY
ASHBURTON
SEATON GDNS
TORRINGTON RD
6
Sacred Heart RC Prim Sch
Recn Gd
Allot Gdns
WEST END RD
NARBOROUGH CL
HASLAM CL
CRANSTON CL
AYLSHAM DR
MELVILLE CL
HEACHAM AVE
PENTLAND WAY
FINCHAM CL
THORPLAND AVE
TAYFIELD CL
Tenn Cts
Pav
West Ruislip Sch
TWEEDDALE GR
1 ANNANDALE GR
2 NITHSDALE GR
CROSIER WAY
BEECHWOOD AVE
WESTFIELD WAY
HERLWYN AVE
ROXBURN WAY
NORTH VIEW
DOWN CL
CHERRY CL
LAWN CL
ALMOND CL
ROUNDWAYS
BERKELEY CL
BELL CL
NEW POND PAR
New Pond Pl Flds
5
Pav
Works
CHURCH PL
Min Rly
COMMUNITY CL
WILLOWTREE CL
AUSTIN'S LA
HA4
Ruislip Gardens
86
Ickenham
KEMPTON CL
LAWRENCE DR
CROSIER RD
UB10
Ruislip Gardens Prim Sch
STAFFORD RD
BROMLEY CRES
HATHAWAY CL
TREVOR CRES
ACORN GR
BEDFORD RD
CLYFFORD RD
4
Allot Gdns
CLOVELLY CL
GLEBE AVE
CLOVELLY AVE
ST GILES AVE
GLEBE CL
Allot Gdns
35
Glebe Prim Sch
Allot Gdns
LEA CRES
MILVERTON DR
Yeading Brook
BURNHAM AVE
SUSSEX RD
TAVISTOCK RD
62
Tenn Cts
Pl Flds
Ickenham Manor
Long Lane Farm
3
Northolt Aerodrome
Ickenham Marsh
85
2
Freezeland Covert
WESTERN AVE
A437
Allot Gdns
North Hillingdon
Recn Gd
WESTERN AVE
WESTON RD
A40
Gutteridge Wood
Yeading Brook
Allot Gdns
LYNHURST RD
OAKLEIGH RD
LYNHURST CRES
RYEFIELD AVE
FLORISTON AVE
BERKELEY RD
1
UB4
MIDHURST GDNS
PO
84
A
B
09
83
C
D
Ryefield Prim Sch
HAZELDENE
Yeading Brook
Ten Acre (Nature Reserve)
10

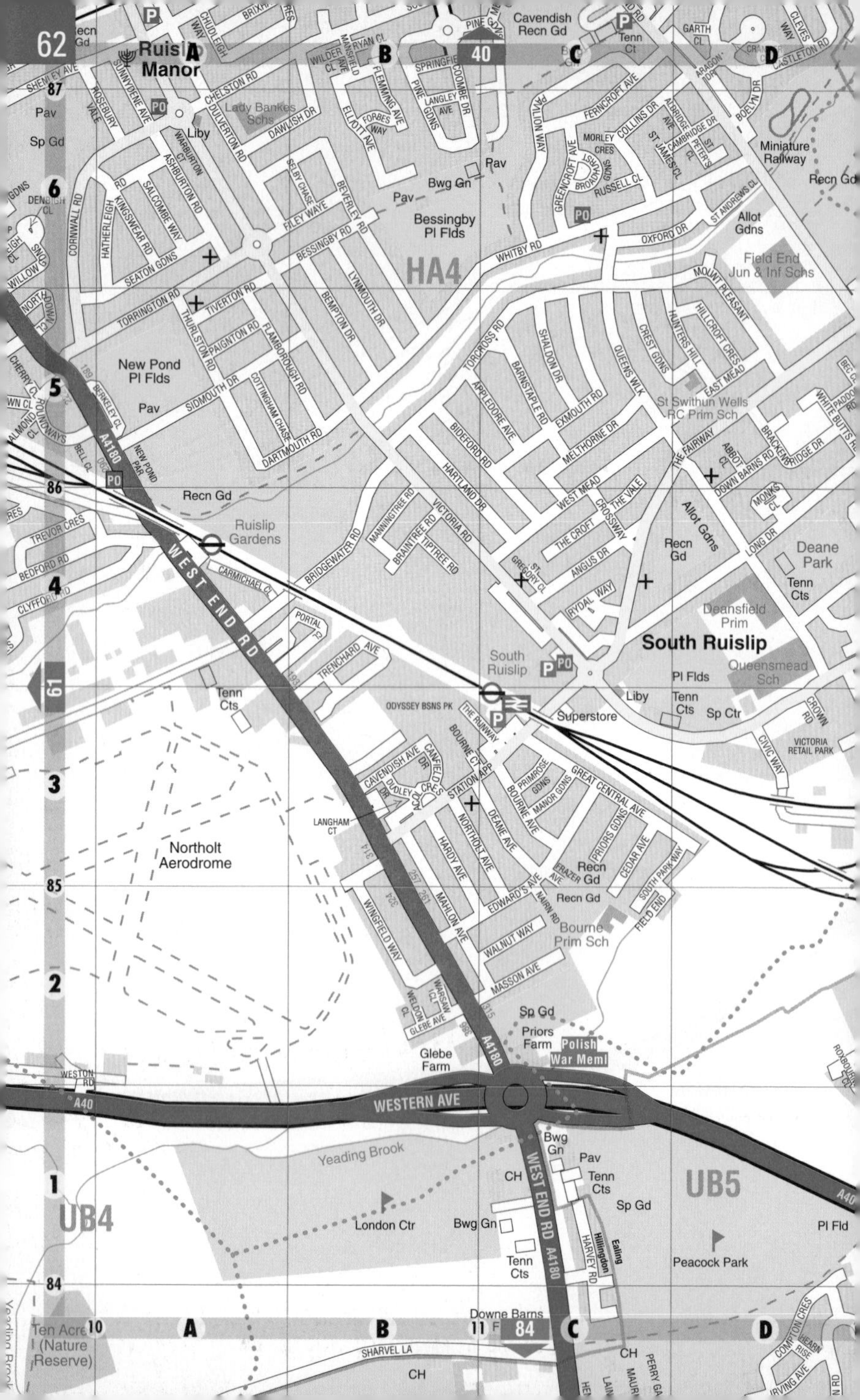

Ruislip Manor
Cavendish Recn Gd
Tenn Ct
40
A
B
C
D
87
Pav
Sp Gd
Lady Bankes Schs
Liby
Miniature Railway
Recn Gd
Pav
Bwg Gn
Pav
Bessingby Pl Flds
Allot Gdns
Field End Jun & Inf Schs
HA4
New Pond Pl Flds
Pav
St Swithun Wells RC Prim Sch
Recn Gd
Ruislip Gardens
Allot Gdns
Recn Gd
Deane Park
Tenn Cts
Deansfield Prim
South Ruislip
Queensmead Sch
South Ruislip
Pl Flds
Liby
Tenn Cts
Sp Ctr
Superstore
ODYSSEY BSNS PK
VICTORIA RETAIL PARK
Tenn Cts
61
Northolt Aerodrome
Recn Gd
Recn Gd
Bourne Prim Sch
Sp Gd
Priors Farm
Polish War Meml
Glebe Farm
WESTERN AVE
A40
A4180
WEST END RD
Yeading Brook
Bwg Gn
Pav
Tenn Cts
CH
Sp Gd
UB5
UB4
London Ctr
Bwg Gn
Tenn Cts
Peacock Park
Pl Fld
Hillingdon
Ealing
HARVEY RD
84
Ten Acre (Nature Reserve)
Downe Barns F
SHARVEL LA
CH
CH
10
11
86
85
6
5
4
3
2
1
SHENLEY AVE
CHUDLEIGH WAY
SUNNYDENE AVE
ROSEBURY VALE
CHELSTON RD
DULVERTON RD
DAWLISH DR
WARBURTON CT
ASHBURTON RD
SALCOMBE WAY
KINGSWEAR RD
HATHERLEIGH RD
CORNWALL RD
SEATON GDNS
TORRINGTON RD
TIVERTON RD
THURLSTON RD
PAIGNTON RD
FLAMBOROUGH RD
SIDMOUTH DR
COTTINGHAM CHASE
DARTMOUTH RD
BESSINGBY RD
BEVERLEY RD
FILEY WAYE
SELBY CHASE
BEMPTON DR
LYNMOUTH DR
WHITBY RD
OXFORD DR
ST ANDREWS CL
MOUNT PLEASANT
FERNCROFT AVE
PAVILION WAY
GREENCROFT AVE
BROADHURST GDNS
RUSSELL CL
COLLINS DR
ST JAMES CL
CAMBRIDGE DR
ST PETERS CL
BOELYN DR
CASTLETON RD
MANSFIELD AVE
FLEMMING AVE
ELLIOTT AVE
FORBES WAY
SPRINGFIELD
COOMBE DR
PINE GDNS
LANGLEY AVE
TORCROSS RD
SHALDON DR
BARNSTAPLE RD
APPLEDORE AVE
BIDEFORD RD
HARTLAND DR
EXMOUTH RD
MELTHORNE DR
QUEENS WLK
CREST GDNS
HUNTERS HILL
HILLCROFT CRES
EAST MEAD
THE FAIRWAY
WEST MEAD
CROSSWAY
THE VALE
THE CROFT
ANGUS DR
RYDAL WAY
ST GREGORY CL
DOWN BARNS RD
BRACKENBRIDGE DR
ABBOT CL
MONKS CL
LONG DR
WHITE BUTTS RD
CROWN RD
CIVIC WAY
MANNINGTREE RD
VICTORIA RD
BRAINTREE RD
TIPTREE RD
BRIDGEWATER RD
CARMICHAEL CL
PORTAL CL
TRENCHARD AVE
TREVOR CRES
BEDFORD RD
CLYFFORD RD
BERKELEY CL
ROUNDWAYS
BELL CL
NEW POND PAR
WEST END RD
THE RUNWAY
BOURNE CT
STATION APP
CAVENDISH AVE
CANFIELD DR
DUDLEY DR
ACOL CRES
LANGHAM CT
PRIMROSE GDNS
MANOR GDNS
BOURNE AVE
GREAT CENTRAL AVE
DEANE AVE
NORTHOLT AVE
HARDY AVE
PRIORS GDNS
CEDAR AVE
SOUTH PARK WAY
FIELD END
FRAZER AVE
NAIRN RD
EDWARD'S AVE
MAHLON AVE
WINGFIELD WAY
WALNUT WAY
MASSON AVE
WELDON CL
WARSAW CL
GLEBE AVE
WESTON RD
COMPTON CRES
HEARN RISE
IRVING AVE
PERRY GA

Rayners Lane
A
B
C
D
41
A4090
RAYNERS LA
WARDEN AVE
OXLEAY RD
OVESDON AVE
CHICHESTER CT
CAPTHORNE AVE
CLITHEROE AVE
DRAKE RD
LUCAS AVE
Tenn Cts
Fbal Gd
Allot Gdns
Grange Schs
Roxbourne Fst & Mid Schs
Newton Farm Fst & Mid Sch
Newton Park
Newton Farm Ecology Pk
Alexandra Sch
The Roxbourne
Pav
HA2
ALEXANDRA AVE
MALVERN AVE
WIDDICOMBE AVE
NEWQUAY CRES
TORBAY RD
EXETER RD
LYNTON RD
KINGS RD
RAVENSWOOD CRES
LULWORTH GDNS
CLOVELLY WAY
DUNSTER WAY
Recn Gd
PARKFIELD CRES
ELIOT DR
DRINKWATER RD
SWIFT CL
COLES CRES
EASTLEIGH AVE
ROXETH GREEN AVE
EASTCOTE AVE
SCOTT CRES
AUSTEN RD
PRIEST PARK AVE
MARYATT AVE
RAYNERS LA
Cemy
REVEREND CL
BEECHWOOD CIRC
BEECHWOOD GDNS
CRANE CL
Liby
EASTCOTE LA
Schs
1 CORNELL HO
2 MEAD FIELD
3 STRADBROOK CL
South Harrow
1 TREGENNA CT
2 PARK GATES
3 ARUNDEL CT
Alexandra Park
TREGENNA AVE
BALMORAL RD
CARLYON AVE
EARLSMEAD
Earlsmead Fst & Mid Sch
ARUNDEL DR
SOMERVELL RD
A312
NORTHOLT RD
Welldon Park Schs
WESTWOOD AVE
Northolt Park
64
Superstores
HA4
Ind Est
VICTORIA RD
STONEFIELD WAY
1 SALISBURY CT
2 FOLKESTONE CT
3 PONTEFRACT CT
4 SEDGEFIELD CT
THE HEIGHTS
WINCANTON CRES
Allot Gdns
Harrow
Ealing
DABBS HILL LA
PERCEVAL CT 1
HILL CT 2
CHURCHILL CT 3
WARWICK CT 4
LANARK CT 5
NEWMARKET AVE
PETT'S HILL
A4090
Sch
EASTCOTE LA
Pl Fld
PLUMPTON CL
HAYDOCK AVE
SUSSEX CRES
UB5
Northolt High Sch
Willow Tree Prim Sch
CONEYGROVE PATH 1
VINCENTS PATH 2
PRIORS FIELD 3
RIDGEWAY WLK 4
SHEPHERDS PATH 5
FORLONG PATH 6
Masts
BLENHEIM RD
Northolt
MANDEVILLE RD
EASTCOTE LA N
Islip Manor Park
BELVUE RD
BELVUE BSNS CTR
CASTLE RD
CARR RD
Grand Union Canal Wlk
NORTHOLT
CHURCH RD
WESTERN AVE
Target Rdbt
A40
Northolt Prim Sch
John Chilton Sch
Walford High Sch
Belvue Park
85
13
14
84
87
86
6
5
4
3
2
1
Golf

A
B
C
D
42
63
86
87
86
85
84
6
5
4
3
2
1
14
15
Harrow on the Hill
Roxeth
Superstore
HA2
HA1
UB6
South Harrow
Orley Farm Sch
Sudbury Hill Harrow
Sudbury Hill
Northolt Park
Greenford
The John Lyon Sch
Bowden House (Private)
The Clementine Churchill
St George's RC Prim Sch
St Dominic's Coll(RC)
Roxeth Recn Gd
Welldon Park Schs
Ealing Northern Sp Ctr
Horsenden Prim Sch
Grand Union Canal Paddington Branch
Grand Union Canal Walk
Grand Union Canal Wlk
Harrow
Ealing
SHAFTESBURY CIRC
SHAFTESBURY AVE
SOUTHDOWN CRES
HILLSIDE CRES
DUDLEY RD
DUDLEY GDNS
JOLLYS LA
GRANGE FARM CL
WESLEY CL
LODGEHILL PARK CL
FRANKLINS MEWS
OSMOND CL
THE CRESCENT
FIELDERS CL
MIDDLE RD
A312
LOWER RD
A4005
ROXETH HILL
WALDRON'S YD
ASHBOURNE AVE
GRANGE RD
BRIGADE CL
HORNBUCKLE CL
ABBOTTS CT
GEORGIAN WAY
ELMFIELD CL
MOUNT PARK AVE
ATHENA CL 1
BRICKFIELDS 2
WEST HILL HALL 3
THE MOAT LO 4
EDWARD CT 5
CHYNGTON CT 6
BRICKFIELDS
GLASFRYN CT
WEST HILL
BYRON HILL RD
CLONMEL CL
CHARTWELL PL
HIGH ST
B458
LONDON RD
HARROW PK
JULIAN HILL
HERGA CT
RAMA CT
WENDERSON CT
GOODWIN CT
SUDBURY HILL
HIGHLAWN HALL
FIRCROFT GDNS
ROWSHAM CT
LABANK CL
HARROW FIELDS GDNS
RUNNELFIELD
CHASEWOOD PK
GRANTCHESTER CL
HERITAGE VIEW
A4127
LANFRANC CT
ASHTON CT
GRANGE CT
ASSISI CT
ST FRANCIS LO
SUDBURY HILL CL
THOMAS A'BECKET CL
SADDLERS MEWS
PRIORY CL
HUSSAIN CL
KIDMORE CL
NEW RD
A4000
Sudbury Hill Pl Flds
Tenn Cts
Allot Gdns
ROXETH GREEN AVE
EASTCOTE AVE
MAPLE AVE
THE ARCHES
BREMBER RD
STANLEY RD
PITT RD
ROSE CT
SHERWOOD RD
BARNABY CL
THE VIADUCT
THE GREENWOODS
ST MARGARET'S AVE
COWEN AVE
INGLEBY DR
MOUNT PARK RD
BERMUDA HO
BROOKE AVE
ASHNEAL GDNS
RENKETH CL
SACKVILLE CL
ARDEN CL
SOUTH HILL AVE
ORLEY FARM RD
HILL CL
SOUTH VALE
SOUTH HILL GR
GRENVILLE CT
TYRELL CL
HARTINGTON CL
CAVENDISH AVE
ROSEBANK AVE
FERNBANK AVE
1 HUTTON CL
2 BRASHER CL
3 HEMERY RD
4 TESSA SANDERSON WAY
5 HAMMOND CL
Toll Gates
BEECHWOOD CIRC
BEECHWOOD GDNS
BEECHWOOD AVE
CRANE CL
PARKFIELD RD
EASTCOTE RD
WHITBY RD
WARGRAVE RD
SCARSDALE RD
KINGSLEY RD
WYVENHOE RD
VALENTINE
Liby
A312 NORTHOLT RD
ROXETH GR
CORBIN'S LA
BARNETTS CT
BRENDON GDNS
WOOD END AVE
WESTWOOD AVE
RAGLAN CT
CADOGAN CL
STROUD GATE
ACOCK GR
HALSBURY RD E
HALSBURY RD W
CASSANDRA CL
WOOD END RD
KILLOWEN AVE
RUSSELL RD
CLAUSON AVE
STATION PAR
DORCHESTER
READING RD
FLORISTON
MORTON CT
WOOD END GDNS
WOOD END WAY
WOOD END
MARY PETERS DR
BANNISTER CL
BEDSER DR
RAMSEY CL
LILIAN BOARD WAY
HAPGOOD CL
LARWOOD CL
HENDREN CL
MATTHEWS RD
DIMMOCK DR
VERNON RISE
THOMAS HEWLETT HO 1
JEM PATERSON CT 2
GREENBANKS 3
LYDIA LO 4
WALTON CROFT 5
GREENFORD RD
HORSENDEN AVE
HIGHFIELD AVE
HORSENDEN CRES
RIDDING LA
GAINSBORO GDNS
ROSEHILL GDNS
NORTHOLT GDNS
MORDEN GDNS
NORTHWOOD GDNS
A4090
QUANTOCK CT
SHERIDAN TERR
MILDRED AVE
MERTON AVE
KEBLE CL
PILGRIMS CL
WHITTON AVE W
CARLTON CL
NEWNHAM GDNS
NEWNHAM CL
ORCHARD CL
OLDFIELDS CIR
GRAINGER CL
BAYSHILL RISE
LANCASTER RD
EGGARDON CT
Masts
BLENHEIM RD
SIVERST CL
GONVILLE CRES
CASTLE RD
ORIEL WAY
WADHAM GDNS
HADDEN WAY
MALDEN AVE
OLDFIELD CL
OLDFIELD LA N
RUGBY AVE
WORCESTER GDNS
CURREY AVE
CLARE RD
ROTHESAY AVE
SURREY RD
GIRTON RD
GIRTON CL
RAGLAN WAY
THE FAIRWAY
GLAMIS WAY
BERKELEY AVE
ENNISMORE AVE
SHERWOOD AVE
MELVILLE AVE
CAMBRIDGE AVE
BOURNE VIEW
DREW GDNS
HORSENDEN LA N
LINDEN CRES
ELTON AVE
BURWELL AVE
HAVERSHAM CT
SHEPPARD'S CT
ROBIN HOOD WAY
The Ball Box (PH)
Bwg Gn
Pl Fld
Recn Gd
CARR RD
CHERRY GDNS
AURIOL DR
OLDFIELD LA N
FAIRWAY DR
STATION APP
ALLINGTON CL
HILL RISE
BELLE VUE
STATION VIEW
ROCKWARE AVE
WESTWAY CROSS
TAUNTON RD
HALIFAX RD
BIRKBECK AVE
BIRKBECK WAY
HILLBECK WAY
WEST GREEN PL
UNEEDA DR
Running Tk
Pl Flds
Pav
Ass Rms
Sch
Schs
Sp Gds

Northwick Park
Rugby Fball Gds
A
B
43
C
D
South Kenton
Byron Court Sch
Preston Park Rec Gd
Tenn Cts
Pav
Bwg Gn
Park Sch
PO
ENNERDALE GDNS
WINDERMERE GR
ALLONBY GDNS
MONTPELIER RISE
COLLEGE RD
GLENDALE
WOODS
CARLTON AVE E
FERNLEIGH CT
87
1 SIMPSON HO
2 AYRTON HO
3 WINTOUR HO
4 STEVENSON HO
LOGAN RD
Bwg Gn
WALTON GD
PELLATT
6
Sp Gd
CHAMBERLAYNE AVE
EDISON DR
NORVAL RD
AUDREY GDNS
SPENCER RD
NATHANS RD
Harrow
Brent
A404
PEBWORTH RD
THE GREEN
ABBOTTS DR
North Wembley
THIRD AVE
SECOND AVE
FIRST AVE
WARREN CL
STRATHCONA RD
LOWESWATER CL
ESKDALE CL
PENARTH PL
THE CRESCENT
CARLTON AVE W
THE FAIRWAY
LANGHAM GDNS
AMERY RD
MULGRAVE RD
A4127
PAXFORD RD
OLDBOROUGH RD
EAST CT
WESTLAKE RD
MAGNET RD
GEC EST
LILIMEN RD
WEMBLEY COMMERCIAL CTR
POPLAR VIEW
BELL LA
TILLING WAY
OSRAM RD
SUDBURY COURT DR
BENGEWORTH RD
BLOCKLEY RD
SHELLEY GDNS
WEST CT
GARDEN CT
KEATS CT
BYRON RD
ADA RD
PEEL RD
LOWER LA
MAIN DR
OUTRAM RD
KENELM CL
HILL RD
PASTURE RD
Recn Gd
CAMPDEN CRES
DEAN CT
HOLT RD
STAPENHILL RD
Tenn Cts
Wembley High Sch
DICKENS CT
COURTENAY RD
1 LOCKIER WLK
2 LAMBERT WLK
5
SUDBURY COURT RD
ST GEORGES CL
CORNERWAYS
PASTURE CL
EAST LA
Pav
A4088
Allot Gdns
Recn Gd
THE SPINNEY
PRIORY CRES
ROWAN CL
ELMWOOD CT
WILLOW WAY
ASPEN DR
COURT PAR
CECIL CT
ROSEN CT
STILECROFT GDNS
HA0
Pav
Vale Farm Sp Gd
WOODFIELD AVE
VALE CT
CONIFER WAY
APPLE LO
ASH WLK
Allot Gdns
North Wembley
SOVEREIGN GR
WADE CT
WAYLETT PL
EVERTON CT
HARWOOD CL
LLANOVER RD
PEMBROKE RD
HUTCHINSON TERR
WINTHROP WLK
EVERARD WAY
Sch
86
CLARENDON GDNS
ROSSLYN CRES
GREENS CT
WATFORD RD
MONTAGUE FELL
PRIORY GDNS
PRIORY HL
LOTHIAN CL
ST ANDREWS AVE
ELMS LA
DYSON CT
PERRIN RD
Allot Gdns
Sp Arena
T Cts
Tenn Cts
Pav
Allot Gdns
RUSTIC PL
REGAL CT
BEDFORD CT
SUDBURY AVE
CIRCLE CT
LANCELOT AVE
MEADOW WAY
THE GLEN
CASTLETON AVE
4
Sudbury
FOXLEES
Sudbury Jun & Inf Schs
Vale Farm Sp Ctr
CHILCOTT CL
HASTINGS CL
Pav
COMPTON AVE
ETON CT
SHELLEY CT
MARLOES CL
CODLING WAY
HARROWDENE RD
LANCELOT CRES
King Ed VII P
CHERRY TREE CL
PRIORY PARK RD
CHURCH GDNS
Tenn Cts
968
HARROW RD
HOMEFIELD RD
Allot Gdns
Fball Gd
DENISE CT
ETON AVE
REPTON AVE
ELMS GDNS
ELMS PARK AVE
MEDWAY GDNS
ASH GR
Butler's Gn
852
A404
RUGBY AVE
BEAUMONT AVE
HARROWDENE CL
BRAMLEY LO
ANDER CL
ALLIANCE CL
GOODMAN'S CT
ST JOHN'S RD
MEDWAY GDNS
BUTLER CT
BRENTRY CL
AVON CT
MAYBANK AVE
GAUNTLETT CT
CHESTNUT CT
CHESTNUT AVE
CHARTERHOUSE AVE
MILFORD GDNS
LANCELOT RD
WINDMORE CL
THE CHINE
THE DELL
SUDBURY CRES
PETTSGROVE AVE
SYLVESTER RD
BEAUMONT CT
RAYNERS CL
Bwg G
KES
MAYBANK AVE
Brent
Ealing
CHESTNUT GR
PERKIN CL
ELTON AVE
THE CROFT
Tenn Cts
ST JO
ACACIA AVE
GREENBANK AVE
Allot Gdns
Maybank Open Space
ROUNDTREE RD
HARROW RD
Sudbury & Harrow Road
Barham Park
COPLAND CL
CRAWFORD AVE
LANTERN CL
ST ANNE'S RD
3
SUDBURY
TWICKENHAM GDNS
THE RISE
HEIGHTS AVE
SAUNDERTON RD
CENTRAL RD
MARNHAM CT
Old Court (Mus & Liby)
DUDLEY CT
ROSECROFT WLK
THURLOW GDNS
ELSPETH RD
TURTON RD
ECCLESTONE
Colls
Mkt
EASTCOTE AVE
DISTRICT RD
THE PARADE
A404
COPLAND AVE
OAKLANDS CL
ROKESBY PL
HARROW RD
CURTIS
243
BRACEWELL
ROSEWOOD AVE
Allot Gdns
200
ODEON PAR
ALLENDALE RD
STATION CRES
STATION APP
A4005
FERNWOOD AVE
COLYTON CL
HARROW RD
DALMENY CL
NEWLANDS CL
LINTHORPE AVE
NORFOLK CT
TURNER CL
HARLEY CL
CHASE CT
NAPIER RD
RANELAGH RD
A4089
85
UNION RD
WHITTON AVE E
WHITTON DR
WOODLAND APP
GREENGATE
Sudbury Town
BARHAM CL
Wembley
FAIRVIEW AVE
BUCKINGHAM CT
OAKWOOD CRES
WOODLAND RISE
WOODCROFT
ASHNESS GDNS
WELLGARTH
CROSSGATE
ORCHARD GATE
CHAPLIN RD
CHAPLIN CL
LINCOLN RD
2
Liby
FARM AVENUE HO
Barham Prim Sch
DANETHORPE RD
WEMBLEY
SCARLE RD
SWINDERBY RD
Coll
HOLLAND RD
BASSINGHAM RD
NORTON RD
THURLBY RD
FARM AVE
WHITTON CL
A4090
CH
CH
Horsenden Hill
84
Horsenden Hill
BRIDGEWATER CT 1
SUNNYDENE GDNS 2
ATHERTON HTS 3
BRIDGEWATER RD
STAPLEFORD RD
QUEEN VICTORIA AVE
EAGLE RD
EALING RD
HAYNES
BOWRONS AVE
1
Sudbury
UB6
Grand Union Canal Paddington Branch
Grand Union Canal Walk
EMPIRE RD
LYNMOUTH GDNS
LAUNCESTON GDNS
TORRINGTON GDNS
Alperton Cemy
Rec Gd
BRAEMAR AVE
HA0
53
Allot Gdns
ST JAMES' GDNS
84
WYAT CT
Horsenden Farm
WOODROW CL
JUBILEE RD
Allot Gdns
GEORGE V WAY
17
87
JORDAN RD
LEE RD
DEVON CL
CLIFFORD RD
BURNSIDE CRES
A4005
Alperton Lower Sch
18
Alperton
A4089
Recn Gd
Liby

Preston
A
B
C
D
44
87
6
5
86
4
65
3
85
2
1
84
18
19
88
WOODFORD PL
GLENDALE GDNS
LONGFIELD AVE
CARLTON AVE E
CARLTON PAR
FERNLEIGH CT
PRINCESS AVE
WEST CL
THE AVENUE
CHARLTON RD
HILLVIEW CL
BASING HILL
EAST HILL
BARN HILL
MIDHOLM
BARN RISE
WICKLIFFE GDNS
BARN WAY
PILGRIMS WAY
PADDOCKS GN
LOGAN RD
Bwg Gn
WALTON GDNS
AYLANDS CL
ORCHID CT
PELLATT RD
SECOND AVE
FIRST AVE
WARREN CL
ELMSTEAD AVE
Tenn Cts
Sp Gd
Preston Manor High Sch
CENTURY HO 1
TAVERNERS CT 2
MAYFIELDS CL
MAYFIELDS
LAWNS CT
SOUTH GDNS
CORRINGHAM RD
THE CROSSWAYS
EVERSLEY AVE
GRENDON GDNS
MASON CT
NEWLAND CT
GRAND PAR
PO
FORTY LA
KINGS DR
CAMEL CT
KINGS CT
GREENHILL WAY
THE PADDOCKS
ADAMS CL
TH
LUMEN RD
MAGNET RD
WESTLAKE RD
GEC EST
BELL LA
TILLING WAY
EDISON DR
CHAMBERLAYNE AVE
ASHLEY GDNS
PRESTON RD
BOWLING GREEN CT
HOLLYCROFT AVE
PERRIN GRANGE
FORTY AVE
PARGRAVES CT
Tenn Cts
Sp Gd
Bwg Gn
Pav
Superstore
FARNBOROUGH CL
COFERS CIRC
CHALKHILL RD
HAVENWOOD
OSRAM RD
QUAD RD
MAIN DR
TOWER LA
COURTENAY RD
ST AUGUSTINE'S AVE
BLENHEIM GDNS
HIGHFIELD AVE
TALISMAN WAY
GABRIELLE CL
RICHMOND CT
FORTY CL
CROWN WLK
BROOK AVE
Wembley Park
BRIDGE RD A4089
GREENRIGG WLK
REDCLIFFE WLK
WINDSOR CRES
CHALKHILL RD
ROOK CL
RAWLINGS CRES
1 LOCKIER WLK
2 LAMBERT WLK
MARSH HALL
THE MARTINS
THE BROADWAY
OAKINGTON AVE
ELLIOT CL
St Christopher's Sch
WAYSIDE CT
ELMSIDE RD
THE BOBBY MOORE BRIDGE
WALTON AVE
ANTON PL
A4088
GREENS CT
PEMBROKE RD
HUTCHINSON TERR
WINTHROP WLK
EVERARD WAY
Sch
CASTLETON GDNS
PADFIELD CT
BEECHCROFT GDNS
HOMEFIRS HO
BALMORAL CT
A4089
WEMBLEY PARK DR
EMPIRE PAR
A479
WEMBLEY STADIUM IND EST
STADIUM RET PK
DANES CT
EMPIRE CT
NORTH END RD
ALBION WAY
Chalkhill Prim Sch
STADIUM BSNS CTR
WEMBLEY BSNS CTR
WATKIN RD
Wembley Manor Schs
MORELLO CT
THE GABLES
RAGLAN CT
FULTON RD
RUTHERFORD WAY
LLANOVER RD
ROSSLYN CRES
CLARENDON GDNS
QUEENSCOURT
WEMBLEY HILL RD
PARK CHASE
HILLCROFT CRES
MANOR DR
RAGLAN CT
IMPERIAL CT
Wembley Park
PALACE OF IND
OLYMPIC WAY
Superstore
OLYMPIC RET PK
Superstore
FOURTH WAY
FIFTH WAY
MEADOW WAY
THE GLEN
CASTLETON AVE
THE DENE
KINGSWAY
HILLSIDE AVE
ADA LEWIS HO
ALEXANDRA CT
EMPIRE WAY
HA9
ENGINEERS WAY
Wembley Arena
WEMBLEY STADIUM IND EST
METRO TRAD CTR
CANNON TRAD EST
FIRST WAY
SECOND WAY
THIRD WAY
THE MIRAGE CTR
Tenn Cts
King Edward VII Park
Park Lane Sch
Tenn Cts
ROSKILD CT
HIGH ST
PARK PL
DAGMAR AVE
LAKESIDE WAY
Conference Centre
Wembley Market
STADIUM WAY
Hotel
Exhibition Halls
ROYAL ROUTE
Wembley Stadium (site)
CAREY WAY
PARK LA
GOODMANS CT
ALLIANCE CL
MILFORD GDNS
LANCELOT RD
KESWICK GDNS
ST JOHN'S RD
Bwg Gn
PRINCES CT
CORINIUM CL
LEA GDNS
LINDEN LAWNS
DENNIS AVE
LINDEN AVE
MOSTYN AVE
B4557
SOUTH WAY
PARK CT
Copland Sch & Tech Ctr
WEMBLEY HILL RD
Wembley Stadium
PARK VIEW
ST JOHN'S CL
ACACIA AVE
ELM RD
A4089
ECCLESTON PL
JUNIPER CL
NEELD PAR
Sherrans Farm Open Space
Oakington Manor Sch
LANTERNS CT
ROSECROFT WLK
THURLOW GDNS
ELSPETH RD
TURTON RD
Colls
Mkt
ECCLESTONE MEWS
HIGH RD
ROSEMEAD AVE
BEATRICE AVE
LONSDALE AVE
CECIL AVE
ELIZABETH HO
St Joseph's RC Schs
CHATSWORTH AVE
WAVERLEY AVE
VIVIAN GDNS
GRAND AVE
NEELD CRES
OAKINGTON MANOR DR
ST MICHAEL'S AVE
TUDOR CT N
TUDOR CT S
GRAND AVE E
CHIPPENHAM AVE
A404
CURTIS LA
Wembley Central
WALROND AVE
NEELD CT
NEELD CT
VIVIAN AVE
VICTORIA AVE
WYLD WAY
CHALFONT AVE
BRENT WAY
WEMBLEY WAY
TALBOT RD
CHASE CT
NAPIER RD
RANELAGH RD
A4089
COPLAND RD
STATION GR
LONDON RD
Allot Gdns
Pl Flds
STANLEY RD
JESMOND AVE
T Cts
CORSHAM HO
VICTORIA CT
UNION RD
PARK RD
BERKHAMSTED AVE
NETTLEDEN AVE
GEORGIAN CT
BABINGTON RISE
ELSLEY CT
Liby
WEMBLEY
Coll
SCARLE RD
SWINDERBY RD
THE CLOSE
Elsley Prim Sch
GADDESDEN AVE
NORTHCHURCH RD
TRING AVE
HARROW RD
Tokyngton
STONEBRIDGE WAY
Allot Gdns
NORTON RD
THURLBY RD
CHRISTCHURCH GN
CHRISTCHURCH AVE
LYON PARK AVE
BRIDGEWAY
HILLFIELD AVE
VALLEY GDNS
TOKYNGTON AVE
FLAMSTED AVE
BOVINGDON AVE
WIGGINTON AVE
ALDBURY AVE
GRITTLETON AVE
Liby
Recn Gd
MONKS PARK GDNS
EAGLE RD
DOUGLAS AVE
WESTBURY AVE
WESTBURY RD
HAYNES CL
CLAYTON AVE
EALING RD
Allot Gdns
CHAMEAD CRES
Allot Gdns
SYLVIA GDNS
DEREK AVE
POINT PL
SYLVIA CT
A404
BOWRONS AVE
VICTOR GR
KATHLEEN AVE
DOROTHY AVE
NEWTON RD
LOMOND CL
Stonebridge Park
ARGENTA WAY
Stonebridge Park
BRENTFIELD
BRAEMAR AVE
HA0
STANLEY CL
EGERTON RD
VINCENT RD
LYON ROWLEY CL
MARQUIS CL
HEATHER PARK PAR
Alperton Com Sch
Lyon Park Jun & Inf Schs
Pl Flds
THE GRANGE
HEATHER PARK DR
KENMERE GDNS
ST JAMES' GDNS
STANLEY AVE
RUSSELL CT
ANNE CARVER LO
WOODSTOCK RD
STANLEY PARK
LYON PARK AVE
HIGHCROFT AVE
Allot Gdns
Alperton Lower Sch
WYATT CT
ORCHARD CL
LIGHTLEY CL
MOUNT PLEASANT
BELMONT AVE
MOUNT PLEASANT
NEWCOMBE PK
CRAIGMUIR PK
BERESFORD AVE
WYCOMBE RD
A406
A4089
MOUNT PLEASANT
A4005
Alperton
WOODSIDE CL
WOODSIDE AVE
ABBEY MANUFACTURING EST
Liby
LIBERTY CTR
NORTHFIELD IND EST

Welsh Harp
45
Brent Resr
Sailing Club
Sp Gd
Neasden Recn Gd
Pav
St Nicholas Sch
Gower Sch
SALMON ST
A4140
BLACKBIRD HILL
NEASDEN LA
B454
Sports Gd
Tenn Cts
Pl Fld
Wykeham Prim Sch
Braintcroft Prim Sch
John Kelly Tech Colls
Allot Gdns
St Margaret Clitherow Sch
HA9
WEMBLEY STADIUM IND EST
HALLMARK TRAD CTR
Neasden Depot
Neasden Junction
The Grange Mus
A4088
B453
Neasden
GREAT CENTRAL WAY
DRURY WAY
Vernon House Sch
Superstore
NORTH CIRCULAR RD
A406
B4557
Northview Prim Sch
FALCON PK IND EST
DUDDEN HILL LA
Dudden Hill
The Coll of NW London (Willesden Ctr)
Church End
Pav
Bwg Gn
River Brent
Tokyngton Recn Gd
Mitchell Brook Prim Sch
Gibbons Recn Gd
Neasden Temple
Brentfield Prim Sch
The Swaminarayan Sch
Games Ct
Power Sta
St Mary's Sch
HIGH RD
A407
CHURCH RD
WILLESDEN
NW10
Willesden New Cemy
Leopold Prim Sch
Brahma Kumaris World Spiritual Univ
Willesden Jewish Cemy
Newfield Prim Sch
Canal Feeder
HILLSIDE
A404
Recn Gd
Stonebridge
Our Lady of Lourdes RC Sch
89
Harlesden
Roundwood Park
Glads
68
A
B
C
D
1
2
3
4
5
6

68
Staples Corner (West)
46
A
B
C
D
JVC BSNS PK
LONDON GROUP BSNS PK
STAPLES CORNER BSNS PK
A406
A5
THE HARP BSNS CTR
WELLINGTON PARK EST
THE APSLEY CTR
PHOENIX PK
APSLEY WAY
STREAKES FIELD RD
WATERLOO RD
DELTA CT
COLES GREEN CT
KELCEDA CL
EYHURST CL
ATLAS BSNS CTR
OXGATE CTR
OXGATE LA
Ind Est
HORSESHOE CL
THE EDGE BSNS CTR
MILLENIUM BSNS CTR
HUMBER RD
TANKRIDGE RD
CHIPSTEAD GDNS
WALTON CL
ANEURIN BEVAN CT
SEYMOUR CT
COLES GREEN RD
OXGATE CT PAR
BALLARDS RD
TADWORTH RD
CREST RD
SELSDON RD
PADDOCK RD
BROOK RD
NUTFIELD RD
HEATHER RD
WARREN RD
ALDER GR
BYRON RD
OXGATE GDNS
CONWAY RD
Superstores
GERON WAY
EDGWARE RD
GLADSTONE PAR
Brent Sidings
Our Lady of Grace Inf Sch
CLAREMONT
CLITTERHOUSE CRES
CLITTERHOUSE RD
CLAREMONT RD
Clitterhouse Pl Flds
Hendon Fball Gd
Clitterhouse Jun & Inf Schs
COTSWOLD GDNS
BRENT TERR
QUANTOCK GDNS
CANEY MEWS
CLAREMONT RD
ROMNEY ROW
CLEVELAND GDNS
PENNINE DR
CHILTERN GDNS
WOODVALE WAY
WORLEY CT 1
DRAYCOTT CL 2
JOY CT 3
HAYFORD CT 4
SHANNON CL
HANDLEY GR
John Kelly Tech Colls
Allot Gdns
DOLLIS HILL EST
RYLANDES RD
AINSWORTH CL
FLOWERS CL
HILLCREST GDNS
ROSECROFT GDNS
HAWARDEN HILL
ORCHARD CL
HOMESTEAD PK
VINCENT GDNS
FORBES CL
COMMER CL
LEDALLE HO
WORCESTER CL
NEWFIELD RISE
MIDWOOD CL
APPLEWOOD CL
CONNOLLY CT
PIPPIN CL
RUSSET CT
BRAMLEY CT
Pav
Tenn Cts
NW2
DOLLIS HTS
LANE CL
THE CRESCENT
COLWYN RD
DOLLIS HILL AVE
MOUNT RD
GLADSTONE PARK GDNS
OXLEYS RD
BADGER CT
DEBHAM CT
PINEMARTIN CL
KATRINE CT
SHOBROKE CL
COPPERMEAD CL
BROADFIELD CL
MASCOTTS CL
SANCROFT CL
WESTMEATH HO
NEVILLE'S CT
DOLLIS HILL LA
Sch
ANDREW'S CL
HILL CL
PARK CL
PARK SIDE
Dollis Hill
Pl Fld
Games Ct
CAMPBELL GORDON WAY
Allot Gdns
Superstores
DORCHESTER CT
RUSPER CL
LONGLEY WAY
WILLIAM HO
STOLL CL
OSWALD TERR
TEMPLE RD
ANGTON RD
NEWTON RD
WOTTON RD
Mora Prim Sch
ST MICHAEL'S RD
BRIAR RD
MORA RD
LARCH RD
PINE RD
HASSOP RD
CEDAR RD
Cricklewood
NEEDHAM TERR
JOHNSTON TERR
MIDLAND TERR
GRATTON TERR
CAMPION TERR
KARA WAY
CRICKLEWOOD BROADWAY
DEPOT APP
Superstore
Cricklewood
86
Tenn Cts
Bwg Gn
Gladstone Park
HILL LA
PARK VIEW RD
LENNOX GDNS
MULGRAVE RD
Tenn Cts
Liby
OMAN CT
MACMILLAN HO
OMAN AVE
DICEY AVE
SNEYD RD
WREN AVE
DAWSON RD
BLACKSTONE RD
HEBER RD
IVY RD
AGAVE RD
OLIVE RD
ASHFORD RD
ASHFORD CT
OAKLANDS RD
OAKLANDS PAS
HOWARD RD
ROCKHALL RD
CHICHELE RD
SYLVAN GR
SHELDON RD
Ind Est
OAKLANDS MEWS 1
ACER CT 2
MAPLE CT 3
KEYES RD
67
DUDDEN HILL LA
CORNMOW DR
LANCASTER RD
KENDAL RD
Dudden Hill
ABERDEEN RD
HAMILTON RD
GEARY RD
HELENA RD
FLEETWOOD RD
ELLESMERE RD
DEWSBURY RD
BURNLEY RD
CULLINGWORTH RD
GLADSTONE CT
PARK AVE N
TRACEY AVE
HENSON AVE
GARDINER AVE
JAMES AVE
MEREDITH AVE
ASTLEY AVE
ANSON RD
Anson Prim Sch
HAVERSHAM LO
GERARD CT
MELROSE AVE
WALM LA
Gladstone Park Sch
SHERRICK GREEN RD
GAY CL
KEMPE RD
NETH CRES
CHANDOS RD
CRANHURST RD
CLOVELLY CT
BLENHEIM GDNS
STANLEY GDNS
GROSVENOR GDNS
ST GABRIEL'S RD
TEIGNMOUTH RD
Dollis Hill
SHORTCROFT MEAD CT
COOPER RD
GRIFFIN CL
CHURCHILL CT
JEYMER AVE
PARK AVE
MARLEY WLK
ELVIS RD
LENNON RD
CASSANORA CT
CARLTON CT
STATION PAR
CHAPTER RD
DEACON RD
85
BRENTHURST RD
SAPCOTE TRAD CTR
KINGSLEY CT
WESTLY CT
LYDFORD RD
DARTMOUTH RD
Willesden Green
COLIN RD
BELTON RD
VILLIERS RD
SANDRINGHAM RD
WINDSOR RD
CHURCHILL RD
OSBORNE RD
BUXTON RD
ADYS LAWN
ACLAND RD
ST PAUL'S AVENUE
GROVE RD
DEAN RD
A4088
A407
METRICK RD
CHAPLIN RD
PRESTON RD
PRESTON PL
Sch
BALMORAL RD
LECHMERE RD
HUDDLESTONE RD
FAITH CT
LINACRE RD
Schs
PARK AVE
RUTLAND PK
MAPESHILL PL
1 RUTLAND PARK GDNS
2 RUTLAND PARK MANS
3 QUEENS PAR
PHARAMOND
CHATSWORTH ROAD
BELVEDERE CT
YATES CT
2
BEACONSFIELD RD
GLEBE RD
CHURCHMEAD RD
BERTIE RD
HIGH RD
A4003
WILLESDEN LA
STRODE RD
EURO CL
LITCHFIELD
MAYBURY GDNS
GOWAN RD
Coll
ST ANDREW'S RD
CORNWALL GDNS
GRANGE RD
RICHMOND AVE
Super store
HEATHFIELD PK
KNIGHTLEAS CT
BRONDESBURY CT
HENLEY CT
MANOR LO
DEERHURST RD
WILLESDEN
NW10
Willesden New Cemy
SHANNON CT
LIFFEY CT
BOYNE CT
NORE CT
KASMIN CT
UNITY CL
POUND LA
CLARE RD
STERLING CL
BELDANES LO
HAWTHORN RD
PARKFIELD RD
HARLESDEN RD
Liby
VICTORIA MANS
Tenn Cts
HONEYMAN CL
MARLOW CT
EDEN LO
BRONDESBURY PARK
BRAMERTON
Brahma Kumaris World Spiritual Univ
PAMELA CT
TOWER RD
NORMAN CT
GRANGE HO
KINGS RD
ROWDON AVE
BRYAN AVE
DOBREE AVE
ALEXANDER AVE
PETER AVE
STAVERTON ROAD
ALVERSTONE RD
SIDMOUTH ROAD
Bwg Gn
Crkt Gd
Pav
ELSTOW GRANGE
LAWNFIELD
COVERDALE RD
1 HUGH GAITSKELL HO
2 KEIR HARDIE HO
3 CLEMENT ATTLEE HO
1
Willesden Jewish Cemy
Min Rly
Cemy
The Willesden Com
Summer Theatre
Allot Gdns
Newfield Prim Sch
ROBSON AVE
H
Tenn Cts
THE OAKS
DONNINGTON CT
FRONTENAC
CHAMBERS LANE
CLARENDON CT
SIDMOUTH PAR
Pav
MILVERTON RD
CHUDLEIGH RD
CLEMENT CL
MANOR HOUSE DR
ALAN PREECE CT
Malorees Jun & Inf Sch
ST HILDA'S CL
84
LONGSTONE AVE
Roundwood Park
Allot Gdns
DONNINGTON RD
Donnington Prim Sch
Tenn Cts
Sp Stad
SLANEY CT
MOUNT PLEASANT RD
AYLESTONE AVE
Queens Park Com Sch
ROSEDENE
GROSVENOR CT
CHRISTCHURCH AVE
CHADWICK RD
FRED NUNN HO
FRY RD
22
23
90
Bwg Gn
HARLESDEN RD
HERSANT CL
GEOFFREY JONES CT
ELLERSLIE GDNS
UFFINGTON RD
SHALFORD
Willesden High Sch
Willesden Sp Ctr
HENLEY RD
HANOVER RD
Brondesbury
JOHN BUCK HO
Allot

Basing Hill Park
Child's Hill Park
Golders Hill Park
Leg of Mutton Pond
West Heath
Child's Hill
NW3
NW2
NW6
West Hampstead
Hampstead Cemy
Fortune Green
Hampstead Sch
King's Coll London
St Margaret's Sch
Brondesbury
Brondesbury Park
HAMPSTEAD
South Hampstead
Kilburn
Kilburn Grange Park Sch
Beckford Prim Sch
Child's Hill Prim Sch
All Saints' CE Prim Sch
St Agnes RC Sch
King Alfred Sch
Finchley Road & Frognal
West Hampstead Thameslink
Islamia Schs
HENDON WAY
CRICKLEWOOD LA
FINCHLEY RD
FORTUNE GREEN RD
WEST END LA
SHOOT-UP HILL
WILLESDEN LA
IVERSON RD
BELSIZE RD
NORTH END WAY
WEST HEATH RD
BLACKBURN RD
BROADHURST GDNS
ABERDARE GDNS
CANFIELD GDNS
MILL LA
MAYGROVE RD
LIDDELL RD
SUMATRA RD
FROGNAL LA
REDINGTON RD
OAKHILL AVE
PLATT'S LA
HOLLYCROFT AVE
ROSECROFT AVE
FERNCROFT AVE
KIDDERPORE AVE
WEST HEATH DR
GOLDERS GREEN
A41
A598
A407
A502
B510
B520
B507
B509
A4003
A5
Barnet
Camden
Brent
47
70
91
84
85
86
87

70
Spaniards Inn (PH)
48
A
B
C
D
Open Air Stage
Ken Wood
Tenn Cts
Bwg Gn
Allot Gdns
North End
Mast
Tenn Ct
Hampstead Heath
Parliament Hill
Highgate Ponds
West Heath
East Heath
Vale of Health
NW3
Hampstead Ponds
SPANIARDS RD
NORTH END WAY
NORTH END RD
NORTH END AVE
INVERFORTH CL
INVERFORTH HO
HEATH BROW
WEST HEATH RD
WHITESTONE LA
BELL MOOR
Queen Mary's
HEATH ST
EAST HEATH RD
THE PRYORS
SOUTH HILL PK
SOUTH HILL PK GDNS
TANZA RD
PARLIAMENT HILL
NASSINGTON RD
Pav
Allot Gdns
SAVERNAKE RD
Hampstead Heath
KEATS GR
Mus
Liby
WILLOW RD
DENNING RD
CARLINGFORD RD
KEMPLAY RD
DOWNSHIRE HILL
HAMPSTEAD HIGH ST
ROSSLYN HILL
FLEET RD
MANSFIELD
AGINCOURT RD
CONSTANTINE RD
POND ST
Royal Free
HAMPSTEAD
CHURCH ROW
FROGNAL
FROGNAL WAY
University College Sch
ARKWRIGHT RD
LYNDHURST RD
St Mary's Sch Hampstead
FITZJOHN'S AVE
Belsize New Tunnel
Belsize Tunnel
BELSIZE AVENUE
BELSIZE PARK GARDENS
HAVERSTOCK HILL
Maitland Park
Belsize Park
LAMBOLLE RD
LANCASTER GR
Finchley Road & Frognal
Finchley Road
FINCHLEY RD
The Freud Mus
NW6
South Hampstead
CANFIELD GDNS
GREENCROFT GDNS
FAIRHAZEL GDNS
GOLDHURST TERR
Swiss Cottage
Swiss Cottage Liby
ADELAIDE RD
AVENUE RD
The Central Sch of Speech & Drama
ETON AVE
Primrose Hill
Primrose Hill Tunnels
St Paul's CE Prim Sch
BELSIZE RD
ABBEY
229
92
230
26
27
84
85
86
87

71
Tenn Cts
Waterlow Park
Highgate Cemy
St Joseph's RC Prim Sch
The Whittington
Highgate Cemy
Brookfield Prim Sch
Archway
Upper Holloway
Whittington Park
Yerbury Prim Sch
N19
Dartmouth Park
La Saint Union RC Sec Sch
William Ellis Sch
Parliament Hill Sch
Athletics Gd
Sw Pool
Gospel Oak
Acland Burghley Sch
Tufnell Park
Univ of North London (Tufnell Park Hall)
Sp Gd
N7
Tufnell Park Prim Sch
Holloway Sch
HM Prison
NW5
City Farm
Carlton Prim Sch
Kentish Town
Kentish Town West
Jews Free Sch
The Camden Sch for Girls
Chalk Farm
Roundhouse Theatre
Superstore
CAMDEN TOWN
NW1
Camden Mkt
Britannia Junction
N1
Freightliner Terminal
Fball Gd
HIGHGATE HILL
HOLLOWAY RD
JUNCTION RD
DARTMOUTH PARK HILL
FORTESS RD
KENTISH TOWN RD
BRECKNOCK RD
CAMDEN RD
CAMDEN PARK RD
YORK WAY
HIGHGATE RD
GORDON HOUSE RD
MALDEN RD
CHALK FARM RD
PRINCE OF WALES RD
TUFNELL PARK RD
LEIGHTON RD
ST JOHN'S GR
DARTMOUTH PARK RD
MAGDALA AVE
OAKESHOTT AVE
MAKEPEACE AVE
LANGBOURNE AVE
SWAIN'S LA
HIGHGATE WEST HILL
AGAR GR
ROYAL COLLEGE ST
CAMDEN ST
GLOUCESTER AVE
A
B
C
D
1
2
3
4
5
6
49
231
93
232
72
28
29
30
84
85
86
87

Finsbury Park
Highbury
ISLINGTON
Lower Holloway
Barnsbury
Nags Head
N19
N4
N7
N5
N1
STROUD GREEN RD
SEVEN SISTERS RD
HOLLOWAY RD
HORNSEY RD
TOLLINGTON RD
PARKHURST RD
CAMDEN RD
CALEDONIAN RD
LIVERPOOL RD
UPPER STREET
BLACKSTOCK RD
HIGHBURY PK
HIGHBURY GR
YORK WAY
CANONBURY RD
ISLEDON RD
HM Prison
Caledonian Park
Paradise Park
Highbury Fields
Highbury Pool
Arsenal
Arsenal Fball Gd
Gillespie Park
Drayton Park
Holloway Road
Caledonian Road
Caledonian Road & Barnsbury
Highbury & Islington
Highbury Corner
Copenhagen Junction
Freightliner Terminal
50
233
94
234
71
32

STOKE NEWINGTON
Abney Park Cemy
Clissold Park
Bwg Gn
Tenn Cts
N4
N16
N5
N1
E8
Shacklewell
Canonbury
Kingsland
Dalston
De Beauvoir Town
Essex Road
Ridley
Dalston Kingsland
Dalston Jct
Stoke Newington
Rectory Road
West Resr
LORDSHIP PK
BROWNSWOOD RD
GREEN LANES
STOKE NEWINGTON CHURCH ST
STOKE NEWINGTON HIGH ST
STOKE NEWINGTON RD
KINGSLAND HIGH ST
KINGSLAND RD
RECTORY RD
EVERING RD
MANSE RD
ALBION RD
NEWINGTON GREEN RD
ST PAUL'S RD
BALLS POND RD
ESSEX RD
SOUTHGATE RD
QUEENSBRIDGE RD
MANOR RD
MILDMAY GR N
MILDMAY GR S
MILDMAY PK
HIGHBURY NEW PK
HIGHBURY QUADRANT
HIGHBURY GRANGE
CLISSOLD CRES
CLISSOLD RD
SHACKLEWELL LA
FOULDEN RD
DOWNHAM RD
BALMES RD
CANAL WLK
A105
A10
A104
A1199
A1200
A1207
B104
B105
B111
B102
B108
51
95
235
74
32
33
34
84
85
86
87
A
B
C
D
1
2
3
4
5
6

Upper Clapton
52
A
B
C
D
Lea Valley Riding Sch
Pl Fld
Leyton Marshes
River Lea or Lee
Leeside Wharf
Lea Valley Ice Ctr
Stoke Newington
N16
UPPER CLAPTON RD
NORTHWOLD RD
LEA BRIDGE RD
Clapton
Recn Gd
E5
Nature Reserve
Lea Valley Wlk
Lea Bridge
Mandeville JMI Sch
Rectory Road
RECTORY RD
A104
A107
A102
B111
Shacklewell
Hackney Downs
CRICKETFIELD RD
PEMBURY RD
LOWER CLAPTON RD
Lower Clapton
Clapton Park
Clapton Girls Tec Coll
The Community Coll
Homerton
73
DALSTON LA
AMHURST RD
HOMERTON HIGH ST
MORNING LA
Hackney Central
A1207
GRAHAM RD
Superstore
B113
WICK RD
Dalston
E8
HACKNEY
MARE ST
London Fields
B108
QUEENSBRIDGE RD
A106
WELL ST
CASSLAND RD
Homerton
E9
Well Street Common
VICTORIA PARK RD
34
35
96
Royal
87
86
85
84
6
5
4
3
2
1

53
E10
Inf Sch Annexe
Church Mead Jun Sch
The Lammas Sch
St Joseph's RC Inf Sch
LAMMAS RD
ELM PARK RD
PERTH RD
CLEMENTINA RD
SEYMOUR RD
VIKING PL
RADLIX RD
PARK RD
GRANGE RD
PRIMROSE RD
GRANGE PARK RD
CRAWLEY RD
FAIRWAYS BSNS PK
CONNAUGHT CL
MARSH LA
LEYTON BSNS CTR
ORIENT IND PK
CHURCH RD
VILLIERS CL
IVE FARM LA
IVE FARM CL
ALLANSON CT 1
ETON MANOR CT 2
SLADE TWR 3
CRESCENT RD
GOLDSMITH RD
CARLISLE RD
ALMSHOUSES
GLEBE LANDS
JOHN STRYPE CT
TENNYSON RD
HIGH ROAD LEYTON
A1006
A112
GRANGE PARK RD
BUCKLAND RD
LINDLEY RD
SEDGWICK RD
Dawlish Prim Sch
DAWLISH RD
87
6
PO
Pl Flds
E10
ORIENT WAY
Waltham Forest
Hackney
INSKIP CL
WILMOT RD
ROSEDENE TERR
SALWAY HO
RYDER CT
ROBINIA CRES
MAGNOLIA CL
LARCH RD
WALNUT RD
THORNHILL RD
WINDSOR RD
BALMORAL RD
BRISBANE RD
OSBORNE RD
BUCKINGHAM RD
LYTTELTON RD
TYNDALL RD
HUXLEY RD
SIDMOUTH RD
TERENCE MESSENGER TWR
TUPELO RD
PINE CL
PALM CL
OSIER WAY
OLIVER RD
Allot Gdns
Bwg Gn
Tenn Cts
Leyton Orient Fball Gd
Bndstd
YORK RD
DUNEDIN RD
ADELAIDE RD
TH
Liby
5
GATEWAY RD
AUCKLAND RD
Recn Gd
Allot Gdns
New Spitalfields Market
RUCKHOLT RD
RUCKHOLT CL
MARSHALL RD
WITHAM CT
Superstore
86
P
COW BRIDGE
E5
P
WILLINGTON CT
MANDEVILLE ST
HAZELWOOD CL
SUNNYHILL CL
1 ASHBOURNE CT
2 MELBORNE CT
3 KEDLESTON CT
4 MONSAL CT
Hackney Marsh
Recn Gds
Lea Valley Wlk
KEYWORTH CL
RUDDINGTON CL
GILPIN RD
SHERRIN RD
River Lea or Lee
1 IRONSIDE HO
2 EDRED HO
3 ETHELBERT HO
4 TEMPLEMEAD HO
5 RUNNYMEDE HO
6 FAIRMEAD HO
7 KINGSMEAD HO
8 EDWY HO
9 ATHELSTAN HO
10 WATERMEAD HO
11 MALMSMEAD HO
12 ASHMEAD HO
13 RIVERMEAD HO
River Lee Navigation Hackney Cut
OSWALD'S MEAD
EDWIN'S MEAD
LINDISFARNE WAY
PENDA'S MEAD
OFFA'S MEAD
KINGSMEAD WAY
JARROW WAY
SUDBURY CT
Kingsmead Prim Sch
Recn Gd
4
EASTWAY
QUARTERMILE LA
Lee Valley Sp Ctr
Tenn Cts
Recn Gd
TEMPLE MILLS RD
A106
A12
COLNE RD
DAUBENEY RD
DURRINGTON RD
TOWER MEWS
CHARLES BURTON CT
MEESON ST
ASHENDEN RD
ADLEY ST
TREHURST ST
EGBERT HO
EDGAR HO
ALFRED HO
HOMERTON RD
B112
Lea Int
201
76
POPLAR MARSHGATE BRIDGE
LOCKGATE CL
CROWFOOT CL
LEE CONSERVANCY RD
Temple Mills
CLAYS LA
CRABTREE CT 1
BAMFORD CT 2
TEMPLARS HO 3
TRAFFORD CL
CLAYS LANE CL
3
1 TWEED
2 TAYL
3 SMIT
4 HOW
5 HOLT
6 COO
7 DALY
8 BRO
RODING RD
COHEN CL
BOSCOMBE CL
CROFTON TERR
LYNEHAM WLK
YATESBURY CT
MARSH HILL
B112
1 CASTLE CL
2 BRENTON CT
3 TYNTE CT
4 SALISBURY CT
5 HILLYFIELD CL
E9
Fball Gds
SEMLEY GATE
Hackney Marsh
EAST CROSS ROUTE
WATERDEN CRES
Allot Gdns
Channelsea River
Cycle Circuit
STUDLEY CL 2
NEWBURY CT 3
HUMBERTON CL
CHEVET ST
KEMEYS ST
SWINNERTON ST
MABLEY ST
BERESFORD CT
LONGLAND CT
AVRO CT
OLDBURY CT
Hackney Wick
Sch
H
KENWORTHY RD
EDMESTON CL
1 SOUTHMOOR WAY
2 WINDSOR WHARF
Stadium
EASTWAY
SHALBOURNE SQ
CHISLEDON WLK
MEADOW CL
Recn Gd
Gainsborough Prim Sch
SILK MILLS SQ
DAINTRY WAY
CORSELEY WAY
OSBORNE RD
WATERDEN RD
Depot
85
ORIEL RD
HASSETT RD
TRAFALGAR MEWS
BUXHALL CRES
INGLESHAW
LAVINGTON CL
BRINKWORTH WAY
BERKSHIRE RD
LEABANK SQ
Hackney
Newham
Hackney Wick
Container Terminal
2
BUSHBERRY RD
BENN ST
BALLANCE RD
BARTRIP ST
A102
B113
WICK RD
HEDGERS GR
HARTLAKE RD
BROOKFIELD RD
A106
Liby
BEANACRE CL
TROWBRIDGE RD
PRINCE EDWARD RD
FELSTEAD ST
WALLIS RD
CHAPMAN RD
Allot Gdns
EAST CROSS CTR
E15
Hackney
Tower Hamlets
MAIN YD
QUEENS YD
KINGS YD
COWDRY RD
DANESDALE RD
LYNNETT RD
ANNIS RD
CHRISTIE RD
HARROWGATE RD
BRADSTOCK RD
B113
A115
WHITE POST LA
HEPSCOTT RD
ROTHBURY RD
TREGO RD
DAVEY RD
HAMLET IND EST
CARPENTER'S RD
Waterworks River
CADOGAN TERR
CADOGAN CL 1
VICTORIA PARK IND CTR 2
CARPENTERS BSNS PK
BOW IND PK
ROACH WORKS
River Lea or Lee
MARSHGATE LA
City Mill River
1
QUEENS GATE VILLAS
Tenn Cts
Bwg Gn
GUINNESS CL
ST MARK'S GATE
WANSBECK RD
REMUS RD
WYKE RD
MONIER RD
BEACHY RD
ROACH RD
SMEED RD
STOUR RD
BREAM ST
WICK LA
WINFORD HO
Sp Gd
Tower Hamlets
Newham
Lea Valley Wlk
84
JODRELL RD
OLLERTON GN
DACE RD
Victoria Park
A12
Swan Wharf
Wharf
A
B
37
97
C
D
38
36
Victoria Fntn
Gunmakers Gate
Hertford Union Canal
SYCAMORE AV
CEDAR CL
OSHEA GR
RUSTON ST
CANAL ST
WENDON ST
CROWN CL
WICK LA
MAVERTON RD
E3
KNOBS HILL RD
Stratford Marsh
EAST

Leytonstone
Leyton
LEYTON
Stratford New Town
STRATFORD
E10
E11
E7
E15
54
75
98
A
B
C
D
1
2
3
4
5
6
HIGH ROAD LEYTON
FRANCIS RD
GROVE GREEN RD
A106 WARREN RD
CATHALL RD
HARROW RD
HARROW GN B161
LEYTON RD
MAJOR RD
ANGEL LA A112
GREAT EASTERN RD
ROMFORD RD
BROADWAY
WEST HAM LA
VICARAGE LA
CARPENTER'S RD
PORTWAY
LEYTONSTONE RD
HIGH ROAD LEYTONSTONE
CANN HALL RD
FOREST LA
HAM PARK RD
TEMPLE MILLS LA
RUCKHOLT RD
LANGTHORNE RD
CHOBHAM RD
HENNIKER RD
MARYLAND RD
BUXTON RD
WATER LA
THE GROVE
St Patrick's RC Cemy
West Ham Cemy
Wanstead Flats
Forest Lane Park
Leyton Orient Fball Gd
Leyton Town Ctr
Superstore
Tenn Cts
Recn Gd
Cycle Circuit
Container Terminal
International Freight Terminal
Waterworks River
Univ of East London
Newham Coll (Stratford Campus)
Sarah Bonnell Sch
Colegrave Prim Sch
Maryland Sch
Jenny Hammond Sch
Tom Hood Sch
Cann Hall Sch
Dawlish Prim Sch
Newport Schs
Noor Ul Islam Prim Sch
Mayville Prim Sch
Davies Lane Jun & Inf Sch
Leytonstone High Road
Earlham Prim Sch
Park Prim Sch
Langthorne
Waltham Forest
Newham
Redbridge
1 TWEEDALE CT
2 TAYLOR CT
3 SMITHIES CT
4 HOWARTH CT
5 HOLT CT
6 COOPER CT
7 DALY CT
8 BROOK CT
1 MOHMMAD KHAN
2 ST JOHN'S CT
3 HARVEY GDNS
4 ST MARY'S CT
THEATRE SQ 1
GERRY RAFFLES SQ 2
STRATFORD CIR 3
Stratford Marsh
Maryland
Stratford

Reservoir Wood
Boat House
Aldersbrook Prim Sch
JACKSON CT
JOSEPH LISTER LODGE
WOODLANDS AVE
NORTHUMBERLAND AVE
55
A
B
C
D
Allot Gdns
87
Redbridge
Newham
BLAKE HALL CRES
QUEENSWOOD GDNS
ST GABRIEL'S CL
BRADING CRES
BURDEN WAY
ALDERS CL
PARK RD
INGATESTONE RD
ALBURY MEWS
HARPENDEN RD
MARGARETTING RD
CLAVERING RD
ARRAN DR
MARK WADE CL
WESTMORLAND CL
SUNDERLAND WAY
BELGRAVE RD
WINDSOR RD
RICHMOND WAY
LAKE HOUSE RD
A116
A114
HOOD LO
BUXTON LO
DOVER RD
HERONGATE RD
B Gn
HIGHFIELD CT
ST MARGARET'S RD
EMPRESS AVE
WANSTEAD PARK AVE
E12
6
HEATHERWOOD CL
ALDERSBROOK RD
Aldersbrook
ST JAMES CT
MERLIN RD
Wanstead Flats
CENTRE RD
P
PO
Crem
City of L Cem
5
1 BROXBOURNE RD
2 HESKETH RD
Centenary Walk
E7
A117
FOREST DR
DAMES RD
SIDNEY RD
KNIGHTON RD
1 CAPEL POINT
2 FOREST SIDE
3 CURWEN AVE
Redbridge Horse Ride
CAPEL RD
86
Manor Park
PEVENSEY RD
WINCHELSEA RD
VANSITTART RD
FOWLER RD
FIELD POINT
TALBOT RD
INGESTRE RD
STRODE RD
FOREST RD
BECTIVE RD
WOODFORD RD
Newham
BARWICK RD
CHESTNUT AVE
HORACE RD
CRANMER RD
LATIMER RD
GODWIN RD
LORNE RD
TYLNEY RD
RIDLEY RD
The Manor Park Cemy & Crem
CENTRE DR
THE CHASE
MORTLOCK CT
MANOR HO
COMET CL
WHITTA RD
KELLER CRES
GLADDING RD
FOREST VIEW RD
4
STATION RD
CARLYLE RD
ERIC CL
ERIC RD
CLARE GDNS
WOODER GDNS
LEONARD RD
BIGNOLD RD
B161
CLINTON RD
STATION RD
Wanstead Park
Godwin Sch
Manor Park
CUMBERLAND RD
MANOR PARK RD
BARNES CL
THE BIRCHES
MACDONALD RD
STRACEY RD
MOORE WLK
DIMOND CL
STATION APP
AVENUE RD
Woodgrange Sch
SEBERT RD
KUBRICK BSNS EST
DURHAM RD
WENTWORTH RD
ALBANY RD
CARLTON RD
CLARENCE RD
A118
78
HERBERT RD
FIELD RD
DEAN ST
SUFFOLK ST
NORFOLK ST
ESSEX ST
FOREST ST
BROOKWAY
KUHN WAY
HAMPTON RD
BALMORAL RD
SAINTS DR
CRANBOURNE RD
SALISBURY RD
SNOWSHILL RD
Sch
Schs
OSBORNE RD
RICHMOND RD
CLAREMONT RD
WOODGRANGE RD
Forest Gate
KEBBELL TERR
WINDSOR RD
THE LUMIERE BLDG
Woodgrange Park
BLUEBELL AVE
QUEENSBERRY PL
3
EARLHAM GR
SPROWSTON RD
FOREST POINT
POINT TERR
ROMFORD RD
TEMBURY CL
Woodgrange Park Cemy
Forest Gate
POST OFFICE APP
Liby
DONALD HUNTER HO
DAVIDSON TERRS
WESTBURY CT
GREEN ST
B167
B109
ROSEDALE RD
BIRCHDALE RD
NIGEL RD
QUAKER'S PL
NORWICH RD
CLOVA RD
SPROWSTON MEWS
JACKSON CT
PALMERSTON RD
WESTBURY RD
ST JOHN'S TERR
FINDEN RD
RATCLIFF RD
SANDRINGHAM RD
ST DUNSTANS RD
HENDERSON RD
SHERRARD RD
THE ELMS
85
ATHERTON MEWS
NURSERY LA
SYLVAN RD
VALE RD
WESTBURY TERR
HALLEY RD
Monega Sch
Plashet
1 SYCAMORE CT
2 FYFFIELD CT
CROSBY RD
MARGERY PARK RD
DISRAELI RD
GLENPARKE RD
MONEGA RD
Plashet Jewish Cemy
2
OLD SCHOOL CRES
CHAUCER RD
WHYTEVILLE RD
WHYTEVILLE HO
STRONE RD
SHREWSBURY RD
COLSTON RD
CLIFTON RD
KNOX RD
GOWER RD
STUDLEY RD
William Davies Sch
YORK RD
WYATT RD
KITCHENER RD
BATH RD
SALISBURY RD
DUNBAR RD
GROSVENOR RD
CHESHUNT RD
BRISTOL RD
LINCOLN RD
STORK RD
SKELTON RD
SOUTH ESK RD
KATHERINE RD
Tenn Cts
REGINALD RD
Fball Gd
MACARTHUR CL
St Angela's Sch
Stratford Sch
STAFFORD RD
WOODHOUSE GR
ST GEORGE'S RD
MARLBOROUGH RD
ROTHSAY RD
DERBY RD
UPTON LA
ISMAILIA RD
BEAUCHAMP RD
WOLSELEY RD
BELTON RD
ST GEORGE'S SQ
ST GEORGE'S AVE
JEPHSON RD
LANSDOWNE RD
Plashet Park
WORDSWORTH AVE
TENNYSON RD
DORIS RD
VERONA RD
UPTON AVE
OAKDALE RD
FERNDALE RD
WOODSTOCK RD
PRESTBURY RD
RUTLAND RD
East Ham Meml
Bwg Gn
Stratford Sch
KINGSLEY RD
ELMHURST RD
CROMWELL RD
CHESTER RD
B165
West Ham Park
JOSEPH LISTER CT
LANCASTER RD
Elmhurst Sch
UPTON PARK RD
SHAFTESBURY RD
ASHLEY RD
RED POST HO
DURBAN CT
EDITH RD
PLASHET GR
COWPER AVE
1
Plashet Sch
St Bonaventure's Sch
ST ANTONY'S RD
Upton
STUKELEY RD
CARLTON TERR
DORSET RD
HILDA RD
MILTON AVE
THE FIRS
BOLEYN RD
ST STEPHENS RD
WHITTAKER RD
WYNDHAM RD
WORTLEY RD
Bndstd
NEVILLE RD
ST STEPHENS PAR
WASHINGTON RD
WATERLOO RD
WALPOLE RD
WHITFIELD RD
FRY RD
HEIGHAM RD
Tenn Cts
A114
PLASHET RD
ELIZABETH RD
84
B109
LAWRENCE RD
UPTON CROSS
B165
PLASEL CT
BISHOPS AVE
CHURSTON AVE
LUCAS AVE
41
99
C
VICTORIA AVE
D
GRANGEWOOD ST
EVERSLEIGH RD
GROSVENOR RD
SPENCER RD
42
OUTRAM RD
MALVERN RD
TEMPLE RD
STAMFORD RD
PARK RD
PARK GR
VICAR
DACRE
CLAUDE RD
LAWRENCE RD
GOLDINE AVE
KING'S RD
CEARNS HO
WILLIAM
Upton Park

Prim Sch
A
B
C
D
56
CH
PO
SEYMOUR
KENSINGTON GDNS
ENDSLEIGH GDNS
DE VERE GDNS
COURTLAND AVE
MAYFAIR AVE
EMPRESS AVE
WESTBURY RD
NORTHBROOK RD
BELGRAVE RD
ARGYLE RD
MANSFIELD RD
BEAL RD
SELBORNE RD
GREENWAY
VALENTINES
INGLEBY RD
MELBOURNE RD
COVENTRY RD
WARWICK GDNS
AIRLIE GDNS
WELLESLEY RD
PARK AVE
Park Sch
GRANVILLE RD
BATHURST RD
Coll
MORLAND RD
HERON CT
BALFOUR RD
IG1
HAINAULT ST
LEY ST
MYRTLE RD
THE EXCHANGE
HAVELOCK ST
RIGBY MEWS
HERON MEWS
Ilford
ILFORD
YORK RD
YORK MEWS
YORK PL
STATION RD
HIGH RD
CHADWICK
OAKFIELD RD
Lib
TH
Mus
CLEMENTS RD
CLEMENTS LA
A118
A123
A406
ILFORD HILL
CHAPEL RD
WINSTON WAY
Mkt
PRIOR RD
MILL RD
Maytime Sch
Alders Brook
Ilford Interchange
Coll
LUGG APP
RODEN ST
READS CL
AUDREY RD
BRITANNIA RD
RIVERDENE RD
BEDFORD RD
CLEVELAND RD
RUTLAND RD
Schs
DUDLEY RD
NORTH CIRCULAR RD
FALAIZE AVE
AGNES AVE
KENNETH AVE
NIGEL MEWS
BENGAL RD
FERNWAYS
CECIL RD
HAMILTON RD
HOWARD RD
MADRAS RD
MADRAS HO
ILFORD LA
Rec Gd
ELTISLEY RD
THORNTON RD
SANDYHILL RD
LOWBROOK RD
NATAL RD
MAY TERR
JERSEY RD
PAGET RD
MAYVILLE RD
HICKLING RD
ST LUKE'S AVE
BADEN RD
PRETORIA RD
DAFFODIL GDNS
BAXTER RD
WINGATE RD
Uphall Prim Sch
KHARTOUM RD
FORSYTHIA CL
HUNTERS RD
Pl Fld
HARVEY RD
WISTERIA CL
LAVENDER PL
AZALEA CL
JASMINE CL
TULIP GDNS
DAHLIA GDNS
UPHALL RD
NORMAN RD
SAXON RD
CONIFER CT
BLUEBELL WAY
LUPIN CRES
ROSE CT
HYACINTH CL
ROMAN RD
FAIRFIELD RD
Redbridge
VICTORIA RD
WEST HO
LOXFORD HO
3 HONEYSUCKLE CT
4 BERBERIS CT
Barking & Dagenham
Newham
GURNEY CL
CROWS RD
HARTS LA
NORTH ST
MERSEA HO 1
COLNE HO 2
CAPE CL
COWBRIDGE LA
A124
IG11
RIVERSIDE WORKS
River Roding
WHITING AVE
HERTFORD RD
LONDON RD
Superstore
ABBEY RD
Pl Fld
Barking Flyover
HIGHBRIDGE RD
Recn Gd
100
43
ST OLAVE'S RD
Allot Gdns
MORLAND CL
87
Redbridge
Newham
ERLAND WAY
Ilford
6
Crem
City of London Cemy
5
A117
FOREST DR
A116
86
Manor Park
MANOR HO
GLADDING RD
KELLER CRES
FOREST VIEW RD
THE WARREN
RABBITS RD
WASHINGTON AVE
MICHIGAN AVE
OREGON AVE
TORONTO RD
WORCESTER RD
GLOUCESTER RD
LANE MEWS
COLCHESTER AVE
ALDERSBROOK LA
DAINES CL
B165
EIGHTH AVE
Sch
MARINER RD
WARRIOR SQ
SELBORNE AVE
SALLY MURRAY CL
FLORENCE
ELSON CL
BANKS WAY
GRANTHAM RD
WALTON RD
WOLFERTON RD
JACK CORNWELL ST
Little Ilford Park
Wks
4
Park
STATION RD
ROMFORD RD
Liby & Mus
FIFTH AVE
SEVENTH AVE
LITTLE ILFORD LA
CARLYLE RD
HASLER CT
THE BIRCHES
Prim Sch
SCHOOL RD
SIXTH AVE
FOURTH AVE
VERNON AVE
TREVELYAN AVE
BRANCASTER RD
DERSINGHAM AVE
LAWRENCE AVE
PARKHURST RD
ALVERSTONE RD
BARNES CL
MANOR PARK
HERBERT RD
SECOND AVE
THIRD AVE
HARCOURT AVE
SHERINGHAM AVE
CHURCH RD
ALBANY RD
77
A118
CRANBOURNE RD
GREENHILL GR
SNOWSHILL RD
Avenue Prim Sch
MEANLEY RD
FIRST AVE
NINE ACRES CL
E12
Sch
ST WINEFRIDE'S AVE
ST MARY'S APP
LANDSEER AVE
GAINSBOROUGH AVE
Little Ilford
SALISBURY RD
3
BLUEBELL AVE
QUEENSBERRY PL
dgrange Park Cemy
WARWICK RD
PIXSEN RD
CHURCH RD
LEAMINGTON CL
MORRIS AVE
MANPREET CT
MALLARD CT
RECTORY RD
ELSENHAM RD
DORE AVE
LEIGHTON AVE
LEADER AVE
REYNOLDS AVE
Allot Gdns
BERKELEY RD
STANLEY RD
SHERIDAN RD
Essex Prim Sch
CHESTERFORD RD
MILLAIS AVE
REESLAND CL
85
THE ELMS
COLERIDGE AVE
Monega Sch
RUSKIN AVE
ESSEX RD
FRANK BAILEY WLK
BARRINGTON RD
Pl Fld
Plashet
Plashet Jewish Cemy
HIGH ST N
GOLDSMITH AVE
BROWNING RD
RUSKIN AVE
HATHAWAY CRES
2
ROSEBERY AVE
ROSEBERY AVE
SHAKESPEARE CRES
KEMP HO
STEVENAGE RD
CLIFTON RD
SHELLEY AVE
LINCOLN RD
BYRON AVE
Sports Gd
Tenn Cts
WOODHOUSE GR
KENSINGTON AVE
Kensington Prim Sch
Plashet Park
WORDSWORTH AVE
GLADSTONE AVE
THE BEECHES
East Ham Meml
Bwg Gn
TENNYSON AVE
EAST AVE
SOUTHEND RD
SHOEBURY RD
SPRINGFIELD RD
NORTHFIELD RD
ASHFORD RD
LEIGH RD
Bwg Gn
H
B165
SIBLEY GR
BRIDGE RD
WATSON AVE
BURGESS CT
1
PLASHET GR
COWPER AVE
MILTON AVE
THE FIRS
Plashet Sch
East Ham
E6
LYDEARD RD
BURGES RD
LATHOM RD
CLEMENTS RD
WALL END RD
BURGES RD
Pl Fld
THE WILLOWS
HART CT
Sch
HEIGHAM RD
ACORN CT
BENDISH RD
CAULFIELD RD
CALEDON RD
HOLLAND RD
84
B109
LAWRENCE RD
A117
RON LEIGHTON WAY
KEPPEL RD
ALTMORE AVE
COURTNEY RD
HOLME RD
ORIA AVE
OUTRAM RD
TEMPLE RD
42
EVERSLEIGH RD
MALVERN RD
STAMFORD RD
SKEFFINGTON RD
KEMPTON RD
HALL RD
NORFOLK RD
BEDFORD
Sch
Park

Christchurch Prim Sch
Allot Gdns
57
Palmer RC Sch
HIGH RD
GREEN LA
Cemy
1 FRANCIS ST
2 FRANCIS RD
3 ELIZABETH AVE
Cricklefield Ath Gd
ILFORD RET PK
REDBRIDGE ENT CTR
A118
A1083
WINSTON WAY
BELMONT RD
IG1
CONNAUGHT MEWS
TA Ctr
HOMES OF REST
Bwg Gn
The Lake
South Park
SOUTH PARK TERR
SOUTH PARK DR
Knox Sp Fld
South Park Prim Sch
IG3
PARKWAY
LEVETT GDNS
DAWLISH DR
Hyleford Sch
Allot Gdns
Woodlands Jun & Inf Schs
Loxford Sch of Science & Tech
Loxford
Loxford Park
1 DURHAM PL
2 LANCASTER PL
1 POWLE TERR
2 FULLER TERR
Redbridge
Barking & Dagenham
Loxford Water
Pl Fld
Barking Abbey Comp Sch
A124
80
Fair Cross
LONGBRIDGE RD
MARQUIS CT 1
CROMWELL LODGE 2
FAIRCROSS PAR 3
1 HEENAN CL
2 BATEMAN CL
3 THE ALMSHOUSES
4 THE WAKERINGS
5 THE CLEVELANDS
6 THE BLOOMFIELDS
Tenn Cts
Barking Park
Bwg Gn
THE TRIANGLE
FANSHAWE AVE A123
NORTHERN RELIEF RD
IG11
Eastbury Comp Sch
Schs
Barking
Upney
Boating Lakes
THE VICARAGE FIELDS SH CTR
BARKING
Liby
TH
St Joseph RC Prim Sch
45
101
46
A123
A
B
C
D
1
2
3
4
5
6
84
85
86
87

58
102
79
Castle Green
Fair Cross
Goodmayes Park
Mayesbrook Park
Parsloes Park
Becontree
IG3
IG11
RM8
RM9
GREEN LA
GOODMAYES LA
LONGBRIDGE RD
PORTERS AVE
LODGE AVE
BENNETT'S CASTLE LA
BECONTREE AVE
VALENCE AVE
A1083
A124
A123
A1153
B177
B191
KINFAUNS RD
ASHGROVE RD
KILDOWAN RD
CASTLETON RD
MAYFIELD RD
BROADVIEW HO
CLARIDGE RD
INSKIP RD
GREENSIDE
BURNSIDE
CHADWAY
GREENWAY
CHITTY'S LA
BARON RD
ROWALLEN PAR
PEACOCK CL
FOSSWAY
ROYAL OAK CT
DONNE RD
WALDEGRAVE RD
ALLEYNDALE RD
WINTERBOURNE RD
KNIGHT CL
THOMAS CT
HYNTON RD
HAYDON RD
BROCKELBANK LO
MANOR SQ
CORIES CL
BONHAM GDNS
NEVILLE RD
BONHAM RD
HENSHAWE RD
MARGERY RD
SEABROOK RD
SHIPTON CL
LAKE CL
WINDING WAY
LINDISFARNE RD
BERRYMAN CL
BROOKING CL
FARMWAY
CROSSWAY
LACEY DR
LINDSEY RD
KILMARNOCK GDNS
BURFORD CL
LINKWAY
GROVEWAY
BUSHWAY
BUSHGROVE RD
AGNES GDNS
RAVENSFIELD CL
HEYNES RD
NOEL SQ
BRYCE RD
CAMPDEN CRES
FIELDWAY
FULLER RD
HAMMONDS CL
LICHFIELD RD
SCHOOL WAY
STEVENS RD
DUNKELD RD
MILNER RD
FELBRIDGE RD
KENILWORTH GDNS
CHARLBURY GDNS
LYNFORD GDNS
NUTFIELD GDNS
TALBOT GDNS
WOODSTOCK GDNS
ARUNDEL GDNS
CARDIGAN GDNS
GRANTON RD
BROOMHILL RD
ALLOA RD
AIRTHRIE RD
HAZELDENE RD
COLINTON RD
ABERDOUR RD
ABBOTSFORD RD
BREAMORE CT
BREAMORE RD
KILMARTIN RD
MELDRUM RD
BUDOCH CT
BUDOCH DR
BROWNLEA GDNS
TRESCO GDNS
WESTROW GDNS
GYLLYNGDUNE GDNS
TRENANCE GDNS
OAKLEIGH LO
ANCHOR HO
SANDON CT
POOLES CT
LEVETT GDNS
DAWLISH DR
FORTERIE GDNS
ASHBURTON AVE
MAYESBROOK RD
HOLDEN CL
Becontree Prim Sch
GAINSBOROUGH RD
BUTLER RD
VICAR'S WLK
SYLVAN WAY
EARLS WLK
LONGBRIDGE HO
GAINSBOROUGH HO
SANDHURST DR
ABINGER
RADLEY AVE
CAPEL GDNS
WATERSIDE CL
LOVELACE GDNS
Univ of East London
AMIDAS GDNS
STONARD RD
DOROTHY GDNS
HIGHGROVE RD
GORING GDNS
COTESMORE GDNS
BABINGTON RD
BOWES RD
MARTIN RD
MARTIN GDNS
HEWETT RD
GARDINER CL
HOBART RD
KINGSLEY MEWS
ELIOT RD
HASKARD RD
DURELL RD
DURELL GDNS
WREN GDNS
WREN RD
CHRISTOPHER GDNS
The Sydney Russell Sch
PEARTREE GDNS
MARLBOROUGH RD
LOWRY RD
HOGARTH RD
FITZSTEPHEN RD
RUTLAND GDNS
DRONFIELD GDNS
EXTON GDNS
CONSTABLE MEWS 1
ROSETTI TERR 2
STUBBS MEWS 3
BEARDSLEY TERR 4
BACON TERR 5
WHISTLER MEWS 6
ILCHESTER RD
HARROLD RD
IVINGHOE RD
Dorothy Barley Schs
CORNWORTHY RD
HEDINGHAM RD
DAVINGTON RD
DAVINGTON GDNS
MARKYATE RD
EASEBOURNE RD
KIRKLEES RD
LILLECHURCH RD
NEASHAM RD
SHERINGHAM DR
BRADFIELD DR
HEPWORTH GDNS
HEPWORTH CT
SOUTHWOLD DR
WOODBRIDGE RD
DEREHAM RD
SANDRINGHAM RD
WESTROW DR
Fball Gd
Sp Gd
Tenn Cts
Pl Fld
Allot Gdns
Liby
Sch
Schs
Bwg Gn
L Ctr
BREWOOD RD
BROMHALL RD
BRAGG CL
AMBLEY RD
BLITHBURY RD
KILSBY WLK
FYFIELD HO
BASEDALE RD
ROWNEY RD
ROWNEY GDNS
CANNINGTON RD
CLEMENTHORPE RD
WATERBEACH RD
THICKET GR
WYKEHAM AVE
RUSPER RD
Jo Richardson Com Sch
RUGBY GDNS
RUGBY RD
MAPLAS RD
GALE ST
SHEPPEY RD
SHEPPEY GDNS
CARROW RD
DENNY GDNS
WOODWARD GDNS
WOODWARD RD
WAGSTAFF GDNS
COTTON CL
HAMELTON TERR
SETON GDNS
BILLINGS CL
STOCKER GDNS
FLAMSTEAD RD
FLAMSTEAD GDNS
ELLERTON GDNS
ELLERTON RD
CANONSLEIGH RD
ROSEDALE RD
ROSEDALE GDNS
CAMPSEY RD
CAMPSEY GDNS
STAMFORD RD
STAMFORD GDNS
ROTHWELL GDNS
ROTHWELL RD
GREENFIELD RD
GREENFIELD GDNS
GORESBROOK RD
AMESBURY RD
POLESWORTH RD
ARDEN CRES
LANGLEY GDNS
LANGLEY CRES
STUDLEY RD
ROMSEY GDNS
ROMSEY RD
WIX RD
BURNHAM RD
PINLEY GDNS
Monteagle Prim Sch
SURMANS CL
ACONBURY RD
MAPLESTEAD RD
MOORE CRES
BASSETT HO
INGRAVE HO
DUNMOW HO
Cemy
Boating Lakes
THE DRIVE
CLARE GDNS
CORNWALL CL
MANOR RD
OAKLEY AVE
EDGEFIELD AVE
Upney
MEADOW RD
MERTON RD
BRIDGEWAY
STRATFORD CL
MARGARET BONDFIELD AVE
LANSBURY AVE
BEVAN AVE
BEN TILLET CL
KEIR HARDIE WAY
Sp Gds

59
103
VII
A
B
C
D
87
6
5
86
4
3
85
2
1
84
49
50
RM8
RM9
RM10
Becontree
DAGENHAM
Central Park
Civic Ctr
1 HAWKWELL HO
2 BUTLER CT
3 LABURNUM HO
4 PEVEREL HO
Robert Clack Lower Sch
All Saints RC Sch
Upper Sch
Grafton Jun & Inf Schs
Becontree Day
Valence House Mus
Valence Park
Five Elms Prim Sch
Trinity Sch
Becontree Pl Fld
Pl Fld
Schs
Bwg Gn
Allot Gdns
Eastbrook Comp Sch
Parkside HO
Redif HO
Midas Bsns Ctr
Sterling Ind Est
Dagenham & Redbridge Fball Gd
Hunters Hall Prim Sch
Rec Gd
Dagenham East
Dagenham Heathway
Godwin Prim Sch
Thomas Arnold Prim Sch
Goresbrook Park
Old Dagenham Park
Sp Arena
Tenn Ct
Liby
Morland Road Day
Dagenham Priory Sch
Catherine Godfrey HO
Min Glf Crs
RUSH GREEN RD
WOOD LA
A124
A1083
A1112
A1240
RAINHAM RD N
RAINHAM RD S
A1112 Dagenham East
HEATHWAY
BALLARDS RD
B178
MERRY FIDDLERS
THE BROADWAY
CINEMA PAR
MEADWAY CT
TURNAGE RD
LAMBERHURST RD
WINIFRED RD
GERALD RD
ROSS AVE
TENTERDEN RD
FORDYKE RD
JOAN GDNS
GRAFTON GDNS
DAVID RD
JOAN RD
HITHERFIELD RD
BENTRY RD
BENTRY CL
STOCKDALE RD
GREEN LA
MORRIS RD
DANETTE GDNS
BECONTREE AVE
HOMESTEAD RD
ROWLANDS RD
STONE CL
GRAFTON RD
BOULTON RD
BLOMVILLE RD
ELEANOR GDNS
STANHOPE GDNS
STANHOPE RD
NICHOLAS RD
COOTE RD
COOTE GDNS
BRITTAIN RD
GRAND CT
VEYSEY GDNS
OGLETHORPE RD
VALENCE WOOD RD
CHARLECOTE RD
WINDSOR RD
DARE GDNS
LUCY GDNS
WINMILL RD
WEYLOND RD
VALENCE CIR
HALBUTT GDNS
THOMPSON RD
NORTHFIELD PATH
FIVE ELMS RD
BOXOLL RD
HALBUTT ST
WESTON RD
AIDAN CL
ELMS GDNS
WESTON GN
HUMPHRIES CL
JOYNERS CL
CONNOR RD
BAINBRIDGE RD
ROBINSON RD
MAXEY GDNS
BEVERLEY RD
KIDD HO
ST GEORGES RD
NORTHFIELD RD
OXLOW LA
NORTHFIELD GDNS
KEPPEL RD
CORNWALLIS RD
CAREY RD
VERNEY GDNS
VERNEY RD
MAXEY RD
OSBORNE SQ
EASTFIELD RD
WESTFIELD RD
ST GEORGES RD
RAYDONS GDNS
RAYDONS RD
PASTURE RD
CHERRY GDNS
SPINNEY GDNS
SPRINGPOND RD
PAGE CL
HALBUTT ST
OSBORNE RD
ALBION RD
PARSLOES AVE
MONMOUTH RD
FANSHAWE CRES
BARNMEAD GDNS
BARNMEAD RD
HARRIS RD
KINGSMILL RD
SINGLETON RD
KINGSMILL GDNS
TERRACE WLK
MEADOW WLK
MEADOW RD
AYLOFFE RD
SHORTCROFTS RD
VINERIES CL
SPURLING RD
IVY WLK
IVYHOUSE RD
HUNSDON CL
TILNEY RD
COLEMAN RD
HEDGEMANS WAY
HEDGEMANS RD
TALBOT RD
LLOYD RD
BRETT GDNS
EATON GDNS
WALFREY GDNS
FINNYMORE RD
CARTWRIGHT RD
SHELDON RD
HATFIELD RD
LULLINGTON RD
MORDAUNT GDNS
CHAPLIN RD
PETER BRADLEY CT
DAGENHAM AVE
VINCENT RD
ELSTOW GDNS
ELSTOW RD
TRESWELL RD
GORESBROOK RD
STARMANS CL
THETFORD GDNS
FORD RD
COMYNS RD
DOWNING RD
ROWDOWNS RD
COMBES RD
ARNOLD RD
MORGAN CL
ARMSTEAD WLK
BROAD ST
CAUSTON SQ
BLUEBIRD LA
MORLAND RD
SCHOOL RD
ORCHARD RD
PEARLSTONES CT
GREEN RD
TERLING RD
ALTHORNE WAY
BRADWELL AVE
STOUR RD
TREFGARNE RD
CALVERLEY CRES
STANSGATE RD
MARSTON CL
MARSTON AVE
BRAINTREE RD
UVEDALE RD
KERSHAW RD
LISTOWEL RD
RUSHOLME AVE
DUNBAR AVE
BOYNE RD
NASEBY RD
WYTHENSHAWE RD
BOSWORTH RD
GLENCOE DR
SEDGEMOOR DR
EDGEHILL GDNS
FRIZLANDS LA
POWELL GDNS
EASTFIELD GDNS
HUNTERS SQ
CROPPATH RD
WAYSIDE GDNS
STERRY CRES
STERRY RD
ALIBON RD
ALIBON GDNS
HUNTERS HALL RD
LAKE GDNS
PETTIT'S RD
PETTIT'S PL
BERRY CL
ROGERS RD
ROGERS GDNS
WATERS GDNS
STANDFIELD RD
WITHAM RD
DUNBAR GDNS
HOLGATE RD
STERRY GDNS
STANDFIELD GDNS
ROCKWELL RD
PONDFIELD RD
1 HOLGATE GDNS
2 WHITE GDNS
3 STATION PAR
4 MILLARD TERR
1 ROCK GDNS
2 WELLS GDNS
3 REEDE GDNS
REEDE RD
REEDE WAY
BULL LA
TANNERY CL
SPARROW GN
LAWRENCE CRES
HAMDEN CRES
FELS CL
HICKS CT
CRESCENT RD
PEMBROKE GDNS
TED HENNEM HO
WRIGHTS CL
WEBBSCROFT RD
JORDANS CL
MUGGERIDGE RD
KINGSLEY CL
1 JACOBS CL
2 TED HENNEM HO
3 VENABLES CL
WOODSHIRE RD
CENTRAL PARK AVE
MACDONALD AVE
GREENWOOD AVE
DAGENHAM RD
DELVERS MEAD
EASTBROOK AVE
BURY RD
VICTORIA RD
SURREY RD
NORFOLK RD
SUFFOLK RD
KENT RD
FOXLANDS CRES
CAMBEYS RD
SHAFTER RD
KITCHENER RD
DEWEY RD
EXETER RD
COOPERS CL
LEWIS WAY
RADLEYS MEAD
PAVET CL
BLACKBORNE RD
HARESFIELD RD
HARRISON RD
INGLEBY RD
CHARLOTTE RD
BUTTFIELD CL
HONEY CL
PLUMTREE CL
SALISBURY RD
CROWN ST
WYHILL WLK
CRANE CL
HUNTINGS RD
MANNING RD
CHURCH ELM LA
RECTORY RD
VICARAGE RD
HOLLIDGE WAY
JOHN PARKER CL
CHURCH ST
ST GILES AVE
ST GILES CL
SISTER WAY
CHURCH LA
LANGHORNE RD
MOSS RD
DUNCHURCH HO
THAXTED HO
BROOK AVE
WILTHORNE GDNS
ACRE RD
ROOKERY CRES
BEECH GDNS
BOLEYN GDNS
SANDOWN CT
SOWN AVE
CROWN ST
HIGHLANDS
HARDIE RD
SWELL CL
BALLARDS CL

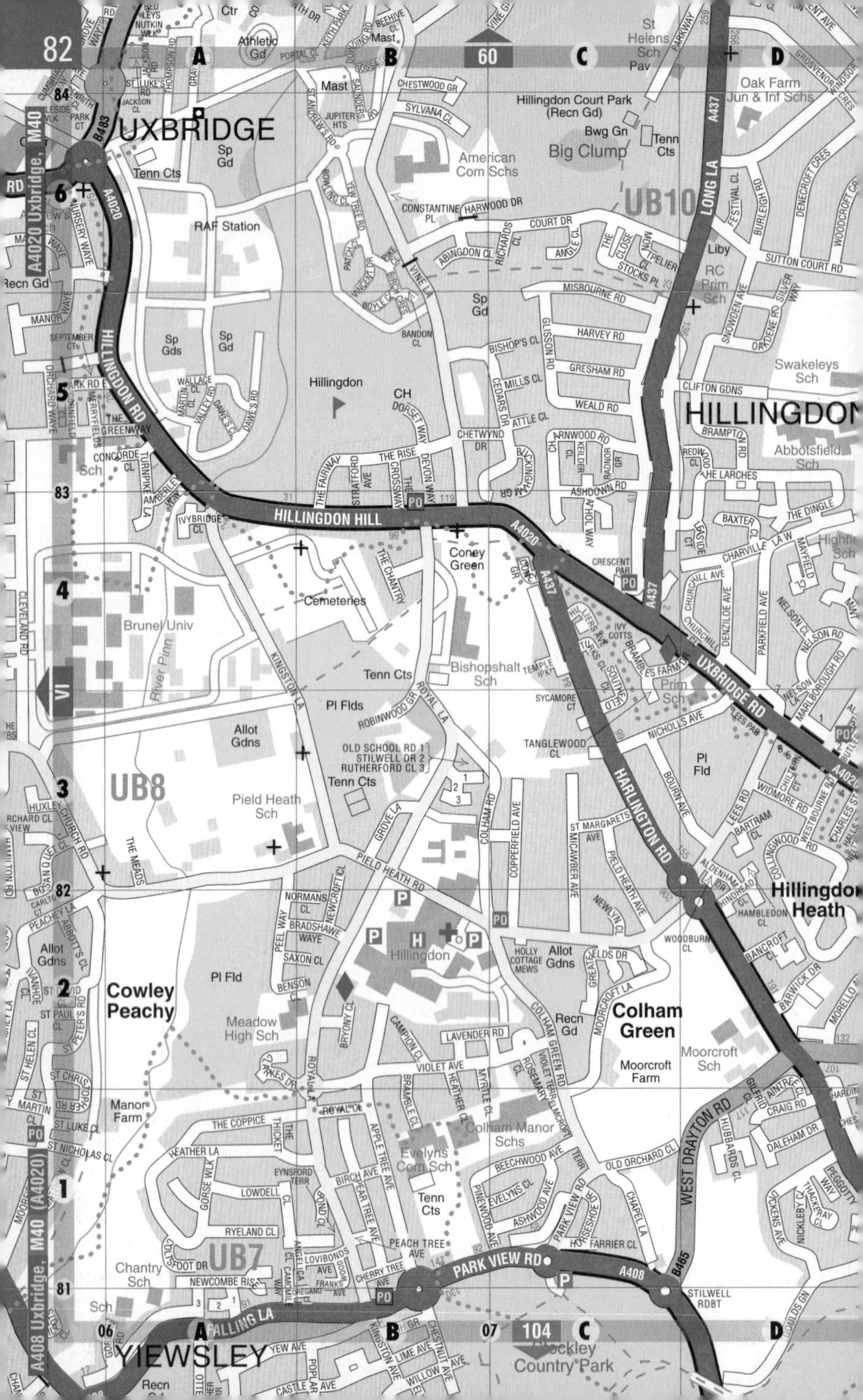
UXBRIDGE
HILLINGDON
Hillingdon Heath
Colham Green
Cowley Peachy
YIEWSLEY
UB10
UB8
UB7
60
104
A4020 Uxbridge, M40
A408 Uxbridge, M40 (A4020)
HILLINGDON RD
HILLINGDON HILL
UXBRIDGE RD
HARLINGTON RD
LONG LA
PARK VIEW RD
FALLING LA
WEST DRAYTON RD
Athletic Gd
St Helens Sch Pav
Hillingdon Court Park (Recn Gd)
Big Clump
American Com Schs
Oak Farm Jun & Inf Schs
RAF Station
Hillingdon CH
Swakeleys Sch
Abbotsfield Sch
Brunel Univ
Cemeteries
Coney Green
Bishopshalt Sch
Pield Heath Sch
Allot Gdns
Hillingdon
Meadow High Sch
Manor Farm
Chantry Sch
Colham Manor Schs
Evelyns Com Sch
Moorcroft Sch
Moorcroft Farm
Stockley Country Park
COURT DR
MISBOURNE RD
HARVEY RD
GRESHAM RD
WEALD RD
SUTTON COURT RD
CLIFTON GDNS
CHARVILLE LA W
NICHOLLS AVE
PIELD HEATH RD
KINGSTON LA
ROYAL LA
COLHAM GREEN RD
VIOLET AVE
THE COPPICE
HEATHER LA
OLD ORCHARD CL
CHAPEL LA
STILWELL RDBT

A
B
61
C
D
84
6
5
4
3
82
2
1
81
10
09
105
UB10
UB4
UB3
UB8
Ryefield Prim Sch
The Gorse
Yeading Brook
Ten Acres (Nature Reserve)
Westways Farm
Lane Covert
Recn Gd
Home Covert
Tenn Cts
Rugby Fball Gd
Hare Plantation
Charville Prim Sch
Ealing
Hillingdon
Allot Gdns
Liby
Hedgewood Specl Sch
Pl Fld
Sp Fld
Hayes Shrub
Hayes Park
Hayes Park Sch
Home Farm
Mellow Lane Sch
Tenn Ct
The Paddocks Farm
Hayes End
Grange Park Jun & Inf Schs
Wood End Green
Pav
Bwg Gn
Beck Theatre
Sp Ctr
Bot Gdns
Wood End
Crkt Gd
Hayes Manor Sch
Sp Stad
HAYES
Town Hall Park
Bndstd
Dr Triplett's CE Prim Sch
Wood End Park Jun & Inf Sch
Fball
RYEFIELD AVE
FLORISTON AVE
BERKELEY RD
MIDHURST GDNS
WILKINSON CL
LEYBOURNE RD
HAZELDENE GDNS
PETWORTH GDNS
COWDRAY RD
LANDSEER CT
GAINSBOROUGH RD
ROMNEY RD
HAYMAN CRES
RAEBURN RD
HEATHERWOOD DR
CHARVILLE LA
ROMNEY PAR
LAWRENCE RD
HOPPNER RD
THE OAKS
TURNER CL
CONSTABLE CL
POLE HILL RD
HARROW VIEW
MELLOW LA W
MELLOW LA E
1 SHERIDAN CL
2 ADDISCOMBE CT
KENDAL CL
ULLSWATER CL
LANGDALE DR
RAYNTON DR
HAYSTALL CL
GROSVENOR AVE
BURY AVE
GOSHAWK GDNS
TRENT WAY
POOLE WAY
SALCOMBE WAY
WEALD WAY
EXMOUTH RD
KENTON WAY
PORTLAND RD
TRURO WAY
BRADENHAM RD
WEYMOUTH RD
LANSBURY DR
DORSET AVE
DORSET CL
KENMORE CRES
ADELPHI CRES
ADELPHI WAY
CHESIL WAY
PERCY GDNS
KINGSHILL AVE
LYNTON WLK 1
KINGSBRIDGE WAY 2
BYRON WAY
DALE DR
BOURNEMEAD CL
CLYDE
KEIR HARDIE
TOWERS CT
STAR RD
STAR CT
BYRON PAR
HEATH RD
SANDRINGHAM CT
HEWENS RD
MEADOW VIEW RD
BLACKLANDS DR
HAYES END DR
DALTON CL
HAYES END RD
MEAD HOUSE LA
FROGMORE GDNS
BLACKPOOL GDNS
WELWYN WAY
PARK LA
MANSFIELD DR
FROGMORE AVE
RAYNTON CL
WOODROW AVE
WARWICK CRES
FEDORA AVE
LEAMINGTON PL
FAIRHOLME CRES
PINE PL
LANSBURY DR
PAGET RD
DE SALIS RD
RUSSET CL
FULHAM CL
CONNAUGHT CL
NEW RD
SIBLEY CT
WEST DRAYTON RD
B465
FOUNTAIN CL
GREEN LA
WILMAR CL
PILLIONS LA
HAYES END CL
NEWPORT RD
WESTCOMBE PARK LO
DERWENT DR
HAVEN CL
HURSTFIELD CRES
WRAYS WAY
BALMORAL DR
CAVENDISH CL
WESTACOTT CL
STOCKDOVE WAY
BURNS CL
MELROSE CL
TITHE CL
GLEDWOOD AVE
GLEDWOOD GDNS
GLEDWOOD DR
GLEDWOOD CRES
GLEDWOOD CT
WHITTINGTON AVE
KEWLWOOD GDNS
WARLEY RD
MARSHALL DR
ABBEYFIELD DR
REGENTS CL
PARK RD
UXBRIDGE RD
A4020
MORGAN'S LA
ROSSLYN CL
ANGEL LA
MELINA CL
DAWSON CL
CHURCH CL
SOUTH WLK
WOODSTOCK HO
PRONTO TRAD EST
KINGSWAY
WAYLANDS
MIDDLETON RD
ROSEDALE AVE
NORTH RD
WOOD END GREEN RD
SAXONY PAR
TUDOR SQ
CAVALIER CIRC
HANOVER GDNS
STUART CRES
NORMANDY DR
TUDOR RD
CRANMER RD
VICTORIA CL
CROMWELL RD
COMMONWEALTH AVE
LANCASTER WLK
BISHOP'S RD
YORK AVE
WHITE HEART AVE
WEST DRAYTON RD
LONSDALE CL
CROMER CL
LANSDOWNE RD
CORWELL LA
TITMUS CL
CORWELL GDNS
ST JEROME'S GR
GRANGE CL
GRANGE RD
ELM AVE
ALBION RD
QUEENS RD
WOOD END
LEVEN WAY
BOTWELL CRES
BOTWELL LA
CHURCH WLK
PARSONAGE CL
SWIFT CL
ACACIA AVE
FULWOOD CL
CEDAR AVE
ELM AVE
RECTORY RD
ADDISON WAY
MANOR RD
BELMORE
COLERIDGE WAY
ARLINGTON RD
A437
1 PEAR TREE HO
2 CONFERENCE HO
JUDGE HEATH LA
BURBAGE CL
LILAC GDNS
PARK PAR
BARRA HALL CIRC
CHURCH RD
LYCH GATE WLK
KELF GR
HEMMEN LA
KERSTIN CL
ST MARY'S CRES
CHAPEL CT
ST MARY'S RD
CHILDS CT
WHEATLEY CRES
NORTH HYDE
PRINCES PARK AVE
PRINCES PARK CL
PRINCES PARK PAR
PRINCES PARK LA
VOLTAIRE WAY 1
MARRINER CT 2
ASH GR
BEECHWOOD AVE
DALLEGA CL
DAWLEY PAR
LIME GR
JUNIPER
BARRA
SYCAMORE AVE
PARKSIDE
FREEMANS LA
MANTON CL
ORCHARD
Uxbridge Coll

A
B
62
C
D
London Ctr
Bwg Gn
Tenn Cts
Sp Gd
Peacock Park
Pl Fld
WEST END RD
Hillingdon
Ealing
HARVEY RD
Yeading Brook
Ten Acres (Nature Reserve)
UB4
Downe Barns Farm
SHARVEL LA
CH
UB5
COMPTON CRES
HEARN RISE
IRVING AVE
LAUGHTON RD
HENSON PL
LAING DEAN
MAURIER CL
PERRY GARTH
Westways Farm Lane Covert
Lime Tree Park
VANBROUGH CRES
ARLISS WAY
BANCROFT CT
THORNDIKE AVE
West London Shooting Grounds
RUISLIP RD
LAUDER CL
RUBENS RD
LYNNE WAY
HAWTREY AVE
NEWDENE AVE
Allot Gdns
BEVERLEY CT 1
POPLAR CT 2
1 BUTTS PIECE
2 BOURNEMEAD WAY
3 ELGIN HO
4 HARTFIELD HO
BOWER CL
OLD RUISLIP RD
GRANGE CT
St Raphael's RC Prim Sch
TREVOR GDNS
BARN CL
EDWARD RD
TANGMERE GDNS
WATERY LA
NUTFIELD GDNS
A4180
A312
White Hart Rdbt
B455
PO
TOWNSON WAY
BOURNEMEAD AVE
HARTFIELD AVE
TOWNSON AVE
TITHE BARN WAY
DOWN CL
REDMAN CL
RUSHDENE CL
BANKSIDE AVE
LONGHOOK GDNS
DOWN WAY
RAYNERS GDNS
RUSHDENE CRES
WEST END GDNS
BEAUVAIS TERR
BOURNEMEAD CL
Sp Fld
Pl Fld
KINGSHILL AVE
RAYNERS CRES
Downe Manor Prim Sch
GURNEY RD
HUGHENDEN GDNS
BROOMCROFT AVE
RADCLIFFE WAY
KNOLE CT
Viking Fst & Mid Sch
ATTLEE RD
ATTLEE CL
AYLES CT
PHILLIPS CT
BONDFIELD AVE
WEBBS RD
MORRISON RD
OWEN RD
BRYANT RD
HUGHENDEN RD
YEADING LA
CANBERRA DR
AUDLEY CT
UFTON CT
DEHAVILLAND CL
CLYNES HO 1
KEIR HARDIE WAY 2
HENDERSON RD
BEVIN RD
AYLES RD
WOLFE CL
Belmore Prim Sch
Sch
MAPLE RD
MAPLE CL
KINGSHILL AVE
RAYNTON DR
JASON HO 1
OWEN CL 2
OWEN CT 3
ATTLEE CT 4
MILNER HO 5
GROVES HO 6
OTTAWA HO 7
MONTCALM CL 8
MONTREAL HO 9
ALBERTA HO 10
MELBOURNE HO 1
HAWKE CT 2
SYDNEY CT 3
NAPIER CT 4
CHRISTCHURCH CT 5
AUCKLAND CT 6
LYTTLETON CT 7
WESTPORT CT 8
BARNHILL CT
VANCOUVER RD
GREENWAY
WELBECK AVE
BARNHILL LA
BARNHILL RD
PERTH AVE
Brookside Prim Sch
HOBART DR
HOBART LA
HOBART RD
HOBART CL
LEAMINGTON PL
FAIRHOLME CRES
WINNIPEG HO 1
WELBECK CT 2
GREENWAY CT 3
SHERWOOD AVE
STRATFORD RD
CRIPPS GN
CHATSWORTH RD
WESTBOURNE CL
MASEFIELD LA
YEADING CT
DUNEDIN WAY
NORWOOD GDNS
MIDDLE WAY
DOUGLAS CRES
Yeading
FREDORA AVE
PINE PL
BARNARD GDNS
ERROL GDNS
REYNOLDS RD
HARRIES RD
NORCOTT CL
MARIAN CL
FRIAR RD
LANSBURY DR
Grange Park Jun & Inf Schs
Allot Gdns
SHAKESPEARE AVE
AVON CL
WILLOW TREE LA
WILLOW TREE CL
HOMEFIELD CL
CEDAR HO
YEADING HO
ROSE PARK CL
YEADING FORK
ELGAR HO
MIMOSA RD
HORNBEAM RD
SULLIVAN CL
LARCH CRES
NORTHCOTE AVE
BEECH HO
BURNS CL
MIMOSA HO 1
HAMBROUGH HO 2
FEATHERSTONE HO 3
WAKLOW HO 4
LARCH HO
MELROSE CL
SHELLEY CL
MARVELL AVE
KEATS CL
LOTHIAN AVE
UB4
THE PARKWAY
Vehicle Testing Sta & Driving Test Ctr
TITHE CL
GLEDWOOD DR
GLEDWOOD AVE
BALMORAL DR
JONSON CL
WYATT CL
RALEIGH AVE
FINDHORN AVE
WARREN CL
Yeading Brook
DORMERS WELLS HO
PINTAIL WAY
1 EIDER CL
2 HARLEQUIN CL
3 CURLEW WAY
4 SPOONBILL WAY
GLEDWOOD CRES
GLEDWOOD GDNS
WARLEY RD
CHAUCER AVE
SHAKESPEARE AVE
SELAN GDNS
EDMUNDS CL
Allot Gdns
Pl Fld
KITTIWAKE WAY
SAWBILL CL
BITTERN CL
BURNDELL WAY
MARSHALL
ABBEYFIELD DR
SPENCER AVE
DUNBAR CL
YEADING GDNS
CARLYON RD
Yeading Jun & Inf Schs
WEPHAM CL
HOLLYWOOD GDNS
BEDFORD AVE
Liby
YEADING LA
SHAFTESBURY WAYE
Warren Park
CYGNET WAY
WHIMBREL WAY
PLOVER WAY
MANDARIN WAY
A4020
WARLEY AVE
MILTON CL
BELMORE AVE
COLERIDGE WAY
CHEDDAR WAYE
SHEARWATER WAY 1
GREBE AVE 2
LAPWING WAY 3
IBIS WAY 4
End
SWIFT CL
ACACIA AVE
CRAVEN CL
THE WARREN
FORSTERS WAY
WIMBORNE AVE
LULWORTH WAYE
SHERBORNE CL
STURMINSTER CL
CARLYON RD
Grand Union Canal Walk
WIGEON WAY
Pl Fld
Dr Triplett's CE Prim Sch
CEDAR AVE
ELM CL
ADDISON WAY
SUTCLIFFE HO
LANGWORTH DR
DORCHESTER WAYE
CORFE CL
BLANDFORD WAYE
SWANAGE WAYE
Pav
Tenn Cts
RECTORY RD
MANOR RD
UB3
HARROW VIEW
UXBRIDGE RD
A4020
CRANBORNE WAYE
MINTERNE WAYE
ASHFORD AVE
ASHFORD AVE
HEMMEN LA
WESLEY RD
DEVONSHIRE WAY
A312
DORCHESTER WAYE
BERWICK AVE
BERWICK AVE
KERSTIN CL
ST MARY'S CRES
CHILDS CT
HESA RD
HARDING HO
LOMBARDY RET PK
CRANBORNE WAYE
BROOKSIDE RD
QUEBEC RD
CAMDEN AVE
CHAPEL CT
WHEATLY CRES
NORTHOLT AVE
MABEL EVETTS CT
ST CHRISTOPHER'S DR
Superstore
11
106
CERNE CL
LONGFORD CL
DELAMERE RD
TOLLGATE DR
ST MARY'S WLK
Uxbridge Coll
DAMSON DR
COLLEGE WAY
ORCHARD
OSSIE GARVIN RDBT
UXBRIDGE RD
Academy Gdns
Gallery Gdns
Parkfield
Delta Gr
Javelin Way
Friendship Wlk
Fellowes
Paddington Cl
Brentford Cl
Glencoe Rd
Repens Way
Stipularis Dr
Ramulis Dr
Lapponum Wlk
Pendula Dr
Triandra Way
Capreaa Cl

NORTHOLT
GREENFORD
Dormer's Wells
63
107
84
83
98
82
81
A
B
C
D
1
2
3
4
5
6
UB5
UB6
UB1
A40
A312
B455
A4127
CHURCH RD
WESTERN AVE
RUISLIP RD
Target Rdbt
John Chilton Sch
Walford High Sch
Belvue Park
Belvue Sch
Golf Range
Grand Union Canal Paddington Branch
Grand Union Canal Wk
Smith's Farm
Superstore
Fball Gd
Pl Fld
Pav
Rectory Park
Gifford Prim Sch
CH
Ravenor Prim Sch
Ravenor Park
Greenford High Sch
Sp Ctr
Crkt Gd
King George's Field
Tenn Cts
Sp Fld
Allot Gdns
T Ct
Liby
Schs
Recn Gd
Cemy
Lady Margaret Prim Sch
Durdans Park Prim Sch
Jubilee Park
Marina
Sp Gd
Mini Glf Crs
Bwg Gn
Ath Gd
Allenby Inf Sch
Dormer's Wells High Sch
Mount Pleasant L Gdns
Tudor Prim Sch
Hillingdon
Ealing
PO
1 JACQUELINE CL
2 HAWTHORN FARM AVE
3 ASHLEY CT
4 BEECH CT
5 CHICHESTER CT
6 PENTLAND PL
7 BUCKINGHAM CT
8 KENTFORD WAY
1 LINGFIELD CT
2 HERMES WLK
3 BANBURY WLK
4 MERSEY WLK
5 STAR PATH
6 CONDOR PATH
7 HAMBLE WLK
8 CATHAY WLK
1 ARROW SCOUT WLK
2 CHIPMUNK GR
3 CONCORD CL
4 DAKOTA GDNS
5 MONTGOLFIER WLK
6 BEAVER GR
7 FLAMINGO GDNS
8 SEALAND WLK
9 GEMINI GR
10 NEWSTEAD CT
11 PINE CT
12 REDWOOD CT
13 MAYTREE CT
1 WILSTONE CL
2 DUNSMORE CL
3 NAPTON CL
4 HELMSDALE CL
5 PIKESTONE CL
6 COULTER CL
7 CHIRK CL
8 BLISWORTH CL
1 PRESTWICK CT
2 DENHAM CT
3 FULWELL CT
4 BRAMLEY CT
5 SAUNTON CT
6 ST ANDREW'S TWR
DUKES
HAREWOOD CL
HAREWOOD AVE
OR AVE
NEY GDNS
VICARAGE
KINGSTON CL
CARISBROOKE CT
ESKDALE AVE
RECTORY GDNS
MOWBRAY GDNS
WESTWAY CT
EALING RD
FARM RD
FORT RD
ROWDELL RD
TAUNTON RD
FAIRWAY DR
DERBY RD
GREENFORD IND EST
HALIFAX RD
BRIDPORT RD
NORWICH RD
BRISTOL RD
FIELD WAY
LONG DR
CHARTWELL CL
STANLEY AVE
LINCOLN CL
JEYMER DR
OLYMPIC WAY
NORSEMAN WAY
BISHOPS DR
MOORLANDS
GODFREY AVE
GARDEN CL
HINDHEAD GDNS
NIGEL CL
SARAH CT
GULLIVER CL
CANFORD AVE
LILLIPUT AVE
SYCAMORE CL
CLIFFORD RD
MAKEPEACE RD
HUXLEY CL
JAMES CT
PARKFIELD CL
PARKFIELD RD
MULBERRY CL
HAZELMERE WLK
HAZELMERE CL
HAZELMERE RD
HAZELMERE DR
DOLPHIN RD
SWALLOW DR
KENSINGTON RD
HORSE SHOE CRES
STABLE CL
PADDOCK CL
MEADOW CL
OLD BRIDGE CL
FARRIER RD
HOTSPUR RD
UNION RD
LEANDER RD
BRABAZON RD
PUMP CL
GREENHILL TERR
GREENHILL GDNS
ELM TREE CL
TOWNEY MEAD
TOWNEY MEAD CT
SHADWELL CT
RECTORY PARK AVE
SHADWELL DR
WATERSIDE CL
HOME CL
COURT MEAD
THORN CL
CRAWFORD GDNS
MARLEY CL
FISHER CL
GOSLING CL
ROSEDENE AVE
FERRYMEAD AVE
FERRYMEAD DR
GREENWAY GDNS
CROSSMEAD AVE
BEECHWOOD AVE
EASTMEAD AVE
DACRE CL
EVESHAM CL
CHESTERTON CL
NICHOLAS CL
BLEDLOW RISE
MELROSE AVE
MELROSE CL
ALEXANDRA CT
MARNHAM CRES
MILLET RD
CHINNOR CRES
WEST RIDGE GDNS
FERRYMEAD GDNS
HEDGERLEY GDNS
PENN CL
BARNHAM RD
GREENFORD GDNS
RAVENOR PARK RD
ARGUS WAY
HIGHVIEW
BYRON WAY
INVICTA GR
ABBEY CL
BRUNEL CL
TAYWOOD RD
DOWNSIDE WLK
HAZELTREE LA
ASPEN LA
STAR RD
FARER RD
WOODSTOCK AVE
ADRIENNE AVE
CORALINE CL
KENILWORTH GDNS
HADFIELD CL
FRESHWATER CT
STICKLETON CL
MAGNOLIA CT
HARCASTLE CL
SENTINEL CL
BRAUNSTON DR
BROADMEAD RD
HASTOE CL
BERRYDALE RD
DOVER
FRENSHAM CL
NEAL AVE
BALMORAL DR
ENMORE RD
TOWERS RD
ALLENBY CL
ALLENBY RD
VERULAM RD
LYNDHURST RD
PEMBROKE RD
ANDOVER CL
RUISLIP CL
RAVENOR CT
AVON CT
AVON RD
BRAUND AVE
HILLSIDE RD
CRESSAGE CL
LAWSON RD
ROSE GDNS
LYRIC DR
WARREN DR
GARRICK RD
DARRIS CL
STRONE WAY
RODWELL CL
WESTLAKE CL
DITCHFIELD RD
ACER AVE
LABURNUM GR
RUTLAND RD
WESTBURY AVE
SELBY GDNS
ROSECROFT RD
UPPER TOWN RD
MORNINGTON RD
ELLESMERE RD
BYCROFT RD
SUNNYCROFT RD
FERMOY RD
MANSELL RD
PURCELL RD
PORTLAND CRES
MAPLE GR
DEVONSHIRE RD
WINDERMERE RD
CEDAR GR
ASH GR
WINDMILL LA
KENNET DR
TELFORD WAY
MARSWORTH CL
GLENORCHY CL
FOSSDYKE CL
KILPATRICK WAY
CAMBUS CL
SHARPNESS CL
ENCOE RD
AIRDRIE CL
PATCHING WAY
WEST QUAY DR
MARINA APP
LYMINSTER CL
ASCOT GDNS
HART GR
SOMERSET RD
DORELL CL
LADY MARGARET RD
CORNWALL AVE
ST PETER'S RD
JUBILEE GDNS
DALES RD
KEATS WAY
HURLEY RD
CANTERBURY CL
BARBICAN RD
BASSETT WAY
QUEEN'S AVE
THE GROVE
PRINCE'S AVE
KING'S AVE
KINGSBRIDGE CRES
CRANLEIGH GARDENS IND EST
CRAVEN AVE
LYNWOOD GDNS
ST STEPHEN'S CL
ST CRISPIN'S CL
ST URSULA RD
DERWENT RD
LONGBOAT ROW
CRANLEIGH GDNS
FAIRFIELD RD
SUTHERLAND RD
EVELYN GR
TRING AVE
DENBIGH CL
STRATTON GDNS
ALLENDALE AVE
KELVIN GDNS
MANATON CRES
WAXLOW CRES
DENBIGH RD
DURDANS RD
DORMER'S AVE
LOVELL RD
WHITTLE CL
WALLIS RD
SWAN RD
DARWIN DR
HOWARD RD
NEWCOMEN RD
FLEMING RD
EDISON DR
MARCONI WAY
LONGRIDGE LA
DORMERS RISE
WHITECOTE RD
LANE RD
REDCROFT RD
CRANLEIGH CT
CHEPSTOW GDNS
BRITTEN DR
PURCELL HO
MOUNT AVE
THURSTON RD
TELFORD RD
FARADAY RD
SHELLEY CRES
NORTH PAR
GREENFIELDS
MASEFIELD AVE
DORMER'S WELLS LA
FARM
BRINDLEY WAY
PANHARD PL
SHERINGHAM TWR
BAIRD AVE
ORCHID CL
SPIKES BRIDGE RD
SAHARA CT
MARIGOLD CL
FOXGLOVE CL
HONEYSUCKLE CL
LANCASTER RD
JASMINE CL
VIKING RD
NORMAN AVE
CARLYLE AVE
CARLYLE GDNS
WEST AVE
SAXON GDNS
EAST AVE
SOUTHALL CT
FREDERICK HO
NORTH RD
WOODLANDS
NORTH AVE
BURNS AVE
WAVERLEY RD
KENTON AVE
LOWDEN RD
DANE RD
Dormer's Wells

A
B
C
D
64
108
84
85
6
5
4
3
2
1
83
82
81
14
15
Greenford
GREENFORD
Ravenor Park
UB6
W7
FAIRWAY DR
STATION APP
ALLINGTON CL
HILL RISE
BELLE VUE
STATION VIEW
OLDFIELD LA N
ROCKWARE AVE
A4127
WESTWAY CROSS SH PK
Grand Union Canal Walk
Perivale Wood
TAUNTON RD
HALIFAX RD
NORWICH RD
BRISTOL RD
LONG DR
CHARTWELL CL
STANLEY AVE
LINCOLN CL
JEYMER DR
BIRKBECK AVE
BIRKBECK WAY
HILLBECK WAY
PEACE CL
WEST GREEN PL
UNEEDA DR
Allot Gdns
Tenn Cts
Pav
Oldfield Recn Gd
Sp Gd
Fball Gd
Bwg Gn
OLYMPIC WAY
NORSEMAN WAY
COMMUNITY RD
OLDFIELD FARM GDNS
INGRAM WAY
BENNETTS AVE
LYON WAY
LEGION RD
COURTHOPE RD
DOWNING DR
MIDDLETON AVE
A40
DACRE CL
NICHOLAS CL
Oldfield Prim Sch
CHARTRES CT
KAROLINE GDNS
Greenford Rdbt
WESTERN AVE
DARYNGTON DR
RUNNYMEDE GDNS
CAYTON RD
CONWAY CRES
Selborne Prim Sch
WOODHOUSE CL
WOODHOUSE AVE
TEES AVE
THAMES AVE
MEDWAY DR
SUEZ AVE
HODDER DR
BARMOUTH AVE
CALDER AVE
COLWYN AVE
WELLAND GDNS
MELROSE AVE
CHINNOR CRES
BLEDLOW RISE
WEST CL
HENLEY CL
EAST CL
FAIRLIGHT CT
MILLET RD
MARNHAM CRES
WEST RIDGE GDNS
FERRYMEAD GDNS
ORMESBY GDNS
GORING WAY
HEDGERLEY GDNS
PENN CL
Edward Betham Prim Sch
Coston Prim Sch
Pl Fld
WORDSWORTH AVE
BLENHEIM CL
WESSEX LA
WHITEOAKS LA
LEAVER GDNS
DAVID AVE
ANTHONY RD
HICKS AVE
South Greenford
MILL CL
RIBCHESTER AVE
WYRESDALE CRES
B452
BARNHAM RD
FARNDALE CRES
T Ct
GREENFORD GDNS
OLDFIELD LA S
BROOKFIELD CT
COSTONS LA
SILVERTREE LA
COWGATE RD
PENIFATHER LA
HOWCROFT LA
COSTONS AVE
SHELLEY AVE
SHELLEY CL
1 CARROWAY LA
2 DEEPWOOD LA
Sp Arena
CH
STOCKDOVE WAY
PEEL CT
RAVENOR PARK RD
Litten Nature Reserve
CROYDE AVE
Liby
PARK RD
STANHOPE PARK RD
GREENFORD RD
OAKFIELD GDNS
WEDMORE RD
BETHAM RD
Perivale Park
Gurnell Swimming Pool
L Ctr
PEMBROKE RD
ANDOVER CL
B455
THE BROADWAY
LOCARNO RD
CLIFTON RD
RUISLIP RD E
GURNELL GR
Bwg Gn
LYRIC DR
WARREN DR
GARRICK RD
Schs
OTTER RD
PO
Sch
BRENTSIDE CL
ANGLESEY CT
Brentside High Sch
Brentside Prim Sch
HARP RD
KENNEDY PATH
BRANTS WLK
Recn Gd
ELLESMERE RD
BINGLEY RD
FERMOY RD
MANSELL RD
PORTLAND CRES
STANHOPE RD
WINDMILL LA
The Cardinal Wiseman RC Sch
Depot
BROOKBANK AVE
ELMBANK WAY
CUCKOO DENE
GIFFORD GDNS
BEECHMOUNT AVE
BERESFORD AVE
MAYFIELD GDNS
BRIDGE AVE
KENNEDY RD
ELFWINE RD
LAURIE RD
HILLYARD RD
ROLLAND HO
BORDARS WLK
BORDARS RD
CUCKOO AVE
UPFIELD RD
GREATDOWN RD
COPLEY CL
Prim Sch
Castle Bar Park
ELLIS CT
TEMPLEMAN RD
WAKELING RD
WESTCOTT CRES
ALCOTT CL
LALE CRES
BENHAM RD
HALE WLK
HALL DR
SHARPE CL
RADNOR CT
SHROPSHIRE CT
SOMERSET CT
STAFFORD CT
WARWICK CT
WORCESTER CT
Drayton Green
HURLEY RD
Cemy
CANTERBURY CL
BARBICAN RD
PRINCE'S AVE
QUEEN'S AVE
THE GROVE
KING'S AVE
Mayfield Prim Sch
COLNE CT 1
DEE CT 2
HUMBER CT 3
IRWELL CT 4
TEES CT 5
HIGH LA
HOBBAYNE RD
HANWAY RD
LYTTE CT
TWEED CT
HIGHLAND AVE
STUDLAND RD
THOMAS CT
GREENFORD AVE
STEPHENSON RD
LITTLEJOHN RD
HOMEFARM RD
FRAMFIELD RD
BROWNING AVE
WESTVIEW
GROVE AVE
River Brent
DARWIN DR
HOWARD RD
OSBORNE RD
EDISON DR
MARCONI WAY
FLEMING RD
LONGRIDGE LA
DORMERS RISE
WHITECOTE RD
HALDANE RD
REDROFT RD
HAWTHORNE MEWS
Brent Valley
Hobbayne Prim Sch
Drayton Manor High Sch
DRYDEN AVE
ELMWOOD GDNS
DRAYTON BRIDGE RD
PARK RD
COWPER RD
SHAKESPEARE RD
MILTON RD
FARADAY RD
PANHARD PL
SHERINGHAM TWR
BAIRD AVE
Sp Gd
ADHILL
CHURCH RD
CUCKOO LA
APRIL CL
BRENT CT
GLEBE CT
SPRING CT
BRIERLEY CT
OAKLEY
LIME TERR
HIGHTREES
GOLDEN
1 PRESTWICK CT
2 DENHAM CT
3 FULWELL CT
4 BRAMLEY CT
5 SAUNTON CT
6 ST ANDREW'S TWR
Dormer's Wells

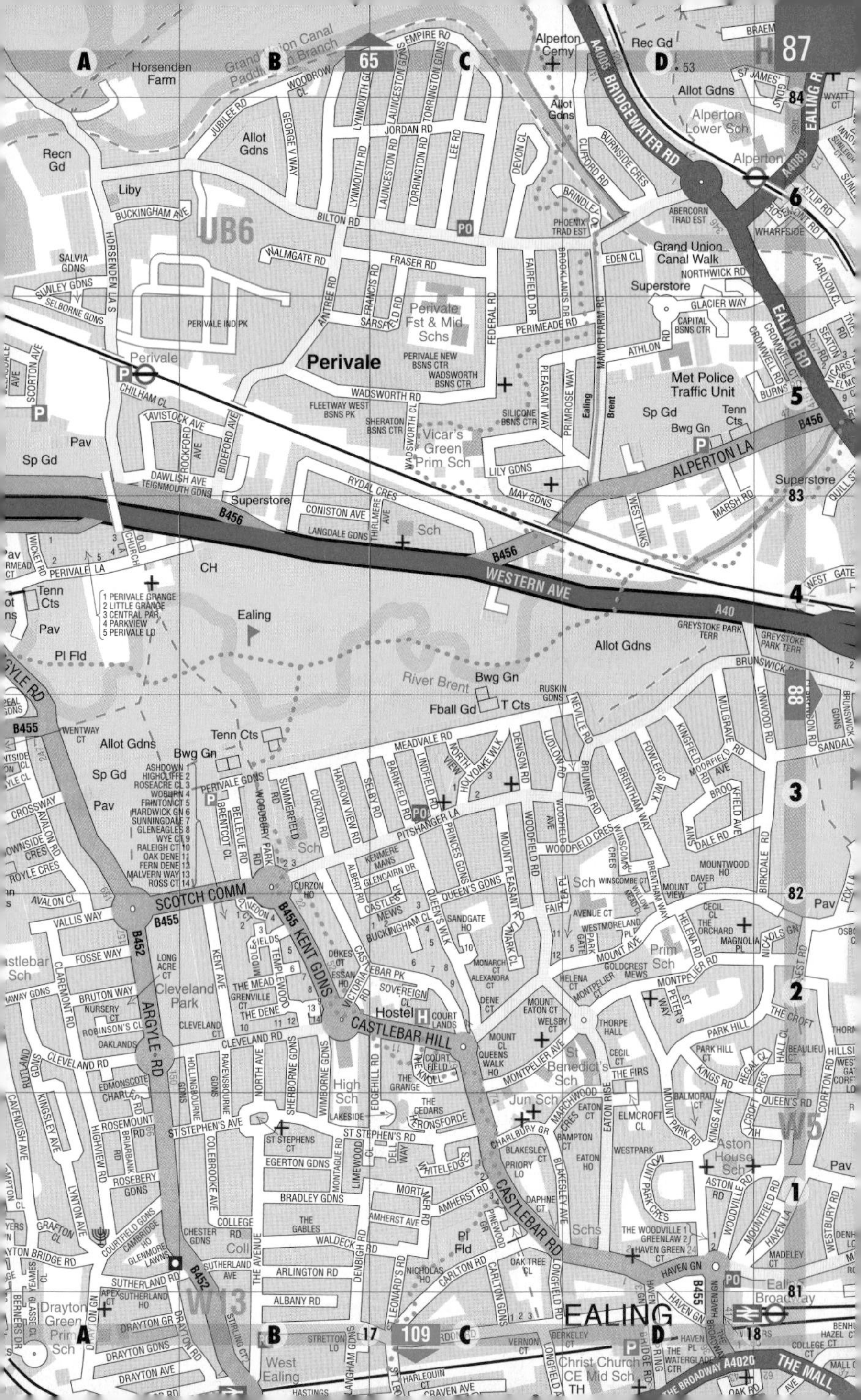

A
B
C
D
65
Horsenden Farm
Grand Union Canal Paddington Branch
Alperton Cemy
Rec Gd
53
Allot Gdns
Alperton Lower Sch
Alperton
EMPIRE RD
WOODROW CL
JUBILEE RD
GEORGE V WAY
LYNMOUTH RD
LAUNCESTON GDNS
TORRINGTON GDNS
JORDAN RD
LAUNCESTON RD
TORRINGTON RD
LEE RD
DEVON CL
A4005 BRIDGEWATER RD
BURNSIDE CRES
CLIFFORD RD
BRINDLEY CL
EALING RD
A4089
ATLIP RD
ROSEMONT RD
WHARFSIDE
ST JAMES' GDNS
WYATT CT
84
Recn Gd
Liby
BUCKINGHAM AVE
UB6
BILTON RD
PO
PHOENIX TRAD EST
ABERCORN TRAD EST
Grand Union Canal Walk
EDEN CL
NORTHWICK RD
Superstore
GLACIER WAY
CAPITAL BSNS CTR
ATHLON RD
CARLYON CL
SALVIA GDNS
SUNLEY GDNS
SELBORNE GDNS
HORSENDEN LA S
WALMGATE RD
FRASER RD
ANTREE RD
FRANCIS RD
SARSFIELD RD
Perivale Fst & Mid Schs
FEDERAL RD
FAIRFIELD DR
BROOKLANDS DR
MANOR FARM RD
PERIMEADE RD
PERIVALE IND PK
Perivale
PERIVALE NEW BSNS CTR
WADSWORTH BSNS CTR
WADSWORTH RD
FLEETWAY WEST BSNS PK
SHERATON BSNS CTR
WADSWORTH CL
SILICONE BSNS CTR
PLEASANT WAY
PRIMROSE WAY
Ealing
Brent
Met Police Traffic Unit
Sp Gd
Tenn Cts
Bwg Gn
CROMWELL RD
SEATON CL
VICARS BRIDGE CL
BURNS
5
B456
ALPERTON LA
SCORTON AVE
CHILHAM CL
TAVISTOCK AVE
ROCKFORD AVE
BIDEFORD AVE
Pav
Sp Gd
Vicar's Green Prim Sch
LILY GDNS
MAY GDNS
WEST LINKS
MARSH RD
Superstore
83
QUILL ST
DAWLISH AVE
TEIGNMOUTH GDNS
Superstore
RYDAL CRES
CONISTON AVE
THIRLMERE AVE
LANGDALE GDNS
Sch
B456
WESTERN AVE
A40
OLD CHURCH LA
WICKET RD
PERIVALE LA
CH
4
WEST GATE
Tenn Cts
1 PERIVALE GRANGE
2 LITTLE GRANGE
3 CENTRAL PAR
4 PARKVIEW
5 PERIVALE LO
Ealing
Pav
Pl Fld
GREYSTOKE PARK TERR
Allot Gdns
River Brent
Bwg Gn
RUSKIN GDNS
BRUNSWICK RD
Fball Gd
T Cts
88
ARGYLE RD
B455
WENTWAY CT
Allot Gdns
Tenn Cts
Bwg Gn
MEADVALE RD
NORTH VIEW
HOLYOAKE WLK
DENISON RD
LUDLOW RD
NEVILLE RD
BRUNNER RD
BRENTHAM WAY
FOWLER'S WLK
KINGSFIELD RD
MULGRAVE RD
LYNWOOD RD
MOORFIELD RD
BROOKFIELD AVE
AINSDALE RD
3
Sp Gd
Pav
ASHDOWN 1
HIGHCLIFFE 2
ROSEACRE CL 3
WOBURN 4
FRINTON CT 5
HARDWICK GN 6
SUNNINGDALE 7
GLENEAGLES 8
WYE CT 9
RALEIGH CT 10
OAK DENE 11
FERN DENE 12
MALVERN WAY 13
ROSS CT 14
PERIVALE GDNS
WOODBURY PARK RD
SUMMERFIELD RD
CURZON RD
HARROW VIEW RD
SELBY RD
BARNFIELD RD
LINDFIELD RD
PITSHANGER LA
PRINCES GDNS
MOUNT PLEASANT RD
WOODFIELD RD
WOODFIELD CRES
WINSCOMBE CRES
BRENTCOT CL
BELLEVUE RD
Sch
CROSSWAY
AVALON RD
DOWNSIDE CRES
ROYLE CRES
AVALON CL
VALLIS WAY
SCOTCH COMM
B455
CURZON HO
KENMERE MANS
GLENCAIRN DR
ALBERT RD
CASTLEBAR MEWS
QUEEN'S GDNS
SANDGATE HO
Sch
WINSCOMBE CT
MOUNT VIEW
DAVER CT
MOUNTWOOD HO
BIRKDALE RD
82
Pav
B452
FOSSE WAY
LONG ACRE CT
KENT AVE
B455 KENT GDNS
TEMPLEWOOD
BUCKINGHAM CL
QUEEN'S WLK
MONARCH CT
ALEXANDRA CT
AVENUE CT
WESTMORELAND PL
MOUNT AVE
GOLDCREST MEWS
Prim Sch
HELENA RD
CECIL CL
THE ORCHARD
MAGNOLIA PL
Castlebar Sch
CLAREMONT RD
BRUTON WAY
NURSERY CT
ROBINSON'S CL
OAKLANDS
Cleveland Park
THE MEAD
GRENVILLE CT
THE DENE
DUKES CT
ESSAN HO
CASTLEBAR PK
SOVEREIGN CL
Hostel
COURTLANDS
DENE CT
HELENA CT
MONTPELIER CT
MONTPELIER RD
ST PETER'S WAY
2
THE CROFT
CLEVELAND CT
CLEVELAND RD
CASTLEBAR HILL
MOUNT EATON CT
WELSBY CT
THORPE HALL
PARK HILL
PARK HILL CT
HALL CL
BEAULIEU CT
RUTLAND GDNS
CLEVELAND RD
ARGYLE RD
HOLLINGBOURNE GDNS
RAVENSBOURNE GDNS
NORTH AVE
SHERBORNE GDNS
WIMBORNE GDNS
EDGEHILL RD
COURTFIELD
THE KNOLL
THE GRANGE
MOUNT CL
QUEENS WALK HO
MONTPELIER AVE
St Benedict's Sch
CECIL CT
THE FIRS
KINGS RD
REGAL CT
QUEEN'S WALK
CORFTON RD
EDMONSCOTE
CHARLES RD
High Sch
LAKESIDE
THE CEDARS
HERONSFORDE
Jun Sch
MARCHWOOD CRES
EATON CT
EATON RISE
ELMCROFT CL
BALMORAL CT
KINGS AVE
LYNCROFT CRES
CAVENDISH AVE
KINGSLEY AVE
HIGHVIEW RD
ROSEMOUNT RD
BRIARBANK RD
ST STEPHEN'S AVE
COLEBROOKE AVE
ST STEPHENS CT
ST STEPHEN'S RD
CHARLBURY GR
BAMPTON CT
WESTPARK
MOUNT PARK RD
W5
Aston House Sch
ROSEBERY GDNS
EGERTON GDNS
MONTAGUE RD
LIMEWOOD CL
DELL WAY
WHITELEDGES
BLAKESLEY CT
PRIORY LO
EATON HO
MOUNT PARK CRES
ASTON RD
WOODVILLE RD
MOUNTFIELD RD
HAVEN LA
WESTBURY RD
Pav
1
LYNTON AVE
BRADLEY GDNS
MORTIMER RD
AMHERST RD
CASTLEBAR RD
DAPHNE CT
BLAKESLEY AVE
GRAFTON CL
COURTFIELD GDNS
CAMBRIDGE HO
CHESTER GDNS
COLLEGE RD
THE GABLES
AMHERST AVE
WALDECK RD
Pl Fld
PINEWOOD GR
Schs
THE WOODVILLE 1
GREENLAW 2
HAVEN GREEN CT
MADELEY CT
DRAYTON BRIDGE RD
GLENMORE LAWNS
SUTHERLAND AVE
Coll
THE AVENUE
ARLINGTON RD
DENBIGH RD
NICHOLAS HO
CARLTON RD
CARLTON GDNS
OAK TREE CL
LONGFIELD RD
HAVEN GN
B455
PO
Ealing Broadway
81
SUTHERLAND RD
APEX CT
SUTHERLAND HO
Drayton Green Prim Sch
DRAYTON GN
W13
B452
ALBANY RD
ST LEONARD'S RD
EALING
HAVEN GN
HAVEN GN
THE BROADWAY
DRAYTON GR
DRAYTON RD
STIRLING CT
DRAYTON GDNS
DRAYTON AVE
STRETTON LO
LANGHAM GDNS
17
109
VERNON CT
BERKELEY CT
SPRING BRIDGE RD
HAVEN PL
THE WATERGLADE CTR
18
COLLEGE CT
HAZEL CT
BENHALE CT
MALL CT
West Ealing
HARLEQUIN CT
CRAVEN AVE
HASTINGS
Christ Church CE Mid Sch
TH
THE BROADWAY A4020
THE MALL
OAK RD
BERNERS DR
YEAMES CL
GLASSE CL

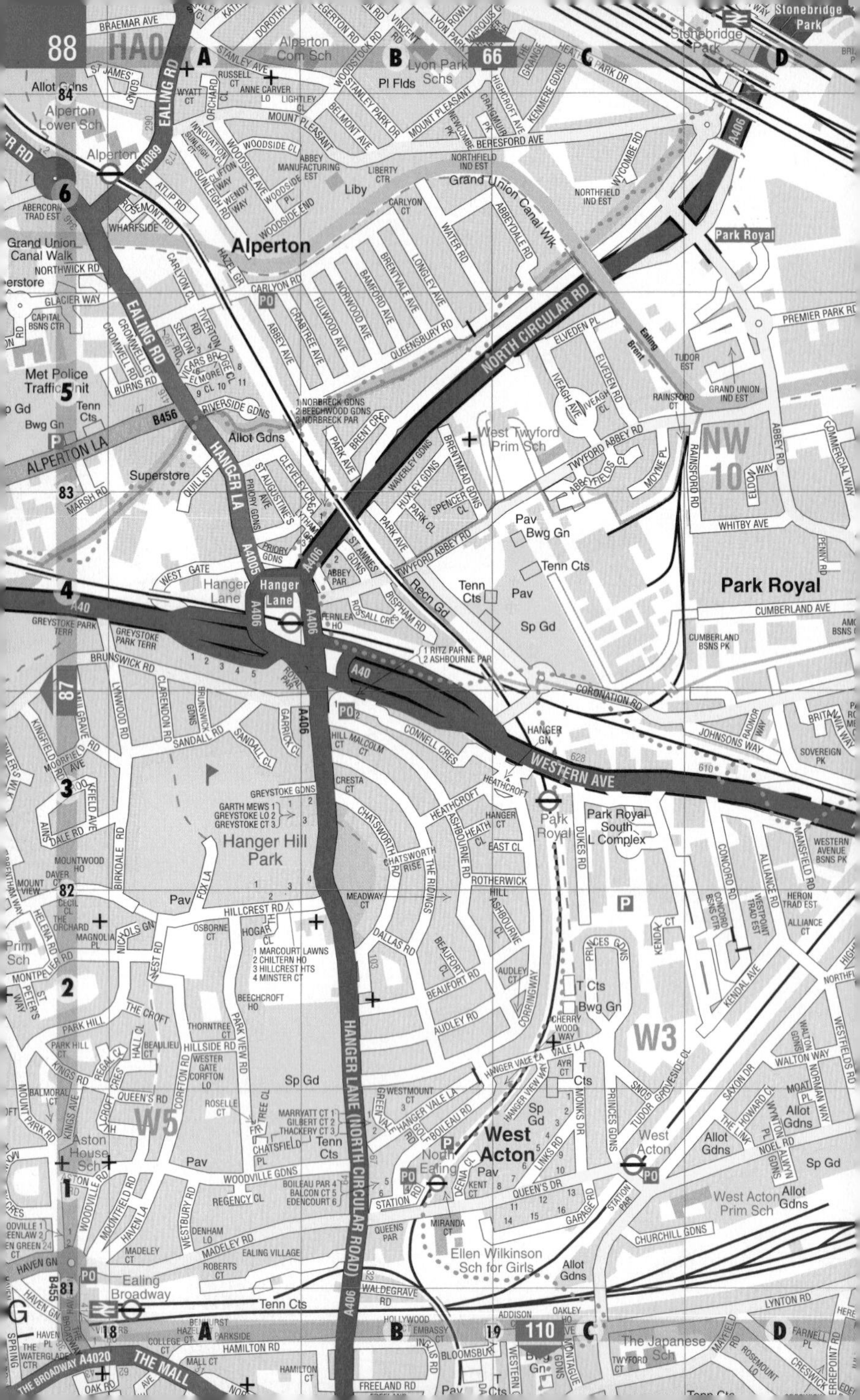

HA0
A
B
C
D
66
Stonebridge Park
Braemar Ave
Alperton Com Sch
Lyon Park Schs
Pl Flds
St James' Gdns
Allot Gdns
84
Alperton Lower Sch
Alperton
Ealing Rd
A4089
Stanley Ave
Russell Ct
Anne Carver Lo
Wyatt Ct
Orchard Cl
Lightley Cl
Mount Pleasant
Woodstock Rd
Stanley Park Dr
Belmont Ave
Mount Pleasant
Newcombe Pk
Craigmuir Pk
Highcroft Ave
Kenmere Gdns
Heather Park Dr
Beresford Ave
Woodside Cl
Woodside Ave
Innovation Cl
Sunleigh Rd
Clifton Way
Wendy Way
Woodside Pl
Woodside End
Abbey Manufacturing Est
Liberty Ctr
Liby
Northfield Ind Est
Wycombe Rd
Grand Union Canal Wlk
Carlyon Ct
Abercorn Trad Est
Semont Rd
Atlip Rd
Wharfside
6
Alperton
Grand Union Canal Walk
Northwick Rd
Glacier Way
Capital Bsns Ctr
Carlyon Rd
Carlyon Cl
Hazel Gr
PO
Abbey Ave
Crabtree Ave
Fulwood Ave
Norwood Ave
Bamford Ave
Brentvale Ave
Longley Ave
Water Rd
Abbeydale Rd
Queensbury Rd
North Circular Rd
A406
Park Royal
Premier Park Rd
Elveden Pl
Elveden Rd
Iveagh Ave
Iveagh Cl
Tudor Est
Grand Union Ind Est
Rainsford Ct
Ealing
Brent
Ealing Rd
Cromwell Rd
Seaton Rd
Tiverton Rd
Vicars Bridge Cl
Elmore Cl
Burns Rd
Met Police Traffic Unit
5
Tenn Cts
Bwg Gn
B456
Alperton La
Riverside Gdns
Allot Gdns
1 Norbreck Gdns
2 Beechwood Gdns
3 Norbreck Par
Brent Cres
Park Ave
Waverley Gdns
Brentmead Gdns
West Twyford Prim Sch
Twyford Abbey Rd
Abbeyfields Cl
Moyne Pl
Rainsford Rd
NW10
Eldon Way
Abbey Rd
Commercial Way
Whitby Ave
Penny Rd
Superstore
Quill St
Hanger La
St Augustine's Ave
Priory Gdns
Cleveley Cres
Lytham Gr
83
Marsh Rd
Huxley Gdns
Park Cl
Spencer Cl
St Annes Gdns
Abbey Par
Park Ave
Twyford Abbey Rd
Pav
Bwg Gn
Tenn Cts
Tenn Cts
Pav
Recn Gd
Sp Gd
Park Royal
Cumberland Ave
Cumberland Bsns Pk
West Gate
Hanger Lane
Priory Gdns
A4005
4
A40
Hanger Lane
Rossall Cres
Bispham Rd
Fernlea Ho
Greystoke Park Terr
Greystoke Park Terr
Brunswick Rd
1 Ritz Par
2 Ashbourne Par
87
Royal Par
A40
Coronation Rd
Lynwood Rd
Clarendon Rd
Brunswick Gdns
Sandall Rd
Sandall Cl
Garrick Cl
PO
Hill Ct
Malcolm Ct
Connell Cres
Hanger Gn
Johnsons Way
Radnor Way
Britannia Way
Kingfield Rd
Millgrave Rd
Moorfield Rd
3
Sovereign Pk
Western Ave
628
610
Cresta Ct
Greystoke Gdns
Garth Mews 1
Greystoke Lo 2
Greystoke Ct 3
Heathcroft
Heathcroft
Park Royal
Park Royal South L Complex
Hanger Ct
Heath Cl
East Cl
Ashbourne Rd
Dukes Rd
Concord Rd
Alliance Rd
Mansfield Rd
Western Avenue Bsns Pk
Dale Rd
Birkdale Rd
Hanger Hill Park
Chatsworth Rd
Chatsworth Rise
The Ridings
Rotherwick Hill
Mountwood Ho
Daver Ct
Mount View
82
Cecil Cl
The Orchard
Helena Rd
Magnolia Pl
Nicholas Gdns
Fox La
Pav
Hillcrest Rd
Osborne Ct
Hogarth Cl
Meadway Ct
Dallas Rd
Beaufort Cl
Ashbourne Cl
Concord Bsns Ctr
Westpoint Trad Est
Heron Trad Est
Alliance Ct
Kendal Ct
Princes Gdns
P
Prim Sch
Montpelier Rd
St Peter's Way
2
West Rd
1 Marcourt Lawns
2 Chiltern Ho
3 Hillcrest Hts
4 Minster Ct
Beechcroft Ho
Beaufort Rd
Audley Ct
Corringway
T Cts
Bwg Gn
Kendal Ave
103
The Croft
Park Hill
Park Hill Ct
Hall Cl
Beaulieu Ct
Thorntree Ct
Hillside Rd
Park View Rd
Audley Rd
Cherry Wood Way
Vale La
W3
Walton Gdns
Walton Way
Westfields Rd
Kings Rd
Regal Cres
Westergate
Corfton Lo
Corfton Rd
Sp Gd
Hanger Vale La
Hanger View Way
Ayr Ct
T Cts
Saxon Dr
Howard Cl
Moat Pl
Norman Way
Balmoral Ct
Queen's Rd
Rosselle Ct
Fir Tree Cl
Westmount Ct
Green Vale
Hanger Vale La
Boileau Rd
Sp Gd
Monks Dr
Princes Gdns
Tudor Gdns
Groveside Cl
The Link
Wynton Pl
Allot Gdns
Mount Park Rd
Kings Ave
W5
Marryatt Ct 1
Gilbert Ct 2
Thackery Ct 3
Chatsfield Pl
Tenn Cts
Golf Cl
West Acton
Links Rd
Allot Gdns
Noel Rd
Alwyn Gdns
Sp Gd
Aston House Sch
Woodville Rd
Pav
Woodville Gdns
Boileau Par 4
Balcon Ct 5
Edencourt 6
P
North Ealing
PO
Deena Cl
Pav
Kent Ct
West Acton
PO
1
Mountfield Rd
Haven La
Westbury Rd
Regency Cl
Station Rd
Queen's Dr
Garage Rd
Station Par
West Acton Prim Sch
Allot Gdns
Queens Par
Miranda Ct
Churchill Gdns
Denham Lo
Madeley Rd
Madeley Ct
Ealing Village
Roberts Ct
Ellen Wilkinson Sch for Girls
Allot Gdns
Haven Gn
81
PO
B455
Ealing Broadway
Haven Gn
Waldegrave Rd
Tenn Cts
Hanger Lane (North Circular Road)
A406
Lynton Rd
G
18
Benhurst Ct
Hazel Ct
Parkside
Hollywood Ct
Embassy Ct
Inglis Rd
Addison Ct
Oakley Ct
19
110
Haven Pl
The Waterglade Ctr
A
B
C
D
College Ct
Hamilton Rd
Mall Ct
Hamilton Ct
Bloomsbury
Western
Montague Gdns
The Japanese Sch
Twyford Ct
Mayfield Rd
Rosemount Lo
Farnell Pl
Creswick Rd
The Broadway
A4020
The Mall
Oak Rd
Freeland Rd
Pav

Stonebridge
Recn Gd
Our Lady of Lourdes RC Sch
Harlesden
Lower Place
Central Middlesex
North Acton
Old Oak Common
Old Oak Common Sidings
Old Oak Sidings
Freightliner Terminal
Willesden Junction
NW10
W3
Gipsy Corner
Acton Main Line
East Acton
Savoy Circus
Roundwood Park
Summer Theatre
HM Prison Wormwood Scrubs
Old Oak Prim Sch
John Perryn Prim Sch
Coll CE Prim Sch
Newfield Prim Sch
Grand Union Canal (Paddington Branch)
Grand Union Canal Wlk
Superstore
Hypermarket
Cemy
Allot Gdns
HILLSIDE
CRAVEN PK
CRAVEN PARK RD
MANOR PARK RD
HIGH STREET HARLESDEN
STATION RD
OLD OAK LA
ACTON LA
VICTORIA RD
PARK ROYAL RD
WESTERN AVE
WESTWAY
HORN LA
WALES FARM RD
OLD OAK COMMON LA
NORTH ACTON RD
CHURCH RD
A404
A407
A400
A4000
A40
B4492
67
111
A
B
C
D
1
2
3
4
5
6
81
82
83
84
90

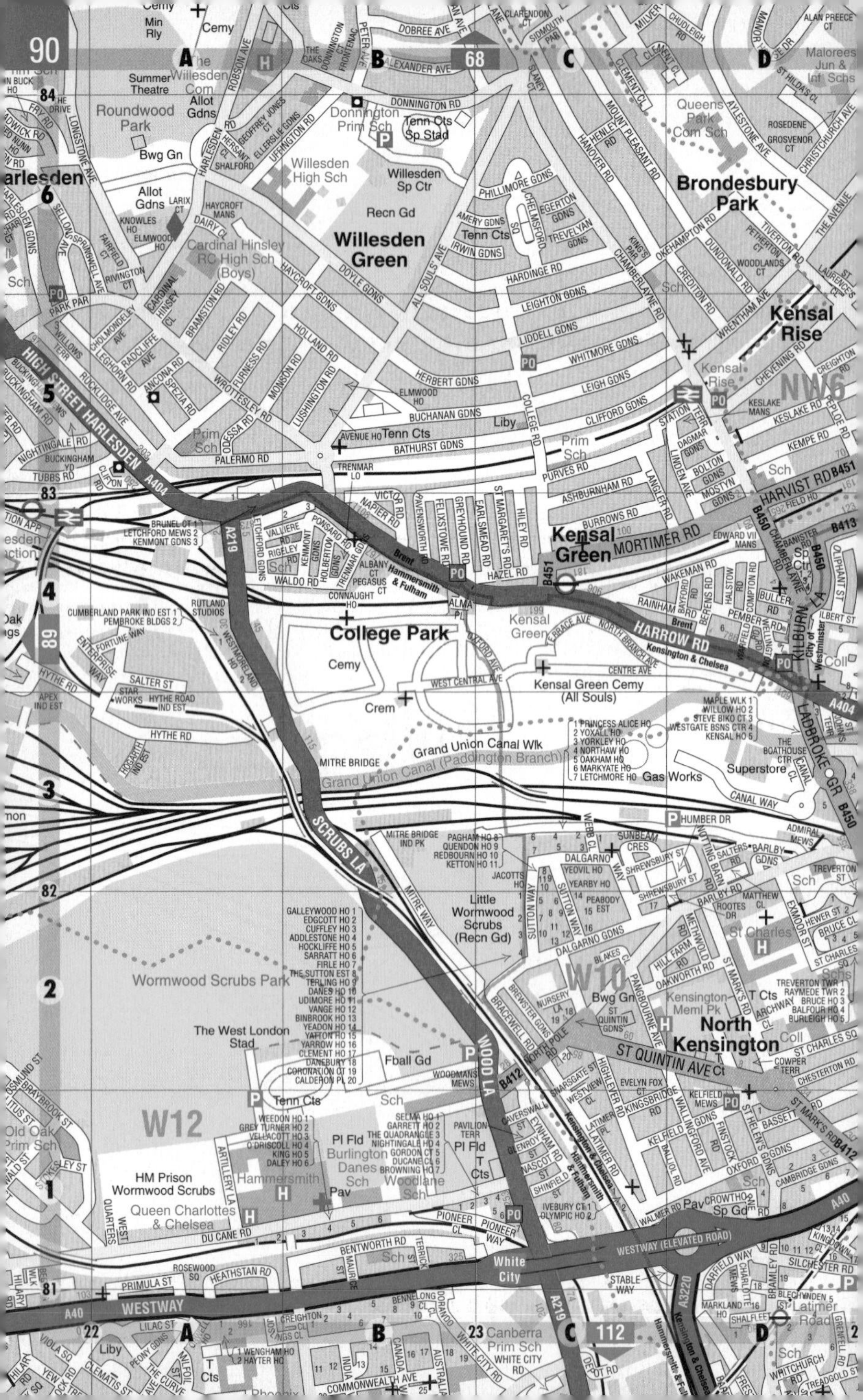
68
112
89
A
B
C
D
1
2
3
4
5
6
81
82
83
84
22
23
Willesden Green
Brondesbury Park
Kensal Rise
Kensal Green
College Park
North Kensington
arlesden
NW6
W10
W12
Roundwood Park
Willesden High Sch
Willesden Sp Ctr
Recn Gd
Donnington Prim Sch
Tenn Cts Sp Stad
Cardinal Hinsley RC High Sch (Boys)
Queens Park Com Sch
Malorees Jun & Inf Schs
Summer Theatre
The Willesden Com
Allot Gdns
Bwg Gn
Kensal Green Cemy (All Souls)
Cemy
Crem
Grand Union Canal Wlk
Grand Union Canal (Paddington Branch)
Gas Works
Superstore
Little Wormwood Scrubs (Recn Gd)
Wormwood Scrubs Park
The West London Stad
Fball Gd
HM Prison Wormwood Scrubs
Queen Charlottes & Chelsea
Hammersmith
Burlington Danes Sch
Woodlane Sch
Kensington Meml Pk
White City
Latimer Road
Canberra Prim Sch
Old Oak Prim Sch
HIGH STREET HARLESDEN
HARROW RD
SCRUBS LA
WOOD LA
WESTWAY
WESTWAY (ELEVATED ROAD)
MORTIMER RD
ST QUINTIN AVE
LADBROKE GR
KILBURN LA
CHAMBERLAYNE RD
DU CANE RD
HYTHE RD
A404
A219
A40
A3220
B450
B451
B412
B413
Brent
Hammersmith & Fulham
Kensington & Chelsea
City of Westminster

A
B
C
D
69
84
83
82
81
229
92
236
244
113
245
25
26
6
5
4
3
2
1
NW6
NW8
W9
W10
W11
W2
Kilburn
Kensal Rise
West Kilburn
Kensal Town
Maida Vale
PADDINGTON
Westbourne Green
Queen's Park
Brondesbury Park
Paddington Cemy
Salusbury Prim Sch
Islamia Schs
Kilburn High Road
Kilburn Park
Paddington Recn Gd
Royal Oak
Westbourne Park
Ladbroke Grove
Portobello Rd
Instituto Espanol
Isaac Newton Ctr
Paddington Com
WILLESDEN LA
KILBURN HIGH RD
BRONDESBURY RD
BRONDESBURY VILLAS
HARVIST RD
KILBURN LA
CARLTON VALE
KILBURN PARK RD
MAIDA VALE
ABBEY RD
BELSIZE RD
SHIRLAND RD
WALTERTON RD
HARROW RD
ELGIN AVE
WARWICK AVE
CLIFTON GDNS
GREAT WESTERN RD
WESTWAY (ELEVATED RD)
WESTBOURNE PARK RD
WESTBOURNE PARK VILLAS
WESTBOURNE GR
PORCHESTER RD
BISHOP'S BRIDGE RD
CHEPSTOW RD
LADBROKE GR
KENSINGTON PARK RD
QUEENSWAY
PEMBRIDGE VILLAS
A5
A404
A40
A4207
A4206
B507
B509
B510
B451
B413
B414
B411
B412
B415
B450

A
B
C
D
70
230
229
236
91
114
237
NW6
NW3
NW8
NW1
W9
W2
South Hampstead
Primrose Hill
Primrose Hill Tunnels
Barrow Hill
St John's Barracks
St John's Wood
Marlborough Day
SS John & Elizabeth
Wellington (North)
Wellington (South)
Lord's (MCC & Middlesex Cty Crkt Gd)
Crkt Mus
Maida Vale
Maida Vale Psychiatric
Tenn Cts
Tenn Ct
Winfield House
Boating Lake
London Business Sch
Lisson Green
Lisson Grove
St Mary's Gardens Coll
Little Venice
Warwick Avenue
Marylebone
Govt Offices
Charter Nightingale
Edgware Road
Antq Mkt
PADDINGTON
Paddington Basin
Marylebone Flyover
St Mary's
Paddington
Royal Oak
Bayswater
Speakers' Corner
Marble Arch
Victoria Gate
Baker Street
BELSIZE RD
ABBEY RD
BOUNDARY RD
AVENUE RD
FINCHLEY RD
WELLINGTON RD
PRINCE ALBERT RD
(Regent's Canal)
Grand Union Canal
OUTER CIRCLE
PARK RD
MAIDA VALE
GROVE END RD
ST JOHN'S WOOD ROAD
LISSON GR
CLIFTON GDNS
HARROW RD
WESTWAY (ELEVATED) HARROW RD (UNDER)
A40 MARYLEBONE FLYOVER
MARYLEBONE RD
EDGWARE RD
GLOUCESTER PL
BISHOP'S BRIDGE RD
PRAED ST
SUSSEX GDNS
BAYSWATER RD
NORTH CARRIAGE DR
NORTH RIDE
QUEENSWAY
WESTBOURNE TERR
DORMAN WAY
LOUDOUN ROAD
MARLBOROUGH HILL
HAMILTON TERR
RANDOLPH AVE
WARWICK AVE
SUTHERLAND AVE
WARRINGTON CRES
ST JOHN'S WOOD HIGH ST
ST JOHN'S WOOD TERR
TOWNSHEND ROAD
ROSSMORE RD
SUSSEX PL
CHAGFORD ST
BOSTON PL
UPPER MONTAGU ST
BRYANSTON ST
SEYMOUR ST
CONNAUGHT ST
OXFORD SQ
HYDE PARK CRES
LONDON ST
CRAVEN RD
LANCASTER GATE
PORCHESTER TERR

CAMDEN TOWN
A
B
C
D
231
71
232
Superstore
Camden Mkt
Camden Town
Britannia Junc
Freightliner Terminal
N1
Depot
6
5
4
3
2
1
London Zoo
Regents Park Barracks
NW1
Regent's Park
Refreshment Room
Cumberland Gate
Open Air Theatre
Queen Mary's Gardens
New Lodge
Royal Coll of Physicians
Regent's Coll
Royal Acad of Music
Pav
Tenn Cts
St Pancras
Ct St Pancras Gardens
Mornington Crescent
Somers Town
The British Liby
Euston
Govt Offices
Euston Underpass
Great Portland Street
Warren Street
Euston Square
University Coll London
RADA
Bloomsbury
British Mus
Fitzrovia
BT Twr
Goodge Street
Tottenham Court Road
Oxford Circus
Soho
Berwick St
MARYLEBONE
Bond Street
W1
Grosvenor Sq Gardens
Leicester Square
Piccadilly
CAMDEN HIGH ST
CAMDEN ST
ROYAL COLLEGE ST
ST PANCRAS WAY
PANCRAS RD
EUSTON ROAD
HAMPSTEAD RD
ALBANY ST
EVERSHOLT ST
GOWER ST
TOTTENHAM COURT RD
BLOOMSBURY ST
PORTLAND PL
GREAT PORTLAND ST
MORTIMER ST
OXFORD ST
NEW OXFORD ST
WIGMORE ST
REGENT ST
CHARING CROSS RD
BAKER ST
MARYLEBONE HIGH ST
PARK CRES
OUTER CIRCLE
INNER CIRCLE
CHESTER RD
BROAD WLK
YORK BRIDGE
DELANCEY ST
PARKWAY
OAKLEY SQ
CROWNDALE RD
Grand Union Canal
Regent's Canal
CAMLEY ST
WHARF RD
RUSSELL SQ
ST GILES HIGH ST
CAVENDISH SQUARE
DEVONSHIRE ST
WEYMOUTH ST
GOODGE ST
93
94
84
83
82
81
238
29
115
239
30
28

A
B
C
D
233
72
234
84
6
5
4
3
2
1
93
82
81
30
31
240
116
241
Freightliner Terminal
N1
Depot
YORK WAY
B514 COPENHAGEN ST
CALEDONIAN RD
RC Prim Sch
Barnard Park
LIVERPOOL RD
UPPER ST
ESSEX RD
Bsns Design Ctr
Camden Pas
King's Cross
ISLINGTON
Chapel Mkt
Pentonville
PENTONVILLE RD
Angel
St Pancras
The British Liby
FINSBURY
ROSEBERY AVE
GOSWELL RD
The City Univ
Eastman Dental
WC1
Tenn Ct
Sp Gd
Coram's Fields
GUILFORD ST
GRAY'S INN RD
FARRINGDON RD
ST JOHN ST
CLERKENWELL RD
Clerkenwell
Russell Square
Russell Square Garden
Bloomsbury
SOUTHAMPTON ROW
THEOBALD'S RD
Gray's Inn
Leather Lane
Holborn
Smithfield Mkt
British Mus
HIGH HOLBORN
HOLBORN VIADUCT
NEW OXFORD ST
St Giles
Lincoln's Inn Fields
KINGSWAY
CHANCERY LA
Public Record Office
Royal Courts of Justice
ALDWYCH
Covent Garden
LONG ACRE
CHARING CROSS
Somerset House
STRAND
VICTORIA EMBANKMENT
Inner Temple Garden
Blackfriars
City Thameslink
LUDGATE HILL

73
235
A
B
C
D
Essex Road
SHOREDITCH
Hoxton
Haggerston
St Luke's
Broadgate
Spitalfields
Whitechapel
N1
E8
E2
EC1
EC2
EC3
EC4
E1
NEW NORTH RD
KINGSLAND RD
QUEENSBRIDGE RD
CITY RD
EAST RD
OLD ST
GREAT EASTERN ST
SHOREDITCH HIGH ST
HACKNEY RD
COLUMBIA RD
BETHNAL GREEN RD
CHESHIRE ST
BRICK LA
COMMERCIAL ST
BISHOPSGATE
LONDON WALL
ALDERSGATE ST
CHISWELL ST
BUNHILL ROW
BATH ST
SHEPHERDESS WLK
PITFIELD ST
CURTAIN RD
LEVER ST
WHITECHAPEL HIGH ST
MINORIES
UPPER THAMES ST
CANNON ST
GRACECHURCH ST
FENCHURCH ST
LEADENHALL ST
HOUNDSDITCH
CAMOMILE ST
LIVERPOOL ST
MOORGATE
Grand Union Canal
(Regent's Canal)
Kingsland Basin
City Road Basin
Shoreditch Park
Haggerston Park
Columbia Rd
Old Street
Brick Lane Shoreditch
Old Spitalfields
Petticoat Lane
Liverpool Street
Barbican Arts & Con Ctr
Barbican
Moorgate
Guildhall
Tower 42
Bank
Mansion House
Cannon Street
Lloyds Bldg
Fenchurch Street
Aldgate
Aldgate East
Tower Hill
Tower Gateway
St Paul's Cath
Monument
Bunhill Row
Burial Gd
Pl Fld
Govt Offices
Art Gall
Mus
Liby
Sch
Coll
Tech Coll
Univ
CITY OF
242
117
243
96
5
4
3
2
1
6

96
74
118
A
B
C
D
HACKNEY
E8
E9
South Hackney
BETHNAL GREEN
E2
E1
STEPNEY
Haggerston
Haggerston Park
Spitalfields
Globe Town
Columbia Rd
Cambridge Heath
Bethnal Green
Stepney Green
Whitechapel
Shadwell
Victoria Park Rd
Mile End Rd
Whitechapel Rd
Commercial Rd
Hackney Rd
Bethnal Green Rd
Old Bethnal Green Rd
Roman Rd
Old Ford Rd
Cambridge Heath Rd
Sewardstone Rd
Bishop's Way
Queensbridge Rd
Brick La
Vallance Rd
New Rd
Cannon Street Rd
Globe Rd
Cheshire St
Dunbridge St
Gosset St
Well St
Mare St
Cable St
Royal Mint St
Leman St
Regent's Canal
Weavers Fields
Meath Gardens
Royal Gate East
Royal Gate West
Crown Gate East
Crown Gate West
The Royal London (Mile End)
Morpeth Sec Sch
Swanlea Sec Sch
London Chest
Stepney Way
Jubilee St
Sidney St
Watney
Whitechapel High St
Lavender Gr
Middleton Rd
Albion Dr
Shrubland Rd
Brownlow Rd
Whiston Rd
Dove Row
Teale St
Coate St
Emma St
Columbia Rd
Quilter St
Wellington Row
Florida St
Derbyshire St
Bacon St
Buxton St
Woodseer St
Hanbury St
Fieldgate St
Ashfield St
Varden St
Nelson St
Tarling St
Burslem St
Boyd St
Chapman St
Martha St
Hindmarsh
Glamis Pl
Ernest St
Harford St
Bancroft Rd
Longnor Rd
Moody St
Portman Pl
Malcolm Rd
Wickford St
Buckhurst St
Coventry Rd
Collingwood St
Headlam St
Cleveland Way
Anchor Ret Pk
City Gate
Trinity Gn
Adelina Gr
Redman's Rd
Smithy St
Lindley St
Wickham Cl
Ewhurst Cl
Clark St
Musbury St
Cornwood Dr
Aylward St
Head St
Chudleigh St
Walter Terr
Senrab St
Bromley St
Westport St
Barnardo St
White Horse La
Rectory Sq
Trafalgar Gdns
Stepney High St
Shandy St
Twig Folly Bridge
Wennington Green
Cricketers Bridge
Bonner Hall Bridge
Gore Rd
Lauriston Rd
Wetherell Rd
Groombridge Rd
Penshurst Rd
Kingshold Rd
Skipworth Rd
Sharon Gdns
King Edward's Rd
Northiam St
Wadeson St
Mowlem St
Parmiter St
Russia La
Robinson Rd
Approach Rd
Cyprus St
Bonner St
Mace St
Knottisford
Usk St
Walter St
Grantley St
Massingham St
Tollet St
Holton St
Alderney Rd
Ifor Evans Pl
Cephas Ave
Boyton

A
B
C
D
75
119
84
83
82
81
98
37
38
1
2
3
4
5
6
Victoria Park
Victoria Fntn
Gunmakers Gate
Hertford Union Canal
Old Ford
BOW
Bromley
Mile End
Univ of London
Mile End Park
Mile End Park (South)
TOWER HAMLETS
Stratford Marsh
Pudding Mill Lane
St Clement's Wharf
Swan Wharf
Crown Wharf
Iceland Wharf
Vulcan Wharf
Meeson's Wharf
Tredegar Wharf
Grove Hall Park
Four Seasons Green
Bow Church
Bow Road
Devons Road
Allot Gdns
The Royal London (St Clements)
Tower Hamlets Cemy
Coll (Annexe)
E3
Gas Works
Bow Common
Hackney Coll
Langdon Park
Bartlett Park
Brickfield Gardens
East London Stadium
Shandy Park
Halley Prim Sch
POPLAR
Limehouse
Limehouse Basin
Limehouse Cut
Regent's Canal
River Lea or Lee
Bow Back River
City Mill River
EAST CROSS ROUTE
BOW RD
GROVE RD
BURDETT RD
EAST INDIA DOCK RD
BLACKWALL TUNNEL NORTHERN APPROACH
DEVONS RD
ST PAUL'S WAY
FAIRFIELD RD
PARNELL RD
OLD FORD RD
BRUCE RD
COMMERCIAL ROAD
WEST INDIA DOCK RD
A12
A11
A13
A1205
A1261
A101
B118
B119
B140
B142
Lea Valley Wlk
Wick La
Marshgate La

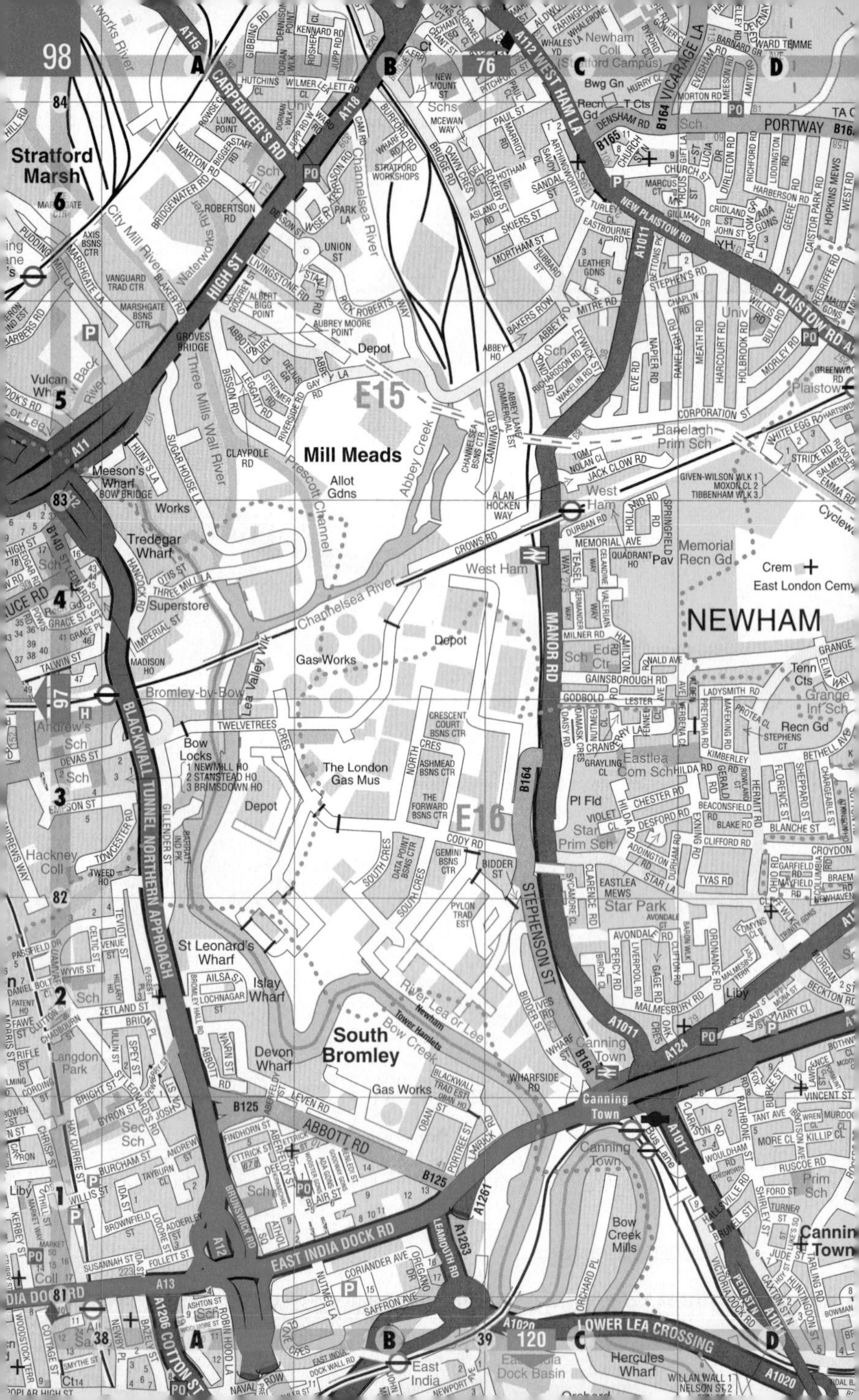
A
B
C
D
76
84
Stratford Marsh
6
5
4
3
2
1
83
82
81
97
120
38
39
CARPENTER'S RD
HIGH ST
A115
A118
A112 WEST HAM LA
B164 VICARAGE LA
B165
A1011
NEW PLAISTOW RD
PLAISTOW RD
PORTWAY
DENSHAM RD
Newham Coll (Stratford Campus)
Bwg Gn
Recn Gd
T Cts
CHURCH ST
CHURCH ST N
GIBBINS RD
DENNISON POINT
KENNARD RD
ROSHER CL
JUPP RD
HUTCHINS CL
WILMER LEA
LETT RD
DORAN WLK
Univ
LUND POINT
ROWSE CL
WARTON RD
BIGGERSTAFF RD
BRIDGEWATER RD
ROBERTSON RD
CAM RD
BURFORD RD
WHARF RD
STRATFORD WORKSHOPS
Channelsea River
NEW MOUNT ST
Schs
MCEWAN WAY
BRIDGE RD
DAWN CRES
PAUL ST
MARRIOTT RD
HOTHAM ST
ROKEBY ST
SANDAL ST
ASLAND RD
SKIERS ST
MORTHAM ST
HUBBARD ST
ARTHINGWORTH ST
TURLEY CL
EASTBOURNE RD
LEATHER GDNS
BETTONS PK
STEPHEN'S RD
CHAPLIN RD
MARCUS ST
GILLMAN DR
CRIDLAND ST
JOHN ST
PLAISTOW GR
ADA GDNS
HARBERSON RD
CAISTOR PARK RD
HOPKINS MEWS
WEST RD
DIRLETON RD
RICHFORD RD
LIDDINGTON RD
GEERE RD
REDRIFFE RD
WILLIS RD
BULL RD
MAUD GDNS
MORLEY RD
GREENWOOD RD
Plaistow
City Mill River
Waterworks River
PUDDING MILL LA
MARSHGATE LA
AXIS BSNS CTR
VANGUARD TRAD CTR
MARSHGATE BSNS CTR
BLAKER RD
DEASON ST
WISE RD
PARK LA
UNION ST
LIVINGSTONE RD
STANLEY RD
RICK ROBERTS WAY
GODFREY ST
ALBERT BIGG POINT
AUBREY MOORE POINT
Depot
ABBOTSBURY CL
DELIUS GR
ABBEY LA
GAY RD
STREIMER RD
LEGGATT RD
RIVERSIDE RD
BISSON RD
GROVES BRIDGE
Three Mills Wall River
E15
Mill Meads
Allot Gdns
Abbey Creek
Prescott Channel
BAKERS ROW
ABBEY RD
MITRE RD
LEYWICK ST
ABBEY HO
POND RD
RICHARDSON RD
WAKELIN RD
ABBEY LANE COMMERCIAL EST
CANNING RD
CHANNELSEA BSNS CTR
EVE RD
NAPIER RD
RANELAGH RD
MEATH RD
HARCOURT RD
HOLBROOK RD
CORPORATION ST
Ranelagh Prim Sch
WHITELEGG RD
STRIDE RD
RUDOLPH RD
SALMEN RD
EMMA RD
TOM NOLAN CL
JACK CLOW RD
GIVEN-WILSON WLK 1
MOXON CL 2
TIBBENHAM WLK 3
West Ham
ALAN HOCKEN WAY
DURBAN RD
HOLLAND RD
SPRINGFIELD RD
MEMORIAL AVE
QUADRANT HO
Pav
Memorial Recn Gd
Crem
East London Cemy
Cyclew
NEWHAM
Vulcan Wharf
Bow Back River
River Lee
A11
Meeson's Wharf
BOW BRIDGE
HUNT'S LA
SUGAR HOUSE LA
CLAYPOLE RD
Works
Tredegar Wharf
HANCOCK RD
OTIS ST
THREE MILL LA
Superstore
IMPERIAL ST
MADISON HO
CROWS RD
Channelsea River
West Ham
Depot
Gas Works
Lea Valley Wlk
MANOR RD
TEASEL WAY
GERMANDER WAY
CELANDINE WAY
VALERIAN WAY
MILNER RD
HAMILTON RD
Sch
Ed Ctr
RONALD AVE
GAINSBOROUGH RD
GODBOLD RD
LESTER AVE
ALDEN AVE
VERBENA CL
LADYSMITH RD
GRANGE RD
ELM WAY
Tenn Cts
Grange Inf Sch
Recn Gd
PRETORIA RD
MAFEKING RD
PROTEA CL
STEPHENS CT
KIMBERLEY RD
BETHELL AVE
DAISY RD
DAMASK CRES
NUTMEG CL
CRANBERRY LA
FENNEL CL
GRAYLING CL
Eastlea Com Sch
HILDA RD
GERALD RD
ROWLAND CT
HERMIT RD
FLORENCE ST
SHEPPARD ST
CHARGEABLE ST
Pl Fld
VIOLET CL
CHESTER RD
BEACONSFIELD RD
BLAKE RD
BLANCHE ST
DESFORD RD
Star Prim Sch
EXNING RD
CLIFFORD RD
CROYDON RD
ADDINGTON RD
DURHAM RD
STAR LA
TYAS RD
GARFIELD RD
MAYFIELD RD
BRAEMAR
NEWHAVEN
OHIO RD
COLUMBIA RD
CLARENCE RD
SYCAMORE CL
EASTLEA MEWS
Star Park
AVONDALE CT
AVONDALE RD
CLIFTON RD
BARON WLK
ORDNANCE RD
MORGAN ST
BECKTON RD
BIRCH CL
PERCY RD
LIVERPOOL RD
GAGE RD
MALMESBURY RD
MALMESBURY TERR
OAK CRES
Liby
MARY CL
E16
HIGH ST
B140
ST LEONARD'S ST
GRACE ST
GRACE PL
TALWIN ST
Bromley-by-Bow
BLACKWALL TUNNEL NORTHERN APPROACH
Andrew's Sch
TWELVETREES CRES
Bow Locks
1 NEWMILL HO
2 STANSTEAD HO
3 BRIMSDOWN HO
The London Gas Mus
Depot
CRESCENT COURT BSNS CTR
NORTH CRES
ASHMEAD BSNS CTR
THE FORWARD BSNS CTR
CODY RD
B164
DEVAS ST
Sch
EMPSON ST
TOWCESTER RD
Hackney Coll
TWEED HO
GILLENDER ST
BARRATT IND PK
SOUTH CRES
DATA POINT BSNS CTR
GEMINI BSNS CTR
BIDDER ST
PYLON TRAD EST
STEPHENSON ST
TEVIOT ST
CELTIC ST
VENUE ST
WYVIS ST
St Leonard's Wharf
AILSA ST
LOCHNAGAR ST
BROMLEY HALL RD
Islay Wharf
River Lea or Lee
Bow Creek
Tower Hamlets
Newham
IVES RD
ZETLAND ST
BRION PL
SPEY ST
ABBOTT RD
NAIRN ST
South Bromley
Devon Wharf
Canning Town
WHARFSIDE RD
A1011
A124
Langdon Park
Sec Sch
BYRON ST
ST LEONARD'S RD
BRIGHT ST
B125
LEVEN RD
Gas Works
BLACKWALL TRAD EST
OBAN ST
OBAN HO
LANRICK RD
PORTREE ST
A1261
BURCHAM ST
TAYBURN CL
ANDREW ST
FINDHORN ST
ETTRICK ST
ABERFELDY ST
BLAIR ST
WILLIS ST
IDA ST
BROWNFIELD ST
LODORE ST
ADDERLEY ST
SUSANNAH ST
FOLLETT ST
Liby
A12
BRUNSWICK RD
EAST INDIA DOCK RD
LEAMOUTH RD
A1263
CORIANDER AVE
OREGANO DR
NUTMEG LA
SAFFRON AVE
Bow Creek Mills
ORCHARD PL
Canning Town
Bus Lane
CLARKSON RD
RATHBONE ST
TANT AVE
MORE CL
KILLIP CL
RUSCOE RD
Prim Sch
WOULDHAM RD
HALLSVILLE RD
FORD ST
TURNER ST
BRUNEL ST
JUDE ST
SHIRLEY ST
VICTORIA DOCK RD
CAXTON ST N
HUNTINGDON ST
Canning Town
VINCENT ST
PELLY ST
A13
ASHTON ST
ROBIN HOOD LA
A1206 COTTON ST
A1020
LOWER LEA CROSSING
East India
East India Dock Basin
Hercules Wharf
WILLAN WALL 1
NELSON ST 2
EAST INDIA DOCK WALL RD
NAVAL ROW
NEWPORT AVE
CHRISP ST
HAY CURRIE ST
KERBEY ST
MARKET SQ
Coll
WOODSTOCK TERR
COTTAGE ST
SMYTHE ST
NEWBY PL
BAZELY ST
POPLAR HIGH ST
EAST INDIA DOCK RD

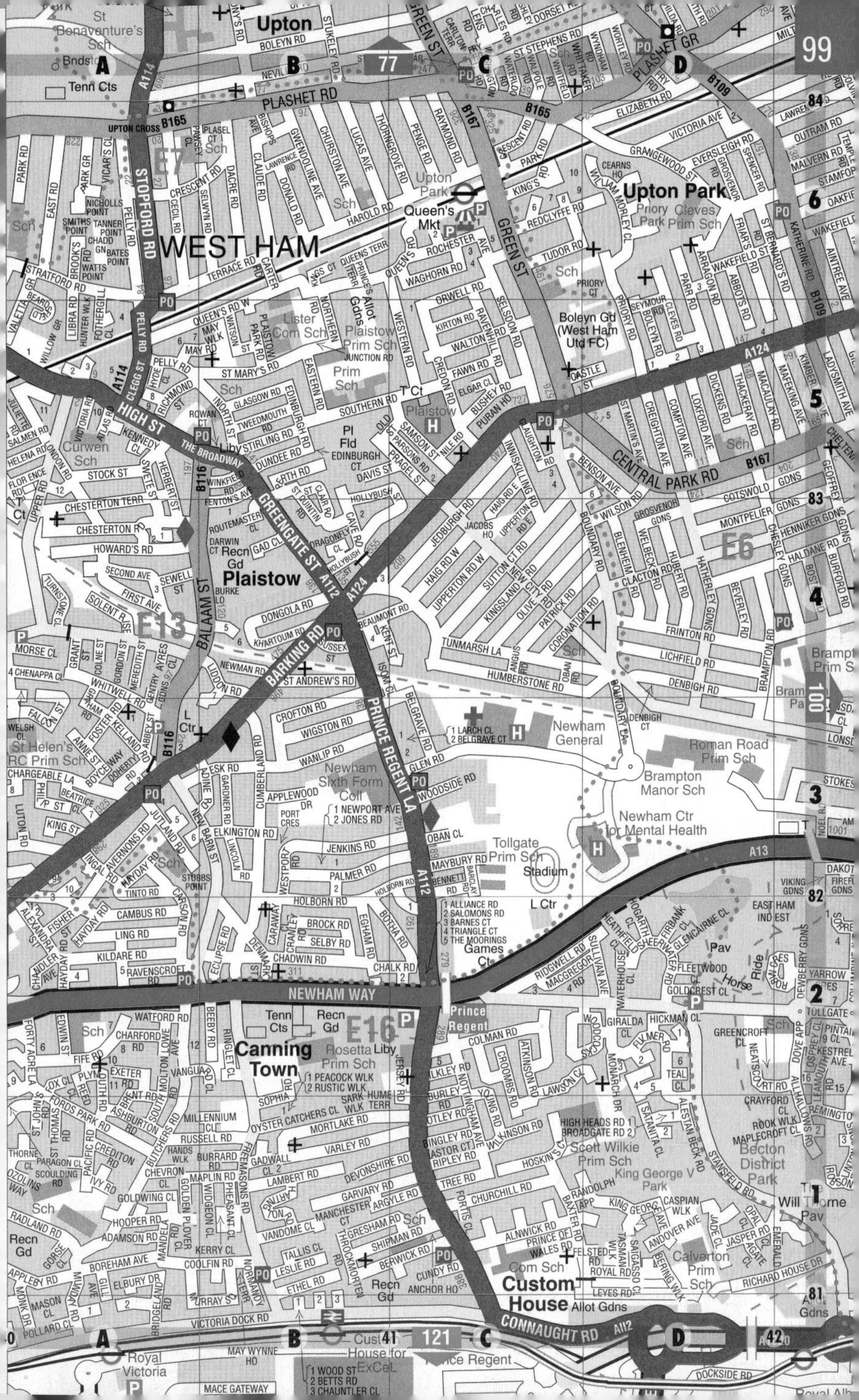
Upton
Upton Park
WEST HAM
Plaistow
Canning Town
Custom House
E7
E13
E6
E16
Upton Park
Queen's Mkt
Boleyn Gd (West Ham Utd FC)
Newham General
Brampton Manor Sch
Newham Ctr for Mental Health
Newham Sixth Form Coll
Tollgate Prim Sch
Stadium
Roman Road Prim Sch
East Ham Ind Est
Becton District Park
King George V Park
Scott Wilkie Prim Sch
Rosetta Prim Sch
Prince Regent
Custom House for ExCeL
Royal Victoria
St Bonaventure's Sch
Lister Com Sch
Plaistow Prim Sch
Priory Park
Cleves Prim Sch
St Helen's RC Prim Sch
Curwen Sch
Calverton Prim Sch
PLASHET RD
PLASHET GR
GREEN ST
STOPFORD RD
HIGH ST
THE BROADWAY
GREENGATE ST
BARKING RD
BALAAM ST
PRINCE REGENT LA
CENTRAL PARK RD
NEWHAM WAY
CONNAUGHT RD
KATHERINE RD
A114
A124
A112
A13
B165
B167
B109
B116
77
100
121
41
42
84
83
82
81
6
5
4
3
2
1
A
B
C
D

EAST HAM
E6
Wallend
Beckton
Central Park
Flanders Pl Fld
East Ham Jewish Cemy
Brampton Prim Sch
Brampton Park
Roman Road Prim Sch
Langdon Sch
Gooseley's Pl Flds
Allot Gdns
Recn Gd
Barking Flyover
Superstore
River Roding
BECKTON TRIANGLE RET PK
GATEWAY RET PK
Beckton Alps
Ski Ctr
Nat Res
TA Ctr
Golf Range
North Beckton Prim Sch
ALPINE BSNS CTR
THE LONDON IND PK
EAST BECKTON DIST CTR
MARY ROSE MALL
Kingsford Com Sch
Becton District Park
The Will Thorne Pav
New Becton Park
Winsor Prim Sch
EAST HAM IND EST
Gallions Reach
Cyprus
Beckton Park
BARKING RD
A124
A117
A13
A406
A1020
B167
B109
HIGH ST S
HIGH ST N
RON LEIGHTON WAY
NORTH CIRCULAR RD
ROYAL DOCKS RD
NEWHAM WAY
WOOLWICH MANOR WAY
EAST HAM MANOR WAY
ROYAL ALBERT WAY
ROYAL ALBERT RD
ABBEY RD
RANCLIFFE RD
CENTRAL PARK RD
LONSDALE AVE
ROMAN RD
STOKES RD
TOLLGATE RD
ALPINE WAY
EASTBURY RD
RODING RD
HENRY ADDINGTON CL
WINSOR TERR
STONEWALL
VICARAGE LA
GOOSELEY LA
WHITE HORSE RD
MARKET ST
LANGDON RD
NELSON ST
SUSSEX RD
KATHERINE RD
CALEDON RD
SKEFFINGTON RD
1 MALDON CT
2 WALL END CT
3 TRAFALGAR CT
1 ATHELSTAN CT
2 WADHURST CT
SIDNEY ELSON WAY 1
MATHEWS AVE 2
SANDFORD CL 1
ST GEORGES CT 2
ST MARYS CT 3
1 MANBROUGH AVE
2 MAGDALENE GDNS
3 MASEFIELD GDNS
4 HARTSHORN GDNS
AMY WARNE CL 1
IRIS CL 2
A B C D
1 2 3 4 5 6
78
122
99
84 83 82 81
42 43 44

BARKING
GREENSLADE RD
THE VICARAGE FIELDS SH CTR
JAMES
LONDON RD
THE ARCADE
HARVEY HO
SOWER HO
A
B
C
D
79
GREAVES CL
CONISTON CL
LAMBOURNE RD
MEADOW
MERTON RD
BRIDGEWAY
DIGBY RD
TRESHAM RD
DAWSON AVE
STUART RD
TUDOR RD
JOHN BURNS DR
LANCASTER AVE
KENDAL AVE
SURREY RD
NORFOLK RD
SUFFOLK RD
ESSEX RD
Schs
Sch
Liby
RIPPLE RD
VICARAGE DR
EAST ST
CLOCKHOUSE AVE
BROADWAY
AXE ST
A123
A124
TH
St Joseph's RC Prim Sch
ST PAULS RD
SUNNINGDALE AVE
ST ERKENWALD RD
ST ERKENWALD MEWS
ST AWDRY'S RD
CRANBORNE RD
WESTBURY RD
BAMBER HO
ST MARGARETS
ST ANN'S
COBHAM HO
EASTBURY AVE
EASTBURY CT
SISLEY RD
EAST BURY SQ
DENHAM WAY
PELHAM AVE
STERRY RD
MAYESBROOK RD
BLAKE AVE
Mayes Brook
MELLISH CL
DEVON RD
HARROW RD
ELDRED RD
WEDDERBURN RD
MORLEY RD
HOWARD RD
JACKSON RD
BOUNDARY RD
PERTH RD
KING EDWARD'S RD
GREATFIELDS RD
KEITH RD
MOVERS LA
GORDON RD
SPARSHOLT RD
KENNEDY RD
ST JOHN'S RD
TOM MANN CL
SUTTON RD
FELTON RD
SAXHAM RD
ALFRED'S GDNS
Greatfields Park
IG11
LINSDELL RD
TOMLINS ORCH
HARDWICKE
PERRYMAN HO
Gascoigne Prim Sch
THE SHAFTESBURYS
THE CLARKSONS
GASCOIGNE RD
BOUNDARY RD
ABBEY RD
ABBEY PARK IND EST
ST MARYS
THE CO
SE MEAD
WHEELERS CROSS
DOVEHOUSE
FISKE CT
LONGREACH CT
NEW ENGLAND EST
Cuckold's Haven
ALFRED'S WAY (EAST HAM AND BARKING BY-PASS)
A13
ALFRED'S WAY
RIVERSIDE COTTS
1 ANDERSON HO
2 ROOKWOOD HO
3 TASKER HO
4 CRISPE HO
5 OBAN HO
6 EARLSDOWN HO
KINGSBRIDGE RD
KINGSBRIDGE IND EST
WESTMINSTER GDNS
WAVERLEY GDNS
CRAVEN GDNS
Allot Gdns
1 SUTTON GDNS
2 FELTON GDNS
3 SUTTON GN
LYON BSNS PK
BARKING IND PK
ALFRED'S WAY IND EST
WAYSIDE COMMERCIAL EST
CHARLTON CRES
SUGDEN WAY
MAUD GDNS
ROYCRAFT AVE
BASTABLE AVE
STANLEY AVE
LOW HO
MAYBURY RD
ROWE GDNS
RAY GDNS
ENDEAVOUR
Liby
PO
Thames View Inf Sch
Thames View Jun Sch
Pl Fld
THAMES VIEW LODGE
HOCKLEY MEWS
Sp Gd
CURZON CRES
ENTERPRISE HO
RADFORD WAY
BARKING BSNS CTR
THAMES RD
KATELLA TRAD EST
RIVER ROAD BSNS PK
CROMWELL BSNS CTR
BANKSIDE PK
CROSSNESS RD
CREEK RD
Allot Gdns
102
CREEKMOUTH IND PK
LONG REACH RD
RIVER RD
JENKINS LA
SPUR RD
ERIC CLARKE LA
Barking & Dagenham
Newham
Barking Creek
Sewage Works
TRAFALGAR BSNS CTR
ANGLIAN IND EST
Creekmouth
IG11
BALMORAL TRAD EST
ATCOST RD
BUZZARD CREEK IND EST
River Roding
Barking Barrier
Horse End
Superstore
Pier
Jetty
Depot
E6
ARMADA WAY
Margaret or Tripcock Ness
Mast
Newham
Greenwich
45
123
46
THAMESMEAD SH CTR
84
83
82
81
6
5
4
3
2
1

A
B
C
D
80
84
6
5
83
4
101
3
82
2
1
81
46
47
124
BEN TILLET CL
KEIR HARDIE WAY
STRATFORD CL
LODGE AVE
ROSEDALE RD
ROSEDALE GDNS
CAMPSEY RD
CAMPSEY GDNS
CANONS
ELLERTON GDNS
ELLERTON RD
BILLINGS CL
STOCKER GDNS
FLAMSTEAD GDNS
FLAMSTEAD RD
STAMFORD RD
STAMFORD GDNS
ROTHWELL GDNS
ROTHWELL RD
LANGLEY GDNS
LANGLEY CRES
ARDEN CRES
STUDLEY RD
ROMSEY GDNS
ROMSEY RD
WIX RD
GREENFIELD RD
GREENFIELD GDNS
GORESBROOK RD
Cemy
PINLEY GDNS
BURNHAM RD
Monteagle Prim Sch
SURMANS CL
ACONBURY RD
MAPLESTEAD RD
MOORE CRES
CASTLE RD
BASSETT HO
INGRAVE HO
DUNMOW HO
Castle Green
RM9
Sp Gds
L Ctr
Rec Gd
Ripple Road
A123
A1153
PO
BARKING IND PK
Mayes Brook
ALFRED'S WAY
(EAST HAM AND BARKING BY-PASS)
A13
MELLISH CL
Works
RIPPLE RD
ALFRED'S WAY IND EST
THE INVICTA CTR
WAYSIDE COMMERCIAL EST
DAVENPORT CTR
STEELE APP
RIPPLESIDE COMMERCIAL EST
PORTLAND COMMERCIAL EST
MAYBELLS COMMERCIAL EST
JULIA GDNS
LEVINE GDNS
SUGDEN WAY
LOW HO
MAYBURY RD
ROWE GDNS
FARR AVE
RAY GDNS
Liby
ENDEAVOUR WAY
STEBBING WAY
WIVENHOE RD
ROXWELL RD
BOX LA
CHELMER CRES
CROUCH AV
ABRIDGE WAY
GILSTEAD HO 1
NAVESTOCK HO 2
STANFORD HO 3
ST AIDANS CT 4
BASTABLE AVE
GLENMORE WAY
Thames View Inf Sch
Thames View Jun Sch
Pl Fld
ALDERMAN AVE
TRIUMPH HO
ADMIRAL CT
LIBERTY CT
FORTUNE CT
STERN CL
GREAT FLEETE WAY
KEEL CL
CALEDONIA CT
Freightliner Terminal
BLESSING WAY
SOVEREIGN RD
CHOATS RD
RENWICK RD
WANDERER DR
GREAT GALLEY CL
HAVERING WAY
STAPLEFORD WAY
BARKING BSNS CTR
RIVERSIDE IND EST
TWINE CL
ESTUARY CL
5 BRECO HO
6 BELLINGHAM CT
7 ARNCROFT CT
THAMES RD
BANKSIDE PK
CROSSNESS RD
CROMWELL CTR
GALLIONS CL
SEAGULL CL
City Farm & Eco Pk
SPINNAKER CL
ANCHOR CL
IG11
PUFFIN CL
MARINE DR
SHEARWATER CL
SCHOONER CL
TRAFALGAR HO
GALLEONS DR
MALLARDS RD
GREBE CL
ATLANTIS CL
HORNBEAM CL
VICTORY CT
Allot Gdns
ALGAR
RIVER RD
ANGLIAN IND EST
BALMORAL TRAD EST
ATCOST RD
BUZZARD CREEK IND EST
Pier
Barking or False Point
Barking Reach
River Thames
Barking & Dagenham
Greenwich
Bexley
ST MELLION CL
Cross Ness
ST ANDREWS CL
BIRKDALE CL
ARDEN CL
CARNOUSTIE DR
REDBOURNE DR
ST GEORGES CL
Crossway Lake Nature Reserve
WENTWORTH
VOYAGERS
THAMESBANK PL
Castilion Prim Sch
COPPERFIELD RD
DRAKE CRES
OULTON CL 1
SALHOUSE CL 2
WATERSMEET WAY
WOBURN CL
TURNBURY CL
DOLPHIN CL
POINTER CL
EASTGATE CL
SUMMERTON WAY
CHERBURY CL
TEMPLAR DR
Green Chain Wlk
NICKELBY CL
GREENHAVEN DR
LUDHAM CL
HOVETON RD
ROLLESBY WAY
GRANGE CRES
MANORDENE RD
CROSSWAY
SURLINGHAM CL
LONGWORTH CL
MANOR CL
KINGFISHER CL
WROXHAM
ORMESBY
COURTLAND GR
FLEMING WAY
HODGKINS CL
Ppg Sta
Linton Mead Prim Sch
Bishop John Robinson Sch
BERTRAND WAY
CENTRAL WAY
THAMESMEAD SH CTR
THAMESMERE DR
JOYCE DAWSON WAY
DOWFORD
TAWNEY RD
ATTLEE
HASLER CL
HOLT CL
FAIRHER RD
LIPTON
WOODP
WHIMBREL CL
GOLDCREST CL
FIELDFARE RD
GARGANEY WLK
CURLEW CL
WALSHAM CL
BAYLISS AVE
SANDERLING

DAGENHAM
Old Dagenham Park
Goresbrook Park
Thomas Arnold Prim Sch
81
A
B
C
D
84
6
5
83
4
3
82
2
1
81
48
49
50
125
RM10
RM9
RM13
SE28
A1240
A1306
RIPPLE RD
NEW RD
A13
B178
BALLARDS RD
A1306 Rainham
Heathway
Allot Gdns
Morland Road Day
Dagenham Priory Sch
SCHOOL RD
ORCHARD RD
PEARLSTONES CT
OVAL RD N
BEAM AVE
THIRD AVE
CENTRE RD
SECOND AVE
FIRST AVE
OVAL RD S
EAST ENTRANCE
SIERRA DR
Marsh Green Prim Sch
Motor Works
Dagenham Dock
LC
CHEQUERS LA
CHOATS MANOR WAY
BREACH LA
THAMES GATEWAY PK
HINDMANS WAY
Dagenham Breach
KENT AVE
Horse Shoe Corner
Power Sta
Ind Est
THUNDERER RD
Jetties
Works
Beam River
THAMES AVE
FIESTA DR
River Thames
Jetty
Barking & Dagenham
Havering
Bexley
Halfway Reach
Crossness Pumping Station
Drv Rng
CHART HILLS CL
FAIRWAY DR
LYTHAM CL
SUNNINGDALE CL
Riverside
MERRIELANDS CRES
MERRIELANDS RET PK
GORE'S BRIDGE
CHEQUERS PAR
SCRATTONS TERR
SHAW AVE
SHAW GDNS
MORRISON RD
HORSEBRIDGE CL
GORESBROOK RD
STARMANS CL
TRESWELL RD
CATHERINE GODFREY HO
VINCENT RD
ELSTOW GDNS
ELSTOW RD
THETFORD GDNS
DAGENHAM AVE
T Cts
Sch
PO
ARNOLD RD
MORLAND RD
DIGBY GDNS
LOWER BROAD ST
D'ARCY GDNS
NUTBROWNE RD
COOMBES RD
ROWDOWNS RD
DOWNING RD
BUTTERIDGES CL
BURDETTS RD
WHITEBARN LA
REVIEW RD
CROSBY RD
SOUTH CL
NORTH CL
PRINCESS PAR
LINK RD
MORGAN CL
CAUSTON SQ
BROAD ST
MARSH GREEN RD
BADDOW CL
Schs

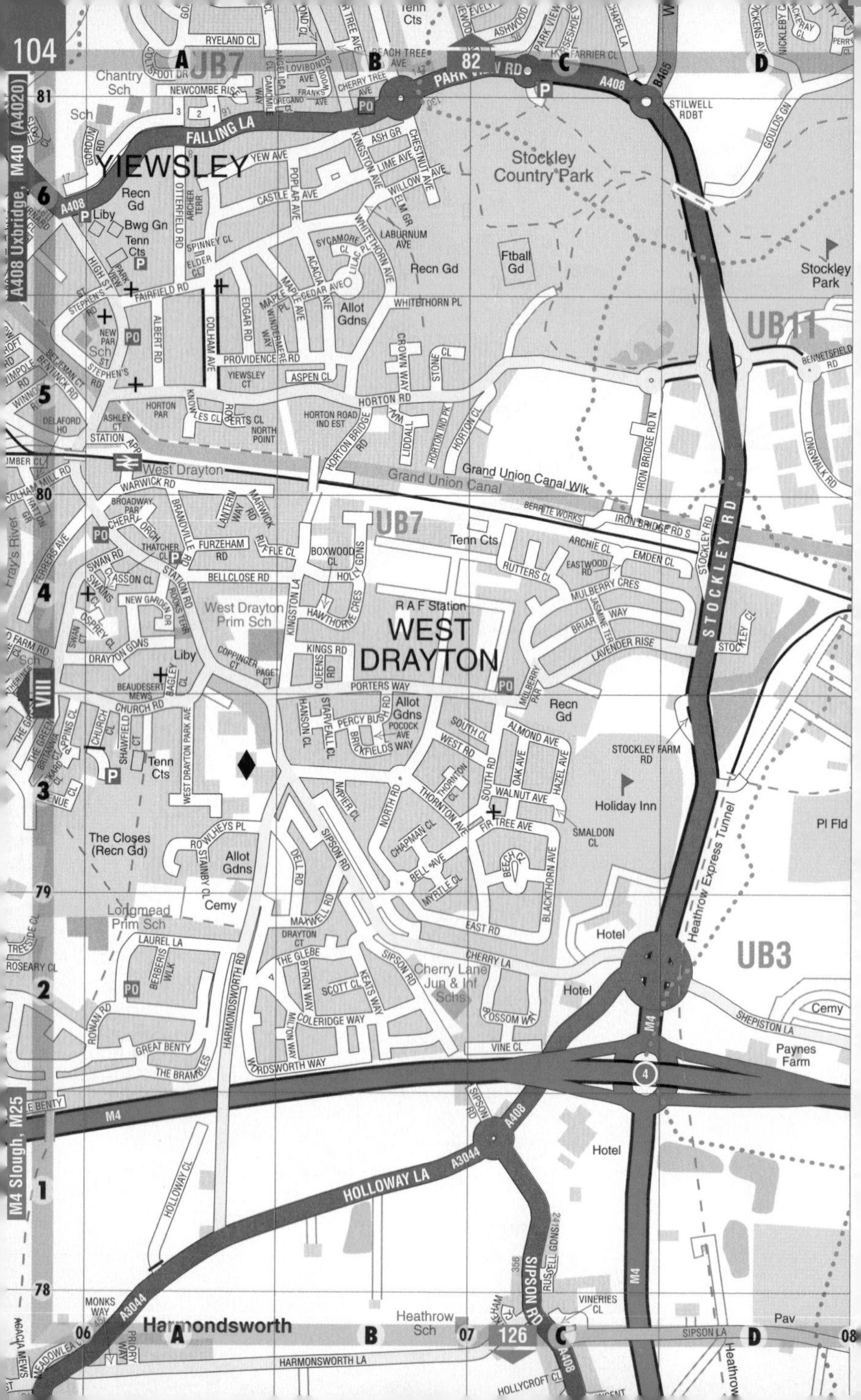

M40 (A4020) A408 Uxbridge
M4 Slough, M25
UB7
UB11
UB3
YIEWSLEY
WEST DRAYTON
Harmondsworth
RYELAND CL
Chantry Sch
NEWCOMBE RISE
FALLING LA
COLTSFOOT DR
ANGELICA
LOVIBONDS AVE
CAMOMILE WAY
FRANKS AVE
OREGANO CL
BEACH TREE AVE
CHERRY TREE AVE
PARK VIEW RD
ASHWOOD
HORSESHOE
FARRIER CL
CHAPEL LA
PARK VIEW
STILWELL RDBT
GOULDS GN
Stockley Country Park
Stockley Park
Ftball Gd
KINGSTON AVE
CHESTNUT AVE
ASH GR
LIME AVE
WILLOW AVE
ELM GR
YEW AVE
CASTLE AVE
POPLAR AVE
WHITETHORN AVE
LABURNUM AVE
SYCAMORE CL
LILAC PL
ACACIA AVE
CEDAR AVE
MAPLE PL
WINDERMERE WAY
Recn Gd
Allot Gdns
WHITETHORN PL
CROWN WAY
STONE CL
GORDON RD
OTTERFIELD RD
ARCHER TERR
SPINNEY CL
ELDER CL
Liby
Bwg Gn
Tenn Cts
HIGH ST
PARK VIEW
FAIRFIELD RD
ST STEPHEN'S RD
NEW PAR
Sch
ALBERT RD
COLHAM AVE
EDGAR RD
PROVIDENCE RD
YIEWSLEY CT
ASPEN CL
HORTON RD
HORTON PAR
KNOWLES CL
ROBERTS CL
NORTH POINT
HORTON ROAD IND EST
HORTON BRIDGE RD
LIDDALL WAY
HORTON IND PK
HORTON CL
BENNETSFIELD RD
LONGWALK RD
IRON BRIDGE RD N
IRON BRIDGE RD S
BETJEMAN CT
BENTINCK RD
WIMPOLE RD
WINNOCK RD
DELAFORD HO
ASHLEY CT
STATION APP
West Drayton
Grand Union Canal
Grand Union Canal Wlk
BERRITE WORKS
HUMBER CL
COLHAM MILL RD
HATTON GR
WARWICK RD
BROADWAY PAR
CHERRY ORCH
BRANDVILLE RD
LANTERN WAY
MARWICK
RUFFLE CL
BOXWOOD CL
HOLLY GDNS
Tenn Cts
ARCHIE CL
EMDEN CL
EASTWOOD RD
RUTTERS CL
MULBERRY CRES
JASMINE TER
BRIAR WAY
LAVENDER RISE
STOCKLEY CL
STOCKLEY RD
Fray's River
FERRERS AVE
SWAN RD
THATCHER CL
FURZEHAM RD
STATION RD
BELLCLOSE RD
ASSON CL
SWAINS CL
NEW GARDEN DR
OSPREY CL
SWAN CT
ROOKS TERR
West Drayton Prim Sch
KINGSTON LA
HAWTHORNE CRES
R A F Station
DRAYTON GDNS
COPPINGER CT
PAGET CT
KINGS RD
QUEENS RD
PORTERS WAY
MULBERRY PAR
FARM RD
BEAUDESERT MEWS
BAGLEY CL
CHURCH RD
THE GREEN
BRITANNIA CL
PIPPINS CL
CHURCH CL
SHAWFIELD CT
WEST DRAYTON PARK AVE
HANSON CL
STARVEALL CL
PERCY BUSH RD
POCOCK AVE
BRICKFIELDS WAY
SOUTH CL
WEST RD
ALMOND AVE
OAK AVE
HAZEL AVE
SOUTH RD
STOCKLEY FARM RD
Holiday Inn
NAPIER CL
NORTH RD
THORNTON CL
THORNTON AVE
WALNUT AVE
FIR TREE AVE
SMALDON CL
Pl Fld
Heathrow Express Tunnel
The Closes (Recn Gd)
ROWLHEYS PL
STAINBY CL
DELL RD
SIPSON RD
CHAPMAN CL
BELL AVE
MYRTLE CL
BEECH CL
BLACKTHORN AVE
Cemy
Longmead Prim Sch
MAXWELL RD
DRAYTON CT
EAST RD
Hotel
TRESIDE CL
ROSEARY CL
LAUREL LA
BERBERIS WLK
HARMONDSWORTH RD
THE GLEBE
BYRON WAY
SCOTT CL
KEATS WAY
CHERRY LA
Cherry Lane Jun & Inf Schs
BLOSSOM WAY
SHEPISTON LA
Paynes Farm
ROWAN RD
GREAT BENTY
COLERIDGE WAY
MILTON WAY
VINE CL
THE BRAMBLES
WORDSWORTH WAY
BENTY
M4
A408
A3044
HOLLOWAY LA
HOLLOWAY CL
SIPSON RD
RUSSELL GDNS
MONKS WAY
MEADOWLEA CL
PRIORY WAY
Heathrow Sch
VINERIES CL
Pav
SIPSON LA
HARMONSWORTH LA
HOLLYCROFT CL
ACACIA MEWS
B465
82
126
VIII

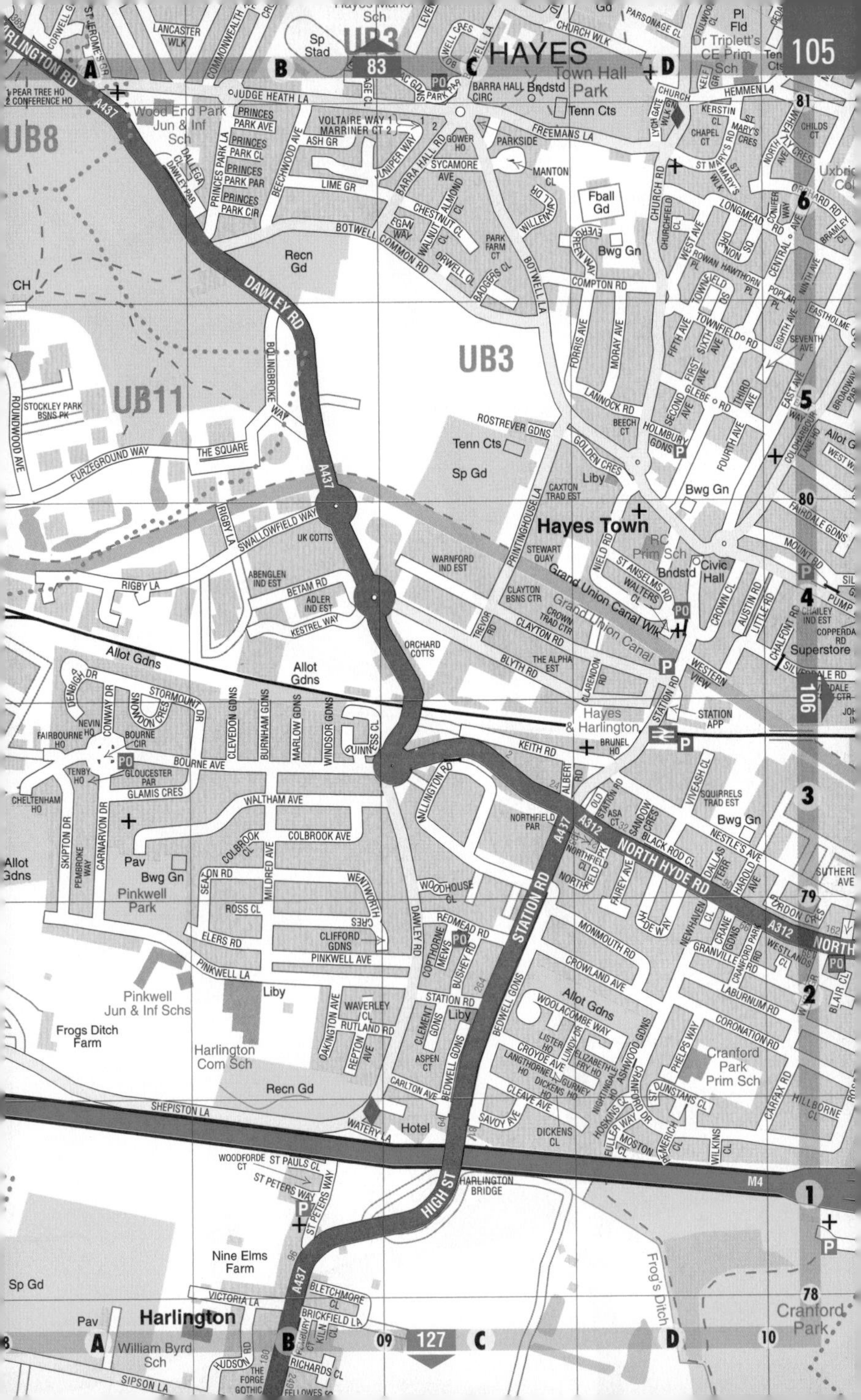
HAYES
UB3
UB8
UB11
A
B
C
D
83
127
Town Hall Park
Barra Hall Circ
Bndstd
Tenn Cts
Church Wlk
Parsonage Cl
Pl Fld
Dr Triplett's CE Prim Sch
Hemmen La
Kerstin Cl
Chapel Ct
St Mary's Rd
St Mary's Cres
Childs Ct
Freemans La
Parkside
Manton Cl
Judge Heath La
Pear Tree Ho
Conference Ho
Wood End Park Jun & Inf Sch
Princes Park Ave
Princes Park Cl
Princes Park Par
Princes Park Cir
Dawley Par
Dallega Cl
Lancaster Wlk
Commonwealth
St Jerome's Gr
Corwell Gdns
Sp Stad
Voltaire Way 1
Marriner Ct 2
Ash Gr
Lime Gr
Beechwood Ave
Juniper Way
Barra Hall Rd
Gower Ho
Sycamore Ave
Almond Cl
Chestnut Cl
Walnut Cl
Egan Way
Orwell Cl
Park Farm Ct
Badgers Cl
Botwell Common Rd
Botwell La
Willenhall Dr
Evergreen Way
Fball Gd
Bwg Gn
Church Rd
Churchfield Cl
West Ave
Longmead Rd
Dene Non Sq
Rowan Pl
Hawthorn Pl
Conifer Way
Central Ave
Orchard Rd
Bramley Cl
North Ave
Wheatley Cres
Ninth Ave
Poplar Pl
Eighth Ave
Eastholme
Seventh Ave
Townfield Rd
Townfield Sq
Fifth Ave
Sixth Ave
First Ave
Second Ave
Third Ave
Fourth Ave
Glebe Rd
East Ave
Broadway
Coldharbour La
Allot Gdns
West Way
Fairdale Gdns
Mount Rd
Pump
Chailey Ind Est
Copperdale
Superstore
Silverdale Rd
106
Recn Gd
CH
Dawley Rd
A437
Bolingbroke Way
Stockley Park Bsns Pk
Roundwood Ave
Furzeground Way
The Square
Compton Rd
Forris Ave
Moray Ave
Lannock Rd
Beech Ct
Holmbury Gdns
Rostrever Gdns
Golden Cres
Tenn Cts
Sp Gd
Liby
Caxton Trad Est
Hayes Town
RC Prim Sch
Printinghouse La
Stewart Quay
Nield Rd
St Anselms Rd
Walters Cl
Bndstd
Civic Hall
Crown Cl
Austin Rd
Little Rd
Chalfont Rd
Rigby La
Swallowfield Way
UK Cotts
Abenglen Ind Est
Betam Rd
Adler Ind Est
Kestrel Way
Warnford Ind Est
Clayton Bsns Ctr
Crown Trad Ctr
Grand Union Canal Wlk
Grand Union Canal
Trevor Rd
Clayton Rd
Blyth Rd
The Alpha Est
Clarendon Rd
Orchard Cotts
Western View
Station Rd
Station App
Hayes & Harlington
Brunel Ho
Keith Rd
Allot Gdns
Denbigh Dr
Conway Dr
Snowdon Cres
Stormount Dr
Nevin Ho
Fairbourne Ho
Bourne Cir
Tenby Ho
Gloucester Par
Cheltenham Ho
Bourne Ave
Glamis Cres
Clevedon Gdns
Burnham Gdns
Marlow Gdns
Windsor Gdns
Guinness Cl
Waltham Ave
Colbrook Ave
Colbrook Cl
Mildred Ave
Seaton Rd
Wentworth Cres
Ross Cl
Elers Rd
Clifford Gdns
Pinkwell Ave
Pinkwell La
Skipton Dr
Pembroke Way
Carnarvon Dr
Pav
Bwg Gn
Pinkwell Park
Willington Rd
Albert Rd
Old Station Rd
Northfield Par
Asa Ct
Sandow Cres
Viveash Cl
Squirrels Trad Est
Bwg Gn
Nestle's Ave
Black Rod Cl
Dallas Terr
Harold Ave
Sutherland Ave
Gordon Cres
79
A312
North Hyde Rd
Northfield Pk
Northfield Cl
Fairey Ave
Hyde Way
Woodhouse Cl
Redmead Rd
Copthorne Mews
Bushey Rd
Station Rd
Monmouth Rd
Crowland Ave
Newhaven Cl
Crane Gdns
Cranford Park Rd
Granville Rd
Westlands Cl
Laburnum Rd
Blair Cl
Coronation Rd
Carfax Rd
Hillborne Cl
Woolacombe Way
Lister Ho
Lundy Dr
Elizabeth Fry Ho
Croyde Ave
Langthorne Ho
Dickens Ho
Gurney
Cleave Ave
Savoy Ave
Dickens Cl
Nightingale Ho
Ashwood Gdns
Phelps Way
Cranford Park Prim Sch
Hoskins Cl
Fuller Way
Moston Cl
Cranford Dr
St Dunstans Cl
Pamerich Cl
Wilkins Cl
Pinkwell Jun & Inf Schs
Frogs Ditch Farm
Liby
Harlington Com Sch
Oakington Ave
Waverley Cl
Rutland Rd
Repton Ave
Clement Gdns
Aspen Ct
Bedwell Gdns
Station Rd
Liby
Carlton Ave
Recn Gd
Shepiston La
Watery La
Hotel
M4
Harlington Bridge
High St
Woodforde Ct
St Pauls Cl
St Peters Way
Nine Elms Farm
Frog's Ditch
Sp Gd
Bletchmore Cl
Victoria La
Brickfield La
Kiln Cl
Pav
Harlington
William Byrd Sch
Hudson Rd
The Forge
Richards Cl
Sipson La
Cranford Park
09
10
78
80
81
1
2
3
4
5
6

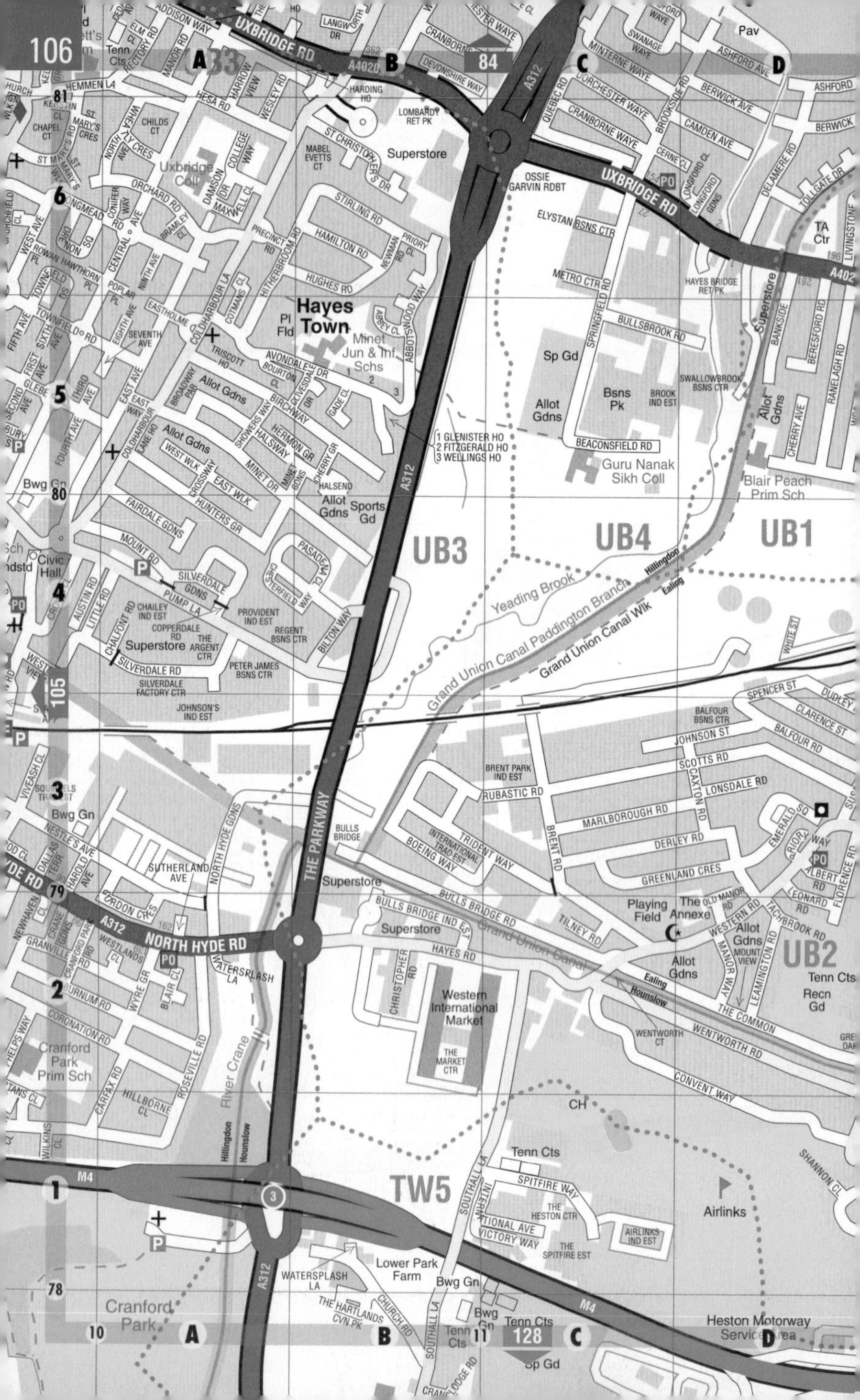
UXBRIDGE RD
A4020
84
ADDISON WAY
MANOR RD
RECTORY RD
HEMMEN LA
HESA RD
HARROW VIEW
WESLEY RD
HARDING HO
LOMBARDY RET PK
Superstore
DEVONSHIRE WAY
CRANBORNE
MINTERNE WAYE
DORCHESTER WAYE
CRANBORNE WAYE
QUEBEC RD
SWANAGE WAYE
ASHFORD AVE
BERWICK AVE
CAMDEN AVE
BROOKSIDE RD
CERNE CL
LONGFORD CL
DELAMERE RD
TOLLGATE DR
LIVINGSTONE
TA Ctr
A312
OSSIE GARVIN RDBT
ELYSTAN BSNS CTR
METRO CTR
SPRINGFIELD RD
BULLSBROOK RD
HAYES BRIDGE RET PK
BANKSIDE
BERESFORD RD
RANELAGH RD
Sp Gd
Bsns Pk
BROOK IND EST
SWALLOWBROOK BSNS CTR
Allot Gdns
CHERRY AVE
BEACONSFIELD RD
Guru Nanak Sikh Coll
Blair Peach Prim Sch
UB4
UB1
UB3
Uxbridge Coll
DAMSON DR
COLLEGE WAY
MAXWELL CL
CHILDS CT
ST MARY'S CRES
CHAPEL CT
WHEATLEY CRES
ORCHARD RD
MABEL EVETTS CT
ST CHRISTOPHER'S DR
STIRLING RD
HAMILTON RD
HUGHES RD
PRIORY CL
ABBOTSWOOD WAY
HITHERBROOM RD
PRECINCT RD
Hayes Town
Pl Fld
Minet Jun & Inf Schs
AVONDALE DR
BOURTON CL
CLIVESDALE DR
GADE CL
1 GLENISTER HO
2 FITZGERALD HO
3 WELLINGS HO
COLDHARBOUR LA
COTMANS CL
TRISCOTT HO
EASTHOLME
SEVENTH AVE
EIGHTH AVE
NINTH AVE
CENTRAL AVE
BRAMLEY CL
LONGMEAD RD
ROWAN
HAWTHORN
POPLAR
TOWNFIELD RD
FIFTH AVE
SIXTH AVE
FIRST AVE
SECOND AVE
THIRD AVE
FOURTH AVE
EAST AVE
BROADWAY PAR
Allot Gdns
SHOWERS WAY
BIRCHWAY
HERMON GR
HALSWAY
MINET DR
MINET GDNS
CHERRY GR
HALSEND
Sports Gd
WEST WLK
EAST WLK
CROSSWAY
HUNTERS GR
FAIRDALE GDNS
MOUNT RD
Bwg Gn
Civic Hall
PASADENA CL
CHESTERFIELD WAY
BILTON WAY
SILVERDALE GDNS
PUMP LA
CHAILEY IND EST
COPPERDALE RD
THE ARGENT CTR
PROVIDENT IND EST
REGENT BSNS CTR
Superstore
AUSTIN RD
LITTLE RD
CHALFONT RD
SILVERDALE RD
SILVERDALE FACTORY CTR
PETER JAMES BSNS CTR
JOHNSON'S IND EST
105
Yeading Brook
Grand Union Canal Paddington Branch
Grand Union Canal Wlk
Hillingdon
Ealing
WHITE ST
SPENCER ST
DUDLEY
CLARENCE ST
BALFOUR BSNS CTR
BALFOUR RD
JOHNSON ST
SCOTTS RD
CAXTON RD
LONSDALE RD
BRENT PARK IND EST
RUBASTIC RD
MARLBOROUGH RD
EMERALD SQ
PRIORY WAY
DERLEY RD
BRENT RD
GREENLAND CRES
ALBERT RD
LEONARD RD
FLORENCE RD
TRIDENT WAY
INTERNATIONAL TRAD EST
BOEING WAY
BULLS BRIDGE
THE PARKWAY
VIVEASH CL
Bwg Gn
NESTLE'S AVE
DALLAS TERR
HAROLD AVE
SUTHERLAND AVE
NORTH HYDE GDNS
Superstore
BULLS BRIDGE IND EST
BULLS BRIDGE RD
TILNEY RD
Playing Field
The Annexe
OLD MANOR RD
WESTERN RD
TACHBROOK RD
Allot Gdns
MANOR WAY
MOUNT VIEW
LEAMINGTON RD
UB2
Tenn Cts
Recn Gd
NORTH HYDE RD
A312
GORDON CRES
WESTLANDS CL
NEWHAVEN CL
CRANE GDNS
CRANFORD PARK RD
GRANVILLE RD
WATERSPLASH LA
Superstore
HAYES RD
Grand Union Canal
Ealing
Hounslow
CHRISTOPHER RD
Western International Market
THE MARKET CTR
THE COMMON
WENTWORTH CT
WENTWORTH RD
CONVENT WAY
BURNUM RD
WYRE GR
BLAIR CL
CORONATION RD
Cranford Park Prim Sch
ROSEVILLE RD
CARFAX RD
HILLBORNE CL
River Crane
Hillingdon
Hounslow
WILKINS CL
CH
Tenn Cts
SHANNON CL
M4
3
TW5
SOUTHALL LA
SPITFIRE WAY
INTERNATIONAL AVE
VICTORY WAY
THE HESTON CTR
THE SPITFIRE EST
AIRLINKS IND EST
Airlinks
Lower Park Farm
WATERSPLASH LA
THE HARTLANDS CVN PK
CHURCH RD
Bwg Gn
Cranford Park
Tenn Cts
Sp Gd
128
Heston Motorway Service Area
LODGE RD
78
79
80
81
10
11
A
B
C
D
1
2
3
4
5
6

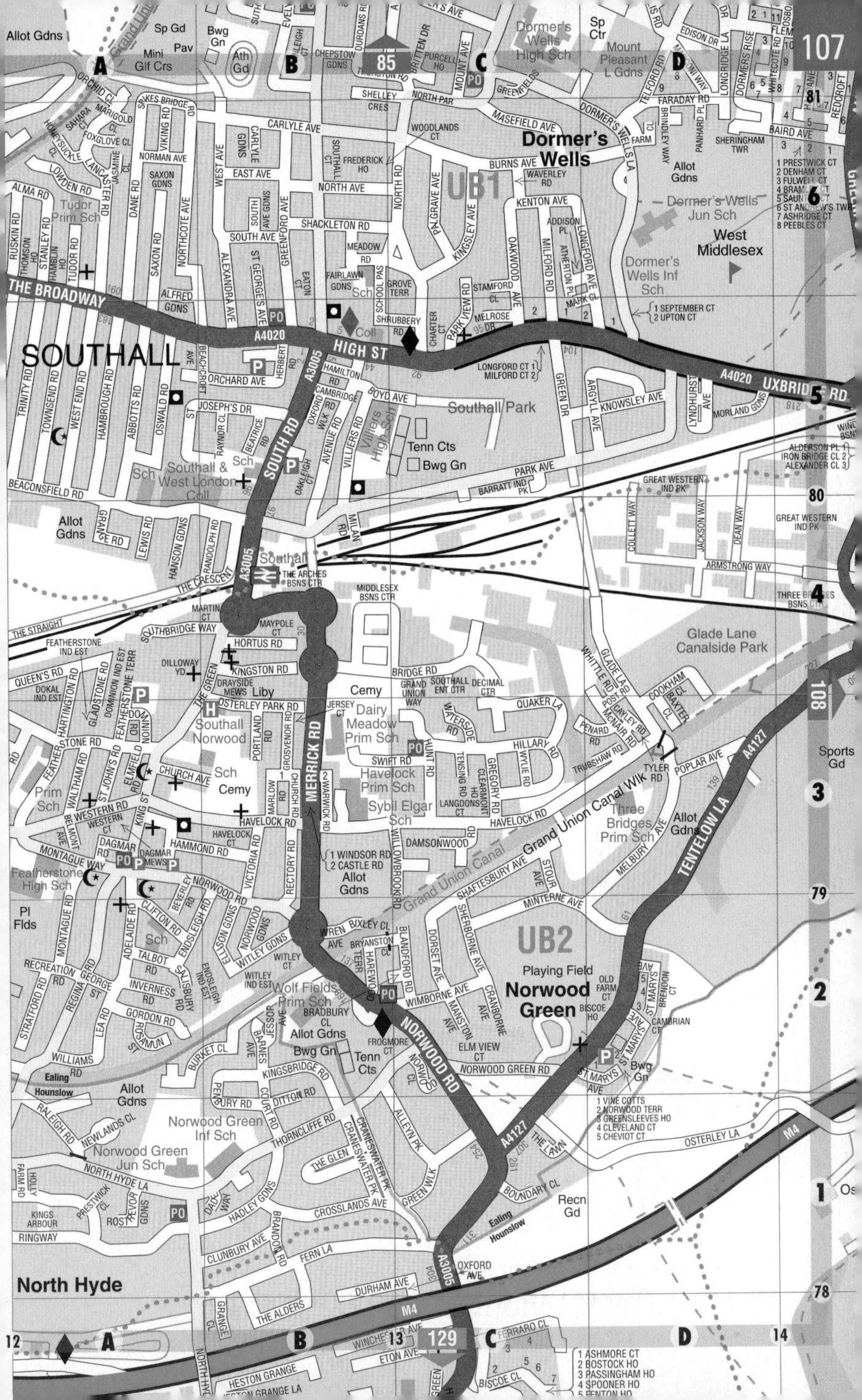
85
108
129
A
B
C
D
1
2
3
4
5
6
12
13
14
78
79
80
81
SOUTHALL
Dormer's Wells
Norwood Green
North Hyde
UB1
UB2
THE BROADWAY
HIGH ST
A4020
UXBRIDGE RD
SOUTH RD
A3005
MERRICK RD
NORWOOD RD
TENTELOW LA
A4127
Grand Union Canal
Grand Union Canal Wlk
M4
Southall Park
Glade Lane Canalside Park
West Middlesex
Allot Gdns
Sp Gd
Bwg Gn
Mini Glf Crs
Pav
Ath Gd
Mount Pleasant L Gdns
Sp Ctr
Dormer's Wells High Sch
Dormer's Wells Jun Sch
Dormer's Wells Inf Sch
Tudor Prim Sch
Villiers High Sch
Southall & West London Coll
Tenn Cts
Cemy
Liby
Southall Norwood
Dairy Meadow Prim Sch
Havelock Prim Sch
Sybil Elgar Sch
Three Bridges Prim Sch
Featherstone High Sch
Pl Flds
Prim Sch
Wolf Fields Prim Sch
Playing Field
Norwood Green Inf Sch
Norwood Green Jun Sch
Recn Gd
Sports Gd
MIDDLESEX BSNS CTR
THE ARCHES BSNS CTR
GREAT WESTERN IND PK
THREE BRIDGES BSNS CTR
FEATHERSTONE IND EST
DOKAL IND EST
WITLEY IND EST
ENDSLEIGH IND EST
BARRATT IND PK
SOUTHALL ENT CTR
DECIMAL CTR
CARLYLE AVE
EAST AVE
NORTH AVE
SOUTH AVE
BURNS AVE
KENTON AVE
MASEFIELD AVE
FARADAY RD
BAIRD AVE
PARK AVE
ARMSTRONG WAY
THE STRAIGHT
THE CRESCENT
SOUTHBRIDGE WAY
BRIDGE RD
HAVELOCK RD
WESTERN RD
NORWOOD GREEN RD
OSTERLEY LA
MINTERNE AVE
SHAFTESBURY AVE
POPLAR AVE
CROSSLANDS AVE
FERN LA
DURHAM AVE
THE ALDERS
RINGWAY
NORTH HYDE LA
HESTON GRANGE
HESTON GRANGE LA
BISCOE CL
FERRARO CL
ETON AVE
WINCHESTER AVE
1 PRESTWICK CT
2 DENHAM CT
3 FULWELL CT
7 ASHRIDGE CT
8 PEEBLES CT
1 SEPTEMBER CT
2 UPTON CT
LONGFORD CT 1
MILFORD CT 2
ALDERSON PL 1
IRON BRIDGE CL 2
ALEXANDER CL 3
1 WINDSOR RD
2 CASTLE RD
1 VINE COTTS
2 NORWOOD TERR
3 GREENSLEEVES HO
4 CLEVELAND CT
5 CHEVIOT CT
1 ASHMORE CT
2 BOSTOCK HO
3 PASSINGHAM HO
4 SPOONER HO
Ealing
Hounslow

A
B
C
D
86
Brent Valley
W7
HAWTHORNE MEWS
FLEMING RD
WHITECOTE RD
HALDANE RD
REDCROFT RD
BAIRD AVE
SHERINGHAM TWR
PANHARD PL
1 PRESTWICK CT
2 DENHAM CT
3 FULWELL CT
4 BRAMLEY CT
5 SAUNTON CT
6 ST ANDREW'S TWR
7 ASHRIDGE CT
8 PEEBLES CT
West Middlesex
GREENFORD RD
A4127
CH
Sp Gd
HIGH LA
ELMWOOD GDNS
GROVE AVE
HOMEFARM
FRAMFIELD RD
WARWICK CT
WORCESTER CT
Hobbayne Prim Sch
Drayton Manor High Sch
Drayton Green
DRYDEN AVE
DRAYTON BRIDGE RD
COWPER RD
SHAKESPEARE RD
MILTON RD
ALLINGHAM CL
TENNYSON RD
PARK RD
MADGE HILL
CHURCH RD
CUCKOO LA
APRIL CL
OAKLEY CL
LIME TERR
SPRING CT
GLEBE CT
BRENT CT
BRIERLEY CT
HIGHTREES CT
COURT RD
GOLDEN CT
TESTWOOD CT
MANOR CT
BRENTMEAD CL
GOLDEN MANOR
BLAGDON CT
CAMPBELL CT
CAMPBELL RD
ALWYNE RD
Churchfields Recn Gd
T Cts
Bwg Gn
Hanwell
1 SHERIDAN CT
2 KIPLING CT
YORK AVE
Schs
Cemy
HOLLY PARK RD
NETHERAVON RD
AZALEA CT
SHIRLEY GDNS
BAKER HO
NIGHTINGALE RD
UB1
UXBRIDGE RD
A4020
WHARNCLIFFE DR
BRENTVALE AVE
BLACKMORE AVE
Allot Gdns
River Brent
CONOLLY RD
LAWN GDNS
MYRTLE GDNS
LAUREL GDNS
HALF ACRE RD
STATION RD
SPRINGFIELD RD
YORK CL
BALFOUR AVE
CLAIRVILLE GDNS
CHERINGTON RD
BROADWAY
Liby
PO
HAYDON HO
FILANCO CT
BARCHESTER CL
MICHAEL GAYNOR CL
LYNDHURST AVE
MORLAND GDNS
TRIANGLE CTR
WINDMILL BSNS CTR
ALDERSON PL
IRON BRIDGE CL
ALEXANDER CL
ELLIS RD
CUBITT SQ
HALLIDAY SQ
WEST PARK RD
WINDMILL AVE
WILLIAM CL
LOCK CL
GRAND DR
CHEVY RD
OSTERLEY GDNS
OSTERLEY VIEWS
Ealing
H
A4001 BOSTON RD
JESSAMINE RD
GEORGE ST
WESTMINSTER RD
WILMOT
FACTORY YD
WALKER CL
THE HEATH
MONTAGUE AVE
ST GEORGE'S RD
City of Westminster Cemy
LOWER BOSTON RD
ADELAIDE CT
Sch
MOUNT OLIVE CT
GREEN LA
BISHOP'S RD
ST ANDREW'S RD
ST MARK'S RD
BOSTONTHORPE RD
ST DUNSTAN'S RD
ROSEBANK RD
OSTERLEY PARK VIEW RD
OSTERLEY GRANGE RD
MONTAGUE RD
DEAN'S RD
CAMBRIDGE RD
DENE CT
SOUTHFIELD COTTS
EDINBURGH RD
OAKLANDS RD
CUMBERLAND RD
A3002
80
JACKSON WAY
DEAN WAY
GREAT WESTERN IND PK
ARMSTRONG WAY
THREE BRIDGES BSNS CTR
WINDMILL LA
NAVIGATOR DR
RIVER CL
Grand Union Canal Wlk
1 WATER LILY CL
2 COMER CRES
3 TULIP CL
WINDMILL BRIDGE
Glade Lane Canalside Park
OAK COTTS
ST MARGARET'S RD
BILLETTS HART CL
STUDLEY GRANGE RD
HUMES AVE
LAMBOURN CL
ROSEDALE CL
BELVEDERE RD
TRUMPERS WAY
TOWNHOLM CRES
Bnstd
Elthorne Park
107
B454
WOLSEY CL
UB2
1 QUEEN TERR COTTS
2 THORNWELL CT
3 ST MARK'S CT
4 DU BURSTOW TERR
5 CHURCHFIELD RD
6 MALLARD CL
WATERSIDE TRAD CTR
Sports Gd
Sp Ctr
Pl Fld
W7
Elthorne Park High Sch
BOSTON BSNS PK
RIVER BRENT BSNS PK
The Aviary
River Brent
Grand Union Canal
79
WINDMILL LA
Osterley Lock
M4
Trumper's Wood
OSTERLEY LA
OSTERLEY LA
Hare & Hounds (PH)
Osterley Park Farm
TW7
Bwg Gn
Tenn Cts
Wyke Green
Osterley Park
Osterley Park House
Sp Gd
78
CH
B454 SYON LA
14
15
130
16
T Cts
P
Pav

EALING
West Ealing
BRENTFORD
W5
TW7
TW8
87
110
131
UXBRIDGE RD
BROADWAY
NEW BROADWAY
THE BROADWAY
THE MALL
A4020
B452
B455
B4491
M4 (ELEVATED)
A3002
A4
HIGH ST
BOND ST
EALING GN
ST MARY'S RD
SOUTH EALING RD
EALING RD
NORTHFIELD AVE
DRAYTON GREEN RD
LITTLE EALING LA
WINDMILL RD
BOSTON RD
BOSTON MANOR RD
Walpole Park
Lammas Park
BBC Television Film Studios
Mus & Art Gall
Christ Church CE Mid Sch
Thames Valley Univ
YMCA
Drayton Green Prim Sch
Fielding Prim Sch
Gunnersbury RC Sch
Northfields Recn Gd
South Ealing Cemy
Boston Manor Pl Flds
Boston Manor Park
Boston Manor
Northfields
South Ealing
Ealing Broadway
Grand Union Canal Wlk
Grand Union Canal
Depot
Allot Gdns
B Sky B HQ
Griffin Park Fball Gd
Brentford Sch for Girls
Phoenix Trad Pk
Ealing Road Trad Est
Reynard Mills Trad Est
A
B
C
D
1
2
3
4
5
6

A
B
C
D
88
Ealing Broadway
West Acton Prim Sch
Ellen Wilkinson Sch for Girls
Allot Gdns
Tenn Cts
CHURCHILL GDNS
LYNTON RD
THE BROADWAY
A4020
THE MALL
UXBRIDGE RD
NORTH COMMON RD
HAMILTON RD
A406
WALDEGRAVE RD
HOLLYWOOD CT
OAKLEY AVE
The Japanese Sch
Bwg Gn
Pav
Coll
Sp Gd
Ealing Common
Ealing Common
W5
W3
W4
TW8
GRANGE RD
THE GROVE
GROVE RD
OXFORD RD
WINDSOR RD
FLORENCE RD
WARWICK RD
ELM AVE
ELM GROVE RD
GUNNERSBURY AVENUE (NORTH CIRCULAR ROAD)
GUNNERSBURY LA
A4000
Twyford CE High Sch
TWYFORD CRES
HIGH ST
Acton High Sch
Acton Town
South Acton
BOLLO BRIDGE RD
BOLLO LA
Pl Fld
Sp Gd
Allot Gdns
POPE'S LA
B4491
Gunnersbury Park
Gunnersbury Park Mus
Bwg Gns
Tenn Cts
International Sch of London
Gunnersbury Cemy
Gunnersbury
Lionel Road Jun & Inf Sch
LIONEL ROAD N
South Ealing Cemy
Claypoonds
M4 (ELEVATED)
GREAT WEST RD (UNDER)
CHISWICK HIGH RD
A315
Chiswick Rdbt
Superstore
Brentford Fountain L Ctr
WELLESLEY RD A3000
A3000
A205
KEW BRIDGE RD
Kew Bridge
Mus
Sch
BRENTFORD
Brentford Ait
Strand on the Green
EALING RD
B455
Griffin Park Fball Gd
CHISWICK PK
109
132
6
5
4
3
2
1

A
B
C
D
89
WESTERN AVE
WESTWAY
A40
Savoy Circus
Superstore
King Fahed Acad
W3
East Acton
Prim Sch
Allot Gdns
Recn Gd
ACTON
Acton Central
Acton Park
HIGH ST
THE VALE
A4020
B408
ASKEW RD
HORN LA
A4000
Bedford Park
THE AVENUE
SOUTHFIELD RD
B491
BATH RD
B409
STAMFORD BROOK RD
GOLDHAWK RD
A402
W4
Turnham Green
TURNHAM GREEN TERR
Stamford Brook
Acton Green
SOUTH PAR
B490
ACTON LA
Chiswick Common
Chiswick Park
CHISWICK HIGH RD
A315
KING ST
HEATHFIELD TERR
A3000
CHISWICK LA
A316
CHISWICK
A4 GREAT WEST RD
CEDARS RD
GREAT WEST RD
Hogarth Roundabout
Thames Path
CHISWICK MALL
112
133
80
81
79
78
6
5
4
3
2
1
21
22

Queen Charlottes & Chelsea
DU CANE RD
PIONEER WAY
WESTWAY (ELEVATED ROAD)
WESTWAY
A40
White City
90
A
B
C
D
PRIMULA ST
ROSEWOOD SQ
HEATHSTAN RD
BENTWORTH RD
Canberra Prim Sch
WHITE CITY RD
Phoenix High Sch
Wormholt Park Prim Sch
Wormholt Park
BRYONY RD
COMMONWEALTH AVE
RC Sch
WHITE CITY EST
SOUTH AFRICA RD
TA Ctr
W12
BBC Television Ctr
WOOD LA
A219
White City
Latimer Road
WEST CROSS ROUTE
Kensington & Chelsea
Hammersmith & Fulham
SILCHESTER RD
Shepherd's Bush
QPR Fball Gd
SAWLEY RD
DUNRAVEN RD
ELLERSLIE RD
ALDBOURNE RD
UXBRIDGE RD
A4020
Shepherd's Bush
Shepherd's Bush (Central Line)
Rail Depot
W11
QUEENSDALE CRES
Holland Park Rdbt
A402
Shepherd's Bush Common
SHEPHERD'S BUSH GN
CONCORD CTR
Tenn Cts
ASKEW RD
B408
GOLDHAWK RD
Goldhawk Road
SHEPHERD'S BUSH RD
W14
Brook Green
BROOK GN
ASHCHURCH TERR
A402
PADDENSWICK RD
Ravenscourt Park
Stamford Brook
GOLDHAWK RD
DALLING RD
GLENTHORNE RD
A315
HAMMERSMITH
W6
BEADON RD
HAMMERSMITH RD
KING ST
Hammersmith Broadway
TALGARTH RD
Hammersmith Flyover
GREAT WEST RD
A4
River Thames
Thames Path
UPPER MALL
LOWER MALL
HAMMERSMITH BRIDGE RD
Hammersmith & Fulham
Richmond upon Thames
HAMMERSMITH BRIDGE
St Paul's Sch
Tenn Cts
CASTELNAU
LONSDALE RD
B350
FULHAM PALACE RD
Charing Cross
Cemy
MARGRAVINE GDNS
CHISWICK MALL
78
79
80
81
111
22
23
134

A
B
C
D
91
245
244
254
114
135
255
W11
W8
W14
SW5
W6
Notting Hill
Kensington
West Kensington
Earl's Court
West Brompton
Holland Park
Ladbroke Square Gardens
Avondale Park
Holland Park Tenn Gd
Holland Park Sch
Kensington Palace
Kensington Palace Green
Round Pond
Diana, Princess of Wales Memorial Walk
Queensway Black Lion Gate
Orme Square Gate
Inverness Terrace Gate
Palace Gate
Notting Hill Gate
Holland Park
High Street Kensington
Kensington Olympia
Olympia Ex Ctr
Gall & Mus
Earl's Court Ex Ctr
Barons Court Cemy
The Queen's Club
Kensington Village
The Grange
Bayswater
Queensway
West Brompton
Gibbs Gn
Notting Hill Gate
Kensington Park Rd
Ladbroke Gr
Holland Park Ave
Kensington Church St
Kensington High St
Addison Rd
Holland Rd
Hammersmith Rd
North End Rd
West Cromwell Rd
Talgarth Rd
Warwick Rd
Warwick Gdns
Pembroke Rd
Earl's Court Rd
Cromwell Rd
Old Brompton Rd
Finborough Rd
Redcliffe Gdns
Holland Walk
Campden Hill Rd
Phillimore Gdns
Abingdon Rd
Pembridge Villas
Pembridge Rd
Pembridge Gdns
Pembridge Sq
Palace Gardens Terr
Palace Green
The Broad Walk
Hyde Park Gate
Gloucester Rd
Victoria Rd
Lexham Gdns
Cornwall Gdns
Kenway Rd
Hogarth Rd
Nevern Sq
Philbeach Gdns
Russell Rd
Olympia Way
Addison Cres
Edith Rd
Baron's Court Rd
Gliddon Rd
Palliser Rd
Portobello Rd
Westbourne Gr
Colville Terr
Moscow Rd
Porchester Terr
Queensborough Terr
Inverness Terr
Lansdowne Rd
Clarendon Rd
Portland Rd
Walmer Rd
Princedale Rd
Queensdale Rd
Royal Cres
Elsham Rd
Russell Gdns Mews
Sinclair Rd
Blythe Rd
Hazlitt Rd
Addison Bridge Pl
Avonmore Rd
Lisgar Terr
Castletown Rd
Comeragh Rd
Perham Rd
Star Rd
Archel Rd
Chesson Rd
Kensington Palace Gdns
Campden Hill
Sheffield Terr
Bedford Gdns
Peel St
Edge St
Uxbridge St
Hillgate Pl
Kensington Pl
Aubrey Wlk
Duchess of Bedford's Wlk
Melbury Rd
Ilchester Pl
Oakwood Ct
Abbotsbury Rd
Woodsford Sq
Redlynch Ct
Edwardes Sq
Pembroke Sq
Scarsdale Villas
Stratford Rd
Marloes Rd
Allen St
Wright's La
Iverna Gdns
Kensington Sq
Derry St
Young St
St Alban's Gr
Kelso Pl
Eldon Rd
Kynance Mews
Courtfield Gdns
Collingham Rd
Harrington Gdns
Bramham Gdns
Barkston Gdns
Earl's Court Sq
Penywern Rd
Trebovir Rd
Longridge Rd
Templeton Pl
Logan Pl
Redcliffe Sq
Coleherne Rd
Harcourt Terr
The Little Boltons
Eardley Cres
Empress Pl
Beaumont Ave
Beaumont Cres
North End Ho
Gunterstone Rd
Gwendwr Rd
Barons Keep
Challoner St
Charleville Rd
Fairholme Rd
Mund St
Sun Rd
Thaxton Rd
Greyhound Rd
Normand Rd
Turneville Rd
Bramber Rd
Seagrave Rd
Ongar Rd
Fawcett St
A402
A4206
A4204
A315
A3220
A3218
A4
B450
B415
B411
B405
B316
B317
B325
B410
Tenn Cts
Sch
Coll
Liby
PO
TH
YH
Pav

246
92
247
Bayswater
Queensway
Bayswater Rd
A402
Sussex Gdns
Westbourne St
Lancaster Gate
Marble Arch
Cumberland Gate
Speakers' Corner
North Carriage Dr
North Ride
Victoria Gate
Westbourne Gate
The Fountains
Marlborough Gate
North Flower Wlk
North Wlk
Queensway Black Lion Gate
Inverness Terrace Gate
W2
The Long Water
West Carriage Dr
Buck Hill Wlk
Bird Sanctuary
Nursery
New Lodge
Diana Princess of Wales Memorial Walk
Hyde Park
Ranger's Lodge
Ranger's Cottage
Serpentine Lodge
Serpentine Rd
The Serpentine
The Lido
Holocaust Memorial
The Dell Garden
Temple Lodge
Serpentine Bridge
Round Pond
Kensington Gardens
The Broad Wlk
Lancaster Wlk
Budge's Wlk
Bndstd
Serpentine Gall
The Flower Wlk
Coalbrookdale Gate
Albert Meml
Palace Gate
Queen's Gate
Alexandra Gate
Prince of Wales' Gate
Rotten Row
Fball Gds
Tenn Cts
Bwg Gn
Pav
Edinburgh Gate
Albert Gate
New Ride
South Carriage Dr
Scotch House
Barracks
W8
The Dial Wlk
Kensington Rd
Kensington Gore
Hyde Park Gate
Knightsbridge
A315
113
The Albert Hall
Prince Consort Rd
Imperial College Rd
Exhibition Rd
Science Mus
Natural History Mus
Victoria & Albert Mus
Brompton
Brompton Oratory
The Oratory
Brompton Rd
SW7
Cromwell Rd
Cromwell Gdns
Gloucester Rd
Gloucester Road
Queen's Gate
Sloane St
Pont St
Hans Cres
Beauchamp Pl
Cadogan Sq
Thurloe Pl
Thurloe Sq
South Kensington
Onslow Sq
Pelham St
Sydney St
Royal Marsden
Royal Brompton
Old Brompton Rd
South Kensington
The Boltons
SW10
SW3
Chelsea
King's Rd
Fulham Rd
Duke of York's HQ
Burton's Court
Royal Hospital Rd
Redcliffe Gdns
Finborough Rd
256
136
257

MARYLEBONE
248
93
249
A
B
C
D
OXFORD ST
Bond Street
ORCHARD ST
Mayfair
Grosvenor Sq Gardens
GROSVENOR SQ
NEW BOND ST
CONDUIT ST
REGENT ST
A4201
CARNABY ST
Govt Offices
SHAFTESBURY AVE
CHARING CROSS RD
CAMBRIDGE CIR
GERRARD ST
LISLE ST
CRANBOURN ST
Leicester Square
Piccadilly Circus
PICCADILLY CIR
Eros
National Gallery
TRAFALGAR
Nelson's Mon
Charing Cross
COCKSPUR ST
PALL MALL E
HAYMARKET
Royal Academy of Arts
PICCADILLY
St James
PALL MALL
ST JAMES'S ST
JERMYN ST
Admiralty Arch
Art Galls
St James's Palace
Clarence House
THE MALL
(CLOSED TO TRAFFIC ON SUNDAYS)
Green Park
SW1
Diana, Princess of Wales Memorial Walk
Duck Island
St James's Park Lake
St James's Park
Horse Guards Parade
WHITEHALL
Govt Offices
DOWNING ST
KING CHARLES ST
Cabinet War Rooms
PARLIAMENT ST
GREAT GEORGE ST
A3214
PARK LA
A4202
Hyde Park Corner
Mus
Horse Ride
CONSTITUTION HILL
(CLOSED TO TRAFFIC ON SUNDAYS)
Queen Victoria Meml
Buckingham Palace Gardens
Buckingham Palace
WESTMINSTER
BIRDCAGE WLK
Wellington Barracks
Queens Gall
The Royal Mews
BUCKINGHAM GATE
PETTY FRANCE
St James's Park
BROADWAY
New Scotland Yard
Westminster Abbey
Meth Hall
TOTHILL ST
Guildhall
116
GROSVENOR PL
A302
GROSVENOR CRES
B310
Tenn Ct
BELGRAVE SQ
LR GROSVENOR PL
GROSVENOR GDNS
VICTORIA ST
Strutton Ground
GREAT PETER ST
GREAT SMITH ST
ABINGDON ST
MILLBANK
KING'S RD
ECCLESTON ST
BUCKINGHAM PALACE RD
Victoria
WILTON RD
VAUXHALL BRIDGE RD
HORSEFERRY RD
MARSHAM ST
Belgravia
Victoria Coach
Sloane Square
PIMLICO RD
WARWICK WAY
BELGRAVE RD
JOHN ISLIP ST
Tate Britain
Chelsea Barracks
Pimlico
BESSBOROUGH ST
BESSBOROUGH GDNS
Royal Hospital (Army Pensioners)
Ranelagh Gardens (Site of Chelsea Flower Show)
CHELSEA BRIDGE RD
Lister
Dock
CHURCHILL GARDENS RD
Wharves
VAUXHALL BRIDGE
CHELSEA EMBANKMENT
258
137
GROSVENOR RD
259
A3212
CHELSEA BRIDGE
GROSVENOR BRIDGE
River Thames
City of Westminster
Kensington & Chelsea
1
2
3
4
5
6

250
94
251
Royal Courts of Justice
Covent Garden
ALDWYCH
Strand
STRAND
Somerset House
Leicester Square
LONG ACRE
Old Covent Garden
CROSS RD
CHARING
Inner Temple Garden
VICTORIA EMBANKMENT
A3211
Temple Pier
BLACKFRIARS UNDERPASS
BLACKFRIARS BRIDGE
Blackfriars
River Bus Route
WATERLOO BRIDGE
King's Reach
River Thames
National Gallery
TRAFALGAR
Nelson's Mon
Charing Cross
Cleopatra's Needle
Festival Pier
National Theatre
Embankment Pier
Embankment
Gallery
PALL MALL E
COCKSPUR ST
NORTHUMBERLAND AVE
Admiralty Arch
Art Galls
STAMFORD ST
SOUTHWARK
HUNGERFORD BRIDGE (FOOT and RAIL)
Royal Festival Hall
Govt Offices
Horse Guards Parade
WHITEHALL
HORSEGUARDS AVE
Jubilee Gdns
Cinema
Waterloo
Waterloo East
THE CUT
BLACKFRIARS RD
Duck Island
DOWNING ST
London Eye
Old County Hall
South Bank
YORK RD
Waterloo Int
WATERLOO RD
Cabinet War Rooms
KING CHARLES ST
Westminster
GREAT GEORGE ST
BRIDGE ST
WESTMINSTER BRIDGE RD
A302
New Palace Yard
LAMBETH
Mus
Lambeth North
BAYLIS RD
ST GEORGE'S CIR
BOROUGH RD
Meth Hall
New Scotland Yard
Westminster Abbey
Houses of Parliament
Old Palace Yard
St Thomas'
LAMBETH PALACE RD
Albert Embankment
Cath
LONDON RD
Elephant & Castle
Archbishop's Park
Lambeth Palace
LAMBETH RD
Geraldine Mary Harmsworth Park
Imperial War Mus
MILLBANK
MARSHAM ST
LAMBETH BRIDGE
A3203
KENNINGTON RD
Recn Gd
Tate Britain
JOHN ISLIP ST
Thames Path
ALBERT EMBANKMENT
SE11
Newington
NEWINGTON BUTTS
KENNINGTON PARK RD
Vauxhall
VAUXHALL BRIDGE
BRIDGEFOOT
Spring Gardens
KENNINGTON LA
Kennington
Vauxhall Cross
Wharves
Wharf
New Covent Garden
260
138
261
The Oval (Surrey Cnty Crkt Gd)
Bnstand
Tenn Cts
SE17
115

CITY OF LONDON
EC4
EC3
St Paul's Cath
Mansion House
Cannon Street
Bank
Aldgate
Whitechapel
Fenchurch Street
Tower Hill
Tower Gateway
Monument
Custom House
Swan Lane Pier
City of London
Southwark
Bankside Pier
The Globe Theatre
London Bridge
The London Dungeon Mus
London Bridge City Pier
Tower Millennium Pier
The Tower
Traitors Gate
Thames Path
River Bus Route
TOWER BRIDGE
St Katharine Docks
St Katharine Pier
Tower Hamlets
Southwark
Butler's Wharf Pier
Tower Bridge Wharf
City Hall
Guy's
Borough
The Borough
BERMONDSEY
Bermondsey (New Caledonian)
Caledonian Market
Bricklayers Arms
Elephant & Castle
Walworth
Burgess Park
Cobourg Jun & Inf Sch
Superstore
SE1
SE16
SE17
SE15
E1
UPPER THAMES ST
LOWER THAMES ST
SOUTHWARK BRIDGE RD
SOUTHWARK ST
BOROUGH HIGH ST
TOOLEY ST
ST THOMAS ST
CRUCIFIX LA
BERMONDSEY ST
LONG LA
GREAT DOVER ST
TOWER BRIDGE RD
ABBEY ST
GRANGE RD
NEW KENT RD
OLD KENT RD
SOUTHWARK PARK RD
WALWORTH RD
DUNTON RD
ROLLS RD
ALBANY RD
EAST SMITHFIELD
ROYAL MINT ST
MINORIES
UNION ST
A
B
C
D
252
95
253
118
263
262
139
33
34
80
79
78
1
2
3
4
5
6

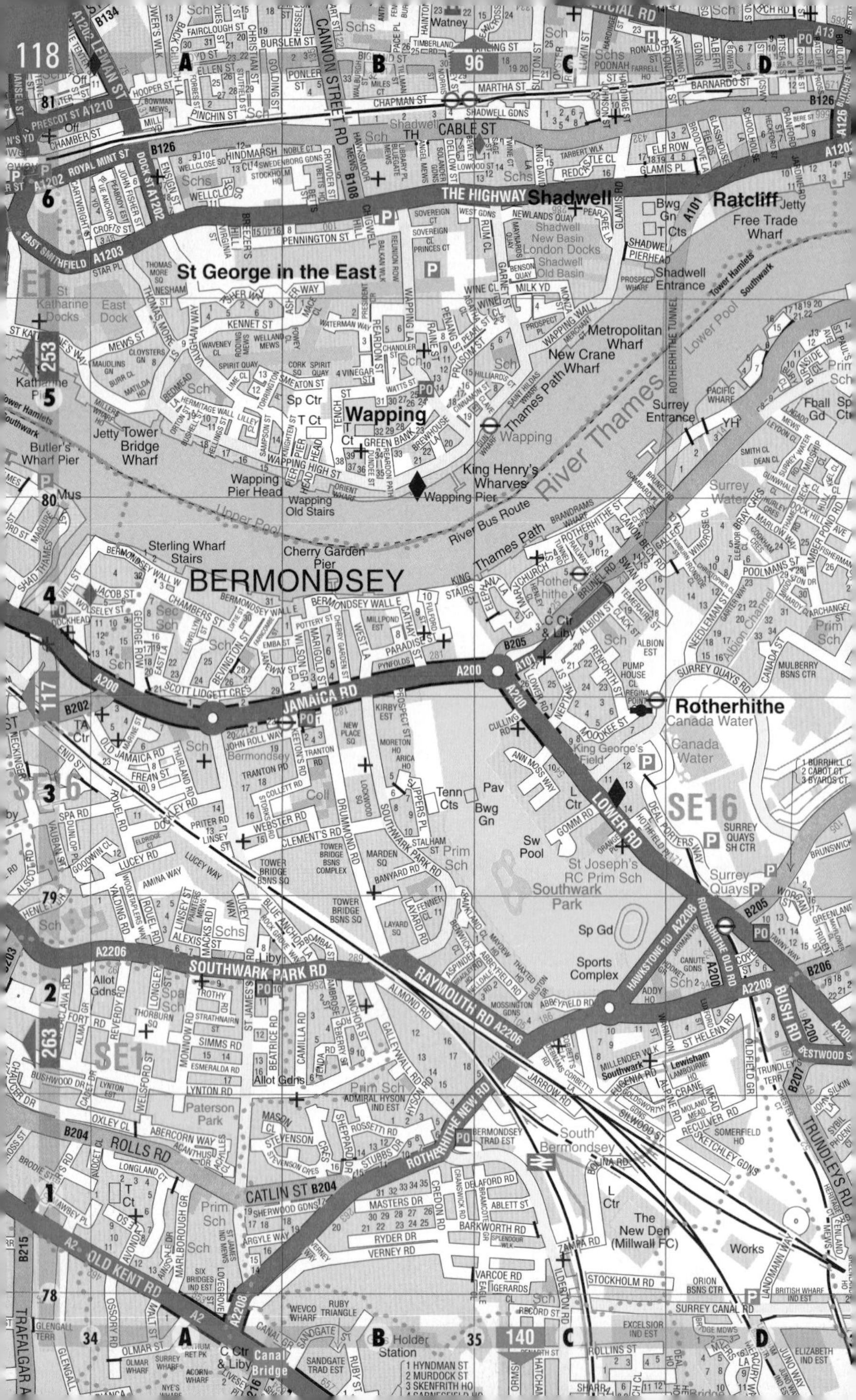

A
B
C
D
96
LEMAN ST
A1202
B134
CANNON STREET RD
Watney
CABLE ST
Shadwell
TH
Schs
Sch
PRESCOT ST A1210
CHAMBER ST
ROYAL MINT ST
DOCK ST A1202
B126
HINDMARSH CL
WELLCLOSE SQ
SWEDENBORG GDNS
CHAPMAN ST
MARTHA ST
BARNARDO ST
SHADWELL GDNS
FAIRCLOUGH ST
BURSLEM ST
HOOPER ST
PINCHIN ST
ELLEN ST
PONLER ST
TIMBERLAND RD
POONAH ST
RONALD ST
TARBERT WLK
REDCASTLE CL
GLAMIS PL
ELF ROW
SCHOOLHOUSE LA
CRANFORD ST
GLASSHOUSE FIELDS
BROADLOVE LA
EAST SMITHFIELD A1203
A1203
THE HIGHWAY
Shadwell
Ratcliff
Free Trade Wharf
Jetty
PENNINGTON ST
SOVEREIGN CT
PRINCES CT
WEST GDNS
NEWLANDS QUAY
PEARTREE LA
GLAMIS RD
A101
Bwg Gn
T Cts
SHADWELL PIERHEAD
Shadwell New Basin
London Docks
Shadwell Old Basin
Shadwell Entrance
PROSPECT WHARF
Tower Hamlets
Southwark
E1
St Katharine Docks
East Dock
St George in the East
THOMAS MORE SQ
NESHAM ST
ASHER WAY
KENNET ST
WAPPING LA
WINE CL
MILK YD
WAPPING WALL
Metropolitan Wharf
New Crane Wharf
Lower Pool
ROTHERHITHE TUNNEL
ST KATHARINE'S WAY
253
MEWS ST
VAUGHAN WAY
THOMAS MORE ST
WAVENEY CL
SPIRIT QUAY
CORK SQ
WATERMAN WAY
REARDON ST
RAINE ST
CHANDLER ST
PRUSOM ST
PENANG ST
HILLIARDS CT
Thames Path
Wapping
Sp Ctr
T Ct
Wapping
WAPPING HIGH ST
GREEN BANK
BREWHOUSE LA
Katharine Pier
Jetty
Tower Bridge Wharf
Butler's Wharf Pier
Wapping Pier Head
Wapping Old Stairs
Wapping Pier
King Henry's Wharves
River Thames
Upper Pool
River Bus Route
Surrey Entrance
PACIFIC WHARF
YH
Fball Gd
Surrey Water
80
Mus
Sterling Wharf Stairs
Cherry Garden Pier
BERMONDSEY
BERMONDSEY WALL W
BERMONDSEY WALL E
KING STAIRS CL
Thames Path
ROTHERHITHE ST
BRANDRAMS WHARF
CANON BECK RD
SWAN RD
BRUNEL RD
Rotherhithe
JACOB ST
WOLSELEY ST
DOCKHEAD
CHAMBERS ST
GEORGE ROW
EMBA ST
MARIGOLD ST
WILSON GR
CHERRY GARDEN ST
MILLPOND EST
WEST LA
CATHAY ST
PARADISE ST
PULFORD
ALBION ST
TEMERAIRE ST
ALBION EST
NEEDLEMAN ST
Albion Channel
POOLMANS ST
SURREY QUAYS RD
MULBERRY BSNS CTR
CANADA ST
B205
PYNFOLDS
SCOTT LIDGETT CRES
A200
JAMAICA RD
A101
C Ctr & Liby
RENFORTH ST
LOWER RD
PUMP HOUSE CL
REGINA POINT
Rotherhithe
Canada Water
Canada Water
KING GEORGE'S FIELD
MOODKEE ST
117
B202
TA Ctr
OLD JAMAICA RD
FREAN ST
THURLAND RD
JOHN ROLL WAY
KEETON'S RD
TRANTON RD
Bermondsey
NEW PLACE SQ
KIRBY EST
PROSPECT ST
MORETON HO
ARICA HO
CULLING RD
ANN MOSS WAY
SE16
ENID ST
NECKINGER
COLLETT RD
WEBSTER RD
CLEMENT'S RD
DRUMMOND RD
LOCKWOOD SQ
SLIPPERS PL
SOUTHWARK PARK RD
Tenn Cts
Pav
Bwg Gn
L Ctr
LOWER RD
GOMM RD
Sw Pool
HOTHFIELD PL
DEAL PORTERS WAY
SE16
SURREY QUAYS SH CTR
Surrey Quays
SPA RD
DUNLOP PL
ROUEL RD
DOCKLEY RD
PRITER RD
LINSEY ST
LUCEY RD
LUCEY WAY
TOWER BRIDGE BSNS SQ
TOWER BRIDGE BSNS COMPLEX
MARDEN SQ
BANYARD RD
STALHAM ST
Prim Sch
St Joseph's RC Prim Sch
Southwark Park
Sp Gd
AMINA WAY
YALDING RD
VAUBAN ST
GOODWIN CL
79
BLUE ANCHOR LA
BOMBAY ST
LAYARD SQ
FENNER CL
B205
WORGAN ST
A2206
SOUTHWARK PARK RD
ALEXIS ST
Liby
RAYMOUTH RD A2206
Sports Complex
HAWKSTONE RD A2208
ROTHERHITHE OLD RD
A200
A2208
BUSH RD
B206
ABBEYFIELD RD
Allot Gdns
2
ALMOND RD
CLAVA RD
FORT RD
THORBURN SQ
STRATHNAIRN ST
SIMMS RD
ESMERALDA RD
SE1
263
BEATRICE RD
CAMILLA RD
ANCHOR ST
GALLEYWALL RD
MOSSINGTON GDNS
ST HELENA RD
MILLENDER WLK
Southwark
Lewisham
LAMBOURNE HO
CRANE
OLDFIELD GR
TRUNDLEY'S TERR
BESTWOOD ST
B207
BUSHWOOD DR
LYNTON RD
Allot Gdns
Prim Sch
ADMIRAL HYSON IND EST
HYSON RD
JARROW RD
CORBETT'S LA
EUGENIA RD
ALPINE RD
MEAD
RECULVER RD
SOMERFIELD HO
TRUNDLEYS RD
JOHN SILKIN LA
CHAUCER DR
Paterson Park
OXLEY CL
ABERCORN WAY
MASON CL
STEVENSON CRES
ROSSETTI RD
STUBBS DR
ROTHERHITHE NEW RD
BERMONDSEY TRAD EST
SILWOOD ST
SKETCHLEY GDNS
B204
ROLLS RD
LONGLAND CT
CATLIN ST B204
South Bermondsey
BOLINA RD
1
T Ct
Prim Sch
MASTERS DR
CREDON RD
DELAFORD RD
ABLETT ST
BARKWORTH RD
L Ctr
The New Den (Millwall FC)
Works
LANDMANN WAY
SHERWOOD GDNS
ARGYLE WAY
RYDER DR
VERNEY RD
MARLBOROUGH GR
AVONDALE SQ
OLD KENT RD
A2
Sch
SIX BRIDGES IND EST
LOVEGROVE ST
VARCOE RD
GERARDS CL
ZAMPA RD
STOCKHOLM RD
ORION BSNS CTR
BRITISH WHARF IND EST
B215
78
TRAFALGAR AV
OSSORY RD
MALT ST
A2208
WEVCO WHARF
RUBY TRIANGLE
RECORD ST
ILDERTON RD
SURREY CANAL RD
EXCELSIOR IND EST
34
OLMAR ST
A
GLENGALL TERR
C Ctr & Liby
Canal Bridge
SANDGATE ST
B
Gas Holder Station
SANDGATE TRAD EST
RUBY ST
35
140
C
ROLLINS ST
D
ELIZABETH IND EST
JUNO WAY
MERCURY WAY
1 HYNDMAN ST
2 MURDOCK ST
1 BURRHILL CT
2 CABOT CT
3 BYARDS CT

POPLAR
Limehouse
Limehouse Basin
EAST INDIA DOCK RD
WEST INDIA DOCK RD
LIMEHOUSE LINK
LIMEHOUSE CAUSEWAY
NARROW ST
ROTHERHITHE ST
Limehouse Reach
Thames Path
WESTFERRY CIR
WESTFERRY RD
Canary Wharf
E14
West India Quay
Billingsgate Mkt
North Quay
Columbus Court Yard
Canary Wharf Pier (River Bus)
Docklands Heritage Mus
Cuckold's Point
Rotherhithe Holiday Inn Pier
Nelson Docks
Heron Quays
West India Dock South
West India and Millwall Docks
South Quay
MARSH WALL
Harbour Island
Millwall Inner Dock
Russia Dock Woodland
Bacon's Coll
Redriff Prim Sch
St John's RC Prim Sch
Surrey Docks Farm
Barnard's Wharf
Express Wharf
Sir John McDougal Gardens
Arnhem Wharf Prim Sch
Millwall
Crossharbour & London Arena
Millwall Outer Dock
Greenland Pier
Klein's Wharf
Surrey Commercial Docks
Greenland Dock
South Dock (Marina)
St George's Wharf
PLOUGH WAY
REDRIFF RD
Greenwich Reach
Cubitt Town
Mudchute
ISLE OF DOGS
Island Gardens
Pepys Park
Slipway
Louis Wharf
Burrell's Wharf
Great Eastern Pier
Convoys Wharf
Palmer's Wharf
Payne's Wharf
Borthwick Wharf
Deptford Park
New Baltic Wharf
Victoria Wharf
Crown Wharf
Blackhorse Wharf
EVELYN ST
GROVE ST
SE8
Locke's Wharf
Dreadnought Wharf
Dowell's Wharf
Folkestone Gardens
A1206
A1261
A200
97
141
120

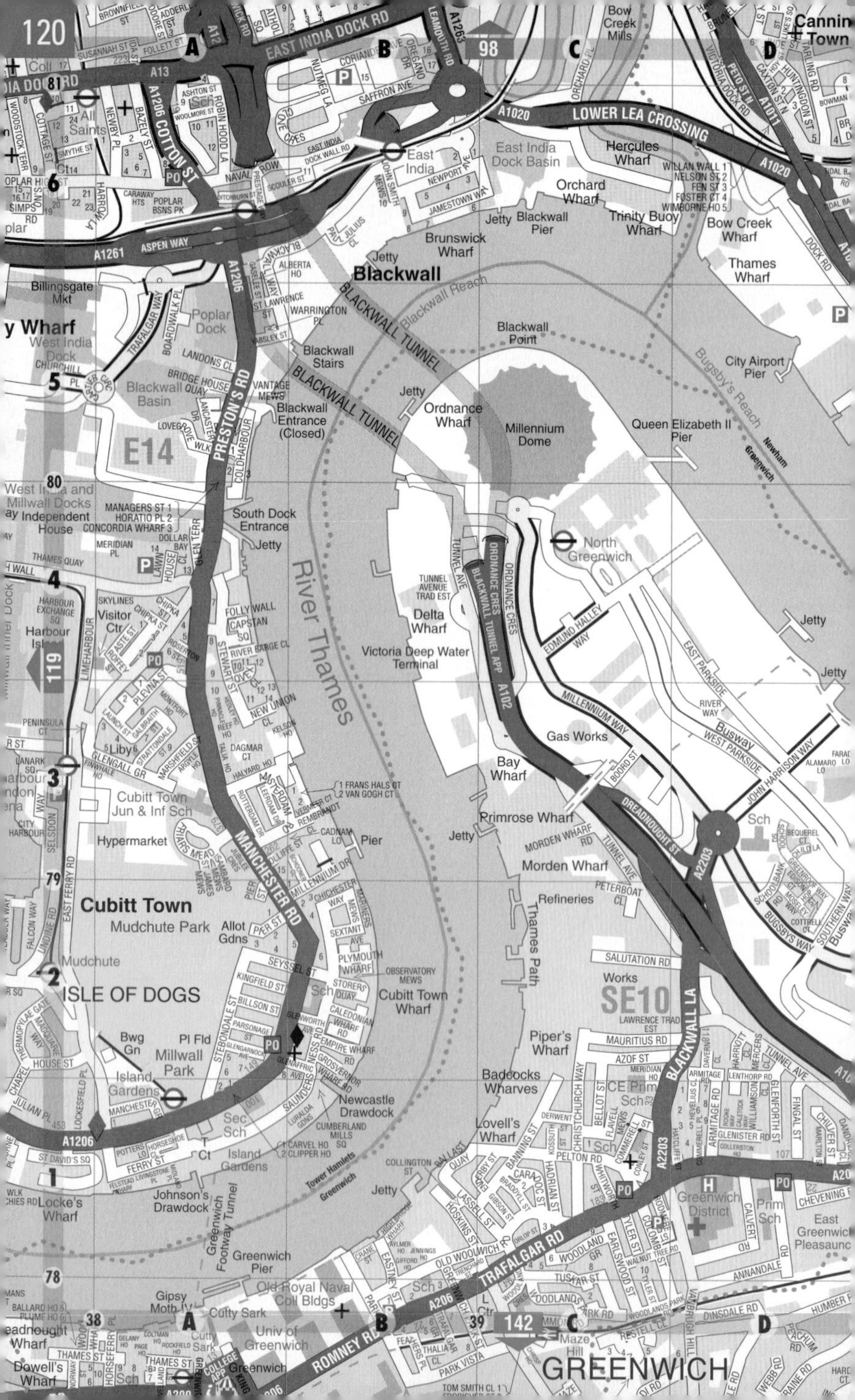

98
EAST INDIA DOCK RD
LEAMOUTH RD
A1261
A1020
LOWER LEA CROSSING
Bow Creek Mills
Canning Town
All Saints
East India
East India Dock Basin
Hercules Wharf
Orchard Wharf
Trinity Buoy Wharf
Bow Creek Wharf
Thames Wharf
Blackwall Pier
Brunswick Wharf
Blackwall
ASPEN WAY
COTTON ST
ROBIN HOOD LA
SAFFRON AVE
NUTMEG LA
POPLAR HIGH ST
POPLAR BSNS PK
Billingsgate Mkt
West India Dock
Poplar Dock
Blackwall Basin
E14
PRESTON'S RD
BLACKWALL TUNNEL
Blackwall Stairs
Blackwall Entrance (Closed)
Blackwall Reach
Blackwall Point
Ordnance Wharf
Millennium Dome
Queen Elizabeth II Pier
City Airport Pier
Bugsby's Reach
Newham
Greenwich
North Greenwich
West India and Millwall Docks
Independent House
South Dock Entrance
THAMES QUAY
River Thames
Delta Wharf
Victoria Deep Water Terminal
TUNNEL AVENUE TRAD EST
ORDNANCE CRES
BLACKWALL TUNNEL APP
A102
EDMUND HALLEY WAY
MILLENNIUM WAY
EAST PARKSIDE
WEST PARKSIDE
JOHN HARRISON WAY
Busway
Gas Works
Bay Wharf
Primrose Wharf
Morden Wharf
Refineries
Thames Path
DREADNOUGHT ST
A2203
SALUTATION RD
Works
SE10
Harbour Exchange SQ
Visitor Ctr
LIMEHARBOUR
119
Cubitt Town Jun & Inf Sch
Hypermarket
MANCHESTER RD
Cubitt Town
Mudchute Park
Mudchute
ISLE OF DOGS
Allot Gdns
Cubitt Town Wharf
Millwall Park
Island Gardens
A1206
Newcastle Drawdock
Tower Hamlets
Greenwich
Johnson's Drawdock
Greenwich Footway Tunnel
Greenwich Pier
Locke's Wharf
Piper's Wharf
Badcocks Wharves
Lovell's Wharf
BLACKWALL LA
TUNNEL AVE
TRAFALGAR RD
Greenwich District
East Greenwich Pleasaunce
Old Royal Naval Coll Bldgs
Gipsy Moth IV
Cutty Sark
Univ of Greenwich
ROMNEY RD
142
Maze Hill
GREENWICH
Dowell's Wharf
Dreadnought Wharf
A
B
C
D
1
2
3
4
5
6

99
Custom House
CONNAUGHT RD
A112
A1020
VICTORIA DOCK RD
Royal Victoria
Custom House for ExCeL
Prince Regent
MAY WYNNE HO
1 WOOD ST
2 BETTS RD
3 CHAUNTLER CL
MACE GATEWAY
ExCel Exhibition Ctr
DOCKSIDE RD
Royal Albert
CONNAUGHT RD
Royal Victoria Dock
E16
CONNAUGHT BRIDGE
ROYAL CONNAUGHT APPS
HARTMANN RD
CAMEL RD
FITZWILLIAM MEWS
HANOVER AVE
SOUTHEY MEWS
KEATS AVE
FAIRFAX MEWS
CONSTABLE AVE
SOUTHAMPTON MEWS
PORTSMOUTH MEWS
WESLEY AVE
EVELYN RD
Mill
AIRPORT RDBT
NORTH WOOLWICH RD
NORTH WOOLWICH RDBT
THAMES RD
Prim Sch
BOXLEY ST
FORT ST
MILL RD
BURT RD
CHARLES ST
ST MARKS IND EST
ORIENTAL RD
Silvertown
KNIGHTS RD
GREENSHIELDS IND EST
BRADFIELD RD
Tenn Cts
BARRIER POINT RD
Thames Barrier Park
THAMESIDE IND EST
THAMES ROAD IND EST
Lyle Park
KIERBECK BSNS COMPLEX
Wharves
The Thames Barrier
Woolwich Reach
Bugsby's Reach
Newham
Greenwich
River Thames
Barrier Gdns Pier
Thames Barrier Visitor Ctr
122
MELLISH IND EST
BYWATER HO
HARRINGTON WAY
UNITY WAY
Mast
BOWATER RD
WESTMINSTER IND EST
Thames Path
Wharf
GREENWICH
RIVERSIDE
ANCHORAGE POINT IND EST
HERRINGHAM RD
NEW LYDENBURG ST COMM EST
ASHLEIGH COMM EST
HOLGATE ST
WESTMOOR ST
EASTMOOR ST
WESTFIELD ST
HARWICK MANS
Coll
SE10
PEARTREE WAY
HORN LINK WAY
LOMBARD WALL
MERIDIAN TRAD EST
LOMBARD TRAD EST
DERRICK GDNS
ATLAS GDNS
VIP TRAD EST
MIRFIELD ST 1
EASTMOOR PL 2
FARADAY WAY 3
STONE LAKE IND PK
STONE LAKE RET PK
PENHALL RD
A206
BROCKLEBANK ROAD IND EST
BROCKLEBANK RD
WILLOUGHBY WAY
SE7
ANCHOR & HOPE LA
ROPERY BSNS EST
New Charlton
Tenn Cts
Maryon Park
Green Chain Wlk
ANGERSTEIN BSNS PK
HORN LA
PENINSULAR PARK RD
Superstore
GREENWICH IND EST
MARITIME IND EST
GALLIONS RD
WOOLWICH RD
HICKIN CL
PRENTISS CT
GALLON CL
HARVEY GDNS
POUND PARK RD
Thorntree Inf Sch
RAMAC IND EST
RAMAC WAY
FEARON ST
ALDEBURGH ST
FELLTRAM WAY
Charlton
BARNEY CL
TROUGHTON RD
The Valley (Charlton Athletic Fball Club)
HASTED RD
COXMOUNT RD
THORNTREE RD
Maryon Wilson Park
RAINTON RD
HARDMAN RD
DUPREE RD
FAIRTHORN RD
FLOYD RD
DELAFIELD RD
VALLEY GR
SAM BARTRAM CL
CHARLTON LA
LANSDOWNE MEWS
WOLFE CRES
Liby
COMBEDALE RD
KEMSING RD
GURDON RD
RATHMORE RD
SUNDORNE RD
1 PLANE TREE HO
2 VALLEYSIDE
3 ST PAUL'S CL
ORMISTON RD
Westcombe Park
SE3
STATION CRES
BERNARD ASHLEY DR
FOSSDENE RD
INVERINE RD
SWALLOWFIELD RD
PRIOLO RD
WELLINGTON GDNS
NADINE ST
CHARLTON CHURCH LA
LANSDOWNE LA
THE HEIGHTS
McCALL CRES
Sch
CALYDON RD
THE BIRCHES
VICTORIA WAY
ELLISCOMBE RD
COUTTS HO
JOYCE PAGE CL
BEACHAM CL
GUILD RD
ST ALFEGE RD
A102
WESTCOMBE HILL
EASTCOMBE AVE
SANDTOFT RD
143
FLETCHING RD
THE VILLAGE
FAIRFIELD GR
CHARLTON PARK RD
B210
EVERSLEY RD
Allot Gdns
MULBERRY CL
Charlton
Pav
Charlton Park Sch
KIRKSIDE RD
BRAMSHOT AVE
HIGHCOMBE
Charlton House
Green Chain Wlk

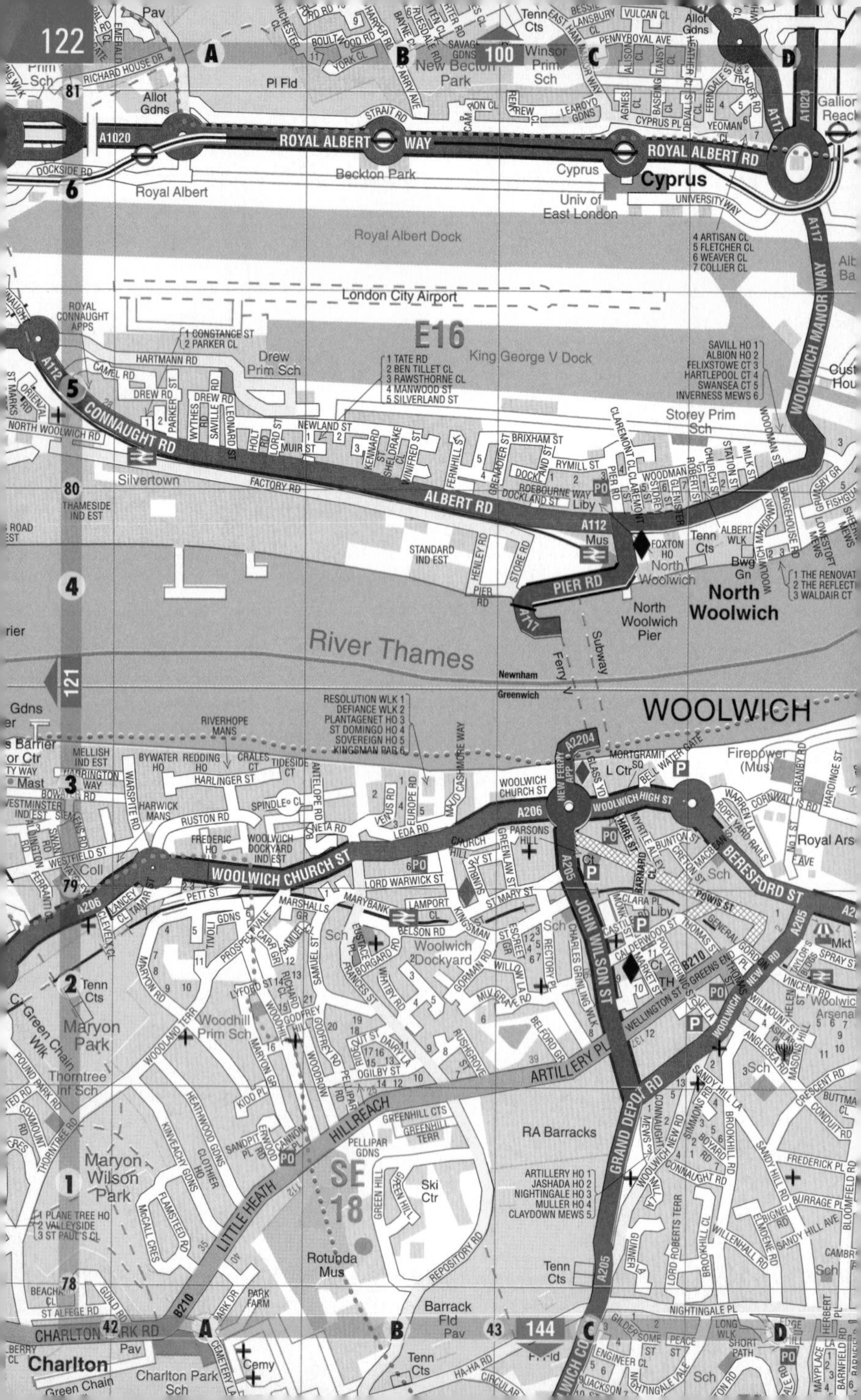
A
B
C
D
100
81
6
5
80
4
121
3
79
2
1
78
42
43
144
Pav
Prim Sch
Allot Gdns
RICHARD HOUSE DR
Pl Fld
New Becton Park
Winsor Prim Sch
Tenn Cts
LANSBURY
VULCAN CL
PENNYROYAL AVE
BOULTWOOD RD
YORK CL
STRAIT RD
CYPRUS PL
YEOMAN
Gallions Reach
A1020
ROYAL ALBERT WAY
ROYAL ALBERT RD
DOCKSIDE RD
Royal Albert
Beckton Park
Cyprus
Univ of East London
UNIVERSITY WAY
A117
Royal Albert Dock
4 ARTISAN CL
5 FLETCHER CL
6 WEAVER CL
7 COLLIER CL
London City Airport
ROYAL CONNAUGHT APPS
1 CONSTANCE ST
2 PARKER CL
E16
King George V Dock
WOOLWICH MANOR WAY
HARTMANN RD
CAMEL RD
Drew Prim Sch
1 TATE RD
2 BEN TILLET CL
3 RAWSTHORNE CL
4 MANWOOD ST
5 SILVERLAND ST
SAVILL HO 1
ALBION HO 2
FELIXSTOWE CT 3
HARTLEPOOL CT 4
SWANSEA CT 5
INVERNESS MEWS 6
A112
CONNAUGHT RD
DREW RD
NORTH WOOLWICH RD
NEWLAND ST
MUIR ST
BRIXHAM ST
RYMILL ST
Storey Prim Sch
Silvertown
FACTORY RD
ALBERT RD
DOCKLAND ST
ROEBOURNE WAY
Liby
Mus
THAMESIDE IND EST
STANDARD IND EST
FOXTON HO
Tenn Cts
ALBERT WLK
Bwg Gn
North Woolwich
PIER RD
North Woolwich Pier
1 THE RENOVAT
2 THE REFLECT
3 WALDAIR CT
River Thames
Ferry
Subway
Newnham
Greenwich
WOOLWICH
RESOLUTION WLK 1
DEFIANCE WLK 2
PLANTAGENET HO 3
ST DOMINGO HO 4
SOVEREIGN HO 5
KINGSMAN PAR 6
RIVERHOPE MANS
MELLISH IND EST
HARRINGTON WAY
BYWATER HO
REDDING HO
CRALES HO
TIDESIDE CT
HARLINGER ST
A2204
NEW FERRY APP
MORTGRAMIT SQ
BELL WATER GATE
L Ctr
Firepower (Mus)
WOOLWICH CHURCH ST
A206
WOOLWICH HIGH ST
CORNWALLIS RD
Royal Ars
BERESFORD ST
HARWICK MANS
RUSTON RD
SPINDLE CL
LEDA RD
FREDERIC HO
WOOLWICH DOCKYARD IND EST
PARSONS HILL
A205
JOHN WILSON ST
POWIS ST
WESTFIELD ST
LORD WARWICK ST
PETT ST
MARSHALLS GR
MARYBANK
LAMPORT CL
BELSON RD
ST MARY ST
Sch
Liby
Woolwich Dockyard
CALDERWOOD ST
B210
TH
WELLINGTON ST
GREENS END
Woolwich Arsenal
Tenn Cts
Maryon Park
Green Chain Wlk
Thorntree Inf Sch
Woodhill Prim Sch
LYFORD ST
ARTILLERY PL
GRAND DEPOT RD
HILLREACH
GREENHILL CTS
GREENHILL TERR
RA Barracks
PELLIPAR GDNS
SE 18
Ski Ctr
Maryon Wilson Park
1 PLANE TREE HO
2 VALLEYSIDE
3 ST PAUL'S CL
LITTLE HEATH
ARTILLERY HO 1
JASHADA HO 2
NIGHTINGALE HO 3
MULLER HO 4
CLAYDOWN MEWS 5
FREDERICK PL
Rotunda Mus
REPOSITORY RD
LORD ROBERTS TERR
Tenn Cts
Sch
Barrack Fld
Pav
NIGHTINGALE PL
PARK FARM
CHARLTON PARK RD
ST ALFEGE RD
Charlton
Pav
Cemy
Charlton Park Sch
Green Chain
Tenn Cts
HA-HA RD
CIRCULAR
ENGINEER CL
SHORT PATH
MAYPLACE LA
BARNFIELD RD

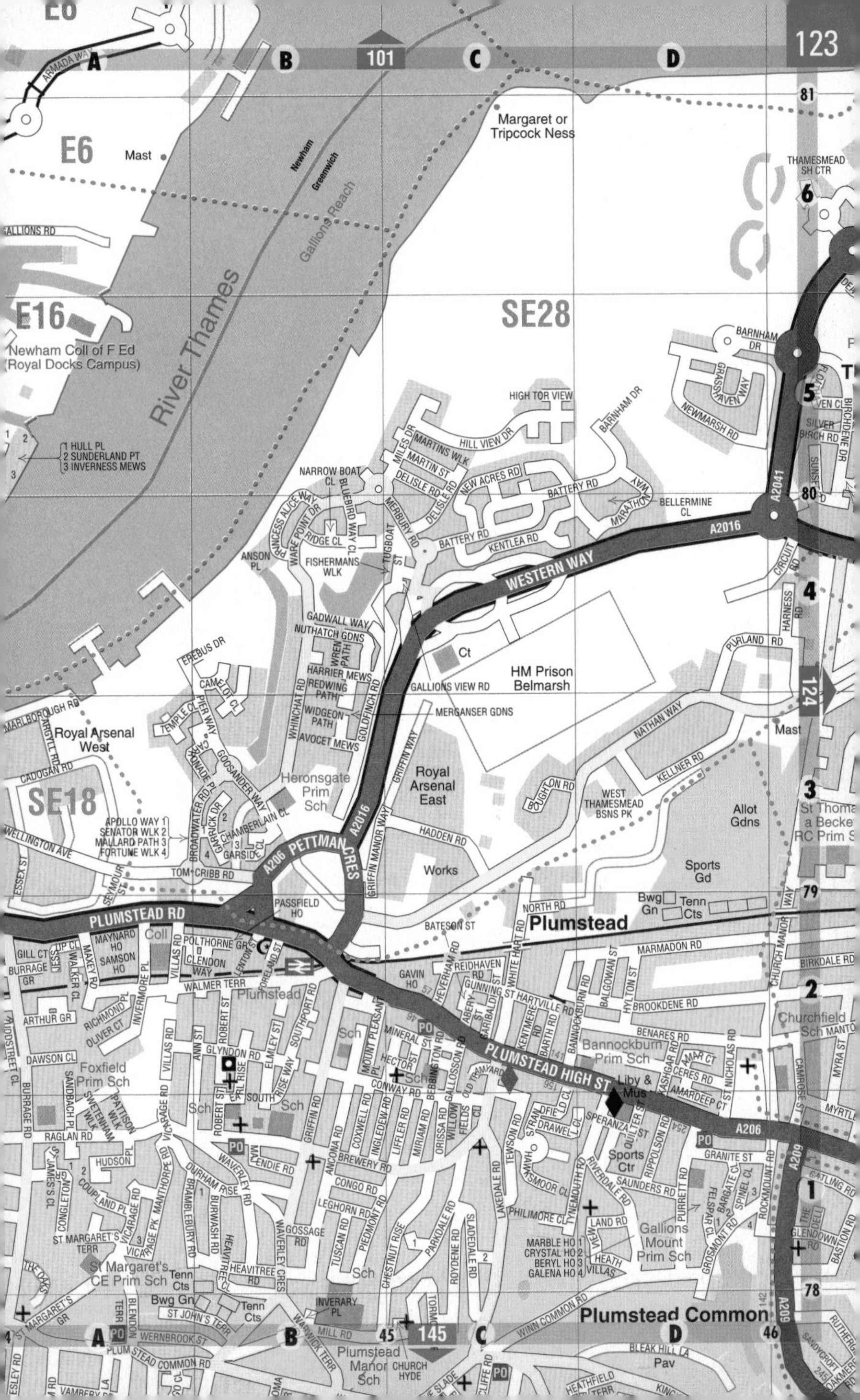
A
B
101
C
D
E6
Mast
Newham
Greenwich
Gallions Reach
Margaret or
Tripcock Ness
THAMESMEAD SH CTR
GALLIONS RD
River Thames
E16
Newham Coll of F Ed
(Royal Docks Campus)
SE28
1 HULL PL
2 SUNDERLAND PT
3 INVERNESS MEWS
BARNHAM DR
GRASSHAVEN WAY
NEWMARSH RD
HIGH TOR VIEW
HILL VIEW DR
MARTINS WLK
MARTIN ST
MILES DR
DELISLE RD
NEW ACRES RD
BATTERY RD
MARATHON WAY
BELLERMINE CL
NARROW BOAT CL
PRINCESS ALICE WAY
WARE POINT DR
BLUEBIRD WAY CL
RIDGE CL
MERBURY RD
TUGBOAT ST
KENTLEA RD
A2016
A2041
WESTERN WAY
ANSON PL
FISHERMANS WLK
CIRCUIT WAY
HARNESS RD
PURLAND RD
GADWALL WAY
NUTHATCH GDNS
WREN PATH
HARRIER MEWS
REDWING PATH
WIDGEON PATH
AVOCET MEWS
WHINCHAT RD
GOLDFINCH RD
Ct
HM Prison
Belmarsh
GALLIONS VIEW RD
MERGANSER GDNS
EREBUS DR
CAMELOT CL
TEMPLE CL
PIER WAY
CARRONADE PL
GOOSANDER WAY
MARLBOROUGH RD
ARGYLL RD
Royal Arsenal
West
CADOGAN RD
SE18
Heronsgate
Prim Sch
GRIFFIN WAY
Royal
Arsenal
East
NATHAN WAY
KELLNER RD
BOUGHTON RD
WEST THAMESMEAD BSNS PK
Mast
Allot
Gdns
St Thomas a Becket RC Prim Sch
APOLLO WAY 1
SENATOR WLK 2
MALLARD PATH 3
FORTUNE WLK 4
BROADWATER RD
GARRICK DR
CHAMBERLAIN CL
GARSIDE CL
WELLINGTON AVE
ESSEX ST
SEYMOUR ST
TOM CRIBB RD
A206
PETTMAN CRES
GRIFFIN MANOR WAY
HADDEN RD
Works
Sports Gd
Bwg Gn
Tenn Cts
NORTH RD
PASSFIELD HO
PLUMSTEAD RD
Coll
BATESON ST
Plumstead
CHURCH MANOR WAY
MAYNARD HO
SAMSON HO
POLTHORNE GR
CLENDON WAY
LENTON ST
FORELAND ST
GILL CT
JESSUP CL
MAXEY RD
BURRAGE GR
WALKER CL
INVERMORE PL
WALMER TERR
Plumstead
GAVIN HO
HEVERHAM RD
REIDHAVEN RD
GUNNING ST
HARTVILLE RD
WHITE HART RD
MARMADON RD
BIRKDALE RD
BALGOWAN ST
HYLTON ST
BROOKDENE RD
ARTHUR GR
RICHMOND PL
OLIVER CT
VILLAS RD
ROBERT ST
ANN ST
ELMLEY ST
SOUTHPORT RD
MOUNT PLEASANT
MINERAL ST
HECTOR ST
ABERY ST
GARIBALDI ST
KENTMERE RD
BARTH RD
BANNOCKBURN RD
BENARES RD
Bannockburn Prim Sch
Churchfield Sch
MANTO
WIDDSTREET CL
DAWSON CL
Foxfield
Prim Sch
GLYNDON RD
EARL RISE
RISE WAY
Sch
PLUMSTEAD HIGH ST
Liby & Mus
ASHGAR RD
AMAR CT
CERES RD
AMARDEEP CT
ST NICHOLAS RD
CAMROSE ST
MYRA ST
MYRTLE
SANDBACH PL
SWETENHAM WLK
PATTISON WLK
BURRAGE RD
VICARAGE RD
CONWAY RD
BEBBINGTON RD
GALLOSSON RD
OLD TRAMYARD
Sch
SPERANZA ST
QUILTER ST
DRAWELL CL
A206
RAGLAN RD
HUDSON PL
ST JAMES'S CL
GRIFFIN RD
ANCONA RD
COXWELL RD
INGLEDEW RD
LIFFLER RD
MIRIAM RD
ORISSA RD
WILLOW FIELDS CL
TEWSON RD
HAWKSMOOR CL
Sports Ctr
RIPPOLSON RD
GRANITE ST
A209
WAVERLEY RD
ENDIE RD
BREWERY RD
CONGO RD
LEGHORN RD
SAUNDERS RD
PURRETT RD
FELSPAR CL
BARGATE CL
SPINEL CL
ROCKMOUNT RD
GATLING RD
THE DELL
CONGLETON GR
COUPLAND PL
VICARAGE PL
MANTHORPE RD
DURHAM RISE
BRAMBLEBURY RD
BURWASH RD
HEAVITREE CL
WAVERLEY CRES
GOSSAGE RD
TUSCAN RD
PIEDMONT RD
CHESTNUT RISE
PARKDALE RD
ROYDENE RD
SLADEDALE RD
LAKEDALE RD
PHILIMORE CL
TYNEMOUTH RD
RIVERDALE RD
LAND RD
Gallions Mount Prim Sch
GROSMONT RD
GLENDOWN RD
BASTION RD
ST MARGARET'S TERR
MARBLE HO 1
CRYSTAL HO 2
BERYL HO 3
GALENA HO 4
HEATH VILLAS
St Margaret's
CE Prim Sch
Tenn Cts
HEAVITREE RD
Sch
THE OAKS
Bwg Gn
Tenn Cts
ST JOHN'S TERR
INVERARY PL
TORMOUNT RD
WINN COMMON RD
Plumstead Common
RUTHERGLEN RD
ST MARGARET'S GR
WERNBROOK ST
MILL RD
45
145
46
PLUMSTEAD COMMON RD
WARWICK TERR
Plumstead Manor Sch
CHURCH HYDE
THE SLADE
CLIFFE RD
BLEAK HILL LA
Pav
SANDYCROFT
OAKMERE RD
HEATHFIELD TERR
KING
VAMBERY RD
ESLEY RD
81
6
5
80
4
124
3
79
2
1
78
SILVER BIRCH RD
BIRCHDENE DR
SUNSET RD

A
B
C
D
102
146
123
81
80
79
78
6
5
4
3
2
1
Ppg Sta
Linton Mead Prim Sch
THAMESMEAD SH CTR
THAMESMERE DR
JOYCE DAWSON WAY
MEADOWFORD CL
CENTRAL WAY
TAWNEY RD
SAUNDERS WAY
ATTLEE RD
ORIOLE WAY
TITMUSS AVE
CLOCK TOWER MEWS
Hawksmoor Sch
BOOTH CL
APPLEGARTH RD
ARNOTT CL
CARLYLE RD
WALDSTOCK RD
DEAN RD
HUTCHINS RD
Woolwich Poly Sch for Boys
Thamesmead
BARNHAM DR
GRASSHAVEN WAY
NEWMARSH RD
FLOATHAVEN CL
BIRCHDENE DR
SILVER BIRCH RD
PITFIELD CRES
ROMAN SQ
AMHURST WLK
SORREL CL
CAMPION PL
COURTAULDS CL
SUNSET RD
LAKESIDE AVE
Lake
HAMPSTEAD SQ
WATERFIELD CL
GALSWORTHY CL
CELANDINE DR
CHERVIL MEWS
WOOLF CL
SOUTHWOOD RD
BENTHAM RD
AUSTEN CL
COLE CL
SHAW CL
Windrush Prim Sch
St Margaret Clitherow RC Prim Sch
OWEN CL
BYRON CL
DISRAELI CL
EASTERN WAY
A2016
A2041
ERMINE CL
SALHOUSE CL
GREENHAVEN DR
NICKELBY CL
LUDHAM CL
ROLLESBY WAY
BERTRAND WAY
Bishop John Robinson Prim Sch
HASLER CL
HOLT CL
BLYTH RD
FAIRFIELD WAY
LIPTON CL
WOODPECKER RD
GOLDCREST CL
LINNET CL
SLOCUM CL
SABBARTON ST
SANDERLING CT
WHIMBREL CL
Green Chain Wlk
GRANGE CRES
KINGFISHER CL
FIELDFARE RD
GARGANEY WLK
CURLEW CL
MANORSIDE
DOLPHIN CL
POINTER CL
EASTGATE CL
CROSSWAY
SURLINGHAM CL
WROXHAM RD
ORMESBY DR
WALSHAM CL
FLEMING WAY
HODGKINS CL
BAYLISS AVE
HALDANE RD
WALLACE CL
SUMMERTON WAY
TURNBULL CL
CHERBURY
LONGWORTH CL
BIGLOW CL
CROWDEN WAY
GLENDALE WAY
KINDER CL
HOWDEN CL
WHERNSIDE CL
POPLAR PL
Jubilee Prim Sch
Pl Flds
Tenn Cts
1 MARTHAM CL
2 CHADWICK WAY
3 LISTER WLK
4 BERNAL CL
SE28
Pav
BELVEDERE RD
THE LAKESIDE COMPLEX
South Mere
HARROW MANOR WAY
BINSEY WLK
PORTMEADOW WLK
HARTSLOCK DR
ST EDMUNDS CL
ST BRIDES CL
ST MICHAEL'S CL
ST MARTINS CL
SEACOURT RD
Southlake Prim Sch
TAVY BRIDGE
Liby
WOLVERCOTE RD
AMPLEFORTH RD
TICKFORD CL
SEWELL RD
STANBROOK RD
MOUNTJOY CL
GROVEBURY RD
GODSTOW RD
ANDWELL CL
PETERSTONE RD
De Lucy Prim Sch
CIRCUIT WAY
HARNESS RD
PURLAND RD
DEVENISH RD
LITTLEMORE RD
PANFIELD RD
COOKHILL RD
Mast
MANISTER RD
Pl Fld
ROSEDALE CL
EYNSHAM DR
FINCHALE RD
BYLANDS CL
PENMON RD
CHALCOMBE RD
EDINGTON RD
BOXGROVE RD
THROWLEY CL
THISTLEBROOK
Greenwich
Bexley
Abbey Prim Sch
HINKSEY PATH
LENSBURY WAY
OVERTON RD
SEDGEMERE RD
SYDNEY RD
LANRIDGE RD
DALBERG WAY
RUSHDENE
Boxgrove Prim Sch
Abbey Wood
SE2
LUFFIELD RD
LYNDEAN IND EST
FELIXSTOWE RD
PYNHAM CL
BROMHOLM RD
BRIMPSFIELD CL
Allot Gdns
St Thomas a Beckett RC Prim Sch
Abbey Wood Sch
COMBWELL CRES
Sports Gd
Tenn Cts
MOTTISFONT RD
CHURCH MANOR WAY
GAYTON RD
ABBEY TERR
WILTON RD
FLORENCE RD
FENDYKE RD
ROSSINGTON RD
BRIGHT CL
BUCKLES CT
BUCKWHEAT CT
TEESWATER CT
MARAN WAY
SHARMAN CT
REDPOLL WAY
BRACONDALE RD
BRINKBURN CL
ABBEY GR
DE LUCY ST
BOSTALL MANOR WAY
CAERLEON TERR
GLOVER CL
CONFERENCE RD
ABBEY WOOD RD
B213
Lesnes Abbey (remains of)
MANORSIDE CL
MONKS CL
Lesnes Abbey Park
WOODLAND WAY
BIRKDALE RD
BLITHDALE RD
SMITHIES RD
BRODRICK GR
OWENITE ST
CHANCELOT RD
SHIELDHALL ST
GREENING ST
CONGRESS RD
CRUMPSALL ST
KNEE HILL CRES
Churchfield Sch
MANTON RD
MYRA ST
WOODHURST RD
BENDMORE AVE
BASILDON RD
McLEOD RD
OPENSHAW RD
Bwg Gn
FEDERATION RD
ST NICHOLAS RD
CAMROSE ST
CASSILDA RD
HOWARTH RD
ROCHDALE RD
VIOLA AVE
DAHLIA RD
BOSTALL LA
WILLROSE CRES
MITCHELL CL
COMMONWEALTH WAY
MYRTLEDENE RD
FUCHSIA ST
CARNATION ST
COLTNESS CRES
Alexander McLeod Sch
SHORNELLS WAY
Co-operative Woods
KNEE HILL
NEW RD
Green Chain Wlk
A206
A209
GRANITE ST
SPINEL CL
FELSPAR CL
GROSMONT RD
ROCKMOUNT RD
GATLING RD
THE DELL
GLENDOWN RD
BASTION RD
OLD PARK RD
BOSTALL HILL
1 ALEXANDER TERR
2 DIANTHUS CL
Bostall Heath
Cottage Hospice
DIXON HO
1 HUXLEY HO
2 HURST HO
3 COLYER HO
4 BELL HO
5 STEPHENSON HO
6 LISTER HO
HURST LA
PRIORY DR
FRIARS WAY
HARVEL CRES
WOOLWICH RD
Common
Bostall Woods
Bwg Gn
RUTHERGLEN RD
OAKMERE RD
SANDYCROFT
1 SOUTHLAND RD
2 PRESTWOOD CL
MARTYN HO 1
HURST PL 2
SENCLER HO 3
ARRAS HO 4
HEATH VIEW DR 5
PINEWOOD RD 6
Bexley Coll
BURCHARBRO RD
AMBERLEY RD
West Heath
GLENVIEW

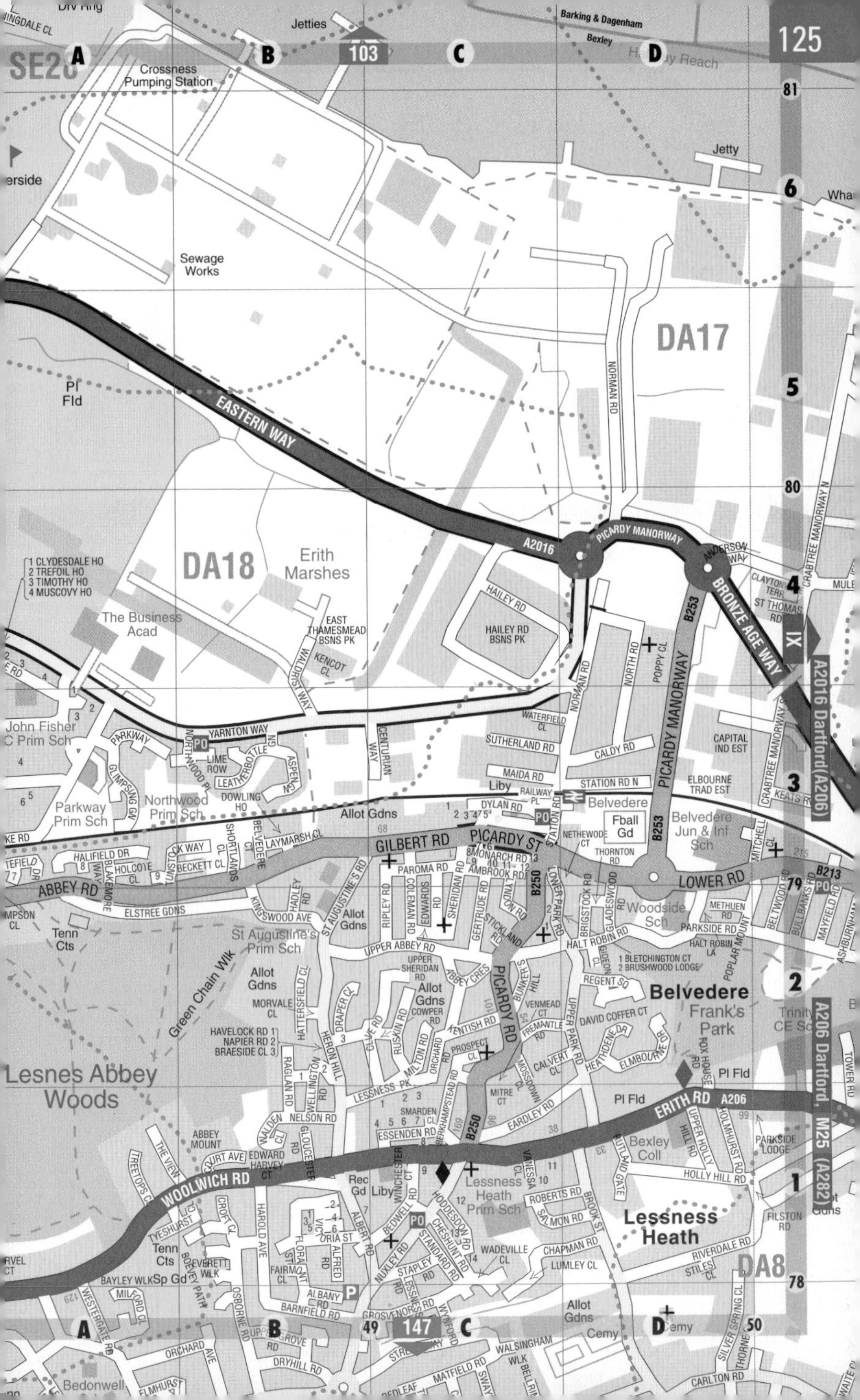

103
Jetties
Barking & Dagenham
Bexley
Halfway Reach
A
B
C
D
SE28
81
Crossness Pumping Station
Jetty
6
Sewage Works
DA17
5
NORMAN RD
Pl Fld
EASTERN WAY
80
DA18
Erith Marshes
A2016
PICARDY MANORWAY
ANDERSON WAY
CRABTREE MANORWAY N
1 CLYDESDALE HO
2 TREFOIL HO
3 TIMOTHY HO
4 MUSCOVY HO
HAILEY RD
HAILEY RD BSNS PK
4
CLAYTON TERR
ST THOMAS RD
MULBERRY
IX
The Business Acad
EAST THAMESMEAD BSNS PK
KENCOT CL
WALDRIST WAY
BRONZE AGE WAY
B253
POPPY CL
NORTH RD
A2016 Dartford (A206)
John Fisher C Prim Sch
PARKWAY
YARNTON WAY
WATERFIELD CL
SUTHERLAND RD
CALDY RD
CAPITAL IND EST
CRABTREE MANORWAY
LIME ROW
LEATHERBOTTLE GN
ASPEN GN
CENTURIAN WAY
MAIDA RD
STATION RD N
ELBOURNE TRAD EST
3
KEATS RD
Parkway Prim Sch
Northwood Prim Sch
DOWLING HO
Liby
RAILWAY PL
Belvedere
DYLAN RD
Allot Gdns
Fball Gd
Belvedere Jun & Inf Sch
GILBERT RD
PICARDY ST
STATION RD
LAYMARSH CL
SHORTLANDS CL
BELVEDERE CT
TUNSTOCK WAY
BECKETT CL
HALIFIELD DR
HOLCOTE CL
BLAKEMORE WAY
ABBEY RD
MONARCH RD
PAROMA RD
AMBROOK RD
NETHEWODE CT
THORNTON RD
LOWER RD
B213
79
PO
MITCHELL CL
ELSTREE GDNS
KINGSWOOD AVE
HADLEY RD
ST AUGUSTINE'S RD
Allot Gdns
RIPLEY RD
COLEMAN RD
EDWARDS RD
SHERIDAN RD
GERTRUDE RD
STICKLAND RD
LYNDON RD
B250
LOWER PARK RD
BRIGSTOCK RD
GLADESWOOD RD
Woodside Sch
METHUEN RD
BELTWOOD RD
BULLBANKS RD
MAYFIELD RD
ASHBURNHAM
PARKSIDE RD
HALT ROBIN RD
HALT ROBIN LA
POPLAR MOUNT
Tenn Cts
St Augustine's Prim Sch
UPPER ABBEY RD
UPPER SHERIDAN RD
ABBEY CRES
GIDEON CL
1 BLETCHINGTON CT
2 BRUSHWOOD LODGE
REGENT SQ
2
Green Chain Wlk
Allot Gdns
MORVALE CL
HATTERSFIELD CL
DRAPER CL
Allot Gdns
COWPER RD
BUNKERS HILL
PICARDY RD
VENMEAD CT
UPPER PARK RD
Belvedere
DAVID COFFER CT
Frank's Park
Trinity CE Sch
A206 Dartford, M25 (A282)
HAVELOCK RD 1
NAPIER RD 2
BRAESIDE CL 3
HERON HILL
CLIVE RD
RUSKIN RD
MILTON RD
ORCHARD RD
KENTISH RD
PROSPECT CL
FREMANTLE RD
HEATHDENE DR
ELMBOURNE DR
FOX HOUSE RD
Lesnes Abbey Woods
RAGLAN RD
WELLINGTON RD
LESSNESS PK
BERKHAMPSTEAD RD
MOSSDOWN CL
CALVERT CL
Pl Fld
TOWER RD
MITRE CT
ERITH RD
A206
EARDLEY RD
Pl Fld
UPPER HOLLY HILL RD
HOLMHURST RD
WALDEN CL
NELSON RD
SMARDEN CL
ABBEY MOUNT
ESSENDEN RD
COURT AVE
EDWARD HARVEY CT
GLOUCESTER RD
WINCHESTER CT
B250
VANESSA CL
Bexley Coll
RUTLAND GATE
PARKSIDE LODGE
TREETOPS CL
THE VIEW
WOOLWICH RD
Rec Gd
Liby
HODDESDON RD
Lessness Heath Prim Sch
ROBERTS RD
HOLLY HILL RD
1
TYESHURST CL
CROFT CL
HAROLD AVE
VICTORIA ST
ALBERT RD
BEDWELL CT
CHESHUNT RD
SALMON RD
BROOK ST
Lessness Heath
FILSTON RD
Tenn Cts
BOEVEY PATH
EVERETT WLK
FLORA ST
ALFRED RD
NUXLEY RD
STANDARD RD
WADEVILLE CL
CHAPMAN RD
RIVERDALE RD
FAIRMONT CL
STAPLEY RD
LUMLEY CL
STILES CL
DA8
BAYLEY WLK
Sp Gd
MILFORD CL
ALBANY RD
P
78
WESTERGATE RD
OSBORNE RD
BARNFIELD RD
LESSNESS AVE
GROSVENOR RD
WYNFORD WAY
Allot Gdns
SILVER SPRING CL
A
B
49
147
C
Cemy
D
50
UPPER GROVE RD
ORCHARD AVE
STREAMWAY
WALSINGHAM WLK
DRYHILL RD
THORNE CL
Bedonwell
ELMHURST
MATFIELD RD
SWAY
BELLRING
CARLTON RD

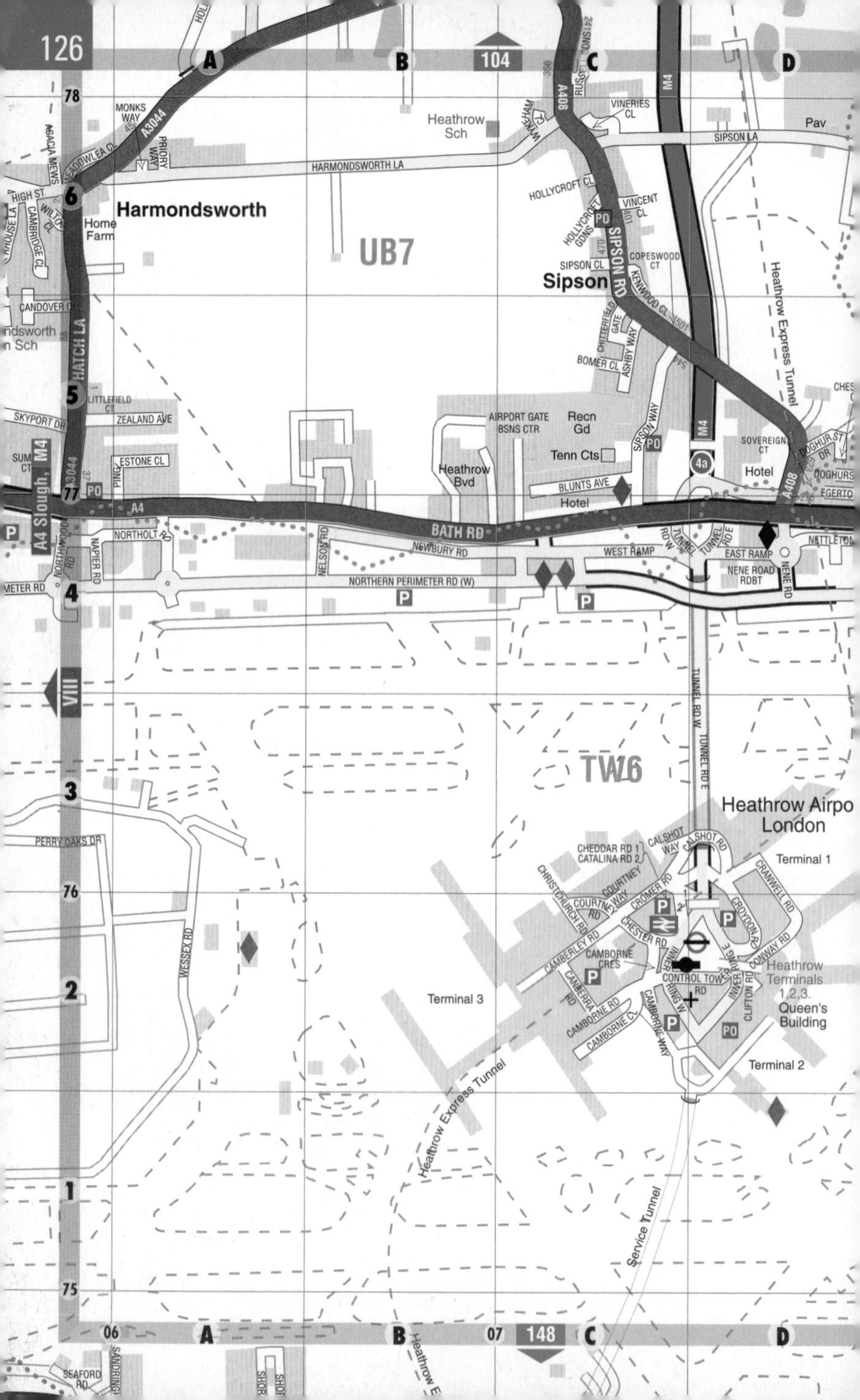
A
B
104
C
D
78
MONKS WAY
A3044
PRIORY WAY
MEADOWLEA CL
ACACIA MEWS
Heathrow Sch
WYKEHAM CL
A408
RUSSELL GDNS
VINERIES CL
M4
SIPSON LA
Pav
HARMONDSWORTH LA
6
HIGH ST
CAMBRIDGE CL
WILTON CL
Harmondsworth
Home Farm
UB7
HOLLYCROFT CL
HOLLYCROFT GDNS
VINCENT CL
SIPSON RD
PO
COPESWOOD CT
SIPSON CL
Sipson
KENWOOD CL
CANDOVER CL
HATCH LA
CHITTERFIELD GATE
ASHBY WAY
BOMER CL
Heathrow Express Tunnel
5
LITTLEFIELD CT
ZEALAND AVE
SKYPORT DR
AIRPORT GATE BSNS CTR
Recn Gd
SIPSON WAY
Tenn Cts
SOVEREIGN CT
Hotel
ESTONE CL
Heathrow Bvd
BLUNTS AVE
A4 Slough, M4
77
A4
BATH RD
4a
NORTHOLT RD
NEWBURY RD
NELSON RD
NAPIER RD
NORTHWOOD RD
TUNNEL RD W
TUNNEL RD E
WEST RAMP
EAST RAMP
NENE ROAD RDBT
NENE RD
NORTHERN PERIMETER RD (W)
4
P
VIII
TW6
3
Heathrow Airport London
CHEDDAR RD 1
CATALINA RD 2
CALSHOT WAY
CALSHOT RD
Terminal 1
PERRY OAKS DR
CHRISTCHURCH RD
COURTNEY RD
COURTNEY WAY
CROMER RD
CRANWELL RD
CROYDON RD
76
CHESTER RD
WESSEX RD
CAMBERLEY RD
CAMBORNE CRES
INNER RING E
CONWAY RD
Heathrow Terminals 1,2,3.
2
CONTROL TOWER RD
CANBERRA RD
INNER RING W
CLIFTON RD
Queen's Building
Terminal 3
CAMBORNE RD
CAMBORNE CL
CAMBORNE WAY
Terminal 2
Heathrow Express Tunnel
1
Service Tunnel
75
06
07
148
SEAFORD RD

HIGH ST
105
A
B
C
D
Nine Elms Farm
ST PETER
rts Gd
Pav
William Byrd Sch
VICTORIA LA
BLETCHMORE CL
BRICKFIELD LA
PEMBURY CT
KILN CL
Hotel
HUDSON RD
RICHARDS CL
THE FORGE
GOTHIC CT
FELLOWES CT
SHORTLANDS
SIPSON LA
A437
Harlington
PO
HIGH ST
FELBRIDGE CT
MANOR LA
MANSE CL
PONDSIDE CL
GILPIN WAY
PROVIDENCE LA
THE CRESCENT
WEST END LA
FIELD CL
RAYWOOD CL
TASKER CL
CROFT CL
HARLINGTON CL
GRAVES RD
BROWNING
NEW RD
Sp Gd
GRAMPIAN CL
PENNINE WAY
QUANTOCK CL
WARNER CL
BRENDON CL
CHEVIOT CL
MENDIP CL
HEATH CL
HALL LA
HIGH STREET HARLINGTON
Poultry Farm
LITTLE ELMS
MARLBOROUGH CRES
DAVID CL
CAROLINE PL
NOBEL DR
MONDIAL WAY
Hotel
Hotels
TRIUMPH CL
Hotels
Harlington Cnr
Hotel
Hotel
Gravel Pits
Frog's Ditch
CRANFORD LA
The White House
ACORN GR
SAUNTON AVE
PENDELL AVE
STRATHEARN AVE
LANGLEY CRES
ETON RD
OXFORD AVE
WINCHESTER RD
WINDSOR PARK RD
MALVERN RD
CRANESWATER
BATH RD
A4
The White Hart (PH)
Cranford Park
UB3
The
Tenn C
Avenue Park
SHE
PARK LA
78
6
5
77
4
3
76
2
1
75
Visitor Ctr
WORLD BSNS CTR
NEWALL RD
NEPTUNE RD
toms ouse
HATTON RD N
NORTHROP RD
NORTHERN PERIMETER RD
DUDSET LA
WAYE
P
CRANFORD LA
Hounslow
Hillingdon
128
ENFIELD ROAD RDBT
ENFIELD RD
ELGIN CRES
ELY RD
ESHER CRES
EPSOM SQ
EASTERN PERIMETER RD
EASTERN BSNS PK
EASTCHURCH ROAD RDBT
EXETER WAY
VANGAURD WAY
EXETER RD
EXETER RD
EASTCHURCH RD
TW6
EASTERN PERIMETER RD
ELECTRA AVE
EAGLE RD
ELMDON RD
CRANFORD LA
HATTON CROSS RDBT
EASTERN PERIMETER RD
A30
VISCOUNT WAY
Hatton Cross
LITHGOW'S RD
DICK TURPIN WAY
GREAT SOUTH-WEST RD
SOUTHERN PERIMETER
STEAM FARM LA
DOCKWELL CL
GREEN MAN LA
HATTON GN
FAGG'S RD
ST THERESA'S RD
ST ANTHONY'S WAY
RADIUS PK
HATTON RD
Hatton
MYRTLE AVE
WELLINGTON RD
SOUTHERN PERIMETER RD
09
149
10
Tenn Cts
Fball
Cemy

A
B
C
D
M4
106
Airlinks
THE HESTON CTR
VICTORY WAY
AIRLINKS IND EST
THE SPITFIRE EST
Bower Park Farm
WATERSPLASH LA
THE HARTLANDS CVN PK
CHURCH RD
SOUTHALL LA
Bwg Gn
Tenn Cts
Heston Motorway Service Area
Sp Gd
CRANE LODGE RD
Cranford Park
Cranford Comm Coll
REDWOOD EST
NORTH RD
PARKWAY TRAD EST
HESTON PHOENIX DISTRIBUTION PK
SOUTH RD
AERODROME WAY
HARLECH GDNS
PHOENIX WAY
NORTH FIELD RD
NORTH FIELD CL
FAIRMEAD CL
UB3
A312
78
6
5
4
3
2
1
75
76
77
The Cedars Prim Sch
Avenue Park
KEYSHAM AVE
SHEEPCOTE CL
QUINTON CL
HIGH ST
BRUNEL CL
The Queen's Head (PH)
Rectory Farm
Allot Gdns
CRANFORD LA
PEGG RD
BLERIOT RD
DE HAVILLAND RD
COBHAM RD
SOPWITH RD
WRIGHT RD
WHITTLE RD
JOHNSON RD
ALCOCK RD
BRABAZON RD
ARMYTAGE RD
NORMAN CRES
SCOTT GDNS
ASH GR
ACORN GR
SAUNTON AVE
PENDELL AVE
STRATHEARN AVE
LANGLEY CRES
CRANESWATER
PARK LA
The White Hart (PH)
A4
HAWTHORN CL
AVENUE GDNS
COLE GDNS
SANDRINGHAM GDNS
THE AVENUE
AVENUE CL
PINE TREE CL
FIRS DR
ROYSTON CL
MORNINGTON CRES
LYNCHEN CL
BLOOMSBURY CT
TREFUSIS CT
THE PARKWAY
TW5
DUDSET LA
WAYE AVE
SANDOWN CL
COMMUNITY CL
MEADOWBANK GDNS
CLEVEDON GDNS
BURNHAM GDNS
Liby
REGENT CL
FIELD CL
WESTWICK GDNS
Cranford
Waggoners Rdbt
BATH RD
BROWNING WAY
CHAILEY CL
MARCHSIDE CL
BROADWELL CT
ALL SAINTS CT
BURNS WAY
SHELLEY CRES
PARKLANDS PAR
Henleys Rdbt
HURN CT
PARKLANDS CT
HURN COURT RD
SPRINGWELL CL
A3006
Hounslow
Hillingdon
127
EASTERN PERIMETER RD
BERKELEY AVE
BYRON AVE
CHAUCER AVE
WOODFIELD RD
RECTORY RD
STANSFIELD RD
ACTON GN
WINDSOR RD
CEDAR RD
HASLEMERE AVE
TRAVELLERS WAY
A30
LANCASTER PL
ANN PARKES CT
LELA AVE
KEVIN CL
LEGRACE AVE
BATH RD
FRANCIS RD
Allot Gdns
Cranford Jun Sch
GRANTLEY RD
ST DUNSTAN'S RD
SILVER JUBILEE WAY
CRANEBANK
THE HASLEMERE & HEATHROW EST
TW6
River Crane
GREAT SOUTH-WEST RD
Recn Gd
CHINCHILLA DR
MUSQUASH WAY
BADGER CL
RACCOON WAY
SABLE CL
ERMINE CL
OPOSSUM WAY
SQUIRREL CL
MINK CT
MARMOT RD
WILTON RD
VINCENT RD
BASILDENE RD
MANOR AVE
ROSEMARY AVE
IVANHOE RD
CLIFFORD RD
CHESTER RD
ELY RD
WARWICK RD
ARUNDEL RD
Beavers Comm Prim Sch
LICHFIELD RD
SALISBURY RD
BEAVERS LA
MARNELL WAY
Hounslow West
Barracks
TW4
ARIEL WAY
HEATHROW CAUSEWAY EST
HEATHROW INTERNATIONAL TRAD EST
WALLBROOK BSNS CTR
SUN LIFE TRAD EST
GIRLING WAY
CAUSEWAY
PROLOGIS PK
Sp Gd
Resr
TW14
STEYNING WAY
GREEN LA
Beavers Lane Camp
CAVALRY CRES
BEAVERS CRES
HINTON AVE
LAWRENCE EST
LAWRENCE RD
MAPLE GR BSNS CTR
PULBOROUGH WAY
TAMIAN IND EST
TAMIAN WAY
Allot Gdns
CLEMENTS CT
CENTRAL PK EST
CARDINGTON SQ
DICK TURPIN WAY
DOCKWELL CL
FAGG'S RD
GREEN MAN LA
HATTON GN
THERESA'S RD
ST ANTHONY'S WAY
HERON WAY
NORTH FELTHAM TRAD EST
SPUR RD
RIVER GDNS BSNS CTR
HASLEMERE IND EST
FREEHOLD IND CTR
AMBERLEY WAY
FAIRWAY EST
ISLAY GDNS
10
11
150
ARMADALE RD
SPACE WAYE
PIER RD
DELL RD
North Feltham

North Hyde
UB2
Heston
TW5
HOUNSLOW
TW3
Lampton
Thorncliffe House (Hotel)
KINGS ARBOUR
RINGWAY
CROSSLANDS AVE
HADLEY GDNS
BRANDON RD
CLUNBURY AVE
DURHAM AVE
OXFORD AVE
THE ALDERS
GRANGE CL
M4
A3005
107
WINCHESTER AVE
ETON AVE
FERRARO CL
BISCOE CL
1 ASHMORE CT
2 BOSTOCK HO
3 PASSINGHAM HO
4 SPOONER HO
5 FENTON HO
6 BELLAMY HO
7 ROTHWELL HO
8 WESTBOURNE HO
HESTON GRANGE
HESTON GRANGE LA
WEST PARK CL
WORTHING RD
NORTH HYDE LA
Heston Park
Allot Gdns
Bwg Gn
Liby
Tenn Cts
WALNUT TREE RD
THE GREEN
HOPES CL
OLD COTE DR
WHEATLANDS
Rosary RC Jun & Inf Schs
THE VALE
SOMERSET WAYE
BLOSSOM WAYE
MEADOW WAYE
HESTON AVE
DAVENPORT LO
THE CROFT
TA Ctr
MEMORIAL CL
NEW HESTON RD
HESTON IND MALL
1 CENTRAL PAR
2 STANWORTH CT
YEOMAN CT
HOUSTOUN CT
HOGARTH CT
Heston Jun Inf & Com Schs
Pl Fld
Pav
LOVAT WLK
CRANFORD LA
A3063
CHURCH RD
ELDON AVE
HESTON RD
Andrew Ewing Jun & Inf Sch
BEECHCROFT CL
BEECH HO
SPEART LA
ORCHARD AVE
VICARAGE FARM CT
THE WARREN
DEVON WAYE
WESTBROOK RD
HOGARTH GDNS
SONIA GDNS
Allot Gdns
OAK AVE
BLACKTHORN CT
BLACKBERRY FARM CL
DORSET WAYE
NUFFIELD CT
OLD PARK MEWS
SUTTON HALL RD
SARK CL
GUERNSEY CL
ALDERNEY AVE
LULWORTH AVE
STUCLEY RD
Springwell Jun & Inf Schs
THE CROSSWAYS
UPPER SUTTON LA
SUTTON RD
LIME TREE RD
ST LEONARD'S GDNS
BEAUFORT GDNS
SUMMERHOUSE AVE
VICTORIA GDNS
QUEEN'S GDNS
WEST WAY
SUTTON SQ
SUTTON WAY
PALMER CL
CAMBORNE WAY
HARDWICKE AVE
NOBLE CNR
CHANNEL CL
SKINNERS LA
PERCY BILTON CT
A4
BRACKENDALE CL
SPRING GROVE CRES
SEFTON CT
CLAIRVALE RD
ADELAIDE RD
SHENLEY RD
CLAYPOLE DR
GREENCROFT RD
VICARAGE FARM RD
GREAT WEST RD
HARRIS CL
WILLOW GDNS
Tenn Cts
Lampton Sch
NORTH DENE
BERWYN AVE
LAMPTON CT
LAMPTON AVE
SUTTON DENE
BALMAIN CT
THE BEECHES
HIGHLANDS CL
B363
LANLOCK PL
KING'S AVE
BROAD WLK
PROSPECT CL
STRATTON CL
SARSEN AVE
BURTON GDNS
KINGSWOOD AVE
QUEENSWOOD AVE
Pl Fld
NEVILLE CL
BROOKWOOD RD
ELMSWORTH AVE
DENBIGH RD
COLWYN CRES
ADDISON
POOLE COURT RD
POOLE CT
SCOTT
TRIMMER WLK
JOHN ST
ELMDON RD
RENFREW RD
RENFREW CT
WIDMER CT
ROSARY CL
MOULTON AVE
CHARLES ST
GEORGE ST
C Ctr
AVONWICK RD
SUNNYCROFT RD
Alexandra Jun & Inf Sch
130
TIVERTON
DALCROSS RD
BATH RD
AMBASSADOR CL
WESLEY AVE
SUTTON LA
HARTE RD
Lampton Park
Tenn Cts
CLOVELLY RD
LAMPTON RD
ALEXANDRA CT
ALEXANDRA GDNS
ELLINGTON RD
GARLAND DR
MYRTLE RD
Hounslow West
Wellington Prim Sch
Bwg Gn
Pav
Cemy
Allot Gdns
Bwg Gn
LAMPTON PARK RD
ALEXANDRA RD
CAVENDISH PAR
CRANSTON CL
ALDERGROVE GDNS
SIDDELEY DR
HARRIER CT
ST PAUL'S CL
JOHN BARTER HO
COOPER HO
Sp Gd
THAMESVALE CL
CONCORDE CL
Hounslow Manor Sch
PRINCE REGENT
DAWN CL
DALE AVE
SOLWAY CL
ST PAUL'S CT
CHURCH CL
DENE AVE
BULSTRODE AVE
QUEEN'S RD
LANSDOWNE RD
Hounslow Central
Bwg Gn
HOLLOWAY ST
CROWN YARD
Tenn Cts
RAVENSDALE RD
FERNDALE AVE
NOEL CT
MAITLAND CL
BOSWOOD CT
TRAFALGAR CT
BULSTRODE GDNS
BULSTRODE RD
CLIPSTONE RD
CORBAN RD
PRIORY CT
BALFOUR RD
YORK RD
MONTAGUE RD
HIGH ST
FAIR ST
RAVENSDALE GDNS
HUSSARS CL
MARTINDALE RD
STANDARD RD
ST PAUL'S CT
National Wks
WELLINGTON RD N
EDE CL
GARDNER CT
BATH RD
CHESTNUT CT
A3006
STEVE BIKO WAY
THE HOUNSLOW CTR
TRINITY PAR
DOUGLAS RD
FAIRFIELDS
EVERGREEN
HEATHDALE AVE
Hounslow Heath Jun & Inf Schs
The Hounslow Ed Ctr (Specl Sch)
CLARE RD
BELGRAVE RD
LOGAN CL
Prim Sch
GROSVENOR RD
OSBORNE RD
STRAFFORD RD
St Mark's RC Sch
HOSPITAL RD
BLENHEIM HO
UPTON RD
Liby
TREATY CTR
JUBILEE CT
BRISTOW RD
CHAPEL RD
BEAVERS LA
SELWYN CL
TRINITY CL
STAINES RD
OLD FARM CL
GROVE CT
GROVE RD
BELL RD
A315
JUNIPER CT
LIVINGSTONE
CAMBRIDGE RD
CRANBROOK RD
ASHTON GDNS
TOAD LA
THE GREENWAY
WIVENHOE CT
SMOOTHFIELD
CROMWELL ST
WAREHAM CL
HANWORTH RD
B361
HOLLY RD
TEMPLE RD
GORDON RD
INWOOD RD
CORPORATION AVE
DUKES AVE
HARTER CRES
BOWNESS DR
IVY LA
FULSTONE CL
ESTRIDGE CL
BENSON CL
GROVE RD
PRINCES MEWS
MAUVEINE GDNS
PERKINS CT
HIBERNIA RD
THOMPSON AVE
ENTON PL
VINE PL
IND EST
HANWORTH TER
TA Ctr
POWNALL RD
POWNALL GDNS
LAYTON RD
Allot Gdns
BARRACK RD
TIVOLI RD
LAUREL GDNS
FIR TREE RD
APSLEY HO
BEVERLEY MANS
BEVERLEY AVE
HOLLYGROVE CL
LABURNUM GR
INVERNESS RD
Prim Sch
ALBERT RD
CAMBRIA CL
HOUNSLOW BSNS PK
ALICE WAY
ANDERSON'S PL
CROSS LANCES
1 BRAMLEY HO
2 RUSSET HO
3 BEVERLEY CT
GLOUCESTER RD
SYCAMORE CT
CONNAUGHT AVE
MIDSUMMER AVE
COBBS RD
BENHAM GDNS
CROMWELL RD
NICHOLES RD
ALBION RD
NEW RD UNITS
STATION RD
THE HEATH BSNS CTR
IVY RD
INWOOD BSNS PK
MASWELL PARK RD
MASWELL PARK CRES
MUNSTER AVE
CRESTWOOD WAY
YALE CL
DRAYTON CL
ROSEHEATH RD
MARSHALL CL
The Orchard Jun & Inf Sch
ROSSINDEL RD
RESTORMEL CL
COOMBE
PARKSIDE RD
HIBERNIA GDNS
Hounslow
WHITTON RD
HOUNSLOW AVE
Allot Gdns
HEATHLANDS WAY
BEAULIEU CL
BROMPTON CL
WELLINGTON AVE
PENDEREL RD
151
A
B
C
D
1
2
3
4
5
6

Farm
TW7
A
B
C
D
108
Osterley Park
Osterley Park House
Tenn Cts
Bwg Gn
Sp Gd
Wyke Green
CH
B454
78
6
P
Tenn Cts
Sp Gd
Pav
SYON LA
OAKLANDS AVE
GOWER RD
MACFARLANE LA
CROWNTREE CL
STAGS WAY
WYKE CL
ASHLEY DR
RIDGEWAY RD N
LINGWOOD GDNS
BRAYBOURNE DR
Allot Gdns
SYON PARK GDNS
Pl Fld
Pav
5
JERSEY RD
HERM CL
BASSETT GDNS
CRANMORE AVE
THISTLEWORTH CL
Osterley
Liby
ST MARY'S CRES
Bwg Gn
Tenn Cts
Pav
LEIGHAM DR
766
A4
PENWERRIS AVE
PEVENSEY CL
BASSETT GDNS
OSTERLEY AVE
Osterley
PO
Pav
690
721
Running Tk
Tenn Cts
Isleworth & Syon Sch for Boys
Brunel Univ Coll Osterley Campus
ROXBOROUGH AVE
ALBURY AVE
GREAT WEST RD
STUCLEY RD
PENWERRIS CT
WEST CT
THORNBURY AVE
ORCHARD CT
CAROLINE CL
CHURCH RD
THORNBURY CT
HAREWOOD RD
NORTHUMBERLAND AVE
CAMPION RD
77
LULWORTH AVE
OSTERLEY CT
Campion House (Seminary)
FAIRACRE
1 OSTERLEY LO
2 ST ANDREW'S CL
3 PARKFIELD
BOROUGH RD
OSTERLEY CRES
PO
516
A4
T Cts
Pav
Bwg Gn
Sp Gd
1 FOXTAIL HO
2 MARYGOLD HO
3 CLOVER HO
4 SORREL HO
5 GRESHAM CT
6 BALDWIN GDNS
7 CHAMBERLAIN GDNS
Sp Gd
THORNBURY AVE
MORETON AVE
DEBORAH CL
OSTERLEY RD
APLIN WAY
Tenn Cts
RIDGEWAY RD
HIGHFIELD RD
MUSGRAVE RD
NORTHUMBERLAND AVE
PARKWOOD RD
BRACKENDALE CL
Lampton
SPRING GROVE CRES
GRESHAM RD
GLADSTONE GDNS
PALMERSTON RD
SPENCER RD
KILBERRY CL
OAKLEY CL
DAVIES WLK
THE BROOKLANDS
ST CHRISTOPHER'S CL
THE GROVE
RAVENSWOOD GDNS
COLLEGE RD
T Cts
Pav
Pav
Sp Gd
LC
4
B363
LANLOCK
TAYLOR CL
BURLINGTON RD
EVERSLEY CRES
HARVARD RD
West Thames Coll
NASEBY CL
COPPER BEECHES
VINCENT RD
WITHAM RD
WESTON GDNS
GROVE RD
AVENUE RD
PARKLAND GR
HARTHAM
129
COLWYN CRES
SPRING GROVE RD
176
STANLEY CL
STANLEYCROFT
230
4 FAIRWAYS
5 GRANWOOD CT
6 GROVEWOOD CT
HEMLEY CL
A315
ADDISON AVE
TENNYSON RD
TAUNTON AVE
KINGSLEY AVE
THE CLOSE
WORTON GDNS
BANKS HO
VILLIERS RD
WAYSIDE CT
468
WIGHTON MEWS
B363
PO
Isleworth
1 OVERTON CL
2 BEECHEN CLIFF WAY
3 THURZA CT
Pav
Sp Gd
DENBIGH RD
Alexandra Jun & Inf Sch
TIVERTON RD
KINGSLEY RD
WORTON WAY
OFFLEY PL
DRAPER CL
CLIFTON RD
PEMBROKE PL
Spring Grove
CRAWFORD CL
SIDMOUTH AVE
METRO IND CTR
LORING RD
NEWTON RD
CASTLE WAY
LINKFIELD RD
SMALLBERRY AVE
RAYBELL CT
3
ALEXANDRA GDNS
STIRLING GR
THE DRIVE
Spring Grove Prim Sch
THE ORCHARD
NORTH DR
HONNOR GDNS
MEON CT
AYLETT RD
ST JOHN'S RD
NOTTINGHAM RD
COPPER MILL DR
GRAINGER RD
ELLINGTON RD
GARLAND DR
P
Hounslow East
RICHENS CL
STAR RD
LONDON RD
621
Tenn Cts
Pav
Pl Fld
TW7
ST JOHN'S CT
THE WOODLANDS
WOODLANDS GR
BRADDOCK
94
MYRTLE RD
PO
DERWENT LO
KELVIN CT 1
HAWKFIELD CT 2
COOPERS CT 3
WOODLANDS RD
ISLEWORTH BSNS COMPLEX
OCTAVIA RD
76
P
Hounslow Manor Sch
CECIL RD
PRINCE REGENT RD
P
746
BIRCH CL
ALDERWICK DR
STANBOROUGH RD
GREENHAM HO
FARNELL'S ALMSHOUSES
HOWARD RD
2 3 PANKHURST CL
DRAYMANS WAY
MALTING WAY
CLYDESDALE CL
SHIRE HORSE WAY
Bwg Gn
Central
HOLLOWAY ST
CROWN YARD
GILBERT ST
A315
P
P
Hounslow Town Prim Sch
DEPOT RD
WOODLAND GDNS
Pav
T Cts
GREENWOOD RD
MORRIS RD
KENNET RD
Woodlands
CLOCK TOWER RD
2
HIGH ST
FAIR ST
SCHOOL RD
DEVONSHIRE HO
PEARS RD
HYDE HO
JAMES ST
GLENWOOD RD
BRIDGE RD
RIVERSIDE WLK
UNWIN RD
WHEATLEY RD
DOUGLAS
63
FAIRFIELDS
EVERGLADES
INWOOD AVE
Allot Gdns
Oaklands Sch
ELMER GDNS
GIBSON CL
SUSSEX AVE
ABINGER GDNS
ESSEX AVE
CHRISTABEL CL
RUSKIN RD
JUBILEE CT
BRISTOW RD
Tenn Cts
Inwood Park
1 DASHWOOD CT
2 VERNEY HO
3 HANNING LO
4 MACDONALD CT
TW3
CHAPEL RD
LIVINGSTONE RD
CHATSWORTH CRES
FARNELL RD
PAGET LA
CLAYTON RD
WORTON RD
1 LESTOR CT
2 TRIMMER CT
3 STEINMAN CT
4 WILKINSON HO
5 BOOTHROYD HO
6 RICHARDSON HO
7 ALLCOTT HO
8 ANTHONY CT
9 OLIVER CT
10 WOODALL HO
Bwg Gn
Tenn Cts
HOLLY RD
TEMPLE RD
GORDON RD
STANLEY RD
DALMENY CRES
HEIDMANN CL
WORTON RD
WORTON CT
Allot Gdns
OAK LA
WEAVERS CL
THE VICTORY BSNS CTR
FLEMING WAY
MEADOWBROOK CT
Redlees Park
B361
LAYTON RD
INWOOD RD
DETHERICK CT 5
AUGUSTUS CT 6
CAMERON LO 7
Chatsworth Inf Sch
TUDOR RD
Duke of Northumberland's River
1
POWNALL RD
Allot Gdns
ELLERDINE RD
WORTON HALL IND EST
Allot Gdns
POWNALL GDNS
HEATH RD
ATCHAM RD
LEIGH RD
CATHERINE GDNS
PO
Chatsworth Jun Sch
Allot Gdns
LYNTON CL
THE HEATH BSNS CTR
WOLSEY CL
LYNCROFT GDNS
NORBURY AVE
EATON RD
Sewage Works
IVY RD
INWOOD BSNS PK
PARK CRES
CENTRAL AVE
WAINWRIGHT GR
BANKSIDE CL
75
MASWELL PARK RD
MASWELL PARK CRES
BRACKEN END
HARVESTERS CL
1453
Hounslow
HOUNSLOW GDNS
CHURCH STATION
14
A
B
Allot Gdns
15
152
C
D
TREVOR CL
HILLARY RD
BRIAR CL
MANN'S CL
A310
WHITTON RD
HOUNSLOW AVE
Allot Gdns
PRIORY RD
LEAMINGTON CL
Allot Gdns
REAPERS WAY
HALL RD
HEATHER CL
GLEN WLK
BEAUMONT PL
MOGDEN LA
IVYBRIDGE
PARK RD

BRENTFORD
B Sky B HQ
Allot Gdns
River Brent
Grand Union Canal
CENTAURS BSNS PK
WEST CROSS CTR
Superstore
BRENTSIDE EXECUTIVE CTR
GREAT WEST TRAD EST
GREAT WEST RD
TW8
Gillette Cnr
SYON LA
B454
A4
A3002
M4
M4 (ELEVATED)
BOSTON MANOR RD
Brentford
Griffin Park Fball Gd
Brentford Sch for Girls
Liby
Recn Gd
Allot Gdns
HALF ACRE
HIGH ST
A315
EALING RD
B455
B452
BRENTFORD BSNS CTR
COUNTY PAR
Marina
BRENTWATERS BSNS PK
Tenn Cts
Brentford End
London Butterfly House
SYON PARK COTTS
Syon Lane
Pl Fld
The Green Sch for Girls
SPUR RD
LONDON RD
A310
NORTHUMBERLAND AVE
John Busch Sch
Syon Park
Syon House
Thames Path
River Thames
Hounslow
Richmond upon Thames
Arboretum
132
Queen Charlotte's Cottage
King's Steps Gate
1 JODRELL CL
2 HOLDERNESSE RD
3 FINNEY LA
4 HANOVER TERR
5 DARCY RD
6 BLENHEIM WAY
7 MILESTONE CT
8 POYNDER LO
1 FERNEY MEADE WAY
2 TOWN FIELD WAY
3 TECK CL
4 THACKERAY CL
Cemy
West Middlesex Univ
HELIX HO
MILL PLAT
B363
TW9
Royal Mid-Surrey
Old Deer Park
Kew Observatory
Isleworth Ait
TW7
ISLEWORTH
TWICKENHAM RD
SOUTH ST
A3004
RICHMOND RD
Old Deer Park Recn Gd
Brunel Univ Coll (Twickenham Campus)
TW1
Richmond Lock
Richmond Athletic Gd
Richmond Coll
T Cts
The Hamlet (Day)
Bwg Gn Coll
THE GATEWAYS 1
FITZWILLIAM HO 2
PORTLAND TERR 3
PEMBROKE VILLAS 4
LITTLE GN 5
A316
Richmond Circus
TWICKENHAM RD
RICHMOND
THE QUADRANT
A307
A305
GEORGE ST
RED LION ST
PARADISE RD
Allot Gdns
A
B
C
D
109
153
1
2
3
4
5
6
75
76
77
78

A
B
C
D
110
BRENTFORD
Strand on the Green
Kew
Kew Bridge
Kew Green
Kew Pier
Brentford Ait
Lots Ait
Herbarium Liby
Thames Path
Kew Palace
Royal Botanic Gardens
Palm House
Temperate House
Pagoda
Arboretum
Public Record Office
KEW RET PK
MARLBOROUGH TRAD EST
Kew Gardens
North Sheen
North Sheen Cemy (Fulham)
Chalkers Cnr
Manor Circus
Richmond Circus
Richmond Athletic Gd
The Hamlet (Day)
Old Deer Park
Holy Trinity CE Jun Sch
TW9
RICHMOND
HIGH ST
KEW RD
MORTLAKE RD
SANDYCOMBE RD
LOWER MORTLAKE RD
LOWER RICHMOND RD
CLIFFORD AVE
SHEEN RD
MANOR RD
KEW BRIDGE RD
EALING RD
GREEN DRAGON LA
WELLESLEY RD
M4
A315
A205
A307
A316
A305
A3003
B353
B455
B322
131
154
77
76
78
75
18
19
1
2
3
4
5
6
1 WATCOMBE COTTS
2 CAMBRIDGE COTTS
3 WILLOW COTTS
4 THETIS TERR
1 SANDSTONE
2 BROADLANDS CT
3 FABYC HO
4 ASPEN CT
BLENHEIM CT 1
WOBURN CT 2
FINUCANE CT 3
TRINITY COTTS 4
1 ARUNDEL HO
2 MARLBOROUGH HO
3 BUCKINGHAM HO
4 OSBOURNE HO
5 YORK HO
6 SANDRINGHAM HO
7 KENT HO
8 NORFOLK HO
9 RUNNYMEDE HO
10 CARISBROOKE HO

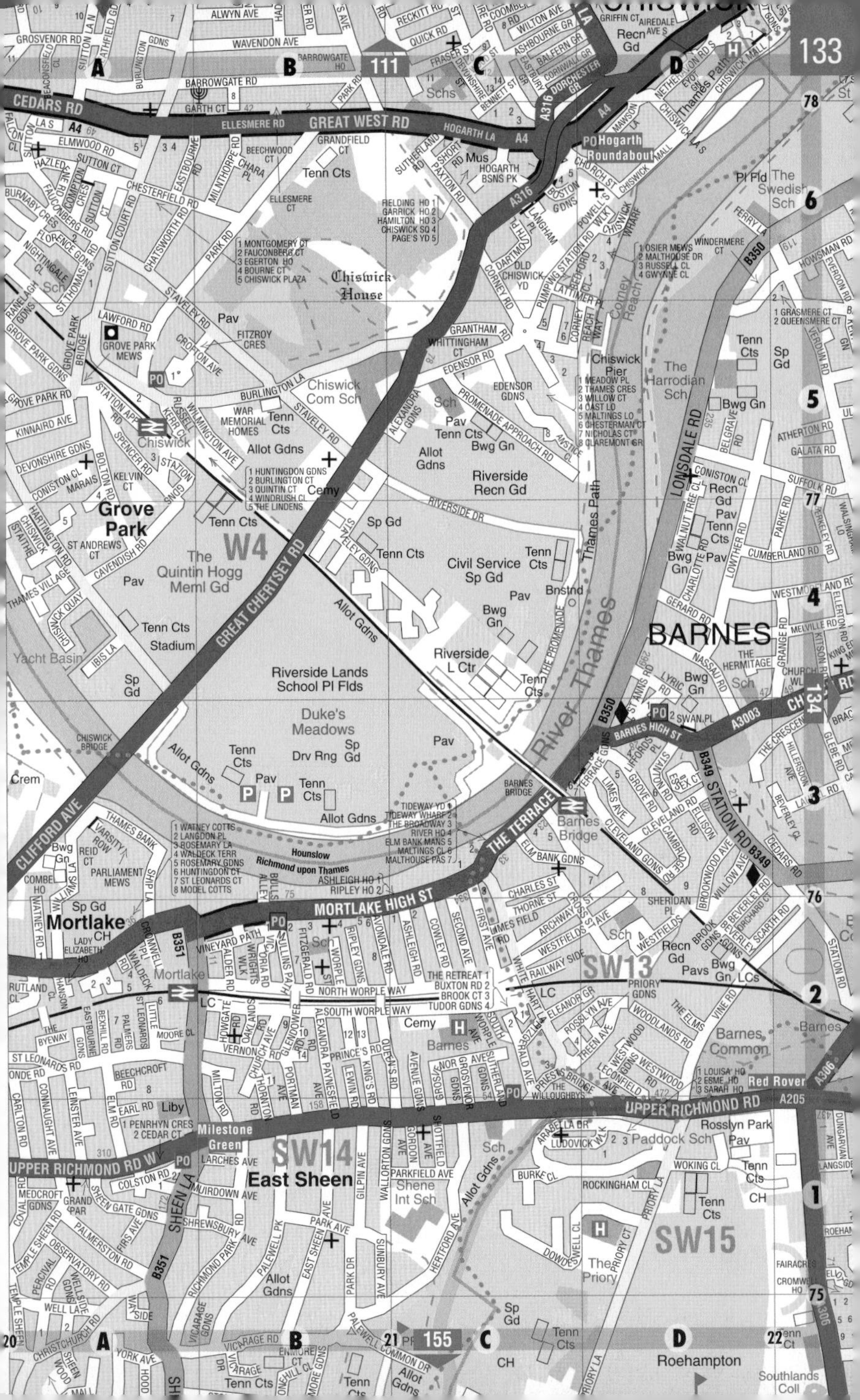
CHISWICK
111
A
B
C
D
CEDARS RD
GREAT WEST RD
ELLESMERE RD
HOGARTH LA
A4
A316
Hogarth Roundabout
BARROWGATE RD
WAVENDON AVE
ALWYN AVE
GROSVENOR RD
SUTTON LA N
DORCHESTER GR
Chiswick House
Tenn Cts
Chiswick Com Sch
Chiswick
Grove Park
W4
GREAT CHERTSEY RD
The Quintin Hogg Meml Gd
Stadium
Yacht Basin
Riverside Lands School Pl Flds
Duke's Meadows
Civil Service Sp Gd
Riverside Recn Gd
Riverside L Ctr
Allot Gdns
Chiswick Pier
Corney Reach
Thames Path
River Thames
The Harrodian Sch
LONSDALE RD
BARNES
B350
BARNES HIGH ST
A3003
B349
STATION RD
THE TERRACE
Barnes Bridge
BARNES BRIDGE
CHISWICK BRIDGE
CLIFFORD AVE
Hounslow
Richmond upon Thames
MORTLAKE HIGH ST
Mortlake
B351
SW13
SW14
SW15
East Sheen
UPPER RICHMOND RD
UPPER RICHMOND RD W
A205
A306
Milestone Green
SHEEN LA
Barnes Common
Red Rover
Rosslyn Park
Paddock Sch
Shene Int Sch
The Priory
Roehampton
Southlands Coll
155
134
78
77
76
75
6
5
4
3
2
1
20
21
22

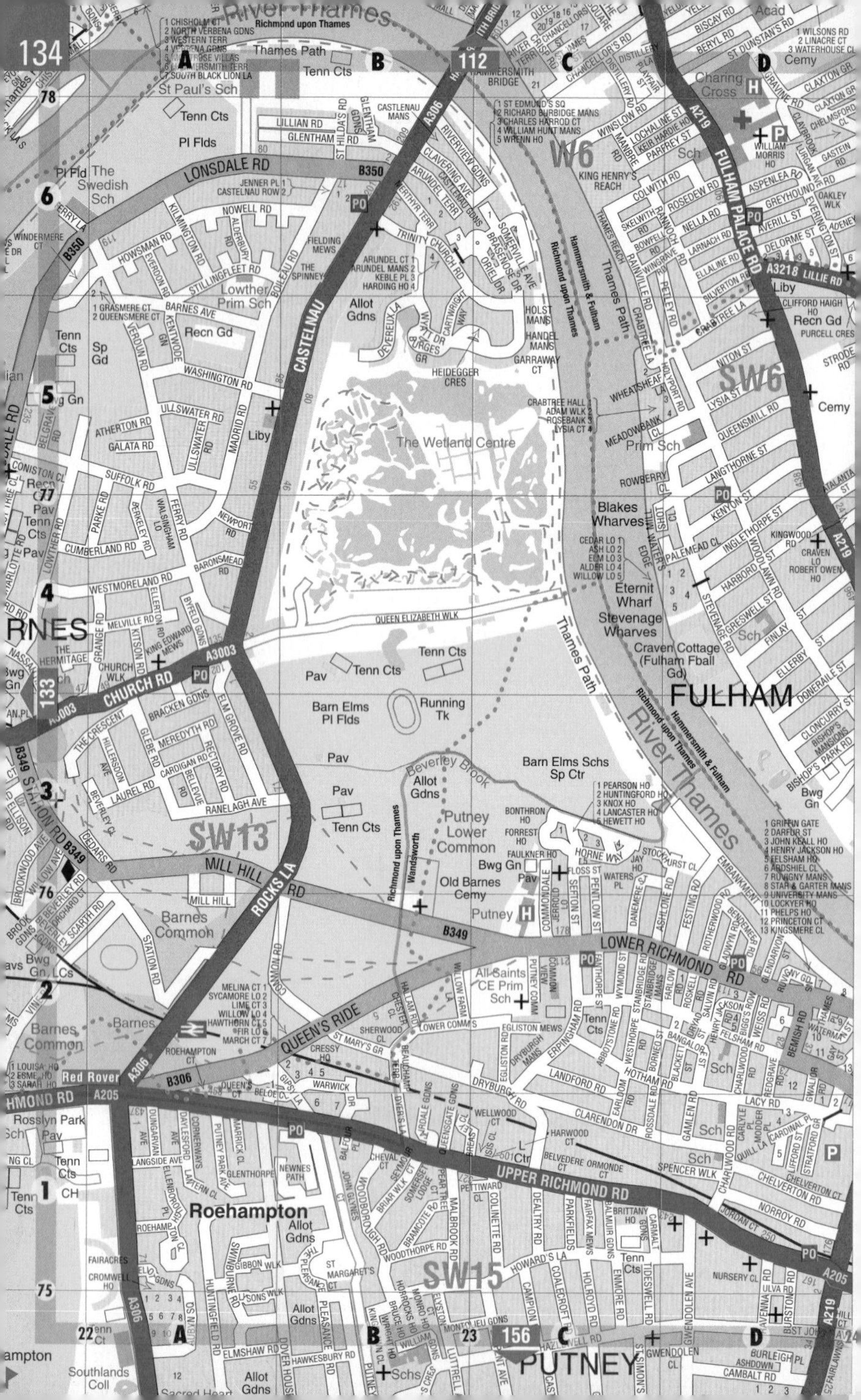
River Thames
Richmond upon Thames
Thames Path
Tenn Cts
St Paul's Sch
112
Hammersmith Bridge
Castelnau Mans
Lillian Rd
Glentham Rd
Lonsdale Rd
B350
Pl Flds
Pl Fld
The Swedish Sch
W6
King Henry's Reach
Charing Cross
Fulham Palace Rd
A219
Cemy
Kilmington Rd
Nowell Rd
Howsman Rd
Stillingfleet Rd
Lowther Prim Sch
Barnes Ave
Recn Gd
Washington Rd
Castelnau
A306
Allot Gdns
Arundel Terr
Trinity Church Rd
Somerville Ave
Holst Mans
Handel Mans
Garraway Ct
Heidegger Cres
The Wetland Centre
Hammersmith & Fulham
Crabtree La
Lysia St
SW6
Queensmill Rd
Meadowbank Cl
Prim Sch
Langthorne St
Rowberry Cl
Kenyon St
Blakes Wharves
Thames Reach
A3218 Lillie Rd
Liby
Recn Gd
Ullswater Rd
Atherton Rd
Galata Rd
Suffolk Rd
Madrid Rd
Ferry Rd
Cumberland Rd
Westmoreland Rd
Baronsmead Rd
Eternit Wharf
Stevenage Wharves
Craven Cottage (Fulham Fball Gd)
Queen Elizabeth Wlk
RNES
Church Rd
A3003
Barn Elms Pl Flds
Running Tk
Pav
FULHAM
Barn Elms Schs Sp Ctr
Beverley Brook
Putney Lower Common
SW13
Mill Hill Rd
Rocks La
Old Barnes Cemy
Putney
Horne Way
Lower Richmond Rd
B349
Station Rd
Barnes Common
Queen's Ride
Red Rover
A205
Upper Richmond Rd
Roehampton
SW15
Howard's La
Rosslyn Park
PUTNEY
156
Southlands Coll
Embankment
Bishop's Park Rd
Bwg Gn
A B C D
1 2 3 4 5 6

A
B
C
D
113
Queen's Club
Earl's Court Ex Ctr
West Brompton
Brompton Cemy
NORTH END RD B317
LILLIE RD
Normand Park
DAWES RD
FULHAM RD
FULHAM BROADWAY
Fulham Broadway
Walham Green
Stamford Bridge Stad (Chelsea F'ball Club)
HARWOOD RD B318
KING'S RD
FINBOROUGH RD
REDCLIFFE GDNS
Parsons Green
Eel Brook Common
NEW KING'S RD
FULHAM PALACE RD
Fulham Palace
All Saints CE Prim Sch
Bishop's Park
FULHAM HIGH ST
Putney Bridge
SW6
South Park
Hurlingham Park
Hurlingham House
Hurlingham & Chelsea Sec Sch
Chelsea Coll of Art & Design
Thames Path
River Thames
Hammersmith & Fulham
Wandsworth
Hurlingham Wharf
WANDSWORTH BRIDGE RD
Wandsworth Bridge
Sands End
Gas Works
Fulham Wharf
Gargoyle Wharf
SW15
PUTNEY HIGH ST
PUTNEY BRIDGE RD
Putney Pier
Wandsworth Park
River Wandle
Wandsworth Town
SWANDON WAY A217
Wandsworth Gyratory
A217 ARMOURY WAY
UPPER RICHMOND RD
East Putney
Putney
157
136
264
265
1
2
3
4
5
6
75
76
77
78
25
26

SW10
CHELSEA
A
B
C
D
114
Burton's Court
FULHAM RD
REDCLIFFE GDNS
FINBOROUGH RD
KING'S RD
Chelsea & Westminster
GUNTER GR
EDITH GR
OLD CHURCH ST
BEAUFORT ST
OAKLEY ST
ROYAL HOSPITAL RD
CHELSEA EMB
Thames Path
Cadogan Pier
Chelsea Reach
ALBERT BRIDGE (SUSPENSION)
Terrace Wlk
THE PARADE
CHEYNE WLK
CREMORNE RD
Kensington & Chelsea
Wandsworth
BATTERSEA BRIDGE
Bridge Wharf
Ransome's Dock
Fountain Lake
Old Ferry Wharf
Chelsea Wharf
Cremorne Wharf
River Thames
Hammersmith & Fulham
BATTERSEA BRIDGE RD
ALBERT BRIDGE RD
Festival Pleasure Gardens
SW11
BATTERSEA
Gas Works
Chelsea Creek
CHELSEA HARBOUR DR
WESTBRIDGE RD
VICARAGE CRES
HARBOUR AVE
135
Chelsea Harbour Pier
266
267
Regent Wharf
PRINCE OF WALES DR
BATTERSEA PARK RD
LOMBARD RD
BATTERSEA HIGH ST
Heliport
Battersea Reach
Superstore
Sands End
Fulham Wharf
Sherwood Wharf
WANDSWORTH BRIDGE
Gargoyle Wharf
PIER TERR
YORK RD
FALCON RD
LATCHMERE RD
Falcon Park
Christ Church CE Prim Sch
THE VILLAGE
Clapham Junction
ST JOHN'S HILL
ELSPETH RD
LAVENDER GDNS
SWANDON WAY
Wandsworth Town
EAST HILL
NORTH SIDE WANDSWORTH COMM
BATTERSEA RISE
158
Belleville Prim Sch
CLAPHAM COMMON
A3220
A3217
A308
A304
A3212
A3031
A3207
A3205
A217
A214
A3036
A205
B304
B305
B302
B229
B234
1
2
3
4
5
6

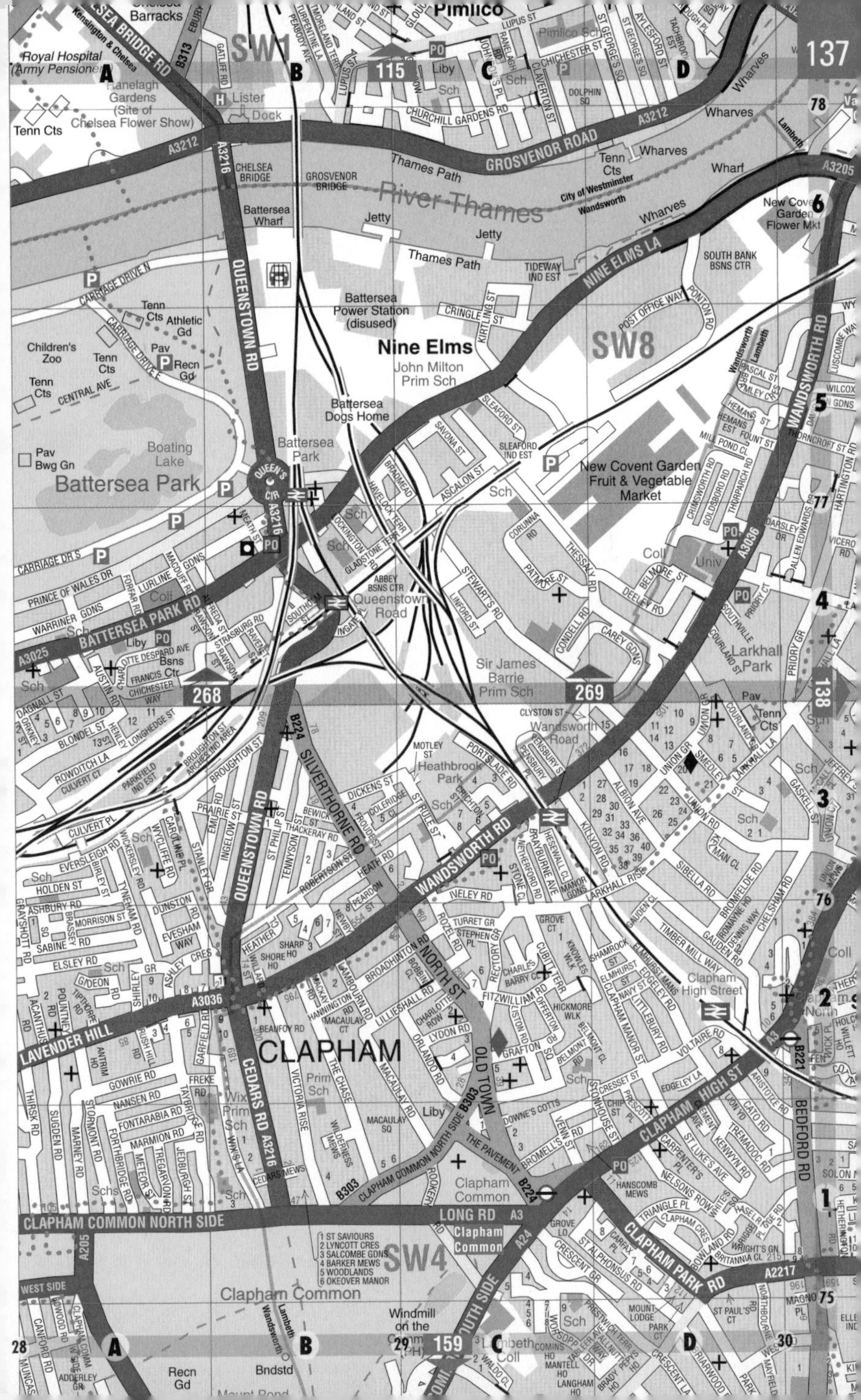
Pimlico
SW1
Royal Hospital (Army Pensioners)
Ranelagh Gardens (Site of Chelsea Flower Show)
Tenn Cts
Lister
Dock
CHELSEA BRIDGE RD
A3212
A3216
GROSVENOR ROAD
CHELSEA BRIDGE
GROSVENOR BRIDGE
Thames Path
River Thames
City of Westminster
Wandsworth
Wharves
Wharf
A3205
New Covent Garden Flower Mkt
Battersea Wharf
Jetty
NINE ELMS LA
TIDEWAY IND EST
SOUTH BANK BSNS CTR
Battersea Power Station (disused)
Nine Elms
SW8
John Milton Prim Sch
Battersea Dogs Home
QUEENSTOWN RD
Children's Zoo
Athletic Gd
CARRIAGE DRIVE N
CARRIAGE DRIVE E
CENTRAL AVE
Boating Lake
Battersea Park
QUEEN'S CIR
CARRIAGE DR S
New Covent Garden Fruit & Vegetable Market
WANDSWORTH RD
A3036
PRINCE OF WALES DR
BATTERSEA PARK RD
A3025
Queenstown Road
Larkhall Park
268
269
138
Sir James Barrie Prim Sch
Wandsworth Road
Heathbrook Park
SILVERTHORNE RD
B224
CLAPHAM
LAVENDER HILL
CEDARS RD
NORTH ST
OLD TOWN
Clapham High Street
CLAPHAM HIGH ST
B221
BEDFORD RD
CLAPHAM PARK RD
A2217
CLAPHAM COMMON NORTH SIDE
LONG RD
A3
A24
B303
Clapham Common
SW4
1 ST SAVIOURS
2 LYNCOTT CRES
3 SALCOMBE GDNS
4 BARKER MEWS
5 WOODLANDS
6 OKEOVER MANOR
WEST SIDE
A205
Windmill on the Common (PH)
159
Lambeth Coll
Recn Gd
Bndstd
A B C D
28 29 30

Vauxhall Bridge
Spring Gardens
Kennington
Kennington La
116
261
SE17
SE11
Vauxhall Cross
Wharves
Wharf
78
6
New Covent Garden Flower Mkt
South Bank Bsns Ctr
The Oval (Surrey Cnty Crkt Gd)
Kennington Oval
Harleyford Rd
Kennington Pk Rd
Kennington Park
Fball Gd
Govt Offices
Bnstnd
Tenn Cts
Vauxhall Park
Bwg Gn
Fentiman Rd
Cottingham Rd
Wandsworth Rd
South Lambeth Rd
Clapham Rd
Brixton Rd
Camberwell New Rd
Wyvil Rd
Parry St
Bondway
Miles St
Trenchold St
Harleyford Rd
Bonnington Sq
Langley La
Lawn La
Ebbisham Dr
Durham St
Oval Way
Handforth Rd
Crewdson Rd
South Island Pl
Mowll St
Vassall Rd
Caldwell St
Cranmer Rd
Minerva Cl
Holland Gro
Foxley Rd
Perseverance Pl
Chryssell Rd
Mandela St
Hanworth Ho
Kendal Cl
Cadman Cl
Frederick Cres
Lothian Rd
Halsmere Rd
Calais St
Myatt's Fields Pk
Heyford Ave
Meadow Pl
Richborne Terr
Oval Pl
Dorset Rd
Carroun Rd
Bolney St
Wilkinson St
Albert Sq
Aldebert Terr
Thorne Rd
Wilcox Rd
Thorncroft St
Hartington Rd
Davidson Gdns
Walton Cl
Luscombe Way
Liby
Sch
5
77
SW8
Viceroy Rd
Lansdowne Gdns
St Barnabas Villas
Guildford Rd
Tradescant Rd
Hampson Way
Portland Gro
Liberty St
Morat St
Hackford Rd
Southey Rd
Cranworth Gdns
Hillyard St
Gosling Way
Mansion Cl
Cowley Rd
Normandy Rd
Fountain
Mostyn Gdns
Akerman Rd
Cormont Rd
Tenn Cts
Bnstand
Lansdowne Way
4
South Lambeth
Larkhall Park
Priory Gro
Larkhall La
Binfield Rd
Stockwell Park Sch
Groveway
Allot Gdns
Mostyn Rd
Lorn Rd
Ingleton St
Robsart St
Stockwell
Studley Rd
Paradise Rd
SW4
137
3
Gaskell St
Union Ct
Clapham Rd
Stockwell Park Cres
St Michael's Rd
Sidney Rd
Aytoun Rd
Aytoun Pl
Stockwell Rd
YMCA
SW9
Evandale Rd
Fiveways Rd
Loughborough Rd
Lilford Rd
Marcella Rd
Hampden Ho
Marston Ho
Ireton Ho
Newbury Ho
Elmore Ho
Prim Sch
Mostyn Rd
Templar St
Penford St
Myatt Ho
Burton Rd
Claribel Rd
Chelsham Rd
76
Rhodesia Rd
Grantham Rd
Kimberley Rd
Mayflower Rd
Edithna St
Landor Rd
Nealden St
Combermere Rd
Burgoyne Rd
Romero Cl
Stansfield Rd
Mordaunt St
Rumsey Rd
Villa Rd
Peckford Pl
Angell Rd
BRIXTON
Loughborough Junc
Coll
Allot Gdns
Stockwell
Clapham North
2
Lambeth
H
Hargwyne St
Dalyell Rd
Chantrey Rd
Gateley Rd
Pulross Rd
Bellefields Rd
Stockwell Park Wlk
St John's Cres
St James's Cres
Wiltshire Rd
Gresham Rd
Canterbury Cres
Barrington Rd
Millbrook Rd
Coldharbour La
Ridgway Rd
Brixton Station Rd
Brixton
Atlantic Rd
Electric Ave
Bedford Rd
SW4
Sandmere Rd
Ferndale Rd
Tintern St
Medwin St
Nursery Rd
Tunstall Rd
Brighton Terr
Trinity Gdns
Solon New Rd
Kepler Rd
Corrance Rd
Ballater Rd
Raeburn St
Concanon Rd
Rushcroft Rd
Saltoun Rd
Kellett Rd
Mervan Rd
Somerleyton Rd
Southwyck Ho
Clarewood Wlk
Tenn Cts
Loughborough Pk
Milkwood Rd
Shakespeare Rd
1
Acre La
Works
Baytree Rd
Arlington Lo
St Matthew's Rd
Effra Rd
Eurolink Bsns Ctr
Sudbourne Rd
Ellerslie Ind Est
Sandhurst Ct
Magnolia Pl
75
30
A
B
31
160
C
D
32
Hayter Rd
Kildoran Rd
Margate Rd
Winslade Rd
Winterwell Rd
Strathleven Rd
Branksome Rd
Barnwell Rd
Mayall Rd
Railton Rd
Derek Walcott Cl

262
117
263
A
B
C
D
CAMBERWELL
SE15
SE5
CAMBERWELL
Burgess Park
ALBANY RD
B214
CAMBERWELL RD
A215
CAMBERWELL CHURCH ST
PECKHAM RD
A202
SOUTHAMPTON WAY
B217
TRAFALGAR AVE
B215
PECKHAM HILL ST
B216
OLD KENT RD
A2
COMMERCIAL WAY
WILLOWBROOK RD
ST GEORGE'S WAY
WELLS WAY
NEW CHURCH RD
WYNDHAM RD
BETHWIN RD
SULTAN ST
MEDLAR ST
Camberwell Green
COLDHARBOUR LA
A2217
DENMARK HILL
A2216
CHAMPION PK
GROVE LA
DOG KENNEL HILL
GROVE VALE
A2214
EAST DULWICH GR
HERNE HILL
The Maudsley
King's College
William Booth Meml Trng Coll
Ruskin Park
St Saviour's Sch
Lucas Gdns
Warwick Park Sch
Cobourg Jun & Inf Sch
Gloucester Prim Sch
Allot Gdns
Superstore
East Dulwich
Dulwich
Bessemer Grange Prim Sch
Goose Green
Peckham Rye
Herne Hill
Recn Gd
BELLENDEN ROAD BSNS CTR
PRINT VILLAGE IND EST
CHADWICK RD
CHOUMERT RD
AVONDALE RISE
LYNDHURST WAY
LYNDHURST GR
RYE LA
140
161
78
77
76
75
33
34
6
5
4
3
2
1

A
B
C
D
118
162
78
77
76
75
139
6
5
4
3
2
1
34
35
OLD KENT RD A2
OLD KENT RD
TRAFALGAR AVE
Canal Bridge
Gas Holder Station
1 HYNDMAN ST
2 MURDOCK ST
3 SKENFRITH HO
4 SARNESFIELD HO
5 PETERCHURCH HO
The New Den (Millwall FC)
STOCKHOLM RD
ORION BSNS CTR
BRITISH WHARF IND EST
SURREY CANAL RD
EXCELSIOR IND EST
ELIZABETH IND EST
ROLLINS ST
Bridge House Meadows
COLDBLOW LA
DEPTFORD
SE15
SE14
PECKHAM PARK RD
PECKHAM HILL ST
Recn Gd
COMMERCIAL WAY
Caroline Gardens
Brimmington Park
CLIFTON CRES
MEETING HOUSE LA
Ecklington Gardens
New Cross
KENDER ST
POMEROY ST
BESSON ST
New Cross Gate
Peckham
PECKHAM HIGH ST
QUEEN'S RD
Queen's Road
THE AYLESHAM CTR
HANOVER PK
Tuke Sch
LAUSANNE RD
Peckham Rye
RYE LA
EVELINA RD
GELLATLY RD
DRAKEFELL RD
Telegraph Hill Park
Nunhead
NUNHEAD LA
Cemy
ABBOTSBURY MEWS
1 MEDINA HO
2 FROME HO
3 WELLAND HO
Allot Gdns
EAST DULWICH RD
PECKHAM RYE
1 STRICKLAND CT
2 GATEFIELD CT
3 WARBURTON CT
Peckham Rye
Peckham Rye Park
East Dulwich
NORTH CROSS RD
Bwg Gn
Waverley Sch
Ppg Sta
Sp Gd
Tenn Cts
Lewisham
Southwark
A202
A2208
A2215
A2214
A2216
B216
B215
B2227
B2142
B219
B238

141
119
163
142
SE8
SE14
SE13
SE4
River Thames
Convoys Wharf
Palmer's Wharf
Payne's Wharf
Borthwick Wharf
Deptford Park
Blackhorse Wharf
Dreadnought Wharf
Dowell's Wharf
Folkestone Gardens
EVELYN ST
CREEK RD
DEPTFORD CHURCH ST
DEPTFORD HIGH ST
NORMAN RD
GREENWICH HIGH RD
GREENWICH SOUTH ST
NEW CROSS RD
DEPTFORD BROADWAY
BLACKHEATH RD
SANFORD ST
PAGNELL ST
AMERSHAM VALE
LEWISHAM WAY
LOAMPIT HILL
LOAMPIT VALE
THURSTON RD
BROOKMILL RD
MALPAS RD
BROCKLEY RD
ENDWELL RD
ADELAIDE AVE
LADYWELL RD
LEWISHAM HIGH ST
MOLESWORTH ST
LEWISHAM RD
HILLY FIELDS CRES
VICARS HILL
ELLERDALE ST
Fordham Park
Goldsmiths' Coll Univ of London
New Cross
New Cross Gate
Deptford
Greenwich
Deptford Bridge
St Johns
Elverson Road
Brockley
Brockley Cemy
Ladywell Cemy
Hilly Fields Park
Ladywell
Prendergast Sch
A
B
C
D
1
2
3
4
5
6
36
37
38
75
76
77
78

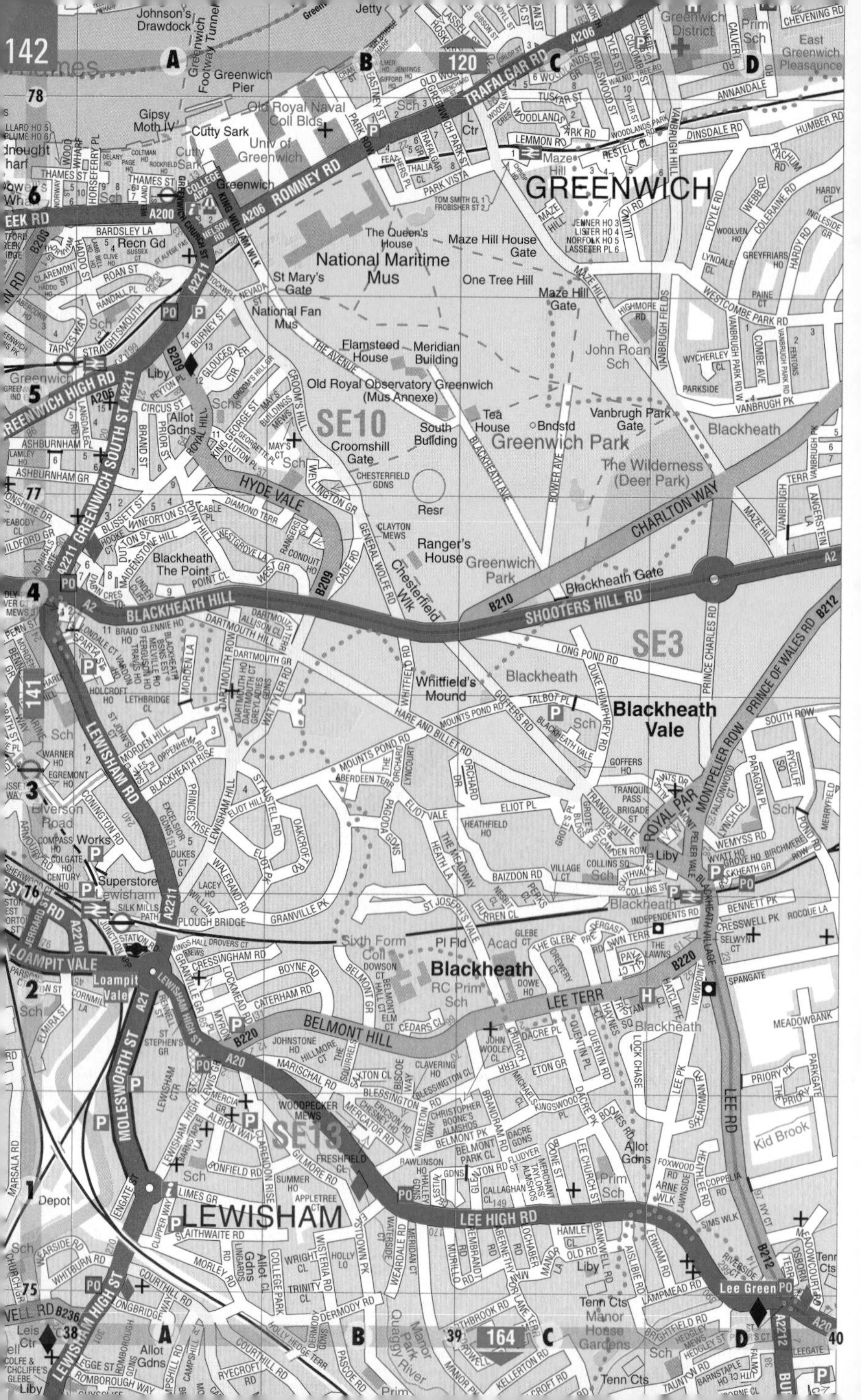
A
B
120
C
D
Johnson's Drawdock
Greenwich Footway Tunnel
Greenwich Pier
Jetty
Gipsy Moth IV
Cutty Sark
Old Royal Naval Coll Blds
Univ of Greenwich
Greenwich District
East Greenwich Pleasaunce
TRAFALGAR RD
ROMNEY RD
GREENWICH
National Maritime Mus
The Queen's House
Maze Hill House Gate
St Mary's Gate
One Tree Hill
Maze Hill Gate
National Fan Mus
Flamsteed House
Meridian Building
Old Royal Observatory Greenwich (Mus Annexe)
The John Roan Sch
SE10
Tea House
Bndstd
Vanbrugh Park Gate
South Building
Greenwich Park
Blackheath
The Wilderness (Deer Park)
Croomshill Gate
CHARLTON WAY
Resr
Ranger's House
Chesterfield Wlk
Blackheath Gate
SHOOTERS HILL RD
BLACKHEATH HILL
GREENWICH HIGH RD
GREENWICH SOUTH ST
HYDE VALE
Blackheath The Point
SE3
Whitfield's Mound
Blackheath Vale
LEWISHAM RD
PRINCE OF WALES RD
MONTPELIER ROW
ROYAL PAR
Elverson Road
Works
Superstore
Lewisham
LOAMPIT VALE
Loampit Vale
Sixth Form Coll
Pl Fld
Blackheath RC Prim Sch
LEE TERR
BELMONT HILL
Blackheath
SE13
MOLESWORTH ST
LEWISHAM
LEE HIGH RD
LEE RD
Kid Brook
Allot Gdns
Prim Sch
Tenn Cts
Manor House Gardens
Lee Green
Quaggy River
Manor Park
LEWISHAM HIGH ST
Depot
Allot Gdns
141
164
78
77
76
75
38
39
40
6
5
4
3
2
1

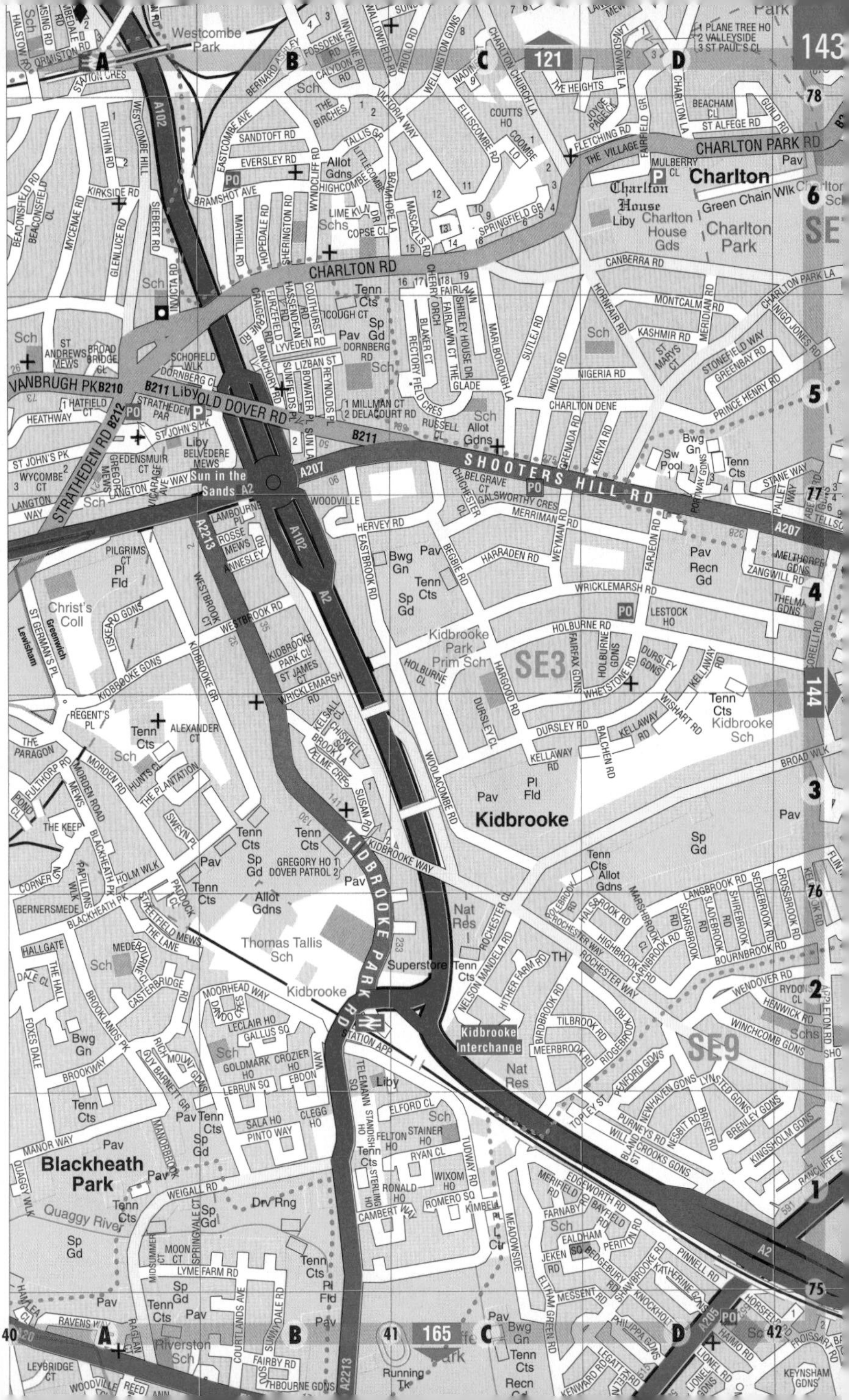
Westcombe Park
Charlton
Charlton House
Charlton House Gds
Charlton Park
Kidbrooke
Blackheath Park
Kidbrooke Park Prim Sch
Christ's Coll
Thomas Tallis Sch
Kidbrooke Interchange
Sun in the Sands
Riverston Sch
Quaggy River
Running Tk
SE3
SE9
SE7
Lewisham
Greenwich
CHARLTON RD
CHARLTON PARK RD
SHOOTERS HILL RD
OLD DOVER RD
VANBRUGH PK
STRATHEDEN RD
KIDBROOKE PARK RD
KIDBROOKE WAY
WESTCOMBE HILL
CHARLTON CHURCH LA
THE VILLAGE
CANBERRA RD
CHARLTON PARK LA
MONTCALM RD
MERIDIAN RD
KASHMIR RD
STONEFIELD WAY
GREENBAY RD
PRINCE HENRY RD
INIGO JONES RD
NIGERIA RD
CHARLTON DENE
INDUS RD
SUTLEJ RD
MARLBOROUGH LA
HORNFAIR RD
KENYA RD
GRENADA RD
WEYMAN RD
FARJEON RD
MERRIMAN RD
HARRADEN RD
WRICKLEMARSH RD
HOLBURNE RD
HOLBURNE GDNS
HOLBURNE CL
FAIRFAX GDNS
WHETSTONE RD
DURSLEY GDNS
DURSLEY RD
DURSLEY CL
KELLAWAY RD
WISHART RD
BALCHEN RD
HARGOOD RD
WOOLACOMBE RD
BROAD WLK
LESTOCK HO
ZANGWILL RD
MELTHORPE GDNS
THELMA GDNS
CORELLI RD
STANE WAY
PALLET WAY
EASTBROOK RD
HERVEY RD
BEGBIE RD
WOODVILLE
GALSWORTHY CRES
BELGRAVE CT
CHICHESTER CL
RUSSELL CL
ROCHESTER WAY
ROCHESTER CL
NELSON MANDELA RD
HITHER FARM RD
BIRDBROOK RD
TILBROOK RD
MEERBROOK RD
RIDGEBROOK RD
HIGHBROOK RD
HALSBROOK RD
COLEBROOK RD
MARSHBROOK CL
CANBROOK RD
SCARSBROOK RD
SLADEBROOK RD
SHIREBROOK RD
SEDGEBROOK RD
CROSSBROOK RD
LANGBROOK RD
BOURNBROOK RD
WENDOVER RD
RYDONS CL
HENWICK RD
WINCHCOMB GDNS
APPLETON RD
PENFORD GDNS
LYNSTED GDNS
NEWHAVEN GDNS
PURNEYS RD
NESBIT RD
BRISET RD
BRENLEY GDNS
KINGSHOLM GDNS
TOPLEY ST
CROOKS GDNS
RANCLIFFE GDNS
EDGEWORTH RD
MERIFIELD RD
FARNABY RD
BAYFIELD RD
PERITON RD
EALDHAM SQ
JEKEN RD
BEDGEBURY RD
SHAWBROOKE RD
KATHERINE GDNS
PINNELL RD
KNOCKHOLT RD
MESSENT RD
ELTHAM GREEN RD
PHILIPPA GDNS
MEADOWSIDE
HORSFELD RD
FROISSART RD
HAIMO RD
LIONEL RD
KEYNSHAM GDNS
LEGATT RD
KENWARD RD
SUSAN RD
DELME CRES
BROOK LA
CHISWELL SQ
KELSALL CL
WRICKLEMARSH RD
ST JAMES CT
KIDBROOKE PARK CL
WESTBROOK RD
WESTBROOK CT
KIDBROOKE GR
KIDBROOKE GDNS
LISKEARD GDNS
ST GERMAN'S PL
REGENT'S PL
ALEXANDER CT
THE PARAGON
FULTHORP RD
MORDEN RD
MORDEN ROAD MEWS
THE PLANTATION
HUNTS CL
SWEYN PL
POND RD
THE KEEP
BLACKHEATH PK
HOLM WLK
PAPILLONS WLK
CORNER GN
BERNERSMEDE
PADDOCK CT
STREETFIELD MEWS
THE LANE
HALLGATE
THE HALL
DALE CL
FOXES DALE
MEDEBOURNE CL
CASTERBRIDGE RD
BROOKLANDS PK
BROOKWAY
RICH MOUNT GDNS
GUY BARNETT GR
MANOR WAY
MANORBROOK
WEIGALL RD
QUAGGY WLK
SPRINGVALE CT
MIDSUMMER CT
MOON CT
LYME FARM RD
COURTLANDS AVE
SUNNINGDALE RD
FAIRBY RD
RAVENS WAY
HAMLEA CL
LEYBRIDGE CT
WOODVILLE
REED
MOORHEAD WAY
DANDO CRES
LECLAIR HO
GALLUS SQ
GOLDMARK HO
CROZIER HO
EBDON WAY
LEBRUN SQ
CLEGG HO
SALA HO
PINTO WAY
TELEMANN SQ
STANDISH HO
FELTON HO
STAINER HO
ELFORD CL
RYAN CL
STERLING HO
RONALD HO
WIXOM HO
ROMERO SQ
KIMBELL PL
CAMBERT WAY
TUDWAY RD
STATION APP
GREGORY HO
DOVER PATROL
Superstore
Kidbrooke
Nat Res
LAMBOURNE PL
ROSSE MEWS
ANNESLEY RD
PILGRIMS CT
Pl Fld
LANGTON WAY
ST JOHN'S PK
WYCOMBE CT
EDENSMUIR CT
GREGOR MEWS
BELVEDERE MEWS
VICARAGE AVE
STRATHEDEN PAR
HEATHWAY
HATFIELD CT
DORNBERG CL
DORNBERG RD
SCHOFIELD WLK
BROAD BRIDGE CL
ST ANDREWS MEWS
BANCHORY RD
SUNFIELDS PL
BOWATER PL
LIZBAN ST
REYNOLDS PL
SUN LA
MILLMAN CT
DELACOURT RD
CRAIGERNE RD
FURZEFIELD RD
HASSENDEAN RD
COUTHURST RD
COUGH CT
LYVEDEN RD
CHERRY ORCH
BLAKER CT
RECTORY FIELD CRES
FAIRLAWN
FAIRLAWN CT
SHIRLEY HOUSE DR
THE GLADE
INVICTA RD
SIEBERT RD
GLENLUCE RD
MYCENAE RD
BEACONSFIELD RD
BEACONSFIELD CL
KIRKSIDE RD
RUTHIN RD
HALSTOW RD
ORMISTON RD
STATION CRES
BERNARD ASHLEY DR
EASTCOMBE AVE
SANDTOFT RD
EVERSLEY RD
BRAMSHOT AVE
MAYHILL RD
HOPEDALE RD
SHERINGTON RD
WYNDCLIFF RD
HIGHCOMBE
LITTLECOMBE
BRAMHOPE LA
TALLIS GR
LIME KILN DR
COPSE CL
MASCALLS RD
VICTORIA WAY
THE BIRCHES
FOSSDENE RD
CALYDON RD
INVERINE RD
WALLOWFIELD RD
PRIOLO RD
WELLINGTON GDNS
NADINE ST
ELLISCOMBE RD
COUTTS HO
COOMBE LO
SPRINGFIELD GR
THE HEIGHTS
JOYCE PAGE CL
FLETCHING RD
FAIRFIELD GR
LANSDOWNE LA
CHARLTON LA
BEACHAM CL
ST ALFEGE RD
GUILD RD
MULBERRY CL
Green Chain Wlk
ST MARYS CT
1 PLANE TREE HO
2 VALLEYSIDE
3 ST PAUL'S CL
121
144
165
A2
A102
A207
A2213
A205
B210
B211
B212
A
B
C
D
1
2
3
4
5
6
40
41
42
75
76
77
78

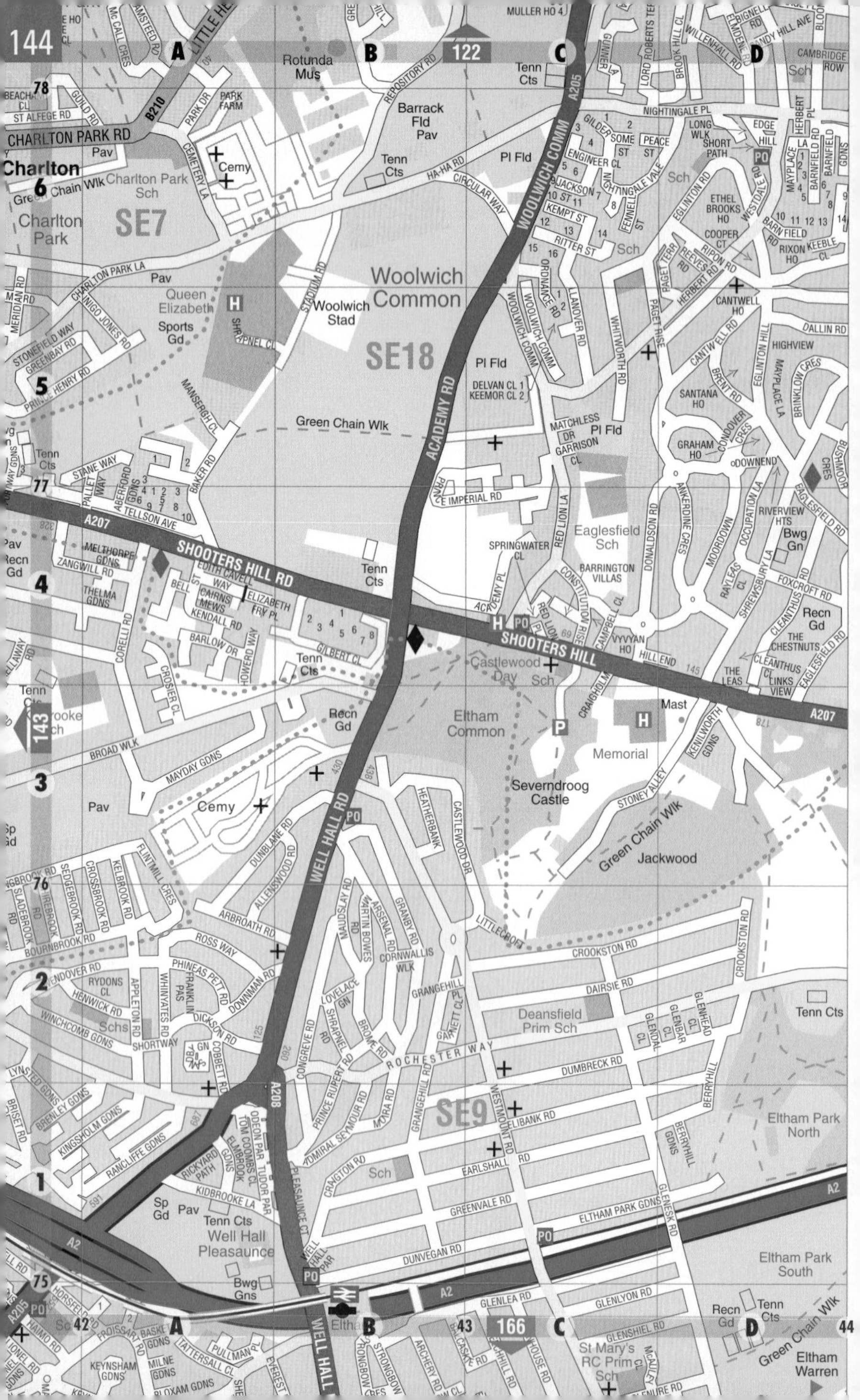
A
B
C
D
122
Rotunda Mus
Tenn Cts
MULLER HO
Mc CALL CRES
LITTLE HEATH
B210
BEACHAM CL
78
GUILD RD
ST ALFEGE RD
CHARLTON PARK RD
PARK DR
PARK FARM
CEMETERY LA
Cemy
Pav
Charlton
Green Chain Wlk
Charlton Park Sch
6
Charlton Park
SE7
REPOSITORY RD
Barrack Fld Pav
HA-HA RD
CIRCULAR WAY
Pl Fld
A205
WOOLWICH COMM
GUNNER LA
LORD ROBERTS TER
BROOK HILL CL
WILLENHALL RD
BIGNELL RD
ELMDENE RD
SANDY HILL AVE
CAMBRIDGE ROW
Sch
NIGHTINGALE PL
GILDERSOME ST
PEACE ST
ENGINEER CL
NIGHTINGALE VALE
JACKSON ST
KEMPT ST
RITTER ST
FENNELL ST
LONG WLK
SHORT PATH
EDGE HILL
HERBERT PL
MAYPLACE LA
BARNFIELD RD
BARNFIELD GDNS
EGLINTON RD
WESTDALE RD
ETHEL BROOKS HO
COOPER CT
BARNFIELD RD
RIXON HO
KEEBLE CL
PAGET TERR
REEVES RD
RIPON RD
HERBERT RD
CANTWELL HO
CHARLTON PARK LA
Queen Elizabeth
H
Sports Gd
MERIDIAN RD
INIGO JONES RD
STONEFIELD WAY
GREENBAY RD
PRINCE HENRY RD
5
STADIUM RD
Woolwich Stad
Woolwich Common
SHRAPNEL CL
SE18
ORDNANCE RD
WOOLWICH COMM
LLANOVER RD
WHITWORTH RD
PAGET RISE
DALLIN RD
HIGHVIEW
CANTWELL RD
EGLINTON HILL
MAYPLACE LA
BRINKLOW CRES
BRENT RD
SANTANA HO
MANSERGH CL
ACADEMY RD
DELVAN CL
KEEMOR CL
Green Chain Wlk
MATCHLESS DR
Pl Fld
GARRISON CL
GRAHAM HO
CONDOVER CRES
DOWNEND
BUSHMOOR CRES
Tenn Cts
STANE WAY
PALLET WAY
ABERFORD GDNS
BAKER RD
77
A207
TELLSON AVE
PRINCE IMPERIAL RD
ANKERDINE CRES
DONALDSON RD
RED LION LA
OCCUPATION LA
RIVERVIEW HTS
EAGLESFIELD RD
Eaglesfield Sch
Bwg Gn
Pav
Recn Gd
MELTHORPE GDNS
ZANGWILL RD
SHOOTERS HILL RD
EDITH CAVELL WAY
Tenn Cts
SPRINGWATER CL
BARRINGTON VILLAS
MOORDOWN
RAYLEAS CL
SHREWSBURY LA
FOXCROFT RD
4
THELMA GDNS
BELL ST
CAIRNS MEWS
ELIZABETH FRY PL
KENDALL RD
BARLOW DR
HOWERD WAY
CORELLI RD
GILBERT CL
ACADEMY PL
CONSTITUTION RISE
RED LION PL
CAMPBELL CL
VYVYAN HO
H
PO
SHOOTERS HILL
HILL END
CLEANTHUS RD
Recn Gd
THE CHESTNUTS
CLEANTHUS CL
THE LEAS
LINKS VIEW
Tenn Cts
CROSIER CL
Castlewood Day Sch
CRAIGHOLM
Mast
Eltham Common
Recn Gd
P
H
Memorial
KENILWORTH GDNS
A207
143
BROAD WLK
MAYDAY GDNS
3
Pav
Cemy
Severndroog Castle
STONEY ALLEY
Green Chain Wlk
Jackwood
WELL HALL RD
PO
HEATHERBANK
CASTLEWOOD DR
DUNBLANE RD
ALLENSWOOD RD
FLINTMILL CRES
SEDGEBROOK RD
CROSSBROOK RD
KELBROOK RD
76
SLADEBROOK RD
BIREBROOK RD
BOURNBROOK RD
ARBROATH RD
ROSS WAY
MAUDSLAY RD
MARTIN BOWES RD
ARSENAL RD
GRANBY RD
CORNWALLIS WLK
LITTLECROFT
CROOKSTON RD
2
WENDOVER RD
RYDONS CL
HENWICK RD
APPLETON RD
WHINYATES RD
PHINEAS PETT RD
FRANKLIN PAS
DOWNMAN RD
LOVELACE GN
SHRAPNEL RD
GRANGEHILL PL
DAIRSIE RD
Deansfield Prim Sch
GLENDAL CL
GLENBAR CL
GLENHEAD CL
Tenn Cts
WINCHCOMB GDNS
Schs
SHORTWAY
DICKSON RD
COBBETT RD
CONGREVE RD
BROME RD
ROCHESTER WAY
GARNETT CL
DUMBRECK RD
BERRYHILL
LYNSTED GDNS
BRENLEY GDNS
BRISET RD
KINGSHOLM GDNS
RANCLIFFE GDNS
A208
ODEON PAR
TOM COOMBS CL
TUDOR PAR
PRINCE RUPERT RD
ADMIRAL SEYMOUR RD
MOIRA RD
GRANGEHILL RD
SE9
WESTMOUNT RD
ELIBANK RD
BERRYHILL GDNS
Eltham Park North
1
RICKYARD PATH
ELMBROOK GDNS
CRAIGTON RD
Sch
EARLSHALL RD
GLENESK RD
KIDBROOKE LA
PLEASAUNCE CT
Sp Gd
Pav
Tenn Cts
Well Hall Pleasaunce
GREENVALE RD
ELTHAM PARK GDNS
A2
PO
DUNVEGAN RD
WELL HALL PAR
PO
Bwg Gns
A2
Eltham Park South
75
A205
PO
GLENLEA RD
GLENLYON RD
Recn Gd
Tenn Cts
Green Chain Wlk
42
HORSFELD RD
FROISSART RD
BASKET GDNS
TATTERSALL CL
PULLMAN PL
EVEREST
WELL HALL
Eltham
43
166
GLENSHIEL RD
St Mary's RC Prim Sch
McCAULEY CL
Eltham Warren
44
HAIMO RD
LIONEL RD
KEYNSHAM GDNS
MILNE GDNS
SLOXAM GDNS
STRONGBOW
ARCHERY RD
BALCASKIE RD

A
B
C
D
123
Plumstead Common
St Margaret's CE Prim Sch
Tenn Cts
Bwg Gn
Plumstead Manor Sch
Gallions Mount Prim Sch
MARBLE HO 1
CRYSTAL HO 2
BERYL HO 3
GALENA HO 4
WINN COMMON RD
BLEAK HILL LA
Pav
KING'S HIGHWAY
REVELL RISE
GILBOURNE RD
KINGSDALE RD
Rockliffe Manor Prim Sch
Cemy
The William Barefoot Garden
CAMDALE RD
SOUTHLAND RD
Pl Fld
Tenn Cts
Allot Gdns
East Wickham Open Sp
PLUMSTEAD COMMON RD
WERNBROOK ST
ST JOHN'S TERR
MACOMA RD
MACOMA TERR
TUAM RD
Liby
VAMBERY RD
ISLA RD
PALMERSTON CRES
UPTON RD
HINSTOCK RD
ROWTON RD
PLUM LA
CHELSWORTH DR
CLOTHWORKERS RD
DOTHILL RD
Green Chain Wlk
Shrewsbury Park
SE18
MOUNTBATTEN CL
KIRKHAM ST
MELLING ST
MALTON MEWS
SWINGATE LA
IRWIN AVE
THORNHILL AVE
EASTVIEW AVE
DUNCROFT
WELTON RD
HIGHMEAD
EDISON GR
COMBESIDE
Pav
DRYDEN RD
MILTON RD
KEATS RD
TENNYSON CL
WORDSWORTH RD
CHAUCER RD
BURNS CL
BLENHEIM DR
WYCLIFFE CL
EDISON RD
GLENMORE RD
PEREGRINE CT
ROSEMARY RD
East Wickham Schs
Willow Dene Sch
Allot Gdns
Cemy
Shooters Hill
Woodlands Farm
DOVER RD
DA16
Greenwich
Bexley
PETERS CL
WICKHAM CT
MARINA DR
SANDRINGHAM DR
WICKHAM ST
EXETER RD
TIDFORD RD
CAMBORNE RD
NEWLYN RD
BALTIMORE PL
MARYVILLE
LULWORTH RD
CLEVELAND RD
VAUGHAN RD
MONKTON RD
AWLISCOMBE RD
CENTRAL AVE
BELLEGROVE RD
A207
STATION APP
RUSKIN AV
Oxleas Wood
Nature Reserve
Eastcote Prim Sch
FALCONWOOD AVE
SUNDRIDGE AVE
BELMONT AVE
SHERWOOD RD
ASHMORE GR
SOUTHCROFT AVE
MONTROSE CL
MONTROSE AVE
WELLING WAY
CONISTON AVE
NORTHUMBERLAND AVE
WESTMORELAND AVE
CORNWALL AVE
CUMBERLAND AVE
CAMBRIDGE AVE
DORSET AVE
YORKLAND AVE
WESTWOOD LA
GLOUCESTER AVE
SOMERSET AVE
KENT AVE
KELVIN RD
CAVENDISH AVE
TYNDALL RD
HUXLEY RD
MAXWELL RD
MARNE AVE
FARADAY RD
HOOK LA
Falconwood Field
Falconwood
SE9
SHEPHERDS LEAS
LINGFIELD CRES
MILLBROOK AVE
BRAYWOOD RD
WINCROFTS DR
Westwood Prim Sch
Coll
Falconwood
BUCKINGHAM AVE
THE GREEN
FALCONWOOD PAR
SUTHERLAND AVE
Tenn Ct
EAST ROCHESTER WAY
Cemy
RIEFIELD RD
COLEPITS WOOD RD
Crown Woods Sch
167
RIDGEWAY
DA15
A2
146
78
77
76
75
46
45
6
5
4
3
2
1

A
B
C
D
124
1 ALEXANDER TERR
2 DIANTHUS CL
BOSTALL HILL
Co-operative Woods
Cottage Hospice
5 STEPHENSON HO
6 LISTER HO
A2041
HURST LA
PRIORY DR
HARVEL CRES
DIXON HO
WOOLWICH RD
A209
78
THE DELL
GLENDOWN RD
BASTION RD
OLD PARK
Allot Gdns
Bostall Woods
Pav
Bwg Gn
Green Chain Wlk
ommon
RUTHERGLEN RD
SANDYCROFT
OAKMERE RD
WATERDALE RD
1 SOUTHLAND RD
2 PRESTWOOD CL
3 DOEBURY WLK
Pl Fld
WICKHAM LA
SE2
H
Goldie Leigh
MARTYN HO 1
HURST PL 2
SENCLER HO 3
ARRAS HO 4
HEATH VIEW DR 5
PINEWOOD RD 6
Bexley Coll
BURCHARBRO RD
AMBERLEY
West Heath
GLENVIEW
WEST HEATH RD
Bostall Heath
LONGLEIGH LA
Bwg Gn
HEATH AVE
CANBERRA RD
MARLEY AVE
POWYS CL
LESSNESS AVE
ABBOTT'S WK
6
Sch
BRICKFIELD COTTS
RADNOR CRES
VERDUN RD
VILLACOURT RD
LITTLEDALE
WOODBROOK RD
STREAMDALE
ALLIANCE RD
GRASDENE RD
CEMETERY RD
ELMSTED CRES
LANGLEY RD
DOWNE CL
SANDGATE RD
HARTLEY RD
HADLOW RD
FIRST AVE
MADISON GDNS
LANSDOWNE AVE
SOUTHLAND RD
Cemy
The William Barefoot Garden
BOURNEWOOD RD
PINECROFT
Cemy
LODGE HILL
KESTON CL
DENTON RD
HILLSGROVE CL
Hillsgrove Prim Sch
MADISON CRES
DA7
THE QUADRANT
5
SE18
East Wickham
HIGHBANKS CL
Greenwich
Bexley
TOTNES RD
SIDMOUTH RD
PLYMSTOCK RD
BIDEFORD RD
EXMOUTH RD
SEATON RD
BUDLEIGH CRES
Allot Gdns
East Wickham Open Space
CHALKSTONE CL
PATRICIA CT
OKEHAMPTON CRES
77
Allot Gdns
ELMFIELD CT 1
BRAMLEY CT 2
ALICIA HO 3
ST MICHAEL'S RISE 4
TEVIOT CL
STUART RD
AXMINSTER CRES
TOR RD
COLYTON CL
TENBY RD
BRIXHAM RD
BOGNOR RD
PRESTON DR
BERKELEY AVE
MAYFAIR AVE
4
Allot Gdns
BEAL CL
DARENTH RD
RIDLEY RD
UPPER WICKHAM LA
KAY ST
BRUCE CL
DOUGLAS RD
LYME RD
CHARMOUTH RD
TAVISTOCK RD
SALTASH RD
Stevens Park
SELSEY CRES
Sch
East Wickham Schs
RIPPERSLEY RD
YEW TREE CL
ANTHONY RD
LINTON CL
BERWICK RD
ROSEMARY RD
Welling Sch
Tenn Cts
TEIGNMOUTH RD
WROTHAM RD
145
Pl Fld
WICKHAM ST
DOVEDALE CL
Allot Gdns
QUEEN'S RD
CHURCH RD
SWANLEY RD
NORMANHURST AVE
MONKTON RD
AWLISCOMBE RD
CENTRAL AVE
MERTON CT
VICTORIA BSNS CTR
EAST RD
FARNHAM RD
TIDFORD RD
NORFOLK PL
LOVEL AVE
BURNELL AVE
OLYFFE AVE
LEIGH PL
BALLIOL RD
ELSA RD
GIPSY RD
WINCHESTER RD
ALEXANDER RD
Brampton Prim Sch
3
DUNSTALL WELLING EST
SOMERHILL RD
KENMERE RD
HAZELDENE RD
IVEDON RD
AVONDALE RD
SUTCLIFFE RD
HOLMESDALE RD
LULWORTH RD
CLEVELAND RD
VAUGHAN RD
BENNETT CL
GRAVES EST
Allot Gdns
LYNMERE RD
STEVEDALE RD
FAIRLAWN AVE
Barrington Prim Sch
STATION APP
FOSTERS OLD SCH
RACKHAM CL
NORTHDOWN RD
BARRINGTON RD
Welling Sch
RUSKIN GR
RUSKIN AVE
RUSKIN DR
NEW RD
Foster's Prim Sch
FOX HOLLOW DR
76
A207
DEEPDENE RD
EDMUND RD
COTON RD
SPRINGFIELD RD
ORCHARD RD
CARLTON RD
WESTBROOKE RD
WESTBROOKE CRES
MARLBOROUGH RD
KELVIN RD
Welling
BULL ALLEY
PALMEIRA RD
CHURCHFIELD RD
Liby
Hook Lane Prim Sch
FARADAY RD
WELLING HIGH ST
CLIFTON RD
WARWICK RD
LEWIS RD
GRANVILLE RD
BETHEL RD
SOUTH GIPSY RD
Westbrooke Sch
2
DAR WIN CT
ST VALENTINE RD
CAVENDISH AVE
MARNE AVE
NEWTON RD
MARWOOD CL
ST JOHN'S RD
ST MICHAEL'S RD
PENPOOL LA
PARK VIEW RD
PARK VIEW
LANGMORE CT 1
GAINSBOROUGH SQ 2
QUEEN ANNE GATE 3
HANOVER WAY
TYNDALL RD
HUXLEY RD
MAXWELL RD
DANSON CRES
ROSEACRE RD
Crook Log Sports Ctr
Welling F.C Fball Gd
Tenn Cts
DANSON MEAD
CROOK LOG
HOOK LA
MONMOUTH CL
PORTHKERRY AVE
LANCELOT RD
SELWYN CRES
PARK APP
1 EMBASSY CT
2 NAG'S HEAD LA
3 SCHOOL LA
4 JOHN NEWTON CT
1 MOAT CROFT
2 DENHAM CL
3 SHARNBROOKE CL
4 STUART EVANS CL
Sw Pool
TURNPIKE CT 1
BRUNSWICK CL 2
MERLIN RD N
CLINTON AVE
DANSINGTON RD
DANSON LA
DA16
PP
Crook Log Prim Sch
WESTWOOD LA
BRADENHAM AVE
Danson Prim Sch
LAKEVIEW RD
Old English Garden
A221
NORTH CL
BALCOMBE CL
DALLIN RD
1
YORKLAND AVE
FAIRWATER AVE
Bwg Gns
THE GROVE
SYDNEY RD
BEXLEY
SOUTH CL
GLOUCESTER AVE
SOMERSET AVE
BIRCH GR
MERLIN RD
Tenn Cts
Bexley Gram Sch
Danson Park
ASKERN CL
BEAN RD
KENT AVE
75
WENDOVER WAY
COWPER CL
Pl Fld
DANSON RD
DA6
COBHAM
46
47
168
The Lake
Allot Gdns
IVERHURST CL
SUTHERLAND AVE
INGLETON AVE
RADNOR AVE
A2
GROOMBRIDGE
Allot Gdns
GREEN WALK
ALERS RD

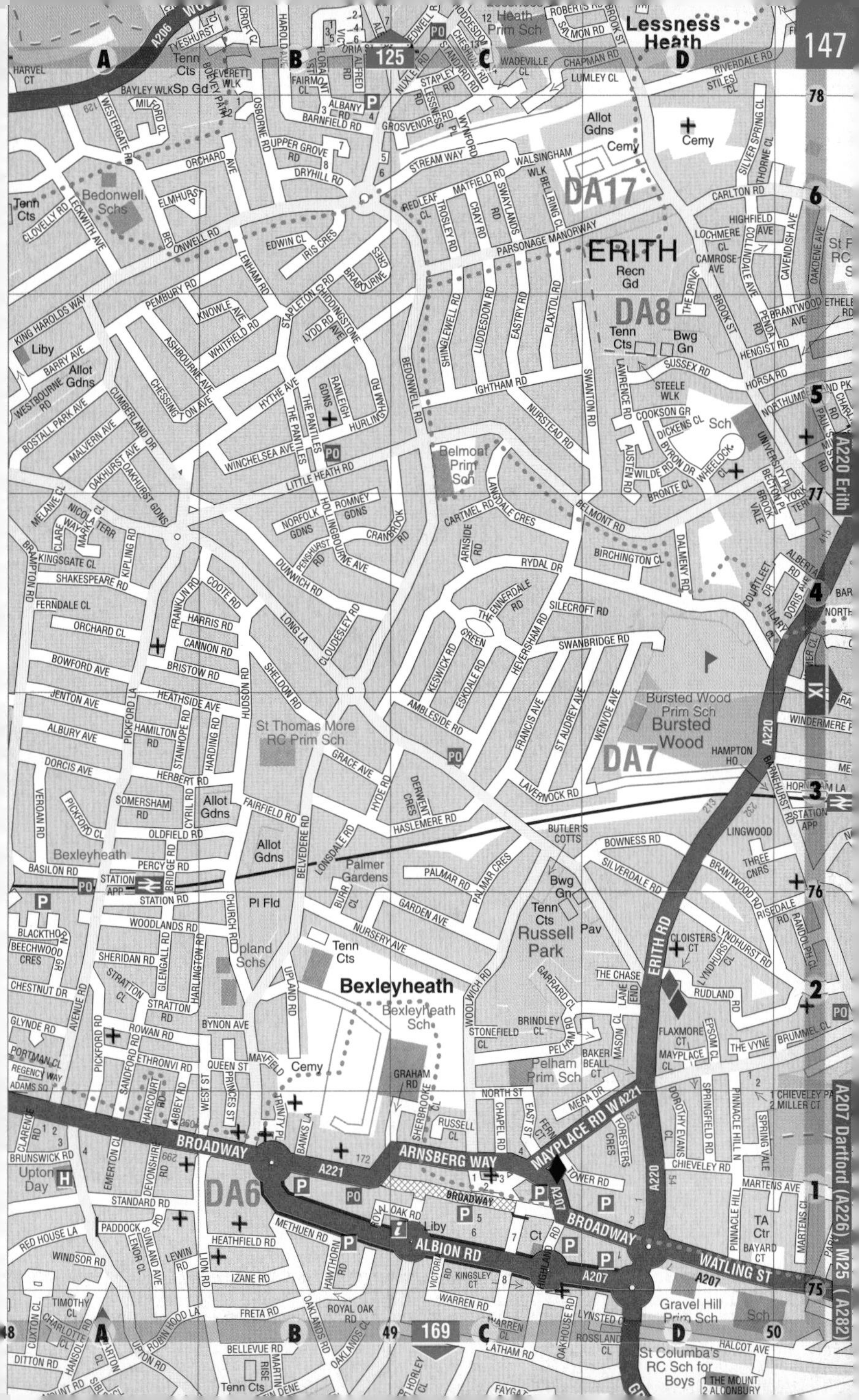
Lessness Heath
ERITH
DA17
DA8
DA7
DA6
Bexleyheath
125
169
A206
A220 Erith
A207 Dartford (A226), M25 (A282)
A221
A207
A220
78
77
76
75
6
5
4
3
2
1
48
49
50
A
B
C
D
HARVEL CT
TYESHURST
CROFT CL
HAROLD AVE
FLORA ST
VICTORIA ST
ALFRED RD
NUXLEY RD
HODDESDON RD
CHESHUNT RD
STANDARD RD
STAPLEY RD
LESSNESS RD
Heath Prim Sch
ROBERTS RD
SALMON RD
BROOK ST
WADEVILLE CL
CHAPMAN RD
LUMLEY CL
RIVERDALE RD
STILES CL
Tenn Cts
Sp Gd
BAYLEY WLK
BOEVEY PATH
EVERETT WLK
FAIRMONT CL
ALBANY RD
BARNFIELD RD
GROSVENOR RD
WYNFORD PL
MILFORD CL
WESTERGATE RD
OSBORNE RD
UPPER GROVE RD
DRYHILL RD
STREAM WAY
WALSINGHAM WLK
Allot Gdns
Cemy
SILVER SPRING CL
THORNE CL
ORCHARD AVE
Bedonwell Schs
ELMHURST
CLOVELLY RD
LECKWITH AVE
BEDONWELL RD
REDLEAF CL
MATFIELD RD
TROSLEY RD
CRAY RD
SWAYLANDS RD
BELLRING CL
CARLTON RD
HIGHFIELD AVE
COLINDALE AVE
CAVENDISH AVE
OAKDENE AVE
LOCHMERE CL
CAMROSE AVE
EDWIN CL
IRIS CRES
LENHAM RD
BRABOURNE CRES
PARSONAGE MANORWAY
Recn Gd
THE DRIVE
BROOK ST
PENDA RD
BRANTWOOD AVE
ETHELBERT RD
KING HAROLDS WAY
PEMBURY RD
STAPLETON RD
CHIDDINGSTONE AVE
SHINGLEWELL RD
LUDDESDON RD
EASTRY RD
PLAXTOL RD
SWANTON RD
Tenn Cts
Bwg Gn
HENGIST RD
Liby
KNOWLE AVE
WHITFIELD RD
LYDD RD
BARRY AVE
ASHBOURNE AVE
CHESSINGTON AVE
SUSSEX RD
HORSA RD
LAWRENCE RD
STEELE WLK
NORTHUMBERLAND PK
WESTBOURNE RD
BOSTALL PARK AVE
CUMBERLAND DR
HYTHE AVE
THE PANTILES
RANLEIGH GDNS
HURLINGHAM RD
IGHTHAM RD
NURSTEAD RD
COOKSON GR
DICKENS CL
Sch
UNIVERSITY PL
MALVERN AVE
OAKHURST AVE
OAKHURST GDNS
WINCHELSEA AVE
PO
LITTLE HEATH RD
Belmont Prim Sch
AUSTEN RD
WILDE RD
BYRON DR
WHEELOCK CL
BRONTE CL
BECTON PL
BROOK VALE
YORK TERR
MELANIE CL
NICOLA TERR
MARK CL
CLARE WAY
HOLLINGBOURNE AVE
ROMNEY GDNS
NORFOLK GDNS
PENSHURST RD
CRANBROOK RD
CARTMEL RD
LANGDALE CRES
BELMONT RD
DALMENY RD
BRAMPTON RD
KINGSGATE CL
KIPLING RD
SHAKESPEARE RD
DUNWICH RD
ARNSIDE RD
RYDAL DR
BIRCHINGTON CL
COURTLEET DR
ALBERTA RD
DORIS AVE
HILARY CL
FERNDALE CL
FRANKLIN RD
COOTE RD
HARRIS RD
CANNON RD
ORCHARD CL
LONG LA
CLOUDESLEY RD
THE GREEN
ENNERDALE RD
SILECROFT RD
HEVERSHAM RD
SWANBRIDGE RD
BOWFORD AVE
BRISTOW RD
HUDSON RD
SHELDON RD
KESWICK RD
ESKDALE RD
JENTON AVE
HEATHSIDE AVE
PICKFORD LA
HAMILTON RD
STANHOPE RD
HARDING RD
St Thomas More RC Prim Sch
AMBLESIDE RD
FRANCIS AVE
ST AUDREY AVE
WENVOE AVE
Bursted Wood Prim Sch
Bursted Wood
HAMPTON HO
WINDERMERE RD
ALBURY AVE
DORCIS AVE
HERBERT RD
GRACE AVE
HYDE RD
DERWENT CRES
LAVERNOCK RD
BARNEHURST RD
HORNBEAM LA
STATION APP
VEROAN RD
PICKFORD CL
SOMERSHAM RD
CYRIL RD
FAIRFIELD RD
HASLEMERE RD
BUTLER'S COTTS
BOWNESS RD
LINGWOOD
OLDFIELD RD
BELVEDERE RD
LONSDALE RD
SILVERDALE RD
BRANTWOOD RD
THREE CNRS
Bexleyheath
BASILON RD
PERCY RD
BRIDGE RD
Palmer Gardens
PALMAR RD
PALMAR CRES
RISEDALE RD
RANDOLPH CL
STATION APP
STATION RD
Pl Fld
BURR CL
GARDEN AVE
Russell Park
Pav
BLACKTHORN GR
BEECHWOOD CRES
WOODLANDS RD
CHURCH RD
NURSERY AVE
CLOISTERS CT
LYNDHURST RD
LYNDHURST CL
ERITH RD
SHERIDAN RD
GLENGALL RD
HARLINGTON RD
Upland Schs
Tenn Cts
CHESTNUT DR
STRATTON CL
STRATTON RD
UPLAND RD
Bexleyheath Sch
WOOLWICH RD
GARRARD CL
THE CHASE
LANE END
RUDLAND RD
GLYNDE RD
AVENUE RD
ROWAN RD
BYNON AVE
STONEFIELD CL
BRINDLEY CL
PELHAM RD
MASON CL
FLAXMORE CT
EPSOM CL
THE VYNE
BRUMMEL CL
PORTMAN CL
REGENCY WAY
ADAMS SQ
PICKFORD RD
SANDFORD RD
ETHRONVI RD
QUEEN ST
MAYFIELD
Cemy
GRAHAM RD
Pelham Prim Sch
BAKER BEALL CT
MAYPLACE CL
HARCOURT RD
ABBEY RD
WEST ST
PRINCES ST
TRINITY PL
NORTH ST
CHAPEL RD
EAST ST
MERA DR
DOROTHY EVANS CL
SPRINGFIELD RD
PINNACLE HILL N
1 CHIEVELEY PDE
2 MILLER CT
SPRING VALE
CLARENCE RD
BRUNSWICK RD
EMERTON CL
DEVONSHIRE RD
BROADWAY
BANKS LA
SHERBROOKE CL
RUSSELL CL
ARNSBERG WAY
MAYPLACE RD W
FERN CT
FORESTERS CRES
CHIEVELEY RD
Upton Day
STANDARD RD
OAK RD
TOWER RD
MARTENS AVE
PINNACLE HILL
MARTENS CL
PADDOCK CL
RED HOUSE LA
LENOR CL
SUNLAND AVE
LEWIN RD
HEATHFIELD RD
METHUEN RD
ROYAL OAK RD
Liby
ALBION RD
Ct
HIGHLAND RD
TA Ctr
BAYARD CT
WINDSOR RD
IZANE RD
LION RD
HAWTHORN RD
VICTORIA RD
KINGSLEY CT
WATLING ST
TIMOTHY CL
CHARLOTTE CL
CUXTON CL
FRETA RD
OAKLANDS RD
WARREN RD
OAKHOUSE RD
LYNSTED CT
Gravel Hill Prim Sch
ROSSLAND CL
LATHAM RD
HALCOT AVE
DITTON RD
HANSOL RD
UPTON RD
ROBIN HOOD LA
BELLEVUE RD
MARTIN RISE
OAKLANDS CL
St Columba's RC Sch for Boys
1 THE MOUNT
2 ALCONBURY
Tenn Cts
FAYGATE

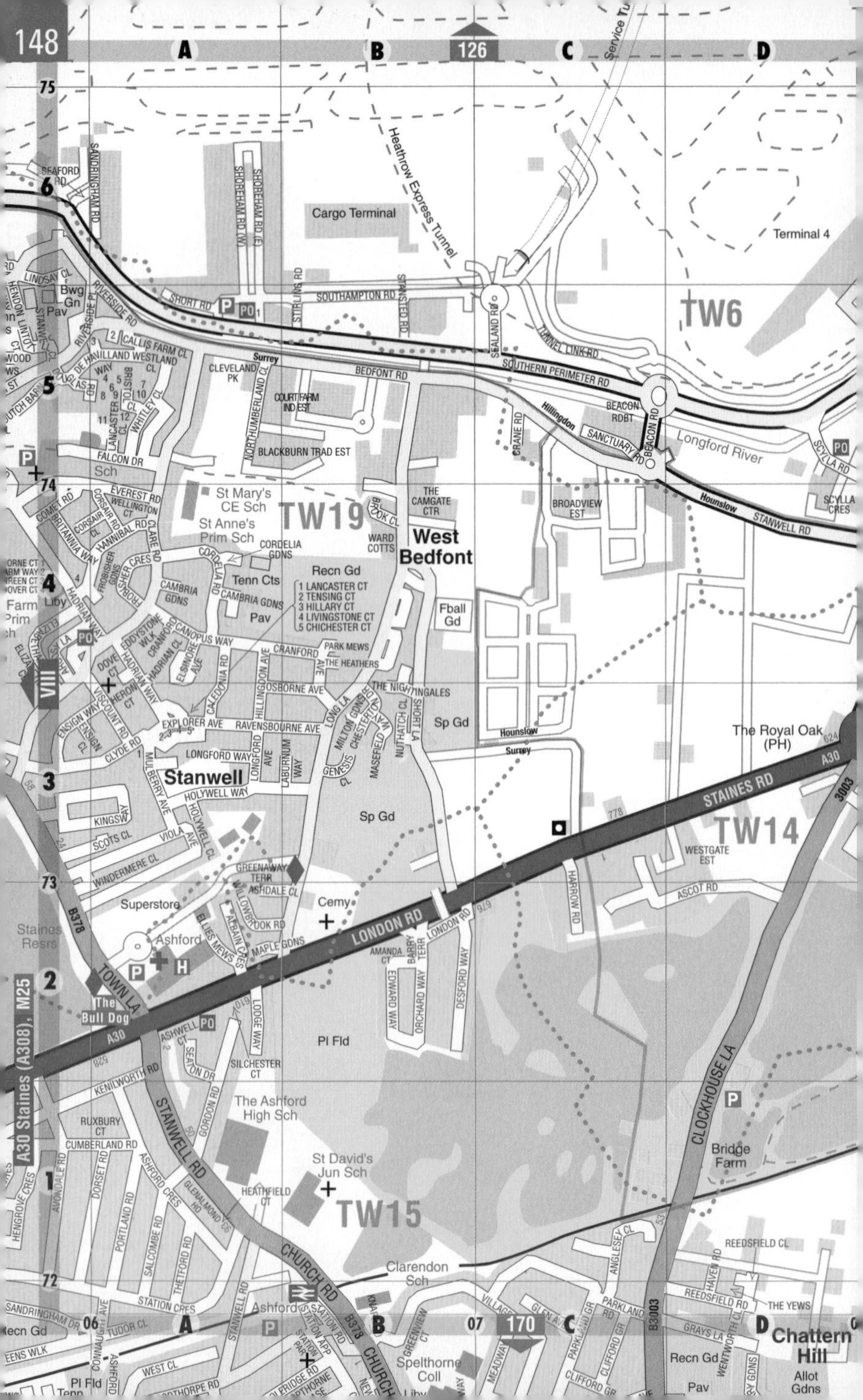
A
B
126
C
D
Heathrow Express Tunnel
Service Tu
Cargo Terminal
Terminal 4
TW6
SANDRINGHAM RD
SEAFORD RD
SHOREHAM RD (W)
SHOREHAM RD (E)
STIRLING RD
STANSTED RD
SOUTHAMPTON RD
SHORT RD
SEALAND RD
TUNNEL LINK RD
SOUTHERN PERIMETER RD
RIVERSIDE RD
RIVERSIDE PL
LINDSAY CL
HENDON
Bwg Gn
Pav
CALLIS FARM CL
DE HAVILLAND WESTLAND CL
WAY
BRISTOL CL
WHITLEY CL
LANCASTER CL
DOUGLAS RD
DUTCH BARN CL
Surrey
BEDFONT RD
CLEVELAND PK
NORTHUMBERLAND CL
COURT FARM IND EST
BLACKBURN TRAD EST
Hillingdon
CRANE RD
SANCTUARY RD
BEACON RD
BEACON RDBT
Longford River
SCYLLA RD
SCYLLA CRES
Hounslow
STANWELL RD
FALCON DR
Sch
St Mary's CE Sch
St Anne's Prim Sch
TW19
EVEREST RD
WELLINGTON CT
COMET RD
CORSAIR RD
CORSAIR CL
BRITANNIA WAY
HANNIBAL RD
CLARE RD
BROOK CL
THE CAMGATE CTR
BROADVIEW EST
WARD COTTS
West Bedfont
CORDELIA GDNS
CORDELIA RD
FROBISHER GDNS
FROBISHER CRES
HADRIAN WAY
Liby
Farm Prim
Tenn Cts
Recn Gd
1 LANCASTER CT
2 TENSING CT
3 HILLARY CT
4 LIVINGSTONE CT
5 CHICHESTER CT
CAMBRIA GDNS
Pav
Fball Gd
EDDYSTONE WLK
CRANFORD CL
CANOPUS WAY
HADRIAN CL
ELSINORE AVE
CALEDONIA RD
HILLINGDON AVE
CRANFORD AVE
PARK MEWS
THE HEATHERS
OSBORNE AVE
THE NIGHTINGALES
DOVE CT
HERON CT
VISCOUNT RD
ENSIGN WAY
ENSIGN CL
EXPLORER AVE
RAVENSBOURNE AVE
LONG LA
MILTON GDNS
CHESTERTON DR
WAINWRIGHT DR
NUTHATCH CL
SHORT LA
Sp Gd
Hounslow
Surrey
The Royal Oak (PH)
CLYDE RD
LONGFORD WAY
LONGFORD AVE
LABURNUM WAY
GENESIS CL
MASEFIELD
Stanwell
HOLYWELL WAY
MULBERRY AVE
KINGSWAY
SCOTS CL
VIOLA AVE
HOLYWELL CL
Sp Gd
STAINES RD
A30
TW14
WESTGATE EST
HARROW RD
ASCOT RD
WINDERMERE CL
GREENAWAY TERR
ASHDALE CL
WILLOWBROOK RD
Cemy
Superstore
Staines Resrs
B378
Ashford
ELLIES MEWS
ALBAIN CRES
MAPLE GDNS
LONDON RD
AMANDA CT
BARRY TERR
EDWARD WAY
ORCHARD WAY
DESFORD WAY
H
TOWN LA
The Bull Dog
ASHWELL CT
SEATON DR
LODGE WAY
SILCHESTER CT
Pl Fld
A30 Staines (A308), M25
KENILWORTH RD
RUXBURY CT
CUMBERLAND RD
GORDON RD
The Ashford High Sch
STANWELL RD
ASHFORD CRES
HENGROVE CRES
AVONDALE RD
DORSET RD
PORTLAND RD
SALCOMBE RD
THETFORD RD
GLENALMOND HO
HEATHFIELD CT
St David's Jun Sch
TW15
CHURCH RD
CLOCKHOUSE LA
Bridge Farm
ANGLESEY CL
REEDSFIELD CL
HAVEN RD
REEDSFIELD RD
THE YEWS
Clarendon Sch
STATION CRES
SANDRINGHAM DR
Ashford
STATION RD
STATION APP
B378
KNAPP RD
GREENVIEW CT
VILLAGE WAY
GLEN AVE
PARKLAND GR
CLIFFORD GR
PARKLAND RD
WENTWORTH CL
GRAYS LA
B3003
Recn Gd
Pav
Chattern Hill
Allot Gdns
06
07
170
TUDOR CL
CONNAUGHT AVE
WEST CL
Spelthorne Coll
MEADWAY
Pl Fld
75
74
73
72
6
5
4
3
2
1

127
A
B
C
D
Hatton
RADIUS PK
ST THERESA'S RD
ST ANTHONY'S WAY
GREAT SOUTH-WEST RD
SOUTHERN PERIMETER RD
HATTON RD
A30
75
6
5
4
3
2
1
74
73
72
TW6
TW14
TW15
TW13
Hounslow
Hillingdon
MYRTLE AVE
WELLINGTON RD
Playground
Tenn Cts
Fball Gd
Cemy
Bwg Gn
Pav
Recn Gd
Allot Gdns
Masts
Superstore
DUKES
SHEFFIELD WAY
SWINDON RD
HATFORD RD
SNOWDON RD
SHEFFIELD RD
Heathrow Terminal 4
Hotel
SWANSEA RD
SHREWSBURY RD
SCARBOROUGH RD
1 SHETLAND RD
2 TERMINAL RDBT
CAIN'S LA
UNWIN AVE
IVERNA GDNS
EDWARD RD
ORCHARD AVE
HATTON RD
Marjory Kinnon Sch
Bedfont Jun Sch
THE GARDENS
HAZELMERE CL
MARRIOTT CL
Duke of Northumberland's River
ENGLEHEART DR
ELMCROFT CL
TURPIN RD
WHITE BRIDGE CL
WELWYN AVE
KINGSTON AVE
PENTELOW GDNS
CLIV
A315
TENNYSON CL
PENINSULAR CL
REGIS CT
NORTHUMBERLAND CRES
TARGET CL
RICHMOND AVE
LONGFORD AVE
ROWAN HO
THACKERY LO
BEDFONT CL
MONTROSE RD
BENSINGTON CT
NORTH RD
NORTH CL
NEW RD
BRAMLEY CT
DORCHESTER DR
HORSHAM RD
BISHOPS DR
PAGE RD
BETHANY WAVE
Allot Gdns
RUSKIN AVE
SHAKESPEARE AVE
CASSIOBURY AVE
Longford Sch
Pl Fld
LETCHWORTH AVE
TACHBROOK RD
LINK RD
FRUEN RD
EDWARD PAULING HO
SYDNEY
Felth Aren
BEDFONT LA
B3377
PO
P
BENEDICT DR
WEST RD
EAST RD
Wks
STANWELL RD
LONGLEAT WAY
PATES MANOR DR
BURLINGTON CL
STAINES RD
WARFIELD RD
GOULD RD
COLONIAL RD
IMPERIAL RD
WEST VIEW
SPINNEY DR
VICARAGE CT
ST MARY'S DR
Liby
FAIRHOLME
GROVESTILE WAYE
MONARCH CL
WALKER CL
STONE CRES
Bwg Gn
T Cts
VEITCH CL
OWEN HO
SHORE CL
GLEBELAND
LINDSEY GDNS
NATALIE CL
ELM RD
SHERBORNE RD
BEECH RD
SOUTHVILLE RD
SOUTHVILLE CL
RUSCOMBE WAY
CHURCHILL CL
150
A315
Clockhouse Rdbt
HATCHETT RD
BEDFONT RD
FAWNS MANOR CL
FAWNS MANOR RD
CEDAR RD
BRIDLEPATH WAY
CHANDLERS CL
BEATTIE CL
ALLCOT CL
POPE CL
Southville Jun Sch
PACIFIC CL
WESTMINSTER CL
ASHMEAD RD
DUDLEY RD
PEACOCK AVE
PADBURY CT
KILLROSS RD
CLEEVE CT
BOWDEN CL
ROUTH CT
SLEDMERE CT
LOXWOOD CL
SOUTHVILLE CRES
INVICTA CL
OAK WAY
ASH GR
SANDY DR
ANDOVER CL
TREVITHICK CL
RADLEY CL
BEDFONT GREEN CL
GRAFTON CT
ELDRICK CT
CRAMOND CT
ELSWORTH CL
WATERMEAD
ENNERDALE CL
WINDERMERE CL
GRASMERE CL
NINE ELMS CL
JUBILEE WAY
ELDRIDGE
Fairholme Jun & Inf Schs
East Bedfont
KENDAL CL 1
APPLEBY GDNS 2
DERWENT CL 3
MISSENDEN CL 4
BUTTERMERE CL 5
AMBLESIDE DR
WESTMACOTT DR
WATERLOO CL
NELSON CL
ST CATHERINES CT
HARVEY CT
TAYLORS CT
Cemy
PADSTOW WLK
Edward Pauling Prim Sch
ROSEMEAD AVE
Pav
T Cts
Grosvenor Park
GUILDFORD AVE
SOUTHCOTE AVE
GRANVILLE AVE
CRAVEN
Bedfont Lakes Country Park
Ind Est
BEDFONT RD
Vineyard Nurseries
BEDFORD CL
RALEIGH RD
LANCING RD
ROCHESTER AVE
VERNON RD
PERCIVAL RD
PRINCES RD
AVENUE RD
WESTBOURNE RD
FRANCIS AVE
ROSS
HM Young Offender Ctr
THE HERMITAGE 1
SPRING CNR 2
QUEENS PARK GDNS 3
ST DUNSTAN'S RD
244
A244
PO
SHERRINGHAM AVE
HAYLING AVE
CRAIGWELL AVE
HARVEST RD
PARK
Feltham Hill Jun Sch
Lower Feltham
Recn Gd
The Sawyers Arms (PH)
SPRING RD
BEDFONT IND PK N
CHALLENGE RD
B377
ASHFORD RD
LARKHAM CL
Cemy
BRIARWOOD CL
WALTON GDNS
SHELSON AVE
SUNBURY RD
LUDLOW RD
RYLAND CL
SUNBURY CRES
Recn Gd
FIELD VIEW
ASHFORD IND EST
MERESIDE PK
PORTLAND CRES
CLUMPS
ALLIANCE CT
SHIELD RD
DUKES
FERN
ELLINGTON RD
DENISON RD
09
171
10
Surrey

150
A
B
128
C
D
75
6
5
74
4
3
73
2
1
72
10
11
172
GREEN MAN LA
HATTON GN
HERON WAY
A312
NORTH FELTHAM TRAD EST
SPUR RD
MAPLE GR BSNS CTR
DULBOROUGH WAY
TAMIAN IND EST
TAMIAN WAY
Allot Gdns
CLEMENTS CT
CENTRAL PK EST
CARDINGTON SQ
RIVER GDNS BSNS CTR
Allot Gdns
HASLEMERE IND EST
ARMADALE RD
PIER RD
DELLBOW RD
FREEHOLD IND CTR
AMBERLEY WAY
FAIRWAY EST
ISLAY GDNS
A315
DOCKWELL'S IND EST
SPACE WAYE
North Feltham
Cemy
FAGG'S RD
CHALMERS WAY
CENTRAL WAY
FALCON WAY
WILLOW HO
RIVER GDNS
Superstore
FAIRWAY CT
MERCURY CTR
ROMAN CL
CH
Superstore
Duke of Northumberland's River
Masts
DUKES GREEN AVE
MILL WAY
STAINES RD
BABER BRIDGE
BABER BRIDGE PAR
THE GRIFFIN CTR
THE VALE
A244
BYWARD AVE
BEESTON WAY
Hounslow Heath
River
WHITE BRIDGE CL
ENGLEHEART DR
MINIMAX CL
PENTELOW GDNS
CLIVE RD
LANSBURY AVE
GARDNER PL
BABER DR
TURPIN RD
CHANDLER CT
PO
A315
TENNYSON CL
BURNS AVE
ROSSLYN AVE
BUCKINGHAM AVE
BECKETTS CL
FIELD RD
Allot Gdns
VIOLA AVE
Allot Gdns
Allot Gdns
RUSKIN AVE
SHAKESPEARE AVE
SHAFTESBURY AVE
GLADSTONE AVE
HARLINGTON RD W
Pl Fld
CARLTON AVE
CHICHESTER WAY
DENHAM RD
FAREHAM RD
SPARROW FARM DR
Longford Sch
TW14
HELEN AVE
THE DELL
WALSHAM RD
HOUNSLOW RD
CLYMPING DENE
1 FRANK TOWELL CT
2 BRASSEY CL
3 EASTLEIGH WAY
4 ORCHARD RD
5 PEACH RD
6 ALMOND CL
7 HAZEL GR
8 HUNTER HO
9 HAWTHORNE RD
10 TILLEY RD
11 PLUM CL
13 MAGNOLIA CT
14 LEMON GR
15 BELVEDERE HO
16 FELBRIDGE CT
Sparrow Farm Schs
THE DRIVE
T Cts
Bwg Gn
PO
CENTRAL PAR
FINCH DR
CYGNET AVE
TACHBROOK RD
FRUEN RD
LINK
SYDNEY
Feltham Arena
Pl Fld
BRAINTON AVE
CAMBRIA CT
Pl Fld
Bwg Gn
T Cts
NURSERY CL
FERN GR
PARK WAY
DURHAM RD
SHORE CL
OWEN HO
GLEBELANDS RD
HAWKES RD
STATION PAR
149
B3377
HILL CL
BEDFONT LA
STATION ESTATE RD
HARLINGTON RD E
NORFOLK RD
Southville Jun Sch
PACIFIC CL
WESTMINSTER CL
ASHMEAD RD
PROCTORS CL
LOCOMOTIVE DR
MANOR PL
NEW RD
Feltham
QUEEN'S RD
GLOUCESTER RD
HEREFORD RD
Tenn Cts
ANDOVER CL
SOUTHERN AVE
TYNAN CL
SANDYCOMBE RD
SYDNEY RD
LC
CROMWELL RD
Ct
SALISBURY RD
BOUNDARIES RD
NINE ELMS CL
TREVITHICK
JUBILEE WAY
ELDRIDGE CL
RAILWAY TERR
B3377
B3377
BEAUCLERK CL
HANWORTH RD
KINGS RD
Tenn Cts
WYATT CL
NELSON CL
WATERLOO CL
ST CATHERINES CT
NORY CT
Sch
CARDINAL RD
FLORENCE RD
ASHFIELD AVE
B3377
DE BROOME RD
SLATTERY RD
NEW CHAPEL SQ
The Victoria Jun Sch
DANESBURY RD
CAMDEN AVE
ALFRED RD
ELTHORNE CT
HANOVER AVE
TAYLORS CT
HIGHFIELD RD
BOWSLEY CT
VICTORIA RD
WILTON WLK
MONOLA
LAFONE AVE
WIGLEY RD
GUILDFORD AVE
Pav
T Cts
Grosvenor Park
Liby
THE CENTRE
THE GREEN
Sch
DEVONSHIRE CT
ASTRID HO
BROWELLS LA
Feltham Comm Sch
MARLBOROUGH RD
AMESBURY RD
EASTBOURNE
UXBRIDGE RD
Superstore
SOUTHCOTE AVE
CRAVAN AVE
GRANVILLE AVE
WILTON PAR
AIR PARK WAY
BROWELLS LA
FELTHAM BSNS COMPLEX
ROCHESTER AVE
MANOR LA
MOSS GDNS
FELTHAM
Tenn Cts
VERNON RD
CAVENDISH TERR
HIGH ST
ROSE GDNS
1 PARKFIELD PAR
2 ROCHESTER PAR
3 THE VINEYARDS
4 CHERVIL CL
Tenn Cts
PERCIVAL RD
Sp Gd
Sp Ctr
AVENUE RD
FRANCIS AVE
VINEYARD RD
ORDNANCE CL
MAPLE IND EST
MAPLE WAY
ELMWOOD AVE
FOREST RD
Hanworth Park House
ST DUNSTAN'S RD
CHARLESTON CL
TAWNY CL
PARKFIELD AVE
FELTHAM CORPORATE CTR
OLAF PALME HOUSE
SANDALWOOD RD
PINEWOOD RD
Hanworth Park
Pav
Recn Gd
A244
SHERRINGHAM AVE
PO
PARKFIELD RD
POPLAR WAY
PLANE TREE CRES
FELTHAMBROOK IND EST
ROOKERIES CL
HAYLING AVE
CRAIGWELL AVE
PARKFIELD CRES
ASPEN WAY
CHESTNUT WAY
TW13
HOUNSLOW RD
APRIL CL
TANGLEWOOD WAY
CLIFTON AVE
Cemy
HARVEST RD
BROOKSIDE
SYCAMORE CL
BADGER CL
FOXWOOD CL
PINKCOAT CL
Allot Gdns
ELMGATE AVE
CAMROSE AVE
RYLAND CL
SUNBURY CRES
SUNBURY RD
LUDLOW RD
DEERHURST CL
ROEBUCK CL
HUNTSMAN CL
FELTHAMBROOK WAY
KERNSIDE AVE
CLIFTON PAR
PO
PARR CT
TUDOR CT
1 BLAKEWOOD CL
2 SHAKESPEARE WAY
THE HOLLANDS
Pav
Hanworth
Bwg Gn
T Cts
A314
DENISON RD
CASTLE WAY

129
173
152
A
B
C
D
1
2
3
4
5
6
72
73
74
75
TW2
TW3
TW4
TW13
Hounslow Heath
Nature Reserve
The Heathland
Sch
The Orchard
Jun &
Inf Sch
WELLINGTON RD S
A3063
A314
A315
A316
A305
A312
B358
B361
HANWORTH RD
HOUNSLOW RD
NELSON RD
HOSPITAL BRIDGE RD
WHITTON RD
GREAT CHERTSEY RD
STAINES RD
TWICKENHAM RD
HAMPTON RD W
HAMPTON RD E
Hospital Bridge
Rdbt
Apex
Cnr
River Crane
Crane
Park
Fulwell
Park
Heathfield
Jun & Inf
Schs
Bishop Perrin
CE Prim Sch
St Edmund's
RC Prim Sch
Nelson
Prim Sch
Crane Park
Prim Sch
Oriel
Prim Sch
Whitton
Sch
Hounslow
Richmond upon Thames
Crem
Cemy
Nursery
Recn
Gd
Tenn Cts
Pav
Sp Gd
Allot
Gdns
Liby
Games
Ct
Pl Fld
CH
Twickenham
Drv Rng
Superstore
MILL FARM
BSNS PK
HAMPTON
FARM
IND EST
HANWORTH
TRAD EST
LINKS
IND EST
INWOOD
BSNS PK
HOUNSLOW
BSNS PK
SHERIDAN CT 1
PICKWICK CL 2
HEATHLANDS CT 3
BRAMLEY WAY 4
BODICEA MEWS 1
SHELBURNE DR 2
FOUR SQUARE CT 3
SLADE HO 1
JAMIESON HO 2
ATHERLEY WAY 1
DUNLEARY CL 2
DANIEL CL 3
1 MALLARD CL
2 BRUNEL WLK
3 BRACKEN CL
4 HEATHER WLK
1 TOWFIELD CT
2 NORMAN HO
3 RIVER CRANE WAY
1 WHITELY CT
2 BUTTS COTTS
1 EDWIN STRAY HO
2 CRANE HO
3 GLEBE HO
4 CHERTSEY HO
5 WHITELEYS HO
6 BUTTS HO
7 GLEBE COTTS
1 BRAMLEY HO
LAUREL GDNS
FIR TREE RD
CONNAUGHT AVE
MUNSTER AVE
MIDSUMMER AVE
COBBS RD
ROSEHEATH RD
MARSHALL CL
BROMPTON CL
BERESFORD GDNS
YEW TREE WLK
AVONDALE GDNS
VICTORIA AVE
WELLINGTON AVE
ROSEVILLE AVE
GRANVILLE AVE
ST AUBYN'S AVE
ST HELIERS AVE
CARLTON HO
NELSON GDNS
WYNDHAM CRES
MEADOW CL
CONWAY RD
STEPHENSON RD
RODNEY RD
COLLINGWOOD CL
VINCAM CL
HARVEY RD
MOORLAND CL
GERARD AVE
HEDLEY RD
REDFERN AVE
HEATHSIDE
THE BIRCHES
LEA CL
BIRD WLK
GODFREY WAY
CURTIS RD
MILLFIELD RD
FARM RD
MILL FARM CRES
GRAFTON CL
PEMBRIDGE AVE
CHESTER AVE
GLASBROOK AVE
ALBEMARLE AVE
VILLIERS AVE
CHEYNE AVE
SHERINGHAM AVE
LYNDHURST AVE
WAVERLEY AVE
POWDER MILL LA
CHILTERN AVE
ELLERMAN AVE
SPRINGFIELD RD
GOSTLING RD
COBBETT RD
WARBURTON RD
LONGFORD RD
STIRLING RD
MONTROSE AVE
BRYANSTON AVE
BLANDFORD AVE
FAIRFIELD AVE
RYECROFT AVE
STRATHEARN AVE
PERCY WAY
PERCY RD
ROSS RD
ROSS HO
SELKIRK RD
GILPIN CRES
RUNNYMEDE GDNS
RUNNYMEDE RD
EVELYN CL
CAMELLIA PL
ASHDALE WAY
ASHDALE CL
CONSTANCE RD
TRANMERE RD
MELROSE AVE
MAYFAIR AVE
WILLOWDENE CL
NELSON RD
ST EDMUND'S LA
BRITANNIA LA
HIGH ST
WHITTON WAYE
WILLS CRES
GRASMERE AVE
RYDAL GDNS
DERWENT RD
CONISTON RD
KESWICK RD
ST VINCENT RD
HOUNSLOW RD
VICARAGE
CEDAR AVE
COLONIAL AVE
PARK AVE
ARGYLE AVE
HAMILTON CRES
CARRINGTON AVE
MURRAY AVE
SANDRA CL
DEAN RD
SHIRLEY DR
SHIRLEY CL
MILLWOOD RD
PARK RD
HOUNSLOW AVE
HOWSLOW GDNS
MASWELL PARK RD
MASWELL PARK CRES
IVY RD
KINGFISHER CT
LANIGAN DR
LINDEN AVE
PARKSIDE RD
ST STEPHEN'S RD
THE AVENUE
ARGYLE RD
HIBERNIA GDNS
RESTORMEL CL
PENDEREL RD
ROSSINDEL RD
ROLLIT CRES
CAMBRIA CL
ALBERT RD
ALBION RD
CROMWELL RD
CROSS LANCES
NEW RD UNITS
STATION RD
PEVENSEY RD
BEXHILL CL
MEADOW RD
LITTLE PARK DR
OAKS AVE
SUNNINGDALE AVE
CANTERBURY RD
BRAID CL
TOWFIELD RD
NORMAN AVE
LORDS CL
BARNLEA CL
SAXON AVE
EDMUND GR
HILL GR
GARDNER HO
EXETER HO
GATFIELD HO
SHORE GR
GATFIELD GR
WATERMILL WAY
BASDEN GR
EVANS GR
BEACH GR
FOUNTAINS CL
FOUNTAINS AVE
CHURCHFIELDS AVE
SEKHON TERR
BIDEFORD CL
EXETER RD
WINCHESTER RD
LINCOLN WAY
YORK WAY
SUNRISE CL
BELLA
NENE GDNS
RIVER WAY
ELM CL
BEECH WAY
GLEBE WAY
WHITELEYS WAY
BUTTS CRES
SOUTH CL
COURT CL
RIVERMEADS AVE
COURT CLOSE AVE
WILLOW WAY
BYEWAYS
WARWICK LO
CRANE PARK RD
WOODLAWN CRES
FULWELL PARK AVE
MANOEL RD
PORTUGAL GDNS
MARKET PAR
NEWGATE CL
THE LION CTR
LONGFORD CL
WEBB HO
SWIFT RD
DEVONSHIRE
OGDEN HO
SWINFIELD CL
CROSBY CL
CRESSWELL
WINSLOW WAY
REX HO
WILLOW COTTS
STOURTON AVE
FAIRLAWN CL
AUGUSTUS CT
BROADLANDS
LONGFORD HO
CROSS RD
WORDSWORTH RD
RISPEN RD
MILLBOURNE RD
GRAHAM RD

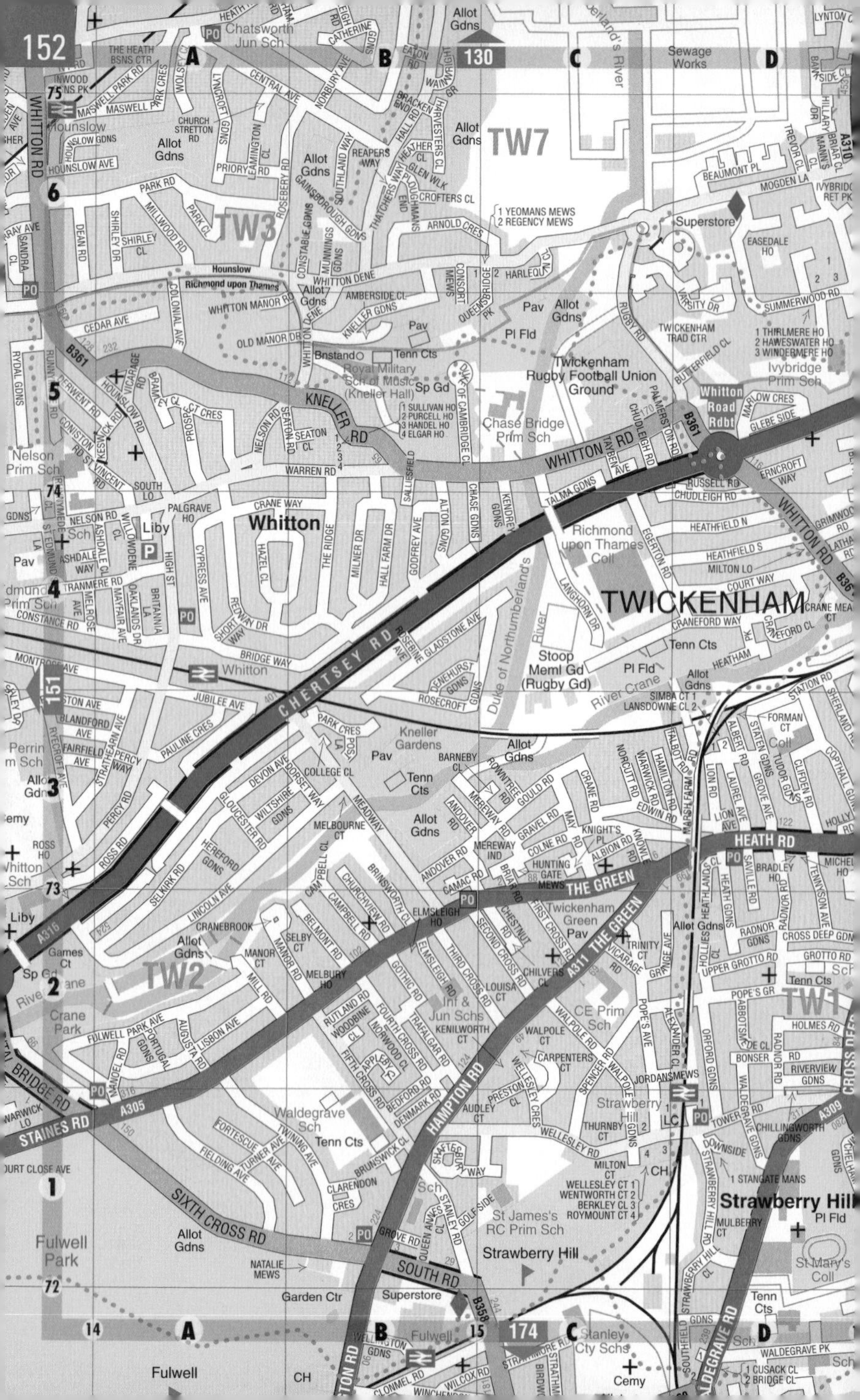
130
174
151
A
B
C
D
6
5
4
3
2
1
75
74
73
72
14
15
TW7
TW3
TW2
TW1
Hounslow
Richmond upon Thames
Whitton
TWICKENHAM
Strawberry Hill
Fulwell
Chatsworth Jun Sch
THE HEATH BSNS CTR
INWOOD BSNS PK
MASWELL PARK RD
MASWELL PK CRES
HOUNSLOW GDNS
HOUNSLOW AVE
WHITTON RD
CHURCH STRETTON RD
LYNCROFT GDNS
LEAMINGTON CL
PRIORY RD
CENTRAL AVE
NORBURY AVE
CATHERINE GDNS
ROSEBERY RD
SOUTHLAND WAY
REAPERS WAY
THATCHERS WAY
HALL RD
BRACKEN END
HARVESTERS CL
HEATHER CL
GLEN WLK
PLOUGHMANS END
CROFTERS CL
WAINWRIGHT GR
EATON RD
Sewage Works
Allot Gdns
PARK RD
MILLWOOD RD
SHIRLEY DR
SHIRLEY CL
DEAN RD
PARK CL
GAINSBOROUGH GDNS
CONSTABLE GDNS
MUNNINGS GDNS
ARNOLD CRES
1 YEOMANS MEWS
2 REGENCY MEWS
CONSORT MEWS
QUEENSBRIDGE PK
HARLEQUIN CL
Superstore
MOGDEN LA
BEAUMONT PL
TREVOR CL
HILLARY DR
MANNS CL
BRIAR CL
BANKSIDE CL
LYNTON CL
IVYBRIDGE RET PK
EASEDALE HO
SUMMERWOOD RD
VARSITY DR
TWICKENHAM TRAD CTR
BUTTERFIELD CL
1 THIRLMERE HO
2 HAWESWATER HO
3 WINDERMERE HO
Ivybridge Prim Sch
Whitton Road Rdbt
MARLOW CRES
GLEBE SIDE
RUGBY RD
Twickenham Rugby Football Union Ground
Pav
Pl Fld
WHITTON DENE
WHITTON MANOR RD
AMBERSIDE CL
KNELLER GDNS
OLD MANOR DR
Tenn Cts
Bnstand
Royal Military Sch of Music (Kneller Hall)
Sp Gd
DUKE OF CAMBRIDGE CL
1 SULLIVAN HO
2 PURCELL HO
3 HANDEL HO
4 ELGAR HO
Chase Bridge Prim Sch
CEDAR AVE
RYDAL GDNS
RUNNYMEDE RD
DERWENT RD
CONISTON RD
KESWICK RD
HOUNSLOW RD
VICARAGE RD
BRAMLEY CL
PROSPECT CRES
COLONIAL AVE
KNELLER RD
NELSON RD
SEATON RD
SEATON CL
WARREN RD
SALLIESFIELD
CHASE GDNS
KENDREY GDNS
TAYBEN AVE
CHUDLEIGH RD
PALMERSTON RD
WHITTON RD
B361
ERNCROFT WAY
RUSSELL RD
TALMA GDNS
Nelson Prim Sch
ST VINCENT RD
SOUTH LO
PALGRAVE HO
CRANE WAY
Liby
HIGH ST
WILLOWDENE CL
ASHDALE CL
ASHDALE WAY
ST EDMUNDS LA
TRANMERE RD
MELROSE AVE
MAYFAIR AVE
OAKLANDS DR
BRITANNIA LA
CONSTANCE RD
CYPRESS AVE
HAZEL CL
THE RIDGE
MILNER DR
HALL FARM DR
GODFREY AVE
ALTON GDNS
REDWAY DR
SHORT WAY
BRIDGE WAY
Whitton
Richmond upon Thames Coll
EGERTON RD
HEATHFIELD N
HEATHFIELD S
MILTON LO
COURT WAY
GRIMWOOD RD
LATHAM CL
LANGHORN DR
CRANEFORD WAY
CRANEFORD CL
CRANE MEAD CT
HEATHAM PK
Stoop Meml Gd (Rugby Gd)
River Crane
Duke of Northumberland's River
CHERTSEY RD
ROSEBINE AVE
GLADSTONE AVE
DENEHURST GDNS
ROSECROFT GDNS
MONTROSE AVE
JUBILEE AVE
BLANDFORD AVE
FAIRFIELD AVE
STRATHEARN AVE
PERCY WAY
PERCY RD
PAULINE CRES
RYECROFT AVE
Perrin Prim Sch
PARK CRES
Kneller Gardens
COLLEGE CL
DEVON AVE
DORSET WAY
WILTSHIRE GDNS
GLOUCESTER RD
HEREFORD GDNS
MEADWAY
MELBOURNE CT
SIMBA CT 1
LANSDOWNE CL 2
STATION RD
SHERLAND RD
FORMAN CT
Coll
BARNEBY CL
ROWNTREE RD
GOULD RD
CRANE RD
NORCUTT RD
WARWICK RD
HAMILTON RD
EDWIN RD
TALBOT RD
MARSH FARM RD
LION RD
ALBERT RD
STATEN GDNS
LAUREL AVE
GROVE AVE
TUDOR GDNS
CLIFDEN RD
COPTHALL GDNS
LION AVE
HEATH RD
HOLLY RD
ROSS RD
ROSS HO
Whitton Sch
SELKIRK RD
LINCOLN AVE
CAMPBELL CL
CHURCHVIEW RD
BRINSWORTH CL
CAMPBELL RD
ANDOVER RD
MEREWAY RD
MEREWAY IND
GRAVEL RD
MAY RD
KNIGHT'S PL
COLNE RD
ALBION RD
KNOWLE RD
HUNTING GATE MEWS
GAMAC RD
BRIAR RD
THE GREEN
Twickenham Green
HEATHLANDS CL
HEATH GDNS
SAVILLE RD
BRADLEY HO
TENNYSON AVE
RADNOR RD
MICHEL HO
CRANEBROOK
MANOR CT
MANOR RD
SELBY CT
BELMONT RD
ELMSLEIGH HO
ELMSLEIGH RD
THIRD CROSS RD
SECOND CROSS RD
CHESTNUT RD
FIRST CROSS RD
CHILVERS CL
A311 THE GREEN
TRINITY CT
VICARAGE RD
GRANGE AVE
HOLLIES RD
RADNOR GDNS
CROSS DEEP GDNS
UPPER GROTTO RD
GROTTO RD
A316
Games Ct
Sp Gd
Crane Park
MILL RD
MELBURY HO
GOTHIC RD
LOUISA CT
Inf & Jun Schs
KENILWORTH CT
WALPOLE CT
WALPOLE RD
CE Prim Sch
POPE'S AVE
ALEXANDER CL
ORFORD GDNS
ABBOTSMEDE CL
POPE'S GR
HOLMES RD
BONSER RD
RIVERVIEW GDNS
CROSS DEEP
FULWELL PARK AVE
PORTUGAL GDNS
MANOEL RD
AUGUSTA RD
LISBON AVE
RUTLAND RD
WOODBINE CL
FOURTH CROSS RD
NORWOOD CL
TRAFALGAR RD
APPLEBY CL
FIFTH CROSS RD
BEDFORD RD
DENMARK RD
HAMPTON RD
CARPENTERS CT
PRESTON CL
WELLESLEY CRES
SPENCER RD
WALPOLE GDNS
JORDANS MEWS
AUDLEY CT
THURNBY CT
WELLESLEY RD
TOWER RD
CHILLINGWORTH GDNS
WALDEGRAVE GDNS
DOWNSIDE
A309
WARWICK LO
BRIDGE RD
STAINES RD
A305
FORTESCUE AVE
TWINING AVE
TURNER AVE
FIELDING AVE
Waldegrave Sch
BRUNSWICK CL
SHAFTESBURY WAY
MILTON CT
WELLESLEY CT 1
WENTWORTH CT 2
BERKLEY CL 3
ROYMOUNT CT 4
1 STANGATE MANS
COURT CLOSE AVE
SIXTH CROSS RD
CLARENDON CRES
Sch
GOLFSIDE
QUEEN ANNES CL
STANLEY RD
St James's RC Prim Sch
STRAWBERRY HILL RD
STRAWBERRY HILL CL
MULBERRY CT
St Mary's Coll
Fulwell Park
NATALIE MEWS
GROVE RD
SOUTH RD
Garden Ctr
B358
Stanley Cty Schs
SOUTHFIELD GDNS
WALDEGRAVE RD
WALDEGRAVE PK
1 CUSACK CL
2 BRIDGE CL
WELLINGTON GDNS
CLONMEL RD
WILCOX RD
STRATHMORE RD
Cemy
CH
LC
PO
P

RICHMOND
TW7
TW1
TW10
St Margarets
Cambridge Park
Ham
Twickenham
Richmond Lock
131
154
175
A
B
C
D
1
2
3
4
5
6
72
73
74
75
River Thames
River Crane
Eel Pie Island
Marble Hill Park
Marble Hill
Ham House
Orleans Park Sec Sch
York House
Clifton Lodge
St Helena Pier
Deutsche Schule
The Russell Prim Sch
Strathmore Sch
The Russell Sch
Grey Court Sch
St Catherine's Convent Girls Prep & Senior Schs
Meadlands Prim Sch
Moor Mead Gd
Thames Path
Ferry P
Sudbrook
Allot Gdns
Tenn Cts
Pl Fld
Sp Gd
Liby
Liby Mus
Bwg Gn
Cemy
Sch
St Margarets Rdbt
London Road Rdbt
TWICKENHAM BRIDGE
TWICKENHAM RD
RICHMOND BRIDGE
RICHMOND RD
THE AVENUE
ST MARGARET'S RD
CHERTSEY RD
LONDON RD
CROSS DEEP
STRAWBERRY VALE
PETERSHAM RD
HAM ST
SANDY LA
HAM COMM
KING ST
YORK ST
CROWN RD
HILL RISE
HILL ST
GEORGE ST
PARADISE RD
RED LION ST
RIVERSIDE
THE EMBANKMENT
A305
A307
A310
A316
A3004
B321
B352
1 CAMBRIDGE PARK CT
2 MEADOWSIDE
1 SUTHERLAND HO
2 SCOTT HO
3 WIGGINS LA
1 HAWKESLEY CL
2 CLAVERING CL
3 CHATSWORTH PL
4 WOODVILLE CL
5 MARLOW HO
6 FAIRWATER HO
7 REGATTA HO
8 FAIRMILE HO
9 ADMIRAL HO

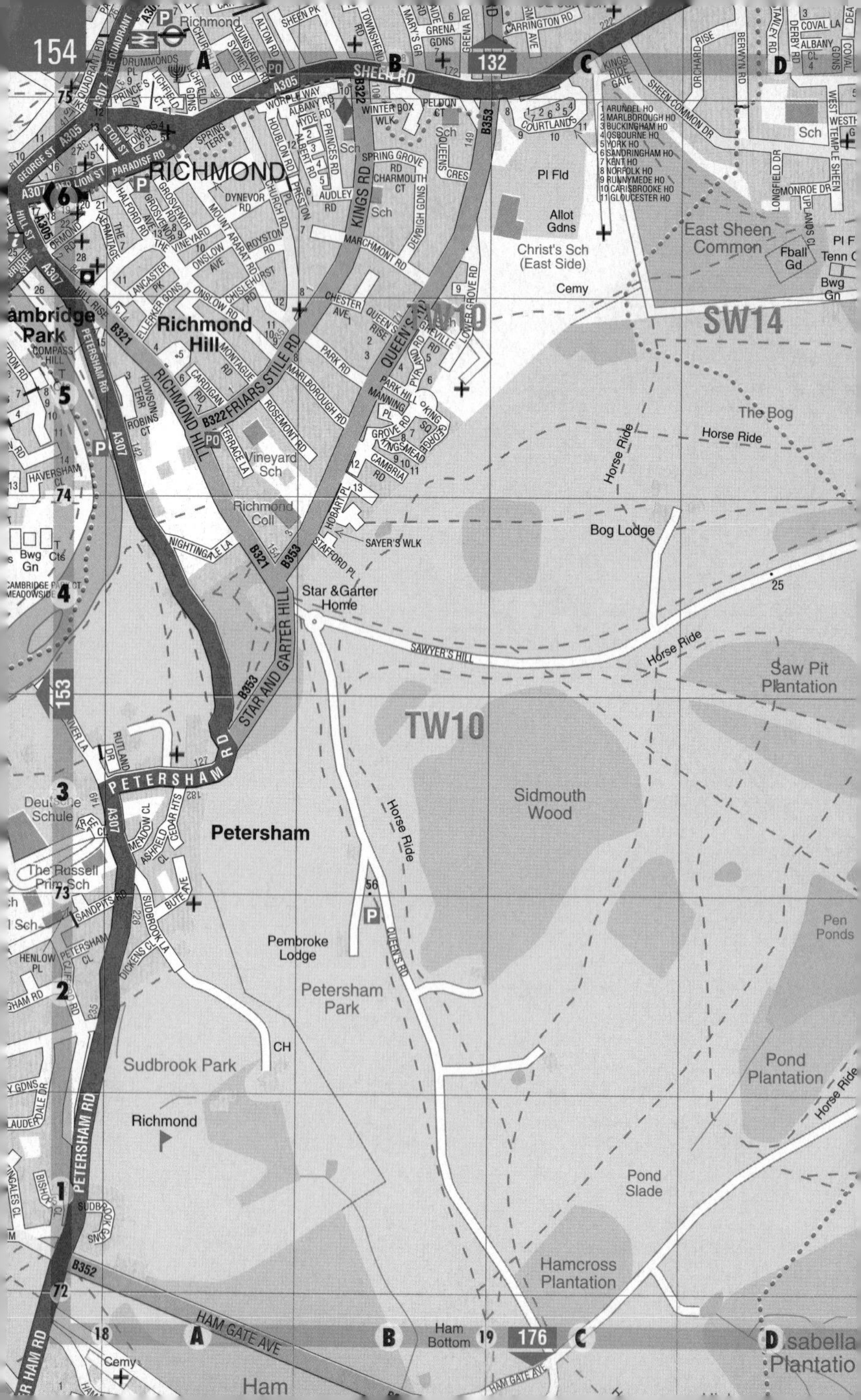
RICHMOND
Richmond Hill
Petersham
Richmond
Sheen Rd
Kings Rd
Queen's Rd
Richmond Hill
Friars Stile Rd
Petersham Rd
Star and Garter Hill
Sawyer's Hill
Ham Gate Ave
Kings Ride Gate
Sheen Common Dr
1 Arundel Ho
2 Marlborough Ho
3 Buckingham Ho
4 Osbourne Ho
5 York Ho
6 Sandringham Ho
7 Kent Ho
8 Norfolk Ho
9 Runnymede Ho
10 Carisbrooke Ho
11 Gloucester Ho
Pl Fld
Allot Gdns
Christ's Sch (East Side)
Cemy
East Sheen Common
Fball Gd
Tenn Ct
Bwg Gn
SW14
TW10
The Bog
Horse Ride
Bog Lodge
Star & Garter Home
Saw Pit Plantation
Sidmouth Wood
Vineyard Sch
Richmond Coll
Pembroke Lodge
Petersham Park
Sudbrook Park
Pen Ponds
Pond Plantation
Pond Slade
Hamcross Plantation
Ham Bottom
Isabella Plantation
Deutsche Schule
The Russell Prim Sch
Cambridge Park
Ham
132
153
176
A
B
C
D
1
2
3
4
5
6

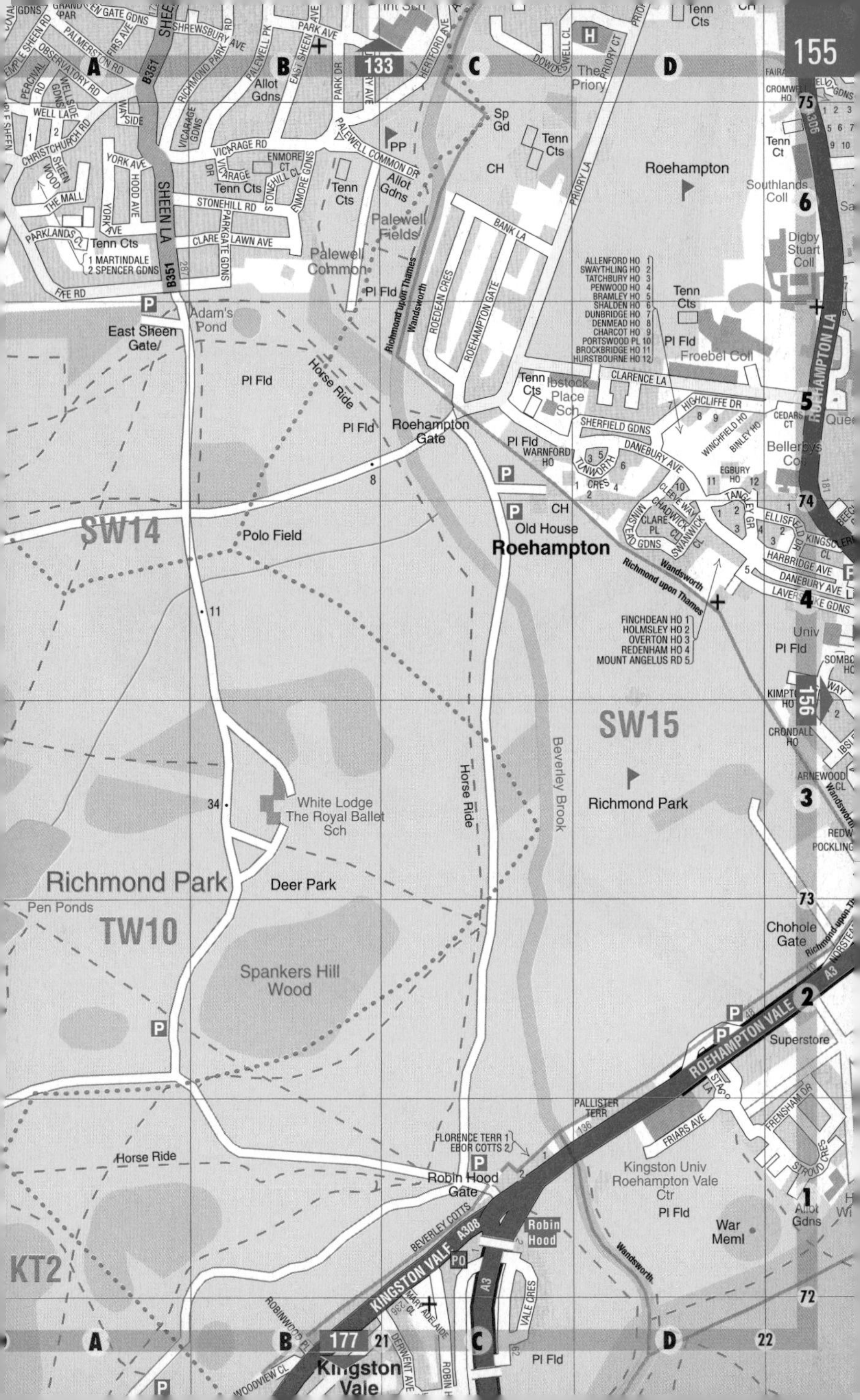

A
B
C
D
133
177
SHEEN LA
B351
EAST SHEEN AVE
PALEWELL PK
RICHMOND PARK RD
SHREWSBURY AVE
PARK AVE
HERTFORD AVE
PARK DR
PALMERSTON RD
FIRS AVE
OBSERVATORY RD
PERCIVAL RD
WELLSIDE GDNS
WELL LA
WAYSIDE
CHRISTCHURCH RD
SHEEN WOOD
THE MALL
YORK AVE
HOOD AVE
VICARAGE GDNS
VICARAGE RD
VICARAGE DR
ENMORE CT
ENMORE GDNS
STONEHILL CL
STONEHILL RD
PARKGATE GDNS
CLARE LAWN AVE
PARKLANDS CL
1 MARTINDALE
2 SPENCER GDNS
FIFE RD
PALEWELL COMMON DR
Allot Gdns
Tenn Cts
PP
Palewell Fields
Palewell Common
Pl Fld
Sp Gd
CH
H
DOWDESWELL CL
PRIORY CT
PRIORY LA
The Priory
BANK LA
ROEDEAN CRES
ROEHAMPTON GATE
Roehampton
Southlands Coll
Digby Stuart Coll
Froebel Coll
ALLENFORD HO 1
SWAYTHLING HO 2
TATCHBURY HO 3
PENWOOD HO 4
BRAMLEY HO 5
SHALDEN HO 6
DUNBRIDGE HO 7
DENMEAD HO 8
CHARCOT HO 9
PORTSWOOD PL 10
BROCKBRIDGE HO 11
HURSTBOURNE HO 12
CLARENCE LA
Ibstock Place Sch
HIGHCLIFFE DR
SHERFIELD GDNS
WARNFORD HO
TUNWORTH CRES
DANEBURY AVE
WINCHFIELD HO
BINLEY HO
CEDARS CT
Bellerbys Coll
EGBURY HO
TANGLEY GR
CLEEVE WAY
CHADWICK CL
CLARE PL
MINSTEAD GDNS
SWANWICK CL
ELLISFIELD DR
KINGSCLERE CL
HARBRIDGE AVE
LAVERSTOKE GDNS
ROEHAMPTON LA
A306
CROMWELL HO
Richmond upon Thames
Wandsworth
East Sheen Gate
Adam's Pond
Horse Ride
Roehampton Gate
Old House
Roehampton
SW14
Polo Field
FINCHDEAN HO 1
HOLMSLEY HO 2
OVERTON HO 3
REDENHAM HO 4
MOUNT ANGELUS RD 5
Univ Pl Fld
KIMPTON HO
CRONDALL HO
156
SW15
Beverley Brook
Richmond Park
White Lodge
The Royal Ballet Sch
ARNEWOOD CL
Richmond Park
Deer Park
Pen Ponds
TW10
Spankers Hill Wood
Chohole Gate
A3
ROEHAMPTON VALE
Superstore
STAG LA
FRIARS AVE
FRENSHAM DR
STROUD CRES
PALLISTER TERR
FLORENCE TERR 1
EBOR COTTS 2
Robin Hood Gate
Kingston Univ Roehampton Vale Ctr
War Meml
Allot Gdns
BEVERLEY COTTS
A308
KINGSTON VALE
Robin Hood
PO
KT2
ROBINWOOD PL
MARY ADELAIDE CL
DERWENT AVE
VALE CRES
WOODVIEW CL
Kingston Vale
75
74
73
72
21
22
6
5
4
3
2
1

Roehampton
PUTNEY
SW15
Putney Heath
Tibbet's Corner
Roehampton Lane
Jerry's Hill
King's Mere
Queen Mary's Univ
Digby Stuart Coll
Froebel Coll
Southlands Coll
Bellerbys Coll
Sacred Heart RC Prim Sch
Granard Prim Sch
Elliott Sch
Roehampton CE Prim Sch
KINGSTON RD
ROEHAMPTON LA
ROEHAMPTON VALE
PUTNEY HILL
TIBBET'S RIDE
WIMBLEDON PARK SIDE
PARKSIDE
WEST HILL
Chohole Gate
Crem
Cemy
Superstore
Putney Vale
Queen's Mere
Wimbledon Windmill Mus
Heathlands Sch
SW19
London Scottish
War Meml
Hall Sch Wimbledon
Parkside
Wimbledon Common
Wandsworth
Merton
Richmond upon Thames
134
155
178
A
B
C
D
22
23
72
73
74
75

WANDSWORTH
West Hill
Southfields
SW15
SW18
SW19
Wimbledon Park
Wimbledon Park Lake
The All England Lawn Tennis & Croquet Club
Wimbledon Lawn Tennis Mus
Wandsworth Gyratory
PUTNEY BRIDGE RD
UPPER RICHMOND RD
WANDSWORTH HIGH ST
WEST HILL
A217 ARMOURY WAY
SWANDON WAY
MERTON RD
DURNSFORD RD
GARRATT LA
BUCKHOLD RD
WIMBLEDON PARK RD
East Putney
Royal Hospl
Whitelands Coll, Roehampton Univ of Surrey
King George's Park
Southfields Com Coll
Earlsfield
Athletics Gd
Wandle Prim Sch
Albermarle Prim Sch
Sheringdale Prim Sch
Riversdale Prim Sch
Linden Lodge Sch
ADT Coll
Visitor Ctr
Wandsworth
Merton
River Wandle
135
158
179
A
B
C
D
1
2
3
4
5
6

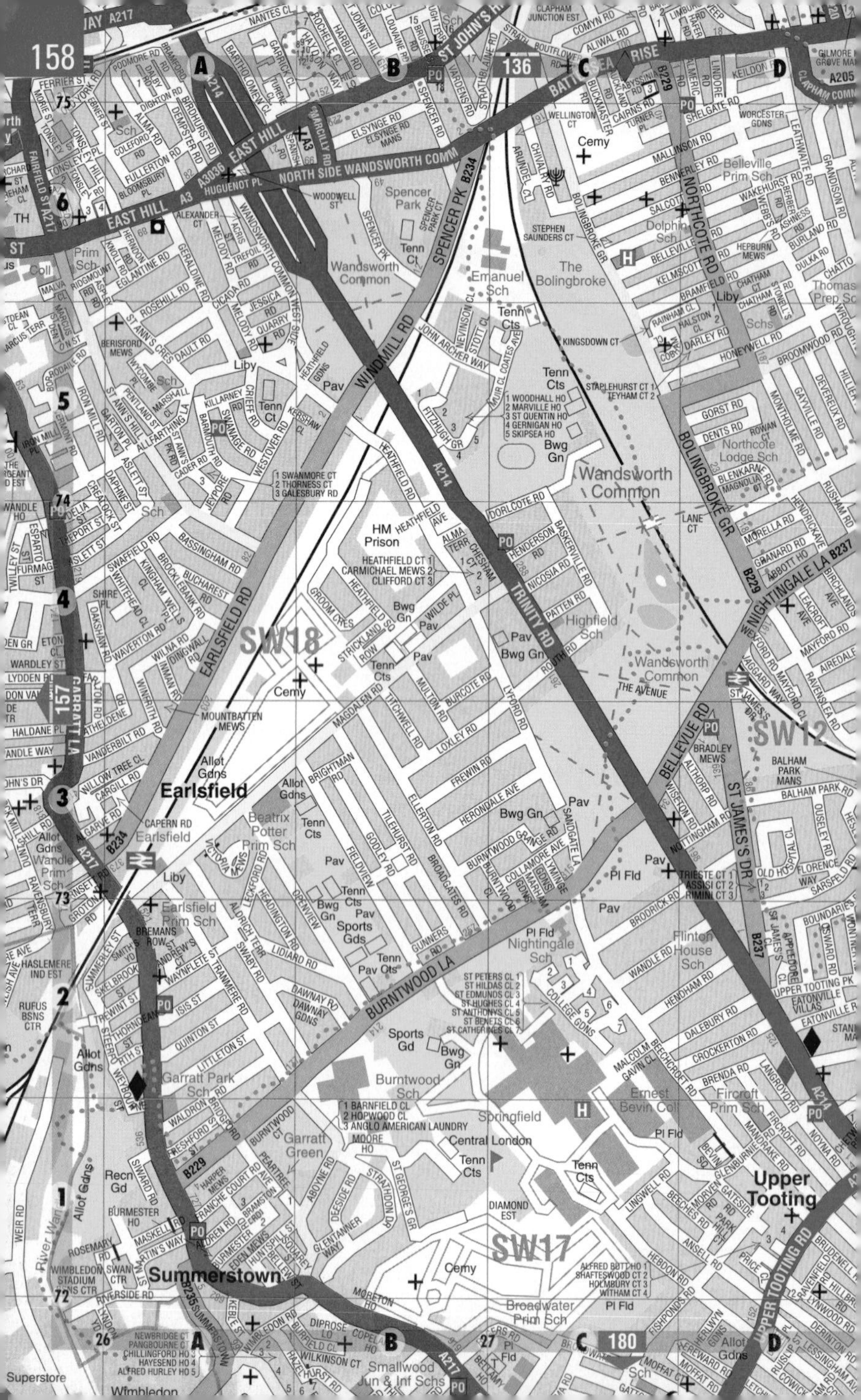
A
B
C
D
136
157
180
1
2
3
4
5
6
SW18
SW12
SW17
Earlsfield
Summerstown
Upper Tooting
Wandsworth Common
Spencer Park
The Bolingbroke
Emanuel Sch
HM Prison
Cemy
Springfield
Central London
Ernest Bevin Coll
Burntwood Sch
Garratt Green
Beatrix Potter Prim Sch
Earlsfield Prim Sch
Garratt Park Sch
Nightingale Sch
Flinton House Sch
Highfield Sch
Fircroft Prim Sch
Broadwater Prim Sch
Smallwood Jun & Inf Schs
Belleville Prim Sch
Dolphin Sch
Northcote Lodge Sch
Wandsworth Stadium Bsns Ctr
Haslemere Ind Est
Rufus Bsns Ctr
Diamond Est
Wimbledon
Superstore
River Wandle
EAST HILL
NORTH SIDE WANDSWORTH COMM
BATTERSEA RISE
ST JOHN'S HILL
SPENCER PK
WINDMILL RD
TRINITY RD
EARLSFIELD RD
GARRATT LA
BURNTWOOD LA
NIGHTINGALE LA
BELLEVUE RD
BOLINGBROKE GR
NORTHCOTE RD
ST JAMES'S DR
UPPER TOOTING RD
SUMMERSTOWN
MAGDALEN RD
WANDSWORTH COMMON WEST SIDE
HEATHFIELD RD
ALLFARTHING LA
WIMBLEDON RD
A3
A214
A217
A3036
B229
B234
B235
B237
A205

CLAPHAM COMMON NORTH SIDE
LONG RD
A3
Clapham Common
A205
A
B
C
D
137
1 ST SAVIOURS
2 LYNCOTT CRES
3 SALCOMBE GDNS
4 BARKER MEWS
5 WOODLANDS
6 OKEOVER MANOR
Clapham Common
Windmill on the Common (PH)
Recn Gd
Bndstd
Mount Pond
Lambeth
Wandsworth
CLAPHAM PARK RD
A2217
CLAPHAM COMMON SOUTH SIDE
A24
THE AVENUE
WINDMILL DR
SW4
CAVENDISH PAR
Clapham South
B237
CAVENDISH RD
A205
Lambeth Coll
Sch
Tenn Ct
ELMS RD
ABBEVILLE RD
CRESCENT LA
Clapham Park
KINGS AVE
RODENHURST RD
CLARENCE AVE
POYNDERS RD
NIGHTINGALE LA
BALHAM HILL
HAZELBOURNE RD
CATHLES RD
DAGNAN RD
YUKON RD
Sch
Liby
CATKINS RD
SCRUTTON CL
A205
SW12
BALHAM NEW RD
OLD DEVONSHIRE RD
St Bernadette RC Jun Sch
Grange Mills
HYDETHORPE RD
CAMBRAY RD
MIDMOOR RD
BURNBURY RD
St Bede's RC Inf Sch
Tenn Cts
Telferscot Prim Sch
THORNTON AVE
160
Balham
B242
Mkt
BALHAM STATION RD
FERNLEA RD
EMMANUEL RD
HEATHWOOD CT
Streatham Hill
TELFORD AVE
B221
STERNHOLD AVE
Fball Gd
BALHAM HIGH RD
Ravenstone Prim Sch
BEDFORD HILL
ELMFIELD RD
Wandsworth
Lambeth
Recn Gd
Tenn Cts
Pav
Streatham & Clapham High Sch
SW16
The Woodfield Ctr
Tooting Bec
A24
Tooting Bec Common
SW17
DR JOHNSON AVE
Tenn Cts
GARRAD'S RD
Horse Ride
FISHERS CL 1
SAXONCROFT HO 2
WELLINGTON MEWS 3
Streatham Park
TOOTING BEC RD
29
181
30
B242
TOOTING BEC GDNS
STREATHAM HIGH RD
A23
1 BRUCE LAWNS
2 BRUCE HALL MEWS

160
A
B
C
D
138
159
182
ACRE LA
A2217
Works
SALTOUN RD
KELLETT RD
MERVAN RD
ST MATTHEW'S RD
EFFRA RD
BAYTREE RD
SUDBOURNE RD
EFFRA CT
HAYTER RD
Prim Sch
Lambeth Coll
EUROLINK BSNS CTR
EFFRA ROAD RET PK
FITCH CT
DALBERG RD
RAILTON RD
MAYALL RD
SHAKESPEARE RD
MILKWOOD RD
DEREK WALCOTT CL
1 FARMLEIGH HO
2 HOLMBURY HO
MAGNOLIA PL
ST PAUL'S CT
WEST RD
ELLERSLIE IND EST
GLENELG RD
STRATHLEVEN RD
BRANKSOME RD
KILDORAN RD
MARGATE RD
MAULEVERER RD
MANDRELL RD
WINSLADE RD
WINTERWELL RD
HAYCROFT RD
TRENT RD
DRAY GDNS
BRIXTON WATER LA
MORVAL RD
TRELAWN RD
A2214
DULWICH RD
SPENSER RD
MILTON RD
MUMFORD RD
REGENT RD
B223
Sch
TA Ctr
PRAGUE PL
GLANVILLE RD
LAMBERT RD
ST SAVIOUR'S RD
JOSEPHINE AVE
CRESCENT CT
RODENHURST CT
CLAUDIA JONES WAY
RAMILLES CL
Allot Gdns
BLENHEIM GDNS
HELIX GDNS
ARODENE RD
HELIX RD
APPACH RD
ARLINGFORD RD
BRAILSFORD RD
Brockwell Lido
PARK VIEW HO 1
HERNE HILL HO 2
Pav
Bwg Gn
Tenn Cts
Brockwell Park
SE24
PINEWOOD CT
MAPLE CL
KINGS AVE
BOWATER CL
LOATS RD
OAKFIELD CT
PETER'S CT
ROSEBERY RD
JOHN ASHBY CL
LYHAM RD
Sp Gd
CHERRY LAUREL WLK
WATERWORKS RD
RALEIGH GDNS
FAIRMOUNT RD
BEECHDALE RD
CALIDORE CL
VIRGINIA WLK
LEANDER RD
WASHBROOK HO
IRBY HO
HOLT HO
TENDRING HO
TULSE HO
POVEY HO
BARTELL HO
BROCKWELL PARK ROW
JEBB AVE
THORNCLIFFE CT
HM Prison
RENTON CL
BEWLEY CT
ENDYMION RD
TUDOR CL
ELM PK
MERREDENE ST
THORNBURY RD
WINGFORD RD
LYHAM CL
CLARENCE CRES
HELBY RD
B221
DUMBARTON RD
CHALE RD
SOMERS RD
HYPERION HO
MEDORA RD
HEADLAM RD
TILSON HO
KINGSWOOD RD
DOVERFIELD RD
FELSBERG RD
MORLEY HO
SAXBY RD
BRIXTON HILL PL
DEEPDENE GDNS
FAIRVIEW PL
WIMBART RD
BRADING RD
OSTADE RD
CRASTER RD
CRAIGNAIR RD
TULSE HILL
PAPWORTH WAY
CROSBY WLK
NEW PARK RD
MORRISH RD
RODMILL LA
SULINA RD
TILSON GDNS
FORSTER RD
A205
STREATHAM PL
HOLMEWOOD RD
HOLMEWOOD GDNS
BROCKHAM DR
REDLANDS WAY
MAPLESTEAD RD
CLAVERDALE RD
ATHLONE RD
MACKIE RD
HILLWORTH RD
HAMBRIDGE WAY
HARDEL WLK
Tulse Hill
BODLEY MANOR WAY
BROCKWELL PARK GDNS
TRINITY RISE
1 DUTTON HO
2 CONSTANTINE HO
3 POULLETT HO
4 AXFORD HO
LANGHOLM CL
TENBURY CT
ASPINALL HO
HAYES CT
FORTROSE GDNS
TIERNEY RD
MONTRELL RD
VIBART GDNS
SAXONFIELD CL
ROMAN RISE
UPPER TULSE HILL
EWEN CRES
ATWATER CL
BANNISTER CL
Liby
SKIFFINGTON CL
CHALLICE WAY
MARNFIELD CRES
HUGGINS PL
RICKARD CL
GAYWOOD CL
TA Ctr
TERRY HO
SCOLES CRES
DERONDA RD
BERWYN RD
TRUST WLK
COTHERSTONE RD
GARDEN LA
ROUPELL RD
LIMETREE CL
CHRISTCHURCH RD
ABBOTS PK
HIGH TREES
MORRISON HO
JARRETT CL
ABBOTS CL
DEERBROOK RD
ROMOLA RD
NORWOOD RD
ST FAITH'S RD
KIRKSTALL GDNS
KIRKSTALL RD
TIERNEY TERR
PULLMAN CT
SW2
DAYSBROOK RD
ARDFIELD CL
BARSTOW CRES
DUCAVEL HO
COBURG CRES
Streatham Hill
TELFORD AVE
STREATHAM HILL
CORNER FIELDE
BATY HO
PRESENTATION MEWS
PONTON HO
ROYCROFT CL
MASKALL CL
A204
COPPIN CT
THORNTON AVE
SALFORD RD
CRIFFEL AVE
BELLASIS AVE
KILLIESER AVE
BARRHILL RD
Sch
WAVERTREE RD
WYATT PARK RD
NORMANHURST RD
NUTHURST AVE
BUSHELL CL
PALACE RD
CHALNER HO
HARDEL RISE
PERRAN RD
STATION RISE
Tulse Hill
A205
GOODMAN CRES
Tenn Cts
BLAIRDERRY RD
ARDWELL RD
DOWNTON AVE
REDHILL CT
LANERCOST RD
LANERCOST CL
PROBYN RD
LUPIN CL
PARADE MEWS
AVENUE PARK RD
MALEY AVE
FAWLEY CT
ELMCOURT RD
HILLSIDE RD
HANNAY WLK
DORRIEN WLK
B221
STERNHOLD AVE
CRICKLADE AVE
BARCOMBE AVE
FAYGATE RD
HILLSIDE GDNS
ULVERSTONE RD
ORFORD CT
DREWSTEAD RD
AMESBURY AVE
KINGSMEAD RD
MAYTREE WLK
NORTHSTEAD RD
KINFAUNS RD
WILLIAM BROWN CT
LANCASTER AVE
COLIN CT
Bwg Gn
Streatham Hill
Bwg Gn
STREATHAM CL
HALSHAM AVE
LYDHURST AVE
1 DESPARD HO
2 PALACE CT
ST MARTIN'S CT
PENRITH PL
HARPENDEN RD
ULLSWATER RD
BROADLANDS AVE
DE MONTFORT RD
Inst
Prim Sch
LEIGHAM VALE
ADARE WLK
KEYMER RD
HITHERFIELD RD
The Woodfield Ctr
WOODFIELD AVE
CHALCOT MEWS
CROMER CT
ALBANS CL
MOUNTEARL GDNS
STOCKFIELD RD
CANUTE CT
TRAEMORE CT
KNOLLY'S RD
KNOLLY'S CL
CAMBRIAN CL
YORK HILL
SNOW HO
DALTON ST
MOUNT EPHRAIM LA
BRANCASTER RD
BLAKEMORE RD
MOORCROFT RD
STREATHAM CT
MANOR CT
CHERRY TREE DR
GARDEN FLATS
BELENOYD CT
MOUNT NOD RD
BARNARD CT
TINA CT
PEVENSEY CT
PORTAL CL
ROYAL CIR
WAYLETT PL
NORFOLK HOUSE RD
LEIGHAM AVE
LEIGHAM COURT RD
ROSEDENE AVE
KINGSCOURT RD
WOODBOURNE CL
STREATHAM HIGH RD
THE HIGH PAR
WOODLEIGH GDNS
CONIFER GDNS
CULVERHOUSE GDNS
LEIGH ORCHARD CL
ROMEYN RD
THURLOW TOWERS
BROXHOLM RD
LANSDOWNE HILL
CHARTHAM GR
PYRMONT GR
WALDECK GR
MOUNT VILLAS
CANTERBURY GR
BLOOM GR
A215
WOODBOURNE AVE
Tenn Cts
STEEP HILL
OCKLEY RD
Dunraven Sch
LEITHCOTE PATH
GLENNIE RD
EGREMONT RD
IVYMOUNT RD
YEOMAN CL
GLYN CT
CANTERBURY GR
TRIAD MEWS
PRIORESS RD
DODBROOKE RD
HAINTHORPE RD
PI Fld
GRACEFIELD GDNS
IVYDAY GR
MILFORD MEWS
CAROLINE CL
CAREW HO
ST PETER'S GDNS
CHICHESTER MEWS
THURLESTONE RD
SELSDON RD
FRANKLIN CL
NETTLEFOLD PL
BUTTERWORTH CT
PENDENNIS RD
NEWCOMBE GDNS
LEITHCOTE GDNS
WOLFINGTON RD
COTSWOLD ST
BECMEAD AVE
Liby
PINFOLD RD
ASTORIA PAR
A23
SAMUEL JOHNSON CL
LEIGHAM CL
ROCKHAMPTON RD
UFFINGTON RD
BEADMAN PL
KNIGHT'S HILL SQ
SE27
UNEHAM
PRENTIS RD
FARM AVE
ANGLES RD
UJIMA HO
UJIMA CT
SCARBOROUGH RD
SOUTH OAK RD
Sp Gd
THE GLEBE
SHRUBBERY
TOOTING BEC GD
SUNNYHILL
Julians
FARM RD
ERNEST
1
2
3
4
5
6
72
73
74
75
30
31

139
183
162
A
B
C
D
6
5
4
3
2
1
75
74
73
72
Herne Hill
HERNE HILL
A215
Lambeth
Southwark
A2214
HALF MOON LA
VILLAGE WAY
EAST DULWICH GR
LORDSHIP LA
A2216
B219
SE22
SE24
SE21
SE27
East Dulwich
North Dulwich
King's Coll
Herne Hill Stadium
Dulwich Hamlet Sch
Sunray Gdns
Alleyn's Sch
Girls Sch
CE Inf Sch
Dulwich Village
Dulwich College
Dulwich Park
Belair Park
Rosendale Prim Sch & Turney Sch
Oakfield Sch
Art Gall
DULWICH COMM
A205
CROXTED RD
A2199
SOUTH CROXTED RD
THURLOW PARK RD
West Dulwich
Dulwich Coll (Endowed)
Dulwich & Sydenham
COLLEGE RD
GRANGE LA
Knight's Hill
Knight's Hill Tunnel
West Norwood
Cemy
Crem
Elm Wood Prim Sch
Dulwich Coll Prep Sch
Kingsdale Sch
Dulwich
Sydenham Hill
Dulwich Wood
LOW CROSS WOOD LA
CROXTED MEWS
BURBAGE RD
TURNEY RD
COURT LA
WOODWARDE RD
TOWNLEY RD
CALTON AVE
DULWICH VILLAGE
GALLERY RD
FRANK DIXON WAY
HUNTS SLIP RD
TOLLGATE DR
CARVER RD
RED POST HILL
GREEN DALE
MELBOURNE GR
ASHBOURNE GR
CHESTERFIELD GR
PLAYFIELD CRES
BARRY RD
DEKKER RD
DRUCE RD
EASTLANDS CRES
COURT LANE GDNS
EYNELLA RD
GIANT ARCHE RD
PICKWICK RD
ROSEWAY
LAIRDALE CL
ROSENDALE RD
DALMORE RD
LANCASTER AVE
CHATSWORTH WAY
ROBSON RD
CHESTNUT RD
PARK HALL RD
ACACIA GR
ALLEYN PK
ALLEYN RD
CLIVE RD
GAINSBOROUGH CT
WOODHALL AVE
PECKARMANS WOOD
CROUCHMANS CL
KINGSDALE
LYALL AVE
NORWOOD RD

A
B
C
D
140
East Dulwich
Peckham Rye Park
Waverley Sch (Lower)
Honor Oak
Camberwell New Cemy
SE22
Camberwell Old Cemetery
Brenchley Gardens
One Tree Hill (Recn Gd)
Honor Oak Park
HONOR OAK PK
FOREST HILL RD
BARRY RD
A2216
B219
B238
Fairlawn Prim Sch
SE23
Horniman Sch
Horniman Mus
LONDON RD
The Grove
161
A205
WALDRAM PARK RD
Forest Hill
DARTMOUTH RD
PERRY VALE
B227
Dulwich & Sydenham
Dulwich Wood
Sydenham Hill Wood (Nat Res)
SE26
Eliot Bank Prim Sch
Sydenham Sec Sch
Forest Hill Sec Sch
Sydenham Wells Park
Mayow Park
184
6
5
4
3
2
1
75
74
73
72
34
35

Brockley
Ladywell
CATFORD
Forest Hill
Bellingham
Bell Green
Lewisham Park
SE6
141
164
185
37
A
B
C
D
1
2
3
4
5
6
72
73
74
75
38
BROCKLEY RD
BROCKLEY RISE
STONDON PK
STANSTEAD RD
CATFORD HILL
PERRY HILL
PERRY RISE
BELL GN
RUSHEY GN
BROMLEY RD
LEWISHAM HIGH ST
ADELAIDE AVE
LADYWELL RD
CATFORD RD
CATFORD BR
B236
B218
B238
B227
A21
A205
A212
A2218
Brockley Cemy
Ladywell Cemy
Brockley Prim Sch
Crofton Park
Crofton L Ctr
Crofton Sch
Ladywell Fields
Greyhound Stadium
Ladywell Arena
Lewisham
Guy's Hospital Athletic Gd
Stillness Jun & Inf Schs
Holbeach Prim Sch
St Dunstan's Coll
Catford Bridge
Catford Gyratory
Rushey Green Prim Sch
Rathfern Prim Sch
Kilmorie Prim Sch
Greenvale Sch
Adamsrill Prim Sch
Athelney Prim Sch
Elfrida Sch
Bromley Ret Pk
Bellingham Trad Est
Superstore
Stanton Sq
STANTON WAY
Pool River
Ravensbourne River
Liby
PO
Allot Gdns
Tenn Cts
Pav

LEWISHAM
LEE HIGH RD
142
A
B
C
D
SLAITHWAITE RD
MORLEY RD
WRIGHT CL
HOLLY LO
TRINITY CL
COLLEGE PARK
DERMODY RD
HOLLY HEDGE TERR
WEARDALE RD
MERIDAN CT
HAMLET CL
OLD RD
Liby
BANKWELL RD
AISLIBIE RD
LENHAM RD
LAMPMEAD RD
SIMS WLK
B212
Lee Green
PO
ST PETER'S CT
A20
A2212
LEEGATE
BURNT ASH RD
CARSTON CL
Tenn Cts
Manor House Gardens
BRIGHTFIELD RD
HEDGLEY MEWS
HEDGLEY ST
Sch
TAUNTON RD
BARNSTAPLE HO
WIMBORNE CL
MERRIDALE
EFFINGHAM RD
Brindishe Prim Sch
RC Inf Sch
HANDEN RD
MICHELDEVER RD
SE12
SOUTHBROOK RD
SOUTHBROOK MEWS
CHILTONIAN IND EST
SYCAMORE CT
HOLME LACEY RD
DALLINGER RD
LUCORN CL
RC Jun Sch
Lee
KIMBOLTON CL
LANAIN CT
NEWSTEAD RD
ANNE COMPTON MEWS
BIRCH GR
WILDWOOD CL
STONEY CROFT CL
PARKCROFT RD
MANOR LA
MILBOROUGH CRES
Allot Gdns
A205
ST MILDREDS RD
KENDALL HO
HELDER GR
RAYFORD AVE
LINCHMERE RD
WAITE DAVIES RD
SUMMERFIELD ST
IVVER RD
NORTHBROOK RD
CORDWELL RD
WOLFRAM CL
KELLERTON RD
CHALCROFT RD
THORNWOOD RD
GUARDIAN CT
MANOR PK
Manor Park
Quaggy River
Prim Sch
STAPLEHURST RD
LONGHURST RD
LEAMINGTON VILLAS
HEREFORD GDNS
LEAHURST RD
FERNBROOK RD
Lee Manor Sch
Hither Green
MANOR LA
Hither Green
LEWISHAM HIGH ST
LADYWELL RD
B236
Leis Ctr
Ladywell
COLFE & HATCHCLIFFE'S GLEBE
LONGBRIDGE WAY
COURTHILL RD
Allot Gdns
LEGGE ST
ROMBOROUGH WAY
ROMBOROUGH GDNS
CAMPSHILL RD
CAMPSHILL PL
GUYSCLIFF RD
Sch
CHIDDING STONE
MONUMENT GDNS
BENDEN HO
CANADA GDNS
KEMPS GDNS
THORNFORD RD
RYECROFT RD
MERBURY CL
KNOWLES HILL CRES
BROMLEY CT
ENNERSDALE RD
NIGHTINGALE GR
SE13
HOLLYDENE
HOLM HURST
SWITHUNS CL
MAYTHORNE COTTS
PASCOE RD
CANTERBURY
Lewisham Park
KEMSLEY
MALLING
BREDGAR
Lewisham
H
HARVARD RD
FORDYCE RD
LITTLEWOOD
RADFORD RD
LANIER RD
MOUNT FIELD CT
BEACON RD
ARDMERE RD
BRIGHTSIDE RD
MALLET RD
ELTHRUDA RD
THEODORE RD
LEWISHAM PK
PLUMMER CT
MOUNT PLEASANT RD
ROXLEY RD
ALDWORTH GR
GEORGE LA
LARA CL
SPRINGRICE RD
HITHER GREEN LA
DUNCRIEVIE RD
SPRINGBANK RD
BLAGDON RD
5
6
75
74
73
72
4
3
2
1
DAVENPORT RD
SYCAMORE GR
ROSENTHAL RD
Bwg Gn
STONE LA
OAKLEY DR
ULLUNDA RD
HIGHFIELD CL
HOSPITAL WAY
ATHER CL
WELLMEADOW RD
FARLEY RD
HONLEY RD
FAIRFIELDS
CUDHAM ST
RINGSTEAD RD
Mountsfield Park
CARSWELL RD
Pl Fld
MELBOURNE MEWS
REDFERN RD
BRITTON CL
MOUNTFIELD CL
STAINTON RD
THE WOODLANDS
WOODLANDS ST
BENIN ST
BLASHFORD ST
A21
A205
LALEHAM RD
BROWNHILL RD
295
308
PLASSY RD
163
Catford Story
BOWNESS RD
JUTLAND RD
ELMER RD
FLEET TERR
SPORTSBANK ST
ENGLEHEART RD
HARRIS LO
SANGLEY RD
WINDSOR MEWS
CULVERLEY RD
Allot Gdns
SHORNDEAN ST
ST FILLANS RD
ARNGASK RD
FORDEL RD
GLENFARG RD
SANDHURST MKT
SANDHURST RD
TORRIDON RD
ARDGOWAN RD
MINARD RD
Sandhurst Jun & Inf Schs
WELLMEADOW RD
FURTHER GREEN RD
Holy Cross RC Prim Sch
Rushey Green Prim Sch
KILLEARN RD
BRAIDWOOD RD
BROADFIELD RD
PASTURE RD
SOUTH PARK CRES
SEDGEWAY
CUMBERLAND PL
PENERLEY RD
BARGERY RD
BURLEIGH WLK
INCHMERY RD
SAMBRUCK MEWS
THORNSBEACH RD
PENBERTH RD
MUIRKIRK RD
DOWANHILL RD
Pl Fld
Pav
ABBOTSHALL RD
BALLOCH RD
BIRKHALL RD
ARDFILLAN RD
HAFTON RD
VERDANT LA
Cemy
ARRAN RD
NEWQUAY RD
SE6
MERCHISTON RD
ARDOCH RD
LUNCIES MEWS
Allot Gdns
Torridon Inf & Jun Sch
HAZELBANK RD
Allot Gdns
CRANTOCK RD
PENDERRY RISE
Bwg Gn
GREENSIDE CL
Pav
WENTLAND CL
WENTLAND RD
MORDRED RD
BAUDWIN RD
CASTILLON RD
WINGROVE RD
EVANS RD
CRUTCHLEY RD
DOWNHAM ENT CTR
Crem
CALLANDER RD
DANEBY RD
MELIOT RD
ECTOR RD
PELLINORE RD
PERSANT RD
BOUNDFIELD RD
BELLINGHAM RD
Pav
Pl Fld
Tenn Cts
Catford Girls' Sch
Forster Park
BATTERSBY RD
LONGHILL RD
SCARLET RD
HEXAL RD
GILTON RD
Forster Park Prim Sch
WATERS RD
JENNIFER RD
ROUNDTABLE RD
BROMLEY RD
235
WOODHAM RD
DANESWOOD AVE
1 NEWNHAM HO
2 WHITCHURCH HO
PASSFIELDS
CARSTAIRS RD
BOSBURY RD
ARKINDALE RD
COMSBOROUGH CRES
WHITEFOOT TERR
LINCOMBE RD
BIDEFORD RD
ILFRACOMBE RD
LENTMEAD RD
UNDERSHAW RD
SHAW RD
SHAW PATH
WOODBANK RD
SHROFFOLD RD
NORTHOVER
CRANMORE RD
WHITEFOOT LA
Pav
Pl Fld
Green Chain Wlk
NUBIA WAY
FORSTER HO
FALKLAND HO
LEEDS CT
ORFORD CT
ALLERFORD RD
WATERBANK RD
38
A
St John Baptist Sch
Southend
COTTON HILL
B
39
186
C
New Woodlands Sch
D
BROCKMAN RISE
SOUTHVIEW RD
HADDINGTON RD
OAKSHADE RD
DOWNDERRY RD
Downderry Prim Sch
CHURCHDOWN
MOORSIDE RD
CAPSTONE RD
LAMEROCK RD
TRISTRAM RD
CAMLAN RD
GITTENS CL
BEACHBOROUGH
Allot Gdns
WATERMEAD RD
NAYLAND HO
A2218
A21
Sch
RAVENSCAR RD

A
B
C
D
143
75
6
5
74
4
166
3
73
2
1
72
42
41
187
40
Quaggy River
Sutcliffe Park
Running Tk
Riverston Sch
ELTHAM RD
A20
A210
A2213
A205
A2
ELTHAM HILL
WESTHORNE AVE
Eltham Green
Yorkshire Grey
Eltham Green Sch
Eltham Hill Coll for Girls
Moatbridge Sch
Cliftons Roundabout
Colfe's Sch
Colfe's Prep Sch
Lee
ELTHAM PALACE RD
Lewisham
Greenwich
Bromley
Horn Park
SE12
SE9
Mottingham Farm
Hadlow Coll
The Grange (Eltham Coll Jun Sch)
Eltham Coll
Mottingham
Green Chain Wlk
GROVE PARK RD
Grove Park
Northbrook Park
BARING RD
A2212
A221
CHINBROOK RD
B226
Malory Sch
SIDCUP RD
LYME FARM RD
RAVENS WAY
UPWOOD RD
CROWN CT
PITFOLD CL
PITFOLD RD
WOODSTOCK CT
JASMINE CT
HORNCASTLE RD
WOODYATES RD
SIMNEL RD
SIBTHORPE RD
GAVESTONE RD
ALNWICK RD
HORSA RD
PASTON CRES
HENGIST RD
MOTTINGHAM LA
WINN RD
MELROSE CL
GUIBAL RD
BURNT ASH HILL
EXFORD RD
ASHDALE RD
JEVINGTON WAY
WESTDEAN AVE
SENLAC RD
FARMCOTE RD
ASHWATER RD
HEATHER RD
KINGSAND RD
PRAGNELL RD
COOPERS LA
SANDSTONE RD
SOMERTREES AVE
BALDER RISE
LE MAY AVE
LUFFMAN RD
MARVELS LA
ALICE THOMPSON CL
EDWARD TYLER RD
PENNINGTON WAY
HALL VIEW
CEDAR MOUNT
CARTERS HILL CL
KIPPINGTON DR
WEST HALLOWES
THE CROSSWAY
SILVERDALE DR
LULWORTH RD
ELMHURST RD
COURT FARM RD
DUNKERY RD
CASTLETON RD
DUDDINGTON CL
CLAYHILL CRES
RIDDONS RD
ROSEVEARE RD
LEAFY OAK RD
DYNELEY RD
LAMBSCROFT AVE
ALDERSGROVE AVE
CHARLES FIELD
MIRROR PATH
ROBINS CT
MEADOW LA
AMBLECOTE RD
AMBLECOTE MDW
CHINBROOK CRES
PULLMAN MEWS
IVORYDOWN
GARETH GR
GERAINT RD
GALAHAD RD
DOWNHAM WAY
RIVERBANK RD
PENDRAGON RD
BEDIVERE RD
BALLAMORE RD
REIGATE RD
STRATFIELD HO
BARING CL
PALACE VIEW
PEGLEY GDNS
HOSER AVE
OAK APPLE CT
BRAMDEAN CRES
ASHGROVE
HARLAND RD
GORDON HO
RATCLIFFE CL
KINGSHURST RD
ELWYN GDNS
CORONA RD
DANESCOMBE
1 DIANNE CT
2 ELLESMERE CT
3 NICHOLAS CT
4 CLIFTONVILLE CT
5 WESTGATE CT
GILLAN CT 1
NAPIER CT 2
ROTHESAY CT 3
MERRYFIELD HO 1
RYDENS HO 2
BUSHEY HO 3
CHURCHBURY RD
CAMPFIELD RD
FERNDOWN RD
GLASBROOK RD
MIDDLE PARK AVE
NEWMARKET GN
GREGORY CRES
JOAN CRES
CUFF CRES
THE VISTA
QUEENSCROFT RD
KINGSGROUND
BLANN CL
ALWOLD CRES
RYELANDS CRES
ABERGELDIE RD
STRATHAVEN RD
SCOTSDALE RD
CRATHIE RD
CEDARHURST DR
SHELDON CL
HORN PARK LA
HORN PARK CL
ADDISON
JEFFREY ROW
LILIAN BARKER CL
ANN STROUD CT
REED CL
WOODVILLE CL
LEYBRIDGE CT
OSBERTON RD
CAMBRIDGE DR
ROSE WAY
SILK CL
DORVILLE RD
ALANTHUS CL
BUCKDEN CL
LEEWOOD CL
LEYLAND RD
COURTLANDS AVE
SUNNYDALE RD
FAIRBY RD
SOUTHBOURNE GDNS
MIDSUMMER AV
MOON CT
SPRINGVALE CT
CAMBERT WAY
KIMBELL PL
MEADOWSIDE
ELTHAM GREEN RD
FARNABY RD
BAYFIELD RD
EALDHAM SQ
PERITON RD
BEDGEBURY RD
JEKEN RD
MESSENT RD
SHAWBROOKE RD
KATHERINE GDNS
KNOCKHOLT RD
PHILIPPA GDNS
LEGATT RD
KENWARD RD
HORSFIELD RD
HAIMO RD
LIONEL RD
LIONEL GDNS
MAYERNE RD
GREEN WAY
FROISSART RD
KEYNSHAM GDNS
KEYNSHAM RD
VANDYKE CROSS
PRINCE JOHN RD
Pav
Sp Gd
Tenn Cts
Allot Gdns
Sch
PO
Bwg Gn
Recn Gd
Pl Fld
Nat Res
L Ctr
Liby
TA Ctr
THOMAS DINWIDDY RD

A
B
C
D
144
188
165
42
43
44
75
74
73
72
1
2
3
4
5
6
A2
A20
A205
A208
A210
A211
B226
B263
ELTHAM
SE9
Well Hall Pleasaunce
Tenn Cts
Sp Gd
Pav
Bwg Gns
Eltham
Eltham Park South
GREENVALE RD
ELTHAM PARK GDNS
DUNVEGAN RD
GLENLEA RD
GLENLYON RD
GLENSHIEL RD
GLENURE RD
Recn Gd
Green Chain Wlk
Eltham Warren
CH
St Mary's RC Prim Sch
WELL HALL RD
STRONGBOW RD
STRONGBOW CRES
ARCHERY RD
BALCASKIE RD
BEECHILL RD
GLENHOUSE RD
ELSTOW CL
ELSTOW RD
DOBELL RD
GOUROCK RD
FRIARS MEWS
BLUNTS RD
ORANGERY LA
FIFTEENPENNY FIELDS
LABURNHAM PL
ELDERSLIE RD
HAMLET HO
GREENHOLM RD
McAULEY CL
HORSFIELD RD
FROISSART RD
BASKETT GDNS
PULLMAN PL
TATTERSALL CL
KEYNSHAM GDNS
MILNE GDNS
KEYNSHAM RD
BLOXAM GDNS
EVEREST RD
SHERARD RD
LASSA RD
JOHN RD
PRINCE JOHN RD
VANDYKE CROSS
LILBURNE RD
LILBURNE GDNS
CARNECKE GDNS
ROLANDE GDNS
SOWERBY CL
HAIMO RD
LIONEL RD
LIONEL GDNS
DAVERNE RD
ELTHAM HILL
Tenn Cts
Eltham Hill Tech Coll for Girls
Eltham Hill Sch
QUEENSCROFT RD
BEACH CT
CEDAR CT
GROVE MARKET PL
RUSKIN CT
WYTHFIELD RD
KING'S ORCH
1 WEATHERSFIELD CT
2 PHILPOT PATH
ELTHAM HIGH ST
ELIZABETH TERR
PASSEY PL
PHILIPOT ALMSHO
ST MARY'S PL
POUND PL
MESSETER PL
WOODINGTON CL
MARLOWE GDNS
PIPPENHALL
WYTHENS WLK
SOUTHEND CRES
SOUTHEND CL
OAKWAYS
BUTTERFLY LA
Allot Gdns
Nursery
Liby
TH
Sch
Bwg Gn
TRINITY CT
NORTH PK
WENSLEY CL
WOLSEY CT
PALACE CT
CHAUNDRYE CL
COURTYARD
MOAT CT
TILT YARD APP
GREENACRES
DARWIN CT
ELMSLIE CT
LADYSMITH RD
HALONS RD
ENSLIN RD
Allot Gdns
KINGSGROUND
KING JOHN'S WLK
Green Chain Wlk
Eltham Palace
CUFF CRES
LASBROOK RD
THE VISTA
NEWMARKET GN
MIDDLE PARK AVE
Pl Fld
King John's Wlk
JOAN CRES
Green Chain Wlk
1 BRITTAIN CT
2 BRITTAIN HO
WOODLANDS
COURT RD
TARNWOOD PK
Mottingham
The Tarn
SHRUBSALL CL
STATION APP
1 POPE STREET CT
2 MOTTINGHAM CT
3 PICKWICK CT
4 ROYAL CT
Royal Blackheath
Tenn Cts
Tenn Ct
WICA DR
Pavs
CLARE CNR
FOOTSCRAY RD
CAMBRIDGE GN
CASTLEFORD AVE
IVOR GR
HAINAULT ST
BLANMERLE RD
Sp Gd
SIDCUP RD
KIPPINGTON DR
MOTTINGHAM GDNS
LAYZELL WLK
WEST HALLOWES
LUXFIELD RD
PRIORY LEAS
HINTON CL
WEST PK
CROSSMEAD
COLLEGE VIEW
HIGHCOMBE CL
SYCAMORE CL
Tenn Cts
Fairy Hill
BROAD LAWN
New Eltham
PARK VIEW RD
EDITH POND CT
St Olaves Prep Sch
HARTSMEAD RD
DOWNLEYS CL
LEYSDOWN RD
MIMSTRY WAY
BILL HAMLING CL
PORCUPINE CL
L Ctr
GREEN LANE BSNS PK
Greenacres Prim Sch & Language Impairment Unit
Games Cts
Coldharbour Sp Ctr
BROOKS CL
Altash Gardens
ALTASH WAY
DEVONSHIRE RD
DORSET RD
PORTLAND RD
THE CROSSWAY
GROVE PARK RD
SILVERDALE DR
CLARENCE RD
LULWORTH RD
MARGARET GARDNER DR
BOWMEAD
BIRBETTS RD
CHAPEL FARM RD
LAVIDGE RD
AVONDALE RD
Fiveways
SOUTHWOOD RD
SOUTHWOOD HO
CADWALLON RD
COLYER CL
LARCHWOOD RD
GREEN LA
CHARLDANE RD
FELHAMPTON RD
CHANCTONBURY WAY
MONTBELLE RD
HIGH POINT
Montbelle Prim Sch
DOMONIC DR
ELMHURST RD
MODEL FARM CL
ALBERT RD
SHOTTERY CL
BLANCHARD CL
GEFFREY'S CT
BELVOIR CL
NUNNINGTON CL
MOTTINGHAM RD
THE UNDERWOOD
WITHERSTON WAY
WYNFORD WAY
WOODCROFT
BROMHEDGE
LITTLEMEDE
1 THE LINK
2 THE MOUND
3 COLDHARBOUR CREST
4 JAMES NEWMAN CT
PARTRIDGE GN
BAREFOOT DR
LEAS DALE
BADGERS CROFT
THE COURSE
CROUCH CROFT
COLEMANS HEATH
KINGSLEY WOOD DR
LONGCROFT
SANDLING RISE
SOUTHOLD RISE
SPEKEHILL
WILLIAM BAREFOOT DR
GREAT HARRY DR
HOLME LACEY
Tenn Cts
Allot Gdns
COURT FARM RD
Recn Gd
SENNEN WLK
WIDECOMBE RD
THURSLEY RD
RAVENSWORTH RD
RAVENSCROFT CRES
BUCKLER GDNS
Pl Fld
DUNKERY RD
HARTING RD
BEACONSFIELD RD
HASSOP WLK
KERSEY GDNS
HORNING CL
FRAMLINGHAM CRES
TENTERDEN CL
KIMMERIDGE RD
SMARDEN GR
SWITHLAND GDNS
BEAUMANOR GDNS
MILVERTON WAY
ADDERLEY GDNS
BEANSHAW
SHALLONS RD
BROWNSPRING DR
Greenwich
Bromley
CALCOTT WLK
CUDDINGTON CL

A
B
C
D
145
Cemy
THE GREEN
FALCONWOOD PAR
PO
Tenn Ct
SUTHERLAND AVE
GLOUCESTER AVE
SOMERSET AVE
KENT AVE
75
EAST ROCHESTER WAY
RIEFIELD RD
COLEPITS WOOD RD
Crown Woods Sch
FAIROAK DR
CROWN WOODS WAY
RENNETS WOOD RD
RENNETS CL
BOUNDARY RD
ORCHARD RISE W
RIDGEWAY W
DA15
GORDON RD
CHESTER RD
RIDGEWAY E
LEECHCROFT AVE
ORCHARD RISE E
BURLEIGH AVE
CURRAN AVE
LYNDON AVE
SUTHERLAND AVE
A2
6
WYNN'S AVE
GLOUCESTER PAR
A210
BLACKFEN RD
BEXLEY RD
LEMONWELL CT
LEMONWELL DR
PACKMORES RD
BLAIR CL
BUSHEY LEES
ALEXANDER CL
MONTGOMERY CL
WAVELL DR
QUEENSWOOD RD
CHRISTOPHER CL
HAWTHORN TERR
LIME GR
SYCAMORE AVE
ASHCROFT AVE
WILLOW AVE
Univ of Greenwich Avery Hill Campus Mansion Site
B2214
AVERY HILL RD
RESTONS CRES
RIDER CL
KIRKLAND CL
PARISH GATE DR
RAEBURN RD
RONALDSTONE RD
FEN GR
FAIRFIELD CL
HARMAN DR
DAYS LA
5
Pav
Avery Hill
DORLAND HO 1
WOOTTON HO 2
WAYFIELD LINK 3
TEYNHAM HO 4
OSPRINGE CT 5
TRINITY MEWS 6
Avery Hill Park
ANSTRIDGE RD
ALDERWOOD RD
RAINHAM CL
Sch
LYDDEN CT
PERPINS RD
LINSTED CT
THANINGTON CT
COPSEWOOD CL
HOLBEACH GDNS
CLOVERDALE GDNS
Our Lady of the Rosary RC Prim Sch
CAITHNESS GDNS
ELMCROFT AVE
ASHCROFT
Allot Gdns
74
SE9
Univ of Greenwich Avery Hill Campus Southwood Site
RESTONS CRES
BERWICK CRES
Hollyoak Wood Park
Liby
CEDAR AVE
BEECH AVE
HADDON GR
NORFOLK CRES
RADFIELD WAY
SOUTHSPRING
GREENHITHE CL
ROSEBERY AVE
HARBOROUGH AVE
OAKLANDS AVE
4
Tenn Cts
Bwg Gn
Sparrow's Farm L Ctr
Valley L Ctr
CROYDE CL
HAMBLEDOWN RD
OVERMEAD
ARLINGTON CL
CORBYLANDS RD
BEVERLEY AVE
SHUTTLE CL
ANNANDALE RD
Willersley Park
Green Chain Wlk
FOREST WAY
MERRILEES RD
WILLERSLEY AVE
WHITE OAK GDNS
LACEBARK CL
168
Sp Gd
Greenwich
Bexley
WOODBINE RD
CORBYLAND RD
CYPRESS TREE CL
ACACIA WAY
ROWANWOOD AVE
ALVERSTONE GDNS
TIVERTON DR
SPARROWS LA
CAMBRIA CL
WOODLANDS AVE
WYNCHAM AVE
ELDER CL
WILLERSLEY CL
Allot Gdns
Works
CROMBIE RD
HALFWAY ST
BRAUNTON AVE
3
AVERY HILL RD
SIDEWOOD RD
ELLISON RD
WEST TERR
EAST TERR
BRENTWOOD CL
LANNOY RD
CRADLEY RD
VALLIERS WOOD RD
MAPLE LEAF DR
Burnt Oak Jun Sch
REVENTLOW RD
GAITSKELL
NOVAR RD
EASTNOR RD
MERCHLAND RD
KEIGHTLEY DR
ROBERTS CL
BEAVERBANK RD
VINCENT CL
LONGMEADOW RD
BROOKEND RD
BRINDLE GATE
FIRSIDE GR
BAYTREE CL
LARCH GR
MARRABON CL
HOLLIES AVE
PINEWOOD AVE
OAKLEY DR
MILNER WLK
LAMORBEY CL
LINGEY CL
OLD FARM RD W
73
PO
Liby
ELLIS CL
OLD FARM AVE
B2214
New Eltham
Allot Gdns
DA15
BERCTA RD
BISHOPS CL
Dulverton Prim Sch
BURSDON CL
OLD FARM RD E
2
DULVERTON RD
RUTLAND CT
AGATON RD
CRAYBURY END
EMMINGTON RD
BRENDON RD
CHARTWELL CL
TELFORD RD
FRENSHAM RD
BROOKLANDS AVE
WESTBROOKE RD
Allot Gdns
King George's Field
Pl Fld
LONGLANDS CT 1
THE FIRS 2
SANDALWOOD HO 3
BUCKTHORN HO 4
MOAT CT 5
Sidcup
KINGSMEAD
YORK AVE
GLOUCESTER AVE
LITTLE BIRCHES
RUSHBROOK RD
GERDA RD
CADWALLON RD
THAXTED RD
CLAYFARM RD
MERVYN AVE
CORNWALLIS AVE
HARLAND AVE
GULLIVER RD
MARLWOOD CL
LONGLANDS PARK CRES
SIDCUP RD
CEDRIC RD
COUNTY GATE
ALDWICK CL
BLENHEIM CT
ST MARGARETS AVE
MARECHAL NIEL AVE
LONGLANDS RD
Allot Gdns
AUSTRAL CL
RANGEWORTH PL
GRANGE CL
MANOR RD
KENDALL CT
MOLESCROFT
BRAEMAR GDNS
MARECHAL NIEL PAR
PARKHILL RD
CROFT WAY
KNOLE GATE
WOODSIDE CRES
WOODSIDE RD
BEDFORD RD
CHYNGTON CL
Recn Gd
PRIESTLANDS PARK RD
STUDLAND CL
CRESCENT RD
1
West Lodge Sch
Tenn Cts
A20
MAIN RD
PO
Longlands Prim Sch
CURZON CT
BROWNSPRING DR
BR7
Drv Rng
Longlands
PEATFIELD CL
SHIRLEY RD
LYDD CL
APPLEDORE CRES
ALDER RD
ROWAN RD
TAYLORS CL
LARKFIELD RD
CHRISTCHURCH RD
SANDHURST RD
DANEHILL WLK
VICTORIA RD
A222
GRAVELWOOD CL
EDGEBURY WLK
IMPERIAL WAY
Mulligan's
Bwg Gn
Pav
Sp Gd
Tenn Cts
SIDCUP BY PASS RD
WOODCHURCH CL
PARTRIDGE RD
HERON
LYMINGE CL
NEVILLE CL
72
STANHOPE RD
HAMILTON RD
SLADES DR
EDGEHILL RD
45
189
MINERVA CL
LINDEN CT
GILLIES CT
ORCHARD RD
EDWIN ARNOLD CT
46
CLIFTON RD
STAFFORD RD
CHELSITER CT
BERENS CT
A211
CAMBRIDGE RD
PRESTON CT
Tenn

BEXLEY
146
A
B
C
D
Tenn Cts
Bexley Gram Sch
Danson Park
Pl Fld
The Lake
DA6
Allot Gdns
DANSON RD
SYDNEY RD
ASKERN CL
SOUTH CL
BEAN RD
COBHAM P
IVERHURST CL
ALERS RD
GREEN VALE
BRASTED CL
SANDHURST RD
PENGARTH RD
PENN LA
BROOK LA
WELLINGTON RD
LODGE LA
CORONATION CL
MARGARET RD
DANSON RD
Danson Intc
A221
LAKESIDE CL
EAST ROCHESTER WAY
WOODSIDE LA
B2210
BLENDON RD
BANWELL RD
CEDAR GR
BEECHWAY
BLENDON DR
THE SANCTUARY
THE CRESCENT
THE AVENUE
THE DRIVE
DA5
BLADINDON DR
Tenn Cts
MONTPELIER AVE
DORCHESTER AVE
CROFTON AVE
ALBANY CL
ALBANY RD
HOWARD AVE
SHIRLEY AVE
Recn Gd
Hurst Prim Sch
PENFOLD LA
SHOREHAM CL
STANSTED CRES
A222
CARISBROOKE AVE
RUTLAND CL
COTLEIGH AVE
STEYNTON AVE
Cemy
Albany Park
LONGMEAD DR
CHERRYDOWN RD
GOODWIN DR
EATON RD
ONSLOW DR
KIMBERLEY DR
NORMAN PAR
HAREFIELD RD
MAYLANDS DR
ROYAL RD
PRINCES CL
CLEVE RD
LADBROOKE CRES
ST ANDREWS RD
Cleeve Park Sch
North Cray Wood
DA14
FAIRWATER
MERLIN RD
WENDOVER WAY
COWPER CL
KENT AVE
SOMERSET
SUTHERLAND AVE
INGLETON AVE
RADNOR AVE
Allot Gdns
GROOMBRIDGE CL
TYRRELL AVE
WELLAN CL
A2
LYNDON AVE
CURRAN AVE
BURLEIGH AVE
WYNN'S AVE
A210
GLOUCESTER PAR
WELLINGTON PAR
GWILLIM CL
MERINO PL
OVERCOURT CL
PARK MEAD
WESTERHAM DR
BLACKFEN RD
HAWTHORN TERR
LIME GR
SYCAMORE AVE
ASHCROFT AVE
WILLOW AVE
MAPLE CRES
WELLINGTON AVE
PENSHURST AVE
BURNS AVE
CLAYWORTH CL
FOUNTAIN CT
BLACKFEN PAR
Blackfen Sch for Girls
Sherwood Park Prim Sch
BLEDDYN CL 1
DANSON UNDERPASS 2
KESTLAKE RD 3
SHERWOOD CL
HARCOURT AVE
PENHILL RD
ELMCROFT AVE
ASHCROFT CRES
Blackfen
BOWES CL
PORTLAND AVE
SHERWOOD PARK AVE
RAMILLIES RD
DAYS LA
Sch
Allot Gdns
Hollyoak Wood Park
Liby
CEDAR AVE
BEECH AVE
THE OVAL
BURNT OAK LA
MEADOW VIEW
Allot Gdns
Penhill Park
Pav
HADDON GR
RUTLAND AVE
CAVENDISH AVE
SOMERHILL AVE
ROWLEY AVE
167
Willersley Park
Tenn Cts
MONTROSE AVE
HILL CREST
DENE AVE
OAKLEY PK
THE RISE
DA15
LACEBARK CL
Sch
REDWOOD CL
Marlborough Park
Pav
River Shuttle
CYPRESS TREE CL
ACACIA WAY
ROWANWOOD AVE
MARLBOROUGH PARK AVE
COLLINDALE AVE
BURNT OAK LA
VIEWFIELD RD
CHATSWORTH AVE
Chatsworth Inf Sch
Sidcup
Tenn Cts
Hurstmere Sch for Boys
WELBECK AVE
Tenn Cts
Burnt Oak Jun Sch
MARRABON CL
Rose Bruford Coll of Speech & Drama
Lamorbey Park
HURST RD
COTTAGE FIELD CL
EYNSFORD CRES
FESTIVAL CL
FOOTS CRAY LA
CHAUCER RD
BLENHEIM RD
Holy Trinity CE Prim Sch
LARCH GR
CHESTNUT CL
Chislehurst & Sidcup Gram Sch
ABBEYHILL RD
OLD FARM RD
B2214
Pl Fld
CANTERBURY AVE
OLD FARM RD E
A222
Allot Gdns
Abbeyhill Park
GREENWOOD CL
Pl Fld
Sidcup
KINGSMEAD CL
JUBILEE WAY
FARADAY AVE
HEMMINGS CL
CLEEVE PARK GDNS
PARKSIDE
MELVILLE RD
HATHERLEY CRES
TUDOR CT
Birkbeck Prim Sch
ALMA RD
GRANGE CL
MANOR RD
KENDALL CT
Waring Park
LUTON RD
LEWIS RD
HEATHERSIDE RD
ROSEWOOD CL
BIRCHWOOD AVE
THE CHEVENINGS
STATION RD
LAUREL CL
GRESSWELL CL
BECKS RD
LANSDOWN RD
DAMON CT
DAMON CL
Tenn Cts
WALTON RD
WREN RD
BEXLEY LA
CRESCENT RD
STUDLAND CL
CHRISTCHURCH RD
West Lodge Sch
LANGFORD PL
HATHERLEY RD
BIRKBECK RD
CLARENCE RD
CLARENCE CRES
DENBERRY DR
CAMBORNE RD
SANDHURST RD
DANEHILL WLK
STANLEY RD
CHERRY CT
TARLING CL
EMBASSEY CT
VICTORIA RD
A222
SHELBURY CL
ASTON CL
ASH CL
COLEBROOKE CT
WARREN RD
STANHOPE RD
GLEN CT
GRANVILLE MEWS
GRANVILLE RD
GATEACRE CT
HIGHVIEW RD
ST JOHN'S RD
THE DRIVE
FARWELL RD
NEVILLE CL
HAMILTON RD
BELTON RD
HADLOW RD
REBECCA CT
47
190
Pl Fld
A211
HIGH ST
Liby
MIRIAM CT
CHARLES CL
THE LAWNS
BEXLEY LA
Foots Cray Place
NELSON RD
1 CHUDLEIGH
6
5
4
3
2
1
75
74
73
72
46
48

147
191
A
B
C
D
75
6
5
74
4
3
73
2
1
72
48
49
50
DA5
DA6
DA14
STANDARD RD
PADDOCK
SUNLAND AVE
LENOR CL
RED HOUSE LA
WINDSOR
LEWIN RD
HEATHFIELD RD
LION RD
METHUEN RD
IZANE RD
HAWTHORN RD
ALBION RD
Liby
OAK RD
ROYAL OAK RD
VICTORIA RD
KINGSLEY CT
WARREN RD
WARREN CL
HIGHLAND RD
Ct
BROADWAY
WATLING ST
A207
PINNACLE
TA Ctr
BAYARD CT
Gravel Hill Prim Sch
Sch
LYNSTED CL
OAKHOUSE RD
ROSSLAND CL
HALCOT AVE
St Columba's RC Sch for Boys
1 THE MOUNT
2 ALCONBURY
3 GROVEBURY CT
4 CHRISTIE HO
5 NESBITT HO
6 CAREY CT
GRAVEL HILL
GRAVEL HILL CL
TIMOTHY CL
CHARLOTTE CL
CUXTON CL
HANSOL RD
BARTON CL
DITTON RD
MOUNT RD
MOUNT DR
SIBLEY CL
CH
ROBIN HOOD LA
UPTON RD
FRETA RD
BELLEVUE RD
MARTIN RISE
Tenn Cts
MARTIN DENE
OAKLANDS RD
OAKLANDS CL
FAIRWAY
GROSVENOR RD
OLRON CRES
Pl Fld
MEADOW CL
TOWNLEY RD
HIGHFIELD RD
HORSHAM RD
PETWORTH RD
HORLEY CL
MIDHURST HILL
LATHAM RD
FAYGATE CRES
BROOMFIELD RD
DASHWOOD CL
BROOMHILL RISE
BROOM MEAD
Upton Prim Sch
Townley Sch
Bexleyheath
IRIS AVE
UPTON CL
ARUNDEL CL
ROCHESTER DR
HENFIELD CL
CRANLEIGH CL
NEWICK CL
RYE CL
Black Prince Intc
A223
TUDOR WLK
EAST ROCHESTER WAY
Hall Place
A2
Beths Gram Sch
TORBROOK CL
BASING DR
OAKWAY CL
ARBUTHNOT LA
ARCADIAN AVE
ARCADIAN CL
ARCADIAN RD
GRESHAM CL
MEADOWVIEW RD
SOUTH VIEW CL
BROOKDALE RD
WILLOW CL
RIVERDALE RD
HARTLANDS CL
BAYNHAM CL
FINSBURY WAY
UPTON RD S
Allot Gdns
LOVE LA
KNOLL RD
HARTFORD RD
FARM VALE
OTFORD CL
ELMINGTON CL
SOUTHWOLD RD
A220
BOURNE RD
Sp Gd
BRIDGEN RD
VENTURE CL
KEMSING CL
CHARTER DR
ELMWOOD DR
THE RIDGE
SHUTTLEMEAD
BACK LA
PARKHURST RD
HARBEX CL
LESLEY CL
Recn Gd
CROSS LA
UNIVERSITY GDNS
ST THOMAS CT
DANE CL
BRADBOURNE RD
ALBERT RD
HURSTBOURNE COTTS
OLD BEXLEY BSNS PK
BOURNE PAR
ASCOT CT 1
KESTON CT 2
BALMORAL GDNS 3
WEDGEWOOD CT 4
WARWICK CL 5
PARKHILL RD
B2210
CHILHAM CL
THANET RD
KENLEY CL
Old Bexley
Church Wood
Bexley Woods
Pl Fld
PARKWOOD RD
A222
PO
OXFORD MEWS
TAN YARD LA
NORTH GLADE
EAST WOODSIDE
WEST WOODSIDE
CAMDEN RD
WOODSTOCK CL
GRANGEWOOD
SOUTH GLADE
MAIDEN ERLEGH AVE
MURCHISON AVE
SELBORNE AVE
HURSTWOOD AVE
RAVENSWOOD
HENGROVE CT
GREENSIDE
Old Bexley CE Prim Sch
MANOR WAY
SALISBURY RD
Bexley
BEXLEY HIGH ST
CLARENDON MEWS
MANOR RD
Cemy
HURST RD
GLENHURST AVE
Pav
River Cray
PELHAM COTTS
A2018
VICARAGE RD
HILL CRES
ESHER CL
DENISTON AVE
VALENTINE AVE
HURST SPRINGS
BRENT CL
ALTON CL
Pinewood Cottage
The Grove
BETTERTON DR
DAVENPORT RD
FRINTON RD
RIVERSIDE RD
PEMBURY CRES
BURNHAM RD
Woollett Hall Farm
WATERY LA
JAQUETS CT
Mount Mascal Farm
Home Close Farm
Hurst Grid Sub Sta
Caveys Spring
Keeper's Cottage
Sports Gd
Loring Hall
PH
NORTH CRAY RD
Royal Park Prim Sch
North Cray
Little Mascal Farm
BUNKERS HILL
Bunkers Hill
LEAFIELD LA
COCKSURE LA
Bexley
Dartford
Faesten Dic
FIVE ARCH BRIDGE
GATTONS
Joyden's Wood
Gattons Plantation
A207 Dartford (A226), M25 (A282)
A2 Rochester (M2), M25
A2018 Dartford, A2

148
A
B
C
D
Clarendon Sch
Ashford
Spelthorne Coll
Liby
Chattern Hill
Recn Gd
Pav
T Cts
Allot Gdns
Tenn Cts
Pl Fld
Sp Ctr
Allot Gdns
Recn Gd
St Michael's RC Prim Sch
Echelford Cty Prim Sch
Ashford Sch
Ashford Manor
CH
ASHFORD
Fordbridge Roundabout
Tenn Cts
Bwg Gn
Works
River Ash
Gravel Pit
Staines Reservoirs Aqueduct
School Road
Queen Mary Resr
TW15
TW18
TW17
STAINES BY-PASS
KINGSTON RD
A308
B377
B378
B3003
CHURCH RD
FORDBRIDGE RD
CLOCKHOUSE LA
CONVENT RD
SCHOOL RD
ASHFORD RD
FELTHAM RD
FELTHAM HILL RD
TOWN TREE RD
WOODTHORPE RD
CHESTERFIELD RD
STANWELL RD
MANOR RD
FONTMELL PK
STATION CRES
STATION RD
SANDRINGHAM DR
CONNAUGHT AVE
PORTLAND RD
SALCOMBE RD
LANCASTER CL
TUDOR CL
WEST CL
ASHFORD CL
HEATHFIELD CT
VILLAGE WAY
GLEN AVE
MEADWAY
PARKLAND GR
PARKLAND RD
CLIFFORD GR
ANGLESEY CL
REEDSFIELD RD
REEDSFIELD CL
THE YEWS
GRAYS LA
WENTWORTH CL
HAVEN RD
ROSA AVE
ECHELFORDE DR
EXEFORDE AVE
CHESTNUT RD
CHATTERN HILL
WYE CL
ST MARGARETS AVE
CHALMERS RD
OAKFIELD RD
CONVENT LO
MUNCASTER RD
MUNCASTER CL
SABAH CT
BROWNRIGG RD
ELMCROFT DR
PERCY AVE
NORMANHURST
FONTMELL CL
LIMES CL
ST MICHAELS RD
HAWLEY WAY
ELMSWAY
METCALF RD
ELM TREE CL
DINGLE RD
WORCESTER RD
WORCESTER CT
NURSERY PL
OLD
THE COPPICE
REDLEAVES AVE
SOUTHFIELDS AVE
GREENLEAVES CT
COURTFIELD RD
MAYFIELD CL
DENMAN DR
CAROLINE CT
PIPPINS CT
LANDON WAY
FAIRWAYS
LINKSCROFT AVE
LUCIE AVE
SYDNEY CRES
ASHFORD AVE
REX AVE
BANCROFT CL
GILMORE CRES
FAIRVIEW CT
ASHTREE CT 1
MORGAN CT 2
VAUGHAN ALMSHOS 3
ROWLAND HILL ALMSHOS 4
ROXETH CT 5
THE ELMS 6
BOURNE HO 7
ST MATTHEW'S CT 8
DENCLIFFE 9
KNAPP RD
GREENVIEW CT
COLLEGE WAY
CHURCH PAR
STATION APP
STATION PAR
QUEENS LA
NEW PAR
CLARENDON RD
COLERIDGE RD
COPTHORNE CHASE
CHAUCER RD
CANTERBURY CT
WOLSEY RD
FORD RD
DUDLEY RD
ALBERT RD
PRINCE WILLIAM CT
PRINCES RD
STANLEY RD
SPRINGFIELD RD
ARLINGTON RD
GABLES AVE
BADGERS CL
PERKINS CT
FAIRHOLME RD
THE CRESCENT
PERRIN CL
STANLEY RD
CHRISTOPHER CT
TENNYSON RD
NELSON RD
LINKS RD
ETHEL RD
ST HILDA'S AVE
WELLINGTON RD
WELLINGTON CT
WARWICK RD
TOWNSEND RD
MARLBOROUGH RD
ADELAIDE RD
FERNDALE RD
TALBOT RD
CHESTERFIELD MEWS
THE WICKETS
SOVEREIGN HO
ASHVIEW CL
ASHVIEW GDNS
FORDBRIDGE CT
FREEHEAD CL
FORD CL
KINGSTON RD
GLOUCESTER CRES
BOOTH DR
A308 Staines, M25 (A30)
VIII
192
06
07
72
71
70
69
6
5
4
3
2
1
ASTLEHAM RD 1
ASTLEHAM WAY 2
OBERON WAY
KORDA CL
LION CL
STUDIOS RD
The Green
NEW RD

149
172
193
A
B
C
D
1
2
3
4
5
6
69
70
71
72
09
10
TW13
TW15
TW16
Lower Feltham
Felthamhill
Ashford Common
Sunbury Common
Littleton Common
Charlton
Upper Halliford
Sunbury
The Sawyers Arms (PH)
Hounslow
Surrey
BEDFONT IND PK N
ASHFORD IND EST
MERESIDE PK
Recn Gd
Allot Gdns
Sp Gd
Cemy
Works
Bwg Gn
Meadhurst Sports Club
Tenn Cts
Spelthorne Cty Inf Sch
Spelthorne Sports Club
The Shears
Liby
Wks
Windmill Trad Est
Windmill Bsns Village
Sunbury Int Bsns Ctr
Superstore
Water Works
Springfield Prim Sch
Leisure Ctr
Bishop Wand CE Sec Sch
Hawkedale Fst Sch
Pl Fld
Mast
Pav
Sunbury Cross
West Surrey Est
The Dolphin Est
Windmill Lo
Felthamhill Brook
ASHFORD RD
FELTHAM RD
CHERTSEY RD
CADBURY RD
STAINES RD W
WINDMILL RD
UPPER HALLIFORD RD
A244
A308
B377
M3
CHALLENGE RD
PORTLAND CRES
THE CLUMPS
SOUTH GATE AVE
FIELD VIEW
SHIELD RD
ALLIANCE CT
DUKES CL
ANDERSON DR
JOHNS CL
CHATTERN RD
FERNHURST RD
SANDELLS AVE
WRENS AVE
LARKHAM CL
BRIARWOOD CL
WALTON GDNS
SHELSON AVE
RYLAND CL
SUNBURY CRES
SUNBURY RD
LUDLOW RD
DENISON RD
ELLINGTON RD
CRANLEIGH RD
HAMILTON RD
HIGHLAND PK
HAMILTON CL
LYNE GROVE AVE
SUNDOWN RD
CHALMERS
COOLGARDIE RD
ST PAUL'S CL
KENNEDY CT
NEW PARK RD
ASPEN GDNS
POPLAR RD
BURLEIGH GDNS
ROMNEY CL
BEAUMONT DR
NEIL CL
NEWHAVEN CRES
ASHGROVE RD
PRIORY GDNS
MORNINGTON RD
PEARSTREE RD
BEECH CL
STAINFORD CL
MEADOW RD
CHESTER CL
RIPSTON RD
LYNN CL
JUNCTION RD
MONTROSE CL
APPROACH RD
GOFFS RD
DORIS RD
FELTHAM HILL RD
WOODLANDS PAR
GARDEN CL
ORCHARD AVE
ORCHARD CL
HOGARTH AVE
DANE RD
SAXON RD
ELGIN AVE
TUDOR RD
HENDON TERR
SAVILLE CRES
ALEXANDRA CT
TEMPLECROFT
STAVELEY RD
GLENFIELD RD
STROUD WAY
CAREW RD
SELBY RD
CONWAY DR
HUGHES RD
CECIL RD
MAXWELL RD
NORMAN RD
DENNIS CL
CECIL CL
STAINES RD W
THE DRIVE
CHEYNE RD
NAPIER RD
SQUIRES WLK
NAPIER WLK
ALEXANDRA RD
WARREN RD
WARREN
HYDE TERR
HYDE CL
BEARD'S RD
CHAPLIN CRES
ROSSLYN CL
MEADHURST PK
SCOTT'S AVE
CARDINAL'S WLK
SCOTT'S WAY
CHESSHOLME CT
TASMAN CT
OAKHALL CT
OAKHALL DR
KINROSS DR
KINROSS CL
CUMBERNAULD GDNS
GROVELEY RD
KING GEORGE CL
CAMILLA CL
CHESTNUT CL
BRACKEN CL
KING'S AVE
THE ROWANS
CAVENDISH CL
CAVENDISH RD
CAVENDISH CT
MARLIN CL
BROAD OAK
BURGOYNE RD
GREEN CT
CLEVES WAY
CATHERINE DR
HOWARD CL
GREEN LA
GREEN LEAS
GREEN LEAS CL
WOLSEY RD
JUNIPER GDNS
WOLSEY
CARLTON RD
VICARAGE RD
BRYONY WAY
BEECHWOOD
HEATHERLANDS
WYCHWOOD
BRYAN CL
SEYMOUR WAY
ARAGON CL
AVON RD
SADDLEBROOK PK
HELGIFORD GDNS
CADBURY CL
SHEARS CT
PRINCE ALBERT CT
DALE RD
THE HEATH GR
HEATHCROFT AVE
THE PARADE
OXFORD CL
BENJAMIN CT
CAMBRIDGE RD
ASHDENE CL
CORNERSIDE
ASHFORD RD
BRIDGE GDNS
LITTLETON RD
ROWLAND WAY
THORNE CL
1 ALEXANDRA CL
2 REDWOOD MEWS
WILLOW CT 1
KILLIGREW HO 2
GRANTHAM HO 3
WINDMILL CL
CEDAR WAY
CASTLE CL
MILL FARM AVE
PERCY BRYANT RD
ESCOT RD
SPELTHORNE GR
CEDAR HO
FOREST DR
CROSSWAYS
ACTION CT
SPELTHORNE LA
BROOKLANDS CL
BROOKLANDS
MILLFIELD
LINCOLN WAY
CRAYONNE CL
DOLPHIN RD N
DOLPHIN RD W
DOLPHIN RD
DOLPHIN RD S
HARRIS WAY
HOMEWATERS AVE 1
ALMSHOS 2
EVELYN CRES
EVELYN WAY
BEVERLEY RD
RAVENSCOURT
NURSERY RD
NURSERY GDNS
SUTHERLAND AVE
SUTHERLAND GDNS
RAVENDALE RD
STRATTON RD
PEREGRINE RD
LAYTON'S LA
FALCON WAY
MANOR GDNS
MANOR DR WAY
GREEN ST
ROOKSMEAD RD
THE RIDINGS
SPRING
DOWNSIDE CT
BENWELL
BRACKENWOOD
MEADOWS END
GENEVA CL
KELLY CL
HASLETT RD
BIRCH GR
QUEEN MARY RD
CHARLTON RD
HETHERINGTON RD
HARROW WAY
LODGE WAY
HETHERINGTON
WALNUT TREE RD
ALMOND CL
CROSSWELL CL
ORCHARD DR
GRANGE FARM CVN PK
CROYSDALE AVE
AIRLAWNS
PARKWOOD GR
SUNMEAD RD

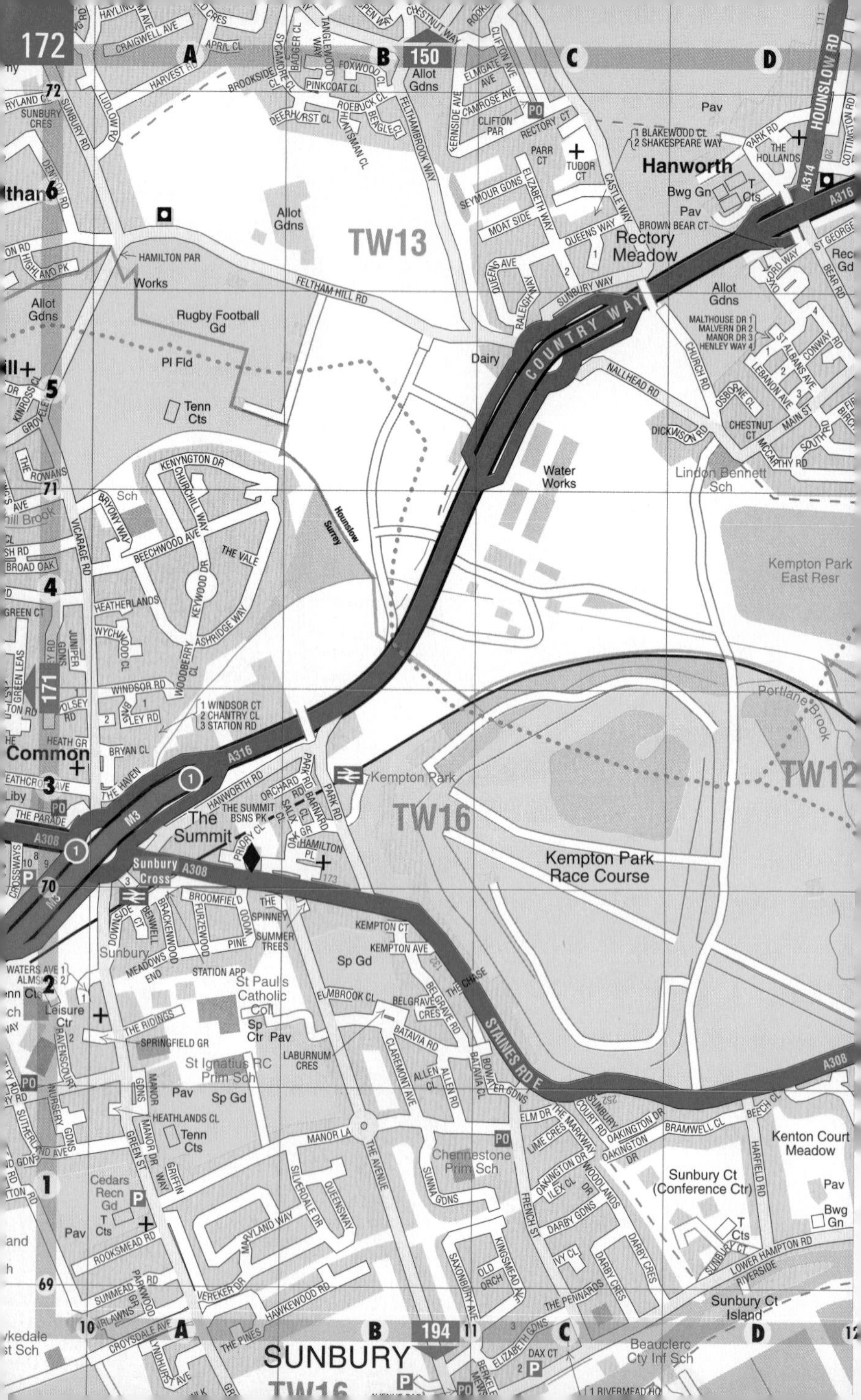
A
B
C
D
150
Allot Gdns
Hanworth
TW13
Rectory Meadow
Allot Gdns
Rugby Football Gd
Pl Fld
Tenn Cts
Works
Dairy
Water Works
COUNTRY WAY
A316
M3
A308
HOUNSLOW RD
A314
Lindon Bennett Sch
Kempton Park East Resr
Portlane Brook
TW12
Kempton Park
TW16
The Summit
Sunbury Cross
Kempton Park Race Course
STAINES RD E
Common
Sunbury
St Pauls Catholic Coll
St Ignatius RC Prim Sch
Leisure Ctr
Sp Gd
Chennestone Prim Sch
Sunbury Ct (Conference Ctr)
Kenton Court Meadow
Cedars Recn Gd
Sunbury Ct Island
Beauclerc Cty Inf Sch
SUNBURY
194
171
173

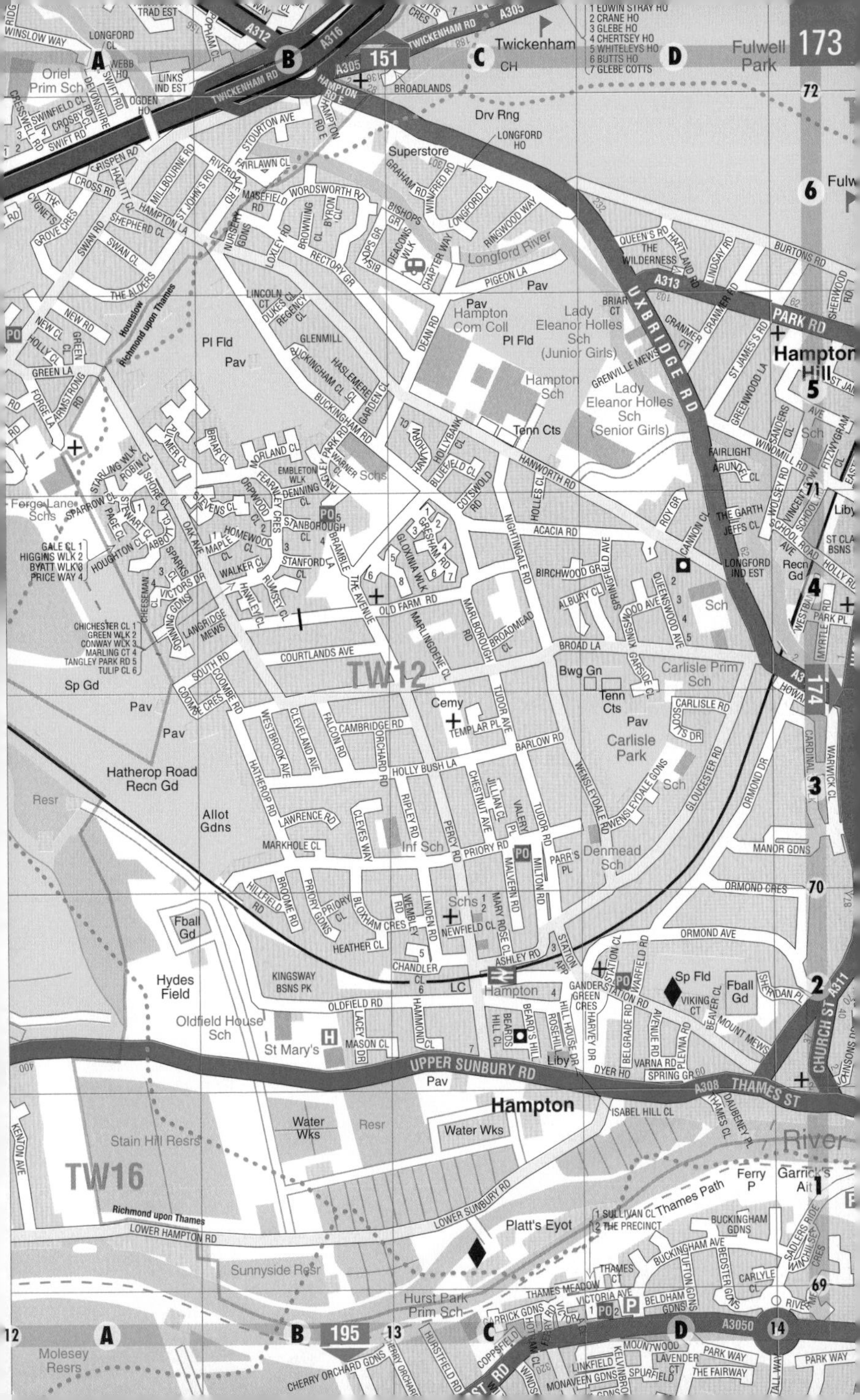
1 EDWIN STRAY HO
2 CRANE HO
3 GLEBE HO
4 CHERTSEY HO
5 WHITELEYS HO
6 BUTTS HO
7 GLEBE COTTS
Twickenham
CH
Fulwell Park
TWICKENHAM RD
A305
A312
A316
151
HAMPTON RD E
BROADLANDS
LONGFORD CL
WINSLOW WAY
Oriel Prim Sch
WEBB HO
SWIFT RD
DEVONSHIRE RD
OGDEN HO
LINKS IND EST
CRESSWELL RD
SWINFIELD CL
CROSBY RD
Drv Rng
LONGFORD HO
Superstore
STOURTON AVE
FAIRLAWN CL
CRISPEN RD
HAZLITT CL
CROSS RD
MILLBOURNE RD
ST JOHN'S RD
RIVERDALE RD
MASEFIELD RD
WORDSWORTH RD
BYRON CL
BROWNING CL
LOXLEY RD
NURSERY GDNS
GRAHAM RD
WINIFRED RD
LONGFORD CL
RINGWOOD WAY
BISHOPS GR
DEACONS WLK
CHAPTER WAY
Longford River
PIGEON LA
RECTORY GR
HAMPTON LA
SHEPHERD CL
SWAN RD
SWAN CL
THE CYGNETS
GROVE CRES
THE ALDERS
Hounslow
Richmond upon Thames
NEW RD
NEW CL
HOLLY CL
GREEN CL
GREEN LA
FORGE LA
ARMSTRONG RD
PO
Pl Fld
Pav
LINCOLN CT
DUKES CL
REGENCY CL
GLENMILL
BUCKINGHAM CL
HASLEMERE CL
GARDEN CL
BUCKINGHAM RD
DEAN RD
Hampton Com Coll
Lady Eleanor Holles Sch (Junior Girls)
Hampton Sch
Lady Eleanor Holles Sch (Senior Girls)
Tenn Cts
QUEEN'S RD
THE WILDERNESS
HARTLAND RD
LINDSAY RD
BURTONS RD
A313
UXBRIDGE RD
BRIAR CT
CRANMER CT
CRANMER RD
PARK RD
ST JAMES'S RD
Hampton Hill
GRENVILLE MEWS
GREENWOOD LA
SANDERS CL
WINDMILL RD
FITZWYGRAM CL
FAIRLIGHT
ARUNDEL CL
Sch
72
6
5
71
4
3
70
2
1
69
Fulwell
Liby
ST CLARE BSNS PK
HOLLY RD
Recn Gd
PARK PL
MYRTLE RD
WOLSEY RD
VINCENT ROW
SCHOOL ROAD AVE
THE GARTH
JEFFS CL
LONGFORD IND EST
ROY GR
CANNON CL
HANWORTH RD
HOLLES CL
NIGHTINGALE RD
COTSWOLD RD
BLUEFIELD CL
HOLLYBANK CL
HAWTHORN CL
TANGLEY PARK RD
WARNER CL
Schs
EMBLETON WLK
DENNING CL
FEARNLEY CRES
MORLAND CL
BRIAR CL
AYLMER CL
ORPWOOD CL
STANBOROUGH CL
STANFORD CL
BRAMBLE LA
GRESHAM RD
GLOXINIA WLK
STARLING WLK
ROBIN CL
SHORE CL
SPARROW CL
STEWART CL
PAGE CL
ABBOTT CL
Forge Lane Schs
GALE CL 1
HIGGINS WLK 2
BYATT WLK 3
PRICE WAY 4
HOUGHTON CL
SPARKS CL
STEVENS CL
HOMEWOOD CL
MAPLE CL
WALKER CL
OAK AVE
VICTORS DR
CHEESEMAN CL
SONNING GDNS
LANGRIDGE MEWS
HAWLEY CL
RUMSEY CL
THE AVENUE
OLD FARM RD
ACACIA RD
BIRCHWOOD GR
SPRINGFIELD AVE
ALBURY CL
KINGSWOOD AVE
QUEENSWOOD AVE
CHICHESTER CL 1
GREEN WLK 2
CONWAY WLK 3
MARLING CT 4
TANGLEY PARK RD 5
TULIP CL 6
COURTLANDS AVE
MARLINGDENE CL
MARLBOROUGH RD
BROADMEAD CL
BROAD LA
TW12
Bwg Gn
Tenn Cts
GARSIDE CL
Carlisle Prim Sch
CARLISLE RD
SCOTTS DR
Carlisle Park
A3
174
HOWARD
CARDINAL
WARWICK CL
SOUTH RD
COOMBE RD
COOMBE CRES
Sp Gd
Pav
Cemy
TEMPLAR PL
TUDOR AVE
BARLOW RD
CAMBRIDGE RD
FALCON RD
ORCHARD RD
CLEVELAND AVE
WESTBROOK AVE
HOLLY BUSH LA
CHESTNUT AVE
JILLIAN CL
VALERY PL
TUDOR RD
WENSLEYDALE RD
WENSLEYDALE GDNS
GLOUCESTER RD
ORMOND DR
Hatherop Road Recn Gd
HATHEROP RD
Resr
Allot Gdns
LAWRENCE RD
RIPLEY RD
CLEVES WAY
PERCY RD
MARKHOLE CL
Inf Sch
PRIORY RD
PO
MILTON RD
PARR'S PL
Denmead Sch
MANOR GDNS
ORMOND CRES
HILLFIELD RD
BROOME RD
PRIORY GDNS
PRIORY CL
BLOXHAM CRES
WEMBLEY RD
LINDEN RD
Schs
MALVERN RD
MARY ROSE CL
NEWFIELD CL
HEATHER CL
STATION APP
ORMOND AVE
ASHLEY RD
Fball Gd
CHANDLER CL
KINGSWAY BSNS PK
LC
Hampton
STATION CL
WARFIELD RD
Sp Fld
Fball Gd
SHERIDAN PL
A311
GANDER GREEN CRES
STATION RD
VIKING CT
BEAVER CL
MOUNT MEWS
Hydes Field
OLDFIELD RD
LACEY DR
HAMMOND CL
BEARDS HILL CL
BEARD'S HILL
ROSEHILL
HILL HOUSE DR
HARVEY DR
BELGRADE RD
AVENUE RD
PLEVNA RD
CHURCH ST
Oldfield House Sch
St Mary's
MASON CL
UPPER SUNBURY RD
Liby
DYER HO
VARNA RD
SPRING GR
Pav
A308
THAMES ST
Hampton
ISABEL HILL CL
THAMES CL
DAUBENEY PL
River
KENTON AVE
Water Wks
Resr
Water Wks
Stain Hill Resrs
TW16
Ferry P
Garrick's Ait
Thames Path
LOWER SUNBURY RD
Richmond upon Thames
LOWER HAMPTON RD
Platt's Eyot
1 SULLIVAN CL
2 THE PRECINCT
BUCKINGHAM GDNS
BUCKINGHAM AVE
BEDSTER GDNS
SADLERS RIDE
WINCHILSEY CRES
Sunnyside Resr
THAMES CT
TUFTON GDNS
CARLYLE CL
THAMES MEADOW
VICTORIA AVE
BELDHAM GDNS
Hurst Park Prim Sch
CARRICK GDNS
A3050
14
A
B
195
13
C
D
12
Molesey Resrs
CHERRY ORCHARD GDNS
HURSTFIELD RD
COPPSFIELD
MOUNTWOOD
LAVENDER CT
PARK WAY
LINKFIELD
MONAVEEN GDNS
SPURFIELD
THE FAIRWAY

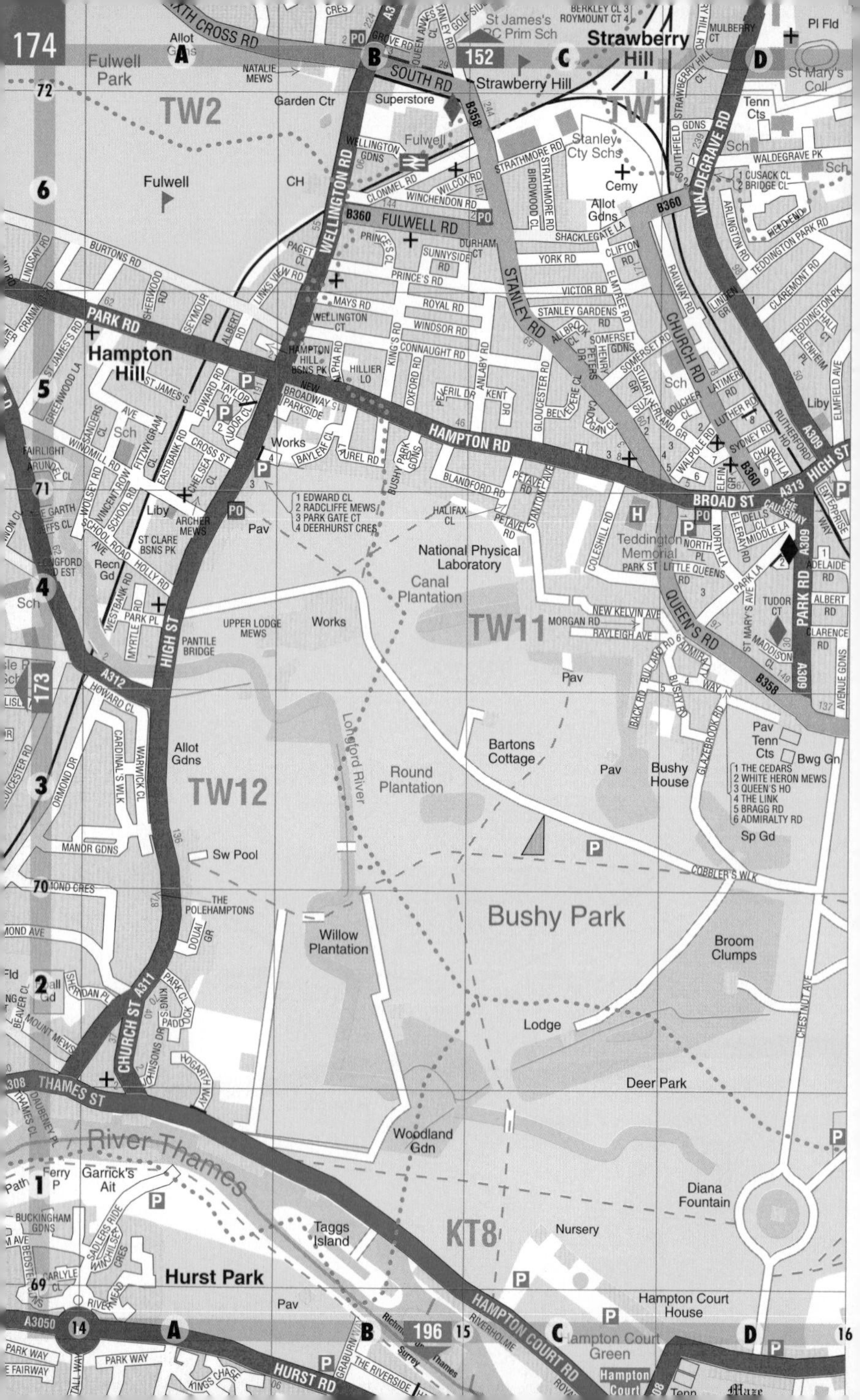

A
B
C
D
152
Strawberry Hill
Fulwell Park
Allot Gdns
TW2
TW1
TW11
TW12
KT8
Garden Ctr
Superstore
Fulwell
Stanley Cty Schs
Cemy
Allot Gdns
St James's RC Prim Sch
St Mary's Coll
Pl Fld
Tenn Cts
Sch
MULBERRY CT
BERKLEY CL 3
ROYMOUNT CT 4
NATALIE MEWS
SOUTH RD
GROVE RD
QUEEN ANNES CL
STANLEY RD
GOLF SIDE
B358
WELLINGTON GDNS
WELLINGTON RD
CLONMEL RD
WILCOX RD
WINCHENDON RD
STRATHMORE RD
BIRDWOOD CL
SOUTHFIELD GDNS
STRAWBERRY HILL CL
WALDEGRAVE RD
WALDEGRAVE PK
1 CUSACK CL
2 BRIDGE CL
FIELD END
ARLINGTON RD
TEDDINGTON PARK RD
Fulwell
CH
B360
FULWELL RD
PRINCE'S CL
SUNNYSIDE RD
DURHAM CT
SHACKLEGATE LA
YORK RD
CLIFTON RD
B360
PAGET CL
LINKS VIEW RD
PRINCE'S RD
VICTOR RD
ELMTREE RD
RAILWAY RD
LINDEN GR
CLAREMONT RD
TEDDINGTON PK
MAYS RD
ROYAL RD
STANLEY GARDENS RD
CHURCH RD
HALL CT
BLENHEIM PL
BURTONS RD
LINDSAY RD
PARK RD
SHERWOOD RD
SEYMOUR RD
ALBERT RD
WELLINGTON CT
WINDSOR RD
KING'S RD
ALLBROOK CL
SOMERSET GDNS
HENRY PETERS DR
SOMERSET RD
Hampton Hill
ST JAMES'S RD
GREENWOOD LA
ST JAMES'S
HAMPTON HILL BSNS PK
NEW BROADWAY
PARKSIDE
HILLIER LO
ALPHA RD
CONNAUGHT RD
OXFORD RD
ANLABY RD
ERIL DR
KENT DR
GLOUCESTER RD
BELVEDERE CL
CADOGAN CL
STUART GR
SUTHERLAND GR
BOUCHER CL
LATIMER RD
LUTHER RD
RUTHERFORD WAY
Liby
ELMFIELD AVE
EDWARD RD
TAYLOR CL
TUDOR CL
SANDERS CL
AVE
Sch
WINDMILL RD
FITZWYGRAM CL
EASTBANK RD
CROSS ST
Works
BAYLEAF CL
LAUREL RD
BUSHY PARK GDNS
HAMPTON RD
WALPOLE RD
SYDNEY RD
CHURCH LA
A309
HIGH ST
FAIRLIGHT
ARUNDEL CL
WOLSEY RD
VINCENT ROW
SCHOOL RD
CHELSEA CL
BLANDFORD RD
PETAVEL RD
STANTON AVE
B360
A313
BROAD ST
THE CAUSEWAY
ENTERPRISE WAY
THE GARTH
RIFFS CL
Liby
ARCHER MEWS
1 EDWARD CL
2 RADCLIFFE MEWS
3 PARK GATE CT
4 DEERHURST CRES
HALIFAX CL
PETAVEL RD
COLESHILL RD
Teddington Memorial
ELFIN GR
ELLERAY RD
DELLS CL
MIDDLE LA
NORTH LA
NORTH PL
PARK ST
LITTLE QUEENS RD
SCHOOL ROAD AVE
ST CLARE BSNS PK
Pav
National Physical Laboratory
Canal Plantation
PARK LA
ADELAIDE RD
LONGFORD RD EST
Recn Gd
HOLLY RD
WESTBANK RD
PARK PL
MYRTLE RD
Sch
UPPER LODGE MEWS
Works
PANTILE BRIDGE
HIGH ST
NEW KELVIN AVE
MORGAN RD
RAYLEIGH AVE
QUEEN'S RD
ST MARY'S AVE
TUDOR CT
PARK RD
ALBERT RD
CLARENCE RD
MADDISON CL
A312
173
HOWARD CL
Pav
BULLARD RD
ADMIRALTY WAY
BUSHY RD
BACK RD
GLAZEBROOK RD
B358
A309
AVENUE GDNS
CARDINAL'S WLK
WARWICK CL
Allot Gdns
Longford River
Bartons Cottage
Round Plantation
Pav
Bushy House
Pav
Tenn Cts
Bwg Gn
1 THE CEDARS
2 WHITE HERON MEWS
3 QUEEN'S HO
4 THE LINK
5 BRAGG RD
6 ADMIRALTY RD
Sp Gd
ORMOND DR
MANOR GDNS
Sw Pool
COBBLER'S WLK
ORMOND CRES
ORMOND AVE
THE POLEHAMPTONS
Willow Plantation
Bushy Park
Broom Clumps
DOUAI GR
SHERIDAN PL
PARK CL
KING'S PADDOCK
CHESTNUT AVE
BEAVER CL
MOUNT MEWS
CHURCH ST
A311
JOHNSONS DR
HOGARTH WAY
Lodge
Deer Park
A308
THAMES ST
THAMES CL
DAUBENEY PL
River Thames
Woodland Gdn
Ferry P
Garrick's Ait
Diana Fountain
BUCKINGHAM GDNS
SADLERS RIDE
WINCHILSEA CRES
Taggs Island
Nursery
KT8
BEDSTER GDNS
CARLYLE CL
RIVERMEAD
Hurst Park
Pav
Hampton Court House
A3050
14
A
B
196
15
C
D
16
Hampton Court Green
HAMPTON COURT RD
RIVERHOLME
PARK WAY
FAIRWAY
PARK WAY
KINGS CHASE
HURST RD
GRABURN WAY
THE RIVERSIDE
Richmond upon Thames
Surrey
Hampton Court
Maze
72
6
5
71
4
3
70
2
1
69

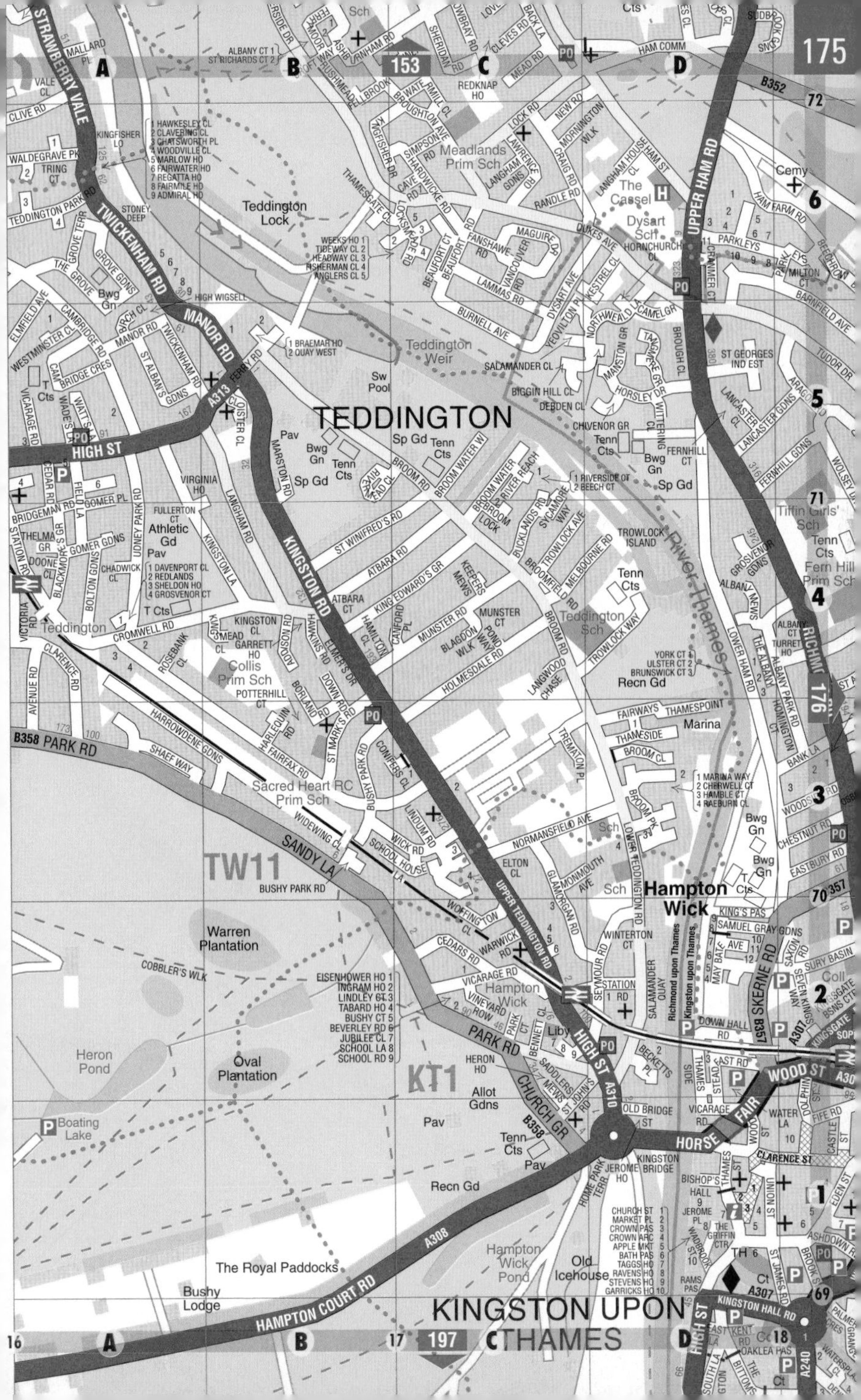
TEDDINGTON
KINGSTON UPON THAMES
Hampton Wick
TW11
KT1
Teddington Lock
Teddington Weir
River Thames
Meadlands Prim Sch
The Cassel
Dysart Sch
Teddington Sch
Collis Prim Sch
Sacred Heart RC Prim Sch
Tiffin Girls' Sch
Fern Hill Prim Sch
Warren Plantation
Oval Plantation
Heron Pond
Boating Lake
The Royal Paddocks
Bushy Lodge
Hampton Wick Pond
Old Icehouse
Athletic Gd
Recn Gd
Allot Gdns
Marina
Trowlock Island
St Georges Ind Est
Salamander Quay
Kingston Bridge
Teddington
Cemy
STRAWBERRY VALE
TWICKENHAM RD
MANOR RD
HIGH ST
KINGSTON RD
UPPER TEDDINGTON RD
UPPER HAM RD
HAMPTON COURT RD
PARK RD
SANDY LA
BROOM RD
LOWER TEDDINGTON RD
LOWER HAM RD
FERRY RD
CROMWELL RD
STATION RD
VICTORIA RD
CLARENCE RD
HORSE FAIR
WOOD ST
CLARENCE ST
KINGSTON HALL RD
CHURCH GR
HAM COMM
COBBLER'S WLK
Richmond upon Thames
Kingston upon Thames
A313
A310
A308
A307
A240
B358
B352
B357
153
176
197
A B C D
1 2 3 4 5 6

A
B
154
C
D
TW10
Ham Gate Ave
B352
Hamcross Plantation
Ham Bottom
Isabella Plantation
Upper Ham Rd
Ham Common
Cemy
Horse Ride
High Wood
Park Gate House
Richmond Park
HM Remand Ctr
Ham Ridings
Allot Gdns
Thatchedhouse Lodge
Queen's Rd
Church Rd
The Shires
Garthside
Barnfield Gdns
Barnfield Ave
Beechrow
Milton Ct
Parkleys
Ham Farm Rd
Cranmer Ct
St Georges Ind Est
Tudor Dr
Aragon Rd
Lancaster Gdns
Cranmer Rd
Bainbridge Cl
Latchmere Cl
Anne Boleyn's Wlk
Garth Rd
Beard Rd
Sopwith Cl
Hatch Pl
Wilmer Cl
Wilmer Cres
Parkfields Rd
Park Rd
Park Gdns
Woodcote Cl
Liby
PO
Fernhill Gdns
Wolsey Dr
Cardinal Ave
Hollybush Rd
Latchmere La
Tiffin Girls' Sch
Tenn Cts
Fern Hill Prim Sch
Recn Gd
Latchmere Jun & Inf Schs
Aldersbrook Dr
Cranleigh Gdns
Wingfield Rd
King Clump
Canbury Sch
Ladderstile Ride
Warboys Rd
Warboys App
Astor Cl
Parkgate Cl
A308
Magnolia Cl
Grosvenor Gdns
Albany Mews
Lower Ham Rd
Richmond Rd
Durlston Rd
Studland Rd
St Albans Rd
Latchmere Rd
St Agatha's Dr
Sp Gd
St Agatha's RC Prim Sch
Kelvedon Cl
Upper Park Rd
Haygreen Cl
Kingsnympton Pk
Heatherdale Cl
Dutch Gdns
Windmill Rise
Winchester Cl
Morecoombe Cl
Albany Ct
Turret Ho
The Albany
Albany Park Rd
Homington Ct
175
Marina
1 Walton Ho
2 Berkeley Cl
3 Canbury Ct
Earle Gdns
Stanton Rd
The Keep
Dinton Rd
Bockhampton Rd
Bertram Rd
Liverpool Rd
Crescent Rd
Cumberland Ho
Deer Park Cl
Beaumont Cl
Boyd Cl
Eaton Dr
Berystede
Blenheim Gdns
Bank La
Archer Cl
Park Farm Rd
Chesfield Rd
Wyndham Rd
New Rd
Tudor Rd
Cherrywood
Rosewood Ct
1 Marina Way
2 Chervel Ct
3 Hamble
4 Raebu...
Woodside Rd
Osborne Rd
Windsor Rd
Thorpe Rd
Burton Rd
King's Rd
Shortlands Rd
Cross Rd
Alexandra Rd
Elm Rd
York Rd
Schs
B351
Bwg Gn
Chestnut Rd
Bearfield Rd
Eastbury Rd
Richmond Park Rd
Princes Rd
T Cts
Pav
Gibbon Rd
Hardings Cl
Acre Rd
Lowther Rd
Clifton Rd
Park Cl
Glenville Rd
Craigside
Fairview Ct
Forsyte Ct
Badminton
Galsworthy Rd
Wolsey Cl
B357
King's Pas
Samuel Gray Gdns
May Bate Ave
Skerne Rd
Saxon Rd
Sury Basin
Seven Kings Way
Coll
East Rd
David Twigg Cl
Waights Ct
Sch
Canbury Ave
Craven Rd
Willoughby Rd
Beresford Rd
Deacon Rd
Elton Rd
Brunswick Rd
Audric Cl
Wolverton Ave
Carlisle Cl
Manorgate Rd
Manor Ct
Kingston
Kingsgate Bsns Ctr
Kingsgate Rd
Sopwith Way
A307
Cowleaze Rd
Elm Cres
Elm Gr
Canbury Park Rd
Boswell Ct
Down Hall Rd
Gordon Rd
Burnham St
Station Rd
Coombe Rd
Andhurst Ct
Dumbleton Ct
Revell Rd
Thames St
Wood St
A308
Cromwell Rd
John Austin Cl
Queen Elizabeth Rd
Tithe Barn Cl
Birkenhead Ave
Norbiton Hall
A238
Sylvestrus Cl
Jemmett Cl
Wessex Cl
Norbiton
1 Brackendale
2 Woodstock Ct
3 Pinkerton Ct
4 Lambourne Gr
5 Maryland Ct
Fair
Water La
Dolphin St
Fife Rd
Castle St
Clarence St
Hardman Rd
Lovekyn Cl
Riverstone Ct
Tiffin Sch
London Rd
Chesham Rd
Cobham Rd
Chatham Rd
Norbiton Ave
Neville Rd
Homersham Rd
Gloucester Rd
Chester Ho
Kenley Rd
Orme Rd
Union St
Eden St
Weston Pk
Fairfield N
Fairfield W
Caversham Rd
Minerva Rd
Church Rd
A2043
Clevedon Rd
Aycliffe Ct
Norbiton
KT1
Cambridge Gdns
Cambridge Rd
Porchester Rd
Ernest Sq
Ernest Rd
Rosebery Sq
Rosebery Rd
Douglas Rd
Charter Sq
Charter Rd
The Griffin Ctr
TH
Ashdown Rd
Brook St
Wheatfield Way
Mus
Ctr
Liby
Fairfield Rd
Pav
Univ
Victoria Rd
Albert Rd
Hawks Rd
Linden Cres
Portman Rd
Excelsior Cl
Washington Rd
St Peters Rd
Burritt Rd
Waters Rd
Waters Sq
St James Rd
Ct
Orchard Rd
Recn Gd
Littlefield Ho
Somerset Rd
Vincent Rd
Hampden Rd
Fairfield S
Kingston Hall Rd
A307
Falconry Ct
Millfield
Kingsworthy Cl
Rowlls Rd
Franklin Cl
Bonner Hill Rd
Willow Ct
Lime Ct
Boundary Cl
Norbiton Common Rd
Fleetwood
King Henry's Rd
Archdale
East
Kent Rd
Oaklea Pas
South La
The Bittoms
A240
Palmer Cres
Grange Rd
Watersplash
Knights Pk
Avenue Rd
Mill St
Green Leas
Dudley Rd
Athena Cl
Mill Pl
Livesey Cl
Winery La
Vineyard Cl
Dawson Rd
Fairfield Pl
Concord Ct
Cemy
Gladstone Rd
Dolllary
18
19
198
20
Gro
Cambridge Gro Rd

A
B
C
D
155
199
178
72
6
5
71
4
3
70
2
1
69
21
22
Kingston Vale
Kingston Hill
Coombe
KT2
KT3
SW15
SW19
SW20
A308
A3
A238
B283
KINGSTON VALE
KINGSTON HILL
ROBIN HOOD WAY
KINGSTON BY PASS
COOMBE LA W
TRAPS LA
COOMBE RD
BEVERLEY WAY
Robin Hood
BEVERLEY COTTS
Pl Fld
War Meml
Wandsworth
VALE CRES
ROBINWOOD PL
MARY ADELAIDE CL
DERWENT AVE
ROBIN HOOD LA
GRASMERE AVE
ULLSWATER CL
ULLSWATER CRES
WOODVIEW CL
CEDAR CL
KINGSTON HILL PL
Walkden Hall
(Hall of Residence)
WINDERMERE RD
ROBIN HOOD LA
BOWNESS CRES
RYDAL GDNS
KESWICK AVE
Sch
Coombe Hurst
Kingston Univ
Horse Ride
Richmond upon Thames
Kingston upon Thames
Merton
Pav
Tenn Cts
Allot Gdns
COOMBE PL
COOMBE WOOD RD
RANDOLPH CL
COOMBE PK
CORSCOMBE CL
COOMBE RIDINGS
PAGET PL
Warren House
THE WATERGARDENS
FAIRLAWN CL
COTSWOLD CL
Coombe Hill
Mill Corner
WARREN PK
WARREN RD
HIGH COOMBE PL
WARREN CUTTING
THE LEIGH
Nat Res
ELLERTON
Coombe Wood
RENFREW RD
STOKE RD
GEORGE RD
COOMBE NEVILLE
EDGECOMBE CL
GOLF CLUB DR
CH
COOMBE HILL RD
GREENWOOD PK
HEMLEY DR
BEVERLEY LA
COOMBE HILL GLADE
COOMBE END
MOOR PARK GDNS
DEVEY CL
WARBANK LA
PRESTON RD
BARTON RD
HOOD RD
Holy Cross Prep RC Sch
THE DRIVE
GATEHOUSE CL
Schs
BALLARD CL
LORD CHANCELLOR WLK
FITZGEORGE AVE
WARREN RISE
COOMBE HOUSE CHASE
COOMBE RIDGE
OAKCOMBE CL
COOMBE BANK
WONFORD CL
H
New Victoria
Coombe Lane
COOMBE LANE FLYOVER 1
BEVERLEY CT 2
BEVERLEY AVE
HOLLAND AVE
PO
MELVILLE AVE
BURDETT AVE
COTTENHAM PARK RD
WESTCOOMBE AVE
Pl Flds
BROOK GDNS
COOMBE RISE
ORCHARD RISE
WEST RD
SOUTHWOOD AVE
NEVILLE AVE
THE FAIRWAY
THE CHESTERS
THE MOAT
Coombe Hill Jun & Inf Schs
CROWN RD
BURGHLEY AVE
ALBION RD
CARDINAL CRES
BEECHCROFT AVE
WOODLANDS AVE
BRANKSOME WAY
MATLOCK WAY
HIGH DR
CROMFORD WAY
BUXTON DR
SOAMES WLK
BADGERS WLK
Coombe Girls Sch
BAKEWELL WAY
DARLEY DR
Coombe Brook
Malden
ELY CL
ABOYNE DR
1 PERTH CL
2 HUNTLEY WAY
ARUNDEL RD
DICKERAGE RD
OVERDALE AVE
OAK RD
LANGLEY GR
Allot Gdns
CLARENCE AVE
OLIVER RD
MYRTLE GR
THE CLOSE
THE CRESCENT
LABURNUM GR
ASH CL
BARTON GN
CARLTON RD
SELBORNE RD
GOLFSIDE CL
DELL WLK
Sp Gd
LINKSIDE
CAMBRIDGE AVE
BURBERRY CL
WOODSIDE RD
THE TRIANGLE
MUYBRIDGE RD
MIDLETON RD
DICKERAGE HILL
ASHCOMBE SQ
LONG WLK
THE GREEN
POPLAR GDNS
LAWN CL
ROWAN CL
BEACONSFIELD RD
SALISBURY RD
SYCAMORE GR
EDGAR CT
FORSYTH CT
ORCHARD AVE
ROSEBERY AVE
HOPPINGWOOD AVE
Bwg Gn
WARWICK RD
LINCOLN RD
ROSEMARY
MOUNT PLEASANT RD
Corpus Christi RC Prim Sch
MOUNT
BEECH GR
ELM RD
POPLAR GR
LIME GR
ST MICHAELS CT
CHESTNUT GR
CHESTNUT GROVE CT
ALRIC AVE
VANFAME CT
STAFFORD RD
Beverley

Allot Gdns
Wimbledon
London Scottish
A
B
156
C
D
A219
LINCOLN AVE
MARLBOROUGH HO
SALISBURY HO
SPENCER HO
SOMERSET RD
COACH HOUSE LA
CEDAR CT
LAWSON CL
GREENOAK WAY
NEWSTEAD WAY
ATHERTON DR
CALONNE RD
72
SW15
WINDMILL RD
Horse Ride
Wimbledon Common
PARKSIDE
The Buddhapadipa Temple
PARKSIDE GDNS
LAMPTON HOUSE CL
DEEPDALE
6
Gravelly Hill
SW19
MARGIN DR
WINDY RIDGE CL
PARKSIDE AVE
PEEK CRES
MARRYAT RD
LANCASTER AVE
SUNSET RD
5
NORTH VIEW
CAMP VIEW
WEST PL
CAMP RD
B281
CANNIZARO RD
THE CAUSEWAY
THE GREEN
RUSHMERE PL
HIGH ST
Caesar's Camp
KINSELLA GDNS
EVERSLEY PK
CH
Allot Gdns
The Study Prep Sch
THE KEIR
WEST SIDE COMM
MASON'S YD
71
LINGFIELD RD
LINGFIELD CT
THE GRANGE
SOUTHSIDE COMM
Royal Wimbledon
Cannizaro Park
CHESTER RD
BEECH CL
SYCAMORE RD
LORDELL PL
CINQUE COTTS
WILBERFORCE WAY
LAURISTON RD
MURRAY RD
GRANGE LO
CORBIERE CT
THORNTON RD E
4
Crooked Billet
STRACHAN PL
WOODHAYES RD
SOUTH VIEW
CLIFTON RD
NUTBORN HO
DENMARK RD
THORNTON RD
HILLSIDE
DUNSTALL RD
King's Coll Sch
Tenn Cts
Pav
RIDGWAY
BERKELEY PL
RIDGWAY CT
RIDGWAY GDNS
177
WOOL RD
MCKAY RD
PEREGRINE WAY
Wimbledon Common Prep Sch
Pl Fld
ELLERTON RD
WOLSEY CL
GRANGE PARK PL
ERNLE RD
RYDON MEWS
HANNAH CT
Pl Fld
Wimbledon Coll
THACKERAY
Tenn Cts
DRAX AVE
ALMER RD
THURSTAN RD
ROKEBY PL
BARHAM RD
KINGSDOWN
HIGH RANGE
COPSE HILL
THE FIRS
EDGE HILL
3
PRESTON RD
H
PROSPECT PL
COTTENHAM PL
COTTENHAM DR
HIGH CEDAR DR
COTTENHAM PARK RD
THE DRIVE
ARTERBERRY RD
LANSDOWNE RD
THE DOWNS
SOUTHRIDGE PL
OAKHILL CT
DARLASTON
Atkinson Morley
LANDIS
FARNE RD
HOOD RD
MELVILLE AVE
Copse Hill
CRANFORD CL
HEIGHTS CL
HILL VIEW
HAMPTON CL
DURRINGTON AVE
Norwegian Sch
LANSDOWNE CL
SOUTHDOWN DR
Sch
EDGE HILL CT
WORPLE AVE
Pl Fld
Pav
70
HOLLAND AVE
BEVERLEY AVE
A3
Tenn Cts
Sp Gd
COTTENHAM PARK RD
ORCHARD LA
DURRINGTON PARK RD
Ursuline High Sch
CRESCENT RD
Hall Sch
SAVONA CT
B235
ALBERT
BURDETT AVE
MELBURY GDNS
Tenn Cts
HUNTER RD
CONWAY RD
PO
OAKWOOD RD
Tenn Cts
Bwg Gn
PANMUIR RD
Hollymount Prim Sch
ARTERBERRY RD
MASON CT
DAYTONE HO
ETHELBERT RD
Kingston upon Thames
2
COTTENHAM PARK RD
St Matthew's CE Fst Sch
Allot Gdns
LAUREL RD
CAMBRIDGE CL
CAMBRIDGE CT
DEVAS RD
MONTANA RD
A238
SW20
CAMBRIDGE RD
DURHAM RD
PENDARVES RD
PEPYS RD
DUNMORE RD
WORPLE RD
SOUTHDOWN RD
BEVERLEY WAY
KINGSTON BY PASS
WEST COOMBE AVE
Pl Flds
Cottenham Park
LYNNE CT
Bwg Gn
TOTHAM LO
SPENCER CT
KENWYN RD
ROSEVINE RD
LAMBTON RD
TOLVERNE RD
TREWINCE RD
LANGHAM RD
DELAMERE RD
ABBOTT AVE
COOMBE GDNS
RICHMOND RD
SPENCER RD
AMITY GR
SURREY LO
STANTON RD
Bwg Gn
Tenn Cts
PARKFIELDS AVE
COOMBE LA
AVENUE RD
HOLLY LO
COTTENHAM PAR
B281
PO
B235
PEPYS CT
WYKE RD
1 STATION BLDGS
2 LANGHAM CT
KINGSTON RD
RICHMOND CT 1
DURHAM CL 2
ROWAN CT 3
CRANLEIGH HO 4
ELY CL
Tenn Cts
CAMBERLEY AVE
MILBURN HO
P
A238
APPROACH RD
PRINCE GEORGE'S AVE
CARLTON PARK AVE
VERNON AVE
EDNA RD
DORIEN RD
DUPONT RD
SYDNEY RD
CHESTNUT RD
1
Sp Gd
SOMERSET AVE
TAUNTON AVE
B282
Raynes Park
Liby
CLIFTON PARK AVE
ASTON RD
GORE RD
ABOYNE DR
1 PERTH CL
2 HUNTLEY WAY
Tenn Cts
Bwg Gn
GRAYSWOOD GDNS
RAINBOW IND EST
FIRSTWAY
BUSHEY RD
MERTON MANS
B286
FARNHAM GDNS
POLESDEN GDNS
69
BEVERLEY WAY
STOURHEAD GDNS
SAVILL GDNS
HIDCOTE GDNS
WEST BARNES LA
BUSHEY CT
B279
P
Sports Ctr
Allot Gdns
Bushey Mead
22
A
Sp Gd
BODNANT GDNS
Bushey Mead
B
23
200
C
D
Superstore
Tenn Cts
VANFAME CT
Beverley
Drv Rng
A298
BARNSCROFT
Sp Gd
Raynes Park
CHURCH WLK
MICHAEL MAS
1 PETWORTH GDNS
Pl Fld

The All England Lawn Tennis & Croquet Club
Wimbledon Lawn Tennis Mus
Wimbledon Park
157
WIMBLEDON
Wimbledon
SW19
South Wimbledon
MERTON
Merton Park
SW20
Superstore
Wimbledon Stadium
Cemy
Allot Gdns
Park House Sch
Ricards Lodge Sch
Bishop Gilpins Sch
Wimbledon High Sch
Priory Sch
Holy Trinity Sch
South Park Gdns
St Mary's Sch
Dundonald Road
Dundonald Prim Sch
Croydon Tramlink
Merton Park
Nelson
Rutlish Sch (Boys)
Merton Park First Sch
Wimbledon Chase
Morden Road
Joseph Hood Fst Sch
Kendor Gdns
NELSON TRAD EST
LOMBARD BSNS PK
JUBILEE WKS
WIMBLEDON STADIUM BSNS CTR
DURNSFORD RD
GAP RD
ALEXANDRA RD
WIMBLEDON HILL RD
WORPLE RD
THE BROADWAY
MERTON RD
MERTON HIGH ST
KINGSTON RD
HARTFIELD RD
HAYDONS RD
PLOUGH LA
MORDEN RD
DORSET RD
QUEEN'S RD
A219
A218
A238
A24
A298
B235
B285
180
201
A
B
C
D
1
2
3
4
5
6
Morden

SW17
158
Summerstown
A
B
C
D
72
6
5
71
4
3
70
2
1
69
26
27
202
179
Wimbledon Stadium
Superstore
Allot Gdns
Crem
Cemy
Plough La
Burnsford Rd
Haydons Road
Recn Gd
Wandle Meadow
Garfield First Sch
South Wimbledon
Haydon's Rd
All Saints CE First Sch
Wandle Park
Colliers Wood
Merton High St
Merantun Way
Hypermarket
Priory Ret Pk
Merton Abbey Mills
Merton Ind Pk
Windsor Ave
Jubilee Way
Saxon Bsns Ctr
Harland Fst Sch
Haslemere Fst Sch
SW19
Morden Rd
Morden Hall
Lombard Bsns Pk
Jubilee Wks
Garratt La
Smallwood Prim Sch
Broadwater Prim Sch
Tooting Broadway
Tooting Mkts
Tooting Gdns
St George's
Tooting Graveney
Tooting High St
Upper Tooting Rd
High Street Colliers Wood
Mitcham Rd
Sellincourt Jun & Inf Schs
Collier's Wood
Tooting
Singlegate First Sch
Christchurch Rd
Western Rd
CR4
Lavender Pk
Liberty Mid Sch
Bond Fst Sch
London Rd
Tandem Ctr
College Fields Bsns Ctr
Chelsea Fields
Recn Gd
Liby
Pl Fld

Tooting Bec Common
159
Streatham Park
TOOTING BEC RD
Horse Ride
GARRAD'S RD
FISHERS CL 1
SAXONCROFT HO 2
WELLINGTON MEWS 3
WOODBOURNE AVE
TARRINGTON CL
BECMEAD AVE
NUNEHAM
PRENTIS RD
PINKERTON PL
SHEPLEY CT
TOOTING BEC GDNS
THE GLEBE
AMBLESIDE AVE
Furzedown
Athletics Gd
OLDFIELD HO
Bwg Gn
PRINGLE GDNS
ULLATHORNE RD
NUGENT CT
BUSBY HO
BOYCE HO
GRIERSON HO
SHENSTONE HO
THE ALDERS
FURZEDOWN RD
CLAIRVIEW RD
BIRCHWOOD RD
CHURCH LA
SW17
RECTORY LA
MACMILLAN WAY
MOLYNEUX DR
LISLE CL
FRANCISCAN RD
1 BRUCE LAWNS
2 BRUCE HALL MEWS
Tenn Cts
Bwg Gns
Graveney Sch
Inst
WELHAM RD
BECLANDS RD
SOUTHCROFT RD
Links Sch
LINKS RD
KNAPTON MEWS
LINKS WAY
MITCHAM LA
SW16
FAYLAND AVE
COLWYN CL
SWALLOW GDNS
BABINGTON RD
CONAL CT 1
LYNN CT 2
BABINGTON CT 3
CLIVE CT 4
FAIRMILE AVE
Streatham
Ice Rink
STREATHAM HIGH RD
STANEDGE CT
STANTHORPE
WESTCOTE RD
RACKHAM MEWS
BLEGBOROUGH RD
Eardley Sch
POTTER'S LA
SOMERVILLE CT
BARROW RD
PATHFIELD RD
GREYHOUND LA
Superstore
182
Streatham Common
Streatham Vale
STREATHAM VALE
THE BUNGALOWS
BROOKSIDE CT
RIDGE RD
MASKANI WLK 1
SUMMERENE CL 2
Allot Gdns
Merton
Lambeth
Wandsworth
CR4
STREATHAM RD
ASHBOURNE RD
GORRINGE PARK AVE
MELROSE AVE
GARDEN AVE
ELMHURST AVE
BEECHOLME AVE
MITCHAM IND EST
Beecholme Prim Sch
Fball Gd
SHERWOOD AVE
WOODMANSTERNE RD
Woodmansterne Prim Sch
RUNNYMEDE CRES
New Stanford Prim Sch
Norbury Manor Prim Sch
Sp Gd
Pl Fld
Pav
Streatham Vale T Cts
Caplan Est
Mitcham Vale High Sch
Lonesome Prim Sch
Recn Gd
Crem
Cemy
Rowan High Sch
ROWAN RD
GREYHOUND TERR
LONGTHORNTON RD
LYMINGTON CL
WINDERMERE RD
MITCHAM
203
Tamworth Manor Sch
The Alfred Mizen
William
A
B
C
D
1
2
3
4
5
6
69
70
71
72

STREATHAM
Streatham Common
SW16
SE27
CR7
Norbury
Norbury Park
Norwood Grove
Streatham Vale
STREATHAM HIGH RD
STREATHAM COMM N
STREATHAM COMM S
CROWN LA
GREEN LA
LONDON RD
KNIGHT'S HILL
GREYHOUND LA
WESTWELL ROAD
A23
A214
A215
A216
B272
B273
160
181
204
1 ELPHINSTONE CT
2 RIDLEY CT
3 BLADON CT
4 COMMONSIDE CT
5 SANDERS HO
6 BYBON CL
Horse Ride
Bishop Thomas Grant RC Sec Sch
St Andrews RC Prim Sch
Sunnyhill Prim Sch
Julians Prim Sch
Crown Lane Prim Sch
St Joseph's RC Coll
Norbury Manor Girl's High Sch
Norbury Manor Prim Sch
New Stanford Prim Sch
Kensington Avenue Jun & Inf Schs
St James The Great RC Prim Sch
Tamworth Manor Sch
Immanuel Sch
Superstore
Ice Rink
Dunraven Sch
NORBURY TRAD EST
Allot Gdns
Tenn Cts
Bwg Gn
Pl Fld
Sp Gd
Recn Gd
Pav
Liby
Lambeth
Croydon

West Norwood
Cemy
Crem
Elm Wood Prim Sch
West Norwood
Kingsdale Sch
Sydenham Hill
161
A2199
SOUTH CROXTED RD
CLEVEDON CT 1
EMMANUEL HO 2
PARK HALL ROAD TRAD EST
TRITTON RD
ATWOOD HO 1
BARKER HO 2
BLACKSTONE HO 3
BERESFORD HO 4
BRADLORD HO 5
BRODERICK HO 6
BUCHANAN HO 7
10 GARRAWAY HO
11 BREAKSPEARE
LOW CROSS WOOD LA
OAKS
Tenn Cts
72
ST CLEMENT'S HEIGHTS
PILGRIM HILL
CARNAC ST
CHALFORD RD
NELLO JAMES GDNS
MOUNT PLEASANT
DURBAN RD
AUCKLAND HILL
EAST PL
WARING ST
NORWOOD HIGH ST B232
Allot Gdns
THE WINDSOR CTR
ADVANCE RD
WINDSOR GR
WINDSOR CL
BALMORAL CT
CLYTHA CT
ST CLOUD RD
DENIS RD
ST GOTHARD RD
ST LOUIS RD
BERRY LA
BURTWELL LA
HAMILTON RD
HAMILTON RD IND EST
ST SAVIOUR'S COLL
ROMMANY RD
GIPSY RD
ROMMANY CT
SURREY MEWS
PAXTON PL
ALLEYN PK
LITTLE BORNES
ROUSE GDNS
BAIRD GDNS
BOWEN DR
KINSEY HO
JULIAN HO
Liby
PO
LYALL AVE
SEELEY DR
KINGSWOOD DR
HITHERWOOD CT
HITHERWOOD DR
COLLEGE RD
GREAT BROWNINGS
WOODSYRE
SYDENHAM HILL
MOUNTACRE CL
TALISMAN SQ
DOME HILL PK
ROCK HILL
CHESTNUT PL
Lewisham
Southwark
BLUEBELL CL
FOUNTAIN DR
HOGARTH CT
WAVEL PL
THE GRADIENT
HIGH LEVEL DR
VIGILANT CL
6
HILLCREST CL
1 SHAMROCK
2 CAMBRIA HO
3 TARQUIN HO
4 PEMBERTON
5 LONGHEDGE
DULWICH WOOD PK A2199
COLLEGE RD
GLEBE HYRST
GILES COPPICE
WICKERS OAKE
LYMER AVE
TYLNEY AVE
HUNTERS MDW
BELL MDW
ROCKWELL GDNS
RUSHOLME GR
DULWICH WOOD AVE
GRAZELEY CT
HILLVIEW CT
OAKS AVE
CHARTERS CL
BENTON'S LA
AUBYN HILL
FINCH AVE
BENTON'S RISE
SUMMERSELL HO
Kingswood Prim Sch
ANTIGUA WLK 1
CLAYLANDS CT 2
EYLEWOOD RD
MORTON HO
NORWOOD PARK RD
GIPSY ROAD GDNS
Allot Gdns
Sch
ELDER RD
B232
TIVOLI RD
WOODVALE WLK
LONGMEAD HO
Games Ct
1 LEVEHURST HO
2 HALLANE HO
3 PONDEFIELD HO
4 WHITTAM HO
5 ELDERWOOD PL
Norwood Park
Lambeth
STARLEE MEWS
UNITY CL
Allot Gdns
Norwood Sch
KINGSTON SQ
ST KITTS TERR
MONTSERRAT CL
BERRIDGE RD
SALTER'S HILL
WHITELEY RD
BRISTOW RD
SAINSBURY RD
Gipsy Hill
GIPSY HILL
GARVENS
KNOLL CT
LOWOOD CT
COLBY RD
DRAKE CT
CRYSTAL CT
FARQUHAR RD
Mast
5
Crystal Palace
Crystal Palace Park
71
Bromley
CRYSTAL PALACE PAR
A212
ALEXANDRA DR
DURNING RD
BLOOMHALL RD
GIBBS SQ
GIBBS AVE
GIBBS CL
FORBES CT
GOULD CT
BECONDALE RD
CAWNPORE ST
Sch
WOODLAND RD
BOWLEY LA
SPINNEY GDNS
BOWLEY CL
JASPER RD
VICTORIA CRES
HIGHLANDS CT
NEW GREEN PL
HIGHLAND RD
WOODLAND HILL
WOODLAND CL
CAMDEN HILL RD
1 GLENHURST CT
2 MARLOWE CT
3 GRENVILLE CT
4 RALEIGH CT
5 BEECHWOODS CT
6 BURNTWOOD VIEW
1 NIGHTINGALE CT
2 MOLLIE DAVIS CT
3 TELFORD CL
4 BRUNEL CL
P
4
CROWN DALE
Croydon
Norwood
WYCHWOOD WAY 1
LAMBETH PROSPECT 2
ROMANY PROSPECT 3
ESSEX CT 4
ILKLEY CL 5
MOUNT RD 6
CENTRAL HILL
ROMAN RISE
HAWKE RD
OAKWOOD DR
LUNHAM RD
VICARS OAK RD
WESTOW HILL
COOPERS YD
BEARDELL ST
Liby
PO
Mus
ANERLEY HILL
GROSVENOR CT
LEDRINGTON RD
CRYSTAL PALACE STATION
184
St Joseph's RC Jun & Inf Schs
Norwood New Town
H
OXFORD RD
NASEBY RD
CRYSTAL TERR
DOVER RD
EAGLE HILL
ESSEX GR
TROY RD
HANCOCK RD
TRELOAR GDNS
SURRIDGE GDNS
ROCKMOUNT RD
HIGH VIEW RD
VERMONT RD
ORLEANS RD
CHEVENING RD
COURTNEY CL
SOUTH VALE
GATESTONE RD
HAYNES LA
PADDOCK GDNS
LOVETT CL
WESTOW ST
ST AUBYN'S RD
PATTERSON RD
CINTRA CT
MILESTONE RD
PATTERSON CT
CINTRA PK
PLEYDELL AVE
PLEYDELL PALACE RD
VICTORY PL
BEAUMONT RD
RYEFIELD RD
HERMITAGE RD
WEDGWOOD WAY
CONVENT HILL
PYTCHLEY CRES
HERMITAGE GDNS
FOUNDERS GDNS
Pav
Rockmount Prim Sch
BEDWARDINE RD
COXWELL RD
SE19
Upper Norwood
Recn Gd
Tenn Cts
EVERSLEY RD
ELIZABETH WAY
HAROLD RD
NESBITT SQ
ROSETTA CT
SILVERTON LO
ALMA PL
RAMA LA
TUDOR RD
LANSDOWNE PL
PALACE SQ
DRGTE CL
CHIPSTEAD CL
BELVEDERE RD
ANERLEY GR
WALDEGRAVE RD
HAMLET RD
ANERLEY VALE
HAMLOW PL
3
A214
Downsview Prim Sch
BEULAH HILL
THE WOODLANDS
PRIORY CRES
MENLO GDNS
MATILDA CL
ELLERY RD
COLLEGE GN
ESKMONT RIDGE
RUSHDEN CL
HIGHFIELD HILL
RAVENSDALE GDNS
WAKEFIELD GDNS
FITZROY GDNS
EFFRA CT
HOMELANDS DR
HAMLYN GDNS
CHURCH RD
AUGUSTUS CT
BRAYBROOKE GDNS
JENSON WAY
SUMMIT WAY
TELFORD RISE
REYNARD DR
FOX HILL
FOX HILL GDNS
Pl Fld
Bromley
PALACE GR
SUTTON CT
Croydon
COPPER CL
MBERLY CT
MABERLEY CRES
VERSAILLES RD
DOWNSVIEW GDNS
GLENHURST RISE
Pl Fld
1 SOUTH VIEW CT
2 WHITEOAK HO
Tenn Cts
Westwood Language Coll
STAMBOURNE WAY
BUCKLEIGH WAY
LIME KILN PL
Allot Gdns
MOWBRAY CT
MOWBRAY RD
70
Anerley Sch for Boys
WADDINGTON WAY
WESTWOOD AVE
SPURGEON RD
SPURGEON AVE
FREETHORPE CL
UPPER BEULAH HILL
TURKEY OAK CL
SOUTHHOLME CL
TREEVIEW CL
SYLVAN HILL
THE DELL
Harris City Tech Coll
BEDFORD CT
DOWNS RD
Allot Gdns
DALE PARK RD
SPA HILL
All Saint's Schs
CRANBROOK HO 1
RAVENSROOST 2
WINDSOR CT 3
BLENHEIM CT 4
SCORESDALE 5
AUCKLAND RISE
AUCKLAND GDNS
AUCKLAND RD
KITLEY GDNS
SYLVAN RD
Lewis Sp & L Ctr
2
INGRAM RD
SPRINGFIELD RD
David Livingstone Prim Sch
THE LAWNS
LUPUS CT
TEMPLETON CL
A212
FORSYTE CRES
Mast
TV Sta
1 EVEREST CT
2 BRAE CT
AUCKLAND CL
ACORN GDNS
CANTLEY GDNS
Allot Gdns
1 ROLAND CT
2 CARLTON CT
3 ENDERLEY HO
St Cyprian's Prim Sch
BEAUCHAMP RD
PO
SPA CL
HILLTOP CT
KINGS
DORRINGTON CT
Cypress Inf Sch
Pav
Pl Fld
South Norwood Lake
OSTERLY GDNS
WESTBROOK RD
HOWBERRY RD
CRANBROOK RD
UPTON RD
PO
NORTHWOOD RD
PENRITH RD
BURLINGTON RD
MOFFAT RD
LAYARD RD
FLAXMORE CT
MERSHAM PL
GRANGE HILL
TEESDALE GDNS
GRANGE AVE
GRANGECLIFFE GDNS
GRANGE GDNS
A215
TUMMONS GDNS
HAZEL BANK
CYPRESS LO
CYPRESS RD
SUNSET GDNS
HIGH VIEW CL
Cypress Jun Sch
Tenn Cts
Bwg Gn
1 WETHERBY CT
2 THE BIRCHES
3 HARDING CT
4 FRANCES CT
Pav
LAKESIDE CL
1
OSBORNE GDNS
DAIRY CL
OSBORNE GDNS
WESTMINSTER CT
ROSEBERY AVE
BYRON CT
NEWNHAM CL
LAKEMAN CT
SPEKE RD
LIVINGSTONE RD
MERSHAM RD
LENHAM RD
HYTHE RD
Spurgeon's Coll
WHARNCLIFFE GDNS
WHARNCLIFFE RD
FALKLAND PARK AVE
PIERREPOINT RD
SOUTH NORWOOD HILL
STUART LO
HOWDEN CT
HOWDEN RD
WOODVALE AVE
ROCHESTER CT
ROCHESTER AVENUE GDNS
WARMINSTER RD
69
BEULAH CRES
BEULAH AVE
NORBURY RD
FOUNTAIN DR
SANDFIELD PL
PARK LAWN
QUEENSBURY CT
ATHOLE TERR
BENSHAM GR
PARCHMORE RD
PO
Beulah Schs
FURZE RD
HAMILTON RD
HEATH RD
KITCHENER RD
ANNSWORTHY CRES
GRANGE RD
33
205
Grangewood Park
Pav
Bwg Gn
BAKERS
CUTHBERT GDNS
ARDENT CL
CRANLEIGH
Tenn Cts
B266
WOODVALE CT
COURT RD
SUNDIAL AVE
LANCASTER RD
34
PITTVILLE GDNS
SPRINGFIELD
NUGENT
A
B
C
D
A
B
C
D

A
B
C
D
162
206
183
SE26
SE20
SE19
Upper Sydenham
Sydenham
Crystal Palace
Crystal Palace Park
Crystal Palace National Sports Ctr
Penge East
Penge West
PENGE
Anerley
Elmers End
Birkbeck
Sydenham Wells Park
Mayow Park
Betts Park
South Norwood Lake
Forest Hill Sec Sch
Alexandra Jun Sch
Malcolm Prim Sch
James Dixon Prim Sch
Anerley Sch for Boys
Anerley Prim Sch
Orchard School Sp Ctr
Royston Prim Sch
Harris City Tech Coll
Lewis Sp & L Ctr
Avenue Road
Croydon Tramlink
Green Chain Walk
Hospice
Mast
Crem
WESTWOOD HILL
SYDENHAM RD
KIRKDALE
CRYSTAL PALACE PARK RD
CRYSTAL PALACE PAR
COLLEGE RD
ANERLEY HILL
ANERLEY RD
CROYDON RD
HIGH ST
NEWLANDS PK
PARISH LA
GREEN LA
ELMERS END RD
PENGE RD
A212
A213
A214
A234
A2216
Lewisham
Southwark
Bromley
Croydon

Bell Green
SE26
Superstore
Stanton Sq
STANTON WAY
SYDENHAM RD
A2218
Lower Sydenham
Lower Sydenham
New Beckenham
New Beckenham
Pool River
Bellingham
SE6
SOUTHEND LA
SOUTHEND RD
BECKENHAM HILL RD
Beckenham Hill
Beckenham Place
Sedgehill Sch
Cator Park Sch for Girls
Green Chain Wlk
Kent House
Beckenham Junction
Beckenham Green
RECTORY RD
BECKENHAM RD
Clock House
BR3
BROMLEY RD
MANOR RD
HIGH ST
BECKENHAM
Beckenham
Kelsey Park
WICKHAM RD
Lewisham
Bromley
163
186
207
72
71
70
69
38
37
6
5
4
3
2
1
A
B
C
D

A
B
164
C
D
Southend
SE6
St John Baptist CE Prim Sch
Bonus Pastor RC Sch
New Woodlands Sch
Downderry Prim Sch
Downham Fields
Good Shepherd RC Prim Sch
Beckenham Hill
BECKENHAM HILL RD
A21
A2218
A2015
BR1
Rangefield Prim Sch
Downham
BROMLEY HILL
Shaftesbury Park
Cemy
Beckenham Place
Beckenham Place Park
Beckenham Place Pk
185
Ravensbourne River
Lewisham
Bromley
BR3
Ravensbourne
St Mary's RC Prim Sch
BR2
Sp Gds
LONDON RD
Bromley Park
BROMLEY
Sloane
BROMLEY RD
A222
BECKENHAM LA
Bishop Challoner Sch
St Christopher's Sch
Shortlands
Clare House Prim Sch
Valley Prim Sch
Recn Gd
WICKHAM RD
208
38
39
SOUTHEND RD
DOWNHAM WAY
RANGEFIELD RD
FARNABY RD
BROMLEY AVE
RAVENSBOURNE AVE
WARREN AVE
SHORTLANDS RD
STATION RD
FOXGROVE RD
THE AVENUE
ALBEMARLE RD
BRANGBOURNE RD
OAKRIDGE RD
WINLATON RD
OLDSTEAD RD

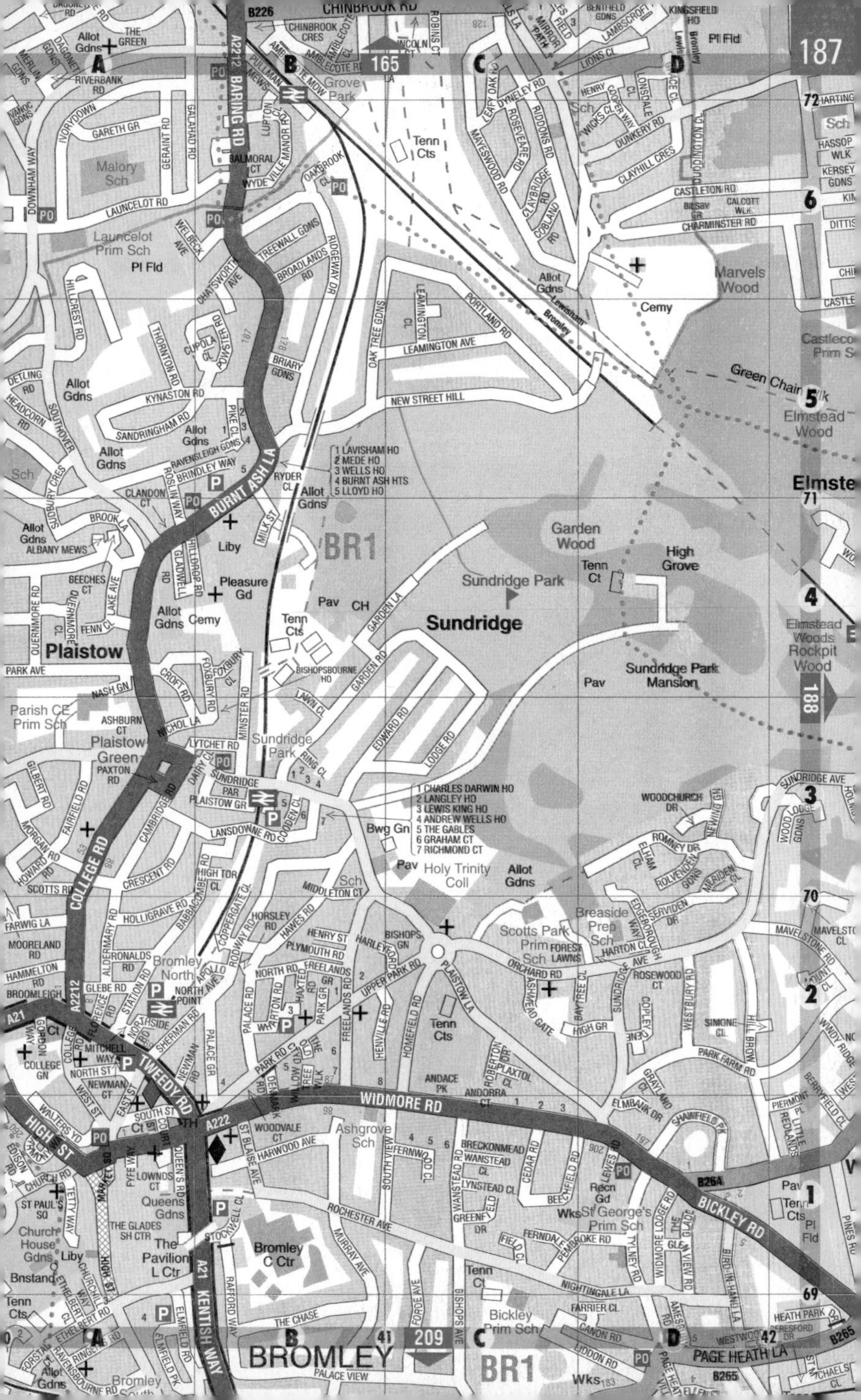
CHINBROOK RD
B226
CHINBROOK CRES
AMBLECOTE RD
165
ROBINS CT
A2212
BARING RD
Allot Gdns
THE GREEN
RIVERBANK RD
DAGONET GDNS
MERLIN GDNS
PULLMAN MEWS
Grove Park
BENTHEIELD GDNS
KINGSFIELD HO
LAMBSCROFT
MIRROR PATH
LIONS CL
Pl Fld
HARTING
Sch
HASSOP WLK
KERSEY GDNS
IVORYDOWN
GARETH GR
GERAINT RD
GALAHAD RD
LUPTON CL
Tenn Cts
LEAFY OAK RD
DYNELEY RD
HENRY COOPER WAY
LONSDALE CL
WICKS CL
DUNKERY RD
Malory Sch
BALMORAL CT
WYDE VILLE MANOR RD
OAKBROOK CL
MAYESWOOD RD
ROSEVEARE RD
RIDDONS RD
CLAYHILL CRES
CLAYBRIDGE RD
COBLAND RD
CASTLETON RD
BILSBY GR
CALCOTT WLK
CHARMINSTER RD
DITTIS
DOWNHAM WAY
LAUNCELOT RD
PO
Launcelot Prim Sch
Pl Fld
WELBECK AVE
TREEWALL GDNS
BROADLANDS RD
RIDGEWAY DR
Allot Gdns
Cemy
Marvels Wood
CHI
CASTLE
HILLCREST RD
CHATSWORTH AVE
THORNTON RD
CUPOLA CL
POWSTER RD
BRIARY GDNS
LEAMINGTON CL
LEAMINGTON AVE
PORTLAND RD
OAK TREE GDNS
Lewisham
Bromley
Castlecombe Prim Sch
Green Chain Wk
DETLING RD
HEADCORN RD
SOUTHOVER
Allot Gdns
KYNASTON RD
SANDRINGHAM RD
PIKE CL
RAVENSLEIGH GDNS
BRINDLEY WAY
ROSLIN WAY
NEW STREET HILL
Elmstead Wood
1 LAVISHAM HO
2 MEDE HO
3 WELLS HO
4 BURNT ASH HTS
5 LLOYD HO
RYDER CL
BURNT ASH LA
Sch
SUDBURY CRES
CLANDON CT
Elmste
Allot Gdns
BROOK LA
ALBANY MEWS
MILK ST
Liby
BR1
Garden Wood
High Grove
Tenn Ct
HILLDROP RD
GLADWELL RD
Pleasure Gd
Sundridge Park
BEECHES CT
QUERNMORE RD
QUERNMORE CL
LAKE AVE
FENN CL
Allot Gdns
Cemy
Pav
CH
GARDEN LA
Sundridge
Elmstead Woods
Rockpit Wood
Plaistow
PARK AVE
FOXBURY CL
FOXBURY RD
CROFT RD
Tenn Cts
BISHOPSBOURNE HO
GARDEN RD
Sundridge Park Mansion
Pav
NASH GN
Parish CE Prim Sch
ASHBURN CT
NICHOL LA
MINSTER RD
LAWN CL
EDWARD RD
LODGE RD
188
Plaistow Green
LYTCHET RD
DAIRY CL
Sundridge Park
RING CL
PAXTON RD
SUNDRIDGE PAR
PLAISTOW GR
GOODEN CT
CAMBRIDGE RD
1 CHARLES DARWIN HO
2 LANGLEY HO
3 LEWIS KING HO
4 ANDREW WELLS HO
5 THE GABLES
6 GRAHAM CT
7 RICHMOND CT
SUNDRIDGE AVE
WOODCHURCH DR
NEWING GN
WOOD LODGE GDNS
GILBERT RD
FAIRFIELD RD
MORGAN RD
HOWARD RD
COLLEGE RD
LANSDOWNE RD
Bwg Gn
ROMNEY DR
ELHAM CL
ROLVENDEN GDNS
MERIDEN CL
SCOTTS RD
CRESCENT RD
HIGH TOR CL
BABBACOMBE RD
Pav
Holy Trinity Coll
Allot Gdns
MIDDLETON CT
Sch
FARWIG LA
HOLLIGRAVE RD
COPPERGATE CL
HORSLEY RD
HAWES RD
Breaside Prep Sch
SERVIDEN DR
EDGEBOROUGH WAY
MAVELSTONE RD
MAVELSTONE CL
MOORELAND RD
HAMMELTON RD
ALDERMARY RD
RONALDS RD
Bromley North
APOLLO AVE
RODWAY RD
HENRY ST
PLYMOUTH RD
HARLEYFORD
BISHOPS GN
Scotts Park Prim Sch
FOREST LAWNS
HARTON CL
BROOMLEIGH
GLEBE RD
STATION RD
NORTH POINT
NORTH RD
FREELANDS RD
UPPER PARK RD
PLAISTOW LA
ORCHARD RD
ASHMEAD GATE
BAYTREE CL
SUNDRIDGE AVE
ROSEWOOD CT
WESTBURY RD
MOUNT CL
A21
GORDON WAY
COLLEGE GN
MITCHELL WAY
NORTHSIDE
SHERMAN RD
PALACE RD
PALACE GR
WHARTON RD
HAXTED RD
PARK GR
HENVILLE RD
HOMEFIELD RD
Tenn Cts
HIGH GR
COPLEY DENE
SIMONE CL
HILL BROW
WINDY RIDGE
NORTH ST
NEWMAN CT
WEST ST
EAST ST
TWEEDY RD
NEWMAN RD
PARK RD
DENMARK RD
WILLOW CT
OLD TREE CT
LIME WLK
ROBERTON DR
PLAXTOL CL
ANDACE PK
ANDORRA CT
PARK FARM RD
BERRYFIELD CL
PIERMONT PL
LITTLE REDLANDS
WALTERS YD
SOUTH ST
COURT ST
A222
WIDMORE RD
GRAYLAND CL
ELMBANK DR
SHAWFIELD PK
HIGH ST
EDISON RD
PO
FYFE WAY
QUEEN'S RD
WOODVALE CT
ST BLAISE AVE
HARWOOD AVE
Ashgrove Sch
SOUTH VIEW
FERNWOOD CT
BRECKONMEAD
WANSTEAD CL
CEDAR RD
BEECHFIELD RD
LEWES RD
B264
BICKLEY RD
CHURCH RD
TETTY WAY
MARKET SQ
LOWNDS CT
Queens Gdns
WANSTEAD RD
LYNSTEAD CL
GREENFIELD DR
Recn Gd
St George's Prim Sch
WIDMORE LODGE RD
THE GLADE
GLEN VIEW RD
Pav
Tenn Cts
Pl Fld
PINES RD
ST PAUL'S SQ
Church House Gdns
THE GLADES SH CTR
The Pavilion L Ctr
STOCKWELL CL
ROCHESTER AVE
Bromley C Ctr
MURRAY AVE
FIELD CL
FERNDALE
PEMBROKE RD
TYLNEY RD
BIRD-IN-HAND LA
Liby
CHURCHILL WAY
HIGH ST
Bnstand
A21
KENTISH WAY
RAFFORD WAY
FORDE AVE
BISHOPS AVE
Tenn Ct
NIGHTINGALE LA
Tenn Cts
ETHELBERT CL
ETHELBERT RD
ELMFIELD RD
THE CHASE
Bickley Prim Sch
FARRIER CL
CANON RD
AMESBURY RD
HEATH PARK DR
BERESFORD RD
WESTWOOD
B265
CORSTAN
RINGERS RD
RAVENSBOURNE RD
ELMFIELD PK
Allot Gdns
Bromley South
BROMLEY
209
PALACE VIEW
BR1
LIDDON RD
PO
PAGE HEATH VIL
PAGE HEATH LA
B265
Wks
ST MICHAELS CL
A
B
C
D
1
2
3
4
5
6
72
71
70
69
41
42

A
B
C
D
166
210
187
72
6
5
71
4
3
70
2
1
69
42
43
Elmstead
Chislehurst West
Widmore
Bickley
BR7
Marvels Wood
Castlecombe Prim Sch
Green Chain Wlk
Elmstead Wood
Elmstead Woods
Rockpit Wood
Ravensbourne Coll
Babington House Sch
Bullers Wood Sch
Red Hill Prim Sch
Camden Park
Chislhurst
Montbelle Prim Sch
Bickley Park Sch
Chislehurst
Caves
Allot Gdns
Tenn Cts
Pav
Sch
Liby
PO
Recn Gd
Pl Fld
Crkt Gd
CH
WHITE HORSE HILL
RED HILL
CHISLEHURST HIGH ST
GREEN LA
A208
B263
B264
B265
A222
BICKLEY RD
BICKLEY PARK RD
CHISLEHURST RD
OLD HILL
SUMMER HILL
BROMLEY RD
PAGE HEATH LA
DUNKERY RD
HARTING RD
BEACONSFIELD RD
HORLEY RD
HASSOP WLK
KERSEY GDNS
KIMMERIDGE RD
CASTLETON RD
CALCOTT WLK
BILSBY GR
CHARMINSTER RD
DITTISHAM RD
ESCOTT GDNS
ICKLETON RD
CHILHAM RD
CASTLECOMBE RD
CATTISTOCK RD
OLD MANOR WAY
HORNING CL
TENTERDEN CL
ST KEVERNE RD
FRAMLINGHAM CRES
RAVENSWORTH RD
THURSLEY RD
WIDECOMBE
SENNEN WLK
FARM RD
BUCKLER GDNS
SMARDEN GR
PRESTBURY SQ
OFFENHAM RD
STEYNING GR
MELLS CRES
MORSTON GDNS
WAYSIDE GR
JAY GDNS
LOUIS GDNS
WALDEN AVE
CROFT CL
BROADHEATH DR
FENTON CL
CRANMORE RD
ELMSTEAD AVE
OAKDENE AVE
ELMSTEAD LA
FOSTERS CL
DOWNS AVE
HALLAM CL
MELANDA CL
FREWING CL
WALDEN RD
ELMSTEAD GLADE
ELMLEE CL
KNOWLE LO
THE WEALD
ROBIN HILL DR
WOOD DR
BENNETTS COPSE
GRANGE DR
DENBIGH CL
CLIFFORD AVE
MELBURY CL
STATION APP
SANDY RIDGE
OAKWOOD CL
GROVE VALE
SELBY CL
SYLVESTER AVE
SOUTH HILL
YESTER PK
SOUTHILL RD
YESTER RD
GREATWOOD
BEECHCROFT
PINE WOOD
FOXHOME CL
WOODHAYES
WILLOW GR
WILLOW VALE
LYNDHURST
PINEHURST
WRRAL WOOD CL
FURZEFIELD
NURSERY GDNS
EMPRESS DR
QUEEN'S PAS 1
POND PATH 2
CAMDEN GR
KINGSLEY MEWS
HOLLINGTON CT
MAXWELL HO
WILDERNESS RD
PRINCE IMPERIAL RD
CAMDEN WAY
CAMDEN PARK RD
1 KNIGHTSBRIDGE MEWS
2 LUBBOCK CT
3 ROSS CT
4 BURLINGTON LO
HATTON CT
LUBBOCK RD
BONCHESTER CL
RAGGLESWOOD
EUGENIE MEWS
HANGMANS CNR
CRICKET GROUND RD
ONSLOW CRES
PAGET GDNS
NORLANDS CRES
RAVENSHILL
SHERIDAN CRES
PENN GDNS
CROMLIX CL
THISTLEMEAD
LINDENFIELD
HEATHERBANK
LONGMEAD
ROUNDWOOD
MILL PL
SUSAN WOOD
ISLEHURST CL
OAKLEIGH PARK AVE
WOODCLYFFE DR
TIMBER CL
FOREST CL
IMPERIAL PL
CAVESIDE CL
RUTLAND CT
DEVEMA CL
BRENCHLEY CL
ROOKERY DR
CONISCLIFFE CL
ENDERFIELD CT
ABBEY GDNS
PORRINGTON CL
KINCRAIG
CLARE CT
LOWER CAMDEN
OAKHURST CL
TUDOR CL
MERLEWOOD DR
PRIORY CL
HUNTS MEAD CL
BRUTON CL
BULLERS CL
WOOD DR
YESTER DR
SQUIRES WOOD DR
BONAR PL
SUNDRIDGE AVE
HOLMBURY PK
WOOD LODGE GDNS
NEWING GN
MERIDEN CL
LOGS HILL
HIGHGROVE CL
MAVELSTONE CL
MAVELSTONE RD
MOUNT CL
LOGS HILL CL
ST NICOLAS LA
KINGSMERE
NORTHFIELD CL
WINDY RIDGE
WESTLEIGH DR
BERRYFIELD CL
PIERMONT PL
LITTLE REDLANDS
PARK FARM RD
HILL BROW
SIMONE CL
WESTBURY RD
HAWFIELD PK
WOODKNOLL DR
MERRYDOWN WAY
ST GEORGES RD W
BEECH COPSE
THE SPINNEYS
ASPEN COPSE
CEDAR COPSE
SPINNEY OAK
OAK CT
DENBRIDGE RD
VALE RD
WYTHES CL
WELLANDS CL
WELLS RD
EASTMEAD CL
INGLEWOOD COPSE
WOODLANDS RD
WOODLANDS CL
HARTLEY CL
PINES RD
FARO CL
COATES HILL RD
GOSSHILL RD
HEVER GDNS
WELLSMOOR GDNS
REYNARD CL
SHORNEFIELD CL
HEATH PARK DR
BERESFORD
WESTWOOD
ST MICHAELS CL
STRATFORD HOUSE AVE
CHARLOTTE PARK AVE
ST GEORGES RD
ST MATTHEWS DR
OTFORD CL
GLADE
VIEW RD
BIRD-IN-HAND LA
ELLEN CL
WILLIAM BAREFORD
SANDLING RI
SOUTHOLD RISE
LONGCROFT
KINGSLEY WOOD
GREAT HARRY DR
BADGERS CR
THE COURSE
LEVERHOLME GDNS
JASON WLK
BIDDENDEN WAY
SWITHLAND GDNS
THE KNOLE
HATHERN GDNS
BEANSHAW
BEAUMANOR GDNS
LAMBARDE AVE
ADDERLEY GDNS
MILVERTON WAY
CROCKHAM WAY
HEVER CROFT
MAINRIDGE RD
LYDSTEP RD
HILLVIEW RD
WALKDEN RD
EILEEN CT
GREENWAY
FARMLAND WLK
HILL CL
BUSHELL WAY
INVICTA CL
VICTORIA RD
INGLEBY WAY
BARHAM RD
BARHAM CL
MEADOW CL
MARSHAM CL
TOWNSHEND RD
DEGEMA RD
BELMONT RD
ALBANY RD
ADELAIDE RD
EDWARD RD
WEST BROW 1
LORAINE CT 2
ALEXANDER RD
PARK RD
QUEEN'S MEWS
SHALLONS RD
DOMONIC DR
BROWNSPRING DR
EDGEBURY
TOYNBEC CL
GOSSINGTON
BEECHWOOD RISE
STEWART CL
WINDSOR CL
GARRARD CL
WESTHURST DR
Greenwich
Bromley

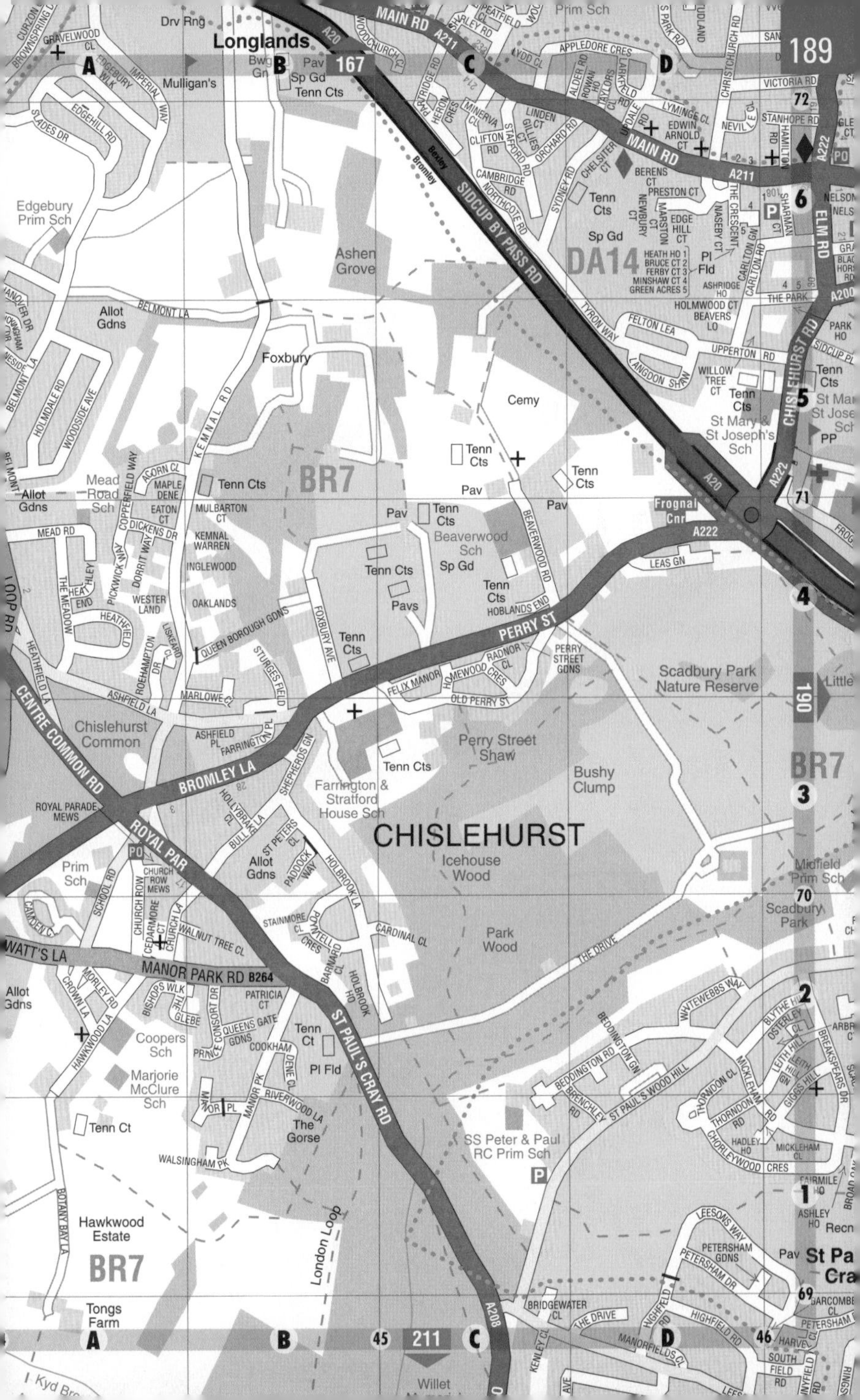

Longlands
Drv Rng
Mulligan's
Bwg Gn
Pav
Sp Gd
Tenn Cts
167
A
B
C
D
MAIN RD
A211
A20
WOODCHURCH CL
GRAVELWOOD CL
EDGEBURY WLK
IMPERIAL WAY
EDGEHILL RD
SLADES DR
BROWNSPRING DR
CURZON
PARTRIDGE RD
HERON CRES
MINERVA CL
CLIFTON RD
STAFFORD RD
LINDEN CT
GILLIES CT
ORCHARD RD
CAMBRIDGE RD
NORTHCOTE RD
SIDCUP BY PASS RD
Bexley
Bromley
LYDD CL
APPLEDORE CRES
ALDER RD
ROWAN HO
TAYLORS CL
LARKFIELD RD
UPDALE RD
LYMINGE CL
EDWIN ARNOLD CT
CHELSITER CT
BERENS CT
PRESTON CT
NEWBURY CT
MARSTON CT
EDGE HILL CT
SYDNEY RD
Tenn Cts
Sp Gd
DA14
HEATH HO 1
BRUCE CT 2
FERBY CT 3
MINSHAW CT 4
GREEN ACRES 5
Pl Fld
ASHRIDGE HO
HOLMWOOD CT
BEAVERS LO
THE CRESCENT
NASEBY CT
CARLTON GN
CARLTON RD
THE PARK
CHRISTCHURCH RD
VICTORIA RD
STANHOPE RD
NEVILLE CL
HAMILTON RD
SHARMAN CT
ELM RD
A222
A200
72
6
NELSON
189
Edgebury Prim Sch
Ashen Grove
Allot Gdns
BELMONT LA
HANOVER DR
Foxbury
KEMNAL RD
HOLMDALE RD
WOODSIDE AVE
BELMONT LA
Cemy
Tenn Cts
Pav
TYRON WAY
FELTON LEA
LANGDON SHAW
UPPERTON RD
WILLOW TREE CT
Tenn Cts
St Mary & St Joseph's Sch
CHISLEHURST RD
SIDCUP PL
PARK HO
5
PP
71
Frognal Cnr
A20
A222
LEAS GN
4
Mead Road Sch
BR7
ACORN CL
MAPLE DENE
EATON CT
COPPERFIELD WAY
MULBARTON CT
DICKENS DR
KEMNAL WARREN
INGLEWOOD
OAKLANDS
MEAD RD
PICKWICK WAY
DORRIT WAY
THE MEADOW
HEATHLEY END
HEATHFIELD
WESTER LAND
LISKEARD CL
ROEHAMPTON DR
QUEEN BOROUGH GDNS
STURGES FIELD
FOXBURY AVE
Pav
Tenn Cts
Beaverwood Sch
Sp Gd
BEAVERWOOD RD
Pavs
HOBLANDS END
PERRY ST
FELIX MANOR
HOMEWOOD CRES
RADNOR CL
PERRY STREET GDNS
OLD PERRY ST
Scadbury Park Nature Reserve
190
Little
LOOP RD
HEATHFIELD LA
CENTRE COMMON RD
ASHFIELD LA
MARLOWE CL
Chislehurst Common
ASHFIELD PL
FARRINGTON PL
BROMLEY LA
SHEPHERDS GN
HOLLYBRAKE CL
BULL LA
Tenn Cts
Perry Street Shaw
Farrington & Stratford House Sch
Bushy Clump
BR7
3
ROYAL PARADE MEWS
ROYAL PAR
PO
CHISLEHURST
Icehouse Wood
Prim Sch
SCHOOL RD
CHURCH ROW
CHURCH ROW MEWS
CEDARMORE CT
CHURCH LA
WALNUT TREE CL
Allot Gdns
ST PETERS CL
PADDOCK WAY
HOLBROOK LA
STAINMORE CL
POYNTELL CRES
CARDINAL CL
Midfield Prim Sch
70
Scadbury Park
Park Wood
THE DRIVE
CAMDEN CL
WATT'S LA
MANOR PARK RD
B264
BARNARD CL
HOLBROOK HO
MORLEY RD
CROWN LA
HAWKWOOD LA
BISHOPS WLK
THE GLEBE
PATRICIA CT
PRINCE CONSORT DR
QUEENS GATE GDNS
COOKHAM DENE CL
ST PAUL'S CRAY RD
Tenn Ct
Pl Fld
WHITEWEBBS WAY
BEDDINGTON GN
BEDDINGTON RD
2
BLYTHE HILL
OSTERLEY CL
LEITH HILL
LEITH HILL GN
BREAKSPEARS DR
ARBRO
Allot Gdns
Coopers Sch
Marjorie McClure Sch
MANOR PK
MANOR PL
RIVERWOOD LA
The Gorse
BRENCHLEY RD
ST PAUL'S WOOD HILL
THORNDON CL
MICKLEHAM RD
THORNDON RD
GIGGS HILL
Tenn Ct
WALSINGHAM PK
SS Peter & Paul RC Prim Sch
P
CHORLEYWOOD CRES
HADLEY HO
MICKLEHAM CL
FAIRMILE HO
1
ASHLEY HO
Recn
BOTANY BAY LA
Hawkwood Estate
London Loop
BR7
LEESONS WAY
PETERSHAM GDNS
PETERSHAM DR
Pav
St Pa Cra
69
BARCOMBE CL
PETERSHAM
Tongs Farm
BRIDGEWATER CL
THE DRIVE
HIGHFIELD RD
HIGHFIELD RD
MANORFIELDS CL
HARVEST
SOUTHFIELD RD
KENLEY CL
A208
45
211
46
A
B
C
D
Kyd Bro
Willet

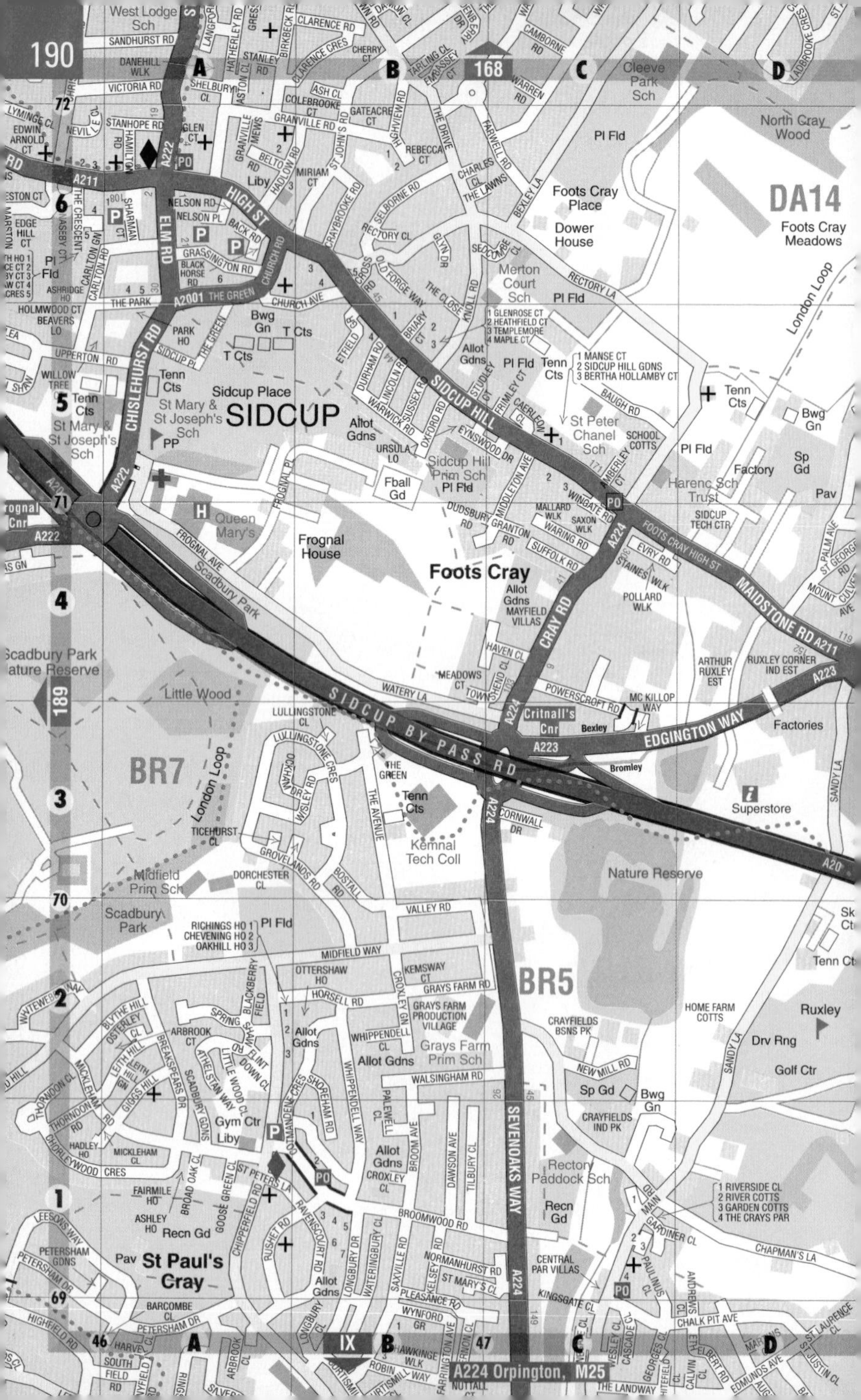

168
189
A
B
C
D
1
2
3
4
5
6
72
71
70
69
46
47
IX
SIDCUP
Foots Cray
St Paul's Cray
BR7
BR5
DA14
West Lodge Sch
SANDHURST RD
DANEHILL WLK
VICTORIA RD
SHELBURY CL
STANHOPE RD
HAMILTON RD
GLEN CT
EDWIN ARNOLD CT
LYMINGE CL
NEVILLE CL
LANGFORD
HATHERLEY RD
GRESHAM
BIRKBECK RD
CLARENCE RD
CLARENCE CRES
STANLEY RD
ASTON CL
ASH CL
COLEBROOKE CT
GRANVILLE RD
GRANVILLE MEWS
BELTON RD
HADLOW RD
Liby
MIRIAM CT
ST JOHN'S RD
GATEACRE CT
HIGHVIEW RD
REBECCA CT
CHERRY CT
TARLING CL
EMBASSEY CT
THE DRIVE
FARWELL RD
WARREN RD
CAMBORNE RD
Cleeve Park Sch
North Cray Wood
Pl Fld
Foots Cray Place
Dower House
Foots Cray Meadows
London Loop
BEXLEY LA
CHARLES CL
THE LAWNS
SELBORNE RD
RECTORY CL
GLYN DR
SEDCOMBE CL
RECTORY LA
Merton Court Sch
CRAYBROOKE RD
A211
A222
A2001
HIGH ST
ELM RD
NELSON RD
NELSON PL
BACK RD
CHURCH RD
GRASSINGTON RD
BLACK HORSE RD
THE GREEN
THE PARK
CHURCH AVE
ESTON CT
MARSTON
EDGE HILL CT
THE CRESCENT
SHARMAN CT
CARLTON GN
CARLTON RD
ASHRIDGE HO
HOLMWOOD CT
BEAVERS LO
UPPERTON RD
WILLOW TREE CT
Tenn Cts
CHISLEHURST RD
PARK HO
SIDCUP PL
Bwg Gn
T Cts
Sidcup Place
St Mary & St Joseph's Sch
PP
OLD FORGE WAY
CROSS RD
THE CLOSE
KNOLL RD
BRIARY CT
ETFIELD GR
DURHAM RD
LINCOLN RD
SUSSEX RD
WARWICK RD
OXFORD RD
SIDCUP HILL
1 GLENROSE CT
2 HEATHFIELD CT
3 TEMPLEMORE
4 MAPLE CT
Allot Gdns
STUDLEY CT
FRIMLEY CT
CAERLEON CL
1 MANSE CT
2 SIDCUP HILL GDNS
3 BERTHA HOLLAMBY CT
BAUGH RD
St Peter Chanel Sch
SCHOOL COTTS
AMBERLEY CT
Harenc Sch Trust
Factory
Sp Gd
Pav
Bwg Gn
URSULA LO
EYNSWOOD DR
Sidcup Hill Prim Sch
Fball Gd
MIDDLETON AVE
WINGATE RD
MALLARD WLK
SAXON WLK
WARING RD
DUDSBURY RD
GRANTON RD
SUFFOLK RD
SIDCUP TECH CTR
FOOTS CRAY HIGH ST
MAIDSTONE RD
PALM AVE
ST GEORGE'S RD
MOUNT CULVER AVE
A224
EVRY RD
STAINES WLK
POLLARD WLK
Frognal Cnr
A20
Queen Mary's
H
FROGNAL PL
FROGNAL AVE
Frognal House
Scadbury Park
Scadbury Park Nature Reserve
Little Wood
London Loop
MAYFIELD VILLAS
HAVEN CL
CRAY RD
ARTHUR RUXLEY EST
RUXLEY CORNER IND EST
A223
MEADOWS CT
WATERY LA
TOWNSHEND CL
POWERSCROFT RD
MC KILLOP WAY
Critnall's Cnr
Bexley
Bromley
EDGINGTON WAY
Factories
SIDCUP BY PASS RD
LULLINGSTONE CL
LULLINGSTONE CRES
OCKHAM DR
WISLEY RD
THE GREEN
THE AVENUE
Tenn Cts
Kemnal Tech Coll
CORNWALL DR
Superstore
SANDY LA
Nature Reserve
TICEHURST CL
GROVELANDS RD
DORCHESTER CL
BOSTALL RD
Midfield Prim Sch
VALLEY RD
RICHINGS HO 1
CHEVENING HO 2
OAKHILL HO 3
MIDFIELD WAY
OTTERSHAW HO
KEMSWAY CT
GRAYS FARM RD
CROXLEY GN
HORSELL RD
GRAYS FARM PRODUCTION VILLAGE
Grays Farm Prim Sch
WHIPPENDELL CL
Allot Gdns
WHITEWEBBS WAY
BLYTHE HILL
OSTERLEY CL
SPRING SHAW RD
BLACKBERRY FIELD
ARBROOK CT
FLINT DOWN CL
LITTLE WOOD CL
ATHELSTAN WAY
SCADBURY GDNS
BREAKSPEARS DR
LEITH HILL
LEITH HILL GN
GIGGS HILL
MICKLEHAM CL
THORNDON CL
THORNDON RD
HADLEY HO
CHORLEYWOOD CRES
Gym Ctr
Liby
SHOREHAM RD
COTMANDENE CRES
WHIPPENDELL WAY
WALSINGHAM RD
PALEWELL CL
BROOM AVE
DAWSON AVE
TILBURY CL
SEVENOAKS WAY
CRAYFIELDS BSNS PK
NEW MILL RD
HOME FARM COTTS
Ruxley
Drv Rng
Golf Ctr
Sp Gd
Bwg Gn
CRAYFIELDS IND PK
Rectory Paddock Sch
Recn Gd
MAIN RD
1 RIVERSIDE CL
2 RIVER COTTS
3 GARDEN COTTS
4 THE CRAYS PAR
GARDINER CL
CHAPMAN'S LA
Sk Ct
Tenn Ct
FAIRMILE HO
BROAD OAK CL
GOOSE GREEN CL
CHIPPERFIELD RD
ST PETERS LA
ASHLEY HO
Recn Gd
RUSHET RD
RAVENSCOURT RD
LONGBURY DR
WATERINGBURY CL
BROOMWOOD RD
SAXVILLE RD
KELSEY RD
NORMANHURST RD
ST MARY'S CL
PLEASANCE RD
CROXLEY CL
Allot Gdns
CENTRAL PAR VILLAS
KINGSGATE CL
PAULINUS CL
LEESONS WAY
PETERSHAM GDNS
PETERSHAM DR
Pav
BARCOMBE CL
HIGHFIELD RD
HARVEL
SOUTHFIELD RD
ARBROOK CL
LONGBURY CL
WYNFORD GR
HAWKINGE WLK
ROBIN WAY
FARRINGTON AVE
A224 Orpington, M25
NUTTALL
WESLEY CL
CASCADE CL
GEORGE'S CL
CALVIN CL
ELBERT RD
EDMUNDS AVE
CHALK PIT AVE
ANDREWS CL
MARINUS
ST LAURENCE CL
ST JUSTIN CL
THE LANDWAY

North Cray
Little Mascal Farm
BUNKERS HILL
169
Bunkers Hill
A
B
C
D
Bexley
Kent
72
Faesten Dic
LEAFIELD LA
A223
FIVE ARCH BRIDGE
River Cray
GATTONS WAY
Home Wood
COCKSURE LA
Gattons Plantation
Joyden's Wood
6
THE GROVE
PARSONAGE LA
THE SPINNEY
ST JAMES WAY
NORTH CRAY RD
Manor Farm
HIGH BEECHES
PO
5
DA14
ELLENBOROUGH RD
BULLERS CL
BEDENS RD
BURDETT CL
1 THURSLAND RD
2 FOWLER CL
3 CHANTREY CL
ARVILL RD
ODDOCKS CL
CALVERT CL
HONEYDEN RD
CORNELL CL
71
Schs
BARTON RD
Chalk Wood
STONEHILL WOODS PK
4
Glf Drv Rng
WHITNEY WLK
B2173
RUXLEY CNR
IX
Upper Ruxley Farm
Ruxley Wood
Ruxley
1 VICTOR MILLS COTTS
2 THE CAMP SITE
Stone Far
3
Ruxley Manor Nursery
OLD MAIDSTONE RD
MAIDSTONE RD
Bexley
Upper Ruxley
Timbertops Farm
Mast
VICTORIA BGLWS
Bromley
70
Birchwood Corner
BIRCHWOOD TERR 1
JESSAMINE TERR 2
2
COOKHAM RD
Upper Hockden
B2173 LONDON
CH
BR8
A20
A20 Swanley (B2173), M20, M25
Burnt House Farm
Cray Valley
1
KIDDENS
HOCKENDEN LA
Barnfield Bank
CHAPMANS END
CHAPMAN'S LA
69
Hockenden
49
50
Pauls Cray Hill Park
Hockenden House

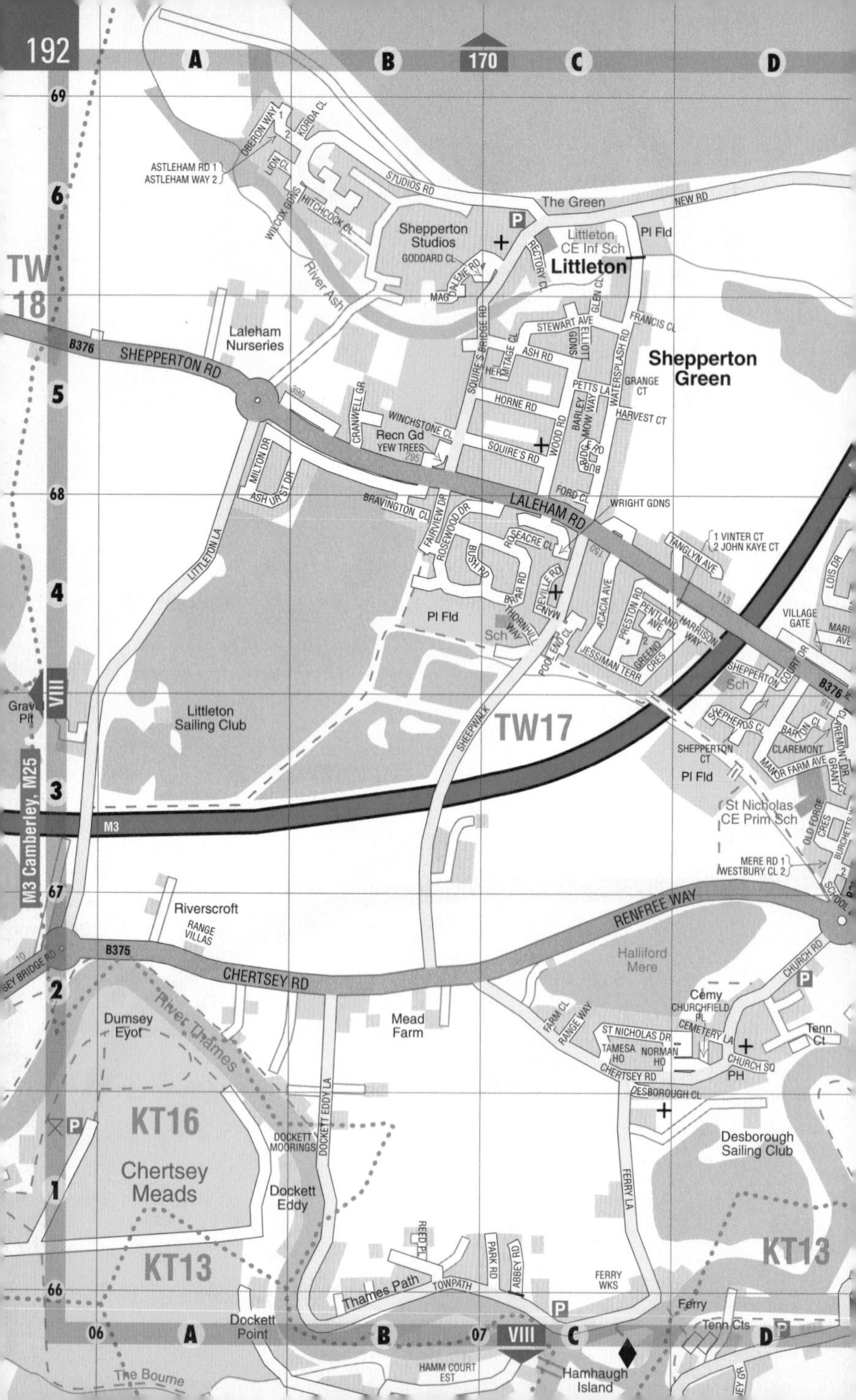

A
B
170
C
D
69
6
5
68
4
3
67
2
1
66
06
07
VIII
TW 18
TW17
KT16
KT13
ASTLEHAM RD 1
ASTLEHAM WAY 2
OBERON WAY
KORDA CL
LION CL
WILCOX GDNS
HITCHCOCK CL
STUDIOS RD
The Green
NEW RD
Shepperton Studios
GODDARD CL
DALENE RD
MAG
River Ash
Littleton CE Inf Sch
Littleton
RECTORY CL
Pl Fld
GLEN CL
FRANCIS CL
STEWART AVE
ELLIOT GDNS
ASH RD
MITAGE CL
HER
SQUIRE'S BRIDGE RD
WATERSPLASH RD
Shepperton Green
GRANGE CT
PETTS LA
BARLEY MOW WAY
HORNE RD
HARVEST CT
Laleham Nurseries
B376
SHEPPERTON RD
399
CRANWELL GR
WINCHSTONE CL
Recn Gd
YEW TREES
295
SQUIRE'S RD
WOOD RD
BURBIDGE RD
MILTON DR
ASHURST DR
FORD CL
BRAVINGTON CL
LALEHAM RD
WRIGHT GDNS
FAIRVIEW DR
ROSEWOOD DR
SEACRE CL
1 VINTER CT
2 JOHN KAYE CT
TANGLYN AVE
BUSH RD
BRIAR RD
DEVILLE RD
MANN
ACACIA AVE
PRESTON RD
PENTLAND AVE
LOIS DR
LITTLETON LA
Pl Fld
Sch
THORNHILL WAY
POOL END CL
JESSIMAN TERR
GREENO CRES
HARRISON WAY
113
VILLAGE GATE
MARIA AVE
SHEPPERTON COURT DR
Sch
B376
Gravel Pit
VIII
Littleton Sailing Club
SHEEPWALK
SHEPHERDS CL
BARTON CL
CLAREMONT DR
CLAREMONT
GRANT CL
SHEPPERTON CT
MANOR FARM AVE
Pl Fld
St Nicholas CE Prim Sch
OLD FORGE CRES
BURCHETTS WAY
M3
M3 Camberley, M25
MERE RD 1
WESTBURY CL 2
SCHOOL
RENFREE WAY
Riverscroft
RANGE VILLAS
CHERTSEY BRIDGE RD
B375
CHERTSEY RD
Halliford Mere
CHURCH RD
Cemy
CHURCHFIELD PL
CEMETERY LA
FARM CL
RANGE WAY
ST NICHOLAS DR
TAMESA HO
NORMAN HO
Tenn Ct
CHURCH SQ
CHERTSEY RD
PH
DESBOROUGH CL
Dumsey Eyot
River Thames
Mead Farm
Chertsey Meads
DOCKETT MOORINGS
DOCKETT EDDY LA
Dockett Eddy
Desborough Sailing Club
FERRY LA
REED PL
PARK RD
ABBEY RD
Thames Path
TOWPATH
FERRY WKS
Ferry
Dockett Point
Tenn Cts
HAMM COURT EST
Hamhaugh Island
The Bourne

Charlton
Upper Halliford
Lower Halliford
Shepperton
Sunbury
Hazelwood
Vicarage Farm
Watersplash Farm
Desborough Island
Thames Meadow
Ashley Park
TW16
TW17
KT12
KT13
171
194
VIII
A3050 Weybridge
A244
A3050
B3366
B375
B376
B365
UPPER HALLIFORD RD
GASTON BRIDGE RD
WALTON BRIDGE RD
NEW ZEALAND AVE
OATLANDS DR
CHURCH ST
HEPWORTH WAY
BRIDGE ST
GREEN LA
RUSSELL RD
WALTON LA
HALLIFORD RD
FORDBRIDGE RD
CHARLTON LA
HIGH ST
GASTON WAY
GOVETT AVE
DUPPAS CL
STATION APP
MANYGATE LA
RICHMOND DR
WESTERN DR
DURRELL WAY
LINDSAY DR
GORDON RD
GORDON DR
BROADLANDS AVE
BRUCE AVE
COPTHORNE CL
KILMISTON AVE
KILMISTON HO
GROVE RD
THURLESTONE CL
THURLESTONE PAR
GLEBELAND GDNS
CLIVEDEN PL
MEADOWVIEW
MERVYN RD
DUNBOE PL
HAMESFIELD CT
WADHAM CL
SANDHILLS MDW
MULBERRY TREES
CASSOCKS SQ
RIVERVIEW
MITRE CL
CLERICS WLK
THE MALYONS
BISHOP DUPPAS PK
SHERBOURNE GDNS
DUNALLY PK
OLD CHARLTON RD
CRESCENT RD
LINDEN WAY
BUXLEY GDNS
SAMPSON CT
STATION RD
CATLIN CRES
RODD EST
SHEPPERTON BSNS PK
NUTTY LA
WALNUT TREE RD
HARROW WAY
HETHERINGTON RD
ALMOND CL
CROSSWELL CL
HASLETT RD
BIRCH GR
VINCENT DR
HALLIFORD CL
BLACKBERRY CL
BRAMBLE CL
HAWTHORN WAY
CHERRY WAY
WALLACE CL
ST ANDREW'S CL
ANNETT CL
HOLMBANK DR
FREEMAN CL
THE CROFTS
MINSTERLEY AVE
CHESTNUT WLK
HOME FARM CL
DORLY CL
ROXFORD CL
GASTON BRIDGE
GRANGE FARM CVN PK
ORCHARD DR
KESWICK AVE
ALLINGTON AVE
PEAR AVE
COXS AVE
BRAMLEY AVE
RUSSET AVE
STERLING AVE
PARK AVE
PEREGRINE RD
STRATTON RD
SUNMEAD RD
PARKWOOD GR
FAIRLAWNS
CROYSDALE AVE
LYNDHURST
SCHOOL WLK
MARTINGALE CL
GREEN WAY
ST MARY'S
LOUDWATER RD
TADMOR CL
HIGHFIELD RD
THE CREEK
LONGWOOD BSNS PK
CAMPASPS BSNS PK
BEASLEY'S AIT LA
BEASLEY'S AIT
LITTLE HALLIARDS
FELIX LA
THE CRESCENT
SULLIVANS REACH
STONEBANKS
MANOR RD
BERKELEY GDNS
HILLRISE
RIVER MOUNT
THAMES ST
DALE RD
HARVEY RD
MAYO RD
BRIDGE CL
MOUNT PL
RIDGEWAY
ORCHARD CT
WELLINGTON CL
HURST GR
SANDY WAY
THE CENTRE
ASHLEY CL
ASHLEY PARK AVE
ASHLEY PARK CRES
WOODSIDE
ASHLEY RD
ST CLEMENTS HO
PENNY LA
RIVERSIDE
SWAN WLK
WINDMILL TERR
WALTON BRIDGE
THAMES MDW
CHASELEY CT
ANARTH CT
TREGLOS CT
ALBANY CT
BECKWORTH
OAKHILL
RIDGEMOUNT
TOWER GR
PARK CL
LINDEN GR
SILVERDALE AVE
Recn Gd
Sports Gd
Allot Gdns
Pl Fld
Bishop Wand CE Sec Sch
Hawkedale Fst Sch
Thamesmead Sec Sch
Halliford Sch
Tenn Cts
Bwg Gn
Bishop Duppas Park
Pav
Liby
Cemy
Nursery
Marina
Gravel Pit
Las Palmas Est
Works
River Ash
River Thames
Engine River
Desborough Channel
Thames Path
PH
PO
A
B
C
D
1
2
3
4
5
6
66
67
68
69
08
09
10

A
B
C
D
172
69
6
5
68
4
193
3
67
2
1
66
10
11
12
VIII
SUNBURY
TW16
WALTON-ON-THAMES
KT12
Hawkedale Fst Sch
Pav
Gd
T Cts
ROOKSMEAD RD
MARYLAND WAY
VEREKER DR
SUNMEAD RD
PARKWOOD
FAIRLAWNS
CROYSDALE AVE
LYNDHURST AVE
HAWKEWOOD RD
THE PINES
KINGSMEAD AV
OLD ORCH
SUNBURY AVE
DARBY GDNS
DARBY CRES
THE PENNARDS
ELIZABETH GDNS
DAX CT
BERKELEY MEWS
AVENUE PAR
PO
Sunbury Ct Island
Beauclerc Cty Inf Sch
1 RIVERMEAD HO
2 CASTLE WLK
3 ELIZABETH CT
Tenn Cts
The Walled Garden
THAMES ST
SCHOOL WLK
GREEN ST
Cemy
Allot Gdns
ANVIL RD
BRIDLE CL
FORGE LA
FORGE MEWS
CHURCH VILLA
CHURCH ST
Sunbury Lock
FARRIER CL
STILE PATH
MONTFORD RD
MARTINGALE CL
ST MARY'S
GREEN WAY
CUMBERLAND PL
HALLIFORD RD
River Thames
PARKE RD
LOUDWATER CL
LOUDWATER RD
FORDBRIDGE RD
WILLOW WAY
Nursery
THE CREEK
Wheatley's Ait
Fball Gd
Leisure Ctr
WATERSIDE DR
Apps Court Farm
HURST RD
A3050
Knight Resr
Rivernook Farm
SUNNYSIDE
RIVERNOOK CL
Bramble Hill Farm
B369
WALTON RD
ARMSTRONG RD
BEASLEY'S AIT LA
TUMBLING BAY
RIVER WLK
DUNSMORE RD
FRANKLYN RD
HALLIARDS
WEIR RD
SUNBURY LA
LITTLE HALLIARDS
FELIX RD
FRANKLIN RD
SUNBURY CL
CAMBRIDGE RD
Thamesfield Farm
Allot Gdns
Sch
KILSHA RD
SPICER CL
THORNEYCROFT CL
1 LUSHINGTON HO
2 LYNDE HO
3 CROXALL HO
4 KIRBY WAY
Recn Gd
RUSSELL RD
TERRACE RD
TANNERS CL
TITHE CL
FIRST AVE
SANDY LA
VICARAGE FIELDS
VINERS CL
VANBRUGH DR
THAMES VIEW HO
THAMES MEAD
DUDLEY RD
SECOND AVE
Queen Elizabeth 2 Storage Resr
SULLIVANS REACH
ANNETT RD
ENTERPRISE HO
THE GROVE
GARDEN RD
GROVE HO
ORCHARD CL
CARLTON RD
TELFORD DR
EMMELINE CT
STONEBANKS
LANCASTER CT
KINGSBRIDGE RD
GROVE CRES
KIMBERLEY WLK
PANKHURST RD
PAXTON CL
VANBRUGH MEWS
MANOR RD
BISHOPS HILL
BERKELEY GDNS
1 COURTLANDS
2 MANOR PL
ALPINE RD
COTTIMORE TERR
NIGHTINGALE RD
FLORENCE CL
FOX GR
FLORENCE RD
CROWN CL
HARVEY RD
DALE RD
MAYO RD
THAMES ST
FIR CL
MONTAGUE CL
WILLOWHAYNE DR
EGMONT RD
COTTIMORE CRES
COTTIMORE LA
BRAYCOURT AVE
SHAW DR
BRIDGE ST
ORCHARD CT
WELLINGTON CL
CHURCH ST
Cemy
REGNOLRUF CT
CHURCHFIELD RD
ESHER AVE
ROYSTON CL
SIDNEY RD
FAIRFAX CL
MONKS CRES
HILLARY CRES
REGENCY GDNS
ST CLEMENTS HO
HIGHFIELD RD
NELSON CL
COTTIMORE AVE
CROMWELL CL
MISTY'S FIELD
NORTH WAY
HIGH ST
CHURCH WLK
WINCHESTER RD
OSBORNE RD
Allot Gdns
Recn Gdns
STUART AVE
Swansmere Sch
LANGPORT CT
1 RODNEY CL
2 EDGEHILL CT
3 WORCESTER CT
4 DUNBAR CT
Sch
HOLLY AVE
BRASSEY HO
NEW ZEALAND AVE
THE CENTRE
COLBY RD
Bwg Gn
1 RYLTON HO
2 BLATCHFORD CT
KINGS CL
PRESTON CT
STRATTON CL
NEWARK CT
COTTIMORE LA
CARDINAL DR
RYDENS RD
ASHLEY PARK AVE
ASHLEY RD
HIGH ST
ASHLEY PARK CRES
WOODSIDE
A244
HERSHAM RD
OAKFIELDS
T Cts
KINGS RD
MARSTON CT
LANSDOWN CL
CHERITON CT
AMBLESIDE AVE
WINDSOR WLK
KING GEORGE AVE
WOLSEY DR
TUDOR DR
NORMANHURST RD
Liby
THE CHESTNUTS
CRUTCHFIELD LA
CROMWELL RD
ST JOHNS DR
RODNEY RD
WILTON GDNS
BRANKSOME CL
Ashley Park
B365
RED HOUSE LA
ALEY CT
BOWES RD
CLEMENTS CT
NOSEBY CT
INWOOD CT
THE FURROWS
MEADOWSIDE
BROOKE CT
LINDEN GR
GRANGE CT
A244 Esher
Rydens
STOMPOND LA
HURLEY CL
MIDWAY
Walton Comm
H
NEWHALL GDNS
GLADSMUIR CL
RYDENS AVE
RYDENS PK
WALTON PARK LA
YORK GDNS
Bwg Gn

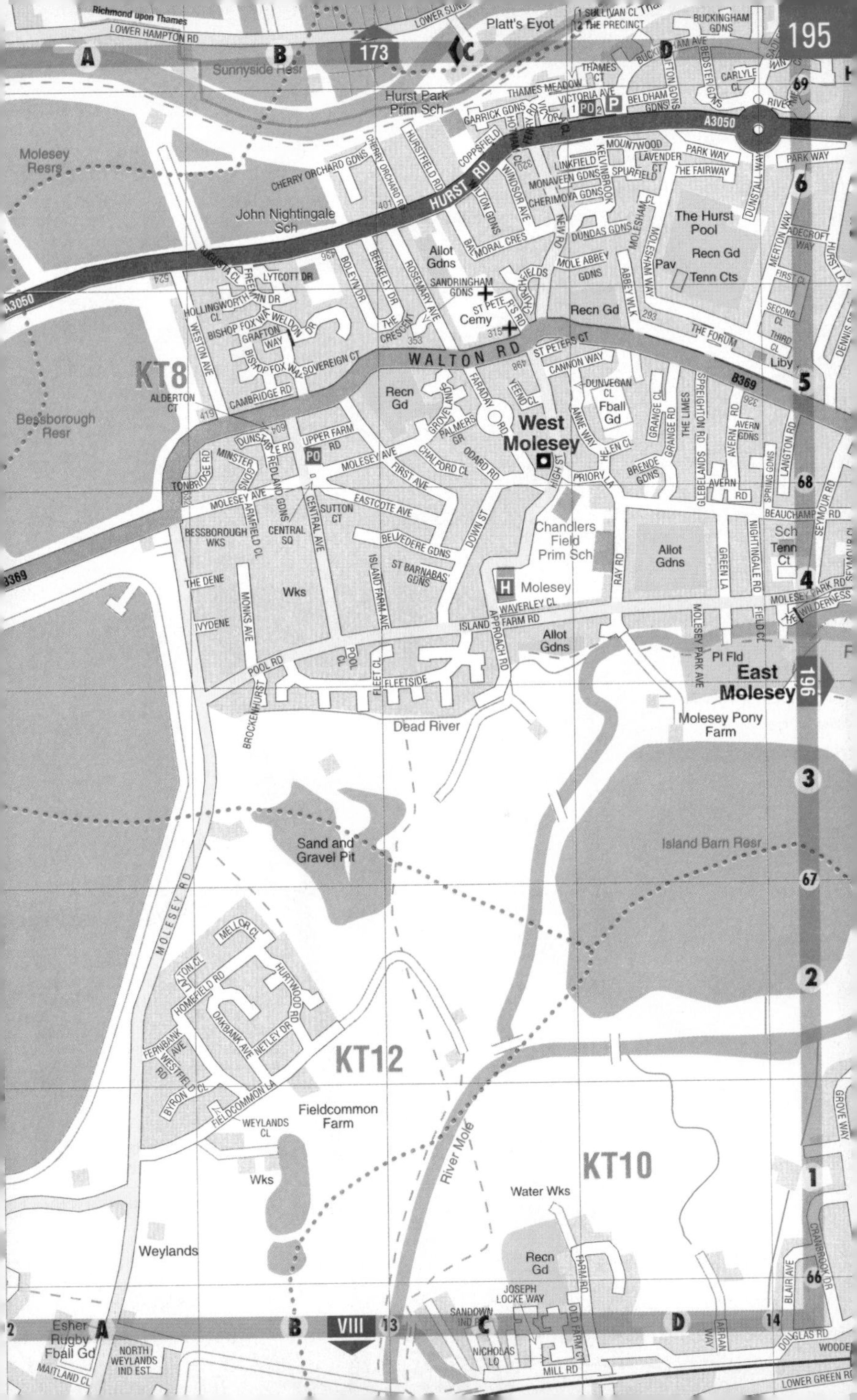
Richmond upon Thames
LOWER HAMPTON RD
LOWER SUNBURY
173
Platt's Eyot
1 SULLIVAN CL
2 THE PRECINCT
BUCKINGHAM GDNS
A
B
C
D
Sunnyside Resr
THAMES CT
THAMES MEADOW
VICTORIA AVE
PO
P
BELDHAM GDNS
BUCKINGHAM AVE
BEDSTER GDNS
CARLYLE CL
RIVERSIDE
69
Hurst Park Prim Sch
GARRICK GDNS
COPPSFIELD
HOTHAM CL
FERRY RD
A3050
MOUNTWOOD
LAVENDER CT
PARK WAY
KELVINBROOK
LINKFIELD
SPURFIELD
THE FAIRWAY
DUNSTALL WAY
Molesey Resrs
CHERRY ORCHARD GDNS
CHERRY ORCHARD RD
HURSTFIELD RD
HURST RD
WALTON GDNS
WINDSOR AVE
MONAVEEN GDNS
CHERIMOYA GDNS
MOLESHAM CL
MOLESHAM WAY
The Hurst Pool
6
MERTON WAY
ADECROFT WAY
HURST LA
John Nightingale Sch
BOLEYN DR
BERKELEY DR
ROSEMARY AVE
Allot Gdns
BALMORAL CRES
DUNDAS GDNS
NEW RD
MOLE ABBEY GDNS
ABBEY WLK
Recn Gd
Pav
Tenn Cts
FIRST CL
SECOND CL
THIRD CL
AUGUSTA CL
FREEMAN DR
LYTCOTT DR
SANDRINGHAM GDNS
CHURCHFIELDS
ST PETER'S RD
Cemy
Recn Gd
THE FORUM
DENNIS RD
HOLLINGWORTH CL
WESTON AVE
BISHOP FOX WAY
WELDON DR
GRAFTON WAY
THE CRESCENT
WALTON RD
ST PETERS CT
CANNON WAY
Liby
B369
5
KT8
SOVEREIGN CT
CAMBRIDGE RD
ALDERTON CT
Recn Gd
GROVELANDS
FARADAY RD
VEEND CL
DUNVEGAN CL
Fball Gd
GRANGE CL
GRANGE RD
THE LIMES
SPREIGHTON RD
AVERN RD
AVERN GDNS
LANGTON RD
Bessborough Resr
DUNSTABLE RD
MINSTER GDNS
TONBRIDGE RD
REDLAND GDNS
UPPER FARM RD
PO
MOLESEY AVE
FIRST AVE
PALMERS GR
CHALFORD CL
ODARD RD
West Molesey
HIGH ST
ANNE WAY
HELEN CL
PRIORY LA
BRENDE GDNS
GLEBELANDS RD
AVERN RD
SPRING GDNS
68
MOLESEY AVE
ARMFIELD CL
CENTRAL AVE
SUTTON CT
EASTCOTE AVE
DOWN ST
Chandlers Field Prim Sch
BEAUCHAMP RD
SEYMOUR RD
BESSBOROUGH WKS
CENTRAL SQ
BELVEDERE GDNS
ST BARNABAS' GDNS
ISLAND FARM AVE
RAY RD
Allot Gdns
GREEN LA
NIGHTINGALE RD
Sch
Tenn Ct
B369
THE DENE
MONKS AVE
Wks
H
Molesey
4
MOLESEY PARK RD
WAVERLEY CL
THE WILDERNESS
IVYDENE
ISLAND FARM RD
APPROACH RD
Allot Gdns
MOLESEY PARK AVE
FIELD CL
POOL RD
POOL CL
FLEET CL
FLEETSIDE
Pl Fld
East Molesey
196
BROCKENHURST
Dead River
Molesey Pony Farm
3
Sand and Gravel Pit
Island Barn Resr
67
MOLESEY RD
MELLOR CL
LAXTON CL
HOMEFIELD RD
HURTWOOD RD
2
OAKBANK AVE
NETLEY DR
FERNBANK AVE
WESTFIELD RD
KT12
BYRON CL
FIELDCOMMON LA
Fieldcommon Farm
WEYLANDS CL
GROVE WAY
Wks
River Mole
KT10
Water Wks
1
Weylands
Recn Gd
FARM RD
BLAIR AVE
CRANBROOK DR
66
JOSEPH LOCKE WAY
Esher Rugby Fball Gd
A
B
VIII
13
SANDOWN IND EST
C
D
ARRAN WAY
14
DOUGLAS RD
OLD FARM CT
NORTH WEYLANDS IND EST
NICHOLAS LO
MILL RD
MAITLAND CL
LOWER GREEN RD
WOODE

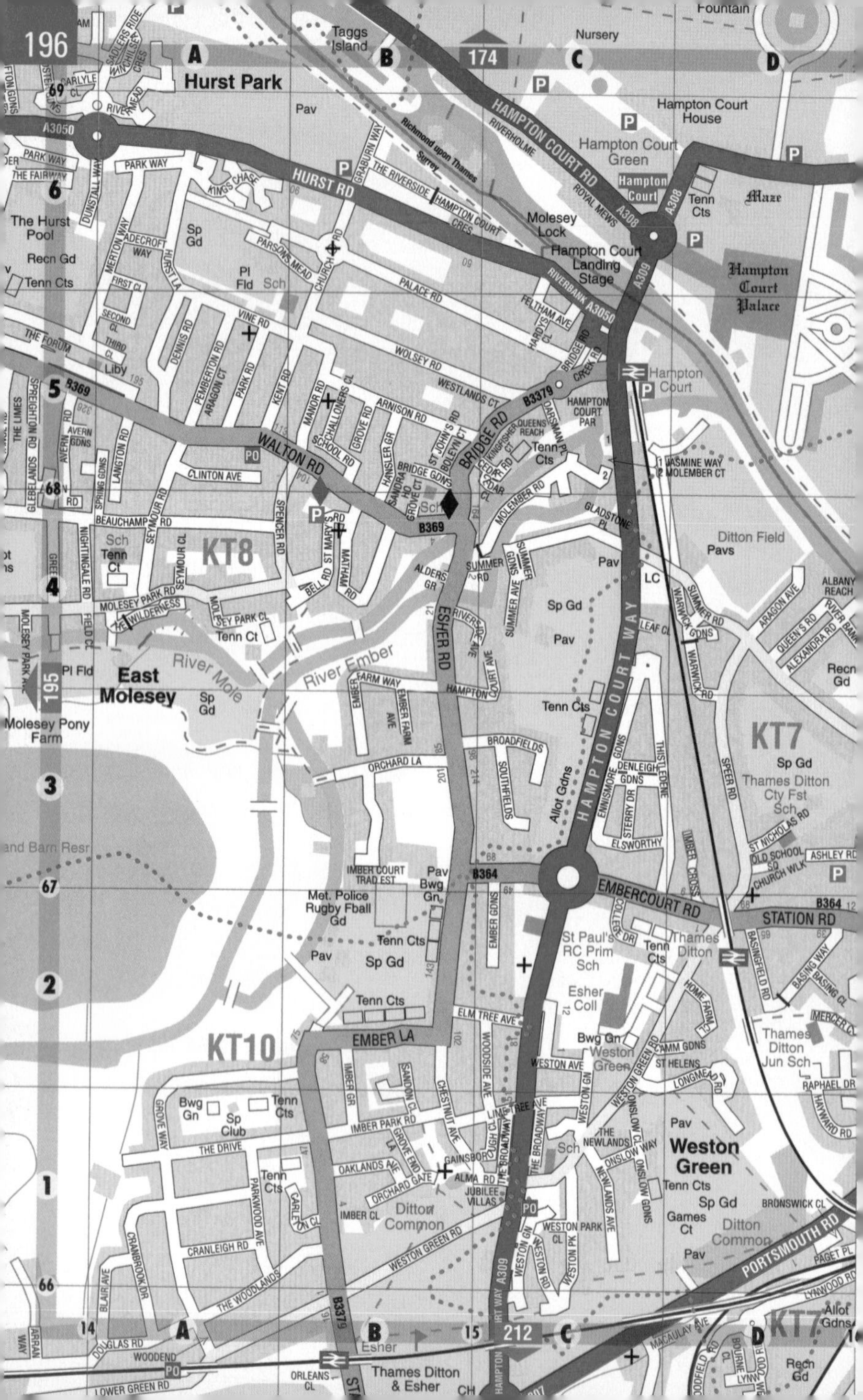
Taggs Island
174
Nursery
Fountain
A
B
C
D
Hurst Park
Pav
HAMPTON COURT RD
Hampton Court House
Hampton Court Green
Hampton Court
A3050
PARK WAY
THE FAIRWAY
HURST RD
Richmond upon Thames
Surrey
THE RIVERSIDE
HAMPTON COURT CRES
RIVERHOLME
ROYAL MEWS
A308
Tenn Cts
Maze
The Hurst Pool
Recn Gd
Tenn Cts
Sp Gd
MERTON WAY
ADECROFT WAY
HURST LA
PARSONS MEAD
CHURCH RD
Molesey Lock
Hampton Court Landing Stage
Hampton Court Palace
FIRST CL
SECOND CL
THIRD CL
Pl Fld
Sch
PALACE RD
RIVERBANK
A309
VINE RD
FELTHAM AVE
HARDYS CL
THE FORUM
Liby
DENNIS RD
PEMBERTON RD
ARAGON CT
PARK RD
KENT RD
WOLSEY RD
BRIDGE RD
CREEK RD
Hampton Court
B369
THE LIMES
SPREIGHTON RD
AVERN GDNS
LANGTON RD
MANOR RD
CHALLONERS CL
GROVE RD
ARNISON RD
WESTLANDS CT
B3379
HAMPTON COURT PAR
WALTON RD
SCHOOL RD
ST JOHN'S RD
BOLEYN CT
KINGFISHER CT
QUEENS REACH
DARSMAN PL
Tenn Cts
1 JASMINE WAY
2 MOLEMBER CT
GLEBELANDS
SPRING GDNS
CLINTON AVE
PO
HANSLER GR
BRIDGE GDNS
SANDRA HO
GROVE CT
CEDAR RD
MOLEMBER RD
GLADSTONE PL
BEAUCHAMP RD
SEYMOUR RD
SPENCER RD
ST MARY'S RD
Sch
Ditton Field
Pavs
KT8
Tenn Ct
NIGHTINGALE RD
SEYMOUR CL
BELL RD
MATHAM RD
ALDERS GR
SUMMER RD
SUMMER GDNS
Pav
LC
ALBANY REACH
ARAGON AVE
MOLESEY PARK RD
THE WILDERNESS
MOLESEY PARK CL
Tenn Ct
ESHER RD
RIVERSIDE AVE
SUMMER AVE
Sp Gd
LEAF CL
WARWICK GDNS
QUEEN'S RD
ALEXANDRA RD
RIVER BANK
MOLESEY PARK AVE
FIELD CL
Pl Fld
East Molesey
River Mole
River Ember
EMBER FARM WAY
EMBER FARM AVE
HAMPTON COURT AVE
Pav
HAMPTON COURT WAY
WARWICK RD
Recn Gd
195
Sp Gd
Molesey Pony Farm
Tenn Cts
KT7
BROADFIELDS
ORCHARD LA
SOUTHFIELDS
Allot Gdns
ENNISMORE GDNS
DENLEIGH GDNS
THISTLEDENE
STERRY DR
SPEER RD
Sp Gd
Thames Ditton Cty Fst Sch
ST NICHOLAS RD
ELSWORTHY
IMBER CROSS
Island Barn Resr
IMBER COURT TRAD EST
Pav
Bwg Gn
Met. Police Rugby Fball Gd
B364
EMBERCOURT RD
OLD SCHOOL SQ
ASHLEY RD
CHURCH WLK
STATION RD
EMBER GDNS
COLLEGE DR
St Paul's RC Prim Sch
Thames Ditton
Tenn Cts
BASINGFIELD RD
BASING WAY
BASING CL
Tenn Cts
Pav
Sp Gd
Esher Coll
HOME FARM CL
MERCER CL
Tenn Cts
ELM TREE AVE
Thames Ditton Jun Sch
KT10
EMBER LA
WOODSIDE AVE
Bwg Gn
Weston Green
WESTON AVE
WESTON GREEN RD
AMM GDNS
ST HELENS
LONGMEAD RD
RAPHAEL DR
HAYWARD RD
IMBER GR
SANDON CL
CHESTNUT AVE
LIME TREE AVE
THE BROADWAY
WESTON GN
ONSLOW RD
Bwg Gn
Sp Club
Tenn Cts
GROVE WAY
IMBER PARK RD
GROVE END LA
GAINSBOROUGH CL
THE NEWLANDS
ONSLOW WAY
Pav
Weston Green
THE DRIVE
OAKLANDS AVE
ORCHARD GATE
ALMA RD
JUBILEE VILLAS
Sch
NEWLANDS AVE
ONSLOW GDNS
Tenn Cts
Tenn Cts
PARKWOOD AVE
CARLETON CL
IMBER CL
Ditton Common
PO
Sp Gd
Games Ct
BRUNSWICK CL
WESTON PARK CL
WESTON PK
WESTON RD
Ditton Common
PORTSMOUTH RD
PAGET PL
CRANLEIGH RD
WESTON GREEN RD
Pav
LYNWOOD RD
CRANBROOK DR
BLAIR AVE
THE WOODLANDS
A309
Allot Gdns
B3379
KT7
ARRAN WAY
14
15
212
MACAULAY AVE
DOUGLAS RD
WOODEND
Esher
PO
ORLEANS CL
Thames Ditton & Esher
LOWER GREEN RD
BOURNE CL
LYNWOOD RD
Recn Gd
6
5
4
3
2
1
69
68
67
66

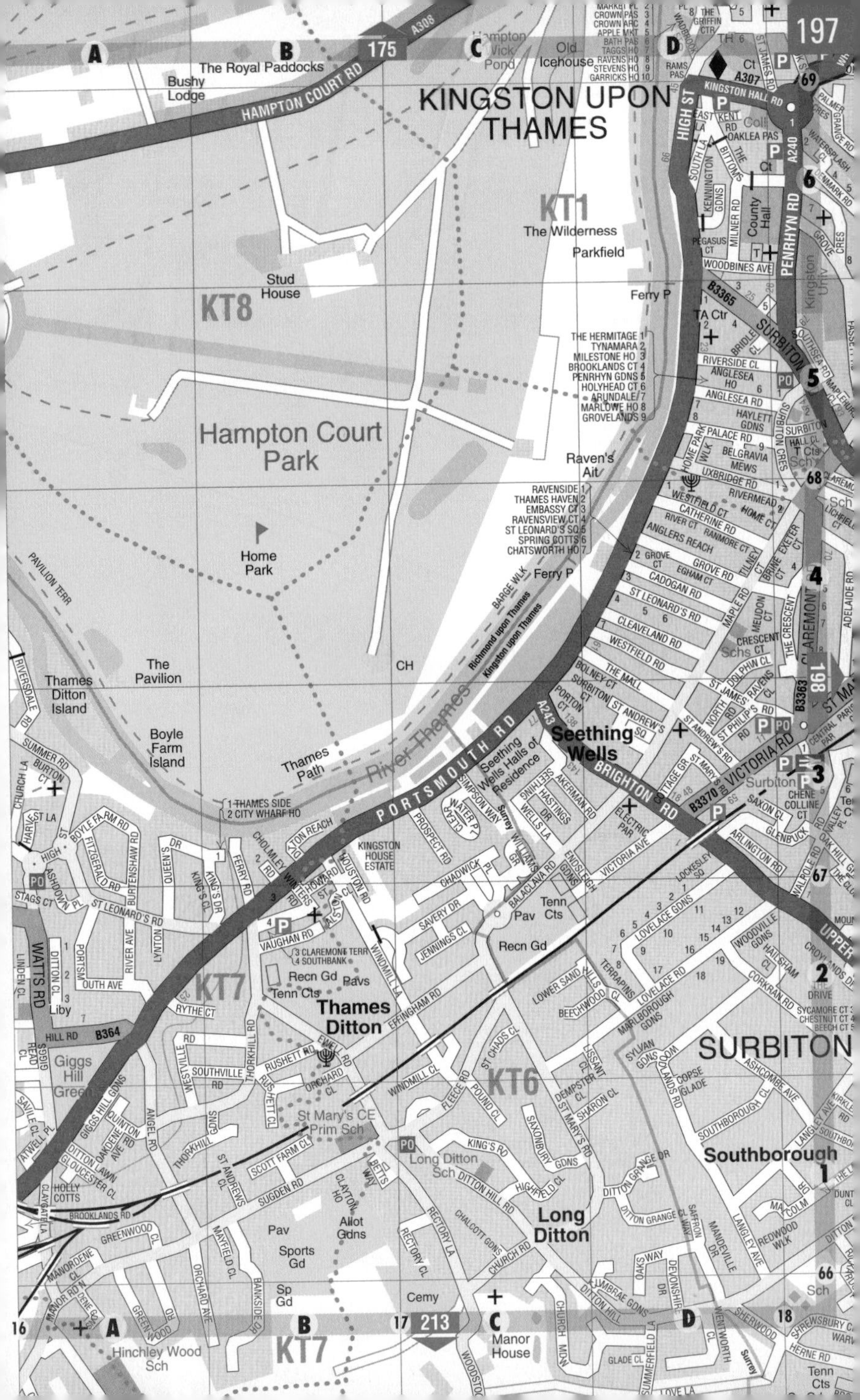
175
213
198
KINGSTON UPON THAMES
THAMES
KT1
KT8
KT7
KT6
Hampton Court Park
Home Park
The Royal Paddocks
Bushy Lodge
Stud House
Hampton Wick Pond
Old Icehouse
The Wilderness
Parkfield
Ferry P
The Pavilion
Thames Ditton Island
Boyle Farm Island
Thames Path
River Thames
Raven's Ait
CH
Richmond upon Thames
Kingston upon Thames
HAMPTON COURT RD
A308
PORTSMOUTH RD
A243
BRIGHTON RD
VICTORIA RD
B3370
B3363
B3365
SURBITON RD
A307
A240
PENRHYN RD
HIGH ST
KINGSTON HALL RD
County Hall
Kingston Univ
MARKET PL 2
CROWN PAS 3
CROWN ARC 4
APPLE MKT 5
BATH PAS 6
TAGGS HO 7
RAVENS HO 8
STEVENS HO 9
GARRICKS HO 10
THE HERMITAGE 1
TYNAMARA 2
MILESTONE HO 3
BROOKLANDS CT 4
PENRHYN GDNS 5
HOLYHEAD CT 6
ARUNDALE 7
MARLOWE HO 8
GROVELANDS 9
RAVENSIDE 1
THAMES HAVEN 2
EMBASSY CT 3
RAVENSVIEW CT 4
ST LEONARD'S SQ 5
SPRING COTTS 6
CHATSWORTH HO 7
1 THAMES SIDE
2 CITY WHARF HO
3 CLAREMONT TERR
4 SOUTHBANK
SYCAMORE CT
CHESTNUT CT
BEECH CT
Seething Wells
Seething Wells Halls of Residence
Thames Ditton
Long Ditton
SURBITON
Southborough
Giggs Hill Green
KINGSTON HOUSE ESTATE
St Mary's CE Prim Sch
Long Ditton Sch
Hinchley Wood Sch
Manor House
Cemy
Allot Gdns
Sports Gd
Recn Gd
Tenn Cts
WATTS RD
HILL RD
B364
CLAYGATE LA
Surrey

A
B
C
D
176
197
214
KT1
KT5
KT6
Berrylands
SURBITON
Southborough
Surbiton
Tolworth
CAMBRIDGE RD
KINGSTON HALL RD
PENRHYN RD
SURBITON RD
SURBITON HILL RD
CLAREMONT RD
ST MARK'S HILL
VICTORIA RD
UPPER BRIGHTON RD
KINGSDOWNE RD
EWELL RD
HOOK RD
DITTON RD
TOLWORTH PARK RD
TOLWORTH RISE N
TOLWORTH RISE S
BROADWAY
WARREN DR N
ALEXANDRA DR
KINGS DR
QUEENS DR
MANOR DR
BERRYLANDS RD
SURBITON HILL PK
LOWER MARSH LA
Thames Down Link
London Loop
Sewage Works
Cemy
Crem
Recn Gd
Allot Gdns
Sp Gd
Nat Res
County Hall
Kingston Univ
Hollyfield Sch
Christ Church CE Prim Sch
Dysart Sch
Tolworth Jun & Inf Schs
FAIRFIELD IND EST
KINGSMILL BSNS PK
A240
A307
A3210
A3
B3363
B3364
B3365
B3370

177
200
215
NEW MALDEN
Old Malden
Malden Manor
New Malden
KT3
KT4
KT5
A
B
C
D
1
2
3
4
5
6
KINGSTON RD
KINGSTON BY PASS
MALDEN WAY
KINGSTON BY-PASS
COOMBE RD
HIGH ST
MALDEN RD
BURLINGTON RD
CHURCH RD
B283
B282
B284
A3
A2043
Hogsmill River
London Loop & Thames Down Link
Corpus Christi RC Prim Sch
Richard Challoner Sch
Malden CE Prim Sch
Grand Avenue Prim Sch
Knollmead Prim Sch
Beverley Sch
The Study Sch
Beverley Park
Beverley Brook
Manor Pk
Shannon Cnr
Superstore
Allot Gdns
Recn Gd
Sp Gd
Bwg Gn
Pl Fld
Tenn Cts
Pav
Liby
PO
Sch
MOUNT PLEASANT RD
STAFFORD RD
CHESTNUT GR
ACACIA GR
LIME GR
SYCAMORE GR
POPLAR GR
BEECH GR
ELM RD
MOUNT RD
DUKES AVE
PRINCES
ST ANDREW'S CT
MALDEN HILL
KINGS AVE
COOMBE GDNS
BLAGDON RD
EGMONT RD
EGERTON RD
ONSLOW RD
ALRIC AVE
ROSEBERY AVE
ORCHARD AVE
CAMBRIDGE RD
CAMBRIDGE AVE
SUSSEX RD
CONNAUGHT RD
CLEVELAND RD
MONTEM RD
ALBANY RD
PENRITH RD
WESTBURY RD
SELWYN RD
ETON AVE
LYNTON RD
NELSON RD
THETFORD RD
COTSFORD AVE
WINDSOR AVE
POTTERS GR
FRANKS AVE
SOUTH PARK GR
GREEN LA
SOUTH LA
CAVENDISH RD
CROMWELL AVE
WALTON AVE
QUEEN'S RD
GEORGE RD
ALBERT RD
COLLEGE GDNS
OAKFIELD CL
SOMERSET CL
WILTON GR
FIR GR
BLAKES AVE
NIGHTWOOD CRES
BRAMSHAW RISE
AMBERWOOD RISE
MALDEN PK
WENDOVER DR
MINSTEAD WAY
ALDRIDGE RISE
WAVERLEY CRES
LYNDHURST DR
HOLMSLEY CL
GLEBE GDNS
HOLLINGTON CRES
PORTLAND AVE
BROADLANDS WAY
PURBECK AVE
ROMNEY RD
TURNER RD
LANDSEER RD
GAINSBOROUGH RD
VAN DYCK AVE
LAWRENCE AVE
KNELLER RD
REYNOLDS RD
MILLAIS RD
MANOR DR N
SHEEPHOUSE WAY
NEWHOUSE CL
BROCKENHURST AVE
STROUDES CL
COLUMBIA AVE
BURFORD RD
BROADMEAD AVE
MALDEN GREEN AVE
MAYFAIR AVE
FULLBROOKS AVE
AVONDALE AVE
FOREST SIDE
THE HOLLANDS
THE MANOR DR
MANOR CL
VICARAGE CL
PADDOCK CL
LEYFIELD
HIGHDOWN
COLLINGWOOD AVE
OAKDENE DR
SOUTHWOOD DR
RALEIGH DR
ELMDENE
WARREN DR S
KNOLLMEAD
ALPINE AVE
ELMBRIDGE AVE
BERESFORD RD
BERESFORD AVE
SPRINGFIELD PL
GEORGIA RD
WILLOW RD
6 TREVELYAN CT
7 MARLFIELD CT
8 RYEHILL CT
9 COLUMBIA CT
NEVADA CL 1
OREGON CL 2
CKWOOD CT 3
WINDRUSH 4

178
216
199
A
B
C
D
69
6
5
68
4
3
67
2
1
66
22
23
BUSHEY RD
B286
MERTON MANS
Allot Gdns
Bushey Mead
Sports Ctr
Tenn Cts
Pl Fld
SW20
Fball Gd
Cannon Hill Common
Allot Gdns
Cannon Hill
Raynes Park
RAINBOW IND EST
WEST BARNES LA
BUSHEY CT
GORE RD
GEORGE'S
PARK AVE
B279
RECTORY CL
CHURCH WLK
MICHAELMAS CL
COPPICE CL
FAIRWAY
1 PETWORTH GDNS
2 NYMANS GDNS
3 TRAFALGAR CT
4 MALDEN CT
T Cts
Sp Gd
RAYNESFIELD
BLENHEIM RD
BLENHEIM CL
CANNON CL
BERRYLANDS
PADDOCK CT
HEATH DR
ORCHARD CL
GRAND DR
ELM CL
Sp Gd
Tenn Cts
GREENWAY
MEADWAY
MEADOW CL
WOODLANDS
ELM WLK
PARKWAY
CROSSWAY
OAKWAY
SOUTHWAY
WESTWAY
MEADOWSWEET CL
Tenn Cts
Pl Fld
Pav
THORNTON CT
CANNON HILL LA
GLENTHORPE RD
QUEEN MARY AVE
EDINBURGH CT
CAMBORNE RD
St Catherine's RC Mid Sch
West Barnes
St John Fisher RC Prim Sch
Pav
Sp Gd
Allot Gdns
DERWENT RD
CONISTON CL
BUTTERMERE CL
TUDOR DR
B279
CRANMER
Crem
Morden Cemy
SM4
ALLGOOD CL
CARLINGFORD RD
WYDELL CL
ROSEBERY CL
ESSEX CL
GARTH CL
ARAGON RD
Schs
Pyl Brook
KINGSBRIDGE RD
SEYMOUR AVE
LYNMOUTH AVE
BEVERLEY TRAD EST
CLEVELAND
Merton & Sutton Joint Cemy
AMENITY WAY
GARTH RD
METRO CTR
Merton
Sutton
1 HANDSIDE CL
2 STANTON CL
SALCOMBE DR
DUNSTER AVE
CONRAD DR
CHARMINSTER RD
TRAFALGAR AVE
INVERNESS RD
ROSE END
SOUTHWOOD CL
CARTERS CL
CRESTON WAY
CLARKE'S AVE
St Anthony
St Cecilia's RC Prim Sch
AMESBURY
BOSCOMBE RD
BISLEY CL
BUCKLAND WAY
MERRILANDS RD
DELCOMBE AVE
DORCHESTER RD
WIMBORNE CL
Sch
MENDIP
CHILTERN
HAMBLETON CL
ANDREWS CL
LANGLEY AVE
DORKING CL
COTSWOLD WAY
North
Allot Gdns
Recn Gd
Sewage Works
KT4
GREEN LA
Green Lane Prim Sch
Allot Gdns
Pl Fld
Bwg Gn
Tenn Cts
Pav
Tenn Cts
Pav
Sp Gd
Motspur Park
Kingston upon Thames
Allot Gdns
KINGSHILL AVE
HUGHENDEN RD
RISBOROUGH DR
PRIMROSE CT
CAVERLEIGH WAY
PEMBURY AVE
SUTHERLAND
LINCOLN RD
GREEN LA
HAZLEMERE GDNS
LONGFELLOW RD
CALDBECK AVE
WASHINGTON RD
BROWNING AVE
BRINKLEY RD
DALEWOOD GDNS
ST PHILIP'S AVE
GLENAVON CT
LINDSAY RD
Cemy
RUSKIN DR
Tenn Cts
Bwg Gn
Beverley Park
Beverley Brook
Sp Gd
Drv Rng
Superstore
BEVERLEY WAY KINGSTON BY-PASS
A298
Bushey Mid Sch
Bushey Fst Sch
Sch
Superstore
STOURHEAD GDNS
POLESDEN GDNS
SAVILL GDNS
HIDCOTE GDNS
BODNANT GDNS
GRAYSWOOD GDNS
FARNHAM GDNS
1 PERTH CL
2 HUNTLEY WAY
BARNSCROFT
WESTWAY
LINKWAY
BROOK CL
LC
Blagdon House
THE WYVERN EST
Kingston upon Thames
Merton
SHANNON COMMERCIAL CTR
Shannon Cnr
Sch
BURLINGTON RD
B282
NEW MALDEN
VANFAME CT
HILLBROW
PARK VIEW
MALDEN HILL GDNS
THE MOUNT
EGMONT RD
EGERTON RD
ALVERSTONE RD
ONSLOW RD
BEVERLEY RD
ROOKWOOD AVE
SHANNON CNR RET PK
ALBERT RD
GEORGE RD
QUEEN'S RD
MALDEN WAY
A3
BYFIELD CT
SHELLEY CT
ERROL GDNS
BARNARD GDNS
BELMONT AVE
CAVENDISH AVE
CLAREMONT AVE
KT3
GRESHAM HO
ESTELLA AVE
SEAFORTH AVE
DOUGLAS AVE
ADELA AVE
PHYLLIS AVE
WEST BARNES LA
KINGSWAY
TENNYSON AVE
Motspur Park
CONSFIELD AVE
COBHAM AVE
BYRON AVE
STANLEY AVE
BLAKES TERR
BARNES END
Liby
STATION RD
MARINA AVE
ARTHUR RD
LC
COLLEGE GDNS
Beverley Sch
THE GRANGE
BLAKES LA
Athletic Gd
Tenn Cts
MOTSPUR PK
HOPTON GDNS
APPLETON GDNS
CHILMARK GDNS
ANCASTER CRES
HOLLINGTON CRES
BARGATE CL
PURBECK AVE
PORTLAND AVE
GREENLAW GDNS
Pav
T Cts
Manor Pk
Bwg Gn
CHELSEA CL
BURFORD RD
BROADMEAD AVE
ASHDOWN
IDMISTON RD
MALDEN GREEN AVE
MAYFAIR AVE
MARLFIELD CL
LOWER GREEN GDNS
T Cts
Bwg Gn
Worcester Park
Sp Gd
A2043
MALDEN RD
CENTRAL RD
DOWNFIELD
KEBLE CL
HOLLANDS
ORCHARD
PARK TERR
Surrey
BADGERS COPSE
SQUIRRELS GN
RUSHMERE CT
AVON CL
KNIGHT
STONE PL
Allot
Liby
PO

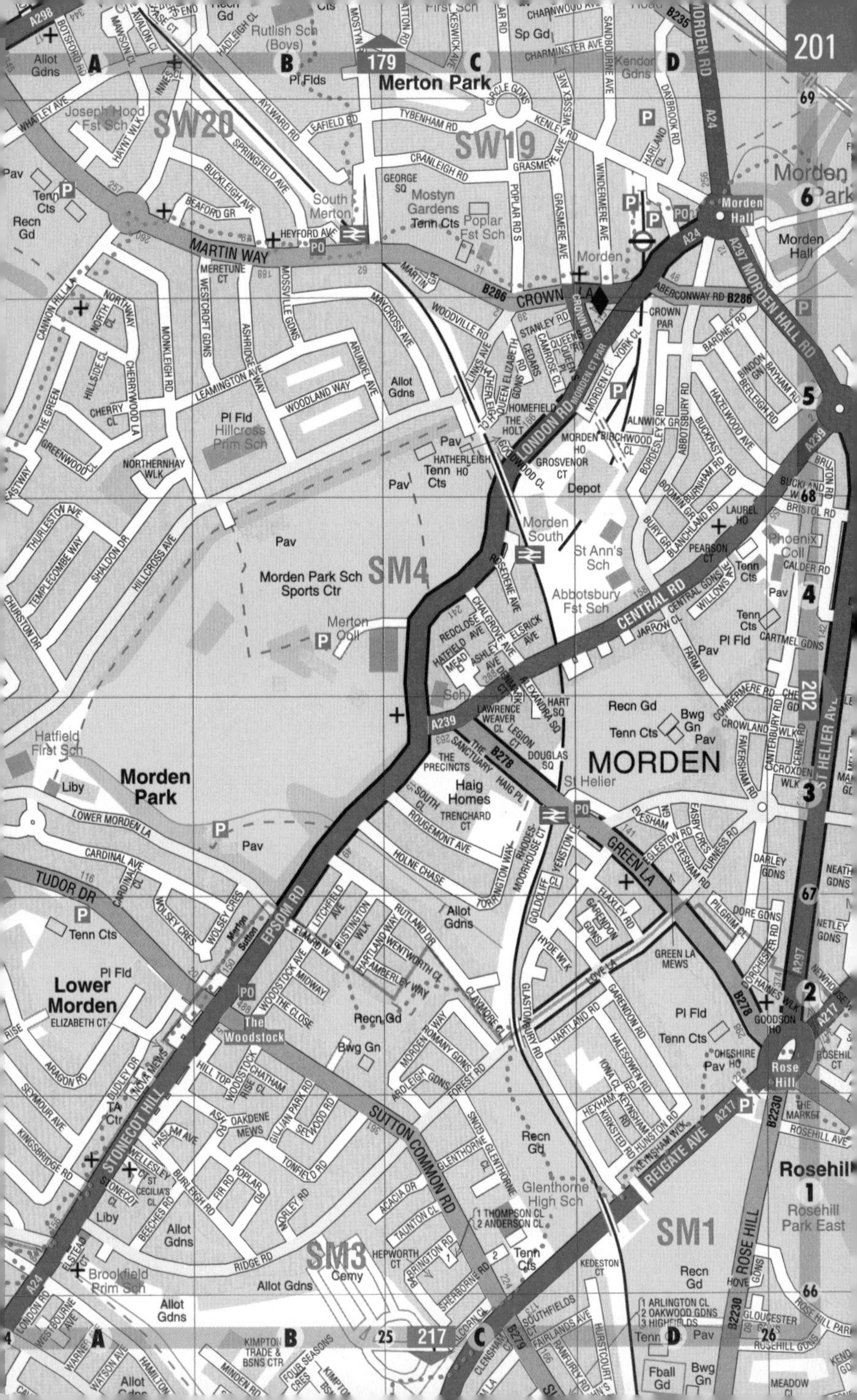
179
Merton Park
SW20
SW19
SM4
SM3
SM1
MORDEN
Morden Park
Lower Morden
Rosehill
Morden Hall
Morden Hall Park
Morden
Morden South
St Helier
South Merton
MARTIN WAY
CROWN LA
LONDON RD
MORDEN RD
MORDEN HALL RD
CENTRAL RD
EPSOM RD
STONECOT HILL
SUTTON COMMON RD
GREEN LA
REIGATE AVE
ROSE HILL
TUDOR DR
LOWER MORDEN LA
CARDINAL AVE
ST HELIER AVE
ABERCONWAY RD
KENLEY RD
GRASMERE AVE
WINDERMERE AVE
POPLAR RD S
CRANLEIGH RD
TYBENHAM RD
LEAFIELD RD
AYLWARD RD
SPRINGFIELD AVE
BUCKLEIGH AVE
WHATLEY AVE
BOTSFORD RD
MONKLEIGH RD
LEAMINGTON AVE
WOODLAND WAY
ARUNDEL AVE
MAYCROSS AVE
HILLCROSS AVE
SHALDON DR
TEMPLECOMBE WAY
THURLESTON AVE
CHURSTON DR
CHERRYWOOD LA
CANNON HILL LA
NORTHERNHAY WLK
Joseph Hood Fst Sch
Rutlish Sch (Boys)
Mostyn Gardens
Poplar Fst Sch
Hillcross Prim Sch
Morden Park Sch Sports Ctr
Merton Coll
Hatfield First Sch
St Ann's Sch
Abbotsbury Fst Sch
Phoenix Coll
Haig Homes
Glenthorne High Sch
Brookfield Prim Sch
The Woodstock
Rosehill Park East
Kendor Gdns
Allot Gdns
Recn Gd
Tenn Cts
Pl Fld
Pav
Bwg Gn
Depot
Cemy
Liby
Sch
A24
A297
A239
A217
A298
B286
B278
B279
B2230
B235
A
B
C
D
1
2
3
4
5
6
66
67
68
69
25
26
202
217
KIMPTON TRADE & BSNS CTR
1 THOMPSON CL
2 ANDERSON CL
1 ARLINGTON CL
2 OAKWOOD GDNS
3 HIGHFIELDS

SW19
Morden Hall Park
Morden Hall
Croydon Tramlink
Phipps Bridge
Benedict Fst & Prim Schs
Belgrave Walk
MORDEN HALL RD
MORDEN RD
DENVALE TRADE PK
Ravensbury Park
River Wandle
CR4
Cricket Green Sch
Melrose Sch
MITCHAM
SS Peter & Paul's RC Prim Sch
LONDON RD
CRICKET GN
MADEIRA RD
CRANMER RD
The Canons L Ctr
Tenn Cts
Cranmer Mid Sch
Mitcham
TRAMWAY PATH
THE BEECHES
BROOKFIELDS AVE
RIVERSIDE DR
Phoenix Coll
ST HELIER AVE
ABBEY IND EST
CAPITAL IND EST
CONNAUGHT BSNS CTR
GRACE BSNS CTR
EAGLE TRAD EST
WANDLE TRAD EST & TECH PK
Pav
Sp Gd
Merton
Sutton
Poulter Park
Moreton Green Fst Sch
Watermeads High Sch
SM4
Moreton Gn
Malmesbury Schs
BISHOPSFORD RD
Games Ct
Green Wrythe Prim Sch
St Helier
MIDDLETON RD
Sutton Arena
Tweeddale Schs
Liby
Wandle Valley Sch
Rose Hill
Rosehill
Rosehill Park East
SM1
WRYTHE LA
St Helier
SM5
Greenshaw High Sch
Muschamp
Recn Gd
Pl Fld
Allot Gdns
180
218
201
A
B
C
D
1
2
3
4
5
6
A24
A297
A239
A217
A236
B278
B2230

181
204
219
A
B
C
D
1
2
3
4
5
6
MITCHAM
CR4
CR0
SM6
Mitcham Common
Mitcham Junction
Croydon Tramlink
Merton
Sutton
Beddington Lane
Beddington Corner
Beddington Farm
Beddington Sewage Treatment Works
Hackbridge
Mill House
Sherwood Prim Sch
Rowan High Sch
Tamworth Manor Sch
The Alfred Mizen Sch
William Morris Sch
Greenwood Sch
Soho Mills
UPPER GN E
CARSHALTON RD
LONDON RD
CROYDON RD
WINDMILL RD
MANOR RD
BEDDINGTON LA
COMMONSIDE EAST
TAMWORTH LA
SHERWOOD PARK RD
CRANMER RD
RED HOUSE RD
ROCHFORD WAY
COOMBER WAY
THERAPIA LA
MILE RD
BROOKMEAD RD
JESSOPS WAY
BROOKMEAD IND EST
MILL GREEN BSNS PK
FELNEX TRAD EST
PIONEERS IND PK
HACKBRIDGE RD
A236
A237
A239
B272
B277
Pl Flds
Tenn Cts
Allot Gdns
Recn Gd
Pav
Sp Gd
CH
LC
PO

Recn Gd
A
B
C
D
182
Sp Gd
Pav
Cts
Liby
St James The Great RC Prim Sch
NORTHBOROUGH RD
NORBURY COURT RD
NEWLANDS
GRANDEN RD
OSPREY
SOLENT CT
KINTYRE CL
DALMENY AVE
DUNBAR AVE
COUNTY RD
BEATRICE AVE
BEECH RD
NORBURY CROSS
NORBURY RISE
ELGAR AVE
POLLARDS WOOD RD
ENA RD
POLLARDS HILL N
POLLARDS HILL E
SOMERSET GDNS
EDERLINE AVE
ARDFERN AVE
MELROSE AVE
KILMARTIN AVE
STRATHYRE AVE
BRAEMAR AVE
BRIDPORT RD
CAMDEN GDNS
CAMDEN WAY
SANDFIELD GDNS
MELFORT RD
WELFONT AVE
Tamworth Manor Sch
William Morris Sch
Recn Gd
65
SW16
HILL OR
SHIRLEY CT
POLLARDS CRES
CRANBOURNE CL
RECREATION WAY
CHESHIRE CL
CAERNARVON CL
GLAMORGAN CL
BRECON CL
WIDE WAY
HOLLY WAY
ORIEL CL
FERN AVE
ELM GDNS
DAHLIA GDNS
Liby
PO
HILL VIEW
CONWAY GDNS
NINETEENTH RD
SOUTH LODGE AVE
HUNTINGDON CL
KENT CL
LINDSEY CL
MONMOUTH CL
Croydon
Merton
HIGHDAUN DR
DORSET GDNS
BRIAR RD
POLLARDS HILL W
POLLARDS HILL S
FORREST GDNS
TALL TREES
LONSDALE GDNS
WHARFEDALE GDNS
WALDEN GDNS
HEADCORN PL
HEADCORN RD
NIMMON DR
GALPIN'S RD
ST STEPHEN'S CRES
ST CHRISTOPHERS GDNS
WARWICK RD
WARWICK GDNS
OAKLANDS AVE
TOTTON RD
WILTSHIRE RD
GOSTON GDNS
WINTERBOURNE RD
STRATFORD RD
Winterbourne Jun & Inf Schs
LANGDALE RD
HEATHVIEW RD
Pav
Recn Gd
CR7
Bwg Gn
Pav
RICHMOND RD
BEECHWOOD AVE
LINDEN AVE
FOXLEY RD
WARLINGHAM RD
QUADRANT RD
ELLIOTT RD
NUTFIELD RD
KENLEY GDNS
CHIPSTEAD AVE
WOODCOTE AVE
CHESSELL CL
Liby
BLETCHINGLEY CL
BEVERSTONE RD
MAPLETHORPE RD
WOODLAND RD
WEYBRIDGE RD
MALVERN RD
LYNDHURST RD
DOVERCOURT AVE
COLLIERS WATER LA
QUEEN'S CT
BRIGSTOCK RD
B266
THORNTON ROW
RAYMEAD AVE
HASLEMERE RD
CHALET CT
PENSHURST RD
NORMAN RD
TOLL GATE RD
LAKEHALL RD
LAKEHALL GDNS
WELDON CT
HEATH HO
Pav
Sp Gd
MEADOW VIEW RD
FRANT RD
BUXTON RD
QUEENSWOOD AVE
KINGSWOOD AVE
EARLSWOOD AVE
ALMA PL
Thornton Heath
Mayday
H
JAMAICA RD
WOODCROFT RD
FORD CL
BENSHAM LA
FAIRGREEN
KIMBERLEY
FREDERICK GDNS
PO
CHESTNUT GR
HAZEL CL
CARISBROOKE RD
TAVISTOCK CRES
LEICESTER AVE
EIGHTEENTH RD
MONTGOMERY CL
SHROPSHIRE CL
RADNOR CL
YORKSHIRE RD
BERKSHIRE WAY
HERTFORD WAY
WESTMORLAND WAY
LANCASTER AVE
SUSSEX RD
MIDDLESEX RD
SOUTHAMPTON GDNS
NORTHUMBERLAND GDNS
COMMONSIDE E
MATTHEW CT
ALMOND WAY
BEECH GR
69
68
6
5
4
3
2
1
67
66
MAYFIELD CRES
MAYFIELD RD
SILVERLEIGH RD
LEANDER RD
GOLDWELL RD
REDFORD AVE
ASHLEY RD
FAIRLANDS AVE
JUBILEE CT
GROVE RD
SILCHESTER CT
KIRKLEES RD
WILLETT PL
WILLETT RD
BLAKEMORE RD
TRAFFORD RD
Bwg Gn
GONVILLE RD
LIMPSFIELD AVE
Pav
Allot Gdns
Pl Fld
Gonville Prim Sch
Crem
CR7
Sp Gd
Fball Gd
Pav
Cemy
Thornton Heath Pond
A23
A235
COLVIN RD
WHITEHALL RD
BROUGHTON RD
1 LANCASTER AVE
2 BERKSHIRE SQ
3 HERTFORD SQ
4 WESTMORLAND SQ
5 BUCKINGHAM RD
6 BUCKINGHAM CT
7 LINCOLN CT
8 SUSSEX CT
9 LINCOLN RD
203
WINGATE CRES
MOYS CL
HOUSE RD
Pl Fld
The Archbishop Lanfranc Sch
Cemy
A236
AURELIA GDNS
AURELIA RD
SHAMROCK RD
THORNTON RD
RAMSEY RD
CURZON RD
KESTON RD
KENMARE RD
HARCOURT RD
DUNHEVED CL
DUNHEVED RD N
DUNHEVED RD W
DUNHEVED RD S
IRVINE CT
LAUNCESTON CT
CHELTENHAM VILLAS
SHARLAND CL
LONDON RD
CROSSLAND
MAYDAY RD
FIVEACRE CL
Broad Green
CAMERON RD
Elmwood Schs
FRANCIS RD
CONSTANCE RD
LODGE RD
ROCHFORD WAY
PO
TANKERTON TERR
LAVENDER RD
PEALL RD
MARDEN CRES
MARDEN RD
FURTHERFIELD CL
SOUTHWELL RD
STANLEY GR
LYNTON RD
OAKWOOD RD
OAKWOOD PL
OAKWOOD GR
BOSTON RD
STANLEY RD
COLCHESTER VILLAS
CAMPBELL RD
BROAD GREEN AVE
KELLING GDNS
DARTMOUTH HO
ELMWOOD RD
BRADING RD
THORNTON AVE
ROSECOURT RD
CECIL RD
Sch
SAFFRON CL
THERAPIA LA
ROSEMARY CL
CINNAMON CL
ALFRISTON AVE
STONECROFT WAY
WESTCOMBE AVE
BEDDINGTON TERR
Lombard Rdbt
LANCING RD
DONALD RD
WORTLEY RD
YORK RD
PO
CANTERBURY RD
MIDHURST AVE
THE TRAMSHEDS
COOMBER WAY
PEPPERMINT CL
RINGWOOD AVE
ROSEDENE AVE
DACRE RD
ENDEAVOUR WAY
THERAPIA LA
Therapia Lane
Liby
Recn Gd
GREENSIDE RD
FAIRHOLME RD
WENTWORTH RD
SUTHERLAND RD
PRIORY RD
PEMDEVON RD
WELLINGTON RD
ST JAMES CT
PO
A236
MITCHAM RD
DRAKE RD
PURLEY WAY CRES
OCKLEY RD
LOMBARD BSNS PK
Croydon Tramlink
BEDDINGTON CROSS
STIRLING WAY
Sutton
Croydon
FRANKLIN WAY
KELVIN GDNS
BRAZIL CL
Ampere Way
EFFINGHAM RD
FAIRMEAD RD
PO
ONSLOW RD
BRIGHTWELL CL
DENNETT RD
LONGLEY RD
BISHOP'S RD
HANDCROFT RD
SUMNER RD
A213
HATHAWAY
KIDDERMINSTER PL
A21
MAXWELL CL
NEWMAN RD
PIONEERS IND PK
BEDDINGTON FARM RD
WIMSHURST CL
CHESTERMAN WAY
VOLTA WAY
FARADAY WAY
AMPERE WAY
PURLEY WAY
ALLEN RD
Sch
CHAPMAN RD
KINGSLEY RD
THOMSON CRES
HATTON RD
ADDINGTON RD
LAMBETH RD
CROYDON GR
SUMNER GDNS
EASTNEY RD
DENMEAD RD
LEIGHTON GDNS
CAVENDISH RD
ZODIAC CT
CHATFIELD RD
MONTAGUE RD
PANTON
B272
Ind Est
DANIELL WAY
GALVANI WAY
WADDON MARSH WAY
Superstore
GURNEY CRES
MILLER RD
EUSTON RD
SUMNER RD S
BUTE RD
GRAFTON RD
LEIGHTON ST
ALBION ST
GARDENERS RD
VANGUARD CL
NELSON CL
PARSON'S MEAD
RODNEY CL
RENOWN CL
HOOD CL
DERBY RD
BATH HOUSE RD
PYLON WAY
LATHAM'S WAY
MARTIN CRES
ENTERPRISE CL
Ind Est
Waddon Marsh
TA Ctr
THE PILTON EST
ANSWELL
CLARENDON
FACTORY LA
PITLAKE
A23
30
31
220
MARLOWE WAY
BEDDINGTON FARM RD
PETERWOOD
PETERWOOD PK
Beddington
TRAFALGAR WAY
WESTFIELD RD 1
LOWER CHURCH ST 2
BOURNE ST 3
THEOBALD RD
CORNWALL
33

South Norwood
Selhurst
SE25
CR0
Thornton Heath
West Croydon
East Croydon
Norwood Junction
Wellesley Road
Lebanon
Selhurst Park (Crystal Palace & Wimbledon Fball Clubs)
Grangewood Park
Croydon Coll
Selhurst Performing Arts & Tech Sch
Heavers Farm Prim Sch
Davidson Jun & Inf Schs
Broadmead Jun & Inf Schs
Ecclesbourne Jun & Inf Schs
Bensham Manor Sch
Oval Prim Sch
St Mary's Jun & Inf Schs
Woodside Jun & Inf Sch
Beulah Schs
Selhurst Works
Cemy
Allot Gdns
Recn Gd
Croydon Tramlink
GRANGE RD
WHITEHORSE RD
WHITEHORSE LA
SELHURST RD
SOUTH NORWOOD HILL
HIGH ST
NORTHCOTE RD
WINDMILL RD
ST JAMES'S RD
LOWER ADDISCOMBE RD
MORLAND RD
CHERRY ORCHARD RD
WELLESLEY RD
PARCHMORE RD
A212
A213
A215
A222
A232
B243
B266
B273
183
206
221
A
B
C
D
1
2
3
4
5
6
32
33
34
66
67
68
69

184
SE20
Birkbeck
Elmers End
South Norwood Country Park
SE25
Norwood Junction
Woodside
Harrington Road
Sports Arena
Ryelands Prim Sch
Golf Ctr
Arena
Long Lane Wood Nat Res
Monks Orchard Sch
Churchfields Prim Sch
Superstore
CROYDON ROAD IND EST
Woodside
Ashburton Park
Blackhorse Lane
Ashburton Com Sch
Shirley Oaks
CR0
Addiscombe
Shirley
222
205
PENGE RD
HIGH ST
MANOR RD
PORTLAND RD
ELMERS END RD
LONG LA
SPRING LA
WOODSIDE GN
LOWER ADDISCOMBE RD
SHIRLEY RD
ADDISCOMBE RD
Croydon Tramlink
A
B
C
D
1
2
3
4
5
6
66
67
68
69
34
35
36

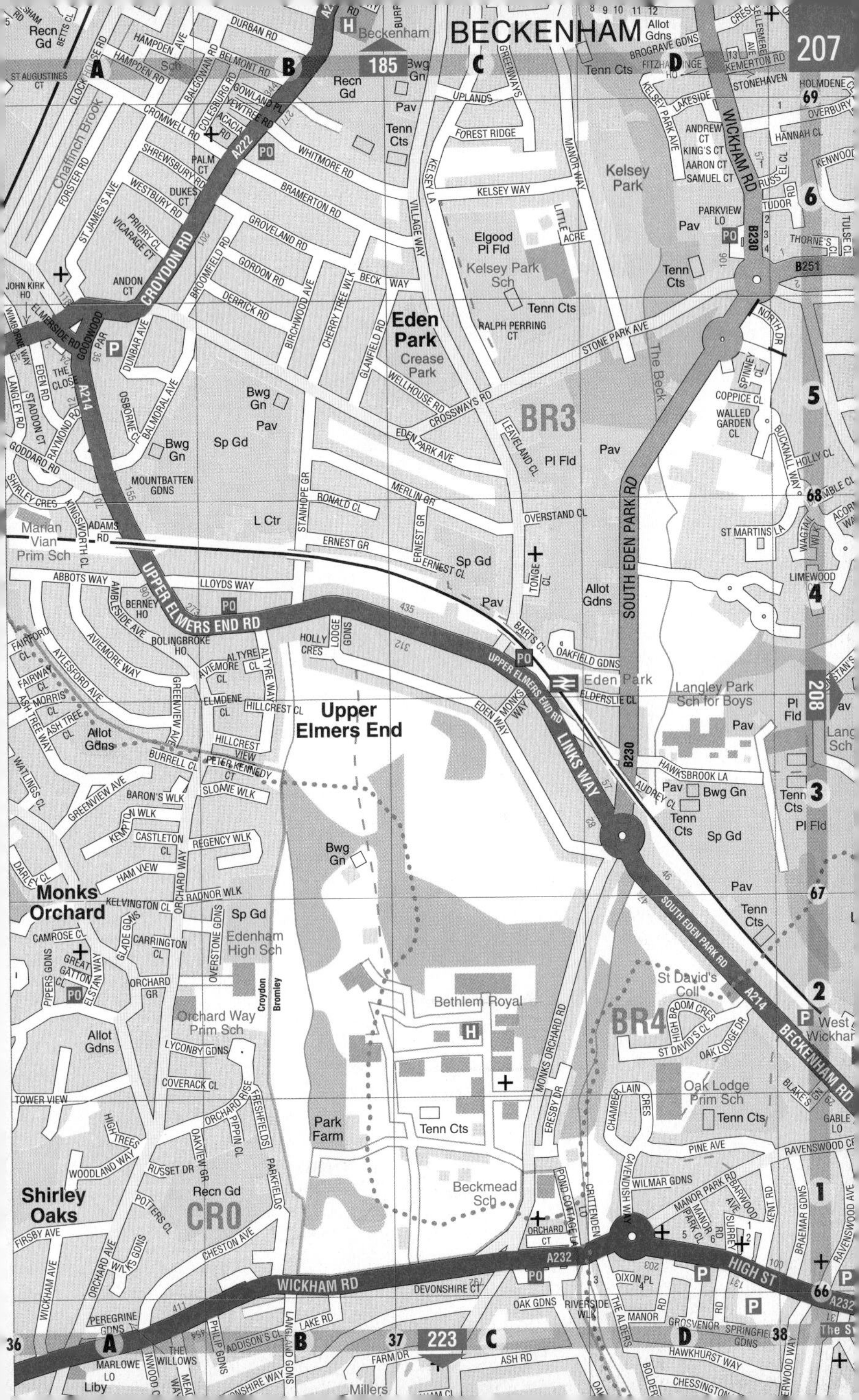
BECKENHAM
185
A
B
C
D
Beckenham
Recn Gd
Allot Gdns
DURBAN RD
HAMPDEN AVE
HAMPDEN RD
BELMONT RD
ST AUGUSTINES CT
CLOCK HOUSE RD
BETTS CL
Sch
Bwg Gn
Pav
Tenn Cts
UPLANDS
GREENWAYS
BROGRAVE GDNS
FITZHARDINGE HO
KEMERTON RD
ELLESMERE AVE
STONEHAVEN
HOLMDENE CL
69
OVERBURY
BALGOWAN RD
COLESBURG RD
GOWLAND PL
YEWTREE RD
ACACIA RD
CROMWELL RD
Chaffinch Brook
FORSTER RD
SHREWSBURY RD
PALM CT
A222
PO
WHITMORE RD
FOREST RIDGE
KELSEY LA
MANOR WAY
Kelsey Park
KELSEY PARK AVE
LAKESIDE
ANDREW CT
KING'S CT
AARON CT
SAMUEL CT
WICKHAM RD
HANNAH CL
KENWOOD
RUSSELL CL
6
WESTBURY RD
DUKES CT
ST JAMES'S AVE
PRIORY CL
VICARAGE CT
BRAMERTON RD
VILLAGE WAY
KELSEY WAY
LITTLE ACRE
Elgood Pl Fld
Kelsey Park Sch
PARKVIEW LO
TUDOR
B230
THORNE'S CL
TULSE CL
B251
GROVELAND RD
GORDON RD
BROOMFIELD RD
CROYDON RD
ANDON CT
JOHN KIRK HO
WIMBORNE WAY
ELMERSIDE RD
GOODWOOD PAR
DERRICK RD
BIRCHWOOD AVE
CHERRY TREE WLK
BECK WAY
GLANFIELD RD
Eden Park
Crease Park
Tenn Cts
RALPH PERRING CT
STONE PARK AVE
NORTH DR
The Beck
SPINNEY CL
COPPICE CL
WALLED GARDEN CL
5
DUNBAR AVE
A214
THE CLOSE
EDEN RD
LANGLEY RD
STADDON CT
RAYMOND RD
GODDARD RD
SHIRLEY CRES
OSBORNE CL
BALMORAL AVE
Bwg Gn
Sp Gd
MOUNTBATTEN GDNS
WELLHOUSE RD
CROSSWAYS RD
EDEN PARK AVE
LEAVELAND CL
BR3
Pl Fld
Pav
BUCKNALL WAY
HOLLY CL
BRAMBLE CL
68
KINGSWORTH CL
ADAMS RD
Marian Vian Prim Sch
L Ctr
STANHOPE GR
RONALD CL
MERLIN GR
ERNEST GR
ERNEST CL
OVERSTAND CL
SOUTH EDEN PARK RD
ST MARTINS LA
WAGTAIL WLK
ACORN WAY
Sp Gd
TONGE CL
Allot Gdns
LIMEWOOD
4
ABBOTS WAY
AMBLESIDE AVE
BERNEY HO
LLOYDS WAY
UPPER ELMERS END RD
BOLINGBROKE HO
HOLLY CRES
LODGE GDNS
BARTS CL
OAKFIELD GDNS
FAIRFORD CL
AYLESFORD AVE
AVIEMORE WAY
FAIRWAY CL
MORRIS CL
ASH TREE CL
ASH TREE WAY
ALTYRE CL
AVIEMORE CL
ALTYRE WAY
ELMDENE CL
HILLCREST CL
Upper Elmers End
Eden Park
ELDERSLIE CL
Langley Park Sch for Boys
EDEN WAY
MONKS WAY
208
Pl Fld
Pav
Allot Gdns
GREENVIEW AVE
HILLCREST VIEW
BURRELL CL
PETER KENNEDY CT
LINKS WAY
HAWKSBROOK LA
WATLINGS CL
BARON'S WLK
SLOANE WLK
AUDREY CL
Bwg Gn
Tenn Cts
3
Pl Fld
KEMPTON WLK
CASTLETON CL
REGENCY WLK
Sp Gd
DARLEY CL
HAM VIEW
RADNOR WLK
67
Monks Orchard
KELVINGTON CL
ORCHARD WAY
OVERSTONE GDNS
Edenham High Sch
CAMROSE CL
GLADE GDNS
CARRINGTON CL
PIPERS GDNS
GREAT GATTON CL
ELSTAN WAY
ORCHARD GR
Croydon
Bromley
St David's Coll
HIGH BROOM CRES
ST DAVID'S CL
OAK LODGE DR
A214
2
West Wickham
BECKENHAM RD
Allot Gdns
Orchard Way Prim Sch
Bethlem Royal
BR4
LYCONBY GDNS
COVERACK CL
TOWER VIEW
HIGH TREES
ORCHARD RISE
FRESHFIELDS
PIPPIN CL
OAKVIEW GR
MONKS ORCHARD RD
ERESBY DR
CHAMBERLAIN CRES
Oak Lodge Prim Sch
Tenn Cts
BLAKE'S GN
GABLE LO
Park Farm
Tenn Cts
PINE AVE
RAVENSWOOD CRES
WOODLAND WAY
RUSSET DR
Shirley Oaks
Recn Gd
CR0
PARKFIELDS
POTTERS CL
Beckmead Sch
POND COTTAGE LA
CRITTENDEN LO
CAVENDISH WAY
WILMAR GDNS
MANOR PARK RD
MANOR PARK CL
BARWOOD AVE
KENT RD
BRAEMAR GDNS
RAVENSWOOD AVE
1
FIRSBY AVE
ORCHARD AVE
WILKS GDNS
CHESTON AVE
ORCHARD CT
A232
HIGH ST
SURREY RD
DIXON PL
WICKHAM AVE
WICKHAM RD
DEVONSHIRE CT
OAK GDNS
RIVERSIDE WLK
THE ALDERS
MANOR RD
GROSVENOR RD
SPRINGFIELD GDNS
66
PEREGRINE GDNS
PHILIP GDNS
ADDISON'S CL
LANGLAND GDNS
LAKE RD
36
37
223
38
THE WILLOWS
MARLOWE LO
INWOOD CL
FARM DR
ASH RD
HAWKHURST WAY
BOLDERO
CHESSINGTON
Liby
Millers

186
224
207
A
B
C
D
Shortlands
Park Langley
Hayes
West Wickham
BR2
BR3
BR4
Langley Park
Pickhurst Green
Clare House Prim Sch
Highfield Inf Sch
Highfield Jun Sch
Langley Park Sch for Girls
Pickhurst Jun Sch
Pickhurst Inf Sch
Hawes Down Schs
Glebe Sch
Oak Lodge Prim Sch
Cupola Wood
Langley Manor
West Wickham
Hayes
WICKHAM RD
B230
B251
B228
B257
A214
A232
HAYES LA
WESTMORELAND RD
PICKHURST LA
BECKENHAM RD
STATION RD
HIGH ST
HAYES WAY
WHITECROFT CL
WHITECROFT WAY
ELWILL WAY
MALMAINS WAY
MALMAINS CL
STYLES WAY
BRABOURNE RISE
WOODMERE WAY
OVERHILL WAY
BUSHEY WAY
BARNFIELD WOOD RD
BARNFIELD WOOD CL
FAIRWAY GDNS
HAYES CHASE
GOODHART WAY
THE CRESCENT
WEST WAY
THE AVENUE
WICKHAM CHASE
LANGLEY WAY
THE DRIVE
PICKHURST RISE
RED LODGE RD
HAWKSBROOK LA
ST DUNSTAN'S LA
WICKHAM WAY
KINGSWOOD AVE
ROMANHURST AVE
ROMANHURST GDNS
HENGIST WAY
DRUIDS WAY
TOP PK
TOOTSWOOD RD
SOUTH HILL RD
HIGHFIELD DR
CUMBERLAND RD
ST MARY'S AVE
DEN RD
DEN CL
FYFIELD CL
SHORTLANDS RD
SHORTLANDS GR
BROMLEY GR
KINGSWOOD RD
CHURCH RD
HAZELWOOD HO
DEEPDENE CT
CASTLE CL
DARRELL CT
EVERGLADES
MAYS HILL RD
IDEN CL
VALLEY RD
FARLEY CROFT
COLEBROOK RISE
QUEEN ANNE AV
HILLSIDE RD
DYKES WAY
WINCHESTER PK
WINCHESTER RD
DURHAM RD
DURHAM AVE
MADISON GDNS
BAYDON CT
MERLIN CT
PINE TREE LO
SPRUCE PK
CHILTERN GDNS
CAYGILL CL
MORLEY CT
FLORIDA CT
LANCASTER CL
BROOKWOOD CL
STAMFORD DR
BODIAM CT
OAKHAM DR
RUTLAND GATE
LANGHAM PK PL
DEEPDALE AVE
KINGSLEIGH WLK
TALL ELMS CL
STONE RD
BRANSCOMBE CT
BROADOAKS WAY
WOODLEA DR
PICKHURST PK
BRAMBLEDOWN CL
CULVERSTONE CL
BARNHILL AVE
HURST GN
PENSHURST
HESFORD PARK DR
MEREWORTH CL
ELVINGTON GN
STANSTEAD CL
BRENCHLEY CL
EASTRY AVE
DRAVEN CL
SEDGEWOOD CL
MALLING WAY
BOUGHTON AVE
PEMBURY
PICKHURST GN
PICKHURST MEAD
MOUNTHURST RD
CONSTANCE CRES
CREST RD
HILLDOWN RD
COURTLANDS AVE
PONDFIELD RD
HAYES MEAD RD
HAYES HILL
HAYES HILL RD
HEPBURN GDNS
BRIAR GDNS
HURSTDENE AVE
DENE CL
SAVILLE ROW
BOURNE WAY
PRICKLEY WOOD
CHATSWORTH CL
MARWELL CL
TIEPIGS LA
RYDAL DR
HEYDON CT
WINDERMERE RD
KESWICK RD
HAWES LA
MARTINS CL
LINDEN LEAS
THE MEAD
LINKS RD
HAWES LA
RAYS RD
RED LO
GABLE LO
BLAKE'S GN
OAK LODGE DR
LONG MEADOW CL
HAZELWOOD LO
RAVENSWOOD CRES
RAVENSWOOD AVE
BRAEMAR GDNS
KENT RD
CROFT AVE
OAK GR
ASH GR
GLEBE WAY
WICKHAM CRES
ROSE WLK
CHATSWORTH
SPRINGFIELD GDNS
HOLLAND WAY
HOLLAND CL
KEMSING CL
HILLSIDE LA
NORTH DR
SPINNEY CL
WALLED GARDEN CL
BUCKNALL WAY
HOLLY CL
BRAMBLE CL
ACORN WAY
WAGTAIL WLK
ST MARTINS LA
LIMEWOOD CL
STONEHAVEN
HOLMDENE CL
OVERBURY AVE
BROADWAY
HANNAH CL
KENWOOD DR
RUSSELL CL
TUDOR
THORNE'S CL
TULSE CL
QUINTON CL
FERGUSON CL
OATES CL
FOXES DALE
WALDRON GDNS
WESTPOINT
SPRINGPARK DR
STANLEY AVE
HOWARDS CREST CL
OAKWOOD AVE
COURTENAY DR
OAKWAY
SCOTTS LA
DAWN WLK
MORDEN
BARTON CT
BLADON CT
FRANKLIN HO
GREEN CL
FIRTREE CT
OCTOBER CT
CELTIC AVE
VALAN LEAS
PUMP HOUSE CL
QUEEN'S MEAD RD
RAVENS CL
BROMLEY CRES
BROMLEY GDNS
RIDLEY RD
Allot Gdns
Tenn Cts
Recn Gd
Pl Fld
Pav
Sp Gd
Bwg Gn
Sw Pool
Liby
CH
PO
P

187
A
B
C
D
BROMLEY
BR1
BR2
Bromley C Ctr
The Pavilion L Ctr
THE GLADES SH CTR
Church House Gdns
Liby
Bromley South
St Mark's Sch
KENTISH WAY
A21
STOCKWELL
RAFFORD WAY
THE CHASE
PALACE VIEW
MURRAY AVE
FORDE AVE
BISHOPS AVE
Tenn Ct
Bickley Prim Sch
NIGHTINGALE LA
FARRIER CL
CANON RD
LIDDON RD
PAGE HEATH LA
PAGE HEATH VILLAS
AMESBURY RD
WESTWOOD CL
HEATH PARK DR
BERESFORD DR
B265
ELLEN CL
Wks
WENDOVER CT
SIWARD RD
GODWIN RD
LANGDON RD
WALDO IND EST
WALDO RD
BROMLEY IND EST
CHARTWELL BSNS CTR
BEACONSFIELD RD
THE AVENUE
CLARENCE RD
WINDSOR CT
MORNINGTON AVE
GLANVILLE RD
GUNDULPH RD
HOMESDALE RD
OLD HOMESDALE RD
WOLDHAM RD
MASONS HILL
B228
WESTMORELAND RD
B2212
H
Bromley
CROMWELL AVE
CROMWELL CL
PINEWOOD RD
SANDFORD RD
STREAMSIDE CL
Recn Gd
Pav
Allot Gdns
HAVELOCK RD
GREAT ELMS RD
MARLBOROUGH RD
RAGLAN RD
NELSON RD
JAFFRAY RD
BOURNE RD
FASHODA RD
ELLIOTT RD
HAYWOOD RD
BATHS RD
SOUTHLANDS RD
TREDWELL CL
GAINSBOROUGH CT
FLETCHERS CL
VINCENT CL
Tenn Cts
Raglan Prim Sch
COWPER RD
COWPER CL
Bwg Gn
WHITEHALL RD
BROOKLYN RD
HERBERT RD
BALFOUR RD
ALBERT RD
VICTORIA RD
CROWN CT
CROWN LA
SALISBURY MEWS
SALISBURY RD
SUNNINGDALE RD
ADDISON RD
BLOOMFIELD RD
CHANTRY LA
CHATTERTON RD
WALPOLE RD
POPE RD
UNION RD
DRYDEN HO
JOHNSON RD
WAVERLEY CL
MOSSLEA RD
HOOK FARM RD
BOSWELL HO
BROMLEY COMM
NEWTON TERR
CROWN LANE SPUR
Sp Gd
210
HAYES RD
HAYES LA
Ravensbourne Sch
Pl Fld
Ravens Bourne
Fball Gd
Fisher's Wood
Norman Park
Athletics Tk
Scrogginhill Wood
ROOKERY LA
Bromley Coll of F & H Ed
Rookery Lake
Bromley Common
BONNINGTON TWR
CHELDWICH TERR
APPLEDORE CL
CAMERON RD
HURSTFIELD
BEADON RD
LETCHWORTH CL
LETCHWORTH DR
HERITON AVE
CORNFORD
FAIR ACRES
WOLFE CL
MONTCALM CL
CRANBROOK CL
HAZELMERE WAY
MARDEN AVE
KINGSDOWN WAY
OAKMEAD AVE
NORTHBOURNE
KECHILL GDNS
CLUB GARDENS RD
DARTMOUTH RD
EASTWAY
SOUTHWAY
SOUTHBOURNE
PITTSMEAD AVE
Brook Wood
Hayes Street Farm
Mazzards Wood
Oakley House
BARHAM CT
A233
Hayes
CHATHAM AVE
STUART AVE
CHERRY WLK
HAMBRO AVE
CECIL WAY
STANHOPE AVE
HUSSEYWELL CRES
ALEXANDER CL
Recn Gds
B251
HAYES ST
GEORGIAN CL
GEORGE LA
Old Rectory Gdns
Hayes Prim Sch
HAYES WOOD AVE
GLEBE HOUSE DR
HOPTON CT
FORGE CL
THE KNOLL
HAYES GARDEN
STATION APP
RIDGEWAY
BURWOOD AVE
WARREN RD
GROVE CL
Hayes Sch
225
41
42
66
67
68
69
Tenn Cts
Pl Fld
Sp Gd
CROSS RD

Bickley
BICKLEY PARK RD
A222
188
A
B
C
D
WOODLANDS RD
HARTLEY
COPSE
PINES RD
Pl Fld
Pav
HEATH PARK DR
BERESFORD DR
WESTWOOD CL
PAGE HEATH LA
B265
STRATFORD HOUSE AVE
ST MICHAELS CL
Tenn Cts
PO
CHARLOTTE PARK AVE
Bickley Park Sch
ST GEORGES RD
ST MATTHEWS DR
SYLVAN WLK
ELLEN CL
WINDSOR CT
ABINGER CL
THE PANTILES
BEACONSFIELD RD
THE AVENUE
SOUTHLANDS GR
HOLMDENE CT
RUSHMORE CL
LINDSEY CL
ARMSTRONG
CHADD DR
CLARENCE RD
BICKLEY CRES
CLARENCE AVE
FALCON AVE
LIME CL
COOMBE LEA
HAWTHORNE CL
HAWTHORNE RD
WYNCROFT CL
SOUTHWARK PL
ROSEMOUNT DR
HURSTWOOD DR
MEADOW CROFT
ALBA FIELD
NEWMANS CL
AYCLIFFE CL
REYNARD CL
WELLSMOOR GDNS
HEVER GDNS
SHORNEFIELD CL
COATES HILL RD
FARO CL
GOSSHILL RD
BARFIELD RD
OTFORD CL
GOLF RD
THORNET WOOD RD
Allot Gdns
BR1
NORTHUMBERLAND GDNS
BLACKBROOK LA
Recn Gd
Bwg Gn
BATHS RD
SOUTHLANDS RD
TREDWELL CL
DRAPER CT
OLDFIELD RD
TANGLEBERRY CL
SOUTHBOROUGH RD
SPRINGFIELD RD
OLDFIELD CL
SOUTHWOOD CL
PARKSIDE AVE
PARK HILL
SPRINGFIELD GDNS
Bromley High Sch for Girls
WHITE'S MDW
Thornet Wood
Jubilee Country Park
COWPER CL
BLENHEIM RD
CLAREMONT RD
HIGHFIELD RD
FAIRMEAD CL
FAIRMEAD
BURFORD RD
WALDEGRAVE RD
SUNNINGDALE RD
MAYFIELD RD
WESTCOTT CL
RINGMER WAY
RIPLEY CL
THE FAIRWAY
BROOKMEAD AVE
HOMEMEAD RD
WOODSIDE RD
WHITEHALL RD
BROOKLYN RD
UNION RD
POPE RD
HERBERT RD
BALFOUR RD
SALISBURY RD
ST AUGUSTINE'S AVE
BIRDHAM CL
MOORCROFT GDNS
CLOISTERS AVE
MOSSLEA RD
ALBERT RD
VICTORIA RD
CROWN CT
SALISBURY MEWS
DUXBERRY CL
AUSTIN AVE
SOUTHBOROUGH LA
Liby
MAGPIE HALL LA
WILLOW CL
HOLMCROFT WAY
HOLBROOK WAY
PARKFIELD WAY
FONTWELL DR
St James RC Prim Sch
MAYBURY CL
MERTON GDNS
Southborough Prim Sch
BR2
209
COMM
LAVENDER CL
NEWTON TERR
CROWN LANE SPUR
Sp Gd
BONNINGTON TWR
SHELDWICH TERR
GREEN WAY
SUNRAY AVE
SOVEREIGN CT
RUSKIN WLK
STILES CL
Parkfield Recn Gd
Cemy
OXHAWTH CRES
LANGLEY GDNS
CHESHAM AVE
THORNSCL
LOVELACE AVE
MONS WAY
BROOM CL
NARROW WAY
MANOR WAY
SHELL CL
Bromley Common
Southborough
THE OAKS
WHITEBEAM AVE
ASH ROW
HAZEL WLK
HORNBEAM WAY
BIRCH ROW
FARINGDON AVE
PRESCOTT AVE
FELTON CL
ROLLESTON AVE
HOLLINGWORTH RD
ley Coll & H Ed
RAYFIELD CL
TURPINGTON LA
MOSUL WAY
MAGPIE HALL CL
TURPINGTON CL
LINK WAY
COBHAM CL
CH
Bromley
LARCH WAY
LABURNUM WAY
ROLLESTON CL
FAIROAK CL
A21
BROMLEY COMM
Tenn Cts
Pl Fld
Recn Gd
Prince's Plain Prim Sch
ALMOND WAY
ALMOND CL
Sparrow Wood
London Loop
Oakley House
Allot Gdns
Prince's Plain
BR5
CHURCH LA
BARHAM CT
COTTAGE AVE
PRINCE'S PLAIN
A233
BREWERY RD
CREDENHALL DR
Scrubs Farm
Crofton Heath
BROMLEY CL
Pl Fld
CAPEL CT
BARHAM CL
LOWER GRAVEL RD
ARAGON CL
SEYMOUR DR
LENNARD RD
RANDOLPH RD
LANSDOWNE AVE
TRINITY CL
RIBSTON CL
JACKSON RD
BRADFORD CL
HATHAWAY CL
DAERWOOD CL
DRAYTON AVE
BROMLEY
66
ST ANTHONY'S CT
ROSE DALE
LIME GR
Knowl Wood
CHERRY ORCHARD RD
JACKSON RD
COPTHORNE AVE
42
43
226
BIRCH MEAD
JASMINE CL
FAIRBANK AVE
POPLAR AVE
WISTARIA CL
MORLEY CL
KNOWLE RD
Knowlehill Wood
WOOD WAY
HAZEL
CROSS RD
HASTIN
1
2
3
4
5
6
67
68
69

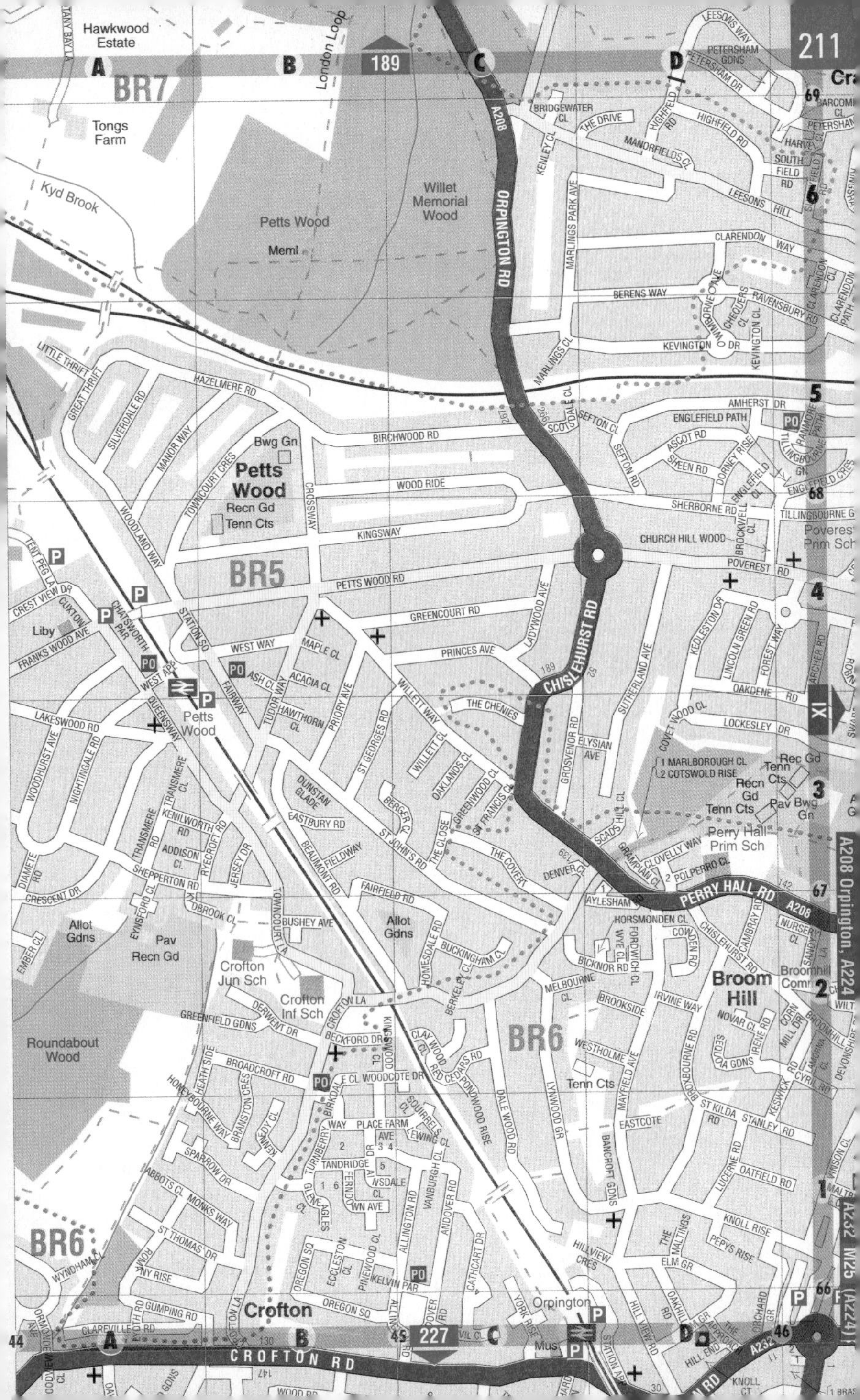
Hawkwood Estate
TANY BAY LA
A
B
189
C
D
London Loop
BR7
Tongs Farm
Kyd Brook
Petts Wood
Meml
Willet Memorial Wood
A208
ORPINGTON RD
BRIDGEWATER CL
THE DRIVE
KENLEY CL
HIGHFIELD RD
PETERSHAM GDNS
PETERSHAM DR
LEESONS WAY
MANORFIELDS CL
SOUTH FIELD RD
LEESONS HILL
HARVEY
PETERSHAM
BARCOMBE CL
69
6
MARLINGS PARK AVE
CLARENDON WAY
BERENS WAY
WIMBORNE AVE
CHEQUERS CL
RAVENSBURY RD
KEVINGTON CL
KEVINGTON DR
CLARENDON CL
CLARENDON PATH
MARLINGS CL
5
LITTLE THRIFT
GREAT THRIFT
HAZELMERE RD
SILVERDALE RD
MANOR WAY
TOWNCOURT CRES
Bwg Gn
BIRCHWOOD RD
Petts Wood
Recn Gd
Tenn Cts
WOOD RIDE
CROSSWAY
KINGSWAY
WOODLAND WAY
SCOTSDALE CL
SEFTON CL
SEFTON RD
AMHERST DR
ENGLEFIELD PATH
ASCOT RD
SHEEN RD
DORNEY RISE
ENGLEFIELD CL
SHERBORNE RD
RANMORE PATH
TILLINGBOURNE GN
ENGLEFIELD CRES
68
TILLINGBOURNE GN
BROCKWELL CL
CHURCH HILL WOOD
Poverest Prim Sch
POVEREST RD
4
BR5
PETTS WOOD RD
GREENCOURT RD
LADYWOOD AVE
CHISLEHURST RD
TENT PEG LA
CREST VIEW DR
CUXTON
Liby
FRANKS WOOD AVE
CHATSWORTH PAR
STATION SQ
WEST WAY
MAPLE CL
PRINCES AVE
ACACIA CL
ASH CL
WEST APP
FAIRWAY
TUDOR WAY
HAWTHORN CL
PRIORY AVE
WILLETT WAY
LAKESWOOD RD
QUEENSWAY
Petts Wood
WOODHURST AVE
NIGHTINGALE RD
ST GEORGES RD
WILLETT CL
OAKLANDS CL
THE CHENIES
GREENWOOD CL
ST FRANCIS CL
GROSVENOR RD
ELYSIAN AVE
SUTHERLAND AVE
KEDLESTON DR
LINCOLN GREEN RD
FOREST WAY
ARCHER RD
OAKDENE RD
COVET WOOD CL
LOCKESLEY DR
IX
1 MARLBOROUGH CL
2 COTSWOLD RISE
Rec Gd
Tenn Cts
Recn Gd
Tenn Cts
Pav Bwg Gn
3
TRANSMERE CL
TRANSMERE RD
KENILWORTH RD
ADDISON CL
RYECROFT RD
JERSEY DR
DUNSTAN GLADE
EASTBURY RD
BERGER CL
THE CLOSE
THE COVERT
SCADS HILL CL
GRAMPIAN CL
CLOVELLY WAY
Perry Hall Prim Sch
POLPERRO CL
DENVER CL
A208 Orpington, A224
DIAMETER RD
CRESCENT DR
SHEPPERTON RD
EYNSFORD CL
DBROOK CL
TOWNCOURT LA
BEAUMONT RD
FIELDWAY
ST JOHN'S RD
FAIRFIELD RD
PERRY HALL RD
A208
AYLESHAM
67
NURSERY CL
SANDY
EMBER CL
Allot Gdns
Pav
Recn Gd
BUSHEY AVE
Allot Gdns
HOMESDALE RD
BUCKINGHAM CL
HORSMONDEN CL
WYE CL
FORDWICH CL
COWDEN RD
CHISLEHURST RD
CAMBRAY RD
Crofton Jun Sch
BERKELEY CL
BICKNOR RD
MELBOURNE CL
Broom Hill
Broomhill Comm
2
Crofton Inf Sch
CROFTON LA
BROOKSIDE
IRVINE WAY
NOVAR CL
IRENE RD
CORN MILL DR
BROOMHILL
GREENFIELD GDNS
DERWENT DR
BECKFORD DR
KINGSWOOD
CLAY WOOD CL
BR6
WESTHOLME
SEQUOIA GDNS
Roundabout Wood
HEATH SIDE
BROADCROFT RD
WOODCOTE DR
RED CEDARS RD
MAYFIELD AVE
BROWNSBOURNE RD
CYRIL RD
KESWICK RD
LYNWOOD GR
Tenn Cts
HONEYBOURNE WAY
BRANSTON CRES
KENNEDY CL
TURNBERRY WAY
PLACE FARM AVE
SQUIRRELS CL
EWING CL
PONDWOOD RISE
DALE WOOD RD
ST KILDA RD
STANLEY RD
SPARROW DR
TANDRIDGE DR
EASTCOTE
BANCROFT GDNS
LUCERNE RD
OATFIELD RD
ABBOTS CL
MONKS WAY
GLENEAGLES CL
FERNDOWN AVE
ALLINGTON RD
VANBURGH CL
ANDOVER RD
1
KNOLL RISE
A232 M25 (A224)
ST THOMAS' DR
THE MALTINGS
PEPYS RISE
BR6
WYNDHAM CL
OREGON SQ
ECCLESTON CL
PINEWOOD CL
KELVIN PAR
CATHCART DR
HILLVIEW CRES
ELM GR
Orpington
66
OAKHILL RD
HILL VIEW RD
ORCHARD GR
GUMPING RD
Crofton
OREGON SQ
YORK RISE
CLAREVILLE RD
CROFTON LA
227
Mus
APPROACH
HILL END
A232
46
44
A
B
45
C
D
CROFTON RD
STATION APP
KNOLL CT
30

A
B
C
D
196
Ditton Common
Games Ct
Pav
IMBER CL
CRANLEIGH RD
WESTON GREEN RD
WESTON PARK
PORTSMOUTH RD
THE WOODLANDS
CRANBROOK DR
BLAIR AVE
DOUGLAS RD
WOODEND
LOWER GREEN RD
ARRAN WAY
PO
66
6
B3379
Esher
ORLEANS CL
STATION RD
Thames Ditton & Esher
CH
HAMPTON COURT WAY A309
WESTON GN
WESTON RD
MACAULAY AVE
KT7
WOODFIELD RD
BOURNE CL
LYNWOOD RD
WESSEX CL
Recn Gd
Allo Gdns
Allot Gdns
Sandown Park
Race Course
YEW TREE COTTS
GRANTS COTTS
SANDOWN GATE
A307
Scilly Isles
COUCHMORE AVE
WESTMONT RD
SOUTHMONT RD
MONTGOMERY AVE
EASTMONT RD
Hinchley Wood
ROYSTON CT
COTSWOLD CL
MANOR RD N
HILLMONT RD
GIBSON CT
KINGSTON BY-PASS
Hinchley Wood
STATION APP
MEADOW CL
MANOR DR
A309
5
Littleworth Common
WESTWOOD CL
LITTLEWORTH COMMON RD
HEATHSIDE CL
HEATHSIDE
MEDINA AVE
HAREFIELD
HINCHLEY DR
HILLCREST GDNS
HINCHLEY CL
Allot Gdns
The Warren
65
PEMBERTON PL
CARRICK GATE
HILLBROW CT
HILLBROW RD
P
PENATES
GREENWAYS
Telegraph Hill
A244 Walton-on-Thames
A307 Cobham, A3(A245)
ELLISFORD
WARREN CL
ESHER GN
ASHBURNHAM PK
SANDOWN RD
LITTLEWORTH PL
LITTLEWORTH LA
LITTLEWORTH RD
MANOR RD S
Semaphore House
4
Civic Office
Liby
Bwg Gn
NEW RD
MARTINEAU CL
CH
Rugby Gd
OLD CHURCH PATH
WOOTTON
WILLOWMERE
LITTLEMEAD
HIGH ST
ESHER
Tenn Cts
Sp Gd
Sp Gd
Tenn Cts
VICTORIA PL
CARRINGTON PL
SANDOWN AVE
KT10
TELEGRAPH LA
GRANTLEY PL
CLAREMONT LA
SIMMONS GATE
ESHER PARK AVE
BROOMFIELDS
LITTLEWORTH AVE
Bwg Gn
STOCKFIELD RD
CAVENDISH DR
OAKEN LA
BROOM CL
CRANFORD RISE
ACORNS WAY
ROSEBRIARS
HOMESTEAD GDNS
3
Tenn Cts
RYTHE RD
Allot Gdns
Slough Farm
FIR TREE CL
Esher Church Sch
LYNNE WLK
HEATHERSET CL
RALEIGH DR
ROSE COTTS
ASTON RD
SIMMIL RD
CLARE HILL
BRACONDALE
Tenn Cts
MILBOURNE LA
CHADWORTH WAY
LOSEBERRY RD
STATION RD
NORFOLK RD
APPLEGARTH
64
COMPTON CL
THE AVENUE
VIII
Jun Sch
ARBROOK LA
JUDGE WLK
MEADOW RD
WOODBOURNE DR
THE ROUNDWAY
Pl Fld
ORCHARD WAY
BRENDON CL
The Rythe
WESTBURY AVE
HAYMEADS DR
BRENDON DR
HARE LA
Tenn Cts
OAKEN DR
BROOKFIELD GDNS
TORRINGTON RD
2
HOME FARM CL
HIGH GARTH
ARBROOK CHASE
THE PARADE
TORRINGTON CL
CEDAR WLK
WOODWARD CL
Milbourne Lodge Sen Sch
Claygate
DERWENT CL
ELM RD
ST LEONARD'S RD
LAKESIDE DR
THE WILLOWS
SYDNEY TERR
SYDNEY COTTS
SIM'S COTTS
THE GREEN
COPSEM DR
MILLBROOK
ALBANY CRES
ATHLONE
HURSTBOURNE
COPSEM WAY
FIRS CL
FAWCUS CL
DALMORE AVE
FOLEY COTTS
ELM GDNS
CLAREMONT END
THE FIRS
ARBROOK HALL
CHURCH RD
BLAKEDEN DR
Loseberry Farm
FOLEY RD
FOLEY MEWS
THE ELMS
Stable Pond
COPSEM LA
GORDON RD
KINGS MEAD PK
Claygate Prim Sch
THE CAUSEWAY
Claremont Park
Recn Gd
CORNWALL AVE
Rowan Prep Sch
CLAREMONT RD
Claygate
FEE FARM RD
1
FOLEY RD
MEADWAY
FITZALAN RD
WOODLANDS CL
Arbrook Common
BEACONSFIELD RD
Rowan Prep Sch
BEACONSFIELD GDNS
COVERTS RD
A244
CLAYGATE LODGE CL
QUEEN ANNE DR
VALE RD
FOXWARREN
VALE CROFT
LANE GDNS
63
Allot Gdns
Esher Common
14
15
VIII
A244 Leatherhead, A3
Horringdon Farm

Long Ditton
197
KT7
KT6
KT10
KT9
A
B
C
D
66
6
5
65
4
3
64
2
1
63
16
17
18
VIII
214
Hinchley Wood Sch
Hinchley Wood Prim Sch
Hill Park Nurseries
Cemy
Manor House
Ditton Hill Nurseries
Sp Gd
Pav
Allot Gdns
KINGSTON BY-PASS
A309
A3
A243
The Waffrons
CH
Surbiton
Manor Farm
Elm Farm
Lower Wood
Barwell
Claygate Common
Nursery
Pl Fld
Tenn Cts
Bwg Gn
Recn Gd
Lovelace Prim Sch
Kingston upon Thames
Surrey
St Philip's Sch
Ellingham Prim Sch
Chessington South
Chessington Com Coll
Chessington
St Paul's Sch
Liby
PO
HOOK RD
LEATHERHEAD RD
WOODSTOCK LA S
WOODSTOCK LA N
CLAYTON RD
SOMERSET AVE
VALLIS WAY
SELWOOD RD
MANSFIELD RD
GARRISON LA
BOLTON RD
ELLINGHAM RD
SHERWOOD
LOVE LA
DITTON HILL
CHURCH RD
RECTORY LA
MANDEVILLE DR
LANGLEY AVE
SUMMERFIELD LA
CLAYGATE LA
OLD CLAYGATE LA
RED LA
COMMON LA
COMMON RD
HILL VIEW RD
RUXLEY CRES
MERLING CL 1
GOLDING CL 2
NICHOLS CL 3
WITHERS CL 4
MITFORD CL 5
VIDLER CL 6
SMEATON CL 7
HUBBARD DR 8
WHITEHALL CRES 1
TREWENNA DR 2
CHESSINGTON PAR 3
A3 Guildford, M25
A243 Leatherhead, M25

198
A
B
C
D
Tolworth Jun & Inf Schs
DENNAN RD
BAKERY MEWS
GRAND PAR
BURWOOD CL
BROADWAY
TOLWORTH CL
EWELL RD
WARREN
DUNTON CL
MALCOLM
KEDWOOD WLK
DITTON RD
HOOK RD
MALVERN RD
COTTERILL RD
ELLERTON RD
DOUGLAS RD
PICTON PL
PYNE RD
IVY RD
HANOVER HO
RED LION RD
SCHOOL LA
LENELBY RD
RICKARDS CL
OAKLEIGH CT
BOND RD
RAVENSCAR RD
TOLWORTH PARK RD
MAYROYD AVE
KINGSMEAD AVE
PRINCES AVE
OAKLEIGH AVE
BROAD OAKS
A240
A3
TOLWORTH RISE S
TOLWORTH RISE N
SHERWOOD
WENTWORTH CL
Surrey
Sch
THE CLIFTON
SHREWSBURY CL
WARWICK CT
HERNE RD
WATERSIDE CL
VALE RD N
VALE ROAD S
CULSAC RD
THORNHILL AVE
THORNHILL RD
TANKERTON RD
Tolworth
KT6
CLIVE CT
HAMILTON AVE
BARNSBURY LA
Tenn Cts
Sp Gd
BROOK RD
DIANA GDNS
AGAR CL
BADEN POWELL CL
FULLERS AVE
RED LION RD
ST GEORGE'S GDNS
HOOK RISE N
TOLWORTH UNDERPASS
HOOK RISE S
TOBY WAY
DONALD WOODS GDNS
LARGEWOOD AVE
LADYWOOD RD
GLADSTONE RD
SYDNEY CT
VERONA DR
KENT WAY
TOLWORTH RD
HAYCROFT RD
Southborough Sch
Hook
A243
CARNEGIE CL
RAVENSWOOD AVE
SELBOURNE AVE
Allot Gdns
ROYSTON CT
KINGSTON BY-PASS
RONELEAN RD
FULLERS WAY N
RED LION BSNS CTR
Pl Fld
CRANBORNE AVE
SUNDIAL CT 1
WOODLAND WAY 2
BELL CT 3
DRAYTON CT 4
LANSDOWNE CL 5
HOOK RISE N
BIDMEAD CT
SWALLOW PK
CHAFFINCH CL
HOOK UNDERPASS
Tolworth Girls' Sch
KELVIN GR
KING EDWARD DR
ACE PAR
ELMCROFT CL
ELMCROFT DR
KINGSTON BSNS CTR
RANYARD CL
ASHCROFT RD
QUEEN MARY CL
Bwg Gn
Tenn Cts
Recn Gd
Allot Gdns
WILLCOCKS CL
CONISTON CT
CONISTON WAY
PRIORY RD
FULLERS WAY S
GLEN RD
CUMBERLAND DR
BEECHCROFT RD
1 CURLEW CT
2 LAPWING CT
ARGENT CT
Fball Gd
King Georges Field
Recn Gd
Pav
JUBILEE WAY
St Paul's Sch
HUNTERS RD
LYNTON CL
CEDARCROFT RD
OAKCROFT VILLAS
OAKCROFT RD
FIRCROFT RD
OAKCROFT BSNS CTR
KING GEORGE'S TRAD EST
DAVIS RD
MACDONOUGH CL
GRANGE RD
APPLE GR
ORCHARD RD
Hook
GOSBURY HILL
COX LA
HAWKHURST GDNS
ROSEMARY GDNS
ORCHARD GDNS
DURBIN RD
THE CAUSEWAY
CECIL CL
ST PAUL'S CL
Liby
GREEN END
ELM RD
ROMNEY CL
TUDOR CL
COUTTS AVE
SANGER AVE
Buckland Inf Sch
LION PARK AVE
CHESSINGTON PK
FOXGLOVE LA
ROEBUCK RD
FINLAYS CL
LOCKWOOD WAY
HURST CL
PEMBERLEY CHASE 1
PEMBERLEY CL 2
GREENLANDS
PEMBERLEY HO
IRIS RD
COX LA
213
MEADOW WAY
RHODRONS AVE
SHERBORNE RD
MOORFIELD RD
MOOR LA
STATION RD
BRAY CT
BUCKLAND RD
MOUNT RD
DRAKE RD
WOLSEY WAY
CHANTRY RD
ANGUS CL
Kingston upon Thames
Surrey
DEREK CL
STANTON CL
RUXLEY CL
RUXLEY MEWS
GATLEY AVE
HOLMWOOD RD
SHERE CL
ALBURY RD
FRIMLEY RD
Chessington North
SOPWITH AVE
NORTH PAR
OSBORNE WAY
Moor Lane Jun Sch
1 ROSEBERRY CT
2 INVICTA CT
3 PADLEY CL
PEARTREE CL
CHESSINGTON HILL PK
DEREK AVE
DEVON WAY
AMIS AVE
JASMINE RD
LAVENDER RD
BRIDGE RD
MELFORD CL
MOOR LA
JUNIPER CL
WOODLAND WLK
64
BOLTON CL
BOLTON RD
PARBURY RISE
COMPTON CRES
MARSTON AVE
WILSON RD
CHURCH RISE
RUTLAND CL
Allot Gdns
CHESSINGTON RD
ORCHARD CL
CARNFORTH CL
HEADLEY CL
B284
LARCH CRES
NIGHTINGALE DR
ST CATHERINES
SALMONS RD
CARLTON CL
ELLINGHAM RD
Recn Gd
Bwg Gn
KT9
Chessington
COXWOLD PATH 1
WETHERBY WAY 2
Allot Gdns
St Mary's Sch
CHURCH LA
HEMSBY RD
GILDERS RD
THRIGBY RD
Thames Down Link
ASHBY AVE
MALTBY RD
KELVIN CL
HARTFORD RD
COLLIER CL
St Philip's Sch
Ellingham Prim Sch
BRANSBY RD
STOKESBY RD
FILBY RD
ROLLESBY RD
Butchers Grove
CRAYKE HILL
YORK WAY
REYNOLDS AVE
CLIPPESBY CL
BILLOCKBY CL
Castle Hill
Chessington South
GARRISON LA
HALFORD CT
ST MARY'S CL
LEAS CL
GREEN VIEW
Allot Gdns
KT19
VIVIEN CL
LARA CL
LINDSAY CL
SELBY CL
HUNTING GATE DR
Chessington Com Coll
Chessington
GREEN LA
Horton Country Park
Horton Country Park
63
18
19
VIII
Sp Gd
Tenn Cts
HORTON LA
66
65
6
5
4
3
2
1

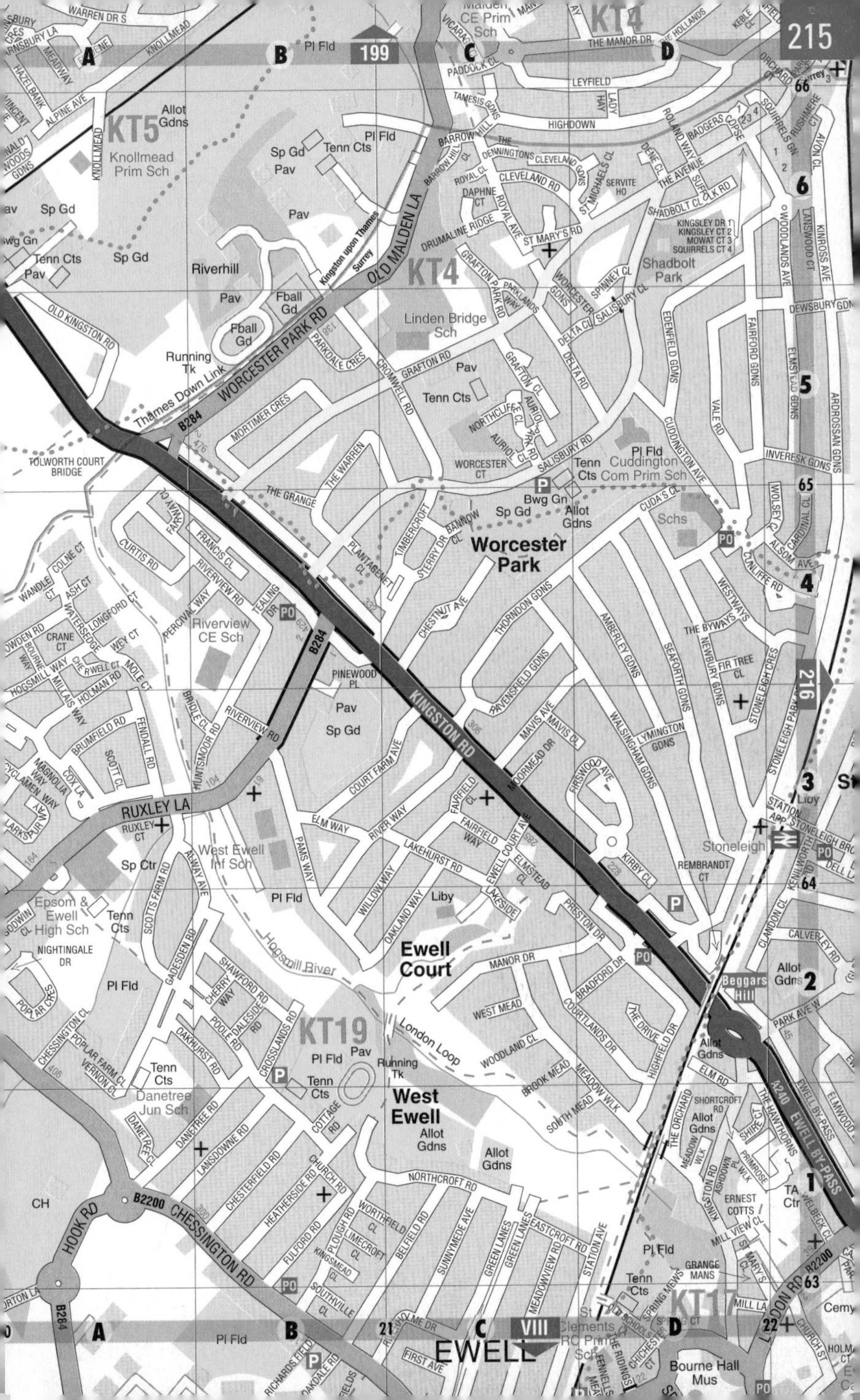

KT4
KT5
KT19
KT17
199
216
VIII
A
B
C
D
1
2
3
4
5
6
21
22
63
64
65
66
Malden CE Prim Sch
THE MANOR DR
THE HOLLANDS
KEBLE CL
WARREN DR S
RANSBURY LA
MEADWAY
HAZELBANK
ALPINE AVE
KNOLLMEAD
Pl Fld
Allot Gdns
Knollmead Prim Sch
Sp Gd
Tenn Cts
Pav
Bwg Gn
Riverhill
Fball Gd
Running Tk
Kingston upon Thames
Surrey
OLD MALDEN LA
WORCESTER PARK RD
Thames Down Link
B284
OLD KINGSTON RD
TOLWORTH COURT BRIDGE
VICARAGE CL
PADDOCK CL
LEYFIELD
LADY HAY
TAMESIS GDNS
HIGHDOWN
BARROW HILL
BARROW HILL CL
THE DENNINGTONS
CLEVELAND GDNS
CLEVELAND RD
ROYAL CL
ROYAL AVE
DAPHNE CT
DRUMALINE RIDGE
ST MARY'S RD
ST MICHAELS CL
SERVITE HO
THE AVENUE
DENE CL
ROLAND WAY
BADGERS COPSE
SQUIRRELS GN
RUSHMERE CT
AVON CL
SUFFOLK RD
SHADBOLT CL
KINGSLEY DR 1
KINGSLEY CT 2
MOWAT CT 3
SQUIRRELS CT 4
Shadbolt Park
WOODLANDS AVE
LANSWOOD CT
KINROSS AVE
DEWSBURY GDNS
Linden Bridge Sch
GRAFTON PARK RD
PARKLANDS WAY
WORCESTER GDNS
SPINNEY CL
SALISBURY CL
DELTA CL
DELTA RD
EDENFIELD GDNS
FAIRFORD GDNS
ELMSTEAD GDNS
ARDROSSAN GDNS
VALE RD
CUDDINGTON AVE
INVERESK GDNS
PARKDALE CRES
CROMWELL RD
GRAFTON RD
GRAFTON CL
AURIOL CL
AURIOL PARK RD
NORTHCLIFFE CL
MORTIMER CRES
WORCESTER CT
SALISBURY RD
Pl Fld
Tenn Cts
Cuddington Com Prim Sch
WOLSEY CR
CARDINAL CL
ALSOM AVE
CUNLIFFE RD
THE WARREN
THE GRANGE
FARM WAY CL
FRANCIS CL
CURTIS RD
TIMBERCROFT
BANNOW CL
STERRY DR
PLANTAGENET CL
Sp Gd
Allot Gdns
Worcester Park
CUDA'S CL
Schs
PO
WESTWAYS
THE BYWAYS
WANDLE CT
COLNE CT
ASH CT
WATERSEDGE
LONGFORD CT
CRANE CT
WEY CT
MOLE CT
HOGSMILL WAY
CHERWELL CT
HOLMAN RD
MILLAIS WAY
BOURNE WAY
BOWDEN RD
RIVERVIEW RD
PERCIVAL WAY
TEALING DR
Riverview CE Sch
CHESTNUT AVE
THORNDON GDNS
AMBERLEY GDNS
SEAFORTH GDNS
NEWBURY GDNS
FIR TREE CL
STONELEIGH CRES
PINEWOOD PL
KINGSTON RD
RAVENSFIELD GDNS
WALSINGHAM GDNS
LYMINGTON GDNS
STONELEIGH PARK RD
BRUMFIELD RD
FENDALL RD
SCOTT CL
BRIDLE CL
HUNTSMOOR RD
COURT FARM AVE
MAVIS AVE
MAVIS CL
MOORMEAD DR
FIRSWOOD AVE
MAGNOLIA WAY
CYCLAMEN WAY
LARKSPUR WAY
COX LA
RUXLEY LA
RUXLEY CT
ELM WAY
RIVER WAY
FAIRFIELD CL
FAIRFIELD WAY
EWELL COURT AVE
ELMSTEAD CL
KIRBY CL
STATION APP
STONELEIGH BROADWAY
Stoneleigh
Liby
DELL LA
KENILWORTH
ALWAY AVE
SCOTS FARM RD
West Ewell Inf Sch
Sp Ctr
PAMS WAY
WILLOW WAY
LAKEHURST RD
OAKLAND WAY
LAKESIDE
PRESTON DR
REMBRANDT CT
CLANDON CL
CALVERLEY RD
Epsom & Ewell High Sch
NIGHTINGALE DR
GADESDEN RD
SHAWFORD RD
CHERRY WAY
Hogsmill River
Ewell Court
MANOR DR
BRADFORD DR
Beggars Hill
POPLAR CRES
DALESIDE RD
POOLE RD
OAKHURST RD
CROSSLANDS RD
WEST MEAD
COURTLANDS DR
THE DRIVE
HIGHFIELD DR
PARK AVE W
CHESSINGTON CL
POPLAR FARM CL
VERNON CL
London Loop
WOODLAND CL
Allot Gdns
ELM RD
EWELL BY-PASS
A240
ELMWOOD
Danetree Jun Sch
DANETREE CL
DANETREE RD
LANSDOWNE RD
COTTAGE RD
West Ewell
BROOK MEAD
MEADOW WALK
SOUTH MEAD
THE ORCHARD
SHORTCROFT RD
THE HAWTHORNS
SHIRE CT
MEADOW WLK
PRIMROSE WLK
ASHDOWN RD
KINGSTON RD
ERNEST COTTS
MILL VIEW CL
TA Ctr
WELBECK CL
CH
CHESTERFIELD RD
HEATHERSIDE RD
CHURCH RD
NORTHCROFT RD
HOOK RD
B2200
CHESSINGTON RD
FULFORD RD
PLOUGH RD
LIMECROFT CL
KINGSMEAD CL
WORTHFIELD CL
BELFIELD RD
SUNNYMEDE AVE
GREEN LANES
EASTCROFT RD
MEADOWVIEW RD
STATION AVE
SOUTHVILLE CL
ST MARY'S CL
GRANGE MANS
SPRING MEWS
OLD SCHOOLS LA
MILL LA
LONDON RD
CHURCH ST
Cemy
RICHARDS FIELD
OAKDALE RD
FIRST AVE
RUTHERFORD MEWS
St Clements RC Prim Sch
THE RIDINGS
CHICHESTER CT
FENNELLS MEAD
Bourne Hall Mus
EWELL
HOLMAN CT
B284

200
North Cheam
Stoneleigh
Nonsuch Park
KT4
KT17
SM3
SM2
CENTRAL RD
A2043
CHEAM COMMON RD
MALDEN RD
LONDON RD
EWELL BY-PASS
A240
A24
B2200
EWELL RD
A232
CHEAM RD
DORCHESTER RD
WASHINGTON RD
CALDBECK AVE
BRINKLEY RD
DERWENT LO
DALEWOOD GDNS
ST PHILIP'S AVE
GLENAVON CT
LINDSAY RD
RUSKIN DR
EBBISHAM RD
BEVERLEY RD
MORNINGSIDE RD
COLBORNE WAY
BEDFORD RD
HILL CRES
BURNHAM DR
GARETH CL
QUANTOCK DR
COTSWOLD WAY
HAMBLETON CL
BRECON CL
MENDIP CL
CHILTERN CL
WIMBORNE CL
ANDREWS CL
LANGLEY AVE
DORKING CL
CLARKE'S AVE
STAINES AVE
EDWARDS CL
ALLERTON RD
LONDON RD
MARLOW DR
CAMBERLEY CL
GLYN RD
LLOYD RD
COURTENAY RD
LAVENDER AVE
GRANDISON RD
FARM WAY
ELM WAY
TRENT WAY
WOODBINE GR
LA SHRUBLAND GR
KINGSMEAD AVE
PACKHAM CT
LINGFIELD RD
HUNTINGDON GDNS
WELLINGTON AVE
WILLOWHAYNE GDNS
QUEENSFIELD CT
HAYLING CT
YARDLEY CT
BRIAR CT
BROOK CT
LEICESTER CL
FAIRLIGHT CL
ENNOR CT
SENHOUSE RD
HILBERT RD
WRAYFIELD RD
HAYES CRES
CHURCH HILL RD
D'ARCY RD
HEMINGFORD RD
PRIORY CRES
PRIORY AVE
WORDSWORTH DR
KENLEY WLK
THE SPINNEY
PALMER AVE
NEWBOLT AVE
WICKHAM AVE
ASHMERE CL
NETLEY CL
Superstore
Tenn Cts
Bwg Gn
Recn Gd
POLLARD HO
OAKS AVE
TUDOR AVE
KILLESTER GDNS
DUNDELA GDNS
THE MOUNT
SPARROW FARM RD
LATIMER CL
ST CLAIR DR
DALMENY RD
HOBART RD
KNOLLS CL
BRAEMAR RD
SANDRINGHAM RD
HAYMER GDNS
BALMORAL RD
BALMORAL CT
GRIFFITHS CL
THE RETREAT
Schs
Liby
Cemy
HAMPTON RD
MORETON RD
DONNINGTON RD
WINDSOR RD
STONE PL
Allot Gdns
LYNWOOD DR
KNIGHT HO
Park
Sp Gd
Sch
St Anthony
St Cecilia's RC Prim Sch
CRESTON WAY
SOUTHWOOD
ROSE END
MERRILANDS
WELCOMBE AVE
Surrey
PARK TERR
ORCHARD CT
SQUIRRELS GN
RUSHMERE CT
AVON CL
BADGERS COPSE
ROLAND WAY
THE AVENUE
KINGSLEY DR
KINGSLEY CT
MOWAT CT
SQUIRRELS CT
WOODLANDS AVE
LANSWOOD CT
KINROSS AVE
DEWSBURY GDNS
FAIRFORD GDNS
ELMSTEAD GDNS
ARDROSSAN GDNS
STONELEIGH AVE
BRIDGEWOOD RD
INVERESK GDNS
VALE RD
CUDDINGTON AVE
WOLSEY CL
CARDINAL CL
ALSOM AVE
CUNLIFFE RD
THE BYWAYS
BYWAYS
TREE CL
STONELEIGH CRES
STONELEIGH PARK RD
SEAFORTH GDNS
215
Pav
RICHLANDS AVE
ROSEDALE RD
GAYFERE RD
WOODSTONE AVE
BRADSTOCK RD
WAVERLEY RD
CHADACRE RD
Nonsuch Prim Sch
Stoneleigh
STATION APP
STONELEIGH BROADWAY
KENILWORTH RD
DELL LA
DELL RD
THE GLADE
REMBRANDT CT
CLANDON CL
CALVERLEY RD
BRIARWOOD RD
GLENWOOD RD
RUTHERWYKE CL
CUMNOR GDNS
PARK AVE E
PARK AVE W
Beggars Hill
ELM RD
SHORTCROFT RD
THE ORCHARD
THE HAWTHORNS
SHIRE CT
PRIMROSE
MEADOW WLK
KINGSTON RD
ERNEST COTTS
TA Ctr
WELBECK CL
MILL VIEW CL
ST MARY'S CL
GRANGE MANS
MILL LA
EWELL PARK WAY
EWELL PARK GDNS
ELMWOOD DR
ELMWOOD CL
CEDAR CL
PARRY CL
BLUEGATES
Organ Crossroads
BEAUFORT WAY
CASTLE PAR
CHURCH ST
Cemy
A24 Epsom
Ewell Castle Sch
Bourne Hall Mus
CASTLE AVE
CLEVES AVE
CASTLEMAINE AVE
VIII
THE AVENUE
FIR WLK
Nursery
Sutton
Cheam Park
Nonsuch High Sch for Girls
Harefield Bridge
JUBILEE RD
ROBERTS CL
HOLMWOOD CL
A232 Epsom (A24)
A
B
C
D
1
2
3
4
5
6
22
23
63
64
65
66

SM3
201
SM1
A
B
C
D
Liby
Brookfield Prim Sch
Allot Gdns
Cemy
Tenn Cts
Recn Gd
ROSE HILL
RIDGE RD
KIMPTON TRADE & BSNS CTR
KIMPTON LINK BSNS CTR
FOUR SEASONS CRES
MINDEN RD
SANDIFORD RD
KIMPTON RD
WEALDSTONE RD
Superstore
Cheam Park Farm Inf Sch
Cheam Park Farm Jun Sch
OLDFIELDS RD
A217
B279
SUTTON COMMON RD
Sutton Common
Fball Gd
Bwg Gn
ANGEL HILL
B2230
Westbourne Prim Sch
OLDFIELDS TRAD EST
STAYTON RD
SM1
F Ball Gd
West Sutton
Allot Gdns
KILLICK HO
CROWN RD
HIGH ST
ST NICHOLAS WAY
THROWLEY WAY
218
Schs
Manor Park
Cheam
Pl Fld
Homefield Prep Sch
CHEAM RD
A232
C Ctr
Coll
Liby
Sutton
Games Ct
ST DUNSTAN'S HILL
St Dunstans
HIGH ST
MALDEN RD
THE BROADWAY
A2043
Cheam Village
B283
STATION WAY
Cheam
Bwg Gn
Tenn Cts
Sch
Cheam High Sch
Cheam Fields Prim Sch
Works
SM2
BELMONT RISE
BURDON LA
BRIGHTON RD
Belmont
Pav
Henderson
Sp Gd
Cuddington Croft Cty Fst & Mid Sch
Ambleside Sch
25
VIII
26
A217 Banstead, M25
Tenn

SM1
A
B
202
C
D
Rosehill Park East
St Helier
B278
Recn Gd
The Wrythe
Greenshaw High Sch
Muschamp Jun & Inf Schs
Allot Gdns
Benhilton
Royston Park
Rushy Meadow Prim Sch
Carshalton High Sch for Girls
CARSHALTON
Carshalton
Carshalton Coll
WRYTHE LA
NIGHTINGALE RD
NORTH ST
WEST ST
POUND ST
St Philomena's Sch
St Mary's RC Jun Sch
CARSHALTON RD
A232
SUTTON
Sutton
Superstore
THROWLEY WAY
ANGEL HILL
B2230
BRIGHTON RD
Manor Park
SM5
PARK HILL
THE BEECHES AVE
Carshalton Beeches
War Memorial
Stanley Park Jun & Inf Sch
Barrow Hedges Prim Sch
WOODMANSTERNE RD
SM2
VIII
217
6
5
4
3
2
1
66
65
64
63
26
27
DOWNSIDE RD
WESTMEAD RD
GORDON RD
STANLEY PARK RD
MULGRAVE RD
CAVENDISH RD
CHRISTCHURCH PK
DEVONSHIRE AVE
CHALGROVE RD
CROSSWAYS
EAST DR
DINGWALL

203
A
B
C
D
66
6
5
4
3
2
1
65
64
63
30
29
220
VIII
Soho Mills
Sch
Hackbridge
Hackbridge
FELNEX TRAD EST
CR0
Be
CRISPIN CL
HARRINGTON CL
BEDDINGTON LA
B272
THE ORION
CRISPIN CRES
MALLINSON RD
DERRY RD
MELLER CL
1 CENTURION CT
2 GREENACRE PL
3 KILLBURNS MILL CL
4 ROYAL WLK
Sp Gd
Tenn Cts
Pav
PARK RD
WANDLE RD
ELMWOOD CL
HERALD GDNS
LONDON RD
PRINCE CHARLES WAY
REGAL CRES
Allot Gdns
BIRCHWOOD AVE
MEADOW WLK
GRANGE CT
CARAWAY PL
Beddington Park
River Wandle
BEDDINGTON PARK COTTS
Carew Manor Sch
Beddington Park Prim Sch
BARONS CT
CHURCH PADDOCK CT
CHURCH RD
CHURCH LA
WHELAN WAY
GUY RD
ARCHWAY
THE BRANDRIES
HILLIER'S LA
WANDLE BANK
WANDLE COURT GDNS
HALLOWELL AVE
BRIDGES LA
Sherwood Park Sch
STREETERS LA
GISBOURNE CL
MANATEE PL
HACKBRIDGE RD
B277
THE GREEN
LODGE CL
LINK RD
CORBET CL
SENGA RD
ELM RD
LANGFIELD AVE
MILE RD
FURLONG CL
NIGHTINGALE RD
NIGHTINGALE CL
THE CAUSEWAY
MILL CL
ROSSIGNOL GDNS
SHEPLEY CL
RIVER GDNS
STRAWBERRY LA
VICTORIA AVE
LYNDON AVE
CURRAN AVE
ST MARY AVE
BURLEIGH AVE
WANDLE SIDE
BOWMAN'S MDW
RIVERSIDE CL
LAKE GDNS
ELM GROVE PAR
LEECHCROFT RD
BUTTER HILL
PARKFIELDS CL
CALEDON RD
WESTCROFT RD
MILL LA
PAPERMILL CL
ARCADIA CL
Westcroft Sports Ctr
Pl Fld
Recn Gd
Bwg Gn
T Cts
SCAWEN CL
BEACON GR
THE GREEN
Wallington Cty Gram Sch
Pl Fld
Pav
LAKESIDE
DEREK AVE
QUINTON CL
MANOR RD N
Wallington Green
ACRE LA
HIGH ST
Liby
LAVENDER CL
LAVENDER RD
WHITEHALL PL
WIGHTS ROW
BERNARD RD
MINT RD
LODGE RD
DANBURY MEWS
HARCOURT FIELD
HARCOURT AVE
HARCOURT RD
ALCESTER RD
CROYDON RD
BERKELEY CT
BAMPFYLDE CL
PASTON CL
BLOXWORTH CL
THE HOLT
THE CEDARS
BOND GDNS
RECTORY CT
MARLESFORD CT
DELL CL
EVELYN WAY
LYTTON GDNS
GREEN LEAF AVE
SANDHILLS
FERRERS AVE
RALEIGH AVE
ROOKWOOD AVE
QUEEN ELIZABETH'S WLK
ROYSTON AVE
IBERIAN AVE
GOIDEL CL
BROADWAY
A232
Liby
COLLYER
Holy Trinity Sch
Inf Sch
THE MANOR WAY
Allot Gdns
STANNET WAY
CLIFFORD AVE
NORTHWAY
DARCY AVE
SOUTHWAY
GRASSWAY
EASTWAY
GREENWAY
RECTORY LA
ST MARY'S CT
Recn Gd
ARRAN CL
HIGHLAND COTTS
BUTE RD
MONTAGU GDNS
QUEENSWOOD AVE
DEMESNE RD
CRICHTON AVE
THE BRIDLE WAY
Cemy
Bandonhill
PLOUGH LANE CL
MALDON RD
MALDON CT
BRABROOK CT
MANOR CT
MANOR HO
FAIRLAWNES
QUEEN'S CL
QUEEN'S RD
PARKGATE RD
MORTON GDNS
PARK RD
BUTE CT
SM6
OSMOND GDNS
1 BANFOR CT
2 YORK CT
3 JEFTON CT
SPOONER WLK
CLOUSTON CL
BROOKSIDE
THE SQUARE
CARSHALTON PL
ROTHERFIELD RD
Sch
TALBOT RD
SEYMOUR RD
RUSKIN RD
PARK LA
Tenn Cts
ST GEORGE'S RD
GATEWAYS CT
ORCHARD CT
SPRINGFIELD CT
SPRINGFIELD RD
TAYLOR RD
CLIFTON RD
BELMONT RD
ORFORD CT
ST CHRISTOPHER'S MEWS
BUTE GDNS
BUTE GDNS W
THARP RD
BEDDINGTON GR
SANDY LA N
UPPER RD
Carshalton Park
SM5
WOODSTOCK RD
CLARENCE RD
DENMORE CT
MELBOURNE RD
OXFORD CT
SPRING GDNS
BRAMLEY CT
MELLOWS RD
MILLBANK
Tenn Cts
Pav
Mellows Park
Bwg Gn
ASHCOMBE RD
GROSVENOR RD
RAILWAY APP
ROSS PAR
ROSS RD
RUSSELL CT
TEAL CT
BANDON RISE
WALLINGTON
Bwg Gn
Wallington
CLARENDON RD
ST MICHAEL'S RD
CLYDE RD
ROBIN CT
CAREW RD
WALETON ACRES
B271
MELROSE TUDOR
PARK CT
HASLEMERE CL
ABINGER CT
PARK AVE
GROSVENOR AVE
ROSSWOOD GDNS
ELGIN RD
STAFFORD RD
1 PENNY ROYAL
2 HILLARD CT
LINK LA
CHALICE CL
LONGACRE PL
BEDDINGTON GDNS
BOUNDARY RD
HOLMWOOD GDNS
SHOTFIELD
WOODCOTE MEWS
CHARLOTTE RD
FRANCIS RD
HINTON RD
MILTON RD
LAVENDER VALE
SANDY LANE S
Bandon Hill Prim Sch
THE MEAD
Sp Gd
Bwg Gn
Pav
NORTHWOOD RD
ANGLESEY COURT RD
WOODFIELD AVE
ANGLESEY GDNS
Stanley Park High Sch
STANLEY PARK RD
Ct
Liby
South Beddington
COWPER GDNS
WORDSWORTH RD
WATERER RISE
Foresters Prim Sch
REDFORD AVE
COBHAM CL
BARLOW CL
OLLEY CL
STANLEY PARK RD
RALEIGH CT
BURNS CT
STANLEY GDNS
HANNAH MEWS
COSDACH AVE
HERMES WAY
CARTER CL
SHAW WAY
DEFIANT WAY
STANLEY CT
HAWTHORN RD
TURPIN WAY
LARKSPUR CT
WILLOW
WOODCOTE RD
CRANLEY GDNS
MARLBOROUGH
GROSVENOR GDNS
Tenn Cts
Pav
BLENHEIM GDNS
PLUMTREE CL
FORESTERS CL
FORESTERS DR
POWELL CL
BROWN CL
FIREFLY CL
ALCOCK CL
CODY CL
BARNARD CL
METEOR WAY
HAWTHORNE AVE
HEATHDENE RD
WOODBOURNE GDNS
DERWENT WLK
PARK HILL RD
ONSLOW GDNS
HILLSIDE GDNS
BLENHEIM CL
SOUTHVIEW GDNS
SANDY LA S
OAKLANDS WAY
TUDOR CL
COURT CL
Liby
STANLEY GDNS
WINDBOROUGH RD
DALMENY RD
STANHOPE RD
THE AVENUE
BOUNDARY RD
DINORBEN
BRAMBLEDOWN RD
BIRDHURST CT
HOLLY CT
THE NEWLANDS
Tenn Cts
Pav
LINDBERGH RD
CAYLEY CL
BRABAZON AVE
GULL CL
MOORE CL
LAWFORD CL
Carshalton on the Hill
WOODCOTE AVE
AVENUE RD
NADINE CT
MARCHMONT RD
INGLEBY WAY
CARLETON AVE
BUCKINGHAM WAY
DIANA CL
ALEXANDRA GDNS
STANLEY RD
PINE RIDGE
MOUNT PK
WOODCOTE HALL
HALL RD
ELYSTAN CL
MALLARD WAY
SUNKIST WAY
APELDOORN DR
HARMONY CL
CLARICE
Allot Gdns
CRANFIELD RD E
SANDOWN DR
SOUTHDOWN RD
THE WOODLANDS
GLEN ROAD END
HARDING
SANDY HILL
DOWER AVE
GALLINGTON GR
A237 Coulsdon, A23
A237

A
B
C
D
204
Beddington
Waddon
Roundshaw
Waddon Marsh
Wandle Park
Wandle Pk
Croydon Tramlink
CR0
SM6
Fiveways
Ind Est
PYLON WAY
BATH HOUSE RD
DANIELL WAY
WADDON MARSH WAY
LATHAM'S WAY
MARTIN CRES
ENTERPRISE CL
EUSTON RD
SUMNER RD
BUTE RD
GRAFTON RD
ALBION ST
NELSON CL
RENOWN CL
RODNEY CL
HOOD CL
TA Ctr
FACTORY LA
DERBY RD
THE PILTON EST
PITLAKE
CLARENDON RD
BEDDINGTON FARM RD
MARLOWE WAY
PETERWOOD WAY
PETERWOOD PK
PROGRESS WAY
BROADFIELD CL
PROGRESS BSNS PK
TRAFALGAR WAY
TURNER'S WAY
DRURY CRES
Bwg Gn
Tenn Cts
Pav
THEOBALD RD
WESTFIELD RD 1
LOWER CHURCH ST 2
BOURNE ST 3
CORNWALL RD
CUTHBERT RD
ROMAN WAY
MILES CT
Reeves Cnr
CRISPIN CL
HARRINGTON CL
BEDDINGTON LA
B272
CRISPIN CRES
MALLINSON RD
THE ORION CTR
ANCHOR BSNS PK
1 WINDSOR GDNS
2 KINGSTON GDNS
3 PETERSHAM TERR
4 OLD FORD HO
5 WANDLE CT
6 WANDLE CT
7 BEACON PL
COMMERCE WAY
TROJAN WAY
JENNETT RD
LATIMER RD 1
CROMWELL HO 2
VICARAGE RD
SIDDONS RD
WADDON NEW RD
RECTORY GR
SYLVERDALE RD
ST JOHN'S RD
RAMSEY CT
OLD TOWN
Beddington Park Prim Sch
Allot Gdns
DERRY RD
MELLER CL
TWICKENHAM CL
MILL LANE TRAD EST
RIGBY CL
WADDON CL
KEMBLE RD
WADDON RD
ELAND PL
ELAND RD
HARRISON'S RISE
ABBEY RD
HANOVER ST
BARONS CT
WHELAN WAY
CHURCH LA
GUY RD
ARCHWAY CL
STREETERS LA
GISBOURNE CL
THE BRANDRIES
MANATEE PL
HILLIER'S LA
WANDLE BANK
WANDLE CT GDNS
WANDLE RD
RICHMOND RD
MORTLAKE CL
CHISWICK CL
RICHMOND GN
BLANDFORD CL
BRIDLE PATH
MILL LA
LIMES AVE
WANDLE SIDE
LODGE AVE
COURTNEY PL
COURTNEY RD
GODSON RD
BENSON RD
THE PRIORY
BOROUGH HILL
WARRINGTON RD
RAVENSWOOD RD
DUPPAS HILL TERR
THE RIDGEWAY
BRIDGES LA
CEDARS RD
SALCOTT RD
LAVINGTON RD
ALDWICK RD
TRITTON AVE
HALLOWELL AVE
GARRATT CL
Link Prim Sch
COURT DR
ALTON RD
WADDON PARK AVE
PENFOLD CL
EPSOM RD
ST LEONARD RD
ARUNDEL CL
DUPPAS RD
LUDFORD CL
WAYNFLETE AVE
Schs
Pl Fld
SANDHILLS
QUEEN ELIZABETH'S WLK
ROYSTON AVE
IBERIAN AVE
GOIDEL CL
THE BROADWAY
CROYDON RD
A232
COLLYER RD
COLLYER AVE
OAKLEY AVE
NICHOLAS RD
WILLOUGHBY AVE
Link Sec Sch
CHERRY HILL GDNS
LYNWOOD GDNS
DUPPAS HILL RD
St Andrew's High Sch
MERIDIAN CT
FERNLEIGH CL
STAFFORD RD
WRANGTHORNE WLK
BRADLEY CT
OLD SCHOOL PL
Recn Gd
PHYLLIS HO
ASHLEY LA
LAWDON GDNS
LENNOX GDNS
HYRSTDENE
HILLSIDE RD
GRINDAL CL
QUEENSWOOD AVE
BRISTOW RD
CLAYDON DR
BEDLOW WAY
Playing Field
PLOUGH LANE CL
PLOUGH LA
HINDHEAD WAY
BANSTEAD WAY
KINGSWOOD AVE
GOMSHALL AVE
REIGATE WAY
GUILDFORD WAY
SHEEN WAY
GODALMING AVE
HEADLEY AVE
MEREBANK LA
STAFFORD GDNS
B271
B275
Red Gates Sch
DENNING AVE
COOPER RD
KING GDNS
PRICE RD
COSEDGE CRES
PAGE CRES
RAGLAN CT
HEIGHTON GDNS
VIOLET LA
CLOUSTON CL
SPOONER WLK
SANDY LA N
UPPER RD
BEDDINGTON GDNS
AMBERWOOD CL
CENTRAL AVE
THE CHASE
FRIMLEY AVE
HIGH VIEW AVE
CAPEL AVE
EAST AVE
WEST AVE
KINGS WAY
THE PARADE
Waddon Inf Sch
COLDHARBOUR RD
STAPLETON GDNS
HILLIER GDNS
LAYTON CRES
CROWLEY CRES
Duppas Jun Sch
CHARLES COBB GDNS
FLEMING CT
BEVAN CT
COLDHARBOUR WAY
PURLEY WAY
FOSS AVE
CHASEMORE GDNS
THORNELOE GDNS
GOODWIN RD
VIOLET GDNS
OAKLANDS
HALING PARK RD
GARDEN CL
ABINGER CL
Tenn Cts Pav
Mellows Park
STAFFORD CROSS
HORATIUS WAY
PRINCESS WAY
QUEENS WAY
BATES CRES
WILLIAMS TERR
BURGOS CL
BARROW RD
HOULDER CRES
GOODWIN GDNS
HEATH CL
HALING PARK GDNS
MELROSE TUDOR 1
PARK CT 2
HASLEMERE CL 3
ABINGER CL 4
1 PENNY ROYAL
2 HILLARD CT
LINK LA
Wilson's Sch
HANNIBAL WAY
LYSANDER RD
WADDON WAY
Bandon Hill Prim Sch
THE MEAD
Sp Gd
EAGLE CL
St Elphege's RC Jun & Inf Schs
CROYDON AIRPORT IND EST
IMPERIAL WAY
Hotel
Purley Way Pl Fld
WATERER RISE
Foresters Prim Sch
BEDFORD AVE
COBHAM CL
BARLOW CL
OLLEY CL
MCINTOSH CL
DOUGLAS CL
ROE WAY
MERLIN CL
NEW BARN CL
CONNAUGHT BSNS CTR
PEGASUS RD
St Giles Sch
HERMES WAY
CARTER CL
SHAW WAY
BRANCKER CL
DEFIANT WAY
DAIMLER WAY
AVRO WAY
MOLLISON DR
BRACKLEY CL
DOVE CL
HURRICANE RD
VICKERS CL
SWIFT CTR
GULLIVER CT
COLUMBINE AVE
FENWICK PL
POWELL CL
ALCOCK CL
BROWN CL
FIREFLY CL
CODY CL
METEOR WAY
GOLIATH CL
VANGUARD WAY
AMY CL
STIRLING AVE
HANDLEY PAGE RD
DAKOTA CL
SPITFIRE RD
Haling Manor High Sch
KENDRA HALL RD
Amy Johnson Prim Sch
Liby
LINDBERGH RD
CAYLEY CL
GULL CL
BRABAZON AVE
LANCASTRIAN RD
MORTON CL
JEAN BATTEN CL
MOTH CL
1 ROUNDSHAW CTR
2 HERACLES CL
Roundshaw Park
ALDER WAY
JOSHUA CL
HURSTVIEW GRANGE
KNIGHTON CL
MOORE CL
BRISTOL CL
LAWFORD CL
MARIETTE WAY
Haling Manor High Sch (Pampisford Wing)
HAMOND CL
SUNKIST WAY
PLESMAN WAY
HARMONY CL
APELDOORN DR
RHEINGOLD WAY
CLARICE WAY
FORESTERS DR
IX
A23 Redhill, M23, M25
Cumnor House
BLACKFORD CL
A23
A236
A232
Croydon
Sutton
Waddon
66
65
64
63
6
5
4
3
2
1
30
31
219

CROYDON
East Croydon
Wellesley Road
George St
Tramway
Lebanon Road
Sandilands
Lloyd Park
Coombe Park
Park Hill
South Croydon
Croham Hurst
Breakneck Hill
Haling Park
Whitgift Sch
Croham Hurst Sch
Park Hill Inf & Jun Schs
CE High Sch
Howard Prim Sch
Oval Prim Sch
Whitgift Ctr
Centrale Ctr
Drummond Ctr
Church Street
Selsdon Road Ind Est
Croydon Tramlink
Vanguard Way
CRO
WELLESLEY RD
A212
A232
A222
A235
A236
B243
B274
B275
B269
FAIRFIELD RD
BARCLAY RD
CHEPSTOW RD
ADDISCOMBE RD
COOMBE RD
PARK LA
PARK HILL RD
SOUTH PARK HILL RD
ST PETER'S RD
BRIGHTON RD
SELSDON RD
UPPER SELSDON RD
LOWER COOMBE ST
SOUTHBRIDGE RD
WARHAM RD
CROHAM RD
CROHAM MANOR RD
HURST VIEW RD
CARLTON AVE
MAYFIELD RD
SANDERSTEAD
ADDISCOMBE GR
NORTH END
HIGH ST
GEORGE ST
PUMP PAIL N
PUMP PAIL S
THE CROYDON FLYOVER
SOUTH END
205
222
IX
A235 Purley, A23
Sanderstead
A
B
C
D
1
2
3
4
5
6
33
34
63
64
65
66

Addiscombe
Shirley
206
A
B
C
D
HAMILTON CT
Tenn Cts
Recn Gd
ASHBURTON CL
MULBERRY LA
66
ELGIN RD
HAVELOCK RD
CREED CT
OUTRAM RD
ASHBURTON GDNS
ASHBURTON RD
Croydon Tramlink
NORTHAMPTON RD
CARLYLE RD
CHEYNE WLK
HARRIET GDNS
ANNANDALE RD
FRYSTON AVE
SEFTON RD
COMPTON RD
ASHBURTON
SELWOOD RD
BIRCH TREE WAY
WHITETHORN GDNS
ASHURST WLK
GREEN COURT GDNS
GREEN COURT AVE
CRAIGEN
A215
PO
SHIRLEY RD
VALLEY WLK
BARNFIELD AVE
SHIRLEY AVE
SHIRLEY OAKS RD
VERDAYNE AVE
ALISON CL
ANGELICA
BURDOCK
IVY HO
TULIP CL
ROSSWOOD LO
WICKHAM RD
A232
ADDISCOMBE RD
CH
Trinity Sch
ELDON AVE
WEST
6
LYNDEN HYRST
Sandilands
WOODBURY CL
1 SONNING CT
2 COLLEGE CT
3 FURZE CT
4 WALCOT CT
FITZJAMES AVE
UPFIELD
MAPLEDALE AVE
Pav
Pl Fld
Tenn Cts
CRANWELL CT
NURSERY AVE
NURSERY CL
BARMOUTH RD
SPRING PARK RD
THE VALE
CANON'S WLK
CE Prim Sch
Bwg Gn
SAVILE GDNS
RADCLIFFE RD
ROWAN GDNS
DIGBY PL
HARDING CL
DELMEY CL
SANDILANDS
HARLAND AVE
Bwg Gn
Shirley Park
OAKS LA
TANGLEWOOD CL
VIEW GDNS
MILL
UPPER SHIRLEY RD
ARDINGLY CL
DANECOURT GDNS
DEEPDENE AVE
5
GRIMWADE AVE
Sp Gd
Oaks Farm
Windmill (dis)
POSTMILL CL
Shirley High Sch
Coloma Convent Girls' Sch
RANMORE AVE
GROVE
65
THE DENE
SANDPITS RD
FARRER'S PL
BIRKDALE GDNS
ROCK PL
Upper Shirley
Lloyd Park
Coombe Park
Coombe Farm
Pl Fld
BADGERS HOLE
SPRUCEDALE GDNS
4
ALWEN COTTS
CR0
PINE COOMBE
OAKS RD
Addington Hills
Vanguard Way
132
P
221
A212
COOMBE RD
BLOSSOM
Hotel
Croydon Tramlink
CONDUIT LA
BIRCH HILL
SHIRLEY HILLS RD
3
MELVILLE AVE
BALLATER RD
PILGRIM'S WAY
Coombe Lane
COOMBE LA
SUNKEN RD
64
BENCHFIELD
Royal Russell Sch
Sp Gd
110
152
BALLARDS WAY
HOLLINGSWORTH RD
RIESCO DR
BALLARDS RISE
BALLARDS FARM RD
2
CH
Heathfield
Bramley Bank
Nat Res
GRAVEL HILL
London Loop
PRIORS
RUFFETTS CL
CREST RD
THE RUFFETTS
CHAPEL VIEW
CHESTNUT GR
THE GALLOP
CROHAM VALLEY RD
1
Croham Hurst
144
FARLEY RD
BROADCOOMBE
WARREN AVE
SHEPHERDS WAY
TEDDER RD
EDGECOOMBE
Selsdon High Sch
LITTLEHEATH RD
CR2
MOSS GDNS
FREELANDS AVE
63
Littleheath Woods
HEATHER WAY
34
35
IX
FOXEARTH RD
INGHAM RD
BRENT RD

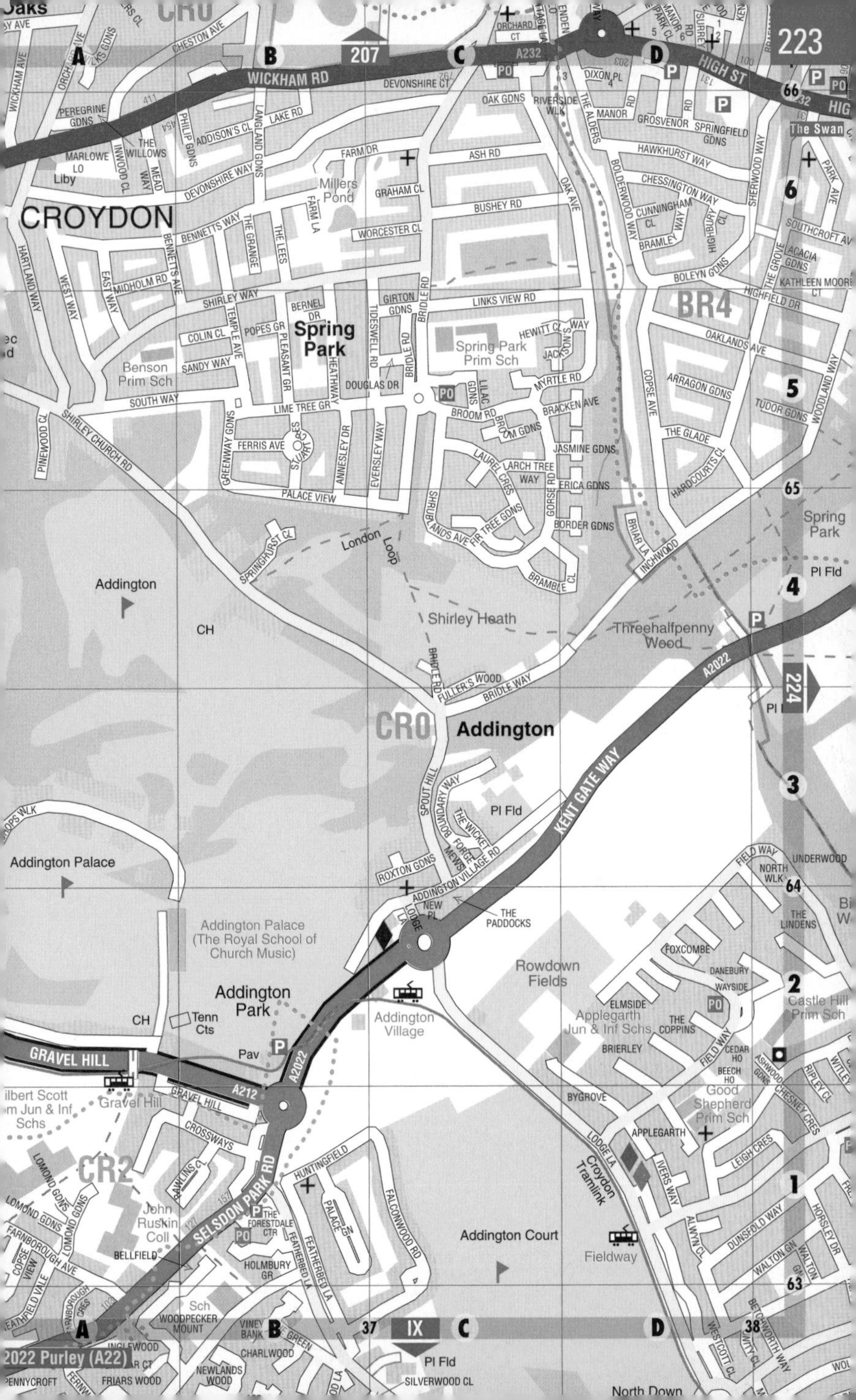

A
B
C
D
207
WICKHAM RD
A232
HIGH ST
CROYDON
Spring Park
CR0
BR4
CR2
Addington
Shirley Heath
Threehalfpenny Wood
Addington Palace
Addington Palace (The Royal School of Church Music)
Addington Park
Addington Village
Rowdown Fields
Addington Court
Croydon Tramlink
Fieldway
Gravel Hill
GRAVEL HILL
A212
A2022
KENT GATE WAY
SELSDON PARK RD
SHIRLEY CHURCH RD
London Loop
Benson Prim Sch
Spring Park Prim Sch
Millers Pond
Liby
CH
Pav
Tenn Cts
Pl Fld
Applegarth Jun & Inf Schs
Good Shepherd Prim Sch
Castle Hill Prim Sch
John Ruskin Coll
Sch
The Swan
Spring Park
CHESTON AVE
WICKHAM AVE
ORCHARD AVE
PEREGRINE GDNS
MARLOWE
THE WILLOWS
INWOOD CL
MEAD WAY
PHILIP GDNS
ADDISON'S CL
LANGLAND GDNS
LAKE RD
DEVONSHIRE WAY
DEVONSHIRE CT
FARM DR
FARM LA
GRAHAM CL
ASH RD
BUSHEY RD
WORCESTER CL
OAK GDNS
OAK AVE
RIVERSIDE WLK
ORCHARD CT
DIXON PL
MANOR RD
THE ALDERS
GROSVENOR RD
SPRINGFIELD GDNS
HAWKHURST WAY
CHESSINGTON WAY
CUNNINGHAM CL
BRAMLEY WAY
HIGHBURY CL
BOLDERWOOD WAY
SHERWOOD WAY
BOLEYN GDNS
SOUTHCROFT AVE
ACACIA GDNS
THE GROVE
KATHLEEN MOORE CT
HIGHFIELD DR
PARK AVE
OAKLANDS AVE
COPSE AVE
ARRAGON GDNS
TUDOR GDNS
WOODLAND WAY
THE GLADE
HARDCOURTS CL
INCHWOOD
BRIAR LA
HARTLAND WAY
WEST WAY
EAST WAY
MIDHOLM RD
BENNETTS WAY
BENNETTS AVE
THE GRANGE
THE LEES
SHIRLEY WAY
TEMPLE AVE
COLIN CL
SANDY WAY
POPES GR
PLEASANT GR
BERNEL DR
TIDESWELL RD
GIRTON GDNS
BRIDLE RD
LINKS VIEW RD
HEWITT CL
JACKSON'S WAY
MYRTLE RD
HEATHWAY
DOUGLAS DR
LILAC GDNS
BROOM RD
BROOM GDNS
BRACKEN AVE
JASMINE GDNS
LARCH TREE WAY
LAUREL CRES
ERICA GDNS
GORSE RD
BORDER GDNS
SHRUBLANDS AVE
FIR TREE GDNS
BRAMBLE CL
SOUTH WAY
LIME TREE GR
PINEWOOD CL
GREENWAY GDNS
FERRIS AVE
STUART CRES
ANNESLEY DR
EVERSLEY WAY
PALACE VIEW
SPRINGHURST CL
FULLER'S WOOD
BRIDLE WAY
SPOUT HILL
BOUNDARY WAY
THE WICKET
FORGE MEWS
ADDINGTON VILLAGE RD
ROXTON GDNS
LODGE LA
NEW PL
THE PADDOCKS
FIELD WAY
NORTH WLK
UNDERWOOD
THE LINDENS
FOXCOMBE
DANEBURY
WAYSIDE
ELMSIDE
THE COPPINS
BRIERLEY
CEDAR HO
BEECH HO
ASHWOOD GDNS
CHESNEY CRES
RIPLEY CL
BYGROVE
APPLEGARTH
LEIGH CRES
IVERS WAY
ALWYN CL
DUNSFOLD WAY
HORSLEY DR
WALTON GN
WALTON
BETCHWORTH WAY
WESTCOTT CL
North Down
CROSSWAYS
RAWLINS CL
LOMOND GDNS
FARNBOROUGH AVE
COPSE VIEW
FAIRFIELD VALE
FARNBOROUGH CRES
BELLFIELD
THE FORESTDALE CTR
HOLMBURY GR
FEATHERBED LA
HUNTINGFIELD
PALACE GN
FALCONWOOD RD
WOODPECKER MOUNT
VINEY BANK
THE GREEN
CHARLWOOD
INGLEWOOD
NEWLANDS WOOD
FRIARS WOOD
PENNYCROFT
SILVERWOOD CL
A2022 Purley (A22)
224
IX
37
38
63
64
65
66
1
2
3
4
5
6

208
A
B
C
D
6
5
4
3
2
1
66
65
64
63
38
39
223
IX
HIGH ST
A232
A214
LINKS RD
THE MEAD
HAWES LA
HAYES HILL
HEPBURN GDNS
HURSTDENE AVE
SAVILLE ROW
CROFT AVE
OAK GR
ASH GR
MARTINS CL
Fld
Hawes Down Schs
LINDEN LEAS
Liby
The Swan
GLEBE WAY
WICKHAM CRES
ROSE WLK
WICKHAM COURT RD
CHATSWORTH
SHERWOOD WAY
RAVENSWOOD AVE
BRAEMAR GDNS
KENT
SPRINGFIELD GDNS
GROSVENOR
HAWKHURST WAY
HESSINGTON WAY
CUNNINGHAM
HIGHBURY CL
PARK AVE
SOUTHCROFT AVE
ACACIA GDNS
THE GROVE
KATHLEEN MOORE CT
BOLEYN GDNS
HIGHFIELD DR
OAKLANDS AVE
ARRAGON GDNS
TUDOR GDNS
WOODLAND WAY
THE GLADE
HARDCOURTS CL
ABERDARE CL
STAMBOURNE WAY
WOOD LODGE LA
CORKSCREW HILL
Pl Fld
Tenn Cts
Bwg Gn
Pav
Sp Gd
ATKINS DR
PALMER CL
BENCURTIS PK
SILVER LA
Glebe Sch
Allot Gdns
PHOENIX CL
HAWES LA
HIGH MEAD
MOUNT CT
KESWICK RD
WINDERMERE RD
RYDAL DR
HEYDON CT
West Wickham
SEABROOK DR
LITTLE CT
ADDINGTON RD
LENNARD CL
LENNARD AVE
DUKES WAY
PRIORY LO
CONEY HILL RD
PRICKLEY WOOD
BOURNE WAY
HILLSIDE
HOLLAND WAY
HOLLAND CL
WESTLAND DR
SANDILANDS CRES
ABBOTSBURY RD
TIEPIGS LA
DEER PARK WAY
CHATSWORTH CL
MARWELL CL
Tenn Cts
Coney Hill Sch
Pav
Sp
Coney Hall Rdbt
A2022
COURTFIELD RISE
GLEBE WAY
CROYDON RD
CROYDON RD
ROSSLYN CL
FARM CL
SOUTH WLK
CONEY HALL PAR
CHURCH DR
West Wickham Common
Coney Hall
COLIN CL
KINGSWAY
PRINCES WAY
QUEENSWAY
PP
Pav
Sparrows Den Sp Gd
Tenn Cts
Bwg Gn
ADDINGTON RD
BR4
Wickham Court
Schiller International Sch
St John Rigby RC Coll
Coney Hall Recn Gd
SYLVAN WAY
HAWTHORN DR
CHESTNUT AVE
BIRCH TREE AVE
CHERRY TREE WLK
LIME TREE WLK
Spring Park
Pl Fld
Threehalfpenny Wood
Pl Fld
Fox Hill
Wickham Court Farm
LAYHAMS RD
Well Wood
FIELD WAY
UNDERWOOD
NORTH WLK
THE LINDENS
Birch Wood
OAK BANK
Bromley
Croydon
FOXCOMBE
DANEBURY
WAYSIDE
CR0
Castle Hill Prim Sch
THE COPPINS
CEDAR HO
BEECH HO
Good Shepherd Prim Sch
DUNLEY DR
ABINGER CL
WITLEY CRES
BURFORD WAY
MERROW WAY
PIRBRIGHT CRES
CLAYGATE CRES
ALFORD GN
RIPLEY CL
CHESNEY CRES
ASHWOOD GDNS
HEADLEY DR
NETLEY CL
LEIGH CRES
FRIMLEY CL
FRIMLEY CRES
THURSLEY CRES
BROCKHAM CRES
MICKLEHAM WAY
Castlehill Ruffs
DUNSFOLD WAY
HORSLEY DR
FRENSHAM DR
WALTON GN
CASTLE HILL AVE
GOLDCREST WAY
Allot Gdns
Wolsey Jun & Inf Schs
New Addington
ALWYN CL
TILFORD AVE
BETCHWORTH WAY
WESTCOTT CL
KING HENRY'S DR
KESTREL WAY
WOLSEY CRES
Rowdown Wood
Bradmanshill Wood
BR2
129
Mast

209
A
B
C
D
B251
B265
Cts
HAYES WOOD
GLEBE HOUSE DR
HOPTON CT
FORGE CL
THE KNOLL
HAYES GARDEN
STATION APP
PO
Recn Gds
RIDGEWAY
STATION HILL
BURWOOD AVE
Pl Fld
Hayes Sch
WARREN RD
GROVE CL
1 LARKFIELD CL
2 WENTWORTH CL
3 HAWTHORNDENE CL
4 HAWTHORNDENE RD
5 WARREN WOOD CL
H
The Priory
HAYES CL
Bwg Gn
Pav
Sp Gd
Tenn Cts
REDGATE DR
Tenn Cts
Pav
Baston Sch
Pl Fld
Pav
Tenn Cts
PRESTONS RD
BASTON RD
FIVE ELMS RD
Pav
Pl Fld
BARNET WOOD RD
Barnet Wood
Keston Mark
Pav
Pl Fld
Ravens Wood Sch
Ravens Bourne
Sp Gd
Pav
OAKLEY RD
A233
66
WEALD
CROSS RD
6
DOVES CL
THE LIMES
Recn Gd
Allot Gdns
GRAVEL RD
OAKLEY DR
CEDAR CL
5
CHEYNE CL
CEDAR
Hayes Court
WEST COMMON RD
Hayes Common
SIMPSON'S COTTS
Colyers Wood
THE DRIFT
Allot Gdns
THE AVENUE
145
A232
CROYDON RD
HARVEST BANK RD
ROBINS GR
HARTFIELD CRES
HARVEST BANK RD
HARTFIELD RD
RODNEY GDNS
LAWRENCE RD
BASTON MANOR RD
GATES GREEN RD
QUIET NOOK
PHOENIX DR
THANET DR
THE DALE
Keston Mark
65
RUSHLEY CL
MARK CL
LONGDON WOOD
BEECHWOOD DR
4
BROCKDENE DR
HASSOCK WOOD
Wickham Common Prim Sch
Pl Fld
BR4
Hast Hill
Baston Manor
P
P
COMMONSIDE
OAKFIELD LA
STOUR CL
KESTON GDNS
WINDMILL DR
Keston
SWIRES SHAW
COLLIERS WOOD
POULTERS WOOD
ROLANSDEN WAY
226
LAKES RD
PH
PO
FOX LA
HERITAGE HILL
HEATHFIELD CL
LEAFY GR
KESTON AVE
Keston CE Prim Sch
GREYS PARK CL
REGENTS DR
3
Rouse Farm
FISHPONDS RD
London Loop
HEATHFIELD RD
WESTERHAM RD
BR2
Windmill
Keston Common
P
64
Nash
NORTH POLE LA
NASH LA
JACKASS LA
2
P
B265
Fuller's Wood
James's Wood
Tenn
ROMAN MAUSOLEUM
1
Keston Court
RECTORY RD
A233
CHURCH RD
Milchden
BLACKNESS LA
63
A
B
41
IX
C
D
42
DOWNE RD
A233 Biggin Hill

A
B
C
D
210
BROMLEY
66
6
5
65
4
225
3
64
2
1
63
42
43
IX
A233 Biggin Hill
Sp Gd
Keston Mark
Pav
Pl Fld
Ravens Wood Sch
Allot Gdns
The Limes Recn Gd
Knowlehill Wood
Knowl Wood
BR2
Hollydale Recn Gd
Keston Mark
The Fantail
Locksbottom
Tenn Cts
Recn Gd
Pav
Allot Gdns
Darrick Wood Sec Sch
Darrick Wood Inf Sch
Darrick Wood Jun Sch
Farnborough
BR6
Lake Wood
Ninhams Wood
Tenn Cts
Caesar's Camp
Broom Bank
The Larches
Holwood
Tenn Cts
Lower Hook Farm
North End Farm
London Loop
Holwood Farm
Farthing Street
A233
A232
A21
B2158
OAKLEY RD
WESTERHAM RD
HASTINGS RD
FARNBOROUGH COMM
CROYDON RD
CROFTON RD
PARK AVE
THE GLEN
MEADOW WAY
ELM WLK
FIR DENE
PRINCESS PAR
PALLANT WAY
STARTS CL
WILLOW WLK
STARTS HILL RD
WELLBROOK RD
HILDA VALE RD
WINTON RD
BASSETTS WAY
ROYAL CL
ASHTREE CL
ACORN WAY
ARDEN GR
PINECREST GDNS
LYNDHURST
ROMSEY
MADA RD
RED OAK CL
GLYNDEBOURNE PK
WINDERMERE CL
GRASMERE AVE
GRASMERE GDNS
LANGDALE CL
LOVIBONDS AV
BURLINGTON CL
HAZEL GR
MERESIDE
MERE CL
MUNNERY WAY
NUTFIELD WAY
LARCH DENE
SUNNYDALE
WOOD WAY
BIRCH MEAD
ST ANTHONY'S CT
JASMINE CL
FAIRBANK AVE
POPLAR AVE
ROSE DALE
LIME GR
WISTARIA CL
HENSON CL
PERCIVAL RD
DRAYTON AVE
LANSDOWNE AVE
JACKSON RD
COPTHORNE AVE
KNOWLE RD
CHERRY ORCHARD RD
WEALD CL
CROSS RD
DOVES CL
GRAVEL RD
BARNET DR
BEVERLEY RD
OAKLEY DR
KEMBLE DR
CEDAR CL
CEDAR CRES
CHEYNE CL
LAKESIDE DR
ROWAN WLK
HOLLYDALE DR
KESTON PARK CL
EBURY CL
FOREST DR
FOREST RIDGE
BEECH DELL
PINE GLADE
HOLWOOD PARK AVE
NINHAMS WOOD
LONGDON WOOD
RUSHLEY CL
MARK CL
BEECHWOOD DR
BROCKDENE DR
HASSOCK WOOD
SWIRES SHAW
COLLIERS WOOD
ROLINSDEN WAY
THE DRIFT
THE AVENUE
PHOENIX DR
THANET DR
THE DALE
PONDS RD
RECTORY RD
DOWNE RD
NEW ROAD HILL
FARTHING ST
BOGEY LA
SHIRE LA
NORTH END LA
ORCHARD RD
WOLDS DR
THE BIRCHES
CLAREMONT CL
SCOTNEY CL
DENNARD WAY
HILDA VALE CL
BASSETTS CL
SUMMERLANDS LO 1
FLEETWOOD CT 2
TUGMUTTON CL 1
HARLANDS GR 2
ELGAL CL 1
LIMES ROW 2
BARHAM CL
LOWER GRAVEL RD
RIBSTON CL
BRADFORD CL
JACKSON RD
DAERWOOD CL
RANDOLPH RD
PO
P
H

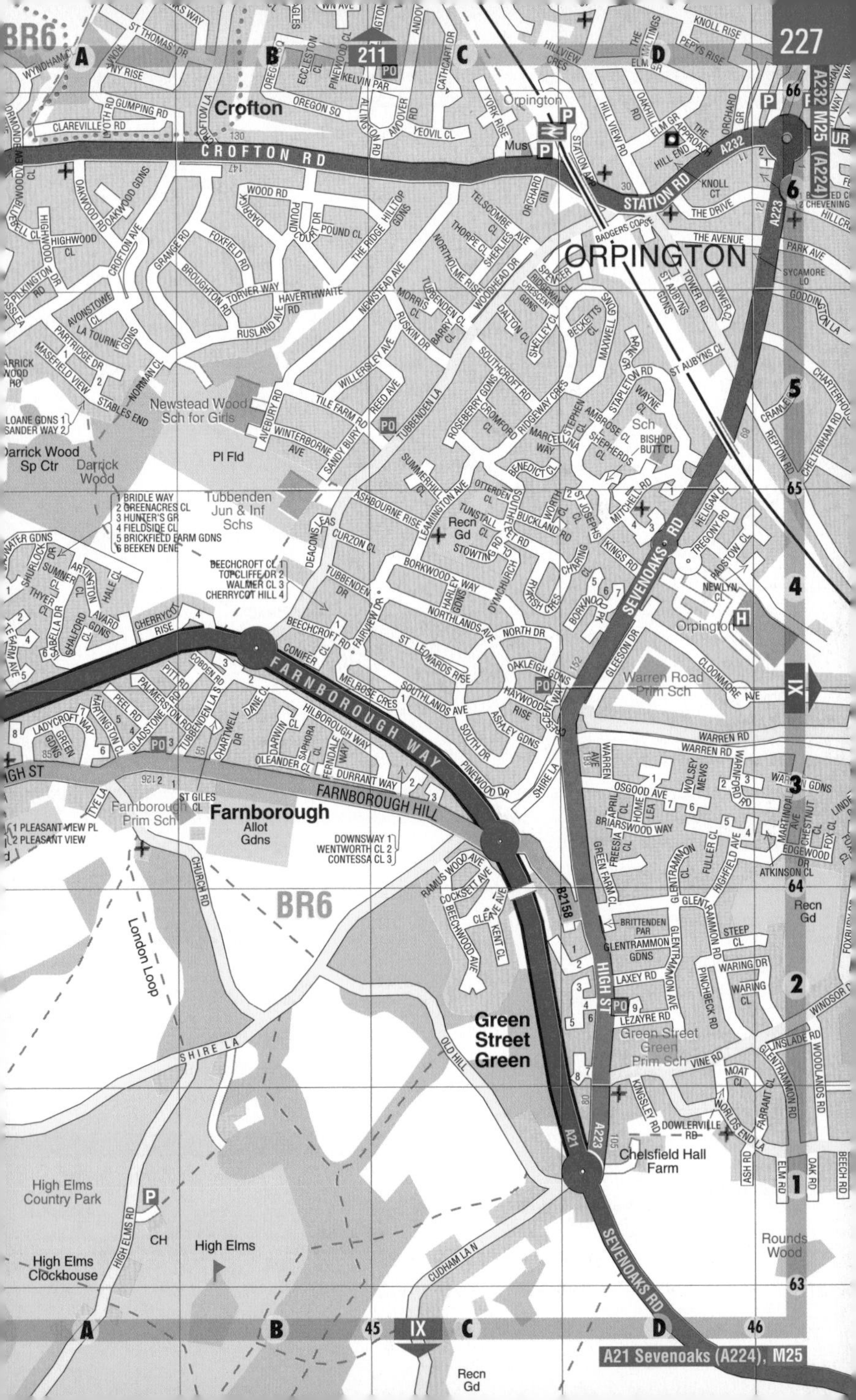
BR6
211
Crofton
CROFTON RD
Orpington
ORPINGTON
STATION RD
A232
A223
A232 M25 (A224)
SEVENOAKS RD
FARNBOROUGH WAY
FARNBOROUGH HILL
HIGH ST
Farnborough
Newstead Wood Sch for Girls
Darrick Wood Sp Ctr
Darrick Wood
Pl Fld
Tubbenden Jun & Inf Schs
Recn Gd
Warren Road Prim Sch
WARREN RD
Farnborough Prim Sch
Allot Gdns
Green Street Green
Green Street Green Prim Sch
Chelsfield Hall Farm
London Loop
SHIRE LA
High Elms Country Park
High Elms
High Elms Clockhouse
CH
Rounds Wood
B2158
A21
CUDHAM LA N
OLD HILL
A21 Sevenoaks (A224), M25
1 BRIDLE WAY
2 GREENACRES CL
3 HUNTER'S GR
4 FIELDSIDE CL
5 BRICKFIELD FARM GDNS
6 BEEKEN DENE
BEECHCROFT CL 1
TOPCLIFFE DR 2
WALMER CL 3
CHERRYCOT HILL 4
DOWNSWAY 1
WENTWORTH CL 2
CONTESSA CL 3
1 PLEASANT VIEW PL
2 PLEASANT VIEW
LOANE GDNS 1
SANDER WAY 2
A B C D
45 IX 46
63 64 65 66

Key to enlarged map pages

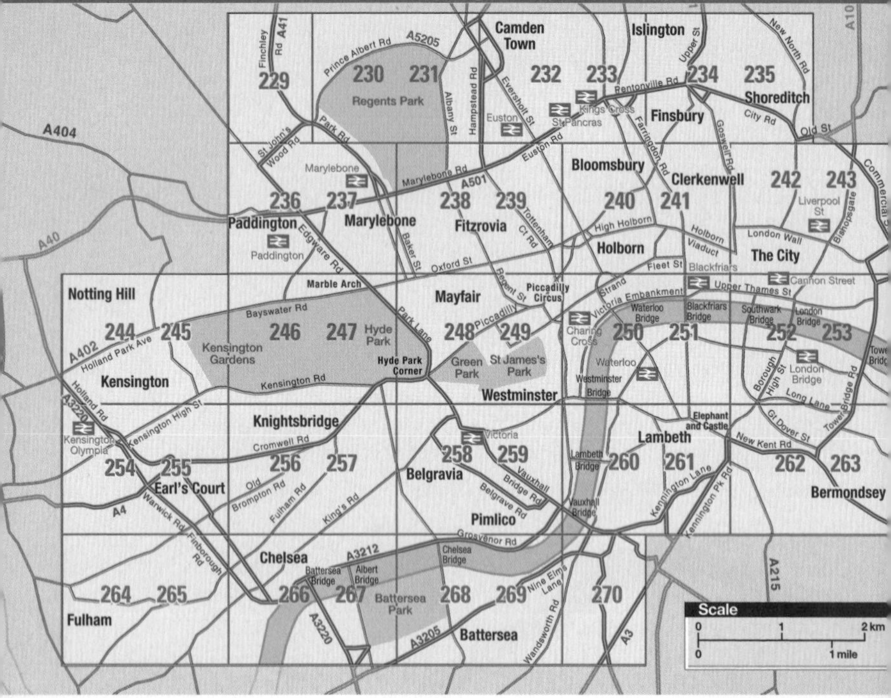

Camden Town
Islington
229
230
231
232
233
234
235
Regents Park
Prince Albert Rd
A5205
Finchley Rd
A41
Albany St
Hampstead Rd
Eversholt St
Upper St
New North Rd
A10
Pentonville Rd
Kings Cross
St Pancras
Euston
Finsbury
Shoreditch
City Rd
Old St
Farringdon Rd
Goswell Rd
A404
St John's Wood Rd
Park Rd
Marylebone
Marylebone Rd
A501
Euston Rd
Bloomsbury
Clerkenwell
236
237
238
239
240
241
242
243
Liverpool St
Commercial St
Bishopsgate
Paddington
Marylebone
Fitzrovia
Tottenham Ct Rd
High Holborn
Holborn
Holborn Viaduct
London Wall
The City
A40
Edgware Rd
Baker St
Oxford St
Regent St
Fleet St
Blackfriars
Cannon Street
Notting Hill
Marble Arch
Mayfair
Piccadilly Circus
Strand
Upper Thames St
Victoria Embankment
Bayswater Rd
Waterloo Bridge
Blackfriars Bridge
Southwark Bridge
London Bridge
244
245
246
247
248
249
250
251
252
253
Hyde Park
Park Lane
Piccadilly
Charing Cross
Tower Bridge
A402
Holland Park Ave
Kensington Gardens
Hyde Park Corner
Green Park
St James's Park
Waterloo
London Bridge
Kensington
Kensington Rd
Westminster Bridge
Borough High St
Long Lane
Tower Bridge Rd
Holland Rd
A3220
Westminster
Kensington High St
Knightsbridge
Victoria
Elephant and Castle
Kensington Olympia
Cromwell Rd
Lambeth
Gt Dover St
New Kent Rd
254
255
256
257
258
259
260
261
262
263
Earl's Court
Old Brompton Rd
Fulham Rd
Belgravia
Vauxhall Bridge Rd
Lambeth Bridge
Kennington Lane
Kennington Pk Rd
Bermondsey
A4
Warwick Rd
King's Rd
Belgrave Rd
Pimlico
Vauxhall Bridge
Grosvenor Rd
Finborough Rd
Chelsea
A3212
Chelsea Bridge
A215
Battersea Bridge
Albert Bridge
Nine Elms Lane
264
265
266
267
268
269
270
Battersea Park
Fulham
A3220
A3205
Battersea
Wandsworth Rd
A3
Scale
0
1
2 km
0
1 mile

Additional symbols on enlarged maps

For all other symbols see page X

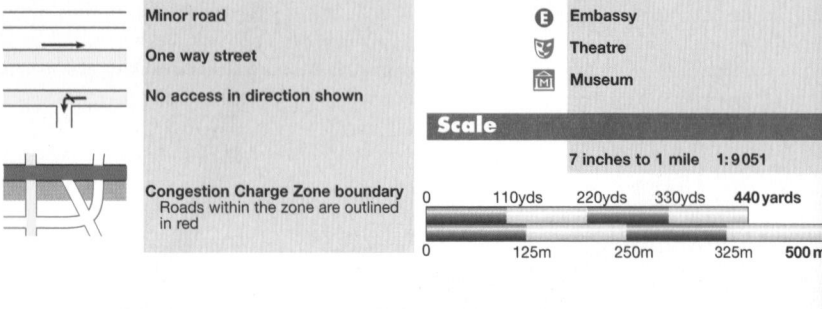

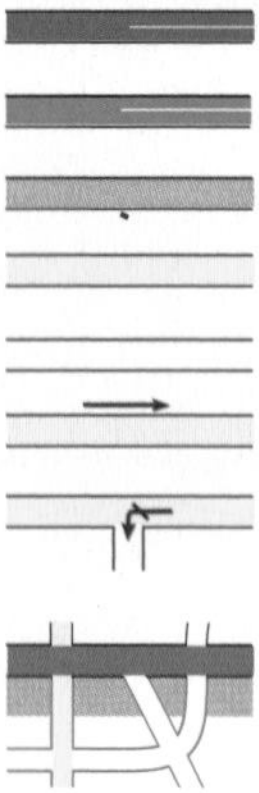

Primary route
– single, dual carriageway

A road – single, dual carriageway

B road

Through-route

Minor road

One way street

No access in direction shown

Congestion Charge Zone boundary
Roads within the zone are outlined in red

Public building

Railway or bus station building

Place of interest

Embassy

Theatre

Museum

Scale

7 inches to 1 mile 1:9051

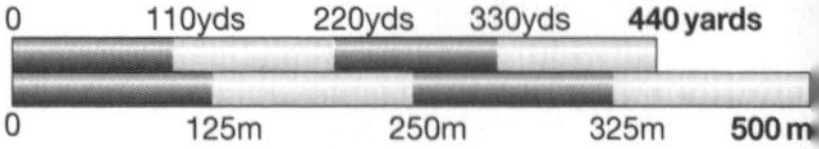

0
110yds
220yds
330yds
440 yards
0
125m
250m
325m
500 m

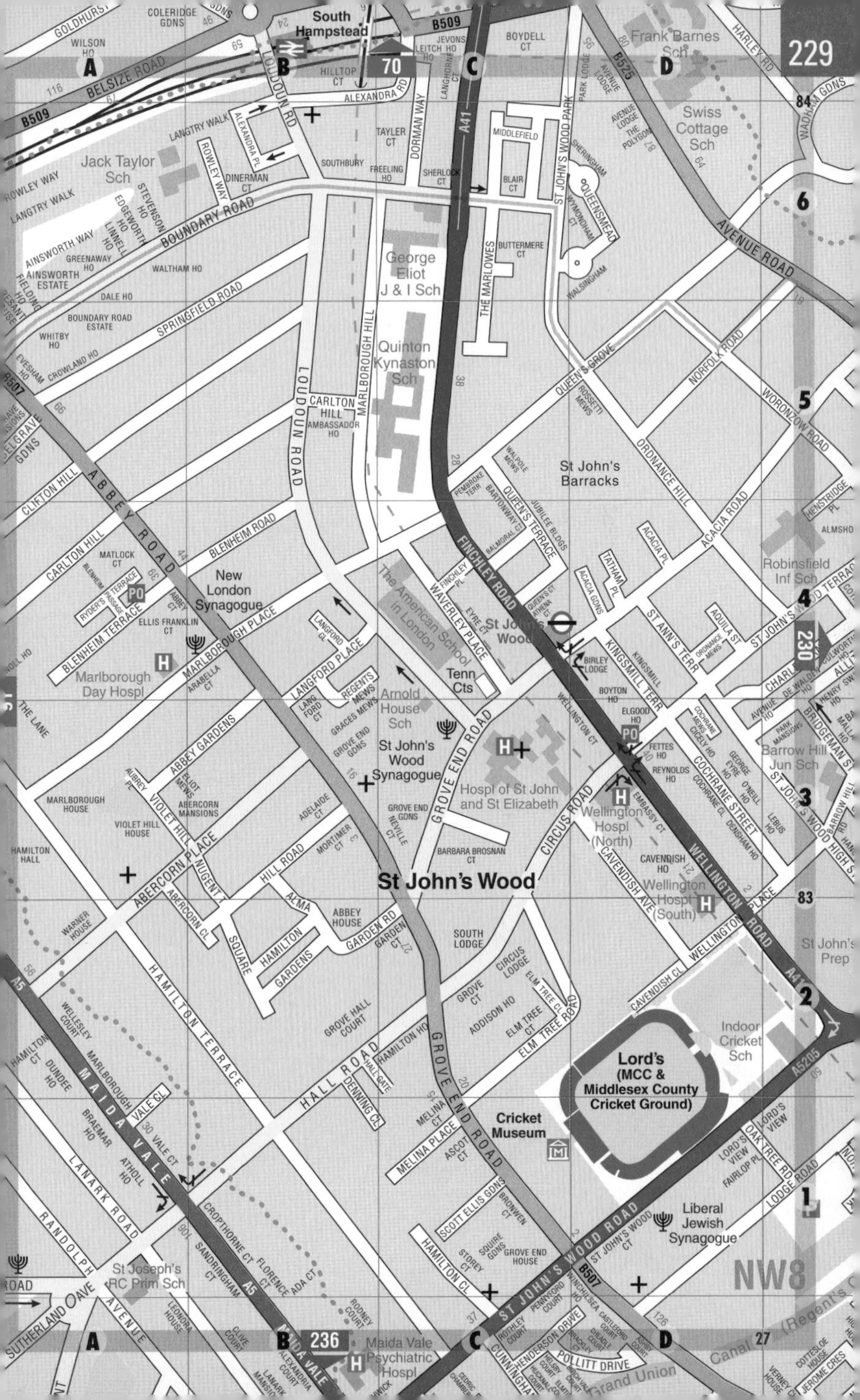
South Hampstead
70
B509
BELSIZE ROAD
Jack Taylor Sch
BOUNDARY ROAD
SPRINGFIELD ROAD
LOUDOUN ROAD
MARLBOROUGH HILL
George Eliot J & I Sch
Quinton Kynaston Sch
A41
Frank Barnes Sch
Swiss Cottage Sch
AVENUE ROAD
QUEEN'S GROVE
NORFOLK ROAD
ORDNANCE HILL
St John's Barracks
ACACIA ROAD
WORONZOW ROAD
Robinsfield Inf Sch
230
ABBEY ROAD
BLENHEIM ROAD
New London Synagogue
MARLBOROUGH PLACE
Marlborough Day Hospl
CARLTON HILL
CLIFTON HILL
FINCHLEY ROAD
The American School in London
St John's Wood
Tenn Cts
Arnold House Sch
St John's Wood Synagogue
GROVE END ROAD
Hospl of St John and St Elizabeth
CIRCUS ROAD
Wellington Hospl (North)
Wellington Hospl (South)
WELLINGTON ROAD
COCHRANE STREET
Barrow Hill Jun Sch
ST JOHN'S WOOD HIGH ST
St John's Wood
ABERCORN PLACE
HILL ROAD
HAMILTON TERRACE
GARDEN RD
CAVENDISH AVE
WELLINGTON PLACE
St John's Prep
Lord's (MCC & Middlesex County Cricket Ground)
Indoor Cricket Sch
Cricket Museum
HALL ROAD
MAIDA VALE
A5
LANARK ROAD
RANDOLPH AVENUE
ST JOHN'S WOOD ROAD
B507
Liberal Jewish Synagogue
St Joseph's RC Prim Sch
NW8
236
Maida Vale Psychiatric Hospl
POLLITT DRIVE
Grand Union Canal (Regent's)
LODGE ROAD
OAK TREE RD
A52205

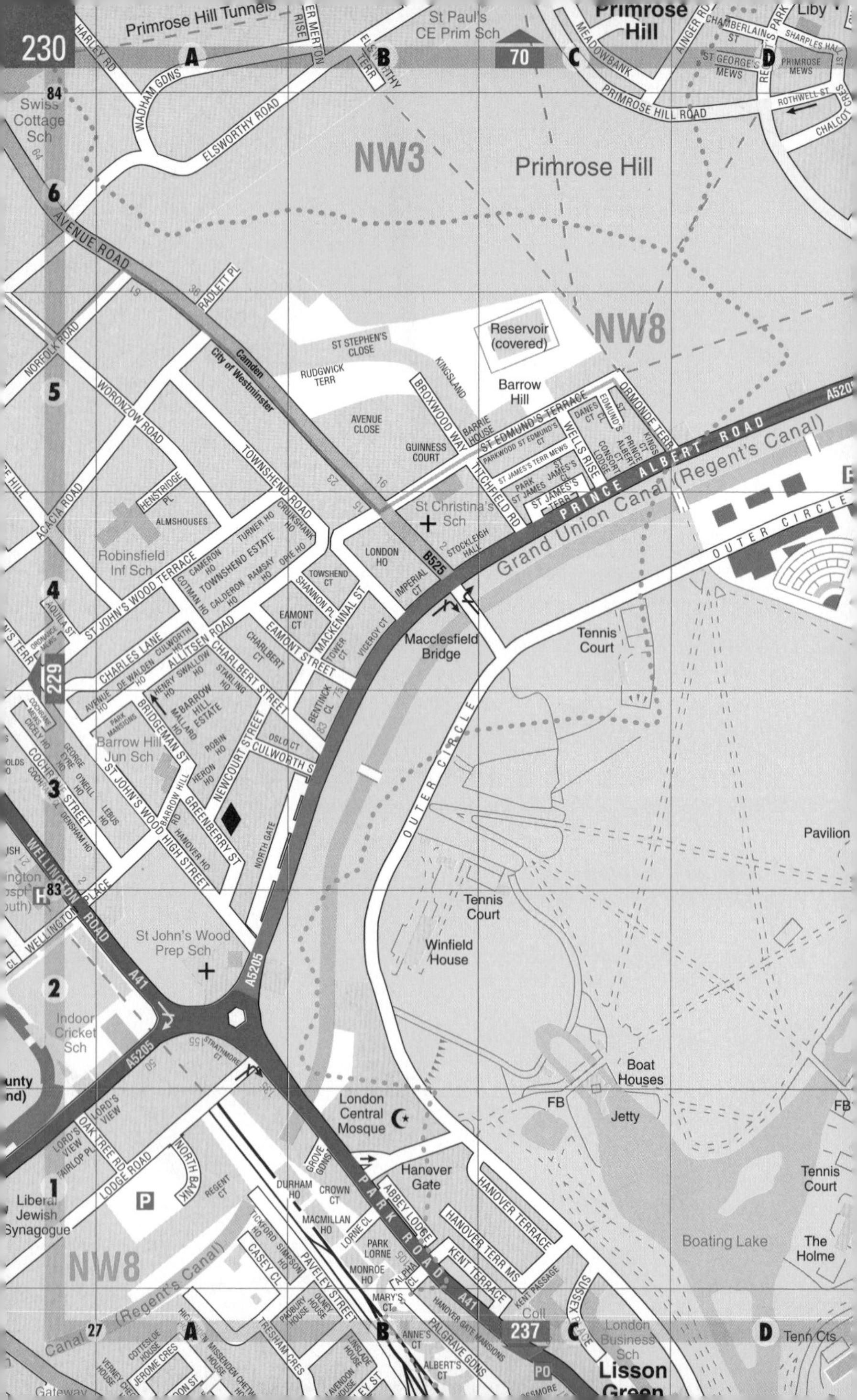
Primrose Hill Tunnels
Primrose Hill
St Paul's CE Prim Sch
Liby
A
B
70
C
D
HARLEY RD
WADHAM GDNS
ELSWORTHY ROAD
ELSWORTHY TERR
MEADOWBANK
AINGER RD
CHAMBERLAINS ST
ST GEORGE'S MEWS
PRIMROSE MEWS
SHARPLES HALL ST
PRIMROSE HILL ROAD
ROTHWELL ST
CHALCOT CRES
REGENT'S PARK
84
Swiss Cottage Sch
NW3
Primrose Hill
6
AVENUE ROAD
RADLETT PL
NORFOLK ROAD
Camden
City of Westminster
ST STEPHEN'S CLOSE
RUDGWICK TERR
Reservoir (covered)
NW8
KINGSLAND
Barrow Hill
BROXWOOD WAY
AVENUE CLOSE
GUINNESS COURT
BARRIE HOUSE
ST EDMUND'S TERRACE
PARKWOOD ST EDMUND'S CT
ST JAMES'S TERR MEWS
DANES CT
ST EDMUND'S CL
WELLS RISE
ORMONDE TERR
PRINCE ALBERT CT
KINGS CT
CONSORT LODGE
5
WORONZOW ROAD
TOWNSHEND ROAD
HENSTRIDGE PL
ALMSHOUSES
ACACIA ROAD
TITCHFIELD RD
PARK ST JAMES
ST JAMES'S CL
ST JAMES'S TERR
PRINCE ALBERT ROAD
A5205
Grand Union Canal (Regent's Canal)
OUTER CIRCLE
St Christina's Sch
STOCKLEIGH HALL
B525
LONDON HO
IMPERIAL CT
Robinsfield Inf Sch
ST JOHN'S WOOD TERRACE
CAMERON HO
TURNER HO
CRUIKSHANK HO
TOWNSHEND ESTATE
COTMAN HO
CALDERON HO
RAMSAY HO
OPIE HO
TOWSHEND CT
SHANNON PL
4
AQUILA ST
ORDNANCE MEWS
EAMONT CT
MACKENNAL ST
VIGEROY CT
Macclesfield Bridge
Tennis Court
CHARLES LANE
DE WALDEN HO
CULWORTH HO
ALLITSEN ROAD
CHARLBERT CT
EAMONT STREET
TOWER CT
229
AVENUE HO
HENRY HO
SWALLOW HO
STARLING HO
CHARLBERT STREET
BENTINCK CL
BARROW HILL ESTATE
MALLARD HO
PARK MANSIONS
BRIDGEMAN ST
Barrow Hill Jun Sch
OSLO CT
CULWORTH ST
COCHRANE MEWS
CICELY HO
GEORGE EYRE HO
O'NEILL HO
ROBIN HO
HERON HO
NEWCOURT STREET
3
COCHRANE STREET
ST JOHN'S WOOD
BARROW HILL RD
GREENBERRY ST
LEBUS HO
DENSHAM HO
HANOVER HO
HIGH STREET
NORTH GATE
Pavilion
WELLINGTON ROAD
WELLINGTON PLACE
83
Tennis Court
Winfield House
St John's Wood Prep Sch
2
Indoor Cricket Sch
A41
A5205
STRATHMORE CT
Boat Houses
FB
Jetty
FB
LORD'S VIEW
OAK TREE RD
FAIRLOP PL
LODGE ROAD
NORTH BANK
REGENT CT
London Central Mosque
GROVE GDNS
Hanover Gate
1
Liberal Jewish Synagogue
DURHAM HO
CROWN CT
PARK ROAD
ABBEY LODGE
HANOVER TERRACE
HANOVER TERR MS
Tennis Court
MACMILLAN HO
LORNE CL
PARK LORNE
TICKFORD HO
SIMPSON HO
CASEY CL
MONROE HO
ALPHA CL
KENT TERRACE
KENT PASSAGE
SUSSEX PLACE
Boating Lake
The Holme
NW8
(Regent's Canal)
PAVELEY STREET
MARY'S CT
HANOVER GATE MANSIONS
Coll
London Business Sch
27
A
B
237
C
D
Tenn Cts
Canal
COTTESLOE HOUSE
JEROME CRES
MISSENDEN HOUSE
TRESHAM CRES
PADBURY HOUSE
OLNEY HOUSE
LINSLADE HOUSE
ANNE'S CT
PALGRAVE GDNS
ALBERT'S CT
VERNEY HOUSE
AVENDON HOUSE
PO
Lisson Green
Gateway

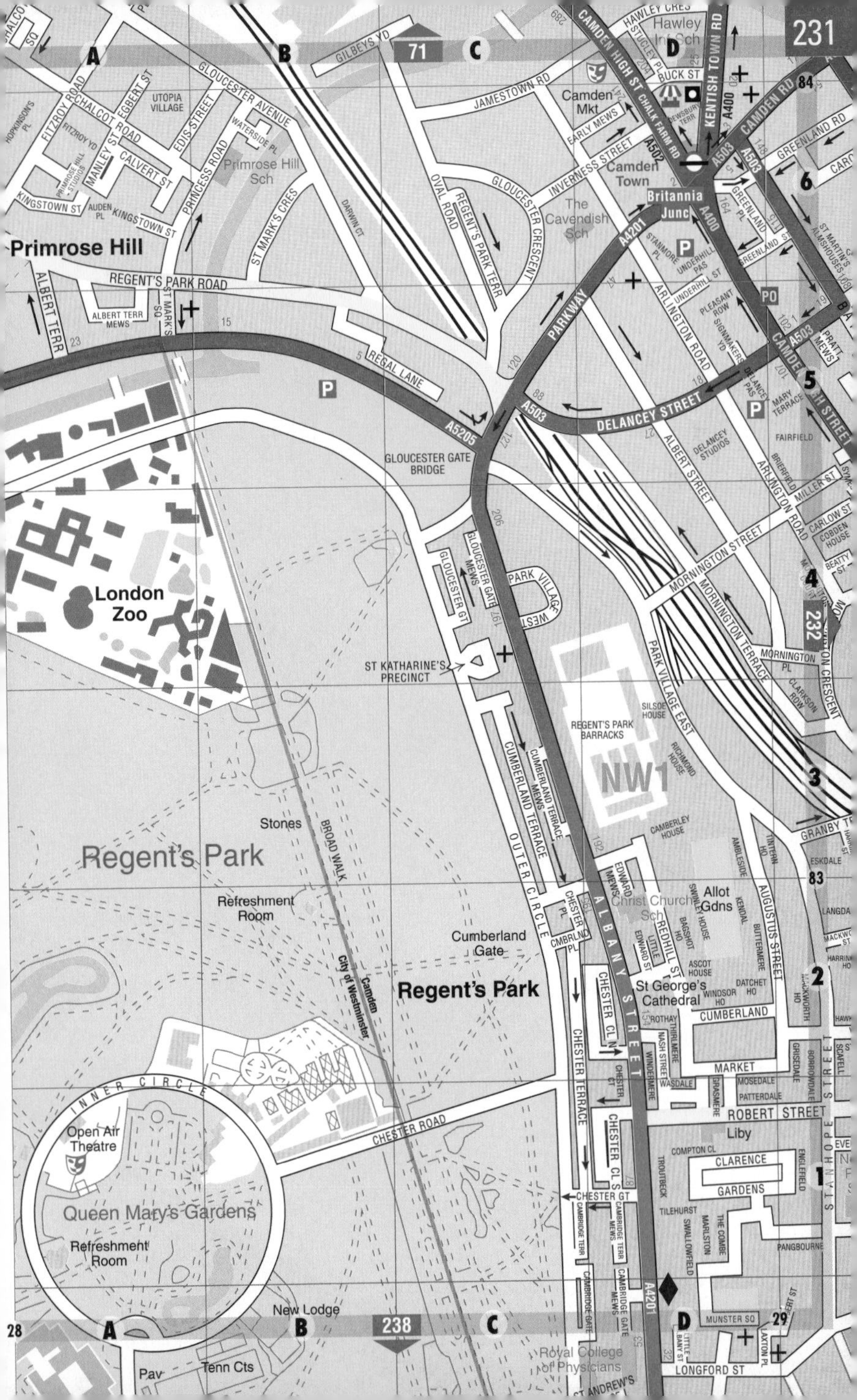
A
B
C
D
71
238
232
Primrose Hill
Primrose Hill Sch
Utopia Village
Gloucester Avenue
Chalcot Road
Fitzroy Road
Egbert St
Edis Street
Manley St
Calvert St
Princess Road
Kingstown St
Auden Pl
Regent's Park Road
Albert Terr
Albert Terr Mews
St Mark's Sq
St Mark's Cres
Gilbeys Yd
Jamestown Rd
Oval Road
Regent's Park Terr
Gloucester Crescent
Inverness Street
Early Mews
Camden Mkt
Camden Town
The Cavendish Sch
Britannia Junc
Camden High St
Chalk Farm Rd
Kentish Town Rd
Hawley Cres
Hawley Inf Sch
Buck St
Camden Rd
Greenland Rd
Greenland Pl
Greenland St
A400
A502
A503
A4201
A5205
Parkway
Arlington Road
Delancey Street
Albert Street
Pleasant Row
Underhill St
Regal Lane
London Zoo
Gloucester Gate Bridge
Gloucester Gate Mews
Gloucester Gt
Park Village West
Park Village East
St Katharine's Precinct
Mornington Street
Mornington Terrace
Mornington Pl
Mornington Crescent
Millers St
Carlow St
Regent's Park Barracks
NW1
Cumberland Terrace
Cumberland Terrace Mews
Outer Circle
Broad Walk
Stones
Regent's Park
Refreshment Room
Cumberland Gate
Camden
City of Westminster
Chester Pl
Cmbrlnd Pl
Chester Cl
Chester Terrace
Chester Road
Chester Gt
Cambridge Terr
Cambridge Terr Mews
Cambridge Gate
Albany Street
Edward Mews
Christ Church Sch
Redhill St
St George's Cathedral
Allot Gdns
Augustus Street
Cumberland Market
Robert Street
Liby
Clarence Gardens
Stanhope Street
Granby Terr
Inner Circle
Open Air Theatre
Queen Mary's Gardens
Refreshment Room
New Lodge
Pav
Tenn Cts
Royal College of Physicians
Munster Sq
Longford St
1
2
3
4
5
6
28
29
83
84

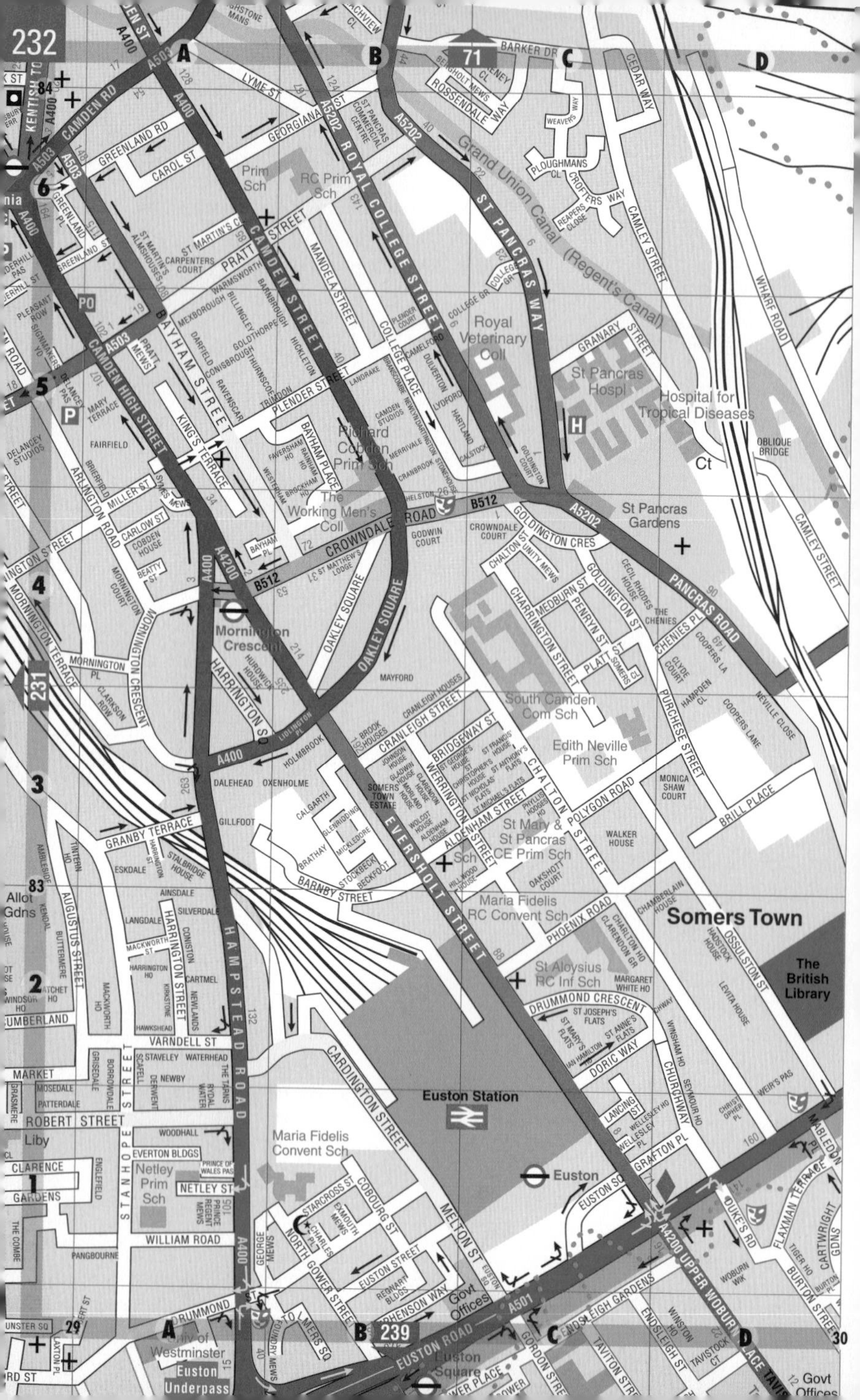
A
B
C
D
71
Camden Rd
Kentish Town Rd
Lyme St
Georgiana St
Greenland Rd
Carol St
Greenland Pl
Greenland St
Barker Dr
Rossendale Way
Cedar Way
Weavers Way
Ploughmans Cl
Crofters Way
Reapers Close
Camley Street
Royal College Street
St Pancras Commercial Centre
St Pancras Way
Grand Union Canal (Regent's Canal)
Prim Sch
RC Prim Sch
Pratt Street
St Martin's Cl
St Martin's Almshouses
Carpenters Court
Camden Street
Mandela Street
College Gr
Royal Veterinary Coll
Granary Street
St Pancras Hospl
Hospital for Tropical Diseases
Wharf Road
Oblique Bridge
Pleasant Row
Signmakers Yd
PO
Camden High Street
Bayham Street
Pratt Mews
Mexborough
Billingley
Barnsbrough
Hickleton
Darfield
Goldthorpe
Conisbrough
Thurnscoe
Ravenscar
Trimdon
Plender Street
College Place
Camelford
Dulverton
Lydford
Hartland
Calstock
Landrake
Bayham Place
Camden Studios
Richard Cobden Prim Sch
The Working Men's Coll
Merrivale
Cranbrook
Stoneshouse
Helston
Goldington Court
Delancey St
Mary Terrace
Fairfield
Delancey Studios
King's Terrace
Arlington Road
Miller St
Symes Mews
Carlow St
Cobden House
Beatty St
Bayham Pl
Crowndale Road
B512
St Matthew's Lodge
Godwin Court
Crowndale Court
Goldington Cres
Unity Mews
Chalton St
A5202
St Pancras Gardens
Pancras Road
Camley Street
Mornington Street
Mornington Terrace
Mornington Court
Mornington Crescent
Mornington Pl
Clarkson Row
A400
A4200
Oakley Square
Harrington Sq
Hurdwick House
Mayford
Medburn St
Penryn St
Goldington St
Cecil Rhodes House
The Chenies
Chenies Pl
Coopers La
Clyde Court
Charrington Street
Platt St
Somers Cl
Hampden Cl
Coopers Lane
Neville Close
South Camden Com Sch
Edith Neville Prim Sch
231
Cranleigh Houses
Cranleigh Street
Bridgeway St
Brook Houses
Holmbrook
Dalehead
Oxenholme
Lidlington Pl
Somers Town Estate
Calgarth
Glenridding
Mickledore
Brathay
Stockbeck
Beckfoot
Johnson House
Werrington Street
Chalton Street
Polygon Road
Monica Shaw Court
Purchese Street
Brill Place
Aldenham Street
St Mary & St Pancras CE Prim Sch
Sch
Walker House
Granby Terrace
Gillfoot
Eskdale
Stalbridge House
Ainsdale
Silverdale
Langdale
Harrington Street
Coniston
Mackworth St
Barnby Street
Oakshott Court
Maria Fidelis RC Convent Sch
Phoenix Road
Charlton Ho
Clarendon Gr
Chamberlain House
Somers Town
Ossulston St
Handstock House
The British Library
Levita House
Allot Gdns
Augustus Street
Ampleside
Kendal
Buttermere
Mackworth Ho
Tintern Ho
Harrington Ho
Cartmel
Newlands
Kirkstone
Hawkshead
Hampstead Road
132
St Aloysius RC Inf Sch
Margaret White Ho
Drummond Crescent
St Joseph's Flats
St Mary's Flats
St Anne's Flats
Doric Way
Churchway
Wrexham Ho
Seymour Ho
Cumberland
Windsor Ho
Varndell St
Staveley
Waterhead
Market
Grisedale
Borrowdale
Newby
Derwent
Mosedale
Patterdale
Rydal Water
The Tarns
Grasmere
Cardington Street
Euston Station
Robert Street
Woodhall
Liby
Stanhope Street
Everton Bldgs
Maria Fidelis Convent Sch
Lancing St
Wellesley Pl
Christopher Pl
Weir's Pas
Clarence Gardens
Netley Prim Sch
Prince of Wales Pas
Netley St
Prince Regent Mews
Englefield
The Combe
William Road
Pangbourne
Starcross St
Exmouth Mews
Cobourg St
Charles Pl
North Gower Street
George Mews
Euston Street
Regnart Bldgs
Melton St
Euston Sq
Euston
Grafton Pl
Mabledon Pl
Flaxman Terrace
Cartwright Gdns
Duke's Rd
Woburn Wlk
Burton Street
Tiger Ho
A4200 Upper Woburn Place
Drummond
Munster Sq
Laxton Pl
Univ of Westminster
Euston Underpass
Tolmers Sq
Foundry Mews
Stephenson Way
Govt Offices
239
Euston Road
A501
Endsleigh Gardens
Endsleigh St
Gordon St
Taviton St
Winston Ho
Tavistock Ct
Euston Square
Tavistock
Govt Offices
Somers Town
1
2
3
4
5
6
29
30
83
84

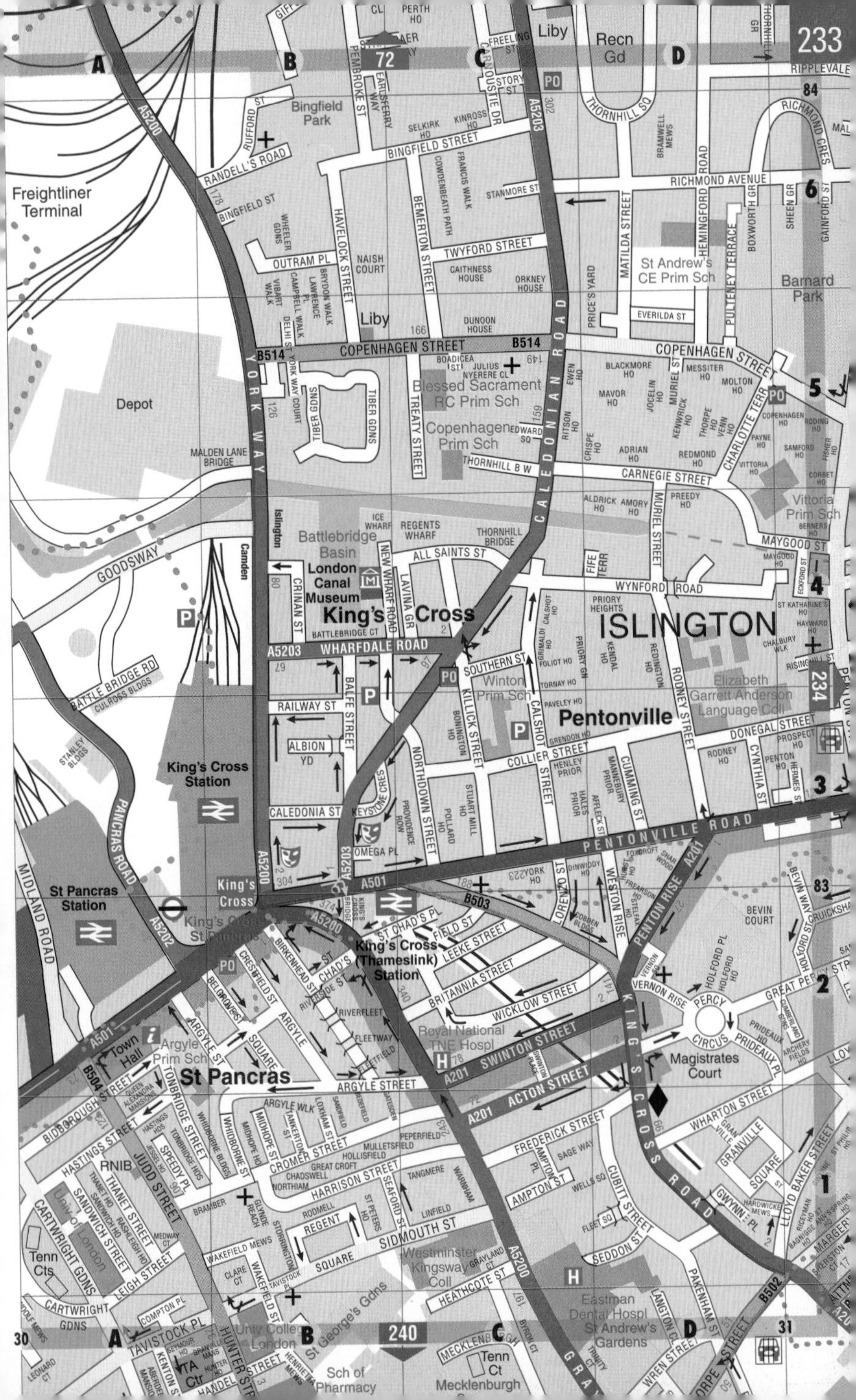

72
240
234
Freightliner Terminal
Depot
Bingfield Park
Recn Gd
Liby
PO
Barnard Park
ISLINGTON
Pentonville
King's Cross
St Pancras
King's Cross Station
St Pancras Station
King's Cross (Thameslink) Station
King's Cross St Pancras
London Canal Museum
Battlebridge Basin
Blessed Sacrament RC Prim Sch
Copenhagen Prim Sch
St Andrew's CE Prim Sch
Vittoria Prim Sch
Winton Prim Sch
Elizabeth Garrett Anderson Language Coll
Argyle Prim Sch
Town Hall
Royal National TNE Hospl
Magistrates Court
Westminster Kingsway Coll
Eastman Dental Hospl
St Andrew's Gardens
Univ of London
Tenn Cts
RNIB
Unity College London
Sch of Pharmacy
Mecklenburgh
St George's Gdns
YORK WAY
CALEDONIAN ROAD
COPENHAGEN STREET
PENTONVILLE ROAD
KING'S CROSS ROAD
PANCRAS ROAD
MIDLAND ROAD
WHARFDALE ROAD
SWINTON STREET
ACTON STREET
ARGYLE STREET
GRAY'S INN ROAD
JUDD STREET
HUNTER STREET
RICHMOND AVENUE
CARNEGIE STREET
WYNFORD ROAD
DONEGAL STREET
COLLIER STREET
BINGFIELD STREET
TWYFORD STREET
HAVELOCK STREET
BEMERTON STREET
CALSHOT STREET
RODNEY STREET
MURIEL STREET
CUMMING ST
WESTON RISE
PENTON RISE
GOODSWAY
BATTLE BRIDGE RD
FREDERICK STREET
CUBITT STREET
WHARTON STREET
LLOYD BAKER STREET
HARRISON STREET
CROMER STREET
SIDMOUTH ST
REGENT SQUARE
LEIGH STREET
CARTWRIGHT GDNS
TAVISTOCK PL
HASTINGS STREET
BIDBOROUGH STREET
TONBRIDGE STREET
WHIDBORNE ST
THANET STREET
SANDWICH STREET
HEATHCOTE ST
MECKLENBURGH
WREN STREET
LANGTON CL
PAKENHAM ST
GWYNNE PL
GREAT PERCY ST
PERCY CIRCUS
VERNON RISE
WICKLOW STREET
BRITANNIA STREET
LEEKE STREET
ST CHAD'S PL
NORTHDOWN STREET
KILLICK STREET
RAILWAY ST
BALFE STREET
CALEDONIA ST
CRINAN ST
NEW WHARF ROAD
ALL SAINTS ST
TREATY STREET
TIBER GDNS
COPENHAGEN STREET
MALDEN LANE BRIDGE
A5200
A5203
A501
A201
A5202
B514
B503
B504
B502
A B C D
1 2 3 4 5 6
30 31 83 84

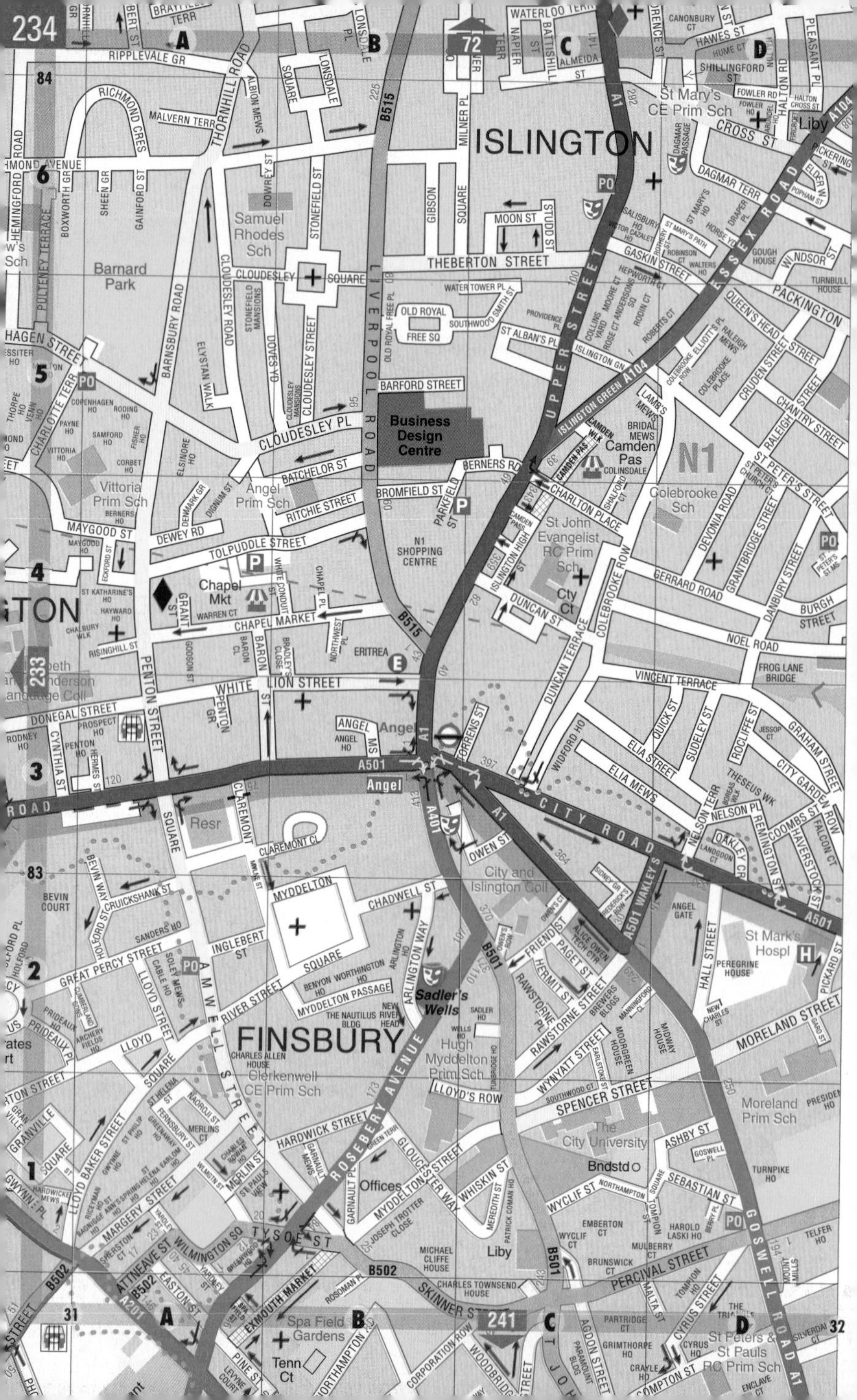

ISLINGTON
FINSBURY
N1
72
233
241
A
B
C
D
84
83
6
5
4
3
2
1
31
32
RIPPLEVALE GR
RICHMOND CRES
MALVERN TERR
THORNHILL ROAD
ALBION MEWS
LONSDALE SQUARE
LONSDALE PL
WATERLOO TERR
NAPIER TERR
BATTISHILL ST
ALMEIDA ST
CANONBURY CT
HAWES ST
HUME CT
SHILLINGFORD ST
FOWLER RD
HALTON RD
PLEASANT PL
HALTON CROSS ST
St Mary's CE Prim Sch
DAGMAR PASSAGE
CROSS ST
Liby
DAGMAR TERR
PICKERING ST
ELDER W
POPHAM ST
ESSEX ROAD
A104
A1
B515
PO
MILNER PL
GIBSON SQUARE
MOON ST
STUDD ST
THEBERTON STREET
SALISBURY HO
VICTOR CAZALET HO
ST MARY'S PATH
ST MARY'S HO
HORSE YD
DRAPER PL
GOUGH HOUSE
WINDSOR ST
GASKIN STREET
ROBINSON CT
WALTERS HO
HEPWORTH CT
TURNBULL HOUSE
PACKINGTON
QUEEN'S HEAD STREET
MOND AVENUE
HEMINGFORD ROAD
BOXWORTH GR
SHEEN GR
GAINFORD ST
DOWREY ST
STONEFIELD ST
Samuel Rhodes Sch
PULTENEY TERRACE
Barnard Park
BARNSBURY ROAD
CLOUDESLEY ROAD
CLOUDESLEY SQUARE
LIVERPOOL ROAD
WATER TOWER PL
OLD ROYAL FREE SQ
OLD ROYAL FREE PL
SOUTHWOOD SMITH ST
PROVIDENCE PL
COLLINS YARD
MOORE CT
ROSE CT
ANDERSONS SQ
RODIN CT
ROBERTS CT
ST ALBAN'S PL
UPPER STREET
ISLINGTON GN
ISLINGTON GREEN
ELLIOTT'S PL
RALEIGH MEWS
COLEBROOKE ROW
COLEBROOKE PLACE
CRUDEN STREET
CHANTRY STREET
HAGEN STREET
STONEFIELD MANSIONS
DOVES YD
ELYSTAN WALK
CLOUDESLEY STREET
CLOUDESLEY MANSIONS
BARFORD STREET
LAMB'S MEWS
BRIDAL MEWS
Camden Pas
CAMDEN WLK
CAMDEN PAS
COLINSDALE
RALEIGH STREET
ST PETER'S STREET
ST PETER'S CHURCH CT
CHARLOTTE TERR
COPENHAGEN HO
RODING HO
PAYNE HO
SAMFORD HO
FISHER HO
VITTORIA HO
CORBET HO
Vittoria Prim Sch
BERNERS HO
CLOUDESLEY PL
ELSINORE HO
Business Design Centre
BATCHELOR ST
BERNERS RD
Angel Prim Sch
DENMARK GR
DIGNUM ST
RITCHIE STREET
BROMFIELD ST
PARKFIELD ST
CHARLTON PLACE
SHALFORD CT
Colebrooke Sch
DEVONIA ROAD
GRANTBRIDGE STREET
MAYGOOD ST
MAYGOOD HO
DEWEY RD
TOLPUDDLE STREET
N1 SHOPPING CENTRE
CAMDEN PASS
ISLINGTON HIGH ST
St John Evangelist RC Prim Sch
DANBURY STREET
ST PETER'S ST MS
ECKFORD ST
WHITE CONDUIT ST
CHAPEL PL
GERRARD ROAD
BURGH STREET
ST KATHARINE'S HO
HAYWARD HO
GRANT ST
Chapel Mkt
WARREN CT
CHAPEL MARKET
DUNCAN ST
Cty Ct
CHALBURY WLK
RISINGHILL ST
BARON CL
BARON ST
BRADLEY'S CLOSE
NORTHWEST PL
ERITREA
NOEL ROAD
DUNCAN TERRACE
FROG LANE BRIDGE
PENTON STREET
GODSON ST
WHITE LION STREET
VINCENT TERRACE
DONEGAL STREET
PROSPECT HO
PENTON GR
ANGEL MS
ANGEL HO
Angel
TORRENS ST
WIDFORD HO
QUICK ST
SUDELEY ST
ROCLIFFE ST
JESSOP CT
GRAHAM STREET
ELIA STREET
ELIA MEWS
CITY GARDEN ROW
RODNEY HO
CYNTHIA ST
PENTON HO
HERMES ST
A501
THESEUS WK
BOREAS WLK
NELSON TERR
NELSON PL
ROAD
CLAREMONT
Resr
A401
OWEN ST
CITY ROAD
OAKLEY CR
LANGDON CT
REMINGTON ST
COOMBS ST
HAVERSTOCK ST
FALCON CT
SQUARE
CLAREMONT CL
MYDDELTON
MYLNE ST
City and Islington Coll
SIDNEY GR
FREDERICK'S ROW
WAKLEY ST
BEVIN WAY
BEVIN COURT
CRUICKSHANK ST
HOLFORD ST
CHADWELL ST
OWEN'S CT
FRIEND ST
ALICE OWEN TECH CTR
ANGEL GATE
HALL STREET
St Mark's Hospl
SANDERS HO
INGLEBERT ST
ARLINGTON WAY
ARLINGTON HO
OWEN'S ROW
PAGET ST
HERMIT ST
PEREGRINE HOUSE
PICKARD ST
HOLFORD PL
GREAT PERCY STREET
CABLE HO
SOLEY MEWS
AMWELL STREET
BENYON WORTHINGTON HO
MYDDELTON PASSAGE
Sadler's Wells
B501
RAWSTORNE PL
RAWSTORNE STREET
BREWERS BLDGS
MANNINGFORD CL
NEW CHARLES ST
MORELAND STREET
GARD ST
PRIDEAUX PL
PRIDEAUX HO
CUMBERLAND HO
LLOYD STREET
RIVER STREET
THE NAUTILUS BLDG
NEW RIVER HEAD
SADLER HO
WELLS HO
MIDWAY HOUSE
MOORGREEN HOUSE
ARCHERY FIELDS HO
LLOYD
WYNYATT STREET
EARLSTOKE ST
CHARLES ALLEN HOUSE
Hugh Myddelton Prim Sch
TUNBRIDGE HO
Clerkenwell CE Prim Sch
LLOYD SQUARE
ROSEBERY AVENUE
LLOYD'S ROW
SOUTHWOOD CT
SPENCER STREET
Moreland Prim Sch
PRESIDENT HO
GRANVILLE SQUARE
ST HELENA HO
NAOROJI ST
FERNSBURY ST
MERLINS CT
GREENAWAY HO
HARDWICK STREET
GREEN TERR
GARNAULT MEWS
GLOUCESTER WAY
The City University
ASHBY ST
GOSWELL PL
LLOYD BAKER STREET
ST PHILIP HO
GWYNNE HO
EARLOM HO
CHARLES ROWAN HO
WILMINGTON ST
MERLIN ST
ST PAULS VIEW
Offices
MYDDELTON STREET
WHISKIN ST
Bndstd
TURNPIKE HO
HARDWICKE MEWS
GWYNNE PL
RIDEYMAN HO
BAGNIGGE HO
AMY SPRING HO
HELENA HO
MARGERY STREET
GARNAULT PL
JOSEPH TROTTER CLOSE
MEREDITH ST
PATRICK COMAN HO
WYCLIF ST
NORTHAMPTON SQUARE
TOMPION ST
SEBASTIAN ST
BERRY PL
HAROLD LASKI HO
TELFER HO
EMBERTON CT
SHERSTON CT
YARDLEY ST
WILMINGTON SQ
TYSOE ST
MICHAEL CLIFFE HOUSE
Liby
WYCLIF CT
MULBERRY CT
BRUNSWICK CT
PERCIVAL STREET
TOMPION HO
GOSWELL ROAD
MOUNT MILLS
B502
ATTNEAVE ST
EASTON ST
A201
EXMOUTH MARKET
ROSOMAN PL
SKINNER STREET
CHARLES TOWNSEND HOUSE
MALTA ST
CYRUS STREET
Spa Field Gardens
NORTHAMPTON RD
CORPORATION ROW
WOODBRIDGE ST
AGDON STREET
PARTRIDGE CT
PARAMOUNT BLDG
GRIMTHORPE HO
CYRUS HO
CRAYLE HO
St Peters & St Pauls RC Prim Sch
SILVERDALE CT
COMPTON ST
ENCLAVE CT
Tenn Ct
PINE ST
LEVYNE COURT
PHOENIX PL

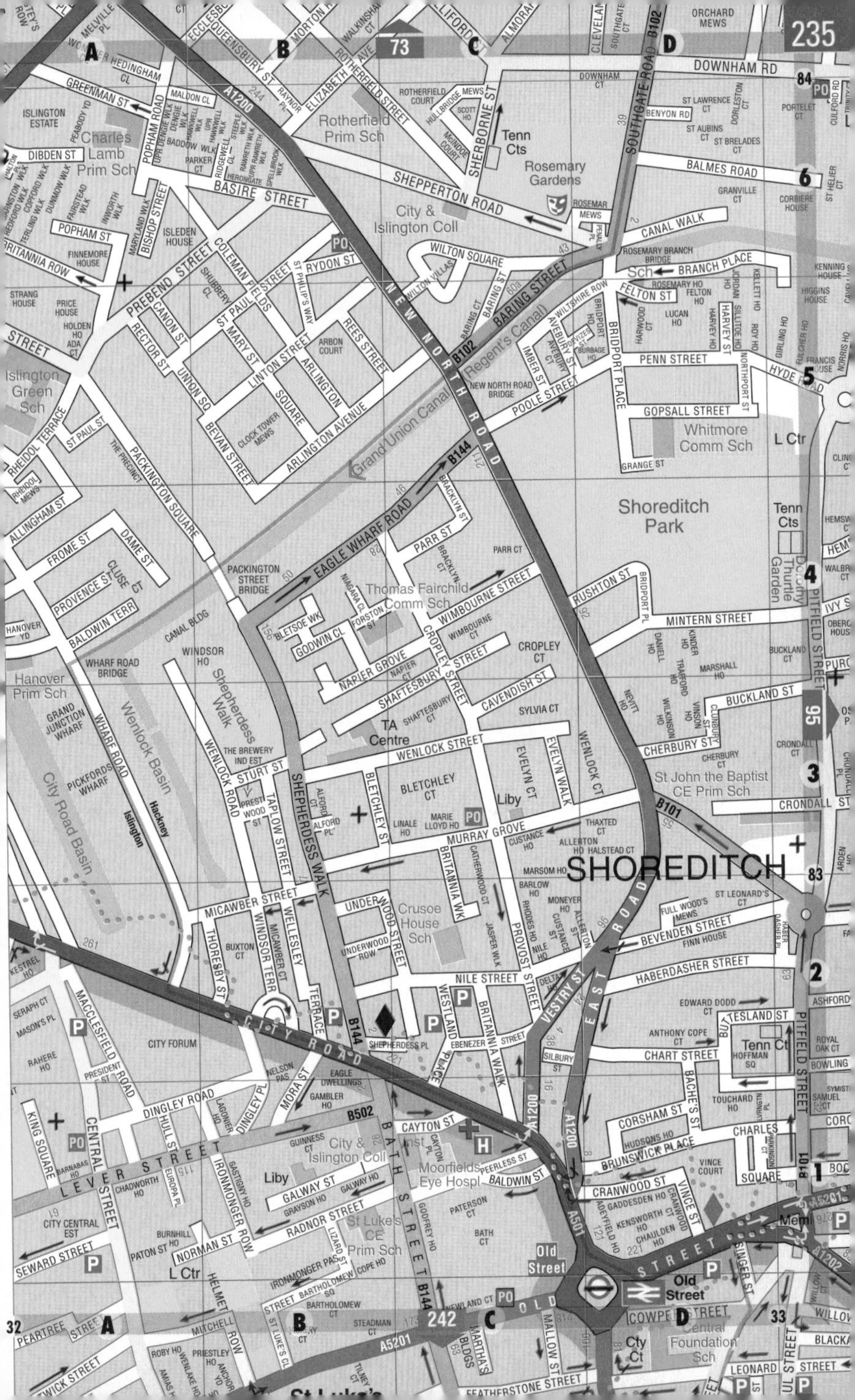
A
B
C
D
73
ORCHARD MEWS
DOWNHAM RD
DOWNHAM CT
84
PO
SOUTHGATE ROAD
SOUTHGATE CT
CLEVELAND
B102
MELVILLE PL
WONTNER
HEDINGHAM CL
GREENMAN ST
QUEENSBURY ST
ECCLESBOURNE
MORTON RD
ROTHERFIELD ST
ELIZABETH AVE
WALKINSHAW CT
CLIFFORD
ALMORAH
ISLINGTON ESTATE
PEABODY YD
Charles Lamb Prim Sch
DIBDEN ST
POPHAM ROAD
MALDON CL
UPR DENGIE WLK
DENGIE WLK
HAWKWELL WLK
STEEPLE CL
RAWRETH WLK
A1200
244
RAYNOR PL
ROTHERFIELD COURT
HULLBRIDGE MEWS
SCOTT HO
McINDOE COURT
SHERBORNE ST
Tenn Cts
Rotherfield Prim Sch
BENYON RD
ST LAWRENCE CT
DORLESTON CT
ST AUBINS CT
ST BRELADES CT
PORTELET CT
CULFORD RD
BALMES ROAD
6
BADDOW WLK
PARKER CT
RIDGEWELL CL
HERONGATE
SPELLBROOK WLK
BASIRE STREET
SHEPPERTON ROAD
Rosemary Gardens
39
GRANVILLE CT
CORBIERE HOUSE
ST HELIER CT
FAIRSTEAD WLK
DUNMOW WLK
COPFORD WLK
TERLING WLK
INWORTH WLK
POPHAM ST
MARYLAND WLK
BISHOP STREET
ISLEDEN HOUSE
City & Islington Coll
ROSEMARY MEWS
PENALLY PL
CANAL WALK
BRITANNIA ROW
FINNEMORE HOUSE
PREBEND STREET
COLEMAN FIELDS
PO
RYDON ST
ST PHILIP'S WAY
WILTON SQUARE
WILTON VILLAS
43
ROSEMARY BRANCH BRIDGE
Sch
BRANCH PLACE
KENNING HOUSE
STRANG HOUSE
PRICE HOUSE
HOLDEN HO
ADA CT
SHUBBERY CL
CANON ST
ST PAUL STREET
MARY ST
NEW NORTH ROAD
BARING ST
BARING CT
BARING STREET
60a
ROSEMARY HO
FELTON ST
FELTON HO
JORDAN HO
SILLITOE HO
KELLETT HO
HIGGINS HOUSE
STREET
RECTOR ST
UNION SQ
LINTON STREET
ARBON COURT
REES STREET
B102
Regent's Canal
WILTSHIRE ROW
DEVIZES ST
AVEBURY ST
AVEBURY CT
BURBAGE HO
BRIDPORT HO
BRIDPORT PLACE
HARWOOD CT
LUCAN HO
HARVEY HO
HARVEY ST
ROY HO
GIRLING HO
FULCHER HO
NORRIS HO
PENN STREET
FRANCIS HOUSE
HYDE ROAD
5
Islington Green Sch
ARLINGTON
SQUARE
IMBER ST
NEW NORTH ROAD BRIDGE
POOLE STREET
NORTHPORT ST
GOPSALL STREET
RHEIDOL TERRACE
ST PAUL ST
THE PRECINCT
PACKINGTON SQUARE
BEVAN STREET
CLOCK TOWER MEWS
ARLINGTON AVENUE
Grand Union Canal
B144
211
Whitmore Comm Sch
L Ctr
GRANGE ST
RHEIDOL MEWS
ALLINGHAM ST
46
BRACKLYN ST
EAGLE WHARF ROAD
Shoreditch Park
Tenn Cts
FROME ST
DAME ST
CLUSE CT
PROVENCE ST
BALDWIN TERR
PACKINGTON STREET BRIDGE
50
28
PARR ST
BRACKLYN CT
PARR CT
Thomas Fairchild Comm Sch
NIAGARA CL
WIMBOURNE STREET
RUSHTON ST
BRIDPORT PL
Dorothy Thurtle Garden
4
PITFIELD STREET
HANOVER YD
CANAL BLDG
156
BLETSOE WK
GODWIN CL
FORSTON ST
WIMBOURNE CT
MINTERN STREET
DANIELL HO
KINDER HO
TRAFFORD HO
MARSHALL HO
BUCKLAND CT
WINDSOR HO
NAPIER GROVE
NAPIER CT
CROPLEY STREET
CROPLEY CT
26
WHARF ROAD BRIDGE
Hanover Prim Sch
Shepherdess Walk
SHAFTESBURY ST
SHAFTESBURY CT
CAVENDISH ST
NEVITT HO
WILKINSON HO
VINSON HO
CLUNBURY ST
BUCKLAND ST
95
GRAND JUNCTION WHARF
WHARF ROAD
Wenlock Basin
TA Centre
SYLVIA CT
CHERBURY ST
CHERBURY CT
CRONDALL CT
3
WENLOCK STREET
THE BREWERY IND EST
WENLOCK ROAD
STURT ST
EVELYN CT
EVELYN WALK
WENLOCK CT
St John the Baptist CE Prim Sch
CRONDALL ST
PICKFORDS WHARF
City Road Basin
Hackney
Islington
PRESTWOOD ST
TAPLOW STREET
SHEPHERDESS WALK
BLETCHLEY ST
BLETCHLEY CT
ALFORD CT
ALFORD PL
LINALE HO
MARIE LLOYD HO
PO
Liby
B101
THAXTED CT
55
MURRAY GROVE
CUSTANCE HO
ALLERTON HO
HALSTEAD CT
BRITANNIA WK
CATHERWOOD CT
MARSOM HO
SHOREDITCH
83
BARLOW HO
MICAWBER STREET
UNDERWOOD STREET
Crusoe House Sch
MONEYER HO
ALLERTON ST
FULL WOOD'S MEWS
ST LEONARD'S CT
HABERDASHER PL
BEVENDEN STREET
FINN HOUSE
WINDSOR TERR
THORESBY ST
MICAWBER CT
WELLESLEY TERRACE
UNDERWOOD ROW
JASPER WALK
PROVOST STREET
RHODES HO
NILE HO
CUSTANCE ST
EAST ROAD
95
261
KESTREL HO
BUXTON CT
NILE STREET
HABERDASHER STREET
2
63
ASHFORD
DELTA ST
VESTRY ST
EDWARD DODD CT
BUTTESLAND ST
ROYAL OAK CT
SERAPH CT
MASON'S PL
MACCLESFIELD ROAD
P
CITY ROAD
B144
SHEPHERDESS PL
WESTLAND PLACE
EBENEZER STREET
BRITANNIA WALK
38
4
SILBURY ST
ANTHONY COPE CT
CHART STREET
Tenn Ct
HOFFMAN SQ
BOWLING
CITY FORUM
RAHERE HO
PRESIDENT ST
NELSON PAS
EAGLE DWELLINGS
GAMBLER HO
MORA ST
221
16
A1200
BACHE'S ST
TOUCHARD HO
SYMISTER CT
SAMUEL CT
KING SQUARE
CENTRAL STREET
DINGLEY ROAD
HULL ST
LAGONIER HO
DINGLEY PL
B502
CAYTON ST
BATH STREET
H
CORSHAM ST
HUDSONS HO
CHARLES SQUARE
PARKINSON CT
BRUNSWICK PLACE
VINCE COURT
PO
BARNABAS HO
LEVER STREET
GUINNESS CT
City & Islington Coll
Inst
CAYTON PL
PEERLESS ST
115
EUROPA PL
CHADWORTH HO
IRONMONGER ROW
GASTIGNY HO
Liby
GALWAY ST
GALWAY HO
Moorfields Eye Hospl
BALDWIN ST
B101
1
BOC
61
CITY CENTRAL EST
GRAYSON HO
RADNOR STREET
GODFREY HO
PATERSON CT
CRANWOOD ST
GADDESDEN HO
ADEYFIELD HO
121
KENSWORTH CT
CRANWOOD ST
VINCE ST
CHAULDEN HO
A5201
Meml
A1202
BURNHILL HO
St Luke's CE Prim Sch
LIZARD ST
BATH CT
A501
SEWARD STREET
PATON ST
NORMAN ST
Old Street
SINGER ST
P
L Ctr
IRONMONGER PAS
COPE HO
OLD STREET
Old Street
HELMET ROW
BARTHOLOMEW
B144
NEWLAND CT
PO
WILLOW
32
BARTHOLOMEW CT
STEADMAN CT
242
COWPER STREET
33
PEARTREE STREET
MITCHELL
STREET
ST LUKE'S CL
MARTHA'S BLDGS
MALLOW ST
Central Foundation Sch
Cty Ct
BLACKALL
LEONARD STREET
ROBY HO
WENLAKE HO
PRIESTLEY HO
ANCHOR YD
AMIAS HO
TILNEY CT
FEATHERSTONE STREET
WICK STREET
St Luke's

229
246
LAUDERDALE ROAD
SUTHERLAND AVE
RANDOLPH AVENUE
St Joseph's RC Prim Sch
MAIDA VALE
ST JOHN'S WOOD ROAD
B507
Liberal Jewish Synagogue
GROVE END HOUSE
HAMILTON CL
SCOTT ELLIS GDNS
SQUIRE GDNS
Maida Vale Psychiatric Hospl
Grand Union Canal
POLLITT DRIVE
HENDERSON DRIVE
CUNNINGHAM PL
Gateway Prim Sch
CAPLAND STREET
A5205
NORTHWICK TERR
ABERDEEN PLACE
CLIFTON ROAD
B413
WARRINGTON CRESCENT
RANDOLPH CRESCENT
W9
CLIFTON GARDENS
FORMOSA STREET
WARWICK AVENUE
Warwick Avenue
CLIFTON VILLAS
BRISTOL GDNS
BRISTOL MEWS
RANDOLPH ROAD
RANDOLPH MEWS
CLARENDON GDNS
MAIDA AVENUE
BLOMFIELD ROAD
WARWICK PLACE
Grand Union Canal Wlk
Little Venice
WARWICK CRESCENT
LAPWORTH COURT
DELAMERE TERRACE
BLOMFIELD VILLAS
WESTBOURNE TERR RD
CROMPTON STREET
HALL PLACE
PARSONS HOUSE
Paddington Green Prim Sch
LYONS PLACE
FISHERTON STREET
ORCHARDSON STREET
FRAMPTON STREET
LUTON STREET
HATTON ST
BOSCOBEL ST
PENFOLD STREET
VENABLES ST
ADPAR STREET
St Mary's Gardens
City of Westminster Coll
PARK PLACE VILLAS
HOWLEY PLACE
ST MARY'S MANSIONS
JOHN AIRD COURT
PORTEUS RD
ST MARY'S TERR
ST MARY'S SQ
FLEMING COURT
PADDINGTON GREEN
NEWCASTLE PL
HARROW RD
HARROW ROAD
A404
A40
A5
WESTWAY (ELEVATED) HARROW RD (UNDER)
PADDINGTON
W2
RANELAGH BRIDGE
WESTBOURNE BRIDGE
BISHOP'S ROAD BRIDGE
(Paddington Branch)
A4206
North Westminster Com Sch
DUDLEY HOUSE
NORTH WHARF ROAD
HARBET ROAD
SIDONS HOUSE
Paddington Basin
SOUTH WHARF ROAD
St Mary's Hospl
Medical Sch
PRAED STREET
BOUVERIE PL
NORFOLK PLACE
NORFOLK SQUARE
Paddington Station
Hilton London Paddington Hotel
Paddington
WINSLAND STREET
WINSLAND MEWS
LONDON ST
LONDON MEWS
SUSSEX GARDENS
BISHOP'S BRIDGE ROAD
A4205
EASTBOURNE TERRACE
EASTBOURNE MEWS
WESTBOURNE TERRACE
GLOUCESTER TERRACE
CHILWORTH STREET
CHILWORTH MEWS
ORSETT TERRACE
PORCHESTER SQUARE
GLOUCESTER GDNS
CLEVELAND TERRACE
CLEVELAND SQUARE
BRECON HOUSE
HALLFIELD
Hallfield Jun & Inf Sch
LEINSTER GDNS
QUEEN'S GARDENS
CRAVEN ROAD
CRAVEN HILL
CRAVEN HILL GDNS
DEVONSHIRE TERR
UPBROOK MEWS
GLOUCESTER MEWS
SPRING ST
CONDUIT MEWS
TALBOT SQUARE
A4209
B410
SUSSEX PLACE
RADNOR MEWS
BATHURST MEWS
HYDE PARK
Bayswater
St James' & St Michael's CE Sch
WESTBOURNE CRES
INVERNESS TERRACE

A
B
C
D
230
W8
(Regent's Canal)
Boating Lake
The Holme
Tenn Cts
NW1
6
5
4
3
2
1
W1
W2
Lisson Green
Lisson Grove
London Business Sch
Coll
Sherlock Holmes Mus
Marylebone Station
Marylebone
Baker Street
Alfie's Antq Mkt
Univ of Westminster
Sylvia Young Theatre Sch
St Edward's RC Prim Sch
Francis Holland CE Sch
Govt Offices
The Charter Nightingale Hosp
The Landmark Hotel
The Western Eye Hosp
Samaritan Hosp for Women
North Westminster Com Sch
Edgware Rd (Bakerloo)
Edgware Road
Marylebone Flyover
Courts
Liby
L Ctr
Hampden Gurney CE Prim Sch
West London Synagogue
West End Great Synagogue
Courtauld Inst of Art
Cumberland Hotel
Marble Arch
Tyburn Tree (site of)
SWITZERLAND
SWEDEN
TONGA
ANGOLA
LITHUANIA
KYRGYZSTAN
HONDURAS
SEYCHELLES
SRI LANKA
BRAZIL
LISSON GROVE
ROSSMORE ROAD
PARK ROAD
MARYLEBONE ROAD
EDGWARE ROAD
OLD MARYLEBONE ROAD
GLOUCESTER PLACE
BAKER STREET
CRAWFORD STREET
GEORGE STREET
SEYMOUR STREET
SEYMOUR PLACE
UPPER BERKELEY STREET
CONNAUGHT STREET
HYDE PARK CRESCENT
HYDE PARK SQ
MARBLE ARCH
CUMBERLAND GATE
OUTER CIRCLE
A41
A40
A5
A501
A4205
A4209
A5204
A404
B507
B524
247
238
27
28
81
82

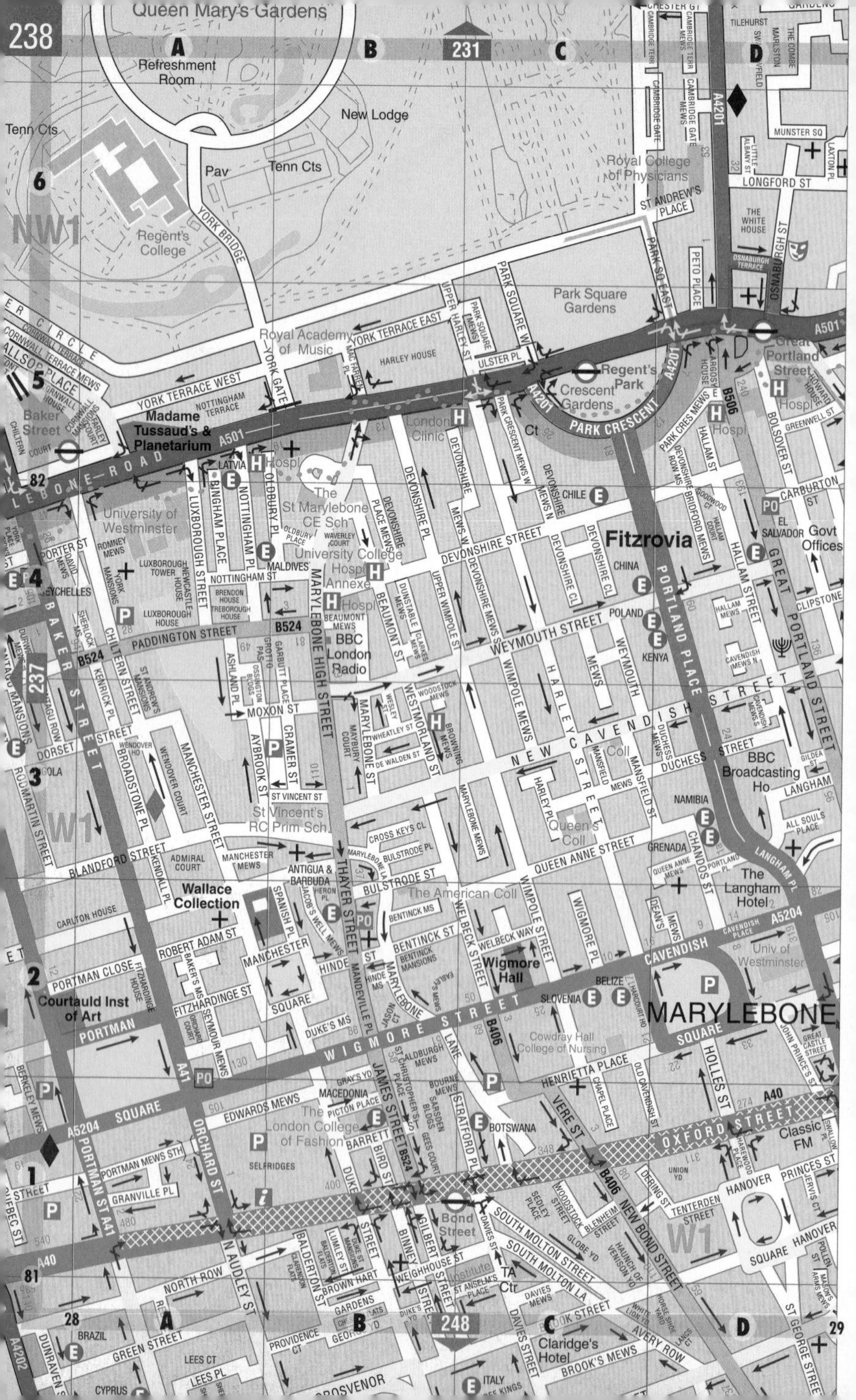

Queen Mary's Gardens
A
B
231
C
D
Refreshment Room
New Lodge
Tenn Cts
Pav
Tenn Cts
6
NW1
Regent's College
YORK BRIDGE
CAMBRIDGE TERR
CAMBRIDGE TERR MEWS
CAMBRIDGE GATE
CAMBRIDGE GATE MEWS
TILEHURST
MARLSTON
THE COMBE
A4201
MUNSTER SQ
LITTLE ALBANY ST
LAXTON PL
Royal College of Physicians
LONGFORD ST
ST ANDREW'S PLACE
THE WHITE HOUSE
OSNABURGH ST
OSNABURGH TERRACE
PARK SQ EAST
PETO PLACE
Park Square Gardens
PARK SQUARE W
UPPER HARLEY ST
PARK SQUARE MEWS
Royal Academy of Music
YORK TERRACE EAST
HARLEY HOUSE
ULSTER PL
A501
Great Portland Street
Regent's Park
Crescent Gardens
PARK CRESCENT
5
YORK TERRACE WEST
NOTTINGHAM TERRACE
YORK GATE
MAC FARREN PL
Madame Tussaud's & Planetarium
Baker Street
CORNWALL TERRACE
CORNWALL TERRACE MEWS
ALLSOP PLACE
CORNWALL MANSIONS
CHILTERN COURT
82
MARYLEBONE ROAD
London Clinic
Hospl
LATVIA
BINGHAM PLACE
NOTTINGHAM PL
OLDBURY PL
The St Marylebone CE Sch
DEVONSHIRE PLACE MEWS
DEVONSHIRE PL
DEVONSHIRE MEWS W
PARK CRESCENT MEWS W
DEVONSHIRE MEWS N
Ct
CHILE
ARGOSY HOUSE
PARK CRES MEWS E
B506
HALLAM ST
DEVONSHIRE ROW MS
BRIDFORD MEWS
GOODWOOD CT
HALLAM COURT
Hospl
BOLSOVER ST
GREENWELL ST
CARBURTON ST
PO
EL SALVADOR
Govt Offices
University of Westminster
PORTER ST
DAVID MEWS
ROMNEY MEWS
YORK MANSIONS
LUXBOROUGH TOWER
NEWCASTLE HOUSE
LUXBOROUGH STREET
NOTTINGHAM ST
MALDIVES
OLDBURY PLACE
WAVERLEY COURT
University College Hospl Annexe
Hospl
DEVONSHIRE STREET
Fitzrovia
DEVONSHIRE CL
CHINA
PORTLAND PLACE
4
SEYCHELLES
BRENDON HOUSE
TREBOROUGH HOUSE
LUXBOROUGH HOUSE
MARYLEBONE HIGH STREET
BEAUMONT MEWS
DUNSTABLE MEWS
CLARKES MEWS
BEAUMONT ST
UPPER WIMPOLE ST
DEVONSHIRE MEWS S
WEYMOUTH STREET
POLAND
KENYA
HALLAM MEWS
HALLAM STREET
CLIPSTONE
GREAT PORTLAND STREET
SHERLOCK MEWS
CHILTERN STREET
PADDINGTON STREET
B524
BBC London Radio
GARBUTT PLACE
GROTTO PAS
OSSINGTON BLDGS
ASHLAND PL
CAVENDISH MEWS N
BAKER STREET
237
KENRICK PL
ST ANDREW'S MANSIONS
WESLEY ST
WESTMORLAND STREET
WOODSTOCK MEWS
WIMPOLE MEWS
HARLEY STREET
WEYMOUTH MEWS
NEW CAVENDISH STREET
CAVENDISH MEWS S
MONTAGU MANSIONS
MONTAGU ROW
DORSET STREET
WENDOVER HO
BROADSTONE PL
WENDOVER COURT
MANCHESTER STREET
MOXON ST
AYBROOK ST
CRAMER ST
MARYLEBONE ST
MAYBURY COURT
WHEATLEY ST
DE WALDEN ST
BROWNING MEWS
MANSFIELD MEWS
DUCHESS MEWS
DUCHESS STREET
Coll
MANSFIELD STREET
BBC Broadcasting Ho
GILDEA ST
LANGHAM
3
W1
RODMARTIN STREET
ST VINCENT ST
St Vincent's RC Prim Sch
MARYLEBONE MEWS
HARLEY PL
Queen's Coll
NAMIBIA
ALL SOULS PLACE
CROSS KEYS CL
MARYLEBONE LA
BULSTRODE PL
QUEEN ANNE STREET
GRENADA
CHANDOS ST
PORTLAND PL
LANGHAM PL
BLANDFORD STREET
ADMIRAL COURT
KENDALL PL
MANCHESTER MEWS
ANTIGUA & BARBUDA
HERON PL
BULSTRODE ST
QUEEN ANNE MEWS
The Langham Hotel
Wallace Collection
CARLTON HOUSE
SPANISH PL
JACOB'S WELL MEWS
THAYER STREET
PO
The American Coll
BENTINCK MS
WIMPOLE STREET
WIGMORE PL
DEAN'S MEWS
CAVENDISH PLACE
A5204
ROBERT ADAM ST
MANCHESTER SQUARE
HINDE ST
BENTINCK ST
BENTINCK MANSIONS
WELBECK WAY
WELBECK STREET
Wigmore Hall
CAVENDISH
Univ of Westminster
2
PORTMAN CLOSE
FITZHARDINGE HOUSE
BAKER'S MS
HINDE MS
EASLEY'S MEWS
MARYLEBONE LANE
BELIZE
P
Courtauld Inst of Art
FITZHARDINGE ST
SEYMOUR MEWS
ORCHARD COURT
JASON CT
SLOVENIA
HARCOURT HO
MARYLEBONE
PORTMAN
DUKE'S MS
MANDEVILLE PL
WIGMORE STREET
B406
Cowdray Hall College of Nursing
SQUARE
HOLLES ST
JOHN PRINCE'S ST
GREAT CASTLE STREET
BERKELEY MEWS
PO
ALDBURGH MEWS
ST CHRISTOPHER'S PLACE
BOURNE MEWS
HENRIETTA PLACE
CHAPEL PLACE
OLD CAVENDISH ST
A40
GRAY'S YD
MACEDONIA
PICTON PLACE
EDWARDS MEWS
SQUARE
A41
ORCHARD ST
The London College of Fashion
JAMES STREET
SARSDEN BLDGS
STRATFORD PL
BOTSWANA
VERE ST
OXFORD STREET
Classic FM
SWALLOW PL
A5204
PORTMAN ST
SELFRIDGES
BARRETT ST
BIRD ST
GEES COURT
B524
HAREWOOD PLACE
UNION YD
HANOVER
PRINCES ST
JERVIS CT
1
PORTMAN MEWS STH
GRANVILLE PL
DUKE ST
Bond Street
DAVIES ST
SEDLEY PLACE
WOODSTOCK STREET
GLOBE YD
BLENHEIM STREET
B406
NEW BOND STREET
DERING ST
TENTERDEN STREET
W1
HANOVER SQUARE
QUEBEC ST
A40
N AUDLEY ST
BALDERTON ST
LUMLEY ST
DUKE ST MANSIONS
GILBERT ST
BINNEY ST
SOUTH MOLTON STREET
SOUTH MOLTON LA
HAUNCH OF VENISON YD
POLLEN ST
MASON'S ARMS MEWS
81
NORTH ROW
CLARENDON FLATS
BALDERTON FLATS
BROWN HART GARDENS
WEIGHHOUSE ST
Institute
ST ANSELM'S PLACE
TA Ctr
DAVIES MEWS
WHITE LION YD
HORSESHOE YARD
LANCASHIRE CT
28
A
B
248
C
D
29
BRAZIL
GREEN STREET
PROVIDENCE CT
DUKE'S YD
BROOK STREET
Claridge's Hotel
BROOK'S MEWS
AVERY ROW
ST GEORGE STREET
A4202
DUNRAVEN ST
LEES CT
LEES PL
CYPRUS
GROSVENOR
ITALY
DAVIES STREET

232
249
240
A
B
C
D
6
5
4
3
2
1
29
30
81
82
Euston Road
Euston Square
Euston Underpass
Euston Twr
Warren Street
Univ of Westminster
Regent's Pl
Triton Sq
Drummond
Tolmers Sq
Foundry Mews
Gower Street
Gower Place
Gower Ct
Stephenson Way
Euston Street
Regnart Bldgs
Govt Offices
Endsleigh Gardens
Endsleigh St
Endsleigh Place
Taviton Street
Gordon Street
Gordon Square
Gordon Square Gdn
Tavistock Square
Tavistock Square Gdn
Tavistock Ct
Upper Woburn Place
Woburn Wlk
Burton Street
Burton Pl
Cartwright Gdns
Flaxman
Duke's Rd
Leonard Ct
Thackeray Ho
Dickens Ho
Coram Ho
Bedford Way
Woburn Square
Torrington Square
Thornhaugh St
Russell Square
Bloomsbury
A4200
Montague Place
Keppel St
Malet Street
Malet Pl
Byng Pl
University College London
Royal Academy of Dramatic Art
RADA
Beaumont Place
Univ Coll Hospl
Elizabeth Garrett Anderson Hospl
Grafton Way
Paramount Ct
University St
Huntley Street
Chenies Mews
Chenies Street
Ridgmount Gdns
Ridgmount Street
Ridgmount Pl
Rosetti Ct
Torrington Place
Mullard Ho
Brock Ho
Tottenham Court Road
A400
Goodge Street
Goodge St A5204
Capper St
Mortimer Market
Shropshire Pl
Queen's Yd
Cypress Pl
Howland Mews E
Howland St
Whitfield St
Whitfield Gdns
Chitty St
Charlotte Mews
Charlotte St
Alfred Ms
Alfred Place
North Cres
South Cr
Store Street
Gower Mews
Tottenham St
Scala St
Kirkman Pl
Bedford Square
Bayley St
B506
Morwell Street
Time Out Magazine
Adeline Pl
Bedford Avenue
Bedford Court Mansions
Bloomsbury Street
British Museum
Great Russell St
Dyott St
Streatham St
Bainbridge St
St Giles' Circus
Barbados
A40
Bucknall
Earnshaw St
Andrew Borde St
St Giles High St
St Giles Ct
Centre Point
Tottenham Court Road
Fitzroy Street
Fitzroy Sq
Fitzroy Ms
Warren Ms
Conway St
Conway Mews
Richardson's Mews
Croatia
Mozambique
St Luke's Hospl
London Foot Hospl
Maple St
Maple Pl
Hertford Pl
Midford Pl
Irvine Ct
Cleveland Street
Cleveland Mews
Clipstone Mews
Holcroft Court
Grafton Way
Brom Ley Pl
BT Tower
University College London
Middlesex Hospl Annexe
Sch of Nursing
All Souls Sch
Middlesex Hospl
Hanson Street
Ogle Street
Foley Street
Candover St
Riding House Street
Nassau St
Bourlet Cl
Great Titchfield St
Gosfield St
Middleton Bldgs
Little Titchfield St
Bywell Pl
Mortimer St
Goodge Pl
Colville Pl
Windmill St
Charlotte Place
Rathbone St
Percy Pas
Percy Street
Percy Mews
Stephen Ms
Stephen St
Gresse St
Birkbeck Coll
Newman Pas
Newman Street
Berners Mews
Berners St
Berners Pl
Wells Street
Wells Mews
Booth's Pl
Law Ct
Liby
Little Portland St
Elsalvador
Margaret Street
Margaret Court
Marylebone Passage
Turkmenistan
Eastcastle Street
Adam and Eve Ct
Winsley St
Market Place
Great Castle St
Rathbone Pl
Evelyn Yd
Hanway Pl
Hanway Street
Perry's Pl
Talk Radio Ltd
Oxford Street
Oxford Circus
Sierra Leone
Oxford Circus Ave
Hills Pl
Ramillies Place
Ramillies St
Argyll St
Little Argyll Street
Great Marlborough Street
Regent Street
A4201
Maddox St
B406
Little Marlborough St
Foubert's Place
Newburgh St
Carnaby Street
Ganton St
Kingly Street
Kingly Ct
Marshall Street
Beak Street
Upper James St
Tenison Ct
New Brlgtn Pl
Poland Street
Noel St
D'Arblay St
Portland Mews
Berwick Street
Livonia St
Sandringham Ct
Dufour's Pl
Broadwick St
Ingestre Place
Lexington St
Silver Pl
Hopkins St
Kemp's Ct
Wardour Street
Wardour Mews
Hollen St
Great Chapel St
Fareham St
Diadem Ct
Sheraton St
Carlisle St
St Anne's Ct
Flaxman Ct
Duck La
Richmond Bldgs
Richmond Mews
Dean Street
Meard St
Soho
Soho Square
Soho St
Falcon Ct
Bateman's Bldgs
Bateman St
Chapone Pl
Royalty Mews
Greek St
Frith St
Manette St
Goslett Yard
Orange Yd
Sutton Row
Denmark Pl
Denmark St
Flitcroft St
Phoenix St
Stacey St
Sch of Art and Design
Charing Cross Road
Cambridge Circus
Moor St
Old Compton Street
Romilly St
Bourchier St
Chancel Ct
Shaftesbury Avenue
Gerrard Pl
Newport Pl
Newport Ct
Horse and Dolphin Yd
Great Newport St
Litchfield Street
Sandringham Flats
West St
Tower St
Seven Dials
Monmouth Street
Upper St Martin's Lane
Shaftesbury Ave
New Compton St
St Giles Pas
Pendrell Ho
B404
Westminster
Soho Parish
Great Pulteney
Peter Street
Green's Ct
Walker's Ct
Winnett St
Globe Ct
Berwick Street
Govt

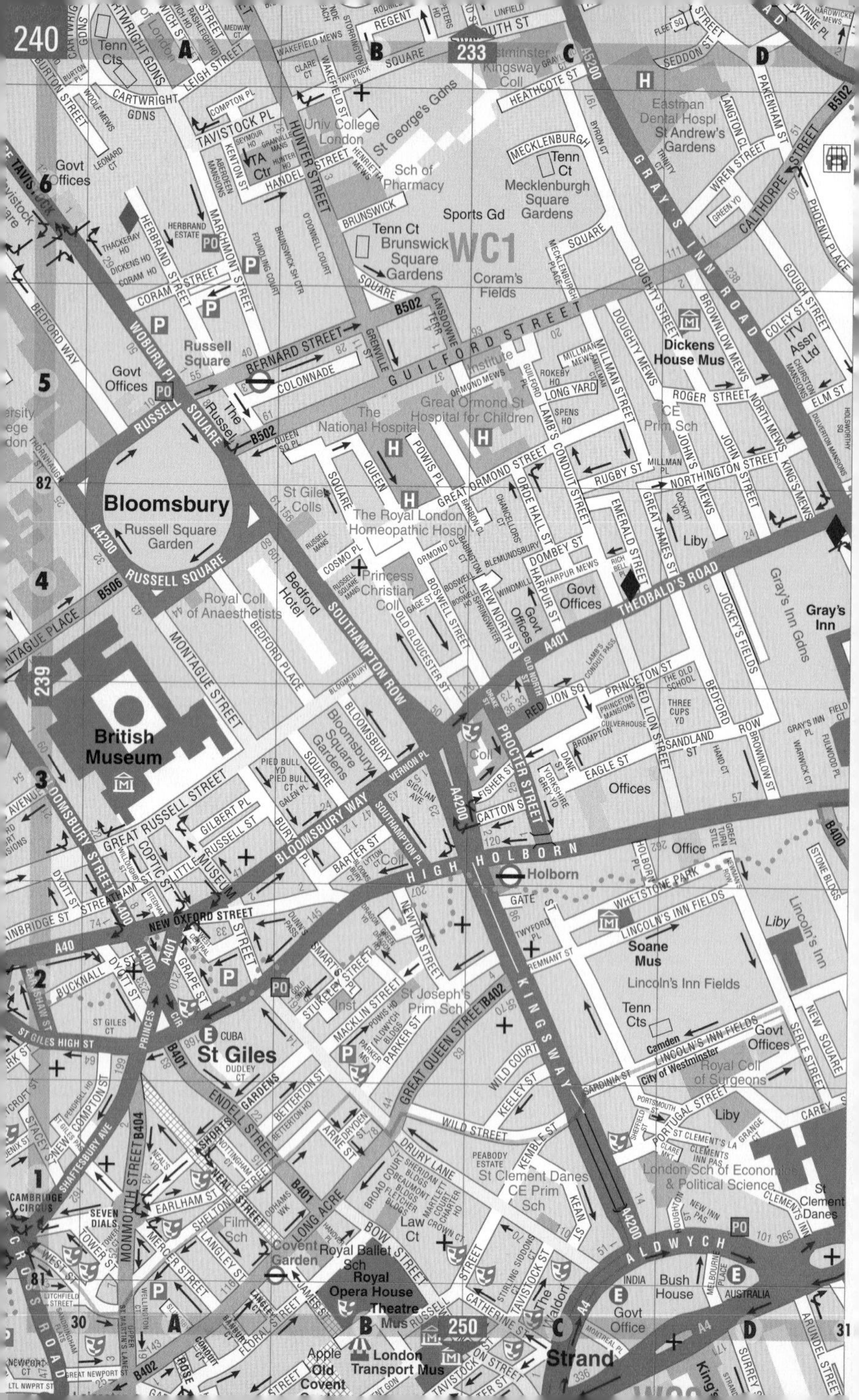

233
A
B
C
D
1
2
3
4
5
6
Tenn Cts
Cartwright Gdns
Burton Street
Leigh Street
Regent Square
Wakefield Mews
Wakefield St
Tavistock Pl
Compton Pl
Kingsway Coll
Heathcote St
Hunter Street
Univ College London
St George's Gdns
Sch of Pharmacy
Handel Street
Henrietta Mews
Brunswick
Kenton St
Marchmont Street
Herbrand Street
Herbrand Estate
Thackeray Ho
Dickens Ho
Coram Ho
Govt Offices
Tavistock Square
Bedford Way
Woburn Pl
Coram Street
Foundling Court
Brunswick Sh Ctr
O'Donnell Court
Tenn Ct
Brunswick Square Gardens
Sports Gd
WC1
Coram's Fields
Mecklenburgh
Mecklenburgh Square Gardens
Mecklenburgh Place
Square
Gray's Inn Road
Eastman Dental Hospl
St Andrew's Gardens
Seddon St
Fleet Sq
Pakenham St
Langton Cl
Wren Street
Calthorpe Street
Phoenix Place
Gough Street
Coley St
ITV Assn Ltd
Green Yd
Doughty Street
Doughty Mews
Dickens House Mus
Brownlow Mews
John Street
John's Mews
Roger Street
North Mews
Elm St
Guilford Street
Bernard Street
Colonnade
Grenville St
Lansdowne Terr
Russell Square
The Russell
Institute
Ormond Mews
Great Ormond St Hospital for Children
The National Hospital
Queen Sq Pl
Queen Square
Powis Pl
Great Ormond Street
Millman Mews
Millman Street
Rokeby Ho
Long Yard
Spens Ho
Lamb's Conduit Street
Guilford Pl
CE Prim Sch
Rugby St
Millman Pl
Northington Street
King's Mews
Cockpit Yd
Great James St
Liby
Orde Hall St
Chancellors Ct
Emerald Street
Dombey St
Blemundsbury
Harpur Mews
Harpur St
Govt Offices
Rich Bell Pl
Theobald's Road
Jockey's Fields
Gray's Inn Gdns
Gray's Inn
Bloomsbury
Russell Square Garden
A4200
B506
B502
St Giles Colls
The Royal London Homeopathic Hospl
Cosmo Pl
Russell Mans
Princess Christian Coll
Ormond Cl
Barbon Cl
Babington Ct
Boswell Ct
Boswell Street
Gage St
Old Gloucester St
New North St
Windmill
Springwater
Govt Offices
Bedford Hotel
Royal Coll of Anaesthetists
Southampton Row
Montague Place
Montague Street
Bedford Place
239
British Museum
Thornhaugh
82
Bloomsbury Pl
Bloomsbury Square Gardens
Bloomsbury Square
A401
Old North St
Lamb's Conduit Pass
Red Lion Sq
Drake St
Princeton St
The Old School
Three Cups Yd
Princeton Mansions
Culverhouse
Red Lion Street
Bedford Row
Brownlow St
Sandland St
Hand Ct
Brompton
Dane St
Eagle St
Offices
Procter Street
Yorkshire Grey Yd
Fisher St
Catton St
Gray's Inn Pl
Field Ct
Warwick Ct
Fulwood Pl
B400
Great Russell Street
Gilbert Pl
Russell St
Little Russell St
Museum Street
Coptic St
Willoughby St
Pied Bull Yd
Pied Bull Ct
Galen Pl
Bury Pl
Bloomsbury Way
Vernon Pl
Sicilian Ave
Southampton Pl
Barter St
Lytton Ct
Bloomsbury Ct
Coll
High Holborn
Holborn
Holborn Pl
Great Turnstile
Office
Stone Bldgs
Whetstone Park
Newman's Row
Lincoln's Inn Fields
Soane Mus
Lincoln's Inn
Liby
Gate St
Twyford Pl
Remnant St
Kingsway
Bloomsbury Street
Streatham St
Dyott St
Avenue
Stedham Pl
New Oxford Street
Dunn's Pass
West Central St
Grape St
Bucknall St
Shaftesbury Ave
Earnshaw St
A40
A400
St Giles Ct
St Giles High St
St Giles Cir
Princes Cir
CUBA
St Giles
Dudley Ct
Endell Street
Gardens
Betterton St
Betterton Ho
Smart's Pl
Stukeley Street
Gold Smith Pl
Inst
Macklin Street
Powis Ho
Aldwych Bldgs
Parker St
Parker Ms
St Joseph's Prim Sch
Great Queen Street
B402
B401
Newton Street
Dragon Yd
Wild Court
Keeley St
Sardinia St
Tenn Cts
Camden
City of Westminster
Lincoln's Inn Fields
Govt Offices
Royal Coll of Surgeons
New Square
Serle Street
Carey St
Portugal Street
Portsmouth St
Sheffield St
St Clement's La
Grange Ct
Clements Inn Pas
Clare Mkt
London Sch of Economics & Political Science
Houghton St
New Inn Pas
St Clement Danes
Clements Inn
Wild Street
Kemble St
Peabody Estate
St Clement Danes CE Prim Sch
Kean St
Drury Lane
Sheridan Bldgs
Beaumont Bldgs
Fletcher Bldgs
Martlett Ct
Charter Ho
Broad Court
Law Ct
Crown Ct
Arne St
Dryden St
Shorts Gardens
Nottingham Ct
Neal's Yd
Neal Street
Earlham St
Shelton St
Film Sch
Langley St
Mercer Street
Monmouth Street
B404
Tower St
Seven Dials
Cambridge Circus
Charing Cross Road
Stacey St
New Compton St
Pendrell Ho
Flitcroft St
Phoenix St
West St
Litchfield Street
Odhams Wk
Long Acre
Covent Garden
Royal Ballet Sch
Royal Opera House
Bow Street
Hanover Pl
James St
Floral Street
Langley Ct
Banbury Ct
Conduit Ct
Rose St
Garrick
Wellington Ct
Upper St Martin's Lane
Earlham Pl
Newport Ct
Great Newport St
Ltl Nwprt St
Theatre Mus
Russell
250
Apple
Old Covent
London Transport Mus
Tavistock St
Catherine St
Stirling Siddons Ct
The Waldorf
Strand
Aldwych
India
Bush House
Melbourne Place
Australia
Govt Office
A4
A4200
Montreal Pl
Surrey St
Arundel St
King's
30
31
81
A5200
B502

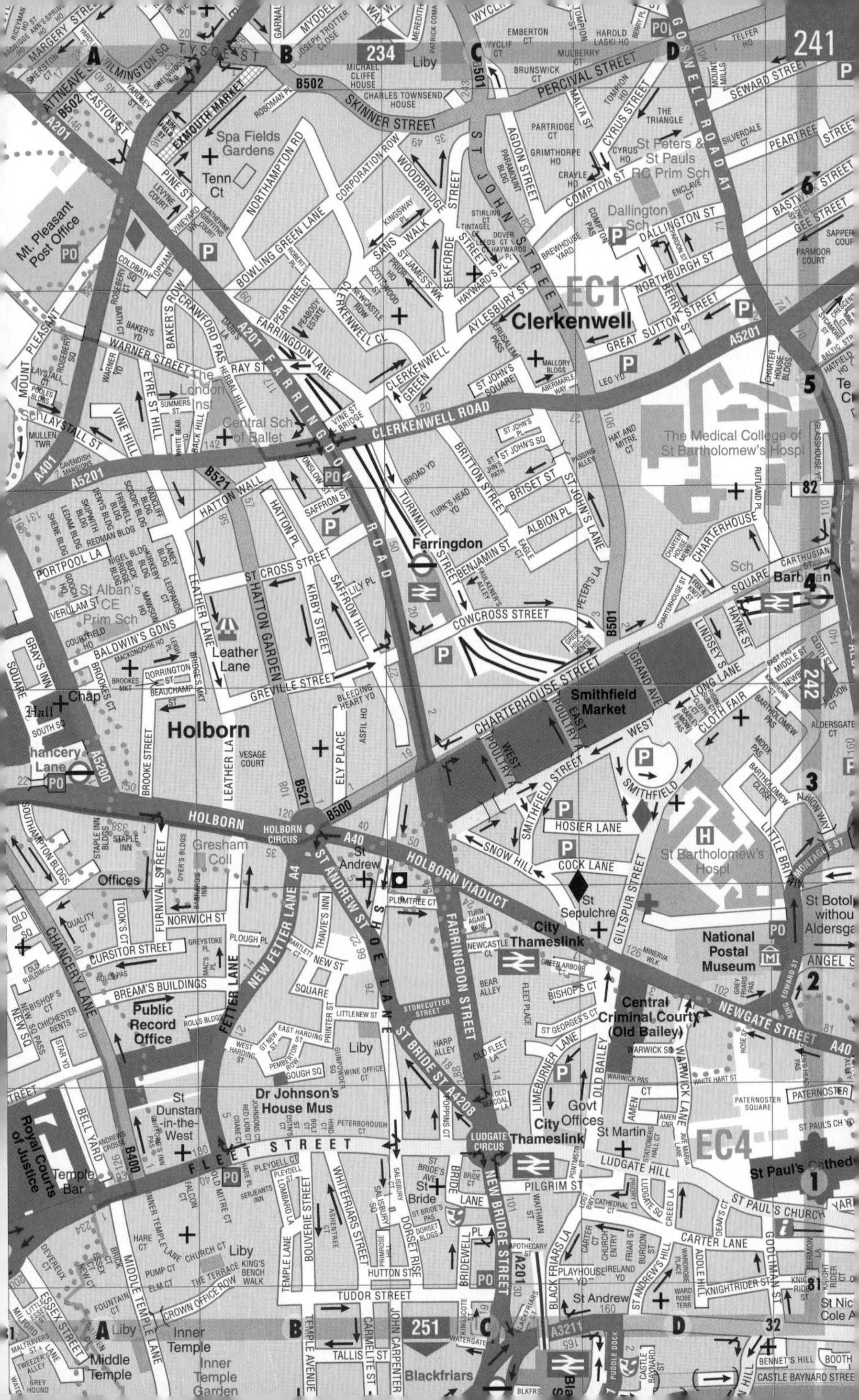
234
242
251
A
B
C
D
1
2
3
4
5
6
Liby
Mt. Pleasant Post Office
Spa Fields Gardens
Tenn Ct
Exmouth Market
Wilmington Sq
Tysoe St
Margery Street
Attneave St
Easton St
Skinner Street
Percival Street
Goswell Road A1
Seward Street
Peartree Street
Compton St
Cyrus Street
St Peters & St Pauls RC Prim Sch
Dallington Sch
Dallington St
Northburgh St
Great Sutton Street
Bastwick Street
Gee Street
St John Street
Agdon Street
Sekforde Street
Woodbridge Street
Corporation Row
Northampton Rd
Bowling Green Lane
Farringdon Lane
Farringdon Road
Clerkenwell Green
Clerkenwell Road
Clerkenwell
EC1
St John's Square
St John's Lane
Britton Street
Briset St
Albion Pl
Turnmill Street
Farringdon
Cowcross Street
Charterhouse Street
Charterhouse Square
Charterhouse
The Medical College of St Bartholomew's Hospl
Barbican
Smithfield Market
Grand Ave
West Poultry Ave
East Poultry Ave
Long Lane
Cloth Fair
Smithfield
Smithfield Street
Hosier Lane
Cock Lane
Snow Hill
St Bartholomew's Hospl
Little Britain
Montague St
Aldersgate St
St Botolph without Aldersgate
National Postal Museum
Angel St
King Edward St
Newgate Street
A40
Central Criminal Court (Old Bailey)
Old Bailey
Warwick Lane
Paternoster Square
St Paul's Cathedral
St Paul's Church Yard
EC4
Ludgate Hill
Ludgate Circus
City Thameslink
St Sepulchre
Giltspur Street
Holborn Viaduct
Holborn
Holborn Circus
St Andrew
Farringdon Street
New Bridge Street
Fleet Street
Shoe Lane
St Andrew St
St Bride St
New Fetter Lane
Fetter Lane
Chancery Lane
Gray's Inn Square
Hatton Garden
Hatton Wall
Leather Lane
Saffron Hill
Kirby Street
Greville Street
St Cross Street
Baldwin's Gdns
Brooke Street
Gresham Coll
Offices
Public Record Office
Dr Johnson's House Mus
St Dunstan-in-the-West
Royal Courts of Justice
Temple Bar
Middle Temple
Inner Temple
Middle Temple Lane
Temple Avenue
John Carpenter St
Tudor Street
Bride Lane
St Bride
Pilgrim St
Black Friars La
Carter Lane
Creed La
Ave Maria Lane
Queen Victoria St
Blackfriars
Puddle Dock
Castle Baynard Street
Bennet's Hill
Godliman St
Knightrider St
Warner Street
Ray St
Rosebery Av
Mount Pleasant
Laystall St
Vine Hill
Central Sch of Ballet
The London Inst
Eyre St Hill
Crawford Pas
Baker's Row
Clerkenwell Cl
Aylesbury St
Hayward's Pl
Mallory Bldgs
Peter's La
Lindsey St
Hayne St
Rutland Pl
Glasshouse Yd
St Alban's CE Prim Sch
Portpool La
Verulam St
Holborn
Southampton Bldgs
Furnival Street
Norwich St
Cursitor Street
Bream's Buildings
Plough Pl
New St Square
Stonecutter Street
Old Fleet La
Limeburner Lane
Govt Offices
St Martin
Warwick Sq
Bishop's Ct
Bell Yard
Essex Street
Devereux Ct
Crown Office Row
Hare Ct
Bouverie Street
Whitefriars Street
Salisbury Sq
Dorset Rise
Hutton St
Carmelite St
Tallis St
Bridewell Pl
Apothecary St
Playhouse Yd
Ireland Yd
St Andrew's Hill
Wardrobe Terr
Addle Hill
Dean's Ct

235
A
B
C
D
CITY CENTRAL EST
SEWARD STREET
PATON ST
NORMAN ST
RADNOR STREET
GALWAY ST
GRAYSON HO
IRONMONGER ROW
L Ctr
HELMET ROW
IRONMONGER PAS
LIZARD ST
COPE HO
BARTHOLOMEW SQ
BARTHOLOMEW CT
GODFREY HO
PATERSON CT
BALDWIN
CRANWOOD ST
GADDESDEN HO
KENSWORTH CT
CHAULDEN HO
VINCE ST
Old Street
Old Street
STREET
COWPER STREET
Central Foundation Sch
City Ct
LEONARD
KIFFEN ST
CLERE PL
CLERE ST
OLIVER'S YARD
PLATINA ST
EPWORTH ST
TABERNACLE STREET
BONHILL ST
Govt Offices
TRITON COURT
FINSBURY
CHRISTOPHER
Bwg Gn
SQUARE
SUN
LACKINGTON ST
WHITECROSS PL
WILSON STREET
DOMINION ST
SOUTH PL
FINSBURY AVENUE
ELDON ST
SOUTH PL MS
FINSBURY
Bndstd
Bwg Gn
London Metropolitan Univ
CIRCUS
BROAD ST PLACE
BLOMFIELD ST
A1211
LONDON WALL
PEARTREE STREET
SILVERDALE CT
MITCHELL STREET
STREET
ST LUKE'S CL
VICKERY CT
STEADMAN CT
NEWLAND CT
PO
OLD
MALLOW ST
MARTHA'S BLDGS
A5201
ROBY HO
PRIESTLEY HO
WENLAKE HO
AMIAS HO
ANCHOR HO
TILNEY CT
St Luke's
BASTWICK STREET
GEE STREET
COTSWOLD COURT
SAPPERTON COURT
PARMOOR COURT
WITHERS PL
FEATHERSTONE STREET
Moorfields Prim Sch
Burial Ground
John Wesley's House & Museum
BUNHILL ROW
CITY ROAD
A501
GARRETT ST
NAGS HEAD CT
BANNER STREET
QUAKER CT
ROSCOE ST
BANNER HO
PEABODY ESTATE
CHEQUER ST
CHEQUER ST
DUFFERIN AVE
DUFFERIN STREET
DUFFERIN CT
ALLEYN HO
The London Inst
BALTIC STREET EAST
BALTIC STREET WEST
CRESCENT ROW
MEMEL ST
Richard Cloudesley Sch
Tenn Cts
BASTERFIELD HO
BAYER HO
GREAT ARTHUR HO
CUTHBERT HARROWING HO
BOWATER HO
FANN ST
GOLDEN LANE
PEABODY CT
PEABODY EST
PEABODY TWR
ST MARY'S TWR
FORTUNE HO
FORTUNE ST
WHITECROSS STREET
ERROL STREET
LAMB'S BLDGS
LAMB'S PAS
WHITBREAD CTR
CHERRY TREE WLK
Prior Weston Prim Sch
SUTTONS WAY
GAVRELLE HOUSE
Playing Field (HAC Ground)
B144
Medical College of St Bartholomew's Hospl
GLASSHOUSE YD
CHARTERHOUSE BLDGS
RUTLAND PL
CHARTERHOUSE SQUARE
CARTHUSIAN ST
Barbican
Sch
BUNYAN CT
JOHN TRUNDLE CT
BRIDGEWATER SQ
BRACKLEY ST
CRIPPLEGATE ST
BRETON HO
VISCOUNT ST
BEECH STREET
B100
CROMWELL TOWER
CHISWELL STREET
SOUTH YD
MILTON ST
MOOR LA
FINSBURY ST
Islington
City of London
ROPEMAKER ST
FINSBURY PAVEMENT
Barbican Arts and Conference Centre
SHAKESPEARE TOWER
DEFOE PL
DEFOE HOUSE
Coroners Court
MILTON CT
SILK STREET
SPEED HO
LAUDERDALE TOWER
City of London Sch for Girls
Guildhall School of Music and Drama
SEDDON HOUSE
THOMAS MORE HOUSE
Barbican
St Giles Cripplegate
GILBERT HO
BRANDON MEWS
WILLOUGHBY HOUSE
ANDREWES HOUSE
MOOR LANE
NEW UNION ST
MOORFIELDS
MOORFIELDS HIGHWALK
Moorgate
MOUNTJOY HO
THE POSTERN
ALDERSGATE STREET
LINDSEY
HAYNE ST
EAST PAS
MIDDLE ST
CLOTH ST
NEWBURY ST
CLOTH FAIR
HALF MOON CT
BARTHOLOMEW PAS
ALDERSGATE ST
241
Museum of London
WALLSIDE
WOOD ST
FORE STREET
MONKWELL SQ
ST ALPHAGE HIGHWALK
ST ALPHAGE GDN
FORE ST AVE
KEATS PL
118
A1211
LONDON WALL
BASSISHAW HIGHWALK
MOORGATE
A501
ALBION WAY
LITTLE BRITAIN
BARTHOLOMEW CLOSE
MONTAGUE ST
Bartholomew's Hospl
H
St Botolph without Aldersgate
St Anne & St Agnes
NOBLE ST
OAT LA
STAINING LA
ADDLE ST
ALDERMANBURY SQ
BASINGHALL AVE
THREE NUN CT
BASINGHALL ST
WHITE HORSE YD
COLEMAN STREET
NUN CT
COLEMAN ST BLDGS
MOORGATE PL
LANG THORN CT
COPTHALL AVENUE
GT SWAN ALLEY
DRAPERS GDNS
THROGMORTON AVE
GREAT WINCHESTER ST
National Postal Museum
ANGEL ST
KING EDWARD ST
NEWGATE STREET
A40
ST MARTIN'S LE GRAND
A1
LOVE LANE
ALDERMANBURY
Guild Hall
Liby
St Lawrence Jewry
GRESHAM STREET
GUILDHALL YD
GUILDHALL BLDGS
MASON'S AVE
Law Court
COPTHALL CL
COPTHALL BLDGS
TELEGRAPH STREET
KING'S ARMS YD
AUSTIN FRIARS
AUSTIN FRIARS SQ
The Dutch Church
FOSTER LANE
CAREY LA
ROSE AND CROWN CT
PRIEST CT
GUTTER LA
WOOD
MILK STREET
MITRE CT
RUSSIA CT
RUSSIA ROW
LAWRENCE LA
TRUMP ST
KING ST
IRONMONGER LANE
ST OLAVE'S CT
OLD JEWRY
FRED ERICK'S PL
PRINCE'S STREET
FOUNDERS CT
TOKENHOUSE YD
LOTHBURY
St Margaret
THROGMORTON ST
OLD BROAD
Stock Exchange
Bank of England
BARTHOLOMEW LA
THREADNEEDLE STREET
Merchant Taylors Ha
St Paul's
St Vedast
GOLDSMITH ST
CHEAPSIDE
St Mary-le-Bow
HONEY LA
ROSE ST
WHITE HART ST
PATERNOSTER SQUARE
PATERNOSTER ROW
ST PAUL'S CH YD
EC4
St Paul's Cathedral
St Paul's Cath Sch
NEW CHANGE
BREAD ST
BOW CHURCHYARD
BOW LANE
CROWN CT
GROVELAND CT
WELL CT
POULTRY
GROCERS' HALL CT
ST MILDRED'S CT
MANSION HO ST
Royal Exchange
FINCH LANE
St Michael
CORNHILL
Mansion Ho
Bank
ST PAUL'S CHURCH YARD
WATLING STREET
PANCRAS LA
SISE LA
BUCKLERSBURY
St Mary Woolnoth
POPE'S HEAD ALLEY
CHANGE AL
COWPER'S CT
BIRCHIN LANE
BALL CT
CASTLE CT
BENGAL CT
ST MICHAEL'S ALLEY
ST PETER'S ALLEY
CORBET CT
BELL INN YD
St Edmund
GEORGE YD
LOMBARD STREET
ARTER LANE
DEAN'S CT
GODLIMAN ST
ADDLE HILL
KNIGHTRIDER ST
KNIGHT RIDER CT
SERMON LA
OLD CHANGE CT
DISTAFF LA
OLD FISH ST HILL
FRIDAY ST
WATLING CT
St Mary Aldermary
Mansion House
CANNON STREET
BUDGE ROW
WALBROOK
BOND CT
ST STEPHEN'S ROW
St Stephen Walbrook
ST SWITHIN'S LANE
SHERBOURNE LA
ABCHURCH LA
NICHOLAS PAS
NICHOLAS LANE
CLEMENT'S LANE
PLOUGH CT
GRACECHURCH
A10
St Nicholas Cole Abbey
QUEEN VICTORIA STREET
BREAD ST HILL
HUGGIN HILL
HUGGIN CT
LITTLE TRINITY LA
GT TRINITY LA
GARLICK HILL
GREAT ST THOMAS APOSTLE
QUEEN STREET
CLOAK LANE
DOBY CT
NEW CSTL CT
COLLEGE HILL
252
Cannon Street
ST MARY ABCHURCH
St Mary
KING WILLIAM
LOMBARD CT
ST CLEMENT'S CT
BENNET'S HILL
BOOTH LA
LAMBETH HILL
CASTLE BAYNARD STREET

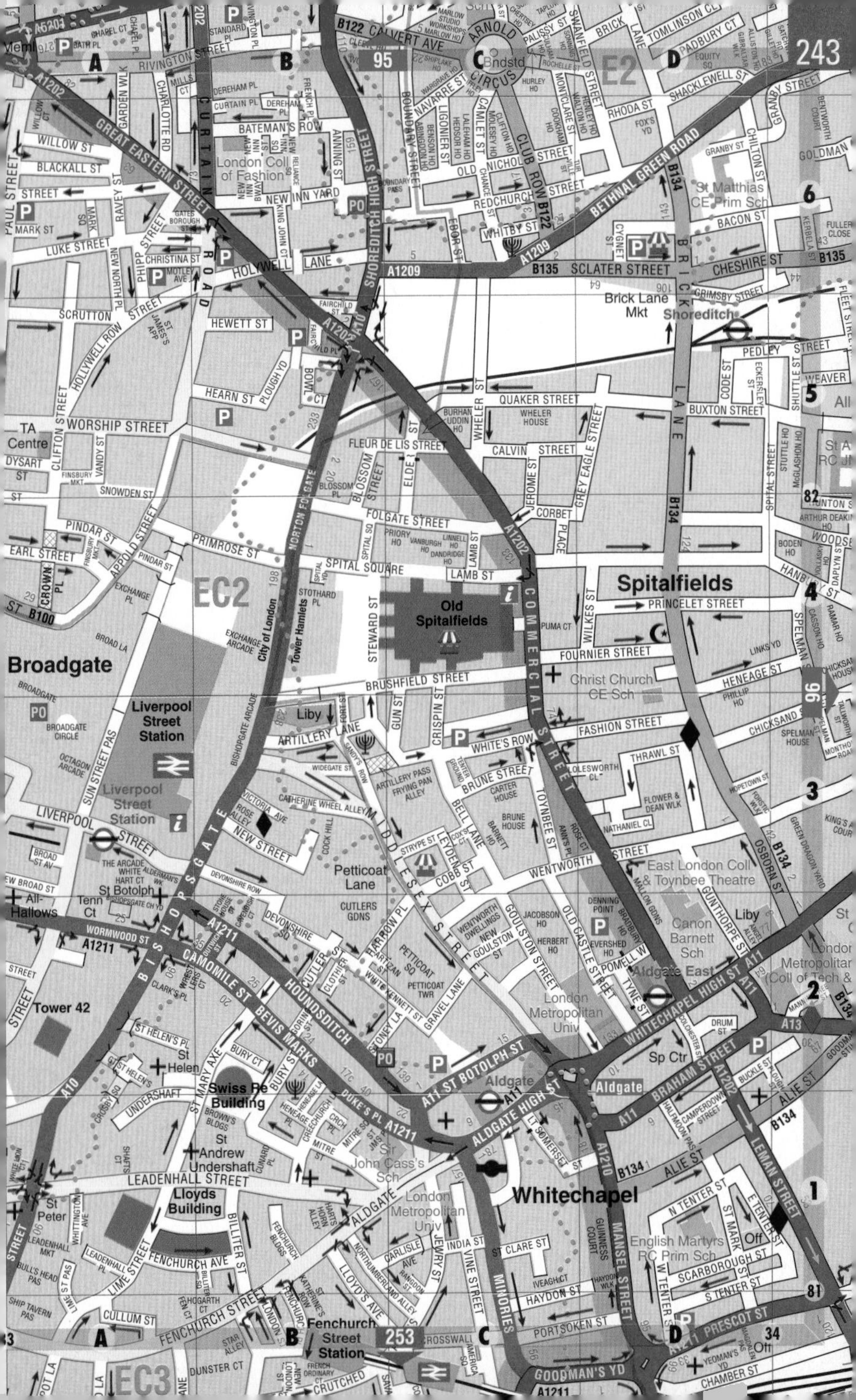

A
B
C
D
E2
95
6
5
4
3
2
1
96
81
82
253
EC2
EC3
RIVINGTON STREET
CALVERT AVE
ARNOLD CIRCUS
Bndstd
SWANFIELD STREET
BRICK LANE
TOMLINSON CL
PADBURY CT
SHACKLEWELL ST
GRANBY STREET
RHODA ST
FOX'S YD
BETHNAL GREEN ROAD
GREAT EASTERN STREET
CURTAIN ROAD
CHARLOTTE RD
GARDEN WALK
WILLOW ST
BLACKALL ST
PAUL STREET
MARK ST
LUKE STREET
RAVEY ST
PHIPP STREET
NEW NORTH PL
CHRISTINA ST
HOLYWELL LANE
BATEMAN'S ROW
London Coll of Fashion
NEW INN YARD
ANNING ST
SHOREDITCH HIGH STREET
BOUNDARY STREET
NAVARRE ST
LIGONIER ST
CAMLET ST
OLD NICHOL STREET
CLUB ROW
REDCHURCH STREET
WHITBY ST
A1209
B135
SCLATER STREET
CHESHIRE ST
BACON ST
St Matthias CE Prim Sch
Brick Lane Mkt
Shoreditch
GRIMSBY STREET
PEDLEY STREET
WEAVER
BUXTON STREET
QUAKER STREET
WHELER HOUSE
WHELER ST
CALVIN STREET
GREY EAGLE STREET
JEROME ST
CORBET PL
FOLGATE STREET
FLEUR DE LIS STREET
BLOSSOM STREET
ELDER ST
NORTON FOLGATE
SCRUTTON STREET
HOLLYWELL ROW
HEWETT ST
HEARN ST
PLOUGH YD
WORSHIP STREET
TA Centre
DYSART ST
CLIFTON STREET
VANDY ST
SNOWDEN ST
PINDAR ST
EARL STREET
APPOLD STREET
PRIMROSE ST
SPITAL SQUARE
LAMB ST
Old Spitalfields
COMMERCIAL STREET
Spitalfields
PRINCELET STREET
FOURNIER STREET
WILKES ST
PUMA CT
Christ Church CE Sch
HENEAGE ST
HANBURY ST
SPELMAN ST
Broadgate
BROADGATE CIRCLE
OCTAGON ARCADE
Liverpool Street Station
SUN STREET PAS
EXCHANGE ARCADE
City of London
Tower Hamlets
STEWARD ST
BRUSHFIELD STREET
Liby
ARTILLERY LANE
GUN ST
CRISPIN ST
WHITE'S ROW
FASHION STREET
THRAWL ST
CHICKSAND ST
BISHOPSGATE
BISHOPSGATE ARCADE
WIDEGATE ST
ARTILLERY PASS
FRYING PAN ALLEY
CATHERINE WHEEL ALLEY
BRUNE STREET
BELL LANE
TOYNBEE ST
FLOWER & DEAN WLK
NATHANIEL CL
OSBORN ST
LIVERPOOL STREET
NEW STREET
MIDDLESEX STREET
Petticoat Lane
WENTWORTH STREET
East London Coll & Toynbee Theatre
GUNTHORPE ST
Canon Barnett Sch
DEVONSHIRE SQ
St Botolph
All-Hallows
Tenn Ct
WORMWOOD ST
A1211
CAMOMILE ST
HOUNDSDITCH
BEVIS MARKS
CUTLER ST
HARROW PL
PETTICOAT SQ
GOULSTON STREET
OLD CASTLE STREET
London Metropolitan Univ
Aldgate East
WHITECHAPEL HIGH ST
A11
Tower 42
ST HELEN'S PL
St Helen
Swiss Re Building
ST MARY AXE
BURY ST
DUKE'S PL
ST BOTOLPH ST
Aldgate
ALDGATE HIGH ST
Sp Ctr
BRAHAM STREET
ALIE ST
LEMAN STREET
B134
UNDERSHAFT
St Andrew Undershaft
MITRE ST
Sir John Cass's Sch
LEADENHALL STREET
Lloyds Building
St Peter
LIME STREET
FENCHURCH AVE
BILLITER ST
ALDGATE
Whitechapel
MANSEL STREET
GUINNESS COURT
English Martyrs RC Prim Sch
SCARBOROUGH ST
S TENTER ST
N TENTER ST
PRESCOT ST
MINORIES
VINE STREET
JEWRY ST
ST CLARE ST
HAYDON ST
PORTSOKEN ST
CULLUM ST
FENCHURCH STREET
Fenchurch Street Station
CROSSWALL
LLOYD'S AVE
DUNSTER CT
CRUTCHED
GOODMAN'S YD
CHAMBER ST
A1210
A1202
A10

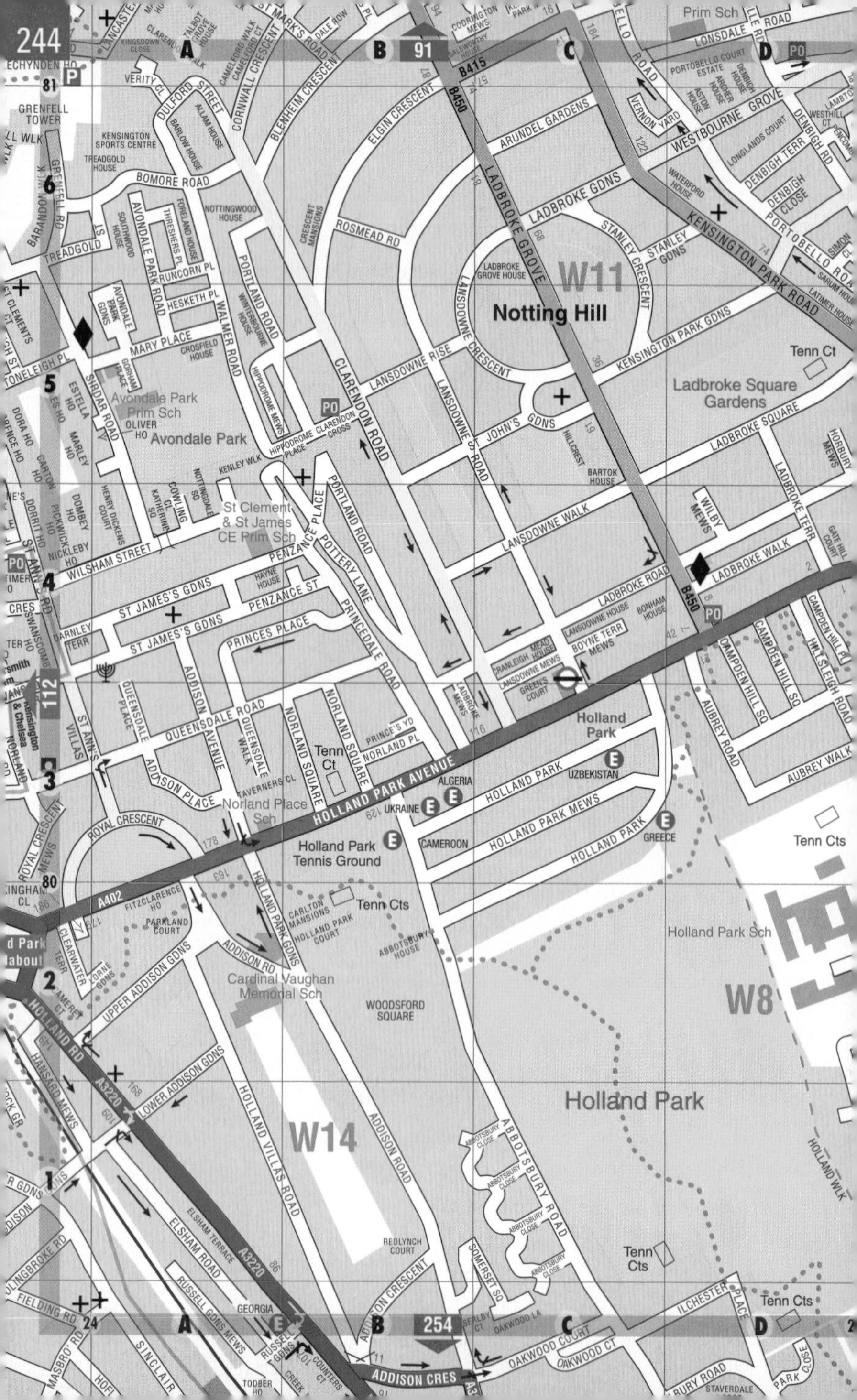
91
254
112
A
B
C
D
1
2
3
4
5
6
W11
Notting Hill
W14
W8
Holland Park
Holland Park Sch
Ladbroke Square Gardens
Tenn Ct
Tenn Cts
Prim Sch
Lonsdale Road
Portobello Court Estate
Archer House
Denbigh House
Aston House
Vernon Yard
Westbourne Grove
Longlands Court
Denbigh Terr
Denbigh Rd
Denbigh Close
Waterford House
Kensington Park Road
Portobello Road
Westhill Ct
Lambton
Simon
Sarum House
Latimer House
Codrington Mews
Galsworthy House
Kensington Park Gdns
B415
B450
Ladbroke Grove
Ladbroke Gdns
Arundel Gardens
Elgin Crescent
Stanley Crescent
Stanley Gdns
Ladbroke Grove House
Lansdowne Crescent
Lansdowne Rise
Lansdowne Road
St John's Gdns
Hillcrest
Bartok House
Ladbroke Square
Horbury Mews
Ladbroke Terr
Wilby Mews
Gate Hill
Ladbroke Walk
Ladbroke Road
Lansdowne Walk
Lansdowne House
Bonham House
Boyne Terr Mews
Mead House
Cranleigh
Lansdowne Mews
Green's Court
Ladbroke Mews
Campden Hill Pl
Campden Hill Sq
Hillsleigh Road
Aubrey Road
Aubrey Walk
Holland Park
Uzbekistan
Algeria
Ukraine
Cameroon
Greece
Holland Park Mews
Holland Park Avenue
Blenheim Crescent
Crescent Mansions
Rosmead Rd
Cornwall Crescent
Camelford Walk
Camelford Ct
St Mark's Road
Dale Row
Talbot Grove House
Lancaster
Clarendon Walk
Kingsdown Close
Lechynden Ho
Grenfell Tower
Verity Cl
Dulford Street
Barlow House
Allam House
Kensington Sports Centre
Treadgold House
Bomore Road
Grenfell Rd
Barandon Wlk
Treadgold St
Southwood House
Avondale Park Road
Threshers Pl
Foreland House
Nottingwood House
Runcorn Pl
Hesketh Pl
Walmer Road
Portland Road
Wintersbourne House
Avondale Park Gdns
Mary Place
Crosfield House
Gorham Place
St Clements
Stoneleigh Pl
Shrdar Road
Estella Ho
Avondale Park Prim Sch
Oliver Ho
Avondale Park
Hippodrome Mews
Hippodrome Place
Clarendon Cross
Clarendon Road
Kenley Wlk
Nottingdale Sq
Katherine Sq
Cowling Cl
Henry Dickens Court
Marley Ho
Dora Ho
Carton Ho
Dorrit Ho
Pickwick Ho
Dombey Ho
Nickleby Ho
St Clement & St James CE Prim Sch
Wilsham Street
Penzance Place
Pottery Lane
Portland Road
Hayne House
Penzance St
St James's Gdns
Princes Place
Princedale Road
St Ann's Rd
Darnley Terr
Swanscombe
Queensdale Place
Addison Avenue
Queensdale Road
Queensdale Walk
Norland Square
Prince's Yd
Norland Pl
St Ann's Villas
Addison Place
Taverners Cl
Norland Place Sch
Royal Crescent
Royal Crescent Mews
Holland Park Tennis Ground
A402
Fitzclarence Ho
Parkland Court
Clearwater Terr
Lorne Gdns
Holland Park Gdns
Carlton Mansions
Holland Park Court
Abbotsbury House
Addison Rd
Upper Addison Gdns
Cardinal Vaughan Memorial Sch
Woodsford Square
Holland Rd
A3220
Hansard Mews
Lower Addison Gdns
Holland Villas Road
Addison Road
Abbotsbury Road
Abbotsbury Close
Holland Wlk
Elsham Terrace
Elsham Road
Russell Gdns Mews
Russell Gdns
Georgia
Redlynch Court
Addison Crescent
Somerset Sq
Serlby Ct
Oakwood La
Oakwood Court
Oakwood Ct
Ilchester Place
Addison Cres
Counters Ct
Todber Ho
Creek
Fielding Rd
Masbro' Rd
Sinclair
Olingbroke Rd
Staverdale
Park Close
Bury Road
Kensington & Chelsea
Hammersmith
Norland
Holland Park Roundabout
Kingham Cl
Camerer Ct

91
246
255
A
B
C
D
1
2
3
4
5
6
80
81
KENSINGTON
W8
Bayswater
Queensway
Notting Hill Gate
High Street Kensington
Kensington Palace
Kensington Palace Green
Diana, Princess of Wales Memorial Walk
THE BROAD WALK
THE DIAL WALK
Clock Tower
Queen Victoria Statue
Orme Square Gate
Queensway Black Lion Gate
Inverness Ter Gate
Pav
New West End Synagogue
College Park Sch
Jun & Inf Sch
Cinema
Fox Prim Sch
St Mary Abbots CE Prim Sch
Kings College London
Tenn Cts
Tenn Ct
Associated Newspapers Ltd
Commonwealth Institute
Richmond Coll
Liby
TH
PO
City of Westminster
Kensington Chelsea
BAYSWATER ROAD
NOTTING HILL GATE
KENSINGTON HIGH STREET
KENSINGTON CHURCH STREET
PEMBRIDGE VILLAS
PEMBRIDGE RD
PEMBRIDGE PLACE
PEMBRIDGE GARDENS
PEMBRIDGE SQUARE
PEMBRIDGE CRES
PEMBRIDGE MEWS
CHEPSTOW VILLAS
CHEPSTOW PLACE
CHEPSTOW CRES
CHEPSTOW COURT
LEDBURY ROAD
LEDBURY MEWS N
LEDBURY MEWS W
WESTBOURNE GROVE MEWS
THORNBURY COURT
RODNEY HOUSE
PORTOBELLO MEWS
KELVIN COURT
HORBURY CRES
DAWSON PLACE
REDE PLACE
HEREFORD ROAD
GARWAY ROAD
LEINSTER SQUARE
PRINCE'S SQUARE
PRINCE'S SQ
PRINCE'S MS
PRINCE EDWARD MANSIONS
PALACE COURT
ILCHESTER GDNS
MOSCOW ROAD
MOSCOW PL
KENSINGTON GDNS SQUARE
KENSINGTON GDNS
BREDAN PLACE
PORCHESTER COURT
PORCHESTER GARDENS
PORCHESTER GDN MEWS
PORCHESTER TERRACE
PORCHESTER GATE
QUEEN'S MEWS
SALEM RD
BEAUMANOR MANSIONS
BURNHAM COURT
WINDSOR COURT
QUEENSWAY
INVERNESS TERRACE
INVERNESS MEWS
INVERNESS PLACE
TENNIEL CL
QUEENSBOROUGH TERRACE
QUEENSBOROUGH MEWS
QUEENS BOROUGH MS
FULTON MS
CHENIES HOUSE
SHAFTESBURY HOUSE
BARK PLACE
POPLAR PLACE
PRINCESS COURT
CAROLINE PLACE
CAROLINE PL MS
CAROLINE CL
CAROLINE HO
LOMBARDY PL
OLYMPIA YD
CONSORT HOUSE
FOSBURY MEWS
QUEEN'S COURT
ST PETERSBURGH MEWS
ST PETERSBURGH PLACE
CHAPEL SIDE
ORME LA
ORME CT
ORME CT MS
ORME SQUARE
LANCASTER CLOSE
SAXON HALL
ST OLAVES COURT
OSSINGTON CL
OSSINGTON STREET
CLANRICARDE GARDENS
VICTORIA GROVE MEWS
THE LIMES
LINDEN GARDENS
LINDEN MEWS
LINDEN GDNS
GARDEN MEWS
PRINCES HOUSE
BULMER MEWS
CAMPTON HILL TOWERS
IVY LODGE
VICTORIA GDNS
UXBRIDGE STREET
FARMER ST
JAMESON ST
NEWCOMBE STREET
CALLCOTT ST
HILLGATE ST
HILLGATE PLACE
FARM PL
KENSINGTON PLACE
EDGE STREET
CAMPDEN HILL MANSIONS
PALMERSTON HOUSE
MELBOURNE HOUSE
CAMPDEN HOUSES
PEEL STREET
PEEL PASS
CAMPDEN STREET
BEDFORD GARDENS
BEDFORD GARDENS HO
THE MOUNT
SHEFFIELD TERRACE
CAMPDEN HOUSE
TOR COURT
TOR GDNS
CAMPDEN HO CL
CAMPDEN HILL
CAMPDEN HILL ROAD
CAMPDEN HILL GDNS
CAMPDEN HILL COURT
CAMPDEN HILL GATE
WATER TOWER HOUSE
KENSINGTON HEIGHTS
AIRLIE GDNS
LAURIE HOUSE
HELDRAKE PLACE
DUCHESS OF BEDFORD HOUSE
DUCHESS OF BEDFORD'S WALK
OBSERVATORY GDNS
HORNTON STREET
HORNTON PLACE
HORNTON COURT
GLOUCESTER WALK
CAMPDEN GROVE
GORDON PLACE
PITT ST
BULLINGHAM MANSIONS
DUKES LANE
CARMEL CT
HOLLAND PL
HOLLAND STREET
GREGORY PL
INGELOW HOUSE
KENSINGTON CHURCH WK
CHURCH WK
KENSINGTON CHURCH CT
DRAYSON MEWS
WEST MALL
RABBIT ROW
KENSINGTON ML
LUCERNE MS
STRATHMORE GARDENS
PALACE GARDEN MEWS
PALACE GARDENS TERRACE
KENSINGTON PALACE GARDENS
BRUNSWICK GARDENS
BERKELEY GARDENS
INVERNESS GARDENS
VICARAGE GATE
VICARAGE GARDENS
VICARAGE COURT
MELON PL
WINCHESTER COURT
HAMILTON HOUSE
CHURCH CLOSE
YORK HOUSE
YORK HOUSE PL
LANCER SQUARE
PALACE GREEN
PALACE AVENUE
OLD COURT PL
OLD COURT HOUSE
UPPER PHILLIMORE GARDENS
PHILLIMORE PLACE
PHILLIMORE GARDENS
PHILLIMORE GDNS CL
PHILLIMORE WALK
PHILLIMORE COURT
ARGYLL ROAD
ESSEX VILLAS
STAFFORD TERRACE
STAFFORD CT
TROY CT
ALLEN HO
ADAM AND EVE
IVERNA CT
WRIGHT'S LANE
DERRY ST
YOUNG ST
KENSINGTON SQUARE
THACKERAY ST
ESMOND CT
ANSDELL ST
ANSDELL TERR
KENSINGTON CT PLACE
KENSINGTON CT
KENSINGTON CT MANS
KENSINGTON COURT
KENSINGTON CT MEWS
KENSINGTON CT GDNS
ST ALBANS MANS
ST ALBAN'S GROVE
SOUTH END
TRAFALGAR GDNS
PRINCE OF WALES TERR
CAMBRIDGE PL
ALBERT PL
VICTORIA ROAD
DOURO PLACE
CANNING PASSAGE
CANNING PL
DE VERE GARDENS
DE VERE COTTS
DE VERE MEWS
LIBERIA
GUYANA
CZECH REPUBLIC
SLOVAK REPUBLIC
LEBANON
NEPAL
RUSSIA
PHILIPPINES
NICARAGUA
ROMANIA
ISRAEL
JORDAN
GEORGIA
AZERBAIJAN
BELARUS
GAMBIA
MONGOLIA
ST CHRISTOPHER & NEVIS / ST VINCENT & THE GRENADINES
VIETNAM
A4207
A4206
A4204
A402
A315
B415
B405
B411

236
245
256
A
B
C
D
1
2
3
4
5
6
Bayswater
TAUNTON HOUSE
LEINSTER PL
LEINSTER GARDENS
LEINSTER SQUARE
CLEVELAND SQUARE
QUEEN'S GARDENS
DEVONSHIRE TERR
UPBROOK MEWS
CRAVEN ROAD
CRAVEN HILL MS
CRAVEN HILL GDNS
CRAVEN HILL
CRAVEN LODGE
SMALLBROOK MEWS
CONDUIT MEWS
WESTBOURNE CRES
SUSSEX GDNS
SUSSEX PLACE
BATHURST MEWS
CLIFTON PL
SUSSEX SQUARE
STANHOPE TERRACE
HYDE PARK GDNS
BROOK ST
HYDE PARK
St James's & St Michael's CE Prim Sch
BROOK MEWS NTH
CRAVEN TERRACE
LANCASTER MEWS
GARSON HO
CERNEY MEWS
MAITLAND COURT
GILRAY HO
A4209
LANCASTER TERR
WESTBOURNE STREET
BATHURST ST
SUSSEX MEWS W
Royal Lancaster Hotel
A402
Victoria Gate
Westbourne Gate
Lancaster Gate
Marlborough Gate
CARROLL HOUSE
ELMS MEWS
COSTA RICA
London Toy & Model Museum
GDNS
SPIRE HOUSE
LANCASTER GATE
LANCASTER COURT
BARRIE HOUSE
LEINSTER MEWS
LEINSTER TERR
B410
HYDE PARK TOWERS
PORCHESTER GATE
PORCHESTER TERRACE
QUEENSBOROUGH TERRACE
QUEENSBOROUGH MEWS
QUEENS BORO PAS
FULTON MS
TENNIEL CL
PORCHESTER GARDENS
INVERNESS TERRACE
INVERNESS PLACE
INVERNESS MEWS
OLYMPIA YD
CONSORT HOUSE
FOSBURY MEWS
B411
BAYSWATER ROAD
NORTH FLOWER WALK
Lancaster Gate
St Agnes' Well
The Fountains
Bayard's Watering Place (site of)
W2
NORTH WALK
Inverness Terrace Gate
Queensway
Black Lion Gate
Speke's Monument
Peter Pan Statue
BUDGE'S WALK
LANCASTER WALK
The Long Water
Diana, Princess of Wales Memorial Walk
Statue
Temple Lodge
Serpentine Bridge
Round Pond
Kensington Gardens
THE BROAD WALK
Queen Victoria Statue
80
Serpentine Gallery
P
Bandstand
Kensington & Chelsea
City of Westminster
THE DIAL WALK
THE FLOWER WALK
Tenn Cts
Bwg Gn
Pav
Albert Memorial
Coalbrookdale Gate
AZERBAIJAN
A315
Palace Gate
Queen's Gate
Alexandra Gate
HYDE PARK GATE
KENSINGTON ROAD
KENSINGTON GORE
PRINCES GATE
BELARUS
KENSINGTON COURT
PRINCE OF WALES TERR
MONGOLIA
ST CHRISTOPHER & NEVIS / ST VINCENT & THE GRENADINES
THORNEY COURT
BROADWALK HOUSE
FIJI
NETHERLANDS
ZAMBIA
RESTON PLACE
B325
Royal College of Art
JAY MEWS
Royal Albert Hall
ALBERT HALL MANSIONS
AFGHANISTAN
Royal Geographical Society
TUNISIA
ETHIOPIA
UNITED ARAB EMIRATES
MONTROSE CT
PRINCES GATE COURT
CAMBRIDGE PL
ALBERT PL
KENSINGTON CT MEWS
VIETNAM
DE VERE GARDENS
CANNING PASSAGE
DE VERE COTTS
PALACE GATE
HYDE PARK GATE MEWS
ESTONIA
CHANCELLOR HOUSE
HYDE PARK GATE
QUEEN'S GATE MEWS
BREMNER RD
Royal College of Science
ALBERT COURT
JAMAICA
PRINCE CONSORT ROAD
PRINCES GARDENS
BULGARIA
Royal College of Music
Tenn Cts
SW7
DOURO PLACE
Richmond Coll
ST ALBANS MANS
BAN'S GROVE
VICTORIA ROAD
CANNING PLACE
KENSINGTON GATE
PO
CALENDAR

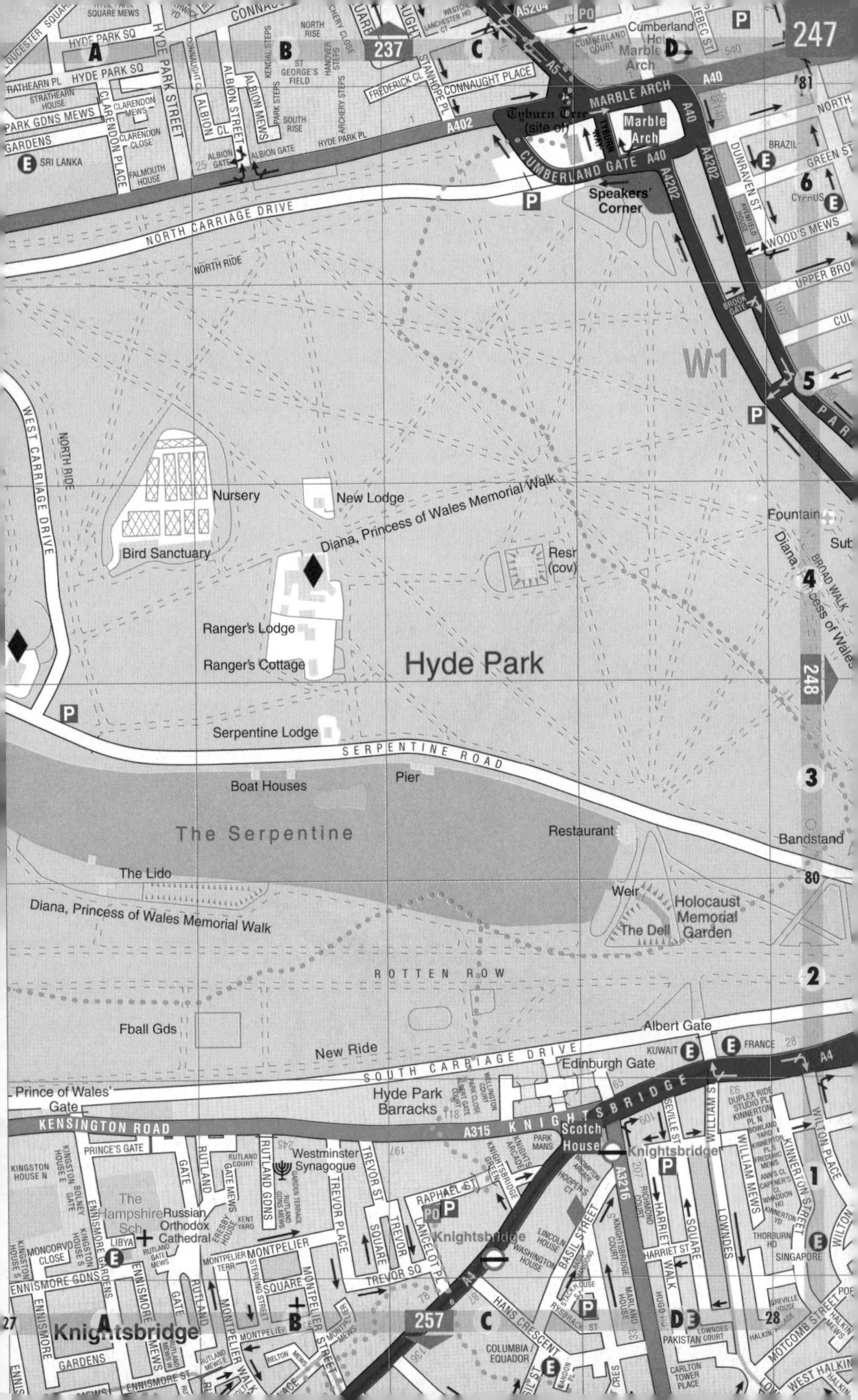
HYDE PARK SQUARE MEWS
CONNAUGHT
GLOUCESTER SQUARE
HYDE PARK SQ
A
B
C
D
237
STRATHEARN PL
STRATHEARN HOUSE
PARK GDNS MEWS
GARDENS
SRI LANKA
CLARENDON PLACE
CLARENDON MEWS
CLARENDON CLOSE
FALMOUTH HOUSE
HYDE PARK STREET
CONNAUGHT CL
ALBION CL
ALBION STREET
ALBION MEWS
ALBION GATE
KENDAL STEPS
PARK STEPS
NORTH RISE
ST GEORGE'S FIELD
SOUTH RISE
HANOVER STEPS
ARCHERY CLOSE
ARCHERY STEPS
HYDE PARK PL
FREDERICK CL
STANHOPE PL
CONNAUGHT PLACE
LANCHESTER HO
A5204
PO
Cumberland Hotel
CUMBERLAND COURT
Marble Arch
A5
A40
MARBLE ARCH
A402
Tyburn Tree (site of)
TYBURN WAY
Marble Arch
CUMBERLAND GATE
A4202
Speakers' Corner
QUEBEC ST
BRAZIL
DUNRAVEN ST
GREEN ST
CYPRUS
WOOD'S MEWS
UPPER BROOK
BROOK GATE
NORTH
W1
5
6
PARK
NORTH CARRIAGE DRIVE
NORTH RIDE
WEST CARRIAGE DRIVE
Nursery
New Lodge
Diana, Princess of Wales Memorial Walk
Bird Sanctuary
Resr (cov)
Ranger's Lodge
Ranger's Cottage
Hyde Park
Fountain
BROAD WALK
4
248
Serpentine Lodge
SERPENTINE ROAD
Boat Houses
Pier
The Serpentine
Restaurant
3
Bandstand
The Lido
Diana, Princess of Wales Memorial Walk
Weir
Holocaust Memorial Garden
The Dell
ROTTEN ROW
2
Fball Gds
Albert Gate
New Ride
KUWAIT
FRANCE
SOUTH CARRIAGE DRIVE
Edinburgh Gate
Prince of Wales' Gate
Hyde Park Barracks
KENSINGTON ROAD
A315
KNIGHTSBRIDGE
A4
Scotch House
Knightsbridge
SEVILLE ST
WILLIAM ST
DUPLEX RIDE
STUDIO PL
KINNERTON PL N
BOWLAND YARD
KINNERTON PL S
WILTON PLACE
KINGSTON HOUSE N
PRINCE'S GATE
RUTLAND GATE
RUTLAND COURT
RUTLAND GDNS
Westminster Synagogue
TREVOR STREET
PARK MANS
KNIGHTSBRIDGE GREEN
BROMPTON ARCADE
HOOPER'S CT
A3216
RICHMOND COURT
HARRIET WALK
LOWNDES SQUARE
WILLIAM MEWS
KINNERTON STREET
1
The Hampshire Sch
Russian Orthodox Cathedral
LIBYA
RUTLAND GATE MEWS
ENNISMORE GARDENS
KINGSTON HOUSE S
MONCORVO CLOSE
ENNISMORE GDNS
ENNISMORE MEWS
MONTPELIER SQUARE
MONTPELIER TERR
MONTPELIER WALK
MONTPELIER STREET
STERLING STREET
TREVOR PLACE
TREVOR SQUARE
TREVOR SQ
RAPHAEL ST
LANCELOT PL
Knightsbridge
LINCOLN HOUSE
WASHINGTON HOUSE
BASIL STREET
KNIGHTSBRIDGE COURT
HARRIET ST
THORBURN HO
SINGAPORE
GREVILLE HOUSE
HALKIN ARCADE
MOTCOMB STREET
HALKIN MEWS
28
27
Knightsbridge
257
HANS CRESCENT
RYSBRACK ST
MARLAND HOUSE
PAKISTAN
LOWNDES COURT
CARLTON TOWER PLACE
COLUMBIA / EQUADOR
ENNISMORE ST
WEST HALKIN

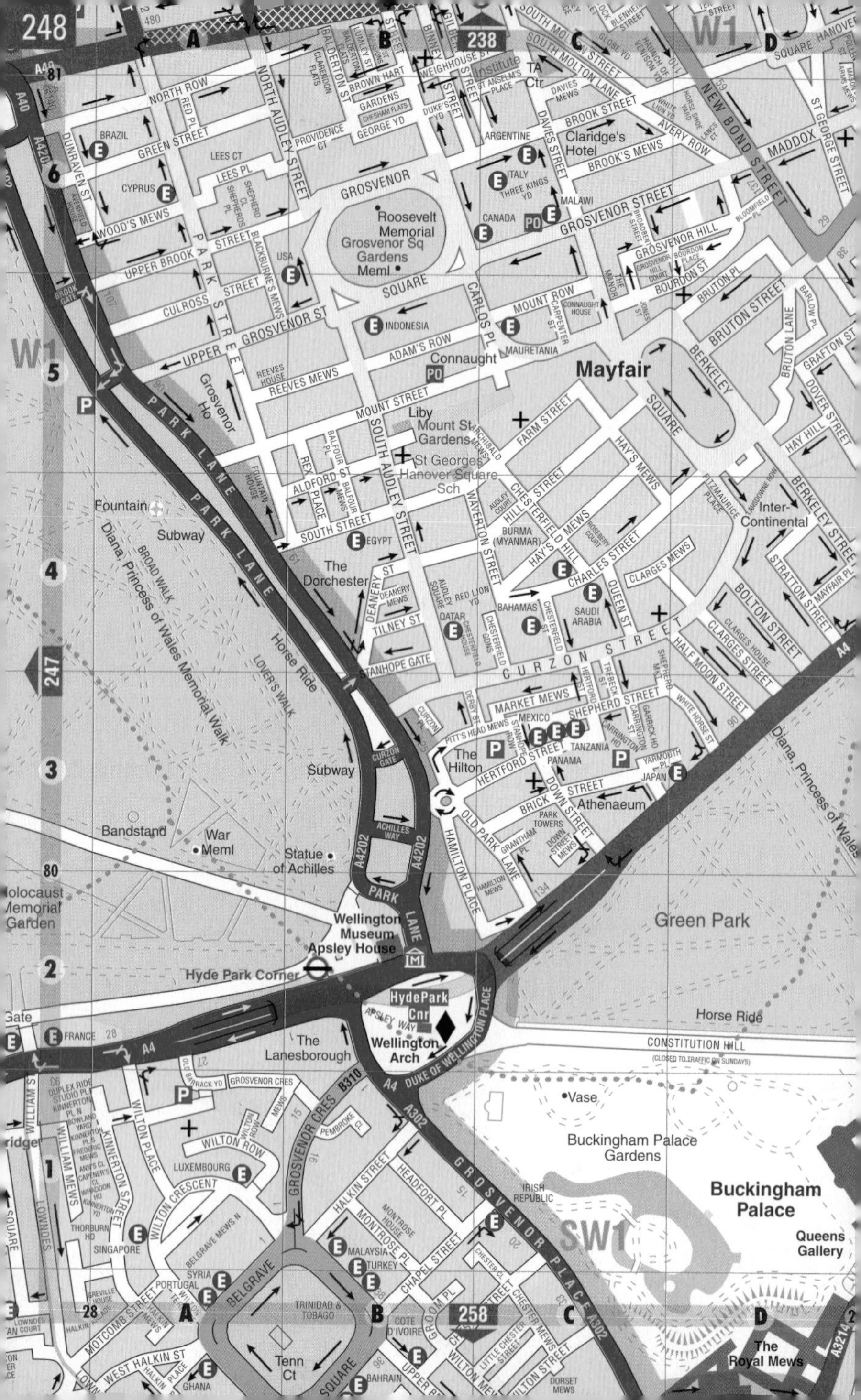

238
W1
A
B
C
D
Mayfair
NORTH ROW
GREEN STREET
NORTH AUDLEY STREET
BALDERTON ST
BROWN HART GARDENS
WEIGHHOUSE ST
BINNEY STREET
DUKE STREET
GILBERT STREET
SOUTH MOLTON STREET
SOUTH MOLTON LANE
DAVIES STREET
BROOK STREET
Claridge's Hotel
AVERY ROW
BROOK'S MEWS
NEW BOND STREET
MADDOX
ST GEORGE STREET
HANOVER SQUARE
GROSVENOR
Roosevelt Memorial
Grosvenor Sq Gardens
Meml
SQUARE
GROSVENOR STREET
GROSVENOR HILL
BOURDON ST
BRUTON PL
BRUTON STREET
BRUTON LANE
GRAFTON ST
DOVER STREET
HAY HILL
BERKELEY STREET
BERKELEY SQUARE
MOUNT ROW
CARLOS PL
ADAM'S ROW
Connaught
UPPER GROSVENOR ST
REEVES MEWS
MOUNT STREET
Grosvenor Ho
PARK STREET
UPPER BROOK STREET
CULROSS STREET
WOOD'S MEWS
DUNRAVEN ST
LEES PL
LEES CT
BLACKBURNE'S MEWS
BRAZIL
CYPRUS
USA
INDONESIA
MAURETANIA
CANADA
ITALY
MALAWI
ARGENTINE
THREE KINGS YD
PO
Liby
Mount St Gardens
St Georges Hanover Square Sch
FARM STREET
HAY'S MEWS
HILL STREET
CHESTERFIELD HILL
CHARLES STREET
QUEEN ST
CLARGES MEWS
CLARGES STREET
BOLTON STREET
STRATTON STREET
Inter-Continental
FITZMAURICE PLACE
LANSDOWNE ROW
MAYFAIR PL
CURZON STREET
HALF MOON STREET
WHITE HORSE ST
SHEPHERD STREET
MARKET MEWS
HERTFORD STREET
BRICK STREET
DOWN STREET
Athenaeum
TANZANIA
PANAMA
JAPAN
MEXICO
BAHAMAS
SAUDI ARABIA
QATAR
BURMA (MYANMAR)
EGYPT
SOUTH AUDLEY STREET
WAVERTON STREET
ALDFORD ST
SOUTH STREET
REX PLACE
DEANERY ST
TILNEY ST
STANHOPE GATE
The Dorchester
PARK LANE
Fountain
Subway
Diana, Princess of Wales Memorial Walk
BROAD WALK
LOVER'S WALK
Horse Ride
CURZON GATE
The Hilton
PITT'S HEAD MEWS
OLD PARK LANE
HAMILTON PLACE
Bandstand
War Meml
Statue of Achilles
A4202
ACHILLES WAY
Holocaust Memorial Garden
Wellington Museum
Apsley House
Hyde Park Corner
HydePark Cnr
APSLEY WAY
Wellington Arch
Green Park
Horse Ride
CONSTITUTION HILL
(CLOSED TO TRAFFIC ON SUNDAYS)
DUKE OF WELLINGTON PLACE
A4
FRANCE
The Lanesborough
GROSVENOR PLACE
A302
Vase
Buckingham Palace Gardens
Buckingham Palace
Queens Gallery
SW1
IRISH REPUBLIC
GROSVENOR CRES
B310
PEMBROKE CL
HALKIN STREET
HEADFORT PL
MONTROSE PL
CHAPEL STREET
WILTON ROW
WILTON PLACE
WILTON CRESCENT
LUXEMBOURG
SINGAPORE
SYRIA
PORTUGAL
MALAYSIA
TURKEY
BELGRAVE
TRINIDAD & TOBAGO
COTE D'IVOIRE
Tenn Ct
BAHRAIN
GHANA
WEST HALKIN ST
MOTCOMB STREET
KINNERTON STREET
WILLIAM MEWS
LOWNDES SQUARE
GROOM PL
CHESTER STREET
CHESTER MEWS
WILTON STREET
DORSET MEWS
The Royal Mews
258
247

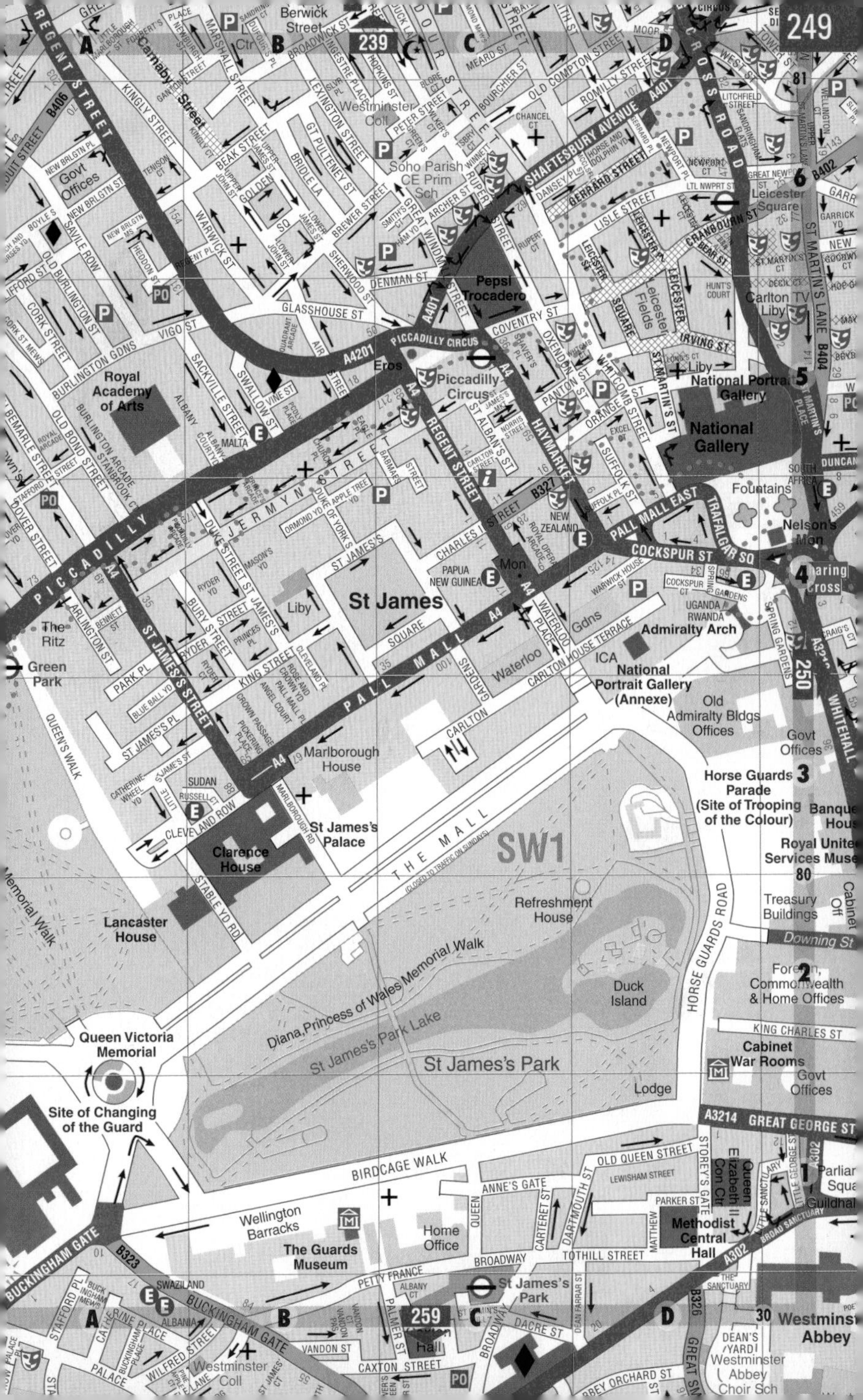

A
B
C
D
239
250
259
Regent Street
Carnaby Street
Berwick Street
Broadwick St
Shaftesbury Avenue
Charing Cross Road
Old Compton Street
Westminster Coll
Soho Parish CE Prim Sch
Govt Offices
Savile Row
Old Burlington St
Cork St
Burlington Gdns
Vigo St
Glasshouse St
Denman St
Piccadilly Circus
Eros
Pepsi Trocadero
Coventry St
Gerrard Street
Lisle Street
Leicester Square
Leicester Fields
Cranbourn St
Irving St
Carlton TV
Liby
St Martin's Lane
National Portrait Gallery
National Gallery
Royal Academy of Arts
Sackville Street
Albany
Swallow St
Vine St
Malta
Haymarket
Jermyn Street
Piccadilly
Duke Street St James's
Charles II Street
Pall Mall East
Trafalgar Sq
Cockspur St
Fountains
Nelson's Mon
Charing Cross
New Zealand
Papua New Guinea
Mon.
St James
St James's Square
Pall Mall
Waterloo Place
Waterloo Gdns
Carlton House Terrace
Admiralty Arch
Uganda
Rwanda
ICA
National Portrait Gallery (Annexe)
Old Admiralty Bldgs Offices
Whitehall
The Ritz
Green Park
Arlington St
St James's Street
King Street
Park Pl
Queen's Walk
Marlborough House
Sudan
Cleveland Row
Clarence House
St James's Palace
The Mall
(Closed to traffic on Sundays)
SW1
Horse Guards Parade (Site of Trooping of the Colour)
Royal United Services Museum
Treasury Buildings
Downing St
Foreign, Commonwealth & Home Offices
Horse Guards Road
King Charles St
Cabinet War Rooms
Lancaster House
Stable Yd Rd
Refreshment House
Duck Island
Diana, Princess of Wales Memorial Walk
St James's Park Lake
St James's Park
Lodge
Queen Victoria Memorial
Site of Changing of the Guard
Birdcage Walk
Old Queen Street
Great George St
A3214
Wellington Barracks
The Guards Museum
Home Office
Queen Anne's Gate
Methodist Central Hall
Queen Elizabeth II Con Ctr
Parliament Square
Tothill Street
Broadway
Petty France
St James's Park
Buckingham Gate
Swaziland
Albania
Westminster Abbey
Dean's Yard
Westminster Abbey Choir Sch
Caxton Street
Vandon St
Palmer St
Dacre St
Great Smith St

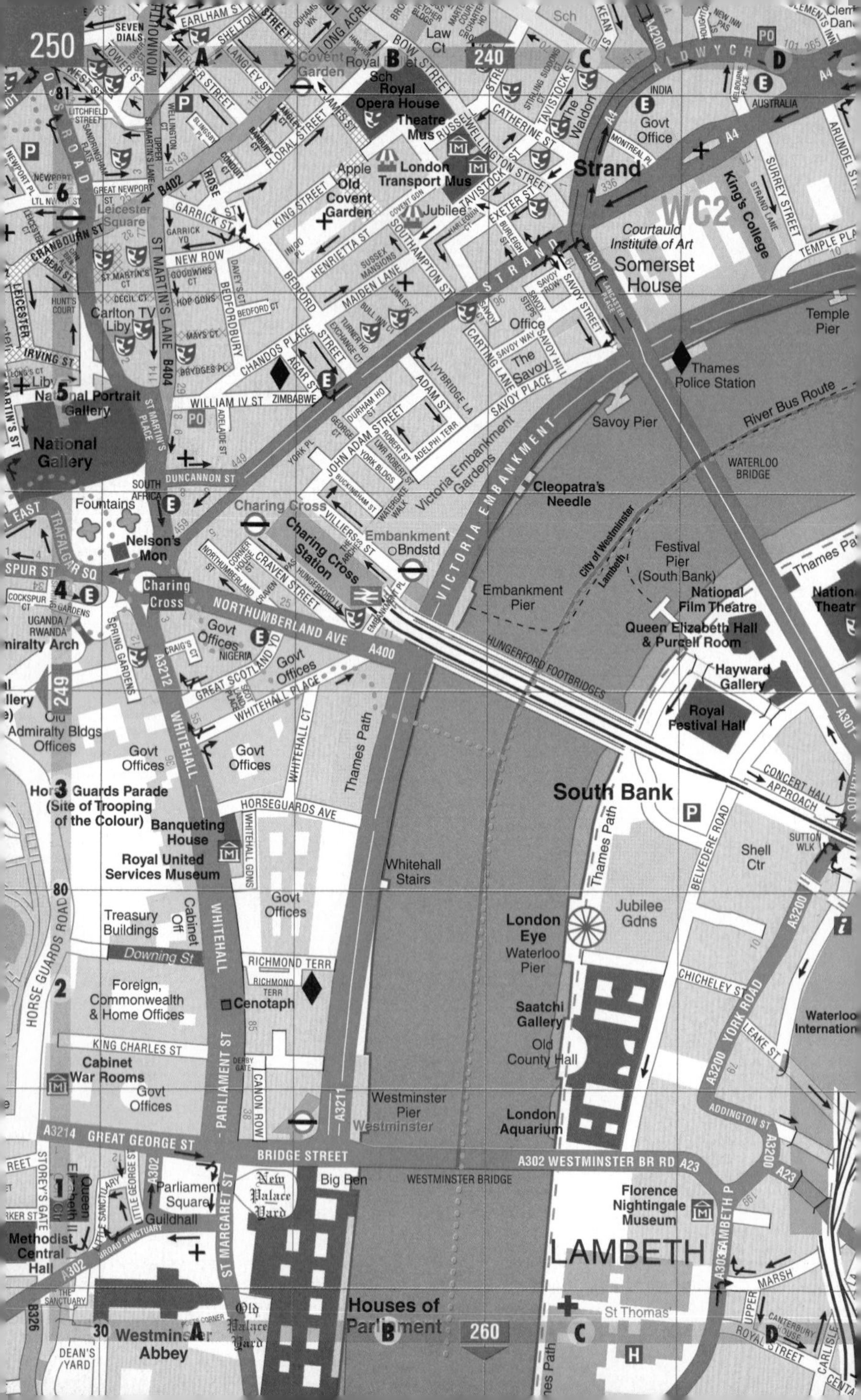
SEVEN DIALS
EARLHAM ST
SHELTON ST
MONMOUTH ST
MERCER STREET
LANGLEY ST
LONG ACRE
Covent Garden
Royal Ballet Sch
BOW STREET
Law Ct
240
Sch
KEAN ST
A4200
ALDWYCH
NEW INN PAS
PO
CLEMENTS INN
TOWER ST
WEST ST
CHARING CROSS ROAD
LITCHFIELD STREET
WELLINGTON CT
SLINGSBY PL
JAMES ST
FLORAL STREET
Royal Opera House
Theatre Mus
RUSSELL
CATHERINE ST
TAVISTOCK ST
The Waldorf
INDIA
AUSTRALIA
Govt Office
MONTREAL PL
A4
ARUNDEL ST
NEWPORT PL
NEWPORT CT
GREAT NEWPORT ST
B402
ROSE ST
CONDUIT CT
UPPER ST MARTIN'S LANE
Apple
Old Covent Garden
London Transport Mus
WELLINGTON STREET
Strand
King's College
SURREY STREET
STRAND LANE
LTL NWPRT ST
Leicester Square
GARRICK ST
KING STREET
COVENT GDN
Jubilee
TAVISTOCK ST
EXETER ST
BURLEIGH ST
WC2
Courtauld Institute of Art
Somerset House
TEMPLE PL
CRANBOURN ST
BEAR ST
GARRICK YD
NEW ROW
GOODWINS CT
INIGO PL
HENRIETTA ST
SOUTHAMPTON ST
SUSSEX MANSIONS
MAIDEN LANE
STRAND
A301
LANCASTER PLACE
SAVOY STREET
SAVOY ROW
LEICESTER ST
HUNT'S COURT
ST MARTIN'S CT
CECIL CT
HOP GDNS
DAVEY'S CT
BEDFORDBURY
BEDFORD CT
BEDFORD ST
BULL INN CT
LUMLEY CT
Carlton TV Liby
MAYS CT
BRYDGES PL
CHANDOS PLACE
AGAR ST
TURNER HO EXCHANGE CT
Office
SAVOY STEPS
SAVOY WAY
CARTING LANE
The Savoy
SAVOY HILL
Temple Pier
Thames Police Station
IRVING ST
Liby
National Portrait Gallery
B404
ST MARTIN'S PLACE
WILLIAM IV ST
ZIMBABWE
ADELAIDE ST
PO
DURHAM HO ST
IVYBRIDGE LA
ADAM ST
JOHN ADAM STREET
GEORGE CT
ROBERT ST
ADELPHI TERR
SAVOY PLACE
Savoy Pier
River Bus Route
National Gallery
DUNCANNON ST
YORK PL
YORK BLDGS
LWR ROBERT ST
Victoria Embankment Gardens
VICTORIA EMBANKMENT
WATERLOO BRIDGE
SOUTH AFRICA
Fountains
Charing Cross
BUCKINGHAM ST
WATERGATE WALK
VILLIERS ST
Cleopatra's Needle
Embankment
Bndstd
City of Westminster
Lambeth
Festival Pier (South Bank)
Thames Path
TRAFALGAR SQ
Nelson's Mon
Charing Cross Station
NORTHUMBERLAND ST
CORNER HOUSE
CRAVEN PAS
CRAVEN STREET
HUNGERFORD LA
THE ARCHES
EMBANKMENT PL
Embankment Pier
National Film Theatre
National Theatre
SPUR ST
COCKSPUR ST
SPRING GARDENS
UGANDA / RWANDA
Admiralty Arch
Charing Cross
NORTHUMBERLAND AVE
A400
Govt Offices
NIGERIA
CRAIG'S CT
GREAT SCOTLAND YD
SCOTLAND PLACE
WHITEHALL PLACE
HUNGERFORD FOOTBRIDGES
Queen Elizabeth Hall & Purcell Room
Hayward Gallery
Royal Festival Hall
A3212
249
Old Admiralty Bldgs
Offices
Govt Offices
WHITEHALL
WHITEHALL CT
Thames Path
A301
Horse Guards Parade (Site of Trooping of the Colour)
HORSEGUARDS AVE
Banqueting House
Royal United Services Museum
WHITEHALL GDNS
South Bank
CONCERT HALL APPROACH
BELVEDERE ROAD
SUTTON WLK
Shell Ctr
Whitehall Stairs
Thames Path
HORSE GUARDS ROAD
Treasury Buildings
Cabinet Off
Govt Offices
Downing St
RICHMOND TERR
London Eye
Waterloo Pier
Jubilee Gdns
A3200
CHICHELEY ST
YORK ROAD
Waterloo International
Foreign, Commonwealth & Home Offices
Cenotaph
Saatchi Gallery
LEAKE ST
KING CHARLES ST
PARLIAMENT ST
DERBY GATE
CANON ROW
Old County Hall
Cabinet War Rooms
Govt Offices
A3211
Westminster Pier
Westminster
London Aquarium
ADDINGTON ST
A3214
GREAT GEORGE ST
BRIDGE STREET
A302 WESTMINSTER BR RD
A23
WESTMINSTER BRIDGE
STOREY'S GATE
Queen Elizabeth II Conf Ctr
LITTLE SANCTUARY
LITTLE GEORGE ST
A302
Parliament Square
Guildhall
ST MARGARET ST
New Palace Yard
Big Ben
Florence Nightingale Museum
LAMBETH PALACE RD
Methodist Central Hall
BROAD SANCTUARY
LAMBETH
MARSH
THE SANCTUARY
B326
POETS CORNER
Westminster Abbey
DEAN'S YARD
Old Palace Yard
Houses of Parliament
260
St Thomas'
Thames Path
UPPER MARSH
CANTERBURY HOUSE
ROYAL STREET
CARLISLE

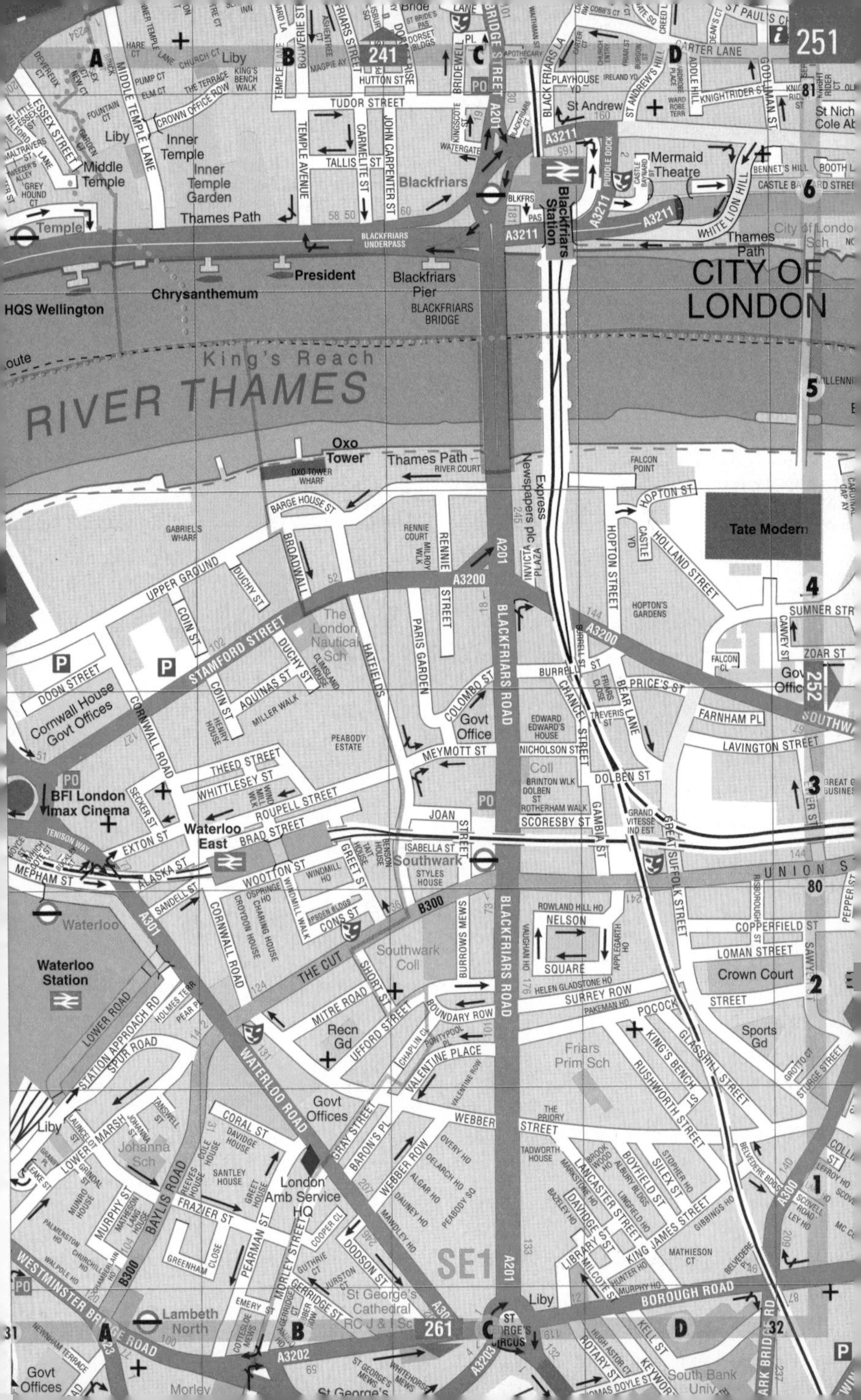
A
B
C
D
241
252
261
6
5
4
3
2
1
81
80
32
Liby
Middle Temple
Inner Temple
Inner Temple Garden
Thames Path
Temple
MIDDLE TEMPLE LANE
ESSEX STREET
CROWN OFFICE ROW
KING'S BENCH WALK
TEMPLE AVENUE
TUDOR STREET
TALLIS ST
CARMELITE ST
JOHN CARPENTER ST
BOUVERIE ST
HUTTON ST
BRIDEWELL PL
NEW BRIDGE STREET
A201
WATERGATE
Blackfriars
BLACKFRIARS UNDERPASS
A3211
BLKFRS PAS
Blackfriars Station
PLAYHOUSE YD
IRELAND YD
St Andrew
ST ANDREW'S HILL
CARTER LANE
ADDLE HILL
GODLIMAN ST
KNIGHTRIDER ST
St Nich Cole Ab
PUDDLE DOCK
Mermaid Theatre
CASTLE BAYNARD ST
WHITE LION HILL
BENNET'S HILL
BOOTH LA
CASTLE BAYNARD STREET
City of London Sch
Thames Path
CITY OF LONDON
President
Chrysanthemum
HQS Wellington
Blackfriars Pier
BLACKFRIARS BRIDGE
King's Reach
RIVER THAMES
Oxo Tower
OXO TOWER WHARF
Thames Path
RIVER COURT
FALCON POINT
Express Newspapers plc
HOPTON ST
Tate Modern
BARGE HOUSE ST
GABRIEL'S WHARF
RENNIE COURT
MILROY WLK
RENNIE STREET
BROADWALL
UPPER GROUND
DUCHY ST
COIN ST
A3200
STAMFORD STREET
The London Nautical Sch
HATFIELDS
PARIS GARDEN
BLACKFRIARS ROAD
INVICTA PLAZA
HOPTON STREET
CASTLE YD
HOLLAND STREET
HOPTON'S GARDENS
SUMNER STREET
CANVEY ST
ZOAR ST
FALCON CL
Govt Offices
BURRELL ST
PRICE'S ST
BEAR LANE
FRIARS CLOSE
TREVERIS ST
FARNHAM PL
SOUTHWARK STREET
LAVINGTON STREET
DOON STREET
Cornwall House Govt Offices
CORNWALL ROAD
AQUINAS ST
MILLER WALK
CLIMSLAND HOUSE
HENRY HOUSE
PEABODY ESTATE
COLOMBO ST
Govt Office
MEYMOTT ST
EDWARD EDWARD'S HOUSE
NICHOLSON ST
Coll
BRINTON WLK
DOLBEN ST
ROTHERHAM WALK
CHANCEL STREET
DOLBEN ST
GRAND VITESSE IND EST
GREAT SUFFOLK STREET
GREAT GUILDFORD BUSINESS
EMERSON ST
THEED STREET
WHITTLESEY ST
WINDMILL WALK
ROUPELL STREET
SECKER ST
BFI London Imax Cinema
Waterloo East
BRAD STREET
EXTON ST
JOAN STREET
SCORESBY ST
GAMBIA ST
ISABELLA ST
TAIT HOUSE
BENSON HOUSE
Southwark
STYLES HOUSE
UNION ST
TENISON WAY
BOYCE ST
MEPHAM ST
ALASKA ST
WOOTTON ST
WINDMILL HO
OSPRINGE HO
GREET ST
SANDELL ST
Waterloo
Waterloo Station
A301
CORNWALL ROAD
CROYDON HOUSE
CHARING HOUSE
IPSDEN BLDGS
CONS ST
B300
THE CUT
Southwark Coll
BURROWS MEWS
ROWLAND HILL HO
NELSON SQUARE
VAUGHAN HO
APPLEGARTH HO
RISBOROUGH ST
COPPERFIELD ST
LOMAN STREET
SAWYER STREET
Crown Court
PEPPER ST
LOWER ROAD
STATION APPROACH RD
HOLMES TERR
PEAR PL
MITRE ROAD
SHORT ST
UFFORD STREET
BOUNDARY ROW
HELEN GLADSTONE HO
SURREY ROW
PAKEMAN HO
POCOCK ST
KING'S BENCH ST
GLASSHILL STREET
Sports Gd
Recn Gd
CHAPLIN CL
PONTYPOOL PL
VALENTINE PLACE
VALENTINE ROW
Friars Prim Sch
RUSHWORTH STREET
GROTTO CT
STURGE STREET
SPUR ROAD
WATERLOO ROAD
Govt Offices
WEBBER STREET
THE PRIORY
TADWORTH HOUSE
GRAY STREET
BARON'S PL
WEBBER ROW
OVERY HO
DELARCH HO
ALGAR HO
DAUNEY HO
PEABODY SQ
MANDLEY HO
LANCASTER STREET
MARKSTONE HO
BROOKWOOD HO
ALBURY BLDGS
BOYFIELD ST
SILEX ST
STOPHER HO
LINGFIELD HO
KING JAMES STREET
GIBBINGS HO
BELVEDERE BLDGS
COLLINSON ST
LEFROY HO
SCOVELL ROAD
LEY HO
A300
Liby
LAUNCELOT ST
LOWER MARSH
JOHANNA ST
Johanna Sch
TANSWELL ST
CORAL ST
DAVIDGE HOUSE
COLE HOUSE
REEVES HOUSE
SANTLEY HOUSE
BAYLIS ROAD
GREET HOUSE
London Amb Service HQ
FRAZIER ST
PEARMAN ST
MORLEY STREET
COOPER CL
DODSON ST
MURPHY ST
MATHESON LANG HOUSE
GRINDAL ST
MUNRO HOUSE
PALMERSTON HO
CHURCHILL HO
CHAMBERLAIN HO
WALPOLE HO
GREENHAM CLOSE
B300
WESTMINSTER BRIDGE ROAD
Lambeth North
EMERY ST
COTTESLOE MEWS
GERRIDGE ST
GUTHRIE CT
JURSTON CT
St George's Cathedral RC J & I Sch
SE1
A201
BAZELEY HO
DAVIDGE ST
LIBRARY ST
MILCOTE ST
HUNTER HO
MURPHY HO
MATHIESON CT
BELVEDERE PL
BOROUGH ROAD
Liby
ST GEORGE'S CIRCUS
A3202
A3203
ST GEORGE'S MEWS
WHITEHORSE MEWS
NEWNHAM TERRACE
Govt Offices
Morley
St George
HUGH ASTOR CT
ROTARY ST
KELL ST
THOMAS DOYLE ST
KEYWORTH ST
South Bank Univ
SOUTHWARK BRIDGE RD
PO
P

CITY OF LONDON
St Nicholas Cole Abbey
Mansion House
Cannon Street
Queen Victoria Street
Castle Baynard Street
White Lion Hill
Lambeth Hill
Upper Thames Street
Thames Path
City of London Sch
Queenhithe Stairs
Southwark Bridge Stairs
City of London
Southwark
Millennium Bridge
Bankside Pier
Bankside
The Globe Theatre
Tate Modern
Southwark Bridge
Jubilee Footbridge
Queen St Pl
A300
St James
St Michael
St Stephen Walbrook
Walbrook
Cloak Lane
College Street
Dowgate Hill
Cannon Street Station
Cousin Lane
Allhallows La
Bush Lane
Laurence Pountney La
Martin Lane
Arthur St
Swan Lane
Angel Pass
Swan Lane Pier
Princess Elizabeth
River Bus Route
London Bridge
St Mary Woolnoth
Lombard Street
St Edmund
King William Street
Gracechurch
St Clement
Monument
The Monument
Fish St H
A3211
A10
A3
St Magnus London Bridge
Old London Bridge (site of)
The Financial Times Ltd
Shakespeare's Globe Theatre (site of)
Park Street
Clink St
Vinopolis
Thames Path
Winchester Sq
Montague Cl
Southwark Cathedral
Borough
Stoney Street
Tooley St
Duke St Hill
A200
The London Dungeon
London Bridge
Railway Approach
London Br St
London Bridge Station
St Thomas Street
Bear Gardens Mus
Sumner Street
Zoar St
Govt Offices
Southwark Street
Southwark Bridge Road
Great Guildford Street
Gatehouse Sq
Perkins Square
Thrale St
Redcross Way
Southwark Bridge Office Village
A3200
Borough High Street
Guy's Hospl Sch
Guy's Hospl
Lavington Street
Farnham Pl
Ewer St
Union Street
B300
Omeara St
Cathedral Sch of St Saviour & St Mary Overie Prim Sch
St Joseph's RC Prim Sch
Ayres Street
Copperfield St
Loman Street
Crown Court
Sawyer St
The Borough
A3201
Marshalsea Road
Little Dorrit Park
Mint St
Lant Street
Great Maze Pond
Newcomen Street
Mermaid Ct
Tennis Street
Liby
Govt Offices
Crosby Row
Snowsfields
City Banking Coll
Weston Street
Guy Street
Porlock St
Kipling Street
Long Lane
Beormund Prim Sch
Charles Dickens Prim Sch
Borough
SE1
A2
A2198
Sudrey St
Great Suffolk Street
Collinson St
Trinity St
Swan Street
Cole Street
Pilgrimage Street
Tabard Gardens
Tabard Street
Mancipl Street
Staple Street
Sports Gd
A3202
Newington Causeway
B240
Inner London & Southwark Crown Cts
Cty Ct
Fball Gd
Great Dover Street
Pardoner Street
Merrick Square
Trinity Church Sq
Brockham St
A
B
C
D
1
2
3
4
5
6
242
251
262

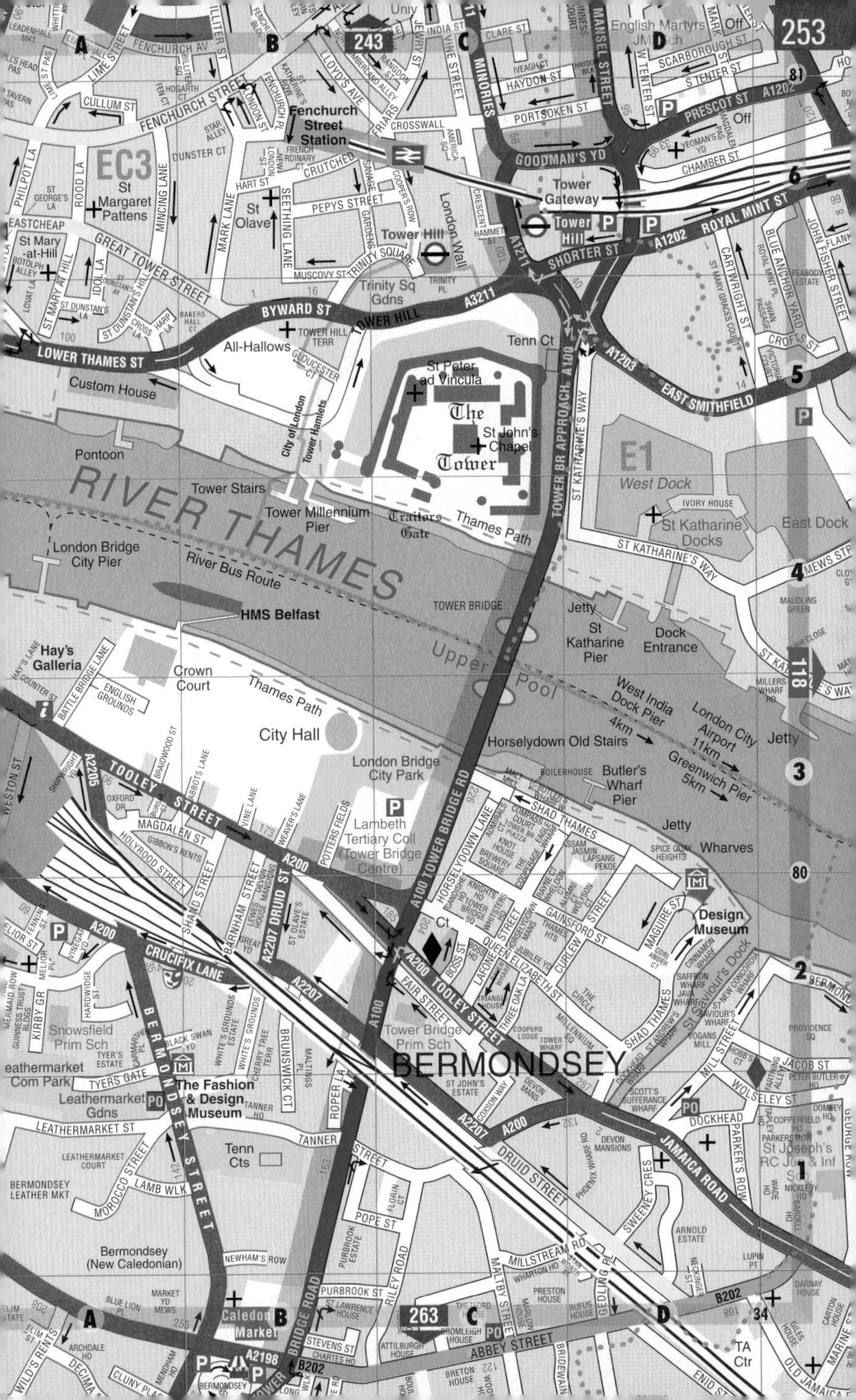
243
263
118
EC3
E1
Fenchurch Street Station
Tower Hill
Tower Gateway
St Olave
St Margaret Pattens
St Mary -at-Hill
Trinity Sq Gdns
All-Hallows
Custom House
LOWER THAMES ST
BYWARD ST
TOWER HILL
GREAT TOWER STREET
FENCHURCH STREET
FENCHURCH AV
MINORIES
MANSEL STREET
GOODMAN'S YD
PRESCOT ST
ROYAL MINT ST
SHORTER ST
EAST SMITHFIELD
TOWER BR APPROACH
ST KATHARINE'S WAY
Tenn Ct
St Peter ad Vincula
The Tower
St John's Chapel
Traitors Gate
Pontoon
Tower Stairs
Tower Millennium Pier
London Bridge City Pier
RIVER THAMES
River Bus Route
Thames Path
HMS Belfast
TOWER BRIDGE
Upper Pool
West Dock
St Katharine Docks
East Dock
IVORY HOUSE
Jetty
St Katharine Pier
Dock Entrance
West India Dock Pier 4km
London City Airport 11km
Greenwich Pier 5km
Horselydown Old Stairs
Butler's Wharf Pier
Wharves
Hay's Galleria
Crown Court
City Hall
London Bridge City Park
Lambeth Tertiary Coll (Tower Bridge Centre)
TOOLEY STREET
TOWER BRIDGE RD
SHAD THAMES
Design Museum
St Saviour's Dock
JAMAICA ROAD
BERMONDSEY
BERMONDSEY STREET
CRUCIFIX LANE
DRUID STREET
Snowsfield Prim Sch
Leathermarket Com Park
Leathermarket Gdns
The Fashion & Design Museum
Tenn Cts
Tower Bridge Prim Sch
St Joseph's RC Jun & Inf Sch
Bermondsey (New Caledonian)
Caledon Market
ABBEY STREET
TOWER BRIDGE ROAD
TA Ctr

A
B
C
D
244
REDLYNCH COURT
ELSHAM ROAD
ELSHAM TERRACE
A3220
RUSSELL GDNS
RUSSELL GDNS MEWS
GEORGIA
ADDISON CRESCENT
ABBOTSBURY CLOSE
ABBOTSBURY CLOSE
Tenn Cts
Tenn Cts
BOLINGBROKE
FIELDING RD
SINCLAIR ROAD
HOFLAND ROAD
SERLBY CT
OAKWOOD LA
OAKWOOD COURT
OAKWOOD CT
ILCHESTER PLACE
PARK CLOSE
ADDISON CRES
COUNTERS CT
CREEK HO
TODBER HO
TARRANT HO
LUDWELL HO
KNOYLE HO
FONTHILL HO
COURTNEY HO
CANN HO
ASHMORE HO
IBBERTON HO
MANSTON HO
OAKEFORD HO
RUSHMORE HO
SHILLINGSTONE HO
HOLLAND ROAD
HOLLAND GDNS
RUSSELL ROAD
MELBURY ROAD
STAVERDALE LODGE
Leighton House (Art Gallery and Museum)
KINGFISHER HO
FARLEY CT
ADDISON ROAD
NAPIER CL
NAPIER ROAD
NAPIER PLACE
MONKTON CT
STRANGWAYS TERR
HOLLAND PARK ROAD
KENBROOK HO
EARLS TERR
ST MARY ABBOTS TERR
ABBOTS HO
Kensington Olympia
MILSON ROAD
RAYBURNE CT
BRADFORD HO
FAROE RD
CEYLON ROAD
PORTEN RD
PORTEN HOS
BRANGWYN CT
GRATTON RD
COLERIDGE CT
ELGAR CT
THACKERAY CT
HAZLITT ROAD
HAZLITT MEWS
MACLISE ROAD
BEACONSFIELD TERRACE RD
OLYMPIA WAY
KENSINGTON HIGH STREET
A3220
ST MARY ABBOTS PL
EDWARDES SQUARE
EDWARDES
PARAGUAY
KENTON CT
A3220
A315
WALPOLE CT
BOSWELL
BLYTHE ROAD
PO
AYNHOE RD
GIRDLERS RD
Olympia Exhibition Centre
ST MARY ABBOT'S CT
PEMBROKE STUDIOS
PEMBROKE
OXFORD GATE
KENSINGTON WEST
HAMMERSMITH ROAD
GLYN MANSIONS
ADDISON BRIDGE PL
WELBECK CT
RADNOR TERR
DURRELS HO
WARWICK GARDENS
WARWICK ROAD
BROADWOOD TERR
WINDSOR WAY
REGENT HO
SANDRINGHAM HO
PALACE MANSIONS
ARGYLL MANSIONS
BISHOP KING'S ROAD
AVONMORE PL
AVONMORE RD
EARSBY ST
Avonmore Prim Sch
STUART HO
BALMORAL HO
TUDOR HO
BROOK GN
LYONS WALK
B317
RUGBY MANSIONS
CUMBERLAND CRES
St James Independent Schs
AVONMORE ROAD
JOSEPH'S HO
112
SOUTHCOMBE ST
CHARLOTTE MEWS
MUNDEN ST
Ct
VERNON STREET
VERNON MEWS
GORLESTON ST
Ct
SAMUEL LEWIS TRUST DWELLINGS
W14
LISGAR TERRACE
THE GRANGE
A3220
BECKFORD CL
FENELON PLACE
A315
NORTH END ROAD
BURNE JONES HO
AVONMORE GDNS
BROADMEAD
AURIOL ROAD
FITZJAMES AVE
FITZ-GEORGE AVE
NORTH END HO
NORTH END PARADE
SAMUEL RICHARDSON HO
MATHESON ROAD
STONOR RD
BEAUMONT
MORE CLOSE
AURIOL MANSIONS
NORTH END CRESCENT
Liby
STANWICK ROAD
CODI HO
KENSINGTON VILLAGE
AVON HO
LILY CL
MORTIMER HO
ABINGDON
COLET GDNS
Ealing, Hammersmith & West London Coll
EDITH ROAD
PELHAM HO
MORNINGTON AVENUE
MORNINGTON AVENUE MANSIONS
GLOUCESTER
WARWICK
West Kensington
CLIFFORD HO
PEMBROKE
GUNTERSTONE ROAD
TREVANION RD
GLAZBURY ROAD
EDITH VILLAS
WEST KENSINGTON CT
FALKLAND HO
WEST CROMWELL ROAD
Gwendwr Gdn
GLIDDON ROAD
BARONS KEEP
GWENDWR ROAD
Tenn Cts
B317
West Kensington
HAMMERSMITH FLYOVER A4
TALGARTH ROAD
Barons Court
BEAUMONT AVE
KENSINGTON HALL GDNS
Gibbs Green Sch
MARGRAVINE GDNS
KNIGHTS HO
BARON'S COURT ROAD
GIBBS GREEN
BARTON CT
BARTON ROAD
COMERAGH MEWS
COMERAGH ROAD
PALLISER CT
PALLISER ROAD
PO
BEAUMONT CRES
WEST KENSINGTON MANSIONS
GARSDALE TERR
CHALLONER STREET
CASTLETOWN RD
CHARLEVILLE CT
CHALLONER MANSIONS
AISGILL AVENUE
MUND STREET
FAIRBURN HO
CHURCHWARD HO
IVATT PL
STANIER CL
Hammersmith Cemetery
VEREKER ROAD
CHARLEVILLE RD
CHARLEVILLE MANSIONS
ROBERT GENTRY HO
CHALLONER CRES
LANFREY PL
MAY ST
BELLAMY CL
FAIRHOLME ROAD
GLEDSTANES ROAD
CHEESEMANS TERR
SUN ROAD
VINE SQ
The Queen's Club
PERHAM ROAD
ORCHARD SQ
SHUTERS SQ
FRANKLIN SQ
CLAXTON GR
HORTON HO
HOLMAN HUNT HO
BARONS COURT MANS
MAY ST
PASSFIELDS
STAR ROAD
MARCHBANK ROAD
AISGILL AVENUE
CLAXTON GR
FIELD ROAD
Pav Tenn Cts
FANE ST
LICKEY HO
CHELMSFORD CL
ALICE GILLIOTT CT
DESBOROUGH HO
ST ANDREW'S ROAD
ST ALBANS TERR
MARY MACARTHUR HO
BROWNING CT
264
TURNEVILLE ROAD
MARGRAVINE RD
COX
MUSCAL
ARCHEL ROAD
THAXTON RD
WILLIAM MORRIS HO
GASTEIN RD
NORMAND
ARCHEL ROAD
6
5
4
3
2
1
79
78

255
245
256
265
A
B
C
D
1
2
3
4
5
6
W8
SW5
Kensington High Street
A315
High Street Kensington
Commonwealth Institute
Phillimore Gardens
Phillimore Pl
Essex Villas
Argyll Road
Stafford Terrace
Phillimore Walk
Phillimore Court
Hornton Court
Hornton Place
Liby
Newspapers Ltd
Kensington Square
Thackeray St
Esmond Ct
Ansdell St
Ansdell Terr
Kensington Ct Place
Kensington Ct Mews
Kensington Ct Gdns
St Christopher Nevis / St Vincent The Grenadines
Cambridge Pl
Albert Pl
Vietnam
Douro Place
Richmond Coll
Victoria Road
Canning Pl
Canning Passage
De Vere Cotts
St Albans Mans
St Alban's Grove
South End
Trafalgar Gdns
South End Row
St Albans Studios
Tenn Ct
Cottesmore Ct
Cottesmore Gdns
Kelso Place
Kelso Pl
Stanford Road
Eldon Road
Kingsley Mews
Stanford Ct
Kynance Mews
Launceston Place
Cornwall Gardens
Cornwall Mews W
Gdns Wlk
Cornwall
Braemar Mans
St John's Villas
Lexham Walk
Osten Mews
Emperor's Gate
McLeod's Mews
Grenville Place
Lexham Gdns Mews
Lexham Gdns
Lexham Gardens
Bosnia & Herzegov
Pennant Mews
Cromwell Hospl
Cromwell Road
A4
Iverna Ct
Iverna Gardens
Wright's Lane
Adam and Eve Mews
Eden Cl
Allen Ho
Phillimore Terr
Wynnstay Gdns
Cheniston Gardens
Armenia
Scarsdale Place
Allendale Sch
Allen Mansions
Allen Street
Abingdon Ct
Abingdon Villas
Abingdon Gdns
Cedar Ho
Zetland Ho
Rutland Ho
Falkland Ho
Sutherland Ho
St Margaret's La
Marloes Road
Senegal
St Mary's Gate
Chantry Sq
St Mary's Pl
Devon Shire Pl
Thomas Pl
Beatrice Pl
Blithfield St
Stratford Studios
Inkerman Terr
Alma Terr
Stratford Road
Radley Mews
Lexham Mews
Sunningdale Gdns
Troy Ct
Phillimore Gdns Cl
Stafford Ct
B316
Ilchester Mansions
Abingdon Mansions
Warwick Chambers
Pater St
Cope Place
Abingdon Road
Pembroke Place
Pembroke Mews
Scarsdale Villas
St Barnabas & St Philip CE Prim Sch
Earls Walk
Pembroke Square
Shaftesbury Mews
Tenn Ct
Pembroke Wlk
Pembroke Villas
Pembroke Gardens Close
Pembroke Sq
Edwardes Sq
South Edwardes Sq
Leonard Ct
A3220
Chatsworth Ct
Pembroke Road
Marlborough Ct
Earl's Court Road
Huntingdon Ho
Logan Place
Logan Mews
Cromwell Cres
Warwick Mansions
Sterton Sq
Savoy Ct
Cromwell Mans
Redfield Lane
Redfield Mews
Wallgrave Rd
Sullivan Ct
Child's St
Child's Walk
Child's Pl
Kenway Road
Hogarth Pl
Hogarth Road
Knaresborough Pl
Collingham Pl
Gaspar Cl
Gaspar Mews
Courtfield Gdns
Astwood Mews
Ashburn Gdns
Courtfield Gardens
Collingham Gardens
Collingham Road
Earl's Court Gardens
Morton Mews
Boston Ho
Courtfield Mews
Colbeck Mews
Harrington
West Cromwell Road
Longridge Road
Templeton Place
Nevern Place
Nevern Road
Nevern Square
Nevern Sq
Nevern Mansions
Spear Ms
Barkston Gdns
Sheridon Ct
Laverton Mews
Laverton Pl
Hesper Mews
Dominica Commonwealth/ St Lucia
Wetherby Gdns
Earl's Court
Trebovir Road
Old Manor Yd
Kensington Mansions
Cluny Mews
Beach Ho
Philbeach Gardens
Warwick Road
Penywern Road
Bramham Gardens
Bolton Gardens
Boltons Ct
Beatrix Ho
A3218
Bousfield Prim Sch
South Bolton Gardens
Bolton Gdns Mews
The Little Boltons
Earl's Court Square
Farnell Mews
Wetherby Mansions
Coleherne Mansions
YH
Earl's Court Exhibition Centre
Eardley Crescent
Kempsford Gdns
Prim Sch
Langham Mansions
Rich Lane
Redcliffe Cl
Richmond Mansions
Old Brompton Road
Sybil Thorndike Casson Ho
Kramer Mews
Hunter Ho
Coleherne Court
Coleherne Road
Coleherne Mews
Wharfdale St
Princess Beatrice Ho
Redcliffe Square
Harcourt Terrace
Redcliffe Mews
Finborough Road
Westgate Ter
Redcliffe Gardens
Redcliffe St
Redcliffe Sch
Tregunter Rd
West Brompton
Lillie Road
Empress Pl
Sharnbrook Ho
Langtry Pl
Rickett St
Roxby Place
Lillie Yd
Seagrave Lodge
Cathcart
Walnut

246
255
266
A
B
C
D
A
B
C
D
6
5
4
3
2
1
SW7
South Kensington
Royal College of Art
Royal Albert Hall
Albert Hall Mansions
Royal Geographical Society
United Arab Emirates
Tunisia
Ethiopia
Fiji
Netherlands
Zambia
Estonia
Thorney Court
Broadwalk House
Reston Place
Palace Gate
De Vere Gardens
Hyde Park Gate
Hyde Park Gate Mews
Queen's Gate Mews
Chancellor House
Jay Mews
Albert Court
Jamaica
Royal College of Science
Bremner Rd
Bulgaria
Prince Consort Road
Princes Gate Court
Montrose Ct
Princes Gardens
Tenn Cts
Royal College of Music
Callendar Rd
Ayrton Rd
Unwin Rd
Exhibition Road
Imperial College of Science, Technology & Medecine
Liby
Wells Way
Armstrong Rd
Imperial College Road
Frankland Road
Science Museum
Geological Museum
Natural History Museum
Victoria Albert Museum
Princes Gate Mews
Royal College of Art
Venezuela
Oman
Albert Pl
Kensington Ct Mews
Vietnam
Douro Place
Canning Passage
De Vere Cotts
Canning Pl Mews
De Vere Mews
Richmond Coll
St Albans Mans
Canning Place
Kensington Gate
Victoria Road
Victoria Grove
Albert Mews
Queen's Gate Mews
Queen's Gate Terrace
Bangladesh
Thailand
Cottesmore Gdns
Launceston Place
St George's Court
Petersham La
Petersham Place
Gore Street
Elvaston Mews
Eldon Road
Kingsley Mews
Kynance Pl
Kynance Mews
Elvaston Place
Gabon
Mauritius
Queen's Gate Pl
Elvaston Mews
Petersham Mews
Cornwall Gardens
Queen's Gate Gdns
Queen's Gate Place
Queen's Gate Place Mews
Campbell Court
Queen's Gate Gardens
Queen's Gate
Gloucester Road
Osten Mews
Cornwall
Mews South
Emperor's Gate
McLeod's Mews
Southwell Gdns
Grenville Place
Morocco
Atherstone Mews
Cromwell Road
A4
B325
Derwent House
Stanhope Gdns
Stanhope Mews E
Yemen
Lycee Francais Charles de Gaulle (French Univ Coll)
Monaco
Cromwell Mews
Cromwell Pl
Thurloe Place
Thurloe Place Ms
Thurloe St
A3218
Queensberry Mews West
Queensberry Pl
Queensberry Way
Gloucester Road
Gloucester Park
Gaspar Cl
Gaspar Mews
Courtfield Gdns
Astwood Mews
Ashburn Gdns
Ashburn Place
Courtfield Road
Stanhope Mews W
Stanhope Gardens
Grenville Mews
Glendower Prep Sch
Harrington Road
Petersham House
Harrington Court
Glendower Place
Bute St
South Kensington
Pelham Street
B304
Old Brompton Road
Malvern Court
Melton Court
Onslow Square
Stanhope Mews South
Clareville Grove Mews
Clareville St
RC Prim Sch
Clareville Court
Clareville Grove
Manson Mews
Manson Pl
Reece Mews
Kendrick Mews
Kendrick Pl
Sumner Place
Sumner Place Mews
St Philip's Sch
Harrington Gardens
Courtfield Mews
Beck Mews
Wetherby Place
Hereford Sq
Barnaby Place
Sussex Mansions
Cranley Pl
Onslow Mews E
Onslow Mews W
Onslow Gardens
Tenn Ct
Sumner Pl
Sydney Close
Sydney Mews
Wetherby Gardens
Gledhow Gdns
Bina Gardens
Rosary Gardens
Dove Mews
Brechin Place
Onslow Gdns
Dominica Commonwealth/ St Lucia
Foulis Terr
Rose Sq
Fulham Road
Royal Marsden Hospl
Cresswell Gdns
Eagle Pl
Roland Way
Roland Gardens
Cranley Mews
Cranley Gardens
Ensor Mews
Neville St
Neville Terr
Selwood Pl
Selwood Terr
Lecky St
Elm Place
Fulham Wing
Royal Brompton Hospl
Dudmaston Mews
South Parade
Beatrix Ho
South Bolton Gardens
Bousfield Prim Sch
Bolton Gdns Mews
The Boltons
The Little Boltons
Cresswell Place
Drayton Gardens
Thistle Grove
Evelyn Gdns
Queen's Elm Square
Chelsea Square
Tenn Ct
Priory Walk
Priory Mansions
Harley Gdns
Drayton Ct
Thistle Grove
Holly Mews
Grove Ct
Elm Park Ho
Elm Park Gardens
Old Church Street
Harcourt Terrace
Redcliffe Mews
Tregunter Road
Gilston Road
Milborne Gr
Onslow Ct
Donovan Ct
A308
Elm Park Lane
Elm Park Road
Carlyle Sq
Bolton Studios
Redcliffe Road
Cavaye Pl
Cavaye Ho
Holmes Pl
Henniker Mews
Mulberry Walk
Redcliffe Gardens
Redcliffe Sch
Cathcart Road
Corbett Ho
Hollywood Mews
Seymour Walk
Cameron House
King's Road

247
258
267
A
B
C
D
1
2
3
4
5
6
Knightsbridge
Brompton
CHELSEA
SW3
The Hampshire Sch
Russian Orthodox Cathedral
LIBYA
The Oratory
Brompton Oratory
URUGUAY
COLUMBIA / EQUADOR
PAKISTAN
PERU
DENMARK
ICELAND
CONGO/ ZAIRE
SINGAPORE
KAZAKHSTAN
Hill House Int Sch
Hellenic Coll of London
Tenn Cts
Sussex House Sch
Holy Trinity CE Prim Sch
St Thomas More RC Sch
St Joseph's RC Prim Sch
Marlborough Prim Sch
Oratory RC Prim Sch
St Luke's Gardens
Royal Brompton Hospl
Sydney Wing
Chelsea Wing
Chelsea Coll of Art & Design
Liby
Sp Ctr
Offices
Kings Coll
Chelsea Synagogue
Burton's Court
Pav
Duke of York's HQ
Running Tk
DUKE OF YORK'S SQ
COLLEGE COURT
National Army Museum
BROMPTON ROAD
A4
B319
BEAUCHAMP PLACE
A308
THURLOE PLACE
SLOANE STREET
A3216
SLOANE SQUARE
LOWER SLOANE ST
A3217
KING'S ROAD
ROYAL HOSPITAL ROAD
SYDNEY STREET
B304
PONT STREET
HANS CRESCENT
HANS ROAD
HANS PLACE
BASIL ST
CADOGAN PLACE
CADOGAN SQUARE
CADOGAN GDNS
CADOGAN GATE
CADOGAN LANE
CADOGAN STREET
LOWNDES SQUARE
LOWNDES STREET
MOTCOMB STREET
ENNISMORE GARDENS
MONTPELIER SQUARE
MONTPELIER STREET
MONTPELIER WALK
TREVOR PLACE
TREVOR SQ
RAPHAEL ST
BROMPTON SQUARE
COTTAGE PLACE
EGERTON GARDENS
EGERTON TERRACE
EGERTON CRESCENT
OVINGTON SQUARE
YEOMAN'S ROW
WALTON STREET
LENNOX GARDENS
MILNER STREET
DRAYCOTT AVENUE
DRAYCOTT PLACE
SLOANE AVENUE
PELHAM STREET
PELHAM CRESCENT
SOUTH TERRACE
THURLOE SQUARE
ALEXANDER SQ
FULHAM ROAD
CALE STREET
ELYSTAN PLACE
ELYSTAN STREET
MARKHAM SQUARE
MARKHAM STREET
JUBILEE PLACE
SMITH STREET
ST LEONARD'S TERRACE
WALPOLE STREET
CHELTENHAM TERR
FRANKLIN'S ROW
TURKS ROW
OAKLEY STREET
FLOOD STREET
SHAWFIELD STREET
RADNOR WALK
TEDWORTH SQUARE
CHRISTCHURCH STREET
TITE STREET
WEST ROAD
ORMONDE GATE
DOVEHOUSE STREET
MANRESA ROAD
CHELSEA MANOR STREET
BRITTEN STREET
ST LUKE'S ST
BURY WALK
POND PLACE

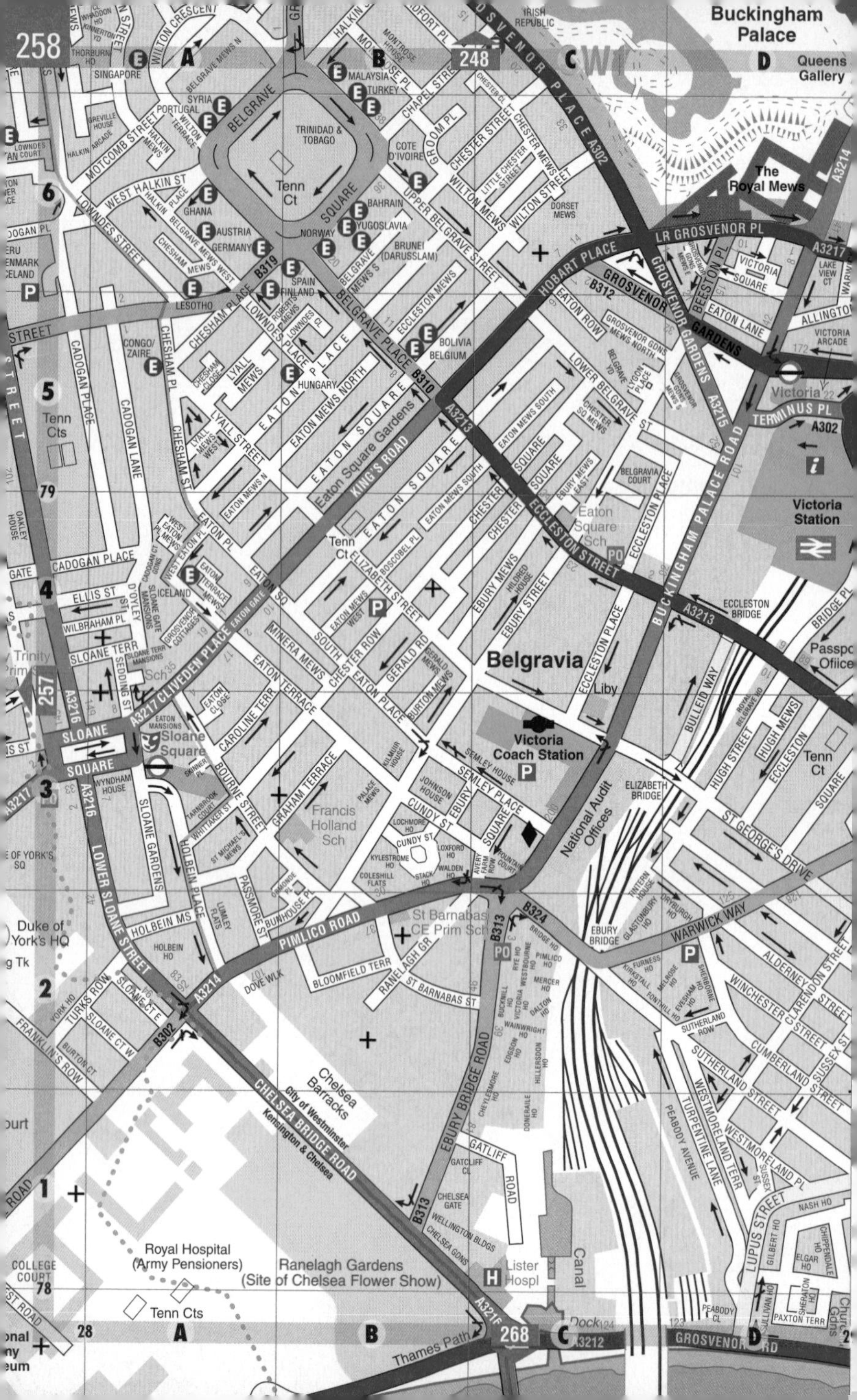
Buckingham Palace
Queens Gallery
The Royal Mews
IRISH REPUBLIC
248
A
B
C
D
WILTON CRESCENT
BELGRAVE MEWS N
SINGAPORE
MALAYSIA
TURKEY
MONTROSE PL
HALKIN ST
CHAPEL ST
GROSVENOR PLACE A302
CHESTER CL
SYRIA
PORTUGAL
WILTON TERRACE
GREVILLE HOUSE
HALKIN ARCADE
MOTCOMB STREET
HALKIN MEWS
BELGRAVE
TRINIDAD & TOBAGO
Tenn Ct
SQUARE
GROOM PL
COTE D'IVOIRE
CHESTER STREET
CHESTER MEWS
LITTLE CHESTER STREET
WILTON MEWS
WILTON STREET
DORSET MEWS
6
LOWNDES STREET
WEST HALKIN ST
HALKIN PLACE
GHANA
BAHRAIN
YUGOSLAVIA
AUSTRIA
NORWAY
BRUNEI (DARUSSLAM)
UPPER BELGRAVE STREET
HOBART PLACE
LR GROSVENOR PL
GROSVENOR GARDENS
BEESTON PL
VICTORIA SQUARE
LAKE VIEW CT
A3217
GERMANY
CHESHAM MEWS
BELGRAVE MEWS WEST
BELGRAVE MEWS S
B319
SPAIN
FINLAND
LESOTHO
CHESHAM PLACE
LOWNDES PLACE
ROBERTS MEWS
LOWNDES CL
ECCLESTON MEWS
BELGRAVE PLACE
GROSVENOR
B312
EATON ROW
GROSVENOR GDNS MEWS NORTH
EATON LANE
ALLINGTON
VICTORIA ARCADE
STREET
CADOGAN PLACE
CONGO/ ZAIRE
CHESHAM PL
CHESHAM CLOSE
LYALL MEWS
HUNGARY
EATON MEWS NORTH
BOLIVIA
BELGIUM
B310
LOWER BELGRAVE ST
BELGRAVE YD
LYGON PLACE
Victoria
TERMINUS PL
A302
5
Tenn Cts
CADOGAN LANE
LYALL STREET
LYALL MEWS WEST
EATON SQUARE
Eaton Square Gardens
KING'S ROAD
A3213
EATON MEWS SOUTH
CHESTER SQ MEWS
BUCKINGHAM PALACE ROAD
A3215
79
CHESHAM ST
EATON MEWS N
EATON MEWS SOUTH
CHESTER SQUARE
EBURY MEWS EAST
BELGRAVIA COURT
ECCLESTON PLACE
Victoria Station
OAKLEY HOUSE
WEST EATON PL MEWS
EATON PL
Tenn Ct
BOSCOBEL PL
ECCLESTON STREET
Eaton Square Sch
PO
CADOGAN PLACE
4
ELLIS ST
D'OYLEY ST
SLOANE GATE MANSIONS
ICELAND
EATON TERRACE MEWS
EATON SQ
ELIZABETH STREET
EATON MEWS WEST
EBURY MEWS
HILDRED HOUSE
EBURY STREET
ECCLESTON BRIDGE
BRIDGE PL
WILBRAHAM PL
GROSVENOR COTTAGES
EATON GATE
MINERA MEWS
SOUTH EATON PLACE
CHESTER ROW
GERALD RD
GERALD MEWS
Belgravia
ECCLESTON PLACE
Liby
Passport Office
SLOANE TERR
SLOANE TERR MANSIONS
Trinity Prim Sch
257
A3216
SEDDING ST
A3217 CLIVEDEN PLACE
EATON CLOSE
CAROLINE TERR
EATON TERRACE
BURTON MEWS
BULLEID WAY
ROYAL BELGRAVE HO
HUGH STREET
HUGH MEWS
SLOANE
EATON MANSIONS
Sloane Square
SQUARE
3
A3216
WYNDHAM HOUSE
SKINNER PL
BOURNE STREET
GRAHAM TERRACE
PALACE MEWS
KILMUIR HOUSE
SEMLEY HOUSE
SEMLEY PLACE
Victoria Coach Station
P
ELIZABETH BRIDGE
ECCLESTON SQUARE
Tenn Ct
TARNBROOK COURT
WHITTAKER ST
ST MICHAEL'S MEWS
Francis Holland Sch
JOHNSON HOUSE
CUNDY ST
EBURY SQUARE
LOCHMORE HO
CUNDY ST
LOXFORD HO
KYLESTROME HO
WALDEN HO
STACK HO
COLESHILL FLATS
AVERY FARM ROW
FOUNTAIN COURT
National Audit Offices
ST GEORGE'S DRIVE
DUKE OF YORK'S SQ
LOWER SLOANE STREET
SLOANE GARDENS
HOLBEIN PLACE
PASSMORE ST
LUMLEY FLATS
ORMONDE PL
BUNHOUSE PL
PIMLICO ROAD
St Barnabas CE Prim Sch
B313
B324
TINTERN HOUSE
GLASTONBURY HO
DRYBURGH HO
WARWICK WAY
Duke of York's HQ
HOLBEIN MS
HOLBEIN HO
DOVE WLK
BLOOMFIELD TERR
RANELAGH GR
ST BARNABAS ST
PO
BRIDGE HO
RYE HO
WESTBOURNE HO
PIMLICO HO
MERCER HO
EBURY BRIDGE
FURNESS HO
KIRKSTALL HO
MELROSE HO
FONTHILL HO
SHERBORNE HO
EVESHAM HO
ALDERNEY STREET
CLARENDON STREET
2
TURKS ROW
SLOANE CT E
A3214
YORK HO
SLOANE CT W
BUCKHILL HO
VICTORIA HO
DALTON HO
WAINWRIGHT HO
SUTHERLAND ROW
WINCHESTER STREET
SUSSEX ST
FRANKLIN'S ROW
BURTON CT
B302
EDGSON HO
HILLERSDON HO
CUMBERLAND STREET
Chelsea Barracks
City of Westminster
Kensington & Chelsea
CHELSEA BRIDGE ROAD
EBURY BRIDGE ROAD
CHEYLESMORE HO
DONERAILE HO
SUTHERLAND STREET
PEABODY AVENUE
TURPENTINE LANE
WESTMORELAND TERR
WESTMORELAND PL
GATLIFF ROAD
GATCLIFF CL
SUSSEX ST
1
ROAD
CHELSEA GATE
WELLINGTON BLDGS
CHELSEA GDNS
B313
LUPUS STREET
NASH HO
GILBERT HO
CHIPPENDALE HO
ELGAR HO
Royal Hospital (Army Pensioners)
COLLEGE COURT
78
Ranelagh Gardens (Site of Chelsea Flower Show)
Lister Hospl
Canal
Tenn Cts
A321F
SULLIVAN HO
SHERATON HO
PAXTON TERR
PEABODY CL
28
A
B
268
C
Dock
A3212
GROSVENOR RD
D
Thames Path

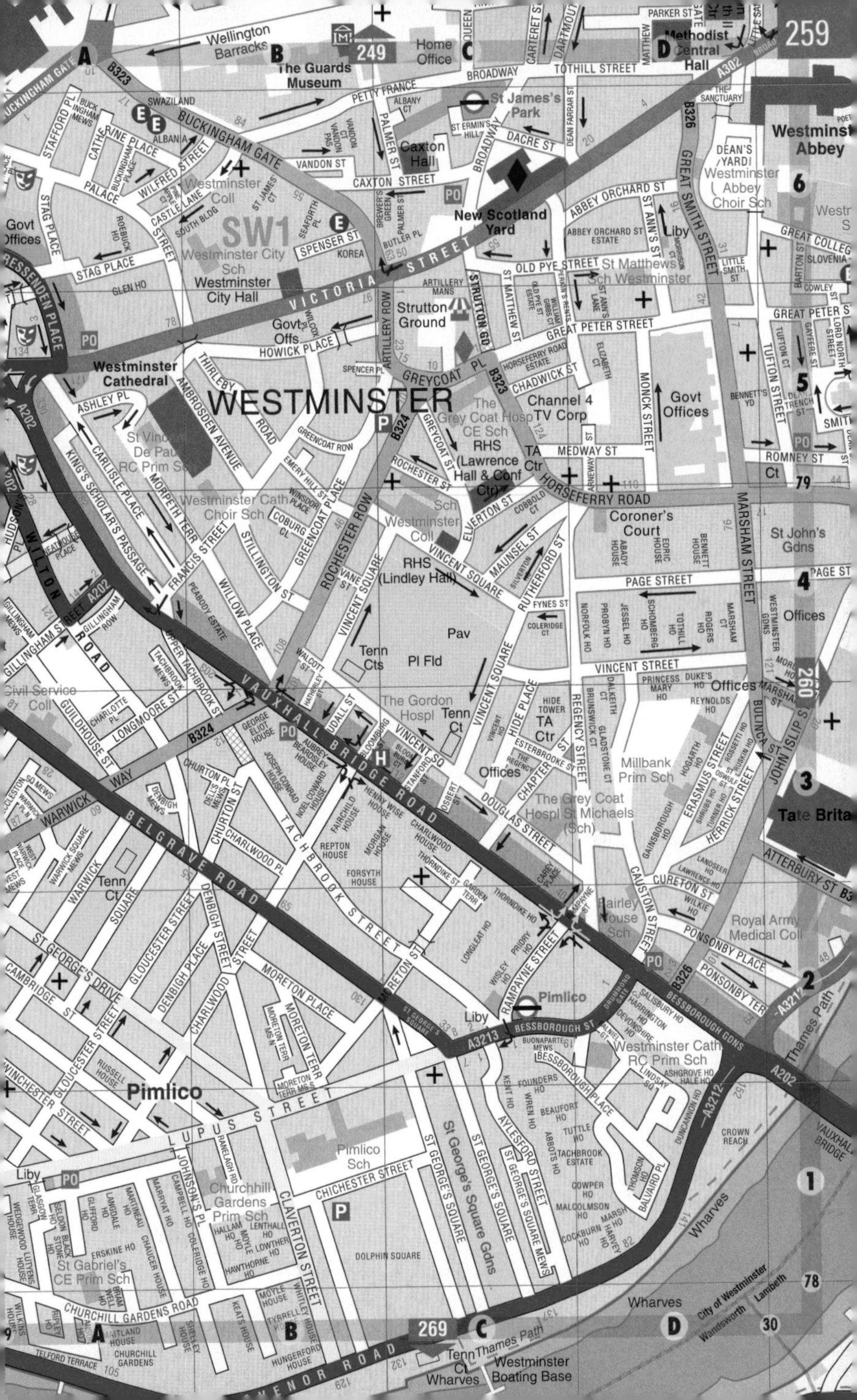

Wellington Barracks
The Guards Museum
249
Home Office
Methodist Central Hall
PARKER ST
BUCKINGHAM GATE
B323
PETTY FRANCE
BROADWAY
TOTHILL STREET
CARTERET ST
DARTMOUTH
MATTHEW
A302
St James's Park
THE SANCTUARY
Westminster Abbey
SWAZILAND
ALBANIA
STAFFORD PL
BUCKINGHAM MEWS
CATHERINE PLACE
BUCKINGHAM PLACE
WILFRED STREET
PALACE
CASTLE LANE
Westminster Coll
SOUTH BLDG
ALBANY CT
VANDON CT
VANDON PAS
VANDON ST
PALMER ST
Caxton Hall
ST ERMIN'S HILL
DACRE ST
DEAN FARRAR ST
CAXTON STREET
New Scotland Yard
ABBEY ORCHARD ST
ST ANN'S ST
GREAT SMITH STREET
DEAN'S YARD
Westminster Abbey Choir Sch
STAG PLACE
Govt Offices
ROEBUCK HO
SW1
Westminster City Sch
Westminster City Hall
SEAFORTH PL
SPENSER ST
KOREA
BREWER'S GREEN
BUTLER PL
VICTORIA STREET
ABBEY ORCHARD ST ESTATE
Liby
GREAT COLLEGE
SLOVENIA
LITTLE SMITH ST
OLD PYE STREET
St Matthews Sch Westminster
GLEN HO
ARTILLERY MANS
STRUTTON GD
ST MATTHEW ST
OLD PYE ST ESTATE
WILLIAM GIBBS CT
PERKIN'S RENTS
ST ANN'S LANE
BARTON ST
COWLEY
GREAT PETER ST
PO
Govt Offs
WILCOX PL
HOWICK PLACE
Strutton Ground
GREAT PETER STREET
HORSEFERRY ROAD ESTATE
ELIZABETH CT
TUFTON CT
GAYFERE ST
LORD NORTH STREET
Westminster Cathedral
THIRLEBY ROAD
AMBROSDEN AVENUE
SPENCER PL
GREYCOAT PL
B323
CHADWICK ST
WESTMINSTER
ASHLEY PL
A202
St Vincent De Paul RC Prim Sch
GREENCOAT ROW
B324
P
The Grey Coat Hosp CE Sch
RHS (Lawrence Hall & Conf Ctr)
Channel 4 TV Corp
Govt Offices
MONCK STREET
BENNETT'S YD
DEAN TRENCH ST
SMITH
CARLISLE PLACE
KING'S SCHOLAR'S PASSAGE
MORPETH TERR
EMERY HILL ST
ROCHESTER ST
GREYCOAT ST
TA Ctr
MEDWAY ST
ROMNEY ST
Ct
HORSEFERRY ROAD
Westminster Cath Choir Sch
WINSOR PLACE
COBURG CL
GREENCOAT PLACE
ROCHESTER ROW
Sch Westminster Coll
ELVERTON ST
COBBOLD CT
Coroner's Court
ABADY HOUSE
EDRIC HOUSE
BENNETT HOUSE
MARSHAM STREET
St John's Gdns
WILTON ROAD
NEATHOUSE PLACE
HUDSON'S PL
FRANCIS STREET
STILLINGTON ST
VINCENT SQUARE
MAUNSEL ST
RUTHERFORD ST
SILVERTON
RHS (Lindley Hall)
PAGE STREET
PAGE ST
WILLOW PLACE
PEABODY ESTATE
VANE ST
FYNES ST
COLERIDGE CT
NORFOLK HO
PROBYN HO
JESSEL HO
SCHOMBERG HO
TOTHILL HO
ROGERS HO
MARSHAM CT
WESTMINSTER GDNS
Offices
GILLINGHAM STREET
GILLINGHAM MEWS
GILLINGHAM ROW
A202
Pav
Tenn Cts
Pl Fld
VINCENT STREET
MORLEY
Civil Service Coll
TACHBROOK MEWS
UPPER TACHBROOK ST
VAUXHALL BRIDGE ROAD
WALCOTT ST
HATHERLEY ST
The Gordon Hospl
Tenn Ct
HIDE PLACE
HIDE TOWER
TA Ctr
DALKEITH CT
BRUNSWICK CT
GLADSTONE CT
PRINCESS MARY HO
DUKE'S HO
REYNOLDS HO
Offices
MARSHAM ST
260
GUILDHOUSE ST
CHARLOTTE PL
LONGMOORE ST
B324
GEORGE ELIOT HOUSE
UDALL ST
BLOOMBURG ST
VINCENT SQ
H
STANFORD ST
ESTERBROOKE ST
CHAPTER ST
REGENCY STREET
Millbank Prim Sch
HOGARTH HO
ERASMUS STREET
ROSSETTI HO
RUSKIN HO
BULINCA ST
JOHN ISLIP ST
WARWICK WAY
DENBIGH MEWS
CHURTON PL
BELL'S MEWS
CHURTON ST
JOSEPH CONRAD HOUSE
AUBREY BEARDSLEY HOUSE
NOEL COWARD HOUSE
FAIRCHILD HOUSE
HENRY WISE HOUSE
OSBERT ST
Offices
DOUGLAS STREET
The Grey Coat Hospl St Michaels (Sch)
GAINSBOROUGH HO
SHRUBS HO
TURNER HO
HERRICK STREET
Tate Britain
WARWICK SQUARE MEWS
BELGRAVE ROAD
CHARLWOOD PL
TACHBROOK STREET
REPTON HOUSE
MORGAN HOUSE
CHARLWOOD HOUSE
THORNDIKE ST
FORSYTH HOUSE
GARDEN TERR
CAREY PLACE
ATTERBURY ST
LANDSEER HO
LAWRENCE HO
CURETON ST
WILKIE HO
Tenn Ct
WARWICK SQUARE
GLOUCESTER STREET
DENBIGH STREET
THORNDIKE HO
RAMPAYNE ST
Fairley House Sch
CAUSTON STREET
Royal Army Medical Coll
ST GEORGE'S DRIVE
CAMBRIDGE ST
DENBIGH PLACE
CHARLWOOD
MORETON ST
LONGLEAT HO
WISLEY HO
PRIORY HO
RAMPAYNE STREET
PONSONBY PLACE
PONSONBY TERR
B326
MORETON PLACE
MORETON TERR
MORETON TERR MS N
ST GEORGE'S SQUARE
Liby
Pimlico
BESSBOROUGH ST
A3213
DRUMMOND GATE
SALISBURY HO
HARRINGTON HO
DEVONSHIRE HO
BESSBOROUGH GDNS
A3212
Thames Path
A202
RUSSELL HOUSE
Pimlico
WINCHESTER STREET
MORETON TERR MS S
BUONAPARTE MEWS
BESSBOROUGH PLACE
Westminster Cath RC Prim Sch
LINDSAY
ASHGROVE HO
HALE HO
LUPUS STREET
JOHNSON'S PL
RANELAGH RD
Pimlico Sch
ST GEORGE'S SQUARE
St George's Square Gdns
AYLESFORD STREET
ST GEORGE'S SQUARE MEWS
KENT HO
FOUNDERS HO
WREN HO
BEAUFORT HO
ABBOTS HO
TUTTLE HO
TACHBROOK ESTATE
DUNCANNON HO
CROWN REACH
VAUXHALL BRIDGE
Liby
PO
CHICHESTER STREET
Churchhill Gardens Prim Sch
GLASGOW TERR
GLIFFORD HO
LANGDALE HO
MARTINEAU HO
MARRYAT HO
CAMPBELL HO
P
THOMSON HO
BALVAIRD PL
COWPER HO
MALCOLMSON HO
COCKBURN HO
HARVEY HO
MARSH HO
Wharves
WEDGEWOOD HOUSE
LUTYENS HOUSE
SELDON HO
BLACKSTONE HO
ERSKINE HO
CHAUCER HOUSE
HALLAM HO
MOYLE HO
LENTHALL HO
LOWTHER HO
HAWTHORNE HO
COLERIDGE HO
CLAVERTON STREET
DOLPHIN SQUARE
St Gabriel's CE Prim Sch
BRAM WELL HO
MOYLE HOUSE
WHITLEY HOUSE
Wharves
City of Westminster
Lambeth
Wandsworth
CHURCHILL GARDENS ROAD
WILKINS HOUSE
RIPLEY HO
MAITLAND HOUSE
SHELLEY HOUSE
KEATS HOUSE
TYRRELL HOUSE
269
A
B
C
D
TELFORD TERRACE
CHURCHILL GARDENS
HUNGERFORD HOUSE
GROSVENOR ROAD
Tenn Ct
Thames Path
Wharves
Westminster Boating Base
1
2
3
4
5
6
78
79
30

260
250
270
259
A
B
C
D
1
2
3
4
5
6
LAMBETH
Houses of Parliament
Westminster Abbey
Old Palace Yard
Palace Yard
Victoria Tower
The Victoria Tower Gardens
Florence Nightingale Museum
St Thomas' Hospl
St Thomas's Hospital Medical School
Lambeth Palace
Mus of Garden History
Archbishop's Park
Lambeth Pier
Fire Brigade Pier
Fire Brigade HQ
Police HQ
RIVER THAMES
Thames Path
Albert Embankment
ALBERT EMBANKMENT
LAMBETH PALACE ROAD
LAMBETH BRIDGE
VAUXHALL BRIDGE
MILLBANK
ABINGDON STREET
ST MARGARET
Guildhall
BROAD SANCTUARY
THE SANCTUARY
DEAN'S YARD
Westminster Abbey Choir Sch
Westminster Sch
GREAT COLLEGE STREET
GREAT SMITH STREET
GREAT PETER STREET
St Johns Concert Hall
SMITH SQ
DEAN STANLEY STREET
ROMNEY ST
St John's Gdns
PAGE STREET
MARSHAM STREET
THORNEY STREET
Offices
Govt Offices
Millbank Tower
Tate Britain
ATTERBURY ST
JOHN ISLIP STREET
Royal Army Medical Coll
PONSONBY PLACE
PONSONBY TER
Gunhouse Stairs (site of)
Vauxhall
Vauxhall Cross
Vauxhall City Farm
Spring Gardens
Pedlers Park
Recn Gd
Lilian Baylis Sch
Vauxhall Prim Sch
St Anne's RC Prim Sch
Superstore
Depot
Tenn Cts
ROYAL STREET
UPPER MARSH
CARLISLE LANE
HERCULES ROAD
LAMBETH HIGH STREET
OLD PARADISE STREET
WHITGIFT ST
NEWPORT STREET
LAMBETH WALK
BLACK PRINCE ROAD
SALAMANCA STREET
RANDALL ROAD
JONATHAN STREET
GLASSHOUSE WALK
LAUD ST
TYERS TERR
VAUXHALL WALK
VAUXHALL STREET
ST OSWALD'S PLACE
SANCROFT STREET
ORSETT STREET
NEWBURN STREET
GODING STREET
DURHAM ST A3204
KENNINGTON LANE
HARLEYFORD
OVAL WAY
FARNHAM ROYAL
ST GEORGE WHARF
Wharves
City of Westminster
Lambeth
Wandsworth
A3212
A3203
A3036
A202
A3204
B323
B326
A302

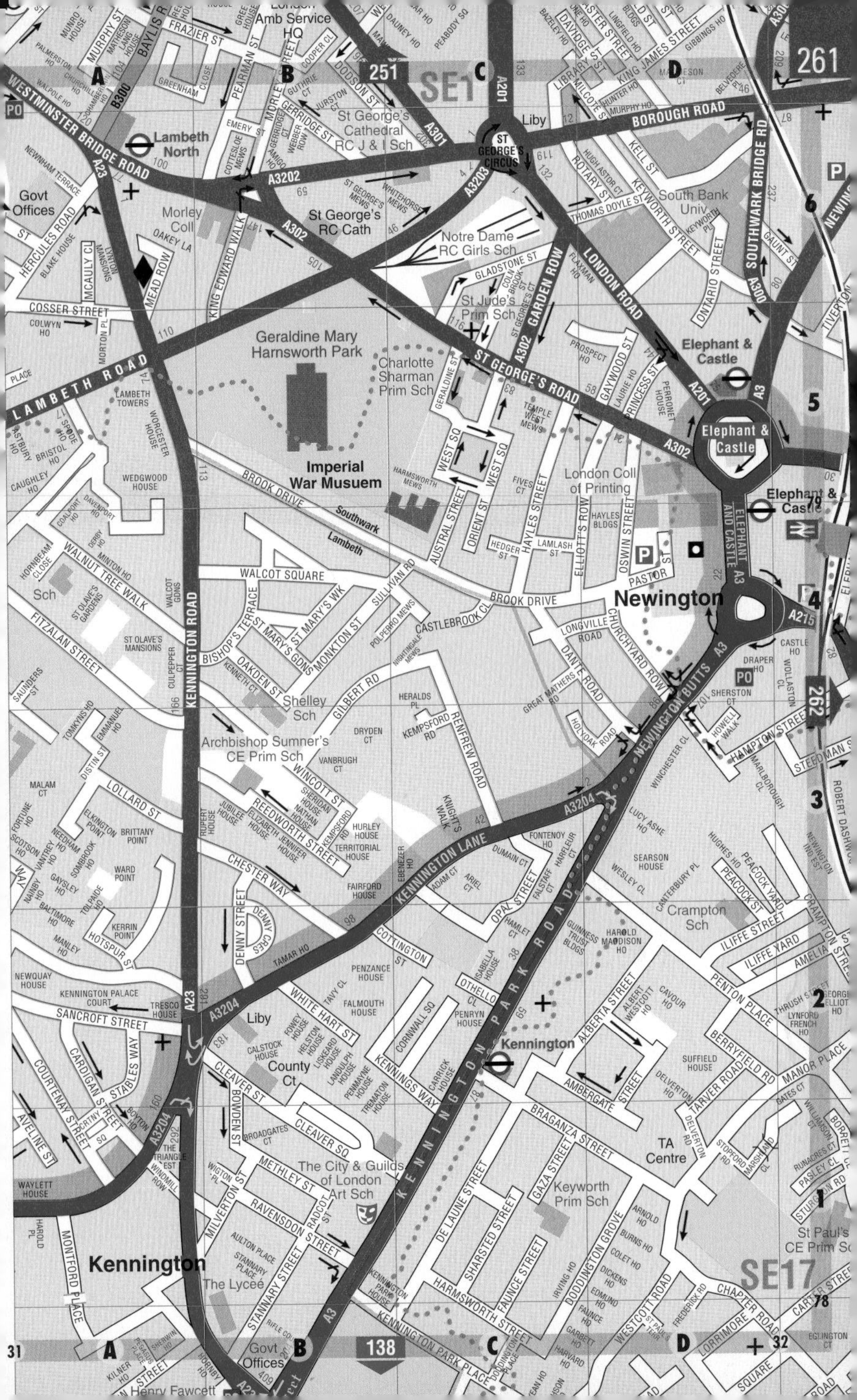

261
251
262
138
SE1
SE17
A
B
C
D
1
2
3
4
5
6
Amb Service HQ
Westminster Bridge Road
B300
Baylis Rd
Frazier St
Murphy St
Matheson Lang House
Greenham Close
Pearman St
Morley St
Cooper Cl
Guthrie Ct
Gerridge St
Gerridge Ct
Amigo Ho
Webber Row
Jurston Ct
Dodson St
Dauney Ho
Peabody Sq
St George's Cathedral RC J & I Sch
Lambeth North
Emery St
Cottesloe Mews
A3202
A301
A201
St George's Circus
Liby
Borough Road
King James Street
Library St
Milcote St
Davidge St
Lingfield Ho
Gibbings Ho
Belvedere Pl
Hunter Ho
Murphy Ho
Kell St
Rotary St
Hugh Astor Ct
Thomas Doyle St
Keyworth Street
Keyworth Pl
South Bank Univ
Southwark Bridge Rd
Gaunt St
A300
Ontario Street
A3203
A302
St George's Mews
Whitehorse Mews
St George's RC Cath
Notre Dame RC Girls Sch
Govt Offices
Newnham Terrace
Hercules Road
Blake House
Lynton Mansions
Mcauly Cl
Morley Coll
Oakey La
Mead Row
King Edward Walk
Cosser Street
Colwyn Ho
Morton Pl
Lambeth Road
Place
Lambeth Towers
Worcester House
Geraldine Mary Harmsworth Park
Charlotte Sharman Prim Sch
Imperial War Musuem
Gladstone St
Colnbrook St
St Jude's Prim Sch
St George's Ct
Garden Row
London Road
Flaxman Ho
Prospect Ho
Gaywood St
Laurie Ho
Princess St
Perronet House
Elephant & Castle
St George's Road
Geraldine St
West Sq
Temple West Mews
Harmsworth Mews
Austral Street
Orient St
Fives Ct
Hayles Street
Hayles Bldgs
London Coll of Printing
Elliott's Row
Oswin Street
Hedger St
Lamlash St
Pastor St
Elephant and Castle
A3
Newington
A215
Castle Ho
Draper Ho
Wollaston Cl
Sherston Ct
Howell Walk
Hampton Street
Steedman St
Robert Dashwood Way
Newington Ind Est
Marlborough Cl
Winchester Cl
Tiverton St
Newington Butts
Churchyard Row
Longville Road
Dante Road
Great Maters Rd
Holyoak Road
Brook Drive
Southwark
Lambeth
Walcot Square
Sullivan Rd
Castlebrook Cl
Polperro Mews
Nightingale Mews
Bishop's Terrace
St Mary's Gdns
St Mary's Wk
Monkton St
Oakden St
Kenneth Ct
Shelley Sch
Gilbert Rd
Heralds Pl
Kempsford Rd
Renfrew Road
Dryden Ct
Vanbrugh Ct
Archbishop Sumner's CE Prim Sch
Wincott St
Sheridan House
Nathan House
Kennington Road
Walcot Gdns
Culpepper Ct
St Olave's Gardens
St Olave's Mansions
Walnut Tree Walk
Fitzalan Street
Hornbeam Close
Sch
Wedgwood House
Caughley Ho
Bristol Ho
Spode Ho
Astbury Ho
Coalport Ho
Davenport Ho
Derby Ho
Minton Ho
Saunders St
Tomkyns Ho
Emmanuel Ho
Distin St
Malam Ct
Lollard St
Fortune Ho
Scotson Ho
Elkington Point
Brittany Point
Needham Ho
Vantrey Ho
Sombrook Ho
Gaysley Ho
Nainby Ho
Baltimore Ho
Ward Point
Tolpaide Ho
Kerrin Point
Manley Ho
Hotspur St
Rupert House
Jubilee House
Elizabeth House
Jennifer House
Reedworth Street
Kempsford Rd
Hurley House
Territorial House
Chester Way
Fairford House
Ebenezer Ho
Knight's Walk
Kennington Lane
A3204
Fontenoy Ho
Harfleur Ct
Dumain Ct
Adam Ct
Ariel Ct
Opal Street
Falstaff Ct
Hamlet Ct
Lucy Ashe Ho
Searson House
Wesley Cl
Canterbury Pl
Hughes Ho
Peacock Yard
Peacock St
Crampton Sch
Crampton Street
Iliffe Street
Iliffe Yard
Amelia St
Denny Street
Denny Cres
Tamar Ho
Cottington St
Penzance House
Tavy Cl
Falmouth House
White Hart St
Cornwall Sq
Isabella House
Othello Cl
Penryn House
Guinness Trust Bldgs
Harold Maddison Ho
Kennington Park Road
Kennington
Alberta Street
Albert Westcott Ho
Cavour Ho
Penton Place
Thrush St
Lynford French Ho
George Elliot Ho
Berryfield Rd
Manor Place
Suffield House
Ambergate Street
Delverton Ho
Delverton Rd
Tarver Road
Gates Ct
Williamson Ct
Borrett Cl
Stopford Rd
Marsland Cl
Runacres Ct
Pasley Cl
Sturgeon Rd
St Paul's CE Prim Sch
TA Centre
Newquay House
Kennington Palace Court
Tresco House
Sancroft Street
Liby
Fowey House
Helston House
Liskeard House
Calstock House
County Ct
Landulph House
Penmayne House
Trematon House
Kennings Way
Carrick House
Braganza Street
Gaza Street
Keyworth Prim Sch
Courtenay Street
Cardigan Street
Stables Way
Aveline St
Crtny Sq
Boyton Ho
The Triangle Est
Windmill Row
Cleaver St
Bowden St
Cleaver Sq
Broadgates Ct
Methley St
Wigton Pl
Milverton St
The City & Guilds of London Art Sch
Radcot St
Ravensdon Street
Aulton Place
Stannary Place
Stannary Street
The Lycee
Waylett House
Harold Pl
Montford Place
Kennington
De Laune Street
Sharsted Street
Faunce Street
Harmsworth Street
Doddington Grove
Irving Ho
Arnold Ho
Burns Ho
Colet Ho
Dickens Ho
Edmund Ho
Faunce Ho
Garrett Ho
Harvard Ho
Westcott Road
Frederick Rd
Chapter Road
Lorrimore Square
Carter Street
Eglington Ct
Kennington Park House
Kennington Park Place
Doddington Place
Rifle Ct
Kilner Ho
Pegasus Place
Sherwin Ho
Hornby Ho
Govt Offices
Henry Fawcett
31
32
78
79

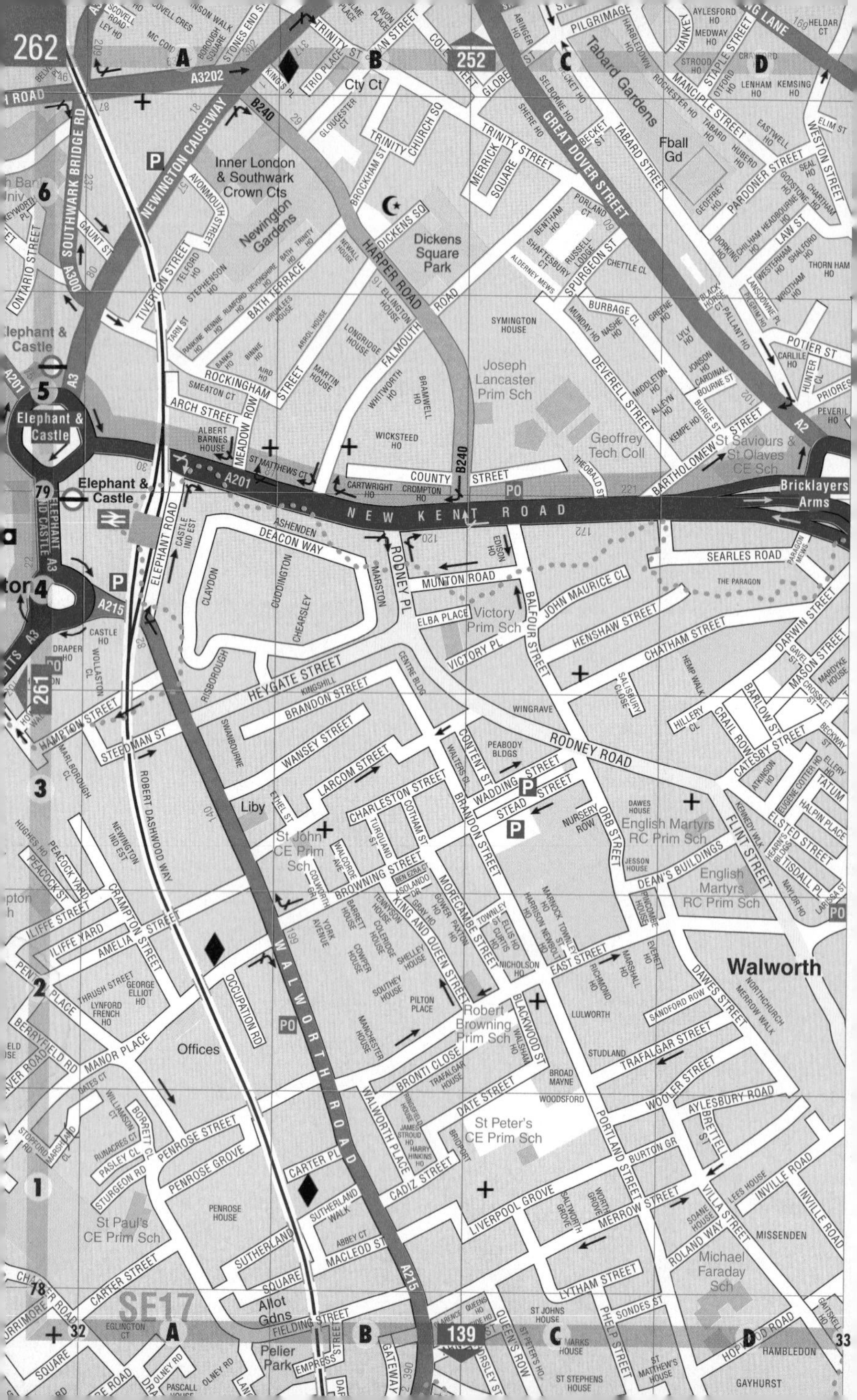
A
B
C
D
252
A3202
NEWINGTON CAUSEWAY
B240
TRINITY PLACE
TRINITY ST
Cty Ct
GLOUCESTER CT
TRINITY CHURCH SQ
BROCKHAM ST
Inner London & Southwark Crown Cts
Newington Gardens
SOUTHWARK BRIDGE RD
A300
ONTARIO STREET
GAUNT ST
TIVERTON STREET
BATH TERRACE
DICKENS SQ
Dickens Square Park
HARPER ROAD
MERRICK SQUARE
TRINITY STREET
GREAT DOVER STREET
Tabard Gardens
TABARD STREET
Fball Gd
PILGRIMAGE
PARDONER STREET
WESTON STREET
LAW ST
MANCIPLE STREET
STAPLE STREET
SPURGEON ST
CHETTLE CL
BURBAGE CL
PORLAND CT
RUSSELL LODGE
SHAFTESBURY CT
ALDERNEY MEWS
SYMINGTON HOUSE
Joseph Lancaster Prim Sch
DEVERELL STREET
Geoffrey Tech Coll
POTIER ST
A2
St Saviours & St Olaves CE Sch
Elephant & Castle
Elephant & Castle
A201
A3
ROCKINGHAM STREET
ARCH STREET
SMEATON CT
MEADOW ROW
FALMOUTH ROAD
WICKSTEED HO
COUNTY STREET
B240
NEW KENT ROAD
PO
Bricklayers Arms
SEARLES ROAD
THE PARAGON
PARAGON MEWS
DEACON WAY
ASHENDEN
CLAYDON
CUDDINGTON
CHEARSLEY
MARSTON
RODNEY PL
MUNTON ROAD
ELBA PLACE
Victory Prim Sch
VICTORY PL
BALFOUR STREET
JOHN MAURICE CL
HENSHAW STREET
CHATHAM STREET
DARWIN STREET
MASON STREET
ELEPHANT ROAD
CASTLE IND EST
A215
HEYGATE STREET
BRANDON STREET
WANSEY STREET
LARCOM STREET
HAMPTON STREET
STEEDMAN ST
ROBERT DASHWOOD WAY
261
RODNEY ROAD
WINGRAVE
PEABODY BLDGS
WADDING STREET
STEAD STREET
CHARLESTON STREET
CONTENT ST
Liby
St John CE Prim Sch
BROWNING STREET
MORECAMBE STREET
KING AND QUEEN STREET
BRANDON STREET
ORB STREET
NURSERY ROW
English Martyrs RC Prim Sch
FLINT STREET
English Martyrs RC Prim Sch
DEAN'S BUILDINGS
CATESBY STREET
CRAIL ROW
BARLOW ST
TATUM
HALPIN PLACE
ELSTED STREET
TISDALL PL
Walworth
EAST STREET
WALWORTH ROAD
OCCUPATION RD
ILIFFE STREET
ILIFFE YARD
AMELIA STREET
CRAMPTON STREET
PEACOCK YARD
PEACOCK ST
PENTON PLACE
MANOR PLACE
BERRYFIELD RD
Offices
PO
Robert Browning Prim Sch
BRONTI CLOSE
TRAFALGAR HOUSE
PILTON PLACE
BLACKWOOD ST
LULWORTH
STUDLAND
TRAFALGAR STREET
DAWES STREET
SANDFORD ROW
NORTHCHURCH
MERROW WALK
WOOLER STREET
AYLESBURY ROAD
BRETTELL ST
BROAD MAYNE
WOODSFORD
St Peter's CE Prim Sch
DATE STREET
WALWORTH PLACE
CADIZ STREET
CARTER PL
PORTLAND STREET
BURTON GR
LIVERPOOL GROVE
MERROW STREET
VILLA STREET
ROLAND WAY
INVILLE ROAD
MISSENDEN
Michael Faraday Sch
PENROSE STREET
PENROSE GROVE
PENROSE HOUSE
St Paul's CE Prim Sch
SUTHERLAND WALK
SUTHERLAND SQUARE
MACLEOD ST
LYTHAM STREET
SONDES ST
CARTER STREET
SE17
Allot Gdns
FIELDING STREET
Pelier Park
EMPRESS STREET
GATEWAY
139
QUEEN'S ROW
PHELP STREET
HOPWOOD ROAD
HAMBLEDON
GAYHURST
ST JOHNS HOUSE
ST STEPHENS HOUSE
1
2
3
4
5
6
32
33
78
79

BERMONDSEY LEATHER MKT
MOROCCO
LAMB WLK
A
B
C
D
Bermondsey (New Caledonian)
NEWHAM'S ROW
253
PURBROOK EST
FLORIN CT
RILEY ROAD
MILLSTREAM RD
WHARTON HO
STANWORTH ST
SWEENEY
ARNOLD ESTATE
LUPIN PT
BLUE LION PL
MARKET YD MEWS
Caledonian Market
PURBROOK ST
ST LAWRENCE HOUSE
TOMSON HOUSE
THETFORD HOUSE
MALTBY STREET
MARLOW HOUSE
PRESTON HOUSE
RUFUS HOUSE
GEDLING PL
NECKINGER ST
B202
DARNAY HOUSE
CARTON HOUSE
GILES HOUSE
ELIM ESTATE
ELIM ST
WILD'S RENTS
ARCHDALE HO
MENDHAM HO
STEVENS ST
CHARTES HO
BROMLEIGH HOUSE
ATTILBURGH HOUSE
ABBEY STREET
PO
TA Ctr
MARINE ST
A2198
B202
BERMONDSEY SQ
CLUNY PLACE
DECIMA STREET
A2205
TROCETTE MANS
TOWER BRIDGE ROAD
LONG WLK
RADCLIFFE RD
BOULOGNE HOUSE
BRETON HOUSE
WOODVILLE HOUSE
BRIDEWAIN ST
NECKINGER
ENID STREET
OLD JAMAICA R
NECKINGER ESTATE
6
MEAKIN ESTATE
ALICE ST
Southwark Coll (Grange Centre)
AYLWIN ESTATE
ST OWEN HOUSE
WALFORD CT
ST VINCENT HOUSE
VALOLS HOUSE
LARNACA HOUSE
GEORGE TINGLE HOUSE
VOYAGER BUSINESS
A2206
GRIGG'S PL
WOOD'S PL
FENDALL ST
GRANGE
THE GRANGE
GRANGE WALK
SKYLINE CT
GRANGE YARD
Liby
SPA ROAD
ROUEL ROAD
DOCK INDUST
ROTHSAY STREET
ALICE ST
GREEN WALK
Grange Prim Sch
GRANGE HOUSE
MARSHALLS PL
VAUBAN ST
DUNLOP PLACE
WEBB STREET
BRIGHTON BLDGS
BUSHBABY CL
SWAN MEAD
HAROLD ESTATE
PAGE'S WALK
CRIMSCOTT STREET
GRANGE ROAD
VAUBAN ESTATE
5
SPA COURT
GOODWIN CL
A100
CREASY ESTATE
STEWART HO
ARUNDEL BLDGS
BACON GROVE
TOWER MANSIONS
CANON MURNANE RD
Bermondsey Spa Gdns
KEYSE RD
ALSCOT ROAD
ALSCOT ROAD IND EST
CADBURY WAY
ROBIN COURT
WOOLSTAPLERS WAY
SPALDING ROAD
ABERDOUR ST
TOWER WLK
LEROY STREET
GUINNESS SQ
PAGE'S WALK
Boutcher CE Prim Sch
KINTORE WAY
HENLEY DRIVE
QUADRANGLE CL
SCHOOL HO
CURTIS STREET
HAZEL WAY
ALSCOT RD
BREWSTER HOUSE
Aylwin Girls Sch
TOWERGATE
CURTIS WAY
WILLOW WALK
SETCHELL WAY
ALSCOT WAY
B203
4
A2206
SETCHELL RD
DHONAU HOUSE
FAIRBY HOUSE
HARTLEY HOUSE
Allot Gdns
118
PRESTON HOUSE
PRESTON CL
TOWNSEND ST
WALERAN FLATS
MANDELA WAY
KINGSLEY FLATS
BUTTERMERE CL
ASH HOUSE
FAWKHAM HOUSE
DARTFORD HOUSE
BALACLAVA ROAD
ALMA GR
FORT ROAD
REVERDY
THORNTON HOUSE
COMUS PLACE
COMUS HOUSE
CONGREVE STREET
BARKER HO
MASSINGER ST
BOARLEY HO
YALDAM HO
DOVER FLATS
AVINGTON COURT
HENDRE HO
HENDRE RD
DUNTON ROAD
LONGFIELD ESTATE
ALFRED SALTER HO
CRAGIE HOUSE
STANSFIELD HOUSE
3
IGHTHAM HO
POVEY HOUSE
OFFHAM HO
PLAXDALE HO
DORMSTONE HO
BROOMFIELD HO
CHELSFIELD HOUSE
STANFORD PL
A2
Liby
MARCIA ROAD
KEATS CL
WORDSWORTH RD
MILTON CL
LONGFELLOW WAY
LYNTON ROAD
BECKWAY ST
HUNTSMAN ST
KNIGHT HO
STAUNTON HO
DENT HO
THOMSON HO
EYNSFORD HO
DETLING HO
CULAND HO
BACKHOUSE PL
PENRY ST
CHAUCER DRIVE
BUSHWOOD DR
BURNHAM CL
ABINGDON CL
CADET DR
LYNTON ESTATE
EAST STREET
EXON ST
CRISPIN CT
MINNOW WLK
OLD KENT ROAD
B203
BURNELL WLK
INNIS HO
DUNNICO HO
FREEMANTLE ST
SURREY TERR
MADRON STREET
PO
106
B204
OXLEY CLOSE
SEDAN WAY
Surrey Square Jun & Inf Schs
SURREY SQUARE
FLINTON ST
LEYSDOWN HO
IFIELD HO
Superstore
HUMPHREY ST
ROLLS ROAD
BROCKLEY HO
ST MARY NEWINGTON CL
ALDBRIDGE ST
HADLOW HO
SWANLEY HO
IVY CHURCH LA
ROWCROSS STREET
LACKLAND HO
MANDERVILLE HO
FITZROY HO
AVOCET CL
2
WOLVERTON
SE17
Surrey Square Park
BARHAM HO
BETHERSDEN HO
SOUTHBOROUGH HO
KINGLAKE STREET
AMERY HO
UPNOR WAY
BENENDEN HO
CUXTON HO
DEAL HO
SHORNCLIFFE RD
B214
B204
BRODIE HO
RIVET HO
BRODIE ST
COOPER'S ROAD
MARCHANT CT
ALSACE RD
ALVEY STREET
TENTERDEN HO
KESTON HO
SMYRK'S ROAD
MINA ROAD
RIDDELL CT
ASTLEY HO
WESSEX HO
CLARE HO
STAFFORD HO
PALAMON CT
YEOMAN HO
ALISON CT
Tenn Cts
WEST POINT
WENDOVER
THURLOW STREET
SURREY GR
FAVERSHAM HO
BAGSHOT STREET
RAVENSTONE
Walworth Sch
Burgess Park
OAKLEY PLACE
MAWBEY PLACE
KENT HOUSE
MAWBEY RD
HARMAN CLOSE
A2
MAWBEY HOUSE
AVONDALE HOUSE
LANARK HOUSE
1
MICHAEL FARADAY HOUSE
BEACONSFIELD ROAD
WINSLOW
PADBURY
NILE TERRACE
B215
TRAFALGAR AVENUE
SE 15
GLENGALL ROAD
AVONDALE
FOXCOTE
ALBANY ROAD
SE5
COBOURG ROAD
PEPLER MEWS
OSSORY ROAD
LATIMER
EMBERTON
B214
CALMINGTON ROAD
Cobourg Jun & Inf Sch
78
DANESFIELD
A
B
139
C
D
34
CALVERTON
WAITE STREET
GLENGALL TERR
LONCROFT ROAD
Pl Fld
Pl Fld

A
B
C
D
254
The Queen's Club
Pav Tenn Cts
HORTON HO
CLAXTON GR
78
CHELMSFORD CL
MARGRAVINE RD
ST ALBANS TERR
COX HO
MUSCAL
WILLIAM MORRIS HO
GASTEIN RD
6
GREYHOUND ROAD
FIELD ROAD
MARY MACARTHUR HO
BARONS COURT MANS
STANES ROAD
FAIRHOLME ROAD
CHEESEMANS TERR
ORCHARD SQ
SUN ROAD
SHUTERS SQ
VINE SQ
MAY ST
PASSFIELDS
STAR ROAD
ST ANDREW'S ROAD
ALICE GILLIOTT CT
FANE ST
LICKEY HO
MARCHBANK RD
DESBOROUGH HO
THAXTON RD
BROWNING CT
TURNEVILLE ROAD
ARCHEL ROAD
NORMAND MEWS
QUEEN'S CLUB GDNS
NORMAND ROAD
CHESSON ROAD
B317
A3218
BEAUFORT MEWS
GEORGE'S SQUARE
PEABODY ESTATE
SPENCER MEWS
TASSO ROAD
KINNOUL ROAD
MUSARD ROAD
QUEEN'S CLUB GARDENS
Tenn Cts
BRAMBER ROAD
Normand Park Prim Sch
Pav
MULGRAVE RD
W6
OAKLEY WLK
EVERINGTON ST
CRAMMOND CL
ABBEY GARDENS
TASSO YD
WENTWORTH CT
ADENEY CL
PAYENS WLK
Normand Park
Bwg Gn
104
CHESTNUT ALLEY
CHESTNUT CT
CHUTER EDE HO
353
St Augustine's RC Prim Sch
Liby
LILLIE ROAD
JIM GRIFFITHS HO
STAFFORD CRIPPS HO
5
ANCILL CL
LAMPETER SQ
LAUNDRY RD
HUMBOLT ROAD
DISBROWE ROAD
MOYLAN ROAD
LITTLE ROAD MANS
TOM WILLIAMS HO
HUGH GAITSKELL CL
ELLEN WILKINSON HO
MANNY HINWELL HO
MARGARET HERBISON HO
HAROLD WILSON HO
COOMER MEWS
COOMER PL
CROWTHER CL
CREFELD CL
BRECON ROAD
LINTAINE CL
284
230
TILTON ST
HERBERT MORRISON HO
CLEM ATTLEE CT
FRANK BESWICK HO
FRANK SOSKICE HO
A3218
CAROLINE WLK
BAYONNE RD
Sir John Lillie Prim Sch
DELAFORD STREET
RYLSTON ROAD
P
DOUGLAS JOHNSTONE HO
JOHN WHEATLEY HO
JOHN STRACHEY HO
MARGARET INGRAM CL
LEN FREEMAN PL
KENNETH YOUNGER HO
BUCKLER'S ALLEY
HALDANE ROAD
330
318
367
PURCELL CRES
TWYNHOLM MANS
PO
A3219
323
320
CHALDON ROAD
WILLIAMS CL
PELLANT ROAD
MENDORA ROAD
JOHN SMITH AVE
GEORGE LINDGREN HO
EDITH SUMMERSKILL HO
NYE BEVAN HO
Recn Ground
STRODE ROAD
4
287
238
CHASEMORE HO
HARTOPP POINT
PROTHERO ROAD
ROCQUE HO
CLYDE FLATS
MATON HO
ESTCOURT ROAD
DONNELLY CT
LANNOY POINT
BEDFORD PAS
ST THOMAS'S WAY
TOURNAY RD
EPIRUS ROAD
MIRABEL ROAD
FABIAN ROAD
HARTISMERE ROAD
ROYAL PAR
245
St Thomas of Canterbury RC Prim Sch
176
152
Fulham Cross Sec Sch
HANNELL ROAD
DAWES ROAD
SHORROLDS RD
PALACE MEWS
BATHS AP
134
AINTREE STREET
ROSALINE ROAD
ROSALINE TERR
SHERBROOKE TERR
SHERBROOKE ROAD
LETTERSTONE RD
SALISBURY MEWS
PARKVILLE ROAD
163
HOMESTEAD ROAD
GOATER'S ALLEY
GIRONDE ROAD
54
57
61
MABLETHORPE ROAD
MUNSTER ROAD
VARNA ROAD
Cemetery
ROWALLAN ROAD
ORBAIN ROAD
ROSAVILLE ROAD
BRONSART ROAD
ALLESTREE ROAD
ST OLAF'S ROAD
BROOKVILLE ROAD
WHEATSHEAF TERR
BURNTHWAITE ROAD
3
THE QUADRANGLE
ST PETER'S TERR
FILMER ROAD
BLOOM PARK RD
LANCASTER CT
KILMAINE ROAD
MARVILLE ROAD
REPORTON RD
KELVEDON RD
DARLAN ROAD
ATALANTA ST
BRANKSEA ST
KINGWOOD ROAD
WYFOLD ROAD
77
241
MARRAYAT SQ
THE CODA CTR
FERNHURST RD
MUNSTER RESIDENCES
BISHOPS RD
CLONMEL RD
ARUNDEL MANSIONS
Henry Compton Sec Sch
DANEHURST ST
WINCHENDON RD
LILYVILLE RD
RADIPOLE RD
CHESILTON RD
FLORENCE MANS
HAZELWOOD MANSIONS
QUENTINGTON MANSIONS
Kensington Prep Sch
Liby
A304
RAVEN LODGE
2
CHILDERLEY ST
CONNAUGHT MANS
St John's CE Prim Sch
ROSTREVOR MANS
PENHURST MANS
FILMER AVONDALE HO
DEEPDENE MANS
FILMER ROAD STUDIOS
604
Al-Muntada Islamic Sch
BERT OWEN HOUSE
A219
309
LAMBROOK TERR
SIDBURY ST
WARDO AVE
GOWAN AVE
SW6
SWIFT ST
ROSTREVOR RD
FINLAY ST
FULHAM
THE COURTYARD
VERA RD
FULHAM RD
PURSERS CROSS RD
EPPLE RD
FULHAM PALACE RD
ELLERBY ST
KIMBELL GDNS
PARK MANSIONS
COLEHILL LA
HORDER RD
FELDEN ST
608
MIMOSA ST
WHITTINGSTALL MANSIONS
WHITTINGSTALL RD
ST MAUR RD
PO
EDGARLEY TERR
FIRTH GDNS
BURNFOOT AVE
CROOKHAM RD
BEACONSFIELD WLK
1
DONERAILE ST
ELY COURT FLATS
RINGMER AVE
DANCER RD
LETTICE ST
WOODLAWN RD
396
399
WALDEMAR AVENUE MANSIONS
COLEHILL GDNS
HESTERCOMBE AVE
DURRELL RD
CLARIDGE CT
WILLIAM BANFIELD HO
HEATHMAN'S RD
CLONCURRY ST
BISHOP'S PARK RD
Tenn Cts
413
LALOR ST
WALDEMAR AVE
DORNCLIFFE RD
WILSTON CT
724
ARTHUR HENDERSON HOUSE
MUNSTER CT
PLATO PL
ST DIONIS RD
BISHOP'S MANSIONS
24
135
MUSTOW PL
EDDISCOMBE RD
GUION RD
DORIA RD
Pav
BISHOP'S AVE
OXBERRY AVE
FULHAM PARK
728

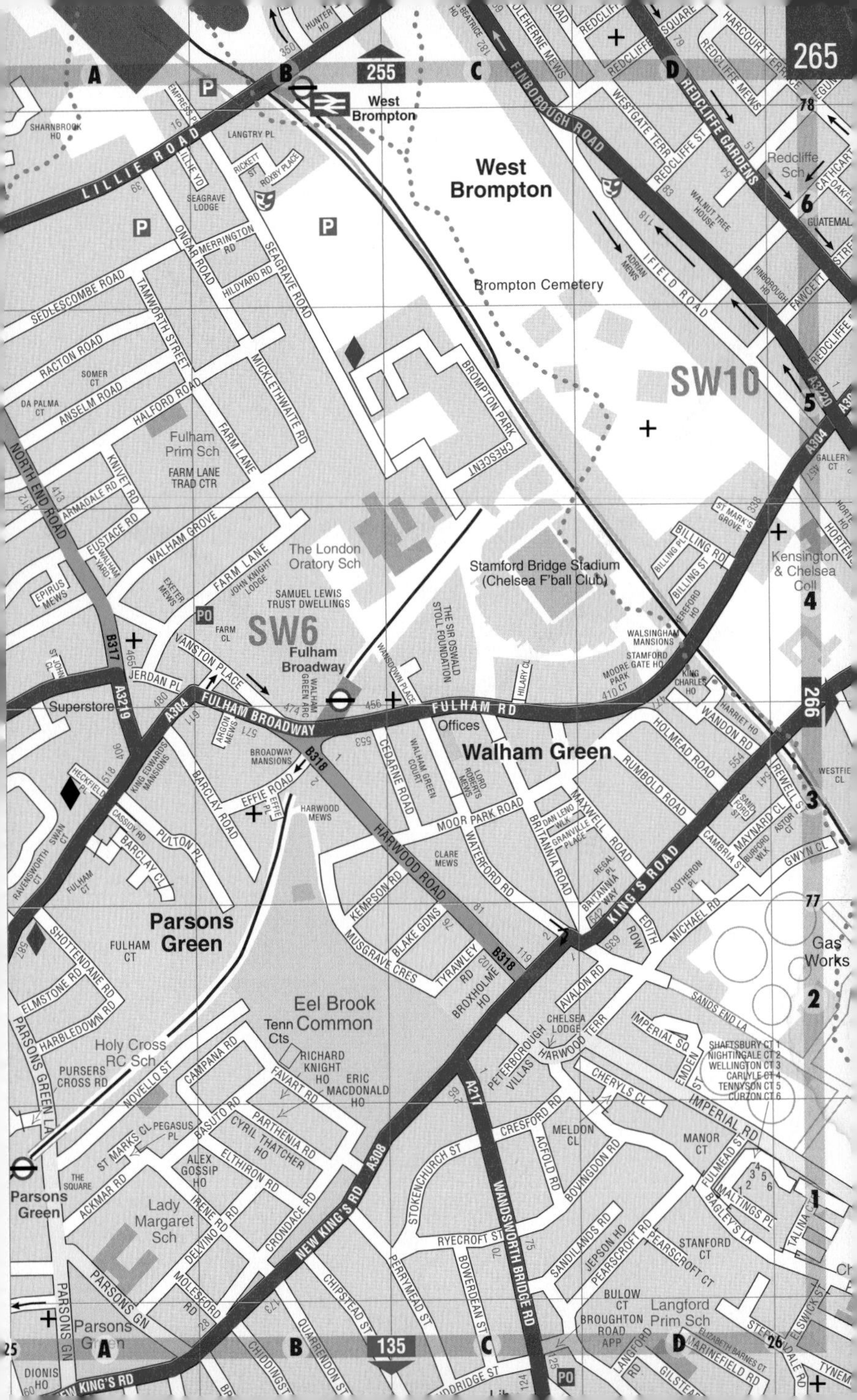

255
135
266
A
B
C
D
1
2
3
4
5
6
West Brompton
West Brompton
Brompton Cemetery
SW10
SW6
Fulham Broadway
Walham Green
Parsons Green
Eel Brook Common
Stamford Bridge Stadium (Chelsea F'ball Club)
The London Oratory Sch
Samuel Lewis Trust Dwellings
The Sir Oswald Stoll Foundation
Fulham Prim Sch
Farm Lane Trad Ctr
Holy Cross RC Sch
Lady Margaret Sch
Langford Prim Sch
Redcliffe Sch
Kensington & Chelsea Coll
Gas Works
Superstore
Offices
Tenn Cts
LILLIE ROAD
FINBOROUGH ROAD
REDCLIFFE GARDENS
IFIELD ROAD
SEAGRAVE ROAD
BROMPTON PARK CRESCENT
NORTH END ROAD
FULHAM BROADWAY
FULHAM RD
KING'S ROAD
NEW KING'S RD
WANDSWORTH BRIDGE RD
HARWOOD ROAD
SEDLESCOMBE ROAD
RACTON ROAD
ANSELM ROAD
HALFORD ROAD
TAMWORTH STREET
MICKLETHWAITE RD
FARM LANE
WALHAM GROVE
ONGAR ROAD
HILDYARD RD
MERRINGTON RD
VANSTON PLACE
JERDAN PL
BARCLAY ROAD
EFFIE ROAD
PULTON PL
CEDARNE ROAD
MOOR PARK ROAD
WATERFORD RD
BRITANNIA ROAD
MAXWELL ROAD
RUMBOLD ROAD
HOLMEAD ROAD
WANDON RD
BILLING RD
MUSGRAVE CRES
KEMPSON RD
BLAKE GDNS
TYRAWLEY RD
SANDS END LA
IMPERIAL RD
HARWOOD TERR
PETERBOROUGH VILLAS
CRESFORD RD
STOKENCHURCH ST
RYECROFT ST
BOWERDEAN ST
PERRYMEAD ST
CHIPSTEAD ST
QUARRENDON ST
BOVINGDON RD
ACFOLD RD
SANDILANDS RD
PEARSCROFT RD
PEARSCROFT CT
BAGLEY'S LA
MALTINGS PL
FULMEAD ST
PARSONS GREEN LA
PARSONS GN
NOVELLO ST
CAMPANA RD
BASUTO RD
FAVART RD
PARTHENIA RD
ELTHIRON RD
IRENE RD
DELVINO RD
MOLESFORD RD
CRONDACE RD
ACKMAR RD
ST MARKS CL
SHOTTENDANE RD
ELMSTONE RD
HARBLEDOWN RD
PURSERS CROSS RD
MICHAEL RD
GWYN CL
CAMBRIA ST
MAYNARD CL
SHAFTSBURY CT 1
NIGHTINGALE CT 2
WELLINGTON CT 3
CARLYLE CT 4
TENNYSON CT 5
CURZON CT 6
A304
A3219
B317
B318
A308
A217
A3220

A
B
C
D
256
136
265
SW10
REDCLIFFE GARDENS
TREGUNTER ROAD
CATHCART ROAD
HOLLYWOOD ROAD
SEYMOUR WALK
REDCLIFFE ROAD
GILSTON ROAD
BOLTON STUDIOS
MILBORNE GR
ONSLOW CT
ELM PARK GARDENS
ELM PARK LANE
ELM PARK ROAD
OLD CHURCH STREET
CARLYLE SQ
MULBERRY WALK
MALLORD STREET
THE VALE
Cameron House Sch
Redcliffe Sch
GUATEMALA ST
OAKFIELD ST
CLIFTON GATE
Servite RC Prim Sch
FULHAM ROAD
NIGHTINGALE PL
Chelsea & Westminster Hospl
HOLMES PL
CAVAYE HO
STANLEY MANSIONS
STANLEY STUDIOS
WINTERTON PL
ELM PARK MANSIONS
THE SANDHILLS
CALLOW STREET
HENNIKER MEWS
LIMERSTON STREET
CAMERA PL
PARK WALK
BEAUFORT
CHELSEA PK GDNS
THE PORTICOS
Park Walk Prim Sch
GERTRUDE STREET
SHALCOMB ST
HOBURY ST
LAMONT ROAD
LANGTON STREET
KING'S ROAD
FAWCETT ST
FINBOROUGH HO
REDCLIFFE PL
BARKER ST
A3220
A308
A304
A3217
A3212
GALLERY CT
NETHERTON GROVE
LITTLE CHELSEA HO
EDITHA MANSIONS
FERNSHAW MANSIONS
FERNSHAW ROAD
GUNTER GROVE
EDITH TERRACE
SLAIDBURN STREET
EDITH GROVE
BRICKBARN CL
HORTENSIA ROAD
COLLEGE PL
HUDSON HO
KNIGHT'S WLK
NEVILL CT
ST MARK'S GROVE
Kensington & Chelsea Coll
IVEAGH HO
CAPLE HO
O'GORMAN HO
WINCH HO
ASHBURTON MANSIONS
CONINGHAM CT
CORNWALL MANSIONS
ASHBURNHAM ROAD
CREMORNE ROAD
WORLD'S END PL
OMEGA HO
EDITH YD
GREAVES TOWER
DARTREY WALK
WHISTLER WLK
DARTREY TOWER
ASHBURNHAM TOWER
WHISTLER TOWER
BLANTYRE TOWER
BLANTYRE WALK
BLANTYRE STREET
BERENGER WLK
BERENGER TOWER
CHELSEA REACH TOWER
WORLD'S END PAS
Ashburnham Com Sch
ANN LANE
APOLLO HO
GILLRAY HO
RILEY ST
BOWLING GREEN HO
BRUNEL HO
MILMAN'S STREET
MORAVIAN PL
ELIZABETH CT
CHELSEA FARM HO
JEAN DARLING HO
MORAVIAN CL
BEAUFORT MANSIONS
ALEXANDRA MANSIONS
LAMONT ROAD PAS
ARGYLL MANSIONS
BEAUFORT HO
MULBERRY CL
PAULTONS SQUARE
PAULTONS STREET
HEREFORD BLDGS
WALDRON MEWS
DANVERS STREET
CADOGAN HO
WINCHESTER HO
SIR THOMAS MORE ESTATE
DACRE HO
BURLEIGH HO
KINGSLEY HO
MORE'S GDN
LAVENDER CL
Lindsey House
CHEYNE WALK
TETCOTT RD
THORNDIKE CL
Westfield Park
WESTFIELD CL
LOTS ROAD
POOLES LANE
TETCOTT ROAD
UPCERNE ROAD
UVERDALE ROAD
TADEMA ROAD
DAMER TERR
ACACIA WLK
BURNABY STREET
PHILADELPHIA CT
STADIUM STREET
KERRIER HO
Cremorne Gdns
Old Ferry Wharf
Chelsea Wharf
Cremorne Wharf
Thames Path
Heatherley Sch of Fine Art
REWELL ST
MAYNARD CL
BURFORD WLK
ASTOR CT
GWYN CL
CAMBRIA ST
Gas Works
SANDS END LA
SHAFTSBURY CT 1
NIGHTINGALE CT 2
WELLINGTON CT 3
CARLYLE CT 4
TENNYSON CT 5
CURZON CT 6
IMPERIAL RD
FULMEAD ST
BAGLEY'S LA
TALINA CTR
Chelsea Coll of Art & Design
ELSWICK ST
ELBE ST
STEPHENDALE RD
ELIZABETH BARNES CT
TYNEMOUTH ST
TOWNMEAD RD
Kensington & Chelsea
Hammersmith & Fulham
Wandsworth
CHELSEA HARBOUR DR
CHELSEA HARBOUR DESIGN CTR
HARBOUR AVE
THE QUADRANGLE
THAMES AVE
ADMIRAL SQ
ADMIRAL CT
KING'S QUAY
THAMES QUAY
THE BELVEDERE
CHELSEA CRES
Chelsea Harbour Pier
RIVER THAMES
THORNEY CRES
WHISTLERS AVENUE
BATTERSEA CHURCH RD
CREWKERNE CT
EXFORD CT
SELWORTHY HO
CHELWOOD CT
SPARKFORD HO
MISTERTON CT
SHEPTON CT
SUNBURY LA
OLD SWAN WHARF
VICARAGE WLK
BLOMFIELD CT 1
BOWSTEAD CT 2
VALIANT HO
GRANFIELD ST
PRICHARD CT
BATTERSEA SQ
ALTHOPE MEWS
HUMPHREY CT
LINDSAY CT
THE RIVERAINS
VICARAGE CRES
COTSWOLD MEWS
Royal Academy of Dance
Thomas's London Day Schs
EATON HO
HAYTHORN HO
ARCHER HO
WHITE HO
WINFIELD HO
RESTORATION SQ
POWRIE HO
COLES CT
BATTERSEA HIGH ST
B305
GROVESIDE CT
VICARAGE CRES
WINDSOR CT
MORGAN CT
Tenn Cts
Fred Wells Gdns
ORVILLE RD
Regent

267
257
268
136
A
B
C
D
1
2
3
4
5
6
78
77
Kings Coll
Liby Sp Ctr
Offices
MANRESA ROAD
A3217
B304
KING'S COURT N
KING'S COURT S
CHELSEA MANOR GDNS
CHELSEA MANOR STREET
CHELSEA TOWERS
SWAN CT
FLOOD WALK
FLOOD STREET
REDESDALE ST
TEDWORTH SQUARE
TEDWORTH GDNS
RALSTON ST
ORMONDE GATE
ROYAL HOSPITAL ROAD
COLLEGE COURT
WEST ROAD
National Army Museum
REDBURN STREET
CHRISTCHURCH STREET
CHRISTCHURCH TERR
CAVERSHAM ST
TITE STREET
ALPHA PL
MANOR STREET ESTATE
MARGARETTA TERR
OAKLEY STREET
GLEBE PLACE
BRAMERTON ST
GROVE HO
OAKLEY GARDENS
PHENE ST
CHESIL CT
ST LOO CT
ST LOO AVE
ROSSETTI GDNS MANSIONS
ROBINSON ST
Christchurch CE Prim Sch
PARADISE WALK
SHELLEY CT
CHELSEA LODGE
PHYSIC PL
CLOVER MEWS
SWAN WALK
CHEYNE CT
The English Gardening Sch
Chelsea Physic Garden
DILKE ST
EMBANKMENT GDNS
CHELSEA CT
A3212
Jamahirya Sch
UPPER CHEYNE ROW
Carlyle's House
ADAIR HO
PIER HO
CHEYNE GDNS
CHEYNE MEWS
B302
Thames Path
CHELSEA EMBANKMENT
Kensington & Chelsea
Wandsworth
OLD CHURCH STREET
JUSTICE WALK
LAWRENCE ST
KING'S MANSIONS
CHELSEA ESTATE
LAWRENCE MANS
LORDSHIP PLACE
CARLYLE MANS
CHEYNE ROW
SHREWSBURY HO
CHEYNE WALK
ROPER'S ORCHARD
PETYT PLACE
A3031
Cadogan Pier
RIVER THAMES
Chelsea Reach
ALBERT BRIDGE (SUSPENSION)
The London Peace Pagoda
Terrace Walk
THE PARADE
Thames Path
BATTERSEA BRIDGE
BridgeWharf
WATERSIDE POINT
ALBION WHARF
RIVERSIDE
THAMES WALK
CRAMBOURNE CT
ANHALT ROAD
GREAT EASTERN WHARF
CARRIAGE DRIVE NORTH
Tennis Courts
Fountain Lake
Pav
Recn Gd
HESTER ROAD
Ransome's Dock
PAVELEY DRIVE
RADSTOCK ST
ELCHO STREET
HOWIE ST
Bsns Ctr
PARKGATE ROAD
ST MARY-LE-PARK CT
ALBANY MANSIONS
Festival Pleasure Gardens
CENTRAL AVENUE
Bwg Gn
MORGAN'S WALK
KINGSWATER PL
BATTERSEA BRIDGE ROAD
Royal Coll of Art Sculpture Sch
Govt Offices
JUIER STREET
ALBERT BRIDGE ROAD
CARRIAGE DRIVE WEST
SW11
CONDRAY PL
PO
SEARLES CL
WORFIELD ST
STAFFORD MANSIONS
B305
Westbridge Prim Sch
MUSGRAVE CT
HENTY CL
HERON HO
MASKELYNE CL
JAGGER HO
ALBERT MANS
BOLINGBROKE WLK
HYDE LA
ETHELBURGA ST
BATTERSEA
CLEVEDON CT
RANDALL CL
ETHELBURGA TOWER
ALBERT STUDIOS
DRAYCOTT CT
WESTBRIDGE RD
WHITGIFT HO
GARDINER HO
VILLIERS CT
HARVEY CT
SANCROFT CT
WATFORD CL
PETWORTH ST
ROSENAU RD
Sports Ground
CARRIAGE DR S
WIGRAM CT
FRASER CT
COMPTON HO
CRANMER HO
BURNETT CT
JACOBSON CT
MACEY HO
MANSEL CT
NORFOLK MANS
OVERSTRAND MANS
PRINCE
PARKHAM ST
SURREY LA
PRINCE OF WALES DR A3220
PARK MANS
SOUDAN RD
KASSALA RD
CYRIL MANS
BEECHMORE RD
BRYNMAER HO
MANDEVILLE CTYD
Salesian Coll
Sch
CONNAUGHT MANS
ROSENAU CRES
CAMBRIDGE MANS
CAMBRIDGE RD
BRYNMAER RD
CHESNEY ST
ORBEL ST
HENNING ST
EDNA ST
URSULA ST
OCTAVIA ST
BRIDGE LA
FOXMORE ST
A3205
BISHOPSTONE HO 1
LODSWORTH HO 2
TELSCOMBE HO 3
Battersea Tech Coll
TROTT ST
SHUTTLEWORTH RD
McCARTHY CT
KERSLEY MEWS
KERSLEY ST
DOVEDALE COTTS
DAGNALL ST
DRESDEN HO
MEECHAM CT
BANBURY ST
STANMER ST
CASTLEMAINE
ORKNEY ST
ROYDON CL
ST JAMES'S GR
REFORM ST
CULVERT RD
WITTERING HO
MACDONALD HO
BERRY HO
HOPKINSON
RUSHLA
McKIERNAN CT
WINDE
GOULDEN HO
INWORTH ST
BULLEN ST
BALFERN ST
COLESTOWN ST
LATCH
Recn Gd
SOUTHSIDE

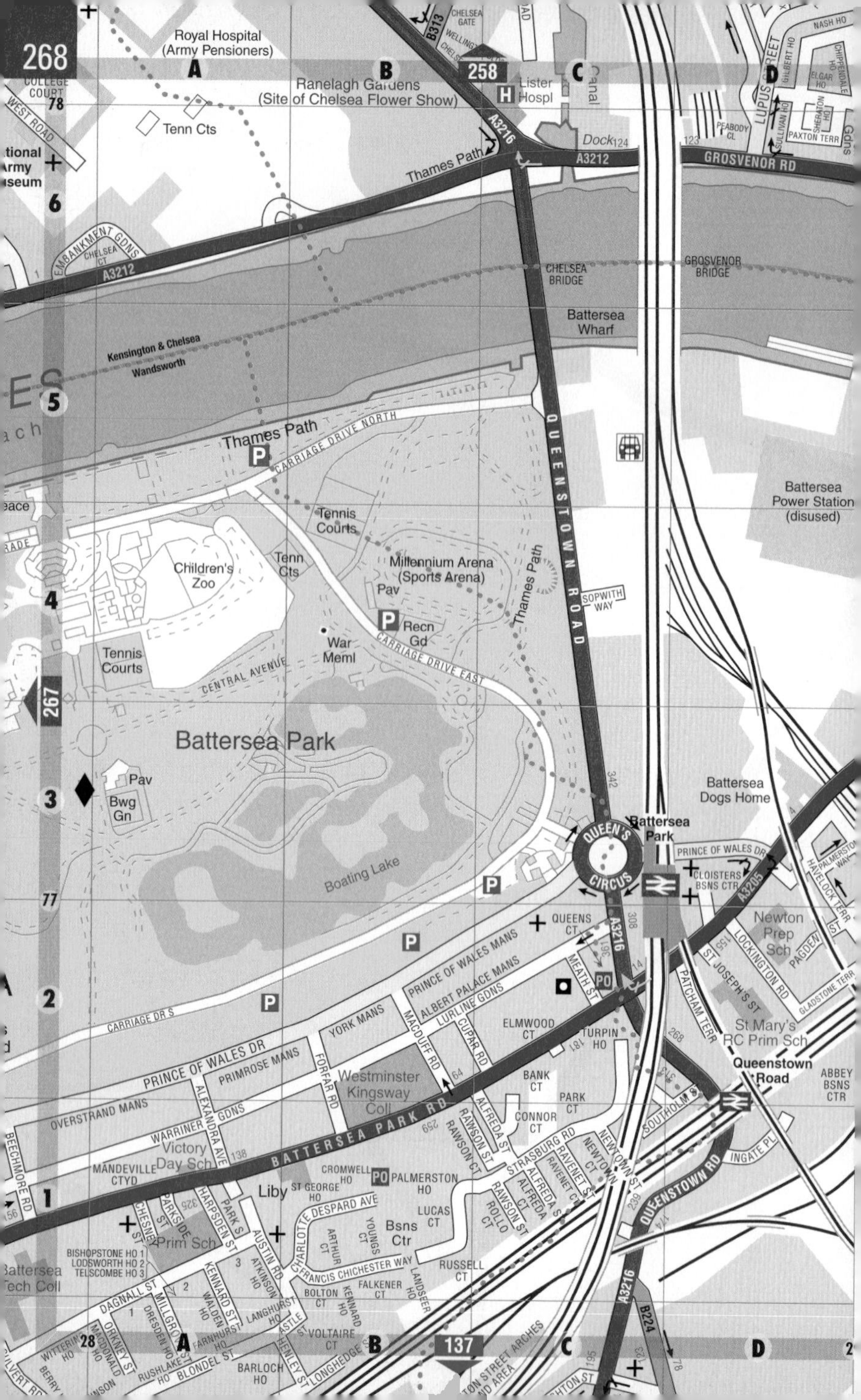

Royal Hospital
(Army Pensioners)
A
B
C
D
258
Ranelagh Gardens
(Site of Chelsea Flower Show)
Lister Hospl
Canal
Dock
124
123
A3212
GROSVENOR RD
COLLEGE COURT
78
WEST ROAD
Tenn Cts
tional
rmy
seum
6
A3216
B373
CHELSEA GATE
NASH HO
LUPUS STREET
GILBERT HO
CHIPPENDALE HO
ELGAR HO
SHERATON HO
SULLIVAN HO
PEABODY CL
PAXTON TERR
Gdns
Thames Path
EMBANKMENT GDNS
CHELSEA CT
A3212
CHELSEA BRIDGE
GROSVENOR BRIDGE
Battersea Wharf
Kensington & Chelsea
Wandsworth
5
Thames Path
CARRIAGE DRIVE NORTH
QUEENSTOWN ROAD
Battersea Power Station (disused)
Tennis Courts
Tenn Cts
Children's Zoo
Millennium Arena
(Sports Arena)
Pav
Recn Gd
Thames Path
SOPWITH WAY
4
War Meml
CARRIAGE DRIVE EAST
Tennis Courts
CENTRAL AVENUE
267
Battersea Park
Pav
Bwg Gn
3
342
Battersea Dogs Home
Battersea Park
QUEEN'S CIRCUS
PRINCE OF WALES DR
CLOISTERS BSNS CTR
A3205
PALMERSTON WAY
HAVELOCK TERR
Boating Lake
77
QUEENS CT
308
A3216
Newton Prep Sch
PAGDEN ST
LOCKINGTON RD
GLADSTONE TERR
ST JOSEPH'S ST
PATCHAM TERR
PRINCE OF WALES MANS
ALBERT PALACE MANS
LURLINE GDNS
MEATH ST
PO
2
CARRIAGE DR S
YORK MANS
MACDUFF RD
CUPAR RD
ELMWOOD CT
TURPIN HO
268
St Mary's RC Prim Sch
Queenstown Road
ABBEY BSNS CTR
PRINCE OF WALES DR
PRIMROSE MANS
FORFAR RD
Westminster Kingsway Coll
BANK CT
PARK CT
SOUTHOLM ST
OVERSTRAND MANS
ALEXANDRA AVE
WARRINER GDNS
BATTERSEA PARK RD
ALFREDA ST
RAWSON ST
CONNOR CT
STRASBURG RD
RAVENET ST
NEWTOWN ST
QUEENSTOWN RD
INGATE PL
Victory Day Sch
BEECHMORE RD
MANDEVILLE CTYD
138
CROMWELL HO
PALMERSTON HO
ST GEORGE HO
Liby
CHARLOTTE DESPARD AVE
LUCAS CT
ROLLO CT
1
CHESNEY ST
PARKSIDE ST
HARPSDEN ST
PARK S
AUSTIN RD
ARTHUR CT
YOUNGS CT
Bsns Ctr
Prim Sch
BISHOPSTONE HO 1
LODSWORTH HO 2
TELSCOMBE HO 3
Battersea Tech Coll
KENNARD ST
ATKINSON HO
FRANCIS CHICHESTER WAY
RUSSELL CT
LANDSEER HO
DAGNALL ST
MILLGROVE ST
WALDEN HO
DRESDEN HO
LANGHURST HO
BOLTON CT
KENNARD HO
FALKENER CT
A3216
B224
28
A
WITTERING HO
MACDONALD HO
ORKNEY ST
FARNHURST HO
RUSHLAKE HO
BLONDEL ST
BARLOCH HO
HENLEY ST
CASTLE
VOLTAIRE CT
LONGHEDGE ST
B
137
C
D
STREET ARCHES
BERRY

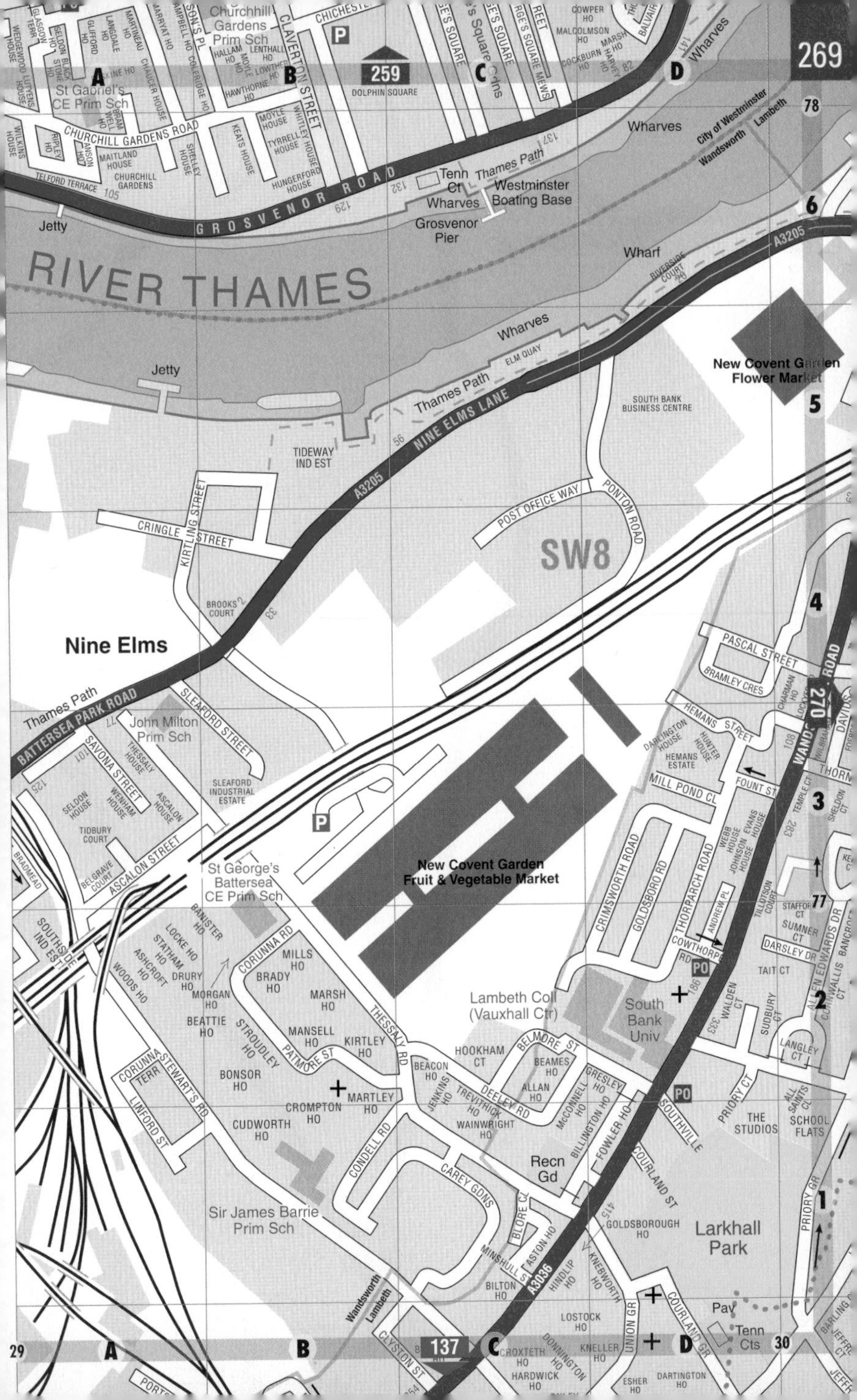

RIVER THAMES
GROSVENOR ROAD
Churchhill Gardens Prim Sch
St Gabriel's CE Prim Sch
CHURCHILL GARDENS ROAD
CHURCHILL GARDENS
TELFORD TERRACE
CLAVERTON STREET
259
DOLPHIN SQUARE
Wharves
City of Westminster
Lambeth
Wandsworth
Tenn Ct
Thames Path
Westminster Boating Base
Wharves
Grosvenor Pier
Jetty
Wharf
A3205
RIVERSIDE COURT
Wharves
ELM QUAY
NINE ELMS LANE
TIDEWAY IND EST
New Covent Garden Flower Market
SOUTH BANK BUSINESS CENTRE
POST OFFICE WAY
PONTON ROAD
SW8
CRINGLE STREET
KIRTLING STREET
BROOKS COURT
Nine Elms
Thames Path
BATTERSEA PARK ROAD
John Milton Prim Sch
SLEAFORD STREET
SAVONA STREET
SLEAFORD INDUSTRIAL ESTATE
ASCALON STREET
TIDBURY COURT
BELGRAVE COURT
SOUTHSIDE IND EST
BRADMEAD
St George's Battersea CE Prim Sch
New Covent Garden Fruit & Vegetable Market
PASCAL STREET
BRAMLEY CRES
HEMANS STREET
HEMANS ESTATE
MILL POND CL
FOUNT ST
CRIMSWORTH ROAD
GOLDSBORO RD
THORPARCH ROAD
COWTHORPE RD
WANDSWORTH ROAD
270
Lambeth Coll (Vauxhall Ctr)
South Bank Univ
CORUNNA RD
THESSALY RD
PATMORE ST
STROUDLEY HO
CORUNNA TERR
STEWART'S RD
LINFORD ST
BELMORE ST
DEELEY RD
CONDELL RD
CAREY GDNS
Recn Gd
COURLAND ST
Sir James Barrie Prim Sch
MINSHULL ST
A3036
Larkhall Park
UNION GR
COURLAND GR
Pav
Tenn Cts
CLYSTON ST
137
PRIORY GR
PRIORY CT
THE STUDIOS
ALL SAINTS CL
SCHOOL FLATS
LANGLEY CT
ALLEN EDWARDS DR
CORNWALLIS
BANCROFT
SUMNER CT
DARSLEY DR
TAIT CT
WALDEN CT
SUDBURY CT
TILLOTSON COURT
STAFFORD CT
TEMPLE CT
SHELDON CT
A
B
C
D
1
2
3
4
5
6
29
30
77
78

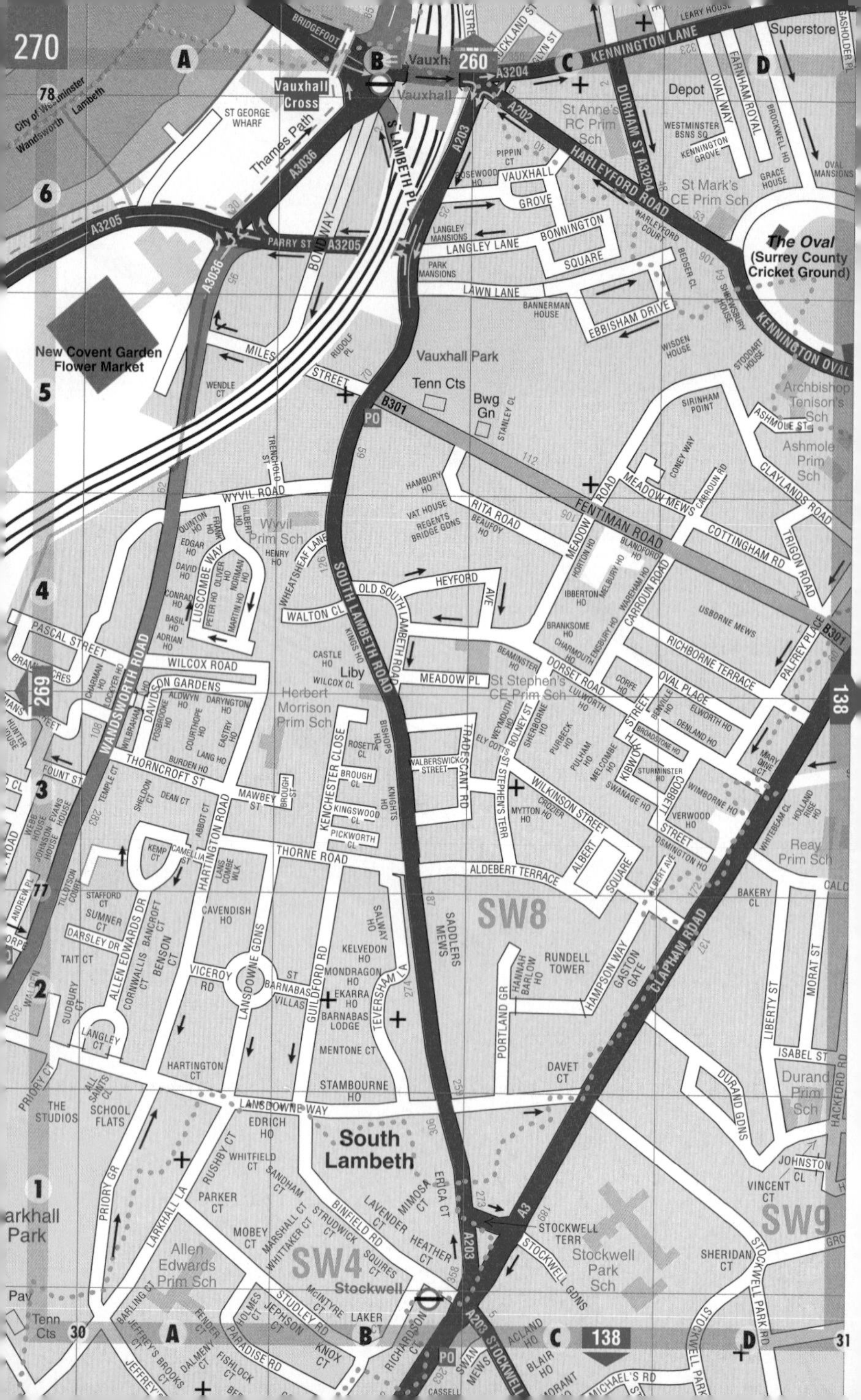
A
B
C
D
6
5
4
3
2
1
78
77
30
31
City of Westminster
Lambeth
Wandsworth
260
269
138
Vauxhall
Vauxhall Cross
BRIDGEFOOT
A3204
KENNINGTON LANE
LEARY HOUSE
Superstore
Depot
OVAL WAY
FARNHAM ROYAL
BROCKWELL HO
WESTMINSTER BSNS SQ
KENNINGTON GROVE
GRACE HOUSE
OVAL MANSIONS
GASHOLDER PL
St Anne's RC Prim Sch
DURHAM ST A3204
HARLEYFORD ROAD
A202
St Mark's CE Prim Sch
The Oval
(Surrey County Cricket Ground)
KENNINGTON OVAL
ST GEORGE WHARF
Thames Path
A3036
A3205
PARRY ST
S LAMBETH PL
A203
BOND WAY
PIPPIN CT
ROSEWOOD HO
VAUXHALL GROVE
BONNINGTON SQUARE
LANGLEY MANSIONS
LANGLEY LANE
PARK MANSIONS
LAWN LANE
BANNERMAN HOUSE
EBBISHAM DRIVE
HARLEYFORD COURT
BEDSER CL
SHREWSBURY HOUSE
WISDEN HOUSE
STODDART HOUSE
New Covent Garden Flower Market
MILES STREET
WENDLE CT
RUDOLF PL
Vauxhall Park
Tenn Cts
Bwg Gn
STANLEY CL
PO
B301
Archbishop Tenison's Sch
SIRINHAM POINT
ASHMOLE ST
Ashmole Prim Sch
CONEY WAY
CLAYLANDS ROAD
MEADOW MEWS
CARROUN RD
MEADOW ROAD
FENTIMAN ROAD
COTTINGHAM RD
TRIGON ROAD
TRENCHOLD ST
WYVIL ROAD
Wyvil Prim Sch
HAMBURY HO
VAT HOUSE
REGENTS BRIDGE GDNS
RITA ROAD
BEAUFOY HO
QUINTON HO
FRANK HO
GILBERT HO
EDGAR HO
DAVID HO
LUSCOMBE WAY
OLIVER HO
NORMAN HO
HENRY HO
WHEATSHEAF LANE
CONRAD HO
PETER HO
MARTIN HO
BASIL HO
ADRIAN HO
SOUTH LAMBETH ROAD
OLD SOUTH LAMBETH RD
HEYFORD AVE
WALTON CL
HORTON HO
BLANDFORD HO
MELBURY HO
WAREHAM HO
CARROUN ROAD
IBBERTON HO
BRANKSOME HO
CHARMOUTH HO
ENSBURY HO
USBORNE MEWS
RICHBORNE TERRACE
PALFREY PLACE
PASCAL STREET
WILCOX ROAD
DAVIDSON GARDENS
CHARMAN HO
LOCKYER HO
WILBRAHAM HO
ALDWYN HO
DARYNGTON HO
FOSBROOKE HO
COURTHOPE HO
EASTRY HO
LANG HO
BURDEN HO
KINGS HO
CASTLE HO
WILCOX CL
Liby
MEADOW PL
St Stephen's CE Prim Sch
Herbert Morrison Prim Sch
BEAMINSTER HO
DORSET ROAD
LULWORTH HO
CORFE HO
OVAL PLACE
BENVILLE HO
ELWORTH HO
DENLAND HO
HUNTER HOUSE
WANDSWORTH ROAD
THORNCROFT ST
FOUNT ST
TEMPLE CT
SHELDON CT
DEAN CT
MAWBEY ST
BROUGH ST
KENCHESTER CLOSE
ROSETTA CL
BROUGH CL
KINGSWOOD CL
PICKWORTH CL
BISHOPS HO
KNIGHTS HO
WALBERSWICK STREET
TRADESCANT RD
WEYMOUTH HO
BOLNEY ST
ELY COTTS
SHERBORNE HO
PURBECK HO
PULHAM HO
MELCOMBE HO
KIBWORTH STREET
BROADSTONE HO
STURMINSTER HO
SWANAGE HO
COBBETT STREET
WIMBORNE HO
VERWOOD HO
MARY DINE CT
WHITEBEAM CL
HOLLAND RISE HO
ST STEPHEN'S TERR
WILKINSON STREET
MYTTON HO
CROZIER HO
OSMINGTON HO
Reay Prim Sch
WEBB HOUSE
JOHNSON HOUSE
EVANS HOUSE
TILLOTSON COURT
ANDREW PL
KEMP CT
CAMELLIA ST
ABBOT CT
HARTINGTON ROAD
LANSCOMBE WLK
THORNE ROAD
ALDEBERT TERRACE
ALBERT SQUARE
ALBERT AVE
BAKERY CL
SW8
STAFFORD CT
SUMNER CT
DARSLEY DR
TAIT CT
ALLEN EDWARDS DR
BANCROFT CT
CORNWALLIS CT
BENSON CT
CAVENDISH HO
SALWAY HO
SADDLERS MEWS
KELVEDON HO
MONDRAGON HO
EKARRA HO
TEVERSHAM LA
BARNABAS LODGE
VICEROY RD
LANSDOWNE GDNS
ST BARNABAS VILLAS
GUILDFORD RD
MENTONE CT
RUNDELL TOWER
HANNAH BARLOW HO
HAMPSON WAY
GASTON GATE
CLAPHAM ROAD
LIBERTY ST
MORAT ST
SUDBURY CT
LANGLEY CT
PORTLAND GR
ISABEL ST
Durand Prim Sch
DURAND GDNS
HACKFORD RD
PRIORY CT
ALL SAINTS CL
THE STUDIOS
SCHOOL FLATS
HARTINGTON CT
STAMBOURNE HO
DAVET CT
LANSDOWNE WAY
EDRICH HO
South Lambeth
WHITFIELD CT
RUSHBY CT
SANDHAM CT
PARKER CT
JOHNSTON CL
VINCENT CT
SW9
arkhall Park
PRIORY GR
LARKHALL LA
MOBEY CT
MARSHALL CT
WHITTAKER CT
STRUDWICK CT
BINFIELD RD
LAVENDER CT
MIMOSA CT
ERICA CT
HEATHER CT
SQUIRES CT
A3
A203
STOCKWELL TERR
Stockwell Park Sch
STOCKWELL GDNS
SHERIDAN CT
STOCKWELL PARK RD
Allen Edwards Prim Sch
SW4
Stockwell
McINTYRE CT
STUDLEY RD
JEPHSON CT
HOLMES CT
BARLING CT
FENDER CT
PARADISE RD
LAKER CT
RICHARDSON CT
KNOX CT
Pav
Tenn Cts
JEFFREY'S BROOKS CT
DALMENY CT
FISHLOCK CT
SWAN MEWS
STOCKWELL
ACLAND HO
BLAIR HO
STOCKWELL PARK
MICHAEL'S RD
CASSELL

Index

Church Rd **6** Beckenham BR2..........**53** C6 **228** C6

Place name
May be abbreviated on the map

Location number
Present when a number indicates the place's position in a crowded area of mapping

Locality, town or village
Shown when more than one place (outside London postal districts) has the same name

Postcode district
District for the indexed place

Standard scale reference
Page number and grid reference for the standard mapping

Enlarged scale reference
Page number and grid reference for the central London enlarged mapping, underlined in red

Public and commercial buildings are highlighted in **magenta**
Places of interest are highlighted in **blue** with a star★

Index of localities, towns and villages

A

Abbey Wood 124 B3
Acton 111 B5
Acton Green 111 A2
Addington 223 C3
Addiscombe 206 A1
Aldborough Hatch ...57 C5
Aldersbrook 77 C6
Alperton 88 A6
Anerley 184 B2
Arkley 12 A6
Ashford 170 B4
Ashford Common 171 B4
Avery Hill 167 B5

B

Balham 159 A3
Bandonhill 219 D3
Barbican 95 A2
Barking 79 B1
Barkingside 57 A6
Barnes 133 D4
Barnet 13 B6
Barnet Gate 11 D5
Barnsbury 72 A1
Battersea 136 D4
Bayswater 114 A6
Beckenham 185 C1
Beckton 100 D2
Becontree 81 A4
Beddington 220 A6
Beddington Corner .203 A2
Bedford Park 111 C3
Belgravia 115 B2
Bell Green 163 B1
Bellingham 185 C5
Belmont 25 B2
Belsize Park 70 C3
Belvedere 125 D2
Benhilton 218 A5
Bermondsey 118 A4
Berrylands 198 C3
Bethnal Green 96 B4
Bexley 146 B1
Bexleyheath 147 B2
Bickley 188 B1
Blackfen 168 A5
Blackheath 142 C2
Blackheath Park ...143 A1
Blackheath Vale ...142 D3
Blackwall 120 B6
Bloomsbury 93 D2
Borehamwood 11 C5
Borough The 117 A4
Bow 97 B5
Bow Common 97 D2
Bowes Park 32 A4
Brent Cross 46 D2
Brentford 131 B6
Brentford End 131 C4
Brimsdown 7 B3
Brixton 138 C2
Broad Green 204 D3
Broadgate 95 C2
Brockley 141 B1
Bromley 186 C2
Bromley
(Tower Hamlets) ...97 D4
Bromley Common ...210 A3
Bromley Park 186 D2
Brompton 114 B3
Brondesbury 69 A2
Brondesbury Park ...90 D6
Brook Green 112 D2
Broom Hill 211 D2
Brunswick Park 15 A1
Buckhurst Hill 21 C2
Burnt Oak 27 B3
Bush Hill Park 17 C5
Bushey 8 A2
Bushey Heath 8 C4
Bushey Mead 200 D6

C

Camberwell 139 A4
Camden Town 71 B1
Canary Wharf 119 D5
Canning Town 99 B1
Canonbury 73 A2
Canons Park 26 A3
Carshalton 218 C4
Carshalton Beeches 218 D1
Carshalton on
the Hill 219 B1
Castle Green 102 C6
Catford 163 C3
Chadwell Heath 58 D4
Charlton
(Greenwich) 143 D6
Charlton (Surrey) .171 B1
Chattern Hill 170 D6
Cheam 217 B3
Chelsea 114 C1
Chertsey Meads 192 A1
Chessington 214 A2
Child's Hill 69 C6
Chingford 20 C3
Chingford Green 20 A4
Chingford Hatch 36 B6
Chipping Barnet 1 B1
Chislehurst 189 C3
Chislehurst West ..188 C4
Chiswick 111 D1
Church End (Barnet) 29 C1
Church End (Brent) .67 D2
City of London 117 A6
Clapham 137 B2
Clapham Common ...137 B1
Clapham Junction ..136 C1
Clapham Park 159 D6
Clapton Park 74 D4
Clay Hill 5 A6
Claygate 212 D1
Clayhall 56 B6
Clerkenwell 94 D3
Cockfosters 2 D1
Colham Green 82 C2
Colindale 45 C6
College Park 90 B4
Collier's Wood 180 C4
Colney Hatch 30 C4
Coney Hall 224 D5
Coombe 177 B3
Copse Hill 178 B3
Cottenham Park 178 B2
Covent Garden 116 A6
Cowley Peachy 82 A2
Cranbrook 56 C1
Cranford 128 C4
Cranley Gardens 49 B5
Creekmouth 101 D2
Cricklewood 68 D4
Crofton 227 B6
Crooked Billet 178 C4
Crouch End 49 D3
Croydon 221 B5
Crystal Palace 184 A5
Cubitt Town 120 A2
Custom House 121 C6
Cyprus 122 C6

D

Dagenham 81 D1
Dalston 74 A2
Dartmouth Park 71 B5
De Beauvoir Town ...73 C1
Deacons Hill 10 C5
Deptford 140 D6
Dollis Hill 68 B5
Dormer's Wells 107 C6
Downham 186 C5
Ducks Island 12 D5
Dudden Hill 68 A3
Dulwich 161 C1
Dulwich Village ...161 C4

E

Ealing 109 D6
Earl's Court 113 C1
Earlsfield 158 A3
East Acton 111 C5
East Barnet 14 D4
East Bedfont 149 C3
East Dulwich 162 A6
East Finchley 48 B5
East Ham 100 A5
East Molesey 196 A4
East Sheen 133 B1
East Wickham 146 A5
Eastbury 22 A5
Eastcote 40 C3
Eastcote Village ...40 B4
Eden Park 207 C5
Edgware 26 C6
Edgware Bury 10 B3
Edmonton 33 D6
Elmers End 206 D6
Elmstead 188 A5
Elstree 10 A5
Eltham 166 B6
Enfield 6 B2
Enfield
Highway 6 C3
Enfield Lock 7 B6
Enfield Town 5 B1
Enfield Wash 6 D5
Erith 147 D6
Esher 212 A4
Euston 93 C4
Ewell 215 C1

F

Fair Cross 79 D3
Falconwood 145 C1
Farnborough 227 B3
Farthing Street ...226 B1
Feltham 150 A3
Felthamhill 171 D5
Finchley 29 D3
Finsbury 94 C4
Finsbury Park 50 D1
Fitzrovia 93 C1
Foots Cray 190 B4
Forest Gate 77 A3
Forest Hill 163 A3
Fortis Green 48 D5
Forty Hill 5 D4
Friday Hill 20 C1
Friern Barnet 31 A6
Fulham 134 D4
Furzedown 181 B6

G

Gants Hill 56 C3
Globe Town 96 D4
Golders Green 47 B4
Goodmayes 58 B1
Gospel Oak 70 D2
Grahame Park 27 C2
Grange Park 16 C6
Green Street
Green 227 C2
Greenford 86 A4
Greenhill 42 D4
Greenwich 142 C6
Grove Park
(Hounslow) 133 A4
Grove Park
(Lewisham) 165 B1
Gunnersbury 110 D2

H

Hackbridge 219 B6
Hackney 74 B2
Hackney Wick 75 C2
Hadley 1 B2
Hadley Wood 2 B5
Haggerston 95 D5
Hale End 36 C4
Ham 153 C1
Hammersmith 112 C2
Hampstead 70 A3
Hampstead
Garden Suburb 47 D4
Hampton 173 C1
Hampton Court 196 C5
Hampton Hill 174 A5
Hampton Wick 175 D3
Hanwell 108 D5
Hanworth 172 D6
Harlesden 89 D6
Harlington 127 A6
Harmondsworth 126 A6
Harringay 50 D4
Harrow 42 B3
Harrow on the Hill ..42 C1
Harrow Weald 24 B2
Hatch End 23 A3
Hatton 127 D1
Hayes (Bromley) ...209 A2
Hayes
(Hillingdon) 83 C1
Hayes End 83 B3
Hayes Town 106 B5
Headstone 41 D5
Hendon 46 C3
Herne Hill 161 A6
Heston 129 B5
High Barnet 1 A2
Higham Hill 35 A2
Highams Park 36 A3
Highbury 72 D4
Highgate 49 A2
Hillingdon 82 D5
Hillingdon Heath ...82 D2
Hinchley Wood 212 D6
Hither Green 164 C5
Holborn 94 C2
Homerton 74 D1
Honor Oak 162 C6
Hook 214 A4
Hornsey 50 A5
Hornsey Vale 50 B4
Hounslow 129 C3
Hounslow West 128 D2
Hoxton 95 C5
Hurst Park 174 A1
Hyde Park 114 D5
Hyde The 45 D4

I

Ickenham 60 C4
Ilford 78 D6
Isle of Dogs 120 A2
Isleworth 131 B2
Islington 72 D2

K

Kennington 116 C1
Kensal Green 90 C4
Kensal Rise 91 A5
Kensal Town 91 A3
Kensington 113 C4
Kentish Town 71 C3
Kenton 43 C3
Keston 225 D4
Keston Mark 225 D6
Kew 132 C6
Kidbrooke 143 C3
Kilburn 91 B6
King's Cross 94 A5
Kingsbury 45 B3
Kingsland 73 C2
Kingston Upon
Thames 197 C6
Kingston Vale 177 B6
Kitts End 1 A5
Knightsbridge 114 C4

L

Ladywell 163 C6
Lambeth 116 B4
Lampton 129 D4
Lea Bridge 74 D5
Lee 74 D5
Lessness Heath 125 D1
Lewisham 142 A1
Leyton 76 B5
Leytonstone 54 D1
Limehouse 119 A6
Lisson Green 92 C3
Lisson Grove 92 B2
Little Heath 58 B5
Little Ilford 78 C3
Little Stanmore 26 B2
Littleton 192 C6
Littleton Common ..171 B3
Locksbottom 226 D5
London City
Airport 122 B5
Long Ditton 197 C1
Longlands 167 B1
Loughton 21 D5
Lower Clapton 74 C4
Lower Edmonton 18 B1
Lower Feltham 149 D1
Lower Green 195 D1
Lower Halliford ...193 C3
Lower Holloway 72 A3
Lower Morden 201 A2
Lower Place 89 A5
Lower Sydenham ...185 A6
Loxford 79 A3

M

Maida Vale 91 D4
Maitland Park 71 A2

Manor Park 78 A4
Marylebone 93 B1
Mayfair 115 B6
Merton 179 C2
Merton Park 179 C1
Mile End 97 A3
Mill Hill 28 B5
Mill Meads 98 B5
Millwall 119 C3
Mitcham 202 D5
Monken Hadley 1 A3
Monks Orchard 207 A3
Morden 201 D3
Morden Park 201 A3
Mortlake 133 A2
Motspur Park 200 A3
Mottingham 165 D2
Muswell Hill 49 A6

N

Nash 225 A2
Neasden 67 B4
New Addington 224 B1
New Barnet 14 A6
New Beckenham ...185 A4
New Charlton 121 C2
New Cross 141 B4
New Cross Gate 140 D4
New Eltham 167 A2
New Malden 199 D5
New Southgate 31 C6
Newbury Park 57 B3
Newham 98 D4
Newington 116 D2
Newyears Green 38 B3
Nine Elms 137 C5
Noel Park 32 D1
Norbiton 176 C1
Norbury 182 C2
North Acton 89 B4
North Cheam 216 C6
North Cray 169 B1
North End 70 A6
North Feltham 150 B6
North Finchley 30 A6
North Harrow 41 D2
North Hillingdon 61 A2
North Hyde 107 A1
North Kensington ...90 D2
North Sheen 132 C3
North Wembley 65 C6
North Woolwich ...122 D4
Northolt 63 C1
Northwood 22 A3
Northwood Hills 22 A1
Norwood Green 107 C2
Norwood New Town 183 A4
Notting Hill 113 B6
Nower Hill 41 B6
Nunhead 140 C1

O

Oakleigh Park 14 B3
Oakwood 15 D6
Old Bexley 169 D4
Old Ford 97 B6
Old Malden 199 C1
Old Oak Common ...89 D3
Orpington 227 D6
Osidge 15 C3
Osterley 130 B5

P

Paddington 92 A2
Palmers Green 16 A1
Park Langley 208 B4
Park Royal 88 D4
Parsons Green 135 C4
Peckham 140 A4
Penge 184 D4
Pentonville 94 B5
Perivale 87 B5
Petersham 153 D3
Petts Wood 211 B5
Pimlico 115 C1
Pinner 41 A6
Pinner Green 22 C1
Pinnerwood Park 22 C3
Plaistow (Bromley) .187 A4
Plaistow (Newham) .99 B4
Plashet 78 A2
Plumstead 123 C2
Plumstead Common 145 D6
Ponders End 18 D6
Poplar 97 C1
Preston 44 A1
Primrose Hill 70 D1
Putney 156 C6
Putney Heath 156 C6
Putney Vale 156 A1

Q

Queensbury 44 B6

R

Ratcliff 118 D6
Rayners Lane 41 B1
Raynes Park 200 C6
Redbridge 55 D3
Regent's Park 93 B4
Richmond 154 A6
Richmond Hill 154 A5
Richmond Park 155 A3
Roehampton 155 C4
Romford 59 C5
Rosehill 202 A1
Rotherhithe 118 D3
Roundshaw 220 B1
Roxeth 64 A6
Ruislip 39 B2
Ruislip Common 39 B4
Ruislip Gardens 61 D5
Ruislip Manor 40 A1
Ruxley 191 A3

S

Sands End 136 A2
Seething Wells 197 D3
Selhurst 205 B4
Selsdon 223 A1
Seven Kings 57 D2
Sewardstonebury ...20 C6
Shacklewell 73 D4
Shadwell 118 C6
Shepherd's Bush ...112 B5
Shepperton 193 A3
Shepperton Green .192 D5
Shirley 206 C1
Shooters Hill 145 A4
Shoreditch 95 B5
Shortlands 208 C6
Sidcup 190 A5
Silvertown 121 C4
Sipson 126 C6
Snaresbrook 54 D6
Soho 93 D1
Somers Town 93 D4
South Acton 110 D3
South Bank 116 B4
South Beddington .219 C2
South Bromley 98 B2
South Croydon 221 B1
South Hackney 96 C6
South Hampstead ...70 A1
South Harrow 63 D5
South Kensington ..114 A1
South Lambeth 138 A4
South Norwood 205 C6
South Oxhey 22 B6
South Ruislip 62 D4
South Tottenham 51 D4
South Wimbledon ..179 D4
Southall 107 A5
Southborough (Bromley) 210 B3
Southborough (Kingston Upon Thames) 197 D1
Southend 186 B6
Southfields 157 C3
Southgate 16 B4
Southwark 117 B5
Spitalfields 95 D2
Spring Grove 130 C3
Spring Park 223 B5
St George in the East 118 A6
St Giles 94 A1
St Helier 202 B2
St James 115 C5
St John's 141 C3
St John's Wood 92 B5
St Luke's 95 A3
St Margarets 153 A5
St Pancras 94 A4
St Paul's Cray 190 A1
Stamford Hill 51 C1
Stanmore 25 B2
Stanwell 148 A3
Stepney 96 D2
Stockwell 138 A2
Stoke Newington 73 C6
Stonebridge 89 A6
Stoneleigh 216 A3
Strand 116 B6
Strand on the Green 132 C6
Stratford 76 A1
Stratford Marsh 97 D6
Stratford New Town 76 A3
Strawberry Hill 152 D1
Streatham 182 A4
Streatham Hill 160 A3
Streatham Park 181 C6
Streatham Vale 181 D3
Stroud Green 50 C3
Sudbury 65 A4
Summerstown 158 A1
Sunbury 194 B6
Sunbury Common ..171 D3
Sundridge 187 C4
Surbiton 198 A2
Sutton 218 A1
Syon Park 131 B4

T

Teddington 175 C5
Temple Mills 75 D3
Thames Ditton 197 B2
Thamesmead 124 A5
Thornton Heath 204 D3
Tokyngton 66 D2
Tolworth 214 C6
Tooting 180 D4
Tooting Graveney ..180 B5
Tottenham 33 D1
Tottenham Hale 52 A6
Totteridge 13 C3
Tower Hamlets 97 B2
Tufnell Park 71 D4
Tulse Hill 160 D4
Twickenham 152 D4

U

Underhill 13 C6
Upper Clapton 52 B1
Upper Edmonton 34 B5
Upper Elmers End ..207 B4
Upper Halliford 193 B5
Upper Holloway 71 D6
Upper Norwood 183 C3
Upper Ruxley 191 C3
Upper Shirley 222 D4
Upper Sydenham ...184 A6
Upper Tooting 158 D1
Upper Walthamstow .54 C6
Upton 77 B1
Upton Park 99 D6
Uxbridge 82 A6

V

Vale of Health 70 B5
Vauxhall 116 A1

W

Waddon 220 D4
Walham Green 135 D5
Wallend 100 C6
Wallington 219 A2
Walthamstow 53 D6
Walton-on-Thames 194 C2
Walworth 117 B1
Wandsworth 157 C5
Wanstead 55 C3
Wapping 118 B5
Waterloo 116 C4
Wealdstone 42 D6
Welling 146 B2
Welsh Harp 45 C1
Wembley 66 A2
Wembley Park 66 C5
West Acton 88 C1
West Barnes 200 C4
West Bedfont 148 C4
West Brompton 135 D6
West Drayton 104 B4
West Dulwich 161 A2
West Ealing 109 B5
West Ewell 215 C1
West Green 51 A5
West Ham 99 B6
West Hampstead 69 C4
West Harrow 42 A2
West Heath 146 D6
West Hendon 45 D3
West Hill 157 B5
West Kensington ...113 A2
West Kilburn 91 A4
West Molesey 195 C5
West Norwood 161 A1
West Ruislip 61 B6
West Wickham 224 C6
Westbourne Green ..91 D3
Westminster 115 C4
Weston Green 196 D1
Whetstone 14 A2
Whitechapel 95 D1
Whitton 152 A4
Widmore 188 A1
Willesden 68 A4
Willesden Green 90 B6
Wimbledon 179 B4
Wimbledon Park ...157 B2
Winchmore Hill 16 D4
Wood End 83 D1
Wood End Green 83 C2
Wood Green 32 B2
Woodford 37 D5
Woodford Green 37 B3
Woodford Wells 21 B1
Woodlands 130 C2
Woodside 206 A4
Woodside Park 29 C6
Woolwich 122 D3
Worcester Park 215 C4
World's End 4 C1
Wrythe The 218 D6

Y

Yeading 84 D3
Yiewsley 104 A6

Abbreviations used in the index

Acad	Academy
App	Approach
Arc	Arcade
Art Gall	Art Gallery
Ave	Avenue
Bglws	Bungalows
Bldgs	Buildings
Bsns Ctr	Business Centre
Bsns Pk	Business Park
Bvd	Boulevard
Cath	Cathedral, Catholic
CE	Church of England
Cemy	Cemetery
Cir	Circus
Circ	Circle
Cl	Close
Cnr	Corner
Coll	College
Com	Community
Comm	Common
Comp	Comprehensive
Con Ctr	Conference Centre
Cotts	Cottages
Cres	Crescent
Cswy	Causeway
Ct	Court
Ctr	Centre
Crkt	Cricket
Ctry Pk	Country Park
Cty	County
Ctyd	Courtyard
Dr	Drive
Ent Ctr	Enterprise Centre
Ent Pk	Enterprise Park
Est	Estate
Ex Ctr	Exhibition Centre
Ex Hall	Exhibition Hall
Fst	First
Gdn	Garden
Gdns	Gardens
Gn	Green
Gr	Grove
Gram	Grammar
Her Ctr	Heritage Centre
Ho	House
Hospl	Hospital
Hts	Heights
Ind Est	Industrial Estate
Inf	Infant
Inst	Institute
Int	International
Intc	Interchange
Jun	Junior
Junc	Junction
La	Lane
L Ctr	Leisure Centre
Liby	Library
Mans	Mansions
Mdw/s	Meadow/s
Meml	Memorial
Mid	Middle
Mix	Mixed
Mkt	Market
Mon	Monument
Mus	Museum
Obsy	Observatory
Orch	Orchard
Par	Parade
Pas	Passage
Pav	Pavilion
Pk	Park
Pl	Place
Prec	Precinct
Prep	Preparatory
Prim	Primary
Prom	Promenade
RC	Roman Catholic
Rd	Road
Rdbt	Roundabout
Ret Pk	Retail Park
Sch	School
Sec	Secondary
Sh Ctr	Shopping Centre
Sp	Sports
Specl	Special
Sports Ctr	Sports Centre
Sq	Square
St	Street, Saint
Sta	Station
Stad	Stadium
Tech	Technical/Technology
Terr	Terrace
Trad Est	Trading Estate
Twr/s	Tower/s
Univ	University
Wlk	Walk
Yd	Yard

ron Ct BR3 207 D6
ron Hill Rd E6 100 C2
ady Ho SW1 259 D4
berley Mews 9
V8 137 B2
berton IG8 37 C5
bess Cl 11 E6 100 A2
eatham SW2 160 D3
beville Mews 3
V4 137 D1
beville Rd N8 49 D5
159 C6
bey Ave HA0 88 A5
bey Bsns Ctr
V8 137 B4 268 D2
bey Cl Hayes UB3 106 B5
rtholt UB5 85 B4
nner HA5 40 C6
bey Cres DA17 125 C2
bey Ct N3 47 C6
V8 229 A4
17 262 B1
W12 111 C3
beydale Ct 6 UB1 85 D1
beydale Rd HA0 88 C6
bey Dr SW17 181 A5
beyfield UB4 83 D2
beyfield Rd SE16 118 C2
beyfields Cl NW10 88 C5
bey Gdns
W8 92 A5 229 B3
SE16 118 A2
6 135 A6 264 A5
hislehurst BR7 188 C2
bey Gr SE2 124 B2
beyhill Rd DA15 168 C2
bey Ho E15 98 C5
W8 229 B2
bey Ind Est CR4 202 D4
bey La E15 98 B5
eckenham BR3 185 C3
bey Lane Commercial Est
5 98 C5
bey Lo NW8 230 B1
Ealing W5 109 C6
bey Manufacturing Est
A0 88 B6
bey Mews E17 53 C4
bey Mount DA17 125 B1
bey Orchard St
W1 115 D3 259 D6
bey Orchard Street Est
W1 259 D6
bey Par Ealing NW10 88 B4
erton SW19 180 A3
bey Park Ind Est
G11 101 A6
bey Pk BR3 185 C3
bey Prim Sch SE2 124 C3
bey Rd E15 98 C5
W8 92 A5 229 A4
arking IG11 100 D6
exley DA6,DA7 147 A1
roydon CR0 220 D5
nfield EN1 17 C6
rith DA17 125 A3
ford IG2 57 B4
ower Halliford TW17 192 C1
erton SW19 180 A2
Vembley NW10 88 D5
bey St E13 99 A3
E1 117 D3 263 C6
bey Terr SE2 124 C2
bey Tutorial Coll W2 91 C1
bey View NW7 11 D1
bey Wlk KT8 195 D5
bey Wood Rd SE2 124 C2
bey Wood Sch SE2 124 A3
bey Wood Sta SE2 124 C3
bot Cl HA4 62 D5
bot Ct SW8 270 A3
bot Ho 18 E14 119 D6
botsbury Cl E15 98 A5
V14 113 B4 244 C1
botsbury Fst Sch
M4 201 D4
botsbury Gdns HA5 40 C3
botsbury Ho W14 244 B2
botsbury Mews
E15 140 C2
botsbury Rd
V14 113 B4 244 C1
oney Hall BR2,BR4 224 D6
lorden SM4 201 D5
bots Cl BR5 211 A1
bots Ct SE25 205 C6
bots Dr HA2 63 C6
botsfield Sch UB10 82 D5
botsford Ave N15 51 A5
botsford Gdns IG8 37 A3
botsford Rd IG3 80 B6
bots Gdns N2 48 B5
bots Gn CR0,CR2 222 D2
botshade Rd 15
E16 118 D5
botshall Ave N14 15 C1

Abbotshall Rd SE6 164 B2
Abbots Ho E17 35 B1
SW1 259 C1
W14 254 C5
Abbots La SE1 117 C5 253 B3
Abbotsleigh Cl SM2 217 D1
Abbotsleigh Rd SW16 181 C5
Abbotsmede Cl TW1 152 D2
Abbots Pk SW2 160 C3
Abbot's Pl NW6 91 D6
Abbots Rd E6 99 D6
HA8 27 B3
Abbot St E8 73 D2
Abbots Terr N8 50 A3
Abbotstone Ho 4 E5 74 A6
Abbotstone Rd SW15 134 C2
Abbots Way BR3 207 A4
Abbotswell Rd SE4 163 B6
Abbotswood Cl 7
DA17 125 A3
Abbotswood Gdns IG5 56 B6
Abbotswood Rd SE22 139 C1
Streatham SW16 159 D1
Abbotswood Way UB3 106 B5
Abbott Ave SW20 178 D2
Abbott Cl
Hampton TW12 173 A4
Northolt UB5 63 B2
Abbott Ho SW12 158 D4
Abbott Rd E14 98 B1
Abbotts Cl N1 73 A2
Romford RM7 59 D6
Woolwich SE28 124 C6
Abbotts Cres
Chingford E4 36 B6
Enfield EN2 4 D3
Abbotts Ct HA2 64 B6
Abbotts Dr HA0 65 B6
Abbotts Park Rd E10 54 A2
Abbotts Rd Barnet EN5 1 D1
Cheam SM3 217 A4
Mitcham CR4 203 C5
Southall UB1 107 A5
Abbott's Wlk DA7 146 D5
Abbyfield Cl CR4 180 C1
Abchurch La
EC2,EC4 117 B6 252 D6
Abchurch Yd EC4 252 C6
Abdale Rd W12 112 B5
Abel Ho 7 SE11 138 C6
Abenglen Ind Est UB3 105 B4
Aberavon Rd E3 97 A4
Abercairn Rd SW16 181 C3
Aberconway Rd SM4 201 D5
Abercorn Cl NW7 29 A3
NW8 92 A4 229 A2
Abercorn Cres HA2 41 D1
Abercorn Gdns
Harrow HA3 43 D2
Ilford RM6 58 B3
Abercorn Gr HA4 39 B5
Abercorn Ho SE10 141 D5
Abercorn Mans NW8 229 B3
Abercorn Mews 10
TW10 132 B1
Abercorn Pl
NW8 92 A5 229 A3
Abercorn Rd NW7 29 A3
Stanmore HA7 25 C3
Abercorn Trad Est HA0 87 D6
Abercorn Way SE1 118 A1
Abercrombie Dr EN1 6 A4
Abercrombie Ho 1
W12 112 B6
Abercrombie St SW11 136 C3
Aberdale Ct 22 SE16 118 D4
Aberdare Cl BR4 224 A6
Aberdare Gdns NW6 69 D1
NW7 28 D3
Aberdare Rd EN3 6 C1
Aberdeen Ct N5 73 A3
W2 236 C5
Aberdeen La N5 73 A3
Aberdeen Mans WC1 240 A6
Aberdeen Par N18 34 B5
Aberdeen Pk N5 73 A3
Aberdeen Pl
NW8 92 B3 236 C6
Aberdeen Rd N5 73 A4
NW10 67 D3
Croydon CR0 221 B4
Edmonton N18 34 B5
Harrow HA3 24 D1
Aberdeen Terr SE3 142 B3
Aberdour Rd IG3 80 B6
Aberdour St
SE1 117 C3 263 A4
Aberfeldy Ho SE5 138 D5
Aberfeldy St E14 98 A1
Aberford Gdns SE18 144 A4
Aberfoyle Rd SW16 181 D4
Abergeldie Rd SE12 165 B5
Abernethy Rd SE13 142 C1
Abersham Rd E8 73 D3
Abery St SE18 123 C2
Abingdon W14 254 D3
Abingdon Cl NW1 71 D2
SE1 263 D2
Hillingdon UB10 82 B6

Abingdon Cl *continued*
Wimbledon SW19 180 A4
Abingdon Ct W8 255 B5
Edgware HA8 26 A6
Abingdon Gdns W8 255 B5
Abingdon Ho E2 243 C6
Abingdon Lo BR2 186 D1
Abingdon Mans W8 255 A6
Abingdon Rd N3 30 A1
W8 113 C3 255 B5
Thornton Heath SW16 182 A2
Abingdon St
SW1 116 A3 260 A6
Abingdon Villas
W8 113 C3 255 B5
Abinger Cl BR1 210 A6
Barking IG11 80 A4
New Addington CR0 224 A2
Wallington SM6 220 A3
Abinger Ct
3 Ealing W5 109 C6
Wallington SM6 220 A3
Abinger Gdns TW7 130 C2
Abinger Gr SE8 141 B6
Abinger Ho SE1 252 C1
2 Kingston KT2 176 D3
Abinger Mews W9 91 C3
Abinger Rd W4 111 C3
Abington Ho NW11 48 A3
Ablett St SE16 118 C1
Abney Gdns 5 N16 73 D6
Abney Park Cemetery★
N16 73 C6
Abney Park Ct N16 73 D6
Aborfield 6 NW5 71 C3
Aboyne Dr SW20 178 A1
Aboyne Rd NW10 67 C5
Wandsworth SW17 158 B1
Abraham Cl WD19 22 B6
Abridge Way IG11 102 B5
Abyssinia Cl SW11 136 C1
Abyssinia Rd SW11 136 C1
Acacia Ave N2 47 D6
Brentford TW8 131 B5
Hayes UB3 83 D1
Littleton TW17 192 C4
Ruislip HA4 40 B2
Tottenham N17 33 B3
Wembley HA9 66 A3
Yiewsley UB7 104 B6
Acacia Bsns Ctr 1 E11 76 C5
Acacia Cl BR5 211 B4
SE8 119 A2
Penge SE20 184 A1
Stanmore HA7 24 C4
Acacia Ct Harrow HA1 41 D3
5 West Norwood
SW16 182 C5
Acacia Dr SM3 201 C1
Acacia Gdns NW8 229 D4
West Wickham BR4 224 A6
Acacia Gr Dulwich SE21 161 B2
Kingston KT3 199 C6
Acacia Ho N16 73 B6
1 New Malden KT3 199 C5
Wood Green N22 32 C2
Acacia Pl NW8 92 B5 229 D4
Acacia Rd E11 76 C6
E17 53 A3
NW8 92 B5 229 D4
W3 111 A6
Beckenham BR3 207 B6
Enfield EN2 5 B4
Hampton TW12 173 C4
Mitcham CR4 181 B1
Thornton Heath SW16 182 A2
Wood Green N22 32 C2
Acacias Lo EN4 14 B6
Acacias The EN4 14 B6
Acacia Way DA15 167 D3
Acacia Wlk SW10 266 B3
Academy Ct 13 E2 96 C4
Academy Gdns
Croydon CR0 205 D1
Northolt UB5 84 D5
Academy Pl SE18 144 C4
Academy Rd SE18 144 B5
Academy The 2 N19 49 C1
Acanthus Dr SE1 118 A1
Acanthus Rd SW11 137 A2
Accadia Ct NW9 67 A6
Accommodation Rd
NW11 47 B1
Ace Par KT9 214 A5
Acer Ave UB4 85 A2
Acer Ct NW2 68 D4
Acfold Rd SW6 265 C1
Achilles Cl SE1 118 A1
Achilles Ho 16 E2 96 B5
Achilles Rd NW6 69 C3
Achilles St SE14 141 A5
Achilles Way W1 248 B3
Acklam Rd W10 91 B2
Acklington Dr NW9 27 C2
Ackmar Rd
SW6 135 C4 265 A1
Ackroyd Dr E3 97 C2
Ackroyd Rd SE23 163 A4

Acland Burghley Sch
NW5 71 B4
Acland Cl SE18 145 B5
Acland Cres SE5 139 B2
Acland Ho SW9 138 B3
Acock Gr UB5 64 A4
Acol Cres HA4 62 B3
Acol Ct 3 NW6 69 C1
Acol Rd NW6 69 D1
Aconbury Rd RM9 102 B6
Acorn Cl Chingford E4 35 D5
Chislehurst BR7 189 A5
Enfield EN2 4 D4
1 Hampton TW12 173 D4
Stanmore HA7 25 B3
Acorn Ct E6 78 A1
Ilford IG2 57 C4
Acorn Gdns W3 89 B2
South Norwood SE19 183 D2
Acorn Gr
Harlington UB3 127 D5
Ruislip HA4 61 D4
Acorn Par 7 SE15 140 B5
Acorn Production Ctr
N7 72 A1
Acorns The 21 SW19 156 D3
Acorns Way KT10 212 A3
Acorn Way
Beckenham BR3 208 A4
Forest Hill SE23 162 D1
Orpington BR6 226 D4
Acorn Wharf SE1 140 A6
Acorn Wlk SE16 119 A5
Acre Dr SE22 140 A1
Acrefield Ho 4 NW4 46 D5
Acre La SW2 138 B1
Wallington SM5 219 A4
Acre Path UB5 63 A2
Acre Rd Dagenham RM10 81 D1
Kingston KT2 176 B2
Mitcham SW19 180 B4
Acre Way HA6 22 A2
Acris St SW18 158 A6
Action Ct TW15 171 A2
Acton Bsns Ctr NW10 89 B3
Acton Central Ind Est 4
W3 110 D5
Acton Central Sta W3 111 B5
Acton Cl N9 18 A2
Acton High Sch W3 110 C4
Acton Hill Mews W3 110 D5
Acton Ho 16 E8 95 D6
5 W3 89 A1
Acton Hospl W3 110 C4
Acton La Acton NW10 89 B5
Acton W3 111 A4
Acton W4 111 A2
Acton Main Line Sta
W3 89 A1
Acton Mews E8 95 D6
Acton Park Est W3 111 B4
Acton St WC1 94 B4 233 C1
Acton Town Sta W3 110 C4
Acton Vale Ind Pk W3 111 D5
Acuba Ho SW18 157 D3
Acuba Rd SW18 157 D2
Acworth Cl N9 18 C4
Acworth Ho 1 SE18 144 D6
Ada Ct N1 235 A5
W9 92 A4 229 B1
Ada Gdns E15 98 D6
South Bromley E14 98 B1
Ada Ho 23 E2 96 A6
Adair Cl SE25 206 B6
Adair Ho SW3 267 B6
Adair Rd W10 91 A3
Adair Twr 7 W10 91 A3
Ada Kennedy Ct 6
SE10 142 A5
Ada Lewis Ho HA9 66 B4
Adam Cl SE6 185 C6
Adam Ct SE11 261 C3
Adam & Eve Ct W1 239 B2
Adam & Eve Mews
W8 113 C3 255 B6
Adamfields NW3 70 B1
Adam Lo N21 16 B6
Adam Rd E4 35 B4
Adams Cl N3 29 C3
NW9 66 D6
Surbiton KT5 198 B3
Adams Ct E17 53 A3
Adams Gardens Est 5
SE16 118 C4
Adams Ho
3 South Bromley E14 98 B1
3 Streatham SW16 181 C5
Adams Mews N22 32 B3
Adamson Ct N2 48 C6
Adamson Rd E16 99 A1
NW3 70 B1
Adams Pl N7 72 B3
Adams Rd
Beckenham BR3 207 A4
Tottenham N17 33 B1
Adamsrill Cl EN1 17 B5
Adamsrill Prim Sch
SE26 163 A1
Adamsrill Rd SE26 185 A6

Adam's Row
W1 115 A6 248 B5
Adams Sq DA6 147 A2
Adam St WC2 116 A6 250 B5
Adams Way CR0 206 A3
Adams Wlk 11 KT1 176 A1
Adam Wlk SW6 134 C5
Ada Pl E2 96 A6
Ada Rd SE5 139 C5
Wembley HA0,HA9 65 D5
Adare Wlk SW16,SW2 160 B2
Ada St E8 96 B6
Adcot Wlk 6 BR6 227 D4
Adderley Gdns SE9 188 C6
Adderley Gr SW11 159 A6
Adderley Rd HA3 24 D2
Adderley St E14 98 A1
Addey Ho SE8 141 B5
Addey & Stanhope Sch
SE14 141 C4
Addington Ct 7 SW14 133 B2
Addington Dr N12 30 B4
Addington Gr SE26 185 A6
Addington Ho 13 SW9 138 B3
Addington Palace (The
Royal Sch of Church
Music) CR9 223 B2
Addington Rd E16 98 C3
E3 97 C4
N4 50 C3
Thornton Heath CR0 204 C1
West Wickham BR4 224 C6
West Wickham BR4,CR0 224 B4
Addington Sq SE5 139 B5
Addington St
SE1 116 B4 250 D1
Addington Village Rd
CR0 223 C3
Addington Village Sta
CR0 223 C2
Addis Cl EN3 6 D4
Addiscombe Ave CR0 206 A2
Addiscombe Cl HA3 43 C4
Addiscombe Court Rd
CR0 221 C6
Addiscombe Ct UB10 83 A3
Addiscombe Rd CR0 222 B6
Addiscombe Sta CR0 206 A1
Addison Ave
W11 113 A5 244 A3
Hounslow TW3 130 A4
Southgate N14 15 C5
Addison Bridge Pl
W14 113 B2 254 C4
Addison Cl
Northwood HA6 22 A2
Orpington BR5 211 A3
Addison Cres
W14 113 A3 254 B6
Addison Ct W5 110 C6
Addison Dr SE12 165 B6
Addison Gdns W14 112 D3
Kingston KT5 198 B5
Addison Gr W4 111 C3
Addison Ho
NW8 92 B4 229 C2
Addison Park Mans 12
W14 112 D4
Addison Pl
W11 113 A5 244 A3
Southall UB1 107 C6
Addison Prim Sch
W14 112 D3
Addison Rd BR2 209 D4
E17 54 A4
W14 113 B3 254 C6
Croydon SE25 206 A5
Enfield EN3 6 D4
Teddington TW11 175 B4
Wanstead E11 55 A3
Addison's Cl CR0 223 B6
Addison Way NW11 47 C5
Hayes UB3 84 A1
Northwood HA6 22 A2
Addle Hill EC4 241 D1
Addle St EC2 242 B3
Addlestone Ho W10 90 C2
Addy Ho SE16 118 C2
Adecroft Way KT8 196 A6
Adela Ave KT3 200 B5
Adela Ho 9 W6 112 C1
Adelaide Ave SE4 141 C1
Adelaide Cl SW9 138 C1
Enfield EN1 5 C5
Stanmore HA7 25 A6
Adelaide Ct NW8 229 B3
W7 108 D4
15 Beckenham BR3 185 C3
Adelaide Gdns RM6 59 A4
Adelaide Gr W12 112 A5
Adelaide Ho E17 53 B6
Adelaide Rd E10 76 A5
NW3 70 C1
2 SW18 157 C6
Ashford TW15 170 A6
Chislehurst BR7 188 D5
Ealing W13 109 A4
Heston TW5 129 A4
Ilford IG1 78 D6

Adelaide Rd *continued*
Kingston KT6 198 A4
Richmond TW9 132 B1
Southall UB2 107 A2
Teddington TW11 174 D4
Adelaide St WC2 250 A5
Adelaide Terr TW8 109 D1
Adela St W10 91 A3
Adelina Gr E1 96 C2
Adelina Mews SW12 159 D3
Adeline Pl WC1 93 D2 239 D3
Adeliza Cl IG11 79 A1
Adelphi Cres UB4 83 D4
Adelphi Ct 20 SE16 118 D4
Adelphi Terr WC2 250 B5
Adelphi Way UB4 83 D4
Adeney Cl W6 134 D6
Aden Gr N16 73 B4
Aden Ho 12 E1 96 D2
Aden Lo N16 73 B4
Adenmore Rd SE6 163 C4
Aden Rd Enfield EN3 7 A1
Ilford IG1 57 A2
Adeyfield Ho EC1 235 D1
Adhara Rd HA6 22 A5
Adie Rd W6 112 C3
Adine Rd E13 99 B3
Adisham Ho 4 E5 74 B3
Adler Ind Est UB3 105 B4
Adler St E1 96 A1
Adley St E5 75 A3
Adlington Cl N18 33 C5
Admaston Rd SE18 145 A6
Admiral Ct NW4 46 A4
SW10 136 A4 266 B2
W1 238 A3
Barking IG11 102 C5
Carshalton SM5 202 C1
Admiral Ho TW11 175 A6
Admiral Hyson Ind Est
SE16 118 B1
Admiral Mews W10 90 D3
Admiral Pl SE16 119 A5
Admirals Cl E18 55 B5
Admirals Ct 3 E6 100 D1
SE1 253 C3
32 Putney SW19 156 D3
Admiral Seymour Rd
SE9 144 B1
Admirals Gate SE10 141 D4
Admiral Sq
SW10 136 A4 266 B2
Admiral St SE8 141 C4
Admirals Way E14 119 C4
Admiral's Wlk NW3 70 A5
Admiralty Arch★
SW1 249 D4
Admiralty Cl 1 SE8 141 C4
Admiralty Rd TW11 174 D4
Admiralty Way TW11 174 D4
Admiral Wlk W9 91 C2
Adolf St SE6 185 D6
Adolphus Rd N4 50 D1
Adolphus St SE8 141 B5
Adomar Rd RM8 81 A5
Adpar St W2 92 B2 236 C4
Adrian Ave NW2 46 B1
Adrian Bolt Ho 2 E2 96 B4
Adrian Ho N1 233 D5
SW8 270 A4
Adrian Mews SW10 265 D6
Adriatic Bldg 18 E14 ....
Adriatic Ho 18 E1 96 D3
Adrienne Ave UB1 85 B4
Adron Ho 9 SE16 118 C2
Adstock Ho 5 N1 72 D1
ADT Coll SW15 157 B6
Advance Rd SE27 183 A6
Adventurers Ct 4 E14 120 B6
Advent Way N18 34 D5
Adys Lawn NW2 68 B2
Adys Rd SE15 139 D2
Aerodrome Rd NW4,
NW9 45 D6
Aerodrome Way TW5 128 C6
Aeroville NW9 27 C1
Affleck St N1 233 D3
Afghan Rd SW11 136 C3
Agamemnon Rd NW6 69 B3
Agar Cl KT6 214 B6
Agar Gr NW1 71 D1
Agar Ho 6 KT1 198 A6
Agar Pl NW1 71 C1
Agar St WC2 250 B5
Agate Cl E16 99 D1
Agate Ho
New Malden KT4 199 C1
12 Penge SE26 184 B5
Agate Rd W6 112 C3
Agatha Cl E1 118 C5
Agaton Rd BR7,SE9 167 A2
Agave Rd NW2 68 C4
Agdon St EC1 94 D3 241 C6
Agincourt E11 54 D3
Agincourt Rd NW3 70 D4
Agnes Ave IG1 78 D4

Agnes Cl E6 122 C6
Agnes Ct 11 SW18 136 B1
Agnesfield Cl N12 30 C4
Agnes Gdns RM8 80 D4
Agnes Ho 13 W11 112 D6
Agnes Rd W3 111 D4
Agnes St E14 97 B1
Agnew Rd SE23 162 D4
Agricola Pl EN1 17 D6
Aidan Cl RM8 81 A4
Aidans Ct N12 30 C5
Aigburth Mans 5
SW9 138 C5
Ailantus Ct HA8 26 B5
Aileen Wlk E15 76 D1
Ailsa Ave TW1 153 B6
Ailsa Rd TW1 153 B6
Ailsa St E14 98 A2
Ainger Rd NW3 70 D1
Ainsdale NW1 232 A2
Ainsdale Cl BR6 211 B1
Ainsdale Cres HA5 41 C6
Ainsdale Dr SE1 118 A1
Ainsdale Rd W5 87 D3
Ainsley Ave RM7 59 D3
Ainsley Cl N9 17 C3
Ainsley St E2 96 B4
Ainsley Wood Prim Sch
E4 35 D5
Ainslie Ct 2 HA0 88 A5
Ainslie Wood Cres E4 35 D5
Ainslie Wood Gdns E4 35 D5
Ainslie Wood Rd E4 35 D5
Ainsty St 14 SE16 118 C4
Ainsworth Cl NW2 68 A5
SE5 139 C3
Ainsworth Est
NW8 92 A6 229 A6
Ainsworth Ho NW8 91 D6
Ainsworth Rd E9 74 C1
Croydon CR0 220 D6
Ainsworth Way
NW8 92 A6 229 A6
Aintree Ave E6 100 A6
Aintree Cl UB8 82 D2
Aintree Ho SE26 184 B4
Aintree Rd UB6 87 B5
Aintree St
SW6 135 A5 264 B4
Airborne Ho 10 SM6 219 B4
Air Call Bsns Ctr NW9 45 C6
Aird Ho SE1 262 A5
Airdrie Cl N1 72 B1
Hayes UB4 85 A2
Airedale Ave W4 111 D1
Airedale Ave S W4 111 D1
Airedale Rd W5 109 D3
Balham SW12 158 D4
Airlie Gdns
W8 113 C5 245 A3
Ilford IG1 56 D1
Airlinks Ind Est TW5 106 C1
Air Park Way TW13 150 B2
Airport Gate Bsns Ctr
UB7 126 B5
Airport Rdbt E16 121 D5
Air St W1 249 B5
Airthrie Rd IG3 80 B6
Aisgill Ave
SW5 113 B1 254 D1
Aisher Rd SE28 124 C6
Aislibie Rd SE12 142 C1
Aislobie Ho N21 17 B5
Aiten Pl W6 112 A2
Aithan Ho 9 E14 97 B1
Aitken Cl E8 96 A6
Carshalton CR4 202 D2
Aitken Rd Barnet EN5 12 C6
Catford SE6 163 D2
Ajax Ave NW9 45 C6
Ajax Ho 15 E2 96 B5
Ajax Rd NW6 69 C3
Akabusi Cl SE25 206 A3
Akbar Ho 7 E14 119 D2
Akehurst St SW15 156 A4
Akenside Ct 3 NW3 70 B3
Akenside Rd NW3 70 B3
Akerman Rd SW9 138 D4
Kingston KT6 197 C3
Akintaro Ho 7 SE8 141 B6
Akiva Sch N3 29 D1
Alabama St SE18 145 C5
Alacross Rd W5 109 D4
Alamaro Lo SE10 120 D3
Alandale Dr HA5 22 B2
Aland Ct SE16 119 A3
Alander Mews E17 54 A5
Alan Dr EN5 13 A5
Alan Gdns RM7 59 C2
Alan Hocken Way E15 98 C5
Alan Lo N3 29 C2
Alan Preece Ct NW6 68 D1
Alan Rd SW19 179 A5
Alanthus Cl SE12 165 A5
Alaska St SE1 251 A3
Alba Cl UB4 84 D3
Albacore Cres SE13 163 D5
Alba Gdns NW11 47 A3
Albain Cres TW15 148 A2
Alba Mews SW18,
SW19 157 C2
Alban Ho NW3 70 A2
Albans Cl SW16 160 A1
Albany N12 29 D4
W1 249 A5
Albany Cl N15 50 D5
Bushey WD23 8 B5
Ickenham UB10 60 C3
Mortlake SW14 132 D1
Sidcup DA5 168 D4
Albany Coll The NW4 46 C4
Albany Cres
Claygate KT10 212 C2
Edgware HA8 26 C3
Albany Ct E10 53 C2
HA8 27 B2
NW10 90 B4
SW1 259 C6
Kingston KT2 176 A4
Richmond TW10 153 B1
Chingford E4 19 D5
Albany Ctyd W1 249 B5
Albany Ho E5 74 C6
6 Brentford TW8 132 A6
Albany Mans SW11 267 B3
Albany Mews BR1 187 A4
N1 72 C1
SE5 139 A6
Kingston KT2 175 D4
Sutton SM1 217 D3
Albany Par 4 TW8 132 A6
Albany Park Ave EN3 6 D4
Albany Park Rd KT2 176 A4
Albany Park Sta DA14 168 D2
Albany Pas 12 TW10 154 A6
Albany Pl N7 72 C4
Brentford TW8 131 D6
Albany Rd E10 53 C2
E12 77 D4
E17 53 A3
N18 34 C5
N4 50 C3
SE5 139 C6
Brentford TW8 131 D6
Chislehurst BR7 188 D5
Dagenham RM6 59 B3
Ealing W13 109 B6
Enfield EN3 6 D5
Erith DA17 147 B6
New Malden KT3 199 B5
Richmond TW10 154 A6
Sidcup DA5 168 C4
Wimbledon SW19 179 D5
Albany Reach KT7 196 D4
Albany Sch EN3 6 D5
Albany St NW1 93 B4 231 D2
Albany Terr 6 TW10 154 B6
Albany The
Kingston KT2 175 D4
Woodford IG8 36 D6
Albany View IG9 21 A3
Albany Wlk N15 50 D5
Alba Pl W11 91 B1
Albatross 31 NW9 27 D1
Albatross St SE18 145 C5
Albemarle SW19 156 D2
Albemarle App IG2 56 D3
Albemarle Ave TW2 151 B3
Albemarle Gdns
Ilford IG2 56 D3
New Malden KT3 199 B5
Albemarle Ho SE8 119 B2
Albemarle Lo SE26 185 A5
Albemarle Mans NW3 69 D4
Albemarle Pk
Beckenham BR3 185 D2
Stanmore HA7 25 C5
Albemarle Prim Sch
SW19 157 A2
Albemarle Rd
Beckenham BR2,BR3 186 A2
East Barnet EN4 14 C4
Albemarle St
W1 115 C6 249 A5
Albemarle Way EC1 241 C5
Albermarle Ho 3
SW9 138 C2
Alberon Gdns NW11 47 B5
Alberta Ave SM1 217 B3
Alberta Ct 1 TW10 154 B6
Alberta Ho E14 120 A5
Hayes UB4 84 B4
Alberta Rd Bexley DA7 147 D4
Enfield EN1 18 A5
Alberta St
SE17 116 D1 261 D2
Albert Ave SW8 270 C3
Chingford E4 35 C6
Albert Barnes Ho SE1 262 A5
Albert Bigg Point E15 98 A6
Albert Bridge Rd
SW11 136 D5 267 C3
Albert Carr Gdns
SW16 182 A5
Albert Cl 11 E9 96 B6
Albert Cl *continued*
N22 31 D2
Albert Cotts 2 E1 96 A2
Albert Cres E4 35 C6
Albert Ct SW7 246 C1
5 Putney SW19 157 A3
Albert Dr SW19 157 A3
Albert Emb
SE1 116 A2 260 B3
Albert Gate Ct SW1 247 C1
Albert Gdns E1 96 D1
Albert Gr SW20 178 D2
Albert Gray Ho SW10 266 C4
Albert Hall Mans
SW7 114 B4 246 C1
Albert Ho 5 E18 55 B6
Albert Mans N8 50 A2
SW11 267 C2
Albert Memorial*
SW7 114 B4 246 C1
Albert Mews W8 256 A6
Albert Palace Mans
SW11 268 B2
Albert Pl N3 29 C2
W8 113 D4 245 D1
Albert Rd BR2 209 D4
E10 54 A1
E17 53 C4
N15 51 C3
N4 50 B2
NW4 46 D5
NW6 91 B5
NW7 27 D5
Ashford TW15 170 B5
Buckhurst Hill IG9 21 D2
Chislehurst SE9 166 A1
Croydon SE25 206 B5
Dagenham RM8 59 C1
Ealing W5 87 B3
East Barnet EN4 2 A1
Erith DA17 125 B1
Hampton TW12 174 A5
Harrow HA2 42 A6
Hayes UB3 105 C3
Hounslow TW3 129 C1
Ilford IG1 79 A5
Kingston KT1 176 B1
Mitcham CR4 202 D6
Newham E16 122 B4
New Malden KT3 199 D5
Penge SE20 184 D4
Richmond TW10 154 B6
Sidcup DA5 169 D4
Southall UB2 106 D3
Sutton SM1 218 B3
Teddington TW11 174 D4
Twickenham TW1 152 D3
4 Wanstead E18 55 B6
Wood Green N22 31 C2
Yiewsley UB7 104 A5
Albert's Ct NW1 237 B6
Albert Sq E15 76 C3
SW8 138 B5 270 C3
Albert St N12 30 A5
NW1 93 B6 231 D5
Albert Starr Ho 7
SE8 118 D2
Albert Studios SW11 267 C2
Albert Terr NW10 89 A6
NW1 93 A6 231 A5
Buckhurst Hill IG9 21 D2
Albert Terr Mews
NW1 231 A5
Albert Victoria Ho N22 32 C2
Albert Way SE15 140 B5
Albert Westcott Ho
SE17 261 D2
Albert Whicher Ho 3
E17 54 A5
Albert Wlk E16 122 D4
Albion Ave N10 31 A2
SW8 137 D3
Albion Cl W2 247 B6
Albion Ct 2 SE7 122 A2
7 W6 112 B2
Sutton SM2 218 B1
Albion Dr E8 74 A1
Albion Est SE16 118 C4
Albion Gate W2 247 B6
Albion Gdns 1 W6 112 B2
Albion Gr N16 73 C4
Albion Hill IG10 21 D6
Albion Ho E16 122 D5
Albion Mews N1 234 A6
W2 114 C6 247 B6
6 W6 112 B2
Albion Pk IG10 21 D6
Albion Pl EC1 241 C4
EC2 242 D3
W6 112 B2
South Norwood SE25 206 A6
Albion Prim Sch SE16 118 C4
Albion Rd E17 54 A6
N16 73 B4
Bexley DA6 147 C1
Dagenham RM10 81 B3
Hayes UB3 83 C1
Hounslow TW3 129 C1
Kingston KT2 177 A2
Albion Rd *continued*
Sutton SM2 218 B1
Tottenham N17 34 A1
Twickenham TW2 152 C3
Albion Sq E8 73 D1
Albion St SE16 118 C4
W2 114 C6 247 B6
Thornton Heath CR0 204 D1
Albion Terr E8 73 D1
Sewardstone E4 7 D1
Albion Villas Rd SE23,
SE26 162 C1
Albion Way EC1 242 A3
SE13 142 A1
Wembley HA9 66 C5
Albion Wharf SW11 267 A4
Albion Yd N1 233 B3
Albon Ho SE14 141 B4
Wandsworth SW18 157 D5
Albrighton Rd SE5,
SE22 139 C2
Albuhera Cl EN2 4 C4
Albury Ave DA7 147 A3
Hounslow TW7 130 D5
Albury Bldgs SE1 251 D1
Albury Cl TW12 173 D4
Albury Ct
4 Croydon CR0 221 A4
Mitcham CR4 180 B1
6 Northolt UB5 84 C4
Sutton SM1 218 A4
Albury Dr HA5 22 D3
Albury Lo 7 SW2 160 B4
Albury Mews E12 77 C6
Albury Rd KT9 214 A3
Albury St SE8 141 C6
Albyfield BR1 210 B6
Albyn Rd SE8 141 C4
Alcester Cres E5 74 B6
Alcester Ct 4 SM6 219 B4
Alcester Rd SM6 219 B4
Alcock Cl SM6 219 D1
Alcock Rd TW5 128 D5
Alconbury DA6 169 D6
Alconbury Rd E5 74 A6
Alcorn Cl SM3 217 C6
Alcott Cl W7 86 D2
Aldborough Ct
Chingford E4 19 D1
Ilford IG2 57 D4
Aldborough Rd IG2 57 D6
Aldborough Rd N IG2 57 D4
Aldborough Rd S IG3 57 C2
Aldbourne Rd W12 112 A5
Aldbridge St
SE17 117 C1 263 B2
Aldburgh Mews W1 238 B2
Aldbury Ave HA9 66 D1
Aldbury Ho SW3 257 A3
Aldbury Mews N9 17 B4
Aldebert Terr
SW8 138 B5 270 C3
Aldeburgh Cl 16 E5 74 B6
Aldeburgh Pl IG8 37 A6
Aldeburgh St SE10 121 A1
Alden Ave E15 98 D4
Alden Ct
South Croydon CR0 221 C5
Wimbledon SW19 179 C4
Aldenham Ctry Pk WD6 9 B6
Aldenham Dr UB8 82 D3
Aldenham Ho NW1 232 B3
Aldenham Rd WD6 9 C6
Aldenham St
NW1 93 D5 232 C3
Alden Ho E8 96 B6
Aldensley Rd W6 112 B3
Alderbrook Prim Sch
SW12 159 B4
Alderbrook Rd SW12 159 B5
Alderbury Rd SW13 134 A6
Alder Ct N11 48 B6
3 West Norwood
SW16 182 C5
Alder Gr NW2 68 B6
Aldergrove Gdns TW4 129 A3
Aldergrove Ho 3 E5 74 B6
Alder Ho 1 NW3 70 D2
SE15 139 D6
SE4 141 C2
Alderley Ho 36 SW8 137 D3
Alder Lo SW6 134 D4
Alderman Ave IG11 102 A4
Aldermanbury
EC2 95 A1 242 B2
Aldermanbury Sq EC2 242 B3
Alderman Judge Mall 6
KT1 176 A1
Alderman's Hill N13 32 B6
Alderman's Wlk EC2 243 A3
Aldermary Rd BR1 187 A2
Aldermead 2 TW3 129 D2
Alder Mews 9 N19 71 C6
Aldermoor Rd SE6 163 B1
Alderney Ave TW5 129 D5
Alderney Gdns UB5 63 B1
Alderney Ho 16 N1 73 A2
Enfield EN3 6 D5
Alderney Mews SE1 262 C6
Alderney Rd E1 96 D3
Alderney St
SW1 115 B1 258 D2
Alder Rd DA14 167 D1
Mortlake SW14 133 B2
Alders Ave IG8 36 C4
Aldersbrook Ave EN1 5 C3
Aldersbrook Dr KT2 176 B4
Aldersbrook House Coll of
Railway Tech E12 78 C5
Aldersbrook La E12 78 B5
Aldersbrook Prim Sch
E12 77 C6
Aldersbrook Rd E11,E12 77 C6
Alders Cl HA8 27 A5
W5 109 D3
Wanstead E11 77 B6
Alders Ct N17 52 B5
Aldersey Gdns IG11 79 B2
Aldersford Cl SE4 140 D1
Aldersgate Ct EC1 242 A3
Aldersgate St
EC1 95 A2 242 A3
Alders Gr KT8 196 B4
Aldersgrove Ave SE9,
SE12 165 D1
Aldershot Rd NW6 91 B6
Aldersmead Ave CR0 206 D3
Aldersmead Rd BR3 185 A3
Alderson Pl UB2 108 A5
Alderson St W10 91 A3
Alders Rd HA8 27 A5
Alders The
Feltham TW13 173 A6
Heston TW5 129 B6
Southgate N21 16 C5
Streatham SW16 181 C6
West Wickham BR4 223 D6
Alderton 9 KT2 176 D2
Alderton Cl NW10 67 B5
Alderton Cres NW4 46 B4
Alderton Ct KT8 195 B5
Alderton Rd SE24 139 A2
Croydon CR0 206 A2
Alderton Way NW4 46 B4
Alderville Rd SW6 135 B3
Alderwick Ct N7 72 B2
Alderwick Dr TW3 130 B2
Alderwood Prim Sch
SE9 167 C5
Alderwood Rd SE9 167 B5
Aldford St W1 115 A5 248 B4
Aldgate EC3 95 C1 243 B1
Aldgate East Sta
E1 95 D1 243 D2
Aldgate High St
EC3 95 D1 243 C1
Aldgate Sta EC3 95 D1 243 C1
Aldham Hall 1 E11 55 A3
Aldham Ho SE4 141 B4
Aldine Ct W12 112 C5
Aldine St W12 112 C4
Aldington Cl RM8 58 C1
Aldington Ct 1 E8 74 A1
Aldington Rd SE18 121 D3
Aldis Mews
Holdbrook EN3 7 C6
Upper Tooting SW17 180 C5
Aldis St SW17 180 C5
Aldred Rd NW6 69 C3
Aldren Rd SW17 158 A1
Aldriche Way E4 36 A4
Aldrich Gdns SM3 217 B5
Aldrich Terr SW18 158 A2
Aldrick Ho N1 233 D4
Aldridge Ave
Edgware HA8 10 D1
Holdbrook EN3 7 C5
Ruislip HA4 62 D6
Stanmore HA7 26 A2
Aldridge Ct W11 91 B2
Aldridge Rd Villas W11 91 B2
Aldridge Rise KT3 199 C3
Aldridge Wlk N14 16 A4
Aldrington Rd SW16 181 C6
Aldsworth Cl W9 91 D3
Aldwick Cl BR7 167 B1
Aldwick Ct N12 30 A6
Aldwick Rd CR0 220 B4
Aldworth Gr SE13 164 A5
Aldworth Rd E15 76 C1
Aldwych WC2 94 B1 240 D1
Aldwych Ave IG6 57 A5
Aldwych Bldgs WC2 240 B2
Aldwyn Ho SW8 270 A3
Alers Rd DA6 168 D6
Alesia Cl N22 32 A3
Alestan Beck Rd E16 99 D1
Alexander Ave NW10 68 B1
Alexander Cl Barnet EN4 2 B1
Hayes BR2 209 A1
Sidcup DA15 167 C5
Southall UB2 108 A5
Twickenham TW2 152 D2
Alexander Ct SW18 158 A6
Beckenham BR3 186 B2
Greenwich SE3 143 B3
Stanmore HA7 44 B6
14 Surbiton KT6 197 D2
Alexander Evans Mews
SE23 162
Alexander Ho 9 E14 119
Alexander McLeod Jun S
SE2 124
Alexander McLeod Prim
Sch SE2 124
Alexander Mews 2
W2 91
Alexander Pl SW7 257
Alexander Rd N19 72
Bexley DA16 146
Chislehurst BR7 188
Alexander Sq
SW3 114 C2 257
Alexander St W2 91
Alexander Terr SE2 124
Alexandra Ave N22 31
SW11 268
Harrow HA2 63
Southall UB1 107
Sutton SM1 217
Alexandra Bsns Ctr EN3 6
Alexandra Cl SE8 141
Ashford TW15 171
Harrow HA2 63
Alexandra Cotts SE14 141
Penge SE20 184
Alexandra Cres BR1 186
Alexandra Ct 4 N16 73
5 W12 112
W9 236
Ashford TW15 171
Ealing W5 87
Greenford UB6 85
Hounslow TW3 129
Southgate N14 15
Wembley HA9 66
Alexandra Dr
Surbiton KT5 198
West Norwood SE19 183
Alexandra Gdns N10 49
Chiswick W4 133
Hounslow TW3 129
Wallington SM5 219
Alexandra Gr N12 29
N4 50
Alexandra Ho 13 W6 112
Alexandra Inf Sch
Kingston KT2 176
Penge BR3 184
Alexandra Jun & Inf Sch
TW3 129
Alexandra Jun Sch
SE26 184
Alexandra Mans
6 NW6 69
SW3 266
Alexandra Mews N2 48
Alexandra National Ho
N4 72
Alexandra Palace*
N22 31
Alexandra Palace Sta
N22 32
Alexandra Palace Way
N10 49
Alexandra Park Rd N10,
N22 31
Alexandra Park Sch
N22 31
Alexandra Pl
NW8 92 A6 229
Croydon CR0 205
South Norwood SE25 205
Alexandra Prim Sch
N22 32
Alexandra Rd E10 76
E17 53
N10 31
N15 51
N8,N22 50
NW4 46
NW8 70
W4 111
Ashford TW15 171
10 Brentford TW8 131
Croydon CR0 205
Dagenham RM6 59
Edmonton N9 18
Enfield EN3 6
Hounslow TW3 129
Kingston KT2 176
Mitcham SW19 180
Mortlake SW14 133
Penge SE26 184
Richmond TW9 132
Thames Ditton KT7 196
Twickenham TW1 153
Wallend E6 100
Wanstead E18 55
Wimbledon SW19 179
Alexandra Sch HA2 63
Alexandra Sq SM4 201
Alexandra St E16 99
5 SE14 141
Alexandra Wlk 8
SE19 183
Alexandria Rd W13 109

lex Gossip Ho SW6 .265 A1
lexis St SE16 .118 A2
lfearn Rd E5 .74 C4
lford Ct N1 .235 B3
5 Belmont SM2 .217 D1
lford Gn CR0 .224 B2
lford Ho N6 .49 C3
6 SE18 .144 D6
lford Pl N1 .235 B3
lfoxton Ave N8,N15 .50 D5
lfreda Ct SW11 .268 C1
lfreda St
SW11 .137 B4 268 C1
lfred Butt Ho SW17 .158 D1
lfred Cl W4 .111 B2
lfred Findley Ho N22 .32 D1
lfred Gdns UB1 .107 A6
lfred Ho E9 .75 A3
lfred Hurley Ho
SW17 .180 A6
lfred Mews W1,WC1 .239 C4
lfred Mizen Prim Sch The
CR4 .203 D6
lfred Nunn Ho NW10 .89 D6
lfred Pl WC1 .93 D2 239 C4
lfred Prior Ho 6 E12 .78 C4
lfred Rd E15 .76 D3
W2 .91 C2
W3 .111 A5
Buckhurst Hill IG9 .21 D2
Croydon SE25 .206 A4
Erith DA17 .125 B1
Feltham TW13 .150 C2
Kingston KT1 .198 B6
Sutton SM1 .218 A3
lfred Salter Ho SE1 .263 D3
lfred Salter Prim Sch
SE16 .118 D4
Alfred's Gdns IG11 .101 C5
Alfred St E3 .97 B4
Alfred's Way (East Ham & Barking By-Pass)
IG11 .101 B5
Alfred's Way Ind Est
IG11 .102 A6
Alfred Villas 9 E17 .54 A5
Alfreton Cl SW19 .156 D1
Alfriston KT5 .198 B3
Alfriston Ave
Harrow HA2 .41 C2
Thornton Heath CR0 .204 A2
Alfriston Cl KT5 .198 B3
Alfriston Rd SW11 .158 D6
Algar Cl Isleworth TW7 .131 A2
Stanmore HA7 .24 D5
Algar Ho SE1 .251 C1
Algar Rd TW7 .131 A2
Algarve Rd SW18 .157 D3
Algernon Rd NW4 .46 A3
NW6 .91 C6
SE13 .141 D1
Algers Cl IG10 .21 D6
Algers Rd IG10 .21 D6
Alghers Mead IG10 .21 D6
Algiers Rd SE13 .141 C1
Alguin Ct HA7 .25 C3
Alibon Gdns RM10 .81 C3
Alibon Rd RM10 .81 C3
Alice Ct SW15 .135 B1
Alice Gilliott Ct W14 .264 D6
Alice La E3 .97 B6
Alice Mews 8 TW11 .174 D5
Alice Owen Tech Ctr
EC1 .234 C2
Alice Shepherd Ho 7
E14 .120 A4
Alice St SE1 .117 C3 263 A5
Alice Thompson Cl
SE12 .165 C2
Alice Walker Cl 8
SE24 .138 D1
Alice Way TW3 .129 D1
Alicia Ave HA3 .43 C5
Alicia Cl HA3 .43 C5
Alicia Gdns HA3 .43 C5
Alicia Ho DA16 .146 B4
Alie St E1 .95 D1 243 D1
Alington Cres NW9 .45 A1
Alison Cl E6 .100 C1
Croydon CR0 .206 D1
Alison Ct 1 SE1 .118 A1
Aliwal Rd SW11 .136 C1
Alkerden Rd W4 .111 C1
Alkham Rd N16 .73 D6
Allam Ho W11 .244 A6
Allan Barclay Cl N15 .51 D3
Allanbridge N16 .51 C2
Allan Cl KT3 .199 B4
Allandale Ave N3 .47 B6
Allan Ho SW8 .269 C2
Allanson Ct E10 .75 C6
Allan Way W3 .89 A2
Allard Cres WD23 .8 A2
Allard Gdns SW4 .159 D6
Allardyce St SW4,SW9 .138 B1
Allbrook Cl TW11 .174 C5
Allbrook Ho 4 SW15 .156 A4
Allcot Cl TW14 .149 D3
Allcott Ho TW7 .130 D2
Allcroft Rd NW5 .71 A2
Allder Way CR2 .220 D1
Allenby Cl UB6 .85 C4
Allenby Inf Sch UB1 .85 D1
Allenby Rd
Forest Hill SE23 .163 A1
Southall UB1 .85 C3
Allen Cl Streatham CR4 .181 C2
Sunbury TW16 .172 B2
Allen Ct E17 .53 C3
Allendale Ave UB1 .85 C1
Allendale Cl SE5 .139 B4
Forest Hill SE26 .184 D5
Allendale Rd UB6 .65 B2
Allendale Sch
W8 .113 C3 255 B6
Allen Edwards Dr
SW8 .138 A4 270 A2
Allen Edwards Prim Sch
SW4 .138 A4 270 A1
Allenford Ho 1 SW15 155 D5
All England Lawn Tennis & Croquet Club The
SW19 .157 A1
Allen Ho W8 .255 B6
Allen Mans W8 .255 B6
Allen Rd E3 .97 B5
N16 .73 C4
Penge BR3 .184 D1
Sunbury TW16 .172 B1
Thornton Heath CR0 .204 C1
Allensbury Pl NW1 .72 A1
7 NW1 .71 D1
Allens Rd EN3 .18 C6
Allen St W8 .113 C3 255 B5
Allenswood 12 SW19 .157 A3
Allenswood Rd SE9 .144 B3
Allerdale Ho 7 N4 .51 B2
Allerford Ct
Catford SE6 .163 D1
Harrow HA2 .42 A4
Allerford Rd SE6 .185 D6
Allerton Ct 5 NW4 .28 D1
North Cheam SM3 .216 D6
Allerton Ho N1 .235 D3
4 Merton SW19 .180 A3
Allerton Rd N16 .73 A6
Allerton St N1 .235 D2
Allerton Wlk 11 N7 .72 B6
Allestree Rd
SW6 .135 A5 264 A3
Alleyn Cres SE21 .161 B2
Alleyndale Rd RM8 .80 C6
Alleyn Ho EC1 .242 B5
SE1 .262 C5
Alleyn Pk Dulwich SE21 161 C1
Southall UB2 .107 C1
Alleyn Rd SE21 .161 C1
Alleyn's Sch SE22 .161 C6
Allfarthing La SW18 .158 A5
Allfarthing Prim Sch
SW18 .158 A5
Allgood Cl SM4 .200 D3
Allgood St 10 E2 .95 D5
Allhallows La EC4 .252 C5
Allhallows Rd E6 .100 A1
All Hallows Rd N17 .33 C2
Alliance Cl HA0 .65 D4
Alliance Ct Acton W3 .88 D2
Ashford TW15 .171 A6
Alliance Rd Acton W3 .88 D3
Newham E16 .99 C2
Woolwich SE18 .146 A5
Allied Ind Est W3 .111 C5
Allied Way W3 .111 C4
Allingham Cl W7 .108 D6
Allingham Ct NW3 .70 C3
Allingham St
N1 .95 A5 235 A4
Allington Ave
Tottenham N17 .33 C4
Upper Halliford TW17 .193 C6
Allington Cl
Greenford UB6 .64 A1
3 Wimbledon SW19 .178 D5
Allington Ct 6 SW8 .137 C3
Croydon CR0 .206 C3
Allington Rd NW4 .46 B3
W10 .91 A5
Harrow HA2 .42 A4
Orpington BR6 .211 C1
Allington St SW1 .258 D5
Allison Cl SE10 .142 A4
Allison Gr SE21 .161 C3
Allison Rd N8 .50 D4
W3 .111 A6
Alliston Ho 27 E2 .95 D4
Allitsen Rd
NW8 .92 C5 230 A4
Allnutt Way SW4 .159 D6
Alloa Ct N14 .15 C2
Alloa Rd SE8 .119 A1
Ilford IG3 .80 A6
Allom Ct 11 SW4 .138 A3
Allonby Dr HA4 .38 D2
Allonby Gdns HA9 .43 C1
Allonby Ho E14 .97 A2
Alloway Rd E3 .97 A4
Allport Ho SE5 .139 B2
Allport Mews 38 E1 .96 C3
All Saints' Benhilton CE Prim Sch SM1 .217 D5
All Saints CE First Sch
SW19 .180 A3
All Saint's CE Jun Sch SE19 ..
All Saints' CE Prim Sch
N20 .14 B2
NW2 .69 B5
SE3 .142 C3
All Saints CE Prim Sch
SW15 .134 C2
All Saints' CE Prim Sch
SM5 .219 A3
All Saints' Cl N9 .18 A2
All Saints Ct 9 E1 .118 C6
E5 .74 C4
Heston TW5 .128 D4
All Saints Dr SE3 .142 D3
All Saint's Inf Sch SE19 ......
All Saints Mews HA3 .24 C4
All Saints Pas SW18 .157 C6
All Saints RC Sch RM8 .59 C1
All Saints Rd W11 .91 B1
All Saints' Rd W3 .111 A3
All Saints Rd
Merton SW19 .180 A3
Sutton SM1 .218 A5
All Saints St N1 94 B5 233 C4
All Saints Sta E14 .119 D6
All Saints Twr 18 E10 .53 D2
Allsop Pl NW1 .92 D3 237 D5
All Souls' Ave NW10 .90 B6
All Souls CE Prim Sch
W1 .93 C2 239 A4
All Souls Pl W1 .238 D3
Allum La WD6 .10 A6
Allum Way N20 .14 A3
Allwood Cl SE26 .184 D6
Alma Ave E4 .36 A3
Alma Birk Ho 1 NW6 .69 B1
Almack Rd E5 .74 C4
Alma Cl N10 .31 B2
Alma Cres SM1 .217 A3
Alma Gr SE1 .117 D2 263 D3
Alma Ho E5 .74 B5
7 Brentford TW8 .132 A6
2 Edmonton N9 .34 A6
Alma Pl NW10 .90 B4
Penge SE19 .183 D3
Thornton Heath CR7 .204 C4
Alma Prim Sch SE16 .118 A2
Enfield EN3 .18 D6
Alma Rd N10 .31 B3
SW18 .158 A6
Carshalton SM5 .218 C3
Enfield EN3 .7 A1
Sidcup DA14 .168 A1
Southall UB1 .107 A6
Thames Ditton KT10,KT7 196 C1
Alma Row HA3 .24 B2
Alma Sq NW8 .92 A4 229 B2
Alma St E15 .76 B2
NW5 .71 B2
Alma Terr W8 .255 B5
Wandsworth SW18 .158 B4
Almeida St 10 N1 .72 D1
Almeric Rd SW11 .136 D1
Almer Rd SW20 .178 A3
Almington St N4 .50 B1
Almond Ave W5 .110 A3
Carshalton SM5 .218 D6
Uxbridge UB10 .60 D5
West Drayton UB7 .104 C3
Almond Cl BR2 .210 C2
SE15 .140 A3
Charlton TW17 .171 A1
Hayes UB3 .105 C6
Ruislip HA4 .61 D5
Feltham TW14 .150 A3
Almond Gr TW8 .131 B5
Almond Ho SE4 .141 B3
Almond Rd SE16 .118 B2
Tottenham N17 .34 A3
Almonds Ave IG9 .21 A2
Almond Way BR2 .210 C2
Harrow HA2 .24 A1
Mitcham CR4 .203 D5
Almorah Rd N1 .73 B1
Heston TW5 .128 D4
Almshouse La EN1 .6 B6
Almshouses E10 .75 D6
Sunbury TW16 .171 D2
Almshouses The IG11 .79 A2
Al-Muntada Islamic Sch
SW6 .135 B4 264 D2
Alnmouth Ct 10 UB1 .86 A1
Alnwick 8 N17 .34 B3
Alnwick Gr SM4 .201 D5
Alnwick Rd
Eltham SE12 .165 B4
Newham E16 .99 C1
Alonso Ct 4 DA17 .125 C1
Alperton Com Lower Sch
HA0 .87 D6
Alperton Com Sch HA0 66 B1
Alperton La UB6 .87 C5
Alperton St W10 .91 B3
Alperton Sta HA0 .88 A6
Alphabet Gdns SM5 .202 B3
Alphabet Sq E3 .97 C2
Alpha Bsns Ctr E17 .53 B4
Alpha Cl NW8 .92 C4 230 B1
Alpha Ct 6 NW5 .71 B2
Alpha Est The UB3 .105 C4
Alpha Gr E14 .119 C4
Alpha Ho NW6 .91 C5
NW8 .237 B5
19 SW4 .138 B1
Alpha Pl NW6 .91 C5
SW3 .136 C6 267 B6
Alpha Rd SE14 .141 B4
Chingford E4 .19 D1
Croydon CR0 .205 C1
Edmonton N18 .34 A4
Enfield EN3 .7 A1
Hillingdon UB10 .82 D3
Surbiton KT5 .198 B3
Teddington TW12 .174 B5
Alpha St SE15 .140 A3
Alphea Cl SW19 .180 C3
Alpine Ave KT5 .215 A6
Alpine Bsns Ctr E6 .100 C2
Alpine Cl CR0 .221 C5
Alpine Copse 2 BR1 .188 C1
Alpine Gr 36 E9 .74 C1
Alpine Rd SE16 .118 D1
Walton-on-T KT12 .194 A2
Alpine View SM1 .218 C3
Alpine Way E6 .100 C2
Alpine Wlk HA7 .8 C2
Alric Ave NW10 .67 B1
Kingston KT3 .199 D6
Alroy Rd N4 .50 C2
Alsace Rd
SE17 .117 C1 263 A2
Al Sadiq & Al Zahra Schs
NW6 .91 A6
Alscot Rd SE1 .117 D3 263 D5
Alscot Road Ind Est
SE1 .263 D5
Alscot Way SE1 .263 C4
Alsike Rd DA18 .125 A3
Alsom Ave KT19,KT4 .216 A4
Alston Cl KT7 .197 B2
Alston Ct EN5 .1 A2
Alston Rd Barnet EN5 .1 A2
Edmonton N18 .34 B5
Upper Tooting SW17 .180 B6
Altair Cl N17 .33 D4
Altash Way SE9 .166 C2
Altenburg Ave W13 .109 B3
Altenburg Gdns SW11 136 D1
Alt Gr SW19 .179 A3
Altham Rd HA5 .23 A3
Althea St SW6 .135 D2
Althorpe Mews SW11 .266 D1
Althorne Gdns E18 .54 D5
Althorne Way RM10 .81 C6
Althorp Cl EN5 .12 A4
Althorpe Rd HA1 .42 A4
Althorp Rd SW17 .158 D3
Altior Ct N6 .49 C3
Altmore Ave E6 .100 B6
Altmore Inf Sch E6 .100 B6
Alton Ave HA7 .24 D3
Alton Cl DA5 .169 A3
Isleworth TW7 .130 D3
Alton Ct 18 BR3 .185 C3
Alton Gdns
Beckenham BR3 .185 C3
Twickenham TW2 .152 B4
Alton Ho 3 E3 .97 D4
Alton Rd N17 .51 B6
Croydon CR0 .220 C5
Richmond TW10,TW9 .132 A1
Roehampton SW15 .156 A3
Alton St E14 .97 D2
Altyre Cl BR3 .207 B4
Altyre Rd CR0 .221 B6
Altyre Way BR3 .207 B4
Alum Ct KT5 .198 B3
Alumni Ct SE1 .253 D2
Alvanley Ct NW3 .69 D3
Alvanley Gdns NW6 .69 D3
Alvanley Ho 14 SW9 .138 C4
Alverstone Ave
East Barnet EN4 .14 C4
Wimbledon SW18,SW19 157 C2
Alverstone Gdns SE9 .167 A3
Alverstone Ho 11
SE11 .138 C6
Alverstone Rd NW2 .68 C1
Little Ilford E12 .78 C4
New Malden KT3 .199 D5
Wembley HA9 .44 B1
Alverston Gdns SE25 .205 C4
Alverton St SE8 .141 B6
Alveston Ave HA3 .43 B6
Alvey St SE17 .263 A2
Alvia Gdns SM1 .218 A4
Alvington Cres E8 .73 D3
Alway Ave KT19 .215 B3
Alwen Cotts CR0
Alwold Cres SE12 .165 C5
Alwyn Ave W4 .111 B1
Alwyn Cl
Borehamwood WD6 .10 B5
Alwyn Cl *continued*
New Addington CR0 .223 D1
Alwyne La N1 .72 D1
Alwyne Pl N1 .73 A1
Alwyne Rd N1 .73 A1
Ealing W7 .108 C6
Wimbledon SW19 .179 B4
Alwyne Sq N1 .73 A2
Alwyne Villas N1 .72 D1
Alwyn Gdns NW9 .46 A5
Acton W3 .88 D1
Alyn Ct N8 .49 D3
Alyth Gdns NW11 .47 C3
Alzette Ho 11 E2 .96 D5
Amalgamated Dr TW8 131 B6
Amanda Ct TW15 .148 B2
Amar Ct SE18 .123 D2
Amardeep Ct SE18 .123 D1
Amazon St E1 .96 B1
Ambassador Cl TW3 .129 A3
Ambassador Ct NW4 .46 D4
9 NW6 .69 C3
Ambassador Gdns E6 .100 B2
Ambassador Ho NW8 .229 B5
Ambassador Sq E14 .119 D2
Amber Ave E17 .35 A2
Amber Ct N7 .72 C2
NW9 .45 C6
Mitcham CR4 .202 C5
Amberden Ave N3 .47 C6
Ambergate St
SE17 .116 D1 261 D2
Amber Gr NW2 .46 D1
Amberley Cl
2 Orpington BR6 .227 D3
Pinner HA5 .41 B6
Amberley Ct 2 SW9 .138 D2
Sidcup DA14 .190 C5
Sutton SM2 .218 A1
Amberley Gdns
Enfield EN1 .17 C4
Worcester Park KT19 .215 D4
Amberley Gr
Croydon CR0 .205 D2
Penge SE26 .184 B5
Amberley Ho EN5 .1 D1
Amberley Rd E10 .53 D2
SE2 .146 D6
W9 .91 C2
Buckhurst Hill IG9 .21 C3
Enfield EN1 .17 D5
Palmers Green N13 .16 B2
Amberley Way
Heston TW4 .150 C6
Morden SM4 .201 B2
Romford RM7 .59 D5
Uxbridge UB10 .82 A5
Amberside Cl TW2 .152 B5
Amber Wharf 29 E2 .95 D6
Amberwood Cl SM6 .220 A3
Amberwood Rise KT3 .199 C3
Amblecote Cl SE12 .165 B1
Amblecote Mdw SE12 165 B1
Amblecote Rd SE12 .165 B1
Ambler Prim Sch N4 .72 D6
Ambler Rd N4 .72 D5
Ambleside NW1 .231 D3
Catford BR1 .186 B4
13 Putney SW19 .157 A3
Ambleside Ave
Beckenham BR3 .207 A4
Streatham SW16 .181 D6
Walton-on-T KT12 .194 C1
Ambleside Cl E10 .53 D2
E9 .74 C3
Ambleside Cres EN3 .6 D2
Ambleside Dr TW14 .149 D3
Ambleside Gdns
Redbridge IG4 .56 A4
Streatham SW16 .181 D5
Sutton SM2 .218 A2
Wembley HA9 .43 D1
Ambleside Jun Sch
KT12 .194 C1
Ambleside Point 1
SE15 .140 C5
Ambleside Rd DA7 .147 C3
NW10 .67 D1
Ambrook Rd DA17 .125 C3
Ambrosden Ave
SW1 .115 C3 259 B5
Ambrose Ave NW11 .47 B3
Ambrose Cl 6 E6 .100 B2
Orpington BR6 .227 D5
Ambrose Ho 9 E14 .97 C2
Ambrose Mews 2
SW11 .136 D3
Ambrose St SE16 .118 B2
Ambrose Wlk E3 .97 C5
AMC Bsns Ctr NW10 .88 D4
Amelia Cl W3 .110 D4
Amelia Ho 5 W6 .112 C1
Amelia St
SE17 .117 A1 262 A2
Amen Cnr EC4 .241 D1
Streatham SW17 .181 A4
Amen Ct EC4 .94 D1 241 D1
Amenity Way SM4 .200 C2
American Coll The
W1 .93 A1 238 B2
American Com Schs
UB10 .82 B6
American Sch in London The NW8 .92 B5 229 C4
America Sq EC3 .253 C6
America St SE1 .252 A3
Amerland Rd SW18 .157 B5
Amersham Ave N18 .33 B4
Amersham Gr SE14 .141 B5
Amersham Rd SE14 .141 B4
Thornton Heath CR0 .205 B3
Amersham Vale SE14,
SE8 .141 B5
Amery Gdns NW10 .90 B6
Amery Ho SE17 .263 B2
Amery Rd HA1 .65 A6
Amesbury Ave SW2 .160 B2
Amesbury Cl KT4 .200 C1
Amesbury Ct EN2 .4 C3
Amesbury Dr E4 .19 D5
Amesbury Rd BR1 .209 D6
Dagenham RM9 .80 D1
Feltham TW13 .150 D2
Amesbury Twr 4
SW8 .137 C3
Ames Cotts 14 E3 .97 A2
Ames Ho 10 E2 .96 D5
Amethyst Cl N11 .31 D3
Amethyst Rd E15 .76 B4
Amherst Ave W13 .87 C1
Amherst Dr BR5 .211 D5
Amherst Gdns 2 W13 .87 C1
Amherst Prim Sch E8 .74 A3
Amherst Rd W13 .87 C1
Amhurst Ct N4 .51 B2
Amhurst Gdns TW7 .131 A3
Amhurst Par N16 .51 D2
Amhurst Pk N4,N16 .51 C2
Amhurst Rd E8,N16 .74 A4
Amhurst Terr E8 .74 A4
Amhurst Wlk SE28 .124 A5
Amias Ho EC1 .242 A6
Amidas Gdns RM8 .80 B4
Amiel St 17 E1 .96 C3
Amies St SW11 .136 D2
Amigo Ho SE1 .261 B6
Amina Way SE16 .118 A3
Amis Ave KT19 .214 D3
Amity Gr SW20 .178 C2
Amity Rd E15 .76 D1
Ammanford Gn NW9 .45 C3
Amner Rd SW11 .159 A5
Amor Rd W6 .112 C3
Amory Ho N1 .233 D4
Amott Rd SE15 .140 A2
Amoy Pl E14 .119 C6
Ampleforth Rd SE2 .124 C4
Ampton Pl WC1 .233 C1
Ampton St WC1 94 B4 233 C1
Amroth Cl SE23 .162 B3
Amroth Gn NW9 .45 C3
Amstel Ct 11 SE15 .139 D5
Amsterdam Rd E14 .120 A3
Amundsen Ho 5 NW10 67 B1
Amwell Cl EN2 .17 B6
Amwell St EC1 .94 C4 234 A2
Amyand Cotts 12 TW1 153 B5
Amyand Park Gdns 2
TW1 .153 B4
Amyand Park Rd TW1 153 B4
Amy Cl SM6 .220 A1
Amy Johnson Ho HA8 .26 D1
Amy Johnson Prim Sch
SM6 .220 A1
Amyruth Rd SE4 .163 C6
Amy Warne Cl E6 .100 A3
Anarth Ct KT13 .193 C1
Anatola Rd N19 .71 C6
Ancaster Cres KT3 .200 A3
Ancaster Rd BR3 .206 D6
Ancaster St SE18 .145 C5
Anchorage Cl SW19 .179 C5
Anchorage Point E14 .119 C4
Anchorage Point Ind Est
SE7 .121 C3
Anchor Bsns Pk CR0,
SM6 .220 A5
Anchor Cl IG11 .102 B4
Anchor Ct 5 EN1 .17 C6
Anchor Ho EC1 .242 A6
Ilford IG3 .80 A5
Newham E16 .99 C1
Anchor & Hope La
SE7 .121 C2
Anchor Mews SW12 .159 B5
Anchor Ret Pk E1 .96 C3
Anchor St SE16 .118 B2
Anchor Terr SE1 .252 B4
Anchor Yd EC1 .242 B6
Ancill Cl W6 .135 A6 264 A5
Ancona Rd NW10 .90 A5
SE18 .123 B1
Andace Pk BR1 .187 C2
Andalus Rd SW9 .138 A2

Andaman Ho 3 E1 97 A2
Ander Cl HA0 65 D4
Anderson Cl W3 89 B1
Morden SM3 201 C1
Southgate N21 16 B6
Anderson Ct NW2 46 C2
Anderson Dr TW15 171 A6
Anderson Ho 10 E14 120 A6
Barking IG11 101 B5
Upper Tooting SW17 180 B5
Anderson Rd E9 74 D2
Redbridge IG8 55 D6
Anderson's Pl TW3 129 D1
Andersons Sq N1 234 C5
Anderson St SW3 257 C2
Anderson Way
Erith DA17 125 D4
Erith DA17 125 D4
Anderton Cl SE5 139 B2
Anderton Ct N22 31 D1
Andhurst Ct KT2 176 D2
Andon Ct BR3 207 A6
Andorra Ct BR1 187 C2
Andover Ave E16 99 D1
Andover Cl
East Bedfont TW14 149 D3
Greenford UB6 85 D3
Andover Ho 5 N7 72 B6
Andover Pl NW6 91 D5
Andover Rd N7 72 B6
Orpington BR6 211 C1
Twickenham TW2 152 B3
Andoversford Ct 7
SE15 139 C6
Andreck Ct BR3 186 A1
Andre St E8 74 A3
Andrew Borde St
WC2 239 D2
Andrew Ct
Beckenham BR3 207 D6
Forest Hill SE23 162 D2
Andrewes Gdns E6 100 A1
Andrewes Ho EC2 242 B3
Sutton SM1 217 C4
Andrew Ewing Jun & Inf
Sch TW5 129 B4
Andrew Ho SE4 141 B3
Putney SW15 156 A6
Andrew Marvell Ho 12
N16 73 C4
Andrew Pl SW8 269 D2
Andrew Reed Ho
SW18 157 A4
Andrews Cl BR5 190 D1
Buckhurst Hill IG9 21 C2
Harrow HA1 42 B2
North Cheam KT4 216 D6
Andrews Crosse WC2 241 A1
Andrews Ct 2 W7 108 C5
Andrew's Rd E8 96 B6
Andrew St E14 98 A1
Andrews Wlk SE17 138 D6
Andrew Wells Ho BR1 187 B3
Andringham Lo 4
BR1 187 B2
Andrula Ct N22 32 D2
Andwell Cl SE2 124 B4
Anerley Ct SE20 184 B3
Anerley Gr SE19 183 D3
Anerley Hill SE19 183 D4
Anerley Park Rd SE20 184 B3
Anerley Pk SE20 184 B3
Anerley Prim Sch
SE20 184 A2
Anerley Rd SE20 184 B2
Anerley Sch for Boys
SE20 184 A2
Anerley Sta SE20 184 B2
Anerley Station Rd
SE20 184 B2
Anerley Vale SE19 184 A3
Aneurin Bevan Ct NW2 68 B6
Aneurin Bevan Ho N11 31 D3
Anfield Cl SW12 159 C4
Angel EC1 94 C5 234 B3
Angela Ct 2 SE23 162 C3
Angela Davis Ind Est 21
SW9 138 D1
Angel Alley E1 243 D2
Angel Cl N18 34 A6
Angel Corner Par 6
N18 34 A6
Angel Ct EC2 242 D2
SW1 249 B3
Angel Edmonton N18 34 A5
Angelfield TW3 151 D6
Angel Gate EC1 234 D2
Angel Hill SM1 217 D5
Angel Hill Dr SM1 217 D5
Angel Ho N1 234 B3
Angelica Cl UB7 82 B1
Angelica Dr E6 100 C2
Angelica Gdns CR0 206 D1
Angelina Ho 2 SE15 140 A4
Angel La E15 76 B2
Hayes UB3 83 B2
Angell Park Gdns 5
SW9 138 C2
Angell Rd SW9 138 D2
Angel Mews N1 234 B3
Putney SW15 156 A4
Stepney E1 118 B6
Angel Pas EC4 117 B6 252 C5
Angel Pl SE1 252 C2
1 Edmonton N18 34 A5
Angel Prim Sch
N1 94 C5 234 B4
Angel Rd Harrow HA1 42 C3
Thames Ditton KT7 197 A1
Angel Rd (North Circular
Rd) N18 34 B5
Angel Rd Works N18 34 C5
Angel Road Sta N18 34 C5
Angel St EC1 95 A1 242 A2
Angel Sta EC1 94 C5 234 B3
Angel Wlk W6 112 C2
Angerstein Bsns Pk
SE10 121 A2
Angerstein La SE3 142 D4
Anglebury 5 W2 91 C1
Angle Cl UB10 82 C6
Angle Gn RM8 58 C1
Anglers Cl TW10 175 C6
Anglers La NW5 71 B2
Anglers Reach KT6 197 D4
Anglesea Ave 4 SE18 122 D2
Anglesea Ho KT1 197 D5
Anglesea Rd SE18 122 D2
Kingston KT1 197 D5
Anglesey Cl TW15 148 C1
Anglesey Court Rd
SM5 219 A2
Anglesey Ct W7 86 D3
Anglesey Gdns SM5 219 A2
Anglesey Ho 9 E14 97 C1
Anglesey Rd Enfield EN3 6 B1
South Oxhey WD19 22 C5
Anglesmede Cres HA5 41 C6
Anglesmede Way HA5 41 C6
Angles Rd SW16 182 A6
Anglia Cl N17 34 B3
Anglia Ho 15 E14 97 A1
Anglian Ind Est IG11 101 D2
Anglian Rd E11 76 B5
Anglo American Laundry
SW17 158 A1
Anglo Rd 24 E3 97 B5
Angrave Ct 4 E8 95 D6
Angrave Pas 5 E8 95 D6
Angus Cl KT9 214 C3
Angus Dr HA4 62 C4
Angus Gdns NW9 27 B2
Angus Ho 12 SW12 159 D4
Angus Rd E13 99 C4
Angus St SE14 141 A5
Anhalt Rd
SW11 136 C5 267 B4
Ankerdine Cres SE18 144 D4
Anlaby Rd TW11 174 C5
Anley Rd W14 112 D4
Anmersh Gr HA7 25 D2
Annabel Cl E14 97 D1
Anna Cl E8 95 D6
Annandale Gr UB10 61 A5
Annandale Prim Sch
SE10 120 D1
Annandale Rd DA15 167 D4
SE10 120 D1
W4 111 C1
Croydon CR0 222 A6
Anna Neagle Cl 2 E7 77 A4
Anne Boleyn's Wlk
Belmont SM3 217 A1
Kingston KT2 176 A5
Anne Carver Lo HA0 66 A1
Anne Compton Mews
SE12 164 D4
Anne Goodman Ho 3
E1 96 C1
Anne Kerr Ct 18 SW15 156 D5
Anne's Ct NW8 237 B6
Annesley Ave NW9 45 B6
Annesley Cl NW10 67 C5
Annesley Dr CR0 223 B5
Annesley Ho 15 SW9 138 C5
31 SW9 138 C4
Annesley Rd SE3 143 B4
Annesley Wlk N19 71 C6
Anne St E13 99 A3
Annett Cl TW17 193 C5
Annette Cl HA3 24 C1
Annette Cres 9 N1 73 A1
Annette Ct N7 72 B5
Annette Rd N7 72 B4
Annett Rd KT12 194 A2
Anne Way KT8 195 D5
Annie Besant Cl E3 97 B6
Annie Taylor Ho 1 E12 78 C4
Anning St E2 243 B6
Annington Rd N2 48 D6
Annis Rd E9 75 A2
Ann La SW10 136 B6 266 C5
Ann Moss Way SE16 118 C3
Ann Parkes Ct TW5 128 D3
Ann's Cl SW1 248 A1
Ann's Pl E1 243 C3
Ann St SE18 123 B2
Ann Stroud Ct SE12 165 A6
Annsworthy Ave CR7 205 B6
Annsworthy Cres CR7 183 B1
Annunciation RC Inf Sch
The HA8 27 B2
Annunciation RC Jun Sch
The HA8 27 B4
Ansar Gdns E17 53 B4
Ansdell Rd SE15 140 C3
Ansdell St W8 113 D3 255 D6
Ansdell Terr
W8 113 D3 255 D6
Ansell Gr SM5 203 A1
Ansell Ho E1 96 C2
Ansell Rd SW17 158 D1
Anselm Cl CR0 221 D5
Anselm Rd
SW6 135 C6 265 A5
Pinner HA5 23 B3
Ansford Rd BR1,SE6 186 B6
Ansleigh Pl W11 112 D6
Anslie Wlk 8 SW12 159 B4
Anson 30 NW9 27 D1
Anson Ho 6 E1 97 A3
SW1 269 A6
Anson Pl SE28
Anson Prim Sch NW2 68 D3
Anson Rd N7 71 D4
NW2 68 C3
Anstey Ct 6 W3 110 D4
Anstey Ho 8 E9 96 C6
Anstey Lo EN1 17 C5
Anstey Rd SE15 140 A2
Anstey Wlk N15 51 A5
Anstice Cl W4 133 C5
Anstridge Rd SE9 167 B5
Antelope Rd SE18 122 B3
Antenor Ho 11 E2 96 B5
Anthony Cl NW7 27 C6
Anthony Cope Ct N1 235 D2
Anthony Ct TW7 130 D2
Anthony Ho NW8 237 A5
Anthony Rd DA16 146 A4
Croydon SE25 206 A3
Greenford UB6 86 C4
Anthony St E1 96 B1
Antigua Wlk SE19 183 B5
Antilles Bay 7 E14 120 A4
Antill Rd E3 97 A4
N15 52 A5
Antill Terr 5 E1 96 D1
Antlers Hill E4 19 D6
Anton Cres SM1 217 C5
Antoneys Cl HA5 22 D1
Anton Pl HA9 66 D5
Anton St E8 74 A3
Antony Ho 4 SE14 140 D5
2 SE16 118 C2
Antrim Gr NW3 70 D2
Antrim Ho SW11 137 A2
Antrim Mans NW3 70 D2
Antrim Rd NW3 70 D2
Antrobus Cl SM1 217 B3
Antrobus Rd W4 111 A3
Anvil Cl SW16 181 C3
Anvil Ho 10 N9 18 A1
Anvil Rd TW16 194 A6
Anworth Cl IG8 37 B4
Apex Cl BR3 185 D2
Apex Cnr NW7 27 B6
Twickenham TW13 151 B1
Apex Ct W13 87 A1
Apex Ind Est NW10 89 D3
Aphrodite Ct 2 E14 119 C2
Aplin Way TW7 130 C4
Apollo Ave BR1 187 B2
Moor Park HA6 22 A5
Apollo Bldg 20 E14 119 C2
Apollo Ho 31 E2 96 B5
N6 48 D2
SW10 266 C5
Apollo Ind Bsns Ctr 29
SE8 140 D6
Apollo Pl E11 76 C5
SW10 266 C4
Apollo Studios 18 NW5 71 D3
Apollo Way SE18 123 B3
Apostle Way CR7 182 D1
Apothecary St EC4 241 C1
Appach Rd SW2 160 C5
Appin Ct HA1 42 C2
Appleby Cl N15 51 B4
Chingford E4 36 A4
Twickenham TW2 152 B2
Appleby Gdns TW14 149 D3
Appleby Rd E16 99 A1
E8 74 A1
Appleby St E2 95 D5
Appledore Ave HA4 62 C5
Appledore Cl BR2 209 A4
Edgware HA8 26 C2
Upper Tooting SW12,
SW17 158 D2
Appledore Cres DA14,
DA15 167 D1
Appleford 8 NW5 71 C3
Appleford Ho 6 W10 91 A3
Appleford Rd W10 91 A3
Applegarth
Claygate KT10 212 D3
New Addington CR0 223 D1
Apple Garth TW8 109 D2
Applegarth Dr IG2 57 D5
Applegarth Ho SE1 251 D2
8 SE15 140 A5
Applegarth Inf Sch
CR0 223 D2
Applegarth Jun Sch
CR0 223 D2
Applegarth Rd W14 112 D3
Woolwich SE28 124 C6
Apple Gr
Chessington KT9 214 A4
Enfield EN1 5 C2
Apple Lo HA0 65 C5
Apple Mkt* WC2 250 B6
Kingston KT1 175 D1
Apple Rd E11 76 C5
Appleshaw Ho 4 SE5 139 C2
Appleton Gdns KT3 200 A3
Appleton Rd SE9 144 A2
Appleton Sq CR4 180 C2
Apple Tree Ave UB7 82 B1
Appletree Cl 5 SE20 184 B2
Appletree Ct SE13 142 B1
Appletree Gdns EN4 2 C1
Apple Tree Yd SW1 249 B4
Applewood Cl N20 14 C3
NW2 68 B5
Ickenham UB10 60 A4
Applewood Dr E13 99 B3
Appold St EC2 95 C2 243 A4
Apollo Ct 7 SW9 138 C4
Apprentice Way 6 E5 74 B4
Approach Cl N16 73 C4
Approach La NW7 29 A5
Approach Rd E2 96 C5
Ashford TW15 171 A4
East Molesey KT8 195 C4
Edgware HA8 26 C4
Merton SW20 178 C1
New Barnet EN4,EN5 2 B1
Approach The BR6 227 D6
NW4 46 D4
W3 89 B1
Enfield EN1 6 B3
Aprey Gdns NW4 46 C5
April Cl Ealing W7 108 C6
Feltham TW13 150 A1
Orpington BR6 227 D3
April Ct 20 E2 96 A5
April Glen SE23 162 D1
April St E8 73 D4
Apsley Cl HA2 42 A4
Apsley Ct SM2 218 A2
Apsley Ctr The NW2 68 A6
Apsley Ho E1 96 C2
Hounslow TW4 129 B1
Apsley Rd
Croydon SE25 206 B5
Kingston KT3 199 A6
Apsley Way NW2 68 A6
W1 248 B2
Aquarius TW1 153 B3
Aquarius Way HA6 22 A6
Aquila St NW8 92 B5 229 D4
Aquinas St
SE1 116 C5 251 B3
Arabella Ct NW8 229 B4
Arabella Dr SW15 133 C1
Arabia Cl E4 20 B4
Arabian Ho 3 E1 97 A3
Arabin Rd SE4 141 B1
Aragon Ave KT7 196 D4
Aragon Cl BR2 210 B1
Ashford TW16 171 D3
Enfield EN2 4 B5
Aragon Ct
Beckenham BR3 186 A2
East Molesey KT8 196 A5
Aragon Dr HA4 40 D1
Aragon Rd
Kingston KT2 176 A5
West Barnes SM4 200 D3
West Barnes SM4 201 A2
Aragon Twr SE8 119 B2
Arakan Ho 4 N16 73 B4
Aral Ho 14 E1 96 D3
Arandora Cres RM6 58 B2
Aranya Ct E17 35 A1
Arapiles Ho 6 E14 98 B1
Arbery Rd E3 97 A5
Arbon Ct N1 235 B5
Arbor Cl BR3 185 D1
Arbor Ct N16 73 B6
Arborfield Ho 6 E14 119 C6
Arbor Rd E4 20 B1
Arbourfield Cl SW2 160 B3
Arbour Ho 3 E1 96 D1
Arbour Rd EN3 6 D2
Arbour Sq E1 96 D1
Arbroath Rd SE9 144 A2
Arbrook Chase KT10 212 A2
Arbrook Ct BR5 190 A2
Chessington KT9 213 D3
Arbrook Hall KT10 212 D2
Arbrook La KT10 212 B2
Arbury Terr 3 SE26 162 B1
Arbuthnot La DA5 169 A5
Arbuthnot Rd SE14 140 D3
Arbutus St E8 95 D6
Arcade Ho 7 NW11 47 B4
Arcade The E17 53 C5
EC2 243 A3
1 N7 72 A4
2 SE9 166 C5
Barking IG11 79 A1
Arcadia Ave N3 29 C2
Arcadia Cl SM5 219 A4
Arcadian Ave DA5 169 A5
Arcadian Cl DA5 169 A5
Arcadian Gdns N22 32 C3
Arcadian Rd DA5 169 A5
Arcadia St E14 97 C1
Archangel St SE16 118 D4
Archbishop Lanfranc Sch
The CR0 204 A3
Archbishop Michael
Ramsey Tech Coll
SE5 138 D5
Archbishop's Pl 1
SW2 160 B4
Archbishop Sumner's CE
Prim Sch
SE11 116 C2 261 B3
Archbishop Tenison's CE
High Sch CR0 221 D5
Archbishop Tenison's Sch
SE11 138 B6 270 D5
Archdale Ct W12 112 B5
Archdale Ho SE1 263 A6
Archdale Pl KT3 198 D6
Archdale Rd SE22 139 D1
Archdeacon Cambridge's
CE Prim Sch TW2 152 C2
Archel Rd W14 135 B6 264 C6
Archer Cl KT2 176 A3
Archer Ho 25 N1 95 C6
1 SW11 136 B3
W11 244 D6
Ealing W13 109 B5
Archer Mews TW12 174 A4
Archer Rd SE25 206 B5
Archers Dr EN3 6 C3
Archers Lo 14 SE16 118 A1
Archer Sq SE14 141 A6
Archer St W1 249 C6
Archer Terr UB7 104 A6
Archery Cl W2 237 B1
Harrow HA3 42 D6
Archery Fields Ho
WC1 234 A2
Archery Rd SE9 166 B6
Archery Steps W2 247 B6
Arches Bsns Ctr The
UB2 107 B4
Arches The WC2 250 B4
Harrow HA2 63 D6
Archibald Mews W1 248 C5
Archibald Rd N7 71 D4
Archibald St E3 97 C4
Archie Cl UB7 104 C4
Arch St SE1 117 A3 262 A5
Archway N19 71 C6
Archway Bsns Ctr 5
N19 71 D5
Archway Cl W10 90 D2
Wallington SM6 220 A5
Wimbledon SW19 179 D6
Archway Hts 5 N19 49 C1
Archway Mews SW15 135 A1
Archway Rd N6 49 B2
Archway St SW13,
SW14 133 C2
Archway Sta N19 71 C6
Arcola St E8 73 D3
Arctic St NW5 71 B3
Arcus Rd BR1 186 C4
Ardbeg Rd SE24 161 B6
Arden 17 SW19 156 D3
Arden Cl Bushey WD23 8 D4
Erith SE28 102 D1
Harrow HA1 64 B5
Arden Court Gdns N2 48 B3
Arden Cres E14 119 C2
Dagenham RM9 80 D1
Arden Gr BR6 226 D4
Arden Grange N12 30 A6
Arden Ho 21 N1 95 C5
SE11 260 C3
29 SW9 138 A3
Arden Mhor HA5 40 B5
Arden Rd N3 47 B6
Ealing W13 109 C6
Ardent Cl SE25 205 C6
Ardent Ho 28 E3 97 A5
Ardfern Ave SW16 204 C6
Ardfillan Rd SE6 164 B2
Ardgowan Rd SE6 164 C3
Ardilaun Rd N5 73 A4
Ardingly Cl CR0 222 D5
Ardleigh Gdns SM3 201 C2
Ardleigh Rd E17 35 B2
N1 73 C2
Ardleigh Terr E17 35 B2
Ardley Cl NW10 67 C
Forest Hill SE6 163 A
Ruislip HA4 39 A
Ardlui Rd SE27 161 A
Ardmay Gdns KT6 198 A
Ardmere Rd SE13 164 B
Ardmore La IG9 21 B
Ardmore Pl IG9 21 B
Ardoch Rd SE6 164 B
Ardra Rd N9 18 D
Ardrossan Gdns KT4 216 A
Ardshiel Cl SW15 134 D
Ardwell Ave IG6 57 A
Ardwell Rd SW2 160 A
Ardwick Rd NW2 69 C
Arena Bsns Ctr N4 51 A
Arena Est N4 50 D
Arena Sta SE25 206 C
Arena The EN3 7 B
Ares Ct 8 E14 119 C
Arethusa Ho 8 E14 119 D
Argall Ave E10 52 D
Argall Ho 3 DA18 125 A
Argall Way E10 53 A
Argenta Way NW10 66 D
Argent Ct KT6 214 C
Argent Ctr The UB3 106 A
Argon Mews SW6 265 B
Argon Rd N18 34 D
Argos Ct 5 SW9 138 C
Argos Ho 8 E2 96 B
Argosy Ho SE8 119 A
W1 238 D
Argus Way UB5 85 A
Argyle Cl W13 87 A
Argyle Ho E14 120 A
Sutton SM2 218 A
Argyle Pl W6 112 B
Argyle Prim Sch WC1 233 A
Argyle Rd E1 96 D
E15 76 C
N12 29 C
Ealing W13 87 A
Edmonton N18 34 A
Harrow HA2 41 D
Hounslow TW3 151 D
Ilford IG1 78 C
Newham E16 99 B
Tottenham N17 34 A
Argyle Sq WC1 94 A4 233 B
Argyle St WC1 94 A4 233 B
Argyle Way SE16 118 A
Argyle Wlk WC1 233 B
Argyll Ave UB1 107 D
Argyll Cl SW9 138 B
Argyll Ct 15 SW2 160 A
Argyll Gdns HA8 26 D
Argyll Mans SW3 266 D
W14 254 B
Argyll Rd SE18 123 A
W8 113 C4 245 B
Argyll St W1 93 C1 239 A
Arica Ho SE16 118 B
Arica Rd SE4 141 A
Ariel Ct SE11 261 C
W12 112 A
5 Belvedere DA17 125 C
Ariel Rd NW6 69 C
Ariel Way W12 112 C5
Hounslow TW4 128 B2
Aristotle Rd SW4 137 D2
Arkansas Ho 21 N19 49 D2
Arkell Gr SW16 182 D
Arkindale Rd SE6 164 A
Arkley Cres E17 53 B4
Arkley Dr EN5 12 B6
Arkley Pk EN5 11 B5
Arkley Rd E17 53 B4
Arklow Ho SE17 139 B6
Arklow Mews 4 KT6 214 A6
Arklow Rd SE14 141 B6
Arklow Road Trad Est
SE14 141 B6
Arkwright Ho 23 SW2 160 A4
Arkwright Mans NW3 70 A3
Arkwright Rd NW3 70 A3
Arlesey Cl SW15 157 A6
Arlesford Rd SW9 138 A2
Arless Ho 8 HA1 42 D4
Arlingford Rd SW2 160 C5
Arlington N12 13 C
Arlington Ave
N1 95 A6 235 B5
Arlington Cl DA15 167 C4
Sutton SM1 217 C6
Twickenham TW1 153 C5
Arlington Ct N6 49 A3
4 Twickenham TW1 153 C5
Arlington Dr
Carshalton SM5 218 D6
Ruislip HA4 39 B3
Arlington Gdns W4 111 A1
Ilford IG1 56 C1
Arlington Ho EC1 234 B2
3 SE8 141 B6
W12 112 B5
Arlington Lo SW2 138 B1
Arlington Park Mans 1
W4 111 A1

ngton Pl 7 SE10 ...142 A5
ngton Rd N14 ...15 C3
/1 ...93 B6 231 D5
hford TW15 ...170 B5
ing W13 ...87 B1
chmond TW10 ...153 D2
rbiton KT6 ...197 D3
ddington TW11 ...174 D6
ickenham TW1 ...153 C5
oodford IG8 ...37 B3
ngton Sq N1 95 A6 235 B5
ngton St
/1 ...115 C5 249 A4
ington Way
1 ...94 C4 234 B2
iss Way UB5 ...84 C6
ow Rd N21 ...16 C3
nada Ct 11 SE8 ...141 C6
nadale Cl N17 ...52 B5
nadale Rd SW6 ...265 A5
tham TW14 ...150 A6
nada St 10 SE8 ...141 C6
nada Way E6 ...101 A1
nagh Rd E3 ...97 B6
neston KT3 ...199 B2
nfield Cl KT8 ...195 B4
nfield Cotts 3
/19 ...180 D1
nfield Cres CR4 ...180 D1
nfield Rd EN2 ...5 B4
ninger Rd W12 ...112 B5
nitage Ho
/1 ...92 C2 237 B4
nitage Rd NW11 ...47 B1
10 ...120 D1
nitice Gdns SE25 ...206 A6
nour Cl N7 ...72 B2
noury Rd SE8 ...141 D3
noury Way SW18 ...157 C6
nsby Ho 15 E1 ...96 C2
nstead Wlk RM10 ...81 C1
nstrong Ave IG8 ...36 C4
nstrong Cl BR1 ...210 A6
agenham RM8 ...58 D2
ewham E6 ...100 B1
nner HA5 ...40 A3
alton-on-T KT12 ...194 A3
nstrong Cres EN4 ...2 B2
nstrong Ho 8
/15 ...156 D5
nstrong Rd SW7 ...256 C5
3 ...111 D5
eltham TW13 ...173 A5
nstrong Way UB2 ...107 D4
nytage Rd TW5 ...128 D5
nal Cres SW18 ...157 A4
ncliffe NW6 ...91 D6
ncliffe Cl N11 ...31 A4
ncroft Ct IG11 ...102 B4
ne Gr BR6 ...227 D5
ne Ho SE11 ...260 C2
ne St WC2 ...94 A1 240 B1
nett Sq E4 ...35 B4
neways Ave RM6 ...58 D6
neway St SW1 ...259 D5
ne Wlk SE3 ...142 D1
newood Cl SW15 ...156 A3
ney's La CR4 ...203 A3
ngask Rd SE6 ...164 B4
nhem Pl E14 ...119 C3
nhem Way 3 SE22 ...161 C6
nhem Wharf E14 ...119 C3
nhem Wharf Prim Sch
4 ...119 C3
nison Rd KT8 ...196 B5
nold Ave E EN3 ...7 C5
nold Ave W EN3 ...7 B5
nold Cir E2 ...95 D4
nold Cl HA3 ...44 B2
nold Cres TW7 ...152 B6
nold Ct E18 ...36 D2
nold Dr KT9 ...213 D2
nold Est SE1 ...253 D1
nold Gdns N13 ...32 D5
nold Ho 9 N16 ...73 C5
E17 ...261 D1
nold House Sch
W8 ...92 B5 229 C3
nold Rd E3 ...97 C4
15 ...51 D6
agenham RM10 ...81 C1
itcham SW17 ...180 D3
ortholt UB5 ...63 A2
nos Gr N14 ...15 D1
nos Grove Ct 4 N11 ...31 C5
nos Grove Sta N11 ...31 C6
nos Rd N11 ...31 C6
not Ho 27 SE5 ...139 A5
nott Cl SE28 ...124 C5
/4 ...111 B2
nould Ave SE5 ...139 B1
nsberg Way DA7 ...147 C1
nside Gdns HA9 ...43 D1
nside Ho 2 SE17 ...139 B6
nside Rd DA7 ...147 C4
nside St SE17 ...139 A6
nulf St SE6 ...185 D6
null's Rd SW16 ...182 D4
odene Rd SW2 ...160 B5
Arosa Rd 4 TW1 ...153 D5
Arragon Gdns
Streatham SW16 ...182 A3
West Wickham BR4 ...223 D5
Arragon Rd E6 ...99 D6
Wandsworth SW18 ...157 C3
Arran Cl SM6 ...219 C4
Arran Ct NW10 ...67 B5
32 NW9 ...27 D1
Arrandene Ho 3 BR5 ...190 B1
Arran Dr Stanmore HA7 ...25 C6
Wanstead E12 ...77 D6
Arran Ho N16 ...51 D1
Arran Mews W5 ...110 B5
Arran Rd SE6 ...164 A2
Arran Wlk N1 ...73 A1
Arras Ave SM4 ...202 A4
Arras Ho SE2 ...146 D6
Arrol Ho SE1 ...262 B5
Arrol Rd BR3 ...206 D6
Arrowe Ct 7 E5 ...74 B4
Arrowhead Ct E11 ...54 B3
Arrow Ho 24 N1 ...95 C6
Arrow Rd E3 ...97 D4
Arrow Scout Wlk UB5 ...85 A4
Arrowsmith Ho SE11 ...260 C2
Arsenal Rd SE9 ...144 B2
Arsenal Sta N5 ...72 C5
Artemis Ct 6 E14 ...119 C2
Arterberry Rd SW20,
SW19 ...178 D2
Artesian Cl NW10 ...67 B1
Artesian Gr EN5 ...2 A1
Artesian Rd W2 ...91 C1
Arthingworth St E15 ...98 C6
Arthur Ct SW11 ...268 B1
10 W10 ...90 D1
W2 ...91 D1
South Croydon CR0 ...221 B5
Arthur Deakin Ho 1
E1 ...96 A2
Arthurdon Rd SE4 ...163 C6
Arthur Gr SE18 ...123 A2
Arthur Henderson Ho
9 N19 ...49 D2
9 Fulham SW6 ...135 B3
Arthur Newton Ho 20
SW11 ...136 B2
Arthur Rd E6 ...100 B5
N7 ...72 B4
Dagenham RM6 ...58 D3
Edmonton N9 ...17 D2
6 Kingston KT2 ...176 C3
West Barnes KT3 ...200 B4
Wimbledon SW19 ...179 C6
Arthur Ruxley Est
DA14 ...190 D4
Arthur St EC4 ...117 B6 252 D6
Arthur Wade Ho 7 E2 ...95 D4
Arthur Walls Ho 3 E12 78 C5
Artichoke Hill 8 E1 ...118 B6
Artichoke Mews 5
SE5 ...139 B4
Artichoke Pl SE5 ...139 B4
Artillery Cl IG2 ...57 A3
Artillery Ho SE18 ...122 C1
Artillery La E1 ...95 C2 243 B3
W12 ...90 A1
Artillery Pass E1 ...243 B3
Artillery Pl SE18 ...122 C2
Harrow HA3 ...24 A3
Artillery Row SW1 ...259 C5
Artington Cl BR6 ...227 A4
Artisan Cl E16 ...122 D6
Artizan St E1 ...243 B2
Arton Wilson Ho 12
SW15 ...156 A6
Arts Educational Sch The
W4 ...111 C2
Arundale KT1 ...197 D5
Arundel Ave SM4 ...201 B5
Arundel Bldgs SE1 ...263 B5
Arundel Cl E15 ...76 C4
SW11 ...158 C6
Croydon CR0 ...220 D5
Hampton TW12 ...173 D5
Sidcup DA5 ...169 B5
Arundel Ct 2 DA6 ...147 A1
N12 ...30 C4
SW3 ...257 B2
Barnes SW13 ...134 B6
4 Beckenham BR2 ...186 C1
Harrow HA2 ...63 C4
Putney SW15 ...156 D6
Tottenham N17 ...34 A2
Arundel Dr Harrow HA2 ...63 C4
Woodford IG8 ...37 A3
Arundel Gdns HA8 ...27 B3
W11 ...113 B6 244 C6
Ilford IG3 ...80 A6
Southgate N21 ...16 C3
Arundel Gr N16 ...73 C3
Arundel Ho N1 ...94 D6 234 D6
3 W3 ...110 D4
Croydon CR0 ...221 B3
Arundel Lo N3 ...29 B1
Arundel Mans SW6 ...264 D2
Barnes SW13 ...134 B6
Arundel Pl N1,N7 ...72 C2
Arundel Rd
Belmont SM2 ...217 B1
Cockfosters EN4 ...2 C2
Hounslow TW4 ...128 C2
Kingston KT1 ...177 A1
Thornton Heath CR0 ...205 B3
Arundel Sq N7 ...72 C2
Arundel St
WC2 ...116 B6 250 D6
Arundel Terr SW13 ...134 B6
Arun Ho 5 KT2 ...175 D2
Arvon Rd N5 ...72 C3
Asa Ct UB3 ...105 D3
Asaph Ho SE14 ...141 B4
Asbaston Terr IG11 ...79 A2
Ascalon Ct 16 SW2 ...160 B4
Ascalon Ho SW8 ...269 A3
Ascalon St
SW8 ...137 C5 269 A3
Ascham Dr E4 ...35 C3
Ascham End E17 ...35 A2
Ascham St NW5 ...71 C3
Aschurch Rd CR0 ...205 D2
Ascot Cl
Borehamwood WD6 ...10 C6
Northolt UB5 ...63 C3
Ascot Ct DA5 ...169 B4
NW8 ...229 C1
8 SW4 ...138 A1
Ascot Gdns Enfield EN3 ...6 C6
Southall UB1 ...85 C2
Ascot Ho NW1 ...231 D2
6 W4 ...111 A1
1 W9 ...91 C2
Penge SE26 ...184 B4
Ascot Lo NW6 ...91 D5
Ascot Par 9 SW4 ...138 A1
Ascot Rd E6 ...100 B4
N15 ...51 B4
East Bedfont TW14 ...148 D2
Edmonton N18 ...34 A6
Orpington BR5 ...211 D5
Streatham SW17 ...181 A4
Ascott Ave W5 ...110 A4
Ascott Ct HA5 ...40 A5
Asfil Ho EC1 ...241 B3
Ashbourne Ave DA7 ...147 A5
N20 ...14 D2
NW11 ...47 B4
Harrow HA2 ...64 B6
Wanstead E18 ...55 B5
Ashbourne Cl N12 ...29 D6
Ealing W5 ...88 C2
Ashbourne Ct E5 ...75 A4
11 N12 ...29 D6
Beckenham BR3 ...186 A2
Ashbourne Gr NW7 ...27 B5
SE22 ...139 D1
W4 ...111 C1
Ashbourne Par
2 NW11 ...47 B5
Ealing W5 ...88 B3
Ashbourne Rd
Ealing W5 ...88 B3
Mitcham CR4 ...181 A3
Ashbourne Rise BR6 ...227 C4
Ashbourne Terr 1
SW19 ...179 C3
Ashbourne Way NW11 ...47 B4
Ashbridge Rd E11 ...54 D2
Ashbridge St
NW8 ...92 C3 237 A5
Ashbrook HA8 ...26 B4
Ashbrook Rd N19 ...71 D6
Dagenham RM10 ...81 D5
Ashburn Ct BR1 ...187 A3
Ashburn Gdns SW7 ...256 A4
Ashburnham Ave HA1 ...42 D3
Ashburnham Cl N2 ...48 B5
Ashburnham Com Sch
SW10 ...266 C4
Ashburnham Gdns HA1 42 D3
Ashburnham Gr SE10 ...141 D5
Ashburnham Pk KT10 ...212 A4
Ashburnham Pl SE10 ...141 D5
Ashburnham Rd NW10 ...90 C5
SW10 ...136 A5 266 B3
Richmond TW10 ...153 B1
Ashburnham Retreat 6
SE10 ...141 D5
Ashburnham Twr
SW10 ...266 C4
Ashburn Pl
SW7 ...114 A2 256 A3
Ashburton Ave
Croydon CR0 ...206 B1
Ilford IG3 ...79 D4
Ashburton Cl CR0 ...206 A1
Ashburton Com Sch
CR9 ...206 B2
Ashburton Gdns CR0 ...222 A6
Ashburton Gr N7 ...72 C4
Ashburton Ho EN3 ...6 D2
Ashburton Jun & Inf Sch
CR0 ...206 B3
Ashburton Mans
SW10 ...266 B4
Ashburton Rd E16 ...99 A1
Croydon CR0 ...222 A6
Ashburton Rd *continued*
Ruislip HA4 ...62 A6
Ashburton Terr 2 E13 ...99 A5
Ashbury Ct N21 ...16 A6
Ashbury Dr UB10 ...60 D5
Ashbury Gdns RM6 ...58 D4
Ashby Ave KT19,KT9 ...214 C2
Ashby Ct NW8 ...236 D6
Ashby Gr N1 ...73 A1
Ashby Grange 7 SM6 219 C2
Ashby Ho 8 N1 ...73 A1
6 SW9 ...138 D3
Ashby Mews SE4 ...141 B3
Ashby Rd N15 ...52 A4
SE4 ...141 B3
Ashby St EC1 ...94 D4 234 D1
Ashby Way UB7 ...126 C5
Ashby Wlk CR0 ...205 A3
Ashchurch Ct W12 ...112 A3
Ashchurch Gr W12 ...112 A3
Ashchurch Park Villas
W12 ...112 A3
Ashchurch Terr W12 ...112 A3
Ash Cl BR5 ...211 B4
HA8 ...27 A6
Carshalton SM5 ...218 D6
Kingston KT3 ...177 B1
Penge SE20 ...184 C1
Sidcup DA14 ...168 B1
Stanmore HA7 ...25 A4
Ashcombe Ave KT6 ...197 D2
Ashcombe Ct 4 SW15 157 A6
Ashcombe Gdns HA8 ...26 C6
Ashcombe Ho 39 E3 ...97 D4
Ashcombe Pk NW2 ...67 C5
Ashcombe Rd
Wallington SM5 ...219 A2
Wimbledon SW19 ...179 C5
Ashcombe Sq KT3 ...199 A6
Ashcombe St SW6 ...135 D3
Ashcroft N14 ...15 D2
Pinner HA5 ...23 C4
Ashcroft Ave DA15 ...168 A5
Ashcroft Cres DA15 ...168 A5
Ashcroft Ct N20 ...14 B2
5 SE9 ...166 C5
Ashcroft Ho SW8 ...269 A2
Ashcroft Rd E3 ...97 A4
Chessington KT9 ...214 B5
Ashcroft Sq W6 ...112 C2
Ash Ct N19 ...71 C6
SE12 ...165 A4
SW11 ...159 A6
W1 ...237 C2
Chingford E4 ...20 B4
Romford RM7 ...59 D3
West Ewell KT19 ...215 A4
2 West Norwood
SW16 ...182 C5
Woodford E18 ...37 C2
Ashdale Cl
Stanwell TW19 ...148 A2
Twickenham TW2 ...152 A4
Ashdale Gr HA7 ...24 D4
Ashdale Ho N4 ...51 B2
Ashdale Rd SE12 ...165 B3
Ashdale Way TW2 ...151 D4
Ashdene 6 SE15 ...140 B5
Pinner HA5 ...40 C6
Ashdene Cl TW15 ...171 A3
Ashdon Cl IG8 ...37 B4
Ashdown Ealing W13 ...87 B2
Putney SW15 ...156 D6
Ashdown Cl 13 BR3 ...185 D1
Ashdown Cres NW5 ...71 A3
Ashdown Ct
New Malden KT4 ...199 D2
Sutton SM2 ...218 A2
Ashdowne Ct N17 ...34 A2
Ashdown Ho 7 E5 ...74 A6
Ashdown Pl
Ewell KT17 ...215 D1
Thames Ditton KT7 ...197 A2
Ashdown Rd NW10 ...89 D6
Enfield EN3 ...6 C3
Hillingdon UB10 ...82 C5
Kingston KT1 ...176 A1
Ashdown Way SW17 ...159 A2
Ashdown Wlk 15 E14 ...119 C2
Ashe Ho 8 TW1 ...153 D5
Ashen E6 ...100 C1
Ashenden SE17 ...262 B4
Ashenden Rd E5 ...75 A3
Ashen Gr SW19 ...157 C2
Ashentree Ct EC4 ...241 B1
Asher Loftus Way N11 ...30 D4
Asher Way E1 ...118 A6
Ashfield Ave
Bushey WD23 ...8 A4
Feltham TW13 ...150 B3
Ashfield Cl
Beckenham BR3 ...185 C3
Richmond TW10 ...154 A3
Ashfield Ho 5 N5 ...73 A3
Ashfield La BR7 ...189 A3
Ashfield Par N14 ...15 D3
Ashfield Pl BR7 ...189 B3
Ashfield Rd N14 ...15 C1
N4 ...51 A3
Ashfield Rd *continued*
W3 ...111 D5
Ashfield St E1 ...96 C2
Ashford Ave N8 ...50 A5
Ashford TW15 ...170 D4
Hayes UB4 ...84 D1
Ashford CE Prim Sch
TW15 ...170 D4
Ashford Cl E17 ...53 B3
Ashford TW15 ...170 A6
Ashford Cres
Ashford TW15 ...148 A1
Enfield EN3 ...6 C3
Ashford Ct NW2 ...68 D4
Edgware HA8 ...10 D1
Ashford Gn WD19 ...22 D5
Ashford High Sch The
TW15 ...148 A1
Ashford Ho 11 SE8 ...141 B6
14 SW9 ...138 D1
Ashford Hospl TW15 ...148 A2
Ashford Ind Est TW15 ...171 A6
Ashford Rd NW2 ...68 D4
Feltham TW13,TW15 ...171 B6
Littleton TW15,TW17 ...171 A3
Staines TW18 ...170 A4
Wallend E6 ...78 C1
Woodford E18 ...37 B1
Ashford St N1 ...95 C4
Ash Gr E8 ...96 B6
NW2 ...69 A4
W5 ...110 A3
East Bedfont TW14 ...149 C3
Edmonton N13 ...17 A1
Enfield EN1 ...17 C4
Hayes UB3 ...105 B6
Heston TW5 ...128 D5
Penge SE20 ...184 C1
Southall UB1 ...85 C2
Wembley HA0 ...65 A4
West Wickham BR4 ...208 A1
Yiewsley UB7 ...104 B6
Ashgrove SE12 ...165 A3
Ashgrove Ct 2 W9 ...91 C2
Ashgrove Ho SW1 ...259 D2
Ashgrove Rd
Ashford TW15 ...171 B5
Catford BR1 ...186 B4
Ilford IG3 ...58 A1
Ashgrove Sch BR1 ...187 B1
Ash Hill Dr HA5 ...40 C6
Ash Ho 3 E14 ...120 A4
SE1 ...263 D3
Ashingdon Cl E4 ...20 A1
Ashington 1 NW5 ...71 B2
Ashington Ho 16 E1 ...96 B3
Ashington Rd SW6 ...135 B3
Ashlake Rd SW16 ...182 A6
Ashland Pl W1 ...238 A4
Ashlar Ct N2 ...48 C6
Ashlar Pl SE18 ...122 D2
Ashleigh Commercial Est
SE7 ...121 D3
Ashleigh Ct N14 ...15 C4
W5 ...109 D2
Penge SE26 ...184 B4
Ashleigh Gdns SM1 ...217 D6
Ashleigh Ho SW14 ...133 C2
Ashleigh Point 8
SE26 ...162 D1
Ashleigh Rd
Mortlake SW14 ...133 C2
Penge SE20 ...206 B6
Ashley Ave SM4 ...201 C4
Ashley CE Prim Sch
KT12 ...194 A1
Ashley Cl NW4 ...28 C1
Oatlands Park KT12,
KT13 ...193 D1
Pinner HA5 ...22 B1
Ashley Cres SW11 ...137 A2
Wood Green N22 ...32 C1
Ashley Ct 19 N16 ...73 C3
NW3 ...69 D3
NW4 ...28 C1
New Barnet EN5 ...14 A6
Northolt UB5 ...85 A6
Yiewsley UB7 ...104 A5
Ashley Dr
Borehamwood WD6 ...11 B6
Hounslow TW7 ...130 C6
Twickenham TW2 ...151 D3
Ashley Gdns
Edmonton N13 ...33 A6
Orpington BR6 ...227 C3
Richmond TW10 ...153 D2
Wembley HA9 ...66 A6
Ashley Ho BR5 ...190 A1
Ashley La NW4 ...28 C1
NW7 ...28 D3
Croydon CR0 ...220 D4
Ashley Park Ave KT12 193 D1
Ashley Park Cres
KT12 ...194 A1
Ashley Pl SW1 115 C3 259 A5
Ashley Rd E7 ...77 C1
N17 ...52 A6
N19 ...50 A2
Chingford E4 ...35 C4
Ashley Rd *continued*
Enfield EN3 ...6 C3
Hampton TW12 ...173 C2
Richmond TW9 ...132 A2
Thames Ditton KT7 ...196 D3
Thornton Heath CR7 ...204 B5
Walton-on-T KT12 ...194 A1
Wimbledon SW19 ...179 D4
Ashley Wlk NW7 ...28 D3
Ashling Rd CR0 ...206 A1
Ashlin Rd E15 ...76 B4
Ash Lo
2 Ashford TW16 ...171 D3
Fulham SW6 ...134 D4
Ashlone Rd SW15 ...134 D2
Ashlyns Way KT9 ...213 D2
Ashmead 4 N14 ...15 C6
Ashmead Bsns Ctr E16 ...98 B3
Ashmead Gate BR1 ...187 C2
Ashmead Ho E9 ...75 A3
Ashmead Prim Sch
SE8 ...141 C3
Ashmead Rd SE8 ...141 C3
East Bedfont TW14 ...150 A3
Ashmere Ave BR3 ...186 B1
Ashmere Cl SM3 ...216 D3
Ashmere Gr 11 SW2,
SW4 ...138 A1
Ashmere Ho 10 SW2 ...138 A1
Ashmill Ct CR0 ...205 A3
Ashmill St NW8 92 C2 237 A4
Ashmole Prim Sch
SW8 ...138 B6 270 D5
Ashmole Sch N14 ...15 C3
Ashmole St SW8 ...270 D5
Ashmoor Lo NW7 ...27 B4
Ashmore NW1 ...71 D1
Ashmore Cl SE15 ...139 D5
Ashmore Ct N11 ...30 D4
Heston TW5 ...129 C6
Ashmore Gr DA16 ...145 C2
Ashmore Ho W14 ...254 B5
Ashmore Rd W9 ...91 B4
Ashmount Prim Sch N6 49 C2
Ashmount Rd N15 ...51 D4
N19 ...49 D2
Ashmount Terr W5 ...109 D2
Ashneal Gdns HA1 ...64 B5
Ashness Gdns UB6 ...65 B2
Ashness Rd SW11 ...158 D6
Ashpark Ho 4 E14 ...97 B1
Ash Rd E15 ...76 D3
Cheam SM3 ...201 B1
Croydon CR0 ...223 C6
Littleton TW17 ...192 C5
Orpington BR6 ...227 D1
Ashridge Cl HA3 ...43 C3
Ashridge Cres SE18 ...145 A5
Ashridge Ct
Southall UB1 ...108 A6
Southgate N14 ...15 C6
Ashridge Dr WD19 ...22 C5
Ashridge Gdns
Bowes Park N13 ...32 A5
Pinner HA5 ...41 A5
Ashridge Ho DA14 ...189 D6
Ashridge Way
Ashford TW16 ...172 A4
Merton SM4 ...201 B5
Ash Row BR2 ...210 C3
Ashtead Ct 15 SW19 ...156 D3
Ashtead Rd E5 ...52 A2
Ashton Cl SM1 ...217 C4
Ashton Ct
1 Beckenham BR3 ...185 B2
Harrow HA1 ...64 D5
Ashton Gdns
Dagenham RM6 ...59 A3
Hounslow TW4 ...129 B1
Ashton Ho 13 SW9 ...138 C5
Roehampton SW15 ...156 B4
Ashton Rd E15 ...76 B3
Ashton St E14 ...120 A6
Ashtree Ave CR4 ...180 B1
Ashtree Cl BR6 ...226 D4
Ash Tree Cl
Croydon CR0 ...207 A3
1 Surbiton KT6 ...198 A1
Ashtree Ct TW15 ...170 D5
Ash Tree Dell NW9 ...45 B4
Ash Tree Way CR0 ...207 A3
Ashurst Cl SE20 ...184 B2
Ashurst Dr
Ilford IG2,IG6 ...57 A4
Littleton TW17 ...192 A4
Ashurst Lo N5 ...72 D3
Ashurst Rd N12 ...30 C5
Cockfosters EN4 ...14 D6
Ashurst Wlk CR0 ...222 B6
Ashvale Rd SW17 ...180 D5
Ashview Cl TW15 ...170 A5
Ashview Gdns TW15 ...170 A5
Ashville Rd E11 ...76 B6
Ashwater Rd SE12 ...165 A3
Ashway Ctr 5 KT2 ...176 A2
Ashwell Cl 8 E6 ...100 A1

Ashwell Ct TW15 ....148 A2
Ashwin St E8 ....73 D2
Ash Wlk HA0 ....65 C4
Ashwood Ave UB8 ....82 C1
Ashwood Gdns
Hayes UB3 ....105 D2
New Addington CR0 ....224 A2
Ashwood Ho 5 NW4 ....46 C5
Ashwood Lo N21 ....16 B5
Ashwood Pk 6 SM2 ....217 C1
Ashwood Rd E4 ....20 B1
Ashworth Cl SE5 ....139 B3
Ashworth Mans W9 ....91 D4
Ashworth Rd W9 ....91 D4
Aske Ho 2 N1 ....95 C4
Asker Ho N7 ....72 A4
Askern Cl DA6 ....146 D1
Aske St N1 ....95 C4
Askew Cres W12 ....112 A4
Askew Mans 14 W12 ....112 A4
Askew Rd W12 ....112 A4
Askham Ct W12 ....112 A5
Askham Lo 5 SE12 ....165 A4
Askham Rd W12 ....112 A5
Askill Dr SW15 ....157 A6
Asland Rd E15 ....98 B6
Aslett St SW18 ....158 A4
Asmara Rd NW2 ....69 A3
Asmuns Hill NW11 ....47 C4
Asmuns Pl NW11 ....47 B4
Asolando Dr SE17 ....262 B3
Aspen Cl 10 N19 ....71 C6
W5 ....110 B4
Yiewsley UB7 ....104 B5
Aspen Copse BR1 ....188 B1
Aspen Ct E8 ....73 D2
Hayes UB3 ....105 C2
Richmond TW9 ....132 C5
Aspen Dr HA0 ....65 A5
Aspen Gdns W6 ....112 B1
Ashford TW15 ....171 A5
Mitcham CR4 ....203 A4
Aspen Gn DA18 ....125 B3
Aspen Ho 2 DA15 ....168 A1
4 NW3 ....70 D2
8 SE15 ....140 C6
Southgate N21 ....16 B6
Aspen La UB5 ....85 A4
Aspenlea Rd W6 ....134 D6
Aspen Way E14 ....120 A6
Feltham TW13 ....150 B1
Aspern Gr NW3 ....70 C3
Aspinall Ho SW12 ....160 A3
Aspinall Rd SE4 ....140 D2
Aspinden Rd SE16 ....118 B2
Aspire Bld SW15 ....157 B6
Aspley Rd SW18 ....157 D6
Asplins Rd N17 ....34 B2
Asquith Cl RM8 ....58 C1
Asquith Court Sch HA3 43 C3
Assam SE1 ....253 D3
Assam St E1 ....96 A1
Assata Mews N1 ....72 D2
Assembly Pas E1 ....96 C2
Assembly Wlk SM5 ....202 C2
Assheton-Bennett Ho 15
KT6 ....198 A4
Ass House La HA3 ....23 D6
Assisi Ct
Upper Tooting SW12 ....158 D3
Wembley HA0 ....64 D5
Astall Cl HA3 ....24 C2
Astbury Ho SE11 ....261 A5
Astbury Rd SE15 ....140 C4
Astell St SW3 .114 C1 257 B2
Aste St E14 ....120 A4
Astey's Row 3 N1 ....73 A1
Asthall Gdns IG6 ....57 A5
Astins Ho 4 E17 ....53 D5
Astleham Rd TW17 ....192 A6
Astleham Way TW17 ....192 A6
Astle St SW11 ....137 A3
Astley Ave NW2 ....68 C3
Astley Ho SE1 ....263 D2
30 W2 ....91 C2
8 West Norwood SE27 .183 A6
Aston Ave HA3 ....43 C2
Aston Cl Bushey WD23 ....8 A5
Sidcup DA14 ....168 A1
Aston Gn TW5 ....128 C3
Aston Ho SW8 ....269 C1
W11 ....244 D6
Aston House Sch W5 ....87 D1
Aston Mews RM6 ....58 C2
Aston Pl SW16 ....182 D4
Aston Rd Claygate KT10 212 C3
Ealing W5 ....87 D1
Merton SW20 ....178 C1
Aston St E14 ....97 A2
Astonville St SW18 ....157 C3
Astor Ave RM7 ....59 D3
Astor Cl KT2 ....176 D4
Astor Ct SW6 ....266 A3
Newham E16 ....99 C1
Astoria Mans 13 SW16 160 A1
Astoria Par SW16 ....160 A1
Astoria Wlk SW9 ....138 C2
Astra Ct W13 ....109 A5
Astra Ho 4 E3 ....97 B4
N4 ....50 B2
Astrid Ho TW13 ....150 C2
Astrop Mews W6 ....112 C3
Astrop Terr W6 ....112 C4
Astwood Mews SW7 ..256 A4
Asylum Rd SE15 ....140 B5
Atalanta St
SW6 ....134 D5 264 A3
Atbara Ct TW11 ....175 B4
Atbara Rd TW11 ....175 B4
Atcham Rd TW3 ....130 A1
Atcost Rd IG11 ....102 A2
Atheldene Rd SW18 ....158 A3
Athelney Prim Sch
SE6 ....163 C1
Athelney St SE6 ....163 C1
Athelstan Ct E6 ....100 C5
Athelstane Gr E3 ....97 B5
Athelstane Mews N4 ....50 C1
Athelstan Gdns 6 NW6 69 A1
Athelstan Ho E9 ....75 B3
N16 ....73 C4
Kingston KT1 ....198 B5
Athelstan House Sch
TW12 ....173 C2
Athelstan Rd KT1 ....198 B5
Athelstan Way BR5 ....190 A2
Athelstone Rd HA3 ....24 B1
Athena Cl Harrow HA2 ..64 C6
Kingston KT1 ....198 B6
Athena Ct NW8 ....229 C4
Athenaeum Pl 3 N10 ....49 B6
Athenaeum Rd N20 ....14 B3
Athenia Ho 7 E14 ....98 B1
Athenlay Rd SE15 ....162 D6
Athenoeum Ct N5 ....73 A4
Athens Gdns W9 ....91 C3
Atherden Rd E5 ....74 C4
Atherfield Ct SW18 ....157 D5
Atherfold Rd SW9 ....138 A2
Atherley Way TW4 ....151 B4
Atherstone Ct W2 ....91 D2
Atherstone Mews
SW7 ....114 A2 256 B4
Atherton Dr SW19 ....178 D6
Atherton Ho CR2 ....221 C2
Atherton Hts HA0 ....65 C2
Atherton Mews E7 ....77 A2
Atherton Pl Harrow HA2 42 B6
Southall UB1 ....107 C6
Atherton Rd E7 ....76 D2
Barnes SW13 ....134 A5
Atherton St SW11 ....136 C3
Athlone KT10 ....212 C2
Athlone Cl 24 E5 ....74 B3
Athlone Ct E17 ....54 B6
Athlone Ho 9 E1 ....96 C1
16 NW5 ....71 A2
Athlone House (The
Middlesex Hospl) N6 .48 D1
Athlone Rd SW2 ....160 C4
Athlone St NW5 ....71 A2
Athlon Rd HA0 ....87 D5
Athol Cl HA5 ....22 B2
Athole Gdns EN1 ....17 C6
Athole Terr CR7 ....183 A1
Athol Gdns HA5 ....22 B2
Atholl Ho W9 ....229 A1
Atholl Rd IG3 ....58 A2
Athol Sq E14 ....98 A1
Athol Way UB10 ....82 C4
Atkins Ct 8 E3 ....97 B6
Atkins Dr BR4 ....224 B6
Atkinson Ct 3 E10 ....53 D2
Atkinson Ho E13 ....98 D3
13 E2 ....96 A5
SE17 ....262 D3
SW11 ....268 A1
Atkinson Morley Hospl
SW20 ....178 B3
Atkinson Rd E16 ....99 C2
Atkins Rd E10 ....53 D3
Streatham SW4,SW12 ..159 D4
Atlanta Ct CR7 ....205 A6
Atlantic Ct 6 E14 ....120 B6
Atlantic Ho 4 E1 ....97 A2
4 Putney SW15 ....157 B6
Atlantic Rd SW2,SW9,
SE24 ....138 C1
Atlantis Cl IG11 ....102 B4
Atlas Bsns Ctr NW2 ....68 B6
Atlas Gdns SE7 ....121 C2
Atlas Mews E8 ....73 D2
Atlas Rd E13 ....99 A5
N11 ....31 A4
NW10 ....89 C4
Wembley HA9 ....67 A4
Atley Rd E3 ....97 C6
Atlip Rd HA0 ....88 A6
Atney Rd SW15 ....135 A1
Atria Rd HA6 ....22 A5
Atterbury Rd N4 ....50 D3
Atterbury St
SW1 ....116 A2 260 A3
Attewood Ave NW10 ....67 C5
Attewood Rd UB5 ....63 A2
Attfield Cl N20 ....14 B2
Attilburgh Ho SE1 ....263 C6
Attleborough Ct 4
SE21 ....162 B2
Attle Cl UB10 ....82 C5
Attlee Cl Hayes UB4 ....84 B4
Thornton Heath CR7 ....205 A4
Attlee Ct UB4 ....84 B4
Attlee Rd SE28 ....124 B6
Hayes UB4 ....84 B4
Attlee Terr 3 E17 ....53 D5
Attneave St WC1 ....234 A1
Atwater Cl SW2 ....160 C3
Atwell Cl E10 ....53 D3
Atwell Pl KT7 ....197 A1
Atwell Rd 4 SE15 ....140 A3
Atwood Ave TW9 ....132 C3
Atwood Ho SE21 ....161 C1
Atwood Rd W6 ....112 B2
Aubert Ct N5 ....72 D4
Aubert Pk N5 ....72 D4
Aubert Rd N5 ....72 D4
Aubrey Beardsley Ho
SW1 ....259 B3
Aubrey Mans NW1 ....237 A4
Aubrey Moore Point
E15 ....98 A5
Aubrey Pl NW8 ....229 A3
Aubrey Rd E17 ....53 D6
N8 ....50 A4
W14 ....113 B5 244 D3
Aubrey Wlk
W14 ....113 B5 244 D3
Auburn Cl SE14 ....141 A5
Aubyn Hill SE27 ....183 B6
Aubyn Sq SW15 ....156 A6
Auckland Cl Enfield EN1 ..6 B6
South Norwood SE19 ....183 D2
Auckland Ct UB4 ....84 C3
Auckland Gdns SE19 ..183 D2
Auckland Hill SE27 ....183 A6
Auckland Ho 11 W12 ....112 B6
Auckland Rd E10 ....75 D5
SW11 ....136 C1
Ilford IG1 ....57 A2
Kingston KT1 ....198 B5
South Norwood SE19 ....183 D2
Auckland Rise SE19 ....183 C2
Auckland St SE11 ....260 C1
Audax 29 NW9 ....27 D1
Auden Pl NW1 ....231 A6
Audley Cl N10 ....31 B3
Audley Ct E11,E18 ....54 D5
W1 ....248 C4
Ealing W5 ....88 C2
Northolt UB5 ....84 C4
Pinner HA5 ....22 C1
Surbiton KT5 ....198 B3
Twickenham TW2 ....152 B1
Audley Dr 3 E16 ....121 B5
Audley Gdns IG3 ....79 D6
Audley Ho 11 E5 ....74 C6
N8 ....50 A5
Audley Pl SM2 ....217 D1
Audley Rd NW4 ....46 B3
Ealing W5 ....88 B2
Enfield EN2 ....4 D3
Richmond TW10 ....154 B6
Audley Sq W1 ....248 B4
Audrey Cl BR3 ....207 D3
Audrey Gdns HA0 ....65 B6
Audrey Rd IG1 ....78 D5
Audrey St E2 ....96 A5
Audric Cl KT2 ....176 C2
Augurs La 8 E13 ....99 B4
Augusta Cl KT8 ....195 B6
Augusta Rd TW2 ....152 A2
Augustas Cl W12 ....112 B3
Augustine Rd W14 ....112 D3
Harrow HA3 ....24 A2
Augustines Ct E9 ....74 C3
Augustus Cl TW8 ....131 D5
Augustus Ct
Isleworth TW3 ....130 A1
8 Putney SW19 ....157 A3
South Norwood SE19 ....183 C3
Streatham SW16 ....159 D2
Augustus Rd SW19 ....157 A3
Augustus St
NW1 ....93 B4 231 D2
Aultone Way
Carshalton SM5 ....218 D5
Sutton SM1 ....218 A6
Aultone Yd Ind Est
SM5 ....218 D5
Aulton Pl SE11 ....261 B1
Aurelia Gdns CR0 ....204 B3
Aurelia Rd CR0 ....204 B3
Auriga Mews N1 ....73 B3
Auriol Cl KT4 ....215 C5
Auriol Dr Greenford UB6 .64 B1
Hillingdon UB10 ....60 D2
Auriol Jun Sch KT19 ....215 D4
Auriol Mans W14 ....254 A3
Auriol Park Rd KT4 ....215 C5
Auriol Rd W14 113 A2 254 A3
Aurora Ct IG8 ....36 D6
Austell Gdns NW7 ....11 C1
Austell Hts NW7 ....11 C1
Austen Cl SE28 ....124 B5
Austen Ho 2 NW6 ....91 C4
Austen Rd DA8 ....147 D5
Harrow HA2 ....63 D6
Austin Ave BR1,BR2 ....210 A4
Austin Cl
Forest Hill SE23 ....163 B4
Twickenham TW1 ....153 C6
Austin Ct 10 E6 ....99 C6
9 Enfield EN1 ....17 C6
Austin Friars EC2 ....242 D2
Austin Friars Sq EC2 ..242 D2
Austin Ho 1 SE14 ....141 B5
6 SW2 ....160 B6
19 Kingston KT6 ....198 A4
Austin Rd
SW11 ....137 A4 268 A1
Hayes UB3 ....105 D4
Austins Ct SE15 ....140 A2
Austin's La UB10 ....61 A5
Austin St E2 ....95 D4
Austral Cl DA15 ....167 D1
Australia Rd W12 ....112 B6
Austral St
SE11 ....116 D2 261 C4
Austyn Gdns KT5 ....198 D1
Autumn Cl Enfield EN1 ....6 A4
Wimbledon SW19 ....180 A4
Autumn Lo CR2 ....221 C4
Autumn St E3 ....97 C6
Avalon Cl Ealing W13 ....87 A2
Enfield EN2 ....4 C3
Merton SW20 ....179 A1
Avalon Rd
SW6 ....135 D4 265 C2
Ealing W13 ....87 A3
Avard Gdns BR6 ....227 A4
Avarn Rd SW17 ....180 D4
Avebury Ct N1 ....235 C5
Avebury Rd BR6 ....227 B5
E11 ....54 B1
Merton SW19 ....179 B2
Avebury St N1 ....235 C5
Aveley Ct 15 E5 ....74 B6
Aveley Mans 1 IG11 ....78 D1
Aveline St
SE11 ....116 C1 261 A1
Aveling Park Rd E17 ....35 C1
Aveling Park Sch E17 ....35 C1
Ave Maria La EC4 ....241 D1
Avenell Mans N5 ....72 D4
Avenell Rd N5 ....72 D5
Avenfield Ho W1 ....247 D6
Avening Rd SW18 ....157 C4
Avening Terr SW18 ....157 C4
Avenue Cl NW8 .92 C6 230 B5
Cranford TW5 ....128 B4
Southgate N14 ....15 C5
Avenue Cres W3 ....110 D4
Cranford TW5 ....128 B5
Avenue Ct NW2 ....69 A5
SW3 ....257 C3
Ealing W5 ....87 D2
Penge SE20 ....184 C2
Redbridge IG5 ....56 A6
Avenue Elmers KT6 ....198 A4
Avenue Gate IG10 ....21 C5
Avenue Gdns W3 ....110 D4
Cranford TW5 ....128 B5
Mortlake SW14 ....133 C2
South Norwood SE25 ....184 A1
Teddington TW11 ....174 D4
Avenue Hall N6 ....49 D3
Avenue Ho N16 ....74 A6
NW10 ....90 B5
NW8 ....230 A3
Avenue Ind Est E4 ....35 B4
Avenue Lo 12 NW8 ....70 B1
Avenue Mans N10 ....31 C1
NW3 ....69 D3
Avenue Mews N10 ....49 B6
Avenue Par
Southgate N21 ....17 B4
Sunbury TW16 ....194 B6
Avenue Park Rd SE21,
SE27 ....160 D2
Avenue Prim Sch E12 ....78 A3
Avenue Rd E7 ....77 B4
N12 ....30 A6
N15 ....51 B4
N6 ....49 D2
NW10 ....89 D5
NW8 ....92 C6 230 A6
W3 ....110 D4
Bexley DA6,DA7 ....147 A2
Brentford TW8 ....109 C1
Feltham TW13 ....149 D1
Hampton TW12 ....173 D2
Hounslow TW7 ....130 D4
Ilford RM6 ....58 C2
Kingston KT1 ....198 A6
Mitcham SW16 ....181 D1
New Malden KT3 ....199 C5
Pinner HA5 ....41 A6
Southall UB1 ....107 B5
Southgate N14 ....15 C5
South Norwood SE25 ....184 A1
South Norwood, Elmers End
BR3,SE20 ....184 D2
Avenue Rd *continued*
Teddington TW11 ....175 A4
Wallington SM6 ....219 C1
Wimbledon SW20 ....178 B1
Woodford IG8 ....37 C4
Avenue Rd Sta BR3 ....184 D1
Avenue S KT5 ....198 C2
Avenue Sch The NW6 ....69 A1
Avenue Terr Ilford IG2 ..57 C3
Kingston KT3 ....199 A6
Avenue The BR1 ....209 D6
BR6 ....227 D6
N10 ....31 C1
N11 ....31 B5
N8 ....50 C6
NW6 ....91 A6
SE10 ....142 B5
SW4 ....159 A6
W4 ....111 C3
Barnet EN5 ....1 A2
Beckenham BR3 ....186 A2
8 Buckhurst Hill IG9 ....21 C2
Chingford E4 ....36 B5
Claygate KT10 ....212 C3
Cranford TW5 ....128 A4
Ealing W13 ....87 B1
Finchley N3 ....29 C1
Hampton TW12 ....173 B4
Hounslow TW3 ....151 D6
Isleworth TW1 ....153 B6
Keston Mark BR2 ....225 D5
Loughton IG10 ....21 D5
4 New Malden KT4 ....200 A1
Pinner HA5 ....23 B4
Pinner HA5 ....41 B3
Richmond TW9 ....132 B3
Sidcup DA5 ....168 D4
South Croydon CR0 ....221 C5
Stoneleigh KT17,SM3 ....216 C1
St Paul's Cray BR5 ....190 B3
Sunbury TW16 ....172 B1
Surbiton KT5 ....198 B3
Tottenham N17 ....33 C1
Uxbridge UB10 ....60 D5
Wallington SM5 ....219 A1
Wandsworth SW18,
SW12 ....158 C4
Wanstead E11 ....55 B4
Wembley HA9 ....44 B1
West Wickham BR4 ....208 C2
Worcester Park KT4 ....215 D6
Averil Gr SW16 ....182 D4
Averill St W6 ....134 D6
Avern Gdns KT8 ....195 D5
Avernons Rd E13 ....99 A3
Avern Rd KT8 ....195 D5
Avery Ct SE20 ....184 B3
Avery Farm Row SW1 .258 C3
Avery Gdns IG2 ....56 B4
Avery Hill Coll (Mile End
Annexe) E3 ....97 B3
Avery Hill Rd SE9 ....167 B3
Avery Row W1 115 B6 248 D6
Aviary Cl E16 ....98 D2
Aviemore Cl BR3 ....207 B4
Aviemore Way BR3 ....207 A4
Avigdor (Jewish) Prim Sch
N16 ....73 B6
Avignon Rd SE4 ....140 D2
Avington Ct SE1 ....263 B3
Avington Gr SE20 ....184 C3
Avion Cres NW7,NW9 ....28 A2
Avis Sq E1 ....96 D1
Avoca Rd SW17 ....181 A6
Avocet Cl SE1 ....118 A1
Avocet Mews SE28 ....123 B3
Avon Cl Hayes UB4 ....84 C3
Sutton SM1 ....218 A4
Worcester Park KT4 ....216 A6
Avon Ct N12 ....29 D5
1 W3 ....89 A1
Greenford UB6 ....85 D3
11 Putney SW15 ....157 A6
Wembley HA0 ....65 A4
Avondale Ave N12 ....29 D5
NW2 ....67 C5
Barnet, London EN4 ....14 D3
Hinchley Wood KT10 ....213 A5
New Malden KT4 ....199 D1
Avondale Cres
Enfield EN3 ....7 A2
Redbridge IG4 ....55 D4
Avondale Ct E11 ....54 C1
E16 ....98 C2
9 Sutton SM2 ....218 A1
Woodford E18 ....37 B2
Avondale Dr UB3 ....106 B5
Avondale Gdns TW4 ....151 B6
Avondale Ho 10 SE1 ....118 A1
6 Mortlake SW14 ....133 B2
Avondale Mans SW6 ....264 C2
Avondale Park Gdns
W11 ....113 A6 244 A5
Avondale Park Prim Sch
W11 ....113 A6 244 A5
Avondale Park Rd
W11 ....113 A6 244 A6
Avondale Rd E16 ....98 C2
E17 ....53 C2
Avondale Rd *continued*
N15 5
N3 3
Bexley DA16 14
Bromley BR1 18
Chislehurst SE9 16
Harrow HA3 4
Mortlake SW14 13
South Croydon CR2 22
Southgate N13 1
Wimbledon SW19 17
Avondale Rise SE15 139
Avondale Sq SE1 118
Avonfield Ct E17 5
Avon Ho 14 N16 7
W14 25
7 Kingston KT2 17
Southgate N21 1
Avon House Sch IG8 3
Avonhurst Ho NW6 6
Avonley Rd SE14 14
Avon Mews HA5 2
Avonmore Gdns W14 25
Avonmore Pl W14 25
Avonmore Prim Sch
W14 ....113 A2 25
Avonmore Rd
W14 ....113 B2 25
Avonmouth St SE1 26
Avon Pl SE1 25
Avon Rd E17 5
SE4 14
Ashford TW16 17
Greenford UB6 85
Avonstowe Cl BR6 227
Avon Way E18 55
Avonwick Rd TW3 12
Avril Way E4 36
Avriol Ho W12 11
Avro Ct E9 7
Avro Way SM6 22
Awlfield Ave N17 33
Awliscombe Rd DA16 14
Axe St IG11 10
Axford Ho SW2 16
Axholm Ave HA8 2
Axis Bsns Ctr E15 97
Axminster Cres DA16 14
Axminster Rd N7 72
Aybrook St W1 .93 A2 238
Aycliffe Cl BR1 21
Aycliffe Ct KT1 176
Aycliffe Rd W12 112
Ayerst Ct 1 E10 5
Aylands Cl HA9 66
Aylesbury Cl E7 76
Aylesbury Ct SM1 21
Aylesbury Ho 13 SE15 14
Aylesbury Rd BR2 20
SE17 ....117 B1 262
Aylesbury St
EC1 ....94 D3 24
NW10 6
Ayles Ct UB4 84
Aylesford Ave BR3 207
Aylesford Ho SE1 252
Aylesford St
SW1 ....115 D1 25
Aylesham Cl NW7 2
Aylesham Ctr The
SE15 14
Aylesham Rd BR6 211
Ayles Rd UB4 84
Aylestone Ave NW6 90
Aylett Rd Croydon SE25 20
Isleworth TW7 13
Ayley Croft EN1 1
Aylmer Cl HA7 25
Aylmer Ct N2 48
Aylmer Dr HA7 25
Aylmer Ho SE10 120
Aylmer Rd E11 54
N2 48
W12 111
Dagenham RM8 81
Ayloffe Rd RM9 81
Aylsham Dr UB10 61
Aylton Est 22 SE16 11
Aylward Fst & Mid Sch
HA7 25
Aylward Rd
Forest Hill SE23 162
Merton SW20 20
Aylward Sch N18 33
Aylwards Rise HA7 25
Aylward St E1 96
Aylwin Est SE1 263
Aylwin Girls Sch
SE1 ....117 D2 263
Aynhoe Mans W14 112
Aynhoe Rd W14 112
Ayr Ct W3 88
Ayres Cl E13 99
Ayres Cres NW10 67
Ayres St SE1 ..117 A4 252
Ayrsome Rd N16 73
Ayrton Gould Ho 9 E2 96
Ayrton Ho HA9 65

ton Rd
W7 114 B3 256 C6
garth Ct SM1 217 D5
garth Rd SE21 161 C4
ston Ho 19 SE8 118 D2
on Ho SE5 139 B5
oun Ct 17 SW9 138 B3
oun Pl SW9 138 B3
oun Rd SW9 138 B3
lea Cl Ealing W7 108 D5
ord IG1 78 D3
lea Ct W7 108 D5
lea Ho SE14 141 B5
lea Wlk HA5 40 B3
lea Ct IG8 36 C3
enby Rd SE15 139 D3
of St SE10 120 C2
ov Ho 9 E1 97 A3

B

albec Rd N5 72 D3
bbacombe Cl KT9 213 D3
bbacombe Gdns IG4 56 A5
bbacombe Rd BR1 187 A2
ber Bridge Par
W14 150 C5
ber Dr TW14 150 C5
bington Ct WC1 240 B4
reatham SW16 181 D5
bington Ho SE1 252 B2
bington House Sch
7 188 B4
bington Rd NW4 46 B5
agenham RM8 80 C4
reatham SW16 181 D5
bington Rise HA9 66 C2
bmaes St SW1 249 C5
cchus Wlk 12 N1 95 C5
che's St N1 95 B4 235 D1
ck Church La E1 96 A1
ck Hill EC1 241 B5
ckhouse Pl SE1 263 B3
ck La HA8 27 A2
8 50 A4
W3 70 A4
rentford TW8 131 D6
agenham RM6 59 A2
ichmond TW10 153 C2
idcup DA5 169 C4
ckley Gdns SE25 206 A3
ck Rd Sidcup DA14 190 A6
eddington TW11 174 C5
con Gr SE1 117 D3 263 C5
con La NW9 44 D5
dgware HA8 26 C2
con's Coll SE16 119 A4
con's La N6 49 A1
con St E2 95 D3 243 D6
con Terr RM8 80 B3
cton NW5 71 A3
cton St E2 96 C4
ddeley Cl EN3 7 C6
ddeley Ho SE11 260 D2
ddow Cl
agenham RM10 103 C6
Woodford IG8 37 D4
ddow Wlk N1 235 A6
den Ct N11 31 D3
den Pl SE1 252 C2
den Powell Cl
agenham RM9 103 A6
urbiton KT6 214 B6
den Powell Ho 11
A17 125 C3
den Powell Sch E5 74 B5
den Rd N8 49 D5
lford IG1 78 D3
dger Cl
eltham TW13 150 B1
ounslow TW4 128 C2
lford IG2 57 A2
dger Ct NW2 68 C5
dgers Cl
Ashford TW15 170 B5
Enfield EN2 4 D2
Harrow HA1 42 B3
Hayes UB3 105 C6
dgers Copse BR6 227 D6
Worcester Park KT4 215 D6
dgers Croft SE9 166 C1
Barnet N20 13 A3
dgers Hole CR0
dgers Wlk KT3 177 C1
dlis Rd E17 53 C6
dma Cl N9 18 C1
dminton KT2 176 D2
dminton Cl
Harrow HA1 42 C5
Northolt UB5 63 C2
dminton Ct 9 N4 51 A2
dminton Ho SE22 139 C1
dminton Mews 10
E16 121 A5
dminton Rd SW12 159 A5
dric Ct SW11 136 B3
dsworth Rd 3 SE5 139 A4
agley Cl UB7 104 A4

Bagley's La
SW6 135 D4 265 D1
Bagleys Spring RM6 59 A5
Bagnigge Ho WC1 234 A1
Bagshot Ho NW1 231 D2
Bagshot Rd EN1 17 D5
Bagshot St
SE17 117 C1 263 B1
Baildon 28 E2 96 C5
Baildon St SE8 141 B5
Bailey Cl N11 31 D3
Chingford E4 36 A6
Bailey Cres KT9 213 D1
Bailey Ct 9 W12 112 A4
4 Chingford E4 36 B5
Bailey Ho 11 SE26 184 B5
Bailey Mews W4 132 D6
Bailey Pl SE26 184 D4
Bainbridge cl KT2 176 A5
Bainbridge Rd RM9 81 B4
Bainbridge St WC1 239 D2
Baines Cl CR2 221 B3
Bain Ho 23 SW9 138 A3
Baird Ave UB1 108 A6
Baird Cl E10 53 C1
NW9 45 A3
Baird Gdns SE19 183 C6
Baird Ho 20 W12 112 B6
12 Belvedere DA17 125 C3
Baird Rd EN1 6 B1
Baird St EC1 242 B6
Baizdon Rd SE3 142 C3
Baker Beal Ct DA7 147 D2
Baker Ct E11 76 B5
Baker Ho 12 E3 97 D4
Ealing W7 108 D5
Baker La CR4 203 A6
Baker Rd NW10 89 C6
SE18 144 A4
Bakers' Almshouses
E10 53 D3
Bakers Ave E17 53 D3
Bakers Ct SE25 205 C6
Bakers End SW20 179 A1
Bakers Field N7 72 A4
Bakers Gdns SM5 218 C6
Bakers Hall Ct EC3 253 B5
Bakers Hill E5 52 C1
Barnet EN5 1 D3
Bakers Ho W5 109 D5
Baker's La N6 48 D3
Bakers Mews 9 BR6 227 D2
Baker's Mews W1 238 A2
Bakers Rents 18 E2 95 D4
Bakers Row E15 98 C5
Baker's Row
EC1 94 C3 241 A5
Baker St W1 92 D2 237 D4
Enfield EN1 5 B4
Baker Street
W1 92 D2 237 D4
Baker Street Sta
NW1 92 D3 237 D5
Baker's Yd EC1 241 A5
Bakery Cl SW9 270 D3
Bakery Mews KT6 198 C1
Bakewell Way KT3 177 C1
Balaam Ho SM1 217 C4
Balaams La N14 15 D2
Balaam St E13 99 B4
Balaclava Rd
SE1 117 D2 263 D3
Kingston KT6 197 C2
Balcaskie Rd SE9 166 B6
Balchen Rd SE3 143 D3
Balchier Rd SE22 162 B5
Balcombe Cl DA6 146 D1
Balcombe Ho NW1 237 C6
3 Streatham SW2 160 B3
Balcombe St
NW1 92 D3 237 C5
Balcon Ct W5 88 B1
Balcorne St E9 74 C1
Balder Rise SE12 165 B2
Balderton Flats W1 238 B1
Balderton St
W1 93 A1 238 B1
Baldewyne Ct N17 34 A2
Baldock Ho 32 SE5 139 A3
Baldock St E3 97 D5
Baldrey Ho 1 SE10 120 D1
Baldry Gdns SW16 182 B4
Baldwin Cres SE5 139 A4
Baldwin Gdns TW3 130 A4
Baldwin Ho 15 SW2 160 C3
Baldwin's Gdns
EC1 94 C2 241 A4
Baldwin St EC1 235 C1
Baldwin Terr
N1 95 A5 235 A4
Baldwyn Gdns W3 111 B6
Bale Rd E1 97 A2
Bales Coll W10 90 D4
Balfern Gr W4 111 C1
Balfern St SW11 136 C3
Balfe St N1 94 A5 233 B3
Balfour Ave W7 108 D5
Balfour Bsns Ctr UB2 106 D3
Balfour Gr N20 14 D1

Balfour Ho W10 90 D2
Balfour Mews W1 248 B4
Edmonton N9 18 A1
Balfour Pl W1 248 B5
Putney SW15 134 B1
Balfour Rd BR2 209 D4
N5 73 A4
W13 109 B4
W3 89 A2
Croydon SE25 206 A5
Harrow HA1 42 B4
Hounslow TW3 129 D2
Ilford IG1 57 A1
Merton SW19 179 D3
Southall UB2 106 D3
Wallington SM5 218 D1
Balfour St
SE17 117 B2 262 C4
Balfron Twr 2 E14 98 A1
Balgonie Rd E4 20 B3
Balgowan Cl KT3 199 C5
Balgowan Prim Sch
BR3 185 A1
Balgowan Rd BR3 185 B1
Balgowan St SE18 123 D2
Balham Gr SW12 159 A4
Balham High Rd
SW12,SW17 159 A3
Balham Hill SW12 159 B5
Balham New Rd SW12 159 B4
Balham Park Mans
SW12 158 D3
Balham Park Rd SW12,
SW17 159 A3
Balham Rd N9 18 A2
Balham Sta SW12 159 B3
Balham Station Rd
SW12 159 B3
Balin Ho SE1 252 C2
Balkan Wlk E1 118 B6
Balladier Wlk E14 97 D2
Ballamore Rd BR1 165 A1
Ballance Rd E9 75 A2
Ballantine St SW18 136 A1
Ballantrae Ho NW2 69 B4
Ballard Cl KT2 177 B3
Ballard Ho SE10 141 D6
Ballards Cl RM10 103 D6
Ballards Farm Rd CR0,
CR2 222 A2
Ballards La N3 29 D3
Ballards Mews HA8 26 C4
Ballards Rd NW2 68 A6
Dagenham RM10 103 D6
Ballards Rise CR2 222 A2
Ballards Way CR0,CR2 222 B2
Ballast Quay SE10 120 B1
Ballater Cl WD19 22 C6
Ballater Rd SW2,SW4 138 A1
South Croydon CR2 221 D3
Ball Ct EC3 242 D1
Ballina St SE23 162 D4
Ballin Ct 9 E14 120 A4
Ballingdon Rd SW11 159 A5
Ballinger Point 18 E3 97 D4
Balliol Ave E4 36 C6
Balliol Ho 11 SW15 156 D5
Balliol Rd DA16 146 B3
W10 90 D1
Tottenham N17 33 C2
Balloch Rd SE6 164 B2
Ballogie Ave NW10 67 C4
Ballow Cl 23 SE5 139 C5
Ball's Pond Pl 3 N1 73 B2
Ball's Pond Rd N1 73 C2
Balmain Cl W5 109 D5
Balmain Ct TW3 129 D4
Balman Ho 3 SE16 118 D2
Balmer Rd E3 97 B5
Balmes Rd N1 95 B6 235 D6
Balmoral Ave N11 31 B5
Beckenham BR3 207 A5
Balmoral Cl 1 SW15 156 D5
Balmoral Cres KT8 195 C6
Balmoral Ct NW8 229 C4
SE12 187 B6
21 SE16 118 D5
11 Belmont SM2 217 C1
Ealing W5 87 D1
Edgware HA8 26 D6
North Cheam KT4 216 B6
Wembley HA9 66 B5
West Norwood SE27 183 A6
Balmoral Dr
Borehamwood WD6 11 B6
Hayes UB4 83 D3
Southall UB1 85 B3
Balmoral Gdns DA5 169 B4
W13 109 A3
Ilford IG3 57 D1
Balmoral Gr N7 72 B2
Balmoral Ho E17 35 B1
N4 51 A1
W14 254 A4
Balmoral Mews W12 111 D3
Balmoral Rd E10 75 D6
E7 77 C3
NW2 68 B2
Harrow HA2 63 C4

Balmoral Rd *continued*
Kingston KT1 198 B5
North Cheam KT4 216 B6
Balmoral Trad Est
IG11 101 D2
Balmore Cres EN4 15 A6
Balmore St N19 71 B6
Balmuir Gdns SW15 134 C1
Balnacraig Ave NW10 67 C4
Balniel Gate SW1 259 D2
Balsam Ho 8 E14 119 D6
Baltic Cl SW19 180 B3
Baltic Ho 7 SE5 139 A3
Baltic St E EC1 95 A3 242 A5
Baltic St W EC1 95 A3 242 A5
Baltimore Ho SE11 261 A2
Baltimore Pl DA16 145 D3
Balvaird Pl SW1 259 D1
Balvernie Gr SW18 157 C4
Bamber Ho 5 IG11 101 A6
Bamborough Gdns 12
W12 112 C4
Bamburgh 9 N17 34 B3
Bamford Ave HA0 88 B5
Bamford Ct E15 75 D3
Bamford Rd
Barking IG11 79 A2
Catford BR1 186 B5
Bampfylde Cl SM6 219 C5
Bampton Ct W5 87 D1
Bampton Dr NW7 28 A3
Bampton Rd SE23 162 D1
Banavie Gdns BR3 186 A2
Banbury Cl EN2 4 D4
Banbury Ct W13 109 A3
WC2 250 A6
8 Belmont SM2 217 C1
Banbury Ho 5 E9 74 D1
Banbury Rd E17 35 A3
E9 74 D1
Banbury St 3 SW11 136 C3
Banbury Wlk UB5 85 B5
Banchory Rd SE3 143 B5
Bancroft Ave N2 48 C4
Woodford IG9 21 A2
Bancroft Cl
Ashford TW15 170 C5
Hillingdon UB8 82 D2
Bancroft Ct SW8 270 A2
Northolt UB5 84 C6
Bancroft Gdns BR6 211 D1
Harrow HA3 24 A2
Bancroft Ho 10 E1 96 C3
Bancroft Rd E1 96 D3
Harrow HA3 24 A1
Bancrofts Sch IG8 21 A1
Bandon Cl UB10 82 B5
Bandon Hill Prim Sch
SM6 219 D2
Bandon Rise SM6 219 D3
Banff Ho 1 NW3 70 C2
Banfield Rd SE15 140 B2
Banfor Ct SM6 219 C3
Bangabandhu Prim Sch
E2 96 C4
Bangalore St SW15 134 D2
Bangor Cl UB5 63 D3
Banim St W6 112 B2
Banister Ho E9 74 D3
SW8 269 B2
15 W10 91 A4
Banister Rd W10 90 D4
Bank Ave CR4 180 B1
Bank Ct SW11 268 C2
Bank End SE1 252 B4
Bankfoot Rd BR1 186 C6
Bankhurst Rd SE6 163 B4
Bank La Kingston KT2 176 A3
Roehampton SW15 155 C6
Bank Mews SM1 218 A2
Bank of England★
EC2 242 C1
Bank Par N11 31 B5
Banks Ho SE1 262 A5
Isleworth TW7 130 C3
Banksia Rd N18 34 D5
Bankside SE1 117 A6 252 A5
SE1 252 B4
Enfield EN2 4 D4
Southall UB1 106 D5
South Croydon CR2 221 D2
Bankside Ave UB5 84 A5
Bankside Cl
Carshalton SM5 218 C2
Isleworth TW7 130 D1
Bankside Dr KT7 213 B6
Bankside Pier
SE1 117 A6 252 A5
Bankside Pk IG11 102 A4
Bankside Rd IG1 79 B3
Bankside Way 6 SE19 183 C4
Banks La DA6 147 B1
Bank Sta EC3 95 B1 242 D1
Banks Way E12 78 C4
Bank The N6 49 B1
Bankton Rd SW2 138 C1
Bankwell Rd SE13 142 C1
Banner Ho EC1 242 B5
Bannerman Ho SW8 270 C5

Banner St EC1 95 A3 242 B6
Banning Ho 4 SW19 156 D3
Banning St SE10 120 C1
Bannister Cl
Greenford UB6 64 B3
Streatham SW2 160 C3
Bannister Ho 28 SE14 140 D6
Bannister Sports Ctr The
HA3 24 A4
Bannockburn Prim Sch
SE18 123 D2
Bannockburn Rd SE18 123 D2
Bannow Cl KT19 215 C4
Banqueting House★
SW1 250 A3
Banstead Ct N4 51 A1
Banstead Gdns N9 17 C1
Banstead Rd SM2,SM5 218 C1
Banstead St SE15 140 C2
Banstead Way SM6 220 A3
Banstock Rd HA8 26 D4
Banting Dr N21 16 B6
Banting Ho 6 NW2 68 A5
Bantock Ho 14 W10 91 A4
Banton Cl EN1 6 B3
Bantry Ho 18 E1 96 D3
Bantry St SE5 139 B5
Banwell Rd DA5 168 D5
Banyan Ho 8 NW3 69 D2
Banyard Rd SE16 118 B3
Baptist Gdns NW5 71 A2
Barandon Wlk 6 W11 112 D6
Barbanel Ho 19 E1 96 C3
Barbara Brosnan Ct
NW8 229 C3
Barbara Cl TW17 192 D4
Barbara Hucklesbury Cl
N22 32 D1
Barbara Martin Ho 1
N11 31 C5
Barbara Ward Ct 3
E11 76 C6
Barbauld Rd N16 73 C5
Barber Beaumont Ho 21
E1 96 D4
Barber Cl N21 16 C4
Barbers Alley 1 E13 99 B4
Barbers Rd E15 97 D5
Barbican★ EC2 95 A2 242 B3
Barbican Arts & Con Ctr★
EC2 95 A2 242 B4
Barbican Rd UB1 85 D1
Barbican Sta
EC1 95 A2 242 A4
Barb Mews W6 112 C3
Barbon Cl WC1 240 C4
Barbot Cl N9 18 A1
Barbrook Ho E9 74 C2
Barchard St SW18 157 D6
Barchester Cl W7 108 D5
Barchester Lo N12 29 D6
Barchester Rd HA3 24 B1
Barchester St E14 97 D2
Barclay Cl
SW6 135 C5 265 A3
Barclay Ct N12 30 A5
Barclay Ho 21 E9 74 C1
Barclay Jun & Inf Schs
E10 54 B3
Barclay Oval IG8 37 A6
Barclay Rd E11 54 D1
E13 99 C3
E17 54 A4
SW6 135 C5 265 B3
Edmonton N18 33 B4
South Croydon CR0 221 B5
Barcombe Ave SW2 160 B2
Barden Ho 14 SE1 118 A4
Barden St SE18 145 C5
Bardfield Ave RM6 58 D6
Bardney Rd SM4 201 D5
Bardolph Rd N7 72 A4
Richmond TW9 132 B2
Bard Rd W10 112 D6
Bardsey Pl 35 E1 96 C3
Bardsey Wlk 2 N1 73 A2
Bardsley Cl CR0 221 D5
Bardsley Ho 5 SE10 142 A6
Bardsley La SE10 142 A6
Barents Ho 10 E1 96 D3
Barfett St W10 91 B3
Barfield Ave N20 14 D2
Barfield Rd BR1,BR7 210 C6
E11 54 D1
Barfleur Ho SE8 119 B2
Barford Cl NW4 28 A2
Barford Ho 19 E3 97 B5
Barford St N1 94 C6 234 B5
Barforth Rd SE15 140 B2
Barfreston Way SE20 184 B2
Bargate Cl SE18 123 D1
New Malden KT3 200 A2
Bargehouse Rd E16 122 D4
Barge House St SE1 251 B4
Bargery Rd SE6 163 D3
Barge Wlk KT1,KT6,KT7 197 C3
Bargrove Cl 8 SE20 184 A3
Bargrove Cres SE6 163 B2

Barham Cl
Chislehurst BR7 188 D5
Keston Mark BR2 210 A1
Wembley HA0 65 C2
Barham Ct N12 29 B5
8 Croydon CR2 221 A4
Keston Mark BR2 210 A1
Wembley HA0 65 C2
Barham Ho SE17 263 B2
Barham Prim Sch HA0 65 C2
Barham Rd
Chislehurst BR7 188 D5
Croydon CR2 221 A3
Wimbledon SW20 178 A3
Baring Cl SE12 165 A2
Baring Ct N1 235 C5
Baring Ho 11 E14 97 C1
Baring Prim Sch SE12 165 A4
Baring Rd SE12 165 A2
Barnet EN4 2 B2
Croydon CR0 206 A1
Baring St N1 95 B6 235 C5
Barker Cl KT3 198 D5
Barker Dr NW1 71 D1
Barker Ho N15 50 D5
SE17 263 A3
Dulwich SE21 161 C1
Barker Mews SW4 137 B1
Barker St SW10 266 A6
Barker Wlk SW16 159 D1
Barkham Rd N17 33 C3
Barking Abbey Comp Sch
IG11 79 D2
Barking Abbey Comp Sch
(Lower Sch) IG11 79 C3
Barking Bsns Ctr IG11 102 A4
Barking Flyover IG11 78 D1
Barking Hospl IG11 79 D1
Barking Ind Pk IG11 102 A6
Barking Rd E13 99 B4
E6 100 B6
Barkingside Sta IG6 57 B6
Barking Sta IG11 79 A1
Bark Pl W2 113 D6 245 C6
Barkston Gdns
SW5 113 D2 255 C3
Barkway Ct N4 73 A6
Barkwith Ho 27 SE14 140 D6
Barkworth Rd SE16 118 C1
Barlborough St SE14 140 D5
Barlby Gdns W10 90 D3
Barlby Prim Sch W10 90 D3
Barlby Rd W10 90 D2
Barley Cl WD23 8 A6
Barleycorn Way E14 119 B6
Barleyfields Cl RM6 58 C2
Barley La IG3 58 B3
Barley Lane Prim Sch
RM6 58 B2
Barley Mow Pas EC1 241 D3
W4 111 B1
Barley Mow Way
TW17 192 C5
Barling 6 NW1 71 B1
Barling Ct 1 SW4 138 A3
Barlings Ho 2 SE4 140 D1
Barloch Ho 13 SW11 137 A3
Barlow Cl SM6 220 A1
Barlow Dr SE18 144 A4
Barlow Ho N1 235 C2
14 SE16 118 B2
W11 244 A6
Barlow Pl W1 248 D5
Barlow Rd NW6 69 B2
Acton W3 110 D5
Hampton TW12 173 C3
Barlow St
SE17 117 B2 262 D3
Barmeston Rd SE6 163 D2
Barmor Cl HA2 23 D1
Barmouth Ave UB6 86 D5
Barmouth Ho 6 N7 72 B6
Barmouth Rd SW18 158 A5
Croydon CR0 222 D6
Barnabas Ct N21 16 D6
Barnabas Ho EC1 235 A1
Barnabas Lo SW8 270 B2
Barnabas Rd E9 74 D3
Barnaby Cl HA2 64 A6
Barnaby Ct NW9 45 C6
Barnaby Pl SW7 256 C3
Barnard Cl
Chislehurst BR7 189 B2
Sunbury TW16 172 B3
Wallington SM6 219 D1
Woolwich SE18 122 C3
Barnard Ct SW16 160 B1
Barnard Gdns
Hayes UB4 84 B3
West Barnes KT3 200 A5
Barnard Gr E15 76 D1
Barnard Hill N10 31 B2
Barnard Ho 17 E2 96 B4
Barnard Lo 10 W9 91 C2
New Barnet EN5 2 A1
Barnard Mews SW11 136 C1

Barnardo Dr IG6 57 A5
Barnardo Gdns 1 E1 118 D6
Barnardo St E1 96 D1
Barnard Rd SW11 136 C1
Enfield EN1 6 B3
Mitcham CR4 181 A1
Barnard's Inn EC4 241 B2
Barnbrough NW1 232 A5
Barnby Sq 1 E15 98 C6
Barnby St 2 E15 98 C6
NW1 93 C4 232 B2
Barn Cl 19 NW5 71 D3
Ashford TW15 170 D5
Northolt UB5 84 C5
Barn Cres HA7 25 C4
Barn Croft Sch E17 53 A3
Barneby Cl TW2 152 C3
Barnehurst Rd DA7 147 D3
Barnersbury Ho N7 72 A4
Barnes Ave
Barnes SW13 134 A5
Southall UB2 107 B2
Barnes Bridge Sta
SW13 133 C3
Barnes Cl E12 77 D4
Barnes Common★
SW13 134 A2
Barnes Ct N1 72 C1
Barnet EN5 1 D1
Newham E16 99 C2
South Norwood CR7 205 A6
Woodford IG8 37 D5
Wood Green N22 32 A3
Barnes End KT3 200 A4
Barnes High St SW13 133 D3
Barnes Ho 14 E2 96 C5
N19 50 A2
28 SE14 140 D6
8 Barking IG11 101 B6
Barnes Hospl SW14 133 C2
Barnes Rd N18 34 C6
Ilford IG1 79 A3
Barnes St E14 97 A1
Barnes Sta SW13 134 A2
Barnes Terr SE8 119 B1
Barnes Wallis Ct HA9 67 A5
Barnet Coll EN4 15 A3
Barnet Coll of F Ed EN5 1 B1
Barnet Dr BR2 226 A6
Barnet Gate La EN5 11 D4
Barnet Gr E2 96 A4
Barnet Hill EN5 1 C1
Barnet Hill JMI Prim Sch
EN5 13 B6
Barnet Ho 38 SE5 139 A3
Barnet La
Barnet EN5,N20 13 B4
Borehamwood WD6 10 B5
Barnet Mus★ EN5 1 A1
Barnet Rd Barnet EN5 1 B5
Edgware EN5 11 C5
Barnett Ho E1 243 C3
Barnett Homestead
NW11 47 C5
Barnet Trad Est EN5 1 B2
Barnetts Ct HA2 63 D5
Barnett St 8 E1 96 B1
Barnet Way (Barnet
By-Pass) EN5,NW7,
WD6 11 B3
Barnet Wood Rd BR2 225 C6
Barney Cl SE7 121 C1
Barn Field NW3 70 D3
Barnfield KT3 199 C3
Barnfield Ave
Croydon CR0 222 C6
Kingston KT2 176 A5
Mitcham CR4 203 B6
Barnfield Cl N4 50 A2
Wandsworth SW17 158 A1
Barnfield Gdns SE18 144 D6
Kingston KT2 176 A5
Barnfield Pl E14 119 C2
Barnfield Prim Sch
HA8 27 A2
Barnfield Rd HA8 27 A2
SE18 144 D6
Ealing W5 87 C3
Erith DA17 147 B6
Barnfield Wood Cl
BR3 208 B3
Barnfield Wood Rd
BR3 208 B3
Barnham Dr SE28 123 D5
Barnham Rd UB6 86 A4
Barnham St SE1 253 B2
Barnhill HA5 40 C4
Barn Hill HA9 44 D1
Barnhill Ave BR2 208 D4
Barnhill Com High Sch
UB4 84 C4
Barnhill Ct UB4 84 B4
Barnhill La UB4 84 B3
Barnhill Rd Hayes UB4 84 C3
Wembley HA9 67 A5
Barnhurst Path WD19 22 C5
Barningham Way NW9 45 B3
Barnlea Cl TW13 151 A2
Barnmead Gdns RM9 81 B3
Barnmead Rd
Dagenham RM9 81 B3
Penge BR3 185 A2
Barn Rise HA9 66 C6
Barnsbury Cl KT3 199 A5
Barnsbury Cres KT5 199 A1
Barnsbury Gr N7 72 B1
Barnsbury Ho 12 SW4 159 D5
Barnsbury La KT5 199 A1
Barnsbury Pk N1 72 C1
Barnsbury Rd
N1 94 C6 234 A5
Barnsbury Sq N1 72 C1
Barnsbury St N1 72 C1
Barnsbury Terr N1 72 B1
Barnscroft SW20 200 B6
Barnsdale Ave E14 119 C2
Barnsdale Rd W9 91 B3
Barnsley St E1 96 B3
Barn St N16 73 C6
Barnstaple Ho SE12 164 D6
Barnstaple La SE13 142 A1
Barnstaple Rd HA4 62 C5
Barnston Wlk N1 235 A6
Barnview Lo HA3 24 C2
Barn Way HA9 66 C6
Barnwell Ho 1 SE5 139 C4
Barnwell Rd SW2 160 C6
Barnwood Cl W9 91 D3
Barnet N20 13 B3
Ruislip HA4 61 B6
Baron Cl N1 234 A4
N11 31 B5
Baron Ct CR4 202 C5
Baroness Rd 5 E2 95 D4
Baronet Gr N17 34 A2
Baronet Rd N17 34 A2
Baron Gdns IG6 57 A6
Baron Gr CR4 202 C5
Baron Rd RM8 58 D1
Barons Court Mans
W14 254 B1
Baron's Court Rd
W14 113 A1 254 B2
Barons Court Sta
W14 113 A1 254 A2
Barons Ct NW9 45 B3
Ilford IG1 79 B6
Wallington SM6 219 D5
Baronsfield Rd TW1 153 B5
Barons Gate 13 W4 111 A3
East Barnet EN4 14 C5
Barons Keep
W14 113 A1 254 A2
Barons Lo 8 E14 120 A2
Barons Mead HA1 42 C5
Baronsmead Rd SW13 134 A4
Baronsmede W5 110 B4
Baronsmere Ct 7 EN5 1 A1
Baronsmere Rd N2 48 C5
Baron's Pl SE1 116 C4 251 B1
Baron St N1 94 C5 234 A4
Barons The TW1 153 B5
Baron's Wlk CR0 207 A3
Baron Wlk E16 98 D2
Barque Mews SE8 141 C6
Barrack Rd TW4 129 A1
Barra Hall Cir UB3 83 C1
Barra Hall Rd UB3 105 C6
Barras Cl EN3 7 C6
Barratt Ave N22 32 B1
Barratt Ho 15 N1 72 D1
Barratt Ind Pk E3 98 A3
Southall UB1 107 C5
Barratt Way HA3 42 B6
Barr Beacon SE23 162 C4
Barrenger Rd N10 30 D1
Barret Ho NW6 91 C6
Barrett Rd E17 54 A5
Barrett's Gr N16 73 C3
Barrett's Green Rd
NW10 89 B5
Barrett St W1 93 A1 238 B1
Barrhill Rd SW2 160 A2
Barrie Ct EN5 14 A6
Barriedale SE14 141 A3
Barrie Ho 8 N16 73 C5
NW8 230 B5
W2 246 B5
Acton W3 111 A4
Edmonton N9 18 B4
Barrier Gdns Pier E16 121 D3
Barringer Sq SW17 181 A6
Barrington Cl NW5 71 A3
Barrington Ct 4 N10 31 B1
NW5 71 A3
31 SW9 138 A3
Barrington Prim Sch
DA16 146 D3
Barrington Rd N8 49 D4
SW9 138 D2
Bexley DA16 146 D3
Cheam SM3 201 C1
Little Ilford E12 78 C2
Barrington Villas
SE18 144 C4
Barrington Wlk 9
SE19 183 C4
Barrow Ave SM5 218 D1
Barrow Cl N21 16 D2
Barrow Ct 6 SE6 164 D3
Barrowdene Cl HA5 23 A1
Barrowell Gn N21 17 A2
Barrowfield Cl N9 18 C1
Barrowgate Ho W4 111 B1
Barrowgate Rd W4 111 B1
Barrow Hedges Cl
SM5 218 C1
Barrow Hedges Prim Sch
SM5 218 C1
Barrow Hedges Way
SM5 218 C1
Barrow Hill KT4 215 C6
Barrow Hill Cl KT4 215 C6
Barrow Hill Est
NW8 92 C5 230 A3
Barrow Hill Jun Sch
NW8 92 C5 230 A3
Barrow Hill Rd NW8 230 A3
Barrow Point Ave HA5 23 A1
Barrow Point La HA5 23 A1
Barrow Rd
Croydon CR0 220 C3
Streatham SW16 181 D4
Barrow Wlk TW8 109 C1
Barrs Rd NW10 67 B1
Barry Ave DA7 147 A5
N15 51 D3
Barry Cl BR6 227 C5
Barry Ct SW4 159 C5
Barrydene N20 14 B2
Barrydene Ct EN2 4 D2
Barry Ho 4 SE16 118 B1
Barry Lo N4 50 B2
Barry Par SE22 140 A1
Barry Rd E6 100 A1
NW10 67 A1
SE22 162 A6
Barry Terr TW15 148 B2
Barset Rd SE15 140 C2
Barsons Cl SE20 184 C3
Barston Rd SE27 161 A1
Barstow Cres SW2 160 B3
Bartell Ho SW2 160 C5
Barter St WC1 94 A2 240 B3
Bartholomew Cl EC1 242 A3
SW18 136 A1
Bartholomew Ct EC1 242 B6
Edgware HA8 25 D3
5 Poplar E14 120 B6
Bartholomew Ho
23 SE5 139 A3
Enfield EN3 7 A6
Enfield EN3 7 B6
Bartholomew La EC2 242 D1
Bartholomew Pas EC1 241 D3
Bartholomew Pl EC1 242 A3
Bartholomew Rd NW5 71 C2
Bartholomew Sq 18 E1 96 B3
Bartholomew St
SE1 117 B3 262 D5
Bartholomew Villas
NW5 71 C2
Barth Rd SE18 123 C2
Bartle Ave E6 100 A5
Bartle Rd W11 91 A1
Bartlett Cl E14 97 C1
Bartlett Ct EC4 241 B2
Bartletts Ho 10 RM10 81 D2
Bartlett St CR2 221 B3
Bartok Ho W11 244 C5
Bartolomew Sq EC1 242 B6
Barton Ave RM7 59 D1
Barton Cl E9 74 C3
NW4 46 A5
SE15 140 B2
Bexley DA6 169 A6
2 Newham E6 100 B1
Shepperton TW17 192 D3
Barton Ct 10 SW4 138 A3
W14 254 B2
Beckenham BR2 208 B6
Barton Gn KT3 177 B1
Barton Ho 8 E3 97 D4
N1 72 D1
SW6 135 D2
Barton Mdws IG6 57 A5
Barton Rd
W14 113 A1 254 B1
Sidcup DA14 191 A4
Barton St SW1 260 A6
Bartons The WD6 9 D5
Bartonway NW8 229 C4
Bartram Cl UB8 82 D3
Bartram Rd SE4 163 A5
Bartrams La EN4 2 A5
Bartrip St E9 75 B2
Barts Cl BR3 207 C4
Barville Cl SE4 141 A1
Barwell Ho 6 E2 96 A3
Barwick Dr UB8 82 D2
Barwick Ho 7 W3 111 A4
Barwick Rd E7 77 B4
Barwood Ave BR4 207 D1
Bascome St 13 SW2 160 C5
Basden Gr TW13 151 C2
Basedale Rd RM9 80 B1
Baseing Cl E6 122 C6
Basevi Way SE8 141 D6
Bashley Rd NW10 89 B3
Basil Ave E6 100 A4
Basildene Rd TW4,
TW5 128 D2
Basildon Rd SE2 124 A1
Basil Gdns
Croydon CR0 206 D1
West Norwood SE27 183 A5
Basil Ho 14 E1 96 A1
SW8 270 A4
Basil Mans SW1 247 C1
Basilon Rd DA7 147 A3
Basil Spence Ho N22 32 B2
Basil St SW1 114 D3 247 C1
SW1,SW3 114 D3 257 C6
Basin App 22 E14 97 A1
Basing Cl KT7 196 D2
Basing Ct 12 SE15 139 D4
Basingdon Way SE5 139 B1
Basing Dr DA5 169 B5
Basingfield Rd KT7 196 D2
Basinghall Ave
EC2 95 B1 242 C2
Basinghall St
EC2 95 B1 242 C2
Basing Hill NW11 47 B1
Wembley HA9 44 C1
Basing Ho
7 Barking IG11 101 B6
Catford SE6 185 C6
Basing House Yd 23 E2 95 C4
Basing Pl E2 95 C4
Basing St W11 91 B1
Basing Way N3 47 D6
Thames Ditton KT7 196 D2
Basire St N1 95 A6 235 B6
Baskerville Gdns NW10 67 C4
Baskerville Rd SW18 158 C4
Basket Gdns SE9 166 A6
Baslow Cl HA3 24 B2
Baslow Wlk E5 74 D4
Basnett Rd 8 SW11 137 A2
Basque Ct 21 SE16 118 D4
Bassano St SE22 161 D6
Bassant Rd SE18 145 D6
Bassein Park Rd W12 111 D4
Bassett Gdns TW7 130 A5
Bassett Ho RM9 102 B6
Bassett Rd W10 90 D1
Bassetts Cl BR6 226 D4
Bassett St NW5 71 A2
Bassetts Way BR6 226 D4
Bassett Way UB1 85 D1
Bassingbourn Ho 3
N1 72 D1
Bassingham Rd
Wandsworth SW18 158 A4
Wembley HA0 65 D2
Bassishaw Highwalk
EC2 242 C3
Basswood Cl SE15 140 B2
Bastable Ave IG11 102 A5
Basterfield Ho EC1 242 A5
Bastion Rd SE18,SE2 124 A1
Baston Manor Rd BR2,
BR4 225 B4
Baston Rd BR2 225 B5
Baston Sch BR2 225 B6
Bastwick St EC1 95 A3 242 A6
Basuto Rd
SW6 135 C4 265 B1
Batavia Cl TW16 172 C2
Batavia Ho 1 SE14 141 A5
Batavia Mews 3 SE14 141 A5
Batavia Rd SE14 141 A5
Sunbury TW16 172 B2
Batchelor St N1 94 C6 234 B5
Bateman Cl IG11 79 A2
Bateman Ho 8 SE17 138 D6
Bateman Rd E4 35 C4
Bateman's Bldgs W1 239 C1
Bateman's Row
EC2 95 C3 243 B6
Bateman St W1 93 D1 239 C1
Bates Cres
Croydon CR0 220 C3
Streatham SW16 181 C3
Bateson St SE18 123 C2
Bates Point E13 99 A6
Bate St 10 E14 119 B6
Bath Cl SE15 140 B5
Bath Ct EC1 235 C1
EC1 241 A5
3 Forest Hill SE26 162 A1
Bathgate Ho 8 SW9 138 D4
Bathgate Rd SW19 156 D1
Bath Gr E2 96 A5
Bath Ho E2 96 A3
SE1 262 B6
Bath House Rd CR0 204 A1
Bath Pas KT1 175 D1
Bath Pl 11 EC2 95 C4
14 W6 112 C1
Barnet EN5 1 B2
Bath Rd E7 77 D2
Bath Rd *continued*
N9 18 C2
W4 111 C2
Cranford TW3,TW4,TW5 128 C4
Dagenham RM6 59 A3
Harlington TW6,UB7,
TW5 127 B4
Harmondsworth TW6,
UB7 126 B4
Baths App
SW6 135 B5 264 D4
Baths Rd BR1,BR2 209 D5
Bath St EC1 95 B4 235 C1
Bath Terr SE1 117 A3 262 A6
Bathurst Ave SW19 179 D2
Bathurst Gdns NW10 90 B5
Bathurst Ho 2 W12 112 B6
Bathurst Mews
W2 114 B6 246 D6
Bathurst Rd IG1 56 D1
Bathurst St W2 246 D6
Bathway 17 SE18 122 C2
Batley Cl CR4 202 D2
Batley Pl 3 N16 73 D5
Batley Rd N16 73 D5
Enfield EN2 5 B4
Batman Cl W12 112 B5
Batoum Gdns W6 112 C3
Batson Ho 21 E1 96 A1
Batson St W12 112 A4
Batsworth Rd CR4 202 B6
Battenberg Wlk 10
SE19 183 C5
Batten Cl E6 100 B1
Batten Ho 8 E17 53 D6
7 SW4 159 C6
13 W10 91 A4
Batten St SW11 136 C2
Battersby Rd SE6 164 B1
Battersea Bridge Rd
SW11 136 C5 267 A3
Battersea Church Rd
SW11 136 B4 266 D2
Battersea Dogs Home
SW8 137 B5 268 D3
Battersea Park★
SW11 137 A5 268 A3
Battersea Park Rd
SW11,SW8 267 D1
Battersea Park Sta
SW8 137 B5 268 C3
Battersea Power
Station(dis)★
SW8 137 B6 268 D6
Battersea Rise SW11 136 C1
Battersea Sq SW11 266 D1
Battersea Tech Coll
SW11 136 D4 267 D1
Battery Rd SE28 123 C4
Battishill St 9 N1 72 D1
Battlebridge Ct NW1 233 B4
Battle Bridge Ctr
NW1 233 A4
Battle Bridge La
SE1 117 C5 253 A3
Battle Bridge Rd
NW1 94 A5 233 A4
Battle Cl SW19 180 A4
Battledean Rd N5 72 D3
Battle Ho 8 SE15 140 A6
Battle of Britain Mus★
NW9 27 D1
Batty St E1 96 A1
Baty Ho SW2 160 B3
Baudwin Rd SE6 164 C2
Baugh Rd DA14 190 C5
Baulk The SW18 157 C4
Bavant Rd SW16 182 B1
Bavaria Rd N19 72 A6
Bavent Rd SE5 139 A3
Bawdale Rd SE22 161 D6
Bawdsey Ave IG2 57 D5
Bawtree Rd SE14 141 A5
Bawtry Rd N20 14 D1
Baxendale N20 14 A2
Baxendale St E2 96 A4
Baxter Cl
Hillingdon UB10 82 D4
Southall UB2 107 D3
Baxter Ho 11 E3 97 D4
Baxter Rd N1 73 B2
Edmonton N18 34 B6
Ilford IG1 78 D3
Newham E16 99 C1
Bayard Ct DA7 147 D1
Baycliffe Ho 8 E9 74 D2
Baycroft Cl HA5 40 C6
Bay Ct 7 E1 96 D3
W5 110 A3
Baydene Mews NW4 46 B5
Baydon Ct BR2 208 D6
Bayer Ho EC1 242 A5
Bayes Ct NW3 70 D1
Bayeux Ho 10 SE7 143 C6
Bayfield Ho 3 SE4 140 D1
Bayfield Rd SE9 143 D1
Bayford Rd NW10 90 D4
Bayford St 5 E8 74 B1
Bayford St Ind Ctr 4
E8 74
Bayham Pl NW1 93 C6 232
Bayham Rd W4 111
Ealing W13 109
Morden SM4 202
Bayham St NW1 93 C6 232
Bayhurst Lo N4 51
Bayhurst Wood Countrysi
Park UB9 38
Bayleaf Cl TW12 174
Bayley St WC1 239
Bayley Wlk SE2 125
Baylis Mews TW1 153
Baylis Rd SE1 116 C4 251
Bayliss Ave SE28 124
Bayliss Cl N21 16
Bayne Cl E6 100
Baynes Cl EN1 6
Baynes Mews 2 NW3 70
Baynes St NW1 71
Baynham Cl DA5 169
Bayon Ho 27 N19 49
Bayonne Rd W6 264
Bays Cl SE26 184
Bays Ct HA8 26
Bayshill Rise UB5 63
Bayston Rd N16 73
Bayswater Rd
W2 114 B6 246
Bayswater Sta
W2 113 D6 245
Baythorne St 5 E3 97
Bayton Ct 2 E8 74
Baytree Cl DA15 167
Bromley BR1 187
Baytree Ho E4 19
Baytree Rd SW2 138
Bazalgette Cl KT3 199
Bazalgette Gdns KT3 199
Bazalgette Ho NW8 236
Bazeley Ho SE1 251
Bazely St E14 120
Bazile Rd N21 16
BBC Television Ctr
W12 112
Beacham Cl SE7 143
Beachborough Rd
BR1 186
Beachcroft Ave UB1 107
Beachcroft Rd E11 76
Beach Ct SE9 166
Beach Gr TW13 151
Beach Ho SW5 255
Beachy Rd E3 75
Beaconfield Terrace Rd
W14 254
Beacon Gate SE14 140
Beacon Gr SM5 219
Beacon Hill N7 72
Beacon Ho 19 SE5 139
SW8 269
10 Penge SE26 184
Beacon House Sch
W5 110
Beacon Pl CR0 220
Beacon Rd SE13 164
Harlington TW19,TW6 148
Beacon Rdbt TW6 148
Beacons Cl 10 E6 100
Beaconsfield Cl N11 31
SE3 143
W4 111
Beaconsfield Ct N11 31
Beaconsfield Gdns
KT10 212
Beaconsfield Par 1
SE9 188
Beaconsfield Prim Sch
UB2 107
Beaconsfield Rd BR1 209
E10 76
E16 98
E17 53
N11 31
N15 51
NW10 67
SE17 117 C1 263
SE9 188
W4 111
W5 109
Claygate KT10 212
Edmonton N9 18
Enfield EN3 6
Greenwich SE3 143
Hayes UB4 106
Kingston KT3 177
Southall UB1 107
Surbiton KT5 198
Thornton Heath CR0 205
Twickenham TW1 153
Beaconsfield Wlk
SW6 135 B4 264
Beaconshaw BR1 186
Beacontree Ave E17 36
Beacontree Rd E11 54
Beadle Ct CR4 202
Beadlow Cl SM4 202
Beadman Pl SE27 182

eadman St SE27 182 D6
eadnell Rd SE23 162 D3
eadon Rd BR2 209 A4
V6 112 C2
eaford Gr SW20 201 B6
eagle Cl TW13 172 B6
eak St W1 115 C6 249 B6
eal Cl DA16 146 A4
eale Cl N13 32 D5
eale Ho 7 SW9 138 B3
eale Pl E3 97 B5
eale Rd E3 97 B6
eal High Sch IG5 56 A5
eal Rd IG1 78 C6
eam Ave RM10 103 D6
eames Ho SW8 269 C2
eaminster Ct N15 51 B4
eaminster Gdns IG6 56 D6
eaminster Ho SW8 270 C4
eamish Dr WD23 8 A3
eamish Ho 5 SE16 118 C2
eamish Rd N9 18 A3
eanacre Cl E9 75 B2
ean Rd DA6 146 D1
eanshaw SE9 188 C6
eansland Gr RM6 59 A6
ear Alley EC4 241 C2
ear Cl RM7 59 D3
ear Croft Ho 6 SW6 135 B3
eardell St SE19 183 D4
eardow Gr N14 15 C5
eard Rd TW10 176 B5
eardsfield E13 99 A5
eard's Hill TW12 173 C2
eards Hill Cl TW12 173 C2
eardsley Terr RM8 80 B3
eardsley Way W3 111 B4
eard's Rd TW15,TW16 171 C4
earfield Rd KT2 176 A3
ear Gardens Mus*
SE1 117 A5 252 A4
ear Gdns SE1 117 A5 252 A4
ear La SE1 116 D5 251 D3
ear Rd TW13 172 D6
ear St WC2 249 D6
earstead Rise SE4 163 B6
earsted Terr 2 BR3 185 C2
easley's Ait TW17 193 D3
easley's Ait La TW16,
TW17 193 D3
eaton Cl SE15 139 D4
eatrice Ave
Thornton Heath SW16 182 B1
Wembley HA9 66 A3
eatrice Cl E13 99 A3
Pinner HA5 40 A5
eatrice Ct NW4 46 C4
Buckhurst Hill IG9 21 D2
eatrice Ho 1 SW2 160 B6
4 W6 112 C1
eatrice Pl W8 255 C5
eatrice Rd E17 53 C4
N4 50 C2
N9 18 C4
SE1 118 A2
2 Richmond TW10 154 B6
Southall UB1 107 B5
eatrice Tate Sch E2 96 B4
eatrice Webb Ho 3
E3 97 A5
eatrix Ho SW5 255 D2
eatrix Potter Prim Sch
SW18 158 A3
eattie Cl TW14 149 D3
eattie Ho SW8 269 B2
eattock Rise N10 49 B5
eatty Rd N16 73 C4
Stanmore HA7 25 C4
eatty St NW1 232 A4
eattyville Gdns IG6 56 D5
eauchamp Cl 16 W4 111 A3
eauchamp Ct HA7 25 C5
eauchamp Pl
SW3 114 C3 257 B5
eauchamp Rd E7 77 B1
SW11 136 D1
East Molesey KT8 196 A4
South Norwood SE19 183 B2
Sutton SM1 217 C4
Twickenham TW1 153 A4
eauchamp St EC1 241 A3
eauchamp Terr
SW15 134 B2
eauclerc Cty Inf Sch
TW16 194 C6
eauclerc Rd W6 112 B3
eauclere Ho 1 SM2 218 A1
eauclerk Cl TW13 150 B3
eauclerk Ho 10
SW16 160 A1
eaudesert Mews
UB7 104 A4
eaufort E6 100 C2
eaufort Ave HA3 43 B6
eaufort Cl Chingford E4 35 D4
Ealing W5 88 B2
Putney SW19 156 B4
eaufort Ct N11 31 B5
New Barnet EN5 14 A6

Beaufort Ct *continued*
Richmond TW10 175 C6
Beaufort Dr NW11 47 C5
Beaufort Gdns NW4 46 C3
SW3 114 C3 257 B6
Heston TW5 129 A4
Ilford IG1 56 C1
South Norwood SW16 182 B3
Beaufort Ho 7 N15 51 D5
NW11 48 A3
SW1 259 C1
SW11 136 C3
SW3 266 D5
1 Wimbledon SW20 178 D2
Beaufort Mans SW3 266 D5
Beaufort Mews SW6 264 D6
Beaufort Pk NW11 47 C5
Beaufort Rd Ealing W5 88 B2
Kingston KT1,KT5,KT6 198 A5
Richmond TW10 175 C6
Ruislip HA4 61 B6
Twickenham TW1 153 C4
Beaufort St
SW3 136 B6 266 C6
Beaufort Way KT17 216 A1
Beaufoy Ho SW8 270 C4
3 West Norwood SE27 160 D1
Beaufoy Rd 11 SW8 137 B2
Tottenham N17 33 C3
Beaufoy Wlk
SE11 116 B2 260 D3
Beaulieu Ave 1 E16 121 B5
Forest Hill SE26 184 B6
Beaulieu Cl NW9 45 C5
SE5 139 B2
Hounslow TW4 151 B6
Mitcham CR4 181 A2
13 Twickenham TW1 153 D5
Beaulieu Ct W5 88 A2
Beaulieu Dr HA5 40 D2
Beaulieu Gdns N21 17 A4
Beaulieu Ho NW4 28 D1
Beaulieu Pl W4 111 A3
Beaumanor Gdns SE9 188 C6
Beaumanor Mans W2 245 D6
Beaumaris 4 N11 32 A4
Beaumaris Dr IG8 37 D3
Beaumaris Gn NW9 45 C3
Beaumaris Twr 2 W3 110 D4
Beaumont W14 254 D3
Putney SW15 157 A6
Beaumont Ave
W14 113 B1 254 C2
Harrow HA2 41 D3
Richmond TW9 132 B2
Wembley HA0 65 C4
Beaumont Bldgs WC2 240 B1
Beaumont Cl KT2 176 C3
Beaumont Cres
W14 113 B1 254 C1
Beaumont Ct E5 74 B5
16 NW9 27 D1
10 W4 111 A1
6 Mitcham CR4 181 A1
Wembley HA0 65 C3
16 Wimbledon SW19 178 D3
Beaumont Dr TW15 171 B5
Beaumont Gdns NW3 69 C5
Beaumont Gr E1 96 D3
Beaumont Ho 11 E10 53 D2
1 Streatham SW2 160 A3
Wimbledon SW19 157 C1
Beaumont Pl
NW1,WC1,W1 93 C3 239 B6
Barnet EN5 1 B4
Isleworth TW7 152 D6
Beaumont Rd E10 53 D2
E13 99 B4
W4 111 A3
Orpington BR5,BR6 211 B3
Putney SW15,SW19 157 A4
South Norwood SE19 183 A4
Beaumont Rise N19 49 D1
Beaumont Sch The E10 53 D1
Beaumont Sq E1 96 D2
Beaumont St W1 238 B4
Beaumont Terr 1
SE13 164 C4
Beaumont Wlk NW3 70 D1
Beauvais Terr UB5 84 D4
Beauvale 6 NW1 71 A1
Beauval Rd SE22 161 D5
Beaverbank Rd DA15,
SE9 167 B3
Beaver Cl
Hampton TW12 173 D2
9 Penge SE20 184 A3
Beaver Gr UB5 85 A4
Beavers Comm Prim Sch
TW4 128 C2
Beavers Cres TW4 128 D1
Beavers La TW4 128 C2
Beavers Lo DA14 189 D5
Beaverwood Rd BR7 189 C4
Beaverwood Sch for Girls
BR7 189 C4
Beavis Ho N16 73 C5
Beavor La W6 112 A1
Bebbington Rd SE18 123 C2

Beblets Cl 4 BR6 227 D3
Bec Cl HA4 62 D5
Beccles Dr IG11 79 D2
Beccles St E14 119 B6
Bechervaise Ct 2 E10 53 D1
Beck Cl SE13 141 D4
Beck Ct BR3 206 D6
Beckenham Bsns Ctr
BR3 185 A4
Beckenham Ct BR3 185 C2
Beckenham Gdns N9 17 C1
Beckenham Gr BR2 186 B1
Beckenham Hill Rd
BR3,SE6 186 A5
Beckenham Hill Sta
SE6 186 A5
Beckenham Hospl
BR3 185 B1
Beckenham Junction Sta
BR3 185 C2
Beckenham La BR1,
BR2 186 D1
Beckenham Place Pk
BR3 185 D3
Beckenham Rd
Penge BR3 185 A2
West Wickham BR3,BR4 208 A2
Beckenham Rd Sta
BR3 185 A2
Beckers The N16 74 A4
Becket Ave E6 100 C4
Becket Cl Croydon SE25 206 A3
2 Merton SW19 179 D2
Becket Fold HA1 42 D4
Becket Ho SE1 252 C1
Becket Rd N18 34 C6
Becket St SE1 262 C6
Beckett Cl DA17 125 B3
NW10 67 C2
Streatham SW16 159 D2
Beckett Ho 12 E1 96 C2
28 SW9 138 A3
Becketts Cl
Feltham TW14 150 B5
Orpington BR6 227 D5
Becketts Pl KT1 175 D2
Beckett Wlk BR3 185 A4
Beckfoot NW1 232 B3
Beckford Cl W14 254 D3
Beckford Dr BR5,BR6 211 B2
Beckford Ho 18 N16 73 C3
Beckford Prim Sch
NW6 69 B3
Beckford Rd CR0 205 D3
Beckham Ho SE11 260 D3
Beck Ho N16 73 C5
4 Edmonton N18 34 A5
Beckington 18 NW5 71 A2
Beck La BR3 206 D6
Beckley Ho E3 97 B3
Becklow Mews 7
W12 112 A4
Becklow Rd W12 112 A4
Beckmead Sch BR3 207 C1
Beck Rd E8 96 B6
Beck River Pk 3 BR3 185 C2
Becks Rd DA14 168 A1
Beckton Alps E6 100 C3
Beckton Alps Ski Ctr
E6 100 C3
Beckton Park Sta E16 122 B6
Beckton Rd E16 98 D2
Beckton Sta E6 100 C2
Beckton Triangle Ret Pk
E6 100 D3
Beck Way BR3 207 B6
Beckway Rd SW16 181 D1
Beckway St
SE17 117 C2 263 A3
Beckwith Ho 22 E2 96 B5
Beckwith Rd SE24 161 B6
Beclands Rd SW17 181 A4
Becmead Ave
Harrow HA3 43 B4
Streatham SW16 181 D6
Becondale Rd SE19 183 C5
Becontree Ave RM8 80 C5
Becontree Day RM8 81 A6
Becontree Prim Sch
RM8 80 B5
Becontree Sta RM9 80 D2
Bective Pl SW15 135 B1
Bective Rd E7 77 A4
Putney SW15 135 B1
Becton Pl
Erith DA7,DA8 147 D5
Erith DA8 147 D5
Bedale Rd EN2 5 A5
Bedale St SE1 252 C3
Beddington Cross
CR0 204 A2
Beddington Farm Rd
CR0 204 A1
Beddington Gdns SM5,
SM6 219 A2
Beddington Gn BR5 189 D2
Beddington Gr SM6 219 D3
Beddington Inf Sch
SM6 219 C4

Beddington La
Wallington CR0 220 A6
Wallington CR0 203 D2
Beddington Lane Sta
CR0 203 C3
Beddington Manor
SM2 218 B2
Beddington Park Cotts
SM6 219 D5
Beddington Park Prim Sch
CR0 219 D5
Beddington Rd BR5 189 D2
Ilford IG3 57 D2
Beddington Terr CR0 204 B2
Bede Cl HA5 22 D2
Bedefield WC1 233 B1
Bede Ho SE14 141 B4
5 Putney SW15 156 D5
Bedelsford Sch KT1 198 A6
Bedens Rd DA14 191 A5
Bede Rd RM6 58 C3
Bedfont Cl
East Bedfont TW14 149 A5
Mitcham CR4 181 A1
Bedfont Green Cl
TW14 149 A3
Bedfont Ind Pk N
TW15 149 A1
Bedfont Jun Sch
TW14 149 C5
Bedfont La TW14,
TW13 149 D4
Bedfont Lakes Ctry Pk
TW14 149 A2
Bedfont Rd
East Bedfont TW13,
TW14 149 B2
Stanwell TW19 148 B5
Bedford Ave
WC1 93 D2 239 D3
Barnet EN5 13 B6
Hayes UB4 84 B1
Bedfordbury
WC2 116 A6 250 A5
Bedford Cl N10 31 A3
Chiswick W4 133 D6
Bedford Cnr 3 W4 111 C2
Bedford Court Mans
WC1 239 D3
Bedford Ct WC2 250 A5
6 Richmond TW9 132 B1
South Norwood SE19 183 D2
Wembley HA0 65 D4
Bedford Gardens Ho
W8 245 B3
Bedford Gdns
W8 113 C5 245 B3
Bedford Hill SW12 159 B2
Bedford Ho 7 SW4 138 A1
2 W4 111 C2
Bedford Park Cnr 5
W4 111 C2
Bedford Park Mans
W4 111 B2
Bedford Pas SW6 264 B4
Bedford Pk CR0 205 A1
Bedford Pl WC1 94 A2 240 A4
Croydon CR0 205 B1
Bedford Rd E17 53 C6
N15 51 C5
N2 48 C6
N8 49 D3
NW7 11 C1
SW2,SW4 138 A1
W4 111 C3
Barking E6 100 C6
Ealing W13 109 B6
Edmonton N9 18 B4
Harrow HA1 42 A3
Ilford IG1 78 D5
North Cheam KT4 216 C6
Ruislip HA4 61 D4
Sidcup DA15 167 C1
Twickenham TW2 152 B1
Woodford E18 37 A1
Wood Green N22 32 A1
Bedford Row
WC1 94 B2 240 D3
Bedford Sq
WC1 93 D2 239 D3
Bedford St
WC2 116 A6 250 B5
Bedford Terr SM2 218 A2
Bedford Way
WC1 93 D3 239 D5
Bedgebury Gdns
SW19 157 A2
Bedgebury Rd SE9 143 D1
Bedivere Rd BR1 165 A1
Bedlow Cl NW8 236 D4
Bedlow Way CR0 220 B4
Bedonwell Inf Sch
SE2 147 A6
Bedonwell Jun Sch
DA17 147 A6
Bedonwell Rd
Bexley DA7,DA17 147 A6
Erith DA7 147 C5
Bedser Cl SE11 270 D6

Bedser Cl *continued*
South Norwood CR7 205 A6
Bedser Ct 7 SW4 138 A3
Bedser Dr UB6 64 B3
Bedster Gdns KT8 195 D6
Bedwardine Rd SE19 183 C3
Bedwell Ct 4 RM6 58 D2
Bedwell Gdns UB3 105 C2
Bedwell Ho 10 SW9 138 C3
Bedwell Rd
Belvedere DA17 125 C1
Tottenham N17 33 C2
Beeby Rd E16 99 B2
Beech Ave N20 14 C3
W3 111 C5
Brentford TW8 131 B5
Chigwell IG9 21 B2
Ruislip HA4 40 B1
Sidcup DA15 168 A4
Beech Cl SE8 141 B6
Ashford TW15 171 B5
Carshalton SM5 218 D6
Enfield N9 18 B5
Putney SW15 156 A4
Sunbury TW16 172 D1
West Drayton UB7 104 C3
Wimbledon SW19 178 C4
Beech Copse BR1 188 B1
South Croydon CR2 221 C3
Beechcroft BR7 188 C3
3 Kingston KT2 176 D2
Beechcroft Ave NW11 47 B2
Harrow HA2 41 C2
Kingston KT1,KT3 177 A1
Beechcroft Cl BR6 227 B4
Heston TW5 129 A5
Streatham SW16 182 B5
Beechcroft Ct 6 N12 29 D6
3 NW11 47 B2
Beech Croft Ct N5 72 D4
Beechcroft Gdns HA9 66 B5
Beechcroft Ho W5 88 A2
Beechcroft Lo 6 SM2 218 A1
Beechcroft Mans
SW16 182 B5
Beechcroft Rd BR6 227 B4
Chessington KT9 214 B5
Mortlake SW14 133 A2
Upper Tooting SW17 158 C2
Woodford E18 37 B1
Beechcroft Way N19 49 D1
Beech Ct E17 54 B6
NW2 69 B6
W1 237 C2
43 W2 91 C2
Beckenham BR3 185 B3
3 Buckhurst Hill IG9 21 D2
Hayes UB3 105 D5
6 Ilford E12 78 C5
Northolt UB5 85 A6
Surbiton KT6 198 A2
Teddington TW11 175 C4
4 West Norwood
SW16 182 C5
Beechdale N21 16 B2
Beechdale Rd SW2 160 B5
Beech Dell BR2,BR6 226 B4
Beechdene 4 SE15 140 B4
Beech Dr N2 48 D6
Beechen Cliff Way
TW7 130 D3
Beechen Gr HA5 41 B6
Beechen Pl SE23 162 C2
Beeches Ave The SM5 218 C1
Beeches Cl SE20 184 C2
Beeches Ct BR1 187 A4
Beeches Rd
Cheam SM3 201 A1
Upper Tooting SW17 158 D1
Beeches The E12 78 B1
1 N19 50 A1
N20 14 C2
Hounslow TW3 129 D4
Mitcham CR4 202 C4
Beechey Ho 30 E1 118 B5
Beech Farm Cotts IG8 36 B3
Beechfield Cotts 3
BR1 187 C1
Beechfield Ct 7 CR2 221 A4
Beechfield Rd BR1 187 C1
N4 51 A3
Forest Hill SE6 163 B3
Beech Gdns W5 110 A3
Dagenham RM10 81 D1
Beech Gr Kingston KT3 199 B6
Mitcham CR4 203 D5
Beech Hall Cres E4 36 B3
Beech Hall Rd E4 36 B3
Beech Hill EN4 2 C5
Beech Hill Ave EN4 2 B4
Beechhill Rd SE9 166 C6
Beech Ho 7 DA15 168 A1
5 N16 73 B6
6 NW3 70 D2
16 SE16 118 C4
Hayes UB4 84 D2
Heston TW5 129 A5
New Addington CR0 223 D2
Beech House Rd CR0 221 B5

Beech La IG9 21 B2
Beech Lawns N12 30 B5
Beechmont Cl BR1 186 C5
Beechmore Gdns SM3 216 D6
Beechmore Rd
SW11 136 D4 267 D1
Beechmount Ave W7 86 C2
Beecholme 13 N12 29 D6
Beecholme Ave CR4 181 B2
Beecholme Est E5 74 B5
Beecholme Prim Sch
CR4 181 B2
Beech Rd
Bowes Park N11 32 A4
East Bedfont TW14 149 C4
Thornton Heath SW16 204 B6
Beechrow KT2 176 A6
Beech St EC2 95 A2 242 B4
Beech Tree Cl N1 72 C1
Stanmore HA7 25 C5
Beech Tree Glade E4 20 D3
Beech Tree Pl SM1 217 D3
Beechvale Cl N12 30 C5
Beechway DA5 168 D5
Beech Way NW10 67 B1
Twickenham TW2 151 C1
Beech Wlk NW7 27 C4
Beechwood Ave N3 47 C6
Ashford TW16 172 A4
Greenford UB6 85 D4
Harrow HA2 63 D5
Hayes UB3 105 B6
Hillingdon UB8 82 C1
Orpington BR6 227 C2
Richmond TW9 132 C4
Ruislip HA4 61 D6
Thornton Heath CR7 204 D5
Beechwood Circ HA2 63 D5
Beechwood Cl N2 48 D5
NW7 27 C5
Surbiton KT6 197 D2
Beechwood Cres DA7 147 A2
Beechwood Ct N16 51 C2
Carshalton SM5 218 D4
Chiswick W4 133 B6
Sutton SM1 217 C3
Beechwood Dr
Keston BR2 225 D4
Woodford IG8 36 D5
Beechwood Gdns
Ealing NW10 88 B4
Harrow HA2 63 D5
Ilford IG5 56 C5
Beechwood Gr W3 111 C6
Beechwood Hall N3 47 B6
Beechwood Ho 22 E2 96 A5
Beechwood Mews 2
N9 18 A2
Beechwood Pk E18 55 A6
Beechwood Rd E8 73 D2
N8 50 A5
South Croydon CR2 221 C1
Beechwood Rise BR7 188 D6
Beechwoods Ct SE19 183 D5
Beechworth Cl NW3 69 C6
Beecroft Rd SE4 163 A6
Beehive Cl E8 73 D1
Elstree WD6 9 D5
Hillingdon UB10 60 B1
Beehive Ct IG1 56 B3
Beehive La IG1 56 B3
Beehive Pl SW9 138 C2
Beehive Prep Sch IG4 56 B4
Beeken Dene BR6 227 A4
Beeleigh Rd SM4 201 D5
Beeston Cl 3 E8 74 A3
South Oxhey WD19 22 D6
Beeston Pl SW1 258 D6
Beeston Rd EN4 14 B5
Beeston's Ho SE15 140 B2
Beeston Way TW14 150 C5
Beethoven Rd WD6 9 D5
Beethoven St W10 91 A4
Beeton Cl HA5 23 C3
Begbie Ho SW9 138 B3
Begbie Rd SE3 143 C4
Beggars Hill KT17 215 D2
Beggar's Roost La
SM1,SM2 217 C2
Begonia Cl E6 100 B3
Begonia Pl 1 TW12 173 C4
Begonia Wlk W12 89 D1
Beira St SW12 159 B4
Beis Rachel D'Satmar Girls
Sch N16 51 C2
Beis Yaakov Prim Sch
NW9 45 B6
Bekesbourne St 19 E14 97 A1
Belcroft Cl BR1 186 D3
Beldanes Lo NW10 68 A1
Beldham Gdns KT8 195 D6
Belenoyd Ct SW16 160 B1
Belfairs Dr RM6 58 C2
Belfairs Gn WD19 22 D5
Belfast Rd N16 73 D6
Croydon SE25 206 B5

Belfield Rd KT19 ... 215 C1
Belfont Wlk N7 ... 72 A4
Belford Gr SE18 ... 122 C2
Belford Ho 7 E8 ... 95 D6
Belfort Rd SE15 ... 140 C3
Belfry Cl 33 SE16 ... 118 B1
Belgrade Ho N16 ... 73 C4
Belgrade Rd N16 ... 73 C4
Hampton TW12 ... 173 D2
Belgrave Cl NW7 ... 27 B5
1 Acton W3 ... 111 A4
Southgate N14 ... 15 C6
Belgrave Cres TW16 ... 172 B2
Belgrave Ct E13 ... 99 C3
SE3 ... 143 C5
SW8 ... 269 A3
8 W4 ... 111 A1
Belgrave Gdns NW8 ... 91 D6
Southgate N14 ... 3 D1
1 Stanmore HA7 ... 25 C5
Belgrave Mans NW8 ... 229 A5
Belgrave Mews N
SW1 ... 248 A1
Belgrave Mews S
SW1 ... 115 A3 258 B6
Belgrave Mews W
SW1 ... 258 A6
Belgrave Pl
SW1 ... 115 A3 258 B5
Belgrave Rd E10 ... 54 A1
E13 ... 99 C3
E17 ... 53 C3
SW1 ... 115 C2 259 A3
Barnes SW13 ... 133 D5
Hounslow TW4 ... 129 B2
Mitcham CR4 ... 202 B6
Redbridge IG1 ... 56 B1
South Norwood SE25 ... 205 D5
Sunbury TW16 ... 172 B2
Wanstead E11 ... 55 A1
Belgrave Sq
SW1 ... 115 A3 258 A6
Belgrave St E1 ... 96 D1
Belgrave Terr IG8 ... 21 A1
Belgrave Wlk CR4 ... 202 B6
Belgrave Wlk Sta CR4 202 B5
Belgrave Yd SW1 ... 258 C5
Belgravia Cl EN5 ... 1 B2
Belgravia Ct SW1 ... 258 C5
Belgravia Gdns BR1 ... 186 C4
Belgravia Ho 11 SW4 ... 159 D5
Teddington TW11 ... 175 C3
Belgravia Mews KT1 ... 197 D5
Belgrove St WC1 ... 233 B2
Belham Wlk 13 SE5 ... 139 B4
Belinda Rd 8 SW9 ... 138 D2
Belitha Villas N1 ... 72 C1
Bel La TW13 ... 151 B1
Bellamy Cl 7 E14 ... 119 C4
HA8 ... 11 A1
SW5 ... 254 D1
Uxbridge UB10 ... 60 C5
Bellamy Ct HA7 ... 25 B2
Bellamy Dr HA7 ... 25 B2
Bellamy Ho Harrow HA3 44 A2
Heston TW5 ... 129 C6
Upper Tooting SW17 ... 180 B6
Bellamy Rd Chingford E4 35 D4
Enfield EN2 ... 5 B3
Bellamy's Ct 16 SE16 ... 118 D5
Bellamy St SW12 ... 159 B4
Bellasis Ave SW2 ... 160 A2
Bell Ave UB7 ... 104 B3
Bell Cl Pinner HA5 ... 40 C6
Ruislip HA4 ... 61 D5
Bellclose Rd UB7 ... 104 A4
Bell Ct NW4 ... 46 C5
Tolworth KT5 ... 214 D6
Bell Dr SW18 ... 157 A4
Bellefields Rd SW9 ... 138 B2
Bellegrove Cl DA16 ... 145 D3
Bellegrove Par DA16 ... 145 D2
Bellegrove Rd DA16 ... 145 D3
Bellenden Rd SE15 ... 139 D3
Bellenden Rd Ret Pk
SE15 ... 140 A4
Bellenden Sch SE15 ... 140 A3
Bellendon Road Bsns Ctr
SE15 ... 139 D3
Bellerbys Coll SW15 ... 156 A5
Bellermine Cl SE28 ... 123 D4
Belle Staines Pleasaunce
E4 ... 19 C2
Belleville Prim Sch
SW11 ... 158 D6
Belleville Rd SW11 ... 158 D6
Belle Vue UB6 ... 86 B6
Belle Vue Gdns SW9 ... 138 A3
Belle Vue La WD23 ... 8 B3
Bellevue Pk CR7 ... 205 A5
Bellevue Pl E1 ... 96 C3
Bellevue Rd DA6 ... 169 B6
N11 ... 31 A5
Barnes SW13 ... 134 A3
Ealing W13 ... 87 B3
Kingston KT1 ... 198 A6

Bellevue Rd *continued*
Upper Tooting SW17 ... 158 D3
Belle Vue Rd E17 ... 36 B1
Bellew St SW17 ... 158 A1
Bellfield CR0 ... 223 B1
Bellfield Ave HA3 ... 24 B4
Bellflower Cl 2 E6 ... 100 A2
Bellgate Mews NW5 ... 71 B5
Bell Gn SE26 ... 185 B6
Bell Green La SE26 ... 185 B6
Bellhill 6 CR0 ... 221 A6
Bell Ho SE10 ... 142 A6
SE2 ... 124 D1
6 Dagenham RM10 ... 81 D2
15 Streatham SW2 ... 160 C4
Bellina Mews NW5 ... 71 C4
Bell Ind Est 2 W4 ... 111 A2
Bellingham 10 N17 ... 34 B3
Bellingham Ct IG11 ... 102 B4
Bellingham Gn SE6 ... 163 C1
Bellingham Rd SE6 ... 164 A1
Bellingham Sta SE6 ... 163 D1
Bellingham Trad Est
SE6 ... 163 D2
Bell Inn Yd EC3 ... 242 D1
Bell La E1 ... 95 D2 243 C3
E16 ... 121 A5
NW4 ... 46 D5
Enfield EN3 ... 6 D5
Twickenham TW1 ... 153 A3
Wembley HA9 ... 65 D6
Bell Lane Prim Sch
NW4 ... 46 D5
Bellmaker Ct 19 E3 ... 97 C2
Bell Mdw SE19 ... 183 C6
Bell Moor NW3 ... 70 A5
Bellmore Ct 5 CR0 ... 205 D1
Bello Cl SE24,SW2 ... 160 D3
Bellot Gdns 1 SE10 ... 120 C1
Bellot St SE10 ... 120 C1
Bell Rd
East Molesey KT8 ... 196 B4
Enfield EN1 ... 5 B4
Hounslow TW3 ... 129 D1
Bellring Cl DA17 ... 147 C6
Bells Hill EN5 ... 12 D6
Bell St NW1 ... 92 C2 237 A4
SE18 ... 144 A4
Bell The E17 ... 53 C6
Belltrees Gr 1 SW16 ... 182 C5
Bell View BR3 ... 185 B3
Bell View Manor HA4 ... 39 C2
Bellview Mews N11 ... 31 A5
Bell Water Gate SE18 ... 122 C3
Bell Wharf La EC4 ... 252 B6
Bellwood Rd SE15 ... 140 D1
Bell Yd WC2 ... 94 C1 241 A1
Belmont Ave DA16 ... 145 C2
N17 ... 51 A6
Bowes Park N13 ... 32 B5
Cockfosters EN4 ... 14 D6
Edmonton N9 ... 18 A3
Southall UB2 ... 107 A3
Wembley HA0 ... 88 B6
West Barnes KT3 ... 200 A5
Belmont Circ HA3 ... 25 B2
Belmont Cl N20 ... 13 D3
SW4 ... 137 C2
Chingford E4 ... 36 B5
Cockfosters EN4 ... 2 D1
Uxbridge UB8 ... 60 A2
Woodford IG8 ... 37 B6
Belmont Ct 6 N16 ... 51 C1
N5 ... 73 A4
NW11 ... 47 B4
Belmont Gr SE13 ... 142 B2
W4 ... 111 B2
Belmont Hall Ct SE13 ... 142 B2
Belmont Hill SE13 ... 142 B2
Belmont Jun & Inf Schs
N22 ... 51 A6
Belmont La
Chislehurst BR7 ... 189 A5
Stanmore HA7 ... 25 C3
Belmont Lo Harrow HA3 24 B3
Stanmore HA7 ... 25 C6
Belmont Mews SW19 ... 156 D2
Belmont Mid Sch HA3 ... 24 D1
Belmont Mill Hill Jun Sch
NW7 ... 12 A1
Belmont Par 2 NW11 ... 47 B4
Chislehurst BR7 ... 189 A5
Belmont Park Cl SE13 142 C1
Belmont Park Rd E10 ... 53 D3
Belmont Pk SE13 ... 142 C1
Belmont Prim Sch W4 111 B2
Erith DA7 ... 147 C5
Belmont Rd N15,N17 ... 51 A5
SW4 ... 137 C2
W4 ... 111 B2
Beckenham BR3 ... 185 B1
Chislehurst BR7 ... 188 D5
Croydon SE25 ... 206 B4
Erith DA8 ... 147 D4
Harrow HA3 ... 43 A6
Ilford IG1 ... 79 A5
Twickenham TW2 ... 152 B2
Uxbridge UB8 ... 60 A2
Wallington SM6 ... 219 C3

Belmont Rise SM1,SM2 217 B1
Belmont St NW1 ... 71 A1
Belmont Terr W4 ... 111 B2
Belmor WD6 ... 10 C5
Belmore Ave UB4 ... 84 A1
Belmore Ho N7 ... 71 D3
Belmore Prim Sch UB4 84 B4
Belmore St
SW8 ... 137 D4 269 C2
Beloe Cl SW15 ... 134 A1
Belsham St E9 ... 74 C2
Belsize Ave NW3 ... 70 C3
W13 ... 109 B3
Bowes Park N13 ... 32 B4
Belsize Court Garages 1
NW3 ... 70 B3
Belsize Cres NW3 ... 70 B2
Belsize Ct NW3 ... 70 B3
Belsize Gdns SM1 ... 217 D4
Belsize Gr NW3 ... 70 C2
Belsize La NW3 ... 70 B3
Belsize Mews NW3 ... 70 B2
Belsize Park Gdns NW3 70 C2
Belsize Park Mews 1
NW3 ... 70 B2
Belsize Park Sta NW3 ... 70 C3
Belsize Pk NW3 ... 70 B2
Belsize Pl NW3 ... 70 B3
Belsize Rd NW6 ... 91 D6
NW8 ... 229 A6
Harrow HA3 ... 24 B3
Belsize Sq NW3 ... 70 B2
Belsize Terr NW3 ... 70 B2
Belson Rd SE18 ... 122 B2
Beltane Dr SW19 ... 156 D1
Belthorn Cres SW12 ... 159 C4
Belton Rd E11 ... 76 C4
E7 ... 77 B1
N17 ... 51 C6
NW2 ... 68 A2
Sidcup DA14 ... 190 A6
Belton Way E3 ... 97 C2
Beltran Rd SW6 ... 135 D3
Belvedere Ave SW19 ... 179 A5
Belvedere Bldgs SE1 ... 251 D1
Belvedere Cl TW11 ... 174 C5
Belvedere Ct DA17 ... 125 B3
N2 ... 48 B4
NW2 ... 68 D2
7 SW4 ... 159 D5
8 Kingston KT2 ... 176 C3
Putney SW15 ... 134 C1
Belvedere Dr SW19 ... 179 A5
Belvedere Gdns KT8 ... 195 C4
Belvedere Gr SW19 ... 179 A5
Belvedere Heights
NW8 ... 237 A6
Belvedere Ho TW14 ... 150 A3
Belvedere Jun & Inf Sch
DA17 ... 125 D3
Belvedere Mews SE15 140 C2
SE3 ... 143 B5
Belvedere Pl SE1 ... 251 D1
18 SW2 ... 138 B1
Belvedere Rd
SE1 ... 116 B4 250 D3
W7 ... 108 D3
Bexley DA7 ... 147 B3
Erith SE28 ... 124 D5
Penge SE19 ... 183 D3
Walthamstow E10 ... 53 A1
Belvedere Sq SW19 ... 179 A5
Belvedere Sta DA17 ... 125 D3
Belvedere Strand NW9 ... 27 D1
Belvedere The SW10 ... 266 B1
Belvedere Way HA3 ... 44 A3
Belvoir Cl SE9 ... 166 A1
Belvoir Lo SE22 ... 162 A4
Belvoir Rd SE22 ... 162 A4
Belvue Bsns Ctr UB5 ... 63 D1
Belvue Cl UB5 ... 63 C1
Belvue Rd UB5 ... 63 C1
Belvue Sch UB5 ... 85 C6
Bembridge Cl NW6 ... 69 A1
Bembridge Gdns HA4 ... 61 B6
Bembridge Ho 8 SE8 119 B2
Wandsworth SW18 ... 157 D5
Bemersyde Point 6
E13 ... 99 B4
Bemerton St N1 94 B6 233 C6
Bemish Rd SW15 ... 134 D2
Bempton Dr HA4 ... 62 B5
Bemsted Rd E17 ... 53 B6
Benabo Ct 6 E8 ... 74 A3
Benares Rd SE18,SE2 ... 123 D2
Benbow Ct W6 ... 112 B3
Benbow Ho 12 SE8 ... 141 C6
Benbow Rd W6 ... 112 B3
Benbow St SE8 ... 141 C6
Benbury Cl BR1 ... 186 A5
Bence Ho 13 SE8 ... 119 A2
Bench Field CR2 ... 221 D3
Bencroft Rd SW16 ... 181 C3
Bencurtis Pk BR4 ... 224 B6
Bendall Mews NW1 ... 237 B4
Bendemeer Rd SW15 ... 134 D2
Benden Ho SE13 ... 164 A6
Bendish Rd E6 ... 78 A1
Bendmore Ave SE2 ... 124 A2

Bendon Valley SW18 ... 157 D4
Benedict Cl BR6 ... 227 C5
9 Erith DA17 ... 125 A3
Benedict Ct RM9 ... 59 B3
Benedict Dr TW14 ... 149 B4
Benedict Fst Sch CR4 ... 202 B6
Benedict Prim Sch
CR4 ... 202 B6
Benedict Rd SW9 ... 138 B2
Mitcham CR4 ... 202 B6
Benedict Way N2 ... 48 A6
Benedict Wharf CR4 ... 202 C6
Benenden Gn BR2 ... 209 A4
Benenden Ho SE17 ... 263 B2
Benett Gdns SW16 ... 182 A1
Ben Ezra Ct SE17 ... 262 B3
Benfleet Cl SM1 ... 218 A5
Benfleet Ct 6 E8 ... 95 D6
Benfleet Way N11 ... 15 A2
Bengal Ct EC3 ... 242 D1
Bengal Ho E1 ... 96 D2
Bengal Rd IG1 ... 78 D5
Bengarth Dr HA3 ... 24 B1
Bengarth Rd UB5 ... 85 A6
Bengeo Gdns RM6 ... 58 C3
Bengeworth Rd SE5 ... 139 A2
Harrow HA1 ... 65 A5
Ben Hale Cl HA7 ... 25 B5
Benham Cl 1 SW11 ... 136 B2
Chessington KT9 ... 213 C2
Benham Gdns TW3,
TW4 ... 151 B6
Benham Rd W7 ... 86 C2
Benham's Pl 8 NW3 ... 70 A4
Benhill Ave SM1 ... 218 A4
Benhill Rd SE5 ... 139 B4
Sutton SM1 ... 218 B4
Benhill Wood Rd SM1 218 A4
Benhilton Gdns SM1 ... 217 D5
Benhurst Ct Ealing W5 ... 110 A6
12 Penge SE20 ... 184 B2
West Norwood SW16 ... 182 C5
Benhurst La SW16 ... 182 C5
Benin St SE13 ... 164 B4
Benjafield Cl N18 ... 34 B6
Benjamin Cl E8 ... 96 A6
Benjamin Ct
4 Ealing W7 ... 108 C5
4 Erith DA17 ... 147 B6
Littleton TW15 ... 171 A3
Benjamin St EC1 ... 241 C4
Ben Jonson Ct 30 N1 ... 95 C5
Ben Jonson Prim Sch
E1 ... 97 A3
Ben Jonson Rd E1 ... 97 A2
Benledi St E14 ... 98 B1
Bennelong Cl W12 ... 90 B1
Bennerley Rd SW11 ... 158 D6
Bennetsfield Rd UB11 104 D5
Bennet's Hill EC4 ... 251 D6
Bennets Lo EN2 ... 5 A2
Bennett Cl DA16 ... 146 A3
Teddington KT1 ... 175 C2
Bennett Ct N7 ... 72 B5
NW6 ... 69 D2
7 W3 ... 110 D4
Bennett Gr SE13 ... 141 D4
Bennett Ho SW1 ... 259 D4
2 Streatham SW4 ... 159 D4
Bennett Pk SE3 ... 142 D2
Bennett Rd E13 ... 99 C3
Dagenham RM6 ... 59 A2
Bennetts Ave
Croydon CR0 ... 223 A6
Greenford UB6 ... 86 C6
Bennett's Castle La
RM8 ... 80 D5
Bennetts Cl
Mitcham CR4,SW16 ... 181 B2
Tottenham N17 ... 33 D4
Bennetts Copse BR7 ... 188 A4
Bennett St SW1 ... 249 A4
W4 ... 111 C1
Bennetts Way CR0 ... 223 B6
Bennett's Yd SW1 ... 259 D5
Benn Ho 7 SE7 ... 121 C1
Benningholme Rd HA8 ... 27 C4
Bennington Rd
Chingford IG8 ... 36 C3
Tottenham N17 ... 33 C2
Benn St E9 ... 75 A2
Benns Wlk 8 TW9 ... 132 A1
Bensbury Cl SW15 ... 156 C4
Bensham Cl CR7 ... 205 A5
Bensham Gr CR7 ... 183 A1
Bensham La CR0,CR7 ... 204 D3
Bensham Manor Rd
CR7 ... 205 A5
Bensham Manor Sch
CR7 ... 205 A4
Bensington Ct TW14 ... 149 B5
Bensley Cl 7 N11 ... 30 D5
Ben Smith Way 21
SE16 ... 118 A3
Benson Ave E13,E6 ... 99 D5
Benson Cl Hillingdon UB8 82 A2
Hounslow TW3 ... 129 C1
Benson Ct 1 N19 ... 71 C4
SW8 ... 270 A2

Benson Ct *continued*
Holdbrook EN3 ... 7 C5
Benson Ho E2 ... 243 C6
SE1 ... 251 B3
Benson Prim sch CR0 223 A5
Benson Quay E1 ... 118 C6
Benson Rd
Croydon CR0 ... 220 C5
Forest Hill SE23 ... 162 C3
Bentall Sh Ctr The 10
KT2 ... 176 A1
Bentfield Gdns SE9 ... 165 D1
Benthal Ct N16 ... 74 A5
Benthal Prim Sch N16 ... 74 A5
Benthal Rd N16 ... 74 A5
Bentham Ct 10 N1 ... 73 A1
Bentham Ho SE1 ... 262 C6
Bentham Rd E9 ... 74 D2
Woolwich SE28 ... 124 B5
Bentham Wlk NW10 ... 67 A3
Ben Tillet Cl
Barking IG11 ... 80 A1
Newham E16 ... 122 B5
Ben Tillet Ho N15 ... 50 D6
Bentinck Cl NW8 ... 230 B3
Bentinck Ho 4 W12 ... 112 B6
Bentinck Mans W1 ... 238 B2
Bentinck Mews W1 ... 238 B2
Bentinck Rd UB7 ... 104 A5
Bentinck St W1 93 A1 238 B2
Bentley Cl SW19 ... 157 C1
Bentley Dr IG2 ... 57 A3
Bentley Ho 4 SE5 ... 139 C4
6 Bow E3 ... 97 C3
Bentley Lo WD23 ... 8 C2
Bentley Mews EN1 ... 17 B5
Bentley Rd N1 ... 73 C2
Bentley Way
Stanmore HA7 ... 25 A5
Woodford IG8 ... 21 A1
Bentley Wood High Sch
HA7 ... 24 D5
Benton Rd Ilford IG1,IG2 57 B1
South Oxhey WD19 ... 22 D5
Benton's La SE27 ... 183 A6
Benton's Rise SE27 ... 183 B5
Bentry Cl RM8 ... 81 A6
Bentry Rd RM8 ... 81 B6
Bentworth Ct 1 E2 ... 96 A3
Bentworth Prim Sch
W12 ... 90 B1
Bentworth Rd W12 ... 90 B1
Benville Ho SW8 ... 270 D3
Benwell Ct TW16 ... 172 A2
Benwell Rd N7 ... 72 C3
Benwick Cl SE16 ... 118 B2
Benwick Ct SE20 ... 184 C2
Benwood Ct SM1 ... 218 A5
Benworth St E3 ... 97 B4
Benyon Ho EC1 ... 234 B2
Benyon Rd N1 ... 95 B6 235 D6
Beormund Prim Sch
SE1 ... 117 B4 252 D1
Bequerel Ct SE10 ... 120 D3
Berberis Ct IG1 ... 78 D2
Berberis Ho 15 E3 ... 97 C2
Berberis Wlk UB7 ... 104 A2
Berber Pl 15 E14 ... 119 C6
Berber Rd SW11 ... 158 D6
Berberry Cl HA8 ... 27 A6
Bercta Rd SE9 ... 167 A2
Berebinder Ho 17 E3 ... 97 B5
Berenger Twr SW10 ... 266 C4
Berenger Wlk SW10 ... 266 C4
Berens Ct DA14 ... 189 D6
Berens Rd NW10 ... 90 D4
Berens Way BR5,BR7 ... 211 D6
Beresford Ave N20 ... 14 D2
Ealing W7 ... 86 C2
Tolworth KT5 ... 199 A2
Twickenham TW1 ... 153 C5
Wembley HA0 ... 88 C6
Beresford Ct E9 ... 75 A3
11 Twickenham TW1 ... 153 C5
Beresford Dr BR1 ... 210 A6
Woodford IG8 ... 37 C6
Beresford Gdns
Dagenham RM6 ... 59 A4
Enfield EN1 ... 5 C1
Hounslow TW4 ... 151 B6
Beresford Ho 14 SW4 ... 138 A1
Dulwich SE21 ... 161 C1
Beresford Lo N4 ... 73 B3
Beresford Rd N2 ... 48 C6
N5 ... 73 B3
N8 ... 50 D4
Belmont SM2 ... 217 B1
Chingford, Chingford Green
E4 ... 20 C3
Chingford, Highams Park
E17 ... 35 D2
Harrow HA1 ... 42 B4
Kingston KT2 ... 176 B2
New Malden KT3 ... 199 A5
Southall UB1 ... 106 D5
Beresford Sq 1 SE18 ... 122 D2
Beresford St SE18 ... 122 D3
Beresford Terr 3 N5 ... 73 A3
Bere St E1 ... 118 D6

Berestede Rd 4 W6 ... 111
Bergen Ho 1 SE5 ... 139
Bergen Sq SE16 ... 119
Berger Cl BR5 ... 211
Berger Prim Sch E9 ... 74
Berger Rd E9 ... 74
Berghem Mews W14 ... 112
Bergholt Ave IG4 ... 56
Bergholt Cres N16 ... 51
Bergholt Mews 4 NW1 71
Berglen Ct E14 ...
Bering Sq E14 ... 119
Bering Wlk E16 ... 99 D
Berisford Mews SW18 158
Berkeley Ave DA16 ... 146 D
Cranford TW4 ... 128
Northolt UB6 ... 64
Berkeley Cl
Borehamwood WD6 ... 10
Kingston KT2 ... 176
Orpington BR5,BR6 ... 211
Ruislip HA4 ... 62
Berkeley Cres EN4 ... 14
Berkeley Ct N3 ... 29 D
NW1 ... 237 D
1 NW11 ... 47 B
Ealing W5 ... 109 C
Edgware HA8 ... 26 D
16 Streatham SW2 ... 160 C
Wallington SM6 ... 219 C
Berkeley Dr KT8 ... 195 C
Berkeley Gdns W8 ... 245 B
Claygate KT10 ... 213
Southgate N21 ... 17 B
Walton-on-T KT12 ... 193 D
Berkeley Ho 17 E3 ... 97 C
8 SE8 ... 119 B
11 Brentford TW8 ... 131 D
Berkeley Lo Enfield EN2 ... 4 C
New Malden KT3 ... 199 C
Berkeley Mews W1 ... 237 D
Sunbury TW16 ... 194 C
Berkeley Pl SW19 ... 178 D
Berkeley Prim Sch
TW5 ... 128 D
Berkeley Rd E12 ... 78 A
N15 ... 51 B
N8 ... 49 D
NW9 ... 44 C
Barnes SW13 ... 134 A
Hillingdon UB10 ... 61 A
Berkeley Sq
W1 ... 115 B6 248 D
Berkeley St
W1 ... 115 B5 248 D
Berkeleys The SE25 ... 206 A
Berkeley The NW11 ... 47 D
Berkeley Waye TW5 ... 128 D
Berkeley Wlk 1 N7 ... 72 B
Berkerley Ct SW15 ... 156 D
Berkhampstead Rd
DA17 ... 125 C
Berkhamsted Ave HA9 66 C
Berkley Cl TW2 ... 152 C
Berkley Ct 6 TW1 ... 153 A
Berkley Gr NW1 ... 71 A
Berkley Rd NW1 ... 70 D
Berkshire Ct 1 W7 ... 86 D
Berkshire Gdns
Edmonton N13 ... 32 C
Edmonton N18 ... 34 B
Berkshire Ho SE6 ... 185 C
Berkshire Rd E9 ... 75 B
Berkshire Sq CR4 ... 204 A
Berkshire Way CR4 ... 204 A
Berleley Ct NW10 ... 67 C
Bermans Way NW10 ... 67 D
Bermondsey Leather Mkt
SE1 ... 253 A
Bermondsey Mkt*
SE1 ... 117 C3 263 B
Bermondsey Sq SE1 ... 263 B
Bermondsey St
SE1 ... 117 C4 253 A
Bermondsey Sta SE16 118 A
Bermondsey Trad Est
SE16 ... 118 C
Bermondsey Wall E
SE16 ... 118 B
Bermondsey Wall W
SE1,SE16 ... 118 A
Bermuda Ho HA1 ... 64 B
Bernal Cl SE28 ... 124 D
Bernard Angell Ho 4
SE10 ... 142 B
Bernard Ashley Dr
SE7 ... 121 B
Bernard Ave W13 ... 109 B
Bernard Cassidy St 4
E16 ... 98 D
Bernard Gdns SW19 ... 179 B
Bernard Rd N15 ... 51 D
Wallington SM5,SM6 ... 219 B
Bernard Shaw Ct 3
NW1 ... 71 C
Bernard Shaw Ho 2
NW10 ... 89 B
Bernard St WC1 94 A3 240 B
Bernays Cl HA7 ... 25 C

nay's Gr SW9 138 B1
nel Dr CR0 223 B5
ne Rd CR7 205 A4
ners Dr W13 109 A6
ners Ho N1 234 A4
nersmede SE3 143 A2
ners Mews
93 C2 239 B3
ners Pl W1 239 B2
ners Rd N1 234 C5
od Green N22 32 C1
ners St W1 93 C1 239 B2
ner Terr 30 E1 96 A1
ney Ho BR3 207 A4
ney Rd CR0 205 B2
nhart Cl HA8 27 A3
nwell Rd E4 20 C1
nwood Ho 6 N4 51 B2
ridge Gn HA8 26 C3
ridge Mews NW6 69 C3
ridge Rd SE19 183 C5
riman Rd N7 72 B5
rite Works UB7 104 C4
riton Rd HA2 41 B1
rybank Cl 4 E4 20 A2
ry Cl NW10 67 C1
genham RM10 81 C3
uthgate N21 16 D3
ry Ct TW4 151 B6
rydale Rd UB4 85 A3
ryfield Cl BR1 188 A1
ry Field Cl 8 E17 53 D5
ryfield Rd
17 116 D1 261 D2
ryhill SE9 144 D1
ry Hill HA7 25 D6
ryhill Gdns SE9 144 D1
ry Ho 25 E1 96 B3
SW11 136 D3
ry La SE21 183 B6
rylands
rbiton KT5 198 C3
est Barnes SW20 200 C5
rylands Ct 7 SM2 217 D1
rylands Rd KT5 198 B3
rylands Sta KT5 198 D5
ryman Cl RM8 80 C5
ryman's La SE26 184 D6
rymead Gdns W3 111 A4
rymede Inf Sch
3 110 D4
rymede Jun Sch
3 110 D4
rymede Rd W4 111 B3
rry Pl EC1 234 D1
rry St EC1 241 D5
rry Way W5 110 A3
rtal Rd SW17 180 B6
rtha Hollamby Ct
A14 190 C5
rtha Neubergh Ho 1
5 139 A4
rthan Gdns E17 54 B4
rthon St SE8 141 C6
rtie Rd NW10 68 A2
enge SE26 184 D4
rtram Cotts SW19 179 C3
rtram Rd NW4 46 A3
field EN1 6 A1
ngston KT2 176 C3
rtram St N19 71 B6
rtrand Ho 11 SW16 160 A1
rtrand St SE13 141 D2
rtrand Way SE28 124 C6
rt Rd CR7 205 A4
t Reilly Ho 1 SE18 123 B1
rtrum House Sch
W17 159 A2
rt Way EN1 5 D1
rwick Ave UB4 106 D6
rwick Cl HA7 24 D4
rwick Cres DA15 167 C5
rwick Ho 10 N2 30 B1
rwick Rd DA16 146 B4
ewham E16 99 C1
ottenham N22 32 D2
rwick St W1 93 C1 239 B1
rwyn Ave TW3 129 D4
rwyn Ho 3 N16 51 D1
rwyn Rd
ortlake SW14,TW10 132 D1
reatham SE24 160 D3
ryl Ave E6 100 A2
ryl Harding Ho 3
W19 178 D3
ryl Ho SE18 123 D1
ryl Rd W6 112 D1
rystede KT2 176 D3
sant Cl NW2 69 A5
sant Ct N1 73 B3
3 SE28 124 B6
sant Ho NW8 229 A5
sant Rd NW2 69 A4
sant Way NW10 67 A3
sant Wlk N7 72 B6
sford Ho 25 E2 96 A5
sley St SW16 181 C4
ssant Dr TW9 132 D4

Bessborough Gdns
SW1 115 D1 259 D2
Bessborough Pl
SW1 115 D1 259 D2
Bessborough Rd
Harrow HA1 42 B1
Roehampton SW15 156 A3
Bessborough St
SW1 115 D1 259 C2
Bessborough Wks
KT8 195 B4
Bessemer Ct 5 NW1 71 C1
Bessemer Grange Prim Sch
SE5 139 C1
Bessemer Park Ind Est 3
SE24 138 D1
Bessemer Rd SE5 139 A3
Bessie Lansbury Cl E6 100 C1
Bessingby Rd HA4 62 B6
Bessingham Wlk SE4 162 D6
Besson St SE14 140 D4
Bessy St E2 96 C4
Bestwood St SE8 118 D2
Beswick Mews 1 NW6 69 D2
Betam Rd UB3 105 B4
Beta Pl 20 SW4 138 B1
Betchworth Cl SM1 218 B3
Betchworth Ho 8 N7 71 D3
Betchworth Rd IG3 79 C5
Betham Rd UB6 86 B4
Bethany Waye TW14 149 C4
Bethecar Rd HA1 42 C4
Bethell Ave E13,E16 98 D3
Ilford IG1 56 C2
Bethel Rd DA16 146 C2
Bethersden Cl BR3 185 B3
Bethersden Ho SE17 263 B2
Bethesda Ct 8 SE20 184 C3
Beth Jacob Gram Sch
NW4 46 D5
Bethlehem Ho 13 E14 119 B6
Bethlem Royal Hospl
BR3 207 C2
Bethnal Green Mus of
Childhood* E2 96 C4
Bethnal Green Rd
E1,E2 96 A4 243 D6
Bethnal Green Sta E1 96 B3
E2 96 C4
Bethnal Green Tech Coll
E2 95 D4
Beths Gram Sch DA5 169 D5
Bethune Ave N11 30 D6
Bethune Rd N16 51 C2
NW10 89 B3
Bethwin Rd SE5 139 A5
Betjeman Cl HA5 41 C5
Betony Cl CR0 206 D1
Betoyne Ave E4 36 C6
Betsham Ho SE1 252 C2
Betspath Ho 6 N11 31 C5
Betstyle Ho 2 N10 31 A3
Betstyle Rd N11 31 B6
Betterton Dr DA14 169 A2
Betterton Ho WC2 240 B1
Betterton St
WC2 94 A1 240 B1
Bettons Pk E15 98 C6
Bettridge Rd SW6 135 B3
Betts Cl BR3 185 A1
Betts Ho E1 118 B6
Betts Mews E17 53 B3
Betts Rd E16 121 B6
Betts St E1 118 B6
Betts Way
Long Ditton KT6 197 B1
Penge SE20 184 B2
Bettswood Ct 18 SE20 184 B2
Betty Layward Prim Sch
N16 73 B5
Betty May Gray Ho 1
E14 120 A2
Beulah Ave CR7 183 A1
Beulah Cl HA8 10 D1
Beulah Cres CR7 183 A1
Beulah Gr CR0 205 A3
Beulah Hill SE19 183 A3
Beulah Inf Sch CR7 205 A6
Beulah Jun Sch CR7 205 A6
Beulah Rd E17 53 D4
Merton SW19 179 B3
South Norwood CR7 205 A6
Sutton SM1 217 C4
Beuleigh Ct E17 54 B4
Bevan Ave IG11 80 A1
Bevan Ct Croydon CR0 220 C3
9 Twickenham TW1 153 D5
Bevan Rd SE2 124 B1
Cockfosters EN4 2 D1
Bevan St N1 95 A6 235 B5
Bev Callender Cl 4
SW8 137 B2
Bevenden St
N1 95 B4 235 D2
Bevercote Wlk 1
DA17 147 B6
Beveridge Ct 1 SE28 124 B6
Southgate N21 16 A6
Beveridge Rd 1 NW10 67 C1

Beverley Ave DA15 167 D4
Hounslow TW4 129 B1
Wimbledon SW20 177 D2
Beverley Cl 6 SW11 136 B1
Barnes SW13 134 A3
Chessington KT9 213 C4
Edmonton N21 17 A3
Enfield EN1 5 C1
Beverley Cotts SW15 155 C1
Beverley Cres IG8 37 B2
Beverley Ct N14 15 C4
N2 48 D5
N5 72 D2
SE4 141 B2
5 W12 111 C4
9 W4 111 A1
Harrow HA2 42 B6
Hounslow TW4 129 B1
Northolt UB5 84 C5
Wimbledon SW20 177 D2
Beverley Dr HA8 44 C6
Beverley Gdns NW11 47 A2
Barnes SW13 133 D2
2 New Malden KT4 200 A1
Stanmore HA7 25 A2
Wembley HA9 44 C1
Beverley Ho 5 BR1 186 B5
Beverley Hyrst 10 CR0 221 D6
Beverley La KT2 177 C3
Beverley Lo 6 TW10 154 A6
Beverley Mans TW4 129 B1
Beverley Path 9
SW13 133 D3
Beverley Rd BR2 226 A6
E6 99 D4
W4 111 D1
Barnes SW13 133 D2
Chingford E4 36 B4
Dagenham RM9 81 A4
Mitcham CR4 203 D5
North Cheam KT4 216 C6
Penge SE20 184 B1
Ruislip HA4 62 B6
Southall UB2 107 A3
Sunbury TW16 171 D2
Teddington KT1 175 C2
West Barnes KT3 200 A5
Beverley Sch KT3 200 A4
Beverley Trad Est
SM4 200 D2
Beverley Way KT3,
SW20,KT2 177 D2
Beverley Way (Kingston By
Pass) KT3,SW20 200 A6
Beverly Ct HA3 43 C5
Beversbrook Rd N19 71 D5
Beverstone Rd SW2 160 B6
Thornton Heath CR7 204 D5
Beverston Mews NW1 237 C3
Bevill Allen Cl SW17 180 D5
Bevill Cl SE25 206 A6
Bevin Cl SE16 119 A5
Bevin Ct WC1 233 D2
Bevington Prim Sch
W10 91 A2
Bevington Rd W10 91 A2
Beckenham BR3 185 D1
Bevington St SE16 118 A4
Bevin Ho 35 E2 96 C4
7 E3 97 C4
Bevin Rd UB4 84 B4
Bevin Sq SW17 158 D1
Bevin Way WC1 234 A2
Bevis Marks
EC3 95 C1 243 B2
Bewcastle Gdns EN2 4 A1
Bew Ct SE21 162 A4
Bewdley Ho N4 51 A2
Bewdley St N1 72 C1
Bewick Mews SE15 140 B5
Bewick St SW8 137 B3
Bewley Ct SW2 160 B5
Bewley Ho 7 E1 118 B6
Bewley St Stepney E1 118 B6
Wimbledon SW19 180 A4
Bewlys Rd SE27 182 D5
Bexhill Cl TW13 151 A2
Bexhill Rd N11 31 D5
SE4 163 B5
Mortlake SW14 133 A2
Bexhill Wlk 8 E15 98 C6
Bexley Coll SE2 146 D6
Bexley Coll (Erith Rd
Campus) DA17 125 D1
Bexley Gdns
Edmonton N9 17 B1
Ilford RM6 58 B4
Bexley Gram Sch
DA16 146 B1
Bexleyheath Sch DA6 147 C2
Bexleyheath Sta DA7 147 A3
Bexley High St DA5 169 D3
Bexley Ho SE4 141 A1
Bexley La DA14 168 C1
Bexley Rd SE9 167 A6
Bexley Sta DA5 169 C3
Beynon Rd SM5 218 D3
BFI London Imax Cinema
SE1 116 C5 251 A3

Bianca Rd SE1,SE15 140 A6
Bibsworth Lo N3 29 B1
Bibsworth Rd N3 29 B1
Bicester Rd TW9 132 D2
Bickenhall Mans W1 237 D4
Bickenhall St
W1 92 D2 237 D4
Bickersteth Rd SW17 180 D4
Bickerton Rd N19 71 C6
Bickley Cres BR1 210 A5
Bickley Ct 1 HA7 25 C6
Bickley Park Rd BR1,
BR7 210 B6
Bickley Park Sch BR1 210 A6
Bickley Prim Sch BR1 209 C6
Bickley Rd BR1 187 D1
E10 53 D2
Bickley St SW17 180 D5
Bickley Sta BR1 210 A6
Bicknell Ho 23 E1 96 A1
Bicknell Rd SE5 139 A2
Bicknoller Rd EN1 5 D4
Bicknor Ho 2 E5 74 B3
Bicknor Rd BR6 211 D2
Bidborough Cl 3 BR2 208 D4
Bidborough St
N1,WC1 94 A4 233 A1
Biddenden Way SE9 188 C6
Biddenham Ho 18
SE16 118 D2
Bidder St E16 98 C2
Biddesden Ho SW3 257 C3
Biddestone Rd N7 72 B4
Biddulph Ho 23 SE18 122 B2
Biddulph Mans W9 91 D4
Biddulph Rd W9 91 D4
Bideford Ave UB6 87 B5
Bideford Cl
Edgware HA8 26 C2
Twickenham TW13 151 B1
Bideford Gdns EN1 17 C4
Bideford Rd DA16 146 B5
Catford BR1 164 D1
Enfield EN3 7 B5
Ruislip HA4 62 B5
Bidmead Ct KT6 214 A5
Bidwell Gdns N11 31 C3
Bidwell St SE15 140 B4
Big Ben* SW1 250 B1
Bigbury Cl N17 33 C3
Biggerstaff Rd E15 98 A6
Biggerstaff St N4 72 C6
Biggin Ave CR4 180 D2
Biggin Hill SE19 182 D3
Biggin Hill Cl KT2 175 C5
Biggin Way SE19 183 A3
Bigginwood Rd SW16 182 D2
Bigg's Row SW15 134 D2
Big Hill E5 52 B1
Bigland Green Prim Sch
E1 96 B1
Bigland St E1 96 B1
Bignell Rd SE18 122 D1
Bignold Rd E7 77 A4
Bigwood Ct NW11 47 D4
Bigwood Rd NW11 47 D3
Bilberry Ho 13 E3 97 C2
Billet Rd E17 35 B2
Ilford RM6 58 C6
Billetts Hart Cl W7 108 C4
Bill Hamling Cl SE9 166 B2
Billingford Cl SE4 140 D1
Billing Ho 6 E1 96 D1
Billingley NW1 232 A5
Billing Pl
SW10 135 D5 265 D4
Billing Rd
SW10 135 D5 265 D4
Billings Cl RM9 80 C1
Billingsgate Mkt E14 119 D5
Billing St
SW10 135 D5 265 D4
Billington Ho SW8 269 D1
Billington Rd SE14 140 D5
Billiter Sq EC3 243 B1
Billiter St EC3 95 C1 243 B1
Bill Nicholson Way N17 33 D3
Billockby Cl KT9 214 B2
Billsley Ct SE25 205 C5
Billson St E14 120 A2
Bilsby Gr SE9 187 D6
Bilton Ho SW8 269 C1
Bilton Rd UB6 87 B6
Bilton Twrs W1 237 D1
Bilton Way Enfield EN3 7 B5
Hayes UB3 106 B4
Bina Gdns
SW5 114 A2 256 A3
Binbrook Ho W10 90 C2
Bincote Rd EN2 4 B2
Binden Rd W12 111 D3
Bindon Gn SM4 201 D5
Binfield Ct SE5 139 A3
Binfield Rd
SW4 138 A4 270 B1
South Croydon CR2 221 D3
Bingfield St N1 94 B6 233 C6
Bingham Cnr CR0 206 A1
Bingham Pl W1 93 A2 238 A4

Bingham Point 11
SE18 122 D2
Bingham Rd CR0 206 B1
Bingham St N1 73 B2
Bingley Rd
Ashford TW16 172 A3
Newham E16 99 C1
Southall UB6 86 A2
Binley Ho SW15 155 D5
Binney St W1 93 A1 238 B1
Binnie Ho SE1 262 A5
Binns Rd W4 111 C1
Binns Terr 3 W4 111 C1
Binsey Wlk 1 SE2 124 C4
Binstead Cl UB4 85 A2
Binstead Ho SW18 157 D5
Binyon Cres HA7 24 D5
Binyon Ho 8 N16 73 C4
Birbetts Rd SE9 166 B2
Bircham Path SE4 140 D1
Birchanger Rd SE25 206 A4
Birch Ave Edmonton N13 17 A1
Hillingdon UB7 82 B1
Birch Cl E16 98 C2
N19 71 C6
SE15 140 A3
Brentford TW8 131 B5
Buckhurst Hill IG9 21 D1
Hounslow TW3 130 B3
Romford RM7 59 D6
Teddington TW11 175 A5
Birch Cres UB10 82 B6
Birch Ct E7 76 D4
Chingford E4 35 D4
Sutton SM1 218 A4
9 Wallington SM6 219 B4
Birchdale Gdns RM6 58 D2
Birchdale Rd E7 77 C3
Birchdene Dr SE28 124 A5
Birchdown Ho 32 E3 97 D4
Birchen Cl NW9 67 B6
Birchend Cl CR2 221 B2
Birchen Gr NW9 67 B6
Birches Cl
Mitcham CR4 202 D6
Pinner HA5 41 A4
Birches The E12 78 A4
SE5 139 C3
2 Beckenham BR2 208 D5
Bushey WD23 8 A6
Greenwich SE7 143 B6
Orpington BR6 226 C4
Southgate N21 16 B5
South Norwood SE25 183 D1
Twickenham TW4 151 B4
Birchfield Ho 2 E14 119 C6
Birchfield St E14 119 C6
Birch Gn NW9 27 C3
Birch Gr E11 76 C5
Acton W3 110 C6
Bexley DA16 146 A1
Lewisham SE12 164 D4
Upper Halliford TW17 171 C1
Birch Hill CR0 222 D3
Birch Ho SE14 141 B4
8 SW2 160 C5
Birchington Cl DA7 147 D4
Birchington Ct N8 49 D3
2 NW6 91 C6
Birchington Ho 1 E5 74 B3
Birchington Rd N8 49 D3
NW6 91 C6
Surbiton KT5 198 B2
Birchin La EC3 242 D1
Birchlands Ave SW12 158 D4
Birch Mead BR2,BR6 226 C6
Birchmead Ave HA5 40 C5
Birchmere Lo 18 SE16 118 B1
Birchmere Row SE3 142 D3
Birchmore Wlk N5 73 A5
Birch Pk HA3 24 A3
Birch Rd Feltham TW13 172 D5
Romford RM7 59 D6
Birch Row BR2 210 C3
Birch Tree Ave BR4 224 D4
Birch Tree Ho 18 SE7 143 C6
Birch Tree Way CR0 222 B6
Birch Vale Ct NW8 236 D6
Birchway UB3 106 A5
Birch Wlk CR4 181 B2
Birchwood Ave N10 49 A6
Beckenham BR3 207 B5
Hackbridge SM5,SM6 219 B5
Sidcup DA14 168 C1
Birchwood Cl SM4 201 D5
Birchwood Ct HA8 27 A1
Edmonton N13 32 D5
Birchwood Dr NW3 69 D5
Birchwood Gr TW12 173 C4
Birchwood Rd
Orpington BR5 211 C5
Streatham SW17 181 B5
Birdbrook Rd SE3,SE9 143 C2
Birdcage Wlk
SW1 115 D4 249 C1
Birdham Cl BR1 210 A4
Birdhurst Ave CR2 221 B4
Birdhurst Ct SM6 219 C1
Birdhurst Gdns CR2 221 B4

Birdhurst Rd SW18 158 A6
Mitcham SW19 180 C4
South Croydon CR2 221 C3
Birdhurst Rise CR2 221 C3
Bird In Bush Rd SE15 140 A5
Bird-in-Hand La BR1 187 D1
Bird-In-Hand Pas
SE23 162 C2
Bird In Hand Yd 14
NW3 70 A4
Birdsall Ho 5 SE5 139 C2
Birdsfield La E3 97 B6
Bird St W1 238 B1
Bird Wlk TW2 151 B3
Birdwood Cl TW11 174 C6
Birkbeck Ave W3 111 A6
Greenford UB6 86 A6
Birkbeck Coll
W1 93 D1 239 C2
Birkbeck Ct W3 111 B5
Birkbeck Gdns IG8 21 A2
Birkbeck Gr W3 111 B4
Birkbeck Hill SE21 160 D3
Birkbeck Mews 5 E8 73 D3
Birkbeck Pl SE21 161 A2
Birkbeck Prim Sch
DA14 168 B1
Birkbeck Rd E8 73 D3
N12 30 A5
N8 50 A5
NW7 27 D5
W3 111 B5
W5 109 C2
Enfield EN2 5 B5
Ilford IG2 57 B4
Penge BR3 184 D1
Sidcup DA14 168 A1
Tottenham N17 33 D2
Wimbledon SW19 179 D4
Birkbeck St E2 96 B4
Birkbeck Sta SE20 206 C6
Birkbeck Way UB6 86 B6
Birkdale Ave HA5 41 C6
Birkdale Cl BR6 211 B2
30 SE16 118 B1
Erith SE28 102 D1
Birkdale Ct 3 UB1 86 A1
Birkdale Gdns CR0 222 D4
Birkdale Rd SE2 124 A2
Ealing W5 88 A3
Birkenhead Ave KT2 176 B2
Birkenhead Ho 11 N7 72 C3
Birkenhead St
WC1 94 A4 233 B2
Birkhall Rd SE6 164 B2
Birkwood Cl SW12 159 D4
Birley Lo NW8 229 D4
Birley Rd N20 14 A2
Birley St SW11 137 A3
Birnam Rd N4 72 B6
Birnbeck Ct NW11 47 B4
Birrell Ho 9 SW9 138 B3
Birse Cres NW10 67 C4
Birstal Gn WD19 22 D6
Birstall Rd N15 51 C4
Birtwhistle Ho 15 E3 97 B6
Biscay Ho 11 E1 96 D3
Biscay Rd W6 112 D1
Biscoe Cl TW5 129 C6
Biscoe Ho UB2 107 D2
Biscoe Way SE13 142 B2
Biscott Ho 3 E3 97 D3
Bisenden Rd CR0 221 C6
Bisham Cl CR4 202 D1
Bisham Gdns N6 49 A1
Bishop Butt Cl BR6 227 D5
Bishop Challoner Collegiate
Sch
E1 118 A6
E1 96 C1
Bishop Challoner Sch
BR2 186 B1
Bishop Ct 20 SW2 160 C5
Bishop Douglass RC High
Sch N2 48 A6
Bishop Duppa's Almshouses
7 TW10 154 A6
Bishop Duppas Pk
TW17 193 C2
Bishop Fox Way KT8 195 B5
Bishopgate 32 N1 95 C6
Bishop Gilpins Prim Sch
SW19 179 B5
Bishop John Robinson CE
Prim Sch SE28 124 C6
Bishop Ken Rd HA3 24 D2
Bishop King's Rd
W14 113 A2 254 B4
Bishop Perrin CE Prim Sch
TW2 151 D3
Bishop Ramsey CE Sch
HA4 40 A2
Bishop Ramsey CE Sch
(Annexe) HA4 39 D2
Bishop Rd N14 15 B4
Bishops Ave BR1 209 C6

Bishops Ave *continued*
E13 .... 99 B6
Borehamwood WD6 .... 10 B6
Ilford RM6 .... 58 C3
Bishop's Ave SW6 .... 135 A3
Bishops Ave The N2 .... 48 B3
Bishopsbourne Ho
BR1 .... 187 B3
Bishop's Bridge Rd
W2 .... 92 A1 236 A2
Bishops Cl SE9 .... 167 A2
W4 .... 111 A1
Bishop's Cl E17 .... 53 D5
N19 .... 71 C5
Bishops Cl Barnet EN5 .... 12 D5
Enfield EN1 .... 6 B3
Richmond TW10 .... 153 D1
Sutton SM1 .... 217 C5
Bishop's Cl UB10 .... 82 C5
Bishopscourt 8 CR0 .... 221 D6
Bishops Ct N2 .... 48 C5
12 W2 .... 91 D1
Bishop's Ct EC4 .... 241 C2
WC2 .... 241 A2
Bishops Ct
1 Ashford TW16 .... 171 D3
Romford RM7 .... 59 D5
Bishopsdale Ho 8
NW6 .... 91 C6
Bishops Dr
East Bedfont TW14 .... 149 B5
Northolt UB5 .... 85 A6
Bishopsford Rd SM4 .... 202 B3
Bishopsgate
EC2 .... 95 C1 243 A2
Bishopsgate Arcade
E1 .... 243 B3
Bishopsgate Church Yd
EC2 .... 243 A2
Bishops Gn BR1 .... 187 C2
Bishops Gr N2 .... 48 C3
Feltham TW12 .... 173 B6
Bishop's Hall KT1 .... 175 D1
Bishopshalt Sch UB8 .... 82 B4
Bishops Hill KT12 .... 194 A2
Bishops Ho SW8 .... 270 B3
Bishop's Mans SW6 .... 134 D3
Bishops Mead SE5 .... 139 A5
Bishops Park Rd
SW16 .... 182 A2
Bishop's Park Rd SW6 134 D3
Bishop's Pl SM1 .... 218 A3
Bishops Rd N6 .... 49 A3
Bishop's Rd W7 .... 108 C4
Bishops Rd SW6 .135 264 C2
Bishop's Rd Hayes UB3 .83 A1
Thornton Heath CR0 .... 204 D2
Bishop St N1 .... 95 A6 235 A6
Bishop's Terr
SE11 .... 116 C2 261 B4
Bishopsthorpe Rd
SE26 .... 184 D6
Bishopstone Ho 4
SW11 .... 137 A3
Bishop Stopford's Sch
EN1 .... 6 B3
Bishop's Way E2 .... 96 C5
Bishops Wlk
Chislehurst BR7 .... 189 A2
South Croydon CR0,CR9 .223 A3
Bishopswood Rd N6 .... 48 D2
Bishop Thomas Grant RC
Sec Sch SW16 .... 182 B5
Bishop Wand CE Sec Sch
TW16 .... 171 D1
Bishop Way NW10 .... 67 C1
Bishop Wilfred Wood Cl
SE15 .... 140 A3
Bishop Wilfred Wood Ct 2
E13 .... 99 C5
Bishop Winnington-Ingram
CE Sch HA4 .... 39 B2
Bisley Cl KT4 .... 200 C1
Bisley Ho SW19 .... 156 D2
Bispham Rd NW10 .... 88 B4
Bissextile Ho SE13 .... 141 D3
Bisson Rd E15 .... 98 A5
Bistern Ave E17 .... 54 B6
Bittacy Bsns Ctr NW7 .... 29 A3
Bittacy Cl NW7 .... 28 D4
Bittacy Ct NW7 .... 29 A3
Bittacy Hill NW7 .... 28 D4
Bittacy Park Ave NW7 .28 D5
Bittacy Rd NW7 .... 28 D4
Bittacy Rise NW7 .... 28 D4
Bittern Cl UB4 .... 84 D2
Bittern Ct NW9 .... 27 C1
8 SE8 .... 141 C6
Chingford E4 .... 20 B4
Bittern Ho SE1 .... 252 A1
Bittern St SE1 .... 252 A1
Bittoms The KT1 .... 197 D6
Bixley Cl UB2 .... 107 B2
Blackall St EC2 .... 243 A6
Blackberry Cl TW17 .... 193 C5
Blackberry Farm Cl
TW5 .... 129 A5
Blackberry Field BR5 .190 A2
Blackbird Ct NW9 .... 67 B5
Blackbird Hill NW9 .... 67 B5
Blackborne Rd RM10 .... 81 D2
Black Boy La N15 .... 51 A4
Blackbrook La BR1,
BR2 .... 210 C5
Blackburn 28 NW9 .... 27 D1
Blackburn Ct 21 SW2 .160 C5
Blackburne's Mews
W1 .... 248 A5
Blackburn Rd NW6 .... 69 D2
Blackburn Trad Est
TW19 .... 148 B5
Blackbush Ave RM6 .... 58 D4
Blackbush Cl SM2 .... 217 D1
Blackcap Ct NW9 .... 27 C1
Blackdown Cl N2 .... 30 A1
Blackdown Ho E8 .... 74 A4
Blackenham Rd SW17 180 D6
Blackett St SW15 .... 134 D2
Black Fan Cl EN2 .... 5 A4
Blackfen Par DA15 .... 168 A5
Blackfen Rd DA15 .... 168 B5
Blackfen Sch for Girls
DA15 .... 168 B5
Blackford Rd WD19 .... 22 D5
Blackfriars Bridge
EC4 .... 251 C5
Blackfriars Ct EC4 .... 251 C6
Black Friars La
EC4 .... 94 D1 241 C1
Blackfriars Pas EC4 .... 251 C6
Blackfriars Pier EC4 .... 251 C6
Blackfriars Rd
SE1 .... 116 D4 251 C3
Blackfriars Sta
EC4 .... 116 D6 251 C6
Blackfriars Underpass
EC4 .... 116 C6 251 B6
Blackham Ho SW19 .... 179 A4
Blackheath★ SE3 .... 142 C4
Blackheath Ave SE3 .... 142 C5
Blackheath Bluecoat CE Sch
SE3 .... 143 B5
Blackheath Bsns Est
SE10 .... 142 A4
Blackheath Gr SE3 .... 142 D3
Blackheath High Sch
SE3 .... 143 A5
Blackheath High Sch (Girls)
SE3 .... 142 D3
Blackheath High Sch
GPDST (Jun Dept)
SE3 .... 143 A3
Blackheath Hill SE10 .142 A4
Blackheath Hospl SE3 142 C2
Blackheath Pk SE3 .... 143 A2
Blackheath Rd SE10 .... 141 D4
Blackheath Rise SE13 .142 A3
Blackheath Sta SE3 .... 142 D2
Blackheath Vale SE3 .... 142 C3
Blackheath Village
SE3 .... 142 D3
Black Horse Ct SE1 .... 262 D6
Blackhorse La E17 .... 34 D1
Croydon CR0 .... 206 A2
Blackhorse La Sta
CR0 .... 206 A2
Blackhorse Mews E17 .52 D6
Black Horse Par HA5 .... 40 B4
Blackhorse Rd E17 .... 53 A5
SE8 .... 141 A6
Black Horse Rd DA14 .190 A6
Blackhorse Road E17 .... 52 D5
Blackhorse Road Sta
E17 .... 52 D5
Blacklands Dr UB4 .... 83 A3
Blacklands Rd SE6 .... 186 A6
Blacklands Terr SW3 .... 257 D3
Black Lion La W6 .... 112 A2
Black Lion Mews 4
W6 .... 112 A2
Blackmore Ave UB1 .... 108 B5
Blackmore Ho N1 .... 233 D5
2 SW18 .... 157 D6
Forest Hill SE23 .... 163 B3
Blackmore's Gr TW11 .175 A4
Blackmore Twr 1 W3 111 A3
Blackness La BR2 .... 225 D1
Blackpool Gdns UB4 .... 83 C3
Blackpool Rd SE15 .... 140 B3
Black Prince Intc DA5 169 D5
Black Prince Rd
SE1,SE11 .... 116 B2 260 D3
Black Rod Cl UB3 .... 105 D3
Black Roof Ho 9 SE5 138 D4
Blackshaw Rd SW17 .... 180 B5
Blacksmith Cl RM6 .... 58 C3
Blacksmiths Ho 7 E17 .53 C5
Black's Rd W6 .... 112 C2
Blackstock Ho N5 .... 72 D5
Blackstock Mews N4 .... 72 D5
Blackstock Rd N4,N5 .... 72 D5
Blackstone Ho SW1 .... 259 A1
Dulwich SE21 .... 161 C1
Blackstone Rd NW2 .... 68 C4
Black Swan Yd SE1 .... 253 A2
Blackthorn Ave UB7 .... 104 C3
Blackthorn Ct 4 E15 .... 76 B4
19 SE15 .... 139 D5
Heston TW5 .... 129 A5
6 West Norwood
SW16 .... 182 C5
Blackthorne Ave CR0 .206 C1
Blackthorne Dr E4 .... 36 B6
Blackthorn Gr DA7 .... 147 A2
Blackthorn St E3 .... 97 C3
Blacktree Mews 12
SW9 .... 138 C2
Blackwall Sta E14 .... 120 A6
Blackwall Trad Est E14 .98 B2
Blackwall Tunnel E14,
SE10 .... 120 B5
Blackwall Tunnel App
SE10 .... 120 C4
Blackwall Tunnel Northern
Approach E14,E3 .... 98 A3
Blackwall Way E14 .... 120 A6
Blackwater Cl E7 .... 76 D4
Blackwater Ho NW8 .... 236 D4
Blackwater St SE22 .... 161 D6
Blackwell Cl 10 E5 .... 74 D4
Harrow HA3 .... 24 B3
Blackwell Gdns HA8 .... 10 C1
Blackwell Ho 3 SW4 .159 D5
Blackwood Ho 11 E1 .... 96 B3
Blackwood St
SE17 .... 117 B1 262 C2
Blade Mews SW15 .... 135 B1
Bladen Ho 4 E1 .... 96 D1
Blades Ct SW15 .... 135 B1
Blades Ho 18 SE11 .... 138 C6
Blades Lo 16 SW2 .... 160 C5
Bladindon Dr DA5 .... 168 D4
Bladon Ct
Beckenham BR2 .... 208 C6
Streatham SW16 .... 182 A4
Bladon Gdns HA2 .... 41 D3
Blagden's Cl N14 .... 15 D2
Blagden's La N14 .... 15 D2
Blagdon Ct W7 .... 108 C6
Blagdon Rd SE13 .... 163 D5
New Malden KT3 .... 199 D5
Blagdon Wlk TW11 .... 175 C4
Blagrove Rd 1 W10 .... 91 B2
Blair Ave NW9 .... 45 C2
Thames Ditton KT10 .... 212 A6
Blair Cl DA15 .... 167 C6
N1 .... 73 A2
Hayes UB3 .... 106 A2
Blair Ct NW8 .... 229 C6
Beckenham BR3 .... 185 D2
7 Catford SE6 .... 164 D3
Blairderry Rd SW2 .... 160 A2
Blair Ho SW9 .... 138 B3
Blair Peach Prim Sch
UB1 .... 106 D5
Blair St E14 .... 98 B1
Blake Ave IG11 .... 101 D6
Blake Cl DA16 .... 145 C4
Carshalton SM5 .... 202 C1
Blake Ct NW6 .... 91 C4
8 SE16 .... 118 B1
Blakeden Dr KT10 .... 212 D2
Blake Gdns
SW6 .... 135 D4 265 C2
Blake Hall Cres E11 .... 55 A1
Blakehall Rd SM5 .... 218 D2
Blake Hall Rd E11 .... 55 A2
Blake Ho 14 N16 .... 73 C4
1 N19 .... 71 D3
SE1 .... 261 A6
2 SE8 .... 141 C6
6 Beckenham BR3 .... 185 D4
Blake Lo N3 .... 29 B1
Blake Mews 14 TW9 .... 132 C4
Blakemore Rd
Streatham SW16 .... 160 A1
Thornton Heath CR7 .... 204 B4
Blakemore Way DA17 .125 A3
Blakeney Ave BR3 .... 185 B2
Blakeney Cl 4 E8 .... 74 A3
N20 .... 14 A3
5 NW1 .... 71 D1
Blakeney Ct EN2 .... 17 B6
Blakeney Rd BR3 .... 185 B2
Blakenham Ct W12 .... 112 A5
Blakenham Rd SW17 .... 180 D6
Blaker Ct SE7 .... 143 C5
Blake Rd E16 .... 98 D3
N11 .... 31 C3
Croydon CR0 .... 221 C6
Mitcham CR4 .... 202 C6
Blaker Rd E15 .... 98 A6
Blakes Ave KT3 .... 199 D3
Blakes Cl W10 .... 90 C2
Blake's Gn BR4 .... 208 A1
Blakes La KT3 .... 199 D4
Blakesley Ave W5 .... 87 C1
Blakesley Ct W5 .... 87 C1
Blakesley Ho 4 E12 .... 78 C5
Blake's Rd SE15 .... 139 C5
Blakes Terr KT3 .... 200 A4
Blakesware Gdns N9 .... 17 B4
Blakewood Cl TW13 .... 172 C6
Blakewood Ct SE20 .... 184 B3
Blanca Ho 16 N1 .... 95 C5
Blanchard Cl SE9 .... 166 A1
Blanchard Gr EN3 .... 7 D5
Blanchard Ho 7 TW1 153 D5
Blanchard Way E8 .... 74 A2
Blanch Cl SE15 .... 140 C5
Blanchedowne SE5 .... 139 B1
Blanche Ho NW8 .... 237 A5
Blanche Nevile Sch The
N15 .... 51 D6
Blanche St E16 .... 98 D3
Blanchland Rd SM4 .... 201 D4
Blandfield Rd SW12 .... 159 A4
Blandford Ave
2 Beckenham BR3 .... 185 A1
Twickenham TW2 .... 151 D3
Blandford Cl N2 .... 48 A5
Romford RM7 .... 59 D5
Wallington CR0 .... 220 A5
Blandford Cres E4 .... 20 A4
Blandford Ct 6 N1 .... 73 C1
NW6 .... 69 A1
Blandford Ho SW8 .... 270 C4
Blandford Rd W4 .... 111 C3
W5 .... 109 D4
Penge BR3 .... 184 D1
Southall UB2 .... 107 C2
Teddington TW11 .... 174 C5
Blandford Sq NW1 .... 237 B5
Blandford St
W1 .... 93 A2 238 A3
Blandford Waye UB4 .... 84 C1
Bland Ho SE11 .... 260 D2
Bland St SE9 .... 143 D1
Blaney Cres E6 .... 100 D4
Blanmerle Rd SE9 .... 166 D3
Blann Cl SE9 .... 165 D5
Blantyre St
SW10 .... 136 B5 266 C4
Blantyre Twr SW10 .... 266 C4
Blantyre Wlk
SW10 .... 136 B5 266 C4
Blashford NW3 .... 70 D1
Blashford St SE13 .... 164 B4
Blasker Wlk E14 .... 119 D1
Blatchford Ct KT12 .... 194 A1
Blatchford Ho 8 RM10 81 C5
Blawith Rd HA1 .... 42 D5
Blaxland Ho 12 W12 .... 112 B6
Blaydon Cl HA4 .... 39 C2
Blaydon Ct 4 UB5 .... 63 C2
Blaydon Wlk N17 .... 34 B3
Bleak Hill La SE18 .... 145 D6
Blean Gr SE20 .... 184 C3
Bleasdale Ave UB6 .... 87 A5
Blechynden Ho 17 W10 90 D1
Blechynden St W10 .... 112 D6
Bleddyn Cl DA15 .... 168 C5
Bledlow Cl SE28 .... 124 C6
Bledlow Rise UB6 .... 86 A5
Bleeding Heart Yd
EC1 .... 241 B3
Blegborough Rd
SW16 .... 181 C4
Blemundsbury WC1 .... 240 C4
Blendon Dr DA5 .... 168 D5
Blendon Path 7 BR1 .186 D3
Blendon Rd DA5 .... 168 D5
Blendon Terr SE18 .... 145 A6
Blendworth Point 4
SW15 .... 156 B3
Blenheim 28 SW19 .... 156 D3
Blenheim Ave IG2 .... 56 C3
Blenheim Bsns Ctr
CR4 .... 180 D1
Blenheim Cl
Edmonton N21 .... 17 A3
Greenford UB6 .... 86 B5
Wallington SM6 .... 219 C1
West Barnes SW20 .... 200 C6
Blenheim Cres
W11 .... 113 A6 244 B6
W11 .... 91 A1
Ruislip HA4 .... 61 B6
South Croydon CR2 .... 221 A1
Blenheim Ct DA15 .... 167 B1
N19 .... 72 A6
N7 .... 72 A2
17 SE16 .... 118 D5
Harrow HA3 .... 43 A3
Richmond TW9 .... 132 B2
South Norwood SE19 .... 183 C2
Sutton SM2 .... 218 A2
Blenheim Dr DA16 .... 145 D4
Blenheim Gdns NW2 .... 68 C3
SW2 .... 160 B5
Kingston KT2 .... 176 D3
Wallington SM6 .... 219 C1
Wembley HA9 .... 66 A5
Blenheim Gr SE15 .... 140 A3
Blenheim Ho
6 Edmonton N9 .... 18 A1
Hounslow TW3 .... 129 C2
Blenheim Par 2 UB10 .82 D3
Blenheim Park Rd
CR2 .... 221 A1
Blenheim Pas NW8 .... 229 A4
Blenheim Pl TW11 .... 174 D5
Blenheim Rd E15 .... 76 C4
E17 .... 53 A6
E6 .... 99 D4
NW8 .... 92 A5 229 B4
W4 .... 111 C3
Bromley BR1,BR2 .... 210 A5
Harrow HA2 .... 41 D3
Northolt UB5 .... 63 D2
Penge SE20 .... 184 C3
Sidcup DA15 .... 168 C3
Sutton SM1 .... 217 D5
West Barnes SW20 .... 200 C6
Blenheim Rise N15 .... 51 D5
Blenheim St W1 .... 238 C1
Blenheim Terr
NW8 .... 92 A5 229 A4
Blenheim Way TW7 .... 131 A4
Blenkarne Rd SW11 .... 158 D5
Bleriot 27 NW9 .... 27 D1
Bleriot Rd TW5 .... 128 C5
Blessbury Rd HA8 .... 27 A2
Blessed Dominic RC Prim
Sch NW9 .... 27 D1
Blessed John Roche RC Sch
The E14 .... 97 C1
Blessed Sacrament RC Prim
Sch N1 .... 94 B6 233 C5
Blessington Cl SE13 .... 142 B2
Blessington Rd SE13 .... 142 B1
Blessing Way IG11 .... 102 C5
Bletchingley Cl CR7 .... 204 D5
Bletchington Ct DA17 .125 C2
Bletchley Ct N1 .... 235 C3
Bletchley St N1 95 A5 235 B3
Bletchmore Cl
Hayes UB3 .... 105 B1
Hayes UB3 .... 127 B6
Bletsoe Wlk N1 .... 235 B4
Blewbury Ho 3 SE2 .... 124 C4
Blick Ho 1 SE16 .... 118 C3
Bligh Ho 4 SE27 .... 183 A6
Blincoe Cl SW19 .... 156 D2
Blind Cnr SE25 .... 206 C5
Blissett St SE10 .... 142 A4
Blissland Ct N12 .... 30 A4
Bliss Mews 17 W10 .... 91 A4
Blisworth Cl UB4 .... 85 A3
Blisworth Ho 12 E2 .... 96 A6
Blithbury Rd RM9 .... 80 B2
Blithdale Rd SE2 .... 124 A2
Blithfield St W8 .... 255 C5
Blockley Rd HA0 .... 65 B6
Bloemfontein Ave
W12 .... 112 B5
Bloemfontein Rd W12 112 B6
Blomfield Ct SW11 .... 266 D2
W9 .... 236 B6
Blomfield Mans W12 .112 C5
Blomfield Rd
W9 .... 92 A2 236 A4
Blomfield St
EC2 .... 95 B2 242 D3
Blomfield Villas W2 .... 91 D2
W9 .... 236 A4
Blomville Rd RM8 .... 81 A5
Blondel St SW11 .... 137 A3
Blondin Ave W5 .... 109 C3
Blondin St E3 .... 97 C5
Bloomburg St SW1 .... 259 B3
Bloomfield Cres IG2 .... 56 D3
Bloomfield Ct N6 .... 49 A3
Bloomfield Ho 17 E1 .... 96 A2
Bloomfield Pl W1 .... 248 D6
Bloomfield Rd BR2 .... 209 D4
N6 .... 49 A3
SE18 .... 122 D1
Kingston KT1 .... 198 A6
Bloomfields The IG11 .... 79 A2
Bloomfield Terr
SW1 .... 115 A1 258 B2
Bloom Gr SE27 .... 160 D1
Bloomhall Rd SE19 .... 183 B5
Bloom Park Rd SW6 .... 264 C3
Bloomsbury Cl NW7 .... 28 A3
Ealing W5 .... 110 B6
Bloomsbury Ct E11 .... 54 B1
WC1 .... 240 B3
Cranford TW5 .... 128 B4
Pinner HA5 .... 41 B6
Bloomsbury Ho 10
SW4 .... 159 D5
Bloomsbury Pl SW18 .... 158 A6
WC1 .... 240 B3
Bloomsbury Sq
WC1 .... 94 A2 240 B3
Bloomsbury St
WC1 .... 93 D2 239 D3
Bloomsbury Way
WC1 .... 94 A2 240 B3
Blore Cl SW8 .... 269 C1
Blore Ct W1 .... 249 C6
Blossom Cl W5 .... 110 A4
Dagenham RM9 .... 103 B6
South Croydon CR2 .... 221 D3
Blossom La EN2 .... 5 A4
Blossom Pl E1 .... 243 B5
Blossom St E1 .95 C3 243 B5
Blossom Way
Hillingdon UB10 .... 60 B1
Blossom Way *continued*
West Drayton UB7 10
Blossom Waye TW5 12
Blount St E14 9
Bloxam Gdns SE9 16
Bloxhall Rd E10 5
Bloxham Cres TW12 17
Bloxworth Cl SM6 21
Blucher Rd SE5 13
Blue Anchor Alley 4
TW9 13
Blue Anchor La SE16 .11
Blue Anchor Yd E1 11
Blue Ball Yd SW1 24
Bluebell Ave E12 7
Bluebell Cl 16 E9 9
Forest Hill SE26 18
Hackbridge SM6 20
Orpington BR6 22
Bluebell Way IG1 7
Blueberry Cl IG8 3
Bluebird La RM10 8
Bluebird Way Cl SE28 ....
Bluefield Cl TW12 17
Blue Gate Fields Jun & In
Schs E1 11
Bluegate Mews E1 11
Bluegates
Stoneleigh KT17 21
Wimbledon SW19 17
Bluehouse Rd E4 2
Blue Lion Pl SE1 26
Blue Point Ct 2 HA1 4
Blue Sch The TW7 13
Blundell Rd HA8 2
Blundell St N7 7
Blunden Cl RM8 5
Blunt Rd CR0 22
Blunts Ave UB7 12
Blunts Rd SE9 16
Blurton Rd E5 7
Blydon Ct N21 1
Blyth Cl 4 E14 12
Twickenham TW1 152
Blythe Cl SE23 16
Blythe Hill BR5 19
Forest Hill SE6 16
Blythe Hill La SE6 16
Blythe Ho 8 SE11 13
Blythe Mews 2 W14 .112
Blythendale Ho 31 E2 9
Blythe Rd W14 112 D3 25
Blythe St E2 9
Blythe Vale SE6 16
Blyth Rd E17 5
Bromley BR1 18
Hayes UB3 10
Woolwich SE28 12
Blyth's Wharf E14 11
Blythswood Rd IG3 5
Blythwood Pk 10 BR1 .18
Blythwood Rd N4 5
Pinner HA5 22
Boadicea St N1 23
Boadoak Ho 18 NW6 91
Boardman Ave E4 1
Boardman Cl EN5 1
Boardwalk Pl E14 12
Boarhound 25 NW9 27
Boarley Ho SE17 263
Boathouse Ctr The
W10 90
Boat Lifter Way 19
SE16 11
Bob Anker Cl 1 E13 9
Bobbin Cl SW4 137
Bobby Moore Bridge The
HA9 66
Bobington Ct
WC1 .... 94 A2 24
Bob Marley Way 11
SE24 138
Bockhampton Rd KT2 17
Bocking St E8 96
Boddicott Cl SW19 157
Boddington Ho SE14 .140
Bodeney Ho 10 SE5 139
Boden Ho 4 E1 96
Bodiam Cl EN1 5
Bodiam Ct BR2 208
Bodiam Rd SW16 18
Bodicea Mews TW4 151
Bodington Ct 2 W12 .112
Bodley Cl KT3 19
Bodley Manor Way
SE24 160
Bodley Rd KT3 199
Bodmin 26 NW9 27
Bodmin Cl HA2 6
Bodmin Gr SM4 201
Bodmin St SW18 157
Bodnant Gdns SW20 200
Bodney Mans 14 E8 74
Bodney Rd E5,E8 74
Boeing Way UB2 106
Boelyn Dr HA4 62
Boevey Path
Erith DA17 125
2 Erith DA17 147

ɔgnor Gdns WD19 ....22 C5
ɔgnor Rd DA16 .....146 D4
ɔhemia Pl 1 E8 ......74 B2
ɔhn Rd E1 ....97 A2
ɔhun Gr EN4 ....14 D5
ɔileau Par W5 ....88 B1
ɔileau Rd
Barnes SW13 ....134 B6
Ealing W5 ....88 B1
ɔilerhouse SE1 ......253 C3
ɔisseau Ho 27 E1 .....96 C2
ɔlden St SE8 ....141 D3
ɔldero Pl NW8 ......237 A5
ɔlderwood Way BR4 223 D6
ɔldmere Rd HA5 .....40 C2
ɔleyn Ave EN1 ....6 B4
ɔleyn Ct E17 ....53 C5
Beckenham BR3 ....186 A2
Buckhurst Hill IG9 ......21 B3
East Molesey KT8 ......196 B5
ɔleyn Dr KT8 ....195 B6
ɔleyn Gdns BR4 .....223 D6
ɔleyn Ground(Upton Park)
West Ham United FC)
13,E6 ....99 D5
ɔleyn Rd E6 ....99 D5
7 ....77 B1
N16 ....73 C3
ɔleyn Way EN5 ....2 A2
ɔlina Rd SE16 ....118 C1
ɔlingbroke Gr SW11 .158 D5
ɔlingbroke Ho
Beckenham BR3 ....207 A4
Catford BR3 ....185 D5
ɔlingbroke Hospl The
SW11 ....158 C6
ɔlingbroke Rd W14 .112 D3
ɔlingbroke Way UB3,
UB11 ....105 B5
ɔlingbroke Wlk
SW11 ....136 C4 267 A2
ɔllo Bridge Rd W3 ..111 A4
ɔllo Ct 2 W3 ....111 A3
ɔllo La W3 ....110 D3
ɔlney Ct KT6 ....197 D4
ɔlney Gate SW7 .....247 A1
ɔlney St SW8 138 B5 270 C3
ɔlsover St W1 93 B3 238 D5
ɔlstead Rd CR4 .....181 B2
ɔlster Gr N22 ....31 D2
ɔlt Ct EC4 ....241 B1
ɔltmore Cl NW4 ......46 D6
ɔlton Cl
Chessington KT9 ......214 A2
Penge SE20 ....184 A1
ɔlton Cres SE5 ......138 D5
ɔlton Ct SW11 ....268 B1
ɔlton Gdns NW10 .....90 D5
SW5 ....113 D1 255 D2
Bromley BR1 ....186 D4
Teddington TW11 .....175 A4
ɔlton Gdns Mews
SW10 ....256 A2
ɔlton Ho 4 SE10 ....120 C1
ɔlton Rd E15 ....76 D2
NW10 ....89 C6
NW8 ....91 D6
Chessington KT9 ......214 A2
Chiswick W4 ....133 A5
Edmonton N18 ....33 D5
Harrow HA1 ....42 B5
ɔltons Ct SW5 ......255 D2
ɔlton's La TW6,UB7 ..127 A5
ɔlton St W1 .115 B5 248 D4
ɔltons The
SW10 ....114 A1 256 A2
Wembley HA0 ....64 D4
Woodford IG8 ....37 A6
ɔlton Studios SW10 .256 B1
ɔlton Wlk N7 ....72 B6
ɔmbay St SE16 ......118 B2
ɔmer Cl UB7 ....126 C5
ɔmore Rd
W11 ....113 A6 244 A6
ɔnar Pl BR7 ....188 A3
ɔnar Rd SE15 ....140 A5
ɔnchester Cl BR7 ....188 C3
ɔnchurch Cl SM2 ...217 D1
ɔnchurch Rd W10 ....91 A2
Ealing W13 ....109 B5
ɔnd Cl UB7 ....82 B1
ɔnd Ct EC4 ....242 C1
ɔndfield Ave UB4 .....84 A4
ɔndfield Rd 4 E6 ....100 B2
ɔnd Fst Sch CR4 ....180 D1
ɔnd Gdns SM6 ......219 C4
ɔnd Ho 4 NW6 ......91 B5
ɔnding Yard Wlk
SE16 ....119 A3
ɔnd Rd Mitcham CR4 .180 D1
Surbiton KT6 ....214 B6
ɔnd St E15 ....76 C3
Ealing W5 ....109 D6
ɔnd Street Sta
W1 ....93 B1 238 B1
ɔndway SW8 138 A6 270 B6
ɔneta Rd SE18 ......122 B3
ɔnfield Rd SE13 ....142 A1
ɔnham Gdns RM8 ....80 D6
Bonham Ho W11 .....244 C4
Bonham Rd SW2 .....160 B6
Dagenham RM8 ....80 D5
Bonheur Rd W4 ......111 B4
Bonhill St EC2 ..95 B3 242 D5
Boniface Gdns HA3 ....23 D3
Boniface Rd UB10 .....60 D5
Boniface Wlk HA3 .....23 D3
Bonington Ho N1 ....233 C3
Enfield EN1 ....18 A6
Bonita Mews SE15 ....140 D2
Bonne Marche Terr Mews
18 SE27 ....183 C6
Bonner Hill Rd KT1 ..198 C6
Bonner Ho 3 SW15 ..156 A6
Bonner Prim Sch E2 ..96 C4
Bonner Rd E2 ....96 C5
Bonnersfield Cl HA1 ...43 A3
Bonnersfield La
Harrow HA1 ....42 D3
Harrow HA1,HA3 ....43 A3
Bonner St E2 ....96 C5
Bonneville Gdns SW4 .159 C5
Bonneville Prim Sch
SW4 ....159 C5
Bonnington Ct 15 UB5 .84 D5
Bonnington Sq
SW8 ....138 B6 270 C6
Bonnington Twr BR2 ..210 A3
Bonny St NW1 ....71 C1
Bonser Rd TW1 ......152 D2
Bonsor Ho SW8 .....269 B2
Bonsor St SE5 ......139 C5
Bonthron Ho SW15 ...134 C3
Bonus Pastor RC Sch
BR1 ....186 C6
Bonville Gdns 17 NW4 .46 A5
Bonville Rd BR1 ......186 D5
Bookbinder Cotts N20 .14 D1
Booker Cl 15 E3 ....97 B2
Booker Rd 5 N18 ......34 A5
Bookham Ct CR4 .....202 B6
Boone Ct N9 ....18 C1
Boones Rd SE13 .....142 C1
Boone St SE13 ....142 C1
Boord St SE10 ....120 C3
Boothby Ct E4 ....20 A1
Boothby Ho 2 SW16 .181 C5
Boothby Rd N19 ....71 D6
Booth Cl 10 E9 ....96 B6
SE28 ....124 B6
Booth Ho 2 SW2 ....160 C4
Booth La EC4 ....252 A6
Boothman Ho HA3 .....43 D6
Booth Rd NW9 ....27 C1
Croydon CR0 ....220 D6
Boothroyd Ho TW7 ...130 D2
Booth's Pl W1 ....239 B3
Boot Par HA8 ....26 C4
Boot St N1 ....95 C4
Bordars Rd W7 ....86 D2
Bordars Wlk W7 ....86 C2
Borden Ave EN1 ....17 B5
Border Cres SE26 .....184 B5
Border Gate CR4 .....180 D2
Border Gdns CR0 .....223 D4
Border Rd SE26 ......184 B5
Bordesley Rd SM4 ...201 D5
Bordeston Ct TW8 ...131 C2
Bordon Wlk 5 SW15 .156 A4
Boreas Wlk N1 ......234 D3
Boreham Ave E16 ......99 A1
Boreham Cl E11 ....54 A1
Boreham Rd N22 ......33 A1
Boreman Ho 10 SE10 .142 A6
Borgard Ho 3 SE18 ..144 A4
Borgard Rd SE18 .....122 B2
Borkwood Pk BR6 ....227 D4
Borkwood Way BR6 ..227 C4
Borland Rd SE15 ....140 C1
Teddington TW11 ......175 B3
Borneo St SW15 .....134 C2
Borough High St
SE1 ....117 B5 252 C2
Borough Hill CR0 ....220 D5
Borough Mkt* SE1 ..252 C3
Borough Rd
SE1 ....116 D3 261 D6
Hounslow TW7 ....130 D4
7 Kingston KT2 ....176 C3
Mitcham CR4 ....180 C1
Borough Sq SE1 .....252 A1
Borough Sta The
SE1 ....117 A4 252 B1
Borrett Cl
SE17 ....117 A1 262 A1
Borrodaile Rd SW18 ..157 D5
Borrowdale NW1 .....232 A1
Borrowdale Ave HA3 ..25 A1
Borrowdale Cl IG4 .....56 A5
Borrowdale Ct EN2 .....5 A4
Borthwick Mews E15 ..76 C4
Borthwick Rd E15 .....76 C4
NW9 ....45 D3
Borthwick St SE8 .....119 C1
Borwick Ave E17 ....53 B6
Bosbury Rd SE6 ......164 A1
Boscastle Rd NW5 .....71 B5
Boscobel Ho 4 E8 ....74 B2
Boscobel Pl SW1 ....258 B4
Boscobel St
NW8 ....92 B3 236 D5
Boscombe Ave E10 ....54 B2
Boscombe Cl E5 ....75 A3
Boscombe Gdns
SW16 ....182 A4
Boscombe Ho CR0 ...205 B1
Boscombe Rd W12 ...112 A4
Merton SW19 ....179 D2
North Cheam KT4 .....200 D1
Streatham SW17 ......181 A4
Bose Cl N3 ....29 A2
Bosgrove E4 ....20 A2
Boss Ho SE1 ....253 C2
Boss St SE1 ....253 C2
Bostall Hill SE2 .....124 B1
Bostall La SE2 ......124 B1
Bostall Manor Way
SE2 ....124 B2
Bostall Park Ave DA7 .147 A5
Bostall Rd BR5 ......190 B3
Bostock Ho TW5 .....129 C6
Boston Bsns Pk W7 ..108 C3
Boston Ct
South Norwood SE25 ..205 D5
Sutton SM2 ....218 A1
Boston Gdns
Brentford TW8 ....109 B2
Chiswick W4 ....133 C6
Boston Gr HA4 ....39 A3
Boston Ho NW1 .....237 C6
25 SE5 ....139 A3
SW5 ....255 D3
Boston Manor Ho
TW8 ....109 B1
Boston Manor Rd
TW8 ....109 B1
Boston Manor Sta
TW8 ....109 A2
Boston Par W7 ......109 A2
Boston Park Rd TW8 .109 C1
Boston Pl NW1 .92 D3 237 C5
Boston Rd E6 ....100 A4
HA8 ....27 A3
Ealing W7 ....109 A3
Thornton Heath CR0 ..204 C3
Bostonthorpe Rd W7 .108 C4
Boston Vale W7 ......109 A2
Bosun Cl 8 E14 .....119 C4
Boswell Ct 9 W14 ...112 D3
WC1 ....240 B4
Kingston KT2 ....176 C2
Boswell Ho BR2 .....209 D4
WC1 ....240 B4
5 Streatham SW16 ....181 C5
Boswell Rd CR7 .....205 A5
Boswell St WC1 94 A2 240 B4
Boswood Ct TW4 ....129 B2
Bosworth Cl E17 ......35 B2
Bosworth Ho 4 W10 ..91 A3
Bosworth Rd N11 .....31 D4
W10 ....91 A3
Barnet EN5 ....1 C2
Dagenham RM10 ....81 C5
Botany Bay La BR7 ...189 A1
Botany Cl EN4 ....2 C1
Boteley Cl E4 ....20 B2
Botham Cl 6 HA8 .....27 A3
Botha Rd E13 ....99 C2
Bothwell Cl E16 ....98 D2
Bothwell St 4 W6 ...134 D6
Botolph Alley EC3 ...253 A6
Botolph La EC3 .....253 A6
Botsford Rd SW20 ...179 A1
Bott's Mews W2 ....91 C1
Botwell Common Rd
UB3 ....105 C6
Botwell Cres UB3 ......83 C1
Botwell House RC Prim Sch
UB3 ....105 D4
Botwell La UB3 ......105 C6
Boucher Cl TW11 ....174 D5
Bouchier Ho 6 N2 ....30 B1
Bough Beech Ct EN3 ....6 D6
Boughton Ave BR2 ...208 D2
Boughton Ho SE1 ...252 C2
Boughton Rd SE28 ...123 C3
Boulcott St E1 ....96 D1
Boulevard The 4
SW17 ....159 A2
Boullen Ct SM1 ......218 A4
Boulogne Ho SE1 ...263 C6
Boulogne Rd CR0 ....205 A3
Boulter Ho SE14 .....140 C4
Boulton Ho TW8 .....110 A1
Boulton Rd RM8 ....81 B6
Boultwood Rd E6 ....100 B1
Bounces La N9 ....18 B2
Bounces Rd N9 ....18 C2
Boundaries Mans 3
SW12 ....159 A3
Boundaries Rd
Feltham TW13 ....150 C3
Upper Tooting SW12 ..159 A3
Boundary Ave E17 .....53 B2
Boundary Bsns Ct CR4 202 B6
Boundary Cl Barnet EN5 ..1 B4
Ilford IG3 ....79 C4
Boundary Cl *continued*
Kingston KT1 ....198 D6
Penge SE20 ....184 A1
Southall UB2 ....107 C1
Boundary Ct 3 N18 ...33 D4
Boundary Ho 1 SE5 ..139 A5
Balham SW12 ....159 B3
Isleworth TW1 ....153 B6
Boundary La E13,E6 ...99 D3
SE17 ....139 A6
Boundary Pas E2 ....243 C6
Boundary Rd DA15 ...167 C6
E13 ....99 D4
E17 ....53 C3
N9 ....18 C5
NW8 ....92 A6 229 B6
Boundary Rd N2 ......30 B2
Boundary Rd
Mitcham SW19 ....180 B4
Pinner HA5 ....40 D2
Tottenham N22 ....33 A1
Wallington SM5,SM6 ..219 A1
Boundary Road Est
NW8 ....92 A6 229 A5
Boundary Row SE1 ..251 C2
Boundary St E2 95 D3 243 C6
Boundary Way CR0 ..223 C3
Boundfield Rd SE6 ..164 C2
Bounds Green Ct N11 .31 D4
Bounds Green Ind Est
N11 ....31 C4
Bounds Green Jun & Inf
Schs N11 ....32 A3
Bounds Green Rd N11 .31 D4
Wood Green N22 ....32 A2
Bounds Green Sta N11 .31 D3
Bourbon Ho 9 SE6 ...186 A6
Bourchier St W1 .....249 C6
Bourdillon Ct 2 SE9 .166 A2
Bourdon Pl W1 ......248 D6
Bourdon Rd SE20 ....184 C1
Bourdon St
W1 ....115 B6 248 D5
Bourke Cl NW10 ....67 C2
SW4 ....160 A5
Bourlet Cl W1 ......239 A3
Bourn Ave N15 ....51 B5
Hillingdon UB8 ....82 C3
New Barnet EN4 ....14 B6
Bournbrook Rd SE3,
SE9 ....143 D2
Bourne Ave Hayes UB3 105 B3
Palmers Green N14 .....16 A2
Ruislip HA4 ....62 C3
Bourne Cir UB3 ......105 A3
Bourne Cl KT7 ....212 D6
Bourne Ct Chiswick W4 133 A6
Ruislip HA4 ....62 B3
Wanstead E11 ....55 A4
Woodford IG8 ....37 D1
Bourne Dr CR4 ......180 B1
Bourne Gdns E4 ....35 D6
Bourne Hill N13 ....16 B2
Bourne Ho 1 NW2 .....68 A5
5 SW4 ....137 C1
Ashford TW15 ....170 C5
Buckhurst Hill IG9 ......21 D1
Bournemead Ave UB5 ..84 A5
Bournemead Cl UB5 ..84 A4
Bournemead Way UB5 .84 B5
Bourne Mews W1 ....238 B1
Bournemouth Cl SE15 140 A3
Bournemouth Rd
SE15 ....140 A3
Merton SW19 ....179 C2
Bourne Par DA5 .....169 D4
Bourne Pl W4 ....111 B1
Bourne Prim Sch HA4 .62 C2
Bourne Rd DA5 ......169 D5
E7,E11 ....76 D5
N8 ....50 A3
Bromley BR2 ....209 D5
Bournes Ho 4 N15 ....51 C3
Bourneside 5 N14 ....15 D3
Bourneside Cres 6
N14 ....15 D3
Bourneside Gdns SE6 .186 A5
Bourne St
SW1 ....115 A2 258 A3
Croydon CR0 ....220 D6
Bourne Terr W2 ....91 D2
Bourne The N14 ....16 A2
Bourne Vale BR2 ....208 D1
Bournevale Rd SW16 .182 A6
Bourne View UB6 .....64 D3
Bourne Way
Cheam SM1 ....217 B3
Coney Hall BR2,BR4 ..224 D6
West Ewell KT19 .....215 A4
Bournewood Rd SE18,
SE2 ....146 A5
Bournville Rd SE6 ..163 C4
Bournwell Cl EN4 ....2 D3
Bourton Cl UB3 ......106 A5
Bousfield Prim Sch
SW10 ....114 A1 256 A2
Bousfield Rd SE14 ...140 D3
Boutcher CE Prim Sch
SE1 ....117 D2 263 C4
Boutflower Rd SW11 .136 C1
Bouverie Gdns HA3 ....43 D3
Bouverie Mews N16 ...73 C6
Bouverie Pl W2 .....236 D2
Bouverie Rd N16 ......73 C6
Harrow HA1 ....42 A3
Bouverie St EC4 94 C1 241 B1
Bouvier Rd EN3 ....6 C5
Boveney Rd SE23 ....162 D4
Bovill Rd SE23 ......162 D4
Bovingdon Ave HA9 ...66 C2
Bovingdon Cl 3 N19 ..71 C6
Bovingdon La NW9 ....27 C2
Bovingdon Rd
SW6 ....135 D4 265 D1
Bovril Ho EN1 ....5 C2
Bowater Cl NW9 ......45 B4
SW2 ....160 A5
Bowater Gdns TW16 ..172 B2
Bowater Ho EC1 .....242 B5
Bowater Pl SE3 .....143 B5
Bowater Rd SE18 ....121 D3
Bow Brook The 20 E2 ..96 D5
Bow Church Sta E3 ....97 C4
Bow Churchyard EC2,
EC4 ....242 B1
Bow Common La E3 ...97 B3
Bowden Cl TW14 ....149 C3
Bowden Ho 28 E3 .....97 D4
Bowden House Hospl
(Private) HA1 ....64 C6
Bowden St
SE11 ....116 C1 261 B1
Bowditch SE8 ....119 B1
Bowdon Rd E17 ....53 C2
Bowen Ct 2 N5 ....72 D4
Bowen Dr SE21 ......161 C1
Bowen Rd HA1 ....42 A2
Bowen St E14 ....97 D1
Bower Ave SE3 ......142 C5
Bower Cl UB5 ....84 C5
Bowerdean St SW6 ...135 D3
Bower Ho SE14 ......140 D4
Bowerman Ave SE14 .141 A6
Bowerman Ct 1 N19 ..71 D6
Bowers Ho 5 IG11 ....78 D1
Bower St E1 ....96 D1
Bowers Wlk 1 E6 ....100 B1
Bowes Cl DA15 ......168 B5
Bowes Park Sta N22 ..32 A3
Bowes Prim Sch N11 ..31 D5
Bowes Rd N11 ....31 C5
W3 ....111 C6
Dagenham RM8 ....80 C4
Walton-on-T KT12 .....194 B1
Bowes Rd (North Circular
Rd) N13 ....32 A5
Bowfell Rd W6 ......134 C6
Bowford Ave DA7 ....147 A4
Bowhill Cl SW9 ......138 C5
Bowie Cl SW4 ....159 D4
Bow Ind Pk E15 ....75 C1
Bow La EC2,EC4 .95 A1 242 B1
N12 ....30 A3
Bowland Ho N4 ....51 A2
Bowland Rd SW4 ....137 D1
Woodford IG8 ....37 C4
Bowland Yd SW1 ....247 D1
Bowl Ct EC2 ....243 B5
Bowles Ct N12 ....30 C3
Bowles Rd 1 SE1 ....140 A6
Bowley Cl SE19 .....183 D4
Bowley Ho 6 SE16 ...118 A3
Bowley La SE19 .....183 D5
Bowling Cl UB10 ......82 B6
Bowling Green Cl
SW19 ....156 B4
Bowling Green Ct HA9 .66 B6
Bowling Green Ho
SW10 ....266 C4
Bowling Green La
EC1 ....94 C3 241 B6
Bowling Green Pl SE1 252 C2
Bowling Green Row 1
SE18 ....122 B2
Bowling Green St
SE11 ....138 C6
Bowling Green Wlk N1 95 C4
Bowls Cl HA7 ....25 B5
Bowman Ave E16 ....120 D6
Bowman Mews E1 ...118 A6
Wandsworth SW18 ....157 B3
Bowmans Cl W13 ....109 B5
Bowmans Lea SE23 ..162 C4
Bowman's Meadow
SM6 ....219 B5
Bowman's Mews N7 ...72 A5
Bowman's Pl N7 ....72 A5
Bowmead SE9 ....166 B2
Bowmore Wlk NW1 ...71 D1
Bowness Cl 5 E8 .....73 D2
Bowness Cres KT2,
SW15 ....177 C5
Bowness Dr TW4 ....129 A1
Bowness Ho SE15 ...140 C5
Bowness Rd DA7 ....147 D3
Catford SE6 ....163 D4
Bowood Rd SW11 ....159 A6
Enfield EN3 ....6 D3
Bow Rd E3 ....97 C4
Bowring Gn WD19 .....22 C5
Bow Road Sta E3 ......97 C4
Bowrons Ave HA0 .....65 D1
Bowry Ho 14 E14 .....97 B2
Bow Sch E3 ....97 C4
Bowsley Ct TW13 ....150 A2
Bowsprit Point 5 E14 119 C3
Bow St E15 ....76 C3
WC2 ....94 A1 240 B1
Bowstead Ct SW11 ..266 D1
Bow Triangle Bsns Ctr
E3 ....97 C3
Bowyer Cl E6 ....100 B2
Bowyer Ct 4 E4 ....20 A3
Bowyer Ho 28 N1 .....95 C6
Wandsworth SW18 ....157 D5
Bowyer Pl SE5 ......139 A5
Bowyer St 15 SE5 ...139 A5
Boxall Rd SE21 .....161 C5
Boxgrove Prim Sch
SE2 ....124 C3
Boxgrove Rd SE2 ....124 C3
Box La IG11 ....102 C5
Boxley Ho 3 E5 ....74 B3
Boxley Rd SM4 ......202 A5
Boxley St E16 ....121 B5
Boxmoor Ho 16 E2 ....96 A6
9 W11 ....112 D5
Boxmoor Rd HA3 ......43 B5
Boxoll Rd RM9 ....81 B5
Boxshall Ho 7 SE18 ..144 D6
Box Tree Ho SE8 ....119 A1
Boxtree La HA3 ....24 B3
Boxtree Rd HA3 ....24 B3
Boxwood Cl UB7 .....104 B4
Boxworth Cl N12 ......30 B5
Boxworth Gr
N1 ....94 B6 233 D6
Boyard Rd SE18 ....122 D1
Boyce Ho 1 W10 ......91 B4
Streatham SW16 ......181 C5
Boyce St SE1 ....251 A3
Boyce Way E13 ....99 A3
Boycroft Ave NW9 .....45 A3
Boyd Ave UB1 ....107 B5
Boyd Cl KT2 ....176 C3
Boyd Ct SW15 ....156 C5
Boydell Ct NW8 ....70 B1
Boyden Ho 8 E17 .....54 A6
Boyd Rd SW19 ....180 B4
Boyd St E1 ....96 A1
Boyfield St
SE1 ....116 D4 251 D1
Boyland Rd BR1 .....186 D5
Boyle Ave HA7 ....25 A4
Boyle Cl UB10 ....82 B5
Boyle Farm Rd KT7 ..197 A3
Boyle Ho 13 DA17 ...125 C3
Boyle St W1 ....249 A6
Boyne Ave NW4 ....46 D5
Boyne Ct NW10 ....68 A1
Boyne Ho 10 E5 ....74 B6
Boyne Rd SE13 ......142 B2
Dagenham RM10 ....81 C5
Boyne Terr Mews
W11 ....113 B5 244 C4
Boyson Rd 10 SE17 ..139 B6
Boyton Cl E1 ....96 D3
N8 ....50 A6
Boyton Ho NW8 .....229 D4
SE11 ....261 A1
Boyton Rd N8 ....50 A6
Brabant Rd N22 ....32 B1
Brabazon Ave SM6 ...220 A1
Brabazon Rd
Heston TW5 ....128 D5
Northolt UB5 ....85 C5
Brabazon St E14 ......97 D2
Brabner Ho 2 E2 ......96 A4
Brabourne Cl 7 SE19 183 C5
Brabourne Cres DA7 .147 B6
Brabourne Hts NW7 ...11 C1
Brabourne Rise BR3 ..208 B4
Brabourn Gr SE15 ...140 C3
Brabrook Ct SM6 ....219 B3
Brabstone Ho 2 UB6 ..86 D5
Bracer Ho 1 N1 ....95 C5
Bracewell Ave UB6 ....65 A2
Bracewell Rd W10 .....90 C2
Bracewood Gdns CR0 221 D5
Bracey St N4 ....72 A6
Bracken Ave
Balham SW12 ....159 A4
Croydon CR0 ....223 C5
Brackenbridge Dr HA4 .62 D5
Brackenbury N4 ....50 B1
Brackenbury Gdns
W6 ....112 B3
Brackenbury Prim Sch
W6 ....112 B3
Brackenbury Rd N2 ...48 A6
W6 ....112 B3
Bracken Cl E6 ....100 B2
Ashford TW16 ....171 D4
Twickenham TW4 .....151 C4

Brackendale
Kingston KT1 176 D1
Southgate N21 16 B2
Brackendale Cl TW5 129 D4
Brackendale Ct 2
BR3 185 C3
Bracken End TW7 152 B6
Brackenfield Cl E5 74 B5
Bracken Gdns SW13 134 A3
Brackenhill HA4 63 A4
Bracken Hill Cl 5
BR1 186 D2
Bracken Hill La BR1 186 D2
Bracken Ho 14 E3 97 C2
Bracken Mews
Chingford E4 20 A3
Romford RM7 59 D3
Brackens BR3 185 C3
Brackens The EN1 17 C4
Bracken The E4 20 A2
Brackenwood TW16 172 A2
Brackenwood Lo EN5 1 C1
Brackley Cl SM6 220 A1
Brackley Ct NW8 236 D6
Brackley Rd W4 111 C1
Beckenham BR3 185 C3
Brackley Sq IG8 37 D3
Brackley St EC1 242 B4
Brackley Terr 6 W4 111 C1
Bracklyn Ct N1 235 C4
Bracklyn St N1 235 C4
Bracknell Cl N22 32 C2
Bracknell Gate NW3 69 D3
Bracknell Gdns NW3 69 D4
Bracknell Way NW3 69 D4
Bracondale KT10 212 A3
Bracondale Rd SE2 124 A2
Bradbeer Ho 24 E2 96 C4
Bradbourne Rd DA5 169 C4
Bradbourne St SW6 135 C3
Bradbury Cl UB2 107 B2
Bradbury Ct 2 SE3 143 A5
Bradbury Ho E1 243 D2
Bradbury St 28 N16 73 C3
Bradby Ho NW8 91 D5
Braddock Cl TW7 130 D3
Braddock Ho 9 NW6 91 D6
Braddon Rd TW9 132 B2
Braddyll St SE10 120 C1
Bradenham 11 SE17 139 B6
Bradenham Ave DA16 146 A1
Bradenham Cl SE17 139 B6
Bradenham Rd
Harrow HA3 43 B5
Hayes UB4 83 C4
Braden St W9 91 D3
Bradfield Ct 10 NW1 71 B1
Bradfield Dr IG11 80 A3
Bradfield Ho 15 SW8 137 D3
Bradfield Rd E16 121 B4
Ruislip HA4 63 A3
Bradford Cl BR2 210 B1
Forest Hill SE26 184 B6
Tottenham N17 33 D4
Bradford Dr KT19 215 D2
Bradford Ho 4 W14 112 D3
Bradford Rd W3 111 C4
Ilford IG1 57 C1
Bradgate Rd SE6 163 D5
Brading Cres E11 77 B6
Brading Rd
Streatham SW2 160 B4
Thornton Heath CR0 204 B3
Brading Terr W12 112 A3
Bradiston Rd W9 91 B4
Bradley Cl N7 72 B2
Bradley Ct CR0 220 C4
Bradley Gdns W13 87 B1
Bradley Ho 4 E2 96 B5
1 E3 97 D4
SE16 118 B2
Twickenham TW1 152 D3
Bradley Mews SW12 158 D3
Bradley Rd Enfield EN3 7 A6
South Norwood SE19 183 A4
Wood Green N22 32 B1
Bradley's Cl N1 234 B4
Bradley Stone Rd E6 100 B2
Bradlord Ho SE21 161 C1
Bradman Row 7 HA8 27 A3
Bradmead
SW8 137 C5 269 A3
Bradmore Park Rd
W6 112 B2
Bradon 24 NW9 27 D1
Bradshaw Cl SW19 179 C4
Bradshawe Waye UB8 82 B2
Bradshaws Cl SE25 206 A6
Bradsole Ho 13 BR3 185 C3
Brad St SE1 116 C5 251 B3
Bradstock Ho E9 75 A1
Bradstock Rd E9 74 D2
Stoneleigh KT17 216 B3
Bradwell Ave RM10 81 C6
Bradwell Cl E18 54 D5
Bradwell Ho 9 E17 53 D6
Bradwell Ho *continued*
6 NW6 91 D6
Bradwell Mews 5 N18 34 A6
Brady Ct RM8 58 D1
Brady Ho SW4 159 D6
SW8 269 B2
Bradymead E6 100 D1
Brady St E1 96 B3
Braeburn Ct 1 EN4 2 C1
Brae Ct
2 Kingston KT2 176 C2
South Norwood SE25 183 C2
Braefoot Ct SW15 156 D6
Braemar SW15 156 D5
Braemar Ave NW10 67 B6
Thornton Heath CR7 204 D6
Wembley HA0 66 A1
Wimbledon SW18,SW19 157 C2
Wood Green N22 32 A2
Braemar Ct
4 Brentford TW8 131 D6
5 Catford SE6 164 D3
Braemar Gdns DA15 167 B1
NW9 27 B2
West Wickham BR4 208 A1
Braemar Ho W9 229 A1
Richmond TW11 175 B5
Braemar Mans W8 255 D5
Braemar Rd E13 98 D3
N15 51 C4
Brentford TW8 131 D6
North Cheam KT4 216 B5
Braemore Ct EN4 3 A1
Braemore Ho 21 SE15 140 A5
Braeside BR3 185 D5
Braeside Ave SW19 179 A2
Braeside Cl HA5 23 C3
Braeside Rd SW16 181 C3
Braeside Sch
Buckhurst Hill IG9 21 B3
Buckhurst Hill IG9 21 C2
Braes St N1 72 D1
Braesyde Cl DA17 125 B2
Brafferton Rd CR0 221 A4
Braganza St
SE17 116 D1 261 C1
Bragg Cl RM8 80 B2
Bragg Rd TW11 174 D4
Braham Ho SE11 260 D1
Braham St E1 243 D2
Brahma Kumaris World
Spiritual Univ NW10 68 A1
Braid Ave W3 89 C1
Braid Cl TW13 151 B2
Braid Ho SE10 142 A4
Braidwood Rd SE6 164 B3
Braidwood St
SE1 117 C5 253 A3
Braikenridge Ho N21 17 B5
Brailsford Cl SW19 180 C3
Brailsford Rd SW2 160 C5
Braintcroft Prim Sch
NW2 67 D5
Brainton Ave TW14 150 C4
Braintree Ave IG4 56 A5
Braintree Ho 5 E1 96 C3
Braintree Rd
Dagenham RM10 81 C5
Ruislip HA4 62 B4
Braintree St E2 96 C4
Braithwaite Ave RM7 59 C2
Braithwaite Gdns HA7 25 C2
Braithwaite Ho EC1 242 C6
14 South Bromley E14 98 B1
Braithwaite Rd EN3 7 B2
Braithwaite Twr W2 236 C4
Bramah Gn SW9 138 C4
Bramall Cl E15 76 D3
Bramall Ct N7 72 B2
Bramber WC1 233 A1
Bramber Ct TW8 110 A2
Bramber Rd N12 30 C5
W14 135 B6 264 C6
Bramble Acres Cl
SM2 217 C1
Bramblebury Rd SE18 123 A1
Bramble Cl N15 52 A5
Beckenham BR3 208 A4
Croydon CR0 223 D4
Hillingdon UB8 82 B1
Stanmore HA7 25 D3
Upper Halliford TW17 193 B6
Brambledown 4 N4 50 A2
Brambledown Cl BR2,
BR4 208 C4
Brambledown Rd
South Croydon CR2 221 C1
Wallington SM5,SM6 219 B1
Bramble Gdns W12 111 D6
Bramble Ho 12 E3 97 C2
Bramble La TW12 173 B4
Brambles Cl TW7,TW8 131 B5
Brambles Farm Dr
UB10 82 C4
Brambles The
West Drayton UB7 104 A2
8 Wimbledon SW19 179 B5
Bramblewood Cl SM5 202 C1
Brambling Ct 25 SE8 141 B6
Bramblings The E4 36 B6
Bramcote Ave CR4 202 D5
Bramcote Ct CR4 202 D5
Bramcote Gr SE16 118 C1
Bramcote Rd SW15 134 B1
Bramdean Cres SE12 165 A3
Bramdean Gdns SE12 165 A3
Bramerton NW6 68 D1
Bramerton Rd BR3 207 B6
Bramerton St
SW3 136 C6 267 A6
Bramfield Ct N4 73 A6
Bramfield Rd SW11 158 D6
Bramford Ct N14 15 D2
Bramford Rd SW18 136 A1
Bramham Gdns
SW5 113 D1 255 D2
Chessington KT9 213 D4
Bramham Ho SE22 139 C1
Bramhope La SE7 143 B6
Bramlands Cl SW11 136 C2
Bramlea Cl N6 49 A3
Bramley Ave TW17 193 C6
Bramley Cl E17 35 A1
Croydon CR2 221 A3
East Barnet N14 15 B6
Hayes UB3 106 A6
Orpington BR6 210 D1
Pinner HA5 39 D6
Twickenham TW2 152 A5
Woodford IG8 37 C3
Bramley Cres
SW8 137 D5 269 D4
Ilford IG2 56 C3
Bramley Ct DA16 146 B4
NW2 68 B5
2 Barnet EN4 2 C1
9 Chingford E4 20 A3
Feltham TW14 149 C5
Mitcham CR4 180 B1
Southall UB1 108 A6
Wallington SM6 219 C3
Bramley Gdns WD19 22 C5
Bramley Hill CR2 221 A4
Bramley Ho 18 W10 90 D1
Hounslow TW3 129 B1
Ilford IG2 56 C3
1 Kingston KT2 176 D3
5 Roehampton SW15 155 D5
Bramley House Ct EN2 5 B6
Bramleyhyrst CR2 221 A3
Bramley Lo HA0 65 D4
Bramley Rd W10 90 D1
W5 109 C3
Southgate N14 15 C6
Sutton SM1 218 B3
Bramley Way
Hounslow TW4 151 B6
West Wickham BR4 223 D6
Brampton Cl 14 E5 74 B6
Brampton Ct NW4 46 B5
Brampton Gr NW4 46 C5
Harrow HA3 43 B5
Wembley HA9 44 C1
Brampton La 4 NW4 46 C5
Brampton Manor Sch
E6 99 D3
Brampton Park Rd N22 50 C6
Brampton Prim Sch
E6 100 A4
Bexley DA16 146 D3
Brampton Rd DA7 147 A4
E6 99 D4
N15 51 A4
NW9 44 C5
Croydon CR0 205 D3
Hillingdon UB10 82 D5
Bramshaw Gdns WD19 22 D5
Bramshaw Rd E9 74 D2
Bramshaw Rise KT3 199 C3
Bramshill Gdns NW5 71 B5
Bramshill Rd NW10 89 D5
Bramshot Ave SE7 143 B6
Bramshott Ct 3 KT6 198 A3
Bramshurst NW8 91 D6
Bramston Rd NW10 90 A5
Wandsworth SW17 158 A1
Bramwell Cl TW16 172 D1
Bramwell Ho SE1 262 B5
SW1 269 A6
Bramwell Mews N1 233 D6
Brancaster Dr NW7 28 A3
Brancaster Ho 22 E1 96 D4
N5 72 D3
Brancaster Rd
Ilford E12 78 B4
Ilford IG2 57 C3
Streatham SW16 160 A1
Brancepeth Gdns IG9 21 A2
Branch Hill NW3 70 A5
Branch Pl N1 95 B6 235 D6
Branch Rd E14 119 A6
Branch St SE15 139 C5
Brancker Cl SM6 220 A1
Brancker Rd HA3 43 D6
Brancroft Way EN3 7 B4
Brand Cl N4 50 D1
Brandlehow Rd SW15 135 B1
Brandon Ho BR3 185 D5
Brandon Mews EC2 242 C4
Brandon Rd E17 54 A6
N7 72 A1
Southall UB2 107 B1
Sutton SM1 217 D4
Brandon St
SE17 117 A2 262 B3
Brandram Rd SE13 142 C1
Brandrams Wharf
SE16 118 C4
Brandreth Ct HA1 42 D3
Brandreth Rd
Newham E6 100 B1
Upper Tooting SW17 159 B2
Brandries The SM6 219 D5
Brand St SE10 142 A5
Brandville Gdns IG6 56 D5
Brandville Rd UB7 104 A4
Brandy Way SM2 217 C1
Brangbourne Rd BR1 186 A5
Brangton Rd SE11 260 D1
Brangwyn Cres SW19 180 B1
Brangwyn Ct W14 254 A5
Branham Ho 1 SE18 122 D1
Branksea St
SW6 135 A3 264 A3
Branksome Ave N18 33 D5
Branksome Cl KT12 194 D1
Branksome Ct 6 N2 48 A6
Branksome Ho SW8 270 C4
Branksome Rd SW2 160 A6
Merton SW19 179 C2
Branksome Way
Harrow HA3 44 B3
Kingston KT3 177 B2
Bransby Ct 4 N16 73 C4
Bransby Rd KT9 214 A2
Branscombe NW1 232 B5
Branscombe Ct BR2 208 C4
Branscombe Gdns N21 16 C4
Branscombe St SE13 141 D2
Bransdale Cl NW6 91 C6
Bransgrove Rd HA8 26 B3
Branston Cres BR5 211 B1
Branstone Ct 9 TW9 132 B4
Branstone Rd TW9 132 B4
Branston Ho N7 72 C3
Brants Wlk W7 86 C3
Brantwood Ave DA8 147 D5
Isleworth TW7 131 A1
Brantwood Cl E17 53 D6
Brantwood Gdns
Enfield EN2 16 A6
Redbridge IG4 56 A5
Brantwood Ho 9 SE5 139 A5
Brantwood Rd DA7 147 D2
SE24 161 A6
Tottenham N17 34 A4
Brasenose Dr SW13 134 C6
Brasher Cl UB6 64 B3
Brassett Point 3 E15 98 C6
Brassey Cl TW14 150 A3
Brassey Ho 1 E14 119 D2
Walton-on-T KT12 194 A1
Brassey Rd NW6 69 B2
Brassey Sq SW11 137 A2
Brassie Ave W3 89 C1
Brass Talley Alley 31
SE16 118 D4
Brasted Cl DA6 168 D6
Forest Hill SE26 184 C6
Brasted Lo 11 BR3 185 C3
Brathay NW1 232 B3
Brathway Rd SW18 157 C4
Bratley St 12 E1 96 A3
Bratten Ct CR0 205 B3
Braund Ave UB6 85 D3
Braundton Ave DA15 167 D3
Braunston Dr UB4 85 A3
Bravington Cl TW17 192 B4
Bravington Pl W9 91 B3
Bravington Rd W9 91 B4
Brawne Ho 12 SE17 138 D6
Braxfield Rd SE4 141 B1
Braxted Pk SW16 182 B4
Bray NW3 70 C1
Brayard's Rd SE15 140 B3
Braybourne Dr TW7 130 D5
Braybrooke Gdns
SE19 183 C3
Braybrook St W12 89 D1
Brayburne Ave SW4 137 C3
Braycourt Ave KT12 194 C2
Bray Cres SE16 118 D4
Bray Ct Chessington KT9 214 B3
Streatham SW16 182 A5
Braydon Rd N16 52 A1
Bray Dr E16 120 D6
Brayfield Terr N1 72 C1
Brayford Sq 12 E1 96 C1
Bray Pl SW3 114 D2 257 C3
Bray Rd NW7 28 D4
Brayton Gdns EN2 3 D1
Braywick Ct 9 KT2 176 C3
Braywood Rd SE9 145 B1
Brazil Cl CR0 204 A2
Breach La RM9 103 C4
Bread St EC2,EC4 242 B1
Breakspeare SE21 161 D1
Breakspear Jun & Inf Schs
UB10 60 C6
Breakspear Rd HA4,UB9 38 D3
Breakspear Rd N UB9 38 B5
Breakspear Rd S UB9,
UB10 38 C1
Breakspears Dr BR5 190 A2
Breakspears Mews
SE4 141 C3
Breakspears Rd SE4 141 C2
Breakwell Ct 16 W10 91 A3
Bream Cl N17 52 B5
Bream Gdns E6 100 C4
Breamore Cl SW15 156 A3
Breamore Ct IG3 80 A6
Breamore Rd IG3 79 D6
Bream's Bldgs
EC4 94 C1 241 A2
Bream St E3 75 C1
Breamwater Gdns
TW10 153 B1
Brearley Cl HA8 27 A3
Uxbridge UB8 60 A2
Breaside Prep Sch
BR1 187 D2
Breasley Cl SW15 134 B1
Brechin Pl
SW7 114 A2 256 B3
Brecknock Prim Sch
NW1 71 D2
Brecknock Rd N19 71 D3
Breckonmead BR1 187 C1
Breco Ho IG11 102 B4
Brecon Cl Mitcham CR4 204 A6
North Cheam KT4 216 C6
Brecon Ct N12 14 A1
7 SE9 166 C5
Brecon Gn NW9 45 C3
Brecon Ho N16 51 D1
W2 236 A2
Wandsworth SW18 157 C4
Brecon Rd W6 135 A6 264 B5
Enfield EN3 6 C1
Brede Cl E6 100 C4
Bredel Ho 1 E14 97 C2
Bredgar SE13 163 D6
Bredgar Rd N19 71 C6
Bredhurst Cl SE20 184 C4
Bredinghurst SE22 162 A4
Bredinghurst Sch
SE15 140 D1
Bredon Ct HA8 26 B6
Bredon Rd CR0 205 D2
Breer St SW6 135 D2
Breezer's Ct 15 E1 118 A6
Breezer's Hill E1 118 A6
Bremans Row SW18 158 A2
Brember Rd HA2 64 A6
Bremer Mews E17 53 D5
Bremner Rd SW7 256 B6
Brenchley Cl
Chislehurst BR7 188 C2
Hayes BR2 208 D3
Brenchley Gdns SE15,
SE22,SE23 162 D5
Brenchley Rd BR5 189 D1
Brenda Rd SW17 158 D2
Brende Gdns KT8 195 D5
Brendon Ave NW10 67 C4
Brendon Cl Esher KT10 212 A2
Harlington UB7 127 A5
Brendon Ct UB2 107 D2
Brendon Dr KT10 212 A2
Brendon Gdns
Harrow HA2 63 D4
Ilford IG2 57 C4
Brendon Gr N2 30 A1
Brendon H SM2 218 A2
Brendon Ho W1 238 A4
Brendon Rd BR7 167 B2
Dagenham RM8 59 C1
Brendon St W1 92 C1 237 B2
Brendon Villas N21 17 A3
Brendon Way EN1 17 C4
Brenley Cl CR4 203 A6
Brenley Gdns SE9 143 D1
Brenley Ho SE1 252 C2
Brent Cl DA5 169 A3
Brentcot Cl W13 87 B3
Brent Cres NW10 88 B5
Brent Cross Flyover
NW2,NW4 46 D2
Brent Cross Gdns NW4 46 D3
Brent Cross Interchange
NW2,NW4 46 D2
Brent Cross Sh Ctr
NW4 46 C2
Brent Cross Sta NW11 46 D2
Brent Ct NW11 46 D2
5 W12 111 C3
Ealing W7 108 B6
Brentfield NW10 66 D1
Brentfield Cl NW10 67 B2
Brentfield Gdns NW2 46 D2
Brentfield Ho 6 NW10 67 B1
Brentfield Prim Sch
NW10 67 B2
Brentfield Rd NW10 67 B2
Brentford Bsns Ctr
TW8 131
Brentford Cl UB4 84
Brentford Fountain Leisure
Centre W4 110
Brentford Ho 6 TW1 153
Brentford Sch for Girls
TW8 131
Brentford Sta TW8 131
Brent Gn NW4 46
Brentham Way W5 87
Brent Ho 15 E9 74
3 Catford BR1 186
Brenthouse Rd E9 74
Brenthurst Rd NW10 67
Brent Knoll Sch SE26 162
Brent Lea TW8 131
Brent Mans NW4 46
Brentmead Cl W7 108
Brentmead Gdns NW10 88
Brentmead Pl NW11 46
Brent New Ent Ctr
NW10 67
Brenton Ct E9 75
Brenton St E14 97
Brent Park Ind Est
UB2 106
Brent Park Rd NW4 46
Brent Pl EN5 13
Brent Rd E16 99
Brentford TW8 131
Southall UB2 106
Woolwich SE18 144
Brent Side TW8 131
Brentside Cl W13 87
Brentside Executive Ctr
TW8 131
Brentside High Sch W7 86
Brentside Prim Sch W7 86
Brent St NW4 46
Brent Trad Est NW10 67
Brentvale Ave
Southall UB1 108
Wembley HA0 88
Brent View Rd NW9 46
Brentwaters Bsns Pk
TW8 131
Brent Way N3 29
Brentford TW8 131
Wembley HA9 66
Brentwick Gdns TW8 110
Brentwood Cl SE9 167
Brentwood Ho 2
SE18 143
Brentwood Lo NW4 46
Brereton Ho 4 SW2 160
Brereton Rd N17 33
Bressenden Pl
SW1 115 C3 259
Bressey Ave EN1 6
Bressey Gr E18 36
Bretherton Ct CR2 221
Breton Ho EC2 242
SE1 263
Brett Cl N16 73
15 Northolt UB5 84
Brett Cres NW10 89
Brett Ct N9 18
Brettell St SE17 262
Brettenham Ave E17 35
Brettenham Prim Sch
N18 34
Brettenham Rd
Chingford E17 35
Edmonton N18 34
Brett Gdns RM9 81
Brett Ho 1 SW15 156
Brett House Cl 2
SW15 156
Brettinghurst 7 SE1 118
Brett Manor E8 74
Bretton Ho N19 50
Brett Pas 28 E8 74
Brett Rd E8 74
Barnet EN5 12
Brewers Bldgs EC1 234
Brewers Ct W2 234
Brewer's Gn SW1 259
Brewers La 11 TW9 153
Brewer St W1 115 C6 249
Brewery Cl HA0 65
Brewery Ind Est The
N1 235
Brewery Mews Bsns Ctr 1
TW7 131
Brewery Rd N7 72
SE18 123
Keston Mark BR2 210
Brewery Sq SE1 253
Brewhouse La E1 118
Brewhouse Rd 3
SE18 122
Brewhouse St SW15 135
Brewhouse Wlk SE16 119
Brewhouse Yd EC1 241
Brewood Rd RM8 80
Brewster Gdns W10 90
Brewster Ho E14 119
SE1 263

ewster Rd E10 ... 53 D1
an Ct N10 ... 31 B2
an Rd RM6 ... 58 C4
ant Ho SE1 ... 260 D5
ants Cl HA5 ... 23 B1
ant St SE14 ... 140 D5
iar Ave SW16 ... 182 B3
iarbank Rd W13 ... 87 A1
iar Cl N2 ... 30 A1
uckhurst Hill IG9 ... 21 D2
dmonton N13 ... 17 A1
ampton TW12 ... 173 B5
sleworth TW7 ... 152 D6
iar Cres UB5 ... 63 D2
iar Ct E11 ... 54 B2
8 ... 73 D1
heam SM3 ... 216 C4
ampton TW12 ... 173 D5
iardale HA8 ... 27 B6
andsworth SW19 ... 157 B3
iardale Gdns NW3 ... 69 C5
iardale Ho N16 ... 51 C1
iarfield Ave N3 ... 29 D1
iar Gdns BR2 ... 208 D1
iaris Cl [11] N17 ... 34 B3
iar La CR0 ... 223 D4
iar Lo E18 ... 37 C2
iar Rd NW2 ... 68 C4
arrow HA3 ... 43 C4
ittleton TW17 ... 192 C4
hornton Heath SW16 ... 204 B6
wickenham TW2 ... 152 C3
iars The WD23 ... 8 C4
iarswood Way BR6 ... 227 D3
iarview Ct E4 ... 36 B4
iar Way UB7 ... 104 C4
iar Wlk HA8 ... 27 A3
W10 ... 91 A3
utney SW15 ... 134 B1
iarwood Cl NW9 ... 45 A3
eltham TW13 ... 149 C1
iarwood Ct [5] KT4 ... 200 A1
iarwood Dr HA6 ... 22 A1
iarwood Rd SW4 ... 159 D6
Stoneleigh KT17 ... 216 A2
riary Cl NW3 ... 70 C1
riary Ct DA14 ... 190 B5
riary Gdns BR1 ... 187 B5
riary Gr HA8 ... 26 D1
riary La N9 ... 17 D1
riary Lo BR3 ... 186 A2
rickbarn Cl SW10 ... 266 B4
rick Ct EC4 ... 241 A1
rickett Cl HA4 ... 39 A4
rick Farm Cl TW9 ... 132 D4
rickfield Cl TW8 ... 131 C5
rickfield Cotts SE18 ... 145 D6
rickfield Farm Gdns
BR6 ... 227 A4
Brickfield La
Edgware EN5 ... 11 D5
Harlington UB3 ... 127 B6
Brickfield Rd
South Norwood CR7,
SW16 ... 182 D2
Wimbledon SW19 ... 179 D6
Brickfields HA2 ... 64 B6
Brickfields Way UB7 ... 104 B3
Brick La E1 ... 95 D3 243 D5
E2 ... 95 D4
Enfield EN1 ... 6 B3
Stanmore HA7 ... 25 D3
Bricklayers Arms SE1 262 D5
Brick St W1 ... 115 B5 248 C3
Brickwall La HA4 ... 39 D1
Brickwood Cl SE26 ... 162 B1
Brickwood Rd CR0 ... 221 C6
Brickworth Ho [26]
SW9 ... 138 C4
Bridal Mews N1 ... 234 C5
Brideale Cl SE15 ... 139 D6
Bride Ct EC4 ... 241 C1
Bride La EC4 ... 94 D1 241 C1
Bride St N7 ... 72 B2
Bridewain St SE1 ... 263 C6
Bridewell Pl [20] E1 ... 118 B5
EC4 ... 241 C1
Bridford Mews W1 ... 238 D4
Bridge App NW3 ... 71 A1
Bridge Ave W6 ... 112 C1
Ealing W7 ... 86 B2
Bridge Avenue Mans [1]
W6 ... 112 C1
Bridge Cl [13] W10 ... 90 D1
Enfield EN1 ... 6 B3
Teddington TW11 ... 174 D6
Walton-on-T KT12 ... 193 D1
Bridge Ct E10 ... 53 B2
Bridge Dr N13 ... 32 B6
Bridge End E17 ... 36 A2
Bridge Field Ho [7] W2 . 91 D1
Bridgefield Rd SM1,
SM2 ... 217 C2
Bridgefoot
SE1 ... 116 A1 260 B1
Bridge Gate N21 ... 17 A4
Bridge Gdns
East Molesey KT8 ... 196 B5
Littleton TW15 ... 171 A3
Bridge Ho E9 ... 74 D3
[1] NW1 ... 71 A1
SE4 ... 141 B1
TW8 ... 109 A2
Bridge Ho S TW8 ... 109 A2
Bridge House Quay
E14 ... 120 A5
Bridge La NW11 ... 47 B4
SW11 ... 136 C4 267 B1
Bridgeland Rd E16 ... 121 A6
Bridgeman Ho [19] E9 ... 74 C1
Bridgeman Rd N1 ... 72 B1
Teddington TW11 ... 175 A4
Bridgeman St
NW8 ... 92 C5 230 A3
Bridge Meadows
SE14 ... 140 D6
Bridgend Rd SW18 ... 136 A1
Bridgenhall Rd EN1 ... 5 D4
Bridgen Ho [15] E1 ... 96 B1
Bridgen Rd DA5 ... 169 A4
Bridge Par N21 ... 17 A4
Bridge Pk [7] SW18 ... 157 C6
Wembley NW10 ... 66 D1
Bridge Pl SW1 115 B2 258 D4
Croydon CR0 ... 205 B1
Bridgeport Pl [4] E1 ... 118 A5
Bridge Rd DA7 ... 147 A3
E15 ... 98 B6
E17 ... 53 B2
E6 ... 78 B1
NW10 ... 67 C2
Beckenham BR3 ... 185 B3
Chessington KT9 ... 214 A3
East Molesey KT8 ... 196 C5
Edmonton N9 ... 18 A1
Hounslow TW3 ... 130 B2
Isleworth TW3,TW7 ... 130 B2
Southall UB2 ... 107 C4
Sutton SM2 ... 217 D2
Twickenham TW1 ... 153 B5
Wallington SM6 ... 219 C3
Wembley HA9 ... 66 C5
Wood Green N22 ... 32 A2
Bridge Row CR0 ... 205 B1
Bridges Ct SW11 ... 136 B3
Bridges Ho [15] SE5 ... 139 B5
Bridges La CR0 ... 220 A4
Bridges Rd
Stanmore HA7 ... 24 D5
Wimbledon SW19 ... 179 D4
Bridges Road Mews
SW19 ... 179 D4
Bridge St SW1 116 A4 250 B1
W4 ... 111 B2
Pinner HA5 ... 41 A6
Richmond TW10 ... 153 D6
Walton-on-T KT12 ... 193 D2
Bridge Terr E15 ... 76 B1
Bridge The HA3 ... 42 D5
Bridgetown Cl [5]
SE19 ... 183 C5
Bridgeview [2] W6 ... 112 C1
Bridgewater Cl BR5,
BR7 ... 211 C6
Bridgewater Ct HA0 ... 65 C2
Bridgewater Gdns HA8 . 26 B1
Bridgewater Rd E15 ... 98 A6
Ruislip HA4 ... 62 B4
Wembley HA0 ... 65 C1
Bridgewater Sq EC2 ... 242 A4
Bridgewater St EC2 ... 242 A4
Bridge Way NW11 ... 47 B4
Bridgeway Barking IG11 79 D1
Wembley HA0 ... 66 B1
Bridge Way
Twickenham TW2 ... 152 A4
Uxbridge UB10 ... 60 D3
Bridgeway St
NW1 ... 93 C5 232 B3
Bridge Wharf [18] E2 ... 96 D5
Bridge Wharf Rd TW7 131 B2
Bridgewood Cl SE20 ... 184 B3
Bridgewood Rd
North Cheam KT17,KT4 . 216 A4
Streatham SW16 ... 181 D3
Bridge Yd SE1 ... 252 D4
Bridgford St SW17,
SW18 ... 158 A1
Bridgman Rd W4 ... 111 A3
Bridgnorth Ho [10]
SE15 ... 140 A6
Bridgwater Ho W2 ... 236 A2
Bridle Cl Enfield EN3 ... 7 B6
Kingston KT1 ... 197 D5
Sunbury TW16 ... 194 A6
West Ewell KT19 ... 215 B3
Bridle La W1 ... 115 C6 249 B6
Twickenham TW1 ... 153 B5
Bridle Path CR0 ... 220 A5
Bridle Path The IG8 ... 36 C3
Bridlepath Way TW14 . 149 C3
Bridle Rd
Addington CR0 ... 223 C4
Claygate KT10 ... 213 B2
Croydon CR0 ... 223 C5
Pinner HA5 ... 40 C4
Bridle Way BR6 ... 227 A4
Addington CR0 ... 223 C3
Bridle Way The SM6 ... 219 C3
Bridlington Ho SW18 . 136 A1
Bridlington Rd N9 ... 18 B4
Bridport SE17 ... 262 B1
Bridport Ave RM7 ... 59 D3
Bridport Ho N1 ... 235 D5
[6] Edmonton N18 ... 34 A5
Bridport Pl N1 . 95 B6 235 D5
Bridport Rd
Edmonton N18 ... 33 D5
Greenford UB6 ... 85 D6
Thornton Heath CR7 ... 204 D6
Bridstow Pl W2 ... 91 C1
Brief St SE5 ... 138 D4
Brierfield NW1 ... 232 A5
Brierley CR0 ... 223 D2
Brierley Ave N9 ... 18 C3
Brierley Cl SE25 ... 206 A5
Brierley Ct W7 ... 108 C6
Brierley Rd E11 ... 76 B4
Upper Tooting SW12 ... 159 C2
Brierly Gdns E2 ... 96 C5
Brigade Cl HA2 ... 64 B6
Brigade St SE3 ... 142 D3
Brigadier Ave EN2 ... 5 A4
Brigadier Hill EN2 ... 5 A5
Briggeford Cl [5] E5 ... 74 A6
Briggs Cl CR4 ... 181 B2
Briggs Ho [20] E2 ... 95 D4
Bright Cl DA17 ... 124 D2
Bright Ct [8] SE28 ... 124 C5
Brightfield Rd SE12 ... 164 D6
Brightling Rd SE4 ... 163 B5
Brightlingsea Pl [5]
E14 ... 119 B6
Brightman Rd SW18 ... 158 B3
Brighton Ave E17 ... 53 B4
Brighton Bldgs SE1 ... 263 A5
Brighton Cl UB10 ... 60 D1
Brighton Ct SW15 ... 157 B5
Brighton Dr [3] UB5 ... 63 C2
Brighton Gr SE14 ... 141 A4
Brighton Ho [7] SE5 ... 139 B4
Brighton Rd N16 ... 73 C4
N2 ... 30 A1
Belmont SM2 ... 217 D1
South Croydon CR2 ... 221 B2
Surbiton KT6 ... 197 D3
Sutton SM2 ... 218 A1
Wallend E6 ... 100 C4
Brighton Terr SW9 ... 138 B1
Brightside Rd SE13 ... 164 B5
Brightside The EN3 ... 7 A4
Bright St E14 ... 97 D2
Brightwell Cl CR0 ... 204 C1
Brightwell Cres SW17 180 D5
Brightwell Ct N7 ... 72 B3
Brightwells [1] SW6 ... 135 D3
Brig Mews SE8 ... 141 C6
Brigstock Ho SE5 ... 139 A3
Brigstock Rd
Belvedere DA17 ... 125 D2
Thornton Heath CR7 ... 204 D4
Brill Ho NW10 ... 67 B5
Brill Pl NW1 ... 93 D5 232 D3
Brim Hill N2 ... 48 B5
Brimpsfield Cl SE2 ... 124 B3
Brimsdown Ave EN3 ... 7 A4
Brimsdown Ho E3 ... 98 A3
Brimsdown Jun & Inf Sch
EN3 ... 6 D2
Brimsdown Sta EN3 ... 7 A3
Brimstone Ho [8] E15 ... 76 C1
Brindishe Prim Sch
SE12 ... 164 D6
Brindle Gate DA15 ... 167 C3
Brindley Cl DA7 ... 147 C2
Wembley HA0 ... 87 D6
Brindley Ho [37] W2 ... 91 C2
[22] Streatham SW12 ... 160 A4
Brindley St SE14 ... 141 B4
Brindley Way BR1 ... 187 B5
Southall UB1 ... 107 D6
Brindwood Rd E4 ... 19 C1
Brine Ct KT6 ... 197 D4
Brine Ho [10] E3 ... 97 A5
Brinkburn Cl SE2 ... 124 A2
Edgware HA8 ... 44 D6
Brinkburn Gdns HA8 ... 44 C6
Brinkley [18] KT1 ... 176 C1
Brinkley Rd KT4 ... 216 B6
Brinklow Cres SE18 ... 144 D5
Brinklow Ho W2 ... 91 D2
Brinkworth Rd IG5 ... 56 A6
Brinkworth Way E9 ... 75 B2
Brinsdale Rd NW4 ... 46 D6
Brinsley Ho [17] E1 ... 96 C1
Brinsley Rd HA3 ... 24 B1
Brinsley St [29] E1 ... 96 B1
Brinsworth Cl TW2 ... 152 B2
Brinton Wlk SE1 ... 251 C3
Brion Pl E14 ... 98 A2
Brisbane Ave SW19 ... 179 D2
Brisbane Ct N10 ... 31 B3
Brisbane Ho [3] W12 ... 112 B6
Brisbane Rd E10 ... 75 D6
Ealing W13 ... 109 A4
Ilford IG1 ... 57 A1
Brisbane St SE5 ... 139 B5
Briscoe Cl E11 ... 76 D6
Briscoe Rd SW19 ... 180 B4
Briset Rd SE9 ... 143 D1
Briset St EC1 ... 94 D3 241 C5
Briset Way N7 ... 72 B6
Bristol Cl
Stanwell TW19 ... 148 A5
Wallington SM6 ... 220 A1
Bristol Ct [11] TW19 ... 148 A5
Bristol Gdns W9 ... 91 D3
Bristol Ho SE11 ... 261 A5
[1] Barking IG11 ... 80 A1
Bristol Mews W9 ... 91 D3
Bristol Park Rd [1] E17 . 53 A5
Bristol Rd E7 ... 77 D2
Greenford UB6 ... 85 D6
Morden SM4 ... 202 A4
Briston Gr N8 ... 50 A3
Briston Mews NW7 ... 28 A3
Bristow Rd DA7 ... 147 A4
Hounslow TW3 ... 130 A2
Wallington CR0 ... 220 A4
West Norwood SE19 ... 183 C5
Britannia Cl SW4 ... 137 D1
Northolt UB5 ... 84 D4
Britannia Gate [12] E16 121 A5
Britannia Junc NW1 ... 231 D6
Britannia La TW2 ... 152 A4
Britannia Rd [11] E14 ... 119 C2
N12 ... 14 A1
SW6 ... 135 D5 265 C3
Ilford IG1 ... 78 D5
Surbiton KT5 ... 198 B2
Britannia Row
N1 ... 95 A6 235 A6
Britannia St
WC1 ... 94 B4 233 C2
Britannia Way
Acton NW10 ... 88 D3
Stanwell TW19 ... 148 A4
Britannia Wlk N1 ... 235 C2
British Gr W4 ... 111 D1
British Grove Pas [2]
W4 ... 111 D1
British Grove S [3] W4 111 D1
British Home & Hospl for
Incurables SE27 ... 182 D5
British Legion Rd E4 ... 20 D2
British Library (Newspaper
Library) NW9 ... 45 C6
British Library The*
WC1 ... 93 D4 232 D2
British Mus*
WC1 ... 94 A2 240 A3
British St E3 ... 97 B4
British Wharf Ind Est
SE14 ... 140 D6
Britley Ho [10] E14 ... 97 B1
Brittain Ct SE9 ... 166 A3
Brittain Ho SE9 ... 166 A3
Brittain Rd RM8 ... 81 B5
Brittany Ho SW15 ... 134 C1
Brittany Point SE11 ... 261 A3
Britten Cl NW11 ... 47 D1
Elstree WD6 ... 9 D5
Brittenden Cl [1] BR6 . 227 D2
Brittenden Par BR6 ... 227 D2
Britten Dr UB1 ... 85 C1
Britten Ho SW3 ... 257 B2
Britten St SW3 114 C1 257 A2
Britton Cl SE6 ... 164 B4
Britton St EC1 ... 94 D2 241 C5
Brixham Cres HA4 ... 40 A1
Brixham Gdns IG3 ... 79 C3
Brixham Rd DA16 ... 146 D4
Brixham St E16 ... 122 C5
Brixton Day Coll SW9 . 138 A2
Brixton Hill SW2 ... 160 B5
Brixton Hill Ct [5] SW2 160 B6
Brixton Hill Pl SW2 ... 160 A4
Brixton Mkt* SW9 ... 138 C1
Brixton Oval [7] SW2 ... 138 C1
Brixton Rd SW9 ... 138 C4
Brixton Sta SW9 ... 138 C1
Brixton Station Rd
SW9 ... 138 C2
Brixton Water La SW2 160 B6
Broadacre Cl UB10 ... 60 D5
Broadbent Cl N6 ... 49 B1
Broadbent St W1 ... 248 C6
Broad Berry Ct N18 ... 34 B5
Broad Bridge Cl SE3 ... 143 A5
Broad Common Est
N16 ... 52 A1
Broadcoombe CR2 ... 222 D1
Broadcroft Ave HA7 ... 25 D1
Broadcroft Rd BR5 ... 211 B2
Broad Ct WC2 ... 240 B1
Broadfield NW6 ... 69 D2
Broadfield Cl NW2 ... 68 C5
Croydon CR0 ... 220 B6
Broadfield Ct WD23 ... 8 C2
Broadfield La NW1 ... 72 A1
Broadfield Rd SE6 ... 164 C3
Broadfields Harrow HA2 23 D1
Thames Ditton KT8 ... 196 C3
Broadfields Ave
Edgware HA8 ... 10 D1
Southgate N21 ... 16 C4
Broadfields Hts HA8 ... 26 D6
Broadfields Inf Sch
HA8 ... 10 C2
Broadfields Jun Sch
HA8 ... 10 D2
Broadfield Sq EN1 ... 6 B3
Broadfields Way NW10 . 67 D3
Broadfield Way IG9 ... 21 C1
Broadford Ho [11] E1 ... 97 A3
Broadgate EC2 . 95 C2 243 A4
Broadgate Circ
EC2 ... 95 C2 243 A3
Broadgate Rd E16 ... 99 D1
Broadgates Ave EN4 ... 1 D4
Broadgates Ct SE11 ... 261 B1
Broadgates Rd SW18 . 158 B3
Broad Green Ave CR0 . 204 D2
Broadhead Strand
NW9 ... 27 D2
Broadheath Dr BR7 ... 188 B5
Broadhinton Rd SW4 . 137 C2
Broadhurst Ave
Edgware HA8 ... 26 D6
Ilford IG3 ... 79 D4
Broadhurst Cl NW6 ... 70 A2
[9] Richmond TW10 ... 154 B6
Broadhurst Gdns NW6 . 69 D2
Ruislip HA4 ... 62 C6
Broadhurst Mans NW6 . 69 D2
Broad La EC2 ... 243 A4
N15 ... 51 D5
N15 ... 52 A5
N8 ... 50 B4
Hampton TW12 ... 173 C4
Broadlands N6 ... 49 A2
Feltham TW13 ... 151 C1
Broadlands Ave
Enfield EN3 ... 6 B2
Shepperton TW17 ... 193 A3
Streatham SW16 ... 160 A2
Broadlands Cl N6 ... 49 A2
Enfield EN3 ... 6 C2
Streatham SW16 ... 160 A2
Broadlands Ct TW9 ... 132 C5
Broadlands Lo N6 ... 48 D2
Broadlands Mans [2]
SW16 ... 160 A2
Broadlands Rd BR1 ... 187 B6
N6 ... 48 D2
Broadlands Way KT3 . 199 D3
Broad Lawn SE9 ... 166 C3
Broadlawns Ct HA3 ... 24 D2
Broadley St
NW8 ... 92 C2 237 A4
Broadley Terr
NW1 ... 92 C3 237 B5
Broadmayne SE17 ... 262 C2
Broadmead W14 ... 254 A3
Catford SE6 ... 163 C1
Broadmead Ave KT4 ... 200 A2
Broadmead Cl
Hampton TW12 ... 173 C4
Pinner HA5 ... 23 A3
Broadmead Ct [6] IG8 ... 37 A4
Broadmead Inf Sch
CR0 ... 205 B2
Broadmead Jun Sch
CR0 ... 205 B3
Broadmead Rd
Northolt UB5 ... 85 A3
Woodford IG8 ... 37 B3
Broad Oak
Ashford TW16 ... 171 D4
Woodford IG8 ... 37 B5
Broad Oak Cl BR5 ... 190 A1
Chingford E4 ... 35 C5
Broadoak Ct [9] SW9 ... 138 C2
Broadoak Ho [18] NW6 ... 91 D6
Broad Oaks KT6 ... 214 D6
Broadoaks Way BR2 ... 208 D4
Broad Sanctuary SW1 250 A1
Broad St
Dagenham RM10 ... 81 C1
Teddington TW11 ... 174 D4
Broad St Ave EC2 ... 243 A3
Broadstone Ho SW8 ... 270 C3
Broadstone Pl W1 ... 238 A3
Broad St Pl EC2 ... 242 D3
Broadview NW9 ... 44 C3
Broadview Est TW19 ... 148 C4
Broadview Ho RM8 ... 58 D1
Broadview Rd SW16 ... 181 D3
Broadwalk E18 ... 54 D6
Harrow HA2 ... 41 D4
Broadwalk Ho SW7 ... 246 A1
Broadwalk La NW11 ... 47 B2
Broadwalk Sh Ctr The
HA8 ... 26 D4
Broadwall SE1 116 C5 251 B4
Broadwater Farm Prim Sch
N17 ... 33 B1
Broadwater Gdns BR6 227 A4
Broadwater Prim Sch
SW17 ... 180 C6
Broadwater Rd SE18 ... 123 B3
Tottenham N17 ... 33 C1
Upper Tooting SW17 ... 180 C6
Broadway DA6 ... 147 B1
E15 ... 76 B1
Broadway *continued*
SW1 ... 115 D3 259 C6
Barking IG11 ... 101 A6
Bexley DA6,DA7 ... 147 C1
Ealing W13 ... 109 A5
Ealing W7 ... 108 C5
Tolworth KT6 ... 198 D1
Broadway Arc [3] W6 . 112 C2
Broadway Ave
Thornton Heath CR0 ... 205 B4
Twickenham TW1 ... 153 B5
Broadway Bldgs [5]
W7 ... 108 C5
Broadway Cl IG8 ... 37 B4
Broadway Ct
Beckenham BR3 ... 208 A6
Wimbledon SW19 ... 179 C4
Broadway Ctr Adult Coll
SW17 ... 180 C6
Broadway Gdns
Mitcham CR4 ... 202 C5
Woodford IG8 ... 37 B4
Broadway Ho [2] E8 ... 96 B6
Broadway Mans SW6 . 265 B3
Broadway Market E8 ... 96 B6
Broadway Market Mews [21]
E8 ... 96 A6
Broadway Mews E5 ... 51 D2
Southgate N21 ... 16 D3
Bowes Park N13 ... 32 B5
Broadway Par N8 ... 50 A3
Chingford E4 ... 36 A4
Hayes UB3 ... 106 A5
West Drayton UB7 ... 104 A4
Broadway Pl SW19 ... 179 B4
Broadway Sh Ctr [5]
DA6 ... 147 C1
Broadway The E13 ... 99 B5
N11 ... 31 A5
[2] N14 ... 15 D3
N8 ... 50 A3
NW7 ... 27 D5
W3 ... 110 C4
Barnes SW13 ... 133 C3
Cheam SM3 ... 217 A2
Chingford E4 ... 36 B4
Dagenham RM8 ... 81 C6
Ealing W5 ... 109 D6
Edmonton N9 ... 18 A1
Greenford UB6 ... 86 A3
Harrow HA3 ... 24 D1
Merton SW19 ... 179 C3
Pinner HA5 ... 23 B3
Southall UB1 ... 107 A6
Stanmore HA7 ... 25 C5
Sutton SM1 ... 218 A4
Thames Ditton KT10 ... 196 C1
Tolworth KT6 ... 198 C1
Wallington SM6 ... 220 A4
Wembley HA9 ... 66 A5
Woodford IG8 ... 37 B4
Wood Green N22 ... 32 C1
Broadwell Ct TW5 ... 128 D4
Broadwick St
W1 ... 93 C1 239 B1
Broad Wlk NW1 93 A5 231 B3
W1 ... 115 A5 248 A4
Eltham SE3,SE18 ... 144 A3
Heston TW5 ... 129 A4
Richmond TW9 ... 132 B5
Southgate N21 ... 16 B3
Broad Wlk The
W8 ... 113 D5 245 D3
Broadwood Ave HA4 ... 39 C3
Broadwood Terr W14 . 254 D4
Broad Yd EC1 ... 241 C5
Brocas Cl NW3 ... 70 C1
Brockbridge Ho [11]
SW15 ... 155 D5
Brockdene Dr BR2 ... 225 D4
Brockdish Ave IG11 ... 79 D3
Brockelbank Lo RM8 ... 80 D6
Brockenhurst KT8 ... 195 B3
Brockenhurst Ave KT4 199 C1
Brockenhurst Gdns
NW7 ... 27 C5
Ilford IG1 ... 79 A3
Brockenhurst Mews [9]
N18 ... 34 A6
Brockenhurst Rd CR0 . 206 B2
Brockenhurst Way
SW16 ... 181 D1
Brocket Ho [16] SW8 ... 137 D3
Brockham Cl SW19 ... 179 B5
Brockham Cres CR0 ... 224 B1
Brockham Ct [6] SM2 ... 217 D1
Brockham Dr Ilford IG2 . 57 A4
Streatham SW2 ... 160 B4
Brockham Ho NW1 ... 232 B5
[11] Streatham SW2 ... 160 B4
Brockham St SE1 ... 262 B6
Brock Ho WC1 ... 239 C4
Brockhurst Cl HA7 ... 24 D4
Brockhurst Ho N4 ... 51 B2
Brockill Cres SE4 ... 141 A1

Brocklebank Ho 7
E16 ... 122 C5
Brocklebank Rd SE7 ... 121 B2
Wandsworth SW18 ... 158 A4
Brocklebank Road Ind Est
SE7 ... 121 A2
Brocklehurst St SE14 . 140 D5
Brocklesby Rd SE25 ... 206 B5
Brockley Ave HA7 ... 10 A1
Brockley Cl HA7 ... 26 A6
Brockley Cross SE4 ... 141 B2
Brockley Cross Bsns Ctr
SE4 ... 141 A2
Brockley Gdns SE4 ... 141 B3
Brockley Gr SE4 ... 163 B6
Brockley Hall Rd SE4 . 163 A6
Brockley Hill HA7,HA8 ... 9 D2
Brockley Hill Ho HA7 ... 9 C3
Brockley Ho SE17 ... 263 A2
Brockley Mews SE4 ... 163 A6
Brockley Pk SE23 ... 163 A4
Brockley Prim Sch
SE4 ... 163 B6
Brockley Rd SE4 ... 163 B6
Brockley Rise SE23 ... 163 A4
Brockleyside HA7 ... 26 A6
Brockley Sta SE4 ... 141 A2
Brockley View SE23 ... 163 A4
Brockley Way SE4 ... 163 A6
Brockman Rise BR1 ... 186 B6
Brockmer Ho 5 E1 ... 118 B6
Brock Pl E3 ... 97 D3
Brock Rd E13 ... 99 B2
Brocks Dr SM3 ... 217 A5
Brockshot Cl 1 TW8 . 131 D6
Brock St SE15 ... 140 C2
Brockway Cl E11 ... 76 C6
Brockweir 29 E2 ... 96 C5
Brockwell Cl BR5 ... 211 D4
Brockwell Ct 2 SW2 . 160 C6
Brockwell Ho SE11 ... 270 D6
Brockwell Park*
SE24 ... 160 D5
Brockwell Park Gdns
SE24 ... 160 D4
Brockworth 8 KT2 ... 176 D2
Broderick Ho SE21 ... 161 C1
Brodia Rd N16 ... 73 C5
Brodick Ho 11 E3 ... 97 B5
Brodie Ho SE1 ... 263 D2
7 Wallington SM6 ... 219 B4
Brodie Rd Chingford E4 . 20 A2
Enfield EN2 ... 5 A5
Brodie St SE1 . 117 D1 263 D2
Brodlove La E1 ... 118 D6
Brodrick Gr SE2 ... 124 B2
Brodrick Rd SW17 ... 158 C2
Brograve Gdns BR3 ... 185 D1
Broken Wharf EC4 ... 252 A6
Brokesley St E3 ... 97 B4
Broke Wlk E8 ... 95 D6
1 E8 ... 96 A6
Bromar Rd SE5 ... 139 C2
Bromborough Gn
WD19 ... 22 C5
Bromefield HA7 ... 25 C2
Bromehead St 8 E1 ... 96 C1
Brome Ho 5 SE18 ... 144 A4
Bromell's Rd SW4 ... 137 C1
Brome Rd SE9 ... 144 B2
Bromfelde Rd SW4 ... 137 D3
Bromfield Ct 20 SE16 . 118 A3
Bromfield St N1 ... 234 B4
Bromhall Rd RM8 ... 80 B2
Bromhedge SE9 ... 166 B1
Bromholm Rd SE2 ... 124 B3
Bromleigh Ct 1 SE21,
SE22 ... 162 B2
Bromleigh Ho SE1 ... 263 C6
Bromley Ave BR1 ... 186 C3
Bromley-by-Bow Sta
E3 ... 97 D4
Bromley Coll of F & H Ed
BR2 ... 209 D3
Bromley Comm BR2 . 209 D4
Bromley Cres
Beckenham BR2 ... 208 D6
Ruislip HA4 ... 61 D4
Bromley Ct SE13 ... 164 B6
Bromley BR1 ... 186 D3
Bromley Gdns BR2 ... 208 D6
Bromley Gr BR2 ... 186 B1
Bromley Hall Rd E14 ... 98 A2
Bromley High Sch for Girls
BR1 ... 210 C5
Bromley High St E3 ... 97 D4
Bromley Hill BR1 ... 186 C4
Bromley Hospl BR1 ... 209 B5
Bromley Ind Est BR1 . 209 D6
Bromley La BR7 ... 189 B3
Bromley Lo 2 W3 ... 89 A1
Bromley Manor Mans 3
BR1 ... 209 A6
Bromley North Sta
BR1 ... 187 A2
Bromley Pk 11 BR1 ... 186 D2
Bromley Pl W1 ... 239 A4
Bromley Rd BR7 ... 188 D2
E10 ... 53 D3
E17 ... 53 C6
Beckenham BR2,BR3 ... 186 B1
Beckenham BR3 ... 185 D2
Catford SE6 ... 163 D1
Edmonton N18 ... 17 B1
Tottenham N17 ... 34 A2
Bromley Rd Ret Pk
SE6 ... 163 D2
Bromley Road Inf Sch
BR3 ... 185 D2
Bromley South Sta
BR2 ... 209 A6
Bromley St E1 ... 96 D1
Brompton WC1 ... 240 C3
Brompton Arc SW1 ... 247 D1
Brompton Cl
Hounslow TW4 ... 151 B6
Penge SE20 ... 184 A1
Brompton Ct 4 HA7 ... 25 C6
Brompton Gr N2 ... 48 C5
Brompton Ho 3 N9 ... 34 A6
Brompton Oratory*
SW3 ... 114 C3 257 A5
Brompton Park Cres
SW6 ... 135 D6 265 C5
Brompton Pl
SW3 ... 114 C3 257 B6
Brompton Rd
SW3 ... 114 C3 257 A5
Brompton Sq
SW3 ... 114 C3 257 A6
Bromstone Ho 10
SW9 ... 138 C4
Bromwich Ave N6 ... 71 A6
Bromwich Ho 3
TW10 ... 154 A5
Bromyard Ave W3 ... 111 C6
Bromyard Ho 3 SE15 . 140 B5
Bron Ct NW6 ... 91 C6
Brondesbury Coll for Boys
NW6 ... 69 A1
Brondesbury Ct NW2 ... 68 D2
Brondesbury Mews 11
NW6 ... 69 C1
Brondesbury Park Sta
NW6 ... 91 A6
Brondesbury Pk NW2 ... 68 D1
Brondesbury Rd NW6 ... 91 C5
Brondesbury Sta NW6 . 69 B1
Brondesbury Villas
NW6 ... 91 C5
Bronhill Terr N17 ... 34 A2
Bronsart Rd
SW6 ... 135 A5 264 A3
Bronson Rd SW20 ... 179 A1
Bronte Cl DA8 ... 147 D5
1 E7 ... 77 A4
Ilford IG2 ... 56 C5
Bronte Ct 8 W14 ... 112 D3
Bronte Ho 6 N16 ... 73 C3
NW6 ... 91 C4
Bronti Cl SE17 117 A1 262 B2
Bronwen Ct NW8 ... 229 C1
Bronze Age Way DA17 125 D4
Bronze St SE8 ... 141 C5
Brook Ave
Dagenham RM10 ... 81 D1
Edgware HA8 ... 26 D4
Wembley HA9 ... 66 C5
Brook Bank EN1 ... 6 B6
Brookbank Ave W7 ... 86 B2
Brookbank Rd SE13 ... 141 D2
Brook Cl Acton W3 ... 110 C5
Finchley N12 ... 29 A3
Ruislip HA4 ... 39 C2
Stanwell TW19 ... 148 B4
Upper Tooting SW17 ... 159 A2
West Barnes SW20 ... 200 B6
Brook Cres Chingford E4 35 D6
Edmonton N9 ... 34 B6
Brook Ct 2 E11 ... 76 C5
E15 ... 76 A3
E17 ... 53 A6
Beckenham BR3 ... 185 B2
5 Brentford TW8 ... 131 D6
Cheam SM3 ... 216 C4
Edgware HA8 ... 26 D5
Mortlake SW14 ... 133 C2
Brookdale N11 ... 31 C6
Brookdale Rd DA5 ... 169 A5
E17 ... 53 C6
SE6 ... 163 D5
Catford SE6 ... 163 D4
Brookdales The NW4 ... 47 A5
Brookdene N12 ... 29 D6
Brookdene Rd SE18,
SE2 ... 123 D2
Brook Dr SE11 116 D2 261 C4
Harrow HA1 ... 42 A5
Ruislip HA4 ... 39 C2
Brooke Ave HA2 ... 64 A5
Brooke Cl WD23 ... 8 A4
Brooke Ct 7 KT2 ... 175 D6
Brookehowse Rd SE6 . 163 D1
Brookend Rd DA15 ... 167 C3
Brooke Rd E17 ... 54 A5
Brooke Rd continued
E5,N16 ... 74 A5
Brookes Ct EC1 ... 241 A4
Brookes Mkt EC1 ... 241 A4
Brooke's Mkt EC1 ... 241 B4
Brooke St EC1 ... 94 C2 241 A3
Brooke Way WD23 ... 8 A4
Brookfield 1 N4 ... 72 C6
N6 ... 71 A5
Brookfield Ave E17 ... 54 A5
NW7 ... 28 B4
Carshalton SM1,SM5 ... 218 C5
Ealing W5 ... 87 D3
Brookfield Cl NW7 ... 28 B4
Brookfield Cres NW7 ... 28 B4
Harrow HA3 ... 44 A4
Brookfield Ct 1 N12 ... 29 D6
Greenford UB6 ... 86 A4
Brookfield Gdns KT10 212 D2
Brookfield House Sch
IG8 ... 36 C4
Brookfield Path IG8 ... 36 C4
Brookfield Pk NW5 ... 71 B5
Brookfield Prim Sch
N19 ... 71 B6
Cheam SM3 ... 201 A1
Brookfield Rd E9 ... 75 A2
W4 ... 111 B4
Edmonton N9 ... 18 B1
Brookfields EN3 ... 6 D1
Brookfields Ave CR4 ... 202 C4
Brookgate N16 ... 73 B6
Brook Gate
W1 ... 114 D6 247 D5
Brook Gdns
Barnes SW13 ... 133 D2
Chingford E4 ... 35 D6
Kingston KT2 ... 177 A2
Brook Gn W6 ... 112 D2
Brook Green Flats 11
W14 ... 112 D3
Brookhill Cl SE18 ... 122 D1
East Barnet EN4 ... 14 C6
Brookhill Ct 2 EN4 ... 14 C5
Brookhill Rd SE18 ... 122 D1
East Barnet EN4 ... 14 C6
Brook Ho 3 SW4 ... 159 C6
W3 ... 110 C4
4 W6 ... 112 C2
3 Edmonton N9 ... 18 A1
3 Twickenham TW1 ... 153 A4
Brook Hos NW1 ... 232 B3
Brookhouse Gdns E4 ... 36 C6
Brook House Sixth Form
Coll The E5 ... 74 B5
Brook Ind Est UB4 ... 106 C5
Brooking Cl RM8 ... 80 C5
Brooking Rd E7 ... 77 A3
Brook La BR1 ... 187 A4
DA5 ... 168 D5
Greenwich SE3 ... 143 B3
Brookland Cl NW11 ... 47 C5
Brookland Garth NW11 47 D5
Brookland Hill NW11 ... 47 D5
Brookland Jun & Inf Schs
NW11 ... 47 D5
Brookland Rise NW11 ... 47 C5
Brooklands Ave DA15 . 167 B2
Wandsworth SW18 ... 157 D2
Brooklands Cl TW16 ... 171 C2
Brooklands Court
Apartments 3 NW6 ... 69 B1
Brooklands Ct 2 NW6 . 69 B1
Enfield N21 ... 17 B6
Kingston KT1 ... 197 D5
2 Mitcham CR4 ... 180 B1
Brooklands Dr UB6 ... 87 D6
Brooklands Pk SE3 ... 143 A2
Brooklands Prim Sch
SE3 ... 143 A2
Brooklands Rd KT7 ... 197 A1
Brooklands The TW7 ... 130 B4
Brook Lane Bns Ctr
TW8 ... 109 D1
Brooklea Cl NW9 ... 27 C2
Brook Lo N8 ... 49 D3
NW4 ... 46 D4
Brooklyn SE20 ... 184 A3
Brooklyn Ave SE25 ... 206 B5
Brooklyn Cl SM5 ... 218 C6
Brooklyn Ct W12 ... 112 C5
Brooklyn Gr SE25 ... 206 B5
Brooklyn Rd BR2 ... 210 A4
Croydon SE25 ... 206 B5
Brookmarsh Ind Est
SE10 ... 141 D5
Brook Mdw N12 ... 13 D1
Brook Mead KT19 ... 215 C2
Brookmead Ave BR1,
BR2 ... 210 B4
Brookmead Ct N20 ... 14 A2
Brookmead Ind Est
CR4 ... 203 C3
Brook Meadow Cl IG8 . 36 C4
Brookmead Rd CR0 ... 203 C3
Brook Mews N
W2 ... 114 B6 246 B6
Brookmill Rd SE8 ... 141 C4
Brook Park Cl N21 ... 16 D6
Brook Pl EN5 ... 13 C6
Brook Rd N12 ... 30 C3
N22 ... 50 B6
N8 ... 50 A5
NW2 ... 68 A6
Buckhurst Hill IG9 ... 21 A3
Ilford IG2 ... 57 C3
South Norwood CR7 ... 205 A5
Surbiton KT6 ... 214 A6
Twickenham TW1 ... 153 A5
Brook Rd S TW8 ... 131 D6
Brooks Ave E6 ... 100 B3
Brooksbank Ho 7 E9 ... 74 C2
Brooksbank St 9 E9 ... 74 C2
Brooksby Mews N1 ... 72 C1
Brooksby St N1 ... 72 C1
Brooksby's Wlk E9 ... 74 D3
Brooks Cl SE9 ... 166 C2
Brookscroft Rd E17 ... 35 D2
Brooks Ct 3 SW4 ... 138 A3
SW8 ... 269 B4
Brookshill HA3 ... 24 B5
Brookshill Ave HA3 ... 24 C5
Brookshill Dr HA3 ... 24 B5
Brooks Ho 6 SW2 ... 160 C3
Brookside BR6 ... 211 D2
East Barnet EN4 ... 14 C5
Southgate N21 ... 16 B5
Wallington SM5 ... 219 A3
Brookside Cl Barnet EN5 13 A5
Feltham TW13 ... 150 A1
Harrow HA3 ... 43 D4
South Harrow HA2,HA4 ... 63 A4
Brookside Cres 1
KT4 ... 200 A1
Brookside Ct SW16 ... 181 C3
Brookside Gdns EN1 ... 6 C6
Brookside Ho N17 ... 33 C1
Brookside Prim Sch
UB4 ... 84 C4
Brookside Rd N19 ... 71 C6
NW11 ... 47 B3
Edmonton N9 ... 34 B6
Hayes UB4 ... 106 C6
Brookside S EN4 ... 15 A4
Brookside Way
Croydon CR0 ... 206 D3
Hillingdon UB10 ... 60 B1
Brooks La W4 ... 132 C6
Brook's Mans 5 IG3 ... 58 B1
Brook's Mews
W1 ... 115 B6 248 C6
Brook's Par 6 IG3 ... 58 B1
Brooks Rd W4 ... 110 C1
Brook's Rd E13 ... 99 A6
Brook St DA8 ... 147 D5
W1 ... 115 B6 248 C6
W2 ... 114 B6 246 D6
Kingston KT1 ... 176 A1
5 Tottenham N17 ... 33 D1
Brookstone Ct SE15 ... 140 B1
Brooksville Ave NW6 ... 91 A6
Brook Vale DA7,DA8 ... 147 D4
Brookview Ct 11 EN1 ... 17 C6
Brookview Rd SW16 ... 181 C5
Brookville Rd
SW6 ... 135 B5 264 C3
Brookway SE3 ... 143 A2
Brook Wlk HA8 ... 27 B4
N2 ... 30 B2
Brookwood Ave SW13 133 D3
Brookwood Cl BR2 ... 208 D5
Brookwood Ho SE1 ... 251 D1
Brookwood Rd
Hounslow TW3 ... 129 D4
Wandsworth SW18 ... 157 C3
Broom Ave BR5 ... 190 B1
Broom Cl BR2 ... 210 A3
Teddington KT1,TW11 ... 175 D3
Broomcroft Ave UB5 ... 84 C4
Broome Ct 3 TW9 ... 132 C4
Broome Ho 7 E5 ... 74 B3
Broome Rd TW12 ... 173 B2
Broome Way SE5 ... 139 B5
Broomfield E17 ... 53 B2
7 NW1 ... 71 A1
Sunbury TW16 ... 172 A2
Broomfield Ave N13 ... 32 B5
Broomfield Cotts N13 ... 32 A5
Broomfield Ct N13 ... 32 A5
Broomfield Ho 4 BR5 190 B1
SE17 ... 263 A3
Stanmore HA7 ... 9 A1
Broomfield House Sch
TW9 ... 132 B4
Broomfield La N13 ... 32 B6
Broomfield Pl W13 ... 109 B5
Broomfield Rd DA6 ... 169 C6
Beckenham BR3 ... 207 B6
Bowes Park N13 ... 32 A5
Dagenham RM6 ... 58 D2
Ealing W13 ... 109 B5
Richmond TW9 ... 132 B4
Surbiton KT5 ... 198 B1
Teddington TW11 ... 175 C4
Broomfields KT10 ... 212 A3
Broomfield Sch N14 ... 31 D5
Broomfield St E14 ... 97 D2
Broom Gdns CR0 ... 223 C5
Broomgrove Gdns HA8 . 26 C2
Broomgrove Rd SW9 . 138 B3
Broomhill Ct 2 IG8 ... 37 A4
Broomhill Rd BR6 ... 211 D2
SW18 ... 157 C6
Ilford IG3 ... 80 A6
Woodford IG8 ... 37 A4
Broomhill Rise DA6 ... 169 C6
Broomhill Wlk IG8 ... 36 D3
Broomhouse La SW6 . 135 C2
Broomhouse Rd SW6 . 135 C3
Broomleigh BR1 ... 187 A2
Broomleigh Bsns Pk
SE26 ... 185 B5
Broomloan La SM1 ... 217 C6
Broom Lock TW11 ... 175 C4
Broom Mead DA6 ... 169 C6
Broom Pk KT1 ... 175 D3
Broom Rd Croydon CR0 223 C5
Richmond TW11 ... 175 C5
Teddington KT1,TW11 ... 175 C4
Broomsleigh St NW6 ... 69 B3
Broom Water TW11 ... 175 C5
Broom Water W TW11 175 C5
Broomwood Cl CR0 ... 206 D4
Broomwood Hall Sch
SW12 ... 159 A4
Broomwood Rd BR5 ... 190 B1
SW11 ... 159 A6
Broseley Gr SE26 ... 185 A5
Broster Gdns SE25 ... 205 D6
Brougham Rd E8 ... 96 A6
W3 ... 89 A1
Brougham St SW11 ... 136 D3
Brough Cl SW8 ... 270 B3
Kingston KT2 ... 175 D5
Brough St SW8 ... 270 B3
Broughton Ave N3 ... 47 A6
Richmond TW10 ... 175 C6
Broughton Ct W13 ... 109 B6
Broughton Dr 20 SW9 138 D1
Broughton Gdns N6 ... 49 C3
Broughton Rd SW6 ... 135 D3
Ealing W13 ... 109 B6
Orpington BR6 ... 227 B6
Thornton Heath CR7 ... 204 C3
Broughton Road App 2
SW6 ... 135 D3
Broughton St SW8 ... 137 B3
Broughton Street Arches
Ind Area SW11 ... 137 A3
Brouncker Rd W3 ... 111 A4
Browells La TW13 ... 150 B2
Brown Bear Ct TW13 . 172 D6
Brown Cl SM6 ... 220 A1
Browne Ho 13 SE8 ... 141 C5
9 Penge SE26 ... 184 B5
Brownfield St E14 ... 98 A1
Brownflete Ho SE4 ... 141 A1
Browngraves Rd UB7 . 127 A5
Brown Hart Gdns W1 . 248 B6
Brownhill Rd SE6 ... 164 A4
Browning Ave
Carshalton SM1 ... 218 C4
Ealing W7 ... 86 D1
North Cheam KT4 ... 200 B1
Browning Cl DA16 ... 145 C4
E17 ... 54 A5
W9 ... 236 B5
Feltham TW12 ... 173 B6
Browning Ct W14 ... 264 C6
Browning Ho 10 N16 ... 73 C4
W12 ... 90 C1
Browning Mews W1 ... 238 B3
Browning Rd E11 ... 54 D2
E12 ... 78 B2
Enfield EN2 ... 5 B5
Browning St
SE17 ... 117 A2 262 B3
Browning Way TW5 ... 128 D4
Brownlea Gdns IG3 ... 80 A6
Brownlow Cl EN4 ... 14 B6
Brownlow Ct N2 ... 48 A4
1 Bowes Park N11 ... 32 A4
Brownlow Ho 7 SE16 118 A4
Brownlow Mews
WC1 ... 94 B3 240 D5
Brownlow Rd 3 E7 ... 77 A4
E8 ... 96 A6
N3 ... 29 D3
NW10 ... 67 C1
Bowes Park N11 ... 32 A4
6 Ealing W13 ... 109 A5
South Croydon CR0 ... 221 D4
Brownlow St
WC1 ... 94 B2 240 D3
Brownrigg Rd TW15 ... 170 C6
Brown's Bldgs EC3 ... 243 B1
Brownspring Dr SE9 ... 166 D1
Brown's Rd E17 ... 53 C6
Surbiton KT5,KT6 ... 198 B2
Brown St W1 ... 92 D1 237 C2
Brownswell Rd N2 ... 30 B1
Brownswood Rd N4 ... 73 A6
Broxash Rd SW11 ... 159 A5
Broxbourne Ave E18 ... 55 B5
Broxbourne Ho 1 E3 ... 97 D3
Broxbourne Rd BR6 . 211 D2
Wanstead E7 ... 77 A5
Broxholme Ho SW6 ... 265
Broxholm Rd SE27,
SW16 ... 160
Broxted Rd SE6 ... 163
Broxwood Way
NW8 ... 92 C6 230
Bruce Ave TW17 ... 193
Bruce Castle Ct N17 ... 33
Bruce Castle Mus*
N17 ... 33
Bruce Castle Rd N17 ... 33
Bruce Cl DA16 ... 146
W10 ... 90
Bruce Ct DA15 ... 189
Bruce Gdns N20 ... 14
Bruce Glasier Ho 13
N19 ... 49
Bruce Gr N17 ... 33
Bruce Grove N17 ... 33
Bruce Grove Prim Sch
N17 ... 33
Bruce Grove Sta N17 ... 33
Bruce Hall Mews
SW17 ... 181
Bruce Ho 4 SW4 ... 159
W10 ... 90
5 Harrow HA1 ... 42
Harrow HA3 ... 44
Putney SW15 ... 156
Bruce Lawns SW17 ... 181
Bruce Rd E3 ... 97
NW10 ... 67
Barnet EN5 ... 1
Harrow HA3 ... 24
Mitcham CR4 ... 181
South Norwood SE25 ... 205
Bruckner St W10 ... 91
Brudenell Rd SW17 ... 181
Bruffs Meadow UB5 ... 63
Bruges Pl 13 NW1 ... 71
Brumfield Rd KT19 ... 215
Brune Ho E1 ... 243
Brunel Cl Cranford TW5 128
Northolt UB5 ... 85
Penge SE19 ... 183
Brunel Ct NW10 ... 90
Brunel Est W2 ... 91
Brunel Ho E14 ... 119
4 NW5 ... 71
SW10 ... 266
Hayes UB3 ... 105
25 Streatham SW2 ... 160
Brunel Pl 8 UB1 ... 85
Brunel Rd E17 ... 53
SE16 ... 118
W3 ... 89
Brunel St E16 ... 98
Brunel Univ UB8 ... 82
Brunel Univ Coll Osterley
Campus TW7 ... 130
Brunel Univ Coll
(Twickenham Campus)
TW1 ... 131
Brunel Wlk N15 ... 51
Twickenham TW4 ... 151
Brune St E1 ... 95 D2 243
Brunlees Ho SE1 ... 262
Brunner Cl NW11 ... 48
Brunner Ho 6 SE6 ... 186
Brunner Rd E17 ... 53
Ealing W5 ... 87
Bruno Pl NW9 ... 67
Brunswick Ave N11 ... 15
Brunswick Cl DA6 ... 146
Pinner HA5 ... 41
Thames Ditton KT7 ... 196
Twickenham TW2 ... 152
Brunswick Cres N11 ... 15
Brunswick Ct EC1 ... 234
SE1 ... 117 C4 253
SW1 ... 259
Kingston KT2 ... 175
New Barnet EN4 ... 14
2 Penge SE19 ... 184
2 Wimbledon SW19 ... 179
Brunswick Gdns
W8 ... 113 C5 245
Ealing W5 ... 88
Brunswick Gr N11 ... 15
Brunswick Ho 4 E2 ... 95
N3 ... 29
NW1 ... 237
Brunswick Lo 6 E4 ... 20
Brunswick Manor
SM1 ... 218
Brunswick Mews W1 . 237
Streatham SW16 ... 181
Brunswick Park Gdns
N11 ... 15
Brunswick Park Prim Sch
N14 ... 15
SE5 ... 139
Brunswick Park Rd
N11 ... 15
Brunswick Pk SE5 ... 139
Brunswick Pl
N1 ... 95 B4 235
Penge SE19 ... 184
Brunswick Quay SE16 118

unswick Rd DA6 147 A1
10 54 A1
14 98 A1
15 51 C5
aling W5 88 A4
oldbrook EN3 7 C5
ingston KT2 176 C2
utton SM1 217 D4
unswick Sh Ctr
VC1 94 A3 240 B6
unswick Sq
VC1 94 A3 240 B6
ottenham N17 33 D4
unswick St E17 54 A4
unswick Villas 2
E5 139 C4
runswick Way N11 31 B6
runton Pl E14 97 A1
rushfield St
1 95 D2 243 C4
rushwood Ho 4 E14 97 D2
rushwood Lo DA17 125 C2
russels Rd SW11 136 B1
ruton Cl BR7 188 B3
ruton La W1 115 B6 248 D5
ruton Pl W1 115 B6 248 D5
ruton Rd SM4 202 A5
ruton St W1 115 B6 248 D5
ruton Way W13 87 A2
ryan Ave NW10 68 B1
ryan Cl TW16 172 A3
ryan Ct W1 237 C2
ryan Ho SE16 119 B4
ryan Rd SE16 119 B4
ryanston Ave TW2 151 D3
ryanston Cl UB2 107 B2
ryanston Ct W1 237 C2
ryanstone Ct SM1 218 A5
ryanstone Rd N8 49 D4
ryanston Ho 11 SE15 139 D4
ryanston Mans W1 237 C4
ryanston Mews E
W1 237 C3
ryanston Mews W
W1 92 D1 237 C2
ryanston Pl
W1 92 D2 237 C3
ryanston Sq
W1 92 D1 237 C2
Bryanston St
W1 92 D1 237 D1
Bryant Cl EN5 13 B6
Bryant Ct E2 95 D5
Bryant Rd UB5 84 C4
Bryant St E15 76 C1
Bryantwood Rd N5,N7 72 C3
Brycedale Cres N14 15 D1
Bryce Ho 25 SE14 140 D6
Bryce Rd RM8 80 C4
Brydale Ho 2 SE16 118 D2
Bryden Cl SE26 185 A5
Brydges Pl WC2 250 A5
Brydges Rd E15 76 B3
Brydon Wlk N1 233 B6
Bryer Ct EC2 242 A4
Bryett Rd N7 72 A5
Bryher Ho W4 111 A1
Brymay Cl E3 97 C5
Brymon Ct W1 237 D3
Brynmaer Ho SW11 267 D1
Brynmaer Rd
SW11 136 D4 267 D1
Bryn-y-Mawr Rd EN1 5 D1
Bryony Cl UB8 82 B2
Bryony Rd W12 112 A6
Bryony Way TW16 172 A4
B Sky B Hq TW7 131 A6
BT Telecom Twr*
W1 93 C2 239 A4
Buccleuch Ho E5 52 A2
Buchanan Cl N21 16 B6
Buchanan Ct 16 SE16 118 D2
Buchanan Gdns NW10 90 B5
Buchanan Ho
Dulwich SE21 161 C1
Wandsworth SW18 157 C4
Buchan Ho W3 110 D4
Buchan Rd SE15 140 C2
Bucharest Rd SW18 158 A4
Buckden Cl N2 48 D5
SE12 165 A5
Buckfast Ct W13 109 A6
Buckfast Ho N14 15 C6
Buckfast Rd SM4 201 D5
Buckfast St E2 96 A4
Buck Hill Wlk
W2 114 B6 246 D5
Buckhold Rd SW18 157 C5
Buckhurst Ave CR4,
SM5 202 D1
Buckhurst Hill Ho IG9 21 B2
Buckhurst Hill Sta IG9 21 D2
Buckhurst Ho 15 N7 71 D3
Buckhurst St E1 96 B3
Buckhurst Way IG9 21 D1
Buckingham Ave
DA16 145 C1
N20 14 B4
East Molesey KT8 173 D1

Buckingham Ave *continued*
Feltham TW14 150 B5
South Norwood CR7 182 C2
Wembley UB6 87 A6
Buckingham Cl BR5 211 C2
Ealing W5 87 C2
Enfield EN1 5 C3
Hampton TW12 173 B5
Buckingham College Sch
HA1 42 C4
Buckingham Ct NW4 46 A6
2 Ealing W7 86 D3
Mitcham CR4 204 A4
Northolt UB5 85 A6
Wembley HA0 65 C2
Buckingham Dr BR7 189 A5
Buckingham Gate
SW1 115 C3 259 B6
Buckingham Gdns
East Molesey KT8 173 D1
Edgware HA8 26 B3
South Norwood CR7 182 C1
Buckingham Gr UB10 82 C5
Buckingham Ho N4 51 A1
1 Acton W3 88 C1
Richmond TW10 154 C6
Buckingham La SE23 163 A4
Buckingham Lo N10 49 C5
Buckingham Mans
NW6 69 D3
Buckingham Mews
7 N1 73 C2
NW10 89 D5
SW1 259 A6
Buckingham Palace*
SW1 115 C4 249 A1
Buckingham Palace Rd
SW1 115 B2 258 D4
Buckingham Pl SW1 259 A6
Buckingham Prim Sch
TW12 173 B5
Buckingham Rd E10 75 D5
E15 76 D3
N1 73 C2
NW10 89 D5
Edgware HA8 26 B3
Hampton TW12,TW13 173 B5
Harrow HA1 42 B4
Ilford IG1 79 B6
Kingston KT1 198 B5
Mitcham CR4 204 A4
Richmond TW10 153 D2
Wanstead E11 55 C4
Woodford E18 36 D2
Wood Green N22 32 A2
Buckingham St WC2 250 B5
Buckingham Way
SM6 219 C1
Buckingham Yd NW10 89 D5
Buck La NW9 45 B4
Buckland Cres NW3 70 B2
Buckland Ct 6 N1 95 C5
Uxbridge UB10 61 A6
Buckland Inf Sch KT9 214 B4
Buckland Rd BR6 227 C4
E10 76 A6
Chessington KT9 214 B3
Buckland Rise HA5 22 D2
Bucklands Rd TW11 175 C4
Buckland St N1 95 B5 235 D3
Buckland Way KT4 200 C1
Buckland Wlk
2 Acton W3 111 A4
Morden SM4 202 A5
Buckleigh Ave SW20 201 B6
Buckleigh Ho SW17 180 B5
Buckleigh Rd SW16 182 A3
Buckleigh Way SE19 183 D3
Buckler Gdns SE9 166 B1
Buckler's Alley SW6 264 D4
Bucklersbury EC2,EC4 242 C1
Bucklers' Way SM5 218 D5
Buckles Ct DA17 124 D2
Buckle St E1 243 D2
9 E1 96 A1
Buckley Cl SE23 162 B4
Buckley Ct 5 NW6 69 B1
Buckley Rd NW6 69 B1
Buckley St SE1 251 A3
Buckmaster Cl SE17 262 B1
11 SW9 138 C2
Buckmaster Ho 1 N7 72 B4
Buckmaster Rd SW11 136 C1
Bucknall St WC1 240 A2
Bucknall Way BR3 208 A5
Bucknell Cl SW2 138 B1
Buckner Rd SW2 138 B1
Buckrell Rd E4 20 B2
Buckridge Bldg EC1 241 A4
Buckshead Ho 19 W2 91 C2
Buck St NW1 71 B1
Buckstone Cl SE23 162 C5
Buckstone Rd N18 34 A5
Buckters Rents SE16 119 A5
Buckthorne Rd SE4 163 A6
Buckthorn Ho DA15 167 D1
Buckwheat Ct DA18 124 D3
Budd Cl N12 29 D6
Buddings Circ HA9 67 A5

Bude Cl E17 53 B4
Budge La CR4 202 D2
Budge Row EC4 242 C1
Budge's Wlk
W2 114 A5 246 B4
Budleigh Cres DA16 146 C4
Budleigh Ho 10 SE15 140 A5
Budoch Ct IG3 80 A6
Budoch Dr IG3 80 A6
Buer Rd SW6 135 A3
Bugsbys Way SE10 120 D2
Bugsby's Way SE7,
SE10 121 B2
Buick Ho 4 E3 97 C3
Bulbarrow NW8 91 D6
Bulganak Rd CR7 205 A5
Bulinca St
SW1 115 D2 259 D3
Bullace Row SE5 139 B4
Bull Alley DA16 146 B2
Bullard Rd TW11 174 D4
Bullards Pl 13 E2 96 D4
Bull Dog The (Juct)
TW15 148 A2
Bulleid Way
SW1 115 B2 258 D3
Bullen Ho 13 E1 96 B3
Bullen St SW11 136 C3
Buller Cl SE15 140 A5
Buller Rd NW10 90 D4
Barking IG11 79 C1
South Norwood CR7 205 B6
Tottenham N17 34 A1
Wood Green N22 32 C1
Bullers Cl DA14 191 A5
Bullers Wood Dr BR7 188 B3
Bullers Wood Sch
BR7 188 B2
Bullescroft Rd HA8 10 D1
Bullfinch Ct 3 SE21 161 B2
Bullingham Mans W8 245 B2
Bull Inn Ct WC2 250 B5
Bullivant St 9 E14 120 A6
Bull La BR7 189 B3
Dagenham RM10 81 D5
Edmonton N18 33 C5
Bull Rd E15 98 D5
Bullrush Cl
Carshalton SM5 218 D6
Thornton Heath CR0 205 C3
Bulls Alley SW14 133 B3
Bulls Bridge Ind Est
UB2 106 B2
Bulls Bridge Rd UB2 106 B2
Bullsbrook Rd UB4 106 C5
Bull's Cross EN1,EN2 6 A6
Bull's Gdns SW3 257 B4
Bulls Head Pas EC3 243 A1
Bull Yd SE15 140 A4
Bulmer Gdns HA3 43 D2
Bulmer Mews
W11 113 C5 245 A4
Bulow Ct 3 SW6 135 D3
Bulstrode Ave TW3 129 C2
Bulstrode Gdns TW3 129 C2
Bulstrode Pl W1 238 B3
Bulstrode Rd TW3 129 C2
Bulstrode St
W1 93 A1 238 B2
Bulwer Court Rd E11 54 B1
Bulwer Ct E11 54 B1
Bulwer Gdns EN5 2 A1
Bulwer Rd E11 54 B1
Edmonton N18 33 C6
New Barnet EN5 2 A1
Bulwer St W12 112 C5
Bunbury Ho SE15 140 A5
Bunces La IG8 36 D3
Bungalow Rd SE25 205 C5
Bungalows The E10 54 A3
Mitcham SW16 181 B3
Bunhill Row
EC1 95 B3 242 C5
Bunhouse Pl SW1 258 B2
Bunkers Hill DA14 169 B1
NW11 48 A2
Bunker's Hill DA17 125 C2
Bunning Ho N7 72 A4
Bunning Way N7 72 B1
Bunn's La NW7 27 D4
Bunsen Ho 1 E3 97 A5
Bunsen St 2 E3 97 A5
Buntingbridge Rd IG2 57 B4
Bunting Cl N9 18 D3
Mitcham CR4 202 D4
Bunting Ct NW9 27 C1
Bunton St SE18 122 C3
Bunyan Ct EC2 242 A4
Bunyan Rd E17 53 A6
Buonaparte Mews
SW1 259 C2
BUPA Bushey Hospl
WD23 8 D3
Burbage Cl
SE1 117 B3 262 C5
Hayes UB3 83 B1
Burbage Ho N1 235 D5
16 SE14 140 D6
Burbage Rd SE21,SE24 161 B4

Burbage Sch N1 95 C5
Burbank KT3 199 D6
Burberry Cl KT3 177 C1
Burbidge Rd TW17 192 C5
Burbridge Way N17 34 A1
Burcham St E14 98 A1
Burcharbro Rd SE2 146 D6
Burchell Ct WD23 8 A4
Burchell Ho SE11 260 D2
Burchell Rd E10 53 D1
SE15 140 B4
Burchetts Way TW17 192 D3
Burchett Way RM6 59 B3
Burcote Rd SW18 158 B4
Burden Cl TW8 109 C1
Burden Ho SW8 270 A3
Burdenshott Ave
TW10 132 D1
Burden Way E11 77 B6
Burder Cl N1 73 C2
Burder Rd N1 73 C2
Burdett Ave SW20 178 A2
Burdett Cl DA14 191 A5
2 Ealing W7 108 D5
Burdett Coutts &
Townshend CE Prim Sch
SW1 115 D2 259 D3
Burdett Mews 4 W2 91 D1
Burdett Rd E3 97 B2
Richmond TW9 132 B2
Thornton Heath CR0 205 B3
Burdetts Rd RM9 103 B6
Burdock Cl CR0 206 D1
Burdock Rd N17 52 A6
Burdon La SM2 217 A1
Burdon Pk SM2 217 B1
Bure Ct 10 EN5 13 D6
Burfield Cl SW17 180 B6
Burford Cl
Dagenham RM8 80 C5
Ickenham UB10 60 A4
Ilford IG6 57 A5
Burford Gdns N13 16 B1
Burford Ho 11 SW9 138 B3
1 Brentford TW8 110 A1
Burford Rd BR1 210 A5
E15 98 B6
E6 100 A4
Brentford TW8 110 A1
Forest Hill SE6 163 B2
New Malden KT4 200 A2
Sutton SM1 217 C6
Burford Way CR0 224 A2
Burford Wlk SW6 265 D3
Burgate Ct 10 SW9 138 C2
Burges Gr SW13 134 B5
Burges Rd E6 78 B1
Burgess Ave NW9 45 B3
Burgess Cl 4 TW13 173 A6
Burgess Ct
3 Southall UB1 85 D1
Wallend E12 78 C1
Burgess Hill NW2 69 C4
Burgess Ho 3 SE5 139 A5
Burgess Ind Pk SE5 139 B5
Burgess Mews SW19 179 D4
Burgess Park Mans
NW6 69 C4
Burgess Rd E15 76 C4
Sutton SM1 217 D4
Burgess St E14 97 C2
Burge St SE1 262 D5
Burghill Rd SE26 185 A6
Burghley Ave
Borehamwood WD6 11 A6
Kingston KT3 177 B2
Burghley Hall Cl
SW19 157 A3
Burghley Ho SW19 157 A1
Burghley Pl CR4 202 D5
Burghley Rd E11 54 C1
N8 50 C6
NW5 71 B4
Wimbledon SW19 179 A6
Burghley Twr W3 111 D6
Burgh St N1 94 D5 234 D4
Burgon St EC4 241 D1
Burgos Cl CR0 220 C2
Burgos Gr SE10 141 D4
Burgoyne Rd N4 50 D3
SW9 138 B2
Ashford TW16 171 D4
South Norwood SE25 205 D5
Burham Cl SE20 184 C3
Burhan Uddin Ho E1 243 C5
Burhill Gr HA5 23 A1
Buriton Ho 9 SW15 156 B3
Burke Cl SW15 133 C1
Burke Ho 1 SW11 136 B1
Burke Lo E13 99 B4
Burke St E16 98 D2
Burket Cl UB2 107 B2
Burland Rd SW11 158 D6
Burleigh Ave DA15 167 D6
Hackbridge SM6 219 B5
Burleigh Ct N17 34 A4
Burleigh Gdns N14 15 C3
Ashford TW15 171 A5
Burleigh Ho SW3 266 D5

Burleigh Ho *continued*
W10 90 D2
Enfield EN1 18 A6
Burleigh Par N14 15 D3
Burleigh Pl SW15 156 D6
Burleigh Rd
Cheam SM3 201 A1
Enfield EN1 5 C1
Hillingdon UB10 82 D6
Burleigh St WC2 250 C6
Burleigh Way EN2 5 B2
Burleigh Wlk SE6 164 A3
Burley Cl Chingford E4 35 C5
Mitcham SW16 181 D1
Burley Ho E1 96 D1
Burley Rd E16 99 C2
Burlington Arc W1 249 A5
Burlington Ave
Richmond TW9 132 C4
Romford RM7 59 D3
Burlington Cl 5 E6 100 A1
W9 91 C3
East Bedfont TW14 149 B4
Orpington BR6 226 D6
Pinner HA5 40 B6
Burlington Ct W4 133 A5
Burlington Danes Sch
W12 90 B1
Burlington Gate SW20 179 A1
Burlington Gdns
W1 115 C6 249 A5
W3 111 A5
W4 111 A1
Dagenham RM6 59 A2
Fulham SW6 135 A3
Burlington Ho NW3 70 B3
Burlington Jun Sch
KT3 199 D5
Burlington La W4 133 B5
Burlington Lo BR7 188 B3
Burlington Mews W3 111 A5
1 Putney SW15 157 B6
Burlington Pl
Fulham SW6 135 A3
Woodford IG8 21 A1
Burlington Rd N10 49 A6
W4 111 A1
Enfield EN2 5 B4
Fulham SW6 135 A3
Hounslow TW7 130 B4
New Malden KT3 199 D5
South Norwood CR7 183 B1
Tottenham N17 34 A2
Burlington Rise EN4 14 D4
Burma Rd N16 73 B4
Burmarsh 6 NW5 71 A2
Burmarsh Ct SE20 184 C2
Burma Terr 11 SE19 183 C5
Burmester Ho SW17 158 A1
Burmester Rd SW17 158 A1
Burnaby Cres W4 133 A6
Burnaby Ct 27 SE16 118 A4
Burnaby Gdns W4 132 D6
Burnaby St
SW10 136 A5 266 B3
Burnand Ho 3 W14 112 D3
Burnaston Ho 5 E5 74 A5
Burnbrae Cl N12 29 D4
Burnbury Rd SW12 159 C3
Burncroft Ave EN3 6 C3
Burndell Way UB4 84 D2
Burne Jones Ho W14 254 B3
Burnell Ave DA16 146 A3
Richmond TW10 175 C5
Burnell Gdns HA7 25 D1
Burnell Ho 19 SW2 160 C3
Burnell Rd SM1 217 D4
Burnell Wlk SE1 263 D2
Burnels Ave E6 100 C4
Burness Cl N7 72 B2
Burne St NW1 237 A4
Burnett Cl E9 74 C3
Burnett Ct SW11 267 A1
Burnett Ho 5 SE13 142 A3
Burney Ave KT5 198 B4
Burney Ho 4 SW16 181 C5
Burney St SE10 142 A5
Burnfoot Ave
SW6 135 A4 264 B1
Burnham NW3 70 C1
Burnham Ave UB10 61 A4
Burnham Cl NW7 28 A3
SE1 263 D3
Enfield EN1 5 C5
Harrow HA3 43 A5
Burnham Cres E11 55 C5
Burnham Ct NW4 46 C5
W2 245 D6
Burnham Dr KT4 216 D6
Burnham Est 8 E2 96 C4
Burnham Gdns
Cranford TW4 128 B4
Croydon CR0 205 D2
Hayes UB3 105 B3
Burnham Rd DA14 169 A2
E4 35 B5
Dagenham RM9 102 B6
Morden SM4 201 D5
Burnham St E2 96 C4

Burnham St *continued*
Kingston KT2 176 C2
Burnham Way W13 109 B3
Penge SE26 185 B5
Burnhill Ho EC1 235 A1
Burnhill Rd BR3 185 C1
Burnley Cl WD19 22 C5
Burnley Rd NW10 68 A3
SW9 138 B3
Burnsall St
SW3 114 C1 257 B2
Burns Ave DA15 168 B5
Feltham TW14 150 A5
Ilford RM6 58 C2
Southall UB1 107 C6
Burns Cl DA16 145 D4
Hayes UB4 84 A2
Mitcham SW17 180 B4
Burns Ct SM6 219 B1
Burns Ho 18 E2 96 C4
11 N16 73 C4
N7 72 B2
SE17 261 D1
Burn's Ho NW10 89 C6
Burnside RM8 58 C1
Burnside Ave E4 35 B4
Burnside Cl SE16 118 D5
Barnet EN5 1 C2
Twickenham TW1 153 A5
Burnside Cres HA0 87 D6
Burns Rd SW11 136 D3
W13 109 B4
Burn's Rd NW10 89 D6
Burns Rd HA0 88 A5
Burns Way TW5 128 D4
Burnt Ash Hill SE12 164 D5
Lewisham SE12 165 A3
Burnt Ash Hts BR1 187 B5
Burnt Ash La BR1,SE12 187 B5
Burnt Ash Prim Sch
BR1 187 A5
Burnt Ash Rd SE12 164 D6
Burnthwaite Rd
SW6 135 B5 264 D3
Burnt Oak Broadway
HA8 26 D2
Burnt Oak Fields HA8 27 A2
Burnt Oak Jun Sch
DA15 168 A3
Burnt Oak La DA15 168 B3
Burnt Oak Sta HA8 27 A2
Burntwood Cl SW18 158 C3
Burntwood Ct SW17 158 A1
Burntwood Grange Rd
SW18 158 C3
Burntwood La SW17 158 B2
Burntwood Sch SW17 158 B2
Burntwood View SE19 183 D5
Buross St E1 96 B1
Burpham Cl UB4 84 D2
Burrage Ct 17 SE16 118 D2
Burrage Gr SE18 123 A2
Burrage Pl SE18 122 D1
Burrage Rd SE18 123 A1
Burrard Ho 11 E2 96 C5
Burrard Rd NW6 69 C4
Newham E16 99 B1
Burr Cl DA7 147 B2
E1 118 A5
Burrell Ct HA1 42 B2
Burrell Cl Croydon CR0 207 A3
Edgware HA8 10 D2
Burrell Ho 4 TW1 153 B4
Burrell Row BR3 185 C1
Burrells 9 BR3 185 D1
Burrell St SE1 116 D5 251 C4
Burrell's Wharf Sq
E14 119 D1
Burrell Twrs E10 53 C2
Burrhill Ct SE16 118 D3
Burritt Rd KT1 176 C1
Burrmead Ct NW2 67 D5
Burroughs Gdns NW4 46 B5
Burroughs The NW4 46 B5
Burrow Ho 10 SW9 138 B3
Burrow Rd SE22 139 C1
Burrows Mews SE1 251 C2
Burrows Rd NW10 90 C4
Burrow Wlk SE21 161 A4
Burr Rd SW18 157 C4
Bursar St SE1 253 A3
Bursdon Cl DA15 167 D2
Bursland Rd EN3 6 D1
Burslem St E1 96 A1
Bursted Wood Prim Sch
DA7 147 D3
Burstock Rd SW15 135 A1
Burston Rd SW15 156 D6
Burstow Rd SW20 179 A2
Burtenshaw Rd KT7 197 A3
Burtley Cl N4 51 A1
Burton Bank N1 73 B1
Burton Cl
Chessington KT9 213 D1
South Norwood CR7 205 B6
Burton Ct SW3 257 D2

Burton Ct *continued*
Thames Ditton KT7 .....197 A3
Burton Dr EN3 .....7 C6
Burton Gdns TW5 ....129 B4
Burton Gr SE17 ....262 C1
Burton Ho 6 SE16 ......118 B4
SE5 ......138 D4
Penge SE26 ......184 B5
Burtonhole Cl NW7 ....28 D6
Burtonhole La NW7 ....28 D6
Burton Lo 5 SW15 ....157 B6
Burton Mews SW1 ....258 B3
Burton Pl WC1 ......232 D1
Burton Rd NW6 ......69 B1
SW9 ......138 D3
8 SW9 ......138 C3
Kingston KT2 ......176 A3
Wanstead E18 ......55 B6
Burtons Ct E15 ......76 B1
Burtons Rd TW12 .....174 A6
Burton St WC1 .93 D3 239 D6
Burtonwood Ho N4 ....51 B2
Burt Rd E16 ......121 C5
Burtt Ho 6 N1 ......95 C4
Burtwell La SE21,SE27 .183 B6
Burwash Ho SE1 .....252 D1
Burwash Rd SE18 ......123 B1
Burwell 2 KT1 ......176 C1
Burwell Ave UB6 ......64 C2
Burwell Cl 25 E1 ......96 B1
Burwell Rd E10 ......53 A1
Burwell Wlk 14 E3 ......97 C3
Burwood Ave BR2 ....225 B6
Pinner HA5 ......40 C4
Burwood Cl KT6 ......198 C1
Burwood Ct SE23 ......162 C4
Burwood Ho 11 SW9 .138 D1
Burwood Pl W2 ......237 B2
Bury Ave Hayes UB4 ....83 C5
Ruislip HA4 ......39 A3
Bury Cl SE16 ......118 D5
Bury Ct EC3 ......243 B2
Bury Gr SM4 ......201 D4
Bury Hall Villas N9 ......17 D4
Bury Pl WC1 ...94 A2 240 B3
Bury Rd N22 ......50 C6
Chingford E4 ......20 C6
Dagenham RM10 ......81 D3
Buryside Cl IG2 ......57 D5
Bury St EC3 ....95 C1 243 B2
SW1 ......115 C5 249 B4
Edmonton N9 ......18 A3
Ruislip HA4 ......39 B3
Bury St W N9 ......17 C4
Bury Wlk SW3 114 C1 257 A2
Burywood Ct EN3 ......6 C3
Busbridge Ho 16 E14 ...97 C2
Busby Ho SW16 ......181 C6
Busby Pl NW5 ......71 D2
Busch Cl TW7 ......131 B4
Busch Cnr TW7 ......131 B4
Bushbaby Cl SE1 ......263 A5
Bushberry Rd E9 ......75 A2
Bush Cl IG2 ......57 B4
Bush Cotts 12 SW18 ..157 C6
Bush Ct N14 ......15 C3
7 W12 ......112 D4
Bushell Cl SW2 ......160 B2
Bushell Gn WD23 ......8 B2
Bushell Ho 3 SE27 ...183 A6
Bushell St E1 ......118 A5
Bushell Way BR7 ......188 C5
Bushey Ave BR5 ......211 B2
E18 ......54 D6
Bushey Cl Chingford E4 ..20 A1
Ickenham UB10 ......60 C6
Bushey Ct SW20 ......178 B1
Bushey Down SW12 ...159 B2
Bushey Fst Sch KT3 ...200 B6
Bushey Hall SE5 ......139 D4
Bushey Heath Prim Sch
WD23 ......8 B3
Bushey Hill Rd SE5 ...139 D4
Bushey Ho SE12 ......165 C1
Bushey La SM1 ......217 C4
Bushey Lees DA15 ....167 D5
Bushey Meads Sch
WD23 ......8 A6
Bushey Mid Sch SW20 200 B6
Bushey Rd E13 ......99 C5
N15 ......51 C3
Croydon CR0 ......223 C6
Hayes UB3 ......105 C2
Ickenham UB10 ......60 C6
Sutton SM1 ......217 C4
West Barnes SW20 ....178 D1
Bushey Way BR3 ......208 B4
Bush Fair Ct N14 ......15 B5
Bushfield Cl HA8 ......10 D2
Bushfield Cres HA8 ....10 D2
Bushfield Ho N5 ......73 A3
Bush Gr NW9 ......45 A2
Stanmore HA7 ......25 D2
Bushgrove Rd RM8 ....80 D5
Bush Hill N21 ......17 A5
Bush Hill Par EN1 ......17 B4
Bush Hill Park Prim Sch
EN1 ......18 A6
Bush Hill Park Sta EN1 17 D5
Bush Hill Rd Enfield N21 17 B5
Harrow HA3 ......44 B3
Bush Ind Est NW10 ....89 B3
Bush La EC4 ..117 B6 252 C6
Bushmead Cl 6 N15 ...51 D5
Bushmoor Cres SE18 .144 D5
Bushnell Rd SW17 ....159 B1
Bush Rd E8 ......96 B6
SE8 ......118 D2
Littleton TW17 ......192 B4
Richmond TW9 ......132 B6
Wanstead E11 ......55 A2
Woodford IG9 ......37 D6
Bushway RM8 ......80 D5
Bushwood E11 ......55 A1
Bushwood Dr
SE1 ......117 D2 263 D3
Bushwood Rd TW9 ...132 C6
Bushy Ct KT1 ......175 C2
Bushy Park Gdns
TW12 ......174 B5
Bushy Park Rd TW11 .175 B3
Bushy Rd TW11 ......174 D3
Business Acad The
DA18 ......125 A4
Business Design Ctr*
N1 ......94 C6 234 B5
Buspace Studios 3
W10 ......91 A3
Butcher Row E1 ......96 D1
Butchers Rd E16 ......99 A1
Bute Ave TW10 ......154 A2
Bute Ct SM6 ......219 C3
Bute Gdns W6 ......112 D2
Wallington SM6 ......219 C3
Bute Gdns W SM6 ....219 C3
Bute House Prep Sch
W6 ......112 D2
Bute Rd Ilford IG6 ......56 D4
Thornton Heath CR0 ....204 C1
Wallington SM6 ......219 C4
Bute St SW7 ..114 B2 256 C4
Butfield Ho 6 E9 ......74 C2
Butler Ave HA1 ......42 B2
Butler Ct Dagenham RM8 81 C6
Wembley HA0 ......65 A4
Butler Ho 18 E14 ......97 B1
32 E2 ......96 C4
6 SW9 ......138 D4
Butler Pl SW1 ......259 C6
Butler Rd NW10 ......67 D1
Dagenham RM8 ......80 B4
Harrow HA1 ......42 A2
Butler's Cotts DA7 ....147 C3
Butler St 33 E2 ......96 C4
Hillingdon UB10 ......82 D3
Butler's Wharf W SE1 .253 C3
Butley Ct 7 E3 ......97 A5
Butterfield Cl 1 SE16 118 B4
Tottenham N17 ......33 A4
Twickenham TW1 ......152 D5
Butterfield Row EN2 ....5 A2
Butterfields E17 ......54 A4
Butterfield Sq 10 E6 ...100 B1
Butterfly La SE9 ......166 D5
Butterfly Wlk 2 SE5 ...139 B4
Butter Hill SM5,SM6 ...219 A4
Butteridges Cl RM9 ....103 B6
Buttermere NW1 ......231 D2
Buttermere Cl E11 ......76 B4
SE1 ......263 C3
East Bedfont TW14 ......149 D3
West Barnes SM4 ......200 D3
Buttermere Ct NW8 ...229 C6
Buttermere Dr SW15 .157 A6
Buttermere Ho 11 E3 ...97 B4
N12 ......30 C5
Buttermere Wlk 9 E8 .73 D2
Butterwick W6 ......112 C2
Butterworth Ct SW16 .160 A1
Butterworth Gdns IG8 .37 A5
Buttesland St
N1 ......95 B4 235 D2
Buttfield Cl RM10 ......81 D2
Buttmarsh Cl SE18 ....122 D1
Buttsbury Rd IG1 ......79 A3
Butts Cotts TW13 ......151 B1
Butts Cres TW13 ......151 C1
Butts Ho TW13 ......151 C1
Butts Piece UB5 ......84 B5
Butts Rd BR1 ......186 C5
Butts The TW8 ......131 D6
Buxhall Cres E9 ......75 B2
Buxlow Prep Sch HA9 ..66 A5
Buxted Rd E8 ......73 D1
N12 ......30 C5
SE22 ......139 C1
Buxton Cl N9 ......18 C2
Woodford IG8 ......37 D4
Buxton Cres SM3 ....217 A4
Buxton Ct N1 ......235 B2
Buxton Dr E11 ......54 C5
Kingston KT3 ......177 B1
Buxton Gdns W3 ......110 D6
Buxton Ho E11 ......54 C5
3 SW11 ......136 B1
Buxton Lo E11 ......77 B6
Buxton Rd E15 ......76 C3
E17 ......53 A5
E6 ......100 A4
N19 ......49 D1
NW2 ......68 B2
Chingford E4 ......20 B4
Ilford IG2 ......57 C3
Mortlake SW14 ......133 C2
Thornton Heath CR7 ....204 D4
Buxton St E1 ...96 A3 243 D5
Buzzard Creek Ind Est
IG11 ......102 A2
Byam Shaw Sch of Art
N19 ......71 D6
Byam St SW6 ......136 A3
Byards Croft SW16 ...181 D2
Byards Ct SE16 ......118 D3
Byas Ho 6 E3 ......97 B4
Byatt Wlk TW12 ......173 A4
Bychurch End 9
TW11 ......174 D5
Bycroft Rd UB1 ......85 C3
Bycroft St SE20 ......184 D3
Bycullah Ave EN2 ......4 D3
Bycullah Rd EN2 ......4 D3
Byefield Cl SE16 ......119 A4
Byelands Cl 12 SE16 ..118 D5
Bye The W3 ......89 C1
Byeways TW2 ......151 D1
Byeways The KT5 ......198 D4
Byeway The SW14 ....133 A2
Bye Way The HA3 ......24 D2
Byfeld Gdns SW13 ....134 A4
Byfield Ct KT3 ......200 A5
Byfield Rd TW7 ......131 A2
Byford Cl E15 ......76 C1
Bygrove CR0 ......223 D1
Bygrove Ct SW19 ......180 B4
Bygrove Prim Sch E14 .97 D1
Bygrove Rd SW19 ....180 B4
Bygrove St E14 ......97 D1
Byland Cl N21 ......16 B4
Bylands Cl SE2 ......124 B3
Byne Rd
Carshalton SM5 ......218 C6
Forest Hill SE26 ......184 C5
Bynes Rd CR2 ......221 B1
Byng Pl WC1 ...93 D3 239 C5
Byng St E14 ......119 C4
Bynon Ave DA7 ......147 B2
Byre Rd N14 ......15 B5
Byrne Ho 11 SW2 ....160 B6
Byrne Rd SW12 ......159 B2
Byron Ave E12 ......78 A2
NW9 ......44 D6
Borehamwood WD6 ......10 C6
Cranford TW4 ......128 B3
Sutton SM1 ......218 B4
West Barnes KT3 ......200 A4
Woodford E18 ......36 D1
Byron Ave E SM1 ......218 B4
Byron Cl E8 ......96 A6
SE28 ......124 C5
Feltham TW12 ......173 B6
Forest Hill SE26 ......185 A6
Streatham SW16 ......182 A4
Walton-on-T KT12 ......195 A1
Byron Court Prim Sch
HA0 ......65 C6
Byron Ct 3 NW6 ......70 A1
SW3 ......257 B3
W7 ......109 A2
W9 ......91 C3
WC1 ......240 C6
Dulwich SE21 ......162 A3
Enfield EN2 ......4 D3
Harrow HA1 ......42 C3
1 Richmond TW10 ....175 D6
South Norwood CR7 ....183 A1
11 Wanstead E11 ......55 A5
Woodford E18 ......37 B2
Byron Dr DA8 ......147 D5
N2 ......48 B3
Byron Gdns SM1 ......218 B4
Byron Hill Rd HA1,HA2 .64 C6
Byron Ho 5 BR3 ......185 D4
Byron Mews NW3 ......70 C4
Byron Par UB10 ......83 A3
Byron Rd E10 ......53 D1
E17 ......53 C6
NW2 ......68 B6
NW7 ......28 A5
Ealing W5 ......110 B5
Harrow HA1 ......42 C3
Harrow HA3 ......24 D1
Wembley HA0 ......65 C5
Byron St E14 ......98 A1
Byron Way Hayes UB4 ..83 D3
Northolt UB5 ......85 A4
West Drayton UB7 ......104 B2
Bysouth Cl N15 ......51 B5
Bythorn St SW9 ......138 B1
Byton Rd SW17 ......180 D4
Byward Ave TW14 ....150 C5
Byward St EC3 117 C6 253 B5
Bywater Ho SE18 ......122 A3
Bywater Pl SE16 ......119 A5
Bywater St
SW3 ......114 D1 257 C2
Byways The KT19 ....215 D4
Bywell Pl W1 ......239 A3
Bywood Ave CR0 ....206 D3
Bywood Terr CR0 ....206 C3
Byworth Wlk N19 ......50 A1

C

Cabbell St NW1 92 C2 237 A3
Cabinet Off SW1 ....250 A2
Cabinet War Rooms*
SW1 ......115 D4 249 D2
Cabinet Way E4 ......35 B4
Cable Ho WC1 ......234 A2
Cable Pl SE10 ......142 A4
Cable St E1 ......118 B6
Cabot Ct SE16 ......118 D3
Cabot Sq E14 ......119 C5
Cabot Way 3 E6 ......99 D6
Cabul Rd SW11 ......136 C3
Cactus Cl SE5 ......139 C3
Cactus Wlk W12 ......89 D1
Cadbury Cl
Ashford TW16 ......171 C3
Isleworth TW7 ......131 A4
Cadbury Rd TW16 ....171 C4
Cadbury Way 1 SE16 .118 A2
Caddington Cl EN4 ....14 C6
Caddington Rd NW2 ...69 A5
Caddis Cl HA7 ......24 D3
Cadell Cl E2 ......95 D5
Cadell Ho 12 E2 ......95 D5
Cade Rd SE10 ......142 B4
Cader Rd SW18 ......158 A5
Cadet Dr SE1 .117 D1 263 D2
Cade Tyler Ho 10
SE10 ......142 A4
Cadiz St SE17 .117 A1 262 B1
Cadley Terr SE23 ......162 C2
Cadman Cl SW9 ......138 D5
Cadmer Cl KT3 ......199 C5
Cadmore Ho 4 N1 ....72 D1
Cadmus Cl 9 SW4 ...137 D2
Cadmus Ct 6 SW9 ...138 C4
Cadnam Lo E14 ......120 B3
Cadnam Point 15
SW15 ......156 B3
Cadogan Cl E9 ......75 B1
Beckenham BR3 ......186 B1
Harrow HA2 ......63 D4
Teddington TW11 ......174 C5
Cadogan Ct SW3 ......257 C3
Sutton SM2 ......217 D2
New Malden KT3 ......199 C5
Cadogan Ct Gdns
SW1 ......258 A4
Cadogan Gate
SW1 ......114 D2 257 D4
Cadogan Gdns N3 ......29 D2
SW3 ......114 D2 257 D3
Southgate N21 ......16 C6
Wanstead E18 ......55 B6
Cadogan Ho SW3 ....266 D5
Cadogan La
SW1 ......115 A3 258 A5
Cadogan Pl
SW1 ......114 D3 257 D5
Cadogan Rd SE18 ....123 A3
Kingston KT6 ......197 D4
Cadogan Sq
SW1 ......114 D3 257 D5
Cadogan St
SW3 ......114 D2 257 C3
Cadogan Terr E9 ......75 B1
Cadoxton Ave 3 N15 ..51 D3
Cadwallon Rd SE9 ....167 A2
Caedmon Rd N7 ......72 B4
Caerleon Cl
Claygate KT10 ......213 B1
Sidcup DA14 ......190 C5
Caerleon Terr SE2 ....124 B2
Caernarvon Cl CR4 ...204 A6
Caernarvon Ct 3 KT5 198 B4
Caernarvon Ho W2 ...236 A2
Caesar Ct 25 E2 ......96 D5
Caesar's Way TW17 ..193 B3
Caesars Wlk CR4 ....202 D4
Cahill St EC1 ......242 B5
Cahir St E14 ......119 D2
Cain Ct 2 W5 ......87 C2
Caine Ho W3 ......110 D4
Cain's La TW14 ......149 C6
Caird St W10 ......91 B4
Cairn Ave W5 ......109 D5
Cairndale Cl BR1 ....186 D3
Cairnfield Ave NW2 ...67 D5
Cairnfield Ct NW2 ....67 C5
Cairns Ho 3 N7 ......72 B4
Cairns Mews SE18 ...144 A4
Cairns Rd SW11 ......158 C6
Cairn Way HA7 ......24 D4
Cairo New Rd CR0 ...220 D6
Cairo Rd E17 ......53 C5
Caister Ho N7 ......72 B2
10 Balham SW12 ......159 B4
Caistor Ho 5 E15 ....98 D6
Caistor Mews SW12 ..159 B4
Caistor Park Rd E15 ..98 D6
Caistor Rd SW12 ......159 B4
Caithness Gdns DA15 .167 D5
Caithness Ho N1 ......233 C6
Caithness Rd W14 ....112 D3
Mitcham CR4 ......181 B3
Calabria Rd N5 ......72 D3
Calais Gate SE5 ......138 D4
Calais St SE5 ......138 D4
Calbourne Rd SW12 ..159 A4
Calcott Wlk SE9 ......187 D6
Calcraft Ho 10 E2 ......96 C5
Caldbeck Ave KT4 ....200 B1
Caldecot Ct SE5 ......139 A3
Caldecote 3 KT1 ....176 C1
Caldecote Gdns WD23 ..8 C4
Caldecote La WD23 ....8 D5
Caldecot Rd SE5 ......139 A3
Caldecott Way E5 ......74 D5
Calder Ave UB6 ......86 D5
Calder Cl EN1 ......5 C2
Calder Ct SE16 ......119 B5
Calder Gdns HA8 ......44 C6
Calderon Ho NW8 ....230 A4
Calderon Pl W10 ......90 C2
Calderon Rd E11 ......76 B5
Calder Rd SM4 ......202 A4
Caldervale Rd SW4 ...159 D6
Calderwood St SE18 ..122 C2
Caldew Ct NW7 ......28 A3
Caldew St SE5 ......139 B5
Caldicote Gn NW9 ......45 C3
Caldwell Rd WD19 ......22 D6
Caldwell St
SW9 ......138 B5 270 D3
Caldy Rd DA17 ......125 D3
Caldy Wlk 15 N1 ......73 A2
Caleb St SE1 ......252 B2
Caledonia Ct IG11 ....102 C5
Caledonia Ho 17 E14 ...97 A1
Caledonian Cl 1 IG3 ...58 B1
Caledonian Market
SE1 ......117 C3 263 B6
Caledonian Rd
N1 ......94 B6 233 C5
N7 ......72 B2
Caledonian Road &
Barnsbury Sta N7 ....72 B1
Caledonian Road Sta
N7 ......72 B2
Caledonian Wharf Rd
E14 ......120 B2
Caledonia Rd TW19 ...148 A3
Caledonia St N1 ......233 B3
Caledon Rd E6 ......78 B1
Hackbridge SM5,SM6 ...219 A4
Cale St SW3 ..114 C1 257 A2
Caletock Way SE10 ...120 D1
Calgarth NW1 ......232 B3
Calgary Ct 24 SE16 ...118 C4
Caliban Twr 9 N1 ......95 C5
Calico Ho 4 SW11 ...136 A2
Calico Row 5 SW11 ..136 A2
Calidore Cl SW2 ......160 B5
California La WD23 .....8 B3
California Rd KT3 ....199 A6
Callaby Terr 11 N1 ......73 B2
Callaghan Cl SE13 ....142 C1
Callahan Cotts 8 E1 ...96 C2
Callander Rd SE6 ......164 A2
Callanders The WD23 ....8 C3
Callard Ave N13 ......32 D6
Callcott Ct NW6 ......69 B1
Callcott Rd NW6 ......69 B1
Callcott St W8 ......245 A4
Callendar Rd SW7 ....256 C6
Callingham Cl 17 E14 ..97 B2
Callingham Ho 1
SW4 ......138 A2
Callis Farm Cl TW19 ..148 A5
Callis Rd E17 ......53 B3
Callonfield 3 E17 ......53 A5
Callow St SW3 136 B6 266 C6
Calmington Rd SE5 ...139 C6
Calmont Rd BR1 ......186 C4
Calonne Rd SW19 ....178 D6
Calshot Ho N1 ......233 C4
Calshot Rd TW6 ......126 D3
Calshot St N1 ..94 B5 233 C3
Calshot Way Enfield EN2 .4 D2
Harlington TW6 ......126 C3
Calstock NW1 ......232 C5
Calstock Ho SE11 ....261 B2
Calthorpe Gdns
Edgware HA8 ......26 B5
Sutton SM1 ......218 A5
Calthorpe St
WC1 ......94 B3 240 D6
Calton Ave SE21 ......161 C5
Calton Rd EN5 ......14 B5
Calver 13 NW5 ......71 B4
Calver Ct E17 ......54 B6
Calverley Cl BR3 ....185 D4
Calverley Cres RM10 ...81 C6
Calverley Gr N19 ......49 D1
Calverley Rd KT17 ....216 A2
Calvert Ave E2 ......95 D4
Calvert Cl
Belvedere DA17 125
Sidcup DA14 191
Calvert Ct 1 N19 49
5 Richmond TW9 132
Calvert Ho 9 W12 112
Calverton SE5 139
Calverton Prim Sch
E16 99
Calverton Rd E6 100
Calvert Rd SE10 120
Calvert's Bldgs SE1 ...252
Calvert St NW1 .93 A6 231
Calvin St E1 ...95 D3 243
Calydon Rd SE7 121
Calypso Cres 5 SE15 .139
Calypso Way SE8,SE16 .119
Camac Rd TW2 152
Camarthen Gn NW9 45
Cambalt Ho 3 SW15 .156
Cambalt Rd SW15 156
Cambell Inf Sch RM9 ..80
Cambell Jun Sch RM9 .80
Cambell Wlk N1 233
Camber Ho 4 SE15 ..140
Camberley Ave
Enfield EN1 5
Wimbledon SW20 178
Camberley Cl SM3 216
Camberley Ct 8 SM2 .217
Camberley Ho NW1 ..231
Camberley Rd TW6 ...126
Cambert Way SE9 143
Camberwell Church St
SE5 139
Camberwell Coll of Arts
SE15 139
SE5 139
Camberwell Glebe
SE5 139
Camberwell Gn SE5 ..139
Camberwell Gr SE5 ...139
Camberwell Green
SE5 ......139 A
Camberwell New Rd
SW9 ......138 D
Camberwell Rd SE5 ..139 A
Camberwell Station Rd
SE5 ......139 A
Camberwell Trad Est
SE5 ......139 A
Cambeys Rd RM10 ....81 D
Cambisgate SW19 ....179 A
Camborne Ave W13 ..109 C
Camborne Cl TW6 ....126 C
Camborne Cres TW6 .126 C
Camborne Rd DA16 ...145 D
Belmont SM2 ......217 D
Croydon CR0 ......206 A
Sidcup DA14 ......168 C
Wandsworth SW18 ....157 C
West Barnes SM4 ......200 D
Harmondsworth TW6 ...126 C
Camborne Way
Harlington TW6 ......126 C
Heston TW5 ......129 C
Cambourne Ave N9 ....18 D
Cambourne Mews 6
W11 ......91 A
Cambray Rd BR6 ......211 D
Streatham SW12 ......159 C
Cambria 6 BR3 ......185 D
Cambria Cl DA15 ......167 C
Hounslow TW3 ......129 C
Cambria Ct TW14 ......150 B
Cambria Gdns TW19 ..148 A
Cambria Ho 16 E14 ....97 A
Forest Hill SE26 ......184 A
Cambrian Ave IG2 ......57 C
Cambrian Cl SE27 ....160 D
Cambrian Ct UB2 ......107 D
Cambrian Gn NW9 ......45 C
Cambrian Rd E10 ......53 C
Richmond TW10 ......154 B5
Cambria Rd SE5 ......139 A2
Cambria St
SW6 ......135 D5 265 D
Cambridge Ave DA16 .145 D
NW6 ......91 C5
Greenford UB6 ......64 D3
Kingston KT3,SW20 ....177 D
Cambridge Barracks Rd 12
SE18 ......122 B
Cambridge Cir
WC2 ......93 D1 239 D
Cambridge Cl E17 ......53 B
NW10 ......67 A5
Hounslow TW4 ......129 A
Wimbledon SW20 ......178 B2
Wood Green N22 ......32 C2
Cambridge Cotts TW9 132 C6
Cambridge Cres 20 E2 .96 B5
Teddington TW11 ......175 A5
Cambridge Ct 25 E2 ...96 B5
N16 ......51 C2
2 NW6 ......91 C5
Wimbledon SW20 ......178 B2
Cambridge Dr SE12 ...165 A6
Ruislip HA4 ......62 D6

Cambridge Gate NW1 238 C6
Cambridge Gate Mews
NW1 238 D6
Cambridge Gdns N10 31 B2
NW6 91 C5
W10 91 A1
Enfield EN1 6 A3
Kingston KT1 176 C1
Southgate N21 17 B4
Tottenham N17 33 B3
Cambridge Gn SE9 166 D3
Cambridge Gr W6 112 B2
Penge SE20 184 B2
Cambridge Grove Rd
Kingston KT1 198 C6
13 Kingston KT1 176 C1
Cambridge Heath Rd
E1,E2 96 B4
Cambridge Heath Sta
E2 96 B5
Cambridge Ho
Ealing W13 87 A1
Fulham SW6 135 A2
2 Teddington TW11 175 A5
7 Woolwich SE18 122 B2
Cambridge Mans
SW11 267 C1
Cambridge Par EN1 6 A4
Cambridge Park Ct
TW1 153 D4
Cambridge Park Rd
E11 55 A2
Cambridge Pas 9 E9 74 C1
Cambridge Pk
Twickenham TW1 153 D5
Wanstead E11 55 A3
Cambridge Pl W8 245 D1
Cambridge Rd BR1 187 A3
E11 54 D3
NW6 91 C4
NW6 91 C5
SW11 136 D4 267 C1
W7 108 D4
Barking IG11 79 A1
Barnes SW13 133 D3
Carshalton SM5 218 C3
3 Chingford E4 20 B3
East Molesey KT8 195 B5
Hampton TW12 173 B3
Harrow HA2 41 C4
Hounslow TW4 129 A1
Ilford IG3 57 C1
Kingston KT1 176 C1
Littleton TW15 171 A3
Mitcham CR4 203 C6
New Malden KT3 199 C5
Penge SE20 206 B6
Richmond TW9 132 C5
Sidcup DA14 189 C6
Southall UB1 107 B5
Teddington TW11 175 A5
Twickenham TW1 153 D5
Walton-on-T KT12 194 B3
Wimbledon SW20 178 B2
Cambridge Rd N W4 110 D1
Cambridge Rd S 3
W4 110 D1
Cambridge Row SE18 122 D1
Cambridge Sch W6 112 B2
Cambridge Sq
W2 92 C1 237 A2
Cambridge St
SW1 115 C1 259 A2
Cambridge Terr NW1 231 C1
Edmonton N9 17 D4
Cambridge Terr Mews
NW1 231 D1
Cambstone Cl N11 15 A2
Cambus Cl UB4 85 A2
Cambus Rd E16 99 A2
Cam Ct 2 SE15 139 D6
Camdale Rd SE18 145 D5
Camden Ave
Feltham TW13 150 C3
Hayes UB4 106 D6
Camden Cl BR7 189 A2
Camden Ct 9 DA17 125 C1
Camden Gdns NW1 71 B1
Sutton SM1 217 D3
Thornton Heath CR7 204 D6
Camden Gr BR7 188 D4
Camden High St
NW1 93 C6 232 A5
Camden Hill Rd SE19 183 C4
Camden Ho 6 SE8 119 B1
Camdenhurst St E14 97 A1
Camden Jun Sch SM5 218 D4
Camden Lock Pl NW1 71 B1
Camden Mews NW1 71 D2
Camden Mkt*
NW1 93 B6 231 D6
Camden Park Rd BR7 188 C3
NW1 71 D2
Camden Pas N1 94 D6 234 C5
Camden Rd DA5 169 B4
E17 53 B3
NW1 71 D2 231 D6
Carshalton SM5 218 D4
Sutton SM1 217 D3
Camden Rd *continued*
Wanstead E11 55 B3
Camden Road Sta NW1 71 C1
Camden Row SE3 142 C3
Camden Sch for Girls The
NW5 71 C2
Camden Sq NW1 71 D2
Camden St
NW1 93 C6 232 B5
Camden Studios NW1 232 B5
Camden Town Sta
NW1 93 B6 231 D6
Camden Way BR7 188 C3
Thornton Heath CR7 204 D6
Camden Wlk N1 234 C5
Cameford Ct 20 SW12 160 A4
Camel Ct HA9 66 D6
Camelford NW1 232 B5
Camelford Ct 7 W11 91 A1
Camelford Wlk 8 W11 91 A1
Camel Gr KT2 175 D5
Camelia Ct IG8 36 C4
Camellia Ct 20 BR3 185 C3
Camellia Ho SE8 141 B5
Camellia Pl TW2 151 D4
Camellia St SW8 270 A3
Camelot Cl SE18 123 B4
Wimbledon SW19 179 C6
Camelot Ho 6 NW1 71 D2
Camelot Prim Sch
SE15 140 B6
Camel Rd E16 121 D5
Camera Pl SW10 266 C6
Cameret Ct 6 W11 112 D4
Cameron Cl N20 14 C2
Edmonton N18 34 B5
Cameron Ct 3 SW19 157 A3
Cameron Ho NW8 230 A4
SE5 139 A5
8 Bromley BR1 186 D2
Cameron House Sch
SW10 266 D5
Cameron Lo TW3 130 A1
Cameron Rd BR2 209 A4
Forest Hill SE6 163 B2
Ilford IG3 57 C1
Thornton Heath CR0 204 D3
Cameron Sq CR4 180 C2
Camerton Cl 8 E8 73 D2
Camfrey Ct N8 50 A5
Camgate Ctr The
TW19 148 B4
Camilla Cl TW16 171 D4
Camilla Ct 14 SM2 217 C1
Camilla Rd SE16 118 B2
Camille Cl SE25 206 A6
Camlan Rd BR1 186 D6
Camlet St E2 243 C6
Camlet Way EN4 1 D4
Camley St NW1 93 D5 232 D4
Camm 23 NW9 27 D1
Camm Gdns
5 Kingston KT1 176 B1
Thames Ditton KT7 196 D2
Camomile Ave CR4 180 D2
Camomile St
EC3 95 C1 243 B2
Camomile Way UB7 82 A1
Campaign Ct W9 91 B3
Campana Rd
SW6 135 C4 265 B2
Campasps Bsns Pk
TW16 193 D4
Campbell Ave IG6 57 A5
Campbell Cl SE18 144 C4
Ruislip HA4 40 A3
Streatham SW16 181 D6
Twickenham TW2 152 B3
Campbell Croft HA8 26 C5
Campbell Ct NW9 45 A3
SW7 256 A5
Dulwich SE21 162 A3
Ealing W7 108 C6
Tottenham N17 33 D2
Campbell Gordon Way
NW2 68 B4
Campbell Ho SW1 259 A1
30 W12 112 B6
W2 236 C5
6 Wallington SM6 219 B4
Campbell Rd E15 76 D4
E17 53 B5
E3 97 C4
E6 100 A6
Ealing W7 108 C6
Thornton Heath CR0 204 D3
Tottenham N17 34 A2
Twickenham TW2 152 B2
Campdale Rd N7 71 D5
Campden Cres
Dagenham RM8 80 C4
Wembley HA0 65 B5
Campden Gr
W8 113 C4 245 B2
Campden Hill
W8 113 C4 245 A2
Campden Hill Ct W8 245 B2
Campden Hill Gate
W8 245 A2
Campden Hill Gdns
W8 245 A4
Campden Hill Mans
W8 245 B4
Campden Hill Pl W14 244 D4
Campden Hill Rd
W8 113 C4 245 A2
Campden Hill Sq
W14 113 B5 244 D4
Campden Ho 4 NW6 70 B1
W8 245 B3
Campden Hos W8 245 A3
Campden House Cl
W8 245 B2
Campden Rd
Ickenham UB10 60 B4
South Croydon CR2 221 C3
Campden St
W8 113 C5 245 A3
Campe Ho 1 N10 31 A3
Campen Cl SW19 157 A2
Camperdown St E1 243 D1
Campfield Rd SE9 165 D4
Campion Cl Harrow HA3 44 B3
Hillingdon UB8 82 B2
Newham E6 122 B6
South Croydon CR2 221 C4
Campion Ct 10 HA0 88 A5
Campion Gdns IG8 37 A5
Campion Ho 15 N16 73 C3
Campion House (Seminary)
TW7 130 B4
Campion Pl SE28 124 B5
Campion Rd
Hounslow TW7 130 D4
Putney SW15 156 C6
Campion Terr NW2 68 D5
Campion Way HA8 27 A6
Camplin Rd HA3 44 A4
Camplin St SE14 140 D5
Camp Rd SW19 178 C5
Campsbourne Ho 3
N8 50 A5
Campsbourne Jun & Inf
Schs N8 50 A6
Campsbourne The N8 50 A5
Campsey Gdns RM9 80 B1
Campsey Rd RM9 80 B1
Campsfield Ho N8 50 A6
Campsfield Rd N8 50 A6
Campshill Pl SE13 164 A6
Campshill Rd SE13 164 A6
Camp Site The BR8 191 C3
Campton Hill Twrs
W8 245 A4
Campus Rd E17 53 B3
Camp View SW19 178 B5
Cam Rd E15 98 B6
Camrose Ave DA8 147 D6
Edgware HA8 26 B2
Feltham TW13 172 C6
Camrose Cl
Croydon CR0 207 A2
Morden SM4 201 C5
Camrose St SE2 124 A2
Camsey Ho 8 SW2 160 B6
Canada Ave N18 33 A4
Canada Cres W3 89 A3
Canada Gdns SE13 164 A6
Canada Rd W3 89 A2
Canada Sq E14 119 D5
Canada St SE16 118 D4
Canada Way W12 112 B6
Canadian Ave SE6 163 D3
Canal App SE8 141 A6
Canal Bldg N1 235 A4
Canal Bridge SE15 140 A6
Canal Cl E1 97 A3
W10 90 D3
Canal Gr SE15 140 B6
Canal Head Public Sq
SE15 140 A4
Canal Path 22 E2 95 D6
Canalside Studios 31
N1 95 C6
Canal St SE5 139 B6
Canal Way W10 90 D3
Canal Wlk N1 95 B6 235 D6
Croydon CR0 205 D3
Forest Hill SE26 184 C5
Canary Wharf* E14 119 D5
Canary Wharf Pier River
Bus) E14 119 B5
Canary Wharf Sta E14 119 C5
Canberra Cl NW4 46 A6
Canberra Dr UB4 84 C4
Canberra Prim Sch
W12 112 B6
Canberra Rd E6 100 B6
SE7 143 D6
Erith DA7 146 D6
Harlington TW6 126 C2
Canbury 2000 Bsns Pk 3
KT2 176 A2
Canbury Ave KT2 176 B2
Canbury Ct KT2 176 A3
Canbury Mews SE26 162 A1
Canbury Park Rd KT2 176 B2
Canbury Sch KT2 176 D4
Cancell Rd SW9 138 C4
Candahar Rd SW11 136 C3
Candida Ct 9 NW1 71 B1
Candishe Ho SE1 253 C2
Candler Mews TW1 153 A4
Candler St N15 51 B3
Candover St W1 239 A3
Candy St E3 97 B6
Caney Mews NW2 68 D6
Canfield Dr HA4 62 B3
Canfield Gdns NW6 69 D1
Canfield Ho N15 51 C3
Canfield Pl NW6 70 A2
Canford Ave UB5 85 A6
Canford Cl EN2 4 C3
Canford Gdns KT3 199 C3
Canford Pl TW11 175 C4
Canford Rd SW11 159 A6
Canham Rd W3 111 C4
South Norwood SE25 205 C6
Canmore Gdns SW16 181 C3
Cann Hall Prim Sch
E11 76 D5
Cann Hall Rd E11 76 D4
Cann Ho W14 254 B5
Canning Cres N22 32 B2
Canning Cross SE5 139 C3
Canning Ct N22 32 B2
Canning Ho 23 W12 112 B6
Canning Pas
W8 114 A3 256 A6
Canning Pl
W8 114 A3 256 A6
Canning Pl Mews W8 256 A6
Canning Rd E15 98 C5
E17 53 A6
N5 72 D5
Croydon CR0 221 D6
Harrow HA3 42 D6
Cannington 14 NW5 71 A2
Cannington Rd RM9 80 C2
Canning Town E16 98 C2
Canning Town Sta E16 98 C2
Cannizaro Rd SW19 178 D5
Cannock Ho N4 51 B2
Cannock Lo EN1 17 C5
Cannonbury Ave HA5 40 D3
Cannon Cl
Hampton TW12 173 D4
West Barnes SW20 200 C6
Cannon Dr E14 119 C6
Cannon Hill NW6 69 C3
Palmers Green N14 16 A1
Cannon Hill La SM4,
SW20 201 A5
Cannon Hill Mews N14 16 A1
Cannon Ho SE11 260 D3
Penge SE26 184 B4
Cannon La NW3 70 B5
Pinner HA5 41 A3
Cannon Pl NW3 70 B5
SE7 122 A1
Cannon Rd DA7 147 B4
Palmers Green N14 16 A1
Cannon St EC4 117 B6 252 B6
Cannon Street Rd E1 96 B1
Cannon Street Sta
EC4 117 B6 252 C6
Cannon Trad Est HA9 66 D4
Cannon Way KT8 195 D5
Cannon Wharf Bsns Ctr 12
SE8 119 A2
Canon Ave RM6 58 C4
Canon Barnett CE Prim Sch
E1 95 D1 243 D2
Canon Beck Rd SE16 118 C4
Canonbie Rd SE23 162 C4
Canonbury Cres N1 73 A1
Canonbury Ct 21 N1 72 D1
Canonbury Gr N1 73 A1
Canonbury La N1 72 D1
Canonbury Pk N N1 73 A2
Canonbury Pk S N1 73 A2
Canonbury Pl N1 72 D2
Canonbury Prim Sch
N1 72 D2
Canonbury Rd N1 72 D1
Enfield EN1 5 C4
Canonbury Sq N1 72 D1
Canonbury St N1 73 A1
Canonbury Sta N1,N5 73 A3
Canonbury Villas N1 72 D1
Canon Lane Fst & Mid Schs
HA5 40 D3
Canon Mohan Cl N14 15 B5
Canon Murnane Rd
SE1 263 C5
Canon Palmer RC Sch
IG3 57 C1
Canon Rd BR1 209 D6
Canon Row
SW1 116 A4 250 A1
Canons Cl N2 48 B2
Edgware HA8 26 B4
Canons Cnr HA8 26 A6
Canons Ct HA8 26 B4
Canons Dr HA8 26 B4
Canons High Sch HA8 26 B1
Canons L Ctr The CR4 202 D5
Canonsleigh Rd RM9 80 B1
Canons Park Cl HA8 26 A3
Canons Park Sta HA8 26 A3
Canon St N1 95 A6 235 A5
Canon's Wlk CR0 222 D5
Canopus Way
Moor Park HA6 22 A6
Stanwell TW19 148 A4
Canrobert St E2 96 B4
Cantelowes Ho EN5 12 D6
Cantelowes Rd NW1 71 D2
Canterbury SE13 164 A6
Canterbury Ave
DA14,DA15 168 C2
Redbridge IG1 56 A2
Canterbury Cl 16 SE5 139 A3
Beckenham BR3 185 D2
7 Newham E6 100 B1
Southall UB6 85 D2
Canterbury Cres SW9 138 C2
Canterbury Ct NW11 47 A3
NW6 91 C5
15 NW9 27 D1
W3 111 C5
Ashford TW15 170 B6
South Croydon CR2 221 A1
Canterbury Gr SE27,
SW16 160 C1
Canterbury Ho 6 E3 97 D4
SE1 260 D6
2 Barking IG11 80 A1
Canterbury Ind Pk 15
SE15 140 C6
Canterbury Mans NW6 69 D2
Canterbury Pl SE17 261 D3
Canterbury Rd E10 54 A3
NW6 91 C5
Feltham TW13 151 A2
Harrow HA1,HA2 42 A4
Morden SM4 202 A3
Thornton Heath CR0 204 C2
Canterbury Terr NW6 91 C5
Cantium Ret Pk SE1 140 A6
Cantley Gdns Ilford IG2 57 A3
South Norwood SE19 183 D2
Cantley Rd W7 109 A3
Canton St E14 97 C1
Cantrell Rd E3 97 C3
Cantwell Ho SE18 144 D5
Cantwell Rd SE18 144 D5
Canute Ct SW16 160 C1
Canute Gdns SE16 118 D2
Canvey St SE1 252 A4
Cape Cl IG11 78 D1
Cape Henry Ct 7 E14 120 B6
Capel KT5 198 B2
Capel Ave SM6 220 B3
Capel Cl N20 14 A1
Keston Mark BR2 210 A1
Capel Ct SE20 184 C2
Capel Gdns Ilford IG3 79 D4
Pinner HA5 41 B5
Capel Ho 17 E9 74 C1
South Oxhey WD19 22 D6
Capella Ho SE7 143 B6
Capel Lo
5 Richmond TW9 132 B4
12 Streatham SW2 160 B4
Capel Point E7 77 B4
Capel Rd E7,E12 77 C4
East Barnet EN4 14 C5
Capener's Cl SW1 248 A1
Cape Rd N17 52 A6
Capern Rd SW18 158 A3
Capital Bsns Ctr HA0 87 D5
Capital Ind Est
Belvedere DA17 125 D3
Mitcham CR4 202 D4
Capital Interchange Way
TW8 110 C1
Capital Wharf 15 E1 118 A5
Capitol Way NW9 45 A6
Capland Ho NW8 236 D6
Capland St
NW8 92 B3 236 D6
Caplan Est CR4 181 C2
Caple Ho SW10 266 B4
Caple Rd NW10 89 D5
Capper St WC1 93 C3 239 B5
Caprea Cl UB4 84 D2
Capricorn Ctr RM8 59 B2
Capri Ho E17 35 B1
Capri Rd CR0 205 D2
Capstan Cl RM6 58 B3
Capstan Ho 5 E14 120 A2
Capstan Rd SE8 119 B2
Capstan Ride EN2 4 C3
Capstan Sq E14 120 A4
Capstan Way SE16 119 A5
Capstone Rd BR1 186 D6
Capthorne Ave HA2 41 B1
Capuchin Cl HA7 25 B4
Capulet Mews 1 E16 121 A5
Capworth St E10 53 D2
Caradoc Cl W2 91 C1
Caradoc Evans Cl 1
N11 31 B5
Caradoc St SE10 120 C1
Caradon Ct E11 54 C1
Caradon Ct *continued*
7 Twickenham TW1 153 C5
Caradon Way N15 51 B5
Caranday Villas 5
W11 112 D5
Caravel Cl E14 119 C3
Caravelle Gdns 1 UB5 84 D4
Caravel Mews 10 SE8 141 C6
Caraway Cl E13 99 B2
Caraway Hts E14 120 A6
Caraway Pl SM6 219 B5
Carberry Rd 12 SE19 183 C4
Carbery Ave W3 110 B4
Carbis Cl E4 20 B3
Carbis Rd E14 97 B1
Carbroke Ho 10 E9 96 C6
Carburton St
W1 93 B3 238 D5
Cardale St 1 E14 120 A3
Cardamom Ct 7 E12 78 C4
Carden Rd SE15 140 B2
Cardiff Ho 9 SE15 140 A6
Cardiff Rd Ealing W7 109 A3
Enfield EN3 6 B1
Cardiff St SE18 145 C5
Cardigan Ct 3 W7 86 D3
Cardigan Gdns IG3 80 A6
Cardigan Rd E3 97 B5
Barnes SW13 134 A3
Richmond TW10 154 A5
Wimbledon SW19 180 A4
Cardigan St
SE11 116 C1 261 A2
Cardigan Wlk 12 N1 73 A1
Cardinal Ave
Kingston KT2 176 A4
West Barnes SM4 201 A3
Cardinal Bourne St
SE1 262 D5
Cardinal Cap Alley
SE1 252 A4
Cardinal Cl HA8 27 B3
Chislehurst BR7 189 B2
West Barnes SM4 201 A3
Worcester Park KT19,
KT4 216 A4
Cardinal Cres KT3 177 A1
Cardinal Dr KT12 194 D1
Cardinal Hinsey Cl
NW10 90 A5
Cardinal Hinsley RC High
Sch (Boys) NW10 90 A6
Cardinal Pl SW15 134 D1
Cardinal Pole RC Sch
E9 75 A3
E9 74 D1
Cardinal Rd
Feltham TW13 150 B3
Ruislip HA4 40 D1
Cardinal Road Inf Sch
TW13 150 B3
Cardinals Way N19 49 D1
Cardinal's Wlk
Ashford TW16 171 C4
Hampton TW12 174 A3
Cardinal Vaughan Memorial
Sch W14 244 A2
Cardinal Way HA3 42 C6
Cardinal Wiseman RC High
Sch UB6 86 A3
Cardinal Wiseman RC Sch
The UB6 86 A2
Cardine Mews SE15 140 B5
Cardington Sq TW4 128 D1
Cardington St
NW1 93 C4 232 B1
Cardozo Rd N7 72 A3
Cardrew Ave N12 30 B5
Cardrew Cl N12 30 B5
Cardrew Ct N12 30 B5
Cardross St W6 112 B3
Cardwell Prim Sch
SE18 122 B2
Cardwell Rd N7 72 A4
Career Ct 11 SE16 118 D4
Carew Cl N7 72 B6
Carew Ct 15 SE14 140 D6
Carew Ho 24 SE18 122 B2
West Norwood SW16 160 C1
Carew Manor Sch
SM6 219 D5
Carew Rd W13 109 C4
Ashford TW15 171 A4
Mitcham CR4 181 A1
Thornton Heath CR7 204 D5
Tottenham N17 34 A1
Wallington SM6 219 C2
Carew St SE5 139 A3
Carey Ct DA6 169 D6
20 SE5 139 A5
Carey Gdns
SW8 137 D4 269 C1
Carey Ho E5 74 B5
Carey La EC2 242 A2
Carey Pl SW1 259 C3
Carey Rd RM9 81 A4

Carey St WC2 ..94 B1 240 D1
Carey Way HA9 ...66 D4
Carfax Pl SW4 ...137 D1
Carfax Rd UB3 ...106 A2
Carfree Cl 3 N1 ...72 C1
Cargill Rd SW18 ...158 A3
Cargreen Pl SE25 ...205 D5
Cargreen Rd SE25 ...205 D5
Cargrey Ho 9 HA7 ...25 C5
Carholme Rd SE23 ...163 B3
Carillon Ct W5 ...109 D6
Carinthia Ct 5 SE8 ...119 A2
Carisbrook 2 N10 ...31 B1
Carisbrook Cl EN1 ...5 D4
Carisbrook Ct 1
SW16 ...160 B1
Carisbrooke Ave DA5 .168 D3
Carisbrooke Cl HA7 ...25 D1
Carisbrooke Ct
Acton W3 ...111 A4
Belmont SM2 ...217 B1
Northolt UB5 ...85 B6
Carisbrooke Gdns
SE15 ...139 D5
Carisbrooke Ho TW10 154 C6
Carisbrooke Rd E17 ...53 A4
Bromley BR2 ...209 C5
Mitcham CR4 ...204 A5
Carleton Ave SM6 ...219 D1
Carleton Cl KT10 ...196 B1
Carleton Gdns N19 ...71 C3
Carleton Rd N7 ...71 D4
Carlile Cl E3 ...97 B5
Carlile Ho SE1 ...262 D5
Carlina Gdns IG8 ...37 B5
Carlingford Gdns CR4 181 A3
Carlingford Rd N15 ...50 D6
NW3 ...70 B4
West Barnes SM4 ...200 D3
Carlisle Ave EC3 ...243 C1
W3 ...89 C1
Carlisle Cl KT2 ...176 C2
Carlisle Gdns
Harrow HA3 ...43 D2
Redbridge IG1 ...56 A3
Carlisle Ho IG1 ...56 A3
Carlisle La
SE1 ...116 B3 260 D6
Carlisle Pl N11 ...31 B6
SW1 ...115 C3 259 A5
Carlisle Prim Sch
TW12 ...173 D4
Carlisle Rd E10 ...53 C1
N4 ...50 C2
NW6 ...91 A6
NW9 ...45 A6
Cheam SM1 ...217 B2
Hampton TW12 ...173 D3
Carlisle St W1 .93 D1 239 C1
Carlisle Way SW17 ...181 A5
Carlisle Wlk 6 E8 ...73 D2
Carlos Pl W1 ..115 B6 248 C5
Carlow St NW1 ...232 A4
Carlton Ave
Feltham TW14 ...150 C5
Harrow HA3 ...43 B4
Hayes UB3 ...105 C2
South Croydon CR2 ...221 C1
Southgate N14 ...15 D6
Carlton Ave E HA9 ...44 A1
Carlton Ave W HA0 ...65 B6
Carlton Cl NW3 ...69 C6
Chessington KT9 ...213 D2
Edgware HA8 ...26 C5
Northolt UB5 ...64 A3
Carlton Cres SM3 ...217 A4
Carlton Ct NW2 ...68 C2
NW6 ...91 D5
SW9 ...138 D4
Ilford IG6 ...57 B6
11 Penge SE20 ...184 B2
South Norwood SE19 ...183 D2
Carlton Dr Ilford IG6 ...57 B6
Putney SW15 ...157 A6
Carlton Gdns
SW1 ...115 D5 249 C3
Ealing W5 ...109 C6
Carlton Gn DA14 ...189 D6
Carlton Gr SE15 ...140 B4
8 SE15 ...140 B5
Carlton Hill
NW8 ...92 A5 229 A4
Carlton Ho NW6 ...91 C5
8 NW6 ...91 B5
W1 ...237 D2
Cheam SM1 ...217 B2
Edmonton N21 ...17 A3
Hounslow TW4 ...151 C5
Carlton House Terr
SW1 ...115 D5 249 D4
Carlton Lo N4 ...50 C2
Carlton Mans N16 ...51 D1
7 NW6 ...69 C1
SW9 ...138 C1
W14 ...244 B2
W9 ...91 D4
Carlton Par HA9 ...44 A1
Carlton Park Ave
SW20 ...178 D1
Carlton Prim Sch NW5 .71 A3
Carlton Rd DA14 ...189 D6
DA16 ...146 B2
DA8 ...147 D6
E11 ...54 D1
E12 ...77 D4
E17 ...35 A2
N11 ...31 A5
N4 ...50 C2
W4 ...111 B4
Ashford TW16 ...171 D3
Ealing W5 ...87 C1
Kingston KT3 ...177 C1
Mortlake SW14 ...133 A1
South Croydon CR2 ...221 B1
Walton-on-T KT12 ...194 B2
Carlton Sq E1 ...96 D3
Carlton St SW1 ...249 C5
Carltons The 5 SW15 157 A6
Carlton Terr E7 ...77 C1
Edmonton N18 ...33 B6
Forest Hill SE26 ...162 C1
Wanstead E11 ...55 B4
Carlton Tower Pl SW1 257 D6
Carlton Twrs SM5 ...218 D5
Carlton Vale NW6 ...91 C5
Carlton Vale Inf Sch
NW6 ...91 B4
Carlwell St SW17 ...180 C5
Carlyle Ave BR1 ...209 D6
Southall UB1 ...107 B6
Carlyle Cl N2 ...48 A3
NW10 ...89 B6
East Molesey KT8 ...173 D1
Carlyle Ct SW6 ...265 D1
Carlyle Gdns UB1 ...107 B6
Carlyle Ho 12 N16 ...73 C5
4 SE5 ...139 A5
SW3 ...266 D6
W5 ...109 D2
Carlyle Mans SW3 ...267 A5
Carlyle Mews E1 ...96 D3
Carlyle Pl SW15 ...134 D1
Carlyle Rd E12 ...78 A4
W5 ...109 C2
Croydon CR0 ...222 A6
Woolwich SE28 ...124 C6
Carlyle's Ho* SW3 ...267 A5
Carlyle Sq
SW3 ...114 B1 256 D1
Carlyon Ave HA2 ...63 C4
Carlyon Cl HA0 ...88 A6
Carlyon Ct HA0 ...88 B6
Carlyon Mans 1 HA0 ...88 A5
Carlyon Rd HA0 ...88 A6
Carlys Cl BR3 ...184 D1
Carmalt Gdns SW15 ..134 C1
Carmarthen Ct 4 W7 ..86 D3
Carmarthen Ho 8
SW15 ...156 C4
Carmarthen Pl SE1 ...253 A2
Carmel Ct W8 ...245 C2
Carmelite Cl HA3 ...24 A2
Carmelite Rd HA3 ...24 A1
Carmelite St
EC4 ...116 C6 251 B6
Carmelite Way HA3 ...24 A1
Carmelite Wlk HA3 ...24 A2
Carmen St E14 ...97 D1
Carmichael Cl
9 SW11 ...136 B2
Ruislip HA4 ...62 A4
Carmichael Ct 5
SW13 ...133 D3
Carmichael Ho 6 E14 120 A6
17 Dulwich SE21 ...183 C6
Carmichael Mews
SW18 ...158 B4
Carmichael Rd SE25 ..206 A5
Carminia Rd SW17 ...159 B2
Carnaby St*
W1 ...93 C1 239 A1
Carnac St SE21,SE27 ..161 B1
Carnanton Rd E17 ...36 B2
Carnarvon Ave EN1 ...5 D3
Carnarvon Dr UB3 ...105 A3
Carnarvon Rd E10 ...54 A4
E15 ...76 D2
Barnet EN5 ...1 A2
Woodford E18 ...36 D2
Carnation St SE2 ...124 B1
Carnbrook Rd SE3 ...143 D2
Carnecke Gdns SE9 ...166 A6
Carnegie Cl
Holdbrook EN3 ...7 D5
Surbiton KT6 ...214 B6
Carnegie Ho NW3 ...70 B5
Carnegie Pl SW19 ...156 D1
Carnegie St N1 .94 B6 233 D5
Carnforth Cl KT19 ...214 D2
Carnforth Rd SW16 ...181 D3
Carnicot Ho 9 SE15 ...140 B4
Carnoustie Cl SE28 ...102 D1
Carnoustie Dr N1 ...72 B1
Carnwath Ho SW6 ...135 D2
Carnwath Rd SW6 ...135 D2
Caroe Ct N9 ...18 B3
Carole Ho 18 SE20 ...184 B2
Carolina Cl E15 ...76 C3
Carolina Rd CR7 ...183 A2
Caroline Cl N10 ...31 B1
W2 ...245 D5
Hounslow TW7 ...130 C5
South Croydon CR0 ...221 C4
Streatham SW16 ...160 B1
Caroline Ct NW11 ...47 A3
Ashford TW15 ...170 D4
Catford SE6 ...186 B6
Stanmore HA7 ...25 A4
17 Surbiton KT6 ...197 D2
Caroline Gdns E2 ...95 C4
Caroline Ho W2 ...245 D5
20 W6 ...112 C1
Caroline Martyn Ho 8
N19 ...49 D2
Caroline Pl SW11 ...137 A3
W2 ...245 D5
Harlington UB3 ...127 C5
Caroline Pl Mews W2 245 D5
Caroline Rd SW19 ...179 B3
Caroline St E1 ...96 D1
Caroline Terr
SW1 ...115 A2 258 A3
Caroline Wlk W6 ...264 A5
Carol St NW1 ..93 C6 232 A6
Caronia Ct 4 SE16 ...119 A2
Carpenter Gdns N21 ...16 D2
Carpenter Ho 10 E14 ...97 C2
6 N19 ...71 D4
NW11 ...48 A3
Carpenters Bsns Pk
E15 ...75 D1
Carpenters Cl EN5 ...13 D5
Carpenters Ct NW1 ...232 A6
5 Dagenham RM10 ...81 D2
Twickenham TW2 ...152 C2
Carpenter's Pl SW4 ...137 D1
Carpenters Prim Sch
E15 ...98 A6
Carpenter's Rd E15 ...75 D1
Carpenter St W1 ...248 C5
Carrara Wharf SW6 ...135 A2
Carrara Wlk 19 SW9 ...138 D1
Carr Gr SE18 ...122 A2
Carriage Dr E
SW11 ...137 A5 268 B4
Carriage Drive E
SW11 ...137 A5 268 B4
Carriage Drive N
SW11,SW8 ...137 A6 268 B5
Carriage Dr N
SW8,SW11 ...136 D5 267 C4
SW8,SW11 ...137 A6 268 B5
Carriage Dr S
SW11 ...137 A4 268 A2
Carriage Dr W
SW11 ...136 D5 267 C3
Carriage Mews IG1 ...79 A6
Carrick Cl TW7 ...131 A2
Carrick Gate KT10 ...212 A5
Carrick Gdns N17 ...33 C3
Carrick Ho N7 ...72 B2
SE11 ...261 C2
Carrick Mews SE8 ...141 C6
Carrill Way DA17 ...124 D3
Carrington Ave
Borehamwood WD6 ...10 D6
Hounslow TW3 ...151 D6
Carrington Cl
Barnet EN5 ...12 A6
Borehamwood WD6 ...11 A6
Croydon CR0 ...207 A2
Carrington Ct SW11 ...136 C1
Carrington Gdns 4 E7 .77 A4
Carrington Ho W1 ...248 C3
Wimbledon SW19 ...179 C3
Carrington Lo 3
TW10 ...154 A6
Carrington Pl KT10 ...212 A4
Carrington Rd TW10 ...132 C1
Carrington Sq HA3 ...24 A3
Carrington St W1 ...248 C3
Carrol Cl NW5 ...71 B4
Carroll Cl E15 ...76 D3
Carroll Ho W2 ...246 C6
Carronade Pl SE18 ...123 B3
Carron Cl E14 ...97 D1
Carroun Rd
SW8 ...138 B5 270 C4
Carroway La UB6 ...86 B4
Carrow Rd RM9 ...80 B1
Carr Rd Chingford E17 ...35 C1
Northolt UB5 ...64 A1
Carrs La N21 ...17 B6
Carr St E14 ...97 A2
Carshalton, Beddington &
Wallington War Memorial
Hospl SM5 ...218 D2
Carshalton Beeches Sta
SM5 ...218 D2
Carshalton Coll SM5 ...218 D5
Carshalton Gr SM1 ...218 B3
Carshalton High Sch for
Boys SM5 ...218 C6
Carshalton High Sch for
Girls SM5 ...218 C5
Carshalton Park Rd
SM5 ...218 D3
Carshalton Pl SM5 ...219 A3
Carshalton Rd
Mitcham CR4 ...203 A4
Sutton SM1,SM5 ...218 B3
Carshalton Sta SM5 ...218 D4
Carslake Rd SW15 ...156 C5
Carson Rd E16 ...99 A2
Cockfosters EN4 ...2 D1
Dulwich SE21 ...161 B2
Carstairs Rd SE6 ...164 A1
Carswell Cl IG4 ...55 D5
Carswell Rd SE6 ...164 A4
Carter Cl SM6 ...219 D1
Carter Ct EC4 ...241 D1
Carteret Ho 8 W12 ...112 B6
Carteret St SW1 ...249 C1
Carteret Way SE8 ...119 A2
Carterhatch Jun & Inf Schs
EN1 ...6 B4
Carterhatch La EN1 ...6 A4
Carterhatch Rd EN3 ...6 D4
Carter Ho E1 ...243 C3
11 SW2 ...160 C6
Carter La EC4 ..94 D1 241 D1
Carter Pl SE17 117 A1 262 B1
Carter Rd E13 ...99 B6
Mitcham SW19 ...180 B4
Carters Cl 2 NW5 ...71 D2
North Cheam KT4 ...200 D1
Carters Hill Cl SE9 ...165 C3
Carters Rd N2 ...30 C3
Carter St SE17 117 A1 262 A1
Carter's Yd SW18 ...157 C6
Carthew Rd W6 ...112 B3
Carthew Villas W6 ...112 B3
Carthusian St EC1 ...242 A4
Cartier Circ E14 ...120 A5
Carting La
WC2 ...116 A6 250 B5
Cart La E4 ...20 C3
Cartmel NW1 ...232 A2
Cartmel Cl N17 ...34 B3
Cartmel Ct
Beckenham BR2 ...186 C1
Northolt UB5 ...63 A2
Cartmel Gdns SM4 ...202 A4
Cartmel Rd DA7 ...147 C4
Carton Ho 2 NW2 ...68 A5
4 SE16 ...118 A3
12 W11 ...112 D6
Cartwright Gdns
WC1 ...94 A4 233 A1
Cartwright Ho SE1 ...262 B5
Cartwright Rd RM9 ...81 B1
Cartwright St
E1 ...117 D6 253 D5
Cartwright Way SW13 134 B5
Carvel Ho E14 ...120 A1
Carver Cl 15 W4 ...111 A3
Carver Rd SE24 ...161 A5
Carville Cres TW8 ...110 A2
Caryl Ho 6 SW19 ...156 D3
Cary Rd E11 ...76 C5
Carysfort Rd N16 ...73 B4
N8 ...49 D4
Casby Ho 7 SE16 ...118 A3
Cascade Ave N10 ...49 C5
Cascade Cl IG9 ...21 D2
Cascade Rd IG9 ...21 D2
Casella Rd SE14 ...140 D5
Casewick Rd SE27 ...182 D6
Casey Cl NW8 ..92 C4 230 B1
Casimir Rd E5 ...74 C5
Casino Ave SE24 ...161 B6
Caspian Ho 7 E1 ...96 D2
Caspian St SE5 ...139 B5
Caspian Wlk E16 ...99 D1
Cassandra Cl UB5 ...64 B4
Cassanora Ct NW2 ...68 C2
Casselden Rd NW10 ...67 B1
Cassel Hospl TW10 ...175 D6
Cassell Ho 21 SW9 ...138 A3
Casserley Ho W4 ...111 B3
Cass Ho 23 E9 ...74 D2
Cassidy Rd SW6 ...265 A3
Cassilda Rd SE2 ...124 A2
Cassilis Rd TW1 ...153 B5
Cassinghurst SE24 ...161 B6
Cassiobury Ave TW14 ..149 D4
Cassiobury Rd E17 ...53 A4
Cassland Rd E9 ...74 D2
South Norwood CR7 ...205 B5
Casslee Rd SE6 ...163 B4
Cassocks Sq TW17 ...193 B2
Casson Ho 10 E1 ...96 A2
Casson St E1 ...96 A2
Castalia Sq 6 E14 ...120 A4
Castellain Mans W9 ...91 D3
Castellain Rd W9 ...91 D3
Castellane Cl HA7 ...24 D3
Castell Ho 11 SE8 ...141 C5
Castello Ave SW15 ...156 C6
Castelnau SW13 ...134 B5
Casterbridge NW6 ...91 D6
3 W11 ...91 C1
Casterbridge Rd SE3 .143 A2
Casterton St E8 ...74 B2
Castile Rd SE18 ...122 C2
Castilion Prim Sch
SE28 ...102 C1
Castillon Rd SE6 ...164 C2
Castlands Rd SE6 ...163 B2
Castleacre W2 ...237 A1
Castle Ave Chingford E4 .36 B5
Yiewsley UB7 ...104 B6
Castlebar Ct 5 W5 ...87 C2
Castlebar Hill W5 ...87 C2
Castlebar Mews W5 ...87 C2
Castle Bar Park Sta
W7 ...86 D2
Castlebar Pk W5 ...87 B2
Castlebar Rd W5 ...87 C1
Castlebar Sch W13 ...87 A2
Castle Baynard St
EC4 ...117 A6 252 A6
Castlebrook Cl
SE11 ...116 D2 261 C4
Castle Cl E9 ...75 A3
W3 ...110 D4
Ashford TW16 ...171 C3
Beckenham BR2 ...208 C6
Wimbledon SW19 ...156 D1
Castlecombe Dr SW19 156 D4
Castlecombe Prim Sch
SE9 ...188 A5
Castlecombe Rd SE9 ..188 A6
Castle Ct EC3 ...242 D1
Belmont SM2 ...217 C2
Forest Hill SE26 ...185 A6
Morden SM4 ...202 B4
Castleden Ho NW6 ...70 B1
Castledine Rd SE20 ...184 B3
Castle Dr IG4 ...56 A3
Castleford Ave SE9 ...166 D3
Castleford Cl N17 ...33 D4
Castleford Ct NW8 ...236 D6
Castlefrank Ho 21 N1 ..95 C4
Castlegate TW9 ...132 B2
Castlehaven Rd NW1 ...71 B1
Castle Hill Ave CR0 ...224 A1
Castle Hill Prim Sch
CR0 ...224 A2
Castle Ho SE1 ...262 A4
SW8 ...270 B4
10 Belmont SM2 ...217 C1
3 Chingford E4 ...36 B5
Castleigh Ct EN2 ...17 B6
Castle Ind Est SE17 ...262 A4
Castle La SW1 115 C3 259 A6
Castlemaine 8 SW11 ..136 D3
Castlemaine Ave CR2 ..221 D3
Castle Mead SE5 ...139 A5
Castle Mews N12 ...30 A5
NW1 ...71 B2
Castlenau Gdns SW13 134 B6
Castlenau Mans SW13 134 B6
Castlenau Row SW13 ..134 B6
Castle Par KT17 ...216 A1
Castle Pl 8 W4 ...111 C2
Castle Point 3 E13 ...99 C5
Castle Rd N12 ...30 B5
NW1 ...71 B2
Dagenham RM9 ...102 B6
Enfield EN3 ...7 A5
Isleworth TW7 ...130 D3
Northolt UB5 ...63 D1
Southall UB2 ...107 B3
Castlereagh St W1 ...237 C2
Castle St E6 ...99 C5
Kingston KT2 ...176 A1
Castleton Ave HA9 ...66 A4
Castleton Cl CR0 ...207 A3
Castleton Ct KT5 ...198 B4
Castleton Gdns HA9 ...66 A5
Castleton Ho 2 E14 ...120 A2
Castleton Rd SE12,SE9 187 D6
Chingford E17 ...36 B1
Ilford IG3 ...58 B1
Mitcham CR4 ...203 D5
Ruislip HA4 ...40 D1
Castletown Rd
W14 ...113 A1 254 B1
Castleview Cl N4 ...73 A6
Castle View Gdns IG1 ..56 B3
Castle Way
Feltham TW13 ...172 C6
Wimbledon SW19 ...156 D1
Castle Wlk TW16 ...194 C6
Castlewood Day Hospl
SE18 ...144 C4
Castlewood Dr SE9 ...144 B3
Castlewood Rd N16 ...52 A3
Barnet EN4 ...2 B2
Castle Yd N6 ...49 A2
SE1 ...251 D4
17 Richmond TW10 ...153 D6
Castor La E14 ...119 D6
Catalina Rd TW6 ...126 C2
Caterham Rd SE13 ...142 B2
Catesby Ho 25 E9 ...74 C1
Catesby St
SE17 ...117 B2 262 D3
Catford Br SE6 ...163 C4
Catford Bridge Sta
SE6 ...163
Catford Broadway
SE6 ...163
Catford Girls' Sch SE6 164
Catford Gyratory SE6 .163
Catford Hill SE6 ...163
Catford Rd SE6 ...163
Catford Sta SE6 ...163
Cathall Rd E11 ...76
Cathay Ho SE16 ...118
Cathay St 9 SE16 ...118
Cathay Wlk UB5 ...85
Cathcart Dr BR6 ...211
Cathcart Hill N19 ...71
Cathcart Rd
SW10 ...136 A6 266
Cathcart St NW5 ...71
Cathedral Ct EC4 ...241
Cathedral Sch of St Saviou
& St Mary Overie Prim Sc
SE1 ...117 A4 252
Cathedral St
SE1 ...117 B5 252
Catherall Rd N5,N16 ..73
Catherine Baird Ct 12
SW12 ...159
Catherine Ct
1 Ilford IG2 ...57
2 Southgate N14 ...15
3 Wimbledon SW19 ...179
Catherine Dr
Ashford TW16 ...171
Richmond TW9 ...132
Catherine Gdns TW3 ..130
Catherine Godfrey Ho
RM9 ...103
Catherine Gr SE10 ...141
Catherine Griffiths Ct
EC1 ...241
Catherine Ho 16 N1 ...95
Isleworth TW7 ...131
Catherine Pl
SW1 ...115 C3 259
Harrow HA1 ...42
Catherine Rd Enfield EN3 .7
Kingston KT6 ...197
Catherine St
WC2 ...116 B6 250
Catherine Wheel Alley
E1 ...243
Catherine Wheel Rd
TW8 ...131
Catherine Wheel Yd
SW1 ...249
Catherwood Ct N1 ...235
Cat Hill EN4 ...14
Cathles Rd SW12 ...159
Cathnor Rd W12 ...112
Catisfield Rd EN3 ...7
Catlin Cres TW17 ...193
Catling Cl SE23 ...162
Catlin's La HA5 ...40
Catlin St SE16 ...118
Catman Ho N4 ...50
Caton Ct BR2 ...186
Cato Rd SW4 ...137
Cator La BR3 ...185
Cator Park Sch for Girls
BR3 ...185
Cator Rd
Penge SE20,SE26 ...184
Wallington SM5 ...218
Cator St SE15 ...139
SE15 ...139
Cato St W1 ...92 C1 237
Catsey La WD23 ...8
Catsey Wood WD23 ...8
Catterick Cl N11 ...31
Cattistock Rd SE9 ...188
Cattley Cl EN5 ...1
Catton St WC1 ...240
Caughley Ho SE11 ...261
Caulfield Ct 12 NW1 ...71
Caulfield Rd E6 ...78
SE15 ...140
Causeway TW14,TW4 ..128
Causeway The N2 ...48
SW18 ...157
Carshalton SM5 ...219
Chessington KT9 ...214
Claygate KT10 ...212
Teddington TW11 ...174
Wimbledon SW19 ...178
Causeyware Rd N9 ...18
Causton Cotts 3 E14 ..97
Causton Ho SE5 ...139
Causton Rd N6 ...49
Causton Sq RM10 ...81
Causton St
SW1 ...115 D1 259
Cautley Ave SW4 ...159
Cavalier Cl RM6 ...58
Cavalier Gdns UB3 ...83
Cavalry Cres TW4 ...128
Cavalry Gdns SW15 ...157
Cavan Pl HA5 ...23
Cavaye Ho SW10 ...266
Cavaye Pl SW10 ...256

vell Dr EN2 ....4 C3
vell Ho 8 N1 ....95 C6
vell Rd N17 ....33 B3
vell St E1 ....96 B2
vendish Ave DA16 ..145 D2
3 ....29 C1
W8 ....92 B5 229 D3
aling W13 ....87 A1
arrow HA1 ....64 C4
uislip HA4 ....62 B3
'dcup DA15 ....168 A4
Vest Barnes KT3 ....200 B5
Voodford IG8 ....37 B3
vendish Cl NW6 ....69 B2
W8 ....92 B4 229 D2
shford TW16 ....171 D4
dmonton N18 ....34 B5
ayes UB4 ....83 C2
3 Putney SW15 ....157 A6
vendish Cres
orehamwood WD6 ....10 C6
orehamwood WD6 ....10 C6
vendish Ct EC2 ....243 B2
shford TW16 ....171 D4
5 Chingford E4 ....20 C4
vendish Dr E11 ....54 B1
laygate KT10 ....212 C3
dgware HA8 ....26 B4
vendish Gdns SW4 .159 C5
arking IG11 ....79 D3
agenham RM6 ....59 A4
lford IG1 ....56 C1
vendish Ho N12 ....30 A6
IW8 ....229 D3
W8 ....270 A2
wickenham TW1 ....153 A5
vendish Mans E5 ....74 C3
C1 ....241 A5
8 NW6 ....69 C3
2 SW12 ....159 C5
avendish Mews N
V1 ....238 D4
avendish Mews S
V1 ....238 D3
avendish Par
Balham SW12 ....159 B5
Hounslow TW4 ....129 A3
avendish Pl W1 ....238 D2
avendish Prim Sch
V4 ....133 C5
avendish Rd N4 ....50 D3
NW6 ....69 B1
SW12 ....159 C5
Ashford TW16 ....171 D4
Chingford E4 ....36 A4
Chiswick W4 ....133 A4
Edmonton N18 ....34 B5
Mitcham SW19 ....180 C3
New Malden KT3 ....199 D5
Sutton SM2 ....218 A1
Thornton Heath CR0 ....204 D1
avendish Sch The
NW1 ....93 B6 231 D6
avendish Sq
W1 ....93 B1 238 D2
avendish St
N1 ....95 B5 235 C3
avendish Terr 10 E3 ....97 B4
Feltham TW13 ....150 A2
avendish The NW11 ....47 D2
avendish Way BR4 ....207 D1
avenham Gdns IG1 ....79 B5
ave Rd E13 ....99 B4
Richmond TW10 ....175 C6
averleigh Way KT4 ....200 B2
averley Gdns HA3 ....43 D2
aversham Ave
Cheam SM3 ....217 A6
Palmers Green N13 ....16 C1
Caversham Ct N11 ....15 A1
Caversham Ho N15 ....51 A5
7 SE15 ....140 A6
8 Kingston KT1 ....176 A1
aversham Rd N15 ....51 A5
NW5 ....71 C2
Kingston KT1 ....176 B1
Caversham St
SW3 ....136 D6 267 C6
Caverswall St W12 ....90 C1
Caveside Cl BR7 ....188 C2
Cavour Ho SE17 ....261 D2
Cawdor Cres W7 ....109 A2
Cawnpore St SE19 ....183 C5
Cawston Ct 6 BR1 ....186 D3
Caxton Gr E3 ....97 C4
Caxton Hall SW1 ....259 C6
Caxton Rd W12 ....112 D4
Southall UB2 ....106 D3
Wimbledon SW19 ....180 A5
Wood Green N22 ....32 B1
Caxton St SW1 115 D3 259 C6
Caxton St N E16 ....98 D1
Caxton Trad Est UB3 ....105 C5
Cayford Ho 1 NW3 ....70 D3
Caygill Cl BR2 ....208 D5
Cayley Cl SM6 ....220 A1
Cayley Prim Sch E14 ....97 A1
Cayley Rd UB2 ....107 D3
Cayton Pl EC1 ....235 C1
Cayton Rd UB6 ....86 C5
Cayton St EC1 ....235 C1
Cazenove Mans 1 N16 74 A6
Cazenove Rd N16 ....74 A6
Chingford E17 ....35 C2
Cearns Ho E6 ....99 D6
Cecil Ave Barking IG11 ..79 B1
Enfield EN1 ....5 D1
Wembley HA9 ....66 B3
Cecil Cl
Chessington KT9 ....213 D4
Ealing W5 ....87 D2
Littleton TW15 ....171 A3
Cecil Ct NW6 ....69 D1
SW10 ....266 A6
WC2 ....250 A5
12 Croydon CR0 ....221 D6
Ealing W5 ....87 D2
Cecile Pk N8 ....50 A3
Cecil Ho 6 E5 ....74 C6
Chingford E17 ....35 C2
Cecilia Cl N2 ....48 A6
Cecilia Rd E8 ....74 A3
Cecil Lo KT9 ....213 D4
Cecil Mans 2 SW17 ..159 A2
Cecil Pk HA5 ....41 A5
Cecil Pl CR4 ....202 D4
Cecil Rd E11 ....76 C5
E13 ....99 A6
N10 ....31 B1
N14 ....15 C3
NW10 ....89 C6
NW9 ....45 C6
W3 ....89 A2
Ashford TW15 ....171 A4
Cheam SM1,SM2 ....217 B2
Chingford E17 ....35 C2
Dagenham RM6 ....58 D2
Enfield EN2 ....5 B1
Harrow HA3 ....42 C6
Hounslow TW3 ....130 A3
Ilford IG1 ....78 D4
Merton SW19 ....179 D3
Thornton Heath CR0 ....204 B3
Cecil Rhodes Ho NW1 232 C4
Cecil Rosen Ct HA0 ....65 B5
Cecil Way BR2 ....209 A1
Cedar Ave
Dagenham RM6 ....59 A4
East Barnet EN4 ....14 C4
Enfield EN3 ....6 C3
Hayes UB3 ....84 A1
Ruislip HA4 ....62 C3
Sidcup DA15 ....168 A4
Twickenham TW2 ....152 A5
Yiewsley UB7 ....104 B6
Cedar Cl Bow E3 ....97 B6
Buckhurst Hill IG9 ....21 D2
East Molesey KT8 ....196 C5
Keston Mark BR2 ....226 A5
Kingston KT2 ....177 B6
Wallington SM5 ....218 D2
West Norwood SE21 ....161 A2
Cedar Copse BR1 ....188 B1
Cedar Cres BR2 ....226 A5
Cedarcroft Rd KT9 ....214 B4
Cedar Ct HA8 ....11 A1
1 N10 ....31 B1
N1 ....73 A1
5 N11 ....31 C5
N20 ....14 B3
N3 ....29 C3
19 SE7 ....143 C6
W1 ....237 B2
7 Brentford TW8 ....131 D6
Eltham SE9 ....166 A5
Mortlake SW14 ....133 A1
Stoneleigh KT17 ....216 A1
3 Sutton SM2 ....218 A2
6 Wanstead E11 ....55 B4
Wimbledon SW19 ....156 D1
5 Woodford E18 ....37 A2
Cedar Dr N2 ....48 C5
Pinner HA5 ....23 C4
Cedar Gdns SM2 ....218 A2
Cedar Gr DA5 ....168 D5
W5 ....110 A3
Southall UB1 ....85 C2
Cedar Grange 10 EN1 ....17 C6
Cedar Ho 5 E14 ....120 A4
SE14 ....140 D4
16 SE16 ....118 D4
W8 ....255 C6
Ashford TW16 ....171 D3
Hayes UB4 ....84 C3
New Addington CR0 ....223 D2
Wood Green N22 ....32 C2
Cedar Hts NW2 ....69 B2
Richmond TW10 ....154 A3
Cedarhurst Dr SE9 ....165 C6
Cedar Lawn Ave EN5 ....13 A6
Cedar Lo SW6 ....134 D4
Cedarmore Ct BR7 ....189 A2
Cedar Mount SE9 ....165 D3
Cedarne Rd
SW6 ....135 D5 265 C3
Cedar Park Gdns RM6 .58 D2
Cedar Park Rd EN2 ....5 A5
Cedar Pl 3 SE7 ....121 C1
Cedar Rd BR1 ....187 C1
NW2 ....68 C4
Cranford TW5 ....128 C3
Croydon CR0 ....221 C6
East Bedfont TW14 ....149 B3
East Molesey KT8 ....196 C5
Enfield EN2 ....5 A5
Sutton SM2 ....218 A2
Tottenham N17 ....33 D2
Cedar Rise N14 ....15 A4
Cedars Ave E17 ....53 C4
Mitcham CR4 ....203 A6
Cedars Cl NW4 ....46 D6
SE13 ....142 B2
Cedars Ct Edmonton N9 .17 D2
Putney SW15 ....156 A5
Cedars Dr UB10 ....82 C5
Cedars Fst & Mid Schs
HA3 ....24 A2
Cedars Ho 15 E17 ....53 D6
21 SW2 ....138 B1
5 West Norwood
SW27 ....182 D5
Cedars Mews SW4 ....137 B1
Cedars Prim Sch The
TW5 ....128 A5
Cedars Rd E15 ....76 C2
SW4 ....137 B1
W4 ....111 C1
Barnes SW13 ....134 A3
Beckenham BR3 ....185 B1
Edmonton N21 ....16 D2
4 Edmonton N9 ....18 A2
Morden SM4 ....201 C5
Teddington KT8 ....175 C2
Wallington CR0 ....220 A4
Cedars The E9 ....74 D1
Buckhurst Hill IG9 ....21 A3
Ealing W13 ....87 C1
4 Kingston KT2 ....176 D2
Teddington TW11 ....174 D4
Wallington SM6 ....219 C4
Cedar Terr
9 Dagenham RM8 ....58 D2
Richmond TW9 ....132 A1
Cedar Tree Ct SE5 ....139 A4
Cedar Tree Gr SE27 ....182 D5
Cedarville Gdns SW16 182 B4
Cedar Way
NW1 ....71 D1 232 C6
Ashford TW16 ....171 C3
Cedar Wlk KT10 ....212 D2
Cedarwood BR3 ....185 B3
Cedarwood Ho EN2 ....4 D3
Cedra Ct N16 ....52 A1
Cedric Chambers
NW8 ....236 C6
Cedric Rd SE9 ....167 A1
Celadon Cl EN3 ....7 A2
Celandine Cl E3,E14 ....97 C2
Celandine Dr E8 ....73 D1
Woolwich SE28 ....124 B5
Celandine Way E15 ....98 C4
Celbridge Mews W2 ....91 D1
Celendine Ct E4 ....19 D1
Celestial Gdns SE13 ....142 B1
Celia Ct 7 TW9 ....132 B4
Celia Ho 10 N1 ....95 C5
Celia Rd N19 ....71 C4
Celtic Ave BR2 ....208 C6
Celtic St E14 ....97 D2
Cemetery La
Lower Halliford TW17 ..192 D2
Woolwich SE7 ....144 A6
Cemetery Rd E7 ....76 D4
Tottenham N17 ....33 C3
Woolwich SE2 ....146 B5
Cenacle Cl NW3 ....69 C5
Cenotaph* SW1 ....250 A2
Centaur Ct 3 TW8 ....110 A1
Centaurs Bsns Pk
TW7 ....131 A6
Centaur St
SE1 ....116 B3 260 D6
Centenary Rd EN3 ....7 B1
Centennial Ave WD6 ....9 C4
Centennial Ct WD6 ....9 C4
Centennial Pk HA7,WD6 .9 C4
Central Ave DA16 ....146 A3
E11 ....76 B6
N2 ....30 B1
N2 ....47 D6
SW11 ....136 D5 267 D3
East Molesey KT8 ....195 B4
Edmonton N9 ....17 D1
Enfield EN1 ....6 B3
Hayes UB3 ....106 A6
Isleworth TW3,TW7 ....130 A1
Pinner HA5 ....41 B2
Wallington SM6 ....220 A3
Central Bsns Ctr NW10 .67 C3
Central Cir NW4 ....46 B4
Central Criminal Court (Old
Bailey)* EC4 .94 D1 241 D2
Central Ct 2 SE18 ....122 D2
Centrale Ctr CR0 ....221 A6
Central Foundation Lower
Sch E3 ....97 A4
Central Foundation Sch
EC2 ....95 B3 242 D6
Central Foundation Upper
Sch E3 ....97 B4
Central Gdns SM4 ....201 D4
Central Hill SE19 ....183 B4
Central Mans 8 NW4 ....46 B4
Central Middlesex Hospl
NW10 ....89 A4
Central Par 8 E17 ....53 C5
W3 ....110 D4
Ealing UB6 ....87 A4
Enfield EN3 ....6 C3
Feltham TW14 ....150 C4
Harrow HA1 ....42 D4
Heston TW5 ....129 C5
Ilford IG2 ....57 B3
Penge SE20 ....184 D3
Surbiton KT6 ....198 A3
Central Park Ave RM10 81 D5
Central Park Prim Sch
E6 ....99 D5
Central Park Rd E6 ....99 D5
Central Par Villas BR5 190 C1
Central Pk Est TW4 ....128 D1
Central Public Health
Laboratories NW9 ....45 C6
Central Rd
Morden SM4 ....201 D4
Wembley HA0 ....65 B3
Worcester Park KT4 ....216 A6
Central Sch of Speech &
Drama The NW3 ....70 B1
Central School of Ballet
EC1 ....94 C3 241 B5
Central Sq NW11 ....47 D3
East Molesey KT8 ....195 B5
4 Wembley HA9 ....66 A3
Central St EC1 .95 A4 235 A1
Central St Martins Coll of
Art & Design (The London
Inst) WC1 ....94 B2 240 C3
Central St Martin's Sch of
Art & Design
W1 ....93 D1 239 D1
Central Terr BR3 ....206 D6
Central Way NW10 ....89 A4
SE28 ....124 B6
Feltham TW14 ....150 B6
Sutton SM5 ....218 C1
Centre Ave N2 ....30 C1
NW10 ....90 C4
W3 ....111 B5
Centre Bldg SE17 ....262 B4
Centre Common Rd
BR7 ....189 A3
Centre Ct N20 ....14 B2
Centre Dr E7 ....77 C4
Centre Hts 5 NW3 ....70 B1
Centre Point 3 SE1 ....118 A1
Centre Rd
Dagenham RM10 ....103 D5
Wanstead E7,E11 ....77 A6
Centre St E2 ....96 B5
Centre The
Feltham TW13 ....150 B2
Walton-on-T KT12 ....193 D1
Centre Way N9 ....18 D2
Centreway IG1 ....79 A6
Centurian Way DA18 ....125 C3
Centurion Cl N7 ....72 B1
Centurion Ct SM6 ....219 B6
Centurion Ho 2 RM10 .81 D2
Centurion La E3 ....97 B5
Century Cl NW4 ....46 D4
Century Ho SE13 ....141 D3
Wembley HA9 ....66 B6
Century Rd E17 ....53 A6
Century Yd SE23 ....162 C2
Cephas Ave E1 ....96 C3
Cephas Ho 8 E1 ....96 C3
Cephas St E1 ....96 C3
Ceres Rd SE18 ....123 D2
Cerise Rd SE15 ....140 A4
Cerne Cl UB4 ....106 C6
Cerne Rd SM4 ....202 A3
Cerney Mews W2 ....246 C6
Cervantes Ct 11 W2 ....91 D1
Ceylon Rd W14 ....254 A5
6 W14 ....112 D3
Chace Com Sch EN1 ....5 C4
Chadacre Ave IG5 ....56 B6
Chadacre Ho 10 SW9 .138 D1
Chadacre Rd KT17 ....216 B3
Chadbourn St E14 ....97 D2
Chadbury Ct NW7 ....28 A2
Chad Cres N9 ....18 C1
Chadd Dr BR1 ....210 A6
Chadd Gn E13 ....99 A6
Chadston Ho 17 N1 ....72 D1
Chadswell WC1 ....233 B1
Chadview Ct 2 RM6 ....58 D2
Chadville Gdns RM6 ....58 D4
Chadway RM8 ....58 C1
Chadwell Ave RM6 ....58 B2
Chadwell Heath Foundation
Sch The RM6 ....58 B3
Chadwell Heath Hospl
RM6 ....58 B4
Chadwell Heath Ind Pk
RM8 ....58 D1
Chadwell Heath La
RM6 ....58 C3
Chadwell Heath Sta
RM6 ....58 D2
Chadwell Prim Sch
RM6 ....58 C2
Chadwell St
EC1 ....94 C4 234 B2
Chadwick Ave
Chingford E4 ....36 B6
Wimbledon SW19 ....179 C4
Chadwick Cl
12 Ealing W7 ....86 D2
Roehampton SW15 ....
Teddington TW11 ....175 A4
Chadwick Ct 4 SE28 .124 B5
Chadwick Pl KT6 ....197 C3
Chadwick Rd E11 ....54 D3
NW10 ....89 D6
SE15 ....139 D3
Ilford IG1 ....78 D5
Chadwick St
SW1 ....115 D3 259 C5
Chadwick Way SE28 .124 D6
Chadwin Rd E13 ....99 B2
Chadworth Ho EC1 ..235 A1
N4 ....51 A1
Chadworth Way KT10 .212 B3
Chaffey Ho 6 SE7 ....121 C1
Chaffinch Ave CR0 ....206 D3
Chaffinch Cl N9 ....18 D3
Croydon CR0 ....206 D3
Tolworth KT6 ....214 C5
Chaffinch Rd BR3 ....185 A2
Chafford Way RM6 ....58 C5
Chagford Ct SW19 ....180 C3
Chagford Ho 38 E3 ....97 D4
NW1 ....237 C5
Chagford St
NW1 ....92 D3 237 D5
Chailey Ave EN1 ....5 D3
Chailey Cl TW5 ....128 D4
Chailey Ind Est UB3 ....106 A4
Chailey St E5 ....74 C5
Chalbury Ho 8 SW9 ..138 B1
Chalbury Wlk N1 ....234 A4
Chalcombe Rd SE2 ....124 B3
Chalcot Cl SM2 ....217 C1
Chalcot Cres
NW1 ....92 D6 230 D6
Chalcot Gdns NW3 ....70 D2
Chalcot Mews SW16 ....160 A1
Chalcot Rd
NW1 ....93 A6 231 A6
Chalcot Sch NW1 ....71 B1
Chalcot Sq NW1 ....71 A1
Chalcott Gdns KT6 ....197 C1
Chalcroft Rd SE13 ....164 C6
Chaldon Rd
SW6 ....135 A5 264 B4
Chale Rd SW2 ....160 A5
Chalet Ct CR7 ....204 D4
Chalfont Ave HA9 ....66 D2
Chalfont Ct NW1 ....237 D5
NW9 ....45 D6
3 Belvedere DA17 ....125 C1
12 Harrow HA1 ....42 D3
Chalfont Gn N9 ....17 C1
Chalfont Ho NW10 ....67 B5
2 SE16 ....118 B3
Chalfont Rd
Edmonton N9 ....17 D1
Hayes UB3 ....106 A4
South Norwood SE25 ....205 D6
Chalfont Way W13 ....109 B3
Chalfont Wlk 3 HA5 ....22 C1
Chalford 7 NW3 ....70 A2
Chalford Cl KT8 ....195 C5
Chalford Ct Ilford IG2 .56 D4
15 Putney SW15 ....156 D5
Surbiton KT6 ....198 B2
Chalford Rd SE21 ....183 B6
Chalford Wlk IG8 ....37 D3
Chalgrove Ave SM4 ....201 C4
Chalgrove Gdns N3 ....47 A6
Chalgrove Prim Sch N3 47 A6
Chalgrove Rd
Sutton SM2 ....218 B1
Tottenham N17 ....34 B2
Chalice Cl SM6 ....219 D2
Chalice Ct N2 ....48 C5
Chalkenden Cl SE20 ....184 B3
Chalkers Cnr TW9 ....132 D2
Chalk Farm Rd
NW1 ....71 A1 231 D6
Chalk Farm Sta NW3 ....71 A1
Chalkhill Prim Sch HA9 66 D5
Chalk Hill Rd W6 ....112 D2
Chalkhill Rd HA9 ....67 A5
Chalk La EN4 ....2 D1
Chalklands HA9 ....67 A5
Chalkley Cl CR4 ....181 A1
Chalkmill Dr EN1 ....6 B2
Chalk Pit Ave BR5 ....190 C1
Chalk Pit Rd SM1 ....218 A3
Chalk Rd E13 ....99 C2
Chalkstone Cl DA16 ....146 A4
Chalkwell Ho 9 E1 ....96 D1
Chalkwell Park Ave EN1 .5 C1
Challenge Cl NW10 ....89 C6
Challenge Rd TW15 ....149 B1
Challenger Ho 7 E14 119 A6
Challice Way SW2 ....160 B3
Challiner Ct HA1 ....43 A4
Challin St 1 SE20 ....184 C2
Challis Rd TW8 ....109 D1
Challoner Cl N2 ....30 B1
Challoner Cres W14 .254 C1
Challoner Ct BR2 ....186 B1
Challoner Mans W14 .254 C1
Challoners Cl KT8 ....196 B5
Challoner St
W14 ....113 B1 254 C1
Chalmers Ho E17 ....53 D4
13 SW11 ....136 A2
Chalmers Rd TW15 ....170 D5
Chalmers Rd E TW15 .171 A5
Chalmers Way TW14 ..150 B6
Chalmer's Wlk 14
SE17 ....138 D6
Chalner Ho SW2 ....160 C3
Chaloner Ct SE1 ....252 C2
Chalsey Rd SE4 ....141 B1
Chalton Dr N2 ....48 B3
Chalton St NW1 93 D5 232 C3
Chamberlain Cl SE18 .123 B3
Chamberlain Cotts
SE5 ....139 B4
Chamberlain Cres
BR4 ....207 D1
Chamberlain Gdns
TW3 ....130 A4
Chamberlain Ho 5
E1 ....118 C6
Chamberlain La HA5 ....40 A5
Chamberlain Pl E17 ....53 A6
Chamberlain Rd N2 ....30 A1
Ealing W13 ....109 A4
Edmonton N9 ....18 A2
Chamberlain St 7
NW1 ....70 D1
Chamberlain Way
Pinner HA5 ....40 B6
Surbiton KT6 ....198 A2
Chamberlain Wlk 5
TW13 ....173 A6
Chamberlayne Mans 3
NW10 ....90 D4
Chamberlayne Rd
NW10 ....90 C6
Chambers Gdns N2 ....30 B2
Chambers Ho 2
SW16 ....181 C6
Chambers La NW10 ....68 C1
Chambers Pl CR2 ....221 B1
Chambers Rd N7 ....72 A4
Chambers St SE16 ....118 A4
Chamber St
E1 ....117 D6 253 D6
Chambon Pl 7 W6 ....112 A2
Chambord Ho 24 E2 ....95 D4
Chambord St E2 ....95 D4
Chamomile Ct E17 ....53 C3
Champion Cres SE26 .185 A6
Champion Gr SE5 ....139 B2
Champion Hill SE5 ....139 B2
Champion Pk SE5 ....139 B3
Champion Rd SE26 ....185 A6
Champlain Ho 26 W12 112 B6
Champness Cl 9
SE27 ....183 B6
Champness Rd IG11 ....79 D1
Champneys Cl SM2 ....217 B1
Chancel Ct W1 ....249 C6
Chancellor Gr SE21 ....161 A1
Chancellor Ho 29 E1 ....118 B5
SW7 ....256 B6
Chancellor Pas E14 ....119 C5
Chancellor Pl NW9 ....27 D1
Chancellors' Ct WC1 ..240 C4
Chancellor's Rd W6 ..112 C1
Chancellors St W6 ....112 C1
Chancellors Wharf 21
W6 ....112 C1
Chancelot Rd SE2 ....124 B2
Chancel St
SE1 ....116 D5 251 C3
Chancery Bldgs 13 E1 118 C6
Chancery La
EC4 ....94 C1 241 A2
Beckenham BR3 ....185 D1
Chancery Lane Sta
WC1 ....94 C2 241 A3
Chance St E2 ....243 C6
Chanctonbury Cl SE9 .166 D1
Chanctonbury Gdns
SM2 ....217 D1
Chanctonbury Way N12 29 C6
Chandler Ave E16 ....99 A2
Chandler Cl TW12 ....173 C2
Chandler Ct
Feltham TW14 ....150 A5
2 Tolworth KT5 ....198 D1

Chandler Ct *continued*
8 Wallington SM6 .....219 B2
Chandlers Cl TW14 ...149 D4
Chandlers Field Prim Sch
KT8 .....195 C4
Chandlers Mews E14 .119 C4
Chandler St E1 .....118 B5
Chandlers Way 11
SE24 .....160 C4
Chandler Way SE15 ..139 D5
Chandon Lo SM2 .....218 A1
Chandos Ave N14 .....15 C1
N20 .....14 B3
W5 .....109 D2
Chingford E17 .....35 C1
Chandos Cl IG9 .....21 B2
Chandos Cres HA8 .....26 C3
Chandos Ct N14 .....15 D2
Chandos Pl
WC2 .....116 A6 250 A5
Chandos Rd E15 .....76 B3
N2 .....30 C1
NW10 .....89 C3
NW2 .....68 C3
Harrow HA1 .....42 A4
Pinner HA5 .....40 D2
Tottenham N17 .....33 C1
Chandos St W1 93 B2 238 D3
Chandos Way NW11 ...47 D1
Change Alley EC3 ....242 D1
Channel Cl TW5 .....129 C4
Channel Ho E14 .....97 A2
Channelsea Bsns Ctr
E15 .....98 B5
Channing Sch N6 .....49 B1
Channon Ct 3 KT6 ...198 A4
Chantrey Cl DA14 ....191 A5
Chantrey Rd SW9 .....138 B2
Chantries The HA7 .....25 A5
Chantry Cl W9 .....91 B3
Edgware NW7 .....11 D4
Enfield EN2 .....5 A5
Harrow HA3 .....44 B4
Sunbury TW16 .....172 A3
Chantry Cres NW10 ...67 D2
Chantry Ct SW6 .....135 A2
Chantry Ct Ind Est
SM5 .....218 C5
Chantry La BR2 .....209 D4
Chantry Pl HA3 .....23 D2
Chantry Rd
Chessington KT9 .....214 C3
Harrow HA3 .....23 D2
Chantry Sch UB7 .....104 A6
Chantry Sq
W8 .....113 D3 255 C5
Chantry St N1 ..94 D6 234 D5
Chantry The
3 Chingford E4 .....20 A3
Hillingdon UB8 .....82 B4
Chantry Way CR4 .....202 B6
Chant Sq E15 .....76 B1
Chant St E15 .....76 B1
Chapel Cl NW10 .....67 D2
Chapel Ct 12 EC2 .....95 C4
N2 .....48 C6
SE1 .....252 C2
Hayes UB3 .....105 D6
Chapel End Ho E17 ....35 D2
Chapel End Inf Sch E17 35 D2
Chapel End Jun Sch
E17 .....35 D2
Chapel Farm Rd SE9 ..166 B2
Chapel Hill N2 .....30 C1
Chapel House St E14 .119 D2
Chapel La
5 Dagenham RM6 .....58 D2
Hillingdon UB8 .....82 C1
Pinner HA5 .....40 D6
Chapel Market
N1 .....94 C5 234 A4
Chapel Pl 13 EC2 .....95 C4
N1 .....234 B4
W1 .....238 C1
Tottenham N17 .....33 D3
Chapel Rd DA7 .....147 C1
Ealing W13 .....109 B5
Hounslow TW3 .....129 D2
Ilford IG1 .....78 D5
Twickenham TW1 .....153 B4
West Norwood SE27 ...182 D6
Chapel Side
W2 .....113 D6 245 C5
Chapel St NW1 .92 C2 237 A3
SW1 .....115 A4 248 B1
Enfield EN2 .....5 B2
Chapel View CR2 .....222 C1
Chapel Wlk NW4 .....46 C5
Chapleton Ho SW2 ...160 C6
Chaplin Cl SE1 .....251 C2
Wembley HA0 .....65 D2
Chaplin Cres TW16 ...171 C4
Chaplin Ho 6 SW9 ...138 C1
Chaplin Rd E15 .....98 D6
2 N17 .....51 D6
NW2 .....68 A2

Chaplin Rd *continued*
Dagenham RM9 .....81 A1
Wembley HA0 .....65 D2
Chapman Cl UB7 ....104 B3
Chapman Cres HA3 ....44 B4
Chapman Gn N22 .....32 C2
Chapman Ho 26 E1 ....96 B1
2 West Norwood SE27 160 D1
Chapman Rd E9 .....75 B2
Belvedere DA17 .....125 D1
Thornton Heath CR0 ...204 C1
Chapmans End BR5 ..191 A1
Chapman's La BR5 ...190 D1
Chapmans Park Ind Est
NW10 .....67 D2
Chapman Sq SW19 ...156 D2
Chapman St E1 .....118 B6
Chapone Pl W1 .....239 C1
Chapter Cl 15 W4 ....111 A3
Hillingdon UB10 .....60 B1
Chapter Rd NW2 .....68 A3
SE17 .....116 D1 261 D1
Chapter St SW1 .....259 C3
Chapter Way TW12 ...173 C6
Chara Pl W4 .....133 B6
Charcot Ho 9 SW15 ..155 D5
Charcroft Ct 11 W14 ..112 D4
Charcroft Gdns EN3 .....6 D1
Chard Ho 7 N7 .....72 B6
Chardin Ho 30 SW9 ...138 C4
Chardin Rd 11 W4 ...111 C2
Chardmore Rd N16 ....52 A1
Chardwell Cl E6 .....100 B1
Charecroft Way W12 .112 D4
Charfield Ct W9 .....91 D3
Charford Rd E16 .....99 A2
Chargeable La E13 ....99 A3
Chargeable St E16 ....98 D3
Chargrove Cl 24 SE16 .118 D4
Charing Cl BR6 .....227 D4
Charing Cross
SW1 .....116 A5 250 A4
Charing Cross Hospl
W6 .....112 D1
Charing Cross Rd
WC2 .....93 D1 239 D1
Charing Cross Sta
WC2 .....116 A5 250 B4
Charing Ct BR2 .....186 C1
Charing Ho SE1 .....251 B2
Charlbert Ct NW8 ....230 A4
Charlbert St
NW8 .....92 C5 230 A4
Charlbury Ave HA7 ....25 D5
Charlbury Gdns IG3 ...79 D6
Charlbury Gr W5 .....87 C1
Charlbury Ho 1 E12 ...78 C5
Charlbury Rd UB10 ....60 B5
Charldane Rd SE9 ....166 D1
Charlecote Gr SE26 ..162 B1
Charlecote Rd RM8 ....81 A5
Charlemont Rd E6 ....100 C4
Charles Allen Ho EC1 .234 A2
Charles Auffray Ho 26
E1 .....96 C2
Charles Babbage Cl
KT9 .....213 C1
Charles Barry Cl SW4 .137 C2
Charles Bradlaugh Ho 2
N17 .....34 B3
Charles Burton Ct E5 ..75 A4
Charles Cl DA14 .....190 B6
Charles Cobb Gdns
CR0 .....220 C3
Charles Coveney Rd 4
SE15 .....139 D4
Charles Cres HA1 .....42 B2
Charles Ct N3 .....29 D1
Charles Darwin Ho
8 E2 .....96 B4
Bromley BR1 .....187 B3
Charles Dickens Ct
SE25 .....206 A5
Charles Dickens Ho 1
E2 .....96 B4
Charles Dickens Prim Sch
SE1 .....117 A4 252 A1
Charles Edward Brooke Sch
SW9 .....138 D4
Charlesfield SE12 ....165 C1
Charles Grinling Wlk
SE18 .....122 C2
Charles Haller St 25
SW2 .....160 C4
Charles Harrod Ct
SW13 .....134 C6
Charles Ho 1 N17 ....33 D3
Charles Hobson Ho
NW10 .....67 C1
Charles Hocking Ho 8
W3 .....111 A4
Charles II Pl
SW3 .....114 D1 257 C1
Charles II St
SW1 .....115 D5 249 C4
Charles La NW8 92 C5 230 A4
Charles Lamb Prim Sch
N1 .....95 A6 235 A6
Charles Lesser KT9 ..213 D3

Charles Mackenzie Ho 7
SE16 .....118 A2
Charles Mills Ct SW16 182 A4
Charles Pl NW1 .....232 B1
Charles Rd E7 .....77 C1
Dagenham RM6 .....58 D3
Ealing W13 .....87 A1
Merton SW19 .....179 C2
Charles Rowan Ho
WC1 .....234 A1
Charles Sevright Dr
NW7 .....28 D5
Charles Sq N1 .95 B4 235 D1
Charles St E16 .....121 C5
W1 .....115 B5 248 C4
Barnes SW13 .....133 C3
Croydon CR0 .....221 A5
Enfield EN1 .....17 D6
Hillingdon UB10 .....82 D3
Hounslow TW3 .....129 B3
Charles Staunton Ho 3
SE27 .....183 B6
Charleston Cl TW13 ..150 A1
Charleston St SE17 ..262 B3
Charles Townsend Ho
EC1 .....241 C6
Charles Winchup Rd 2
E16 .....121 B5
Charlesworth Ho 2
E14 .....97 C1
Charleville Cir SE26 ..184 A5
Charleville Ct SW5 ...254 C1
Charleville Mans W14 254 B1
Charleville Rd
W14 .....113 A1 254 C1
Charlie Browns Rdbt
E18 .....37 C1
Charlmont Rd SW17 ..180 D4
Charlotte Cl DA6 .....169 A6
Charlotte Ct N8 .....49 D3
Ilford IG2 .....56 C3
5 Wembley HA0 .....66 A2
Charlotte Ho 12 W6 ..112 C1
Charlotte Mews W10 ..90 D1
W1 .....239 B4
W14 .....254 A4
Charlotte Park Ave
BR1 .....210 A6
Charlotte Pl SW1 ....259 A3
W1 .....239 B3
Charlotte Rd
EC2 .....95 C3 243 A6
Barnes SW13 .....133 D4
Dagenham RM10 .....81 D2
Wallington SM6 .....219 C2
Charlotte Row SW4 ..137 C2
Charlotte Sharman Prim
Sch SE11 ....116 D3 261 C5
Charlotte Sq 5 TW10 .154 B5
Charlotte St W1 93 C2 239 B4
Charlotte Terr
N1 .....94 B6 233 D5
Charlow Cl SW6 .....136 A3
Charlton Church La
SE7 .....121 C1
Charlton Cl UB10 .....60 D6
Charlton Cres IG11 ...101 D5
Charlton Ct 25 E2 .....95 D6
E6 .....100 B4
17 N7 .....71 D3
Charlton Dene SE7 ...143 D5
Charlton Ho NW1 ....232 C2
5 Brentford TW8 ....132 A6
Charlton King's Rd
NW5 .....71 D3
Charlton La SE7 .....121 D1
Upper Halliford TW17 ..193 B5
Upper Halliford TW17 ..193 C5
Charlton Lo 1 NW11 ...47 B3
Charlton Manor Prim Sch
SE7 .....143 D5
Charlton Park La SE7 .144 A6
Charlton Park Rd SE7 143 D6
Charlton Park Sch
SE7 .....144 A6
Charlton Pl N1 .94 D5 234 C4
Charlton Rd N9 .....18 D4
NW10 .....89 C6
SE3,SE7 .....143 B6
Charlton TW17 .....171 A1
Harrow HA3 .....43 D5
Wembley HA9 .....44 B1
Charlton Way SE10,
SE3 .....142 C4
Charlwood Cl HA3 ....24 C4
Charlwood Ho SW1 ...259 C3
1 Streatham SW2 ....160 B3
Charlwood Pl
SW1 .....115 C2 259 B3
Charlwood Rd SW15 ..134 D1
Charlwood Sq CR4 ...202 B6
Charlwood St
SW1 .....115 C1 259 B2
Charlwood Terr 5
SW15 .....134 D1
Charman Ho 18 SW2 .160 C5
SW8 .....270 A4
Charmian Ave HA7 ....25 D1
Charmian Ho 19 N1 ...95 C5

Charminster Ave
SW19 .....179 D1
Charminster Ct 3
KT6 .....197 D2
Charminster Rd
SE12,SE9 .....187 D6
North Cheam KT4 .....200 D1
Charmouth Ct TW10 ..154 B6
Charmouth Ho SW8 ..270 C4
Charmouth Rd DA16 ..146 C4
Charnock Ho 22 W12 .112 B6
Charnock Rd E5 .....74 B5
Charnwood Ave SW19 179 D1
Charnwood Cl KT3 ...199 C5
Charnwood Dr E18 ....55 B5
Charnwood Gdns E14 .119 C2
Charnwood Ho 9 E5 ...74 B6
Charnwood Pl N20 ....14 A1
Charnwood Rd
Hillingdon UB10 .....82 C5
South Norwood SE25 ..205 B5
Charnwood St E5 .....74 B6
Charrington Rd 2
CR0 .....221 A6
Charrington St
NW1 .....93 D5 232 C4
Charsley Rd SE6 .....163 D2
Chart Cl Bromley BR2 ..186 C2
Croydon CR0 .....206 C3
Mitcham CR4 .....202 D5
Charter Ave IG2 .....57 B2
Charter Cres TW4 ....129 A1
Charter Ct N4 .....50 C1
W1 .....237 B3
Kingston KT3 .....199 C6
Southall UB1 .....107 C5
Charter Dr DA5 .....169 A4
Charter Ho WC2 .....240 B1
Charterhouse Ave HA0 .65 C3
Charterhouse Bldgs
EC1 .....242 A5
Charterhouse Mews
EC1 .....241 D4
Charterhouse Rd E8 ...74 A3
Charterhouse Sq
EC1 .....94 D2 241 D4
Charterhouse Square Prim
Sch The EC1 ..94 D2 241 D3
Charterhouse St EC1 .241 C3
Charteris Rd N4 .....50 C1
NW6 .....91 B6
Woodford IG8 .....37 B4
Charter Nightingale Hospl
The NW1 .....92 C2 237 B4
Charter Rd KT1 .....198 D6
Charter Rd The IG8 ...36 D4
Charter Sch The SE24 .161 B6
Charters Cl SE19 .....183 C5
Charter Sq KT1 .....176 D1
Charter Way NW3 .....47 B5
Southgate N14 .....15 D5
Chartes Ho SE1 .....263 B6
Chartfield Ave SW15 ..156 C6
Chartfield Sch SW15 ..156 B6
Chartfield Sq SW15 ..156 D6
Chartham Ct 13 SW9 .138 C2
Chartham Gr SE27 ...160 D1
Chartham Ho SE1 ....262 D6
Chartham Rd SE25 ...206 B6
Chart Hills Cl SE28 ..103 A1
Chartley Ave NW2 .....67 C5
Harrow HA7 .....24 D4
Charton Cl 5 DA17 ..147 B6
Chartres Ct UB6 .....86 B5
Chartridge SE17 .....139 B6
Chartridge Cl
Barnet EN5 .....12 A6
Bushey WD23 .....8 A5
Chartridge Ct 6 HA7 ..25 C5
Chart St N1 .....95 B4 235 D2
Chartwell 25 SW19 ...156 D3
Chartwell Bsns Ctr
BR1 .....209 D6
Chartwell Cl
2 Croydon CR0 .....205 B1
Greenford UB6 .....85 D6
Sidcup BR7,DA15 .....167 B2
Chartwell Ct
8 Barnet EN5 .....1 A1
2 Woodford IG8 .....37 A3
Chartwell Dr BR6 ....227 B3
Chartwell Gdns SM3 ..217 A4
Chartwell Lo 5 BR3 ..185 C3
Chartwell Pl
Cheam SM3 .....217 B4
Harrow HA2 .....64 B6
Chartwell Way 3
SE20 .....184 B2
Charville Ct 8 HA1 ....42 D3
Charville La UB4 .....83 C5
Charville La W UB10 ..82 D4
Charville Prim Sch UB4 83 C5
Charwood SW16 .....182 C6
Chase Bridge Prim Sch
TW2 .....152 C5
Chase Court Gdns EN2 ..5 A2
Chase Ct SW3 .....257 C5
Isleworth TW7 .....131 A3
Merton SW20 .....179 A1

Chase Ct *continued*
Southgate N14 .....15 C5
Wembley HA0 .....65 D2
Chase Ctr The NW10 ...89 B4
Chase Farm Hospl EN2 ..4 C5
Chasefield Rd SW17 ..180 D6
Chase Gdns
Chingford E4 .....35 C6
Twickenham TW2 .....152 B4
Chase Gn EN2 .....5 A2
Chase Green Ave EN2 ..5 A3
Chase Hill EN2 .....5 A2
Chase La IG6 .....57 B4
Chase Lane Inf Sch E4 .35 B6
Chase Lane Jun Sch E4 35 B6
Chaseley Ct W4 .....110 D1
Oatlands Park KT13 ...193 C1
Chaseley St E14 .....97 A1
Chasemore Cl CR4 ...202 D2
Chasemore Gdns CR0 220 C3
Chasemore Ho SW6 ..264 B4
Chase Rd NW10 .....89 B3
Southgate N14 .....15 D5
Chase Ridings EN2 .....4 C3
Chase Road Trad Est
NW10 .....89 B3
Chase Side N14 .....15 B4
Enfield EN2 .....5 A3
Chaseside Ave SW20 .179 A1
Chase Side Ave EN2 .....5 A3
Chase Side Cres EN2 ....5 A4
Chase Side Pl EN2 .....5 A3
Chase Side Prim Sch
EN2 .....5 A3
Chase The DA7 .....147 D2
E12 .....77 D4
SW4 .....137 B2
Bromley BR1 .....209 B6
Edgware HA8 .....26 D2
Ickenham UB10 .....60 C3
Loughton IG10 .....21 D4
Pinner HA5 .....40 C3
Pinner HA5 .....41 B5
South Norwood SW16 ..182 C3
Stanmore HA7 .....25 A4
Sunbury TW16 .....172 B2
Wallington CR0,SM6 ...220 B3
Dagenham RM6 .....59 A3
Chaseville Par N21 .....16 B6
Chaseville Park Rd N21 16 B6
Chase Way N14 .....15 C3
Chasewood Ave EN2 ....4 D3
Chasewood Ct NW7 ....27 B5
Chasewood Pk HA1 ....64 C5
Chater Ho 6 E2 .....96 D4
Chatfield Rd SW11 ...136 A2
Thornton Heath CR0 ...204 D1
Chatham Ave BR2 ....209 A2
Chatham Cl NW11 .....47 C4
Cheam SM3 .....201 B2
Chatham Ct SW11 ....158 D6
Chatham Ho 22 SE18 .122 B2
7 SE5 .....139 C3
Chatham Pl E9 .....74 C2
Chatham Rd E17 .....53 A6
SW11 .....158 D6
Kingston KT1,KT2 ....176 C1
1 Woodford E18 .....36 D1
Chatham St
SE17 .....117 B2 262 D4
Chatsfield Pl W5 .....88 A1
Chatsworth Ave BR1 ..187 B6
DA15 .....168 A3
NW4 .....28 C1
Merton SW20 .....179 A1
Wembley HA9 .....66 B3
Chatsworth Cl NW4 ....28 C1
Coney Hall BR2,BR4 ..224 D6
Chatsworth Cres TW3,
TW7 .....130 B2
Chatsworth Ct E5 .....74 D4
W8 .....255 A4
5 Stanmore HA7 .....25 C5
Chatsworth Dr EN1 ....18 A5
Chatsworth Est E5 .....74 D4
Chatsworth Gdns
Acton W3 .....110 D5
Harrow HA2 .....41 D1
New Malden KT3 .....199 D4
Chatsworth Ho
2 BR2 .....209 A5
Kingston KT6 .....197 D4
Chatsworth Inf Sch
DA15 .....168 A3
Isleworth TW3 .....130 A1
Chatsworth Jun Sch
TW3 .....130 A1
Chatsworth Lo 1 W4 .111 B1
West Wickham BR4 ...224 A6
Chatsworth Par BR5 ..211 A4
Chatsworth Pl
Mitcham CR4 .....202 D6
Teddington TW11 .....175 A6
Chatsworth Rd E15 ....76 D3
E5 .....74 D4
NW2 .....68 D2
Cheam SM3 .....217 A4
Chiswick W4 .....133 A6
Ealing W5 .....88 B3

Chatsworth Rd *continued*
Hayes UB4 84
South Croydon CR0 221
Chatsworth Rise W5 ..88
Chatsworth Way SE27 161
Chattenden Ho 8 N4 ..51
Chattern Hill TW15 ..170
Chattern Rd TW15 ...171
Chatterton Ct TW9 ...132
Chatterton Rd BR2 ...209
N4 72
Chatton Ct 5 NW9 ...46
Chatto Rd SW11 158
Chaucer Ave
Cranford TW4 128
Hayes UB4 84
Richmond TW9 132
Chaucer Cl N11 31
Chaucer Ct 17 N16 ...73
12 New Barnet EN5 ...13
Chaucer Dr
SE1 .....117 D2 263
Chaucer Gdns SM1 ...217
Chaucer Gn CR0 206
Chaucer Ho SW1 259
Harrow HA2 41
Sutton SM1 217
2 West Norwood SE27 .183
Chaucer Rd DA16 145
E7 77
SE24 160
W3 111
Ashford TW15 170
Chingford E17 36
Sidcup DA15 168
Sutton SM1 217
Wanstead E11 55
Chaucer Way SW17 ..180
Chaulden Ho EC1 235
Chauncey Cl N9 18
Chaundrye Cl SE9 ...166
Chauntler Cl E16 121
Chaville Ct N11 31
Cheadle Ct NW8 236
Cheadle Ho 11 E14 ...97
Cheam Common Inf Sch
KT4 216
Cheam Common Jun Sch
KT4 216
Cheam Common Rd
KT4 216
Cheam Court Flats 1
SM3 217
Cheam Fields Prim Sch
SM3 217
Cheam High Sch SM3 217
Cheam Mans SM3 217
Cheam Park Farm Inf Sch
SM3 217
Cheam Park Farm Jun Sch
SM3 217
Cheam Park Way SM3 217
Cheam Rd
Belmont SM2,SM3 216
Cheam SM1 217
Cheam St 4 SE15 140
Cheam Sta SM2 217
Cheam Village SM3 ..217
Cheapside EC2 .95 A1 242
Edmonton N13 33
Chearsley SE17 262
Cheddar Cl N11 31
Cheddar Rd TW6 126
Cheddar Waye UB4 ...84
Cheddington Ho 9 E2 .96
Cheddington Rd N18 ..33
Chedworth Cl E16 98
Chedworth Ho 2 E5 ..74
N15 .....51 B5
Cheeseman Cl TW12 .173
Cheesemans Terr
W14 .....254 C1
Chelford Rd BR1 ....186 B5
Chelmer Cres IG11 ..102 B5
Chelmer Rd E9 .....74 D3
Chelmsford Cl W6 ...134
Newham E6 100
Chelmsford Ct N14 ...15 D4
Chelmsford Gdns IG1 ..56 B2
Chelmsford Ho 5 N7 .72 B4
Chelmsford Rd E11 ...54 B1
E17 .....53 C3
N14 .....15 C4
Woodford E18 .....36 D2
Chelmsford Sq NW10 ..90 C6
Chelsea Barracks*
SW1 .....115 A1 258 B1
Chelsea Bridge
SW1 .....137 B6 268 C6
Chelsea Bridge Rd
SW1 .....115 A1 258 B1
Chelsea Cl NW10 .....89 B6
Edgware HA8 .....26 C1
Hampton TW12 .....174 A5
New Malden KT4 .....200 A2
Chelsea Cloisters
SW3 .....257 B3

helsea Coll of Art &
Design
SW3 .. 114 C1 257 A1
W12 .. 112 C4
helsea Cres SW10 .. 266 B1
helsea Ct SW3 .. 268 A6
8 Chingford E4 .. 20 A3
helsea Emb
SW3 .. 136 D6 267 C5
helsea Est SW3 .. 267 A5
helsea Farm Ho
SW10 .. 266 D5
Chelsea Fields SW19 .. 180 B2
helsea Gate SW1 .. 258 B1
helsea Gdns SW1 .. 258 B1
Cheam SM3 .. 217 A4
Ealing W13 .. 86 D2
Chelsea Harbour Design Ctr
SW10 .. 266 B2
Chelsea Harbour Dr
SW10 .. 136 A4 266 B2
Chelsea Harbour Pier
SW10 .. 266 C1
Chelsea Lo SW3 .. 267 D6
SW6 .. 265 C2
Chelsea Manor Ct
SW3 .. 267 B6
Chelsea Manor Gdns
SW3 .. 257 B1
Chelsea Manor St
SW3 .. 114 C1 257 B1
Chelsea Manor Studios
SW3 .. 257 B1
Chelsea Park Gdns
SW3 .. 136 B6 266 C6
Chelsea Physic Gdn*
SW1 .. 267 C6
Chelsea Reach Twr
SW10 .. 266 C4
Chelsea Sq
SW3 .. 114 B1 256 D1
Chelsea Twrs SW3 .. 267 B6
Chelsea & Westminster
Hospl SW10 .. 136 A6 266 B5
Chelsfield Ave N9 .. 18 D4
Chelsfield Gdns SE26 .. 162 C1
Chelsfield Gn N9 .. 18 D4
Chelsfield Ho SE17 .. 263 A3
Chelsfield Point 3 E9 .. 74 D1
Chelsham Ho 1 SW4 .. 137 D2
Chelsham Rd SW4 .. 137 D2
South Croydon CR2 .. 221 B2
Chelsiter Ct DA14 .. 189 D6
Chelston Ct 2 E11 .. 55 B4
Chelston Rd HA4 .. 40 A1
Chelsworth Dr SE18 .. 145 B6
Cheltenham Ave 8
TW1 .. 153 A4
Cheltenham Cl
Kingston KT3 .. 199 A6
Northolt UB5 .. 63 D2
Cheltenham Ct 8 HA7 .. 25 C5
Cheltenham Gdns E6 .. 100 A5
Cheltenham Ho UB3 .. 105 A3
Cheltenham Pl 1 W3 .. 110 D4
Harrow HA3 .. 44 A5
Cheltenham Rd E10 .. 54 A3
SE15 .. 162 C6
Cheltenham Terr
SW3 .. 114 D1 257 D2
Cheltenham Villas
CR7 .. 204 C3
Chelverton Ct SW15 .. 134 D1
Chelverton Rd SW15 .. 134 D1
Chelwood N20 .. 14 B2
NW5 .. 71 A3
Chelwood Cl E4 .. 19 D5
Chelwood Ct SW11 .. 266 D2
Chelwood Gdns TW9 .. 132 C3
Chelwood Ho W2 .. 236 D1
Chenappa Cl E13 .. 99 A4
Chenduit Way HA7 .. 24 D5
Chene Colline Ct KT6 .. 198 A3
Cheney Ct SE23 .. 162 D3
Cheney Row E17 .. 35 B2
Cheneys Rd E11 .. 76 C5
Cheney St HA5 .. 40 C4
Chenies Ho W2 .. 245 C6
Chenies Mews WC1 .. 239 C5
Chenies Pl NW1 .. 232 D4
Chenies St WC1 .. 93 D2 239 C4
Chenies The NW1 .. 232 D4
Orpington BR5,BR6 .. 211 C3
Cheniston Gdns W8 .. 255 C6
Chennestone Cty Prim Sch
TW16 .. 172 B1
Chepstow Cl SW15 .. 157 A6
Chepstow Cres
W11 .. 113 C6 245 A6
Ilford IG3 .. 57 C3
Chepstow Ct W11 .. 245 A6
Chepstow Gdns UB1 .. 85 B1
Chepstow Pl
W2 .. 113 C6 245 B6
Chepstow Rd W2 .. 91 C1
Croydon CR0 .. 221 D6
Ealing W7 .. 109 A3
Chepstow Rise CR0 .. 221 C5
Chepstow Villas
W11 .. 113 C6 245 A6
Chequers IG9 .. 21 B3
Chequers Cl NW9 .. 45 C6
Orpington BR5 .. 211 D5
Chequers Ct EC1 .. 242 C5
7 Croydon CR0 .. 205 D1
Chequers Ho NW8 .. 237 A6
Chequers La RM9 .. 103 C5
Chequers Par
Dagenham RM9 .. 103 C6
Edmonton N13 .. 33 A5
Chequer St EC1 .. 95 A3 242 B5
Chequers The HA5 .. 40 D6
Chequers Way N13 .. 32 D5
Cherbury Cl SE28 .. 102 D1
Cherbury Ct N1 .. 235 D3
Cherbury St N1 .. 95 B5 235 D3
Cherchefells Mews
HA7 .. 25 B5
Cherimoya Gdns KT8 .. 195 D6
Cherington Rd W7 .. 108 D5
Cheriton Ave BR2 .. 209 A4
Cheriton Cl
Cockfosters EN4 .. 2 D1
10 Ealing W5 .. 87 C2
Cheriton Ct 4 SE12 .. 165 A4
South Norwood SE25 .. 205 C4
Walton-on-T KT12 .. 194 C1
Cheriton Dr SE18 .. 145 B6
Cheriton Ho 9 E5 .. 74 B3
Cheriton Sq SW17 .. 159 A2
Cherry Ave UB1 .. 106 D5
Cherry Blossom Cl N13 .. 32 D5
Cherry Cl E17 .. 53 D4
W5 .. 109 D3
Carshalton SM5 .. 218 D6
Merton SM4 .. 201 A5
Ruislip HA4 .. 61 D5
1 Streatham SW2 .. 160 C4
Cherrycot Hill BR6 .. 227 B4
Cherrycot Rise BR6 .. 227 A4
Cherry Cres TW8 .. 131 B5
Cherry Croft Gdns 2
HA5 .. 23 B3
Cherry Ct W3 .. 111 C5
Ilford IG6 .. 56 D6
Pinner HA5 .. 22 D2
Sidcup DA14 .. 168 B1
Cherrydeal Ct E11 .. 54 B2
Cherrydown Ave E4 .. 19 C1
Cherrydown Cl E4 .. 19 C1
Cherrydown Rd DA14 .. 168 D2
Cherry Garden Ho 5
SE16 .. 118 B4
Cherry Garden Sch
SE16 .. 118 A2
Cherry Garden St
SE16 .. 118 B4
Cherry Garth TW8 .. 109 D1
Cherry Gdns
Dagenham RM9 .. 81 B3
Northolt UB5 .. 63 D1
Cherry Gr Hayes UB3 .. 106 B5
Hillingdon UB8 .. 83 A2
Cherry Hill
New Barnet EN5 .. 13 D5
Stanmore HA3 .. 24 C4
Cherry Hill Gdns CR0 .. 220 B4
Cherry Hills WD19 .. 23 A5
Cherry La UB7 .. 104 C2
Cherrylands Cl NW9 .. 67 A6
Cherry Lane Jun & Inf Schs
UB7 .. 104 B2
Cherry Laurel Wlk
SW2 .. 160 B5
Cherry Orch SE7 .. 143 C6
West Drayton UB7 .. 104 A4
Cherry Orchard Gdns
7 Croydon CR0 .. 205 B1
East Molesey KT8 .. 195 B6
5 South Croydon CR0 .. 221 B6
Cherry Orchard Prim Sch
SE7 .. 143 C5
Cherry Orchard Rd
BR2 .. 226 A6
Croydon CR0 .. 205 C1
East Molesey KT8 .. 195 C6
Cherry Rd EN3 .. 6 C5
Cherry Tree Ave UB7 .. 82 B1
Cherry Tree Cl 17 E9 .. 96 C6
Wembley HA0 .. 65 A4
Cherrytree Ct NW9 .. 45 A5
Cherry Tree Ct 17 SE7 .. 143 C6
3 Woodford E18 .. 36 D1
Cherry Tree Dr SW16 .. 160 A1
Cherrytree Ho 8 W10 .. 90 D4
Cherry Tree Ho SE14 .. 141 B3
Cherry Tree Rd E15 .. 76 C3
N2 .. 48 D5
Cherry Tree Ri IG9 .. 37 D6
Cherry Trees Sch The
E3 .. 97 C4
Cherry Tree Terr SE1 .. 253 B2
Cherry Tree Way HA7 .. 25 B4
Cherry Tree Wlk EC1 .. 242 B5
Beckenham BR3 .. 207 B5
Coney Hall BR4 .. 224 D4
Cherry Way
Upper Halliford TW17 .. 193 C5
West Ewell KT19 .. 215 B2
Cherry Wlk BR2 .. 209 A1
Cherrywood Cl E3 .. 97 A4
Kingston KT2 .. 176 C3
Cherrywood Ct 1
TW11 .. 175 A5
Cherrywood Dr SW15 .. 156 D6
Cherrywood La SM4,
SW20 .. 201 A5
Cherry Wood Way W5 .. 88 C2
Chertsey Ct SW14 .. 132 D2
Chertsey Dr SM3 .. 217 A6
Chertsey Ho 37 E2 .. 95 D4
Feltham TW13 .. 151 C1
Chertsey Rd E11 .. 76 B6
Ashford TW15,TW16 .. 171 B4
Feltham TW13,TW16 .. 171 C6
Ilford IG1 .. 79 B4
Lower Halliford TW17 .. 192 C2
Shepperton TW17 .. 192 A2
Twickenham TW2 .. 152 B4
Chertsey St SW17 .. 181 A5
Chervil Cl TW13 .. 150 A1
Chervil Mews SE28 .. 124 B5
Cherwell Ct
Teddington KT1 .. 175 D3
West Ewell KT19 .. 215 A4
Cherwell Ho NW8 .. 236 D5
Cherwell Way HA4 .. 39 A3
Cheryls Cl
SW6 .. 135 D4 265 D2
Cheseman St SE26 .. 162 B1
Chesfield Rd KT2 .. 176 A3
Chesham Ave BR2,BR5 .. 210 D3
Chesham Cl SW1 .. 258 A5
Chesham Cres SE20 .. 184 C2
Chesham Ct SW18 .. 158 B4
Chesham Flats W1 .. 248 B6
Chesham Mews SW1 .. 258 A6
Chesham Pl
SW1 .. 115 A3 258 A5
Chesham Rd
Kingston KT1,KT2 .. 176 C1
Penge SE20 .. 184 C2
Chesham St NW10 .. 67 B5
SW1 .. 115 A3 258 A5
Chesham Terr W13 .. 109 B4
Cheshire Cl
Chingford, Highams Park
E17 .. 35 D2
Mitcham CR4,SW16 .. 204 A6
Cheshire Gdns KT9 .. 213 D2
Cheshire Ho SM4 .. 201 D2
Cheshire Rd N22 .. 32 B4
Cheshire St E2 .. 95 D3 243 D6
Cheshir Ho NW4 .. 46 C5
Chesholm Rd N16 .. 73 C5
Cheshunt Ho 7 NW6 .. 91 D6
Cheshunt Rd E7 .. 77 B2
Belvedere DA17 .. 125 C1
Chesil Ct 18 E2 .. 96 C5
SW3 .. 267 B6
Chesilton Rd
SW6 .. 135 B4 264 C2
Chesil Way UB4 .. 83 D4
Chesley Gdns E6 .. 100 A4
Chesney Cres CR0 .. 224 A1
Chesney Ct W9 .. 91 C3
Chesney Ho SE13 .. 142 B1
Chesney St SW11 .. 268 A1
Chesnut Gr N17 .. 51 D6
Chesnut Rd N17 .. 51 D6
Chessell Cl CR7 .. 204 D5
Chessholme Ct TW16 .. 171 C3
Chessholme Rd TW15 .. 171 A4
Chessing Ct N2 .. 48 D6
Chessington Ave DA7 .. 147 A5
N3 .. 47 B6
Chessington Cl KT19 .. 215 A2
Chessington Com Coll
KT9 .. 213 D1
Chessington Ct N3 .. 47 B6
Pinner HA5 .. 41 B5
Chessington Hall Gdns
KT9 .. 213 D1
Chessington Hill Pk
KT9 .. 214 C3
Chessington Ho 19
SW8 .. 137 D3
Chessington Lo N3 .. 47 B6
Chessington Mans E10 .. 53 C2
E11 .. 54 C2
Chessington North Sta
KT9 .. 214 A3
Chessington Par KT9 .. 213 D3
Chessington Park KT9 .. 214 C4
Chessington Pk KT9 .. 214 C4
Chessington Rd KT19 .. 215 B1
Chessington South Sta
KT9 .. 213 D1
Chessington Way BR4 .. 223 D6
Chesson Rd
W14 .. 135 B6 264 D6
Chesswood Way HA5 .. 22 D1
Chestbrook Ct 12 EN1 .. 17 C6
Chester Ave
Richmond TW10 .. 154 B5
Chester Ave *continued*
Twickenham TW2 .. 151 B3
Chester Cl SW1 .. 248 C1
Ashford TW15 .. 171 B5
Barnes SW13 .. 134 B2
Hayes UB8 .. 82 D1
1 Richmond TW10 .. 154 B5
Sutton SM1 .. 217 C6
Chester Close N NW1 .. 231 D2
Chester Close S NW1 .. 231 D1
Chester Cres E8 .. 73 D3
Chester Ct NW1 .. 231 D1
NW5 .. 71 A4
4 SE5 .. 139 B5
SE8 .. 118 D1
2 Acton W3 .. 88 C1
Chester Dr HA2 .. 41 C3
Chesterfield Ct KT6 .. 198 A4
Chesterfield Dr KT10 .. 213 A6
Chesterfield Flats EN5 .. 12 D6
Chesterfield Gdns N4 .. 50 D4
SE10 .. 142 B5
W1 .. 248 C4
Chesterfield Gr SE22 .. 161 D6
Chesterfield Hill
W1 .. 115 B5 248 C4
Chesterfield Ho W1 .. 248 B4
6 Streatham SW16 .. 181 C5
Chesterfield Jun & Inf Sch
EN3 .. 7 A6
Chesterfield Lo N21 .. 16 B4
Chesterfield Mews N4 .. 50 D4
Ashford TW15 .. 170 A6
Chesterfield Rd E10 .. 54 A3
N3 .. 29 C4
Ashford TW15 .. 170 A5
Barnet EN5 .. 12 D6
Chiswick W4 .. 133 A6
Enfield EN3 .. 7 A6
West Ewell KT19 .. 215 B1
Chesterfield St W1 .. 248 C4
Chesterfield Way
SE15 .. 140 C5
Hayes UB3 .. 106 A4
Chesterford Gdns NW3 .. 69 D4
Chesterford Ho 4
SE18 .. 143 D5
Chesterford Rd E12 .. 78 B3
Chester Gate NW1 .. 231 D1
Chester Gdns
Ealing W13 .. 87 B1
Enfield EN3 .. 18 B5
Morden SM4 .. 202 A3
Chester Ho N19 .. 71 B6
1 SE8 .. 141 B6
Kingston KT1 .. 176 D1
Chesterman Ct W4 .. 133 C5
Chester Mews SW1 .. 258 C6
Chester Pl NW1 .. 231 C2
Chester Rd DA15 .. 167 C6
E16 .. 98 C3
E17 .. 52 D4
E7 .. 77 D1
N17 .. 51 C6
N19 .. 71 B6
NW1 .. 93 B4 231 C2
Edmonton N9 .. 18 B3
Harlington TW6 .. 126 C2
Hounslow TW4 .. 128 B2
Ilford IG3 .. 57 D2
Wanstead E11 .. 55 B3
Wimbledon SW19,SW20 .. 178 C4
Chester Row
SW1 .. 115 A2 258 B4
Chester Sq
SW1 .. 115 B2 258 C4
Chester Sq Mews
SW1 .. 258 C5
Chester St E2 .. 96 A3
E2 .. 96 A6
SW1 .. 115 A3 258 B6
Chesters The KT3 .. 177 C2
Chester Terr
NW1 .. 93 B4 231 C2
Chesterton Cl SW18 .. 157 C6
Greenford UB6 .. 85 D5
Chesterton Dr TW19 .. 148 B3
Chesterton Ho
21 SW11 .. 136 B2
3 W10 .. 91 A2
Chesterton Prim Sch
SW11 .. 137 A4 268 A1
Chesterton Rd E13 .. 99 A4
W10 .. 91 A2
Chesterton Sq W8 .. 255 A3
Chesterton Terr E13 .. 99 A4
6 Kingston KT1 .. 176 C1
Chester Way
SE11 .. 116 C2 261 B3
Chesthunte Rd N17 .. 33 A2
Chestnut Alley SW6 .. 264 D5
Chestnut Ave E7 .. 77 B4
N8 .. 50 A4
Brentford TW8 .. 109 D2
Buckhurst Hill IG9 .. 21 D1
Coney Hall BR4 .. 224 C4
Edgware HA8 .. 26 B4
Hampton TW12 .. 173 C3
Chestnut Ave *continued*
Hampton, Hampton Court
KT8,KT11 .. 174 D2
11 Mortlake SW14 .. 133 B2
Thames Ditton KT10 .. 196 B1
Wembley HA0 .. 65 B3
Worcester Park KT19 .. 215 C4
Yiewsley UB7 .. 104 B6
Chestnut Ave N E17 .. 54 B5
Chestnut Ave S E17 .. 54 B4
Chestnut Cl DA15 .. 168 A2
1 N16 .. 73 B6
SE14 .. 141 B4
Ashford TW15 .. 170 D6
Ashford TW16 .. 171 D4
Buckhurst Hill IG9 .. 21 D2
Carshalton SM5 .. 202 D1
Catford SE6 .. 186 A6
Harlington UB7 .. 126 D5
Hayes UB3 .. 105 C6
Southgate N14 .. 15 D6
West Norwood SW16 .. 182 C6
Chestnut Ct N8 .. 49 D3
N8 .. 50 A4
SW6 .. 264 D6
Beckenham BR3 .. 185 C3
5 Croydon CR0 .. 221 A4
Feltham TW13 .. 172 D5
Hounslow TW3 .. 129 C2
Kingston KT3 .. 199 C6
Surbiton KT6 .. 198 A2
Wembley HA0 .. 65 B3
Chestnut Dr DA7 .. 147 A2
Harrow HA3 .. 24 D2
Pinner HA5 .. 41 A3
Wanstead E11 .. 55 A3
Chestnut Gr W5 .. 109 D3
Cockfosters EN4 .. 14 D6
Isleworth TW7 .. 131 A1
Kingston KT3 .. 199 B6
Mitcham CR4 .. 203 D5
Penge SE20 .. 184 C3
South Croydon CR2 .. 222 B1
Upper Tooting SW12 .. 159 A3
Wembley HA0 .. 65 B3
Chestnut Grove Sch
SW12 .. 159 A3
Chestnut Ho 7 NW3 .. 70 D2
SE4 .. 141 B2
1 W4 .. 111 C2
West Norwood SE27 .. 161 A1
Chestnut La N20 .. 13 A3
Chestnut Pl SE19 .. 183 D6
Chestnut Rd
Ashford TW15 .. 170 D6
Kingston KT2 .. 176 A3
Twickenham TW2 .. 152 C2
West Barnes SW20 .. 178 D1
West Norwood SE21,
SE27 .. 161 A1
Chestnut Rise SE18 .. 123 C1
Chestnut Row N3 .. 29 C3
Chestnuts Ct 3 E17 .. 54 A6
Chestnuts The N2 .. 48 D4
1 N5 .. 72 D4
NW9 .. 45 C6
SE18 .. 144 D4
3 Erith DA17 .. 125 B1
Penge BR3 .. 206 D6
Uxbridge UB10 .. 60 A1
Walton-on-T KT12 .. 194 B1
Chestnut Way TW13 .. 150 B1
Chestnut Wlk
Upper Halliford TW17 .. 193 C5
Woodford IG8 .. 37 A5
Cheston Ave CR0 .. 207 B1
Chestwood Gr UB10 .. 60 B1
Chettle Cl SE1 .. 262 C6
Chettle Ct N8 .. 50 C3
Chetwode Ho NW8 .. 237 A6
Chetwode Rd SW17 .. 158 D1
Chetwood Wlk 13 E6 .. 100 A2
Chetwynd Ave EN4 .. 14 D3
Chetwynd Dr UB10 .. 82 B5
Chetwynd Rd NW5 .. 71 B5
Cheval Ct SW15 .. 134 B1
Chevalier Cl HA7 .. 26 A6
Cheval Pl SW7 .. 114 C3 257 B6
Cheval St E14 .. 119 C3
Cheveney Wlk 2 BR2 .. 209 A6
Chevening Ho BR5 .. 190 A2
Chevening Rd NW6 .. 91 A6
SE10 .. 120 D1
South Norwood SE19 .. 183 B4
Chevenings The DA14 .. 168 C1
Cheverell Ho 24 E2 .. 96 A5
Cheverton Rd N19 .. 49 D1
Chevet St E9 .. 75 A3
Chevington NW2 .. 69 B2
Cheviot 4 N17 .. 34 B3
Cheviot Cl Bushey WD23 .. 8 A5
Enfield EN1 .. 5 B3
Harlington UB3 .. 127 B5
Cheviot Ct 16 SE14 .. 140 C5
Enfield EN2 .. 5 B3
Southall UB2 .. 107 D2
Cheviot Gate NW2 .. 69 A6
Cheviot Gdns NW2 .. 69 A6
West Norwood SE27 .. 182 D6
Cheviot Ho N16 .. 51 D1
Cheviot Rd SE27 .. 182 D5
Cheviots Hostel EN1 .. 5 B3
Cheviot Way IG2 .. 57 C5
Chevron Cl E16 .. 99 A1
Chevy Rd UB2 .. 108 A4
Chewton Rd E17 .. 53 A5
Cheylesmore Ho SW1 .. 258 C2
Cheyne Ave E18 .. 54 D6
Twickenham TW2 .. 151 B3
Cheyne Cl 6 NW4 .. 46 B4
Keston Mark BR2 .. 226 A5
Cheyne Ct SW3 .. 267 C6
1 Croydon CR0 .. 221 D6
4 Wallington SM6 .. 219 B2
Cheyne Gdns
SW3 .. 136 C6 267 B5
Cheyne Hill KT5 .. 198 B5
Cheyne Mews
SW3 .. 136 C6 267 B5
Cheyne Path W7 .. 86 D1
Cheyne Rd TW15 .. 171 B4
Cheyne Row
SW3 .. 136 C6 267 A5
Cheyne Wlk NW4 .. 46 C3
SW10 .. 136 B5 266 C4
Croydon CR0 .. 222 A6
Southgate N21 .. 16 D6
Cheyney Ho 2 E9 .. 74 D2
Cheyneys Ave HA8 .. 25 D4
Chichele Gdns CR0 .. 221 C4
Chichele Rd NW2 .. 68 D3
Chicheley Gdns HA3 .. 24 A3
Chicheley Rd HA3 .. 24 A3
Chicheley St SE1 .. 250 D2
Chichelle Ho HA8 .. 26 B6
Chichester Ave HA4 .. 61 B6
Chichester Cl E6 .. 100 A1
SE3 .. 143 C4
Hampton TW12 .. 173 B4
Chichester Ct
Edgware HA8 .. 26 C4
Harrow HA2 .. 41 B1
Northolt UB5 .. 85 A6
3 Sidcup DA5 .. 169 C4
Stanmore HA7 .. 44 A6
Stanwell TW19 .. 148 A3
Chichester Gdns IG1 .. 56 B2
Chichester Ho NW6 .. 91 C5
2 Kingston KT2 .. 176 D2
Chichester Mews
SE27 .. 182 C6
Chichester Rd E11 .. 76 C5
NW6 .. 91 C5
W2 .. 91 D2
Edmonton N9 .. 18 A3
South Croydon CR0 .. 221 C5
Chichester Rents WC2 .. 241 A2
Chichester St
SW1 .. 115 C1 259 B1
Chichester Way E14 .. 120 B2
Feltham TW14 .. 150 C4
Chicksand Ho 13 E1 .. 96 A2
Chicksand St
E1 .. 95 D2 243 D3
Chiddingfold N12 .. 13 C1
Chiddingstone SE13 .. 164 A6
Chiddingstone Ave
DA7 .. 147 B5
Chiddingstone St
SW6 .. 135 C3
Chieveley Par DA7 .. 147 D2
Chieveley Rd DA7 .. 147 D1
Chignell Pl 7 W13 .. 109 A5
Chigwell Hill E1 .. 118 B6
Chigwell Hurst Ct HA5 .. 40 D6
Chigwell Rd
Wanstead E18 .. 55 B6
Woodford IG8 .. 37 D3
Chilam Ho 5 SE15 .. 140 C6
Chilchester Ct 13 BR3 .. 207 D6
Chilcombe Ho 6
SW15 .. 156 A4
Chilcot Cl 13 E14 .. 97 D1
Chilcott Cl HA0 .. 65 C4
Child Ct E11 .. 54 B2
Childebert Rd SW17 .. 159 B2
Childeric Prim Sch
SE14 .. 141 A5
Childeric Rd SE14 .. 141 A5
Childerley St
SW6 .. 135 A4 264 A2
Childerly KT1 .. 198 C6
Childers St SE8 .. 141 B6
Child La SE10 .. 120 D3
Childs Ct UB3 .. 106 A6
Child's Hill Prim Sch
NW2 .. 69 A5
Childs La 11 SE19 .. 183 C4
Child's Pl SW5 .. 255 B3
Child's St SW5 .. 255 B3
Childs Way NW11 .. 47 B4
Child's Wlk SW5 .. 255 B3
Chilham Cl DA5 .. 169 B4
Wembley UB6 .. 87 A5
Chilham Ct 14 SW9 .. 138 C2

Chilham Ho SE1 262 D6
Chilham Rd SE9 188 A6
Chilham Way BR2 209 A2
Chillerton Rd SW17 181 B5
Chillingford Ho SW17 180 A6
Chillingworth Gdns
TW1 152 D1
Chillingworth Rd N7 72 C3
Chilmark Gdns KT3 200 A3
Chilmark Rd SW16 181 D2
Chiltern Ave
Bushey WD23 8 A5
Twickenham TW2 151 C3
Chiltern Cl
Ickenham UB10 60 C6
North Cheam KT4 216 C6
South Croydon CR0 221 C5
Bushey WD23 8 A5
Chiltern Ct N10 31 A1
NW1 237 D5
[15] SE14 140 C5
[11] SE9 166 C5
Harrow HA1 42 B4
Hillingdon UB8 82 D3
New Barnet EN5 14 A6
Chiltern Dene EN2 4 B1
Chiltern Dr KT5 198 D4
Chiltern Gdns NW2 68 D5
Beckenham BR2 208 D5
Chiltern Ho [5] N16 51 D1
SE17 139 B6
[4] W10 91 A2
Ealing W5 88 A2
[5] Edmonton N9 18 A1
Chiltern Rd Bow E3 97 C3
Ilford IG2 57 C4
Pinner HA5 40 C4
Chiltern St W1 93 A2 238 A4
Chiltern Way IG8 21 A1
Chilthorne Cl SE6 163 B4
Chilton Ave W5 109 D2
Chilton Gr SE8 119 A2
Chiltonian Ind Est
SE12 164 D5
Chilton Rd Edgware HA8 26 C4
Richmond TW9 132 C2
Chilton St E2 95 D3 243 D6
Chiltons The [1] E18 37 A1
Chilvers Cl TW2 152 C2
Chilver St SE10 120 D1
Chilwell Gdns WD19 22 C6
Chilworth Ct [8] SW19 156 D3
Chilworth Gdns SM1 218 A5
Chilworth Mews
W2 92 B1 236 C1
Chilworth St
W2 92 A1 236 B1
Chimes Ave N13 32 D6
Chimney Ct [23] E1 118 B5
Chimneys Ct [2] SW19 178 C3
China Ct [1] E1 118 B5
China Mews [17] SW2 160 B4
Chinbrook Cres SE12 165 B1
Chinbrook Rd SE12 165 B1
Chinchilla Dr TW4 128 C3
Chindit Ho [11] N16 73 B4
Chine The N10 49 C5
Southgate N21 16 D6
Wembley HA0 65 B3
Ching Ct E4 20 C1
Chingdale Rd E4 20 C1
Chingford Ave E4 19 D2
Chingford CE Inf Sch
E4 20 B3
Chingford CE Jun Sch
E4 20 B3
Chingford Foundation Sch
E4 19 D3
Chingford Hall Com Prim
Sch E4 35 B4
Chingford Hospl E4 20 A1
Chingford Ind Ctr E4 35 A5
Chingford La IG8 36 D5
Chingford Mount Rd
E4 35 C5
Chingford Rd
Chingford E17 35 D1
Chingford E4 35 C3
Chingford Sch E4 19 D3
Chingford Sta E4 20 C4
Chingley Cl BR1 186 C4
Ching Way E4 35 B4
Chinnery Cl EN1 5 D4
Chinnocks Wharf E14 119 A6
Chinnor Cres UB6 86 A5
Chipka St E14 120 A4
Chipley St SE14 141 A6
Chipmunk Gr UB5 85 A4
Chippendale Ho SW1 258 D1
Chippendale St E5 74 D5
Chippenham [4] KT1 176 B1
Chippenham Ave HA9 66 D3
Chippenham Cl HA5 39 D5
Chippenham Gdns
NW6 91 C4
Chippenham Mews W9 91 C3
Chippenham Rd W9 91 C3
Chipperfield Rd BR5 190 A1
Chipping Cl EN5 1 A2
Chip St SW4 137 D1
Chipstead Ave CR7 204 D5
Chipstead Cl SE19 183 D3
Chipstead Gdns NW2 68 B6
Chipstead Ho [4] SW2 160 A3
Chipstead St SW6 135 C3
Chirk Cl UB4 85 A3
Chisenhale Prim Sch
E3 97 A5
Chisenhale Rd E3 97 A5
Chisholm Ct W6 112 A1
Chisholm Rd
Croydon CR0 221 C6
[13] Richmond TW10 154 B5
Chisledon Wlk E9 75 B2
Chislehurst Ave N12 30 A3
Chislehurst High St
BR7 188 D4
Chislehurst Rd BR6 211 D2
Bromley BR1,BR7 188 A2
Orpington,Petts Wood
BR5,BR6,BR7 211 C4
Richmond TW10 154 A6
Sidcup DA14 190 A5
Chislehurst & Sidcup Gram
Sch DA15 168 B2
Chislehurst Sta BR7 188 C1
Chislehurst St Nicholas CE
Prim Sch BR7 189 A3
Chislet [5] NW5 71 A2
Chislet Cl BR3 185 C3
Chisley Rd [5] N15 51 C3
Chiswell Sq SE3 143 B3
Chiswell St EC1 95 B2 242 C4
Chiswick & Bedford Park
Prep Sch W4 111 C2
Chiswick Cl CR0 220 B5
Chiswick Common Rd
W4 111 B2
Chiswick Com Sch
W4 133 B5
Chiswick Ct HA5 41 B6
Chiswick Green Studios [1]
W4 111 A2
Chiswick High Rd W4 111 C2
Chiswick High Road (North Circular Rd) W4 110 C1
Chiswick Ho* W4 133 B6
Chiswick La W4 111 C1
Chiswick La S W4 133 D6
Chiswick Mall W4 111 D1
Chiswick Maternity Hospl
W4 111 D1
Chiswick Park Sta W4 111 A2
Chiswick Pier W4 133 D5
Chiswick Pk W4 110 D2
Chiswick Plaza W4 133 A6
Chiswick Quay W4 133 A4
Chiswick Rd Acton W4 111 A2
Edmonton N9 18 A2
Chiswick Rdbt W4 110 C1
Chiswick Sq W4 133 C6
Chiswick Sta W4 133 A5
Chiswick Staithe W4 133 A4
Chiswick Terr [6] W4 111 A2
Chiswick Village W4 132 D6
Chiswick Wharf W4 133 D6
Chitterfield Gate UB7 126 C5
Chitty's La RM8 80 D6
Chitty St W1 93 C2 239 B4
Chivalry Rd SW11 158 C6
Chivelston [27] SW19 156 D3
Chivenor Gr KT2 175 D5
Chivers Rd E4 35 D6
Choats Rd IG11 102 D4
Chobham Gdns SW19 156 D2
Chobham Rd E15 76 B3
Cholmeley Cres N6 49 B2
Cholmeley Ct N12 30 A6
Cholmeley Lo N6 49 B1
Cholmeley Pk N6 49 B2
Cholmley Gdns NW6 69 C3
Cholmley Rd KT7 197 B3
Cholmondeley Ave
NW10 90 A5
Cholmondeley Wlk
TW9 153 C6
Chopin's Ct [13] E1 118 B5
Chopwell Cl E15 76 B1
Chorleywood Cres
BR5 190 A1
Choumert Gr SE15 140 A3
Choumert Mews SE15 140 A3
Choumert Rd SE15 139 D3
Choumert Sq [2] SE15 140 A3
Chow Sq [2] E8 73 D3
Chrisp Ho SE10 142 C6
Chrisp St E14 97 D1
Christabel Cl TW7 130 C2
Christchurch Ave N12 30 A4
NW6 69 A1
Harrow HA3 42 D5
Harrow HA3 43 A5
[4] Teddington TW11 175 A5
Wembley HA0 66 A2
Christ Church Bentinck CE
Prim Sch NW1 92 C2 237 B4
Christ Church CE Mid Sch
W5 109 D6
Christchurch CE Prim Sch
SW3 136 D6 267 C6
Christ Church CE Prim Sch
NW6 69 B1
SE10 120 C1
SE18 144 C4
SW11 136 C2
Forest Hill SE23 162 D2
Kingston KT3 199 C6
Christ Church CE Sch
E1 95 D2 243 D3
Christ Church CE Sec Sch
N12 30 B5
Christchurch Cl N12 30 B3
Enfield EN2 5 A3
Mitcham SW19 180 B3
Christ Church Ct NW10 89 C6
NW6 69 A1
Christchurch Ct UB4 84 C3
Christchurch Gdns HA3 43 A5
Christchurch Gn HA0 66 A2
Christchurch Hill NW3 70 B4
Christchurch Ho [2]
SW2 160 A3
Christ Church La EN5 1 A3
Christchurch Lo EN4 2 D1
Christchurch Pas NW3 70 A5
Christchurch Pk SM2 218 A1
Christ Church Prim Sch,
Hampstead NW3 70 B5
Christchurch Rd DA15 167 D1
Christ Church Rd N8 50 A3
Christchurch Rd
Harlington TW6 126 C2
Ilford IG1 57 A1
Mitcham SW19 180 B3
Mortlake SW14 155 A6
Surbiton KT5 198 B3
Christ Church Rd [1]
BR3 185 C1
Christ Church Sch
NW1 93 B4 231 D2
Christ Church Sq [4] E9 96 C6
Christchurch St
SW3 136 D6 267 C6
Christ Church Streatham CE
Prim Sch SW2 160 B3
Christchurch Terr
SW3 267 C6
Christchurch Way
SE10 120 C1
Christian Ct SE16 119 B5
Christian Fields SW16 182 C3
Christian St E1 96 A1
Christie Ct [1] N19 72 A6
NW3 70 C3
Christie Dr SE25 206 A4
Christie Gdns RM6 58 B2
Christie Ho DA6 169 D6
[2] SE10 120 D1
[4] West Wickham BR4 207 D1
Christie Rd E9 75 A2
Christina Sq N4 50 D1
Christina St EC2 243 A6
Christine Worsley Cl
N21 16 D3
Christopher Ave W7 109 A3
Christopher Boone's Almshouses SE13 142 B1
Christopher Cl DA15 167 D6
SE16 118 D4
Christopher Ct
Ashford TW15 170 A5
Barnet EN5 1 D1
[6] Croydon CR0 206 A1
Christopher Gdns RM9 80 D3
Christopher Hatton Prim
Sch EC1 94 C3 241 A5
Christopher Lo [2] N6 49 D2
Christopher Pl NW1 232 D1
Christopher Rd UB2 106 B2
Christopher St
EC2 95 B3 242 D5
Christ's Coll NW11 47 D6
SE3 143 A4
Christ's Coll Upper Sch
N3 29 B1
Christ's Sch (East Side)
TW10 154 C6
Christ's Sch (West Side)
TW10 154 B6
Christ the King RC Fst Sch
TW19 148 A5
Christ the King RC Prim Sch
N4 72 B6
Christ the King RC Sixth
Form Coll SE13 142 B2
Chryssell Rd SW9 138 C5
Chubworthy St SE14 141 A6
Chudleigh [1] DA14 190 B6
Chudleigh Cres IG3 79 C4
Chudleigh Gdns SM1 218 A5
Chudleigh Rd NW6 68 D1
SE4 163 C6
Twickenham TW1,TW2 152 D4
Chudleigh St E1 96 D1
Chudleigh Way HA4 40 A1
Chulsa Rd SE26 184 B5
Chumleigh Gdns SE5 139 C6
Chumleigh St SE5 139 C6
Chumleigh Wlk KT5 198 B5
Church App SE21 161 B1
Church Ave DA14 190 B5
N2 30 B2
NW1 71 B2
Beckenham BR3 185 C2
Chingford E4 36 B4
Mortlake SW14 133 B2
Northolt UB5 63 B1
Pinner HA5 41 B3
Ruislip HA4 39 B1
Southall UB2 107 A3
Churchbank E17 53 C5
Churchbury Cl EN1 5 C3
Churchbury La EN1 5 C3
Churchbury Rd SE9 165 D4
Enfield EN1 5 C3
Church Cl HA8 27 A5
N20 14 C1
W8 245 C2
Hayes UB4 83 B2
Hounslow TW4 129 B3
West Drayton UB7 104 A3
Church Cres E9 74 D1
N10 49 B5
N20 14 C1
N3 29 B2
Churchcroft Cl SW12 159 A4
Church Ct EC4 241 B1
N2 48 B6
Forest Hill SE26 185 A5
[27] Richmond TW10 153 D6
Churchdale Ct [1] W4 110 D1
Churchdown BR1 186 C6
Church Dr NW9 45 B1
Coney Hall BR4 224 C5
Harrow HA2 41 C3
Church Elm La RM10 81 C2
Church End E17 53 D5
Hendon NW4 46 B6
Church Entry EC4 241 D1
Church Estate Almshouses
[8] TW9 132 B1
Church Farm House Mus*
NW4 46 B6
Church Farm La SM3 217 A2
Churchfield Ave N12 30 B4
Churchfield Cl
Harrow HA2 42 A5
Hayes UB3 105 D6
Churchfield Ho W2 236 C5
Churchfield Mans [5]
SW6 135 B3
Churchfield Pl TW17 192 D2
Churchfield Prim Sch
N9 17 D3
Churchfield Rd DA16 146 A2
W3 111 A5
W7 108 C4
Ealing W13 109 C5
Walton-on-T KT12 194 A1
Churchfields SE10 142 A6
East Molesey KT8 195 C6
Woodford E18 37 A2
Churchfields Ave
TW13 151 C1
Churchfields Sch SE2 124 A2
Churchfields Inf Sch
E18 37 A2
Churchfields Prim Sch
BR3 206 D6
Churchfields Rd BR3 185 A1
Churchfield Way N12 30 A4
Church Garth [3] N19 71 D6
Church Gate N20 14 C2
Fulham SW6 135 A2
Church Gdns W5 109 D4
Wembley HA0 65 A4
Church Gn [4] SW9 138 C3
Hayes UB3 83 D1
Church Gr SE13 163 D6
Teddington KT1 175 C1
Church Hill E17 53 D5
SE18 122 B3
Harrow HA1 42 C1
Southgate N21 16 C4
Wallington SM5 218 D3
Wimbledon SW19 179 B5
Church Hill Prim Sch
EN4 14 D4
Church Hill Rd E17 53 D5
Cheam SM1,SM3 217 A4
East Barnet EN4 14 D4
Kingston KT6 198 A4
Church Hill Wood
BR5 211 D4
Church Hyde SE18 145 C6
Churchill Ave
Harrow HA3 43 B3
Hillingdon UB10 82 D4
Churchill Cl
East Bedfont TW14 149 D3
Hillingdon UB10 82 D4
Churchill Ct [4] BR6 227 A3
Churchill Ct *continued*
N4 50 C2
NW2 68 B3
Edmonton N9 17 B3
Harrow HA2 41 D4
[7] Ilford IG1 78 D5
Northolt UB5 63 C3
Churchill Gardens Prim Sch
SW1 115 C1 259 B1
Churchill Gdns
SW1 137 C6 269 A6
Acton W3 88 C1
Churchill Gdns Rd
SW1 137 C6 269 A6
Churchill Ho TW8 109 C1
Churchill Lo IG8 36 D4
Churchill Mews IG8 36 D4
Churchill Pl E14 119 D5
Harrow HA1 42 C5
Churchill Rd NW2 68 B2
NW5 71 B4
Edgware HA8 26 C4
Newham E16 99 C1
South Croydon CR2 221 A1
Churchill Terr E4 19 C1
Churchill Way BR1 187 A1
Ashford TW16 172 A4
Churchill Wlk E9 74 C3
Church La E11 54 C1
E17 53 D5
N2 48 B6
N8 50 B5
NW9 45 B2
W5 109 D4
Chessington KT9 214 B2
Chislehurst BR7 189 A2
Dagenham RM10 81 D1
Edmonton N9 18 A2
Enfield EN1 5 B2
Harrow HA3 24 D2
Keston Mark BR2 210 A1
Pinner HA5 41 B6
Teddington TW11 174 D5
Thames Ditton KT7 197 A3
Tottenham N17 33 C2
Twickenham TW1 153 A3
Upper Tooting SW17 181 A5
Wallington SM6 219 D5
Merton SW19 179 C2
Churchley Rd SE26 184 B6
Churchley Villas SE26 184 B6
Church Lo UB5 63 B1
Church Manor Way
SE18,SE2 124 A2
Church Mdw KT6 213 C6
Church Mead SE5 139 A5
Churchmead Cl EN4 14 C5
Church Mead Inf Sch
E10 53 C1
Church Mead Jun Sch
E10 53 C1
Churchmead Rd NW10 68 A2
Churchmore Rd SW16 181 D2
Church Mount N2 48 B4
Church Paddock Ct
SM6 219 D5
Church Par TW15 170 B6
Church Path E17 53 D5
W4 111 A3
Merton SW19 179 C1
Mitcham CR4 202 C6
Wanstead E11 55 A4
Church Pl SW1 249 B5
W5 109 D4
Mitcham CR4 202 C6
Uxbridge UB10 61 A5
Church Rd BR1,BR2 187 A1
BR6 227 B3
DA16 146 B3
E10 75 C6
E12 78 A3
E17 35 A1
[21] N1 73 A2
N6 49 A3
NW10 67 C1
NW4 46 C5
Acton W3 111 A4
Ashford TW15 170 B6
Barking IG11 79 A2
Barnes SW13 134 A4
Beckenham BR2 208 C6
Bexley DA6,DA7 147 B2
Buckhurst Hill IG9 21 B3
Cheam SM3 217 A2
Claygate KT10 212 D1
Croydon CR0 221 A5
Ealing W7 108 C6
East Molesey KT8 196 B6
Enfield EN3 18 C6
Feltham TW13 172 D5
Hayes UB3 105 D6
Heston TW5 128 B6
Heston TW5 129 C5
Hillingdon UB8 82 A3
Hounslow TW7 130 C5
Ilford IG2 57 C3
Keston BR2 225 D1
Kingston KT1 176 B1
Long Ditton KT6 197 C1
Church Rd *continued*
Lower Halliford TW17 192 D
Mitcham CR4,SW19 180 B
New Malden KT4 199 C
Northolt UB5 85 A
Richmond TW10,TW9 154 A
Richmond, Ham Common
TW10 176 A
Sidcup DA14 190 A
Southall UB2 107 B
South Norwood SE19 183 C
Stanmore HA7 25 B
Teddington TW11 174 D
Tottenham N17 33 D
Wallington SM6 219 D
West Drayton UB7 104 A
West Ewell KT19 215 B
Wimbledon SW19 179 A
Mitcham CR4 202 C
Church Rd N N2 30 B
Church Rd S N2 30 B
Church Rise
Chessington KT9 214 B
Forest Hill SE23 162 D
Church Row NW3 70 A
Chislehurst BR7 189 A
Church Row Mews
BR7 189 A
Church Sq TW17 192 D
Church St E15 98 D6
E16 122 D5
NW8 92 C3 237 A5
Chiswick W4 133 D6
Croydon CR0 221 A6
Dagenham RM10 81 D2
Edmonton N9 17 C2
Enfield EN2 5 B2
Hampton TW12 174 A2
Isleworth TW7 131 B3
Kingston KT1 175 D
Sunbury TW16 194 B6
Twickenham TW1 153 A3
Walton-on-T KT12 194 A2
Church St N E15 98 C6
Church Stretton Rd
TW3 152 A6
Church St Sta CR0 221 A6
Church Terr SE13 142 C2
Hendon NW4 46 B6
[20] Richmond TW10 153 D6
Church Vale N2 48 D6
Forest Hill SE23 162 D2
Churchview Rd TW2 152 B2
Church Villa TW16 194 B6
Churchward Ho SE17 138 D6
SW5 254 D1
Churchway NW1 232 D2
Church Way N20 14 C1
Churchway EN4 2 D1
Church Wlk N16 73 B4
NW2 69 B5
NW9 67 B6
Barnes SW13 134 A4
Brentford TW8 131 C6
Hayes UB3 83 D1
Mitcham SW16 181 C1
[15] Richmond TW10 153 D6
Thames Ditton KT7 196 D3
Walton-on-T KT12 194 A1
West Barnes SW20 200 C6
Churchwood Gdns IG8 37 A6
Churchyard Row
SE11 116 D2 261 D4
Churnfield [2] N4 72 C6
Churston Ave E13 99 B6
Churston Cl [17] SW2 160 C3
Churston Dr SM4 201 A4
Churston Gdns N11 31 C4
Churston Mans WC1 240 D5
Churton Pl SW1 259 B3
Brentford W4 132 D6
Churton St
SW1 115 C2 259 B3
Chute Ho [10] SW9 138 C3
Chuter Ede Ho SW6 264 D5
Chyngton Cl DA15 167 D1
Chyngton Ct HA1 64 C6
Cibber Rd SE23 162 D2
Cicada Rd SW18 158 A6
Cicely Ho NW8 229 D3
Cicely Rd SE15 140 A4
Cinderford Way BR1 186 C6
Cinema Par RM8 81 B6
Cinnabar Wharf Central [17]
E1 118 A5
Cinnabar Wharf East [16]
E1 118 A5
Cinnabar Wharf West [18]
E1 118 A5
Cinnamon Cl [8] SE15 139 D5
Thornton Heath CR0 204 A2
Cinnamon Row [3]
SW11 136 A2
Cinnamon St E1 118 B5
Cinnamon Wharf SE1 253 D2
Cinque Cotts SW19 178 C4
Cintra Ct SE19 183 D4
Cintra Pk SE19 183 D3
Circle Ct HA0 65 D4

rcle Gdns SW19 ....179 C1
rcle Ho 12 E14 ....98 B1
rcle The NW2 ....67 C5
W7 ....27 B4
E1 ....253 D2
rcuit Rd SE28 ....124 A4
rcuits The HA5 ....40 C5
ircular Rd N17 ....51 D6
N2 ....30 B2
rcular Way SE18 ....144 C6
rcus Lo NW8 ....229 C2
rcus Mews W1 ....237 C4
rcus Pl EC2 ....242 D3
rcus Rd NW8 .92 B5 229 C3
rcus St SE10 ....142 A5
irencester St W2 ......91 D2
irrus 17 NW9 ....27 D1
issbury Ho 6 SE26 ..162 A1
issbury Rd N15 ....51 B4
issbury Ring N N12 ...29 C5
issbury Ring S N12 ...29 B5
itizen Ho N7 ....72 C4
itizen Rd N7 ....72 C4
itron Terr 3 SE15 ....140 B2
itrus Ho 14 SE8 .....119 B1
ity Airport Pier E16 .120 D5
ity and Islington Coll
EC1 ....94 D4 234 C1
ity Banking Coll
SE1 ....117 B4 252 D2
ity Bsns Ctr 26 SE16 .118 C4
ity Central Est EC1 ..235 A1
ity Forum EC1 95 A4 235 A2
ity Garden Row
N1 ....94 D5 234 D3
ity Gate E1 ....96 C3
ity & Guilds of London Art
Sch The SE11 116 C1 261 B1
ity Harbour E14 .....119 D3
City & Islington Coll
N1 ....95 B6 235 C6
N4 ....72 D6
City Literature Inst The
WC2 ....94 A1 240 B2
City of London Sch
EC4 ....117 A6 252 A6
City of London Sch for Girls
EC2 ....95 A2 242 B4
City of Westminster Coll
NW1 ....92 C2 237 B4
W2 ....92 B2 236 C4
City of Westminster Coll,
Maida Vale Ctr W9 ...91 D4
City of Westminster Coll,
Queens Park Ctr W9 ..91 C4
City Prospect 5 SE19 183 C4
City Rd EC1 .....95 A4 235 B2
City Thameslink Sta
EC4 ....94 D1 241 C1
City Wharf Ho KT7 ....197 B3
Civic Way Ilford IG6 .....57 A5
Ruislip HA4 ....62 D3
Civil Service Coll
SW1 ....115 C2 259 A3
Clabon Mews
SW1 ....114 D2 257 C4
Clack St SE16 ....118 C4
Clacton Rd E17 ....53 A3
E6 ....99 D4
Tottenham N17 ....33 D1
Claigmar Gdns N3 .....29 D2
Claire Ct N12 ....14 A1
NW2 ....69 A2
Bushey WD23 ....8 B3
Claire Gdns HA7 ....25 C5
Claire Pl E14 ....119 C3
Clairvale Rd TW5 ......129 A4
Clairview Rd SW16 ...181 B5
Clairville Gdns W7 ...108 C5
Clairville Point 12
SE23 ....162 D1
Clamp Hill HA7 ....24 C5
Clancarty Rd SW6 .....135 C3
Clandon Cl W3 ....110 D4
Stoneleigh KT17 ....216 A2
Clandon Ct BR1 ....187 A4
Sutton SM2 ....218 B2
Clandon Gdns N3 ......47 C6
Clandon Ho N3 ....47 C6
12 Kingston KT2 ....176 D4
Clandon Rd IG3 ....79 C6
Clandon St SE8 ....141 C3
Clanfield Ho 12 SW15 .156 A3
Clanricarde Gdns
W2 ....113 C6 245 B5
Clapham Common*
SW4 ....137 C1
Clapham Common North
Side SW4 ....137 A1
Clapham Common South
Side SW4 ....159 C6
Clapham Common Sta
SW4 ....137 C1
Clapham Common West
Side
SW11 ....159 A6
SW4,SW11 ....136 D1
Clapham Court Terr 2
SW4 ....160 A6
Clapham Cres SW4 ...137 D1
Clapham Ct 3 SW4 ...160 A6
Clapham High St SW4 137 D1
Clapham High Street Sta
SW4 ....137 D2
Clapham Junction Est
SW11 ....136 C1
Clapham Junction Sta
SW11 ....136 C1
Clapham Manor Ct 1
SW4 ....137 C2
Clapham Manor Prim Sch
SW4 ....137 C2
Clapham Manor St
SW4 ....137 D2
Clapham Mans SW4 ..159 B5
Clapham North Sta
SW4 ....138 A2
Clapham Park Rd
SW4 ....137 D1
Clapham Park Terr 4
SW2 ....160 A6
Clapham Rd
SW9 ....138 B4 270 D2
Clapham South Sta
SW4 ....159 B5
Claps Gate La E6 .....100 D3
Clapton Comm E5 ......52 A2
Clapton Girls Tec Coll
E5 ....74 C4
Clapton Ho 7 E5 ....74 C6
Clapton Pas E5 ....74 C3
Clapton Sq E5 ....74 C3
Clapton Sta E5 ....74 B6
Clapton Terr E5 ....52 A1
Clapton Way E5 ....74 A5
Clara Grant Prim Sch The
E3 ....97 C3
Clara Pl SE18 ....122 C2
Clare Cl N2 ....48 A6
Borehamwood WD6 .....10 B5
Clare Cnr SE9 ....166 D4
Clare Ct BR7 ....188 B2
WC1 ....233 B1
Wimbledon SW19 .....179 A4
Claredale Ct SM2 .....218 A1
Claredale Ho 3 E2 .....96 B5
Claredale St E2 ....96 A5
Clare Gdns E7 ....77 A4
W11 ....91 A1
Barking IG11 ....80 A1
Clare Grant Ho 3 E14 119 C3
Clare Ho 6 E3 ....97 B6
4 HA8 ....27 A1
SE1 ....263 D2
Clare House Prim Sch
BR3 ....186 A1
Clare La N1 ....73 A1
Clare Lawn Ave SW14 .155 B6
Clare Mews SW6 .....265 C3
Clare Mkt WC2 ....240 D1
Claremont
1 Putney SW15 ....157 A6
Shepperton TW17 ......192 D3
Claremont Ave
Harrow HA3 ....44 A4
Sunbury TW16 ....172 B2
West Barnes KT3 ......200 B4
Claremont Cl E16 .....122 C5
N1 ....94 C5 234 B3
Orpington BR6 ....226 C4
4 Streatham SW2 .....160 B3
Claremont Ct 1 W9 ...91 B5
Claremont Dr TW17 ..192 D3
Claremont Gdns
Ilford IG3 ....79 C6
Kingston KT6 ....198 A4
Claremont Gr
Chiswick W4 ....133 C5
Woodford IG8 ....37 C4
Claremont High Sch
HA3 ....44 A4
Claremont Hts EN2 ....4 D1
Claremont La KT10 ...212 A3
Claremont Pk N3 ....29 A2
Claremont Rd BR1 ....210 B5
E17 ....35 A1
E7 ....76 B5
E7 ....77 C3
N6 ....49 C2
W9 ....91 B5
Claygate KT10 ....212 C1
Croydon CR0 ....206 A1
Ealing W13 ....87 A2
Hadley Wood EN4 ....2 B6
Harrow HA3 ....24 C1
Hendon NW2 ....68 D6
Kingston KT6 ....198 A4
Teddington TW11 .....174 D6
Twickenham TW1 .....153 C5
Claremont Sq
N1 ....94 C5 234 A3
Claremont St E16 .....122 C4
SE10 ....141 D6
Edmonton N18 ....34 A4
Claremont Terr KT7 ..197 B2
Claremont Way NW2 ...46 C1
Claremont Way Ind Est
NW2 ....46 C1
Clarence Ave SW4 ....159 D5
Bromley BR1,BR2 .....210 A5
Ilford IG2 ....56 C3
Kingston KT3 ....177 B1
Clarence Cl Bushey WD23 8 D4
New Barnet EN4 ....14 B6
Clarence Cres DA14 ..168 B1
Clarence Ct NW7 ....27 D5
10 W6 ....112 B2
Clarence Gate Gdns
NW1 ....237 D5
Clarence Gdns
NW1 ....93 B4 231 D1
Clarence Ho SE17 .....139 A6
Clarence Ho*
SW1 ....115 C5 249 B3
Clarence La SW15 ....155 D5
Clarence Mews E5 .....74 B3
1 SE16 ....118 D5
Balham SW12 ....159 B4
Clarence Pl 25 E5 ......74 B3
Clarence Rd DA6 ......147 A1
E12 ....77 D3
E16 ....98 C3
E17 ....34 D1
E5 ....74 B4
N15 ....51 A4
NW6 ....69 B1
W4 ....110 C1
Bromley BR1,BR2 .....210 A6
Chislehurst SE9 ....166 A2
Enfield EN3 ....18 C6
Richmond TW9 ....132 C4
Sidcup DA14 ....168 B1
Sutton SM1 ....217 D3
Teddington TW11 .....175 A4
Thornton Heath CR0 ..205 B2
Wallington SM6 ....219 B3
Wimbledon SW19 .....179 D4
Wood Green N22 ....32 A3
Clarence St
Kingston KT1,KT2 .....176 A1
5 Richmond TW9 ......132 A1
Southall UB2 ....106 D3
Clarence Terr NW1 ...237 D6
Hounslow TW3 ....129 D1
Clarence Way NW1 ....71 B1
Clarence Wlk 9 SW4 .138 A3
Clarendon CE Infants Sch
TW15 ....170 B6
Clarendon Cl W2 ......247 A6
37 Hackney E9 ....74 C1
Clarendon Cres TW2 ..152 B1
Clarendon Cross W11 .244 B5
Clarendon Ct NW11 ....47 B5
NW2 ....68 C1
W9 ....236 B6
1 Richmond TW9 ......132 C4
Clarendon Dr SW15 ..134 C1
Clarendon Flats W1 ..238 B1
Clarendon Gdns
W9 ....92 A3 236 B5
Hendon NW4 ....46 B6
Redbridge IG1 ....56 B2
Wembley HA9 ....66 A4
Clarendon Gr NW1 ...232 C2
Mitcham CR4 ....202 D6
Clarendon Ho N12 ......30 A5
NW1 ....232 B3
Clarendon Mews DA5 169 D3
W2 ....247 A6
Clarendon Pl
W2 ....114 C6 247 A6
Clarendon Rd E11 ......54 B1
E17 ....53 D3
N15 ....51 A5
N8 ....50 B6
W11 ....113 A6 244 B5
Ashford TW15 ....170 B6
Croydon CR0 ....220 D6
Ealing W5 ....88 A3
Edmonton N18 ....34 A5
Harrow HA1 ....42 C3
Hayes UB3 ....105 D4
Mitcham SW19 ....180 C3
Wallington SM6 ....219 C2
Wanstead E18 ....55 A6
Wood Green N22 ....32 B1
Clarendon Rise SE13 .142 A1
Clarendon Sch TW12 .173 D4
Clarendon St
SW1 ....115 B1 258 D2
Clarendon Terr W9 ...236 B6
Clarendon Way
BR5,BR7 ....211 D6
Enfield N21 ....17 A5
Clarendon Wlk 10 W11 .91 A1
Clarens St SE6 ....163 B2
Clare Pl SW15 ....156 A4
Clare Point NW2 ....46 D1
Clare Rd E11 ....54 B3
NW10 ....68 A1
SE14 ....141 B4
Hounslow TW4 ....129 B2
Northolt UB6 ....64 B2
Stanwell TW19 ....148 A4
Clare St E2 ....96 B5
Claret Gdns SE25 .....205 C5
Clareville Ct SW7 .....256 B3
Clareville Gr
SW7 ....114 A2 256 B3
Clareville Grove Mews
SW7 ....256 B3
Clareville Rd BR5,BR6 .227 A6
Clareville St
SW7 ....114 A2 256 B3
Clare Way DA7 ....147 A4
Clarewood Ct W1 .....237 C3
Clarewood Wlk SW9 ..138 C1
Clarges Ho W1 ....248 D4
Clarges Mews
W1 ....115 B5 248 C4
Clarges St W1 115 B5 248 D4
Claribel Rd SW9 ......138 D3
Clarice Ct NW4 ....46 B6
Claridge Ct SW6 ......264 C1
Claridge Rd RM8 ....58 D1
Clarissa Ho 7 E14 .....97 D1
Clarissa Rd RM6 ....58 D2
Clarissa St E8 ....95 D6
Clark Ct NW10 ....67 A1
Clarke Ho 2 SW4 .....137 C2
Clarke Mans 8 IG11 ...79 D1
Clarke Mews N9 ....18 B1
Clarke Path N16 ....52 A1
Clarke's Ave KT4,SM3 .216 D6
Clarkes Dr UB8 ....82 A2
Clarkes Mews W1 .....238 B4
Clark Lawrence Ct 11
SW11 ....136 B2
Clarks Mead WD23 ....8 B4
Clarkson Ho SW11 ...136 B1
Clarkson Rd E16 ....98 D1
Clarkson Row NW1 ..232 A3
Clarkson St E2 ....96 B4
Clarksons The IG11 ..101 A5
Clark's Pl EC2 ....243 A2
Clark's Rd IG1 ....79 B6
Clark St E1 ....96 C2
Clark Way TW5 ....128 D5
Classic Mans 33 E9 ....74 C1
Classinghall Ho 14
SW15 ....156 D5
Classon Cl UB7 ....104 A4
Claude Rd E10 ....54 A1
E13 ....99 B6
SE15 ....140 B3
Claude St E14 ....119 C2
Claudia Jones Way
SW2 ....160 A5
Claudia Pl SW19 ......157 A3
Claughton Rd E13 ......99 C5
Clauson Ave UB5 ....64 A3
Clavell St 7 SE10 ....142 A6
Claverdale Rd SW2 ..160 C4
Clavering Ave SW13 ..134 B6
Clavering Cl TW1 .....175 A6
Clavering Ho SE13 ...142 B1
Clavering Rd E12 ....77 D6
Claverings Ind Est N9 ..18 C2
Claverley Gr N3 ....29 D2
Claverley Villas N3 .....29 D3
Claverton St
SW1 ....115 C1 259 B1
Clave St E1 ....118 C5
Claxton Gr W6 112 D1 254 A1
Clay Ave CR4 ....181 B1
Claybank Gr SE13 ....141 D2
Claybourne Mews 2
SE19 ....183 D3
Claybridge Rd SE12 ..187 C6
Claybrook Cl N2 ....48 B6
Claybrook Rd W6 .....134 D6
Claybury Broadway
IG5 ....56 A6
Clay Ct E17 ....54 B6
Claydon SE17 ....262 A4
Claydon Dr CR0 ....220 A4
Claydon Ho NW4 ....28 D1
Claydown Mews SE18 122 C1
Clayfarm Rd SE9 .....167 A2
Claygate Cres CR0 ...224 B2
Claygate La
Hinchley Wood KT10 ..213 A6
Thames Ditton KT7 ....197 A1
Claygate Lodge Cl
KT10 ....212 C1
Claygate Prim Sch
KT10 ....212 C1
Claygate Rd W13 .....109 B3
Claygate Sta KT10 ...212 C2
Clayhall Ct 16 E3 ....97 B5
Clay Hill EN2 ....5 B6
Clayhill Cres SE12,SE9 187 D6
Clay La WD23 ....8 C4
Claylands Ct SE19 ...183 B5
Claylands Pl SW8 ....138 C5
Claylands Rd
SW8 ....138 B6 270 D5
Claymill Ho 2 SE18 ..123 A1
Claymore Ct SM3,SM4 .201 C2
Claypole Ct E17 ....53 C4
Claypole Dr TW5 ......129 A4
Claypole Rd E15 ....98 A5
Claypoinds Ave TW8 ..110 A2
Clayponds Gdns W5 ..109 D2
Clayponds Hospl & Day
Treatment Ctr TW8 ..110 A2
Clayponds La TW8 ....110 A1
Clays Ct N16 ....51 D1
Clays La E15 ....75 D3
Clays Lane Cl E15 ......75 D3
Clay St W1 .....92 D2 237 D3
Clayton 22 NW9 ....27 D1
Clayton Ave HA0 ....66 A1
Clayton Bsns Ctr UB3 .105 C4
Clayton Cl 3 E6 ....100 B1
Clayton Cres TW8 ....109 D1
Clayton Ct E17 ....35 A1
N16 ....52 A2
Clayton Field NW9 .....27 C2
Clayton Ho 22 E9 ....74 C1
Long Ditton KT7 ....197 B1
Clayton Mews SE10 ..142 B4
Clayton Rd SE15 ......140 A4
Chessington KT10,KT9 ..213 D4
Hayes UB3 ....105 C4
Isleworth TW7 ....130 C2
Clayton St SE11 ......138 C6
Clayton Terr UB4 ....84 D2
Claytonville Terr
DA17 ....125 D4
Clay Wood Cl BR6 ....211 C2
Clayworth Cl DA15 ...168 B5
Cleanthus Cl SE18 ...144 D4
Cleanthus Rd SE18 ..144 D4
Clearbrook Way 13 E1 .96 C1
Clearmont Ho UB2 ...107 C3
Clearwater Ho 9
TW10 ....154 A6
Clearwater Pl KT6 ...197 C3
Clearwater Terr 4
W11 ....112 D4
Clearwell Dr W9 ....91 D3
Cleave Ave Hayes UB3 .105 C2
Orpington BR6 ....227 C2
Cleaveland Rd KT6 ..197 D4
Cleaver Ho 6 NW3 ....70 D1
Cleaverholme Cl SE25 206 B3
Cleaver Sq
SE11 ....116 C1 261 B1
Cleaver St
SE11 ....116 C1 261 B2
Cleave's Almshos 1
KT2 ....176 A1
Cleeve Ct N10 ....31 B3
East Bedfont TW14 ...149 C3
Cleeve Hill SE23 ......162 B3
Cleeve Ho 16 E2 ....95 C4
Cleeve Park Gdns
DA14 ....168 B2
Cleeve Park Sch DA14 168 C1
Cleeve Way SW15 ....
Clegg Ho SE3 ....143 B1
Clegg St 16 E1 ....118 B5
E13 ....99 A5
Cleland Ho 20 E2 ......96 C5
Clematis Gdns IG8 .....37 A5
Clematis St W12 ......112 A6
Clem Attlee Ct
SW6 ....135 B6 264 D5
Clemence St E14 ....97 B2
Clement Attlee Ho
NW10 ....67 D1
Clement Ave SW4 ....137 D1
Clement Cl NW6 ....68 C1
W4 ....111 B2
Clement Gdns UB3 ...105 C2
Clement Ho 14 SE8 ..119 A2
W10 ....90 C2
Clementhorpe Rd RM9 .80 C2
Clementina Rd E10 ....53 B1
Clementine Churchill Hospl
The HA1 ....64 D5
Clementine Cl W13 ..109 B4
Clement Rd Penge BR3 184 D1
Wimbledon SW19 .....179 A5
Clements Ave 1 E16 .121 A6
Clements Ct
Hounslow TW4 ....128 D1
5 Ilford IG1 ....78 D5
Clements Inn
WC2 ....94 B1 240 D1
Clements Inn Pas
WC2 ....240 D1
Clement's La
EC2,EC4 .....117 B6 252 D6
Clements La IG1 ....78 D5
Clements Pl TW8 .....109 D1
Clements Rd E6 ....78 B1
Clement's Rd SE16 ...118 B3
Clements Rd IG1 ....78 D5
Clemson Ho 9 E8 ......95 D6
Clendon Way SE18 ..123 B2
Clenham St SE1 ......252 B2
Clensham Ct SM3 ....217 C6
Clensham La SM1 ...217 C6
Clenston Mews W1 ..237 C2
Clent Ho 4 N16 ....51 D1
Cleopatra's Needle*
WC2 ....116 B5 250 C5
Clephane Rd 6 N1 ....73 A2
Clephane Rd N N1 .....73 A2
Clephane Rd S N1 .....73 B2
Clere Pl EC2 ....242 D6
Clere St EC2 ...95 B3 242 D6
Clerics Wlk TW17 ....193 B3
Clerkenwell Cl
EC1 ....94 C3 241 B5
Clerkenwell Gn
EC1 ....94 D3 241 C5
Clerkenwell Parochial CE
Prim Sch EC1 .94 C4 234 A2
Clerkenwell Rd
EC1 ....94 D3 241 C5
Clermont Rd E9 ....96 C6
Cleveden Ct CR2 ......221 C3
Clevedon Ct SW11 ...267 A2
Dulwich SE21 ....161 B1
Clevedon Gdns
Cranford TW5 ....128 B4
Hayes UB3 ....105 B3
Clevedon Mans NW5 ...71 A4
Clevedon Rd
Kingston KT1 ....176 C1
Penge SE20 ....184 D2
Twickenham TW1 .....153 D5
Cleve Ho NW6 ....69 D1
Cleveland Ave W4 ....111 D2
Hampton TW12 ....173 B3
Merton SW20 ....179 B1
Cleveland Cres WD6 ...11 A6
Cleveland Ct Ealing W13 87 B2
Southall UB2 ....107 D2
Cleveland Gdns N4,N15 51 A4
W2 ....92 A1 236 A1
Barnes SW13 ....133 D3
Hendon NW2 ....68 D6
Worcester Park KT4 ..215 D6
Cleveland Gr 33 E1 ....96 C3
Cleveland Ho 7 N2 ....30 B1
Cleveland Inf Sch IG1 .78 D5
Cleveland Jun Sch IG1 78 D5
Cleveland Mans
4 NW6 ....69 B1
3 SW9 ....138 C5
W9 ....91 C3
Cleveland Mews W1 ..239 A4
Cleveland Park Ave
E17 ....53 C5
Cleveland Park Cres
E17 ....53 C5
Cleveland Pk TW19 ...148 A5
Cleveland Pl SW1 ....249 B4
Cleveland Rd DA16 ..145 D3
N1 ....73 B1
14 W4 ....111 A3
Barnes SW13 ....133 D3
Ealing W13 ....87 B2
Edmonton N9 ....18 B4
Ilford IG1 ....78 D5
Isleworth TW7 ....131 A1
New Malden KT3 .....199 C5
Wanstead E18 ....55 A6
Worcester Park KT4 ..215 C6
Cleveland Rise SM4 .200 D2
Cleveland Row
SW1 ....115 C5 249 B3
Cleveland Sq
W2 ....92 A1 236 A1
Cleveland St
W1 ....93 C3 239 A5
Clevelands The IG11 ...79 A2
Cleveland Terr
W2 ....92 A1 236 B2
Cleveland Way E1 ......96 C3
Cleveley Cres W5 ......88 B5
Cleveleys Rd E5 ....74 B5
Clevely Cl SE7 ....121 D2
Clevendon Cl N16 ......73 D5
Cleve Rd DA14 ....168 D1
NW6 ....69 D1
Cleverly Cotts W12 ..111 D5
Cleverly Est W12 .....112 A6
Cleves Ct KT6 ....198 A3
Cleves Prim Sch E6 ...99 D6
Cleves Rd E6 ....99 D5
Richmond TW10 ....153 C1
Cleves Way
Ashford TW16 ....171 D4
Hampton TW12 ....173 B3
Ruislip HA4 ....40 D1
Clewer Cres HA3 ....24 B2
Clewer Ct 2 E10 ....53 C1
Clewer Ho 8 SE2 .....124 D4
Cley Ho SE4 ....140 D1
Clichy Ho 22 E1 ....96 C2
Clifden Centre (Richmond
Adult & Com Coll)
TW1 ....152 D3
Clifden Ho 6 TW8 ...131 D6
Clifden Rd E5 ....74 D3
Brentford TW8 ....131 D6
Twickenham TW1 .....152 D3
Cliff Ct 5 NW1 ....71 D2
Cliffe Ho 4 SE10 .....120 D1
Cliffe Rd CR2 ....221 B3
Cliffe Wlk 2 SM1 ....218 A3
Clifford Ave BR7 ......188 B4
Mortlake SW14 ....133 A3
Wallington SM6 ....219 C4
Clifford Cl UB5 ....85 A6
Clifford Ct NW10 ....67 C4

Clifford Ct *continued*
W2 91 D2
Wandsworth SW18 158 B4
Clifford Dr SW9 138 D1
Clifford Gdns NW10 90 C5
Hayes UB3 105 B2
Clifford Gr TW15 170 C6
Clifford Haigh Ho
SW6 134 D5
Clifford Ho W14 254 C3
2 Beckenham BR3 185 D4
Clifford Rd E16 98 D3
N9 18 C5
Barnet EN5 1 D2
Chingford E17 36 A1
Croydon SE25 206 A5
Hounslow TW4 128 D2
Richmond TW10 153 D2
Wembley HA0 87 D6
Clifford's Inn Pas EC4 241 A1
Clifford St W1 115 C6 249 A5
Clifford Way NW10 67 D4
Cliff Rd NW1 71 D2
Cliffsend Ho 23 SW9 138 C4
Cliff Terr SE8 141 C3
Cliffview Rd SE13 141 C2
Cliff Villas NW1 71 D2
Cliff Wlk E16 98 D2
Clifton Ave E17 52 D6
N3 29 B2
Feltham TW13 150 C1
Shepherd's Bush W12 111 D5
Stanmore HA7 25 B1
Wembley HA9 66 B2
Clifton Cl 8 BR6 227 A3
Clifton Cres SE15 140 B5
Clifton Ct N4 72 C6
NW8 236 C6
SE15 140 B5
2 Beckenham BR3 185 D2
Putney SW15 156 D6
South Norwood SE25 205 C4
9 Stanwell TW19 148 A5
Surbiton KT5 198 B2
3 Woodford IG8 37 A4
Clifton Gate SW10 266 A6
Clifton Gdns N15 51 D3
2 NW11 47 B3
W4 111 B2
W9 92 A3 236 A5
Enfield EN2 16 A6
Hillingdon UB10 82 D5
Clifton Gr E8 74 A2
Clifton Hill
NW8 92 A6 229 A5
Clifton Ho E11 76 C6
E2 243 C6
Clifton Lodge (Brunel Univ Coll Twickenham Campus)
TW1 153 B6
Clifton Mans 4 SW9 138 C1
Clifton Mews SE25 205 C5
Clifton Par TW13 172 C6
Clifton Park Ave
SW20 178 C1
Clifton Pl SE16 118 C4
W2 236 D1
Clifton Prim Sch UB2 107 A2
Clifton Rd E16 98 C2
E7 77 D2
N3 30 A2
N8 49 D3
NW10 90 A5
W9 92 A3 236 B6
Bexley DA16 146 C2
Greenford UB6 86 B3
Harlington TW6 126 D2
Harrow HA3 44 B4
Ilford IG2 57 B3
Isleworth TW7 130 C3
Kingston KT2 176 B2
Sidcup DA14 189 C6
Southall UB2 107 A2
South Norwood SE25 205 C5
Teddington TW11 174 C6
Wallington SM6 219 B3
Wimbledon SW19 178 D4
Wood Green N22 31 C2
Clifton Rise SE14 141 A5
Cliftons Roundabout
SE9,SE12 165 C5
Clifton St EC2 95 C3 243 A5
Clifton Terr N4 72 C6
Clifton The KT6 214 A6
Clifton Villas
W9 92 A2 236 A4
Cliftonville Ct SE12 165 A3
Clifton Way SE15 140 C5
Wembley HA0 88 A6
Climsland Ho SE1 251 B4
Clinch Ct 11 E16 99 A2
Cline Ho SW15 156 A6
Cline Rd N11 31 C4
Clinger Ct N1 95 C6
Clink St SE1 117 B5 252 C4
Clinton Ave
Bexley DA16 146 A1
East Molesey KT8 196 A5
Clinton Ho
New Malden KT3 199 B1
6 Surbiton KT6 197 D2
Clinton Rd E3 97 A4
E7 77 A4
N15 51 B5
Clipper Cl 3 SE16 118 D4
Clipper Ho E14 120 A1
Clipper Way SE13 142 A1
Clippesby Cl KT9 214 B2
Clipstone Ho 10 SW15 156 A6
Clipstone Mews W1 239 A4
Clipstone Rd TW3 129 C2
Clipstone St
W1 93 C2 239 A4
Clissold Cl N2 48 D6
Clissold Cres N16 73 B4
Clissold Ct N4 73 A6
Clissold Ho 4 N16 73 B6
Clissold Rd N16 73 B5
Clitheroe Ave HA2 41 C1
Clitheroe Gdns WD19 22 D6
Clitheroe Rd SW9 138 A3
Clitherow Ave W7 109 A3
Clitherow Rd TW8 109 C1
Clitterhouse Cres NW2 46 C1
Clitterhouse Jun & Inf Schs
NW2 68 D6
Clitterhouse Rd NW2 46 C1
Clive Ave N18 34 A4
Clive Ct W9 236 B6
Streatham SW16 181 D5
Tolworth KT6 214 C6
Cliveden Cl N12 30 A6
Cliveden Pl
SW1 115 A2 258 A4
Shepperton TW17 193 A3
Cliveden Rd SW19 179 B2
Clivedon Ct W13 87 B2
Clivedon Rd E4 36 C5
Clive Ho SE10 142 A6
18 SW8 137 D3
3 Croydon CR0 205 D1
Clive Lloyd Ho N15 51 A4
Clive Lo NW4 46 D3
Clive Rd
Belvedere DA17 125 C2
Enfield EN1 6 A1
Feltham TW14 150 A5
Mitcham SW19 180 C4
Teddington TW1 175 A6
West Norwood SE21,
SE27 161 B1
Clivesdale Dr UB3 106 B5
Clive Way EN1 6 A1
Cloak La EC4 117 B6 252 C6
Clochar Ct NW10 89 D6
Clock Ct E11 55 B5
Clock Ho E17 54 B5
N16 51 D2
Clock Ho The EN2 5 D6
Clockhouse Ave IG11 101 A6
Clockhouse Cl SW19 156 C2
Clock House Ct 1
BR3 185 A1
Clockhouse Junc N13 32 C5
Clockhouse La TW14,
TW15 148 D2
Clockhouse Par N13 32 C5
Clock House Par E11 55 B3
Clockhouse Pl SW15 157 A5
Clock House Rd BR3 185 A1
Clockhouse Rdbt
TW14 149 A3
Clock House Sta BR3 185 A2
Clockhouse The SW19 156 C1
Clock Tower Mews
N1 235 B5
Thamesmead SE28 124 B6
Clock Tower Pl N7 72 A2
Clock Tower Rd TW7 130 D2
Cloister Cl TW11 175 B5
Cloister Gdns HA8 27 A5
Croydon SE25 206 B3
Cloister Rd NW2 69 B6
W3 89 A2
Cloisters Ave BR1,BR2 210 B4
Cloisters Ct DA7 147 D2
N6 49 B1
Cloisters The 22 SW9 138 C4
Clonard Way HA5 23 C4
Clonbrock Rd N16 73 C4
Cloncurry St SW6 134 D3
Clone Ct 4 W12 111 C3
Clone The 5 KT2 176 D3
Clonmel Cl HA2 42 B1
Clonmell Rd N17 51 B6
Clonmel Rd TW11 174 B6
Fulham SW6 135 B4 264 D2
Clonmore St SW18 157 B3
Cloonmore Ave BR6 227 D4
Clorane Gdns NW3 69 C5
Close The BR5 211 C3
DA14 190 B5
N10 31 B1
N14 15 D2
Close The *continued*
N20 13 B2
Beckenham BR3 207 A5
Cheam SM3 201 B2
Chingford E4 36 A3
Cockfosters EN4 14 D6
Croydon SE25 206 A3
Dagenham RM6 59 A3
Hillingdon UB10 82 C6
Hounslow TW7 130 B3
Ilford IG2 57 C3
Kingston KT3 177 A1
Mitcham CR4 202 D5
Mortlake TW9 132 D2
Pinner HA5 40 C2
Pinner HA5 41 B2
1 Sidcup DA5 169 C4
Surbiton KT6 198 A3
Wembley HA0 66 A2
Wembley HA9 67 A5
Cloth Ct EC1 241 D3
Cloth Fair EC1 94 D2 241 D3
Clothier Ho SE7 122 A1
Clothier St EC3 243 B2
Cloth St EC1 95 A2 242 A4
Clothworkers Rd SE18 145 B5
Cloudesdale Rd SW17 159 B2
Cloudesley Mans N1 234 B5
Cloudesley Pl
N1 94 C6 234 B5
Cloudesley Rd DA7 147 B4
N1 94 C6 234 A5
Cloudesley Sq
N1 94 C6 234 B6
Cloudesley St
N1 94 C6 234 B5
Clouston Cl SM6 220 A3
Clova Rd E7 77 A3
Clove Cres E14 120 B6
Clovelly Ave NW9 45 D5
Uxbridge UB10 61 A4
Clovelly Cl Pinner HA5 40 C6
Uxbridge UB10 61 A4
Clovelly Ct NW2 68 C3
Clovelly Gdns EN1 17 C4
Clovelly Ho W2 236 A2
Clovelly Rd DA7 147 A6
N8 49 D5
W4 111 B4
W5 109 C4
Hounslow TW3 129 C3
Clovelly Way BR6 211 D3
E1 96 C1
Harrow HA2 63 B6
Clover Cl E11 76 B6
Cloverdale Gdns DA15 167 D5
Clover Ho TW3 130 A4
Cloverleys IG10 21 D6
Clover Mews SW3 267 D6
Clover Way SM6 203 A1
Clove St 9 E13 99 A3
Clowders Rd SE6 163 B1
Clowes Ho 3 SW4 138 A1
Clowser Cl 4 SM1 218 A3
Cloysters Gn E1 118 A5
Cloyster Wood HA8 25 D4
Club Gardens Rd BR2 209 A2
Club Row E2 95 D3 243 C6
Clumps The TW15 171 B6
Clunbury Ave UB2 107 B1
Clunbury St N1 235 D3
Clunie Ho SW1 257 D6
Cluny Mews SW5 255 A3
Cluny Pl SE1 117 C3 263 A6
Cluse Ct N1 235 A4
Clutton St E14 97 D2
Clydach Rd EN1 5 D1
Clyde Cir N15 51 C5
Clyde Ct NW1 232 D4
Clyde Flats SW6 264 C4
Clyde Ho 9 KT2 175 D2
Clyde Pl E10 53 D2
Clyde Rd N15 51 C5
N22 31 D2
Croydon CR0 221 D6
Stanwell TW19 148 A3
Sutton SM1 217 C3
Wallington SM6 219 C2
Clydesdale EN3 6 D1
Clydesdale Ave HA7 43 D6
Clydesdale Cl
Borehamwood WD6 11 B6
Isleworth TW7 130 D2
Clydesdale Ct N20 14 B3
Clydesdale Gdns
TW10 132 D1
Clydesdale Ho DA18 125 A4
4 W11 91 B1
Clydesdale Path WD6 11 B6
Clydesdale Rd W11 91 B1
Clyde St SE8 141 B6
Clyde Terr SE23 162 C2
Clyde Vale SE23 162 C2
Clyfford Rd HA4 61 D4
Clymping Dene TW14 150 B4
Clynes Ho 3 E2 96 D4
6 Dagenham RM10 81 C5
Hayes UB4 84 A4
Clyro Ct N4 50 B1
Clyston St SW8 137 C3
Clytha Ct SE27 183 A6
Coach & Horses Yd
W1 249 A6
Coach House La N5 72 D4
Wimbledon SW19 156 D1
Coach House Mews
SE23 162 D5
Coach House Yd NW3 70 B4
Coachmaker Mews 5
SW9 138 A2
Coachman Lo N12 30 A5
Coalbrook Mans 3
SW12 159 B3
Coaldale Wlk SE21 161 A4
Coalecroft Rd SW15 156 C6
Coalport Ho SE11 261 A4
Coal Wharf Rd W12 112 D5
Coates Ave SW18 158 C5
Coates Ct NW3 70 C3
Coates Hill Rd BR1 188 C1
Coates Rd WD6 9 D4
Coate St E2 96 A5
Coates Wlk TW8 110 A1
Cobbett Rd SE9 144 A2
Twickenham TW2 151 C3
Cobbetts Ave IG4 55 D4
Cobbett St
SW8 138 B5 270 D3
Cobble La N1 72 D1
Cobble Mews N4,N5 73 A5
Cobbler's Wlk
Teddington KT1,TW11 175 A2
Teddington TW11 174 D3
Cobblestone Pl CR0 205 A1
Cobbold Ct SW1 259 C4
Cobbold Ind Est NW10 67 D2
Cobbold Mews W12 111 D4
Cobbold Rd E11 76 D5
NW10 67 D2
W12 111 D4
Cobb's Hall 1 SW6 134 D6
Cobbs Rd TW4 129 B1
Cobb St E1 243 C3
Cob Cl WD6 11 A6
Cobden Bldgs WC1 233 C2
Cobden Ct 9 SE28 124 C5
Cobden Ho 7 E2 96 A4
NW1 232 A4
Cobden Mews SE26 184 B5
Cobden Rd BR6 227 B4
E11 76 C6
Croydon SE25 206 A4
Cobham 21 NW9 27 D1
Cobham Ave KT3 200 A4
Cobham Cl 2 DA15 168 B5
SW11 158 C5
Bromley BR2 210 A2
Edgware HA8 26 D1
Enfield EN1 6 A2
Wallington SM6 220 A2
Cobham Ct CR4 180 B1
Cobham Ho IG11 101 A6
Cobham Mews 3 NW1 71 D1
Cobham Pl DA6 168 D6
Cobham Rd N22 50 D6
Chingford E17 36 A2
Heston TW5 128 C5
Ilford IG3 79 C5
Kingston KT1,KT2 176 C1
Cobland Rd SE12 187 C6
Coborn Mews 9 E3 97 B4
Coborn Rd E3 97 B4
Coborn St E3 97 B4
Cobourg Prim Sch
SE5 139 D6
Cobourg Rd SE5 139 D6
Cobourg St
NW1 93 C4 232 B1
Coburg Cl SW1 259 B4
Coburg Cres SW2 160 C3
Coburg Dwellings 10
E1 118 C6
Coburg Gdns IG5 37 D1
Coburg Rd N22 32 B1
Cochrane Cl NW8 229 D3
Cochrane Ct 3 E10 53 C1
Cochrane Mews
NW8 92 B5 229 D3
Cochrane Rd SW19 179 B3
Cochrane St
NW8 92 B5 229 D3
Coci Ho W14 254 D3
Cockburn Ho SW1 259 D1
Cockerell Rd E17 53 A3
Cockfosters Par EN4 3 A1
Cockfosters Rd EN4 2 D3
Cockfosters Sta EN4 3 A1
Cock Hill E1 243 B3
Cock La EC1 94 D2 241 D3
Cockpit Yd WC1 240 D4
Cocks Cres KT3 199 D5
Cocksett Ave BR6 227 C2
Cockspur Ct SW1 249 D4
Cockspur St
SW1 115 D5 249 D4
Cocksure La DA14 191 C6
Coda Ctr The
SW6 135 A4 264 B2
Code St E1 95 D3 243 D5
Codicote Ho 22 SE8 118 D2
Codicote Terr N4 73 A6
Codling Cl 13 E1 118 A5
Codling Way HA0 65 D4
Codrington Ct SE16 119 A5
Codrington Hill SE23 163 A4
Codrington Ho 7 E1 96 B3
Codrington Mews W11 91 A1
Cody Cl Harrow HA3 43 D6
Wallington SM6 219 D1
Cody Rd E16 98 B3
Coe Ave SE25 206 A3
Coerdale Ct EN3 7 A6
Coe's Alley EN5 1 A1
Cofers Circ HA9 66 D5
Coffey St SE8 141 C5
Cogan Ave E17 35 A2
Cohen Ho NW7 28 A6
Cohen Lo E5 75 A3
Coin St SE1 116 C5 251 A4
Coity Rd NW5 71 A2
Cokers La SE21 161 B3
Coke St E1 96 A1
Colab Ct N22 32 C2
Colas Mews 7 NW6 91 C6
Colbeck Mews
SW5 113 D2 255 D3
Colbeck Rd HA1 42 A2
Colberg Pl N16 51 D2
Colbert 1 SE5 139 D4
Colborne Ho 7 E14 119 C6
Colborne Way KT4 216 C6
Colbrook Ave UB3 105 B3
Colbrook Cl UB3 105 B3
Colburn Ave HA5 23 A4
Colburn Way SM1 218 B5
Colby Rd
Walton-on-T KT12 194 A1
West Norwood SE19 183 C5
Colchester Ave E12 78 B5
Colchester Dr HA5 40 D4
Colchester Ho 17
SW8 137 D3
Colchester Rd E10 54 A2
E17 53 C3
HA8 27 A3
Pinner HA6 22 A1
Colchester St E1 243 D2
Colchester Villas CR7 204 C3
Coldbath Sq EC1 241 A6
Coldbath St SE13 141 D3
Coldblow La SE14 140 D6
Coldershaw Rd W13 109 A4
Coldfall Ave N10 31 A1
Coldfall Prim Sch N10 30 D1
Coldham Ct N22 32 D2
Coldham Gr EN3 7 A6
Coldharbour E14 120 A5
Coldharbour Crest
SE9 166 C1
Coldharbour Ind Est
SE5 139 A3
Coldharbour La SW9 138 D2
Bushey WD23 8 A6
Hayes UB3 106 A5
Coldharbour Lane Ho
UB3 106 A5
Coldharbour Pl SE5 139 B3
Coldharbour Rd CR0 220 C3
Coldharbour Sports Ctr
SE9 166 C2
Coldharbour Way CR0 220 C3
Coldstream Gdns
SW18 157 B5
Colebeck Mews N1 72 D2
Colebert Ave E1 96 C3
Colebert Ho 20 E1 96 C3
Colebrook Cl SW19 156 D4
Colebrook Ct SW3 257 B3
Colebrooke Ave W13 87 B1
Colebrooke Ct DA14 190 B6
Colebrooke Dr E11 55 C2
Colebrooke Pl N1 234 D5
Colebrooke Row
N1 94 D5 234 C4
N1 234 C5
Colebrooke Sch
N1 94 D5 234 D4
Colebrook Ho 1 E14 97 D1
Colebrook Rd SW16 182 A2
Colebrook Rise BR2 186 C1
Colebrook Way N11 31 B5
Coleby Path 21 SE5 139 B5
Colechurch Ho 8 SE1 118 A1
Cole Cl SE28 124 B5
Cole Court Lo 7 TW1 153 A4
Coledale Dr HA7 25 C2
Coleford Rd SW18 158 A6
Cole Gdns TW5 128 A5
Colegrave Prim Sch
E15 76 B3
Colegrave Rd E15 76 B3
Colegrove Rd SE15 139 D6
Coleherne Ct
SW10 113 D1 255 D1
Coleherne Mans SW5 255 D2
Coleherne Mews
SW10 113 D1 255 C1
Coleherne Rd
SW10 113 D1 255
Colehill Gdns SW6 264
Colehill La
SW6 135 A4 264
Cole Ho SE1 251
Coleman Cl SE25 184
Coleman Ct SW18 157
Coleman Fields
N1 95 A6 235
Coleman Mans N19 50
Coleman Rd SE5 139
Belvedere DA17 125
Dagenham RM9 81
Colemans Heath SE9 166
Coleman St EC2 95 B1 242
Coleman St Bldgs EC2 242
Colenso Dr NW7 28
Colenso Rd E5 74
Ilford IG2 57
Cole Park Gdns TW1 153
Cole Park Rd TW1 153
Cole Park View 2
TW1 153
Colepits Wood Rd SE9 167
Coleraine Park Prim Sch
N17 34
Coleraine Rd N8,N22 50
SE3 142
Cole Rd TW1 153
Coleridge Ave E12 78
Carshalton SM1 218
Coleridge Cl SW8 137
Coleridge Ct W14 112
11 New Barnet EN5 13
2 Richmond TW10 175
Coleridge Gdns NW6 70
Coleridge Ho SE17 262
SW1 259
Coleridge Prim Sch N8 49
Coleridge Rd E17 53
N12 30
N4,N7 72
N8 49
Ashford TW15 170
Croydon CR0 206
Coleridge Sq W13 87
Coleridge Way
Hayes UB4 84
West Drayton UB7 104
Coleridge Wlk NW11 47 C
Colerne Ct NW4 29 A
Colesburg Rd BR3 185 B
Coles Cres HA2 63 D
Coles Ct SW11 266 D
Coles Gn WD23 8 A
Coles Green Ct NW2 68 A
Coles Green Rd NW2 68 B
Coleshill Flats SW1 258 B
Coleshill Rd TW11 174 C
Cole St SE1 117 A4 252 B
Colestown St 4 SW11 136 C
Coleswood N20 14 C
Colesworth Ho 1 HA8 27 A
Colet Cl N13 32 D
Colet Gdns W14 112 D
Colet Ho SE17 261 D
Colette Ct 5 SE16 118 D
Coley St WC1 94 B3 240 D
Colfe & Hatchcliffe's Glebe
SE13 163 D
Colfe Rd SE23 163 A3
Colfe's Prep Sch SE12 165 A5
Colfe's Sch SE12 165 B5
Colgate Ct EN5 13 A6
Colgate Ho SE13 141 D3
Colgate Pl EN3 7 C6
Colham Ave UB7 104 A5
Colham Green Rd UB8 82 C2
Colham Manor Jun & Inf
Schs UB8 82 C1
Colham Rd UB8 82 B3
Colina Mews N8,N15 50 D5
Colina Rd N8,N15 50 D4
Colin Blanchard Ho
SE4 141 C3
Colin Cl NW9 45 C5
Coney Hall BR4 224 D5
Croydon CR0 223 B5
Colin Cres NW9 45 D5
Colin Ct SW16 159 D2
Colindale Ave NW9 45 C6
Colindale Hospl NW9 45 C6
Colindale Prim Sch
NW9 45 D5
Colindale Sta NW9 45 C6
Colindeep Gdns NW4 46 A5
Colindeep La NW9,NW4 45 D5
Colin Dr NW9 45 D4
Colinette Rd SW15 134 C1
Colin Gdns NW9 45 D5
Colin Par NW9 45 C5
Colin Park Rd NW9 45 C5
Colin Rd NW10 68 A2
Colinsdale N1 234 C5
Colinton Rd IG3 80 B6
Colin Winter Ho 37 E1 96 C3
Coliston Pass SW18 157 C4
Coliston Rd SW18 157 C4

ollamore Ave SW18 .158 C3
ollapit Cl HA1 ...41 D3
ollard Pl NW1 ...71 B1
ollege App SE10 ...142 A6
ollege Ave HA3 ...24 C2
ollege Cl E5 ...74 C3
Edmonton N18 ...33 D5
Harrow HA3 ...24 C3
Twickenham TW2 ...152 B3
ollege Cres NW3 ...70 B2
ollege Cross N1 ...72 C1
ollege Ct NW3 ...70 B2
SW3 ...114 D1 257 D1
3 W6 ...112 C1
Croydon CR0 ...222 A6
Ealing W5 ...110 A6
Enfield EN3 ...18 C6
ollege Dr Ruislip HA4 ..40 A2
Thames Ditton KT7 ...196 C2
ollege Fields Bsns Ctr
SW19 ...180 C2
College Gdns
Chingford E4 ...20 A3
Dulwich SE21 ...161 C3
Edmonton N18 ...34 A5
Enfield EN2 ...5 B4
New Malden KT3 ...199 D4
Redbridge IG4 ...56 A4
Upper Tooting SW17 ...158 C2
College Gn BR1 ...187 A2
South Norwood SE19 ...183 C3
College Gr NW1 ...232 C6
College Hill EC4 ...252 B6
College Hill Rd HA3 ...24 C3
College La NW5 ...71 B4
College Park Cl SE13 .142 B1
College Park Rd N17 ..33 D4
College Park Sch W2 ..91 D1
College Pl E17 ...54 C5
NW1 ...93 C6 232 B5
SW10 ...266 A4
College Pt E15 ...76 D2
College Rd BR1 ...187 A3
E17 ...54 A4
NW10 ...90 C5
Dulwich SE19,SE21 ...161 C2
Ealing W13 ...87 B1
Enfield EN2 ...5 B3
Harrow HA1 ...42 C3
Harrow HA3 ...24 C2
Hounslow TW7 ...130 D4
Mitcham SW19 ...180 B4
South Croydon CR0 ...221 B6
Southgate N21 ...16 C2
Tottenham N17 ...33 D4
Wembley HA9 ...43 D1
College Rdbt 1 KT1 ..198 A6
College St EC4 117 A6 252 B6
College Terr E3 ...97 B4
N3 ...29 B1
College View SE9 ...165 D3
College Way
Ashford TW15 ...170 B6
Hayes UB3 ...106 A6
College Wlk 10 KT1 ...198 A6
Collent Ho 12 E9 ...74 C2
Collent St E9 ...74 C2
Collerston Ho SE10 ...120 D1
Colless Rd N15 ...51 D4
Collette Ct SE25 ...205 C4
Collette Ho N16 ...51 D1
Collett Rd SE16 ...118 A3
Collett Way UB2 ...107 D4
Colley Ho 12 N7 ...71 D3
Collier Cl E16 ...122 D6
West Ewell KT19 ...214 D2
Collier Dr HA8 ...26 B1
Collier St N1 ...94 B5 233 C3
Colliers Water La CR7 204 C4
Colliers Wood BR2 ...225 D3
Mitcham SW19 ...180 B3
Collier's Wood Sta
SW19 ...180 B3
Collindale Ave DA15 ..168 A3
DA8 ...147 D6
Collingbourne Rd
W12 ...112 B5
Collingham Gdns
SW5 ...113 D2 255 D3
Collingham Pl
SW5 ...113 D2 255 D4
Collingham Rd
SW5 ...113 D2 255 D3
Collings Cl N22 ...32 B4
Collington Ho SE7 ...143 B6
Collington St SE10 ...120 B1
Collingtree Rd SE26 ..184 C6
Collingwood Ave N10 ..49 A5
Tolworth KT5 ...199 A1
Collingwood Cl
2 Penge SE20 ...184 B2
Twickenham TW2,TW4 ..151 C4
Collingwood Ct NW4 ...46 C4
New Barnet EN5 ...13 D6
Collingwood Ho 27 E1 .96 B3
Collingwood Rd N15 ...51 C5
Hillingdon UB8 ...82 D3
Mitcham CR4 ...202 C6
Sutton SM1 ...217 C4
Collingwood Sch SM6 219 B3
Collingwood St E1 ...96 B3
Collins Ave HA7 ...26 A1
Collins Ct E8 ...74 A2
Collins Dr HA4 ...62 C6
Collins Ho 4 E14 ...120 A6
6 SE10 ...120 D1
8 Barking IG11 ...78 D1
Collinson Ct SE1 ...252 A1
Edgware HA8 ...26 B6
Collinson Ho 13 SE15 .140 A5
Collinson St SE1 ...252 A1
Collinson Wlk SE1 ...252 A1
Collins Rd N5,N16 ...73 A4
Collins Sq SE3 ...142 D3
Collins St SE3 ...142 C3
Collins Yd N1 ...234 C5
Collinwood Ave EN3 ...6 C1
Collinwood Gdns IG5 ..56 C5
Collis Prim Sch TW11 .175 B4
Coll of Liberal Arts
SM1 ...217 D3
Coll of North East London
The
N11 ...31 D3
N15 ...51 D5
Coll of NW London
(Willesden Centre) The
NW10 ...67 D3
Coll Sharp Ct 42 E2 ...95 D4
Coll's Rd SE15 ...140 C4
Collyer Ave CR0 ...220 A4
Collyer Pl SE15 ...140 A4
Collyer Rd CR0 ...220 A4
Colman Ct N12 ...30 A4
Stanmore HA7 ...25 B4
Colman Rd E16 ...99 C2
Colmans Wharf 6 E14 .97 D2
Colmar Cl 3 E1 ...96 D3
Colmer Pl HA3 ...24 B3
Colmer Rd SW16 ...182 A3
Colmore Mews SE15 ..140 B4
Colmore Rd EN3 ...6 C1
Colnbrook Ct SW17 ...180 B6
Colnbrook St SE1 ...261 C6
Colne Ct Ealing W7 ...86 B1
West Ewell KT19 ...215 A4
Colne Ho NW8 ...236 D5
Barking IG11 ...78 D2
Colne Rd E5 ...75 A4
Southgate N21 ...17 B4
Twickenham TW1,TW2 ..152 C3
Colne St E13 ...99 A4
Colney Hatch N10 ...31 A3
Colney Hatch La N10 ...31 A3
Cologne Rd SW11 ...136 B1
Coloma Convent Girls Sch
CR0 ...222 D5
Colombo Rd IG1 ...57 A2
Colombo St SE1 ...251 C3
Colomb St SE10 ...120 C1
Colonades The 4 SE5 139 B4
Colonels Wlk EN2 ...4 D2
Colonial Ave TW2 ...152 A5
Colonial Dr W4 ...111 A2
Colonial Rd TW14 ...149 C4
Colonnade WC1 ...240 B5
Colonnades The 6 E8 ..74 B2
Colonnade The 11 SE8 119 B2
Colosseum Ct N3 ...29 B1
Colroy Ct NW4 ...47 A4
Colson Rd CR0 ...221 C6
Colson Way SW16 ...181 C6
Colstead Ho 23 E1 ...96 B1
Colsterworth Rd N15 ..51 D5
Colston Ave SM1,SM5 .218 C4
Colston Ct SM5 ...218 D4
Colston Rd E7 ...77 D2
Mortlake SW14 ...133 A1
Colthurst Cres N4 ...73 A6
Colthurst Dr N9 ...18 B1
Coltman Ho 1 E14 ...97 A1
SE10 ...142 A6
Colt Mews EN3 ...7 C6
Coltness Cres SE2 ...124 B1
Colton Gdns N17 ...51 A6
Colton Rd HA1 ...42 C4
Coltsfoot Dr UB7 ...82 A1
Columba Ho SE14 ...141 B4
Columbas Dr NW3 ...48 B1
Columbia Ave
Edgware HA8 ...26 D2
New Malden KT4 ...199 D2
Ruislip HA4 ...40 B1
Columbia Ct KT3 ...199 D2
Columbia Ho 16 E3 ...97 C4
Columbia Point 7
SE16 ...118 C3
Columbia Prim Sch E2 .95 D4
Columbia Rd E13 ...98 D3
E2 ...95 D4
Columbine Ave E6 ...100 A2
Croydon CR2 ...220 D1
Columbus Gdns HA6 ...22 A2
Colveiw Ct SE9 ...165 D3
Colverson Ho 11 E1 ...96 C2
Colvestone Cres E8 ...73 D3
Colvestone Prim Sch
E8 ...73 D3
Colville Gdns W11 ...91 B1
Colville Ho 33 E2 ...96 C5
W11 ...91 B1
Colville Mews W11 ...91 B1
Colville Pl W1 ...239 B3
Colville Prim Sch W11 .91 B1
Colville Rd E11 ...76 A5
E17 ...35 A1
W11 ...91 B1
W3 ...110 D3
Edmonton N9 ...18 B3
Colville Sq W11 ...91 B1
Colville Sq Mews 6
W11 ...91 B1
Colville Terr W11 ...91 B1
Colvin Cl SE26 ...184 C5
Colvin Gdns
Chingford E4 ...20 A1
Wanstead E11 ...55 B5
Colvin Rd E6 ...78 A1
Thornton Heath CR7 ...204 C4
Colwall Gdns IG8 ...37 A5
Colwall Ho 18 SW9 ...138 B3
Colwell Rd SE22 ...161 D6
Colwick Cl N6 ...49 D2
Colwith Rd W6 ...134 C6
Colwood Gdns SW19 ..180 B3
Colworth Gr SE17 ...262 B3
Colworth Rd E11 ...54 C2
Croydon CR0 ...206 A1
Colwyn Ave UB6 ...86 D5
Colwyn Cl SW16 ...181 C5
Colwyn Cres TW3 ...130 A4
Colwyn Gn NW9 ...45 C3
Colwyn Ho SE1 ...261 A5
Colwyn Rd NW2 ...68 B5
Colyer Cl SE9 ...166 D2
Colyer Ho SE2 ...124 D1
Colyton Cl DA16 ...146 D4
Wembley HA0 ...65 C2
Colyton Rd SE22 ...162 B6
Colyton Way N18 ...34 A5
Combe Ave SE3 ...142 D5
Combedale Rd SE10 ..121 A1
Combe Ho 20 W2 ...91 C2
Mortlake SW14 ...133 A3
Combe Hurst KT2 ...177 A5
Combe Lane Sta CR0 .222 C3
Combemartin Rd
SW18 ...157 A3
Combe Mews 4 SE3 ..142 D5
Comber Cl NW2 ...68 B6
Comber Gr SE5 ...139 A5
Comber Grove Prim Sch
SE5 ...139 A5
Comber Ho SE5 ...139 A5
Combermere Rd SW9 .138 B2
Morden SM4 ...201 D4
Comberton 10 KT1 ...176 C1
Comberton Rd E5 ...74 B6
Combeside SE18 ...145 D5
Combes Rd RM9 ...81 B1
Combe The NW1 ...231 D1
Combwell Cres SE2 ..124 A3
Comely Bank Rd E17 ..54 A4
Comeragh Mews W14 254 B1
Comeragh Rd
W14 ...113 A1 254 B1
Comer Cres UB2 ...108 A4
Comerford Rd SE4 ...141 B1
Comet Cl E12 ...77 D4
Comet Pl SE8 ...141 C5
Comet St SE8 ...141 C5
Comins Ho SW4 ...159 C6
Commerce Est E18 ...37 C1
Commerce Rd
Brentford TW8 ...131 C5
Wood Green N22 ...32 B2
Commerce Way CR0 ..220 B6
Commercial Rd E1 ...96 C1
Edmonton N18 ...33 C4
Commercial St
E1 ...95 D2 243 C4
Commercial Way
SE15 ...140 A5
Wembley NW10 ...88 D5
Commerell Pl SE10 ...120 D1
Commerell St SE10 ...120 C1
Commodore Ct SE8 ...141 C4
Commodore Ho 7
E14 ...120 A6
Commodore St E1 ...97 A3
Commondale SW15 ...134 C2
Common La KT10 ...213 A1
Common Rd
Barnes SW13 ...134 A2
Claygate KT10 ...213 A1
Stanmore HA7 ...8 C1
Commonside BR2 ...225 C4
Commonside Ct SW16 182 A4
Commonside E CR4 ...203 B6
Common The
Ealing W5 ...110 A5
Southall UB2 ...106 D2
Stanmore HA7 ...8 D2
Common View SW15 ..134 C2
Commonwealth Ave
21 W12 ...112 B6
Hayes UB3 ...83 B1
Commonwealth Rd
N17 ...34 A3
Commonwealth Way
SE2 ...124 C1
Community Cl
Cranford TW5 ...128 B4
Uxbridge UB10 ...61 A5
Community Coll The
E9 ...74 D3
E9 ...96 D6
Community Rd E15 ...76 B3
Greenford UB6 ...86 A6
Como Rd SE23 ...163 A2
Compania Bldg 12 E1 118 D6
Compass Ct SE1 ...253 C3
Compass Hill TW10 ...153 D5
Compass Ho SE8 ...141 D3
W2 ...91 D1
Compass Point 9 E14 119 C6
Compayne Gdns NW6 ..69 D1
Compton Ave E6 ...99 D5
N1 ...72 D2
N6 ...48 C2
Wembley HA0 ...65 C4
Compton Cl 5 HA8 ...27 A3
NW1 ...231 D1
NW11 ...68 D5
SE15 ...139 D5
Ealing W13 ...87 A1
Esher KT10 ...212 B3
Compton Cres
Chessington KT9 ...214 A2
Chiswick W4 ...133 A6
Northolt UB5 ...84 D6
Tottenham N17 ...33 A3
Compton Ct
Sutton SM1 ...218 A4
9 West Norwood SE19 .183 C5
Compton High Sch & Sports
Coll UB5 ...85 A6
Compton Ho SW11 ...267 A2
Compton Lo N21 ...16 D3
Compton Pas EC1 ...241 D6
Compton Pl WC1 ...240 A6
South Oxhey WD19 ...23 A6
Compton Rd N1 ...72 D2
NW10 ...90 D4
Croydon CR0 ...206 B1
Hayes UB3 ...105 D6
Southgate N21 ...16 D3
Wimbledon SW19 ...179 B4
Compton Rise HA5 ...41 B4
Compton Sch The N12 .30 C4
Compton St
EC1 ...94 D3 241 D6
Compton Terr N1 ...72 D2
Southgate N21 ...16 C3
Comreddy Cl EN2 ...4 D4
Comus Ho SE17 ...263 A3
Comus Pl
SE17 ...117 C2 263 A3
Comyn Rd SW11 ...136 C1
Comyns Cl E16 ...98 D2
Comyns Rd RM9 ...81 C1
Comyns The WD23 ...8 A3
Conal Ct SW16 ...181 D5
Conant Ho SE11 ...138 D6
Conant Mews 1 E1 ...118 A6
Concanon Rd SW2,
SW4 ...138 B1
Concert Hall App
SE1 ...116 B5 250 D3
Concord Bsns Ctr W3 ..88 D2
Concord Cl UB5 ...85 A4
Concord Ct KT1 ...198 B6
Concord Ctr W12 ...112 D4
Concorde Cl
Hounslow TW3 ...129 D3
Uxbridge UB10 ...82 A5
Concorde Dr E6 ...100 B2
Concord Ho
Kingston KT3 ...199 C6
5 Tottenham N17 ...33 D3
Concordia Wharf E14 .120 A5
Concord Rd Acton W3 ..88 D3
Enfield EN3 ...18 C6
Concourse The 7 N9 ...18 A2
Condell Rd
SW8 ...137 C4 269 B1
Conder St E14 ...97 A1
Condor Path UB5 ...85 C5
Condover Cres SE18 ..144 D5
Condray Pl SW11 ...267 A3
Conduit Ct WC2 ...250 A6
Conduit Ho SE10 ...142 B4
Conduit La N18 ...34 C5
South Croydon CR0 ...222 A3
Conduit Mews
W2 ...92 B1 236 C1
Conduit Pas W2 ...236 C1
Conduit Pl W2 ...236 C1
Conduit Rd SE18 ...122 D1
Conduit St W1 115 C6 249 A6
Conduit Way NW10 ...67 A1
Conewood St N5 ...72 D5
Coney Acre SE21 ...161 A3
Coney Burrows E4 ...20 C2
Coney Gr UB8 ...82 C4
Coneygrove Path UB5 ..63 A2
Coney Hall Par BR4 ..224 C5
Coney Hall Rdbt BR4 .224 C5
Coney Hill Rd BR4 ...224 D6
Coney Hill Sch BR2 ..224 D5
Coney Way SW8 ...270 D5
Conference Cl 3 E4 ...20 A2
Conference Ho UB8 ...83 A1
Conference Rd SE2 ...124 C2
Congers Ho SE8 ...141 C5
Congleton Gr SE18 ...123 A1
Congo Rd SE18 ...123 B1
Congress Rd SE2 ...124 C2
Congreve Ho 10 N16 ...73 C3
Congreve Rd SE9 ...144 B2
Congreve St
SE17 ...117 C2 263 A3
Congreve Wlk 6 E16 ...99 D2
Conical Cnr EN2 ...5 A3
Conifer Cl BR6 ...227 B4
Conifer Ct Ilford IG1 ...78 D2
23 Putney SW19 ...156 D3
Conifer Gdns
Enfield EN1 ...17 C5
Streatham SW16 ...160 B1
Sutton SM1 ...217 D6
Conifer Ho SE4 ...141 B1
Conifers Cl TW11 ...175 C3
Conifer Way
Hayes UB3 ...106 A6
Wembley HA0 ...65 C5
Coniger Rd SW6 ...135 C3
Coningham Ct SW10 ..266 B4
Coningham Mews
W12 ...112 A5
Coningham Rd W12 ...112 B4
Coningsby Cotts W5 ..109 D4
Coningsby Ct 4 CR4 ..181 A1
Coningsby Gdns E4 ...35 D4
Coningsby Rd N4 ...50 D2
W5 ...109 D4
Conington Rd SE13 ...142 A3
Conisbee Ct 3 N14 ...15 C6
Conisborough Cres
SE6 ...164 A1
Conisbrough NW1 ...232 A5
Coniscliffe Cl BR7 ...188 C2
Coniscliffe Rd N13 ...17 A1
Coniston NW1 ...232 A2
Coniston Ave DA16 ...145 C2
Barking IG11 ...79 C1
Ealing UB6 ...87 B4
Coniston Cl N20 ...14 A1
Barking IG11 ...79 C1
Barnes SW13 ...133 D5
Chiswick W4 ...133 A5
West Barnes SM4 ...200 D3
Coniston Ct 6 SE16 ..118 D4
W2 ...237 B1
Beckenham BR3 ...186 A2
Chessington KT9 ...214 A5
Edgware HA8 ...26 B5
Penge SE26 ...184 B4
3 Wallington SM6 ...219 B4
Conistone Way N7 ...72 A1
Coniston Gdns N9 ...18 C3
NW9 ...45 B4
Pinner HA5 ...40 A5
Redbridge IG4 ...56 A5
Sutton SM2 ...218 B2
Wembley HA9 ...43 C1
Coniston Ho 13 E3 ...97 B4
18 SE5 ...139 A5
Coniston Rd N10 ...31 B1
Catford BR1 ...186 C4
Croydon CR0 ...206 A2
Tottenham N17 ...34 A4
Twickenham TW2 ...151 D5
Coniston Way KT9 ...214 A5
Coniston Wlk E9 ...74 C3
Conlan St W10 ...91 A3
Conley Rd NW10 ...67 C2
Conley St SE10 ...120 C1
Connaught Ave
Ashford TW15 ...170 A6
Barnet, London EN4 ...14 D3
Chingford E4 ...20 B4
Enfield EN1 ...5 C3
Hounslow TW4 ...129 A1
Mortlake SW14 ...133 A1
Connaught Bsns Ctr
NW9 ...45 D4
Mitcham CR4 ...202 D4
Wallington CR0 ...220 B2
Connaught Cl E10 ...75 A6
W2 ...237 B1
Carshalton SM1 ...218 B6
Enfield EN1 ...5 C3
Hillingdon UB8 ...83 A3
Connaught Ct 10 E17 ..53 D5
1 Chingford E4 ...20 C4
Connaught Day Hospl
E11 ...54 C3
Connaught Dr NW11 ...47 C5
Connaught Gdns N10 ..49 B4
Edmonton N13 ...32 D6
Morden SM4 ...202 A5
Connaught Grange
N13 ...32 D6
Connaught Ho N10 ...49 B4
Connaught Ho *continued*
NW10 ...90 B4
W1 ...248 C5
Connaught La IG1 ...79 B6
Connaught Lo N4 ...50 C2
Connaught Mans
15 N16 ...73 B4
SW11 ...267 B1
SW6 ...264 A2
3 SW9 ...138 C1
Connaught Mews
SE18 ...122 C1
Ilford IG1 ...79 B6
Connaught Pl W2 ...237 C1
Connaught Rd E11 ...54 B1
E16 ...121 D5
E17 ...53 C4
N4 ...50 C2
NW10 ...89 C5
SE18 ...122 D1
Barnet EN5 ...12 D5
Carshalton SM1 ...218 B6
Chingford, Chingford Green
E4 ...20 C3
Ealing W13 ...109 B6
Harrow HA3 ...24 D2
Ilford IG1 ...79 B6
New Malden KT3 ...199 C5
5 Richmond TW10 ...154 B6
Teddington TW11,TW12 .174 B5
Connaught Sch for Girls
E11 ...54 C1
Connaught Sch for Girls
(Annexe) E11 ...76 C6
Connaught Sq
W2 ...92 D1 237 C1
Connaught St
W2 ...92 C1 237 B1
Connaught Way N13 ...32 D6
Connell Cres W5 ...88 B3
Connell Ct 6 SE14 ...140 D6
Connell Ho 6 SM6 ...219 C2
Connemara Cl WD6 ...11 B5
Connett Ho 5 E2 ...96 B5
Connington 5 KT1 ...176 C1
Connington Cres E4 ...20 B1
Connoly Ct NW2 ...68 B5
Connop Rd EN3 ...6 D5
Connor Cl E11 ...54 C2
Connor Ct SW11 ...268 C1
Connor Rd RM9 ...81 B4
Connor St E9 ...96 D6
Conolly Rd W7 ...108 C5
Conrad Dr KT4 ...200 D1
Conrad Ho 12 N16 ...73 C3
8 SE16 ...119 A6
SW8 ...270 A4
Consfield Ave KT3 ...200 A4
Consolata Missionary Coll
N20 ...13 C1
Consort Ho NW7 ...27 D5
W2 ...245 D5
Consort Lo NW8 ...230 C5
Consort Mews TW7 ...152 B6
Consort Rd SE15 ...140 B3
Cons St SE1 ...251 B2
Constable Ave E16 ...121 B5
Constable Cl NW11 ...47 D3
Hayes UB4 ...83 A5
Constable Cres N15 ...52 A4
Constable Ct 11 SE16 .118 B1
Constable Gdns
Edgware HA8 ...26 C1
Isleworth TW7 ...152 B6
Constable Ho NW3 ...70 D1
Enfield EN1 ...18 A6
14 Northolt UB5 ...84 D5
Constable Mews RM8 ..80 B4
Constable Wlk SE21 ..161 C1
Constance Cres BR2 .208 D1
Constance Rd
Enfield EN1 ...17 C5
Sutton SM1 ...218 A4
Thornton Heath CR0 ..204 D2
Twickenham TW2 ...151 D4
Constance St E16 ...122 A5
Constant Ho 23 E14 ..119 D6
Constantine Ho SW2 ..160 D3
Constantine Pl UB10 ...82 B6
Constantine Rd NW3 ...70 C4
Constitution Hill
SW1,W1 ...115 B4 248 D2
Constitution Rise
SE18 ...144 C4
Consul Ho 5 E3 ...97 C3
Content St
SE17 ...117 B2 262 C3
Contessa Cl BR6 ...227 C3
Control Tower Rd
TW6 ...126 D2
Convair Wlk 11 UB5 ...84 D4
Convent Cl BR3 ...186 A3
Convent Gdns W11 ...91 B1
W5 ...109 C2
Convent Hill SE19 ...183 A4
Convent Lo TW15 ...170 D5

Convent of Jesus & Mary Language Coll NW10 89 D6
Convent of Jesus & Mary RC Inf Sch NW2 68 C2
Convent Rd TW15 170 D5
Convent Way UB2 106 D2
Conway Cl HA7 25 A4
Conway Cres
Dagenham RM6 58 C3
Greenford UB6 86 C5
Conway Dr
Ashford TW15 171 A4
Hayes UB3 105 A3
Sutton SM2 217 D2
Conway Gdns Enfield EN2 5 C5
Mitcham CR4 204 A5
Wembley HA9 43 C2
Conway Gr W3 89 B2
Conway Ho 5 E14 119 D2
6 Streatham SW2 160 A3
Conway Mews W1 239 A5
Conway Prim Sch SE18 123 C2
Conway Rd N15 51 A4
NW2 68 C6
SE18 123 C2
Feltham TW13 172 D5
Harlington TW6 126 D2
Palmers Green N14 16 A1
Twickenham TW4 151 C4
Wimbledon SW20 178 C2
Conway St W1 93 C3 239 A5
Conway Wlk TW12 173 B4
Conybeare NW3 70 C1
Conyers Cl IG8 36 C4
Conyer's Rd SW16 181 D5
Conyer St 19 E3 97 A5
Cooden Cl BR1 187 B3
Cookes Cl E11 76 D6
Cookes La SM3 217 A2
Cookham Cl UB2 107 D4
Cookham Cres SE16 118 D4
Cookham Dene Cl BR7 189 B2
Cookham Ho E2 243 C6
Cookham Rd BR8 191 C2
Cookhill Rd SE2 124 B3
Cooks Ferry N18 34 D5
Cook's Hole Rd EN2 5 A5
Cookson Gr DA8 147 D5
Cook's Rd E15 97 D5
SE17 138 D6
Coolfin Rd E16 99 B1
Coolgardie Ave E4 36 B5
Coolgardie Rd TW15 171 A5
Coolhurst Rd N8 49 D3
Cool Oak La NW9 45 D2
Coomassie Rd W9 91 B3
Coombe Ave CR0 221 C4
Coombe Bank KT2,KT3 177 C2
Coombe Cl Edgware HA8 26 B1
Hounslow TW3 129 C1
Coombe Cnr N21 16 D3
Coombe Cres TW12 173 A3
Coombe Ct
2 Beckenham BR3 185 B2
3 Croydon CR0 221 B4
Coombe Dr HA4 40 B1
Coombe End KT2 177 B3
Coombefield Cl KT3 199 C4
Coombe Gdns
New Malden KT3 199 D5
Wimbledon SW20 178 A2
Coombe Girls Sch KT3 177 B1
Coombe Hill Glade KT2 177 C3
Coombe Hill Inf Sch KT3 177 B2
Coombe Hill Jun Sch KT3 177 B2
Coombe Hill Rd KT2 177 C3
Coombe Ho 13 N7 71 D3
Coombe House Chase KT3 177 B2
Coombehurst Cl EN4 2 D3
Coombe La CR0 222 B3
Coombe Lane Flyover SW20 177 D2
Coombe La W KT2 177 B2
Coombe Lea BR1 210 A6
Coombe Lo SE7 143 C6
Coombe Neville KT2 177 B3
Coombe Pk KT2 177 B5
Coombe Pl KT2 177 A5
Coombe Rd NW10 67 B5
W13 109 B3
W4 111 C1
Bushey WD23 8 B4
Forest Hill SE26 184 B6
Hampton TW12 173 B4
Kingston KT2 176 C2
Kingston KT3 199 C6
South Croydon CR0,CR2 221 C4
Wood Green N22 32 C2
Coomber Ho SW6 135 D2
Coombe Ridings KT2 177 A5
Coombe Rise KT2 177 A2
Coombes Rd RM9 103 B6
Coombe Wlk SM1 217 D5
Coombewood Dr RM6 59 B3
Coombe Wood Rd KT2 177 A5
Coombs St N1 234 D3
Coomer Mews SW6 264 D5
Coomer Pl SW6 135 B6 264 D5
Cooms Wlk HA8 27 A2
Cooperage Cl 5 N17 33 D4
Cooperage The SE1 253 C3
Cooper Ave E17 35 A2
Cooper Cl SE1 251 B1
Cooper Cres SM5 218 D5
Cooper Ct E15 76 A3
SE18 144 D6
Cooper Ho NW8 236 C5
Hounslow TW4 129 B2
7 West Norwood SW27 182 D5
Cooper Rd NW10 68 A3
NW4 46 D3
Croydon CR0,CR9 220 D4
Coopersale Cl 3 IG8 37 C3
Coopersale Rd E9 74 D3
Coopers Cl E1 96 C3
Dagenham RM10 81 D2
Coopers Ct E3 97 B3
9 W3 111 A5
Isleworth TW7 130 D3
Coopers La NW1 232 D3
SE12 165 B2
Cooper's La E10 54 A1
Coopers' Lane Prim Sch SE12 165 B2
Coopers Lodge SE1 253 C2
Cooper's Rd SE1 117 D1 263 D2
Cooper's Row EC3 117 D6 253 C6
Coopers Sch BR7 189 A2
Cooper St 10 E16 98 D2
Cooper's Yd SE19 183 C4
Coote Gdns RM8 81 B5
Coote Rd DA7 147 B4
Dagenham RM8 81 B5
Cope Ho EC1 235 B1
Copeland Dr E14 119 C2
Copeland Ho SE11 260 D5
Upper Tooting SW17 180 B6
Copeland Rd E17 53 D3
SE15 140 B3
Copelands BR3 185 B3
Copeman Cl SE26 184 C5
Copenhagen Gdns W4 111 B4
Copenhagen Ho N1 234 A5
Copenhagen Pl E14 97 B1
Copenhagen Prim Sch N1 94 B6 233 C5
Copenhagen St N1 94 B6 233 C5
Cope Pl W8 113 C3 255 A5
Copers Cope Rd BR3 185 B3
Cope St SE16 118 D2
Copeswood Ct UB7 126 C5
Cope Yd 6 E1 118 A5
Copford Wlk N1 235 A6
Copinger Wlk HA8 26 D2
Copland Ave HA0 65 D3
Copland Cl HA0 65 C3
Copland Com Sch & Tech Ctr HA9 66 B3
Copland Mews 3 HA0 66 A2
Copland Rd HA0 66 A2
Copleston Rd SE15 139 D2
Copley Cl 15 SE17 138 D6
Ealing W7 86 D2
Copley Dene BR1 187 D2
Copley Pk SW16 182 B4
Copley Rd HA7 25 C5
Coppard Gdns KT9 213 C2
Coppedhall 1 SE21 161 B2
Coppelia Rd SE3 142 D1
Coppen Rd RM8 59 B2
Copperas St SE8 141 D6
Copper Beech N6 49 A2
Copperbeech Cl NW3 70 B3
Copper Beech Ct N20 14 A1
Copper Beeches TW7 130 B4
Copper Cl SE19 183 D3
Copperdale Rd UB3 106 A4
Copperfield Ave UB8 82 C3
Copperfield Dr N15 51 D5
Copperfield Ho 10 SE1 118 A4
Copperfield Mews N18 33 C5
Copperfield Rd SE28 102 C1
Stepney E3 97 A2
Copperfields
5 Beckenham BR3 186 A2
Harrow HA1 42 C2
Copperfields Ct W3 110 C4
Copperfield St SE1 117 A4 252 A2
Copperfield Way BR7 189 A4
Pinner HA5 41 B5
Coppergate Cl BR1 187 B2
Coppermead Cl NW2 68 C5
Copper Mill Dr TW7 130 D3
Coppermill La E17 52 D4
Copper Mill La SW17 180 A6
Coppermill Prim Sch E17 52 D4
Copperwood Lo EN2 4 D3
Coppetts Cl N12 30 D3
Coppetts Ctr★ N12 30 D3
Coppetts Rd N10 30 D2
Coppetts Wood Prim Sch N10 31 A2
Coppice Cl
Beckenham BR3 207 D5
Harrow HA7 24 D4
Ruislip HA4 39 B3
West Barnes SW20 200 C6
Coppice Dr SW15 156 B5
Coppice The
Ashford TW15 170 D4
Enfield EN2 4 D1
Hillingdon UB7 82 A1
New Barnet EN5 13 D5
Coppice Way E18 54 D6
Coppice Wlk N20 13 C1
Coppies Gr N11 31 B6
Copping Cl CR0 221 C4
Coppinger Ct UB7 104 A4
Coppin Ho SW2 160 D3
Coppins The
New Addington CR0 223 D2
Stanmore HA3 24 C4
2 Ilford RM6 58 B2
Coppock Cl SW11 136 C3
Coppsfield KT8 195 C6
Copse Ave BR4 223 D5
Copse Cl SE7 143 B6
Copse Ct SW15 157 A6
Copse Glade KT6 197 D1
Copse Hill
Belmont SM2 217 D1
Wimbledon SW20 178 B3
Copsem Dr KT10 212 A2
Copsem La KT10 212 A1
Copsem Way KT10 212 A2
Copse The N2 48 D6
Chingford E4 20 D3
Copse View CR2 223 A1
Coptefield Dr DA17 125 A3
Copthall Ave EC2 95 B1 242 D2
Copthall Bldgs EC2 242 D2
Copthall Cl EC2 242 C2
Copthall Dr NW7 28 A4
Copthall Gdns NW7 28 A3
Twickenham TW1 152 D3
Copthall Rd E UB10 60 C5
Copthall Rd W UB10 60 C6
Copthall Sch NW7 28 B3
Copthall Sports Ctr NW4 28 B2
Copthorne Ave BR2 226 B6
Streatham SW12 159 D4
Copthorne Chase TW15 170 B6
Copthorne Cl TW17 193 A3
Copthorne Mews UB3 105 C2
Coptic St WC1 94 A2 240 A3
Copton Cl E3 97 C2
Copwood Cl N12 30 B6
Coral Cl RM6 58 C6
Coral Ho 5 E1 97 A3
Coraline Cl UB1 85 B4
Coralline Wlk 4 SE2 124 C4
Coral Row 14 SW11 136 A2
Coral St SE1 116 C4 251 B1
Coram Ho 9 W4 111 C1
WC1 240 A6
Coram St WC1 94 A3 240 A5
Coran Cl N9 18 D4
Corban Rd TW3 129 C2
Corbar Cl EN4 2 B4
Corbden Cl SE15 139 D4
Corbet Cl CR4,SM6 219 A6
Corbet Ct EC3 242 D1
Corbet Ho N1 234 A5
Corbet Pl E1 95 D2 243 C4
Corbett Ct SE26 185 B6
Corbett Gr N22 32 A3
Corbett Ho SW10 266 A6
Corbett Rd E17 54 A6
Wanstead E11 55 C3
Corbett's La SE16 118 C2
Corbett Villas RM8 58 C1
Corbicum E11 54 C2
Corbidge Ct SE8 141 D6
Corbiere Ct SW19 178 D4
Corbiere Ho 5 N1 95 C6
Corbin Ho 7 E3 97 D4
Corbin's La HA2 63 D5
Corbridge 5 N17 34 B3
Corbridge Cres E2 96 B5
Corby Cres EN2 4 A1
Corbyland Rd DA15 167 C3
Corbylands Rd DA15 167 C4
Corbyn St N4,N19 50 A1
Corby Rd NW10 89 B5
Corby Way E3 97 C3
Cordelia Cl SE24 138 D1
Cordelia Gdns TW19 148 A4
Cordelia Ho 26 N1 95 C5
Cordelia Rd TW19 148 A4
Cordelia St E14 97 D1
Cordell Ho N15 51 D4
Cordingley Rd HA4 61 B6
Cording St E14 97 D2
Cordwainers Coll E8 74 B1
Cordwainers Ct 18 E9 74 C1
Cordwainers Wlk 9 E13 99 A5
Cordwain Ho 7 N18 34 A5
Cord Way 7 E14 119 C3
Cordwell Rd SE13 164 C6
Corefield Cl N11 15 A2
Corelli Rd SE3 144 A4
Corfe Ave HA2 63 C4
Corfe Cl UB4 84 C1
Corfe Ho SW8 270 C4
Corfe Lo SE21 161 B2
Corfe Twr 6 W3 111 A4
Corfield Rd N21 16 B6
Corfield St E2 96 B4
Corfton Lo W5 88 A2
Corfton Rd W5 88 A2
Coriander Ave E14 98 B1
Coriander Ct SE1 253 D2
Cories Cl RM8 80 D6
Corigan Ct 5 E11 76 C6
Corinium Cl HA9 66 B4
Corinne Rd N19 71 C4
Corkscrew Hill BR4 224 B5
Cork Sq E1 118 B5
Cork St W1 115 C6 249 A5
Cork St Mews W1 249 A5
Cork Tree Ho 3 SW27 182 D5
Cork Tree Ret Pk N18 35 A4
Cork Tree Way E4 35 A5
Corlett St NW1 237 A4
Cormont Rd SE5 138 D4
Cormorant Cl E17 35 A3
Cheam SM1 217 B3
Cormorant Ct 34 SE8 141 B6
12 Dulwich SE21 161 B2
Cormorant Ho EN3 18 D6
Cormorant Rd E7 76 D3
Cornbury Ho 5 SE8 141 B6
Cornbury Rd HA8 25 D3
Cornel Ho 4 DA15 168 A1
Cornelia St N7 72 B2
Cornell Cl DA14 191 A4
Cornell Ho HA2 63 B5
Corner Fielde SW2 160 B3
Corner Gn SE3 143 A3
Corner House St WC2 250 A4
Corner Mead NW9 27 D2
Cornerside TW15 171 A3
Cornerways Harrow HA1 65 A5
Putney SW15 134 A1
Corney Rd W4 133 C6
Corney Reach Way W4 133 C5
Cornflower La CR0 206 D1
Cornflower Terr SE22 162 B5
Cornford Cl BR2 209 A4
Cornford Gr SW12 159 B2
Cornhill EC3 95 B1 242 D1
Cornhill Dr EN3 7 A6
Cornick Ho 7 SE16 118 B3
Cornish Ct N9 18 B4
Cornish Gr SE20 184 B2
Cornish Ho 7 SE17 138 D6
Brentford TW8 110 B1
Cornmill La SE13 142 A2
Cornmow Dr NW10 68 A3
Cornshaw Rd RM8 58 D1
Cornthwaite Rd E5 74 C5
Cornwall Ave DA16 145 D2
E2 96 C4
N3 29 C3
Claygate KT10 212 D1
Southall UB1 85 C2
Wood Green N22 32 A2
Cornwall Cl
Barking IG11 79 D2
3 Pinner HA5 23 B3
Cornwall Cres W11 91 A1
Cornwall Ct 5 W7 86 D3
Cornwall Dr BR5 190 C3
Cornwall Gdns NW10 68 B2
SW7 113 D3 255 D5
Cornwall Gdns Wlk SW7 255 D5
Cornwall Gr W4 111 C1
Cornwall Ho NW1 237 D5
3 Putney SW15 156 C4
Cornwallis Ave DA15 167 B2
N9 18 C2
Cornwallis Ct SW8 270 A2
Cornwallis Gr N9 18 C2
Cornwallis Ho 24 W12 112 B6
Cornwallis Rd N19 72 A6
SE18 122 D3
Dagenham RM9 81 A4
Edmonton N9 18 B2
Walthamstow E17 52 D5
Cornwallis Sq N19 72 A6
Cornwallis Wlk SE9 144 B2
Cornwall Mans NW1 237 D5
SW10 266 B4
Cornwall Mews S SW7 256 A5
Cornwall Mews W SW7 255 D5
Cornwall Rd N15 51 B4
N4 50 C2
SE1 116 C5 251 B2
Belmont SM2 217 B1
Croydon CR0 220 D6
Edmonton N18 34 A5
Harrow HA1 42 A3
Pinner HA5 23 B3
Ruislip HA4 61 D6
Twickenham TW1 153 A3
Cornwall Sq SE11 261 D2
Cornwall St 4 E1 118 B6
Cornwall Terr NW1 237 D5
Cornwall Terr Mews NW1 237 D5
Corn Way E11 76 C5
Cornwell Ct 21 E10 53 D2
Cornwood Cl N2 48 B5
Cornwood Dr E1 96 C1
Cornworthy Rd RM8 80 C3
Corona Rd SE12 165 A4
Coronation Ave 1 N16 73 D4
Coronation Cl DA5 168 D5
Ilford IG6 57 A5
Coronation Ct E15 76 D2
W10 90 C2
Coronation Rd E13 99 C4
Acton NW10 88 C3
Hayes UB3 105 D2
Coronet Par 4 HA0 66 A2
Coronet St N1 95 C4
Corporation Ave TW4 129 A1
Corporation Row EC1 241 B6
Corporation St E15 98 D5
N7 72 A3
Corpus Christi RC Prim Sch SW2 160 B6
Kingston KT3 199 A6
Corrance Rd SW2,SW4 138 A1
Corri Ave N14 31 D6
Corrib Ct N13 16 B1
Corrib Dr SM1 218 C3
Corrib Hts N8 49 D3
Corrigan Cl NW4 46 C6
Corringham Ct NW11 47 C2
Corringham Ho 10 E1 96 D1
Corringham Rd NW11 47 C2
Wembley HA9 66 C6
Corringway NW11 47 D2
Ealing W5 88 C2
Corris Gn NW9 45 C3
Corry Dr SW9 138 D1
Corry Ho 2 E14 119 D6
Corsair Cl TW19 148 A4
Corsair Rd TW19 148 A4
Corscombe Cl KT2 177 A5
Corsehill St SW16 181 C4
Corseley Way E9 75 B2
Corsham Ho HA9 66 C2
Corsham St N1 95 B4 235 D1
Corsica St N5 72 D2
Cortayne Rd SW6 135 B3
Cortis Rd SW15 156 B5
Cortis Terr SW15 156 B5
Corunna Rd SW8 137 C4 269 B2
Corunna Terr SW8 269 A2
Corvette Sq 5 SE10 142 B6
Corwell Gdns UB8 83 A1
Corwell La UB8 83 A1
Coryton Path W9 91 B3
Cosbycote Ave SE24 161 A6
Cosdach Ave SM6 219 D1
Cosedge Cres CR0,CR9 220 D3
Cosgrove Cl
Edmonton N21 17 A2
Hayes UB4 84 D3
Cosgrove Ho 11 E2 96 A6
Cosmo Pl WC1 240 B4
Cosmur Cl W12 111 D3
Cossall Wlk SE15 140 B4
Cossar Mews 10 SW2 160 C6
Cosser St SE1 116 C3 261 A6
Costa St SE15 140 A3
Coston Prim Sch UB6 86 A4
Costons Ave UB6 86 B4
Costons La UB6 86 B4
Coston Wlk 4 SE4 140 D1
Cosway Ho NW11 48 A3
Cosway Mans NW1 237 B4
Cosway St NW1 92 C2 237 B4
Cotall St E14 97 C2
Coteford Cl HA5 40 A4
Coteford Inf Sch HA5 40 A3
Coteford Jun Sch HA5 39 D4
Coteford St SW17 181 A6
Cotelands CR0 221 C5
Cotesbach Rd E5 74 C5
Cotes Ho NW8 237 A5
Cotesmore Gdns RM8 80 C4
Cotford Rd CR7 205 A5
Cotham St SE17 262 B3
Cotherstone Rd SW2 160 B3
Cotleigh Ave DA5 168
Cotleigh Rd NW6 69
Cotman Cl NW11 48
Putney SW15 156
Cotman Ct BR3 185
Cotmandene Cres BR5 190
Cotman Gdns HA8 26
Cotman Ho NW8 230
6 Northolt UB5 84 D
Cotmans Cl UB3 106
Coton Rd DA16 146
Cotsford Ave KT3 199
Cotswold Ave WD23 8
Cotswold Cl
Hinchley Wood KT10 212 D
Kingston KT2 177
Cotswold Ct EC1 242
N11 31
3 Wembley UB6 86
Cotswold Gate NW2 47
Cotswold Gdns E6 99
Hendon NW2 68 D
Ilford IG2 57
Cotswold Gn EN2 4
Cotswold Ho N16 51 D
Cotswold Mews SW11 266 D
Cotswold Rd TW12 173 C
Cotswold Rise BR6 211 D
Cotswold St SE27 182 D
Cotswold Way Enfield EN2 4 B
North Cheam KT4 216 C
Cottage Ave BR2 210 A
Cottage Cl HA4 39 B
Cottage Field Cl DA5, DA15 168 C
Cottage Gn SE5 139 B
Cottage Gr SW9 138 A
Surbiton KT6 197 D
Cottage Pl SW3 114 C3 257 A
Cottage Rd KT19 215 B
Cottage St E14 119 D
Cottages The UB10 60 D
Cottage Wlk 2 N16 73 D
Cottenham Dr NW9 45 D
Wimbledon SW20 178 B
Cottenham Ho 4 N19 72 A
Cottenham Par SW20 178 B
Cottenham Park Rd SW20 178 C
Cottenham Pl SW20 178 B
Cottenham Rd E17 53 B
Cotterill Rd KT6 198 B
Cottesbrook St 9 SE14 141 A
Cottesloe Ho NW8 237 A
Cottesloe Mews SE1 261 B
Cottesmore Ct W8 255 D
Cottesmore Gdns W8 113 D3 255 D
Cottimore Ave KT12 194 B
Cottimore Cres KT12 194 B
Cottimore Terr KT12 194 B
Cottingham Chase HA4 62 A
Cottingham Rd SW8 138 B5 270 D
Penge SE20 184 D
Cottington Rd TW13 172 D
Cottington St SE11 261 C
Cotton Ave W3 89 B
Cotton Cl RM9 80 C
Cottongrass Cl 1 CR0 206 D
Cotton Hill BR1 186 B
Cotton Ho W12 111 D
18 Streatham SW12 160 A
Cotton Row SW11 136 B
Cotton's Gdns E2 95 C
Cottons La SE1 252 D
Cotton St E14 120 A
Cottrell Ct SE10 120 D
Cotts Cl 13 W7 86 D
Couchman Ho 6 SW4 159 C
Couchmore Ave KT10 212 C
Coulgate St SE4 141 A
Coulsdon Ct 3 N8 49 D
Coulsdon Ho 5 SW2 160 A
Coulson Cl RM8 58 C
Coulson St SW3 114 D1 257 C
Coulter Cl UB4 85 A
Coulter Rd W6 112 B
Coulthurst Ct SW16 182 A
Coults Cres NW5 71 A
Councillor St SE5 139 A
Counters Ct W14 254 B
Counter St SE1 253 A
Countess Rd NW5 71 C
Countisbury Ave EN1 17 D
Countisbury Ho SE26 162 A
Country Way TW13, TW16 172 C
County Gate BR7 167 A
New Barnet EN5 13 D
County Gr SE5 139 A
County Ho 9 SW9 138 C
County Par TW8 131 D
County Rd Newham E6 100 D
South Norwood CR7 182 D

unty St SE1 117 A3 262 B5
oupland Pl SE18 123 A1
ourcy Rd N8,N22 50 C6
ourier Ho 17 SW2 160 C4
ourland Gr SW8 137 D3
ourland St
W8 137 D4 269 D1
ourse The SE9 166 C1
ourtauld Galleries*
WC2 250 C6
ourtauld Ho 11 E2 84 A5
ourtauld Inst of Art
W1 237 D2
ourtauld Rd N19 50 A1
ourtaulds Cl SE28 124 A5
ourt Ave DA17 125 B1
ourt Cl Harrow HA3 44 A6
wickenham TW13,TW2 151 D1
Wallington SM6 219 D1
ourt Close Ave TW13,
TW2 151 D1
ourt Cres KT9 213 D2
ourt Downs Rd BR3 185 D1
ourt Dr
Carshalton SM1 218 C4
Hillingdon UB10 82 C6
Stanmore HA7 26 A6
Wallington CR0 220 B4
ourtenay Ave N6 48 C2
Harrow HA3 24 A2
ourtenay Dr BR3 186 B1
ourtenay Gdns HA3 24 A1
ourtenay Mews E17 53 A4
ourtenay Pl E17 53 A4
ourtenay Rd E11 76 D5
North Cheam KT4,SM3 216 C5
Penge BR3,SE20 184 D4
Walthamstow E17 52 D5
Wembley HA9 65 D5
ourtenay Sq SE11 261 A1
ourtenay St
SE11 116 C1 261 A2
ourtens Mews HA7 25 C3
ourt Farm Ave KT19 215 B3
ourt Farm Ind Est
TW19 148 B5
ourt Farm Rd
Chislehurst SE9 166 A1
Northolt UB5 63 C1
ourtfield W13 87 C2
ourtfield Ave HA1 42 D4
ourtfield Cres HA1 42 D4
ourtfield Gdns
SW5 113 D2 255 D3
Ealing W13 87 A1
Ruislip HA4 61 D6
ourtfield Ho EC1 241 A4
ourtfield Mews SW7 255 D3
ourtfield Rd
SW7 114 A2 256 A3
Ashford TW15 170 D4
ourtfield Rise BR4 224 B5
Court Gdns N7 72 C2
ourthill Rd SE13 142 A1
ourthope Ho
14 SE16 118 C3
SW8 270 A3
Courthope Rd NW3 70 D4
Greenford UB6 86 B5
Wimbledon SW19 179 A5
Courthope Villas
SW19 179 A3
Court House Gdns N3 29 C4
Court House Rd N12 29 D4
Court La SE21 161 D4
Courtland Ave NW7 11 C1
Chingford E4 20 D2
Redbridge IG1 78 B6
South Norwood SW16 182 B3
Courtland Gr SE28 124 D6
Courtland JMI Sch
NW7 11 C2
Courtland Rd E6 100 A6
Courtlands 5 E5 52 B1
11 Beckenham BR3 185 D1
10 Belmont SM2 217 D1
Ealing W5 87 C2
Richmond TW10 154 C6
Walton-on-T KT12 194 A2
Courtlands Ave SE12 165 B6
Hampton TW12 173 B4
Hayes BR2 208 D1
Richmond TW9 132 D3
Courtlands Cl HA4 39 D2
Courtlands Dr KT19 215 D2
Courtlands Rd KT5 198 C2
Court Lane Gdns SE21 161 C4
Courtleet Dr DA7 147 D4
Courtleigh 6 NW11 47 B4
Courtleigh Ave EN4 2 B5
Courtleigh Gdns NW11 47 A5
Court Lo 11 DA17 125 C1
Courtman Rd N17 33 A3
Court Mans 8 W6 112 A2
Court Mead UB5 85 B4
Courtmead Cl SE24 161 A5
Courtnell St W2 91 C1
Courtney Cl SE19 183 C4
Courtney Cres SM5 218 D1
Courtney Ct N7 72 C3
Courtney Ho 1 NW4 46 C5
W14 254 B6
Courtney Pl CR0 220 C5
Courtney Rd N7 72 C3
Croydon CR0 220 C5
Harlington TW6 126 C2
Mitcham SW19 180 C3
Courtney Way TW6 126 C2
Court Par HA0 65 B5
Courtrai Rd SE23 163 A5
Court Rd Eltham SE9 166 B4
Southall UB2 107 B1
South Norwood SE25 205 D6
Uxbridge UB10 60 D4
Court Royal SW15 157 A6
Courtside N8 49 D3
Forest Hill SE23 162 C1
Court St BR1 187 A1
E1 96 B2
Courts The SW16 182 A3
Court The N10 49 C5
Ruislip HA4 63 A4
Courtville Ho 11 W10 91 A4
Court Way NW9 45 C5
W3 89 A2
Courtway IG8 37 C5
Court Way Ilford IG6 57 A6
Twickenham TW1,TW2 152 D4
Courtyard The N1 72 B1
13 SW18 136 B1
Fulham SW6 135 A4 264 A1
Court Yd SE9 166 B5
Cousin La EC4 117 B6 252 C5
Cousins Cl 2 UB7 104 A6
Cousins Ct 2 NW9 46 A5
Couthurst Rd SE3 143 B5
Coutts Ave KT9 214 A3
Coutts Ho SE7 143 C6
Couzens Ho 9 E3 97 B2
Coval Gdns SW14 132 D1
Coval La SW14 132 D1
Coval Rd SW14 133 A1
Covelees Wall E6 100 C1
Covell Ct 15 SE8 141 C5
Covent Garden Sta
WC2 94 A1 240 B1
Covent Gdn*
WC2 116 A6 250 B6
Coventry Cl NW6 91 C6
9 Newham E6 100 B1
Coventry Rd E1 96 B3
Croydon SE25 206 A5
Ilford IG1 56 D1
Coventry St W1 249 C5
Coverack Cl
Croydon CR0 207 A2
Southgate N14 15 C5
Coverdale Cl HA7 25 B5
Coverdale Gdns CR0 221 D5
Coverdale Pl NW6 68 D1
Coverdale Rd N11 31 A4
NW2 69 A2
W12 112 B4
Coverdales The IG11 101 B5
Coverham Ho 5 SE4 140 D1
Coverley Cl E1 96 A2
Coverley Point SE11 260 C3
Coverton Rd SW17 180 C5
Coverts Rd KT10 212 D1
Covert The BR5,BR6 211 C3
Covert Way EN4 2 A3
Covet Wood Cl BR5 211 D3
Covey Cl SW19 179 D1
Covington Gdns SW16 182 D3
Covington Way
South Norwood SW16 182 C3
South Norwood SW16 182 D3
Cowan Cl E6 100 A2
Cowan Ct NW10 67 B1
Cowbridge La IG11 78 D1
Cowbridge Rd HA3 44 B5
Cowcross St
EC1 94 D2 241 C4
Cowdenbeath Path
N1 233 C6
Cowden Rd BR6 211 D2
Cowden St SE6 185 C6
Cowdray Hall Coll of
Nursing W1 93 B1 238 C2
Cowdray Ho 23 SE22 139 C2
Cowdray Rd UB10 83 A6
Cowdrey Cl EN1 5 C3
Cowdrey Rd SW19 180 A5
Cowdry Rd E9 75 B2
Cowell Lo E4 36 D5
Cowen Ave HA2 64 B6
Cowen Ho 4 SE18 144 D6
Cowgate Rd UB6 86 B4
Cowick Rd SW17 180 D6
Cowings Mead UB5 63 A2
Cowland Ave EN3 6 C1
Cow Leaze E6 100 C1
Cowleaze Rd KT2 176 A2
Cowley La E11 76 C5
Cowley Pl NW4 46 C4
Cowley Rd SW9 138 C4
16 SW9 138 C5
W3 111 D5
Cowley Rd continued
Mortlake SW14 133 C2
Redbridge IG1 56 B2
Wanstead E11 55 B4
Cowley St SW1 260 A5
Cowling Cl W11 244 A4
Cowper Ave E6 78 A1
Sutton SM1 218 B4
Cowper Cl Bexley DA16 168 A6
Bromley BR2 209 D5
Cowper Gdns
Southgate N14 15 C5
Wallington SM6 219 C2
Cowper Ho SE17 262 B2
SW1 259 D1
Cowper Rd N14 15 B3
N16 73 C4
W3 111 B5
Belvedere DA17 125 C2
Bromley BR2 209 D5
Ealing W7 108 D6
Edmonton N18 34 A5
Richmond TW10 176 B5
Wimbledon SW19 180 A4
Cowper's Ct EC3 242 D1
Cowper St EC1,
EC2 95 B3 242 D6
Cowper Terr W10 90 D2
Cowslip Cl UB10 60 A1
Cowslip Rd E18 37 B1
Cowthorpe Rd SW8 269 D2
Cox Ct 3 EN4 2 C1
Coxe Pl HA3 43 A5
Cox Ho W6 264 A6
Cox La Chessington KT9 214 B4
West Ewell KT19 215 A3
Coxmount Rd SE7 121 D1
Coxs Ave TW17 193 C6
Cox's Ct E1 243 C3
Coxson Way SE1 253 C1
Coxwell Rd SE18 123 B1
South Norwood SE19 183 C3
Coxwold Path KT9 214 A1
Coysh Ct 8 SW15 157 A6
Crabbs Croft Cl 7
BR6 227 A3
Crab Hill BR3 186 B3
Crabtree Ave
Dagenham RM6 58 D5
Wembley HA0 88 B5
Crabtree Cl 2 E2 95 D5
Crabtree Ct E15 75 D3
Crabtree Hall SW6 134 C5
Crabtree La SW6 134 D5
Craddock Rd EN1 5 D2
Craddock St NW5 71 A2
Cradley Rd DA15,SE9 167 B3
Craig Dr UB8 82 D1
Craigen Ave CR0 206 B1
Craigerne Rd SE3 143 B5
Craig Gdns E18 36 D1
Craigholm SE18 144 C4
Craigie Ho SE1 263 D3
Craigleith SW15 156 D5
Craigmuir Pk HA0 88 B6
Craignair Rd SW2 160 C4
Craignish Ave SW16 182 B1
Craig Park Rd N18 34 B6
Craig Rd TW10 175 C6
Craig's Ct SW1 250 A4
Craigside KT2 176 D2
Craigton Rd SE9 144 B1
Craigweil Cl HA7 25 D5
Craigweil Dr HA7 25 D5
Craigwell Ave TW13 150 A1
Craik Ct NW6 91 B5
Crail Row
SE17 117 B2 262 D3
Crales Ct SE18 122 A3
Cramer Ct KT3 199 A6
Cramer St W1 93 A2 238 B3
Crammond Cl W6 264 A5
Cramond Ct TW14 149 C3
Crampton Rd SE20 184 C4
Crampton Sch
SE17 116 D1 261 D2
Crampton St
SE17 117 A1 262 A2
Cranberry Cl 2 UB5 84 D5
Cranberry La E16 98 C3
Cranborne Ave
Southall UB2 107 C2
Tolworth KT6,KT9 214 C5
Cranborne Rd IG11 101 B6
Cranborne Waye
Hayes UB4 106 C6
Hayes UB4 84 B1
Cranbourn Alley WC2 249 D6
Cranbourne Cl SW16 204 A6
Cranbourne Ct N2 47 D6
SW11 267 B4
Wanstead E18 55 B5
Cranbourne Dr HA5 40 D4
Cranbourne Gdns
NW11 47 B4
Ilford IG6 57 A6
Cranbourne Rd E12 78 A3
E15 76 A4
N10 31 B1
Cranbourne Rd continued
Northwood HA6 39 D6
Cranbourn Ho 4 SE16 118 B4
Cranbourn St
WC2 115 D6 249 D6
Cranbrook NW1 232 B5
Cranbrook Cl BR2 209 A3
Cranbrook Coll (Boys)
IG1 78 C6
Cranbrook Ct 8 TW8 131 D6
Cranbrook Dr
Thames Ditton KT10 196 A1
Twickenham TW2 151 D3
Cranbrook Ho 5 E5 74 B3
South Norwood SE19 183 B2
Cranbrook La N11 31 B6
Cranbrook Mews E17 53 B4
Cranbrook Pk N22 32 C2
Cranbrook Rd DA7 147 B4
SE8 141 C4
W4 111 C1
Hounslow TW4 129 B1
Ilford IG1,IG2 56 C3
New Barnet EN4 14 B5
South Norwood CR7 183 A1
Wimbledon SW19 179 A3
Cranbrook Rise IG1 56 B2
Cranbrook St E2 96 D5
Cranbury Rd SW6 135 D3
Crandale Ho 8 E5 74 B3
Crandley Ct SE8 119 A2
Crane Ave W3 111 A6
Isleworth TW7 153 A6
Cranebrook TW2 152 A2
Crane Cl
Dagenham RM10 81 C2
Harrow HA2 64 A5
Crane Ct EC4 241 B1
7 W12 111 C4
West Ewell KT19 215 A4
Craneford Cl TW2 152 D4
Craneford Way TW2 152 D4
Crane Gdns UB3 105 D2
Crane Gr N7 72 C2
Crane Ho 22 E3 97 A5
9 SE15 139 D4
9 Catford BR1 186 B5
Feltham TW13 151 C1
Crane Lodge Rd TW5 128 B6
Crane Mead SE16 118 D2
Crane Mead Ct TW1 152 D4
Crane Park Prim Sch
TW13 151 B2
Crane Park Rd TW2 151 D2
Crane Rd
Stanwell TW19 148 C5
Twickenham TW2 152 C3
Cranes Dr KT5 198 B5
Cranes Park Ave KT5,
KT6 198 B5
Cranes Park Cres KT5 198 B5
Cranes Pk KT5,KT6 198 A4
Crane St SE10 120 B1
5 SE15 139 D4
Craneswater TW6 127 D5
Craneswater Pk UB2 107 B1
Cranes Way WD6 11 A6
Crane Way TW2 152 A4
Cranfield Ct NW1 237 B3
2 Woodford IG8 37 A6
Cranfield Dr NW9 27 C3
Cranfield Rd SE4 141 B2
Cranford Ave
Bowes Park N13 32 A5
Stanwell TW19 148 B4
Cranford Cl
Stanwell TW19 148 A4
Wimbledon SW20 178 B3
Cranford Comm Coll
TW5 128 B6
Cranford Cotts 8 E1 118 D6
Cranford Ct SM1 218 A4
Cranford Dr UB3 105 D2
Cranford Jun Sch
TW4 128 B3
Cranford La
Harlington UB3 127 C5
Hatton TW6 127 D4
Hatton, Hatton Cross
TW6 127 D2
Heston TW5 128 C5
Cranford Lo SW19 156 D2
Cranford Park Prim Sch
UB3 105 D2
Cranford Park Rd UB3 105 D2
Cranford Rise KT10 212 A3
Cranford St E1 118 D6
Cranford Way N8 50 C4
Cranhurst Rd NW2 68 C3
Cranleigh W11 244 C4
Cranleigh Cl DA5 169 D5
Penge SE20 184 B1
Cranleigh Ct 4 N16 51 C1
Mitcham CR4 202 B6
Richmond TW9 132 C2
Southall UB1 85 B1
Cranleigh Gardens Ind Est
UB1 85 B2
Cranleigh Gdns
Barking IG11 79 B2
Harrow HA3 44 A4
Kingston KT2 176 B3
Southall UB1 85 B1
Southgate N21 16 C6
South Norwood SE25 205 C6
Sutton SM1 217 D6
Cranleigh Ho SW20 178 B1
Cranleigh Hos NW1 232 B3
Cranleigh Mews
SW11 136 D3
Cranleigh Rd N15 51 A4
Feltham TW13 171 D6
Merton SW19 201 C6
Thames Ditton KT10 196 A1
Cranleigh St
NW1 93 C5 232 B3
Cranley Dene Ct N10 49 B5
Cranley Dr Ilford IG2 57 A2
Ruislip HA4 61 D6
Cranley Gdns N10 49 B5
SW7 114 B1 256 C2
Palmers Green N13 16 B1
Wallington SM6 219 C1
Cranley Mews
SW7 114 A1 256 B2
Cranley Par 2 SE9 188 A6
Cranley Pl
SW7 114 B2 256 C3
Cranley Rd E13 99 B2
Ilford IG2 57 A2
Cranmer Ave W13 109 B3
Cranmer Cl Ruislip HA4 40 D1
Stanmore HA7 25 C3
West Barnes SM4 200 D3
Cranmer Ct N3 29 A1
SW3 257 B3
Hampton TW12 173 D5
Kingston KT2 175 D6
Cranmer Farm Cl CR4 202 D5
Cranmer Ho SW11 267 A2
Cranmer Mid Sch CR4 202 D5
Cranmer Rd E7 77 B4
SW9 138 C5
Croydon CR0 221 A5
Edgware HA8 10 D1
Hampton TW12 173 D5
Hayes UB3 83 B1
Kingston KT2 176 A5
Mitcham CR4 202 D5
Cranmer Terr SW17 180 B5
Cranmore Ave TW7 130 A5
Cranmore Rd BR7 188 B5
Catford BR1 164 D1
Cranmore Way N10 49 C5
Cranston Cl
Hounslow TW3,TW4 129 A3
Uxbridge UB10 61 B6
Cranston Gdns E4 35 D4
Cranston Rd SE23 163 A2
Cranswick Rd SE16 118 B1
Crantock Rd SE6 164 A2
Cranwell Cl E3 97 D3
Cranwell Ct 6 NW9 27 D3
Croydon CR0 222 D6
Cranwell Gr TW17 192 B5
Cranwell Rd TW6 126 D3
Cranwich Ave N21 17 B4
Cranwich Rd N16 51 C2
Cranwood Ct EC1 235 D1
Cranwood St
EC1 95 B4 235 D1
Cranworth Cres 7 E4 20 B3
Cranworth Gdns SW9 138 C4
Cranworth Ho 6 N7 72 B4
Craster Rd SW2 160 B4
Craston Ho 2 SE5 139 C3
Crathie Rd SE12 165 B5
Crathorne Ho N2 30 B1
Cravan Ave TW13 150 A2
Craven Ave Ealing W5 109 C6
Southall UB1 85 B2
Craven Cl N16 52 A2
Hayes UB4 84 A1
Craven Cottage (Fulham
FC) SW6 134 D4
Craven Ct NW10 89 C6
Dagenham RM6 59 A3
Edgware HA8 26 B6
Craven Gdns
Barking IG11 101 C5
Ilford IG6 57 B6
Wimbledon SW19 179 D5
Craven Hill
W2 114 A6 246 B6
Craven Hill Gdns
W2 114 A6 246 A6
Craven Hill Mews W2 246 B6
Craven Ho 13 N2 30 B1
2 Mortlake SW14 133 B2
Craven Lo W2 246 B6
Fulham SW6 134 D4
Craven Mews 6
SW11 137 A2
Craven Park Mews
NW10 89 C6
Craven Park Rd N15 52 A3
NW10 89 C6
Craven Park Sch N16 52 A3
Craven Pas WC2 250 A4
Craven Pk NW10 89 C6
Craven Rd NW10 89 B6
W2 92 A1 236 B1
Croydon CR0 206 B1
Ealing W5 109 C6
Kingston KT2 176 B2
Craven St
WC2 116 A5 250 A4
Craven Terr
W2 114 A6 246 B6
Craven Wlk E5,N16 52 A2
Crawford Ave HA0 65 D3
Crawford Bldgs NW1 237 B3
Crawford Cl TW7 130 C3
Crawford Gdns
Edmonton N13 16 D1
Northolt UB5 85 B4
Crawford Mews W1 237 C3
Crawford Pas EC1 241 B5
Crawford Pl W1 92 C2 237 B3
Crawford Place Dwellings
NW1 237 B3
Crawford Point 4 E16 98 D1
Crawford Prim Sch
SE5 139 A4
Crawford Rd SE5 139 A3
Crawford St
W1 92 D2 237 C3
Crawley Rd E10 53 D1
Enfield EN1 17 D4
Tottenham N22 33 A1
Crawshay Ct SW9 138 C4
Crawshay Ho 13 N16 73 B4
Crawthew Gr SE22 139 D1
Craybrooke Rd DA14 190 B6
Craybury End SE9 167 A2
Crayfields Bsns Pk
BR5 190 C2
Crayfields Ind Pk BR5 190 C1
Crayford Cl E6 100 A1
Crayford Ho N7 72 A4
SE1 252 D1
Crayford Rd N7 72 A4
Crayke Hill KT9 214 A1
Crayle Ho EC1 241 D6
Crayonne Cl TW16 171 C2
Cray Rd DA17 147 C6
Sidcup DA14 190 C4
Crays Par The BR5 190 C1
Crealock Gr IG8 36 D5
Crealock St SW18 157 D5
Creasy Est SE1 263 A5
Crebor St SE22 162 A5
Credenhall Dr BR2 210 B1
Credenhill Ho 2 SE15 140 B5
Credenhill St SW16 181 C4
Crediton Hill NW6 69 D3
Crediton Ho EN3 6 D2
Crediton Rd E16 99 A1
NW10 90 D6
Crediton Way KT10 213 A3
Credon Rd E13 99 C5
SE16 118 B1
Creechurch La EC3 243 B1
Creechurch Pl EC3 243 B1
Creed Ho SE15 140 B2
Creed La EC4 241 D1
Creek Ho W14 254 B6
Creekmouth Ind Pk
IG11 101 D3
Creek Rd SE10,SE8 141 D6
Barking IG11 101 D4
East Molesey KT8 196 C5
Creekside SE8 141 D5
Creek The TW16 194 A4
Creeland Gr SE6 163 B3
Crefeld Cl W6 135 A6 264 A5
Creffield Rd W3,W5 110 C6
Creighton Ave E6 99 D5
N2,N10 30 D1
Creighton Cl W12 112 B6
Creighton Ho N2 48 C6
Creighton Rd NW6 90 D5
W5 109 D3
Tottenham N17 33 C3
Cremer Bsns Ctr 8 E2 95 D5
Cremer Ho 9 SE8 141 C5
Cremer St E2 95 D5
Cremorne Rd
SW10 136 B5 266 C4
Creon Ct 3 SW9 138 C4
Crescent EC3 253 C6
Crescent Court Bsns Ctr
E16 98 B3
Crescent Ct 14 DA15 168 A1
SW4 159 D6
Kingston KT6 197 D4
Crescent Dr BR5 211 A3
Crescent E EN4 2 A5
Crescent Gdns
Ruislip HA4 40 B2
Wimbledon SW19 157 C1
Crescent Gr SW4 137 C1
Mitcham CR4 202 C5

Crescent Ho SE13 ... 141 D3
5 Wimbledon SW20 ... 178 D2
Crescent La SW4 ... 159 D6
Crescent Mans N5 ... 72 D3
W11 ... 244 B6
Crescent Par UB10 ... 82 C4
Crescent Pl SW3 ... 257 B4
Crescent Rd BR1 ... 187 A3
DA15 ... 167 D1
E10 ... 75 D6
E13 ... 99 A6
E6 ... 99 C6
N11 ... 30 D6
N15 ... 50 D6
N22 ... 31 D2
N3 ... 29 B2
N8 ... 49 D3
SE18 ... 122 D2
Beckenham BR3 ... 185 D1
Chingford E4 ... 20 C4
Dagenham RM10 ... 81 D5
East Barnet EN4 ... 14 C6
Edmonton N9 ... 18 A3
Enfield EN2 ... 4 D1
Kingston KT2 ... 176 D3
Shepperton TW17 ... 193 A4
Wimbledon SW20 ... 178 D2
Woodford E18 ... 37 C2
Crescent Rise N22 ... 31 D2
N3 ... 29 B2
3 N3 ... 29 C2
East Barnet EN4 ... 14 C6
Crescent Row EC1 ... 242 A5
Crescent St N1 ... 72 B1
Crescent Stables
SW15 ... 157 A6
Crescent The DA14 ... 189 D6
E17 ... 53 A4
N11 ... 31 A6
N2 ... 47 D6
NW2 ... 68 B5
W3 ... 89 C1
Ashford TW15 ... 170 B5
Barnes SW13 ... 134 A3
Barnet EN5 ... 1 D3
Beckenham BR3 ... 185 C2
East Molesey KT8 ... 195 C5
Harlington UB7 ... 127 B5
Harrow HA2 ... 42 A1
Ilford IG2 ... 56 C3
Kingston KT3 ... 177 A1
Kingston KT6 ... 198 A4
Loughton IG10 ... 21 D5
Lower Halliford TW17 ... 193 D2
Sidcup DA5 ... 168 C4
Southall UB1 ... 107 A4
Sutton SM1 ... 218 B3
Thornton Heath CR0 ... 205 B3
Wembley HA0 ... 65 B6
West Wickham BR4 ... 208 C3
Wimbledon SW19 ... 157 C1
Crescent View IG10 ... 21 D6
Crescent W EN4 ... 2 A5
Crescent Way N12 ... 30 C4
SE4 ... 141 C2
Orpington BR6 ... 227 C3
South Norwood SW16 ... 182 C3
Crescent Wood Rd
SE21,SE26 ... 162 A1
Cresford Rd
SW6 ... 135 D4 265 C1
Crespigny Rd NW4 ... 46 B3
Cressage Cl UB1 ... 85 C3
Cressage Ho 9 TW8 ... 132 A6
Cressall Ho 8 E14 ... 119 C3
Cresset Ho 8 E9 ... 74 C2
Cresset Rd E9 ... 74 C2
Cresset St SW4 ... 137 D2
Cressfield Cl NW5 ... 71 A3
Cressida Rd N19 ... 49 D1
Cressingham Ct 1
DA17 ... 125 C3
Cressingham Gr SM1 ... 218 A4
Cressingham Rd HA8 ... 27 B3
SE13 ... 142 A2
Cressington Cl 4 N16 ... 73 C3
Cress Mews BR1 ... 186 B5
Cresswell Gdns SW5 ... 256 A2
Cresswell Pk SE3 ... 142 D2
Cresswell Pl
SW10 ... 114 A1 256 B2
Cresswell Rd
Croydon SE25 ... 206 A5
Feltham TW13 ... 173 A6
Twickenham TW1 ... 153 D5
Cresswell Way N21 ... 16 C4
Cressy Ct 6 E1 ... 96 C2
W6 ... 112 B3
Cressy Ho SW13 ... 134 B2
Cressy Hos 7 E1 ... 96 C2
Cressy Pl E1 ... 96 C2
Cressy Rd NW3 ... 70 D4
Cresta Ct W5 ... 88 B3
Cresta Ho NW6 ... 70 B1
7 Bow E3 ... 97 C3
Crestbrook Ave N13 ... 16 D1
Crestbrook Pl N13 ... 16 D1
Crest Ct NW4 ... 46 C4
Crest Dr EN3 ... 6 C5
Crestfield St N1,WC1 ... 233 B2
Crest Gdns HA4 ... 62 C5
Creston Way KT4 ... 200 D1
Crest Rd NW2 ... 68 A6
Hayes BR2 ... 208 D2
South Croydon CR2 ... 222 B1
Crest The NW4 ... 46 C4
Edmonton N13 ... 32 C6
Surbiton KT5 ... 198 C4
10 West Norwood
SW27 ... 182 D5
Crestview NW5 ... 71 B5
Crest View HA5 ... 40 D5
Crest View Dr BR5 ... 211 A4
Crestway SW15 ... 156 B5
Crestwood Way TW4 ... 151 A6
Creswick Ct W3 ... 110 D6
Creswick Rd W3 ... 110 D6
Creswick Wlk 6 E3 ... 97 C4
NW11 ... 47 B5
Creton St SE18 ... 122 C3
Crewdson Rd SW9 ... 138 C5
Crewe Pl NW10 ... 89 D4
Crewkerne Ct SW11 ... 266 D2
Crews St E14 ... 119 C2
Crewys Rd NW2 ... 69 B6
SE15 ... 140 B3
Crichton Ave SM6 ... 219 D4
Crichton Rd SM5 ... 218 D1
Crichton St SW8 ... 137 C3
Cricketers Arms Rd EN2 ... 5 A3
Cricketers Cl N14 ... 15 C4
Chessington KT9 ... 213 D4
Cricketers Mews 4
SW18 ... 157 D6
Cricketers Wlk SE26 ... 184 C5
Cricketfield Rd E5 ... 74 B4
Cricket Gn CR4 ... 202 D5
Cricket Green Sch
CR4 ... 202 C6
Cricket Ground Rd
BR7 ... 188 D2
Cricket La BR3 ... 185 A4
Cricket Row N2 ... 48 B6
Cricklade Ave SW2 ... 160 B2
Cricklewood Broadway
NW2 ... 68 D4
Cricklewood La NW2 ... 69 B5
Cricklewood Sta NW2 ... 68 D4
Cridland St E15 ... 98 D6
Crieff Ct TW11,KT8 ... 175 C3
Crieff Rd SW18 ... 158 A5
Criffel Ave SW2 ... 159 D3
Crimscott St
SE1 ... 117 C3 263 B5
Crimsworth Rd
SW8 ... 137 D5 269 D3
Crinan St N1 ... 94 A5 233 B4
Cringle St
SW8 ... 137 C5 269 A4
Cripplegate St EC1 ... 242 B4
Cripps Gn UB4 ... 84 B3
Crispe Ho N1 ... 233 D5
Barking IG11 ... 101 B5
Crispen Rd TW13 ... 173 A6
Crispian Cl NW10 ... 67 C4
Crispin Cl SM6 ... 220 A6
Crispin Cres SM6 ... 219 D6
Crispin Ct SE17 ... 263 A3
Crispin Rd HA8 ... 27 A4
Crispin St E1 ... 95 D2 243 C3
Crisp Rd W6 ... 112 C1
Cristowe Rd SW6 ... 135 B3
Criterion Mews N19 ... 71 D6
Crittall's Cnr DA14 ... 190 C3
Crittenden Lo BR4 ... 207 C1
Crockerton Rd SW17 ... 158 D2
Crockham Way SE9 ... 188 C6
Crocus Cl CR0 ... 206 D1
Crocus Field EN5 ... 13 B5
Croft Ave BR4 ... 208 A1
Croft Cl BR7 ... 188 B5
NW7 ... 11 C1
Erith DA17 ... 125 B1
Harlington UB7 ... 127 A5
Hillingdon UB10 ... 60 C1
Croft Ct HA4 ... 39 D1
Croftdown Rd NW5 ... 71 B5
Crofters Cl TW7 ... 152 B6
Crofters Ct 9 SE8 ... 119 A2
Crofters Way
NW1 ... 93 D6 232 C6
Croft Gdns W7 ... 109 A4
Ruislip HA4 ... 39 D1
Croft Ho 12 W10 ... 91 A4
Putney SW15 ... 157 A5
Croft Lodge Cl IG8 ... 37 B4
Croft Mews N12 ... 14 A1
Crofton Ave
Chiswick W4 ... 133 B5
Orpington BR6 ... 227 A6
Sidcup DA5 ... 168 D4
Crofton Gate Way SE4 163 A6
Crofton Gr E4 ... 36 B6
Crofton Inf Sch BR5 ... 211 B2
Crofton Jun Sch BR5 ... 211 B2
Crofton La BR5,BR6 ... 211 B2
Crofton L Ctr SE4 ... 163 C5
Crofton Park Rd SE4 ... 163 B5
Crofton Park Sta SE4 ... 163 B6
Crofton Rd BR6 ... 226 C5
BR6 ... 226 D5
E13 ... 99 B3
SE5 ... 139 C3
Crofton Sch SE4 ... 163 C5
Crofton Terr E5 ... 75 A3
Richmond TW9 ... 132 B1
Crofton Way Enfield EN2 ... 4 C3
New Barnet EN5 ... 13 D5
Croft Rd BR1 ... 187 A4
Carshalton SM1 ... 218 C3
Enfield EN3 ... 7 A4
Merton SW19 ... 180 A3
South Norwood SW16 ... 182 C3
Crofts Ho 10 E2 ... 96 A5
Croftside The SE25 ... 206 A6
Crofts La N22 ... 32 C3
Crofts Rd HA1 ... 43 A4
Crofts St E1 ... 118 A6
Croft St SE8 ... 119 A2
Crofts The TW17 ... 193 C5
Croft The NW10 ... 89 D5
Barnet EN5 ... 1 A1
Chingford E4 ... 20 C2
Ealing W5 ... 88 A2
Edgware HA8 ... 26 D3
Heston TW5 ... 129 A5
New Malden KT3 ... 199 C4
Pinner HA5 ... 41 B2
Ruislip HA4 ... 62 C4
Wembley HA0 ... 65 C3
Croft Villas HA1 ... 43 A3
Croft Way
Richmond TW10 ... 153 B1
Sidcup DA15 ... 167 C1
Crogsland Rd NW1 ... 71 A1
Croham Cl CR2 ... 221 C1
Croham Hurst Sch
CR2 ... 221 D3
Croham Manor Rd
CR2 ... 221 C2
Croham Mount CR2 ... 221 C1
Croham Park Ave CR2 221 D3
Croham Rd CR2 ... 221 C3
Croham Valley Rd
CR2 ... 222 B1
Croindene Rd SW16 ... 182 A2
Crokesley Ho 2 HA8 ... 27 A1
Cromartie Rd N19 ... 49 D2
Cromarty Ct 5 BR1 ... 187 C1
Cromarty Ho 8 E1 ... 97 A2
Cromarty Rd HA8 ... 10 D2
Cromberdale Ct N17 ... 34 A2
Crombie Cl IG4 ... 56 B4
Crombie Mews 5
SW11 ... 136 C3
Crombie Rd DA15 ... 167 B3
Cromdale Ct N16 ... 51 D2
Crome Ho UB5 ... 85 A5
Cromer Cl UB8 ... 83 A1
Cromer Ct
7 Southall UB1 ... 85 D1
Streatham SW16 ... 160 A1
Wandsworth SW18 ... 157 B5
Cromer Pl 5 BR6 ... 211 B1
Cromer Rd E10 ... 54 B2
Barnet EN5 ... 2 A2
Croydon SE25 ... 206 B6
Dagenham RM6 ... 59 A3
Harlington TW6 ... 126 C3
Streatham SW17 ... 181 A4
Tottenham N17 ... 34 A1
Woodford IG8 ... 37 A6
Cromer Road Prim Sch
EN5 ... 2 A2
Cromer St WC1 . 94 A4 233 B1
Cromer Terr E8 ... 74 A3
Cromer Villas Rd
SW18 ... 157 B5
Cromford Cl BR6 ... 227 C5
Cromford Path 1 E5 ... 74 D4
Cromford Rd SW18 ... 157 C6
Cromford Way KT3 ... 177 B2
Cromlix Cl BR7 ... 188 D1
Crompton Ct SW3 ... 257 A4
Crompton Ho SE1 ... 262 B5
SW8 ... 269 B1
W2 ... 236 C5
Crompton Pl EN3 ... 7 C5
Crompton St
W2 ... 92 B3 236 C5
Cromwell Ave BR2 ... 209 B5
N6 ... 49 B1
W6 ... 112 B2
New Malden KT3 ... 199 D4
Cromwell Bsns Ctr
IG11 ... 101 C4
Cromwell Cl N2 ... 48 B5
W3 ... 111 A5
2 W4 ... 110 D1
Bromley BR2 ... 209 B5
Walton-on-T KT12 ... 194 B1
Cromwell Cres
SW5 ... 113 C2 255 A4
Cromwell Ct Enfield EN3 18 D6
Cromwell Ct *continued*
15 Kingston KT2 ... 176 C3
Wembley HA0 ... 88 A5
Cromwell Ctr NW10 ... 89 B4
Barking IG11 ... 102 A4
Cromwell Ctr The RM8 . 59 B2
Cromwell Est E10 ... 53 A1
Cromwell Gdns
SW7 ... 114 B3 256 D5
Cromwell Gr W6 ... 112 C3
Cromwell Ho SW11 ... 268 B1
Croydon CR0 ... 220 D5
Putney SW15 ... 134 A1
Cromwell Hospl
SW5 ... 113 D2 255 C4
Cromwell Lo 36 E1 ... 96 C3
Barking IG11 ... 79 C3
Cromwell Mans SW5 ... 255 B4
Cromwell Mews SW7 ... 256 D4
Cromwell Pl N6 ... 49 B1
SW7 ... 114 B2 256 D4
5 W3 ... 111 A5
Mortlake SW14 ... 133 A2
Cromwell Rd E17 ... 54 A4
E7 ... 77 C1
N10 ... 31 A3
N3 ... 30 A2
SW7 ... 256 B4
SW9 ... 138 D4
Beckenham BR3 ... 207 A6
Feltham TW13 ... 150 B3
Hayes UB3 ... 83 B1
Hounslow TW3 ... 129 C1
Kingston KT2 ... 176 A2
Teddington TW11 ... 175 A4
Thornton Heath CR0 ... 205 B2
Walton-on-T KT12 ... 194 B1
Wembley HA0 ... 88 A5
Wimbledon SW19 ... 179 D5
Worcester Park KT4 ... 215 C5
Cromwell St TW3 ... 129 C1
Cromwell Twr EC2 ... 242 B4
Crondace Rd
SW6 ... 135 C4 265 B1
Crondall Ct 7 N1 ... 95 C5
Crondall Ho SW15 ... 156 A3
Crondall Pl 15 N1 ... 95 C5
Crondall St N1 ... 95 C5
Crone Ct 5 NW6 ... 91 B5
Cronin St SE15 ... 139 D5
Crooked Billet E4 ... 35 C3
Crooked Billet Yd 19
E2 ... 95 C4
Crooked Usage N3 ... 47 A6
Crooke Rd SE8 ... 119 A1
Crookham Rd
SW6 ... 135 B4 264 C1
Crook Log DA6 ... 146 D1
Crook Log Prim Sch
DA6 ... 146 D1
Crook Log Sports Ctr
DA16 ... 146 D2
Crookston Rd SE9 ... 144 C2
Croombs Rd E16 ... 99 C2
Croom's Hill SE10 ... 142 B5
Croom's Hill Gr SE10 . 142 A5
Cropley Ct N1 ... 235 C4
Cropley St N1 .. 95 B5 235 C4
Croppath Rd RM10 ... 81 C4
Cropthorne Ct W9 ... 229 B1
Crosbie 10 NW9 ... 27 D1
Crosbie Ho 20 E17 ... 53 D6
Crosby Cl TW13 ... 173 A6
Crosby Ct N2 ... 48 A5
SE1 ... 252 C2
Crosby Rd E7 ... 77 A2
Dagenham RM10 ... 103 D6
Crosby Row
SE1 ... 117 B4 252 C2
Crosby Sq EC3 ... 243 A2
Crosby Wlk 3 E8 ... 73 D2
Streatham SE24 ... 160 C4
Crosfield Ct 3 W10 ... 90 D1
Crosfield Ho W11 ... 244 A5
Crosier Cl SE3 ... 144 A3
Crosier Rd UB10 ... 61 A4
Crosier Way HA4 ... 61 C5
Crosland Pl 5 SW11 ... 137 A2
Crossbow Ho 15 N1 ... 95 C6
Ealing W13 ... 109 B5
Crossbrook Rd SE3 ... 144 A2
Cross Cl SE15 ... 140 B3
Cross Ct 11 SE28 ... 124 B6
SE5 ... 139 B2
Cross Deep TW1 ... 153 A2
Cross Deep Gdns
TW1 ... 152 D2
Crossfield Rd N17 ... 51 A6
NW3 ... 70 B2
Crossfield St SE8 ... 141 C5
Crossford St SW9 ... 138 B3
Crossgate Edgware HA8 . 10 C1
Wembley UB6 ... 65 B2
Crossharbour & London
Arena Sta E14 ... 119 D3
Cross Keys Cl W1 ... 238 B3
5 Edmonton N9 ... 18 A2
Cross La DA5 ... 169 B4
EC3 ... 253 A5
Cross La *continued*
N8 ... 50 B5
Cross Lances Rd TW3 129 D1
Crossland Rd CR7 ... 204 D3
Crosslands Ave
Ealing W5 ... 110 B5
Southall UB2 ... 107 B1
Crosslands Rd KT19 ... 215 B2
Crossleigh Ct 3 SE14 . 141 B5
Crosslet St SE17 ... 262 D4
Crosslet Vale SE10 ... 141 D4
Crossley St N7 ... 72 C2
Crossman Hos 19
SW12 ... 160 A4
Crossmead SE9 ... 166 B3
Crossmead Ave UB6 ... 85 C4
Crossmount Ho 13
SE5 ... 139 A5
Crossness Rd IG11 ... 101 D4
Cross Rd BR2 ... 226 A6
N11 ... 31 B5
N2 ... 30 C1
SE5 ... 139 C3
Chingford, Chingford Green
E4 ... 20 C3
Croydon CR0 ... 205 B1
Enfield EN1 ... 5 C1
Feltham TW13 ... 173 A6
Harrow HA1 ... 42 B4
Harrow HA2 ... 63 D5
Harrow HA3 ... 25 A1
Ilford RM6 ... 58 C2
Kingston KT2 ... 176 B3
Merton SW19 ... 179 C3
Romford RM7 ... 59 C6
Sidcup DA14 ... 190 B6
Sutton SM1 ... 218 B3
Wood Green N22 ... 32 C3
Cross St N1 ... 94 D6 234 D6
2 Edmonton N18 ... 34 A5
Hampton TW12 ... 174 A5
Mortlake SW13 ... 133 C2
Crossthwaite Ave SE5,
SE24 ... 139 B1
Crosswall EC3 117 D6 253 C6
Crossway BR5 ... 211 B4
E8,N16 ... 73 C3
N12 ... 30 B4
NW9 ... 45 D5
SE28 ... 102 D1
Dagenham RM8 ... 80 C5
Ealing W13 ... 87 A3
Enfield EN1 ... 17 C4
Hayes UB3 ... 106 A5
Pinner HA5 ... 22 B1
Ruislip HA4 ... 62 C4
West Barnes KT3,SW20 . 200 C5
Woodford IG8 ... 37 C6
Crossway Ct SE4 ... 141 A3
Crossway Par N22 ... 32 D3
Crossways
Ashford TW16 ... 171 D3
South Croydon CR2 ... 223 B1
Sutton SM2 ... 218 B1
Crossways Rd
Beckenham BR3 ... 207 C5
Mitcham CR4 ... 203 B6
Crossways The
Heston TW5 ... 129 B5
Wembley HA9 ... 66 C6
Crossway The
Chislehurst SE9 ... 165 D2
Hillingdon UB10 ... 82 B5
Tottenham N22 ... 32 D3
Cross Way The HA3 ... 24 C1
Crosswell Cl TW17 ... 171 A1
Croston St E8 ... 96 A6
Crothall Cl N13 ... 16 B1
Crouch Ave IG11 ... 102 B5
Crouch Cl BR3 ... 185 C4
Crouch Croft SE9 ... 166 C1
Crouch End Hill N8 ... 49 D2
Crouch Hall Ct N19 ... 50 A1
Crouch Hall Rd N8 ... 49 D3
Crouch Hill N4,N8,N19 .. 50 A2
Crouchmans Cl SE21,
SE26 ... 162 A1
Crouch Rd NW10 ... 67 B1
Crowborough Ct W13 109 C6
Crowborough Path
WD19 ... 22 D6
Crowborough Rd
SW17 ... 181 A5
Crowden Way SE28 ... 124 C6
Crowder St E1 ... 118 B6
Crowfield Ho N5 ... 73 A4
Crowfoot Cl E9 ... 75 B3
Crowhurst SE25 ... 206 A6
Crowhurst Cl SW9 ... 138 C3
Crowhurst Ct N17 ... 34 B2
Crowhurst Ho 21 SW9 138 B3
Crow La RM7,RM8 ... 59 D2
Crowland Ave UB3 ... 105 D2
Crowland Gdns N14 ... 16 A4
Crowland Ho NW8 ... 229 A5
Crowland Prim Sch
N15 ... 52 A4
Crowland Rd N15 ... 51 D4
South Norwood CR7 ... 205 B5
Crowlands Ave RM7 ... 59
Crowland Terr N1 ... 73
Crowland Wlk SM4 ... 202
Crowley Cres CR0 ... 220
Crowline Wlk 1 N1 ... 73
Crowmarsh Gdns
SE23 ... 162
Crown Arc KT1 ... 175
Crown Bldgs 4 E4 ... 20
Crownbourne Ct SM1 . 217
Crown Cl E3 ... 97
NW6 ... 69
NW7 ... 11
Hayes UB3 ... 105
Walton-on-T KT12 ... 194
Crown Close Bsns Ctr
E3 ... 97
Crown Ct EC4 ... 242
6 N10 ... 31
NW8 ... 230
SE12 ... 165
WC2 ... 240
Bromley BR1 ... 209
4 Putney SW15 ... 134
3 Twickenham TW1 ... 153
Crown Dale SE19 ... 183
Crowndale Ct NW1 ... 232
Crowndale Rd
NW1 ... 93 C5 232
Crownfield Ave IG2 ... 57
Crownfield Rd E15 ... 76
Crown Hill CR0 ... 221
Crownhill Rd NW10 ... 89
Crown Ho HA4 ... 40
Crown La BR2 ... 209
N14 ... 15
Chislehurst BR7 ... 189
Merton SM4 ... 201
South Norwood SE19,
SW16 ... 182 C
Crown Lane Gdns
SE27 ... 182 C
Crown Lane Prim Sch
SE27 ... 182 D
Crown Lane Spur BR2 209 D
Crownleigh Ct SW2 ... 160 C
Crown Lo SW3 ... 257
Crownmead Way RM7 . 59 D
Crown Mews 3 E13 ... 99 C
Crown Office Row
EC4 ... 251 A
Crown Par N14 ... 15 C
Morden SM4 ... 201 D
South Norwood SE19 ... 182 D
Crown Pas SW1 ... 249 B
Kingston KT1 ... 175 D
Crown Pl EC2 ... 243 A
NW5 ... 71 B
Crown Point SE19 ... 182 D
Crown Rd N10 ... 31 A
Enfield EN1 ... 6 B
Ilford IG6 ... 57 B
Kingston KT3 ... 177 A
Morden SM4 ... 201 D
Ruislip HA4 ... 62 D
Sutton SM1 ... 217 D
Twickenham TW1 ... 153 B
Crown Reach SW1 ... 259 D
Crown St SE5 ... 139 A
Acton W3 ... 110 D
Dagenham RM10 ... 81 D
Harrow HA2 ... 42 C
Crownstone Ct 1
SW2 ... 160 C
Crownstone Rd SW2 ... 160 C
Crown Terr TW9 ... 132 B
Crown Trad Ctr UB3 ... 105 C
Crowntree Cl TW7 ... 130 D
Crown Way UB7 ... 104 B
Crown Wlk HA9 ... 66 B
Crown Woods Sch
SE9 ... 167 A
Crown Woods Way
SE9 ... 167 B
Crown Yard TW3 ... 130 A
Crowshott Ave HA7 ... 25 D
Crows Rd E15 ... 98 B
Barking IG11 ... 78 D2
Crowther Ave TW8 ... 110 A2
Crowther Cl
SW6 ... 135 B6 264 D5
Crowther Rd SE25 ... 206 A5
Crowthorne Cl SW18 ... 157 B3
Crowthorne Rd W10 ... 90 D1
Croxall Ho KT12 ... 194 C3
Croxden Cl HA8 ... 44 C6
Croxden Wlk SM4 ... 202 A3
Croxford Gdns N22 ... 32 D3
Croxley Cl BR5 ... 190 B1
Croxley Gn BR5 ... 190 B2
Croxley Rd W9 ... 91 B4
Croxted Cl SE21 ... 161 A4
Croxted Mews SE24 ... 161 A5
Croxted Rd SE21,SE24 . 161 B3
Croxteth Ho 11 SW8 ... 137 D3
Croxton 17 KT1 ... 176 C1
Croyde Ave
Greenford UB6 ... 86 A4
Hayes UB3 ... 105 C2

oyde Cl SE9 167 B4
oydon N17 33 B1
oydon Airport Ind Est
R0 220 B2
oydon Central Sta
R0 221 A6
oydon Coll CR0 221 B6
oydon Coll Annexe
R0 205 B1
oydon Coll (Selhurst
ertiary Ctr) SE25 205 B4
oydon Flyover The
R0 221 A5
oydon Gr CR0 204 D1
oydon Ho SE1 251 B2
oydon Rd E13 98 D3
eckenham BR3 207 A6
oney Hall BR2,BR4 224 D5
arlington TW6 126 D2
eston Mark BR2,BR4,
BR6 225 C5
Aitcham CR0,CR4 203 C4
enge SE20 184 C2
Vallington CR0 220 B4
Vallington CR0,SM5,
SM6 219 C5
oydon Rd Ind Est
3R3 206 D5
royland Rd N9 18 A3
roylands Dr KT6 198 A2
roysdale Ave TW16 194 A6
rozier Ho SE3 143 B2
SW8 270 C3
rozier Terr E9 74 D3
rucible Cl RM6 58 B3
rucifix La
SE1 117 C4 253 A2
ruden Ho 23 E3 97 B5
11 SE17 138 D6
ruden St N1 94 D6 234 D5
ruickshank St WC1 234 A2
ruikshank Ho NW8 230 B4
ruikshank Rd E15 76 C3
rummock Gdns NW9 45 C4
rumpsall St SE2 124 C2
rundale Ave NW9 44 C4
runden Rd CR2 221 B1
rusader Gdns CR0 221 C5
rusader Ind Est N4 51 A3
rusoe House Sch
N1 95 B4 235 C2
rusoe Mews N16 73 B6
rusoe Rd CR4 180 D3
Crutched Friars
EC3 117 C6 253 B6
Crutchfield La KT12 194 B1
Crutchley Rd SE6 164 C2
Crystal Ct SE19 183 D5
Crystal Ctr The 1 HA1 42 D4
Crystal Ho SE18 123 D1
Crystal Palace Mus★
SE19 183 D4
Crystal Palace National
Sports Ctr SE20 184 A4
Crystal Palace Par
SE19 183 D5
Crystal Palace Park Rd
SE26 184 B5
Crystal Palace Rd
SE22 162 A6
Crystal Palace Sta
SE19 184 A4
Crystal Palace Station Rd
SE19 184 A4
Crystal Terr SE19 183 B4
Crystal View Ct BR1 186 B6
Crystal Way
Dagenham RM8 58 C1
Harrow HA1 42 D4
Cuba Dr EN3 6 C3
Cuba St E14 119 C4
Cubitt Ho 4 SW4 159 C5
Cubitt Sq UB2 108 A5
Cubitt St WC1 94 B4 233 D1
Cubitt Terr SW4 137 C2
Cubitt Town Jun & Inf Sch
E14 120 A3
Cuckoo Ave W7 86 C3
Cuckoo Dene W7 86 B2
Cuckoo Hall La N9 18 D4
Cuckoo Hall Prim Sch
N9 18 C4
Cuckoo Hill HA5 40 C6
Cuckoo Hill Dr HA5 40 C6
Cuckoo Hill Rd HA5 40 D5
Cuckoo La W7 108 C6
Cuda's Cl KT19 215 D4
Cuddington SE17 262 B4
Cuddington Ave KT19,
KT4 215 D5
Cuddington Com Prim Sch
KT4 215 D5
Cudham La N BR6 227 C1
Cudham St SE6 164 A4
Cudworth Ho SW8 269 B1
Cudworth St E1 96 B3
Cuff Cres SE9 165 D5
Cuffley Ho W10 90 C2
Cuff Point 12 E2 95 D4
Culand Ho SE17 263 A3
Culford Gdns
SW3 114 D2 257 D3
Culford Gr N1 73 C2
Culford Mans SW3 257 D3
Culford Mews N1 73 C2
Culford Rd N1 73 C2
N1 95 C6
Culgaith Gdns EN2 4 A1
Culham Ho 33 E2 95 D4
21 W2 91 C2
Cullen Ho W9 91 B5
Cullen Way NW10 89 A3
Culling Rd SE16 118 C3
Cullington Cl HA3 43 A5
Cullingworth Rd NW10 68 B3
Culloden Cl 15 SE16 118 A1
Culloden Prim Sch E14 98 A1
Culloden Rd EN2 4 D3
Cullum St EC3 253 A6
Culmington Mans
W13 109 C6
Culmington Par W13 109 C6
Culmington Rd
Ealing W13,W5 109 C5
South Croydon CR2 221 A1
Culmore Rd SE15 140 C5
Culmstock Rd SW11 159 A6
Culpepper Ct SE11 261 A4
Culross Bldgs NW1 233 A4
Culross Cl N15 51 A5
Culross St W1 115 A6 248 A5
Culsac Rd KT6 214 A6
Culver Ct SW18 157 D5
Culverden Rd SW12 159 C2
Culver Gr HA7 25 C1
Culverhouse WC1 240 C3
Culverhouse Gdns
SW16 160 B1
Culverlands Cl HA7 25 B6
Culverley Rd SE6 164 A3
Culvers Ave SM5,CR4 218 D6
Culvers House Prim Sch
CR4 203 A1
Culvers Retreat SM5 218 D6
Culverstone Cl BR2 208 D4
Culvers Way SM5 218 D6
Culvert Ct SW11 137 A3
Culverton Ct 5 DA14 190 A6
Culvert Pl SW11 137 A3
Culvert Rd N15 51 C4
SW11 136 D3
Culworth Ho NW8 230 A4
Culworth St NW8 230 A3
Cumber Ho SW18 157 C3
Cumberland Ave
DA16 145 D1
Wembley NW10 88 D4
Cumberland Bsns Pk
NW10 88 D4
Cumberland Cl E8 73 D2
2 Twickenham TW1 153 B5
8 Wimbledon SW20 178 D3
Cumberland Cres
W14 254 B4
Cumberland Ct W1 237 D1
4 Croydon CR0 205 B1
Woodford IG8 37 B3
Cumberland Dr DA7 147 A5
Chessington KT9 214 B5
Hinchley Wood KT10 213 A6
Cumberland Gate
W1 114 D6 247 D6
Cumberland Gdns NW4 29 A1
WC1 234 A2
Cumberland Ho N9 18 C3
Kingston KT2 176 D3
1 Putney SW15 156 C4
Cumberland Mans
7 NW6 69 C3
W1 237 C2
Cumberland Market
NW1 93 B4 231 D2
Cumberland Mills Sq
E14 120 B1
Cumberland Park Ind Est
NW10 90 A4
Cumberland Pk W3 111 A6
Cumberland Pl NW1 231 C2
Catford SE6 164 D3
Sunbury TW16 194 A5
Cumberland Rd E12 77 D4
E13 99 B3
E17 35 A1
N9 18 C3
W3 111 A6
W7 108 D4
Ashford TW15 148 A1
Barnes SW13 134 A4
Beckenham BR2 208 D6
Croydon SE25 206 B3
Harrow HA1 41 D4
Richmond TW9 132 C5
Stanmore HA7,HA8 44 B6
Wood Green N22 32 B1
Cumberland Sch E16 98 D2
Cumberland St
SW1 115 B1 258 D2
Cumberland Terr
NW1 231 C3
Cumberland Terrace Mews
NW1 231 C3
Cumberland Villas
W3 111 A6
Cumberlow Ave SE25 206 A6
Cumbernauld Gdns
TW16 171 D5
Cumberton Rd N17 33 B2
Cumbrae Gdns KT6 213 D6
Cumbria Ho 2 SW15 157 B6
Cumbrian Gdns NW2 69 A6
Cumming St N1 233 D3
Cumnor Cl 23 SW9 138 B3
Cumnor Gdns KT17 216 A2
Cumnor Rd SM2 218 A2
Cunard Cres N21 17 B5
Cunard Pl EC3 243 B1
Cunard Rd NW10 89 B4
Cunard Wlk 3 SE16 119 A2
Cundy Rd E16 99 C1
Cundy St SW1 115 A2 258 B3
Cunliffe Rd KT19 215 D4
Cunliffe St SW16 181 C4
Cunningham Cl
Dagenham RM6 58 C4
West Wickham BR4 223 D6
Cunningham Ct W2 236 C5
Cunningham Ho 16
SE5 139 B5
Cunningham Pk HA1 42 B4
Cunningham Pl
NW8 92 B3 236 C6
Cunningham Rd N15 52 A5
Cunnington St W4 111 A2
Cupar Rd SW11 268 B2
Cupola Cl BR1 187 B5
Cureton St
SW1 115 D2 259 D3
Curie Gdns NW9 27 C1
Curie Ho 1 HA9 67 A5
Curlew Cl SE28 124 D6
Curlew Ct KT6 214 C5
Curlew Ho 6 SE15 139 D4
SE4 141 A1
Enfield EN3 18 D6
Curlew St SE1 117 D4 253 D2
Curlew Way UB4 84 D2
Curnick's La SE27 183 A6
Curran Ave DA15 167 D6
Hackbridge SM6 219 A5
Curran Ho SW3 257 A3
Currey Rd UB6 64 B2
Curricle St W3 111 C5
Currie Hill Cl SW19 179 B6
Currie Ho 13 SW12 159 D4
Curry Rise NW7 28 D4
Cursitor St EC4 94 C1 241 A2
Curtain Pl EC2 243 B6
Curtain Rd EC2 95 C3 243 B6
Curthwaite Gdns EN2 15 D6
Curtis Dr W3 89 B1
Curtis Field Rd SW16 182 C6
Curtis Ho 7 N11 31 C5
SE17 262 C2
Curtis La HA0 66 A3
Curtis Rd
Twickenham TW4 151 B4
West Ewell KT19 215 A4
Curtis St SE1 117 D2 263 C4
Curtis Way SE1 263 C4
7 SE28 124 B6
Curtlington Ho 3 HA8 27 A1
Curve The W12 112 A6
Curwen Ave E7 77 B4
Curwen Rd W12 112 A4
Curwen Sch E13 99 A5
Curzon Ave Enfield EN3 18 D6
Stanmore HA7 25 A2
Curzon Cl BR6 227 B4
Curzon Cres NW10 67 C1
Barking IG11 101 D4
Curzon Ct SE9 167 A1
SW6 265 D1
Curzon Gate W1 248 B3
Curzon Ho W5 87 B3
Curzon Pl W1 248 B3
Pinner HA5 40 C4
Curzon Rd N10 31 B1
Ealing W5 87 B3
Thornton Heath CR7 204 C3
Curzon St W1 115 B5 248 C4
Cusack Cl TW1 174 D6
Custance Ho N1 235 C3
Custance St N1 235 C2
Custom House★
EC3 117 C6 253 A5
Custom House for ExCeL
Sta E16 121 B6
Custom House Reach
SE16 119 B3
Cutbush Ho N7 71 D3
Cutcombe Mans 22
SE5 139 A3
Cutcombe Rd SE5 139 A3
Cuthberga Cl IG11 79 A1
Cuthbert Gdns SE25 205 C6
Cuthbert Harrowing Ho
EC1 242 A5
Cuthbert Ho W2 236 C4
Cuthbert Rd E17 54 A6
Croydon CR0 220 D6
8 Edmonton N18 34 A6
Cuthbert St W2 236 C5
Cuthill Wlk 3 SE5 139 B4
Cutlers Gdns EC2 243 B2
Cutlers Sq E14 119 C2
Cutler St EC2 243 B2
Cut The SE1 116 C4 251 B2
Cutty Sark★ SE10 142 A6
Cutty Sark Sta SE10 142 A6
Cuxton BR5 211 A4
Cuxton Cl DA6 169 A6
Cuxton Ho SE17 263 B2
Cyclamen Cl 4 TW12 173 C4
Cyclamen Way KT19 215 A3
Cyclops Mews 9 E14 119 C2
Cygnet Ave TW14 150 D4
Cygnet Cl NW10 67 B3
Cygnet St E1 243 D6
Cygnets The TW13 173 A6
Cygnet Way UB4 84 D2
Cygnus Bsns Ctr NW10 67 D2
Cymbeline Ct 6 HA1 42 D3
Cyns Ct 5 E11 55 A3
Cynthia St N1 233 D3
Cypress Ave N2 47 D6
Twickenham TW2 152 A4
Cypress Ct 5 E11 76 B4
Cheam SM1 217 C2
7 West Norwood
SW16 182 C5
Cypress Gdns SE4 163 A6
Cypress Ho SE14 140 D4
Cypress Inf Sch SE25 183 C1
Cypress Jun Sch SE25 183 C1
Cypress Lo SE25 183 C1
Cypress Pl W1 239 B5
Cypress Rd Harrow HA3 24 B1
South Norwood SE25 183 C1
Cypress Tree Cl DA15 167 D3
Cyprus Ave N3 29 A1
Cyprus Cl N4 50 C3
Cyprus Gdns N3 29 A1
Cyprus Pl 24 E2 96 C5
E6 122 C6
Cyprus Rd N3 29 B1
Edmonton N9 17 D2
Cyprus St E2 96 C5
Cyprus Sta E6 122 C6
Cyrena Rd SE22 161 D6
Cyril Jackson Prim Sch
(North Bldg) E14 119 B6
Cyril Jackson Prim Sch
(South Bldg) E14 119 B6
Cyril Lo 2 DA14 190 A6
Cyril Mans SW11 267 D1
Cyril Rd DA7 147 A3
Cyril Smith Ho N13 32 B5
Cyril Thatcher Ho
SW6 265 B1
Cyrus Ho EC1 241 D6
Cyrus St EC1 94 D3 241 D6
Czar St SE8 141 C6

D

Dabbs Hill La UB5 63 C3
Dabb's La EC1 241 B5
Dabin Cres SE10 142 A4
Dacca St SE8 141 B6
Dace Rd E3 97 C6
Dacre Cl UB6 85 D5
Dacre Gdns SE13 142 C1
Borehamwood WD6 11 B6
Dacre Ho SW3 266 D5
Dacre Pk SE13 142 C1
Dacre Pl SE13 142 C2
Dacre Rd E11 54 D1
E13 99 B6
Thornton Heath CR0 204 A2
Dacres Rd SE23 162 D1
Dacre St SW1 115 D3 259 C6
Dade Way UB2 107 B1
Daerwood Cl BR2 210 B1
Daffodil Cl CR0 206 D1
Daffodil Gdns IG1 78 D3
Daffodil Pl 7 TW12 173 C4
Daffodil St W12 111 D6
Dafforne Rd SW17 159 A1
Dagenham Ave RM9 103 A6
Dagenham Dock Sta
RM9 103 B5
Dagenham East Sta
RM10 81 D3
Dagenham Heathway Sta
RM9 81 B2
Dagenham Priory Comp
Sch RM10 103 D6
Dagenham Rd E10 53 B1
Dagenham RM10 81 D4
Dagger La WD23,WD6 9 A6
Dagmar Ave HA9 66 B4
Dagmar Ct E14 120 A3
Dagmar Gdns NW10 90 D5
Dagmar Mews UB2 107 A3
Dagmar Pas N1 234 D6
Dagmar Rd N15 51 B5
N22 31 D2
N4 50 C2
SE5 139 C4
4 Kingston KT2 176 C3
Southall UB2 107 A3
South Norwood SE25 205 C4
Dagmar Terr
N1 94 D6 234 D6
Dagnall Pk SE25 205 C4
Dagnall Rd SE25 205 C4
Dagnall St
SW11 137 A4 268 A1
Dagnan Rd SW12 159 C4
Dagobert Ho 25 E1 96 C2
Dagonet Gdns BR1 165 A1
Dagonet Rd BR1 165 A1
Dahlia Gdns Ilford IG1 78 D2
Mitcham CR4 203 D5
Dahlia Rd SE2 124 B2
Dahomey Rd SW16 181 C4
Daiglen Sch The IG9 21 C2
Daimler Ho 8 E3 97 C3
Daimler Way SM6 220 A1
Daines Cl E12 78 B5
Dainford Cl BR1 186 B5
Dainton Cl 2 BR1 187 B2
Dainton Ho 22 W2 91 C2
Daintry Cl HA3 43 A5
Daintry Way E9 75 B2
Dairsie Ct 2 BR1 187 C1
Dairsie Rd SE9 144 C2
Dairy Cl BR1 187 B3
South Norwood CR7 183 A1
Dairy La SE18 122 B2
Dairyman Cl NW2 69 A5
Dairy Meadow Prim Sch
UB2 107 B3
Daisy Cl CR0 206 D1
Daisy Dormer Ct 11
SW9 138 B1
Daisy La SW6 135 C2
Daisy Rd E16 98 C3
Woodford E18 37 B1
Dakota Cl SM6
Dakota Gdns
Newham E6 100 A3
Northolt UB5 85 A4
Dalberg Rd SW2 160 C6
Dalberg Way SE2 124 D3
Dalbury Ho 6 SW9 138 B1
Dalby Rd SW18 136 A1
Dalbys Cres N17 33 C4
Dalby St NW5 71 B2
Dalcross Rd TW4,TW5 129 A3
Dale Ave Edgware HA8 26 B1
Hounslow TW4 129 A2
Dalebury Rd SW17 158 D2
Dale Cl SE3 143 A2
New Barnet EN5 13 D5
Pinner HA5 22 B2
Dale Croft N4 73 A5
Dale Ct N8 49 C5
3 Kingston KT2 176 B3
Woodford E18 37 A1
Dale Dr UB4 83 D4
Dalefield IG9 21 D3
Dale Gdns IG8 37 B6
Dale Gr N12 30 A5
Dale Green Rd N11 15 B1
Dalehaed NW1 232 A3
Daleham Dr UB8 82 D1
Daleham Gdns NW3 70 B2
Daleham Mews NW3 70 B2
Dale Ho NW8 229 A6
SE4 141 A1
Dale Lo N6 49 C3
Dalemain Ho 5 SW8 137 D3
Dalemain Mews 13
E16 121 A5
Dale Park Ave SM5 218 D6
Dale Park Rd SE19 183 B2
Dale Rd NW5 71 A3
SE17 138 D6
Ashford TW16 171 D3
Cheam SM1 217 B4
Southall UB6 85 D2
Walton-on-T KT12 193 D2
Dale Row W11 91 A1
Daleside Rd
Streatham SW17 181 B5
West Ewell KT19 215 B2
Dales Path WD6 11 B6
Dales Rd WD6 11 B6
Dale St W4 111 C1
Dale The BR2 225 D4
Dale View Ave E4 20 A2
Dale View Cres E4 20 A1
Dale View Gdns E4 20 B1
Daleview Rd N15 51 C3
Dalewood Gdns KT4 216 B6
Dale Wood Rd BR6 211 C1
Daley Ho W12 90 B1
Daley St E9 74 D2
Daley Thompson Way 7
SW8 137 B2
Dalgarno Gdns W10 90 C2
Dalgarno Way W10 90 C3
Daling Way E3 97 A5
Dalkeith Ct SW1 259 D3
Dalkeith Gr HA7 26 A5
Dalkeith Ho 6 SW9 138 D4
Dalkeith Rd Ilford IG1 79 A5
West Norwood SE21 161 A4
Dallas Rd NW4 46 A2
Cheam SM3 217 A2
Ealing W5 88 B2
Forest Hill SE26 162 B1
Dallas Terr UB3 105 D3
Dallega Cl UB3 105 B6
Dallinger Rd SE12 164 D5
Dalling Rd W6 112 B2
Dallington Sch
EC1 94 D3 241 D6
Dallington St
EC1 94 D3 241 D6
Dallin Rd DA6 146 D1
Woolwich SE18 144 D5
Dalmain Prim Sch
SE23 163 A3
Dalmain Rd SE23 162 D3
Dalmally Rd CR0 206 A2
Dalmeny Ave N7 71 D4
Thornton Heath SW16 182 C1
Dalmeny Cl HA0 65 C2
Dalmeny Cres TW3 130 B1
Dalmeny Ct 4 SW4 138 A3
Dalmeny Rd DA7,DA8 147 D4
N7 71 D4
New Barnet EN5 14 A5
North Cheam KT4 216 B5
Wallington SM5 219 A1
Dalmeyer Rd NW10 67 D2
Dalmore Ave KT10 212 D2
Dalmore Rd SE21 161 A2
Dalrymple Cl N14 15 D4
Dalrymple Rd SE4 141 A1
Dalston Gdns HA7 26 A1
Dalston Jct E8 73 D2
Dalston Kingsland Sta
E8 73 D3
Dalston La E8 74 A3
Dalton Ave CR4 180 C1
Dalton Cl BR6 227 C5
Hayes UB4 83 B3
Dalton Ho 9 E3 97 A5
19 SE14 140 D6
Dalton St SE27 160 D1
Dalwood St SE5 139 C4
Daly Ct E15 76 A3
Dalyell Rd SW9 138 B2
Damascene Wlk SE21 161 A3
Damask Cres E16 98 C3
Damer Ho 9 TW10 154 B5
Damer Terr SW10 266 B3
Dames Rd E7 77 A5
Dame St N1 95 A5 235 A4
Damien Ct 20 E1 96 B1
Damien St E1 96 B1
Damon Cl DA14 168 B1
Damon Ct DA14 168 B1
Damory Ho 1 SE16 118 C2
Damson Dr UB3 106 A6
Damsonwood Rd UB2 107 C3
Danbrook Rd SW16 182 A3
Dan Bryant Ho 5
SW12 159 C4
Danbury Cl RM6 58 D6
Danbury Mans 3 IG11 78 D1
Danbury Mews SM5,
SM6 219 B4
Danbury St N1 94 D5 234 D4
Danbury Way IG8 37 C4
Danby Ct EN2 5 A2
Danby Ho 23 E9 74 C1
3 W10 91 B4
Danby St SE15 139 D2
Dancer Rd
Fulham SW6 135 B4 264 C1
Richmond TW9 132 C2
Dando Cres SE3 143 B2
Dandridge Cl SE10 120 D1
Dandridge Ho E1 243 C4
Danebury W10 90 C2
New Addington CR0 223 D2
Danebury Ave SW15 155 D5
Daneby Rd SE6 164 A2
Dane Cl BR6 227 B3
Sidcup DA5 169 C4
Danecourt Gdns CR0 221 D5
Danecroft Rd SE24 161 B6
Danegrove Prim Sch
EN4 14 C5
Danegrove Sch EN4 14 D5
Danehill Wlk DA14 168 A1
Dane Ho 15 SE5 139 A3
Danehurst TW8 131 C5
Danehurst Gdns IG4 56 B4
Danehurst St
SW6 135 A4 264 A2
Daneland EN4 14 D5
Danemead Gr UB5 63 D3
Danemere St SW15 134 C2

Dane Pl E3 .... 97 B5
Dane Rd N18 .... 18 C1
Ashford TW15 .... 171 B4
Ealing W13 .... 109 C5
Ilford IG1 .... 79 A3
Merton SW19 .... 180 A2
Southall UB1 .... 107 A6
Danesbury Rd TW13 .. 150 B3
Danescombe SE12 .... 165 A3
Danescourt Cres SM1 218 A6
Danescroft NW4 .... 46 D4
Danescroft Ave NW4 .. 46 D4
Danescroft Gdns NW4 .. 46 D4
Danes Ct NW8 .... 230 C5
Wembley HA9 .... 66 D5
Danesdale Rd E9 .... 75 A2
Danesfield SE5 .... 139 C6
Danes Gate HA1 .... 42 C6
Danes Ho W10 .... 90 C2
Dane St WC1 .... 240 C3
Daneswood Ave SE6 .. 164 A1
Danethorpe Rd HA0 .. 65 D2
Danetree Cl KT19 .... 215 A1
Danetree Jun Sch
KT19 .... 215 A1
Danetree Rd KT19 .... 215 A1
Danette Gdns RM8 .... 81 B6
Daneville Rd SE5 .... 139 B4
Danford Ho 9 N11 .... 31 C5
Dangan Rd E11 .... 55 A3
Daniel Bolt Cl E14 .... 97 D2
Daniel Cl N18 .... 34 C6
Twickenham TW4 .... 151 B4
Upper Tooting SW17 .. 180 C4
Daniel Ct 8 NW9 .... 27 C2
W3 .... 111 C6
3 Beckenham BR3 .... 185 C3
Daniel Gdns SE15 .... 139 D5
Daniell Ho N1 .... 235 D4
Daniell Way CR0 .... 204 B1
Daniel Pl NW4 .... 46 B2
Daniel Rd W5 .... 110 B6
Daniel's Rd SE15 .... 140 C2
Dan Leno Wlk SW6 .. 265 C3
Dansey Pl W1 .... 249 C6
Dansington Rd DA16 .. 146 A1
Danson Cres DA16 .... 146 B2
Danson Intc DA5,DA6 .. 168 C5
Danson La DA16 .... 146 B1
Danson Mead DA16 .. 146 C2
Danson Prim Sch
DA16 .... 146 A1
Danson Rd DA5,DA6,
DA15 .... 168 D6
Danson Underpass
DA15 .... 168 C5
Dante Rd SE11 116 D2 261 C4
Danube Ct 12 SE15 .. 139 D5
Danube St
SW3 .... 114 C1 257 B2
Danvers Ho 22 E1 .... 96 A1
Danvers Rd N8 .... 49 D5
Danvers St
SW3 .... 136 B6 266 D5
Da Palma Ct SW6 .... 265 A5
Daphne Ct Ealing W5 .. 87 C1
Worcester Park KT4 .. 215 C6
Daphne Gdns E4 .... 20 A1
Daphne Ho N22 .... 32 C2
Daphne St SW18 .... 158 A5
Daplyn St 6 E1 .... 96 A2
D'arblay St W1 . 93 C1 239 B1
Darby Cres TW16 .... 172 C1
Darby Gdns TW16 .... 172 C1
Darcy Ave SM6 .... 219 C4
Darcy Cl N20 .... 14 B2
D'arcy Dr HA3 .... 43 D5
D'arcy Gdns
Dagenham RM9 .... 103 B6
Harrow HA3 .... 44 A5
Darcy Ho E8 .... 96 B6
D'arcy Pl BR2 .... 209 A5
Darcy Rd
Isleworth TW7 .... 131 A4
Thornton Heath SW16 .. 182 A1
D'arcy Rd SM3 .... 216 D4
Dare Ct 2 E10 .... 54 A2
Dare Gdns RM8 .... 81 A5
Darell Prim Sch TW9 .. 132 C2
Darell Rd TW9 .... 132 C2
Daren Ct N7 .... 72 A4
Darent Ho NW8 .... 236 D4
4 Catford BR1 .... 186 B5
Darenth Rd DA16 .... 146 A4
N16 .... 51 D1
Darfield NW1 .... 232 A5
Darfield Rd SE4 .... 163 B6
Darfield Way W10 .... 90 D1
Darfur St SW15 .... 134 D2
Dargate Cl SE19 .... 183 D3
Darien Ho 8 E1 .... 96 D2
17 SW11 .... 136 B2
Darien Rd SW11 .... 136 B2
Daring Ho 21 E3 .... 97 A5
Darland Ct SW15 .... 157 B5
Darlands Dr EN5 .... 12 D6

Darlan Rd
SW6 .... 135 B5 264 D3
Darlaston Rd SW19 .. 179 A3
Darley Cl CR0 .... 207 A3
Darley Dr KT3 .... 177 B1
Darley Gdns SM4 .... 201 D3
Darley Ho SE11 .... 260 C1
Darley Rd SW11 .... 158 D5
Edmonton N9 .... 17 D3
Darling Ho 5 TW1 .... 153 D5
Darling Rd SE4 .... 141 C2
Darling Row E1 .... 96 B3
Darlington Ct 8 SE6 .. 164 D3
Darlington Ho SW8 .... 269 D3
2 Surbiton KT6 .... 197 D2
Darlington Rd SE27 .. 182 D5
Darmaine Cl CR2 .... 221 A1
Darnay Ho 3 SE16 .... 118 A3
Darndale Cl E17 .... 35 B1
Darnell Ho 4 SE10 .... 142 A4
9 SE10 .... 142 A5
Darnley Ho 9 E14 .... 97 A1
Darnley Rd E9 .... 74 C2
Woodford IG8 .... 37 B2
Darnley Terr 12 W11 .. 112 D5
Darrell Ct BR2 .... 208 C6
Darrell Rd SE22 .... 162 A6
Darren Cl N4 .... 50 B2
Darrick Wood Ho BR6 227 A5
Darrick Wood Inf Sch
BR6 .... 226 D5
Darrick Wood Jun Sch
BR6 .... 226 D4
Darrick Wood Rd BR6 227 B6
Darrick Wood Sec Sch
BR6 .... 226 D5
Darrick Wood Sports Ctr
BR6 .... 227 C6
Darris Cl UB4 .... 85 A3
Darsley Dr
SW8 .... 138 A4 270 A2
Dartford Ave N9 .... 18 D5
Dartford Gdns RM6 .... 58 B4
Dartford Ho SE1 .... 263 D4
Dartford St SE17 .... 139 A6
Dartington NW1 .... 232 B5
Dartington Ho
7 SW8 .... 137 D3
W2 .... 91 D2
Dartle Ct 26 SE16 .... 118 A4
Dartmoor Wlk 17 E14 .. 119 C2
Dartmouth Cl W11 .... 91 C1
Dartmouth Ct SE10 .. 142 A4
Dartmouth Gr SE10 .. 142 A4
Dartmouth Hill SE10 .. 142 A4
Dartmouth Ho N19 .... 71 B6
Lewisham SE10 .... 142 A3
Thornton Heath CR0 .. 204 D2
Dartmouth Park Ave
NW5 .... 71 B5
Dartmouth Park Hill
N19 .... 71 B6
Dartmouth Park Rd
NW5 .... 71 B5
Dartmouth Pl
Chiswick W4 .... 133 C6
Forest Hill SE23 .... 162 C2
Dartmouth Rd NW2 .... 68 D2
NW4 .... 46 A3
Forest Hill SE23,SE26 .. 162 C1
Hayes BR2 .... 209 A2
Ruislip HA4 .... 62 A5
Dartmouth Row SE10 . 142 A4
Dartmouth St
SW1 .... 115 D4 249 D1
Dartmouth Terr SE10 . 142 B4
Dartnell Rd CR0 .... 205 D2
Darton Ct W3 .... 111 A5
Dartrey Twr SW10 .... 266 C4
Dartrey Wlk
SW10 .... 136 A5 266 B4
Dart St W10 .... 91 B4
Darville Rd N16 .... 73 D5
Darwell Cl E6 .... 100 C5
Darwen Pl E2 .... 96 B6
Darwin Cl BR6 .... 227 B3
N11 .... 15 B1
Darwin Ct E13 .... 99 B4
NW1 .... 231 B6
SE9 .... 166 C5
Darwin Dr UB1 .... 85 D1
Darwin Gdns WD19 .... 22 C5
Darwin Ho 2 HA9 .... 67 A5
Darwin Rd DA16 .... 145 D2
W5 .... 109 C2
Tottenham N22 .... 32 D1
Darwin St
SE17 .... 117 B2 262 D4
Daryngton Dr UB6 .... 86 C5
Daryngton Ho SW8 .... 270 A3
Dashwood Cl DA6 .... 169 C6
Dashwood Ct TW3 .... 130 A1
Dashwood Ho SE21 .... 161 D1
Dashwood Rd N8 .... 50 B3
Dassett Rd SE27 .... 182 D5
Data Point Bsns Ctr
E16 .... 98 B3
Datchelor Pl 14 SE5 .. 139 B4
Datchet Ho NW1 .... 231 D2

Datchet Rd SE6 .... 163 B2
Datchett Ho 40 E2 .... 95 D4
Datchwood Ct N4 .... 73 A5
Datchworth Ct 7 EN1 .. 17 C6
Datchworth Ho 8 N1 .. 72 D1
Date St SE17 .. 117 B1 262 C1
Daubeney Gdns N17 .. 33 A3
Daubeney Pl TW12 .. 173 D1
Daubeney Prim Sch E5 75 A4
Daubeney Rd E5 .... 75 A4
Tottenham N17 .... 33 A3
Daubeney Twr 2 SE8 . 119 B1
Dault Rd SW18 .... 158 A5
Dauney Ho SE1 .... 251 C1
Dave Adams Ho 7 E3 . 97 B5
Davenant Ho 18 E1 .... 96 A2
Davenant Rd N19 .... 71 D6
Croydon CR0,CR9 .... 220 D4
Davenant St E1 .... 96 A2
Davenport Cl TW11 .. 175 A4
Davenport Ctr IG11 .. 102 B5
Davenport Ho SE11 .. 261 A5
Davenport Lo TW5 .... 129 A5
Davenport Rd DA14 .. 169 A2
SE6 .... 164 A5
Daventer Dr HA7 .... 24 D3
Daventry Ave E17 .... 53 C3
Daventry St
NW1 .... 92 C2 237 A4
Dave Porter Hts SW19 157 A4
Daver Ct SW3 .... 257 B1
Ealing W5 .... 87 D3
Davern Cl SE10 .... 120 D2
Davet Ct SW8 .... 270 C2
Davey Cl N7 .... 72 B2
Bowes Park N13 .... 32 B5
Davey Lo 2 N1 .... 72 C1
Davey Rd E9 .... 75 C1
Davey's Ct WC2 .... 250 A6
Davey St SE15 .... 139 D6
David Ave UB6 .... 86 C5
David Cl UB3 .... 127 C5
David Coffer Ct DA17 . 125 D2
David Devine Ho 7 E8 74 A3
Davidge Ho SE1 .... 251 B1
Davidge St
SE1 .... 116 D4 251 D1
David Ho 3 E14 .... 97 D2
SW8 .... 270 A4
8 Putney SW15 .... 156 A6
South Norwood SE25 .. 206 A6
David Lee Point 4 E15 98 C6
David Livingstone Prim Sch
CR7 .... 183 A2
David Mews W1 .... 237 D4
David Rd RM8 .... 81 A6
Davidson Gdns
SW8 .... 138 A5 270 A4
Davidson Ho 7 N19 .... 71 C4
Davidson Inf Sch CR0 205 D2
Davidson Jun Sch
CR0 .... 205 D2
Davidson Lo CR0 .... 205 C2
Davidson Rd CR0 .... 205 D3
Davidson Terrs E7 .... 77 B3
Davidson Twr BR1 .... 187 B5
David's Rd SE23 .... 162 C3
David St E15 .... 76 B3
David Twigg Cl KT2 .. 176 A2
Davies Cl CR0 .... 206 A3
Davies La E11 .... 76 D6
Davies Lane Jun & Inf Sch
E11 .... 76 D6
Davies Mews W1 .... 248 C6
Davies St W1 . 115 B6 248 C6
Davies Walk TW7 .... 130 B4
Da Vinci Ct 12 SE16 .. 118 B1
Davington Gdns RM8 .. 80 B3
Davington Rd RM8 .... 80 B3
Davis Ho W12 .... 112 B6
Davis Rd W3 .... 111 D4
Chessington KT9 .... 214 C4
Davis St E13 .... 99 B5
Davisville Rd W12 .... 112 A4
Davmor Ct TW8 .... 109 C1
Davy Ho HA9 .... 67 A6
Dawes Ave TW7 .... 131 A1
Dawe's Cl UB10 .... 82 A5
Dawes Ho SE17 .... 262 C3
Dawes Rd
SW6 .... 135 B5 264 C4
Dawe's Rd UB10 .... 82 A5
Dawes St SE17 117 B1 262 D2
Dawley Ave UB8 .... 83 A1
Dawley Par UB3 .... 105 A6
Dawley Rd Hayes UB3 . 105 B6
Hayes UB3 .... 105 C2
Dawlish Ave
Bowes Park N13 .... 32 A5
Wandsworth SW18 .... 157 D2
Wembley UB6 .... 87 A5
Dawlish Dr Ilford IG3 .. 79 D4
Pinner HA5 .... 41 A3
Ruislip HA4 .... 62 B6
Dawlish Prim Sch E10 . 54 A1
Dawlish Rd E10 .... 76 A6
N17 .... 52 A6
NW2 .... 68 D2
Dawnay Gdns SW18 .... 158 B2

Dawnay Rd SW17,
SW18 .... 158 B2
Dawn Cl TW4 .... 129 A2
Dawn Cres E15 .... 98 B6
Dawn Wlk BR2 .... 186 B1
Dawpool Rd NW2 .... 67 D6
Daws Ho 35 W12 .... 112 B6
Daws La NW7 .... 28 A5
Dawson Ave BR5 .... 190 B1
Barking IG11 .... 79 D1
Dawson Cl SE18 .... 123 A2
Hayes UB3 .... 83 B2
Dawson Gdns 9 IG11 .. 79 D1
Dawson Ho 23 E2 .... 96 C4
5 SE5 .... 139 C4
Dawson Pl W2 113 C6 245 B6
Dawson Rd NW2 .... 68 C4
Kingston KT1 .... 198 B6
Dawson St E2 .... 95 D5
Dawson Terr N9 .... 18 C4
Dax Ct TW16 .... 194 C6
Daybrook Rd SW19 .. 201 D6
Day Ho SE5 .... 138 D5
2 SE5 .... 139 A5
Daylesford Ave SW15 . 134 A1
Daymer Gdns HA5 .... 40 C5
Daynor Ho 4 NW6 .... 91 C6
Daysbrook Rd SW2 .. 160 B3
Days La DA15 .... 167 C4
Days Lane Prim Sch
DA15 .... 167 D5
Daytone Ho SW20 .. 178 D2
Dayton Gr SE15 .... 140 C4
Deaconess Ct 4 N15 .. 51 D5
Deacon Ho SE11 .... 260 D3
Deacon Mews N1 .... 73 B1
Deacon Rd NW2 .... 68 A2
Kingston KT2 .... 176 B2
Deacons Cl HA5 .... 22 B1
Deacon's Hill Rd WD6 .. 10 C6
Deacons Hts WD6 .... 10 C5
Deacons Leas BR6 .... 227 B4
Deacons Rise N2 .... 48 B4
Deacons Wlk TW12 .. 173 C6
Deacon Way
SE17 .... 117 A2 262 B4
Deal Ct 13 NW9 .... 27 D1
7 Southall UB1 .... 86 A1
Deal Ho SE15 .... 140 D6
SE17 .... 263 B2
Deal Porters Way
SE16 .... 118 D3
Deal Rd SW17 .... 181 A4
Deal St E1 .... 96 A2
Dealtry Rd SW15 .... 134 C1
Deal Wlk 3 SW9 .... 138 C5
Dean Bradley St SW1 . 260 A5
Dean Cl E9 .... 74 C3
SE16 .... 118 D5
Hillingdon UB10 .... 60 B1
Deancross St E1 .... 96 C1
Dean Ct SW8 .... 270 A3
Edgware HA8 .... 26 D4
10 Kingston KT2 .... 176 C3
Wembley HA0 .... 65 B5
Dean Dr HA7 .... 26 A1
Deane Ave HA4 .... 62 C3
Deane Croft Rd HA5 .. 40 C3
Deanery Cl N2 .... 48 C5
Deanery Mews W1 .... 248 B4
Deanery Rd E15 .... 76 C2
Deanery St
W1 .... 115 A5 248 B4
Deane Way HA4 .... 40 B3
Dean Farrar St SW1 .. 259 D6
Deanfield Gdns CR0 .. 221 B4
Dean Gdns E17 .... 54 B5
Deanhill Ct 2 SW14 .. 132 D1
Deanhill Rd SW14 .... 132 D1
Dean Ho 10 E1 .... 96 C1
N16 .... 51 D1
N4 .... 51 A2
SE14 .... 141 B5
Ruislip HA4 .... 39 B1
Dean Rd NW2 .... 68 C2
Croydon CR0 .... 221 B4
Hampton TW12 .... 173 C5
Hounslow TW3 .... 151 D6
Thamesmead SE28 .... 124 A6
Dean Ryle St SW1 .... 260 A4
Dean's Bldgs
SE17 .... 117 B2 262 D3
Deansbrook Cl HA8 .... 27 A3
Deansbrook Jun & Inf Schs
HA8,NW7 .... 27 A4
Deansbrook Rd HA8 .... 27 B4
Edgware HA8 .... 26 D3
Deans Cl HA8 .... 27 A4
Chiswick W4 .... 132 D6
South Croydon CR0 .. 221 D5
Deanscroft Ave NW9 .. 45 A1
Dean's Ct EC4 .... 241 D1
Dean's Dr HA8 .... 27 B5
Deans Dr N13 .... 32 D4
Deansfield Prim HA4 .. 62 D4
Deansfield Prim Sch
SE9 .... 144 C2
Deans Gate Cl SE23 .. 162 D1

Deanshanger Ho 21
SE8 .... 118 D2
Dean's La HA8 .... 27 A4
Dean's Mews W1 .... 238 D2
Dean's Rd W7 .... 108 D4
Deans Rd SM1 .... 217 D5
Dean St E7 .... 77 A3
W1 .... 93 D1 239 C1
Dean Stanley St SW1 . 260 A5
Deansway N2 .... 48 B5
Deans Way HA8 .... 27 A5
Deansway N9 .... 17 C1
Deanswood N11 .... 31 D4
Dean's Yd SW1 .... 259 D6
Dean Trench St SW1 . 260 A5
Dean Way UB2 .... 107 D4
Dean Wlk HA8 .... 27 B3
Dearmer Ho 6 SW2 .. 160 C4
Dearne Cl HA7 .... 25 A5
De'arn Gdns CR4 .... 202 C6
Dearsley Rd EN1 .... 6 A2
Deason St E15 .... 98 A6
Deauville Ct 4 SE16 . 118 D4
14 SW4 .... 159 C5
Deauville Mans 13
SW4 .... 159 C5
De Barowe Mews N5 .. 72 D3
Debdale Ho 20 E2 .... 96 A6
Debden N17 .... 33 B1
Debden Cl
Kingston KT2 .... 175 D5
Woodford IG8 .... 37 D3
De Beauvoir Cres N1 .. 95 C6
De Beauvoir Ct N1 .... 73 B1
De Beauvoir Pl 5 N1 .. 73 C2
De Beauvoir Prim Sch
N1 .... 73 C2
De Beauvoir Rd N1 .... 73 C1
De Beauvoir Sq N1 .... 73 C1
Debenham Ct E8 .... 96 A6
Barnet EN5 .... 12 C6
Debham Ct NW2 .... 68 C5
Debnams Rd SE16 .... 118 C2
De Bohun Ave N14 .... 15 B5
De Bohun Prim Sch
N14 .... 15 B6
Deborah Cl TW7 .... 130 C4
Deborah Cres HA4 .... 39 B2
Deborah Ct 7 E18 .... 55 B6
De Broome Rd TW13 .. 150 C3
De Burgh Ho 10 SW19 180 A3
Deburgh Rd SW19 .... 180 A3
Debussy 9 NW9 .... 27 D1
Decimal Ctr UB2 .... 107 C4
Decima St SE1 117 C3 263 A6
Decimus Cl CR7 .... 205 B5
Deck Cl SE16 .... 118 D5
Decoy Ave NW11 .... 47 A5
De Crespigny Pk SE5 .. 139 B3
Dedham Ho 1 SE6 .... 186 A6
Dee Ct W7 .... 86 B1
Deeley Rd
SW8 .... 137 D4 269 C2
Deena Cl W3 .... 88 B1
Deepdale N4 .... 72 D5
Wimbledon SW19 .... 178 D6
Deepdale Ave BR2 .... 208 D5
Deepdale Cl N11 .... 31 A4
Deepdale Ct 4 CR0 .. 221 B4
Deepdene N12 .... 30 C6
Deepdene Ave CR0 .. 221 D5
Deepdene Cl E11 .... 55 A5
Deepdene Ct
Beckenham BR2 .... 208 C6
Southgate N21 .... 16 D5
Deepdene Gdns SW2 .. 160 B4
Deepdene Ho N16 .... 51 B1
Deepdene Lo 5 SW2 .. 160 B4
Deepdene Mans SW6 .. 264 C2
Deepdene Point 9
SE26 .... 162 D1
Deepdene Rd DA16 .. 146 A2
SE5,SE24 .... 139 B1
Deepwell Cl TW7 .... 131 A4
Deepwood La UB6 .... 86 B4
Deerbrook Rd SE24,
SW2 .... 160 D3
Dee Rd TW9 .... 132 B1
Deerdale Rd SE24 .... 139 A1
Deerhurst 9 KT2 .... 176 D2
Deerhurst Cl TW13 .. 172 B6
Deerhurst Cres TW12 . 174 A5
Deerhurst Ho 6 SE15 140 A6
Deerhurst Rd NW2 .... 68 D2
Streatham SW16 .... 182 B5
Deerings Dr HA5 .... 40 A4
Deerleap Gr E4 .... 19 D6
Deer Lo SW6 .... 135 A2
Deer Park Cl KT2 .... 176 D3
Deer Park Gdns CR4 .. 202 B5
Deer Park Rd SW19 .. 180 A1
Deer Park Way BR4 .. 224 D6
Deeside Rd SW17 .... 158 B1
Dee St E14 .... 98 A1
Defiance Wlk SE18 .. 122 B3
Defiant 18 NW9 .... 27 D1
Defiant Way SM6 .... 220 A1
Defoe Ave TW9 .... 132 C5
Defoe Cl SW17 .... 180 C4

Defoe Ho EC2 242
5 N16 73
Defoe Pl EC2 242
Upper Tooting SW17 .. 180
Defoe Rd N16 73
SE16 119
De Frene Rd SE26 .. 163
De Gama Pl E14 119
Degema Rd BR7 188
Dehar Cres NW9 46
Dehavilland Cl UB5 .. 84
De Havilland Rd
Edgware HA8 26
Heston TW5 128
De Havilland Way
TW19 148
Dekker Ho 19 SE5 139
Dekker Rd SE21 161
Delacourt Rd SE3 143
Delafield Ho 18 E1 96
Delafield Rd SE7 121
Delaford Rd SE16 118
Delaford St
SW6 .... 135 B6 264
Delamare Cres CR0 .. 206
Delamere Gdns NW7 .. 27
Delamere Ho 4 N4 51
Delamere Rd W5 110
Hayes UB4 106
Wimbledon SW20 178
Delamere St W2 236
Delamere Terr W2 91
Delancey Pas NW1 .. 231
Delancey St
NW1 .... 93 B6 231
Delancey Studios
NW1 231
Delany Ho SE10 142
Delarch Ho SE1 251
De Laune St
SE17 .... 116 D1 261
Delaware Rd W9 91
Delawyk Cres SE24 .. 161
Delcombe Ave KT4 .. 200
Delft Ho 8 KT2 176
Delft Way 2 SE22 161
Delhi Rd EN1 17
Delhi St N1 .... 94 A6 233
Delia St SW18 157
Delisle Rd SE28 123
Delius Cl WD6 9
Delius Gr E15 98
Dellafield N4 72
Della Path E5 74
Dellbow Rd TW14 150
Dell Cl E15 98
Wallington SM6 219
Woodford IG8 21
Dellfield Cl BR3 186
Dell La KT17 216
Dellors Cl EN5 12
Dellow Cl IG2 57
Dellow Ho 6 E1 118
Dellow St E1 118
Dell Rd Enfield EN3 .... 6 C5
Stoneleigh KT17 .... 216 A2
West Drayton UB7 .... 104 B3
Dells Cl Chingford E4 .... 19 D4
Teddington TW11 .... 174 D4
Dell's Mews SW1 .... 259 B3
Dell The SE2 .... 124 A1
Brentford TW8 .... 131 C6
Feltham TW14 .... 150 B4
Pinner HA5 .... 22 D1
South Norwood SE19 .. 183 D2
Wembley HA0 .... 65 B3
Woodford IG8 .... 21 B1
Dell Way W13 .... 87 C1
Dell Wlk KT3 .... 177 C1
Dellwood Gdns IG5 .... 56 C6
Delme Cres SE3 .... 143 B3
Delmey Cl CR0 .... 221 D5
Deloraine Ho SE8 .... 141 C4
Deloraine St SE8 .... 141 C4
Delorme St W6 .... 134 D6
Delphian Ct 5 SW16 .. 182 C6
Delroy Ct N20 .... 14 A4
Delta Bldg 4 E14 .... 98 A1
Delta Cl KT4 .... 215 D5
Delta Ct NW2 .... 68 A6
Delta Gr UB5 .... 84 D4
Delta Ho N1 .... 235 D2
Delta Pk SW18 .... 135 D1
Delta Rd KT4 .... 215 C5
Delta St 3 E2 .... 96 A4
De Lucy Prim Sch SE2 124 B4
De Lucy St SE2 .... 124 B2
Delvan Cl SE18 .... 144 C5
Delverton Ho SE17 .. 261 D2
Delverton Rd SE17 .. 261 D1
Delvino Rd
SW6 .... 135 C4 265 B1
De Mandeville Ct E4 .. 35 A6
De Mandeville Gate EN1 6 B1
Demesne Rd SM6 .... 219 D4
Demeta Cl HA9 .... 67 A5
De Montfort Par 1
SW16 .... 160 A1
De Montfort Rd SW16 160 A2

e Morgan Rd SW6 135 D2
empster Cl KT6 197 C1
empster Rd SW18 158 A6
enberry Dr DA14 168 B1
enbigh Cl BR7 188 B4
NW10 67 C1
W11 113 B6 244 D6
Cheam SM1 217 B3
Ruislip HA4 61 D6
Southall UB1 85 B1
enbigh Ct E6 99 D4
1 Ealing W7 86 D2
enbigh Dr UB3 105 A4
enbigh Gdns TW10 154 B6
enbigh Ho SW1 257 D6
W11 244 D6
7 W11 91 B1
enbigh Mews SW1 259 A3
enbigh Pl
SW1 115 C1 259 A2
enbigh Rd E6 99 D4
W11 113 B6 244 D6
Ealing W13 87 B1
Hounslow TW3 129 D3
Southall UB1 85 B1
enbigh St
SW1 115 C1 259 B2
Denbigh Terr
W11 113 B6 244 D6
Denbridge Rd BR1,BR7 188 B1
Denbury Ho 48 E3 97 D4
Denby Ct SE11 260 D4
Dence Ho 20 E2 96 A4
Denchworth Ho 15
SW9 138 C3
Den Cl BR2,BR3 208 B6
Dencliffe TW15 170 C5
Dendridge Cl EN1 6 B6
Dendy St SW12 159 A3
Dene Ave DA15 168 B4
Hounslow TW3 129 B2
Dene Cl SE4 141 A1
Hayes BR2 208 D1
Worcester Park KT4 215 D6
Denecroft Cres UB10 82 D6
Dene Ct W7 108 D4
Ealing W5 87 C2
Dene Gdns
Hinchley Wood KT7 213 A6
Stanmore HA7 25 C5
Dene Ho N14 15 D4
Denehurst Gdns NW4 46 C3
Acton W3 110 D5
Richmond TW10 132 C1
Twickenham TW2 152 B4
Woodford IG8 37 B6
Dene Mans 1 NW6 69 C2
Dene Rd N11 14 D2
Buckhurst Hill IG9 21 D3
Denesmead SE24 161 A6
Dene The Ealing W13 87 B2
East Molesey KT12,KT8 195 B4
South Croydon CR0 222 D4
Wembley HA9 66 A4
Denewood EN5 14 A6
Denewood Rd N6 48 D2
Dengie Wlk N1 235 A6
Denham Cl DA16 146 C2
Denham Cres CR4 202 D5
Denham Ct
Forest Hill SE26 162 B1
Southall UB1 108 A6
Denham Dr IG2 57 A3
Denham Ho 32 W12 112 B6
Denham Lo W5 88 A1
Denham Rd N20 14 D1
Feltham TW14 150 C4
Denham St SE10 121 A1
Denham Way IG11 101 D6
Denholme Rd W9 91 B4
Denise Ct HA0 65 C4
Denison Cl N2 48 A6
Denison Ho 8 E14 97 C1
Denison Rd Ealing W5 87 C3
Feltham TW13 171 D6
Mitcham SW19 180 B4
Deniston Ave DA5 169 A3
Denland Ho SW8 270 D3
Denleigh Ct N14 15 D4
Denleigh Gdns
Southgate N21 16 C4
Thames Ditton KT7 196 C3
Denman Dr NW11 47 C4
Ashford TW15 170 D4
Claygate KT10 213 A3
Denman Dr N NW11 47 C4
Denman Dr S NW11 47 C4
Denman Ho N16 73 C6
Denman Rd SE15 139 D3
Denman St W1 249 C5
Denmark Ave SW19 179 A3
Denmark Ct SM4 201 C4
Denmark Gdns SM5 218 D5
Denmark Gr N1 234 A4
Denmark Hill SE5 139 B3
Denmark Hill Dr NW9 46 A6
Denmark Hill Sta SE5 139 B3
Denmark Ho 9 SE7 122 A2
Denmark Mans 14
SE5 139 A3
Denmark Pl WC2 239 D2
Denmark Rd BR1 187 B2
N8 50 C5
NW6 91 B5
SE5 139 A3
Carshalton SM5 218 D5
Croydon SE25 206 B4
Ealing W13 109 B6
Kingston KT1 198 A6
Twickenham TW2 152 B1
Wimbledon SW19 178 D4
Denmark St 6 E11 76 C5
E13 99 B2
WC2 239 D2
Tottenham N17 34 B3
Denmark Terr NW2 48 D6
Denmead Ho 8 SW15 155 D5
Denmead Rd CR0 204 D1
Denmead Sch TW12 173 D3
Denmead Upper Sch
TW12 173 D3
Denmore Ct SM6 219 B3
Dennan Rd KT6 198 B1
Dennard Way BR6 226 C4
Denner Rd E4 19 C2
Denne Terr E8 95 D6
Dennett Rd CR0 204 C2
Dennett's Gr SE14 140 D3
Dennett's Rd SE14 140 C4
Denning Ave CR0 220 C3
Denning Cl
NW8 92 A4 229 B1
Hampton TW12 173 B5
Denning Point E1 243 D2
Denning Rd NW3 70 B4
Dennington Cl 17 E5 74 B6
Dennington Park Rd
NW6 69 C2
Denningtons The KT4 215 C6
Dennis Ave HA9 66 B3
Dennis Cl TW15 171 B3
Dennis Ct E17 36 B1
Dennis Gdns HA7 25 C5
Dennis Ho 4 E3 97 B5
Sutton SM1 217 C4
Dennis La HA7 25 B6
Dennison Point E15 76 A1
Dennis Par 1 N14 15 D3
Dennis Park Cres
SW20 179 A2
Dennis Rd KT8 196 A5
Dennis Reeve Cl CR4 180 D2
Dennis Way SW4 137 D2
Denny Cl 15 E6 100 A2
Denny Cres SE11 261 B2
Denny Gdns RM9 80 B1
Denny Rd N9 18 B3
Denny St SE11 116 C1 261 B2
Den Rd BR2 208 B6
Densham Ho NW8 229 D3
Densham Rd E15 98 C6
Densole Cl BR3 185 A2
Denstone Ho 5 SE15 140 A6
Densworth Gr N9 18 C2
Dent Ho SE17 263 A3
Denton NW1 71 A2
Denton Cl EN5 12 C6
Denton Ho N1 72 D1
Denton Rd N8 50 B3
Bexley DA16 146 C5
Edmonton N18 33 C6
Twickenham TW1 153 D5
Denton St SW18 157 D5
Denton Way E5 74 D5
Dents Rd SW11 158 D5
Denvale Trade Pk CR4 202 B5
Denver Cl BR6 211 C3
Denver Rd N16 51 C2
Denwood SE23 162 D1
Denyer Ho 1 NW5 71 B4
Denyer St
SW3 114 C2 257 B4
Denys Bldg EC1 241 A4
Denziloe Ave UB10 82 D4
Denzil Rd NW10 67 D3
Deodar Rd SW15 135 A1
Deodora Cl N20 14 D1
Depot App NW2 68 D4
Depot Rd W12 112 C6
Isleworth TW3,TW7 130 B2
Depot St SE5 139 B6
Deptford Bridge SE8 141 C4
Deptford Bridge Sta
SE8 141 C4
Deptford Broadway
SE8,SE14 141 C4
Deptford Church St
SE8 141 C5
Deptford Ferry Rd 12
E14 119 C2
Deptford Gn SE8 141 C6
Deptford Green Sch
SE14 141 B5
Deptford Green Sch
(Annexe) SE14 141 A5
Deptford High St SE8 141 C5
Deptford Park Prim Sch
SE8 119 A1
Deptford Sta SE8 141 C5
Deptford Trad Est SE8 141 A6
Deptford Wharf SE8 119 B2
Dept of Transport &
Environment SW1 259 D5
De Quincey Mews 3
E16 121 A5
De Quincey Rd N17 33 B2
Derby Ave N12 30 A5
Harrow HA3 24 B2
Romford RM7 59 D3
Derby Ct 8 E5 74 D4
Woodford E18 36 D2
Derby Gate SW1 250 A2
Derby Hill SE23 162 C2
Derby Hill Cres SE23 162 C2
Derby Ho NW4 46 C6
SE11 261 A4
Pinner HA5 22 D1
Derby Lo N3 29 B1
Derby Rd E7 77 D1
E9 96 D6
N18 34 C5
Cheam SM1,SM2 217 B2
Enfield EN3 18 C6
Greenford UB6 85 D6
Hounslow TW3 129 D1
Merton SW19 179 C3
Mortlake SW14 132 D1
Surbiton KT5,KT6 198 C1
Thornton Heath CR0 204 D1
Woodford E18 36 D2
Derby Rd Ind Est TW3 129 D1
Derbyshire St E2 96 A4
Derby St W1 248 B3
Dereham Ho 7 SE4 140 D1
Dereham Pl EC2 243 B6
Dereham Rd IG11 79 D3
Derek Ave
Chessington KT19 214 D3
Wallington SM6 219 B4
Wembley HA9 66 D1
Derek Cl KT19 214 D3
Derek Walcott Cl
SE24 160 D6
Dericote St E8 96 B6
Deri Dene Cl 2 TW19 148 A5
Derifall Cl E6 100 B2
Dering Pl CR0 221 A4
Dering Rd CR0 221 A4
Dering St W1 238 D1
Derinton Rd SW17 181 A6
Derley Rd UB2 106 D3
Dermody Gdns SE13 164 B6
Dermody Rd SE13 164 B6
Deronda Rd SE24,SW2 160 D3
Deroy Cl SM5 218 D2
Deroy Ct SM5 218 D2
Derrick Gdns SE7 121 C2
Derrick Ho 13 SW2 160 C3
Derrick Rd BR3 207 B5
Derrycombe Ho W11 91 B2
18 W2 91 C2
Derry Rd CR0,SM6 220 A5
Derry St W8 113 D4 245 C1
Dersingham Ave E12 78 C4
Dersingham Inf Sch
E12 78 C3
Dersingham Rd NW2 69 A5
Derwent NW1 232 A1
Derwent Ave NW7 27 B4
NW9 45 C4
Barnet, London EN4 14 D3
Edmonton N18 33 B5
Kingston SW15 177 C6
Pinner HA5 23 A4
Uxbridge UB10 60 C5
Derwent Cl
Claygate KT10 212 D2
East Bedfont TW14 149 D3
Derwent Cres DA7 147 C3
N20 14 A1
Stanmore HA7 25 C1
Derwent Ct N8 50 A3
8 SE16 118 D4
2 W6 112 A2
Derwent Dr BR5 211 B2
Hayes UB4 83 C2
Derwent Gdns
Redbridge IG4 56 A5
Wembley HA9 43 C2
Derwent Gr SE22 139 D1
Derwent Ho E3 97 B3
SW7 256 B4
Penge SE20 184 B1
Derwent Lo
Hounslow TW7 130 B3
North Cheam KT4 216 B6
Derwent Rd W5 109 C3
Palmers Green N13 16 B1
Penge SE20 184 B1
Southall UB1 85 B1
Twickenham TW2 151 D5
West Barnes SM4 200 D3
Derwent Rise NW9 45 C3
Derwent St SE10 120 C1
Derwentwater Mans 2
W3 111 A5
Derwentwater Prim Sch
W3 111 A5
Derwentwater Rd W3 111 A5
Derwent Wlk SM6 219 B1
Derwent Yd W5 109 C3
De Salis Rd UB10 83 A3
Desborough Cl W2 91 D2
Lower Halliford TW17 192 C2
Desborough Ct SE25 206 B5
Desborough Ho W14 264 D6
Desenfans Rd SE21 161 C5
Desford Rd E16 98 C3
Desford Way TW15 148 B2
Design Mus*
SE1 117 D4 253 D2
Desmond Ho 4 EN4 14 C5
Desmond St SE14 141 A6
Despard Ho SW2 160 C2
Despard Rd N19 49 C1
Dessouter 19 NW9 27 D1
Detherick Ct TW3 130 A1
Dethick Ct E3 97 A6
Detling Ho SE17 263 A3
Detling Rd BR1 187 A5
Detmold Rd E5 74 C6
Deutsche Schule
TW10 153 D3
Devalls Cl E6 122 C6
Devana End SM5 218 D5
Devas Rd SW20 178 C2
Devas St E3 97 D3
Devema Cl BR7 188 C2
Devenay Rd E15 76 D1
Devenish Rd SE2 124 A4
Deventer Cres 8
SE22 161 C6
De Vere Cotts W8 256 A6
De Vere Gdns
W8 114 A4 246 A1
Redbridge IG1 56 B1
Deverell St
SE1 117 B3 262 C5
De Vere Mews W8 256 A6
Devereux Ct WC2 241 A1
Devereux Ho 7 SW15 156 A6
Devereux La SW13 134 B5
Devereux Rd SW11 158 D5
Deverill Ct SE20 184 C2
Devey Cl KT2 177 B5
Devitt Ho 4 E14 119 D6
Devizes St N1 235 D5
Devon Ave TW2 152 A3
Devon Cl N17 51 D6
Chigwell IG9 21 B2
Wembley UB6 87 C6
Devoncroft Gdns TW1 153 A4
Devon Ct 3 Acton W3 88 C1
2 Ealing W7 86 D2
Devon Gdns N4 50 D3
Devon Ho E17 35 B1
Penge SE20 184 B3
5 Wanstead E11 55 A4
Devonhurst Pl 4 W4 111 B1
Devonia Gdns N18 33 A4
Devonia Rd N1 94 D5 234 D4
Devon Mans SE1 253 B2
Devon Par HA3 43 C4
Devonport W2 237 A2
Devonport Gdns IG1 56 B3
Devonport Ho 23 W2 91 C2
Devonport Rd W12 112 B4
Devonport St E1 96 D1
Devon Rd IG11 101 C6
Devon Rise N2 48 B5
Devonshire Ave SM2 218 A1
Devonshire Cl E15 76 C4
W1 238 C4
Edmonton N13 32 C6
Devonshire Cres NW7 28 D3
Devonshire Ct
Croydon CR0 207 C1
Feltham TW13 150 B2
6 Richmond TW9 132 B4
Tottenham N17 33 A4
Devonshire Dr SE10 141 D4
Long Ditton KT6 213 D6
Devonshire Gdns
Chiswick W4 133 A5
Edmonton N21 17 A4
Tottenham N17 33 A4
Devonshire Gr SE15 140 B6
Devonshire Hall 14 E9 74 C2
Devonshire Hill La N17 33 A4
Devonshire Hill Prim Sch
N17 33 B4
Devonshire Ho N12 14 A1
NW6 69 B2
SE1 262 A6
SW1 259 D2
W2 236 D4
14 Balham SW12 159 B4
Hounslow TW3 130 A2
2 Putney SW15 156 C4
10 Sutton SM2 218 A1
Devonshire Hospl
W1 93 A2 238 B4
Devonshire House Prep Sch
NW3 70 B3
Devonshire House Sch
NW3 70 A3
Devonshire Mews 2
W4 111 C1
Devonshire Mews N
W1 238 C4
Devonshire Mews S
W1 238 C4
Devonshire Mews W
W1 238 B4
Devonshire Pl NW2 69 C5
W1 93 A2 238 B4
W8 255 C5
Devonshire Place Mews
W1 238 B4
Devonshire Prim Sch
SM2 218 A1
Devonshire Rd DA6 147 A1
E17 53 C3
N9 18 C3
NW7 28 D3
W4 111 C1
W5 109 C3
Chislehurst SE9 166 A2
Edmonton N13 32 C6
Feltham TW13 173 A6
Forest Hill SE23 162 C4
Hackbridge SM5,SM6 219 A4
Harrow HA1 42 B3
Ilford IG2 57 C2
Mitcham SW17,SW19 180 C3
Newham E16 99 B1
Pinner HA5 23 B2
Pinner HA5 40 C2
Southall UB1 85 C2
Sutton SM2 218 A1
Thornton Heath CR0 205 B2
Tottenham N17 33 A4
Devonshire Row EC2 243 B3
Devonshire Row Mews
W1 238 D5
Devonshire Sq BR2 209 B5
EC2 95 C1 243 B2
Devonshire St
W1 93 B2 238 C4
W4 111 C1
Devonshire Terr
W2 92 A1 236 B1
Devonshire Way
Croydon CR0,CR9 223 B6
Hayes UB4 84 B1
Devons Rd E3 97 D3
Devons Road Sta E3 97 D3
Devon St SE15 140 B6
Devon Way
Chessington KT19 214 D3
Chessington KT9 213 C3
Hillingdon UB10 82 B5
Devon Waye TW5 129 B5
De Walden Ho NW8 230 A4
De Walden St W1 238 B3
Dewar Ho 2 SW17 180 C5
Dewar St SE15 140 A2
Dewberry Gdns E6 100 A2
Dewberry St E14 98 A2
Dewey Rd N1 94 C5 234 A4
Dagenham RM10 81 D2
Dewey St SW17 180 D5
Dewhurst Rd W14 112 D3
Dewlands Ct NW4 28 D1
Dewsbury Cl HA5 41 A3
Dewsbury Ct 5 W4 111 A2
Dewsbury Gdns KT4 216 A5
Dewsbury Rd NW10 68 A3
Dewsbury Terr NW1 231 D6
Dexter Ho 2 DA18 125 A3
Dexter Rd EN5 12 D5
Deyncourt Rd N17 33 A2
Deynecourt Gdns E11 55 C5
D'eynsford Rd SE5 139 B4
Dhonau Ho SE16 263 D4
Diadem Ct W1 239 C2
Dial Wlk The
W8 113 D4 245 D2
Diameter Rd BR5 211 A3
Diamond Cl RM8 58 C1
Diamond Est SW17 158 C1
Diamond Ho 20 E3 97 A5
Diamond Rd HA4 63 A4
Diamond St SE15 139 C5
13 NW10 67 B1
Diamond Terr SE10 142 A4
Diana Cl 45 SE8 141 B6
Woodford E18 37 B2
Diana Ct SM5 219 A1
Diana Gdns KT6 214 B6
Diana Ho 4 SW2 160 B6
Diana, Princess of Wales
Mml Wlk W2 114 A5 246 A3
Diana Rd E17 53 B6
Dianne Ct SE12 165 A3
Dianne Way EN4 2 C1
Dianthus Cl SE2 124 B1
Dibden Ho 16 SE5 139 C5
Dibden St N1 95 A6 235 A6
Dibdin Cl SM1 217 C5
Dibdin Ho W9 91 D5
Dibdin Rd SM1 217 C6
Dicey Ave NW2 68 C4
Dickens Ave N3 30 A2
Hayes UB8 82 D1
Dickens Cl DA8 147 D5
Hayes UB3 105 C2
Richmond TW10 154 A2
Dickens Ct
10 Wanstead E11 55 A5
Wembley HA0 65 C5
Dickens Dr BR7 189 A4
Dickens Ho NW6 91 C4
NW8 236 D6
SE17 261 D1
WC1 240 A6
3 Erith DA17 125 B1
Hayes UB3 105 C2
Dickens House Mus*
WC1 94 B3 240 D5
Dickens La N18 33 C5
Dickenson Cl N9 18 A3
Dickenson Ho N8 50 B3
Dickenson Rd N8 50 A2
Dickenson's La SE25 206 A3
Dickenson's Pl SE25 206 A3
Dickens Rd E6 99 D5
Dickens Sq
SE1 117 A3 262 B6
Dickens St SW8 137 B3
Dickens Wood Cl
SE19 182 D3
Dickerage Hill
Kingston KT3 199 A6
Kingston KT3 177 A1
Dickerage La KT3 199 A6
Dickerage Rd KT1,KT2,
KT3 177 A1
Dickinson Ho 21 E2 96 A4
Dickinson Rd TW13 172 D5
Dicksee Ho NW8 236 C5
Dick Shepherd Ct 17
SW2 160 C5
Dickson Fold HA5 40 D5
Dickson Ho 13 E1 96 B1
9 SE18 144 A4
Dickson Rd SE9 144 A2
Dick Turpin Way
TW14 127 D1
Didbin Ho N7 72 B6
Didsbury Cl E6 100 B6
Digby Bsns Ctr E9 74 D2
Digby Cres N4 73 A6
Digby Gdns RM10 103 C6
Digby Mans W6 112 C1
Digby Pl CR0 221 D5
Digby Rd E9 74 D2
Barking IG11 79 D1
Digby St E2 96 C4
Digby Stuart Coll
SW15 156 A6
Diggon St 16 E1 96 D2
Dighton Ct SE17 139 A6
Dighton Rd SW18 136 A1
Dignum St N1 234 A4
Digswell St N7 72 C2
Dilhorne Cl SE12 165 B1
Dilke St SW3 136 D6 267 D6
Dilloway Yd UB2 107 A4
Dillwyn Cl SE26 185 A6
Dilston Cl 1 UB5 84 C4
Dilston Gr SE16 118 C2
Dilton Gdns SW15 156 B3
Dilwyn Ct E17 35 A1
Dimes Pl 9 W6 112 B2
Dimmock Dr UB6 64 B3
Dimond Cl E7 77 A4
Dimsdale Dr NW9 45 A1
Enfield EN1 18 A5
Dimsdale Wlk 4 E13 99 A5
Dimson Cres E3 97 C4
Dinerman Ct NW8 229 B6
Dingle Cl EN5 11 D5
Dingle Gdns E14 119 C6
Dingle Rd TW15 170 D5
Dingle The UB10 82 D4
Dingley La SW16 159 D2
Dingley Pl EC1 95 A4 235 B1
Dingley Rd EC1 95 A4 235 A1
Dingwall Ave CR0 221 A6
Dingwall Gdns NW11 47 C3
Dingwall Rd
South Croydon CR0 221 B6
Wandsworth SW18 158 A4
Dinmont Ho 28 E2 96 A5
Dinmont St 1 E2 96 B5
Dinmore Ho 7 E9 96 C6
Dinnington Ho 17 E1 96 B3
Dinorben SM6 219 C1
Dinsdale Ct EN5 13 D6
Dinsdale Gdns
New Barnet EN5 13 D6
South Norwood SE25 205 C4
Dinsdale Rd SE3 142 D6
Dinsmore Rd SW12 159 B4
Dinton Ho NW8 237 A6
Dinton Rd Kingston KT2 176 B3

Dinton Rd *continued*
Mitcham SW19 ...180 B4
Dinwiddy Ho N1 ...233 C3
Diploma Ave N2 ...48 C5
Diploma Ct N2 ...48 C5
Dirleton Rd E15 ...98 D6
Disbrowe Rd
W6 ...135 A6 264 B5
Discovery Bsns Pk 13
SE16 ...118 A3
Discovery Ho 1 E14 ..120 A6
Dishforth La NW9 ...27 C2
Disley Ct 2 UB1 ...85 D1
Disney Pl SE1 ...252 B2
Disney St SE1 ...252 B2
Dison Cl EN3 ...6 D4
Disraeli Cl SE28 ...124 C5
W4 ...111 B2
Disraeli Gdns SW15 ..135 B1
Disraeli Rd E7 ...77 A2
Acton NW10 ...89 B5
Ealing W5 ...109 D5
Putney SW15 ...135 A1
Diss St E2 ...95 D4
Distaff La EC4 ...252 A6
Distillery La W6 ...112 C1
Distillery Rd W6 ...112 C1
Distillery Wlk 14 TW8 .132 A6
Distin St SE11 .116 C2 261 A3
District Rd HA0 ...65 B3
Ditchburn St E14 ...120 A6
Ditchfield Rd UB4 ...85 A3
Dittisham Rd SE9 ...188 A6
Ditton Cl KT7 ...197 A2
Dittoncroft Cl CR0 ...221 C4
Ditton Grange Cl KT6 .197 D1
Ditton Grange Dr KT6 197 D1
Ditton Hill KT6 ...213 D6
Ditton Hill Rd KT6 ...197 C1
Ditton Ho 10 E5 ...74 B3
Ditton Lawn KT7 ...197 A1
Ditton Pl 6 SE20 ...184 B2
Ditton Rd Bexley DA6 ..169 A6
Southall UB2 ...107 B1
Surbiton KT6 ...198 B1
Ditton Reach KT7 ...197 B3
Divis Way SW15 ...156 B5
Dixon Cl 4 E6 ...100 B1
Dixon Clark Ct N1 ...72 D2
Dixon Ct N4 ...50 C3
Dixon Ho SE2 ...124 C1
Dixon Pl BR4 ...207 D1
Dixon Rd SE14 ...141 A4
South Norwood SE25 ..205 D6
Dobbin Cl HA3 ...25 A1
Dobell Rd SE9 ...166 B6
Dobree Ave NW10 ...68 B1
Dobson Cl NW6 ...70 B1
Dobson Ho 18 SE14 ..140 D6
SE5 ...139 B5
Doby Ct EC4 ...252 B6
Dockers Tanner Rd 19
E14 ...119 C2
Dockett Eddy La KT16,
TW17 ...192 B1
Dockett Moorings
KT16 ...192 B1
Dockhead SE1 117 D4 253 D1
Dockhead Wharf SE1 .253 D2
Dock Hill Ave SE16 ..118 D4
Docklands Heritage Mus*
SE16 ...119 B5
Docklands Mus (Museum in
Docklands)* E14 ..119 C6
Dockland St E16 ...122 C5
Dockley Rd SE16 ...118 A3
Dockley Road Ind Est 11
SE16 ...118 A3
Dock Offices 12 SE16 .118 C3
Dock Rd E16 ...120 D6
Brentford TW8 ...131 D5
Dockside Rd E16 ...121 D6
Dock St E1 ...118 A6
Dockwell Cl TW14 ...128 A1
Dockwell's Ind Est
TW14 ...150 C6
Doctors Cl SE26 ...184 C5
Doctor Spurstowe Almshos
9 E8 ...74 B2
Docura Ho N7 ...72 B6
Docwra's Bldgs N1 ...73 C2
Dodbrooke Rd SE27 ..160 D1
Dodd Ho 10 SE16 ...118 B2
Doddington Gr
SE17 ...116 D1 261 D1
Doddington Pl 4
SE17 ...138 D6
Dodsley Pl N9 ...18 C1
Dodson St SE1 116 C4 251 B1
Dod St E14 ...97 C1
Doebury Wlk SE18 ...146 A6
Doel Cl SW19 ...180 A3
Doggett Rd SE6 ...163 C4
Doggetts Ct EN4 ...14 C6
Doghurst Ave UB3 ...126 D5
Doghurst Dr UB7 ...126 D5
Dog Kennel Hill SE22 .139 C2
Dog Kennel Hill Sch
SE22 ...139 C2
Dog La NW10 ...67 C4
Dogrose Ct 14 NW9 ...46 A5
Doherty Rd E13 ...99 A3
Dokal Ind Est UB2 ...107 A4
Doland Ct SW17 ...180 D4
Dolben Ct SE8 ...119 B2
Dolben St SE1 116 D5 251 D3
Dolby Rd SW6 ...135 B3
Dolland Ho SE11 ...260 D1
Dolland St SE11 ...260 D1
Dollar Bay E14 ...120 A4
Dollary Ct KT3 ...198 D6
Dollis Ave N3 ...29 B2
Dollis Brook Wlk EN5 ..13 A5
Dollis Cres HA4 ...40 C1
Dolliscroft NW7 ...29 A3
Dollis Ct N3 ...29 B2
Dollis Hill Ave NW2 ...68 B5
Dollis Hill Est NW2 ...68 A5
Dollis Hill La NW2 ...68 A5
Dollis Hill Sta NW2 ...68 A3
Dollis Hts NW2 ...68 B5
Dollis Jun & Inf Schs
NW7 ...28 C3
Dollis Mews N3 ...29 C2
Dollis Pk N3 ...29 B2
Dollis Rd N3,NW7 ...29 B3
Dollis Valley Way EN5 ..13 B5
Dolman Cl N3 ...30 A1
Dolman Rd W4 ...111 B2
Dolman St SW4 ...138 B1
Dolphin Cl 2 SE16 ...118 D4
SE28 ...102 D1
Kingston KT6 ...197 D4
Dolphin Ct N7 ...71 D4
NW11 ...47 A3
Harrow HA3 ...24 C1
Merton SW19 ...179 C3
2 Wallington SM6 ...219 B2
Dolphin Est The TW16 171 B2
Dolphin La E14 ...119 D6
Dolphin Rd
Charlton TW16 ...171 C2
Northolt UB5 ...85 B5
Dolphin Rd N TW16 ...171 C2
Dolphin Rd S TW16 ...171 C2
Dolphin Rd W TW16 ...171 C2
Dolphin Sch SW11 ...158 D6
Dolphin Sq SW1 ...259 B1
Dolphin St KT2 ...176 A2
Dolphin Twr 21 SE8 ...141 B6
Dombey Ho 9 SE1 ...118 A4
4 W11 ...112 D5
Dombey St WC1 ...240 C4
Dome Hill Pk SE26 ...183 D6
Domelton Ho SW18 ...157 D5
Domett Cl SE5 ...139 B1
Domfe Pl E5 ...74 C4
Domingo St EC1 ...242 A5
Dominica Cl 6 E6 ...99 D5
Dominion Bsns Pk N9 .18 D2
Dominion Ind Est UB2 107 A4
Dominion Par HA1 ...42 D4
Dominion Rd
Croydon CR0 ...205 D2
Southall UB2 ...107 A3
Dominion St
EC2 ...95 B2 242 D4
Dominion Wks RM8 ...59 A1
Domonic Dr SE9 ...166 D1
Domville Cl N20 ...14 B2
Donaghue Cotts 13 E14 97 A2
Donald Dr RM6 ...58 C4
Donald Lynch Ho CR4 180 D1
Donald Rd E13 ...99 B6
Thornton Heath CR0 ...204 B2
Donaldson Rd NW6 ...91 B6
SE18 ...144 C4
Donald Woods Gdns
KT5 ...215 A6
Doncaster Dr UB5 ...63 B3
Doncaster Gdns N4 ...51 A3
Northolt UB5 ...63 B3
Doncaster Gn WD19 ...22 C5
Doncaster Rd N9 ...18 B4
Doncel Ct E4 ...20 B4
Donegal Ho 2 E1 ...96 C3
Donegal St N1 .94 B5 233 D3
Doneraile Ho SW1 ...258 C1
Doneraile St SW6 ...134 D4
Dongola Rd E1 ...97 A2
E13 ...99 B4
N17 ...51 C6
Dongola Rd W 5 E13 ...99 B4
Donington Ave IG6 ...57 A4
Donkey Alley SE22 ...162 A5
Donkey La EN1 ...6 A3
Donkin Ho 15 SE16 ...118 B2
Donne Ct SE24 ...161 A5
Donnefield Ave HA8 ...26 A3
Donne Ho 7 E14 ...97 C1
18 N16 ...73 B4
14 SE14 ...140 D6
Donnelly Ct SW6 ...264 B4
Donne Pl SW3 114 C2 257 B4
Mitcham CR4 ...203 B5
Donne Rd RM8 ...80 C6
Donnington Ct NW10 ..68 B1
11 NW1 ...71 B1
Donnington Ho 12
SW8 ...137 D3
Donnington Prim Sch
NW10 ...90 B6
Donnington Rd NW10 ..90 B6
Harrow HA3 ...43 D3
Worcester Park KT4 ...216 A6
Donnybrook Rd SW16 181 D3
Donovan Ave N10 ...31 C1
Donovan Ct SW7 ...256 C1
Donovan Ho 3 E1 ...118 C6
Donovan Pl N21 ...16 B6
Don Phelan Cl SE5 ..139 B4
Doone Cl TW11 ...175 A4
Doon St SE1 ..116 C5 251 A4
Doradus Ct 20 SW19 ..156 D3
Dora Ho 1 E14 ...97 B1
11 W11 ...112 D6
Doral Way SM5 ...218 D3
Doran Ct E6 ...100 B5
Dorando Cl W12 ...112 B6
Doran Gr SE18 ...145 C5
Doran Manor N2 ...48 D4
Doran Wlk E15 ...76 A1
Dora Rd SW19 ...179 C6
Dora St E14 ...97 B1
Dorcas Ct 9 SW18 ..136 B1
Dorchester Ave
Edmonton N13 ...33 A6
Harrow HA2 ...42 A3
Sidcup DA5 ...168 D4
Dorchester Cl
Northolt UB5 ...63 D3
St Paul's Cray BR5 ...190 B3
Dorchester Ct 1 N10 ..49 B6
1 N1 ...73 C1
N14 ...15 B4
NW2 ...68 D5
SE24 ...161 A6
SW1 ...257 D5
5 Streatham SW16 ..160 A2
2 Woodford E18 ...36 D2
Dorchester Dr SE24 ..161 A6
Feltham TW14 ...149 C5
Dorchester Gdns NW11 47 C5
Chingford E4 ...35 C6
Dorchester Gr W4 ...111 D1
Dorchester Mews
New Malden KT3 ...199 B5
Twickenham TW1 ...153 C5
Dorchester Prim Sch
KT4 ...200 C1
Dorchester Rd
Cheam SM4 ...202 A2
North Cheam KT4 ...200 C1
Northolt UB5 ...63 D3
Dorchester Way HA3 ..44 B3
Dorchester Waye
Hayes UB4 ...84 B1
Hayes UB4 ...84 C1
Dorcis Ave DA7 ...147 A3
Dordrecht Rd W3 ...111 C5
Dore Ave E12 ...78 C3
Doreen Ave NW9 ...45 B1
Doreen Capstan Ho 3
E11 ...76 C5
Dore Gdns SM4 ...201 D2
Dorell Cl UB1 ...85 B2
Doria Rd SW6 ...135 B3
Doric Ho 7 E2 ...96 D5
Doric Way NW1 93 D4 232 C2
Dorien Rd SW20 ...178 D1
Doris Emmerton Ct
SW18 ...136 A1
Doris Rd E7 ...77 A1
Ashford TW15 ...171 B4
Dorking Cl SE8 ...141 B6
North Cheam KT4 ...216 D6
Dorking Ct N17 ...34 A2
Dorking Ho SE1 ...262 D6
Dorland Ho SE9 ...167 B5
Dorlcote Rd SW18 ...158 C4
Dorleston Ct N1 ...235 D6
Dorly Cl TW17 ...193 C4
Dorman Pl 6 N9 ...18 A2
Dorman Way
NW8 ...92 B6 229 C6
Dorman Wlk NW10 ...67 B2
Dorma Trad Pk E10 ...52 D1
Dormay St SW18 ...157 D6
Dormer Cl E15 ...76 D2
Barnet EN5 ...12 D6
Dormer's Ave UB1 ...85 C1
Dormers Lo EN4 ...2 D3
Dormers Rise UB1 ...85 D1
Dormer's Wells High Sch
UB1 ...85 C1
Dormers Wells Ho UB4 84 C2
Dormer's Wells Inf Sch
UB1 ...107 D6
Dormer's Wells Jun Sch
UB1 ...107 D6
Dormer's Wells La
UB1 ...107 C5
Dormstone Ho SE17 ..263 A3
Dormywood HA4 ...39 D4
Dornan Wlk E15 ...98 A6
Dornberg Cl SE3 ...143 A5
Dornberg Rd SE3 ...143 B5
Dorncliffe Rd SW6 ..135 A3
Dorney NW3 ...70 C1
Dorney Ct SW6 ...135 A2
Dorney Rise BR5 ...211 D5
Dorney Way TW4 ...151 A6
Dornfell St NW6 ...69 B3
Dornoch Ho 25 E3 ...97 B5
Dornton Rd
South Croydon CR2 ...221 C3
Upper Tooting SW12,
SW17 ...159 C2
Dorothy Ave HA0 ...66 A1
Dorothy Barley Inf Sch
RM8 ...80 B3
Dorothy Barley Jun Sch
RM8 ...80 B3
Dorothy Charrington Ho 1
SE22 ...162 A6
Dorothy Evans Cl DA7 147 D1
Dorothy Gdns RM8 ...80 B4
Dorothy Rd SW11 ...136 D2
Dorrien Wlk SW16 ...159 D2
Dorrington Ct SE25 ..183 C1
Dorrington Point 20 E3 97 D4
Dorrington St EC1 ...241 A4
Dorrit Ho 2 W11 ...112 D5
Dorrit Mews N18 ...33 C5
Dorrit St SE1 ...252 B2
Dorrit Way BR7 ...189 A4
Dorryn Ct SE26 ...184 D5
Dors Cl NW9 ...45 B1
Dorset Ave DA16 ...145 D1
Hayes UB4 ...83 C4
Southall UB2 ...107 C2
Dorset Bldgs EC4 ...241 C1
Dorset Cl NW1 ...237 C4
Hayes UB4 ...83 C4
Dorset Ct 3 N1 ...73 C1
3 Ealing W7 ...86 D2
Dorset Dr HA8 ...26 B4
Dorset Gdns SW16 ...204 B5
Dorset Ho 1 SE20 ...184 B2
Dorset Mans 2 W6 ..134 D6
Dorset Mews N3 ...29 C2
SW1 ...258 C6
Dorset Pl E15 ...76 B2
Dorset Rd E7 ...77 C1
N15 ...51 B5
SW8 ...138 B5 270 C4
W5 ...109 D3
Ashford TW15 ...148 A1
Chislehurst SE9 ...166 A2
Harrow HA1 ...42 A3
Merton SW19 ...179 C1
Mitcham CR4 ...180 C1
Penge BR3 ...206 D6
Wood Green N22 ...32 A2
Dorset Rise EC4 94 D1 241 C1
Dorset Road Inf Sch
SE9 ...166 A2
Dorset Sq NW1 .92 D3 237 C5
Dorset St W1 .92 D2 237 D3
Dorset Way
Hillingdon UB10 ...82 B5
Twickenham TW2 ...152 B3
Dorset Waye TW5 ...129 B5
Dorton Cl 6 SE15 ...139 C5
Dorville Cres W6 ...112 B3
Dorville Rd SE12 ...165 A6
Dothill Rd SE18 ...145 A5
Douai Gr TW12 ...174 A2
Douay Martyrs RC Sch
(Annexe) The UB10 ...60 D3
Doughty Ct 11 E1 ...118 B5
Doughty Mews
WC1 ...94 B3 240 C5
Doughty St
WC1 ...94 B3 240 C5
Douglas 20 NW9 ...27 D1
Douglas Ave
Chingford E17 ...35 C2
Wembley HA0 ...66 A1
West Barnes KT3 ...200 B5
Douglas Bader Ho N3 .29 D4
Douglas Bldgs SE1 ..252 B2
Douglas Cl
Stanmore HA7 ...25 A5
Wallington SM6 ...220 A2
Douglas Cres UB4 ...84 D3
Douglas Ct N3 ...29 D1
5 NW6 ...69 C1
Douglas Dr CR0 ...223 C5
Douglas Gracey Ho
SW18 ...157 A4
Douglas Ho
Isleworth TW1 ...153 B6
Putney SW15 ...156 A5
Douglas Johnstone Ho
SW6 ...264 C5
Douglas Mews NW2 ...69 A5
Douglas Rd DA16 ...146 B4
5 E16 ...99 A2
N1 ...73 A1
NW6 ...91 B6
Chingford, Chingford Green
E4 ...20 C3
Douglas Rd *continued*
Hounslow TW3 ...129 D2
Ilford IG3 ...58 A3
Kingston KT1 ...176 D1
Stanwell TW19 ...148 A5
Surbiton KT6 ...198 B1
Thames Ditton KT10 ...212 A6
Wood Green N22 ...32 C2
Douglas Rd N N1 ...73 A2
Douglas Rd S N1 ...73 A2
Douglas Robinson Ct
SW16 ...182 A3
Douglas Sq SM4 ...201 C3
Douglas St
SW1 ...115 D2 259 C3
Douglas Terr E17 ...35 B2
Douglas Waite Ho NW6 69 D1
Douglas Way SE8 ...141 B5
Doulton Ho SE11 ...260 D4
Doulton Mews 4 NW6 .69 D2
Dounesforth Gdns
SW18 ...157 D3
Douro Pl W8 .113 D3 255 D6
Douro St E3 ...97 C5
Douthwaite Sq 12 E1 .118 A5
Dove App E6 ...100 A2
Dove Cl NW7 ...27 D3
Northolt UB5 ...84 D3
Wallington SM6 ...
Dovecot Cl HA5 ...40 C4
Dovecote Gdns 8
SW14 ...133 B2
Dove Ct Enfield EN3 ...18 B6
Stanwell TW19 ...148 A4
Dovedale Ave HA3 ...43 C3
Dovedale Cl DA16 ...146 A3
Dovedale Cotts 6
SW11 ...136 D3
Dovedale Ho N16 ...51 B2
Dovedale Rd SE22 ...162 B5
Dovedale Rise CR4 ...180 D3
Dovedon Cl N14 ...16 A2
Dove House Gdns E4 ..19 C2
Dovehouse Mead
IG11 ...101 B5
Dovehouse St
SW3 ...114 C1 257 A1
Dove Mews
SW7 ...114 A2 256 B2
Dove Pk HA5 ...23 C3
Dover Cl NW2 ...68 D6
Dovercourt Ave CR7 ..204 C5
Dovercourt Gdns HA7 ..26 A5
Dovercourt La SM1 ..218 A5
Dovercourt Rd SE22 ..161 D5
Dover Ct EC1 ...241 C5
SE10 ...141 D4
Dove Rd N1 ...73 B2
Doverfield Rd SW2 ...160 A4
Dover Flats SE1 ...263 B3
Dover Gdns SM5 ...218 D5
Dover Ho 11 SE15 ...140 C6
SE5 ...138 D4
7 Beckenham BR3 ...185 C3
14 Penge SE20 ...184 B2
Dover House Rd SW15 156 B6
Doveridge Gdns N13 ...32 D6
Dover Mans 17 SW9 ..138 C2
Dove Row E2 ...96 A6
Dover Park Dr SW15 ..156 B5
Dover Patrol SE3 ...143 C3
Dover Rd N9 ...18 C2
Dagenham RM6 ...59 A3
South Norwood SE19 ..183 B4
Wanstead E12 ...77 C6
Woolwich SE18 ...145 A3
Dover St W1 ..115 C5 249 A4
Dover Terr TW9 ...132 C3
Dover Yd W1 ...249 A4
Doves Cl BR2 ...226 A6
Doves Yd N1 ..94 C6 234 A5
Doveton Ho 6 E1 ...96 C3
Doveton Rd CR2 ...221 B3
Doveton St 7 E1 ...96 C3
Dove Wlk SW1 ...258 A2
Dowanhill Rd SE6 ...164 B3
Dowdeswell Cl SW15 .133 C1
Dowding Ho N6 ...49 A2
Dowding Pl HA7 ...25 A4
Dowding Rd UB10 ...60 B1
Dowe Ho SE3 ...142 C2
Dowell Ho SE21 ...161 D1
Dowes Ho 13 SW16 ...160 A1
Dowgate Hill EC4 ...252 C6
Dowland Ho EN1 ...5 D5
Dowland St W10 ...91 A4
Dowlas St SE5 ...139 C5
Dowler Ct 2 KT2 ...176 B2
Dowlerville Rd BR6 ..227 D2
Dowling Ho DA17 ...125 B3
Dowman Cl 2 SW19 .179 D3
Downage NW4 ...46 C6
Downalong WD23 ...8 B3
Down Barns Rd HA4 ..62 D5
Downbarton Ho 11
SW9 ...138 C4
Downbury Mews 13
SW18 ...157 C6
Down Cl UB5 ...84 B5
Downderry Prim Sch
BR1 ...186
Downderry Rd BR1 ...186
Downe Cl DA16 ...146
Downe Ho 9 SE7 ...143
Downe Manor Prim Sch
UB5 ...84
Downend SE18 ...144
Downend Ct 8 SE15 .139
Downe Rd CR4 ...180 D
Downer's Cotts SW4 ..137
Downes Cl TW1 ...153
Downes Ct N21 ...16
Downey Ho 6 E1 ...96
Downfield KT4 ...200
Downfield Cl W9 ...91 D
Downfield Ho KT3 ...199 B
Down Hall Rd KT2 ...175 D
Downham Ct N1 ...73 B
Downham Ent Ctr SE6 164 D
Downham La BR1 ...186 B
Downham Rd N1 ...73
Downham Way BR1 ...186 C
Downhills Ave N17 ...51 B
Downhills Jun & Inf Schs
N15 ...51 B
Downhills Park Rd N17 51 A
Downhills Way N17 ...33 A
Downhurst Ave NW7 ...27 B
Downhurst Ct NW4 ...46 C
Downing Cl HA2 ...42 A
Downing Ct N12 ...29 D
Downing Dr UB6 ...86 C
Downing Ho 2 W10 ...90 D
3 Merton SW19 ...179 C
4 Putney SW15 ...156 A
Downing Rd RM9 ...81 B
Downings E6 ...100 C
Downing St*
SW1 ...116 A4 250 A
Downland Cl N20 ...14 A
Downland Ct E11 ...76 C
Downleys Cl SE9 ...166 B
Downman Rd SE9 ...144 A
Down Pl W6 ...112 B
Down Rd TW11 ...175 B
Downs Ave BR7 ...188 B
Pinner HA5 ...41 B
Downs Bridge Rd BR3 186 B
Downs Ct 16 E8 ...74 B
12 Wimbledon SW19 ...178 D
Downsell Jun & Inf Schs
E15 ...76 B
Downsell Rd E15 ...76 B
Downsfield Rd E17 ...53 A
Downshall Ave IG3 ...57 C
Downshall Ct IG3 ...57 C
Downs Hill BR2,BR3 ...186 B
Downshire Hill NW3 ...70 B
Downside
2 Putney SW15 ...157 A6
Sunbury TW16 ...172 A2
Twickenham TW1 ...152 D1
Downside Cl SW19 ...180 A4
Downside Cres NW3 ...70 C3
Ealing W13 ...87 A3
Downside Rd SM2 ...218 C2
Downside Wlk UB5 ...85 B4
Downs La 3 E5 ...74 B4
Downs Park Rd E5,E8 ..74 A3
Downs Rd E5,N16 ...74 A4
Beckenham BR3 ...185 D1
Enfield EN1 ...5 C1
South Norwood CR7 ...183 A2
Downs Side JMI Sch
E5 ...74 A4
Down St W1 ..115 B5 248 C3
East Molesey KT8 ...195 C4
Downs The SW19,
SW20 ...178 D3
Down St Mews W1 ..248 C3
Downs View TW7 ...131 A4
Downsview Gdns
SE19 ...183 A3
Downs View Lo 9
KT6 ...198 A3
Downsview Prim Sch
SE19 ...183 A3
Downsview Rd SE19 ..183 A3
Downsview Sch E5 ...74 B4
Downsway BR6 ...227 C3
Downsway The SM2 ..218 A1
Downton Ave SW2 ...160 B2
Downtown Rd SE16 ...119 A4
Downway N12 ...30 C3
Down Way UB5 ...84 B4
Dowrey St N1 ...234 A6
Dowsett Rd N17 ...34 A1
Dowson Cl SE5 ...139 B1
Dowson Ct SE13 ...142 B2
Dowson Ho 7 E1 ...96 D1
Doyce St SE1 ...252 A2
Doyle Gdns NW10 ...90 B6
Doyle Ho W3 ...110 D4
Doyle Rd SE25 ...206 A5
D'Oyley St SW1 ...258 A4
Doynton St N19 ...71 B6
Draco St SE17 ...139 A6
Dragonfly Cl E13 ...99 B4

agon Rd SE15 139 C6
agon Yd WC1 240 B2
agoon Rd SE8 119 B1
agor Rd NW10 89 A3
ake Cl 30 SE16 118 D4
ake Cres SE28 102 C1
ake Croft N16 73 B6
ake Ct 5 W12 112 B4
ulwich SE19 183 D5
ngston KT5 198 B5
akefell Rd SE4,SE14 140 D2
akefield Rd SW17 159 A1
ake Ho 17 E1 96 C2
4 E14 119 A6
akeley Ct N5 72 D4
ake Rd SE4 141 C2
essington KT9 214 C3
arrow HA2 63 B6
itcham CR4 203 A3
ornton Heath CR0 204 B2
akes Ct SE23 162 C3
akes Ctyd NW6 69 B1
ake St WC1 240 C3
nfield EN2 5 B4
akes Wlk E6 100 B6
akewood Rd SW16 181 D3
aldo Ho 6 SW15 157 A6
aper Cl DA17 125 B2
ounslow TW7 130 B3
aper Ct BR1 210 A5
aper Ho SE1 261 D4
aper Pl N1 234 D6
apers Almshouses 4
3 97 C4
aper's Cottage Homes
W7 28 A6
apers Gdns EC2 242 D2
rapers Rd E15 76 B4
17 51 D6
nfield EN2 4 D4
rappers Way 8
E16 118 A2
aven Cl BR2 208 D2
awell Cl SE18 123 C1
ax Ave SW20 178 A3
axmont SW19 179 A4
aycot Rd
olworth KT6 198 C1
Vanstead E11 55 B2
aycott Ave
W3 114 C2 257 B3
arrow HA3 43 C3
aycott Cl NW2 68 D5
arrow HA3 43 B3
raycott Ct SW11 267 A2
raycott Ho SW3 257 C3
raycott Pl
W3 114 D2 257 C3
raycott Terr
W3 114 D2 257 D3
rayford Cl W9 91 B3
ray Gdns SW2 160 B6
raymans Ct 4 SW9 138 B2
raymans Way TW7 130 D2
rayside Mews UB2 107 B4
rayson Mews
W8 113 C4 245 B1
rayton Ave
Ealing W13 109 A6
Orpington BR6 210 D1
rayton Bridge Rd
Ealing W13 87 A1
Ealing W7,W13 108 D6
rayton Cl
Hounslow TW4 151 B6
lford IG1 57 B1
rayton Ct SW10 256 B1
Tolworth KT5 214 D6
West Drayton UB7 104 B2
rayton Gdns
SW10 114 A1 256 B1
Ealing W13 109 A6
Southgate N21 16 D4
West Drayton UB7 104 A4
rayton Gn W13 109 A6
rayton Gr W13 109 A6
rayton Green Prim Sch
W13 109 A6
rayton Green Rd
W13 109 B6
rayton Green Sta W7 86 D1
rayton Ho E11 54 B1
14 SE5 139 B5
Drayton Manor High Sch
W7 86 D1
Drayton Park Prim Sch
N5 72 C3
Drayton Park Sta N5 72 C3
Drayton Pk N5,N7 72 C4
Drayton Rd E11 54 B1
NW10 89 D6
Croydon CR0 220 D6
Ealing W13 109 B6
Tottenham N17 33 C1
Drayton Sch The N15 52 A3
Drayton Waye HA3 43 B3
Dreadnought St SE10 120 C3
Drenon Sq UB3 105 D6
Dresden Cl NW6 69 D2
Dresden Ho SE11 260 D4
5 SW11 137 A3
Dresden Rd N19 49 D1
Dressington Ave SE4 163 C5
Drew Ave NW7 29 A4
Drewery Ct SE3 142 C2
Drewett Ho 19 E1 96 A1
Drew Gdns UB6 64 D2
Drew Ho 12 SW16 160 A1
Drew Prim Sch E16 122 A5
Drew Rd E16 122 A5
Drewstead Rd SW16 159 D2
Driffield Ct 4 NW9 27 C2
Driffield Rd E3 97 A5
Drift The BR2 225 D5
Driftway Ho 15 E3 97 B5
Driftway The CR4 181 A2
Drinkwater Ho 11 SE5 139 B5
Drinkwater Rd HA2 63 D6
Drive Mans SW6 135 A3
Drive The BR6 227 D6
BR7 189 D2
DA8 147 D6
E17 53 D6
HA9 67 A6
N11 31 D4
N3 29 C3
N6 48 D4
N7 72 B2
NW10 89 D6
NW11 47 A2
W3 89 A1
Ashford TW15 171 B3
Barking IG11 79 D1
Barnet EN5 1 A2
Beckenham BR3 185 C2
Buckhurst Hill IG9 21 C4
Chingford E4 20 B4
Edgware HA8 26 C5
Enfield EN2 5 B4
Feltham TW14 150 C4
Harrow HA2 41 C2
Hounslow TW3,TW7 130 B3
Ickenham UB10 60 A5
Kingston KT2 177 A3
Morden SM4 202 B4
New Barnet EN5 14 A5
Redbridge IG1 56 B2
Sidcup DA14 190 B6
Sidcup DA5 168 D4
South Norwood CR7 205 B5
St Paul's Cray BR7 211 D6
Surbiton KT6 198 A2
Thames Ditton KT10 196 A1
Wanstead E18 55 A6
West Ewell KT19 215 D2
West Wickham BR4 208 B2
Wimbledon SW19,SW20 178 C3
Barking IG11 80 A2
Dr Johnson Ave SW17 159 B1
Dr Johnson's House★
EC4 241 B1
Droitwich Cl SE26 162 A1
Dromey Gdns HA3 24 D3
Dromore Rd SW15 157 A5
Dronfield Gdns RM8 80 C3
Dron Ho E1 96 C2
Droop St W10 91 A3
Drovers Ct SE13 142 A2
3 Kingston KT1 176 A1
Drovers Pl SE15 140 B5
Drovers Rd CR2 221 B3
Dr Triplett's CE Prim Sch
UB3 83 D1
Druce Rd SE21 161 C5
Druid St SE1 117 D4 253 C1
Druids Way BR2 208 B5
Drumaline Ridge KT4 215 C6
Drummer Lo N7 72 B5
Drummond Castle Ct
E7 76 D4
Drummond Cres
NW1 93 D4 232 C2
Drummond Ct N12 30 C3
Drummond Ctr CR0 221 A6
Drummond Dr HA7 24 D3
Drummond Gate SW1 259 D2
Drummond Ho 12 E2 96 A5
N2 30 A1
Drummond Rd SE16 118 B3
Croydon CR0 221 A6
Wanstead E11 55 C3
Drummonds Pl TW9 132 A1
Drummond St
NW1 93 C3 239 A6
Drummonds The IG9 21 B2
Drum St E1 243 D2
Drury Cres CR0 220 C6
Drury Ho SW8 269 A2
Drury La WC2 94 A1 240 B1
Drury Rd HA1 42 A2
Drury Way NW10 67 B3
Dryad St SW15 134 D2
Dryburgh Gdns NW9 44 C6
Dryburgh Ho SW1 258 D2
Dryburgh Mans SW15 134 C2
Dryburgh Rd SW15 134 C2
Dryden Ave W7 86 D1
Dryden Ct SE11 261 B3
Dryden Ct *continued*
11 Richmond TW10 175 D6
Dryden Ho BR2 209 D4
16 N16 73 C5
6 SE5 139 C4
Dryden Rd DA16,SE18 145 D4
Enfield EN1 17 D5
Harrow HA3 24 D2
Wimbledon SW19 180 A4
Dryden St WC2 240 B1
Dryer's Bldgs EC1 241 A3
Dryfield Cl NW10 67 A2
Dryfield Rd HA8 27 A4
Dryfield Wlk 1 SE8 141 C6
Dryhill Rd DA17 147 B6
Dryland Ave 5 BR6 227 D4
Drylands Rd N8 50 A3
Drysdale Ave E4 19 D5
Drysdale Flats 3 E8 73 D3
Drysdale Ho 20 E2 95 C4
Drysdale Pl N1 95 C4
Drysdale St N1 95 C4
Dublin Ave E8 96 A6
Du Burstow Terr W7 108 C4
Ducal St 25 E2 95 D4
Ducane Cl W12 90 C1
Du Cane Ct SW12 159 A3
Du Cane Rd W12 90 A1
Ducavel Ho SW2 160 B3
Duchess Cl N11 31 B5
Sutton SM1 218 A4
Duchess Gr IG9 21 B2
Duchess Mews W1 238 D3
Duchess of Bedford Ho
W8 245 A2
Duchess of Bedford's Wlk
W8 113 C4 245 A1
Duchess St W1 93 B2 238 D3
Duchy Rd EN4 2 B5
Duchy St SE1 116 C5 251 B4
Ducie Ho 8 SE7 143 C6
2 Putney SW15 156 C6
Ducie St SW4 138 B1
Duckett Mews N4 50 D3
Duckett Rd N4 50 D3
Duckett St E1 97 A2
Duck La W1 239 C1
Duck Lees La EN3 7 A1
Ducks Hill Rd HA4,HA6 39 A5
Duck's Wlk TW1 153 C6
Du Cros Dr HA7 25 D4
Du Cros Rd W3 111 C5
Dudden Hill La NW10 67 D3
Duddington Cl SE9 187 D6
Dudley Ave HA3,HA7 43 C6
Dudley Ct NW11 47 B5
W1 237 C1
WC2 240 A2
9 Wanstead E11 55 A4
Wembley HA0 65 D3
Dudley Dr Ruislip HA4 62 B3
West Barnes SM4 201 A2
Dudley Gdns W13 109 B4
Harrow HA2 42 B1
Dudley Ho 14 SW9 138 C3
W2 236 C3
Dudley Mews 14 SW2 160 C5
Dudley Rd N3 29 D1
NW6 91 B5
Ashford TW15 170 B6
Chingford E17 35 C1
East Bedfont TW14 149 B3
Harrow HA2 64 A6
Ilford IG1 78 D4
Kingston KT1 198 B6
Richmond TW9 132 B3
Southall UB2 106 D3
Walton-on-T KT12 194 A2
Wimbledon SW19 179 C4
Dudley St W2 236 C3
Dudlington Rd E5 74 C6
Dudmaston Mews
SW3 256 D2
Dudsbury Rd DA14 190 B4
Dudset La TW5 128 A4
Duffell Ho SE11 260 D1
Dufferin Ave EC1 242 C5
Dufferin Ct EC1 242 C5
Dufferin St EC1 95 A3 242 B5
Duffield Cl HA1 42 D4
Duffield Dr N15 51 D5
Duffield Ho N4 51 A2
Duff St E14 97 D1
Dufour's Pl W1 239 B1
Dugdale Ho 10 N7 71 D3
Duke Gdns IG6 57 B5
Duke Humphrey Rd
SE3 142 C3
Duke Of Cambridge Cl
TW2 152 B5
Duke Of Edinburgh Rd
SM1 218 B6
Duke of Wellington Pl
SW1,W1 248 B2
Duke Of York's Sq
SW3 114 D2 258 A4
Duke of York St SW1 249 B4
Duke Rd W4 111 B1
Ilford IG6 57 B5
Dukes Ave N10 49 C6
N3 29 D2
Duke's Ave W4 111 B1
Dukes Ave Edgware HA8 26 B5
Harrow HA1 42 C5
Harrow HA2,HA5 41 B3
Hounslow TW4 129 A1
Kingston KT3 199 D6
Northolt UB5 63 A1
Richmond KT2,TW10 175 D6
Dukes Cl Ashford TW15 171 A6
Hampton TW12 173 B5
Dukes Ct SE13 142 A3
SE22 162 A3
SE22 162 B6
Barking E6 100 C6
Beckenham BR3 207 A6
Ealing W13 87 B2
Dukes Gate 4 W4 111 A2
Dukes Green Ave
TW14 150 A6
Dukes Head Yd N6 49 B1
Duke's Ho SW1 259 D4
Duke Shore Wharf
E14 119 B6
Dukes La W8 113 D4 245 C2
Dukes Mews N10 49 B6
Duke's Mews W1 238 B2
Duke's Pl EC3 95 C1 243 B1
Dukes Point N6 49 B1
Duke's Rd WC1 93 D4 232 D1
Dukes Rd Acton W3 88 C3
Barking E6 100 C6
Dukes Ride UB10 60 A4
Duke St W1 93 A1 238 B1
Richmond TW10,TW9 153 D6
Sutton SM1 218 B4
Duke St Hill SE1 252 D4
Dukesthorpe Rd SE26 184 D6
Duke St Mans W1 238 B1
Duke St St James's
SW1 115 C5 249 B4
Dukes Way BR4 224 C5
Duke's Yd W1 248 B6
Dulas St N4 50 B1
Dulford St
W11 113 A6 244 A6
Dulka Rd SW11 158 D6
Dulverton NW1 232 B5
Dulverton Ct 12 KT6 198 A4
Dulverton Mans WC1 240 D5
Dulverton Prim Sch
DA15 167 B2
Dulverton Rd
DA15,DA15 167 B2
Ruislip HA4 62 A6
Dulwich Bsns Ctr
SE23 162 D3
Dulwich Coll (Endowed)
SE21 161 C2
Dulwich Coll Picture Gall★
SE21 161 C4
Dulwich Coll Prep Sch
SE21 161 C1
Dulwich Comm SE21 161 C3
Dulwich Ct SE22 162 B3
Dulwich Hamlet Jun Sch
SE21 161 B5
Dulwich High Sch for Boys
SE24 161 B6
Dulwich Hospl SE22 139 C1
Dulwich Mead SE24 161 A5
Dulwich Mews 1
SE22 139 D1
Dulwich Oaks The
SE21 161 D1
Dulwich Rd SE24 160 D5
Dulwich Village SE21 161 C5
Dulwich Village CE Inf Sch
SE21 161 C5
Dulwich Wood Ave
SE19 183 C5
Dulwich Wood Pk
SE19 183 C6
Dumain Ct SE11 261 C3
Du Maurier Ho 2 NW3 70 D3
Dumbarton Ct 16 SW2 160 A4
Dumbarton Rd SW2 160 A5
Dumbleton Cl KT2 176 D2
Dumbreck Rd SE9 144 C2
Dumont Rd N16 73 C5
Dumphreys Ho 5
SW4 159 D4
Dumpton Pl NW1 71 A1
Dunally Pk TW17 193 B2
Dunbar Ave
Beckenham BR3 207 A5
Dagenham RM10 81 C5
Thornton Heath SW16 182 C1
Dunbar Cl UB4 84 A2
Dunbar Ct 3 N12 29 D6
Sutton SM1 218 B3
Walton-on-T KT12 194 C1
Dunbar Gdns RM10 81 D3
Dunbar Rd E7 77 A2
New Malden KT3 199 A5
Tottenham N22 32 D2
Dunbar St SE27 161 A1
Dunbar Wharf 20 E14 119 B6
Dunblane Rd SE9 144 A3
Dunboe Pl TW17 193 A2
Dunboyne Rd NW3 70 D3
Dunbridge Ho 7
SW15 155 D5
Dunbridge St E2 96 B3
Duncan Cl EN5 2 A1
Duncan Ct 3 E14 98 A2
Southgate N21 16 D3
Duncan Gr W3 89 C1
Duncan Ho 3 NW3 70 D1
Duncannon Ho SW1 259 D1
Duncannon St WC2 250 A5
Duncan Rd E8 96 B6
Richmond TW9 132 A1
Duncan St N1 94 D5 234 C4
Duncan Terr
N1 94 D5 234 C4
Dunch St 30 E1 96 B1
Dunchurch Ho RM10 81 C1
Duncombe Hill SE23 163 A4
Duncombe Ho 7
SW19 156 D3
Duncombe Prim Sch
N19 50 A1
Duncombe Rd N19 49 D1
Duncrievie Rd SE13 164 B5
Duncroft SE18 145 C5
Dundalk Ho 2 E1 96 C1
Dundalk Rd SE4 141 A2
Dundas Gdns KT8 195 D6
Dundas Ho 12 E2 96 C5
Dundas Rd SE15 140 C3
Dundee Ct 36 E1 118 B5
Dundee Ho W9 229 A2
Dundee Mews EN3 7 C6
Dundee Rd E13 99 B5
Croydon SE25 206 B4
Dundee St E1 118 B5
Dundee Way EN3 7 A2
Dundee Wharf E14 119 B6
Dundela Gdns KT17,
KT4 216 B4
Dundonald Cl 6 E6 100 A1
Dundonald Prim Sch
SW19 179 B3
Dundonald Rd NW10 90 D6
Merton SW19 179 B3
Dundonald Road Sta
SW19 179 B3
Dundry Ho 8 SE26 162 A1
Duneaves HA1 64 C5
Dunedin Rd E10 75 D5
Ilford IG1 57 A1
Dunedin Way UB4 84 C3
Dunelm Gr SE27 161 A1
Dunelm St E1 96 D1
Dunfield Gdns SE6 185 D5
Dunfield Rd SE6 185 D5
Dunford Rd N7 72 B4
Dungarvan Ave SW15 134 A1
Dungeness Ho SW18 136 A1
Dunheved Cl CR7 204 C3
Dunheved Rd N CR7 204 C3
Dunheved Rd S CR7 204 C3
Dunheved Rd W CR7 204 C3
Dunhill Point 12 SW15 156 B3
Dunholme Gn N9 17 D1
Dunholme La N9 17 D1
Dunholme Rd N9 17 D1
Dunkeld Ho 13 E14 98 B1
Dunkeld Rd
Dagenham RM8 80 C6
South Norwood SE25 205 B5
Dunkery Rd SE9 166 A1
Dunkirk St 12 SE27 183 A6
Dunlace Rd E5 74 D4
Dunleary Cl TW4 151 B4
Dunley Dr CR0 224 A2
Dunlin Ct 11 SE21 161 B2
Dunlin Ho 13 SE16 118 D2
Dunloe Ave N17 51 B6
Dunloe Ct 7 E2 95 D5
Dunloe St E2 95 D5
Dunlop Pl
SE16 117 D3 263 D5
Dunlop Point 10 E16 121 B5
Dunmore Point 15 E2 95 D4
Dunmore Rd NW6 91 A6
Wimbledon SW20 178 D2
Dunmow Cl
Dagenham RM6 58 C4
3 Feltham TW13 173 A6
Dunmow Ho SE11 260 D2
Dagenham RM9 102 B6
Dunmow Rd E15 76 B4
Dunmow Wlk N1 235 A6
Dunnage Cres SE16 119 A2
Dunnet Ho 26 E3 97 B5
Dunnico Ho SE17 263 A2
Dunn Mead NW9 27 D3
Dunnock Cl N9 18 D3
Dunnock Ct 10 SE21 161 B2
Dunnock Rd E6 100 A1
Dunn's Pas WC1 240 B2
Dunn St E8 73 D3
Dunollie Pl NW5 71 C3
Dunollie Rd NW5 71 C3
Dunoon Gdns SE23 162 D4
Dunoon Ho N1 233 C5
Dunoon Rd SE23 162 C4
Dunraven Dr EN2 4 C3
Dunraven Ho 12 TW9 132 B4
Dunraven Rd W12 112 A5
Dunraven St
W1 114 D6 247 D6
Dunraven Upper Sch
SW16 160 B1
Dunrobin Ct NW3 69 D3
Dunsany Rd W14 112 D3
Dunsfold Ct 9 SM2 217 D1
Dunsfold Ho
10 Kingston KT2 176 D4
4 Streatham SW2 160 B4
Dunsfold Way CR0 223 D1
Dunsford Ct 4 HA5 23 B3
Dunsford Way SW15 156 B5
Dunsmore Cl
Bushey WD23 8 B5
Hayes UB4 85 A3
Dunsmore Rd KT12 194 B3
Dunsmore Way WD23 8 B5
Dunsmure Rd N16 51 C1
Dunstable Ct 3 SE3 143 A5
Dunstable Mews W1 238 B4
Dunstable Rd
East Molesey KT8 195 B5
Richmond TW10,TW9 132 A1
Dunstall Ho 9 SE15 140 A4
Dunstall Rd SW19,
SW20 178 C4
Dunstall Way KT8 195 D6
Dunstall Welling Est
DA16 146 B3
Dunstan Cl 2 N2 48 A6
Dunstan Glade BR5 211 B3
Dunstan Ho SE4 141 B3
Dunstan Hos 5 E1 96 C2
Dunstan Rd NW11 47 C1
Dunstan's Gr SE22 162 B5
Dunstan's Rd SE22 162 A5
Dunster Ave SM4 200 D1
Dunster Ct EC3 253 B6
Dunster Dr NW9 45 A1
Dunster Gdns NW6 69 B1
Dunster Ho SE6 163 D1
Dunsterville Way SE1 252 D1
Dunster Way
Carshalton CR4 203 A1
Harrow HA2 63 A5
Dunston Rd E8 95 D6
SW11 137 A3
Dunston St E8 95 D6
Dunton Cl KT6 198 A1
Dunton Ct 5 SE26 162 B2
Dunton Ho 14 SW16 160 A1
Dunton Rd E10 53 D2
SE1 117 D2 263 C3
Duntshill Rd SW18 157 D3
Dunvegan Cl KT8 195 D5
Dunvegan Rd SE9 144 B1
Dunwich Rd DA7 147 B4
Dunworth Mews W11 91 B1
Duplex Ride SW1 247 D1
Dupont Rd SW20 178 D1
Duppas Ave CR0 220 D4
Duppas Cl TW17 193 B4
Duppas Ct CR0 220 D5
Duppas Hill La CR0 220 D4
Duppas Hill Rd CR0 220 D4
Duppas Hill Terr CR0 220 D5
Duppas Jun Sch CR0 220 D3
Duppas Rd CR0 220 D5
Dupree Rd SE7 121 B1
Dura Den Cl BR3 185 D3
Durand Cl SM5 202 D1
Durand Gdns
SW9 138 B4 270 D1
Durand Prim Sch
SW9 138 B4 270 D1
Durand Way NW10 67 A1
Durants Lo EN3 6 D2
Durants Park Ave EN3 6 D1
Durants Rd EN3 6 D1
Durants Sch EN3 6 C4
Durant St E2 96 A4
Durban Ct E7 77 D1
Durban Ho 28 W12 112 B6
Durban Rd E15 98 C4
E17 35 B2
Beckenham BR3 185 B1
Ilford IG2 57 C1
Tottenham N17 33 D4
West Norwood SE27 183 B6
Durbin Ho 13 N9 18 A1
Durbin Rd KT9 214 B4
Durdans Ho 1 NW1 71 C1
Durdans Park Prim Sch
UB1 85 B2
Durdans Rd UB1 85 B1
Durell Gdns RM9 80 D3
Durell Rd RM9 80 D3
Durfey Ho SE5 139 B5
Durford Cres SW15 156 B3

Durham Ave
Beckenham BR2 208 D5
Hounslow TW5 107 B1
Woodford IG8 37 D5
Durham Cl SW20 178 B1
Durham Ct 3 NW6 91 C5
Teddington TW11 174 C6
Durham Hill BR1 186 D6
Durham Ho NW8 230 B1
3 Barking IG11 80 A1
Durham House St
WC2 250 B5
Durham Pl SW3 257 C1
Ilford IG1 79 A4
Durham Rd DA14 190 B5
E12 77 D4
E16 98 C3
N2 48 D6
N4,N7 72 B6
W5 109 D3
Beckenham BR2 208 D6
Edmonton N9 18 A2
Feltham TW14 150 C4
Harrow HA1 41 D4
Wimbledon SW20 178 B2
Durham Rise SE18 123 B1
Durham Row E1 97 A2
Durham St
SE11 138 B6 270 C6
Durham Terr W2 91 D1
Durley Ave HA5 41 A3
Durley Rd N16 51 C2
Durlock Ho 16 SW9 138 C4
Durlston Rd E5 74 A6
Kingston KT2 176 A4
Durnford Ho SE6 163 D1
Durnford St N15 51 C4
3 SE10 142 A6
Durning Rd SE19 183 B5
Durnsford Ave SW18,
SW19 157 C2
Durnsford Rd N11 31 D3
Wimbledon SW18,SW19 157 C1
Durrant Ct HA3 24 C2
Durrant Way BR6 227 B3
Durrell Rd SW6 264 C1
Durrell Way TW17 193 B3
Durrels Ho W14 254 D4
Durrington Ave SW20 178 C3
Durrington Park Rd
SW20 178 C2
Durrington Rd E5 75 A4
Durrington Twr 3
SW8 137 C3
Durrisdeer Ho NW2 69 B4
Dursley Cl SE3 143 C3
Dursley Gdns SE3 143 D4
Dursley Rd SE3 143 C3
Durston NW5 71 A3
Durston House Middleton's
Sch W5 87 D1
Durston House Prep Sch
W5 87 D1
Durward St E1 96 B2
Durweston Mews W1 237 D4
Durweston St W1 237 D3
Dury Rd EN5 1 B3
Dutch Gdns KT2 176 D4
Dutch Yd SW18 157 C6
Dutton Ho SW2 160 D3
Dutton St SE10 142 A4
Duxberry Cl BR2 210 A4
Duxford 21 KT1 176 C1
Duxford Ho 12 SE2 124 D4
Dwight Ct SW6 135 A3
Dycer Ho 19 E9 74 D2
Dye House La E3 97 C6
Dyer Ho TW12 173 D2
Dyers Hall Rd E11 54 C1
E11 76 B6
Dyer's La SW15 134 B1
Dykes Ct 11 SW2 160 B3
Dykes Way BR2 208 D6
Dylan Cl WD6 9 D4
Dylan Rd 2 SE24 138 D1
Belvedere DA17 125 C3
Dylan Thomas Ho N8 50 B5
Dylways SE5 139 B1
Dymchurch Cl BR6 227 C4
Ilford IG5 56 C6
Dymchurch Ho 12 E5 74 B3
Dymes Path SW19 156 D2
Dymock St SW6 135 D2
Dyneley Rd SE12 165 C1
Dyne Rd NW6 69 B1
Dynevor Rd N16 73 D5
Richmond TW10 154 A6
Dynham Rd NW6 69 C1
Dyott St WC1 239 D2
WC1,WC2 94 A1 240 A2
Dysart Ave KT2,TW10 175 C6
Dysart Sch
Kingston KT2 175 D6
Surbiton KT6 198 B2
Dysart St EC2 95 C3 243 A5
Dyson Ct NW2 46 C2
Dyson Ct *continued*
Wembley HA0 65 A4
Dyson Ho 3 SE10 120 D1
Dyson Rd E11 54 C3
E15 76 D2
Dyson's Rd N18 34 B4

E

Eade Rd N4 51 A2
Eagans Cl N2 48 B6
Eagle Ave RM6 59 A3
Eagle Cl SE16 118 C1
Enfield EN3 6 C1
Wallington SM6 220 A2
Eagle Ct EC1 241 C4
9 Dulwich SE21 161 B2
Edmonton N18 33 D4
6 Wanstead E11 55 A5
Eagle Dr NW9 27 C1
Eagle Dwellings EC1 235 B2
Eagle Hill SE19 183 B4
Eagle Ho 22 E1 96 B3
Eagle Hts 10 SW11 136 C2
Eagle La E11 55 A5
Eagle Lo E11 54 D5
NW11 47 B2
Eagle Mans N16 73 D3
Eagle Mews N1 73 C2
Eagle Pl SW1 249 B5
SW7 114 A1 256 B2
Eagle Rd Hatton TW6 127 D2
Wembley HA0 65 D1
Eaglesfield Rd SE18 144 D4
Eaglesfield Sch SE18 144 C4
Eagle St WC1 94 B2 240 C3
Eagle Terr IG8 37 B3
Eagle Trad Est CR4 202 D3
Eagle Wharf SE1 253 C3
Eagle Wharf Rd
N1 95 A5 235 B4
Ealcom Ct W5 110 B5
Ealdham Prim Sch
SE9 143 C1
Ealdham Sq SE9 143 C1
Ealing Almshouses
W5 109 D4
Ealing Broadway Ctr
W5 109 D6
Ealing Broadway Sta
W5 109 D6
Ealing Coll W13 87 B1
Ealing Common W5 110 B6
Ealing Common Sta
W5 110 B5
Ealing Gn W5 109 D5
Ealing,Hammersmith &
West London Coll
W14 113 A1 254 B1
Ealing Hospl UB1,UB2 108 B4
Ealing Park Gdns W5 109 C2
Ealing Park Mans W5 109 D3
Ealing Rd
Brentford TW8 109 D2
Northolt UB5 63 C1
Wembley HA0 66 A1
Ealing Road Trad Est
TW8 109 D1
Ealing Tertiary Coll
Acton W3 110 D5
Ealing W5 109 D5
Ealing Village W5 88 A1
Eamann Casey Ho 34
SW9 138 C4
Eamont Cl HA4 38 D2
Eamont Ct NW8 230 B4
Eamont St NW8 92 C5 230 B4
Eardley Cres
SW5 113 C1 255 B1
Eardley Point 9 SE18 122 D2
Eardley Prim Sch
SW16 181 C4
Eardley Rd
Belvedere DA17 125 C1
Streatham SW16 181 C4
Earl Cl N11 31 B5
Earldom Rd SW15 134 C1
Earle Gdns KT2 176 A3
Earlham Gr E7 77 A3
Wood Green N22 32 B3
Earlham Prim Sch E7 76 D3
Earlham Prim Schs
N22 32 C3
Earlham St
WC2 94 A1 240 A1
Earl Ho NW1 237 B5
Earlom Ho WC1 234 A1
Earl Rd SW14 133 A1
Earl Rise SE18 123 B2
Earl's Court Ex Ctr
SW5 255 A1
Earl's Court Gdns
SW5 113 D2 255 C3
Earl's Court Rd
SW5,W8 113 C2 255 B4
Earl's Court Sq
SW5 113 D1 255 C2
Earl's Court Sta
SW5 113 C2 255 B3
Earls Cres HA1 42 C5
Earlsdown Ho IG11 101 B5
Earlsferry Way N1 72 A1
Earlsfield Prim Sch
SW18 158 A2
Earlsfield Rd SW18 158 A4
Earlsfield Sta SW18 158 A3
Earlshall Rd SE9 144 C1
Earlsmead HA2 63 B4
Earlsmead Fst & Mid Sch
HA2 63 B4
Earlsmead Prim Sch
N15 51 D5
Earlsmead Rd N15 51 D4
NW10 90 C4
Earl St EC2 95 C2 243 A4
Earls Terr W8 254 D5
Earlsthorpe Mews 3
SW12 159 A5
Earlsthorpe Rd SE26 184 D6
Earlstoke St EC1 234 C2
Earlston Gr E9 96 B6
Earls Wlk W8 113 C3 255 A5
Dagenham RM8 80 B4
Earlswood Ave CR7 204 C4
Earlswood Cl 10 SE10 120 C1
Earlswood Gdns IG5 56 C6
Earlswood Ho 2 SW2 160 B3
Earlswood St SE10 120 C1
Early Mews NW1 231 D6
Earnshaw St WC1,WC2 239 D2
Earsby St W14 254 B4
Easby Cres SM4 201 D3
Easebourne Rd RM8 80 C3
Easedale Ho TW7 152 D6
Eashing Point 5
SW15 156 B3
Easleys Mews W1 238 B2
East Acton Arc W3 89 D1
East Acton Ct W3 111 C6
East Acton La W3 111 C6
East Acton Prim Sch
W3 111 C6
East Acton Sta W12 89 D1
East Arbour St E1 96 D1
East Ave E12 78 A1
E17 53 D5
NW2 48 A6
Croydon CR0 220 B3
Hayes UB3 106 A5
Southall UB1 107 B6
East Bank N16 51 C2
Eastbank Rd TW12 174 A5
East Barnet Main Sch
Barnet EN4 2 B2
East Barnet EN4 14 D5
East Barnet Rd EN4 2 B1
East Beckton District Ctr
E6 100 B2
East Block 5 E1 118 D6
Eastbourne Ave W3 89 B1
Eastbourne Gdns
SW14 133 A2
Eastbourne Mews
W2 92 A1 236 B2
Eastbourne Rd E15 98 C6
N15 51 C3
Brentford TW8 109 D1
Chiswick W4 133 A6
Feltham TW13 150 D2
Streatham SW17 181 A4
Wallend E6 100 C4
Eastbourne Terr
W2 92 A1 236 B2
Eastbournia Ave N9 18 B1
Eastbrook Ave N9 18 C4
Eastbrook Rd SE3 143 B4
Eastbury Ave
Barking IG11 101 C6
Enfield EN1 5 D4
Moor Park HA6 22 A5
Eastbury Ct
Barking IG11 101 C6
New Barnet EN5 14 A6
Eastbury Gr W4 111 C1
Eastbury Inf Sch IG11 79 D1
Eastbury Rd E6 100 C3
Kingston KT2 176 A3
Eastbury Sq IG11 101 D6
Eastbury Terr E1 96 D3
Eastcastle St
W1 93 C1 239 B2
Eastcheap EC3 117 C6 253 A6
East Churchfield Rd
W3 111 B5
Eastchurch Rd TW6 127 C2
Eastchurch Road Rdbt
TW6 127 C3
East Cl W5 88 C3
Cockfosters EN4 3 A1
Greenford UB6 86 A5
Eastcombe Ave SE7 143 B6
Eastcote BR6 211 D1
Eastcote Ave
East Molesey KT8 195 C4
Greenford UB6 65 A3
Harrow HA2 64 A6
Eastcote Ind Est HA4 40 C2
Eastcote La Harrow HA2 63 C5
Northolt UB5 63 B2
Eastcote La N UB5 63 C2
Eastcote Pl HA5 40 B3
Eastcote Prim Sch
DA16 145 B2
Eastcote Rd DA16 145 B3
Harrow HA2 64 A5
Pinner HA5 40 D4
Ruislip HA4 40 A3
Eastcote St SW9 138 B3
Eastcote Sta HA5 40 C2
Eastcote View HA5 40 C5
Eastcourt Ind Sch IG3 58 A1
East Cres N11 30 D6
Enfield EN1 17 D6
Eastcroft Rd KT19 215 C1
East Cross Ctr E15 75 C2
East Cross Route E3 97 C6
E9 75 B3
East Croydon Sta CR0 221 B6
East Ct HA0 65 C6
Eastdown Ho E8 74 A4
Eastdown Pk SE13 142 B1
East Duck Lees La EN3 7 B1
East Dulwich Gr SE22 161 C6
East Dulwich Rd SE15,
SE22 140 A1
East Dulwich Sta SE22 139 C1
East End Rd N2 48 A6
N2,N3 47 D6
N3 29 C1
East End Way HA5 41 A6
East Entrance RM10 103 D5
Eastern Ave
Ilford IG1,IG2,IG4, 56 B3
Ilford IG1,IG2,IG4 56 C3
Ilford IG2 57 B3
Pinner HA5 40 D2
Wanstead E11 55 C3
Eastern Ave W RM7 59 C5
Eastern Bsns Pk
TW16 127 D3
Eastern Perimeter Rd
TW14 127 D3
Eastern Rd E13 99 B5
E17 54 A4
N2 48 D5
SE4 141 C1
Wood Green N22 32 A2
Easternville Gdns IG2 57 A3
Eastern Way SE28 124 B4
East Ferry Rd E14 119 D2
Eastfield Gdns RM10 81 C4
Eastfield Prim Sch EN3 6 D5
Eastfield Rd E17 53 C5
N8 50 A6
Dagenham RM10 81 C4
Dagenham RM9 81 B4
Enfield EN3 6 D5
Eastfields HA5 40 C4
Eastfields Rd W3 89 A2
Mitcham CR4 181 A1
Eastfield St E14 97 A2
East Finchley Sta N2 48 C5
Eastgate Cl SE28 102 D1
East Gdns SW17 180 C4
Eastglade HA5 41 B6
Eastham Cl EN5 13 B6
East Ham Ind Est E6 100 A2
East Ham Manor Way
E6 100 C1
East Ham Meml Hospl
E7 77 D1
East Ham Sta E6 78 A1
East Harding St EC4 241 B2
East Heath Rd NW3 70 B5
East Hill SW18 158 A6
Wembley HA9 44 C1
Eastholm NW11 47 D5
Eastholme UB3 106 A5
East India Bldgs 8
E14 119 C6
East India Dock Basin
E14 120 C6
East India Dock Rd
E14 119 D6
East India Dock Road
Tunnel 17 E14 98 B1
East India Dock Wall Rd
E14 120 B6
East India Sta E14 120 B6
East La SE16 118 A4
Kingston KT1 197 D6
Wembley HA0,HA9 65 D5
Eastlake Ho NW8 236 D5
Eastlake Rd SE5 139 A3
Eastlands Cres SE21 161 D5
Eastlea Com Sch E16 98 C3
Eastlea Mews E16 98 C3
Eastleigh Ave HA2 63 D6
Eastleigh Cl NW2 67 C5
Belmont SM2 217 D1
Eastleigh Rd E17 35 B1
Eastleigh Way TW14 150 A3
Eastleigh Wlk 9
SW15 156 A4
East London Coll & Toynbee
Theatre E1 95 D2 243 D3
East London Stadium
E3 97 B2
Eastman Dental Hospl
WC1 94 B4 240 C6
Eastman Ho 7 SW4 159 C5
Eastman Rd W3 111 B4
East Mascalls 15 SE7 143 C6
Eastmead IG3 58 A2
East Mead HA4 62 D5
Eastmead Ave UB6 85 D4
Eastmead Cl BR1 188 A1
Eastmearn Rd SE21,
SE27 161 A2
East Molesey Inf sch
KT8 196 B5
Eastmont Rd KT10 212 D6
Eastmoor Pl SE7 121 D3
Eastmoor St SE7 121 D3
East Mount St E1 96 B2
Eastney Rd CR0 204 D1
Eastney St SE10 120 B1
Eastnor Rd SE9 167 A3
Easton Ho 4 SE27 160 D1
Easton St WC1 241 A6
East Park Cl RM6 59 A4
East Parkside SE10 120 D4
East Pas EC1 242 A4
East Pl SE27 183 A6
East Point 4 SE1 118 A1
Eastpole Cotts N14 3 D1
East Poultry Ave EC1 241 C3
East Putney Sta SW15 157 A6
East Ramp TW6 126 D4
East Rd DA16 146 B3
E15 99 A6
HA8 27 A2
N1 95 B4 235 D2
N2 30 C2
Dagenham RM6 59 A4
East Barnet EN4 15 A3
East Bedfont TW14 149 B4
Enfield EN3 6 C5
Kingston KT2 176 A2
West Drayton UB7 104 C2
Wimbledon SW19 180 A4
East Rochester Way
DA5,DA15,DA16,SE9 168 C5
East Row W10 91 A3
Wanstead E11 55 A3
Eastry Ave BR2 208 D3
Eastry Ho SW8 270 A3
Eastry Rd DA8 147 C5
East Sheen Ave SW14 133 B1
East Sheen Prim Sch
SW14 133 C1
Eastside Rd NW11 47 B5
East Smithfield
E1 117 D6 253 D5
East St BR1 187 A1
DA7 147 C1
SE17 117 B1 262 C2
Barking IG11 79 A1
Brentford TW8 131 C5
East Surrey Gr SE15 139 D5
East Tenter St
E1 95 D1 243 D1
East Terr DA15 167 C3
East Thamesmead Bsns Pk
DA18 125 B4
East Towers HA5 40 D3
Eastvale W3 111 D5
East View NW3 70 B6
Barnet EN5 1 B2
Chingford E4 36 A5
Eastview Ave SE18 145 C5
Eastville Ave NW11 47 B3
Eastway E3,E9 97 A6
E9,E10 75 C4
Hayes BR2 209 A2
Merton SM4,SW20 201 A5
Wallington SM6 219 C4
Wanstead E11 55 B4
East Way Croydon CR0 223 A5
Hayes UB3 106 A5
Ruislip HA4 40 A1
Eastwell Cl BR3 185 A2
Eastwell Ho SE1 262 D6
Eastwick Ct 2 SW19 156 D3
East Wickham Inf Sch
DA16 145 D4
East Wickham Jun Sch
DA16 146 A4
East Wlk East Barnet EN4 15 A3
Hayes UB3 106 A5
Eastwood Cl
7 Tottenham N17 34 B3
Woodford E18 37 A1
Eastwood Rd N10 31 A1
Ilford IG3 58 A2
West Drayton UB7 104 C4
Woodford E18 37 A1
East Woodside DA5 169 A3
Eastwood St SW16 181 C4
Eatington Rd E10 54 B4
Eaton Cl SW1 258 A3
Stanmore HA7 25 B6
Eaton Ct BR7 189 A4
Eaton Ct *continued*
Ealing W5 87
Edgware HA8 26
Southall UB1 107
Sutton SM2 218
Eaton Dr SW9 138 [illegible]
Kingston KT2 176
Eaton Gate
SW1 115 A2 258
Eaton Gdns RM9 81
Eaton Ho SW11 266
Ealing W5 87
Eaton House The Manor
Sch SW4 137
Eaton La SW1 115 B3 258
Eaton Mans SW1 258
Eaton Mews N
SW1 115 A3 258
Eaton Mews S
SW1 115 B3 258
Eaton Mews W SW1 258
Eaton Park Rd N13 16
Eaton Pl SW1 115 A3 258
Eaton Rd DA14 168
NW4 46
Enfield EN1 5
Isleworth TW3,TW7 130
Sutton SM2 218
Eaton Rise Ealing W5 87
Wanstead E11 55
Eaton Row
SW1 115 B3 258
Eatons Mead E4 19
Eaton Sq SW1 115 A3 258
Eaton Square Sch
SW1 115 B2 258
Eaton Terr E3 97
SW1 115 A2 258
Eaton Terr Mews SW1 258
Eatonville Rd SW17 158
Eatonville Villas SW17 158
Ebbisham Dr
SW8 138 B6 270
Ebbisham Rd KT4 216
Ebbsfleet Rd NW2 69
Ebdon Way SE3 143
Ebenezer Ho SE11 261
Ebenezer Mussel Ho 5
E2 96
Ebenezer St N1 235
Ebenezer Wlk CR4 181
Ebley Cl SE15 139
Ebner St SW18 157
Ebony Ho 10 NW3 69
Ebor Cotts SW15 155
Ebor St E1,E2 243
Ebrington Rd HA3 43 D
Ebsworth St SE23 162 D
Eburne Rd N7 72 A
Ebury Bridge Rd
SW1 115 A1 258
Ebury Cl BR2 226 A
Ebury Mews
SW1 115 B2 258 C
Ebury Mews E SW1 258 C
Ebury Sq SW1 258
Ebury St SW1 115 B2 258 C
Ecclesbourne Cl N13 32 C
Ecclesbourne Gdns
N13 32 C
Ecclesbourne Inf Sch
CR7 205 A
Ecclesbourne Jun Sch
CR7 205 A
Ecclesbourne Prim Sch
N1 73 B
Ecclesbourne Rd N1 73 A
Thornton Heath CR7 205 A
Eccleshill 3 BR2 208 D
Eccles Rd SW11 136 D
Eccleston Cl BR6 211 B
Cockfosters EN4 2 D
Eccleston Cres RM6 58 B
Ecclestone Ct HA9 66 A
Ecclestone Mews HA9 66 B
Ecclestone Pl HA9 66 B
Eccleston Ho 1 SW2 160 C
Eccleston Mews
SW1 115 A3 258 B
Eccleston Pl
SW1 115 B2 258 C
Eccleston Rd W13 109 A
Eccleston Sq
SW1 115 B2 258 D
Eccleston Sq Mews
SW1 259 A
Eccleston St
SW1 115 B2 258 C
Echelford Cty Prim Sch
TW15 170 D
Echelforde Dr TW15 170 C
Echo Hts E4 19 D
Eckersley St E1 243 D
8 E2 96 A
Eckford St N1 234 A
Eckington Ho N15 51 B
Eckstein Rd SW11 136 C
Eclipse Rd E13 99 B
Ector Rd SE6 164 C

dam Ct 1 DA14 …168 A1
ans Ct W12 …111 D4
brooke Rd W9 …91 C3
disbury Ho 7 SE26 162 A1
discombe Rd SW6 .135 B3
ddy Cl RM7 …59 D3
dystone Rd SE4 …163 A6
dystone Twr SE8 …119 A1
dystone Wlk TW19 .148 A4
de Cl TW4 …129 B2
denbridge Cl 29
SE16 …118 B1
denbridge Rd E9 …74 D1
Enfield EN1 …17 C5
den Cl NW3 …69 C6
W8 …255 B6
Wembley HA0 …87 D6
dencourt W5 …88 B1
dencourt Rd SW16 …181 B4
dendale W3 …110 D6
denfield Gdns KT4 …215 D5
den Gr E17 …53 D4
N7 …72 B3
denham High Sch
CR0 …207 B2
denham Way W10 …91 B2
den Ho NW8 …237 A5
15 SW11 …136 C2
denhurst Ave SW6 …135 B2
den Lodge NW6 …68 D1
den Mews SW17 …158 A1
den Park Ave BR3 …207 C4
den Park Sta BR3 …207 C4
den Rd E17 …53 D4
Croydon CR0 …221 B4
Penge BR3 …185 A2
West Norwood SE27 …182 D5
densmuir Ct SE3 …143 A5
densor Gdns W4 …133 C5
densor Rd W4 …133 C5
den St KT1,KT2 …176 A1
denvale Cl CR4 …181 A3
denvale Rd CR4 …181 A3
denvale St SW6 …136 A3
den Way BR3 …207 C3
den Wlk 5 KT1 …176 A1
derline Ave SW16 …182 C1
dgar Ct KT3 …199 C6
dgar Ho E9 …75 A3
SW8 …270 A4
Wanstead E11 …55 A2
dgar Kail Way SE22 .139 C1
dgarley Terr SW6 …264 A1
dgar Rd E3 …97 D4
Dagenham RM6 …58 D2
Twickenham TW4 …151 B4
Yiewsley UB7 …104 A5
dgcott Ho W10 …90 C2
dgeborough Way
BR1 …187 D2
dge Bsns Ctr The
NW2 …68 B6
dgebury BR7,SE9 …188 D6
dgebury Prim Sch
BR7 …189 A6
Edgebury Wlk BR7 …167 A1
Edgecombe Cl KT2 …177 B3
Edgecombe Ho
4 SE5 …139 C3
Putney SW19 …157 A4
Edgecoombe CR2 …222 C1
Edgecote Cl 7 W3 …111 A5
Edgecot Gr N15 …51 C4
Edgecumbe Ct 2 CR0 206 A1
Edgefield Ave IG11 …79 D1
Edgefield Ct 2 IG11 …79 D1
Edge Hill SE18 …144 D6
Wimbledon SW19 …178 D3
Edge Hill Ave N3 …47 C5
Edge Hill Ct DA14 …189 D6
Edgehill Ct KT12 …194 C1
Edge Hill Ct SW19 …178 D3
Edgehill Gdns RM10 …81 C4
Edgehill Ho 4 SW9 …138 D3
Edgehill Rd BR7 …189 A6
Ealing W13 …87 C2
Mitcham CR4 …181 B2
Edgeley La SW4 …137 D2
Edgeley Rd SW4 …137 D2
Edgel St SW18 …135 D1
Edge Point Cl SE27 …182 D5
Edge St W8 …113 C5 245 B4
Edgewood Dr BR6 …227 D3
Edgewood Gn CR0 …206 D1
Edgeworth Ave NW4 …46 A4
Edgeworth Cl NW4 …46 A4
Edgeworth Cres NW4 .46 A4
Edgeworth Ct 10 EN4 …2 C1
Edgeworth Ho NW8 …229 A6
Edgeworth Rd SE9 …143 D1
Barnet EN4 …2 C1
Edgington Rd SW16 …181 D4
Edgington Way DA14 .190 D3
Edgson Ho SW1 …258 C2
Edgwarebury Ct HA8 …26 C5
Edgwarebury Gdns
HA8 …26 C5
Edgwarebury La HA8 …10 C2
Edgware Community Hospl
HA8 …26 D3
Edgware Ct HA8 …26 C4
Edgware Jun & Inf Schs
HA8 …26 C4
Edgware Rd NW2 …68 C6
W1,W2,NW1,
NW8 …92 C2 237 A3
Edgware Rd Burnt Oak
Broadway HA8 …26 D3
Edgware Rd High St
HA8 …26 C4
Edgware Road Sta
(Bakerloo)
NW1 …92 C2 237 A3
Edgware Road Sta
(Met,Distr,Circle)
NW1 …237 B3
Edgware Road The Hyde
NW9 …45 C5
Edgware Road West
Hendon Broadway
NW9 …46 A2
Edgware Sch The HA8 .26 B6
Edgware Sta HA8 …26 D4
Edgware Way (Watford
By-Pass) HA8 …26 C6
Edinburgh Cl 7 E2 …96 C5
Uxbridge UB10 …60 D4
Edinburgh Ct E13 …99 B5
10 SE16 …118 D5
1 Catford SE6 …164 D3
2 Kingston KT1 …198 A6
West Barnes SM4 …200 D4
Edinburgh Dr UB10 …60 D4
Edinburgh Ho NW4 …46 C6
3 W3 …89 B1
W9 …91 D4
Edinburgh Prim Sch
E17 …53 B4
Edinburgh Rd E13 …99 B5
E17 …53 C4
W7 …108 D4
Carshalton SM1 …218 B6
Edmonton N18 …34 A5
Edington 20 NW5 …71 A2
Edington Rd SE2 …124 B3
Enfield EN3 …6 C3
Edison Bldg 11 E14 …119 C4
Edison Cl E17 …53 C4
Edison Ct SE10 …120 D3
Edison Dr UB1 …85 D1
Edison Gr SE18 …145 D5
Edison Ho SE1 …262 C4
10 Wembley HA9 …67 A5
Edison Rd DA16 …145 D4
N8 …49 D3
Brimsdown EN3 …7 B3
Bromley BR2 …187 A1
Edis St NW1 …93 A6 231 B6
Editha Mans SW10 …266 A5
Edith Cavell Cl 6 N19 .50 A2
Edith Cavell Way SE18 144 A4
Edith Gdns KT5 …198 D2
Edith Gr SW10 136 A5 266 B4
Edith Ho 6 W6 …112 C1
Edithna St SW9 …138 A2
Edith Neville Prim Sch
NW1 …93 D5 232 C3
Edith Pond Ct SE9 …166 D2
Edith Ramsay Ho 2 E1 97 A2
Edith Rd E15 …76 B3
E6 …77 D1
N11 …31 D3
W14 …113 A2 254 B3
Dagenham RM6 …58 D2
South Norwood SE25 …205 B4
Wimbledon SW19 …179 D4
Edith Row SW6 …265 D2
Edith St E2 …96 A5
Edith Summerskill Ho
SW6 …264 C4
Edith Terr
SW10 …136 A5 266 A4
Edith Villas
W14 …113 B2 254 C2
Edith Yd SW10 …266 B4
Edmansons' Cl N17 …33 D2
Edmeston Cl E9 …75 A2
Edmond Ct SE14 …140 C4
Edmonscote W13 …87 A2
Edmonton Coll of F Ed
EN3 …6 C4
Edmonton Ct 5 SE16 .118 C3
Edmonton Cty Lower Sch
N9 …17 C3
Edmonton Cty Upper Sch
EN1 …17 D4
Edmonton Green Sh Ctr
N9 …18 B2
Edmonton Green Sta
N9 …18 A2
Edmonton Wharf N18 …34 D4
Edmund Gr TW13 …151 B2
Edmund Halley Way
SE10 …120 C4
Edmund Ho SE14 …141 B4
SE17 …261 D1
Edmund Hurst Dr E6 .100 D2
Edmund Rd DA16 …146 A2
Mitcham CR4 …202 C6
Edmundsbury Ct Est 16
SW9 …138 B1
Edmunds Cl UB4 …84 C2
Edmund St SE5 …139 B5
Edmunds Wlk N2 …48 C5
Edmund Waller Prim Sch
SE14 …140 D3
Ednam Ho SE15 …140 A6
Edna Rd SW20 …178 D1
Edna St SW11 .136 C4 267 A1
Edred Ho E9 …75 A4
Edrich Ho SW4 …270 A1
Edric Ho SW1 …259 D4
Edrick Rd HA8 …27 A4
Edrick Wlk HA8 …27 A4
Edric Rd SE14 …140 D5
Edridge Cl WD23 …8 A6
Edridge Ho 9 SE27 …160 D1
Edridge Rd CR0 …221 B5
Edward Alleyn Ho
SE21 …161 C4
Edward Ave
Chingford E4 …35 D4
Morden SM4 …202 B4
Edward Betham CE Prim
Sch UB6 …86 A5
Edward Cl Edmonton N9 .17 D4
Hampton TW12 …174 A5
Edward Ct 2 E16 …99 A2
2 Ealing W5 …87 B3
Harrow HA1 …64 C6
Edward Dodd Ct N1 …235 D2
Edward Edward's Ho
SE1 …251 C3
Edwardes Sq
W8 …113 B3 254 D5
Edward Friend Ho 6
N16 …73 C5
Edward Gr EN4 …14 B6
Edward Harvey Ct
DA17 …125 B1
Edward Ho SE11 …260 D2
W2 …236 C5
Edward Kennedy Ho 18
W10 …91 A3
Edward Mann Cl 12 E1 .96 D1
Edward Mans 7 IG11 .79 D1
Edward Mews NW1 …231 D3
Edward Pauling Ho
TW14 …149 D4
Edward Pauling Prim Sch
TW13 …149 C2
Edward Pinner Ct 5
KT6 …214 A6
Edward Pl SE8 …141 B6
Edward Rd E17 …52 D4
Bromley BR1 …187 C3
Chislehurst BR7 …188 D5
Croydon CR0 …205 C2
Dagenham RM6 …59 A3
Hampton TW12 …174 A5
Harrow HA2 …42 A6
Hatton TW14 …149 C6
New Barnet EN4 …14 B6
Northolt UB5 …84 C5
Penge SE20 …184 D4
Edward Redhead Jun & Inf
Sch E17 …53 A6
Edward Robinson Ho 3
SE14 …140 D5
Edward's Ave HA4 …62 C2
Edwards Cl KT4 …216 D6
Edward's Cotts 11 N1 …72 D1
Edwards Dr N11 …31 D3
Edward's La N16 …73 C6
Edwards Language Sch
W5 …110 A6
Edwards Mews N1 …72 C1
W1 …93 A1 238 A1
Edward Sq N1 …233 C5
SE16 …119 A5
Edwards Rd DA17 …125 C2
Edward St 10 E16 …99 A3
SE14 …141 B5
Edward Temme Ave
E15 …76 D1
Edward Tyler Rd SE12 .165 C2
Edward VII Mans NW10 90 D4
Edward Way TW15 …148 B2
Edward Wilson Prim Sch
W2 …91 D2
Edwina Ct SM1 …217 D4
Edwina Gdns IG4 …56 A4
Edwin Arnold Ct DA15 189 D6
Edwin Ave E6 …100 C5
Edwin Cl DA7 …147 B6
Edwin Ho SE15 …140 A5
Edwin Rd HA8 …27 B4
Twickenham TW1,TW2 …152 C3
Edwin's Mead E9 …75 A4
Edwin St E1 …96 C3
E16 …99 A2
Edwin Stray Ho TW13 .151 C1
Edwin Ware Ct 2 HA5 .22 C1
Edwy Ho E9 …75 B4
Edwyn Cl EN5 …12 D5
Edwyn Ho SW18 …157 D5
Eel Pie Island★ TW1 .153 A3
Effie Pl SW6 …265 B3
Effie Rd SW6 …135 C5 265 B3
Effingham Cl SM2 …217 D1
Effingham Ct SW19 …180 C3
Effingham Ho 37 SW8 137 D3
9 Kingston KT2 …176 D4
Effingham Lo 1 KT6 .198 A4
Effingham Rd N8 …50 C5
SE12 …164 D6
Thames Ditton KT6,KT7 .197 C2
Thornton Heath CR0 …204 B2
Effort St SW17 …180 C5
Effra Ct SW2 …160 B6
South Norwood SE19 …183 C3
Effra Mans SW2 …160 C6
Effra Par SW2 …160 C6
Effra Rd SW2 …160 C6
Wimbledon SW19 …179 D4
Effra Road Ret Pk
SW2 …160 C6
Egan Way UB3 …105 C6
Egbert Ho E9 …75 A3
Egbert St NW1 .93 A6 231 A6
Egbury Ho SW15 …155 D5
Egerton Cl HA5 …40 A5
Egerton Cres
SW3 …114 C2 257 B4
Egerton Ct E11 …54 B2
5 Richmond TW10 …154 A6
Egerton Dr SE10 …141 D4
Egerton Gdns NW4 …46 B5
SW3 …114 C3 257 A5
Ealing W13 …87 B1
Ilford IG3 …79 D5
Willesden NW10 …90 C6
Egerton Gdns Mews
SW3 …257 B5
Egerton Ho W4 …133 A6
Egerton Pl SW3 …257 B5
Egerton Rd N16 …51 D2
New Malden KT3 …199 D5
South Norwood SE25 …205 C6
Twickenham TW2 …152 C4
Wembley HA0 …66 B1
Egerton Terr
SW3 …114 C3 257 B5
Egerton Way UB3 …126 D5
Eggardon Ct UB5 …64 A2
Egham Cl Cheam SM3 .217 A6
Putney SW19 …157 A2
Egham Cres SM3 …217 A6
Egham Ct KT6 …197 D4
Egham Rd E13 …99 B2
Eglantine Rd SW18 …158 A6
Egleston Rd SM4 …201 D3
Eglington Ct SE17 …139 A6
Eglington Rd E4 …20 B4
Eglinton Hill SE18 …144 D5
Eglinton Prim Sch
SE18 …144 C6
Eglinton Rd SE18 …144 D6
Egliston Mews SW15 .134 C2
Egliston Rd SW15 …134 C2
Egmont Ave KT6 …198 B1
Egmont Rd
New Malden KT3 …199 D5
Sutton SM2 …218 A1
Tolworth KT6 …198 C1
Walton-on-T KT12 …194 B2
Egmont St SE14 …140 D5
Egremont Ho SE13 …141 D3
Egremont Rd SE27 …160 C1
Egret Ho 11 SE16 …118 D2
Egret Way UB4 …84 D2
Eider Cl E7 …76 D3
Hayes UB4 …84 D2
Eider Ct 39 SE8 …141 B6
Eighteenth Rd CR4 …204 A5
Eighth Ave Hayes UB3 .106 A5
Ilford E12 …78 B4
Eileen Ct BR7 …188 C5
Eileen Rd SE25 …205 B4
Eindhoven Cl SM5 …203 A1
Einstein Ho HA9 …67 A5
Eisenhower Dr E6 …100 A2
Eisenhower Ho KT8 …175 C2
Ekarra Ho SW8 …270 B2
Elaine Ct 13 NW3 …70 D2
Elaine Gr NW5 …71 A3
Elaine Ho N4 …50 A1
Elam Cl SE5 …138 D3
Elam St SE5 …138 D3
Elan Ct E1 …96 B2
Eland Pl CR0 …220 D5
Eland Rd SW11 …136 D2
Croydon CR0 …220 D5
Elba Pl SE17 …117 A2 262 B4
Elberon Ave CR0 …203 C3
Elbe St SW6 …136 A3
Elborough Rd SE25 …206 A4
Elborough St SW18 …157 C3
Elbourne Trad Est
DA17 …125 D3
Elbury Dr E16 …99 A1
Elcho St SW11 136 C5 267 B3
Elcot Ave SE15 …140 B5
Eldenwall Ind Est RM8 .59 B1
Elder Ave N8 …50 A4
Elderberry Gr 10 SE27 183 A6
Elderberry Rd W5 …110 A4
Elder Cl DA15 …167 D3
HA8 …27 A5
Barnet N20 …13 D3
Yiewsley UB7 …104 A6
Elder Ct WD23 …8 C2
Elderfield Ho 3 E14 .119 C6
Elderfield Pl SW17 …181 B6
Elderfield Rd E5 …74 C4
Elderfield Wlk E11 …55 B4
Elderflower Way E15 …76 C1
Elder Gdns 9 SE27 …183 A6
Elder Oak Cl SE20 …184 B2
Elder Rd SE27 …183 A5
Elderslie Cl BR3 …207 D3
Elderslie Rd SE9 …166 C6
Elder St E1 …95 D3 243 C5
Elderton Rd SE26 …185 A6
Eldertree Pl CR4 …181 C2
Eldertree Way CR4 …181 C2
Elder Wlk N1 …234 D6
Elderwood Pl SE27 …183 A5
Eldon Ave Croydon CR0 222 C6
Heston TW5 …129 C5
Eldon Ct NW6 …91 C6
Eldon Gr NW3 …70 B3
Eldon Ho SW9 …138 D2
Eldon Jun & Inf Schs
N9 …18 C3
Eldon Pk SE25 …206 B5
Eldon Rd E17 …53 B5
N9 …18 C3
W8 …113 D3 255 D5
Tottenham N22 …32 D2
Eldon St EC2 …95 B2 242 D3
Eldon Way NW10 …88 D5
Eldred Rd IG11 …101 C6
Eldrick Ct TW14 …149 B3
Eldridge Cl TW14 …150 A3
Eldridge Ct SE16 …118 A3
Eleanor Cl N15 …51 D6
SE16 …118 D4
Eleanor Cres NW7 …28 D6
Eleanor Ct 13 E2 …96 A6
Eleanor Gdns
Barnet EN5 …12 D6
Dagenham RM8 …81 B6
Eleanor Gr
Mortlake SW13 …133 C2
Uxbridge UB10 …60 D5
Eleanor Ho 1 NW5 …71 C3
18 W6 …112 C1
6 Merton SW19 …179 D2
Eleanor Palmer Prim Sch
NW5 …71 C4
Eleanor Rathbone Ho 1
N6 …49 D2
Eleanor Rd E15 …76 D2
Bowes Park N11 …32 A4
Eleanor Smith Sch E13 .99 B5
Eleanor St E3 …97 C4
Eleanor Wlk 25 SE18 …122 B2
Electra Ave TW6 …127 D2
Electric Ave SW9 …138 C1
Enfield EN3 …7 B6
Electric Ho 12 E3 …97 C4
Electric La 2 SW9 …138 C1
Electric Mans 1 SW9 138 C1
Electric Par Ilford IG3 .57 D1
Surbiton KT6 …197 D3
Woodford E18 …37 A1
Elephant & Castle
SE1 …261 D4
SE1 …117 A3 261 D5
Elephant & Castle Sta
SE1 …116 D3 261 D5
SE17 …117 A2 262 A4
Elephant La SE16 …118 C4
Elephant Rd
SE17 …117 A2 262 A4
Elers Rd W13 …109 C4
Hayes UB3 …105 B2
Eley Rd N18 …34 D5
Eley's Est N18 …34 D6
Elfindale Rd SE24 …161 A6
Elfin Gr TW11 …174 D5
Elford Cl SE9 …143 C1
Elfort Rd N5 …72 C4
Elfrida Cres SE6 …185 C6
Elfrida Prim Sch SE6 .185 C6
Elf Row E1 …118 C6
Elfwine Rd W7 …86 C2
Elgal Cl BR6 …226 D3
Elgar N8 …50 A6
Elgar Ave NW10 …67 B2
W5 …110 A4
Thornton Heath SW16 .204 A6
Tolworth KT5,KT6 …198 D2
Elgar Cl E13 …99 C5
SE8 …141 C5
Buckhurst Hill IG9 …21 D2
Elstree WD6 …9 D4
Ickenham UB10 …60 C6
Elgar Ct W14 …254 A5
Elgar Ho NW6 …70 A1
SW1 …258 D1
Hayes UB4 …84 C2
Isleworth TW2 …152 B5
Elgar St SE16 …119 A3
Elgin Ave W12 …112 B3
W9 …91 D3
Ashford TW15 …171 A4
Harrow HA3 …25 B1
Elgin Cres
W11 …113 A6 244 B6
Hatton TW6 …127 C3
Elgin Ct W9 …91 D3
6 Croydon CR0 …221 A4
Elgin Ho 8 E14 …97 D1
Northolt UB5 …84 B5
Elgin Mans W9 …91 D4
Elgin Mews W11 …91 A1
Elgin Mews N W9 …91 D4
Elgin Mews S W9 …91 D4
Elgin Rd N22 …31 C1
Croydon CR0 …221 D6
Ilford IG3 …57 C2
Sutton SM1 …218 A5
Wallington SM6 …219 C2
Elgood Ave HA6 …22 A3
Elgood Ho NW8 …229 D3
Elham Cl BR1 …187 D3
Elham Ho 13 E5 …74 B3
Elia Mews N1 …94 D5 234 C3
Elias Pl SW8 …138 C6
Elia St N1 …94 D5 234 C3
Elibank Rd SE9 …144 C1
Elim Est SE1 …263 A6
Elim St SE1 …263 A6
Elim Way E13 …98 D4
Eliot Bank SE23,SE26 …162 B2
Eliot Bank Prim Sch
SE23 …162 B2
Eliot Ct SW18 …157 D5
Eliot Dr HA2 …63 D6
Eliot Gdns SW15 …134 A1
Eliot Hill SE13 …142 A3
Eliot Ho 10 TW10 …154 B5
Eliot Mews NW8 …229 A3
Eliot Pk SE13 …142 A3
Eliot Pl SE3 …142 C3
Eliot Rd RM9 …80 D4
Eliot Vale SE3 …142 B3
Elizabethan Ct N3 …47 A6
Elizabeth Ave
N1 …73 B1 235 B6
Enfield EN2 …4 D2
Ilford IG1 …79 B6
Elizabeth Barnes Ct 5
SW6 …135 D3
Elizabeth Blackwell Ho
N22 …32 C2
Elizabeth Cl 12 E14 …97 D1
W9 …236 B5
Cheam SM1 …217 B6
Elizabeth Clyde Cl N15 .51 C5
Elizabeth Cotts 5
TW9 …132 C4
Elizabeth Ct NW8 …237 B6
SE22 …140 A1
SW10 …266 D5
SW1 …259 D5
Buckhurst Hill IG9 …21 B3
Sunbury TW16 …194 C6
3 Teddington TW11 …174 C5
West Barnes SM4 …201 A2
6 Woodford E18 …37 A2
2 Woodford IG8 …37 C3
Elizabeth Finn Ho
W12 …112 A3
Elizabeth Fry Ho UB3 .105 D2
Elizabeth Fry Pl SE18 .144 A4
Elizabeth Garrett Anderson
Ho 9 DA17 …125 C3
Elizabeth Garrett Anderson
Hospl NW1 …93 C3 239 B6
Elizabeth Garrett Anderson
Language Coll
N1 …94 B5 233 C3
Elizabeth Gdns W3 …111 D5
Stanmore HA7 …25 C5
Sunbury TW16 …194 C6
Elizabeth Ho 46 E3 …97 D4
N20 …14 D1
SE11 …261 B3
15 W6 …112 C1
Wembley HA9 …66 B3
Elizabeth Ind Est SE14 140 D6
Elizabeth Kenny Ho N1 73 A2
Elizabeth Mews NW3 .70 D2
Elizabeth Pl N15 …51 B5
Elizabeth Rd E6 …99 D6
N15 …51 C4
Elizabeth Ride N9 …18 B4
Elizabeth Selby Inf Sch
E2 …96 A4
Elizabeth Sq 13 SE16 .119 A6
Elizabeth St
SW1 …115 A2 258 B4
Elizabeth Terr SE9 …166 B5
Elizabeth Way
Feltham TW13 …172 C6
South Norwood SE19 …183 B3
Elkanette Mews N20 …14 A2

Elkington Point SE11 261 A3
Elkington Rd E13 99 B3
Elkstone Rd W10 91 B2
Ellacombe Ho 1 SW2 160 C4
Ellaline Rd W6 134 D6
Ella Mews NW3 70 D4
Ellanby Cres N18 34 B5
Elland Ho 12 E14 97 B1
Elland Rd SE15 140 C1
Ella Rd N4,N8 50 A2
Ellement Cl HA5 40 D4
Ellena Ct N14 16 A1
Ellenborough Ct N22 32 D2
Ellenborough Ho 5
W12 112 B6
Ellenborough Pl
SW15 134 A1
Ellenborough Rd
DA14 191 A5
Tottenham N22 33 A2
Ellen Cl BR1 209 D6
Ellen Ct N9 18 C2
6 Chingford E4 20 A3
Ellen Miller Ho 2 E17 54 A4
Ellen St E1 96 A1
Ellen Webb Dr HA3 42 C6
Ellen Wilkinson Ho
7 E2 96 D4
SW6 264 D5
12 Dagenham RM10 81 C5
Ellen Wilkinson Prim Sch
E6 100 A2
Ellen Wilkinson Sch for
Girls W3 88 B1
Elleray Rd TW11 174 D4
Ellerby St SW6 134 D4
Ellerdale Cl 22 NW3 70 A4
Ellerdale Rd NW3 70 A3
Ellerdale St SE13 141 D2
Ellerdine Rd TW3 130 B1
Ellerker Gdns TW10 154 A5
Ellerman Ave TW2,
TW4 151 B3
Ellerslie Ct 6 SM6 219 B2
Ellerslie Gdns NW10 90 A6
Ellerslie Ind Est SW2 160 A6
Ellerslie Rd W12 112 B5
Ellerton Ct W3 110 D4
Ellerton Gdns RM9 80 C1
Ellerton Lo N3 29 C1
Ellerton Rd
Barnes SW13 134 A4
Dagenham RM9 80 C1
Surbiton KT6 198 B1
Wandsworth SW17,
SW18 158 B3
Wimbledon SW20 178 A3
Ellery Ho SE17 262 D3
Ellery Rd SE19 183 B3
Ellery St SE15 140 B3
Ellesborough Cl WD19 22 C5
Ellesmere Ave NW7 11 B1
Beckenham BR3 185 D1
Ellesmere Cl E11 54 D4
Ruislip HA4 39 A2
Ellesmere Ct
Chiswick W4 133 B6
Lewisham SE12 165 A3
Penge SE20 184 B1
Ellesmere Gdns IG4 56 A3
Ellesmere Gr EN5 13 B6
Ellesmere Rd E3 97 A5
NW10 68 A3
Chiswick W4 133 B6
Greenford UB6 86 A3
Twickenham TW1 153 C5
Ellesmere St E14 97 D1
Ellies Mews TW15 148 A2
Ellingfort Rd E8 74 B1
Ellingham Prim Sch
KT9 213 D1
Ellingham Rd E15 76 B4
W12 112 A4
Chessington KT9 213 D2
Ellington Ct N14 15 D2
Ellington Ho SE1 262 B5
Ellington Rd N10 49 B5
Feltham TW13 171 D6
Hounslow TW3 129 D3
Ellington St N7 72 C2
Elliot Cl E15 76 C1
Wembley HA9 66 C5
Elliot Ct 5 N15 51 D5
Elliot Rd NW4 46 B3
SW9 138 D5
Elliott Ave HA4 62 B6
Elliott Gdns TW17 192 C5
Elliott Rd SW9 138 D4
W4 111 C2
Bromley BR2 209 D5
Stanmore HA7 25 A4
Thornton Heath CR7 204 D5
Elliott Sch SW15 156 C5
Elliott's Pl N1 234 D5
Elliott Sq NW3 70 C1
Elliott's Row
SE11 116 D2 261 D4
Ellis Cl HA8 27 C4
NW10 68 C2
SE9 167 A2
Elliscombe Mount 11
SE7 143 C6
Elliscombe Rd SE7 143 C6
Ellis Ct W7 86 D2
Ellisfield Dr SW15 156 A4
Ellis Franklin Ct NW8 229 A4
Ellis Ho E17 54 A4
SE17 262 C2
Ellison Gdns UB2 107 B2
Ellison Ho 1 SE13 142 A3
Ellison Rd DA15 167 B3
Barnes SW13 133 D3
Streatham SW16 182 A3
Ellis Rd Mitcham CR4 202 D3
Southall UB2 108 A5
Ellis St SW1 115 A2 258 A4
Elliston Ho 14 SE18 122 C2
Ellora Rd SW16 181 D5
Ellswood Ct 18 KT6 197 D2
Ellsworth St E2 96 B4
Ellwood Ct 1 W9 91 D3
Elmar Rd N15 51 B5
Elm Ave Ealing W5 110 B5
Ruislip HA4 40 B2
Elmbank N14 16 A4
Elmbank Dr BR1 187 D1
Elm Bank Gdns SW13 133 C3
Elm Bank Mans SW13 133 C3
Elmbank Way W7 86 B2
Elmbourne Dr DA17 125 D2
Elmbourne Rd SW17 159 B1
Elmbridge Ave KT5 199 A3
Elmbridge Cl HA4 40 A3
Elmbridge Dr HA4 40 A3
Elmbridge Wlk E8 74 A1
Elmbrook 2 E18 55 A6
Elmbrook Cl TW16 172 B2
Elmbrook Gdns SE9 144 A1
Elmbrook Rd SM1 217 B4
Elm Cl N19 71 C6
NW4 46 D4
Buckhurst Hill IG9 21 D2
Carshalton SM5 202 D1
Harrow HA2 41 D3
Hayes UB3 84 A1
South Croydon CR2 221 C2
Tolworth KT5 199 A2
Twickenham TW13,TW2 151 D2
Wanstead E11 55 B3
West Barnes SW20 200 C5
Elmcote HA5 22 D1
Elmcourt Rd SE21,
SE27 160 D2
Elm Court Sch SE27 161 A2
Elm Cres W5 110 A4
Kingston KT2 176 A2
Elmcroft N6 49 C2
N8 50 B4
Elmcroft Ave DA15 168 A5
NW11 47 B2
Enfield N9 18 B5
Wanstead E11 55 B5
Elmcroft Cl
Chessington KT9 214 A5
Ealing W5 87 D1
Feltham TW14 149 D5
Wanstead E11 55 B5
Elmcroft Cres NW11 47 A2
Harrow HA2 41 C6
Elmcroft Dr
Ashford TW15 170 C5
Chessington KT9 214 A5
Elmcroft Gdns NW9 44 C4
Elmcroft St E5 74 C4
Elmcroft Terr UB8 82 C1
Elm Ct EC4 251 A6
4 N3 29 C2
SE13 142 B2
SW9 138 C4
42 W2 91 C2
5 Ashford TW16 171 D3
Catford SE6 163 D3
Chingford E4 36 A4
Mitcham CR4 180 D1
Elmdale Rd N13 32 B5
Elmdene KT5 199 A1
Elmdene Cl BR3 207 B4
Elmdene Rd SE18 122 D1
Elmdon Rd
Hatton, Hatton Cross
TW6 127 D2
Hounslow TW5 129 A3
Elm Dr Harrow HA2 41 D3
Sunbury TW16 172 C1
Elmer Cl EN2 4 B2
Elmer Ct SW6 135 A3
Elmer Gdns
Edgware HA8 26 D3
Isleworth TW7 130 B2
Elmer Ho NW1 237 A4
Elmer Rd SE6 164 A4
Elmer's Dr TW11 175 B4
Elmers End Rd BR3,
SE20 206 C6
Elmers End Sta BR3 206 D5
Elmerside Rd BR3 207 A5
Elmers Rd SE25 206 A2
Elmfield Ave N8 50 A4
Mitcham CR4 181 A2
Teddington TW11 174 D5
Elmfield Cl HA1 64 C6
Elmfield Ct DA16 146 B4
Elmfield Ho 17 N2 30 B1
6 N5 73 A3
W9 91 C3
Elmfield Mans 5
SW17 159 A2
Elmfield Pk BR1 209 A6
Elmfield Rd BR1 209 A6
E17 52 D3
N2 48 B6
Chingford E4 20 B2
Southall UB2 107 A3
Upper Tooting SW17 159 B2
Elmfield Way W9 91 C2
South Croydon CR2 221 D1
Elm Friars Wlk NW1 71 D1
Elmgate Ave TW13 150 C1
Elmgate Gdns HA8 27 B6
Elm Gdns N2 48 A6
Claygate KT10 212 D2
Enfield EN2 5 B5
Mitcham CR4 203 D5
Elm Gn W3 89 C1
Elm Gr BR6 211 D1
N8 50 A3
NW2 68 D4
SE15 140 A3
Harrow HA2 41 C2
Kingston KT2 176 A2
Sutton SM1 217 D4
Wimbledon SW19 179 A3
Woodford IG8 36 D5
Yiewsley UB7 104 B6
Elmgreen Cl 8 E15 98 C6
Elmgrove Cres HA1 43 A4
Elmgrove Fst & Mid Schs
HA3 43 A5
Elmgrove Gdns HA1 43 A4
Elm Grove Par SM6 219 A5
Elm Grove Rd W5 110 A4
Elmgrove Rd
Croydon CR0 206 B2
Harrow HA1 42 D4
Elm Grove Rd SW13 134 A3
Elm Hall Gdns E11 55 B3
Elm Hatch HA5 23 B3
Elm Ho 4 E14 120 A4
2 Kingston KT2 176 B3
Elmhurst DA17 147 A6
Elmhurst Ave N2 48 B6
Mitcham CR4 181 B3
Elmhurst Ct CR0 221 B3
Elmhurst Dr E18 37 A1
Elmhurst Lo 3 SM2 218 A1
Elmhurst Mans SW4 137 D2
Elmhurst Prim Sch E7 77 B1
Elmhurst Rd E7 77 B1
Chislehurst SE9 166 A1
Enfield EN3 6 C6
Tottenham N17 33 D1
Elmhurst Sch CR2 221 B3
Elmhurst St SW4 137 D2
Elmhurst Villas SE15 140 C1
Elmington Cl DA5 169 D5
Elmington Rd SE5 139 B5
Elmira St SE13 141 D2
Elm La SE6 163 B2
Elm Lawn Cl UB8 60 A1
Elmlea Dr UB3 83 D2
Elmlee Cl BR7 188 B4
Elmley Cl 12 E6 100 A2
Elmley St SE18 123 B2
Elm Lo SW6 134 D4
Elmore Cl HA0 88 A5
Elmore Ho SW9 138 D3
Elmore Rd E11 76 B5
Enfield EN3 6 D5
Elmore St N1 73 B1
Elm Park Ave N15 52 A3
Elm Park Ct HA5 40 C6
Elm Park Gdns NW4 46 D4
SW10 114 B1 256 C1
Elm Park Ho SW10 256 C1
Elm Park La
SW3 114 B1 256 C1
Elm Park Mans SW10 266 B6
Elm Park Rd N3 29 B3
SW3 136 B6 266 C6
Edmonton N21 17 A4
Pinner HA5 40 D6
South Norwood SE25 205 D6
Walthamstow E10 53 A1
Elm Pk Stanmore HA7 25 C5
Streatham SW2 160 B4
Elm Pl SW7 114 B1 256 C2
Elm Quay SW8 269 C5
Elm Rd E11 76 B6
E17 54 A4
E7 76 D2
Barnet EN5 1 B1
Beckenham BR3 185 B1
Chessington KT9 214 A4
Elm Rd *continued*
Claygate KT10 212 D2
East Bedfont TW14 149 B4
Hackbridge SM6 203 A1
Kingston KT2 176 B2
Kingston KT3 199 B6
Mortlake SW14 133 A1
Sidcup DA14 190 A6
South Norwood CR7 205 B5
Stoneleigh KT17 215 D2
Tottenham N22 32 D2
Wembley HA9 66 A3
Elm Rd W SM4 201 B2
Elm Row NW3 70 A5
Elms Ave N10 49 B6
NW4 46 D4
Elmscott Gdns N21 17 A5
Elmscott Rd BR1 186 D5
Elms Cotts 1 CR4 180 D1
Elms Cres SW4 159 D5
Elms Ct Merton SW19 179 D3
Wembley HA0 65 A4
Elmsdale Rd E17 53 B5
Elms Gdns
Dagenham RM9 81 B4
Wembley HA0 65 A4
Elmshaw Rd SW15 156 A6
Elmshurst Cres N2 48 B5
Elmside CR0 223 D2
Elmside Rd HA9 66 C5
Elms La HA0 65 A5
Elmsleigh Ave HA3 43 C5
Elmsleigh Ct SM1 217 D5
Elmsleigh Ho TW2 152 B2
Elmsleigh Rd TW2 152 B2
Elmslie Ct SE9 166 C5
Elmslie Point 2 E3 97 B2
Elms Mews W2 246 C6
Elms Park Ave HA0 65 A4
Elms Rd SW4 159 C6
Harrow HA3 24 C3
Elm St WC1 94 B3 240 D5
Elmstead Ave BR7 188 B5
Wembley HA9 66 B6
Elmstead Cl N20 13 C2
West Ewell KT19 215 C3
Elmstead Gdns KT4 216 A5
Elmstead Glade BR7 188 B4
Elmstead La BR7 188 B5
Elmstead Rd IG3 79 D6
Elmstead Woods Sta
BR7 188 A4
Elmsted Cres DA16 146 C6
Elms The E12 78 A2
NW10 89 C5
NW9 45 A3
Ashford TW15 170 C5
Barnes SW13 133 D2
Claygate KT10 212 D1
Croydon CR0 205 A1
Elmstone Rd SW6 265 A2
Elmsway TW15 170 C5
Elmsworth Ave TW3 129 D3
Elm Terr NW2 69 C5
3 SE9 166 C5
Harrow HA3 24 B2
Elmton Ct NW8 236 C6
Elmton Way E5 74 A5
Elm Tree Ave KT10 196 C2
Elm Tree Cl
NW8 92 B4 229 C2
Ashford TW15 170 D5
Northolt UB5 85 B5
Elm Tree Ct NW8 229 C2
5 SE5 139 A4
18 SE7 143 C6
Elm Tree Rd
NW8 92 B4 229 C2
Elmtree Rd TW11 174 C5
Elm View Ct UB2 107 C2
Elm Way N11 31 A4
NW10 67 C4
North Cheam KT4 216 C5
West Ewell KT19 215 B3
Elm Wlk NW3 69 C6
Orpington BR6 226 B5
West Barnes SW20 200 D5
Elmwood Ave
Bowes Park N13 32 A5
Feltham TW13 150 B1
Harrow HA3 43 B3
Elmwood Cl
Hackbridge SM6 219 B6
Stoneleigh KT17 216 A1
Elmwood Cres NW9 45 A5
Elmwood Ct SW11 268 C2
Wembley HA0 65 A5
Elmwood Dr DA5 169 A4
Stoneleigh KT17 216 A1
Elmwood Gdns W7 86 C1
Elmwood Inf Sch CR0 204 D3
Elmwood Jun Sch
CR0 204 D2
Elm Wood Prim Sch
SE27 161 B1
Elmwood Rd SE24 161 B6
Chiswick W4 133 A6
Mitcham CR4 202 D6
Thornton Heath CR0 204 D2
Elmworth Gr SE21 161 B2
Elnathan Mews W9 91 D3
Elphinstone Ct SW16 182 A4
Elphinstone Rd E17 35 B1
Elphinstone St N5 72 D4
Elrington Rd E8 74 A2
Woodford IG8 37 A5
Elsa Ct BR3 185 B2
Elsa Rd DA16 146 C3
Elsa St E1 97 A2
Elsdale St E9 74 C2
Elsden Mews E2 96 C5
Elsden Rd N17 33 D2
Elsenham Rd E12 78 C3
Elsenham St SW18,
SW19 157 B2
Elsfield NW5 71 B3
Elsham Rd E11 76 C4
W14 113 A4 244 A1
Elsham Terr W14 244 A1
Elsiedene Rd N21 17 A4
Elsie Lane Ct W2 91 D2
Elsiemaud Rd SE4 163 B6
Elsie Rd SE22 139 D1
Elsinge Rd EN1 6 B6
Elsinore Ave TW19 148 A4
Elsinore Gdns NW2 69 A5
Elsinore Ho N1 234 A5
12 SE5 139 A3
7 SE7 122 A2
Elsinore Rd SE23 163 A3
Elsinore Way TW9 132 D2
Elsley Ct HA9 66 D2
Elsley Prim Sch HA9 66 B2
Elsley Rd SW11 137 A2
Elsley Sch SW11 137 A2
Elspeth Rd SW11 136 D1
Wembley HA0 66 A3
Elsrick Ave SM4 201 C4
Elstan Way CR0 207 A2
Elstead Ct SM4 201 A1
Elstead Ho 9 SW2 160 B4
Elsted St SE17 117 B2 262 D3
Elstow Cl SE9 166 B6
Ruislip HA4 40 D2
Elstow Gdns RM9 103 A6
Elstow Grange NW6 68 D1
Elstow Rd RM9 103 A6
Elstree Gdns DA17 125 A2
Edmonton N9 18 B3
Ilford IG1 79 A3
Elstree Hill BR1 186 C3
Elstree Hill N WD6 9 D6
Elstree Hill S WD6 9 D4
Elstree Ho 3 HA7 25 C6
Elstree Pk WD6 11 B5
Elstree Rd Bushey WD23 8 C4
Elstree WD6 9 A5
Elswick Rd SE13 141 D3
Elswick St SW6 136 A3
Elsworth Cl TW14 149 C3
Elsworthy KT7 196 C3
Elsworthy Rd
NW3 92 C6 230 A6
Elsworthy Rise NW3 70 C1
Elsworthy Terr NW3 70 C1
Elsynge Rd SW18 158 B6
Elsynge Road Mans
SW18 158 B6
Eltham CE Prim Sch
SE9 166 B6
Eltham Coll SE9 165 D2
Eltham Green Rd SE9 165 C6
Eltham Green Sch
SE9 165 D5
Eltham High St SE9 166 B5
Eltham Hill SE9 166 A6
Eltham Hill Sch SE9 166 A5
Eltham Hill Tech Coll for
Girls SE9 166 A5
Eltham Palace* SE9 166 A4
Eltham Palace Rd SE9 165 D5
Eltham Park Gdns
SE9 144 C1
Eltham Rd SE9,SE12 165 B6
Eltham Sta SE9 166 B6
Elthiron Rd
SW6 135 C4 265 B1
Elthorne Ave W7 109 A4
Elthorne Ct NW9 45 B3
Feltham TW13 150 C3
Elthorne Park High Sch
W7 108 D3
Elthorne Park Rd W7 109 A4
Elthorne Rd N19 71 D6
NW9 45 B2
Elthorne Way NW9 45 B3
Elthruda Rd SE13 164 B5
Eltisley Rd IG1 78 D4
Elton Ave Barnet EN5 13 B6
Wembley HA0 65 B3
Wembley UB6 64 D2
Elton Cl KT1 175 C3
Elton Ho 3 E3 97 B6
Elton Lo 4 W5 110 A6
Elton Pl N16 73 C3
Elton Rd KT2 176 C2
Elton St 11 N16 73 C3
Eltringham St SW18 136 A1
Elvaston Ct EN5 12
Elvaston Mews SW7 256
Elvaston Pl
SW7 114 A3 256
Elveden Ho 17 SW9 138
Elveden Pl NW10 88
Elveden Rd NW10 88
Elvendon Rd N13 32
Elver Gdns 6 E2 96
Elverson Rd SE8 141
Elverson Rd Sta SE8 141
Elverton St
SW1 115 D2 259
Elvin Ct NW9 45
Elvington Gn BR2 208
Elvington La NW9 27
Elvin Ho 2 E9 74
Elvino Rd SE26 185
Elvis Rd NW2 68
Elwill Way BR3 208
Elwin St E2 96
Elwood Ho N5 72
Elwood St N4,N5 72
Elworth Ho SW8 270
Elwyn Gdns SE12 165
Ely Cl SW20 177
Ely Cottages SW8 270
Ely Court Flats SW6 264
Ely Ct KT1 198
Ely Gdns
Borehamwood WD6 11
Redbridge IG1 56
Ely Ho 22 SE15 140
Barnet EN4 2
Elyne Rd N4 50
Ely Pl EC1 94 C2 241
Ely Rd E10 54
Hatton TW6 127
Hounslow TW4 128
Thornton Heath CR0 205
Elysian Ave BR5 211
Elysium Gate 7 SW6 135
Elysium Pl SW6 135
Elysium St SW6 135
Elystan Bsns Ctr UB4 106
Elystan Pl
SW3 114 D1 257
Elystan St
SW3 114 C2 257
Elystan Wlk N1 234
Elyston Ct SW15 156
Emanuel Ave W3 89
Emanuel Ct W3 89
Emanuel Sch SW11 158
Embankment SW15 134
Embankment Gdns
SW3 136 D6 267
Embankment Pier
WC2 116 B4 250
Embankment Pl WC2 250
Embankment Sta
WC2 116 A5 250
Embankment The
TW1 153
Embassey Ct DA14 168
Embassy Ct DA16 146
N11 31
NW8 229
Kingston KT6 197
7 Wallington SM6 219
7 Wanstead E18 55
Ealing W5 110
Embassy Gdns BR3 185
Embassy Ho 2 NW6 69
Embassy Lo N3 29
Emba St SE16 118
Ember Cl BR5 211
Embercourt Rd KT10,
KT7,KT8 196
Ember Ct 14 NW9 27
2 W12 111
Ember Farm Ave KT8 196
Ember Farm Way KT8 196
Ember Gdns KT10,KT8 196
Ember Ho 8 BR1 186
Ember La KT10,KT8 196
Emberson Ho 7 E17 54
Emberton SE5 139
Emberton Ct EC1 234
Embleton Rd SE13 141
Embleton Wlk TW12 173
Embley Point 2 E5 74
Embry Cl HA7 25
Embry Dr HA7 25
Embry Way HA7 25
Emden Cl UB7 104
Emden St SW6 265
Emerald Cl E16 100
Emerald Ct N12 30
Emerald Gdns RM8 59
Emerald Sq UB2 106
Emerald St WC1 94 B2 240
Emerson Gdns HA3 44
Emerson Ho N16 73
Emerson Rd IG1 56
Emerson St
SE1 117 A5 252
Emerton Cl DA6 147
Emery Hill St SW1 259

1ery St SE1 .116 C3 261 B6
nilia Cl EN3 .18 B6
nily Pl N7 .72 C4
nily St 7 E16 .98 D1
nlyn Gdns 3 W12 .111 C3
nlyn Rd W12 .111 D3
nmanuel CE Prim Sch
W6 .69 C3
nmanuel Ct 9 E10 .53 D2
nmanuel Ho SE11 .261 A3
ulwich SE21 .161 B1
nmanuel Rd
treatham SW12 .159 D3
orthwood HA6 .22 A3
nma Rd E13 .98 D5
nma St E2 .96 B5
nmeline Ct KT12 .194 C2
nminster NW6 .91 D6
nmott Ave IG6 .57 A4
nmott Cl E1 .97 A3
W11 .48 A3
nperor's Gate
W7 .114 A2 256 A4
npingham Ho 20
E8 .118 D2
npire Ave N18 .33 A4
npire Ct HA9 .66 D5
npire Ho SW3 .257 A5
dmonton N18 .33 B4
npire Par
dmonton N18 .33 B4
Vembley HA9 .66 C5
npire Rd UB6 .65 C1
npire Sq N19 .72 A5
npire Way HA9 .66 C4
npire Wharf E3 .97 A6
npire Wharf Rd E14 .120 B2
npress Ave
Chingford E4 .35 D3
lford IG1 .78 C6
Vanstead E12 .77 D6
Voodford IG8 .36 D3
npress Dr BR7 .188 D4
npress Mews 37 SE5 139 A3
npress Par E4 .35 C3
npress Pl
W5 .113 C1 255 A1
npress St SE17 .139 A6
mpson St E3 .97 D3
msworth Cl N9 .18 C3
nsworth St SW2 .160 B2
nu Rd SW8 .137 B3
na Rd SW16 .204 A6
nard Ho 27 E3 .97 B5
nbrook St W10 .91 A4
nclave Ct EC1 .241 C6
ndale Cl SM5 .218 D6
ndeavour Way
Barking IG11 .102 A5
Thornton Heath CR0 .204 A2
Vimbledon SW19 .179 D6
ndell St WC2 .94 A1 240 A1
nderby St SE10 .120 C1
nderfield Ct BR7 .188 C2
nderley Cl HA3 .24 C2
nderley Ho SE19 .183 D2
nderley Rd HA3 .24 C2
ndersby Rd EN5 .12 C6
ndersleigh Gdns NW4 46 A5
ndlebury Ct 3 E4 .20 B2
ndlebury Rd E4 .20 A2
ndlesham Ct 2
SW12 .159 A4
ndlesham Rd SW12 .159 A4
ndsleigh Gdns
WC1 .93 D3 239 C6
lford IG1 .56 D1
Kingston KT6 .197 C3
ndsleigh Ind Est UB2 107 B2
ndsleigh Mans 4
SW16 .160 A1
ndsleigh Pl WC1 .239 D6
ndsleigh Rd
Ealing W13 .109 A6
Southall UB2 .107 A2
ndsleigh St
WC1 .93 D3 239 D6
ndway KT5 .198 D2
ndwell Rd SE4 .141 A3
ndymion Rd N4 .50 D2
SW2 .160 B5
nergen Cl NW10 .67 C1
NW10 .67 C2
nfield Chase Sta EN2 .5 A2
nfield Cloisters 7 N1 95 C4
nfield Coll EN3 .6 C2
nfield Gram Sch EN2 .5 B2
nfield Gram Sch Lower
EN1 .5 B3
nfield Ho 24 SW9 .138 A3
nfield Lock Sta EN3 .7 A6
nfield Rd E8,N1 .73 C1
W3 .110 D4
Brentford TW8 .109 D1
Enfield EN2 .4 A2
Hatton TW6 .127 C3
nfield Road Rdbt
TW6 .127 C3
nfield Town Sta EN1 .5 B2
Enfield Wlk TW8 .109 D1
Enford St W1 .92 D2 237 C4
Engadine Cl CR0 .221 D5
Engadine St SW18 .157 C3
Engate St SE13 .142 A1
Engel Pk NW7 .28 C4
Engineer Cl SE18 .144 C6
Engineers Way HA9 .66 C4
England's La NW3 .70 D2
England Way KT3 .199 A5
Englefield NW1 .232 A1
Englefield Cl Enfield EN2 .4 C3
Orpington BR5 .211 D5
Thornton Heath CR0 .205 A3
Englefield Path BR5 .211 D5
Englefield Rd N1 .73 C1
Engleheart Dr TW14 .149 D5
Engleheart Rd SE6 .164 A4
Englewood Rd SW12 .159 C5
English Gardening Sch The
SW3 .136 D6 267 C6
English Grounds SE1 .253 A3
English Martyrs RC Prim
Sch E1 .95 D1 243 D1
English St E3 .97 B3
Enid St SE16 .117 D3 263 D6
Enid Stacy Ho 11 N19 .49 D2
Enmore Ave SE25 .206 A4
Enmore Ct SW14 .155 B6
Enmore Gdns SW14 .155 B6
Enmore Rd
Croydon SE25 .206 A4
Putney SW15 .156 C6
Southall UB1 .85 C3
Ennerdale Ave HA3,HA7 43 C6
Ennerdale Cl
Cheam SM1 .217 B4
East Bedfont TW14 .149 D3
Ennerdale Ct E11 .55 A2
Ennerdale Dr NW9 .45 C4
Ennerdale Gdns HA9 .43 C1
Ennerdale Ho 3 N4 .51 B2
Ennerdale Rd DA7 .147 C4
Richmond TW9 .132 B3
Ennersdale Prim Sch
SE13 .164 B6
Ennersdale Rd SE13 .164 B6
Ennis Ho 16 E14 .97 D1
Ennismore Ave W4 .111 D2
Greenford UB6 .64 C3
Ennismore Gdns
SW7 .114 C3 257 A6
Thames Ditton KT7 .196 C3
Ennismore Gdns Mews
SW7 .114 C3 257 A6
Ennismore Mews
SW7 .114 C3 257 A6
Ennismore St
SW7 .114 C3 257 A6
Ennis Rd N4 .50 C1
SE18 .145 A6
Ennor Ct KT4 .216 C4
Ensbury Ho SW8 .270 C4
Ensign Cl TW19 .148 A3
Ensign Ct 7 E1 .118 A6
Ensign Dr N13 .17 A1
Ensign St E1 .118 A6
Ensign Way TW19 .148 A3
Enslin Rd SE9 .166 C4
Ensor Mews SW7 .256 C2
Enstone Rd Enfield EN3 .7 A2
Ickenham UB10 .60 B5
Enterprise Cl CR0 .204 C1
Enterprise Ho
Barking IG11 .101 D4
Chingford E4 .20 A4
Walton-on-T KT12 .194 B2
Enterprise Row N15 .51 D4
Enterprise Way NW10 .90 A4
SW18 .135 C1
Teddington TW11 .174 D4
Enterprize Way SE8 .119 B2
Enton Pl TW3 .129 D1
Epirus Mews SW6 .265 A4
Epirus Rd SW6 135 B5 264 D4
Epping Cl E14 .119 C2
Romford RM7 .59 D6
Epping Forest* IG10 .21 B6
Epping Glade E4 .20 A5
Epping Ho E5 .74 A6
Epping New Rd IG9 .21 B5
Epping Pl N1 .72 C2
Epping Way E4 .19 D5
Epple Rd SW6 .135 B4 264 D2
Epsom Cl DA7 .147 D2
Northolt UB5 .63 B3
Epsom & Ewell High Sch
KT19 .215 A3
Epsom Rd E10 .54 A3
Croydon CR0 .220 C4
Ilford IG3 .57 D3
Morden SM4 .201 B2
Epsom Sq TW6 .127 D3
Epstein Rd SE28 .124 B5
Epworth Rd TW7,TW8 .131 B5
Epworth St EC2 95 B3 242 D5
Equity Sq 29 E2 .95 D4
Erasmus St
SW1 .115 D2 259 D3
Erconwald St W12 .89 D1
Erebus Dr SE28 .123 B4
Eresby Dr BR3 .207 C1
Eresby Ho SW7 .247 B1
Eresby Pl NW6 .69 C1
Erica Ct SW4 .270 B1
Erica Gdns CR0 .223 D5
Erica Ho SE4 .141 B2
Wood Green N22 .32 C2
Erica St W12 .112 A6
Eric Cl E7 .77 A4
Eric Clarke La IG11 .101 A4
Ericcson Cl SW18 .157 C6
Eric Fletcher Ct 7 N1 .73 A1
Eric Macdonald Ho
SW6 .265 B1
Eric Rd E7 .77 A4
NW10 .67 D2
Dagenham RM6 .58 D2
Eric Shipman Terr 2
E13 .99 A3
Ericson Ho N16 .51 D1
SE13 .142 B1
Eric St E3 .97 B3
Eric Wilkins Ho 13
SE1 .118 A1
Eridge Ho SE22 .139 D2
Eridge Rd W4 .111 B3
Erin Cl BR1 .186 C3
Erindale SE18 .145 B6
Erindale Ct 1 BR3 .185 C2
Erindale Terr SE18 .145 B6
Erith Rd DA7 .147 D2
Belvedere DA17 .125 D1
Erlanger Rd SE14 .140 D3
Erlesmere Gdns W13 .109 A3
Ermine Cl TW4 .128 C3
Ermine Ho 3 N17 .33 D3
Ermine Rd N15 .51 D3
SE13 .141 D1
Ermine Side EN1 .18 A6
Ermington Rd BR7,SE9 167 A2
Ernald Ave E6 .100 A5
Erncroft Way TW1 .152 D5
Ernest Ave SE27 .182 D6
Ernest Bevin Coll
SW17 .158 C2
Ernest Cl BR3 .207 C4
Ernest Cotts KT17 .215 D1
Ernest Gdns W4 .132 D6
Ernest Gr BR3 .207 B4
Ernest Rd KT1 .176 D1
Ernest Richards Twr
E17 .53 B3
Ernest Simmonds Ho
SE14 .140 C3
Ernest Sq KT1 .176 D1
Ernest St E1 .96 D3
Ernle Rd SW20 .178 C3
Ernshaw Pl SW15 .157 A6
Eros (Shaftesbury Meml)*
W1 .115 D6 249 C5
Erpingham Rd SW15 .134 C2
Erridge Rd SW19 .179 C1
Errington Rd W9 .91 B3
Errol Gdns Hayes UB4 .84 B3
West Barnes KT3 .200 A5
Errol St EC1 .95 A3 242 B5
Erskine Cl SM1 .218 C5
Erskine Cres N17 .52 B5
Erskine Hill NW11 .47 C4
Erskine Ho 7 SE7 .143 C6
SW1 .259 A1
Erskine Rd E17 .53 B5
NW3 .70 D1
Carshalton SM1,SM5 .218 B5
Erwood Rd SE7 .122 A1
Esam Way SW16 .182 C5
Escot Rd TW16 .171 C3
Escott Gdns SE9 .188 A6
Escot Way EN5 .12 C6
Escreet Gr SE18 .122 C2
Escuan Lo N5 .73 A3
Esher Ave Cheam SM3 .216 D5
Walton-on-T KT12 .194 A1
Esher Church Sch
KT10 .212 A3
Esher Cl DA5 .169 A3
Esher Coll KT7 .196 C2
Esher Cres TW6 .127 D3
Esher Gdns SW19 .156 D2
Esher Ho 8 SW8 .137 D3
Esher Mews 4 CR4 .202 D6
Esher Park Ave KT10 .212 A3
Esher Rd
East Molesey KT8 .196 B4
Ilford IG3 .79 C5
Esher Sta KT10 .212 B6
Eskdale NW1 .232 A3
Eskdale Ave UB5 .85 B6
Eskdale Cl HA9 .65 D6
Eskdale Rd DA7 .147 C4
Esk Ho E3 .97 B3
Eskmont Ridge SE19 .183 C3
Esk Rd E13 .99 B3
Esmar Cres NW9 .46 A2
Esme Ho SW15 .133 D1
Esmeralda Rd SE1 .118 A2
Esmond Ct W8 .255 D6
Esmond Gdns W4 .111 B2
Esmond Rd NW6 .91 B6
W4 .111 B3
Esmond St SW15 .135 A1
Esparto St SW18 .157 D4
Essan Ho W13 .87 B2
Essenden Rd
Belvedere DA17 .125 C1
South Croydon CR2 .221 C1
Essendine Mans W9 .91 C4
Essendine Prim Sch
W9 .91 C4
Essendine Rd W9 .91 C4
Essex Ave TW7 .130 C2
Essex Cl E17 .53 A5
Romford RM7 .59 D5
Ruislip HA4 .40 D1
West Barnes SM4 .200 D2
Essex Ct EC4 .241 A1
W6 .112 C3
Barnes SW13 .133 D3
South Norwood SE19 .183 B4
Essex Gdns N4 .50 D3
Essex Gr SE19 .183 B4
Essex Ho 2 E14 .97 D1
4 Acton W3 .88 C1
Essex Lo 5 N10 .31 B1
Essex Mans E11 .54 B2
Essex Park Mews W3 .111 C5
Essex Pk N3 .29 D4
Essex Pl W4 .111 A2
Essex Place Sq W4 .111 B2
Essex Prim Sch E12 .78 A3
Essex Rd E10 .54 A3
E12 .78 A2
E17 .53 A3
N1 .73 A1 234 D6
NW10 .67 C1
W3 .111 A6
W4 .111 B2
Barking IG11 .79 B1
Chingford, Chingford Green
E4 .20 C3
Enfield EN2 .5 B1
Ilford RM6 .58 C2
Romford RM7 .59 D5
Woodford E18 .37 B1
Essex Rd S E11 .54 B2
Essex Road Sta N1 .73 A1
Essex St E7 .77 A3
SE18 .123 A3
WC2 .116 C6 251 A6
Essex Twr 4 SE20 .184 B2
Essex Villas
W8 .113 C4 245 A1
Essian St E1 .97 A2
Essington SW15 .157 A5
Essoldo Way HA8 .44 B6
Estate Way E10 .53 B1
Estcourt Rd
SW6 .135 B5 264 C4
Croydon SE25 .206 B3
Estella Ave KT3 .200 B5
Estella Ho W11 .112 D6
Estelle Rd NW3 .70 D4
Esterbrooke St SW1 .259 C3
Este Rd SW11 .136 C2
Esther Cl N21 .16 C4
Esther Rd E11 .54 C2
Estoria Cl 22 SW2 .160 C4
Estreham Rd SW16 .181 D4
Estridge Cl TW3 .129 C1
Estuary Cl IG11 .102 B4
Eswyn Rd SW17 .180 D5
Etal Ho N1 .72 D1
Etchingham Ct N12 .30 A3
Etchingham Park Rd
N3 .29 D3
Etchingham Rd E15 .76 A4
Etfield Gr DA14 .190 B5
Ethelbert Cl BR1 .209 A6
Ethelbert Gdns IG2 .56 C4
Ethelbert Ho E9 .75 A4
Ethelbert Rd
Bromley BR1,BR2 .209 A6
Wimbledon SW20 .178 D2
Ethelbert St SW12 .159 B3
Ethel Brooks Ho SE18 144 D6
Ethelburga St
SW11 .136 C4 267 B2
Ethelburga Twr SW11 .267 B2
Ethel Cotts RM6 .58 D6
Ethel Davis Sch RM6 .58 B4
Etheldene Ave N10 .49 C5
Ethelden Rd W12 .112 B5
Ethel Rankin Ct 8
SW6 .135 B3
Ethel Rd Ashford TW15 .170 A5
Newham E16 .99 B1
Ethel St SE17 .262 B3
Ethelworth Ct 4 SW2 160 C3
Etheridge Rd NW2 .46 C2
Etherley Rd N15 .51 A4
Etherow St SE22 .162 A4
Etherstone Gn SW16 .182 C6
Etherstone Rd SW16 .182 C6
Ethnard Rd SE15 .140 B6
Ethronvi Rd DA7 .147 A2
Etloe Ho E10 .53 C1
Etloe Rd E10 .75 C6
Eton Ave N12 .30 A3
NW3 .70 C1
East Barnet EN4 .14 C5
Heston TW5 .129 C6
New Malden KT3 .199 B5
Wembley HA0 .65 C4
Eton Cl SW18 .157 D4
Eton College Rd NW3 .70 D2
Eton Ct NW3 .70 B1
Wembley HA0 .65 C4
Eton Garages 11 NW3 .70 C2
Eton Gr NW9 .44 C5
SE13 .142 C2
Eton Hall NW3 .70 D2
Eton Ho N5 .72 D4
Eton Manor Ct E10 .75 C6
Eton Pl NW1 .71 A1
Eton Rd NW3 .70 D2
Harlington UB3 .127 D5
Ilford IG1 .79 B4
Eton Rise NW3 .70 D2
Eton St TW10 .154 A6
Eton Villas NW3 .70 D2
Etta St SE8 .141 A6
Ettrick Ho 8 E5 .74 B6
Ettrick St E14 .98 A1
Etwell Pl KT5 .198 B3
Eugene Cotter Ho
SE17 .262 D3
Eugenia Rd SE16 .118 C2
Eugenie Mews BR7 .188 D2
Eureka Rd 8 KT1 .176 C1
Euro Bsns Ctr 3 E15 .98 D6
Euro Cl NW10 .68 A2
Eurolink Bsns Ctr
SW2 .160 C6
Europa Pl EC1 .235 A1
Europe Rd SE18 .122 B3
Eusdon Cl N9 .18 B1
Eustace Ho SE11 .260 C4
Eustace Pl SE18 .122 B2
Eustace Rd E6 .100 A4
SW6 .135 C5 265 A4
Dagenham RM6 .58 D2
Euston Rd NW1 93 D3 239 B6
Thornton Heath CR0 .204 C1
Euston Sq NW1 .232 C1
Euston Square Sta
WC1 .93 C3 239 B6
Euston St NW1 .93 C4 232 B1
Euston Sta
NW1 .93 D4 232 C1
Euston Underpass
NW1 .239 A6
Evandale Rd SW9 .138 C3
Evangelist Rd NW5 .71 B4
Evans Cl E8 .73 D2
Evans Gr TW13 .151 C2
Evans Ho SW8 .269 D3
34 W12 .112 B6
Evans Rd SE6 .164 C2
Evanston Ave E4 .36 A3
Evanston Gdns IG4 .56 A3
Eva Rd RM6 .58 D2
Evelina Mans 8 SE5 .139 B5
Evelina Rd SE15 .140 C3
Penge SE20 .184 D3
Eveline Ct N10 .49 B4
Eveline Lowe Prim Sch
SE1 .118 A1
Eveline Rd CR4 .180 D2
Evelyn Ave NW9 .45 B5
Ruislip HA4 .39 D2
Evelyn Cl TW2 .151 D4
Evelyn Cres TW16 .171 D2
Evelyn Ct E8 .74 A4
N1 .235 C3
W1 .237 C1
Croydon CR0 .206 A2
Evelyn Denington Ct 2
N1 .72 D1
Evelyn Denington Rd
E6 .100 A3
Evelyn Dr HA5 .22 D3
Evelyn Fox Ct W10 .90 C2
Evelyn Gdns
SW7 .114 B1 256 C1
Richmond TW9 .132 A1
Evelyn Gr Ealing W5 .110 B5
Southall UB1 .85 B1
Evelyn Ho 3 SW2 .160 B6
W12 .111 D4
Evelyn Rd E16 .121 B5
E17 .54 A5
W4 .111 B3
Cockfosters EN4 .2 D1
Richmond TW10 .153 C1
Richmond TW9 .132 A2
Wimbledon SW19 .179 D4
Evelyns Cl UB8 .82 C1
Evelyns Com Sch UB7 .82 B1
Evelyn St SE8 .119 A1
Evelyn Terr TW9 .132 A2
Evelyn Way
Sunbury TW16 .171 D2
Wallington SM6 .219 D4
Evelyn Wlk N1 .95 B5 235 C3
Evelyn Yd W1 .239 C2
Evening Hill BR3 .186 A3
Evenlode Ho 5 SE2 .124 C4
Evenwood Cl SW15 .157 A6
Everard Ave BR2 .209 A1
Everard Ct N13 .16 B1
Everard Ho 24 E1 .96 A1
Everard Way HA9 .66 A5
Everatt Cl SW18 .157 B6
Eve Rd E11 .76 C4
E15 .98 C5
N17 .51 C6
Isleworth TW7 .131 A1
Everdale Ct N2 .48 C5
Everdon Rd SW13 .134 A6
Everest Ct
6 Chislehurst SE9 .166 A2
South Norwood SE19 .183 C2
Everest Pl E14 .98 A2
Everest Rd SE9 .166 B6
Stanwell TW19 .148 A4
Everett Cl Bushey WD23 .8 C3
Pinner HA5 .39 D6
Everett Ho N7 .72 C4
SE17 .262 C2
Everett Wlk DA17 .125 B1
Everglade Ho E17 .35 B1
Everglades
Beckenham BR2 .208 C6
Hounslow TW3 .130 A2
Everglade Strand NW9 .27 D2
Evergreen Cl SE20 .184 C3
Evergreen Sq 3 E8 .73 D1
Evergreen Way UB3 .105 D6
Everilda St N1 .233 D5
Evering Rd E5,N16 .74 A5
Everington Rd N10 .30 D1
Everington St W6 .134 D6
Everitt Rd NW10 .89 B4
Everleigh St N4 .50 B1
Eversfield Ct SE12 .165 B2
Eversfield Gdns HA8,
NW7 .27 C3
Eversfield Rd TW9 .132 B3
Evershed Ho E1 .243 D2
Evershed Wlk W4 .111 B2
Eversholt Ct EN5 .14 A6
Eversholt St
NW1 .93 C4 232 B3
Evershot Rd N4 .50 B1
Eversleigh Ct N3 .29 C3
Eversleigh Rd E6 .99 D6
N3 .29 B3
SW11 .137 A3
New Barnet EN5 .14 A6
Eversley Ave HA9 .66 C6
Eversley Cl N21 .16 B5
Eversley Cres
Hounslow TW7 .130 B4
Ruislip HA4 .61 D6
Southgate N21 .16 C5
Eversley Ho 18 E2 .96 A4
Eversley Mount N21 .16 B5
Eversley Park Rd N21 .16 B5
Eversley Pk SW19 .178 B5
Eversley Prim Sch N21 .16 B5
Eversley Rd
Greenwich SE7 .143 B6
Kingston KT5 .198 B4
South Norwood SE19 .183 B3
Eversley Way CR0 .223 C5
Everthorpe Rd SE15 .139 D2
Everton Bldgs NW1 .232 A1
Everton Ct HA0 .65 D4
Everton Dr HA7 .44 A6
Everton Rd CR0 .206 A1
Evesham Ave E17 .35 C1
Evesham Cl
Belmont SM2 .217 C1
Greenford UB6 .85 D5
Evesham Ct
2 Ealing W13 .109 A5
2 Richmond TW10 .154 B5
Evesham Gn SM4 .201 D3
Evesham Ho 1 E2 .96 C5
NW8 .229 A5
SW1 .258 D2
Evesham Rd E15 .76 D1
N11 .31 D5
Morden SM4 .201 D3
Evesham St W11 .112 D6
Evesham Way SW11 .137 A2
Ilford IG5 .56 C6
Evesham Wlk SE5 .139 B3
SW9 .138 C3
Evry Rd DA14 .190 C4
Ewald Rd SW6 .135 B3
Ewanrigg Terr IG8 .37 C5
Ewart Gr N22 .32 C2
Ewart Pl 10 E3 .97 B5
Ewart Rd SE23 .162 D4
Ewe Cl N7 .72 A2
Ewell By-Pass KT17 .216 A1
Ewell Court Ave KT19 .215 C3
Ewell Park Gdns KT17 .216 A1
Ewell Park Way KT17 .216 A1

Ewell Rd
Cheam SM2,SM3 ... 216 D2
Surbiton KT5,KT6 ... 198 B2
Thames Ditton KT6,KT7 . 197 B2
Tolworth KT6 ... 198 D1
Ewelme Rd SE23 ... 162 C3
Ewen Cres SW2 ... 160 C4
Ewen Ho N1 ... 233 C5
Ewer St SE1 .. 117 A5 252 A3
Ewhurst 10 SW15 ... 156 D5
Ewhurst Cl E1 ... 96 C2
Ewhurst Ct CR4 ... 202 B6
Ewhurst Rd SE4 ... 163 B5
Exbury Ho E9 ... 74 C2
4 SW9 ... 138 B1
Exbury Rd SE6 ... 163 C2
Excel Ct WC2 ... 249 D5
Excel Ex Ctr E16 ... 121 B6
Excelsior Cl KT1 ... 176 C1
Excelsior Gdns SE13 ... 142 A3
Excelsior Ind Est SE16 140 C6
Exchange Arc EC2 ... 243 B4
Exchange Cl N11 ... 15 A2
Exchange Ct WC2 ... 250 B5
Exchange Mans 2
NW11 ... 47 B2
Exchange Pl EC2 ... 243 A4
Exchange The IG1 ... 78 D6
Exeforde Ave TW15 ... 170 C6
Exeter Cl E6 ... 100 B1
Exeter Ct NW6 ... 91 C5
Kingston KT6 ... 198 A4
Mitcham SW19 ... 180 C3
Exeter Gdns IG1 ... 56 B1
Exeter Ho 11 SE15 ... 140 A6
W2 ... 236 A2
7 Barking IG11 ... 80 A1
Feltham TW13 ... 151 C2
Putney SW15 ... 156 C5
Exeter Mans NW2 ... 69 A2
Exeter Mews SW6 ... 265 A4
Exeter Rd DA16 ... 145 D3
E16 ... 99 A2
E17 ... 53 C4
N14 ... 15 B4
N9 ... 18 C2
NW2 ... 69 A2
Croydon CR0 ... 205 D2
Dagenham RM10 ... 81 D2
Enfield EN3 ... 6 D2
Harrow HA2 ... 63 A6
Hatton TW6 ... 127 C2
Twickenham TW13 ... 151 B1
Exeter St WC2 116 B6 250 C6
Exeter Way 2 SE14 ... 141 B5
Hatton TW6 ... 127 C3
Exford Ct SW11 ... 266 D2
Exford Gdns SE12 ... 165 B3
Exford Rd SE12 ... 165 B3
Exhibition Cl W12 ... 112 C6
Exhibition Rd
SW7 ... 114 B3 256 D6
Exmoor Ho 23 E3 ... 97 A5
Exmoor St W10 ... 90 D2
Exmouth Ho 6 E14 ... 119 D2
Exmouth Market
EC1 ... 94 C3 241 B6
Exmouth Mews NW1 ... 232 B1
Exmouth Pl E8 ... 74 B1
Exmouth Rd E17 ... 53 B4
Bexley DA16 ... 146 C5
Hayes UB4 ... 83 C4
Ruislip HA4 ... 62 C5
Exmouth St E1 ... 96 C1
Exning Rd E16 ... 98 D3
Exonbury NW8 ... 91 D6
Exon St SE17 .. 117 C2 263 A3
Explorer Ave TW19 ... 148 A3
Express Dr IG3 ... 58 B1
Exton Cres NW10 ... 67 A1
Exton Gdns RM8 ... 80 C3
Exton St SE1 .. 116 C5 251 A3
Eyebright Cl 3 CR0 ... 206 D1
Eyhurst Cl NW2 ... 68 A6
Eylewood Rd SE27 ... 183 A5
Eynella Rd SE21 ... 161 D4
Eynham Rd W12 ... 90 C1
Eynsford Cl BR5 ... 211 A3
Eynsford Cres DA5,
DA14 ... 168 D3
Eynsford Ho SE1 ... 252 C2
12 SE15 ... 140 C6
SE17 ... 263 A3
Eynsford Rd IG3 ... 79 C6
Eynsford Terr UB7 ... 82 B1
Eynsham Dr SE2 ... 124 B3
Eynswood Dr DA14 ... 190 C5
Eyot Gdns W6 ... 111 D1
Eyot Gn W4 ... 111 D1
Eyre Ct NW8 ... 229 C4
Eyre St Hill EC1 94 C3 241 A5
Eysham Ct 8 EN5 ... 13 D6
Eythorne Rd SW9 ... 138 C4
Ezra St E2 ... 95 D4

F

Faber Gdns NW4 ... 46 A4
Fabian Rd
SW6 ... 135 B5 264 D4
Fabian St E6 ... 100 B3
Fabyc Ho TW9 ... 132 C5
Factory La
Croydon CR0 ... 220 D6
Tottenham N17 ... 33 D1
Factory Rd E16 ... 122 A5
Factory Yd W7 ... 108 C5
Fagg's Rd TW14 ... 150 A6
Fairacre Hounslow TW7 130 B4
Kingston KT3 ... 199 C6
Pinner HA5 ... 40 A5
Fair Acres BR2 ... 209 A4
Fairacres Putney SW15 134 A1
Ruislip HA4 ... 39 D2
Fairbairn Gn 1 SW9 ... 138 D4
Fairbank Ave BR6 ... 226 D6
Fairbanks Rd N17 ... 52 A6
Fairbourne Ho UB3 ... 105 A3
Fairbourne Rd N17 ... 51 C6
Fairbridge Rd N19 ... 71 D6
Fairbrook Cl N13 ... 32 C5
Fairbrook Rd N13 ... 32 C4
Fairburn Ct SW15 ... 157 A6
Fairburn Ho 9 N16 ... 51 C1
SW5 ... 254 D1
Fairby Ho SE1 ... 263 D4
Fairby Rd SE12 ... 165 B6
Faircharm Trad Est
SE8 ... 141 D5
Fairchild Cl 6 SW11 ... 136 B3
Fairchild Ho 13 E9 ... 74 C1
5 N1 ... 95 C4
SW1 ... 259 B3
Fairchild Pl EC2 ... 243 B5
Fairchild St EC2 ... 243 B5
Fairclough St E1 ... 96 A1
Faircourt 14 NW3 ... 70 D2
Faircroft N16 ... 51 B1
Forest Hill SE26 ... 184 C6
Faircross Ave IG11 ... 79 A2
Faircross Par IG11 ... 79 C3
Fairdale Gdns
Hayes UB3 ... 106 A4
Putney SW15 ... 134 B1
Fairdene Ct N7 ... 72 A3
Fairey Ave UB3 ... 105 D3
Fairfax Cl KT12 ... 194 B1
Fairfax Gdns SE3 ... 143 C4
Fairfax Ho 12 SW9 ... 138 C3
5 Ealing W5 ... 88 A4
6 Putney SW15 ... 156 A6
Fairfax Mews E16 ... 121 B5
N8 ... 50 D5
Putney SW15 ... 134 C1
Fairfax Pl NW6 ... 70 A1
Fairfax Rd N8 ... 50 C5
NW6 ... 70 A1
W4 ... 111 C3
Teddington TW11 ... 175 B3
Fairfax Way N10 ... 31 A3
Fairfield 4 E1 ... 96 C2
N20 ... 14 B4
NW1 ... 232 A5
Pinner HA6 ... 22 A1
Fairfield Ave NW4 ... 46 B3
Edgware HA8 ... 26 D3
Ruislip HA4 ... 39 A2
Twickenham TW2 ... 151 D3
Fairfield Cl DA15 ... 167 D5
N12 ... 30 A6
Enfield EN3 ... 7 A1
Mitcham SW19 ... 180 C3
West Ewell KT19 ... 215 C3
Fairfield Cres HA8 ... 26 D4
Fairfield Ct NW10 ... 90 A6
1 SW18 ... 157 D6
Ruislip HA4 ... 39 B1
8 Woodford IG8 ... 37 A4
Fairfield Dr SW18 ... 157 D6
Harrow HA2 ... 42 A6
Wembley UB6 ... 87 C6
Fairfield E KT1 ... 176 A1
Fairfield Gdns N8 ... 50 A4
Fairfield Gr SE7 ... 143 D6
Fairfield Ind Est KT1 ... 198 B6
Fairfield N KT1,KT2 ... 176 A1
Fairfield Path CR0 ... 221 B5
Fairfield Pl KT1 ... 198 A6
Fairfield Rd BR1 ... 187 A3
BR5 ... 211 B3
E17 ... 35 A1
E3 ... 97 C5
N8 ... 50 A4
Beckenham BR3 ... 185 C1
Bexley DA7 ... 147 B3
Edmonton N18 ... 34 A6
Ilford IG1 ... 78 D2
Kingston KT1 ... 176 A1
Southall UB1 ... 85 B1
South Croydon CR0 ... 221 C5
Woodford IG8 ... 37 A4
Yiewsley UB7 ... 104 A6
Fairfields SE6 ... 163 D4
Fairfield S KT1 ... 176 B1
Fairfields Cl NW9 ... 45 A4
Fairfields Cres NW9 ... 45 A4
Fairfields Rd TW3 ... 130 A2
Fairfield St SW18 ... 157 D6
Fairfield W KT1 ... 176 A1
Fairfield Way
Barnet EN5 ... 13 C6
West Ewell KT19 ... 215 C3
Fairfoot Rd E3 ... 97 C3
Fairford SE6 ... 163 C3
Fairford Ave CR0 ... 206 D4
Fairford Cl CR0 ... 207 A4
Fairford Ct SM2 ... 217 D1
Fairford Gdns KT4 ... 215 D5
Fairford Ho SE11 ... 261 B3
Fairgreen EN4 ... 2 D2
Fairgreen Ct EN4 ... 2 D2
Fair Green Ct 1 CR4 ... 202 D6
Fairgreen E EN4 ... 2 D2
Fairgreen Rd CR7 ... 204 D4
Fairhall Ct KT6 ... 198 B2
Fairhaven Ave CR0 ... 206 D3
Fairhaven Ct CR2 ... 221 A3
Fairhazel Gdns NW6 ... 70 A1
Fairheathe SW15 ... 156 D5
Fairholme TW14 ... 149 C4
Fairholme Cl N3 ... 47 A5
Fairholme Cres UB4 ... 84 A3
Fairholme Gdns N3 ... 47 A5
Fairholme Ho 3 KT3 ... 199 C5
Fairholme Jun & Inf Schs
TW14 ... 149 B3
Fairholme Rd
W14 ... 113 A1 254 B1
Ashford TW15 ... 170 B5
Cheam SM1 ... 217 B2
Harrow HA1 ... 42 D4
Ilford IG1 ... 56 C2
Thornton Heath CR0 ... 204 C2
Fairholt Cl N16 ... 51 C1
Fairholt Rd N16 ... 51 B1
Fairholt St SW7 ... 257 B6
Fairhurst 4 NW6 ... 70 A2
Fairland Ho BR2 ... 209 B5
Fairland Rd E15 ... 76 D1
Fairlands Ave
Sutton SM1 ... 217 C6
Thornton Heath CR7 ... 204 C4
Woodford IG9 ... 21 A2
Fairlands Ct 6 SE9 ... 166 C5
Fairlawn SE7 ... 143 C6
Fairlawn Ave N2 ... 48 C5
Acton W4 ... 111 A2
Bexley DA16 ... 146 D3
Fairlawn Cl
Claygate KT10 ... 212 D2
Feltham TW13 ... 173 B6
Kingston KT2 ... 177 A4
Southgate N14 ... 15 D5
Fairlawn Ct SE7 ... 143 C5
3 Acton W4 ... 111 A2
Fairlawn Dr IG8 ... 37 A3
Fairlawnes SM6 ... 219 B3
Fairlawn Gdns UB1 ... 107 B6
Fairlawn Gr W4 ... 111 A2
Fairlawn Mans SE14 ... 140 D4
Fairlawn Pk SE26 ... 185 A5
Fairlawn Prim Sch
Forest Hill SE23 ... 162 C4
Forest Hill SE23 ... 162 C3
Fairlawn Rd SW19 ... 179 B3
Fairlawns
3 Bowes Park N11 ... 32 A4
10 Chingford E4 ... 20 A2
Pinner WD19 ... 22 D1
Putney SW15 ... 156 D6
Sunbury TW16 ... 194 A6
Twickenham TW1 ... 153 C5
Fairlea Pl W5 ... 87 D3
Fair Lea Pl W5 ... 87 C2
Fairleas 12 BR3 ... 185 D1
Fairley House Sch
SW1 ... 259 D2
Fairlie Ct 22 E3 ... 97 D4
1 N7 ... 71 D4
Fairlie Gdns SE23 ... 162 C4
Fairlight TW12 ... 173 D5
Fairlight Ave NW10 ... 89 C5
Chingford E4 ... 20 B2
Woodford IG8 ... 37 A4
Fairlight Cl Cheam KT4 216 C4
Chingford E4 ... 20 B2
Fairlight Ct NW10 ... 89 C5
Greenford UB6 ... 86 B5
Fairlight Rd SW17 ... 180 B6
Fairline Ct BR3 ... 186 A1
Fairlop Ct E11 ... 54 C1
Fairlop Pl NW8 ... 229 D1
Fairlop Rd E11 ... 54 B2
Fairmark Dr UB10 ... 60 C2
Fairmead BR1 ... 210 B5
Tolworth KT5,KT6 ... 198 D1
Fairmead Cl BR1 ... 210 B5
Heston TW5 ... 128 D5
Kingston KT3 ... 199 B6
Fairmead Cres HA8 ... 11 A1
Fairmead Ct 3 E4 ... 20 C4
Fairmead Gdns IG4 ... 56 A4
Fairmead Ho E9 ... 75 A4
Fairmead Rd N7,N19 ... 72 A5
Thornton Heath CR0 ... 204 C2
Fairmeadside IG10 ... 21 C6
Fairmile Ave SW16 ... 181 D5
Fairmile Ho BR5 ... 190 A1
Teddington TW11 ... 175 A6
Fairmont Cl DA17 ... 125 B1
Fairmont Ho 1 E3 ... 97 C3
Fairmount Rd SW2 ... 160 B5
Fairoak Cl BR5 ... 210 D2
Fairoak Dr SE9 ... 167 B6
Fairoaks Gr EN3 ... 6 D6
Fairseat Cl WD23 ... 8 C2
Fair St SE1 ... 117 D4 253 C2
Hounslow TW3 ... 130 A2
Fairstead Lo 4 IG8 ... 37 A4
Fairstead Wlk N1 ... 235 A6
Fairthorn Rd SE7,SE10 121 A1
Fairview Ave HA0 ... 65 D2
Fair View Cl E17 ... 35 A2
Fairview Cl SE26 ... 185 A5
Fairview Cres HA2 ... 41 C1
Fairview Ct NW4 ... 28 D1
Ashford TW15 ... 170 C5
Kingston KT2 ... 176 D2
Fairview Dr BR6 ... 227 B4
Littleton TW17 ... 192 B4
Fairview Gdns IG8 ... 37 B2
Fairview Ho 14 SW2 ... 160 B4
Fairview Pl SW2 ... 160 B4
Fairview Rd N15 ... 51 D3
Carshalton SM1,SM5 ... 218 C3
Enfield EN2 ... 4 C4
Thornton Heath SW16 ... 182 B2
Fairview Villas E4 ... 35 D3
Fairview Way HA8 ... 26 C6
Fairwall Ho 9 SE5 ... 139 C4
Fairwater Ave DA16 ... 146 A1
Fairwater Ho TW11 ... 175 A6
Fairway BR5 ... 211 B4
Bexley DA6 ... 169 A6
West Barnes SW20 ... 200 C6
Woodford IG8 ... 37 C5
Fairway Ave NW9 ... 44 D6
Fairway Cl NW11 ... 48 A2
Croydon CR0 ... 207 A4
Hounslow TW4 ... 150 D6
West Ewell KT19 ... 215 A4
Fairway Ct NW7 ... 11 B1
13 SE16 ... 118 D4
12 SE9 ... 166 C5
New Barnet EN5 ... 13 D5
Fairway Dr Erith SE28 ... 103 A1
Greenford UB6 ... 63 D1
Fairway Est TW4 ... 150 C6
Fairway Gdns Ilford IG1 79 A3
West Wickham BR3 ... 208 B3
Fairway Prim Sch NW7 11 B2
Fairways E17 ... 54 A5
Ashford TW15 ... 170 D4
4 Hounslow TW7 ... 130 C4
Stanmore HA7 ... 26 A1
Teddington TW11 ... 175 D3
Fairways Bsns Pk E10 ... 75 A6
Fairway The BR1,BR2 ... 210 B4
NW7 ... 11 B1
W3 ... 89 C1
East Molesey KT8 ... 195 D6
Edmonton N13 ... 17 B1
Hillingdon UB10 ... 82 B5
Kingston KT3 ... 177 B2
New Barnet EN5 ... 13 D5
Northolt UB5 ... 64 A2
Ruislip HA4 ... 62 D5
Southgate N14 ... 15 C5
Wembley HA0 ... 65 B6
Fairweather Cl N15 ... 51 C5
Fairweather Ct N13 ... 32 B6
Fairweather Ho N7 ... 72 A4
Fairweather Rd N16 ... 52 A3
Fairwood Ct E11 ... 54 B2
Fairwyn Rd SE26 ... 185 A6
Faith Ct NW2 ... 68 B2
Faithfull Ho N5 ... 73 A3
Fakenham Cl NW7 ... 28 A3
6 Northolt UB5 ... 63 C2
Fakruddin St E1 ... 96 A3
Falaize Ave IG1 ... 78 D4
Falcon Ave BR1 ... 210 A5
Falconberg Ct W1 ... 239 D2
Falconberg Mews W1 239 D2
Falconbrook Inf Sch
SW11 ... 136 B2
Falcon Cl SE1 ... 251 D4
Chiswick W4 ... 133 A6
Falcon Cres EN3 ... 18 D6
Falcon Ct EC4 ... 241 A1
N1 ... 234 D3
8 Dulwich SE21 ... 161 B2
New Barnet EN5 ... 2 A1
Ruislip HA4 ... 61 C6
6 Wanstead E18 ... 55 B6
Falcon Dr TW19 ... 148 A5
Falconer Ct N17 ... 33 A3
Falconer Wlk 12 N7 ... 72 B6
Falcon Gr SW11 ... 136 C2
Falcon Ho 10 SE15 ... 139 D4
Falconhurst 4 KT6 ... 198 A4
Falcon La SW11 ... 136 C2
Falcon Lo NW3 ... 69 D4
11 W9 ... 91 C2
Falcon Pk Ind Est
NW10 ... 67 C3
Falcon Point SE1 ... 251 D5
Falcon Rd SW11 ... 136 C2
Enfield EN3 ... 18 D6
Hampton TW12 ... 173 B3
Falconry Ct KT1 ... 198 A6
Falcon St E13 ... 99 A3
Falcon Terr SW11 ... 136 C2
Falcon Way E14 ... 119 D2
NW9 ... 27 C1
Feltham TW14 ... 150 B6
Harrow HA3 ... 44 A3
Sunbury TW16 ... 171 C1
Wanstead E11 ... 55 A5
Falconwood Ave DA16 145 C3
Falconwood Ct SE3 ... 142 D3
Falconwood Par DA16 145 D1
Falconwood Rd CR0 ... 223 C1
Falconwood Sta SE9 ... 145 B1
Falcourt Cl SM1 ... 217 D3
Falkener Ct SW11 ... 268 B1
Falkirk Ct 11 SE16 ... 118 D5
Falkirk Gdns WD19 ... 22 D5
Falkirk Ho W9 ... 91 D4
Falkirk St N1 ... 95 C5
Falkland Ave N11 ... 31 B6
N3 ... 29 C3
Falkland Ho W14 ... 254 C2
W8 ... 255 C5
Catford SE6 ... 186 A6
Falkland Park Ave
SE25 ... 183 C1
Falkland Pl 2 NW5 ... 71 C3
Falkland Rd N8 ... 50 C5
NW5 ... 71 C3
Barnet EN5 ... 1 A3
Falladon Ho W11 ... 91 B2
Falling La UB7 ... 104 A6
Falloden Way NW11 ... 47 C5
Fallodon Ho 6 SW8 ... 137 D3
Fallow Court Ave N12 ... 30 A4
Fallow Ct 16 SE16 ... 118 A1
Fallowfield N4 ... 72 B6
Stanmore HA7 ... 9 A1
Fallowfield Ct HA7 ... 9 A1
Fallowfields Dr N12 ... 30 C4
Fallows Cl N2 ... 30 B1
Fallsbrook Rd SW16 ... 181 C4
Falman Cl N9 ... 18 A3
Falmer Rd E17 ... 53 D6
N15 ... 51 B4
Enfield EN1 ... 5 C1
Falmouth Ave E4 ... 36 C5
Falmouth Cl SE12 ... 164 D6
Wood Green N22 ... 32 B3
Falmouth Gdns IG4 ... 55 D5
Falmouth Ho SE11 ... 261 B2
W2 ... 247 A6
Falmouth Rd
SE1 ... 117 A3 262 B5
Falmouth St E15 ... 76 B3
Falmouth Way E17 ... 53 B4
Falstaff Ct SE11 ... 261 C3
Falstaff Ho 18 N1 ... 95 C5
Fambridge Cl SE26 ... 185 B6
Fambridge Rd RM8 ... 59 C1
Fane St W14 ... 264 D6
Fann St EC1 ... 95 A3 242 B5
Fanshawe Ave IG11 ... 79 A2
Fanshawe Cres RM9 ... 81 B3
Fanshawe Rd TW10 ... 175 C6
Fanshaw Ho 6 E17 ... 53 D6
Fanshaw St N1 ... 95 C4
Fantail The BR6 ... 226 B5
Fanthorpe St SW15 ... 134 C2
Faraday Ave DA14 ... 168 B2
Faraday Cl N7 ... 72 B2
Faraday Ho 6 E14 ... 119 B6
6 NW5 ... 71 B4
W10 ... 91 A2
2 Balham SW12 ... 159 B4
4 Belvedere DA17 ... 125 C3
5 Hampton TW12 ... 173 D4
Wembley HA9 ... 67 A5
Faraday Lo SE10 ... 120 D3
Faraday Rd DA16 ... 146 A2
E15 ... 76 D2
W10 ... 91 A2
W3 ... 111 A6
East Molesey KT8 ... 195 C5
Southall UB1 ... 107 D6
Wimbledon SW19 ... 179 D4
Faraday Way SE18 ... 121 D3
Thornton Heath CR0 ... 204 B1
Fareham Ho 13 SW15 ... 156 A3
Fareham Rd TW14 ... 150 C4
Fareham St W1 ... 239 C2
Farewell Pl CR4 ... 180 C2
Faringdon Ave BR2 ... 210 C3
Faringford Rd E15 ... 76 C1
Farjeon Ho NW6 ... 70 B1
Farjeon Rd SE3 ... 143 D4
Farleigh Ave BR2 ... 209 A2
Farleigh Ct CR2 ... 221 A3
Farleigh Ho 7 KT2 ... 176 D4
Farleigh Pl N16 ... 7
Farleigh Rd N16 ... 7
Farleycroft 1 CR0 ... 20
Farley Croft BR2 ... 18
Farley Ct NW1 ... 23
W14 ... 25
Farley Dr IG3 ... 5
Farley Ho SE26 ... 16
Farley Pl SE25 ... 20
Farley Rd Catford SE6 .16
South Croydon CR2 ... 22
Farlington Pl SW15 ... 15
Farlow Rd SW15 ... 13
Farlton Rd SW18 ... 15
Farman Terr HA3 ... 4
Farm Ave NW2 ... 6
Harrow HA2,HA5 ... 4
Streatham SW16 ... 18
Wembley HA0 ... 6
Farm Avenue Ho HA0 .. 6
Farmborough Cl HA1 .. 4
Farm Cl SW6 ... 26
Barnet EN5 ... 1
Buckhurst Hill IG9 ... 2
Coney Hall BR4 ... 22
Lower Halliford TW17 .. 19
Southall UB1 ... 10
Sutton SM2 ... 21
Uxbridge UB10 ... 6
Farmcote Rd SE12 ... 16
Farm Cotts E17 ... 5
Farm Ct NW4 ... 4
Farmdale Rd SE10 ... 12
Sutton SM5 ... 21
Farm Dr CR0 ... 22
Farm End E4 ... 2
Farmer Ho 4 SE16 ... 11
Farmer Rd E10 ... 5
Farmers Rd SE5 ... 13
Farmer St W8 ... 24
Farmfield Rd BR1 ... 18
Farm House Ct NW7 ... 2
Farmhouse Rd SW16 . 18
Farmilo Rd E17 ... 5
Farmington Ave SM1 . 21
Farm La SW6 . 135 C5 26
Croydon CR0 ... 22
East Barnet N14 ... 1
Farmlands Enfield EN2 ...
Pinner HA5 ... 4
Farmlands The UB5 ... 6
Farmland Wlk BR7 ... 188
Farm Lane Trad Ctr
SW6 ... 135 C6 26
Farmleigh N14 ... 1
Farmleigh Ho SW9 ... 16
Farm Pl W8 ... 24
Farm Rd NW10 ... 8
Edmonton N21 ... 17
Morden SM4 ... 201
Sutton SM2 ... 21
Twickenham TW4 ... 15
Thames Ditton KT10 ... 195
Farm St W1 ... 115 B6 248
Farmstead Rd
Catford SE6 ... 185
Harrow HA3 ... 24
Farm Vale DA5 ... 169
Farm View N3 ... 47
Farmway RM8 ... 80
Farm Way
Buckhurst Hill IG9 ... 37
North Cheam KT4 ... 216
Farm Wlk NW11 ... 47
Farnaby Ho 2 W10 ... 91
Farnaby Rd SE9 ... 143
Bromley BR1,BR2 ... 186
Farnan Ave E17 ... 53
Farnan Rd SW16 ... 182
Farnborough Ave E17 .. 53
South Croydon CR2 ... 223
Farnborough Cl HA9 ... 66
Farnborough Comm
Keston Mark BR2,BR6 .. 226
Orpington BR6 ... 226
Farnborough Cres
3 Hayes BR2 ... 208
South Croydon CR2 ... 223
Farnborough Ct 2
BR6 ... 227
Farnborough Hill BR6 227
Farnborough Ho 1
SW15 ... 156
Farnborough Hospl
BR6 ... 226
Farnborough Prim Sch
BR6 ... 227
Farnborough Way
BR6 ... 227
10 SE15 ... 139
Farncombe St SE16 ... 118
Farndale Ave N13 ... 17
Farndale Cres UB6 ... 86
Farndale Ho 1 NW6 ... 91
Farnell Mews SW5 ... 255
Farnell Pl W3 ... 110
Farnell Rd TW7 ... 130
Farnell's Almshouses
TW7 ... 130

rnfield Ho 12 SW2 160 B6
rnham Cl N20 14 A4
rnham Ct 2 N16 51 C1
Cheam SM3 217 A2
Southall UB1 86 A1
rnham Gdns SW20 178 B1
rnham Green Prim Sch
3 58 A3
rnham Ho NW1 237 B5
1 252 A3
rnham Pl SE1 251 D3
rnham Rd
exley DA16 146 C3
ford IG3 57 D2
rnham Royal
E11 116 B1 260 D1
rnhurst Ho 7 SW11 137 A3
rningham Ct SW16 181 D3
rningham Ho 9 N4 51 B2
rningham Rd N17 34 A3
rnley Ho 13 SW8 137 D3
rnley Rd Chingford E4 20 C4
outh Norwood SE25 205 B5
rnsworth Ho 8
W27 182 D5
rnworth Ho 5 E14 120 B2
ro Cl BR1 188 C1
roe Rd W14 112 D3
rorna Wlk EN2 4 C4
rquhar Rd
ulwich SE19 183 D5
Vimbledon SW19 157 C1
rquharson Rd CR0 205 A1
rrance Rd RM6 59 A2
rrance St E14 97 C1
rrans Ct HA3 43 B2
rrant Ave N22 32 D1
rrant Cl BR6 227 D1
rrant Ho 15 SW11 136 B2
rr Ave IG11 102 A5
rrell Ho E1 96 C1
rren Rd SE23 163 A2
rrer Ho SE8 141 C5
rrer Mews N8 49 C5
rrer Rd N8 49 D5
arrow HA3 44 A5
rrer's Pl CR0 222 D4
rrier Cl BR1 209 D6
illingdon UB8 82 C1
unbury TW16 194 A5
rrier Mews SE15 140 C2
rrier Rd UB5 85 C5
rriers Ct
elmont SM2 217 A1
Vimbledon SW19 179 A3
rrier St NW1 71 C1
rriers Way WD6 11 B6
rrier Wlk
W10 136 A6 266 A6
rringdon La
C1 94 C3 241 B5
rringdon Rd
C1 94 C3 241 B5
rringdon St
C4 94 D1 241 C2
rringdon Sta
C1 94 D2 241 C4
rrington Pl BR7 189 B3
rrington & Stratford
House Sch BR7 189 B3
rrins Rents SE16 119 A5
rrow La SE14 140 C5
rrow Pl SE16 119 A3
rr Rd EN2 5 B4
rthingale Wlk E15 76 B1
rthing Alley 5 SE1 118 A4
rthing Fields 8 E1 118 B5
rthings Cl
Chingford E4 20 C1
Pinner HA5 40 B3
rthing St BR6 226 B1
rthings The 1 KT2 176 C2
rwell Rd DA14 190 C6
rwig La BR1 187 A2
ashion & Design Museum
The★ SE1 253 A2
ashion St E1 95 D2 243 D3
ashoda Rd BR2 209 D5
assett Rd E8 74 A2
Kingston KT1 198 A5
assett Sq E8 74 A2
auconberg Ct W4 133 A6
auconberg Rd W4 133 A6
aulkner Cl 6 RM8 58 D2
aulkner Ho SW15 134 C3
aulkner's Alley EC1 241 C4
aulkner St SE14 140 C4
auna Cl RM6 58 C3
aunce Ho 1 SE17 138 D6
aunce St
SE17 116 D1 261 C1
avart Rd SW6 135 C4 265 B2
Ave SE18 122 D3
aversham Ave
Chingford E4 20 D3
Enfield EN1 17 B5
aversham Ho NW1 232 B5
SE17 263 A1
Faversham Rd
Beckenham BR3 185 B1
Forest Hill SE6 163 B3
Morden SM4 201 D3
Fawcett Cl SW11 136 B3
West Norwood SW16 182 C6
Fawcett Est E5 52 A1
Fawcett Ho 25 SW9 138 A3
Fawcett Rd NW10 67 D1
Croydon CR0 221 A5
Fawcett St
SW10 136 A6 266 A6
Fawcus Cl KT10 212 C2
Fawe Park Rd SW15 135 B1
Fawe St E14 97 D2
Fawkham Ho SE1 263 D3
Fawley Ct SE27 160 D2
Fawley Lo 2 E14 120 B2
Fawley Rd NW6 69 D3
Fawnbrake Ave SE24 161 A6
Fawn Rd E13 99 C5
Fawns Manor Cl
TW14 149 A3
Fawns Manor Rd
TW14 149 B3
Fawood Ave NW10 67 B1
Fayetville Ho 26 N19 49 D2
Faygate Cres DA6 169 C6
Faygate Rd SW2 160 B2
Fayland Ave SW16 181 C5
Fazal Laf IG1 79 A6
Fazerley Ct 49 W2 91 C2
Fearnley Cres TW12 173 B4
Fearnley Ho SE5 139 C3
Fearon St SE10 121 A1
Featherbed La CR0 223 B1
Feathers Pl SE10 142 B6
Featherstone Ave 4
SE23 162 C2
Featherstone Ct NW7 28 A3
Featherstone Ho UB4 84 C2
Featherstone Ind Est
UB2 107 A3
Featherstone Prim Sch
UB2 107 A3
Featherstone Rd NW7 28 B4
Southall UB2 107 A3
Featherstone St
EC1 95 B3 242 C6
Featherstone Terr
UB2 107 A3
Featley Rd SW9 138 D2
Federal Rd UB6 87 C5
Federation Rd SE2 124 C2
Fee Farm Rd KT10 212 D1
Felbridge Ave HA7 25 B2
Felbridge Cl SW16 182 C6
Felbridge Ct
Croydon CR2 221 A1
East Bedfont TW14 150 B3
Feltham TW14 150 A3
Harlington UB3 127 B6
Felbridge Ho 22 SE22 139 C2
Felbrigge Rd IG3 57 D1
Felday Rd SE13 163 D5
Felden Cl HA5 23 A3
Felden St SW6 135 B4 264 C1
Feldman Cl N16 52 A1
Felgate Mews 4 W6 112 B2
Felhampton Rd SE9 166 D1
Felhurst Cres RM10 81 D4
Feline Ct 1 EN4 14 C5
Felix Ave N8 50 A3
Felix Ct E17 53 D4
Felix La TW17 193 D3
Felix Manor BR7 189 C4
Felix Neubergh Ct EN1 5 C1
Felix Rd Ealing W13 109 A6
Walton-on-T KT12 194 A3
Felix St 19 E2 96 B5
Felixstowe Ct E16 122 D5
Felixstowe Rd N17 51 D6
NW10 90 B4
SE2 124 B3
Edmonton N9 34 A6
Fellbrigg Rd SE22 161 D6
Fellbrigg St 21 E1 96 B3
Fellbrook TW10 153 B1
Fellmongers Yd 3
CR0 221 A5
Fellowes Cl UB4 84 D3
Fellowes Ct UB3 127 B6
Fellowes Rd SM1,SM5 218 C6
Fellows Ct E2 95 D5
Fellows Rd NW3 70 C1
Fell Rd CR0 221 A5
Fells Haugh 6 W3 89 A1
Felltram Way SE7 121 A1
Fell Wlk HA8 26 D2
Felmersham Cl 2
SW4 137 D1
Felmingham Rd SE20 184 C1
Felnex Trad Est SM6 219 A6
Felsberg Rd SW2 160 A4
Fels Cl RM10 81 D5
Felsham Ho SW15 134 D2
Felsham Rd SW15 134 D2
Felspar Cl SE18 123 D1
Felstead Rd E11 55 A2
Felstead St E9 75 B2
Felstead Wharf E14 120 A1
Felsted Rd E16 99 D1
Feltham Ave KT8 196 C5
Felthambrook Ind Est
TW13 150 B1
Felthambrook Way
TW13 172 B6
Feltham Bsns Complex
TW13 150 B2
Feltham Comm Sch
TW13 150 C2
Feltham Corporate Ctr
TW13 150 B1
Feltham Hill Jun Sch
TW13 149 D1
Feltham Hill Rd
Ashford TW15 171 A4
Feltham TW13 172 B6
Feltham Rd
Ashford TW15 171 A6
Mitcham CR4 181 A1
Feltham Sta TW13 150 B3
Felton Cl BR5 210 D3
Felton Gdns IG11 101 C5
Felton Ho N1 235 D5
SE9 143 C1
Felton Lea DA14 189 D5
Felton Rd W13 109 C4
Barking IG11 101 C5
Felton St N1 95 B6 235 D5
Fenchurch 34 N1 95 C6
Fenchurch Ave
EC3 95 C1 243 A1
Fenchurch Bldgs EC3 243 B1
Fenchurch Pl EC3 253 B6
Fenchurch St
EC3 117 C6 253 B6
Fenchurch Street Sta
EC3 117 C6 253 B6
Fen Ct EC3 253 A6
Fendall Rd KT19 215 A3
Fendall St SE1 117 C3 263 B5
Fender Ct 5 SW4 138 A3
Fendt Cl 8 E16 98 D1
Fendyke Rd SE2,DA17 124 D3
Fenelon Pl
W14 113 B2 254 D3
Fen Gr DA15 167 D5
Fenham Rd SE15 140 B5
Fenman Ct N17 34 B2
Fenman Gdns IG3 58 B1
Fenn Cl BR1 187 A4
Fenn Ct HA1 43 A4
Fennel Cl E16 98 C3
Croydon CR0 206 D1
Fennell St SE18 144 C6
Fenner Cl SE16 118 B2
Fenner Ho 25 E1 118 B5
Fenner Sq 10 SW11 136 B2
Fenning Ct CR4 202 C5
Fenning St SE1 253 A2
Fenn St E9 74 C3
Fen St E16 120 D6
Fenstanton Ave N12 30 B5
Fenstanton Prim Sch
SW2 160 C3
Fentiman Rd
SW8 138 B5 270 C4
Fenton Cl BR7 188 B5
E8 73 D2
SW9 138 B3
Fenton Ho SE14 141 A5
Heston TW5 129 C6
Fenton Rd N17 33 A3
Fentons SE3 142 D5
Fenton's Ave E13 99 B5
Fenton St E1 96 B1
Fenwick Cl 16 SE18 144 C6
Fenwick Gr SE15 140 A2
Fenwick Pl SW9 138 A2
Croydon CR2 220 D1
Fenwick Rd SE15 140 A2
Ferby Ct DA15 189 D6
Ferdinand Ho 1 NW1 71 B1
Ferdinand Pl NW1 71 A1
Ferdinand St NW1 71 A1
Ferguson Ave KT5 198 B4
Ferguson Cl BR2,BR3 208 B6
Ferguson Dr W3 89 B1
Ferguson Ho SE10 142 A4
Ferguson's Cl E14 119 C2
Fergus Rd N5 72 D3
Fermain Ct E N1 95 C6
Fermain Ct N N1 95 C6
Fermain Ct W N1 95 C6
Ferme Park Rd N4,N8 50 B3
Fermor Rd SE23 163 A3
Fermoy Rd W9 91 B3
Greenford UB6 85 D3
Fern Ave CR4 203 D5
Fernbank IG9 21 B3
Fernbank Ave
Walton-on-T KT12 195 A2
Wembley HA0 64 D3
Fernbank Mews SW12 159 C5
Fernbrook Dr HA2 41 D2
Fernbrook Rd SE13 164 C5
Fern Cl 3 N1 95 C5
Ferncliff Rd E8 74 A3
Ferncroft Ave N12 30 D4
NW3 69 C4
Ruislip HA4 62 C6
Fern Ct DA7 147 C1
SE14 140 D3
Chingford E4 36 A4
Ferndale BR1 187 C1
Ferndale Ave E17 54 B4
Hounslow TW4 129 A2
Ferndale Cl DA7 147 A4
Ferndale Ct 3 SE3 142 D5
Ferndale Ho N16 51 B1
Ferndale Rd E11 76 D6
E7 77 B1
N15 51 D4
SW4,SW9 138 B1
Ashford TW15 170 A5
Croydon SE25 206 B4
Enfield EN3 7 A6
Ferndale St E6 100 D1
Ferndale Way BR6 227 A3
Ferndene NW9 45 A4
Fern Dene W13 87 B2
Ferndene Rd SE24 139 A1
Fernden Way RM7 59 D3
Ferndown
5 Kingston KT6 198 A4
Pinner HA6 22 A1
6 Wanstead E18 55 A6
Ferndown Ave BR6 211 B1
Ferndown Cl Pinner HA5 23 A3
Sutton SM2 218 B2
Ferndown Ct 6 UB1 86 A1
Ferndown Lo E14 120 A3
Ferndown Rd SE9 165 D4
South Oxhey WD19 22 C6
Ferney Meade Way
TW7 131 A3
Ferney Rd EN4 15 A3
Fern Gr TW14 150 B4
Fernhall Dr IG4 55 D4
Fernham Rd CR7 205 A6
Fernhead Rd W9 91 B4
Fernhill Ct Chingford E17 36 B1
Kingston KT2 175 D5
Fernhill Gdns KT2 175 A5
Fernhill Ho E5 74 A6
Fern Hill Pl 3 BR6 227 A3
Fern Hill Prim Sch
KT2 176 A4
Fernhill St E16 122 B5
Fernholme Rd SE15 162 D6
Fernhurst Gdns HA8 26 C4
Fernhurst Rd
Ashford TW15 171 A6
Croydon CR0 206 B1
Fulham SW6 135 A4 264 B2
Fernie Ho SE22 139 D2
Fern La TW5 107 B1
Fernlea Ho NW10 88 B4
Fernlea Rd
Balham SW12 159 B3
Mitcham CR4 181 A2
Fernleigh Cl W9 91 B4
Croydon CR0 220 C4
Fernleigh Ct
Harrow HA2 23 D1
Wembley HA9 44 A1
Fernleigh Rd N21 16 D2
Fernley Cl HA5 40 A5
Fern Lo 13 SW16 182 C5
Fernsbury St WC1 234 A1
Fernshaw Mans SW10 266 A5
Fernshaw Rd
SW10 136 A6 266 A5
Fernside IG9 21 B3
Fernside Ave NW7 11 B1
Feltham TW13 172 B6
Fernside Ct NW4 28 D1
Fernside Rd SW12 159 A4
Ferns Rd E15 76 D2
Fern St E3 97 C3
Fernthorpe Rd SW16 181 C4
Ferntower Rd N5 73 B3
Fernways IG1 78 D4
Fern Wlk 17 SE16 118 A1
Fernwood
Wandsworth SW19 157 B3
Wood Green N22 32 A3
Fernwood Ave
Streatham SW16 181 D6
Wembley HA0 65 C2
Fernwood Cl BR1 187 C1
Fernwood Cres N20 14 D1
Ferny Hill EN4 3 A5
Ferranti Cl SE18 121 D3
Ferraro Cl TW5 129 C6
Ferrers Ave
Wallington SM6 219 D4
West Drayton UB7 104 A4
Ferrers Rd SW16 181 D5
Ferrestone Rd N8 50 B5
Ferrey Mews 20 SW9 138 C3
Ferriby Cl N1 72 C1
Ferrier Ind Est SW18 135 D1
Ferrier Point 6 E16 99 A2
Ferrier St SW18 135 D1
Ferring Cl HA2 42 A1
Ferrings SE21 161 C1
Ferris Ave CR0 223 B5
Ferris Rd SE22 140 A1
Ferron Rd E5 74 B5
Ferrour Ct N2 48 B6
Ferrybridge Ho SE11 260 D5
Ferry Ho E5 52 B1
Ferry La N17 52 B5
Barnes SW13 133 D6
Brentford TW8 132 A6
Lower Halliford TW17 192 C1
Richmond TW9 132 B6
Ferry Lane Prim Sch
N17 52 B5
Ferrymead Ave UB6 85 C5
Ferrymead Dr UB6 85 C5
Ferrymead Gdns UB6 86 A5
Ferrymoor TW10 153 B1
Ferry Rd Barnes SW13 134 A4
East Molesey KT8 195 C6
Richmond TW11 175 B5
Thames Ditton KT7 197 B3
Twickenham TW1 153 B3
Ferry Sq 1 TW8 132 A6
Ferry St E14 120 A1
Ferry Wks TW17 192 C1
Festing Rd SW15 134 D2
Festival Cl DA5 168 D3
Hillingdon UB10 82 D6
Festival Pier
SE1 116 B5 250 C4
Festival Pleasure Gdns
SW11 136 D5 267 C3
Fetter La EC4 94 C1 241 B2
Fettes Ho NW8 229 D3
Fews Lo RM6 58 D5
Ffinch St SE8 141 C5
Field Cl BR1 187 C1
Buckhurst Hill IG9 21 C1
Chessington KT9 213 C3
Chingford E4 35 D4
Cranford TW4 128 B4
East Molesey KT8 195 D4
Harlington UB7 127 A5
Ruislip HA4 39 A1
Uxbridge UB10 60 D6
Fieldcommon La KT12 195 B1
Field Ct N7 72 A3
NW3 70 A3
WC1 240 D3
Wimbledon SW19 157 C1
Field End Ruislip HA4 62 C2
Twickenham TW11 174 D6
Field End Jun & Inf Schs
HA4 62 D6
Fieldend Rd SW16 181 C2
Field End Rd HA5,HA4 40 C1
Fielders Cl 2 Enfield EN1 5 C1
Harrow HA2 42 A1
Fieldfare Rd SE28 124 C6
Fieldgate Mans 23 E1 96 A2
Fieldgate St E1 96 A2
Field Ho 4 N9 34 A6
Fieldhouse Cl E18 37 B2
Fieldhouse Rd SW12 159 C3
Fielding Ave TW2 152 A1
Fielding Ho 3 NW6 91 C4
NW8 229 A6
Chiswick W4 133 C6
Fielding Mews SW13 134 B6
Fielding Prim Sch
W13 109 B3
Fielding Rd W14 112 D3
W4 111 C3
Fielding St SE17 139 A6
Fieldings The SE23 162 C3
Fielding Terr W5 110 B6
Field La Brentford TW8 131 C5
Teddington TW11 175 A5
Field Mead NW9,NW7 27 D3
Field Pl KT3 199 D3
Field Point E7 77 A4
Field Rd E7 77 A4
N17 51 C6
W6 135 A6 264 A6
Feltham TW14 150 B5
Fieldsend Rd SM3 217 A3
Fields Est E8 74 A1
Fieldside Cl BR6 227 A4
Fieldside Rd BR1 186 B5
Fields Park Cres RM6 58 D4
Field St WC1 233 C2
Fieldsway Ho N5 72 C3
Fieldview SW17,SW18 158 B3
Field View TW13 171 B6
Fieldview Ct N5 72 D3
NW9 44 C3
Fieldway BR5 211 B3
Field Way NW10 67 A1
Fieldway RM8 80 C4
Field Way
Greenford UB6 85 D6
New Addington CR0 223 D2
Ruislip HA4 39 A1
Fieldway Cres N5,N7 72 C3
Fieldway Sta CR0 223 D1
Fieldwick Ho 14 E9 74 D2
Fiennes Cl RM8 58 C1
Fife Ct 5 W3 88 C1
Fifehead Cl TW15 170 A4
Fife Rd E16 99 A2
Kingston KT2 176 A1
Mortlake SW14 155 A6
Tottenham N22 32 D3
Fife Terr N1 233 D4
Fifield Path SE23 162 D1
Fifteenpenny Fields
SE9 166 C6
Fifth Ave W10 91 A4
Hayes UB3 105 D5
Ilford E12 78 B4
Fifth Cross Rd TW2 152 B2
Fifth Way HA9 66 D4
Figge's Rd CR4 181 A3
Fig Tree Cl NW10 89 C6
Filanco Ct W7 108 D5
Filby Rd KT9 214 B2
Filey Ave N16 52 A1
Filey Cl SM2 218 A1
Filey Ho SW18 136 A1
Filey Waye HA4 62 B6
Filigree Ct SE16 119 B5
Fillebrook Ave EN1 5 D3
Fillebrook Hall E11 54 C2
Fillebrook Rd E11 54 C1
Filmer Ho SW6 264 B2
Filmer Rd SW6 135 B5 264 C3
Filmer Road Studios
SW6 264 B2
Filston Rd DA8 125 D1
Filton Ct 14 SE14 140 C5
Finborough Ho SW10 266 A6
Finborough Rd
SW10 135 D6 265 D6
Upper Tooting SW17 180 D4
Finchale Rd SE2 124 A3
Fincham Cl UB10 61 A5
Finch Ave SE27 183 B6
Finch Cl NW10 67 B2
Barnet EN5 13 C6
Finchdean Ho SW15 155 D4
Finch Dr TW14 150 D4
Finch Gdns E4 35 C5
Finch Ho 1 SE8 141 D5
Finchingfield Ave IG8 37 C3
Finch La EC2,EC3 242 D1
Finchley Cath High Sch
N12 13 D1
Finchley Central Sta
N3 29 C2
Finchley Ct N3 29 D4
Finchley La NW4 46 D5
Finchley Lo N12 29 D5
Finchley Memorial Hospl
N12 30 A3
Finchley Pk N12 30 B6
Finchley Pl NW8 229 C4
Finchley Rd NW11 47 B3
NW3 70 A2
NW8 229 C4
Finchley Road & Frognal
Sta NW3 70 A3
Finchley Road Sta NW3 70 A2
Finchley Way N3 29 C3
Finch Lo 15 W9 91 C2
Finch Mews 3 SE15 139 D4
Finch's Ct 4 E14 119 D6
Finden Rd E7 77 C3
Findhorn Ave UB4 84 B2
Findhorn St E14 98 A1
Findon Cl SW18 157 C5
Harrow HA2 63 D5
Findon Rd W12 112 A4
Edmonton N9 18 B3
Fine Bush La HA4 38 D3
Fineran Ct 16 SW11 136 B1
Fingal St SE10 120 D1
Fingest Ho NW8 237 A6
Finians Cl UB10 60 B1
Finland Rd SE4 141 A2
Finland St SE16 119 A3
Finlays Cl KT9 214 C3
Finlay St SW6 134 D4
Finley Ct 21 SE5 139 A5
Finmere Ho 1 N4 51 A2
Finnemore Ho N1 235 A6
Finney La TW7 131 A4
Finn Ho N1 235 D2
Finnis St E2 96 B3
Finnymore Rd RM9 81 A1
Finsbury Ave EC2 242 D3
Finsbury Cir
EC2 95 B2 242 D3
Finsbury Cotts N22 32 A3
Finsbury Ct EC2 242 C4
Finsbury Ho N22 32 A2
Finsbury Market EC2 243 A4
Finsbury Mkt EC2 243 A5
Finsbury Park Ave N4 51 A3
Finsbury Park Rd N4,
N5 72 D6
Finsbury Park Sta N4 72 C6
Finsbury Pavement
EC2 95 B2 242 D4
Finsbury Rd N22 32 B2

Finsbury Sq
EC2 ....95 B2 242 D4
Finsbury St EC2 ....242 C4
Finsbury Way DA5 ....169 B5
Finsen Rd SE5 ....139 A2
Finstock Rd W10 ....90 D1
Finton House Sch
SW17 ....158 D2
Finucane Ct TW9 ....132 B2
Finucane Rise WD23 ....8 A2
Finwhale Ho E14 ....119 D3
Fiona Ct 9 NW6 ....91 B5
Enfield EN2 ....4 D2
Firbank Cl E16 ....99 D2
Enfield EN2 ....5 A1
Firbank Rd SE15 ....140 B3
Fir Cl KT12 ....194 A2
Fircroft N1 ....94 D6 234 D6
Fircroft Gdns HA1 ....64 C5
Fircroft Prim Sch
SW17 ....158 D1
Fircroft Rd
Chessington KT9 ....214 B4
Upper Tooting SW17 ....158 D1
Fir Dene BR6 ....226 C5
Firdene KT5 ....199 A1
Fire Bell Alley KT6 ....198 A3
Firebell Mews KT6 ....198 A3
Fire Brigade Pier SE1 ....260 B4
Firecrest Dr NW3 ....69 D5
Firefly 7 NW9 ....27 D1
Firefly Cl SM6 ....220 A1
Firefly Gdns E6 ....100 A3
Firemans Cotts N10 ....49 A6
Fireman's Flats N22 ....32 A2
Firepower (The Royal
Artillery Mus)★
SE18 ....122 D3
Fire Station Alley EN5 ....1 A3
Fire Station Mews 3
BR3 ....185 D2
Firethorn Cl HA8 ....27 A6
Fir Gr KT3 ....199 D3
Firhill Rd SE6 ....163 C1
Firle Ho W10 ....90 C2
Fir Lo SW15 ....134 B1
Firmston Ho 9 SW14 ....133 B2
Fir Rd Cheam SM3 ....201 B1
Feltham TW13 ....172 D5
Firs Ave N10 ....49 A5
N11 ....31 A4
Mortlake SW14 ....133 A1
Firsby Ave CR0 ....207 A1
Firsby Rd N16 ....52 A1
Firs Cl N10 ....49 A6
Claygate KT10 ....212 C2
Forest Hill SE23 ....163 A4
Mitcham CR4 ....181 B2
Firscroft N13 ....17 A1
Firs Dr TW5 ....128 B5
Firs Farm Prim Sch
N13 ....17 B1
Firs Ho N22 ....32 C2
Firside Gr DA15 ....167 D3
Firs La N21,N13 ....17 A2
Firs Park Ave N21 ....17 B3
Firs Park Gdns N21 ....17 B3
First Ave E12 ....78 A3
E13 ....99 A4
E17 ....53 D4
N18 ....34 C6
NW4 ....46 C5
W10 ....91 B3
W3 ....111 D5
Bexley DA7 ....146 C5
Dagenham RM10 ....103 D5
Dagenham RM6 ....58 C4
East Molesey KT8 ....195 C5
Enfield EN1 ....17 D6
Hayes UB3 ....105 D5
Mortlake SW14 ....133 C2
Walton-on-T KT12 ....194 B3
Wembley HA9 ....65 D6
First Cl KT8 ....196 A6
First Cross Rd TW2 ....152 C2
First Dr NW10 ....67 A1
Firs The DA15 ....167 D1
E6 ....78 A1
N20 ....14 B3
Belmont SM2 ....217 D1
Claygate KT10 ....212 C2
Ealing W5 ....87 D2
Forest Hill SE26 ....184 C5
2 Penge SE26 ....184 B5
Wimbledon SW20 ....178 A3
Woodford IG8 ....37 C3
First St SW3 ....114 C2 257 B4
Firstway SW20 ....178 C1
First Way HA9 ....66 D4
Firs Wlk IG8 ....37 A5
Firswood Ave KT19 ....215 D3
Firth Gdns
SW6 ....135 A4 264 A1
Firtree Ave CR4 ....181 A1
Fir Tree Ave UB7 ....104 C3
Fir Tree Cl Ealing W5 ....88 A1
Fir Tree Cl *continued*
Esher KT10 ....212 A3
5 Orpington BR6 ....227 D3
Streatham SW16 ....181 C5
Worcester Park KT19 ....215 D4
Firtree Ct BR2 ....208 D6
Fir Tree Gdns CR0 ....223 C4
Fir Tree Gr SM5 ....218 D1
Fir Tree Ho 11 SE14 ....140 C5
Fir Tree Rd TW4 ....129 A1
Fir Trees Cl SE16 ....119 A5
Fir Tree Wlk EN1 ....5 B2
Fir Wlk KT17,SM3 ....216 D2
Fisher Cl Croydon CR0 ....205 D1
Southall UB6 ....85 C4
Holdbrook EN3 ....7 C6
Fisher Ho 8 E1 ....118 C6
N1 ....234 A5
2 N19 ....71 C5
Fisherman Cl TW10 ....175 C6
Fishermans Dr SE16 ....118 D4
Fishermans Wlk SE28 ....123 C4
Fisherman's Wlk E14 ....119 C5
Fisher Rd HA3 ....24 D1
Fishers Cl SW16 ....159 D1
Fishers Ct SE14 ....140 D4
4 Teddington TW11 ....174 D5
Fishersdene KT10 ....213 A1
Fisher's La W4 ....111 B2
Fisher St E16 ....99 A2
WC1 ....240 C3
Fisherton St
NW8 ....92 B3 236 D6
Fisherton Street Est
NW8 ....92 B3 236 D5
Fishguard Way E16 ....122 D5
Fishlock Ct 6 SW4 ....138 A3
Fishponds Rd BR2 ....225 D3
Upper Tooting SW17 ....180 C6
Fish St Hill EC3 ....252 D5
Fiske Ct Barking IG11 ....101 B5
1 Merton SW19 ....180 A3
Sutton SM2 ....218 A1
Tottenham N17 ....34 A2
Fitch Ct SW2 ....160 C6
8 Mitcham CR4 ....181 A1
Fitzalan Rd N3 ....47 B6
Claygate KT10 ....212 C1
Fitzalan St
SE11 ....116 C2 261 A4
Fitzclarence Ho W11 ....244 A2
Fitz-George Ave W14 ....254 A3
Fitzgeorge Ave KT2,
KT3 ....177 B2
Fitzgerald Ave SW14 ....133 C2
Fitzgerald Ct 1 E10 ....53 D1
Fitzgerald Ho 14 E14 ....97 D1
16 SW9 ....138 C3
Hayes UB3 ....106 B5
Fitzgerald Rd
Mortlake SW14 ....133 B2
Thames Ditton KT7 ....197 A3
Wanstead E11 ....55 A4
Fitzhardinge Ho W1 ....238 A2
Beckenham BR3 ....185 D1
Fitzhardinge St W1 ....238 A2
Fitzherbert Ho 11
TW10 ....154 B5
Fitzhugh Gr SW18 ....158 B5
Fitzjames Ave W14 ....254 B3
Croydon CR0 ....222 A6
Fitzjohn Ave EN5 ....1 B1
Fitzjohn's Ave NW3 ....70 B3
Fitzjohns Mans NW3 ....70 A2
Fitzjohns Prim Sch
NW3 ....70 B3
Fitzmaurice Ho 17
SE16 ....118 B2
Fitzmaurice Pl W1 ....248 D4
Fitzneal St W12 ....89 D1
Fitzroy Cl N6 ....48 D1
Fitzroy Cres W4 ....133 B5
Fitzroy Ct N6 ....49 C3
W1 ....239 B5
Fitzroy Gdns SE19 ....183 C3
Fitzroy Ho 14 E14 ....97 B1
SE1 ....263 D2
Fitzroy Lo N21 ....16 D6
Fitzroy Mews W1 ....239 A5
Fitzroy Pk N6 ....48 D1
Fitzroy Rd NW1 ....93 A6 231 A6
Fitzroy Sq W1 ....239 A5
Fitzroy St W1 ....93 C3 239 A5
Fitzroy Yd NW1 ....231 A6
Fitzsimmons Ct 1
NW10 ....89 B6
Fitzstephen Rd RM8 ....80 C3
Fitzwarren Gdns N19 ....49 C1
Fitzwilliam Ave TW9 ....132 B3
Fitzwilliam Ho TW9 ....131 D1
Fitzwilliam Hts 1
SE23 ....162 C2
Fitzwilliam Mews E16 ....121 A5
Fitzwilliam Rd SW4 ....137 C2
Fitzwygram Cl TW12 ....174 A5
Five Acre NW9 ....27 D1
Fiveacre Cl CR7 ....204 C3
Five Elms Prim Sch
RM8 ....81 B5
Five Elms Rd BR2 ....225 C5
Dagenham RM9 ....81 B5
Fives Ct SE11 ....261 C5
Fiveways SE9 ....166 D2
Croydon CR0 ....220 C4
Five Ways Cnr NW4 ....28 A2
Fiveways Rd SW9 ....138 C3
Five Ways Retail Pk
NW7 ....27 D3
Flack Ct 14 E10 ....53 D2
Fladbury Rd N15 ....51 B3
Fladgate Rd E11 ....54 C3
Flag Cl CR0 ....206 D1
Flag Wlk HA5 ....40 A3
Flambard Rd HA1,HA3 ....43 A3
Flamborough Ho 11
SE15 ....140 A4
Flamborough Rd HA4 ....62 A5
Flamborough St E14 ....97 A1
Flamingo Ct 2 SE8 ....141 C5
Flamingo Gdns UB5 ....85 A4
Flamstead Gdns RM9 ....80 C1
Flamstead Rd RM9 ....80 C1
Flamsted Ave HA9 ....66 C2
Flamsteed Ho★ SE10 ....142 B5
Flamsteed Rd SE7 ....122 A1
Flanchford Rd W12 ....111 D3
Flanders Cres SW17 ....180 D4
Flanders Ct E17 ....53 A3
Flanders Mans 1 W4 ....111 D2
Flanders Rd W4 ....111 C2
Wallend E6 ....100 C5
Flanders Way E9 ....74 D2
Flank St 6 E1 ....118 A6
Flansham Ho 2 E14 ....97 B1
Flash La EN2 ....5 A6
Flask Wlk NW3 ....70 B4
Flatford Ho 2 SE6 ....186 A6
Flavell Mews SE10 ....120 C1
Flaxen Cl E4 ....19 D1
Flaxen Rd E4 ....19 D1
Flaxley Rd SM4 ....201 D2
Flaxman Ct W1 ....239 C1
12 Belvedere DA17 ....125 C1
Flaxman Ho SE1 ....261 D6
10 W4 ....111 C1
Flaxman Rd SE5 ....138 D3
Flaxman Terr
WC1 ....93 D4 232 D1
Flaxman Villas N2 ....48 A6
Flaxmore Ct DA7 ....147 D2
South Norwood CR7 ....183 B1
Flaxton Rd SE18 ....145 C5
Flecker Cl HA7 ....24 D5
Flecker Ho 6 SE5 ....139 B5
Fleece Dr N9 ....34 A6
Fleecefield Prim Sch
N18 ....34 A6
Fleece Rd KT6 ....197 C1
Fleece Wlk N7 ....72 A2
Fleeming Cl E17 ....35 B1
Fleeming Rd E17 ....35 B1
Fleet Cl
East Molesey KT8 ....195 B4
Ruislip HA4 ....39 A3
Fleet Ct 1 W12 ....111 C3
Fleetfield WC1 ....233 B2
Fleet Ho 4 E14 ....119 A6
6 SW2 ....160 C6
Fleet Pl EC4 ....241 C2
Fleet Prim Sch NW3 ....70 D3
Fleet Rd NW3 ....70 D3
Fleetside KT8 ....195 C4
Fleet Sq WC1 ....233 D1
Fleet St EC4 ....94 C1 241 B1
Fleet Street Hill 11 E1 ....96 A3
Fleet Terr SE6 ....164 A4
Fleetway WC1 ....233 B2
Fleetway West Bsns Pk
UB6 ....87 B5
Fleet Wood 6 N16 ....73 D6
Fleetwood Cl E16 ....99 D2
Chessington KT9 ....213 D1
South Croydon CR0 ....221 D5
Fleetwood Ct 1 E6 ....100 B2
Orpington BR6 ....226 C4
8 Stanwell TW19 ....148 A5
Fleetwood Rd NW10 ....68 A3
Kingston KT3 ....198 D6
Fleetwood Sq KT3 ....198 D6
Fleetwood St N16 ....73 C6
Fleetwood Way WD19 ....22 C6
Fleming Cl 3 W9 ....91 C3
Fleming Ct W2 ....236 C4
Croydon CR0 ....220 C3
Fleming Dr N21 ....16 B6
Fleming Ho N4 ....51 A1
8 SE16 ....118 A4
8 Wembley HA9 ....67 A5
Fleming Mead CR4 ....180 D3
Fleming Rd SE17 ....138 D6
Southall UB1 ....86 A1
Fleming Way SE28 ....124 D6
Isleworth TW7 ....130 D1
Fleming Wlk NW9 ....27 C1
Flemming Ave HA4 ....62 B6
Flempton Rd E10 ....53 A1
Fletcher Bldgs WC2 ....240 B1
Fletcher Cl E16 ....122 D6
Fletcher Ct 9 NW5 ....71 B4
Fletcher Ho 22 N1 ....95 C6
16 N16 ....73 C4
Fletcher La E10 ....54 A2
Fletcher Path 7 SE8 ....141 C5
Fletcher Rd W4 ....111 A3
Fletchers Cl BR2 ....209 B5
Fletcher St 10 E1 ....118 A6
Fletching Rd E5 ....74 C5
SE7 ....143 D6
Fletton Rd N11 ....32 A3
Fleur Gates 7 SW19 ....156 D4
Flexmere Rd N17 ....33 C2
Flimwell Cl BR1 ....186 C5
Flinders Ho 28 E1 ....118 B5
Flint Cl 8 BR6 ....227 D2
Flint Down Cl BR5 ....190 A2
Flintmill Cres SE3,SE9 ....144 A3
Flinton St
SE17 ....117 C1 263 B2
Flint St SE17 ....117 B2 262 D3
Flitcroft St WC2 ....239 D1
Flitton Ho 7 N1 ....72 D1
Floathaven Cl SE28 ....124 A5
Flock Mill Pl SW18 ....157 D3
Flodden Rd SE5 ....139 A4
Flood La 4 TW1 ....153 A3
Flood St SW3 ....136 C6 267 B6
Flood Wlk
SW3 ....136 C6 267 B6
Flora Cl E14 ....97 D1
Flora Gardens Prim Sch
W6 ....112 B2
Flora Gdns 2 W6 ....112 B2
Dagenham RM6 ....58 C3
Floral St WC2 ....116 A6 250 A6
Flora St DA17 ....125 B1
Florence Ave Enfield EN2 ....5 A2
Morden SM4 ....202 A4
Florence Cl KT12 ....194 B2
Florence Ct 4 E5 ....74 A5
W9 ....229 B1
Wanstead E11 ....55 C5
5 Wimbledon SW19 ....179 A4
Florence Dr EN2 ....5 A2
Florence Elson Cl E12 ....78 C4
Florence Gdns
Chiswick W4 ....133 A6
Ilford RM6 ....58 C2
Florence Ho 20 SE16 ....118 B1
2 SE18 ....144 B4
7 SW18 ....136 B1
2 SW2 ....160 B6
10 W11 ....112 D6
5 Kingston KT2 ....176 B3
Florence Mans 4 NW4 ....46 B4
SW6 ....264 C2
Florence Nightingale Ho 11
N1 ....73 A2
Florence Nightingale Mus★
SE1 ....250 D1
Florence Rd BR1 ....187 A2
E13 ....99 A5
8 E6 ....99 C6
N4 ....50 C2
SE14 ....141 B4
SE2 ....124 C2
W4 ....111 B3
5 Beckenham BR3 ....185 A1
Ealing W5 ....110 A6
Feltham TW13 ....150 B3
6 Kingston KT2 ....176 B3
Southall UB2 ....106 D3
Walton-on-T KT12 ....194 B2
Wimbledon SW19 ....179 D4
Florence Root Ho IG4 ....56 B4
Florence St E16 ....98 D3
N1 ....72 D1
NW4 ....46 C5
Florence Terr SE14 ....141 B4
Kingston SW15 ....155 C1
Florence Way SW12 ....158 D3
Florentine Ho 3 IG1 ....78 D6
Flores Ho 10 E1 ....96 D2
Florfield Rd E8 ....74 B2
Florian SE5 ....139 C4
Florian Ave SM1 ....218 B4
Florian Rd SW15 ....135 A1
Florida Cl WD23 ....8 B2
Florida Ct BR2 ....208 D5
Florida Rd CR7 ....182 D2
Florida St E2 ....96 A4
Florin Ct SE1 ....253 C1
Edmonton N18 ....33 C6
Floris Pl 7 SW4 ....137 C2
Floriston Ave UB10 ....61 A1
Floriston Cl HA7 ....25 B2
Floriston Ct UB5 ....63 D3
Floriston Gdns HA7 ....25 B2
Florys Ct 7 SW19 ....157 A3
Floss St SW15 ....134 C3
Flower & Dean Wlk
E1 ....243 D3
Flower La NW7 ....27 D4
Flower Pot Cl N15 ....51 D3
Flowers Cl NW2 ....68 A5
Flowersmead SW17 ....159 A2
Flowers Mews 1 N19 ....71 C6
Flower Wlk The
SW7 ....114 A4 246 B2
Floyd Rd SE7 ....121 C1
Fludyer St SE13 ....142 C1
Fluer De Lis St E1 ....243 C5
Flynn Ct 12 E14 ....119 C6
Fogerty Cl EN3 ....7 C6
Foley Cotts KT10 ....212 D2
Foley Ho 19 E1 ....96 C1
Foley Mews KT10 ....212 C2
Foley Rd KT10 ....212 C1
Foley St W1 ....93 C2 239 A3
Folgate St E1 ....95 D2 243 C4
Foliot Ho N1 ....233 C4
Foliot St W12 ....89 D1
Folkestone Ct UB5 ....63 D3
Folkestone Rd E17 ....53 D5
Edmonton N18 ....34 A6
Wallend E6 ....100 C4
Folkingham La 6 NW9 ....27 C2
Folkington Cnr N12 ....29 B5
Folland 6 NW9 ....27 D1
Follett Ho SW10 ....266 C4
Follett St E14 ....98 A1
Folly La E17 ....35 A2
E4 ....35 B3
Folly Wall E14 ....120 A4
Fontaine Ct 3 BR3 ....185 B2
Fontaine Rd SW16 ....182 B3
Fontarabia Rd SW11 ....137 A1
Fontenelle SE5 ....139 C4
Fontenoy Ho SE11 ....261 C3
Fontenoy Rd SW12,
SW17 ....159 C2
Fonteyne Gdns IG8 ....37 D1
Fonthill Cl SE20 ....184 A1
Fonthill Ct SE23 ....162 C4
Fonthill Ho SW1 ....258 D2
W14 ....254 B6
Fonthill Mews N4 ....72 B6
Fonthill Rd N4 ....72 C6
Font Hills N2 ....30 A1
Fontley Way SW15 ....156 A4
Fontmell Cl TW15 ....170 C5
Fontmell Pk TW15 ....170 C5
Fontwell Cl Harrow HA3 ....24 C3
Northolt UB5 ....63 C2
Fontwell Dr BR2 ....210 C4
Football La HA1 ....42 C1
Footpath The SW15 ....156 A6
Foots Cray High St
DA14 ....190 D4
Foots Cray La DA5,
DA14 ....168 C3
Footscray Rd SE9 ....166 D3
Forber Ho 25 E2 ....96 C4
Forbes Cl NW2 ....68 A5
Forbes Ct SE19 ....183 C5
Forbes Ho 2 W4 ....110 C1
Forbes St E1 ....96 A1
Forbes Way HA4 ....62 B6
Forburg Rd N16 ....52 A1
Fordbridge Ct TW15 ....170 A4
Fordbridge Rd
Ashford TW15 ....170 B5
Lower Halliford TW16,
TW17 ....193 D3
Sunbury TW16 ....194 A5
Fordbridge Rdbt
TW15 ....170 A4
Ford Cl 11 E3 ....97 A5
Ashford TW15 ....170 A4
Harrow HA1 ....42 B2
Littleton TW17 ....192 C4
Thornton Heath CR7 ....204 D4
Fordcombe 13 NW5 ....71 A2
Forde Ave BR1 ....209 C6
Fordel Rd SE6 ....164 B3
Ford End IG8 ....37 B4
Fordham 4 KT1 ....176 C1
Fordham Cl EN4 ....2 C2
Fordham Rd EN4 ....2 C2
Fordham St 7 E1 ....96 A1
Ford Ho 2 SE18 ....122 D1
2 New Barnet EN5 ....13 D6
Fordhook Ave W5 ....110 C6
Fordingley Rd W9 ....91 B4
Fordington Ho 2
SE26 ....162 B1
Fordington Rd N6 ....48 D5
Fordmill Rd SE6 ....163 C2
Ford Rd E3 ....97 B5
Ashford TW15 ....170 B6
Dagenham RM10 ....81 C1
Ford's Gr N21 ....17 A3
Fords Park Rd E16 ....99 A1
Ford Sq E1 ....96 B2
Ford St E16 ....98 D1
E3 ....97 A5
Fordwich Cl BR6 ....211 D2
Fordwych Ct NW2 ....69 A2
Fordwych Rd NW2 ....69 A3
Fordyce Ho 3 SW16 ....181 C6
Fordyce Rd SE13 ....164 A6
Fordyke Rd RM8 ....81 B6
Foreign, Commonwealth &
Home Offices SW1 ....250 A2
Foreland Ct NW4 ....29 A2
Foreland Ho W11 ....244 A6
Foreland St SE18 123
Foreshore SE8 119
Fore St EC2 ....95 A2 242
Edmonton N18 34
Pinner HA5 40
Forest App Chingford E4 20
Woodford IG8 37
Fore St Ave EC2 242
Forest Ave E4 20
Forest Bsns Pk E17 52
Forest Cl
Chislehurst BR7 188
Wanstead E11 55
Woodford IG8 37
Forest Croft SE23 162
Forest Ct E11 54
12 N12 29
Chingford E4 20
Forestdale N14 31
Forestdale Ctr The
CR0 223
Forest Dene Ct 2
SM2 218
Forest Dr
Ashford TW16 171
Chingford IG8 36
Keston Mark BR2 226
Wanstead E12 77
Forest Dr E E11 54
Forest Dr W E11 54
Forest Edge IG9 21
Forester Rd SE15 140
Foresters Cl SM6 219
Foresters Cres DA7 147
Foresters Dr E17 54
Wallington SM6 219
Foresters Prim Sch
SM6 219
Forest Gate NW9 45
Forest Gate Com Sch
E7 77
Forest Gate Sta E7 77
Forest Gdns N17 33
Forest Glade E11 54
Chingford E4 36
Forest Gr E8 73
Forest Hill SE23 162
Forest Hill Bsns Ctr
SE23 162
Forest Hill Ct 6 SE26 162
Forest Hill Ind Est
SE23 162
Forest Hill Rd SE22 162
Forest Hill Sec Sch
SE23 162
Forest Hill Sta SE23 162
Forest Ho 9 E4 20
Forestholme Cl SE23 162
Forest Hts IG9 21
Forest La E7,E15 76
Forest Lawns BR1 187
Forest Lea E11 54
Forest Lo 1 SE23 162
Forest Mount Rd IG8 36
Forest Point E7 77
Forest Rd E11 54
E17 53
E7 77
E8 73
Edmonton N9 18
Feltham TW13 150
Morden SM3,SM4 201
Richmond TW9 132
Romford RM7 59
Woodford IG8 21
Forest Ridge BR2 226
Beckenham BR3 207
Forest Rise E17 54
Forest Sch E17 54
Forest Side E7 77
Buckhurst Hill IG9 21
Chingford E4 20
New Malden KT4 199
Forest St E7 77
Forest The E11 54
Forest Trad Est E17 52
Forest View E11 54
Chingford E4 20
Forest View Ave E10 54
Forest View Rd E12 78
Chingford E17 36
Forest Way BR5 211
6 N19 71
Sidcup DA15 167
Woodford IG8 37
Forfar Rd
SW11 ....137 A4 268
Tottenham N22 32
Forge Cl BR2 209
Forge Cotts W5 109
Forge Dr KT10 213
Forge La Belmont SM3 217
Feltham TW13 173
Sunbury TW16 194
Forge Lane Inf Sch
TW13 173
Forge Lane Jun Sch
TW13 173

orge Mews
Addington CR0 223 C3
Sunbury TW16 194 A6
orge Pl NW1 71 A2
orge The UB3 127 B6
orlong Path UB5 63 A2
orman Ct TW1 152 D3
orman Gr 2 UB5 84 D4
orman Ho SE4 140 D1
orman Pl N16 73 D4
ormby Ave HA3,HA7 43 C6
ormby Ct 9 N7 72 C3
ormosa Ho 1 E1 97 A3
ormosa St W9 91 D3
ormunt Cl E16 98 D2
orres Gdns NW11 47 C3
orrest Ct N7 72 C2
orrester Path SE26 184 C6
orresters The HA5 40 B3
orrest Gdns SW16 204 B6
orrest Ho SW15 134 C3
orris Ave UB3 105 D5
orset Ct W1 237 B2
orset St W1 92 C1 237 B2
orstal Cl BR2 209 A6
orster Ho SE6 164 B1
orster Park Prim Sch
SE6 164 C1
orster Rd E17 53 A3
N17 51 D6
Beckenham BR3 207 A6
Streatham SW2 160 A4
Thornton Heath CR0 205 A2
orsters Cl RM6 59 B3
orsters Way UB4 84 B1
orstic Wlk E1 243 D3
orston St N1 95 A5 235 B4
orsyte Cres SE19 183 C2
orsyte Ct KT2 176 D2
orsyth Ct KT3 177 C1
orsythe Shades BR3 186 A2
orsyth Gdns SE17 138 D6
orsyth Ho 14 E9 74 C1
SW1 259 B3
orsythia Cl IG1 78 D3
orsythia Ho SE4 141 A2
orsyth Pl EN1 17 C6
orterie Gdns IG3 80 A4
ortescue Ave 1 E8 74 B1
Twickenham TW2 152 A1
ortescue Rd HA8 27 B3
Mitcham SW19 180 B3
ortess Gr NW5 71 C3
ortess Rd NW5 71 C4
ortess Wlk NW5 71 B3
orthbridge Rd SW11 137 A1
orth Ho 28 E3 97 B5
orties The 9 NW5 71 C3
ortior Ct N6 49 C2
ortis Cl E16 99 C1
ortis Ct N10 49 A6
ortis Gn N2,N10 48 D6
ortis Green Ave N2 48 D5
ortis Green Cotts N2 48 D6
ortismere Ave N10 49 A6
ortismere Sch N10 30 D1
ortismere Sch (South
Wing) N10 49 A6
ortnam Rd N19 71 D6
ortnums Acre HA7 24 D4
ort Rd SE1 117 D2 263 D3
Northolt UB5 63 C1
ortrose Gdns SW12,
SW2 160 A3
ort St E1 243 B3
E16 121 B5
ortuna Cl N7 72 B2
ortune Ct IG11 102 B5
Fortune Gate Rd NW10 89 C6
Fortune Green Rd NW6 69 C4
Fortune Ho EC1 242 B5
SE11 261 A3
Fortune La WD6 9 D5
Fortunes Mead UB5 63 A2
Fortune St EC1 95 A3 242 B5
Fortune Way NW10 90 A4
Fortune Wlk SE28 123 B3
Forty Acre La E16 99 A2
Forty Ave HA9 66 B6
Forty Cl HA9 66 B5
Forty Hall★ EN2 5 D6
Forty Hill EN2 5 D5
Forty Hill CE Prim Sch
EN2 6 A6
Forty Hill Ho EN1 5 D5
Forty La HA9 66 D6
Forumside HA8 26 C4
Forum The KT8 195 D5
Forum Way HA8 26 C4
Forval Cl CR4 202 D4
Forward Bsns Ctr The
E16 98 B3
Forward Dr HA3 42 D5
Fosbroke Ho SW8 270 A3
Fosbury Ho 7 SW9 138 B1
Fosbury Mews W2 245 D5
Foscote Mews W9 91 C2
Foscote Rd NW4 46 B3
Foskett Ho 16 N2 30 B1

Foskett Rd SW6 135 B3
Foss Ave CR0,CR9 220 C3
Fossdene Prim Sch
SE7 121 B1
Fossdene Rd SE7 121 B1
Fossdyke Cl UB4 85 A2
Fosse Way W13 87 A2
Fossil Rd SE13 141 C2
Fossington Rd DA17 124 D2
Foss Rd SW17 180 B6
Fossway RM8 80 C6
Foster Ct E16 120 D6
4 NW1 71 C1
NW4 46 C5
Foster Ho SE14 141 B4
Foster La EC2 95 A1 242 A2
Foster Rd E13 99 A3
W3 111 C6
W4 111 B1
Fosters Cl BR7 188 B5
Woodford E18 37 B2
Fosters Old Sch DA16 146 B3
Foster's Prim Sch
DA16 146 C2
Foster St NW4 46 C5
Foster Wlk NW4 46 C5
Fothergill Cl E13 99 A5
Fothergill Dr N21 16 A6
Fotheringham Ct EN1 5 D1
Fotheringham Rd EN1 5 D1
Foubert's Pl W1 239 A1
Foulden Rd N16 73 D4
Foulden Terr N16 73 D4
Foulis Terr
SW7 114 B1 256 D2
Foulser Rd SW17 159 A1
Foulsham Rd CR7 205 B6
Foundary Ho 7 E14 97 D2
Founder Cl 2 E6 100 D1
Founders Ct EC2 242 C2
Founders Gdns SE19 183 A3
Founders Ho SW1 259 C2
Foundling Ct WC1 240 A6
Foundry Cl SE16 119 A5
Foundry Mews NW1 239 B6
Foundry Pl E1 96 C2
Fountain Cl UB8 83 A2
Fountain Ct DA15 168 B5
EC4 251 A6
SW1 258 C3
New Malden KT3 199 A5
Penge SE26 184 C4
Fountain Dr
Dulwich SE19 183 D6
Wallington SM5 218 D1
Fountain Green Sq 31
SE16 118 A4
Fountain Ho 1 NW6 69 A1
30 SE16 118 A4
W1 248 A4
Fountain Mews 1 N5 73 A4
NW3 70 D2
Fountain Pl SW9 138 C4
Fountain Rd
South Norwood CR7 183 A1
Upper Tooting SW17 180 B6
Fountains Ave TW13 151 B1
Fountains Cl TW13 151 B1
Fountains Cres N14 16 A4
Fountains The N3 29 D3
Loughton IG10 21 D4
Fountayne Bsns Ctr
N15 52 A5
Fountayne Rd N15 52 A5
N16 74 A6
Fount St SW8 137 D5 269 D3
Four Acres N12 29 D6
Fouracres EN3 7 A4
Fourland Wlk HA8 27 A4
Fournier St E1 95 D2 243 D4
Four Seasons Cl E3 97 C5
Four Seasons Cres
SM3 217 B6
Four Square Ct TW4 151 C5
Fourth Ave W10 91 A4
Hayes UB3 105 D5
Ilford E12 78 B4
Fourth Cross Rd TW2 152 B2
Fourth Way
Wembley HA9 66 D4
Wembley HA9 67 A4
Four Tubs The WD23 8 B4
Fourways 2 CR0 221 D6
Four Wents The E4 20 B2
Fovant Ct 5 SW8 137 C3
Fowey Ave IG4 55 D4
Fowey Cl E1 118 B5
Fowey Ho SE11 261 B2
Fowler Cl DA14 191 A5
SW11 136 B2
Fowler Ho N1 94 D6 234 D6
N15 51 B4
5 SE5 139 C3
SW8 269 D1
Fowler Rd E7 77 A4
N1 94 D6 234 D6
Mitcham CR4 181 A1
Fowler's Wlk W5 87 D3
Fownes St SW11 136 C2

Foxberry Ct SE4 141 B1
Foxberry Rd SE4 141 A2
Foxborough Gdns SE4 163 C6
Foxbourne Rd SW17 159 A2
Foxbury Ave BR7 189 B4
Foxbury Cl BR1 187 B4
Foxbury Rd BR1 187 B4
Fox Cl E1 96 C3
E16 99 A2
Elstree WD6 9 D5
Foxcombe CR0 223 D2
Foxcombe Cl 1 E6 99 D5
Foxcombe Rd 6
SW15 156 A3
Foxcote SE5 263 B1
Foxcroft N1 233 D3
Foxcroft Rd SE18 144 D4
Foxes Dale SE3 143 A2
Beckenham BR2 208 B6
Foxfield Prim Sch
SE18 123 A2
Foxfield Rd BR6 227 B6
Foxglove Ave BR3 185 D3
Foxglove Cl UB1 107 A6
Foxglove Ct 11 HA0 88 A5
Foxglove Gdns E11 55 C5
Foxglove La KT9 214 C4
Foxglove St W12 111 D6
Foxglove Way SM6 203 B1
Fox Gr KT12 194 B2
Foxgrove N14 16 A1
Foxgrove Path WD19 22 D5
Foxgrove Rd BR3 186 A3
Foxham Rd N19 71 D5
Fox Hill SE19 183 D3
Fox Hill Gdns SE19 183 D3
Fox Ho 2 SW11 136 B1
Foxhole Rd 2 SE9 166 A6
Fox Hollow Cl 1 SE18 123 C1
Fox Hollow Dr DA16 146 D2
Foxholt Gdns NW10 67 A1
Foxhome Cl BR7 188 C4
Fox House Rd DA17 125 D1
Fox & Knot St EC1 241 D4
Fox La BR2 225 C3
Ealing W5 88 A3
Palmers Green N13 16 B1
Foxlands Rd RM10 81 D3
Foxlees HA0 65 A4
Foxley Cl E8 74 A3
Foxley Ct SM2 218 A1
Foxley Ho 4 E3 97 D4
Foxley Rd SW9 138 D5
Thornton Heath CR7 204 D5
Foxley Sq 3 SW9 138 D4
Foxmead Cl EN2 4 B2
Foxmore St SW11 267 C1
Fox Prim Sch
W8 113 C5 245 A3
Fox Rd E16 98 D2
Foxs Path CR4 180 C1
Fox's Yd E2 243 D6
Foxtail Ho TW3 130 A4
Foxton KT1 198 C6
Foxton Gr CR4 180 B1
Foxton Ho E16 122 C4
Foxwarren KT10 212 D1
Foxwell Mews SE4 141 A2
Foxwell St SE4 141 A2
Foxwood Cl NW7 27 C6
Feltham TW13 150 B1
Foxwood Green Cl EN1 17 C5
Foxwood Rd SE3 142 D1
Foyle Rd SE3 142 D6
Tottenham N17 34 A2
Fradel Lo N16 51 B1
Framfield Cl N12 13 C1
Framfield Ct EN1 17 C5
Framfield Rd N5 72 D3
Ealing W7 86 D1
Mitcham CR4 181 A3
Framlingham Cl 2 E5 74 C6
Framlingham Cres
SE9 188 B6
Frampton NW1 71 D1
Frampton Cl SM2 217 C1
Frampton Ct 3 W3 111 A4
Frampton Ho NW8 236 D5
Frampton Park Rd E9 74 C1
Frampton Rd TW4 151 A6
Frampton St
NW8 92 B3 236 D5
Francemary Rd SE4 163 C6
Frances Ct E17 53 C3
South Norwood SE25 183 D1
Frances Grey Ho 18 E1 96 D2
Frances Rd E4 35 C4
Frances St SE18 122 B2
Franche Court Rd
SW17 158 A1
Francis Ave DA7 147 C3
Feltham TW13 150 A1
Ilford IG1 79 B6
Francis Barber Cl
SW16 182 B6
Franciscan Prim Sch
SW17 181 A5
Franciscan Rd SW17 181 A6

Francis Chichester Way
SW11 137 A4 268 B1
Francis Cl 6 E14 120 B2
Littleton TW17 192 C5
West Ewell KT19 215 B4
Francis Ct NW7 27 D5
12 SE14 140 D6
Ealing W5 110 B6
Kingston KT5 198 A5
Francis Gr SW19 179 B4
Francis Ho 11 N1 95 C6
NW10 89 D6
Francis Holland Sch
NW1 92 D3 237 D5
SW1 115 A2 258 B3
Francis Rd E10 76 A6
N2 48 D5
Harrow HA1 43 A4
Hounslow TW4 128 D3
Ilford IG1 79 B6
Pinner HA5 40 C4
Thornton Heath CR0 204 D2
Wallington SM6 219 C2
Wembley UB6 87 C6
Francis Snary Lo 11
SW18 157 C6
Francis St E15 76 C3
SW1 115 C2 259 B4
Ilford IG1 79 B6
Francis Terr N19 71 C5
Francis Wlk N1 233 C6
Francklyn Gdns HA8 10 C1
Franconia Rd SW4 159 D6
Frank Bailey Wlk E12 78 C2
Frank Barnes Prim Sch for
Deaf Children NW3 70 B1
Frank Beswick Ho
SW6 264 D5
Frank Burton Cl 4
SE7 121 B1
Frank Dixon Cl SE21 161 C3
Frank Dixon Way
SE21 161 C3
Frank Douglas Ct W6 112 A2
Frankfurt Rd SE24 161 A6
Frankham Ho 8 SE8 141 C5
Frankham St SE8 141 C5
Frank Ho SW8 270 A4
Frankland Cl SE16 118 B2
Woodford IG8 37 C5
Frankland Ho 4
SW12 159 B4
Frankland Rd
SW7 114 B3 256 C5
Chingford E4 35 C5
Franklin Bldg 6 E14 119 C4
Franklin Cl N20 14 A4
SE13 141 D4
Kingston KT1 198 C6
West Norwood SE27 160 D1
Franklin Cres CR4 203 C5
Franklin Ho 26 E1 118 B5
NW9 45 D2
Beckenham BR2 208 C6
Franklin Ind Est SE20 184 C2
Franklin Pas SE9 144 A2
Franklin Rd DA7 147 A4
Penge SE20 184 C3
Walton-on-T KT12 194 A3
Franklins Mews HA2 64 A6
Franklin Sq SW5 254 D1
Franklin's Row
SW3 114 D1 257 D2
Franklin St 43 E3 97 D4
N15 51 C3
Franklin Way CR0 204 A2
Franklyn Rd NW10 67 D2
Walton-on-T KT12 194 B3
Franks Ave KT3 199 A5
Franks Ho TW7 131 B1
Frank Slater Ho 4 IG3 58 B1
Frank Soskice Ho
SW6 264 D5
Frank St 5 E13 99 A3
Franks Wood Ave BR2,
BR5 211 A4
Frankswood Ave UB7 82 B1
Frank Towell Ct TW14 150 A3
Frank Whymark Ho 4
SE16 118 C4
Franlaw Cres N13 33 A6
Fransfield Gr SE26 162 B1
Frans Hals Ct E14 120 B3
Franshams WD23 8 C2
Frant Cl SE20 184 C3
Franthorne Way SE6 163 D1
Frant Rd CR7 204 D4
Fraserburgh Ho 28 E3 97 B5
Fraser Cl 3 E6 100 A1
Fraser Ct SW11 267 A2
Fraser Ho 3 SE18 122 C2
40 SW8 137 D3
Brentford TW8 110 B1
Fraser Rd E17 53 D3
Edmonton N9 18 B1
Wembley UB6 87 C6
Fraser Regnart Ct 12
NW5 70 D3
Fraser St W4 111 C1

Frating Cres IG8 37 B4
Frazer Ave HA4 62 C3
Frazier St SE1 116 C4 251 A1
Freame Ho N21 17 B5
Frean St SE16 118 A3
Frearson Ho WC1 233 D2
Freda Corbett Cl 9
SE15 140 A5
Frederica Rd E4 20 B4
Frederica St 4 N7 72 B1
Frederic Ho SE7 122 A3
Frederick SE16 119 B5
Frederick Charrington Ho
3 E1 96 C3
Frederick Cl
W2 114 D6 247 C6
Cheam SM1 217 B3
Frederick Cres SW9 138 D5
Enfield EN3 6 C3
Frederick Ct SW6 135 A2
Frederick Gdns
Cheam SM1 217 B3
Thornton Heath CR0 204 D3
Frederick Ho UB1 107 B6
Frederick Pl SE18 122 D1
Frederick Rd SM1 217 B3
Frederick's Pl EC2 242 C1
N12 30 A6
Frederick Sq 11 SE16 119 A6
Frederick's Row EC1 234 C2
Frederick St
WC1 94 B4 233 C1
Frederick Terr E8 73 D1
Frederic Mews SW1 248 A1
Frederic St E17 53 A4
Fredora Ave UB4 83 D4
Fred Wigg Twr E11 76 D6
Freedom Cl E17 53 A5
Freedom St SW11 136 D3
Freegrove Rd N7 72 A3
Freehold Ind Ctr TW4 150 C6
Freeland Ct W5 110 B6
Freeland Pk N3 29 A1
Freeland Rd W5 110 B6
Freelands Ave CR2 222 D1
Freelands Gr BR1 187 B2
Freelands Rd BR1 187 B2
Freeling Ho NW8 229 C6
Freeling St 7 N1 72 B1
Freeman Cl
Northolt UB5 63 A1
Upper Halliford TW17 193 C5
Freeman Dr KT8 195 B5
Freeman Ho 13 SW2 160 A4
Freeman Rd SM4 202 B4
Freemans La UB3 105 C6
Freemantle Ave EN3 18 D6
Freemantle St
SE17 117 C1 263 A2
Freemasons Rd E16 99 B1
Freemason's Rd CR0 205 C1
Freemens Hos 1 SW9 138 B1
Freesia Cl BR6 227 D3
Freethorpe Cl SE19 183 C2
Freezeland Way UB10 60 D2
Freke Rd SW11 137 A2
Fremantle Ho 14 E1 96 B3
Fremantle Rd
Belvedere DA17 125 C2
Ilford IG6 57 A6
Fremont St E9 96 C6
French Ordinary Ct
EC3 253 B6
French Pl E1 243 B6
French St TW16 172 C1
Frendsbury Rd SE4 141 A1
Frensham Cl UB1 85 B4
Frensham Ct N5 73 A3
4 NW9 46 A5
Mitcham CR4 202 B6
Frensham Dr
New Addington CR0 224 A1
Roehampton SW15 156 A2
Frensham Ho 7 KT6 198 A4
Frensham Rd DA15 167 B2
Frensham St SE15 140 A6
Frere St 6 SW11 136 C3
Fresham Ho BR2 208 D6
Freshfield Ave E8 73 D1
Freshfield Cl SE13 142 B1
Freshfield Dr N14 15 B4
Freshfields CR0 207 B1
Freshford St SW17,
SW18 158 A1
Freshwater Cl SW17 181 A4
Freshwater Ct UB1 85 C4
Freshwater Rd
Dagenham RM8 59 A1
Streatham SW17 181 A4
Freshwell Ave RM6 58 C5
Fresh Wharf Est IG11 100 D6
Fresh Wharf Rd IG11 100 D5
Freshwood Cl BR3 185 D2
Freston Gdns EN4 15 A6
Freston Pk N3 29 B1
Freston Rd W10,W11 112 D6
Freswick Ho 6 SE8 119 A2
Freta Rd DA6 169 B6
Freud Mus The★ NW3 70 A2

Frewell Bldg EC1 241 A4
Frewing Cl BR7 188 C5
Frewin Rd SW18 158 B3
Friar Mews SE27 160 D1
Friar Rd UB4 84 D3
Friars Ave N20 30 C6
Roehampton SW15 155 D1
Friars Cl SE1 251 D3
Chingford E4 20 A1
Ilford IG1 57 B1
16 Northolt UB5 84 D4
Friars Ct 5 SM6 219 B4
Friars Gate Cl IG8 37 A6
Friars Gdns W3 89 B1
Friars La TW9 153 D6
Friars Mead E14 120 A3
Friars Mews SE9 166 C6
Friars Place La W3 111 B6
Friars Prim Sch
SE1 116 D4 251 D1
Friar's Rd E6 99 D6
Friars Stile Pl 9
TW10 154 A5
Friars Stile Rd TW10 154 A5
Friar St EC4 241 D1
Friars Way W3 89 B1
Friars Wlk N14 15 B4
SE2 124 D1
Friary Cl N12 30 C5
Friary La IG8 37 A6
Friary Park Ct W3 89 A1
Friary Rd N12 30 C6
SE15 140 A5
W3 89 B1
Friary Way N12 30 C6
Friday Hill E4 20 C1
Friday Hill E E4 20 C1
Friday Hill W E4 20 C2
Friday Rd CR4 180 D3
Friday St EC4 117 A6 252 A6
Frideswide Pl NW5 71 C3
Friendly Pl SE13 141 D4
Friendly St SE8 141 C4
Friendly Street Mews
SE8 141 C3
Friendship Wlk UB5 84 D4
Friends' Rd CR0 221 B5
Friend St EC1 94 D4 234 C2
Friern Barnet La N20 30 C6
Friern Barnet Rd N11 31 A5
Friern Barnet Sch N11 30 D5
Friern Bridge Ret Pk
N11 31 B4
Friern Ct N20 14 B1
Friern Mount Dr N20 14 A4
Friern Pk N12 30 B5
Friern Rd SE22 162 A5
Friern Watch Ave N12 30 B6
Frigate Ho 6 E14 120 A2
Frigate Mews SE8 141 C6
Frimley Ave SM6 220 B3
Frimley Cl
New Addington CR0 224 A1
Putney SW19 157 A2
Frimley Cres CR0 224 A1
Frimley Ct DA14 190 C5
Frimley Gdns CR4 202 C6
Frimley Ho CR4 202 C6
Frimley Rd
Chessington KT9 214 A3
Ilford IG3 79 C5
Frimley Way E1 96 D3
Frinstead Ho 1 W10 112 D6
Frinton Ct W13 87 B2
Frinton Dr IG8 36 B3
Frinton Mews IG2 56 C3
Frinton Rd DA14 169 A2
E6 99 D4
N15 51 C3
Streatham SW17 181 A4
Friston St SW6 135 D3
Friswell Pl 1 DA7 147 C1
Fritham Cl KT3 199 C3
Frith Ct NW7 29 A3
Frith Ho E2 96 A4
NW8 236 D5
Frith La NW7 29 A4
Frith Manor Sch N12 29 B5
Frith Rd E11 76 B4
Croydon CR0 221 A6
Frith St W1 93 D1 239 C1
Frithville Ct W12 112 C5
Frithville Gdns W12 112 C5
Frizlands La RM10 81 D5
Frobisher Cl HA5 40 D2
Frobisher Cres TW19 148 A4
Frobisher Ct NW9 27 C1
1 SE10 142 B6
3 W12 112 C4
Belmont SM2 217 B1
6 Forest Hill SE23 162 B2
Frobisher Gdns TW19 148 A4
Frobisher Ho 27 E1 118 B5
3 Ealing W5 88 A4
Frobisher Mews EN2 5 B1
Frobisher Pas E14 119 C5

Frobisher Pl SE14 ... 140 C4
Frobisher Rd E6 ... 100 B1
N8 ... 50 C5
Frobisher St SE10 ... 142 C6
Froebel Coll SW15 ... 155 D5
Frogley Rd SE22 ... 139 D1
Frogmore SW18 ... 157 C6
Frogmore Ave UB4 ... 83 C3
Frogmore Cl SM3 ... 217 A5
Frogmore Ct UB2 ... 107 B2
Frogmore Est NW10 ... 89 A4
Frogmore Gdns
Cheam SM3 ... 217 A4
Hayes UB4 ... 83 C3
Frogmore Ind Est N5 ... 73 A4
Frognal NW3 ... 70 A3
Frognal Ave DA14 ... 190 A4
Harrow HA1 ... 42 D5
Frognal Cl NW3 ... 70 A3
Frognal Cnr BR7 ... 189 D4
Frognal Ct NW3 ... 70 A2
Frognal Gdns NW3 ... 70 A4
Frognal La NW3 ... 69 D3
Frognal Par NW3 ... 70 A2
Frognal Pl DA14 ... 190 A5
Frognal Rise NW3 ... 70 A4
Frognal Way NW3 ... 70 A4
Froissart Rd SE9 ... 166 A6
Frome Ho SE15 ... 140 C1
Frome Rd N22 ... 50 D6
Frome St N1 ... 95 A5 235 A4
Fromondes Rd SM3 ... 217 A3
Frontenac NW10 ... 68 B1
Frontier Works N17 ... 33 C4
Froude St SW8 ... 137 B3
Fruen Rd TW14 ... 149 D4
Fryatt Rd N17 ... 33 B3
Frye Ct E3 ... 97 B4
Fryent Cl NW9 ... 44 C3
Fryent Cres NW9 ... 45 C3
Fryent Ctry Park HA3,
HA9 ... 44 C2
Fryent Fields NW9 ... 45 C3
Fryent Gr NW9 ... 45 C3
Fryent Prim Sch NW9 ... 45 A2
Fryent Way HA9,NW9 ... 44 D2
Fry Ho E6 ... 77 C1
Frying Pan Alley E1 ... 243 C3
Fry Rd E6 ... 77 D1
NW10 ... 89 D6
Fryston Ave CR0 ... 222 A6
Fuchsia St SE2 ... 124 B1
Fulbeck Dr NW9 ... 27 C2
Fulbeck Ho N7 ... 72 B2
Fulbeck Way HA2 ... 24 A1
Fulbourn 9 KT1 ... 176 C1
Fulbourne Rd E17 ... 36 A1
Fulbourne St E1 ... 96 B2
Fulbrook Rd N19 ... 71 C4
Fulcher Ho 10 N1 ... 95 C6
13 SE8 ... 119 B1
Fulford Mans N19 ... 72 A5
Fulford Rd KT19 ... 215 B1
Fulford St SE16 ... 118 B4
Fulham Broadway
SW6 ... 135 C5 265 B3
Fulham Broadway Sta
SW6 ... 135 C5 265 B4
Fulham Cl UB10 ... 83 A3
Fulham Cross Sec Sch
SW6 ... 135 A5 264 B2
Fulham Ct
SW6 ... 135 C4 265 A2
Fulham High St SW6 ... 135 A3
Fulham Palace★ SW6 135 A3
Fulham Palace Rd
W6 ... 134 D6
Fulham SW6 ... 135 A4 264 A1
Fulham Park Gdns
SW6 ... 135 B3
Fulham Park Rd SW6 ... 135 B3
Fulham Prep Sch
SW6 ... 135 A3
Fulham Prim Sch
SW6 ... 135 C6 265 A5
Fulham Rd
SW10 ... 136 A6 266 B6
Fulham SW6 ... 135 B4 264 D2
Fulke Ho E5 ... 74 B5
Fullbrooks Ave KT4 ... 199 D1
Fuller Cl 3 E2 ... 96 A3
Orpington BR6 ... 227 D3
Fuller Rd RM8 ... 80 C4
Fullers Ave KT6 ... 214 B6
Fuller's Ave IG8 ... 36 D3
Fullers Cotts N22 ... 32 B3
Fullers Ho 6 SW18 ... 157 C6
Fuller's Rd E18 ... 36 D3
Fuller St NW4 ... 46 C5
Fullers Way N KT6 ... 214 B5
Fullers Way S KT9 ... 214 A5
Fuller's Wood CR0 ... 223 C3
Fuller Terr IG1 ... 79 B3
Fullerton Ct TW11 ... 175 A4
Fullerton Rd SW18 ... 158 A6
Croydon CR0 ... 205 D2
Fuller Way UB3 ... 105 D1
Fullwood Prim Sch IG6 57 A5
Fullwood's Mews N1 ... 235 D2
Fulmar Ct
5 Dulwich SE21 ... 161 B2
Surbiton KT5 ... 198 B3
Fulmar Ho NW8 ... 237 B5
12 SE16 ... 118 D2
Fulmead St SW6 ... 265 D1
Fulmer Cl TW12 ... 173 A5
Fulmer Rd E16 ... 99 D2
Fulmer Way W13 ... 109 B3
Fulneck 1 E1 ... 96 C2
Fulready Rd E10 ... 54 B4
Fulstone Cl TW4 ... 129 B1
Fulthorp Rd SE3 ... 143 A3
Fulton Ct EN3 ... 7 C5
Fulton Mews W2 ... 246 A6
Fulton Rd HA9 ... 66 C5
Fulwell Ct UB1 ... 108 A6
Fulwell Park Ave TW2 152 A2
Fulwell Rd TW11,TW12 174 B6
Fulwell Sta TW11 ... 174 B6
Fulwood Ave HA0 ... 88 B5
Fulwood Cl UB3 ... 83 D1
Fulwood Gdns TW1 ... 153 A5
Fulwood Pl WC1 ... 240 D3
Fulwood Wlk SW19 ... 157 A3
Furber St W6 ... 112 B3
Furham Field HA5 ... 23 C3
Furley Ho 7 SE15 ... 140 A5
Furley Rd SE15 ... 140 A5
Furlong Cl SM6 ... 203 B1
Furlong Rd N7 ... 72 C2
Furmage St SW18 ... 157 D4
Furneaux Ave SE27 ... 182 D5
Furness Ho SW1 ... 258 C2
Furness Lo 4 SW14 ... 132 D1
Furness Rd NW10 ... 90 A5
SW6 ... 135 D3
Harrow HA2 ... 41 D1
Morden SM4 ... 201 D3
Furnival St EC4 ... 94 C1 241 A2
Furrow La E9 ... 74 C3
Furrows The KT12 ... 194 C1
Fursby Ave N3 ... 29 C4
Fursecroft W1 ... 237 C2
Further Acre NW9 ... 27 D1
Furtherfield Cl CR0 ... 204 C3
Further Green Rd SE6 164 C3
Furze Cl WD19 ... 22 C5
Furze Ct CR0 ... 222 A6
Furzedown Dr SW17 ... 181 B5
Furzedown Prim Sch
SW17 ... 181 A4
Furzedown Rd SW17 ... 181 B5
Furzefield Cl BR7 ... 188 D4
Furzefield Rd SE3 ... 143 B5
Furzeground Way
UB11 ... 105 A5
Furzeham Rd UB7 ... 104 A4
Furzehill Rd WD6 ... 11 A6
Furze Inf Sch RM6 ... 59 A3
Furzeland Ho 2 KT3 ... 199 C2
Furze Rd CR7 ... 205 A6
Furze St E3 ... 97 C2
Furzewood TW16 ... 172 A2
Fuschia Ct IG8 ... 36 C4
Fyfe Way BR1 ... 187 A1
Fyfield N4 ... 72 C6
Fyfield Cl BR2,BR3 ... 208 B5
Fyfield Ct E7 ... 77 A2
Fyfield Ho RM9 ... 80 B1
Fyfield Rd E17 ... 54 B6
6 SW9 ... 138 C2
Enfield EN1 ... 5 C2
Woodford IG8 ... 37 C3
Fynes St SW1 ... 259 C4

G

Gable Cl HA5 ... 23 C3
Gable Ct SE26 ... 184 B6
Gable Ho 12 W4 ... 111 C2
Gable Lo
Hadley Wood EN4 ... 2 A5
West Wickham BR4 ... 208 A1
Gables Ave TW15 ... 170 B5
Gables Cl SE5 ... 139 C4
Lewisham SE12 ... 165 A3
Gables The BR1 ... 187 B3
N10 ... 49 A6
N12 ... 29 D5
NW3 ... 70 B6
3 SW4 ... 137 C2
Barking IG11 ... 79 A2
Ealing W13 ... 87 B1
Wembley HA9 ... 66 B5
Gabriel Cl 1 TW13 ... 173 A6
Gabriel Ho SE11 ... 260 C4
Gabrielle Cl HA9 ... 66 B5
Gabrielle Ct NW3 ... 70 B2
Gabriel St SE23 ... 163 A4
Gabriel's Wharf★ SE1 251 A4
Gad Cl E13 ... 99 B4
Gaddesden Ave HA9 ... 66 B2
Gaddesden Ho EC1 ... 235 D1
Gade Cl UB3 ... 106 B5
Gadesden Rd KT19 ... 215 A2
Gadsbury Cl NW9 ... 45 D3
Gadsden Ho 6 E9 ... 74 D2
8 W10 ... 91 A3
Gadwall Cl E16 ... 99 B1
Gadwall Way SE28 ... 123 B4
Gagarin Ho SW11 ... 136 B2
Gage Rd E16 ... 98 C2
Gage St WC1 ... 240 B4
Gainford Ho 18 E2 ... 96 B4
Gainford St N1 ... 94 C6 234 A6
Gainsboro Gdns UB6 ... 64 C3
Gainsborough Ave E12 ... 78 C3
Gainsborough Cl
Beckenham BR3 ... 185 C3
Thames Ditton KT10 ... 196 C1
Gainsborough Ct N12 ... 29 D5
6 SE16 ... 118 B1
W12 ... 112 C4
Barnet EN5 ... 1 D1
Bromley BR2 ... 209 C5
Dulwich SE21 ... 161 C2
Gainsborough Gdns
NW11 ... 47 B2
NW3 ... 70 B5
Edgware HA8 ... 26 C1
Isleworth TW7 ... 152 B6
Gainsborough Ho
5 E14 ... 119 A6
N4 ... 50 B1
3 NW3 ... 70 A4
SW1 ... 259 D3
Dagenham RM8 ... 80 B4
Enfield EN1 ... 18 A6
Gainsborough Lo HA1 ... 42 C4
Gainsborough Mews 5
SE26 ... 162 B1
Gainsborough Prim Sch
E15 ... 98 C4
E9 ... 75 C2
Gainsborough Rd E11 ... 54 C2
E15 ... 98 C4
N12 ... 29 D5
W4 ... 111 D2
Dagenham RM8 ... 80 B5
Hayes UB4 ... 83 B5
New Malden KT3 ... 199 B2
Richmond TW9 ... 132 B2
Gainsborough Sq DA7 146 D2
Gainsborough Twr 8
UB5 ... 84 D5
Gainsford Rd E17 ... 53 B5
Gainsford St
SE1 ... 117 D4 253 D2
Gairloch Ho 2 NW1 ... 71 D1
Gairloch Rd SE5 ... 139 C3
Gaisford St NW5 ... 71 C2
Gaitskell Ct SW11 ... 136 C3
Gaitskell Ho 3 E17 ... 53 D6
2 E6 ... 99 D6
SE17 ... 139 B6
Gaitskell Rd SE9 ... 167 A3
Galahad Rd BR1 ... 187 A6
Galata Rd SW13 ... 134 A5
Galatea Sq SE15 ... 140 B2
Galba Ct 1 TW8 ... 131 D5
Galbraith St E14 ... 120 A3
Galdana Ave EN5 ... 2 A2
Galeborough Ave IG8 ... 36 B3
Gale Cl Hampton TW12 ... 173 A4
Mitcham CR4 ... 202 B6
Gale Ho 10 SW2 ... 160 B6
Galena Ho SE18 ... 123 D1
5 W6 ... 112 B2
Galena Rd W6 ... 112 B2
Galen Pl WC1 ... 240 B3
Galesbury Rd SW18 ... 158 A5
Gales Gdns E2 ... 96 B4
Gale St E3 ... 97 C2
Dagenham RM9 ... 80 D1
Galgate Cl 4 SW19 ... 157 A3
Gallants Farm Rd EN4 ... 14 C3
Galleon Cl SE16 ... 118 D4
Galleon Ho 7 E14 ... 120 A2
Galleons Dr IG11 ... 102 A4
Gallery Ct SW10 ... 266 A5
Gallery Gdns UB5 ... 84 D5
Gallery Rd SE21 ... 161 B3
Galleywall Prim Sch
SE16 ... 118 B2
Galleywall Rd SE16 ... 118 B2
Galleywall Road Trad Est 12
SE16 ... 118 B2
Galleywood Ho W10 ... 90 C2
Gallia Rd N5 ... 72 D3
Galliard Cl N9 ... 18 C5
Galliard Ct N9 ... 18 A5
Galliard Rd N9 ... 18 A5
Gallions Cl IG11 ... 102 A4
Gallions Mount Prim Sch
SE18 ... 123 D1
Gallions Rd
Greenwich SE7 ... 121 A2
Newham E16 ... 123 A6
Gallions Reach Sta
E16 ... 122 D6
Gallions View Rd
SE28 ... 123 C4
Gallon Cl SE7 ... 121 C2
Gallop The
South Croydon CR2 ... 222 B1
Sutton SM2 ... 218 A1
Gallosson Rd SE18 ... 123 C2
Galloway Path 5 CR0 221 B4
Galloway Rd W12 ... 112 A5
Gallus Cl N21 ... 16 B5
Gallus Sq SE3 ... 143 B2
Galpin's Rd CR4,CR7 ... 204 B5
Galsworthy Ave E14 ... 97 A2
Ilford RM6 ... 58 B2
Galsworthy Cl SE28 ... 124 B5
Galsworthy Cres SE3 ... 143 C4
Galsworthy Ho 4 W11 ... 91 A1
Galsworthy Rd NW2 ... 69 A4
Kingston KT2 ... 176 D2
Galton Ho 1 SE18 ... 144 B4
Galton St W10 ... 91 A4
Galva Cl EN4 ... 3 A1
Galvani Way CR0 ... 204 B1
Galveston Ho 2 E1 ... 97 A3
Galveston Rd SW15 ... 157 B6
Galway Cl 28 SE16 ... 118 B1
Galway Ho 6 E1 ... 96 D2
EC1 ... 235 B1
Galway St EC1 ... 95 A4 235 B1
Galy 5 NW9 ... 27 D1
Gambetta St 3 SW8 ... 137 B3
Gambia St
SE1 ... 116 D5 251 D3
Gambier Ho EC1 ... 235 B1
Gambole Rd SW17 ... 180 C6
Games Ho 6 SE7 ... 143 C6
Games Rd EN4 ... 2 D2
Gamlen Rd SW15 ... 134 D1
Gamuel Cl E17 ... 53 C3
Gander Green Cres
TW12 ... 173 C2
Gander Green La KT4,
SM1,SM3 ... 217 B5
Gandhi Cl E17 ... 53 C3
Gandolfi st 5 SE15 ... 139 C6
Ganley Ct 19 SW11 ... 136 B2
Gannet Ct 4 SE21 ... 161 B2
Gannet Ho SE15 ... 139 D4
Ganton St W1 ... 239 B1
Ganton Wlk WD19 ... 22 D6
Gants Hill IG2 ... 56 C3
Gants Hill Cres IG2 ... 56 C4
Gants Hill Sta IG2 ... 56 C3
Gap Rd SW19 ... 179 D5
Garage Rd W3 ... 88 C1
Garbett Ho 2 SE17 ... 138 D6
Garbutt Pl W1 ... 238 B3
Garden Ave DA7 ... 147 C2
Mitcham CR4 ... 181 B3
Garden City HA8 ... 26 C4
Garden Cl SE12 ... 165 B1
Ashford TW15 ... 171 A4
Chingford E4 ... 35 C5
Hampton TW12 ... 173 B5
Northolt UB5 ... 85 A6
Roehampton SW15 ... 156 B4
Ruislip HA4 ... 61 D6
Wallington SM6 ... 220 A3
Garden Cotts BR5 ... 190 C1
Garden Ct EC4 ... 251 A6
N12 ... 29 D5
NW8 ... 229 C2
10 SE9 ... 166 C5
12 W4 ... 111 A3
5 Belmont SM2 ... 217 C1
4 Richmond TW9 ... 132 B4
South Croydon CR0 ... 221 D5
4 Stanmore HA7 ... 25 C5
Wembley HA0 ... 65 C5
Gardeners Rd CR0 ... 204 D1
Garden Flats SW16 ... 160 A1
Garden Ho 2 N2 ... 30 B1
12 SW9 ... 138 A3
Garden Hospl The NW4 46 C6
Gardenia Ct 1 BR3 ... 185 C3
Gardenia Rd EN1 ... 17 C5
Gardenia Way IG8 ... 37 A5
Garden La Bromley BR1 187 B4
Streatham SW2 ... 160 B3
Garden Lodge Ct N2 ... 48 B6
Garden Mews W2 ... 245 B5
Garden Pl 28 E2 ... 95 D6
Garden Rd NW8 92 A4 229 B2
Bromley BR1 ... 187 B4
Penge SE20 ... 184 C2
Richmond TW9 ... 132 C2
Walton-on-T KT12 ... 194 B2
Garden Row
SE1 ... 116 D3 261 C6
Garden Royal 16
SW15 ... 156 D5
Garden St E1 ... 96 D2
Gardens The N16 ... 51 D2
SE22 ... 140 A1
Beckenham BR3 ... 186 A2
East Bedfont TW14 ... 149 B5
Harrow HA1,HA2 ... 42 A3
Pinner HA5 ... 41 B3
Garden Suburb Jun & Inf
Schs NW11 ... 47 B4
Garden Terr SW1 ... 259 C2
SW7 ... 247 B1
Garden Way NW10 ... 67 A2
Garden Wlk
EC2 ... 95 C3 243 A6
Beckenham BR3 ... 185 B2
Gardiner Ave NW2 ... 68 C3
Gardiner Cl BR5 ... 190 C1
Dagenham RM8 ... 80 D4
Enfield EN3 ... 18 D5
Gardiner Ct NW10 ... 89 B6
Gardiner Ho 3 SE18 ... 144 A5
SW11 ... 267 A2
Gardner Cl E11 ... 55 B3
Gardner Ct N5 ... 73 A4
Hounslow TW3 ... 129 C2
Tottenham N22 ... 32 D1
Gardner Ho
Feltham TW13 ... 151 B2
Southall UB1 ... 106 D6
Gardner Ind Est SE26 ... 185 B5
Gardner Pl TW14 ... 150 B5
Gardner Rd E13 ... 99 B3
Gardners Cl N11 ... 15 A2
Gardners La EC4 ... 252 A6
Gardnor Mans 10 NW3 ... 70 A4
Gardnor Rd NW3 ... 70 B4
Gard St EC1 ... 234 D2
Garendon Gdns SM4 ... 201 D2
Garendon Rd SM4 ... 201 D2
Garenne Ct 10 E4 ... 20 A3
Gareth Cl KT4 ... 216 D6
Gareth Ct SW16 ... 159 D1
Gareth Gr BR1 ... 187 A6
Garfield Edmonton N9 ... 18 B3
Enfield EN2 ... 17 B6
Garfield First Sch
SW19 ... 180 A4
Garfield Prim Sch N11 ... 31 C5
Garfield Rd E13 ... 98 D3
SW11 ... 137 A2
Chingford E4 ... 20 B3
Enfield EN3 ... 6 C1
2 Twickenham TW1 ... 153 A3
Wimbledon SW19 ... 180 A4
Garford St E14 ... 119 C6
Garganey Ct NW10 ... 67 B2
Gargany Wlk SE28 ... 124 C6
Garibaldi St SE18 ... 123 C2
Garland Dr TW3 ... 130 A3
Garland Ho N16 ... 73 B5
Garland Rd SE18 ... 145 B5
Stanmore HA7 ... 26 A2
Garlands Ct 2 CR0 ... 221 B4
Garlands The HA1 ... 42 D2
Garlick Hill
EC4 ... 117 A6 252 B6
Garlies Rd SE23 ... 163 A1
Garlinge Ho 12 SW9 ... 138 C4
Garlinge Rd NW2 ... 69 B2
Garman Cl N18 ... 33 B5
Garman Rd N17 ... 34 C3
Garnault Mews EC1 ... 234 B1
Garnault Pl EC1 ... 234 B1
Garnault Rd EN1 ... 5 D5
Garner Cl RM8 ... 58 D1
Garner Rd E17 ... 36 A2
Garner St E2 ... 96 A5
Garnet Ho KT4 ... 199 B1
Garnet Rd NW10 ... 67 C2
South Norwood CR7 ... 205 B5
Garnet St E1 ... 118 C6
Garnett Cl SE9 ... 144 B2
Garnett Ho 5 NW3 ... 70 D3
Garnett Rd NW3 ... 70 D3
Garnett Way E17 ... 35 A2
Garnet Wlk 8 E6 ... 100 A2
Garnham Cl 2 N16 ... 73 D6
Garnham St 1 N16 ... 73 D6
Garnies Cl SE15 ... 139 D5
Garrad's Rd SW16 ... 159 D1
Garrard Cl DA7 ... 147 C2
Chislehurst BR7 ... 188 D5
Garrard Wlk NW10 ... 67 C2
Garratt Cl CR0 ... 220 A4
Garratt Ho 8 N16 ... 51 C1
Garratt La
Upper Tooting SW17,
SW18 ... 180 C6
Wandsworth SW18 ... 157 D3
Garratt Park Sch
SW18 ... 158 A1
Garratt Rd HA8 ... 26 C3
Garratts Rd WD23 ... 8 A4
Garratt Terr SW17 ... 180 C6
Garraway Ct SW13 ... 134 C5
Garraway Ho SE21 ... 161 D1
Garrett Cl W3 ... 89 B2
Garrett Ho W12 ... 90 B1
Teddington TW11 ... 175 B4
Garrett St EC1 ... 95 A3 242 B6
Garrick Ave NW11 ... 47 A3
Garrick Cl SW18 ... 136 A1
Ealing W5 ... 88 A3
1 Richmond TW9 ... 153 D6
Garrick Cres CR0 ... 221 C6
Garrick Ct HA8 ... 26 B6
Garrick Dr NW4 ... 28 C1
SE18 ... 123 B3
Garrick Gdns KT8 ... 195 C6
Garrick Ho W1 ... 248 C3
Garrick Ho *continued*
Chiswick W4 ... 133
2 Kingston KT1 ... 198
7 Streatham SW16 ... 181
Garrick Ind Est NW9 ... 45
Garrick Pk NW4 ... 28
Garrick Rd NW9 ... 45
Greenford UB6 ... 85
Richmond TW9 ... 132
Garrick's Ait KT8 ... 174
Garricks Ho KT1 ... 175
Garrick St
WC2 ... 116 A6 250
Garrick Way NW4 ... 46
Garrick Yd WC2 ... 250
Garrison Cl SE18 ... 144
Hounslow TW4 ... 151
Garrison La KT9 ... 214
Garrowsfield EN5 ... 13
Garsdale Cl N11 ... 31
Garsdale Terr SW5 ... 254
Garside Cl SE28 ... 123
Hampton TW12 ... 173
Garsington Mews SE4 141
Garson Ho W2 ... 246
Garston Ho 6 N1 ... 72
Garter Way SE16 ... 118
Garth Cl Kingston KT2 ... 176
Ruislip HA4 ... 40
West Barnes SM4 ... 200
Garth Ct Chiswick W4 ... 133
Harrow HA1 ... 42
Garth Ho NW2 ... 69
Garthland Dr EN5 ... 12
Garth Mews W5 ... 88
Garthorne Rd SE23 ... 162
Garth Rd NW2 ... 69
8 W4 ... 111
Kingston KT2 ... 176
West Barnes SM4 ... 200
Garthside TW10 ... 176
Garth The N12 ... 29
Hampton TW12 ... 173
Harrow HA3 ... 44
Garthway N12 ... 30
Gartmoor Gdns SW19 ... 157
Gartmore Rd IG3 ... 79
Garton Ho 6 N6 ... 49
Garton Pl SW18 ... 158
Gartons Cl EN3 ... 6
Gartons Way SW11 ... 136
Garvary Rd E16 ... 99
Garvens SE19 ... 183
Garway Rd W2 ... 91
Gascoigne Gdns IG8 ... 36
Gascoigne Pl 17 E2 ... 95
Gascoigne Prim Sch
IG11 ... 101
Gascoigne Rd IG11 ... 101
Gascony Ave NW6 ... 69
Gascoyne Ho 2 E9 ... 74
Gascoyne Rd E9 ... 74
Gaselee St E14 ... 120
Gasholder Pl
SE11 ... 116 B1 260
Gaskarth Rd HA8 ... 27
Balham SW12 ... 159
Gaskell Rd N6 ... 48
Gaskell St SW4 ... 138
Gaskin Ho N16 ... 73
Gaskin St N1 ... 94 D6 234
Gaspar Cl SW7 ... 255
Gaspar Mews SW5 ... 255
Gassiot Rd SW17 ... 180
Gassiot Way SM1 ... 218
Gasson Ho 24 SE14 ... 140
Gastein Rd W6 ... 134
Gastigny Ho EC1 ... 235
Gaston Bell Cl TW9 ... 132
Gaston Bridge Rd
TW17 ... 193
Gaston Gate SW8 ... 270
Gaston Rd CR4 ... 203
Gaston Way TW17 ... 193
Gataker Ho 5 SE16 ... 118
Gataker St 6 SE16 ... 118
Gatcliff Cl SW1 ... 258
Gatcombe Ct BR3 ... 185
Gatcombe Ho 20 SE22 139
Gatcombe Mews W5 ... 110
Gatcombe Rd 9 E16 ... 121
N19 ... 71
Gatcombe Way EN4 ... 2
Gateacre Ct DA14 ... 190
Gatebeck Ho 21 SE22 ... 139
Gate End HA6 ... 22
Gatefield Ct SE15 ... 140
Gateforth St NW8 ... 237
Gate Hill Ct W11 ... 244
Gatehill Rd HA6 ... 22
Gate Ho 4 KT6 ... 198
Gatehouse Cl KT2 ... 177
Gatehouse Sch E2 ... 96 D
Gatehouse Sq SE1 ... 252 B
Gateley Ho 6 SE4 ... 140
Gateley Rd SW9 ... 138
Gate Mews
SW7 ... 114 C4 247
Gater Dr EN2 ... 5

tes 4 NW9 27 D1
tesborough St EC2 243 A6
tes Ct SE17 262 A2
tesden WC1 233 B1
tes Green Rd
2,BR4 225 A4
oney Hall BR4 224 D5
teside Rd SW17 158 D1
te St WC2 94 B1 240 C2
testone Ct 10 SE19 183 C4
testone Rd SE19 183 C4
teway SE17 139 A6
teway Mews 4 E8 73 D3
teway Prim Sch
W8 92 B3 236 D6
teway Rd E10 75 D5
teway Ret Pk E6 100 D3
teways KT6 198 A4
teways Ct SM6 219 B3
teways The SW3 257 B3
chmond TW9 131 D1
teway Trad Est
W10 89 D4
tfield Gr TW13 151 C2
tfield Ho TW13 151 C2
thorne Rd N22 32 C2
thorne St 19 E2 96 D5
tley Ave KT19 214 D3
tliff Rd SW1 115 B1 258 C1
tling Rd SE18,SE2 124 A1
tonby St SE15 139 D4
tting Cl HA8 27 A3
tting Way UB8 60 A2
tton Rd SW17 180 C6
ttons Way DA14 191 B6
tward Cl N21 16 D5
tward Gn N9 17 D2
twick Ho 3 E14 97 B1
twick Rd SW18 157 B4
uden Cl SW4 137 D2
uden Rd SW4 137 D2
ugin Ct 13 SE16 118 B1
untlet 1 NW9 27 D1
untlet Cl UB5 63 A1
untlett Ct HA0 65 B3
untlett Rd SM1 218 B3
unt St SE1 262 A6
utrey Rd SE15 140 C3
utrey Sq 5 E6 100 B1
vel St SE17 262 D4
ven Ho N17 33 C1
vestone Cres SE12 165 B4
vestone Rd SE12 165 B4
viller Pl 4 E5 74 B4
vina Cl SM4 202 C4
vin Ho SE18 123 C2
vrelle Ho EC1 242 C5
wber St E2 96 C4
wsworth Cl E15 76 D3
wthorne Ave NW7 29 A5
wthorne Ct E3 97 C5
y Cl NW2 68 B3
ydon Ho W2 91 D2
ydon La NW9 27 C2
yfere Rd
Redbridge IG5 56 B6
Stoneleigh KT17 216 A3
yfere St
SW1 116 A3 260 A5
yford Rd W12 111 D4
y Ho N16 73 C3
yhurst SE17 139 B6
yhurst Ct 9 UB5 84 C4
yhurst Ho NW8 237 B6
yhurst Rd E8 74 A1
yhurst Sch E8 74 A1
ylor Rd UB5 63 B3
ymead NW8 91 D6
ynesford Rd
Forest Hill SE23 162 D2
Wallington SM5 218 D1
y Rd E15 98 B5
aysham Ave IG2 56 D4
aysham Hall IG5 56 D6
aysley Ho SE11 261 A3
ay St SW15 134 D2
ayton Cres NW3 70 B4
ayton Ct
3 Harrow HA1 42 D3
New Malden KT3 199 D4
ayton Ho E3 97 C3
ayton Rd NW3 70 B4
SE2 124 C3
Harrow HA1 43 A3
ayville Rd SW11 158 D5
aywood Cl SW2 160 C3
aywood Rd E17 53 C6
aywood St SE1 261 D5
aza St SE17 116 D1 261 C1
aze Ho 10 E14 98 B1
ean Ct 8 E11 76 B4
earies Inf Sch IG2 56 D4
earies Jun Sch IG2 56 D4
earisville Gdns IG6 56 D5
eary Ho N7 72 B3
eary Rd NW10 68 A3
eary St N7 72 B3
EC Est HA9 65 D6
eddes Pl 3 DA7 147 C1

Gedeney Rd N17 33 A2
Gedge Ct CR4 202 C5
Gedling Ho SE22 139 D2
Gedling Pl SE1 263 D6
Geere Rd E15 98 D6
Gees Ct W1 238 B1
Gee St EC1 95 A3 242 A6
Geffrey's Ct SE9 166 A1
Geffrye Ct N1 95 C5
Geffrye Mus★ E2 95 D5
Geffrye St E2 95 D5
Geldart Rd SE15 140 B5
Geldeston Rd E5 74 A6
Gellatly Rd SE14 140 D3
Gell Cl UB10 60 B5
Gemini Bsns Ctr E16 98 B3
Gemini Gr UB5 85 A4
Gemini Ho SW15 134 D1
Gemma Ct BR3 185 B1
General Gordon Pl
SE18 122 D2
Generals Wlk The EN3 7 A6
General Wolfe Rd
SE10 142 B4
Genesis Cl TW19 148 B3
Genesta Rd SE18 145 A6
Geneva Cl TW17 171 C1
Geneva Ct N16 51 B1
1 Putney SW15 156 D6
Geneva Dr SW9 138 C1
Geneva Gdns RM6 59 A4
Geneva Rd
Kingston KT1 198 A5
Thornton Heath CR7 205 A4
Genever Cl E4 35 C5
Genista Rd N18 34 B5
Genoa Ave SW15 156 C6
Genoa Ho 19 E1 96 D3
Genoa Rd SE20 184 C2
Genotin Rd EN1 5 B2
Genotin Terr EN1 5 B2
Gentleman's Row EN2 5 A2
Gentry Gdns E13 99 A4
Geoffrey Chaucer Tech Coll
SE1 117 B3 262 B5
Geoffrey Cl SE5 139 A3
Geoffrey Ct SE4 141 B2
Geoffrey Gdns E6 100 A5
Geoffrey Ho SE1 262 D6
Geoffrey Jones Ct
NW10 90 A6
Geoffrey Rd SE4 141 B2
Geological Mus★
SW7 114 B3 256 D5
George Akass Ho 3
SE18 123 A1
George Beard Rd 10
SE8 119 B2
George Beare Lo 9
SW4 159 C6
George Belt Ho 8 E2 96 D4
George Comberton Wlk 3
E12 78 C3
George Cres N10 31 A3
George Ct WC2 250 B5
Buckhurst Hill IG9 21 D2
George Downing Est
N16 73 D6
George Eliot Ho SW1 259 B3
George Eliot Jun & Inf Sch
NW8 92 B6 229 C6
George Elliot Ho SE17 262 A2
George Elliston Ho 12
SE1 118 A1
George Eyre Ho NW8 229 D3
George Gange Way
HA3 42 D6
George Green's Sec Sch
E14 120 A1
George Groves Rd
SE20 184 A2
George Ho 8 SE26 184 B5
George Inn Yd SE1 252 C3
George La SE13 164 A5
Hayes BR2 209 B1
Wanstead E18 55 B6
Woodford E18 37 A1
George Lansbury Ho
7 E3 97 B4
NW10 67 C1
Wood Green N22 32 C2
George Lashwood Ct 12
SW9 138 B1
George Leybourne Ho 9
E1 118 A6
George Lindgren Ho
SW6 264 D4
George Loveless Ho 4
E2 95 D4
George Lovell Dr EN3 7 C6
George Mews NW1 232 A1
George Mitchell Com Sch
E10 53 D1
George Orwell Sch N4 50 B1
George Parr Ho N21 16 D4
George Peabody Ct
NW1 237 A4
George Rd Chingford E4 35 C4
Kingston KT2 177 A3

George Rd *continued*
New Malden KT3 199 D4
George Row SE16 118 A4
Georges Mead WD6 10 A5
George Spicer Prim Sch
EN1 5 D2
George Sq SW19 201 C6
George's Rd N7 72 B3
George's Sq SW6 264 D6
George St 6 E16 98 D1
W1 92 D1 237 D2
Barking IG11 79 A1
Ealing W7 108 C5
Hounslow TW3,TW5 129 B3
Richmond TW10 153 D6
Southall UB2 107 A2
South Croydon CR0 221 B6
George Tingle Ho SE1 263 D6
George Tomlinson Prim Sch
E11 54 C1
Georgetown Cl 4
SE19 183 C5
Georgette Pl SE10 142 A5
George Vale Ho 32 E2 96 A5
George V Ave HA2,HA5 41 C6
Georgeville Gdns IG6 56 D5
George V Way UB6 87 B6
George Walter Ho 7
SE16 118 C2
George Wyver Cl
SW18 157 A4
George Yd EC3 242 D1
W1 115 A6 248 B6
Georgiana St
NW1 93 C6 232 B6
Georgian Cl Hayes BR2 209 B1
Ickenham UB10 60 A4
Stanmore HA7 25 A3
Georgian Ct 19 E9 96 C6
3 NW4 46 B4
Croydon CR0 205 B1
Wembley HA9 66 D2
Georgian Lo HA5 40 B4
Georgian Way HA1 64 B6
Georgia Rd
New Malden KT3 199 A5
South Norwood CR7 182 D2
Georgina Ct 5 TW1 153 C5
Georgina Gdns 10 E2 95 D4
Geraint Rd BR1 187 A6
Geraldine Ct 6 NW9 46 A5
Geraldine Rd SW18 158 A6
Brentford W4 132 C6
Geraldine St SE11 261 C5
Gerald Mews SW1 258 B4
Gerald Rd E16 98 D3
SW1 115 A2 258 B4
Dagenham RM8 59 B1
Gerard Ave TW4 151 C4
Gerard Ct NW2 68 D3
Gerard Rd
Barnes SW13 133 D4
Harrow HA1 43 A3
Gerards Cl SE16 118 C1
Gerboa Ct 6 E4 36 B5
Gerda Rd SE9 167 A2
Germander Way E15 98 C4
Gernigan Ho SW18 158 B5
Gernon Rd E3 97 A5
Geron Way NW2 68 C6
Gerrard Gdns HA5 40 A4
Gerrard Ho 5 SE14 140 D5
Gerrard Pl W1 249 D6
Gerrard Rd N1 94 D5 234 D4
Gerrards Cl N14 15 C6
Gerrard's Ct W5 109 D3
Gerrard St W1 115 D6 249 D6
Gerridge Ct SE1 261 B6
Gerridge St
SE1 116 C3 261 B6
Gerry Raffles Sq E15 76 B2
Gertrude Rd DA17 125 C2
Gertrude St
SW10 136 A6 266 B5
Gervase Cl HA9 67 A5
Gervase Rd HA8 27 B2
Gervase St SE15 140 B5
Ghent St SE6 163 C2
Ghent Way E8 73 D2
Giant Arches Rd SE24 161 A5
Giant Tree Hill WD23 8 B3
Gibbards Cott 1 IG11 79 D1
Gibbfield Cl RM6 59 A6
Gibbings Ho SE1 251 D1
Gibbins Rd E15 76 A1
Gibbon Ho NW8 236 D5
Gibbon Rd SE15 140 C3
W3 111 C6
Kingston KT2 176 A3
Gibbons Rd NW10 67 C2
Gibbon's Rents SE1 253 A3
Gibbon Wlk SW15 134 A1
Gibbs Ave SE19 183 B5
Gibbs Cl SE19 183 B5
Gibbs Gn HA8 27 A6
W14 113 B1 254 D2
Gibbs Green Sch
W14 113 B1 254 D2

Gibbs Ho
6 Balham SW12 159 B4
2 Bromley BR1 186 D2
Gibbs Rd N18 34 C6
Gibbs Sq SE19 183 B5
Gibraltar Ho NW10 89 C5
Gibraltar Wlk 28 E2 95 D4
Gibson Bsns Ctr N17 33 D3
Gibson Cl E1 96 C3
Chessington KT9 213 C3
Isleworth TW7 130 B2
Southgate N21 16 C5
Gibson Ct KT10 212 D5
Gibson Gdns N16 73 D6
Gibson Ho
South Croydon CR2 221 A2
Sutton SM1 217 C4
Gibson Rd SE11 260 D3
Dagenham RM8 58 C1
Ickenham UB10 60 B4
Sutton SM1 217 D3
Gibson's Hill
South Norwood SW16 182 C3
South Norwood SW16 182 C4
Gibson Sq N1 94 C6 234 B6
Gibson St SE10 120 C1
Gideon Cl DA17 125 D2
Gideon Mews W5 109 D4
Gideon Rd SW11 137 A2
Giesbach Rd N19 71 D6
Giffard Rd N18 33 C4
Giffen Square Mkt
SE8 141 C5
Giffin St SE8 141 C5
Gifford Gdns W7 86 C2
Gifford Ho SE10 120 B1
5 SW4 137 D1
Gifford Prim Sch UB5 85 B5
Gifford St N1 72 A1
Gift La E15 98 D6
Giggs Hill BR5 190 A2
Giggs Hill Gdns KT7 197 A1
Giggs Hill Rd KT7 197 A2
Gilbert Cl SE18 144 B4
1 Merton SW19 179 D2
Gilbert Ct W5 88 B1
Gilbert Gr HA8 27 B2
Gilbert Ho 5 E17 54 A6
5 E2 96 D4
EC2 242 B3
SE8 141 C6
SW1 258 D1
SW8 270 A4
Gilbert Pl WC1 94 A2 240 A3
Gilbert Rd BR1 187 A3
SE11 116 C2 261 B4
Belvedere DA17 125 C3
Merton SW19 180 A3
Pinner HA5 40 D5
Gilbert Scott Com Inf Sch
CR2 223 A1
Gilbert Scott Com Jun Sch
CR2 223 A1
Gilbert Sheldon Ho
W2 236 D4
Gilbertson Ho 4 E14 119 C3
Gilbert St E15 76 C4
W1 93 A1 238 B1
Enfield EN3 6 C6
Hounslow TW3 130 A2
Gilbey Cl UB10 60 D4
Gilbey Rd SW17 180 C5
Gilbeys Yd NW1 71 A1
Gilbourne Rd SE18 145 D6
Gilby Ho 5 E9 74 D2
Gilda Ave EN3 19 A6
Gilda Cres N16 52 A1
Gilda Ct NW7 28 A2
Gildea Cl HA5 23 C3
Gildea St W1 238 D3
Gilden Cres NW5 71 A3
Gildersome St SE18 144 C6
Gilders Rd KT9 214 B2
Giles Coppice SE19 183 D6
Giles Ho 5 SE16 118 A3
W11 91 C1
Gilesmead SE5 139 B4
Gilfrid Cl UB8 82 D1
Gilkes Cres SE21 161 C5
Gilkes Pl SE21 161 C5
Gillam Ho 6 SE16 118 C2
Gillan Ct SE12 165 B1
Gillan Gn WD23 8 A2
Gillards Mews 6 E17 53 C5
Gillards Way E17 53 C5
Gill Ave E16 99 A1
Gill Ct SE18 123 A2
Gillender St E3 98 A3
Gillespie Prim Sch N5 72 D5
Gillespie Rd N4,N5 72 D5
Gillett Ave E6 100 A5
Gillette Cnr TW7 131 A5
Gillett Ho N8 50 A6
Gillett Pl 27 E8 73 C3
Gillett Rd CR7 205 B5
Gillett St E8,N16 73 C3
Gillfoot NW1 232 A3
Gillham Terr N17 34 A3
Gillian Ho HA3 24 C4

Gillian Park Rd SM3 201 B1
Gillian St SE13 163 D6
Gillies Ct DA14 189 C6
Gillies Ho NW6 70 B1
Gilling Ct 5 NW3 70 C2
Gillingham Mews
SW1 259 A4
Gillingham Rd NW2 69 A5
Gillingham Row SW1 259 A4
Gillingham St
SW1 115 C2 259 A4
Gillings Ct EN5 1 A1
Gillison Wlk 18 SE16 118 A3
Gillman Dr E15 98 D6
Gillman Ho 23 E2 96 A5
Gillray Ho SW10 266 C5
Gill St E14 119 B6
Gillum Cl EN4 14 D3
Gilmore Cl UB10 60 C5
Gilmore Cres TW15 170 C4
Gilmore Ct N11 30 D5
Gilmore Ho SW4 136 D1
Gilmore Rd SE13 142 B1
Gilpin Ave SW14 133 B1
Gilpin Cl CR4 180 C1
Gilpin Cres
Edmonton N18 33 D5
Twickenham TW2 151 D4
Gilpin Ho
9 Edmonton N9 18 A1
New Malden KT3 199 C4
Gilpin Rd E5 75 A4
Gilpin Way UB3 127 B5
Gilray Ho W2 246 C6
Gilsland Rd CR7 205 B5
Gilstead Ho IG11 102 B5
Gilstead Rd SW6 135 D3
Gilston Rd
SW10 114 A1 256 B1
Gilton Rd SE6 164 C1
Giltspur St EC1 94 D1 241 D2
Gilwell Cl E4 7 D1
Gilwell Ct 8 E5 74 B4
Gippeswyck Cl HA5 22 D2
Gipsy Cnr W3 89 B2
Gipsy Hill SE19 183 C5
Gipsy Hill Sta SE19 183 C5
Gipsy La SW15 134 B2
Gipsy Moth IV★ SE10 142 A6
Gipsy Rd Bexley DA16 146 D3
West Norwood SE27 183 B6
Gipsy Road Gdns SE27 183 A6
Giralda Cl E16 99 D2
Giraud St E14 97 D1
Girdlers Rd W14 112 D2
Girdlestone Wlk N19 71 C6
Girdwood Rd SW18,
SW19 157 A4
Girling Ho 9 N1 95 C6
Girling Way TW14 128 A2
Gironde Rd
SW6 135 B5 264 D3
Girtin Ho 5 UB5 84 D5
Girton Ave NW9 44 C6
Girton Cl UB5 64 A2
Girton Gdns CR0 223 C5
Girton Ho SW15 156 D5
Girton Rd
Forest Hill SE26 184 D5
Northolt UB5 64 A2
Girton Villas 6 W10 90 D1
Gisbourne Cl SM6 219 D5
Gisburn Mans N8 50 B5
Gisburn Rd N8 50 B5
Gissing Wlk N1 72 C1
Gistelword Ho 9 TW7 131 A2
Gittens Cl BR1 186 D6
Given-Wilson Wlk E13 98 D5
Glacier Way HA0 87 D5
Gladbeck Way EN2 4 D1
Gladding Rd E12 77 D4
Glade Cl KT6 213 D6
Glade Gdns CR0 207 A2
Glade La UB2 107 D4
Gladeside Croydon CR0 206 D3
Southgate N21 16 B4
Gladeside Cl KT9 213 D1
Gladesmore Com Sch
N15 52 A4
Gladesmore Rd N15 51 D3
Glades Sh Ctr The
BR1 187 A1
Gladeswood Rd DA17 125 D2
Glade The BR1 187 D1
SE7 143 C5
Croydon CR0 206 D3
Enfield EN2 4 C3
Southgate N21 16 B4
Stoneleigh KT17 216 A2
West Wickham BR4 223 D5
Woodford IG8 21 B1
Gladiator St SE23 163 A4
Glading Terr N16 73 D5
Gladioli Cl 6 TW12 173 C4
Gladsdale Dr HA5 40 B5
Gladsmuir Rd N19 49 C1
Barnet EN5 1 A3
Gladstone Ave E12 78 A1
Feltham TW14 150 B5

Gladstone Ave *continued*
Tottenham N22 32 D1
Twickenham TW2 152 B4
Gladstone Ct NW2 68 B3
SW1 259 D3
5 Merton SW19 179 C3
Gladstone Gdns TW3 130 A4
Gladstone Ho 14 E14 97 C1
Gladstone Mews
3 Penge SE20 184 C3
Wood Green N22 32 C1
Gladstone Par NW2 68 C5
Gladstone Park Gdns
NW2 68 B5
Gladstone Park Sch
NW10 68 B3
Gladstone Pl KT8 196 C4
Gladstone Rd BR6 227 A3
W4 111 B3
Buckhurst Hill IG9 21 C3
Kingston KT1 198 C6
Merton SW19 179 C3
Southall UB2 107 A4
Surbiton KT6 214 A6
Thornton Heath CR0 205 B2
Gladstone St SE1 261 C6
Gladstone Terr
SW8 137 B4 268 D2
Gladstone Way HA3 42 C6
Gladwell Rd BR1 187 A4
N8 50 B3
Gladwin Ho NW1 232 B3
Gladwyn Rd SW15 134 D2
Gladys Dimson Ho E7 76 D3
Gladys Rd NW6 69 C1
Glaisher St 2 SE10 142 A5
SE8 141 D6
Glamis Cres UB3 105 A3
Glamis Ct W3 110 D4
Glamis Est 3 E1 118 D6
Glamis Pl E1 118 C6
Glamis Rd E1 118 C6
Glamis Way UB5 64 A2
Glamorgan Cl CR4,
SW16 204 A6
Glamorgan Ct 4 W7 86 D2
Glamorgan Rd KT1 175 C3
Glanfield Rd BR3 207 B5
Glanleam Rd HA7 25 D6
Glanville Ho 4 SW12 159 C4
Glanville Rd SW2 160 A6
Bromley BR2 209 B6
Glasbrook Ave TW2 151 B3
Glasbrook Rd SE9 165 D4
Glasbury Ho 5 SW9 138 B1
Glaserton Rd N16 51 C2
Glasford St SW17 180 D4
Glasfryn Ct HA2 64 B6
Glasgow Ho W9 91 D5
Glasgow Rd E13 99 B5
Edmonton N18 34 B5
Glasgow Terr
SW1 115 C1 259 A1
Glasse Cl W13 109 A6
Glasshill St
SE1 116 D4 251 D2
Glasshouse Fields E1 118 D6
Glasshouse St
W1 115 C6 249 B5
Glasshouse Wlk
SE11 116 B1 260 C2
Glasshouse Yd EC1 242 A5
Glasslyn Rd N8 49 D4
Glassmill La BR2 186 D1
Glass St 4 E2 96 B3
Glass Yd SE18 122 C3
Glastonbury Ave IG8 37 D4
Glastonbury Ct
12 SE14 140 C5
1 Ealing W13 109 A5
Glastonbury Ho SW1 258 C2
Glastonbury Pl 25 E1 96 C1
Glastonbury Rd
Edmonton N9 18 A3
Morden SM4 201 C2
Glastonbury St NW6 69 B3
Glaston Ct W5 109 D5
Glaucus St E3 97 D2
Glazbury Rd
W14 113 A1 254 B2
Glazebrook Cl SE21 161 B2
Glazebrook Rd TW11 174 D3
Glebe Ave Enfield EN2 4 D2
Harrow HA3 44 A6
Mitcham CR4 180 C1
Ruislip HA4 62 B2
Uxbridge UB10 61 A4
Woodford IG8 37 A4
Glebe Cl 1 W4 111 C1
Uxbridge UB10 61 A4
Glebe Cotts TW13 151 C1
Glebe Cres NW4 46 C5
Harrow HA3 44 A6
Glebe Ct SE3 142 C2
Ealing W5 109 D5
Ealing W7 108 B6

Glebe Ct *continued*
Mitcham CR4 ... 202 D6
Palmers Green N13 ... 16 C1
Stanmore HA7 ... 25 C5
Glebe Fst & Mid Sch
HA3 ... 44 A5
Glebe Gdns KT3 ... 199 C2
Glebe Ho 8 SE16 ... 118 B3
7 SE18 ... 122 C2
Feltham TW13 ... 151 C1
Glebe House Dr BR2 ... 209 B1
Glebehyrst SE19 ... 183 C6
Glebe La Barnet EN5 ... 12 A5
Harrow HA3 ... 44 A5
Glebeland Gdns TW17 193 A3
Glebelands E10 ... 75 D6
East Molesey KT8 ... 195 D5
Glebelands Ave
Ilford IG2 ... 57 B2
Woodford E18 ... 37 A1
Glebelands Cl SE5 ... 139 C2
Glebelands Rd TW14 ... 150 A4
Glebe Path CR4 ... 202 D6
Glebe Pl SW3 .136 C6 267 A6
Glebe Prim Sch UB10 ... 61 B4
Glebe Rd BR1 ... 187 A2
E8 ... 73 D1
N3 ... 30 A2
N8 ... 50 B5
NW10 ... 68 A2
Barnes SW13 ... 134 A3
Belmont SM2 ... 217 A1
Dagenham RM10 ... 81 D2
Hayes UB3 ... 105 D5
Stanmore HA7 ... 25 C5
Wallington SM5 ... 218 D2
Glebe Sch BR4 ... 224 B6
Glebe Side TW1 ... 152 D5
Glebe Sq CR4 ... 202 D6
Glebe St W4 ... 111 C1
Glebe Terr 15 E3 ... 97 D4
Glebe The SE3 ... 142 C2
Chislehurst BR7 ... 189 A2
New Malden KT4 ... 199 D1
Streatham SW16 ... 181 D6
West Drayton UB7 ... 104 B2
Glebeway IG8 ... 37 C5
Glebe Way
Feltham TW13 ... 151 C1
West Wickham BR4 ... 224 B6
Gledhow Gdns SW5 ... 256 A3
Gledstanes Rd
W14 ... 113 A1 254 B1
Gledwood Ave UB4 ... 84 A2
Gledwood Cres UB4 ... 83 D2
Gledwood Ct UB4 ... 83 D2
Gledwood Dr UB4 ... 83 D2
Gledwood Gdns UB4 ... 84 A2
Gleed Ave WD23 ... 8 B2
Gleeson Dr BR6 ... 227 D4
Glegg Pl 3 SW15 ... 134 D1
Glenaffric Ave E14 ... 120 B2
Glen Albyn Rd SW19 ... 156 D2
Glenalla Rd HA4 ... 39 D2
Glenalmond Ho
Ashford TW15 ... 148 A1
2 Putney SW15 ... 156 D5
Glenalmond Rd HA3 ... 44 A5
Glenalvon Way 5 SE7 122 A2
Glena Mount SM1 ... 218 A4
Glenarm Coll IG1 ... 78 D6
Glenarm Rd E5 ... 74 D4
Glen Ave TW15 ... 170 C6
Glenavon Cl KT10 ... 213 A1
Glenavon Ct KT4 ... 216 B6
Glenavon Lo 4 E18 ... 55 A6
Glenavon Rd E15 ... 76 C1
Glenbarr Cl SE9 ... 144 D2
Glenbow Rd BR1 ... 186 C5
Glenbrook Inf Sch
SW4 ... 159 D5
Glenbrook Jun Sch
SW4 ... 159 D5
Glenbrook N EN2 ... 4 B1
Glenbrook Rd NW6 ... 69 C3
Glenbrook S EN2 ... 4 B1
Glenbuck Ct 6 KT6 ... 198 A3
Glenbuck Rd KT6 ... 198 A3
Glenburnie Rd SW17 ... 158 D1
Glencairn Dr W5 ... 87 C3
Glencairne Cl E16 ... 99 D2
Glencairn Rd SW16 ... 182 A3
Glen Cl TW17 ... 192 C5
Glencoe Ave IG2 ... 57 C2
Glencoe Dr RM10 ... 81 C4
Glencoe Mans 6 SW9 138 C5
Glencoe Rd UB4 ... 84 D3
Glencorse Gn WD19 ... 22 D6
Glen Cres IG8 ... 37 B4
Glen Ct 5 Bromley BR1 186 D3
9 Penge SE20 ... 184 B2
Sidcup DA14 ... 190 A6
Glendale Ave
Edgware HA8 ... 26 C6
Ilford RM6 ... 58 C2
Wood Green N22 ... 32 C3
Glendale Cl SE9 ... 144 C2
Glendale Dr SW19 ... 179 B5
Glendale Gdns HA9 ... 44 A1
Glendale Mews BR3 ... 185 D2
Glendale Way SE28 ... 124 C6
Glendall St SW9 ... 138 B1
Glendarvon St SW15 ... 134 D2
Glendevon Cl HA8 ... 10 D1
Glendish Rd N17 ... 34 B2
Glendor Gdns NW7 ... 27 B6
Glendower Gdns 10
SW14 ... 133 B2
Glendower Pl SW7 ... 256 C4
Glendower Prep Sch
SW7 ... 114 B2 256 D4
Glendower Rd
Chingford E4 ... 20 B3
Mortlake SW14 ... 133 B2
Glendown Ho 2 E8 ... 74 A3
Glendown Rd SE2 ... 124 A1
Glendun Ct W3 ... 111 C6
Glendun Rd W3 ... 111 C6
Gleneagle Lo BR3 ... 185 C2
Gleneagle Mews
SW16 ... 181 D5
Gleneagle Rd SW16 ... 181 D5
Gleneagles Ealing W13 ... 87 B2
Stanmore HA7 ... 25 B4
Gleneagles Cl BR6 ... 211 B1
21 SE16 ... 118 B1
South Oxhey WD19 ... 22 D6
Gleneagles Ct 3
TW11 ... 175 A5
Gleneagles Gn 1 BR6 211 B1
Gleneagles Twr 2 UB1 ... 86 A1
Gleneldon Mews
SW16 ... 182 A6
Gleneldon Rd SW16 ... 182 A6
Glenelg Rd SW2 ... 160 A6
Glenesk Rd SE9 ... 144 D1
Glenfarg Rd SE6 ... 164 B3
Glenfield Cres HA4 ... 39 B2
Glenfield Rd W13 ... 109 B4
Ashford TW15 ... 171 A4
Streatham SW12 ... 159 C3
Glenfield Terr W13 ... 109 B5
Glenfinlas Way SE5 ... 138 D5
Glenforth St SE10 ... 120 D1
Glengall Gr E14 ... 120 A3
Glengall Pass 2 NW6 ... 91 C6
Glengall Rd DA7 ... 147 A2
NW6 ... 91 B6
SE15 ... 139 D6
Edgware HA8 ... 10 D1
Woodford IG8 ... 37 B4
Glengall Terr SE15 ... 139 D6
Glengarnock Ave E14 ... 120 A2
Glengarry Rd SE22 ... 161 D6
Glen Gdns CR0 ... 220 C4
Glenham Dr IG2 ... 56 D4
Glenhead Cl SE9 ... 144 D2
Glenhill Cl N3 ... 29 C1
Glen Ho 6 E16 ... 122 C5
SW1 ... 259 A6
Glenhouse Rd SE9 ... 166 C6
Glenhurst 4 BR3 ... 186 A2
Glenhurst Ave DA5 ... 169 B3
NW5 ... 71 A4
Ruislip HA4 ... 39 A1
Glenhurst Ct SE19 ... 183 D5
Glenhurst Rd N12 ... 30 B5
Brentford TW8 ... 109 C1
Glenhurst Rise SE19 ... 183 A3
Glenilla Rd NW3 ... 70 C2
Glenister Ho UB3 ... 106 B5
Glenister Park Rd
SW16 ... 181 D3
Glenister Rd SE10 ... 120 D1
Glenister St E16 ... 122 C5
Glenlea Rd SE9 ... 166 C6
Glenloch Ct 2 NW3 ... 70 C2
Glenloch Rd NW3 ... 70 C3
Enfield EN3 ... 6 C3
Glenluce Rd SE3 ... 143 A6
Glenlyon Rd SE9 ... 166 C6
Glenmead IG9 ... 21 C3
Glenmere Ave NW7 ... 28 A4
Glen Mews E17 ... 53 B4
Glenmill TW12 ... 173 B5
Glenmore SW15 ... 156 D5
Glenmore Ho 6 TW10 154 A5
Glenmore Lawns W13 ... 87 A1
Glenmore Rd DA16 ... 145 D4
NW3 ... 70 C2
Glenmore Way IG11 ... 102 A5
Glenmount Path 1
SE18 ... 123 A1
Glennie Ct SE21 ... 162 A3
Glennie Ho SE10 ... 142 A4
Glennie Rd SE27,SW16 160 C1
Glenny Rd IG11 ... 79 A2
Glenorchy Cl UB4 ... 85 A2
Glenparke Rd E7 ... 77 B2
Glen Rd E13 ... 99 C3
E17 ... 53 B4
Chessington KT9 ... 214 A5
Glenridding NW1 ... 232 B3
Glen Rise IG8 ... 37 B4
Glenrosa St SW6 ... 136 A3
Glenrose Ct DA14 ... 190 B5
Glenroy St W12 ... 90 C1
Glensdale Rd SE4 ... 141 B2
Glenshaw Mans 7
SW9 ... 138 C5
Glenshiel Rd SE9 ... 166 C6
Glentanner Way SW17 158 B1
Glen Terr E14 ... 120 A4
Glentham Gdns SW13 ... 134 B6
Glentham Rd SW13 ... 134 B6
Glen The BR6 ... 226 C5
Beckenham BR2 ... 186 C1
Enfield EN2 ... 4 D1
Pinner HA5 ... 40 B4
Pinner HA5 ... 41 A2
Southall UB2 ... 107 B1
South Croydon CR0 ... 222 D5
Wembley HA9 ... 65 D4
Glenthorne Ave CR0 ... 206 C1
Glenthorne Cl SM3 ... 201 C1
Glenthorne Gdns
Cheam SM3 ... 201 C1
Ilford IG6 ... 56 D5
Glenthorne High Sch
SM3 ... 201 C1
Glenthorne Mews W6 112 B2
Glenthorne Rd E17 ... 53 A4
N11 ... 31 A5
W6 ... 112 B2
Kingston KT1 ... 198 B5
Glenthorpe SW15 ... 134 A1
Glenthorpe Rd SM4 ... 200 D4
Glenton Rd SE13 ... 142 C1
Glentrammon Ave
BR6 ... 227 D2
Glentrammon Cl BR6 ... 227 D3
Glentrammon Gdns
BR6 ... 227 D2
Glentrammon Rd BR6 227 D2
Glentworth St
NW1 ... 92 D3 237 D5
Glenure Rd SE9 ... 166 C6
Glenview SE2 ... 146 D6
Glen View Rd BR1 ... 187 D1
Glenville Ave EN2 ... 5 A5
Glenville Gr SE8 ... 141 B5
Glenville Mews SW18 ... 157 C4
Glenville Rd KT2 ... 176 C2
Glen Wlk TW7 ... 152 B6
Glenwood Ave NW9 ... 45 C1
Glenwood Cl HA1 ... 42 D4
Glenwood Ct
4 Sidcup DA14 ... 190 A6
5 Wanstead E18 ... 55 A6
Glenwood Gdns IG2 ... 56 C4
Glenwood Gr NW9 ... 45 A1
Glenwood Ho 3 EN5 ... 13 D6
Glenwood Rd N15 ... 50 D4
NW7 ... 11 C1
Forest Hill SE6 ... 163 C3
Hounslow TW3 ... 130 B2
Stoneleigh KT17 ... 216 A2
Glenwood Way CR0 ... 206 D3
Glenworth Ave E14 ... 120 B2
Gliddon Rd
W14 ... 113 A1 254 A2
Glifford Ho SW1 ... 259 A1
Glimpsing Gn DA18 ... 125 A3
Glisson Rd UB10 ... 82 C5
Globe Pond Rd SE16 ... 119 A5
Globe Prim Sch E2 ... 96 C4
Globe Rd E15 ... 76 D3
E1,E2 ... 96 C3
Woodford IG8 ... 37 C4
Globe St SE1 ... 117 B4 252 C1
Globe Terr 9 E2 ... 96 C4
Globe Theatre The★
SE1 ... 252 A5
Globe View EC4 ... 252 A6
Globe Yd W1 ... 238 C1
Gloster Rd KT3 ... 199 C5
Gloucester
W14 ... 113 B2 254 D3
Gloucester Ave DA16 ... 145 D1
NW1 ... 93 A6 231 B6
Sidcup DA15 ... 167 C2
Gloucester Cir SE10 ... 142 A5
Gloucester Cl NW10 ... 67 B1
Thames Ditton KT7 ... 197 A1
Gloucester Cres
NW1 ... 93 B6 231 C6
Staines TW18 ... 170 A4
Gloucester Ct EC3 ... 253 B5
NW11 ... 47 B2
SE1 ... 262 B6
SE22 ... 162 A3
6 Acton W3 ... 88 C1
5 Ealing W7 ... 86 D2
Harrow HA1 ... 42 C6
Redbridge IG1 ... 56 B2
Richmond TW9 ... 132 C5
8 Surbiton KT6 ... 197 D2
Gloucester Dr N4 ... 72 D6
NW11 ... 47 C5
Gloucester Gate NW1 231 C4
Gloucester Gate Mews
NW1 ... 231 C4
Gloucester Gdns NW11 47 B2
W2 ... 236 A2
Gloucester Gdns *continued*
Cockfosters EN4 ... 15 A6
Redbridge IG1 ... 56 A2
Sutton SM1 ... 217 D6
Gloucester Gr HA8 ... 27 B2
Gloucester Ho NW6 ... 91 C5
Richmond TW10 ... 154 C6
Gloucester Lo 9 CR0 ... 221 D6
Gloucester Mews W2 ... 236 B1
Gloucester Mews W
W2 ... 236 B1
Gloucester Par DA15 ... 168 A6
Hayes UB3 ... 105 A3
Gloucester Pk SW7 ... 256 A4
Gloucester Pl
W1 ... 92 D2 237 D4
Gloucester Pl Mews
W1 ... 92 D2 237 D3
Gloucester Prim Sch
SE15 ... 139 C5
Gloucester Rd E10 ... 53 C2
E17 ... 34 D1
N17 ... 51 B6
SW7 ... 114 A3 256 A4
W5 ... 109 C4
Acton W3 ... 111 A4
Croydon CR0 ... 205 C2
Edmonton N18 ... 33 D5
Enfield EN2 ... 5 A5
Erith DA17 ... 125 B1
Feltham TW13 ... 150 C3
Hampton TW12 ... 173 D3
Harrow HA1 ... 41 D4
Hounslow TW4 ... 129 A1
Ilford E12 ... 78 B4
Kingston KT1,KT2 ... 176 D1
New Barnet EN5 ... 14 A6
Richmond TW9 ... 132 C5
Teddington TW11 ... 174 C5
Twickenham TW2 ... 152 A3
Wanstead E11 ... 55 C4
Gloucester Road Sta
SW7 ... 114 A2 256 A4
Gloucester Sq 6 E2 ... 96 A6
W2 ... 92 C1 237 A1
Gloucester St
SW1 ... 115 C1 259 A2
Gloucester Terr
W2 ... 92 A1 236 B1
Gloucester Way EC1 ... 234 B1
Gloucester Wlk
W8 ... 113 C4 245 B2
Glover Cl SE2 ... 124 C2
Glover Dr N18 ... 34 C4
Glover Ho 2 NW6 ... 70 A1
SE15 ... 140 B1
Glover Rd HA5 ... 40 D3
Glovers Gr HA4 ... 38 D2
Gloxinia Wlk TW12 ... 173 C4
Glycena Rd SW11 ... 136 D2
Glyn Ave EN4 ... 2 B1
Glyn Cl SE25 ... 183 C2
Glyn Ct SE27 ... 160 C1
Glyndale Grange SM2 217 D2
Glyndebourne Ct 5
UB5 ... 84 C4
Glyndebourne Pk BR6 226 D6
Glynde Mews SW3 ... 257 B5
Glynde Rd DA7 ... 147 A2
Glynde Reach WC1 ... 233 B1
Glynde St SE4 ... 163 B5
Glyndon Rd SE18 ... 123 B2
Glyn Dr DA14 ... 190 B6
Glynfield Rd NW10 ... 67 C1
Glyn Mans W14 ... 254 B4
Glynne Rd N22 ... 32 C1
Glyn Rd E5 ... 74 D4
Enfield EN3 ... 6 C1
North Cheam KT4,SM3 ... 216 D6
Glyn St SE11 ... 260 C1
Glynwood Ct SE23 ... 162 C2
Goater's Alley SW6 ... 264 D3
Goat La EN1 ... 5 D5
Goat Rd CR4 ... 202 D2
Goat Wharf TW8 ... 132 A6
Godalming Ave SM6 ... 220 B3
Godalming Rd E14 ... 97 D2
Godbold Rd E15 ... 98 C4
Goddard Cl TW17 ... 192 B6
Goddard Ho SW19 ... 156 D2
Goddard Pl N19 ... 71 C5
Goddard Rd BR3 ... 207 A5
Goddards Way IG1 ... 57 B1
Goddarts Ho E17 ... 53 C6
Godfrey Ave
Northolt UB5 ... 85 A6
Twickenham TW2 ... 152 B4
Godfrey Hill SE18 ... 122 A2
Godfrey Ho EC1 ... 235 C1
Godfrey Rd SE18 ... 122 B2
Godfrey St E15 ... 98 A5
SW3 ... 114 C1 257 B2
Godfrey Way TW4 ... 151 B4
Goding St
SE11 ... 116 A1 260 B1
Godley Rd SW18 ... 158 B3
Godliman St EC4 ... 252 A6
Godman Rd SE15 ... 140 B3
Godolphin Cl N13 ... 32 D4
Godolphin Ho NW3 ... 70 C1
7 Streatham SW2 ... 160 C3
Godolphin & Latymer Sch
W6 ... 112 B2
Godolphin Pl W3 ... 111 B6
Godolphin Rd W12 ... 112 B4
Godson Rd CR0 ... 220 C5
Godson St N1 ... 234 A4
Godstone Ct 1 N16 ... 51 C1
Godstone Ho SE1 ... 262 D6
1 Kingston KT2 ... 176 D4
Godstone Rd
Sutton SM1 ... 218 A4
Twickenham TW1 ... 153 B5
Godstow Rd SE2 ... 124 C4
Godwin Cl N1 ... 235 B4
West Ewell KT19 ... 215 A2
Godwin Ct NW1 ... 232 B4
Godwin Ho 2 E2 ... 95 D5
NW6 ... 91 D5
6 SE18 ... 144 B4
Godwin Jun Sch E7 ... 77 B4
Godwin Prim Sch RM9 ... 81 A1
Godwin Rd BR1,BR2 ... 209 C6
E7 ... 77 B4
Goffers Ho SE3 ... 142 C3
Goffers Rd SE3,SE13 ... 142 C3
Goffs Rd TW15 ... 171 B4
Goffton Ho 14 SW9 ... 138 B3
Goidel Cl SM6 ... 219 D4
Golborne Gdns W10 ... 91 B3
5 W10 ... 91 A3
Golborne Mews 9
W10 ... 91 A2
Golborne Rd W10 ... 91 A2
Golda Cl EN5 ... 12 D5
Goldbeaters Gr HA8 ... 27 C3
Goldbeaters Prim Sch
HA8 ... 27 B2
Goldcliff Cl SM4 ... 201 C2
Goldcrest Cl E16 ... 99 D2
Woolwich SE28 ... 124 C6
Goldcrest Mews W5 ... 87 D2
Goldcrest Way
Bushey WD23 ... 8 A3
New Addington CR0 ... 224 B1
Golden Cres UB3 ... 105 D5
Golden Cross Mews 8
W11 ... 91 B1
Golden Ct 4 Barnet EN4 ... 2 C1
Ealing W7 ... 108 C6
10 Richmond TW9 ... 153 D6
Golden Hind Pl 4 SE8 119 B2
Golden La EC1 .95 A3 242 B5
Golden Manor W7 ... 108 C6
Golden Mews SE20 ... 184 C2
Golden Par 2 E17 ... 54 A6
Golden Plover Cl E16 ... 99 A1
Golden Sq W1 115 C6 249 B6
Golders Cl HA8 ... 26 D5
Golders Ct NW11 ... 47 B2
Golders Gdns NW11 ... 47 B2
Golders Green Coll
NW11 ... 47 B1
Golders Green Cres
NW11 ... 47 C2
Golders Green Rd
NW11 ... 47 A2
Golders Green Sta
NW11 ... 47 C1
Golders Hill Sch NW11 ... 47 C2
Goldersiea NW11 ... 47 C1
Golders Manor Dr
NW11 ... 47 A3
Golders Park Cl NW11 ... 47 C1
Golders Rise NW4 ... 46 D4
Golders Way NW11 ... 47 B2
Golderton 2 NW4 ... 46 C5
Goldfinch Rd SE28 ... 123 B3
Goldhawk Ind Est The
W6 ... 112 B3
Goldhawk Mews 2
W12 ... 112 B4
Goldhawk Rd W12 ... 112 A3
Goldhawk Road Sta
W12 ... 112 C4
Goldhaze Cl IG8 ... 37 D3
Gold Hill HA8 ... 27 B4
Goldhurst Terr NW6 ... 70 A1
Goldie Ho N19 ... 49 D2
Goldie Leigh Hospl
SE2 ... 146 C6
Golding Cl KT9 ... 213 C2
Golding Ct 7 IG1 ... 78 C5
Golding St E1 ... 96 A1
Golding Terr 17 E1 ... 96 A1
Goldington Cres NW1 232 C4
Goldington Ct NW1 ... 232 C5
Goldington St
NW1 ... 93 D5 232 C4
Gold La HA8 ... 27 B4
Goldman Cl E2 ... 96 A3
Goldmark Ho SE3 ... 143 B2
Goldney Rd W9 ... 91 C3
Goldrill Dr N11 ... 15 A2
Goldsboro Rd
SW8 ... 137 D5 269 D3
Goldsborough Cres E4 .20 A2
Goldsborough Ho
SW8 ... 26
Goldsdown Cl EN3
Goldsdown Rd EN3
Goldsmid St 2 SE18 ... 12
Goldsmith Ave E12 ... 7
NW9 ... 4
W3 ... 11
Dagenham RM7 ... 5
Goldsmith Cl HA2 ... 4
Goldsmith Ct WC1 ... 24
Edgware HA8 ... 2
Goldsmith Ho W3 ... 11
Goldsmith La NW9 ... 45
Goldsmith Rd E10 ... 53
E17 ... 34
N11 ... 30
SE15 ... 140
W3 ... 11
Goldsmiths Bldgs W3 ... 11
Goldsmiths Cl W3 ... 11
Goldsmith's Coll, Univ of
London SE14 ... 141
Goldsmith's Ct N6 ... 49
Goldsmith's Pl 4 NW6 ... 91
Goldsmith's Row E2 ... 96
Goldsmith's Sq 16 E2 ... 96
Goldsmith St EC2 ... 242
Goldsworthy Gdns
SE16 ... 118
Goldthorpe NW1 ... 232
Goldwell Ho SE22 ... 139
Goldwell Rd CR7 ... 204
Goldwin Cl SE14 ... 140
Goldwing Cl E16 ... 99
Golf Cl
South Norwood SW16 ... 182
Stanmore HA7 ... 25
Golf Club Dr KT2 ... 177
Golfe Rd IG1 ... 79
Golf Rd BR1 ... 210
Ealing W5 ... 88
Golf Side TW2 ... 152
Golfside Cl N20 ... 14
Kingston KT3 ... 177
Goliath Cl SM6 ... 220
Gollogly Terr 9 SE7 ... 121
Gomer Gdns TW11 ... 175
Gomer Pl TW11 ... 175
Gomm Rd SE16 ... 118
Gomshall Ave SM6 ... 220
Gondar Gdns NW6 ... 69
Gondar Mans NW6 ... 69
Gonson St SE8 ... 141
Gonston Cl SW19 ... 157
Gonville Cres UB5 ... 63
Gonville Ho 6 SW15 ... 156
Gonville Prim Sch
CR7 ... 204
Gonville Rd CR7 ... 204
Gonville St SW6 ... 135
Gooch Ho E5 ... 74
EC1 ... 241
Goodall Ho 10 SE4 ... 140
Goodall Rd E11 ... 76
Goodbehere Ho 7
SE27 ... 183
Gooden Ct HA1 ... 64
Goodenough Rd SW19 179
Goodey Rd IG11 ... 79
Goodfaith Ho 16 E14 ... 119
Goodge Pl W1 ... 239
Goodge St W1 ... 93 C2 239
Goodge Street Sta
W1 ... 93 D2 239
Goodhall St NW10 ... 89
Good Hart Pl E14 ... 119
Goodhart Way BR4 ... 208
Goodhew Rd CR0 ... 206
Goodhope Ho 15 E14 ... 119
Gooding Cl KT3 ... 199
Goodinge Cl N7 ... 72
Goodinge Rd N7 ... 72
Gooding Ho 4 SE7 ... 121
Goodison Cl WD23 ... 8
Goodland Ho 1 KT3 ... 199
Goodman Cres SW2 ... 159
Goodman Rd E10 ... 54
Goodmans Ct HA0 ... 65
Goodman's Stile 12 E1 ... 96
Goodman's Yd
E1,EC3 ... 117 D6 253
Goodmayes Ave IG3 ... 58
Goodmayes Hospl IG3 ... 58
Goodmayes La IG3 ... 80
Goodmayes Prim Sch
IG3 ... 58
Goodmayes Rd IG3 ... 58
Goodmayes Ret Pk
RM6 ... 58
Goodmayes Sta IG3 ... 58
Goodrich Com Sch
SE22 ... 162
Goodrich Ct 9 W10 ... 90
Goodrich Ho 21 E2 ... 96
N16 ... 51
Goodrich Rd SE22 ... 162
Goodridge Ho E17 ... 36

d Shepherd RC Prim
n
ford BR1 ....150 D6
v Addington CR0 ...223 D1
d Shepherd RC Prim
n The W12 ......111 D4
dson Ho SM4 .....202 A2
dson Rd NW10 .....67 C1
dsway NW1 94 A5 233 A4
dway Gdns E14 ....98 B1
dwill Ho 19 E14 ..119 D6
dwin Cl
16 ......117 D3 263 D5
cham CR4 ....202 B6
dwin Ct N8 ....50 A6
st Barnet EN4 ......14 C5
dwin Dr DA14 ....168 D2
dwin Gdns CR0,
2 ....220 D2
dwin Ho N9 ....18 C3
SE15 ....140 B2
dwin Rd N9 ....18 D3
12 ....112 A4
oydon CR0 ....220 D3
dwins Ct WC2 ....250 A6
dwin St N4 ....72 C6
odwood Ave EN3 .....6 C6
odwood Cl
orden SM4 ....201 C5
Stanmore HA7 ....25 C5
odwood Ct W1 ....238 D4
odwood Dr UB5 .....63 C2
odwood Ho 3 W4 .111 A1
enge SE26 ....184 B4
odwood Mans 4
W9 ....138 C2
oodwood Par BR3 ...207 A5
oodwood Rd SE14 ...141 A5
odwyn Ave NW7 ....27 C5
odwyn Sch NW7 ....28 A5
odwyn's Vale N10 ...31 B2
odyear Ho 8 N2 ....30 B1
odyers Gdns NW4 ...46 D4
osander Ct 34 NW9 .27 D1
osander Way SE18,
28 ....123 B3
oseacre La HA3 ....43 D4
oose Green Cl BR5 ..190 A1
oose Green Trad Est
E22 ....140 A1
oseley La E6 ......100 C4
oose Sq 8 E6 ......100 B1
ossens Cl 1 SM1 ..218 A3
ophir La EC4 ......252 C6
opsall St N1 ..95 B6 235 D5
ordon Ave
Chingford E4 ....36 C4
Isleworth TW1 ....153 B6
Mortlake SW14 ....133 C1
Stanmore HA7 ....25 A4
ordonbrock Prim Sch
SE4 ....163 C6
ordonbrock Rd SE4 .163 C6
ordon Cl E17 ....53 C3
ordon Cres
Croydon CR0 ....205 D1
Hayes UB3 ....106 A2
ordon Ct W12 ....90 C1
17 Wimbledon SW20 ..178 D3
ordondale Rd SW18,
SW19 ....157 C2
ordon Dr TW17 .....193 B2
Gordon Gdns HA8 .....26 D1
Gordon Gr SE5 ......138 D3
Gordon Hill EN2 ......5 A4
Gordon Hill Sta EN2 ...4 D4
Gordon Ho 16 E1 ....118 C6
3 SE10 ....141 D5
SE12 ....165 A4
2 Ealing W5 ....88 A4
Gordon Hospl The
SW1 ....115 D2 259 C3
Gordon House Rd NW5 71 A4
Gordon Inf Sch IG1 ...79 B5
Gordon Lo N16 ....51 B1
Gordon Pl W8 .113 C4 245 B2
Gordon Prim Sch SE9 .144 B1
Gordon Rd DA15 .....167 C6
E15 ....76 A4
N11 ....31 D3
N3 ....29 B3
SE15 ....140 B3
Ashford TW15 ....148 A1
Barking IG11 ....101 C6
Beckenham BR3 ....207 B6
Chingford E4 ....20 C4
Chiswick W4 ....132 D6
Claygate KT10 ....212 C1
Dagenham RM6 ....59 B3
Ealing W13 ....109 C6
Edmonton N9 ....18 B2
Enfield EN2 ....5 B3
Harrow HA3 ....42 C6
Ilford IG1 ....79 B5
Isleworth TW3 ....130 A1
Kingston KT2 ....176 B2
Richmond TW9 ....132 B3
Shepperton TW17 .....193 B3
Southall UB2 ....107 A2

Gordon Rd *continued*
Surbiton KT5 ......198 B2
Wallington SM5 ......218 D2
Wanstead E11 ......55 A3
Woodford E18 ....37 B2
Yiewsley UB7 ....104 A6
Gordon Sq WC1 93 D3 239 D6
Gordon St E13 ......99 A4
WC1 ....93 D3 239 C6
Gordon Way BR1 ....187 A2
Barnet EN5 ....1 B1
Gore Ct NW9 ....44 C4
Gorefield Ho NW6 ....91 C5
Gorefield Pl NW6 ....91 C5
Gore Rd E9 ....96 C6
Merton SW20 ....178 C1
Goresbrook Rd RM9 ..102 D6
Gore St SW7 ..114 A3 256 B6
Gorham Ho 12 SW4 ...159 C5
Gorham Pl W11 ......244 A5
Goring Gdns RM8 .....80 C4
Goring Rd N11 ....32 A4
Goring St EC3 ......243 B2
Goring Way UB6 ......86 A5
Gorleston Rd N15 ....51 B4
Gorleston St
W14 ....113 A2 254 B4
Gorman Rd SE18 .....122 B2
Gorringe Park Ave
CR4 ....181 A3
Gorringe Park Prim Sch
CR4 ....181 A2
Gorse Cl E16 ....99 A1
Gorsefield Ho 5 E14 .119 C6
Gorse Rd CR0 ....223 C5
Gorse Rise SW17 ....181 A5
Gorse Wlk UB7 ......82 A1
Gorst Rd NW10 ....89 B3
SW11 ....158 D5
Gorsuch Pl 1 E2 .....95 D4
Gorsuch St E2 ....95 D4
Gosberton Rd SW12 ..159 A3
Gosbury Hill KT9 ....214 A4
Gosfield Rd RM8 .....59 C1
Gosfield St W1 .93 C2 239 A3
Gosford Gdns IG4 ....56 B4
Gosford Ho 21 E3 ....97 B5
Goshawk Gdns UB4 ...83 C5
Goslett Yd WC2 .....239 D2
Gosling Cl UB6 ......85 C4
Gosling Ho 1 E1 ....118 C6
Gosling Way SW9 ....138 C4
Gospatrick Rd N17 ...33 A2
Gospel Oak Prim Sch
NW5 ....71 A4
Gospel Oak Sta NW5 ...71 A4
Gosport Ho 9 SW15 ..156 A3
Gosport Rd E17 ......53 B4
Gosport Wlk N17 .....52 B5
Gossage Rd SE18 ....123 B1
Hillingdon UB10 .....60 B1
Gosset St E2 ....96 A4
Gosshill Rd BR7 .....188 C1
Gossington Cl BR7 ...188 D6
Gosterwood St SE8 ...141 A6
Gostling Rd TW2 ....151 C3
Goston Gdns CR7 ....204 C6
Goswell Pl EC1 .....234 D1
Goswell Rd EC1 94 D4 234 D2
Gothic Ct 17 SE5 ....139 A5
Harlington UB3 .....127 B6
Gothic Rd TW2 ......152 B2
Gottfried Mews NW5 ...71 C4
Goudhurst Ho 10 SE20 184 C3
Goudhurst Rd BR1 ...186 D5
Gough Ho N1 ....234 D6
4 Kingston KT1 ......176 A1
Gough Rd E15 ....76 D4
Enfield EN1 ....6 B3
Gough Sq EC4 ..94 C1 241 B2
Gough St WC1 .94 B3 240 D5
Gough Wlk 10 E14 ....97 C1
Gould Ct SE19 ....183 C5
Goulden Ho SW11 ....136 C3
Goulding Ct N8 ......50 B5
Goulding Gdns CR7 ...183 A1
Gould Rd
East Bedfont TW14 ...149 C4
Twickenham TW2 .....152 C3
Gould's Gn UB8 .....104 D6
Gould Terr 26 E8 ....74 B3
Goulston St E1 .95 D1 243 C2
Goulton Rd E5 ....74 B4
Gourley Pl N15 ......51 C4
Gourley St N15 ......51 C4
Gourock Rd SE9 .....166 C6
Govan St E2 ....96 A6
Gover Ct 8 SW4 ....138 A3
Government Row EN3 ...7 C6
Govett Ave TW17 ....193 A4
Govier Cl E15 ....76 C1
Gowan Ave
SW6 ....135 A4 264 A2
Gowan Ho 22 E2 ......95 D4
Gowan Lea 4 E18 .....55 A5
Gowan Rd NW10 ....68 B2
Gower Cl SW4 ....159 C5
Gower Ct WC1 ....239 C6

Gower Ho 12 E17 .....53 D6
SE17 ....262 B2
Barking IG11 ....79 A1
Hayes UB3 ....105 C6
Upper Tooting SW17 ...180 B4
Gower House Sch NW9 67 A6
Gower Mews WC1 ....239 D4
Gower Pl NW1,
WC1 ....93 D3 239 C6
Gower Rd E7 ....77 A2
Hounslow TW7 ....130 D6
Gower St WC1 .93 D3 239 C5
Gower's Wlk E1 ......96 A1
Gowland Pl BR3 .....185 B1
Gowlett Rd SE15 ....140 A2
Gowrie Rd SW11 ....137 A2
Graburn Way KT8 ....196 B6
Grace Ave DA7 ......147 B3
Grace Bsns Ctr CR4 ..202 D3
Gracechurch St EC2,
EC4 ....252 D6
Grace Cl HA8 ....27 A3
SE9 ....165 D1
Gracedale Rd SW16 ..181 B5
Gracefield Gdns SW16 160 A1
Gracehill 2 E1 ....96 C2
Grace Ho SE11 ......270 D6
Penge SE26 ....184 B5
Grace Jones Cl E8 ....74 A2
Grace Path SE26 ....184 C6
Grace Pl E3 ....97 D4
Grace Rd CR0 ....205 A3
Graces Mews NW8 ....229 B3
Grace's Mews SE5 ...139 C3
Grace's Rd SE5 .....139 C3
Grace St E3 ....97 D4
Gradient The SE26 ...184 A6
Graeme Rd EN1 ....5 C3
Graemesdyke Ave
SW14 ....132 D1
Grafton Cl Ealing W13 ..87 A1
Twickenham TW4 ....151 B3
Worcester Park KT4 ..215 C5
Grafton Cres NW1 ....71 B2
Grafton Ct 10 E8 .....74 A3
East Bedfont TW14 ...149 B3
Grafton Gdns N4 .....51 A3
Dagenham RM8 ....81 A6
Grafton Ho 15 E3 ....97 C4
12 SE8 ....119 B1
Grafton Inf Sch RM8 ..81 B6
Grafton Jun Sch RM8 ..81 B6
Grafton Mews W1 ....239 A5
Grafton Park Rd KT4 .215 C6
Grafton Pl NW1 93 D4 232 D1
Grafton Prim Sch N7 ..72 A5
Grafton Rd NW5 ......71 A3
W3 ....111 A6
Dagenham RM8 ....81 A6
Enfield EN2 ....4 B2
Harrow HA1 ....42 A4
Kingston KT3 ....199 C6
Thornton Heath CR0 ...204 C1
Worcester Park KT4 ..215 C5
Grafton Sq SW4 .....137 C2
Grafton St W1 115 B6 248 D5
Grafton Terr NW5 ....71 A3
Grafton Way W1 .....239 B5
East Molesey KT8 ....195 B5
Grafton Yd NW5 .....71 B2
Graham Ave W13 ....109 B4
Mitcham CR4 ....181 A2
Graham Cl CR0 ......223 C6
Graham Ct BR1 ......187 B3
5 SE14 ....140 D6
Northolt UB5 ....63 B3
Grahame Park Way
NW7,NW9 ....27 D2
Grahame White Ho
HA3 ....43 D6
Graham Gdns KT6 ....198 A1
Graham Ho 7 N19 ....71 D4
N9 ....18 C3
5 Balham SW12 ......159 B4
Woolwich SE18 ......144 D5
Graham Lo NW4 ......46 B3
Graham Mans 2 E8 ...74 B2
11 Barking IG11 .....80 A1
Graham Rd DA7 .....147 C1
E13 ....99 A3
E8 ....74 A2
N15 ....50 D6
NW4 ....46 B3
W4 ....111 B3
Hampton TW12 ....173 C6
Harrow HA3 ....42 C6
Merton SW19 ....179 B3
Mitcham CR4 ....181 A2
Graham St N1 .94 D5 234 D3
Graham Terr
SW1 ......115 A2 258 B3
Grainger Cl UB5 .....64 A3
Grainger Ct 22 SE5 ..139 A5
Grainger Rd
Isleworth TW7 ......130 D3
Tottenham N22 ....33 A2
Gramer Cl E11 ......76 B6
Grampian Cl BR6 ....211 D3
Harlington UB3 ......127 B5

Grampian Cl *continued*
15 Sutton SM2 ......218 A1
Grampian Gdns NW2 ..47 A1
Grampians The 10
W14 ....112 D4
Granada St SW17 ....180 D5
Granard Ave SW15 ...156 B6
Granard Bsns Ctr NW7 .27 C4
Granard Ho 20 E9 ....74 D2
Granard Prim Sch
SW15 ....156 B5
Granard Rd SW11,
SW12 ....158 D4
Granary Cl N9 ....18 C4
Granary Ct 3 RM6 ....58 D2
Granary Rd E1 ....96 B3
Granary St NW1 93 D6 232 C5
Granby Ho 14 SE18 ..122 B2
Granby Pl SE1 ......251 A1
Granby Rd SE18 ....122 D3
SE9 ....144 B2
Granby St E2 ..96 A3 243 D6
Granby Terr
NW1 ....93 C5 232 A3
Grand Arc N12 ....30 A5
Grand Ave EC1 ......241 D4
N10 ....49 A5
Tolworth KT5 ....198 D3
Wembley HA9 ....66 C3
Grand Ave E HA9 .....66 D3
Grand Avenue Prim Sch
KT5 ....199 A3
Grand Ct RM8 ....81 A5
Grand Depot Rd SE18 .122 C1
Grand Dr Southall UB2 .108 A4
West Barnes SM4,SW20 200 C5
Granden Rd SW16 ...182 A1
Grandfield Ct W4 ....133 B6
Grandison Rd SW11 ..158 D6
North Cheam KT4 ....216 C5
Grand Junction Wharf
N1 ....235 A3
Grand Par N4 ....50 D3
Mortlake SW14 ......133 A1
Tolworth KT6 ....198 C1
Wembley HA9 ....66 C6
Grand Union Cl W9 ....91 B2
Grand Union Cres E8 ..96 A6
Grand Union Ind Est
NW10 ....88 D5
Grand Union Way UB2 107 C4
Grand Vitesse Ind Est
SE1 ....251 D3
Granfield St SW11 ...266 D1
Grange Ave N12 ......30 A5
Barnet N20 ....13 A4
Barnet, London EN4 ...14 D3
South Norwood SE25 ..183 C1
Stanmore HA7 ....25 C1
Twickenham TW2 .....152 C2
Woodford IG8 ....37 A3
Grange Cl DA15 .....168 A1
HA8 ....27 A5
East Molesey KT8 ....195 D5
Hayes UB3 ....83 C2
Heston TW5 ....129 B6
Woodford IG8 ....37 A3
Grangecliffe Gdns
SE25 ....183 C1
Grangecourt Rd N16 ..51 C1
Grange Cres SE28 ...102 C1
Grange Ct SE15 ....139 D3
WC2 ....240 D1
Belmont SM2 ....217 D1
Hackbridge SM6 ....219 B5
Littleton TW17 .....192 C5
Loughton IG10 ....21 D6
Northolt UB5 ....84 C5
Pinner HA5 ....41 A6
Harrow HA1 ....64 D5
Grange Dr BR7 .....188 B4
Grange Farm Cl HA2 ..64 A6
Grange Farm Cvn Pk
TW17 ....193 C6
Grangefield NW1 .....72 A1
Grange Fst & Mid Schs
HA2 ....41 D1
Grange Gdns N14 ....15 D3
NW3 ....69 D5
Pinner HA5 ....41 A5
South Norwood SE25 ..183 C1
Grange Gr N1 ....73 A2
Grange Hill HA8 .....27 A5
South Norwood SE25 ..183 C1
Grangehill Pl SE9 ...144 B2
Grangehill Rd SE9 ...144 B1
Grange Ho NW10 .....68 B1
SE1 ....263 C5
6 Barking IG11 .....101 B6
Grange Inf Sch E13 ...98 D4
Grange La SE21 .....161 D2
Grange Lo SW19 ....178 D4
Grange Mans KT17 ...215 D1
Grangemill 11 NW5 ...71 B4
Grangemill Rd SE6 ...163 C2
Grange Mills SW12 ..159 C3
Grangemill Way SE6 ..163 C2
Grange Mus of Community
History The★ NW10 ...67 C4

Grange Park Ave N21 ..17 A5
Grange Park Jun & Inf Schs
UB4 ....83 D3
Grange Park Pl SW20 .178 B3
Grange Park Prep Sch
N21 ....16 D5
Grange Park Rd E10 ...53 D1
South Norwood CR7 ...205 B6
Grange Park Sta N21 ..16 D5
Grange Pk W5 ....110 A5
Grange Pl NW6 ....69 C1
Grange Prim Sch
SE1 ....117 C3 263 A5
W5 ....109 D4
Grange Rd E10 ....53 C1
E13 ....98 D4
E17 ....53 A4
HA8 ....27 B4
N6 ....49 A3
NW10 ....68 B2
SE1 ....117 D3 263 C5
W4 ....110 D1
Barnes SW13 ....134 A4
Belmont SM2 ....217 C1
Borehamwood WD6 ....10 B6
Chessington KT9 ...214 A4
Ealing W5 ....110 A5
East Molesey KT8 ...195 D5
Harrow HA1 ....43 A4
Harrow HA2 ....64 B6
Hayes UB3 ....83 C1
Ilford IG1 ....79 A4
Kingston KT1 ....198 A6
Orpington BR6 .....227 A6
Southall UB1 ......107 A4
South Norwood SE19,
SE25 ....183 B1
Tottenham N17 ......34 A4
Grange St N1 ......235 D5
Grange The 3 E17 ....53 A4
19 NW3 ....70 D2
SE1 ....117 D3 263 C5
W12 ....112 B3
W14 ....113 B2 254 C3
W3 ....110 D4
7 W4 ....110 D1
Cockfosters EN4 ......2 D2
Croydon CR0 ....223 B6
Ealing W13 ....87 C2
3 Wanstead E18 ......55 A6
Wembley HA0 ....66 C1
West Barnes KT3 ....200 A4
West Ewell KT19 ....215 B4
Wimbledon SW19 ....178 D4
Grange The(Eltham Coll
Jun Sch) SE9 ......165 D3
Grange Vale SM2 ....217 D1
Grangeview Rd N20 ...14 A3
Grangeway N12 ....29 D6
NW6 ....69 C1
Woodford IG8 ....37 C6
Grangeway Gdns IG4 ..56 A4
Grangeway The N21 ...16 D5
Grange Wlk
SE1 ....117 D3 263 C5
Grangewood DA5 ....169 B3
Grangewood Cl HA5 ...40 A4
Grangewood Ind Sch
E7 ....77 D1
Grangewood La BR3 ..185 B4
Grangewood Sch HA5 .39 D4
Grangewood St E6 ....99 D6
Grange Yd
SE1 ....117 D3 263 C5
Granham Gdns N9 ....17 D2
Granite St SE18 ....123 D1
Granleigh Rd E11 ....76 C6
Gransden Ave E8 .....74 B1
Gransden Ho 1 SE8 ..119 B1
Gransden Rd W12 ....111 D4
Grantbridge St
N1 ....94 D5 234 D4
Grantchester 12 KT1 ..176 C1
Grantchester Cl HA1 ..64 D5
Grant Cl N14 ....15 C4
Shepperton TW17 ....192 D3
Grant Ct 11 NW9 ......27 D1
2 Chingford E4 ....20 A3
Grantham Cl HA8 .....10 A1
Grantham Ct 9 SE16 .118 D4
Dagenham RM6 ....59 B2
Grantham Gdns RM6 ...59 B2
Grantham Gn WD6 ....11 A6
Grantham Ho 12 SE15 140 A6
Ashford TW16 ......171 C3
Grantham Pl W1 ....248 C3
Grantham Rd SW9 ...138 A3
Chiswick W4 ....133 C5
Little Ilford E12 .....78 C4
Grant Ho 38 SW8 ....137 D3
Grantley Ho 2 SE14 ..140 D6
5 Putney SW19 ......156 D3
Grantley Pl KT10 ...212 A3
Grantley Rd TW4,TW5 .128 C3
Grantley St E1 ......96 D3
Grantock Rd E17 .....36 B2
Granton Prim Sch
SW16 ....181 C3
Granton Rd Ilford IG3 ..58 A1

Granton Rd *continued*
Sidcup DA14 ....190 C4
Streatham SW16 .....181 C2
Grant Pl 2 CR0 .....205 D1
Grant Rd SW11 ......136 C2
Croydon CR0 ....205 D1
Harrow HA3 ....42 D6
Grants Cl NW7 ....28 D3
Grants Cotts KT10 ...212 B6
Grant St E13 ....99 A4
N1 ....234 A4
Grantully Rd W9 .....91 D4
Grant Way TW7 .....131 A6
Granville Ave N9 .....18 C1
Feltham TW13 ......150 A2
Hounslow TW3,TW4 ...151 C6
Granville Cl CR0 ....221 C6
Granville Ct N1 .....235 D6
N4 ....50 B3
8 SE14 ....141 A5
Granville Gdns
Ealing W5 ....110 B5
South Norwood SW16 ..182 B3
Granville Gr SE13 ...142 A2
Granville Ho 13 E14 ...97 C1
Granville Mans
8 W12 ....112 C4
WC1 ....240 A6
Granville Mews
Sidcup DA14 ....190 A6
Stanmore HA7 ....25 A5
Granville Pk SE13 ...142 B2
Granville Pl N12 .....30 A3
SW6 ....265 C3
W1 ....93 A1 238 A1
Pinner HA5 ....40 D6
Granville Point NW2 ..69 B6
Granville Rd E17 .....53 D3
N12 ....30 A3
N4,N8 ....50 B3
NW2 ....69 B6
NW6 ....91 C5
Bexley DA16 ....146 C2
Bowes Park N13 ......32 B4
Hayes UB3 ....105 D2
Hillingdon UB10 .....60 D2
Ilford IG1 ....78 D6
Merton SW19 ....179 C3
Sidcup DA14 ....190 B6
Tottenham N22 ......32 D2
Wandsworth SW18 ...157 B4
Woodford E18 ....37 B1
Granville Sq 8 SE15 ..139 C5
WC1 ....94 B4 233 D1
Granville St WC1 ...233 D1
Granwood Ct 5 TW7 .130 C4
Grape St WC2 ......240 A2
Grapsome Cl KT9 ...213 C1
Grasdene Rd SE18,SE2 146 A5
Grasmere NW1 ......231 D1
Grasmere Ave BR6 ...226 D5
W3 ....111 B6
Kingston SW15 .....177 C6
Merton SW19 ....201 C6
Ruislip HA4 ....39 A2
Twickenham TW3 ....151 D5
Wembley HA9 ....43 D1
Grasmere Cl TW14 ...149 D3
Grasmere Ct
Barnes SW13 ....134 A6
Bowes Park N22 .....32 B4
Forest Hill SE26 ...184 A5
Grasmere Gdns BR6 ..226 D5
Harrow HA3 ....25 A1
Redbridge IG4 ......56 B4
Grasmere Ho 10 N16 ...73 B4
Grasmere JMI Sch N16 73 B4
Grasmere Point 2
SE15 ....140 C5
Grasmere Rd BR6 ...226 D5
3 E13 ....99 A5
N10 ....31 B2
Bromley BR1 ....186 D3
Croydon SE25 ......206 B4
Streatham SW16 ....182 B5
Tottenham N17 ......34 A4
Grasshaven Way SE28 123 D5
Grassington Cl N11 ...31 A4
Grassington Rd DA14 .190 A6
Grassmere Ct 6 EN1 ...17 C6
Grassmount SE23 ...162 B2
Grass Pk N3 ....29 B2
Grassway SM6 ......219 C4
Grasvenor Ave EN5 ...13 C5
Grasvenor Avenue Inf Sch
EN5 ....13 C5
Grately Ho 10 SW15 ..156 B3
Gratton Rd
W14 ....113 A3 254 A5
Gratton Terr NW2 ....68 D5
Graveley 16 KT1 ....176 C1
Graveley Ave WD6 ...11 A6
Graveley Ho 7 SE8 ..119 A2
Gravel Hill DA6 ....169 D6
N3 ....29 B1
South Croydon CR0,CR2 .223 B1

Gravel Hill Cl DA5,DA6 169 D5
Gravel Hill Prim Sch DA6 169 D6
Gravel Hill Sta CR0 223 A2
Gravel La E1 95 D1 243 C2
Gravel Rd BR2 226 A6
Twickenham TW2 152 C3
Gravelwood Cl BR7 167 A1
Gravenel Gdns 5 SW17 180 C5
Graveney Gr SE20 184 C3
Graveney Rd SW17 180 C6
Graveney Sch SW17 181 B5
Gravesend Rd W12 112 A6
Graves Est DA16 146 B3
Gray Ave RM8 59 B1
Gray Ct 8 KT2 175 D6
Grayfriars Pas EC1 241 D2
Grayham Cres KT3 199 B5
Grayham Rd KT3 199 B5
Gray Ho SE17 262 B2
Grayland Cl BR1 187 D2
Grayland Ct WC1 233 C1
Grayling Cl E16 98 C3
Grayling Ct N17 52 B5
Ealing W5 109 D5
Grayling Rd N16 73 B6
Grayling Sq E2 96 A4
Grays Cotts UB9 38 C1
Grayscroft Rd SW16 181 D3
Grays Farm Prim Sch BR5 190 B2
Grays Farm Production Village BR5 190 B2
Grays Farm Rd BR5 190 B2
Grayshott Rd SW11 137 A2
Gray's Inn★ WC1 94 B2 240 D4
Gray's Inn Pl WC1 240 D3
Gray's Inn Rd WC1 94 B3 240 D6
Gray's Inn Sq WC1 94 C2 241 A4
Grays La TW15 170 D6
Grayson Ho EC1 235 B1
Gray's Rd UB10 60 A1
Gray St SE1 116 C4 251 B1
Grayswood Gdns SW20 178 B1
Grayswood Point 14 SW15 156 A3
Gray's Yd W1 238 B2
Graywood Ct N12 30 A3
Grazebrook Prim Sch N16 73 C6
Grazebrook Rd N16 73 B6
Grazeley Ct SE19 183 C5
Great Arthur Ho EC1 242 A5
Great Bell Alley EC2 242 C2
Great Benty UB7 104 A2
Great Brownings SE21 183 D6
Great Bushey Dr N20 13 D3
Great Cambridge Ind Est EN1 18 B6
Great Cambridge Junction N13,N18 33 B6
Great Cambridge Rd
Edmonton N9,N18 17 C3
Enfield EN1 6 A3
Great Castle St W1 239 A2
Great Central Ave HA4 62 C3
Great Central St NW1 92 D2 237 C4
Great Central Way NW10 67 B4
Great Chapel St W1 93 D1 239 C2
Great Chertsey Rd
Chiswick SW14,W4 133 B4
Feltham TW13,TW2 151 C1
Great Church La W6 112 D1
Great College St SW1 116 A3 260 A6
Great Croft WC1 233 B1
Great Cumberland Mews W1 237 C1
Great Cumberland Pl W1 92 D1 237 D1
Great Dover St SE1 117 B3 262 C6
Greatdown Rd W7 86 D2
Great Eastern Bldgs 10 E8 74 B2
Great Eastern Ent Ctr E14 119 D4
Great Eastern Pier E14 119 C1
Great Eastern Rd E15 76 B2
Great Eastern St EC2 95 C3 243 A6
Great Eastern Wharf SW11 267 B3
Great Elms Rd BR2 209 C5
Great Field 7 NW5 71 C3
NW9 27 D2
Greatfield Ave E6 100 B3
Greatfield Cl 4 N19 71 C4
SE4 141 C1
Greatfields Dr UB8 82 C2
Greatfields Rd IG11 101 B5
Great Fleete Way IG11 102 C5
Great Galley Cl IG11 102 C4
Great Gatton Cl CR0 207 A2
Great George St SW1 116 A4 250 A1
Great Guildford St SE1 117 A5 252 A3
Great Guilford Bsns Sq SE1 252 A3
Greatham Wlk 8 SW15 156 A3
Great Harry Dr SE9 166 C1
Great James St WC1 240 C4
Great Marlborough St W1 93 C1 239 A1
Great Mathers Rd SE11 261 C4
Great Maze Pond SE1 117 B4 252 D2
Great Newport St WC2 250 A6
Great New St EC4 94 C1 241 B2
Great North Rd N2 48 C5
Barnet EN5 1 A2
New Barnet EN5 13 D6
Great North Way (Barnet By-Pass) NW4 46 D6
Greatorex Ho 12 E1 96 A2
Greatorex St E1 96 A2
Great Ormond St WC1 94 B3 240 C5
Great Ormond St Hospl for Children WC1 94 B3 240 C5
Great Percy St WC1 94 C4 234 A2
Great Peter St SW1 115 D3 259 D5
Great Portland St W1 93 B2 238 D4
Great Portland Street Sta W1 93 B3 238 D5
Great Pulteney St W1 249 B6
Great Queen St WC2 94 A1 240 B2
Great Russell St WC1 94 A2 240 A3
Great Scotland Yd SW1,WC2 116 A5 250 A4
Great Smith St SW1 115 D3 259 D6
Great South West Rd TW6,TW14,TW4 126 B4
Great South-West Rd TW5 128 B2
Great Spilmans SE22 161 C6
Great St Helen's EC3 243 A2
Greatstone Ho 13 SE20 184 C3
Great Strand NW9 27 D1
Great St Thomas Apostle EC4 252 B6
Great Suffolk St SE1 116 D4 251 D3
Great Sutton St EC1 94 D3 241 D5
Great Swan Alley EC2 242 C2
Great Thrift BR5 211 A5
Great Titchfield St W1 93 C2 239 A3
Great Tower St EC3 117 C6 253 A6
Great Trinity La EC4 252 B6
Great Turnstile WC2 240 D3
Great Western Ind Pk UB2 108 A4
Great Western Rd W2, W9 91 B2
Great West Rd
Brentford TW7,TW8 131 B6
Chiswick W4,W6 133 B6
Heston TW5,TW7 129 B4
Hounslow TW5 129 B4
Hounslow TW5,TW7 130 B5
Great West Road Cedars Rd W4 133 A6
Great West Road Hogarth La W4 133 C6
Great West Trad Est TW8 131 B6
Great Winchester St EC2 95 B1 242 D2
Great Windmill St W1 115 D6 249 C6
Greatwood BR7 188 C3
Great Yd SE1 253 B2
Greaves Cl IG11 79 C1
Greaves Cotts 12 E14 97 A2
Greaves Pl SW17 180 C6
Greaves Twr SW10 266 B4
Grebe 3 NW9 27 D1
Grebe Ave UB4 84 D1
Grebe Cl E17 35 A3
Grebe Cl *continued*
E7 76 D3
Barking IG11 102 A3
Grebe Ct 11 E14 120 A4
Cheam SM1 217 B3
Grebe Terr 4 KT1 198 A6
Grecian Cres SE19 182 D4
Greek Ct W1 239 D1
Greek St W1 93 D1 239 D1
Greenacre Cl Barnet EN5 1 B5
Northolt UB5 63 B3
Greenacre Ct E8 74 A3
Greenacre Gdns E17 54 A5
Greenacre Pl SM6 219 B6
Greenacres N3 29 A1
SE9 166 C5
Green Acres DA14 189 D6
Greenacres WD23 8 B2
Green Acres CR0 221 D5
Greenacres Ave UB10 60 C5
Greenacres Cl BR6 227 A4
Greenacres Dr HA7 25 B3
Greenacres Prim Sch SE9 166 C2
Greenacre Sq 26 SE16 118 D4
Greenacre Wlk N14 15 D1
Green Arbour Ct EC1 241 C2
Green Ave NW7 27 C6
W13 109 B3
Greenaway Gdns NW3 69 D4
Greenaway Ho NW8 229 A6
WC1 234 A1
Greenaway Terr TW19 148 A3
Green Bank E1 118 B5
N12 29 D6
Greenbank Ave HA0 65 A3
Greenbank Cl E4 20 A2
Greenbank Cres NW4 47 A5
Greenbank Lo 2 BR7 188 C2
Greenbanks HA1 64 C4
Greenbay Rd SE7 143 D5
Greenberry St NW8 230 A3
Greenbrook Ave EN4 2 A4
Green CE Prim Sch The N17 51 D6
Green CE Sch Holy Trinity (Infants' Annexe) The N15 51 D5
Green Cl NW11 48 A2
NW9 45 A3
Beckenham BR2 208 C6
Carshalton SM5 218 D6
Feltham TW13 173 A5
Greencoat Ho 13 KT1 176 A1
Greencoat Pl SW1 115 C2 259 B4
Greencoat Row SW1 259 B5
Greencourt Ave HA8 26 D2
Green Court Ave CR0 222 B6
Green Court Gdns CR0 222 B6
Greencourt Ho E1 96 D3
Greencourt Rd BR5 211 C4
Greencroft HA8 27 A5
Greencroft Ave HA4 62 C6
Greencroft Cl E16 99 D2
Greencroft Gdns NW6 70 A1
Enfield EN1 5 C2
Greencroft Rd TW5 129 B4
Green Ct TW16 171 D4
Greendale NW7 27 C6
Green Dale SE22 161 C6
Greendale Cl SE22 161 C6
Greendale Ct CR2 221 A2
Green Dr UB1 107 C5
Green Dragon Ct SE1 252 C3
Green Dragon Ho WC1 240 B2
Green Dragon Jun & Inf Sch TW8 132 A6
Green Dragon La
Brentford TW8 110 B1
Southgate N21 16 D5
Green Dragon Yd 21 E1 96 A2
Greene Ct 20 SE14 140 D6
Greene Ho SE1 262 C5
Green Elms IG6 57 A6
Green End
Chessington KT9 214 A4
Edmonton N21 16 D2
Greenend Rd W4 111 C4
Greener Ho 3 SW4 137 D2
Green Farm Cl BR6 227 D3
Greenfell Mans SE8 141 D6
Greenfield Ave KT5 198 D3
Greenfield Dr BR1 187 C1
N2 48 D5
Greenfield Gdns BR5 211 B2
NW2 69 A5
Dagenham RM9 102 D6
Greenfield Ho 28 SW19 156 D3
Greenfield Rd E1 96 A1
N15 51 C4
Dagenham RM9 102 C6
Greenfields UB1 85 C1
Greenfields JMI Sch WD19 22 C5
Greenfields Sch N10 30 D2
Greenfield Way HA2 41 D6
Greenford Ave
Ealing W7 86 C1
Southall UB1 107 B6
Greenford Gdns UB6 86 A4
Greenford High Sch UB6 85 C4
Greenford Ind Est UB6 85 D6
Greenford Rd
Greenford UB6 86 A3
Greenford, Harrow HA1, UB6 64 C3
Sutton SM1 217 D4
Greenford Rdbt UB6 86 B5
Greenford Sta UB6 86 B6
Greengate UB6 65 B2
Greengate St E13 99 B4
Green Gdns BR6 227 A3
Greenhalgh Wlk N2 48 A5
Greenham Cl SE1 251 A1
Greenham Cres E4 35 B4
Greenham Ho 6 E9 96 C6
Isleworth TW7 130 B2
Greenham Rd N10 31 A1
Greenhaven Dr SE28 102 B1
Greenheath Bsns Ctr 3 E2 96 B3
Green Hedges 8 TW1 153 C5
Greenheys Dr E18 54 D6
Greenhill HA9 66 D6
NW3 70 B4
Buckhurst Hill IG9 21 C3
Sutton SM1 218 A6
Green Hill SE18 122 B1
Greenhill Cts SE7 122 B1
Greenhill Gdns UB5 85 B5
Greenhill Gr E12 78 A4
Greenhill Par EN5 13 D6
Greenhill Pk NW10 89 C6
New Barnet EN5 13 D6
Greenhill Rd NW10 89 C6
Harrow HA1 42 C3
Greenhill's Rents EC1 241 C4
Greenhills Terr 16 N1 73 B2
Greenhill Terr
Northolt UB5 85 B5
Woolwich SE18 122 B1
Greenhill Way HA9 66 D6
Harrow HA1 42 C3
Greenhithe Cl SE9 167 C4
Greenholm Rd SE9 166 D6
Green Ho The 5 SW19 157 A3
Green Hundred Rd SE15 140 A6
Greenhurst Rd SE27 182 C5
Greening St SE2 124 C2
Green La NW4 46 D4
SE9 166 D1
W7 108 C4
Ashford TW16 171 D4
Chessington KT9 214 A1
Dagenham RM8 81 B6
East Molesey KT8 195 D4
Edgware HA8 26 C5
Feltham TW13 173 A5
Hillingdon UB8 83 A2
Hounslow TW4 128 C1
Ilford IG1 79 C6
Ilford IG3 79 C6
Morden SM4 201 D3
New Malden KT3 199 A4
New Malden KT4 200 A1
Penge SE20 184 D3
Shepperton TW17 193 A4
South Norwood CR7, SW16 182 C2
Stanmore HA7 25 B5
Greenland Cres UB2 106 D3
Greenland Ho 4 E1 97 A3
SE8 118 D1
Greenland Mews SE8 118 D1
Greenland Pl NW1 231 D6
Greenland Quay SE16 118 D2
Greenland Rd
NW1 93 C6 232 A6
Barnet EN5 12 C5
Greenlands
Borehamwood WD6 11 B5
Chessington KT19 214 D3
Greenland St NW1 231 D6
Green Lane Bsns Pk SE9 166 C2
Green Lane Cotts HA7 25 B6
Green Lane Gdns CR7 183 A1
Green Lane Mews SM4 201 D3
Green Lane Prim Sch KT4 200 B2
Green Lanes N4,N8,N15 50 D2
Palmers Green N13 16 C1
West Ewell KT19 215 C1
Greenlaw Ct W5 87 D1
Greenlaw Gdns KT3 199 D2
Greenlawns N12 29 D4
Green Lawns 8 SE18 122 D2
Ruislip HA4 40 C1
Greenlaw St SE18 122 C3
Green Leaf Ave SM6 219 D4
Greenleaf Cl 8 SW2 160 C4
Greenleafe Dr IG6 56 D6
Greenleaf Prim Sch E17 53 B6
Greenleaf Rd E17 53 B6
6 E6 99 C6
Greenlea Pk SW19 180 C2
Green Leas
Ashford TW16 171 D4
Kingston KT1 198 A6
Green Leas Cl TW16 171 D4
Greenleaves Ct TW15 170 D4
Green Man Gdns W13 109 A6
Green Man Intc E11 54 D2
Green Man La
Ealing W13 109 A5
Hatton TW14 128 A1
Greenman St N1 95 A6 235 A6
Greenmead Cl SE25 206 A4
Greenmead Sch SW15 156 B6
Green Moor Link N21 16 D4
Greenmoor Rd EN3 6 C3
Greenoak Pl EN4 2 D3
Green Oaks UB2 106 D2
Greenoak Way SW19 178 D6
Greenock Rd 11 W3 111 A3
Mitcham SW16 181 D2
Greeno Cres TW17 192 C4
Green Park★ SW1,W1 115 B4 248 D2
Green Park Sta W1 115 C5 249 A4
Green Pond Cl E17 53 B6
Green Pond Rd E17 53 A6
Green Pt E15 76 C2
Green Rd N20 14 A1
East Barnet N14 15 B5
Green Ride IG10,E4 21 A6
Greenrigg Wlk HA9 66 D5
Greenroof Way SE10 120 D3
Green Sch for Girls The TW7 131 A4
Greens Ct W1 249 C6
Green's Ct W11 244 C3
Greens Ct HA9 65 D5
Greens End SE18 122 D2
Greenshank Cl E17 35 A3
Greenshields Ind Est E16 121 B5
Greenside DA5 169 A3
Dagenham RM8 58 C1
Greenside Cl N20 14 B2
Catford SE6 164 B2
Greenside Prim Sch W12 112 A4
Greenside Rd W12 112 A4
Thornton Heath CR0 204 C2
Greenslade Prim Sch SE18 145 B6
Greenslade Rd IG11 79 B1
Greensleeves Ho UB2 107 D2
Greensleeves Manor SM2 217 D2
Green St E13 99 C6
E7 77 C1
W1 115 A6 248 A6
Enfield EN3 6 D3
Sunbury TW16 172 A1
Greenstead Ave IG8 37 C4
Greenstead Cl IG8 37 C4
Greenstead Gdns
Putney SW15 156 B6
Woodford IG8 37 C4
Greenstone Mews E11 55 A3
Green Street Green Prim Sch BR6 227 D2
Greenstreet Hill SE4 140 D2
Green Terr EC1 234 B1
Green The BR1 165 A1
DA16 145 C1
DA7 147 C4
E15 76 D2
N14 15 D1
W3 89 C1
Chingford E4 20 B3
Claygate KT10 212 D2
Ealing W5 109 D6
Edmonton N9 18 A2
Feltham TW13 150 B2
Hackbridge SM6 219 A6
Hayes BR2 209 A2
Heston TW5 129 C6
Kingston KT3 177 A1
Merton SM4 201 A5
7 Richmond TW9 153 D6
Sidcup DA14 190 A5
Southall UB2 107 B4
Southgate N21 16 C4
St Paul's Cray BR5 190 B3
Sutton SM1 217 D5
Tottenham N17 33 A4
Twickenham TW2 152 C2
Uxbridge UB10 61 A6
Wallington SM5 219 A4
Wanstead E11 55 B3
Wembley HA0 65 A6
Wimbledon SW19 178 D5
Green The *continued*
Woodford IG8 3
Buckhurst Hill IG9 2
Green Vale DA6 16
Ealing W5 8
Greenvale Rd SE9 14
Greenvale Specl Sch SE23 16
Green Verges HA7 2
Green View KT9 21
Greenview Ave CR0 20
Greenview Cl W3 11
Greenview Ct TW15 17
Greenway N20 1
Green Way BR2 21
Greenway
Chislehurst BR7 18
Dagenham RM8 5
Harrow HA3 4
Hayes UB4 8
Palmers Green N14 1
Pinner HA5 2
Wallington SM6 21
West Barnes SW20 20
Woodford IG8 3
Green Way Eltham SE9 16
Sunbury TW16 19
Greenway Ave E17 5
Greenway Cl N11 3
1 N15 5
N20 1
N4 7
NW9 2
Greenway Ct Hayes UB4 8
Ilford IG1 5
Greenway Gdns NW9 2
Croydon CR0 22
Greenford UB6 8
Green Way Gdns HA3 2
Greenways
Beckenham BR3 185
Forest Hill SE26 184
Hinchley Wood KT10 212
Greenways The 1 TW1 153
Greenway The NW9 27
Hounslow TW4 129
Pinner HA5 41
Uxbridge UB10 61
Uxbridge UB8 82
Green Way The HA3 24
Greenwell St W1 238
Greenwich Academy SE10 141
Greenwich Bsns Ctr SE10 141
Greenwich Bsns Pk SE10 141
Greenwich Church St SE10 142
Greenwich Com Coll (Charlton Ctr) SE7 121
Greenwich Cres E6 100
Greenwich Ct 18 E1 96
Greenwich District Hospl SE10 120
Greenwich High Rd SE10 141
Greenwich Hts 2 SE18 144
Greenwich Ind Est
SE10 141
SE7 121
Greenwich Mkt 1 SE10 142
Greenwich Park SE10 142
Greenwich Park Sch SE10 142
Greenwich Park St SE10 142
Greenwich South St SE10 142
Greenwich Sta SE10 141
Greenwich View E14 119
Green Wlk NW4 46
SE1 263
Hampton TW12 173
Ruislip HA4 39
Southall UB2 107
Green Wlk The E4 20
Green Wood NW5 71
Greenwood
8 Putney SW19 156
3 Woodford IG8 37
Greenwood Ave
Dagenham RM10 81
Enfield EN3 7
Greenwood Cl DA15 168
Bushey WD23 8
Merton SM4 201
Orpington BR5,BR6 211
Thames Ditton KT7 197
Greenwood Dr E4 36
Greenwood Gdns N13 16
Greenwood Ho
8 SE4 140
WC1 234
Wood Green N22 32
Greenwood La TW12 173

eenwood Mans 9
11 80 A1
eenwood Pk KT2 177 C3
eenwood Pl NW5 71 B3
eenwood Prim Sch
Mitcham CR4 203 D6
Northolt UB5 64 A3
eenwood Rd E13 98 D5
8 74 A2
Hinchley Wood KT7 213 A6
Isleworth TW7 130 D2
Mitcham CR4 203 D6
Thornton Heath CR0 205 A2
reenwoods The HA2 64 A5
reenwood Terr NW10 89 B5
reen Wrythe Cres
SM5 202 C1
reen Wrythe La SM5 202 C2
reen Wrythe Prim Sch
SM5 202 B3
reen Yd WC1 240 D6
reer Rd HA3 24 A2
reet Ho SE1 251 B1
reet St SE1 116 C5 251 B3
reg Cl E10 54 A3
regor Mews SE3 143 A5
regory Cres SE9 165 D4
regory Ho SE3 143 B3
regory Pl W8 245 C2
regory Rd
Dagenham RM6 58 D5
Southall UB2 107 C3
reig Cl N8 50 A4
reig Terr SE17 138 D6
renaby Ave CR0 205 B2
renaby Rd CR0 205 B2
renada Ho 18 E14 119 B6
renada Rd SE7 143 C5
renade St E14 119 B6
renadier St E16 122 C5
Grena Gdns TW9 132 B1
Grena Rd TW10,TW9 132 B1
Grenard Cl SE15 140 A5
Grendon Gdns HA9 66 C6
Grendon Ho 29 E9 74 C1
N1 233 C3
Grendon Lo HA8 11 A2
Grendon St
NW8 92 C3 237 A6
Grenfell Ct NW7 28 B4
Grenfell Gdns
Harrow HA3 44 A2
Ilford IG2 57 D4
Grenfell Ho SE5 139 A5
Grenfell Rd W11 112 D6
Mitcham CR4,SW17 180 D4
Grenfell Twr 5 W11 112 D6
Grenfell Wlk 4 W11 112 D6
Grengate Lo 2 E13 99 B4
Grennell Cl SM1 218 B6
Grennell Rd SM1 218 A6
Grenoble Gdns N13 32 C4
Grenville Cl N3 29 B2
Tolworth KT5 199 A1
Grenville Ct
Dulwich SE19 183 D5
Ealing W13 87 B2
Edgware HA8 26 D6
Harrow HA1 64 C4
Grenville Gdns IG8 37 C3
Grenville Ho 24 E3 97 A5
4 SE8 141 C6
Grenville Lo N6 49 C2
Grenville Mews SW7 256 A3
Hampton TW12 173 D5
Grenville Pl NW7 27 B5
SW7 114 A2 256 A4
Grenville Rd N19 50 A1
Grenville St WC1 240 B5
Gresham Almshouses 3
SW9 138 B1
Gresham Ave N20 30 D6
Gresham Cl Enfield EN2 5 A2
Sidcup DA5 169 B5
Gresham Coll
EC1 94 C2 241 B3
Gresham Ct TW3 130 A4
Gresham Dr RM6 58 B3
Gresham Gdns NW11 47 A1
Gresham Ho
2 Teddington TW11 174 D5
3 Thames Ditton KT7 197 A2
West Barnes KT3 200 B5
Gresham Rd E6 100 B5
NW10 67 B3
SW9 138 C2
Beckenham BR3 185 A1
Croydon SE25 206 A5
Edgware HA8 26 B4
Hampton TW12 173 C4
Hillingdon UB10 82 C5
Hounslow TW3,TW5 130 A4
Newham E16 99 B1
Gresham St EC2 95 A1 242 B2
Gresham Way SW19 157 C1
Gresham Way Est
SW19 157 D1
Gresley Cl E17 53 A3
N15 51 B5
Gresley Ho SW8 269 D2
Gresley Rd N19 49 C2
Gressenhall Rd SW18 157 B4
Gresse St W1 93 D1 239 C2
Gresswell Cl DA14 168 A1
Greswell St SW6 134 D4
Gretton Ho 2 E2 96 C4
Gretton Rd N17 33 D3
Greville Cl TW1 153 B4
Greville Hall NW6 91 D5
Greville Ho SW1 258 A6
Putney SW15 134 D2
Harrow HA2 42 B1
Greville Lo 14 N12 29 D6
5 W2 91 D1
Greville Mews 3 NW6 91 D6
Greville Pl W9 91 D5
Greville Rd E17 54 A5
NW6 91 D5
Richmond TW10 154 B5
Greville St EC1 94 C2 241 B4
Grey Cl NW11 48 A3
Grey Coat Hospital CE Sch
The SW1 115 D3 259 C5
Grey Coat Hospital St
Michaels The
SW1 115 D2 259 C3
Greycoat Pl
SW1 115 D3 259 C5
Greycoat St
SW1 115 D3 259 C5
Greycot Rd BR3 185 C5
Grey Court Sch TW10 153 C1
Grey Eagle St
E1 95 D3 243 D5
Greyfell Cl HA7 25 B5
Greyfriars 16 SE26 162 A1
Greyfriars Ho SE3 142 D6
Grey Ho 27 W12 112 B6
Greyhound Ct WC2 251 A6
Greyhound Hill NW4 46 B6
Greyhound La SW16 181 D4
Greyhound Rd N17 51 C6
NW10 90 B4
W6 135 A6 264 A6
Sutton SM1 218 A3
Greyhound Terr SW16 181 C2
Greyladies Gdns SE10 142 A3
Greys Park Cl BR2 225 D3
Greystead Rd SE23 162 C4
Greystoke Ave HA5 41 C6
Greystoke Ct W5 88 B3
Greystoke Dr HA4 38 D3
Greystoke Gdns
Ealing W5 88 B3
Enfield EN2 3 D1
Greystoke Ho SE15 140 A6
Greystoke Lo W5 88 B3
Greystoke Park Terr
W5 88 A4
Greystoke Pl EC4 241 B2
Greystone Gdns HA3 43 C3
Greyswood St SW16 181 B4
Grey Turner Ho W12 90 A1
Grice Ct N1 73 A2
Grierson Ho SW16 181 C6
Grierson Rd SE23 162 D4
Griffin Cl NW10 68 B3
Griffin Ct W12 112 B5
W4 111 D1
8 Brentford TW8 132 A6
Griffin Ctr The
Feltham TW14 150 B5
Kingston KT1 175 D1
Griffin Gate SW15 134 D2
Griffin Lo N12 30 A6
Griffin Manor Way
SE28 123 B3
Griffin Park (Brentford FC)
TW8 131 D6
Griffin Rd SE18 123 B1
Tottenham N17 33 C1
Griffin Way
Sunbury TW16 172 A1
Woolwich SE28 123 C3
Griffith Cl RM8 58 C1
Griffiths Cl KT4 216 B6
Griffiths Ho 2 SE18 144 D6
Griffiths Rd SW19 179 D3
Grifton Ho 3 SW11 136 C2
Griggs App IG1 79 A6
Grigg's Pl SE1 263 B5
Griggs Rd E10 54 A3
Grilse Cl N9 34 B6
Grimaldi Ho N1 233 C4
Grimsby Gr E16 122 D5
Grimsby St E2 243 D6
7 E2 96 A3
Grimsdyke Fst & Mid Sch
HA5 23 B4
Grimsdyke Rd HA5 23 A3
Grimsel Path SE5 138 D5
Grimshaw Cl N6 49 A2
Grimston Rd SW6 135 B3
Grimthorpe Ho EC1 241 C6
Grimwade Ave CR0 222 A5
Grimwade Cl SE15 140 C2
Grimwood Rd TW1 152 D4
Grindall Cl CR0 220 D4
Grindall Ho 26 E1 96 B3
Grindal St SE1 251 A1
Grindleford Ave N11 15 A2
Grindley Gdns CR0 205 D3
Grindley Ho 3 E3 97 B2
Grinling Gibbons Prim Sch
SE8 141 B6
Grinling Ho 6 SE18 122 C2
Grinling Pl SE8 141 C6
Grinstead Rd SE8 119 A1
Grisedale NW1 232 A2
Grittleton Ave HA9 66 D2
Grittleton Rd W9 91 C3
Grizedale Terr 8
SE23 162 B2
Grocers' Hall Ct EC2 242 C1
Groombridge Cl DA16 168 A6
Groombridge Ho 1
SE20 184 D3
Groombridge Rd E9 74 D1
Groom Cl BR2 209 B5
Groom Cres SW18 158 B4
Groome Ho SE11 260 D3
Groomfield Cl SW17 181 A6
Groom Pl SW1 115 A3 258 B6
Grooms Dr HA5 40 A4
Grosmont Rd SE18 123 D1
Grosse Way SW15 156 B5
Grosslea SM4 202 B4
Grosvenor Ave N5 73 A3
Harrow HA2 41 D3
Hayes UB4 83 D5
Mortlake SW14 133 C2
Richmond TW10 154 A6
Wallington SM5,SM6 219 A2
Grosvenor Bridge
SW1 137 B6 268 D6
Grosvenor Cotts SW1 258 A4
Grosvenor Cres NW9 44 C5
SW1 115 A4 248 B1
Hillingdon UB10 82 D6
Grosvenor Cres Mews
SW1 248 A1
Grosvenor Ct E10 53 D1
N14 15 C4
NW6 90 D6
NW7 27 B5
W4 110 D1
4 Acton W3 110 C5
3 Ealing W5 110 A6
Morden SM4 201 C5
Penge SE19 183 D4
Putney SW15 157 A6
1 Sutton SM2 218 A2
Teddington TW11 175 A4
3 Wanstead E11 55 B4
2 Wimbledon SW19 179 A4
Grosvenor Ct Mans
W2 237 C1
Grosvenor Gdns E6 99 D4
N10 49 C6
NW11 47 B4
NW2 68 C3
SW1 115 B3 258 D5
Kingston KT2 175 D4
Mortlake SW14 133 C2
Southgate N14 15 D6
Wallington SM6 219 C1
Woodford IG8 37 B4
Grosvenor Gdns Mews E
SW1 258 D6
Grosvenor Gdns Mews N
SW1 258 C5
Grosvenor Gdns Mews S
SW1 258 D5
Grosvenor Hill
W1 115 B6 248 C6
Wimbledon SW19 179 A4
Grosvenor Hill Ct W1 248 C6
Grosvenor Ho E5 52 A1
Grosvenor Lo 4 E18 36 D1
Grosvenor Par 1 W5 110 C5
Grosvenor Park SE5 139 A5
Grosvenor Park Rd E17 53 D4
Grosvenor Pier SW1 269 C6
Grosvenor Pk SE5 139 A6
Grosvenor Pl
SW1 115 B4 248 C1
Grosvenor Rd DA17 147 C6
E10 54 A1
E6 99 D6
E7 77 B2
N10 31 B2
N3 29 C3
SW1 137 C6 269 B6
W4 111 A1
Bexley DA6 169 A6
Brentford TW8 131 D6
Croydon SE25 206 A5
Dagenham RM8 59 B1
Ealing W7 109 A5
Edmonton N9 18 B3
Hounslow TW3,TW4 129 B2
Ilford IG1 79 A5
Orpington BR5,BR6 211 C3
Richmond TW10 154 A6
Southall UB2 107 B3
Twickenham TW1 153 A3
Wallington SM6 219 B3
Grosvenor Rd *continued*
Wanstead E11 55 B4
West Wickham BR4 223 D6
Grosvenor Residences 1
W14 112 D3
Grosvenor Rise E E17 53 D4
Grosvenor Sq
W1 115 A6 248 B6
Grosvenor St
W1 115 B6 248 C6
Grosvenor Terr SE5 139 A6
Grosvenor The NW11 47 D2
Grosvenor Vale HA4 61 D6
Grosvenor Way E5 74 C6
Grosvernor Wharf Rd
E14 120 B2
Grote's Bldgs SE3 142 C3
Grote's Pl SE3 142 C3
Groton Rd SW18 157 D2
Grotto Ct SE1 252 A2
Grotto Pas W1 238 A4
Grotto Rd TW1 152 D2
Grove Ave N10 31 C1
Cheam SM1,SM2 217 C2
Ealing W7 86 C1
Finchley N3 29 C3
Pinner HA5 41 A5
Twickenham TW1 152 D3
Grovebury Ct DA6 169 D6
N14 15 D4
Grovebury Rd SE2 124 B4
Grove Cl BR2 225 A6
N14 15 B4
Forest Hill SE23 163 A3
Ickenham UB10 60 C3
Kingston KT1 198 B5
Grove Cres NW9 45 B5
Feltham TW13 173 A6
Kingston KT1 198 A6
Walton-on-T KT12 194 B2
Woodford E18 36 D1
Grove Crescent Rd E15 76 B2
Grove Ct NW8 229 C2
SE5 139 C3
SW10 256 B1
SW4 137 C2
Barnet EN5 1 B2
Ealing W5 110 A5
East Molesey KT8 196 B4
3 Forest Hill SE26 185 A6
Hounslow TW3 129 C1
8 Kingston KT1 198 A6
Kingston KT3 199 C6
Kingston KT6 197 D4
Penge SE20 184 B3
Grovedale Rd N19 71 D6
Grove Dwellings E1 96 C2
Grove End NW5 71 B4
Woodford E18 36 D1
Grove End Gdns NW8 229 B3
Grove End Ho NW8 229 C1
Grove End La KT10 196 B1
Grove End Rd
NW8 92 B4 229 C1
Grove Farm Ct CR4 202 D4
Grovefield 1 N11 31 B6
Grove Footpath KT5 198 A5
Grove Gdns NW4 46 A5
NW8 92 C4 230 B1
Enfield EN3 6 D5
Teddington TW11 175 A6
Grove Green Rd E11 76 B6
Grove Hall Ct E3 97 C5
NW8 92 A4 229 B2
Grove Hill Harrow HA1 42 C2
Woodford E18 36 D1
Grovehill Ct BR1 186 D4
Grove Hill Rd SE5 139 C2
Harrow HA1 42 D2
Grove Ho N3 46 D6
SE3 142 D3
SW3 267 B6
Walton-on-T KT12 194 B2
Grove House Rd N8 50 A5
Grove La SE5 139 C2
Hillingdon UB8 82 B3
Kingston KT1 198 A5
Groveland Ave SW16 182 B3
Groveland Ct EC4 242 B1
Groveland Rd BR3 207 B6
Grovelands
East Molesey KT8 195 C5
Kingston KT1 197 D5
Grovelands Cl SE5 139 C3
Harrow HA2 63 D5
Grovelands Ct N14 15 D4
Grovelands Priory (Private
Hospl) N14 16 A3
Grovelands Rd BR5 190 A3
N15 52 A3
Palmers Green N13 16 B1
Grovelands Sch KT12 194 B3
Groveland Way KT3 199 B4
Grove Lane Terr SE5 139 B3
Groveley Ho 7 N4 51 A2
Groveley Rd TW13,
TW16 171 D5
Grove Lo SW4 137 C1
Grove Mans 3 N16 52 A1
Grove Mans *continued*
SW4 136 D1
2 W6 112 C4
Grove Market Pl SE9 166 B5
Grove Mews W6 112 C3
Grove Mill Pl SM5 219 A5
Grove Park Ave E4 35 D3
Grove Park Bridge
W4 133 A5
Grove Park Gdns W4 133 A5
Grove Park Mews W4 133 A5
Grove Park Prim Sch
W4 133 A6
Grove Park Rd N15 51 C5
SE9,SE12 165 D2
Chiswick W4 132 D5
Grove Park Sch NW9 45 A5
Grove Park Sta SE12 165 B1
Grove Park Terr W4 132 D6
Grove Pk NW9 45 B5
SE5 139 C3
Wanstead E11 55 B4
Grove Pl NW3 70 B5
W3 111 A5
Balham SW12 159 B5
Grove Prim Sch RM6 58 C4
Grover Ct SE13 141 D3
Grove Rd E11 54 D2
E17 53 D4
E3 97 A5
N11 31 B5
N12 30 B5
N15 51 C4
NW2 68 C2
W3 111 A5
Barnes SW13 133 D3
Belmont SM2 217 C2
Brentford TW8 109 C1
Chingford E4 20 A1
Cockfosters EN4 2 C2
Dagenham RM6 58 C3
Ealing W5 109 D6
East Molesey KT8 196 B5
Edgware HA8 26 C4
8 Erith DA17 147 B6
Hounslow TW3 129 C1
Hounslow TW7 130 C4
Kingston KT6 197 D4
Merton SW19 180 A3
Mitcham CR4 181 B1
Pinner HA5 41 B4
Richmond TW10 154 B5
Shepperton TW17 193 A3
Thornton Heath CR7 204 C5
Twickenham TW2 152 B1
Uxbridge UB8 60 A1
Woodford E18 36 D1
Grove Rd Prim Sch
TW3 129 C1
Grove Rd W EN3 6 C6
Grover Ho SE11 260 D1
4 SW4 159 C6
Groves Ho UB4 84 B4
Groveside Cl Acton W3 88 C1
Carshalton SM5 218 C6
Groveside Ct SW11 136 B3
Groveside Rd E4 20 C1
Grove St SE8 119 B1
Edmonton N18 33 D4
Grovestile Waye TW14 149 B4
Grove Terr NW5 71 B4
Southall UB1 107 C6
Teddington TW11 175 A6
Grove The DA6 146 D1
E15 76 C2
N3 29 C3
N4 50 B2
N6 49 A1
N8 49 D4
NW11 47 A2
NW9 45 B4
Dulwich SE21 162 A3
Ealing W5 110 A5
Edgware HA8 26 D6
Edmonton N13 32 C6
Enfield EN2 4 C3
Hounslow TW7 130 C4
Ickenham UB10 60 C3
Sidcup DA14 191 A6
Southall UB6 86 A1
Teddington TW11 175 A6
1 Twickenham TW1 153 B5
Walton-on-T KT12 194 B2
West Wickham BR4 224 A6
Grove Vale BR7 188 C4
SE22 139 D1
Grove Vale Prim Sch
SE22 139 D1
Groveway
SW9 138 B4 270 D1
Dagenham RM8 80 D4
Grove Way
Thames Ditton KT10 196 A1
Wembley HA9 67 A3
Grovewood 9 TW9 132 C4
Grovewood Ct 6 TW7 130 C4
Grovewood Ho NW2 69 B6
Grummant Rd SE15 139 D4
Grundy St E14 97 D1
Gruneisen Rd N3 29 D3
Guardian Angels RC Prim
Sch E3 97 A4
Guardian Ct SE12 164 C6
Guards Mus The★
SW1 115 C4 249 B1
Gubyon Ave SE24 160 D6
Guerin Sq E3 97 B4
Guernsey Cl TW5 129 C5
Guernsey Gr SE24 161 A4
Guernsey Ho 9 N1 73 A2
Enfield EN3 6 D5
Guernsey Rd E11 54 B1
8 N1 73 A2
Guibal Rd SE12 165 B3
Guildersfield Rd
SW16 182 A3
Guildford Ave TW13 150 A2
Guildford Gr SE10 141 D4
Guildford Ho 24 SE5 139 A3
Guildford Rd
SW8 138 A4 270 B2
Chingford E17 36 A2
Ilford IG3 79 C6
Newham E6 100 B1
Thornton Heath CR0 205 B3
Guildford Way SM6 220 A3
Guild Hall★
EC2 95 A1 242 B2
Guildhall Bldgs EC2 242 C2
Guildhall Sch Music &
Drama EC2 95 A2 242 B4
Guildhall Yd EC2 242 B2
Guildhouse St
SW1 115 C2 259 A3
Guildown Ave N12 29 D6
Guild Rd SE7 143 D6
Guildsway E17 35 B2
Guilford Ave KT5 198 B4
Guilford Pl WC1 240 C5
Guilford St WC1 94 A3 240 B5
Guilfoyle 2 NW9 27 D1
Guillemot Ct 28 SE8 141 B6
Guilsborough Cl NW10 67 C1
Guinness Cl E9 75 A1
Hayes UB3 105 B3
Guinness Ct E1 243 D1
EC1 235 B1
NW8 230 B5
SW3 257 C3
6 Croydon CR0 221 D6
Guinness Sq SE1 263 A4
Guinness Trust Bldgs
7 E2 96 A5
SE1 253 A2
SE11 261 C2
SW3 257 C3
W6 112 C1
Guion Rd SW6 135 B3
Gujarat Ho 1 N16 73 C5
Gulland Cl WD23 8 A6
Gulland Wlk 20 N1 73 A2
Gullane Ho 22 E3 97 B5
Gull Cl SM6 220 A1
Gulliver Cl UB5 85 B6
Gulliver Ct CR2 220 D1
Gulliver Rd DA15 167 C2
Gulliver St SE16 119 B3
Gulston Wlk SW3 257 D3
Gumleigh Rd W5 109 C2
Gumley Gdns TW7 131 A2
Gumley House Convent Sch
for Girls TW7 131 A2
Gumping Rd BR5 227 A6
Gundulph Rd BR2 209 C6
Gunmakers La E3 97 A6
Gunnell Cl SE25 206 A3
Gunnell Ct 3 CR4 180 C2
Gunnels Ct & Hastingwood
Ct 6 IG9 21 C2
Gunner Dr EN3 7 C6
Gunner La SE18 122 C1
Gunnersbury Avenue (North
Circular Rd) W3 110 C3
Gunnersbury Cl 8
W4 110 D1
Gunnersbury Cres W3 110 C4
Gunnersbury Ct 8
W3 110 D4
Gunnersbury Dr W5 110 B4
Gunnersbury Gdns
W3 110 C4
Gunnersbury La W3 110 C4
Gunnersbury Manor
W5 110 B5
Gunnersbury Mews 6
W4 110 D1
Gunnersbury Park W3 110 C3
Gunnersbury Park Mus★
W3 110 C3
Gunnersbury RC Sch
TW8 109 C1
Gunnersbury Sta W4 110 D1
Gunners Gr E4 20 A1
Gunners Rd SW18 158 B2
Gunning St SE18 123 C2

Gunpowder Sq EC4 241 B2
Gun St E1 243 C3
Gunstor Rd N16 73 C4
Gunter Gr HA8 27 B2
SW6 136 A5 266 A4
Gunterstone Rd W14 113 A1 254 B2
Gunthorpe St E1 95 D1 243 D2
Gunton Rd E5 74 B6
Streatham SW17 181 A4
Gunwhale Cl SE16 118 D5
Gun Wharf E1 118 C5
E3 97 A6
Gurdon Ho 3 E14 97 C1
Gurdon Rd SE7 121 A1
Gurnell Gr W13 86 D3
Gurney Cl E15 76 C3
E17 34 D2
Barking IG11 78 D2
Gurney Cres CR0 204 B1
Gurney Dr N2 48 A5
Gurney Ho 14 E2 96 A5
3 W2 91 D1
Hayes UB3 105 C2
Gurney Rd E15 76 C3
SW6 136 A2
Northolt UB5 84 C4
Wallington SM5 219 A4
Guru Nanak Sikh Coll UB4 106 C5
Guthrie Ct SE1 251 B1
Guthrie St SW3 257 A2
Gutter La EC2 95 A1 242 A2
Guyatt Gdns CR4 181 A1
Guy Barnett Gr SE3 143 A2
Guy Rd CR0,SM6 219 D5
Guyscliff Rd SE13 164 A6
Guy's Hospl SE1 117 B5 252 D2
Guy's Hospl Sch SE1 117 B5 252 D3
Guy's Retreat IG9 21 C4
Guy St SE1 117 B4 252 D2
Gwalior Ho N14 15 C5
Gwalior Rd SW15 134 D2
Gwendolen Ave SW15 156 D6
Gwendolen Cl SW15 156 D6
Gwendoline Ave E13 99 B6
Gwendwr Rd W14 113 A1 254 B2
Gwent Ct 13 SE16 118 D5
Gwillim Cl DA15 168 A6
Gwilym Maries Ho 11 E2 96 B4
Gwydor Rd BR3 206 D6
Gwydyr Rd BR2 208 D6
Gwyn Cl SW6 136 A5 266 A3
Gwyn Jones Prim Sch E11 54 B2
Gwynne Ave CR0 206 D2
Gwynne Cl W4 133 D6
Gwynne Ho WC1 234 A1
6 Streatham SW2 160 B3
3 Wanstead E11 55 A4
Gwynne Pl WC1 233 D1
Gwynne Rd SW11 136 B3
Gye Ho 2 SW4 138 A1
Gylcote Cl SE5 139 B1
Gyles Pk HA7 25 C2
Gyllyngdune Gdns IG3 79 D5

H

Haarlem Rd 12 W14 112 D3
Haberdasher Pl 4 N1 95 C4
Haberdasher St N1 95 B4 235 D2
Habington Ho 9 SE5 139 B5
Haccombe Rd SW19 180 A4
Hackbridge Park Gdns SM5 218 D6
Hackbridge Prim Sch SM5 203 A1
Hackbridge Rd SM5, SM6 219 A6
Hackbridge Sta SM6 219 B6
Hackett Cl SE8 119 B2
Hackford Rd SW9 138 C4 270 D2
Hackford Wlk SW9 138 C4
Hackforth Cl EN5 12 B6
Hackington Cres BR3 185 C4
Hackney Central Sta E8 74 B2
Hackney Cl WD6 11 B6
Hackney Coll (Poplar Ctr) E3 97 D3
Hackney Com Coll N1 95 C4
N4 51 A2
Hackney Downs Sch E5,E8 74 A3
Hackney Downs Sta E8 74 B3
Hackney Free & Parochial CE Sch (Secondary) E9 74 C2
Hackney Gr E8 74 B2
Hackney Hospl E9 75 A3
Hackney Rd E2 96 A5
Hackney Wick E9 75 B2
Hackney Wick Sta E9 75 C2
Hackworth Point 24 E3 97 D4
Haddenham Ct SW17 180 B6
Hadden Rd SE28 123 C3
Hadden Way UB6 64 B2
Haddington Ct 4 SE10 141 D5
Haddington Rd BR1 186 B6
Haddo Ho NW5 71 B4
SE10 141 D6
Haddon Cl Enfield EN1 18 A5
New Malden KT3 199 D4
Haddon Ct NW4 46 C6
W3 111 D6
Haddon Gr DA15 168 A4
Haddon Rd SM1 217 D4
Haddo St SE10 142 A6
Haden Ct N4 72 C6
Hadfield Cl UB1 85 B4
Hadfield Ho 26 E1 96 A1
Hadleigh Cl 16 E1 96 C3
Merton SW20 179 B1
Hadleigh Ct 8 E4 20 C4
Hadleigh Ho 15 E1 96 C3
Hadleigh Lo 5 IG8 37 A4
Hadleigh Rd N9 18 B4
Hadleigh St E2 96 C4
Hadleigh Wlk 1 E6 100 A1
Hadley Cl
Borehamwood WD6 10 B5
Southgate N21 16 C5
Hadley Ct N16 52 A1
Hadley Gdns W4 111 B1
Southall UB2 107 B1
Hadley Gn EN5 1 B3
Hadley Gn W EN5 1 B3
Hadley Gr EN5 1 A3
Hadley Green Rd EN5 1 B3
Hadley Hall N21 16 C3
Hadley Highstone EN5 1 B4
Hadley Ho BR5 189 D1
Hadley Rd DA17 125 B2
Barnet EN5 1 D2
Enfield EN2 4 A5
Mitcham CR4 203 D5
Hadley Ridge EN5 1 B2
Hadley St NW1 71 B2
Hadleyvale Ct EN5 1 D2
Hadley Way N21 16 C5
Hadley Wood Prim Sch EN4 2 A5
Hadley Wood Rd
Barnet EN4 2 A3
Barnet EN5 1 C3
Hadley Wood Sta EN4 2 A5
Hadlow Coll (Mottingham Ctr) SE12 165 C3
Hadlow Ho SE17 263 B2
Hadlow Pl SE19 184 A3
Hadlow Rd
Bexley DA16 146 C5
Sidcup DA14 190 A6
Hadrian Cl TW19 148 A4
Hadrian Ct SE4 141 C2
Barnet EN5 1 D1
1 Belmont SM2 217 D1
Hadrian Est 30 E2 96 A5
Hadrian's Ride EN1 17 D6
Hadrian St SE10 120 C1
Hadrian Way TW19 148 A4
Hadstock Ho NW1 232 D2
Hadyn Park Ct 13 W12 112 A4
Hadyn Park Rd W12 112 A4
Hafer Rd SW11 136 D1
Hafton Rd SE6 164 C2
Haggard Rd TW1 153 B4
Hagger Ct E17 54 B6
Haggerston Rd E8 95 D6
Haggerston Sch E2 95 D5
Hague Prim Sch E2 96 B3
Hague St 12 E2 96 A4
Ha-Ha Rd SE7,SE18 144 B6
Haig Ct BR7 188 D5
Haig Ho 4 E2 96 A5
Haig Pl SM4 201 C3
Haig Rd Hillingdon UB8 83 A2
Stanmore HA7 25 C5
Haig Rd E E13 99 C5
Haig Rd W E13 99 C4
Haigville Gdns IG6 56 D5
Hailes Cl SW19 180 A4
Haileybury Ave EN1 17 D5
Hailey Rd DA18 125 C4
Hailey Rd Bsns Pk DA18 125 C4
Hailsham Ave SW2 160 B2
Hailsham Cl KT6 197 D2
Hailsham Dr HA1 42 B6
Hailsham Ho NW8 237 A5
Hailsham Rd SW17 181 A4
Hailsham Terr N18 33 B5
Haimo Prim Sch SE9 165 D6
Haimo Rd SE9 165 D6
Hainault Bldgs E10 54 A1
Hainault Bridge Par 4 IG1 78 D6
Hainault Ct E17 54 B5
Hainault Gore RM6 59 A4
Hainault Rd E11 54 B2
Dagenham RM6 59 B3
Ilford RM6 58 B6
Hainault St SE9 166 D3
Ilford IG1 78 D6
Haines Wlk SM4 201 D2
Hainford Cl SE4 140 D1
Haining Cl 3 W4 110 C1
Hainthorpe Rd SE27 182 D6
Hainton Cl E1 96 B1
Halberd Mews E5 74 B6
Halbutt Gdns RM9 81 B5
Halcomb St N1 95 C6
Halcot Ave DA6 169 D6
Halcrow St E1 96 B2
Halcyon 3 EN1 17 C6
Halcyon Wharf 10 E1 118 A5
Haldane Cl N10 31 B3
Holdbrook EN3 7 D5
Haldane Pl SW18 157 D3
Haldane Rd E6 100 A4
SE28 124 D6
SW6 135 B6 264 D5
Southall UB1 86 A1
Haldan Rd E4 36 A4
Haldon Rd SW18 157 B5
Hale Cl BR6 227 A4
HA8 27 A5
Chingford E4 20 A1
Hale Ct HA8 27 A5
Hale Dr NW7 27 B4
Hale End Cl HA4 40 A3
Hale End Rd E17 36 B2
Halefield Rd N17 34 B2
Hale Gdns N17 52 A6
Acton W3 110 C5
Hale Grove Gdns NW7 27 C5
Hale Ho SW1 259 D2
Enfield EN3 6 D6
Hale La NW7,HA8 27 B5
Hale Lo HA1 42 C2
Hale Rd N17 52 A6
Newham E6 100 A3
Hales Ct 5 TW11 175 A5
Hales Ho 3 SW12 159 B4
Halesowen Rd SM4 201 D2
Hales Prior N1 233 C3
Hales St SE8 141 C5
Hale St E14 119 D6
Halesworth Cl 3 E5 74 C6
Halesworth Rd SE13 141 D2
Hale The N17 52 A6
Chingford E4 36 B3
Hale Wlk W7 86 C2
Haley Rd NW4 46 C3
Half Acre TW8 131 D6
Half Acre Mews TW8 131 D6
Half Acre Rd W7 108 C5
Half Moon Ct EC1 242 A3
Half Moon La SE24 161 A5
Halfmoon Pas E1 243 D1
Half Moon St W1 115 B5 248 D3
Halford Cl HA8 26 D1
Halford Ct KT9 214 A1
Halford Ho 6 SW15 156 D6
Halford Rd E10 54 B4
SW6 135 C6 265 A5
Ickenham UB10 60 C3
Richmond TW10 154 A6
Halfway St DA15 167 C3
Haliburton Rd TW1, TW7 131 A1
Haliday Ho N1 73 B2
Haliday Wlk 4 N1 73 B2
Halidon Cl E9 74 C3
Halifax 8 NW9 27 D1
Halifax Cl TW11 174 C4
Halifax Rd Enfield EN2 5 B3
Greenford UB6 85 D6
Halifax St SE26 162 B1
Halifield Dr DA17 125 A3
Haling Gr CR2 221 A1
Haling Manor High Sch CR2 220 D1
Haling Park Gdns CR2 220 D2
Haling Park Rd CR2 221 A2
Haling Rd CR2 221 B2
Haliwell Ho 8 NW6 91 D6
Halkett Ho 11 E2 96 C6
Halkin Arc SW1 114 D3 257 D6
Halkin Mews SW1 258 A6
Halkin Pl SW1 258 A6
Halkin St SW1 115 A4 248 B1
Hallam Cl BR7 188 B5
Hallam Ct W1 238 D4
Hallam Gdns HA5 23 A3
Hallam Ho SW1 259 B1
17 SW9 138 C4
Hallam Mews W1 238 D4
Hallam Rd N15 50 D5
Hallam Rd *continued*
Barnes SW13 134 B2
Hallam St W1 93 B2 238 D4
Hallane Ho SE27 183 A5
Hall Cl W5 88 A2
Hall Ct TW11 174 D5
Hall Dr Ealing W7 86 C1
Forest Hill SE26 184 C5
Halley Gdns SE13 142 B1
Halley Ho 15 E2 96 A5
8 SE10 120 D1
Halley Prim Sch E14 97 A2
Halley Rd E7,E12 77 D2
Halley St E14 97 A2
Hall Farm Cl HA7 25 B6
Hall Farm Dr TW2 152 B4
Hallfield W2 236 A1
Hallfield Jun & Inf Schs W2 91 D1
Hallgate SE3 143 A2
Hall Gate NW8 92 A4 229 B2
Hall Gdns E4 35 B6
Halliards The KT12 194 A3
Halliday Ho 29 E1 96 A1
Halliday Sq UB2 108 B5
Halliford Cl TW17 193 C6
Halliford Rd
Sunbury TW16 194 A5
Upper Halliford TW16, TW17 193 D5
Halliford Sch TW17 193 A2
Halliford St N1 73 B1
Halling Ho SE1 252 D1
Halliwell Ct 4 SE22 162 A6
Halliwell Rd SW2 160 B5
Halliwick Court Par 2 N12 30 D5
Halliwick Ct 1 N12 30 D5
Halliwick Ho N21 17 B5
Halliwick Rd N10 31 A2
Hall La E4 35 B5
NW4 28 A1
Harlington UB3 127 B5
Hall Lane E4 35 A5
Hallmark Trad Ctr HA9 67 A4
Hallmead Rd SM1 217 D5
Hall Oak Wlk NW6 69 B2
Hallowell Ave CR0 220 A4
Hallowell Cl CR4 203 A6
Hallowfield Way CR4 202 C6
Hall Pl W2 92 B3 236 C5
Hall Rd E15 76 B4
E6 100 B6
NW8 92 A4 229 B2
Dagenham RM6 58 D3
Isleworth TW7 152 B6
Hall Sch SW20 178 D2
Hall Sch The NW3 70 B2
Hall Sch Wimbledon SW15 156 A1
Hallside Rd EN1 5 D5
Hall St EC1 94 D4 234 D2
N12 30 A5
Halls Terr UB10 82 D3
Hallsville Prim Sch E16 99 A1
Hallsville Rd E16 98 D1
Hallswelle Par 1 NW11 47 B4
Hallswelle Rd NW11 47 B4
Hall The SE3 143 A2
Hall Twr W2 236 D4
Hall View SE9 165 D2
Hallywell Cres E6 100 B2
Halons Rd SE9 166 C4
Halpin Pl SE17 117 B2 262 D3
Halsbrook Rd SE3 143 D2
Halsbury Cl HA7 25 B6
Halsbury Ct HA7 25 B6
Halsbury Ho 4 N7 72 B4
Halsbury Rd W12 112 B5
Halsbury Rd E UB5 64 A4
Halsbury Rd W UB5 63 D3
Halsend UB3 106 B5
Halsey St SW3 114 D2 257 C4
Halsham Cres IG11 79 D3
Halsmere Rd SE5 138 D4
Halstead Cl 2 CR0 221 A5
Halstead Ct N1 235 D3
Halstead Gdns N21 17 B3
Halstead Rd
Edmonton N21 17 B3
Enfield EN1 5 C1
Wanstead E11 55 B4
Halston Cl SW11 158 D5
Halstow 12 NW5 71 A2
Halstow Prim Sch SE10 121 A1
Halstow Rd NW10 90 D4
SE3,SE10 121 A1
Halsway UB3 106 A5
Halter Cl WD6 11 B6
Halton Cl N11 30 D4
Halton Cross St N1 94 D6 234 D6
Haltone Ho 1 SW4 137 D3
Halton Ho 23 N1 72 D1
Halton Mans N1 72 D1
Halton Pl N1 235 A6
Halton Rd N1 72 D1 234 D6
Halt Robin La DA17 125 D2
Halt Robin Rd DA17 125 D2
Halyard Ho E14 120 A3
Hamara Ghar 5 E13 99 C6
Hambalt Rd SW4 159 C6
Hamble Cl HA4 61 C6
Hamble Ct KT1 175 D3
Hambledon SE17 139 B6
Hambledon Chase N4 50 A2
Hambledon Cl UB8 82 D3
Hambledon Ct
5 Ealing W5 110 A6
9 Wallington SM6 219 B2
Hambledon Gdns SE25 205 D6
Hambledon Ho E5 74 B4
2 Kingston KT2 176 D4
Hambledon Pl SE21 161 D3
Hambledon Rd SW18 157 B4
Hambledown Rd SE9 167 C4
Hamble St SW6 135 D2
Hambleton Cl KT4 216 C6
Hamble Wlk UB5 85 C5
Hambley Ho 5 SE16 118 B2
Hamblin Ho UB1 107 A6
Hamblyn Ct N16 51 D2
Hambridge Way SW2 160 C4
Hambro Ave BR2 209 A1
Hambrook Ct 12 NW5 71 B4
Hambrook Rd SE25 206 B6
Hambro Rd SW16 181 D5
Hambrough Ho UB4 84 C2
Hambrough Prim Sch UB1 107 B5
Hambrough Rd UB1 107 A5
Hambury Ho SW8 270 B5
Ham Cl TW10 153 C1
Ham Comm TW10 153 D1
Ham Ct 12 NW9 27 D1
Hamden Cres RM10 81 D5
Hamel Cl HA3 43 D5
Hamelton Terr RM9 80 C1
Hamers Ho 19 SW2 160 C4
Hameway E6 100 C3
Ham Farm Rd KT2, TW10 176 A6
Hamfrith Rd E15 76 D2
Ham Gate Ave TW10 176 A6
Ham Ho★ TW10 153 C2
Hamilton Ave
Cheam SM3 217 A6
Edmonton N9 18 A4
Ilford IG6 57 A4
Tolworth KT6,SM3 214 C6
Hamilton Cl N17 51 D6
NW8 92 B4 229 C1
SE16 119 A4
Ashford TW13 171 D5
Cockfosters EN4 2 D1
Teddington TW11 175 B4
Hamilton Cres
Edmonton N13 32 C6
Harrow HA2 63 B5
Hounslow TW3 151 D6
Hamilton Ct W9 229 A2
9 Catford SE6 164 D3
Croydon CR0 206 A1
Ealing W5 110 B6
Hamilton Gdns NW8 92 A4 229 B2
Hamilton Hall NW8 92 A5 229 A3
Hamilton Ho 1 E14 119 B6
19 E3 97 B4
NW8 229 C2
W8 245 C2
Chiswick W4 133 C6
Putney SW15 156 A6
10 Richmond TW9 132 C4
Hamilton La N5 72 D4
Hamilton Lo 32 E1 96 C3
Hamilton Mews W1 248 C2
Hamilton Par TW13 172 A6
Hamilton Pk N5 72 D4
Hamilton Pk W N5 72 D4
Hamilton Pl W1 115 A5 248 B3
Sunbury TW16 172 B3
Tottenham N17 33 D1
Hamilton Rd DA7 147 A3
E15 98 C4
E17 35 A1
N2 48 A6
NW10 68 A3
NW11 47 A2
W4 111 C4
Barnet EN4 2 C1
Brentford TW8 131 D6
Ealing W5 110 A6
Edmonton N9 18 A4
Feltham TW13 171 D6
Harrow HA1 42 C4
Hayes UB3 106 B6
Ilford IG1 78 D4
Merton SW19 179 D3
Sidcup DA15 190 A6
Southall UB1 107 B5
South Norwood CR7 205 B6
Twickenham TW2 152 C3
West Norwood SE27 183 B6
Hamilton Road Ctr E15 98
Hamilton Road Ind Est SE27 183
Hamilton Road Mews 1 SW19 179
Hamilton Sq N12 30
SE1 252
Hamilton St SE8 141
Hamilton Terr NW8 92 A4 229
Hamilton Way N3 29
Edmonton N13 32
Hamlea Cl SE12 165
Hamlet Cl SE13 142
Hamlet Ct SE11 261
1 W6 112
14 Enfield EN1 17
Hamlet (Day) Hospl The TW9 132
Hamlet Gdns W6 112
Hamlet Ho SE9 166
Hamlet Ind Est E9 75
Hamlet Rd SE19 184
Hamlet Sq NW2 69
Hamlets Way E3 97
Hamlet The SE5 139
Hamlet Way SE1 252
Hamlin Cres HA5 40
Hamlyn Cl HA8 10
Hamlyn Gdns SE19 183
Hammelton Ct 4 BR1 186
Hammelton Gn 2 SW9 138
Hammelton Rd BR1 187
Hammers La NW7 28
Hammersley Ho 8 SE14 140
Hammersmith Bridge Rd W6,SW13 112
Hammersmith Broadway 5 W6 112
Hammersmith Flyover W6 112
Hammersmith Gr W6 112
Hammersmith Hospl W12 90
Hammersmith Rd
W14 254
W6 112
Hammersmith Sta W6 112
Hammersmith Terr W6 112
Hammet Cl UB4 84
Hammett St EC3 253
Hammond Ave CR4 181
Hammond Cl
Barnet EN5 13 B6
Greenford UB6 64 B3
Hampton TW12 173 C2
Hammond Ct 1 E10 75 D6
1 E17 53 A4
Hammond Ho E14 119 D3
10 SE14 140 C5
Hammond Lo 6 W9 91 C2
Hammond Rd Enfield EN1 6 B3
Southall UB2 107 A3
Hammonds Cl RM8 80 C5
Hammond St NW5 71 C2
Hammond Way 2 SE28 124 B6
Hamonde Cl HA8 10 D2
Hamond Sq N1 95 C5
Ham Park Rd E15 76 D1
Hampden Ave BR3 185 A1
Hampden Cl NW1 232 D4
Hampden Ct 5 N10 31 A3
Hampden Gurney CE Prim Sch W1 92 C1 237 B2
Hampden Gurney St W1 237 C1
Hampden Ho SW9 138 C3
Hampden La N17 34 A2
Hampden Rd N10 31 A3
N19 71 D6
N8 50 C5
Beckenham BR3 185 A1
Harrow HA3 24 A1
Kingston KT1 198 C6
Tottenham N17 34 A2
Hampden Sq N14 15 B3
Hampden Way N14 15 B2
Hampshire Cl N18 34 B5
Hampshire Ct 6 SW13 133 D3
Hampshire Hog La 11 W6 112 B2
Hampshire Rd N22 32 B3
Hampshire Sch The SW7 114 C4 247 B1
Hampshire St NW5 71 D2
Hampson Way SW8 138 B4 270 C2
Hampstead Cl SE28 124 B5
Hampstead Garden Suburb Inst NW11 47 D4
Hampstead Gate NW3 70 A3
Hampstead Gdns NW11 47 C3
Hampstead Gn NW3 70 C3
Hampstead Gr NW3 70 A5

mpstead Heath★
W3 70 B6
mpstead Heath Sta
W3 70 C4
mpstead High St
W3 70 B4
mpstead Hill Gdns
W3 70 C4
mpstead Hill Sch
W3 70 C3
mpstead Hts N2 48 A6
mpstead La N6 48 C2
mpstead Parochial CE
Prim Sch NW3 70 A4
ampstead Rd
NW1 93 C4 232 A2
ampstead Sch NW2 69 A4
ampstead Sq NW3 70 A5
ampstead Sta NW3 70 A4
ampstead Way NW11 47 C3
ampstead West 4
NW6 69 C2
ampstead Wlk 1 E3 97 B6
ampton Cl N11 31 B5
NW6 91 C4
Wimbledon SW20 178 C3
ampton Com Coll
TW12 173 C5
ampton Court KT8 196 C6
ampton Court Ave
KT8 196 C3
ampton Court Cres
KT8 196 B6
ampton Court Landing
Stage KT8 196 C6
ampton Court Palace★
KT8 196 D6
Hampton Court Par
KT8 196 C5
Hampton Court Rd
KT1,KT8 197 B6
Hampton Court Sta
KT8 196 C5
Hampton Court Way
KT10,KT7,KT8 196 C3
Hampton Ct N1 72 D2
19 SE16 118 D5
Wood Green N22 31 C2
Hampton Farm Ind Est
TW13 151 A1
Hampton Hill Bsns Pk
TW12 174 A5
Hampton Hill Jun Mix Sch
TW12 174 A5
Hampton Ho DA7 147 D3
Hampton Inf Sch
TW12 173 C3
Hampton Jun Sch
TW12 173 C2
Hampton La TW13 173 A6
Hampton Rd E11 54 B1
E4 35 B5
E7 77 C3
Ilford IG1 79 A4
North Cheam KT4 216 B6
Teddington TW11,TW12 174 C5
Thornton Heath CR0 205 A3
Twickenham TW2 152 B1
Hampton Rd E TW13 151 B1
Hampton Rd W TW13 151 A1
Hampton Rise HA3 44 A3
Hampton Road Ind Pk
CR0 205 A3
Hampton Sch TW12 173 C5
Hampton St
SE1 116 D2 261 D3
Hampton Sta TW12 173 C2
Hampton Wick Inf Sch
KT1 175 D3
Hampton Wick Sta
KT1 175 C2
Ham Ridings TW10 176 B5
Ham Shades Cl 1
DA15 168 A1
Ham St TW10 153 C1
Ham The TW8 131 C5
Ham View CR0 207 A3
Ham Yd W1 249 C6
Hanameel St 6 E16 121 A5
7 E16 121 B5
10 E16 121 B5
Hana Mews E5 74 B4
Hanbury Cl NW4 46 C6
Hanbury Ct HA1 42 D3
Hanbury Dr N21 16 B6
Hanbury Ho 6 E1 96 A2
Hanbury Rd W3 110 D4
Tottenham N17 34 B1
Hanbury St E1 96 A2 243 D4
Hancocke Ho 4 E17 53 D6
Hancock Nunn Ho 1
NW3 70 D1
Hancock Rd E3 98 A4
South Norwood SE19 183 B4
Handa Wlk 3 N1 73 A2
Handcroft Rd CR0 204 D1
Hand Ct WC1 240 D3
Handel Cl HA8 26 B4
Handel Ho TW2 152 B5
Handel Mans SW13 134 C5
Handel Pl NW10 67 B2
Handel St WC1 94 A3 240 B6
Handel Way HA8 26 C3
Handen Rd SE12 164 D6
Handforth Rd SW9 138 C5
6 Ilford IG1 78 D5
Handley Gr NW2 68 D5
Handley Page Rd SM6
Handley Rd E9 96 C6
Handowe Cl NW4 46 A5
Handside Cl KT4 200 D1
Hands Wlk E16 99 A1
Handsworth Ave E4 36 B4
Handsworth Prim Sch
E4 36 B4
Handsworth Rd N17 51 B6
Handtrough Way
IG11 100 D5
Hanford Cl SW18 157 C3
Hanger Ct W5 88 C3
Hanger Gn W5 88 C3
Hanger Lane Sta W5 88 A4
Hanger La (North Circular
Rd) W5 88 B2
Hanger Vale La W5 88 B1
Hanger View Way W3 88 C2
Hangmans Cnr BR7 188 D2
Hankey Pl SE1 117 B4 252 D1
Hankins La NW7 11 C1
Hanley Gdns N4 50 B1
Hanley Pl BR3 185 C3
Hanley Rd N4,N19 50 A1
Hanmer Wlk N7 72 B6
Hannah Cl BR3 208 A6
Hannah Ct SW19 178 D3
Hannah Mary Way 15
SE1 118 A2
Hannah Mews SM6 219 C1
Hannan Cl NW10 67 A4
Hannay La N8 49 D2
Hannay Wlk SW16 159 D2
Hannell Rd
SW6 135 A5 264 B4
Hannen Ho SE5 139 B2
Hannen Rd SE27 160 D1
Hannibal Rd E1 96 C2
Stanwell TW19 148 A4
Hannibal Way CR0 220 B2
Hanning Lo TW3 130 A1
Hannington Rd SW4 137 B2
Hanover Ave E16 121 A5
Feltham TW13 150 A2
Hanover Circ UB3 83 B1
Hanover Cl Cheam SM3 217 B4
Richmond TW9 132 C5
Hanover Ct N16 51 D2
NW9 45 C6
W12 112 A5
1 Penge SE19 184 A3
Hanover Dr BR7 189 A6
Hanover Gate Mans
NW1 237 B6
Hanover Gdns SE11 138 C6
Hanover Ho NW8 230 A3
New Barnet EN5 2 A1
Tolworth KT6 198 C1
Hanover Mans 5
SW2 160 C6
Hanover Mead NW11 47 A3
Hanover Pk SE15 140 A4
Hanover Pl 12 E3 97 B4
WC2 240 B1
Hanover Prim Sch N1 235 B4
Hanover Rd N15 51 D5
Merton SW19 180 A3
Willesden NW10 90 C6
Hanover Sq W1 93 B1 238 D1
Hanover St W1 93 B1 238 D1
Croydon CR0 220 D5
Hanover Steps W2 237 B1
Hanover Terr
NW1 92 D4 230 C1
Isleworth TW7 131 A4
Hanover Terr Mews
NW1 92 C4 230 B1
Hanover Way DA7 146 D2
Hanover West Ind Est
NW10 89 B4
Hanover Yd N1 235 A4
Hansard Mews W14 112 D4
Hansart Way EN2 4 C4
Hanscomb Mews 3
SW4 137 C1
Hans Cres
SW1 114 D3 257 C6
Hanselin Cl HA7 24 D5
Hansen Dr N21 16 B6
Hanshaw Dr HA8 27 B2
Hansler Gr KT8 196 B5
Hansler Rd SE22 161 D6
Hansol Rd DA6 169 A6
Hansom Terr 1 BR1 187 B2
Hanson Cl
Balham SW12 159 B4
Beckenham BR3 185 D4
Mortlake SW14 133 A2
West Drayton UB7 104 B3
Hanson Ct E17 53 D3
Hanson Gdns UB1 107 A4
Hanson Ho 2 E1 118 A6
Hanson St W1 93 C2 239 A4
Hans Pl SW1 114 D3 257 C6
Hans Rd SW3 114 D3 257 C6
Hans St SW1 114 D3 257 D5
Hanway Ho 25 SW9 138 C4
Hanway Pl W1 239 C2
Hanway Rd W7 86 C1
Hanway St W1 239 C2
Hanwell Ho 24 W2 91 C2
Hanwell Sta W7 108 C6
Hanworth Ho SE5 138 D5
Hanworth Rd
Ashford TW16 172 A3
Feltham TW13 150 B3
Hampton TW12 173 C5
Hounslow TW3,TW4 129 D1
Twickenham TW4 151 B4
Hanworth Terr TW3 129 D1
Hanworth Trad Est
TW13 151 A1
Hapgood Cl UB6 64 B3
Harben Rd NW6 70 A1
Harberson Rd E15 98 D6
Balham SW12 159 B3
Harberton Rd N19 49 C1
Harbet Rd N18 35 A4
W2 92 B2 236 D3
Harbex Cl DA5 169 D4
Harbinger Prim Sch
E14 119 D2
Harbinger Rd E14 119 D2
Harbin Ho 5 SW2 160 C3
Harbledown Ho SE1 252 C1
Harbledown Rd SW6 265 A2
Harbord Cl SE5 139 B3
Harbord Ho 5 SE16 118 D2
Harbord St SW6 134 D4
Harborne Cl WD19 22 C5
Harborough Ave DA15 167 D4
Harborough Rd SW16 182 B6
Harborough Sch N19 71 D6
Harbour Ave
SW10 136 A4 266 B1
Harbour Exchange Sq
E14 119 D4
Harbour Rd SE5 139 A2
Harbridge Ave SW15 156 A4
Harbury Rd SM5 218 C1
Harbut Rd SW11 136 B1
Harcastle Cl UB4 85 A3
Harcombe Rd N16 73 C5
Harcourt Ave
DA5,DA15 168 C4
E12 78 B3
HA8 11 A1
Wallington SM6 219 B4
Harcourt Cl TW7 131 A2
Harcourt Field SM6 219 B4
Harcourt Ho 27 SW8 137 D3
W1 238 C2
5 Chingford E4 36 B5
Harcourt Lo 2 SM6 219 B4
Harcourt Rd E15 98 D5
N22 31 D2
SE4 141 B2
Bexley DA6,DA7 147 A1
Bushey WD23 8 A6
Merton SW19 179 C3
Thornton Heath CR7 204 C3
Wallington SM6 219 B4
Harcourt St W1 92 C2 237 B3
Harcourt Terr
SW10 113 D1 255 D1
Hardcastle Cl SE25 206 A3
Hardcastle Ho 8
SE15 140 A4
Hardcourts Cl BR4 223 D5
Hard Ct IG8 37 C4
Hardel Rise SW2 160 D3
Hardel Wlk SE24,SW2 160 C4
Harden Ct 1 SE7 122 A2
Harden Ho SE5 139 C3
Harders Rd SE15 140 B3
Hardess St SE24 139 A2
Hardham Ho 5 SW2 160 C5
Hardie Cl NW10 67 B3
Harding Cl SE17 139 A6
South Croydon CR0 221 D5
Harding Ct SE25 183 D1
Hardinge Cl UB8 82 D1
Hardinge Rd
Edmonton N18 33 C4
Willesden NW10 90 C6
Hardinge St E1 96 C1
SE18 122 D3
Harding Ho 16 SE18 122 B2
Barnes SW13 134 B6
Hayes UB3 84 B1
Harding Pl SE23 163 A4
Harding Rd DA7 147 B3
Hardings Cl KT2 176 B2
Hardings La SE20 184 D4
Hardington 2 NW1 71 A1
Hardman Rd SE7 121 B1
Kingston KT2 176 A1
Hardwick Cl 7 HA7 25 C5
Hardwick Ct 8 E11 55 A3
Hardwicke Ave TW5 129 C4
Hardwicke Ho 14 E3 97 D4
Hardwicke Mews
WC1 233 D1
Hardwicke Rd W4 111 B2
Bowes Park N13 32 A4
Richmond TW10 175 C6
Hardwicke St IG11 101 A6
Hardwick Gn W13 87 B2
Hardwick Ho NW8 237 B6
14 SW8 137 D3
Hardwick St
EC1 94 C4 234 B1
Hardwick's Way SW18 157 C6
Hardwidge St SE1 253 A2
Hardy Ave 4 E16 121 A5
Ruislip HA4 62 B3
Hardy Cl SE16 118 D4
Barnet EN5 13 A6
Pinner HA5 40 D2
Hardy Cotts 2 SE10 142 B6
Hardy Ct SE3 142 D6
9 Wanstead E11 55 A5
Hardyng Ho 4 E17 53 A5
Hardy Pas N22 32 C1
Hardy Rd E4 35 B4
SE3 142 D6
Merton SW19 179 D3
Hardys Cl KT8 196 C5
Hardy Way EN2 4 C4
Harebell Dr E6 100 C2
Hare & Billet Rd SE3 142 B3
Harecourt Rd N1 73 A2
Hare Ct EC4 241 A1
Haredale Ho 22 SE16 118 A4
Haredale Rd SE24 139 A1
Haredon Cl SE23 162 D4
Harefield KT10 212 C5
Harefield Cl EN2 4 C4
Harefield Ct 6 SW19 179 C3
Harefield Mews SE4 141 B2
Harefield Rd DA14 168 D1
N8 49 D4
SE4 141 B2
South Norwood SW16 182 B3
Uxbridge UB8 60 A3
Hare La KT10 212 C2
Hare Marsh E2 96 A3
Harenc Sch Trust
DA14 190 C5
Hare Pl EC4 241 B1
Hare Row E2 96 B5
Haresfield Rd RM10 81 C2
Hare St SE18 122 C3
Hare Wlk N1 95 C5
Harewood Ave
NW1 92 C3 237 B5
Northolt UB5 63 B1
Harewood Cl UB5 63 B1
Harewood Ct HA3 24 C2
Harewood Pl W1 238 D1
Harewood Rd
Hounslow TW7 130 D4
Mitcham SW19 180 C4
South Croydon CR2 221 C2
Harewood Row NW1 237 B4
Harewood Terr UB2 107 B2
Harfield Gdns 1 SE5 139 C2
Harfield Rd TW16 172 D1
Harfleur Ct SE11 261 C3
Harford Cl E4 19 D4
Harford Ho SE5 139 A6
W11 91 B2
Harford Rd E4 19 D4
Harford St E1 97 A3
Harford Wlk N2 48 B5
Hargood Cl HA3 44 A3
Hargood Rd SE3 143 C4
Hargrave Mans 2 N19 71 D6
Hargrave Park Prim Sch
N19 71 C6
Hargrave Pk N19 71 C6
Hargrave Pl N7 71 D3
Hargrave Rd N19 71 C6
Hargraves Ho 14 W12 112 B6
Hargwyne St SW9 138 B2
Haringey Pk N8 50 A3
Haringey Rd N8 50 A5
Harington Terr N18 17 B1
Harkett Cl HA3 24 D1
Harkness Ho 20 E1 96 A1
Harland Ave
Sidcup DA15 167 C2
South Croydon CR0 222 A5
Harland Cl SW19 201 D6
Harland Fst Sch CR4 180 B1
Harland Rd SE12 165 A3
Harlands Gr BR6 226 D4
Harlech Ct 1 SE23 162 C3
Harlech Gdns TW5 128 C5
Harlech Rd N14 16 A1
Harlech Twr 5 W3 111 A4
Harlequin Ave TW8 131 A6
Harlequin Cl Hayes UB4 84 D2
Isleworth TW7 152 C6
Harlequin Ct NW10 67 B2
Croydon CR2 221 A1
Ealing W5 109 C6
Harlequin Ho 1 DA18 125 A3
Harlequin Rd TW11 175 B3
Harlescott Rd SE15 140 D1
Harlesden Gdns NW10 89 D6
Harlesden Plaza 2
NW10 89 D5
Harlesden Prim Sch
NW10 89 C5
Harlesden Rd NW10 90 A6
Harlesden Sta NW10 89 B5
Harleston Cl 4 E5 74 C6
Harley Cl HA0 65 D2
Harley Cres HA1 42 B5
Harley Ct N20 14 A1
Wanstead E11 55 A2
Harleyford BR1 187 C2
Harleyford Ct SW8 270 C6
Harleyford Manor 8
W3 111 A5
Harleyford Rd
SE11 138 B6 270 C6
Harleyford St SE11 138 C6
Harley Gdns BR6 227 C4
SW10 114 A1 256 B1
Harley Gr E3 97 B4
Harley Ho E11 54 B2
NW1 238 B5
Harley Pl W1 93 B2 238 C3
Harley Rd NW10 89 C5
NW3 70 B1
Harrow HA1 42 B5
Harley St W1 93 B2 238 C3
Harley Villas NW10 89 C5
Harling Ct 3 SW11 136 D3
Harlinger St SE18 122 A3
Harlington Bridge
UB3 105 C1
Harlington Cl UB7 127 A5
Harlington Cnr UB3 127 B4
Harlington Com Sch
UB3 105 B2
Harlington Rd DA7 147 A2
Hillingdon UB8 82 C3
Harlington Rd E TW13,
TW14 150 C3
Harlington Rd W
TW14 150 B5
Harlowe Ho 13 E8 95 D6
Harlow Mans 2 IG11 78 D1
Harlow Rd N13 17 B1
Harlyn Dr HA5 40 B6
Harlyn Prim Sch HA5 40 B6
Harlynwood 19 SE5 139 A5
Harman Ave IG8 36 D4
Harman Cl NW2 69 A5
9 SE1 118 A1
Chingford E4 36 B6
Harman Dr DA15 167 D5
NW2 69 A4
Harman Rd EN1 17 D6
Harmondsworth La
UB7 126 B6
Harmondsworth Rd
UB7 104 A2
Harmon Ho 6 SE8 119 B2
Harmony Cl NW11 47 A4
Harmony Way BR1 187 A1
NW4 46 C5
Harmood Gr NW1 71 B1
Harmood Ho 2 NW1 71 B1
Harmood St NW1 71 B1
Harmsworth St
SE17 116 D1 261 C1
Harmsworth Way N20 13 C3
Harness Rd SE28 124 A4
Harold Ave Erith DA17 125 B1
Hayes UB3 105 D3
Harold Ct 14 SE16 118 D4
Harold Est SE1 263 B5
Harold Gibbons Ct 12
SE7 143 C6
Harold Ho 16 E2 96 D5
Harold Laski Ho EC1 234 D1
Harold Maddison Ho
SE17 261 D2
Harold Pl SE11 261 A1
Harold Rd E11 54 C1
E13 99 B6
N15 51 D4
N8 50 B5
NW10 89 B4
Chingford E4 20 A1
South Norwood SE19 183 B3
Sutton SM1 218 B4
Woodford IG8 37 A2
Haroldstone Rd E17 53 A4
Harold Wilson Ho
SW6 264 D5
Harp Alley EC4 241 C2
Harp Bsns Ctr The
NW2 68 A6
Harpenden Rd
Wanstead E12 77 C6
West Norwood SE27,
SW16 160 D2
Harpenmead Point
NW2 69 B6
Harper Cl N14 15 C6
Harper Ho 3 SW9 138 D2
Harper Mews SW17 158 A1
Harper Rd SE1 117 A3 262 B6
Newham E6 100 B1
Harper's Yd N17 33 D2
Harp Island Cl NW10 67 B6
Harp La EC3 253 A5
Harpley Sq E1 96 D3
Harpour Rd IG11 79 A2
Harp Rd W7 86 D3
Harpsden St SW11 268 A1
Harpur Mews WC1 240 C4
Harpur St WC1 94 B2 240 C4
Harraden Rd SE3 143 C4
Harrier Ave E11 55 B3
Harrier Ct TW4 129 A3
Harrier Ho 9 SW11 136 C2
Harrier Mews SE28 123 B4
Harrier Rd NW9 27 C1
Harriers Cl W5 110 A6
Harrier Way E6 100 B2
Harries Rd UB4 84 C3
Harriet Cl E8 96 A6
Harriet Gdns CR0 222 A6
Harriet Ho SW6 265 D3
Harriet St
SW1 114 D4 247 D1
Harriet Tubman Cl 21
SW2 160 C4
Harriet Way WD23 8 B4
Harriet Wlk
SW1 114 D4 247 D1
Harringay Gdns N8 50 D5
Harringay Green Lanes Sta
N4 50 D3
Harringay Rd N15 50 D5
Harringay Sta N4 50 C3
Harrington Cl NW10 67 B5
Wallington CR0 220 A6
Harrington Ct SW7 256 D4
9 W9 91 B4
6 South Croydon CR0 221 B6
Harrington Gdns
SW7 114 A2 256 A3
Harrington Hill E5 52 B1
Harrington Hill Prim Sch
E5 52 B1
Harrington Ho E5 52 C1
NW1 232 A2
SW1 259 D2
Harrington Rd E11 54 C1
SW7 114 B2 256 C4
Croydon SE25 206 B5
Harrington Rd Sta
SE25 206 C6
Harrington Sq
NW1 93 C5 232 A3
Harrington St
NW1 93 C4 232 A2
Harrington Way SE18 121 D3
Harriott Cl SE10 120 D2
Harriott Ho 11 E1 96 C1
Harris City Tech Coll
SE19 183 D2
Harris Cl Enfield EN2 4 D4
Heston TW5 129 C4
Harris Cotts 1 E15 98 D6
Harris Ho 10 E3 97 C4
8 SW9 138 C2
Harris Lo SE6 164 A3
Harrison Cl N20 14 C3
Harrison Ho SE17 262 C2
Harrison Rd RM10 81 D2
Harrisons Ct 1 SE14 140 D6
Harrison's Rise CR0 220 D5
Harrison St
WC1 94 A4 233 B1
Harrison Way TW17 192 D4
Harris Rd DA7 147 B4
Dagenham RM9 81 B3
Harris St E17 53 B2
SE5 139 B5
Harris Way TW16 171 C2
Harrodian Sch The
SW13 133 D5
Harrogate Ct 2 SE26 162 A1
Harrold Ho 1 NW3 70 A1
Harrold Rd RM8 80 B3
Harrow Ave EN1 17 D5
Harroway Rd SW11 136 B3
Harrowby St
W1 92 C1 237 B2
Harrow Cl KT9 213 D1
Harrow Coll HA1 42 C2
Harrow Coll (Harrow Weald
Campus) HA3 24 C4
Harrowdene Cl HA0 65 D4
Harrowdene Ct SW19 179 A5
Harrowdene Gdns
TW11 175 A3
Harrowdene Rd HA0 65 D4
Harrow Dr N9 17 D3
Harrowes Meade HA8 10 C1
Harrow Fields Gdns
HA1 64 C5
Harrowgate Ho 22 E9 74 D2
Harrowgate Rd E9 75 A1
Harrow Gn E11 76 C5

Harrow High Sch HA1 43 A3
Harrow Hospl HA2 64 C6
Harrow La E14 120 A6
Harrow Lo SM2 218 B2
Harrow Manor Way
SE2 124 C3
Harrow Mus & Her Ctr★
HA2 42 A6
Harrow-on-the-Hill Sta
HA1 42 C3
Harrow Pk HA1 64 C6
Harrow Pl E1 95 C1 243 B2
Harrow Rd E11 76 D5
2 E6 100 A6
W2 92 A2 236 B3
W2,W9 91 C3
Ashford TW15 148 C2
Barking IG11 101 C6
Carshalton SM1,SM2,
SM5 218 C2
Ilford IG1 79 A4
Wembley HA0 65 A4
Wembley HA0 65 D3
Wembley HA9 66 C2
Harrow Sch HA1 42 C1
Harrow St NW1 237 A4
Harrow View
Harrow HA1,HA2 42 B5
Hayes UB3 84 A1
Hillingdon UB10 83 A4
Harrow View Rd W5 87 B3
Harrow Way
Charlton TW17 171 A1
South Oxhey WD19 23 A6
Harrow Weald Pk HA3 24 B4
Harrow & Wealdstone Sta
HA1 42 C5
Harry Ct 15 NW9 46 A5
Harry Gosling Prim Sch
E1 96 A1
Harry Hinkins Ho
SE17 262 B1
Harry Lambourn Ho 10
SE15 140 B5
Harston 15 KT1 176 C1
Harston Dr EN3 7 C5
Hart Ct E12 78 C1
Harte Rd TW3 129 B3
Hartfield Ave
Borehamwood WD6 10 C6
Northolt UB5 84 B5
Hartfield Cl WD6 10 C6
Hartfield Cres BR4 225 A5
Merton SW19 179 B3
Hartfield Gr SE20 184 C2
Hartfield Ho UB5 84 B5
Hartfield Rd
Chessington KT9 213 D3
Hayes BR4 225 A4
Merton SW19 179 C3
Hartfield Terr E3 97 C5
Hartford Ave HA3 43 B6
Hartford Rd DA5 169 C5
West Ewell KT19 214 D2
Hart Gr Ealing W5 110 C5
Southall UB1 85 C2
Hart Grove Ct 3 W5 110 C5
Hartham Cl N7 72 A3
Isleworth TW7 131 A4
Hartham Rd N7 72 A3
Isleworth TW7 131 A4
Tottenham N17 33 D1
Hart Ho SW2 160 C3
Harting Rd SE9 166 A1
Hartington Cl BR6 227 A3
Harrow HA1 64 C4
Hartington Ct SW8 270 A2
Chiswick W4 132 D5
Hartington Rd E17 53 A3
SW8 138 A5 270 A3
Chiswick W4 133 A4
Ealing W13 109 B6
Newham E16 99 B1
Southall UB2 107 A3
Twickenham TW1 153 B5
Hartismere Rd
SW6 135 B5 264 D4
Hartlake Rd E9 75 A2
Hartland NW1 232 B5
Hartland Cl
Edgware HA8 10 C2
Enfield N21 17 A5
Hartland Ct 5 N11 30 D5
Hartland Dr
Edgware HA8 10 C2
Ruislip HA4 62 B4
Hartland Rd E15 76 D1
N11 30 D5
NW1 71 B1
NW6 91 B6
Cheam SM4 201 D2
Hampton TW12 173 D6
Isleworth TW7 131 A2
Hartlands Cl DA5 169 B5
Hartlands Cvn Pk The
TW5 128 B6
Hartland Way
Croydon CR0 223 A6
Morden SM4 201 B2
Hartlepool Ct E16 122 D5
Hartley Ave E6 100 A6
NW7 27 D5
Hartley Cl BR1 188 B1
NW7 27 D5
Hartley Ct W5 110 C5
Hartley Ho N3 29 D4
SE1 263 D4
Putney SW15 156 A6
Hartley Prim Sch E6 100 A6
Hartley Rd E11 54 D1
Bexley DA16 146 C5
Thornton Heath CR0 205 A2
Hartley St E2 96 C4
Hart Lo EN5 1 A2
Hartmann Rd E16 122 A5
Hartmoor Mews EN3 6 D6
Hartnoll Ho 4 N7 72 C3
Hartnoll St N7 72 B3
Harton Cl BR1 187 D2
Harton Lo 2 SE8 141 C4
Harton Rd N9 18 B2
Harton St SE8 141 C4
Hartopp Ct N16 73 C5
Hartopp Point SW6 264 B4
Hartsbourne Ave WD23 8 B2
Hartsbourne Cl WD23 8 B2
Hartsbourne Ct 5 UB1 86 A1
Hartsbourne Pk WD23 8 C2
Hartsbourne Prim Sch
WD23 8 B2
Hartsbourne Rd WD23 8 B2
Harts Gr IG8 37 A5
Hartshill Cl UB10 60 D2
Hartshorn Alley EC3 243 B1
Hartshorn Gdns E6 100 C3
Hart's La SE14 141 A4
Harts La IG11 78 D2
Hartslock Dr SE2 124 D4
Hartsmead Rd SE9 166 B2
Hart Sq SM4 201 C3
Hart St EC3 253 B6
Hartsway EN3 6 C1
Hartswood Gn WD23 8 B2
Hartswood Ho 10 SW2 160 A3
Hartswood Rd W12 111 D3
Hartsworth Cl E13 98 D5
Hartville Rd SE18 123 C2
Hartwell Dr E4 36 A4
Hartwell Ho 2 SE7 121 B1
Hartwell St E8 73 D2
Harvard Ct NW6 69 D3
9 SE9 166 C5
Harvard Hill W4 132 D6
Harvard Ho 3 SE17 138 D6
Putney SW15 156 D5
Harvard Mans 18
SW11 136 B1
Harvard Rd SE13 164 A6
W4 110 D1
11 W4 111 A1
Hounslow TW7 130 C4
Harvel Cres SE2 124 D1
Harvest Bank Rd BR4 225 A5
Harvest Ct
Beckenham BR3 185 C3
Littleton TW17 192 C5
Harvesters Cl TW7 152 B6
Harvest La
Loughton IG10 21 D4
Thames Ditton KT7 197 A3
Harvest Rd TW13 150 A1
Harvey Ct E17 53 C4
SW11 267 B2
Harvey Dr TW12 173 C2
Harvey Gdns E11 54 D1
SE7 121 C1
Harvey Ho 10 E1 96 B3
N1 235 D5
N8 50 A6
SW1 259 D1
Barking IG11 79 A1
Brentford TW8 110 A1
Dagenham RM6 58 D5
Harvey Lo 8 W9 91 C2
Harvey Mews N8 50 B4
Harvey Point 7 E16 99 A2
Harvey Rd E11 54 D1
N8 50 B4
15 SE5 139 B4
Hillingdon UB10 82 C5
Ilford IG1 78 D3
Ruislip UB5 62 C1
Twickenham TW4 151 B4
Walton-on-T KT12 194 A2
Harvey St N1 235 D5
Harvill Rd DA14 191 A5
UB9 38 A2
Harvil Rd UB9,UB10 38 A2
Harvington Sch W5 87 D1
Harvington Wlk E8 74 A1
Harvist Rd NW6 91 A5
Harwell Cl HA4 39 B1
Harwick Mans SE18 122 A3
Harwood Ave BR1 187 B1
Mitcham CR4 202 C6
Harwood Cl N12 30 C4
Wembley HA0 65 D4
Harwood Ct N1 235 D5
Putney SW15 134 C1
Harwood Dr UB10 82 B6
Harwood Point SE16 119 B4
Harwood Rd
SW6 135 D5 265 C3
Harwoods Yd N21 16 C4
Harwood Terr
SW6 135 D4 265 C2
Hascombe Ho 11
SW15 156 B3
Hascombe Terr 2
SE5 139 B3
Haselbury Rd N9 17 C1
Haseley End SE23 162 C4
Haselrigge Rd SW4 137 D1
Haseltine Prim Sch
SE26 185 B6
Haseltine Rd SE26 185 B6
Haselwood Dr EN2 4 D1
Haskard Rd RM9 80 D4
Hasker St SW3 114 C2 257 B4
Haslam Ave SM3 201 A1
Haslam Cl N1 72 C1
Uxbridge UB10 61 A6
Haslam Ct N11 31 B6
Haslam Ho 1 N1 73 A1
Haslam St SE15 139 D4
Haslemere Ave NW4 46 D3
W13 109 A3
Barnet, London EN4 14 D3
Cranford TW5 128 C3
Mitcham CR4,SW19 180 B1
Wandsworth SW18 157 D2
Haslemere Cl
Hampton TW12 173 B5
Wallington SM6 220 A3
Haslemere Ct 5 N16 51 C1
Haslemere Fst Sch
CR4 180 B1
Haslemere Gdns N3 47 B5
Haslemere & Heathrow Est
The TW4 128 B2
Haslemere Ind Est
Feltham TW14 150 A6
Wandsworth SW18 157 D2
Haslemere Rd DA7 147 C3
N8 50 A2
Ilford IG3 79 D6
Southgate N21 16 D3
Thornton Heath CR7 204 D4
Hasler Cl SE28 124 C6
Hasler Ct E12 78 A4
Haslett Rd TW17 171 C1
Hasluck Gdns EN5 14 A5
Hasmonean High Sch
(Boys) NW4 28 D1
Hasmonean High Sch
(Girls) NW7 28 A2
Hasmonean Prim Sch
NW4 46 D4
Hassard St E2 95 D5
Hassendean Rd SE3 143 B5
Hassett Rd E9 75 A2
Hassocks Cl SE23,SE26 162 B1
Hassocks Rd SW16 181 D2
Hassop Rd NW2 68 D4
Hassop Wlk SE9 188 A6
Hasted Rd SE7 121 D1
Hastings Ave IG6 57 A5
Hastings Cl 16 SE15 140 A5
New Barnet EN5 2 A1
Wembley HA0 65 C4
Hastings Dr KT6 197 C3
Hastings Ho 11 SE18 122 B2
18 W12 112 B6
Ealing W13 109 B6
Enfield EN3 6 C3
Tottenham N17 34 A2
Hastings Hos WC1 233 A1
Hastings Pl 1 CR0 205 D1
Hastings Rd BR2 226 A6
N11 31 D5
N17 51 B6
Croydon CR0 205 D1
Ealing W13 109 B6
Hastings St
WC1 94 A4 233 A1
Hastingwood Ct E17 53 D4
Hastingwood Trad Est
N18 34 D4
N18 35 A4
Hastoe Cl UB4 85 A3
Hatcham Mews Bsns Ctr
SE14 140 D4
Hatcham Park Mews
SE14 140 D4
Hatcham Park Rd
SE14 140 D4
Hatcham Rd SE15 140 C6
Hatchard Rd N19 72 A6
Hatchcroft NW4 46 B6
Hatch End High Sch
HA3 23 D2
Hatch End Sta HA5 23 C3
Hatchett Rd TW14 149 A3
Hatchfield Ho 8 N15 51 C3
Hatch Gr RM6 59 A5
Hatch La E4 20 C1
Hatch Pl TW10 176 B5
Hatch Rd SW16 182 A1
Hatch The EN3 6 D4
Hatchwoods IG8 36 D6
Hatcliffe Almshouses 8
SE10 120 C1
Hatcliffe Cl SE3 142 D2
Hatcliffe St SE10 120 D1
Hatfield Cl SE14 140 D5
Ilford IG6 56 D6
Mitcham CR4 202 B5
Hatfield Ct
Greenwich SE3 143 A5
8 Northolt UB5 84 C4
Hatfield First Sch
SM4 201 A3
Hatfield Ho E11 54 D2
EC1 242 A5
16 Kingston KT6 198 A4
Hatfield Mead SM4 201 C4
Hatfield Rd E15 76 C3
W4 111 B4
Dagenham RM9 81 A1
10 Ealing W13,W7 109 A5
Hatfields SE1 116 C5 251 B4
Hathaway Cl BR2 210 B1
Ruislip HA4 61 D4
Stanmore HA7 25 A5
Hathaway Cres E12 78 C2
Hathaway Gdns
Ealing W13 87 A2
Ilford RM6 58 D4
Hathaway Ho 3 N1 95 C4
Hathaway Prim Sch
W13 86 D2
Hathaway Rd CR0 204 D2
Hatherleigh Cl
Chessington KT9 213 D3
Morden SM4 201 C5
Hatherleigh Ho SM4 201 C5
Hatherleigh Rd HA4 62 A6
Hatherley Cres DA14 168 A2
Hatherley Ct 6 W2 91 D1
Hatherley Gdns E6 99 D4
N8 50 A3
Hatherley Gr W2 91 D1
Hatherley Ho 2 E17 53 C5
Hatherley Mews E17 53 C5
Hatherley Rd E17 53 C5
Richmond TW9 132 B4
Sidcup DA14 168 A1
Hatherley St SW1 259 B3
Hathern Gdns SE9 188 C6
Hatherop Rd TW12 173 B3
Hathersage Ct N1 73 B3
Hathersley Ho 3 SW2 160 C4
Hathorne Cl 3 SE15 140 B3
Hathway Ho 3 SE15 140 C3
Hathway St 4 SE15 140 C3
Hatley Ave IG6 57 A5
Hatley Cl N11 30 D5
Hatley Rd N4,N7 72 B6
Hat & Mitre Ct EC1 241 D5
Hatteraick St 6 SE16 118 C4
Hattersfield Cl DA17 125 B2
Hatton Cl SE18 145 B5
Hatton Cross Rdbt
TW6 127 D2
Hatton Cross Sta TW6 127 D1
Hatton Ct BR7 188 B3
Hatton Gdn EC1 94 C2 241 B4
Hatton Gdns CR4 202 D4
Hatton Gn TW14 128 A1
Hatton Ho 13 E1 118 A6
Hatton Pl EC1 241 B4
Hatton Rd
Hatton TW14,TW6 149 C6
Thornton Heath CR0 204 C1
Hatton Rd N TW6 127 B4
Hatton Row NW8 236 D5
Hatton Sch IG8 55 D6
Hatton St NW8 236 D5
Hatton Wall
EC1 94 C2 241 B4
Haughmond 4 N12 29 D6
Haunch of Venison Yd
W1 238 C1
Hauteville Court Gdns 2
W6 111 D3
Havana Rd SW18,SW19 157 C2
Havannah St E14 119 C4
Havant Rd E17 54 A6
Havelock Cl 13 W12 112 B6
Havelock Ct UB2 107 B3
Havelock Hall 8 CR0 205 D1
Havelock Ho
4 Croydon CR0 205 D1
Forest Hill SE23 162 C3
Havelock Pl HA1 42 C3
Havelock Prim Sch
UB2 107 B3
Havelock Rd DA17 125 B2
Bromley BR2 209 C5
Croydon CR0 221 D6
Harrow HA3 42 C6
Southall UB2 107 C3
Tottenham N17 34 A1
Havelock Rd *continued*
Wimbledon SW19 180 A5
Havelock St N1 94 A6 233 B6
Ilford IG1 78 D6
Havelock Terr
SW8 137 B5 268 D3
Havelock Wlk SE23 162 C2
Haven Cl SE9 166 B1
Hayes UB4 83 C3
Sidcup DA14 190 C4
Wimbledon SW19 156 D1
Haven Ct BR3 186 A1
Haven Gn W5 87 D1
Haven Green Ct W5 87 D1
Havenhurst Rise EN2 4 C3
Haven La W5 88 A1
Haven Lo NW11 47 B4
7 SE18 122 D2
15 Enfield EN1 17 C6
Haven Pl W5 109 D6
Havenpool NW8 91 D6
Haven Rd TW15 148 D1
Haven St 17 NW1 71 B1
Haven The
Ashford TW16 172 A3
East Barnet N14 15 B5
Richmond TW9 132 C2
Havenwood HA9 66 D5
Havercourt 3 NW3 70 C2
Haverfield Gdns TW9 132 C5
Haverfield Rd E3 97 A4
Haverford Way HA8 26 B2
Havergal Villas N15 50 D6
Haverhill Rd
Chingford E4 20 A3
Streatham SW12 159 C3
Havering 8 NW1 71 B1
Havering Gdns RM6 58 D4
Havering Ho N4 51 A2
Havering St E1 96 D1
Havering Way IG11 102 B4
Haverley 14 SW20 178 D3
Haversham Cl TW1 153 D5
Haversham Ct UB6 64 D2
Haversham Lo NW2 68 D3
Haversham Pl N6 70 D6
Haverstock Ct 2 BR5 190 B1
Haverstock Hill NW3 70 D2
Haverstock Rd NW5 71 A3
Haverstock Sch NW1 71 A2
Haverstock St
N1 94 D5 234 D3
Haverthwaite Rd BR6 227 B5
Havilland Ct HA8 26 B6
Havil St SE5 139 C4
Havisham Ho 23 SE16 118 A4
Havisham Pl SW16 182 D3
Hawarden Gr SE24 161 A4
Hawarden Hill NW2 68 A5
Hawarden Rd E17 52 D5
Hawberry Ho N7 72 A2
Hawbridge Rd E11 54 B1
Hawes Down Inf Sch BR4 ....
Hawes Down Jun Sch
BR4 208 B1
Hawes La BR4 224 C6
Hawes Rd BR1 187 B2
Edmonton N18 34 B4
Hawes St N1 72 D1
Haweswater Ho TW1 152 D6
Hawfinch 29 NW9 27 D2
Hawgood St E3 97 C2
Hawkdene E4 20 A5
Hawke Ct UB4 84 C3
Hawkedale Fst Sch
TW16 193 D6
Hawke Ho 20 E1 96 D3
Hawke Park Rd N22 50 D6
Hawke Pl 29 SE16 118 D4
Hawker 28 NW9 27 D2
Hawker Ct 14 KT2 176 C3
Hawke Rd SE19 183 C4
Hawkesbury Rd SW15 156 B6
Hawkesfield Rd SE23 163 B2
Hawkesley Cl TW1 175 A6
Hawkes Rd
Feltham TW14 150 A4
Mitcham CR4 180 D2
Hawkesworth Ho 5
SW4 159 C5
Hawke Twr 4 SE14 141 A6
Hawkewood Rd TW16 194 A6
Hawkfield Ct TW7 130 C3
Hawk Ho 7 SW11 136 C2
Hawkhurst Gdns KT9 214 A4
Hawkhurst Rd SW16 181 D2
Hawkhurst Way
New Malden KT3 199 B4
West Wickham BR4 223 D6
Hawkinge N17 33 B1
Hawkins Cl NW7 27 B5
Harrow HA1 42 B2
Hawkins Ho 3 SE8 141 C6
Hawkins Rd TW11 175 B4
Hawkins Way SE6 185 C5
Hawkley Gdns SE27 160 D2
Hawkridge 19 NW5 71 A2
Hawkridge Cl RM6 58 C3
Hawksbrook La BR3 208 A3
Hawkshead NW1 232
Hawkshead Cl BR1 186
Hawkshead Rd NW10 67
W4 111
Hawkslade Rd SE15 162
Hawksley Rd N16 73
Hawks Mews 10 SE10 142
Hawksmoor Cl 2 E6 100
SE18 123
Hawksmoor Mews E1 118
Hawksmoor Sch SE28 124
Hawksmoor St 5 W6 134
Hawksmouth E4 20
Hawks Rd KT1 176
Hawkstone Rd SE16 118
Hawkswood Sch E4 20
Hawkwell Ct E4 20
Hawkwell Ho RM8 81
Hawkwell Wlk N1 235
Hawkwood Cres E4 19
Hawkwood La BR7 189
Hawkwood Mount 1
E5 52
Hawlands Dr HA5 41 A
Hawley Cl TW12 173
Hawley Cres NW1 71
Hawley Inf Sch NW1 71
Hawley Mews 4 NW1 71
Hawley Rd N18 34 D
3 NW1 71
Hawley St NW1 71
Hawley Way TW15 170 D
Haworth Ct E15 76 A
Haworth Ho 7 SW2 160 C
Hawstead Rd SE6 163 D
Hawsted IG9 21
Hawthorn Ave Bow E3 97 B
Bowes Park N13 32 A
South Norwood CR7 182 D
Hawthorn Cl BR5 211 B
Cranford TW5 128 B
Hampton TW12 173 C
Hawthorn Cres SW17 181 A
Hawthorn Ct
Putney SW15 134 B
Richmond TW9 132 D
8 West Norwood
SW16 182 C
Hawthorn Ctr HA1 43 A
Hawthornden Cl N12 30 C
Hawthorndene Cl BR2 225 A
Hawthorndene Rd
BR2 225 A6
Hawthorn Dr
Coney Hall BR4 224 C4
Harrow HA2 41 C3
Hawthorne Ave
Harrow HA3 43 A3
Mitcham CR4 180 B1
Ruislip HA4 40 B2
Wallington SM5 219 A1
Hawthorne Cl BR1 210 B6
N1 73 C2
Sutton SM1 218 A6
Hawthorne Ct UB7 104 B4
Hawthorne Cres
Chingford E4 35 D4
Ealing W5 110 A5
Pinner HA6 22 A1
Hawthorne Gr NW9 45 A2
Hawthorne Ho SW1 259 B1
Hawthorne Mews UB6 86 A1
Hawthorne Rd BR1 210 B6
E17 53 C6
Edmonton N18 33 D5
Feltham TW14 150 A3
Hawthorne Way N9 17 D2
Hawthorn Farm Ave
UB5 85 A6
Hawthorn Gdns W5 109 D3
Hawthorn Gr
Edgware EN5 11 D5
Enfield EN2 5 B5
Penge SE20 184 B2
Hawthorn Hatch TW8 131 B5
Hawthorn Mews NW7 29 A2
Hawthorn Pl UB3 105 D6
Hawthorn Rd DA6 147 B1
N8 50 A6
NW10 68 A1
Brentford TW8 131 B5
Carshalton SM1,SM2,
SM5 218 C2
Wallington SM5,SM6 219 B1
Woodford IG9 37 D6
Hawthorns IG8 21 A1
Hawthorns The KT17 216 A1
Hawthorn Terr DA15 167 D6
Hawthorn Way TW17 193 B5
Hawthorn Wlk W10 91 A3
Hawtrey Ave UB5 84 D5
Hawtrey Dr HA4 40 A2
Hawtrey Rd NW3 70 C1
Haxted Rd BR1 187 B2
Haybridge Ho 1 E5 74 C6
Hay Cl E15 76 D1
Haycroft Gdns NW10 90 B6
Haycroft Mans NW10 90 A6
Haycroft Rd SW2 160 A6

aycroft Rd *continued*
Surbiton KT6 214 A6
ay Currie St E14 97 D1
ayday Rd E16 99 A2
ayden's Pl W11 91 B1
aydock Ave UB5 63 C2
aydock Gn UB5 63 C2
aydock Green Flats 2
UB5 63 C2
aydon Cl NW9 45 A5
Enfield EN1 17 C6
aydon Ct NW9 45 A5
aydon Dr HA5 40 A5
aydon Ho Ealing W7 108 D5
Teddington TW11 175 C3
aydon Park Rd
SW19 179 D5
aydon Rd RM8 80 C6
aydon Sch HA5 39 D6
aydon's Rd SW19 180 A4
aydons Road Sta
SW19 180 A5
aydon St E1,
EC3 117 D6 253 C6
Haydon Way SW11 136 B1
Haydon Wlk E1 243 D1
Hayes Bridge Ret Pk
UB4 106 D6
Hayes Chase BR4 208 C3
Hayes Cl BR2 225 A6
Hayes Cres NW11 47 B4
Cheam SM3 216 D4
Hayes Ct 23 SE5 139 A5
Streatham SW12 160 A3
Wimbledon SW19 179 A4
Hayes End Cl UB4 83 B2
Hayes End Dr UB4 83 B3
Hayesend Ho SW17 180 A6
Hayes End Rd UB4 83 B3
Hayesford Park Dr
BR2 208 D4
Hayes Garden BR2 209 A1
Hayes & Harlington Sta
UB3 105 D3
Hayes Hill BR2 208 C1
Hayes Hill Rd BR2 208 D1
Hayes La BR2 209 A4
Beckenham BR2,BR3 208 B5
Hayes Manor Sch UB3 83 C1
Hayes Mead Rd BR2 208 C1
Hayes Park Sch UB4 83 D3
Hayes Pl NW1 237 B5
Hayes Prim Sch BR2 209 B1
Hayes Rd BR2 209 A5
Southall UB2 106 B2
Hayes Sch BR2 225 B6
Hayes St BR2 209 B1
Hayes Sta BR2 208 D1
Hayes Way BR3 208 B5
Hayes Wood Ave BR2 209 B1
Hayfield Pas E1 96 C3
Hayford Ct NW2 68 D5
Haygarth Pl 2 SW19 178 D5
Haygreen Cl KT2 176 D4
Hay Hill W1 115 B6 248 D5
Hay La NW9 45 B5
Hayland Cl NW9 45 B5
Hay Lane Sch NW9 45 A5
Hayles Bldgs SE11 261 D4
Hayles St SE11 116 D3 261 C4
Haylett Gdns KT1 197 D5
Hayling Ave TW13 150 A1
Hayling Cl 20 N16 73 C3
Hayling Ct SM3 216 C4
Haymaker Cl UB10 60 B1
Hayman Cres UB4 83 B5
Haymans Point SE11 260 C2
Haymarket
SW1 115 D6 249 C5
Haymeads Dr KT10 212 A2
Haymer Gdns KT4 216 A5
Haymerle Ho 6 SE15 140 A5
Haymerle Rd SE15 140 A6
Haymerle Sch SE15 140 A6
Haymill Cl UB6 86 D4
Hayne Ho W11 244 A4
Hayne Rd BR3 185 B2
Haynes Cl N11 15 A1
SE3 142 C2
Tottenham N17 34 B3
Haynes Dr N9 18 B1
Haynes Ho 3 E9 74 D2
Haynes La SE19 183 C4
Haynes Rd HA0 66 A1
Hayne St EC1 94 D2 241 D4
Haynt Wlk SW20 201 A6
Hay's Galleria SE1 253 A4
Hay's La SE1 253 A4
Haysleigh Gdns SE20 184 A1
Haysleigh Ho SE20 184 B1
Hay's Mews
W1 115 B6 248 C4
Hay St E2 96 A6
Haystall Cl UB4 83 C5
Haystocks E18 55 C6
Hayter Ho W12 112 A6
Hayter Rd SW2 160 B6
Haythorn Ho
SW11 136 B4 266 D1
Hayton Cl 11 E8 73 D2
Hayward Cl SW19 179 D2
Hayward Ct 14 SW4 138 A3
Mitcham CR4 180 B1
Hayward Gallery★
SE1 116 B5 250 D4
Hayward Gdns SW15 156 C5
Hayward Ho E5 74 B5
N1 234 A4
Hayward Rd N20 14 A2
Thames Ditton KT7 196 D1
Haywards Cl RM6 58 C4
Haywards Pl EC1 241 C6
Haywood Cl HA5 22 D1
Haywood Lo N11 31 D4
23 N7 71 D3
Haywood Rd BR2 209 D5
Haywood Rise BR6 227 C3
Hazel Ave UB7 104 C3
Hazelbank KT5 199 A1
Hazel Bank SE25 183 C1
Hazelbank Rd SE6 164 C2
Hazelbourne Rd SW12 159 B5
Hazelbury Cl SW19 179 C1
Hazelbury Gn N9 17 C1
Hazelbury Inf Sch N9 17 C1
Hazelbury Jun Sch N9 17 C1
Hazelbury La N9 17 C1
Hazel Cl N19 71 C6
NW9 27 D1
SE15 140 A3
Brentford TW8 131 B5
Croydon CR0 206 D1
Edmonton N13 17 B1
Mitcham CR4 203 D5
Twickenham TW2 152 A4
Hazelcroft HA5 23 D4
Hazelcroft Cl UB10 60 B1
Hazel Ct Ealing W5 110 A6
9 West Norwood
SW16 182 C5
Hazeldean Rd NW10 67 B1
Hazeldene Dr HA5 40 C6
Hazeldene Gdns UB10 83 A6
Hazeldene Rd
Bexley DA16 146 C3
Ilford IG3 80 B6
Hazeldon Rd SE4 163 A6
Hazel Gdns HA8 26 D6
Hazel Gr Dagenham RM6 59 A6
Enfield EN1 18 A5
Feltham TW14 150 A3
Forest Hill SE26 184 D6
Orpington BR6 226 D6
Wembley HA0 88 A6
Hazelgreen Cl N21 16 D3
Hazel Ho 12 NW3 70 D2
SE4 141 B2
Hazelhurst BR3 186 B2
Hazelhurst Ct SE6 186 A5
Hazelhurst Rd SW17 180 B6
Hazellville Rd N19 49 D1
Hazel Mead EN5 12 B6
Hazelmere Cl
Feltham TW14 149 C5
Northolt UB5 85 B5
Hazelmere Ct 10 SW2 160 B3
Hazelmere Dr UB5 85 B5
Hazelmere Rd BR5 211 B5
NW6 91 B6
Northolt UB5 85 B5
Hazelmere Way BR2 209 A3
Hazelmere Wlk UB5 85 B5
Hazel Rd E15 76 C3
NW10 90 C4
Hazeltree La UB5 85 A4
Hazel Way E4 35 B4
SE1 263 C4
Hazel Wlk BR2 210 C3
Hazelwood IG10 21 D6
Hazelwood Ave SM4 201 D5
Hazelwood Cl E5 75 A5
W5 110 A4
Harrow HA2 41 D5
Hazelwood Cres N13 32 C6
Hazelwood Ct 1 NW10 67 C5
Surbiton KT6 198 A3
Hazelwood Dr HA5 22 B1
Hazelwood Ho 11 SE8 119 A2
Beckenham BR2 208 C6
Edmonton N13 32 D6
Hazelwood Jun & Inf Schs
N13 32 C6
Hazelwood La N13 32 C6
Hazelwood Lo BR4 208 A2
Hazelwood Mans SW6 264 C2
Hazelwood Rd E17 53 A4
Enfield EN1 17 D5
Hazlebury Rd SW6 135 D3
Hazledean Rd CR0 221 B6
Hazledene Rd W4 133 A6
Hazlemere Bsns Ctr
EN1 18 B6
Hazlemere Gdns KT4 200 A1
Hazlewell Rd SW15 156 C6
Hazlewood Cres W10 91 A3
Hazlewood Twr W10 91 B3
Hazlitt Cl TW13 173 A6
Hazlitt Ct 4 SE28 124 C5
Hazlitt Mews W14 254 A5
Hazlitt Rd
W14 113 A3 254 A5
Heacham Ave UB10 61 A5
Headbourne Ho SE1 262 D6
Headcorn 10 NW5 71 A2
Headcorn Pl CR7 204 B5
Headcorn Rd BR1 187 A5
Thornton Heath CR7 204 B5
Tottenham N17 33 D3
Headfort Pl
SW1 115 A4 248 B1
Headington Rd SW18 158 A2
Headlam Rd SW4 159 D4
Headlam St E1 96 B3
Headley App IG2 56 D4
Headley Ave CR0,SM6 220 B3
Headley Cl KT19 214 C2
Headley Ct SE26 184 C5
Headley Dr Ilford IG2 56 D3
New Addington CR0 224 A1
Headley Ho 5 BR5 190 B1
Heads Mews W11 91 C1
Head St E1 96 D1
Headstone Dr HA1,HA3 42 C6
Headstone Gdns HA2 42 A5
Headstone La
Harrow HA2 41 D5
Harrow HA2,HA3 23 D2
Headstone Lane Sta
HA3 23 D2
Headstone Rd HA1 42 C3
Headway Cl TW10 175 C6
Heald St SE8,SE14 141 C4
Healey St NW1 71 B2
Healy Ct EN5 12 D5
Healy Dr 1 BR6 227 D4
Healy Ho 2 E3 97 C3
12 SW9 138 C5
Heanor Ct 4 E5 74 D4
Hearne Rd W4 132 C6
Hearn Rise UB5 84 D6
Hearn's Bldgs SE17 262 D3
Hearn St EC2 95 C3 243 B5
Hearnville Rd SW12 159 A3
Heart Hospl The
W1 93 A2 238 B4
Heatham Pk TW2 152 D4
Heath Ave DA7 146 D6
Heathbourne Rd WD23,
HA7 8 D3
Heathbrook Prim Sch
SW4 137 C3
Heath Brow NW3 70 A5
Heath Bsns Ctr The
TW3 130 A1
Heath Cl NW11 47 D2
Croydon CR2 220 D2
Ealing W5 88 B3
Harlington UB3 127 B5
Heathcote Gr E4 20 A2
Heathcote Rd TW1 153 B6
Heathcote Sch E4 20 C2
Heathcote St
WC1 94 B4 233 C1
Heathcroft NW11 47 D1
Ealing W5 88 B3
Heathcroft Ave TW16 171 D3
Heathcroft Gdns E4 36 B2
Heath Ct E11 54 D3
N16 51 B1
2 NW3 70 A2
Uxbridge UB8 60 A1
Heathdale Ave TW4 129 A2
Heathdene N14 15 C4
Heathdene Dr DA17 125 D2
Heathdene Rd
South Norwood SW16 182 B3
Wallington SM5,SM6 219 B1
Heath Dr SW20 200 C5
Heathedge SE23,SE26 162 B2
Heatherbank BR7 188 C1
SE9 144 B3
Heather Cl E6 100 C1
SW8 137 B2
Hampton TW12 173 B2
Hillingdon UB8 82 B2
Isleworth TW7 152 B6
Heather Ct SW4 270 B1
Heatherdale Cl KT2 176 D3
Heatherdene Cl N12 30 A2
Mitcham CR4 202 C5
Heatherdene Mans 2
TW1 153 D5
Heather Dr EN2 4 D3
Heatherfold Way HA5,
HA6 39 D6
Heather Gdns NW11 47 A3
Belmont SM2 217 C2
Heather Ho 7 E14 98 A1
Heather La UB7 82 A1
Heatherlands TW16 172 A4
Heatherley Ct N16 74 A5
Heatherley Dr IG5 56 B6
Heatherley Sch of Fine Art
SW10 266 B3
Heather Lo N16 51 C1
Heather Park Dr HA0 66 C1
Heather Park Par HA0 66 B1
Heather Rd E4 35 B4
NW2 67 D6
Lewisham SE12 165 A3
Heatherset Cl KT10 212 A3
Heatherset Gdns
SW16 182 B3
Heatherside Rd
Sidcup DA14 168 C1
West Ewell KT19 215 B1
Heathers The TW19 148 B4
Heather Way HA7 24 D4
Heather Wlk W10 91 A3
Edgware HA8 26 D5
Twickenham TW4 151 C4
Heatherwood Cl E12 77 C6
Heatherwood Dr UB4 83 B5
Heathfield BR7 189 A4
Chingford E4 20 A1
Heathfield Ave SW18 158 B4
Heathfield Cl BR2 225 C3
E16 99 D2
Heathfield Ct DA14 190 B5
5 W4 111 B1
Ashford TW15 148 A1
Penge SE20 184 C3
Wandsworth SW18 158 B4
Heathfield Dr CR4 180 C2
Heathfielde N2 48 A4
Heathfield Gdns NW11 46 D3
SW18 158 B5
W4 111 A1
Croydon CR0 221 B4
Heathfield Ho SE3 142 C3
Heathfield Inf Sch
TW2 151 C3
Heathfield Jun Sch
TW2 151 C3
Heathfield La BR7 189 A4
Heathfield N TW1,TW2 152 D4
Heathfield Park Dr
RM6 58 B4
Heathfield Pk NW2 68 C2
Heathfield Rd BR2 225 D3
DA6 147 B1
SW18 158 B5
W3 110 D4
Bromley BR1 186 D3
Croydon CR0 221 B4
Heathfield Rise HA4 39 A2
Heathfield S TW1,TW2 152 D4
Heathfield Sch HA5 40 D2
Heathfield Sq SW18 158 B4
Heathfield Terr SE18 145 D6
W4 111 B1
Heathfield Vale CR2 223 A1
Heathgate NW11 47 D3
Heathgate Pl NW3 70 D4
Heath Gdns TW1 152 D2
Heath Gr Ashford TW16 171 D3
Penge SE20 184 C3
Heath Ho DA15 189 D6
Thornton Heath CR7 204 C4
Uxbridge UB10 60 D4
Heath Hurst Rd NW3 70 C4
Heath La SE3 142 B3
Heathland Rd N16 51 C1
Heathland Sch SW19 156 D1
Heathland Sch The
TW4 151 B5
Heathlands Cl
Sunbury TW16 172 A1
Twickenham TW1 152 D3
Heathlands Ct
Hounslow TW4 151 A6
Mitcham CR4 203 A6
Heathlands Way TW4 151 A6
Heathlee Rd SE3 142 D1
Heathley End BR7 189 A4
Heath Lo WD23 8 B3
Heath Mans 4 NW3 70 A4
Putney SW15 156 D5
Heathman's Rd
SW6 135 B4 264 D1
Heath Mead SW19 156 D1
Heathmere Prim Sch
SW15 156 A3
Heath Park Dr BR1 210 A6
Heath Park Gdns NW3 69 D5
Heathpool Ct 8 E1 96 B3
Heath Rd SW8 137 B3
Dagenham RM6 59 A2
Harrow HA1 42 A2
Hillingdon UB10 83 A3
Isleworth TW3,TW7 130 A1
South Norwood CR7 205 A6
Twickenham TW1 152 D3
Heath Rise Hayes BR2 209 A3
Putney SW15 156 D5
Heathrow Airport London
TW6 126 D3
Heathrow Bvd UB7 126 B5
Heathrow Causeway Est
TW4 128 B2
Heathrow International
Trad Est TW4 128 B2
Heathrow Sch UB7 126 B6
Heathrow Terminal 4 Sta
TW6 149 A5
Heathrow Terminals 1,2,3
TW6 126 D2
Heath Royal SW15 156 D5
Heath's Cl EN1 5 C3
Heathshot 8 TW10 154 A5
Heathside NW3 70 B4
Heath Side BR5 211 A2
Heathside
Hinchley Wood KT10 212 C5
Twickenham TW4 151 B4
Heathside Ave DA7 147 A3
Heathside Cl
Hinchley Wood KT10 212 C5
Ilford IG2 57 B4
Heathside Prep Sch
NW3 70 A4
Heath St NW3 70 A5
Heathstan Rd W12 90 A1
Heath Terr RM6 58 D2
Heath The W7 108 C5
Heath View N2 48 A5
NW5 71 A4
Heath View Cl N2 48 A5
Heathview Ct SW19 156 D2
Heath View Dr SE2 146 D6
Heathview Gdns
SW15 156 C4
Heathview Rd CR7 204 C5
Heath Villas SE18 123 D1
Heathville Rd N4,N19 50 A2
Heathwall St SW11 136 D2
Heathway 6 SE3 142 D5
Croydon CR0 223 B5
Greenwich SE3 143 A5
Woodford IG8 37 C5
Heathway Ct NW3 69 C6
Heathwood Ct
1 Hounslow TW3 129 D1
Streatham SW12 159 C3
Heathwood Gdns SE7 122 A1
Heathwood Point 7
SE26 162 D1
Heaton Cl E4 20 A1
Heaton Ho 6 SE15 140 B3
SW10 266 B6
Heaton Rd SE15 140 B3
Mitcham CR4 181 A3
Heaver Rd 24 SW11 136 B2
Heavers Farm Prim Sch
SE25 205 D4
Heavitree Cl SE18 123 B1
Heavitree Rd SE18 123 B1
Hebden Ct 24 E2 95 D6
Hebden Terr N17 33 C4
Hebdon Rd SW17 158 C1
Heber Prim Sch SE22 161 D5
Heber Rd NW2 68 D4
SE22 161 D5
Hebron Rd W6 112 B3
Hecham Cl E17 35 A2
Heckfield Pl
SW6 135 C5 265 A3
Heckford St E1 118 D6
Hector 31 NW9 27 D2
Hector Ct 1 SW9 138 C4
Putney SW15 156 D6
Hector Ho 14 E2 96 B5
Hector St SE18 123 C2
Heddington Gr N7 72 B3
Heddon Cl TW7 131 A1
Heddon Court Ave EN4 14 D6
Heddon Court Par EN4 15 A6
Heddon Ct EN4 15 A6
Heddon Rd EN4 14 D6
Heddon St W1 249 A6
Hedge Hill EN2 4 D4
Hedge La N13 17 A1
Hedgeley IG4 56 B5
Hedgemans Rd RM9 81 A1
Hedgemans Way RM9 81 A2
Hedgemoor Ct 1 E4 36 B5
Hedgerley Gdns UB6 86 A5
Hedgerow La EN5 12 B6
Hedger's Gr E9 75 A2
Hedger St SE11 261 C4
Hedge Wlk SE6 185 D6
Hedgewood Gdns IG5 56 C4
Hedgewood Specl Sch
UB4 83 C4
Hedgley Mews SE12 164 D6
Hedgley St SE12 164 D6
Hedingham Cl 6 N1 73 A1
Hedingham Rd RM8 80 B3
Hedley Ct SW15 156 D5
Hedley Ho E14 120 A3
Hedley Rd TW4 151 C4
Hedley Row N5,N16 73 B3
Hedsor Ho E2 243 C6
Heenan Cl IG11 79 A2
Heene Rd EN2 5 B4
Heidegger Cres SW13 134 B5
Heigham Rd E6 78 A1
Heighton Gdns CR0 220 D3
Heights Cl SW20 178 B3
Heights The N4 50 C3
NW3 70 A4
SE7 121 C1
Beckenham BR3 186 A3
Northolt UB5 63 C3
Heiron St SE17 138 D6
Helby Rd SW4 159 D5
Heldar Ct SE1 252 D1
Helder Gr SE12 164 D4
Helder St CR2 221 B2
Heldmann Cl TW7 130 B1
Helena Cl EN4 2 B5
Helena Ct W5 87 D2
Helena Rd E13 99 A5
E17 53 C4
NW10 68 B3
Ealing W5 87 D2
Helena Sq 12 SE16 119 A6
Helen Ave TW14 150 B4
Helen Cl N2 48 A6
East Molesey KT8 195 D5
Helen Ct N3 47 A6
Helen Gladstone Ho
SE1 251 C2
Helen Ho 9 E2 96 B5
Helen Mackay Ho 9
E14 98 B1
Helen Peele Cotts 10
SE16 118 C3
Helenslea Ave NW11 47 C1
Helen's Pl E2 96 C4
Helen St SE18 122 D2
Helen Taylor Ho 5
SE16 118 A2
Helford Cl HA4 61 C6
Helgiford Gdns TW16 171 C3
Heligan Cl BR6 227 D4
Helios Rd CR4 203 A1
Heliport Est The
SW11 136 B3
Helix Gdns SW2 160 B5
Helix Ho TW7 131 B3
Helix Rd SW2 160 B5
Hellenic Coll of London
SW1 114 D3 257 C5
Hellings St E1 118 A5
Helme Cl SW19 179 B5
Helmet Row EC1 242 B6
Helmore Rd IG11 79 D1
Helmsdale Cl UB4 85 A3
Helmsdale Ho NW6 91 D5
Helmsdale Rd SW16 181 D2
Helmsley 10 E18 55 A6
Helmsley Pl E8 74 B1
Helmsley St 7 E8 74 B1
Helperby Rd NW10 67 C1
Helsby Ct NW8 236 C6
Helsinki Sq SE16 119 A3
Helston NW1 232 B4
Helston Cl HA5 23 B3
Helston Ct N15 51 C4
Helston Ho SE11 261 B2
Helvetia St SE6 163 B2
Helwys Ct E4 36 A4
Hemans Est
SW8 137 D5 269 D3
Hemans St
SW8 137 D5 269 D3
Hemberton Rd SW9 138 A2
Hemery Rd UB6 64 B3
Hemingford Cl N12 30 B5
Hemingford Rd
N1 72 B1 233 D6
Cheam SM3 216 C4
Heming Rd HA8 26 D3
Hemington Ave N11 30 D5
Hemlock Rd W12 111 D6
Hemmen La UB3 83 D1
Hemming Cl 5 TW12 173 C2
Hemmings Cl DA14 168 B2
Hemmings Ct HA8 27 A3
Hemming St E1 96 A3
Hempstead Cl IG9 21 A2
Hempstead Rd E17 36 B1
Hemp Wlk SE17 262 D4
Hemsby Rd KT9 214 B2
Hemstal Rd NW6 69 C1
Hemswell Dr NW9 27 C2
Hemsworth Ct N1 95 C5
Hemsworth St N1 95 C5
Hemus Pl SW3 257 B1
Henchman St W12 89 D1
Hendale Ave NW4 46 B6
Hendale Ho 13 E5 74 B6
Henderson Cl NW10 67 A2
Henderson Ct NW3 70 B3
8 SE14 140 D6
Henderson Dr
NW8 92 B3 236 C6
Henderson Ho 7 RM10 81 C5
Henderson Rd E7 77 C2
Edmonton N9 18 B3
Hayes UB4 84 A4
Thornton Heath CR0 205 B3
Wandsworth SW18 158 C4
Hendfield Ct 5 SM6 219 B2
Hendham Rd SW17 158 D2
Hendon Ave N3 29 A2
Hendon Central NW4 46 B4
Hendon Central Sta
NW4 46 B4

Hendon Coll NW9 27 D2
Hendon Coll of F Ed NW4 46 A3
Hendon Hall Ct NW4 46 D6
Hendon Ho NW4 46 D4
Hendon La N3 29 B1
Hendon Lo NW4 46 B6
Hendon Park Mans NW4 46 C4
Hendon Park Row NW11 47 B3
Hendon Prep Sch NW4 46 D6
Hendon Rd N9 18 A2
Hendon Sch NW4 46 D4
Hendon Sta NW4 46 A3
Hendon Terr TW15 171 B4
Hendon Way NW2 46 C3
NW2,NW4 46 C3
Hendon Wood La NW7 12 A3
Hendre Ho SE1 263 B3
Hendren Cl UB6 64 B3
Hendre Rd SE1 117 C2 263 B3
Hendrick Ave SW12 158 D4
Heneage La EC3 243 B1
Heneage Pl EC3 243 B1
Heneage St E1 95 D2 243 D4
Henfield Cl DA5 169 C5
N19 49 C1
Henfield Rd SW19, SW20 179 B2
Hengelo Gdns CR4 202 B5
Hengist Rd DA8 147 D5
Eltham SE12 165 B4
Hengist Way BR2,BR3 208 C5
Hengrave Rd SE23 162 D4
Hengrove Ct DA5 169 A3
Henley Ave SM3 217 A5
Henley Cl SE16 118 C4
Greenford UB6 86 A5
Hounslow TW7 130 D4
Henley Ct N14 15 C4
NW2 68 D2
NW4 46 A6
SE15 140 A2
Mitcham CR4 203 A6
Henley Dr SE1 117 D2 263 D4
Kingston KT2 177 D3
Henley Gdns
Dagenham RM6 59 A4
Pinner HA5 40 B6
Henley Ho E2 243 D6
N12 30 B5
Henley Lo E17 53 B4
South Norwood SE25 205 D5
Henley Prior N1 233 C3
Henley Rd
Edmonton N18 33 C6
Ilford IG1 79 B4
Newham E16 122 B4
Willesden NW10 90 C6
Henleys Cnr NW11 47 B5
Henley St SW11 137 A3
Henley Way TW13 172 D5
Henlow Pl TW10 153 D2
Henlys Rdbt TW5 128 C3
Hennel Cl SE23 162 C1
Hennessy Rd N9 18 C2
Henniker Gdns E6 100 A4
Henniker Mews SW3 266 C6
Henniker Point E15 76 C3
Henniker Rd E15 76 B3
Henningham Rd N17 33 B2
Henning St SW11 136 C4 267 A1
Henrietta Barnett Sch NW11 47 D3
Henrietta Cl SE8 141 C6
Henrietta Ho 3 N15 51 C3
11 W6 112 C1
Henrietta Mews WC1 240 B6
Henrietta Pl W1 93 B1 238 C2
Henrietta St E15 76 A3
WC2 116 A6 250 B6
Henriques St E1 96 A1
Henry Addlington Cl E6 100 D2
Henry Cavendish Prim Sch SW12 159 C3
Henry Cl EN2 5 C5
Henry Compton Sec Sch SW6 135 A4 264 A2
Henry Cooper Way SE12 187 D6
Henry Darlot Dr NW7 29 A5
Henry Dent Cl SE5 139 B2
Henry Dickens Ct W11 244 A4
Henry Doulton Dr SW17 181 B6
Henry Fawcett Prim Sch SE11 138 C6
Henry Green Prim Sch RM8 80 D6
Henry Hatch Ct SM2 218 A1
Henry Ho NW8 230 A4
Henry Ho *continued*
SE1 251 B3
SW8 270 A4
Henry Jackson Ho SW15 134 D2
Henry Jackson Rd SW15 134 D2
Henry Maynard Inf Sch E17 54 A4
Henry Maynard Jun Sch E17 54 A4
Henry Peters Dr TW11 174 C5
Henry Rd E6 100 A5
N4 51 A1
New Barnet EN4 14 B6
Henry's Ave IG8 36 D5
Henryson Rd SE4 163 C6
Henry St BR1 187 B2
Henry Tate Mews SW16 182 C5
Henry Wise Ho SW1 259 B3
Hensford Gdns SE26 184 B6
Henshall Point 10 E3 97 D4
Henshall St N1 73 B2
Henshawe Rd RM8 80 D5
Henshaw St SE17 117 B2 262 C4
Henslowe Rd SE22 162 A6
Henslow Ho 11 SE15 140 A5
Henson Ave NW2 68 C3
Henson Cl BR6 226 D6
Henson Ct 3 N5 73 A4
Henson Path HA3 43 D6
Henson Pl UB5 84 C6
Henty Cl SW11 136 C4 267 B2
Henty Wlk SW15 156 B6
Henville Rd BR1 187 B2
Henwick Prim Sch SE9 144 A2
Henwick Rd SE9 144 A2
Hepburn Gdns BR2 208 D1
Hepburn Mews SW11 158 D6
Hepple Cl TW7 131 B3
Hepplestone Cl SW15 156 B5
Hepscott Rd E9 75 C1
Hepworth Ct N1 234 D6
Barking IG11 80 A3
Cheam SM3 201 C1
Hepworth Gdns IG11 80 A3
Hepworth Ho IG8 21 A1
Hepworth Rd SW16 182 A3
Hepworth Way KT12 193 D1
Heracles 30 NW9 27 D2
Heracles Cl SM6 220 A1
Hera Ct 7 E14 119 C2
Herald Gdns SM6 219 B5
Heralds Pl SE11 261 C4
Herald St 5 E2 96 B3
Herbal Hill EC1 241 B5
Herbert Chapman Ct N5 72 D4
Herbert Cres SW1 257 D6
Herbert Gdns NW10 90 B5
Chiswick W4 132 D6
Dagenham RM6 58 D2
Herbert Ho E1 243 C2
Herbert Mews 15 SW2 160 C5
Herbert Morrison Ho SW6 264 C5
Herbert Morrison Prim Sch SW8 138 A5 270 B3
Herbert Pl SE18 144 D6
Herbert Rd BR2 210 A4
DA7 147 A3
E12 78 A4
E17 53 B2
N15 51 D4
NW9 46 A3
SE18 144 D6
Ilford IG3 79 C6
Kingston KT1 198 B6
Merton SW19 179 B3
Southall UB1 107 B5
Wood Green N11 32 A3
Herbert St E13 99 A5
NW5 71 A2
Herbrand Est WC1 94 A3 240 A6
Herbrand St WC1 94 A3 240 A6
Hercies Rd UB10 60 C2
Hercules Pl N7 72 A5
Hercules Rd SE1 116 B3 260 D5
Hercules St N7 72 A5
Hereford Ave EN4 14 D3
Hereford Bldgs SW3 266 D6
Hereford Ct
12 Belmont SM2 217 C1
6 Croydon CR0 205 D1
6 Ealing W7 86 D2
Harrow HA1 42 C6
Hereford Gdns SE13 164 C6
Pinner HA5 41 A4
Redbridge IG1 56 A2
Twickenham TW2 152 A3
Hereford Ho 26 SE5 139 A3
SW10 265 D4
5 SW2 138 C1
Hereford Ho *continued*
SW3 257 B6
7 Acton W3 88 C1
Hereford Mans 10 W2 91 C1
Hereford Mews 11 W2 91 C1
Hereford Pl SE14 141 B5
Hereford Rd
W2 91 C1 245 B6
W3 111 A6
W5 109 C3
Feltham TW13 150 C3
Wanstead E11 55 B4
Hereford Retreat 5 SE15 140 A5
Hereford Sq SW7 114 A2 256 B3
Hereford St E2 96 A3
Hereford Way KT9 213 D3
Herent Dr IG5 56 B6
Hereward Gdns N13 32 C5
Hereward House Sch NW3 70 B2
Hereward Rd SW17 180 D6
Herga Ct HA1 64 C6
Herga Rd HA3 42 D5
Heriot Ave E4 19 C2
Heriot Rd NW4 46 C4
Heriots Cl HA7 25 A6
Heritage Cl SW9 138 D2
Heritage Ct SE8 118 D1
Heritage Hill BR2 225 C3
Heritage Ho 22 SW19 156 D3
Heritage View HA1 64 D5
Herlwyn Ave HA4 61 C5
Herlwyn Gdns SW17 180 D6
Herm Cl TW7 130 A5
Hermes Cl 4 W9 91 C3
Hermes Ct 4 SW9 138 C4
Hermes Ho BR3 185 A2
Hermes St N1 234 A3
Hermes Way SM6 219 D1
Hermes Wlk UB5 85 C5
Herm Ho 10 N1 73 A2
Enfield EN3 6 D5
Hermiston Ave N8 50 A4
Hermitage Cl E18 54 D5
Claygate KT10 213 A2
Enfield EN2 4 D3
Littleton TW17 192 C5
Hermitage Ct 14 E1 118 A5
2 NW2 69 C5
3 Wanstead E18 55 A5
Hermitage Gdns NW2 69 C5
South Norwood SE19 183 A3
Hermitage La NW2 69 C5
Croydon CR0 206 A3
South Norwood SW16 182 B3
Hermitage Prim Sch E1 118 A5
Hermitage Rd N4,N15 51 A3
South Norwood SE19 183 B4
Hermitage Row 9 E8 74 A3
Hermitage St W2 236 C3
Hermitage The
Barnes SW13 133 D4
Feltham TW13 149 D1
Forest Hill SE23 162 C3
Kingston KT1 197 D5
Richmond TW10 154 A6
Uxbridge UB8 60 A2
Hermitage Wall E1 118 A5
Hermitage Way HA7 25 A2
Hermitage Wlk E18 54 D5
Hermit Pl NW6 91 D6
Hermit Rd E16 98 D3
Hermit St EC1 234 C2
Hermon Gr UB3 106 A5
Hermon Hill E11 55 A5
Herndon Rd SW18 158 A6
Herne Cl NW10 67 B3
Herne Ct WD23 8 A4
Herne Hill SE24 139 A1
Herne Hill Ho SE24 160 D5
Herne Hill Mans SE24 161 A5
Herne Hill Rd SE24 139 A1
Herne Hill Sta SE24 160 D5
Herne Hill Stad SE24 161 B5
Herne Mews N18 34 A6
Herne Pl SE24 160 D6
Herne Rd KT6 214 A6
Heron Cl E17 35 B1
NW10 67 C2
Buckhurst Hill IG9 21 A3
Cheam SM1 217 B3
Heron Cres DA14 189 C6
Heron Ct 14 E14 120 A3
Bromley BR2 209 C5
6 Dulwich SE21 161 B2
9 Forest Hill SE23 162 C3
Ilford IG1 78 D6
5 Kingston KT1 198 A6
Ruislip HA4 61 B6
Stanwell TW19 148 A3
Herondale Ave SW18 158 C3
Heron Dr N4 73 A6
Herongate N1 235 B6
Herongate Rd E12 77 C6
Heron Hill DA17 125 B2
Heron Ho NW8 230 A3
Heron Ho *continued*
SE15 139 D4
SW11 267 B2
Ealing W13 87 A3
Teddington KT1 175 C2
Heron Ind Est E15 97 D5
Heron Mead EN3 7 C5
Heron Mews IG1 78 D6
Heron Pl SE16 119 A5
W1 238 B2
Heron Quays E14 119 C5
Heron Quays Sta E14 119 C5
Heron Rd SE24 139 A1
Croydon CR0 221 C6
Isleworth TW1 131 B1
Heronsforde W13 87 C1
Heronsgate HA8 26 C5
Heronsgate Prim Sch SE28 123 B3
Heron's Lea N6 48 D3
Heronslea Dr HA7 26 A5
Herons Pl TW7 131 B2
Heron Sq 25 TW10 153 D6
Herons Rise EN4 2 C1
Herons The E11 54 D3
Heron Trad Est W3 88 D2
Heronway IG8 37 C6
Heron Way TW14 128 A1
Herrick Ct 4 TW10 175 D6
Herrick Ho 17 N16 73 B4
18 SE5 139 B5
Herrick Rd N5 73 A5
Herrick St SW1 115 D2 259 D3
Herries St W10 91 A5
Herringham Rd SE7 121 C3
Herrongate Cl EN1 5 D3
Hersant Cl NW10 90 A6
Herschell Rd SE23 163 A4
Herschell's Mews SE5 139 A2
Hersham Cl SW15 156 A4
Hersham Rd KT12 194 A1
Hershell Ct 1 SW14 132 D1
Hertford Ave SW14 133 C1
Hertford Cl EN4 2 B2
Hertford Ct E6 100 B4
16 SW11 136 C2
Palmers Green N13 16 C1
Hertford Lo 10 SW19 157 A3
Hertford Pl W1 239 B5
Hertford Rd N1 95 C6
N2 48 C6
Barking IG11 78 D1
Barnet EN4 2 A2
Edmonton N9 18 B3
Enfield EN3 6 C5
Ilford IG2 57 C3
Hertford Rd High St EN3 18 C6
Hertford Sq CR4 204 A5
Hertford St W1 115 B5 248 C3
Hertford Way CR4 204 A5
Hertford Wlk 13 DA17 125 C1
Hertmitage The 4 SE13 142 A3
Hertslet Rd N7 72 B5
Hertsmere Rd E14 119 C6
Hertswood Ct 1 EN5 1 A1
Hervey Cl N3 29 C2
Hervey Park Rd E17 53 A5
Hervey Rd SE3 143 B4
Hesa Rd UB3 106 A6
Hesewall Cl SW4 137 C3
Hesketh Pl W11 244 A5
Hesketh Rd E7 77 A5
Heslop Ct 1 SW12 159 A3
Heslop Rd SW12 158 D3
Hesper Mews SW5 113 D2 255 C3
Hesperus Cres E14 119 D2
Hessel Rd W13 109 B4
Hessel St E1 96 B1
Hestercombe Ave SW6 135 B4 264 B1
Hesterman Way CR0 204 B1
Hester Rd SW11 136 C5 267 A3
Edmonton N18 34 A5
Hester Terr TW9 132 C2
Heston Ave TW5 129 A5
Heston Com Sch TW5 129 C5
Heston Ctr The TW5 106 C1
Heston Grange TW5 129 B6
Heston Grange La TW5 129 B6
Heston Ho 5 SE8 141 C4
W4 110 D1
Heston Ind Mall TW5 129 B5
Heston Inf Sch TW5 129 C5
Heston Jun Sch TW5 129 C5
Heston Phoenix Distribution Pk TW5 128 C6
Heston Rd TW5 129 C5
Heston St SE14 141 C4
Hetherington Rd SW2,SW4 138 A1
Charlton TW17 171 A1
Hetherington Way UB10 60 A4
Hethpool Ho W2 236 C5
Hetley Gdns 1 SE19 183 D3
Hetley Rd W12 112 B4
Heton Gdns NW4 46 A5
Hevelius Cl SE10 120 D1
Hever Croft SE9 188 C6
Heverfield Ct CR4 180 D3
Hever Gdns BR1 188 C1
Heverham Rd SE18 123 C2
Hever Ho SE15 140 D6
Heversham Ho SE15 140 C6
Heversham Rd DA7 147 C4
Hewens Rd UB4 83 A3
Hewer Ho 6 SW4 159 C6
Hewer St W10 90 D2
Hewes Ho E17 52 D5
Hewett Cl HA7 25 B6
Hewett Ho 7 SE18 122 D1
Hewett Rd RM8 80 D4
Hewett St EC2 95 C3 243 B5
Hewish Rd N18 33 C6
Hewison St E3 97 B5
Hewitt Ave N22 32 D1
Hewitt Cl CR0 223 C5
Hewitt Ho 2 E4 36 B5
Hewitt Rd N8 50 D4
Hewlett Rd E3 97 A5
Hewling Ho 11 N16 73 C3
Hewtt Ho SW15 134 C3
Hexagon The N6 48 D1
Hexal Rd SE6 164 C1
Hexham Gdns TW7 131 A5
Hexham Rd Barnet EN5 1 D1
Cheam SM4 201 D1
West Norwood SE27 161 A2
Heybourne Rd N17 34 B3
Hey Bridge 9 NW1 71 B2
Heybridge Ave SW16 182 B4
Heybridge Dr IG6 57 B6
Heybridge Way E10 53 B1
Heydon Ct BR4 224 C6
Heydon Ho SE14 140 C4
Heyford Ave SW8 138 A5 270 B4
Merton SW20 201 B6
Heyford Rd CR4 180 C1
Heygate St SE17 117 A2 262 B4
Heylyn Sq E3 97 B4
Heynes Rd RM8 80 C4
Heysham Dr WD19 22 D5
Heysham La NW3 69 D5
Heysham Rd N15 51 B3
Heythorp St SW18 157 B2
Heythrop Dr UB10 60 B4
Heyward Ct SM2 217 C2
Heywood Ave NW9 27 C2
Heywood Ct 2 HA7 25 C5
Heywood Ho 11 SE14 140 D6
6 SW2 160 C5
Heyworth Rd E15 76 D4
E5 74 B4
Hibbert Rd E17 53 B2
Harrow HA3 24 D1
Hibbert St SW11 136 B2
Hibernia Gdns TW3 151 C6
Hibernia Point 11 SE2 124 D4
Hibernia Rd TW3 129 C1
Hibiscus Cl HA8 27 A6
Hibiscus Lo E15 76 C1
Hichisson Rd SE15 162 C6
Hickes Ho 6 NW6 70 B1
Hickey's Almshouses 7 TW9 132 B1
Hickin Cl SE7 121 D2
Hickin St 2 E14 120 A3
Hickleton NW1 232 B5
Hickling Ho 10 SE16 118 B3
Hickling Rd IG1 78 D3
Hickman Ave E4 36 A4
Hickman Cl E16 99 D2
Hickman Rd RM6 58 C2
Hickmore Wlk SW4 137 C2
Hickory Cl N9 18 A4
Hicks Ave UB6 86 C4
Hicks Cl SW11 136 C2
Hicks Ct RM10 81 D5
Hicks St SE8 119 A1
Hidaburn Ct 7 SW16 181 C6
Hidcote Gdns SW20 200 B6
Hidcote Ho 11 SM2 218 A1
Hide E6 100 C1
Hide Pl SW1 115 D2 259 C3
Hide Rd HA1 42 B5
Hide Twr SW1 259 C3
Hieover SE21 161 A2
Higgins Ho 7 N1 95 C6
Higginson Ho 2 NW3 70 D1
Higgins Wlk TW12 173 A4
Higgs Ind Est 9 SE24 138 D2
High Acre EN2 4 D2
Higham Ct 9 IG8 37 A4
Higham Hill Ho E17 34 D2
Higham Hill Rd E17 35 A1
Higham Ho E4 35 C4
Higham Pl E17 53 A6
Higham Rd N17 51 B6
Higham Rd *continued*
Woodford IG8 37 A4
Highams Lodge Bsns Ctr E17 52 D6
Highams Park Sch E4 36 B4
Highams Park Sta E4 36 B4
Higham St E17 53 A6
Higham Station Ave E4 35 D4
Highams The E17 36 A2
High Ashton 11 KT2 176 D3
Highbanks Cl DA16 146 B5
Highbanks Rd HA5 23 D4
Highbank Way N8 50 C3
High Barnet Sta EN5 1 C1
Highbarrow Rd CR0 206 A1
High Beech
South Croydon CR2 221 C1
Southgate N21 16 B5
High Beeches DA14 191 A5
High Birch Ct 7 EN4 2 C1
Highbridge Ct 13 SE14 140 C5
Highbridge Rd IG11 100 D6
High Bridge Wharf SE10 120 B1
Highbrook Rd SE3 143 D2
High Broom Cres BR4 207 D2
Highbury (Arsenal FC) N5 72 D5
Highbury Ave CR7 182 D1
Highbury Cl
New Malden KT3 199 A4
West Wickham BR4 223 D6
Highbury Cnr N5 72 D2
Highbury Corner N5 72 D2
Highbury Cres N5 72 C3
Highbury Fields Sch N5 72 D3
Highbury Gdns IG3 79 C6
Highbury Gr N5 72 D3
Highbury Grange N5 73 A4
Highbury Grove Ct N5 72 D2
Highbury Grove Sch N5 73 A3
Highbury Hill N5 72 D4
Highbury & Islington Sta N1 72 D2
Highbury New Pk N5 73 A4
Highbury Pk N5 72 D4
Highbury Pl N5 72 D3
Highbury Quadrant N5 73 A5
Highbury Quadrant Prim Sch N5 73 A4
Highbury Rd SW19 179 A5
Highbury Station Rd N1 72 C2
Highbury Terr N5 72 D3
Highbury Terrace Mews N5 72 D3
High Cedar Dr SW20 178 B3
Highclere Rd KT3 199 B6
Highclere St SE26 185 A6
Highcliffe
Beckenham BR3 185 D2
Ealing W13 87 B2
Highcliffe Dr SW15 155 D5
Highcliffe Gdns IG4 56 A4
Highcombe SE7 143 B6
Highcombe Cl SE9 166 A3
High Coombe Pl KT2 177 B3
Highcroft N6 49 A3
NW9 45 C4
2 Kingston KT5 198 B4
Highcroft Ave HA0 88 C6
Highcroft Gdns NW11 47 B3
Highcroft Rd N19 50 A2
High Cross Ctr The N15 52 A5
High Cross Rd N17 52 A6
Highcross Way 4 SW15 156 A3
Highdaun Dr SW16 204 B5
High Dene EN2 4 D2
Highdown KT4 215 D6
Highdown Rd SW15 156 B5
High Dr KT2,KT3 177 A1
High Elms IG8 37 A5
High Elms Rd BR6 227 A1
Highenden Ho NW8 237 A6
Highfield WD23 8 C2
Highfield Ave DA8 147 D6
NW11 47 A2
NW9 45 A4
Greenford UB6 64 D3
Orpington BR6 227 D3
Pinner HA5 41 B4
Wembley HA9 66 B5
Highfield Cl NW9 45 A4
SE13 164 B5
Long Ditton KT6 197 C1
Wood Green N22 32 C2
Highfield Ct NW11 47 A3
Mitcham CR4 202 C5
Southgate N14 15 C5
Wanstead E12 77 C6
Highfield Dr
Beckenham BR2 208 D5
Ickenham UB10 60 A5
West Ewell KT19 215 D2
West Wickham BR4 224 A5

ghfield Gdns NW11 ..47 A3
ghfield Gr N6 ....48 D1
ghfield Hill SE19 ..183 C3
ghfield Ho N21 ....16 D3
ghfield Inf Sch BR2 .208 C5
ghfield Jun Sch
R2 ....208 C5
ghfield Prim Sch
dmonton N21 ....17 A3
illingdon UB10 ....82 D4
ghfield Rd BR1 ....210 B5
R5,BR7 ....211 D6
A6 ....169 B6
W11 ....47 A3
/3 ....89 A2
arshalton SM1 ....218 C3
dmonton N21 ....16 D2
ltham TW13 ....150 A2
ounslow TW7 ....130 D4
lworth KT5 ....199 A2
pper Halliford TW16 ..193 D4
Valton-on-T KT12 ....194 A1
ghfields SM1 ....217 C6
ghfield Sch SW18 ..158 C4
gh Foleys KT10 ....213 B1
gh Gables
eckenham BR2 ....186 C1
oughton IG10 ....21 D6
gh Garth KT10 ....212 A2
ghgate Archway N6 .49 C1
ghgate Ave N6 ....49 B2
ghgate Ballet Sch
W11 ....47 D5
ghgate Cemetery*
19 ....71 B6
ghgate Cl N6 ....49 A2
gh Gate Edge N2 ....48 C4
ghgate High St N6 ..49 B1
ghgate Hill N19 ....49 C1
ighgate Ho 11 SE26 .162 A1
ighgate Hts N6 ....49 C3
ighgate Jun Sch N6 ..48 D2
ighgate Prim Sch N6 .48 D3
ighgate Private Hospl
6 ....48 D3
ighgate Rd NW5 ....71 B4
ighgate Sch N6 ....49 A2
ighgate Spinney N8 ..49 D3
ighgate Sta N6 ....49 B3
ighgate West Hill N6 .71 A6
ighgate Wlk SE23 ..162 C2
ighgate Wood Sch N8 49 C4
igh Gr Bromley BR1 ..187 D2
Woolwich SE18 ....145 B4
ighgrove Cl BR7 ....188 A2
11 ....31 A5
ighgrove Ct BR3 ....185 C3
ighgrove Ho HA4 ....40 A3
ighgrove Mews SM5 218 D5
ighgrove Point 2
W3 ....70 A4
ighgrove Rd RM8 ....80 C4
ighgrove Way HA4 ....40 A2
igh Hill Ferry 3 E5 ....52 B1
igh Holborn
WC1 ....94 B2 240 C3
igh La W7 ....86 B1
ighland Ave W7 ....86 C1
ighland Cotts SM6 ..219 C4
ighland Croft BR3 ..185 D4
ighland Ct E18 ....37 B2
ighland Dr WD23 ....8 A4
ighland Lo 3 SE19 ..183 D3
ighland Pk TW13 ....171 D6
ighland Rd
Bexley DA6 ....147 C1
Bromley BR1 ....186 D2
Pinner HA6 ....22 A1
West Norwood SE19 ..183 C4
Highlands N20 ....14 B2
Highlands Ave W3 ....111 A6
Southgate N21 ....16 B6
Highlands Cl N4 ....50 A2
Hounslow TW3 ....129 D4
Highlands Ct SE19 ....183 C4
Highlands Gdns IG1 ....56 B1
Highlands Heath
SW15 ....156 C4
Highlands Prim Sch
IG1 ....56 B1
Highlands Rd EN5 ....13 C6
Highlands Sch N21 ....6 C1
Highlands The
Barnet EN5 ....1 D1
Edgware HA8 ....26 D1
Highlawn Hall HA1 ....64 C5
Highlea Cl NW9 ....27 C2
High Level Dr SE26 ..184 A6
Highlever Rd W10 ....90 C2
High Limes 2 SE19 ..183 C4
High London 5 N6 ....49 D2
Highmead SE18 ....145 D5
9 Edmonton N18 ....34 A5
High Mead Harrow HA1 .42 D4
West Wickham BR4 ....224 C6
Highmead Cres HA0 ..66 B1
High Meadow Cl HA5 ..40 C5
High Meadow Cres
NW9 ....45 B4
High Meads Rd E16 ....99 D1
Highmore Rd SE3 ....142 C5
High Mount NW4 ....46 A3
High Oaks EN2 ....4 B5
High Park Ave TW9 ..132 C4
High Park Rd TW9 ....132 C4
High Par The SW16 ..160 A1
High Path SW19 ....180 A2
High Point N6 ....49 A2
SE9 ....166 D1
Highpoint EN5 ....14 A6
High Range SW20 ....178 C3
High Rd E10 ....53 D3
N11 ....31 B5
N15,N17 ....51 D5
N20 ....14 A4
N2 ....48 C6
N2,N12 ....30 A3
NW10 ....68 A2
Buckhurst Hill IG9,IG10 ..21 C5
Bushey WD23 ....8 B3
Harrow HA3 ....24 C3
Ilford IG1 ....78 D6
Ilford IG1,IG3 ....79 C6
Ilford IG3 ....57 D1
Ilford RM6 ....58 B2
Tottenham N17 ....33 D2
Wembley HA0,HA9 ....66 A3
Woodford E18 ....37 A2
Wood Green N22 ....32 B3
High Ridge N10 ....31 B2
High Road Eastcote
HA5 ....40 B4
High Road, Ickenham
UB10 ....61 A6
High Road Leyton E10 .75 D6
High Road Leytonstone
E11 ....76 C6
High Road Woodford Gn
IG8 ....37 A6
High Sheldon N6 ....48 D3
Highshore Rd SE15 ..139 D3
Highshore Sch SE15 ..139 D4
High Silver IG10 ....21 D6
High St BR1 ....187 A1
BR6 ....227 A3
BR6 ....227 D2
E13 ....99 A5
E15 ....98 A6
E17 ....53 B5
N14 ....15 D2
N8 ....50 B5
NW7 ....28 B5
Acton W3 ....110 D5
Barnet EN5 ....1 B1
Beckenham BR3 ....185 C1
Brentford TW8 ....132 A6
Cheam SM1,KT17 ....217 A2
Claygate KT10 ....212 D2
Cranford TW5 ....128 B5
Croydon CR0 ....221 A5
Croydon SE25 ....206 A5
Ealing W5 ....109 D6
East Molesey KT8 ....195 C5
Elstree WD6 ....9 D5
Feltham TW13 ....150 A2
Hampton TW12 ....174 A4
Harlington UB3 ....127 B6
Harrow HA1 ....42 C1
Harrow HA3 ....42 C6
Hounslow TW3 ....129 D2
Ilford IG6 ....57 A6
Kingston KT1 ....197 D6
New Malden KT3 ....199 C5
Penge SE20 ....184 D3
Pinner HA5 ....41 A6
Ruislip HA4 ....39 C1
Shepperton TW17 ....193 A3
Sidcup DA14 ....190 A6
Southall UB1 ....107 B5
South Norwood CR7 ....205 B6
Sutton SM1 ....217 D4
Sutton SM1,SM2 ....217 D3
Teddington KT1 ....175 D2
Teddington TW11 ....175 A5
Thames Ditton KT7 ....197 A3
Twickenham TW2 ....152 A4
Wallington SM5 ....219 A4
Walton-on-T KT12 ....194 A1
Wanstead E11 ....55 A4
Wembley HA9 ....66 B4
West Wickham BR4 ....207 D1
Wimbledon SW19 ....178 D5
Yiewsley UB7 ....104 A6
High St Mews SW19 ..179 A5
High St N E12 ....78 A2
E6 ....100 A6
Highstone Ave E11 ....55 A3
Highstone Ct E11 ....54 D3
High Street Collier's Wood
SW17,SW19 ....180 B4
High Street Harlesden
NW10 ....89 D5
High Street Harlington
TW6 ....127 B5
High Street Kensington Sta
W8 ....113 D3 245 C1
High St S E6 ....100 B4
High The SW16 ....160 A1
High Timber St EC4 ..252 A6
High Tor Cl BR1 ....187 B3
High Tor View SE28 ..123 C5
High Trees N20 ....14 A1
Croydon CR0 ....207 A1
East Barnet EN4 ....14 C6
Streatham SW2 ....160 C3
Uxbridge UB10 ....61 A6
Hightrees Ct W7 ....108 C6
Hightrees Ho SW12 ..159 A5
Highview N8 ....50 A2
Northolt UB5 ....85 A4
Woolwich SE18 ....144 D5
High View
6 Penge SE19 ....183 D3
Pinner HA5 ....40 C6
Highview Ave HA8 ....27 A6
High View Ave CR0,
SM6 ....220 B3
High View Cl
Loughton IG10 ....21 C6
South Norwood SE19 ..183 D1
Highview Ct 2 SW19 .157 A3
High View Ct HA3 ....24 C3
Highview Gdns HA8 ....27 A6
N11 ....31 C5
N3 ....47 A6
High View Par 1 IG4 ..56 B4
High View Prim Sch
SW11 ....136 B1
Wallington SM6 ....220 A3
High View Rd E18 ....54 D6
N10 ....30 D2
Highview Rd Ealing W13 87 A1
Sidcup DA14 ....190 B6
High View Rd SE19 ....183 B4
Highway Bsns Pk The 7
E1 ....118 D6
Highway The E1 ....118 C6
Stanmore HA7 ....25 A3
Highway Trad Ctr The 6
E1 ....118 D6
High Wigsell TW11 ....175 A5
Highwood Ave N12 ....30 A6
Highwood Cl BR6 ....227 A6
Highwood Ct N12 ....14 A1
Barnet EN5 ....13 C6
Highwood Dr BR6 ....227 A6
Highwood Gdns IG5 ....56 B5
Highwood Gr NW7 ....27 B5
Highwood Hill NW7 ....11 D2
Highwood Rd N19 ....72 A5
High Worple HA2 ....41 B1
Highworth Rd N11 ....31 D5
Highworth St NW1 ....237 B4
Hilary Ave CR4 ....203 A6
Hilary Cl SW6 ....265 C4
Bexley DA7 ....147 D4
Hilary Ct N9 ....18 D3
Hilary Rd W12 ....111 D6
Hilbert Rd SM3 ....216 D5
Hilborough Cl SW19 ..180 A3
Hilborough Ct 1 E8 ..95 D6
Hilborough Rd 1 E8 ..73 D1
Hilborough Way BR6 .227 B3
Hilda Rd E16 ....98 C3
E6 ....77 D1
Hilda Terr 2 SW9 ....138 C3
Hilda Vale Cl BR6 ....226 D4
Hilda Vale Rd BR6 ....226 D4
Hildenborough Gdns
BR1 ....186 D4
Hildenborough Ho BR3 185 B3
Hildenlea Pl BR2 ....186 C1
Hilditch Ho 7 TW10 ..154 B5
Hildred Ho SW1 ....258 C4
Hildreth St SW12 ....159 B3
Hildreth Street Mews 2
SW12 ....159 B3
Hildyard Rd SW6 ....265 B6
Hiley Rd NW10 ....90 C4
Hilfield La WD23 ....8 C6
Hilfield La S WD23 ....8 D5
Hilgrove Rd NW6 ....70 A1
Hiliary Gdns HA7 ....25 C1
Hillard Ct SM6 ....219 D2
Hillary Cres KT12 ....194 C1
Hillary Ct
3 Chislehurst SE9 ....166 A2
Stanwell TW19 ....148 A3
Hillary Dr TW7 ....152 D6
Hillary Ho E14 ....98 A2
Hillary Rd UB2 ....107 C3
Hillary Rise EN5 ....1 C1
Hillbeck Cl SE15 ....140 C5
SE15 ....140 C6
Hillbeck Way UB6 ....86 B6
Hillborne Cl UB3 ....106 A1
Hillboro Ct E11 ....54 B2
1 Woodford E18 ....36 D2
Hillbrook Rd SW17 ....181 A6
Hillbrook Sch SW17 ..181 A6
Hillbrow Kingston KT3 .199 D6
7 Richmond TW10 ....154 A5
Hill Brow BR1 ....187 D2
Hillbrow Ct KT10 ....212 A4
Hillbrow Rd
Catford BR1 ....186 C4
Esher KT10 ....212 A4
Hill Bunker's DA17 ....125 C2
Hillbury Ave HA3 ....43 B4
Hillbury Rd SW17 ....159 B1
Hill Cl NW11 ....47 C3
NW2 ....68 B5
Barnet EN5 ....12 C6
Chislehurst BR7 ....188 D5
Harrow HA1 ....64 C5
Stanmore HA7 ....25 B6
Hillcote Ave SW16 ....182 C3
Hillcourt Ave N12 ....29 D4
Hillcourt Rd SE22 ....162 B5
Hill Cres N20 ....13 D2
Harrow HA1 ....43 A4
Kingston KT5 ....198 B4
North Cheam KT4 ....216 C6
Hillcrest N6 ....49 A2
SE24 ....139 B1
W11 ....244 C5
Hill Crest DA15 ....168 B4
Hillcrest N21 ....16 C4
Hillcrest Ave NW11 ....47 B4
Edgware HA8 ....26 D6
Pinner HA5 ....40 D5
Hillcrest Cl
Beckenham BR3 ....207 B3
Forest Hill SE26 ....184 A6
Hillcrest Ct NW2 ....69 A3
Sutton SM2 ....218 B2
Hillcrest Gdns N3 ....47 A5
NW2 ....68 A5
Hinchley Wood KT10 ....212 D5
Hillcrest Hts W5 ....88 A3
Hillcrest Rd BR1 ....187 A6
Acton W3 ....110 D5
Chingford E17 ....36 B1
Ealing W5 ....88 A2
Loughton IG10 ....21 D5
Woodford E18 ....37 A1
Hillcrest View BR3 ....207 B3
Hillcroft Ave HA5 ....41 B3
Hillcroft Coll KT6 ....198 A3
Hillcroft Cres Ealing W5 87 D1
Ruislip HA4 ....62 D5
Wembley HA9 ....66 B4
Hillcroft Rd E6 ....100 D2
Hillcroome Rd SM2 ....218 B2
Hillcross Ave SM4 ....201 A4
Hillcross Prim Sch
SM4 ....201 B5
Hill Ct NW3 ....70 C4
Barnet EN4 ....2 C1
Ealing W5 ....88 B3
8 Kingston KT2 ....176 D3
14 Kingston KT6 ....198 A4
Northolt UB5 ....63 C3
Putney SW15 ....156 D6
Hilldale Rd SM1 ....217 B4
Hilldown Ct SW16 ....182 A3
Hilldown Rd
Hayes BR2 ....208 D1
South Norwood SW16 ..182 B3
Hill Dr NW9 ....45 A1
Thornton Heath SW16 ..204 B6
Hilldrop Cres N7 ....71 D3
Hilldrop Est 4 N7 ....71 D4
Hilldrop La N7 ....71 D3
Hilldrop Rd N7 ....71 D3
Bromley BR1 ....187 B4
Hill End BR6 ....227 D6
SE18 ....144 C4
Hillersdon Ave
Barnes SW13 ....134 A3
Edgware HA8 ....26 B5
Hillersdon Ho SW1 ....258 C2
Hillery Cl SE17 ....262 D3
Hill Farm Rd W10 ....90 D2
Hillfield Ave N8 ....50 A5
NW9 ....45 C5
Mitcham SM4 ....202 C4
Wembley HA0 ....66 B1
Hillfield Cl HA2 ....42 A5
Hillfield Ct NW3 ....70 C3
Hillfield Ho N5 ....73 A3
Hillfield Mans NW3 ....70 C3
Hillfield Par SM4 ....202 B3
Hillfield Park Mews
N10 ....49 B5
Hillfield Pk N10 ....49 B5
Southgate N21 ....16 C2
Hillfield Rd NW6 ....69 C3
Hampton TW12 ....173 B2
Hillgate Pl W8 113 C5 245 A4
Balham SW12 ....159 B4
Hillgate St W8 ....245 A4
Hill Gr TW13 ....151 B2
Hill Ho E5 ....52 B1
Stanmore HA7 ....9 A1
Hill House Ave HA7 ....24 D3
Hill House Cl N21 ....16 C4
Hill House Dr TW12 ....173 C2
Hill House Rd SW16 ..182 B5
Hill House Sch
SW1 ....114 D3 257 D5
Hilliard Ho 15 E1 ....118 B5
Hilliard's Ct E1 ....118 C5
Hillier Cl EN5 ....13 D5
Hillier Gdns CR0 ....220 C3
Hillier Ho 1 NW1 ....71 D1
Hillier Lo TW12 ....174 B5
Hillier Pl KT9 ....213 D2
Hillier Rd SW11 ....158 D5
Hilliers Ave UB8 ....82 C4
Hillier's La CR0,SM6 ....220 A5
Hillingdon Ave TW19 .148 A3
Hillingdon Circus UB10 60 D2
Hillingdon Hill UB10 ..82 B4
Hillingdon Hospl UB8 ..82 B2
Hillingdon Par 6 UB10 82 D3
Hillingdon Prim Sch
UB10 ....82 D4
Hillingdon Rd UB10 ....82 A5
Hillingdon St SE17 ..138 D6
Hillingdon Sta UB10 ..60 D3
Hillington Gdns IG8 ..37 D1
Hill La HA4 ....39 A1
Hill Lo SW11 ....136 B1
Hillman Cl UB8 ....60 A3
Hillman St E8 ....74 B2
Hillmarton Rd N7 ....72 A3
Hillmead Dr SW9 ....138 D1
Hill Mead Prim Sch
SW9 ....138 D1
Hillmont Rd KT10 ....212 C5
Hillmore Ct SE13 ....142 B2
Hillmore Gr SE26 ....185 A5
Hill Rd N10 ....30 D2
NW8 ....92 A5 229 B3
Carshalton SM5 ....218 C2
Harrow HA1 ....43 A4
Mitcham CR4 ....181 B3
Pinner HA5 ....41 A3
Sutton SM1 ....217 D3
Wembley HA0 ....65 B5
Hillreach SE7,SE18 ....122 B1
Hill Rise NW11 ....47 D5
Hillrise KT12 ....193 D2
Hill Rise Enfield N9 ....18 B5
Forest Hill SE23 ....162 B3
Greenford UB6 ....86 A6
Hinchley Wood KT10 ..213 B6
Richmond TW10 ....153 D6
Ruislip HA4 ....39 B1
Hillrise Mans N19 ....50 A2
Hillrise Rd N19 ....50 A2
Hillsboro Rd SE22 ....161 C6
Hillsborough Ct 11
NW6 ....91 D6
Hillsgrove Cl DA16 ....146 C5
Hillsgrove Prim Sch
DA16 ....146 C5
Hillside N8 ....49 D3
NW10 ....89 B6
NW9 ....45 B5
Barnet EN5 ....14 A6
Wimbledon SW19 ....178 D4
Hill Side EN5 ....14 A6
Hillside Ave N11 ....30 D4
Wembley HA9 ....66 B4
Woodford IG8 ....37 C5
Hillside Cl NW8 ....91 D5
Merton SM4 ....201 A5
Woodford IG8 ....37 C5
Hillside Cres Enfield EN2 .5 B5
Harrow HA2 ....42 A1
Northwood HA6 ....22 A2
Hillside Ct NW3 ....69 D3
7 Kingston KT2 ....176 D3
Hillside Dr HA8 ....26 C5
Hillside Gdns E17 ....54 B6
N6 ....49 B3
Barnet EN5 ....1 A1
Barnet N11 ....31 C4
Edgware HA8 ....26 B6
Harrow HA3 ....44 A2
Northwood HA6 ....22 B2
Streatham SW2 ....160 C2
Wallington SM6 ....219 C1
Hillside Gr N14 ....15 D4
NW7 ....28 A3
Hillside Jun Inf Schs
HA6 ....22 A3
Hillside La BR2 ....224 D6
Hillside Mans EN5 ....1 B1
Hillside Rd N15 ....51 C3
Beckenham BR2 ....208 D6
Belmont SM2 ....217 B1
Croydon CR0 ....220 D4
Ealing W5 ....88 A2
Northwood HA6,HA5 ....22 B3
Southall UB1 ....85 C3
Streatham SW2 ....160 C2
Surbiton KT5 ....198 C4
Hillside Rise HA6 ....22 A3
Hillsleigh Rd
W14 ....113 B5 244 D4
Hills Mews 2 W5 ....110 A6
Hills Pl W1 ....239 A1
Hill's Rd IG9 ....21 B3
Hill St W1 ....115 B6 248 C4
Richmond TW10 ....153 D6
Hillstone Ct 5 E3 ....97 D3
Hillstowe St E5 ....74 C5
Hilltop 7 E17 ....53 D6
Hill Top NW11 ....47 D5
Cheam SM3 ....201 B2
Hilltop Ct NW8 ....70 A1
12 SW18 ....136 B1
Hilltop Ct *continued*
South Norwood SE19 ..183 B2
Hilltop Gdns BR6 ....227 C6
Hilltop Ho 7 N6 ....49 D2
Hilltop Rd NW6 ....69 C1
Hilltop Way HA7 ....9 A1
Hillview SW20 ....178 B3
Hill View CR4 ....204 A5
Hillview Ave HA3 ....44 A4
Hillview Cl Pinner HA5 ..23 B4
Wembley HA9 ....66 B6
Hillview Cres BR6 ....211 D1
Hill View Cres IG1 ....56 B3
Hillview Ct SE19 ....183 C6
Hill View Dr DA16 ....145 C3
Woolwich SE28 ....123 C5
Hillview Gdns NW4 ....46 D5
Hill View Gdns NW9 ....45 B4
Hillview Gdns HA2 ....41 C5
Hillview Rd BR7 ....188 D6
NW7 ....28 D6
Hill View Rd BR6 ....227 D6
Hillview Rd
Carshalton SM1 ....218 B5
Pinner HA5 ....23 B4
Hill View Rd
Claygate KT10 ....213 A1
Twickenham TW1 ....153 A5
Hillway N6 ....71 A6
NW9 ....45 C1
Hill Wood Ho NW1 ....232 C3
Hillworth 7 BR3 ....185 D1
Hillworth Rd SW2 ....160 C4
Hillyard Rd W7 ....86 C2
Hillyard St SW9 ....138 C4
Hillyfield E17 ....35 A1
Hillyfield Cl E9 ....75 A3
Hilly Fields Cres SE4 .141 C2
Hilly Mead SW19 ....179 A3
Hilsea Point 7 SW15 .156 B3
Hilsea St E5 ....74 C4
Hilton Ave N12 ....30 B5
Hilton Ho N7 ....72 A4
9 SE4 ....140 D1
4 Ealing W13 ....87 C1
Hilversum Cres 10
SE22 ....161 C6
Himley Rd SW17 ....180 D4
Hinchley Cl KT10 ....212 D5
Hinchley Dr KT10 ....212 D5
Hinchley Way KT10 ....213 A5
Hinchley Wood Prim Sch
KT10 ....213 A6
Hinchley Wood Sch
KT10 ....213 A6
Hinchley Wood Sta
KT10 ....212 D5
Hinckley Rd SE15 ....140 A1
Hind Ct EC4 ....241 B1
Hinde Mews W1 ....238 B2
Hindes Rd HA1 ....42 C4
Hinde St W1 ....93 A1 238 B2
Hind Gr E14 ....97 C1
Hindhead Cl UB8 ....82 D2
Hindhead Gdns UB5 ....85 A6
Hindhead Gn WD19 ....22 C5
Hindhead Point 6
SW15 ....156 B3
Hindhead Way SM6 ....220 A3
Hind Ho N7 ....72 C4
13 SE14 ....140 D6
Hindhurst Ct NW9 ....45 A5
Hindle Ho E8 ....73 D3
Hindley Ho N7 ....72 B5
Hindlip Ho SW8 ....269 C1
Hindmans Rd SE22 ....162 A6
Hindmans Way RM9 ....103 B3
Hindmarsh Cl E1 ....118 A6
Hindrey Rd E5 ....74 B3
Hindsley's Pl SE23 ....162 C2
Hines Ct HA1 ....43 A4
Hinkler Rd HA3 ....43 D6
Hinksey Path SE2 ....124 D3
Hinstock NW6 ....91 D6
Hinstock Rd SE18 ....145 A5
Hinton Ave TW4 ....128 D1
Hinton Cl SE9 ....166 A3
Hinton Ct 3 E10 ....75 D6
Hinton Rd SE24 ....138 D2
Edmonton N18 ....33 C6
Wallington SM6 ....219 C2
Hippodrome Mews
W11 ....244 A5
Hippodrome Pl W11 ....244 B5
Hiscocks Ho NW10 ....67 A1
Hitcham Rd E17 ....53 B2
Hitchcock Cl TW17 ....192 B6
Hitchin Sq E3 ....97 A5
Hitherbroom Rd UB3 ..106 A6
Hither Farm Rd SE3 ..143 C2
Hitherfield Prim Sch
SW2 ....160 C2
Hitherfield Rd
Dagenham RM8 ....81 A6
Streatham SW16,SW27 .160 C1
Hither Green La SE13 .164 B5

Hither Green Prim Sch
SE13 164 B5
Hither Green Sta SE13 164 C5
Hitherlands SW12 159 B2
Hitherwell Dr HA3 24 B2
Hitherwood Ct SE21 183 D6
Hitherwood Dr SE19 183 D6
Hive Cl WD23 8 B2
Hive Rd WD23 8 C2
HM Prison Wormwood
Scrubs W12 90 A1
HMS Belfast★ SE1 253 B4
Hoadly Rd SW16 159 D2
Hobart Cl N20 14 C2
Hayes UB4 84 D3
Hobart Ct Harrow HA1 42 C2
Woodford IG8 36 D6
Hobart Dr UB4 84 D3
Hobart Gdns CR7 205 B6
Hobart La UB4 84 D3
Hobart Pl SW1 115 B3 258 C6
Richmond TW10 154 B4
Hobart Rd
Dagenham RM9 80 D4
Hayes UB4 84 D3
North Cheam KT4 216 B5
Hobbayne Prim Sch
W7 86 D1
Hobbayne Rd W7 86 B1
Hobbes Wlk SW15 156 B6
Hobb's Ct SE1 253 D2
Hobbs Gn N2 48 A6
Hobbs Mews IG3 79 D6
Hobbs' Pl N1 95 C6
Hobbs Rd 5 SE27 183 A6
Hobday St E14 97 D1
Hobill Wlk KT5 198 B3
Hoblands End BR7 189 C4
Hobsons Pl 7 E1 96 A2
Hobury St
SW10 136 B6 266 C5
Hockenden La BR5,
BR8 191 D1
Hocker St 41 E2 95 D4
Hockington Ct 7 EN5 13 D6
Hockley Ave E6 100 A5
Hockley Ct 2 E18 37 A2
Hockley Ho 6 E9 74 C2
Hockley Mews IG11 101 C5
Hockliffe Ho W10 90 C2
Hockney Ct 1 SE16 118 B1
Hockworth Ho 7 N16 51 C1
Hocroft Ave NW2 69 B5
Hocroft Ct NW2 69 B5
Hocroft Rd NW2 69 B5
Hocroft Wlk NW2 69 B5
Hodder Dr UB6 86 D5
Hoddesdon Rd DA17 125 C1
Hodford Rd NW11 47 B1
Hodgkins Cl SE28 124 D6
Hodister Cl 26 SE5 139 A5
Hodnet Gr SE16 118 D2
Hodson Cl HA2 63 B5
Hodson Pl EN3 7 C5
Hoecroft Ct EN3 6 C5
Hoe La EN1 6 B5
Hoe St E17 53 C4
Hoffman Sq N1 235 D2
Hofland Rd
W14 113 A3 254 A6
Hogan Mews W2 236 C4
Hogan Way E5 74 A6
Hogarth Ave TW15 171 A4
Hogarth Bsns Pk W4 133 C6
Hogarth Cl E16 99 D2
Ealing W5 88 A2
Hogarth Cres
Mitcham SW19 180 B2
Thornton Heath CR0 205 A2
Hogarth Ct 15 E1 96 A1
EC3 253 B6
6 NW1 71 C1
Dulwich SE19 183 D6
Heston TW5 129 A5
Hogarth Gdns TW5 129 C5
Hogarth Hill NW11 47 B5
Hogarth Ho SW1 259 D3
Enfield EN1 18 A6
13 Northolt UB5 84 D5
6 West Norwood SE27 183 A6
Hogarth Ind Est NW10 90 A3
Hogarth La W4 133 C6
Hogarth Pl SW5 255 C3
Hogarth Prim Sch W4 111 C1
Hogarth Rd
SW5 113 D2 255 C3
Barking RM8 80 B3
Edgware HA8 26 C1
Hogarth Roundabout
W4 133 C6
Hogarth Way TW12 174 A2
Hogsmill Way KT19 215 A4
Holbeach Gdns DA15 167 D5
Holbeach Mews 1
SW12 159 B3

Holbeach Prim Sch
SE6 163 C4
Holbeach Rd SE6 163 D4
Holbeck Row SE15 140 A5
Holbein Ho SW1 258 A2
10 Stanmore HA7 25 C5
Holbein Mews
SW1 115 A1 258 A2
Holbein Pl
SW1 115 A2 258 A3
Holberry Ho 5 SE21 183 C6
Holberton Gdns NW10 90 B4
Holborn EC1 94 C2 241 B3
Holborn Cir EC1 94 C2 241 B3
Holborn Pl WC1 240 C3
Holborn Rd E13 99 B3
Holborn Sta
WC1 94 B2 240 C3
Holborn Way CR4 180 D1
Holbrook Cl N19 49 B1
Enfield EN1 6 A5
Holbrooke Ct N7 72 A4
Holbrooke Pl 28 TW10 153 D6
Holbrook Ho W3 89 B2
Chislehurst BR7 189 B2
5 Streatham SW2 160 B3
Holbrook La BR7 189 B3
Holbrook Rd E15 98 D5
Holbrook Way BR2 210 B4
Holburn 33 N1 95 C6
Holburne Cl SE3 143 C4
Holburne Gdns SE3 143 D4
Holburne Rd SE3 143 D4
Holburn Viaduct
EC1 94 D2 241 C3
Holcombe Hill NW7 12 A1
Holcombe Ho SW9 138 A2
Holcombe Rd N17 52 A6
1 N17 51 D6
Ilford IG1 56 C2
Holcombe St W6 112 B2
Holcote Cl DA17 125 A3
Holcroft Ct W1 239 A4
Holcroft Ho SE10 142 A4
SW11 136 B2
Holcroft Rd E9 74 C1
Holden Ave N12 29 D5
NW9 45 A1
Holdenby Rd SE4 163 A6
Holden Cl RM8 80 B5
Holden Ho N1 235 A5
12 SE8 141 C5
Holden Hts N12 13 D1
Holdenhurst Ave N12 30 A3
Holden Lo N11 31 C5
Holden Rd N12 29 D6
Holden St SW11 137 A3
Holdernesse Rd
Isleworth TW7 131 A4
6 Upper Tooting SW17 159 A2
Holderness Ho SE5 139 C2
Holderness Way SE27 182 D5
Holders Hill Ave NW4 46 D6
Holders Hill Cres NW4 28 D1
Holders Hill Dr NW4 28 D1
Holders Hill Gdns NW4 29 A1
Holders Hill Par NW7 29 A2
Holders Hill Rd NW4 28 D1
NW4,NW7 29 A2
Holdsworth Ho 5
SW2 160 C4
Holford Ho 6 SE16 118 B2
WC1 233 D2
Holford Pl WC1 233 D2
Holford Rd NW3 70 A5
Holford St WC1 234 A2
Holgate Ave SW11 136 B2
Holgate Ct HA8 26 B6
Holgate Gdns RM10 81 C2
Holgate Rd RM10 81 C3
Holgate St SE7 121 D3
Hollam Ho N8 50 B5
Holland Ave
Belmont SM2 217 C1
Wimbledon SW20 177 D2
Holland Cl
Coney Hall BR2 224 D6
New Barnet EN5 14 B4
Stanmore HA7 25 B5
Holland Ct 6 E17 54 A5
NW7 28 A4
Holland Dr SE23 163 A1
Holland Gdns W14 254 B6
Holland Gr SW9 138 C5
Holland Ho E4 36 A6
Holland House Sch
HA8 26 D6
Holland Park
W11 113 B5 244 C3
Holland Park Ave
W11 113 A5 244 B3
Ilford IG3 57 D4
Holland Park Ct W14 244 B2
Holland Park Gdns
W14 113 A4 244 A2
Holland Park Mews
W11 113 B5 244 C3
Holland Park Rd
W14 113 B3 254 D5

Holland Park Rdbt
W12 112 D4
Holland Park Sch
W8 113 B4 244 D2
Holland Park Sta
W11 113 B5 244 C3
Holland Pl W8 245 C2
Holland Rd E15 98 C4
NW10 90 B5
W14 113 A3 254 B6
Croydon SE25 206 A4
Wallend E6 78 C1
Wembley HA0 65 D2
Holland Rise Ho SW9 270 D3
Holland St
SE1 116 D5 251 D4
W8 113 C4 245 B2
Hollands The
Feltham TW13 172 D6
New Malden KT4 199 D1
Holland Villas Rd
W14 113 A4 244 A1
Holland Way BR2 224 D6
Holland Wlk N19 49 D1
W14 113 B4 244 D1
Stanmore HA7 25 A5
Hollar Rd N16 73 D5
Hollen St W1 239 C2
Holles Cl TW12 173 C5
Holles Ho 9 SW9 138 C3
Holles St W1 93 B1 238 D2
Holley Rd W3 111 C4
Hollickwood Ave N12 30 D4
Hollickwood Prim Sch
N10 31 B3
Holliday Sq 7 SW11 136 B2
Hollidge Way RM10 81 D1
Hollies Ave DA15 167 D3
Hollies Cl
South Norwood SW16 182 C4
Twickenham TW1 152 D2
Hollies End NW7 28 B5
Hollies Rd W5 109 C2
Hollies The N20 14 B3
Harrow HA3 43 A5
7 Wanstead E11 55 A4
Hollies Way 1 SW12 159 A4
Holligrave Rd BR1 187 A2
Hollingbourne Ave
DA7 147 B4
Hollingbourne Gdns
W13 87 B2
Hollingbourne Rd
SE24 161 A6
Hollingbury Ct 1 E17 53 D6
Hollingsworth Rd CR0 222 B2
Hollington Cres KT3 199 D3
Hollington Ct BR7 188 D4
Hollington Rd E6 100 B4
Tottenham N17 34 A1
Hollingworth Cl KT8 195 B5
Hollingworth Ct 7
KT6 197 D2
Hollingworth Rd BR2,
BR5 210 D2
Hollins Ho N7 72 A4
Hollisfield WC1 233 B1
Hollman Gdns SW16 182 D4
Holloway Cl UB7 104 A1
Holloway La UB7 104 B1
Holloway Rd E11 76 B5
E6 100 B4
N19 71 D6
N7 72 B4
Holloway Road Sta N7 72 B3
Holloway Sch N7 71 D3
Holloway St TW3 129 D2
Hollowfield Wlk UB5 63 A2
Hollow The IG8 36 D6
Holly Ave N2 47 D6
Stanmore HA7 26 A1
Walton-on-T KT12 194 D1
Hollybank Cl TW12 173 C5
Holly Berry La 6 NW3 70 A4
Hollybrake Cl BR7 189 B3
Hollybush Cl
Harrow HA3 24 C2
Wanstead E11 55 A4
Hollybush Gdns E2 96 B4
Hollybush Hill E11 54 D3
Holly Bush Hill 23 NW3 70 A4
Hollybush Ho 23 E2 96 B4
Holly Bush La TW12 173 C3
Hollybush Pl E2 96 B4
Hollybush Rd KT2 176 A4
Hollybush St E13 99 B4
Holly Bush Vale 9
NW3 70 A4
Holly Cl NW10 67 C1
Beckenham BR3 208 A5
Buckhurst Hill IG9 21 D1
Feltham TW13 173 A5
Holly Cott KT7 197 A1
Holly Cottage Mews
UB8 82 C2
Holly Cres
Beckenham BR3 207 B4
Chingford IG8 36 B3
Hollycroft Ave NW3 69 C5

Hollycroft Ave *continued*
Wembley HA9 66 B5
Hollycroft Cl
Harmondsworth UB7 126 C6
South Croydon CR2 221 C3
Hollycroft Gdns UB7 126 C6
Holly Ct N15 51 C5
9 Belmont SM2 217 C1
4 Sidcup DA14 190 B6
Wallington SM6 219 B1
Hollydale Cl UB5 63 D4
Hollydale Dr BR2 226 B5
Holly Dale Prim Sch
SE15 140 C3
Hollydale Rd SE15 140 C3
Hollydene SE13 164 B5
5 SE15 140 B4
Bromley BR1 186 D2
Hollydown Way E11 76 B5
Holly Dr E4 19 D4
Holly Farm Rd UB2 107 A1
Hollyfield Ave N11 30 D5
Hollyfield Rd KT5 198 B2
Hollyfield Sch KT6 198 A4
Holly Gdns UB7 104 B4
Holly Gr NW9 45 A2
SE15 140 A3
Pinner HA5 23 A2
Hollygrove WD23 8 B4
Hollygrove Cl TW3 129 B1
Holly Hedge Terr
SE13 164 B6
Holly Hill NW3 70 A4
Southgate N21 16 B5
Holly Hill Rd DA8,DA17 125 D1
Holly Ho TW8 131 C6
Holly House Hospl IG9 21 B2
Holly Lo SE13 142 B1
Harrow HA1 42 B4
Southgate N21 16 C3
4 Wimbledon SW19 179 A4
Wimbledon SW20 178 B1
Holly Lodge Gdns N6 49 A1
Holly Lodge Mans N6 71 A6
Hollymead SM5 218 D5
Holly Mews SW10 256 B1
Holly Mount NW3 70 A4
Hollymount Cl 9
SE10 142 A4
Hollymount Prim Sch
SW20 178 C2
Holly Park Est N4 50 B2
Holly Park Gdns N3 47 C6
Holly Park Prim Sch
N11 31 A5
Holly Park Rd N11 31 A5
Ealing W7 108 D5
Holly Pk N3 47 C6
N4 50 B2
Holly Pl NW3 70 A4
Holly Rd E11 54 D2
W4 111 B2
Hampton TW12 174 A4
Hounslow TW3 129 D1
Twickenham TW1 153 A3
Holly St E8 73 D1
Holly Terr N6 49 A1
Hollytree Cl SW19 156 D3
Holly Tree Ho SE4 141 B2
Holly Tree Lo EN2 4 D3
Hollyview Cl NW4 46 A3
Holly Village N6 71 B6
Holly Way CR4 203 D6
Hollywell Row
EC2 95 C3 243 A5
Holly Wlk NW3 70 A4
Enfield EN2 5 B2
Hollywood Ct W5 110 B6
Hollywood Gdns UB4 84 B1
Hollywood Mews
SW10 266 A6
Hollywood Rd E4 35 A5
SW10 136 A6 266 A6
Hollywood Way IG8 36 B4
Holman Ho 2 E2 96 D4
Holman Hunt Ho W14 254 A1
Holman Rd SW11 136 B3
West Ewell KT19 215 A3
Holmbank Dr TW17 193 C5
Holmbridge Gdns EN3 6 D1
Holmbrook NW1 232 B3
Holmbrook Dr NW4 46 D4
Holmbury Cl WD23 8 C2
Holmbury Ct
Mitcham SW19 180 C3
Upper Tooting SW17 158 D1
Holmbury Gdns UB3 105 D5
Holmbury Gr CR0 223 B1
Holmbury Ho SW9 160 D6
Holmbury Manor 6
DA14 190 A6
Holmbury Pk BR7 188 A3
Holmbury View 2 E5 52 B1
Holmbush Ct NW4 46 D4
Holmbush Rd SW15 157 A5
Holmcote Gdns N5 73 A3
Holmcroft Ho 9 E17 53 D5
Holmcroft Way BR2 210 B4
Holm Ct SE12 165 B1

Holmdale Gdns NW4 46 D4
Holmdale Rd NW6 69 C3
Chislehurst BR7 189 A5
Holmdale Terr N15 51 C3
Holmdene N12 29 D5
Holmdene Ave NW7 28 A4
SE24 161 A6
Harrow HA2 41 D6
Holmdene Cl BR3 186 A1
Holmdene Ct BR1 210 A6
Holmead Rd
SW6 135 D5 265 D3
Holmefield Ho W10 91 A3
Holme Lacey Rd SE12 164 D5
Holmeleigh Ct EN3 6 C1
Holme Rd E6 100 A6
Holmes Ave E17 53 B6
NW7 29 A5
Holmes Ct 18 SW4 138 A3
17 W4 111 A3
5 Chingford E4 20 B2
Holmesdale Ave
SW14 132 D1
Holmesdale Cl SE25 205 D6
Holmesdale Ho 12 NW6 91 C6
Holmesdale Rd N6 49 B2
Bexley DA16 146 D3
Richmond TW9 132 B4
South Norwood SE25 205 C5
Teddington TW11 175 C4
Thornton Heath CR0 205 B4
Holmesley Rd SE23 163 A5
Holmes Pl SW10 266 B6
Holmes Rd NW5 71 B3
Merton SW19 180 A3
Twickenham TW1 152 D2
Holmes Terr SE1 251 A2
Holmeswood Ct 3 N22 32 C1
Holme Way HA7 24 D4
Holmewood Gdns
SW2 160 B4
Holmewood Rd
South Norwood SE25 205 C6
Streatham SW2 160 B4
Holmfield Ave NW4 46 D4
Holmfield Ct 4 NW3 70 C2
Holmfield Ho E17 54 B5
Holm Gr UB10 60 C1
Holmhurst SE13 164 B5
Holmhurst Rd DA17 125 D1
Holmlea Ct 1 CR0 221 B4
Holmleigh Prim Sch
N16 51 C1
Holmleigh Rd N16 51 C1
Holm Oak Cl SW15 157 B5
Holmoaks Ho BR3 186 A1
Holmsbury Ho 6 N7 71 D3
Holmsdale Ho 21 E14 119 D6
6 N11 31 B6
Holmshaw Cl SE26 185 A6
Holmside Ct SW12 159 A5
Holmside Rd SW12 159 A5
Holmsley Cl KT3 199 D2
Holmsley Ho SW15 155 D4
Holmstall Ave HA8 27 A1
Holmstall Par HA8 27 A1
Holm Wlk SE3 143 A3
Holmwood 2 KT5 198 B3
Holmwood Cl
Cheam SM2 216 D1
Harrow HA2 42 A6
Northolt UB5 63 D2
Holmwood Ct DA14 189 D5
3 N16 51 D2
Kingston KT3 199 B6
Holmwood Gdns N3 29 C1
Wallington SM6 219 B2
Holmwood Gr NW7 27 B5
Holmwood Mans W3 110 C5
Holmwood Rd
Chessington KT9 214 A3
Ilford IG3 79 C6
Holne Chase N2 48 A3
Morden SM4 201 C3
Holness Rd E15 76 D2
Holocaust Meml Gdn★
W2 114 D4 247 D2
Holroyd Rd SW15 156 C6
Holsgrove Ct W3 111 C5
Holstein Way 6 DA18 125 A3
Holst Mans SW13 134 C5
Holstock Rd IG1 79 A6
Holsworth Cl HA2 42 A4
Holsworthy Ho 49 E3 97 D4
Holsworthy Way KT9 213 C3
Holt Cl N10 49 A5
Woolwich SE28 124 C6
Holt Ct E15 76 A3
Holt Ho SW2 160 C5
Holtoake Ct 1 W5 87 C3
Holtoake Ho 8 W5 87 C3
Holton St E1 96 D3
Holt Rd E16 122 A5
Wembley HA0 65 C5
Holt The Morden SM4 201 C5
Wallington SM6 219 C4
Holtwhite Ave EN2 5 A3
Holtwhite's Hill EN2 4 D4
Holwell Pl HA5 41 A5

Holwood Park Ave
BR2,BR6 226
Holwood Pl 7 SW4 137
Holybourne Ave SW15 156
Holy Cross RC Sch
SW6 135 C4 265
Holy Cross Sch The
KT3 199
Holy Family RC Prim Sch
E14 119
SE9 143
Holy Ghost RC Prim Sch
SW12 159
Holyhead Cl E3 97
3 E6 100
Holyhead Ct KT1 197
Holy Innocents RC Prim Sc
BR6 227
Holyoake Ct SE16 119
Holyoake Wlk N2 48
Ealing W5 87
Holyoak Rd
SE11 116 D2 261
Holyport Rd SW6 134
Holyrood Ave HA2 63
Holyrood Gdns HA8 26
Holyrood Ho N4 50
Holyrood Mews 11
E16 121
Holyrood Rd EN5 14
Holyrood St
SE1 117 C5 253
Holy Trinity CE First Sch
SW19 179
Holy Trinity CE Inf Sch
SW17 158
Holy Trinity CE JMI Sch
E8 73
Holy Trinity CE Jun Sch
Richmond TW10 132
Wallington SM6 219
Holy Trinity CE Prim Sch
DA15 168
N2 48
NW3 70
SW1 114 D2 257
SW1 115 A2 258
Forest Hill SE23 162
Streatham SW2 160
Holy Trinity Coll BR1 187
Holy Trinity & St Silas CE
Prim Sch NW1 71
Holywell Cl 35 SE16 118
2 SE3 143
Stanwell TW19 148
Holywell La EC2 243
Holywell Way TW19 148
Homan Ct N12 30
Homan Ho 6 SW4 159
Homebush Ho E4 19
Home Cl
Carshalton SM5 218
Northolt UB5 85
Homecoppice Ho 1
BR1 186
Homecroft Rd
Forest Hill SE26 184
Tottenham N22 33
Home Ct KT6 197
Home Farm Cl
Thames Ditton KT7 196
Upper Halliford TW17 193
Home Farm Cotts BR5 190
Homefarm Rd W7 86
Homefield SM4 201
Home Field EN5 13
Homefield Ave IG2 57
Homefield Cl NW10 67
Hayes UB4 84
Homefield Ct NW4 46
Homefield Gdns N2 48
Mitcham CR4,SW19 180
Homefield Ho SE23 162
Homefield Pk SM1,
SM2 217
Homefield Pl 4 SW19 178
Homefield Prep Sch
SM1 217
Homefield Rd BR1 187
HA8 27
W4 111
Walton-on-T KT12 195
Wembley HA0 65
Wimbledon SW19 179
Homefield St 14 N1 95
Homefirs Ho HA9 66
Homelands Dr SE19 183
Home Lea BR6 227
Homeleigh Ct 8
SW16 160
Homeleigh Rd SE15 162
Homemead SW12 159
Home Mead HA7 25
Homemead Rd BR2 210
Wallington CR0 203
Home Office SW1 249
Home Park Rd SW19 157
Home Park Terr KT1 175
Home Park Wlk KT1 197

ome Rd SW11 .... 136 C3
omer Dr E14 .... 119 C2
omer Rd E9 .... 75 A2
Croydon CR0 .... 206 D3
omer Row W1 .... 237 B3
omersham Rd KT1 .... 176 D1
omer St W1 .. 92 C2 237 B3
omerton Coll of
Technology E9 .... 74 C3
omerton Gr E9 .... 74 D3
omerton High St E9 .... 74 D3
omerton Hospl E9 .... 74 D3
omerton Rd E9 .... 75 B3
omerton Row E9 .... 74 C3
omerton Sta E9 .... 74 D2
omerton Terr E9 .... 74 C2
omesdale Cl E11 .... 55 A4
omesdale Rd
BR1,BR2 .... 209 C6
Orpington BR5,BR6 .... 211 C2
omesfield NW11 .... 47 C4
omes Of Rest (CE
Temperance Society)
IG1 .... 79 B5
omestall Rd SE22 .... 162 C6
omestead Ct EN5 .... 13 C6
omestead Gdns
KT10 .... 212 C3
omestead Paddock
N14 .... 15 B6
omestead Pk NW2 .... 67 D5
omestead Rd
SW6 .... 135 B5 264 D3
Dagenham RM8 .... 81 B6
omesteads The BR3 .... 185 D4
omestead The N11 .... 31 B6
omewalk Ho SE26 .... 184 C6
omewaters Ave
TW16 .... 171 D2
Homewillow Cl N21 .... 16 D5
Homewood Cl TW12 .... 173 B4
Homewood Cres BR7 .... 189 C4
Homewood Gdns
SE25 .... 205 C4
Homewoods 2 SW12 .... 159 C4
Homildon Ho 10 SE26 .... 162 A1
Homington Ct KT2 .... 176 A3
Honduras St EC1 .... 242 A6
Honeybourne Rd NW6 .... 69 D3
Honeybourne Way
BR5 .... 211 B1
Honeybrook Rd SW12,
SW4 .... 159 C4
Honey Cl RM10 .... 81 D2
Honeycroft Hill UB10 .... 60 A1
Honeyden Rd DA14 .... 191 A4
Honeyfield N4 .... 72 C6
Honey Hill UB10 .... 60 B1
Honey La EC2 .... 242 B1
Honeyman Cl NW6 .... 68 D1
Honeypot Bsns Ctr HA7 26 A2
Honeypot Cl NW9 .... 44 B5
Honeypot La HA3,HA7,
NW9 .... 44 B6
Honeysett Rd 1 N17 .... 33 D1
Honeysuckle Cl UB1 .... 107 A6
Honeysuckle Ct
2 SE12 .... 165 A4
Ilford IG1 .... 78 D2
Honeysuckle Gdns
CR0 .... 206 D1
Honeywell Jun & Inf Schs
SW11 .... 158 D5
Honeywell Rd SW11 .... 158 D5
Honeywood Ho 5
SE15 .... 140 A4
Honeywood Rd NW10 .... 89 D5
Isleworth TW7 .... 131 A1
Honeywood Wlk SM5 .... 218 D4
Honister Cl HA7 .... 25 B2
Honister Gdns HA7 .... 25 B2
Honister Pl HA7 .... 25 B2
Honiton Gdns 1 SE15 140 C3
Honiton Ho 30 SE5 .... 139 A3
Honiton Rd DA16 .... 145 D3
NW6 .... 91 B5
Honley Rd SE6 .... 163 D4
Honnor Gdns TW7 .... 130 B3
Honor Oak Park Sta
SE23 .... 162 D5
Honor Oak Pk SE23 .... 162 D5
Honor Oak Rd SE23 .... 162 C4
Honor Oak Rise SE23 .... 162 C5
Honwell Ho W2 .... 91 C2
Hood Ave
East Barnet N14 .... 15 B5
Mortlake SW14 .... 155 A6
Hood Cl CR0 .... 204 D1
Hoodcote Gdns N21 .... 16 D4
Hood Ct N7 .... 72 B5
Hood Ho 17 SE5 .... 139 B5
Hood Lo E11 .... 77 B6
Hood Rd SW20 .... 177 D3
Hook KT6 .... 214 A5
Hooke Ct SE10 .... 142 A4
Hooke Ho 30 E3 .... 97 A5
Hooker's Rd E17 .... 52 D6
Hook Farm Rd BR2 .... 209 D4
Hookham Ct SW8 .... 269 C2

Hook Ho 9 SW27 .... 182 D5
Hooking Gn HA2 .... 41 D4
Hook La DA16 .... 146 A1
Hook Lane Prim Sch
DA16 .... 146 A2
Hook Rd KT19,KT17 .... 215 A1
Hook Rise N
Surbiton KT6 .... 214 A5
Tolworth KT6,KT9 .... 214 D6
Hook Rise S KT6,KT9 .... 214 D6
Hook Rise South KT6 214 A5
Hooks Cl SE15 .... 140 B4
Hookstone Way IG8 .... 37 D3
Hook The EN5 .... 14 B5
Hook Underpass KT6 .... 214 A5
Hook Wlk HA8 .... 27 A4
Hooper Ho 8 SW18 .... 157 B6
Hooper Rd E16 .... 99 A1
Hooper's Ct SW1 .... 247 C1
Hooper's Mews 4 W3 111 A5
Hooper St E1 .... 96 A1
Hoop La NW11 .... 47 C2
Hoover Ho 5 SE6 .... 186 A6
Hope Cl N1 .... 73 A2
SE12 .... 165 B1
2 Brentford TW8 .... 110 A1
Dagenham RM6 .... 58 D5
Sutton SM1 .... 218 A3
1 Woodford IG8 .... 37 C4
Hopedale Rd SE7 .... 143 B6
Hopefield 3 W7 .... 108 D5
Hopefield Ave NW6 .... 91 A5
Hope Pk BR1 .... 186 D3
Hopes Cl TW5 .... 129 C6
Hope St SW11 .... 136 B2
Hopetown St E1 .... 243 D3
Hopewell St SE5 .... 139 B5
Hop Gdns WC2 .... 250 A5
Hopgood St W12 .... 112 C5
Hopkins Cl N10 .... 31 A3
Hopkins Ho 12 E14 .... 97 C1
Hopkins Mews E15 .... 98 D6
Hopkinson Ho 1
SW11 .... 137 A3
Hopkinson's Pl NW1 .... 231 A6
Hopkins St W1 . 93 D1 239 C1
Hoppers Rd N21 .... 16 C2
Hoppett Rd E4 .... 20 C2
Hopping La N1 .... 72 D2
Hoppingwood Ave
KT3 .... 199 C6
Hoppner Rd UB4 .... 83 B5
Hop St SE10 .... 120 D3
Hopton Ct BR2 .... 209 A1
Hopton Gdns KT3 .... 200 A3
Hopton Ho 5 SW9 .... 138 D3
Hopton Rd SW16 .... 182 A5
Hopton's Gdns SE1 .... 251 D4
Hopton St SE1 116 D5 251 D4
Hoptree Cl N12 .... 29 D6
Hopwood Cl SW17 .... 158 A1
Hopwood Rd SE17 .... 139 B6
Hopwood Wlk E8 .... 74 A1
Horace Rd E7 .... 77 B4
Ilford IG6 .... 57 A6
Kingston KT1 .... 198 B6
Horatio Ho 13 E2 .... 95 D5
Horatio Pl E14 .... 120 A5
Horatio St 11 E2 .... 95 D5
Horatius Way CR0 .... 220 B2
Horbury Cres
W11 .... 113 C6 245 A5
Horbury Mews
W11 .... 113 B6 244 D5
Horder Rd
SW6 .... 135 A4 264 B1
Hordle Prom E 14
SE15 .... 139 D5
Hordle Prom N 3
SE15 .... 139 D5
Hordle Prom S 7
SE15 .... 139 D5
Hordle Prom W 13
SE15 .... 139 C5
Horizon Bldg 14 E14 .... 119 C6
Horizon Sch N16 .... 73 C4
Horle Wlk SE5 .... 138 D3
Horley Cl DA6 .... 169 C6
Horley Rd SE9 .... 188 A6
Hormead Rd W9 .... 91 B3
Hornbeam Cl NW7 .... 11 D1
SE11 .... 261 A4
Barking IG11 .... 102 B3
Buckhurst Hill IG9 .... 21 D1
Northolt UB5 .... 63 B3
Hornbeam Cres TW8 .... 131 B5
Hornbeam Gr E4 .... 20 D1
Hornbeam Ho
6 DA15 .... 168 A1
2 NW3 .... 70 D2
Buckhurst Hill IG9 .... 21 D1
Hornbeam La E4 .... 20 C6
Hornbeam Rd
Buckhurst Hill IG9 .... 21 D1
Hayes UB4 .... 84 C2
Hornbeams Rise N11 .... 31 A4
Hornbeam Terr SM5 .... 202 C1
Hornbeam Twr E11 .... 76 B5
Hornbeam Way BR2 .... 210 C3

Hornblower Cl 2
SE16 .... 119 A2
Hornbuckle Cl HA2 .... 64 B6
Hornby Cl NW3 .... 70 B1
Hornby Ho 6 SE11 .... 138 C6
Horncastle Cl SE12 .... 165 A4
Horncastle Rd SE12 .... 165 A4
Hornchurch N17 .... 33 B1
Hornchurch Cl KT2 .... 175 D6
Horndean Cl 3 SW15 156 A3
Horne Ho 7 SE18 .... 144 A4
Horner Ct E11 .... 76 B5
Horne Rd TW17 .... 192 C5
Horner Hos 18 N1 .... 95 C6
Horner La 3 CR4 .... 180 B1
Horne Way SW15 .... 134 C3
Hornfair Rd SE7 .... 143 D5
Horniman Dr SE23 .... 162 C4
Horniman Grange 7
SE23 .... 162 C3
Horniman Mus & Gdns*
SE23 .... 162 B3
Horniman Sch SE23 .... 162 B3
Horning Cl SE9 .... 188 A6
Horn La SE10 .... 121 A2
W3 .... 89 A1
Woodford IG8 .... 37 A3
Horn Link Way SE10 .... 121 A2
Horn Park Cl SE12 .... 165 B6
Horn Park La SE12 .... 165 B5
Horn Park Prim Sch
SE12 .... 165 B4
Hornsby House Sch
SW12 .... 159 A3
Horns End Pl HA5 .... 40 C4
Hornsey Central Hospl
N8 .... 49 D4
Hornsey La N6 .... 49 C2
Hornsey Lane Gdns N6 49 C2
Hornsey Park Rd N8 .... 50 B6
Hornsey Rd N7,N19 .... 72 B6
Hornsey Rise Gdns N19 50 A2
Hornsey Sch for Girls
N8 .... 50 B4
Hornsey St N7 .... 72 B3
Hornsey Sta N8 .... 50 B5
Hornshay St SE15 .... 140 C6
Horns Rd IG2,IG6 .... 57 A4
Hornton Ct W8 .... 245 B1
Hornton Pl W8 .... 245 B1
Hornton St
W8 .... 113 C4 245 B2
Horrocks Ho SW15 .... 156 B6
Horsa Rd DA8 .... 147 D5
Eltham SE12 .... 165 C4
Horsebridge Cl RM9 .... 103 A6
Horsecroft Rd HA8 .... 27 B3
Horse & Dolphin Yd
W1 .... 249 D6
Horse Fair KT1 .... 175 D1
Horseferry Pl SE10 .... 142 A6
Horseferry Rd E14 .... 119 A6
SW1 .... 115 D2 259 D4
Horseferry Rd Est
SW1 .... 259 C5
Horseguards Ave
SW1 .... 116 A5 250 A3
Horse Guards Par*
SW1 .... 115 D5 249 D3
Horse Guards Rd
SW1 .... 115 D4 249 D2
Horse Leaze E6 .... 100 C1
Horsell Rd BR5 .... 190 B2
N5 .... 72 C3
Horselydown La
SE1 .... 117 D5 253 C3
Horselydown Mans
SE1 .... 253 C2
Horsenden Ave UB6 .... 64 D3
Horsenden Cres UB6 .... 64 D3
Horsenden La N UB6 .... 64 D1
Horsenden La S UB6 .... 87 A6
Horsenden Prim Sch
UB6 .... 64 C2
Horsendon Ho 11 N7 .... 71 D3
Horseshoe Cl E14 .... 120 A1
NW2 .... 68 B6
Horse Shoe Cres UB5 .... 85 C5
Horseshoe Dr UB8 .... 82 C1
Horse Shoe Gn SM1 .... 217 D6
Horseshoe La
Barnet N20 .... 12 D3
Enfield EN2 .... 5 A2
Horse Shoe Yd W1 .... 248 D6
Horse Yd N1 .... 234 D6
Horsfeld Gdns 1 SE9 .... 166 A6
Horsfeld Rd SE9 .... 165 D6
Horsfield Ho 2 N1 .... 73 A1
Horsford Rd SW2 .... 160 B6
Horsham Ave N12 .... 30 C5
Horsham Ct N17 .... 34 A2
Horsham Rd DA6 .... 169 C6
East Bedfont TW14 .... 149 A5
Horsley Dr
Kingston KT2 .... 175 D5
New Addington CR0 .... 224 A1
Horsley Ho 11 SE4 .... 140 D1
Horsley Rd BR1 .... 187 B2
Chingford E4 .... 20 A2

Horsley St 3 SE17 .... 139 B6
Horsman Ho SE5 .... 139 A6
Horsman St SE5 .... 139 A6
Horsmonden Cl BR6 .... 211 D2
Horsmonden Rd SE4 .... 163 B5
Horston Ho N4 .... 51 A2
Hortensia Ho SW10 .... 266 A4
Hortensia Rd
SW10 .... 136 A5 266 A4
Horticultural Pl 6
W4 .... 111 B1
Horton Ave NW2 .... 69 A4
Horton Bridge Rd UB7 104 B5
Horton Cl UB7 .... 104 B5
Horton Ctry Pk KT19 .... 214 C1
Horton Ho 13 SE15 .... 140 C6
SW8 .... 270 C4
W14 .... 254 A1
Horton Ind Pk UB7 .... 104 B5
Horton La KT19 .... 215 A1
Horton Par UB7 .... 104 A5
Horton Rd E8 .... 74 B2
Yiewsley UB7 .... 104 B5
Horton Road Ind Est
UB7 .... 104 B5
Horton St SE13 .... 141 D2
Horton Way CR0 .... 206 D4
Hortus Rd Chingford E4 . 20 A2
Southall UB2 .... 107 B4
Horwood Ho 24 E2 .... 96 B4
NW8 .... 237 B6
Hosack Rd SW12,SW17 159 A2
Hoser Ave SE12 .... 165 A2
Hosier La EC1 .. 94 D2 241 D3
Hoskins Cl UB3 .... 105 D1
Hoskin's Cl E16 .... 99 C1
Hoskins St SE10 .... 120 B1
Hospital Bridge Rd
TW2 .... 151 D3
Hospital Bridge Rdbt
TW2 .... 151 D2
Hospital of the Holy Trinity
(Almshouses) 5
CR0 .... 221 A6
Hospital Rd TW3 .... 129 C2
Hospl for Tropical Diseases
NW1 .... 232 C5
Hospl of St John & St
Elizabeth NW8 92 B5 229 C3
Hotham Cl KT8 .... 195 C6
Hotham Prim Sch
SW15 .... 134 D1
Hotham Rd
Merton SW19 .... 180 A3
Putney SW15 .... 134 C2
Hotham Road Mews 12
SW19 .... 180 A3
Hotham St E15 .... 98 C6
Hothfield Pl SE16 .... 118 C3
Hotspur Ind Est N17 .... 34 B4
Hotspur Rd UB5 .... 85 C5
Hotspur St
SE11 .... 116 C1 261 A2
Houblon Rd TW10 .... 154 A6
Houghton Cl 10 E8 .... 73 D2
Hampton TW12 .... 173 A4
Houghton Rd N15 .... 51 D5
Houghton St WC2 .... 240 D1
Houlder Cres CR0 .... 220 D2
Houndsden Rd N21 .... 16 C5
Houndsditch
EC3 .... 95 C1 243 B2
Houndsfield Prim Sch
N9 .... 18 B4
Houndsfield Rd N9 .... 18 B4
Hounslow Ave TW3 .... 151 D6
Hounslow Bsns Pk
TW3 .... 129 D1
Hounslow Central Sta
TW3 .... 129 D2
Hounslow Ctr The
TW3 .... 129 D2
Hounslow East Sta
TW3 .... 130 A3
Hounslow Ed Ctr (Specl
Sch) The TW4 .... 129 A2
Hounslow Gdns TW3 .... 151 D6
Hounslow Heath Jun & Inf
Schs TW4 .... 129 A2
Hounslow Heath Nature
Reserve TW4 .... 151 A5
Hounslow Manor Sch
TW3 .... 130 A2
Hounslow Rd
Feltham TW13 .... 151 A2
Twickenham TW2,TW3 .... 152 A5
Feltham TW14 .... 150 B4
Hounslow Sta TW3 .... 151 D6
Hounslow Town Prim Sch
TW3 .... 130 B2
Hounslow West Sta
TW3 .... 129 A3
Houseman Way 20
SE5 .... 139 B5
Houses of Parliament*
SW1 .... 116 A3 260 B6
Houston Ct 3 CR0 .... 205 C1
Houston Rd
Forest Hill SE23 .... 163 A1

Houston Rd *continued*
Thames Ditton KT6 .... 197 B3
Houstoun Ct TW5 .... 129 B5
Hove Ave E17 .... 53 B4
Hoveden Rd NW2 .... 69 A3
Hove Gdns SM1 .... 201 D1
Hovenden Ho 6 SE21 183 C6
Hoveton Rd SE28 .... 102 C1
Howard Ave DA5 .... 168 C4
Howard Cl N11 .... 15 A2
NW2 .... 69 A4
Acton W3 .... 88 D1
Ashford TW16 .... 171 D4
Bushey WD23 .... 8 C4
Hampton TW12 .... 174 A4
Howard Ct SE15 .... 140 A2
12 Barking IG11 .... 101 B6
Beckenham BR3 .... 186 A1
Howard Ho 8 E5 .... 74 C6
14 SE8 .... 141 B6
7 SW9 .... 138 C2
W1 .... 238 D5
Penge SE20 .... 184 C2
Howard Mans E17 .... 53 D6
Howard Prim Sch CR0 221 A4
Howard Rd BR1 .... 187 A3
E11 .... 76 C5
E17 .... 53 D6
E6 .... 100 B5
N15 .... 51 C3
N16 .... 73 B4
NW2 .... 68 D4
Barking IG11 .... 101 B6
Croydon SE25 .... 206 A3
Ilford IG1 .... 78 D4
Isleworth TW7 .... 130 D2
New Malden KT3 .... 199 D5
Penge SE20 .... 184 C2
Southall UB1 .... 85 D1
Surbiton KT5 .... 198 B3
Howards Cl HA5 .... 22 B1
Howards Crest Cl BR3 186 A1
Howard's La SW15 .... 134 C1
Howard's Rd E13 .... 99 A4
Howard St KT7 .... 197 B3
Howard Way EN5 .... 12 D6
Howard Wlk N2 .... 48 B5
Howarth Rd SE2 .... 124 A2
Howberry Cl HA8 .... 25 D4
Howberry Rd
South Norwood CR7 .... 183 B1
Stanmore HA7,H8 .... 25 D4
Howbury Rd SE15 .... 140 C2
Howcroft Cres N3 .... 29 C3
Howcroft Ho 3 E3 .... 97 B4
Howcroft La UB6 .... 86 B4
Howden Cl SE28 .... 124 D6
Howden Ct SE25 .... 183 D1
Howden Rd SE25 .... 183 D1
Howden St SE15 .... 140 A2
Howell Cl RM6 .... 58 D4
Howell Ct 2 E10 .... 53 D2
Howell Ho 5 N7 .... 71 D3
Howell Wlk SE1 .... 261 D3
Howerd Way SE18 .... 144 A4
Howes Cl N3 .... 47 C6
Howfield Pl N17 .... 51 D6
Howgate Rd SW14 .... 133 B2
Howick Pl
SW1 .... 115 C3 259 B5
Howie St
SW11 .... 136 C5 267 A3
Howitt Cl 6 NW3 .... 70 C2
Howitt Rd NW3 .... 70 C2
Howland Ho 9 SW16 .... 160 A1
Howland Mews E W1 .... 239 B4
Howland St W1 93 C2 239 B4
Howland Way SE16 .... 119 A4
Howletts La HA4 .... 39 A3
Howletts Rd SE24 .... 161 A5
Howley Pl W2 .. 92 A2 236 B4
Howley Rd CR0 .... 221 A5
Howmic Ct 1 TW1 .... 153 C5
Howsman Rd SW13 .... 134 A6
Howson Rd SE4 .... 141 A1
Howson Terr TW10 .... 154 A5
How's St E2 .... 95 D5
Howton Pl WD23 .... 8 B3
Hoxton Mkt 10 N1 .... 95 C4
Hoxton Point EC1 .... 95 C4
Hoxton Sq N1 .... 95 C4
Hoxton St N1 .... 95 C5
Hoylake Cres UB10 .... 60 D6
Hoylake Gdns
Mitcham CR4 .... 203 C6
Ruislip HA4 .... 40 B1
South Oxhey WD19 .... 22 D6
Hoylake Rd W3 .... 89 C1
Hoyland Cl 4 SE15 .... 140 B5
Hoyle Rd SW17 .... 180 C5
Hoy St E16 .... 98 D1
Huan Ct N20 .... 14 C2
Hubbard Dr KT9 .... 213 D2
Hubbard Rd SE27 .... 183 A6
Hubbards Cl UB8 .... 82 D1
Hubbard St E15 .... 98 C6
Hub Buildings The 4
SW12 .... 159 B3
Huberd Ho SE1 .... 262 D6

Hubert Gr SW9 .... 138 A2
Hubert Ho NW8 .... 237 A5
Hubert Rd E6 .... 99 D4
Hucknall Ct NW8 .... 236 C6
Huddart St E3 .... 97 B2
Huddleston Cl E2 .... 96 C5
Huddlestone Rd E7 .... 76 D4
NW2 .... 68 B2
Huddleston Rd N7 .... 71 C4
Hudson 27 NW9 .... 27 D2
Hudson Cl 15 W12 .... 112 B6
Hudson Ct
Croydon SE25 .... 206 A5
4 Merton SW19 .... 179 D2
3 Millwall E14 .... 119 C1
Hudson Ho SW10 .... 266 A4
5 W11 .... 91 A1
Hudson Pl SE18 .... 123 A1
Hudson Rd DA7 .... 147 B4
Harlington UB7 .... 127 B6
Hudsons Ho N1 .... 235 D1
Hudson's Pl
SW1 .... 115 C2 259 A4
Hudson Way N9 .... 18 C2
Huggin Ct EC4 .... 252 B6
Huggin Hill EC4 .... 252 B6
Huggins Ho 8 E3 .... 97 C4
Huggins Pl SW2 .... 160 B3
Hughan Rd E15 .... 76 B3
Hugh Astor Ct SE1 .... 261 D6
Hugh Clark Ho W13 .... 109 A5
Hughenden Ave HA3 .... 43 B4
Hughenden Gdns UB5 .... 84 C4
Hughenden Rd KT4 .... 200 A2
Hughendon EN5 .... 1 D1
Hughendon Terr E15 .... 76 A4
Hughes Cl N12 .... 30 A5
Hughes Ho 26 E2 .... 96 C4
SE17 .... 261 D3
SE5 .... 139 A4
15 SE8 .... 141 C6
Hughes Mans E1 .... 96 A3
Hughes Rd
Ashford TW15 .... 171 A4
Hayes UB3 .... 106 B6
Hughes Terr 6 E16 .... 98 D2
Hughes Wlk CR0 .... 205 A2
Hugh Gaitskell Cl
SW6 .... 264 C5
Hugh Gaitskell Ho N16 . 73 D6
NW10 .... 67 D1
Hugh Herland KT1 .... 198 A6
Hugh Mews SW1 .... 258 D3
Hugh Morgan Ho 5
SW4 .... 137 D2
Hugh Myddelton Prim Sch
EC1 .... 94 C4 234 B1
Hugh Platt Ho 29 E2 .... 96 B5
Hugh St SW1 . 115 B2 258 D3
Hugo Ho SW1 .... 257 D6
Hugon Rd SW6 .... 135 D2
Hugo Rd N19 .... 71 C4
Huguenot Pl SW18 .... 158 A6
Huguenot Sq SE15 .... 140 B2
Hullbridge Mews N1 .... 235 C6
Hull Cl SE16 .... 118 D5
Hull Ct SE5 .... 139 B3
Hull Pl E16 .... 123 A5
Hull St EC1 .... 235 A1
Hulme Pl SE1 .... 252 B1
Hulse Ave IG11 .... 79 C2
Humber Ct W7 .... 86 B1
Humber Dr W10 .... 90 D3
Humber Rd NW2 .... 68 B6
SE3 .... 142 D6
Humberstone Rd E13 .... 99 C4
Humberton Cl E9 .... 75 A3
Humbolt Rd
W6 .... 135 A6 264 A5
Hume Ct N1 .... 72 D1
Hume Ho 14 W11 .... 112 D5
Humes Ave W7 .... 108 D4
Hume Terr E16 .... 99 B1
Hume Way HA4 .... 40 A3
Humphrey Ct SW11 .... 266 D1
Humphrey St
SE1 .... 117 D1 263 C2
Humphries Cl RM9 .... 81 B4
Humphry Ho 10 SW15 156 D6
Hundred Acre NW9 .... 27 D1
Hungerdown E4 .... 20 A3
Hungerford Bridge
WC2 .... 250 C4
Hungerford Ho SW1 .... 269 B6
Hungerford Inf Sch N7 . 72 A2
Hungerford Jun & Inf Schs
N7 .... 71 D2
Hungerford La WC2 .... 250 B4
Hungerford Prim Sch
N7 .... 72 A2
Hungerford Rd N7 .... 72 A3
4 N7 .... 71 D2
Hungerford St 24 E1 .... 96 B1
Hunsdon Cl RM9 .... 81 A2
Hunsdon Ho E5 .... 74 B5
Hunsdon Rd SE14 .... 140 D5

Hunslett St 27 E2 ... 96 C5
Hunstanton Ho NW1 ... 237 B4
Hunston Rd SM4 ... 201 D1
Hunt Ct N14 ... 15 B4
11 Northolt UB5 ... 84 D5
Hunter Cl SE1 ... 262 D5
Borehamwood WD6 ... 11 A6
Upper Tooting SW12 ... 159 A3
Huntercrombe Gdns
WD19 ... 22 C5
Hunter Ct 8 SE5 ... 139 B1
27 Streatham SW2 ... 160 C4
Hunter Ho 1 N19 ... 71 C5
SE1 ... 251 D1
SW5 ... 255 B1
SW8 ... 269 D3
WC1 ... 240 B6
Feltham TW14 ... 150 A3
Hunter Lo 9 W9 ... 91 C2
Hunter Rd
South Norwood CR7 ... 205 B6
Wimbledon SW20 ... 178 C2
Hunters Ct 5 TW9 ... 153 D6
Hunter's Gr BR6 ... 227 A4
Hunters Gr Harrow HA3 ... 43 C5
Hayes UB3 ... 106 A4
Hunters Hall Prim Sch
RM10 ... 81 D3
Hunters Hall Rd RM10 ... 81 C3
Hunters Hill HA4 ... 62 D5
Hunters Lo 10 DA15 ... 168 A1
Hunters Mdw SE19 ... 183 C6
Hunters Rd
Chessington KT9 ... 214 A4
Ilford IG1 ... 78 D3
Hunters Sq RM10 ... 81 C4
Hunter St WC1 ... 94 A3 240 B6
Hunters The 2 BR3 ... 186 A2
Hunters Way Enfield EN2 ... 4 C4
South Croydon CR0 ... 221 C4
Hunter Wlk E13 ... 99 A5
Borehamwood WD6 ... 11 B6
Huntingdon Cl CR4,
SW16 ... 204 A5
Huntingdon Ct SW14 ... 133 A2
Huntingdon Gdns
Chiswick W4 ... 133 A5
North Cheam KT4 ... 216 C5
Huntingdon Ho SW5 ... 255 B4
Huntingdon Rd N2 ... 48 C6
N9 ... 18 C3
Huntingdon St E16 ... 98 D1
N1 ... 72 B1
Huntingfield CR0 ... 223 B1
Huntingfield Rd SW15 ... 156 A6
Huntingford Ho SW15 ... 134 C3
Hunting Gate Cl EN2 ... 4 C2
Hunting Gate Dr KT9 ... 214 A1
Hunting Gate Mews
Sutton SM1 ... 217 D5
Twickenham TW2 ... 152 C3
Huntings Farm IG1 ... 79 C6
Huntings Rd RM10 ... 81 C2
Huntley Ho 7 SE21 ... 183 C6
Huntley St WC1 ... 93 D3 239 C5
Huntley Way SW20 ... 178 A1
Huntly Dr N3 ... 29 C4
Huntly Rd SE25 ... 205 C5
Hunton St E1 ... 96 A2
Hunt Rd UB2 ... 107 C3
Hunts Cl SE3 ... 143 A3
Hunt's Ct WC2 ... 249 D5
Huntshaw Ho 37 E3 ... 97 D4
Hunt's La E15 ... 98 A5
Huntsman Cl TW13 ... 172 B6
Huntsman St SE17 ... 263 A3
Hunts Mead EN3 ... 6 D2
Hunts Mead Cl BR7 ... 188 B3
Huntsmoor Rd KT19 ... 215 B3
Huntspill St SW17 ... 158 A1
Hunts Slip Rd SE21 ... 161 C2
Huntsworth Ct SE6 ... 163 C3
Huntsworth Mews
NW1 ... 92 D3 237 C5
Hurdwick Ho NW1 ... 232 A4
Hurleston Ho 11 SE8 ... 119 B1
Hurley Cres SE16 ... 118 D4
Hurley Ct 1 W5 ... 87 C1
Hurley Ho 34 E2 ... 95 D4
SE11 ... 261 B3
Hurley Lo SE22 ... 162 C5
Hurley Rd UB6 ... 85 D2
Hurlingham Bsns Pk
SW6 ... 135 C2
Hurlingham & Chelsea Sec
Sch SW6 ... 135 C2
Hurlingham Court Mans
SW6 ... 135 C3
Hurlingham Ct SW6 ... 135 B2
Hurlingham Gdns
SW6 ... 135 B2
Hurlingham Rd DA7 ... 147 B5
Fulham SW6 ... 135 B3
Hurlingham Sq SW6 ... 135 D2
Hurlock Ho N5 ... 72 D5
Hurlock St N5 ... 72 D5
Hurlstone Rd SE25 ... 205 C4
Hurn Court Rd TW5 ... 128 D3
Hurn Ct TW5 ... 128 D3
Huron Cl 5 BR6 ... 227 D3
Huron Rd SW17 ... 159 A1
Hurren Cl SE3 ... 142 C2
Hurricane Rd SM6 ... 220 B1
Hurry Cl E15 ... 76 C1
Hursley Ct 11 KT6 ... 197 D2
Hurst Ave N6 ... 49 C3
Chingford E4 ... 19 C1
Hurstbourne KT10 ... 212 D2
Hurstbourne Cotts
DA5 ... 169 D4
Hurstbourne Gdns
IG11 ... 79 C2
Hurstbourne Ho 12
SW15 ... 155 D5
Hurstbourne Priors
CR2 ... 221 C2
Hurstbourne Rd SE23 ... 163 A3
Hurst Cl NW11 ... 47 D3
Chessington KT9 ... 214 C3
Chingford E4 ... 19 C1
Hayes BR2 ... 208 D1
Northolt UB5 ... 63 B3
Hurstcombe IG9 ... 21 A2
Hurstcourt Rd SM1 ... 217 D6
Hurst Ct
Beckenham BR3 ... 185 C3
South Norwood SE25 ... 205 D5
Woodford IG8 ... 37 B4
Hurstdene Ave BR2 ... 208 D1
Hurstdene Gdns N15 ... 51 C2
Hurstfield BR2 ... 209 A4
Hurstfield Cres UB4 ... 83 C2
Hurstfield Rd KT8 ... 195 C6
Hurst Gr KT12 ... 193 D1
Hurst Ho N1 ... 233 D3
SE2 ... 124 D1
7 Penge SE26 ... 184 B5
Hurst La SE2 ... 124 D1
East Molesey KT8 ... 196 A6
Hurst Lo N8 ... 49 D3
Hurstmead Ct HA8 ... 26 D6
Hurstmere Foundation Sch
for Boys DA15 ... 168 C3
Hurst Park Prim Sch
KT8 ... 195 C6
Hurst Pl SE2 ... 146 D6
Hurst Prim Sch DA5 ... 168 D3
Hurst Rd DA5,DA15 ... 168 C3
E17 ... 53 D6
Buckhurst Hill IG9 ... 21 D3
Croydon CR0 ... 221 B3
East Molesey KT8,KT12 ... 195 C6
Southgate N21 ... 16 C3
Walton-on-T KT8&KT12 ... 194 D5
Hurst Rise EN5 ... 1 C2
Hurst Springs DA5 ... 169 A3
Hurst St SE24 ... 160 D5
Hurstview Grange
CR2 ... 220 D1
Hurst View Rd CR2 ... 221 C1
Hurst Way CR2 ... 221 C2
Hurstway Wlk 2 W11 ... 112 D6
Hurstwood Ave DA5 ... 169 A3
Wanstead E18 ... 55 B5
Hurstwood Ct N12 ... 30 C4
NW11 ... 47 B5
Hurstwood Dr BR1 ... 210 B6
Hurstwood Rd NW11 ... 47 B5
Hurtwood Rd KT12 ... 195 B2
Husbourne Ho 8 SE8 ... 119 A2
Huson Cl NW3 ... 70 C1
Hussain Cl HA1 ... 64 D4
Hussars Cl TW4 ... 129 A2
Husseywell Cres BR2 ... 209 A1
Hutching's St E14 ... 119 C4
Hutchings Wlk NW11 ... 47 D5
Hutchins Cl E15 ... 76 A1
Hutchins Ho 8 SW4 ... 159 D4
Hutchinson Ct RM6 ... 58 D5
Hutchinson Ho 9
SE14 ... 140 C5
Hutchinson Terr HA9 ... 65 D5
Hutchins Rd SE28 ... 124 A5
Thamesmead SE28 ... 124 A6
Hutton Cl Greenford UB6 ... 64 B3
Woodford IG8 ... 37 B4
Hutton Ct 3 N4 ... 50 B1
N9 ... 18 C4
1 Ealing W5 ... 87 C2
Hutton Gdns HA3 ... 24 A3
Hutton Gr N12 ... 29 D5
Hutton Ho 22 E2 ... 96 A4
Hutton La HA3 ... 24 A3
Hutton Row 4 HA8 ... 27 A3
Hutton St EC4 ... 241 B1
Hutton Wlk HA3 ... 24 A3
Huxbear St SE4 ... 163 B6
Huxley Cl UB5 ... 85 A6
Huxley Dr RM6 ... 58 B2
Huxley Gdns NW10 ... 88 B5
Huxley Ho NW8 ... 236 D5
SE2 ... 124 D1
4 SW9 ... 138 B3
Huxley Par N18 ... 33 B5
Huxley Pl N13 ... 16 D1
Huxley Rd DA16 ... 145 D2
E10 ... 76 A6
Edmonton N18 ... 33 C6
Huxley Sayze N18 ... 33 B5
Huxley South N18 ... 33 B5
Huxley St W10 ... 91 A4
Hyacinth Cl
3 Hampton TW12 ... 173 C4
Ilford IG1 ... 78 D2
Hyacinth Dr UB10 ... 60 A1
Hyacinth Rd SW15 ... 156 A3
Hyde Cl E13 ... 99 A5
Ashford TW16 ... 171 C4
Barnet EN5 ... 1 B2
Hyde Cres NW9 ... 45 C4
Hyde Ct N20 ... 14 B1
NW9 ... 45 B2
Hounslow TW4 ... 151 B6
Hyde Estate Rd NW9 ... 45 D4
Hyde Farm Mews
SW12 ... 159 D3
Hydefield Cl N21 ... 17 B3
Hydefield Ct N9 ... 17 C2
Hyde Ho TW3 ... 130 A2
Hyde La SW11 ... 136 C4 267 A2
Hyde Park★
W2 ... 114 D5 247 C3
Hyde Park Ave N21 ... 17 B3
Hyde Park Cnr SW1 ... 248 B2
Hyde Park Corner Sta
SW1 ... 115 A4 248 B2
Hyde Park Cres
W2 ... 92 C1 237 A1
Hyde Park Gate Mews
SW7 ... 246 B1
Hyde Park Gdns
W2 ... 114 C6 246 D6
Edmonton N21 ... 17 A3
Hyde Park Gdns Mews
W2 ... 114 C6 247 A6
Hyde Park Mans NW1 ... 237 A3
Hyde Park Pl W2 ... 247 B6
Hyde Park Sq
W2 ... 92 C1 237 A1
Hyde Park Square Mews
W2 ... 237 A1
Hyde Park St
W2 ... 92 C1 237 A1
Hyde Park Twrs W2 ... 246 A5
Hyderabad Way E15 ... 76 C1
Hyde Rd N1 ... 95 C6
Bexley DA7 ... 147 B3
Richmond TW10 ... 154 B6
Hyde Sch The NW9 ... 45 D3
Hydeside Gdns N9 ... 17 D2
Hyde's Pl 12 N1 ... 72 D1
Hyde St SE8 ... 141 C6
Hyde Terr TW15,TW16 ... 171 C4
Hydethorpe Ave N9 ... 17 D2
Hydethorpe Rd SW12 ... 159 C3
Hyde Vale SE10 ... 142 A5
Hyde Way Edmonton N9 ... 17 D2
Hayes UB3 ... 105 D2
Hyde Wlk SM4 ... 201 C2
Hydon Ct N11 ... 30 D5
Hyh Ho E17 ... 35 D2
Hyland House Sch E17 ... 36 B1
Hylands Rd E17 ... 36 B1
Hylda Ct NW5 ... 71 A5
Hyleford Sch IG3 ... 79 C4
Hylton St SE18 ... 123 D2
Hyndewood 14 SE23 ... 162 D1
Hyndman Ho 5 N19 ... 71 D4
5 Dagenham RM10 ... 81 C5
Hyndman St SE15 ... 140 B6
Hynton Rd RM8 ... 80 C6
Hyperion Ho 25 E3 ... 97 A5
Streatham SW2 ... 160 B4
Hyrstdene CR0 ... 220 D4
Hyson Rd SE16 ... 118 B1
Hythe Ave DA7 ... 147 B5
Hythe Cl N18 ... 34 A6
Hythe Ho 7 SE16 ... 118 C4
Hythe Rd NW10 ... 90 A3
South Norwood CR7 ... 183 B1
Hythe Road Ind Est
NW10 ... 90 A3
Hyver Hill NW7 ... 11 B4

I

Ian Ct SE23 ... 162 C2
Ian Hamilton Ho NW1 ... 232 C2
Ian Sq EN3 ... 6 D4
Ibberton Ho SW8 ... 270 C4
W14 ... 254 B6
Ibbotson Ave E16 ... 98 D1
Ibbott St 22 E1 ... 96 C3
Iberia Ho 17 N19 ... 49 D2
Iberian Ave CR0,SM6 ... 220 A4
Ibis Ct 16 SE8 ... 141 B6
Ibis La W4 ... 133 A4
Ibis Way UB4 ... 84 D1
Ibrox Ct 3 IG9 ... 21 C2
Ibsley Gdns SW15 ... 156 A3
Ibsley Way EN4 ... 2 C1
Ibstock Place Sch
SW15 ... 155 C5
Icarus Ho 10 E3 ... 97 B4
Iceland Rd E3 ... 97 C6
Iceland Wharf SE16 ... 119 A2
Ice Wharf NW1 ... 233 B4
Ickburgh Est E5 ... 74 B6
Ickburgh Rd E5 ... 74 B5
Ickburgh Sch E5 ... 74 B5
Ickenham Cl HA4 ... 61 B6
Ickenham Rd HA4 ... 39 B1
Ickenham Sta UB10 ... 61 A4
Ickleton Rd SE9 ... 188 A6
Icknield Dr IG2 ... 56 D4
Ickworth Park Rd E17 ... 53 A5
Icough Ct SE3 ... 143 B5
Ida Rd N15 ... 51 B5
Ida St E14 ... 98 A1
Iden Cl BR2 ... 208 C6
Idlecombe Rd SW17 ... 181 A4
Idmiston Rd E15 ... 76 D3
New Malden KT4 ... 199 D2
West Norwood SE21,
SE27 ... 161 A2
Idmiston Sq KT4 ... 199 D2
Idol La EC3 ... 117 C6 253 A5
Idonia St SE8 ... 141 C5
Iffley Ho 47 E2 ... 95 D4
Iffley Rd W6 ... 112 B3
Ifield Ho SE17 ... 263 B2
Ifield Rd SW10 ... 135 D6 265 D6
Ifor Evans Pl E1 ... 96 D3
Ightham Ho SE17 ... 263 A3
Beckenham BR3 ... 185 B3
Ightham Rd DA8 ... 147 C5
Ilbert St W10 ... 91 A4
Ilchester Gdns W2 ... 245 C6
Ilchester Mans W8 ... 255 A6
Ilchester Pl
W14 ... 113 B3 254 D6
Ilchester Rd RM8 ... 80 C3
Ildersly Gr SE21 ... 161 B2
Ilderton Prim Sch
SE16 ... 118 C1
Ilderton Rd SE15,SE16 ... 140 C6
Ilex Cl TW16 ... 172 C1
Ilex Rd NW10 ... 67 D2
Ilex Way SW16 ... 182 C5
Ilford Hill IG1 ... 78 C5
Ilford Ho 10 N1 ... 73 B2
Ilford Interchange IG1 ... 78 C5
Ilford Jewish Prim Sch
IG6 ... 57 B6
Ilford La IG1 ... 78 D4
Ilford Prep Sch IG3 ... 58 A1
Ilford Ret Pk IG1 ... 79 A6
Ilford Sta IG1 ... 78 D6
Ilford Ursuline High Sch
IG1 ... 78 D6
Ilfracombe Gdns RM6 ... 58 B2
Ilfracombe Rd BR1 ... 164 D1
Iliffe St SE17 ... 116 D1 261 D2
Iliffe Yd SE17 ... 116 D1 261 D2
Ilkeston Ct 7 E5 ... 74 D4
Ilkley Cl SE19 ... 183 B4
Ilkley Ct N11 ... 31 A4
Ilkley Rd Newham E16 ... 99 C2
South Oxhey WD19 ... 22 D5
Illingworth Cl CR4 ... 202 B6
Illingworth Way EN1 ... 17 C6
Ilmington Rd HA3 ... 43 D3
Ilminster Gdns SW11 ... 136 C1
Ilsley Ct 8 SW8 ... 137 C3
Imber Cl N14 ... 15 C4
Thames Ditton KT7 ... 196 B1
Imber Court Trad Est
KT8 ... 196 B3
Imber Cross KT7 ... 196 D3
Imber Ct 4 SE9 ... 166 C5
Imber Gr KT10 ... 196 B2
Imber Park Rd KT10 ... 196 B1
Imber St N1 ... 235 C5
Immanuel Coll WD23 ... 8 C4
Immanuel & St Andrew CE
Prim Sch SW16 ... 182 A4
Impact Ct SE20 ... 184 B1
Imperial Ave 5 N16 ... 73 C4
Imperial Cl HA2 ... 41 C3
Imperial College Rd
SW7 ... 114 B3 256 C6
Imperial Coll of Science,
Technology & Medicine
SW7 ... 114 B3 256 C6
Imperial Ct N20 ... 14 A1
NW8 ... 230 B4
Wembley HA9 ... 66 C5
Harrow HA2 ... 41 C3
Imperial Dr HA2 ... 41 C3
Imperial Gdns CR4 ... 203 B6
Imperial Ho 2 E14 ... 119 B6
E3 ... 97 A4
Imperial Mews 5 E6 ... 99 D5
Imperial Pl BR7 ... 188 C2
Imperial Rd SW6 ... 265 D1
East Bedfont TW14 ... 149 C4
Wood Green N22 ... 32 A2
Imperial Sq SW6 ... 265 D2
Imperial St E3 ... 98 A4
Imperial Twrs 3 NW3 ... 70 A2
Imperial War Mus★
SE1,SE11 ... 116 C3 261 B5
Imperial Way BR7,SE9 ... 167 A1
Croydon CR0,CR9 ... 220 C2
Harrow HA3 ... 44 A3
Impington 19 KT1 ... 176 C1
Imre Cl W12 ... 112 B5
Inca Dr SE9 ... 166 D4
Inchmery Rd SE6 ... 164 A3
Inchwood BR4,CR0 ... 223 D4
Independant Jewish Day
Sch NW4 ... 46 D4
Independant Pl E8 ... 73 D3
Independents Rd SE3 ... 142 D2
Inderwick Rd N8 ... 50 B4
Indescon Ct E14 ... 119 D4
India St EC3 ... 243 C1
India Way W12 ... 112 B6
Indigo Mews N16 ... 73 B5
Indus Ct 15 SE15 ... 139 D5
Indus Rd SE7 ... 143 C5
Ingal Rd E13 ... 99 A3
Ingate Pl SW8 ... 137 B4 268 D1
Ingatestone Rd
Croydon SE25 ... 206 B5
Wanstead E12 ... 55 C1
Woodford IG8 ... 37 B3
Ingelow Ho W8 ... 245 C2
Ingelow St SW8 ... 137 B3
Ingersoll Rd W12 ... 112 B5
Enfield EN3 ... 6 C5
Ingestre Pl W1 ... 239 B1
Ingestre Rd E7 ... 77 A4
NW5 ... 71 B4
Ingham Rd NW6 ... 69 C4
Inglebert St
EC1 ... 94 C4 234 A2
Ingleborough Ct N17 ... 51 D6
Ingleborough St SW9 ... 138 C3
Ingleby Dr HA1 ... 64 B5
Ingleby Rd N7 ... 72 A5
Dagenham RM10 ... 81 D2
Ilford IG1 ... 56 D1
Ingleby Way BR7 ... 188 C5
Wallington SM6 ... 219 D1
Ingle Cl HA5 ... 41 B6
Ingledew Rd SE18 ... 123 B1
Inglefield Sq 12 E1 ... 118 B5
Ingle Ho 3 SW12 ... 159 D3
Inglehurst Gdns IG4 ... 56 B4
Inglemere Ct CR4,
SW17 ... 180 D3
Inglemere Rd
Forest Hill SE23 ... 162 D1
Mitcham CR4,SW17 ... 180 D3
Ingleshaw Wlk E9 ... 75 B2
Ingleside Cl BR3 ... 185 C3
Ingleside Gr SE3 ... 142 D6
Inglethorpe Ho 6 E5 ... 74 A6
Inglethorpe St SW6 ... 134 D4
Ingleton Ave DA16 ... 168 A6
Ingleton Rd N18 ... 34 A4
Ingleton St SW9 ... 138 C3
Ingle Way N12 ... 30 C4
Inglewood BR7 ... 189 B4
Inglewood Cl E14 ... 119 C2
Inglewood Copse BR1 ... 188 B1
Inglewood Ct 3 BR1 ... 186 D3
Inglewood Mans 11
NW6 ... 69 C3
Inglewood Rd NW6 ... 69 C3
Inglis Ct W5 ... 110 B6
Inglis Ho 1 SW15 ... 156 C6
Inglis Rd Croydon CR0 ... 205 D1
Ealing W5 ... 110 B6
Inglis St SE5 ... 138 D4
Ingram Ave NW11 ... 48 A2
Ingram Cl SE11 ... 260 D4
Stanmore HA7 ... 25 C5
Ingram Ct EN1 ... 17 D5
Ingram Ho E3 ... 97 A6
7 Harrow HA1 ... 42 D4
Teddington KT8 ... 175 C2
Ingram Lo 8 SW4 ... 159 D5
Ingram Rd N2 ... 48 C5
South Norwood CR7 ... 183 A2
Ingram Way UB6 ... 86 B6
Ingrave Ho RM9 ... 102 B6
Ingrave St SW11 ... 136 C2
Ingrebourne Ct E4 ... 19 D2
Ingrebourne Ho NW8 ... 236 D4
2 Catford BR1 ... 186 B5
Ingress St 4 W4 ... 111 C1
Inigo Jones Rd SE7 ... 144 A5
Inigo Pl WC2 ... 250 A6
Inkerman Rd NW5 ... 71 B2
Inkerman Terr W8 ... 255 B5
Inks Gn E4 ... 36 A5
Inkster Ho 8 SW11 ... 136 C2
Inkwell Cl N12 ... 14 A1
Inman Rd NW10 ... 89 C6
Wandsworth SW18 ... 158 A4
Inmans Row IG8 ... 37 A6
Inner Circ NW1 ... 93 A4 231 A2
Inner Park Rd SW19 ... 156 D2
Inner Ring E TW6 ... 126 D2
Inner Ring W TW6 ... 126 C2
Inner Temple★ EC4 ... 251 A6
Inner Temple La EC4 ... 241 A1
Innes Cl SW20 ... 179 A1
Innes Gdns SW15 ... 156 B5
Innes Lo SE23 ... 162
Innes Yd CR0 ... 221
Innis Ho SE17 ... 263
Inniskilling Rd E13 ... 99
Innovation Cl HA0 ... 88
Inskip Cl E10 ... 75
Inskip Rd RM8 ... 58
Insley Ho 13 E3 ... 97
Inst for Child Health
WC1 ... 94 B3 240
Institute Pl E8 ... 74
Instituto Espanol Vicente
Canada Blanch W10 ... 91
Inst of Ophthalmology
EC1 ... 235
Integer Gdns E11 ... 54
Interchange The NW5 ... 71
International Ave
TW5 ... 106
International Sch of London
W3 ... 110
International Trad Est
UB2 ... 106
Inveagh Cl E9 ... 96
Inverary Pl SE18 ... 145
Inver Cl E5 ... 74
Inverclyde Gdns RM6 ... 58
Inver Ct W2 ... 91
Inveresk Gdns KT4 ... 216
Inverforth Cl NW3 ... 70
Inverforth Ho NW3 ... 70
Inverforth Rd N11 ... 31 B
Invergarry Ho NW6 ... 91
Inverine Rd SE7 ... 121
Invermore Pl SE18 ... 123
Inverness Ave EN1 ... 5
Inverness Ct
8 Acton W3 ... 88
10 Catford SE6 ... 164 D
Inverness Gdns W8 ... 245
Inverness Mews E16 ... 122 D
W2 ... 245 D
North Woolwich E16 ... 123 A
Inverness Pl W2 ... 245 D
Inverness Rd
Edmonton N18 ... 34 B
Hounslow TW3 ... 129 C
North Cheam KT4 ... 200 D
Southall UB2 ... 107 A
Inverness St NW1 ... 231 D
Inverness Terr
W2 ... 113 D6 245 D
Inverton Rd SE15 ... 140 D
Invicta Cl BR7 ... 188 C
18 E3 ... 97 C
East Bedfont TW14 ... 149 D
Invicta Ct KT9 ... 214 B
Invicta Ctr The IG11 ... 102 A
Invicta Gr UB5 ... 85 B
Invicta Plaza SE1 ... 251 C
Invicta Prim Sch SE3 ... 143 A
Invicta Rd SE3,SE7 ... 143 A
Inville Rd SE17 ... 117 B1 262 D
Inwen Ct SE8 ... 119 A
Inwood Ave TW3 ... 130 A
Inwood Bsns Pk TW3 ... 129 D
Inwood Cl CR0 ... 223 A
Inwood Ct 10 NW1 ... 71 C
Inwood Ho 19 SE22 ... 139 C
Inwood Rd TW3 ... 130 A
Inworth St SW11 ... 136 C3
Inworth Wlk N1 ... 235 A6
Iona Cl Catford SE6 ... 163 C4
Morden SM4 ... 201 D2
Ion Ct 8 E2 ... 96 A5
Ionian Bldg 19 E14 ... 119 A6
Ionian Ho 22 E1 ... 96 D3
Ipsden Bldgs SE1 ... 251 B2
Ipswich Ho SE4 ... 162 D6
Ipswich Rd SW17 ... 181 A4
Irby Ho SW2 ... 160 C5
Ireland Cl E6 ... 100 B2
Ireland Pl N22 ... 32 A3
Ireland Yd EC4 ... 241 D1
Irene Rd BR6 ... 211 D2
SW6 ... 135 C4 265 B1
Ireton Cl N10 ... 31 A3
Ireton Ho SW9 ... 138 C3
Ireton St 12 E3 ... 97 C3
Iris Ave DA5 ... 169 A5
Iris Cl Croydon CR0 ... 206 D1
Newham E6 ... 100 A3
Surbiton KT6 ... 198 B2
Iris Cres DA7 ... 147 B6
Iris Rd KT19 ... 214 D3
Iris Way E4 ... 35 B4
Iris Wlk 1 HA8 ... 27 A6
Irkdale Ave EN1 ... 5 D4
Iroko Ho 7 NW3 ... 69 D2
Iron Bridge Cl NW10 ... 67 C3
Southall UB2 ... 108 A5
Iron Bridge Ho NW3 ... 70 D1
Iron Bridge Rd N
UB11 ... 104 C5
Iron Bridge Rd S UB7 ... 104 C4
Iron Mill Pl SW18 ... 157 D5
Iron Mill Rd SW18 ... 157 D5
Ironmonger La
EC2 ... 95 B1 242 C1

nmonger Pas EC1 235 B1
nmonger Row
C1 95 A4 235 B1
onmonger's Pl 13
14 119 C2
onside Cl SE16 118 D4
onside Ho E9 75 A4
ine Ave HA3 43 B6
ine Cl N20 14 C2
ine Ct W1 239 B5
hornton Heath CR7 204 C3
ine Ho 2 E14 97 D2
7 72 B2
ine Way BR6 211 D2
ving Ave UB5 84 D6
ving Ct N22 32 D2
ving Gr SW9 138 B3
ving Ho SE17 261 C1
ving Mews N1 73 A2
ving Rd W14 112 D3
ving St WC2 249 D5
well Ct W7 86 B1
well Est 25 SE16 118 C4
win Ave SE18 145 C5
win Cl UB10 60 C5
win Gdns NW10 90 B6
abel Hill Cl TW12 173 C2
sabella Cl N14 15 C4
sabella Ct 8 TW10 154 B5
sabella Dr BR6 227 A4
sabella Ho SE11 261 C2
19 W6 112 C1
abella Rd E9 74 C3
abella St SE1 251 C3
abel St SW9 270 D2
ambard Mews E14 120 A3
ambard Pl SE16 118 C5
eldon Ct N7 72 A4
el Way 4 SE22 161 C6
ham Rd SW16 182 A1
sis Cl Putney SW15 134 C1
Ruislip HA4 39 A3
sis Ct W4 132 D5
sis Ho NW8 236 D5
2 Edmonton N18 33 D4
sis St SW18 158 A2
slamia Girls' High Sch
NW6 91 A6
slamia Prim Sch NW6 91 A6
slamic Coll for Advanced
Studies NW10 68 B2
sland Centre Way EN3 7 C6
sland Farm Ave KT8 195 B4
sland Farm Rd KT8 195 C4
sland Gardens Sta
E14 120 A1
sland Ho SW19 202 A5
sland Rd CR4 180 D3
sland Row E14 97 B1
sla Rd SE18 145 A6
slay Gdns TW4 150 D6
sleden Ho N1 235 A6
sledon Rd N4,N7 72 C5
slehurst Cl BR7 188 C2
sleworth Bsns Complex
TW7 130 D3
sleworth Sta TW7 130 D3
sleworth & Syon Sch for
Boys TW7 130 C5
sleworth Town Sch
TW7 131 A3
slington Est N1 95 A6 235 A6
slington Gn N1 94 D6 234 C5
slington Green Sch
N1 95 A6 235 A5
slington High St
N1 94 D5 234 C4
slington Park Mews 1
N1 72 D1
slington Park St N1 72 D1
slington Sixth Form Ctr
N7 72 C4
Islip Gdns HA8 27 B3
Northolt UB5 63 A1
Islip Manor Rd UB5 63 A1
Islip St NW5 71 C3
Ismailia Rd E7 77 B1
Isobel Ho
10 Ashford TW16 171 D3
Harrow HA1 42 D4
Isokon Flats 3 NW3 70 D3
Isom Cl E13 99 B4
Ivanhoe Dr HA3 25 B1
Ivanhoe Ho 32 E3 97 A5
11 Balham SW12 159 B4
Ivanhoe Rd SE5 139 D2
Hounslow TW4 128 D2
Ivatt Pl W14 113 B1 254 D1
Ivatt Way N17 50 D6
Iveagh Ave NW10 88 C5
Iveagh Cl NW10 88 C5
Iveagh Ct EC3 243 C1
4 Beckenham BR3 207 D6
Iveagh Ho SW10 266 B4
2 SW9 138 D3
Ivebury Ct W10 90 C1
Ivedon Rd DA16 146 C3
Ive Farm Cl E10 75 C6
Ive Farm La E10 75 C6
Iveley Rd SW4 137 C3
Iver Ct N1 73 A2
Ivere Dr EN5 13 D5
Iverhurst Cl DA6 168 D6
Iverna Ct W8 255 B6
Iverna Gdns
W8 113 C3 255 B6
Hatton TW14 149 B6
Iverson Rd NW6 69 C2
Ivers Way CR0 223 D1
Ives Rd E16 98 C2
Ives St SW3 114 C2 257 B4
Ivestor Terr SE23 162 C4
Ivimey St E2 96 A4
Ivinghoe Cl EN1 5 C4
Ivinghoe Ho 14 N7 71 D3
Ivinghoe Rd
Barking RM8 80 B3
Bushey WD23 8 B4
Ivor Ct N8 50 A3
NW1 237 C6
Ivor Gr SE9 166 D3
Ivories The N1 73 A1
Ivor Pl NW1 92 D3 237 C5
Ivor St NW1 71 C1
Ivory Ct TW13 150 A3
Ivorydown BR1 187 A6
Ivory Ho E1 253 D4
9 SW11 136 A2
Ivybridge Cl
2 Twickenham TW1 153 A4
Uxbridge UB8 82 A4
Ivybridge Ct 1 BR7 188 C2
Ivybridge Ho 18 SE22 139 C2
Ivybridge La WC2 250 B5
Ivybridge Prim Sch
TW1 152 D5
Ivybridge Ret Pk TW7 152 D6
Ivychurch Cl SE20 184 C3
Ivy Church La SE1,
SE17 263 C2
Ivy Cl Harrow HA2 63 B4
Pinner HA5 40 C2
Sunbury TW16 172 C1
Ivy Cotts UB10 82 C4
Ivy Cres W4 111 A2
Ivy Ct SE13 163 C6
18 SE16 118 A1
SE3 142 D1
Ivydale Prim Sch
SE15 140 D1
Ivydale Rd SE15 140 D1
Carshalton SM5 218 D6
Ivyday Gr SW16 160 B1
Ivydene KT12,KT8 195 B4
Ivydene Cl SM1 218 A4
Ivy Gdns N8 50 A3
Mitcham CR4 203 D6
Ivy Ho 6 E5 52 B1
Croydon CR0 206 D1
Ivyhouse Rd
Dagenham RM9 81 A2
Uxbridge UB10 60 D5
Ivy La TW4 129 B1
Ivy Lo W8 245 A4
Ivymount Rd SE27 160 C1
Ivy Rd E16 99 A1
E17 53 C3
N14 15 D4
NW2 68 C4
SE4 141 C1
Hounslow TW3 129 D1
Tolworth KT6 198 C1
Upper Tooting SW17 180 C5
Ivy St N1 95 C5
Ivy Terr 3 IG2 57 A3
Ivy Wlk RM9 81 A2
Ixworth Pl
SW3 114 C2 257 A3
Izane Rd DA6 147 B1

J

Jacaranda Cl KT3 199 C6
Jacaranda Gr E8 73 D1
Jack Ashley Ct 5 NW9 27 C2
Jackass La BR2 225 C2
Jack Barnett Way N22 32 B1
Jack Clow Rd E15 98 C5
Jack Cook Ho 9 IG11 78 D1
Jack Cornwell St E12 78 C4
Jack Goodchild Way
KT3 198 D6
Jacklin Gn IG8 37 A6
Jackman Ho 24 E1 118 B5
Jackman Mews NW2 67 C5
Jackman St E8 96 B6
Jackson Cl E9 74 D1
Uxbridge UB10 60 A1
Jackson Ct E7 77 B2
Wanstead E11 55 B1
Jackson Ho 16 SW11 136 B2
Jackson Rd BR2 226 B6
N7 72 B4
Barking IG11 101 B6
East Barnet EN4 14 C5
Uxbridge UB10 60 A1
Jackson's La N6 49 B2
Jackson's Pl CR0 205 C1
Jackson St SE18 144 C6
Jackson's Way CR0 223 C5
Jackson Way UB2 107 D4
Jack Taylor Sch
NW8 92 A6 229 A6
Jack Tizard Sch SW6 134 D4
Jack Walker Ct N5 72 D4
Jacob Ho 5 DA18 124 D4
Jacobin Lo N7 72 A3
Jacob Mans 1 E1 96 B1
Jacobs Cl RM10 81 D4
Jacobs Ho E13 99 C4
Jacobson Ct SW11 267 B1
Jacobson Ho E1 243 C2
Jacob St SE1 118 A4
Jacob's Well Mews
W1 238 B2
Jacotts Ho W10 90 C3
Jacqueline Cl UB5 85 A6
Jade Cl E16 99 D1
NW2 46 D2
Dagenham RM8 58 C1
Jaffe Rd IG1 57 B1
Jaffray Rd BR2 209 D5
Jaggard Way SW12 158 D4
Jagger Ho SW11 267 C2
Jago Cl SE18 145 A6
Jago Wlk 22 SE5 139 B5
Jamahiriya Sch
SW3 136 C6 267 A6
Jamaica Rd SE1 253 D1
SE16 118 B3
Thornton Heath CR7 204 D3
Jamaica St E1 96 C2
James Allen's Girls' Sch
SE22 161 C6
James Anderson Ct 29
E2 95 C5
James Ave NW2 68 C3
Dagenham RM8 59 B1
James Bedford Cl HA5 22 C1
James Boswell Cl 1
SW16 182 C6
James Brine Ho 6 E2 95 D4
James Campbell Ho 2
E2 96 C5
James Cl 8 E13 99 A5
NW11 47 A3
James Collins Cl W9 91 B3
James Ct N12 30 C3
NW9 27 C1
4 Chingford E4 20 B2
Northolt UB5 85 A5
3 Woodford E18 37 B1
James Dixon Prim Sch
SE20 184 B3
James Docherty Ho 4
E2 96 C5
James Dudson Ct
NW10 67 A1
James Est CR4 180 D1
James Gdns N22 32 D3
James Hammett Ho 9
E2 95 D5
James Ho E1 97 A3
33 SE16 118 D4
James Joyes Wlk 7
SE24 138 D1
James La E10,E11 54 B3
James Lee Sq EN3 7 C5
James Leicester Hall of
Residence N7 72 A2
James Lind Ho 5 SE8 119 B2
James Middleton Ho 20
E2 96 B4
James Newman Ct
SE9 166 C1
Jameson Ct 6 E2 96 C5
Jameson Ho SE11 260 C2
Jameson Lo N6 49 C3
Jameson Pl 11 W3 111 A4
Jameson St W8 245 B4
James Pl N17 33 D2
James St W1 93 A1 238 B1
WC2 116 A6 250 B6
Barking IG11 79 A1
Enfield EN1 17 D6
Hounslow TW3 130 B2
James Stewart Ho NW6 69 B1
James Stroud Ho
SE17 262 B1
Jamestown Rd
NW1 93 B6 231 C6
Jamestown Way E14 120 B6
James Wolfe Prim Sch
SE10 142 A5
Jamieson Ho TW4 151 B5
Jamuna Cl E14 97 A2
Jane Sabina Colard's
Almshouses 1 E17 54 A4
Jane St E1 96 B1
Janet Ct 4 DA7 147 C1
Janet St E14 119 C3
Janeway Pl 2 SE16 118 B4
Janeway St SE16 118 A4
Janice Mews 3 IG1 78 D5
Jansen Wlk SW11 136 B1
Janson Cl E15 76 C3
Janson Cl *continued*
NW10 67 C5
Janson Rd E15 76 C3
Jansons Rd N15 51 C6
Japan Cres N4 50 B1
Japanese Sch The
W3 110 C6
Japan Rd RM6 58 D3
Jaquets Ct DA5 169 C2
Jardine Rd E1 118 D6
Jarman Ho 13 E1 96 C2
SE16 118 D2
Jarret Ho 1 E3 97 C4
Jarrett Cl SW2 160 D3
Jarrow Cl SM4 201 D4
Jarrow Rd N17 52 B5
SE16 118 C1
Dagenham RM6 58 C3
Jarrow Way E9 75 A4
Jarvis Cl
1 Barking IG11 101 B6
Barnet EN5 12 D6
Jarvis Ct 2 SE10 142 A4
Jarvis Ho 3 SE15 140 A4
Jarvis Rd SE22 139 C1
South Croydon CR2 221 B2
Jashada Ho SE18 122 C1
Jasmin SE1 253 D3
Jasmine Cl Ilford IG1 78 D3
Orpington BR6 226 D6
Southall UB1 107 A6
Jasmine Ct SE12 165 A5
11 Wallington SM6 219 B2
Jasmine Gdns
Harrow HA2 63 C6
West Wickham CR0 223 D5
Jasmine Gr SE20 184 B2
Jasmine Rd KT19 214 D3
Jasmine Terr UB7 104 C4
Jasmine Way KT7 196 C5
Jasmin Ho SE4 141 B2
Jasmin Lo 17 SE16 118 B1
Jason Ct 2 SW9 138 C4
W1 238 B2
Jason Ho UB5 84 B4
Jason Wlk SE9 188 C6
Jasper Cl EN3 6 C5
Jasper Ho KT4 199 B1
Jasper Rd E16 99 D1
Penge SE19 183 D4
Jasper Wlk N1 235 C2
Java Wharf SE1 253 D2
Javelin Way UB5 84 D4
Jawahar Bagh SW16 182 D4
Jaycroft EN2 4 C4
Jay Gdns BR7 188 B6
Jay Ho SW15 134 C3
Jay Mews SW7 114 A4 246 B1
Jayson Ct 7 CR0 206 A1
Jean Batten Cl SM6 220 B1
Jean Darling Ho
SW10 266 C5
Jean Ho 3 SW17 180 C5
Jean Humbert Ho 2
SE27 183 B6
Jean Pardies Ho 21 E1 96 C2
Jebb Ave SW2 160 A5
Jebb St E3 97 C5
Jedburgh Rd E13 99 C4
Jedburgh St SW11 137 A1
Jeddo Mews W12 111 D4
Jeddo Rd W12 111 D4
Jefferies Ho 12 NW10 67 B1
Jefferson Bldg 3 E14 119 C4
Jefferson Cl W13 109 B3
Ilford IG2 56 D4
Jefferson Wlk 13 SE18 144 C6
Jeffrey Row SE12 165 B6
Jeffrey's Ct 2 SW4 138 A3
Jeffrey's Pl NW1 71 C1
Jeffrey's Rd SW4 138 A3
Jeffreys Rd EN3 7 B1
Jeffrey's St NW1 71 C1
Jeffs Cl TW12 173 D4
Jeffs Rd SM1 217 B4
Jefton Ct SM6 219 C3
Jeger Ave E2 95 D6
Jeken Rd SE9 143 C1
Jelf Rd SW2 160 C6
Jellicoe Ct E4 36 B4
Jellicoe Gdns HA7 25 A4
Jellicoe Ho 5 E2 96 A5
11 Putney SW15 156 D6
Jellicoe Rd 4 E13 99 A3
Tottenham N17 33 B3
Jemmett Cl KT2 176 D2
Jemotts Ct 9 SE14 140 D6
Jem Paterson Ct HA1 64 C4
Jengar Cl SM1 217 D4
Jenkins Ho SW8 269 C2
Jenkins La IG11 101 A4
Jenkinson Ho 12 E2 96 D4
Jenkins Rd E13 99 B3
Jenner Ave W3 89 B2
Jenner Ct N21 16 A6
Jenner Ho SE3 142 C6
5 Belvedere DA17 125 C3
Jenner Pl SW13 134 B6
Jenner Rd N16 73 D5
Jennett Rd CR0 220 C5
Jennifer Ho SE11 261 B3
Jennifer Rd BR1 164 D1
Jennings Cl KT6 197 C2
Jennings Ho SE10 120 B1
Jennings Rd SE22 161 D5
Jenny Hammond Cl
E11 76 D5
Jenny Hammond Sch
E11 76 C4
Jensen Ho 10 E3 97 C3
Jenson Way SE19 183 D3
Jenton Ave DA7 147 A3
Jephson Ct 17 SW4 138 A3
Jephson Ho 6 SE17 138 D6
Jephson Rd E7 77 C1
Jephson St SE5 139 B4
Jephtha Rd SW18 157 C5
Jeppo's La CR4 202 D5
Jerdan Pl SW6 265 A4
Jeremiah St 11 E14 97 D1
Jeremy Bentham Ho 9
E2 96 A4
Jeremy's Gn N18 34 C6
Jermyn St
SW1 115 C5 249 B4
Jerningham Ct SE14 141 A4
Jerningham Rd SE14 141 A4
Jerome Cres
NW8 92 C3 237 A6
Jerome Ct 2 N11 31 C5
Jerome Ho NW1 237 B4
Kingston KT1 175 D1
Jerome Pl KT1 175 D1
Jerome St E1 95 D3 243 C5
Jerome Twr 5 W3 110 D4
Jerrard St SE13 141 D2
Jerrold Lo SW15 134 C2
Jerrold St 24 N1 95 C5
Jersey Ave HA7 25 C1
Jersey Ct UB2 107 B3
Jersey Dr BR5 211 B3
Jersey Ho 12 N1 73 A2
Enfield EN3 6 D5
Jersey Rd E11 54 B1
N1 73 A2
W7 109 A4
Hounslow TW5,TW7 130 B5
Ilford IG1 78 D4
Mitcham SW17 181 B4
Newham E16 99 C1
Jersey St E2 96 B4
Jerusalem Pas EC1 241 C5
Jervis Bay Ho 8 E14 98 B1
Jervis Ct W1 238 D1
9 Dagenham RM10 81 D2
Jerviston Gdns SW16 182 C4
Jesmond Ave HA9 66 B2
Jesmond Cl CR4 203 B6
Jesmond Rd CR0 205 D2
Jesmond Way HA7 26 A5
Jessam Ave E5 52 B1
Jessamine Rd W7 108 D5
Jessel Ho SW1 259 D4
WC1 233 A1
Jesse Rd E10 54 A1
Jessica Rd SW18 158 A6
Jessie Blythe La 2
N19 50 A2
Jessie Duffett Ho 11
SE5 139 A5
Jessie's Cotts E17 53 A3
Jessiman Terr TW17 192 C4
Jesson Ho SE17 262 C3
Jessop Ave UB2 107 B2
Jessop Ct N1 234 D3
Jessop Prim Sch SE24 139 A1
Jessop Sq E14 119 C5
Jessops Way CR0 203 C3
Jessup Cl SE18 123 A2
Jeston Ho 10 SE27 160 D1
Jethou Ho 13 N1 73 A2
Jetstar Way UB5 85 A4
Jevington Way SE12 165 B3
Jevons Ho 6 NW8 70 B1
Jewell Ho 3 SW12 159 C4
Jewel Rd E17 53 C6
Jewish Prep Sch The
NW6 91 D5
Jewry St EC3 95 D1 243 C1
Jews Coll NW4 46 D5
Jews Free Sch NW1 71 D2
Jews Row SW18 136 A1
Jews Wlk SE26 184 B6
Jeymer Ave NW2 68 C3
Jeymer Dr UB6 86 A6
Jeypore Rd SW18 158 A5
JFS Sch NW9 44 C3
Jillian Cl TW12 173 C3
Jim Bradley Cl 16
SE18 122 C2
Jim Griffiths Ho SW6 264 D5
Joan Cres SE9 165 D4
Joan Gdns RM8 81 A6
Joanna Ho 7 W6 112 C1
Joan Player Ho EN3 6 D6
Joan Rd RM8 81 A6
Joan St SE1 116 D5 251 C3
Jocelin Ho N1 233 D5
Jocelyn Rd TW9 132 A2
Jocelyn St SE15 140 A4
Jockey's Fields
WC1 94 B2 240 D4
Jodane Rd SE8 119 B2
Jodrell Cl TW7 131 A4
Jodrell Rd E3 75 B1
Joe Hunte Ct 2 SW27 182 D5
Joel St HA5,HA6 40 A5
Johanna Prim Sch
SE1 116 C4 251 A1
Johanna St SE1 251 A1
John Adam St
WC2 116 A6 250 B5
John Aird Ct
W2 92 A2 236 B4
John Archer Way
SW18 158 B5
John Ashby Cl SW2 160 A5
John Austin Cl KT2 176 B2
John Baird Ct SE26 184 D6
John Baird Ho 14
SE20 184 C3
John Ball Prim Sch
SE3 142 C3
John Barker Ct NW6 69 A1
John Barker Ho IG1 79 B6
John Barnes Wlk E15 76 D2
John Barter Ho TW3 129 B3
John Betts' Ho W12 112 A3
John Betts Prim Sch
W6 112 B3
John Bond Ho 2 E3 97 B5
John Bradshaw Rd N14 15 D3
John Brent Ho 8 SE8 118 D2
John Buck Ho NW10 89 D6
John Burns Dr IG11 79 C1
John Burns Prim Sch
SW11 137 A3
John Busch Sch TW7 131 B4
Johnby Cl EN3 7 A6
John Campbell Rd 26
N16 73 C3
John Carpenter St
EC4 251 C6
John Cartwright Ho 7
E2 96 B4
John Chilton Sch UB5 63 A1
John Clifford Ho N8 50 A3
John Conwey Ho 23
SW2 160 C5
John Cornwell VC Ho 5
E12 78 C4
John Dee Ho 3 SW14 133 B2
John Donne Prim Sch
SE15 140 B4
John Drinkwater Cl
E11 54 D2
John Dwight Ho SW6 135 D2
John Felton Rd 16
SE16 118 A4
John Fielden Ho 10 E2 96 B4
John Fisher St E1 118 A6
John F. Kennedy Specl Sch
E15 98 B6
John Glynes Ct SW15 134 B1
John Gooch Dr EN2 4 D4
John Harris Ho SE15 140 A2
John Harrison Way
SE10 120 D3
John Hunt Ct 5 SE9 166 A2
John Islip St
SW1 116 A2 260 A3
John Kaye Ct TW17 192 C4
John Keall Ho SW15 134 D2
John Keats Lo EN2 5 B4
John Keble CE Prim Sch
NW10 89 D6
John Kelly Tech Colls
NW2 67 D5
John Kennedy Ct 1 N1 73 B2
John Kennedy Ho 1
SE16 118 D2
John Kennedy Lo 2
N1 73 B2
John King Ct 4 N19 71 D6
John Kirk Ho 22 SW11 136 B2
Beckenham BR3 207 A5
5 Streatham SW16 160 A1
John Knight Lo SW6 265 B4
John Lamb Ct HA3 24 C2
John Loughborough Sch
The N17 33 D1
John Lyon Sch The
HA2 42 B1
John Masefield Ho N15 51 B3
John Maurice Cl
SE17 117 B2 262 C4
John McDonald Ho 3
E14 120 A3
John McKenna Wlk 17
SE16 118 A3
John Milton Prim Sch
SW8 137 C5 269 A3
John Nettleford Ho 14
E2 96 B4

John Newton Ct DA16 146 B2
John Nightingale Sch KT8 195 B6
John Orwell Sports Ctr E1 118 B5
John Parker Cl RM10 81 D1
John Parker Sq 8 SW11 136 B2
John Parry Ct 28 N1 95 C5
John Paul II Sch SW19 156 D4
John Penn St SE13 141 D4
John Perrin Pl HA3 44 A2
John Perryn Prim Sch W3 89 C1
John Prince's St W1 238 D2
John Pritchard Ho 14 E1 96 A3
John Ratcliffe Ho 5 NW6 91 C4
John Rennie Wlk 1 E1 118 C5
John Roan Sch The SE3 142 C5
John Roll Way SE16 118 A3
John Ruskin Coll CR2 223 A1
John Ruskin Prim Sch SE5 139 A6
John Ruskin St SE5 139 A6
John's Ave NW4 46 C5
Johns Cl TW15 171 A6
John Scurr Ho 20 E14 97 A1
John Scurr Prim Sch E1 96 C3
John Silkin La SE8 118 D1
Johns La SM4 202 A4
John's Mews WC1 94 B3 240 D5
John Smith Ave SW6 135 B5 264 C4
Johnson Cl E8 96 A6
Johnson Ct 10 SW18 136 B1
Johnson Ho 14 E2 96 A4
NW1 232 B3
SW1 258 B3
SW8 269 D3
Johnson Lo 12 W9 91 C2
Johnson Rd BR2 209 D4
NW10 89 B6
Heston TW5 128 C5
Thornton Heath CR0 205 B2
Johnson's Cl SM5 218 D5
Johnsons Ct EC4 241 B1
Johnsons Dr TW12 174 A2
Johnson's Ind Est UB3 106 A3
Johnson's Pl SW1 115 C1 259 A1
Johnson St E1 96 C1
Southall UB2 106 D3
Johnsons Way NW10 88 D3
John Spencer Sq N1 72 D2
John's Pl E1 96 B1
John St E15 98 D6
WC1 94 B3 240 D5
Croydon SE25 206 A5
Enfield EN1 17 D6
Hounslow TW3,TW5 129 A3
John Stainer Com Prim Sch SE4 141 A2
John's Terr CR0 205 C1
Johnston Cl SW9 270 D1
Johnstone Ho SE13 142 B2
Johnstone Rd E6 100 B4
Johnston Rd IG8 37 A5
Johnston Terr NW2 68 D5
John Strachey Ho SW6 264 D5
John Strype Ct E10 53 D1
John Trundle Ct EC2 242 A4
John Tucker Ho 2 E14 119 C3
John Walsh Twr E11 76 D6
John Wesley Ct 5 TW1 153 A3
John Wesley's House & Mus* EC1 242 D6
John Wheatley Ho 14 N19 49 D2
SW6 264 D5
John Williams Cl SE14 140 D6
12 Kingston KT2 175 D2
John Wilson St SE18 122 C2
John Wooley Cl SE13 142 C1
Johsen Ho 5 SW15 156 A6
Joiners Arms Yd 1 SE5 139 B4
Joiner St SE1 252 D3
Joint Rd N10 30 C2
Jolles Ho 9 E3 97 D4
Jollys La Harrow HA2 42 B1
Hayes UB4 84 D2
Jonathan Ct 9 W4 111 C2
Jonathan St SE11 116 B1 260 C2
Jones Ho N16 51 C1
Jones Ho *continued*
4 South Bromley E14 98 B1
Jones Rd E13 99 B3
Jones St W1 248 C5
Jones Wlk 6 TW10 154 B5
Jonquil Gdns 5 TW12 173 C4
Jonson Cl Hayes UB4 84 A2
Mitcham CR4 203 B6
Jonson Ho 16 N16 73 B4
SE1 262 D5
Jordan Cl HA2 63 B5
Jordan Ct SW15 134 D1
Jordan Hill N10 30 C2
Jordan ho N1 235 D5
12 SE4 140 D1
Jordan Rd UB6 87 C6
Jordans Cl RM10 81 D4
Jordans Ho NW8 237 A5
Jordans Mews TW11 152 C2
Jo Richardson Com Sch RM9 80 C2
Joscoyne Ho 14 E1 96 B1
Josef Perrin Ho 1 SE27 183 B6
Joseph Ave W3 89 B1
Joseph Clarke Sch E4 36 B4
Joseph Conrad Ho SW1 259 B3
Joseph Ct N16 51 C2
Joseph Hood Fst Sch SW20 201 A6
Josephine Ave SW2 160 B6
Joseph Irwin Ho 11 E14 119 B6
Joseph Lancaster Prim Sch SE1 117 B3 262 C5
Joseph Lister Ct E7 77 A1
Joseph Lister Lo E11 55 B1
Joseph Powell Cl 1 SW12 159 C5
Joseph Priestley Ho 12 E2 96 B4
Joseph Ray Rd E11 76 C6
Joseph St E3 97 B3
Joseph Trotter Cl EC1 234 B1
Joshua Cl N10 31 B3
Croydon CR2 220 D1
Joshua St E14 98 A1
Joslings Cl W12 112 A6
Joslyn Cl EN3 7 C5
Josseline Ct 8 E3 97 A5
Joubert Mans SW3 257 B2
Joubert St SW11 136 D3
Jowett Ho 27 SW9 138 A3
Jowett St SE15 139 D5
Joyce Ave N18 33 D5
Joyce Butler Ho N22 32 B2
Joyce Dawson Way SE28 124 A6
Joyce Page Cl SE7 143 D6
Joy Ct NW2 68 D5
Joydon Dr RM6 58 B3
Joyners Cl RM9 81 B4
Joystone Ct 8 EN4 2 C1
Jubb Powell Ho N15 51 C3
Jubet Ho 9 N16 73 B4
Jubilee Ave Chingford E4 36 A4
Romford RM7 59 D4
Twickenham TW2 152 A3
Jubilee Bldgs NW8 229 C4
Jubilee Cl NW9 45 B3
Pinner HA5 22 C1
Romford RM7 59 D4
Teddington KT1 175 C2
Jubilee Cres E14 120 A3
Edmonton N9 18 A3
Jubilee Ct Harrow HA3 44 A2
Hounslow TW3 129 D2
Thornton Heath CR7 204 C5
Jubilee Ctry Pk BR2 210 D4
Jubilee Dr HA4 63 A4
Jubilee Gdns UB1 85 C1
Jubilee Ho SE11 261 B3
3 Hampton TW12 173 C2
Jubilee Mans 10 E1 96 C1
Jubilee Mkt WC2 250 B6
Jubilee Par IG8 37 C4
Jubilee Pl SW3 114 C1 257 B2
Jubilee Prim Sch N16 52 A1
SW2 160 C5
Woolwich SE28 124 C6
Jubilee Rd Cheam SM3 216 D1
Wembley UB6 87 B6
Jubilee St E1 96 C2
Jubilee The 2 SE10 141 D5
Jubilee Villas KT10 196 C1
Jubilee Way DA14 168 A2
East Bedfont TW14 150 A3
Merton SW19 179 D2
Tolworth KT4,KT9 214 D5
Jubilee Wks SW19 180 A1
Jubilee Yd SE1 253 C2
Judd St WC1 94 A4 233 A1
Jude St E16 98 D1
Judge Heath La UB3 83 B1
Judges' Wlk NW3 70 A5
Judge Wlk KT10 212 C2
Juer St SW11 136 C5 267 B3
Jules Thorn Ave EN1 6 A1
Julia Ct E17 53 D4
Julia Garfield Mews 4 E16 121 B5
Julia Gdns IG11 102 D5
Juliana Cl N2 48 A6
Julian Ave W3 110 D6
Julian Cl EN5 1 D2
Julian Hill HA1 64 C6
Julian Ho SE21 183 C6
Julian Pl E14 119 D1
Julians Prim Sch SW16 182 C6
Julian Taylor Path 7 SE23 162 B2
Julia St NW5 71 A3
Julie Garfield Mews 4 E16 121 B5
Julien Rd W5 109 C3
Juliet Ho 11 N1 95 C5
Juliette Rd E13 99 A5
Julius Ct TW8 132 A5
Julius Nyerere Cl N1 233 C5
Junction App SE13 142 A2
SW11 136 C2
Junction Mews W2 237 A2
Junction Pl W2 236 D2
Junction Rd E13 99 B5
N17 52 A6
N19 71 C5
Ashford TW15 171 B5
Brentford TW8 109 D2
Croydon CR2 221 B3
Edmonton N9 18 A3
Harrow HA1 42 C3
Junction Rd E RM6 59 A2
Junction Rd W RM6 59 A2
Juniper Cl Barnet EN5 12 D6
Chessington KT9 214 B3
Wembley HA9 66 C3
Juniper Cres NW1 71 A1
Juniper Ct N16 73 B6
Belmont SM2 217 C2
Dagenham RM6 58 C3
12 Ealing W5 87 C2
Harrow HA3 24 D2
Hounslow TW3 129 D1
Juniper Gdns Ashford TW16 171 D4
Streatham CR4 181 C2
Juniper La E6 100 A2
Juniper Rd IG1 78 D4
Juniper St 15 E1 118 C6
Juniper Way UB3 105 C6
Juno Ct 11 SW9 138 C5
Juno Way SE14 140 D6
Juno Way Ind Est SE14 140 D6
Jupiter Ct 10 SW9 138 C5
8 Northolt UB5 84 D4
Jupiter Hts UB10 82 B6
Jupiter Way N7 72 B2
Jupp Rd E15 76 B1
Jupp Rd W E15 98 B6
Jura Ho SE16 119 A2
Jurston Ct SE1 251 B1
Justice Wlk SW3 267 A5
Justin Cl TW8 131 D5
Justin Rd E4 35 B4
Jute La EN3 7 A2
Jutland Cl N19 50 A1
Jutland Ho 4 SE5 139 A3
10 SE7 122 A2
Jutland Rd E13 99 A3
Catford SE6 164 A4
Jutsums Ave RM7 59 D3
Jutsums Ct RM7 59 D3
Jutsums La RM7 59 D2
Juxon Cl HA3 23 D2
Juxon St SE11 116 B2 260 D4
JVC Bsns Pk NW2 46 A1

K

Kaduna Cl HA5 40 B4
Kale Rd DA18 125 A4
Kambala Rd SW11 136 B2
Kangley Bridge Ctr SE26 185 B5
Kangley Bridge Rd SE26 185 B5
Kaplan Dr N21 16 B6
Kara Way NW2 68 D4
Karen Ct 2 SE5 139 C2
Bromley BR1 186 D2
Karen Ho 7 N16 73 B4
Karens Ct EN3 6 D6
Karen Terr E11 76 D6
Ilford IG2 57 B4
Karenza Ct HA9 43 C2
Kariba Cl N9 18 C1
Karoline Gdns UB6 86 B5
Kashgar Rd SE18 123 D2
Kashmir Rd SE7 143 D5
Kasmin Ct NW10 68 A1
Kassala Rd SW11 136 D4 267 D1
Katella Trad Est IG11 101 C4
Kates Cl EN5 12 A6
Katharine Rd 1 TW1 153 A3
Katharine St CR0 221 A5
Katherine Cl 3 SE16 118 D5
Katherine Ct 10 Forest Hill SE23 162 C3
Penge SE20 184 C2
Katherine Gdns SE9 143 D1
Katherine Ho 15 W10 91 A3
Katherine Rd E6,E7 77 C1
Katherine Sq W11 244 A4
Kathleen Ave W3 89 A2
Wembley HA0 66 A1
Kathleen Ferrier Ct 4 N17 33 D3
Kathleen Moore Ct BR4 224 A6
Kathleen Rd SW11 136 D2
Katrine Ct NW2 68 C5
Kayemoor Rd SM2 218 C2
Kay Rd SW9 138 B3
Kays Ct EN3 6 D1
Kay St DA16 146 B4
E2 96 A5
Kean Ho 5 SE17 138 D6
Kean St WC2 94 B1 240 C1
Keates Est N16 73 D6
Keatley Gn E4 35 B4
Keats Ave E16 121 B5
Keats Cl NW3 70 C4
SE1 263 C3
Enfield EN3 18 D6
Hayes UB4 84 A2
Mitcham SW19 180 B4
Wanstead E11 55 B4
Keats Ct HA0 65 C5
Keats Gr NW3 70 C4
Keats Ho 22 E2 96 C4
30 SE5 139 A5
SW1 269 B6
7 Beckenham BR3 185 D4
Keats House Mus* NW3 70 C4
Keats Par 3 N9 18 A2
Keats Pl EC2 242 C3
Keats Rd DA16 145 D4
Keats Way Croydon CR0 206 C3
Southall UB6 85 D2
West Drayton UB7 104 B2
Kebbell Terr E7 77 B3
Keble Cl New Malden KT4 199 D1
Northolt UB5 64 A3
Keble Ho 4 SW15 156 D5
Keble Pl SW13 134 B6
Keble Prep Sch N21 16 C4
Keble St SW17 180 A6
Kechill Gdns BR2 209 A2
Kedeston Ct SM3 201 D1
Kedge Ho 10 E14 119 C3
Kedleston Ct E5 75 A4
Kedleston Dr BR5 211 D4
Kedleston Wlk 21 E2 96 B4
Kedyngton Ho 5 HA8 27 A1
Keeble Cl SE18 144 D6
Keedonwood Rd BR1 186 D5
Keel Cl SE16 118 D5
Barking IG11 102 C5
Keeley St WC2 94 B1 240 C1
Keeling Ho 2 TW11 174 C5
Keeling Rd SE9 165 D6
Keely Cl EN4 14 C6
Keemor Cl SE18 144 C5
Keens Cl SW16 181 D5
Keen's Rd CR0 221 A4
Keen's Yd N1 72 D2
Keepers Mews TW11 175 C4
Keeper Wharf E1 118 D6
Keepier Wharf 15 E1 118 D6
Keep The SE3 143 A3
Forest Hill SE6 163 C3
Kingston KT2 176 B3
Keeton's Rd SE16 118 B3
Keevil Dr SW19 157 A4
Keighley Cl N7 72 A4
Keightley Dr SE9 167 A3
Keilder Cl UB10 82 C5
Keildon Rd SW11 136 D1
Keir Hardie Est E5 52 B1
Keir Hardie Ho 15 N19 49 D2
NW10 67 D1
W6 134 D6
Keir Hardie Way Barking IG11 80 A1
Hayes UB4 84 A4
Keir Hardy Ho 6 DA17 125 C3
Keir The SW19 178 C5
Keith Connor Cl 5 SW8 137 B2
Keith Gr W12 112 A5
Keith Ho NW6 91 D5
Keith Park Rd UB10 60 B1
Keith Rd E17 35 B2
Barking IG11 101 B5
Hayes UB3 105 C3
Keith Sutton Ho 3 SE9 167 A2
Kelbrook Rd SE3 144 A2
Kelby Ho N7 72 B2
Kelceda Cl NW2 68 A6
Kelf Gr UB3 83 D1
Kelfield Ct 1 W10 90 D1
Kelfield Gdns W10 90 D1
Kelfield Mews W10 90 D1
Kelham Ho 10 SE18 144 D6
Kelland Cl 1 N8 49 D4
Kelland Rd E13 99 A3
Kellaway Rd SE3 143 D3
Keller Cres E12 77 D4
Kellerton Rd SE13 164 C6
Kellett Ho N1 235 D5
Kellett Rd SW2 138 C1
Kelling Gdns CR0 204 D2
Kellino St SW17 180 D6
Kellner Rd SE28 123 D3
Kellow Ho SE1 252 C2
Kell St SE1 116 D3 261 D6
Kelly Ave SE15 139 D4
Kelly Cl NW10 67 B5
Upper Halliford TW17 171 C1
Kelly Ct 11 E14 119 C6
Kelly Rd NW7 29 A4
Kelly St NW1 71 B2
Kelly Way RM6 59 A3
Kelman Cl SW4 137 D3
Kelmore Gr SE22 140 A1
Kelmscott 5 SE23 162 D1
Kelmscott Cl E17 35 B2
Kelmscott Ct 2 HA7 25 C6
Kelmscott Gdns W12 112 A3
Kelmscott L Ctr E17 53 B3
Kelmscott Rd SW11 158 D6
Kelmscott Sch E17 53 B3
Kelross Rd N5 73 A4
Kelsall Cl SE3 143 B3
Kelsey Gate 8 BR3 185 D1
Kelsey La BR3 207 C6
Kelsey Park Ave BR3 185 D1
Kelsey Park Rd BR3 185 C1
Kelsey Park Sch BR3 207 C6
Kelsey Rd BR5 190 B1
Kelsey Sq BR3 185 C1
Kelsey St E2 96 A3
Kelsey Way BR3 207 C6
Kelshall Ct N4 73 A6
Kelso Ct SE20 184 B3
Kelso Lo E18 37 B1
Kelson Ho E14 120 A3
Kelso Pl W8 113 D3 255 D6
Kelso Rd SM5 202 A2
Kelvedon Cl KT2 176 C4
Kelvedon Ho SW8 270 B2
Kelvedon Rd SW6 135 B5 264 D3
Kelvin Ave N13 32 B4
Kelvinbrook KT8 195 D6
Kelvin Cl KT19 214 C2
Kelvin Cres HA3 24 C3
Kelvin Ct W11 245 A5
Chiswick W4 133 A5
Isleworth TW7 130 C3
7 Penge SE20 184 B2
8 Twickenham TW1 153 B5
Kelvin Dr TW1 153 B5
Kelvin Gdns Southall UB1 85 C1
Thornton Heath CR0 204 A2
Kelvin Gr Forest Hill SE26 162 B1
Surbiton KT6 214 A5
Kelvin Grove Prim Sch SE26 162 B1
Kelvington Cl CR0 207 A2
Kelvington Rd SE15 162 D6
Kelvin Ho 3 DA17 125 C3
Kelvin Par BR6 211 C1
Kelvin Rd DA16 146 A2
N5 73 A4
Kelyway Ho 20 SW2 160 C4
Kember St N1 72 B1
Kemble Dr BR2 226 A5
Kemble Ho SW9 138 D2
Kemble Rd Croydon CR0 220 D5
Forest Hill SE23 162 D3
Tottenham N17 34 A2
Kemble St WC2 94 B1 240 C1
Kemerton Rd SE5 139 A2
Beckenham BR3 185 D1
Croydon CR0 205 D2
Kemey's St E9 75 A3
Kemnal Rd BR7 189 B5
Kemnal Tech Coll BR5 190 B3
Kemnal Warren BR7 189 B4
Kemp 24 NW9 27 D2
Kemp Ct SW8 270 A3
Kempe Ho SE1 262 D5
Kempe Rd NW6 90 D5
Kemp Gdns CR0 205 A3
Kemp Ho 1 E2 96 D5
Wallend E6 78 C2
Kempis Way 5 SE22 161 C6
Kemplay Rd NW3 70 B4
Kemp Rd RM8 58 D1
Kemps Ct NW2 68 D5
Kemp's Ct W1 239 C1
Kemps Dr E14 119
Kempsford Gdns SW5 113 C1 255
Kempsford Rd SE11 261
Kemps Gdns SE13 164
Kempshott Rd SW16 182
Kempson Rd SW6 135 C5 265
Kempthorne Rd SE8 119
Kempton Ave Northolt UB5 63
Sunbury TW16 172
Kempton Cl UB10 61
Kempton Ct E1 96
Sunbury TW16 172
Kempton Ho 13 N1 95
Kempton Park Race Course TW16 172
Kempton Park Sta TW16 172
Kempton Rd E6 100
Kempton Wlk CR0 207
Kempt St SE18 144
Kemsford Rd SE11 261
Kemsing Cl DA5 169
Coney Hall BR2 224
South Norwood CR7 205
Kemsing Ho SE1 252
Kemsing Rd SE10 121
Kemsley SE13 163 D
Kemsley Ct W13 109 C
Kemsway Ct BR5 190 B
Kenbrook Ho 5 NW5 71 C
W14 254 D
Kenbury Cl UB10 60 C
Kenbury Gdns 10 SE5 139 A
Kenbury Mans 18 SE5 139 A
Kenbury St SE5 139 A
Kenchester Cl SW8 138 A5 270 B
Kencot Cl DA18 125 B
Erith DA18 125 B
Kendal NW1 231 D
Kendal Ave Acton W3 88 D
Barking IG11 101 C
Edmonton N18 33 B
Kendal Cl SE5 138 D
East Bedfont TW14 149 D
Hayes UB4 83 C
Woodford IG8 20 D
Kendal Ct NW2 69 A
Acton W3 88 C
11 Chingford E4 20 A
7 Croydon CR0 205 C
Kendale Rd BR1 186 C
Kendal Gdns Edmonton N18 33 B
Sutton SM1 218 A
Kendal Ho 32 E9 74 C
N1 233 D
5 Croydon CR0 205 C
Penge SE20 184 B
Kendall Ave BR3 185 A
Kendall Ct DA15 168 A
3 SE22 162 A
Mitcham SW19 180 B
5 Penge SE19 183 D
Kendall Ho SE12 164 D
Kendall Lo 5 BR1 187 B
Kendall Pl W1 238 A
Kendall Rd SE18 144 A
Beckenham BR3 185 A
Isleworth TW7 131 A
Kendalmere Cl N10 31 B
Kendal Par N18 33 B
Kendal Pl SW15 157 B
Kendal Rd NW10 68 A
Kendal St W2 92 C1 237 B
Kendal Steps W2 237 B
Kender Prim Sch SE14 140 C
Kender St SE14 140 C
Kendoa Rd 1 SW4 137 D1
Kendon Cl E11 55 B
Kendra Hall Rd CR2 220 D1
Kendrey Gdns TW2 152 C
Kendrick Ct 11 SE15 140 B
Kendrick Mews SW7 256 C
Kendrick Pl SW7 256 C
Kenelm Cl HA1 65 A5
Kenerne Dr EN5 13 A6
Kenilford Rd SW12 159 B
Kenilworth Ave E17 53 C6
Harrow HA2 63 B4
Wimbledon SW19 179 C6
Kenilworth Cres EN1 5 C4
Kenilworth Ct
7 Chingford E4 20 A2
Fulham SW6 135 A2
Twickenham TW2 152 C2
Kenilworth Gdns
Hayes UB4 83 D2
Ilford IG3 79 D6
Southall UB1 85 B4
South Oxhey WD19 22 C5
Woolwich SE18 144 D3
Kenilworth Rd E3 97 A5
HA8 11 A1
NW6 91 B6

enilworth Rd *continued*
Ashford TW15,TW19 ...148 A1
Ealing W5 ...110 A5
Orpington BR5 ...211 A3
Penge SE20 ...184 D2
Stoneleigh KT17 ...216 A3
enilworth Terr 3
SM2 ...217 C1
enley N17 ...33 B1
enley Ave NW9 ...27 C1
enley Cl Barnet EN4 ...2 C1
Sidcup DA5 ...169 C4
St Paul's Cray BR7 ...211 C6
enley Gdns CR7 ...204 D5
enley Ho 6 BR5 ...190 B1
5 Croydon CR0 ...206 A1
enley Rd
Kingston KT1,KT3 ...176 D1
Merton SW19 ...201 C6
Twickenham TW1 ...153 B5
enley Wlk W11 ...244 A5
Cheam SM3 ...216 D4
enlor Rd SW17 ...180 B5
enmare Ct 5 HA7 ...25 C6
enmare Dr CR4 ...180 D3
enmare Gdns N13 ...33 A6
enmare Mans NW6 ...69 B3
enmare Rd CR7 ...204 C3
enmere Gdns HA0 ...88 C6
enmere Mans W5 ...87 C3
enmere Rd DA16 ...146 C3
enmont Gdns NW10 ...90 B4
enmont Prim Sch
NW10 ...90 B4
Kenmore Ave HA3 ...43 A6
Kenmore Cl TW9 ...132 C5
Kenmore Cres UB4 ...83 D4
Kenmore Ct NW6 ...69 C1
Kenmore Gdns HA8 ...26 D1
Kenmore Park Fst & Mid
Schs HA3 ...44 A6
Kenmore Rd HA3 ...43 D5
Kenmure Rd E8 ...74 B3
Kenmure Yd E8 ...74 B3
Kennacraig Cl 7 E16 ...121 A5
Kennard Ho 11 SW11 ...137 A3
Kennard Mans 6 N11 ...30 D5
Kennard Rd E15 ...76 B1
N11 ...30 D5
Kennard St 9 SW11 ...137 A3
Newham E16 ...122 B5
Kennedy Ave EN3 ...18 C5
Kennedy Cl BR5 ...211 B1
E13 ...99 A5
1 Mitcham CR4 ...181 A1
Pinner HA5 ...23 B4
Kennedy Cox Ho 9
E16 ...98 D2
Kennedy Ct TW15 ...171 A5
Kennedy Ho SE11 ...260 C2
Kennedy Path W7 ...86 D3
Kennedy Rd
Barking IG11 ...101 C6
Ealing W7 ...86 C2
Kennedy Wlk SE17 ...262 D3
Kennet Cl SW11 ...136 B1
Kennet Ct 47 W2 ...91 C2
Kennet Dr UB4 ...85 A2
Kenneth Ave IG1 ...78 D4
Kenneth Campbell Ho
NW8 ...236 D6
Kenneth Cres NW2 ...68 B3
Kenneth Ct SE11 ...261 B4
Kenneth Gdns HA7 ...25 A4
Kenneth Moor Rd 4
IG1 ...78 D5
Kennet Ho NW8 ...236 D5
Kenneth Rd RM6 ...59 A2
Kenneth Robbins Ho 1
N17 ...34 B3
Kenneth Younger Ho
SW6 ...264 D5
Kennet Rd W9 ...91 B3
Isleworth TW7 ...130 D2
Kennet Sq CR4 ...180 C2
Kennet St E1 ...118 A5
Kennet Wharf La EC4 ...252 B6
Kenninghall N18 ...34 C5
Kenninghall Rd E5 ...74 B5
N18 ...34 C5
Kenning Ho 6 N1 ...95 C6
Kenning St 12 SE16 ...118 C4
Kennings Way
SE11 ...116 C1 261 B2
Kennington Gdns KT1 197 D6
Kennington Gr SE11 ...270 D6
Kennington La
SE11 ...116 C1 260 D1
Kennington Oval
SE11 ...138 C6 270 D5
Kennington Palace Ct
SE11 ...261 A2
Kennington Park Gdns
SE17 ...138 D6
Kennington Park Ho
SE11 ...261 B1
Kennington Park Pl
SE11 ...138 D6
Kennington Park Rd
SE11 ...116 D1 261 C2
Kennington Rd
SE11 ...116 C2 261 A3
Kennington Sta
SE17 ...116 D1 261 C2
Kennoldes SE21 ...161 B2
Kennyland Lo NW4 ...46 B3
Kenny Rd NW7 ...29 A5
Kenrick Pl W1 ...238 A3
Kensal Green Cemy (All
Souls)* NW10 ...90 C4
Kensal Green Sta
NW10 ...90 C4
Kensal Ho W10 ...90 D3
Kensal Rd W10 ...91 A3
Kensal Rise Prim Sch
NW6 ...90 D5
Kensal Rise Sta NW10 ...90 D5
Kensington Ave E12 ...78 B2
South Norwood CR7 ...182 C2
Kensington Avenue Inf Sch
CR7 ...182 C2
Kensington Avenue Jun Sch
CR7 ...182 C2
Kensington & Chelsea Coll
SW10 ...136 A5 266 A4
W10 ...91 A2
Kensington Church Ct
W8 ...245 C1
Kensington Church St
W8 ...113 C5 245 B3
Kensington Church Wlk
W8 ...245 C1
Kensington Cl N11 ...31 A4
Kensington Court Mans
W8 ...245 D1
Kensington Court Mews
W8 ...255 D6
Kensington Court Pl
W8 ...113 D3 255 D6
Kensington Ct 2 NW7 ...27 B5
W8 ...113 D4 245 D1
Enfield EN2 ...5 C5
Kensington Ct Gdns
W8 ...255 D6
Kensington Dr IG8 ...37 D1
Kensington Gardens*
W2 ...114 A5 246 B3
Kensington Gate
W8 ...114 A3 256 A6
Kensington Gdns IG1 ...56 B1
Kensington Gdns Sq
W2 ...91 D1
Kensington Gore
SW7 ...114 B4 246 C1
Kensington Hall Gdns
W14 ...254 C2
Kensington Hgts HA1 ...42 D3
Kensington High St
W8 ...113 C3 255 B6
Kensington Ho 8 NW5 71 C3
Kensington Hts W8 ...245 A3
Kensington Mall W8 ...245 B4
Kensington Mans
SW5 ...255 B2
Kensington Olympia Sta
W14 ...113 A3 254 A6
Kensington Palace*
W8 ...113 D5 245 D3
Kensington Palace Gdns
W8 ...113 D5 245 C4
Kensington Park Gdns
W11 ...113 B6 244 D5
Kensington Park Mews
W11 ...91 B1
Kensington Park Rd
W11 ...113 B6 244 D6
Kensington Pl
W8 ...113 C5 245 A4
Kensington Prep Sch
SW6 ...135 B4 264 D2
Kensington Prim Sch
E12 ...78 B2
Kensington Rd
SW7 ...114 C4 246 B1
Northolt UB5 ...85 C5
Kensington Sports Ctr
W11 ...244 A6
Kensington Sq
W8 ...113 D4 245 C1
Kensington Terr CR2 ...221 B1
Kensington Village
W14 ...113 B2 254 D3
Kensington W W14 ...254 A4
Kensworth Ho EC1 ...235 D1
Kent Ave Bexley DA16 ...167 D6
Dagenham RM9 ...103 C3
Ealing W13 ...87 B2
Kent Cl
Mitcham CR4,SW16 ...204 A5
Orpington BR6 ...227 C2
Kent Ct 3 E2 ...95 D5
NW9 ...27 C1
Acton W3 ...88 B1
Kent Dr Cockfosters EN4 .15 A6
Teddington TW11 ...174 C5
Kentford Way UB5 ...85 A6
Kent Gate Way CR0 ...223 D3
Kent Gdns Ealing W13 ...87 B2
Ruislip HA4 ...40 B3
Kent Ho SE1 ...263 D1
SW1 ...259 C1
13 W4 ...111 C1
Richmond TW10 ...154 C6
Kent House La BR3 ...185 A5
Kent House Rd BR3 ...185 A4
Kent House Sta BR3 ...185 A2
Kent House Station App
BR3 ...184 D2
Kentish Bldgs SE1 ...252 C3
Kentish Rd DA17 ...125 C2
Kentish Town CE Prim Sch
NW5 ...71 C3
Kentish Town Rd NW1 ...71 B2
Kentish Town Sta NW5 .71 C3
Kentish Town West Sta
NW5 ...71 B2
Kentish Way BR1,BR2 .209 B6
Kentlea Rd SE28 ...123 C4
Kent Lo 9 SW19 ...156 D3
Kentmere Ho SE15 ...140 C6
Kentmere Rd SE18 ...123 C2
Kenton Ave Harrow HA1 42 D2
Southall UB1 ...107 C6
Sunbury TW16 ...173 A1
Kenton Ct W14 ...254 C5
2 Forest Hill SE26 ...185 A6
Harrow HA3 ...43 B3
3 Richmond TW10 ...153 D5
Kenton Gdns HA3 ...43 C4
Kenton Ho 21 E1 ...96 C3
N5 ...72 C5
Kenton La Harrow HA3 ...24 D3
Harrow HA3 ...43 C6
Kenton Park Ave HA3 ...43 D5
Kenton Park Cl HA3 ...43 C4
Kenton Park Cres HA3 ...43 D5
Kenton Park Par HA3 ...43 D4
Kenton Park Rd HA3 ...43 C5
Kenton Rd E9 ...74 D2
Harrow HA3 ...43 C4
Kenton St WC1 ...240 A6
Kenton Sta HA3 ...43 B3
Kenton Way UB4 ...83 C4
Kent Pas NW1 ...237 C6
Kent Rd W4 ...111 A3
Dagenham RM10 ...81 D3
East Molesey KT8 ...196 A5
Kingston KT1 ...197 D6
Richmond TW9 ...132 C5
Southgate N21 ...17 B4
West Wickham BR4 ...207 D1
Kent St E13 ...99 B4
E2 ...95 D5
Kent Terr NW1 ...92 C4 230 B1
Kent Twr SE20 ...184 B3
Kent View Gdns IG3 ...79 C6
Kent Way KT6 ...214 B6
Kentwell Cl SE4 ...141 A1
Kentwode Gn SW13 ...134 A5
Kent Yard SW7 ...247 B1
Kenver Ave N12 ...30 B4
Kenward Rd SE9 ...165 D6
Ken Way HA9 ...67 A5
Kenway Rd
SW5 ...113 D2 255 C3
Ken Wilson Ho 17 E2 ...96 A5
Kenwood EN1 ...17 C5
Kenwood Ave N14 ...15 D6
Kenwood Cl NW3 ...48 B1
Harmondsworth UB7 ...126 C6
Kenwood Ct NW9 ...45 A5
Kenwood Dr BR3 ...208 A6
Kenwood Gdns
Ilford IG2 ...56 C4
2 Wanstead E18 ...55 B6
Kenwood Ho* NW3 ...48 C1
15 SW9 ...138 D1
Kenwood Rd N6 ...48 D3
Edmonton N9 ...18 A3
Kenworthy Rd E9 ...75 A2
Kenwrick Ho N1 ...233 D5
Kenwyn Dr NW2 ...67 D5
Kenwyn Rd SW4 ...137 D1
Wimbledon SW20 ...178 C2
Kenya Rd SE7 ...143 D5
Kenyngton Dr TW16 ...172 A5
Kenyngton Manor Prim Sch
TW16 ...172 A4
Kenyngton Pl HA3 ...43 C4
Kenyon Ho 31 SE5 ...139 A5
Kenyon St SW6 ...134 D4
Keogh Rd E15 ...76 D2
Kepler Ho 9 SE10 ...120 D1
Kepler Rd SW2,SW4 ...138 A1
Keppel Ho 5 SE8 ...119 B1
SW3 ...257 A3
Keppel Rd E6 ...100 B6
Dagenham RM9 ...81 A4
Keppel Row SE1 ...252 A3
Keppel St WC1 ...239 D4
Kerala Ct N17 ...33 D2
Kerbela St 2 E2 ...96 A3
Kerbey St E14 ...97 D1
Kerem Sch N2 ...48 B4
Kerfield Cres SE5 ...139 B4
Kerfield Pl SE5 ...139 B4
Kerridge Ct N1 ...73 C2
Kerrier Ho SW10 ...266 B3
Kerrington Ct 7 W12 112 C4
Kerrin Point SE11 ...261 A2
Kerrison Pl W5 ...109 D5
Kerrison Rd E15 ...98 B6
SW11 ...136 C2
Ealing W5 ...109 D5
Kerrison Villas W5 ...109 D5
Kerry N7 ...72 A2
Kerry Ave HA7 ...25 D6
Kerry Cl Newham E16 ...99 B1
Palmers Green N13 ...16 B2
Kerry Ct HA7 ...25 D6
Kerry Ho 5 E1 ...96 C1
Kerry Path SE8 ...141 B6
Kerry Rd SE8 ...141 B6
Kerscott Ho 30 E3 ...97 D4
Kersey Gdns SE9 ...188 A6
Kersfield Ho SW15 ...156 D5
Kersfield Rd SW15 ...156 D5
Kershaw Cl SW18 ...158 B5
Kershaw Ho 7 SE27 ...160 D1
Kershaw Rd RM10 ...81 C5
Kersley Mews SW11 ...267 C1
Kersley Rd N16 ...73 C5
Kersley St SW11 ...136 D3
Kerstin Cl UB3 ...105 D6
Kerswell Cl N15 ...51 C4
Kerwick Cl 1 N7 ...72 B1
Keslake Mans NW10 ...90 D5
Keslake Rd NW6 ...90 D5
Kessock Cl N17 ...52 B4
Kestlake Rd DA5 ...168 C5
Keston Ave BR2 ...225 C3
Keston CE Prim Sch
BR2 ...225 D3
Keston Cl Bexley DA16 .146 C5
Edmonton N18 ...17 B1
Keston Ct DA5 ...169 B4
Keston Gdns BR2 ...225 C4
Keston Ho SE17 ...263 B2
Keston Mark BR2 ...226 A5
Keston Park Cl BR2 ...226 B5
Keston Rd N17 ...51 B5
SE15 ...140 A2
Thornton Heath CR7 ...204 C3
Kestral Ho EC1 ...235 A2
Kestrel Ave E6 ...100 A2
SE24 ...161 A6
Kestrel Cl NW10 ...67 B3
NW9 ...27 C1
Kingston KT2 ...175 D6
Kestrel Ct E17 ...34 D1
Ruislip HA4 ...61 B6
South Croydon CR2 ...221 A2
Kestrel Ho 4 SW11 ...136 C2
Enfield EN3 ...19 A6
Kestrel Pl SE14 ...141 A6
Kestrel Way UB3 ...105 B4
Keswick Ave
Kingston KT2,SW15 ...177 C5
Merton SW19 ...179 C1
Upper Halliford TW17 ...193 C6
Keswick Cl SM1 ...218 A4
Keswick Ct 2 SE22 ...162 A6
13 Catford SE6 ...164 D3
Keswick Dr EN3 ...6 C6
Keswick Gdns
Redbridge IG4 ...56 A5
Ruislip HA4 ...39 B3
Wembley HA9 ...66 A4
Keswick Ho 8 SE5 ...139 A4
Keswick Hts 9 SW15 .157 A6
Keswick Lo E8 ...73 D2
Keswick Mews W5 ...110 A5
Keswick Rd BR6 ...211 D1
DA7 ...147 C4
Putney SW15 ...157 A6
Twickenham TW2 ...152 A5
West Wickham BR4 ...224 C6
Kettering Ct CR7 ...205 A5
Kettering Rd EN3 ...6 D6
Kettering St SW16 ...181 C4
Kett Gdns SW2 ...160 B6
Kettlebaston Rd E10 ...53 B1
Kettleby Ho SW9 ...138 D2
Kettlewell Cl N11 ...31 A4
Ketton Ho W10 ...90 C3
Kevan Ct 6 E17 ...53 D5
Kevan Ho SE5 ...139 A5
Kevelioc Rd N17 ...33 A2
Kevin Cl TW4 ...128 D3
Kevington Cl BR5 ...211 D5
Kevington Dr BR5,BR7 211 D5
Kew Bridge TW8 ...110 B1
Kew Bridge Ct 8 W4 .110 C1
Kew Bridge Distribution Ctr
TW8 ...110 B1
Kew Bridge Rd TW8 ...110 B1
Kew Bridge Sta TW8 ...110 B1
Kew Bridge Steam Mus*
TW8 ...110 B1
Kew Cres SM3 ...217 B5
Kew Foot Rd TW9 ...132 A2
Kew Gardens Rd TW9 132 C4
Kew Gardens(Royal
Botanic)* TW9 ...132 A4
Kew Gardens Sta TW9 132 C4
Kew Gn TW9 ...132 B6
Kew Green TW9 ...132 C6
Kew Lo 11 TW9 ...132 B4
Kew Obsy* TW9 ...131 C2
Kew Palace* TW9 ...132 A5
Kew Pier TW9 ...132 C6
Kew Rd N2 ...30 C2
Richmond TW9,W4 ...132 B4
Kew Ret Pk TW9 ...132 D4
Key Cl E1 ...96 B3
Keyes Ct SE22 ...162 A6
Keyes Rd NW2 ...68 D3
Keyham Ho 31 W2 ...91 C2
Key Ho 9 SE11 ...138 C6
Keymer Rd SW2 ...160 B2
Keynes Cl N2 ...48 D6
Keynes Ct 9 SE28 ...124 B6
Keynsham Ave IG8 ...36 C6
Keynsham Gdns SE9 ...166 A6
Keynsham Ho 2 N4 ...51 A2
Keynsham Rd SE9 ...166 A6
Cheam SM4 ...201 D1
Keynsham Wlk SM4 ...201 D1
Keyse Rd SE1 .117 D3 263 C5
Keysham Ave TW5 ...128 A4
Keystone Cres N1 ...233 B3
Keywood Dr TW16 ...172 A4
Keyworth Cl E5 ...75 A4
Keyworth Pl SE1 ...261 D6
Keyworth Prim Sch
SE17 ...116 D1 261 C2
Keyworth St
SE1 ...116 D3 261 D6
Kezia St SE8 ...119 A1
Khalsa Ct N22 ...32 D2
Khama Rd SW17 ...180 C6
Khartoum Rd E13 ...99 B4
Ilford IG1 ...78 D3
Upper Tooting SW17 ...180 B6
Khyber Rd SW11 ...136 C3
Kibworth St
SW8 ...138 B5 270 C3
Kidbrooke Gdns SE3 ...143 A4
Kidbrooke Gr SE3 ...143 B4
Kidbrooke Interchange
SE3 ...143 C2
Kidbrooke La SE9 ...144 A1
Kidbrooke Park Cl
SE3 ...143 B4
Kidbrooke Park Prim Sch
SE3 ...143 C4
Kidbrooke Park Rd
SE12,SE3 ...143 B2
Kidbrooke Sch SE3 ...143 D3
Kidbrooke Sta SE3 ...143 B2
Kidbrooke Way SE3 ...143 B3
Kiddens BR8 ...191 D1
Kidderminster Pl CR0 204 D1
Kidderminster Rd CR0 205 A2
Kidderpore Ave NW3 ...69 C4
Kidderpore Gdns NW3 .69 C4
Kidd Ho RM9 ...81 B4
Kidd Pl SE7 ...122 A1
Kidlington Way NW9 ...27 C2
Kierbeck Bsns Complex
E16 ...121 B4
Kiffen St EC2 ...242 D6
Kilberry Cl TW7 ...130 B4
Kilbrennan Ho 5 E14 ...98 A1
Kilburn Bridge 14 NW6 91 C6
Kilburn Gate NW6 ...91 D5
Kilburn High Rd NW6 ...91 C6
Kilburn High Road Sta
NW6 ...91 D6
Kilburn Ho 13 W9 ...91 B4
Kilburn La W10 ...91 A5
Kilburn Park Jun Sch
NW6 ...91 B5
Kilburn Park Rd NW6 ...91 C4
Kilburn Park Sta NW6 ...91 C5
Kilburn Pl NW6 ...91 C6
Kilburn Priory NW6 ...91 D6
Kilburn Sq NW6 ...91 C6
Kilburn Sta NW2 ...69 B2
Kilburn Vale NW6 ...91 D6
Kilburn Vale Est 13
NW6 ...91 C6
Kildare Cl HA4 ...40 C1
Kildare Ct W2 ...91 C1
Kildare Gdns W2 ...91 C1
Kildare Rd E16 ...99 A2
Kildare Terr W2 ...91 C1
Kildare Wlk E14 ...97 C1
Kildoran Rd SW2 ...160 A6
Kildowan Rd IG3 ...58 A1
Kilgour Rd SE23 ...163 A5
Kilkie St SW6 ...136 A3
Killarney Rd SW18 ...158 A5
Killburns Mill Cl SM6 .219 B6
Killearn Rd SE6 ...164 B3
Killester Gdns KT17,
KT4 ...216 B4
Killick Ho SM1 ...217 D4
Killick St N1 ...94 B5 233 C3
Killieser Ave SW2 ...160 A2
Killigrew Ho TW16 ...171 C3
Killip Cl E16 ...98 D1
Killowen Ave UB5 ...64 A3
Killowen Rd E9 ...74 D2
Killross Rd TW14 ...149 B3
Killyon Rd SW8 ...137 C3
Kilmaine Rd
SW6 ...135 A5 264 B3
Kilmarnock Gdns RM8 ...80 C5
Kilmarnock Rd WD19 ...22 D6
Kilmarsh Rd W6 ...112 C2
Kilmartin Ave SW16 ...204 C6
Kilmartin Rd IG3 ...80 A6
Kilmington Rd SW13 ...134 A6
Kilmiston Ave TW17 ...193 A3
Kilmiston Ho TW17 ...193 A3
Kilmore Ho 17 E14 ...97 D1
Kilmorey Gdns TW1 ...131 B1
Kilmorey Rd TW1 ...131 B1
Kilmorie Prim Sch
SE23 ...163 A2
Kilmorie Rd SE23 ...163 A2
Kilmuir Ho SW1 ...258 B3
Kiln Cl UB3 ...127 B6
Kiln Ct E14 ...119 B6
Kilner Ho 3 SE11 ...138 C6
Kilner St E14 ...97 C2
Kiln Mews SW17 ...180 B5
Kiln Pl NW5 ...71 A3
Kilnside KT10 ...213 A1
Kiloh Ct 1 SW11 ...136 C2
Kilpatrick Ct N16 ...51 D1
Kilpatrick Way UB4 ...85 A2
Kilpeck Ho 3 N4 ...51 A2
Kilravock Ho SE25 ...205 C6
Kilravock St W10 ...91 A4
Kilronan 5 W3 ...89 B1
Kilross Rd TW14 ...149 C3
Kilsby Wlk RM9 ...80 B2
Kilsha Rd KT12 ...194 C3
Kilvinton Dr EN2 ...5 B5
Kimbell Gdns
SW6 ...135 A4 264 A1
Kimbell Pl SE9 ...143 C1
Kimber Ctr The SW18 .157 C4
Kimber Ho 11 SE18 ...144 D6
Kimberley Ave E6 ...100 A5
SE15 ...140 C2
Ilford IG2 ...57 C2
Kimberley Dr DA14 ...168 D2
Kimberley Gate 2
BR1 ...186 D3
Kimberley Gdns N4 ...50 D4
Enfield EN1 ...5 D2
Kimberley Ho 7 E14 ...120 A3
Kimberley Ind Est E17 ...35 B2
Kimberley Rd E11 ...76 B6
E16 ...98 D3
E17 ...35 B2
NW6 ...91 A6
SW9 ...138 A2
Chingford, Chingford Green
E4 ...20 C3
Edmonton N18 ...34 B4
Penge BR3 ...184 D1
Thornton Heath CR0 ...204 D3
Tottenham N17 ...34 A1
Kimberley Way E4 ...20 C3
Kimberley Wlk KT12 ...194 B2
Kimber Rd SW18 ...157 D4
Kimble Cres WD23 ...8 A4
Kimble Ho 1 N7 ...72 A3
NW8 ...237 B6
Kimble Rd
Mitcham SW17 ...180 B4
Upper Tooting SW17 ...180 B5
Kimbolton Cl SE12 ...164 D5
Kimbolton Row SW3 ...257 A3
Kimmeridge Gdns 3
SE9 ...188 A6
Kimmeridge Rd SE9 ...188 A6
Kimm Ho 16 E17 ...53 D6
Kimpton Ct 12 SE5 ...139 B4
Kimpton Ho SW15 ...156 A4
Kimpton Link Bsns Ctr
SM3 ...217 B6
Kimpton Rd SE5 ...139 B4
Cheam SM3 ...217 B6
Kimpton Trade & Bsns Ctr
SM3 ...217 B6
Kinburn St SE16 ...118 D4
Kincaid Rd SE15 ...140 B5
Kincardine Gdns W9 ...91 C3
Kinch Gr HA3,HA9 ...44 B2
Kincraig BR7 ...188 C2
Kindell Ho 4 SW14 ...133 B2
Kinder Cl SE28 ...124 D6
Kinder Ho N1 ...235 D4
Kindersley Ho 27 E1 ...96 A1
Kinder St 9 E1 ...96 B1
Kinefold Ho N7 ...72 A2
Kinetic Cres EN3 ...7 B6
Kinfauns Rd Ilford IG3 ...58 B1
Streatham SW2 ...160 C2
King Alfred Ave SE6 ...185 C6
King Alfred Sch NW11 .47 D1
King Arthur Cl SE15 ...140 C5
King Athelstan Prim Sch
KT1 ...198 B6
King Charles Cres KT5 198 B2

King Charles Ho SW6 ... 265 D4
King Charles' Rd KT5, KT6 ... 198 B3
King Charles St SW1 ... 116 A4 250 A2
King Charles Wlk 6 SW19 ... 157 A3
King Ct 15 E10 ... 53 D2
Kingcup Cl CR0 ... 206 D1
King David La E1 ... 118 C6
Kingdon Ho 8 E14 ... 120 A3
Kingdon Rd NW6 ... 69 C2
King Edward Dr KT6 ... 214 A5
King Edward Mans 12 E8 ... 96 B6
King Edward Mews SW13 ... 134 A4
King Edward Rd E10 ... 54 A1
E17 ... 53 A6
Barnet EN5 ... 1 D1
King Edward's Gdns W3 ... 110 C5
King Edward's Gr TW11 ... 175 C4
King Edwards Mans SW6 ... 265 A3
King Edward's Rd E9 ... 96 C6
Barking IG11 ... 101 B5
Edmonton N9 ... 18 B4
Enfield EN3 ... 6 D1
Ruislip HA4 ... 39 B1
King Edward St EC1 ... 242 A2
King Edward The Third Mews 8 SE16 ... 118 B4
King Edward Wlk SE1 ... 116 C3 261 B6
King Fahad Acad The W5 ... 109 C2
King Fahed Acad W3 ... 111 D6
Kingfield Rd W5 ... 87 D3
Kingfield St E14 ... 120 A2
Kingfisher Ave E11 ... 55 B3
Kingfisher Cl
Harrow HA3 ... 24 D3
Woolwich SE28 ... 124 C6
Kingfisher Ct 12 E14 ... 120 A4
11 SW11 ... 136 C2
Cheam SM1 ... 217 B3
East Molesey KT8 ... 196 C5
Enfield EN2 ... 4 B5
Hounslow TW3 ... 151 D6
Merton SW19 ... 179 B3
Putney SW19 ... 157 A2
Kingfisher Dr TW10 ... 175 B6
Kingfisher Ho SE15 ... 139 D4
W14 ... 254 C6
Kingfisher Lo TW11 ... 175 A6
Kingfisher Mews SE13 163 D6
Kingfisher Sports Ctr The 12 KT1 ... 176 A1
Kingfisher Sq 19 SE8 ... 141 B6
Kingfisher St E6 ... 100 A2
Kingfisher Way NW10 ... 67 B3
Croydon CR0 ... 206 D4
Kingfisher Wlk NW9 ... 27 C1
King Frederick IX Ct SE16 ... 119 B3
King Garth Mews SE23 ... 162 C2
King Gdns CR0 ... 220 D3
King George Ave E16 ... 99 D1
Ilford IG2 ... 57 B3
Walton-on-T KT12 ... 194 D1
King George Cl TW16 ... 171 C5
King George Hospl IG3 58 A4
King George Sq TW10 154 B5
King George St SE10 ... 142 A5
King George's Trad Est KT9 ... 214 C4
King George VI Ave CR4 ... 202 D5
Kingham Cl 3 W11 ... 112 D4
Wandsworth SW18 ... 158 A4
King Harolds Way DA7 ... 147 A5
King Henry Mews 7 BR6 ... 227 D3
King Henry's Mews EN3 ... 7 C6
King Henry's Rd NW3 ... 70 C1
Kingston KT1,KT3 ... 198 D6
King Henry's Reach W6 ... 134 C6
King Henry St N16 ... 73 C3
King Henry's Wlk N1 ... 73 C2
King Henry's Yd 5 N16 73 C3
King Ho W12 ... 90 B1
Kinghorn St EC1 ... 242 A3
King James St SE1 ... 116 D4 251 D1
King John Ct EC2 ... 243 B6
King John St E1 ... 96 D2
King John's Wlk SE9 ... 166 A5
Kinglake St SE17 ... 117 C1 263 B2
Kingly Ct W1 ... 249 B6
Kingly St W1 ... 115 C6 249 A6
King & Queen Cl 4 SE9 ... 188 A6
King & Queen St SE17 ... 117 A1 262 B2
Kingsand Rd SE12 ... 165 A2
Kings Arbour UB2 ... 107 A1
King's Arms Ct 22 E1 ... 96 A2
King's Arms Yd EC2 ... 242 C2
Kingsash Dr UB4 ... 85 A3
Kings Ave N10 ... 49 A6
SW4 ... 160 A5
Bromley BR1 ... 186 D4
Dagenham RM6 ... 59 B3
Ealing W5 ... 87 D1
New Malden KT3 ... 199 D5
Wallington SM5 ... 218 D1
King's Ave
Ashford TW16 ... 171 D4
Buckhurst Hill IG9 ... 21 D2
Hounslow TW3,TW5 ... 129 D4
Southall UB1 ... 85 D1
Southgate N21 ... 16 D3
Woodford IG8 ... 37 C5
Kings Avenue Sch SW4 ... 160 A6
King's Bench St SE1 ... 116 D4 251 D2
King's Bench Wlk EC4 241 B1
Kingsbridge N16 ... 51 B1
Kingsbridge Ave W3 ... 110 B4
Kingsbridge Cres UB1 ... 85 B2
Kingsbridge Ct E14 ... 119 C2
Edmonton N21 ... 16 D2
Kingsbridge Ho 10 SE20 ... 184 B2
Kingsbridge Ind Est IG11 ... 101 C4
Kingsbridge Rd W10 ... 90 C1
Barking IG11 ... 101 B5
Southall UB2 ... 107 B2
Walton-on-T KT12 ... 194 B2
West Barnes SM4 ... 200 D2
Kingsbridge Way UB4 ... 83 C4
Kingsbury Green Prim Sch NW9 ... 44 D4
Kingsbury High Sch Annexe NW9 ... 44 D5
Kingsbury Rd N1 ... 73 C2
NW9 ... 44 D4
Kingsbury Sta NW9 ... 44 C4
Kingsbury Terr N1 ... 73 C2
Kingsbury Trad Est NW9 ... 45 B3
Kings Chace View EN2 ... 4 C3
Kings Chase KT8 ... 196 A6
Kings Cl NW4 ... 46 D5
King's Cl E10 ... 53 D2
Kings Cl KT12 ... 194 B1
King's Cl KT7 ... 197 A2
Kingsclere Cl SW15 ... 156 A4
Kingsclere Ct N12 ... 30 C5
New Barnet EN5 ... 14 A6
Kingsclere Pl EN2 ... 5 A3
Kingscliffe Gdns SW19 ... 157 B3
King's Coll SE24 ... 161 B5
WC2 ... 116 B6 250 D6
Kings College Ct NW3 ... 70 C1
King's College Hospl SE5 ... 139 B3
King's College London NW3 ... 69 C4
Kings College Rd NW3 ... 70 B1
Ruislip HA4 ... 39 D3
Kings Coll London W8 ... 245 A2
Kings Coll London (Chelsea Campus) SW3 ... 114 C1 257 A1
King's Coll Sch SW19 ... 178 D4
Kingscote NW11 ... 47 B1
Kingscote Rd W4 ... 111 B3
Croydon CR0 ... 206 B2
Kingston KT3 ... 199 B6
Kingscote St EC4 ... 251 C6
King's Court N SW3 ... 257 A1
Kingscourt Rd SW16 ... 160 A1
King's Court S SW3 ... 257 A1
King's Cres N4,N5 ... 73 A5
Kingscroft SW4 ... 160 A5
Kingscroft Rd NW2 ... 69 B2
King's Cross WC1 ... 94 A4 233 B2
King's Cross Bridge WC1 ... 233 B2
King's Cross Rd WC1 ... 94 B4 233 D1
King's Cross Sta N1 ... 94 A5 233 B3
King's Cross, St Pancras N1 ... 233 A2
King's Cross (Thames Link) Sta WC1 ... 233 B2
Kings Ct E13 ... 99 B6
HA9 ... 66 D6
6 N7 ... 72 B1
NW8 ... 230 C5
SE22 ... 140 A1
W6 ... 112 A2
Kings Ct *continued*
2 Buckhurst Hill IG9 ... 21 D2
16 Kingston KT2 ... 176 C3
10 Putney SW15 ... 156 A4
3 Wallington SM6 ... 219 B2
King's Ct
Beckenham BR3 ... 207 D6
9 Ealing W5 ... 87 C2
Wimbledon SW19 ... 179 C4
Kingsdale Gdns W11 ... 112 D5
Kingsdale Rd SE18 ... 145 D6
Penge SE20 ... 184 D3
Kingsdale Sec Sch SE21 ... 161 C1
Kingsdown 1 SW19 ... 178 D3
Kingsdown Ave W13 ... 109 B4
W3 ... 111 C6
Kingsdown Cl 26 SE16 118 B1
W10 ... 90 D1
11 W11 ... 91 A1
Kingsdown Ct SW11 ... 158 C5
Kingsdowne Rd KT6 ... 198 B2
Kingsdown Ho 1 E8 ... 74 A3
Kingsdown Rd E11 ... 76 C5
3 N19 ... 72 A6
Cheam SM3 ... 217 A3
Kingsdown Way BR2 ... 209 A3
Kings Dr HA9 ... 66 D6
Edgware HA8 ... 26 B6
Surbiton KT5 ... 198 C3
King's Dr KT7 ... 197 B2
Kingsend HA4 ... 39 C1
Kings Farm E17 ... 35 D2
Kings Farm Ave TW10 132 C1
Kingsfield Ave HA1,HA2 42 A4
Kingsfield Ho 18 N16 ... 73 C5
SE9 ... 165 D1
Kingsfield Rd HA1 ... 42 B2
Kingsford Com Sch E13 ... 99 C3
Newham E6 ... 100 B1
Kingsford St NW5 ... 70 D3
Kingsford Way E6 ... 100 B2
Kingsgate HA9 ... 67 A5
Kingsgate Ave N3 ... 47 C6
Kingsgate Bsns Ctr KT2 ... 176 A2
Kingsgate Cl BR5 ... 190 C1
DA7 ... 147 A4
Kingsgate Est N1 ... 73 C2
Kingsgate Ho 28 SW9 ... 138 C4
Kingsgate Pl NW6 ... 69 C1
Kingsgate Prim Sch NW6 ... 69 C1
Kingsgate Rd NW6 ... 69 C1
Kingston KT2 ... 176 A2
King's Gdns 6 NW6 ... 69 C1
Kings Gdns IG1 ... 57 B1
King's Gr SE15 ... 140 B4
SE15 ... 140 B5
Kings Grange HA4 ... 39 D1
Kingsground SE9 ... 166 A5
Kings Hall Mews SE13 142 A2
Kings Hall Rd BR3 ... 185 A2
Kings Head Hill E4 ... 19 D4
King's Head Yd SE1 ... 252 C3
King's Highway SE18, SE2 ... 145 D6
Kingshill SE17 ... 262 B4
Kingshill Ave
Harrow HA3 ... 43 B5
Hayes UB4 ... 83 D4
New Malden KT4 ... 200 B2
Northolt UB5 ... 84 B4
Kingshill Ct 6 EN5 ... 1 A1
Kingshill Dr HA3 ... 43 B6
Kings Ho 19 E14 ... 119 B6
SW8 ... 270 B4
Kingshold Rd E9 ... 74 C1
Kingsholm Gdns SE9 ... 144 A1
King's House Jun Sch TW10 ... 154 B6
King's House Prep Sch TW10 ... 154 B6
Kingshurst Rd SE12 ... 165 A4
Kings Keep KT6 ... 198 A5
King's Keep 6 SW15 ... 156 D6
King's La SM1,SM2 ... 218 B3
Kingsland NW8 ... 92 C6 230 B5
Kingsland Gn 1 E8,N1 ... 73 C2
Kingsland High St E8 ... 73 D3
Kingsland Pas 2 E8 ... 73 C2
Kingsland Rd E13 ... 99 C4
E2 ... 95 C5
Kingsland Sch E8 ... 73 D3
Kingsland Sh Ctr E8 ... 73 D2
Kingslawn Cl SW15 ... 156 B6
Kingslee Ct 12 SM2 ... 217 D1
Kingsleigh Pl CR4 ... 202 D6
Kingsleigh Wlk BR2 ... 208 D5
Kingsley Ave Ealing W13 87 A1
Hounslow TW3 ... 130 A3
Southall UB1 ... 107 C6
Sutton SM1 ... 218 B4
Kingsley Cl N2 ... 48 A4
Dagenham RM10 ... 81 D4
Kingsley Ct E11 ... 54 D3
NW2 ... 68 B2
1 SE28 ... 124 C5
Kingsley Ct *continued*
Bexley DA6 ... 147 C1
Edgware HA8 ... 10 D2
Wood Green N22 ... 32 B3
2 Worcester Park KT4 ... 215 D6
Kingsley Dr 1 KT4 ... 215 D6
Kingsley Flats SE1 ... 263 B3
Kingsley Gdns E4 ... 35 C5
Kingsley Grange 1 E11 ... 55 A4
Kingsley Ho NW11 ... 48 A3
SW3 ... 266 D5
3 SW4 ... 137 D3
8 Kingston KT6 ... 198 A4
Kingsley Mews BR7 ... 188 D4
W8 ... 255 D5
Dagenham RM9 ... 80 D4
Kingsley Pl N6 ... 49 A2
Kingsley Prim Sch CR9 ... 204 C1
Kingsley Rd E7 ... 77 A1
NW6 ... 91 B6
Chingford E17 ... 36 A1
Edmonton N13 ... 32 D6
Harrow HA2 ... 64 A5
Hounslow TW3 ... 130 A3
Orpington BR6 ... 227 D1
Pinner HA5 ... 41 B5
Thornton Heath CR0 ... 204 C1
Wimbledon SW19 ... 179 D5
Kingsley St SW11 ... 136 D2
Kingsley Way N2 ... 48 A4
Kingsley Wood Dr SE9 166 B1
Kings Lo HA4 ... 39 C1
Kingslyn Cres SE19 ... 183 C2
Kings Mall W6 ... 112 C2
Kingsman Par SE18 ... 122 B3
King's Mans SW3 ... 267 A5
Kingsman St SE18 ... 122 B2
Kingsmead Barnet EN5 ... 1 C1
Richmond TW10 ... 154 B5
Kingsmead Ave NW9 ... 45 B2
Edmonton N9 ... 18 B3
Mitcham CR4 ... 203 C6
North Cheam KT4 ... 216 B5
Sunbury TW16 ... 172 C1
Tolworth KT6 ... 214 C6
Kingsmead Cl DA15 ... 168 A2
Teddington TW11 ... 175 B4
West Ewell KT19 ... 215 B1
Kingsmead Ct N6 ... 49 D2
Bromley BR1 ... 186 D3
Kingsmead Dr UB5 ... 63 B1
Kingsmead Ho E9 ... 75 A4
Kingsmead Lo
9 Chingford E4 ... 20 A2
Sutton SM2 ... 218 B2
Kings Mead Pk KT10 ... 212 C1
Kingsmead Prim Sch E9 ... 75 A4
Kingsmead Rd SW2 ... 160 C2
Kingsmead Sch EN1 ... 6 A2
Kingsmead Way E5,E9 ... 75 A4
Kingsmere BR7 ... 188 A2
Catford SE6 ... 163 D3
Kingsmere Cl SW15 ... 134 D2
Kingsmere Ct NW9 ... 44 D1
Kingsmere Pk NW9 ... 45 A1
Kingsmere Pl N16 ... 51 B1
Kingsmere Rd SW19 ... 156 D2
King's Mews 1 SW4 ... 160 A6
WC1 ... 94 B3 240 D5
Kingsmill NW8 ... 92 B5 229 D4
Kingsmill Bsns Pk KT1 198 B6
Kingsmill Gdns RM9 ... 81 B3
Kingsmill Rd RM9 ... 81 B3
Kingsmill Terr NW8 ... 92 B5 229 D4
Kingsnorth Ho 12 W10 ... 90 D1
Kingsnympton Pk KT2 176 D4
Kings Oak RM7 ... 59 C6
Kings Oak Hospl (Private) The EN2 ... 4 C5
King's Orch SE9 ... 166 A5
King's Paddock TW12 ... 174 A2
King's Par W12 ... 112 A3
Willesden NW10 ... 90 C6
Kingspark Ct E18 ... 55 A6
Kings Pas KT2 ... 175 D2
King's Pl SE1 ... 252 A1
Kings Pl Acton W4 ... 111 A2
Buckhurst Hill IG9 ... 21 D2
Loughton IG10 ... 21 D4
King Sq EC1 ... 95 A4 235 A1
King's Quay SW10 ... 266 B2
Kings Rd BR6 ... 227 D4
NW10 ... 68 B1
King's Rd E11 ... 54 C2
E6 ... 99 C6
SW10 ... 136 B6 266 C5
SW3 ... 257 B1
Kings Rd Ealing W5 ... 87 D2
Feltham TW13 ... 150 C3
Harrow HA2 ... 63 B6
Mitcham CR4 ... 203 A6
Richmond TW10,TW9 ... 154 B6
Walton-on-T KT12 ... 194 B1
West Drayton UB7 ... 104 B4
Wood Green N22 ... 32 B2
King's Rd Barking IG11 ... 79 A1
Chingford E4 ... 20 B3
Edmonton N18 ... 34 A6
Kingston KT2 ... 176 B3
Long Ditton KT6 ... 197 C1
Mortlake SW14 ... 133 B2
South Norwood SE25 ... 206 A6
Teddington TW11,TW12 ... 174 B5
Tottenham N17 ... 33 D2
Twickenham TW1 ... 153 B5
Wimbledon SW19 ... 179 C4
Kings Ride Gate TW10 132 C1
Kingsridge SW19 ... 157 A2
Kings Road Bglws HA2 ... 63 B5
King's Scholars' Pas SW1 ... 259 A4
King St E13 ... 98 D3
E13 ... 99 A3
EC2 ... 95 A1 242 B1
N2 ... 48 B6
SW1 ... 115 C5 249 B4
W3 ... 111 A5
W6 ... 112 A2
WC2 ... 250 A6
Richmond TW9 ... 153 D6
Southall UB2 ... 107 A3
Tottenham N17 ... 33 D2
Twickenham TW1 ... 153 A3
King Stairs Cl SE16 ... 118 B4
King's Terr NW1 ... 93 C6 232 A5
8 Isleworth TW7 ... 131 A2
Kingsthorpe Rd SE26 ... 184 D6
Kingston Ave
Cheam SM3 ... 217 A5
Feltham TW14 ... 149 D5
Yiewsley UB7 ... 104 B6
Kingston Bsns Ctr KT9 214 B5
Kingston By-Pass KT6, KT7,KT9 ... 213 C5
Kingston By - Pass KT6 ... 214 C5
Kingston Cl
Dagenham RM6 ... 59 A6
Northolt UB5 ... 85 B6
Teddington TW11 ... 175 B4
Kingston Coll of F Ed KT1 ... 197 D6
Kingston Coll of F Ed (M V Annex) KT2 ... 176 A2
Kingston Cres BR3 ... 185 B2
Kingston Gdns CR0 ... 220 A5
Kingston Gram Sch KT2 ... 176 B1
Kingston Hall Rd KT1 ... 197 D6
Kingston Hill KT2 ... 177 A5
Kingston Hill Ave RM6 ... 59 A6
Kingston Hill Pl KT2, TW10 ... 177 A6
Kingston Ho 2 NW6 ... 69 A1
Kingston Ho E SW7 ... 247 A1
Kingston Ho N SW7 ... 247 A1
Kingston Ho S SW7 ... 247 A1
Kingston Hospl KT2 ... 176 D2
Kingston House Estate KT6 ... 197 B3
Kingston La
Teddington TW11 ... 175 B4
Uxbridge UB8 ... 82 A4
West Drayton UB7 ... 104 B4
Kingston Lo 2 KT3 ... 199 C5
Kingston Mus KT1 ... 176 A1
Kingston Pl HA3 ... 24 D3
Kingston Rd
SW15,SW19 ... 156 B3
Ashford TW15 ... 170 A4
Ashford TW15,TW17 ... 170 B4
Edmonton N9 ... 18 A2
Ilford IG1 ... 79 A4
Kingston KT1,KT3 ... 199 A5
Merton SW19,SW20 ... 179 B1
New Barnet EN4 ... 14 B6
Southall UB2 ... 107 B4
Teddington TW11 ... 175 B4
Ewell KT17 ... 215 D1
Kingston Sq SE19 ... 183 B5
Kingston Sta KT2 ... 176 A2
Kingston Univ
Kingston KT1 ... 198 A6
Kingston KT2 ... 177 B5
Kingston Univ Annex KT1 ... 176 B1
Kingston Univ Roehampton Vale Ctr SW15 ... 155 D1
Kingston Vale SW15 ... 155 C1
Kingstown St NW1 ... 93 A6 231 A6
King Street Cloisters 8 W6 ... 112 B2
King Street Coll W12 ... 112 C4
W6 ... 112 C2
King Street Par 6 TW1 ... 153 A3
Kings View Ct 1 SW20 ... 178 D3
Kingswater Pl SW11 ... 267 A3
Kingsway BR5 ... 211 B4
N12 ... 30 A4
WC2 ... 94 B1 240 C2
Kingsway *continued*
Coney Hall BR4 ... 224 D
Enfield EN3 ... 18 B
Hayes UB3 ... 83 A
Mortlake SW14,TW9 ... 132 D
Stanwell TW19 ... 148 A
Wembley HA9 ... 66 A
West Barnes KT3 ... 200 C
Woodford IG8 ... 37 C
Kings Way Croydon CR0 220 B
Harrow HA1 ... 42 C
Kingsway Bsns Pk TW12 ... 173 B
Kingsway Coll NW5 ... 71 B
Kingsway Cres HA2 ... 42 A
Kingsway Est N18 ... 34 D
Kingsway Pl EC1 ... 241 C
Kingsway Rd SM3 ... 217 A
Kingswear Ho 5 SE23 162 C
Kingswear Rd NW5 ... 71 B
Ruislip HA4 ... 62 A
Kingswood 32 E2 ... 96 C
Kingswood Ave DA17 ... 125 B
NW6 ... 91 A
Beckenham BR2,BR3 ... 208 C
Hampton TW12 ... 173 D
Hounslow TW3,TW5 ... 129 B
Thornton Heath CR7 ... 204 C
Kingswood Cl BR6 ... 211 B
N20 ... 14 A
SW8 ... 270 B
Enfield EN1 ... 17 D
New Malden KT3 ... 199 D
Surbiton KT6 ... 198 A
Kings Wood Ct 4 NW6 69 C1
Kingswood Ct
Chingford E4 ... 35 C5
7 Richmond TW10 ... 154 B6
Kingswood Dr
Carshalton SM5 ... 202 D1
Dulwich SE19,SE21 ... 183 D6
Kingswood Ho 3 KT2 176 D4
Kingswood Pk N3 ... 29 B1
Kingswood Pl SE13 ... 142 C1
Kingswood Prim Sch SE27 ... 183 B5
Kingswood Rd E11 ... 54 C2
W4 ... 111 A3
Beckenham BR2 ... 208 C6
Ilford IG3 ... 58 A2
Merton SW19 ... 179 B2
Penge SE20 ... 184 C4
Streatham SW2 ... 160 A4
Kingswood Terr W4 ... 111 A3
Kingswood Way SM6 ... 220 A3
Kingsworth Cl BR3 ... 207 A4
Kingsworthy Cl KT1 ... 198 B6
Kings Yd E15 ... 75 C2
Kingthorpe Rd NW10 ... 67 B1
Kingthorpe Terr 1 NW10 ... 67 B1
Kington Ho 16 NW6 ... 91 D6
Kingward Ho E1 ... 96 A2
Kingwell Rd EN4 ... 2 B5
King William IV Gdns SE20 ... 184 C4
King William La 3 SE10 ... 120 C1
King William St EC4 ... 117 B6 252 D6
King William Wlk SE10 ... 142 A6
Kingwood Rd SW6 ... 135 A5 264 A3
Kinlet Rd SE18 ... 145 A4
Kinloch Dr NW9 ... 45 C2
Kinloch St N7 ... 72 B5
Kinloss Ct NW3 ... 47 B5
Kinloss Gdns NW3 ... 47 B5
Kinloss Rd SM5 ... 202 A2
Kinnaird Ave
Bromley BR1 ... 186 D4
Chiswick W4 ... 133 A5
Kinnaird Cl BR1 ... 186 D4
Kinnear Ct 2 SW20 ... 178 D2
Kinnear Rd W12 ... 111 D4
Kinnerton Pl N SW1 ... 247 D1
Kinnerton Pl S SW1 ... 247 D1
Kinnerton St SW1 ... 115 A4 248 A1
Kinnerton Yd SW1 ... 248 A1
Kinnoull Mans 10 E5 ... 74 B4
Kinnoul Rd W6 ... 135 A6 264 A6
Kinross Ave KT4 ... 216 A6
Kinross Cl
Ashford TW16 ... 171 D5
Harrow HA3 ... 44 B4
Kinross Ct 1 SE6 ... 164 D2
Kinross Dr TW16 ... 171 D5
Kinross Ho N1 ... 233 C6
Kinross Terr E17 ... 35 B1
Kinsale Rd SE15 ... 140 A2
Kinsella Gdns SW19 ... 178 B5
Kinsey Ho SE21 ... 183 C6
Kinsham Ho 4 E2 ... 96 A3
Kintore Way SE1 ... 263 C4
Kintyre Cl SW16 ... 204 B6
Kintyre Ct 17 SW2 ... 160 A4

Kinveachy Gdns SE7 122 A1
Kinver Ho N4 51 B2
Kinver Rd SE26 184 C6
Kipling Ct W7 108 D6
Kipling Dr SW17 180 B4
Kipling Ho 29 SE5 139 A5
Kipling Pl HA7 24 D4
Kipling Rd DA7 147 A4
Kipling St SE1 117 B4 252 D2
Kipling Terr N9 17 B2
Kipling Twr 3 W3 111 A3
Kippington Dr SE9 165 D3
Kirby Cl KT19 215 D3
Kirby Est SE16 118 B3
Kirby Gr SE1 117 C4 253 A2
Kirby St EC1 94 C2 241 B4
Kirby Way KT12 194 C3
Kirchen Rd W13 109 B6
Kirkby Cl N11 31 A4
Kirkdale SE26 162 B1
Kirkdale Rd E11 54 C2
Kirkeby Bldg EC1 241 A4
Kirkfield Cl W13 109 B5
Kirkham Rd E6 100 A1
Kirkham St SE18 145 C6
Kirk La SE18 145 A6
Kirkland Cl DA15 167 C5
Kirkland Dr EN2 5 A4
Kirkland Wlk 4 E8 73 D2
Kirkleas Rd KT6 198 A1
Kirklees Rd
Dagenham RM8 80 C3
Thornton Heath CR7 204 C4
Kirkley Ho N16 51 C1
Kirkley Rd SW19 179 C2
Kirkman Pl W1 239 C3
Kirkmichael Rd E14 98 A1
Kirk Rd E17 53 B3
Kirk Rise SM1 217 D5
Kirkside Rd SE3 143 A6
Kirk's Pl E3 97 B2
Kirkstall Ave N17 51 B5
Kirkstall Gdns SW2 160 A3
Kirkstall Ho SW1 258 C2
Kirkstall Rd SW2 160 A3
Kirkstead Ct E5 75 A4
Kirksted Rd SM4 201 D1
Kirkstone NW1 232 A2
Kirkstone Way BR1 186 C3
Kirkton Lo SW18 157 D5
Kirkton Rd N15 51 C5
Kirkwall Pl E2 96 C4
Kirkwood Rd SE15 140 B3
Kirn Rd W13 109 B6
Kirrane Cl KT3 199 D4
Kirtley Ho SW8 269 B2
Kirtley Rd SE26 185 A6
Kirtling St
SW8 137 C5 269 A4
Kirton Cl W4 111 B2
Kirton Rd E13 99 C5
Kirton Wlk HA8 27 A3
Kirwin Way SE5 138 D5
Kisharon Day Sch
NW11 47 B3
Kitcat Terr E3 97 C4
Kitchener Rd E7 77 B2
N17 51 C6
N2 48 C6
Chingford, Highams Park
E17 35 D2
Dagenham RM10 81 D2
South Norwood CR7 205 B6
Kite Ho 5 SW11 136 C2
Kitley Gdns SE19 183 D2
Kitson Rd SE5 139 A5
Barnes SW13 134 A4
Kittiwake Ct 26 SE8 141 B6
Kittiwake Pl SM1 217 B3
Kittiwake Rd UB5 84 D4
Kittiwake Way UB4 84 D2
Kitto Rd SE14 140 D3
Kitt's End Rd EN5 1 A6
Kiver Rd N19 72 A6
Klea Ave SW4 159 C5
Kleffens Ct 2 SE3 142 D5
Knaggs Ho 1 TW11 174 C5
Knapdale Cl SE23 162 B2
Knapmill Rd SE6 163 D2
Knapmill Way SE6 163 D2
Knapp Cl NW10 67 C2
Knapp Rd
Ashford TW15 170 B6
Bow E3 97 C3
Knapton Mews SW17 181 A4
Knaresborough Dr
SW18 157 D3
Knaresborough Ho 4
N4 51 A2
Knaresborough Pl
SW5 113 D2 255 C4
Knatchbull Rd NW10 89 B6
SE5 138 D4
Knebworth Ave E17 35 C2
Knebworth Ho 2 N16 73 C4
SW8 269 D1
Chingford E17 35 C2
Knebworth Rd 3 N16 73 C4
Knee Hill SE2 124 C1
Knee Hill Cres SE2 124 C2
Kneller Gdns TW7 152 B5
Kneller Ho 9 SW8 137 D3
4 Northolt UB5 84 D5
Kneller Rd SE4 141 A1
Isleworth TW2 152 B5
New Malden KT3 199 C2
Knight Cl RM8 80 C6
Knight Ct N15 51 C3
1 Chingford E4 20 A3
Knighten St E1 118 B5
Knighthead Point E14 119 C4
Knight Ho SE17 263 A3
Knightland Ho E5 74 B6
Knightland Rd E5 74 B6
Knightleas Ct NW2 68 C2
Knighton Cl
Croydon CR2 220 D1
Woodford IG8 37 B6
Knighton Dr IG8 37 B6
Knighton Gn IG9 21 B2
Knighton La IG9 21 B2
Knighton Park Rd
SE26 184 D5
Knighton Rd E7 77 A4
Knightrider Ct EC4 252 A6
Knightrider St EC4 251 D6
Knights Arc SW1 247 C1
Knight's Ave W5 110 A4
Knightsbridge
SW1,SW7 114 D4 247 C1
Knightsbridge Ct SW1 247 D1
Knightsbridge Gn
SW1 247 C1
Knightsbridge Mews
BR7 188 B3
Knights Cl E9 74 C3
Knights Ct Bushey WD23 8 B3
Kingston KT1 198 A6
Penge BR3 185 A2
Knightshayes Ho NW4 28 D1
Knight's Hill SE19,SE27 182 D6
Knight's Hill Sq SE27 182 D6
Knights Ho SE1 253 C2
SW5 254 C2
SW8 270 B3
Knight's Ho SW10 266 A4
Knight's La N9 18 A1
Knight's Pk KT1 198 A6
Knight's Pl TW2 152 C3
Knights Rd
Newham E16 121 A4
Stanmore HA7 25 C6
Knight's Wlk SE11 261 C3
Knightswood Cl HA8 11 A2
Knightswood Ct N6 49 D2
Knightswood Ho N12 30 A4
Knightwood Cres KT3 199 C3
Knivet Rd SW6 265 A5
Knobs Hill Rd E15 97 D6
Knockholt Rd SE9 165 D6
Knole Cl CR0 206 C3
Knole Ct UB5 84 C4
Knole Gate DA15 167 C1
Knole The SE9 188 C6
Knoll Ct BR6 227 D6
Dulwich SE19 183 D5
Knoll Dr N14 15 A4
Knoll Ho NW8 229 A4
Knollmead KT4,KT5 199 A1
Knollmead Prim Sch
KT5 215 A6
Knoll Rd DA5 169 C5
SW18 158 A6
Sidcup DA14 190 B6
Knoll Rise BR6 211 D1
Knolls Cl KT4 216 B5
Knoll The
Beckenham BR3 185 D2
Ealing W13 87 C2
Hayes BR2 209 A1
Knolly's Cl SE27,SW16 160 C1
Knolly's Rd SE27,SW16 160 C1
Knot Ho SE1 253 C3
Knottisford St E2 96 C4
Knotts Green Mews
E10 54 A3
Knotts Green Rd E10 54 A3
Knowlden Ho 4 E1 118 C6
Knowle Ave DA7 147 B5
Knowle Cl SW9 138 C2
Knowle Lo BR7 188 B4
Knowle Rd BR2 226 A6
Twickenham TW2 152 C3
Knowles Cl UB7 104 A5
Knowles Ct 7 HA1 42 D3
Knowles Hill Cres
SE13 164 B6
Knowles Ho NW10 90 A6
Wandsworth SW18 157 D5
Knowles Wlk SW4 137 C2
Knowl Pk WD6 10 A6
Knowlton Gn 1 BR2 208 D4
Knowlton Ho 32 SW9 138 C4
Knowl Way WD6 10 B6
Knowsley Ave UB1 107 D5
Knowsley Rd SW11 136 D3
Knox Ct 16 SW4 138 A3
Knox Ho SW15 134 C3
Knox Rd E7 77 A2
Knox St W1 92 D2 237 C4
Knoyle Ho W14 254 B5
Knoyle St SE14 141 A6
Kobi Nazrul Prim Sch
E1 96 A1
Koblenz Ho N8 50 A6
Kohat Rd SW19 179 D5
Korda Cl TW17 192 B6
Kossuth St SE10 120 C1
Kotree Way 16 SE1 118 A2
Kramer Mews SW5 255 C1
Kreedman Wlk 8 E8 74 A3
Kreisel Wlk TW9 132 B6
Kuala Gdns SW16 182 B2
Kubrick Bsns Est E7 77 B4
Kuhn Way E7 77 A3
Kwesi Johnson Ct 4
N22 32 C1
Kydbrook Cl BR5 211 A2
Kylemore Cl 3 E6 99 D5
Kylemore Ct 4 W12 112 A4
Kylemore Rd NW6 69 C1
Kylestrome Ho SW1 258 B3
Kymberley Rd HA1 42 C3
Kynance Gdns HA7 25 C2
Kynance Mews
SW7 113 D3 255 D5
Kynance Pl SW7 256 A5
Kynaston Ave CR7 205 A4
Kynaston Cl HA3 24 B3
Kynaston Cres CR7 205 A4
Kynaston Ho 7 SW2 160 B3
Kynaston Rd BR1 187 A5
N16 73 C5
Enfield EN2 5 B4
Thornton Heath CR7 205 A4
Kynaston Wood HA3 24 B3
Kynersley Cl SM5 218 D5
Kynoch Rd N18 34 D6
Kyrle Rd SW11 159 A5
Kyverdale Rd N16 51 D1

L

Laburnam Ct 12 SW16 182 C5
Laburnham Cl 5 SE15 140 C5
Laburnham Ct NW2 69 B6
Laburnham Ho SE4 141 B3
Laburnham Pl SE9 166 C6
Laburnum Ave
Carshalton SM1 218 C5
Edmonton N9 17 D2
Tottenham N17 33 B3
Yiewsley UB7 104 B6
Laburnum Cl E4 35 B4
N11 31 A4
Laburnum Cres TW16 172 B2
Laburnum Ct 26 E2 95 D6
Harrow HA1 41 D3
5 Mitcham CR4 181 A1
Stanmore HA7 25 C6
Laburnum Gdns
Croydon CR0 206 D1
Edmonton N21 17 A2
Laburnum Gr NW9 45 A2
Edmonton N21 17 A2
Hounslow TW3 129 B1
Kingston KT3 177 B1
Ruislip HA4 39 B3
Southall UB1 85 B3
Laburnum Ho 6 N16 73 B6
Dagenham RM10 81 C6
Laburnum JMI Sch E2 95 D6
Laburnum Lo N3 29 B1
Laburnum Rd
Hayes UB3 105 D2
Merton SW19 180 A3
Mitcham CR4 181 A1
Laburnum St E2 95 D6
Laburnums The E6 100 A3
Laburnum Way BR2 210 D2
Stanwell TW19 148 B3
Lacebark Cl DA15 167 D4
Lacey Cl N9 18 A2
Lacey Dr Dagenham RM8 80 C5
Edgware HA8 26 B6
Hampton TW12 173 B2
Lacey Ho 6 SE13 142 A3
Lacey Wlk E3 97 C5
Lacine Ct 12 SE16 118 D4
Lackington St EC2 242 D4
Lackland Ho SE1 263 D2
Lacland Ho SW10 266 C4
Lacock Cl SW19 180 A4
Lacock Ct 3 W13 109 A5
Lacon Rd SE22 140 A1
Lacrosse Way SW16 181 D2
Lacy Rd SW15 134 D1
Ladas Rd SE27 183 A5
Ladbroke Cres W11 91 A1
Ladbroke Gdns
W11 113 B6 244 C6
Ladbroke Gr W10 91 A2
W11 113 B6 244 C6
Ladbroke Grove Ho
W11 244 C6
Ladbroke Grove Sta
W10 91 A1
Ladbroke Mews W11 244 B3
Ladbroke Rd
W11 113 B5 244 C4
Enfield EN1 17 D5
Ladbroke Sq
W11 113 B6 244 D5
Ladbroke Terr
W11 113 B5 244 D4
Ladbroke Wlk
W11 113 B5 244 D4
Ladbrook Cl HA5 41 B4
Ladbrooke Cres DA14 168 D1
Ladbrook Rd SE25 205 B5
Ladderstile Ride KT2,
TW10 176 D5
Ladderswood Way N11 31 C5
Ladlands SE22 162 A4
Lady Aylesford Ave
HA7 25 B5
Lady Bankes Jun & Inf Schs
HA4 62 A6
Lady Booth Rd 7 KT1 176 A1
Ladybower Ct 6 E5 74 D4
Ladycroft Gdns 6
BR6 227 A3
Ladycroft Rd SE13 141 D2
Ladycroft Wlk BR6 227 A3
Ladycroft Wlk HA7 25 D1
Lady Eleanor Holles Sch
The (Jun Girls)
TW12 173 D5
Lady Eleanor Holles Sch
The (Senior Girls)
TW12 173 D5
Lady Elizabeth Ho
SW14 133 A2
Lady Florence Ctyd 14
SE8 141 C5
Ladygate La HA4 39 A3
Lady Hay KT4 215 D6
Lady Margaret Prim Sch
UB1 85 B2
Lady Margaret Rd NW5 71 C3
Southall UB1 85 B2
Lady Margaret Sch
SW6 135 C4 265 A1
Lady Shaw Ct N13 16 B1
Ladysmith Ave E6 100 A5
Ilford IG2 57 C2
Ladysmith Cl NW7 28 A3
Ladysmith Rd E16 98 D4
SE9 166 C5
Edmonton N18 34 B5
Enfield EN1 5 D3
Harrow HA3 24 C1
Tottenham N17 34 A1
Lady Somerset Rd NW5 71 B4
Ladywell Cl SE4 141 C1
Ladywell Ho 7 BR5 190 B1
Ladywell Hts SE4 163 B5
Ladywell Rd SE13 163 D6
Ladywell St 4 E15 98 D6
Ladywell Sta SE13 163 D6
Ladywell Water Twr
SE4 163 C6
Ladywood Ave BR5 211 C4
Ladywood Rd KT6 214 C6
Lafitte Ho 22 N19 49 D2
Lafone Ave TW13 150 C2
Lafone Ho 11 SW2 160 A4
Lafone St SE1 117 D4 253 C2
Lagado Mews SE16 118 D5
Lagonda Ho 11 E3 97 C3
Lagonier Ho EC1 235 B1
Laidlaw Dr N21 16 B6
Laindon Ho 6 N16 51 D1
Laing Dean UB5 84 C6
Laing Ho SE5 139 A5
Laings Ave CR4 180 D1
Laings Cnr CR4 180 D2
Lainlock Pl TW3 129 D4
Lainson St SW18 157 C4
Lairdale Cl SE21 161 A4
Laird Ho SE5 139 A5
Lairs Cl N7 72 A2
Laitwood Rd SW12 159 B3
Lakanal 14 SE5 139 C4
Lake Ave BR1 187 A4
Lake Bsns Ctr N17 34 A3
Lake Cl Dagenham RM8 80 D5
6 Wimbledon SW19 179 B5
Lakedale Rd SE18 123 C1
Lake Dr WD23 8 B2
Lakefield Cl SE20 184 B3
Lakefield Rd N22 32 D1
Lake Gdns
Dagenham RM10 81 C3
Hackbridge SM6 219 B5
Richmond TW10 153 B2
Lakehall Gdns CR7 204 D4
Lakehall Rd CR7 204 D4
Lake Ho SE1 252 A1
4 West Norwood
SW27 182 D5
Lake House Rd E11 77 A6
Lakehurst Rd KT19 215 C3
Lakeland Cl HA3 24 B4
Lakeman Ct CR7 183 A1
Lakenheath N14 15 D6
Laker Ct SW4 138 A3
Lake Rd Croydon CR0 223 B6
Dagenham RM6 58 D5
Dagenham RM9 103 D4
Wimbledon SW19 179 B5
Laker Pl SW15 157 A5
Lakeside
Beckenham BR3 207 D6
Borehamwood WD6 10 C6
Ealing W13 87 C1
Enfield EN2 3 D1
10 Kingston KT2 176 D3
Wallington SM6 219 B4
West Ewell KT19 215 C2
Lakeside Ave SE28 124 A5
Redbridge IG4 55 D5
Lakeside Cl Ruislip HA4 39 B5
Sidcup DA15 168 C6
South Norwood SE25 184 A1
Lakeside Complex The
SE2 124 D5
Lakeside Cres EN4 14 D6
Lakeside Ct N4 51 A1
Lakeside Dr
Esher KT10 212 A2
Keston Mark BR2 226 A5
Lakeside Lo NW4 47 A5
Lakeside Rd W14 112 D3
Palmers Green N13 16 B1
Lakeside Way HA9 66 C4
Lakes Rd BR2 225 C3
Lakeswood Rd BR5 211 A3
Lake The WD23 8 B3
Lakeview 23 E3 96 D5
Lake View HA8 26 B5
Lake View Ct SW1 258 D6
Lakeview Ct E4 36 B4
Lakeview Rd DA16 146 B1
West Norwood SE27 182 D5
Lake View Terr N18 33 D6
Lakis Cl NW3 70 A4
Laleham Ave NW7 11 B1
Laleham Ho E2 243 C6
Laleham Rd
Catford SE6 164 A4
Littleton TW17 192 C4
Lambarde Ave SE9 188 C6
Lamb Ct 18 E14 119 A6
Lamberhurst Ho 14
SE15 140 C6
Lamberhurst Rd
Dagenham RM8 59 B1
West Norwood SE27 182 C5
Lambert Ave TW9 132 D2
Lambert Ho 19 N19 49 D2
17 SW9 138 C3
Lambert Lo TW8 109 D1
Lambert Rd N12 30 B5
SW2 160 B6
Newham E16 99 B1
Lambert's Pl CR0 205 B1
Lambert's Rd KT6 198 B4
Lambert St N1 72 C1
Lambert Way N12 30 A5
Lambert Wlk HA9 65 D5
Lambeth Coll (Brixton Ctr)
SW2 160 B6
Lambeth Coll (Clapham Ctr)
SW4 159 C6
Lambeth Coll (Tower
Bridge Ctr)
SE1 117 C5 253 B3
Lambeth Coll (Vauxhall Ctr)
SW8 137 D4 269 C2
Lambeth Ct 8 SW18 157 C6
Lambeth High St
SE1 116 B2 260 C4
Lambeth Hill EC4 252 A6
Lambeth Hospl SW9 138 B2
Lambeth Inst Strand Ctr
SW2 160 B4
Lambeth North Sta
SE1 116 C3 261 A6
Lambeth Palace★
SE1 116 B3 260 C5
Lambeth Palace Rd
SE1 116 B3 260 C6
Lambeth Pier SE1 260 B5
Lambeth Prospect
SE19 183 B4
Lambeth Rd
SE1 116 C3 261 B5
Thornton Heath CR0 204 D1
Lambeth Twrs SE11 261 A5
Lambeth Wlk
SE11 116 B2 260 D4
Lambfold Ho N7 72 A2
Lamb Ho SE10 142 A6
11 SE5 139 B4
28 SE5 139 A5
Lamb La E8 74 B1
Lamble St NW5 71 A4
Lambley Rd RM9 80 B2
Lambolle Pl NW3 70 C2
Lambolle Rd NW3 70 C2
Lambourn Cl 9 NW5 71 C4
W7 108 D4
Lambourne Ave SW19 179 B6
Lambourne Ct 5 IG8 37 C3
Lambourne Gdns
4 Barking IG11 79 D1
Chingford E4 19 C2
Enfield EN1 5 D3
Lambourne Gr KT1 176 D1
Lambourne Ho NW8 236 D4
SE16 118 D2
Lambourne Pl SE3 143 B4
Lambourne Rd E11 54 A2
Barking IG11 79 D1
Ilford IG3 79 C6
Lambourn Rd SW4 137 B2
Lambrook Ho 12 SE15 140 A4
Lambrook Terr
SW6 135 A4 264 A2
Lamb's Bldgs EC1 242 C5
Lamb's Cl N9 18 A2
Lamb's Conduit Pas
WC1 240 C4
Lamb's Conduit St
WC1 94 B3 240 C5
Lambscroft Ave SE9,
SE12 165 D1
Lambs Mdw IG8 37 D1
Lamb's Mews N1 234 C5
Lamb's Pas EC1 95 B3 242 C5
Lamb St E1 95 D2 243 C4
Lamb's Terr N9 17 B2
Lambs Wlk EN2 5 A3
Lambton Ct 2 N19 50 A1
Lambton Pl W11 244 D6
Lambton Rd N19 50 A1
Wimbledon SW20 178 C2
Lamb Wlk SE1 253 A1
Lamerock Rd BR1 186 D6
Lamerton Lo 10 TW9 132 B4
Lamerton St 9 SE8 141 C6
Lamford Cl N17 33 B3
Lamington St 3 W6 112 B2
Lamlash St SE11 261 C4
Lamley Ho SE10 141 D5
Lammas Ave CR4 181 A1
Lammas Gn SE26 162 B1
Lammas Park Gdns
W5 109 C5
Lammas Park Rd W5 109 D4
Lammas Rd E9 74 D1
Richmond TW10 175 C6
Walthamstow E10 53 A1
Lammas Sch The E10 53 B1
Lammermoor Rd
SW12 159 B4
Lamont Rd
SW10 136 B6 266 C5
Lamont Rd Pas SW10 266 C5
Lamorbey Cl DA15 167 D2
Lamorna Cl E17 36 A2
Lamorna Gr HA7 25 D1
Lampard Gr N16 51 D1
Lampern Sq 8 E2 96 A4
Lampeter Cl NW9 45 C3
Lampeter Sq W6 264 A5
Lamplighter Cl 31 E1 96 C3
Lampmead Rd SE12 142 D1
Lamport Cl SE18 122 B2
Lampson Ho 6 N19 71 C4
Lampton Ave TW5 129 D4
Lampton Ct TW5 129 D4
Lampton House Cl
SW19 178 D6
Lampton Park Rd
TW3 129 D3
Lampton Rd TW3,TW5 129 D3
Lampton Sch TW5 129 C4
Lanacre Ave NW9 27 C2
Lanain Ct SE12 164 D4
Lanark Cl W5 87 C2
Lanark Ct UB5 63 C3
Lanark Ho 11 SE1 118 A1
Lanark Mans 6 W12 112 C4
W9 236 B6
Lanark Pl W9 92 A3 236 B6
Lanark Rd W9 92 A4 229 A1
Lanark Sq E14 119 D3
Lanata Wlk UB4 84 D3
Lanbury Rd SE15 140 D1
Lancashire Ct W1 248 D6
Lancaster Ave
Barking IG11 101 C6
Hadley Wood EN4 2 B5
Wanstead E18 55 B5
West Norwood SE21,
SE27 161 A2
Wimbledon SW19 178 D5
Lancaster Cl 9 N1 73 C1
NW9 27 D3
W2 245 C5
Beckenham BR2 208 D5
Kingston KT2 175 D5
Stanwell TW19 148 A5
Tottenham N17 34 A3
Lancaster Cotts 1
TW10 154 A5
Lancaster Ct SW6 264 D3

Lancaster Ct *continued*
W2 246 B6
1 Belmont SM2 217 C1
Stanwell TW19 148 A3
Walton-on-T KT12 194 B2
West Norwood SE27 160 D2
Lancaster Dr E14 120 A5
NW3 70 C2
Lancaster Gate
W2 114 A6 246 B6
Lancaster Gate Sta
W2 114 B6 246 C6
Lancaster Gdns W13 109 B4
Kingston KT2 175 D5
Wimbledon SW19 179 A5
Lancaster Gr NW3 70 C2
Lancaster Ho Enfield EN2 5 B4
Putney SW15 134 C3
Wandsworth SW18 157 D4
Lancaster House SW1 249 A2
Lancasterian Inf Sch
N17 33 D2
Lancaster Lo 2 W11 91 A1
Lancaster Mews
3 SW18 157 D6
W2 114 A6 246 B6
2 Richmond TW10 154 A5
Lancaster Pk TW10 154 A6
Lancaster Pl
WC2 116 B6 250 C5
Hounslow TW5 128 D3
Ilford IG1 79 A4
Twickenham TW1 153 A4
1 Wimbledon SW19 178 D5
Lancaster Rd E11 76 C6
E17 34 D1
E7 77 A1
N11 31 D4
N4 50 C2
NW10 68 A3
W11 91 A1
Edmonton N18 33 D5
Enfield EN2 5 B4
Harrow HA2 41 C4
New Barnet EN4 14 B6
Northolt UB5 64 A2
Southall UB1 107 A6
South Norwood SE25 206 A6
Wimbledon SW19 178 D5
Lancaster Road Ind Est 2
EN4 14 B6
Lancaster St
SE1 116 D4 251 D1
Lancaster Stables 10
NW3 70 C2
Lancaster Terr
W2 114 B6 246 C6
Lancaster Wlk
W2 114 A5 246 B4
Hayes UB3 83 A1
Lancastrian Rd SM6 220 B1
Lancefield Ct 1 NW6 91 A5
Lancefield Ho SE15 140 B2
Lancefield St W10 91 B4
Lancell St N16 73 C6
Lancelot Ave HA0 65 D4
Lancelot Cres HA0 65 D4
Lancelot Gdns EN4 15 A4
Lancelot Par 4 HA0 65 D3
Lancelot Pl
SW7 114 D4 247 C1
Lancelot Rd DA16 146 A2
Wembley HA0 65 D3
Lance Rd HA1 42 A2
Lancer Sq W8 245 C2
Lancey Cl SE7 122 A2
Lanchester Ct W2 237 C1
Lanchester Rd N6 48 D4
Lancing Gdns N9 17 D3
Lancing Rd Ealing W13 109 B6
Feltham TW13 149 D2
Ilford IG2 57 B2
Thornton Heath CR0 204 B2
Lancing St NW1 232 C1
Lancresse Ct N1 95 C6
Landale Ho 13 SE16 118 C3
Landcroft Rd SE22 161 D5
Landells Rd SE22 162 A5
Lander Ct EN5 14 A6
Landford Rd SW15 134 C2
Landgrove Rd SW19 179 C5
Landin Ho 11 E14 97 C1
Landleys Field 21 N7 71 D3
Landmann Ho 16 SE16 118 B2
Landmann Way SE14 118 D1
Landmark Commercial Ctr
N18 33 C4
Landon Pl SW1 257 C6
Landons Cl E14 120 A5
Landon Way TW15 170 D4
Landon Wlk 14 E14 119 D6
Landor Ct N16 73 C3
Landor Ho 7 SE5 139 B5
Landor Rd SW9 138 A2
Landor Wlk 11 W12 112 A4
Landra Gdns N21 16 D5
Landrake NW1 232 B5
Landridge Dr EN1 6 B5
Landridge Rd SW6 135 B3
Landrock Rd N8 50 B3
Landscape Rd IG8 37 B3
Landseer Ave E12 78 C3
Landseer Cl
Edgware HA8 26 C1
Mitcham SW19 180 B2
Landseer Ct UB4 83 B5
Landseer Ho NW8 236 D6
SW1 259 D3
SW11 268 B1
17 Northolt UB5 84 D5
Landseer Rd N19 72 A6
Cheam SM1,SM2 217 C2
Enfield EN1 18 A6
New Malden KT3 199 B2
Lands' End WD6 9 D5
Landstead Rd SE18 145 B5
Landulph Ho SE11 261 B2
Landward Ct W1 237 B2
Lane Cl NW2 68 B5
Lane Ct SW11 158 D4
Lane End DA7 147 D2
Lane Gdns Bushey WD23 8 C4
Claygate KT10 212 D1
Lane Mews E12 78 B5
Lanercost Cl SW2 160 C2
Lanercost Gdns N14 16 A4
Lanercost Rd SW2 160 C2
Laneside HA8 27 A5
Chislehurst BR7 189 A5
Laneside Ave RM8 59 B2
Lane The NW8 92 A5 229 A3
SE3 143 A2
Laneway SW15 156 B6
Laney Bldg EC1 241 A4
Lanfranc Ct HA1 64 D5
Lanfranc Rd E3 97 A5
Lanfrey Pl W14 254 C1
Langbourne Ave N6 71 A6
Langbourne Ct E17 53 A3
Langbourne Ho 7
SW2 160 C6
Langbourne Mans N6 71 A6
Langbourne Pl E14 119 D1
Langbourne Prim Sch
SE21 161 C1
Langbourne Way
KT10 213 A2
Langbrook Rd SE3 143 D3
Langcroft Cl SM5 218 D5
Langdale NW1 232 A2
Langdale Ave CR4 202 D6
Langdale Cl BR6 226 D5
SE17 139 A6
Dagenham RM8 58 C1
Mortlake SW14 132 D1
Langdale Cres DA7 147 C4
Langdale Ct
3 Ealing W5 87 C2
9 Ilford IG1 78 D5
Langdale Dr UB4 83 C5
Langdale Gdns UB6 87 B4
Langdale Ho SW1 259 A1
Langdale Rd SE10 142 A5
Thornton Heath CR7 204 C5
Langdale St 3 E1 96 B1
Langdon Cres E6 100 C5
Langdon Ct EC1 234 D3
NW10 89 C6
Langdon Dr NW9 45 A1
Langdon Ho 1 E14 98 A1
Langdon Park Rd N6 49 C2
Langdon Park Sec Sch
E14 98 A1
Langdon Pl SW14 133 A2
Langdon Rd Barking E6 100 C6
Bromley BR2 209 B6
Morden SM4 202 A4
Langdon Sch E6 100 D6
Langdons Ct UB2 107 C3
Langdon Shaw DA14 189 D5
Langdon Way 14 SE1 118 A2
Langdon Wlk SM4 202 A4
Langford Cl E8 74 A3
7 N15 51 C3
NW8 229 B4
Langford Cres EN4 2 D1
Langford Ct NW8 229 B3
Langford Gn SE5 139 C2
Langford Ho 5 SE8 141 C6
Langford Pl
NW8 92 A5 229 B4
Sidcup DA14 168 A1
Langford Prim Sch
SW6 135 D3
Langford Rd 4 SW6 135 D3
Cockfosters EN4 2 D1
Woodford IG8 37 C4
Langfords IG9 21 D2
Langham Cl N15 50 D6
Langham Ct NW4 46 D4
Merton SW20 178 C1
4 Putney SW15 156 D6
Ruislip HA4 62 B3
12 Twickenham TW1 153 C5
Langham Dr RM6 58 B3
Langham Gdns HA8 27 A3
Ealing W13 109 B6
Richmond TW10 175 C6
Southgate N21 16 D6
Wembley HA0 65 C6
Langham Ho SW4 159 C6
Langham House Cl
TW10 175 D6
Langham Mans SW5 255 C1
Langham Park Pl BR2 208 D5
Langham Pl N15 50 D6
W1 93 B2 238 D3
Chiswick W4 133 C6
Langham Rd HA8 27 A4
N15 51 A6
Teddington TW11 175 B4
Wimbledon SW20 178 C2
Langham Sch The N15 51 A5
Langham St W1 93 B2 238 D3
Langhedge Cl N18 33 D4
Langhedge La N18 33 D4
Langhedge Lane Ind Est
N18 33 D4
Lang Ho 3 N19 71 C5
SW8 270 A3
Langholm Cl SW12 159 D4
Langholme WD23 8 A3
Langhorn Dr TW2 152 C4
Langhorne Ct 10 NW8 70 B1
Langhorne Ho 5 SE7 143 C6
Langhorne Rd RM10 81 C1
Langhurst Ho 10
SW11 137 A3
Langland Cres HA7 25 D1
Langland Dr HA5 23 A3
Langland Gdns NW3 69 D3
Croydon CR0 223 B6
Langland Ho 10 SE5 139 B5
Upper Tooting SW17 180 B5
Langler Rd NW10 90 C5
Langley Ave
North Cheam KT4,SM3 216 D6
Ruislip HA4 62 B6
Surbiton KT6 198 A1
Langley Cres HA8 11 A1
Dagenham RM9 80 D1
Harlington UB3 127 D5
Wanstead E11 55 C2
Langley Ct SW8 270 A2
WC2 250 A6
Langley Dr W3 110 D4
Wanstead E11 55 B2
Langley Gdns BR5 210 D3
Bromley BR2 209 C5
Dagenham RM9 80 D1
Langley Gr KT3 177 C1
Langley Ho BR1 187 B3
11 E5 74 B3
36 W2 91 C2
Langley La
SW8 138 A6 270 B6
Langley Manor BR3 208 A4
Langley Mans SW8 270 B6
Langley Park Rd SM1,
SM2 218 A1
Langley Park Sch for Boys
BR3 207 D3
Langley Park Sch for Girls
BR3 208 A3
Langley Pk NW7 27 C4
Langley Rd DA16 146 C6
Beckenham BR3 207 A5
Isleworth TW7 130 D3
Merton SW19 179 C2
Surbiton KT6 198 A2
Langley Row EN5 1 B4
Langley St WC2 94 A1 240 A1
Langley Way BR4 208 C2
Langmead Dr WD23 8 B3
Langmead Ho 34 E3 97 D4
Langmead St SE27 183 A6
Langmore Ct DA7 146 D2
Langmore Ho 28 E1 96 A1
Langport Ct KT12 194 C1
Langport Ho 1 SW9 138 D3
Langridge 15 NW5 71 A2
Langridge Mews
TW12 173 B4
Langroyd Rd SW17 158 D2
Langside Ave SW15 134 A1
Langside Cres N14 15 D1
Lang St E1 96 C3
Langston Hughes Cl 5
SE24 138 D1
Langthorn Ct EC2 242 D2
Langthorne Ct 4 SE6 186 A6
Langthorne Ho UB3 105 C2
Langthorne Lo 30
SW2 160 C4
Langthorne Rd E11 76 B5
Langthorne St SW6 134 D5
Langton Ave N20 14 B4
Wallend E6 100 C4
Langton Cl WC1 94 B3 240 D6
Langton Ct SW15 157 B5
Langton Ho SE11 260 D4
5 Streatham SW16 181 C6
Langton Pl SW18 157 C3
Langton Rd NW2 68 C5
Langton Rd *continued*
SW9 138 D5
East Molesey KT8 196 A5
Harrow HA3 24 A3
Langton Rise SE22,
SE23 162 B4
Langton St
SW10 136 A6 266 B5
Langton Way
Greenwich SE3 143 A5
South Croydon CR0 221 C4
Langtry Pl SW6 265 B6
Langtry Rd NW8 91 D6
Northolt UB5 84 D5
Langtry Wlk
NW8 92 A6 229 A6
NW8 91 D6
Langwood Chase
TW11 175 C4
Langworth Dr UB4 84 B1
Langworthy HA5 23 C4
Lanherne Ho 7 SW19 178 D3
Lanhill Rd W9 91 C3
Lanier Rd SE13 164 B5
Lanigan Dr TW3 151 D6
Lankaster Gdns N2 30 B2
Lankers Dr HA2 41 B3
Lankton Cl BR3 186 A2
Lanner Ho 2 SW11 136 C2
Lannock Rd UB3 105 D5
Lannoy Point SW6 264 B4
Lannoy Rd SE9 167 A3
Lanrick Rd E14 98 C1
Lanridge Rd SE2 124 D3
Lansbury Ave
Barking IG11 80 A1
Dagenham RM6 59 A4
Edmonton N18 33 C5
Feltham TW14 150 B5
Lansbury Cl NW10 67 A3
Lansbury Ct 4 SE28 124 B6
Lansbury Dr UB4 83 D3
Lansbury Gdns 1 E14 98 B1
Lansbury Ho 5 DA17 125 B1
Lansbury Rd EN3 6 D4
Lansbury Way N18 33 C5
Lanscombe Wlk SW8 270 A3
Lansdell Rd CR4 181 A1
Lansdown Cl KT12 194 C1
Lansdowne Ave DA7 146 D5
Orpington BR6 210 D1
Lansdowne Cl
Tolworth KT5 214 D6
Twickenham TW1 152 D3
Wimbledon SW20 178 D3
Lansdowne Copse 1
KT4 216 A6
Lansdowne Cres
W11 113 A6 244 B5
Lansdowne Ct 2 KT4 216 A6
Lansdowne Dr E8 74 A1
Lansdowne Gdns
SW8 138 A4 270 A2
Lansdowne Gr NW10 67 C4
Lansdowne Hill SE27 160 D1
Lansdowne Ho W11 244 C4
Enfield EN2 4 C3
Lansdowne La SE7 121 D1
Lansdowne Mews SE7 121 D1
W11 244 C4
Lansdowne Pl SE1 262 D6
Penge SE19 183 D3
Lansdowne Rd BR1 187 B3
E11 76 D6
E17 53 C3
E8 74 A2
N10 31 C1
N3 29 C3
W11 113 A6 244 B5
Chingford E4 19 C2
Croydon CR0 205 B1
Harrow HA1 42 C2
Hayes UB8 83 A1
Hounslow TW3 129 D2
Ilford IG3 57 D2
Stanmore HA7 25 C4
Tottenham N17 34 A2
Wanstead E18 55 A6
West Ewell KT19 215 B1
Wimbledon SW19,SW20 178 C3
Lansdowne Rise
W11 113 A6 244 B5
Lansdowne Row W1 248 D4
Lansdowne Sch SW9 138 B2
Lansdowne Terr WC1 240 B5
Lansdowne Way
SW4,SW8 138 A4 270 B1
Lansdowne Wlk
W11 113 B5 244 C4
Lansdowne Wood Cl 11
SE27 160 D1
Lansdown Ho 29 SE5 139 A3
Lansdown Rd E7 77 C1
Sidcup DA14 168 B1
Lansfield Ave N18 34 A6
Lanson Ct E11 76 D6
Lanson Ho HA8 26 C4
Lanswood Ct KT4 216 A6
Lantern Cl
Putney SW15 134 A1
Wembley HA0 65 D3
Lantern Ct 4 SW20 178 D2
Lantern Ho E14 119 C4
Lanterns Ct E14 119 C3
Lanterns The N12 29 D4
Lantern Way UB7 104 B4
Lant Ho SE1 252 A1
Lantry Ct 1 W3 110 D5
Lant St SE1 117 A4 252 B1
Lanvanor Rd SE15 140 C3
Lanyard Ho 3 SE8 119 B2
Lapford Cl W9 91 B3
Lapponum Wlk UB4 84 D2
Lapsang SE1 253 D3
Lapse Wood Wlk SE22 162 B3
Lapstone Gdns HA3 43 C3
Lapwing Ct NW9 27 C1
Tolworth KT6 214 C5
Lapwing Twr 31 SE8 141 B6
Lapwing Way UB4 84 D1
Lapworth 2 N11 31 B6
Lapworth Ct W2 91 D2
Lara Cl SE13 164 A5
Chessington KT9 214 A1
Larbert Rd SW16 181 C3
Larch Ave W3 111 C5
Larch Cl E13 99 C3
N11 31 A3
7 N19 71 C6
15 SE8 141 B6
Balham SW12 159 B2
Larch Cres Hayes UB4 84 D2
West Ewell KT19 214 D2
Larch Ct 41 W2 91 C2
Larch Dene BR6 226 C6
Larches Ave SW14 133 B1
Larches The
Edmonton N13 17 A1
Hillingdon UB10 82 D5
Larchfield Ho 2 N5 73 A3
Larch Gn NW9 27 C2
Larch Gr DA15 167 D3
Larch Ho 17 SE16 118 C4
Hayes UB4 84 C2
Larchmore Ct N19 72 A6
Larch Rd E10 75 C6
NW2 68 C4
Larch Tree Way CR0 223 C5
Larchvale Ct 4 SM2 217 D1
Larch Way BR2 210 C2
Larchwood Rd SE9 166 D2
Larcombe Cl CR0 221 D4
Larcom St
SE17 117 A2 262 B3
Larden Rd W3 111 C4
La Retraite RC Girls Sch
SW12 159 C4
Largewood Ave KT6 214 C6
Larissa St SE17 262 D3
Larix Ct NW10 90 A6
Larkbere Rd SE26 185 A6
Larken Cl WD23 8 A3
Larken Dr WD23 8 A3
Larkfield Ave HA3 43 B6
Larkfield Cl BR2 225 A6
Larkfield Rd DA14 167 D1
Richmond TW9 132 A1
Lark Hall Inf Sch SW4 137 D3
Lark Hall Jun Sch
SW4 138 A3
Larkhall La
SW4 138 A4 270 A1
Larkhall Rise SW4 137 D3
Larkham Cl TW13 149 C1
Lark Row E2 96 C6
Larksfield Gr EN1 6 B4
Larks Gr IG11 79 C1
Larkshall Bsns Ctr 2
E4 20 B2
Larkshall Cres E4 36 A6
Larkshall Ct E4 36 A5
Larkshall Rd E4 36 B6
Larkspur Cl 4 E6 100 A2
NW9 44 D4
Ruislip HA4 39 A2
Tottenham N17 33 B3
Larkspur Ct SM6 219 B1
Larkspur Gr HA8 27 A6
Larkspur Way KT19 215 A3
Larkswood Ct E4 36 B5
Larkswood Jun & Inf Sch
E4 35 D6
Larkswood Rd E4 35 D6
Larkswood Rise HA5 40 C5
Lark Way SM5 202 C2
Larkway Cl NW9 45 B5
Larmenier & Sacred Heart
RC Prim Sch W6 112 D2
Larnaca Ho SE1 263 C6
Larnach Rd W6 134 D6
Larne Rd HA4 39 D2
Larpent Ave SW15 156 C6
Larwood Cl UB6 64 B3
La Saint Union Rc Sec Sch
NW5 71 A5
Lascelles Ave HA1 42 B2
Lascelles Cl E11 76 B6
Lascelles Ho NW1 237
Lascott's Rd N22 32
Lashford Ho HA8 27 A
Lassa Rd SE9 166
Lassell St SE10 120
Lasseter Pl SE3 142 D
Latchett Rd E18 37 B
Latchingdon Ct E17 52 D
Latchmere Cl KT2,
TW10 176 A
Latchmere Jun & Inf Schs
KT2 176 B
Latchmere La KT2,
TW10 176 B
Latchmere Rd SW11 136 D
Kingston KT2 176
Latchmere St 5
SW11 136 D
Lateward Rd TW8 131 D
Latham Cl E6 100 A
4 Twickenham TW1 153 A
Latham Ct
2 Bowes Park N11 32 A
7 Northolt UB5 84 D
Latham Ho E1 96 D
18 E17 53 D
Latham Rd DA6 169 C
Twickenham TW1 152 D
Latham's Way CR0 220 B
Lathkill Cl EN1 18 A
Lathkill Ct BR3 185 B
Lathom Jun Sch E6 78 A
Lathom Rd E6 78 B
Lathwood Ho 6 SE26 184 B5
Latimer SE17 263 A
Latimer Ave E6 100 B6
Latimer Cl
North Cheam KT4 216 B
Pinner HA5 22 C
Latimer Gdns HA5 22 C2
Latimer Ho 11 E9 74 D2
W11 244 D5
Latimer Pl W10 90 C
Latimer Rd E7 77 B4
N15 51 C3
W10 90 C1
Barnet EN5 1 D2
Croydon CR0 220 D5
Teddington TW11 174 D5
Wimbledon SW19 179 D4
Latimer Road Sta
W10 112 D6
Latona Rd SE15 140 A6
La Tourne Gdns BR6 227 A5
Lattimer Pl W4 133 C6
Latton Cl KT12 195 A2
Latymer All Saints CE Prim
Sch N9 17 D2
Latymer Ct W6 112 D2
Latymer Rd N9 17 D3
Latymer Sch The N9 17 C2
Latymer Upper Sch
W6 112 A1
Latymer Way N9 17 C2
Lauder Cl UB5 84 D5
Lauder Ct N14 16 A4
Lauderdale Dr TW10 153 D1
Lauderdale Mans W9 91 D4
Lauderdale Rd W9 91 D4
Lauderdale Twr EC2 242 A4
Laud St SE11 116 B1 260 C2
Croydon CR0 221 A5
Laughton Ho 11 SW2 160 C5
Laughton Rd UB5 84 D6
Launcelot Prim Sch
BR1 187 A6
Launcelot Rd BR1,
SE12 187 A6
Launcelot St SE1 251 A1
Launceston Ct CR7 204 C3
Launceston Gdns UB6 65 C1
Launceston Pl
W8 114 A3 256 A5
Launceston Rd UB6 87 C6
Launch St E14 120 A3
Laundress La N16 74 A5
Laundry La 15 N1 73 A1
Laundry Mews SE23 162 D4
Laundry Rd
W6 135 A6 264 A5
Laura Cl Enfield EN1 17 C6
Wanstead E11 55 C4
Lauradale Rd N2 48 D5
Laura Pl E5 74 C4
Laurel Ave TW1 152 D3
Laurel Bank Gdns 3
SW6 135 B3
Laurel Bank Rd EN2 5 B4
Laurel Cl 5 N19 71 C6
Sidcup DA14 168 A1
Upper Tooting SW17 180 C5
Laurel Cres CR0 223 C5
Laurel Ct E8 73 D2
2 Putney SW15 156 D6
South Norwood SE25 205 C4
8 Wembley HA0 88 A5
Laurel Dr N21 16 C4
Laurel Gdns NW7 11 B1
Chingford E4 19 D4

urel Gdns *continued*
aling W7 .108 C5
ounslow TW4 .129 A1
urel Gr
orest Hill SE26 .185 A6
enge SE20 .184 C3
urel Ho 5 NW3 .69 D2
9 SE8 .141 B6
Morden SM4 .201 D4
urel La UB7 .104 A2
urel Manor SM2 .218 A1
urel Mead Ct 8 E18 .37 A2
urel Pk HA3 .24 D3
urel Rd Barnes SW13 134 A3
eddington TW12 .174 B5
Wimbledon SW20 .178 B2
urel St E8 .73 D2
urels The 8 BR1 .187 B2
BR2 .209 A5
N3 .29 D4
Bushey WD23 .8 C2
8 Belvedere DA17 .125 C1
Buckhurst Hill IG9 .21 C3
urel View N12 .13 D1
urel Way E18 .54 D5
N20 .13 C1
aurence Ct E10 .53 D2
aurence Mews 12
W12 .112 A4
aurence Pountney Hill
EC4 .252 C6
aurence Pountney La
EC4 .252 D6
aurie Gr SE14 .141 A4
aurie Ho SE1 .261 D5
W8 .113 C5 245 A3
aurie Rd W7 .86 C2
aurier Rd NW5 .71 B5
Croydon CR0 .205 D2
aurimel Cl HA7 .25 B4
aurino Pl WD23 .8 A2
auriston Lo NW6 .69 B2
auriston Rd E9 .74 D1
Wimbledon SW19 .178 D4
Lauriston Sch E9 .96 D6
ausanne Rd N8 .50 C5
SE15 .140 C4
Lavenham Ho E17 .35 D2
Lavell St N16 .73 B4
Lavender Ave NW9 .45 A1
Mitcham CR4 .180 D2
North Cheam KT4,SM3 .216 C5
Lavender Cl BR2 .210 A3
SW3 .266 D5
Wallington SM5 .219 B4
Lavender Ct SW4 .270 B1
East Molesey KT8 .195 D6
Lavender Gdns SW11 .136 D1
Enfield EN2 .4 D4
Stanmore HA3 .24 C4
Lavender Gr E8 .74 A1
Mitcham CR4 .180 C2
Lavender Hill SW11 .137 A2
Enfield EN2 .4 D4
Lavender Ho 14 SE16 .118 D5
Lavender Pl IG1 .78 D3
Lavender Prim Sch EN2 .5 C5
Lavender Rd SE16 .119 A5
SW11 .136 B2
Enfield EN2 .5 B4
Hillingdon UB8 .82 B2
Sutton SM1 .218 B4
Thornton Heath CR0 .204 B3
Wallington SM5 .219 A4
West Ewell KT19 .214 D2
Lavender Rise UB7 .104 C4
Lavender St E15 .76 C2
Lavender Sweep
SW11 .136 D1
Lavender Terr 12
SW11 .136 C2
Lavender Vale SM6 .219 D2
Lavender Way CR0 .206 D3
Lavender Wlk SW11 .136 D1
Lavendon Ho NW8 .237 B6
Lavengro Rd SE27 .161 A2
Lavenham Ho E17 .35 D2
Lavenham Rd SW18 .157 C3
Lavernock Rd DA7 .147 C3
Lavers Rd N16 .73 C5
Laverstoke Gdns
SW15 .156 A4
Laverton Mews SW5 .255 D3
Laverton Pl SW5 .255 D3
Lavidge Rd SE9 .166 B2
Lavina Gr N1 .233 C4
Lavington Cl E9 .75 B2
Lavington Rd
Ealing W13 .109 B5
Wallington CR0 .220 B4
Lavington St
SE1 .116 D5 251 D3
Lavinia Ct BR1 .186 C3
Lavisham Ho BR1 .187 B5
Lawdale Jun Sch E2 .96 A4
Lawdon Gdns CR0 .220 D4
Lawford Cl SM6 .220 A1
Lawford Rd N1 .73 C1
NW5 .71 C2
Lawford Rd *continued*
Chiswick W4 .133 A5
Lawfords Wharf 15
NW1 .71 C1
Lawless Ho 5 E14 .120 A6
Lawless St 11 E14 .119 D6
Lawley Ho 10 TW1 .153 D5
Lawley Rd N14 .15 B4
Lawley St E5 .74 C4
Lawman Ct 2 TW9 .132 B4
Lawn Cl BR1 .187 B3
Edmonton N9 .17 D4
Kingston KT3 .177 C1
Ruislip HA4 .61 D5
Lawn Cres TW9 .132 C3
Lawn Farm Gr RM6 .59 A5
Lawnfield NW6 .68 D1
Lawn Gdns W7 .108 C5
Lawn House Cl E14 .120 A4
Lawn La SW8 .138 B6 270 C6
Lawn Rd NW3 .70 D3
Beckenham BR3 .185 B3
Lawns Ct HA9 .66 C6
Lawnside SE3 .142 D1
Lawns The N16 .73 C3
SE3 .142 D2
Belmont SM2 .217 A1
Chingford E4 .35 C5
Harrow HA5 .23 D3
Sidcup DA14 .190 B6
South Norwood SE19 .183 B2
1 Wimbledon SW19 .179 B5
Lawn Terr SE3 .142 C2
Lawn The UB2 .107 C1
Lawn Vale HA5 .23 A1
Lawrence Ave E17 .34 D2
NW7 .27 D6
Edmonton N13 .32 D6
Little Ilford E12 .78 C4
New Malden KT3 .199 C2
Lawrence Camp Ct N20 14 B1
Lawrence Cl E3 .97 C5
N15 .51 C5
6 W12 .112 B6
Lawrence Cres
Dagenham RM10 .81 D5
Edgware HA8 .26 C1
Lawrence Ct N10 .49 C6
N16 .73 D5
NW7 .27 C5
4 W3 .111 A3
Lawrence Dr UB10 .61 A4
Lawrence Est TW4 .128 C1
Lawrence Gdns NW7 .11 D1
Lawrence Hill E4 .19 C2
Lawrence Ho SW1 .259 D3
Bowes Park N22 .32 B4
Lawrence La EC2 .242 B2
Lawrence Mans SW3 .267 A5
Lawrence Pl N1 .233 B6
Lawrence Rd DA8 .147 D5
E13 .99 B6
E6 .100 A6
N15 .51 C5
W5 .109 D2
Edmonton N18 .34 B6
Hampton TW12 .173 B3
Hayes BR4 .225 A4
Hayes UB4 .83 A5
Hounslow TW4 .128 C1
Pinner HA5 .40 D4
Richmond TW10 .175 C6
South Norwood SE25 .205 D5
Lawrence's Bldgs 1
N16 .73 D5
Lawrence St E16 .98 D2
NW7 .27 D6
SW3 .136 C6 267 A5
Lawrence Trad Est
SE10 .120 C2
Lawrence Way NW10 .67 B5
Lawrence Weaver Cl
SM4 .201 C3
Lawrence Yd N15 .51 C5
Lawrie Ct HA3 .24 D3
Lawrie Park Ave SE26 .184 B5
Lawrie Park Cres
SE26 .184 B5
Lawrie Park Gdns
SE26 .184 B5
Lawrie Park Rd SE26 .184 C5
Lawson Cl Newham E16 .99 C2
Wimbledon SW19 .156 D1
Lawson Ct 1 N4 .50 B1
13 Surbiton KT6 .197 D2
Lawson Gdns HA5 .40 B6
Lawson Ho 1 SE18 .144 C6
17 W12 .112 B6
Lawson Rd Enfield EN3 .6 C4
Southall UB1 .85 C3
Law St SE1 .117 B3 262 D6
Lawton Rd E10 .54 A1
E3 .97 A4
Barnet EN4 .2 B2
Laxcon Cl NW10 .67 B3
Laxey Rd BR6 .227 D2
Laxfield Ct E8 .96 A6
Laxley Cl SE5 .138 D5
Laxton Ct CR7 .205 A5
Laxton Path 1 SE4 .140 D1
Laxton Pl NW1 .238 D6
Layard Rd SE16 .118 B2
Enfield EN1 .5 D4
South Norwood CR7 .183 B1
Layard Sq SE16 .118 B2
Laycock Prim Sch N1 .72 D2
Laycock St N1 .72 C2
Layer Gdns W3 .110 C6
Layfield Cl NW4 .46 B2
Layfield Cres NW4 .46 B2
Layfield Ho 1 SE10 .121 A1
Layfield Rd NW4 .46 B2
Laymarsh Cl DA17 .125 B3
Laymead Cl UB5 .63 A2
Laystall Ct EC1 .241 A5
Laystall St EC1 .241 A5
Layton Cres CR0 .220 D3
Layton Ct TW8 .109 D1
Layton Pl TW9 .132 C4
Layton Rd
Brentford TW8 .109 D1
Hounslow TW3 .129 D1
Layton's La TW16 .171 D1
Layzell Wlk SE9 .165 D3
Lazar Wlk 2 N7 .72 B6
Leabank Cl HA1 .64 C5
Leabank Sq E9 .75 C2
Leabank View N15 .52 A3
Leabourne Rd N16 .52 A2
Lea Bridge Rd E10 .53 C2
Lea Cl TW2 .151 B4
Lea Cres HA4 .61 D4
Leacroft Ave SW12 .158 D4
Leacroft Cl
Southgate N21 .16 D2
3 Yiewsley UB7 .104 A6
Lea Ct 2 E13 .99 A4
3 W12 .111 C4
1 Chingford E4 .20 A2
3 Hillingdon UB10 .82 D3
Leadale Ave E4 .19 C2
Leadale Rd N16 .52 A3
Leadbeaters Cl N11 .30 D5
Leadbetter Ct 10 NW10 .67 B1
Leadenhall Mkt EC3 .243 A1
Leadenhall Pl EC3 .243 A1
Leadenhall St
EC3 .95 C1 243 A1
Leadenham Ct 15 E3 .97 C3
Leader Ave E12 .78 C3
Leadings The HA9 .67 A5
Leaf Cl KT7,KT8 .196 C4
Leaf Gr SE27 .182 C5
Leaf Ho 9 HA1 .42 D4
Leafield Cl SW16 .182 D4
Leafield La DA14 .169 B1
Leafield Rd
Merton SW19,SW20 .201 B6
Sutton SM1 .217 C6
Leafy Gr BR2 .225 C3
Leafy Oak Rd SE12 .165 C1
Leafy Way CR0 .221 D6
Lea Gdns HA9 .66 B4
Leagrave St E5 .74 C5
Lea Hall Gdns E10 .53 C1
Lea Hall Rd E10 .53 C1
Lea Ho E5 .52 C1
NW8 .237 A5
2 Edmonton N9 .18 A1
Leaholme Waye HA4 .39 A3
Leahurst Rd SE13 .164 C6
Lea Int E9 .75 C3
Leake St SE1 .116 B4 250 D2
SE1 .251 A1
Lealand Rd N15 .51 D3
Leamington Ave BR6 .227 C4
E17 .53 C4
Bromley BR1 .187 C5
Merton SM4 .201 B5
Leamington Cl E12 .78 A3
Bromley BR1 .187 C5
Hounslow TW3 .152 A6
Leamington Cres HA2 .63 B5
Leamington Ct W3 .89 B2
4 Forest Hill SE26 .162 A1
Leamington Gdns IG3 .79 D6
Leamington Ho 3 W11 91 B2
Edgware HA8 .26 B5
Leamington Pk W3 .89 B2
Leamington Pl UB4 .83 D3
Leamington Rd UB2 .106 D2
Leamington Rd Villas
W11 .91 B2
Leamington Villas
SE13 .164 C6
Leamore St W6 .112 C2
Leamouth Rd E6 .100 A2
South Bromley E14 .98 B1
Leander Ct 27 E9 .74 C1
7 NW9 .27 C2
SE8 .141 C4
5 Surbiton KT6 .197 D2
Leander Rd SW2 .160 C5
Northolt UB5 .85 C5
Thornton Heath CR7 .204 B5
Lea Rd
2 Beckenham BR3 .185 C1
Enfield EN2 .5 B4
Lea Rd *continued*
Southall UB2 .107 A2
Learner Dr HA2 .63 C6
Learoyd Gdns E6 .122 C6
Leary Ho SE11 .260 D1
Leas Cl KT9 .214 B1
Leas Dale SE9 .166 C1
Leas Gn BR7 .189 D4
Leaside Ave N10 .49 A5
Leaside Bsns Ctr EN3 .7 B3
Leaside Ct UB10 .82 D4
Leaside Ho 4 E5 .52 B1
Leaside Mans N10 .49 A6
Leaside Rd E5 .52 C1
Leasowes Rd E10 .53 C1
Leas The SE18 .144 D4
Leatherbottle Gn
DA18 .125 B3
Leather Cl CR4 .181 A1
Leatherdale St 29 E1 .96 C3
Leather Gdns E15 .98 C6
Leatherhead Cl N16 .51 D1
Leatherhead Rd KT9 .213 D1
Leather La EC1 .94 C2 241 B4
Leathermarket Ct SE1 253 A1
Leathermarket St
SE1 .117 C4 253 A1
Leathersellers Cl EN5 .1 A2
Leathsale Rd HA2 .63 D5
Leathwaite Rd SW11 .158 D6
Leathwell Rd SE8 .141 D3
Lea Valley Prim Sch
N17 .34 A3
Lea Valley Rd EN3 .19 B5
Lea Valley Riding Sch
E10 .52 D1
Lea Valley Technopark
N17 .52 A6
Lea Valley Trad Est
N18 .34 D5
Leaveland Cl BR3 .207 C5
Leaver Gdns UB6 .86 C5
Leavesden Rd HA7 .25 A4
Leaview Ct 7 E4 .20 A3
Lea View Ho E5 .52 B1
Lebanon Ave TW13 .172 D5
Lebanon Ct 10 TW1 .153 B4
Lebanon Gdns SW18 .157 C5
Lebanon Pk TW1 .153 B4
Lebanon Rd SW18 .157 C6
Croydon CR0 .205 C1
Lebanon Road Sta
CR0 .221 C6
Lebrun Sq SE3 .143 B2
Lebus Ho NW8 .230 A3
Le Chateau CR0 .221 B5
Lechmere App IG8 .37 D1
Lechmere Ave IG8 .37 D1
Lechmere Rd NW2 .68 B2
Leckford Rd SW18 .158 A3
Leckhampton Pl 23
SW2 .160 C4
Leckwith Ave DA17 .147 A6
Lecky St SW7 .114 B1 256 C2
Leclair Ho SE3 .143 B2
L'Ecole des Petits
SW6 .135 D3
Leconfield Ave SW13,
SW15 .133 D2
Leconfield Ho SE5 .139 C2
Leconfield Rd N5 .73 B4
Leda Ave EN3 .6 D5
Leda Ct 9 SW9 .138 C5
Ledalle Ho NW2 .68 B5
Ledam Bldg EC1 .241 A4
Leda Rd SE18 .122 B3
Ledbury Ho 12 SE22 .139 C2
Ledbury Mews N W11 .91 C1
Ledbury Mews W
W11 .245 A6
Ledbury Pl 10 CR0 .221 A4
Ledbury Rd W11 .91 C1
Croydon CR0 .221 B4
Ledbury St SE15 .140 A5
Ledo Ho 1 N16 .73 B4
Ledrington Rd SE19 .184 A4
Ledway Dr HA9 .44 B2
Lee Ave RM6 .59 A3
Leechcroft Ave DA15 .167 D6
Leechcroft Rd SM6 .219 A5
Lee Church St SE13 .142 C1
Lee Cl E17 .34 D2
New Barnet EN5 .2 A1
Lee Conservancy Rd E9 75 B3
Leecroft Rd EN5 .1 A1
Leeds Ct EC1 .241 C5
Carshalton SM5 .218 D5
Catford SE6 .163 D1
Leeds Rd IG1 .57 B1
Leeds St N18 .34 A5
Leegate SE12 .164 D6
Lee Green SE12 .142 D1
Lee High Rd SE12,SE13 142 C1
Lee Ho 8 N19 .71 D3
Leeke St WC1 .94 B4 233 C2
Leeland Mans W13 .109 A5
Leeland Rd W13 .109 A5
Leeland Terr W13 .109 A5
Leeland Way NW10 .67 D4
Lee Manor Sch SE13 .164 C5
Leemount Cl NW4 .46 D5
Lee Park Way N9,N18 .19 A1
Lee Pk SE3 .142 D2
Lee Rd NW7 .28 D3
SE3 .142 D1
Enfield EN1 .18 A5
Merton SW19 .179 D2
Wembley UB6 .87 C6
Leerdam Dr E14 .120 A3
Lees Ct W1 .248 A6
Lees Ho SE17 .262 D1
Leeside EN5 .13 A5
Leeside Cres NW11 .47 B4
Leeside Ind Est N17 .34 B3
Leeside Rd N17 .34 B3
Leeside Trad Est N17 .34 C3
Leeside Works N17 .34 C3
Leeson Ho 7 TW1 .153 B4
Leeson Rd 12 SE24 .138 C1
Leesons Hill BR5,BR7 .211 D6
Leesons Way BR5 .189 D1
Lees Par UB10 .82 D3
Lees Pl W1 .115 A6 248 A6
Lees Rd UB8 .82 D3
Lee St E8 .95 D6
Lee Sta SE12 .165 A5
Lees The CR0 .223 B6
Leet Ct N16 .73 B4
Lee Terr SE3 .142 C2
Lee Valley L Ctr N9 .19 A3
Lee Valley Sp Ctr E15 .75 D4
Leeve Ho 7 W9 .91 B4
Lee View EN2 .4 D4
Leeward Ct 3 E1 .118 A5
Leeward Gdns SW19 .179 B5
Leeway SE8 .119 B1
Leeway Cl HA5 .23 B3
Leewood Cl SE12 .165 A5
Lefevre Wlk E3 .97 B6
Leffern Rd W12 .112 A4
Leff Ho 7 NW6 .69 A1
Lefroy Ho SE1 .252 A1
Lefroy Rd W12 .111 D4
Legard Rd N5 .72 D5
Legat Ct N4 .51 A4
Legatt Rd SE9 .165 D6
Leggatt Rd E15 .98 A5
Legge St SE13 .164 A6
Leghorn Rd NW10 .90 A5
SE18 .123 B1
Legion Cl N1 .72 C1
Legion Ct SM4 .201 C3
Legion Rd UB6 .86 A5
Legion Terr E3 .97 C6
Legion Way N12 .30 C3
Legrace Ave TW4,TW5 128 D3
Leicester Ave CR4 .204 A5
Leicester Cl KT4 .216 C4
Leicester Ct 46 W2 .91 C2
WC2 .249 D6
11 Twickenham TW1 .153 D5
Leicester Gdns IG3 .57 C2
Leicester Ho 4 SW9 .138 D2
5 Putney SW15 .156 C4
2 Thames Ditton KT7 .197 A2
Leicester Mews N2 .48 C6
Leicester Pl WC2 .249 D6
Leicester Rd N2 .48 C6
NW10 .67 B1
Barnet EN5 .1 D1
Croydon CR0 .205 C2
Wanstead E11 .55 B4
Leicester Sq★
WC2 .115 D6 249 D5
Leicester Square Sta
WC2 .115 D6 249 D6
Leicester St WC2 .249 D6
Leigham Ave SW16 .160 A1
Leigham Cl SW16 .182 B6
Leigham Court Rd
SW16 .182 C6
Leigham Dr TW7 .130 C5
Leigham Hall 3 SW16 160 A1
Leigham Hall Par 2
SW16 .160 A1
Leigham Vale SE27,
SW16,SW2 .160 C2
Leigh Ave IG4 .55 D5
Leigh Cl KT3 .199 B5
Leigh Cres CR0 .223 D1
Leigh Ct 22 SW2 .160 C5
Harrow HA2 .42 C1
3 Woodford E18 .37 A1
Leighfield Ho 5 N4 .51 A2
Leigh Gdns NW10 .90 C5
Leigh Ho
4 Kingston KT2 .176 D4
9 Putney SW15 .156 A6
Leigh Hunt Dr N14 .15 D3
Leigh Orchard Cl
SW16 .160 B1
Leigh Pl DA16 .146 A3
EC1 .241 A4
Leigh Rd E10 .54 A2
N5 .72 D4
Isleworth TW3 .130 B1
Wallend E6 .78 C2
Leigh St WC1 .94 A4 233 A1
Leigh The KT2 .177 C3
Leighton Ave
Little Ilford E12 .78 C3
Pinner HA5 .41 A6
Leighton Cl HA8 .26 C1
Leighton Cres NW5 .71 C3
Leighton Gdns NW10 .90 C5
Thornton Heath CR0 .204 D1
Leighton Gr NW5 .71 C3
Leighton Ho 7 KT6 .198 A3
Leighton House (Art Gall &
Mus)★ W14 .254 D6
Leighton Pl NW5 .71 C3
Leighton Rd NW5 .71 C3
Ealing W13 .109 A4
Enfield EN1 .18 A6
Harrow HA3 .24 B1
Leighton St CR0 .204 D1
Leila Parnell Pl 14
SE7 .143 C6
Leinster Ave SW14 .133 A1
Leinster Ct NW6 .91 C4
Leinster Gdns
W2 .114 A6 246 A6
Leinster Mews W2 .246 A6
Leinster Pl W2 .236 A1
Leinster Rd N10 .49 B5
Leinster Sq W2 .91 D1
Leinster Terr W2 .246 A6
Leisure Way N12 .30 B3
Leitch Ho 8 NW8 .70 B1
Leith Cl NW9 .45 B1
Leithcote Gdns SW16 .182 B6
Leithcote Path SW16 .160 B1
Leith Hill BR5 .190 A2
Leith Hill Gn BR5 .190 A2
Leith Ho 7 N7 .71 D3
13 Streatham SW2 .160 B4
Leith Mans W9 .91 D4
Leith Rd N22 .32 D2
Leith Towers 11 SM2 .217 D1
Leith Yd 3 NW6 .91 C6
Lela Ave TW4,TW5 .128 C3
Lelitia Cl E8 .96 A6
Lelland Ho 8 SE7 .122 A2
Lely Ho 3 UB5 .84 D5
Leman St E1 .96 A1
Lemark Cl HA7 .25 C4
Le May Ave SE12 .165 B1
Lemmon Rd SE10 .142 C6
Lemna Ct E11 .54 C2
Lemna Rd E11 .54 C2
Le Moal Ho 23 E1 .96 C2
Lemon Gr TW14 .150 A3
Lemonwell Ct SE9 .167 A6
Lemonwell Dr SE9 .167 A6
Lemsford Cl N15 .52 A4
Lemsford Ct N4 .73 A6
Lena Cres N9 .18 C2
Lena Gardens Prim Sch
W6 .112 C3
Lena Gdns W6 .112 C3
Lena Kennedy Cl E4 .36 A4
Len Clifton Ho 13
SE18 .122 B2
Lendal Terr 7 SW4 .137 D2
Lenelby Rd KT6 .198 C1
Len Freeman Pl SW6 .264 C5
Lenham 11 NW5 .71 A2
Lenham Ho SE1 .252 D1
Lenham Rd DA7 .147 B6
SE12 .142 D1
South Norwood CR7 .183 B1
Sutton SM1 .218 A3
Lennard Ave BR4 .224 C6
Lennard Cl BR4 .224 C6
Lennard Rd BR2 .210 B1
Croydon CR0 .205 A1
Penge BR3 .185 A4
Lennon Rd NW2 .68 C2
Lennox Gdns NW10 .67 D4
SW1 .114 D3 257 C5
Croydon CR0 .220 D4
Redbridge IG1 .56 B1
Lennox Gdns Mews
SW1 .257 C4
Lennox Ho 10 E9 .74 C2
7 Belvedere DA17 .125 C3
Lennox Rd E17 .53 C3
N4,N7 .72 C6
Lenor Cl DA6 .147 A1
Lensbury Way SE2 .124 D3
Lens Rd E7 .77 C1
Lenthall Ho SW1 .259 B1
Lenthall Rd E8 .74 A1
Lenthorp Rd SE10 .120 D2
Lentmead Rd BR1 .164 D1
Lenton Rise TW9 .132 A2
Lenton St SE18 .123 B2
Len Williams Ct NW6 .91 C5
Leo Ct 4 TW8 .131 D5
Leof Cres SE6 .185 D5
Leominster Rd SM4 .202 A3
Leominster Wlk SM4 .202 A3
Leonard Ave SM4 .202 A4
Leonard Ct W8 .255 A6

Leonard Ct *continued*
WC1 240 A6
Leonard Day Ho 3
NW5 71 B2
Leonard Pl 6 N16 73 C4
Leonard Rd E7 77 A4
Chingford E4 35 C4
Edmonton N9 18 A1
Mitcham CR4,SW16 181 C2
Southall UB2 106 D2
Leonard Robbins Path 3
SE28 124 B6
Leonard St E16 122 A5
EC2 95 B3 242 D6
Leonora Ho W9 236 A6
Leontine Cl SE15 140 A5
Leopards Ct EC1 241 A4
Leopold Ave SW19 179 B5
Leopold Bldgs 14 E2 95 D4
Leopold Mews E9 96 C6
Leopold Prim Sch
NW10 67 D1
Leopold Rd E17 53 C4
N2 48 B6
NW10 67 C1
Ealing W5 110 B5
Edmonton N18 34 B5
Wimbledon SW19 179 B5
Leopold St E3 97 B2
Leopold Terr SW19 179 C5
Leopold Wlk SE11 260 C1
Leo St SE15 140 B5
Leo Yd EC1 241 D5
Leppoc Rd SW4 159 D6
Leroy St SE1 117 C2 263 A4
Lerry Cl W14 264 D6
Lerwick Ct 4 EN1 17 C6
Lerwick Ho SW18 136 A1
Lescombe Cl SE23 163 A1
Lescombe Rd SE23,
SE6 163 A1
Lesley Cl DA5 169 D4
Lesley Ct 8 SM6 219 B4
Leslie Gdns SM2 217 C1
Leslie Gr CR0 205 C1
Leslie Grove Pl CR0 205 C1
Leslie Park Rd CR0 205 C1
Leslie Rd E11 76 B4
N2 48 B6
Newham E16 99 B1
Leslie Smith Sq 7
SE18 144 C6
Lessar Ave SW4 159 C5
Lessar Ct SW4 159 C5
Lessingham Ave
Ilford IG5 56 C6
Upper Tooting SW17 181 A6
Lessing St SE23 163 A4
Lessness Ave DA7 146 D5
Lessness Heath Prim Sch
DA17 125 C1
Lessness Pk DA17 125 C1
Lessness Rd
Belvedere DA17 125 C1
Morden SM4 202 A4
Lester Ave E16 98 C3
Lester Ct 42 E3 97 D4
Lester Ho IG8 36 B3
Lestock Ho SE3 143 D4
Lestor Ct TW7 130 D2
Leswin Pl N16 73 D5
Leswin Rd N16 73 D5
Letchford Gdns NW10 90 A4
Letchford Mews NW10 90 A4
Letchmore Ho W10 90 C3
Letchworth Ave TW14 149 D4
Letchworth Cl BR2 209 A4
South Oxhey WD19 22 D5
Letchworth Dr BR2 209 A4
Letchworth St SW17 180 D6
Lethaby Ho 15 SW4 138 B1
Lethbridge Cl SE13 142 A3
Letterstone Rd SW6 264 C3
Lettice St SW6 135 B4 264 D1
Lett Rd E15 76 B1
Lettsom St SE5 139 C3
Lettsom Wlk 1 E13 99 A5
Leucha Rd E17 53 A4
Levana Cl SW19 157 A3
Levant Ho 17 E1 96 D3
Levehurst Ho SE27 183 A5
Levehurst Way SW4,
SW9 138 A3
Leven Cl WD19 22 D5
Levendale Rd SE23 163 B2
Leven Rd E14 98 B1
Leven Way UB3 83 C1
Lever Ct 16 E9 74 D2
Leverett St SW3 257 B4
Leverholme Gdns SE9 188 C6
Leverington Pl N1 235 D1
Leverson St SW16 181 C4
Lever St EC1 95 A4 235 A1
Leverstock Ho SW3 257 B2
Leverton Pl NW5 71 C3
Leverton St NW5 71 C3
Levett Gdns IG3 80 A5
Levett Ho 8 SW16 181 C5
Levett Rd IG11 79 C2
Levine Gdns IG11 102 D5
Levison Way 2 N19 49 D1
Levita Ho NW1 232 D2
Levyne Ct EC1 241 A6
Lewes Cl UB5 63 C2
Lewes Ct 3 CR4 202 D6
Lewesdon Cl 13 SW19 156 D3
Lewes Ho SE1 253 B2
SE15 140 A6
Lewes Rd BR1 187 D1
N12 30 C5
Leweston Pl N16 51 D2
Lewey Ho E3 97 B3
Lewgars Ave NW9 45 A3
Lewin Ct SW16 182 A4
Lewing Cl BR6 211 C1
Lewin Rd DA6 147 A1
Mortlake SW14 133 B2
Streatham SW16 181 D4
Lewis Ave E17 35 C2
Lewis Cl N14 15 C4
Lewis Cres NW10 67 B3
Lewis Ct 5 SE16 118 B1
Lewis Gdns N2 30 B1
Lewis Gr SE13 142 A2
Lewisham Bridge Prim Sch
SE13 141 D2
Lewisham Bsns Ctr
SE14 140 D6
Lewisham Coll SE4 141 C3
Lewisham Ctr SE13 142 A2
Lewisham High St
SE13 163 D6
Lewisham Hill SE13 142 A3
Lewisham Hospl SE13 163 D6
Lewisham Pk SE13 164 A5
Lewisham Rd SE13 142 A3
Lewisham St SW1 249 D1
Lewisham Sta SE13 142 A2
Lewisham Way SE4,
SE14 141 B4
Lewis King Ho BR1 187 B3
Lewis Pl E8 74 A3
Lewis Rd Bexley DA16 146 C2
Mitcham CR4 180 C1
18 Richmond TW10 153 D6
Sidcup DA14 168 C1
Southall UB1 107 A4
Sutton SM1 217 D4
Lewis Silkin Ho 9
SE15 140 C6
Lewis Sports & L Ctr
SE19 183 D2
Lewis St NW1 71 B2
Lewis Way RM10 81 D2
Lexden Dr RM6 58 B3
Lexden Rd Acton W3 110 D5
Mitcham CR4 203 D5
Lexfield Ho N5 73 A4
Lexham Gardens Mews
W8 255 D5
Lexham Gdns
W8 113 D2 255 C4
Lexham Ho 9 IG11 101 B6
Lexham Mews
W8 113 C2 255 B4
Lexham Wlk W8 255 D5
Lexington St
W1 115 C6 249 B6
Lexton Gdns SW12 159 D3
Leyborne Ave W13 109 C4
Leyborne Pk TW9 132 C4
Leybourne Cl BR2 209 A3
Leybourne Ho 15 E14 97 B1
19 SE15 140 C6
Leybourne Rd E11 54 D1
16 NW1 71 B1
NW9 44 C4
Hillingdon UB10 83 A6
Leybourne St 5 NW1 71 B1
Leybridge Ct SE12 165 A6
Leyburn Cl E17 53 D5
Leyburn Gdns CR0 221 C6
Leyburn Gr N18 34 A4
Leyburn Ho 1 SE18 144 A5
Leyburn Rd N18 34 B4
Leyden Mans 3 N19 50 A2
Leyden St E1 95 D2 243 C3
Leydon Cl SE16 118 D5
Leyes Rd E16 99 D1
Leyfield KT4 199 D1
Ley Ho SE1 252 A1
Leyland Ave EN3 7 A3
Leyland Gdns IG8 37 C5
Leyland Ho 5 E14 119 D6
Leyland Rd SE12 165 A6
Leylands SW18 157 B5
Leylang Rd SE14 140 D5
Leys Cl HA1 42 B4
Leys Ct 10 SW9 138 C3
Leysdown 9 NW5 71 A2
Leysdown Ho SE17 263 B2
Leysdown Rd SE9 166 B2
Leysfield Rd W12 112 A4
Leys Gdns EN4 15 A6
Leyspring Rd E11 54 D1
Leys Rd E EN3 7 A4
Leys Rd W EN3 7 A4
Ley St Ilford IG1 78 D6
Ilford IG1,IG2 57 B1
Leys The N2 48 A5
Harrow HA3 44 B3
Leyswood Dr IG2 57 C4
Leythe Rd W3 111 A4
Leyton Bsns Ctr E10 75 C6
Leyton Ct SE23 162 C3
Leyton Grange E10 53 C1
Leyton Green Rd E10 54 A3
Leyton Ind Village E10 52 D2
Leyton Midland Road Sta
E10 54 A2
Leyton Park Rd E10 76 A5
Leyton Rd E15 76 B2
Merton SW19 180 A3
Leyton Sixth Form Coll
E10 54 B3
Leyton Sta E11 76 A5
Leyton Stadium (Leyton
Orient FC) E10 75 D5
Leytonstone High Road Sta
E11 76 C6
Leytonstone Rd E15 76 C3
Leytonstone Sch E11 54 C3
Leytonstone Sta E11 54 C1
Leyton Town Ctr E10 76 A5
Leywick St E15 98 C5
Lezayre Rd BR6 227 D2
Liardet St SE14 141 A6
Liberia Rd N5 72 D2
Liberty Ave SW19 180 B2
Liberty Ct IG11 102 C5
Liberty Ctr HA0 88 B6
Liberty Mews SW12 159 B5
Liberty Mid Sch CR4 180 C1
Liberty Pl 18 E1 118 A6
Liberty St SW9 138 B4 270 D2
Libra Ct E4 35 C6
Libra Rd E13 99 A5
6 E3 97 B5
Library Ct N17 51 D6
Library Mans 4 W12 112 C4
Library Par NW10 89 C6
Library Pl E1 118 B6
Library St SE1 116 D4 251 D1
Lichen Ct IG6 56 D6
Lichfield Cl EN4 2 D2
Lichfield Ct
Kingston KT6 198 A4
Richmond TW9 132 A1
Lichfield Gdns TW10,
TW9 154 A6
Lichfield Gr N3 29 C1
Lichfield Ho 28 SE5 139 A3
Lichfield Rd E3 97 A4
E6 99 D4
NW2 69 A4
Dagenham RM8 80 C5
Edmonton N9 18 A2
Hounslow TW4 128 C2
Northwood HA6 40 A6
Richmond TW9 132 B4
Woodford IG8 36 C6
Lichfield Terr 1 TW9 154 A6
Lichlade Cl 7 BR6 227 D4
Lichport Ct N4 50 D1
Lickey Ho W14 264 D6
Lidbury Rd NW7 29 A4
Lidcote Gdns 22 SW9 138 B3
Liddall Way UB7 104 B5
Liddell Cl HA3 43 D6
Liddell Gdns NW10 90 C5
Liddell Rd NW6 69 C2
Lidding Rd HA3 43 D4
Liddington Rd E15 98 D6
Liddlesdale Ho E 6
KT2 176 D2
Liddlesdale Ho W 5
KT2 176 D2
Liddon Rd BR1 209 D6
E13 99 B4
Liden Cl E10,E17 53 B1
Lidfield Rd N16 73 B4
Lidgate Rd 21 SE15 139 D5
Lidiard Rd SW18 158 A2
Lidlington Pl NW1 232 B3
Lido Sq N17 33 B1
Lidyard Rd N19 49 C1
Liffey Ct NW10 68 A1
Liffler Rd SE18 123 C1
Liffords Pl SW13 133 D3
Lifford St SW15 134 D1
Lightcliffe Rd N13 16 C1
Lighter Cl 16 SE16 119 A2
Lighterman Mews 13
E1 96 D1
Lighterman's Rd E14 119 D4
Lighterman's Wlk
SW18 135 C1
Lightfoot Rd N8 50 A4
Lightley Cl HA0 88 B6
Ligonier St E2 243 C6
Lilac Cl E4 35 B4
Lilac Ct 4 E13 99 C6
Lilac Gdns W5 109 D3
Croydon CR0 223 C5
Lilac Gdns *continued*
Hayes UB3 83 C1
Lilac Ho SE4 141 B2
Lilac Pl SE11 116 B2 260 C3
Yiewsley UB7 104 B6
Lilac St W12 112 A6
Lilburn Ct SW15 134 D2
Lilburne Gdns SE9 166 A6
Lilburne Rd SE9 166 A6
Lilburne Wlk NW10 67 A2
Lile Cres W7 86 C2
Lilestone Est NW8 236 D5
Lilestone Ho NW8 236 D6
Lilestone St
NW8 92 C3 237 A6
Lilford Ho 21 SE5 139 A3
Lilford Rd SE5 138 D3
Lilian Barker Cl SE12 165 A6
Lilian Baylis Ho N1 73 A2
Lilian Baylis Sch
SE11 116 B1 260 C2
Lilian Board Way UB6 64 B3
Lilian Gdns IG8 37 B2
Lilian Rd SW16 181 C2
Lilian Rolfe Ho 5
SE27 183 B6
Lillechurch Rd RM8 80 C2
Lilleshall Rd SM4 202 B3
Lilley Cl E1 118 A5
Lillian Ave W3 110 C4
Lillian Cl 14 N16 73 C5
Lillian Rd SW13 134 B6
Lillie Ho N5 72 C3
Lillie Rd SW6 135 B6 264 C5
Lillieshall Rd SW4 137 C2
Lillie Yd SW6 135 C6 265 A6
Lillingston Ho N7 72 C4
Lilliput Ave UB5 85 B6
Lillywhite 21 NW9 27 D2
Lily Cl W14 112 D2
Lily Gdns HA0 87 C5
Lily Pl EC1 241 B4
Lily Rd E17 53 C3
Lilyville Rd
SW6 135 B4 264 C2
Limavady Ho 18 SE18 122 C2
Limberg Ho SE8 119 B2
Limborough Ho 5 E14 97 C2
Limbourne Ave RM8 59 B2
Limburg Rd SW11 136 C1
Lime Ave UB7 104 B6
Limeburner La
EC4 94 D1 241 C2
Lime Cl BR1 210 A5
E1 118 A5
Buckhurst Hill IG9 21 D2
Carshalton SM5 218 D6
Harrow HA3 25 A1
Pinner HA5 39 D6
Lime Cres TW16 172 C1
Limecroft Cl KT19 215 B1
Lime Ct 8 E11 76 C6
9 Harrow HA1 42 D3
Kingston KT3 198 D6
Mitcham CR4 180 B1
Putney SW15 134 B2
Limedene Cl HA5 22 D2
Lime Gr DA15 167 D5
W12 112 C4
Barnet N20 13 B3
Hayes UB3 105 B6
Kingston KT3 199 C6
Orpington BR6 226 D6
Ruislip HA4 40 B2
Twickenham TW1 153 A5
Limeharbour E14 119 D4
Limehouse Cswy E14 119 B6
Limehouse Cut 5 E14 97 D2
Limehouse Fields Est
E14 97 A2
Limehouse Link (Tunnel)
E14 119 B6
Limehouse Sta E14 97 A1
Lime Kiln Dr SE7 143 B6
Limekiln Pl SE19 183 D3
Limekiln Wharf 21
E14 119 B6
Lime Lo 3 TW16 171 D3
Limerick Cl SW12 159 C4
Limerick Ct 1 SW12 159 C4
Lime Row DA18 125 B3
Limerston St
SW10 136 A6 266 B5
Limes Ave N12 30 A6
NW11 47 A2
NW7 27 C4
Barnes SW13 133 D3
Carshalton SM5 202 D1
Croydon CR0 220 C5
Penge SE20 184 B3
Wanstead E11 55 B5
Limes Ave The N11 31 C5
Limes Cl 3 N11 31 C5
Ashford TW15 170 C5
Limes Ct NW6 68 D1
Beckenham BR3 185 D1
Limesdale Gdns HA8 27 A1
Limes Field Rd SW14 133 C2
Limesford Rd SE15 140 D1
Limes Gdns SW18 157 C5
Limes Gr SE13 142 A1
Limes Rd
Beckenham BR3 185 D1
Thornton Heath CR0 205 B2
Limes Row BR6 226 D3
Lime St E17 53 A5
EC3 95 C1 243 A1
Limes The BR2 226 A6
SE5 139 C2
W2 245 B5
East Molesey KT8 195 D5
Lime St Pas EC3 253 A6
Limes Wlk SE15 140 C1
W5 109 D4
Lime Terr W7 108 C6
Lime Tree Ave KT10,
KT7 196 C1
Limetree Cl SW2 160 B3
Lime Tree Ct N2 47 D6
Limetree Ct HA5 23 C3
Lime Tree Ct CR2 221 A2
Lime Tree Gr CR0 223 B5
Lime Tree Pl CR4 181 B2
Lime Tree Rd TW5 129 D4
Limetree Wlk 2
SW17 181 A5
Lime Tree Wlk
Bushey WD23 8 C2
Coney Hall BR4 224 D4
Enfield EN2 5 A5
Lime Wlk 11 E15 98 C6
Limewood Cl E17 53 B5
Beckenham BR3 208 A4
Ealing W13 87 B1
Limewood Ct IG4 56 B4
Limpsfield Ave
Putney SW19 156 D2
Thornton Heath CR7 204 B4
Limscott Ho 35 E3 97 D4
Linacre Cl SE15 140 B2
Linacre Ct W6 112 D1
Linacre Rd NW2 68 B2
Linale Ho N1 235 C3
Linberry Wlk 2 SE8 119 B2
Linchmere Rd SE12 164 D4
Lincoln Ave N14 15 C2
Twickenham TW2 152 A2
Wimbledon SW19 156 D1
Lincoln Cl
Croydon SE25 206 B3
Greenford UB6 86 A6
Harrow HA2 41 B4
Lincoln Cres EN1 17 D6
Lincoln Ct N16 51 B2
NW4 46 B5
SE12 165 C1
Borehamwood WD6 11 B6
Enfield EN2 5 B1
Hampton TW12 173 B5
2 Ilford IG2 57 A3
Mitcham CR4 204 A4
Redbridge IG1 56 B2
Lincoln Gdns IG1 56 A2
Lincoln Green Rd BR5 211 D4
Lincoln Ho SW1 247 C1
10 Putney SW15 157 A6
Lincoln Lo 10 BR3 185 D1
Lincoln Mews NW6 91 B6
Lincoln Rd DA14 190 B5
E13 99 B3
E7 77 D2
N2 48 C6
Croydon SE25 206 B6
Enfield EN1,EN3 18 B6
Harrow HA2,HA5 41 B4
Kingston KT3 199 A6
Mitcham CR4 204 A4
North Cheam KT4 200 B1
Northwood HA6 39 D6
Twickenham TW13 151 B1
Wembley HA0 65 D2
Woodford E18 37 A2
Lincoln's Inn★
WC2 94 B1 240 D2
Lincoln's Inn Fields
WC2 94 B1 240 D2
Lincoln St E11 76 C6
SW3 257 C3
Lincolns The NW7 11 D1
Lincoln Terr 4 SM2 217 C1
Lincoln Way
Charlton TW16 171 C2
Enfield EN1 18 B6
Lincombe Rd BR1 164 D1
Linda Ct KT9 213 D4
Lindal Cres EN2 4 B1
Lindal Ct 1 E18 37 A2
Lindale SW19 157 A2
Lindales The N17 33 D4
Lindal Rd SE4 163 B6
Lindbergh Rd SM6 220 A1
Linden Ave NW10 90 D5
Enfield EN1 6 A4
Hounslow TW3 151 D6
Ruislip HA4 40 A1
Thornton Heath CR7 204 D5
Wembley HA9 66 B3
Linden Bridge Sch
KT4 215
Linden Cl Ruislip HA4 40
Southgate N14 15
Stanmore HA7 25
Thames Ditton KT7 197
Linden Cotts 6 SW19 179
Linden Cres
Kingston KT1 176
Wembley UB6 64
Woodford IG8 37
Linden Ct NW7 27
8 SW18 136
W12 112
1 Beckenham BR3 207
Penge SE20 184
Sidcup DA14 189
Lindenfield BR7 188
Linden Gdns
W2 113 C6 245
W4 111
Enfield EN1 6
Linden Gr SE15 140
Kingston KT3 199
Penge SE20 184
Teddington TW11 174
Linden Ho 10 SE8 141
Linden Lawns HA9 66
Linden Lea N2 48
Lindenlea Ct E17 53
Linden Leas BR4 224
Linden Lodge Sch
SW19 157
Linden Mans N6 49
Linden Mews N1 73
W2 245
Linden Pl CR4 202
Linden Rd N10 49
N11 15
N15 51
Hampton TW12 173
Lindens The 5 E17 53
N12 30
Chiswick W4 133
New Addington CR0 224
Linden Way
Shepperton TW17 193
Southgate N14 15
Lindeth Cl HA7 25
Lindfield Gdns NW3 70
Lindfield Hts NW3 70
Lindfield Rd
Croydon CR0 205
Ealing W5 87
Lindfield St E14 97
Lindhill Cl EN3 6
Lindholme Ct 3 NW9 27
Lindisfarne Rd
Dagenham RM8 80 C5
Wimbledon SW20 178 A3
Lindisfarne Way E9 75 A4
Lindley Ct KT1 175 C2
Lindley Ho 12 SE15 140 A5
Lindley Pl TW9 132 C4
Lindley Rd E10 76 A6
Lindley St E1 96 C2
Lindon Bennett Sch
TW13 172 D5
Lindop Ho 7 E3 97 A3
Lindore Rd SW11 136 D3
Lindores Rd SM5 202 A1
Lindo St SE15 140 C3
Lind Rd SM1 218 A3
Lindrop St SW6 136 A3
Lindsay Cl KT9 214 A1
Lindsay Ct SW11 266 D1
Lindsay Dr Harrow HA3 44 B4
Shepperton TW17 193 B3
Lindsay Ho 2 SE18 122 C2
Lindsay Rd
Hampton TW12 173 D6
North Cheam KT4 216 B6
Lindsay Sq
SW1 115 D1 259 D2
Lindsell St 6 SE10 142 A4
Lindsey Cl BR1 210 A6
Mitcham CR4,SW16 204 A5
Lindsey Ct N13 16 C1
Lindsey Gdns TW14 149 B4
Lindsey Ho★ SW10 266 D4
W5 109 D2
Lindsey Mews 13 N1 73 A1
Lindsey Rd RM8 80 C5
Lindsey St EC1 94 D2 241 D4
Lind St SE8 141 D3
Lindum Rd TW11 175 C3
Lindums The BR3 185 B4
Lindway SE27 182 D5
Lindwood Cl 8 E6 100 B2
Linfield WC1 233 C1
Linfield Cl NW4 46 C5
Linford Ct 1 CR4 180 C2
Linford Ho 17 E2 96 A6
Linford Rd E17 54 A6
Linford St
SW8 137 C4 269 A1
Lingard Ho 9 E14 120 A3
Lingards Rd SE13 142 A1
Lingey Cl DA15 167 D2

ngfield Ave KT1,KT5 198 B5
ngfield Cl EN1 17 C5
ngfield Cres SE9,
DA16 145 B1
ngfield Ct
Northolt UB5 85 C5
Wimbledon SW19 178 D4
ngfield Gdns N9 18 B4
ngfield Ho SE1 251 D1
5 W4 111 A1
Penge SE26 184 B4
ngfield Rd
North Cheam KT4 216 C5
Wimbledon SW19 178 D4
ngham St SW9 138 B3
ngholm Way EN5 12 D6
ng Rd E16 99 A2
ngrove Gdns IG9 21 B2
ing's Coppice SE21 161 B2
ingwell Rd SW17 158 C1
ingwood DA7 147 D3
ingwood Gdns TW7 130 C5
ingwood Rd E5 52 A2
inhope St
NW1 92 D3 237 C5
inkenholt Mans 3
W6 111 D2
inkfield KT8 195 D6
ink Field BR2 209 A3
inkfield Rd TW7 130 D3
ink La SM6 220 A2
inklea Cl NW9 27 C3
ink Prim Sch CR0 220 A4
ink Rd N11 31 A6
Dagenham RM9 103 D5
East Bedfont TW14 149 D4
Hackbridge SM6 203 A1
inks Ave SM4 201 C5
inkscroft Ave TW15 170 D4
inks Ct N20 14 B1
inks Dr N20 13 D3
Link Sec Sch CR0 220 B4
Links Gdns SW16 182 C3
Linkside N12 29 C4
Kingston KT3 177 C1
Linkside Cl EN2 4 C2
Linkside Gdns EN2 4 B2
Links Ind Est TW13 151 A1
Links Prim Sch SW17 181 A4
Links Rd NW2 67 D6
Acton W3 88 C1
Ashford TW15 170 A5
Mitcham SW16,SW17 181 A4
West Wickham BR4 208 A1
Woodford IG8 37 A5
Links Side EN2 4 C2
Link St E9 74 C2
Links The E17 53 A5
Linksview N2 48 D4
Links View N3 29 B3
SE18 144 D4
Links View Cl HA7 25 A4
Links View Rd
Croydon CR0 223 C5
Hampton TW12 174 A6
Linksway NW4 28 D1
Links Way
Beckenham BR3 207 C3
Streatham SW17 181 A4
Links Yd E1 243 D4
9 E1 96 A2
Link The NW2 46 A1
SE9 166 C1
Acton W3 88 D1
Enfield EN3 7 A4
Northolt UB5 63 B3
Pinner HA5 40 C2
Teddington TW11 174 D4
Wembley HA0 43 C1
Linkway N4 51 A2
Dagenham RM8 80 C4
Pinner HA5 22 D2
West Barnes SW20 200 B6
Link Way Bromley BR2 210 A2
Richmond TW10 153 B2
Linkway The EN5 13 D5
Linkwood Wlk NW1 71 D1
Linley Cres RM7 59 D6
Linley Ct
1 Dulwich SE21 183 C6
Sutton SM1 218 A4
Linley Rd N17 33 C1
Linnell Cl NW11 47 D3
Linnell Dr NW11 47 D3
Linnell Ho E1 243 C4
NW8 229 A6
Linnell Rd SE5 139 C3
Edmonton N18 34 A5
Linnet Cl N9 18 D3
Bushey WD23 8 A3
Woolwich SE28 124 C6
Linnet Mews SW12 159 A4
Linnett Cl E4 36 A6
Linom Rd SW4 138 A1
Linscott Rd E5 74 C4
Linsdell Rd IG11 101 A6
Linsey St SE16 118 A2
SE16 118 A3
Linslade Cl
Hounslow TW4 151 A6
Pinner HA5 40 B6
Linslade Ho 10 E2 96 A6
NW8 237 B6
Linstead St 1 NW6 69 C1
Linstead Way SW18,
SW19 157 A4
Linsted Ct SE9,DA15 167 C5
Linster Gr WD6 11 A6
Lintaine Cl W6 264 B5
Linthorpe Ave HA0 65 C2
Linthorpe Rd N16 51 C2
Cockfosters EN4 2 C2
Linton Cl DA16 146 B4
2 SE7 121 C1
Carshalton CR4 202 D2
Linton Gdns E6 100 A1
Linton Gr SE27 183 A5
Linton Ho 2 E3 97 C2
Linton Mead Prim Sch
SE28 124 B6
Linton Rd IG11 79 A1
Linton St N1 95 A6 235 B5
Lintons The IG11 79 A1
Linver Rd SW6 135 C3
Linwood Cl SE5 139 D3
Linwood Cres EN1 6 A4
Linzee Rd N8 50 A5
Lion Ave TW1 152 D3
Lion Cl SE4 163 C5
Littleton TW17 192 A6
Lion Ct 12 NW9 46 A5
Lion Ctr The TW13 151 A1
Lionel Gdns SE9 165 D6
Lionel Ho 5 W10 91 A2
Bowes Park N22 32 B4
Lionel Mans 14 W14 112 D3
Lionel Mews W10 91 A2
Lionel Rd SE9 165 D6
Lionel Road Jun & Inf Sch
TW8 110 A2
Lionel Road N TW8 110 A2
Lionel Road S TW8 110 B1
Lion Gate Gdns TW9 132 B2
Lion Gate Mews SW18 157 C4
Lion Mills 33 E2 96 A5
Lion Park Ave KT9 214 C4
Lion Rd DA6 147 B1
E6 100 B2
Edmonton N9 18 A2
Thornton Heath CR0 205 A4
Twickenham TW1,TW2 152 D3
Lions Cl SE12 165 D1
Lion Way TW8 131 D5
Lion Wharf Rd TW7 131 B2
Lion Yd SW4 137 D1
Liphook Cres SE23 162 C4
Liphook Rd WD19 22 D6
Lipton Cl SE28 124 C6
Lipton Rd 8 E1 96 D1
Lisa Lo 5 EN5 13 D6
Lisbon Ave TW2 152 A2
Lisbon Cl E17 35 B1
Lisburne Rd NW3 70 D4
Lisford St SE15 139 D4
Lisgar Terr
W14 113 B2 254 C4
Liskeard Cl BR7 189 A4
Liskeard Gdns SE3 143 A4
Liskeard Ho SE11 261 B2
Lisle Cl SW17 181 B6
Lisle Ct NW2 69 A5
Lisle St WC2 115 D6 249 D6
Lismirrane Ind Pk WD6 9 B5
Lismore 9 SW19 179 B5
Lismore Cl TW7 131 A3
Lismore Rd N17 51 B6
South Croydon CR2 221 C2
Lismore Wlk 4 N1 73 A2
Lissant Cl KT6 197 D2
Lisselton Ho 3 NW4 46 D5
Lissenden Gdns NW5 71 A4
Lissenden Mans NW5 71 A4
Lisson Cotts NW1 237 B4
Lisson Gr NW1,
NW8 92 C3 237 A6
Lisson Ho NW1 237 A4
Lisson St NW1 92 C2 237 A4
Lister Cl W3 89 B2
Mitcham SW19 180 C2
Lister Com Sch E13 99 B5
Lister Ct N16 73 C6
NW9 27 C1
Lister Gdns N18 33 A5
Lister Ho E1 96 A2
SE2 124 D1
SE3 142 C6
Hayes UB3 105 C2
9 Wembley HA9 67 A5
Lister Hospl
SW1 115 B1 258 C1
Lister Mews N7 72 B4
Lister Rd E11 54 D1
Lister Wlk SE28 124 D6
Liston Ho N21 16 B6
Liston Rd SW4 137 C2
Tottenham N17 34 A2
Liston Way 1 IG8 37 C3
Listowel Cl 2 SW9 138 C5
Listowel Rd RM10 81 C5
Listria Lo N16 73 D6
Listria Pk N16 73 D6
Litcham Ho 23 E1 96 D4
Litchfield Ave E15 76 C2
Morden SM4 201 B2
Litchfield Ct E17 53 C3
Litchfield Gdns NW10 68 A2
Litchfield Rd SM1 218 A4
Litchfield St WC2 249 D6
Litchfield Way NW11 48 A4
Lithgow's Rd TW14,
TW6 127 D1
Lithos Rd NW3 70 A2
Little Acre BR3 207 C6
Little Albany St NW1 238 D6
Little Argyll St W1 239 A1
Little Birches DA15 167 C2
Little Boltons The
SW10 255 D1
Little Bornes SE21 183 C6
Littlebourne 2 SE13 164 C4
Little Britain EC1 242 A3
Littlebrook Cl CR0 206 D3
Little Brownings SE23 162 B2
Littlebury Rd SW4 137 D2
Little Bury St N9 17 C4
Little Bushey La WD23 8 B5
Little Cedars N12 30 A6
Little Chelsea Ho
SW10 266 B5
Little Chester St SW1 258 C6
Little College St SW1 260 A6
Littlecombe SE7 143 B6
Little Combe Cl 13
SW15 156 D5
Little Common HA7 9 A1
Littlecote Cl SW19 157 A4
Littlecote Pl HA5 23 B2
Littlecroft SE9 144 C2
Little Ct BR4 224 C6
Littledale SE2 146 A6
Little Dimocks SW12 159 B2
Little Dorrit Ct SE1 252 B2
Little Ealing La W5 109 C2
Little Ealing Prim Sch
W5 109 C3
Little Edward St NW1 231 D2
Little Elms UB3 127 B5
Little Essex St WC2 251 A6
Little Ferry Rd TW1 153 B3
Littlefield Cl N19 71 C4
9 Kingston KT1 176 A1
Littlefield Ct UB7 126 A5
Littlefield Ho KT1 176 A1
Littlefield Rd HA8 27 A3
Little Friday Rd E4 20 C2
Little Gearies IG6 56 D5
Little George St SW1 250 A1
Little Gn TW9 131 D1
Little Grange UB6 87 A4
Little Green St NW5 71 B4
Littlegrove EN4 14 C5
Littlegrove Ct 3 EN4 14 C5
Little Halliards KT12 194 A3
Little Heath SE7 122 A1
Ilford RM6 58 B5
Little Heath Rd DA7 147 B5
Littleheath Rd CR2 222 B1
Little Heath Sch RM6 58 B5
Little Holt 8 E11 55 A4
Little Ilford La E12 78 B4
Little Ilford Sch E12 78 B3
Littlejohn Rd W7 86 D1
Little Larkins EN5 13 A5
Little Marlborough St
W1 239 A1
Littlemead KT10 212 B4
Littlemede SE9 166 B1
Littlemoor Rd IG1 79 B5
Littlemore Rd SE2 124 A4
Little Moss La HA5 23 A1
Little Newport St
WC2 249 D6
Little New St EC4 241 B2
Little Orchard Cl HA5 23 A1
Little Oxhey La WD19 23 A6
Little Park Dr TW13 151 A2
Little Park Gdns EN2 5 B2
Little Pluckett's Way
IG9 21 D3
Little Portland St W1 239 A2
Little Potters WD23 8 C4
Little Queens Rd
TW11 174 D4
Little Rd UB3 105 D4
Little Redlands BR1 188 A1
Little Road Mans SW6 264 B5
Littlers Cl SW19 180 B2
Little Russell St WC1 240 A3
Little Sanctuary SW1 250 A1
Little Smith St SW1 259 D6
Little Somerset St E1 243 C1
Little Stanmore Fst & Mid
Sch HA8 26 B2
Little St James's St
SW1 249 A3
Little St Leonards
SW14 133 A2
Littlestone Cl BR3 185 C4
Little Strand NW9 27 D1
Little Thrift BR5 211 A5
Little Titchfield St W1 239 A3
Littleton Ave E4 20 D3
Littleton CE Inf Sch
TW17 192 C6
Littleton Cres HA1 64 D6
Littleton La TW17,
TW18 192 A4
Littleton Rd Harrow HA1 64 D6
Littleton TW15,TW17 171 A3
Littleton St SW18 158 A2
Little Trinity La EC4 252 B6
Little Venice★
W9 92 A2 236 A4
Littlewood SE13 164 A5
Littlewood Cl W13 109 B3
Little Wood Cl BR5 190 A2
Littleworth Ave KT10 212 B3
Littleworth Common Rd
KT10 212 B5
Littleworth La KT10 212 B4
Littleworth Pl KT10 212 B4
Littleworth Rd KT10 212 C4
Livermere Ct 3 E8 95 D6
Livermere Rd E8 95 D6
Liverpool Gr
SE17 117 B1 262 C1
Liverpool Ho N7 72 C2
Liverpool Rd E10 54 A3
E16 98 C2
N1 234 B5
N1,N7 72 C1
W5 109 D4
Kingston KT2 176 C3
South Norwood CR7 205 A6
Liverpool St
EC2 95 C2 243 A3
Liverpool Street Sta
EC2 95 C2 243 A3
Livesey Cl KT1 198 B6
Livesey Mus★ SE15 140 B6
Livesey Pl SE15 140 A6
Livingstone Ct E10 54 A3
Barnet EN5 1 A3
Stanwell TW19 148 A3
Livingstone Ho 16 SE5 139 A5
Livingstone Lo 13 W9 91 C2
Livingstone Pl E14 120 A1
Livingstone Prim Sch
EN4 2 B2
Livingstone Rd E15 98 A6
E17 53 D3
14 SW11 136 B2
Bowes Park N13 32 A5
Isleworth TW3 130 A1
Southall UB1 106 D6
South Norwood CR7 183 B1
Livity Sch The SW2 160 A6
Livonia St W1 239 B1
Lizard St EC1 95 A4 235 B1
Lizban St SE3 143 B5
Llandovery Ho 1 E14 120 A4
Llanelly Rd NW2 69 B6
Llanover Ct HA9 65 D4
Llanover Rd SE18 144 C5
Wembley HA9 65 D5
Llanthony Rd SM4 202 B4
Llanvanor Rd NW2 69 B6
Llewellyn Ct SE20 184 C2
Llewellyn St SE16 118 A4
Lloyd Ave SW16 182 A2
Lloyd Baker St
WC1 94 C4 234 A1
Lloyd Ct SE13 163 D6
Pinner HA5 40 D4
6 West Norwood SE27 160 D1
Lloyd Ho N16 73 B5
3 Beckenham BR3 185 D4
Bromley BR1 187 B5
Lloyd Mews EN3 7 C5
Lloyd Park Ave CR0 221 D4
Lloyd Park Ho E17 53 C6
Lloyd Park Sta CR0 221 D4
Lloyd Rd E6 100 B6
Dagenham RM9 81 B1
North Cheam KT4,SM3 216 D5
Walthamstow E17 52 D5
Lloyd's Ave EC3 243 B1
Lloyd's Bldg★
EC3 95 C1 243 A1
Lloyd's Pl SE3 142 C3
Lloyd Sq WC1 94 C4 234 A2
Lloyd's Row
EC1 94 D4 234 C1
Lloyd St WC1 94 C4 234 A2
Lloyds Way BR3 207 B4
Lloyd Villas SE4 141 C3
Loampit Hill SE13 141 D3
Loampit Vale SE13 142 A2
Loanda Cl 17 E8 95 D6
Loanda Ho SE15 140 C2
Loats Rd SW2 160 A5
Lobelia Cl 5 E6 100 A2
Locarno Rd 6 W3 111 A5
Greenford UB6 86 B3
Lochaber Rd SE13 142 C1
Lochaline St W6 134 C6
Lochan Cl UB4 85 A3
Lochbie 5 N4 50 A2
Lochinvar St SW12 159 B4
Lochleven Ho 9 N2 30 B1
Lochmere Cl DA8 147 D6
Lochmore Ho SW1 258 B3
Lochnagar St E14 98 A2
Lockbridge Ct 3 W9 91 C2
Lock Chase SE3 142 C2
Lock Cl UB2 108 A4
Locke Ho SW8 269 A2
Lockesfield Pl E14 119 D1
Lockesley Dr BR5 211 D3
Lockesley Sq KT6 197 D3
Locket Rd HA3 24 D1
Lockfield Ave EN3 7 B4
Lockgate Cl E9 75 B3
Lockhart Cl N7 72 B2
Enfield EN3 18 B6
Lockhart Lo 4 E4 20 C4
Lockhart St E3 97 B3
Lock Ho N16 51 D1
Lockhurst St E5 74 D4
Lockier Wlk HA9 65 D5
Lockington Rd
SW8 137 B4 268 D2
Lockmead Rd N15 52 A3
SE13 142 A2
Lock Rd TW10 175 C6
Lockside 17 E14 119 A6
Lock's La CR4 181 A1
Locksley St E14 97 B2
Locksmeade Rd TW10 175 C6
Lock View Ct 9 E14 119 A6
Lockwood Cl SE26 184 D6
Lockwood Ct KT3 199 A5
Lockwood Ho 10 SE11 138 C6
Lockwood Ind Pk N17 52 B6
Lockwood Sq SE16 118 B3
Lockwood Way E17 34 D1
Chessington KT9 214 C3
Lockyer Est SE1 252 D1
Lockyer Ho 7 SE10 120 D1
SW8 270 A4
Putney SW15 134 D2
Lockyer St SE1 252 D1
Locomotive Dr TW14 150 A3
Locton Gn 4 E3 97 B6
Lodden Lo 13 SM2 218 A1
Loddiges Ho 5 E9 74 C1
Loddiges Rd E9 74 C1
Loddon Ho NW8 236 D5
Loder St SE15 140 C5
Lodge Ave
Borehamwood WD6 10 B6
Croydon CR0 220 C5
Dagenham RM8,RM9,IG11 80 B3
Harrow HA3 44 A5
Lodge Cl Edgware HA8 26 C4
Edmonton N18 33 A5
Hackbridge SM6 203 A1
Isleworth TW7 131 B4
Lodge Ct 3 HA0 66 A3
Lodge Dr N13 32 C6
Lodge Gdns BR3 207 B4
Lodge Hill DA16 146 B5
Redbridge IG4 56 A5
Lodgehill Park Cl HA2 63 D6
Lodge La DA5 168 D5
N12 30 A5
New Addington CR0 223 D1
Lodge Pl SM1 217 D3
Lodge Rd NW4 46 C5
NW8 92 C4 230 A1
Bromley BR1 187 C3
Sutton SM1 217 D3
Thornton Heath CR0 204 D2
Wallington SM6 219 B3
Lodge Villas IG8 36 D4
Lodge Way
Charlton TW17 171 A1
Stanwell TW15 148 A2
Lodore Gdns NW9 45 C4
Lodore Gn UB10 60 A5
Lodore St E14 98 A1
Lodsworth Ho SW11 268 A1
Lofthouse Pl KT9 213 C2
Loftie St SE16 118 A4
Lofting Rd N1 72 C1
Lofts on the Park 24 E9 74 D2
Loftus Rd W12 112 B5
Loftus Rd (Queens Park
Rangers FC) W12 112 B5
Logan Cl Enfield EN3 6 D4
Hounslow TW4 129 B2
Logan Mews W8 255 A4
Logan Pl W8 113 C2 255 A4
Logan Rd Edmonton N9 18 B2
Wembley HA9 66 A6
Loggetts SE21 161 C2
Logs Hill BR1,BR7 188 A2
Logs Hill Cl BR7 188 A2
Lohmann Ho 5 SE11 138 C6
Lois Dr TW17 192 D4
Lolesworth Cl E1 243 D3
Lollard St
SE11 116 C2 261 A3
Loman St SE1 116 D4 251 D2
Lomas Cl CR0 224 A1
Lomas St E1 96 A2
Lombard Ave Enfield EN3 6 C4
Ilford IG3 57 C1
Lombard Bsns Pk
Merton SW19 179 D1
Thornton Heath CR0 204 B2
Lombard Ct EC3 252 D6
Lombard Ho 4 SE10 142 A5
Lombard La EC4 241 B1
Lombard Rd N11 31 B5
SW11 136 B3
Merton SW19 179 D1
Lombard Rdbt CR0 204 B2
Lombard St EC3 95 B1 242 D1
Lombard Trad Est SE7 121 B2
Lombard Wall SE7 121 B2
Lombardy Pl W2 245 D5
Lombardy Ret Pk UB3 106 B6
Lomley Ho 10 SW2 160 C5
Lomond Cl N15 51 C4
Wembley HA0 66 B1
Lomond Ct HA3 42 D6
Lomond Gdns CR2 223 A1
Lomond Gr SE5 139 B5
Lomond Ho 10 SE5 139 B4
Loncroft Rd SE5 139 C6
Londale Ct SE10 142 A4
Londesborough Ho 1
N16 73 C4
Londesborough Rd
N16 73 C4
London Aquarium★
SE1 250 C1
London Bridge
EC4,SE1 117 B6 252 D5
London Bridge City Pier
SE1 117 C5 253 A4
London Bridge Hospl
SE1 117 B5 252 D4
London Bridge St
SE1 117 B5 252 D3
London Bridge Sta
SE1 117 B5 252 D3
London Business Sch
NW1 92 D3 237 C6
London Butterfly Ho★
TW8 131 B4
London Canal Mus★
N1 94 A5 233 B4
London Central Mosque★
NW8 92 C4 230 B1
London Chest Hospl E2 96 C5
London City Airport
E16 122 B5
London Clinic
NW1 93 A3 238 B5
London Coll of Fashion
EC2 95 C3 243 B6
London Coll of Fashion The
W1 238 B1
London Coll of International
Business Studies
WC1 240 B3
London Coll of Printing
SE11 116 D3 261 D5
London Ct 3 SW18 157 C6
London Docklands Visitor
Ctr E14 120 A4
London Dungeon The★
SE1 117 B5 252 D4
London Eye (Millennium
Wheel)★ SE1 116 B4 250 C2
London Fields East Side
E8 74 B1
London Fields Prim Sch
E8 96 B6
London Fields Sta E8 74 B1
London Fields West Side
E8 74 A1
London Foot Hospl
W1 93 C3 239 A5
London Gas Mus The★
E3,E16 98 B3
London Group Bsns Pk
NW2 46 A1
London Ho NW8 230 B4
Edgware HA8 26 A6
London Hospital Dental Inst
E1 96 B2
London Independent Hospl
The E1 96 D2
London Ind Pk The E6 100 C2
London Inst The W1 238 C1
Streatham SW17 181 B5
London International Film
Sch WC2 94 A1 240 B1
London La E8 74 B1
Bromley BR1 186 D3
London Metropolitan Univ
E1 95 D1 243 D2
London Metropolitan Univ
(Carleton Grange Hall) 2
N7 71 D4

London Metropolitan Univ (Central Ho) E1 ....96 A1
London Metropolitan Univ (Coll of Tech & Design) E1 ....96 A1
London Metropolitan Univ (Commercial Rd) E1 ..96 A1
London Metropolitan Univ (Ladbrook Ho) N5 ....72 D3
London Metropolitan Univ (Moorgate) EC2 ....95 B2 242 C3
London Metropolitan Univ (North London Campus) N7 ....72 C3
London Metropolitan Univ (Tufnel Park Hall) N7 .71 C5
London Metropolitian Univ (Spring Ho) N7 ....72 C2
London Mews W2 ....236 D2
London Nautical Sch The SE1 ....116 C5 251 B4
London Oratory Sch The SW6 ....135 C5 265 B4
London Peace Pagoda★ SW3 ....267 D4
London Rd E13 ....99 A5
SE1 ....116 D3 261 D6
Ashford TW15,TW18, TW19,TW14 ....148 B2
Brentford TW7,TW8 ....131 B4
Bromley BR1 ....186 D3
Enfield EN2 ....5 B1
Forest Hill SE22,SE23 ..162 C3
Hackbridge SM6,CR4 ..219 B6
Harrow HA1 ....64 C6
Hounslow TW3,TW7, TW1,TW8 ....130 B3
Kingston KT1,KT2 ....176 B1
Morden SM4 ....201 C5
Romford RM7,RM8 ....59 C3
Stanmore HA7 ....25 D6
Stoneleigh KT17 ....216 B3
Stoneleigh KT17,KT4, SM3 ....216 B3
Thornton Heath CR0, CR7,SW16 ....204 C3
Twickenham TW1 ....153 A4
Wembley HA9 ....66 A2
Carshalton CR4 ....203 A2
London Road Rdbt TW1 ....153 A5
London Sch of Economics & Political Science WC2 ....94 B1 240 D1
London St EC3 ....253 B6
W2 ....92 B1 236 C1
London Stile 5 W4 ....110 C1
London Terr 1 E2 ....96 A5
London Theological Seminary at Kensit Memorial Coll N3 ....29 A1
London Toy & Model Mus★ W2 ....114 A6 246 A6
London Transport Mus★ WC2 ....250 B6
London Wall EC2 ....95 B2 242 D3
London Wharf 4 E2 ....96 B6
London Zoo★ NW1 ....93 A5 231 A4
Lonesome Prim Sch CR4 ....181 B1
Lonesome Way CR4 ....181 C2
Long Acre WC2 .94 A1 240 B1
Long Acre Ct W13 ....87 A2
Longacre Pl SM5 ....219 A2
Longacre Rd E17 ....36 B2
Longbeach Rd SW11 .136 D2
Longberrys NW2 ....69 B5
Longboat Row UB1 ....85 B1
Longbow Ho 20 N1 ....95 C6
Longbridge Ho RM8 ....80 B4
Longbridge Rd
Barking IG11 ....79 C3
Dagenham RM8 ....80 B4
Longbridge Way SE13 164 A6
Longbury Dr BR5 ....190 B1
Longcliffe Ho SW18 ....157 D6
Longcroft SE9 ....166 C1
Longcrofte Rd HA8 ....25 D3
Longdale Sq N1 ....234 B6
Long Deacon Rd E4 ....20 C3
Long Ditton Cty Inf Sch KT6 ....197 C1
Longdon Wood BR2 ....226 A4
Longdown Rd SE6 ....185 C6
Long Dr W3 ....89 C1
Greenford UB6 ....85 D6
Ruislip HA4 ....62 D4
Long Elmes HA3 ....24 A2
Longfellow Rd E17 ....53 B3
North Cheam KT4 ....200 B1
Longfellow Way SE1 ..263 D3
Long Field NW9 ....27 D3
Longfield
3 Bromley BR1 ....186 D2
Loughton IG10 ....21 C6
Longfield Ave E17 ....53 A5
NW7 ....28 A3
Ealing W5 ....109 C6
Enfield EN3 ....6 C5
Hackbridge SM6 ....203 A1
Wembley HA9 ....44 A1
Longfield Cres SE23, SE26 ....162 C1
Longfield Ct 4 N2 ....48 A6
Longfield Dr
Mitcham SW19 ....180 C2
Mortlake SW14 ....154 D6
Longfield Est SE1 ....263 D3
Longfield Fst & Mid Schs HA2 ....41 C3
Longfield Ho E17 ....53 B4
Ealing W5 ....109 C6
Longfield Rd W5 ....87 C1
Longfield St SW18 ....157 C4
Longford Ave
Feltham TW14 ....149 D5
Southall UB1 ....107 D6
Stanwell TW19 ....148 A3
Longford Cl
Feltham TW13 ....151 A1
Hampton TW12 ....173 C6
Hayes UB4 ....106 D6
Longford Ct 2 E5 ....74 D4
6 NW4 ....46 C5
1 W12 ....111 C4
Southall UB1 ....107 C5
West Ewell KT19 ....215 A4
Longford Gdns
Hayes UB4 ....106 D6
Sutton SM1 ....218 A6
Longford Ho 7 E1 ....96 C1
1 Catford BR1 ....186 B5
Hampton TW12 ....173 C6
Longford Ind Est TW12 ....173 D4
Longford Rd TW2 ....151 D3
Longford Sch TW14 ..149 D4
Longford St NW1 ....93 B3 238 D6
Longford Way TW19 ..148 A3
Longford Wlk 9 SW2 160 C4
Longhayes Ave RM6 ....58 D5
Longhayes Ct RM6 ....58 D5
Longheath Gdns CR0 .206 C4
Longhedge Ho SE26 ..184 A6
Longhill Rd SE6 ....164 B1
Longhook Gdns UB5 ....84 B4
Longhope Cl SE15 ....139 D6
Longhurst Ho 8 W9 ....91 B4
Longhurst Rd SE13 ....164 C6
Croydon CR0 ....206 B3
Long La DA7 ....147 B4
EC1 ....94 D2 241 D4
N2 ....48 B6
N3 ....29 D2
SE1 ....117 B4 252 D1
Croydon CR0 ....206 C3
Hillingdon UB10 ....60 D1
Stanwell TW15,TW19 ....148 B3
Longland Ct E9 ....75 A3
SE1 ....118 A1
Longland Dr N20 ....13 D2
Longlands Ct DA15 ..167 D1
E17 ....35 A2
W11 ....244 D6
Mitcham CR4 ....181 A2
Longlands Park Cres DA15 ....167 C2
Longlands Prim Sch DA15 ....167 C1
Longlands Rd DA15 ..167 D1
Longleat Ho SW1 ....259 C2
Longleat Rd EN1 ....17 C6
Longleat Villas 3 DA6 ....147 A1
Longleat Way TW14 ..149 B4
Longleigh Ho 8 SE5 .139 C4
Longleigh La SE2 ....146 C6
Longlents Ho 3 NW10 .89 B6
Longley Ave HA0 ....88 B6
Longley Ho 5 N19 ....71 C4
Longley Rd Harrow HA1 .42 B5
Thornton Heath CR0 ..204 D2
Upper Tooting SW17 ..180 D4
Long Leys E4 ....36 A4
Longley St SE1 ....118 A2
Longley Way NW2 ....68 C5
Longman Ho 9 E2 ....96 D5
10 E8 ....95 D6
Long Mark Rd 5 E16 ....99 D2
Longmead BR7 ....188 C1
Long Mead NW9 ....27 D2
Longmead Dr DA14 ..168 D2
Longmead Ho SE27 ..183 A5
Long Meadow 20 N7 ....71 D3
Long Meadow Cl BR3, BR4 ....208 A2
Longmeadow Rd DA15 ....167 C3
Longmead Prim Sch UB7 ....104 A2
Longmead Rd
Hayes UB3 ....105 D6
Thames Ditton KT7 ....196 D2
Upper Tooting SW17 ....180 D5
Longmoor Point 14 SW15 ....156 B3
Longmore Ave EN4,EN5 .14 B5
Longmore St SW1 ....115 C2 259 A3
Longnor Rd E1 ....96 D4
Long Pond Rd SE3 ....142 C4
Long Rd SW4 ....137 C1
Longreach Ct IG11 ....101 B5
Long Reach Rd IG11 ..101 D3
Longridge Ho SE1 ....262 B5
Longridge La UB1 ....85 D1
Longridge Rd SW5 ....113 C2 255 B3
Long Ridges N2 ....49 A6
Long's Ct W1 ....249 D5
Longs Ct 2 TW9 ....132 B1
Longshaw Prim Sch E4 20 B1
Longshaw Rd E4 ....20 B1
Longshore SE8 ....119 B2
Long St E2 ....95 D4
Longstaff Cres SW18 .157 C4
Longstaff Rd SW18 ..157 C5
Longstone Ave NW10 ..89 D6
Longstone Rd SW17 ..181 B5
Longthorne Ho 20 E3 ..97 B4
Longthornton Rd SW16 ....181 D1
Longton Ave SE26 ....184 A6
Longton Gr SE26 ....184 B6
Longville Rd SE11 ....261 D4
Longwalk Rd UB11 ....104 D5
Long Wlk SE1 ....263 B6
SE18 ....144 D6
Kingston KT3 ....199 A6
Longwood Bsns Pk TW16 ....193 D4
Longwood Dr SW15 ..156 A5
Longwood Gdns IG2, IG6,IG5 ....56 C6
Longwood Par IG6 ....56 D6
Longworth Cl SE28 ..102 D1
Long Yd WC1 ..94 B3 240 C5
Loning The NW9 ....45 D5
Enfield EN3 ....6 C5
Lonsdale Ave
Newham E6 ....100 A3
Wembley HA9 ....66 A3
Lonsdale Cl SE12 ....165 D1
Edgware HA8 ....26 B5
Hillingdon UB8 ....83 A2
Newham E6 ....100 A3
Pinner HA5 ....23 A2
Lonsdale Cres IG2 ....56 D3
Lonsdale Dr EN2 ....16 A6
Lonsdale Dr N EN2 ....4 A1
Lonsdale Gdns CR7, SW16 ....204 B5
Lonsdale Ho 6 N4 ....51 A2
SW6 ....135 C2
Lonsdale Mews W11 ..91 B1
4 Richmond TW9 ....132 C4
Lonsdale Pl N1 ....72 C1
Lonsdale Rd E11 ....54 D2
NW6 ....91 B6
W11 ....91 B1
W4 ....111 D2
Barnes SW13 ....133 D5
Bexley DA7 ....147 B3
Croydon SE25 ....206 B5
Southall UB2 ....106 D3
Lonsdell Ho 9 SW2 ..160 C5
Loobert Rd N15 ....51 C6
Looe Gdns IG6 ....56 D6
Loop Rd BR7 ....189 A4
Lopen Rd N18 ....33 C6
Lopen Works N18 ....33 C6
Lopez Ho 4 SW9 ....138 A2
Lorac Ct 13 SM2 ....217 C1
Loraine Cl EN3 ....18 C6
Loraine Ct BR7 ....188 D5
Loraine Ho 1 SM5 ....219 B4
Loraine Rd N7 ....72 B4
Chiswick W4 ....132 D6
Lord Ave IG5 ....56 B6
Lord Chancellor Wlk KT2 ....177 A2
Lord David Pitt Ho 8 SE24 ....138 C1
Lordell Pl SW19 ....178 C4
Lorden Wlk 25 E2 ....96 A4
Lord Gdns IG5 ....56 B5
Lord Hills Rd W2 ....91 D2
Lord Holland La 5 SW9 ....138 C3
Lord Knyvetts Ct 3 TW19 ....148 A5
Lord Napier Pl W6 ....112 A1
Lord North St SW1 ....260 A5
Lord Roberts Mews SW6 ....265 C3
Lord Roberts Terr SE18 ....122 C1
Lords Cl Feltham TW13 .151 A2
West Norwood SE21 ..161 A2
Lord's Cricket Mus★ NW8 ....92 B4 229 D1
Lords Ct 3 HA8 ....27 A3
Lordship Gr N16 ....73 B6
Lordship Ho 3 N16 ....73 B6
Lordship La SE22 ....161 D5
Tottenham N22 ....33 B2
Lordship Lane Prim Sch N22 ....33 A2
Lordship Park Mews N16 ....73 A6
Lordship Pk N16 ....73 B6
Lordship Pl SW3 ....267 A5
Lordship Rd N16 ....73 B6
Northolt UB5 ....63 A1
Lordship Terr N16 ....73 B6
Lord's Indoor Cricket Sch NW8 ....229 D2
NW8 ....230 A2
Lord's (MCC & Middlesex Cty Cricket Ground)★ NW8 ....92 B4 229 D2
Lordsmead Rd N17 ....33 C1
Lord St E16 ....122 A5
Lord's View NW8 ....229 D1
Lord Warwick St SE18 122 B3
Loreburn Ho 2 N7 ....72 B4
Lorenzo St N1,WC1 ....233 C2
Loretto Gdns HA3 ....44 A5
Lorian Cl N12 ....29 D6
Loring Rd N20 ....14 C2
Isleworth TW7 ....130 D3
Loris Rd W6 ....112 C3
Lorn Ct SW9 ....138 C3
Lorne Ave CR0 ....206 D2
Lorne Cl NW8 ..92 C4 230 B1
Lorne Ct SW15 ....156 D5
Lorne Gdns 5 W11 ..112 D4
Croydon CR0 ....206 D2
Wanstead E11 ....55 C5
Lorne Ho 7 E1 ....97 A2
3 N11 ....31 B5
Lorne Rd E17 ....53 C4
E7 ....77 C4
N4 ....50 B1
Harrow HA3 ....24 D1
3 Richmond TW10 ....154 B6
Lorn Rd SW9 ....138 C3
Lorraine Ct 10 NW1 ....71 B1
Beckenham BR3 ....186 A2
Lorraine Pk HA3 ....24 C3
Lorrimore Rd SE17 ..138 D6
Lorrimore Sq SE17 ..138 D6
Lorton Ho 9 NW6 ....91 C6
Loseberry Rd KT10 ..212 B3
Lostock Ho 10 SW8 ..137 D3
Lothair Rd W5 ....109 D4
Lothair Rd N N4 ....50 D3
Lothair Rd S N4 ....50 D2
Lothbury EC2 ..95 B1 242 C2
Lothian Ave UB4 ....84 B2
Lothian Cl HA0 ....65 A5
Lothian Rd SW9 ....138 D4
Lothrop St W10 ....91 A4
Lots Rd SW10 .136 A5 266 B3
Loubet St SW17 ....180 D4
Loudoun Ave IG6 ....56 D4
Loudoun Rd NW8 ....92 A6 229 B5
Loudwater Cl TW16 ..194 A5
Loudwater Rd TW16 ..194 A5
Loughborough Ct 7 SW9 ....138 D2
Loughborough Junction Sta SW9 ....138 D2
Loughborough Pk SW9 ....138 D1
Loughborough Prim Sch SW9 ....138 D3
Loughborough Rd SE5,SW9 ....138 D3
Loughborough St SE11 ....116 B1 260 D1
Lough Rd N7 ....72 B2
Loughton Way IG9 ....21 D3
Louisa Cl E9 ....96 D6
Louisa Ct TW2 ....152 C2
Louisa Gdns E1 ....96 D3
Louisa Ho SW15 ....133 D1
Louisa St E1 ....96 D3
Louis Ct 3 RM10 ....81 D2
Louise Bennett Cl 9 SE24 ....138 D1
Louise Ct
4 Wanstead E11 ....55 B4
Wood Green N22 ....32 C2
Louise De Marillac Ho 18 E1 ....96 C2
Louise Graham Ho 5 IG11 ....101 B6
Louise Rd E15 ....76 C2
Louise White Ho 1 N19 ....49 D1
Louis Gdns BR7 ....188 B6
Louis Mews N10 ....31 B2
Louisville Rd SW17 ..159 A1
Lousada Lo N14 ....15 C5
Louvaine Rd SW11 ....136 B1
Lovage App E6 ....100 A2
Lovat Cl NW2 ....67 D5
Lovat La EC3 ....253 A5
Lovatt Cl HA8 ....26 D4
Lovatt Ct SW12 ....159 B3
Lovatt Dr HA4 ....39 D4
Lovat Wlk TW5 ....129 A5
Loveday Ho 2 SW2 ..160 C3
Loveday Rd W13 ....109 B5
Lovegrove St SE1 ....140 A6
Lovegrove Wlk E14 ..120 A5
Lovekyn Cl KT2 ....176 B1
Love La DA5 ....169 C5
EC2 ....95 A1 242 B2
SE18 ....122 D2
Cheam SM3 ....217 A2
Cheam SM4 ....201 D2
Croydon SE25 ....206 B6
Long Ditton KT6 ....213 D6
Mitcham CR4 ....202 C6
Pinner HA5 ....41 A6
Tottenham N17 ....33 D3
Lovelace Ave BR2 ....210 C3
Lovelace Gdns
Barking IG11 ....80 A4
Surbiton KT6 ....197 D2
Lovelace Gn SE9 ....144 B2
Lovelace Ho 12 E8 ....95 D6
Lovelace Prim Sch KT9 ....213 C3
Lovelace Rd
East Barnet EN4 ....14 C4
Surbiton KT6 ....197 D2
West Norwood SE21 ..161 A3
Loveland Mans 6 IG11 79 D1
Lovel Ave DA16 ....146 A3
Lovelinch Cl SE15 ....140 C6
Lovell Ho E8 ....96 A6
4 Merton SW19 ....180 A2
Lovell Pl SE16 ....119 A3
Lovell Rd
Richmond TW10 ....153 C1
Southall UB1 ....85 D1
Loveridge Mews NW6 ..69 B2
Loveridge Rd NW6 ....69 B2
Lover's Wlk W1 ....115 A5 248 A3
Lovett Dr SM5 ....202 B2
Lovette Ho 3 E3 ....97 C4
Lovett Way NW10 ....67 A3
Love Wlk SE5 ....139 B3
Lovibonds Ave BR6 ..226 D5
Hillingdon UB7 ....82 B1
Lowbrook Rd IG1 ....78 D4
Low Cross Wood La SE21 ....161 D1
Lowdell Cl UB7 ....82 A1
Lowden Rd SE24 ....139 A1
Edmonton N9 ....18 B3
Southall UB1 ....107 A6
Lowder Ho 6 E1 ....118 B5
Lowe Ave E16 ....99 A2
Lowell Ho 10 SE5 ....139 A5
Lowell St E14 ....97 A1
Lower Addiscombe Rd CR0 ....205 C1
Lower Addison Gdns W14 ....113 A4 244 A1
Lower Belgrave St SW1 ....115 B3 258 C5
Lower Boston Rd W7 .108 C4
Lower Broad St RM10 .103 C6
Lower Camden BR7 ..188 B2
Lower Church St CR0 .220 D6
Lower Clapton Rd E5 ..74 C4
Lower Clarendon Wlk 12 W11 ....91 A1
Lower Comm S SW15 .134 B2
Lower Coombe St CR0 ....221 A4
Lower Downs Rd SW20 ....178 D2
Lower Fosters NW4 ....46 C4
Lower George St 13 TW10 ....153 D6
Lower Gn W CR4 ....202 C6
Lower Gravel Rd BR2 .210 B1
Lower Green Gdns KT4 ....200 A1
Lower Green Rd KT10 212 A6
Lower Grosvenor Pl SW1 ....115 B3 258 D6
Lower Grove Rd TW10 154 B6
Lower Hall La E4 ....35 A6
Lower Hampton Rd TW12,TW16 ....172 D1
Lower Ham Rd KT2 ..175 D4
Lower James St W1 ..249 B6
Lower John St W1 ..249 B6
Lower Kenwood Ave EN2 ....16 A6
Lower Lea Crossing E14,E16 ....120 C6
Lower Maidstone Rd N11 ....31 C4
Lower Mall W6 ....112 B1
Lower Marsh SE1 ....116 C4 251 A1
Lower Marsh La KT1, KT5 ....198 C5
Lower Merton Rise NW3 70
Lower Morden La SM4 201
Lower Mortlake Rd TW9 132
Lower Park Rd N11 31
Belvedere DA17 125
Loughton IG10 21
Lower Pk 5 SW15 156
Lower Place Bsns Ctr NW10 89
Lower Queen's Rd IG9 .21
Lower Rd N2 30
SE16 118
Belvedere DA17 125
Harrow HA2 42
Sutton SM1 218
Lower Richmond Rd
Mortlake SW14,TW9 ....132 D
Putney SW15 ....134 C
Lower Robert St WC2 .250 B
Lower Sand Hills KT6 .197 C
Lower Sloane St SW1 ....115 A1 258 A
Lower Strand NW9 27
Lower Sunbury Rd TW12 ....173 C
Lower Sydenham Sta SE26 ....185 B
Lower Teddington Rd KT1 ....175 D
Lower Terr NW3 ....70 A
Lower Thames St EC3 ....117 C6 253 A
Lower Tub WD23 ....8 B
Lowerwood Ct W11 ....91 A
Lower Wood Rd KT10 .213 B
Lowestoft Cl 5 E5 ....74 C
Lowestoft Mews E16 .122 D
Loweswater Cl HA9 ....65 D
Loweswater Ho E3 ....97 B
Lowfield Rd NW6 ....69 C
W3 ....89 A
Low Hall Cl E4 ....19 D
Low Hall La E17 ....53 A
Low Ho IG11 ....102 A
Lowick Rd HA1 ....42 C
Lowland Gdns RM7 ....59 D
Lowlands NW3 ....70 C
Lowlands Rd
Harrow HA1 ....42 C
Pinner HA5 ....40 C
Lowman Rd N7 ....72 B
Lowndes Cl SW1 ....258 B
Lowndes Ct SW1 ....257 D6
Lowndes Lo EN5 ....1 D2
Lowndes Pl SW1 ....115 A3 258 A5
Lowndes Sq SW1 ....114 D4 247 D1
Lowndes St SW1 ....115 A3 258 A6
Lownds Ct BR1 ....187 A1
Lowood Ct SE19 ....183 D5
Lowood Ho 11 E1 ....118 C6
Lowood St E1 ....118 B6
Lowry Cres CR4 ....180 C1
Lowry Ct 3 SE16 ....118 B1
Lowry Ho N17 ....33 D2
Lowry Lo 2 HA0 ....65 D3
Lowry Rd RM8 ....80 B3
Lowther Cl WD6 ....10 B6
Lowther Dr EN2 ....4 A1
Lowther Hill SE23 ....163 A4
Lowther Ho 11 E8 ....95 D6
SW1 ....259 B1
Lowther Prim Sch SW13 ....134 A6
Lowther Rd E17 ....35 A1
N7 ....72 C3
Barnes SW13 ....133 D4
Kingston KT2 ....176 B2
Stanmore HA7 ....44 B6
Lowth Rd SE5 ....139 A3
Loxdon Ct RM6 ....58 B3
Loxford Ave E6 ....99 D5
Loxford Ho SW1 ....258 B3
Loxford La IG1 ....79 B3
Loxford Rd IG11 ....78 D2
Loxford Sch of Science & Tech IG1 ....79 B3
Loxham Rd E4 ....35 D3
Loxham St WC1 ....233 B1
Loxley Cl SE26 ....184 D5
Loxley Rd
Feltham TW12 ....173 B6
Wandsworth SW18 ....158 B3
Loxton Rd SE23 ....163 A3
Loxwood Cl TW14 ....149 C3
Loxwood Rd N17 ....51 C6
Loyola Prep Sch IG9 ..21 C3
Lubavitch House Gram Sch N2 ....48 A4
Lubbock Ct BR7 ....188 B3
Lubbock Ho 18 E14 ..119 D6
Lubbock Rd BR7 ....188 B3
Lubbock St SE14 ....140 C5
Lucan Ho N1 ....235 D5

ucan Pl SW3 114 C2 257 B3
ucan Rd EN5 1 A2
ucas Ave E13 99 B6
Harrow HA2 63 C6
ucas Ct SW11 268 B1
Forest Hill SE26 185 A5
ucas Gdns N2 30 A1
ucas Ho 2 SW8 137 C3
ucas Rd SE20 184 C4
ucas Sq NW11 47 C3
ucas St SE4,SE8 141 C4
ucas Vale Prim Sch
SE8 141 C4
ucerne Cl N14 16 A1
ucerne Ct 5 DA18 125 A3
8 Beckenham BR3 185 C3
ucerne Gr E17 54 B5
ucerne Mews W8 245 B4
ucerne Rd BR6 211 D1
N5 72 D4
South Norwood CR7 205 A5
ucey Rd SE16 118 A3
ucey Way SE16 118 A2
ucie Ave TW15 170 D4
ucien Rd
Upper Tooting SW17 181 A6
Wandsworth SW18 157 D2
ucille Ho SE26 184 B4
ucknow St SE18 145 C5
ucorn Cl SE12 164 D5
ucraft Ho 12 SW2 160 A4
uctons Ave IG9 21 C3
ucy Ashe Ho SE17 261 D3
ucy Brown Ho SE1 252 B3
ucy Cres W3 89 A3
ucy Gdns RM8 81 A5
uddesdon Rd DA8 147 C5
udford Cl NW9 27 C1
Croydon CR0 220 D4
udgate Broadway
EC4 241 D1
udgate Cir
EC4 94 D1 241 C1
udgate Hill
EC4 94 D1 241 D1
udgate Sq EC4 241 D1
udham NW5 70 D3
udham Cl SE28 102 C1
udlow Cl BR2 209 A6
Harrow HA2 63 B4
udlow Ct W3 111 A4
udlow Rd Ealing W5 87 C3
Feltham TW13 172 A6
udlow St EC1 242 A6
udlow Way N2 48 A5
Ludovick Wlk SW15 133 C1
Ludwell Ho W14 254 B6
Ludwick Mews SE14 141 A5
Luffield Rd SE2 124 B3
Luffman Rd SE12 165 B1
Lugard Ho W12 112 B5
Lugard Rd SE15 140 B4
Lugg App E12 78 C5
Luke Ho 31 E1 96 B1
Lukes Ct N3 47 C6
Luke St EC2 95 C3 243 A6
Lukin Cres E4 20 B1
Lukin St E1 96 C1
Lullingstone Cl BR5 190 B3
Lullingstone Cres BR5 190 B3
Lullingstone Ho 20
SE15 140 C6
Lullingstone La SE13 164 B5
Lullingstone Rd 3
DA17 147 B6
Lullington Garth N12 29 B5
Borehamwood WD6 10 D6
Bromley BR1 186 C3
Lullington Rd
Dagenham RM9 81 A1
Penge SE20 184 A3
Lulot Gdns N19 71 B6
Lulworth NW1 71 D1
SE17 262 C2
Lulworth Ave
Hounslow TW5,TW7 130 A5
Wembley HA9 43 C2
Lulworth Cl HA2 63 B5
Lulworth Cres CR4 180 C1
Lulworth Ct N14 16 A1
Lulworth Dr HA5 41 A2
Lulworth Gdns HA2 63 B6
Lulworth Ho SW8 270 C3
Lulworth Rd DA16 145 D3
SE15 140 B3
Chislehurst SE9 166 A2
Lulworth Waye UB4 84 B1
Lumen Rd HA9 65 D6
Lumiere Bldg The E7 77 D3
Lumiere Ct SW17 159 A2
Lumley Cl DA17 125 C1
Lumley Ct WC2 250 B5
Lumley Flats SW1 258 A2
Lumley Gdns SM3 217 A3
Lumley Ho KT3 199 B1
Lumley Rd SM1,SM3 217 A3
Lumley St W1 238 B1
Lumsdon NW8 91 D6
Lunan Ho 12 E3 97 B5
Luna Rd CR7 205 A6
Lundin Wlk WD19 22 D6
Lund Point E15 98 A6
Lundy Dr UB3 105 C2
Lunham Rd SE19 183 C4
Lupin Cl Croydon CR0 206 D1
Streatham SW2 160 D2
Lupin Cres IG11 78 D2
Lupino Ct SE11 260 C4
Lupin Point SE1 253 D1
Lupton Cl SE12 187 B6
Lupton St NW5 71 C4
Lupus Ct SE19 183 B2
Lupus St SW1 115 C1 259 B1
Luralda Gdns E14 120 B1
Lurgan Ave W6 134 D6
Lurline Gdns
SW11 137 A4 268 B2
Luscombe Ct BR2 186 C1
Luscombe Ho SW18 157 B6
Luscombe Way
SW8 138 A5 270 A4
Lusher Ho SW15 156 D5
Lushington Ho KT12 194 C3
Lushington Rd NW10 90 B5
Catford SE6 185 D5
Lushington Terr 11 E8 74 A3
Lutea Ho SM2 218 A1
Luther Cl HA8 11 A2
Luther King Cl E17 53 A3
Luther Rd TW11 174 D5
Luton Pl SE10 142 A5
Luton Rd E13 99 A3
E17 53 B6
Sidcup DA14 168 C1
Luton St NW8 92 B3 236 D5
Luttrell Ave SW15 156 B6
Lutwyche Rd SE6 163 B2
Lutyens Ho SW1 259 A1
Luxborough Ho W1 238 A4
Luxborough St
W1 93 A2 238 A4
Luxborough Twr W1 238 A4
Luxemburg Gdns W6 112 D2
Luxfield Rd SE9 166 A3
Luxford St SE16 118 D2
Luxmore St SE4 141 B4
Luxor St SE5 139 A2
Lyall Ave SE21 183 D6
Lyall Mews
SW1 115 A3 258 A5
Lyall Mews W SW1 258 A5
Lyall St SW1 115 A3 258 A5
Lyal Rd E3 97 A5
Lycée Francais Charles de
Gaulle (French Univ Coll)
SW7 114 B2 256 C4
Lyceé The SE11 116 C1 261 B1
Lycett Ho 10 SW2 160 A4
Lycett Pl 3 W12 112 A4
Lychgate Manor HA1 42 C2
Lych Gate Wlk UB3 105 D6
Lyconby Gdns CR0 207 A2
Lydd Cl DA15 167 C1
Lydden Ct SE9 167 C5
Lydden Gr SW18 157 D4
Lydden Rd SW18 157 D4
Lydd Rd DA7 147 B5
Lydeard Rd E6 78 B1
Lydford NW1 232 B5
Lydford Cl 22 N16 73 C3
Lydford Rd N15 51 B4
NW2 68 D2
W9 91 B3
Lydgate Ho 8 N16 73 C3
Lydhurst Ave SW2 160 B2
Lydia Lo HA1 64 C4
Lydney Cl SE15 139 C5
Putney SW19 157 A2
Lydon Rd SW4 137 C2
Lydstep Rd BR7 188 C6
Lydwell Ho 29 SW8 137 D3
Lyford Rd SW18 158 C3
Lyford St SE7 122 A2
Lygoe Ho 18 N6 49 D2
Lygoe Rd N2 30 B2
Lygon Ho 1 E2 96 A4
Lygon Pl SW1 258 C5
Lyham Cl SW2 160 A5
Lyham Rd SW2 160 A5
Lyle Cl CR4 203 A2
Lyly Ho SE1 262 D5
Lyme Farm Rd SE12 143 B1
Lyme Gr E9 74 C1
Lyme Grove Ho 2 E9 74 C1
Lymer Ave SE19 183 D5
Lyme Rd DA16 146 B4
Lymescote Gdns SM1 217 C6
Lyme St NW1 71 C1 232 A6
Lyminge Cl DA14 189 D6
Lyminge Gdns SW17,
SW18 158 C3
Lymington Ave N22 32 D1
Lymington Cl 2 E6 100 B2
Mitcham SW16 181 D1
Lymington Ct SM1 218 A5
Lymington Dr HA4 61 B6
Lymington Gdns KT19 215 D3
Lymington Mans NW6 69 D2
Lymington Rd NW6 69 D2
Dagenham RM8 58 D1
Lyminster Cl UB4 85 A2
Lympne N17 33 B1
Lympstone Gdns SE15 140 A5
Lynbridge Gdns N13 32 D6
Lynch Cl SE3 142 D3
Lynchen Cl TW5 128 B4
Lynch Wlk 2 SE8 141 B6
Lyncott Cres SW4 137 B1
Lyncourt SE3 142 B3
Lyncroft Ave HA5 41 A4
Lyncroft Gdns NW6 69 C3
Ealing W13 109 C5
Hounslow TW3 152 A6
Lyncroft Mans 4 NW6 69 C3
Lyndale NW2 69 B5
Lyndale Ave NW2 69 B5
Lyndale Cl SE3 142 D6
Lyndean Ind Est SE2 124 C3
Lynde Ho 2 SW4 137 D2
Walton-on-T KT12 194 C3
Lynden Gate SW15 156 B4
Lynden Hyrst CR0 221 D6
Lyndhurst BR7 188 D4
Lyndhurst Ave N12 30 D4
NW7 27 C4
Mitcham SW16 181 D1
Pinner HA5 22 B2
Southall UB1 107 D5
Sunbury TW16 194 A6
Tolworth KT5 198 D1
Twickenham TW2,TW4 151 C3
Lyndhurst Cl DA7 147 D2
NW10 67 B5
Orpington BR6 226 D4
South Croydon CR0 221 D5
Lyndhurst Ct
7 Belmont SM2 217 C1
11 Woodford E18 37 A2
Lyndhurst Dr E10 54 A2
New Malden KT3 199 D2
Lyndhurst Gdns N3 29 A2
NW3 70 B3
Barking IG11 79 C2
Enfield EN1 5 C1
Ilford IG2 57 B3
Pinner HA5 22 B2
Lyndhurst Gr SE5,SE15 139 D3
Lyndhurst Ho 2
SW15 156 A4
Lyndhurst House Prep Sch
NW3 70 B3
Lyndhurst Lo 3 E14 120 B2
Lyndhurst Rd DA7 147 D2
NW3 70 B3
Chingford E4 36 A3
Edmonton N18 34 A6
Greenford UB6 85 D3
Thornton Heath CR7 204 C5
Tottenham N22 32 C4
Lyndhurst Sch SE5 139 B3
Lyndhurst Sq SE15 139 D4
Lyndhurst Terr NW3 70 B3
Lyndhurst Way SE15 139 D3
Belmont SM2 217 C1
Lyndon Ave DA15 167 D6
Hackbridge SM6 219 A5
Pinner HA5 23 A4
Lyndon Rd DA17 125 C2
Lyndon Yd SW17 179 D6
Lyndum Ct N22 32 C2
Lyne Cres E17 35 B2
Lyne Ct NW9 45 B2
Lynegrove Ave TW15 171 A5
Lyneham Wlk E5 75 A3
Pinner HA5 39 D6
Lynette Ave SW4 159 C5
Lynfield Ct SE23 162 D4
Lynford Cl HA8 27 A2
Edgware EN5 11 D6
Lynford French Ho
SE17 262 A2
Lynford Gdns
Edgware HA8 10 D1
Ilford IG3 79 D6
Lynford Terr N9 17 D3
Lynhurst Cres UB10 61 B1
Lynhurst Rd UB10 61 A1
Lynmere Rd DA16 146 B3
Lynmouth Ave
Enfield EN1 17 D5
West Barnes SM4 200 D2
Lynmouth Dr HA4 62 B5
Lynmouth Gdns
Heston TW5 128 D4
Wembley UB6 65 B1
Lynmouth Rd E17 53 A4
N16 51 D1
N2 48 D5
Wembley UB6 87 B6
Lynn Cl Ashford TW15 171 B5
Harrow HA3 24 B1
Lynn Ct SW16 181 D5
Lynne Cl 7 BR6 227 D2
Lynne Ct NW6 69 D1
Forest Hill SE23 163 B4
South Croydon CR2 221 C4
Wimbledon SW20 178 B2
Lynnett Ct E9 75 A2
Lynnett Rd RM8 58 D1
Lynne Way NW10 67 C2
Northolt UB5 84 D5
Lynne Wlk KT10 212 A3
Lynn Ho SE15 140 A6
Lynn Mews E11 76 C6
Lynn Rd E11 76 C5
Balham SW12 159 B4
Ilford IG2 57 B2
Lynn St EN2 5 B4
Lynstead Cl BR1 187 C1
Lynsted Cl DA6 169 D6
Lynsted Ct 4 BR3 185 A1
Lynsted Gdns SE9 143 D2
Lynton KT7 197 A2
Lynton Ave N12 30 B6
NW9 45 D5
Ealing W13 87 A1
Lynton Cl NW10 67 D3
Chessington KT9 214 A4
Isleworth TW7 130 D1
Lynton Cres IG2 56 D3
Lynton Ct 9 W3 89 A1
Bowes Park N13 32 A5
Penge SE20 184 B2
Sutton SM2 218 A2
Lynton Est SE1 118 A2
Lynton Gdns N11 31 D4
Enfield EN1 17 C4
Lynton Grange N2 48 D6
Lynton Ho 15 W2 91 D1
Lynton Lo N5 72 D3
Lynton Mans SE1 261 A6
Lynton Mead N20 13 D2
Lynton Rd N8 50 A4
NW6 91 B5
SE1 118 D3263
Acton W3 110 D6
Chingford E4 35 D5
Harrow HA2 63 A6
New Malden KT3 199 B4
Thornton Heath CR0 204 C3
Lynton Terr 4 W3 89 A1
Lynton Wlk UB4 83 C4
Lynwood Cl Harrow HA2 63 A5
Woodford E18 37 C2
Lynwood Dr KT4 216 A6
Lynwood Gdns
Southall UB1 85 B1
Wallington CR0 220 B4
Lynwood Gr
Orpington BR6 211 C1
Southgate N21 16 C3
Lynwood Rd Ealing W5 88 A3
Thames Ditton KT7 196 D1
Upper Tooting SW17 180 D6
Lyon Bsns Pk IG11 101 C5
Lyon Ct HA4 39 D1
Lyon Ho NW8 237 A5
Lyon Meade HA7 25 C2
Lyon Park Ave HA0 66 B2
Lyon Park Jun & Inf Schs
HA0 66 B1
Lyon Rd Harrow HA1 42 D3
Merton SW19 180 A2
Lyonsdown Ave EN5 14 A5
Lyonsdown Ct EN5 14 A6
Lyonsdown Rd EN5 14 A6
Lyonsdown Sch EN5 14 A6
Lyons Pl NW8 92 B3 236 C5
Lyon St N1 72 B1
Lyons Wlk W14 254 A4
Lyon Way UB6 86 C6
Lyoth Rd BR5 227 A6
Lyric Dr UB6 85 D3
Lyric Mews SE26 184 C6
Lyric Rd SW13 133 D4
Lysander 20 NW9 27 D2
Lysander Gdns KT5 198 B3
Lysander Gr N19 49 D1
Lysander Ho 10 E2 96 B5
Lysander Rd Ruislip HA4 61 B6
Wallington CR0 220 B2
Lysander Way BR6 227 A5
Lysia Ct SW6 134 D5
Lysias Rd SW12 159 B5
Lysia St SW6 134 D5
Lysons Wlk SW15 156 A6
Lytchet Rd BR1 187 B3
Lytchet Way EN3 6 C4
Lytchgate Cl CR2 221 C1
Lytcott Dr KT8 195 B6
Lytcott Gr SE22 161 D6
Lytham Ave WD19 22 D5
Lytham Cl SE28 103 A1
Lytham Ct 5 UB1 85 D1
Lytham Gr W5 88 B4
Lytham St
SE17 117 B1 262 C1
Lyttelton Cl NW3 70 C1
Lyttelton Ct N2 48 A4
Lyttelton Rd E10 76 A5
N2 48 A4
Lytten Ct 6 W12 112 A4
Lyttleton Ct UB4 84 C3
Lyttleton Ho 10 E9 74 C1
Lyttleton Rd N8 50 C6
Lytton Ave Enfield EN3 7 A5
Lytton Ave *continued*
Southgate N13 16 C2
Lytton Cl N2 48 B4
Northolt UB5 63 B1
Lytton Ct WC1 240 B3
Lytton Gdns SM6 219 D4
Lytton Gr SW15 157 A5
Lytton Ho 3 TW12 173 D4
Lytton Rd E11 54 C2
New Barnet EN5 2 A1
Pinner HA5 23 A3
Lytton Strachy Path 8
SE28 124 B6
Lyveden Rd SE3 143 B5
Mitcham SW17,SW19 180 D4

M

Mabbett Ho 2 SE18 144 C6
Mabel Evetts Ct UB3 106 B6
Mabel Thornton Ho 12
N16 73 B4
Maberley Cres SE19 184 A3
Maberley Ct SE19 184 A3
Maberley Rd SE19 182 C2
Mabledon Pl NW1,
WC1 232 D1
Mablethorpe Rd SW6 264 A3
Mabley St E9 75 A3
Mcadam Dr EN2 4 D3
Macallister Ho 8
SE18 144 D6
Macaret Cl N20 14 A4
Macarthur Cl E7 77 A2
MacArthur Ho 4 SW2 160 A4
Macaulay Ave KT10 212 C6
Macaulay CE Prim Sch
SW4 137 B1
Macaulay Ct SW4 137 B2
Macaulay Ho 10 N16 73 C5
2 W10 91 A2
Macaulay Rd E6 99 D5
SW4 137 B2
Macaulay Sq SW4 137 B1
Macaulay Way 2
SE28 124 B5
McAuley Cl
SE1 116 C3 261 A6
SE9 166 C6
Macbean St SE18 122 D3
Macbeth Ho 4 N1 95 C5
Macbeth St W6 112 B1
McBride Ho 5 E3 97 B5
McCall Cl SW4 138 A3
McCall Cres SE7 122 A1
McCall Ho N7 72 A4
Mccarthy Ct SW11 267 B1
McCarthy Rd TW13 172 D5
Macclesfield Rd
EC1 95 A4 235 A2
Croydon SE25 206 C4
Macclesfield St W1 249 D6
McClintock Pl EN3 7 C6
McCoid Way SE1 252 A1
Mcconnell Ho SW8 269 C1
McCormick Ho 9
SW2 160 C3
McCrone Mews 3
NW3 70 B2
McCullum Rd E3 97 B6
McDermott Cl SW11 136 C2
McDermott Rd SE15 140 A2
Macdonald Ave RM10 81 D5
Macdonald Ct TW3 130 A1
Macdonald Ho 2
SW11 137 A3
McDonald Ho 1 KT2 176 B3
Macdonald Rd E7 77 A4
N11 30 D5
N19 71 C6
Chingford E17 36 A1
McDonough Cl KT9 214 A4
McDougall Ct TW9 132 C3
McDowall Cl E16 98 D2
McDowall Rd SE5 139 A4
Macduff Rd
SW11 137 A4 268 B2
Mace Cl E1 118 B5
Mace Gateway E16 121 B6
Mace Ho 2 E17 53 D6
McEntee Ave E17 35 A2
Mace St E2 96 D5
McEwan Way E15 98 B6
Macey Ho 9 SE10 142 A6
SW11 267 A1
Macfarlane La TW7 131 A6
Macfarlane Rd W12 112 C5
Macfarren Ho 9 W10 91 A4
MacFarren Pl NW1 238 B5
McGlashon Ho 10 E1 96 A3
McGrath Rd E15 76 D2
McGregor Ct 8 N1 95 C4
MacGregor Ho 2
SW12 159 D3
McGregor Rd W11 91 B2
Macgregor Rd E16 99 C2
Mcguffie Ct E17 53 B6
Machell Rd SE15 140 C2
McIndoe Ct N1 235 C6
McIntosh Cl SM6 220 A1
McIntosh Ho 11 SE16 118 C2
McIntyre Ct 19 SW4 138 A3
Mackay Ho 33 W12 112 B6
Mackay Rd SW4 137 B2
McKay Rd SW20 178 C4
McKellar Cl WD23 8 A2
McKenna Ho 18 E3 97 B5
Mackennal St
NW8 92 C5 230 B4
Mackenzie Cl 7 W12 112 B6
Mackenzie Ct 1 N8 50 A5
Mackenzie Ho 5 NW2 68 A5
Mackenzie Rd N7 72 B2
Penge BR3 184 D1
Mackenzie Wlk E14 119 C5
McKerrell Rd SE15 140 A4
Mackeson Rd NW3 70 D4
Mackie Ho SW2 160 C4
Mackie Rd 18 SW2 160 C4
McKiernan Ct 2
SW11 136 C3
Mc Killop Way DA14 190 C3
McKinlay Ct BR3 185 B1
McKinnon Wood Ho 23
E2 96 A4
Mackintosh La E9 74 D3
Macklin Ho SE23 162 B2
Macklin St WC2 94 A1 240 B2
Mackonochie Ho EC1 241 A4
Mackrow Wlk 11 E14 120 A6
Macks Rd SE16 118 A2
Mackworth Ho NW1 232 A2
Mackworth St NW1 232 A2
Maclean Rd SE23 163 A5
Mcleod Ct SE21 162 A3
Macleod Ho 4 SE18 144 A4
McLeod Ho 3 SE23 162 C2
McLeod Rd SE2 124 B2
Macleod Rd N21 16 A6
McLeod's Mews
SW7 113 D2 255 D4
Macleod St
SE17 117 A1 262 B1
Maclise Rd
W14 113 A3 254 A5
McManus Ho 3 SW11 136 B2
McMillan Ct 2 SE6 164 D3
Macmillan Ct HA2 41 C1
Mcmillan Ho SE4 141 A2
Macmillan Ho NW4 68 B4
NW8 230 A1
McMillan St SE8 141 C6
Macmillan Way SW17 181 B6
Mcmorran Ho N7 72 A4
McNair Rd UB2 107 D3
Macnamara Ho SW10 266 C4
Mcneil Rd SE5 139 C3
McNicol Dr NW10 89 A5
Macoma Rd SE18 145 B6
Macoma Terr SE18 145 B6
Maconochies Rd E14 119 D1
Macquarie Way E14 119 D2
McRae La CR4 202 D2
Macready Ho W1 237 B3
Macready Pl 2 N7 72 A4
Macroom Ho W9 91 B4
Macroom Rd W9 91 B4
Mac's Pl EC4 241 B2
Madame Tussaud's★
NW1 93 A3 238 A5
Mada Rd BR6 226 D5
Maddams St E3 97 D3
Maddison Cl TW11 174 D4
Maddocks Cl DA14 191 A5
Maddocks Ho 3 E1 118 B6
Maddock Way SE17 138 D6
Maddox Ct 1 E4 20 B3
Maddox St W1 248 D6
Madeira Ave BR1 186 C3
Madeira Gr IG8 37 C4
Madeira Rd E11 54 C1
Edmonton N13 16 D1
Mitcham CR4 202 D5
Streatham SW16 182 A5
Madeley Ct W5 88 A1
Madeley Rd W5 88 A1
Madeline Gr IG1 79 B3
Madeline Rd SE20 184 A3
Madge Gill Way 4 E6 100 A6
Madge Hill W7 108 C6
Madinah Rd E8 74 A3
Madingley 11 KT1 176 C1
Madingley Ct TW1 153 C6
Madison Cres DA7 146 C5
Madison Gdns
Beckenham BR2 208 D6
Bexley DA7 146 C5
Madison Ho E3 98 A4
Madras Ho IG1 78 D4
Madras Pl N7 72 C2
Madras Rd IG1 78 D4
Madrid Rd SW13 134 A5
Madron St
SE17 117 C1 263 B2

Mafeking Ave E6 ... 100 A5
Brentford TW8 ... 132 A6
Ilford IG2 ... 57 B2
Mafeking Rd E16 ... 98 D3
Enfield EN1 ... 5 D2
Tottenham N17 ... 34 A1
Magdala Ave N19 ... 71 C6
Magdala Rd
Isleworth TW7 ... 131 A2
South Croydon CR2 ... 221 B1
Magdalen Ct SE25 ... 206 A4
Magdalene Cl 7 SE15 140 B3
Magdalene Gdns E6 ... 100 C3
Magdalene Ho 7
SW15 ... 156 D5
Magdalene Rd TW17 ... 192 B6
Magdalen Pas E1 ... 253 D6
Magdalen Rd SW18 ... 158 B3
Magdalen St SE1 ... 253 A3
Magee St SE11 ... 138 C6
Magellan Ct 9 NW10 ... 67 B1
Magellan Ho 16 E1 ... 96 D3
Magellan Pl 10 E14 ... 119 C2
Magnaville Rd WD23 ... 8 D4
Magnet Rd HA9 ... 65 D6
Magnin Cl 5 E8 ... 96 A6
Magnolia Cl E10 ... 75 C6
Kingston KT2 ... 176 D4
Magnolia Ct 2 N12 ... 29 D6
SW11 ... 158 D5
3 Belmont SM2 ... 217 D1
Feltham TW14 ... 150 A3
Forest Hill SE26 ... 184 C5
Harrow HA3 ... 44 B2
Hillingdon UB10 ... 60 D2
Northolt UB5 ... 85 A3
Richmond TW9 ... 132 D4
Magnolia Ho 13 SE8 ... 141 B6
Magnolia Lo E4 ... 19 D1
Magnolia Pl SW4 ... 160 A6
Ealing W5 ... 87 D2
Magnolia Rd W4 ... 132 D6
Magnolia Way KT19 ... 215 A3
Magnolia Wharf W4 ... 132 D6
Magpie Cl E7 ... 76 D3
NW9 ... 27 C1
Enfield EN1 ... 6 A4
Magpie Hall Cl BR2 ... 210 A3
Magpie Hall La BR2 ... 210 B3
Magpie Hall Rd WD23 ... 8 C2
Magpie Ho 7 E3 ... 97 B6
Magpie Pl SE14 ... 141 A6
Maguire Dr TW10 ... 175 C6
Maguire St
SE1 ... 117 D4 253 D2
Mahatma Gandhi Ind Est 11
SE24 ... 138 D1
Mahlon Ave HA4 ... 62 B2
Mahogany Cl SE16 ... 119 A5
Mahon Cl EN1 ... 5 D4
Mahoney Ho SE14 ... 141 B4
Maida Ave W2 ... 92 A3 236 B5
Chingford E4 ... 19 D4
Maida Rd DA17 ... 125 C3
Maida Vale W9 ... 92 A4 229 A1
Maida Vale Psychiatric
Hospl W9 ... 92 A3 236 B6
Maida Vale Sta W9 ... 91 D4
Maida Way E4 ... 19 D4
Maiden Erlegh Ave
DA5 ... 169 A3
Maiden La NW1 ... 71 D1
SE1 ... 117 A5 252 B4
WC2 ... 116 A6 250 B6
Maiden Rd E15 ... 76 C1
Maidenstone Hill
SE10 ... 142 A4
Maids of Honour Row 4
TW9 ... 153 D6
Maidstone Bldgs SE1 ... 252 C3
Maidstone Ho 4 E14 ... 97 D1
Maidstone Rd N11 ... 31 D4
Ruxley DA14 ... 191 C3
Mail Coach Yd 24 E2 ... 95 C4
Main Ave EN1 ... 17 D6
Main Dr HA9 ... 65 D5
Main Rd BR5 ... 190 C1
Sidcup DA14,DA15 ... 167 C1
Mainridge Rd BR7,SE9 188 C6
Main St TW13 ... 172 D5
Mainwaring Ct 3 CR4 181 A1
Main Yd E9 ... 75 C2
Mais Ho SE26 ... 162 B2
Maismore St SE15 ... 140 A6
Maison Alfort HA3 ... 24 C2
Maisonettes The SM1 ... 217 B3
Maitland Cl 5 SE10 ... 141 D5
Hounslow TW4 ... 129 B2
Maitland Ct W2 ... 246 C6
Maitland Ho 17 E2 ... 96 C5
SW1 ... 269 A6
Maitland Park Rd NW3 70 D2
Maitland Park Villas
NW3 ... 70 D2
Maitland Pl E5 ... 74 C4
Maitland Rd E15 ... 76 D2

Maitland Rd *continued*
Penge SE26 ... 184 D4
Majendie Rd SE18 ... 123 B1
Majestic Ct N4 ... 50 D1
Majestic Way CR4 ... 180 D1
Major Rd E15 ... 76 B3
22 SE16 ... 118 A3
Makepeace Ave N6 ... 71 A6
Makepeace Mans N6 ... 71 A6
Makepeace Rd
Northolt UB5 ... 85 A6
Wanstead E11 ... 55 A5
Makinen Ho IG9 ... 21 C3
Makins St SW3 ... 257 B3
Malabar Ct 20 W12 ... 112 B6
Malabar St E14 ... 119 C4
Malam Ct SE11 ... 261 A3
Malam Gdns 3 E14 ... 119 D6
Malatia CR2 ... 221 A2
Malay Ho 2 E1 ... 118 C5
Malbrook Rd SW15 ... 134 B1
Malcolm Cl SE20 ... 184 C3
Malcolm Cres NW4 ... 46 A3
Malcolm Ct E7 ... 76 D2
NW4 ... 46 A3
Ealing W5 ... 88 B3
Stanmore HA7 ... 25 C5
Malcolm Dr KT6 ... 198 A1
Malcolm Gavin Cl
SW17 ... 158 C2
Malcolm Ho 13 N1 ... 95 C5
Malcolm Pl E2 ... 96 C3
Malcolm Prim Sch
SE20 ... 184 C3
Malcolm Rd E1 ... 96 C3
Croydon SE25 ... 206 A3
Ickenham UB10 ... 60 B4
Penge SE20 ... 184 C3
Wimbledon SW19 ... 179 A4
Malcolmson Ho SW1 ... 259 D1
Malcolms Way N14 ... 15 C6
Malcolm Way E11 ... 55 A5
Malden Ave
Croydon SE25 ... 206 B6
Northolt UB6 ... 64 C2
Malden CE Prim Sch
KT4 ... 199 C1
Malden Cres NW1 ... 71 A2
Malden Ct N4 ... 51 A3
West Barnes KT3 ... 200 B6
Malden Green Ave
KT4 ... 200 A1
Malden Hill KT3 ... 199 D6
Malden Hill Gdns KT3 199 D6
Malden Junc KT3 ... 199 D4
Malden Manor Prim Sch
KT3 ... 199 C2
Malden Manor Sta
KT3 ... 199 C2
Malden Pk KT3 ... 199 D3
Malden Pl NW5 ... 71 A3
Malden Rd NW5 ... 71 A2
Cheam KT4,SM3 ... 216 D4
New Malden KT3,KT4 ... 199 D2
Malden Way KT3 ... 200 A5
**Malden Way (Kingston By
Pass)** KT3,KT5 ... 199 C4
Maldon Cl E15 ... 76 B3
N1 ... 235 B6
SE5 ... 139 C2
Maldon Ct Barking E6 ... 100 C6
Wallington SM6 ... 219 C3
Maldon Rd W3 ... 111 A6
Edmonton N9 ... 17 D1
Wallington SM6 ... 219 B3
Maldon Wlk IG8 ... 37 C4
Malet Pl WC1 ... 239 C5
Malet St WC1 ... 93 D2 239 D4
Maley Ave SE27 ... 160 D2
Malford Ct E18 ... 37 A1
Malford Gr E18 ... 54 D6
Malfort Rd SE5 ... 139 C2
Malham Cl N11 ... 31 A4
Malham Rd SE23 ... 162 D3
Malham Road Ind Est
SE23 ... 162 D3
Malins Cl EN5 ... 12 C6
Mallams Mews 1
SW9 ... 138 D2
Mallard Cl E9 ... 75 B2
NW6 ... 91 C6
W7 ... 108 C4
New Barnet EN5 ... 14 B5
Twickenham TW4 ... 151 C4
Mallard Ct E12 ... 78 B3
E17 ... 54 B6
NW9 ... 45 A2
Chingford E4 ... 20 B4
Ilford IG1 ... 79 A6
18 Richmond TW10 ... 153 D5
Mallard Ho NW8 ... 230 A3
7 SE15 ... 139 D4
Mallard Path SE28 ... 123 B3
Mallard Pl TW1 ... 153 A1
Mallard Point 5 E3 ... 97 C4
Mallards E11 ... 55 A2
Mallards Rd
Barking IG11 ... 102 A3
Woodford IG8 ... 37 B3

Mallard Way NW9 ... 45 A2
Mallard Wlk
Beckenham BR3 ... 206 D4
Sidcup DA14 ... 190 C4
Mall Ct W5 ... 110 A6
Mallet Dr UB5 ... 63 B3
Mallet Ho 11 SW15 ... 156 A6
Mallet Rd SE13 ... 164 B5
Malling SE13 ... 163 D6
Malling Cl CR0 ... 206 C3
Malling Gdns SM4 ... 202 A3
Malling Ho 9 BR3 ... 185 C3
Malling Way BR2 ... 208 D2
Mallinson Ct 2 E11 ... 76 C6
Mallinson Rd SW11 ... 158 D6
Wallington SM6 ... 219 D5
Mallon Gdns E1 ... 243 D3
Mallord St
SW3 ... 136 B6 266 D6
Mallory Bldgs EC1 ... 241 C5
Mallory Cl SE4 ... 141 A1
Mallory Gdns EN4 ... 15 A4
Mallory Ho E14 ... 98 A2
Mallory St NW8 92 C3 237 B6
Mallow Cl CR0 ... 206 D1
Mallow Mead NW7 ... 29 A3
Mallow St EC1 ... 242 C6
Mallows The UB10 ... 60 D5
Mall Rd W6 ... 112 B1
Mall Studios 9 NW3 ... 70 D3
Mall The 4 BR1 ... 209 A6
SW1 ... 115 D5 249 C3
6 Bexley DA6 ... 147 C1
Brentford TW8 ... 131 D6
Ealing W5 ... 110 A6
Harrow HA3 ... 44 B3
Kingston KT6 ... 197 D4
Mortlake SW14 ... 155 A6
Palmers Green N14 ... 16 A1
Mall The (Prep Sch)
TW2 ... 152 B1
Malmains Cl BR3 ... 208 B5
Malmains Way BR3 ... 208 B5
Malmesbury 31 E2 ... 96 C5
Malmesbury Cl HA5 ... 40 A5
Malmesbury Fst Sch
SM4 ... 202 A2
Malmesbury Mid Sch
SM4 ... 202 A3
Malmesbury Prim Sch
E3 ... 97 B4
Malmesbury Rd E16 ... 98 C2
E3 ... 97 B5
Morden SM4 ... 202 A3
Woodford E18 ... 36 D2
Malmesbury Terr E16 ... 98 D2
Malmsey Ho SE11 ... 260 D2
Malmsmead Ho E9 ... 75 A3
Malorees Jun & Inf Schs
NW6 ... 68 D1
Malory Sch BR1 ... 187 A6
Malpas Dr HA5 ... 40 D4
Malpas Rd E8 ... 74 B2
SE4 ... 141 B3
Dagenham RM9 ... 80 D2
Malta Rd E10 ... 53 C2
Malta St EC1 ... 241 D6
Maltby Dr EN1 ... 6 B5
Maltby Rd KT9 ... 214 C2
Maltby St SE1 ... 117 D3 263 C6
Maltham Terr N18 ... 34 B4
Malthouse Dr
Chiswick W4 ... 133 D6
Feltham TW13 ... 172 D5
Malthouse Pas SW13 ... 133 C3
Malthus Path 7 SE28 ... 124 C5
Malting Ho E14 ... 119 B6
Maltings W4 ... 110 C1
Maltings Cl SW13 ... 133 C3
Maltings Lo W4 ... 133 C5
Maltings Pl SE1 ... 253 B2
SW6 ... 265 D1
Maltings The BR6 ... 211 D1
Malting Way TW7 ... 130 D2
Malt Mill SE1 ... 253 C3
Malton Ho SE25 ... 205 C5
Malton Mews SE18 ... 145 C6
1 W10 ... 91 A1
Malton Rd W10 ... 91 A1
Malton St SE18 ... 145 C6
Maltravers St WC2 ... 251 A6
Malt St SE1 ... 140 A6
Malva Cl SW18 ... 157 D6
Malvern Ave DA7 ... 147 A5
Chingford E4 ... 36 B3
Harrow HA2 ... 63 B5
Malvern Cl W10 ... 91 B2
Ickenham UB10 ... 60 C6
Mitcham CR4 ... 203 C6
Penge SE20 ... 184 A1
Surbiton KT6 ... 198 A1
Malvern Court SW7 ... 256 D4
Malvern Ct
Belmont SM2 ... 217 C1
3 Surbiton KT6 ... 198 A1
Malvern Dr
Feltham TW13 ... 172 D5
Ilford IG3 ... 79 D4
Woodford IG8 ... 37 C6

Malvern Gdns NW2 ... 69 A6
Harrow HA3 ... 44 A5
Malvern Ho N16 ... 51 D1
Malvern Lo N12 ... 30 B6
Malvern Mews NW6 ... 91 C4
Malvern Pl NW6 ... 91 B4
Malvern Rd E11 ... 76 D6
E6 ... 100 A6
E8 ... 74 A1
N17 ... 52 A6
N19 ... 49 D1
N8 ... 50 C6
NW6 ... 91 C4
Enfield EN3 ... 7 A6
Hampton TW12 ... 173 C3
Harlington UB3 ... 127 C5
Surbiton KT6 ... 198 A1
Thornton Heath CR7 ... 204 C5
Malvern Terr N1 ... 234 A6
Edmonton N9 ... 17 D3
Malvern Way W13 ... 87 B2
Malwood Rd SW12 ... 159 B5
Malyons Rd SE13 ... 163 D6
Malyons Terr SE13 ... 163 D6
Malyons The TW17 ... 193 B3
Managers St E14 ... 120 A5
Manatee Pl SM6 ... 219 D5
Manaton Cl SE15 ... 140 B2
Manaton Cres UB1 ... 85 C1
Manbey Gr E15 ... 76 C2
Manbey Park Rd E15 ... 76 C2
Manbey Rd E15 ... 76 C2
Manbey St E15 ... 76 C2
Manbre Rd W6 ... 134 C6
Manbrough Ave E6 ... 100 C4
Manchester Ct E16 ... 99 B1
Manchester Dr W10 ... 91 A3
Manchester Gr E14 ... 120 A1
Manchester Ho SE17 ... 262 B2
Manchester Mans N19 ... 49 D2
Manchester Mews
W1 ... 238 A3
Manchester Rd E14 ... 120 A3
N15 ... 51 B3
South Norwood CR7 ... 205 A6
Manchester Sq
W1 ... 93 A1 238 B2
Manchester St
W1 ... 93 A2 238 A3
Manchester Way RM10 ... 81 D4
Manchuria Rd SW11 ... 159 A5
Manciple St
SE1 ... 117 B3 262 D6
Mandalay Ho 6 N16 ... 73 B4
Mandalay Rd SW4 ... 159 C6
Mandarin Ct NW10 ... 67 B2
6 SE8 ... 141 C6
Mandarin Way UB4 ... 84 D1
Mandela Cl NW10 ... 67 A1
36 W12 ... 112 B6
Mandela Ho 18 E2 ... 95 D4
Mandela Rd E16 ... 99 A1
Mandela St
NW1 ... 93 C6 232 B6
SW9 ... 138 C5
Mandela Way
SE1 ... 117 C2 263 B4
Manderville Ho SE1 ... 263 D2
Mandeville Cl 5 SE3 ... 142 D5
Merton SW19 ... 179 A2
Mandeville Ct NW3 ... 69 D3
Mandeville Ctyd SW11 268 A1
Mandeville Dr KT6 ... 197 D1
Mandeville Ho 8
SW4 ... 159 C6
Mandeville Pl W1 ... 238 B2
Mandeville Prim Sch
E5 ... 74 D5
Mandeville Rd N14 ... 15 C2
Enfield EN3 ... 7 A6
Isleworth TW7 ... 131 A3
Littleton TW17 ... 192 C4
Northolt UB5 ... 63 C1
Mandeville Sch UB5 ... 63 B2
Mandeville St E5 ... 75 A5
Mandrake Rd SW17 ... 158 D1
Mandrake Way 2 E15 ... 76 C1
Mandrell Rd SW2 ... 160 A6
Manesty Ct N14 ... 15 D4
Manette St W1 ... 239 D1
Manfred Ct 6 SW15 ... 157 B6
Manfred Rd SW15 ... 157 B6
Manger Rd N7 ... 72 A2
Mangold Way 4 DA18 125 A3
Manilla St E14 ... 119 C4
Manister Rd SE2 ... 124 A3
Manitoba Ct 23 SE16 ... 118 C4
Manitoba Gdns 6
BR6 ... 227 D2
Manley Ct N16 ... 73 D5
Manley Ho SE11 ... 261 A2
Manley St NW1 ... 231 A6
Manly Dixon Dr EN3 ... 7 A6
Mann Cl 1 CR0 ... 221 A5
Mannebury Prior N1 ... 233 D3
Mannering Ho 16 SW2 160 B6
Manning Ct 3 SE28 ... 124 B5
Manningford Cl EC1 ... 234 C2
Manning Gdns HA3 ... 43 D2

Manning Ho 6 E17 ... 54 A6
3 W11 ... 91 A1
Manning Pl TW10 ... 154 B5
Manning Rd E17 ... 53 A4
Dagenham RM10 ... 81 C1
Manningtree Cl SW19 157 A3
Manningtree Rd HA4 ... 62 B4
Manningtree St 1 E1 ... 96 A1
Mannin Rd RM6 ... 58 B2
Mannock Rd N22 ... 50 D6
Mann's Cl TW7 ... 152 D6
Manns Rd HA8 ... 26 C4
Manny Shinwell Ho
SW6 ... 264 D5
Manoel Rd TW2 ... 152 A2
Manor Ave SE4 ... 141 B3
Hounslow TW4 ... 128 D3
Northolt UB5 ... 63 B1
Manorbrook SE12,SE3 ... 143 A1
Manor Circus TW9 ... 132 C2
Manor Cl E17 ... 35 A1
NW7 ... 27 B5
NW9 ... 44 D4
SE28 ... 102 C1
Barnet EN5 ... 1 A1
New Malden KT4 ... 199 C1
Ruislip HA4 ... 39 D1
Manor Cottages App
N2 ... 30 A1
Manor Cotts N2 ... 30 A1
Manor Court Rd W7 ... 108 C6
Manor Cres KT5 ... 198 C3
Manor Ct E10 ... 53 D1
N14 ... 15 D2
N20 ... 14 D1
N2 ... 48 D4
SE15 ... 139 D4
7 SW2 ... 160 B6
SW6 ... 265 D1
W3 ... 110 C2
3 Barking IG11 ... 79 D1
Chingford, Chingford Green
E4 ... 20 C3
Harrow HA1 ... 42 D3
Kingston KT2 ... 176 C2
Streatham SW16 ... 160 A1
Surbiton KT5 ... 198 C3
Twickenham TW2 ... 152 A2
5 Wembley HA9 ... 66 A3
Manordene Cl KT7 ... 197 A1
Manordene Rd SE28 ... 102 D1
Manor Dr N14 ... 15 B3
N20 ... 14 D1
NW7 ... 27 B5
Feltham TW13 ... 172 D5
Hinchley Wood KT10 ... 213 A5
Sunbury TW16 ... 172 A1
Surbiton KT5 ... 198 C3
Wembley HA9 ... 66 B4
West Ewell KT19 ... 215 C2
Manor Dr N KT3,KT4 ... 199 B2
Manor Dr The KT4 ... 199 D1
Manor Farm Ave
TW17 ... 192 D3
Manor Farm Cl KT4 ... 199 C1
Manor Farm Ct E6 ... 100 B4
Manor Farm Dr E4 ... 20 C1
Manor Farm Rd
Thornton Heath CR7,
SW16 ... 182 C1
Wembley HA0 ... 87 D5
Manorfield Cl 3 N19 ... 71 C4
Manorfield Prim Sch
E14 ... 97 D2
Manorfields Cl BR7 ... 211 D6
Manor Gate UB5 ... 63 A1
Manorgate Rd KT2 ... 176 C2
Manor Gdns N7 ... 72 A5
SW4 ... 137 C3
W3 ... 110 C2
8 W4 ... 111 C1
Hampton TW12 ... 174 A3
Merton SW20 ... 179 B1
Richmond TW10,TW9 ... 132 B1
Ruislip HA4 ... 62 C3
South Croydon CR2 ... 221 D2
Sunbury TW16 ... 172 A1
Manor Gr SE15 ... 140 C6
Beckenham BR3 ... 185 D1
Richmond TW9 ... 132 C2
Manor Gt SW15 ... 157 A6
Manor Hall Ave NW4 ... 28 D1
Manor Hall Dr NW4 ... 28 D1
Manor Hall Gdns E10 ... 53 C1
Manor Ho E12 ... 77 D4
N14 ... 15 D3
NW1 ... 237 B4
Brentford TW8 ... 109 C1
Wallington SM6 ... 219 B3
Manor House Ct W9 ... 236 A5
Manor House Dr NW6 ... 68 D1
Manor House Est HA7 ... 25 B5
Manor House Sch W7 108 C6
Manor House Way
TW7 ... 131 B2
Manor Inf Sch IG11 ... 79 D2
Manor Jun Sch IG11 ... 79 D2
Manor La SE12 ... 164 C5
Feltham TW13 ... 150 A2

Manor La *continued*
Harlington UB3 ... 127
Sunbury TW16 ... 172
Sutton SM1 ... 218
Manor Lane Terr SE13 164
Manor Lodge NW2 ... 68
Manor Mans N7 ... 72
7 NW3 ... 70
Manor Mead Sch
TW17 ... 192
Manor Mews NW6 ... 91
SE4 ... 141
Manor Mount SE23 ... 162
Manor Oak Mans SE22 162
Manor Par N16 ... 73
Harrow HA1 ... 42
Manor Park Cl BR4 ... 207
Manor Park Cres HA8 ... 26
Manor Park Dr HA2 ... 41
Manor Park Gdns HA8 ... 26
Manor Park Prim Sch
SM1 ... 218
Manor Park Rd E12 ... 77
N2 ... 48
NW10 ... 89
Chislehurst BR7 ... 189
Sutton SM1 ... 218
West Wickham BR4 ... 207
Manor Park Sta E12 ... 77
Manor Pk SE13 ... 164
Chislehurst BR7 ... 189
Richmond TW9 ... 132
Manor Pl BR7 ... 189
SE17 ... 117 A1 262
East Bedfont TW14 ... 150
Mitcham CR4 ... 203
Sutton SM1 ... 217
Walton-on-T KT12 ... 194
Manor Prim Sch E15 ... 98
Manor Rd DA15 ... 168
DA5 ... 169
E10 ... 53
E15,E16 ... 98
E17 ... 35
N16 ... 51
Ashford TW15 ... 170
Barking IG11 ... 79
Barnet EN5 ... 1
Beckenham BR3 ... 185
Belmont SM2 ... 217
Bowes Park N22 ... 32
Dagenham RM6 ... 58
Ealing W13 ... 109
East Molesey KT8 ... 196
Enfield EN2 ... 5
Harrow HA1 ... 43
Hayes UB3 ... 84
Loughton IG10 ... 21
Merton SW20 ... 179
Mitcham CR4 ... 203 C
Richmond TW10,TW9 ... 132 B
Richmond TW11 ... 175 B
Ruislip HA4 ... 39
South Norwood SE25 ... 206
Tottenham N17 ... 34
Twickenham TW2 ... 152
Wallington SM5,SM6 ... 219
Walton-on-T KT12 ... 193
West Wickham BR4 ... 223
Manor Rd N
Hinchley Wood KT7 ... 213
Wallington SM5,SM6 ... 219
Manor Rd S KT10 ... 212
Manor Sch NW10 ... 90
Manorside EN5 ... 1
Manorside Cl SE2 ... 124
Manorside Prim Sch
N3 ... 30
Manor Sq RM8 ... 80
Manor Street Est SW3 267
Manor The W1 ... 248
Manor Vale TW8 ... 109
Manor View N3 ... 29
Manor Way BR2 ... 210
BR5 ... 211
DA5 ... 169 C3
NW9 ... 45 C5
W3 ... 110 C2
Manorway Enfield EN1 ... 17
Woodford IG8 ... 37
Manor Way
Beckenham BR3 ... 207
Chingford E4 ... 36 B6
Greenwich SE3 ... 143
Harrow HA2 ... 41 D5
Mitcham CR4 ... 203 C6
New Malden KT4 ... 199 D1
Ruislip HA4 ... 39 D1
Southall UB2 ... 106 D2
South Croydon CR2 ... 221 D2
Manor Waye UB8 ... 82 A6
Manor Way The SM6 ... 219 B4
Manpreet Ct E12 ... 78 B3
Manresa Rd
SW3 ... 114 C1 257 A1
Mansard Beeches
SW17 ... 181 A5
Mansard Cl HA5 ... 40 D6

Mansard Manor 4
SM2 218 A1
Manse Cl UB3 127 B6
Manse Ct DA14 190 C5
Mansel Ct SW11 267 B1
Mansel Gr E17 35 C2
Mansell Ho SW8 269 B2
Mansell Rd W3 111 B4
Southall UB6 85 D2
Mansell St E1 95 D1 243 D1
Mansel Rd SW19 179 B4
Manse Rd N16 73 D5
Mansergh Cl SE18 144 A5
Mansfield Ave N15 51 B5
East Barnet EN4 15 A5
Ruislip HA4 40 B1
Mansfield Cl N9 18 A5
Mansfield Ct 27 E2 95 D6
Mansfield Dr UB4 83 C3
Mansfield Hill E4 19 D3
Mansfield Ho SW15 156 D5
Mansfield Hts N2 48 D4
Mansfield Mews W1 238 C3
Mansfield Pl 11 NW3 70 A4
Mansfield Rd E17 53 B5
NW3 70 D4
Acton W3 88 D3
Chessington KT9 213 D3
Ilford IG1 78 C6
South Croydon CR2 221 B2
Wanstead E11 55 B3
Mansfield St
W1 93 B2 238 C3
Mansford St E2 96 A5
Manship Rd CR4 181 A2
Mansion Cl SW9 138 C4
Mansion Gdns NW3 69 D5
Mansion House★ EC4 242 C1
Mansion House Pl
EC3,EC4 242 C1
Mansion House St
EC2 242 C1
Mansion House Sta
EC4 117 A6 252 B6
Mansions The NW6 69 B3
Manson Mews
SW7 114 B2 256 C3
Manson Pl
SW7 114 B2 256 C3
Manstead Gdns RM6 58 C2
Manston NW1 71 C1
Tottenham N17 33 B1
Manston Ave UB2 107 C2
Manston Cl SE20 184 C2
Manstone Rd NW2 69 A3
Manston Gr KT2 175 D5
Manston Ho W14 254 B5
Mantell Ho SW4 159 C6
Manthorpe Rd SE18 123 A1
Mantilla Rd SW17 181 A6
Mantle Rd SE4 141 A2
Mantlet Cl SW16 181 C3
Mantle Way E15 76 C1
Manton Ave W7 109 A4
Manton Cl UB3 105 C6
Manton Ho N16 73 B5
Manton Rd SE2 124 A2
Holdbrook EN3 7 C5
Mantua St 23 SW11 136 B2
Mantus Cl E1 96 C3
Mantus Rd E1 96 C3
Manus Way N20 14 A3
Manville Gdns SW17 159 B1
Manville Rd SW17 159 B1
Manwood Rd SE4 163 B5
Manwood St E16 122 B5
Manygate La TW17 193 A3
Many Gates SW12 159 B2
Mapesbury Ct NW2 69 A3
Mapesbury Rd NW2 69 A2
Mapeshill Pl NW2 68 C2
Mapes Ho 5 NW6 69 A1
Mape St E2 96 B3
Maple Ave E4 35 B4
W3 111 C5
Harrow HA2 63 D6
Yiewsley UB7 104 B6
Maple Cl BR5 211 B4
N16 52 A3
N3 29 C4
SW4 159 D5
Buckhurst Hill IG9 21 D1
Hampton TW12 173 B4
Hayes UB4 84 D4
Mitcham CR4 181 B2
Ruislip HA4 40 B3
Maple Cres DA15 168 A5
Maplecroft Cl E6 100 A1
Maple Ct E6 100 C2
NW2 68 D4
Catford SE6 163 D3
2 Croydon CR0 221 A4
7 Dagenham RM8 58 D2
Kingston KT3 199 B6
4 Pinner HA5 22 C1
Sidcup DA14 190 B5
11 West Norwood
SW16 182 C5
Mapledale Ave CR0 222 A5
Mapledene BR7 189 A5
Mapledene Est E8 74 A1
Mapledene Rd E8 74 A1
Mapledown Sch NW2 46 C2
Maple Gdns HA8 27 C3
Stanwell TW19 148 A2
Maple Gr NW9 45 A2
W5 109 D3
Brentford TW8 131 B5
Southall UB1 85 B2
Maple Gr Bsns Ctr
TW4 128 C1
Maple Ho 13 E17 53 D6
11 NW3 70 D2
5 SE8 141 B5
2 Kingston KT6 198 A4
Maplehurst 2 BR2 186 C1
Maplehurst Cl KT1 198 A5
Maple Ind Est TW13 150 A1
Maple Inf Sch KT6 197 D4
Maple Leaf Dr DA15 167 D3
Mapleleafe Gdns IG6 56 D6
Maple Leaf Sq 27
SE16 118 D4
Maple Lo NW9 67 B6
Putney SW15 157 A5
Maple Mews NW6 91 D5
Streatham SW16 182 B5
Maple Pl W1 239 B5
Tottenham N17 34 A3
Yiewsley UB7 104 B6
Maple Rd E11 54 C3
Hayes UB4 84 D4
Kingston KT6 197 D4
Penge SE20 184 C2
Maples Pl E1 96 B2
Maple St W1 93 C3 239 B5
Maplestead Rd
Dagenham RM9 102 B6
Streatham SW2 160 B4
Maples The KT8 175 C3
Maplethorpe Rd CR7 204 D5
Mapleton Cl BR2 209 A3
Mapleton Cres
Enfield EN3 6 C5
Wandsworth SW18 157 D5
Mapleton Rd
Chingford E4 20 A1
Enfield EN1 6 B3
Wandsworth SW18 157 D5
Maple Way TW13 150 B1
Maple Wlk W10 90 D3
Maplin Cl N21 16 B5
Maplin Ho 9 SE2 124 D4
Maplin Rd E16 99 B1
Maplin St E3 97 B4
Mapperley Cl 3 E11 55 A3
Mapperley Dr IG8 36 C3
Marada Ho NW6 69 A1
Marais W4 133 A5
Maran Way DA18 124 D3
Marathon Way SE28 123 D4
Marban Rd W9 91 B4
Marble Arch★
W1 114 D6 247 D6
Marble Arch Sta
W1 92 D1 237 D1
Marble Cl W3 110 D5
Marble Dr NW2 46 D2
Marbleford Ct 4 N6 49 D2
Marble Hill★ TW1 153 C4
Marble Hill Cl TW1 153 B4
Marble Hill Gdns TW1 153 B4
Marble Ho SE18 123 D1
W9 91 B3
Marbrook Ct SE12 165 C1
Marcella Rd SW9 138 C3
Marcellina Way BR6 227 D5
March 23 NW9 27 D2
Marchant Ct SE1 263 D2
Marchant Ho 18 SW2 160 B6
Marchant Rd E11 76 B6
Marchant St SE14 141 A6
Marchbank Rd
W14 135 B6 264 D6
March Ct SW15 134 B1
Marchmont Ho 10
SW16 181 C5
Marchmont Rd
Richmond TW10 154 B6
Wallington SM6 219 C1
Marchmont St
WC1 94 A3 240 A6
March Rd 5 TW1 153 A4
Marchside Cl TW5 128 D4
Marchwood Cl 17 SE5 139 C5
Marchwood Cres W5 87 D1
Marcia Rd SE1 117 C2 263 B3
Marcilly Rd SW18 158 B6
Marcon Ct 23 E8 74 B3
Marconi Pl N11 31 B6
Marconi Rd E10 53 C1
Marconi Way UB1 85 D1
Marcon Pl E8 74 B3
Marco Rd W6 112 C3
Marcourt Lawns W5 88 A3
Marcus Ct E15 98 C6
Brentford TW8 132 A5
Marcus Garvey Mews
SE22 162 B6
Marcus Garvey Way 9
SE24 138 C1
Marcus Ho 13 SE15 139 D4
Marcus St E15 98 D6
Wandsworth SW18 157 D5
Marcus Terr SW18 157 D5
Mardale Ct NW7 28 A3
Mardale Dr NW9 45 B4
Mardell Rd CR0 206 D4
Marden Ave BR2 209 A3
Marden Cres CR0 204 B3
Marden Ho 6 E8 74 B3
Marden Rd
Thornton Heath CR0 204 B3
Tottenham N17 33 C1
Marden Sq SE16 118 B3
Marder Rd W13 109 A4
Mardyke Ho SE17 262 D4
Marechal Niel Ave
DA15 167 B1
Marechal Niel Par
DA15 167 B1
Maresby Ho E4 19 D2
Maresfield CR0 221 C5
Maresfield Gdns NW3 70 A2
Mare St E8 74 B2
E8,E2 96 B6
Marfleet Cl SM5 218 C6
Margaret Ave E4 19 D5
Margaret Bondfield Ave
IG11 80 A1
Margaret Bondfield Ho
4 E3 97 A5
22 N7 71 D3
Margaret Ct W1 239 A2
Barnet EN4 2 B1
Margaret Gardner Dr
SE9 166 B2
Margaret Herbison Ho
SW6 264 D5
Margaret Hill Ho N8 50 A4
Margaret Ho 16 W6 112 C1
Margaret Ingram Cl
SW6 264 C5
Margaret Lockwood Cl
KT5 198 B5
Margaret Mcmillan Ho 10
N19 49 D2
Margaret Rd DA5 168 D5
N16 51 D1
Barnet EN4 2 B1
Margaret's Ct E11 54 B2
SE1 252 C3
Margarets Ct HA8 26 D5
Margaret St W1 93 C1 239 A2
Margaretta Terr
SW3 136 C6 267 B6
Margaretting Rd E12 55 C1
Margaret Way IG4 56 A3
Margaret White Ho
NW1 232 C2
Margate Rd SW2 160 A6
Margery Fry Ct N7 72 A5
Margery Park Rd E7 77 A2
Margery Rd RM8 80 D5
Margery St
WC1 94 C4 234 A1
Margetson Ho N16 51 D3
Margin Dr SW19 178 D6
Margravine Gdns W14 254 A2
W6 112 D1
Margravine Rd
W6 112 D1 264 A6
Marham Gdns
Morden SM4 202 A3
Wandsworth SW17,
SW18 158 C3
Mar Ho 4 SE7 143 C6
Maria Cl 10 SE1 118 A2
Maria Fidelis RC Convent
Sch NW1 93 D4 232 C2
Maria Ho 18 SW9 138 C4
Marian Cl UB4 84 D3
Marian Ct E9 74 C3
Sutton SM1 217 D3
Marian Lo 5 SW20 178 D3
Marian Pl E2 96 B5
Marian Rd SW16 181 C2
Marian Sq E2 96 B5
Marian St 2 E2 96 B5
Marian Vian Prim Sch
BR3 207 A4
Marian Way NW10 67 D1
Maria Terr E1 96 D3
Maria Theresa Cl KT3 199 B4
Maribor 18 SE10 142 A5
Maricas Ave HA3 24 B2
Marie Curie SE5 139 C4
Marie Lloyd Ct 13
SW9 138 B1
Marie Lloyd Gdns 1
N19 50 A2
Marie Lloyd Ho N1 235 C3
Marien Ct E4 36 B5
Marigold Cl UB1 107 A6
Marigold Rd N17 34 C3
Marigold St SE16 118 B4
Marigold Way CR0 206 D1
Marilea Ct W5 109 D4
Marina App UB4 85 A2
Marina Ave KT3 200 B4
Marina Cl 1 BR2 209 A6
Marina Ct 11 E3 97 C4
Marina Dr DA16 145 C3
Marina Gdns RM7 59 D4
Marina Way TW11 175 D3
Marine Dr 5 SE18 122 B2
Barking IG11 102 B4
Marinefield Rd SW6 135 D3
Marinel Ho 25 SE5 139 A5
Mariner Gdns TW10 153 C1
Mariner Rd E12 78 C4
Mariners Mews E14 120 B2
Marine St SE16 118 A3
Marine Twr 29 SE8 141 B6
Marion Ave TW17 192 D4
Marion Ct 4 SW17 180 C5
Marion Gr IG8 36 C6
Marion Rd NW7 28 A5
Thornton Heath CR0 205 B4
Marion Richardson Prim
Sch E1 96 D1
Marischal Rd SE13 142 B2
Maritime Ho 5 SW4 137 C2
Maritime Ind Est SE7 121 B2
Maritime Quay 6 E14 119 C1
Maritime St E3 97 B3
Marius Mans 3 SW17 159 A2
Marius Rd SW17 159 A2
Marjorie Gr SW11 136 D1
Marjorie McClure Sch
BR7 189 A2
Marjory Kinnon Sch
TW14 149 C6
Markab Rd HA6 22 A5
Mark Ave E4 19 D5
Mark Cl BR2 226 A4
DA7 147 A4
Southall UB1 107 D5
Markeston Gn WD19 22 D6
Market Ct W1 239 A2
Market Ctr The UB2 106 B2
Market La HA8 27 A2
Market Mews
W1 115 B5 248 C3
Market Par E10 53 D3
E17 53 B6
Croydon SE25 206 A5
1 Edmonton N9 18 A2
Feltham TW13 151 A2
Market Pl 2 DA7 147 C1
N2 48 C6
1 SE16 118 B2
W1 239 A2
3 W3 111 A5
Brentford TW8 131 C5
Enfield EN2 5 B2
Kingston KT1 175 D1
Market Pl The NW11 47 D5
Market Rd N7 72 A2
Richmond TW9 132 C2
Market Sq BR1 187 A1
E14 97 D1
Market Sq The N9 18 B2
Market St SE18 122 C2
Wallend E6 100 C5
Market The SM1,SM5 202 A1
Market Way E14 97 D1
1 Wembley HA0 66 A3
Market Yd Mews SE1 263 A6
Markfield Gdns E4 19 D4
Markfield Ho N15 52 A5
Markfield Rd N15 52 A4
Markham Ct NW4 46 C6
Markham Ho
1 Dagenham RM10 81 C5
9 Dulwich SE21 183 C6
Markham Pl SW3 257 C2
Markham Sq
SW3 114 D1 257 C2
Markham St
SW3 114 C1 257 B2
Mark Ho 8 E2 96 D5
Markhole Cl TW12 173 B3
Markhouse Ave E17 53 A3
Markhouse Pas E17 53 B3
Markhouse Rd E17 53 B3
Mark La EC3 117 C6 253 B6
Markland Ho W10 112 D6
Mark Lo 9 EN4 2 C1
Markmanor Ave E17 53 B2
Mark Mans W12 112 A4
Mark Rd N22 32 D1
Marksbury Ave TW9 132 C2
Marks Gate Inf Sch
RM6 59 A6
Marks Gate Jun Sch
RM6 59 A6
Mark Sq EC2 243 A6
Mark St E15 76 C1
EC2 243 A6
Markstone Ho SE1 251 C1
Mark Wade Cl E12 55 D1
Markway The TW16 172 C1
Markwell Cl SE26 184 B6
Markyate Ho W10 90 C3
Markyate Rd RM8 80 B3
Marland Ho SW1 257 D6
Marlands Rd IG5 56 B6
Marlang Ct BR3 186 B2
Marlborough W9 229 A2
11 Putney SW19 156 D3
Marlborough Ave
3 E8 96 A6
N14 15 C1
Edgware HA8 10 D1
Ruislip HA4 39 B3
Marlborough Cl BR6 211 D3
N20 14 D1
SE17 261 D3
Mitcham SW19 180 C4
Marlborough Cres
W4 111 C3
Harlington UB3 127 B5
Marlborough Ct W8 255 A4
7 Buckhurst Hill IG9 21 C2
Harrow HA1 42 B5
Wallington SM6 219 C1
Marlborough Day Hospl
NW8 92 A5 229 A4
Marlborough Dr IG5 56 A6
Marlborough Flats
SW3 257 B4
Marlborough Fst & Mid Sch
HA1 42 C5
Marlborough Gdns N20 14 D1
Surbiton KT6 197 D2
Marlborough Gr SE1 118 A1
Marlborough Hill
NW8 92 A6 229 B5
Harrow HA1 42 C5
Marlborough Ho N4 51 A1
NW8 229 A3
Richmond TW10 154 C6
Wimbledon SW19 156 D1
Marlborough House
SW1 249 B3
Marlborough La SE7 143 C5
Marlborough Mans 5
NW6 69 C3
Marlborough Mews
SW2 138 B1
Marlborough Par 1
UB10 82 D3
Marlborough Park Ave
DA15 168 A3
Marlborough Pl
NW8 92 A5 229 B4
Marlborough Prim Sch
SW3 114 C2 257 B3
Marlborough Rd DA16 146 D2
E15 76 C4
E7 77 C1
N19 72 A6
SE18 123 A3
SW1 115 C5 249 B3
W4 111 A1
W5 109 D4
Ashford TW15 170 A5
Bowes Park N22 32 B4
Brentford TW7 131 B5
Bromley BR2 209 C5
Chingford E4 35 D4
Dagenham RM8 80 C4
Edmonton N9 18 A3
Feltham TW13 150 D2
Hampton TW12 173 C4
Hillingdon UB10 82 D4
Mitcham SW19 180 C4
Richmond TW10 154 B5
Romford RM7 59 D5
Southall UB2 106 C3
South Croydon CR2 221 A1
Sutton SM1 217 C6
Wanstead E18 55 A6
Marlborough Sch
Isleworth TW7 131 A4
Sidcup DA15 168 A4
Marlborough St
SW3 114 C2 257 B3
Marlborough Trad Est
TW9 132 D4
Marlborough Yd N19 71 D6
Marlbury NW8 91 D6
Marler Rd SE23 163 B3
Marlesford Ct SM6 219 C4
Marley Ave DA7 146 D6
Marley Cl N15 50 D5
Southall UB6 85 C4
Marley Ho 14 W11 112 D6
Marley Wlk NW2 68 C3
Marlfield Cl KT4 200 A1
Marlfield Ct KT3 199 D2
Marlin Cl TW16 171 C4
Marling Ct TW12 173 B4
Marlingdene Cl TW12 173 C4
Marlings Cl BR7 211 C5
Marlings Park Ave
BR7 211 C6
Marlin Ho SW15 157 A6
Marlins Cl 3 SM1 218 A3
Marloes Cl HA0 65 D4
Marloes Rd
W8 113 D3 255 C5
Marlow Cl SE20 206 B6
Marlow Cres TW1 152 D5
Marlow Ct N14 15 C4
NW6 68 D1
NW9 45 D6
1 Ealing W7 108 C5
Marlow Dr SM3 216 D5
Marlowe Bsns Ctr 2
SE14 141 A5
Marlowe Cl BR7 189 B4
Marlowe Ct SW3 257 B3
Dulwich SE19 183 D5
6 Kingston KT2 175 D6
Marlowe Gdns SE9 166 C5
Marlowe Ho 15 N16 73 C4
SE8 119 B1
Kingston KT1 197 D5
Marlowe Lo CR0 223 A6
Marlowe Rd E17 54 A5
Marlowe Sq CR4 203 C5
Marlowes The
NW8 92 B6 229 C6
Marlowe Way CR0 220 A6
Marlow Gdns UB3 105 B3
Marlow Ho 44 E2 95 D4
SE1 263 C6
14 W2 91 D1
Teddington TW11 175 A6
Marlow Rd E6 100 B4
Penge SE20 184 B1
Southall UB2 107 B3
Marlow Studio Workshops
43 E2 95 D4
Marlow Way SE16 118 D4
Marl Rd SW18 136 A1
Marlston NW1 231 D1
Marlton St SE10 120 D1
Marlwood Cl DA15 167 C2
Marmadon Rd SE18,
SE2 123 D2
Marmion App E4 35 C6
Marmion Ave E4 35 B6
Marmion Cl E4 35 B6
Marmion Ho 13 SW12 159 B4
Marmion Mews 4
SW11 137 A2
Marmion Rd SW11 137 A1
Marmont Rd SE15 140 A5
Marmora Ho E1 97 A2
Marmora Rd SE22 162 C5
Marmot Rd TW4 128 D2
Marne Ave DA16 146 A2
N11 31 B6
Marnell Way TW4 128 D2
Marner Prim Sch E3 97 D3
Marne St W10 91 A4
Marney Rd SW11 137 A1
Marnfield Cres SW2 160 B3
Marnham Ave NW2 69 A4
Marnham Cres UB6 85 D5
Marnham Ct HA0 65 C3
Marnock Ho SE17 262 C2
Marnock Rd SE4 163 B6
Maroon St E14 97 A2
Maroons Way SE6 185 C5
Marqueen Twrs SW16 182 B3
Marquess Rd N1 73 B2
Marquess Rd N N1 73 B2
Marquess Rd S 17 N1 73 A2
Marquis Cl HA0 66 B1
Marquis Ct N4 50 B1
Barking IG11 79 C3
1 Kingston KT1 198 A5
Marquis Rd N4 50 C1
NW1 71 D2
Bowes Park N22 32 B4
Marrabon Cl DA15 168 A3
Marrayat Sq SW6 264 A2
Marrick Cl SW15 134 A1
Marrick Ho 17 NW6 91 D6
Marrilyne Ave EN3 7 B5
Marriner Ct UB3 105 C6
Marriott Cl TW14 149 B5
Marriott Ho 8 SE6 186 A6
Marriott Rd E15 98 C6
N10 30 D2
N4 50 B1
Marriotts Cl NW9 45 D3
Marryat Ct 12 W6 112 B2
Marryat Ho SW1 259 A1
Marryat Pl SW19 179 A6
Marryat Rd SW19 179 A6
Marryatt Ct W5 88 B1
Marsala Rd SE13 141 D1
Marsalis Ho 2 E3 97 C4
Marsden Rd SE15 139 D2
Edmonton N9 18 B2
Marsden St NW5 71 A2
Marsden Way 2 BR6 227 D4
Marshall Cl N11 15 B1
SW18 158 A5
Harrow HA1 42 B2
Hounslow TW4 151 B6
Marshall Ct SW4 270 B1
Marshall Dr UB4 83 D2
Marshall Ho N1 235 D4
NW6 91 B5

Marshall Ho *continued*
SE17 262 C2
4 New Malden KT3 199 C5
Marshall Path 10 SE28 124 B6
Marshall Rd Leyton E10 75 D4
Tottenham N17 33 B2
Marshalls Gr SE18 122 A2
Marshall's Pl SE16 263 D5
Marshall's Rd SM1 217 D4
Marshall St W1 93 C1 239 B1
Marshalsea Rd
SE1 117 A4 252 B2
Marsham Cl BR7 188 D5
Marsham Ct SW1 259 D4
19 Putney SW19 156 D3
Marsham St
SW1 115 D2 259 D4
Marsh Ave CR4 181 A1
Marshbrook Cl SE3 143 D2
Marsh Cl NW7 11 D1
Marsh Ct E8 74 A2
3 Merton SW19 180 A2
Marsh Dr NW9 45 D3
Marsh Farm Rd TW2 152 D3
Marshfield St E14 120 A3
Marshgate Bsns Ctr
E15 98 A5
Marshgate Ctr The E15 97 D6
Marshgate La E15 75 D1
Marsh Green Prim Sch
RM10 103 C5
Marsh Green Rd RM10 103 C6
Marsh Hall HA9 66 B5
Marsh Hill E9 75 A3
Marsh Ho SW1 259 D1
SW8 269 B2
Marsh La E10 75 C6
NW7 11 C1
Stanmore HA7 25 C4
Tottenham N17 34 B2
Marsh Rd Pinner HA5 41 A5
Wembley HA0 87 D5
Marshside Cl N9 18 C3
Marsh St E14 119 D2
Marsh Wall E14 119 D4
Marshwood Ho 10 NW6 91 C6
Marsland Cl SE17 261 D1
Marsom Ho N1 235 C3
Marston SE17 262 B4
Marston Ave
Chessington KT9 214 A2
Dagenham RM10 81 C5
Marston Cl NW6 70 A1
Dagenham RM10 81 C5
Marston Ct DA14 189 D6
Walton-on-T KT12 194 C1
Marston Ho SW9 138 C3
Marston Rd TW11 175 B5
Marston Way SE19 183 A3
Marsworth Ave HA5 22 D2
Marsworth Cl UB4 85 A2
Marsworth Ho 8 E2 96 A6
Martaban Rd N16 73 D6
Martello St E8 74 B1
Martello Terr E8 74 B1
Martell Rd SE21 161 B1
Martel Pl E8 73 D2
Marten Rd E17 35 C1
Martens Ave DA7 147 D1
Martham Cl SE28 124 D6
Martha Rd E15 76 C2
Martha's Bldgs EC1 242 C6
Martha St E1 96 C1
Marthorne Cres HA3 24 B1
Martin Bowes Rd SE9 144 B2
Martinbridge Trad Est
EN1 18 B6
Martin Cl N9 18 D3
Uxbridge UB10 82 A5
Martin Cres CR0 204 C1
Martin Ct 10 E14 120 A4
Merton SW19 179 C3
Southall UB2 107 B4
Martindale SW14 155 A6
Martindale Ave 2
E16 121 A6
Martindale Ho 20 E14 119 D6
Martindale Rd
Balham SW12 159 B4
Hounslow TW4 129 A2
Martin Dene DA6 169 B6
Martin Dr UB5 63 B3
Martineau Cl KT10 212 B4
Martineau Ho SW1 259 A1
Martineau Mews N5 72 D4
Martineau Rd N5 72 D4
Martingale Cl TW16 194 A5
Martingales Cl TW10 153 D1
Martin Gdns RM8 80 D4
Martin Gr SM4 201 C6
Martin Ho SE1 262 B5
SW8 270 A4
6 New Malden KT3 199 C5
Martini Dr EN3 7 C6
Martin La EC4 252 D6
Martin Prim Sch N2 30 C1
Martin Rd RM8 80 D4
Martin Rise DA6 169 B6
Martins Cl BR4 224 B6
Martins Mount EN5 1 D1
Martin's Rd BR2 186 D1
Martin St SE28 123 C5
Martins The
Penge SE26 184 B5
Wembley HA9 66 B5
Martins Wlk N10 31 A2
Woolwich SE28 123 C5
Martin Way SW19,
SW20,SM4 201 B6
Martlesham N17 33 C1
Martlet Gr 5 UB5 84 D4
Martlett Ct WC2 240 B1
Martlett Lo NW3 69 D4
Martley Dr IG2 56 D4
Martley Ho SW8 269 B2
Martock Cl HA3 43 A5
Martock Ct 10 SE15 140 B4
Martock Gdns N11 31 A5
Marton Cl SE6 163 C1
Marton Rd 2 N16 73 C5
Martyn Ct HA8 26 B6
Martyn Ho SE2 146 D6
Martynside 22 NW9 27 D2
Marvel Ho 5 SE5 139 B5
Marvell Ave UB4 84 A2
Marvels Cl SE12 165 B2
Marvels La SE12 165 C1
Marvels Lane Prim Sch
SE12 187 D6
Marville Ho SW18 158 B5
Marville Rd
SW6 135 B5 264 C3
Marvin Ho 9 SE18 144 D6
Marvin St 3 E8 74 B2
Marwell Cl BR4 224 D6
Marwick Rd UB7 104 B4
Marwood Cl DA16 146 B2
Mary Adelaide Cl
Kingston SW15 155 C1
Kingston SW15 177 C6
Mary Adelaide Ho W2 236 D4
Mary Ann Bldgs SE8 141 C6
Maryatt Ave HA2 63 D6
Marybank SE18 122 B2
Mary Batchelor Sch (Girls)
SE5 139 B4
Mary Cl HA7 44 B5
Mary Datchelor Cl
SE5 139 B4
Mary Dine Ct SW8 270 D3
Mary Gn NW8 91 D6
Marygold Ho TW3 130 A4
Mary Ho 6 SW9 138 B3
8 W6 112 C1
Mary James Ho 29 E2 96 A5
Mary Jones Ho 13 E14 119 C6
Maryland Ct KT1 176 D1
Maryland Pk E15 76 C3
Maryland Point E15 76 C2
Maryland Prim Sch E15 76 C3
Maryland Rd E15 76 B3
W9 91 C3
South Norwood CR7 182 D2
Tottenham N22 32 C4
Marylands Ind Est E15 76 C3
Maryland Sq E15 76 C3
Marylands Rd W9 91 D3
Maryland St E15 76 C3
Maryland Sta E15 76 C2
Maryland Way TW16 172 A1
Maryland Wlk N1 235 A6
Mary Lawrenson Pl 1
SE3 143 A5
Marylebone Flyover
NW1 92 C2 237 A3
Marylebone High St
W1 93 A2 238 B4
Marylebone La
W1 93 A1 238 B2
Marylebone Mews
W1 238 C3
Marylebone Pas W1 239 B2
Marylebone Rd
NW1 92 D2 237 D4
Marylebone St
W1 93 A2 238 B3
Marylebone Sta
NW1 92 D3 237 C5
Marylee Way
SE11 116 B2 260 D3
Mary Macarthur Ho
18 E2 96 D4
W14 264 A6
11 Belvedere DA17 125 C3
11 Dagenham RM10 81 C5
Mary McArthur Ho 12
N19 49 D2
Marymount International
Sch KT2 177 A3
Maryon Gr SE7 122 A2
Maryon Mews NW3 70 C4
Maryon Rd SE7 122 A2
Mary Peters Dr UB6 64 B3
Mary Pl W11 113 A6 244 A5
Mary Rose Cl TW12 173 C2
Mary Rose Mall E6 100 B2
Maryrose Way N20 14 B3
Mary's Ct NW8 237 B6
Mary Secole Cl 21 E8 95 D6
Mary St 5 E16 98 D2
N1 95 A6 235 B5
Mary's Terr TW1 153 A4
Mary Terr NW1 232 A5
Maryville DA16 145 D3
Mary Wharrie Ho 4
NW3 70 D1
Masbro' Rd W14 112 D3
Mascalls Ct 13 SE7 143 C6
Mascalls Rd SE7 143 C6
Mascotte Rd 2 SW15 134 D1
Mascotts Cl NW2 68 B5
Masefield Ave
Borehamwood WD6 10 D6
Southall UB1 107 C6
Stanmore HA7 24 D5
Masefield Cres N14 15 C5
Masefield Ct N5 73 B3
New Barnet EN5 2 A1
10 Surbiton KT6 197 D2
Masefield Gdns E6 100 C3
Masefield Ho 1 NW6 91 C4
Masefield La UB4 84 C3
Masefield Rd TW13 173 B6
Masefield View BR6 227 A5
Masefield Way TW19 148 B3
Masham Ho 6 DA18 124 D4
Mashie Rd W3 89 C1
Maskall Cl SW2 160 C3
Maskani Wlk SW16 181 C3
Maskell Rd SW17 158 A1
Maskelyne Cl
SW11 136 C4 267 B2
Mason Cl DA7 147 D2
E16 121 A6
SE16 118 A1
Hampton TW12 173 B2
Wimbledon SW20 178 D2
Mason Ct
4 Penge SE19 183 D3
Wembley HA9 66 C6
Mason Ho 16 E9 74 C1
8 N11 31 C5
13 SE1 118 A2
Mason Rd Sutton SM1 217 D3
Woodford IG8 36 C6
Mason's Arms Mews
W1 248 D6
Mason's Ave EC2 242 C2
Masons Ave HA3 42 D5
Mason's Ave CR0 221 A5
Masons Hill BR2 209 B5
SE18 122 D2
Mason's Pl EC1 235 A2
Mitcham CR4 180 D2
Mason St SE17 117 B2 262 D4
Mason's Yd SW1 249 B4
Wimbledon SW19 178 D5
Massey Cl N11 31 B5
Massey Ct 7 E6 99 C6
Massie Rd E8 74 A2
Massingberd Way
SW17 181 B6
Massinger St SE1,SE17 263 A3
Massingham St E1 96 D3
Masson Ave HA4 62 C2
Mast Ct 17 SE16 119 A2
Master Gunner's Pl 1
SE18 144 A4
Masterman Ho 1 SE5 139 B5
Masterman Rd E6 100 A4
Masters Cl SW16 181 C4
Masters Ct HA4 61 C6
Masters Dr SE16 118 B1
Masters Lo 22 E1 96 C1
Master's St 14 E1 96 D2
Mast House Terr E14 119 C2
Mastin Ho SW18 157 C3
Mastmaker Rd E14 119 C4
Maswell Park Cres
TW3 152 A6
Maswell Park Rd TW3 130 A1
Matcham Rd E11 76 D5
Matching Ct 13 E3 97 C4
Matchless Dr SE18 144 C5
Matfield Cl BR2 209 A4
Matfield Rd DA17 147 C6
Matham Gr SE22 139 D1
Matham Rd KT8 196 B4
Mathart Ct E4 36 B4
Matheson Lang Ho
SE1 251 A1
Matheson Rd
W14 113 B2 254 C3
Mathews Ave E6 100 C5
Mathews Park Ave E15 76 D2
Mathieson Ct SE1 251 D1
Mathieson Ho 10 E4 20 C4
Matilda Cl SE19 183 B3
Matilda Ho E1 118 A5
Matilda Marks-Kennedy
Jewish Prim Sch NW7 27 B5
Matilda St N1 94 B6 233 D6
Matlock Cl SE24 139 A1
Barnet EN5 12 D6
Matlock Cres SM3 217 A4
Matlock Ct NW8 229 A4
7 SE5 139 B1
Matlock Gdns SM1,
SM3 217 A4
Matlock Pl SM1,SM3 217 A4
Matlock Rd E10 54 A3
Matlock St E14 97 A1
Matlock Way KT3 177 B2
Maton Ho SW6 264 C4
Matson Ct IG8 36 C3
Matson Ho 16 E9 74 D2
9 SE16 118 B3
Matthew Cl W10 90 D3
Matthew Ct 4 E17 54 A6
Mitcham CR4 203 D4
Matthew Parker St
SW1 249 D1
Matthews Ct N5 73 A4
Matthews Ho 3 E14 97 C2
Matthews Rd UB6 64 B3
Matthews St SW11 136 D3
Matthias Ct 12 TW10 154 A5
Matthias Ho 2 N16 73 C3
Matthias Rd N16 73 C3
Mattingly Way 4
SE15 139 D5
Mattison Rd N4 50 D3
Mattock La W5,W13 109 C5
Maud Cashmore Way
SE18 122 B3
Maude Ho 3 E2 96 A5
Maude Rd E17 53 A4
SE5 139 C4
Maudesville Cotts W7 108 C5
Maude Terr E17 53 A5
Maud Gdns E13 98 D5
Barking IG11 101 D5
Maudlins Gn E1 118 A5
Maud Rd E10 76 A5
E13 98 D5
Maudslay Rd SE9 144 B2
Maudsley Ho TW8 110 A1
Maudsley Hospl The
SE5 139 B3
Maud St E16 98 D2
Maugham Ct 5 W3 111 A3
Mauleverer Rd SW2 160 A6
Maundeby Wlk NW10 67 C2
Maunder Rd 4 W7 108 D5
Maunsel St
SW1 115 D2 259 C4
Mauretania Bldg 11
E1 118 D6
Maurice Ave N22 32 D1
Maurice Browne Cl
NW7 28 D4
Maurice Ct 3 TW8 131 D5
Maurice Ho 1 SW9 138 B3
Maurice St W12 90 B1
Maurice Wlk NW11 48 A5
Maurier Cl UB5 84 C6
Mauritius Rd SE10 120 C2
Maury Rd N16 74 A5
Mauveine Gdns TW3 129 C1
Mavelstone Cl BR1 188 A2
Mavelstone Rd BR1 188 A2
Maverton Rd E3 97 C6
Mavery Ct 4 BR1 186 D3
Mavis Ave KT19 215 C3
Mavis Cl KT19 215 C3
Mavis Ct 33 NW9 27 D1
Mavis Wlk 9 E6 100 A2
Mavor Ho N1 233 D5
Mawbey Ho SE1 263 D1
Mawbey Pl
SE1 117 D1 263 D1
Mawbey Rd SE1 263 D1
Mawbey St SW8 270 A3
Mawdley Ho SE1 251 B1
Mawney Cl RM7 59 D6
Mawney Rd RM7 59 D6
Mawson Cl SW20 179 A1
Mawson Ho EC1 241 A4
Mawson La W4 133 D6
Maxden Ct SE15 140 A2
Maxey Gdns RM9 81 A4
Maxey Rd SE18 123 A2
Dagenham RM9 81 A4
Maxfield Cl N20 14 A4
Maxim Rd N21 16 C5
Maxted Pk HA1 42 C2
Maxted Rd SE15 139 D2
Maxwell Cl
Croydon CR0 204 A1
Hayes UB3 106 A6
Maxwell Ct SE21 162 A3
Maxwell Gdns BR6 227 D5
Maxwell Ho 12 SE18 144 D6
Bowes Park N22 32 B4
Chislehurst BR7 188 D3
Maxwell Rd DA16 146 A2
SW6 135 D5 265 D3
Ashford TW15 171 A4
West Drayton UB7 104 B2
Maxwelton Ave NW7 27 B5
Maxwelton Cl NW7 27 B5
Maya Cl SE15 140 B3
Mayall Cl EN3 7 C5
Mayall Rd SE24 160 D6
Maya Pl N11 31 D3
Maya Rd N2 48 A5
Maybank Ave
Wembley HA0 65 A3
Woodford E18 37 B1
Maybank Gdns HA5 40 A4
Maybank Rd E18 37 C2
May Bate Ave KT2 175 D2
Maybells Commercial Est
IG11 102 D5
Mayberry Pl KT5 198 B2
Maybourne Cl SE26 184 B5
Maybourne Grange
CR0 221 C6
Maybury Cl BR5 210 D4
Enfield EN1 6 B5
Maybury Ct W1 238 B3
Beckenham BR3 185 B3
Harrow HA1 42 B3
Maybury Gdns NW10 68 B2
Maybury Mews N6 49 C2
Maybury Rd E13 99 C3
Barking IG11 102 A5
Maybury St SW17 180 C5
Maychurch Cl HA7 25 D3
May Cl KT9 214 B2
Maycroft 2 Hayes BR2 208 D1
Pinner HA5 22 B1
Maycross Ave SM4 201 C5
May Ct 2 SW19 180 A2
Mayday Gdns SE3 144 A3
Mayday Rd CR0,CR7 204 D3
Mayday University Hospl
CR7 204 D3
Maydeb Ct RM6 59 B3
Maydew Ho SE16 118 C2
Maydwell Ho 6 E14 97 C2
Maye Angelou Ct E4 36 A6
Mayefield Rd CR7 204 B4
Mayerne Rd SE9 165 D6
Mayers Ct E8 74 A4
Mayesbrook Rd
Barking IG11 101 D6
Dagenham RM8,IG3 80 B5
Mayesford Rd RM6 58 C2
Mayespark Prim Sch
IG3 80 A5
Mayeswood Rd SE12 187 C6
Mayfair Ave DA16 146 D4
Dagenham RM6 58 D3
Ilford IG1 56 C1
New Malden KT4 200 A1
Twickenham TW2 152 A4
Mayfair Cl
Beckenham BR3 185 D2
Surbiton KT6 198 A1
Mayfair Ct
1 Beckenham BR3 185 D2
7 Croydon CR0 221 D6
1 Wimbledon SW19 179 A3
Mayfair Gdns
Tottenham N17 33 B4
Woodford IG8 37 A3
Mayfair Pl W1 248 D4
Mayfair Terr N14 15 D4
Mayfield DA7 147 B2
Mayfield Ave BR6 211 D2
N12 30 B6
N14 15 D2
W13 109 B4
W4 111 C2
Harrow HA3 43 B4
Woodford IG8 37 A4
Mayfield Cl E8 73 D2
SW4 159 D6
Ashford TW15 170 D4
Hillingdon UB10 82 D4
Long Ditton KT7 197 B1
Penge SE20 184 B2
Mayfield Cres Enfield N9 18 B5
Thornton Heath CR7 204 B4
Mayfield Ct SM2 218 A1
Mayfield Dr HA5 41 B5
Mayfield Gdns NW4 46 D3
Ealing W7 86 C2
Mayfield Ho 30 E2 96 B5
N16 51 C2
Mayfield Mans SW15 157 B6
Mayfield Prim Sch W7 86 B1
Mayfield Rd BR1 210 A4
E13 98 D3
E17 35 A1
E8 73 D1
N8 50 B3
W12 111 C4
Acton W3 110 D6
Chingford E4 20 B2
Dagenham RM8 58 C1
Enfield EN3 6 D3
Merton SW19 179 B2
South Croydon CR2 221 B1
Sutton SM2 218 B2
Mayfields HA9 66 C6
Mayfield Sch & Coll
RM8 58 C1
Mayfields Cl HA9 66 C6
Mayfield Villas DA14 190 C4
Mayflower Cl SE16 118 D2
Mayflower Cl *continued*
Ruislip HA4 39
Mayflower Ho 2 IG11 101
Mayflower Lo N10 31
N3 47
Mayflower Prim Sch
E14 97
Mayflower Rd SW9 138
Mayflower St 1 SE16 118
Mayfly Cl HA5 40
Mayfly Gdns 12 UB5 84
Mayford NW1 232
Mayford Cl
Balham SW12 158
Penge BR3 206
Mayford Rd SW12 159
May Gdns Elstree WD6 9
Wembley HA0 87
Maygood Ho N1 234
Maygood St N1 94 C5 234
Maygrove Rd NW6 69
Mayhew Cl E4 19
Mayhew Ct 2 SE5 139
Mayhill Rd Barnet EN5 13
Greenwich SE7 143
Mayland Mans 4 IG11 78
Maylands Dr DA14 168
Maylands Ho SW3 257
Maylands Rd WD19 22
Maynard Cl N15 51
SW6 135 D5 265
Maynard Ct EN3 7
Maynard Ho E1 97
SE18 123
Maynard Rd E17 54
Maynards Quay E1 118
Maynooth Gdns CR4 202
Mayo Ct W13 109
Mayola Rd E5 74
Mayo Rd NW10 67
Thornton Heath CR0 205
Walton-on-T KT12 194
Mayow Rd SE23,SE26 184
Mayplace Cl DA7 147
Mayplace La SE18 144
Mayplace Rd W DA7 147
Maypole Ct UB2 107
May Rd E13 99
Chingford E4 35
Twickenham TW2 152
Mayroyd Ave KT6 214
May's Buildings Mews
SE10 142
Mays Ct WC2 250
May's Ct SE10 142
May's Hill Rd BR2 208
Mays La EN5 12
Maysoule Rd SW11 136
Mays Rd TW11,TW12 174
Mayston Mews 3
SE10 121
May Terr IG1 78
Maythorne Cotts SE13 164
Maytime Prep Sch IG1 78
Mayton St N7 72
Maytree Cl HA8 11
Maytree Ct
Mitcham CR4 203
Northolt UB5 85
May Tree Ho SE4 141
Maytree La HA7 24
Maytree Wlk SW2 160
Mayville Prim Sch E11 76
Mayville Rd E11 76
Ilford IG1 78
Mayward Ho 7 SE5 139
May Wlk E13 99
Maywood Cl BR3 185
May Wynne Ho E16 99
Maze Hill SE10,SE3 142
Maze Hill Lo 8 SE10 142
Maze Hill Specl Sch
SE10 142
Maze Hill Sta SE10 142
Mazenod Ave NW6 69
Maze Rd TW9 132
Mead Cl 3 NW1 71
Harrow HA3 24
Mead Cres
Carshalton SM1 218
Chingford E4 36
Meadcroft Ho 4 KT3 199
Meadcroft Rd SE17 138
Mead Ct NW9 45
Meade Cl W4 132
Meader Ct SE14 140
Meadfield HA8 10
Mead Field HA2 63
Meadfield Gn HA8 10
Meadfoot Rd SW16 181
Mead Gr RM6 58
Mead Ho W11 244
Mead House La UB4 83
Meadhurst Pk TW16 171
Mead Inf Sch The
KT19 215
Meadlands Dr TW10 153
Meadlands Prim Sch
TW10 175

ad Lo W4 .....111 B4
adow Ave CR0 .....206 D3
adowbank NW3 .....70 D1
3 .....142 D2
uthgate N21 .....16 B5
rbiton KT5 .....198 B3
adow Bank 7
/15 .....157 B6
adowbank Cl SW6 .134 C5
adowbank Gdns
V5 .....128 B4
adowbank Rd NW9 .45 B2
adowbanks EN5 .....12 A6
adowbrook Ct
V7 .....130 D2
adow Cl DA6 .....169 B6
 .....75 B3
rnet EN5 .....13 B5
tford SE6 .....185 C5
ingford E4 .....19 D3
hislehurst BR7 .....188 D5
field EN3 .....7 A5
nchley Wood KT10 ...212 D5
rtholt UB5 .....85 C5
chmond TW10 .....154 A3
uislip HA4 .....39 D3
itton SM1 .....218 A6
est Barnes SW20 .....200 C5
ounslow TW4 .....151 C5
adowcourt Rd SE3 142 D1
adowcroft 9 W4 ..110 C1
adow Croft BR1 ...210 B6
adowcroft Rd N13 ..16 C2
adow Dr N10 .....49 B6
W4 .....28 C1
adowford Cl SE28 .124 A6
adow Garth NW10 ..67 B2
adowgate Sch SE4 141 A2
adow Gdns HA8 .....27 A4
adow High Sch UB8 82 A2
adow Hill KT3 .....199 C3
adow La SE12 .....165 B1
adow Mews SW8 ..270 C5
adow Pl
W8 .....138 A5 270 B4
hiswick W4 .....133 C5
adow Rd
W8 .....138 B5 270 C4
shford TW15 .....171 B5
arking IG11 .....80 A1
eckenham BR2 .....186 C1
arshalton SM1 .....218 C3
laygate KT10 .....212 C2
agenham RM9 .....81 B2
eltham TW13 .....151 A2
oughton IG10 .....21 D6
Merton SW19 .....180 A3
Pinner HA5 .....41 A5
Southall UB1 .....107 B6
eadow Row SE1 .....262 A5
eadows Cl E10 .....75 C6
eadows Ct DA14 .....190 B4
eadows End TW16 ..172 A2
eadowside SE9 .....143 C1
Twickenham TW1 .....153 D4
eadow Stile CR0 .....221 A5
eadowsweet Cl
3 E16 .....99 D2
West Barnes KT3 .....200 C5
eadow The BR7 .....189 A4
eadow View DA15 ...168 B4
eadowview TW17 ...193 A2
eadow View HA1 .....42 C1
eadowview Rd
Catford SE6 .....185 C5
Sidcup DA5 .....169 B5
West Ewell KT19 .....215 C1
eadow View Rd
Hayes UB4 .....83 B3
Thornton Heath CR7 ...204 D4
eadow Way BR6 .....226 C5
NW9 .....45 B4
Chessington KT9 .....214 A3
Ruislip HA4 .....40 B3
Wembley HA9 .....65 D4
eadow Waye TW5 ..129 A5
eadow Way The HA3 .24 C2
eadow Wlk
Dagenham RM9 .....81 B2
Ewell KT17 .....215 D1
Hackbridge SM6 .....219 B5
Wanstead E18 .....55 A5
West Ewell KT17,KT19 ..215 D1
eadow Wood Sch
WD23 .....8 A6
ead Pl E9 .....74 C2
Croydon CR0 .....205 A1
ead Plat NW10 .....67 A2
ead Rd BR7 .....189 A4
Edgware HA8 .....26 C4
Richmond TW10 .....153 C1
ead Road Inf Sch
BR7 .....189 A4
ead Row
SE1 .....116 C3 261 A6
eads Ct E15 .....76 D2
eadside Cl BR3 .....185 A2
eads La IG3 .....57 D2
eads Rd Enfield EN3 ....7 A4
Meads Rd *continued*
Tottenham N22 .....32 D1
Meads The HA8 .....27 B4
Cheam SM3 .....217 A5
Hillingdon UB8 .....82 A3
Mead The N2 .....30 A1
Beckenham BR3 .....186 A2
Ealing W13 .....87 B2
Ickenham UB10 .....60 C6
Wallington SM6 .....219 D2
West Wickham BR4 ....208 B1
Meadvale Rd
Croydon CR0 .....206 A3
Ealing W5 .....87 C3
Meadway NW11 .....47 D3
Ashford TW15 .....170 C6
Barnet EN5 .....1 C1
Beckenham BR3 .....186 A2
Enfield EN3 .....6 D6
Palmers Green N14 .....16 A2
Tolworth KT5 .....199 A1
Twickenham TW2 .....152 B3
West Barnes SW20 ....200 C5
Woodford IG8 .....37 C5
Mead Way CR0 .....223 A6
Meadway KT10 .....212 A1
Mead Way Hayes BR2 .209 A3
Hayes BR2,BR4 .....208 D3
Ilford IG3 .....79 C4
Ruislip HA4 .....39 B3
Meadway Cl NW11 .....47 D3
Barnet EN5 .....1 C1
Pinner HA5 .....23 D4
Meadway Ct NW11 .....47 D3
Dagenham RM8 .....81 B6
Ealing W5 .....88 B2
Meadway Gate NW11 ..47 C3
Meadway Gdns HA4 ....39 B3
Meadway The SE3 ....142 B3
Buckhurst Hill IG9 .....21 D3
Meaford Way SE20 ....184 B3
Meakin Est SE1 .....263 A6
Meakin Ho N7 .....72 B3
Meanley Rd E12 .....78 A3
Meard St W1 .....239 C1
Meath Ho SE24 .....160 D5
Meath Rd E15 .....98 D5
Ilford IG1 .....79 A5
Meath St
SW11 .....137 B4 268 C2
Mecklenburgh Pl
WC1 .....240 C6
Mecklenburgh Sq
WC1 .....94 B3 240 C6
Medburn St NW1 .....232 C4
Medcalf Rd EN3 .....7 B6
Medcroft Gdns SW14 .133 A1
Medebourne Cl SE3 ..143 A2
Mede Ho BR1 .....187 B5
Medesenge Way N13 ..32 D4
Medfield St SW15 .....156 B4
Medhurst Cl 17 E3 .....97 A5
Median Rd E5 .....74 C3
Medical Coll of St Bartholomew's Hospl The
EC1 .....94 D3 241 D5
Medina Ave KT10 .....212 C5
Medina Ct N7 .....72 C5
Medina Gr N7 .....72 C5
Medina Ho SE15 .....140 C1
Medina Rd N7 .....72 C5
Medland Cl CR4 .....203 A1
Medlar Cl 1 UB5 .....84 D5
Medlar Ho 3 DA15 ...168 A1
Medlar St SE5 .....139 A4
Medley Rd NW6 .....69 C2
Medora Rd SW2 .....160 B4
Medresco Ho NW3 .....70 B3
Medusa Rd SE6,SE13 ..163 D5
Medway Bldgs E3 .....97 A5
Medway Cl
Croydon CR0 .....206 C3
Ilford IG1 .....79 A3
Medway Ct WC1 .....233 A1
South Norwood SE25 ...205 C4
Medway Dr UB6 .....86 D5
Medway Gdns HA0 .....65 A4
Medway Ho N16 .....73 B4
NW8 .....237 A4
SE1 .....252 D1
6 Kingston KT2 .....175 D2
Medway Mews 33 E3 ..97 A5
Medway Par 1 UB6 ...86 D5
Medway Rd E3 .....97 A5
Medway St
SW1 .....115 D3 259 D5
Medwin St SW4 .....138 B1
Meecham Ct 1 SW11 136 C3
Meerbrook Rd SE3,
SE9 .....143 C2
Meeson Rd E15 .....76 D1
Meeson St E5 .....75 A4
Meeting House Alley 7
E1 .....118 B5
Meeting House La
SE15 .....140 B5
Mehetabel Rd E9 .....74 C3
Meister Cl IG1 .....57 B1
Melanda Cl BR7 .....188 B5
Melanie Cl DA7 .....147 A4
Melba Ct E8 .....73 D1
Melbourne Ave
Bowes Park N13 .....32 B4
Ealing W13 .....109 A5
Pinner HA2,HA5 .....41 D6
Melbourne Cl BR6 ....211 C2
Ickenham UB10 .....60 C4
Wallington SM6 .....219 C3
Melbourne Ct E5 .....75 A4
N10 .....31 B3
W9 .....236 B6
Penge SE20 .....184 A3
Twickenham TW2 .....152 B3
Melbourne Gdns RM6 ..59 A4
Melbourne Gr SE22 ...139 D1
Melbourne Ho W8 ....245 A3
Hayes UB4 .....84 C3
Melbourne Mews
SW9 .....138 C4
Catford SE6 .....164 A4
Melbourne Pl WC2 ...240 D1
Melbourne Rd E10 .....53 D2
E17 .....53 A5
E6 .....100 B5
Ilford IG1 .....56 D1
Merton SW19 .....179 C2
Teddington TW11 .....175 C4
Wallington SM6 .....219 C3
Melbourne Sq 21 SW9 138 C4
Melbourne Way EN1 ...17 D5
Melbrook Ho 11 SE22 .139 C2
Melbury Ave UB2 .....107 D3
Melbury Cl BR7 .....188 B4
Claygate KT10 .....213 B2
Melbury Ct
W8 .....113 B3 254 D6
Melbury Dr SE5 .....139 C5
Melbury Gdns SW20 ..178 B2
Melbury Ho SW8 .....270 C4
Twickenham TW2 .....152 B2
Melbury Rd
W14 .....113 B3 254 D6
Harrow HA3 .....44 B4
Melchester 3 W11 .....91 B1
Melchester Ho 1 N19 .71 D5
Melcombe Ct NW1 ...237 C4
Melcombe Gdns HA3 ..44 B3
Melcombe Ho SW8 ...270 C3
Melcombe Pl NW1 ...237 C4
Melcombe Prim Sch
W6 .....134 D6
Melcombe St
NW1 .....92 D3 237 D5
Meldex Cl NW7 .....28 C4
Meldon Cl SW6 .....265 D2
Meldone KT3 .....199 B1
Meldone Cl KT5 .....198 D3
Meldrum Rd IG3 .....80 A6
Melfield Gdns SE6 ....186 A5
Melfont Ave CR7 .....204 D6
Melford Ave IG11 .....79 D2
Melford Cl KT9 .....214 B3
Melford Ct E5 .....74 B5
Dulwich SE22 .....162 A4
2 Sutton SM2 .....218 A1
Melford Rd E11 .....76 C6
E17 .....53 B5
E6 .....100 B4
Dulwich SE21,SE22 ....162 A3
Ilford IG1 .....79 B6
Melfort Rd CR7 .....204 D6
Melgund Rd N5 .....72 C3
Melina Cl UB3 .....83 B2
Melina Ct NW8 .....229 C1
Putney SW15 .....134 A2
Melina Pl NW8 .92 B4 229 C1
Melina Rd W12 .....112 B4
Melior Ct N6 .....49 C3
Melior Pl SE1 .....253 A2
Melior St SE1 .117 C4 253 A2
Meliot Rd SE6 .....164 B2
Melisa Ct N6 .....49 D2
Meller Cl SM6 .....220 A5
Melling Dr EN1 .....6 A4
Melling St SE18 .....145 C6
Mellington Ct 2 N16 ..74 A5
Mellis Ave TW9 .....132 D4
Mellish Cl IG11 .....101 D6
Mellish Ct KT6 .....198 A3
Mellish Flats E10 .....53 C2
Mellish Gdns IG8 .....37 A5
Mellish Ho 12 E1 .....96 B1
Mellish Ind Est E16 ...121 D3
Mellish St E14 .....119 C3
Mellison Rd SW17 ....180 C5
Mellitus St W12 .....89 D1
Mellor Cl KT12 .....195 B2
Mellor Ct 2 SW19 ....180 A3
Mellor Ho 2 SE21 ....183 C6
Mellow La E UB4 .....83 A3
Mellow Lane Sch UB4 .83 A3
Mellow La W UB10 .....83 A4
Mellows Rd
Redbridge IG5 .....56 B6
Wallington SM6 .....219 D3
Mells Cres SE9 .....188 B6
Mell St 6 SE10 .....120 C1
Melody Rd SW18 .....158 A6
Melon Pl W8 .....245 B2
Melon Rd E11 .....76 C5
SE15 .....140 A4
Melrose Ave NW2 .....68 C3
Borehamwood WD6 .....10 D6
Greenford UB6 .....85 D5
Mitcham CR4 .....181 B3
Thornton Heath SW16 ..204 C6
Tottenham N22 .....32 D2
Twickenham TW2 .....151 D4
Wimbledon SW19 .....157 C1
Melrose Cl SE12 .....165 B3
Greenford UB6 .....85 D5
Hayes UB4 .....84 A2
Melrose Cres BR6 ....227 B3
Melrose Ct
5 Ealing W13 .....109 A5
Wandsworth SW18 ....157 B5
Melrose Dr UB1 .....107 C5
Melrose Gdns W6 ....112 C3
Edgware HA8 .....26 D1
Kingston KT3 .....199 B6
Melrose Ho NW6 .....91 C4
SW1 .....258 D2
Melrose Rd
1 Barnes SW13 .....133 D3
Merton SW19 .....179 C2
Pinner HA5 .....41 B5
Wandsworth SW18 ....157 B5
Melrose Sch CR4 .....202 C6
Melrose Terr W6 .....112 C3
Melrose Tudor SM6 ...220 A3
Melsa Rd SM4 .....202 A3
Melthorne Dr HA4 .....62 C5
Melthorpe Gdns SE3 ..144 A4
Melton Cl HA4 .....40 C1
Melton Ct SW7 .....256 D3
11 Croydon CR0 .....221 D6
Sutton SM2 .....218 A1
1 Twickenham TW1 ...153 B4
Melton Ho E5 .....74 A6
Melton St NW1 .93 D4 232 C1
Melville Ave
Greenford UB6 .....64 D3
South Croydon CR2 ....221 D3
Wimbledon SW20 .....178 A3
Melville Cl UB10 .....61 B5
Melville Court Flats
W12 .....112 B4
Melville Ct SE8 .....119 A2
4 W4 .....110 C1
Melville Gdns N13 .....32 D5
Melville Ho SE10 .....142 A4
New Barnet EN5 .....14 B5
Melville Pl 4 N1 .....73 A1
Melville Rd E17 .....53 B6
NW10 .....67 B1
Barnes SW13 .....134 A4
Sidcup DA14 .....168 C2
Melville Villas Rd W3 .111 B5
Melvin Ct 11 TW9 .....132 C4
Melvin Rd SE20 .....184 C2
Melwood Ho 22 E1 .....96 B1
Melyn Cl N7 .....71 C4
Memel Ct EC1 .....242 A5
Memel St EC1 .....242 A5
Memess Path 4 SE18 144 C6
Memorial Ave E15 .....98 C4
Memorial Cl TW5 .....129 B6
Memorial Hospl SE18 .144 C3
Mendham Ho SE1 ....263 A6
Mendip Cl
Forest Hill SE26 .....184 C6
Harlington UB3 .....127 B5
North Cheam KT4 .....216 C6
Mendip Ct SE14 .....140 C6
12 SW11 .....136 A2
Mendip Dr NW2,NW11 ..69 A6
Mendip Ho 2 N4 .....51 B2
Mendip Hos 12 E2 .....96 C4
Mendip Rd SW11 .....136 A2
Bushey WD23 .....8 A5
Ilford IG2 .....57 C4
Mendora Rd
SW6 .....135 B5 264 C4
Menelik Rd NW2 .....69 B4
Menlo Gdns SE19 .....183 B3
Mennie Ho 5 SE18 ...144 B4
Menon Dr N9 .....18 B1
Menora Foundation Sch
HA8 .....27 A3
Menorah Gram Sch
NW11 .....47 A2
Menorah Prim Sch
NW11 .....47 A2
Menotti St 5 E2 .....96 A3
Menteath Ho 5 E14 ...97 C1
Mentmore Cl HA3 .....43 C3
Mentmore Terr E8 .....74 B1
Mentone Ct SW8 .....270 B2
Meon Ct TW7 .....130 C3
Meon Rd W3 .....111 A4
Meopham Rd CR4,
SW16 .....181 C2
Mepham Cres HA3 .....24 A3
Mepham Gdns HA3 .....24 A3
Mepham St
SE1 .....116 C5 251 A3
Mera Dr DA7 .....147 D1
Merantun Way SW19 .180 A2
Merbury Cl SE13 .....164 B6
Merbury Rd SE28 .....123 C4
Merbury St SE18 .....122 D3
Mercator Pl E14 .....119 C1
Mercator Rd SE13 ....142 B1
Mercer Cl KT7 .....196 D2
Merceron Ho 3 E2 ....96 C4
Merceron St E1 .....96 B3
Mercer Pl HA5 .....22 C1
Mercers Cl SE10 .....120 D2
Mercer's Cotts 10 E3 ...97 A1
Mercers Pl W6 .....112 D2
Mercers Rd N19 .....71 D5
Mercer St WC2 .94 A1 240 A1
Merchant Ct E1 .....118 C5
Merchants Cl SE25 ...206 A5
Merchants Lo 5 E17 ..53 C5
Merchant St E3 .....97 B4
Merchant Taylors' Almshouses SE13 ...142 C1
Merchant Taylors Hall★
EC3 .....242 D1
Merchiston Rd SE6 ...164 B2
Merchland Rd SE9 ....167 A3
Merchon Ho N7 .....71 C4
Mercia Gr SE13 .....142 A1
Mercia Ho 9 SE5 .....139 A3
Mercier Rd SW15 .....157 A6
Mercury 25 NW9 .....27 D2
Mercury Ct 3 E14 ....119 C2
8 SW9 .....138 C4
Mercury Ctr TW14 ....150 B6
Mercury Ho TW8 .....109 D1
Mercury Rd TW8 .....109 C1
Mercury Way SE14 ...140 D6
Mercy Terr SE13 .....163 D6
Merebank La CR0,SM6 220 B3
Mere Cl Orpington BR6 .226 D6
Putney SW15,SW19 ....156 D4
Meredith Ave NW2 .....68 C3
Meredith Cl HA5 .....22 D3
Meredith Ho 17 N16 ...73 C3
Meredith Mews SE4 ..141 B1
Meredith St E13 .....99 A4
EC1 .....234 C1
Meredyth Rd SW13 ...134 A3
Mere End CR0 .....206 D2
Mere Rd TW17 .....192 D3
Mereside BR6 .....226 C6
Meretone Cl SE4 .....141 A1
Meretune Ct SM4 .....201 B6
Merevale Cres SM4 ...202 A3
Mereway Industry
TW2 .....152 C3
Mereway Rd TW2 ....152 C3
Merewood Cl 1 BR1 .188 C1
Mereworth Cl BR2 ....208 D4
Mereworth Dr SE18 ...145 A5
Mereworth Ho 3
SE15 .....140 C6
Merganser Ct 17 SE8 .141 B6
Merganser Gdns SE28 123 B3
Meridan Ct SE13 .....142 B1
Meriden Cl BR1 .....187 D3
Meriden Ct SW3 .....257 A1
Meriden Ho 26 N1 .....95 C6
3 Barnet EN5 .....1 A1
Meridian Building
SE10 .....142 B5
Meridian Ct
4 Catford SE6 .....164 D3
Croydon CR0 .....220 C4
Meridian Ho SE10 ....120 C2
Meridian Pl E14 .....120 A4
Meridian Prim Sch
SE10 .....142 B6
Meridian Rd SE7 .....143 D5
Meridian Sq E15 .....76 B1
Meridian Trad Est SE7 121 B2
Meridian Way N9,N18 ..18 D1
Enfield EN3 .....19 A5
Meridian Wlk N17 .....33 C4
Merifield Rd SE9 .....143 C1
Merino Cl E11 .....55 C5
Merino Pl DA15 .....168 A6
Merioneth Ct 7 W7 ...86 D2
Merivale Rd Harrow HA1 42 A2
Putney SW15 .....135 A1
Merlewood Dr BR7 ...188 B2
Merley Ct NW9 .....45 A1
Merlin 26 NW9 .....27 D2
Merlin Cl Mitcham CR4 .202 C6
4 Northolt UB5 .....84 C4
South Croydon CR0 ....221 C4
Wallington SM6 .....220 B2
Merlin Cres HA8 .....26 B2
Merlin Ct
Beckenham BR2 .....208 D5
6 Ealing W7 .....86 D3
Ruislip HA4 .....61 B6
Wood Green N22 .....32 C2
Merling Cl KT9 .....213 D3
Merlin Gdns BR1 .....165 A1
Merlin Gr BR3 .....207 C4
Merlin Ho NW3 .....69 D4
7 W4 .....111 B1
Enfield EN3 .....18 D6
Merlin Prim Sch BR1 .165 A1
Merlin Rd Bexley DA16 .146 A1
Wanstead E12 .....77 D6
Merlin Rd N DA16 .....146 A1
Merlins Ave HA2 .....63 B5
Merlins Ct WC1 .....234 A1
Merlin St EC1 ..94 C4 234 A1
Mermaid Ct N4 .....50 C3
SE1 .....117 B4 252 C2
SE16 .....119 B5
Mermaid Ho 8 E14 ..120 A6
Mermaid Twr 22 SE8 ..141 B6
Meroe Ct N16 .....73 C6
Merredene St SW2 ...160 B5
Merriam Ave 3 E9 ....75 B2
Merriam Cl E4 .....36 A5
Merrick Rd UB2 .....107 B3
Merricks Ct 5 SW14 .132 D1
Merrick Sq
SE1 .....117 B3 262 C6
Merridale SE12 .....164 D6
Merridene N21 .....16 D5
Merrielands Cres RM9 103 B5
Merrielands Ret Pk
RM9 .....103 B5
Merrilands Rd KT4 ...200 C1
Merrilees Rd DA15 ...167 C4
Merrilyn Cl KT10 .....213 A2
Merriman Rd SE3 .....143 C4
Merrington Rd SW6 ..265 B6
Merrion Ave HA7 .....25 D5
Merritt Gdns KT9 .....213 C2
Merritt Rd SE4 .....163 B6
Merrivale NW1 .....232 B5
Southgate N14 .....15 D6
Merrivale Ave IG4 .....55 D5
Merrow Ct CR4 .....180 B1
Merrow St
SE17 .....117 B1 262 C1
Merrow Way CR0 .....224 A2
Merrow Wlk SE17 ....262 D2
Merrydown Way BR7 .188 B2
Merry Fiddlers RM8 ....81 B6
Merryfield SE3 .....142 D3
Merryfield Gdns HA7 ..25 C5
Merryfield Ho SE12 ...165 C1
Merryhill Cl E4 .....19 D4
Merry Hill Rd WD23 .....8 A3
Merry Hill Sch WD23 ....8 A4
Merryhills Ct N14 .....15 C6
Merryhills Dr EN2 .....4 A1
Merryhills Prim Sch EN2 4 B1
Merryweather Ct 1
KT3 .....199 C4
Mersea Ho IG11 .....78 D2
Mersey Ct 10 KT2 .....175 D2
Mersey Ho 10 N7 .....72 C3
Mersey Rd E17 .....53 B6
Mersey Wlk UB5 .....85 C5
Mersham Dr NW9 .....44 D4
Mersham Pl
Penge SE20 .....184 B2
South Norwood CR7 ....183 B1
Mersham Rd CR7 .....183 B1
Merstone Ho SW18 ...157 D5
Merten Rd RM6 .....59 A2
Merthyr Terr SW13 ....134 B6
Merton Abbey Mills
Merton SW19 .....180 A2
Wandsworth SW18 ....157 D3
Merton Abbey Prim Sch
SW19 .....179 D2
Merton Ave W4 .....111 D2
Hillingdon UB10 .....60 D1
Northolt UB5 .....64 A3
Merton Coll SM4 .....201 B4
Merton Court Sch
DA14 .....190 C6
Merton Ct DA16 .....146 B3
Merton Gdns BR5 ....210 D4
Merton Hall Gdns
SW20 .....179 A2
Merton Hall Rd SW19 .179 A2
Merton High St SW19 .180 A3
Merton Ho SW18 .....157 C3
Merton Ind Pk SW19 ..180 A2
Merton La N6 .....70 D6
Merton Lo EN5 .....14 A6
Merton Mans SW20 ..178 D1
Merton Park Fst Sch
SW19 .....179 C1
Merton Park Par
SW19 .....179 B2
Merton Park Sta
SW19 .....179 C2
Merton Pl 9 SW19 ...180 A3
Merton Rd E17 .....54 A3
Barking IG11 .....79 D1
Croydon SE25 .....206 A4
Enfield EN2 .....5 B5
Harrow HA2 .....42 A1
Ilford IG3 .....57 D2
Merton SW19 .....179 D3
Wandsworth SW18 ....157 C4
Merton Rise NW3 .....70 C1
Merton Road Ind Est
SW18 .....157 C4

Merton Way
East Molesey KT8 196 A6
Hillingdon UB10 60 D1
Merttins Rd SE15 162 D6
Meru Cl NW5 71 A3
Mervan Rd SW2 138 C1
Mervyn Ave BR7,SE9 167 A2
Mervyn Rd W13 109 A3
Shepperton TW17 193 A2
Mervyn Stockwood Ho 1
SE9 167 A2
Messaline Ave W3 89 A1
Messent Rd SE9 165 D6
Messeter Pl SE9 166 C5
Messina Ave NW6 69 C1
Messiter Ho N1 233 D5
Metcalfe Ho 28 SW8 137 D3
Metcalfe Wlk 2 TW13 173 A6
Metcalf Rd TW15 170 D5
Meteor St SW11 137 A1
Meteor Way SM6 220 A1
Metford Cres EN3 7 C5
Metherell Ho N21 17 B5
Metheringham Way
NW9 27 C2
Methley Ho 8 N7 72 B6
Methley St
SE11 116 C1 261 B1
Methodist Central Hall★
SW1 115 D4 249 D1
Methuen Cl HA8 26 C3
Methuen Pk N10 49 B6
Methuen Rd DA6 147 B1
Belvedere DA17 125 D2
Edgware HA8 26 C3
Methwold Rd W10 90 D2
Metro Bsns Ctr The
SE26 185 B5
Metro Ctr Hayes UB4 106 C6
West Barnes SM4 200 D2
Metro Ind Ctr TW7 130 C3
Metropolitan Benefit Societies Almshs 3
N1 73 C2
Metropolitan Cl 17 E14 97 C2
Metropolitan Police Cadet Training Sch NW9 45 C6
Metro Trad Ctr HA9 66 D4
Meudon Ct KT6 197 D4
Mews Pl IG8 37 A6
Mews St E1 118 A5
Mews The N8 50 C5
Beckenham BR3 185 C2
Redbridge IG4 55 D4
Thornton Heath SW16 182 B2
Mexborough NW1 232 A5
Mexfield Rd SW15 157 B6
Meyer Gn EN1 6 A5
Meyer Ho 1 SW12 159 B4
Meymott St
SE1 116 D5 251 C3
Meynell Cres E9 74 D1
Meynell Gdns E9 74 D1
Meynell Rd E9 74 D1
Meyrick Ho 8 E14 97 C2
Meyrick Rd NW10 68 A2
SW11 136 C2
Miah Terr 10 E1 118 A5
Miall Wlk SE26 185 A6
Micawber Ave UB8 82 C3
Micawber Ct N1 235 B2
Micawber Ho 24 SE16 118 A4
Micawber St N1 95 A4 235 B2
Michael Cliffe Ho EC1 234 B1
Michael Faraday Ho
SE17 262 D1
Michael Faraday Sch
SE17 117 B1 262 D1
Michael Gaynor Cl
W7 108 D5
Michael Marshall Ho 2
SE9 167 A2
Michaelmas Cl SW20 200 C6
Michael Rd E11 54 D1
SW6 135 D4 265 D2
South Norwood SE25 205 C6
Michaels Cl SE13 142 C1
Michael Sobell Sinai Sch
HA3 44 C3
Michaelson Ho 4
SE21 183 C6
Michelangelo Ct 14
SE16 118 B1
Micheldever Rd SE12 164 D5
Michelham Gdns TW1 152 D1
Michelle Ct N12 30 A5
W3 111 B6
Michell Ho TW1 152 D3
Michels Almshouses 11
TW10 154 A6
Michelsdale Dr 3
TW9 132 A1
Michelson Ho SE11 260 D3
Michel's Row 2 TW9 132 A1
Michigan Ave E12 78 B4
Michigan Ho E14 119 C3
Michleham Down N12 29 B6
Mickledore NW1 232 B3
Mickleham Cl BR5 190 A1
Mickleham Gdns SM3 217 A2
Mickleham Rd BR5 190 A1
Mickleham Way CR0 224 B1
Micklethwaite Rd
SW6 135 C6 265 B5
Mickleton Ho 30 W2 91 C2
Midas Bsns Ctr RM10 81 D4
Midcroft HA4 39 C1
Middle Dene NW7 11 B1
Middlefield
NW8 92 B6 229 C6
Middlefielde W13 87 B2
Middlefield Gdns IG2 56 D3
Middle Green Cl 3
KT5 198 B3
Middleham Gdns N18 34 A4
Middleham Rd N18 34 A4
Middle La N8 50 A4
Teddington TW11 174 D4
Middle Lane Mews N8 50 A4
Middle Mill KT5 198 B6
Middle Park Ave SE9 165 D4
Middle Park Prim Sch
SE9 165 D4
Middle Rd 12 E13 99 A5
N10 30 C2
East Barnet EN4 14 C5
Harrow HA2 42 B1
Mitcham SW16 181 D1
Middle Row W10 91 A3
Middle Row Prim Sch
W10 91 A3
Middlesborough Rd
N18 34 A4
Middlesex Bsns Ctr
UB2 107 B4
Middlesex Coll of Computing & Tech
HA9 66 A3
Middlesex Ct 5 W4 111 D2
Harrow HA1 42 D4
Middlesex Cty Cricket Sch
N3 29 D1
Middlesex Ho 6 SE20 184 C3
Middlesex Hospl
W1 93 C2 239 B3
Middlesex Hospl Annexe
W1 239 B4
Middlesex Pas EC1 241 D3
Middlesex Pl 13 E9 74 C2
Middlesex Rd CR4 204 A4
Middlesex St
E1 95 D2 243 C2
Middlesex Univ N17 33 D4
Middlesex Univ (Bounds Green) N11 31 C4
Middlesex Univ (Cat Hill)
EN4 15 A6
Middlesex Univ (Enfield Campus) EN3 18 C6
Middlesex Univ (Hendon Campus) NW4 46 B5
Middlesex Univ Trent Park
EN4 3 C3
Middle St EC1 242 A4
Croydon CR0 221 A5
Middle Temple★
EC4 116 C6 251 A6
Middle Temple La
EC4 116 C6 251 A6
Middleton Ave E4 19 B1
Greenford UB5 86 B5
Sidcup DA14 190 C5
Middleton Bldgs W1 239 A3
Middleton Cl E4 19 B1
Middleton Ct BR1 187 B3
Middleton Dr SE16 118 D4
Pinner HA5 40 A6
Middleton Gdns IG2 56 D3
Middleton Gr N7 72 A3
Middleton Ho E8 73 D1
SE1 262 C5
Middleton Mews N7 72 A3
Middleton Rd E8 73 D1
NW11 47 C2
Carshalton CR4,SM5 202 B2
Hayes UB3 83 B2
Middleton St E2 96 B4
Middleton Way SE13 142 B1
Middleway NW11 47 D4
Middle Way Hayes UB4 84 C3
Mitcham SW16 181 D1
Middle Way The HA3 24 D1
Midfield Prim Sch
BR5 190 A3
Midfield Way BR5 190 B2
Midford Ho 1 NW4 46 D5
Midford Pl W1 239 B5
Midholm NW11 47 D5
Wembley HA9 44 C1
Midholm Cl NW11 47 D5
Midholm Rd CR0 223 A6
Midhope Ho WC1 233 B1
Midhope St WC1 233 B1
Midhurst SE26 184 C4
Midhurst Ave N10 49 A6
Midhurst Ave *continued*
Thornton Heath CR0 204 C2
Midhurst Ct N8 50 A2
Midhurst Gdns UB10 61 A1
Midhurst Hill DA6 169 C6
Midhurst Ho 6 E14 97 B1
Midhurst Par N10 49 A6
Midhurst Rd W13 109 A3
Midhurst Way E5 74 A4
Midland Pl E14 120 A1
Midland Rd E10 54 A2
NW1 94 A5 233 A3
Midland Terr NW10 89 C3
NW2 68 D5
Midleton Rd KT3 177 A1
Midlothian Rd E3 97 B3
Midmoor Rd
Merton SW19 179 A2
Streatham SW12 159 C3
Midship Cl SE16 118 D5
Midship Point E14 119 C4
Midstrath Rd NW10 67 C4
Midsummer Apmts 15
SM2 217 C1
Midsummer Ave TW4 129 B1
Midsummer Ct SE12 143 A1
Midway SM3 201 B2
Midway Ho EC1 234 D2
Midwinter Cl 3 DA16 146 A2
Midwood Cl NW2 68 B5
Mighell Ave IG4 55 D4
Milan Ct N11 31 D2
Milan Rd UB1 107 B4
Milborne Gr SW10 256 B1
Milborne Ho 11 E9 74 C2
Milborne St E9 74 C2
Milborough Cres SE12 164 C5
Milbourne La KT10 212 A3
Milbourne Lodge Jun Sch
KT10 212 B2
Milbourne Lodge Sen Sch
KT10 212 B2
Milbrook KT10 212 A2
Milburn Dr 1 UB7 104 A6
Milburn Ho SW20 178 B1
Milcote St SE1 251 D1
Milday Gr N N1 73 B3
Mildenhall Rd E5 74 C5
Mildmay Ave N1 73 B2
Mildmay Ct N1 73 B3
Mildmay Gr N N1 73 B3
Mildmay Ho 6 SW15 156 C6
Mildmay Mission Hospl
E2 95 D4
Mildmay Pk N1 73 B3
Mildmay Rd N1 73 C3
Ilford IG1 78 D5
Mildmay St N1 73 B2
Mildon Ho EN3 6 C3
Mildred Ave
Hayes UB3 105 B3
Northolt UB5 63 D3
Mildura Ct N8 50 B5
Mile End Pl E1 96 D3
Mile End Rd E1,E3 96 D3
Mile End Sta E3 97 B4
Mile End The E17 34 D2
Mile Rd
Hackbridge SM6 203 A1
Wallington CR0, CR4,
CR9 203 D1
Miles Bldgs NW1 237 A4
Miles Coverdale Prim Sch
W12 112 C4
Miles Ct E1 96 B1
Croydon CR0 220 D6
Miles Dr SE28 123 C5
Miles Ho 5 SE10 120 C1
Miles Lo E15 76 B3
Harrow HA1 42 B4
Milespit Hill NW7 28 C5
Miles Pl NW8 236 D4
Miles Rd N8 50 A6
Mitcham CR4 202 C6
Miles St SW8 138 A6 270 B5
Milestone Cl
Edmonton N9 18 A2
Sutton SM2 218 B1
Milestone Ct TW7 131 A4
Milestone Green
SW14 133 B1
Milestone Ho KT1 197 D5
Milestone Rd SE19 183 D4
Miles Way N20 14 C2
Milfoil St W12 112 A6
Milford Cl SE2 147 A6
Milford Ct 3 N16 51 C1
Southall UB1 107 C5
Milford Gdns
Croydon CR0 206 D4
Edgware HA8 26 C3
Wembley HA0 65 D3
Milford Gr SM1 218 A4
Milford La
WC2 116 C6 251 A6
Milford Mews SW16 160 B1
Milford Rd Ealing W13 109 B5
Southall UB1 107 C6
Milk St E16 122 D5
Milk St *continued*
EC2 95 A1 242 B2
Bromley BR1 187 B4
Milkwell Gdns IG8 37 B3
Milkwell Yd SE5 139 A4
Milkwood Rd SE24 138 D1
Milk Yd E1 118 C6
Millais Ave E12 78 C3
Millais Ct 10 UB5 84 D5
Millais Gdns HA8 26 C1
Millais Rd E11 76 B4
Enfield EN1 17 D6
New Malden KT3 199 C2
Millais Way KT19 215 A4
Milland Ho 11 SW15 156 A3
Millard Cl 21 N16 73 C3
Millard Ho SE8 119 B1
Millard Terr RM10 81 C2
Millbank SW1 116 A2 260 A3
Wallington SM6 219 D3
Millbank Ho KT6 198 B2
Millbank Prim Sch
SW1 115 D2 259 D3
Millbank Way SE12 165 A6
Millbourne Rd TW13 173 A6
Mill Bridge EN5 13 B5
Millbrook 1 E18 55 A6
Millbrook Ave DA16 145 B1
Millbrooke Ct 7
SW15 157 A6
Millbrook Gdns RM6 59 A3
Millbrook Ho 4 SE15 140 A6
Millbrook Rd SW9 138 D2
Edmonton N9 18 B3
Mill Cl SM5 219 A6
Mill Cnr EN5 1 B4
Millcroft Ho SE6 185 D6
Mill Ct E10 76 A5
NW7 29 A2
14 SE28 124 B6
Millender Wlk SE16 118 C2
Millennium Bsns Ctr
NW2 68 B6
Millennium Bridge★
SE1,EC4 252 A5
Millennium Dome★
SE10 120 C5
Millennium Dr E14 120 B2
Millennium Harbour
E14 119 C4
Millennium Pl 27 E2 96 B5
Millennium Prim Sch
SE10 120 D3
Millennium Sq SE1 253 D2
Millennium Way SE10 120 C3
Miller Ave EN3 7 C5
Miller Cl
Carshalton CR4 202 D2
Pinner HA5 22 C1
Miller Ct DA7 147 D2
8 NW9 46 A5
Miller Ho N15 50 D5
9 Streatham SW2 160 A4
Miller Rd
Mitcham SW19 180 B4
Thornton Heath CR0 204 C1
Miller's Ave E8,N16 73 D3
Millers Cl NW7 28 A6
Miller's Ct 1 W4 111 D1
Millers Ct 3 HA0 88 A5
Millers Green Cl EN2 4 D2
Millers Mead Ct SW19 180 B3
Miller St NW1 232 A4
Miller's Terr 1 E8 73 D3
Miller's Way W6 112 C4
Millers Wharf Ho E1 118 A5
Millers Yd N3 29 D3
Miller Wlk SE1 251 B3
Millet Rd UB6 85 D5
Mill Farm Ave TW16 171 C3
Millfarm Bsns Pk TW4 151 A4
Mill Farm Cl HA5 22 C1
Mill Farm Cres TW4 151 A3
Millfield N4 72 C6
Charlton TW16 171 B2
Kingston KT1 198 B6
Millfield Ave E17 35 B2
Millfield La N6 70 D6
Millfield Pl N6 71 A6
Millfield Rd HA8 27 A1
Twickenham TW4 151 B3
Millfields Com Sch E5 74 C4
Millfields Rd E5 74 C5
Mill Gdns SE26 162 B1
Mill Gn CR4 203 A2
Mill Green Bsns Pk
CR4 203 A2
Mill Green Rd CR4 203 A2
Millgrove St 6 SW11 137 A3
Millharbour E14 119 D4
Millhaven Cl RM6 58 B3
Mill Hill SW13 134 A2
Mill Hill Broadway Sta
NW7 27 C4
Mill Hill Circus NW7 27 D5
Mill Hill Cty High Sch
NW7 11 C2
Mill Hill East Sta NW7 29 A3
Mill Hill Gr 11 W3 110 D5
Mill Hill Ind Est NW7 27 D4
Mill Hill Rd W3 110 D4
Barnes SW13 134 A3
Mill Hill Sch NW7 28 B6
Mill Hill Terr 9 W3 110 D5
Mill Ho IG8 36 D5
Millhouse Pl SE27 182 D6
Millicent Fawcett Ct
N17 33 D2
Millicent Preston Ho 4
IG11 101 B6
Millicent Rd E10 53 B1
Milligan St E14 119 B6
Milling Rd HA8 27 B3
Millington Ho N16 73 B5
Millington Rd UB3 105 C3
Mill La NW6 69 B3
SE18 122 C1
Carshalton SM5 219 A5
Croydon CR0 220 C5
Dagenham RM6 59 A3
Sewardstone E4 7 D2
Woodford IG8 36 D5
Mill Lane Trad Est
CR0 220 B5
Millman Ct SE3 143 B5
WC1 240 C5
Millman Mews WC1 240 C5
Millman Pl WC1 240 D5
Millman St WC1 94 B3 240 C5
Millmark Gr SE14 141 A3
Millmarsh La EN3 7 B3
Millmead Bsns Ctr N17 52 B6
Millmead Ind Ctr N17 52 B6
Mill Mead Rd N17 52 B6
Millner Ct SE4 141 B3
Mill Pl BR7 188 D2
E14 97 A1
Kingston KT1 198 B6
Mill Plat TW7 131 A3
Mill Plat Ave TW7 131 A3
Mill Pond Cl
SW8 137 D5 269 D3
Millpond Est SE16 118 B4
Mill Rd E16 121 B5
Ilford IG1 78 C5
Merton SW19 180 A3
Twickenham TW2 152 A2
Mill Ridge HA8 26 C5
Mill River Trad Est EN3 7 A1
Mill Row N1 95 C6
Mills Cl UB10 82 C5
Mills Ct 7 E11 76 C5
Mills Gr 1 E14 98 A2
NW4 46 D6
Mills Ho E17 54 B6
SW8 269 B2
Millshot Cl SW6 134 C4
Millside SM5 218 D6
Millside Pl TW7 131 B3
Millson Cl N20 14 B2
Mills Row W4 111 B2
Mill St SE1 117 D4 253 D2
W1 249 A6
Kingston KT1 198 A6
Millstream Cl N13 32 C5
Millstream Rd
SE1 117 D4 253 C1
Mill Trad Est The NW10 89 A4
Mill Vale BR2 186 D1
Mill View Cl KT17 215 D1
Mill View Gdns CR0 222 D5
Millwall Dock Rd E14 119 C3
Millward Wlk 14 SE18 144 C6
Mill Way NW7 27 C5
Feltham TW14 150 B6
Millway Gdns UB5 63 B2
Millwood Rd TW3,TW7 152 A6
Millwood St 10 W10 91 A2
Mill Yd E1 118 A6
Milman Cl HA5 40 D6
Milman Rd NW6 91 A5
Milman's Ho SW10 266 C5
Milman's St
SW10 136 B6 266 C5
Milne Ct 4 E18 37 A2
Milne Field HA5 23 C3
Milne Gdns SE9 166 A6
Milne Ho 15 SE18 122 B2
Milner Dr TW2 152 B4
Milner Ho 2 SW11 136 B2
Hayes UB4 84 B4
Milner Pl N1 94 C6 234 B6
Milner Rd E15 98 C4
Dagenham RM8 80 C6
Kingston KT1 197 D6
Merton SW19 179 D2
Morden SM4 202 B4
South Norwood CR7 205 B6
Milner Sq N1 72 D1
Milner St SW3 114 D2 257 C4
Milner Wlk DA15 167 B3
Milnthorpe Rd W4 133 B6
Milo Rd SE22 161 D5
Milrood Ho 4 E1 96 D2
Milroy Wlk SE1 251 C4
Milson Rd
W14 112 D3 254 A6
Milsted Ho 23 E5 74 B3
Milton Ave E6 78
N6 49
NW10 89
NW9 45
Barnet EN5 13
Carshalton SM1 218
Thornton Heath CR0 205
Milton Cl N2 48
SE1 117 D2 263
Carshalton SM1 218
Hayes UB4 84
Milton Court Rd SE14 141
Milton Cres IG2 57
Milton Ct EC2 242
NW11 47
SE14 141
9 SW18 157
Fulham SW6 135
Ilford RM6 58
Kingston KT2 176
Twickenham TW2 152
Uxbridge UB10 60
Milton Dr
Borehamwood WD6 10
Littleton TW17 192
Milton Gdns TW19 148
Milton Gr N11 31
N16 73
Milton Ho 19 E2 96
2 SE5 139
12 Beckenham BR3 185
5 Kingston KT2 176
Sutton SM1 217
Milton House Mans E8 73
Milton Lo
3 Sidcup DA14 190
Southgate N21 16
Twickenham TW1 152
Milton Pk N6 49
Milton Pl 3 N7 72
Milton Rd DA16 145
E17 53
N15 50
N6 49
NW7 28
1 NW9 46
SE24 160
W3 111
Belvedere DA17 125
Ealing W7 108
Harrow HA1 42
Mitcham CR4 181
Mortlake SW14 133
Sutton SM1 217
Thornton Heath CR0 205
Uxbridge UB10 60
Wallington SM6 219
Wimbledon SW19 180
Hampton TW12 173
Milton St EC1,
EC2 95 B2 242
Milton Way UB7 104
Milverton NW5 71
Milverton Dr UB10 61
Milverton Gdns IG3 79
Milverton Ho SE23 163
Milverton Rd NW6 68
Milverton St
SE11 116 C1 261
Milverton Way SE9 188
Milward St E1 96
Mimosa N15 51
Mimosa Ct SW4 270
Mimosa Ho UB4 84
Mimosa Rd UB4 84
Mimosa St
SW6 135 B4 264
Mina Rd SE17 117 C1 263
Merton SW19 179
Minard Rd SE6 164
Minchenden Cres N14 15
Minchenden Ct N14 15
Minchin Ho 6 E14 97
Mincing La
EC3 117 C6 253
Minden Rd Cheam SM3 217
Penge SE20 184
Minehead Ct HA2 63
Minehead Rd
Harrow HA2 63
Streatham SW16 182
Mineral St SE18 123
Minera Mews SW1 258
Minerva Cl SW9 138
Sidcup DA14 189
Minerva Rd NW10 89
Chingford E4 35
Kingston KT1 176
Minerva St E2 96
Minerva Wlk EC1 241
Minet Ave NW10 89
Minet Dr UB3 106
Minet Gdns NW10 89
Hayes UB3 106
Minet Jun & Inf Schs
UB3 106
Minet Rd SE5,SW9 138
Minford Gdns W14 112
Mingard Wlk N7 72

Ming St E14 119 C6
Minimax Cl TW14 150 A5
Ministry Way SE9 166 B2
Mink Ct TW4 128 C3
Minniedale KT5 198 B4
Minnow Wlk SE17 263 B3
Minories EC3 117 D6 253 C6
Minshaw Ct DA14 189 D6
1 Sidcup DA14 190 A6
Minshull Pl 23 BR3 185 C3
Minshull St SW8 269 C1
Minson Rd E9 96 D6
Minstead Gdns SW15 155 D4
Minstead Way KT3 199 C3
Minster Ave SM1 217 C6
Minster Dr CR0 221 C4
Minster Gdns KT8 195 B5
Minsterley Ave TW16, TW17 193 C5
Minster Rd BR1 187 B3
NW2 69 A3
Minster Wlk N8 50 A5
Minstrel Ct HA3 24 C1
Minstrel Gdns KT5 198 B5
Mint Bsns Pk 12 E16 99 A2
Mint Cl UB10 82 D4
Mintern Cl N13 16 D1
Minterne Ave UB2 107 C2
Minterne Rd HA3 44 B4
Minterne Waye UB4 84 C1
Mintern St N1 95 B5 235 D4
Minton Ho SE11 261 A4
Minton Mews 3 NW6 69 D2
Mint Rd SM5,SM6 219 B4
Mint St SE1 252 B2
Mint Wlk CR0 221 A5
Mirabel Rd SW6 135 B5 264 D4
Mirage Ctr The HA9 66 D4
Miranda Cl 16 E1 96 C2
Miranda Ct W3 88 B1
Miranda Ho 17 N1 95 C5
6 Belvedere DA17 125 C1
Miranda Rd N19 49 C1
Mirfield Ct SE20 184 A1
Mirfield St SE7 121 D3
Miriam Ct DA14 190 B6
Miriam Rd SE18 123 C1
Mirravale Trad Est RM6 59 A2
Mirren Cl HA2 63 B5
Mirror Path SE12 165 C1
Misbourne Rd UB10 82 C6
Missenden SE17 262 D1
Missenden Cl TW14 149 D3
Missenden Gdns SM4 202 A3
Missenden Ho NW8 237 A6
Mission Gr E17 53 A4
Mission Grove Prim Sch E17 53 B5
Mission Pl SE15 140 A4
Mission Sq 13 TW8 132 A6
Misterton Ct SW11 266 D2
Mistletoe Cl CR0 206 D1
Mistley Thorn IG1 56 C2
Mistral SE5 139 C4
Mistral Ct E4 19 D1
Mistys Field KT12 194 C1
Mitali Pas 13 E1 96 A1
Mitcham Garden Village CR4 203 A4
Mitcham Ho 9 SE5 139 A4
Mitcham Ind Est CR4 181 A2
Mitcham Junction Sta CR4 203 A4
Mitcham La SW16 181 C5
Mitcham Pk CR4 202 D5
Mitcham Rd E6 100 A4
Ilford IG3 57 D2
Upper Tooting SW17 180 D5
Mitcham Sta CR4 202 C5
Mitcham Vale High Sch CR4 181 B1
Mitchell 10 NW9 27 D2
Mitchell Brook Prim Sch NW10 67 C2
Mitchellbrook Way NW10 67 B2
Mitchell Cl SE2 124 C2
Belvedere DA17 125 D3
Mitchell Ct 20 E10 53 D2
Mitchell Ho 31 W12 112 B6
W4 110 D1
Mitchell Rd BR6 227 D4
Edmonton N13 33 A5
Mitchell's Pl SE21 161 C4
Mitchell St EC1 95 A3 242 B6
Mitchell Way NW10 67 A2
Bromley BR1 187 A2
Mitchell Wlk E6 100 B2
Mitchison Rd N1 73 B2
Mitchley Rd N17 52 A6
Mitford Cl KT9 213 C2
Mitford Rd N19 72 A6
Mitre Bridge Ind Pk W10 90 B3
Mitre Cl
Shepperton TW17 193 B3
Sutton SM2 218 B1
Mitre Ct EC2 242 B2
Mitre Ct *continued*
Belvedere DA17 125 C1
1 Ilford RM6 58 B2
9 Woodford E18 37 A2
Mitre Ho RM7 59 D5
Mitre Rd E15 98 C5
SE1 116 C4 251 B2
Mitre Sq EC3 243 B1
Mitre St EC3 95 C1 243 B1
Mitre The 9 E14 119 B6
Mitre Way W10 90 B2
Moatbridge Sch SE9 165 D5
Moat Cl BR6 227 D2
Moat Cres N3 47 D6
Moat Croft DA16 146 C2
Moat Ct DA15 167 D1
9 DA15 168 A1
SE9 166 B5
Moat Dr 4 E13 99 C5
Harrow HA1 42 B5
Ruislip HA4 39 C2
Moat Farm Rd UB5 63 B1
Moatfield NW6 69 A1
Moat Lo The HA1 64 C6
Moat Pl SW9 138 B2
Acton W3 88 D1
Moat Side Enfield EN3 6 D1
Feltham TW13 172 C6
Moat The KT3 177 C2
Moberly Rd SW4 159 D4
Mobey Ct SW4 270 A1
Moblin Lo IG9 21 C3
Moby Dick RM6 59 B5
Mocatta Ho 9 E1 96 B3
Modbury Gdns NW5 71 A2
Modder Pl SW15 134 D1
Model Cotts SW14 133 A2
Model Farm Cl SE9 166 A1
Modling Ho 8 E2 96 D5
Moelwyn Hughes Ct N7 71 D3
Moelyn Mews HA1 43 A4
Moffat Ct
Upper Tooting SW17 180 C6
Wimbledon SW19 179 C5
Moffat Ho 24 SE5 139 A5
Moffat Rd
Bowes Park N13 32 A4
South Norwood CR7 183 B1
Upper Tooting SW17 180 D6
Mogden La TW7 152 D6
Mohawk Ho 31 E3 97 A5
Mohmmad Khan Rd E11 54 D1
Mohr Ct N22 32 B3
Moineau 18 NW9 27 D2
Moira Cl N17 33 C1
Moira Ct SW17 159 A2
Moira Rd SE9 144 B1
Moland Mead SE16 118 D1
Molasses Ho 1 SW11 136 A2
Molasses Row 2 SW11 136 A2
Mole Abbey Gdns KT8 195 D6
Mole Ct 2 W12 111 C4
West Ewell KT19 215 A4
Mole Ho NW8 236 D5
Molember Ct KT7 196 C5
Molember Rd KT8 196 C4
Molescroft SE9 167 A1
Molesey Ave KT12,KT8 195 B4
Molesey Dr SM3 217 A5
Molesey Ho E2 243 C6
Molesey Hospl KT8 195 C4
Molesey Park Ave KT8 195 D4
Molesey Park Cl KT8 196 A4
Molesey Park Rd KT8 196 A4
Molesey Rd KT12 195 A2
Molesford Rd SW6 265 A1
Molesham Cl KT8 195 D6
Molesham Way KT8 195 D6
Molesworth Ho 9 SE17 138 D6
Molesworth St SE13 142 A2
Moliner Ct 4 BR3 185 C3
Mollie Davis Ct SE19 183 D4
Mollison Ave EN3 7 B5
Mollison Dr SM6 220 A1
Mollison Way HA8 26 C1
Molly Huggins Cl SW12 159 C4
Molton Ho N1 233 D5
Molyneux Dr SW17 181 B6
Molyneux St W1 92 C2 237 B3
Monarch Cl
Coney Hall BR4 224 D4
East Bedfont TW14 149 C4
Monarch Ct N2 48 A4
Ealing W5 87 C2
Monarch Dr E16 99 D2
Monarch Mews E17 53 D3
West Norwood SW16 182 C5
Monarch Par CR4 180 D1
Monarch Pl IG9 21 C2
Monarch Rd DA17 125 C3
Monarchs Ct 1 NW7 27 B5
Monarch's Way HA4 39 C1
Mona Rd SE15 140 C3
Mona St E16 98 D2
Monastery Gdns EN2 5 B3
Monaveen Gdns KT8 195 D6
Monck's Row SW18 157 B5
Monck St SW1 115 D3 259 D5
Monclar Rd SE5 139 B1
Moncorvo Cl SW7 114 C4 247 A1
Moncrieff Cl 4 E6 100 A1
Moncrieff St SE15 140 A3
Mondial Way UB7 127 A5
Mondragon Ho SW8 270 B2
Monega Prim Sch E12 77 D2
Monega Rd E7,E12 77 D2
Monet Ct 15 SE16 118 B1
Moneyer Ho N1 235 C2
Monica James Ho 12 DA14 168 A1
Monica Shaw Ct NW1 232 D3
Monier Rd E3 75 C1
Monivea Rd BR3 185 B3
Monk Ct W12 112 A5
Monk Dr E16 121 A6
Monken Hadley CE Prim Sch EN4 1 C4
Monkfrith Ave N14 15 B5
Monkfrith Cl N14 15 B4
Monkfrith Prim Sch N14 15 A4
Monkfrith Way N14 15 B4
Monkham's Ave IG8 37 B5
Monkham's Dr IG8 37 B5
Monkham's La IG8 37 B6
Monkleigh Rd SM4, SW20 201 A5
Monkridge 3 N8 49 D2
Monks Ave
East Molesey KT8 195 B4
New Barnet EN5 14 A5
Monks Cl SE2 124 D2
Enfield EN2 5 A3
Harrow HA2 63 D6
Ruislip HA4 62 D4
Monks Cres KT12 194 B1
Monksdene Gdns SM1 217 D5
Monks Dr W3 88 C1
Monksfield N4 72 C6
Monks Orchard Rd BR3,CR0 207 C2
Monks Orchard Sch CR0 206 D4
Monks Park Gdns HA9 66 D1
Monks Pk HA9 67 A2
Monks Rd EN2 5 A3
Monk St SE18 122 C2
Monks Way BR5 211 B1
NW11 47 B5
Beckenham BR3 207 C3
Harmondsworth UB7 126 A6
Monkswell Ct N10 31 A2
Monkswood Gdns
Borehamwood WD6 11 B6
Ilford IG5 56 C6
Monkton Ct W14 254 C6
Monkton Ho 22 E5 74 B3
32 SE16 118 D4
Monkton Rd DA16 145 D3
Monkton St SE11 116 C2 261 B4
Monkville Ave NW11 47 B5
Monkville Par 1 NW11 47 B5
Monkwell Sq EC2 242 B3
Monmouth Ave
Teddington KT1 175 C3
Wanstead E18 55 B6
Monmouth Cl W4 111 B3
Bexley DA16 146 A1
Mitcham CR4,SW16 204 A5
Monmouth Ct 9 W7 86 D2
Monmouth Gr TW8 110 A2
Monmouth Ho 5 NW5 71 B2
SW18 157 C5
Monmouth Pl W2 91 D1
Monmouth Rd E6 100 B4
N9 18 C2
W2 91 C1
Dagenham RM9 81 B3
Hayes UB3 105 D2
Monmouth St WC2 94 A1 240 A1
Monnery Rd N19 71 C5
Monnow Rd SE1 118 A2
Mono La TW13 150 B2
Monoux Almshouses E17 53 D5
Monoux Gr E17 35 C2
Monro Dr N11 31 C4
Monroe Cres EN1 6 B4
Monroe Dr SW14 154 D6
Monroe Ho 16 N19 49 D2
NW8 230 A1
Monro Gdns HA3 24 C3
Monro Ho 21 NW3 70 A4
Putney SW15 156 B6
Monro Way E5 74 A4
Monsal Ct E5 75 A4
Monsell Rd N4,N5 72 D5
Monson Prim Sch SE14 140 D5
Monson Rd NW10 90 B5
SE14 140 D5
Mons Way BR2 210 A3
Montacute Rd
Bushey WD23 8 C4
Carshalton SM4 202 B3
Forest Hill SE6 163 B4
Montagu Cres N18 34 B6
Montagu Ct W1 237 D3
Montague Ave SE4 141 C1
Ealing W7 108 D5
Montague Cl SE1 252 C4
Walton-on-T KT12 194 A2
Montague Fell HA0 65 A4
Montague Gdns W3 110 C6
Montague Pl WC1 93 D2 239 D4
Montague Rd E11 76 D6
E8 74 A3
N15 52 A5
N8 50 B4
W7 108 D4
Ealing W13 87 B1
Hounslow TW3 129 D2
Merton SW19 179 D3
Richmond TW10 154 A5
Southall UB2 107 A2
Thornton Heath CR0 204 D1
Uxbridge UB8 60 A1
Montague Sq SE15 140 C5
Montague St WC1 94 A2 240 A4
Montague Street EC1 242 A3
Montague Terr 1 BR2 209 A5
Montague Way UB2 107 A3
Montagu Gdns
Edmonton N18 34 B6
Wallington SM6 219 C4
Montagu Ind Est N18 34 C6
Montagu Mans W1 92 D2 237 D3
Montagu Mews N W1 237 D3
Montagu Mews S W1 237 D2
Montagu Mews W W1 237 D2
Montagu Pl W1 92 D2 237 D3
Montagu Rd N9,N18 18 C1
NW4 46 A3
Montagu Row W1 237 D3
Montagu Sq W1 92 D1 237 D2
Montagu St W1 92 D1 237 D2
Montalt Ho IG8 36 D6
Montalt Rd IG8 36 D5
Montana Gdns
Penge SE26 185 B5
5 Sutton SM1 218 A3
Montana Rd
Upper Tooting SW17 159 A1
Wimbledon SW20 178 C2
Montbelle Prim Sch SE9 166 D1
Montbelle Rd SE9 166 D1
Montcalm Cl
Hayes BR2 209 A3
Hayes UB4 84 B4
Montcalm Ho E14 119 C3
Montcalm Rd SE7 143 D5
Montclare St E2 95 D3 243 C6
Monteagle Ave IG11 79 A2
Monteagle Ct 27 N1 95 C5
Monteagle Prim Sch RM9 102 B6
Monteagle Way E5 74 A5
SE15 140 B2
Montefiore Ct 2 N16 51 D1
Montefiore St 2 SW8 137 B3
Montem Prim Sch N7 72 B5
Montem Rd
Forest Hill SE23 163 B4
New Malden KT3 199 C5
Montem St N4 50 B1
Montenotte Rd N8 49 C4
Montesole Ct 5 HA5 22 C1
Montesquieu Terr 3 E16 98 D1
Montessori Coll SW19 179 C4
Montford Pl SE11 116 C1 261 A1
Montford Rd TW16 194 A5
Montfort Ho E14 120 A3
4 E2 96 C4
Montfort Pl SW19 156 D3
Montgo Cl 10 SW2 138 C1
Montgolfier Wlk UB5 85 A4
Montgomery Ave KT10 212 C6
Montgomery Cl DA15 167 D5
Mitcham CR4 204 A5
Montgomery Ct W4 133 A6
Montgomery Ho 5 SW14 133 B2
Montgomery Lo 34 E1 96 C3
Montgomery Rd
Acton W4 111 A2
Edgware HA8 26 B4
Montholme Rd SW11 158 D5
Monthorpe Rd 16 E1 96 A2
Montolieu Gdns SW15 156 B6
Montpelier Ave
Ealing W5 87 C2
Sidcup DA5 168 D4
Montpelier Cl UB10 82 C6
Montpelier Ct
5 Beckenham BR2 208 D5
Ealing W5 87 D2
Montpelier Gdns E6 99 D4
Ilford RM6 58 C2
Montpelier Gr NW5 71 C3
Montpelier Mews SW7 257 B6
Montpelier Pl 21 E1 96 C1
SW7 257 B6
Montpelier Prim Sch W5 87 D2
Montpelier Rd N3 30 A2
SE15 140 B4
Ealing W5 87 D2
Sutton SM1 218 A4
Montpelier Rise NW11 47 A2
Wembley HA9 43 D1
Montpelier Row SE3 142 D3
Twickenham TW1 153 C4
Montpelier Sq SW7 114 C4 247 B1
Montpelier St SW7 114 C3 257 B6
Montpelier Terr SW7 247 B1
Montpelier Vale SE3 142 D3
Montpelier Way NW11 47 A2
Montpelier Wlk SW7 114 C3 257 B6
Montrave Rd SE20 184 C3
Montreal Ho UB4 84 B4
Montreal Pl WC2 250 C6
Montreal Rd IG1 57 A2
Montrell Rd SW2 160 A3
Montrose Ave DA16 145 C2
HA8 27 B2
NW6 91 A5
Sidcup DA15 168 A4
Twickenham TW2 151 D4
Montrose Cl DA16 145 D2
Ashford TW15 171 A5
Woodford IG8 37 A6
Montrose Cres N12 30 A4
1 Wembley HA0 66 A2
Montrose Ct NW11 47 B5
NW9 27 A1
SW7 114 B4 246 D1
2 Catford SE6 164 D2
Montrose Gdns
Mitcham CR4 180 D1
Sutton SM1 217 D6
Montrose Ho E14 119 C3
SW1 248 B1
Montrose Pl SW1 115 A4 248 B1
Montrose Rd
East Bedfont TW14 149 B5
Harrow HA3 24 D1
Montrose Villas W6 112 A1
Montrose Way SE23 162 D3
Montserrat Ave IG8 36 B3
Montserrat Cl SE19 183 B5
Montserrat Rd SW15 135 A1
Montway Hts SW19 179 D3
Monument Gdns SE13 164 A6
Monument St EC3 117 B6 252 D6
Monument Sta EC3 117 B6 252 D6
Monument The★ EC3 252 D6
Monument Way N17 51 D6
Monza St E1 118 C6
Moodkee St SE16 118 C3
Moody Rd SE15 139 D4
Moody St E1 96 D4
Moon Ct SE12 143 A1
Moon La EN5 1 B2
Moon St N1 94 D6 234 C6
Moorcroft HA8 26 D2
Moorcroft Gdns BR1 210 A4
Moorcroft La UB8 82 C2
Moorcroft Rd SW16 160 A1
Moorcroft Sch UB8 82 D2
Moorcroft Way HA5 41 A4
Moordown SE18 144 D4
Moore Cl Mitcham CR4 181 B1
Mortlake SW14 133 A2
Wallington SM6 220 A1
Moore Cres RM9 102 B6
Moore Ct N1 234 C5
Moorefield Rd N17 33 D1
Moore Ho 6 E1 118 C6
16 E2 96 C4
N8 50 A5
5 SE10 120 D1
Wandsworth SW17 158 B1
1 West Norwood SE27 183 A6
Mooreland Rd BR1 187 A2
Moore Park Ct SW6 265 D4
Moore Park Rd SW6 135 D5 265 C3
Moore Rd SE19 183 A4
Moore St SW3 114 D2 257 C4
Moore Wlk E7 77 A4
Moorey Cl 2 E15 98 D6
Moorfield Ave W5 87 D3
Moorfield Rd
Chessington KT9 214 A3
Enfield EN3 6 C4
Moorfields EC2 95 B2 242 C3
Moorfields Ct 6 SW16 181 C6
Moorfields Eye Hospl EC1 95 B4 235 C1
Moorfields Highwalk EC2 242 C3
Moorfields Prim Sch EC1 95 B3 242 C6
Moorgate EC2 95 B2 242 C3
Moorgate Pl EC2 242 C2
Moorgate Sta EC2 95 B2 242 C3
Moorgreen Ho EC1 234 C2
Moorhead Way SE3 143 B2
Moorhouse 17 NW9 27 D2
Moorhouse Rd W2 91 C1
Harrow HA3 43 D6
Moorings The E16 99 C2
Moor La EC2 95 B2 242 C3
Chessington KT9 214 A3
Moorland Cl TW4 151 C4
Moorland Rd SW9 138 D1
Moorlands UB5 85 A6
Moorlands Ave NW7 28 B4
Moor Lane Jun Sch KT9 214 B3
Moormead Dr KT19 215 C3
Moor Mead Rd TW1 153 A5
Moor Park Gdns KT2 177 C3
Moor Pl EC2 242 C3
Moorside Rd BR1 186 D6
Moor St W1 239 D1
Moortown Rd WD19 22 C6
Moot Ct NW9 44 C4
Morant Ho SW9 138 B3
Morant Pl N22 32 B2
Morant St E14 119 C6
Mora Prim Sch NW2 68 C4
Mora Rd NW2 68 C4
Mora St EC1 95 A4 235 B1
Morat St SW9 138 B4 270 D2
Moravian Cl SW3 266 D5
Moravian Pl SW10 136 B6 266 D5
Moravian St 10 E2 96 C4
Moray Ave UB3 105 D5
Moray Cl HA8 10 D2
Moray Ho 8 E1 97 A3
11 Kingston KT6 198 A4
Moray Mews N4,N7 72 B6
Moray Rd N4,N7 72 B6
Mordaunt Gdns RM9 81 A1
Mordaunt Ho 4 NW10 89 B6
34 SW8 137 D3
Mordaunt Rd NW10 89 B6
Mordaunt St SW9 138 B2
Morden Court Par SM4 201 D5
Morden Ct SM4 201 D5
Morden Gdns
Greenford UB6 64 D3
Mitcham CR4 202 B5
Morden Hall SW19 201 D6
Morden Hall Rd SM4 202 A5
Morden Hill SE13 142 A3
Morden Ho 19 SW2 160 C5
Morden SM4 201 C5
Morden La SE13 142 A4
Morden Lo BR2 186 B1
Morden Mount Prim Sch SE13 141 D3
Morden Park Sch Sports Ctr SM4 201 B4
Morden Prim Sch SM4 201 C4
Morden Rd SE3 143 A3
Dagenham RM6 59 A2
Merton SW19 179 D1
Mitcham CR4,SM4 202 B5
Morden Road Mews SE3 143 A3
Morden Road Sta SW19 179 D1
Morden South Sta SM4 201 C4
Morden St SE13 141 D4
Morden Sta SW19 201 D6
Morden Way SM3 201 C2
Morden Wharf Rd SE10 120 C3
Mordern Ho NW1 237 B5
Mordon Rd IG3 57 D2
Mordred Rd SE6 164 C2
Morecambe Cl 2 E1 96 D2
Morecambe Gdns HA7 25 D6
Morecambe St SE17 117 B2 262 B2
Morecambe Terr N18 33 B6

More Cl E16 98 D1
W14 113 A2 254 A3
Morecoombe Cl KT2 176 D3
Moredown Ho 3 E8 74 A3
Moree Way N18 34 A6
More House Sch
SW1 114 D3 257 D5
Moreland Ct 3 NW2 69 C5
Moreland Prim Sch
EC1 94 D4 234 D1
Moreland St
EC1 94 D4 234 D2
Moreland Way E4 20 A1
Morella Rd SW11,
SW12 158 D4
Morell Ho 5 SW9 138 B3
Morello Ave UB8 82 D2
Morello Ct HA9 66 B5
Moremead Rd SE6 185 C6
Morena St SE6 163 D4
Moresby Ave KT5 198 D2
Moresby Rd E5 52 B1
Moresby Wlk 6 SW8 137 B3
More's Gdn SW3 266 D5
Moreton Ave TW7 130 C4
Moreton Cl E5 52 C1
N15 51 B3
NW7 28 C4
Moreton Green Fst Sch
SM4 202 B4
Moreton Ho SE16 118 B3
Upper Tooting SW17 180 B6
Moreton Pl
SW1 115 C1 259 B2
Moreton Rd N15 51 B3
Croydon CR2 221 B3
North Cheam KT4 216 B6
Moreton St
SW1 115 D1 259 C2
Moreton Terr
SW1 115 C1 259 B2
Moreton Terr Mews N
SW1 259 B2
Moreton Terr Mews S
SW1 259 B2
Moreton Twr 3 W3 110 D5
Morford Cl HA4 40 B2
Morford Way HA4 40 B2
Morgan Ave E17 54 B5
Morgan Cl RM10 81 C1
Morgan Ct 5 SW11 136 B3
Ashford TW15 170 D5
Morgan Ho SW1 259 B3
SW8 269 B2
Morgan Rd BR1 187 A3
N7 72 C3
W10 91 B2
Teddington TW11 174 C4
Morgan's La UB3 83 B2
Morgan St E16 98 D2
E3 96 D4
Morgan's Wlk SW11 267 A3
Morgan Terr RM6 58 C4
Moriah Jewish Day Sch The
HA5 41 A1
Moriatry Cl N7 72 A4
Morie St SW18 157 D6
Morieux Rd E10 53 B1
Moring Rd SW17 181 A6
Moriss Ho 5 E5 74 B6
Morkyns Wlk SE21 161 C1
Morland Ave CR0 205 C1
Morland Cl NW11 47 D1
Hampton TW12 173 B5
Mitcham CR4 202 C6
Morland Ct W12 112 B4
Morland Est E8 74 A1
Morland Gdns NW10 67 B1
Southall UB1 107 D5
Morland Ho NW1 232 B3
NW6 91 C6
SW1 260 A4
W11 91 A1
Morland Mews N1 72 C1
Morland Rd E17 52 D4
Croydon CR0 205 D2
Dagenham RM10 81 C3
Harrow HA3 44 A5
Ilford IG1 78 D6
Penge SE20 184 D4
Sutton SM1 218 A3
Morland Road Day Hospl
RM10 103 C6
Morley Ave Chingford E4 36 B3
Edmonton N18 34 A6
Tottenham N22 32 D1
Morley Cl BR6 226 D6
Morley Coll
SE1 116 C3 261 B6
Morley Cres HA8 11 A2
Ruislip HA4 62 C6
Morley Cres E HA7 43 D6
Morley Cres W HA7 43 C6
Morley Ct E4 35 B5
Beckenham BR2 208 D5
Beckenham BR3 186 B2
Morley Hill EN2 5 B5
Morley Ho N16 74 A6
Streatham SW2 160 A4
Morley Rd E10 54 A1
E15 98 D5
SE13 142 A1
Barking IG11 101 B6
Cheam SM3 201 B1
Chislehurst BR7 189 A2
Dagenham RM6 59 A4
Twickenham TW1 153 D5
Morley St SE1 116 C4 251 B1
Morna Rd SE5 139 A3
Morning La E9 74 C2
Morningside Prim Sch
E9 74 C2
Morningside Rd KT4 216 C6
Mornington Ave BR1 209 D6
W14 113 B2 254 C3
Ilford IG1 56 C2
Mornington Avenue Mans
W14 254 C3
Mornington Cl IG8 37 A6
Mornington Cres
NW1 93 C5 232 A4
Cranford TW5 128 B4
Mornington Crescent Sta
NW1 93 C5 232 A4
Mornington Ct NW1 232 A4
Mornington Gr E3 97 C4
Mornington Mews 2
SE5 139 A4
Mornington Pl NW1 232 A4
4 SE8 141 B5
Mornington Rd E11 54 D1
SE14,SE8 141 B5
Ashford TW15 171 A5
Chingford E4 20 B4
Greenford UB6 85 D3
Woodford IG8 36 D6
Mornington St
NW1 93 B5 231 D4
Mornington Terr
NW1 93 B5 231 D4
Mornington Wlk
TW10 175 C6
Morocco St
SE1 117 C4 253 A1
Morpeth Gr E9 96 D6
Morpeth Rd E9 96 D6
Morpeth Sec Sch E2 96 C4
Morpeth St E2 96 D4
Morpeth Terr
SW1 115 C3 259 A4
Morpeth Wlk N17 34 B3
Morrab Gdns IG3 79 D5
Morrel Cl EN5 2 A2
Morrel Ct 10 E2 96 A5
Morris Ave E12 78 B3
Morris Blitz Ct 2 N16 73 D4
Morris Cl BR6 227 C5
Croydon CR0 207 A4
Morris Ct 3 SE5 139 B1
Chingford E4 19 D1
Morris Gdns SW18 157 C4
Morris Ho 17 E2 96 C4
10 N19 71 C4
NW8 237 A5
1 SW4 138 A1
Morrish Rd SW2 160 A4
Morrison Ave N17 51 C6
Morrison Bldgs 3 E1 96 A1
Morrison Ct N12 30 C3
5 Barnet EN5 1 A1
Morrison Ho SW2 160 C3
Morrison Rd
Barking IG11 103 A5
Hayes UB4 84 B4
Morrison St SW11 137 A2
Morrison Yd N17 33 D1
Morris Pl N4 72 C6
Morris Rd E15 76 C4
Dagenham RM8 81 B6
Isleworth TW7 130 D2
Morriss Ho 7 SE16 118 B4
Morris St E1 96 B1
E14 97 D2
Morriston Cl WD19 22 C5
Morritt Ho 3 HA0 65 D3
Morse Cl E13 99 A4
Morshead Mans W9 91 C4
Morshead Rd W9 91 C4
Morson Rd EN3 19 A5
Morston Gdns SE9 188 B6
Mortain Ho 9 SE16 118 B2
Morten Cl SW4 159 D5
Morteyne Rd N17 33 B2
Mortgramit Sq SE18 122 C3
Mortham St E15 98 C6
Mortimer Cl 1 NW2 69 B5
Streatham SW16 159 D2
Mortimer Cres NW6 91 D6
Worcester Park KT4 215 B5
Mortimer Ct NW8 229 B3
Mortimer Dr EN1 17 C6
Mortimer Est NW6 91 D6
Mortimer Ho 6 W11 112 D5
W14 254 B3
Mortimer Lo 11 SW19 157 A3
Mortimer Market WC1 239 B5
Mortimer Pl NW6 91 D6
Mortimer Rd E6 100 B4
N1 73 C1
NW10 90 C4
Ealing W13 87 C1
Mitcham CR4 180 D2
Mortimer Sq W11 112 D6
Mortimer St W1 93 C2 239 B3
Mortimer Terr NW5 71 B4
Mortlake Cl CR0 220 A5
Mortlake Dr CR4 180 C2
Mortlake High St
SW14 133 B2
Mortlake Rd Ilford IG1 79 B4
Newham E16 99 B1
Richmond SW14,TW9 132 C4
Mortlake Sta SW14 133 A2
Mortlock Cl SE15 140 B4
Mortlock Ct E12 77 D4
Morton Cl SM6 220 B1
Morton Cres N14 31 D6
Morton Ct UB5 64 A3
Morton Gdns SM6 219 C3
Morton Ho SE17 138 D6
West Norwood SE27 183 B5
Morton Mews SW5 255 C3
Morton Pl SE1 261 A5
Morton Rd E15 76 D1
N1 73 A1
Morden SM4 202 B4
Morton Way N14 31 D6
Morvale Cl DA17 125 B2
Morval Rd SW2 160 C6
Morven Rd SW17 158 D1
Morville St E3 97 C5
Morwell St WC1 239 D3
Moscow Pl W2 245 C6
Moscow Rd
W2 113 D6 245 C6
Mosedale NW1 231 D1
Moseley Way SE10 120 D3
Moselle Ave N22 32 C1
Moselle Cl N8 50 B6
Moselle Ho 2 N17 33 D3
Moselle Pl N17 33 D3
Moselle Sch N17 51 A6
Tottenham N17 33 C1
Moselle St N17 33 D3
Mosque Terr E1 96 A2
Mosque Tower 24 E1 96 A2
Mossborough Cl N12 29 D4
Mossbury Rd SW11 136 C2
Moss Cl E1 96 A2
Pinner HA5 23 A1
Mossdown Cl DA17 125 C2
Mossford Ct IG6 56 D6
Mossford Gn IG6 57 A6
Mossford St E3 97 B3
Moss Gdns
Feltham TW13 150 A2
South Croydon CR2 222 D1
Moss Hall Cres N12 30 A4
Moss Hall Ct N12 29 D4
Moss Hall Gr N12 29 D4
Moss Hall Jun & Inf Schs
N12 29 D4
Mossington Gdns
SE16 118 C2
Moss La HA5 23 A1
Mosslea Rd BR2 209 D4
BR6 227 A5
Penge SE20 184 C4
Mossop St
SW3 114 C2 257 B4
Moss Rd RM10 81 C1
Mossville Gdns SM4 201 B5
Mosswell Ho 4 N10 31 A3
Moston Cl UB3 105 D1
Mostyn Ave HA9 66 B3
Mostyn Gdns NW10 90 D5
Mostyn Gr E3 97 C5
Mostyn Lo N5 73 A4
Mostyn Rd HA8 27 C3
SW9 138 C4
Bushey WD23 8 A6
Merton SW19 179 B1
Mosul Way BR2 210 A3
Motcomb St
SW1 115 A3 258 A6
Moth Cl SM6 220 A1
Mothers Sq The 13 E5 74 B4
Motley Ave EC2 243 A6
Motley St SW8 137 C3
Motspur Park Sta KT3 200 B4
Motspur Pk KT3 200 A3
Mottingham Ct SE9 166 B3
Mottingham Gdns
SE9 165 D3
Mottingham Prim Sch
SE9 166 B1
Mottingham Rd N9 18 D4
SE9 166 B1
Mottingham Sta SE9 166 B3
Mottisfont Rd SE2 124 B2
Moules Ct SE5 139 A5
Moulins Rd E9 74 C1
Moulsford Ho 5 N7 72 A3
32 W2 91 C2
Moulton Ave TW3,TW5 129 B3
Moundfield Rd N16 52 A3
Mound The SE9 166 C1
Mounsey Ho 10 W10 91 A4
Mountacre Cl SE26 183 D6
Mount Adon Pk SE21,
SE22 162 A4
Mountague Pl 2 E14 120 A6
Mountain Ho SE11 260 C2
Mountaire Ct NW9 45 B4
Mount Angelus Rd
SW15 155 D4
Mount Ararat Rd
TW10 154 A6
Mount Arlington 3
BR2 186 C1
Mount Ash Rd SE26 162 B1
Mount Ave Chingford E4 19 D1
Ealing W5 87 D2
Southall UB1 85 C1
Mountbatten Cl SE18 145 C6
6 West Norwood SE19 183 C5
Mountbatten Ct IG9 21 D2
Mountbatten Gdns
BR3 207 A5
Mountbatten Ho N6 49 A2
Mountbatten Mews
SW18 158 A3
Mountbel Rd HA7 25 A1
Mount Carmel RC Coll
N19 49 D1
Mount Carmel RC Sec Sch
N7 72 B3
Mount Cl BR1 188 A2
Cockfosters EN4 3 A1
Ealing W5 87 C2
Mountcombe Cl KT6 198 A2
Mountcombe Ho
SW17 180 B5
Mount Ct
6 Kingston KT2 176 D3
West Wickham BR4 224 C6
Mount Culver Ave
DA14 190 D4
Mount Dr HA9 67 A6
Bexley DA6 169 A6
Harrow HA2,HA5 41 B4
Mountearl Gdns SW16,
SW2 160 B1
Mount Eaton Ct W5 87 C2
Mount Echo Ave E4 19 D3
Mount Echo Dr E4 19 D3
Mount Ephraim La
SW16 159 D1
Mount Ephraim Rd
SW16 159 D1
Mount Felix KT12 193 D1
Mountfield NW2 69 B6
Mountfield Cl SE6 164 B4
Mountfield Ct SE13 164 B5
Mountfield Rd N3 47 C6
Ealing W5 88 A1
Wallend E6 100 C4
Mountford Ho EN2 4 D1
Mountford St 4 E1 96 A1
Mountfort Cres N1 72 C1
Mountfort Terr 1 N1 72 C1
Mount Gdns SE26 162 B1
Mount Gr HA8 27 B6
Mountgrove Rd N5 73 A5
Mount House (St Martha's
Senior Sch) The EN4 1 C4
Mounthurst Rd BR2 208 D2
Mountington Park Cl
HA3 43 D3
Mountjoy Cl SE2 124 B4
Mountjoy Ho EC2 242 A3
Mount Lo N6 49 C3
Mount Lodge SW4 137 D1
Mount Mews TW12 173 D2
Mount Mills EC1 234 D1
Mount Nod Rd SW16,
SW2 160 B1
Mount Olive Ct W7 108 C4
Mount Park Ave HA1 64 C6
Mount Park Cres W5 87 D1
Mount Park Rd
Ealing W5 87 D1
Harrow HA1 64 B5
Pinner HA5 40 A4
Mount Pk SM5 219 A1
Mount Pl 7 W3 110 D5
Mount Pleasant N14 15 D4
WC1 94 C3 241 A5
Cockfosters EN4 2 D1
Ilford IG1 79 A3
Ruislip HA4 62 D6
Wembley HA0 88 B6
West Norwood SE27 183 A6
Mount Pleasant Cres
N4 50 B2
Mount Pleasant Hill E5 74 C6
Mount Pleasant La E5 52 B1
Mount Pleasant Pl
SE18 123 B2
Mount Pleasant Rd E17 35 A1
SE13 164 A5
Ealing W5 87 C3
Kingston KT3 199 A6
Mount Pleasant Rd *continued*
Tottenham N17 33 C1
Willesden NW10 90 C6
Mount Pleasant Villas
N4 50 B2
Mount Prim Sch The
KT3 199 A6
Mount Rd NW2 68 C5
NW4 46 A3
Bexley DA6 169 A6
Chessington KT9 214 B3
Dagenham RM8 59 B1
East Barnet EN4 14 C6
Feltham TW13 151 A1
Hayes UB3 106 A4
Kingston KT3 199 B6
Mitcham CR4 180 C1
South Norwood SE19 183 B4
Wimbledon SW18,SW19 157 D2
Mount Row
W1 115 B6 248 C5
Mount Sch NW7 28 C5
Mountside HA7 25 A2
Mounts Pond Rd SE3,
SE13 142 B3
Mount Sq The NW3 70 A5
Mount St W1 115 A6 248 B5
Mount Stewart Ave
HA3 43 D2
Mount Stewart Jun & Inf
Schs HA3 43 D2
Mount Terr E1 96 B2
Mount The DA6 169 D6
E5 74 B6
HA9 67 A6
N20 14 A2
N2 30 C1
NW3 70 A5
W8 245 A3
Croydon CR2 221 A3
Kingston KT3 199 D6
North Cheam KT4 216 B4
Northolt UB5 63 D3
Mount Tyndal NW3 48 B1
Mount Vernon NW3 70 A4
Mountview NW7 11 B1
5 Streatham SW16 160 B1
Mount View Ealing W5 87 D3
Enfield EN2 4 B5
Southall UB2 106 D2
Northwood HA6 22 A4
Mountview Cl NW11 48 A1
Mountview Ct N8 50 D5
Mount View Rd N4 50 B3
NW9 45 B4
Chingford E4 20 B4
Claygate KT10 213 B1
Mountview Theatre Sch
N8 50 A3
Mount Villas SE27 160 D1
Mountwood KT8 195 D6
Mountwood Ho W5 87 D3
Mourne Ho NW3 70 A2
Movers La IG11 101 C6
Mowat Ct 3 KT4 215 D6
Mowatt Cl N19 49 D1
Mowbray Ct
South Norwood SE19 183 D2
Wood Green N22 32 C2
Mowbray Gdns UB5 85 C6
Mowbray Ho 5 N2 30 B1
Mowbray Rd NW6 69 A1
Edgware HA8 26 C6
New Barnet EN5 14 A6
Richmond TW10 153 C1
South Norwood SE19 183 D2
Mowlem Prim Sch E2 96 C5
Mowlem St E2 96 B5
Mowlem Trad Est N17 34 C3
Mowll St SW9 138 C5
Moxon Cl E13 98 D5
Moxon St W1 93 A2 238 A3
Barnet EN5 1 B2
Moye Cl 9 E2 96 A5
Moyers Rd E10 54 A2
Moylan Rd W6 135 A6 264 B5
Moyle Ho SW1 269 B6
Moyne Ho 16 SW9 138 D1
Moyne Pl NW10 88 C5
Moynihan Dr N21 16 A6
Moys Cl CR0 204 A3
Moyser Rd SW16 181 B5
Mozart St W10 91 B4
Mt Carmel RC Prim Sch
W5 109 C3
Muchelney Rd SM4 202 A3
Mudchute Sta E14 119 D2
Mudie Ho 8 SW2 160 A4
Muggeridge Cl CR2 221 B3
Muggeridge Rd RM10 81 D4
Muir Cl SW18 158 C5
Muirdown Ave SW14 133 B1
Muirfield W3 89 C1
Muirfield Cl 23 SE16 118 B1
South Oxhey WD19 22 C6
Muirfield Cres E14 119 D3
Muirfield Gn WD19 22 C6
Muirfield Rd WD19 22 C6
Muirkirk Rd SE6 164 A3
Muir Rd E5 74 A
Muir St E16 122 A
Mulbarton Ct BR7 189 B
Mulberry Ave TW19 148 A
Mulberry Bsns Ctr
SE16 118 D
Mulberry Cl N8 50 A
NW3 70 B
NW4 46 C
SE22 162 A
SE7 143 D
SW3 266 D
Barnet EN4 2 B
Chingford E4 19 C
Northolt UB5 85 A
Streatham SW16 181 C
Mulberry Cres
Brentford TW8 131 C
West Drayton UB7 104 C
Mulberry Ct 1 E11 76 B
EC1 234 D
N5 72 D
NW10 67 B
10 W9 91 B
Barking IG11 79 D
4 Surbiton KT6 197 D
Twickenham TW1 152 D
Mulberry Ho 1 E2 96 C
8 SE8 141 B
Mulberry House Sch
NW2 69 A3
Mulberry La CR0 205 D1
Mulberry Mews SE14 141 B4
2 Wallington SM6 219 C2
Mulberry Par UB7 104 C4
Mulberry Pl W6 112 A1
Mulberry Rd E8 73 D1
Mulberry Sch for Girls
E1 96 B1
Stepney E1 118 B6
Mulberry St 8 E1 96 A1
Mulberry Trees TW17 193 B2
Mulberry Way Ilford IG6 57 A5
Woodford E18 37 B1
Mulberry Wlk
SW3 136 B6 266 D6
Mulgrave Chambers
SM2 217 D2
Mulgrave Hall SM2 217 D2
Mulgrave Ho 20 SE18 122 B2
Mulgrave Manor SM2 217 D2
Mulgrave Prim Sch
SE18 122 D3
Mulgrave Rd NW10 67 D4
SE18 122 C2
W14 264 C6
Belmont SM2 217 C2
Ealing W5 87 D3
Harrow HA1 65 A6
South Croydon CR0 221 B5
Mulholland Cl CR4 181 B1
Mulkern Rd N19 49 D1
Mullard Ho WC1 239 C4
Mullards Cl CR4 202 D1
Mullens Ho 7 SW15 156 C6
Mullen Twr EC1 241 A5
Muller Ho SE18 122 C1
Mullet Gdns 5 E2 96 A4
Mulletsfield WC1 233 B1
Mull Ho 13 E3 97 B5
Mullins Path SW14 133 B2
Mullion Cl HA3 23 D2
Mullion Wlk WD19 22 D6
Mulready St NW8 237 A5
Multi Way W3 111 C4
Multon Ho E9 74 C1
Multon Rd SW18 158 B4
Mulvaney Way SE1 252 D1
Mumford Rd SE24 160 D6
Muncaster Cl TW15 170 C6
Muncaster Rd SW11 159 A6
Ashford TW15 170 D5
Muncies Mews SE6 164 A2
Mundania Ct SE22 162 B5
Mundania Rd SE22 162 C5
Munday Ho SE1 262 C5
Munday Rd E16 121 A6
Munden Ho 5 E3 97 D4
Munden St
W14 113 A2 254 A4
Mundesley Cl WD19 22 C6
Mundford Rd E5 74 C6
Mundon Gdns IG1 57 B1
Mund St W14 113 B1 254 D1
Mundy Ho 8 W10 91 A4
Mundy St N1 95 C4
Mungo-Park Cl WD23 8 A2
Munnery Way BR6 226 D6
Munnings Gdns TW7 152 B6
Munro Ho SE1 251 A1
SE1 252 D1
Munro Mews W10 91 A2
Munro Rd WD23 8 A6
Munslow Gdns SM1 218 B4
Munstead Ct 12 SM2 218 A1
Munster Ave TW4 151 A6
Munster Ct
Fulham SW6 135 B3
Teddington TW11 175 C4

ıster Gdns N13 33 A6
ıster Rd
'6 135 A4 264 B2
ldington TW11 175 C4
ınster Residences
'6 264 B2
ınster Sq
V1 93 B3 238 D6
ınton Rd
l,SE17 117 A2 262 B4
ırchison Ave DA5 169 A3
ırchison Ho 1 W10 91 A2
ırchison Rd E10 76 A6
ırdoch Ho 4 SE16 118 C3
ırdock Cl E16 98 D1
ırdock St SE15 140 B6
ırfett Cl SW19 157 A2
ıriel Ct 17 E10 53 D2
ıriel St N1 94 B6 233 D4
ırillo Rd SE13 142 C1
ırley Ct N21 17 A4
ırphy Ho SE1 261 D6
ırphy St SE1 116 C4 251 A1
ırray Ave BR1 187 B1
ounslow TW3 151 D6
ırray Cres HA5 22 D2
ırray Ct 5 HA1 42 D3
ırray Gr N1 95 B5 235 C3
ırray Ho 21 SE18 122 B2
ırray Mews NW1 71 D1
ırray Rd W5 109 C2
ichmond TW10 153 C2
Vimbledon SW19 178 D4
ırray Sq E16 121 B6
ırray St NW1 71 D1
ırray Terr NW3 70 B4
usard Rd W6 135 A6 264 B6
usbury St E1 96 C1
uscal W6 264 A6
uscatel Pl SE5 139 C4
uschamp Inf Sch
SM5 218 C6
uschamp Jun Sch
SM5 218 C6
uschamp Rd SE15 139 D2
Carshalton SM1,SM5 218 C6
uscott Ho 15 E2 96 A6
uscovy Ho DA18 125 A4
uscovy St EC3 253 B6
useum Ho 7 E2 96 C4
useum in Docklands*
E14 119 C6
useum St
WC1 94 A1 240 A2
usgrave Cl EN4 2 A4
usgrave Cres
SW6 135 C4 265 B2
usgrave Ct SW11 267 A2
usgrave Rd TW7 130 D4
usgrove Ho 1 E9 74 D2
usgrove Rd SE14 141 A4
usical Mus The*
TW8 132 A6
usjid Rd 7 SW11 136 B3
uslim Coll The W5 110 C6
us of Garden History*
SE1 260 C5
us of London*
EC2 95 A2 242 A3
us of Richmond*
TW10 153 D6
us of the Great Eastern
Railway* E16 122 C4
Musquash Way TW4 128 C3
Muston Rd E5 74 B6
Mustow Pl 2 SW6 135 B3
Muswell Ave N10 31 B1
Muswell Hill N10 49 C6
Muswell Hill Bdwy N10 49 B6
Muswell Hill Jun & Inf Schs
N10 49 B6
Muswell Hill Pl N10 49 B5
Muswell Hill Rd N10 49 A4
Muswell Mews N10 49 B6
Muswell Rd N10 31 B1
Mutrix Rd NW6 91 C6
Mutton Pl NW1 71 A2
Muybridge Rd KT3 177 A1
Myatt Ct SE4 141 B3
Myatt Garden Prim Sch
SE4 141 B3
Myatt Ho SE5 138 D3
Myatt Rd SW9 138 D4
Myatts Field Ct SE5 139 A4
Mycenae Rd SE3 143 A6
Mychell Ho 8 SW19 180 A3
Myddelton Ave EN1 5 C5
Myddelton Cl EN1 5 D4
Myddelton Gdns N21 17 A4
Myddelton Ho N8 50 A6
Myddelton Pas
EC1 94 C4 234 B2
Myddelton Pk N20 14 B2
Myddelton Rd N8 50 A5
Myddelton Sq
EC1 94 C4 234 B2
Myddelton St
EC1 94 C4 234 B1
Myddleton Ave N4 73 A6
Myddleton Mews N22 32 A3
Myddleton Rd N22 32 B3
Myers Ho 5 SE5 139 A5
Myers La SE14 140 D6
Mylis Cl SE26 184 B6
Mylius Cl SE14 140 C4
Mylne Cl W6 112 A1
Mylne Ho N21 17 B5
Mylne St EC1 234 A3
Mynterne Ct 16 SW19 156 D3
Myra St SE2 124 A2
Myrdle Ct 8 E1 96 A1
Myrdle St E1 96 A1
Myrna Cl SW19 180 C3
Myron Pl SE13 142 A2
Myrtle Alley SE18 122 C3
Myrtle Ave
Hatton TW14 149 C6
Ruislip HA4 40 B2
Myrtle Cl
Barnet, London EN4 14 D3
Hillingdon UB8 82 B2
West Drayton UB7 104 B3
Myrtledene Rd SE2 124 A1
Myrtle Gdns W7 108 C5
Myrtle Gr Enfield EN2 5 B5
Kingston KT3 177 A1
Myrtle Ho SE14 140 D4
Myrtle Rd E17 53 A3
E6 100 A6
W3 111 A5
Croydon CR0 223 C5
Edmonton N13 17 B1
Hampton TW12 174 A4
Hounslow TW3 130 A3
Ilford IG1 78 D6
Sutton SM1 218 A3
Myrtle Wlk 20 N1 95 C5
Mysore Rd SW11 136 D1
Myton Rd SE21 161 B1
Mytton Ho SW8 270 C3

N

N1 Shopping Ctr
N1 94 C5 234 B4
Nadine St SE7 121 C1
Nadir Ct E11 55 A2
Naffenton Rise IG10 21 D6
Nagle Cl E17 36 B1
Nags Head N7 72 B4
Nags Head Ct EC1 242 B5
Nag's Head La DA16 146 B2
Nags Head Rd EN3 6 D1
Nainby Ho SE11 261 A3
Nairn Ct
3 Wallington SM6 219 C2
Wimbledon SW19 179 D4
Nairne Gr SE5,SE24 139 B1
Nairn Rd HA4 62 C2
Nairn St E14 98 A2
Naish Ct N1 233 B6
Nallhead Rd TW13 172 C5
Nalton Ho 4 NW6 70 A1
Namba Roy Cl SW16 182 B6
Namton Dr CR7,SW16 204 B5
Nan Clark's La NW7 11 D2
Nankin St E14 97 C1
Nansen Ct 1 E11 76 C6
Nansen Ho 7 NW10 67 B1
Nansen Rd SW11 137 A2
Nansen Village 5 N12 29 D6
Nant Ct NW2 69 B6
Nantes Cl SW18 136 A1
Nant Rd NW2 69 B6
Nant St E2 96 B4
Naoroji St WC1 234 A1
Napier 15 NW9 27 D2
Napier Ave E14 119 C1
Fulham SW6 135 B2
Napier Cl SE14,SE8 141 B5
W14 254 C6
West Drayton UB7 104 B3
Napier Ct N1 235 C4
SE12 165 B1
13 Croydon CR0 221 D6
Fulham SW6 135 B2
Hayes UB4 84 C3
1 Surbiton KT6 197 D2
Napier Gr N1 95 A5 235 B4
Napier Lo TW15 171 B4
Napier Pl W14 113 B3 254 C5
Napier Rd BR2 209 B5
DA17 125 B2
E11 76 C5
E15 98 C5
N17 51 C6
NW10 90 B4
W14 113 B3 254 C5
Ashford TW15 171 B3
Croydon SE25 206 B5
Enfield EN3 18 D6
Isleworth TW7 131 A1
South Croydon CR2 221 B1
Wallend E6 100 C5
Wembley HA0 65 D2
Napier Terr N1 72 D1
Napier Wlk TW15 171 B3
Napoleon Rd E5 74 B5
Twickenham TW1 153 B4
Napton Cl UB4 85 A3
Narbonne Ave SW4 159 C6
Narborough Cl UB10 61 A6
Narborough St SW6 135 D3
Narcissus Rd NW6 69 C3
Nardini 12 NW9 27 D2
Naresby Fold HA7 25 C4
Narford Rd E5 74 A6
Narrow Boat Cl SE28 123 B4
Narrow St E14 119 A6
6 Acton W3 110 D5
Narrow Way BR2 210 A3
Nascot St W12 90 C1
Naseby Cl NW6 70 A1
Hounslow TW7 130 C4
Naseby Ct DA14 189 D6
Naseby Rd
Dagenham RM10 81 C5
South Norwood SE19 183 B4
Nash Cl SM1 218 B5
Nash Ct HA3 43 B3
Nashe Ho SE1 262 C5
Nash Gn BR1 187 A4
Nash Ho 1 E17 53 D5
SW1 258 D1
Nash La BR2 225 A2
Nash Rd N9 18 C2
SE4 163 A6
Dagenham RM6 58 D5
Nash Street NW1 231 D2
Nash Way HA3 43 B3
Nasmyth St W6 112 B3
Nassau Path 6 SE28 124 C5
Nassau Rd SW13 133 D4
Nassau St W1 239 A3
Nassington Rd NW3 70 D4
Natalie Cl TW14 149 B4
Natalie Mews TW2 152 B1
Natal Rd Bowes Park N11 32 A4
Ilford IG1 78 D4
South Norwood CR7 205 B6
Streatham SW16 181 D4
Nathan Ct N9 18 C4
Nathan Ho SE11 261 B3
Nathaniel Cl E1 243 D3
Nathaniel Ct E17 53 A3
Nathans Rd HA0 65 C6
Nathan Way SE28,SE18 123 D3
National Army Mus*
SW3 136 D6 267 D6
National Fan Mus*
SE10 142 A5
National Film Theatre*
SE1 250 D4
National Gallery*
W1 115 D6 249 D5
National Hospital for
Neurology & Neurosurgery
N2 48 C5
National Hospl The
WC1 94 A3 240 B5
National Maritime Mus*
SE10 142 B6
National Physical
Laboratory TW11 174 C4
National Portrait Gallery*
W1 115 D6 249 D5
National Portrait Gallery
(Annexe)*
SW1 115 D5 249 D4
National Postal Mus*
EC1 95 A1 242 A2
National Theatre
SE1 116 B5 250 D4
National Wks TW4 129 B2
Nation Way E4 20 A3
Natural History Mus*
SW7 114 B3 256 C5
Nat West Twr* EC2 243 A2
Nautilus Bldg The EC1 234 B2
Naval Row E14 120 A6
Navarino Gr E8 74 A2
Navarino Mans E8 74 A2
Navarino Rd E8 74 A2
Navarre Rd E6 100 A5
Navarre St E2 243 C6
Navenby Wlk 13 E3 97 C3
Navestock Cl E4 20 A1
Navestock Ho IG11 102 B5
Navigator Dr UB2 108 A4
Navy St SW4 137 D2
Nayland Ho SE6 186 A6
Naylor Gr EN3 18 D6
Naylor Ho SE17 262 D2
33 SW8 137 D3
5 W10 91 B4
Naylor Rd N20 14 A2
SE15 140 B5
Nazareth Cl SE15 140 B3
Nazrul St E2 95 D4
Neal Ave UB1 85 B3
Neal Cl HA6 22 A2
Nealden St SW9 138 B2
Neale Cl N2 48 A6
Neale Ct N10 31 B3
Neal St WC2 94 A1 240 A1
Neal's Yd WC2 240 A1
Near Acre NW9 27 D2
Neasden Cl NW10 67 C3
Neasden Junc NW10 67 C4
Neasden La NW10 67 B5
NW10 67 C3
Neasden La N NW10 67 C5
Neasden Sta NW10 67 C3
Neasham Rd RM8 80 B3
Neate St SE5 139 C6
SE5 139 D6
Neath Gdns SM4 202 A3
Neathouse Pl SW1 259 A4
Neats Acre HA4 39 B2
Neatscourt Rd E16 99 D2
Nebraska St
SE1 117 B4 252 C1
Neckinger
SE16 117 D3 263 D6
Neckinger Est SE16 263 D6
Neckinger St SE1 263 D6
Nectarine Way SE13 141 D3
Nedahall Ct 4 NW11 47 B2
Needham Ho SE11 261 A3
Needham Rd W11 91 C1
Needham Terr NW2 68 D5
Needleman St SE16 118 D4
Needwood Ho N4 51 A1
Neela Cl UB10 60 D4
Neeld Cres NW4 46 B4
Wembley HA9 66 C3
Neeld Ct HA9 66 C3
Neeld Par HA9 66 B3
Neil Cl TW15 171 A5
Neilson-Terry Ct 9
SW9 138 B1
Neil Wates Cres 18
SW2 160 C3
Nelgarde Rd SE6 163 C4
Nelland Ct SE6 163 B2
Nella Rd W6 134 D6
Nelldale Rd SE16 118 C2
Nellgrove Rd UB10 82 D3
Nell Gwynne Ave
TW17 193 B3
Nell Gwynn Ho SW3 257 B3
Nello James Gdns
SE27 183 B6
Nelson Cl 9 NW6 91 C4
East Bedfont TW14 149 D3
Hillingdon UB10 82 D4
Thornton Heath CR0 204 D1
Walton-on-T KT12 194 B1
Nelson Ct SE16 119 B5
Carshalton SM5 218 D5
Nelson Gdns E2 96 A4
Twickenham TW3,TW4 151 C5
Nelson Grove Rd
SW19 180 A2
Nelson Ho 1 W5 88 A4
Nelson Hospl SW20 179 B1
Nelson La UB10 82 D4
Nelson Mandela Cl N10 31 A1
Nelson Mandela Rd
SE3 143 C2
Nelson Pas EC1 235 B2
Nelson Pl N1 234 D3
Sidcup DA14 190 A6
Nelson Prim Sch
Twickenham TW2 151 D5
Wallend E6 100 C5
Nelson Rd N15 51 C5
N8 50 B3
SE10 142 A6
Ashford TW15 170 A5
Bromley BR2 209 C5
Chingford E4 35 D4
Edmonton N9 18 B2
Enfield EN3 18 D5
Erith DA17 125 B1
Harmondsworth TW6 126 B4
Harrow HA1 42 C1
Hillingdon UB10 82 D4
Merton SW19 180 A3
New Malden KT3 199 B4
Sidcup DA14 190 A6
Stanmore HA7 25 C4
Twickenham TW2,TW4 151 C5
Wanstead E11 55 B5
Nelson's Monument*
WC2 250 A4
Nelson Sq SE1 116 D4 251 C2
Nelsons Row SW4 137 D1
Nelson St E1 96 B1
E16 120 D6
E6 100 B5
Barking E6 100 C6
Nelson Terr N1 234 D3
Nelson Trad Est SW19 179 D2
Nemoure Rd W3 111 A6
Nene Gdns TW13 151 B2
Nene Rd TW6,UB7 126 D4
Nene Road Rdbt TW6 126 D4
Nepaul Rd 17 SW11 136 C2
Nepean St SW15 156 A4
Neptune Ct 5 E14 119 C2
Neptune Ho 14 N16 73 C3
2 SE16 118 C3
Neptune Rd
Harlington TW6 127 A4
Neptune Rd *continued*
Harrow HA1 42 B3
Neptune St SE16 118 C3
Nero Ct 6 TW8 131 D5
Nesbit Cl SE3 142 C2
Nesbit Rd SE9 143 D1
Nesbitt Ho DA6 169 D6
Nesbitt Sq SE19 183 C3
Nesham Ho 14 N1 95 C6
Nesham St E1 118 A5
Ness St 9 SE16 118 A3
Nesta Rd IG8 36 D4
Nestle's Ave UB3 105 D3
Nestor Ave N21 16 D5
Nestor Ho 13 E2 96 B5
Netheravon Rd W4 111 D1
Ealing W7 108 D5
Netheravon Rd S W4 111 D1
Netherbury Rd W5 109 D3
Netherby Gdns EN2 4 A1
Netherby Ho 23 SW8 137 D3
Netherby Rd SE23 162 C4
Nether Cl N3 29 C3
Nethercombe Ho 1
SE3 143 A6
Nethercott Ho 27 E3 97 D4
Nethercourt Ave N3 29 C4
Netherfield Gdns IG11 79 B1
Netherfield Rd N12 29 D5
Upper Tooting SW17 159 A1
Netherford Rd SW4 137 C3
Netherhall Gdns NW3 70 A3
Netherhall Way NW3 70 A3
Netherlands Rd EN5 14 B5
Netherleigh Cl N6 49 B1
Nether St N12 30 A5
N3 29 D4
Netherton Gr
SW10 136 A6 266 B5
Netherton Rd N15 51 B3
Isleworth TW1 153 B6
Netherwood 19 N2 30 B1
Netherwood Rd W14 112 D4
Netherwood St NW6 69 C2
Nethewode Ct DA17 125 D3
Netley 13 SE5 139 C4
Netley Cl Cheam SM3 216 D3
New Addington CR0 224 A1
Netley Ct IG2 57 B4
Netley Dr KT12 195 B2
Netley Gdns SM4 202 A2
Netley Prim Sch
NW1 93 C4 232 A1
Netley Rd E17 53 B4
Brentford TW8 132 A6
Cheam SM4 202 A2
Ilford IG2 57 B4
Netley Rd (W) TW6 127 B4
Netley St NW1 93 C4 232 A1
Nettlecombe NW1 71 D1
Nettleden Ave HA9 66 C2
Nettleden Ho SW3 257 B3
Nettlefold Pl SE27 160 D1
Nettlestead Cl 16 BR3 185 C3
Nettleton Rd SE14 140 D4
Harlington TW6 126 D4
Ickenham UB10 60 B4
Nettlewood Rd SW16 181 D3
Neuchatel Rd SE6 163 B2
Nevada Cl KT3 199 A5
Nevada St SE10 142 A6
Nevena Ct 3 SW2 160 C6
Nevern Mans SW5 255 A2
Nevern Pl SW5 113 C2 255 B3
Nevern Rd SW5 255 A3
Nevern Sq
SW5 113 C2 255 B3
Nevil Ho 7 SW9 138 D3
Nevill Ct SW10 266 A4
Neville Ave KT3 177 B2
Neville Cl DA15 189 D6
E11 76 D5
NW1 232 D3
NW6 91 B5
SE15 140 A4
17 SE15 140 A5
Acton W3 111 A4
Hounslow TW3 129 D3
Neville Ct 10 SW12 159 C4
Neville Dr N2 48 A3
Neville Gdns RM8 80 D5
Neville Gill Cl SW18 157 D5
Neville Ho N11 31 A6
Neville Pl N22 32 B2
Neville Rd E7 77 B1
NW6 91 B5
Dagenham RM8 80 D5
Ealing W5 87 D3
Kingston KT1 176 C1
Richmond TW10 153 C2
Thornton Heath CR0 205 B2
Neville's Ct NW2 68 A5
Neville St SW7 114 B1 256 C2
Neville Terr SW7 256 C2
Neville Wlk SM5 202 C2
Nevill Rd N16 73 C5
Nevin Dr E4 19 D3
Nevin Ho UB3 105 A3
Nevinson Cl SW18 158 B5
Nevis Rd SW17 159 A2
Nevitt Ho N1 235 D3
New Acres Rd SE28 123 C5
Newall Ho SE1 262 B6
Newall Rd TW6 127 A4
Newark Cres NW10 89 B4
Newark Ct KT12 194 C1
Newark Ho 3 SW9 138 D3
Newark Knok E6 100 C2
Newark Par NW4 46 A6
Newark Rd CR2 221 B2
Newark St E1 96 B2
Newark Way NW4 46 A6
New Ash Cl N2 48 B6
New Barn Cl SM6 220 B2
New Barnet Sta EN5 14 B6
New Barns Ave CR4 203 D5
New Barn St E13 99 B3
New Beckenham Sta
BR3 185 B3
New Belmont Ho 4
SE23 162 C3
New Bentham Ct 11 N1 73 A1
Newbery Ho N1 73 A1
Newbiggin Path WD19 22 C6
Newbold Cotts 4 E1 96 C1
Newbolt Ave SM3 216 D3
Newbolt Ho SE17 262 C2
Newbolt Rd HA7 24 D5
New Bond St
W1 115 B6 248 D6
Newborough Gn KT3 199 B5
Newborough Ho
SW19 180 B3
New Brent St NW4 46 C4
Newbridge Ct SW17 180 A6
Newbridge Point 3
SE23 162 D1
New Bridge St
EC4 94 D1 241 C1
New Broad St
EC2 95 C2 243 A3
New Broadway
Ealing W5 109 D6
7 Hillingdon UB10 82 D3
Teddington TW12 174 B5
New Bsns Ctr The
NW10 89 D4
Newburgh Rd W3 111 A5
Newburgh St W1 239 B1
New Burlington Mews
W1 249 A6
New Burlington Pl
W1 249 A6
New Burlington St
W1 249 A6
Newburn Ho SE11 260 D2
Newburn St
SE11 116 B1 260 D2
Newbury Ave EN3 7 B6
Newbury Cl UB5 63 B2
Newbury Cotts 4 IG2 57 A3
Newbury Ct DA14 189 D6
E5 75 A3
7 Wanstead E11 55 A5
Newbury Gdns KT19 215 D4
Newbury Ho SW9 138 D3
13 W2 91 D1
Wood Green N22 32 A2
Newbury Mews NW5 71 A2
Newbury Park Prim Sch
IG2 57 B3
Newbury Park Sta IG2 57 B3
Newbury Rd BR2 209 A6
Chingford E4 36 A4
Harmondsworth TW6 126 B4
Ilford IG2 57 C3
Newbury St EC1 242 A4
Newbury Way UB5 63 B2
New Butt La SE8 141 C5
Newby NW1 232 A2
Newby Cl EN1 5 C3
Newby Pl E14 120 A6
Newby St SW8 137 B2
New Caledonian Wharf
SE16 119 B3
New Campden Ct 7
NW3 70 A4
Newcastle Cl EC4 241 C2
Newcastle Ct EC4 252 B6
Newcastle Ho W1 238 A4
Newcastle Pl
W2 92 B2 236 D4
Newcastle Row EC1 241 B5
New Cavendish St
W1 93 B2 238 C3
New Change
EC4 95 A1 242 A1
New Chapel Sq TW13 150 B3
New Charles St EC1 234 D2
New Church Ct 3
SE19 184 A3
New Church Rd SE5 139 B6
32 SE5 139 A5
New City Prim Sch E13 99 C4
New City Rd E13 99 C4

New Cl Feltham TW13 ... 173 A5
Morden SW19 ... 202 A6
New Colebrooke Ct SM5 ... 219 A1
New College Ct 6 NW3 ... 70 A2
New College Mews 4 N1 ... 72 C1
New College Par 1 NW3 ... 70 B1
Newcombe Ho N5 ... 73 A3
Newcombe Pk NW7 ... 27 C5
Wembley HA0 ... 88 B6
Newcombe Rise UB7 ... 82 A1
Newcombe St W8 ... 245 B4
Newcome Gdns SW16 182 A6
Newcome Ho E5 ... 74 B5
Newcomen Ho 5 NW5 ... 71 B4
Newcomen Rd E11 ... 76 D5
SW11 ... 136 B2
Newcomen St SE1 ... 117 B4 252 C2
New Compton St WC2 ... 94 A1 240 A1
New Concordia Wharf SE1 ... 253 D2
Newcourt Ho 20 E2 ... 96 B4
Newcourt St NW8 ... 92 C5 230 A3
New Covent Garden Flower Market SW8 ... 138 A6 270 A5
New Covent Garden Fruit & Vegetable Mkt SW8 ... 137 D5 269 C3
New Crescent Yd 1 NW10 ... 89 D5
Newcroft Cl UB8 ... 82 B2
New Cross SE14 ... 141 B5
New Cross Gate SE14 ... 140 D4
New Cross Gate Sta SE14 ... 141 A5
New Cross Hospl SE14 ... 140 C5
New Cross Rd SE14 ... 141 A4
New Cross Sta SE14 ... 141 B5
New Ct EC4 ... 241 A1
N16 ... 51 B1
13 NW3 ... 70 A4
Northolt UB5 ... 63 D3
Newdales Cl N9 ... 18 A2
Newdene Ave UB5 ... 84 D5
New Den (Millwall FC) The SE16 ... 118 C1
Newdigate Ho 5 E14 ... 97 B1
6 Kingston KT2 ... 176 D4
Newell St E14 ... 97 B1
New Eltham Sta SE9 ... 166 D3
New End NW3 ... 70 A5
New End Prim Sch NW3 ... 70 A4
New End Sq NW3 ... 70 B4
New England Est IG11 101 A5
Newent Cl SE15 ... 139 C5
Carshalton SM5 ... 202 D1
New Farm Ave BR2 ... 209 A5
New Ferry App SE18 ... 122 C3
New Fetter La EC4 ... 94 C1 241 B2
Newfield Cl TW12 ... 173 C2
Newfield Prim Sch NW10 ... 67 D1
Newfield Rise NW2 ... 68 B5
New Furness Prim Sch The NW10 ... 90 A5
Newgale Gdns HA8 ... 26 B2
New Garden Dr UB7 ... 104 A4
Newgate CR0 ... 205 A1
Newgate Cl TW13 ... 151 A1
Newgate St EC1 ... 94 D1 241 D2
Chingford E4 ... 20 C1
New Globe Wlk SE1 ... 252 A4
New Goulston St E1 ... 243 C2
New Green Pl SE19 ... 183 C4
Newham Acad of Music E6 ... 100 A6
Newham Coll of FE E6 ... 100 B5
Newham Coll of F Ed (Royal Docks Campus) E16 ... 123 A5
Newham Ctr for Mental Health E16 ... 99 D3
Newham General Hospl E13 ... 99 C3
Newham Gn N22 ... 32 C2
Newham Ho IG10 ... 21 D5
Newham Sch of Nursing E3 ... 97 D3
Newham Sixth Form Coll E13 ... 99 B3
Newham's Row SE1 ... 253 B1
Newham Way E13 ... 99 B2
E6 ... 100 B3
Newhaven Cl UB3 ... 105 D2
Newhaven Cres TW15 ... 171 B5
Newhaven Gdns SE9 ... 143 D1
Newhaven La 3 E16 ... 99 A2
Newhaven Rd SE25 ... 205 B4
New Heston Rd TW5 ... 129 B5
Newhouse 5 KT3 ... 199 C2
Newhouse Ave RM6 ... 58 D6
Newhouse Cl KT3 ... 199 C2
Newhouse Wlk SM4 ... 202 A2
Newick Cl DA5 ... 169 D5
Newick Rd E5 ... 74 C5
Newing Gn BR1 ... 187 D3
Newington Barrow Way N7 ... 72 B5
Newington Butts SE1,SE11 ... 116 D2 261 D3
Newington Cswy SE1 ... 117 A3 262 A6
Newington Green Mans N16 ... 73 B3
Newington Green Prim Sch N16 ... 73 B3
Newington Green Rd N1 ... 73 B3
Newington Ind Est SE17 ... 262 A3
New Inn Broadway EC2 ... 243 B6
New Inn Pas WC2 ... 240 D1
New Inn Sq EC2 ... 243 B6
New Inn St EC2 ... 243 B6
New Inn Yd EC2 95 C3 243 B6
New James Ct SE15 ... 140 B2
New Jubilee Ct 1 IG8 ... 37 A3
New Kelvin Ave TW11 ... 174 C4
New Kent Rd SE1 ... 117 A2 262 B4
New King's Prim Sch SW6 ... 135 B3
New Kings Rd SW6 ... 135 C3
New King's Rd SW6 ... 135 C3 265 B1
New King St SE8 ... 141 C6
Newland Cl HA5 ... 23 B4
Newland Ct EC1 ... 242 C6
Wembley HA9 ... 66 C6
Newland Dr EN1 ... 6 B4
Newland Gdns W13 ... 109 A4
Newland Ho N8 ... 50 A6
17 SE14 ... 140 D6
Newland House Sch TW1 ... 174 D6
Newland House Sch Annex TW1 ... 174 D6
Newland Rd N8 ... 50 A6
Newlands NW1 ... 232 A2
Newlands Ave KT7 ... 196 C1
Newlands Cl
Edgware HA8 ... 10 A1
Southall UB2 ... 107 A1
Wembley HA0 ... 65 C2
Newlands Croft SE20 ... 184 D4
Newlands Ct 8 SE9 ... 166 C5
Streatham SW16 ... 182 A5
Newlands Pk SE26 ... 184 D5
Newlands Pl EN5 ... 12 D6
Newlands Quay E1 ... 118 C6
Newlands Rd
Thornton Heath SW16 ... 182 A1
Woodford IG8 ... 20 D2
Newland St E16 ... 122 B5
Newlands The
Thames Ditton KT7 ... 196 C1
Wallington SM6 ... 219 D1
Newlands Way KT9 ... 213 C3
Newling Cl E6 ... 100 B1
New London St EC3 ... 253 B6
New Lydenburg Commercial Est E16 ... 121 C3
New Lydenburg St SE7 ... 121 C3
Newlyn NW1 ... 232 B5
Newlyn Cl Hillingdon UB8 82 C2
Orpington BR6 ... 227 D4
Newlyn Gdns HA2 ... 41 B2
Newlyn Rd DA16 ... 145 D3
Barnet EN5 ... 1 B1
Tottenham N17 ... 33 D2
New Malden Sta KT3 ... 199 C6
Newman Ct BR1 ... 187 A2
Newman Pas W1 ... 239 B3
Newman Rd BR1 ... 187 A2
E13 ... 99 B4
E17 ... 52 D4
Hayes UB3 ... 106 B6
Thornton Heath CR0 ... 204 B1
Newman's Ct EC3 ... 242 D1
Newman's Row WC2 ... 240 D3
Newman St W1 93 C2 239 B3
Newman's Way EN4 ... 2 A4
Newmarket Ave UB5 ... 63 D3
Newmarket Gn SE9 ... 165 D4
Newmarsh Rd SE28 ... 123 D5
Newmill Ho E3 ... 98 A3
New Mill Rd BR5 ... 190 C2
Newminster Rd SM4 ... 202 A3
Newmount NW3 ... 70 B3
New Mount St E15 ... 76 B1
Newnes Path SW15 ... 134 B1
Newnham Ave HA4 ... 40 C1
Newnham Cl
Loughton IG10 ... 21 D5
Northolt UB5 ... 64 A2
South Norwood CR7 ... 183 A1
Newnham Gdns UB5 ... 64 A2
Newnham Ho
Catford SE6 ... 164 A1
9 Putney SW15 ... 156 D5
Newnham Jun & Inf Schs HA4 ... 40 C1
Newnham Lo 10 DA17 125 C1
Newnham Rd N22 ... 32 C2
Newnhams Cl BR1 ... 210 B6
Newnham Terr SE1 ... 261 A6
Newnham Way HA3 ... 44 A4
New North Pl EC2 ... 243 A6
New North Rd N1 ... 95 B6 235 C5
New North Road Bridge N1 ... 235 C5
New North St WC1 ... 94 B2 240 C4
Newnton Cl N4 ... 51 B2
New Oak Rd N2 ... 30 A1
New Oxford St WC1 ... 94 A1 240 A2
New Palace Yd SW1 ... 116 A4 250 A1
New Par Ashford TW15 ... 170 B6
Yiewsley UB7 ... 104 A5
New Park Ave N13 ... 17 B1
New Park Cl UB5 ... 63 A2
New Park Ct 26 SW2 ... 160 A4
New Park Est N18 ... 34 C5
New Park Ho N13 ... 32 B6
New Park Par 14 SW2 160 A4
New Park Rd
Ashford TW15 ... 171 A5
Streatham SW2 ... 160 A4
New Pl CR0 ... 223 C2
New Place Sq SE16 ... 118 B3
New Plaistow Rd E15 ... 98 C6
New Pond Par HA4 ... 62 A5
Newport Ave E13 ... 99 B3
E14 ... 120 B6
Newport Cl EN3 ... 7 A6
Newport Ct WC2 ... 249 D6
Newport Ho E3 ... 97 A4
Newport Jun & Inf Schs E10,E11 ... 76 A6
Newport Lo 2 EN1 ... 17 C6
Newport Mead WD19 ... 22 D6
Newport Pl WC2 ... 249 D6
Newport Rd E10 ... 76 B6
E17 ... 53 A5
Barnes SW13 ... 134 A4
Harmondsworth TW6 ... 126 C4
Hayes UB4 ... 83 B2
Newport St SE11 ... 116 B2 260 D4
New Priory Ct 9 NW6 ... 69 C1
Newquay Cres HA2 ... 63 A6
Newquay Ho SE11 ... 261 A2
Newquay Rd SE6 ... 164 A2
New Quebec St W1 ... 237 D1
New Rd DA16 ... 146 B3
E1 ... 96 B2
N10 ... 30 C2
N8 ... 50 A4
NW7 ... 29 A3
SE2 ... 124 D1
Brentford TW8 ... 109 D1
Carshalton CR4 ... 203 A1
Chingford E4 ... 36 A6
Dagenham RM10 ... 103 D5
East Bedfont TW14 ... 149 B5
East Bedfont TW14 ... 150 B3
East Molesey KT8 ... 195 C6
Edmonton N9 ... 18 A2
Elstree WD6 ... 9 D5
Esher KT10 ... 212 A4
Feltham TW13 ... 173 A5
Harlington TW6,UB7 ... 127 A5
Harrow HA1 ... 64 D4
Hillingdon UB8 ... 83 A2
Hounslow TW3 ... 129 D1
Ilford IG3 ... 79 C6
Kingston KT2 ... 176 C3
Littleton TW17 ... 192 D6
Richmond TW10 ... 175 C6
Tottenham N22 ... 33 A2
New Rd Units TW3 ... 129 D1
New River Cres N13 ... 32 D6
New River Ct N5 ... 73 B4
New River Sports & Recreation Ctr N22 ... 32 D3
New River Way N4 ... 51 B2
New Row WC2 116 A6 250 A6
Newry Rd TW1 ... 153 A6
Newsam Ave N15 ... 51 B4
New Scotland Yard* SW1 ... 115 D3 259 C6
Newsholme Dr N21 ... 16 B6
New Southgate Ind Est 10 N11 ... 31 C5
New Southgate Sta N11 ... 31 B5
New Spring Gdns Wlk SE11 ... 260 B1
New Sq WC2 ... 94 B1 240 D2
East Bedfont TW14 ... 149 A3
New Sq Pas WC2 ... 241 A2
New St EC2 ... 95 C2 243 B3
New Stanford Prim Sch SW16 ... 181 D2
Newstead Ave BR6 ... 227 C6
Newstead Cl N12 ... 30 C4
Newstead Ct UB5 ... 85 A4
Newstead Rd SE12 ... 164 D4
Newstead Way SW19 ... 178 D6
Newstead Wlk SM5 ... 202 A2
Newstead Wood Sch for Girls BR6 ... 227 B5
New Street Hill BR1 ... 187 C5
New St Sq EC4 94 C1 241 B2
Newton Ave N10 ... 31 B2
Acton W3 ... 111 A4
Newton Cl E17 ... 53 A3
Harrow HA2 ... 63 C6
Newton Farm Fst & Mid Sch HA2 ... 63 B6
Newton Gr W4 ... 111 C2
Newton Ho 10 E17 ... 54 A6
NW8 ... 91 D6
22 SW8 ... 137 D3
1 Stepney E1 ... 118 B6
Newton Pl E14 ... 119 C2
Newton Point 1 E16 ... 98 D1
Newton Prep Sch SW8 ... 137 B4 268 D2
Newton Rd DA16 ... 146 A2
E15 ... 76 B3
N15 ... 52 A4
NW2 ... 68 C5
W2 ... 91 D1
Harrow HA3 ... 24 C1
Isleworth TW7 ... 130 D3
Wembley HA0 ... 66 B1
Wimbledon SW19 ... 179 A3
Newton St WC2 94 A1 240 B2
Newton's Yd 14 SW18 ... 157 C6
Newton Terr BR2 ... 209 D3
Newton Way N18 ... 33 A5
Newton Wlk HA8 ... 26 D2
New Tower Bldgs 21 E1 ... 118 B5
Newtown Ct SW11 ... 268 C1
SW4 ... 159 B6
New Trinity Rd 1 N2 ... 30 B1
New Union Cl E14 ... 120 A3
New Union St EC2 ... 242 C3
New Victoria Hospl KT3 ... 177 C2
New Wanstead E11 ... 55 A3
New Way Rd NW9 ... 45 C5
New Wharf Rd N1 ... 94 A5 233 B4
New Woodlands Sch BR1 ... 186 C6
Newyears Green La UB9 ... 38 B3
New Zealand Ave KT12 ... 193 D1
Niagara Ave W5 ... 109 C2
Niagara Cl N1 ... 235 B4
Niagara Ct 6 SE16 ... 118 C3
Niagara Ho W5 ... 109 C2
Nibthwaite Rd HA1 ... 42 C4
Nicholas Cl UB6 ... 85 D5
Nicholas Ct
Chiswick W4 ... 133 C5
Lewisham SE12 ... 165 A3
Nicholas Gdns W5 ... 109 D4
Nicholas Ho Ealing W13 ... 87 C1
Penge SE26 ... 184 B4
2 Putney SW15 ... 156 A6
Nicholas La EC2,EC4 ... 252 D6
Nicholas Pas EC3 ... 252 D6
Nicholas Rd E1 ... 96 C3
Borehamwood WD6 ... 10 B6
Dagenham RM8 ... 81 B5
Wallington CR0 ... 220 A4
Nicholas Stacey Ho 3 SE7 ... 121 B1
Nicholay Rd N19 ... 49 D1
Nichol Cl N14 ... 15 D3
Nicholes Rd TW3 ... 129 C1
Nichol La BR1 ... 187 A3
Nicholl Ho N4 ... 51 A1
Nicholls Ave UB8 ... 82 C3
Nicholls Point E15 ... 99 A6
Nicholl St E2 ... 96 A6
Nichols Cl N4 ... 50 C1
Chessington KT9 ... 213 C2
Nichols Ct E2 ... 95 D5
Nichols Gn W5 ... 88 A2
Nicholson Dr WD23 ... 8 A2
Nicholson Ho SE17 ... 262 C2
2 SE18 ... 144 A4
Nicholson Rd CR0 ... 205 D1
Nicholson St SE1 ... 251 C3
Nickelby Cl SE28 ... 102 C1
Nickleby Cl UB8 ... 82 D1
Nickleby Ho 15 SE1 ... 118 A4
7 W11 ... 112 D5
Nicola Cl Harrow HA3 ... 24 B1
South Croydon CR2 ... 221 A2
Nicola Terr DA7 ... 147 A4
Nicol Cl 6 TW1 ... 153 B5
Nicole Ho SE25 ... 206 A6
Nicoll Ct N10 ... 31 B3
NW10 ... 89 C6
Nicoll Pl NW4 ... 46 B2
Nicoll Rd NW10 ... 89 C6
Nicoll Way WD6 ... 11 B6
Nicolson 14 NW9 ... 27 D2
Nicosia Rd SW18 ... 158 C4
Niederwald Rd SE26 ... 185 A6
Nield Rd UB3 ... 105 D4
Nigel Bldg EC1 ... 241 A4
Nigel Cl UB5 ... 85 A6
Nigel Ct N3 ... 29 D3
Nigel Fisher Way KT9 ... 213 D1
Nigel Mews IG1 ... 78 D4
Nigel Playfair Ave W6 112 B1
Nigel Rd E7 ... 77 C3
SE15 ... 140 A2
Nigeria Rd SE7 ... 143 D5
Nighthawk 16 NW9 ... 27 D2
Nightingale Ave
Chingford E4 ... 36 C5
Harrow HA1 ... 43 B1
Nightingale Cl
Carshalton SM5 ... 219 A6
Chingford E4 ... 36 C6
Chiswick W4 ... 133 A6
Pinner HA5 ... 40 C4
Nightingale Ct 12 E14 120 A3
N4 ... 72 B6
SW6 ... 265 D1
1 Harrow HA1 ... 42 D3
Penge SE19 ... 183 D4
Sutton SM1 ... 218 A3
1 Wanstead E11 ... 55 B4
Nightingale Dr KT19 ... 214 D2
Nightingale Gr SE13 ... 164 B6
Nightingale Ho 7 E1 ... 118 A5
21 E1 ... 95 C6
SE18 ... 122 C1
W12 ... 90 C1
Hayes UB3 ... 105 D2
Nightingale La BR1 ... 187 D1
N8 ... 50 A6
Balham SW11,SW12 ... 159 A5
Richmond TW10 ... 154 A4
Wanstead E11 ... 55 B4
Nightingale Lo 5 W9 ... 91 C2
Nightingale Mews SE11 ... 261 D4
Nightingale Pl SE18 ... 144 D6
SW10 ... 136 A6 266 B6
Nightingale Prim Sch SE18 ... 122 D1
Wanstead E18 ... 55 C5
Wood Green N22 ... 32 B2
Nightingale Rd E5 ... 74 B5
N9 ... 18 C4
NW10 ... 89 D5
Carshalton SM5 ... 219 A6
Ealing W7 ... 108 D5
East Molesey KT8 ... 195 D4
Hampton TW12 ... 173 C4
Orpington BR5 ... 211 A3
Walton-on-T KT12 ... 194 B2
Wood Green N22 ... 32 B3
Nightingale Sch SW17 158 C2
Nightingale Sq SW12 ... 159 A4
Nightingales The TW19 ... 148 B3
Nightingale Vale SE18 144 C6
Nightingale Way E6 ... 100 A2
Nightingale Wlk SW18, SW4 ... 159 B5
Nile Cl N16 ... 73 D5
Nile Dr N9 ... 18 C2
Nile Ho N1 ... 235 C2
Nile Path 6 SE18 ... 144 C6
Nile Rd E13 ... 99 C5
Nile St N1 ... 95 B4 235 C2
Nile Terr SE1, SE15 ... 117 D1 263 D1
Nimegen Way 9 SE22 161 C6
Nimmo Dr WD23 ... 8 B4
Nimrod 9 NW9 ... 27 C2
Nimrod Cl UB5 ... 84 D4
Nimrod Pas 4 N1 ... 73 C2
Nimrod Rd SW16 ... 181 B5
Nina Mackay Cl 10 E15 ... 98 C6
Nine Acres Cl E12 ... 78 A3
Nine Elms Cl TW14 ... 149 D3
Nine Elms La SW8 ... 137 D6 269 C5
Nineteenth Rd CR4 ... 204 A5
Ninhams Wood BR6 ... 226 C4
Ninth Ave UB3 ... 106 A6
Nisbet 10 NW9 ... 27 C2
Nisbet Ho E9 ... 74 D3
Nita Ct SE12 ... 165 A3
Nithdale Rd SE18 ... 145 A5
Nithsdale Gr UB10 ... 61 A5
Niton Cl EN5 ... 12 D5
Niton Rd TW9 ... 132 C2
Niton St SW6 ... 134 D5
No 1 St SE18 ... 122 D3
Noam Prim Sch N12 ... 29 D6
Nobel Dr TW6 ... 127 C5
Nobel Ho 8 SE5 ... 139 A3
Nobel Rd N18 ... 3
Noble Cnr TW5 ... 12
Noble Ct Mitcham CR4 ... 18
Stepney E1 ... 11
Noblefield Hts N2 ... 4
Noble Ho 12 E1 ... 11
Noble St EC2 ... 95 A1 24
Noel 13 NW9 ... 2
Noel Baker Ct 4 E11 ... 7
Noel Coward Ho SW1 ... 25
Noel Ct TW4 ... 12
Noel Dene W5 ... 10
Noel Ho 3 NW3 ... 7
Noel Park Prim Schs N22 ... 3
Noel Park Rd N22 ... 3
Noel Rd N1 ... 94 D5 23
Acton W3 ... 88
Newham E6 ... 10
Noel Sq RM8 ... 8
Noel St W1 ... 93 C1 23
Noel Terr SE23 ... 16
Nolan Way E5 ... 7
Noll Ho N7 ... 7
Nolton Pl HA8 ... 2
Nonsuch Ct SM3 ... 217
Nonsuch High Sch for Gir SM3 ... 21
Nonsuch Prim Sch KT17 ... 21
Noor Ul Islam Prim Sch E10 ... 76
Nora Gdns NW4 ... 46
Norbiton Ave KT1,KT2 ... 176
Norbiton Common Rd KT1,KT3 ... 198
Norbiton Hall KT2 ... 17
Norbiton Rd E14 ... 97
Norbiton Sta KT1 ... 176
Norbreck Gdns NW10 ... 88
Norbreck Par NW10 ... 88
Norbroke St W12 ... 111
Norburn St W10 ... 91
Norbury Ave
Isleworth TW3 ... 130
Thornton Heath CR7, SW16 ... 182
Norbury Cl SW16 ... 182
Norbury Court Rd SW16 ... 182
Norbury Cres SW16 ... 182
Norbury Cross SW16 ... 204
Norbury Gdns RM6 ... 58
Norbury Gr NW7 ... 11
Norbury Hill SW16 ... 182
Norbury Manor Girls High Sch CR7 ... 182
Norbury Manor Prim Sch SW16 ... 182
Norbury Rd Chingford E4 35
South Norwood CR7 ... 205
Norbury Rise SW16 ... 204
Norbury Sch HA1 ... 42
Norbury Sta SW16 ... 182
Norbury Trad Est SW16 ... 182
Norcombe Gdns HA3 ... 43
Norcombe Ho 2 N19 ... 71
Norcott Cl UB4 ... 84
Norcott Rd N16 ... 74
Norcroft Gdns SE22 ... 162
Norcutt Rd TW2 ... 152
Norden Ho 25 E2 ... 96
Norden Point NW2 ... 46
Nore Ct NW10 ... 68
Norfolk Ave N15 ... 51
Edmonton N13 ... 32
Norfolk Cl N2 ... 48
Cockfosters EN4 ... 3
Edmonton N13 ... 32
5 Twickenham TW1 ... 153
Norfolk Cres DA15 ... 167
W2 ... 92 C1 237
Norfolk Ct 4 Barnet EN5 ... 1
Surbiton KT5 ... 198
Wembley HA0 ... 65
Norfolk Gdns DA7 ... 147
Norfolk Ho E8 ... 73
EC4 ... 252
SE3 ... 142
SE8 ... 141
SW1 ... 259
13 Acton W3 ... 88
11 Merton SW19 ... 180
Penge SE20 ... 184
4 Putney SW15 ... 156
Richmond TW10 ... 154
2 South Croydon CR0 ... 221
3 Stanmore HA7 ... 25
Norfolk House Rd SW16 ... 160
Norfolk House Sch N10 31
Norfolk Mans SW11 ... 267
10 SW18 ... 157
Norfolk Mews 12 W10 ... 91
Norfolk Pl DA16 ... 146
W2 ... 92 B1 236
Norfolk Rd E17 ... 34
E6 ... 100

olk Rd continued
10 67 C1
3 92 B6 229 D5
king IG11 79 C1
net EN5 1 C2
gate KT10 212 C3
enham RM10 81 D3
eld EN3 18 B6
ham TW13 150 C3
row HA1 41 D4
d IG3 57 C2
ham SW19 180 C4
th Norwood CR7 205 A6
folk Row
,SE11 116 B2 260 C4
folk Sq W2 92 B1 236 D2
olk Sq Mews W2 236 D1
olk St E7 77 A3
grove St SW12 159 A4
hyrst Ave SE25 205 D6
land Ho 13 W11 112 D5
land Pl
1 113 A5 244 B3
land Place Sch
1 113 A5 244 A3
land Rd W11 112 D5
lands Cres BR7 188 D2
land Sq
1 113 A5 244 B3
ley Vale SW15 156 A3
lington Rd E10,E11 54 B1
lington Sch for Boys
) 54 B1
man Ave
tham TW13 151 B2
uthall UB1 107 A6
tenham N22 33 A2
ckenham TW1 153 C4
man Butler Ho 10
0 91 A3
manby Cl SW15 157 B6
manby Rd NW10 67 D4
man Cl BR6 227 A5
ttenham N22 33 A2
man Cres
ston TW5 128 D5
ner HA5 22 C2
man Ct N4 50 C2
V10 68 A1
lwich SE22 162 A4
Hampton TW12 173 C2
ord IG2 57 B2
est Norwood SW16 182 C5
oodford IG8 37 B5
mand Mews W14 264 B6
mand Park Prim Sch
14 135 B6 264 D6
mand Rd
14 135 B6 264 C6
rmandy Ave EN5 1 B1
rmandy Cl SE26 163 A1
rmandy Dr UB3 83 A1
rmandy Ho 4 NW4 28 D1
rmandy Rd SW9 138 C4
rmandy Terr E16 99 B1
rman Gr E3 97 A5
rman Ho 6 E11 76 C6
W8 270 A4
ltham TW13 151 B2
wer Halliford TW17 192 C2
rmanhurst TW15 170 C5
rmanhurst Ave
A16 146 D4
rmanhurst Dr TW1 153 B6
rmanhurst Rd BR5 190 B1
reatham SW2 160 B2
alton-on-T KT12 194 D1
rmanhurst Sch E4 20 B4
rman Par DA14 168 D2
rman Rd E11 76 C6
5 100 B3
15 51 D4
E10 141 D5
shford TW15 171 B4
ford IG1 78 D3
erton SW19 180 A3
utton SM1 217 C3
hornton Heath CR7 204 D4
rmans Cl NW10 67 B2
illingdon UB8 82 A2
rmansfield Ave KT1,
T8 175 C3
rmanshire Dr E4 35 D6
rmans Mead NW10 67 B2
rman St EC1 95 A4 235 B1
rmanton Ave SW18,
W19 157 C2
rmanton Ct CR2 221 C3
rmanton Ho 6
W4 159 C5
rmanton Pk E4 20 C2
rmanton Rd CR2 221 C2
rmanton St SE23 162 D2
rman Way Acton W3 88 D1
almers Green N14 16 A2
rmington Cl SW16 182 C5
rrice Lea N2 48 B4
rris 11 NW9 27 D2
rris Ho 22 E9 96 C6

Norris Ho continued
12 N1 95 C6
Norris St SW1 249 C5
Norroy Rd SW15 134 D1
Norrys Cl EN4 2 D1
Norrys Rd EN4 2 D1
Norse Ho 13 SE5 139 A3
Norseman Cl 3 IG3 58 B1
Norseman Way UB6 85 D6
Norstead Pl SW15 156 A2
North Access Rd E17 52 D3
North Acre NW9 27 C2
North Acton Rd NW10 89 B4
North Acton Sta W3 89 B2
Northampton Gr N1 73 B3
Northampton Pk N1 73 B2
Northampton Rd
EC1 94 C3 241 B6
Croydon CR0 222 A6
Enfield EN3 7 A1
Northampton Sq
EC1 94 D4 234 C1
Northampton St N1 73 A1
Northanger Rd SW16 182 A4
North Audley St
W1 115 A6 248 A6
North Ave Ealing W13 87 B2
Edmonton N18 34 A6
Harrow HA2 41 D3
Hayes UB3 106 A6
8 Richmond TW9 132 C4
Southall UB1 107 B6
Wallington SM5 219 A1
Northaw Ho W10 90 C3
North Bank
NW8 92 C4 230 A1
Northbank Rd E17 36 A1
North Beckton Prim Sch
E6 100 B2
North Birkbeck Rd E11 76 B5
North Block 18 E1 118 C6
Northborough Rd
SW16 182 A1
Northbourne BR2 209 A2
Northbourne Ho 21 E5 74 B3
N14 15 D4
Northbourne Rd SW4 159 D6
North Branch Ave
NW10 90 C4
Northbrook CE Sch
SE12 164 D6
Northbrook Rd SE13 164 C6
Barnet EN5 13 A5
Ilford IG1 78 C6
Thornton Heath CR0 205 B4
Wood Green N22 32 A3
Northburgh St
EC1 94 D3 241 D6
Northbury Jun & Inf Sch
IG11 79 A2
North Carriage Dr
W2 114 C6 247 B6
Northchurch SE17 262 D2
North Church Ho 19 E2 96 A6
Northchurch Rd N1 73 B1
Wembley HA9 66 C2
Northchurch Terr N1 73 C1
North Circular Rd N2 30 B2
N3,NW2,NW4 47 A4
NW10 67 C3
NW2 67 C3
Chingford, Highams Park
E17 35 D2
Edmonton N13 32 C5
Ilford IG1,E12 78 C4
Woodford E18 37 C1
North Cl DA6 146 D1
Barnet EN5 12 C6
Dagenham RM10 103 C6
East Bedfont TW14 149 B5
Merton SM4 201 A5
Northcliffe Cl KT4 215 C5
Northcliffe Dr N20 13 B3
North Colonnade E14 119 C5
North Common Rd
Ealing W5 110 A6
Uxbridge UB8 60 A3
Northcote 1 HA5 22 C1
Northcote Ave
Ealing W5 110 A6
Isleworth TW7 153 A6
Southall UB1 107 A6
Tolworth KT5 198 D2
Northcote Ho UB4 84 D2
Northcote Lodge Sch
SW11 158 D5
Northcote Rd E17 53 A5
NW10 67 C1
SW11 158 D6
Isleworth TW7 153 A6
Kingston KT3 199 B6
Sidcup DA14 189 C6
Thornton Heath CR0 205 B3
Northcott Ave N22 32 A2
North Countess Rd E17 35 B2
Northcourt W1 239 B4
North Cray Prim Sch
DA14 191 A4
North Cray Rd DA14 191 A5

North Cres E16 98 B3
N3 29 B1
WC1 239 C4
Northcroft Ct 8 W12 112 A4
Northcroft Rd W13 109 B3
West Ewell KT19 215 C1
North Crofts SE21 162 B3
North Cross Rd SE22 162 A6
Ilford IG6 57 A5
North Ct SW1 260 A5
North Dene NW7 11 B1
Hounslow TW5 129 D4
Northdene Gdns N15 51 D3
Northdown Cl HA4 61 D5
Northdown Gdns IG2 57 C4
Northdown Rd DA16 146 C3
Northdown St
N1 94 B5 233 C3
North Dr BR6 227 C4
Beckenham BR3 207 D5
Hounslow TW3,TW7 130 A3
Ruislip HA4 39 C2
Streatham SW16 181 C6
North Dulwich Sta
SE21 161 B6
North Ealing Prim Sch
W5 87 B3
North Ealing Sta W3 88 B1
North End NW3 70 A6
Buckhurst Hill IG9 21 C4
Croydon CR0 221 A6
North End Ave NW3 70 A6
North End Cres
W14 113 B2 254 C3
North End Ho
W14 113 A2 254 B3
North End La BR6 226 D1
North End Par W14 254 B3
North End Rd NW11 47 D1
W14 113 B1 254 D1
Wembley HA9 66 D5
North End Way NW3 70 A6
Northern Ave N9 17 D2
Northernhay Wlk SM4 201 A5
Northern Hts N8 49 D2
Northern Perimeter Rd
TW6 127 C4
Northern Perimeter Road
(W) TW6 126 B4
Northern Rd E13 99 B5
Northern Relief Rd
IG11 79 A2
Northesk Ho 6 E1 96 B3
North Eyot Gdns 5
W6 111 D1
Northey St E14 119 A6
North Farm IG10 21 C5
North Feltham Trad Est
TW14 128 B1
Northfield IG10 21 D6
Northfield Ave
W13,W5 109 B4
Pinner HA5 40 D5
Northfield Cl BR1 188 A2
Hayes UB3 105 D3
Northfield Cres SM3 217 A4
Northfield Gdns RM9 81 B4
Northfield Hall N6 49 A2
Northfield Ho 3 SE15 140 A6
Northfield Ind Est HA0 88 C6
Northfield Par UB3 105 D3
Northfield Path RM9 81 B4
Northfield Pk UB3 105 D3
Northfield Rd E6 78 B1
N16 51 C2
W13 109 B4
Cockfosters EN4 2 C2
Dagenham RM9 81 B4
Enfield EN3 18 B6
Heston TW5 128 D5
Northfields SW18 135 C1
Northfields Prospect
SW18 135 C1
Northfields Rd W3 89 A2
Northfields Sta W5 109 C3
Northfleet Ho SE1 252 C2
North Flower Wlk
W2 114 246 C5
North Gate
NW8 92 C5 230 A3
Northgate Bsns Ctr EN1 6 B1
Northgate Ct 15 SW9 138 C2
Northgate Dr NW9 45 C3
North Gates N12 30 A2
North Gdns SW19 180 B3
North Glade DA5 169 B3
North Gn NW9 27 C3
North Gower St
NW1 93 C4 232 B1
North Gr N15 51 B4
N6 49 A2
North Greenwich Sta
SE10 120 C4
North Haringay Jun & Inf
Sch N8 50 C5
North Harrow Sta HA2 41 D4
North Hill N6 49 A3
North Hill Ave N6 48 D3
North Hill Ct N6 49 A2

North Ho 3 SE8 119 B1
North Hyde Gdns UB3 106 A2
North Hyde La UB2 107 A1
North Hyde Rd UB3 105 D3
Northiam N12 29 C6
WC1 233 B1
Northiam St E9 96 B6
Northington St
WC1 94 B3 240 D5
North La TW11 174 D4
Northlands Ave BR6 227 C4
Northlands St SE5 139 A3
Northleigh Ho 36 E3 97 D4
North Lo N22 31 D1
New Barnet EN5 14 A6
North Lodge Cl SW15 156 D6
North London Boys Sch
N16 52 A1
North London Collegiate
Sch HA7,HA8 26 A5
North London Collegiate
Sch The HA7,HA8 26 A5
North London Nuffield
Hospl EN2 4 C3
North Mall The N9 18 B2
North Mews
WC1 94 B3 240 D5
North Middlesex Hospl
N18 33 C5
Northmoor 4 SE23 162 D1
North Mount N20 14 A2
Northolm HA8 27 B6
Northolme Gdns HA8 26 C2
Northolme Rd N5 73 A4
Northolme Rise BR6 227 C6
Northolt N17 33 C1
Northolt Ave HA4 62 B3
Northolt Gdns UB6 64 D3
Northolt High Sch UB5 63 B2
Northolt Park Inf Sch
UB5 63 D3
Northolt Park Sta HA2 63 D4
Northolt Prim Sch UB5 63 A1
Northolt Rd
Harmondsworth TW6 126 A4
Harrow HA2 64 A5
Northolt Sta UB5 63 C2
Northover BR1 164 D1
North Par
Chessington KT9 214 B3
Edgware HA8 26 C1
Southall UB1 85 C1
North Pas SW18 157 C6
North Pk SE9 166 C5
North Pl Mitcham SW19 180 D3
Teddington TW11 174 D4
Northpoint BR1 187 A2
North Point UB7 104 A5
North Pole La BR2 225 A2
North Pole Rd W10 90 C2
Northport St N1 235 D5
North Prim Sch UB1 107 B6
North Rd BR1 187 B2
N2 30 C2
N6 49 A2
N7 72 A2
SE18 123 C2
W5 109 D3
Brentford TW8 132 A6
Dagenham RM6 59 A4
East Bedfont TW14 149 B5
Edgware HA8 26 D2
Edmonton N9 18 B3
Erith DA17 125 D4
Hayes UB3 83 B2
Heston TW5 128 C6
Ilford IG3 79 C6
Richmond TW9 132 C3
Southall UB1 107 C6
Surbiton KT6 197 D3
West Drayton UB7 104 B3
1 West Wickham BR4 207 D1
Wimbledon SW19 180 A4
North Residence IG3 58 B4
North Ride
W2 114 C6 247 A5
North Rise W2 237 B1
Northrop Rd TW6 127 C4
North Row W1 115 A6 248 A6
North Sheen Sta
TW10 132 C1
Northside Prim Sch
N12 30 A5
Northside Rd BR1 187 A2
North Side Wandsworth
Comm SW18 158 B6
Northspur Rd SM1 217 C5
North Sq NW11 47 C4
Edmonton N9 18 B2
North St BR1 187 A2
DA7 147 C1
E13 99 B5
NW4 46 C4
SW4 137 C2
Barking IG11 79 A1
Carshalton SM5 218 D4
Isleworth TW7 131 A2
Northstead Rd SW2 160 C2
North Tenter St E1 243 D1

North Terr SW3 257 A5
Northumberland Alley
EC3 243 B1
Northumberland Ave
DA16 145 C2
WC2 116 A5 250 A4
Enfield EN1 6 B4
Hounslow TW7 130 D4
Wanstead E12 55 C1
Northumberland Cl
TW19 148 A5
Northumberland Cres
TW14 149 C5
Northumberland Ct
3 Hounslow TW3 129 D1
South Croydon CR2 221 C3
Northumberland Gdns
BR1 210 C5
Brentford TW7 131 A5
Edmonton N9 17 D1
Mitcham CR4 203 D4
Northumberland Gr
N17 34 B3
Northumberland Heath
Prim Sch DA8 147 D5
Northumberland Ho
NW5 71 C2
Northumberland Mans
E5 74 C4
Northumberland Park Com
Sch N17 34 A3
Northumberland Park Ind
Est N17 34 B3
Northumberland Park
Sports Ctr N17 34 A3
Northumberland Park Sta
N17 34 B3
Northumberland Pk
DA8 147 D5
Tottenham N17 34 A3
Northumberland Pl W2 91 C1
26 Richmond TW10 153 D6
Northumberland Rd
E17 53 C2
E6 100 A1
Harrow HA2 41 C4
New Barnet EN5 14 A4
Northumberland St
WC2 250 A4
Northumbria St E14 97 C1
North Verbena Gdns
W6 112 A1
Northview 1 N7 72 A5
North View Ealing W5 87 C3
Pinner HA5 40 C2
Wimbledon SW19 178 C5
Northview Cres NW10 67 D4
Northview Dr IG8 37 D1
Northview Prim Sch
NW10 67 D3
North View Rd N8 49 D6
North Villas NW1 71 D2
Northway NW11 47 D4
North Way N11 31 C4
N9 18 D2
NW9 44 D6
Northway Merton SM4 201 A5
Wallington SM6 219 C4
North Way Pinner HA5 40 D5
Uxbridge UB10 60 A1
Northway Cir NW7 27 B6
Northway Cres NW7 27 C6
Northway Ct NW11 47 D4
NW7 27 B6
Northway Rd SE5 139 A2
Croydon CR0 205 D2
Northway Sch NW7 11 B1
Northways Par 2 NW3 70 B1
Northweald La KT2 175 D5
North Wembley Sta
HA0,HA9 65 D5
North Western Ave
(Watford By-Pass)
WD6 9 B5
North Westminster Com
Sch
W2 92 B2 236 D4
W9 91 C3
Northwest Pl N1 234 B4
North Wharf Rd
W2 92 B2 236 C3
Northwick Ave HA3 43 B3
Northwick Circ HA3 43 C3
Northwick Cl
NW8 92 B3 236 C6
Harrow HA1 65 B6
Northwick Ho NW8 236 B6
Northwick Park Hospl
HA1 43 A2
Northwick Park Rd
HA1 42 D3
Northwick Park Sta
HA3 43 B2
Northwick Rd
South Oxhey WD19 22 C6
Wembley HA0 87 D6
Northwick Terr
NW8 92 B3 236 C6
North Wlk W2 114 A6 246 A5

North Wlk continued
New Addington CR0 224 A3
Northwold Dr HA5 40 C6
Northwold Prim Sch
E5 74 A6
Northwold Rd E5,N16 74 A6
Northwood Comp Sch
HA6 22 B2
Northwood Gdns N12 30 B5
Greenford UB6 64 D3
Ilford IG5 56 C5
Northwood Hills Cir
HA6 22 A2
Northwood Hills Sta
HA6 22 A1
North Wood Lo NW3 69 D4
Northwood & Pinner Com
Hospl HA6 22 A2
Northwood Pl DA18 125 B3
Northwood Prim Sch
DA18 125 B3
Northwood Rd N6 49 B2
Forest Hill SE23 163 B3
South Norwood CR7 183 A1
Wallington SM5 219 A2
Northwood Twr 1 E17 54 A5
Northwood Way
Northwood HA6 22 A3
1 West Norwood SE19 183 C4
North Woolwich Rd
E16 121 B5
North Woolwich Rdbt
E16 121 D5
North Woolwich Sta
E16 122 C4
North Worple Way
SW14 133 B2
Norton Ave KT5 198 D2
Norton Cl Chingford E4 35 C5
Enfield EN1 6 B3
Norton Ct
Beckenham BR3 185 B2
Ilford IG2 57 B3
Norton Folgate E1 243 B4
Norton Gdns SW16 182 A1
Norton Ho 33 E1 96 B1
14 E2 96 D5
16 SW9 138 B3
5 New Malden KT3 199 C5
Norton Rd E10 53 B1
Wembley HA0 65 D2
Norval Gn 1 SW9 138 C3
Norval Rd HA0 43 B1
Norvic Ho 5 SE5 139 A3
Norway Gate SE16 119 A3
Norway Pl E14 97 B1
Norway St SE10 141 D6
Norwegian Sch SW19 178 C3
Norwich Ho 6 E14 97 D1
Norwich Mews IG3 58 A1
Norwich Pl 7 DA6 147 C1
Norwich Rd E7 77 A3
Greenford UB6 85 D6
Northwood HA6 39 D6
South Norwood CR7 205 A6
Norwich St EC4 94 C1 241 A2
Norwich Wlk HA8 27 A3
Norwood Ave HA0 88 B5
Norwood Cl
Southall UB2 107 C2
Twickenham TW2 152 B2
Norwood Dr HA2 41 C3
Norwood Gdns
Hayes UB4 84 C3
Southall UB2 107 B2
Norwood Green Inf Sch
UB2 107 B1
Norwood Green Jun Sch
UB2 107 A1
Norwood Green Rd
UB2 107 C2
Norwood Heights Sh Ctr 13
SE19 183 C4
Norwood High St
SE27 183 A6
Norwood Ho 22 E14 119 D6
Norwood Hospl SE19 183 B4
Norwood Junction Sta
SE25 206 A5
Norwood Park Rd
SE27 183 A5
Norwood Rd
Southall UB2 107 C2
West Norwood SE24,
SE27 160 D3
Norwood Terr UB2 107 D2
Notley St SE5 139 B5
Notre Dame RC Girls Sch
SE1 116 D3 261 D5
Notson Rd SE25 206 B5
Notting Barn Rd W10 90 D3
Nottingdale Sq W11 244 A4
Nottingham Ave E16 99 C1
Nottingham Ct WC2 240 A1
Nottingham Ho N4 51 A1
34 SE5 139 A3

Nottingham Pl
W1 ...93 A2 238 A4
Nottingham Rd E10 ...54 A3
Croydon CR2 ...221 A3
Isleworth TW7 ...130 D3
Upper Tooting SW17 ...158 D3
Nottingham St W1 ...238 A4
Nottingham Terr NW1 238 A5
Notting Hill & Ealing High Sch W13 ...87 B2
Notting Hill Gate W11 ...113 C5 245 A4
Notting Hill Gate Sta W11 ...113 C5 245 A4
Nottingwood Ho W11 .244 A6
Nova Bldg 21 E14 ...119 C2
Nova Mews SM4 ...201 A2
Novar Cl BR6 ...211 D2
Nova Rd CR0 ...205 A2
Novar Rd SE9 ...167 A3
Novello St SW6 ...135 C4 265 A2
Nowell Rd SW13 ...134 A6
Nower Ct HA5 ...41 B5
Nower Hill HA5 ...41 B5
Nower Hill High Sch HA5 ...41 C5
Noyna Rd SW17 ...158 D1
Nubia Way SE6 ...164 C1
Nuding Cl SE13 ...141 C2
Nuffield Ct TW5 ...129 B5
Nuffield Lo 14 W9 ...91 C2
Nugent Ct SW16 ...181 C6
Nugent Rd N19 ...50 A1
South Norwood SE25 ...205 D6
Nugents Ct HA5 ...23 A2
Nugent's Pk HA5 ...23 B2
Nugent Terr NW8 ...92 A5 229 B3
Numa Ct TW8 ...131 D5
Nun Ct EC2 ...242 C2
Nuneaton Rd RM9 ...81 A1
Nuneham SW16 ...181 D6
Nunhead Cres SE15 ...140 B2
Nunhead Gr SE15 ...140 C2
Nunhead La SE15 ...140 B2
Nunhead Sta SE15 ...140 C3
Nunnington Cl SE9 ...166 A1
Nunn's Rd EN2 ...5 A3
Nupton Dr EN5 ...12 C5
Nurse Cl HA8 ...27 A2
Nursery Ave DA7 ...147 B2
N3 ...30 A1
Croydon CR0 ...222 D6
Nursery Cl BR6 ...211 D2
SE4 ...141 B3
Croydon CR0 ...222 D6
Dagenham RM6 ...58 D3
Enfield EN3 ...6 D4
Feltham TW14 ...150 B4
Putney SW15 ...134 D1
Woodford IG8 ...37 B5
Nursery Ct Ealing W13 ...87 A2
7 Tottenham N17 ...33 D3
Nursery Gdns BR7 ...188 D4
Enfield EN3 ...6 D4
Hampton TW13 ...173 B6
Hounslow TW4 ...151 B6
Sunbury TW16 ...171 D1
Nursery La E2 ...95 D6
E7 ...77 A2
W10 ...90 C2
Nurserymans Rd N11 ...15 A2
Nursery Rd E9 ...74 C2
N14 ...15 C4
N2 ...30 B2
SW9 ...138 B1
Loughton IG10 ...21 C6
Merton SW19 ...179 D1
Mitcham CR4 ...202 C6
Pinner HA5 ...40 C6
South Norwood CR7 ...205 B5
Sunbury TW16 ...171 D1
Sutton SM1 ...218 A4
Wimbledon SW19 ...179 A3
Nursery Row SE17 ...262 C3
Nursery St N17 ...33 D3
Nursery Walk Ct NW4 .46 B6
Nursery Wlk NW4 ...46 C6
Nurstead Rd DA8 ...147 C5
Nutborn Ho SW19 ...178 D4
Nutbourne St W10 ...91 A4
Nutbrook St SE15 ...140 A2
Nutbrowne Rd RM9 ...103 B6
Nutcroft Rd SE15 ...140 B5
Nutfield Cl
Carshalton SM5 ...218 C5
Edmonton N18 ...34 A4
Nutfield Gdns Ilford IG3 80 A6
Northolt UB5 ...84 C5
Nutfield Rd E15 ...76 A4
NW2 ...68 A5
SE22 ...139 D1
Thornton Heath CR7 ...204 D5
Nutfield Way BR6 ...226 D6
Nutford Pl W1 .92 D1 237 C2
Nuthatch Cl TW19 ...148 B3
Nuthatch Gdns SE28 ...123 B4
Nuthurst Ave SW2 ...160 B2
Nutkin Wlk UB8 ...60 A1
Nutley Terr NW3 ...70 B2
Nutmeg Cl E16 ...98 C3
Nutmeg La E14 ...98 B1
Nuttall St N1 ...95 C5
Nutter La E11 ...55 C4
Nutt Gr HA8 ...9 D2
Nutt St SE15 ...139 D5
Nutty La TW17 ...193 A6
Nutwell St SW17 ...180 C5
Nuxley Rd DA17 ...125 C1
NW London Jewish Day Sch NW6 ...69 A1
Nyanza St SE18 ...145 B6
Nye Bevan Est E5 ...74 D5
Nye Bevan Ho SW6 ...264 C4
Nye's Wharf SE15 ...140 A6
Nylands Ave TW9 ...132 C3
Nymans Gdns SW20 ...200 B6
Nynehead St SE14 ...141 A5
Nyon Gr SE6 ...163 B2
Nyton Cl N19 ...50 A1

O

Oak Apple Ct SE12 ...165 A3
Oak Ave N10 ...31 B3
N8 ...50 A5
Croydon CR0 ...223 D6
Enfield EN2 ...4 B5
Hampton TW12,TW13 ...173 A4
Heston TW5 ...129 A5
Tottenham N17 ...33 C3
Uxbridge UB10 ...60 D6
West Drayton UB7 ...104 C3
Oak Bank CR0 ...224 A2
Oakbank Ave KT12 ...195 B2
Oakbank Gr SE24 ...139 A1
Oakbrook 3 BR3 ...185 D1
Oakbrook Cl BR1 ...187 B6
Oakbury Rd SW6 ...135 D3
Oak Cl N14 ...15 B4
Sutton SM1 ...218 A6
Oakcombe Cl KT3 ...177 C2
Oak Cottage Cl 11 SE6 ...164 D3
Oak Cotts W7 ...108 C4
Oakcourt 16 SE15 ...139 D5
Oak Cres E16 ...98 C2
Oakcroft SE12 ...165 B1
Oakcroft Bsns Ctr KT9 214 B4
Oakcroft Cl HA5 ...22 B1
Oakcroft Ho 3 KT3 ...199 C2
Oakcroft Rd SE13 ...142 B3
Chessington KT9 ...214 B4
Oakcroft Villas KT9 ...214 B4
Oak Ct BR1 ...188 B1
Chingford E4 ...35 D4
Oakdale N14 ...15 B3
Beckenham BR3 ...186 A1
Oakdale Ave
Harrow HA3 ...44 A4
Pinner HA6 ...22 A1
Oakdale Cl WD19 ...22 C6
Oakdale Ct N19 ...72 A6
Oakdale Gdns E4 ...36 A5
Oakdale Inf Sch E18 ...37 B1
Oakdale Jun Sch E18 ...37 B1
Oakdale Lo NW4 ...29 A2
Oakdale Rd E11 ...76 B6
E7 ...77 B1
N4 ...51 B3
SE15 ...140 C2
South Oxhey WD19 ...22 C6
Streatham SW16 ...182 A5
Woodford E18 ...37 B1
Oakdale Way CR4 ...203 A2
Oakdene 3 SE15 ...140 B4
1 West Norwood SE19 .183 C5
Oak Dene W13 ...87 B2
Oakdene Ave BR7 ...188 C5
Thames Ditton KT7 ...197 A1
Oakdene Cl HA5 ...23 B3
Oakdene Dr KT5 ...199 A1
Oakdene Ho N16 ...51 C1
Enfield EN2 ...4 D2
Oakdene Lo SE20 ...184 B3
Oakdene Mews SM3 ...201 B1
Oakdene Pk N3 ...29 B3
Oakdene Rd BR5 ...211 D4
Hillingdon UB10 ...82 D5
Oakden St SE11 ...116 C2 261 B4
Oake Ct SW15 ...157 A6
Oakeford Ho W14 ...254 B5
Oakend Ho 10 N4 ...51 B2
Oaken Dr KT10 ...212 D2
Oakenholt Ho 1 SE2 .124 D4
Oaken La KT10 ...212 C3
Oakenshaw Cl KT6 ...198 A2
Oakes Cl E6 ...100 B1
Oakeshott Ave N6 ...71 A6
Oakey La SE1 ...261 A6
Oak Farm WD6 ...11 A6
Oak Farm Jun & Inf Schs UB10 ...82 D6
Oakfield E4 ...35 D5
Oakfield Ave HA3 ...43 B6
Oakfield Cl
New Malden KT3 ...199 D4
Ruislip HA4 ...39 D3
Oakfield Ct N3 ...29 D2
N8 ...50 A2
NW2 ...46 D2
SW4 ...160 A5
2 Ealing W5 ...110 C5
South Croydon CR2 ...221 A2
Oakfield Gdns
Beckenham BR3 ...207 C4
Carshalton SM5 ...202 D1
Edmonton N18 ...33 C6
Greenford UB6 ...86 B4
3 West Norwood SE19 .183 C5
Oakfield Ho 2 IG1 ...78 D5
Oakfield La BR2 ...225 C4
Oakfield Lo 8 IG1 ...78 D5
Oakfield Prep Sch SE21 ...161 B3
Oakfield Rd E17 ...35 A1
E6 ...100 A6
N3 ...29 D2
N4 ...50 C2
Ashford TW15 ...170 D5
Croydon CR0 ...205 A1
Ilford IG1 ...78 D5
Palmers Green N14 ...16 A2
Penge SE20 ...184 B3
Wimbledon SW19 ...156 D1
Oakfields KT12 ...194 A1
Oakfields Rd NW11 ...47 A3
Oakfield St SW10 ...136 A6 266 A6
Oakford Rd NW5 ...71 C4
Oak Gdns HA8 ...27 A1
Croydon CR0 ...223 C6
Oak Gr NW2 ...69 A4
Ruislip HA4 ...40 B1
Sunbury TW16 ...172 B3
West Wickham BR4 ...208 A1
Oak Grove Rd SE20 ...184 C1
Oakhall Ct
Ashford TW16 ...171 D5
Wanstead E11 ...55 B3
Oakhall Dr TW16 ...171 D5
Oak Hall Rd E11 ...55 B3
Oakham Cl SE6 ...163 B2
Oakham Dr BR2 ...208 D5
Oakham Ho W10 ...90 C3
Oakhampton Rd NW7 ...28 D3
Oakhill KT10 ...213 A2
Oak Hill Chingford IG8 ...36 C3
Surbiton KT6 ...198 A2
Oakhill Ave NW3 ...69 D4
Pinner HA5 ...23 A1
Oak Hill Cl IG8 ...36 B3
Oak Hill Coll N14 ...15 A5
Oak Hill Cres
Chingford IG8 ...36 C3
Surbiton KT6 ...198 A2
Oakhill Ct SE23 ...162 C5
Putney SW15 ...157 B6
8 Surbiton KT6 ...198 A3
Wimbledon SW19 ...178 D3
Oak Hill Ct IG8 ...36 C3
Oak Hill Gdns E4 ...36 C2
Oak Hill Gr KT6 ...198 A3
Oakhill Ho BR5 ...190 A2
Oak Hill Lo NW3 ...69 D4
Oak Hill Park Mews NW3 ...70 A4
Oak Hill Pk NW3 ...69 D4
Oakhill Pl SW15 ...157 C6
Oakhill Prim Sch IG8 ...36 C4
Oakhill Rd BR6 ...227 D6
Beckenham BR3 ...186 A1
Putney SW15 ...157 B6
Sutton SM1 ...218 A5
Thornton Heath SW16 ...182 B2
Oak Hill Rd KT6 ...198 A3
Oak Hill Way NW3 ...70 A4
Oak Ho 13 DA15 ...168 A1
8 E14 ...120 A4
N16 ...73 B6
11 N2 ...30 B1
3 NW3 ...70 D2
Penge SE20 ...184 B1
Wood Green N22 ...32 A3
Oakhouse Rd DA6 ...169 C6
Oakhurst Ave DA7 ...147 A5
East Barnet EN4 ...14 C4
Oakhurst Cl BR7 ...188 B2
E17 ...54 C5
4 Teddington TW11 ...174 C5
Oakhurst Ct E17 ...54 C5
Oakhurst Gdns DA7 ...147 A5
E11,E17 ...54 C5
Chingford E4 ...20 D3
Oakhurst Gr SE22 ...140 A1
Oakhurst Rd KT19 ...215 B2
Oakington 14 KT1 ...176 C1
Oakington Ave
Harrow HA2 ...41 C2
Hayes UB3 ...105 B2
Oakington Ave *continued*
Wembley HA9 ...66 B5
Oakington Dr TW16 ...172 C1
Oakington Manor Dr HA9 ...66 C3
Oakington Manor Prim Sch HA9 ...66 D3
Oakington Rd W9 ...91 C3
Oakington Way N8 ...50 A2
Oak La E14 ...119 B6
N11 ...31 D4
N2 ...30 B1
Isleworth TW7 ...130 C1
Twickenham TW1 ...153 A4
Woodford IG8 ...36 D6
Oakland Pl IG9 ...21 A2
Oakland Rd E15 ...76 C4
Oaklands BR7 ...189 B4
Croydon CR0 ...220 D3
Ealing W13 ...87 A2
Southgate N21 ...16 B2
Oaklands Ave DA15 ...167 D4
Enfield N9 ...18 B5
Hounslow TW7 ...130 D6
Thames Ditton KT10 ...196 B1
Thornton Heath CR7 ...204 C5
West Wickham BR4 ...223 D5
Oaklands Cl BR5 ...211 C3
DA6 ...169 B6
Chessington KT9 ...213 C4
Wembley HA0 ...65 D3
Oaklands Ct NW10 ...89 C6
1 Wembley HA0 ...65 D3
Oaklands Dr TW2 ...152 A4
Oaklands Gr W12 ...112 A5
Oaklands Ho SE4 ...141 B2
Oaklands Mews NW2 ...68 D4
Oaklands Park Ave IG1 79 A6
Oaklands Pas NW2 ...68 D4
Oaklands Pl 3 SW4 ...137 D1
Oaklands Prim Sch W7 ...108 D4
Oaklands Rd DA6 ...169 B6
NW2 ...68 D4
W7,W13 ...109 A4
Barnet N20 ...13 B4
Bromley BR1 ...186 C3
Ealing W7 ...108 D4
Mortlake SW14 ...133 B2
Oaklands Sch
Hounslow TW3 ...130 B2
Loughton IG10 ...21 C6
Oaklands Sec Sch E2 ...96 B4
Oaklands Way SM6 ...219 D1
Oakland Way KT19 ...215 C2
Oakleafe Gdns IG6 ...56 D6
Oaklea Pas KT1 ...197 D6
Oakleigh Ave N20 ...14 C3
Edgware HA8 ...26 D2
Tolworth KT6 ...214 D6
Oakleigh Cl N20 ...14 D1
Oakleigh Cres N20 ...14 C1
Oakleigh Ct HA8 ...27 A1
East Barnet EN4 ...14 C5
Penge SE20 ...184 B3
Southall UB1 ...107 B5
Surbiton KT6 ...214 B6
Oakleigh Gdns BR6 ...227 C4
N20 ...14 B3
Edgware HA8 ...26 B5
Oakleigh Lo IG3 ...80 A5
Oakleigh Mews N20 ...14 A2
Oakleigh Park Ave BR7 ...188 C2
Oakleigh Park Sta EN4 .14 C4
Oakleigh Pk N N20 ...14 B3
Oakleigh Pk S N20 ...14 C3
Oakleigh Rd
Hillingdon UB10 ...61 A1
Pinner HA5 ...23 B4
Oakleigh Rd N N20 ...14 C2
Oakleigh Rd S N11 ...31 A6
Oakleigh Sch N20 ...14 D1
Oakleigh Way
Mitcham CR4 ...181 B2
1 Tolworth KT6 ...198 D1
Oakley Ave Barking IG11 79 D1
Ealing W5 ...110 C6
Wallington CR0 ...220 A4
Oakley Cl 7 E6 ...100 A1
Chingford E4 ...20 A1
Ealing W7 ...108 C6
Hounslow TW7 ...130 B4
Oakley Cres EC1 ...234 D3
Oakley Ct CR4 ...203 A2
Oakley Dr DA15 ...167 B3
SE13 ...164 B5
Keston Mark BR2 ...226 A5
Oakley Gdns N8 ...50 B4
SW3 ...136 C6 267 B6
Oakley Ho SW1 ...257 D4
Ealing W5 ...110 C6
Oakley Pk DA5,DA15 ...168 C4
Oakley Pl SE1 .117 D1 263 C1
Oakley Rd N1 ...73 B1
Croydon SE25 ...206 B4
Harrow HA1 ...42 C3
Keston Mark BR2 ...226 A6
Oakley Sq NW1 .93 C5 232 B4
Oakley St SW3 136 C6 267 A6
Oakley Wlk W6 ...134 D6
Oak Lo
4 Ashford TW16 ...171 D3
Southgate N21 ...16 B5
Wanstead E11 ...55 A2
Oak Lodge Cl HA7 ...25 C5
Oak Lodge Dr BR4 ...207 D2
Oak Lodge Sch N2 ...48 A5
Balham SW12 ...159 A4
Oaklodge Way NW7 ...27 D4
Oakman Ho 29 SW19 .156 D3
Oakmead Ave BR2 ...209 A3
Oakmead Ct HA7 ...25 C6
Oakmeade HA5 ...23 C4
Oakmead Gdns HA8 ...27 B6
Oakmead Pl CR4 ...180 C2
Oakmead Rd
Balham SW12 ...159 B3
Wallington CR0 ...203 D3
Oakmere Rd SE2 ...146 A6
Oakmont Pl 6 BR6 ...211 B1
Oak Park Gdns SW19 .156 D3
Oak Park Mews N16 ...73 D5
Oak Rd Ealing W5 ...109 D6
Kingston KT3 ...177 B1
Oakridge Dr N2 ...48 B6
Oakridge La BR1 ...186 B5
Oakridge Rd BR1 ...186 C6
Oak Rise IG9 ...21 D1
Oak Row CR4 ...181 C1
Oaks Ave
Feltham TW13 ...151 A2
North Cheam KT4 ...216 B4
West Norwood SE19 ...183 C5
Oaksford Ave SE26 ...162 B1
Oaks Gr E4 ...20 C2
Oakshade Rd BR1 ...186 B6
Oakshaw Rd SW18 ...157 D4
Oakshott Ct NW1 ...232 C3
Oaks La Ilford IG2 ...57 C5
South Croydon CR0 ...222 C5
Oaks Park High Sch IG2 ...57 C4
Oaks Rd CR0 ...222 C4
Oaks Sh Ctr The W3 ...111 A5
Oaks The BR2 ...210 C3
N12 ...29 D6
NW10 ...68 B1
NW6 ...68 D1
SE18 ...123 A1
Chingford IG8 ...36 C3
Enfield EN2 ...4 D2
Hayes UB4 ...83 A5
Long Ditton KT6 ...213 C5
Ruislip HA4 ...39 C2
Wimbledon SW19 ...179 A4
Oaks Way Surbiton KT6 197 D1
Wallington SM5 ...218 D1
Oakthorpe Ct N13 ...33 A5
Oakthorpe Prim Sch N13 ...33 A5
Oakthorpe Rd N13 ...32 C5
Oak Tree Ave N2 ...47 D6
Oaktree Ave N13 ...16 D1
Oak Tree Cl Ealing W5 ...87 C1
Stanmore HA7 ...25 C3
Oak Tree Ct 6 SW4 ...160 A6
Acton W3 ...110 D6
Elstree WD6 ...9 D5
Oak Tree Dell NW9 ...45 B4
Oak Tree Dr N20 ...13 D3
Oak Tree Gdns BR1 ...187 B5
Oaktree Gr IG1 ...79 B3
Oak Tree Ho W9 ...91 D3
Oak Tree Rd NW8 ...92 C4 230 A1
Oaktree Sch EN4 ...15 A5
Oakview Gdns N2 ...48 B5
Oakview Gr CR0 ...207 A1
Oakview Lo NW11 ...47 B2
Oakview Rd SE6 ...185 D5
Oak Village NW5 ...71 A4
Oak Way N14 ...15 B4
W3 ...111 C5
Oakway
Beckenham BR2 ...186 B1
West Barnes SW20 ...200 C5
Oak Way Croydon CR0 .206 D3
East Bedfont TW14 ...149 C3
Oakway Cl DA5 ...169 A5
Oakways SE9 ...166 D5
Oakwell Ho 24 SW8 ...137 D3
Oak Wlk CR4 ...203 A1
Oakwood Ave N14 ...15 D4
Beckenham BR2,BR3 ...186 A1
Bromley BR2 ...209 B6
Mitcham CR4 ...180 B1
Southall UB1 ...107 C6
Oakwood Cl BR7 ...188 C4
Southgate N14 ...15 C5
Oakwood Cres
Southgate N21 ...16 B5
Wembley UB6 ...65 B2
Oakwood Ct 1 E6 ...100 A6
W14 ...113 B3 254 C6
Beckenham BR3 ...186 A1
6 Chingford E4 ...20 C4
Oakwood Dr HA8 ...27 A4
Oakwood Dr *continued*
West Norwood SE19 ...18
Oakwood Gdns
Ilford IG3 ...7
Orpington BR6 ...22
Sutton SM1 ...21
Oakwood La
W14 ...113 B3 254
Oakwood Park Rd N14 .1
Oakwood Pl CR0 ...20
Oakwood Rd NW11 ...4
Orpington BR6 ...22
Pinner HA5 ...2
Thornton Heath CR0 ...20
Wimbledon SW20 ...17
Oakwood Sta N14 ...1
Oakwood View N14 ...1
Oakworth Rd W10 ...9
Oarsman Pl KT8 ...19
Oasis The 4 BR1 ...18
Oast Ct 8 E14 ...11
Oast Lo W4 ...13
Oates Cl BR2 ...20
Oatfield Ho 1 N15 ...5
Oatfield Rd BR6 ...211
Oat La EC2 ...95 A1 242
Oatland Rise E17 ...35
Oatlands Ct 3 SW19 .15
Oatlands Dr KT13 ...19
Oatlands Rd EN3 ...6
Oatwell Ho SW3 ...257
Oban Cl E13 ...99
Oban Ho Barking IG11 .101
South Bromley E14 ...98
Oban Rd E13 ...99
South Norwood SE25 ...205
Oban St E14 ...98
Oberon Ho 5 N1 ...95
Oberon Way TW17 ...192
Oberstein Rd 15 SW11 13
Oborne Cl SE24 ...160
O'Brian Ho 10 E1 ...96
Observatory Gdns W8 245
Observatory Mews E14 ...120
Observatory Rd SW14 133
Occupation La SE18 ...144
W5 ...109
Occupation Rd SE17 ...117 A1 262
W13 ...109
Ocean St E1 ...96
Ocean Wharf E14 ...119
Ockbrook 3 E1 ...96
Ockendon Rd N1 ...73
Ockham Dr BR5 ...190
Ockley Ct SM1 ...218
Ockley Ho 8 KT2 ...176
Ockley Rd
Streatham SW16 ...160
Thornton Heath CR0 ...204
Octagon Arc EC2 ...243
Octagon The NW3 ...69
Octavia Cl CR4 ...202
Octavia Ho W10 ...91
Octavia Rd TW7 ...130
Octavia St SW11 ...136 C4 267
Octavia Way 12 SE28 ...124
Octavius St SE8 ...141
October Ct BR2 ...208
October Pl NW4 ...46
Odard Rd KT8 ...195
Odell Cl IG11 ...79
Odeon Ct 1 E16 ...99
NW10 ...89
Odeon Par SE9 ...144
Wembley UB6 ...65
Odessa Inf Sch E7 ...77
Odessa Rd E7 ...76
NW10 ...90
Odessa St SE16 ...119
Odette Ct N20 ...14
Odette Duval Ho 24 E1 .96
Odette Ho 6 SE27 ...183
Odger St SW11 ...136
Odhams Wlk WC2 ...240
Odin Ho 6 SE5 ...139
O'Donnell Ct WC1 ...240
O'Driscoll Ho W12 ...90
Odyssey Bsns Pk HA4 ...62
Offa's Mead E9 ...75
Offenbach Ho 12 E2 ...96
Offenham Rd BR7,SE9 .188
Offers Ct KT1 ...198
Offerton Rd SW4 ...137
Offham Ho SE17 ...263
Offham Slope N12 ...29
Offley Ho 10 E9 ...74
Offley Pl TW7 ...130
Offley Rd SW9 ...138
Offord Cl N17 ...34
Offord Rd N1 ...72
Offord St N1 ...72
Ogden Ho TW13 ...173
Ogilby St SE18 ...122
Ogilvie Ho 11 E1 ...96
Oglander Rd SE15 ...139
Ogle St W1 ...93 C2 239

Oglethorpe Rd RM10 ...81 C5
O'Gorman Ho SW10 ...266 B4
O'Grady Ho 17 E17 ...53 D6
Ohio Rd E13 ...98 D3
Oil Mill La W6 ...112 A1
Okeburn Rd SW17 ...181 A5
Okehampton Cl N12 ...30 B5
Okehampton Cres DA16 ...146 C4
Okehampton Rd NW10 .90 D6
Okeover Manor SW4 ..137 B1
Olaf Palme Ho TW13 ..150 B1
Olaf St W11 ...112 D6
Old Bailey EC4 .94 D1 241 D1
Old Barn Cl SM2 ...217 A1
Old Barrack Yd SW1 ..248 A1
Old Bellgate Wharf E14 ...119 C3
Oldberry Rd HA8 ...27 B4
Old Bethnal Green Rd E2 ...96 B4
Old Bexley Bsns Pk DA5 ...169 D4
Old Bexley CE Prim Sch DA5 ...169 B3
Old Bldgs WC2 ...241 A2
Old Bond St W1 ...115 C6 249 A5
Oldborough Rd HA0 ...65 C5
Old Borrowfield 7 E15 98 C6
Old Brewery Mews NW3 ...70 B4
Old Bridge Cl UB5 ...85 C5
Old Bridge St KT1 ...175 D1
Old Broad St EC2 ...95 B1 242 D2
Old Bromley Rd BR1 ..186 B5
Old Brompton Rd SW5,SW7 ...114 A1 256 B3
Old Burlington St W1 ...115 C6 249 A5
Oldbury Ct E9 ...75 A3
Oldbury Pl W1 .93 A2 238 B4
Oldbury Rd EN1 ...6 A3
Old Castle St E1 ...95 D1 243 D2
Old Cavendish St W1 .238 C1
Old Change Ct EC4 ..242 A1
Old Chapel Pl 2 N10 ...49 B6
Old Charlton Rd TW17 193 A4
Old Chiswick Yd W4 ..133 C6
Old Church Ct N11 ...31 B5
Old Church La NW9 ...67 B6
Ealing UB6 ...87 A4
Stanmore HA7 ...25 C4
Old Church Path KT10 212 A4
Old Church Rd E1 ...96 D1
Chingford E4 ...19 C1
Old Church St SW3 ..256 D1
Old Claygate La KT10 .213 A3
Old Clem Sq 12 SE18 .144 C6
Old Compton St W1 ...93 D1 239 C1
Old Cote Dr TW5 ...129 C6
Old County Hall SE1 ..250 C2
Old Court Ho W8 ...245 C1
Old Court (Mus & Liby) HA0 ...65 C3
Old Court Pl W8 ...113 D4 245 C1
Old Covent Garden WC2 ...250 B6
Old Ctyd The BR1 ...187 B2
Old Dairy Mews 4 NW5 ...71 B2
5 Balham SW12 ...159 A3
Old Deer Park Gdns TW9 ...132 A2
Old Devonshire Rd SW12 ...159 B4
Old Dock Cl TW9 ...132 C6
Old Dover Rd SE3 ...143 B5
Oldegate Ho 1 E6 ...99 D6
Old Farm Ave N14 ...15 C4
Sidcup DA15 ...167 C2
Old Farm Cl TW4 ...129 B1
Old Farm Ct UB2 ...107 D2
Old Farm Rd N2 ...30 B2
Hampton TW12 ...173 C4
Old Farm Rd E DA15 ..168 A2
Old Farm Rd W DA15 .167 D2
Oldfield Cl BR1 ...210 B5
Stanmore HA7 ...25 A5
Oldfield Farm Gdns UB6 ...86 B6
Oldfield Gr SE16 ...118 D2
Oldfield Ho 14 W4 ...111 C1
Streatham SW16 ...181 B6
Oldfield House Sch TW12 ...173 B2
Oldfield Mews N6 ...49 C2
Oldfield Prim Sch UB6 .86 B5
Oldfield Rd BR1 ...210 B5
DA7 ...147 A3
N16 ...73 C5
NW10 ...67 D1
W3,W12 ...111 D4
Hampton TW12 ...173 B2
Wimbledon SW19 ...179 A4
Oldfields Cir UB5 ...64 A2
Oldfields Rd SM1,SM3 .217 C6
Oldfields Trad Est SM1 ...217 C5
Old Fish St Hill EC4 ...252 A6
Old Fleet La EC4 ...241 C2
Old Fold Cl EN5 ...1 B4
Old Fold La EN5 ...1 B4
Old Ford Ho CR0 ...220 A5
Old Ford Prim Sch E3 ..97 B5
Old Ford Rd E2,E3 ...96 D5
Old Ford Trad Ctr E3 ..97 C6
Old Forge Cl HA7 ...25 A6
Old Forge Cres TW17 .192 D3
Old Forge Mews W12 .112 B4
Old Forge Rd EN1 ...5 D5
Old Forge Way DA14 ..190 B6
Old Gloucester St WC1 ...94 A2 240 B4
Old Hall Cl HA5 ...23 A2
Old Hall Dr HA5 ...23 A2
Oldham Ho 10 SE21 ..183 C6
Oldham Terr W3 ...111 A5
Old Hatch Manor HA4 .40 A2
Old Hill Chislehurst BR7 188 C2
Orpington BR6 ...227 C2
Oldhill St N16 ...52 A1
Old Homesdale Rd BR2 ...209 C5
Old Hospital Cl SW12, SW17 ...158 D3
Old House Cl SW19 ..179 A5
Old House Gdns 9 TW1 ...153 C5
Old Howlett's La HA4 ..39 B3
Olding Ho 6 SW12 ..159 C4
Old Jamaica Bsns Est 23 SE16 ...118 A3
Old Jamaica Rd SE16 .118 A3
Old James St SE15 ...140 B2
Old Jewry EC2 .95 B1 242 C1
Old Kenton La NW9 ...44 D4
Old Kent Rd SE1 ...117 C1 263 B2
SE1,SE15 ...140 B6
Old Kingston Rd KT4 .215 A5
Old Laundry The 14 SW18 ...136 B1
Old Lodge Pl 7 TW1 .153 B5
Old Lodge Way HA7 ..25 A5
Old Maidstone Rd BR8,DA14 ...191 B3
Old Malden La KT4 ..215 C6
Oldman Ct SE12 ...165 B2
Old Manor Dr TW7 ...152 A5
Old Manor Rd UB2 ..106 D2
Old Manor Way BR7, SE9 ...188 B5
Old Manor Yd SW5 ..255 C3
Old Market Sq 11 E2 ..95 D4
Old Marylebone Rd NW1 ...92 C2 237 B3
Oldmead Ho 8 RM10 ..81 D2
Old Mill Ct E18 ...55 C6
Old Mill Rd SE18 ...145 B6
Old Mitre Ct EC4 ...241 B1
Old Montague St E1 ..96 A2
Old Nichol St E2 ...95 D3 243 C6
Old North St WC1 ...240 C4
Old Nursery Pl TW15 .170 D5
Old Oak Common La NW10 ...89 C3
Old Oak La NW10 ...89 D4
Old Oak Prim Sch W12 89 D1
Old Oak Rd W3 ...111 D6
Old Orch TW16 ...172 C1
Old Orchard Cl
Hadley Wood EN4 ...2 B5
Hillingdon UB8 ...82 C1
Old Orch The NW3 ...70 D4
Old Palace La TW9 ..153 C6
Old Palace Prim Sch E3 ...97 D4
Old Palace Rd CR0 ..221 A5
Old Palace Sch of John Whitgift CR9 ...220 D5
Old Palace Terr 8 TW9 ...153 D6
Old Palace Yd 2 TW9 153 D6
Old Paradise St SE11 ...116 B2 260 C4
Old Park Ave SW12 ..159 A5
Enfield EN2 ...5 A1
Old Park Gr EN2 ...5 A1
Old Park Ho N13 ...32 B6
Old Park La W1 ...115 B5 248 C3
Old Park Mews TW5 ..129 B5
Old Park Rd SE2 ...124 A1
Enfield EN2 ...4 D2
Palmers Green N13 ...32 B6
Old Park Rd S EN2 ...4 D1
Old Park Ridings N21 .17 A6
Old Park View EN2 ...4 D2
Old Perry St BR7 ...189 C3
Old Pound Cl TW7 ...131 A4
Old Priory UB9 ...38 D2
Old Pye St SW1 ...259 C6
Old Pye Street Est SW1 ...259 C5
Old Quebec St W1 ..237 D1
Old Queen St SW1 ...115 D4 249 D1
Old Rd SE13 ...142 C1
Enfield EN3 ...6 C4
Old Rectory Gdns HA8 .26 C4
Old Redding HA3 ...24 A6
Oldridge Rd SW12 ...159 B4
Old Royal Free Pl N1 .234 B5
Old Royal Free Sq N1 ...94 C6 234 B5
Old Royal Observatory Greenwich (National Maritime Mus Annexe)* SE10 ...142 B5
Old Ruislip Rd UB5 ...84 C5
Old School Cl
3 Beckenham BR3 ...185 A1
Merton SW19 ...179 C1
Old School Cres E7 ...77 A2
Old School Ho The EN2 .4 D2
Old School Pl CR0 ...220 C4
Old School Rd UB8 ...82 B3
Old School Sq 19 E14 ..97 C1
Thames Ditton KT7 ...196 D3
Old School The WC1 ..240 C4
Old Seacoal La EC4 ..241 C1
Old South Lambeth Rd SW8 ...138 A5 270 B4
Old Spitalfields Mkt E1 ...95 D2 243 D2
Old Sq WC2 ...241 A2
Old St E13 ...99 B5
EC1 ...95 B3 242 B6
Old Stable Mews N5 ...73 A5
Old St Andrews Mans NW9 ...67 B6
Old Station Rd UB3 ..105 D3
Oldstead Rd BR1 ...186 B6
Old Street Sta EC1 ...95 B3 242 D6
Old Sun Wharf E14 ..119 A6
Old Swan Wharf SW11 ...266 D2
Old Swan Yd SM5 ...218 D4
Old Theatre Ct SE1 ..252 B4
Old Town SW4 ...137 C2
Croydon CR0 ...220 D5
Old Tramyard SE18 ..123 C2
Old Woolwich Rd SE10 ...120 B1
Old York Rd SW18 ...157 D6
Oleander Cl BR6 ...227 B3
O'Leary Sq E1 ...96 C2
Olga Prim Sch E3 ...97 A5
Olga St 18 E3 ...97 A5
Olinda Rd N16 ...51 D3
Oliphant St W10 ...91 A4
Olive Blythe Ho 14 W10 91 A3
Oliver Ave SE25 ...205 D6
Oliver Bsns Pk NW10 ..89 A5
Oliver Cl W4 ...132 D6
Oliver Ct SE18 ...123 A2
Isleworth TW7 ...130 D2
Olive Rd E13 ...99 C4
NW2 ...68 C4
W5 ...109 D3
3 Merton SW19 ...180 A3
Oliver Gdns E6 ...100 A2
Oliver Goldsmith Prim Sch NW9 ...45 B4
Oliver Goldsmith Prim Schs SE5 ...139 D4
Oliver Gr SE25 ...205 D5
Oliver Ho 19 SE16 ...118 A4
SW8 ...270 A4
W11 ...244 B5
Oliver Mews SE15 ...140 A3
Oliver Rd E10 ...75 D5
E17 ...54 A4
Kingston KT3 ...177 A1
Sutton SM1 ...218 B4
Oliver's Yd EC1 ...242 D6
Olive Tree Ho N4 ...50 C3
7 SE15 ...140 C6
Olivette St 1 SW15 ..134 D1
Olive Waite Ho NW6 ..69 D1
Ollard's Gr IG10 ...21 D6
Ollerton Gn E3 ...97 B6
Ollerton Rd N11 ...31 D5
Olley Cl SM6 ...220 A2
Ollgar Cl W12 ...111 D5
Olliffe St E14 ...120 A3
Olmar St SE1 ...140 A6
Olmar Wharf SE1 ...140 A6
Olney Ho NW8 ...237 B6
Olney Rd SE17 ...139 A6
Olron Cres DA6 ...169 A6
Olven Rd SE18 ...145 A6
Olveston Wlk SM5 ...202 B3
Olwen Mews HA5 ...22 D1
Olyffe Ave DA16 ...146 A3
Olyffe Dr BR3 ...186 A2
Olympia Ex Ctr* W14 ...112 D3 254 A6
Olympian Ct 1 E14 ..119 C2
Olympia Way W14 ...113 A3 254 B5
Olympia Yd W2 ...245 D5
Olympic Ho W10 ...90 C1
Olympic Ret Pk HA9 ..66 D4
Olympic Way
Greenford UB6 ...85 D6
Wembley HA9 ...66 C4
Olympus Sq E5 ...74 A5
Oman Ave NW2 ...68 C4
Oman Ct NW4 ...68 B4
Ombersley Ho N4 ...51 A2
Omeara St SE1 ...252 B3
Omega Cl E14 ...119 D3
Omega Ho SW10 ...266 B4
Omega Pl N1 ...233 B3
Omega St SE14 ...141 C4
Ommaney Rd SE14 ..141 A4
Omnibus Way E17 ...35 C1
Ondine Rd SE15 ...139 D1
Onedin Point 17 E1 ..118 A6
Onega Gate SE16 ...119 A3
O'Neill Ho NW8 ...229 D3
O'Neill Path 11 SE18 ..144 C6
One Tree Cl SE23 ...162 C5
Ongar Cl RM6 ...58 C4
Ongar Ho 15 N1 ...73 B2
Ongar Rd SW6 135 C6 265 B6
Onra Rd E17 ...53 C2
Onslow Ave TW10 ...154 A6
Onslow Avenue Mans 10 TW10 ...154 A6
Onslow Cl Chingford E4 .20 B2
Thames Ditton KT7 ...196 C1
Onslow Cres BR7 ...188 D2
Onslow Ct SW10 ...256 B1
Onslow Dr DA14 ...168 D2
Onslow Gdns N10 ...49 B4
SW7 ...114 B1 256 C2
Southgate N21 ...16 C6
Thames Ditton KT7 ...196 C1
Wallington SM6 ...219 C1
Wanstead E18 ...55 C6
Onslow Ho 1 KT2 ...176 B2
Onslow Lo 28 SW2 ...160 C4
Onslow Mews E SW7 .256 C3
Onslow Mews W SW7 256 C3
Onslow Par N14 ...15 B3
Onslow Rd
Richmond TW10 ...154 A5
Thornton Heath CR0 ...204 C1
West Barnes KT3 ...200 A5
Onslow Sq SW7 ...114 B2 256 D3
Onslow St EC1 ...241 B5
Onslow Way KT7 ...196 C1
Ontario St SE1 116 D3 261 D6
Ontario Way E14 ...119 C6
Onyx Ho KT4 ...199 B1
Opal Cl E16 ...99 D1
Opal Ho KT4 ...199 B1
Opal Mews 2 IG1 ...78 D6
Opal St SE11 ..116 D1 261 C2
Open Air Theatre, Regent's Park NW1 ...231 A1
Openshaw Rd SE2 ...124 B2
Openview SW17,SW18 .158 B2
Operating Theatre Mus & Herb Garret* SE1 ...117 B5 252 D3
Ophelia Gdns NW2 ...69 A5
Ophir Terr SE15 ...140 A4
Opie Ho NW8 ...230 B4
Opossum Way TW4 ...128 C2
Oppenheim Rd SE13 ..142 A3
Oppidans Rd NW3 ...70 D1
Orange Hill Rd HA8 ...27 A3
Orange Pl SE16 ...118 C3
Orangery La SE9 ...166 B6
Orangery The TW10 ..153 C2
Orange St WC2 ...115 D6 249 D5
Orange Yd WC2 ...239 D1
Oratory La SW3 ...256 D2
Oratory RC Prim Sch SW3 ...114 C1 257 A2
Oratory The* SW7 ...114 C3 257 A5
Orbain Rd SW6 ...135 A5 264 B3
Orbel St SW11 136 C4 267 A1
Orb St SE17 ...117 B2 262 C3
Orchard Ave N14 ...15 C4
N20 ...14 B2
N3 ...47 C6
Ashford TW15 ...171 A4
Carshalton CR4 ...203 A1
Croydon CR0 ...207 A1
Erith DA17 ...147 B6
Hatton TW14 ...149 B6
Heston TW5 ...129 A5
Hinchley Wood KT7 ...213 A6
Kingston KT3 ...199 C6
Southall UB1 ...107 B5
Orchard Bsns Ctr SE26 ...185 B5
Orchard Cl DA7 ...147 A4
N1 ...73 A1
NW2 ...68 A5
Orchard Cl *continued*
SE23 ...162 C5
W10 ...91 A2
Ashford TW15 ...171 A4
Bushey WD23 ...8 B3
Chingford E4 ...35 C6
Edgware HA8 ...26 A4
Northolt UB5 ...64 A2
Ruislip HA4 ...39 A2
Thames Ditton KT7 ...197 B2
Walton-on-T KT12 ...194 B2
Wanstead E11 ...55 B5
Wembley HA0 ...88 A6
West Barnes SW20 ...200 C5
West Ewell KT19 ...214 D2
Orchard Cotts UB3 ...105 C4
Orchard Cres HA8 ...27 A5
Enfield EN1 ...5 D4
Orchard Ct E10 ...53 D1
W1 ...238 A2
Barnes SW13 ...133 D2
Croydon BR3 ...207 C1
Edgware HA8 ...26 B5
Hounslow TW7 ...130 B5
New Malden KT4 ...200 A1
Southgate N14 ...15 C5
Wallington SM6 ...219 B3
Walton-on-T KT12 ...193 D1
Wood Green N22 ...32 A3
Orchard Dr SE3 ...142 C3
Edgware HA8 ...26 B5
Upper Halliford TW17 ..193 C6
Orchard Gate NW9 ...45 C5
Thames Ditton KT10 ...196 B1
Wembley UB6 ...65 B2
Orchard Gdns
Chessington KT9 ...214 A4
Sutton SM1 ...217 C3
Orchard Gn BR6 ...227 C6
Orchard Gr BR6 ...211 D1
BR6 ...227 D6
Croydon CR0 ...207 A2
Edgware HA8 ...26 D2
Harrow HA3 ...44 B4
Penge SE20 ...184 A3
Orchard Hill SE13 ...141 D4
Orchard Ho 11 SE16 ..118 C3
SE5 ...139 A4
W12 ...112 A5
Orchard Jun & Inf Sch The TW3 ...151 C6
Orchard La
Thames Ditton KT8 ...196 B3
Wimbledon SW20 ...178 B2
Woodford IG8 ...37 C6
Orchardleigh Ave EN3 ..6 C3
Orchard Lo N12 ...14 A1
Orchard Mead Ho NW11 ...69 C6
Orchardmede N21 ...17 B5
Orchard Mews N1 ...73 B1
Orchard Pl E14 ...120 C6
Tottenham N17 ...33 D3
Orchard Prim Sch E9 ..74 C1
Orchard Rd BR1 ...187 C2
BR6 ...226 D3
DA16 ...146 B2
N6 ...49 B2
Barnet EN5 ...1 B1
Belvedere DA17 ...125 C2
Brentford TW8 ...131 C6
Carshalton CR4 ...203 A1
Chessington KT9 ...214 A4
Dagenham RM10 ...103 C6
Enfield EN3 ...18 C6
Feltham TW14 ...150 A3
Hampton TW12 ...173 B3
Hayes UB3 ...106 A6
Hounslow TW4 ...151 C6
Isleworth TW1 ...153 B6
Kingston KT1 ...176 A1
Richmond TW9 ...132 C2
Sidcup DA14 ...189 C6
Sunbury TW16 ...172 B3
Sutton SM1 ...217 C4
Orchard Rise
Croydon CR0 ...207 B1
Kingston KT2 ...177 A2
Mortlake TW10 ...132 D1
Pinner HA5 ...39 D6
Orchard Rise E DA15 .167 D6
Orchard Rise W DA15 .167 C6
Orchard School Sports Ctr SE20 ...184 A2
Orchardson Ho NW8 .236 D5
Orchardson St NW8 ...92 B3 236 D5
Orchard Sq W14 ...254 C1
Orchard St E17 ...53 A5
W1 ...238 B2
Orchard Terr EN1 ...18 A5
Orchard The N20 ...13 D3
NW11 ...47 C4
SE3 ...142 B3
W4 ...111 B2
Ealing W5 ...87 D2
East Barnet N14 ...15 B6
Enfield N21 ...17 B5
Ewell KT17 ...215 D1
Orchard The *continued*
Hounslow TW3 ...130 A3
Orchard Way
Ashford TW15 ...148 B2
Croydon BR3,CR0 ...207 A3
Enfield EN1 ...5 C2
Esher KT10 ...212 A2
Sutton SM1 ...218 B4
Orchard Way Prim Sch CR0 ...207 A2
Orchid Cl 1 E6 ...100 A2
Chessington KT9 ...213 C1
Southall UB1 ...85 A1
Orchid Ct HA9 ...66 A6
Orchid Grange N14 ...15 C4
Orchid Lo N14 ...15 C4
Orchid Rd N14 ...15 C4
Orchid St W12 ...112 A6
Orde 6 NW9 ...27 D2
Orde Hall St WC1 ...94 B2 240 C4
Orde Ho 10 N16 ...73 B4
Ordell Ct 30 E3 ...97 B5
Ordell Rd E3 ...97 B5
Ordnance Cl TW13 ...150 A2
Ordnance Cres SE10 ..120 C4
Ordnance Hill NW8 ...92 B6 229 D5
Ordnance Mews NW8 229 D4
Ordnance Rd E16 ...98 D2
SE18 ...144 C6
Enfield EN3 ...7 B6
Oregano Cl UB7 ...104 B6
Oregano Dr E14 ...98 B1
Oregon Ave E12 ...78 B4
Oregon Cl KT3 ...199 A5
Oregon Sq BR6 ...211 B1
Orestes Ct 8 E18 ...55 A6
Orestes Mews 1 NW6 .69 C3
Orford Ct Stanmore HA7 .25 C4
Wallington SM6 ...219 C3
West Norwood SE27 ...160 D2
Orford Gdns TW1 ...152 D2
Orford Rd E17 ...53 D4
Catford SE6 ...163 D1
Wanstead E18 ...55 B6
Organ Crossroads KT17 ...216 A1
Oriana Ho 3 E14 ...119 B6
Oriel Cl CR4 ...203 D6
Oriel Ct NW3 ...70 A4
6 Croydon CR0 ...205 B1
Oriel Dr SW13 ...134 C6
Oriel Gdns IG5 ...56 B6
Oriel Jun & Inf Sch TW13 ...151 A1
Oriel Rd E9 ...74 D2
E9 ...75 A2
Oriel Way UB5 ...63 D1
Oriental City NW9 ...45 B6
Oriental Rd E16 ...121 D5
Orient Ind Pk E10 ...75 C6
Orient St SE11 116 D2 261 C4
Orient Way E5 ...74 D5
Oriole Way SE28 ...124 B6
Orion Bsns Ctr SE14 ..118 D1
Orion Ctr The CR0 ...220 A6
Orion Ho 20 E1 ...96 B3
Orion Prim Sch The NW9 ...27 D2
Orion Rd N11 ...31 A4
Orion Way HA6 ...22 A6
Orissa Rd SE18 ...123 C1
Orkney Ho N1 ...233 C6
Orkney St SW11 ...137 A3
Orlando Rd SW4 ...137 C2
Orleans Cl KT10 ...212 B6
Orleans Ct 9 TW1 ...153 B4
Orleans Inf Sch TW1 ..153 B4
Orleans Park Sec Sch TW1 ...153 B4
Orleans Rd
South Norwood SE19 ..183 B4
Twickenham TW1 ...153 C4
Orleston Mews N7 ...72 C2
Orleston Rd N7 ...72 C2
Orley Farm Rd HA1 ...64 C5
Orley Farm Sch HA1 ...64 B5
Orlop St SE10 ...120 C1
Ormanton Rd SE26 ...184 A6
Orme Ct W2 ..113 D6 245 C5
Orme Ct Mews W2 ...245 D5
Orme Ho 8 E8 ...95 D6
Orme La W2 ..113 D6 245 C5
Ormeley Rd SW12 ...159 B3
Orme Rd
Kingston KT1,KT3 ...176 D1
Sutton SM1 ...217 D2
Ormerod Gdns CR4 ...181 A2
Ormesby Cl SE28 ...124 D6
Ormesby Way HA3 ...44 B4
Orme Sq W2 ...245 C5
Ormiston Gr W12 ...112 B5
Ormiston Rd SE10 ...121 A1
Ormond Ave
Hampton TW12 ...173 D2

Ormond Ave *continued*
22 Richmond TW10 ... 153 D6
Ormond Cl WC1 ... 240 B4
Ormond Cres TW12 ... 173 D2
Ormond Dr TW12 ... 173 D3
Ormonde Ave BR6 ... 227 A6
Ormonde Ct SW15 ... 134 C1
Ormonde Gate
SW3 ... 114 D1 257 D1
Ormonde Pl SW1 ... 258 B3
Ormonde Rd SW14 ... 133 A2
Ormonde Rise IG9 ... 21 C3
Ormonde Terr
NW8 ... 92 D6 230 C5
Ormond Ho 7 N16 ... 73 B6
Ormond Mews WC1 ... 240 B5
Ormond Rd N4,N19 ... 50 A1
Richmond TW10 ... 153 D6
Ormond Yd SW1 ... 249 B4
Ormrod Ct W11 ... 91 B1
Ormsby SM2 ... 217 D1
Ormsby Gdns UB6 ... 86 A5
Ormsby Lo 7 W4 ... 111 C3
Ormsby Pl N16 ... 73 D5
Ormsby Point 6 SE18 122 D2
Ormsby St E2 ... 95 D5
Ormside St SE15 ... 140 C6
Ormskirk Rd WD19 ... 22 D5
Ornan Rd NW3 ... 70 C3
Oronsay Rd 18 N1 ... 73 A2
Orpheus Ho 25 N19 ... 49 D2
Orpheus St SE5 ... 139 B4
Orpington Gdns N18 ... 17 C1
Orpington Hospl BR6 . 227 D4
Orpington Mans N21 ... 16 C3
Orpington Rd
Southgate N21 ... 16 D3
St Paul's Cray BR7 ... 211 C6
Orpington Sta BR6 ... 227 C6
Orpwood Cl TW12 ... 173 B4
Orsett Mews
W2 ... 91 D1 236 A2
Orsett St SE11 116 B1 260 D2
Orsett Terr W2 . 92 A1 236 A2
Woodford IG8 ... 37 C3
Orsman Rd N1 ... 95 C6
Orton St E1 ... 118 A5
Orville Rd SW11 ... 136 B3
Orwell Cl UB3 ... 105 C6
Orwell Ct E8 ... 96 A6
N5 ... 73 A4
Orwell Ho W12 ... 112 A6
Orwell Lo 2 E18 ... 55 A5
Orwell Rd E13 ... 99 C6
Osbaldeston Rd N16 ... 52 A1
Osberton Rd SE12 ... 165 A6
Osbert St SW1 ... 259 C3
Osborn Cl E8 ... 96 A6
Osborne Ave TW19 ... 148 B3
Osborne Cl
Beckenham BR3 ... 207 A5
Cockfosters EN4 ... 2 D2
Feltham TW13 ... 172 D5
Osborne Ct 16 E10 ... 53 D2
Ealing W5 ... 88 A2
10 Surbiton KT6 ... 198 A3
Osborne Gdns CR7 ... 183 A1
Osborne Gr E17 ... 53 B5
Osborne Mews E17 ... 53 B5
Osborne Pl SM1 ... 218 B3
Osborne Rd E10 ... 75 D6
E7 ... 77 B3
E9 ... 75 B2
N4 ... 50 C1
NW2 ... 68 B2
W3 ... 110 D4
Buckhurst Hill IG9 ... 21 B3
Dagenham RM9 ... 81 B3
Enfield EN3 ... 7 A3
Erith DA17 ... 147 B6
Hounslow TW3,TW4 ... 129 B2
Kingston KT2 ... 176 A3
Palmers Green N13 ... 16 C1
Southall UB1 ... 86 A1
South Norwood CR7 ... 183 A1
Walton-on-T KT12 ... 194 A1
Osborne Sq RM9 ... 81 B4
Osborne Way KT9 ... 214 B3
Osborn Gdns NW7 ... 28 D3
Osborn La SE23 ... 163 A4
Osborn St E1 . 95 D2 243 D2
Osborn Terr SE3 ... 142 D1
Osbourne Ct HA2 ... 41 D5
Osbourne Ho TW10 ... 154 C6
Osbourne Terr 1
SW17 ... 181 A5
Oscar Faber Pl 8 N1 ... 73 C1
Oscar St SE8 ... 141 C4
Oseney Cres NW5 ... 71 D2
Osgood Ave BR6 ... 227 D3
Osgood Gdns 1 BR6 . 227 D3
O'Shea Gr E3 ... 97 B6
Osidge JMI Sch N14 ... 15 C3
Osidge La N14 ... 15 B3
Osier Cres N10 ... 30 D2
Osier Ct E1 ... 96 D3
Osier Mews W4 ... 133 D6
Osiers Ct 3 KT1 ... 175 D2
Osiers Rd SW18 ... 135 C1
Osier St E1 ... 96 C3
Osier Way E10 ... 75 D5
Mitcham CR4 ... 202 D4
Oslac Rd SE6 ... 185 D5
Oslo Ct NW8 ... 230 A3
Mitcham SW19 ... 180 B3
Oslo Ho 2 SE5 ... 139 A3
Oslo Sq SE16 ... 119 A3
Osman Cl N15 ... 51 B3
Osmani Prim Sch E1 ... 96 A2
Osman Rd W6 ... 112 C3
Edmonton N9 ... 18 A1
Osmington Ho SW8 ... 270 D3
Osmond Cl HA2 ... 64 A6
Osmond Gdns SM6 ... 219 C3
Osmund St W12 ... 89 D2
Osnaburgh St
NW1 ... 93 B3 238 D6
Osnaburgh Terr NW1 . 238 D6
Osney Ho 4 SE2 ... 124 D4
Osney Wlk SM5 ... 202 B3
Osprey 7 NW9 ... 27 D2
Osprey Cl E17 ... 35 A3
E6 ... 100 A2
Cheam SM1 ... 217 B3
Wanstead E11 ... 55 A5
West Drayton UB7 ... 104 A4
Osprey Ct NW3 ... 69 D3
7 Ealing W7 ... 86 D3
Thornton Heath SW16 . 182 B1
Osprey Ho 3 E14 ... 119 A6
E4 ... 35 B4
SE15 ... 139 D4
Osprey Mews EN3 ... 18 B6
Ospringe Cl 9 SE20 ... 184 C3
Ospringe Ct SE9 ... 167 B5
Ospringe Ho SE1 ... 251 B3
Ospringe Rd NW5 ... 71 C4
Osram Ct W6 ... 112 C3
Osram Rd HA9 ... 65 D5
Osric Path 8 N1 ... 95 C5
Ossian Rd N4 ... 50 B2
Ossie Garvin Rdbt
UB4 ... 106 C6
Ossington Bldgs W1 ... 238 A3
Ossington Cl W2 ... 245 B5
Ossington St
W2 ... 113 D6 245 C5
Ossory Rd SE1 ... 140 A6
Ossulston St
NW1 ... 93 D4 232 D2
Ossultan Pl N2 ... 48 A6
Ossulton Way N2 ... 48 A5
Ostade Rd SW2 ... 160 B4
Ostell Cres EN3 ... 7 C5
Osten Mews
SW7 ... 113 D3 255 D5
Osterley Ave TW7 ... 130 B5
Osterley Cl BR5 ... 190 A2
Osterley Cres TW7 ... 130 D4
Osterley Ct
Hounslow TW7 ... 130 B4
7 Northolt UB5 ... 84 C4
Osterley Gdns UB2 ... 108 A4
Osterley Ho 5 E14 ... 97 D1
Osterley La
Isleworth TW7 ... 108 C1
Southall UB2,TW7 ... 107 D1
Osterley Lo 1 TW7 ... 130 C4
Osterley Park* TW7 ... 108 B1
Osterley Park Rd UB2 . 107 B3
Osterley Park View Rd
W7 ... 108 C4
Osterley Rd N16 ... 73 C4
Hounslow TW7 ... 130 C4
Osterley Sta TW7 ... 130 B5
Osterley Views UB2 ... 108 B4
Osterly Gdns CR7 ... 183 A1
Oster Terr E17 ... 52 D4
Ostliffe Rd N13 ... 33 A5
Oswald Rd UB1 ... 107 A5
Oswald's Mead E9 ... 75 A4
Oswald St E5 ... 74 D5
Oswald Terr NW2 ... 68 C5
Osward Pl N9 ... 18 B2
Osward Rd SW12,
SW17 ... 158 D2
Oswell Ho 9 E1 ... 118 B5
Oswin St SE11 116 D2 261 D4
Oswyth Rd SE5 ... 139 C3
Otford Cl BR1 ... 210 C6
DA5 ... 169 D5
Penge SE20 ... 184 C2
Otford Cres SE4 ... 163 B5
Otford Ho SE1 ... 252 D1
6 SE15 ... 140 C6
Otha Ho 13 SW9 ... 138 A3
Othello Cl SE11 ... 261 C2
Otho Ct 5 TW8 ... 131 D5
Otis St E3 ... 98 A4
Otley App IG2 ... 56 D3
Otley Ct N11 ... 31 A4
Otley Dr IG2 ... 56 D3
Otley Ho N5 ... 72 D5
Otley Rd E16 ... 99 C1
Otley Terr E5 ... 74 D5
Ottawa Ho 4 HA4 ... 40 C1
Ottaway Ct E5 ... 74 A5
Ottaway St E5 ... 74 A5
Otterbourne Rd
Chingford E4 ... 20 B1
1 Croydon CR0 ... 221 A6
Otterburn Gdns TW7 . 131 A5
Otterburn Ho 12 SE5 . 139 A5
Otterburn St SW17 ... 180 D4
Otterden Cl BR6 ... 227 C4
Otterden St SE6 ... 185 C6
Otterfield Rd UB7 ... 104 A6
Otter Rd UB6 ... 86 A3
Ottershaw Ho BR5 ... 190 B2
Ottoman Ct W5 ... 109 D2
Otto St SE17 ... 138 D6
Otway Ct N4 ... 50 B3
Otway Gdns WD23 ... 8 C4
Oulton Cl E5 ... 74 C6
Erith SE28 ... 102 C1
Oulton Cres IG11 ... 79 D3
Oulton Rd N15 ... 51 B4
Oulton Way WD19 ... 23 B6
Oundle Ave WD23 ... 8 A5
Our Lady Immaculate RC
Prim Sch KT6 ... 198 D1
Our Lady of Dolours RC
Prim Sch W2 ... 91 D2
Our Lady of Grace RC Inf
Sch NW2 ... 68 C6
Our Lady of Grace RC Jun
Sch NW2 ... 68 B5
Our Lady of Grace Sch
SE7 ... 143 B6
Our Lady of Lourdes RC
Prim Sch
N11 ... 31 C5
N12 ... 30 A2
SE13 ... 142 B2
Our Lady of Lourdes RC Sch
NW10 ... 89 A6
Our Lady of Lourds RC Prim
Sch E11 ... 55 A3
Our Lady of Muswell Prim
Sch N10 ... 49 A6
Our Lady of Muswell RC
Prim Sch N10 ... 31 A1
Our Lady of the Assumption
RC Prim Sch E2 ... 96 C5
Our Lady of the Rosary RC
Prim Sch DA15 ... 167 C5
Our Lady of the Sacred
Heart RC Prim Sch
(Annexe) N7 ... 72 B2
Our Lady of the Sacred
Heart RC Sch N7 ... 72 B3
Our Lady of the Visitation
RC Prim Sch UB6 ... 86 A3
Our Lady of Victories RC
Prim Sch
SW7 ... 114 A2 256 B3
Putney SW15 ... 134 D1
Our Lady Queen of Heaven
RC Sch SW19 ... 156 D4
Our Lady RC Prim Sch
E14 ... 97 B1
NW1 ... 93 C6 232 B5
Our Lady's Convent High
Sch N15,N16 ... 51 C2
Our Lady & St John's RC
Jun & Inf Sch TW8 ... 109 C1
Our Lady & St Joseph RC
Prim Sch N1 ... 73 C2
Our Lady & St Philip Neri
RC Prim Sch SE26 ... 185 A6
Our Lady & St Philip Neri
RC Sch SE26 ... 185 A6
Ouseley Rd SW12 ... 158 D3
Outer Circ NW8 92 C4 230 B3
Outgate Rd NW10 ... 67 D1
Outram Pl N1 . 94 A6 233 B6
Outram Rd E6 ... 100 A6
N22 ... 31 D2
Croydon CR0 ... 221 D6
Outwich St EC3 ... 243 B2
Outwood Ct CR2 ... 221 A1
Outwood Ho 3 SW2 ... 160 B4
Oval Ct HA8 ... 27 A3
Oval Mans SE11 ... 270 D6
Oval Pl SW8 . 138 B5 270 D4
Oval Prim Sch CR0 ... 205 C1
Oval Rd NW1 . 93 B6 231 C6
Croydon CR0 ... 205 C1
Oval Rd N RM10 ... 103 D6
Oval Rd S RM10 ... 103 D5
Oval Sta SE11 ... 138 C6
Oval The E2 ... 96 B5
Sidcup DA15 ... 168 A4
Oval The (Surrey Cnty Crkt
Gd) SE11 ... 138 C6
Oval Way SE11 116 B1 260 D1
Overbrae BR3 ... 185 C5
Overbrook Wlk HA8 ... 26 C3
Overbury Ave BR3 ... 208 A6
Overbury Ct 1 BR3 ... 208 A6
Overbury Ho 3 E5 ... 74 D4
Overbury Rd N4,N15 ... 51 B3
Overbury St E5 ... 74 D4
Overcliff Rd SE13 ... 141 C2
Overcourt Cl DA15 ... 168 B5
Overdale Ave KT3 ... 177 B1
Overdale Rd W5 ... 109 C3
Overdown Rd SE6 ... 185 D6
Overhill Rd SE21,SE22 . 162 A4
Overhill Way BR3 ... 208 B4
Overlea Rd E5 ... 52 A2
Overmead DA15 ... 167 B4
Oversley Ho 17 W2 ... 91 C2
Overstand Cl BR3 ... 207 C4
Overstone Gdns CR0 ... 207 B2
Overstone Ho 17 E14 ... 97 C1
Overstone Rd W6 ... 112 C2
Overstrand Mans
SW11 ... 268 A1
Overton Cl NW10 ... 67 A2
Hounslow TW7 ... 130 D4
Overton Ct E11 ... 55 A2
Overton Dr Ilford RM6 ... 58 C2
Wanstead E11 ... 55 B2
Overton Grange Sch
SM2 ... 217 D1
Overton Ho SW15 ... 155 D4
Overton Rd SE2 ... 124 D3
SW9 ... 138 C3
Belmont SM2 ... 217 C1
Southgate N14 ... 16 A6
Walthamstow E10 ... 53 A1
Overton's Yd CR0 ... 221 A5
Overy Ho SE1 ... 251 C1
Ovesdon Ave HA2 ... 41 B1
Ovett Cl SE19 ... 183 C4
Ovex Cl E14 ... 120 A4
Ovington Ct SW3 ... 257 B5
Ovington Gdns SW3 ... 257 B5
Ovington Mews SW3 ... 257 B5
Ovington Sq
SW3 ... 114 C3 257 B5
Ovington St
SW3 ... 114 C2 257 B4
Owen Cl SE28 ... 124 C5
Hayes UB4 ... 84 B4
Thornton Heath CR0 ... 205 B3
Owen Ct UB4 ... 84 B4
Owen Ho 11 N19 ... 71 C4
Feltham TW14 ... 150 A4
5 Twickenham TW1 ... 153 B4
Owenite St SE2 ... 124 B2
Owen Rd Edmonton N13 . 33 A5
Hayes UB4 ... 84 B4
Owen's Ct EC1 ... 234 C2
Owen's Row EC1 ... 234 C2
Owen St EC1 ... 234 C3
Owens Way SE23 ... 163 A4
Owen Way NW10 ... 67 A3
Owen Wlk 7 SE20 ... 184 A3
Owgan Cl SE5 ... 139 B5
Oxberry Ave SW6 ... 135 A3
Oxbridge Ct 4 W4 ... 110 D1
Oxendon St
SW1,W1 ... 115 D6 249 C5
Oxenford St SE15 ... 139 D2
Oxenham Ho 13 SE8 ... 141 C6
Oxenholme NW1 ... 232 B3
Oxenpark Ave HA9 ... 44 A2
Oxestalls Rd SE8 ... 119 A1
Oxford Ave NW10 ... 90 C4
Harlington TW6 ... 127 D5
Hounslow TW5 ... 107 C1
Merton SW20 ... 179 A1
Oxford & Cambridge Mans
NW1 ... 237 B3
Oxford Cir W1 . 93 C1 239 A1
Oxford Circus Ave W1 239 A1
Oxford Circus Sta
W1 ... 93 C1 239 A1
Oxford Cl Edmonton N9 ... 18 B2
Littleton TW15,TW17 ... 171 A3
Mitcham CR4 ... 203 C6
Oxford Cres KT3 ... 199 B3
Oxford Ct EC4 ... 252 C6
48 W2 ... 91 C2
W4 ... 110 D1
16 Acton W3 ... 88 C1
8 Ealing W7 ... 86 D2
17 Kingston KT6 ... 198 A4
Oxford Dr SE1 ... 253 B1
Ruislip HA4 ... 62 C6
Oxford Gardens Prim Sch
W10 ... 90 D1
Oxford Gate W6 ... 112 D2
Oxford Gdns N20 ... 14 B3
W10 ... 90 D1
Brentford W4 ... 132 C6
Edmonton N21 ... 17 A4
Oxford Mews DA5 ... 169 C4
Oxford Rd DA14 ... 190 B5
E15 ... 76 B2
N4 ... 50 C1
NW6 ... 91 C5
Carshalton SM2,SM5 ... 218 C3
Ealing W5 ... 109 D6
Edmonton N9 ... 18 B2
Enfield EN3 ... 18 B6
Harrow HA1 ... 42 A3
Harrow HA3 ... 42 D6
Ilford IG1 ... 79 A3
Putney SW15 ... 135 A1
South Norwood SE19 ... 183 B4
Oxford Rd *continued*
Teddington TW11,TW12 . 174 B5
Wallington SM6 ... 219 C3
Woodford IG8 ... 37 D5
Oxford Rd N W4 ... 110 D1
Oxford Rd S W4 ... 110 D1
Oxford Sq W2 . 92 C1 237 B1
Oxford St W1 . 93 B1 238 D1
Oxford Way TW13 ... 172 D6
Oxford Wlk UB1 ... 107 B5
Oxgate Ct Par NW2 ... 68 A6
Oxgate Ctr NW2 ... 68 B6
Oxgate Gdns NW2 ... 68 B6
Oxgate La NW2 ... 68 B6
Oxhawth Cres BR2 ... 210 D3
Oxhey Dr HA6,WD19 ... 22 B6
Oxhey La HA5 ... 23 C5
Oxhey Ridge Cl HA6 ... 22 B5
Oxhey Wood JMI Schs
WD19 ... 22 C6
Oxleas E6 ... 100 D1
Oxleas Cl DA16 ... 145 B3
Oxleay Rd HA2 ... 41 C1
Oxleigh Cl KT3 ... 199 C4
Oxley Cl SE1 ... 118 A1
Oxleys Rd NW2 ... 68 B5
Oxlip Cl 2 CR0 ... 206 D1
Oxlow La RM10 ... 81 C4
Oxonian St SE22 ... 139 D1
Oxo Tower SE1 ... 251 B5
Oxo Tower Wharf SE1 251 B5
Oxted Cl CR4 ... 202 B6
Oxted Ct N16 ... 51 C1
Oxtoby Way SW16 ... 181 D2
Oyster Catchers Cl E16 99 B1
Oyster Catcher Terr
IG5 ... 56 C6
Oyster Row E1 ... 96 C1
Ozolins Way E16 ... 99 A1

P

Pablo Neruda Cl 4
SE24 ... 138 D1
Pace Pl E1 ... 96 B1
Pacific Cl TW14 ... 149 D3
Pacific Ho 15 E1 ... 96 D3
Pacific Hts BR3 ... 185 C3
Pacific Rd E16 ... 99 A1
Pacific Wharf SE16 ... 118 D5
Packenham Ho 21 E2 ... 95 D4
24 N19 ... 49 D2
Packham Ct KT4 ... 216 C5
Packington Ho 22
SW9 ... 138 A3
Packington Sq
N1 ... 95 A6 235 A6
Packington St
N1 ... 94 D6 234 D5
Packmores Rd SE9 ... 167 B6
Padbury SE17 ... 263 B1
Padbury Cl TW14 ... 149 B3
Padbury Ct E2 ... 95 D4
Padbury Ho NW8 ... 237 B6
Paddenswick Ct W6 ... 112 B3
Paddenswick Rd W6 ... 112 A3
Paddington Cl UB4 ... 84 D3
Paddington Com Hospl
W9 ... 91 C2
Paddington Ct 10 W7 ... 86 D2
Paddington Gn
W2 ... 92 B2 236 C4
Paddington Green Prim Sch
NW8 ... 92 B3 236 C5
Paddington St W1 ... 238 A4
Paddington Sta
W2 ... 92 B1 236 C2
Paddock Cl SE3 ... 143 A3
Forest Hill SE26 ... 184 D6
New Malden KT4 ... 199 C1
Northolt UB5 ... 85 C5
Orpington BR6 ... 226 D4
Paddock Ct SW20 ... 200 C5
Paddock Gdns SE19 ... 183 C4
Paddock Lo 13 EN1 ... 17 C6
Paddock Rd DA6 ... 147 A1
NW2 ... 68 A6
Ruislip HA4 ... 62 D5
Paddock Sch SW15 ... 133 D1
Paddocks Cl HA2 ... 63 D4
Paddocks Gn NW9 ... 44 D1
Paddocks The HA9 ... 66 D6
Addington CR0 ... 223 C2
Cockfosters EN4 ... 2 D2
Paddock The UB10 ... 60 D4
Paddock Way BR7 ... 189 B3
Padfield Ct HA9 ... 66 B5
Padfield Rd SE5 ... 139 A2
Padley Cl KT9 ... 214 B3
Padnall Ct RM6 ... 58 D6
Padnall Rd RM6 ... 58 D5
Padstow Cl BR6 ... 227 D4
Padstow Ho 12 E14 ... 119 B6
Padstow Rd EN2 ... 4 D4
Padstow Wlk TW14 ... 149 D3
Padua Rd SE20 ... 184 C2
Pagden St SW8 ... 268 D2
Pageant Ave NW9 ... 27 C2
Pageant Cres SE16 ... 119 B5
Pageantmaster Ct
EC4 ... 241 C1
Pageant Wlk CR0 ... 221 C5
Page Cl Dagenham RM9 . 81 A3
Hampton TW12 ... 173 A4
Harrow HA3 ... 44 B3
Page Cres CR0 ... 220 D3
Page Ct NW7 ... 28 A3
Page Green Rd N15 ... 52 A4
Page Green Terr N15 ... 51 D4
Page Heath La BR1 ... 209 D6
Page Heath Villas
BR1 ... 209 D6
Page High N22 ... 50 C6
Page Ho SE10 ... 142 A6
Pagehurst Rd CR0 ... 206 B2
Page Mdw NW7 ... 28 A3
Page Rd TW14 ... 149 B5
Page's Ct N10 ... 31 A1
Page's Hill N10 ... 31 A1
Page's La N10 ... 31 A1
Page St NW7 ... 28 A3
SW1 ... 115 D2 259 D4
Page's Wlk
SE1 ... 117 C3 263 B5
Page's Yd W4 ... 133 C6
Paget Ave SM1 ... 218 B5
Paget Cl TW12 ... 174 B6
Paget Ct UB7 ... 104 A4
Paget Gdns BR7 ... 188 D2
Paget Ho 15 E2 ... 96 C5
Paget La TW7 ... 130 C2
Paget Pl Kingston KT2 . 177 A4
Thames Ditton KT7 ... 196 D1
Paget Rd N16 ... 51 B1
Hillingdon UB10 ... 83 A3
Ilford IG1 ... 78 D4
Paget Rise SE18 ... 144 C5
Paget St EC1 ... 234 C2
Paget Terr SE18 ... 144 D6
Pagham Ho W10 ... 90 C3
Pagin Ho N15 ... 51 C4
Pagitts Gr EN4 ... 1 D4
Pagnell St SE14 ... 141 B5
Pagoda Ave TW9 ... 132 B2
Pagoda Gdns SE3 ... 142 B3
Paignton Rd N15 ... 51 C3
Ruislip HA4 ... 62 A5
Paine Ct SE3 ... 142 D6
Paines Cl HA5 ... 41 A6
Paine's La HA5 ... 23 A1
Pain's Cl CR4 ... 181 B1
Painsthorpe Rd 8 N16 73 C5
Painswick Ct 1 SE15 . 139 D5
Painters Mews SE16 ... 118 A2
Painters Rd IG2,RM6 ... 58 A6
Paisley Rd
Carshalton SM5 ... 202 B1
Tottenham N22 ... 32 D2
Pakeman Ho SE1 ... 251 D2
Pakeman Prim Sch N7 . 72 B5
Pakeman St N7 ... 72 B5
Pakenham Cl SW12 ... 159 A3
Pakenham St
WC1 ... 94 B3 240 D6
Palace Ave
W8 ... 113 D4 245 D2
Palace Court Gdns N10 49 C6
Palace Ct NW3 ... 69 D3
SE9 ... 166 B5
W2 ... 113 D6 245 C5
Harrow HA3 ... 44 A3
South Norwood CR7 ... 205 B5
Streatham SW2 ... 160 C2
Palace Garden Mews
W8 ... 245 B4
Palace Gardens Terr
W8 ... 113 D5 245 C3
Palace Gate
W8 ... 114 A4 246 A1
Palace Gates Rd N22 ... 31 D2
Palace Gdns
Buckhurst Hill IG9 ... 21 D3
Enfield EN2 ... 5 B1
Palace Gdns Mews
W8 ... 113 D5 245 D3
Palace Gn W8 113 D5 245 C3
New Addington CR0 ... 223 B1
Palace Gr BR1 ... 187 B2
Penge SE19 ... 183 D3
Palace Mans W14 ... 254 B4
Palace Mews E17 ... 53 B5
SW1 ... 258 B3
SW6 ... 264 D4
Palace of Ind HA9 ... 66 C4
Palace Par E17 ... 53 C5
Palace Pl SW1 ... 259 A6
Palace Rd BR1 ... 187 B2
N8 ... 49 D4
East Molesey KT8 ... 196 B6
Kingston KT1 ... 197 D5
Penge SE19 ... 183 D3
Ruislip HA4 ... 63 A4
Streatham SE27,SW16,
SW2 ... 160 C2
Wood Green N11 ... 32 A3
Palace Sq SE19 ... 183 D3
Palace St SW1 115 C3 259 A6

ace View SE12 165 A2
omley BR1 209 B6
aydon CR0 223 B4
ace View Rd E4 35 D5
amon Ct SE1 263 D2
amos Rd E10 53 C1
atine Ave N16 73 C4
atine Rd N16 73 C4
emead Cl SW6 134 D4
ermo Rd NW10 90 A5
estine Gr SW19 180 B2
ewell Cl BR5 190 B1
ewell Common Dr
V14 155 B6
ewell Pk SW14 133 B1
frey Pl
V8 138 B5 270 D4
grave Ave UB1 107 C6
grave Gdns NW1 237 A5
grave Ho 4 NW3 70 D3
SE5 139 A5
vickenham TW2 152 A4
lgrave Rd W12 111 D3
lissy St 35 E2 95 D4
llant Ho SE1 262 D5
llant Way BR6 226 C5
llet Way SE18 144 A4
lliser Ct W14 254 A1
lliser Ho 21 E1 96 D3
SE10 142 B6
lliser Rd
/14 113 A1 254 A1
llister Terr SW15 155 D2
ll Mall SW1 115 D5 249 C3
ll Mall E
W1 115 D5 249 D4
ll Mall Pl SW1 249 B3
almar Cres DA7 147 C3
almar Rd DA7 147 C3
alm Ave DA14 190 D4
alm Cl E10 75 D5
alm Ct N16 73 B6
7 SE15 139 D5
Beckenham BR3 207 B6
Wood Green N22 32 B3
almeira Rd DA16 146 D2
almer Ave KT4,SM3 216 C4
almer Cl Heston TW5 129 C4
West Wickham BR4 224 B6
almer Cres KT1 198 A6
almer Ct NW10 89 B6
almer Gdns EN5 12 D6
almer Ho 5 N19 71 C5
8 NW5 71 C4
6 SE14 140 D5
almer Pl N7 72 C3
almer Rd E13 99 B3
Dagenham RM8 58 D1
almer's Ct 11 N11 31 C5
almers Gr KT8 195 C5
almers Green High Sch
N21 16 C2
almers Green Sta N13 32 B6
almers La EN3 6 C4
almers Rd E2 96 D5
almer's Rd N11 31 C5
almers Rd
Mortlake SW14 133 A2
Thornton Heath SW16 182 B1
Palmer St SW1 259 C6
Palmerston Cres SE18 145 A6
Bowes Park N13 32 B5
Palmerston Ct E17 53 B5
22 E3 96 D5
2 Buckhurst Hill IG9 21 C2
9 Surbiton KT6 197 D2
Palmerston Ctr HA3 42 D6
Palmerston Gr 4
SW19 179 C3
Palmerston Ho SW11 268 B1
W8 245 A3
Palmerston Rd BR6 227 A3
E17 53 B5
E7 77 B2
NW6 69 B1
NW6 69 C1
W3 111 A3
Bowes Park N22 32 B4
Buckhurst Hill IG9 21 C3
Harrow HA3 42 D6
Hounslow TW3 130 A4
Merton SW19 179 C3
Mortlake SW14 133 A1
Sutton SM1 218 A3
Thornton Heath CR0 205 B4
Twickenham TW2 152 C5
Wallington SM5 219 A4
Palmerston Way SW8 268 D3
Palm Gr W5 110 A3
Palm Tree Ct 3 N17 33 D1
Palm Tree Ho 2 SE14 140 D5
Pamela Ct N12 29 D4
NW10 68 A1
Pamela Gdns HA5 40 B4
Pamela Ho 14 E8 95 D6
Pamlion Ct N4 50 A2
Pams Way KT19 215 B3
Panama Ho 5 E1 96 D2
Panbro Ho 7 SE18 144 B4
Pancras La EC2 242 C1
Pancras Rd
NW1 93 D5 232 D4
Pandora Ct 4 KT6 198 A3
Pandora Rd NW6 69 C2
Panfield Mews IG2 56 C3
Panfield Rd SE2 124 A3
Pangbourne NW1 232 A1
Pangbourne Ave W10 90 C2
Pangbourne Ct N20 14 A4
Upper Tooting SW17 180 A6
Pangbourne Dr HA7 26 A5
Pangbourne Ho 4 N7 72 A3
Panhard Pl UB1 107 D6
Pank Ave EN5 14 A6
Pankhurst Cl 7 SE14 140 D5
Isleworth TW7 130 D2
Pankhurst Rd KT12 194 C2
Panmuir Rd SW20 178 B2
Panmure Cl N5 72 D4
Panmure Ct 11 UB1 86 A1
Panmure Rd SE26 162 B1
Panorama Ct N6 49 C3
Pansy Gdns W12 112 A6
Panther Dr NW10 67 B3
Pantiles Cl N13 32 D5
Pantiles The BR1 210 A6
DA7 147 B5
NW11 47 B4
Bushey WD23 8 B3
Panton Cl CR0 204 D1
Panton St SW1 249 C5
Panyer Alley EC2 242 A2
Papermill Cl SM5 219 A4
Paper Mill Wharf E14 119 A6
Papillons Wlk SE3 143 A2
Papworth Gdns N7 72 B3
Papworth Way SW2 160 C4
Parade Mans 2 NW4 46 B4
19 SE5 139 A3
Parade Mews SE27,
SW2 160 D2
Parade The
SW11 136 D5 267 D4
Ashford TW16 171 D3
Claygate KT10 212 C2
Croydon CR0 220 B3
Greenford UB6 65 B3
2 Kingston KT2 176 A1
Paradise Pas N7 72 C3
Paradise Pl 15 SE7 122 A2
Paradise Rd SW4 138 A3
Richmond TW10 154 A6
Paradise Row E2 96 B4
Paradise St SE16 118 B4
Paradise Wlk
SW3 136 D6 267 D6
Paragon Cl E16 99 A1
Paragon Ct NW4 29 A2
Paragon Gr KT5 198 B3
Paragon Mews SE1 262 D4
Paragon Pl SE3 142 D3
Surbiton KT5 198 B3
Paragon Rd E9 74 C2
Paragon The SE17 262 C4
SE3 143 A3
Paramount Bldg EC1 241 C6
Paramount Ct WC1 239 B5
Paramount Ho 8 E11 76 C5
Parayhouse Sch W12 112 B5
Parbury Rd SE23 163 A5
Parbury Rise KT9 214 A2
Parchmore Rd CR7 205 A6
Parchmore Way CR7 182 D1
Pardes House & Beis
Yaakov Sch (Boys) N3 29 B1
Pardoner St
SE1 117 B3 262 D6
Pardon St EC1 241 D6
Parfett St E1 96 A1
Parfew Ct 2 SE22 162 B2
Parfitt Cl NW3 48 A1
Parfrey St W6 134 C6
Pargraves Ct HA9 66 C4
Parham Dr IG2 56 D4
Paris Gdn SE1 116 D5 251 C4
Parish CE Prim Sch
BR1 187 A3
Parish Church CE Inf & Jun
Schs CR0 220 D5
Parish Ct KT6 198 A3
Parish Gate Dr DA15 167 C5
Parish La SE20 184 D3
Paris Ho 12 E2 96 B5
Parish Wharf 6 SE7 122 A2
Park App DA16 146 B1
Park Ave BR1 187 A4
BR6 226 C6
E15 76 C2
N3 29 D2
NW11 47 D1
NW2 68 C2
Barking IG11 79 A2
Edmonton N18 34 A6
Enfield EN1 17 C5
Ilford IG1 56 C1
Mitcham CR4 181 B3
Mortlake SW14 133 B1
Palmers Green N13 16 C1
Park Ave *continued*
Ruislip HA4 39 C3
Southall UB1 107 C5
Twickenham TW3 151 D5
Upper Halliford TW17 193 C6
Wallend E6 100 C5
Wallington SM5 219 A2
West Wickham BR4 224 A6
Woodford IG8 37 B5
Wood Green N22 32 B2
Park Ave E KT17 216 A2
Park Ave N N8 49 D5
NW10 68 B3
Park Avenue Mews
CR4 181 B3
Park Avenue Rd N17 34 B3
Park Ave S N8 49 D5
Park Ave W KT17 216 A2
Park Bsns Ctr 4 NW6 91 C4
Park Chase HA9 66 B4
Park Cl 20 E9 96 C6
N12 30 B6
NW2 68 B5
SW1 247 C1
W14 113 B3 254 D6
Ealing NW10 88 B4
Hampton TW12 174 A2
Harrow HA3 24 C2
Isleworth TW3,TW7 152 A6
Kingston KT2 176 C2
Wallington SM5 218 D2
Park Cotts 10 TW1 153 B5
Park Cres N3 30 A3
W1 93 B3 238 C5
Enfield EN2 5 B1
Harrow HA3 24 C2
Twickenham TW2 152 B3
Park Cres Mews E
W1 238 D5
Park Cres Mews W
W1 238 C5
Park Croft HA8 27 A2
Parkcroft Rd SE12 164 D4
Park Ct E17 53 D4
N11 31 D3
N12 30 B5
SW11 268 C2
SW4 159 D6
2 Beckenham BR3 207 D6
2 Chingford E4 20 A2
Dulwich SE21 161 B1
New Barnet EN5 14 B4
New Malden KT3 199 B5
Teddington KT1 175 C2
Upper Tooting SW12 159 A3
Wallington SM6 220 A3
Wembley HA9 66 A3
Parkdale N11 31 D4
Parkdale Cres KT4 215 B5
Parkdale Rd SE18 123 C1
Park Dr NW11 47 D1
Acton W3 110 C3
Enfield N21 17 A5
Harrow HA2 41 C2
Mortlake SW14 133 B1
Stanmore HA3 24 C4
Woolwich SE7 144 A6
Park Dwellings 7 NW3 70 D3
Park End NW3 70 C4
Bromley BR1 186 D2
Parker Cl E16 122 A5
Parker Ct N1 235 B6
SW4 270 A1
Wimbledon SW19 179 A3
Parke Rd Barnes SW13 134 A4
Sunbury TW16 194 A5
Parker Ho 4 SE18 122 D1
Parker Mews WC2 240 B2
Parker Rd CR0 221 A4
Parkers Rd N10 30 C2
Parkers Row 12 SE16 118 A4
Parker's Row SE1 253 D1
Parker St E16 122 A5
WC2 94 A1 240 B2
Park Farm SE7 144 A6
Park Farm Cl N2 48 A6
Pinner HA5 40 B4
Park Farm Ct UB3 105 C6
Park Farm Rd
Bromley BR1 187 D2
Kingston KT2 176 A3
Parkfield 3 TW7 130 C4
Parkfield Ave
Feltham TW13 150 A1
Harrow HA2 24 A1
Hillingdon UB10 82 D4
Mortlake SW14 133 C1
Northolt UB5 84 D5
Parkfield Cl
Edgware HA8 26 D4
Northolt UB5 85 A5
Parkfield Cres
Feltham TW13 150 A1
Harrow HA2 24 A1
Ruislip HA4 63 A5
Parkfield Dr UB5 84 D5
Parkfield Gdns HA2 41 D6
Parkfield Ho HA2 23 D2
Parkfield Ind Est
SW11 137 A3
Parkfield Par TW13 150 A1
Parkfield Prim Sch
NW4 46 B2
Parkfield Rd NW10 68 B1
SE14 141 B4
Feltham TW13 150 A1
Harrow HA2 64 A5
Northolt UB5 85 A5
Uxbridge UB10 60 D6
Parkfields Croydon CR0 207 B1
Putney SW15 134 C1
Parkfields Ave NW9 45 B1
Wimbledon SW20 178 B1
Parkfields Cl SM5 219 A4
Parkfields Rd TW10 176 B5
Parkfield St N1 94 C5 234 B4
Parkfield Way BR2 210 B4
Park Flats N6 48 C2
Parkgate SE3 142 D2
Park Gate N2 48 B6
Ealing W5 87 D2
Southgate N21 16 B4
Parkgate Ave EN4 2 A4
Parkgate Cl KT2 176 D4
Parkgate Cres EN4 2 A4
Park Gate Ct TW12 174 A5
Parkgate Gdns SW14 155 B6
Parkgate House Sch
SW11 137 A1
Park Gate Mans N2 48 B6
Parkgate Mews N6 49 C2
Parkgate Rd
SW11 136 C5 267 B3
Wallington SM5,SM6 219 B3
Park Gates HA2 63 C4
Park Gdns NW9 44 D6
Kingston KT2 176 B5
Park Gr BR1 187 B2
E15 99 A6
N11 31 D3
Edgware HA8 26 B5
Park Grove Rd E11 76 C6
Park Hall Rd N2 48 C5
Dulwich SE21 161 B1
Park Hall Road Trad Est
SE21 161 B1
Parkham Ct BR2 186 C1
Parkham St
SW11 136 C4 267 A1
Parkham Way N10 31 C1
Park High Sch HA7 25 D1
Park Hill BR1 210 B5
SW4 159 D6
Ealing W5 87 D2
Forest Hill SE23 162 C3
Loughton IG10 21 D6
Richmond TW10 154 B5
Wallington SM5 218 D2
Park Hill Cl SM5 218 C3
Park Hill Ct
Croydon CR0 221 C6
Ealing W5 87 D2
Upper Tooting SW17 158 D1
Parkhill Inf Sch IG5 56 C6
Park Hill Inf Sch CR0 221 C5
Parkhill Jun Sch IG5 56 C6
Park Hill Jun Sch CR0 221 C5
Parkhill Rd DA5 169 B4
NW3 70 D3
Chingford E4 20 A4
Sidcup DA15 167 C1
Park Hill Rd
Beckenham BR2 186 C1
South Croydon CR0 221 C5
Wallington SM6 219 B1
Park Hill Rise CR0 221 D5
Park Hill Sch KT2 176 C3
Park Hill Wlk 10 NW3 70 D3
Park Ho 35 E9 74 C1
N4 72 D6
8 SE5 139 B4
Forest Hill SE26 184 A5
Sidcup DA14 190 A5
Southgate N21 16 B4
Parkholme Rd E8 74 A2
Park House Gdns
TW1 153 C6
Park House Mid Sch
SW19 179 B6
Parkhouse St SE5 139 B5
Parkhurst Ct N7 72 A4
Parkhurst Gdns 2
DA5 169 C4
Parkhurst Rd E17 53 A5
N11 31 A5
N7 72 A4
Bowes Park N22 32 B4
Little Ilford E12 78 C4
Sidcup DA5 169 C4
Sutton SM1 218 B4
Tottenham N17 34 A1
Parkin Ho SE20 184 D3
Parkinson Ct EC1 235 D2
N1 235 C1
Parkinson Ho 6 E9 74 C1
Park La E15 98 B6
W1 115 A6 248 A5
Park La *continued*
Cheam SM3 217 A2
Cranford TW5 128 A5
Dagenham RM6 58 D3
Edmonton N9 17 D1
Harrow HA2 63 D5
Hayes UB4 83 C3
Richmond TW9 131 D1
South Croydon CR0 221 B5
Stanmore HA7 9 A1
Teddington TW11 174 D4
Tottenham N17 34 A3
Wallington SM5,SM6 219 A3
Wembley HA9 66 A4
Parkland Ct E15 76 C3
W14 244 A2
Parkland Gdns 12
SW19 156 D3
Parkland Gr
Ashford TW15 170 C6
Hounslow TW7 130 D4
Parkland Rd
Ashford TW15 170 C6
Woodford IG8 37 B3
Wood Green N22 32 B1
Parklands N6 49 B2
SE22 162 B6
Bushey WD23 8 A5
Kingston KT5 198 B4
Parklands Cl
Hadley Wood EN4 2 B5
Ilford IG2 57 A2
Mortlake SW14 155 A6
Parklands Ct TW5 128 D3
Parklands Dr N3 47 A6
Parklands Par TW5 128 D3
Parklands Rd SW16 181 B5
Parklands Way KT4 215 C6
Parkland Wlk N4,N8 50 B2
Park Lane Cl N17 34 B3
Park Lane Prim Sch
HA9 66 A3
Park Lawn CR7 183 A1
Parklea Cl NW9 27 C2
Park Lea Ct N16 51 C2
Parkleigh Ct SW19 179 D1
Parkleigh Rd SW19 179 D1
Parkleys
Richmond KT2,TW10 175 D6
Richmond, Ham Common
TW10 176 A6
Park Lo 10 E1 118 B5
N12 30 A5
NW2 68 C4
11 NW8 70 B1
3 Ealing W5 87 B3
Park Lofts 7 SW4 160 A6
Park Lorne NW8 230 B1
Park Mans 5 NW4 46 B4
NW8 230 A3
SW1 247 C1
SW11 267 C1
SW6 264 B1
SW8 270 B6
W6 111 D3
Forest Hill SE26 162 C1
Park Mead DA15 168 B5
Parkmead SW15 156 B5
Park Mead HA2 63 D5
Parkmead Gdns NW7 27 D4
Park Mews BR7 188 D4
W10 91 A5
Stanwell TW19 148 B4
Parkmore Cl IG8 37 A6
Park Nook Gdns EN2 5 B6
Park Par NW10 89 D5
NW9 45 B6
Acton W3 110 C3
Hayes UB3 83 C1
Park Pl E14 119 C5
SW1 115 C5 249 A4
W3 110 C2
Ealing W5 109 D5
Hampton TW12 174 A4
Wembley HA9 66 B4
Park Place Dr W3 110 C3
Park Place Villas W2 236 B4
Park Prim Sch E15 76 D1
Park Rd BR1 187 B2
BR7 188 D4
E10 53 C1
E15 99 A6
E17 53 B4
E6 99 C6
N11 31 D3
N14 15 D4
N2 48 B6
N8 49 D4
N8,N15 50 D5
NW10 89 C6
NW1,NW8 92 C3 237 B6
NW4 46 B3
NW9 45 B2
Ashford TW15 170 D5
Barnet EN4 2 C1
Barnet EN5 1 B1
Beckenham BR3 185 C3
Cheam SM3 217 A2
Chiswick W4 133 B6
Park Rd *continued*
Ealing W7 108 D6
East Molesey KT8 196 A5
Edmonton N18 34 A6
Feltham TW13 172 D6
Hackbridge SM6 219 B6
Hampton TW12 174 A5
Hayes UB4 83 C2
Ilford IG1 79 B5
Isleworth TW3,TW7 152 A6
Isleworth TW7 131 B3
Kingston KT2,TW10 176 C3
Lower Halliford TW17 192 C1
Mitcham SW19 180 C4
New Malden KT3 199 B5
Richmond TW10 154 B5
South Norwood SE25 205 C5
Sunbury TW16 172 B3
Teddington KT1 175 C2
Teddington TW11 174 D4
Twickenham TW1 153 C5
Uxbridge UB8 60 A2
Wallington SM6 219 B3
Wanstead E12 77 B6
Wembley HA0 66 A2
Park Rd E Acton W3 111 A4
Uxbridge UB10 82 A5
Park Rd N W3 110 D4
W4 111 B1
Park Ridings N8 50 C6
Park Rise
Forest Hill SE23 163 A3
Harrow HA3 24 C2
Park Rise Rd SE23 163 A3
Park Road Ho 3 KT2 176 C3
Park Row SE10 142 B6
Park Royal NW10 88 D6
Park Royal Bsns Ctr
NW10 89 A3
Park Royal Metro Ctr
NW10 88 D3
Park Royal Rd NW10,
W3 89 A3
Park Royal Sta W5 88 C3
Park S SW11 268 A1
Park Sch IG1 56 D1
Park Sheen 3 SW14 132 D1
Parkshot TW9 132 A1
Parkside DA14 168 B2
N3 29 D3
NW7 28 A4
SE3 142 D5
W3 111 C5
Park Side NW2 68 B4
Parkside
1 Beckenham BR3 185 D1
Cheam SM3 217 A2
Ealing W5 110 A6
Hampton TW12 174 A5
Hayes UB3 105 C6
Wimbledon SW19 178 D6
Park Side IG9 21 B2
Parkside Ave BR1 210 A5
Wimbledon SW19 178 D5
Parkside Cl SE20 184 C3
Parkside Cres N7 72 C5
Tolworth KT5 199 A3
Parkside Ct
Bowes Park N22 32 B4
2 Wanstead E11 55 A3
Parkside Dr HA8 10 C1
Parkside Est E9 96 D6
Parkside Gdns
East Barnet EN4 15 A4
Wimbledon SW19 178 D6
Parkside Lo DA17 125 D1
Parkside Rd
Belvedere DA17 125 D2
Hounslow TW3 151 D6
Parkside St SW11 268 A1
Parkside Terr N18 33 B6
Parkside Way HA2 42 A5
Park Sq E NW1 93 B3 238 D6
Park Sq Mews NW1 238 C5
Park Sq W NW1 93 B3 238 C5
Park St SE1 117 A5 252 B4
W1 115 A6 248 A5
Croydon CR0 221 A6
Teddington TW11 174 C4
Parkstead Rd SW15 156 B6
Park Steps W2 247 B6
Park St James NW8 230 C5
Parkstone Ave N18 33 D5
Parkstone Rd E17 54 A6
3 SE15 140 A3
Park Terr
Carshalton SM5 218 C5
Enfield EN3 7 A5
New Malden KT4 200 A1
Park The N6 49 A3
NW11 47 D1
Ealing W5 109 D5
Forest Hill SE23 162 C3
Sidcup DA14 190 A5
Wallington SM5 218 D3
Parkthorne Cl HA2 41 D3

Parkthorne Dr HA2 41 D3
Parkthorne Rd SW12 159 D4
Park Twrs W1 248 C3
Park View N5 73 A4
NW2 68 C4
W3 89 A2
Parkview UB6 87 A4
Park View
Kingston KT3 199 D6
Morden SM4 202 B4
Pinner HA5 23 B2
Southgate N21 16 B4
Wembley HA9 66 D3
Yiewsley UB7 104 A6
Park View Cres N11 31 B6
Park View Ct N12 30 C6
NW9 45 A5
SW18 157 C5
Parkview Ct
Fulham SW6 135 A3
Penge SE20 184 B2
Park View Dr CR4 180 B1
Park View Gdns NW4 46 D4
Redbridge IG4 56 B5
Wood Green N22 32 C2
Park View Ho SE24 160 D5
Parkview Lo BR3 207 D6
Park View Mews 24
SW9 138 B3
Park View Rd DA16 146 D2
N3 29 D2
NW10 67 D4
SE9 166 D2
Parkview Rd CR0 206 A1
Park View Rd Ealing W5 88 A2
Hillingdon UB8 82 C1
Pinner HA5 22 B3
Southall UB1 107 C5
Tottenham N17 34 A1
Park Village E
NW1 93 B5 231 D3
Park Village W
NW1 93 B5 231 C4
Park Villas RM6 58 D3
Parkville Rd
SW6 135 B5 264 C3
Park Vista SE10 142 B6
Park Walk Prim Sch
SW10 136 B6 266 C5
Parkway DA18 125 A3
NW1 93 B6 231 C5
Park Way N20 30 D6
NW11 47 A4
W3 110 C2
Parkway Hillingdon UB10 60 D1
Ilford IG3 79 D5
Palmers Green N14 16 A2
West Barnes SW20 200 D5
Woodford IG8 37 C5
Park Way
East Molesey KT8 195 D6
Edgware HA8 26 D2
Enfield EN2 4 C3
Feltham TW14 150 B4
Ruislip HA4 40 A1
Park Way Ct HA4 39 D1
Parkway Prim Sch
DA18 125 A3
Parkway The
Cranford TW5 128 B5
Hayes UB2,UB3,UB4,
TW5 106 B3
Hayes UB4 84 D2
Parkway Trad Est
TW5 128 C6
Park West W2 92 C1 237 B1
Park West Pl
W1,W2 92 C1 237 B2
Park Wlk
SW10 136 B6 266 C6
Parkwood N20 14 D2
NW8 230 C5
Beckenham BR3 185 C3
Parkwood Ave KT10 196 A1
Parkwood Gr TW16 194 A6
Parkwood Mews N6 49 B3
Parkwood Prim Sch
N4 72 D6
Parkwood Rd DA5 169 B4
Hounslow TW7 130 D4
Wimbledon SW19 179 B5
Parliament Ct NW3 70 C4
Parliament Hill NW3 70 C4
Parliament Hill Mans
NW5 71 A4
Parliament Hill Sch
NW5 71 A4
Parliament Mews
SW14 133 A3
Parliament Sq*
SW1 116 A4 250 A1
Parliament St
SW1 116 A4 250 A2
Parliament View
Apartments SE11 260 B4
Parma Cres SW11 136 D1
Parminter Ind Est 23
E2 96 B5
Parmiter St E2 96 B5
Parmoor Ct EC1 242 A6
Parnall Ho 11 SE19 183 C6
Parnell Cl HA8 27 A6
W12 112 B3
Parnell Rd E3 97 B6
Parnham St E14 97 A1
Parolles Rd N19 49 C1
Paroma Rd DA17 125 C3
Parr Cl N9 34 B6
Parr Ct N1 235 C4
Feltham TW13 172 C6
Parrington Ho 1
SW4 159 D5
Parr Pl W4 111 D2
Parr Rd E6 99 D6
Stanmore HA7 26 A2
Parr's Pl TW12 173 C3
Parr St N1 95 B5 235 C4
Parry Ave E6 100 B1
Parry Cl KT17 216 A1
Parry Ho 32 E1 118 B5
Parry Pl SE18 122 D2
Parry Rd W10 91 A4
South Norwood SE25 205 C6
Parry St SW8 138 A6 270 B6
Parsifal Coll NW3 69 C4
Parsifal Ho NW3 69 C4
Parsifal Rd NW6 69 C3
Parsley Gdns CR0 206 D1
Parsloes Ave RM9 81 A3
Parsloes Prim Sch RM9 81 B2
Parsonage Cl UB3 83 D1
Parsonage Gdns EN2 5 A3
Parsonage La DA14 191 B6
Enfield EN2 5 B3
Parsonage Manorway
DA8,DA17 147 C6
Parsonage St E14 120 A2
Parson Ct SE13 141 D2
Parsons Gn
SW6 135 C3 265 A1
Parsons Gr HA8 10 C1
Parsons Green La
SW6 135 C4 265 A2
Parsons Green Sta
SW6 135 C4 265 A1
Parsons Hill SE18 122 C3
Parsons Ho W2 236 C5
21 Streatham SW12 160 A4
Parsons Lo NW6 69 D1
Parsons Mead KT8 196 A6
Parson's Mead CR0 204 D1
Parsons Rd E13 99 C5
Edgware HA8 10 C1
Parson St NW4 46 C6
Parthenia Rd
SW6 135 C4 265 B1
Partingdale La NW7 28 D5
Partington Cl N19 49 D1
Partridge Cl 1 E16 99 D2
Barnet EN5 12 C5
Bushey WD23 8 A3
Stanmore HA7 26 A6
Partridge Ct EC1 241 C6
Partridge Dr BR6 227 A5
Partridge Gn SE9 166 C1
Partridge Ho 20 E3 97 B5
Partridge Rd
8 Hampton TW12 173 C4
Sidcup DA14 189 C6
Partridge Sq 3 E6 100 A2
Partridge Way N22 32 A2
Pasadena Cl UB3 106 B4
Pascall Ho SE17 139 A6
Pascal St SW8 137 D5 269 D4
Pascoe Rd SE13 164 B6
Pasley Cl SE17 262 A1
Pasquier Rd E17 53 A6
Passey Pl SE9 166 B5
Passfield Dr E14 97 D2
Passfield Ho SE18 123 B2
Passfield Path 13
SE28 124 B6
Passfields W14 254 C1
Catford SE6 164 A1
Passing Alley EC1 241 D5
Passingham Ho TW5 129 C6
Passmore Gdns N11 31 D4
Passmore Ho 12 N9 18 A1
Passmores Edwards Ho
N11 31 D3
Passmore St
SW1 115 A1 258 A2
Pasteur Cl NW9 27 C1
Pasteur Gdns N18 33 A5
Paston Cl SM6 219 C5
Paston Cres SE12 165 B4
Pastor Ct N6 49 C3
Pastor St SE1,
SE11 116 D2 261 D4
Pasture Cl Bushey WD23 8 A4
Wembley HA0 65 B5
Pasture Rd Catford SE6 164 D3
Dagenham RM9 81 B3
Wembley HA0 65 B5
Pastures Mead UB10 60 C2
Pastures The N20 13 B3
Patcham Terr SW8 268 D2
Patch Cl UB10 82 B6
Patching Way UB4 85 A2
Patent Ho E14 97 D2
Paternoster Row
EC2,EC4 95 A1 242 A1
Paternoster Sq
EC4 94 D1 241 D2
Pater St W8 113 C3 255 A5
Pates Manor Dr TW14 149 B4
Pathfield Rd SW16 181 D4
Path The SW19 179 D2
Patience Rd SW11 136 C3
Patio Cl SW4 159 D5
Patmore Ho 9 N16 73 C3
Patmore St
SW8 137 C4 269 B2
Paton Cl E3 97 C4
Paton Ho 3 SW9 138 B3
Paton St EC1 235 A1
Patricia Ct
Chislehurst BR7 189 B2
Woolwich SE2 146 B5
Patricia Villas N17 34 B2
Patrick Coman Ho
EC1 234 C1
Patrick Connolly Gdns 41
E3 97 D4
Patrick Rd E13 99 C4
Patriot Sq E2 96 B5
Patrol Pl SE6 163 D5
Pat Shaw Ho 2 E1 96 D3
Patshull Pl NW5 71 C2
Patshull Rd NW5 71 C2
Patson Cl E5 74 D5
Pattenden Rd SE6 163 B3
Patten Ho N4 51 A1
Patten Rd SW18 158 C4
Patterdale NW1 231 D1
Patterdale Cl BR1 186 C4
Patterdale Rd SE15 140 C5
Patterson Ct SE19 183 D4
Patterson Rd SE19 183 D4
Pattina Wlk SE16 119 A5
Pattinson Point 10 E16 99 A2
Pattison Ho 1 E1 96 D1
SE1 252 B2
Pattison Rd NW2 69 C5
Pattison Wlk SE18 123 A1
Paul Byrne Ho 3 N2 48 A6
Paul Cl E15 76 C1
Paul Ct N3 29 A1
7 Edmonton N18 34 A6
Paulet Rd SE5 138 D4
Paul Gdns CR0 221 D6
Paulhan Rd HA3 43 D5
Paul Ho 13 W10 91 A3
Paulin Dr N21 16 C4
Pauline Cres TW2 152 A3
Pauline Ho 19 E1 96 A2
Paulinus Cl BR5 190 C1
Paul Julius Cl E14 120 B6
Paul Robeson Cl E6 100 C4
Paul's Ho E3 97 B2
Paulson Ho 7 IG11 78 D1
Paul St E15 98 C6
EC2 95 C3 243 A6
Paultons Ho SW3 266 D6
Paultons Sq
SW3 136 B6 266 D6
Paultons St
SW3 136 B6 266 D5
Pauntley Ho 6 N19 49 C1
Pauntley St 4 N19 49 C1
Pavan Ct 29 E2 96 C4
Paved Ct 9 TW9 153 D6
Paveley Dr
SW11 136 C5 267 A3
Paveley Ho N1 233 C3
Paveley St NW8 92 C3 237 B6
Pavement Mews 1
RM6 58 D2
Pavement Sq CR0 206 A1
Pavement The E11 54 A1
SW4 137 C1
W5 110 A3
11 West Norwood SE27 183 A6
Pavet Cl RM10 81 D2
Pavilion Ct NW3 70 B3
5 NW3 70 A4
8 NW6 91 C4
3 Wimbledon SW19 179 A3
Pavilion L Ctr The
BR1 187 A1
Pavilion Lo HA2 42 B1
Pavilion Mans 10 SW9 138 B1
Pavilion Mews N3 29 C1
Pavilion Rd
SW1 114 D3 257 D5
Redbridge IG1 56 B2
Pavilion St SW1 257 D5
Pavilion Terr W12 90 C1
Hampton KT1 197 A4
Pavilion Way HA8 27 A3
Ruislip HA4 62 C6
Pawleyne Cl SE20 184 C3
Pawsey Cl E13 99 A6
Pawson's Rd CR0 205 A4
Paxford Rd HA0 65 B6
Paxton Cl
Richmond TW9 132 B3
Walton-on-T KT12 194 C2
Paxton Ct SE9 165 C1
1 Forest Hill SE26 185 A6
Mitcham CR4 180 D1
Paxton Ho SE17 262 B2
Paxton Pl SE27 183 C6
Paxton Prim Sch SE19 183 C4
Paxton Rd BR1 187 A3
Forest Hill SE23 163 A1
Tottenham N17 34 A3
Chiswick W4 133 C6
Paxton Terr SW1 268 D6
Payens Wlk
W6 135 A6 264 A5
Paymal Ho 28 E1 96 C2
Payne Cl IG11 79 D1
Payne Ho N1 233 D5
Paynell Ct SE3 142 C2
Payne Rd E3 97 D5
Paynesfield Ave SW14 133 B2
Paynesfield Rd WD23 8 D4
Payne St SE8 141 B6
Payzes Gdns IG8 36 D5
Peabody Ave
SW1 115 B1 258 D1
Peabody Bldgs SE17 262 C3
6 SE5 139 B4
Peabody Cl SW1 268 D6
Croydon CR0 206 C1
Peabody Cotts N17 33 C2
Peabody Ct EC1 242 B5
9 SE5 139 B4
Peabody Est E1 118 A6
4 E1 118 D6
18 E2 96 B5
EC1 241 B5
EC1 242 B5
SE1 251 B3
SE1 252 A3
SW1 259 B4
SW6 135 B6 264 D6
W10 90 C2
17 W6 112 C1
WC2 240 C1
Streatham SE24 161 A4
Peabody Hill SE21 161 A3
Peabody Sq SE1 251 C1
Peabody Twr EC1 242 B5
Peabody Yd N1 235 A6
Peace Cl East Barnet N14 15 B6
Greenford UB6 86 B6
South Norwood SE25 205 C5
Peace Ct 10 NW9 46 A5
Peace Gr HA9 66 D6
Peace St SE18 144 C6
Peaches Cl SM2 217 A1
Peach Rd W10 91 A4
Feltham TW14 150 A3
Peach Tree Ave UB7 82 B1
Peachum Rd SE3 142 D6
Peach Walk Mews 23
E3 96 D5
Peacock Ave TW14 149 B3
Peacock Cl RM8 80 C6
Peacock Est N17 33 D3
Peacock St
SE17 116 D2 261 D3
Peacock Wlk E16 99 B1
Peacock Yd SE17 261 D3
Peaketon Ave IG4 55 D4
Peak Hill SE26 184 C6
Peak Hill Ave SE26 184 C6
Peak Hill Gdns SE26 184 C6
Peak Ho N4 51 A1
Peak The SE26 162 C1
Peal Gdns W13 87 A3
Peall Rd CR0 204 B3
Pear Ave TW17 193 C6
Pearce Cl 2 CR4 181 A1
Pearcefield Ave 5
SE23 162 C3
Pearce Ho N19 71 C5
7 Streatham SW2 160 A4
Pear Cl NW9 45 B5
SE14 141 A5
Pearcroft Rd E11 76 B6
Pear Ct 20 SE15 139 D5
Peardon St SW8 137 B3
Peareswood Gdns HA7 25 D2
Pearfield Ho 1 N5 73 A3
Pearfield Rd SE23 163 A1
Pearl Cl E6 100 C1
NW2 46 D2
Pearl Ct 18 NW9 46 A5
Pearl Rd E17 53 C6
Pearl St E1 118 B5
Pearlstones Ct RM10 103 C6
Pearmain Cl TW17 192 D4
Pearman St
SE1 116 C4 251 B1
Pear Pl SE1 251 A2
Pear Rd E11 76 C5
Pearscroft Ct
SW6 135 D4 265 D1
Pearscroft Rd
SW6 135 D4 265 D1
Pearse St 3 SE15 139 C6
Pearson Ct SM4 201 D4
Pearson Ho SW15 134 C3
Pearson's Ave SE8,
SE14 141 C4
Pearson St E2 95 D5
Pears Rd TW3 130 A2
Peartree Ave SW17 158 A1
Pear Tree Ave UB7 82 B1
Pear Tree Cl 23 E2 95 D6
Peartree Cl KT9 214 C3
Pear Tree Cl CR4 180 C1
Pear Tree Ct EC1 241 B5
Putney SW15 134 B1
Peartree Gdns RM8 80 B4
Pear Tree Ho SE4 141 B1
Hayes UB8 83 A1
Peartree La E1 118 C6
Peartree Rd EN1 5 C2
Pear Tree Rd TW15 171 A5
Peartree St EC1 95 A3 242 A6
Peartree Way SE10 121 A2
Peary Ho 3 NW10 67 B1
Peary Pl E2 96 C4
Peas Mead Terr E4 36 A6
Peatfield Cl DA15 167 C1
Pebworth Lo SE25 205 D5
Pebworth Rd HA1 65 A6
Peckarmans Wood
SE21,SE26 162 A1
Peckett Sq 3 N5 72 D4
Peckford Pl SW9 138 C3
Peckham Gr SE15 139 C5
Peckham High St
SE15 140 A4
Peckham Hill St SE15 140 A5
Peckham Park Prim Sch
SE15 140 A5
Peckham Park Rd
SE15 140 A5
Peckham Rd SE5 139 C4
Peckham Rye SE22 140 A1
Peckham SE15,SE22 140 B1
Peckham Rye Prim Sch
SE15 140 B2
Peckham Rye Sta
SE15 140 A3
Peckwater St NW5 71 C3
Pedlars Wlk N7 72 A3
Pedley Rd RM8 58 C1
Pedley St E1 95 D3 243 D5
Pedro St E5 74 D4
Pedworth Gdns 4
SE16 118 C2
Peebles Ct UB1 86 A1
Peek Cres SW19 178 D5
Peel Centre (Metropolitan
Police Training
Establishment) NW9 45 D6
Peel Cl Chingford E4 19 D2
Edmonton N9 18 A1
Peel Ct UB6 86 A4
Peel Dr NW9 45 D6
Redbridge IG5 56 A6
Peel Gr E2 96 C5
Peel Pass W8 245 A3
Peel Pl IG5 37 D1
Peel Prec NW6 91 C5
Peel Rd BR6 227 A3
NW6 91 B4
Harrow HA3 42 D6
Wembley HA0,HA9 65 D5
Woodford E18 36 D2
Peel St W8 113 C5 245 A3
Peel Way UB8 82 A2
Peel Yates Ho 13 SE7 122 A2
Peerglow Est EN3 18 C6
Peerless St EC1 95 B4 235 C1
Pegamoid Rd N18 18 C1
Pegasus Ct NW10 90 B4
Brentford TW8 110 B1
Kingston KT1 197 D6
Pegasus Ho 9 E1 96 D3
Pegasus Rd CR0,CR9 220 C2
Pegasus Way N11 31 B4
Peggotty Way UB8 82 D1
Pegg Rd TW5 128 D5
Peggy Quirke Ct 2
HA0 66 A2
Pegley Gdns SE12 165 A2
Pegwell Ho 19 E5 74 B3
Pegwell St SE18 145 C5
Pekin St E14 97 C1
Pekoe SE1 253 D3
Peldon Ct TW10 154 B6
Pele Ct N17 33 B3
Pelham Ave IG11 101 D6
Pelham Cl SE5 139 C2
Pelham Cotts DA5 169 D3
Pelham Cres SW7 257 A3
Pelham Ct SW3 257 A3
Pelham Ho W14 254 C3
Pelham Pl SW7 257 A3
8 Ealing W7 86 D3
Pelham Prim Sch DA7 147 C2
Pelham Rd DA7 147 C2
N15 51 D5
Ilford IG1 79 B6
Merton SW19 179 C3
Pelham Rd *continued*
Penge BR3,SE20 184
Wanstead E18 55
Wood Green N22 32
Pelham St
SW7 114 B2 256
Pelican Ho 7 SE8 119
Pelier St SE17 139
Pelinore Rd SE6 164
Pella Ho SE11 260
Pellant Rd
SW6 135 A5 264
Pellatt Gr N22 32
Pellatt Rd SE22 161
Wembley HA9 66
Pellerin Rd N16 73
Pellew Ho 15 E1 96
Pelling St E14 97
Pellipar Cl N13 16
Pellipar Gdns SE18 122
Pellipar Rd SE18 122
Pelly Ct 4 E17 54
Pelly Rd E13 99
Pelter St E2 95
Pelton Ct CR2 221
Pelton Rd SE10 120
Pembar Ave E17 53
Pemberley Chase
KT19 214
Pemberley Cl KT19 214
Pemberley Ho KT19 214
Pember Rd NW10 90
Pemberton Ct 18 E1 96
Pemberton Gdns N19 71
Dagenham RM6 59
Pemberton Ho SE26 184
Pemberton Pl 2 E8 74
Esher KT10 212
Pemberton Rd N4 50
East Molesey KT8 196
Pemberton Row EC4 241
Pemberton Terr N19 71 C
Pembridge Ave TW4 151
Pembridge Cres
W11 113 C6 245
Pembridge Gdns
W2 113 C6 245
Pembridge Mews
W11 113 C6 245
Pembridge Pl
1 SW15 157
W2 113 C6 245
Pembridge Rd
W11 113 C6 245
Pembridge Sq
W2 113 C6 245
Pembridge Villas
W11 113 C6 245
Pembroke W14 254
Pembroke Ave
Enfield EN1 6 B
Harrow HA3 43 B
Surbiton KT5 198 D
Pembroke Bldgs NW10 90 A
Pembroke Cl SW1 248 B
Pembroke Ct 11 W7 86 D
Pembroke Gdns
W8 113 C3 254 D
Dagenham RM10 81 D
Pembroke Gdns Cl
W8 255 A
Pembroke Hall NW4 46 C
Pembroke Ho 16 W2 91 D
Acton W3 111 A
Putney SW15 156 A
Upper Tooting SW17 180 B
Pembroke Mews N10 31 A
W8 255 A
Pembroke Pl W8 255 A
Edgware HA8 26 C
Isleworth TW7 130 C
Pembroke Rd BR1 187 D
E17 53 D
E6 100 B
N10 31 A
N15 51 D
N8 50 A5
W8 113 C2 255 A
Edmonton N13 17 A1
Greenford UB6 85 D3
Ilford IG3 57 D2
Mitcham CR4 181 A1
Ruislip HA4 39 D1
South Norwood SE25 205 C5
Wembley HA9 65 D5
Pembroke Sq
W8 113 C3 255 A5
Pembroke St
N1 72 A1 233 B6
Pembroke Studios
W8 254 D5
Pembroke Terr NW8 229 C5
Pembroke Villas W8 255 A4
Richmond TW9 131 D1
Pembroke Way UB3 105 A3
Pembroke Wlk W8 255 A4
Pembrook Lo 2
SW16 160 B1
Pembury Ave KT4 200 A2

Pembury Cl E5 ....74 B3
Hayes BR2 ....208 D2
Pembury Cres DA14 ....169 A2
Pembury Ct UB3 ....127 B6
Pembury Ho SE5 ....139 C3
Pembury Pl 15 E5,E8 ....74 B3
Pembury Rd DA7 ....147 A6
E5 ....74 B3
Croydon SE25 ....206 A5
Tottenham N17 ....33 D1
Pemdevon Rd CR0 ....204 C2
Pemell Cl 27 E1 ....96 C3
Pemell Ho 28 E1 ....96 C3
Pemerich Cl UB3 ....105 D1
Pempath Pl HA9 ....65 D6
Penally Pl N1 ....235 D6
Penang St E1 ....118 B5
Penard Rd UB2 ....107 D3
Penarth Ct SM2 ....218 A1
Penarth St SE15 ....140 C6
Penates KT10 ....212 B4
Penberth Rd SE6 ....164 A3
Penbury Rd UB2 ....107 B1
Penceat Ct SE20 ....184 C1
Pencombe Mews
W11 ....244 D6
Pencraig Way SE15 ....140 B6
Pendall Cl EN4 ....2 C1
Penda Rd DA8 ....147 D5
Pendarves Rd SW20 ....178 C2
Penda's Mead E9 ....75 A4
Pendell Ave UB3 ....127 D5
Pendennis Ho 15 SE8 ....119 A2
Pendennis Rd N17 ....51 B6
Streatham SW16 ....182 A6
Penderel Rd TW3 ....151 C6
Penderry Rise SE6 ....164 B2
Penderyn Way N7 ....71 D4
Pendlebury Gn 8
SE18 ....144 A4
Pendle Ho 13 SE26 ....162 A1
Pendle Rd SW16 ....181 B5
Pendlestone Rd E17 ....53 D4
Pendley Ho 18 E2 ....96 A6
Pendragon Rd BR1 ....165 A1
Pendragon Sec Sch
BR1 ....165 A1
Pendrell Ho WC2 ....239 D1
Pendrell Rd SE4 ....141 A3
Pendrell St SE18 ....145 B6
Pendula Dr UB4 ....84 D3
Penelope Ho 20 SW9 ....138 C4
Penerley Rd SE6 ....163 D3
Penfield Lo 7 W9 ....91 C2
Penfields Ho N7 ....72 A2
Penfold Cl CR0 ....220 C5
Penfold Ct NW8 ....236 D5
7 Mitcham CR4 ....181 A1
Penfold Ho 14 SE18 ....144 D6
Penfold La DA5 ....168 D3
Penfold Pl NW1 92 C2 237 A4
Penfold Rd N9 ....18 D3
Penfold St NW8 92 B3 236 D5
Penford Gdns SE9 ....143 D2
Penford St SE5 ....138 D3
Pengarth Rd DA5 ....168 D5
Penge East Sta SE20 ....184 C4
Penge La SE20 ....184 D3
Penge Rd E13 ....99 C6
South Norwood SE25 ....206 A6
Penge West Sta SE20 ....184 B4
Penhall Rd SE7 ....121 D2
Penhill Rd DA5 ....168 C4
Penhurst Mans SW6 ....264 C2
Penifather La UB6 ....86 B4
Peninsula Ct E14 ....119 D3
Peninsular Cl TW14 ....149 C5
Peninsular Park Rd
SE7 ....121 A2
Penistone Rd SW16 ....182 A3
Penketh Dr HA1 ....64 B5
Penmayne Ho SE11 ....261 B2
Penmon Rd SE2 ....124 A3
Pennack Rd SE15 ....139 D6
Penn Almshouse 1
SE10 ....142 A4
Pennant Mews
W8 ....113 D2 255 C4
Pennant Terr E17 ....35 B1
Pennard Mans 5
W12 ....112 C4
Pennard Rd W12 ....112 C4
Pennards The TW16 ....194 C6
Penn Cl Greenford UB6 ....85 D5
Harrow HA3 ....43 C5
Penn Ct NW9 ....45 B6
Penner Cl SW19 ....157 A2
Penners Gdns KT6 ....198 A2
Pennethorne Cl E9 ....96 C6
Pennethorne Ho
SW11 ....136 B2
Pennethorne Rd SE15 140 B5
Penn Gdns BR7 ....188 D1
Penn Ho NW8 ....237 A5
7 Edmonton N9 ....18 A1
Pennine Dr NW2 ....68 D6
Pennine La NW2 ....69 A6
Pennine Mans NW2 ....69 A6
Pennine Par NW2 ....69 A6
Pennine Way UB7 ....127 B5
Pennington Cl 10
SE27 ....183 B6
Pennington Ct 16 E1 ....118 A6
SE16 ....119 A5
Pennington Dr N21 ....16 A6
Pennington Lo 18 KT5 198 A4
Pennington St E1 ....118 B6
Pennington Way SE12 165 B2
Penniston Cl N17 ....33 A1
Penn La DA5 ....169 A5
Penn Rd N7 ....72 A4
Penn St N1 ....95 B6 235 D5
Penny Ct SW10 ....266 B6
Pennyfields E14 ....119 C6
Pennyford Ct NW8 ....236 C6
Penny La TW17 ....193 C2
Penny Mews SW12 ....159 B4
Pennymore Wlk W9 ....91 B3
Penny Rd NW10 ....88 D4
Penny Royal SM6 ....219 D2
Pennyroyal Ave E6 ....100 C1
Penpoll Rd E8 ....74 B2
Penpool La DA16 ....146 B2
Penrhyn Ave E17 ....35 C2
Penrhyn Cres
Chingford E17 ....35 C2
Mortlake SW14 ....133 A1
Penrhyn Gdns KT1 ....197 D5
Penrhyn Gr E17 ....35 C2
Penrhyn Rd KT1 ....198 A6
Penrith Cl
Beckenham BR3 ....185 D2
Putney SW15 ....157 A6
Penrith Pl SE27 ....160 D2
Penrith Rd N15 ....51 B4
New Malden KT3 ....199 B5
South Norwood CR7 ....183 A1
Penrith St SW16 ....181 C4
Penrose Gr
SE17 ....117 A1 262 A1
Penrose Ho SE17 ....262 A1
Southgate N21 ....16 B6
Penrose St
SE17 ....117 A1 262 A1
Penryn Ho SE11 ....261 C2
Penryn St NW1 93 D5 232 C4
Penry St SE1 ....263 B3
Pensbury Pl SW8 ....137 C3
Pensbury St SW8 ....137 C3
Pensford Ave TW9 ....132 C3
Penshurst 2 NW5 ....71 A2
Penshurst Ave DA15 ....168 A5
Penshurst Gdns HA8 ....26 D5
Penshurst Gn BR2 ....208 D4
Penshurst Ho 1 SE15 140 C6
Penshurst Rd DA7 ....147 B4
E9 ....74 D1
Thornton Heath CR7 ....204 D4
Tottenham N17 ....33 D3
Penshurst Way SM2 ....217 C1
Penshurst Wlk 4 BR2 208 D4
Pensilver Cl EN4 ....2 C1
Penstemon Cl N3 ....29 C4
Pentelow Gdns TW14 ....150 A5
Pentire Rd E17 ....36 B2
Pentland Ave
Edgware HA8 ....10 D2
Littleton TW17 ....192 C4
Pentland Cl N9 ....18 C2
NW11 ....69 A6
Pentland Ho 7 N16 ....51 D1
17 NW5 ....71 A2
Pentland Pl UB5 ....85 A6
Pentland Rd WD23 ....8 A5
Pentlands BR3 ....186 A2
Pentlands Cl CR4 ....203 B6
Pentland St SW18 ....158 A5
Pentland Way UB10 ....61 A5
Pentlow St SW15 ....134 C2
Pentney Rd
5 Chingford E4 ....20 B3
Merton SW19,SW20 ....179 A2
Streatham SW12 ....159 C3
Penton Gr N1 ....234 A3
Penton Ho N1 ....234 A3
3 SE2 ....124 D4
Sutton SM2 ....218 A1
Penton Pl
SE17 ....116 D1 261 D2
Penton Rise
WC1 ....94 B4 233 D2
Penton St N1 ....94 C5 234 A3
Pentonville Rd
N1 ....94 B5 233 C3
Pentrich Ave EN1 ....6 A5
Pentridge St SE15 ....139 D5
Pentyre Ave N18 ....33 B5
Penwerris Ave TW5,
TW7 ....130 A5
Penwerris Ct TW7 ....130 A5
Penwith Rd SW18 ....157 D2
Penwood Ho 4 SW15 155 D5
Penwortham Ct 1 N22 32 C1
Penwortham Prim Sch
SW17 ....181 B4
Penwortham Rd SW16 181 C4
Penylan Pl HA8 ....26 C3
Penywern Rd
SW5 ....113 C1 255 B2
Penzance Ho SE11 ....261 B2
Penzance Pl
W11 ....113 A5 244 B4
Penzance St
W11 ....113 A5 244 A4
Peony Ct IG8 ....36 C3
Peony Gdns W12 ....112 A6
Peperfield WC1 ....233 C1
Pepler Ho 17 W10 ....91 A3
Pepler Mews SE1 ....263 C1
Peploe Rd NW6 ....90 D5
Pepper Cl E6 ....100 B2
Peppermead Sq SE13 163 C6
Peppermint Cl CR0 ....204 A2
Peppermint Pl 5 E11 ....76 C5
Pepper St E14 ....119 D3
SE1 ....252 A2
Peppie Cl N16 ....73 C6
Pepsi Trocadero W1 ....249 C5
Pepys Cl UB10 ....60 D4
Pepys Cres 2 E16 ....121 A5
Barnet EN5 ....12 C6
Pepys Ct SW20 ....178 C1
Pepys Ent Ctr 12 SE8 ....119 B2
Pepys Ho 14 E2 ....96 C4
SW4 ....159 D6
Pepys Rd SE14 ....140 D3
Wimbledon SW20 ....178 C2
Pepys Rise BR6 ....211 D1
Pepys St EC3 ....117 C6 253 B6
Perak Ct KT5 ....199 A2
Perceval Ave NW3 ....70 C3
Perceval Ct UB5 ....63 C3
Percheron Cl TW7 ....130 D2
Percheron Ct 3 SW9 ....138 B2
Percheron Rd WD6 ....11 B5
Perch St E8 ....73 D4
Percival Ct N17 ....33 D3
Percival Gdns RM6 ....58 C3
Percival Rd Enfield EN1 ....5 D1
Feltham TW13 ....149 D2
Mortlake SW14 ....133 A1
Orpington BR6 ....226 D6
Percival St EC1 94 D4 234 D1
Percival Way KT19 ....215 B4
Percy Ave TW15 ....170 C5
Percy Bilton Ct TW5 ....129 D4
Percy Bryant Rd TW16 171 C3
Percy Bush Rd UB7 ....104 B3
Percy Cir WC1 ....94 B4 233 D2
Percy Ct 1 KT5 ....198 B3
Percy Gdns Enfield EN3 ....18 D6
Hayes UB4 ....83 C4
3 Isleworth TW7 ....131 A2
New Malden KT4 ....199 C1
Percy Ho 4 SW16 ....181 C6
Percy Mews W1 ....239 C3
Percy Pas W1 ....239 C3
Percy Rd DA7 ....147 A3
E11 ....54 C2
E16 ....98 C2
N12 ....30 A5
W12 ....112 A4
Carshalton CR4 ....203 A2
Croydon SE25 ....206 A4
Edmonton N21 ....17 A4
Hampton TW12 ....173 C3
Ilford IG3 ....58 A2
Isleworth TW7 ....131 A1
Penge SE20 ....184 D2
Romford RM7 ....59 D6
Twickenham TW2 ....152 A3
Percy St W1 ....93 D2 239 C3
Percy Way TW2 ....152 A3
Peregrine Cl NW10 ....67 B3
Peregrine Ct DA16 ....145 D4
Streatham SW16 ....182 B6
Peregrine Gdns CR0 ....223 A6
Peregrine Ho EC1 ....234 D2
6 SW11 ....136 C2
Peregrine Rd TW16 ....171 D1
Peregrine Way SW19,
SW20 ....178 C3
Performing Arts & Tech Sch
SE25 ....205 B3
Perham Rd
W14 ....113 B1 254 B1
Peridot St E6 ....100 A2
Perifield SE21 ....161 A3
Perimeade Rd UB6 ....87 C5
Periton Rd SE9 ....143 D1
Perivale UB6 ....86 D5
Perivale Fst & Mid Schs
UB6 ....87 C5
Perivale Gdns W13 ....87 B3
Perivale Grange UB6 ....87 A4
Perivale Ind Pk UB6 ....87 B5
Perivale La UB6 ....87 A4
Perivale Lo UB6 ....87 A4
Perivale New Bsns Ctr
UB6 ....87 C5
Perivale Sta UB6 ....87 A5
Perkin Cl
Hounslow TW3 ....129 D1
Wembley HA0 ....65 B3
Perkins Ct TW15 ....170 B5
Perkins Ho 13 E14 ....97 B2
Perkins Rd IG2 ....57 B4
Perkins Rents SW1 ....259 C5
Perkins Sq SE1 ....252 B4
Perks Cl SE3 ....142 C2
Perley Ho 10 E3 ....97 B2
Perotti Ho SW6 ....135 D2
Perpins Rd SE9 ....167 C5
Perran Rd SE24,SW2 ....160 D2
Perren St NW5 ....71 B2
Perrers Rd W6 ....112 B2
Perrin Cl TW15 ....170 B5
Perring Est E3 ....97 C2
Perrin Grange HA9 ....66 B6
Perrin Rd HA0 ....65 B4
Perrin's Ct 17 NW3 ....70 A4
Perrin's La NW3 ....70 A4
Perrin's Wlk NW3 ....70 A4
Perronet Ho SE1 ....261 D5
Perry Ave W3 ....89 B1
Perry Cl UB8 ....82 D1
Perry Ct 2 N15 ....51 C3
5 Millwall E14 ....119 C1
Perryfield Way NW9 ....45 D3
Richmond TW10 ....153 B2
Perry Garth UB5 ....84 C6
Perry Gdns N9 ....17 C1
Perry Hall Prim Sch
BR6 ....211 D3
Perry Hill SE6 ....163 B1
Perry Ho 24 SW2 ....160 A4
Perry How KT4 ....199 D1
Perryman Ho IG11 ....101 A6
Perrymans Farm Rd
IG2 ....57 B4
Perry Mead Bushey WD23 8 A5
Enfield EN2 ....4 D3
Perrymead St
SW6 ....135 D3 265 C1
Perrymount Prim Sch
SE23 ....162 D2
Perryn Ct 1 TW1 ....153 A4
Perryn Ho W3 ....111 C6
Perryn Rd 1 SE16 ....118 B3
W3 ....111 B6
Perry Rise SE23 ....163 A1
Perry's Pl W1 ....239 C2
Perry St BR7 ....189 C4
Perry Street Gdns
BR7 ....189 C4
Perry Vale SE23 ....162 D2
Perrywood Ho 17 E5 ....74 B3
Persant Rd SE6 ....164 C2
Perserverance Pl
SW9 ....138 C5
Perseverance Works 18
E2 ....95 C4
Pershore Cl IG2 ....56 D4
Pershore Gr SM5 ....202 B3
Pert Cl N10 ....31 B4
Perth Ave NW9 ....45 B2
Hayes UB4 ....84 C3
Perth Cl SW20 ....178 A1
Perth Ct 5 SE5 ....139 B1
Perth Ho N1 ....72 B1
12 Acton W3 ....88 C1
Perth Rd E10 ....53 B1
E13 ....99 B5
N4 ....50 C1
Barking IG11 ....101 B6
Beckenham BR3 ....186 A1
Ilford IG2 ....56 D3
Tottenham N22 ....32 D2
Perth Terr IG2 ....57 A2
Perwell Ave HA2 ....41 B1
Perystreete SE23 ....162 C2
Petavel Rd TW11 ....174 C4
Peter Ave NW10 ....68 B1
Peter Best Ho 6 E1 ....96 B1
Peterboat Cl SE10 ....120 C2
Peterborough Ct EC4 241 B1
Peterborough Gdns
IG1 ....56 A2
Peterborough Mews
SW6 ....135 C3
Peterborough Prim Sch
SW6 ....135 C3
Peterborough Rd E10 ....54 B3
SW6 ....135 C2
Carshalton SM5 ....202 C3
Harrow HA1 ....42 D2
Peterborough Villas
SW6 ....265 C2
Peter Bradley Ct RM9 ....81 B1
Peter Butler Ho 6
SE1 ....118 A4
Peterchurch Ho SE15 ....140 B6
Petergate SW11 ....136 A1
Peterhead Ct 12 UB1 ....86 A1
Peter Hills Ho 6 SE16 118 A2
Peter Hills with St Mary's &
St Paul's CE Prim Sch
SE16 ....118 D5
Peter Ho SW8 ....270 A4
Peter James Bsns Ctr
UB3 ....106 A4
Peter Kennedy Ct CR0 207 B3
Peterley Bsns Ctr 21 E2 96 B5
Peters Cl DA16 ....145 C3
Dagenham RM8 ....58 D1
Peters Cl continued
Stanmore HA7 ....25 D4
Peters Ct 9 W2 ....91 D1
Peter's Ct SW4 ....160 A5
Petersfield Cl N18 ....33 A5
Petersfield Rd W3 ....111 A4
Petersfield Rise SW15 156 B3
Petersham Cl
Richmond TW10 ....153 D2
Sutton SM1 ....217 C3
Petersham Dr BR5 ....190 A1
Petersham Gdns BR5 ....189 D1
Petersham Ho SW7 ....256 C4
Petersham La SW7 ....256 A6
Petersham Mews
SW7 ....114 A3 256 B5
Petersham Pl
SW7 ....114 A3 256 B6
Petersham Rd TW10 ....154 A3
Petersham Terr CR0 ....220 A5
Peter's La EC1 ....241 D4
Peter's Lo HA8 ....26 B4
Peter's Path SE26 ....184 B6
Peter St W1 ....115 D6 249 C6
Peterstone Rd SE2 ....124 B4
Peterstow Cl SW19 ....157 A2
Peterwood Pk CR9 ....220 B6
Peterwood Way CR0 ....220 B6
Petherton Ct NW10 ....90 D6
10 Harrow HA1 ....42 D3
Petherton Ho N4 ....51 A1
Petherton Rd N5 ....73 A3
Petiver Cl 26 E9 ....74 C1
Petley Rd W6 ....134 D5
Peto Pl NW1 ....238 D6
Peto St N E16 ....98 D1
Petrel Ct 7 SE21 ....161 B2
Petrie Cl NW2 ....69 A2
Petrie Ho 3 SE18 ....144 C6
Petros Gdns 1 NW3 ....70 A2
Petticoat Lane Mkt★
EC2 ....95 D2 243 C3
Petticoat Sq E1 ....243 C2
Petticoat Twr E1 ....243 C2
Pettit's Pl RM10 ....81 C3
Pettit's Rd RM10 ....81 C3
Pettiward Cl SW15 ....134 C1
Pettman Cres SE18,
SE28 ....123 B3
Pettsgrove Ave HA0 ....65 C3
Pett's Hill UB5 ....63 D3
Petts La TW17 ....192 C5
Pett St SE7 ....122 A2
Petts Wood Rd BR5 ....211 B4
Petts Wood Sta BR5 ....211 A4
Petty France
SW1 ....115 C3 259 C6
Petworth Cl UB5 ....63 B1
Petworth Gdns
Hillingdon UB10 ....83 A6
West Barnes SW20 ....200 B6
Petworth Ho 16 SE22 ....139 C2
Petworth Rd DA6 ....169 C6
N12 ....30 C5
Petworth St
SW11 ....136 C4 267 B2
Petyt Pl SW3 ....136 C6 267 A5
Petyward SW3 114 C2 257 B3
Pevensey Ave N11 ....31 D5
Enfield EN1 ....5 C3
Pevensey Cl TW7 ....130 A5
Pevensey Ct 4 W3 ....110 D4
West Norwood SW16 ....160 C1
10 Woodford E18 ....37 A2
Pevensey Ho 5 E1 ....97 A2
Pevensey Rd E7 ....77 A4
Feltham TW13 ....151 A3
Upper Tooting SW17 ....180 B6
Peverel E6 ....100 C1
Peverel Ho RM10 ....81 C6
Peverett Cl N11 ....31 B5
Peveril Dr TW11 ....174 B5
Peveril Ho SE1 ....262 D5
Pewsey Cl E4 ....35 C5
Pewsham Ho N4 ....51 A1
Pewterers Ct N3 ....29 B2
Peyton Ho N11 ....31 A6
Peyton Pl SE10 ....142 A5
Pharamond NW2 ....68 D2
Pharaoh Cl CR4 ....202 D2
Pheasant Cl E16 ....99 B1
Phelps Ho SW15 ....134 D2
Phelp St SE17 ....139 B6
Phelps Way UB3 ....105 D2
Phene St SW3 ....136 C6 267 B6
Philadelphia Ct SW10 266 B3
Philbeach Gdns
SW5 ....113 C1 255 A2
Phil Brown Pl 3 SW8 137 B2
Philchurch Pl 25 E1 ....96 A1
Phildor Ct NW11 ....47 A3
Philia Ho 2 NW1 ....71 C1
Philimore Cl SE18 ....123 C1
Philip Ct W2 ....236 C4
Enfield EN2 ....5 B4
Philip Gdns CR0 ....223 B6
Philip Ho N20 ....14 D2
10 NW6 ....91 D6
Philip La N15 ....51 C6
Philipot Almshouse
SE9 ....166 B5
Philipot Path SE9 ....166 B5
Philippa Gdns SE9 ....165 D6
Philip Rd SE15 ....140 A2
Philips Cl CR4 ....203 A1
Philip St E13 ....99 A3
Philip Turner Est 28 E9 ....74 C1
Philip Wlk SE15 ....140 B2
Phillimore Ct W8 ....245 B1
Phillimore Gardens Cl
W8 ....113 C3 255 A6
Phillimore Gdns
W8 ....113 C4 245 A1
Willesden NW10 ....90 C6
Phillimore Pl
W8 ....113 C4 245 A1
Phillimore Terr W8 ....255 B6
Phillimore Wlk
W8 ....113 C3 255 B6
Phillip Ho E1 ....243 D3
Phillipp St N1 ....95 C6
Phillips Ct Edgware HA8 ....26 C4
Hayes UB4 ....84 B4
Philpot La EC3 ....253 A6
Philpot Sq SW6 ....135 D2
Philpot St E1 ....96 B1
Phineas Pett Rd SE9 ....144 A2
Phipp's Bridge Rd CR4,
SW19 ....202 B6
Phipps Bridge Sta
CR4 ....202 B6
Phipps Hatch La EN2 ....5 A5
Phipps Ho 1 SE7 ....121 B1
16 W12 ....112 B6
Phipp St EC2 ....95 C3 243 A6
Phoebeth Rd SE4 ....163 C6
Phoenix Bsns Ctr E3 ....97 C2
Phoenix Cl E17 ....35 B1
18 E8 ....95 D6
West Wickham BR4 ....224 C6
Phoenix Coll SM4 ....202 A4
Phoenix Ct E14 ....119 C2
2 SE14 ....141 A6
4 Brentford TW8 ....110 A1
Chingford E4 ....19 D1
Croydon SE25 ....206 A4
Enfield EN3 ....6 C5
Phoenix Dr BR2 ....225 D5
Phoenix High Sch
W12 ....112 A6
Phoenix Ind Est HA1 ....42 D5
Phoenix Lodge Mans 1
W6 ....112 C2
Phoenix Pk NW2 ....68 A6
Phoenix Pl WC1 94 B3 240 D6
Phoenix Rd
NW1 ....93 D4 232 C2
Penge SE20 ....184 C4
Phoenix Sch E3 ....97 B4
Phoenix Sch The NW3 ....70 A2
Phoenix St WC2 ....239 D1
Phoenix Trad Est UB6 ....87 D6
Phoenix Trad Pk TW8 ....109 D1
Phoenix Way TW5 ....128 D6
Phoenix Wharf Rd
SE1 ....253 D1
Phyllis Ave KT3 ....200 B4
Phyllis Ho CR0 ....220 D4
Phyllis Hodges Ho
NW1 ....93 D5 232 C3
Physic Pl SW3 136 D6 267 C6
Picador Ho 1 RM10 ....81 D2
Picardy Manorway
DA17 ....125 D4
Picardy Rd DA17 ....125 C2
Picardy St DA17 ....125 C3
Piccadilly W1 ....115 C5 249 A4
Piccadilly Arc SW1 ....249 A4
Piccadilly Cir★
W1 ....115 D6 249 C5
Piccadilly Circus Sta
SW1 ....115 D6 249 C5
Piccadilly Pl W1 ....249 B5
Pickard St EC1 ....234 D2
Pickering Ave E6 ....100 C4
Pickering Gdns N11 ....31 A4
Croydon SE25 ....205 D3
Pickering Ho N4 ....51 B2
4 SE18 ....122 C2
17 W2 ....91 D1
W5 ....109 C2
Pickering Mews W2 ....91 D1
Pickering Pl SW1 ....249 B3
Pickering St N1 ....234 D6
Pickets Cl WD23 ....8 C3
Pickets St SW12 ....159 B4
Pickett Croft HA7 ....25 D2
Pickett's Lock La N9 ....18 D2
Pickford Cl DA7 ....147 A3
Pickford La DA7 ....147 A3
Pickford Rd DA7 ....147 A2
Pickfords Wharf N1 ....235 A3
Pickhurst Gn BR2 ....208 D2
Pickhurst Inf Sch BR2 208 D3

Pickhurst Jun Sch BR2 208 D3
Pickhurst La BR2,BR3, BR4 208 C2
Pickhurst Mead BR2 208 D2
Pickhurst Pk BR2 208 D4
Pickhurst Rise BR4 208 B1
Pickwick Cl TW4 151 A6
Pickwick Ct SE9 166 B3
Pickwick Ho 18 SE16 118 A4
3 W11 112 D5
Pickwick Mews N18 33 C5
Pickwick Pl HA1 42 C2
Pickwick Rd SE21 161 C4
Pickwick St SE1 252 A1
Pickwick Way BR7 189 A4
Pickworth Cl SW8 270 B3
Picton Ho 1 SW4 160 A4
Picton Pl W1 238 B1
Tolworth KT6 198 C1
Picton St SE5 139 B5
Pied Bull Ct WC1 240 B3
Pied Bull Yd WC1 240 B3
Piedmont Rd SE18 123 B1
Pield Heath Ave UB8 82 C3
Pield Heath Rd UB8 82 B3
Pield Heath Sch UB8 82 A3
Pierhead Wharf 37 E1 118 B5
Pier Ho SW3 267 B5
Piermont Pl BR1 188 A1
Piermont Rd SE22 162 B6
Pier Par 3 E16 122 C5
Pierpoint Bldg 5 E14 119 C4
Pier Rd E16 122 C4
Feltham TW14 150 B6
Pierrepoint SE25 205 C6
Pierrepoint Rd W3 110 D6
Pierson Ho 12 SE19 183 C6
Pier St E14 120 A2
Pier Terr SW18 136 A1
Pier Way SE18 123 B3
Pigeon Ct E4 36 A4
Pigeon La TW12 173 C6
Piggott Ho 2 E2 96 D5
Pigott St E14 97 C1
Pike Cl BR1 187 B5
Hillingdon UB10 82 B6
Pike Rd NW7 27 B6
Pike's End HA5 40 B5
Pikestone Cl UB4 85 A3
Pikethorne SE23 162 D2
Pilgrimage St SE1 117 B4 252 C1
Pilgrim Cl SM4 201 D2
Pilgrim Hill SE27 183 A6
Pilgrim Ho SE1 262 D5
Pilgrims Cl Northolt UB5 64 A3
Palmers Green N13 32 B6
Pilgrims Cloisters 18 SE5 139 C5
Pilgrims Ct SE3 143 A4
Enfield EN1 5 B3
Pilgrim's La NW3 70 B4
Pilgrims Mews E14 120 B6
Pilgrim's Rise EN4 14 C6
Pilgrim St EC4 241 C1
Pilgrims Way 5 E6 100 A6
N19 49 D1
Wembley HA9 44 D1
Pilgrim's Way CR2 221 D3
Pilgrims Way Prim Sch SE15 140 C6
Pilkington Ct 1 NW9 46 A5
Pilkington Rd 4 SE15 140 B3
Orpington BR6 227 A6
Pillar of Fire Society Church & Bible Sch NW4 46 D4
Pillions La UB4 83 B3
Pilot Ind Ctr NW10 89 C3
Pilsden Cl SW19 156 D3
Piltdown Rd WD19 22 D6
Pilton Est The CR0 220 D6
Pilton Pl SE17 262 B2
Pimento Ct W5 109 D3
Pimilico Sta SW1 115 D1 259 C2
Pimlico Rd SW1 115 A1 258 B2
Pimlico Sch SW1 115 C1 259 B1
Pimlico Wlk 1 N1 95 C4
Pinchbeck Rd BR6 227 D2
Pinchin St E1 118 A6
Pincombe Ho SE17 262 C2
Pincott Pl SE4 140 D2
Pincott Rd
8 Bexley DA6 147 C1
Merton SW19 180 A2
Pindar St EC2 95 C2 243 A4
Pindock Mews W9 91 D3
Pine Apple Ct SW1 259 A6
Pine Ave E15 76 B3
West Wickham BR4 207 D1
Pine Cl N14 15 C4
8 N19 71 C6
Pine Cl *continued*
E10 75 D6
3 Penge SE20 184 C2
Stanmore HA7 25 B6
Pine Coombe CR0 222 D4
Pinecrest Gdns BR6 226 D4
Pinecroft DA16 146 A5
Harrow HA3 44 B4
Pinecroft Cres EN5 1 A1
Pine Ct UB5 85 A4
Pinedene 2 SE15 140 B4
Pinefield Cl E14 119 C6
Pine Gdns Ruislip HA4 62 B6
Surbiton KT5 198 C3
Pine Glade BR6 226 B4
Pine Gr N20 13 C3
N4,N19 72 B6
Wimbledon SW19 179 B5
Pine Ho 15 SE16 118 C4
Pinehurst BR7 188 D4
Pinehurst Ct 5 W11 91 B1
Pinehurst Wlk 4 BR6 211 B1
Pinelands Cl 7 SE3 142 D5
Pine Lo SW15 157 A5
Pinemartin Cl NW2 68 C5
Pine Pl UB4 83 D3
Pine Rd N11 15 A2
NW2 68 D4
Pine Ridge SM5 219 A1
Pines Ct 14 SW19 156 D3
Pines Rd BR1 188 A1
Pine St EC1 94 C3 241 A6
Pines The Southgate N14 15 C6
South Norwood SE19 182 D4
Sunbury TW16 194 A6
Woodford IG8 21 A1
Pine Tree Cl TW5 128 B4
Pine Tree Ho SE14 140 D5
Pine Tree Lo BR2 208 D5
Pine Trees Dr UB10 60 A4
Pineview Ct 5 E4 20 A3
Pine Wlk KT5 198 C3
Pinewood BR7 188 C4
Pine Wood TW16 172 A2
Pinewood Ave DA15 167 C3
Hillingdon UB8 82 B1
Pinner HA5 23 D4
Pinewood Cl BR6 211 B1
Croydon CR0 223 A5
Pinner HA5 23 D4
Pinewood Ct SW4 159 D5
Enfield EN2 4 D2
Pinewood Dr BR6 227 C3
Pinewood Gr W5 87 C1
Pinewood Pl KT19 215 B4
Pinewood Rd BR2 209 A5
SE2 146 D6
Feltham TW13 150 B1
Pinfold Rd SW16 182 A6
Pinglestone Cl UB7 126 A5
Pinkcoat Cl TW13 150 B1
Pinkerton Ct KT2 176 D1
Pinkerton Pl SW16 181 D6
Pinkham Mans W4 110 C1
Pinkham Way (North Circular Rd)
N12 30 D3
N12 31 A4
Pinkwell Ave UB3 105 B2
Pinkwell Jun & Inf Schs UB3 105 A2
Pinkwell La UB3 105 B2
Pinley Gdns RM9 102 B6
Pinnacle Hill DA7 147 D1
Pinnacle Hill N DA7 147 D1
Pinnacle Ho E14 120 A3
Pinnell Rd SE9 143 D1
Pinner Ct HA5 41 C5
Pinner Gn HA5 22 C1
Pinner Gr HA5 41 A4
Pinner Hill HA5 22 B3
Pinner Hill Rd HA5 22 C1
Pinner Ho 31 SE5 139 A3
Pinner Park Ave HA2 24 A1
Pinner Park Fst & Mid Schs HA5 41 D6
Pinner Park Gdns HA2 24 A1
Pinner Rd
Harrow HA1,HA2 42 A3
Harrow, Pinner HA2,HA5 41 C5
Pinner HA6 22 A1
Pinner Sta HA5 41 A5
Pinner View HA1,HA2 42 A4
Pinner Wood Fst & Mid Schs HA5 22 C2
Pinn Way HA4 39 C2
Pintail Cl E6 100 A2
Pintail Ct 40 SE8 141 B6
Pintail Rd IG8 37 B3
Pintail Way UB4 84 D2
Pinter Ho 30 SW9 138 A3
Pinto Cl WD6 11 B5
Pinto Way SE3 143 B1
Pioneer Cl W12 90 B1
Pioneers Ind Pk CR0 204 A1
Pioneer St SE15 140 A4
Pioneer Way W12 90 C1
Piper Cl N7 72 B2
Piper Rd KT1 198 C6
Pipers Gdns CR0 207 A2
Pipers Gn NW9 45 A4
Pipers Green La HA8 10 A1
Pipewell Rd SM5 202 C3
Pippenhall SE9 166 D5
Pippin Cl NW2 68 B5
Croydon CR0 207 B1
Pippin Ct 5 EN4 2 C1
Pippins Ct TW15 170 D4
Piquet Rd SE20 184 C1
Pirbright Cres CR0 224 A2
Pirbright Ho 11 KT2 176 D4
Pirbright Rd SW18 157 C3
Pirie St 6 E16 121 B5
Pitcairn Cl RM7 59 C5
Pitcairn Ho 1 E9 74 C1
Pitcairn Rd CR4 180 D3
Pitchford St E15 76 C1
Pitfield Cres SE28 124 A5
Pitfield Ho N5 73 A3
Pitfield St N1 95 C5
Pitfield Way NW10 67 A2
Enfield EN3 6 C4
Pitfold Cl SE12 165 B5
Pitfold Rd SE12 165 A4
Pit Ho NW10 67 B5
Pitlake CR0 220 D6
Pitman Ho 4 SE8 141 C4
Southgate N21 16 B6
Pitmans Coll HA0 65 D2
Pitman St SE5 139 A5
Pitmaston Ho 2 SE13 142 A3
Pitsea Pl E1 96 D1
Pitsea St E1 96 D1
Pitshanger Ct 2 W5 87 C3
Pitshanger La W5 87 C3
Pitshanger Manor Mus & Art Gallery★ W5 109 D5
Pitt Cres SW19 179 D6
Pitt Ho 4 SW11 136 B1
Pittman Gdns IG1 79 A3
Pitt Rd BR6 227 A4
Harrow HA2 64 A6
Thornton Heath CR0, CR7 205 A4
Pitt's Head Mews W1 248 B3
Pittsmead Ave BR2 209 A2
Pitt St W8 113 C4 245 B2
Pittville Gdns SE25 206 A6
Pixfield Ct BR2 186 D1
Pixley St E14 97 B1
Pixton 11 NW9 27 C2
Pixton Way CR2 223 B1
Place Farm Ave BR5, BR6 211 B1
Plains The 7 E4 20 C4
Plaistow Gr BR1 187 B3
E15 98 D6
Plaistow Hospl E13 99 C5
Plaistow La BR1 187 C2
Plaistow Park Rd E13 99 B5
Plaistow Prim Sch E13 99 B5
Plaistow Rd E13,E15 98 D5
Plaistow Sta E13 98 D5
Plane St SE26 162 B1
Planetarium The★ NW1 93 A3 238 A5
Plane Tree Cres TW13 150 B1
Planetree Ct W6 112 D2
Plane Tree Ho SE7 121 D1
SE8 141 A6
Plane Tree Wlk 4 SE19 183 C4
Plantagenet Cl KT19 215 B4
Plantagenet Gdns RM6 58 D2
Plantagenet Ho SE18 122 B3
Plantagenet Pl RM6 58 D2
Plantagenet Rd EN5 2 A1
Plantain Pl SE1 252 C2
Plantation The SE3 143 A3
Plasel Ct E13 99 B6
Plashet Gr E6 77 D1
Plashet Rd E13 77 B1
Plashet Sch E6 78 A1
Plassy Rd SE6 163 D4
Platina St EC2 242 D6
Plato Pl 1 SW6 135 B3
Plato Rd SW2 138 A1
Platt Halls (a) 35 NW9 27 D1
Platt Halls (b) 37 NW9 27 D1
Platt Halls (c) 38 NW9 27 D1
Platt's Eyot TW12 173 C1
Platt's La NW3 69 C5
Platts Rd EN3 6 C4
Platt St NW1 232 C4
Plaxdale Ho SE17 263 A3
Plaxtol Cl BR1 187 C2
Plaxtol Rd DA8 147 C5
Plaxton Ct E11 76 D5
Playfair St W6 112 C1
Playfield Cres SE22 161 D6
Playfield Rd HA8 27 A1
Playford Rd N4 72 B6
N4 72 C6
Playgreen Way SE6 185 C6
Playground Cl BR3 184 D1
Playhouse Yd EC4 241 C1
Plaza Bsns Ctr EN3 7 B3
Pleasance Rd BR5 190 B1
Pleasance Rd *continued*
Putney SW15 156 B6
Pleasance The SW15 134 B1
Pleasant Gr CR0 223 B5
Pleasant Pl N1 72 D1
Pleasant Row NW1 231 D5
Pleasant View BR6 227 A3
Pleasant View Pl BR6 227 A3
Pleasant Way HA0 87 C5
Pleasaunce Ct SE9 144 B1
Plender Ct NW1 232 B5
Plender St NW1 93 C6 232 B5
Pleshey Rd N7 71 D4
Plevna Cres N15 51 C3
Plevna Ho 1 N9 18 A1
Plevna Rd Edmonton N9 18 B1
Hampton TW12 173 D2
Plevna St E14 120 A3
Pleydell Ave W6 111 D2
Penge SE19 183 D3
Pleydell Ct EC4 241 B1
Pleydell Gdns SE19 183 D4
Pleydell St EC4 241 B1
Plimsoll Cl E14 97 D1
Plimsoll Rd N4 72 D5
Plough Ct EC3 252 D6
Plough Farm Cl HA4 39 B3
Plough La SE22 161 D5
Wallington CR0,SM6 220 A3
Wimbledon SW17,SW19 180 A6
Plough Lane Cl CR0, SM6 220 A3
Ploughmans Cl NW1 232 C6
Ploughmans End TW7 152 B6
Plough Pl EC4 241 B2
Plough Rd SW11 136 B1
West Ewell KT19 215 B1
Plough St 10 E1 96 A1
Plough Terr SW11 136 B1
Plough Way SE16 119 A2
Plough Yd EC2 243 B5
Plover Ho 4 SW9 138 C5
Plover Way SE16 119 A3
Hayes UB4 84 D2
Plowman Cl N18 33 B5
Plowman Ho SW19 156 D2
Plowman Way RM8 58 C1
Plumbers Row E1 96 A1
Plumbridge St 7 SE10 142 A4
Plum Cl TW14 150 A3
Plumcroft Prim Sch SE18 145 A6
Plume Ho SE10 141 D6
Plum Garth TW8 109 D2
Plum La SE18 145 A5
Plummer Ct SE13 163 D5
Plummer La CR4 180 D1
Plummer Rd SW4 159 D4
Plumpton Cl UB5 63 C2
Plumpton Way SM5 218 C5
Plumstead Common Rd SE18 145 A6
Plumstead High St SE18,SE2 123 C2
Plumstead Manor Sch SE18 145 B6
Plumstead Rd SE18, SE28 123 A2
Plumstead Sta SE18 123 B2
Plumtree Cl
Dagenham RM10 81 D2
Wallington SM6 219 D1
Plumtree Ct EC4 241 C2
Plymouth Ho 10 IG11 80 A1
Plymouth Rd BR1 187 B2
E16 99 A2
Plymouth Wharf E14 120 B2
Plympton Ave NW6 69 B1
Plympton Cl 8 DA17 125 A3
Plympton Pl NW1 237 A5
Plympton Rd NW6 69 B1
Plympton St NW8 237 A5
Plymstock Rd DA16 146 C5
Pocklington Cl NW9 27 C1
Pocklington Ct SW15 156 A3
Pocock Ave UB7 104 B3
Pocock St SE1 116 D4 251 D2
Podmore Rd SW18 136 A1
Poets Corner SW1 260 A6
Poet's Rd N5 73 B3
Poets Way HA1 42 C5
Pointalls Cl N3 30 A1
Point Cl SE10 142 A4
Pointer Cl SE28 102 D1
Pointer Sch The SE3 143 A5
Pointers Cl E14 119 D1
Point Hill SE10 142 A4
Point Pl HA9 66 D1
Point Pleasant SW18 135 C1
Point Terr E7 77 B3
Poland St W1 93 C1 239 B1
Polebrook Rd SE3 143 C2
Polecroft La SE6 163 B2
Polehamptons The TW12 174 A2
Pole Hill Rd
Chingford E4 20 A4
Hillingdon UB4 83 A4
Polesden Gdns SW20 178 B1
Polesworth Ho 16 W2 91 C2
Polesworth Rd RM9 80 D1
Polish Univ Abroad W6 112 A2
Polish War Meml HA4 62 C2
Pollard Cl E16 121 A6
N7 72 B4
Pollard Ho N1 233 C3
Cheam KT4 216 C4
Pollard Rd N20 14 C2
Morden SM4 202 B4
Pollard Row E2 96 A4
Pollards Cl IG10 21 C6
Pollards Cres SW16 204 A6
Pollards Hill E SW16 204 B6
Pollards Hill N SW16 204 B6
Pollards Hill S SW16 204 B6
Pollards Hill W SW16 204 B6
Pollard St E2 96 A4
Pollards Wood Rd SW16 204 A6
Pollard Wlk DA14 190 C4
Pollen St W1 238 D1
Pollitt Dr NW8 92 B3 236 D6
Pollock Ho W10 91 A3
Polperro Cl BR6 211 D3
Polperro Mans 3 NW6 69 C3
Polperro Mews SE11 261 D4
Polsted Rd SE6 163 B4
Polsten Mews EN3 7 C6
Polthorne Gr SE18 123 B2
Polworth Rd SW16 182 A5
Polygon Rd NW1 93 D5 232 C3
Polygon The NW8 229 D6
1 SW4 137 C1
Polytechnic St SE18 122 C2
Pomell Way E1 243 D2
Pomeroy Ct W11 91 A1
Pomeroy Ho 5 E2 96 D5
Pomeroy St SE14 140 C4
Pomfret Rd SE5 138 D2
Pomoja La N19 72 A6
Pomona Ho 10 SE8 119 A2
Pond Cl N12 30 C4
SE3 143 A3
Pond Cottage La BR3, BR4 207 C1
Pond Cotts SE21 161 C3
Ponders End Ind Est EN3 19 A6
Ponders End Sta EN3 19 A6
Ponder St 5 N7 72 B1
Pond Farm Est E5 74 C5
Pondfield End IG10 21 C4
Pondfield Ho 4 N5 73 A3
West Norwood SE27 183 A5
Pondfield Rd BR6 226 D5
Dagenham RM10 81 D3
West Wickham BR2 208 C1
Pond Gn HA4 61 C6
Pond Hill Gdns SM3 217 A2
Pond Ho SW3 257 A3
Pond Mead SE21 161 B5
Pond Path BR7 188 D4
Pond Pl SW3 114 C2 257 A3
Pond Rd E15 98 C5
SE3 142 D3
Pondside Cl UB3 127 B6
Pond Sq N6 49 A1
Pond St NW3 70 C3
Pond Way TW11 175 C4
Pondwood Rise BR6 211 C2
Ponler St E1 96 B1
Ponsard Rd NW10 90 B4
Ponsford St E9 74 C2
Ponsonby Pl SW1 115 D1 259 D2
Ponsonby Rd SW15 156 B4
Ponsonby Terr SW1 259 D2
Pontefract Ct UB5 63 D3
Pontefract Rd BR1 186 D5
Ponton Ho SW2 160 C3
Ponton Rd SW8 137 D6 269 D5
Pont St SW1 114 D3 257 D5
Pont St Mews SW1 257 C5
Pontypool Pl SE1 251 C2
Pool Cl Beckenham BR3 185 C5
East Molesey KT8 195 B4
Pool Ct SE6 163 C2
Poole Cl HA4 61 C6
Poole Court Rd TW5 129 A3
Poole Ct N1 73 C1
Hounslow TW5 129 A3
Poole Ho SE11 260 D5
Pool End Cl TW17 192 C4
Poole Rd E9 74 D2
West Ewell KT19 215 B2
Pooles Bldgs EC1 241 A5
Pooles Ct IG3 80 A5
Pooles La SW10 266 A3
Pooles Park Prim Sch N4 72 B6
Pooles Pk N4 72 C6
Poole St N1 95 B6 235 C5
Poole Way UB4 83 C4
Pool Ho NW8 236 D4
Poolmans St SE16 118 D4
Pool Rd
East Molesey KT12,KT8 195 B4
Harrow HA1 42 B2
Poolsford Rd NW9 45 C5
Poonah St E1 96 C1
Pope Cl
East Bedfont TW14 149 D3
Mitcham SW17,SW19 180 B4
Pope Ct 10 KT2 175 D6
Pope Ho 7 SE16 118 B2
3 SE5 139 B5
Pope John RC Prim Sch W12 112 B6
Pope Rd BR2 209 D4
Pope's Ave TW2 152 C2
Popes Dr N3 29 C2
Popes Gr CR0 223 B5
Pope's Gr TW1,TW2 152 D2
Pope's Head Alley EC3 242 D1
Pope's La W5 110 A3
Pope's Rd SW9 138 C2
Pope St SE1 253 B1
Pope Street Ct SE9 166 B3
Popham Cl TW13 151 B1
Popham Ct N16 73 C5
Popham Gdns TW9 132 D2
Popham Rd N1 95 A6 235 A6
Popham St N1 234 D6
N1 95 A6 235 A6
Poplar Ave
Mitcham CR4 180 D2
Orpington BR6 226 D6
Southall UB2 107 D3
Yiewsley UB7 104 B6
Poplar Bath St 10 E14 119 D6
Poplar Bsns Pk E14 120 A6
Poplar Cl E9 75 B3
Pinner HA5 22 D2
Poplar Cres KT19 215 A2
Poplar Ct Chingford E4 35 D4
Northolt UB5 84 C5
4 Streatham SW16 160 B1
13 Twickenham TW1 153 C5
Wimbledon SW19 179 C5
Poplar Farm Cl KT19 215 A2
Poplar Fst Sch SW19 201 C6
Poplar Gdns KT3 177 B1
Poplar Gr N11 31 A4
W6 112 C4
Kingston KT3 199 B6
Wembley HA9 67 A5
Poplar High St E14 119 D6
Poplar Ho 19 SE16 118 D4
SE4 141 B1
Poplar Mews W12 112 C5
Poplar Mount DA17 125 D2
Poplar Pl W2 113 D6 245 D6
Hayes UB3 106 A6
Woolwich SE28 124 C6
Poplar Rd SE24 139 A1
Ashford TW15 171 A5
Cheam SM3 201 B1
Merton SW19 179 C1
Poplar Rd S SW19 201 C6
Poplars Cl HA4 39 C1
Poplars Ho 14 E17 53 D6
Poplars Rd E17 53 D3
Poplar Sta E14 119 D6
Poplars The NW5 71 C3
East Barnet N14 15 B6
Poplar View HA9 65 D6
Poplar Way
Feltham TW13 150 B1
Ilford IG6 57 A5
Poplar Wlk SE24 139 A1
Croydon CR0 205 A1
Poppins Ct EC4 241 C1
Poppleton Rd E11 54 C3
Poppy Cl
Belvedere DA17 125 D4
Hackbridge SM6 203 A1
Poppy La CR0 206 C1
Porchester Ct W2 245 D6
Porchester Gate W2 246 A5
Porchester Gdn Mews W2 91 D1
Porchester Gdns W2 113 D6 245 D6
Porchester Mead BR3 185 D4
Porchester Mews W2 91 D1
Porchester Pl W2 237 B1
Porchester Rd W2 91 D1
Kingston KT1 176 D1
Porchester Sq W2 91 D1
Porchester Terr W2 114 A6 246 A6
Porchester Terr N W2 91 D1
Porch Way N20 14 D1
Porcupine Cl SE9 166 A2
Porden Rd SW2 138 B1
Porland Ct SE1 262 C6
Porlock Ave HA1,HA2 42 A1
Porlock Ho 6 SE26 162 A1
Porlock Rd EN1 17 D4
Porlock St SE1 117 B4 252 D2
Porrington Cl BR7 188 C2
Portal Cl Hillingdon UB10 60 B1

tal Cl *continued*
islip HA4 62 B4
est Norwood SE27 160 C1
tbury Cl 16 SE15 140 A4
tchester Cl SE24 139 B1
tchester Ct W2 91 D1
t Cres E13 99 B3
tcullis Lodge Rd EN1 5 B2
te 10 NW9 27 D2
telet Ct 1 N1 95 C6
telet Rd E1 96 D4
ten Hos W14 254 A5
ten Rd W14 254 A5
ter Rd E6 100 B1
ters Ave RM8,RM9 80 C3
ter Sq N19 50 A1
ter St SE1 117 A5 252 B4
1 237 D4
rters & Walters
mshouses N22 32 B3
rters Way UB7 104 B4
rteus Rd W2 236 B4
rtgate Cl W9 91 B3
rthcawe Rd SE26 185 B6
rthkerry Ave DA16 146 A1
rt Ho 6 SW11 136 A2
rtia Ct 12 IG11 80 A1
rtia Way E3 97 B3
rticos The SW3 266 C5
rtinscale Rd SW15 157 B6
rtishead Ho 29 W2 91 C2
rtland Ave DA15 168 A5
16 51 D2
ew Malden KT3 199 D2
rtland Cl RM6 59 A4
rtland Commercial Est
G11 102 C5
rtland Cotts CR0 203 D2
rtland Cres
Chislehurst SE9 166 A2
eltham TW13 171 B6
outhall UB6 86 A2
tanmore HA7 25 D1
rtland Cres W HA7 43 D6
rtland Ct 7 N1 73 C1
SE14 141 A6
rtland Dr EN2 5 C5
rtland Gdns N4 50 D3
lford RM6 58 D4
ortland Gr
SW8 138 B4 270 C2
ortland Ho 20 SW2 160 C3
ortland Hospl for Women
& Children The W1 238 D5
ortland Mans SE25 206 B4
ortland Mews W1 239 B1
ortland Pl W1 93 B2 238 D3
Croydon SE25 206 A5
ortland Rd N15 51 D4
W11 113 A6 244 A5
W11 113 A5 244 B4
Ashford TW15 148 A1
Bromley BR1 187 C5
Chislehurst SE9 166 A2
Croydon SE25 206 B4
Hayes UB4 83 C4
Kingston KT1 198 B6
Mitcham CR4 180 C1
Southall UB2 107 B3
ortland Rise N4 51 A1
ortland Sq 4 E1 118 B5
ortland St
SE17 117 B1 262 C1
ortland Terr TW9 131 D1
ortland Village W6 112 C3
ortman Ave SW14 133 B2
ortman Cl DA7 147 A2
W1 93 A1 238 A2
ortman Dr IG8 37 D1
ortman Gate NW1 237 B5
ortman Gdns NW9 27 B1
Hillingdon UB10 60 C1
ortman Hts 1 NW3 69 C5
ortman Lo N21 16 D6
ortman Mews S W1 238 A1
ortman Pl E2 96 C4
ortman Rd KT1 176 B1
ortman Sq W1 93 A1 238 A2
ortman St W1 93 A1 238 A1
ortman The NW11 47 C2
ortman Twrs W1 237 D2
ortmeadow Wlk SE2 124 D4
ortmeers Cl E17 53 C3
ortnall Rd W9 91 B4
ortobello Ct Est W11 91 B1
ortobello Ho 6
SW27 182 D5
Portobello Mews W11 245 A5
Portobello Rd W10 91 A2
W11 113 B6 244 D6
Portobello Road Mkt★
W10 91 A2
Porton Ct KT6 197 C3
Portpool La
EC1 94 C2 241 A4
Portree Cl N22 32 B3
Portree St E14 98 B1
Port Royal Pl 3 N16 73 C3
Portrush Ct 9 UB1 86 A1

Portsdown HA8 26 C5
Portsdown Ave NW11 47 B3
Portsdown Mews NW11 47 B3
Portsea Hall W2 237 B1
Portsea Ho 3 SW15 156 B3
Portsea Mews W2 237 B1
Portsea Pl W2 237 B1
Portslade Rd SW8 137 C3
Portsmouth Ave KT7 197 A2
Portsmouth Rd
Esher KT10 212 A5
Putney SW15 156 C4
Thames Ditton KT6,KT7 197 C3
Portsmouth St WC2 240 D1
Portsoken St E1,EC3 253 C6
Portswood Pl 10
SW15 155 D5
Portugal Gdns TW2 152 A2
Portugal St
WC2 94 B1 240 D1
Portway E15 98 D6
Portway Gdns SE18 143 D5
Portway Sch E13 98 D6
Poseidon Ct 4 E14 119 C2
Postern Gn EN2 4 C2
Postern The EC2 242 B3
Post La TW2 152 B3
Postmill Cl CR0 222 D5
Post Office App E7 77 B3
Post Office Way
SW8 137 D5 269 C4
Post Rd UB2 107 D3
Postway Mews 1 IG1 78 D5
Potier St SE1 262 D5
Potter Cl CR4 181 B1
Potterhill Ct TW11 175 B3
Potteries The EN5 13 C6
Potterne Cl 5 SW19 156 D4
Potters Cl CR0 207 A1
Pottersfield EN1 5 C1
Potters Fields
SE1 117 C5 253 B3
Potters Gr KT3 199 A5
Potters Heights Cl HA5 22 B3
Potter's La Barnet EN5 1 C1
Streatham SW16 181 D4
Potters Lo E14 120 A1
Potters Mews 4 WD6 9 D5
Potters Rd SW6 136 A3
Potter's Rd EN5 1 D1
Potter St HA5 22 B2
Potter Street Hill HA5 22 B3
Pottery La
W11 113 A5 244 B4
Pottery Rd TW8 132 A6
Pottery St SE16 118 B4
Pott St E2 96 B4
Poulett Gdns TW1 153 A3
Poulett Rd E6 100 B5
Poullett Ho SW2 160 D3
Poulters Wood BR2 225 D3
Poulton Ave SM1,SM5 218 B5
Poulton Cl E8 74 B2
Poultry EC2 95 B1 242 C1
Pound Cl
Long Ditton KT6 197 C1
Orpington BR6 227 B6
Pound Court Dr BR6 227 B6
Pound Green Ct 4
DA5 169 C4
Pound La NW10 68 A2
Pound Park Rd SE7 121 D2
Pound Pl SE9 166 C5
Pound St SM5 218 D3
Pountney Rd SW11 137 A2
Poverest Rd BR5 211 D4
Povey Ho SE17 263 A3
SW2 160 C5
Powder Mill La TW2,
TW4 151 C3
Powell Cl
Chessington KT9 213 D3
Edgware HA8 26 B4
Wallington SM6 220 A1
Powell Ct 18 E17 53 D6
Croydon CR2 221 A4
Powell Gdns RM10 81 C4
Powell Rd E5 74 B5
Buckhurst Hill IG9 21 C4
Powell's Wlk W4 133 D6
Powergate Bsns Pk
NW10 89 B4
Power Ho 12 TW9 132 C4
Power Ho The W4 111 D2
Power Rd W4 110 C2
Powerscroft Rd E5 74 C4
Sidcup DA14 190 C4
Powers Ct TW1 153 D4
Powis Ct Bushey WD23 8 B3
Edgware HA8 26 B6
Powis Gdns NW11 47 B2
W11 91 B1
Powis Ho WC2 240 B2
Powis Mews W11 91 B1
Powis Pl WC1 94 A3 240 B5
Powis Rd E3 97 D4
Powis Sq W11 91 B1
Powis St SE18 122 D2
Powis Terr W11 91 B1

Powlesland Ct 23 E14 97 A1
Powle Terr IG1 79 B3
Powlett Ho NW1 71 B2
Powlett Pl NW1 71 B1
Pownall Gdns TW3 129 D1
Pownall Rd E8 96 A6
Hounslow TW3 129 D1
Pownsett Terr IG1 79 A3
Powrie Ho 4 SW11 136 B3
Powster Rd BR1 187 B5
Powys Cl DA7 146 D6
Powys Ct N11 32 A5
Powys La
Bowes Park N13 32 A5
Palmers Green N14 32 A6
Poynder Ct 3 N7 72 A3
Poynder Lo TW7 131 A4
Poynders Ct 9 SW4 159 C5
Poynders Gdns SW12 159 C4
Poynders Rd SW12,
SW4 159 D4
Poynings Rd N19 71 C5
Poynings Way N12 29 C5
Poyntell Cres BR7 189 B2
Poynter Ct 12 UB5 84 D5
Poynter Ho NW8 236 C6
10 W11 112 D5
Poynter Rd EN1 18 A6
Poynton Rd N17 34 A1
Poyntz Rd SW11 136 D3
Poyser St E2 96 B5
Praed Mews W2 236 D2
Praed St W2 92 B1 236 D2
Pragel St E13 99 C5
Pragnell Rd SE12 165 B2
Prague Pl SW2 160 A6
Prah Rd N4 72 C6
Prairie St SW8 137 B3
Pratt Mews NW1 232 A5
Pratt St NW1 93 C6 232 A6
Pratt Wlk SE1,
SE11 116 B2 260 D4
Prayle Gr NW2 46 D1
Prebend Gdns W4,W6 111 D2
Prebend Mans 4 W4 111 D2
Prebend St N1 95 A6 235 A6
Precinct Rd UB3 106 A6
Precincts The SM4 201 C3
Precinct The N1 235 A5
N5 72 D3
East Molesey KT8 195 D6
Preedy Ho N1 233 D4
Premier Ct EN3 6 D5
Premier Lo N3 29 C2
Premier Park Rd NW10 88 D5
Premier Pl E14 119 C6
Prendergast Ho 7
SW4 159 D4
Prendergast Rd SE3 142 C2
Prendergast Sch SE4 141 C1
Prentice Ct 2 SW19 179 B5
Prentis Rd SW16 181 D6
Prentiss Ct SE7 121 D2
Presburg Rd KT3 199 C4
Prescelly Pl HA8 26 B2
Prescot St E1 117 D6 253 D6
Prescott Ave BR5 210 D3
Prescott Ho 18 SE17 138 D6
Prescott Pl SW4 137 D1
Presentation Mews
SW2 160 B3
President Dr E1 118 B5
President Ho EC1 234 D1
President St EC1 235 A2
Prespa Cl N9 18 C2
Press Ho NW10 67 B5
Press Rd NW10 67 B5
Prestage Way E14 120 A6
Prestbury Rd E7 77 C1
Prestbury Sq SE9 188 B6
Prested Rd SW11 136 C1
Preston Ave E4 36 B4
Preston Cl SE1 263 A4
Twickenham TW2 152 C1
Preston Ct DA14 189 D6
Walton-on-T KT12 194 C1
Preston Dr DA16 146 D4
Wanstead E11 55 C4
West Ewell KT19 215 D2
Preston Gdns NW10 67 C2
Enfield EN3 7 A6
Redbridge IG1 56 A3
Preston Hill HA3 44 B3
Preston Ho SE1 263 A4
SE1 263 C6
1 SE18 122 C2
3 Dagenham RM10 81 C5
Preston Manor High Sch
HA9 66 B6
Preston Park Prim Sch
HA9 43 D1
Preston Pl NW2 68 A2
Richmond TW10 154 A6
Preston Rd E11 54 C3
Littleton TW17 192 C4
South Norwood SE19 182 D4
Wembley HA3,HA9 66 A6
Wimbledon SW20 177 D3
Preston Road Sta HA3 44 A1

Prestons Rd BR2 225 A6
Preston's Rd E14 120 A5
Preston Waye HA3 44 A1
Prestwich Terr SW4 159 D6
Prestwick Cl UB2 107 A1
Prestwick Ct UB1 108 A6
Prestwick Rd WD19 22 D6
Prestwood Ave HA3 43 B5
Prestwood Cl SE18 146 A6
Harrow HA3 43 B5
Prestwood Gdns CR0 205 A2
Prestwood Ho 3
SE16 118 B3
Prestwood St N1 235 B3
Pretoria Ave E17 53 A5
Pretoria Cres E4 20 A3
Pretoria Ho 3 HA4 40 C1
Pretoria Rd E11 54 B1
E16 98 D3
Chingford E4 20 B3
Ilford IG1 78 D3
Streatham SW16 181 C5
Tottenham N17 33 D4
Pretoria Rd N N18 33 D4
Pretty Cnr HA6 22 A5
Prevost Rd N11 15 A2
Priam Ho 17 E2 96 B5
Price Cl NW7 29 A4
Upper Tooting SW17 158 D1
Price Ct HA1 43 A4
Price Ho N1 235 A5
Price Rd CR0 220 D3
Prices Ct SW11 136 B2
Price's St SE1 251 D4
Price's Yd N1 233 D5
Price Way TW12 173 A4
Prichard Ct N7 72 B3
SW11 266 D1
Pricklers Hill EN5 13 D5
Prickley Wood BR2 208 D1
Priddy's Yd 4 CR0 221 A6
Prideaux Ho WC1 233 D2
Prideaux Pl W3 111 B6
WC1 94 B4 233 D2
Prideaux Rd SW9 138 A2
Pridham Rd CR7 205 B5
Priestfield Rd SE23 163 A1
Priestlands Park Rd
DA15 167 D1
Priestley Cl N16 51 D2
Priestley Gdns RM6 58 B3
Priestley Ho EC1 242 B6
2 NW5 71 B2
6 Wembley HA9 67 A5
Priestley Rd CR4 181 A1
Priestley Way E17 52 D6
NW2 46 A1
Priestman Point 25 E3 97 D4
Priestmead Fst & Mid Schs
HA3 43 B6
Priest Park Ave HA2 63 C6
Priests Bridge SW14 133 C2
Priest's Ct EC2 242 A2
Prima Rd SW9 138 C5
Primrose Ave Enfield EN2 5 C4
Ilford RM6 58 B2
Primrose Cl
Catford SE6 186 A5
Hackbridge SM6 203 B1
Harrow HA2 63 B5
Primrose Ct
New Malden KT4 200 A2
11 Streatham SW12 159 D4
Primrose Gdns NW3 70 C2
Ruislip HA4 62 C3
Primrose Hill EC4 241 B1
Primrose Hill★
NW1,NW3 92 D6 230 C6
Primrose Hill Ct NW3 70 D1
Primrose Hill Rd
NW1,NW3 70 D1 230 C6
Primrose Hill Sch
NW1 93 A6 231 B6
Primrose Hill Studios
NW1 231 A6
Primrose Ho 7 SE15 140 A4
1 Richmond TW9 132 B4
Primrose La CR0 206 D1
Primrose Mans SW11 268 A2
Primrose Mews 9
NW1 70 D1
Primrose Rd E10 53 D1
Woodford E18 37 B1
Primrose Sq E9 96 C6
Primrose St
EC2 95 C2 243 B4
Primrose Way HA0 87 D5
Primrose Wlk 6 SE14 141 A5
Ewell KT17 215 D1
Primula St W12 90 A1
Prince Albert Ct NW8 230 C5
Sunbury TW16 171 C3
Prince Albert Rd
NW8 92 D5 230 C5
Prince Arthur Ct 19
NW3 70 A4
Prince Arthur Mews 20
NW3 70 A4
Prince Arthur Rd NW3 70 A3

Prince Charles Dr NW2 46 C2
Prince Charles Rd
SE3 142 D4
Prince Charles Way
SM6 219 B5
Prince Consort Dr
BR7 189 B2
Prince Consort Rd
SW7 114 B3 256 C6
Princedale Rd
W11 113 A5 244 B4
Prince Edward Mans
W2 245 B6
Prince Edward Rd E9 75 B2
Prince George Ave N14 15 D6
Prince George Rd N16 73 C4
Prince George's Ave
SW20 178 C1
Prince Georges Rd
SW19 180 B2
Prince Henry Rd SE7 143 D5
Prince Imperial Rd
SE18 144 B4
Chislehurst BR7 188 D3
Prince John Rd SE9 166 A6
Princelet St E1 95 D2 243 D4
Prince of Orange La 3
SE10 142 A5
Prince Of Wales Cl
NW4 46 B5
Prince of Wales Dr
SW11 137 A4 268 A2
Prince of Wales Mans
SW11 268 B2
SW4 159 B6
Prince of Wales Pas
NW1 232 A1
Prince of Wales Prim Sch
EN3 7 B6
Prince Of Wales Rd
NW5 71 A2
SE3 142 D4
Newham E16 99 C1
Prince Of Wales' Rd
SM1 218 B6
Prince Of Wales Terr
W4 111 C1
W8 245 D1
Prince Rd SE25 205 C4
Prince Regent E16 99 C2
Prince Regent Ct
SE16 119 A5
Prince Regent La E13 99 C3
Prince Regent Mews
NW1 232 A1
Prince Regent Rd
TW3 130 A2
Prince Regent Sta
E16 121 C6
Prince Rupert Rd SE9 144 B1
Princes Arc SW1 249 B4
Princes Ave BR5 211 C4
N10 49 B6
N22 31 D2
N3 29 D2
NW9 44 D5
Acton W3 110 C3
Edmonton N13 32 C5
Tolworth KT6 214 C6
Wallington SM5 218 D1
Woodford IG8 37 C6
Prince's Ave UB1 85 D1
Princes Cir
WC2 94 A1 240 A2
Princes Cl DA14 168 D1
N4 50 D1
NW9 44 C5
Edgware HA8 26 C5
Prince's Cl TW11,TW12 174 B6
Princes Ct NW2 69 A3
NW3 70 B4
Prince's Ct SE16 119 B3
Princes Ct
Kingston KT3 199 D6
Stepney E1 118 B6
Wembley HA9 66 A3
Princes Dr HA1 42 C6
Princes Gate
SW7 114 C4 246 D1
Prince's Gate
SW7 114 C4 247 A1
Princes Gate Ct SW7 246 D1
Princes Gate Mews
SW7 114 B3 256 D6
Princes Gdns
SW7 114 B3 256 D6
Acton W3 88 C2
Ealing W5 87 C3
Princes Ho W11 245 A5
Princes La N10 49 B6
Prince's Mews
W2 113 D6 245 C6
W6 112 B1
Princes Mews TW3 129 C1
Princes Par NW11 47 A3
Princes Park Ave NW11 47 A4
Hayes UB3 105 B6
Princes Park Circ UB3 105 B6
Princes Park Cl UB3 105 B6

Princes Park La UB3 105 B6
Princes Park Par UB3 105 B6
Princes Pl SW1 249 B4
W11 113 A5 244 A4
Prince's Plain BR2 210 A1
Prince's Plain Prim Sch
BR2 210 A2
Princes Rd N18 34 C6
Ashford TW15 170 B5
Buckhurst Hill IG9 21 C2
Ealing W13 109 B5
Feltham TW13 149 D1
Ilford IG6 57 B5
Kingston KT2 176 C3
Penge SE20 184 D4
Richmond TW10 154 B6
Richmond TW9 132 B4
Prince's Rd
Mortlake SW14 133 B2
Teddington TW11,TW12 174 B6
Wimbledon SW19 179 C4
Princes Rise SE13 142 A3
Princes Riverside Rd 7
SE16 118 D5
Princessa Ct EN2 17 B6
Princess Alexandra School
of Nursing The E1 96 B2
Princess Alice Ho W10 90 C3
Princess Alice Way
SE28 123 B4
Princess Ave HA9 66 A6
Princess Beatrice Ho
SW10 255 C1
Princess Christian Coll
WC1 94 A2 240 B4
Princess Cres N4 72 D6
Princess Ct NW6 69 D1
W1 237 C3
W2 245 D6
Catford BR1 186 C4
3 Croydon CR0 221 D6
11 Wimbledon SW19 178 D3
Princess Frederica CE Prim
Sch NW10 90 C5
Princess Grace Hospl The
W1 93 A3 238 A5
Princess La HA4 39 C1
Princess Louise Cl
W2 236 D4
Princess Louise Hospl
W10 90 C2
Princess Mary Ho
SW1 259 D3
Princess May Prim Sch
N16 73 D4
Princess May Rd N16 73 C4
Princess Mews NW3 70 B2
Kingston KT1 198 B6
Princess Par BR6 226 C5
Dagenham RM10 103 C5
Princess Park Manor
N11 31 A5
Prince's Sq
W2 113 D6 245 C6
Princess Rd
NW1 93 A6 231 B6
NW6 91 C5
Thornton Heath CR0 205 A3
Princess St SE1 261 D5
Princes St DA7 147 B2
W1 238 D1
Prince's St EC2 95 B1 242 C1
Princes St Sutton SM1 218 B4
Tottenham N17 33 C4
Prince's St TW10,TW9 154 A6
Prince St SE8 141 B6
Prince's Terr E13 99 B6
Princes Way Acton W3 110 C3
Buckhurst Hill IG9 21 C2
Coney Hall BR4 224 D5
Croydon CR0 220 B3
Putney SW15,SW19 157 A3
Ruislip HA4 63 A4
Princes Yd W11 244 B3
Princethorpe Ho W2 91 D2
Princethorpe Rd SE26 184 D6
Princeton Ct SW15 134 D2
Princeton Mans WC1 240 C3
Princeton Mews 3
KT2 176 C2
Princeton St
WC1 94 B2 240 C4
Prince William Ct
TW15 170 B5
Pringle Gdns SW16 181 C6
Printers Mews E3 97 A6
Printer St EC4 241 B2
Printinghouse La UB3 105 C4
Printing House Yd 17
E2 95 C4
Printon Ho 12 E3 97 B2
Print Village Ind Est
SE15 139 D3
Priolo Rd SE7 121 C1
Prior Ave SM2,SM5 218 C1
Prior Bolton St N1 72 D2

Prioress Ho 2 E3 ... 97 D4
Prioress Rd SE27 ... 160 D1
Prioress St SE1 ... 262 D5
Prior Rd IG1 ... 78 C5
Priors Croft E17 ... 35 B1
Priors Field UB5 ... 63 A2
Priors Gdns HA4 ... 62 C3
Priors Lo 4 TW10 ... 154 A5
Priors Mead EN1 ... 5 C4
Prior St SE10 ... 142 A5
Priorty Ct SE15 ... 140 C1
Prior Weston Prim Sch
EC1 ... 95 A3 242 B5
Priory Ave BR5 ... 211 B3
E17 ... 53 C4
N8 ... 49 D5
W4 ... 111 C3
Cheam SM3 ... 216 D4
Chingford E4 ... 19 C1
Wembley HA0 ... 64 D4
Priory CE Prim Sch
SW19 ... 179 D5
Priory Cl BR7 ... 188 B2
E4 ... 19 B1
N3 ... 29 B2
Ashford TW16 ... 172 A3
Barnet N20 ... 13 B4
Beckenham BR3 ... 207 A6
East Barnet N14 ... 15 B6
Hampton TW12 ... 173 B2
Hayes UB3 ... 106 B6
3 Merton SW19 ... 179 D2
Ruislip HA4 ... 39 D1
Stanmore HA7 ... 8 D1
Wembley HA0 ... 64 D4
Woodford E18 ... 37 A2
Priory Cres
Cheam SM3 ... 216 D4
South Norwood SE19 ... 183 A3
Wembley HA0 ... 65 A5
Priory Ct E17 ... 35 B1
E17 ... 53 B6
E6 ... 99 D6
E9 ... 74 D3
EC4 ... 241 D1
SW8 ... 137 D4 269 D2
Bushey WD23 ... 8 A3
Cheam SM1 ... 217 B3
Cheam SM3 ... 217 A4
Hounslow TW3 ... 129 D2
Ilford RM6 ... 58 B3
Putney SW15 ... 156 C5
Roehampton SW15 ... 133 D1
4 Wembley HA0 ... 88 A5
Priory Dr SE2 ... 124 D1
Stanmore HA7 ... 8 D1
Priory Field Dr HA8 ... 26 D6
Priory Gdns N6 ... 49 B3
6 W4 ... 111 C2
Ashford TW15 ... 171 B5
Barnes SW13 ... 133 D2
Ealing W5 ... 88 A4
Hampton TW12 ... 173 B2
South Norwood SE25 ... 205 D5
Wembley HA0 ... 65 A4
Priory Gn N1 ... 233 C4
Priory Gr SW8 ... 138 A4 270 A1
Priory Grange N2 ... 48 D6
Priory Heights N1 ... 233 D4
Priory Hill HA0 ... 65 A4
Priory Ho E1 ... 243 C4
EC1 ... 241 C6
3 SE7 ... 143 C6
SW1 ... 259 C2
Priory Hospl Hayes Grove
The BR2 ... 225 A6
Priory Hospl The
SW15 ... 133 D1
Priory House Ct SE6 ... 163 D3
Priory La
East Molesey KT8 ... 195 D5
Roehampton SW15 ... 155 D6
Priory Leas SE9 ... 166 A3
Priory Lo 8 W4 ... 110 C1
Coney Hall BR4 ... 224 C5
Ealing W5 ... 87 C1
Priory Mans 17 NW3 ... 70 D2
SW10 ... 256 B1
Priory Park Rd NW6 ... 91 B6
Wembley HA0 ... 65 A4
Priory Pk SE3 ... 142 D2
Priory Rd E6 ... 99 D5
N8 ... 49 D5
NW6 ... 69 D1
W4 ... 111 B3
Barking IG11 ... 79 B1
Cheam SM3 ... 216 D4
Chessington KT9 ... 214 A5
Hampton TW12 ... 173 C3
Hounslow TW3 ... 152 A6
Mitcham SW19 ... 180 B3
Richmond TW9 ... 132 C5
Thornton Heath CR0 ... 204 C2
Priory Ret Pk SW19 ... 180 B3
Priory Sch SE25 ... 205 D5
Priory St 16 E3 ... 97 D4
Priory Terr NW6 ... 91 D6
Priory The N8 ... 49 D5
SE1 ... 251 C1
SE3 ... 142 D1
Croydon CR0 ... 220 C5
21 Kingston KT6 ... 198 A4
Priory View WD23 ... 8 C4
Priory Villas N11 ... 30 D5
Priory Way
Harmondsworth UB7 ... 126 A6
Harrow HA2 ... 41 D5
Southall UB2 ... 106 D3
Priory Wlk
SW10 ... 114 A1 256 B1
Priscilla Ho 8 TW16 ... 171 D3
Pritchard Ho 34 E2 ... 96 A5
Pritchard's Rd E2 ... 96 A5
Pritchett Cl EN3 ... 7 C6
Priter Rd SE16 ... 118 A3
Priter Road Hostel 14
SE16 ... 118 A3
Private Rd EN1 ... 17 C6
Probert Rd SW2 ... 160 C6
Probyn Ho SW1 ... 259 D4
Probyn Rd SW2 ... 160 D2
Procter Ho 12 SE5 ... 139 B5
Procter St WC1 ... 94 B2 240 C3
Proctor Cl CR4 ... 181 A2
Proctor Ho 5 SE1 ... 118 A1
Proctors Cl TW14 ... 150 A3
Prodger 8 NW9 ... 27 D2
Progress Bsns Pk CR9 ... 220 B6
Progress Way
Croydon CR0 ... 220 B6
Enfield EN1 ... 18 A6
Wood Green N22 ... 32 C2
Prologis Pk TW4 ... 128 C1
Prome Ho 3 N16 ... 73 B4
Promenade Approach Rd
W4 ... 133 C5
Promenade Mans HA8 ... 26 C5
Promenade The W4 ... 133 C4
Pronto Trad Est UB4 ... 83 C2
Prospect Cl
Belvedere DA17 ... 125 C2
Forest Hill SE26 ... 184 B6
Hounslow TW5 ... 129 B4
Ruislip HA4 ... 40 D2
Prospect Cotts SW18 ... 135 C1
Prospect Cres TW2 ... 152 A5
Prospect Hill E17 ... 53 D5
Prospect Ho 9 E17 ... 54 A6
1 E8 ... 73 D2
N1 ... 234 A3
SE1 ... 261 D5
14 W10 ... 90 D1
Prospect House Sch
SW15 ... 156 D4
Prospect Pl E1 ... 118 C5
N2 ... 48 B5
4 NW2 ... 69 B5
24 NW3 ... 70 A4
5 SE8 ... 141 B6
2 W4 ... 111 B1
Bromley BR2 ... 209 B6
Tottenham N17 ... 33 C3
Wimbledon SW20 ... 178 B3
Prospect Quay SW18 ... 135 C1
Prospect Rd NW2 ... 69 C5
Barnet EN5 ... 1 D1
Kingston KT6 ... 197 C3
Woodford IG8 ... 37 C5
Prospect Ring N2 ... 48 B6
Prospect St SE16 ... 118 B4
Prospect Vale SE7,
SE18 ... 122 A2
Prospect Wharf E1 ... 118 C6
Prospero Ho 7 DA17 ... 125 C1
Prospero Rd N19 ... 49 D1
Protea Cl E16 ... 98 D3
Protheroe Ho 4 N17 ... 51 D6
Prothero Gdns NW4 ... 46 B4
Prothero Ho NW10 ... 67 B1
Prothero Rd
SW6 ... 135 B5 264 C4
Prout Gr NW10 ... 67 D4
Prout Rd E5 ... 74 B5
Provence St N1 ... 235 A4
Providence Ct W1 ... 248 B6
Providence Ho E9 ... 96 D6
Providence La UB3 ... 127 B5
Providence Pl N1 ... 234 C5
Providence Rd UB7 ... 104 B5
Providence Row N1 ... 233 C3
Providence Sq 4 SE1 ... 118 A4
Providence Twr 1
SE16 ... 118 A4
Provident Ind Est UB3 ... 106 A4
Provincial Terr 2
SE20 ... 184 D3
Provost Ct NW3 ... 70 D2
Provost Rd NW3 ... 70 D1
Provost St N1 ... 95 B4 235 C2
Prowse Ave WD23 ... 8 A2
Prowse Pl NW1 ... 71 C1
Pruden Cl N14 ... 15 C2
Prudent Pas EC2 ... 242 B1
Prusom's Island 8 E1 ... 118 C5
Prusom St E1 ... 118 B5
Pryors The NW3 ... 70 B5
Public Record Office
EC4,WC2 ... 94 C1 241 A2
Richmond TW9 ... 132 D5
Public Record Office Mus★
EC4,WC2 ... 241 A2
Pudding La EC3 ... 252 D6
Pudding Mill La E15 ... 97 D6
Pudding Mill Lane Sta
E15 ... 97 D6
Puddle Dock
EC4 ... 116 D6 251 D6
Puffin Cl Barking IG11 ... 102 B4
Beckenham BR3 ... 206 D4
Puffin Terr IG5 ... 56 C6
Pugin Ct N1 ... 72 C1
Pulborough Rd SW18 ... 157 B4
Pulborough Way TW4 ... 128 C1
Pulford Rd N15 ... 51 B3
Pulham Ave N2 ... 48 B5
Pulham Ho SW8 ... 270 C3
Puller Rd EN5 ... 1 A3
Pulleyns Ave E6 ... 100 A4
Pullman Ct SW2 ... 160 B3
Pullman Gdns SW15 ... 156 C5
Pullman Mews SE12 ... 165 B1
Pullman Pl SE9 ... 166 A6
Pulross Rd SW9 ... 138 B2
Pulteney Cl 13 E3 ... 97 B6
Pulteney Gdns 3 E18 ... 55 B6
Pulteney Rd E18 ... 55 B6
Pulteney Terr
N1 ... 94 B6 233 D6
Pulton Ho SE4 ... 141 A1
Pulton Pl SW6 ... 135 C5 265 A3
Puma Ct E1 ... 243 C4
Pump Alley 8 TW8 ... 131 D5
Pump Cl UB5 ... 85 C5
Pump Ct EC4 ... 241 A1
Pump House Cl SE16 ... 118 C4
Bromley BR2 ... 186 D1
Pumping Station Rd
W4 ... 133 C6
Pump La SE14 ... 140 C5
Hayes UB3 ... 106 A4
Pump Pail N CR0 ... 221 A5
Pump Pail S CR0 ... 221 A5
Punchard Cres EN3 ... 7 D5
Punderson's Gdns E2 ... 96 B4
Puran Ho E13 ... 99 C5
Purbeck Ave KT3 ... 199 D3
Purbeck Dr NW2 ... 68 D6
Purbeck Ho SW8 ... 270 C3
Purbrook Est SE1 ... 253 B1
Purbrook Ho 2 SW15 ... 156 B3
Purbrook St SE1 ... 263 B6
Purcell Cres
SW6 ... 135 A5 264 A4
Purcell Ho SW10 ... 266 C5
Isleworth TW2 ... 152 B5
Southall UB1 ... 85 C1
Purcell Mews NW10 ... 67 C1
Purcell Rd UB6 ... 85 D2
Purcells Ave HA8 ... 26 C5
Purcell St N1 ... 95 C5
Purchese St
NW1 ... 93 D5 232 D3
Purday Ho 4 W10 ... 91 B4
Purdey Ct 3 KT4 ... 200 A1
Purdon Ho 10 SE15 ... 140 A4
Purdy St E3 ... 97 D3
Purland Cl RM8 ... 59 B1
Purland Rd SE28,SE18 ... 123 D4
Purley Ave NW2 ... 69 A6
Purley Oaks Prim Sch
CR2 ... 221 B1
Purley Pl N1 ... 72 D1
Purley Rd Edmonton N9 ... 17 C1
South Croydon CR2 ... 221 B1
Purley View Terr CR2 ... 221 B1
Purley Way
Croydon CR0,CR9 ... 220 C3
Thornton Heath CR0 ... 204 B1
Purley Way Cres CR0 ... 204 B2
Purneys Rd SE9 ... 143 D1
Purrett Rd SE18 ... 123 D1
Purser Ho 3 SW2 ... 160 C5
Pursers Cross Rd
SW6 ... 135 B4 264 D2
Pursewardens Cl W13 ... 109 C5
Pursley Rd NW7 ... 28 B3
Purves Rd NW10 ... 90 C5
Purvis Ho CR0 ... 205 B2
Pusey Ho 18 E14 ... 97 C1
Puteaux Ho 6 E2 ... 96 D5
Putney Bridge App
SW6 ... 135 A2
Putney Bridge Rd
SW15 ... 135 B1
Putney Bridge Sta
SW6 ... 135 B2
Putney Comm SW15 ... 134 C2
Putney Gdns RM6 ... 58 B4
Putney Heath SW15 ... 156 C5
Putney Heath La
SW15 ... 156 D5
Putney High Sch
SW15 ... 156 D6
Putney High St SW15 ... 135 A1
Putney Hill SW15 ... 156 D6
Putney Hospl SW15 ... 134 C2
Putney Park Ave
SW15 ... 134 A1
Putney Park La SW15 ... 156 B6
Putney Pier SW15 ... 135 A2
Putney School of Art &
Design SW15 ... 135 A1
Putney Sta SW15 ... 135 A1
Putney Wharf Twr
SW15 ... 135 A2
Pycombe Cnr N12 ... 29 B6
Pycroft Way N9 ... 34 A6
Pylbrook Rd SM1 ... 217 D5
Pylon Trad Est E16 ... 98 B2
Pylon Way CR0 ... 204 A1
Pym Cl EN4 ... 14 B6
Pymers Mead SE21 ... 161 A3
Pymmes Brook Ho 3
N10 ... 31 A3
Pymmes Cl
Bowes Park N13 ... 32 B5
Tottenham N17 ... 34 B2
Pymmes Gdns N N9 ... 17 D1
Pymmes Gdns S N9 ... 17 D1
Pymmes Green Rd N11 ... 15 C1
Pymmes Rd N13 ... 32 A5
Pymms Brook Dr EN4 ... 2 C1
Pynchester Cl UB10 ... 60 C6
Pyne Rd KT6 ... 198 C1
Pynfolds SE16 ... 118 B4
Pynham Cl SE2 ... 124 B3
Pynnacles Cl HA7 ... 25 B5
Pynnersmead SE24 ... 161 A6
Pyramid Ho N12 ... 30 A6
Pyrford Ho 12 SW9 ... 138 D1
Pyrland Rd N5 ... 73 B3
Richmond TW10 ... 154 B5
Pyrmont Gr SE27 ... 160 D1
Pyrmont Rd W4 ... 132 C6
Pytchley Cres SE19 ... 183 A4
Pytchley Rd SE22 ... 139 C2

Q

Quadrangle Cl SE1 ... 263 A4
Quadrangle Lo SW19 ... 179 C4
Quadrangle The E17 ... 35 B1
SE24 ... 161 A6
SW10 ... 266 B2
SW6 ... 264 A3
W12 ... 90 C1
W2 ... 237 A2
Stanmore HA7 ... 25 C3
Quadrant Arc W1 ... 249 B5
Quadrant Bsns Pk NW6 ... 91 A6
Quadrant Cl NW4 ... 46 B4
Quadrant Gr NW5 ... 70 D3
Quadrant Ho E15 ... 98 C4
Quadrant Rd
Richmond TW9 ... 131 D1
Thornton Heath CR7 ... 204 D5
Quadrant The DA7 ... 146 D5
4 W10 ... 90 D4
Richmond TW9 ... 132 A1
Sutton SM2 ... 218 A2
Wimbledon SW20 ... 179 A2
Quad Rd HA9 ... 65 D5
Quaggy Wlk SE3 ... 143 A1
Quainton Hall Sch HA1 ... 42 C4
Quainton St NW10 ... 67 B5
Quaker Ct EC1 ... 242 B6
Quaker La UB2 ... 107 C3
Quakers Course NW9 ... 27 D2
Quaker's Pl E7 ... 77 D3
Quaker St E1 ... 95 D3 243 C5
Quakers Wlk N21 ... 17 B5
Quality Ct WC2 ... 241 A2
Quantock Cl UB3 ... 127 B5
Quantock Ct UB6 ... 64 C3
Quantock Dr KT4 ... 216 C6
Quantock Gdns NW2 ... 68 D6
Quantock Ho N16 ... 51 D1
Quarrendon St SW6 ... 135 C3
Quarr Rd SM5 ... 202 C3
Quarry Park Rd SM1 ... 217 B2
Quarry Rd SW18 ... 158 A5
Quarry Rise SM1 ... 217 B2
Quarterdeck The E14 ... 119 C4
Quartermain Ho SM4 ... 202 A4
Quartermile La E10,E15 ... 75 D4
Quayside Ct 6 SE16 ... 118 D5
Quay West TW11 ... 175 B5
Quebec & Crown Wharves
E14 ... 97 B1
Quebeck Ind Est SE16 ... 119 A3
Quebec Mews W1 ... 237 D1
Quebec Rd Hayes UB4 ... 84 C1
Ilford IG1 ... 56 D2
Quebec Way SE16 ... 119 A4
Quedgeley Ct 3 SE15 ... 139 D6
Queen Adelaide Ct
SE20 ... 184 C4
Queen Adelaide Rd
SE20 ... 184 C3
Queen Alexandra Mans
WC1 ... 233 A1
Queen Alexandra's Ct 5
SW19 ... 179 B5
Queen Anne Ave BR2 ... 208 D6
Queen Anne Dr KT10 ... 212 C1
Queen Anne Gate
DA7 ... 146 D2
Queen Anne Mews
W1 ... 238 D3
Queen Anne Rd E9 ... 74 D2
Queen Annes Cl TW2 ... 152 B1
Queen Anne's Gate
SW1 ... 115 D4 249 C1
Queen Anne's Gdns
W4 ... 111 C3
W5 ... 110 A4
Enfield EN1 ... 17 C5
Mitcham CR4 ... 202 D6
Queen Anne's Gr W4 ... 111 C3
W5 ... 110 A4
Enfield EN1 ... 17 C5
Queen Anne's Pl EN1 ... 17 C5
Queen Anne St
W1 ... 93 B2 238 C3
Queen Borough Gdns
BR7 ... 189 B4
Queenborough Gdns
IG2 ... 56 C5
Queen Caroline St
W6 ... 112 C1
Queen Charlotte's & Chelsea
Hospl W12 ... 90 A1
Queen Elizabeth College 15
SE10 ... 142 A5
Queen Elizabeth Ct EN5 ... 1 B1
Queen Elizabeth Gdns
SM4 ... 201 C5
Queen Elizabeth Hall &
Purcell Room SE1 ... 250 D4
Queen Elizabeth Hospital
for Children The E2 ... 96 A5
Queen Elizabeth Hospl
SE7 ... 144 A5
Queen Elizabeth II Con Ctr
SW1 ... 249 D1
Queen Elizabeth II Jubilee
Sch W9 ... 91 B3
Queen Elizabeth II Pier
SE10 ... 120 D5
Queen Elizabeth Rd
E17 ... 53 A6
Kingston KT2 ... 176 B1
Queen Elizabeth's Cl
N16 ... 73 B6
Queen Elizabeth's Dr
N14 ... 16 A3
Queen Elizabeth's Girls Sch
EN5 ... 1 B1
Queen Elizabeth's Hunting
Lodge Mus★ E4 ... 20 D4
Queen Elizabeth St
SE1 ... 117 D4 253 C2
Queen Elizabeth's Wlk
N16 ... 73 B6
Wallington SM6 ... 219 D4
Queen Elizabeth Wlk
SW13 ... 134 B4
Queenhithe EC4 ... 252 B6
Queen Margaret Flats 22
E2 ... 96 B4
Queen Margarets Ct
N1 ... 73 C3
Queen Margaret's Gr
N1 ... 73 C3
Queen Mary Ave SM4 ... 200 D4
Queen Mary Cl KT9 ... 214 C5
Queen Mary Rd
Charlton TW17 ... 171 A1
South Norwood SE19 ... 182 D4
Queen Mary's Ave
SM5 ... 218 D1
Queen Mary's Gdns★
NW1 ... 231 A1
Queen Mary's Hospl
DA14 ... 190 A4
NW3 ... 70 A5
Queen Mary's Univ Hospl
SW15 ... 156 A5
Queen Mary, Univ of
London E1 ... 97 A3
Queen of Denmark Ct
SE16 ... 119 B3
Queens Acre SM3 ... 217 A1
Queens Ave N10 ... 49 B6
N20 ... 14 B2
Queen's Ave N3 ... 30 A2
Queens Ave
Feltham TW13 ... 172 C6
Stanmore HA7 ... 25 C1
Queen's Ave
Southall UB1 ... 86 A1
Southgate N21 ... 16 D3
Woodford IG8 ... 37 B5
Queensberry Ho 6
TW9 ... 153 D6
Queensberry Mews W
SW7 ... 256 C4
Queensberry Pl E12 ... 78 A3
SW7 ... 114 B2 256 C4
Queensberry Way
SW7 ... 256
Queensborough Ct N3 ... 47
Queensborough Mews
W2 ... 246
Queensborough Pas
W2 ... 246
Queensborough Terr
W2 ... 113 D6 245
Queensbridge Ct 1 E2 ... 95
Queensbridge Inf Sch
E8 ... 73
Queensbridge Pk
TW7 ... 152
Queensbridge Rd E2,E8 ... 95
E8 ... 73
Queensbury IG9 ... 21
Queensbury Circ Par
HA3 ... 44
Queensbury Ct CR7 ... 183
Queensbury Rd NW9 ... 45
Wembley HA0 ... 88
Queensbury St N1 ... 73
Queensbury Sta HA7,
HA8 ... 44
Queensbury Station Par
HA8 ... 44
Queen's CE Prim Sch The
TW9 ... 132
Queen's Cir
SW11 ... 137 B5 268
Queen's Cl Edgware HA8 ... 26
Wallington SM6 ... 219
Queen's Club Gdns
W14 ... 135 A6 264
Queen's Club The★
W14 ... 113 A1 254
Queen's Coll
W1 ... 93 B2 238
Queenscourt HA9 ... 66
Queen's Cres NW5 ... 71
Queens Cres TW10 ... 154
Queenscroft Rd SE9 ... 165
Queens Ct E10 ... 53
4 E14 ... 119
E17 ... 53
8 NW11 ... 47
SE5 ... 139
SW11 ... 268
Queen's Ct E11 ... 54
NW11 ... 47
NW8 ... 229
W2 ... 245
Queens Ct
Beckenham BR3 ... 185
5 Buckhurst Hill IG9 ... 21
Stanmore HA7 ... 25
Queen's Ct
Barnes SW13 ... 134
Beckenham BR3 ... 185
Croydon CR2 ... 221
8 Ealing W5 ... 87
1 Kingston KT2 ... 176
3 Richmond TW10 ... 154
Thornton Heath CR7 ... 204
Queensdale Cres W11 ... 112
Queensdale Pl W11 ... 244
Queensdale Rd
W11 ... 113 A5 244
Queensdale Wlk W11 ... 244
Queens Down Rd E5 ... 74
Queens Dr E10 ... 53
Queen's Dr N4 ... 72
Queens Dr KT5 ... 198
Queen's Dr Acton W3 ... 88
Thames Ditton KT7 ... 197
Queen's Elm Sq SW3 ... 256
Queensferry Wlk N17 ... 52
Queensfield Ct SM3 ... 216
Queen's Gallery The★
SW1 ... 115 B4 248
Queen's Gate
SW7 ... 114 A3 256
Queens Gate IG4 ... 56
Queensgate Ct N12 ... 29
Queen's Gate Gdns
SW7 ... 114 A3 256
Queensgate Gdns
SW15 ... 134
Queens Gate Gdns
BR7 ... 189
Queen's Gate Mews
SW7 ... 114 A3 256
Queensgate Pl 10 NW6 ... 69
Queen's Gate Pl
SW7 ... 114 A3 256
Queen's Gate Pl Mews
SW7 ... 114 A3 256
Queen's Gate Terr
SW7 ... 114 A3 256
Queens Gate Villas E9 ... 75 A1
Queens Gdns NW4 ... 46
Queen's Gdns
W2 ... 114 A6 246
Ealing W5 ... 87 C3
Heston TW5 ... 129 A4
Queen's Gr
NW8 ... 92 B6 229 D5
Queen's Grove Rd E4 ... 20

Queen's Head Pas
EC2 242 A2
Queen's Head St
N1 94 D6 234 D5
Queen's Head Yd SE1 252 C3
Queens Ho 1 SE17 139 B6
Queen's Ho TW11 174 D4
Queen's Hospl CR0 205 A3
Queen's House The★
SE10 142 B6
Queens Keep 10 TW1 153 C5
Queens La N10 49 B6
Queensland Ave
Edmonton N18 33 A4
Merton SW19 179 D2
Queensland Cl E17 35 B1
Queensland Ct N10 31 B3
Queensland Ho 2
E16 122 C5
Queensland Pl N7 72 C4
Queensland Rd N7 72 C4
Queens Manor Prim Sch
SW6 134 D5
Queens Mans NW4 46 B4
NW6 69 D3
Queen's Mans W6 112 D2
Queensmead
NW8 92 B6 229 D6
Queen's Mead Rd BR2 186 D1
Queensmead Sch HA4 62 D4
Queensmere Cl SW19 156 D2
Queensmere Ct SW13 134 A6
Queensmere Rd SW19 156 D2
Queen's Mews
W2 113 D6 245 C6
Queensmill Rd SW6 134 D5
Queensmill Sch SW6 135 C3
Queen's Mkt 1 E13 99 C6
Queens Par NW2 68 C2
7 NW4 46 B4
Queen's Par 3 N11 30 D5
Queens Par W5 88 B1
Queen's Par N11 32 A3
Queens Parade Cl N11 30 D5
Queens Park Com Sch
NW6 90 D6
Queens Park Ct 5
W10 90 D4
Queens Park Gdns
TW13 149 D1
Queen's Park Prim Sch
W10 91 A3
Queen's Park Sta NW6 91 B5
Queen's Pas BR7 188 D4
Queen's Pl SM4 201 C5
Queen Sq WC1 94 A2 240 B4
Queen Sq Pl WC1 240 B5
Queen's Quay EC4 252 B6
Queen's Rd BR1 187 A1
BR7 188 D4
DA16 146 B3
E11 54 C2
E13 99 C6
E17 53 C3
N3 30 A2
NW4 46 C4
SE14,SE15 140 C4
Queens Rd Hayes UB3 83 C1
Morden SM4 201 C5
Twickenham TW1 153 A3
West Drayton UB7 104 B4
Queen's Rd Barking IG11 79 A2
Beckenham BR3 185 A1
Bowes Park N11 32 A4
Buckhurst Hill IG9 21 C2
Ealing W5 88 A1
Edmonton N9 18 B2
Enfield EN1 5 C1
Feltham TW13 150 B3
Hampton TW12 173 D6
Hounslow TW3 129 D2
Kingston KT2 176 C3
Mitcham CR4 202 B6
Mortlake SW14 133 B2
New Malden KT3 199 D4
Richmond TW10 154 B5
Richmond, Richmond Park
KT2,TW10 176 C5
Southall UB2 107 A4
Teddington TW11 174 D4
Thames Ditton KT7 196 D4
Thornton Heath CR0 205 A3
Wallington SM6 219 B3
Wimbledon SW19 179 C4
Queen's Rd W E13 99 B5
Queens Reach KT8 196 C5
Queen's Ride SW13 134 B2
Queen's Rise TW10 154 B5
Queen's Road Sta
SE15 140 C4
Queen's Row SE17 139 B6
Queen St DA7 147 B2
EC4 117 A6 252 B6
W1 115 B5 248 C4
Croydon CR0 221 A4
Tottenham N17 33 C4
Queens Terr E13 99 B6
NW8 92 B5 229 C4
Queen's Terr TW7 131 A1
Queensthorpe Rd
SE26 184 D6
Queenstown Rd
SW8 137 B5 268 C4
Queenstown Road Sta
SW8 137 B4 268 D2
Queen St Pl EC4 252 B6
Queensville Rd SW12,
SW4 159 D4
Queens Walk Ho W5 87 C2
Queensway
W2 113 D6 245 D6
Queens Way NW4 46 C4
Queensway
Coney Hall BR4 224 D4
Enfield EN3 6 C1
Orpington BR5 211 A3
Sunbury TW16 172 B1
Queens Way
Croydon CR0 220 B3
Feltham TW13 172 C6
Queensway Sta
W2 113 D6 245 D5
Queens Well Ave N20 30 C6
Queenswell Jun & Inf Schs
N20 14 B2
Queens Wlk NW9 67 A6
Queen's Wlk
SW1 115 C5 249 A3
Queens Wlk
Ashford TW15 170 A6
Chingford E4 20 B3
Harrow HA1 42 C5
Ruislip HA4 62 C5
Queen's Wlk W5 87 C2
Queenswood Ave
Chingford E17 36 A2
Hampton TW12 173 D4
Hounslow TW3,TW5 129 B3
Thornton Heath CR7 204 C4
Wallington CR0,SM6 219 D4
Queenswood Ct
5 SW4 160 A6
11 West Norwood SE27 183 B6
Queenswood Gdns E11 55 B1
Queenswood Pk N3 29 A2
Queenswood Rd DA15 167 D5
Queen's Wood Rd N6 49 B3
Queenswood Rd SE23 163 A1
Queens Yd E9 75 C2
Queen's Yd W1 239 B5
Queen Terr Cotts W7 108 C4
Queen Victoria Ave
HA0 65 D1
Queen Victoria Mon★
SW1 249 A2
Queen Victoria St
EC4 117 A6 252 A6
Quelch Ho 2 N19 71 D3
Quemerford Rd N7 72 B3
Quendon Ho W10 90 C3
Quenington Ct 5
SE15 139 D6
Quennel Ho 7 SW12 159 C4
Quentington Mans
SW6 264 C2
Quentin Pl SE13 142 C2
Quentin Rd SE13 142 C2
Quernmore Cl BR1 187 A4
Quernmore Rd BR1 187 A4
N4 50 C3
Querrin St SW6 136 A3
Quested Ct 27 E8 74 B3
Quex Mews NW6 91 C6
Quex Rd NW6 91 C6
Quick Rd W4 111 C1
Quicks Rd SW19 179 D3
Quick St N1 94 D5 234 D3
Quickswood NW3 70 C1
Quiet Nook BR2 225 D5
Quill La SW15 134 D1
Quill St N4 72 C5
Ealing W5 88 A5
Quilp St SE1 252 A2
Quilter Ho 11 W9 91 B4
Quilter St E2 96 A4
SE18 123 D1
Quilting Ct 23 SE16 118 D4
Quinta Dr EN5 12 C6
Quintin Ave SW20 179 B2
Quintin Ct W4 133 A5
Quintock Ho 2 TW9 132 C4
Quinton Cl
Beckenham BR3 208 A6
Cranford TW5 128 B5
Wallington SM6 219 B4
Quinton Ho SW8 270 A4
Quinton Kynaston Sch
NW8 92 B6 229 C5
Quinton Rd KT7 197 A1
Quinton St SW18 158 A2
Quixley St E14 120 B6
Quorn Rd SE22 139 C2

R

Rabbit Row W8 245 B4
Rabbits Rd E12 78 A4
Rabbs Farm Prim Sch
UB7 104 A6
Rabournmead Dr UB5 63 A3
Raby Rd KT3 199 B5
Raby St E14 97 A1
Raccoon Way TW4 128 C3
Rachel Cl IG6 57 B6
Rachel Ct SM2 218 B1
Rachel Point E5 74 A4
Racine 15 SE5 139 C4
Rackham Cl DA16 146 B3
Rackham Mews SW16 181 C4
Racton Rd
SW6 135 C6 265 A5
Radbourne Ave W5 109 C2
Radbourne Cl E5 74 D4
Radbourne Cres E17 36 B1
Radbourne Ct HA3 43 B3
Radbourne Rd SW12 159 D3
Radcliff Bldg EC1 241 A4
Radcliffe Ave NW10 90 A5
Enfield EN2 5 A4
Radcliffe Gdns SM5 218 C1
Radcliffe Ho 10 SE16 118 B2
Radcliffe Mews TW12 174 A5
Radcliffe Path 5 SW8 137 B3
Radcliffe Rd SE1 263 B6
Harrow HA3 25 A1
South Croydon CR0 221 D5
Southgate N21 16 D3
Radcliffe Sq SW15 156 D5
Radcliffe Way UB5 84 D4
Radcot Point 2 SE23 162 D1
Radcot St SE11 261 B1
Raddington Rd W10 91 A2
Radfield Way SE9 167 B4
Radford Ho 8 E14 97 D2
N7 72 B3
Radford Rd SE13 164 A5
Radford Way IG11 101 D4
Radipole Rd
SW6 135 B4 264 C2
Radius Pk TW6 127 D1
Radland Rd E16 99 A1
Radlet Ave SE23 162 B2
Radlett Cl E7 76 D2
Radlett Pl NW8 92 C6 230 A6
Radley Ave IG3 80 A4
Radley Cl TW14 149 D3
Radley Ct 25 SE16 118 D4
3 Catford BR1 186 A6
Radley Gdns HA3 44 A5
Radley Ho NW1 237 C6
13 SE2 124 D4
Radley Lo 30 SW19 156 D3
Radley Mews W8 255 B5
Radley Rd N17 33 C1
Radley's La E18 37 A1
Radleys Mead RM10 81 D2
Radley Sq E5 74 C6
Radley Terr 1 E16 98 D2
Radlix Rd E10 53 C1
Radnor Ave DA16 168 B6
Harrow HA1 42 C4
Radnor Cl BR7 189 C4
Mitcham CR4 204 A5
Radnor Cres
Redbridge IG4 56 B4
Woolwich SE18 146 A5
Radnor Ct Ealing W7 86 D1
6 Forest Hill SE23 162 D1
Harrow HA3 24 D2
Radnor Gdns Enfield EN1 5 C4
Twickenham TW1 152 D2
Radnor Gr UB10 82 C5
Radnor Lo W2 236 D1
Radnor Mews
W2 92 B1 236 D1
Radnor Pl W2 92 C1 237 A1
Radnor Rd NW6 91 A6
SE15 140 A5
Twickenham TW1 152 D2
Radnor St EC1 95 A4 235 B1
Radnor Terr
W14 113 B2 254 C4
Radnor Way NW10 88 D3
Radnor Wlk 14 E14 119 C2
SW3 114 D1 257 C1
Croydon CR0 207 A3
Radstock Ave HA3 43 B6
Radstock Cl N11 31 A4
Radstock St SW11 267 A3
Radway Ho 38 W2 91 C2
Radwell Ho SW2 160 C6
Raebarn Ct 6 SW16 160 A1
Raebarn Gdns EN5 12 B6
Raeburn Ave
Surbiton KT3 198 D3
Tolworth KT5,KT6 198 D3
Raeburn Cl NW11 48 A3
Teddington KT1 175 D3
Raeburn Ho 7 UB5 84 D5
Raeburn Rd
Edgware HA8 26 C2
Hayes UB4 83 B5
Sidcup DA15 167 C5
Raeburn St SW2 138 A1
Raffles Ct HA8 26 B6
Raffles Ho NW4 46 B5
Rafford Way BR1 209 B6
RAF Mus★ NW9 28 A1
Ragate Ho E5 74 A5
Ragged School Mus The★
E3 97 A2
Raggleswood BR7 188 C2
Raglan Cl TW4 151 B6
Raglan Ct SE12 165 A6
SW9 138 C2
Croydon CR0,CR2 220 D3
Wembley HA9 66 C5
Raglan Jun & Inf Schs
EN1 17 C4
Raglan Prim Sch BR2 209 D5
Raglan Rd DA17 125 B2
E17 54 B4
SE18 123 A1
Bromley BR2 209 C5
Enfield EN1 17 D4
Raglan St NW5 71 B2
Raglan Terr HA2 63 D4
Raglan Way UB5 64 A2
Ragley Cl W3 111 A4
Ragwort Ct 1 SE26 184 B5
Rahere Ho EC1 235 A2
Railey Mews NW5 71 C3
Railshead Rd TW1,
TW7 131 B1
Railton Rd SE24 160 D6
Railway App N4 50 C3
SE1 252 D4
Harrow HA1,HA3 42 D5
9 Twickenham TW1 153 A4
Wallington SM6 219 B3
Railway Ave SE16 118 C4
Railway Cotts W6 112 C4
Railway Gr SE14 141 B5
Railway Pl DA17 125 C3
Railway Rd TW11 174 D6
Railway Rise SE22 139 C1
Railway Side SW13 133 C2
Railway St N1 233 B3
Ilford RM6 58 C2
Railway Terr SE13 163 D6
Chingford E17 36 A2
Feltham TW13,TW14 150 A3
Rainborough Cl NW10 67 A2
Rainbow Ave E14 119 D1
Rainbow Ct 3 SE14 141 A6
Rainbow Ind Est SW20 178 B1
Rainbow Quay SE16 119 A3
Rainbow St SE5 139 C5
Rainbow Works N15 52 A4
Raine's Foundation Sch
E2 96 B4
Raines Foundation Sec Sch
E2 96 C5
Raine St E1 118 B5
Rainford Ho 9 N7 72 B6
Rainham Cl SE9 167 C5
SW11 158 C5
Rainham Ho NW1 232 B5
Rainham Rd NW10 90 C4
Rainham Rd N RM10 81 D6
Rainham Rd S RM10 81 D4
Rainhill Way E3 97 C4
Rainsborough Ave
SE8 119 A2
Rainsford Cl HA7 25 C5
Rainsford Ct NW10 88 D5
Rainsford Ho 14 SW2 160 B6
Rainsford Rd NW10 88 D5
Rainsford St W2 237 A2
Rainstar Est N18 34 C6
Rainton Rd SE7 121 A1
Rainville Rd W6 134 C6
Raisins Hill HA5 40 C6
Raith Ave N14 15 D1
Raleigh Ave Hayes UB4 84 B2
Wallington SM6 219 D4
Raleigh Cl NW4 46 C4
Pinner HA5 40 D2
Ruislip HA4 61 D6
Raleigh Ct 2 SE16 118 D5
Beckenham BR3 185 D2
Dulwich SE19 183 D5
Ealing W13 87 B2
Wallington SM6 219 B2
Raleigh Dr N20 14 C1
Esher KT10 212 B3
Tolworth KT5 199 A1
Raleigh Gdns SW2 160 B5
Mitcham CR4 202 D6
Raleigh Ho 30 SW8 137 D3
1 Thames Ditton KT7 197 A2
Raleigh Mews N1 234 D5
6 Orpington BR6 227 D3
Raleigh Rd N10 30 C2
N8 50 C5
Enfield EN2 5 B1
Feltham TW13 149 D2
Penge SE20 184 D3
Richmond TW9 132 B2
Southall UB2 107 A1
Raleigh St N1 94 D6 234 D5
Raleigh Way
Feltham TW13 172 C5
Southgate N14 16 A3
Ralph Ct 8 W2 91 D1
Ralph Perring Ct BR3 207 C5
Ralston St SW3 257 C1
Ramac Ind Est SE7 121 B1
Rama Cl SW16 182 A3
Rama Ct HA1 64 C6
Ramac Way SE7 121 B1
Rama La SE19 183 D3
Ramar Ho 11 E1 96 A2
Rambler Cl SW16 181 C6
Rambler Ct 11 NW9 46 A5
Rame Cl SW17 181 A5
Ramilles Cl SW2 160 A5
Ramillies Pl W1 93 C1 239 A1
Ramillies Rd DA15 168 B5
NW7 11 C2
W4 111 B3
Ramillies St W1 239 A1
Ramney Dr EN3 7 A6
Rampart St E1 96 B1
Rampayne St SW1 259 C2
Rampton Cl E4 19 C1
Ramsay Ho NW8 230 A4
Ramsay Rd E7 76 D4
Acton W3 111 A4
Ramscroft Cl N9 17 C4
Ramsdale Rd SW17 181 A5
Ramsdean Ho 1
SW15 156 B3
Ramsden Rd N11 30 D5
Balham SW12 159 A4
Ramsey Cl NW9 45 D3
Greenford UB6 64 B3
Ramsey Ct N8 49 D4
Croydon CR0 220 D6
Ramsey Ho 14 SW9 138 C5
7 Merton SW19 179 D2
Ramsey Rd CR7 204 B3
Ramsey St E2 96 A3
Ramsey Way N14 15 C4
Ramsfort Ho 4 SE16 118 B2
Ramsgate Cl 8 E16 121 B5
11 E16 121 B5
Ramsgate St E8 73 D2
Ramsgill App IG2 57 D5
Ramsgill Dr IG2 57 D5
Rams Gr RM6 59 A5
Rams Pas KT1 175 D1
Ram St SW18 157 D6
Ramulis Dr UB4 84 D3
Ramus Wood Ave BR6 227 C3
Rance Ho 12 SE7 122 A2
Rancliffe Gdns SE9 144 A1
Rancliffe Rd E6 100 A5
Randal Cremer JMI Sch
E2 95 D5
Randall 9 NW9 27 D2
Randall Ave NW2 67 D5
Randall Cl
SW11 136 C4 267 A2
Randall Ct NW7 28 A3
Randall Pl SE10 142 A5
Randall Rd
SE11 116 B2 260 C3
Randall Row SE11 260 C3
Randell's Rd N1 94 A6 233 B6
Randisbourne Gdns
SE6 163 D1
Randle Rd TW10 175 C6
Randlesdown Rd SE6 163 D1
Randmore Ct 6 BR3 185 C3
Randolph App E16 99 C1
Randolph Ave
W9 92 A4 229 A1
Randolph Cl KT2 177 A5
Randolph Cres
W9 92 A3 236 A6
Randolph Ct HA5 23 C3
Randolph Gdns NW6 91 D5
Randolph Gr RM6 58 C4
Randolph Mews
W9 92 A3 236 B5
Randolph Rd BR2 210 B1
E17 53 D4
W9 92 A3 236 B5
Southall UB1 107 B4
Randolph St NW1 71 C1
Randon Cl HA2 23 D1
Ranelagh Ave
Barnes SW13 134 A3
Fulham SW6 135 B2
Ranelagh Cl HA8 26 C6
Ranelagh Dr
Edgware HA8 26 C6
Twickenham TW1 153 C6
Ranelagh Gardens Mans
SW6 135 A2
Ranelagh Gardens (site of
Chelsea Flower Show)★
SW1 115 A1 258 B1
Ranelagh Gdns 3 W6 111 D3
Chiswick W4 133 A5
Fulham SW6 135 B2
Ilford IG1 56 C1
Wanstead E11 55 C4
Ranelagh Gr
SW1 115 A1 258 B2
Ranelagh Ho SW3 257 C2
Ranelagh Mans 4
SW6 135 B3
Ranelagh Pl KT3 199 C4
Ranelagh Prim Sch E15 98 C5
Ranelagh Rd E11 76 C4
E15 98 C5
N17 51 C6
NW10 89 D5
SW1 115 C1 259 B1
W5 109 D4
Southall UB1 106 D5
Wallend E6 100 C5
Wembley HA0 65 D2
Wood Green N22 32 B2
Ranfurly Rd SM1 217 C6
Rangdon St EC3 243 C1
Rangefield Prim Sch
BR1 186 C5
Rangefield Rd BR1 186 D5
Rangemoor Rd N15 51 D4
Ranger's Rd
Buckhurst Hill IG9,IG10 21 A4
Chingford E4 20 D4
Rangers Sq SE10 142 B4
Range Villas TW17 192 A2
Range Way TW17 192 C2
Rangeworth Pl DA15 167 D1
Rangoon Ho 5 N16 73 B4
Rankin Cl NW9 45 C6
Rankine Ho SE1 262 A5
Ranleigh Gdns DA7 147 B5
Ranmere St SW12 159 B3
Ranmoor Cl HA1 42 B5
Ranmoor Gdns HA1 42 C5
Ranmore Ave CR0 221 D5
Ranmore Ct
Kingston KT6 197 D4
3 Wimbledon SW20 178 D2
Rann Ho 1 SW14 133 B2
Rannoch Cl HA8 10 D2
Rannoch Ct 9 KT6 198 A4
Rannoch Rd W6 134 D6
Rannock Ave NW9 45 C2
Ransford Ho 16 SE21 183 C6
Ransom Rd 1 SE7 121 C1
Ranston St NW1 237 A4
Ranulf Rd NW2 69 B4
Ranwell Cl 11 E3 97 B6
Ranwell Ho 10 E3 97 B6
Ranworth Rd N9 18 C2
Ranyard Cl KT9 214 B5
Raphael Ct 9 SE16 118 B1
Raphael Dr KT7 196 D2
Raphael St SW7 247 C1
Rapide 12 NW9 27 C2
Rapley Ho 19 E2 96 A4
Rashleigh Ct 8 SW8 137 B2
Rashleigh Ho WC1 233 A1
Rasper Rd N20 14 A2
Rastell Ave SW12 159 D3
Ratcliffe Cl SE12 165 A4
Ratcliffe Cross St E1 96 D1
Ratcliffe Ho 12 E14 97 A1
Ratcliffe La 18 E14 97 A1
Ratcliffe Orch 9 E1 118 D6
Ratcliff Rd E7 77 C3
Rathbone Ho 5 E16 98 D1
NW6 91 C6
10 Wimbledon SW19 178 D3
Rathbone Mkt 2 E16 98 D2
Rathbone Pl
W1 93 D1 239 C2
Rathbone Point E5 74 A4
Rathbone St E16 98 D1
W1 93 C2 239 B3
Rathcoole Ave N8 50 B4
Rathcoole Gdns N8 50 B4
Rathfern Prim Sch
SE23 163 B3
Rathfern Rd SE6 163 B3
Rathgar Ave W13 109 C5
Rathgar Cl N3 29 B1
Rathgar Rd SW9 138 D2
Rathmell Dr SW4 159 D5
Rathmore Rd SE7 121 B1
Ratier 18 NW9 27 C2
Rattray Ct 3 SE6 164 D2
Rattray Rd SW2 160 C6
Raul Rd SE15 140 A4
Raveley St NW5 71 C4
Raven Cl NW9 27 C1
Ravendale Rd TW16 171 D1
Ravenet Ct SW11 268 C1
SW4 159 B6
Ravenet St
SW11 137 B4 268 C1
Ravenfield Rd SW17 158 D1
Ravenhill Rd E13 99 C5
Raven Ho 10 SE16 118 D2
Ravenings Par IG3 58 A1
Ravenna Rd SW15 156 D6
Ravenor Ct UB6 85 D3
Ravenor Park Rd UB6 86 A4
Ravenor Prim Sch UB6 85 C4
Raven Rd E18 37 C1
Raven Row E1 96 B2
Ravensbourne 3 TW1 153 C5

Ravensbourne Ave
Bromley BR2,BR3 ... 186 C2
Catford BR2 ... 186 B3
Stanwell TW19 ... 148 A3
Ravensbourne Coll of Design & Communication
BR7 ... 188 B5
Ravensbourne Ct SE6 . 163 C4
Ravensbourne Gdns
W13 ... 87 B2
Ravensbourne Ho
NW8 ... 237 A4
10 Catford BR1 ... 186 B5
Ravensbourne Park Cres
SE6 ... 163 B4
Ravensbourne Pk SE6 163 C4
Ravensbourne Pl
SE13 ... 141 D3
Ravensbourne Rd
Bromley BR1,BR2 ... 209 A6
Forest Hill SE23 ... 163 B3
Twickenham TW1 ... 153 C5
Ravensbourne Sch The
BR2 ... 209 B4
Ravensbourne Sta
BR3 ... 186 B3
Ravensbury Ave SM4 . 202 A4
Ravensbury Ct CR4 .. 202 B5
Ravensbury Gr CR4 .. 202 B5
Ravensbury La CR4 .. 202 B5
Ravensbury Rd
Orpington BR5 ... 211 D5
Wandsworth SW18 ... 157 D2
Ravensbury Terr
SW18 ... 157 D2
Ravenscar NW1 ... 232 A5
Ravenscar Lo 13
SW19 ... 178 D3
Ravenscar Rd
Catford BR1 ... 186 C6
Surbiton KT6 ... 214 B6
Ravens Cl Bromley BR2 186 D1
Enfield EN1 ... 5 C3
Kingston KT6 ... 197 D3
Ravenscourt 1 N16 .. 74 A5
Sunbury TW16 ... 171 D2
Ravenscourt Ave W6 . 112 A2
Ravenscourt Cl HA4 .. 39 A2
Ravenscourt Gdns W6 112 A2
Ravenscourt Park Mans
W6 ... 112 B3
Ravenscourt Park Prep Sch
W6 ... 112 A2
Ravenscourt Park Sta
W6 ... 112 B2
Ravenscourt Pk W6 .. 112 A2
Ravenscourt Pl W6 .. 112 B2
Ravenscourt Rd BR5 .. 190 B1
W6 ... 112 B2
Ravenscourt Sq W6 .. 112 A3
Ravenscourt Theatre Sch
W6 ... 112 B2
Ravenscraig Rd N11 ... 31 C6
Ravenscroft Ave NW11 . 47 B2
Wembley HA9 ... 44 B2
Ravenscroft Cl 4 E16 .. 99 A2
Ravenscroft Cres SE9 . 166 B1
Ravenscroft Ct NW11 .. 47 B2
Ravenscroft Prim Sch
E16 ... 99 A3
Ravenscroft Rd E16 ... 99 A2
Acton W4 ... 111 A2
Penge BR3 ... 184 D1
Ravenscroft Sch N20 .. 13 B4
Ravenscroft St E2 ... 95 D4
Ravensdale Ave N12 ... 30 B6
Ravensdale Com Est
N16 ... 52 A3
Ravensdale Gdns
Hounslow TW4 ... 129 A2
South Norwood SE19 ... 183 B3
Ravensdale Mans N8 .. 50 A3
Ravensdale Rd N16 ... 51 D3
Hounslow TW4 ... 129 A2
Ravensdon St
SE11 ... 116 C1 261 B1
Ravensfield Cl RM9 ... 80 D4
Ravensfield Gdns
KT19 ... 215 C4
Ravenshaw St NW6 ... 69 B3
Ravenshill BR7 ... 188 D2
Ravens Ho KT1 ... 175 D1
Ravenshurst Ave NW4 . 46 C5
Ravenside KT6 ... 197 D4
Ravenside Cl N18 ... 34 D5
Ravenslea Rd SW11,
SW12 ... 158 D4
Ravensleigh Gdns
BR1 ... 187 B5
Ravensmead Rd BR2 .. 186 B3
Ravensmede Way W4 111 D2
Ravensroost SE19 ... 183 B2
Ravenstone
SE17 ... 117 C1 263 B1
Ravenstone Prim Sch
SW12 ... 159 A2
Ravenstone Rd N8 ... 50 C6
NW9 ... 45 D3
Ravenstone St SW12 . 159 A3
Ravensview Ct KT6 .. 197 D4
Ravens Way SE3,SE12 . 165 A6
Ravenswood DA5 ... 169 A3
Ravenswood Ave
Tolworth KT6 ... 214 C6
West Wickham BR4 ... 208 A1
Ravenswood Cres
Harrow HA2 ... 63 B6
West Wickham BR4 ... 208 A1
Ravenswood Gdns
TW7 ... 130 C4
Ravenswood Pk HA6 .. 22 A4
Ravenswood Rd E17 .. 54 A5
Balham SW12 ... 159 B4
Croydon CR0 ... 220 D5
Ravenswood Road Ind Est
5 E17 ... 54 A5
Ravens Wood Sch
BR2 ... 225 D5
Ravensworth Ct SW6 . 265 A3
Ravensworth Rd NW10 . 90 B4
SE9 ... 188 B6
Raven Wharf SE1 ... 253 C2
Ravey St EC2 ... 95 C3 243 A6
Ravine Gr SE18 ... 145 C6
Rav Pinter Cl N16 ... 51 C2
Rawlings Cl 3 BR6 .. 227 D3
Rawlings Cres HA9 ... 66 D5
Rawlings St
SW3 ... 114 D2 257 C4
Rawlins Cl N3 ... 47 A6
South Croydon CR2 ... 223 B1
Rawlinson Ct NW2 ... 46 C2
Rawlinson Ho SE13 .. 142 B1
Rawlinson Point 8
E16 ... 98 D2
Rawnsley Ave CR4 .. 202 C4
Rawreth Wlk N1 ... 235 B6
Rawson Ct SW11 ... 268 B1
Rawson St
SW11 ... 137 B4 268 C1
Rawsthorne Cl E16 .. 122 B5
Rawstone Wlk 5 E13 .. 99 A5
Rawstorne Pl EC1 ... 234 C2
Rawstorne St
EC1 ... 94 D4 234 C2
Raybell Ct TW7 ... 130 D3
Rayburne Ct W14 ... 254 A6
Buckhurst Hill IG9 ... 21 C3
Ray Cl KT9 ... 213 C2
Ray Ct Ealing W13 ... 109 B5
Woodford IG8 ... 37 D4
Raydean Rd EN5 ... 13 D6
Raydons Gdns RM9 ... 81 A3
Raydons Rd RM9 ... 81 A3
Raydon St N19 ... 71 B6
Rayfield Cl BR2 ... 210 A3
Rayford Ave SE12 ... 164 D4
Ray Gdns Barking IG11 . 102 A5
Stanmore HA7 ... 25 B5
Ray Ho 7 W10 ... 90 D1
Rayleas Cl SE18 ... 144 D4
Rayleigh Ave TW11 ... 174 C4
Rayleigh Cl N13 ... 17 B1
Rayleigh Ct
2 Kingston KT1 ... 176 B1
Tottenham N22 ... 33 A2
Rayleigh Rd 5 E16 ... 121 B5
7 E16 ... 121 B5
Edmonton N13 ... 17 B1
Merton SW19 ... 179 B2
Woodford IG8 ... 37 C3
Rayleigh Rise CR2 ... 221 C2
Ray Lodge Prim Sch
IG8 ... 37 D4
Ray Lodge Rd IG8 ... 37 D4
Ray Massey Way 3
E6 ... 100 A6
Raymead Ave CR7 ... 204 C4
Raymede Twr W10 ... 90 D2
Raymere Gdns SE18 .. 145 C5
Raymond Ave W13 ... 109 A3
Woodford E18 ... 36 D1
Raymond Cl SE26 ... 184 C5
Raymond Ct N10 ... 31 A3
Raymond Postgate Ct 5
SE28 ... 124 B6
Raymond Rd E13 ... 99 C6
Beckenham BR3 ... 207 A5
Ilford IG2 ... 57 B2
Wimbledon SW19 ... 179 A4
Raymond Way KT10 ... 213 A2
Raymouth Rd SE16 ... 118 B2
Raynald Ho 15 SW16 .. 160 A1
Rayne Ct E18 ... 54 D5
SE1 ... 253 C2
Rayne Ho 1 SW12 ... 159 A5
W9 ... 91 D3
Rayner Ct 10 W12 ... 112 C4
Rayners Cl HA0 ... 65 D3
Rayners Cres UB5 ... 84 B4
Rayners Gdns UB5 ... 84 B4
Rayners La Harrow HA2 . 63 D6
Pinner HA5 ... 41 D3
Rayners Lane Sta HA5 . 41 B2
Rayner's Rd SW15 ... 157 A6
Rayner Twrs E10 ... 53 C2
Raynes Ave E11 ... 55 C2
Raynes Ct NW2 ... 69 A4
Raynesfield SW20 ... 200 C6
Raynes Park High Sch
KT3 ... 200 B6
Raynes Park Sta
SW20 ... 178 C1
Raynham W2 ... 237 A2
Raynham Ave N18 ... 34 A5
Raynham Ho 1 E1 ... 96 D3
Raynham Prim Sch
N18 ... 34 A5
Raynham Rd W6 ... 112 B2
Edmonton N18 ... 34 A5
Raynham Terr N18 ... 34 A5
Raynor Cl UB1 ... 107 B5
Raynor Pl N1 ... 235 B6
Raynton Cl Harrow HA2 . 41 A2
Hayes UB4 ... 83 D3
Raynton Dr Hayes UB4 .. 83 C5
Hayes UB4 ... 83 D3
Raynton Rd EN3 ... 6 D6
Ray Rd KT8 ... 195 D4
Rays Ave N18 ... 34 C6
Rays Rd N18 ... 34 C6
West Wickham BR4 ... 208 A2
Ray St EC1 ... 241 B5
Ray Wlk N7 ... 72 B6
Raywood Cl UB7 ... 127 A5
Reachview Cl 14 NW1 .. 71 C1
Read Cl KT7 ... 197 A2
Read Ct E17 ... 53 D3
Reade Ct 6 W3 ... 111 A3
Reade Ho 7 SE10 ... 142 B6
Reade Wlk NW10 ... 67 C1
Read Ho N11 ... 30 D6
4 SE11 ... 138 C6
Reading Ho SE15 ... 140 A6
W2 ... 236 A1
Reading La E8 ... 74 B2
Reading Rd
Northolt UB5 ... 64 A3
Sutton SM1 ... 218 A3
Reading Way NW7 ... 29 A5
Readman Ct 8 SE20 .. 184 B2
Reads Cl IG1 ... 78 D5
Reapers Cl NW1 ... 232 C6
Reapers Way TW7 ... 152 B6
Reardon Ho 5 E1 ... 118 B5
Reardon Path 31 E1 .. 118 B5
Reardon St E1 ... 118 B5
Reaston St SE14 ... 140 D5
Reay Prim Sch
SW9 ... 138 B5 270 D3
Rebecca Ct
Beckenham BR3 ... 185 C2
Sidcup DA14 ... 190 B6
Rebecca Ho 10 N12 ... 29 D6
Reckitt Rd W4 ... 111 C1
Record St SE16 ... 140 C6
Recovery St SW17 ... 180 C5
Recreation Rd
Bromley BR2 ... 186 D1
Forest Hill SE26 ... 184 D6
Southall UB2 ... 107 A2
Recreation Way CR4,
SW16 ... 204 A6
Rector St N1 ... 95 A6 235 A5
Rectory Bsns Ctr 5
DA14 ... 190 B6
Rectory Cl N3 ... 29 B2
Chingford E4 ... 19 C1
Littleton TW17 ... 192 C6
Long Ditton KT6 ... 197 C1
Sidcup DA14 ... 190 B6
Stanmore HA7 ... 25 B5
West Barnes SW20 ... 200 C6
Rectory Cres E11 ... 55 C3
Rectory Ct E11 ... 76 D5
Cranford TW5 ... 128 C3
Feltham TW13 ... 172 C6
Wallington SM6 ... 219 C4
Woodford E18 ... 36 D2
Rectory Field Cres
SE7 ... 143 C5
Rectory Gdns N8 ... 50 A5
SW4 ... 137 C2
Beckenham BR3 ... 185 C2
Northolt UB5 ... 85 B6
Rectory Gn BR3 ... 185 B2
Rectory Gr SW4 ... 137 C2
Croydon CR0 ... 220 D6
Hampton TW12,TW13 .. 173 B6
Rectory La DA14 ... 190 C6
Edgware HA8 ... 26 C4
Long Ditton KT6 ... 197 C1
Stanmore HA7 ... 25 B5
Upper Tooting SW17 ... 181 A5
Wallington SM6 ... 219 C4
Rectory Orch SW19 ... 179 A6
Rectory Paddock Sch
BR5 ... 190 C1
Rectory Park Ave UB5 .. 85 B4
Rectory Pl SE18 ... 122 C2
Rectory Rd E12 ... 78 B3
E17 ... 53 D5
N16 ... 73 D5
1 W3 ... 111 A5
Rectory Rd *continued*
Barnes SW13 ... 134 A3
Beckenham BR3 ... 185 C2
Cranford TW5 ... 128 C3
Dagenham RM10 ... 81 D1
Hayes UB3 ... 84 A1
Keston BR2 ... 225 D1
Southall UB2 ... 107 B3
Sutton SM1 ... 217 D5
Rectory Road Sta N16 . 73 D5
Rectory Sq E1 ... 96 D2
Rectory Way UB10 ... 60 D5
Reculver Ho 2 SE15 .. 140 C6
Reculver Mews N18 ... 34 A6
Reculver Rd SE16 ... 118 D1
Red Anchor Cl SW3 ... 267 A5
Redan Pl W2 ... 91 D1
Redan St W14 ... 112 D3
Redan Terr SE5 ... 138 D3
Red Barracks Rd 4
SE18 ... 122 B2
Redberry Gr SE23,SE26 162 C1
Redbourne Ave N3 ... 29 C2
Redbourne Dr SE28 .. 102 D1
Redbourne Ho 7 E14 .. 97 B1
N3 ... 29 C2
Redbourn Ho W10 ... 90 C3
Redbridge Coll RM6 ... 58 B4
Redbridge Ent Ctr IG1 . 79 A6
Redbridge Gdns SE5 .. 139 C5
Redbridge Inf Sch IG4 . 56 A4
Redbridge Jun Sch IG4 56 A4
Redbridge La E IG4 ... 56 A4
Redbridge La W E11 ... 55 C3
Redbridge Rdbt IG4 ... 55 D3
Redbridge Sta IG4 ... 55 D3
Redburn St
SW3 ... 136 D6 267 C6
Redburn Trad Est EN3 .. 18 D5
Redcar Cl UB5 ... 63 D2
Redcar Ho SE26 ... 184 B4
Redcar St SE5 ... 139 A5
Redcastle Cl E1 ... 118 C6
Red Cedars Rd BR6 ... 211 C2
Redchurch St
E2 ... 95 D3 243 C6
Redcliffe Cl SW5 ... 255 C1
Redcliffe Gdns
SW10 ... 135 D6 265 D6
Chiswick W4 ... 132 D5
Ilford IG1 ... 56 C1
Redcliffe Mews SW10 255 D1
Redcliffe Pl SW10 ... 266 A5
Redcliffe Rd
SW10 ... 136 A6 266 B6
Redcliffe Sch
SW10 ... 136 A6 266 B6
Redcliffe Sq
SW10 ... 113 D1 255 D1
Redcliffe St SW10 ... 265 D6
Redcliffe Wlk HA9 ... 66 D5
Redclose Ave SM4 ... 201 C4
Redclyffe Rd E6 ... 99 C6
Redclyffe Terr 2 SM2 217 C1
Redclyf Ho 12 E1 ... 96 C3
Redcroft 5 NW6 ... 69 C2
Redcroft Rd UB1 ... 86 A1
Redcross Way
SE1 ... 117 A5 252 B3
Redding Ho SE18 ... 122 A3
Reddings Ave WD23 ... 8 A6
Reddings Cl NW7 ... 27 D6
Reddings The NW7 ... 11 D1
Reddins Rd SE15 ... 140 A6
Reddons Rd BR3 ... 185 A3
Rede Ho 2 E12 ... 78 C3
Rede Pl W2 ... 113 C6 245 B6
Redesdale Gdns TW7 . 131 A5
Redesdale St SW3 ... 267 C6
Redfern Ave TW2,TW4 151 C4
Redfern Ho 6 E13 ... 98 D6
Redfern Rd NW10 ... 67 C1
Catford SE6 ... 164 A4
Redfield La
SW5 ... 113 D2 255 C4
Redfield Mews SW5 ... 255 B4
Redriff Est SE16 ... 119 B3
Redford Ave
Thornton Heath CR7 ... 204 B5
Wallington SM6 ... 220 A2
Redford Cl TW13 ... 149 D2
Redford Wlk N1 ... 235 A6
Redgate Dr BR2 ... 225 B6
Red Gates Sch CR9 ... 220 C3
Redgate Terr SW15 ... 156 D5
Redgrave Cl SE25 ... 205 D3
Redgrave Rd SW15 ... 134 D2
Red Hill BR7 ... 188 D5
Redhill Ct SW2 ... 160 C2
Redhill Dr HA8 ... 27 A1
Red Hill Prim Sch
BR7 ... 188 D5
Redhill St NW1 . 93 B4 231 D2
Red House La DA6 ... 147 A1
Red House Rd CR0 ... 203 D3
Redif Ho RM10 ... 81 D4
Redington Gdns NW3 .. 69 D4
Redington Ho N1 ... 233 D4
Redington Rd NW3 ... 69 D4
Redknap Ho TW10 ... 153 C1
Red La KT10 ... 213 A2
Redland Gdns KT8 ... 195 B5
Redlands N15 ... 51 B5
Teddington TW11 ... 175 A4
Redlands Ct BR1 ... 186 D3
Redlands Prim Sch E1 . 96 C2
Redlands Rd EN3 ... 7 A4
Redlands The 5 BR3 . 185 D1
Redlands Way SW2 ... 160 B4
Redleaf Cl DA17 ... 147 C6
Redleaves Ave TW15 . 170 D4
Redlees Cl TW7 ... 131 A1
Red Leys UB8 ... 60 A1
Red Lion Bsns Ctr KT6 214 B5
Red Lion Cl 9 SE17 .. 139 B6
Red Lion Ct EC4 ... 241 B1
Red Lion Hill N2 ... 30 B1
Red Lion La SE18 ... 144 C4
Red Lion Pl SE18 ... 144 C4
Red Lion Rd KT6 ... 214 C6
Red Lion Row SE17 .. 139 A6
Red Lion Sq
WC1 ... 94 B2 240 C3
Red Lion St
WC1 ... 94 B2 240 C3
Richmond TW10 ... 153 D6
Red Lion Yd W1 ... 248 B4
Red Lo BR4 ... 208 A2
Red Lodge Rd BR3,BR4 208 B2
Redlynch Ct
W14 ... 113 A4 244 B1
Redlynch Ho 27 SW9 . 138 C4
Redman Bldg EC1 ... 241 A4
Redman Cl UB5 ... 84 C5
Redman Ho SE1 ... 252 B1
Redman's Rd E1 ... 96 C2
Redmayne Ho 15 SW9 138 B3
Redmead La E1 ... 118 A5
Redmead Rd UB3 ... 105 C2
Redmill Ho 24 E1 ... 96 B3
Redmond Ho N1 ... 233 D5
Redmore Rd W6 ... 112 B2
Red Oak Cl BR6 ... 226 D6
Red Pl W1 ... 248 A6
Redpoll Way DA18 ... 124 D3
Red Post Hill SE21,
SE24 ... 161 B6
Red Post Ho E6 ... 77 D1
Redriffe Rd E13 ... 98 D6
Redriff Prim Sch SE16 119 A4
Redriff Rd SE16 ... 119 A3
Redroofs Cl BR3 ... 185 D2
Redrose Trad Ctr 1
EN4 ... 14 B6
Red Rover SW13 ... 134 A2
Redrup Ho 21 SE14 .. 140 D6
Redruth Cl N22 ... 32 B3
Redruth Ho SM2 ... 217 D1
Redruth Rd E9 ... 96 C6
Red Sq The N16 ... 73 B5
Redstart Cl E6 ... 100 A2
SE14 ... 141 A5
Redston Rd N8 ... 49 D5
Redvers Rd N22 ... 32 C1
Redvers St E2 ... 95 C4
Redway Dr TW2 ... 152 A4
Redwing Path SE28 .. 123 B4
Redwood Cl DA15 ... 168 A3
N14 ... 15 D4
SE16 ... 119 A5
Chigwell IG9 ... 21 B2
Hillingdon UB10 ... 82 D5
South Oxhey WD19 ... 22 D6
Redwood Ct N19 ... 49 D2
NW6 ... 69 A1
Northolt UB5 ... 85 A4
10 Surbiton KT6 ... 197 D2
Redwood Est TW5 ... 128 B6
Redwood Gdns E4 ... 19 D5
Redwood Mews
2 SW4 ... 137 B2
Ashford TW15 ... 171 B3
Redwoods SW15 ... 156 A3
Redwood Twr E11 ... 76 B5
Redwood Way EN5 ... 12 D6
Redwood Wlk KT6 ... 197 D1
Reece Mews SW7 ... 256 C4
Reed Ave BR6 ... 227 C5
Reed Cl E16 ... 99 A2
SE12 ... 165 A6
Reede Gdns RM10 ... 81 D3
Reede Rd RM10 ... 81 D2
Reede Way RM10 ... 81 D2
Reedham Cl N17 ... 52 B5
Reedham St SE15 ... 140 A2
Reed Ho SW15 ... 156 A5
Reedholm Villas N16 .. 73 B4
Reed Mans 6 E11 ... 55 A3
Reed Pl Bsns Pk TW17 192 B1
Reed Rd N17 ... 33 D1
Reedsfield Cl TW15 ... 148 D1
Reedsfield Rd TW15 .. 170 D6
Reed's Pl NW1 ... 71 C1
Reedworth St
SE11 ... 116 C2 261 B3
Reef Ho E14 ... 120 A3
Reenglass Rd HA7 ... 25 D6
Rees Dr HA7 ... 26 A6
Rees Gdns CR0 ... 205 D3
Rees Ho 6 N17 ... 33 D3
Reesland Cl E12 ... 78 C2
Rees St N1 ... 95 A6 235 B5
Reets Farm Cl NW9 ... 45 C3
Reeves Ave NW9 ... 45 B2
Reeves Cnr CR0 ... 220 D6
Reeves Cnr Sta CR0 .. 220 D6
Reeves Ho SE1 ... 251 A1
W1 ... 248 A5
Reeves Mews
W1 ... 115 A6 248 B5
Reeves Rd E3 ... 97 D3
SE18 ... 144 D6
Reflection The E16 ... 122 D4
Reform Row N17 ... 33 D1
Reform St SW11 ... 136 D3
Regal Cl E1 ... 96 A2
Ealing W5 ... 87 D2
Regal Cres SM6 ... 219 B5
Regal Ct Edmonton N18 . 33 D5
2 Mitcham CR4 ... 202 D6
Wembley HA0 ... 65 D4
Regal Dr N11 ... 31 B5
Regal La NW1 ... 231 B5
Regal Pl 8 E3 ... 97 B4
SW6 ... 265 D3
Regal Way HA3 ... 44 A3
Regan Ho 1 N18 ... 33 D4
Regan Way N1 ... 95 C5
Regatta Ho TW11 ... 175 A6
Regatta Point TW8 ... 132 B6
Regency Cl Ealing W5 ... 88 A1
Hampton TW12 ... 173 B5
Regency Cres 3 NW4 . 28 D1
Regency Ct 21 E9 ... 96 C6
Enfield EN1 ... 17 B6
4 Kingston KT5 ... 198 B4
4 Penge SE19 ... 184 A3
Sutton SM1 ... 217 D4
Wimbledon SW19 ... 179 B3
Regency Dr HA4 ... 39 C1
Regency Gdns KT12 .. 194 C1
Regency Ho N3 ... 29 B1
Regency Lo NW3 ... 70 B1
1 Buckhurst Hill IG9 ... 21 D2
Regency Mews
1 NW10 ... 68 A2
Beckenham BR3 ... 186 A2
Isleworth TW7 ... 152 C6
Regency St
SW1 ... 115 D2 259 D3
Regency Way DA7 ... 147 A2
Regency Wlk
Croydon CR0 ... 207 B3
8 Richmond TW10 ... 154 A6
Regent Ave UB10 ... 60 D1
Regent Bsns Ctr UB3 . 106 A4
Regent Cl N12 ... 30 A5
Cranford TW4 ... 128 B4
Harrow HA3 ... 44 A3
Regent Ct 1 N16 ... 51 D2
N3 ... 29 D3
NW8 ... 230 A1
South Norwood SE19 ... 182 D4
Regent Gdns IG3 ... 58 A2
Regent Ho W14 ... 254 A4
Regent Lo 9 SW2 ... 160 B3
Regent Pl W1 ... 249 B6
Croydon CR0 ... 205 D1
Wimbledon SW19 ... 180 A5
Regent Rd SE24 ... 160 D6
Surbiton KT5 ... 198 C4
Regents Ave N13 ... 32 C5
Regents Bridge Gdns
SW8 ... 270 B4
Regents Canal Ho 21
E14 ... 97 A1
Regents Cl Hayes UB4 .. 83 C2
South Croydon CR2 ... 221 C2
Regent's Coll
NW1 ... 93 A3 238 A6
Regents Ct E8 ... 96 A6
22 Beckenham BR3 ... 185 C3
Bromley BR1 ... 186 D3
Edgware HA8 ... 26 A6
1 Kingston KT2 ... 176 A2
Regents Dr BR2 ... 225 D3
Regents Gate Ho 20
E14 ... 119 A6
Regents Mews
NW8 ... 92 A5 229 B4
Regent's Park★
NW1 ... 93 A4 231 A3
Regent's Park Barracks
NW1 ... 231 D3
Regent's Park Rd N3 ... 47 B6
NW1 ... 93 A6 231 A6
Regent's Park Sta
NW1 ... 93 B3 238 C5
Regent's Park Terr
NW1 ... 231 C6
Regent's Pl SE3 ... 143 A3
Regents Pl IG10 ... 21 D4
Regents Plaza 2 NW6 . 91 D5
Regent Sq 23 E3 ... 97 D4
WC1 ... 94 A4 233 B1
Belvedere DA17 ... 125 D2
Regent's Row E8 ... 96 A6

gent St W1 .115 C6 249 A6
........110 C1
ents Wharf 3 E2 ..96 B6
........233 C4
ina Coeli RC Prim Sch
2 ....220 D1
ginald Ct BR3 ......186 A2
ginald Pl 6 SE8 ...141 C5
ginald Rd E7 ....77 A2
8 ....141 C5
ginald Sorenson Ct
1 ....54 B2
ginald Sq SE8 ......141 C5
gina Point SE16 ....118 C3
gina Rd N4 ....50 B1
ling W13 ....109 A5
uthall UB2 ....107 A2
uth Norwood SE25 ..206 A6
gina Terr W13 ......109 B5
gis Ct N8 ....50 B5
W1 ....237 C4
ast Bedfont TW14 ....149 B5
itcham SW19 ....180 C2
gis Pl 17 SW2 ......138 B1
gis Rd NW5 ....71 B3
gnart Bldgs NW1 ...232 B1
gnolruf Ct KT12 ...194 A2
id Cl HA5 ....40 A5
id Ct SW14 ....133 A3
eidhaven Rd SE18 ...123 C2
eigate Ave SM3,SM4 .201 D1
eigate Rd BR1,SE12 ..165 A2
atford BR1 ....164 D1
ford IG3 ....79 D6
eigate Way SM6 .....220 A3
eighton Rd E5 ....74 A6
eizel Cl N16 ....51 C1
elay Rd W12 ....112 C5
elf Rd SE15 ....140 A2
eliance Sq E2 ......243 A6
elko Gdns SM1 ......218 B3
elton Mews SW7 .....257 B6
embrandt Cl E14 ....120 B3
embrandt Ct 10 SE16 118 B1
West Ewell KT19 .....215 D2
embrandt Rd SE13 ..142 C1
dgware HA8 ....26 C1
emembrance Ave N2 .47 D6
emington Rd E6 ....100 A1
N15 ....51 B3
emington St
N1 ....94 D5 234 D3
emnant St WC2 .....240 C2
emsted Ho 5 NW6 ....91 D6
emus Rd E3 ....75 C1
enbold Ho 5 SE10 ..142 A4
endlebury Ho 17
SE18 ....122 B2
endle Cl CR0 ....206 A4
endlesham Ho 3 E5,
N16 ....74 A5
endlesham Rd E5 ....74 A5
Enfield EN2 ....4 D4
enforth St SE16 ....118 C4
enfree Way TW17 ...192 C2
enfrew Cl E6 ....122 C6
enfrew Ct TW5 ......129 A3
enfrew Ho E17 ....35 B1
NW6 ....91 D5
Renfrew Rd
SE11 ....116 D2 261 C3
Hounslow TW5 ....129 A3
Kingston KT2 ....177 A3
Renmuir St SW17 ...180 D4
Rennell Ho 18 E9 ....74 D2
Rennell St SE13 ....142 A2
Renness Rd E17 ......53 A6
Rennets Cl SE9 .....167 C6
Rennets Wood Rd SE9 167 B6
Rennie Cotts 24 E1 ...96 C3
Rennie Ct SE1 ......251 C4
Holdbrook EN3 ....7 C5
Rennie Ho SE1 ......262 A5
Rennie St SE1 116 D5 251 C4
Renoir Ct 7 SE16 ...118 B1
Renovation The E16 ..122 D4
Renown Cl CR0 ......204 D1
Rensburg Rd E17 .....52 D3
Rensburg Villas E17 ..52 D4
Renshaw Cl 7 DA17 ..147 B6
Renshaw Ct SW19 ....179 A6
Renshaw Ho 11 SW27 182 D5
Renters Ave NW4 .....46 C3
Renton Cl SW2 ......160 B5
Renwick Rd IG11 ....102 B4
Repens Way UB4 .....84 D3
Rephidim St SE1 ....263 A5
Replingham Rd SW18 .157 C3
Reporton Rd
SW6 ....135 A5 264 B3
Repository Rd SE7,
SE18 ....122 B1
Repton Ave Hayes UB3 .105 B2
Wembley HA0 ....65 C4
Repton Cl SM1,SM5 ..218 C3
Repton Ct BR3 ......185 D2
Repton Ho 2 E14 .....97 A1
SW1 ....259 B3
Repton Rd Harrow HA3 .44 B5
Repton Rd *continued*
Orpington BR6 ......227 D5
Repton St E14 ....97 A1
Re Sassoon Ho SE15 ..140 C4
Reservoir Cl CR7 ....205 B5
Reservoir Rd SE4 ....141 A3
Ruislip HA4 ....39 B5
Southgate N14 ....15 C6
Resolution Wlk SE18 ..122 B3
Restell Cl SE3 ......142 C6
Restmor Way SM5,
SM6 ....219 A6
Reston Pl SW7 ......246 A1
Restons Cres DA15,
SE9 ....167 C5
Restoration Sq SW11 .266 D1
Restormel Cl TW3 ...151 C6
Retcar Pl N19 ....71 B6
Retford St E2 ....95 C5
Retingham Way E4 ....19 D2
Retreat Cl HA3 ......43 C4
Retreat Ho 5 E9 .....74 C2
Retreat Pl E9 ....74 C2
Retreat Rd TW9 .....153 D6
Retreat The NW9 .....45 B4
Harrow HA2 ....41 C2
Mortlake SW14 ......133 C2
North Cheam KT4 ....216 B6
South Norwood CR7 ..205 B5
Surbiton KT5 ....198 B3
Reunion Row E1 .....118 B6
Reveley Sq SE16 ....119 A4
Revell Rd Cheam SM1 .217 B2
Kingston KT1 ....176 D2
Revell Rise SE18 ...145 D6
Revelon Rd SE4 .....141 A2
Revelstoke Rd SW18,
SW19 ....157 C2
Reventlow Rd SE9 ...167 A3
Reverdy Rd SE1 .....118 A2
Reverend Cl HA2 .....63 D5
Revesby Rd SM5 .....202 C3
Review Rd NW2 ....67 D6
Dagenham RM10 .....103 D6
Rewell St SW6 136 A5 266 A3
Rewley Rd SM4 .....202 B3
Rex Ave TW15 ......170 C5
Rex Ho TW13 ....151 A1
Rex Par 2 IG8 ....37 C4
Rex Pl W1 ...115 A5 248 B4
Reydon Ave E11 ......55 C3
Reygate Ct N4 ....51 A3
Reynard Cl BR1 ....210 C6
SE4 ....141 B2
Reynard Dr SE19 ...183 D3
Reynard Mills Trad Est
TW8 ....109 C1
Reynard Pl SE14 ...141 A6
Reynardson Rd N17 ...33 A3
Reynardson's Ct 3 N17 51 D6
Reynolds Ave
Chessington KT9 ....214 A1
Ilford RM6 ....58 C2
Little Ilford E12 ....78 C3
Reynolds Cl NW11 ....47 D2
Carshalton SM5 .....202 D1
Mitcham SW19 ......180 B2
Reynolds Ct E11 .....76 D5
Ilford RM6 ....58 D6
Reynolds Dr HA8 .....44 B6
Reynolds Ho 19 E2 ...96 C5
N4 ....50 A1
NW8 ....229 D3
SW1 ....259 D3
Enfield EN1 ....18 A6
Reynolds Pl SE3 ....143 B5
12 Richmond TW10 ...154 B5
Reynolds Rd SE15 ...140 C1
W4 ....111 A3
Hayes UB4 ....84 C3
New Malden KT3 ....199 B2
Reynolds Way CR0 ...221 C4
Rheidol Mews N1 ...235 A4
Rheidol Terr
N1 ....95 A6 235 A5
Rhein Ho N8 ....50 A6
Rheola Cl N17 ....33 D2
Rhoda St E2 ...95 D3 243 D6
Rhodes Ave N22 ......31 C2
Rhodes Avenue Prim Sch
N22 ....31 C2
Rhodes Ho N1 ......235 C2
Rhodesia Rd E11 ....76 B6
SW9 ....138 A3
Rhodes-Moorhouse Ct
SM4 ....201 C3
Rhodes St N7 ....72 B3
Rhodeswell Rd E14 ...97 A2
Rhodrons Ave KT9 ...214 A3
Rhondda Gr E3 ......97 B4
Rhyl Prim Sch NW5 ...71 A2
Rhyl Rd UB6 ....86 D5
Rhyl St NW5 ....71 A2
Rhys Ave N11 ....31 D3
Rialto Rd CR4 .....181 A1
Ribble Cl IG8 ....37 C4
Ribblesdale Ave N11 ..31 A4
Northolt UB5 ....63 D2
Ribblesdale Ho 11 NW6 91 C6
Ribblesdale Rd N8 ....50 B5
Streatham SW16 ....181 B5
Ribbon Dance Mews
SE5 ....139 B4
Ribchester Ave UB6 ...86 D4
Ribston Cl BR2 .....210 B1
Ribstone Ho 12 E9 ...74 D2
Ricardo Path 5 SE28 .124 C5
Ricardo St E14 ......97 D1
Ricards Lodge High Sch
SW19 ....179 B5
Ricards Rd SW19 ....179 B5
Riccal Ct 2 NW9 ......27 C2
Riceyman Ho WC1 ...234 A1
Richard Alibon Prim Sch
RM10 ....81 C3
Richard Anderson Ct 1
SE14 ....140 D5
Richard Atkins Prim Sch
SW2 ....160 A4
Richard Burbidge Mans
SW13 ....134 C6
Richard Burton Ct 4
IG9 ....21 C2
Richard Challoner Sch
KT3 ....199 B2
Richard Cl SE18 ....122 A2
Richard Cloudesley Sch
EC1 ....95 A3 242 A5
Richard Cobden Prim Sch
NW1 ....93 C6 232 B5
Richard Ct EN5 ....1 A2
Richard Fell Ho 2 E12 .78 C4
Richard Fox Ho N4 ...73 A5
Richard Ho 8 SE16 ..118 C2
Richard House Dr E16 .99 D1
E6 ....100 A1
Richard Knight Ho
SW6 ....265 B2
Richard Neale Ho 2
E1 ....118 B6
Richards Cl Bushey WD23 .8 B4
Harlington UB3 .....127 B6
Harrow HA1 ....43 A4
Hillingdon UB10 .....82 C6
Richards Ct BR3 ....184 D2
Richardson Cl 19 E8 ..95 D6
Richardson Ct 20 SW4 138 A3
Richardson Gdns 12
RM10 ....81 D2
Richardson Ho TW7 ..130 D2
Richardson Rd E15 ...98 C5
Richardson's Mews
W1 ....239 A5
Richards Pl E17 .....53 C6
Richard's Pl SW3 ...257 B4
Richard St 10 E1 ....96 B1
Richard Thornton Ho
SW19 ....179 C1
Richbell Pl WC1 ....240 C4
Richborne Terr
SW8 ....138 B5 270 D4
Richborough Ho 14 E5 .74 B4
10 SE15 ....140 C6
Richborough Rd NW2 ..69 A4
Richens Cl TW3 ....130 B3
Riches Rd IG1 ....79 A6
Richfield Ct 4 BR3 ..185 B2
Richfield Rd WD23 .....8 A4
Richford Gate W6 ...112 C3
Richford Rd E15 .....98 D6
Richford St W6 ....112 C3
Richings Ho BR5 ...190 A2
Rich La SW5 ....255 C2
Richland Ho 4 SE15 ..140 A4
Richlands Ave KT17 ..216 A4
Richman Ho 10 SE8 ..119 B1
Richmond Adult & Com Coll
TW9 ....131 D1
Richmond Ave
N1 ....94 B6 233 D6
NW10 ....68 C2
Chingford E4 ....36 B5
Feltham TW14 ......149 C5
Hillingdon UB10 .....60 D2
Wimbledon SW20 ....179 A2
Richmond Bldgs W1 ..239 C1
Richmond Bridge
TW1 ....153 D5
Richmond Bridge Mans 1
TW1 ....153 D5
Richmond Circus TW9 132 A1
Richmond Cl E17 ....53 B3
Borehamwood WD6 ...11 B6
Richmond Coll
W8 ....113 D3 255 D6
Richmond TW10 .....154 A4
Richmond Cres
N1 ....94 C6 234 A6
Chingford E4 ....36 B5
Edmonton N9 ....18 A3
Richmond Ct BR1 ...187 B3
SW1 ....247 D1
12 Kingston KT2 ....176 C3
Mitcham CR4 ....202 B6
Wembley HA9 ....66 B6
Wimbledon SW20 ....178 B1
Richmond Dr TW17 ..193 B3
Richmond Gdns NW4 ..46 A4
Richmond Gdns *continued*
Harrow HA3 ....24 D3
Richmond Gn CR0 ...220 A5
Richmond Gr N1 .....72 D1
Surbiton KT5 ....198 B3
Richmond Hill TW10 ..154 A5
Richmond Hill Ct 5
TW10 ....154 A5
Richmond Ho NW1 ..231 D3
SE17 ....262 C2
12 Forest Hill SE26 ..162 A1
Richmond Ho(Annexe of
Rectory Sch) TW12 ..173 B5
Richmond International
Bsns Ctr 9 TW9 ....132 B1
Richmond Mans SW5 .255 C2
Putney SW15 ....135 A2
14 Twickenham TW1 ..153 D5
Richmond Mews W1 ..239 C1
Richmond Park★
TW10 ....155 A3
Richmond Park Rd
Kingston KT2 ....176 A3
Mortlake SW14 .....133 B1
Richmond Pk IG10 ....21 D4
Richmond Pl SE18 ..123 A2
Richmond Rd E11 ....76 B6
E7 ....77 B3
E8 ....74 A1
N15 ....51 C3
N2 ....30 A1
W5 ....110 A4
Bowes Park N11 .....32 A4
Chingford E4 ....20 B3
Ilford IG1 ....79 A5
Isleworth TW7 .....131 A2
Kingston KT2 ......176 A4
New Barnet EN5 .....14 A6
Thornton Heath CR7 ..204 D5
Twickenham TW1 ...153 C4
Wallington CR0 ....220 A5
Wimbledon SW20 ...178 B2
Richmond St E13 ....99 A5
Richmond Sta TW9 ..132 A1
Richmond Terr
SW1 ....116 A4 250 A2
Richmond upon Thames
Coll TW2 ....152 C4
Richmond Way
W12,W14 ....112 D4
Wanstead E11 ......77 A6
Richmount Gdns SE3 .143 A2
Rich St E14 ....119 B6
Rickard Cl NW4 .....46 A5
Streatham SW2 ....160 C3
Rickards Cl KT6 ...214 A6
Rickett St SW6 ....265 B6
Rickman Ho 26 E2 ...96 C3
Rickman St 25 E1 ...96 C3
Rickmansworth Rd
HA5 ....22 C1
Rick Roberts Way E15 .98 B5
Rickthorne Rd 6 N19 .72 A6
Rickyard Path SE9 ..144 A1
Riddell Ct SE1 .....263 C2
Ridding La UB6 .....64 D3
Riddons Rd SE12 ...187 C6
Rideout St SE18 ...122 B2
Rider Cl DA15 .....167 C5
Ride The
Brentford TW8 .....109 C1
Enfield EN3 ....6 D2
Ridgdale St E3 .....97 D5
Ridge Ave N21 ......17 B4
Ridgebrook Rd SE3,
SE9 ....143 D2
Ridge Cl NW4 ....28 D1
NW9 ....45 B5
SE28 ....123 B4
Ridge Crest EN2 .....4 B4
Ridge Hill NW11 ....47 A1
Ridge Ho 4 KT2 ....176 D3
Ridgemead Cl N13,N14 .16 A2
Ridgemont Gdns HA8 ..27 A6
Ridgemount Ave CR0 .222 D6
Ridgemount Cl SE20 .184 B3
Ridgemount Gdns EN2 ..4 D3
Ridgeon Ct N22 .....32 B4
Ridge Rd N8 ....50 B3
NW2 ....69 B5
Cheam SM3 ....201 B1
Edmonton N21 ......17 B3
Mitcham CR4 ......181 B3
Ridges The E4 ......35 C6
Ridge Terr N21 .....17 A4
Ridge The DA5 ....169 B4
Barnet EN5 ....13 B6
Orpington BR6 ....227 B6
Surbiton KT5 .....198 C4
Twickenham TW2 ..152 B4
Ridgeview Cl EN5 ...12 D5
Ridgeview Rd N20 ...14 A1
Ridgeway BR2 ....225 A6
11 Richmond TW10 ..154 A5
Walton-on-T KT12 ..193 D1
Woodford IG8 ......37 C6
Ridge Way
Feltham TW13 ....151 A1
7 West Norwood SE19 .183 C4
Ridgeway Ave EN4 ...14 D5
Ridgeway Cres BR6 ..227 C5
Ridgeway Crescent Gdns
BR6 ....227 C5
Ridgeway Ct HA5 ....23 C3
Ridgeway Dr BR1 ..187 B6
Acton W3 ....110 C3
Ridgeway E DA15 ..167 D6
Ridgeway Gdns N6 ...49 C2
Redbridge IG4 ......56 A4
Ridgeway Rd TW7 ..130 C4
Ridgeway Rd N TW7 .130 C5
Ridgeway The N11 ...30 D6
N3 ....29 D3
NW11 ....47 B1
NW7 ....28 B6
NW9 ....45 B5
Acton W3 ....110 C3
Chingford E4 ....20 A3
Enfield EN2 ....4 B5
Harrow HA2 ....41 B4
Harrow HA2 ....41 D3
Harrow HA3 ....43 C3
Palmers Green N14 ..16 A2
Ruislip HA4 ....40 A2
Stanmore HA7 ......25 C4
Wallington CR0 ...220 B5
Ridgeway W DA15 ..167 C6
Ridgeway Wlk UB5 ..63 A2
Ridgewell Cl N1 ..235 B6
Dagenham RM10 ...103 D6
Forest Hill SE26 ..185 B6
Ridgmount Gdns
WC1 ....93 D2 239 C4
Ridgmount Pl WC1 ..239 C4
Ridgmount Rd SW18 .157 D6
Ridgmount St
WC1 ....93 D2 239 C4
Ridgway SW19,SW20 ..178 D4
Ridgway Ct SW19 ..178 D4
Ridgway Gdns SW19 .178 D3
Ridgway Pl SW19 ..179 A4
Ridgway Rd SW9 ..138 D2
Ridgway The SM2 ..218 B1
Ridgwell Rd E16 ....99 C2
Riding House St
W1 ....93 C2 239 A3
Ridings Ave N21 ....17 A6
Ridings Cl N6 ......49 C2
Ridings The EN4 ....14 B4
Ealing W5 ....88 B3
Sunbury TW16 ....172 A2
Surbiton KT5 .....198 C4
Riding The NW11 ...47 B2
Ridler Rd EN1 ....5 C5
Ridley Ave W13 ...109 B3
Ridley Cl IG11 .....79 D1
Ridley Ct SW16 ...182 A4
Ridley Ho 14 SW11 ..136 C2
Ridley Rd DA16 ...146 B4
E7 ....77 C4
E8 ....73 D3
NW10 ....90 A5
Beckenham BR2 ...208 D6
Merton SW19 .....179 D3
Ridley Road Mkt E8 ..73 D3
Ridsdale Rd SE20 ..184 B2
Riefield Rd SE9 ..167 A6
Riesco Dr CR0 ...222 D2
Riffel Rd NW2 .....68 C3
Rifle Ct SE11 ....138 C6
Rifle Pl W11 .....112 D5
Rifle Range La HA1 ..42 D1
Rifle St E14 ......97 D2
Rigault Rd SW6 ..135 A3
Rigby Cl CR0 ....220 C5
Rigby La UB3 ....105 A4
Rigby Mews IG1 ...78 C6
Rigby Pl EN3 ....7 C6
Rigden St E14 .....97 D1
Rigeley Rd NW10 ...90 A4
Rigg App E10 ......53 A1
Riggle Pl SW4 ....137 D1
Rigg Ho 2 SW4 ...160 A4
Riggindale Rd SW16 .181 D6
Rignold Ho 6 SE5 ..139 C3
Rigo Ho 9 E1 ......96 D2
Riley Ho SW10 ...266 C5
9 Bow E3 ....97 C3
1 Streatham SW4 ..159 D4
Riley Rd SE1 ..117 D3 263 C6
Enfield EN3 ....6 C5
Riley St SW10 .136 B5 266 C4
Rill Ho 24 SE5 ...139 C5
Rimini Ct SW12 ..158 D3
Rinaldo Rd SW12 ..159 B4
Ring Cl BR1 .....187 B3
Ringcroft St N7 ...72 C3
Ring Cross Prim Sch
N7 ....72 B3
Ringer's Rd BR1 ..209 A6
Ringford Ho SW18 ..157 B6
Ringford Rd SW18 ..157 C5
Ring Ho 14 E1 ...118 C6
Ringlet Cl E16 ....99 B2
Ringlewell Cl EN1 ...6 B3
Ringmer Ave
SW6 ....135 A4 264 B1
Ringmer Gdns 2 N19 .72 A6
Ringmer Ho 15 SE22 ..139 C2
Ringmer Pl N21 ....17 B6
Ringmer Way BR1 ..210 B4
Ringmore Rise SE23 .162 B4
Ringsfield Ho SE17 ..262 B1
Ringslade Rd N22 ...32 B1
Ringstead Ct SM1 ..218 B3
Ringstead Rd
Catford SE6 .....163 D4
Sutton SM1 ......218 B3
Ring Way N11 ......31 C4
Ringway UB2 .....107 A1
Ringwold Cl BR3 ..185 A3
Ringwood Ave N2 ...48 D6
Thornton Heath CR0 ..204 A2
Ringwood Cl HA5 ...40 C6
Ringwood Gdns
18 E14 ....119 C2
Roehampton SW15 ..156 A3
Ringwood Rd E17 ...53 B3
Ringwood Way
Hampton TW12 ...173 C6
Southgate N21 .....16 D4
Ripley Cl BR1 ....210 B4
New Addington CR0 ..224 A2
Ripley Ct 1 CR4 ..180 B1
Ripley Gdns
Mortlake SW14 ...133 B2
Sutton SM1 ......218 A4
Ripley Ho SW1 ...269 A6
13 Kingston KT2 ..176 D4
Mortlake SW14 ...133 C2
5 Penge SE26 ....184 B5
Ripley Mews E11 ...54 C3
Ripley Rd
Belvedere DA17 ..125 C2
Enfield EN2 ....5 A4
Hampton TW12 ...173 C3
Ilford IG3 ....79 D6
Newham E16 ....99 C1
Riplington Ct SW15 ..156 B4
Ripon Cl UB5 ......63 C2
Ripon Gdns
Chessington KT9 ..213 D3
Redbridge IG1 .....56 A2
Ripon Rd N17 ......51 B6
SE18 ....144 D6
Edmonton N9 ......18 B4
Ripon Way WD6 ....11 B6
Rippersley Rd DA16 .146 A4
Ripple Ct 10 IG11 ..101 B6
Ripple Rd Barking IG11 101 C6
Barking RM9 .....102 A6
Rippleside Commercial Est
IG11 ....102 C5
Ripplevale Gr N1 ...72 B1
Rippolson Rd SE18 ..123 D1
Ripston Rd TW15 ..171 B5
Risborough SE17 ..262 A4
Risborough Cl 4 N10 ..49 B6
Risborough Dr KT4 ..200 A2
Risborough Ho NW8 .237 B6
Risborough St SE1 ..251 D2
Risdon Ho 20 SE16 ..118 C4
Risdon St 21 SE16 ..118 C4
Risedale Rd DA7 ..147 D2
Riseholme Ho 14 SE22 139 C2
Riseldine Rd SE23 ..163 A5
Rise The NW10 .....67 B5
NW7 ....27 D4
Borehamwood WD6 ..10 B6
Buckhurst Hill IG9 ..21 D4
Chingford, Chingford Green
E4 ....20 C3
Edgware HA8 ......26 D5
Edmonton N13 .....32 C6
Greenford HA0,UB6 ..65 A3
Hillingdon UB10 ...82 B5
Sidcup DA5 ......168 C4
Wanstead E11 .....55 A4
Risinghill St N1 ..234 A4
Risingholme Cl HA3 ..24 C2
Risingholme Rd HA3 ..24 C1
Risings The E17 ...54 B5
Rising Sun Ct EC1 ..241 D3
Risley Ave N17 ....33 B2
Risley Avenue Prim Sch
N17 ....33 C2
Risley Ho 7 E9 ....74 D2
Rita Rd SW8 ..138 B5 270 C4
Ritches Rd N15 ....51 A4
Ritchie Ho N19 ....49 D2
8 SE16 ....118 C3
11 South Bromley E14 ..98 B1
Ritchie Rd CR0 ..206 B3
Ritchie St N1 ..94 C5 234 B4
Ritchings Ave E17 ..53 A5
Ritherdon Rd SW17 ..159 B2
Ritson Ho N1 ....233 C5
Ritson Rd E8 ......74 A2
Ritter St SE18 ..144 C6
Ritz Par W5 ....88 B3
Rivaz Pl E9 ....74 C2
Riven Ct 10 W2 ....91 D1
Rivenhall Gdns E11,E18 54 D5
Riverains The SW11 ..266 C1

River Ave Southgate N13 16 D2
Thames Ditton KT7 197 A2
Riverbank KT8 196 C5
River Bank
Edmonton N21 17 A4
Thames Ditton KT7 196 D4
Riverbank Rd BR1 165 A1
Riverbank Way TW8 131 C6
River Barge Cl E14 120 A4
River Brent Bsns Pk
W7 108 C3
River Cl Ruislip HA4 39 D3
Southall UB2 108 A4
Wanstead E11 55 C3
River Cotts BR5 190 C1
Rivercourt Rd W6 112 B1
River Crane Way
TW13 151 B2
River Ct SE1 251 C3
Kingston KT6 197 D4
Wanstead E11 55 C3
Riverdale Dr SW18 157 D3
Riverdale Gdns TW1 153 C6
Riverdale Rd SE18 123 D1
Erith DA8 125 D1
Feltham TW13 173 B6
Sidcup DA5 169 B5
Twickenham TW1 153 C5
Riverdene HA8 11 A1
Riverdene Rd IG1 78 D5
Riverfleet WC1 233 B2
Riverford Ho 28 W2 91 C2
River Front EN1 5 C2
River Gdns
Carshalton SM5 219 A5
Feltham TW14 150 B6
River Gdns Bsns Ctr
TW14 128 B1
River Grove Pk BR3 185 B2
Riverhead Cl E17 34 D1
River Ho Barnes SW13 133 C3
1 Forest Hill SE26 162 B1
Riverholme KT8 196 C6
Riverhope Mans SE18 122 A3
Riverine Lo HA7 25 A5
River La TW10 153 D3
Rivermead
East Molesey KT8 196 A6
Kingston KT6 197 D4
Rivermead Cl TW11 175 B5
Rivermead Ct
Ealing UB6 87 A4
Fulham SW6 135 B2
Rivermead Ho E9 75 A3
Sunbury TW16 194 C6
Rivermeads Ave TW13,
TW2 151 D1
River Mount KT12 193 D2
Rivernook Cl KT12 194 C4
River Park Gdns BR2 186 B3
River Park Rd N22 32 B1
River Pl N1 73 A1
River Rd Barking IG11 101 D3
Buckhurst Hill IG9 21 D3
River Reach TW11 175 C5
River Road Bsns Pk
IG11 101 D4
Riversdale Gdns N22 32 C2
Riversdale Prim Sch
SW18 157 C3
Riversdale Rd N5 73 A5
Thames Ditton KT7 197 A3
Riversdene N5 73 A5
Riversfield Rd EN1 5 C2
Rivers Ho 11 TW8 110 C1
Riverside NW4 46 B2
SW11 267 B4
WC1 233 B2
Forest Hill SE6 185 B6
Greenwich SE7 121 B3
Oatlands Park TW17 193 C2
Sunbury TW16 172 D1
Twickenham TW1 153 B3
Riverside Apartments
N13 32 B5
Riverside Ave KT8 196 B4
Riverside Bsns Ctr
SW18 157 D3
Riverside Bsns Pk
SW19 180 A2
Riverside Cl BR5 190 C1
E5 74 C6
Ealing W7 86 C3
Hackbridge SM6 219 B5
Kingston KT1 197 D5
Riverside Cotts IG11 101 B5
Riverside Ct SE12 142 D1
SW8 269 D6
Chingford E4 19 D5
Richmond TW11 175 C5
Riverside Dr NW11 47 A3
Chiswick W4 133 C4
Mitcham CR4 202 C4
Richmond TW10 153 B1
Riverside Est EN3 19 A5
Riverside Gdns N3 47 A6
Riverside Gdns *continued*
W6 112 B1
Enfield EN2 5 A3
Wembley HA0 88 A5
Riverside Ho N12 29 D6
Morden SW19 202 A5
Riverside Ind Est IG11 102 A4
Riverside Mans 4 E1 118 C5
Riverside Pl N11 15 C1
Stanwell TW19 148 A5
Riverside Prim Sch
SE16 118 A4
Riverside Rd DA14 169 A2
E15 98 A5
N15 52 A3
Stanwell TW19 148 A5
Wandsworth SW17,
SW19 158 A1
Riverside The KT8 196 B6
Riverside West SW18 135 D1
Riverside Wlk
Isleworth TW7 130 C2
3 West Wickham BR4 207 D1
Riverside Works IG11 78 D1
Riverside Workshops
SE1 252 B4
River St EC1 94 C4 234 A2
Riverstone Ct KT2 176 B2
Riverston Sch SE12 165 A6
River Terr W6 112 C1
Riverton Cl W9 91 B4
Riverview TW17 193 B2
River View EN2 5 A2
Riverview CE Sch
KT19 215 B4
Riverview Ct 14 DA17 125 C1
Riverview Gdns
Barnes SW13 134 B6
Twickenham TW1 152 D2
Riverview Gr W4 132 D6
Riverview Hts SE18 144 D5
Riverview Lo NW9 67 B6
Riverview Pk SE6 163 C2
Riverview Prim Sch
KT19 215 B4
Riverview Rd
Chiswick W4 132 D6
West Ewell KT19 215 B4
River Way SE10 120 D3
Riverway N13 32 C6
River Way
Twickenham TW13,TW2 151 D2
West Ewell KT19 215 C3
River Wlk KT12 194 A3
Riverwood La BR7 189 B2
Rivet Ho SE1 263 D2
Rivington Ave IG8 37 D1
Rivington Cres NW7 27 D3
Rivington Ct NW10 90 A6
Rivington Pl EC2 95 C4
Rivington St EC2 95 C4
Rivington Wlk 4 E8 96 A6
Rivulet Rd N17 33 A3
Rixon Ho SE18 144 D6
Rixon St N7 72 C5
Rixsen Rd E12 78 A3
Roach Rd E3 75 C1
Roach Works E3 75 C1
Roads Pl N19 72 A6
Roan Ind Est CR4 180 D2
Roan St SE10 142 A6
Robarts Cl HA5 40 B4
Robbins Hall EN3 18 D5
Robb Rd HA7 25 A4
Robert Adam St W1 238 A2
Roberta St E2 96 A4
Robert Bell Ho 2
SE16 118 A2
Robert Blair Prim Sch
N7 72 A2
Robert Browning Prim Sch
SE17 117 B1 262 C2
Robert Burns Ho N17 34 B3
Robert Cl W9 236 B5
Robert Clack Lower Sch
RM8 81 B6
Robert Clack Upper Sch
RM8 59 C1
Robert Dashwood Way
SE17 262 A3
Robert Gentry Ho
W14 254 B1
Robert Gerard Ho 7
SE27 183 B6
Robert Jones Ho 3
SE16 118 A2
Robert Keen Cl 17
SE15 140 A4
Robert Lowe Cl SE14 140 D5
Roberton Dr BR1 187 C2
Robert Owen Ho 8 E2 95 D4
Fulham SW6 134 D4
Robert Owen Lo 5 E5 74 B4
Robertsbridge Rd
SM5 202 B2
Roberts Cl SE9 167 B3
Cheam SM3 216 D1
Yiewsley UB7 104 A5
Roberts Ct N1 234 D5
Roberts Ct *continued*
NW10 67 C2
Chessington KT9 213 D3
Ealing W5 88 A1
Penge SE20 184 C2
Roberts Ho 2 N11 31 B5
10 SE18 144 A4
5 West Norwood SE27 160 D1
Roberts Mews SW1 258 A5
Robertson Ho 11 SE10 142 A4
4 SE18 144 B4
1 Upper Tooting SW17 180 C5
Robertson Rd E15 98 A6
Robertson St SW8 137 B3
Robert's Pl EC1 241 B6
Roberts Rd NW7 29 A4
Belvedere DA17 125 C1
Chingford, Highams Park
E17 35 D2
Robert St E16 122 D5
NW1 93 B4 231 D1
SE18 123 B2
WC2 250 B5
Croydon CR0 221 A5
Robert Sutton Ho 20
E1 96 C1
Robeson St 8 E3 97 B2
Robina Cl DA6 146 D1
Northwood HA6 22 A2
Robin Cl NW7 11 C1
Hampton TW12 173 A5
Robin Cres E16 99 D2
Robin Ct 13 E14 120 A3
Wallington SM6 219 C2
Robin Gr N6 71 A6
Brentford TW8 131 C6
Harrow HA3 44 B3
Robin Hill Dr BR7 188 A4
Robin Ho NW8 230 A3
Robin Hood SW15 155 C1
Robinhood Cl CR4 203 C6
Robin Hood Ct SM1 217 D3
Robin Hood Dr HA3 24 D3
Robin Hood Gdns 12
E14 120 A6
Robin Hood Inf Sch
SM1 217 C3
Robin Hood Jun Sch
SM1 217 D3
Robin Hood La E14 120 A6
Robinhood La CR4 203 C6
Robin Hood La
Bexley DA6 169 A6
Kingston SW15 177 C6
Sutton SM1 217 D3
Robin Hood Prim Sch
SW15 177 C5
Robin Hood Way UB6 64 D2
Robin Hood Way (Kingston
By Pass) KT2,SW15,
SW20 177 C5
Robinia Cl SE20 184 A2
Robinia Cres E10 75 D6
Robinscroft Mews
SE10 141 D4
Robins Ct SE12 165 C1
Robin's Ct SW4 160 A5
Robins Ct TW10 154 A5
Robin's Ct BR3 186 B1
Robinsfield Inf Sch
NW8 92 C5 230 A4
Robins Gr BR4 225 A5
Robinson Cres WD23 8 A3
Robinson Ct N1 234 D6
4 Richmond TW9 132 B1
Robinson Ho 11 E14 97 C2
4 W10 90 D1
Robinson Rd E2 96 C5
Dagenham RM10 81 C4
Mitcham SW19 180 C4
Robinson's Cl W13 87 A2
Robinson St SW3 267 C6
Robinwood Gr UB8 82 B3
Robinwood Pl SW15 177 B6
Robsart St SW9 138 C3
Robson Ave NW10 68 A1
Robson Cl E6 100 A1
Enfield EN2 4 D3
Robson Ct N12 30 A5
Robson Rd SE21,SE27 161 A1
Roby Ho EC1 242 A6
Roch Ave HA8 26 B1
Rochdale 8 SE19 183 C4
Rochdale Rd E10 53 C2
SE2 124 B2
Rochdale Way 4 SE8 141 C5
Roche Ho 15 E14 119 B6
Rochelle Cl SW11 136 B1
Rochelle Ct 14 E1 96 C1
Beckenham BR3 185 D3
Rochelle St 31 E2 95 D4
Rochemont Wlk 2 E8 96 A6
Roche Rd SW16 182 B2
Rochester Ave BR1 187 B1
E13 99 C6
Feltham TW13 149 D2
Rochester Cl 1 DA15 168 B5
SE3 143 C2
Enfield EN1 5 C4
Rochester Cl *continued*
Streatham SW16 182 A3
Rochester Ct 1 E2 96 B3
7 NW1 71 C1
NW9 45 B4
South Norwood SE25 184 A1
Rochester Dr DA5 169 C5
Pinner HA5 40 D4
Rochester Gdns
Redbridge IG1 56 B2
South Croydon CR0 221 C5
Rochester Ho SE1 252 D1
18 SE15 140 C6
Rochester Mews NW1 71 C1
Rochester Par TW13 150 A1
Rochester Pl NW1 71 C2
Rochester Rd NW1 71 C2
Carshalton SM5 218 D4
Northwood HA6 39 D6
Rochester Row
SW1 115 C2 259 B4
Rochester Sq NW1 71 C1
Rochester St SW1 259 C5
Rochester Terr NW1 71 C2
Rochester Way
SE3,SE9 143 D2
SE9 144 C2
Rochester Wlk SE1 252 C4
Roche Wlk SM5 202 B3
Rochford N17 33 C1
Rochford Ave RM6 58 C4
Rochford Cl 2 E6 99 D5
Rochford Way CR0 204 A3
Rochford Wlk 3 E8 74 A1
Rochfort Ho 4 SE8 119 B1
Rock Ave 13 SW14 133 B2
Rockbourne Rd SE23 162 D3
Rock Cl CR4 180 B1
Rockell's Pl SE22 162 B5
Rockfield Ho 2 NW4 46 D5
SE10 142 A6
Rockford Ave UB6 87 B5
Rock Gdns RM10 81 D3
Rock Grove Way SE16 118 A2
Rockhall Rd NW2 68 D4
Rockhampton Cl 4
SE27 182 C6
Rockhampton Rd
South Croydon CR2 221 C2
West Norwood SE27,
SW16 182 C6
Rock Hill SE19 183 D6
Rockingham Cl SW15 133 D1
Rockingham Ct 19
BR3 185 C3
Rockingham Gate WD23 8 A5
Rockingham St
SE1 117 A3 262 A5
Rockland Rd SW15 135 A1
Rocklands N3 29 B3
Rocklands Dr HA7 25 C1
Rockley Ct 9 W14 112 D4
Rockley Rd W14 112 D4
Rockliffe Manor Prim Sch
SE18 145 D6
Rockmount Prim Sch
SE19 183 B4
Rockmount Rd
SE18,SE2 123 D1
South Norwood SE19 183 B4
Rocks La SW13 134 A2
Rock St N4 72 C6
Rockstraw Ho 5 NW3 70 D1
Rockware Ave UB6 86 C6
Rockways EN5 11 D5
Rockwell Gdns SE19 183 C6
Rockwell Rd RM10 81 D3
Rockwood Ct N16 52 A2
Rocliffe St N1 94 D5 234 D3
Rocombe Cres SE23 162 C4
Rocque Ho SW6 264 C4
Rocque La SE3 142 D2
Rodborough Rd NW11 47 C1
Rodd Est TW17 193 B4
Roden Gdns CR0 205 C3
Rodenhurst Ct SW4 159 D6
Rodenhurst Rd SW4 159 D5
Roden St N7 72 B5
Ilford IG1 78 C5
Roderick Ho 3 SE16 118 C2
Roderick Rd NW3 70 D4
Rodgers Cl WD6 9 D5
Rodgers Ho 4 SW4 159 D4
Rodin Ct N1 234 C5
Roding Ct 6 W12 111 C4
Roding Ho N1 234 A5
Roding Hospl IG4 55 D6
Roding La IG9 21 D3
Roding La N IG8 37 D1
Roding La S IG4 55 D5
Roding Lo IG1 55 D3
Roding Mews E1 118 A5
Roding Prim Sch RM8 80 C3
Roding Rd E5 75 A3
Newham E6 100 D2
Rodings Ct E4 36 B5
Rodings The Barnet EN5 1 A1
4 Woodford IG8 37 C4
Roding Valley Sta IG9 37 D6
Roding View IG9 21 D3
Rodmarton St
W1 92 D2 237 D3
Rodmell WC1 233 B1
Rodmell Cl UB4 85 A3
Rodmell Slope N12 29 B5
Rodmere St SE10 120 C1
Rodmill La SW2 160 A4
Rodney Cl
New Malden KT3 199 C4
Pinner HA5 41 A2
Thornton Heath CR0 204 D1
Walton-on-T KT12 194 C1
Rodney Ct NW8 236 B6
Rodney Gdns
Hayes BR4 225 A4
Pinner HA5 40 C4
Rodney Ho 4 E14 119 D2
N1 233 D3
W11 245 A6
Rodney Pl E17 35 B1
SE17 117 A2 262 B4
Merton SW19 180 A2
Rodney Rd
SE17 117 B2 262 C3
Mitcham CR4 202 C6
New Malden KT3 199 C4
Twickenham TW4 151 C4
Walton-on-T KT12 194 C1
Wanstead E11 55 B5
Rodney St N1 94 B5 233 D3
Rodway Rd BR1 187 B2
Putney SW15 156 A4
Rodwell Cl 2 HA4 40 C1
Rodwell Rd SE22 161 D5
Roe 5 NW9 27 D2
Roebourne Way E16 122 C4
Roebuck Cl
Feltham TW13 172 B6
Tottenham N17 33 D4
Roebuck Ct Chingford E4 36 A3
2 New Malden KT3 199 C4
Roebuck Ho SW1 259 A6
Roebuck La IG9 21 C3
Roebuck Rd KT9 214 C3
Roedean Ave EN3 6 C5
Roedean Cl EN3 6 C4
Roedean Cres SW15 155 C6
Roe End NW9 45 A5
Roe Gn NW9 45 A4
Roe Green Jun & Inf Schs
NW9 44 D5
Roehampton CE Prim Sch
SW15 156 B4
Roehampton Cl SW15 134 A1
Roehampton Ct SW13 134 A2
Roehampton Dr BR7 189 A4
Roehampton Gate
SW15 155 C5
Roehampton High St
SW15 156 A4
Roehampton La
Putney SW15 156 A5
Roehampton SW15 156 B3
Roehampton Vale
SW15 155 D2
Roe La NW9 45 A5
Roe Way SM6 220 A2
Roffey Ct 9 NW9 46 A5
Roffey St E14 120 A4
Roger Ascham Prim Sch
E17 35 B2
Roger Dowley Ct 8 E2 96 C5
Roger's Almshouses 2
SW9 138 B1
Rogers Est 28 E2 96 C4
Rogers Gdns RM10 81 C3
Rogers Ho SW1 259 D4
9 Dagenham RM10 81 C5
Rogers Rd E16 98 D1
Dagenham RM10 81 C3
Upper Tooting SW17 180 C6
Roger St WC1 94 B3 240 D5
Roger Stone Ct NW10 67 B6
Rogers Wlk N12 13 D1
Rojack Rd SE23 162 D3
Rokeby Gdns IG8 37 A2
Rokeby Ho WC1 240 C5
9 Balham SW12 159 B4
Rokeby Pl SW20 178 B3
Rokeby Rd SE4 141 B3
Rokeby Sch E15 76 B1
Kingston KT2 177 A3
Rokeby St E15 98 C6
Rokeland Ho SE4 141 A1
Rokell Ho BR3 185 D5
Roker Park Ave UB10 60 A4
Rokesby Cl DA16 145 B3
Rokesby Pl HA0 65 D3
Rokesly Ave N8 50 A4
Rokesly Jun & Inf Schs
N8 50 A4
Roland Ct SE19 183 D2
Roland Gdns
SW7 114 A1 256 B2
Roland Mews 1 E1 96 D2
Roland Rd E17 54 B5
Roland Way SE17 262 D1
SW7 114 A1 256 B2
Roland Way *continued*
Worcester Park KT4 215
Roles Gr RM6 59
Rolfe Cl EN4 2
Rolfe Ho N11 30
Rolinsden Way BR2 225
Rolland Ho W7 86
Rollesby Rd KT19,KT9 214
Rollesby Way SE28 102
Rolleston Ave BR5 210
Rolleston Cl BR5 210
Rolleston Rd CR2 221
Roll Gdns IG2 56
Rollins St SE15 140
Rollit Cres TW3 151
Rollit Ho N7 72
Rollit St N7 72
Rollo Ct SW11 268
Rolls Bldgs EC4 241
Rollscourt Ave SE24 161
Rolls Park Ave E4 35
Rolls Park Rd E4 35
Rolls Pas EC4 241
Rolls Rd SE1 118 A1 263
Rolt St SE8 141
Rolvenden Gdns BR1 187
Rolvenden Pl N17 34
Roman Cl W3 110
Feltham TW14 150
Romanfield Rd SW2 160
Romanhurst Ave BR2 208
Romanhurst Gdns
BR2,BR3 208
Roman Ind Est CR0 205
Roman Rd E2,E3 96
E3 97
N10 31
N12 30
W4 111
Ilford IG1 78
Newham E6 100
Roman Rise SE19 183
Roman Road Prim Sch
E6 99
Roman Sq SE28 124
Roman Square Mkt 1
E3 97
Roman Way N7 72
4 SE15 140
Croydon CR0 220
Enfield EN1 17
Romany Gdns E17 35
Cheam SM3 201
Romany Ho 8 N9 18
Romany Prospect
SE19 183
Romany Rise BR5 211
Roma Rd E17 53 A
Roma Read Cl SW15 156 B
Romayne Ho SW4 137 D
Romberg Rd SW17 159 A
Romborough Gdns
SE13 164 A
Romborough Way
SE13 164 A
Romeland WD6 9 D
Romer Ho 9 SW2 160 B
12 W10 91 B
Romero Cl SW9 138 B
Romero Sq SE9 143 C
Romey Mews W1 238 A
Romeyn Rd SW16 160 B
Romford Ho 17 N1 73 B
Romford Rd E15 76 D
E7,E12 77 C
Romford St E1 96 B
Romilly Dr WD19 23 A
Romilly Rd N4 72 D
Romilly St W1 249 D
Romily Ct SW6 135 A
Rommany Ct SE27 183 B
Rommany Rd SE27 183 B
Romney Cl NW11 48 A
7 SE14 140 C
Ashford TW15 171 A
Chessington KT9 214 A
Harrow HA2 41 C
Tottenham N17 34 B
Romney Ct 9 NW3 70 C
9 W12 112 C
16 Northolt UB5 84 D
Romney Dr
Bromley BR1 187 D
Harrow HA2 41 C2
Romney Gdns DA7 147 B
Romney Ho EN1 18 A
Romney Par UB4 83 B
Romney Rd SE10 142 B
Hayes UB4 83 B5
New Malden KT3 199 B3
Romney Row NW2 68 D6
Romney St
SW1 116 A3 260 A5
Romola Rd SE24,SW2 160 D3
Romsey Cl BR6 227 A4
Romsey Gdns RM9 102 D6
Romsey Ho 5 SW11 136 B1
Romsey Rd
Dagenham RM9 102 D6

Romsey Rd continued
Ealing W13 ... 109 A6
Romulus Ct 7 TW8 ... 131 D5
Ronald Ave E15 ... 98 C4
Ronald Cl BR3 ... 207 B4
Ronald Ho SE9 ... 143 C1
Ronald Ross Prim Sch
SW19 ... 157 A4
Ronaldshay N4 ... 50 C1
Ronalds Rd BR1 ... 187 A2
N5 ... 72 C3
Ronald St E1 ... 96 C1
Ronaldstone Rd DA15 167 C5
Rona Rd NW3 ... 71 A4
Ronart St HA3 ... 42 D6
Rona Wlk 7 N1 ... 73 B2
Rondu Rd NW2 ... 69 A3
Ronelean Rd KT6 ... 214 B5
Ron Leighton Way E6 100 A6
Ronver Lo E4 ... 20 C1
Ronver Rd SE12 ... 164 D3
Rood La EC3 .. 117 C6 253 A6
Rookby Ct N21 ... 16 D2
Rook Cl HA9 ... 66 D5
Rookeries Cl TW13 ... 150 C1
Rookery Cl NW9 ... 45 D4
Rookery Cotts EN4 ... 3 B2
Rookery Cres RM10 ... 81 D1
Rookery Dr BR7 ... 188 C2
Rookery La BR2 ... 209 D3
Rookery Rd SW4 ... 137 C1
Rookery Way NW9 ... 45 D4
Rookes Heath High Sch
HA2 ... 63 C5
Rooke Way SE10 ... 120 D1
Rookfield Ave N10 ... 49 C5
Rookfield Cl N10 ... 49 C5
Rook Lo IG1 ... 55 D3
Rooksmead Rd TW16 . 172 A1
Rooks Terr UB7 ... 104 A4
Rookstone Rd SW17 .. 180 D5
Rook Wlk E6 ... 100 A1
Rookwood Ave
Wallington SM6 ... 219 D4
West Barnes KT3 ... 200 A5
Rookwood Gdns E4 ... 20 D2
Rookwood Ho IG11 ... 101 B5
Rookwood Rd N16 ... 52 A2
Rootes Dr W10 ... 90 D2
Ropemaker Rd SE16 .. 119 A3
Ropemaker's Fields 7
E14 ... 119 B6
Ropemaker St
EC2 ... 95 B2 242 C4
Roper Ho 13 SE21 ... 183 C6
Roper La SE1 . 117 C4 253 B1
Ropers Ave E4 ... 36 A5
Roper's Orchard SW3 . 267 A5
Roper St 1 SE9 ... 166 C5
Ropers Wlk 13 SE24 ... 160 C4
Roper Way CR4 ... 181 A1
Ropery Bsns Est SE7 . 121 C2
Ropery St E3 ... 97 B3
Rope St SE16 ... 119 A3
Ropewalk Gdns 16 E1 .. 96 A1
Rope Yard Rails SE18 . 122 D3
Ropley St 6 E2 ... 96 A5
Rosa Alba Mews N5 ... 73 A4
Rosa Ave TW15 ... 170 C6
Rosalind Ct 6 IG11 ... 80 A1
Rosalind Ho 25 N1 ... 95 C5
Rosaline Rd
SW6 ... 135 A5 264 B3
Rosaline Terr SW6 ... 264 B3
Rosamond St SE26 ... 162 B1
Rosamund Cl CR2 ... 221 B4
Rosamun St UB2 ... 107 A2
Rosa Parks Ho 8
SW9 ... 138 B3
Rosary Cl TW3,TW5 ... 129 A3
Rosary Gdns
SW7 ... 114 A2 256 B3
Ashford TW15 ... 170 D6
Bushey WD23 ... 8 C4
Rosary RC Inf Sch
TW5 ... 129 C6
Rosary RC Jun Sch
TW5 ... 129 C6
Rosary RC Prim Sch
NW3 ... 70 C3
Rosaville Rd
SW6 ... 135 B5 264 C3
Rosbury SW15 ... 157 A5
Roscoe St EC1 . 95 A3 242 B5
Roscoff Cl HA8 ... 27 A2
Roscommon Ho 2
NW3 ... 70 B3
Roseacre Cl Ealing W13 . 87 B2
Littleton TW17 ... 192 C4
Roseacre Lo EN3 ... 6 C1
Roseacre Rd DA16 ... 146 B2
Rose Alley EC2 ... 243 B3
SE1 ... 252 B4
Rose Ave Mitcham CR4 . 180 D2
Morden SM4 ... 202 A4
Woodford E18 ... 37 B1
Rosebank SW6 ... 134 C5
2 W3 ... 89 B1
Penge SE20 ... 184 B3
Rosebank Ave HA0 ... 64 D4
Rose Bank Cl N12 ... 30 C5
Rosebank Cl TW11 .. 175 A4
Rosebank Gdns E3 ... 97 B5
1 W3 ... 89 B1
Rosebank Gr E17 ... 53 B6
Rosebank Rd E17 ... 53 D3
W7 ... 108 C4
Rosebank Villas E17 ... 53 C5
Rosebank Way W3 ... 89 B1
Rosebank Wlk NW1 ... 71 D1
14 SE7 ... 122 A2
Rose Bates Dr NW9 ... 44 C5
Roseberry Gdns BR6 . 227 C5
N4 ... 50 D3
Roseberry Pl E8 ... 73 D2
Roseberry St SE16 ... 118 B2
Rosebery Ave DA15 ... 167 C4
E12 ... 78 B2
EC1 ... 94 C4 234 B1
Harrow HA2 ... 63 B4
Kingston KT3 ... 199 D6
South Norwood CR7 ... 183 A1
Tottenham N17 ... 34 A1
Rosebery Cl SM4 ... 200 D3
Rosebery Ct EC1 ... 241 A6
W1 ... 248 C4
Chessington KT9 ... 214 B3
Rosebery Gdns N8 ... 50 A4
Ealing W13 ... 87 A1
Sutton SM1 ... 217 D4
Rosebery Ho 22 E2 ... 96 C5
Rosebery Ind Pk N17 ... 34 B1
Rosebery Mews N10 ... 31 C1
Rosebery Rd N10 ... 31 C1
SW2 ... 160 A5
Cheam SM1,SM2 ... 217 B2
Edmonton N9 ... 18 A2
Isleworth TW3,TW7 ... 152 A6
Kingston KT1 ... 176 D1
Rosebery Sq EC1 ... 241 A5
Kingston KT1 ... 176 D1
Rosebine Ave TW2 ... 152 B4
Rosebriars KT10 ... 212 A3
Rose Bruford Coll SE8 141 C6
Rose Bruford Coll of
Speech & Drama
DA15 ... 168 B3
Rosebury Rd SW6 ... 135 D3
Rosebury Vale HA4 ... 62 A6
Rose Bush Ct NW3 ... 70 D3
Rose Cotts KT10 ... 212 B3
Rosecourt Rd CR0 ... 204 B3
Rosecroft N22 ... 32 B2
Rosecroft Ave NW3 ... 69 C5
Rosecroft Gdns NW2 ... 68 A5
Twickenham TW2 ... 152 B3
Rosecroft Rd UB1 ... 85 C3
Rosecroft Wlk
Pinner HA5 ... 40 D4
Wembley HA0 ... 65 D3
Rose & Crown Ct EC2 . 242 A2
Rose & Crown Yd
SW1 ... 249 B3
Rose Ct E1 ... 243 D3
N1 ... 234 D6
Harrow HA2 ... 64 A6
Ilford IG1 ... 78 D2
7 Wembley HA0 ... 88 A5
10 Wimbledon SW19 ... 179 B5
Rose Dale BR6 ... 226 D6
Rosedale Ave UB3 ... 83 B2
Rosedale Cl SE2 ... 124 B3
W7 ... 108 D4
Stanmore HA7 ... 25 B4
Rosedale Ct N5 ... 72 D4
Rosedale Gdns RM9 ... 80 B1
Rosedale Ho N16 ... 51 B1
Rosedale Lo N14 ... 15 B4
Rosedale Rd E7 ... 77 C3
Dagenham RM9 ... 80 B1
Richmond TW9 ... 132 A1
Stoneleigh KT17 ... 216 A3
Rosedale Terr W6 ... 112 B3
Rosedene NW6 ... 90 D6
Rosedene Ave
Morden SM4 ... 201 C4
Southall UB6 ... 85 C4
Streatham SW16 ... 160 B1
Thornton Heath CR0 ... 204 A2
Rosedene Gdns IG2 ... 56 C5
Rosedene Terr E10 ... 75 D6
Rosedew Rd W6 ... 134 D6
Rose End KT4 ... 200 D1
Rosefield Cl SM5 ... 218 C3
Rosefield Ct EN4 ... 2 D1
Rosefield Gdns E14 ... 119 C6
Rose Garden Cl HA8 ... 26 A4
Rose Gdns W5 ... 109 D3
Feltham TW13 ... 150 A2
Southall UB1 ... 85 C3
Rose Glen NW9 ... 45 B5
Rosehart Mews 8 W11 91 C1
Rose Hatch Ave RM6 ... 58 D6
Roseheath Rd TW4 ... 151 B6
Rosehill Claygate KT10 . 213 A2
Hampton TW12 ... 173 C2
Rose Hill
Carshalton SM4,SM5 .. 202 A2
Rose Hill continued
Cheam SM1 ... 201 D1
Rosehill Ave SM1,SM5 . 202 A1
Rosehill Ct SM4 ... 202 A2
Rosehill Gdns
Greenford UB6 ... 64 D3
Sutton SM1 ... 218 A6
Rose Hill Park W SM1 218 A6
Rosehill Rd SW18 ... 158 A6
Rose La RM6 ... 59 A5
Roseland Cl N17 ... 33 B3
Roseland Ho SW6 ... 135 A2
Rose Lawn WD23 ... 8 A3
Roseleigh Ave N5 ... 72 D4
Roseleigh Cl 12 TW1 . 153 D5
Roselle Ct W5 ... 88 A1
Rosemary Ave N3 ... 29 D1
NW2 ... 47 D5
East Molesey KT8 ... 195 C5
Edmonton N9 ... 18 B3
Enfield EN2 ... 5 C4
Hounslow TW4 ... 128 D3
Rosemary Branch Bridge
N1 ... 235 C6
Rosemary Cl
Hillingdon UB8 ... 82 C2
Thornton Heath CR0 ... 204 A3
Rosemary Cotts 3
SW19 ... 178 C3
Rosemary Ct 43 SE8 .. 141 B6
Rosemary Dr
Redbridge IG4 ... 55 D4
15 South Bromley E14 ... 98 B1
Rosemary Gdns
Chessington KT9 ... 214 A4
Dagenham RM8 ... 59 B1
Mortlake SW14 ... 133 A2
Rosemary Ho N1 ... 235 D5
Rosemary La SW14 ... 133 A2
Rosemary Mews N1 .. 235 D6
Rosemary Rd DA16 ... 145 D4
SE15 ... 139 D5
Wandsworth SW17 ... 158 A1
Rosemary Works Sch
N1 ... 235 D5
Rosemead NW9 ... 46 A2
Rosemead Ave
Feltham TW13 ... 149 D2
Mitcham CR4 ... 181 C1
Wembley HA9 ... 66 A3
Rosemead Prep Sch
SE27 ... 161 A2
Rose Mews N18 ... 34 B6
Rosemont Ave N12 ... 30 A4
Rosemont Mans 11
NW3 ... 69 D2
Rosemont Rd NW3 ... 70 A2
Acton W3 ... 110 D6
Kingston KT3 ... 199 A6
Richmond TW10 ... 154 A5
Wembley HA0 ... 88 A6
Rosemoor St
SW3 ... 114 D2 257 C3
Rosemount Ct
2 Acton W3 ... 110 D5
South Norwood SE25 ... 205 C6
Rosemount Dr BR1 ... 210 B5
Rosemount Lo W3 ... 110 D6
Rosemount Point 10
SE23 ... 162 D1
Rosemount Rd W13 ... 87 A1
Rosemount Towers 5
SM6 ... 219 C2
Rosenau Cres SW11 .. 267 C1
Rosenau Rd
SW11 ... 136 D4 267 C2
Rosendale Prim Sch
SE21 ... 161 A4
Rosendale Rd SE21,
SE24 ... 161 A3
Roseneath Ave N21 ... 16 D3
Roseneath Rd SW11 .. 159 A5
Roseneath Wlk EN1 ... 5 C1
Rosens Wlk HA8 ... 10 D1
Rosenthal Rd SE6 ... 164 A5
Rosenthorpe Rd SE15 162 D6
Roserton St E14 ... 120 A4
Rosery The CR0 ... 206 D3
Rose Sq SW7 ... 256 D2
Rose St EC4 ... 241 D1
WC2 ... 116 A6 250 A6
Roses The IG8 ... 36 D3
Rosethorn Cl SW12 ... 159 D4
Rosetta Cl SW8 ... 270 B3
Rosetta Ct SE19 ... 183 C3
Rosetta Prim Sch E16 .. 99 B2
Rosetti Terr RM8 ... 80 B4
Roseveare Rd SE12 ... 187 C6
Roseville N21 ... 16 C3
Roseville Ave TW3,
TW4 ... 151 C6
Roseville Rd UB3 ... 106 A2
Rosevine Rd SW20 ... 178 C2
Roseway SE21 ... 161 B5
Rose Way HA8 ... 27 A6
SE12 ... 165 A6
Rosewell Cl SE20 ... 184 B3
Rose Wlk Surbiton KT5 . 198 D4
West Wickham BR4 ... 224 B6
Rosewood Ave UB6 ... 65 A2
Rosewood Cl DA14 ... 168 C1
Rosewood Ct 2 E11 ... 76 B4
Bromley BR1 ... 187 D2
Dagenham RM6 ... 58 C4
Kingston KT2 ... 176 C3
Rosewood Dr TW17 ... 192 B4
Rosewood Gr SM1 ... 218 A6
Rosewood Sq W12 ... 90 A1
Rosher Cl E15 ... 76 B1
Roshni Ho SW17 ... 180 C4
Rosh Pinah Prim Sch
HA8 ... 10 D1
Rosina Ct SW17 ... 180 C5
Rosina St E9 ... 74 D2
Roskeen Ct 1 SW19 .. 178 C3
Roskell Rd SW15 ... 134 D2
Roskild Ct HA9 ... 66 B4
Roslin Ho 2 E1 ... 118 D6
Roslin Rd W3 ... 110 D3
Roslin Way BR1 ... 187 A5
Roslyn Cl CR4 ... 180 B1
Roslyn Rd N15 ... 51 C4
Rosmead Rd
W11 ... 113 A6 244 B6
Rosoman Pl EC1 ... 241 B6
Rossal Ct SE20 ... 184 B3
Rossall Cres NW10 ... 88 B4
Rossanne Ho N3 ... 29 D3
Ross Ave NW7 ... 29 A5
Dagenham RM8 ... 59 B1
Ross Cl Harrow HA3 ... 24 A3
Hayes UB3 ... 105 B2
Ross Ct BR7 ... 188 B3
NW9 ... 45 C6
Ealing W13 ... 87 B2
4 Putney SW15 ... 156 D4
South Croydon CR2 ... 221 A2
Rossdale SM1 ... 218 C3
Rossdale Dr N9 ... 18 C5
NW9 ... 45 A1
Rossdale Rd SW15 ... 134 C1
Rosse Mews SE3 ... 143 B4
Rossendale Cl EN2 ... 4 D6
Rossendale Ho 7 E5 ... 74 B6
Rossendale St E5 ... 74 B6
Rossendale Way
NW1 ... 93 C6 232 B6
Rossendon Ct 1 SM6 219 C2
Rossetti Ct WC1 ... 239 C4
Rossetti Gdns Mans
SW3 ... 267 C6
Rossetti Ho SW1 ... 259 D3
Rossetti Mews NW8 ... 229 D5
Rossetti Rd SE16 ... 118 B1
Ross Ho 18 E1 ... 118 B5
6 SE18 ... 144 A4
Twickenham TW2 ... 151 D2
Rossignol Gdns SM5 .. 219 A6
Rossindel Rd TW3 ... 151 C6
Rossington Cl EN1 ... 6 B5
Rossington St E5 ... 74 A6
Rossiter Fields EN5 ... 13 B5
Rossiter Rd SW12 ... 159 B3
Rossland Cl DA6 ... 169 D6
Rosslyn Ave
Barnes SW13 ... 133 D2
Chingford E4 ... 20 D2
Dagenham RM8 ... 59 C2
East Barnet EN4 ... 14 C5
Feltham TW14 ... 150 A5
Rosslyn Cl
Ashford TW16 ... 171 C4
Coney Hall BR4 ... 224 D5
Hayes UB3 ... 83 B2
Rosslyn Cres
Harrow HA1 ... 42 D5
Wembley HA9 ... 66 A4
Rosslyn Ct NW3 ... 70 C3
Rosslyn Hill NW3 ... 70 B3
Rosslyn Ho 8 TW9 ... 132 B4
Rosslyn Mans NW6 ... 70 A2
Rosslyn Park Mews
NW3 ... 70 B3
Rosslyn Rd E17 ... 54 A5
Barking IG11 ... 79 B1
Twickenham TW1 ... 153 C5
Rossmore Ct NW1 ... 237 C6
Rossmore Rd
NW1 ... 92 C3 237 B6
Ross Par SM6 ... 219 B2
Ross Rd
South Norwood SE25 ... 205 C6
Twickenham TW2 ... 152 A3
Wallington SM6 ... 219 C3
Ross Way SE9 ... 144 A2
Rossway Dr WD23 ... 8 B6
Rosswood Gdns SM6 . 219 C2
Rosswood Lo CR0 ... 222 D6
Rostella Rd SW17 ... 180 B6
Rostrever Gdns UB3 .. 105 C5
Rostrevor Ave N15 ... 51 D3
Rostrevor Gdns UB2 .. 107 A1
Rostrevor Mans SW6 . 264 C2
Rostrevor Rd
Fulham SW6 ... 135 B4 264 C2
Wimbledon SW19 ... 179 C5
Rotary St SE1 ... 261 D6
Rothay NW1 ... 231 D2
Rothbury Gdns TW7 .. 131 A5
Rothbury Rd E9 ... 75 C1
Rothbury Wlk N17 ... 34 A3
Rotherfield Ct
N1 ... 73 B1 235 C6
Rotherfield Prim Sch
N1 ... 95 A6 235 B6
Rotherfield Rd
Enfield EN3 ... 6 D6
Wallington SM5 ... 219 A3
Rotherfield St
N1 ... 73 A1 235 B6
Rotherham Wlk SE1 .. 251 C3
Rotherhill Ave SW16 .. 181 D4
Rotherhithe SE16 ... 119 B5
Rotherhithe Holiday Inn
Pier SE16 ... 119 B5
Rotherhithe New Rd
SE16 ... 118 B1
Rotherhithe Old Rd
SE16 ... 118 D2
Rotherhithe Prim Sch
SE16 ... 118 D2
Rotherhithe St SE16 .. 118 C4
10 SE16 ... 118 B4
Rotherhithe Sta SE16 . 118 C4
Rotherhithe Tunnel
SE16 ... 118 D5
Rother Ho SE15 ... 140 B1
Rotherwick Hill W5 ... 88 B3
Rotherwick Rd NW11 .. 47 C2
Rotherwood Cl SW20 . 179 A2
Rotherwood Rd SW15 134 D2
Rothery St N1 ... 234 D6
Rothesay Ave
Merton SW20 ... 179 A1
Mortlake SW14,TW10 .. 132 D1
Northolt UB6 ... 64 B2
Rothesay Ct 13 SE11 .. 138 C6
SE12 ... 165 B1
4 Catford SE6 ... 164 D2
Rothesay Rd SE25 ... 205 C5
Rothley Ct NW8 ... 236 C6
Rothsay Rd E7 ... 77 C2
Rothsay St
SE1 ... 117 C3 263 A5
Rothsay Wlk 16 E14 .. 119 C2
Rothschild Rd W4 ... 111 A3
Rothschild St SE27 .. 182 D6
Rothwell Ct HA1 ... 42 D4
Rothwell Gdns RM9 .. 102 C6
Rothwell Ho TW5 ... 129 C6
Rothwell Rd RM9 ... 102 C6
Rothwell St NW1 ... 230 D6
10 NW1 ... 70 D1
Roth Wlk N7 ... 72 B6
Rotten Row★
SW1 ... 114 D4 247 C2
Rotterdam Dr E14 ... 120 A3
Rotunda Mus★ SE18 .. 122 B1
Rouel Rd SE16 ... 118 A2
SE16 ... 118 A3
Rougemont Ave SM4 . 201 C3
Roundabout Ho HA6 ... 22 A2
Roundacre SW19 ... 156 D2
Roundel Cl SE4 ... 141 B1
Roundell Ho 14 SE21 . 183 C6
Rounders Ct 7 RM10 .. 81 D2
Round Gr CR0 ... 206 D2
Roundhay Cl SE23 ... 162 D2
Roundhedge Way EN2 ... 4 B5
Round Hill SE23 ... 162 C1
Roundhill Dr EN2 ... 4 B1
Roundshaw Ctr SM6 .. 220 A1
Roundtable Rd BR1 ... 164 D1
Roundtree Rd HA0 ... 65 B3
Roundways HA4 ... 61 D5
Roundway The
Claygate KT10 ... 212 D2
Tottenham N17 ... 33 B2
Roundwood BR7 ... 188 D1
Roundwood Ave UB11 105 A5
Roundwood Cl HA4 ... 39 B2
Roundwood Rd NW10 .. 67 D1
Rounton Rd E3 ... 97 C3
Roupell Ho 7 KT2 ... 176 B3
Roupell Rd SW2 ... 160 B3
Roupell St SE1 116 C5 251 B3
Rousden St NW1 ... 71 C1
Rouse Gdns SE21 ... 183 C6
Routemaster Cl E13 ... 99 B4
Routh Ct TW14 ... 149 B3
Routh Rd SW18 ... 158 C4
Routh St E6 ... 100 B2
Rover Ho 27 N1 ... 95 C6
Rowallan Ct 3 SE6 .. 164 D3
Rowallan Rd
SW6 ... 135 A5 264 A3
Rowallen Par RM8 ... 58 C1
Rowan N10 ... 31 B1
Rowan Ave E4 ... 35 B4
Rowan Cl W5 ... 110 A4
Harrow HA7 ... 24 D4
Kingston KT3 ... 177 C1
Streatham SW16 ... 181 C2
Wembley HA0 ... 65 A5
Rowan Cres SW16 ... 181 C2
Rowan Ct 18 SE15 ... 139 D5
SW11 ... 158 D5
Rowan Ct continued
Forest Hill SE26 ... 184 C6
11 Kingston KT2 ... 176 C3
Wimbledon SW20 ... 178 B1
Rowan Dr NW9 ... 46 A6
Rowan Gdns CR0 ... 221 D5
Rowan High Sch
SW16 ... 181 C1
Rowan Ho DA14 ... 167 D1
NW10 ... 66 B1
5 NW3 ... 70 D2
East Bedfont TW14 ... 149 B5
Ilford IG1 ... 79 B3
Rowan Pl UB3 ... 105 D6
Rowan Rd DA7 ... 147 A2
W6 ... 112 D2
Brentford TW8 ... 131 B5
Mitcham SW16 ... 181 C1
West Drayton UB7 ... 104 A2
Rowans The
Ashford TW16 ... 171 D5
Edmonton N13 ... 17 A1
Rowan Terr W6 ... 112 D2
Rowantree Cl N21 ... 17 B3
Rowantree Rd
Edmonton N21 ... 17 B3
Enfield EN2 ... 4 D3
Rowan Way RM6 ... 58 C6
Rowan Wlk BR2 ... 226 B5
N19 ... 71 C6
N2 ... 48 A4
W10 ... 91 A3
1 New Barnet EN5 ... 13 D6
Rowanwood Ave
DA15 ... 168 A3
Rowanwood Mews EN2 . 4 D3
Rowben Cl N20 ... 13 D3
Rowberry Cl SW6 ... 134 C5
Rowcross St
SE1 ... 117 D1 263 D2
Rowdell Rd UB5 ... 85 C6
Rowden Par E4 ... 35 C4
Rowden Park Gdns E4 . 35 C4
Rowden Rd
Beckenham BR3 ... 185 B2
Chingford E4 ... 35 D4
West Ewell KT19 ... 215 A4
Rowditch La SW11 ... 137 A3
Rowdon Ave NW10 ... 68 B1
Rowdowns Rd RM9 ... 81 B1
Rowe Gdns IG11 ... 102 A5
Rowe La E9 ... 74 C3
Rowena Cres SW11 .. 136 C3
Rowe Wlk HA2 ... 63 C5
Rowfant Rd SW12,
SW17 ... 159 A2
Rowhill Mans 11 E5 ... 74 B4
Rowhill Rd E5 ... 74 B4
Rowington Cl W2 ... 91 D2
Rowland Ave HA3 ... 43 C6
Rowland Ct E16 ... 98 D3
Rowland Gr SE26 ... 162 B1
Rowland Hill Almshouses
TW15 ... 170 C5
Rowland Hill Ave N17 .. 33 B4
Rowland Hill Ho SE1 . 251 C2
Rowland Hill St NW3 .. 70 C3
Rowlands Ave HA5 ... 23 D4
Rowlands Cl N6 ... 49 A3
NW7 ... 28 A3
Rowlands Rd RM8 ... 81 B6
Rowland Way
Ashford TW15 ... 171 B3
Merton SW19 ... 179 D2
Rowley Ave DA15 ... 168 B4
Rowley Cl HA0 ... 66 B1
Rowley Gdns N4 ... 51 A2
Rowley Green Rd EN5 .. 12 A6
Rowley Ho SE8 ... 141 C6
Rowley Ind Pk W3 ... 110 D3
Rowley La EN5 ... 11 D6
Rowley Rd N15 ... 51 A4
Rowlheys Pl UB7 ... 104 A3
Rowlls Rd KT1 ... 198 B6
Rowney Gdns RM9 ... 80 C2
Rowney Rd RM9 ... 80 B2
Rowntree Cl NW6 ... 69 C2
Rowntree Clifford Cl 7
E13 ... 99 B4
Rowntree Path 1
SE28 ... 124 B5
Rowntree Rd TW2 ... 152 C3
Rowse Cl E15 ... 98 A6
Rowsham Ct HA1 ... 64 C5
Rowsley Ave NW4 ... 46 C6
Rowstock 1 NW5 ... 71 D2
Rowstock Gdns N7 ... 71 D3
Rowton Rd SE18 ... 145 A5
Roxborough Ave
Harrow HA1 ... 42 C2
Hounslow TW7 ... 130 D5
Roxborough Pk HA1 .. 42 C2
Roxborough Rd HA1 .. 42 B3
Roxbourne Cl UB5 ... 62 D2
Roxbourne Fst & Mid Schs
HA2 ... 63 A6

Roxburgh Rd SE27 .. 182 D5
Roxburn Way HA4 .. 61 D5
Roxby Pl SW6 .. 135 C6 265 B6
Roxeth Ct TW15 .. 170 C5
Roxeth Fst & Mid Sch HA2 .. 64 B6
Roxeth Gr HA2 .. 63 D4
Roxeth Green Ave HA2 .. 63 D6
Roxeth Hill HA2 .. 64 C6
Roxeth Manor Fst & Mid Schs HA2 .. 63 C5
Roxeth Mead Sch HA2 .. 64 B6
Roxford Cl TW17 .. 193 C4
Roxford Ho 3 E3 .. 97 D3
Roxley Rd SE13 .. 163 D5
Roxton Gdns CR0 .. 223 C3
Roxwell 10 NW1 .. 71 B2
Roxwell Rd W12 .. 112 A4
Barking IG11 .. 102 A5
Roxwell Trad Pk E10 .. 53 A2
Roxwell Way IG8 .. 37 C3
Roxy Ave RM6 .. 58 C2
Royal Academy of Dramatic Art★ WC1 .. 93 D2 239 C4
Royal Acad of Arts★ W1 .. 115 C6 249 A5
Royal Acad of Dance SW11 .. 266 D1
Royal Acad of Music NW1 .. 238 B5
Royal Albert Hall★ SW7 .. 114 B4 246 C1
Royal Albert Rd E16 .. 122 D6
Royal Albert Sta E16 .. 122 A6
Royal Albert Way E16 .. 122 B6
Royal Arc W1 .. 249 A5
Royal Army Medical Coll SW1 .. 116 A1 260 A2
Royal Ave
SW3 .. 114 D1 257 C2
Worcester Park KT4 .. 215 C6
Royal Avenue Ho SW3 257 C2
Royal Ballet Sch The WC2 .. 240 B1
Royal Brompton Hospl
SW3 .. 114 B1 256 C2
SW3 .. 114 C1 257 B1
Royal Cir SE27 .. 160 D1
Royal Cl BR6 .. 226 D4
N16 .. 51 C1
SE8 .. 141 B6
Hillingdon UB7 .. 82 B1
Ilford IG3 .. 58 A2
Putney SW19 .. 156 D2
Worcester Park KT4 .. 215 C6
Royal College St NW1 .. 93 C6 232 B6
Royal Coll of Anaesthetists WC1 .. 94 A2 240 B4
Royal Coll of Art SW7 .. 114 B4 246 C1
Royal Coll of Art Sculpture Sch SW11 .. 136 C5 267 A3
Royal Coll of Midwives W1 .. 93 B2 238 C3
Royal Coll of Music SW7 .. 114 B3 256 C6
Royal Coll of Obstetricians & Gynaecologists NW1 .. 92 D3 237 C6
Royal Coll of Physicians NW1 .. 93 B3 238 D6
Royal Coll of Science SW7 .. 114 B3 256 C6
Royal Coll of Surgeons WC2 .. 94 B1 240 D2
Royal Connaught Apps E16 .. 121 D5
Royal Courts of Justice WC2 .. 94 C1 241 A1
Royal Cres
W11 .. 113 A5 244 A3
Ruislip HA4 .. 63 A5
Royal Crescent Mews W11 .. 112 D5
Royal Ct SE16 .. 119 B3
SE9 .. 166 B3
Enfield EN1 .. 17 C5
9 Kingston KT2 .. 176 D3
Royal Docks Rd E6 .. 100 D2
Royal Duchess Mews SW12 .. 159 B4
Royal Exchange★ EC3 .. 242 D1
Royal Exchange Ave EC3 .. 242 D1
Royal Exchange Bldgs EC3 .. 242 D1
Royal Festival Hall★ SE1 .. 116 B5 250 D3
Royal Free Hospl NW3 .. 70 C3
Royal Gdns W7 .. 109 A3
Royal Geographical Society SW7 .. 114 B4 246 D1
Royal Hill SE10 .. 142 A5
Royal Horticultural Society (Lawrence Hall & Conf Ctr) SW1 .. 259 D5
Royal Horticultural Society (Lindley Hall) SW1 .. 259 C4
Royal Hospital (Army Pensioners)★ SW1 .. 115 A1 258 A1
Royal Hospital Rd SW3 .. 114 D1 257 D1
Royal Hospl and Home SW15 .. 157 A5
Royal La Hillingdon UB7 .. 82 B1
Hillingdon UB8 .. 82 B3
Royal Langford 3 NW6 91 D5
Royal London Est N17 .. 34 B4
Royal London Est The NW10 .. 89 B5
Royal London Homeopathic Hospl The WC1 .. 94 A2 240 B4
Royal London Hospl (Mile End) The E2 .. 96 D4
Royal London Hospl (St Clements) The E3 .. 97 B4
Royal London Hospl (Whitechapel) The E1 .. 96 B2
Royal Marsden Hospl SW3 .. 114 B1 256 D2
Royal Mews KT8 .. 196 C6
Royal Mews The★ SW1 .. 115 B3 258 D6
Royal Military Sch of Music (Kneller Hall) TW2 .. 152 B5
Royal Mint Pl 5 E1 .. 118 A6
Royal Mint St
E1 .. 117 D6 253 D6
Royal National Orthopaedic Hospl
W1 .. 93 B3 238 D5
Stanmore HA7 .. 9 C2
Royal National TNE Hospl The WC1 .. 94 B4 233 C2
Royal Nat TN&E Hospl The W5 .. 87 C2
Royal Naval Pl SE14 .. 141 B5
Royal Oak Ct 9 N1 .. 95 C4
Dagenham RM8 .. 80 C6
Royal Oak Pl SE22 .. 162 B5
Royal Oak Rd 5 E8 .. 74 B2
Bexley DA6 .. 147 C1
Royal Oak Sta W2 .. 91 D2
Royal Opera Arc SW1 .. 249 C4
Royal Orchard Cl SW18 .. 157 A4
Royal Par BR7 .. 189 A3
SE3 .. 142 D3
SW6 .. 264 A4
Ealing W5 .. 88 A4
11 Dagenham RM10 .. 81 D2
Royal Parade Mews BR7 .. 189 A3
Royal Park Prim Sch DA14 .. 169 A1
Royal Pl 11 SE10 .. 142 A5
Royal Rd DA14 .. 168 D1
E16 .. 99 D1
SE17 .. 138 D6
Teddington TW11 .. 174 B5
Royal Route HA9 .. 66 B4
Royal Russell Sch (Ballards) CR0 .. 222 B3
Royal Sch Hampstead The NW3 .. 70 B4
Royal St SE1 .. 116 B3 260 D6
Royalty Mews W1 .. 239 C1
Royalty Studios W11 .. 91 A1
Royal United Services Mus★ SW1 .. 250 A3
Royal Veterinary Coll NW1 .. 93 D6 232 C5
Royal Victoria Pl E16 .. 121 B5
Royal Victoria Sta E16 121 A6
Royal Victor Pl E3 .. 96 D5
Royal Wlk SM6 .. 219 B5
Roycraft Ave IG11 .. 101 D5
Roycroft Cl
Streatham SW2 .. 160 C3
Woodford E18 .. 37 B2
Roydene Rd SE18 .. 123 C1
Roydon Cl 7 SW11 .. 136 D3
Roy Gdns IG2 .. 57 D4
Roy Gr TW12 .. 173 D4
Roy Ho N1 .. 235 D5
Royle Cres W13 .. 87 A3
Roymount Ct TW2 .. 152 C1
Roy Ridley Ho 6 SW4 137 D2
Roy Sq E14 .. 119 A6
Royston Ave
Carshalton SM1 .. 218 B5
Chingford E4 .. 35 D5
Wallington SM6 .. 219 D4
Royston Cl
Cranford TW5 .. 128 B4
Walton-on-T KT12 .. 194 A1
Royston Ct 1 E13 .. 99 A6
Hinchley Wood KT10 .. 212 D6
Redbridge IG1 .. 55 D3
3 Richmond TW9 .. 132 B4
Royston Ct *continued*
Tolworth KT6 .. 214 C6
Royston Gdns IG1 .. 55 D3
Royston Gr HA5 .. 23 C4
Royston Ho N11 .. 31 A6
14 SE15 .. 140 A6
Royston Par IG1 .. 55 D3
Royston Park Rd HA5 .. 23 C5
Royston Prim Sch SE20 .. 184 D2
Royston Rd
Penge SE20 .. 184 D2
Richmond TW10 .. 154 A6
Royston St 25 E2 .. 96 C5
Roystons The KT5 .. 198 D4
Rozel Ct 3 N1 .. 95 C6
Rozel Rd SW4 .. 137 C2
Rubastic Rd UB2 .. 106 C3
Rubens Rd UB5 .. 84 D5
Rubens St SE6 .. 163 B2
Ruby Pl EN3 .. 7 C6
Ruby Rd E17 .. 53 C6
Ruby St NW10 .. 67 A1
SE15 .. 140 B6
Ruby Triangle SE15 .. 140 B6
Ruckholt Cl E10 .. 75 D5
Ruckholt Rd E10 .. 75 D5
Rucklidge Ave NW10 .. 90 A5
Rudall Cres NW3 .. 70 B4
Rudbeck Ho 10 SE15 .. 140 A5
Ruddington Cl E5 .. 75 A4
Ruddock Cl HA8 .. 27 A3
Ruddstreet Cl SE18 .. 123 A2
Rudge Ho 1 SE16 .. 118 A3
Rudgwick Terr NW8 .. 92 C6 230 B5
Rudhall Ho 4 SW2 .. 160 C5
Rudland Rd DA7 .. 147 D2
Rudloe Rd SW12 .. 159 C4
Rudolf Pl SW8 .. 270 B5
Rudolph Ct SE22 .. 162 B4
Rudolph Rd E13 .. 98 D5
NW6 .. 91 C5
Rudstone Ho 10 E3 .. 97 D4
Rudyard Ct SE1 .. 252 D1
Rudyard Gr NW7 .. 27 A4
Ruegg Ho 5 SE18 .. 144 C6
Ruffetts Cl CR2 .. 222 B1
Ruffetts The CR2 .. 222 B1
Ruffle Cl UB7 .. 104 B4
Rufford Cl HA3 .. 43 A3
Rufford St N1 .. 94 A6 233 B6
Rufford Street Mews N1 .. 72 A1
Rufford Twr 5 W3 .. 110 D5
Rufforth Ct 1 NW9 .. 27 C2
Rufus Bsns Ctr SW18 .. 157 D2
Rufus Cl HA4 .. 63 A5
Rufus Ho SE1 .. 263 D6
Rufus St N1 .. 95 C4
Rugby Ave Edmonton N9 17 D3
Northolt UB6 .. 64 B2
Wembley HA0 .. 65 C4
Rugby Cl HA1 .. 42 C5
Rugby Gdns RM9 .. 80 C2
Rugby Mans W14 .. 254 B4
Rugby Rd NW9 .. 44 D5
W4 .. 111 C4
Dagenham RM9 .. 80 C2
Twickenham TW1,TW2, TW7 .. 152 C5
Rugby St WC1 .. 94 B3 240 C5
Rugg St E14 .. 119 C6
Rugless Ho 2 E14 .. 120 A4
Rugmere 4 NW1 .. 71 A1
Ruislip Cl UB6 .. 85 D3
Ruislip Ct HA4 .. 61 D6
Ruislip Gardens Prim Sch HA4 .. 61 D4
Ruislip Gardens Sta HA4 .. 62 A4
Ruislip Lido★ HA4,HA5 .. 39 B5
Ruislip Lido Railway★ HA4 .. 39 B5
Ruislip Manor Sta HA4 .. 40 A1
Ruislip Rd UB6,UB5 .. 85 C4
Ruislip Rd E
Ealing UB6,W7 .. 86 D3
Greenford UB6 .. 86 B3
Ruislip St SW17 .. 180 D6
Ruislip Sta HA4 .. 39 D1
Rumball Ho 22 SE5 .. 139 C5
Rumbold Rd SW6 .. 135 D5 265 D3
Rum Cl E1 .. 118 C6
Rumford Ho SE1 .. 262 A5
Rumsey Cl TW12 .. 173 B4
Rumsey Rd SW9 .. 138 B2
Runacres Ct SE17 .. 262 A1
Runbury Circ NW9 .. 67 B6
Runcorn Cl N17 .. 52 B5
Runcorn Pl W11 .. 244 A6
Rundell Cres NW4 .. 46 B4
Rundell Twr SW8 .. 270 C2
Runes Cl CR4 .. 202 C5
Runnelfield HA1 .. 64 C5
Running Horse Yd 12 TW8 .. 132 A6
Runnymede SW19 .. 180 B2
Runnymede Cl TW2 .. 151 D4
Runnymede Cres SW16 .. 182 A2
Runnymede Ct 1 SM6 219 B2
Runnymede Gdns
Greenford UB6 .. 86 C5
Twickenham TW2 .. 151 D4
Runnymede Ho E9 .. 75 A4
Richmond TW10 .. 154 C6
Runnymede Rd TW2 .. 151 D5
Runway The HA4 .. 62 C3
Rupack St 3 SE16 .. 118 C4
Rupert Ave 6 HA9 .. 66 A3
Rupert Ct W1 .. 249 C6
Rupert Gdns SW9 .. 138 D3
Rupert Ho SE11 .. 261 B3
Rupert Rd N19 .. 71 D6
NW6 .. 91 B5
W4 .. 111 C3
Rupert St W1 .. 115 D6 249 C6
Rural Way SW16 .. 181 B3
Rusbridge Cl E8 .. 74 A3
Ruscoe Ho 12 SW27 .. 182 D5
Ruscoe Rd E16 .. 98 D1
Ruscombe Way TW14 .. 149 D4
Rusham Rd SW12 .. 158 D4
Rushbrook Cres E17 .. 35 B2
Rushbrook Ho 20 SW8 .. 137 D3
Rushbrook Rd SE9 .. 167 A2
Rushbury Ct 4 TW12 .. 173 C2
Rushby Ct SW4 .. 270 A1
Rush Common Mews 18 SW2 .. 160 B4
Rushcroft Rd
SW2,SW9 .. 138 C1
Chingford E4 .. 35 D3
Rush Croft Sch E4 .. 35 D3
Rushcutters Ct 18 SE16 .. 119 A2
Rushden Cl SE19 .. 183 B3
Rushdene SE2 .. 124 D3
Rushdene Ave EN4 .. 14 C4
Rushdene Cl UB5 .. 84 C5
Rushdene Cres UB5 .. 84 C4
Rushdene Rd HA5 .. 40 D3
Rushden Gdns NW7 .. 28 C4
Ilford IG5 .. 56 C6
Rushen Wlk SM5 .. 202 B1
Rushet Rd BR5 .. 190 A1
Rushett Cl KT7 .. 197 B1
Rushett Rd KT7 .. 197 B2
Rushey Cl KT3 .. 199 B5
Rushey Gn SE6 .. 163 D4
Rushey Green Prim Sch SE6 .. 163 D3
Rushey Hill EN2 .. 4 B1
Rushey Mead SE4 .. 163 C6
Rushford Rd SE4 .. 163 B5
Rush Green Rd RM7, RM8,RM10 .. 59 D1
Rushgrove Ave NW9 .. 45 D5
Rushgrove Ct NW9 .. 45 C4
Rushgrove St SE18 .. 122 B2
Rush Hill Mews 3 SW11 .. 137 A2
Rush Hill Rd SW11 .. 137 A2
Rushlake Ho 3 SW11 .. 137 A3
Rushley Cl BR2 .. 226 A4
Rushman Villas KT3 .. 199 D5
Rushmead 5 E2 .. 96 B4
Richmond TW10 .. 153 B1
Rushmead Cl CR0 .. 221 D4
Rushmere Ct KT4 .. 216 A6
Rushmere Ho 2 SW15 .. 156 A3
Rushmere Pl SW19 .. 178 D5
Rushmon Pl SM3 .. 217 A2
Rushmoor Cl HA5 .. 40 B5
Rushmore Cl BR1 .. 210 A6
Rushmore Cres 9 E5 .. 74 D4
Rushmore Ho 9 N7 .. 71 D3
W14 .. 254 B5
Rushmore Prim Sch E5 74 D4
Rushmore Rd E5 .. 74 D4
E5 .. 75 A4
Rusholme Ave RM10 .. 81 C5
Rusholme Gr SE19 .. 183 C5
Rusholme Rd SW15 .. 157 A5
Rushout Ave HA3 .. 43 B3
Rush The SW20 .. 179 B2
Rushton Ho 26 SW8 .. 137 D3
Rushton St N1 .. 95 B5 235 D4
Rushworth St
SE1 .. 116 D4 251 D1
Rushy Meadow La SM5 .. 218 C5
Rushy Meadow Prim Sch SM5 .. 218 C5
Ruskin Ave DA16 .. 146 A3
E12 .. 78 A2
Feltham TW14 .. 149 D5
Richmond TW9 .. 132 C5
Ruskin Cl NW11 .. 47 D3
Ruskin Ct SE5 .. 139 B2
SE9 .. 166 B5
Southgate N21 .. 16 B4
Ruskin Dr BR6 .. 227 C5
DA16 .. 146 A2
Ruskin Dr *continued*
North Cheam KT4 .. 216 C6
Ruskin Gdns Ealing W5 .. 87 D3
Harrow HA3 .. 44 B5
Ruskin Gr DA16 .. 146 A3
Ruskin Ho SW1 .. 259 D3
Ruskin Par CR0 .. 221 B3
Ruskin Park Ho SE5 .. 139 B2
Ruskin Rd
Belvedere DA17 .. 125 C2
Croydon CR0 .. 220 D6
Isleworth TW7 .. 130 D2
Southall UB1 .. 107 A6
Tottenham N17 .. 33 D2
Wallington SM5 .. 219 A3
Ruskin Way SW19 .. 180 B2
Ruskin Wlk BR2 .. 210 B3
SE24 .. 161 A6
Edmonton N9 .. 18 A2
Rusland Ave BR6 .. 227 B5
Rusland Hts HA1 .. 42 C5
Rusland Park Rd HA1 .. 42 C5
Rusper Cl NW2 .. 68 C5
Stanmore HA7 .. 25 C6
Rusper Ct SW9 .. 138 A3
Rusper Rd N17,N22 .. 51 A6
Dagenham RM9 .. 80 C2
Russel Cl BR3 .. 208 A6
Russel Ct N14 .. 15 D6
Russell Ave N22 .. 32 D1
Russell Cl DA7 .. 147 C1
NW10 .. 67 A1
SE7 .. 143 C5
Chiswick W4 .. 133 D6
Ruislip HA4 .. 62 C6
Russell Ct 4 E10 .. 53 D2
5 SE15 .. 140 B3
SW1 .. 249 B3
SW11 .. 268 B1
Bromley BR1 .. 186 D3
New Barnet EN5 .. 2 A1
Streatham SW16 .. 182 B5
Surbiton KT6 .. 198 A2
Wallington SM6 .. 219 C3
Wembley HA0 .. 66 A1
Russell Gdns N20 .. 14 C2
NW11 .. 47 A3
W14 .. 113 A3 254 A6
Ilford IG2 .. 57 B2
Richmond TW10 .. 153 C2
West Drayton UB7 .. 104 C1
Russell Gdns Mews
W14 .. 113 A3 254 A6
Russell Gr NW7 .. 27 C6
33 SW9 .. 138 C4
Russell Ho 15 E14 .. 97 C1
SW1 .. 259 A2
Russell Kerr Cl W4 .. 133 A5
Russell La N20 .. 14 D2
Russell Lo 5 E4 .. 20 A2
Russell Lodge SE1 .. 262 C6
Russell Mans WC1 .. 240 B4
Russell Par NW11 .. 47 A3
Russell Pickering Ho 2 SW4 .. 138 A2
Russell Pl NW3 .. 70 C3
SE16 .. 119 A3
Russell Prim Sch The TW10 .. 153 D3
Russell Rd E10 .. 53 D3
E17 .. 53 B6
E4 .. 35 B6
N15 .. 51 C4
N20 .. 14 C2
N8 .. 49 D3
NW9 .. 45 D3
W14 .. 113 A3 254 B5
Bowes Park N13 .. 32 B4
Buckhurst Hill IG9 .. 21 C3
Enfield EN1 .. 5 D5
Merton SW19 .. 179 C3
Mitcham CR4 .. 202 C6
Newham E16 .. 99 B1
Northolt UB5 .. 64 A3
Shepperton TW17 .. 193 A2
Twickenham TW1,TW2 .. 152 D5
Walton-on-T KT12 .. 194 A3
Russell Sch The TW10 153 D2
Russell Sq WC1 94 A3 240 A5
Russell Square Mans WC1 .. 240 B4
Russell Square Sta WC1 .. 94 A3 240 A5
Russell St WC2 .. 116 A6 250 B6
Russell's Wharf 2 W9 .. 91 B3
Russell Way SM1 .. 217 D3
Russell Wlk 4 TW10 .. 154 B5
Russet Ave TW16, TW17 .. 193 C6
Russet Cl UB10 .. 83 A3
Russet Cres N7 .. 72 B3
Russet Ct NW2 .. 68 B5
6 Barnet EN4 .. 2 C1
Russet Dr CR0 .. 207 A1
Russet Ho TW3 .. 129 B1
Russet House Sch EN1 .. 6 B4
Russets Cl E4 .. 36 B6
Russett Way SE13 .. 141 D3
Russia Ct EC2 .. 242 B2
Russia Dock Rd SE16 .. 119 A5
Russia La E2 .. 96 C5
Russian Submarine SE18 .. 121 D3
Russia Row EC2 .. 242 B1
Russington Rd TW17 .. 193 B3
Rusthall Ave W4 .. 111 B3
Rusthall Cl CR0 .. 206 C3
Rusthall Mans W4 .. 111 B2
Rustic Ave SW16 .. 181 B3
Rustic Pl HA0 .. 65 D4
Rustic Wlk E16 .. 99 B1
Rustington Wlk SM4 .. 201 B2
Ruston Ave KT5 .. 198 D2
Ruston Gdns N14 .. 15 A5
Ruston Mews W11 .. 91 A1
Ruston Rd SE18 .. 122 A3
Ruston St E3 .. 97 B6
Rust Sq SE5 .. 139 B5
Rutford Rd SW16 .. 182 A5
Ruth Cl HA7 .. 44 B5
Ruth Ct 14 E3 .. 97 A5
Rutherford Cl
Hillingdon UB8 .. 82 B3
Sutton SM2 .. 218 B2
Rutherford Ho 12 E1 .. 96 B3
Teddington TW11 .. 174 D5
7 Wembley HA9 .. 67 A5
Rutherford St
SW1 .. 115 D2 259 C4
Rutherford Twr 10 UB1 .. 85 D1
Rutherford Way
Bushey WD23 .. 8 C3
Wembley HA9 .. 66 C4
Rutherglen Rd SE2 .. 146 A6
Rutherwyke Cl KT17 .. 216 A2
Ruth Ho W10 .. 91 A3
Ruthin Cl NW9 .. 45 C3
Ruthin Rd SE3 .. 143 A6
Ruthven St E9 .. 96 D6
Rutland Ave DA15 .. 168 A4
Rutland Cl DA5 .. 168 D3
Chessington KT9 .. 214 B2
Mitcham SW19 .. 180 C3
Mortlake SW14 .. 133 A2
Rutland Ct SE5 .. 139 B1
SW7 .. 247 B1
15 Acton W3 .. 88 C1
Chislehurst BR7 .. 188 C2
Enfield EN3 .. 18 B6
Sidcup BR7 .. 167 A2
Rutland Dr
Morden SM4 .. 201 C2
Richmond TW10 .. 154 A3
Rutland Gate
SW7 .. 114 C4 247 B1
Beckenham BR2 .. 208 D5
Belvedere DA17 .. 125 D1
Rutland Gate Mews SW7 .. 247 A1
Rutland Gdns N4 .. 51 A3
SW7 .. 114 C4 247 B1
Dagenham RM8 .. 80 C3
Ealing W13 .. 87 A2
South Croydon CR0 .. 221 C4
Rutland Gdns Mews SW7 .. 247 B1
Rutland Gr W6 .. 112 B1
Rutland Ho 18 SE18 .. 122 B2
W8 .. 255 C5
6 Northolt UB5 .. 63 C2
2 Penge SE20 .. 184 C2
10 Putney SW15 .. 156 C4
Tolworth KT6 .. 198 C1
Rutland Lo SE6 .. 163 B2
Rutland Mews E SW7 .. 257 B6
Rutland Mews S SW7 .. 257 A6
Rutland Mews W SW7 257 A6
Rutland Park Gdns NW2 .. 68 C2
Rutland Park Mans NW2 .. 68 C2
Rutland Pk NW2 .. 68 C2
Forest Hill SE6 .. 163 B2
Rutland Pl EC1 .. 241 D4
Bushey WD23 .. 8 B3
Rutland Rd E17 .. 53 C3
E7 .. 77 D1
E9 .. 96 D6
Harrow HA1 .. 42 A3
Hayes UB3 .. 105 B2
Ilford IG1 .. 78 D5
Mitcham SW19 .. 180 C3
Southall UB1 .. 85 C2
Twickenham TW2 .. 152 B2
Wanstead E11 .. 55 B4
Rutland St SW7 .. 257 B6
Rutland Studios NW10 .. 90 A4
Rutland Wlk SE6 .. 163 B2
Rutley Cl SE11 .. 138 D6
Rutlish Rd SW19 .. 179 C2
Rutlish Sch (Boys) SW20 .. 179 B1
Rutter Gdns CR4 .. 202 B5
Rutters Cl UB7 .. 104 C4
Rutt's Terr SE14 .. 140 D4
Rutts The WD23 .. 8 B3
Ruvigny Gdns SW15 .. 134 D2

Ruvigny Mans SW15 ..134 D2
Ruxbury Ct TW15 ..148 A1
Ruxley Cl
Chessington KT19 ..214 D3
Sidcup DA14 ..191 A4
Ruxley Cnr DA14 ..191 A4
Ruxley Corner Ind Est
DA14 ..190 D4
Ruxley Cres KT10 ..213 B1
Ruxley Ct KT19 ..215 A3
Ruxley Gdns TW17 ..193 A4
Ruxley La KT19 ..215 B3
Ruxley Mews KT19 ..214 D3
Ruxley Ridge KT10 ..213 A1
Ryall's Ct N20 ..14 D1
Ryan Cl SE9 ..143 C1
Ruislip HA4 ..40 B1
Ryan Ct SW16 ..182 A3
Ryan Dr TW8 ..131 A6
Ryan Ho 3 HA1 ..42 D4
Ryarsh Cres BR6 ..227 C4
Rycott Path SE22 ..162 A4
Rycroft Way N17 ..51 D6
Ryculff Sq SE3 ..142 D3
Rydal Cl NW4 ..29 A2
Rydal Cres UB6 ..87 C5
Rydal Ct Edgware HA8 ..26 B5
Wembley HA9 ..44 A2
Rydal Dr DA7 ..147 C4
West Wickham BR4 ..224 C6
Rydal Gdns NW9 ..45 C4
Kingston SW15 ..177 C5
Twickenham TW2,TW3 ..151 D5
Wembley HA9 ..43 C1
Rydal Ho 25 SW8 ..137 D3
Rydal Lo N17 ..34 A3
Rydal Rd SW16 ..181 D6
Rydal Water NW1 ..232 A1
Rydal Way Enfield EN3 ..18 C5
Ruislip HA4 ..62 C4
Ryde Ho 1 NW6 ..91 C6
Rydens Ho SE9 ..165 C1
Rydens Rd KT12 ..194 D1
Ryde Pl TW1 ..153 D5
Ryder Cl BR1 ..187 B5
Ryder Ct E10 ..75 D6
SW1 ..249 B4
Ryder Dr SE16 ..118 B1
Ryder Ho 14 E1 ..96 C3
5 Merton SW19 ..179 D2
Ryder St SW1 ..249 B4
Ryder's Terr
NW8 ..92 A5 229 A4
Ryder Yd SW1 ..249 B4
Ryde Vale Rd SW12 ..159 C2
Rydon Mews SW19 ..178 C3
Rydons Cl SE9 ..144 A2
Rydon St N1 ..235 B6
Rydston Cl 2 N7 ..72 B1
Rye Cl DA5 ..169 D5
Ryecotes Mead SE21 ..161 C3
Ryecroft Ave TW2 ..151 D3
Ryecroft Cres EN5 ..12 B6
Ryecroft Rd BR5 ..211 B3
SE13 ..164 A6
South Norwood SW16 ..182 C4
Ryecroft St
SW6 ..135 D4 265 C1
Rye Ct BR3 ..185 B2
Ryedale SE22 ..162 B5
Ryedale Ct 6 TW12 ..173 C2
Ryefield Ave UB10 ..60 D1
Ryefield Cres HA5,HA6 ..22 A1
Ryefield Ct HA6 ..22 A1
Ryefield Path 7
SW15 ..156 A3
Ryefield Prim Sch UB10 83 B6
Ryefield Rd SE19 ..183 A4
Ryegates 2 SE15 ..140 B3
Ryehill Ct KT3 ..199 D2
Rye Hill Pk SE15 ..140 C1
Rye La SE15 ..140 A3
Ryeland Cl UB7 ..82 A1
Ryelands Cres SE12 ..165 C5
Ryelands Prim Sch
SE25 ..206 B4
Rye Rd SE15 ..140 D1
Rye The N14 ..15 C4
Rye Way HA8 ..26 B4
Rye Wlk SW15 ..156 D6
Ryfold Rd SW19 ..157 C1
Ryhope Rd N11 ..31 B6
Ryland Cl TW13 ..171 D6
Ryland Ct EN2 ..5 B1
Rylandes Rd NW2 ..68 A5
Ryland Ho 11 SW16 ..181 C5
Ryland Rd NW5 ..71 B2
Rylett Cres W12 ..111 D3
Rylett Rd W12 ..111 D3
Rylston Rd
SW6 ..135 B6 264 C5
Edmonton N13 ..17 B1
Rylton Ho KT12 ..194 A1
Rymer Rd CR0 ..205 C2
Rymer St SE24 ..160 D5
Rymill St E16 ..122 C5
Rysbrack St SW1 ..257 C6
Rythe Cl KT9 ..213 C1
Rythe Ct KT7 ..197 A2
Rythe Ho 7 BR1 ..186 B5
Rythe Rd KT10 ..212 C3

S

Saatchi Gallery* SE1 ..250 C2
Sabah Ct TW15 ..170 C6
Sabbarton St 9 E16 ..98 D1
Sabella Ct E3 ..97 B5
Sabine Rd SW11 ..137 A2
Sable Cl TW4 ..128 C2
Sable Ct 3 KT3 ..199 C4
Sable St N1 ..72 D1
Sach Rd E5 ..74 B6
Sacketts Ho 24 SW9 ..138 C4
Sackville Ave BR2 ..209 A1
Sackville Cl HA2 ..64 B5
Sackville Gdns IG1 ..56 B1
Sackville Ho N8 ..50 A5
16 Streatham SW16 ..160 A1
Sackville Rd SM2 ..217 C1
Sackville St
W1 ..115 C6 249 B5
Sacred Heart High Sch
W6 ..112 C2
Sacred Heart Jun Sch
W6 ..112 D2
Sacred Heart Prim Sch,
Battersea SW11 ..136 C3
Sacred Heart RC High Sch
The HA3 ..24 C1
Sacred Heart RC Prim Sch
N20 ..14 C2
Putney SW15 ..156 A6
Ruislip HA4 ..61 C6
Teddington TW11 ..175 B3
West Barnes KT3 ..200 A5
Sacred Heart RC Sch The
SE5 ..139 A4
Saddlebrook Pk TW16 171 C3
Saddlers Cl Barnet EN5 ..12 B6
Borehamwood WD6 ..11 B5
Pinner HA5 ..23 C5
Saddlers Mews SW8 ..270 B2
Teddington KT1 ..175 C2
Wembley HA0 ..64 D4
Saddlers Path WD6 ..11 B6
Saddlescombe Way
N12 ..29 C5
Sadler Cl CR4 ..180 D1
Sadler Ho 17 E3 ..97 D4
EC1 ..234 C2
Sadlers Ride KT8 ..174 A1
Saffron Ave E14 ..120 B6
Saffron Cl NW11 ..47 B3
Thornton Heath CR0 ..204 A3
Saffron Ct E15 ..76 C3
10 N1 ..73 B2
Saffron Hill EC1 94 C2 241 B4
Saffron St EC1 ..241 B4
Saffron Way KT6 ..197 D1
Saffron Wharf SE1 ..253 D2
Sage Cl 7 E6 ..100 B2
Sage Mews SE22 ..161 D6
Sage St E1 ..118 C6
Sage Way WC1 ..233 C1
Sage Yd KT6 ..198 B1
Sahara Ct UB1 ..107 A6
Saigasso Cl E16 ..99 D1
Sailmakers Ct SW6 ..136 A2
Sail St SE11 ..116 C3 260 D4
Saimet 3 NW9 ..27 D2
Sainfoin Rd SW17 ..159 A2
Sainsbury Rd SE19 ..183 C5
St Agatha's Dr KT2 ..176 B4
St Agatha's Gr SM5 ..202 D1
St Agatha's RC Prim Sch
KT2 ..176 B4
St Agatha's RC Sch
KT2 ..176 B3
St Agnes Cl E9 ..96 C6
St Agnes Pl SE11 ..138 D6
St Agnes RC Prim Sch
E3 ..97 D4
St Agnes RC Sch NW2 ..69 A5
St Aidans Ct IG11 ..102 B5
St Aidan's Prim Sch N4 50 C2
St Aidan's RC Prim Sch
IG1 ..57 B1
St Aidan's Rd SE22 ..162 B6
W13 ..109 B4
St Albans Ave W4 ..111 B3
Feltham TW13 ..172 D5
St Alban's Ave E6 ..100 C4
St Alban's CE Prim Sch
EC1 ..94 C2 241 A4
St Alban's Cl NW11 ..47 C1
St Albans Cres N22 ..32 C2
St Alban's Cres IG8 ..37 A2
St Alban's Gdns TW11 175 A5
St Alban's Gr
W8 ..113 D3 255 D6
Carshalton SM5 ..202 C2
St Albans Ho 2 SW16 182 C6
St Albans La NW11 ..47 C1
St Albans Mans W8 ..255 D6
St Alban's Pl
N1 ..94 D6 234 C5
St Alban's RC Prim Sch
KT8 ..196 A4
St Alban's Rd NW10 ..89 C6
NW5 ..71 B5
St Albans Rd Barnet EN5 ..1 A3
Cheam SM1 ..217 B4
Ilford IG3 ..57 D2
Kingston KT2 ..176 A4
St Alban's Rd IG8 ..37 A3
St Alban's St SW1 ..249 C5
St Albans Studios W8 255 D6
St Albans Terr W6 ..264 A6
St Alban's Villas NW5 ..71 A5
St Alfege Pas SE10 ..142 A6
St Alfege Rd SE7 ..143 D6
St Alfege with St Peter's CE
Prim Sch SE10 ..142 A6
St Aloysius RC Inf Sch
NW1 ..232 D1
St Aloysius' RC Jun & Inf
Sch NW1 ..232 C2
St Aloysius RC Jun Sch
NW1 ..93 D5 232 D3
St Alphage Ct NW9 ..45 B6
St Alphage Gdn EC2 ..242 B3
St Alphage Highwalk
EC2 ..242 B3
St Alphage Wlk HA8 ..27 A1
St Alphege Rd N9 ..18 C4
St Alphonsus Rd SW4 137 D1
St Amunds Cl SE6 ..185 C6
St Andrews Ave HA0 ..65 A4
St Andrew's CE Prim Sch
N1 ..94 B6 233 D6
N14 ..15 D3
SW9 ..138 A3
Enfield EN1 ..5 C3
St Andrew's CE Sch
N20 ..13 B2
St Andrews Cl 25 SE16 118 B1
St Andrew's Cl N12 ..30 A6
NW2 ..68 B5
St Andrews Cl
Erith SE28 ..102 D1
Hinchley Wood KT7 ..197 B1
Ruislip HA4 ..62 D6
Stanmore HA7 ..25 C1
St Andrew's Cl
2 Hounslow TW7 ..130 C4
Upper Halliford TW17 ..193 B5
St Andrew's Ct E17 ..35 A1
St Andrews Ct W4 ..133 A4
St Andrew's Ct
Kingston KT3 ..199 D6
Wandsworth SW18 ..158 A2
St Andrews Dr HA7 ..25 C2
St Andrew's Gr N16 ..51 B1
St Andrew's Greek Sch
NW1 ..71 C2
St Andrew's High Sch
CR0 ..220 D4
St Andrew's Hill
EC4 ..94 D1 241 D1
St Andrews Ho 11
SE16 ..118 B3
St Andrew's Hospl E3 ..97 D3
St Andrew's Mans W1 238 A3
St Andrew's Mews N16 51 C1
St Andrews Mews
Greenwich SE3 ..143 A5
4 Streatham SW12 ..159 D3
St Andrew's Pl NW1 ..238 D6
St Andrews RC Prim Sch
SW16 ..182 A5
St Andrews Rd DA14 ..168 D1
E17 ..35 A1
N9 ..18 C4
NW9 ..45 B1
St Andrew's Rd E11 ..54 C3
E13 ..99 B4
NW11 ..47 B3
NW2 ..68 B2
W14 ..264 B6
W3 ..89 C1
W7 ..108 C4
St Andrews Rd SM5 ..218 C5
St Andrew's Rd
3 Croydon CR0 ..221 A4
Enfield EN1 ..5 B2
Hillingdon UB10 ..82 B6
Redbridge IG1 ..56 B2
Surbiton KT6 ..197 D3
St Andrew's Sq W11 ..91 A1
Surbiton KT6 ..197 D3
St Andrew's & St Mark's CE
Jun Sch KT6 ..197 D4
St Andrew St EC4 ..241 B3
St Andrews Terr WD19 ..22 C5
St Andrew & St Francis CE
Prim Sch NW2 ..68 A2
St Andrew's Twr UB1 ..108 A6
St Andrews Way E3 ..97 D3
St Andrew's Wharf
SE1 ..253 D2
St Angela's Ursuline
Convent Sch E7 ..77 B2
St Anna Rd EN5 ..12 D6
St Anne RC Prim Sch
E1 ..96 A3
St Annes Catholic High Sch
for Girls (Upper) N13 ..32 C6
St Anne's CE Prim Sch
SW18 ..157 D6
St Anne's Cl N6 ..71 A5
St Annes Cl WD19 ..22 C6
St Anne's Ct NW6 ..91 A6
W1 ..239 C1
St Anne's Flats NW1 ..232 C2
St Annes Gdns NW10 ..88 B4
St Anne's Pas E14 ..97 B1
St Anne's Prim Sch
TW19 ..148 A4
St Anne's RC Prim Sch
SE11 ..138 B6 270 C6
St Anne's Rd E11 ..76 B6
Wembley HA0 ..65 D3
St Anne's Row E14 ..97 B1
St Anne St E14 ..97 B1
St Anne's Trad Est E14 ..97 B1
St Ann's IG11 ..101 A6
St Ann's CE Prim Sch
N15 ..51 B4
St Ann's Cres SW18 ..158 A5
St Ann's Ct NW4 ..46 B6
St Ann's Ctr HA1 ..42 C3
St Ann's Gdns NW5 ..71 A2
St Ann's General Hospl
N4,N15 ..51 A4
St Ann's Hill SW18 ..158 A5
St Ann's Ho WC1 ..234 A1
St Ann's La SW1 ..259 D5
St Ann's Park Rd
SW18 ..158 A5
St Ann's Rd N15 ..51 B4
W11 ..112 D6
St Anns Rd SW13 ..133 D4
St Ann's Rd
2 Barking IG11 ..101 A6
Edmonton N9 ..17 D3
Harrow HA1 ..42 C3
St Ann's Sch Ealing W7 108 C5
Morden SM4 ..201 D4
St Ann's St
SW1 ..115 D3 259 D6
St Ann's Terr
NW8 ..92 B5 229 D4
St Ann's Villas
W11 ..112 D5 244 A3
St Ann's Way CR2 ..220 D2
St Anselm RC Prim Sch
UB2 ..107 B3
St Anselm's Ct SW16 ..182 A5
St Anselm's Pl W1 ..248 C6
St Anselm's RC Prim Sch
Harrow HA1 ..42 C2
Upper Tooting SW17 ..159 A1
St Anselms Rd UB3 ..105 D4
St Anthony's Ave IG8 ..37 C3
St Anthony's Cl 8 E1 ..118 A5
St Anthonys Cl SW17 ..158 C2
St Anthony's Ct
2 SW12 ..159 A5
Orpington BR6 ..226 D6
Upper Tooting SW17 ..159 A2
St Anthony's Flats
NW1 ..232 C3
St Anthony's Hospl
KT4 ..200 D1
St Anthony's RC Prim Sch
E7 ..77 B1
SE22 ..162 A5
Penge SE20 ..184 B2
St Anthony's Way
TW14 ..127 D1
St Antony's RC Prim Sch
IG8 ..37 A6
St Antony's Rd E7 ..77 B1
St Arvans Cl CR0 ..221 C5
St Asaph Ct SE4 ..140 D2
St Asaph Rd SE4 ..140 D2
St Aubins Ct N1 ..235 D6
St Aubyns E18 ..54 D5
St Aubyn's Ave
Hounslow TW3,TW4 ..151 C6
Wimbledon SW19 ..179 B5
St Aubyns Cl BR6 ..227 D5
St Aubyn's Ct SW19 ..179 A4
St Aubyns Gdns BR6 ..227 D6
St Aubyn's Prep Sch
IG8 ..36 D3
St Aubyn's Rd SE19 ..183 D4
St Aubyn's Sch IG8 ..36 D3
St Audrey Ave DA7 ..147 C3
St Augustine's Ave
BR1,BR2 ..210 A4
Ealing W5 ..88 A4
South Croydon CR2 ..221 A1
Wembley HA9 ..66 A5
St Augustine's CE High Sch
NW6 ..91 C5
St Augustine's CE Prim Sch
NW6 ..91 D5
St Augustine's Ct E11 ..54 D1
St Augustines Ct BR3 ..185 A1
St Augustine's Prim Sch
DA17 ..125 B2
St Augustine's RC Prim Sch
W6 ..135 A6 264 B5
St Augustine's RC Prim Sch
continued
Ilford IG2 ..56 D4
St Augustine's Rd
DA17 ..125 B2
NW1 ..71 D1
St Augustines's RC Prim
Sch SE6 ..186 A5
St Austell Cl HA8 ..26 B1
St Austell Rd SE13 ..142 B3
St Awdry's Rd IG11 ..79 B1
St Barnabas CE Prim Sch
SW1 ..115 A1 258 B2
St Barnabas Cl
11 SE22 ..161 C6
Beckenham BR3 ..186 A1
St Barnabas Ct HA3 ..24 A2
St Barnabas' Gdns
KT8 ..195 C4
St Barnabas Rd E17 ..53 C3
Mitcham CR4 ..181 A3
Sutton SM1 ..218 B3
Woodford IG8 ..37 C3
St Barnabas St SW1 ..258 B2
St Barnabas & St Philip's CE
Prim Sch W8 113 C3 255 A5
St Barnabas Terr E9 ..74 D3
St Barnabas Villas
SW8 ..138 A4 270 B2
St Bartholomews CE Prim
Sch SE26 ..162 C1
St Bartholomew's CE Prim
Sch SE26 ..184 C6
St Bartholomew's Cl
SE26 ..184 C6
St Bartholomew's Hospl
EC1 ..94 D2 241 D3
St Bartholomew's Rd
E6 ..100 B5
St Bede's RC Inf Sch
SW12 ..159 D3
St Bede's RC Prim Sch
RM6 ..58 C4
St Benedict's Cl SW17 181 A5
St Benedict's Jun Sch
W5 ..87 C2
St Benedict's Sch W5 ..87 D2
St Benets Cl SW17 ..158 C2
St Benet's Gr SM5 ..202 A2
St Benet's Pl EC3 ..252 D6
St Bernadette RC Jun Sch
SW12 ..159 C4
St Bernadette's RC Fst &
Mid Sch HA3 ..44 B5
St Bernadette's RC Prim
Sch UB10 ..82 D6
St Bernard Ho 6 E14 ..120 A3
St Bernards CR0 ..221 C5
St Bernards Cl 8
SE27 ..183 B6
St Bernards Ho 1
KT6 ..214 A6
St Bernard's Rd E6 ..99 D6
St Blaise Ave BR1 ..187 B1
St Bonaventure's RC Sec
Sch E7 ..77 A1
St Boniface Catholic Prim
Sch SW17 ..180 D5
St Botolph St
E1,EC3 ..95 D1 243 C2
St Brelades Ct N1 ..235 D6
St Bride's Ave EC4 ..241 C1
Edgware HA8 ..26 B2
St Brides Cl DA18 ..124 D4
St Bride's Pas EC4 ..241 C1
St Bride St EC4 ..94 D1 241 C2
St Catherines Cl
Chessington KT9 ..213 D2
Upper Tooting SW17 ..158 C2
St Catherine's Convent Girls
Prep & Senior Schs
TW1 ..153 A2
St Catherine's Ct 8
W4 ..111 C3
St Catherines Ct
TW13 ..150 A3
St Catherine's Dr
SE14 ..140 D3
St Catherines Farm Ct
HA4 ..39 A3
St Catherines Mews
SW3 ..257 C4
St Catherine's RC Mid Sch
SW20 ..200 C4
St Catherine's RC Prim Sch
EN5 ..1 C1
St Catherine's RC Sch for
Girls DA6 ..169 D6
St Catherines Rd
Chingford E4 ..19 C2
Ruislip HA4 ..39 B3
St Cecilia's Cl SM3 ..201 A1
St Cecilia's RC Prim Sch
SM3 ..216 D6
St Chads Cl KT6 ..197 C2
St Chad's Gdns RM6 ..59 A2
St Chad's Pl WC1 ..233 C2
St Chad's RC Prim Sch
SE25 ..205 C4
St Chad's Rd RM6 ..59 A2
St Chad's St WC1 ..233 B2
St Charles' Hospl W10 ..90 D2
St Charles Pl W10 ..91 A2
St Charles RC Prim Sch
W10 ..90 D2
St Charles RC Sixth Form
Coll W10 ..90 D2
St Charles Sq W10 ..90 D2
St Christina's Sch
NW8 ..92 C5 230 A3
St Christopher's Cl
TW7 ..130 C4
St Christophers Dr
UB3 ..106 B6
St Christophers Gdns
CR7 ..204 C6
St Christopher's Ho
NW1 ..232 C3
St Christopher's Hospice
SE26 ..184 C5
St Christopher's Mews
SM6 ..219 C3
St Christopher's Pl
W1 ..238 B2
St Christopher's Sch
NW3 ..70 B3
Beckenham BR3 ..186 A1
Wembley HA9 ..66 B5
St Clair Dr KT4 ..216 B4
St Clair Ho 14 E3 ..97 B4
St Clair Rd E13 ..99 B5
St Clair's Rd CR0 ..221 C6
St Clare Bsns Pk
TW12 ..174 A4
St Clare St EC3 ..243 C1
St Clement Danes CE Prim
Sch WC2 ..94 B1 240 C1
St Clements Ct N7 ..72 B2
7 SE14 ..140 D6
8 W11 ..112 D6
St Clement's Ct EC3 ..252 D6
St Clements Ho KT12 ..194 A2
St Clement's Hts SE26 184 A6
St Clement's La WC2 ..240 D1
St Clements Mans 3
SW6 ..134 D6
St Clements St N7 ..72 C1
St Clement & St James CE
Prim Sch
W11 ..112 D5 244 A3
St Cloud Rd SE27 ..183 B6
St Columba's Ct E15 ..76 C4
St Columbas Ho 2 E17 53 D5
St Columba's RC Sch for
Boys DA6 ..169 D6
St Columb's Ho 11 W10 91 A2
St Crispins Cl NW3 ..70 C4
St Crispin's Cl UB1 ..85 B1
St Cross St EC1 ..94 C2 241 B4
St Cuthberts Gdns 1
HA5 ..23 B3
St Cuthbert's Rd NW2 ..69 B2
St Cuthberts Rd N13 ..32 C4
St Cuthbert with St
Matthias Prim Sch
SW5 ..113 D1 255 C2
St Cyprian's Greek Orthodox
Prim Sch CR7 ..183 A2
St Cyprian's St SW17 ..180 D6
St Davids Cl 27 SE16 ..118 B1
Wembley HA9 ..67 A5
St David's Cl BR4 ..207 D2
St David's Coll BR4 ..207 D2
St David's Ct 1 E17 ..54 A6
St Davids Ct 5 E11 ..55 B4
St David's Ct 8 UB1 ..86 A1
St David's Dr HA8 ..26 B2
St David's Pl NW4 ..46 B2
St David's Sch TW15 ..148 B1
St David's Sq E14 ..119 D1
St Denis Rd SE27 ..183 B6
St Dionis Rd SW6 ..135 B3
St Domingo Ho SE18 ..122 B3
St Dominic RC Prim Sch
NW5 ..70 D3
St Dominics RC Prim Sch
E9 ..75 A2
St Dominic's Sixth Form
Coll (RC) HA1 ..64 C6
St Donatt's Rd SE14 ..141 B4
St Dunstans SM1 ..217 B2
St Dunstan's Alley
EC3 ..253 A5
St Dunstan's Ave W3 ..111 B6
St Dunstan's CE Prim Sch
SM3 ..217 A1
St Dunstans Cl UB3 ..105 D2
St Dunstan's Coll SE6 ..163 C3
St Dunstan's Ct EC4 ..241 B1
St Dunstan's Gdns W3 111 B6
St Dunstan's Hill EC3 ..253 A5
Cheam SM1,SM3 ..217 A3
St Dunstan's La EC3 ..253 A5
Beckenham BR3 ..208 A4
St Dunstans Rd E7 ..77 C2

St Dunstan's Rd W6 ... 112 D1
W7 ... 108 C4
Cranford TW5 ... 128 B3
Feltham TW13 ... 149 D1
South Norwood SE25 ... 205 D5
St Edmund RC Sch E14 ... 119 C2
St Edmunds Ave HA4 ... 39 B3
St Edmunds Cl DA18 ... 124 D4
St Edmund's Cl NW8 ... 230 C5
St Edmunds Cl SW17 ... 158 C2
St Edmund's Ct NW8 ... 230 C5
St Edmunds Dr HA7 ... 25 A2
St Edmund's La TW2 ... 151 D4
St Edmund's RC Prim Sch
Edmonton N9 ... 18 B3
Twickenham TW2 ... 151 D4
St Edmunds Rd N9 ... 18 A4
St Edmund's Rd IG1 ... 56 B3
St Edmund's Sq SW13 134 C6
St Edmund's Terr NW8 ... 92 D6 230 C5
St Edward's CE Comp Sch RM7 ... 59 C3
St Edward's Cl NW11 ... 47 C3
St Edwards Ct 3 E10 ... 54 A2
St Edward's Ct NW11 ... 47 C3
St Edward's RC Prim Sch E6 ... 99 C6
St Edward's RC Prim Sch NW1 ... 92 C3 237 B5
St Egberts Way E4 ... 20 A3
St Elizabeth Ct 8 E10 ... 53 D2
N12 ... 30 A6
St Elizabeth's RC Prim Sch TW10 ... 154 B5
St Elmo Rd W12 ... 111 D4
St Elmos Rd SE16 ... 119 A4
St Elphege's RC Inf Sch SM6 ... 220 A2
St Elphege's RC Jun Sch SM6 ... 220 A2
St Erkenwald Mews IG11 ... 101 B6
St Erkenwald Rd IG11 101 B6
St Ermin's Hill SW1 ... 259 C6
St Ervan's Rd W10 ... 91 B2
St Eugene de Mazenod RC Prim Sch NW6 ... 91 C6
St Faith's CE Prim Sch SW18 ... 158 A6
St Faith's Cl EN2 ... 5 A4
St Faith's Rd SE24 ... 160 D3
St Fillans Rd SE6 ... 164 A4
St Francesca Cabrini Prim Sch SE23 ... 162 C5
St Francis Cl BR6 ... 211 C3
St Francis de Sales RC Jun Sch N17 ... 33 D3
St Francis' Ho NW1 ... 232 C3
St Francis Lo HA0 ... 64 D5
St Francis of Assisi RC Prim Sch W11 ... 112 D6
St Francis RC Prim Sch
E15 ... 76 C3
SE15 ... 140 A5
St Francis Rd SE22 ... 139 C1
St Francis Way IG1 ... 79 B4
St Francis Xavier Sixth Form Coll SW12 ... 159 B5
St Gables Ct N11 ... 31 D3
St Gabriel's CE Prim Sch SW1 ... 115 C1 259 A1
St Gabriel's Cl E11 ... 55 B1
St Gabriel's Rd NW2 ... 68 D3
St George Ho SW11 ... 268 B1
St George's Ave E7 ... 77 B1
N7 ... 71 D4
NW9 ... 45 B5
W5 ... 109 D4
Southall UB1 ... 107 B6
St George's Battersea CE Prim Sch SW8 ... 137 C5 269 B3
St George's Bickley CE Prim Sch BR1 ... 187 D1
St George's Cath NW1 231 D2
St George's Cath RC Jun & Inf Sch SE1 ... 116 D3 261 C6
St George's CE Prim Sch SE5 ... 139 C5
St George's Circ SE1 ... 116 D3 261 C6
St George's Cl NW11 ... 47 B3
St Georges Cl
Erith SE28 ... 102 D1
Wembley HA0 ... 65 A5
St Georges Ct E17 ... 54 B4
E6 ... 100 B3
St George's Ct SE1 ... 261 C5
SW3 ... 257 A4
SW7 ... 256 A5
St Georges Ct
Harrow HA3 ... 43 A3
Penge SE20 ... 184 B2
Putney SW15 ... 135 B1
St George's Dr SW1 ... 115 C1 259 A2
Ickenham UB10 ... 60 B6
South Oxhey WD19 ... 23 A6
St George's Field W2 ... 92 C1 237 B1
St George's Gdns KT6 214 D6
St George's Gr SW17 ... 158 B1
St Georges Hanover Sq Sch W1 ... 115 A6 248 B5
St George's Ho NW1 ... 232 B3
St George's Hospl SW17 ... 180 B5
St Georges Ind Est
Kingston KT2 ... 175 D5
Tottenham N22 ... 32 D3
St George's La EC3 ... 253 A6
St Georges Lo N10 ... 49 C5
St Georges Mews 11 NW1 ... 70 D1
St George's Mews SE1 261 B6
St George's RC Cath SE1 ... 116 C3 261 B6
St George's RC Prim Sch
Enfield EN2 ... 5 B3
Harrow HA1 ... 64 D5
St George's RC Sec Sch W9 ... 91 D5
St Georges Rd BR1 ... 210 B6
BR5 ... 211 B3
W4 ... 111 B4
St George's Rd DA14 ... 190 D4
E10 ... 76 A5
E7 ... 77 B2
NW11 ... 47 B3
SE1 ... 116 D3 261 C5
St Georges Rd RM9 ... 81 A4
St George's Rd
Beckenham BR3 ... 185 D2
Ealing W7 ... 108 D5
Edmonton N9 ... 18 A1
Enfield EN1 ... 5 D5
Feltham TW13 ... 172 D6
Isleworth TW1 ... 153 B6
2 Kingston KT2 ... 176 C3
Mitcham CR4 ... 203 B6
Palmers Green N13 ... 16 B2
Redbridge IG1 ... 56 B2
Richmond TW9 ... 132 B2
Wallington SM6 ... 219 B3
Wimbledon SW19 ... 179 B4
St Georges Rd W BR1 188 A1
St George's Residences 4 SW2 ... 160 C6
St Georges's Ct EC4 ... 241 C2
St Georges Sh & L Ctr HA1 ... 42 C3
St Georges Sq 1 E14 ... 119 A6
St George's Sq E7 ... 77 B1
SE8 ... 119 B2
SW1 ... 115 D1 259 C1
Kingston KT3 ... 199 C6
St George's Square Mews SW1 ... 259 C1
St George St W1 ... 115 B6 248 D6
St Georges Terr NW1 ... 70 D1
St George's Way SE15 139 C6
St George's Wlk CR0 ... 221 A5
St George the Martyr CE Prim Sch WC1 94 B3 240 D5
St Gerards Cl SW4 ... 159 C6
St German's Pl SE3 ... 143 A4
St German's Rd SE23 ... 163 A3
St Gildas' RC Jun Sch N8 ... 50 A3
St Giles Ave
Dagenham RM10 ... 81 D1
Uxbridge UB10 ... 61 A4
St Giles Cir WC1 ... 93 D1 239 D2
St Giles Cl BR6 ... 227 B3
Dagenham RM10 ... 81 D1
St Giles Colls WC1 ... 94 A2 240 B4
St Giles Ct WC2 ... 240 A2
Ealing W13 ... 109 C5
St Giles High St WC2 ... 93 D1 239 D2
St Giles Hospl SE5 ... 139 C4
St Giles Pas WC2 ... 239 D1
St Giles Rd SE5 ... 139 C4
St Giles' Sch CR2 ... 220 D2
St Giles Twr 3 SE5 ... 139 C4
St Gilles Ho 15 E2 ... 96 D5
St Gothard Rd SE21, SE27 ... 183 B6
St Gregory Cl HA4 ... 62 C4
St Gregory RC High Sch HA3 ... 43 D4
St Gregory's RC Prim Sch W5 ... 87 D2
St Helena Ho WC1 ... 234 A1
St Helena Pier TW9 ... 153 D6
St Helena Rd SE16 ... 118 D2
St Helena St WC1 ... 234 A1
St Helena Terr 23 TW9 ... 153 D6
St Helens KT7 ... 196 D2
Saint Helens Coll UB10 60 C1
St Helen's Cres SW16 ... 182 B2
St Helen's Gdns W10 ... 90 D1
St Helen's Pl EC3 ... 243 A2
St Helen's RC Inf Sch E17 ... 54 A4
St Helen's RC Prim Sch
E13 ... 99 A3
SW9 ... 138 C2
St Helens Rd 7 DA18 ... 124 D4
St Helen's Rd
Ealing W13 ... 109 C5
Redbridge IG1 ... 56 B3
Thornton Heath SW16 ... 182 B2
St Helens Sch UB10 ... 60 C1
St Helier Ave SM4 ... 202 A3
St Helier Ct 4 N1 ... 95 C6
St Helier Hospl SM5 ... 202 A1
St Heliers Ave TW3, TW4 ... 151 C6
St Helier's Rd E10 ... 54 A3
St Helier Sta SM4 ... 201 C3
St Hilda's Ave TW15 ... 170 A5
St Hilda's Cl NW6 ... 68 D1
St Hildas Cl SW17 ... 158 C2
St Hilda's Rd SW13 ... 134 B6
St Hildas Wharf E1 ... 118 C5
St Hubert's Ho 1 E14 119 C3
St Hughes Cl SW17 ... 158 C2
St Hugh's Rd SE20 ... 184 B3
St Ignatius Coll EN1 ... 6 B6
St Ignatius' RC Prim Sch N15 ... 51 D3
St Ignatius RC Prim Sch TW16 ... 172 A2
St Ivian Ct 3 N10 ... 31 B1
St James Apartments 2 E17 ... 53 A4
St James Ave N20 ... 14 C1
Sutton SM1 ... 217 C3
St James' Ave W13 ... 109 A5
St James CE Jun Sch E7 ... 77 A3
St James CE Prim Sch EN3 ... 6 C3
St James Cl N20 ... 14 C1
Barnet EN4 ... 2 B1
St James' Cl
New Malden KT3 ... 199 D4
Ruislip HA4 ... 62 C6
St James Ct 11 E2 ... 96 A4
SE3 ... 143 B4
10 W4 ... 110 C1
St James' Ct SW1 ... 259
W4 ... 111 B3
St James Ct
Thornton Heath CR0 ... 204 D2
Wanstead E12 ... 77 C6
St James' Ct 7 KT1 ... 198 A6
St James Gate IG9 ... 21 B3
St James Gdns IG6 ... 58 B5
St James' Gdns HA0 ... 66 A1
St James Hatcham CE Prim Sch SE14 ... 141 A4
St James Independent Schs W14 ... 113 A2 254 A4
St James Ind Mews SE1 ... 118 A1
St James' Mans NW6 ... 69 C1
St James Mews E14 ... 120 A3
St James RC Prim Sch BR5 ... 210 D4
St James' Rd E15 ... 76 D3
St James Rd
Carshalton SM5 ... 218 C5
Kingston KT1 ... 175 D1
Sutton SM1,SM2 ... 217 C3
St James' Rd
Edmonton N9 ... 18 B2
Mitcham CR4 ... 181 A3
Surbiton KT6 ... 197 D3
St James's SE14 ... 141 A4
St James's App EC2 ... 243 A5
St James's Ave E2 ... 96 C5
Beckenham BR3 ... 207 A6
Hampton TW12 ... 174 A5
St James's CE Prim Sch
N10 ... 49 A5
SE16 ... 118 A3
St James School Flats 5 N7 ... 72 C3
St James's Cl NW8 ... 230 C5
SE18 ... 123 A1
Upper Tooting SW17 ... 158 D2
St James's Cloisters 2 SE22 ... 139 D1
St James's Cotts 14 TW10 ... 153 D6
St James's Cres SW9 ... 138 C2
St James's Ct 8 N18 ... 34 A5
St James's Dr
Balham SW12,SW17 ... 158 D4
Upper Tooting SW17 ... 158 D3
St James's Gdns W11 ... 113 A5 244 A4
St James's Gr SW11 ... 136 D3
St James's La N10 ... 49 B5
St James's Lo 4 CR0 ... 205 C1
St James's Market SW1 ... 249 C5
St James's Mews E17 ... 53 A4
St James's Palace★ SW1 ... 115 C5 249 B3
St James's Park★ SW1 ... 249 C2
St James's Park Sta SW1 ... 115 D3 259 C6
St James's Pas EC3 ... 243 B1
St James's Pk CR0 ... 205 A2
St James's Pl SW1 ... 115 C5 249 A3
St James's RC High Sch NW9 ... 27 D2
St James's RC Prim Sch TW2 ... 152 C1
St James's Rd
SE1,SE16 ... 118 A2
Hampton TW12 ... 173 D5
Thornton Heath CR0 ... 205 B2
St James's Sq SW1 ... 115 C5 249 B4
St James's St E17 ... 53 A4
SW1 ... 115 C5 249 A4
St James's & St Michael's CE Prim Sch W2 ... 114 A6 246 A6
St James St W6 ... 112 C1
St James's Terr NW8 ... 230 C4
2 Upper Tooting SW12 ... 159 A3
St James's Terrace Mews NW8 ... 230 C5
St James Street Sta E17 ... 53 A4
St James's Wlk EC1 ... 241 C6
St James The Great RC Prim Sch
SE15 ... 139 D4
South Norwood CR7 ... 182 D1
St James Way DA14 ... 191 A5
St Jerome's Gr UB3 ... 83 A1
St Joachim's RC Prim Sch E16 ... 99 C1
St Joan of Arc RC Prim Sch N5 ... 73 A4
St Joan's Rd N9 ... 17 D2
St John Baptist CE Prim Sch BR1 ... 186 A6
St John CE Prim Sch SE17 ... 117 A2 262 B3
St John Cl SW6 ... 265 A4
St John Evangelist RC Prim Sch N1 ... 94 D5 234 C4
St John Fisher RC Fst & Mid Sch HA5 ... 41 C5
St John Fisher RC Prim Sch
DA18 ... 125 A3
Wembley UB6 ... 87 C4
West Barnes SW20 ... 200 D4
St John of Jerusalem CE Prim Sch E9 ... 74 C1
St John Rigby RC Coll BR4 ... 224 B4
St John's Angell Town CE Prim Sch SW9 ... 138 C3
St John's Ave N11 ... 30 D5
NW10 ... 89 D6
Putney SW15 ... 156 D6
St Johns CE Fst Sch HA7 ... 25 B6
St John's CE Inf Sch NW4 ... 46 B4
St John's CE JMI Sch N11 ... 30 D6
St Johns CE Mid Sch HA7 ... 25 A6
St John's CE Prim Sch
E2 ... 96 C5
N20 ... 14 A2
Buckhurst Hill IG9 ... 21 B3
Fulham SW6 ... 135 A4 264 B1
Kingston KT1 ... 198 A6
Penge SE20 ... 184 C3
St John's Church Rd E9 ... 74 C3
St John's Cl N20 ... 14 A1
St Johns Cl N14 ... 15 C5
St John's Cl HA9 ... 66 A3
St Johns Concert Hall SW1 ... 260 A5
St John's Cotts 2 SE20 ... 184 C3
St John's Cres SW9 ... 138 C2
St Johns Ct 39 E1 ... 118 B5
St John's Ct E11 ... 54 D1
N4 ... 72 D6
N5 ... 72 D4
5 NW3 ... 70 A2
SE13 ... 142 A3
W6 ... 112 B2
Buckhurst Hill IG9 ... 21 B3
2 Harrow HA1 ... 42 D3
Isleworth TW7 ... 130 D3
Kingston KT1 ... 198 A5
St Johns Dr KT12 ... 194 C1
St John's Dr SW18 ... 157 D3
St John's Est SE1 ... 253 C1
St John's Gdns W11 ... 113 B6 244 C5
St John's Gr N19 ... 71 C6
3 Barnes SW13 ... 133 D3
1 Richmond TW9 ... 132 A1
St John's (Highbury Vale) CE Prim Sch N5 ... 72 D5
St John's Hill SW11 ... 136 B1
St John's Hill Gr SW11 136 B1
St Johns Ho 5 SE17 ... 139 B6
St John's La EC1 ... 94 D2 241 D4
St John's Mans E5 ... 74 C3
St John's Par
Ealing W13 ... 109 B5
3 Sidcup DA14 ... 190 B6
St John's Park Mans N19 ... 71 C5
St John's Path EC1 ... 241 C5
St John's Pk SE3 ... 143 A5
St John's Pl EC1 ... 241 C5
St John's Prim Sch W13 ... 109 A6
St John's RC Prim Sch SE16 ... 119 A4
St John's Rd DA16 ... 146 B2
E16 ... 99 A1
E6 ... 100 A6
N15 ... 51 C3
NW11 ... 47 B3
SW11 ... 136 C1
St Johns Rd Ilford IG2 ... 57 C2
Kingston KT3 ... 199 A6
St John's Rd
Barking IG11 ... 101 C6
Carshalton SM5 ... 218 C5
Chingford E17 ... 36 A1
Chingford E4 ... 35 D6
Croydon CR0 ... 220 D5
East Molesey KT8 ... 196 B5
Feltham TW13 ... 173 B6
Harrow HA1 ... 42 D3
Isleworth TW7 ... 130 D3
Orpington BR5,BR6 ... 211 C3
Penge SE20 ... 184 C4
Richmond TW9 ... 132 A1
Sidcup DA14 ... 190 B6
Southall UB2 ... 107 A3
Sutton SM1 ... 217 D6
Teddington KT1 ... 175 C1
Wembley HA9 ... 66 A3
Wimbledon SW19 ... 179 A4
St John's (Shirley) CE Prim Sch CR0 ... 222 D5
St John's Sq EC1 ... 94 D3 241 C5
St Johns Sta SE8 ... 141 C3
St John's & St Clements CE Prim Sch SE15 ... 140 A2
St John St EC1 ... 94 D3 241 C6
St John's Terr E7 ... 77 B2
SE18 ... 145 B6
W10 ... 90 D3
Enfield EN2 ... 5 B6
St John & St James CE Prim Sch
E9 ... 74 C3
Edmonton N18 ... 33 D5
St Johnstone Ho 15 N12 ... 29 D6
St John's (Upper Holloway) Prim Sch N19 ... 71 D6
St John's Vale SE8 ... 141 C3
St John's Village 4 N11 ... 30 D5
St John's Villas N19 ... 71 D6
W8 ... 255 D5
St John's Way N19 ... 49 D1
St John's Wood Ct NW8 ... 229 D1
St John's Wood High St NW8 ... 92 C5 230 A3
St John's Wood Park NW8 ... 92 B6 229 C6
St John's Wood Prep Sch NW8 ... 92 C4 230 A1
St John's Wood Rd NW8 ... 92 B4 229 D1
St John's Wood Sta NW8 ... 92 B5 229 C4
St John's Wood Terr NW8 ... 92 C5 230 A4
St John the Baptist CE Jun Sch KT1 ... 175 D3
St John the Baptist CE Prim Sch N1 ... 95 C5
St John the Divine CE Jun & Inf Sch SE5 ... 138 D5
St John Vianney RC Prim Sch N8 ... 50 D5
St Joseph RC Prim Sch W7 ... 108 C5
St Joseph's Acad SE3 ... 142 C2
St Josephs Cl BR6 ... 227 D4
St Joseph's Cl W10 ... 91 A2
St Joseph's Coll Mill Hill Missionaries NW7 ... 27 D6
St Joseph's Convent Prep Sch KT8 ... 196 A4
St Joseph's Convent Prim Sch NW4 ... 46 B
St Joseph's Convent Sch E11 ... 55 A
St Josephs Ct 19 E10 ... 53 D
3 NW10 ... 89 D
St Joseph's Ct E4 ... 20 B
St Joseph's Dr UB1 ... 107 B
St Joseph's Flats NW1 232 C
St Josephs Gr NW4 ... 46 B
St Joseph's Ho W6 ... 112 D
St Joseph's Hospice E9, E8 ... 96 B
St Joseph's RC Coll SW16 ... 182 D
St Josephs RC Fst & Mid Sch HA3 ... 25 A
St Joseph's RC Inf Sch
E10 ... 75 C
South Norwood SE19 ... 183 A
St Joseph's RC Jun & Inf Sch
SE1 ... 117 A4 252 B
SE16 ... 118 A
SE16 ... 118 C
St Joseph's RC Jun & Inf Schs HA9 ... 66 B
St Joseph's RC Jun Sch
E10 ... 53 D
SE5 ... 139 A
South Norwood SE19 ... 183 A
St Joseph's RC Prim Sch
N19 ... 49 B
NW10 ... 67 C
SE10 ... 120 C
SE8 ... 141 C
SW18 ... 157 C
SW3 ... 114 D2 257 C
W9 ... 92 A4 229 A
WC2 ... 94 A1 240 B
Barking IG11 ... 101 A
Dagenham RM9 ... 81 B
Kingston KT1 ... 176 B
St Joseph's RC Sch BR1 ... 187 B3
St Joseph's Rd N9 ... 18 C3
St Joseph's St SW8 ... 268 D2
St Joseph's Vale SE3 ... 142 B2
St Jude's CE Prim Sch SE24 ... 160 D6
St Judes Ho 6 W10 ... 91 B4
St Jude's Prim Sch SE1 ... 116 D3 261 C5
St Jude's Rd E2 ... 96 B5
St Jude's & St Paul's Prim Sch N1 ... 73 C2
St Jude St N16 ... 73 C3
St Julian's Cl SW16 ... 182 C6
St Julian's Farm Rd SE27,SW16 ... 182 D6
St Julian's Rd NW6 ... 91 C6
St Katharine Docks★ E1 ... 117 D5 253 D4
St Katharine's Ho N1 ... 234 A4
St Katharine's Pier E1 ... 117 D5 253 D4
St Katharine's Way E1 ... 117 D5 253 D4
St Katherine's Prec NW1 ... 231 C4
St Katherines Rd DA18 ... 124 D4
St Katherine's Row EC3 ... 243 B1
St Katherine's Wlk 1 W11 ... 112 D5
St Keverne Rd SE9 ... 188 A6
St Kilda Rd BR6 ... 211 D1
Ealing W13 ... 109 A4
St Kilda's Rd N16 ... 51 C1
Harrow HA1 ... 42 C3
St Kitts Terr SE19 ... 183 C5
St Laurence's Cl NW6 ... 90 D6
St Lawrence CE Jun & Mid Sch KT8 ... 196 B5
St Lawrence Cl HA8 ... 26 B3
St Lawrence Ct N1 ... 235 D6
St Lawrence Dr HA5 ... 40 B4
St Lawrence Ho SE1 ... 263 B6
St Lawrence RC Sch TW13 ... 150 B2
St Lawrence St E14 ... 120 A5
St Lawrence Terr W10 91 A2
St Lawrence Way SW9 ... 138 C3
St Leonards Ave HA3 ... 43 C4
St Leonard's Ave E4 ... 36 B4
St Leonards CE Prim Sch SW16 ... 181 D5
St Leonards Cl 4 DA16 ... 146 A2
St Leonard's Ct N1 ... 235 D2
St Leonards Ct SW14 ... 133 A2
St Leonards Gdns IG1 79 A3
St Leonard's Gdns TW5 ... 129 A4
St Leonard's Hospl N1 ... 95 C5
St Leonard's Rd E14 ... 98 A2
NW10 ... 89 B3

onards Rd SW14 133 A2
onard's Rd
jate KT10 212 D2
don CR0 220 D5
ig W13 109 C6
ston KT6 197 D4
nes Ditton KT7 197 A2
onards Rise BR6 227 C4
onard's Sq NW5 71 A2
ston KT6 197 D4
onard's St E3 97 D4
onard's Terr
114 D1 257 D1
onard's Wlk
6 182 B3
o Ave
136 C6 267 B6
o Ct SW3 267 C6
uis Rd SE27 183 B6
y's Rd N17 51 D6
cia Dr E15 98 D6
ke Ct 5 E10 53 D2
ke's Ave SW4 137 D1
ld EN2 5 B5
d IG1 78 D3
ke's CE Prim Sch
120 B2
ke's CE Prim Sch
235 A2
91 B4
ston KT2 176 B2
mond TW9 132 C4
t Norwood SE27 183 A5
ke's Cl EC1 95 A3 242 B6
don SE25 206 B3
ke's Ct W11 91 B1
ke's Hospl
93 C3 239 A5
ke's Mews W11 91 B1
ke's Path 1 IG1 78 D3
ke's Prim Sch
98 D1
ke's Rd W11 91 B2
idge UB10 60 A1
ke's Sq E16 98 D1
ke's St SW3 257 B2
ke's Woodside Hospl
49 A5
alo Ave N9 18 C1
argaret Clitherow RC
n Sch
0 67 A4
lwich SE28 124 B5
argarets IG11 101 B6
argarets Ave
5 167 B1
14 A3
argaret's Ave N8,
50 D5
argarets Ave
ord TW15 170 D5
gdon UB8 82 C3
argaret's Ave
m SM3 217 A5
row HA2 64 A5
argarets Bsns Ctr 11
153 B5
argaret's CE Prim Sch
123 A1
king IG11 79 A1
argaret's Cres
5 156 B6
argaret's Ct E15 76 C4
ey SW15 134 B1
wickenham TW1 153 B5
argaret's Dr TW1 153 B6
argaret's Gr E11 76 D5
145 A6
kenham TW1 153 A5
argaret's La
113 D3 255 C5
argaret's Lee CE Prim
SE13 142 C1
argarets Lo W3 110 D4
argaret's Rd N17 51 C6
10 90 C4
141 B1
108 C4
argarets Rd
ware HA8 26 D5
lip HA4 39 B3
argaret's Rd
worth TW1 153 B6
stead E12 77 C6
argarets Rdbt
153 B6
argaret's Sch NW3 69 D4
argaret's Sta TW1 153 B5
argaret St SW1 250 A1
argaret's Terr
123 A1
ark's CE Prim Sch
209 A6
138 B6 270 D6
don SE25 206 A5
arks Cl 5 SE10 142 A5
ark's Cl Barnet EN5 1 D2
ow HA1 43 B1

St Mark's Cres NW1 93 A6 231 B6
St Mark's Ct 7 E10 53 D2
W7 108 C4
St Mark's Fst Sch CR4 180 D1
St Marks Gate E9 75 B1
St Mark's Gr
SW10 135 D5 265 D4
St Mark's Hill KT6 198 A3
St Marks Ho 6 SE17 139 B6
St Mark's Ho 8 E17 54 A5
St Mark's Hospl
EC1 94 D4 234 D2
St Marks Ind Est E16 121 D5
St Mark's Pl W11 91 A1
Wimbledon SW19 179 B4
St Mark's Prim Sch
N19 72 A6
W7 108 C4
St Mark's RC Sch TW3 129 C2
St Mark's Rd W10 90 D2
W11 91 A1
W7 108 C4
Bromley BR2 209 B6
Croydon SE25 206 A5
Ealing W5 110 A5
Enfield EN1 17 D6
Mitcham CR4 181 A1
Teddington TW11 175 B3
St Mark's Rise E8 73 D3
St Mark's Sq NW1 231 A5
St Mark St E1 95 D1 243 D1
St Martha's Convent Jun
Sch for Girls EN5 1 A1
St Martin-in-the-Fields
High Sch for Girls
SW2 160 C3
St Martin of Porres RC Prim
Sch N11 31 C4
St Martin's Almshos
NW1 232 A6
St Martin's App HA4 39 C2
St Martin's Ave E6 99 D5
St Martins Cl DA18 124 D4
St Martin's Cl NW1 232 A6
St Martins Cl WD19 22 C6
St Martin's Cl EN1 6 B4
St Martins Ct N1 95 C6
St Martin's Ct WC2 250 A6
West Norwood SE27 160 D2
St Martin's La
WC2 116 A6 250 A5
St Martins La BR3 207 D4
St Martin's Le Grand
EC1 242 A2
St Martin's Pl WC2 250 A5
St Martin's Rd N2 30 B2
SW9 138 B3
Edmonton N9 18 B2
St Martin's Sch NW7 27 B5
St Martin's St WC2 249 D5
St Martin's Way SW17 158 A1
St Mary Abbots CE Prim
Sch W8 113 D4 245 C1
St Mary Abbot's Ct
W14 254 C5
St Mary Abbot's Pl
W8 254 D5
St Mary Abbots Terr
W14 254 D5
St Mary at Hill
EC3 117 C6 253 A5
St Mary Ave SM6 219 B5
St Mary Axe
EC3 95 C1 243 B2
St Marychurch St
SE16 118 C4
St Mary Graces Ct E1 253 D5
St Marylebone CE Sch The
W1 93 A2 238 A3
St Mary le Bow Church★
EC2 242 B1
St Mary- le-Park Ct
SW11 267 B3
St Mary Magdalene CE Prim
Sch
N7 72 C2
SE15 140 B3
W2 91 D2
St Mary Magdalens RC Prim
Sch SE4 141 A1
St Mary Magdalen's RC
Prim Sch SW14 133 B2
St Mary Magdelen's RC Jun
Sch NW2 68 B2
St Mary Newington Cl
SE17 263 B2
St Mary of the Angels RC
Prim Sch W2 91 C1
St Mary RC Prim Sch
W10 91 A3
St Mary Rd E17 53 D5
St Marys IG11 101 B6
St Mary's App E12 78 B3
St Mary's Ave N3 29 B1
St Marys Ave UB2 107 D2
St Mary's Ave
Beckenham BR2 208 C6
Teddington TW11 174 D4

St Mary's Ave *continued*
Wanstead E11 55 B2
St Mary's Bryanston Square
CE Sch W1 92 D2 237 C4
St Mary's CE High Sch
(Lower & Upper) NW4 46 C6
St Mary's CE High Sch
(Middle) NW4 46 C6
St Mary's CE Inf Sch N8 50 B5
St Mary's CE Jun Sch
N8 50 A5
NW4 46 B4
St Mary's CE Prim Sch
E17 53 D5
N1 94 D6 234 D6
N3 29 B3
NW10 67 C2
SE18 122 C2
Chessington KT9 214 B2
East Barnet EN4 14 C5
Long Ditton KT7 197 B1
Putney SW15 134 D2
St Mary's CE Sch
TW19 148 A4
St Mary's Church Sch
TW1 153 A4
St Mary's Cl BR5 190 B1
Chessington KT9 214 B1
Ewell KT17 215 D1
Sunbury TW16 194 A5
Tottenham N17 34 A2
St Mary's Coll TW1 152 D1
St Mary's Cottage Hospl
TW12 173 B2
St Mary's Cres
Hayes UB3 105 D6
Hendon NW4 46 B6
Hounslow TW7 130 C5
St Marys Ct E6 100 B3
SE7 143 D5
St Mary's Ct E11 54 D1
N12 30 A3
W5 109 D4
W6 111 D3
Kingston KT3 199 C6
Wallington SM6 219 C4
St Mary's Dr TW14 149 A4
St Mary's Est 2 SE16 118 C4
St Mary's Flats NW1 232 C2
St Mary's Gate W8 255 C5
St Mary's Gdns SE11 261 B4
St Mary's Gn 1 N2 48 A6
St Mary's Gr N1 72 D2
Barnes SW13 134 B2
Chiswick W4 132 D6
Richmond TW10,TW9 132 B1
St Mary's Ho N1 234 D6
W5 109 D3
St Mary's Hospl
W2 92 B1 236 D2
St Mary's Inf Sch E17 53 D5
St Mary's Kilburn CE Prim
Sch NW6 91 C6
St Mary's Lewisham CE
Prim Sch SE13 163 D6
St Mary's Lo E11 55 B3
St Mary's Mans NW10 89 C6
W2 92 B2 236 C4
St Mary's Medical Sch
W2 92 B1 236 D2
St Mary's Mews NW6 69 D1
St Mary's Path N1 234 D6
St Mary's Pl SE9 166 C5
W5 109 D4
W8 113 D3 255 C5
St Mary's RC High Sch
CR0 205 A1
St Mary's RC Inf Sch
CR0 205 B1
St Mary's RC Jun & Inf Schs
N15 51 B4
St Mary's RC Jun Sch
E17 54 A6
Croydon CR0 205 B1
Wallington SM5 218 D3
St Mary's RC Prim Sch
NW6 91 C5
SE9 166 C6
SW4 159 C6
SW8 137 B4 268 D2
W14 112 D3
Beckenham BR3 186 A3
Chingford E4 20 B3
Chiswick W4 133 C6
Enfield EN3 6 D1
Isleworth TW7 131 A2
Merton SW19 179 C3
St Mary's RC Sch TW7 131 A2
St Mary's Rd E10 76 A6
E13 99 B5
N2 30 B2
N8 50 A5
N9 18 C3
NW10 89 C6
NW11 47 A2
SE15 140 C3
St Marys Rd IG1 79 B6
St Mary's Rd Ealing W5 109 D5
East Barnet EN4 14 D4

St Mary's Rd *continued*
East Molesey KT8 196 B4
Hayes UB3 105 D6
Long Ditton KT6 197 C1
South Norwood SE25 205 C6
Surbiton KT6 197 D3
Wimbledon SW19 179 B5
Worcester Park KT4 215 C6
St Mary's Roman Catholic
Inf Sch SM5 218 D4
St Mary's Sch Hampstead
NW3 70 B3
St Mary's Sq W2 236 C4
W5 109 D4
St Mary's Stoke Newington
CE Prim Sch N16 73 C6
St Mary's & St Peter's CE
Prim Sch TW11 174 D5
St Mary St SE18 122 C2
St Mary's Terr W2 236 C4
St Mary & St Joseph's Sch
DA14 190 A5
St Mary & St Michael Prim
Sch E1 96 C1
St Mary & St Pancras CE
Prim Sch NW1 93 D5 232 C3
St Mary's Twr EC1 242 B5
St Marys View HA3 43 C4
St Mary's Wlk SE11 261 B4
Hayes UB3 105 D6
St Matthew's Ave KT6 198 B1
St Matthew's CE Fst Sch
SW20 178 A2
St Matthew's CE Prim Sch
Enfield EN3 18 C6
Surbiton KT6 198 A2
Yiewsley UB7 104 A5
St Matthews Ct 6 E10 53 D2
E15 76 D1
N10 31 A1
SE1 262 A5
St Matthew's Ct TW15 170 C5
St Matthews Dr BR1 210 B6
St Matthew's Ho 8
SE17 139 B6
St Matthew's Lo NW1 232 B4
St Matthew's Rd SW2 160 B6
Ealing W5 110 A5
St Matthew's Row E2 96 A3
St Matthews Sch
Westminster
SW1 115 D3 259 D6
St Matthew St SW1 259 C5
St Matthias CE Prim Sch
E2 95 D3 243 D6
St Matthias Cl NW9 45 D4
St Matthias's CE Prim Sch
N16 73 C4
St Maur Rd
SW6 135 B4 264 D1
St Mellion Cl SE28 102 D1
St Merryn Cl SE18 145 B5
St Merryn Ct BR3 185 C3
St Michael-at-Bowes CE
Jun Sch N13 32 C4
St Michael's Alley EC3 242 D1
St Michaels Ave N9 18 C4
St Michael's Ave HA9 66 C2
St Michael's CE Jun & Inf
Sch N22 32 B2
St Michael's CE Prim Sch
N6 49 A2
NW1 93 C6 232 A6
Enfield EN2 5 A4
Forest Hill SE26 185 A6
Wandsworth SW18 157 B4
St Michaels Cl BR1 210 A6
4 E16 99 D2
St Michael's Cl DA18 124 D4
N12 30 C5
N3 29 B1
St Michaels Cl KT4 215 D6
St Michael's Cres HA5 41 A3
St Michaels Ct E14 98 A2
St Michael's Ct N11 15 A1
NW11 47 B2
St Michael's East Wickham
CE Sch DA16 146 C4
St Michael's Flats
NW1 232 C3
St Michael's Gdns W10 91 A2
St Michael's Hospl EN2 5 B4
St Michael's RC Gram Sch
N12 30 A5
St Michael's RC Prim Sch
E6 100 B5
Ashford TW15 170 C5
St Michael's RC Sch
SE16 118 A4
St Michael's Rd DA16 146 B2
NW2 68 C4
SW9 138 B3
St Michaels Rd TW15 170 C5
St Michael's Rd
Croydon CR0 205 A1
Wallington SM6 219 C2
St Michael's Rise
DA16 146 B4

St Michael's St
W2 92 C1 237 A2
St Michael's Terr N22 32 A2
St Michael & St Martin RC
Prim Sch TW4 129 B2
St Michael Twr E17 53 B4
St Mildred's Ct EC2 242 C1
St Mildreds Rd SE12,
SE6 164 D4
St Mirren Ct EN5 14 A6
St Monica's RC Prim Sch
N1 95 C4
St Nicholas CE JMI Sch
WD6 9 D5
St Nicholas CE Prim Sch
TW17 192 D3
St Nicholas Cl WD6 9 D5
St Nicholas Ct SE18 123 D1
St Nicholas Ctr SM1 217 D3
St Nicholas Dr TW17 192 C2
St Nicholas Elstree CE Prim
Sch WD6 9 D5
St Nicholas' Flats
NW1 232 C3
St Nicholas Glebe
SW17 181 A4
St Nicholas Ho SE8 141 C6
St Nicholas Rd SE18 123 D2
Sutton SM1 217 D3
Thames Ditton KT7 196 D3
St Nicholas Sch NW9 67 A6
St Nicholas St SE8 141 C4
St Nicholas Way SM1 217 D3
St Nicolas La BR7 188 A2
St Ninian's Ct N20 14 D1
St Norbert Gn SE4 141 A1
St Norbert Rd SE4 141 A1
St Olaf's Rd
SW6 135 A5 264 B3
St Olaves Ct W2 245 C5
St Olave's Ct EC2 242 C1
St Olave's Est SE1 253 B2
St Olave's Gdns SE11 261 A4
St Olave's Mans SE11 261 A4
St Olaves Prep Sch
SE9 166 D2
St Olave's Rd E6 100 C6
St Olave's Wlk SW16 181 D1
St Olav's Sq 27 SE16 118 C4
St Osmund's RC Prim Sch
SW13 133 D4
St Oswald's Pl
SE11 116 B1 260 C1
St Oswald's Rd SW16 182 D2
St Oswulf St SW1 259 D3
St Owen Ho SE1 263 B6
St Pancras Almshouses 13
NW5 70 D3
St Pancras Commercial Ctr
NW1 232 B6
St Pancras Ct N2 30 B1
St Pancras Hospl
NW1 93 D6 232 C5
St Pancras Sta
WC1 94 A4 233 A2
St Pancras Way
NW1 93 C6 232 C6
St Patrick's RC Inf Sch
E1 118 B5
St Patrick's RC Prim Sch
E17 53 A5
NW5 71 B3
SE18 123 B2
St Paul's & All Hallows CE
Jun & Inf Sch N17 34 A3
St Paul's Ave NW2 68 C2
SE16 118 D5
Harrow HA3 44 B5
St Paul's Cath★
EC4 95 A1 242 A1
St Paul's Catholic Coll
TW16 172 A2
St Pauls Catholic Sch
TW16 172 A2
St Paul's Cath Sch
EC4 95 A1 242 A1
St Paul's CE Jun Sch
KT2 176 C3
St Paul's CE Prim Sch
N11 31 B5
NW3 70 D1
NW7 28 B6
SE17 262 B2
W6 112 C1
St Pauls CE Prim Sch
TW8 131 D6
St Paul's CE Prim Sch
Chessington KT9 214 A4
Southgate N21 16 D4
St Paul's Church Yd
EC4 95 A1 242 A1
St Pauls Cl W5 110 B4
St Paul's Cl SE7 121 D1
St Pauls Cl UB3 105 B1
St Paul's Cl
Ashford TW15 171 A5
Carshalton SM5 202 C1
Chessington KT9 213 D4
Hounslow TW3,TW4 129 A3

St Paul's Cray Rd BR7 189 B2
St Pauls Cres NW1 71 D1
St Paul's Ct 5 N19 72 A6
SW4 137 D1
Hounslow TW4 129 A2
St Paul's Dr E15 76 B3
St Paul's Girls' Sch
W6 112 D2
St Pauls Mews NW1 71 D1
St Paul's Pl N1 73 B2
St Paul's RC Prim Sch
Thames Ditton KT7 196 C2
Wood Green N22 32 B1
St Paul's RC Sec Sch
SE2 146 A6
St Paul's Rd N1 73 A2
St Pauls Rd
Barking IG11 101 A6
Richmond TW9 132 B2
St Paul's Rd
Brentford TW8 131 D6
South Norwood CR7 205 A6
Tottenham N17 34 A2
St Pauls Rise N13 32 D4
St Paul's Sch SW13 112 A1
St Paul's Sq BR2 187 A1
St Paul's Sta
EC2 95 A1 242 A2
St Paul St N1 235 B5
St Paul's Terr SE17 138 D6
St Paul's Twr 18 E10 53 D2
St Pauls View WC1 234 A1
St Paul's Way E3 97 C2
N3 29 D3
St Paul's Way Com Sch
E3 97 C2
St Paul's Whitechapel CE
Prim Sch E1 118 A6
St Paul's with St Michael's
Prim Sch E8 96 A6
St Paul's Wood Hill
BR5,BR7 189 D1
St Paul with St Luke CE
Prim Sch E3 97 B2
St Peter Chanel RC Prim
Sch DA14 190 C5
St Peter in Chains RC Inf
Sch N8 50 A3
SS Peter & Paul RC Prim
Sch BR5 189 C1
SS Peter & Paul's RC Prim
Sch
Ilford IG1 79 B5
Mitcham CR4 202 D5
St Peter's Alley EC3 242 D1
St Peters Ave N12 30 C3
St Peter's Ave N18 34 A6
St Petersburgh Mews
W2 245 C6
St Petersburgh Pl
W2 113 D6 245 C5
St Peter's CE Prim Sch
SE17 262 D1
W9 91 C3
St Peter's Church Ct
N1 234 D5
St Peters Cl BR7 189 B3
St Peter's Cl E2 96 A5
St Peters Cl Ilford IG2 57 D5
Upper Tooting SW17 158 C2
St Peter's Cl Barnet EN5 12 B6
Bushey WD23 8 B3
Ruislip HA4 62 D6
St Peters Ct SE12 164 D6
SE4 141 B3
St Peter's Ct NW4 46 C4
St Peters Ct KT8 195 C5
St Peter's Eaton Square CE
Sch SW1 115 B3 258 D5
St Peter's Gdns SE27 160 C1
St Peter's Gr W6 112 A2
St Peters Ho N15 52 A5
WC1 233 B1
St Peter's Ho N16 51 C2
4 SE17 139 B6
St Peters La BR5 190 A1
St Peter's London Docks CE
Prim Sch E1 118 C5
St Peter's Path E17 54 C5
St Peter's Pl W9 91 D3
St Peter's Prim Sch
W6 112 A1
South Croydon CR2 221 C2
St Peter's RC Prim Sch
SE18 122 D2
Dagenham RM9 103 B6
St Peter's Rd W6 112 A1
St Peters Rd KT1 176 C1
St Peter's Rd
Croydon CR0 221 B4
East Molesey KT8 195 C5
Edmonton N9 18 B3
Isleworth TW1 153 B6
Southall UB1 85 C2
St Peter's Sq E2 96 A5
W6 111 D1

St Peter's St N1 94 D6 234 D5
Croydon CR2 221 B3
St Peters & St Pauls RC Prim Sch EC1 94 D3 241 D6
St Peter's Street Mews N1 234 D4
St Peter's Terr SW6 264 B3
St Peter's Villas 5 W6 112 A2
St Peter's Way N1 73 C1
St Peters Way UB3 105 B1
St Peter's Way W5 87 D2
St Philip Ho WC1 234 A1
St Philip's Ave KT4 216 B6
St Philip Sq 1 SW8 137 B3
St Philip's Rd E8 74 A2
Surbiton KT6 197 D3
St Philip's Sch SW7 256 B4
Chessington KT9 213 D2
St Philip St SW8 137 B3
St Philip's Way N1 235 B5
St Philomena's Sch SM5 218 C3
St Quentin Ho SW18 158 B5
St Quentin Rd DA16 145 D2
St Quintin Ave W10 90 D2
St Quintin Gdns W10 90 C2
St Quintin Rd E13 99 B5
St Raphael's RC Prim Sch UB5 84 B5
St Raphael's Way NW10 67 A3
St Regis Cl N10 31 B1
St Regis Hts NW3 69 D5
St Richard of Chichester RC Sec Sch NW1 71 C1
St Richards Ct TW10 153 B1
St Richard's with St Andrew's CE Prim Sch TW10 153 B1
St Ronan's 2 N3 29 C2
St Ronans Cl EN4 2 B5
St Ronans Cres IG8 37 A3
St Rule St SW8 137 C3
St Savior's CE Inf Sch W5 109 D6
St Saviours SW4 137 B1
St Saviour's CE Prim Sch
E14 97 D2
E17 53 B2
SE24 139 A2
W9 91 D3
St Saviour's Coll SE27 183 B6
St Saviours Ct N22 31 D1
Harrow HA1 42 C4
St Saviours Ho 4 SE1 118 A4
St Saviour's RC Prim Sch SE13 142 A1
St Saviour's Rd SW2 160 B6
Thornton Heath CR0 205 A3
St Saviours & St Olaves CE Sch SE1 117 B3 262 D5
St Saviour's Wharf SE1 253 D2
St Scholastica's RC Prim Sch E5 74 A5
Saints Cl SE27 182 D6
Saints Dr E7 77 D3
St Silas Pl NW5 71 A2
St Simon's Ave SW15 156 C6
St Stephen's Ave E17 54 A4
W12 112 B4
Ealing W13 87 B1
St Stephen's CE Prim Sch
SE8 141 C3
SW8 138 B5 270 C4
W12 112 C4
W2 91 C2
St Stephen's Cl E17 53 D4
NW5 70 D3
NW8 230 B5
Southall UB1 85 C2
St Stephen's Cres W2 91 C1
Thornton Heath CR7 204 C6
St Stephens Ct N8 50 B3
Ealing W13 87 B1
St Stephen's Gdns W2 91 C1
3 Putney SW15 157 B6
Twickenham TW1 153 C5
St Stephen's Gr SE13 142 A2
St Stephens Ho 7 SE17 139 B6
St Stephen's Mews 34 W2 91 C2
St Stephens Par E6 77 C1
St Stephens Prim Sch E6 77 C1
St Stephen's RC Prim Sch DA16 146 A3
St Stephens Rd E6 77 C1
St Stephen's Rd E17 53 D4
E3 97 B5
St Stephens Rd EN5 12 D6
St Stephen's Rd
Ealing W13 87 C1
Enfield EN3 6 D6
Hounslow TW3,TW4 151 C6
St Stephen's Rd *continued*
Yiewsley UB7 104 A5
St Stephen's Row EC4 242 C1
St Stephen's Terr SW8 270 C3
St Swithin's La EC4 117 B6 252 C6
St Swithun's Rd SE13 164 B6
St Swithun Wells RC Prim Sch HA4 62 D5
St Teresa RC Prim Sch The RM8 80 C4
St Teresa's RC Fst & Mid Sch HA3 24 A2
St Teresa's RC Prim Sch SM4 202 B3
St Theresa Ct E4 20 B4
St Theresa's RC Sch N3 47 D6
St Thomas a Beckett RC Prim Sch SE2 124 A3
St Thomas Becket RC Prim Sch SE25 206 A3
St Thomas' CE Prim Sch
N16 52 A1
W10 91 A3
St Thomas' Cl KT6 198 B1
St Thomas Ct 10 E10 53 D2
Sidcup DA5 169 C4
St Thomas' Dr BR5 211 A1
Pinner HA5 23 A2
St Thomas' Gdns NW5 71 A2
St Thomas Gdns IG1 79 A2
St Thomas Ho 2 E1 96 D1
St Thomas More RC Prim Sch
SE9 144 A2
Bexley DA7 147 B3
St Thomas More RC Sch
SE9 166 C5
SW3 114 D2 257 C3
East Molesey KT8 196 A4
St Thomas More Sch N22 32 C3
St Thomas of Canterbury RC Mid Sch CR4 203 A6
St Thomas of Canterbury RC Prim Sch SW6 135 B5 264 C4
St Thomas Rd E16 99 A1
N14 15 D4
St Thomas' Rd W4 133 A6
St Thomas's Hospl SE1 116 B3 260 C6
St Thomas's Hospl Medical Sch SE1 116 B3 260 C5
St Thomas's Pl 20 E9 74 C1
St Thomas's Rd N4,N5 72 C5
NW10 89 C6
St Thomas's Sq E9 74 C1
St Thomas St SE1 117 B5 252 D3
St Thomas's Way SW6 135 B5 264 D4
St Thomas the Apostle Coll The SE15 140 C4
St Timothy's Mews 3 BR1 187 B2
St Ursula Gr HA5 41 A4
St Ursula Rd UB1 85 C1
St Ursula's Convent Sch SE10 142 B5
St Vincent Cl SE27 182 D5
St Vincent De Paul Ho 20 E1 96 C2
St Vincent De Paul RC Prim Sch SW1 115 C3 259 B6
St Vincent Ho SE1 263 C6
St Vincent Rd TW2 152 A5
St Vincent's Hospl HA5 39 D6
St Vincents RC Prim Sch SE9 188 A6
St Vincent's RC Prim Sch
W1 93 A2 238 B3
Acton W3 110 D6
Dagenham RM8 80 C6
St Vincent's RC Sch NW7 28 C5
St Vincent St W1 238 B3
St Wilfrid's Cl EN4 14 C6
St Wilfrid's Rd EN4 14 C6
St William of York RC Prim Sch SE23 163 A3
St William of York RC Sec Boys Sch (Upper) N1 72 A1
St Winefride's Ave E12 78 B3
St Winefride's RC Prim Sch E12 78 B3
St Winifred's RC Inf Sch SE12 164 C6
St Winifred's RC Jun Sch SE12 164 D4
St Winifred's Rd TW11 175 B4
Sala Ho SE3 143 B1
Salamanca Pl SE1 260 C3
Salamanca St SE1,SE11 116 B2 260 C3
Salamander Cl KT2 175 C5
Salamander Quay KT1 175 D2
Salcombe Dr
Dagenham RM6 59 B3
North Cheam SM4 200 D1
Salcombe Gdns NW7 28 C4
SW4 137 B1
Salcombe Ho 6 SE23 162 C2
Salcombe Lo NW5 71 A4
Salcombe Pk IG10 21 D6
Salcombe Prep Sch N14 15 B4
Salcombe Rd E17 53 B2
23 N16 73 C3
Ashford TW15 148 A1
Salcombe Villas 13 TW10 154 A6
Salcombe Way
Hayes UB4 83 C4
Ruislip HA4 62 A6
Salcot N4 72 B6
Salcott Rd SW11 158 D6
Wallington CR0 220 B4
Salehurst Cl HA3 44 A4
Salehurst Rd SE4 163 B5
Salem Ho 13 E9 74 D2
Salem Pl CR0 221 A5
Salem Rd W2 113 D6 245 D6
Sale Pl W2 92 C1 237 A2
Salesian Coll SW11 136 C4 267 A1
Sale St E2 96 A3
Salford Ho 4 E14 120 A2
Salford Rd SW12,SW2 159 D3
Salhouse Cl SE28 102 C1
Salisbury Ave N3 47 B6
Barking IG11 79 C1
Cheam SM1,SM2 217 B2
Salisbury Cl SE17 262 C4
Worcester Park KT4 215 D5
Salisbury Ct E9 75 A3
EC4 241 C1
N3 29 B1
15 SE16 118 A3
W4 111 C2
Edgware HA8 26 B6
Enfield EN2 5 B1
Northolt UB5 63 D3
Salisbury Gdns
Buckhurst Hill IG9 21 D2
Wimbledon SW19 179 A3
Salisbury Hall Gdns E4 35 C4
Salisbury Ho 3 E14 97 D1
N1 234 C6
SW1 259 D2
1 Ruislip HA4 40 C1
Stanmore HA7 25 A4
Wimbledon SW19 156 D1
Salisbury Lower Sch N9 18 C4
Salisbury Mans N4,N15 50 D4
Salisbury Mews BR2 210 A4
SW6 264 C3
Salisbury Pl SW9 138 D5
W1 237 C4
Salisbury Prim Sch E12 78 A3
Salisbury Rd BR2 210 A4
DA5 169 C3
E10 76 A6
E12 77 D3
E17 54 A4
E7 77 A2
N4 50 D4
W13 109 B4
Barnet EN5 1 A2
Chingford E4 19 C1
Croydon SE25 206 A3
Dagenham RM10 81 D2
East Bedfont TW6 149 A5
Edmonton N9 18 A1
Enfield EN3 7 B6
Feltham TW13 150 C3
Harrow HA1 42 B4
Hounslow TW4 128 C2
Ilford IG3 79 C6
Kingston KT3 199 B6
Pinner HA5 40 A5
Richmond TW9 132 A1
Southall UB2 107 A2
Tottenham N22 32 D1
Wallington SM5 218 D2
Wimbledon SW19 179 A3
Worcester Park KT4 215 C5
Salisbury Sq EC4 241 B1
Salisbury St NW8 237 A5
10 Acton W3 111 A4
Salisbury Terr SE15 140 C2
Salisbury Upper Sch N9 18 C4
Salisbury Wlk N19 71 C6
Salix Cl TW16 172 B3
Salix Ct N3 29 C4
Salliesfield TW2 152 B5
Sally Murray Cl E12 78 C4
Salmen Rd E13 98 D5
Salmond Cl HA7 25 A4
Salmon La E14 97 A1
Salmon Rd DA17 125 C1
Salmons Rd
Chessington KT9 214 A2
Salmons Rd *continued*
Edmonton N9 18 A3
Salmon St 6 E14 97 B1
NW9 45 A2
Salomons Rd E13 99 C2
Salop Rd E17 52 D3
Saltash Cl SM1 217 B4
Saltash Rd DA16 146 C4
Saltcoats Rd W4 111 C4
Saltcroft Cl HA9 44 D1
Saltdene N4 50 B1
Salter Cl HA2 63 B4
Salterford Rd SW17 181 A4
Salter Ho 8 SW16 181 C6
Salter Rd SE16 119 A5
Salters' Hall Ct EC4 252 C6
Salter's Hill SE19 183 B5
Salters Rd E17 54 B5
W10 90 D3
Salter St 10 E14 119 C6
NW10 90 A4
Salterton Rd N7 72 B5
Salt Hill Cl UB8 60 A3
Saltley Cl E6 100 A1
Saltoun Rd SW2,SW9 138 C1
Saltram Cl N15 51 D5
Saltram Cres W9 91 C4
Saltwell St E14 119 C6
Saltwood Gr SE17 262 C1
Salusbury Prim Sch NW6 91 B6
Salusbury Rd NW6 91 A6
Salutation Rd SE10 120 C2
Salvador SW17 180 D5
Salvatorian RC Coll HA3 24 C1
Salvia Gdns UB6 87 A5
Salvin Rd SW15 134 D2
Salway Cl IG8 37 A3
Salway Ho E10 75 D6
SW8 270 B2
Salway Pl E15 76 C2
Salway Rd E15 76 B2
Salween Ho 2 N16 73 B4
Samantha Cl E17 53 B2
Samantha Ct E11 54 C2
Samaritan Hospl for Women NW1 237 C4
Sam Bartram Cl SE7 121 C1
Sambrooke Ct EN1 17 D6
Sambrook Ho 19 E1 96 C2
Sambruck Mews SE6 163 D3
Samels Ct W6 112 A1
Samford Ho N1 234 A5
Samford St NW8 92 C3 237 A5
Samira Cl E17 53 C3
Sam Manners Ho 7 SE10 120 C1
Sam March Ho 5 E14 98 B1
Samos Rd SE20 184 B1
Sampson Ave EN5 12 D6
Sampson Cl DA17 125 A3
Sampson Ct TW17 193 A4
Sampson St E1 118 A5
Samson Ho SE18 123 A2
Samson St E13 99 C5
Samuel Cl E8 95 D6
SE14 140 D6
SE18 122 A2
Samuel Ct BR3 207 D6
Samuel Gray Gdns KT2 175 D2
Samuel Ho 15 E8 95 D6
Samuel Johnson Cl SW16 182 B6
Samuel Jones Ind Est 15 SE15 139 C5
Samuel Lewis Bldgs N1 72 C2
Samuel Lewis Trust Dwellings
6 SE5 139 A4
SW3 257 A3
SW6 135 C5 265 B4
W14 254 B4
Samuel Lewis Trust Est N15 51 C3
Samuel Rhodes Sch N1 94 C6 234 A6
Samuel Richardson Ho W14 254 C3
Samuel's Cl 2 W6 112 C2
Samuel St 6 SE15 139 D5
SE18 122 B2
Sancroft Cl NW2 68 B5
Sancroft Ct SW11 267 B2
Sancroft Rd HA3 25 A1
Sancroft St SE11 116 C1 260 D2
Sanctuary Rd TW19, TW6 148 C5
Sanctuary St SE1 252 B2
Sanctuary The DA5 168 D5
33 E1 118 B5
SW1 115 D3 259 D6
Morden SM4 201 C3
Sandale Cl N16 73 B5
Sandall Cl W5 88 A3
Sandall Ho 6 E3 97 A5
Sandall Rd NW5 71 C2
Ealing W5 88 A3
Sandal Rd Edmonton N18 34 A5
New Malden KT3 199 C5
Sandal St E15 98 C6
Sandalwood Cl 10 E1 97 A3
Sandalwood Dr HA4 39 A2
Sandalwood Ho DA15 167 D1
6 NW3 69 D2
Sandalwood Rd TW13 150 B1
Sandbach Pl SE18 123 A1
Sandbourne 12 NW8 91 D6
4 W11 91 C1
Sandbourne Ave SW19 179 D1
Sandbourne Rd SE4 141 A3
Sandbrook Cl NW7 27 B4
Sandbrook Rd N16 73 C5
Sandby Ct BR3 185 B2
Sandby Gn SE9 144 A2
Sandby Ho 6 NW6 91 C6
11 SE5 139 C4
Sandcroft Cl N13 32 D4
Sandcroft Ho SE11 260 D2
Sandells Ave
Ashford TW15 171 A6
Ashford TW15 171 A6
Sandell St SE1 251 A2
Sanderling Ct 20 SE8 141 B6
Woolwich SE28 124 C6
Sanders Cl TW12 174 A5
Sanders Ho WC1 234 A2
Streatham SW16 182 A4
Sanders La NW7 28 C3
Sanderson Cl NW5 71 B4
Sanderson Ho 7 SE8 119 B1
Sanderstead Ave NW2 69 A6
Sanderstead Cl SW12 159 C4
Sanderstead Rd
South Croydon CR2 221 B1
Walthamstow E10 53 A1
Sanders Way 3 N19 49 D1
Sandfield WC1 233 B1
Sandfield Gdns CR7 204 D6
Sandfield Pl CR7 205 A6
Sandfield Rd CR7 204 D6
Sandford Ave N22 33 A2
Sandford Cl E6 100 B3
Sandford Ct N16 51 C1
Barnet EN5 1 D2
Sandford Rd BR2 209 A5
E6 100 B4
Bexley DA6,DA7 147 A2
Sandford Row SE17 262 D2
Sandford St SW6 265 D3
Sandford Wlk 4 N16 73 D6
SE14 141 A6
Sandgate Ho 15 E5 74 B4
14 Beckenham BR3 185 C3
Ealing W5 87 C2
Sandgate La SW17, SW18 158 C3
Sandgate Rd DA16 146 C5
Sandgate St SE15 140 B6
Sandgate Trad Est SE15 140 B6
Sandham Ct SW4 270 B1
Sandham Point 10 SE18 122 D2
Sandhills CR0,SM6 219 D4
Sandhills Mdw TW17 193 A2
Sandhills The SW10 266 B6
Sandhurst Ave
Harrow HA2 41 D3
Tolworth KT5 198 D2
Sandhurst Cl NW9 44 C6
South Croydon CR2 221 C1
Sandhurst Ct SW2 138 A1
Sandhurst Dr IG3 79 D4
Sandhurst Ho 10 E1 96 C2
Sandhurst Jun & Inf Sch SE6 164 C3
Sandhurst Mkt SE6 164 A3
Sandhurst Rd DA15 168 A1
HA8,NW9 44 C6
N9 18 D5
Bexley DA5 168 D6
Catford SE6 164 B3
Sandhurst Way CR2 221 C1
Sandifer Dr NW2, NW11 68 D5
Sandiford Rd SM3 217 B6
Sandiland Cres BR2 224 D6
Sandilands CR0 222 A5
Sandilands Rd SW6 135 D4 265 C1
Sandilands Sta CR0 221 D6
Sandison St SE15 140 A2
Sandland St WC1 240 D3
Sandling Rise SE9 166 C1
Sandlings Cl SE15 140 B3
Sandlings The N22 50 D6
5 Wood Green N22 32 C1
Sandmartin Way CR4 203 A1
Sandmere Rd SW4 138 A1
Sandon Cl KT10 196 B1
Sandon Ct IG3 80 A5
Sandon Ho 5 SW2 160 A4
Sandow Cres UB3 105 D3
Sandown Ave KT10
Sandown Cl TW5
Sandown Gate KT10
Sandown Ho 2 W4
Penge SE26
Sandown Park KT10
Sandown Rd
Croydon SE25
Esher KT10
Sandown Way UB5
Sandpiper Cl E17
SE16
Sandpiper Ct 11 E14
1 SE8
Sandpiper Rd SM1
Sandpiper Terr IG5
Sandpit Pl SE7
Sandpit Rd BR1
Sandpits Rd
Richmond TW10
South Croydon CR0
Sandra Cl
Hounslow TW3
Tottenham N17
Sandra Ho KT8
Sandridge Cl HA1
Sandridge Ct N4
Sandridge St 2 N19
Sandringham Ave
SW20
Sandringham Cl
Enfield EN1
Ilford IG6
1 Putney SW19
Sandringham Cres HA2
Sandringham Ct
18 SE16
W1
W9
3 Beckenham BR3
Edgware HA8
Hillingdon UB10
Putney SW15
Sandringham Dr DA16
Ashford TW15
Sandringham Flats
WC2
Sandringham Gdns
N12
N8
Cranford TW5
East Molesey KT8
Ilford IG6
Sandringham Ho W14
Richmond TW10
Sandringham Prim Sch
E7
Sandringham Rd BR1
E10
E7
E8
NW11
NW2
Barking IG11
Northolt UB5
Stanwell TW19,TW6
Thornton Heath CR0
Tottenham N22
Worcester Park KT4
Sandrock Pl CR0
Sandrock Rd SE13
Sands End La
SW6 135 D4
Sandstone TW9
Sandstone Pl N19
Sandstone Rd SE12
Sandtoft Rd SE7
Sandways 6 TW9
Sandwell Cres 2 NW6
Sandwell Mans 3 NW6
Sandwich Ho 9 SE16
WC1
Sandwich St
WC1 94 A4
Sandwick Cl NW7
Sandy Bury BR6
Sandycombe Rd
East Bedfont TW14
Richmond TW9
Sandycoombe Rd
TW1
Sandycroft SE2
Sandy Dr TW14
Sandy Hill Ave SE18
Sandy Hill La SE18
Sandy Hill Rd SE18
Sandyhill Rd IG1
Sandy La BR5
Belmont SM2
Harrow HA3
Mitcham CR4
Moor Park HA6
Richmond TW10
Teddington KT8,TW11
Walton-on-T KT12
Sandy La N SM6
Sandy La S SM6
Sandy Lo N6
Sandymount Ave HA7

dy Rd NW3 69 D6
dy Ridge BR7 188 C4
dy's Row E1 243 B3
dy Way
ydon CR0 223 B5
ton-on-T KT12 193 D1
ford La 3 N16 73 D6
ord St SE14,SE8 141 A6
ord Terr N16 73 D5
ger Ave KT9 214 B4
gley Rd Catford SE6 164 A3
th Norwood SE25 205 C5
gora Rd 17 SW11 136 B1
key Ho 23 E2 96 C5
som Rd E11 76 D6
som St SE5 139 B4
SE5 139 B5
s Wlk EC1 94 D3 241 C6
tana Ho SE18 144 D5
ley Ho SE1 251 B1
ley St SW4 138 B1
os Rd SW18 157 C6
cote Trad Ctr NW10 67 D2
erton Wlk SE11 260 D4
nora Cl BR6 227 B3
berton Ct EC1 242 A6
bhire Cl E6 100 C1
enham RM8 58 C1
bhire Ct 8 E1 118 A6
bhire Rd SE8 119 A2
cen Cl CR0 205 B3
cen St E14 97 C1
h Bonnell Sch E15 76 C2
h Ct UB5 85 B6
h Ho 11 E1 96 B1
nampton SW15 133 D1
h Swift Ho SE1 252 D2
Lane Ct 31 N1 95 C5
toga Rd E5 74 C4
Turnbull Ho 2
3 122 B2
eson Ho 13 SW27 182 D5
inia St WC2 240 C2
ents Hill N2 30 C2
a Cl HA3 24 B1
ant Path SW19 156 D2
Cl TW5 129 C5
Ho 5 N1 73 A2
eld EN3 6 D5
Wlk E16 99 B1
ersfield Ho SE15 140 B6
es Ct 4 N11 31 B6
esfield Rd EN2 5 B2
att Ho W10 90 C2
e Rd NW2 69 B3
den Bldgs W1 238 B1
en Ave TW3 129 C3
eld Rd SW12,
7 158 D3
field Rd UB6 87 C5
or Rd SE15 140 D1
m Hall Sch NW3 70 C1
m Ho W11 244 D5
oon 4 NW9 27 D2
nita Cl E16 99 D1
nell Mead NW9 27 D2
hwell Rd 24 E2 96 A4
Ct 4 SE15 139 D6
s Gn E11 76 C5
ders Cl 14 E14 119 B6
ders Ho 11 SW2 160 C3
ders Ness Rd
120 B2
ders Rd SE18 123 D1
ngdon UB10 82 B6
ders St SE11 261 A4
ders Way SE28 124 B6
derton Rd HA0 65 B3
ton Ave UB3 127 D5
ton Ct UB1 108 A6
ge Gdns EC3 253 B6
ham E6 100 B1
na N16 73 C6
nnah Cl 9 SE15 139 D5
nake Ct HA7 25 B4
nake Ho N4 51 B2
nake Rd NW3 70 D4
eld N9 18 A5
y Dr KT6 197 C2
e Cl
Malden KT3 199 C4
es Ditton KT7 197 A1
e Gdns CR0 221 D6
e Cres TW15 171 B4
e Rd E16 122 A5
111 B3
nham RM6 59 B2
kenham TW1 152 D3
e Row
115 C6 249 A6
ld EN3 6 D3
s BR2 208 D1
Gdns SW20 200 A6
Ho E16 122 D5
W4 159 D5
Row IG8 36 D4
Lo 7 SM2 218 A1
na Cl 15 SW19 178 D3
na Ct SW20 178 D2

Savona St
SW8 137 C5 269 A3
Savoy Ave UB3 105 C1
Savoy Bldgs W12 111 D6
Savoy Circus W3 111 D6
Savoy Cl E15 98 C6
Edgware HA8 26 C5
Savoy Ct SW5 255 B4
WC2 250 B5
Savoy Hill WC2 250 C5
Savoy Par EN1 5 C2
Savoy Pier WC2 250 C5
Savoy Pl WC2 116 B6 250 C5
Savoy Row WC2 250 C6
Savoy St WC2 116 B6 250 C5
Savoy Steps WC2 250 C5
Savoy Way WC2 250 C5
Sawbill Cl UB4 84 D2
Sawkins Cl SW19 157 A2
Sawley Rd W12 112 A5
Sawmill Yd E3 97 A6
Sawtry Cl SM5 202 C2
Sawyer Cl N9 18 A2
Sawyer Ho 15 SE21 183 C6
Sawyer's Hill TW10 154 B4
Sawyers Lawn W13 87 A1
Sawyer St SE1 117 A4 252 A2
Saxby Rd SW2 160 A4
Saxham Rd IG11 101 D5
Saxlingham Rd E4 20 B1
Saxon Ave TW13 151 B2
Saxon Bsns Ctr SW19 180 A2
Saxonbury Ave TW16 172 B1
Saxonbury Cl CR4 202 B6
Saxonbury Ct 2 N7 72 A3
16 N7 71 D3
Saxonbury Gdns KT6 197 C1
Saxon Cl E17 53 C2
Hillingdon UB8 82 A2
Surbiton KT6 197 D3
Saxoncroft Ho SW16 159 D1
Saxon Cty Jun Sch
TW17 192 C4
Saxon Dr W3 88 D2
Saxonfield Cl SW2 160 B4
Saxon Gdns UB1 107 A6
Saxon Hall W2 245 C5
Saxon Ho 4 SW4 137 D1
Feltham TW13 151 B2
Saxon Rd E3 97 B5
E6 100 B3
Ashford TW15 171 B4
Bromley BR1 186 D3
Ilford IG1 78 D3
Kingston KT2 176 A2
Southall UB1 107 A6
South Norwood SE25 205 B4
Tottenham N22 32 D2
Wembley HA9 67 A5
Saxon Way N14 15 D5
Saxon Wlk DA14 190 C4
Saxony Par UB3 83 A2
Saxton Cl SE13 142 B2
Saxville Rd BR5 190 B1
Sayer Ho SE4 141 A1
Sayers Ho 4 N2 30 B1
Sayer's Wlk TW10 154 B4
Sayesbury La N18 34 A5
Sayes Court St SE8 141 B6
Sayes Ct SE8 141 B6
Scadbury Gdns BR5 190 A1
Scadbury Park Nature
Reserve* BR7 189 D4
Scads Hill Cl BR5,BR6 211 D3
Scafell NW1 232 A2
Scala St W1 239 B4
Scales Rd N17 52 A6
Scampston Mews 5
W10 90 D1
Scandrett St 38 E1 118 B5
Scarba Wlk N1 73 B2
Scarborough Rd E11 54 B1
N4 50 C1
N9 18 C4
East Bedfont TW6 149 A5
Scarborough St E1 243 D1
Scarbrook Rd CR0 221 A5
Scardale Ho 12 E5 74 B6
Scarle Rd HA0 65 D2
Scarlet Rd SE6 164 C1
Scarlette Manor Wlk 10
SE24 160 C4
Scarsbrook Ho 2
SW2 160 C5
Scarsbrook Rd SE3 143 D2
Scarsdale Pl W8 255 C6
Scarsdale Rd HA2 64 A5
Scarsdale Villas
W8 113 C3 255 B5
Scarth Rd SW13 133 D2
Scawen Cl SM5 219 A4
Scawen Rd SE8 119 A1
Scawfell St E2 95 D5
Scaynes Link N12 29 C6
Sceptre Ho 9 E1 96 C3
Sceptre Rd E2 96 C4
Schiller International Sch
BR4 224 B4
Schofield Wlk SE3 143 A5

Sch of Nursing
W1 93 C2 239 A4
Sch of Pharmacy
WC1 94 A3 240 B6
Sch of the Douay Martyrs
UB10 60 D4
Scholars Ho 6 E4 20 B3
Scholars Rd
Chingford E4 20 B3
Streatham SW12 159 C3
Scholefield Rd N19 71 D6
Scholey Ho SW11 136 C2
Schomberg Ho SW1 259 D4
Schonfeld Sq N16 51 B1
School App 22 E2 95 C4
Schoolbank Rd SE10 120 D3
School Bell Cloisters 15
E3 97 A5
Schoolbell Mews 16 E3 97 A5
School Cotts DA14 190 C5
School Flats SW8 270 A1
School Ho SE1 263 A4
Schoolhouse La E1 118 D6
School House La
TW11 175 C3
School La DA16 146 B2
Lower Halliford TW17 192 D2
Pinner HA5 41 A5
Surbiton KT6 198 B1
Teddington KT1 175 C2
School of Finance &
Management N7 72 B2
School of St David & St
Katharine The N8 50 A5
School Pas
3 Kingston KT1 176 B1
Southall UB1 107 B6
School Rd BR7 189 A3
NW10 89 B3
Ashford TW15 170 D4
Dagenham RM10 103 D6
East Molesey KT8 196 B5
Hampton TW12 174 A4
Hounslow TW3 130 A2
Ilford E12 78 B4
Littleton TW15 170 D3
Teddington KT1 175 C2
School Road Ave
TW12 174 A4
School Sq SE10 120 D3
Schoolway N12 30 B4
School Way RM8 80 C5
School Wlk TW16 193 D6
Schooner Cl E14 120 B3
1 SE16 118 D4
Barking IG11 102 B4
Schubert Rd Elstree WD6 9 D5
Putney SW15 157 B6
Science Mus*
SW7 114 B3 256 C5
Scilly Isles KT10 212 C6
Sclater St E1 243 D6
Scoles Cres SW2 160 C3
Scope Way KT1 198 A5
Scoresby St SE1 251 C3
Scoresdale SE19 183 C2
Scorton Ave UB6 87 A5
Scorton Ho 2 N1 95 C5
Scotch Comm W13 87 B2
Scotch Ho
SW1 114 D4 247 C1
Scoter Cl IG8 37 B3
Scoter Ct 23 SE8 141 B6
Scot Gr HA5 22 D3
Scotia Bldg 10 E1 118 D6
Scotia Ct 3 SE16 118 C3
Scotia Rd 24 SW2 160 C4
Scotland Gn N17 33 D1
Scotland Green Rd EN3 18 D6
Scotland Green Rd N
EN3 7 A1
Scotland Pl SW1 250 A3
Scotland Rd IG9 21 C3
Scotney Ho E9 74 C2
Scots Cl TW19 148 A3
Scotsdale Cl BR5,BR7 211 C5
Belmont SM3 217 A1
Scotsdale Rd SE12 165 B6
Scotson Ho SE11 261 A3
Scotswood St
EC1 94 C3 241 B6
Scotswood Wlk N17 34 A3
Scott Cl
Thornton Heath SW16 182 B2
West Drayton UB7 104 B2
West Ewell KT19 215 A3
Scott Ct 17 N16 73 C5
4 SW11 137 B3
W4 111 B4
Scott Ellis Gdns
NW8 92 B4 229 C1
Scottes La RM8 58 D1
Scott Farm Cl KT7 197 B1
Scott Gdns TW5 128 D5
Scott Ho 6 E13 99 A5
N1 235 C6
N7 72 B2
2 NW10 67 B1
NW8 237 A5

Scott Ho *continued*
3 Edmonton N18 34 A5
4 Erith DA17 125 B1
Richmond TW10 153 C2
Scott Lidgett Cres
SE16 118 A4
Scott's Ave
Ashford TW16 171 C3
Beckenham BR2 186 B1
Scotts Ct 6 W12 112 B4
Scotts Dr TW12 173 D3
Scotts Farm Rd KT19 215 A2
Scott's La BR2,BR3 186 B1
Scotts Park Prim Sch
BR1 187 C2
Scotts Rd BR1 187 A3
Scott's Rd E10 54 A1
W12 112 B4
Scotts Rd UB2 106 D3
Scott's Sufferance Wharf
SE1 253 D1
Scott St E1 96 B3
Scott's Way TW16 171 C3
Scott's Yd EC4 252 C6
Scott Trimmer Way
TW3 129 A3
Scottwell Dr NW9 45 D4
Scott Wilkie Prim Sch
E16 99 C1
Scoulding Ho 6 E14 119 C3
Scoulding Rd E16 99 A1
Scouler St E14 120 B6
Scout App NW10 67 C4
Scout Way NW7 27 B6
Scovell Cres SE1 252 A1
Scovell Rd SE1 252 A1
Scrattons Terr IG11 103 A5
Scriven Ct 2 E8 95 D6
Scriven St E8 95 D6
Scrooby St SE6 163 D5
Scrope Bldg EC1 241 A4
Scrubs La NW10,W10,
W12 90 B3
Scrutton Cl SW12 159 D4
Scrutton St EC2 95 C3 243 A5
Scudamore La NW9 45 A5
Scutari Rd SE22 162 C6
Scylla Cres
TW6&TW14 148 D4
Scylla Rd SE15 140 B2
East Bedfont TW14,TW6 148 D5
Seabright St 27 E2 96 B4
Seabrook Dr BR4 224 C6
Seabrook Gdns RM7 59 C2
Seabrook Rd RM8 80 D5
Seacole Cl W3 89 B2
Seacole Ct N15 51 D4
Seacole Lo N21 16 B6
Seacourt Rd SE2 124 D4
Seacroft Gdns WD19 22 D6
Seafield Rd N11 31 D6
Seaford Cl HA4 61 B6
Seaford Ho 8 SE16 118 C4
Seaford Rd E17 53 D6
N15 51 C4
Ealing W13 109 B5
Enfield EN1 5 C1
Seaford St WC1 233 B1
Seaforth Ave KT3 200 B5
Seaforth Cres N5 73 A3
Seaforth Gdns
Southgate N21 16 C3
Woodford IG8 37 C5
Worcester Park KT19 215 D3
Seaforth Lo 2 SW13 133 D3
Seaforth Pl SW1 259 B6
Seager Pl E3 97 B2
Seagrave Lo SW6 265 B6
Seagrave Rd
SW6 135 C6 265 B6
Seagrove Cl E1 96 D2
Seagry Rd E11 55 B2
Seagull Cl IG11 102 A4
Sealand Rd TW6 148 C5
Sealand Wlk UB5 85 A4
Seal Ho SE1 262 D6
Seal St E8 73 D4
Searle Ct 2 CR4 180 C2
Searle Pl N4 50 B1
Searles Cl
SW11 136 C5 267 B3
Searles Dr E6 100 D2
Searles Rd SE1 262 D4
Searson Ho SE17 261 D3
Sears St SE5 139 B5
Seasalter Ho 10 SW9 138 C4
Seasprite Cl 10 UB5 84 D4
Seath Ho 4 SE26 184 B5
Seaton Ave IG3 79 D3
Seaton Cl 6 E13 99 A3
Isleworth TW2 152 B5
Roehampton SW15 156 B4
Seaton Dr TW15 148 A2
Seaton Gdns HA4 62 A6
Seaton Point E5 74 A4
Seaton Rd Bexley DA16 146 C5
Hayes UB3 105 B3
Mitcham CR4 180 C1
Twickenham TW2 152 A5

Seaton Rd *continued*
Wembley HA0 88 A5
Seaton Sq NW7 28 D3
Seaton St N18 34 A5
Seavington Ho 3 SE5 139 C2
Sebastian Ct 10 IG11 79 D1
Sebastian Ho 22 N1 95 C5
Sebastian St
EC1 94 D4 234 D1
Sebastopol Rd N9 34 A6
Sebbon St N1 72 D1
Sebergham Gr NW7 28 A3
Sebert Rd E7 77 B4
Sebright Ho 21 E2 96 A5
Sebright Rd EN5 1 A2
Sebright Sch E2 96 A5
Secker Cres HA3 24 A2
Secker Ho SW9 138 D3
Secker St SE1 251 A3
Second Ave E12 78 A3
E13 99 A4
E17 53 C4
N18 34 C6
NW4 46 D5
W10 91 A3
W3 111 D5
Dagenham RM10 103 D5
Dagenham RM6 58 C4
Enfield EN1 17 D6
Hayes UB3 105 D5
Mortlake SW14 133 C2
Walton-on-T KT12 194 B3
Wembley HA9 65 D6
Second Cl KT8 196 A5
Second Cross Rd TW2 152 C2
Second Way HA9 66 D4
Sedan Way
SE17 117 C1 263 A2
Sedcombe Cl DA14 190 C6
Sedcote Rd EN3 18 D6
Sedding St SW1 258 A4
Seddon Ho EC2 242 A4
Seddon Rd SM4 202 B4
Seddon St WC1 94 B4 233 D1
Sedgebrook Rd SE3 143 D2
Sedgecombe Ave HA3 43 C4
Sedgefield Ct UB5 63 D3
Sedgeford Rd W12 111 D5
Sedgehill Rd SE6 185 D5
Sedgehill Sch SE6 185 D5
Sedgemere Ave N2 48 A6
Sedgemere Rd SE2 124 C3
Sedgemoor Dr RM10 81 C4
Sedge Rd N17 34 C3
Sedgeway SE6 164 D3
Sedgewick Ho SW19 156 D2
Sedgewood Cl BR2 208 D2
Sedgley Ho N4 72 B6
Sedgmoor Pl SE5 139 C5
Sedgwick Ave UB10 60 D1
Sedgwick Rd E10 76 A6
Sedgwick St E9 74 D3
Sedleigh Rd SW18 157 B5
Sedlescombe Rd
SW6 135 C6 265 A6
Sedley Cl EN1 6 B5
Sedley Ct SE26 162 B2
Sedley Ho SE11 260 D2
Sedley Pl W1 238 C1
Sedum Cl NW9 44 D4
Seeley Dr SE21 183 C6
Seelig Ave NW9 46 A2
Seely Rd SW17 181 A4
Seething La
EC3 117 C6 253 B6
Seething Wells Halls of
Residence KT6 197 C3
Seething Wells La
KT6 197 C3
Sefton Ave NW7 27 B5
Harrow HA3 24 B2
Sefton Cl BR5 211 D5
Sefton Ct TW5 129 D4
Sefton Lo 2 TW1 153 C5
Sefton Rd Croydon CR0 206 A1
Orpington BR5 211 D5
Sefton St SW15 134 C2
Segal Cl SE23 163 A4
Sekforde St
EC1 94 D3 241 C6
Sekhon Terr TW13 151 C1
Selan Gdns UB4 84 B2
Selbie Ave NW10 67 D3
Selborne 2 SW11 137 A2
Selborne Ave DA5 169 A3
E17 53 B5
Little Ilford E12 78 C4
Selborne Gdns NW4 46 A5
Wembley UB6 87 A5
Selborne Ho SE1 252 C1
Selborne Prim Sch
UB6 86 D5
Selborne Rd E17 53 C4
1 SE5 139 B3
Ilford IG1 78 C6
Kingston KT3 177 C1
Palmers Green N14 16 A1
Sidcup DA14 190 B6
South Croydon CR0 221 D5

Selborne Rd *continued*
Wood Green N22 32 B2
Selborne Wlk E17 53 B5
Selbourne Ave KT6 214 C5
Selby Chase HA4 62 B6
Selby Cl BR7 188 C4
14 E6 100 A2
Chessington KT9 214 A1
Selby Ct TW2 152 B2
Selby Gdns UB1 85 C3
Selby Gn SM5 202 C2
Selby Ho 10 SW4 159 C5
6 W10 91 A4
Selby Rd E11 76 C5
E13 99 B2
Ashford TW15 171 A4
Carshalton SM5 202 C2
Ealing W5 87 C3
Penge SE20 184 A1
Tottenham N17 33 C4
Selby St E1 96 A3
Selden Ho 2 SE15 140 C3
Selden Rd SE15 140 C3
Selden Wlk N7 72 B6
Seldon Ho SW1 259 A1
SW8 269 A3
Selena Ct N20 14 D1
Selfridges W1 238 B1
Selhurst Cl SW19 156 D3
Selhurst New Ct SE25 205 C3
Selhurst New Rd SE25 205 C3
Selhurst Park (Crystal
Palace FC) SE25 205 C5
Selhurst Pl SE25 205 C3
Selhurst Rd
Edmonton N9 17 C1
South Norwood SE25 205 C4
Selhurst Sta SE25 205 C4
Selina Ho NW8 236 D6
Selinas La RM8 59 B2
Selkirk Ct N17 33 C1
Selkirk Ho N1 233 C6
4 N16 73 C5
Selkirk Rd
Twickenham TW2 152 A3
Upper Tooting SW17 180 C6
Sellers Hall Cl N3 29 C3
Sellincourt Inf Sch
SW17 180 C4
Sellincourt Jun Sch
SW17 180 C4
Sellincourt Rd SW17 180 C4
Sellindge Cl BR3 185 B3
Sellons Ave NW10 89 D6
Sellsby Ct N11 31 B5
Sellwood Dr EN5 12 D6
Selma Ho W12 90 B1
Selman Ho 3 E9 75 A2
Selsdon Ave CR2 221 B2
Selsdon Cl KT6 198 A4
Selsdon Ct 4 UB1 85 D1
Selsdon High Sch
CR2 222 D1
Selsdon Park Rd CR0,
CR2 223 B1
Selsdon Rd E13 99 C5
NW2 67 D6
South Croydon CR2 221 B2
Wanstead E11 55 A2
West Norwood SE27 182 D6
Selsdon Road Ind Est
CR2 221 B2
Selsdon Way E14 119 D3
Selsea Pl N16 73 C3
Selsey Cres DA16 146 D4
Selsey St E14 97 C2
Selvage La NW7 27 B6
Selway Cl HA5 40 B6
Selwood Ho 1 N4 51 B2
Selwood Pl
SW7 114 B1 256 C2
Selwood Rd
Cheam SM3 201 B1
Chessington KT9 213 D4
Croydon CR0 206 B1
Selwood Terr SW7 256 C2
Selworthy Cl E11 55 A4
Selworthy Ho SW11 266 D2
Selworthy Rd SE6 163 B1
Selwyn Ave Chingford E4 36 A4
Ilford IG3 57 D3
Richmond TW9 132 B2
Selwyn Cl TW4 129 A1
Selwyn Cres DA16 146 B1
Selwyn Ct E17 53 C4
SE3 142 D2
Edgware HA8 26 D3
8 Richmond TW10 154 B6
Selwyn Ho 3 SW15 156 D5
Selwyn Inf Sch E4 36 A4
Selwyn Jun Sch E4 36 A4
Selwyn Prim Sch E13 99 A6
Selwyn Rd E13 99 B6
E3 97 B5
NW10 67 C1
New Malden KT3 199 B4

Semley Gate E9 75 B2
Semley Ho SW1 258 C3
Semley Pl
SW1 115 B2 258 C3
Semley Rd SW16 182 A1
Senate St SE15 140 C3
Senators Lo 29 E3 97 A5
Senator Wlk SE28 123 B3
Sencler Ho SE2 146 D6
Sendall Ct 13 SW11 136 B2
Seneca Rd CR7 205 A5
Senga Rd SM6 203 A1
Senhouse Rd SM3 216 D5
Senior St W2 91 D2
Senlac Rd SE12 165 B3
Sennen Rd EN1 17 D4
Sennen Wlk SE9 166 A1
Senrab St E1 96 D1
Sentinel Cl UB5 85 A3
Sentinel Ho NW4 46 C5
Sentinel Sq NW4 46 C5
September Ct UB1 107 D5
September Way HA7 25 B4
Sequoia Cl WD23 8 B3
Sequoia Gdns BR6 211 D2
Sequoia Pk HA5 23 D4
Seraph Ct EC1 95 A4 235 A2
Serbin Cl E10 54 A2
Serenaders Rd 21
SW9 138 C3
Sergeant Ind Est The
SW18 157 D5
Serica Ct 14 SE10 142 A5
Serjeants' Inn EC4 241 B1
Serlby Ct W14 254 C6
Serle St WC2 94 B1 240 D2
Sermon La EC4 242 A1
Serpentine Ct 10 SE16 118 D4
Serpentine Gallery★
W2 114 B4 246 D2
Serpentine Rd
W2 114 D5 247 C3
Serpentine The★
W2 114 C5 247 B3
Service Route No 1 E15 76 B1
Service Route No 2 E15 76 B1
Service Route No 3 E15 76 B1
Serviden Dr BR1 187 D2
Servite Ho SE13 141 D4
Beckenham BR3 185 B2
East Barnet N14 15 B6
Penge SE26 184 C4
Worcester Park KT4 215 D6
Servite RC Prim Sch
SW10 136 A6 266 A6
Servius Ct 2 TW8 131 D5
Setchell Rd
SE1 117 D2 263 C4
Setchell Way SE1 263 C4
Seth St 18 SE16 118 C4
Seton Ct 3 NW9 46 A5
Seton Gdns RM9 80 C1
Settle Point 11 E13 99 A5
Settlers Ct 2 E14 120 B6
Settles St E1 96 A1
Settrington Rd SW6 135 D3
Seven Acres
Carshalton SM5 218 C6
Northwood HA6 22 A4
Seven Dials
WC2 94 A1 240 A1
Seven Kings High Sch
IG2 57 B2
Seven Kings Rd IG3 79 D6
Seven Kings Sta IG3 57 C1
Seven Kings Way KT2 176 A2
Seven Mills Prim Sch
E14 119 C4
Sevenoaks Rd BR6 227 D4
SE4 163 B5
Sevenoaks Way BR5 190 C1
Seven Sisters N15 51 D4
Seven Sisters Inf Sch
N15 51 B4
Seven Sisters Rd N4,N7,
N15 51 A2
Seven Sisters Sta N15 51 C4
Seven Stars Cnr W12 112 A3
Seventh Ave
Hayes UB3 106 A5
Ilford E12 78 B4
Seven Ways Par IG2 56 C4
Severnake Cl E14 119 C2
Severn Ct 11 KT2 175 D2
Severn Dr Enfield EN1 6 A5
Hinchley Wood KT10 213 A6
Severn Way NW10 67 D3
Severus Rd SW11 136 C1
Seville Ho 11 E1 118 A5
Seville Mews N1 73 C1
Seville St SW1 247 D1
Sevington Rd NW4 46 B3
Sevington St W9 91 D3
Seward Rd W7 109 A4
Penge BR3 184 D1
Seward St EC1 95 A4 235 A1
Sewardstone Gdns E4 19 D6
Sewardstone Rd E2 96 C5
Chingford E4 19 D6
Sewdley St E5 74 D5
Sewell Ho 7 N16 73 C3
Sewell Rd SE28 124 B4
Sewell St E13 99 A4
Sextant Ave E14 120 B2
Sexton's Ho 4 SE13 142 A6
Seychelle Ct BR3 185 D3
Seymour Ave
Tottenham N17 34 A1
West Barnes SM4 200 D2
Seymour Cl
East Molesey KT8 196 A4
Pinner HA5 23 B2
Seymour Ct N10 31 A1
N16 52 A1
NW2 68 B6
Chingford E4 20 D2
Putney SW15 134 B1
Southgate N21 16 B5
Seymour Dr BR2 210 B1
Seymour Gdns SE4 141 A2
Feltham TW13 172 C6
Kingston KT5 198 B4
Redbridge IG1 56 B1
Ruislip HA4 40 D1
Twickenham TW1 153 B4
Seymour Ho NW1 232 D1
1 SW8 137 C3
WC1 240 A6
Seymour Mews W1 238 A2
Seymour Pl W1 92 D1 237 C2
Croydon SE25 206 B5
Seymour Rd E10 53 B1
E6 99 D6
N3 29 D3
N8 50 D4
Acton W4 111 A2
Carshalton CR4 203 A2
Chingford E4 19 D3
East Molesey KT8 196 A4
Edmonton N9 18 B2
Hampton TW12 174 A5
Teddington KT1 175 D2
Wallington SM5 219 A3
Wandsworth SW18 157 B5
Wimbledon SW19 156 D1
Seymour St SE18 123 A3
W1 92 D1 237 D1
Seymour Terr SE20 184 B2
Seymour Villas SE20 184 A2
Seymour Way TW16 171 C3
Seymour Wlk
SW10 136 A6 266 A6
Seyssel St E14 120 A2
Shaa Rd W3 111 B6
Shacklegate La TW11 174 C6
Shackleton Cl SE23 162 B2
Shackleton Ct 4 W12 112 B4
2 Dulwich SE21 161 B2
4 Millwall E14 119 C1
7 Stanwell TW19 148 A5
Shackleton Ho 5 E1 118 C5
4 NW10 67 B1
Shackleton Rd UB1 107 B6
Shacklewell Ho 3 E8 73 D4
Shacklewell La E8 73 D3
Shacklewell Prim Sch
E8 73 D4
Shacklewell Rd N16 73 D4
Shacklewell Row E8 73 D4
Shacklewell St 30 E2 95 D4
Shadbolt Cl KT4 215 D6
Shad Thames
SE1 117 D4 253 D2
Shadwell Ct UB5 85 B5
Shadwell Dr UB5 85 B4
Shadwell Gdns E1 118 C6
Shadwell Pierhead E1 118 C6
Shadwell Sta E1 118 B6
Shady Bush Cl WD23 8 A4
Shaef Way TW11 175 A3
Shafter Rd RM10 81 D2
Shaftesbury Ave
W1 115 D6 249 D6
Enfield EN3 6 D3
Feltham TW14 150 A5
Harrow HA1,HA2 42 A1
Harrow HA3 44 A3
New Barnet EN5 2 A1
Southall UB2 107 C3
Shaftesbury Circ HA2 42 A1
Shaftesbury Ct N1 235 C3
SE1 262 C6
3 SE28 124 C5
1 SE5 139 B1
Ilford RM6 58 C2
Shaftesbury Gdns
NW10 89 C3
Shaftesbury Ho 13 N16 73 C5
W2 245 D6
Croydon SE25 206 A3
Shaftesbury Lo 9 E14 97 D1
Shaftesbury Mews
W8 255 B5
Shaftesbury Park Chambers
1 SW11 137 A2
Shaftesbury Prim Sch
E7 77 C1
Shaftesbury Rd E10 53 C1
E17 53 D3
E7 77 C1
N4,N19 50 A1
Beckenham BR3 185 B1
Carshalton SM5 202 C2
Chingford E4 20 B3
Edmonton N18 33 D4
Richmond TW9 132 A2
Shaftesbury Sch HA3 23 D2
Shaftesbury St N1 235 C3
Shaftesburys The
IG11 101 A5
Shaftesbury Way TW2 152 B1
Shaftesbury Waye UB4 84 C1
Shafteswood Ct SW17 158 D1
Shafto Mews SW1 257 D5
Shafton Rd E9 96 D6
Shaftsbury Ct E6 100 C1
SW6 265 D1
Shaftsbury Mews 2
SW4 159 C6
Shaftsbury Park Prim Sch
SW11 137 A3
Shafts Ct EC3 243 A1
Shahjalal Ho 18 E2 96 A5
Shakespeare Ave N11 31 C5
NW10 89 B6
Feltham TW14 150 A5
Hayes UB4 84 B2
Shakespeare Cl HA3 44 C2
Shakespeare Cres E12 78 B2
NW10 89 B6
Shakespeare Dr HA3 44 B3
Shakespeare Gdns N2 48 D5
Shakespeare Ho 3 E9 74 C1
N14 15 D2
1 Erith DA17 125 B1
Shakespeare Rd DA7 147 A4
E17 34 D1
N3 29 C2
NW7 28 A6
SE24 138 D1
W3 111 A5
Ealing W7 108 D6
Shakespeare's Globe
Theatre (site of)★
SE1 252 B4
Shakespeare Twr EC2 242 B4
Shakespeare Way
TW13 172 C6
Shakspeare Mews 7
N16 73 C4
Shakspeare Wlk N16 73 C4
Shalbourne Sq E9 75 B2
Shalcomb St
SW10 136 A6 266 B5
Shalden Ho 6 SW15 155 D5
Shaldon Dr Ruislip HA4 62 C5
West Barnes SM4 201 A4
Shaldon Rd HA8 26 B1
Shalfleet Dr W10 112 D6
Shalford NW10 90 A6
3 Woodford IG8 37 C4
Shalford Cl BR6 227 A4
Shalford Ct N1 234 C4
Shalford Ho SE1 262 D6
Shalimar Gdns W3 111 A6
Shalimar Lo W3 111 A6
Shalimar Rd W3 111 A6
Shallons Rd SE9 188 D6
Shalstone Rd SW14,
TW9 132 D2
Shalston Villas KT5,
KT6 198 B3
Shamrock Ho SE26 184 A6
Shamrock Rd CR0 204 B3
Shamrock St SW4 137 D2
Shamrock Way N14 15 B3
Shandon Rd SW4 159 C5
Shand St SE1 117 C4 253 B2
Shandy St E1 96 D3
Shanklin Gdns WD19 22 C6
Shanklin Ho E17 35 B1
Shanklin Rd N15 52 A5
N8 49 D4
Shannon Cl NW2 68 D5
Southall UB2 106 D1
Shannon Cnr KT3 200 A5
Shannon Cnr Ret Pk
KT3 200 A5
Shannon Commercial Ctr
KT3 200 A5
Shannon Ct N16 73 C5
NW10 68 A2
Croydon CR0 205 A1
Shannon Gr SW9 138 B1
Shannon Pl
NW8 92 C5 230 B4
Shannon Way BR3 185 D4
Shanti Ct SW18 157 C3
Shap Cres SM5 202 D1
Shapland Way N13 32 B5
Shapla Prim Sch E1 118 A6
Shapwick Cl N11 30 D5
Shardcroft Ave SE24 160 D6
Shardeloes Rd SE14 141 B3
Shard's Sq SE15 140 A6
Sharebourne Ho SW2 160 C6
Sharland Cl CR7 204 C3
Sharman Ct DA14 190 A6
Sharnbrooke Cl DA16 146 C2
Sharnbrook Ho W6 265 A6
Sharon Cl KT6 197 C1
Sharon Gdns E9 96 C6
Sharon Rd W4 111 B1
Enfield EN3 7 A3
Sharpe Cl W7 86 D2
Sharp Ho SW8 137 B2
Sharples Hall St 8
NW1 70 D1
Sharpness Cl UB4 85 A2
Sharpness Ct 2 SE15 139 D5
Sharps La HA4 39 B2
Sharratt St SE15 140 C6
Sharstead St
SE17 116 D1 261 C1
Sharvel La UB5 84 B6
Sharwell Ho SW18 157 D5
Sharwood WC1 233 D3
Shaver's Pl SW1 249 C5
Shaw Ave IG11 103 A5
Shawbrooke Rd SE9 143 D1
Shawbury Ct SE22 161 D6
Shawbury Rd SE22 161 D6
Shaw Cl Bushey WD23 8 C2
Woolwich SE28 124 B5
Shaw Ct N19 72 A6
12 SW11 136 B2
8 W3 111 A3
Shaw Dr KT12 194 C2
Shawfield Ct UB7 104 A3
Shawfield Pk BR1 187 D1
Shawfield St
SW3 114 C1 257 B1
Shawford Ct 8 SW15 156 A4
Shawford Rd KT19 215 B2
Shaw Gdns IG11 103 A5
Shaw Ho 5 E16 122 C5
6 Erith DA17 125 B1
Shaw Path BR1 164 D1
Shaw Rd SE22 139 C1
Catford BR1 164 D1
Enfield EN3 6 D4
Shaw Sq E17 35 A2
Shaws Wood Cotts EN4 3 C3
Shaw Way SM6 220 A1
Shearing Dr SM4 202 A2
Shearling Way N7 72 A2
Shearman Rd SE3 142 D2
Shears Ct TW16 171 C3
Shearsmith Ho 14 E1 118 A6
Shears The TW16 171 C3
Shearwater Cl IG11 102 A4
Shearwater Ct 24 SE8 141 B6
Shearwater Rd SM1 217 B3
Shearwater Way UB4 84 D1
Sheaveshill Ave NW9 45 C5
Sheaveshill Ct NW9 45 C5
Sheaveshill Par NW9 45 C5
Sheen Common Dr
SW14,TW10 154 C6
Sheen Court Rd TW10 132 C1
Sheen Ct TW10 132 C1
Sheendale Rd TW9 132 B1
Sheenewood SE26 184 B6
Sheen Gate Gdns
SW14 133 A1
Sheen Gr N1 94 C6 234 A6
Sheen La SW14 133 A1
Sheen Mount JMI Sch
SW14 154 D6
Sheen Pk TW10,TW9 132 A1
Sheen Rd
Orpington BR5 211 D5
Richmond TW10,TW9 132 B1
Sheen Way SM6 220 B3
Sheen Wood SW14 155 A6
Sheepcote Cl TW5 128 A5
Sheepcote La SW11 136 D3
Sheepcote Rd HA1 42 D3
Sheepcotes Rd RM6 59 A5
Sheephouse Way KT3 199 C2
Sheep La E8 96 B6
Sheepwalk TW17 192 B3
Sheep Walk Mews 7
SW19 179 A4
Sheerness Mews E16 122 D4
Sheerwater Rd E16 99 D2
Sheffield Ho 14 SE15 139 D4
Sheffield Rd TW14,
TW6 149 A6
Sheffield Sq 2 E3 97 B4
Sheffield St WC2 240 C1
Sheffield Terr
W8 113 C5 245 B3
Sheffield Way TW14,
TW6 149 B6
Shefton Rise HA6 22 A3
Shelbey Ct BR1 186 D2
Shelbourne Cl HA5 41 B6
Shelbourne Ho 20 N19 49 D2
Shelbourne Rd N17 34 B2
Shelburne Ct SW15 156 D6
Shelburne Dr TW4 151 C5
Shelburne Ho 9
SW16 181 C5
Shelburne Rd N7 72 B4
Shelbury Cl DA14 168 A1
Shelbury Rd SE22 162 B6
Sheldon Ave N6 48 D3
Sheldon Cl SE12 165 B6
Penge SE20 184 B2
Sheldon Ct SW8 270 A3
Barnet EN5 1 D1
Sheldon Ho 9 E9 74 D2
Chingford E4 36 C4
Teddington TW11 175 A4
Sheldon Rd DA7 147 B4
NW2 68 D4
Dagenham RM9 81 A1
Edmonton N18 33 C6
Sheldon St CR0 221 A5
Sheldrake Cl E16 122 B5
Sheldrake Ho 15 SE16 118 D2
Sheldrake Pl
W8 113 C4 245 A2
Sheldrick Cl CR4 180 B1
Shelduck Cl E15 76 D3
Shelduck Ct 36 SE8 141 B6
Sheldwich Terr BR2 210 A3
Shelford 20 KT1 176 C1
Shelford Ct 7 E5 52 B1
Shelford Pl N16 73 B5
Shelford Rd EN5 12 C5
Shelford Rise SE19 183 D3
Shelgate Rd SW11 158 D6
Shell Cl BR2 210 A3
Shell Ctr SE1 250 D3
Shellduck Cl NW9 27 C1
Shelley N8 50 A6
Shelley Ave E12 78 A2
Greenford UB6 86 B4
Shelley Cl BR6 227 C5
SE15 140 B3
Edgware HA8 26 C6
Greenford UB6 86 B4
Hayes UB4 84 A2
Shelley Cres
Heston TW5 128 D4
Southall UB1 85 B1
Shelley Ct 12 E10 53 D2
N4 50 B1
SW3 267 D6
9 Kingston KT2 175 D6
8 Wanstead E11 55 A5
Wembley HA0 65 C4
West Barnes KT3 200 A4
Shelley Dr DA16 145 C4
Shelley Gdns HA0 65 C6
Shelley Ho 21 E2 96 C4
9 N16 73 C4
SE17 262 B2
SW1 269 A6
Shelley Rd NW10 89 B6
Shelley Sch
SE11 116 C2 261 B3
Shelley Way SW17 180 B4
Shellgrove Rd N16 73 C3
Shellness Rd E5 74 B3
Shell Rd SE13 141 D2
Shellwood Rd SW11 136 D3
Shelly Lo EN2 5 B4
Shelmerdine Cl E3 97 C2
Shelson Ave TW13 171 D6
Shelton Rd SW19 179 C2
Shelton St WC2 94 A1 240 A1
Shene Bldg EC1 241 A4
Shene Int Sch SW14 133 C1
Shenfield Ho 3 SE18 143 D5
Shenfield Rd IG8 37 B3
Shenfield St N1 95 C5
Shenley Ave HA4 39 D1
Shenley Rd SE5 139 C4
Heston TW5 129 A4
Shenstone W13 109 C5
Shenstone Gdns IG2 57 D4
Shenstone Ho SW16 181 C5
Shepherd Cl W1 248 A6
Feltham TW13 173 A6
Shepherdess Pl N1 235 B2
Shepherdess Wlk
N1 95 A5 235 B3
Shepherd Ho 10 E14 97 D1
N7 72 A2
Shepherd Mkt W1 248 C3
Shepherd's Bush (Central
Line) Sta W12 112 D4
Shepherd's Bush Gn
W12 112 C4
Shepherd's Bush (Hamm &
City) Sta W12 112 C5
Shepherd's Bush Market
W12 112 C4
Shepherd's Bush Pl
W12 112 D4
Shepherd's Bush Rd
W6 112 C3
Shepherd's Cl N6 49 B3
Shepherds Cl
Dagenham RM6 58 D5
Orpington BR6 227 D5
Shepperton TW17 192 D3
Shepherds Ct 8 W12 112 D4
Shepherds Gn BR7 18
Shepherd's Hill N6 4
Shepherd's La E9 7
Shepherds Leas SE9 14
Shepherds Path UB5
Shepherds Pl W1 24
Shepherd St
W1 115 B5 24
Shepherds Way CR2 22
Shepherds Wlk NW2
Shepherd's Wlk NW3
Shepherds Wlk WD23
Shepiston La UB3 10
Shepley Cl SM5 21
Shepley Ct SW16 18
Shepley Mews EN3
Sheppard Cl Enfield EN1
Kingston KT6 19
Sheppard Dr SE16 1
Sheppard Ho 28 E2
18 SW11 1
8 Streatham SW2 16
Sheppard's Ct
Harrow HA1
Wembley UB6
Sheppard St E16
Shepperton Bsns Park
TW17 19
Shepperton Court Dr
TW17 19
Shepperton Ct TW17 19
Shepperton Rd
N1 95 B6 2
Littleton TW17,TW18 19
Orpington BR5 2
Shepperton Sta TW17 19
Shepperton Studios
TW17 1
Sheppey Gdns RM9
Sheppey Ho 16 E5
Sheppey Rd RM9
Sheppey Wlk N1
Shepton Ct SW11 2
Shepton Hos 11 E2
Sherard Ct N19
Sherard Ho 24 E9
Sherard Rd SE9 1
Sheraton Bsns Ctr UB6
Sheraton Cl WD6
Sheraton Ho SW1 2
Sheraton Lo HA3
Sheraton St W1 2
Sheraton The 22 KT6 1
Sherborne Ave
Enfield EN3
Southall UB2 1
Sherborne Cl UB4
Sherborne Cres SM5 2
Sherborne Ct SE20 1
Sherborne Gdns NW9
Ealing W13
Sherborne Ho SW1 2
SW8 2
Sherborne La EC4 2
Sherborne Rd BR5 2
Cheam SM3 2
Chessington KT9 2
East Bedfont TW14 1
Sherborne St
N1 95 B6 2
Sherboro Rd 1 N15
Sherbourne Ct 1
TW12 1
Sherbourne Gdns
TW17 1
Sherbourne Pl HA7
Sherbrooke Cl DA7 1
Sherbrooke Ho 9 E2
Sherbrooke Rd
SW6 135 A5 2
Sherbrooke Terr SW6 2
Sherbrook Gdns N21
Shere Cl KT9 2
Sheredan Rd E4
Shere Ho SE1 2
Shere Rd IG2
Sherfield Cl KT3 1
Sherfield Gdns SW15 1
Sheridan N8
Sheridan Bldgs WC2 2
Sheridan Cl UB10
Sheridan Cres BR7 1
Sheridan Ct NW6
SW9 2
Ealing W7 1
Harrow HA1
Hounslow TW4 1
Sheridan Gdns HA3
Sheridan Ho 16 E1
7 N16
SE11 2
Sheridan Lo EN5
Sheridan Mews E11
Sheridan Pl
Barnes SW13 1
Hampton TW12 1
Harrow HA1
Sheridan Rd DA7 1
E12

ridan Rd continued
76 D5
vedere DA17 125 C2
ton SW19 179 B2
mond TW10 153 C1
ridan St 28 E1 96 B1
ridan Terr UB5 63 D3
ridan Way 5 BR3 185 B2
idan Wlk NW11 47 C3
idon Ct SW5 255 C3
ingdale Prim Sch
18 157 B3
ingham NW8 229 D6
ingham Ave E12 78 B3
thgate N14 15 D5
ckenham TW2 151 C3
ingham Dr IG11 80 A3
ingham Ho NW1 237 B4
ingham Jun Sch
78 B4
ingham Rd N7 72 C2
ge SE20 206 C6
ingham Twr UB1 107 D6
ington Ave HA5 23 C3
ington Prim Sch
143 B6
ington Rd SE7 143 B6
land Rd TW1 152 D3
rleys Ct HA4 61 C6
lies Ave BR6 227 C6
lock Ct NW8 229 C6
lock Holmes Mus*
1 92 D3 237 D5
rlock Mews W1 238 A4
man Gdns RM6 58 C3
man Rd BR1 187 A2
nwood Ho 1 E18 55 A5
rard Rd E7,E12 77 D2
rards Way EN5 13 D5
rrick Green Rd
10 68 B3
riff Ct NW6 69 C2
riff Rd NW6 69 C2
ringham Ave
ham TW13 150 A1
enham N17 34 A1
ringham Ct 1 N3 29 C2
rin Rd E10 75 D4
rock Gdns NW4 46 A5
ry Mews IG11 79 B1
rston Ct SE1 261 D4
1 234 A1
rwin Ho 1 SE11 138 C6
win Rd SE14 140 D4
wood NW6 69 A1
g Ditton KT6 213 D6
wood Ave
enford UB6 64 C3
es UB4 84 B3
ham SW16 181 D2
lip HA4 39 C3
stead E18 55 B6
wood Cl DA5 168 C5
35 B1
es SW13 134 B2
g W13 109 B5
wood Ct SE13 141 D3
SW11 136 A2
237 C3
West Wickham BR4 207 D1
wood Gdns E14 119 C2
5 118 B1
ing IG11 79 B1
wood Hall 7 N2 48 A6
wood Ho N4 51 A2
wood Park Ave
5 168 B5
wood Park Prim Sch
5 168 B5
wood Park Rd
ham CR4 203 D5
on SM1 217 C3
wood Park Sch
219 D5
wood Prim Sch
203 C5
wood Rd DA16 145 C2
46 C6
don CR0 206 B1
pton TW12 174 A5
ow HA2 64 A6
d IG6 57 B5
ton SW19 179 B3
wood St N20 14 B1
249 B6
wood Terr N20 14 B1
wood Way BR4 224 A6
land Cl WD6 11 B5
land Rd E3 97 B5
Bedfont TW6 149 A5
d Dr TW8 131 A6
dhall St SE2 124 C2
d Rd TW15 171 B6
ord Path SE23 162 D1
aker Ct W3 111 D5
ibeer Pl W1 237 B3
ngford Ho 40 E3 97 D4
ngford St 22 N1 72 D1
ngstone Ho W14 254 B5
Shinfield St W12 90 C1
Shinglewell Rd DA8 147 C5
Shinners Cl SE25 206 A4
Shipka Rd SW12 159 B3
Ship La SW14 133 A3
Shiplake Ct SW17 180 B6
Shiplake Ho 45 E2 95 D4
Shipley Ct SE20 184 A1
Shipley Ho 32 SW8 137 D3
Shipman Par SE23 163 A2
Shipman Rd
Forest Hill SE23 162 D2
Newham E16 99 C1
Ship & Mermaid Row
SE1 253 A2
Ship St SE8 141 C4
Ship Tavern Pas EC3 253 A6
Shipton Cl RM8 80 D5
Shipton Ho 14 E2 95 D5
7 NW5 71 A2
Shipton Rd UB8 60 B4
Shipton St E2 95 D4
Shipwright Rd SE16 119 A4
Shipwright Yd SE1 253 A3
Shirburn Cl SE23 162 C4
Shirbutt St E14 119 D6
Shirebrook Rd SE3 143 D2
Shire Ct DA18 124 D3
Ewell KT17 215 D1
Shirehall Cl NW4 46 D3
Shirehall Gdns NW4 46 D3
Shirehall La NW4 46 D3
Shirehall Pk NW4 46 D3
Shire Ho E11 76 D5
Shire Horse Way TW7 130 D2
Shire La
Farthing Street BR6,BR2 227 B2
Orpington BR6 227 C3
Shiremeade WD6 10 B6
Shire Pl SW18 158 A4
Shires The TW10 176 A6
Shirland Mews W9 91 B4
Shirland Rd W9 91 C3
Shirley Ave DA5 168 D3
Carshalton SM1 218 C4
Croydon CR0 206 D1
Shirley Church Rd
CR0 223 A5
Shirley Cl TW3 152 A6
Shirley Cres BR3 207 A5
Shirley Ct NW9 45 B4
8 Ealing W13 109 A5
Ilford IG2 57 B4
Thornton Heath SW16 204 B6
Shirley Dr TW3 152 A6
Shirley Gdns
Barking IG11 79 C2
Ealing W7 108 D5
Shirley Gr N9 18 D4
SW11 137 A2
Shirley High Sch CR0 222 D5
Shirley Hills Rd CR0 222 D3
Shirley Ho 13 SE5 139 B5
Shirley House Dr SE7 143 C5
Shirley Lo 4 SE26 185 A6
Shirley Oaks Hospl
CR0 206 C2
Shirley Oaks Rd CR0 222 D6
Shirley Park Rd CR0 206 C1
Shirley Rd E15 76 C1
W4 111 B4
Croydon CR0 206 B1
Enfield EN2 5 A2
Sidcup DA15 167 C1
Shirleys Cl E17 53 D4
Shirley St E16 98 D1
Shirley Way CR0 223 B5
Shirlock Rd NW3 70 D4
Shobden Rd N17 33 B2
Shobroke Cl NW2 68 C5
Shoebury Rd E6 78 B1
Shoe La EC4 94 C1 241 B2
Shoelands Ct NW9 45 B6
Shooters Ave HA3 43 C5
Shooters Hill SE18 144 C4
Shooters Hill Rd
SE18,SE3,SE7 143 D5
SE3,SE10 142 C4
Shooters Rd EN2 4 D4
Shoot-Up Hill NW2 69 A2
Shore Bsns Ctr 31 E9 74 C1
Shore Cl Feltham TW14 150 A4
Hampton TW12 173 A5
Shorediche Cl UB10 60 B5
Shoreditch Ct 2 E8 73 D1
Shoreditch High St
E2 95 C3 243 B6
Shoreditch Sta
E1 95 D3 243 D5
Shore Gr TW13 151 C2
Shoreham Cl DA5 168 D3
SW18 157 D6
Croydon CR0 206 C3
Shoreham Rd BR5 190 B1
Shoreham Rd (E)
TW6 148 A6
Shoreham Rd (W)
TW6 148 A6
Shoreham Way BR2 209 A3
Shore Ho SW8 137 B2
Shore Mews 30 E9 74 C1
Shore Pl E9 74 C1
Shore Rd E9 74 C1
Shorncliffe Rd
SE1 117 D1 263 C2
Shorndean St SE6 164 A3
Shorne Cl 3 DA15 168 B5
Shornefield Cl BR1 210 C6
Shornells Way SE2 124 C1
Shorrolds Rd
SW6 135 B5 264 D4
Shortcroft Mead Ct
NW10 68 A3
Shortcroft Rd KT17 215 D1
Shortcrofts Rd RM9 81 B2
Shorter St
EC3 117 D6 253 D6
Shortgate N12 29 B6
Short La TW15,TW19 148 B3
Shortlands W6 112 D2
Harlington UB3 127 B6
Shortlands Cl DA17 125 B3
Edmonton N18 17 B1
Shortlands Gdns BR2 186 C1
Shortlands Gr BR2 208 B6
Shortlands Rd E10 53 D2
Beckenham BR2,BR3 208 C6
Kingston KT2 176 B3
Shortlands Sta BR2 186 C1
Short Path SE18 144 D6
Short Rd E11 76 C6
Chiswick W4 133 C6
Stanwell TW19 148 A5
Shorts Croft NW9 44 D5
Shorts Gdns
WC2 94 A1 240 A1
Shorts Rd SM5 218 C3
Short St 7 NW4 46 C5
SE1 251 B2
Shortway SE9 144 A2
Short Way N12 30 C4
Twickenham TW2 152 A4
Shotfield SM6 219 B2
Shott Cl SM1 218 A3
Shottendane Rd
SW6 135 C4 265 A2
Shottery Cl SE9 166 A1
Shottfield Ave SW14 133 C1
Shottsford 1 W11 91 C1
Shoulder of Mutton Alley 10
E14 119 A6
Shouldham St
W1 92 C2 237 B3
Showers Way UB3 106 A5
Shrapnel Cl SE18 144 A5
Shrapnel Rd SE9 144 B2
Shreveport Ho 23 N19 49 D2
Shrewsbury Ave
Harrow HA3 44 A5
Mortlake SW14 133 B1
Shrewsbury Cl KT6 214 A6
Shrewsbury Cres NW10 89 B6
Shrewsbury Ho SE11 270 D5
SW3 267 A5
Shrewsbury House Sch
KT6 214 A6
Shrewsbury La SE18 144 D4
Shrewsbury Mews 33
W2 91 C2
Shrewsbury Rd E7 77 D2
N11 31 D4
W2 91 C1
Beckenham BR3 207 A6
Carshalton SM5 202 C2
Harlington TW14,TW6 149 B5
Shrewsbury St W10 90 C3
Shrewsbury Wlk 7
TW7 131 A2
Shrewton Rd SW17 180 D3
Shroffold Rd BR1 164 D1
Shropshire Cl CR4 204 A5
Shropshire Ct W7 86 D1
Shropshire Pl WC1 239 B5
Shropshire Rd N22 32 B3
Shroton St NW1 92 C2 237 B4
Shrubberies The
Ilford IG2 57 D4
Woodford E18 37 A1
Shrubbery Gdns N21 16 D4
Shrubbery Rd
Edmonton N9 18 A1
Southall UB1 107 C5
Streatham SW16 182 A6
Shrubbery The
2 Surbiton KT6 198 A1
7 Wanstead E11 55 B4
Shrubland Gr KT4 216 C5
Shrubland Rd E10 53 C2
E8 96 A6
Walthamstow E10 53 C4
Shrublands Ave CR0 223 C4
Shrublands Cl N20 14 B2
Forest Hill SE26 162 C1
Shrubsall Cl SE9 166 A3
Shrubs Ho SW1 259 D3
Shubbery Cl N1 235 B5
Shurland Ave EN4 14 B5
Shurland Gdns SE15 139 D5
Shurlock Dr BR6 227 A4
Shuters Sq W14 254 C1
Shuttle Cl DA15 167 D4
Shuttlemead DA5 169 B4
Shuttle St E1 96 A3
Shuttleworth Rd
SW11 136 C3
Sibella Rd SW4 137 D3
Sibford Ct 5 CR4 202 D6
Sibley Cl DA6 169 A6
Sibley Ct UB8 83 A2
Sibley Gr E12 78 A1
Sibthorpe Rd SE12 165 C4
Sibthorp Rd 2 CR4 180 D1
Sibton Rd SM5 202 C2
Sicilian Ave WC1 240 B3
Sidbury St
SW6 135 A4 264 A2
Sidcup By Pass Rd
Sidcup DA14 189 C6
St Paul's Cray BR5,BR7 190 B3
Sidcup Hill DA14 190 B5
Sidcup Hill Gdns
DA14 190 C5
Sidcup Hill Prim Sch
DA14 190 B5
Sidcup Pl DA14 190 A5
Sidcup Rd SE9 166 A3
Sidcup Sta DA14,DA15 168 A2
Sidcup Tech Ctr DA14 190 D4
Siddeley Dr TW4 129 A3
Siddons Ct WC2 240 C1
Siddons Ho 8 NW3 70 D3
W2 236 D3
Siddons La
NW1 92 D3 237 D5
Siddons Rd
Croydon CR0 220 D5
Forest Hill SE23 163 A2
Tottenham N17 34 A2
Side Rd E17 53 B4
Sidewood Rd DA15,
SE9 167 B3
Sidford Ho SE1 260 D5
Sidford Pl SE1 116 B3 260 D5
Sidgwick Ho 26 SW9 138 A3
Sidings Mews N7 72 C4
Sidings The E11 54 A1
Sidlaw Ho N16 51 D1
Sidmouth Ave TW7 130 C3
Sidmouth Dr HA4 62 A5
Sidmouth Ho 18 SE15 140 A5
W1 237 B2
26 Streatham SW2 160 C4
Sidmouth Par NW2 68 C1
Sidmouth Rd E10 76 A5
NW2 68 C1
Bexley DA16 146 C5
Sidmouth St
WC1 94 B4 233 C1
Sidney Ave N13 32 B5
Sidney Boyd Ct NW6 69 C1
Sidney Elson Way E6 100 C5
Sidney Gdns TW8 131 D6
Sidney Godley (VC) Ho 31
E2 96 C4
Sidney Gr EC1 234 C3
Sidney Ho 4 E2 96 D5
3 SE18 144 B4
Sidney Miller Ct 8
W3 110 D5
Sidney Rd SW9 138 B3
Beckenham BR3 185 A1
Croydon SE25 206 A4
Harrow HA2 42 A6
Twickenham TW1 153 B5
Walton-on-T KT12 194 B1
Wanstead E7 77 A5
Wood Green N22 32 B3
Sidney Sq E1 96 C2
Sidney St E1 96 C2
Sidworth St 6 E8 74 B1
Siebert Rd SE3 143 A6
Siedle Ho 9 SE18 144 C6
Siege Ho 21 E1 96 B1
Siemens Rd SE18 121 D3
Sierra Dr RM9 103 D5
Sigdon Rd E8 74 A3
Sigers The HA5 40 B3
Signmakers Yd NW1 231 D5
Sigrist Sq 4 KT2 176 A2
Silbury Ave CR4 180 C2
Silbury Ho 9 SE26 162 A1
Silbury St N1 235 C2
Silchester Ct
Stanwell TW15 148 A2
Thornton Heath CR7 204 C5
Silchester Rd W10 90 D1
Silecroft Rd DA7 147 C4
Silesia Bldgs E8 74 B1
Silex St SE1 116 D4 251 D1
Silicone Bsns Ctr UB6 87 C5
Silk Cl SE12 165 A5
Silkfield Rd NW9 45 C4
Silk Ho NW9 45 B6
Silk Mills Path SE13 142 A2
Silk Mills Sq E9 75 B2
Silks Ct E11 54 C1
Silk St EC2 95 A2 242 B4
Silkstream Par HA8 27 A2
Silkstream Rd HA8 27 A2
Sillitoe Ho N1 235 D5
Silsoe Ho NW1 231 D3
Silsoe Rd N22 50 B6
Silver Birch Ave E4 35 B4
Silver Birch Cl N11 31 A4
Forest Hill SE6 163 B1
Ickenham UB10 60 A4
Silver Birch Ct EN3 18 D6
Silver Birch Gdns E6 100 B3
Silver Birch Rd SE28 124 A5
Silverbirch Wlk 1
NW3 71 A2
Silverburn Ho 4 SW9 138 D4
Silver Cl SE14 141 A5
Harrow HA3 24 B3
Silvercliffe Gdns EN4 2 C1
Silver Cres W4 110 D2
Silver Ct N19 71 C5
Silverdale NW1 232 A2
Enfield EN2 4 A1
Forest Hill SE26 184 C6
Silverdale Ave IG3 57 D4
Silverdale Cl
Cheam SM1 217 B4
1 Ealing W7 108 D5
Northolt UB5 63 B3
Silverdale Ct EC1 241 D6
Silverdale Dr
Chislehurst SE9 166 A2
Sunbury TW16 172 B1
Silverdale Factory Ctr
UB3 106 A4
Silverdale Gdns UB3 106 A4
Silverdale Par IG3 57 D4
Silverdale Rd BR5 211 A5
DA7 147 D3
Chingford E4 36 B4
Hayes UB3 106 A4
Silverhall St TW7 131 A2
Silverholme Cl HA3 44 A2
Silver Ind Est N17 33 D1
Silver Jubilee Way
TW4 128 B3
Silver La BR4 224 B6
Silverland St E16 122 B5
Silverleigh Rd CR7 204 B4
Silvermead 7 E18 37 A2
Silvermere Rd SE6 163 D5
Silver Pl W1 249 B6
Silver Rd W12 112 D6
Silvers IG9 21 C3
Silver Spring Cl DA8 147 D6
Silver St Edmonton N18 33 C6
Enfield EN1 5 B2
Silverstone Ct 6 BR1 187 C1
Silverston Way HA7 25 C4
Silver Street Sta N18 33 D5
Silverthorn 15 NW6 91 D6
Silverthorne Rd SW8 137 B3
Silverthorn Gdns E4 19 C2
Silverton Lo SE19 183 C3
Silverton Rd W6 134 D6
Silvertown Sta E16 122 A5
Silvertown Way E16 121 A5
Silvertree La UB6 86 B4
Silver Way
Hillingdon UB10 82 D5
Romford RM7 59 D6
Silver Wlk SE16 119 B5
Silverwood Cl BR3 185 C3
Silvester Ho 17 E1 96 B1
27 E2 96 C4
2 W11 91 B1
Pinner HA5 40 A5
Silvester Rd SE22 161 D6
Silvester St SE1 252 C1
Silwood St SE16 118 C1
Simba Ct TW1 152 D3
Simla Ho SE1 252 D1
Simmil Rd KT10 212 C3
Simmons Cl N20 14 C3
Chessington KT9 213 C2
Simmons Gate KT10 212 A3
Simmons Ho 16 E2 96 A4
N7 72 B6
Simmons La E4 20 B2
Simmons Rd SE18 122 D1
Simmons' Way N20 14 C2
Simms Cl SM5 218 C6
Simms Ct SW6 135 A2
Simms Gdns N2 30 A1
Simms Rd SE1 118 A2
Simnel Rd SE12 165 B4
Simon Cl W11 113 B6 244 D6
Simon Ct W9 91 C4
5 Woolwich SE28 124 B5
Simonds Rd E10 75 C6
Simone Cl BR1 187 D2
Simon Lo 31 SW19 156 D3
Simon Marks (Jewish) Prim
Sch N16 73 D6
Simon Peter Ct EN2 4 D3
Simons Wlk E15 76 B3
Simpson Cl N21 16 B6
Simpson Dr W3 89 B1
Simpson Ho NW8 230 A1
SE11 260 C1
Simpson Ho continued
Wembley HA9 65 D6
Simpson Rd
Hounslow TW4 151 B5
Richmond TW10 175 C6
Simpson's Cotts BR2 225 C5
Simpson's Rd BR2 209 A6
E14 119 D6
Simpson St SW11 136 C3
Simpson Way KT6 197 C3
Sim's Cotts KT10 212 D2
Sims Wlk SE3 142 D1
Sinclair Ct N5 73 A2
21 Beckenham BR3 185 C3
5 Croydon CR0 221 D6
Sinclair Gdns W14 112 D4
Sinclair Gr NW11 46 D3
Sinclair Ho 1 SW12 159 D3
Sinclair Mans 13 W12 112 D4
Sinclair Rd E4 35 B5
W14 113 A3 254 A6
Sinclairs Ho 14 E3 97 B5
Sinclare Cl EN1 5 D4
Singapore Rd W13 109 A5
Singer St EC2 235 D1
Singlegate First Sch
SW19 180 B3
Singleton Cl
Mitcham SW17,SW19 180 D3
Thornton Heath CR0 205 A2
Singleton Rd RM9 81 B3
Singleton Scarp N12 29 C5
Sinnott Rd E17 34 D2
Sion Ct TW1 153 B3
Sion-Manning RC Sch for
Girls
W10 90 D2
W10 91 A2
Sion Rd TW1 153 B3
Sippetts Ct IG1 57 B1
Sipson Cl UB7 126 C6
Sipson La UB3,UB7 126 D6
Sipson Rd
Harmondsworth UB7 126 C6
West Drayton UB7 104 B2
West Drayton UB7 104 C1
Sipson Way UB7 126 C5
Sir Abraham Dawes Cotts
SW15 135 A1
Sir Alexander Cl W3 111 D5
Sir Alexander Rd W3 111 D5
Sir Cyril Black Way 2
SW19 179 C3
Sirdar Rd W11 113 A6 244 A5
Mitcham CR4 181 A4
Tottenham N22 33 A1
Sir Francis Drake Prim Sch
SE8 119 A1
Sir George Monoux Sixth
Form Coll E17 35 D1
Sir Henry Floyd Ct HA7 9 B2
Sirinham Point SW8 270 D5
Sirius Bldg 13 E1 118 D6
Sir James Barrie Prim Sch
SW8 137 C4 269 B1
Sir John Cass Foundation &
Redcoat CE Sec Sch
E1 96 D2
Sir John Cass's Prim Sch
EC3 95 C1 243 A1
Sir John Heron Prim Sch
E12 78 B4
Sir John Kirk Cl 33
SE5 139 A5
Sir John Lillie Prim Sch
SW6 135 A6 264 B5
Sir Martin Bowes Ho 15
SE18 122 C2
Sir Oswald Stoll Foundation
The SW6 265 C4
Sir Thomas Abney Sch
N16 51 B1
Sir Thomas More Est
SW3 136 B6 266 D5
Sirus Rd HA6 22 A5
Sir William Burrough Prim
Sch E14 97 A1
Sir William Powell's
Almshos SW6 135 A2
Sise La EC4 242 C1
Siskin Ho 14 SE16 118 D2
Sisley Rd IG11 101 D6
Sispara Gdns SW18 157 B5
Sissinghurst Cl BR1 186 C5
Sissinghurst Ho 17
SE15 140 C6
Sissinghurst Rd CR0 206 A2
Sissulu Ct 9 E6 99 C6
Sister Mabel's Way 14
SE15 140 A5
Sisters Ave SW11 136 D1
Sistova Rd SW12 159 B3
Sisulu Pl SW9 138 C2
Site of Changing of the
Guard* SW1 249 A1
Sittingbourne Ave EN1 17 B5

Sitwell Gr HA7 24 D5
Siverst Cl UB5 63 D2
Sivill Ho 9 E2 95 D4
Siviter Way RM10 81 D1
Siward Rd Bromley BR2 209 C6
Tottenham N17 33 B2
Wandsworth SW17 158 A1
Six Bridges Ind Est SE1 118 A1
Sixth Ave W10 91 A4
Hayes UB3 105 D5
Ilford E12 78 B4
Sixth Cross Rd TW2 152 A1
Skardu Rd NW2 69 A3
Skeena Hill SW18, SW19 157 A4
Skeffington Rd E6 100 B6
Skeggs Ho 5 E14 120 A3
Skegness Ho 3 N7 72 B1
Skelbrook St SW18 158 A2
Skelgill Rd SW15 135 B1
Skelley Rd E15 76 D1
Skelton Cl 7 E8 73 D2
Skelton Ho N16 73 C3
Skelton Rd E7 77 A2
Skelton's La E10 53 D2
Skelwith Rd W6 134 C6
Skenfrith Ho SE15 140 B6
Skerne Rd KT2 175 D2
Sketchley Gdns SE16 118 D1
Sketty Rd EN1 5 D2
Skiers St E15 98 C6
Skiffington Cl SW2 160 C3
Skinner Ct E17 53 C4
Skinner Pl SW1 258 A3
Skinners Almshouses N13 16 C1
Skinners Company Sch (Upper) N16 51 D2
Skinner's Company's Lower Sch E5 52 B1
Skinners La EC4 252 B6
Hounslow TW5 129 D4
Skinner St EC1 94 C3 241 B6
Skipsea Ho SW18 158 B5
Skipsey Ave E6 100 B4
Skipton Cl N11 31 A4
Skipton Dr UB3 105 A3
Skipton Ho SE4 141 A1
Skipwith Bldg EC1 241 A4
Skipworth Rd E9 96 C6
Skua Ct 42 SE8 141 B6
Skyline Ct SE1 263 C5
Skylines E14 120 A4
Sky Peals Rd IG8 36 B3
Sladebrook Rd SE3 143 D2
Slade Ct NW2 69 A3
Barnet EN5 1 D2
Sladedale Rd SE18 123 C1
Slade Ho TW4 151 B5
Sladen Pl 12 E5 74 B4
Slades Cl EN2 4 C2
Slades Dr BR7 189 A6
Slades Gdns EN2 4 C2
Slades Hill EN2 4 C2
Slades Rise EN2 4 C2
Slade The SE18 145 C6
Slade Twr E10 75 C6
Slade Wlk SE17 139 A6
Slagrove Pl SE13 163 D6
Slaidburn St SW10 136 A6 266 B5
Slaithwaite Rd SE13 142 A1
Slaney Ct NW10 68 C1
Slaney Pl 1 N7 72 C3
Slater Cl 13 SE18 122 C2
Slater Ho 4 N16 51 D3
Slatter 1 NW9 27 D2
Slattery Rd TW13 150 C3
Sleaford Ho 16 E3 97 C3
Sleaford Ind Est SW8 137 C5 269 B3
Sleaford St SW8 137 C5 269 B3
Sleat Ho 9 E3 97 B5
Sledmere Ct TW14 149 C3
Slievemore Cl 8 SW4 137 D2
Sligo Ho 8 E1 96 D3
Slingsby Pl WC2 250 A6
Slippers Pl SE16 118 B3
Sloane Ave SW3 114 C2 257 B3
Sloane Avenue Mans SW3 257 C3
Sloane Ct E SW3 258 A2
Sloane Ct W SW3 258 A2
Sloane Gate Mans SW1 258 A4
Sloane Gdns BR6 227 A5
SW1 115 A2 258 A3
Sloane Ho 7 E9 74 C1
Sloane Hospl BR3 186 B2
Sloane Sq SW1 257 D3
Sloane Square Sta SW1 115 A2 258 A3
Sloane St SW1 114 D3 257 D5
Sloane Terr SW1 258 A4
Sloane Terr Mans SW1 258 A4
Sloane Wlk CR0 207 B3
Slocum Cl SE28 124 C6
Slomon Ho 2 W10 91 A4
Slough La NW9 45 A3
Sly St 7 E1 96 B1
Smaldon Cl UB7 104 C3
Smallberry Ave TW7 130 D3
Smallberry Green Prim Sch TW7 131 A4
Smallbrook Mews W2 236 C1
Smalley Cl N16 73 D5
Smallwood Prim Sch SW17 180 B6
Smallwood Rd SW17 180 B6
Smarden Cl DA17 125 C1
Smarden Gr SE9 188 B6
Smart's Pl WC1,WC2 240 B2
Edmonton N18 34 A5
Smart St E2 96 D4
Smeaton Cl KT9 213 D2
Smeaton Ct SE1 262 A5
Smeaton Rd
Holdbrook EN3 7 C6
Wandsworth SW18 157 C4
Smeaton St E1 118 B5
Smedley St SW4 137 D3
Smeed Rd E3 75 C1
Smiles Pl SE13 142 A3
Smith Cl SE16 118 D5
Smithers Ho 3 SE20 184 D3
Smithfield Mkt EC1 241 D3
Smithfield St EC1 94 D2 241 C3
Smithies Ct E15 76 A3
Smithies Rd SE2 124 B2
Smith's Ct W1 249 C6
Smithson Rd N17 33 B2
Smiths Point E13 99 A6
Smith Sq SW1 116 A3 260 A5
Smith St SW3 114 D1 257 C1
Surbiton KT5 198 B3
Smith's Yd SW18 158 A2
Smith Terr SW3 114 D1 257 C1
Smithwood Cl SW19 157 A2
Smithy St E1 96 C2
Smithy Street Sch E1 96 C2
Smock Wlk CR0 205 A3
Smoothfield TW3 129 C1
Smugglers Way SW18 135 D1
Smyrk's Rd SE17 117 C1 263 B1
Smyrna Mans 8 NW6 69 C1
Smyrna Rd NW6 69 C1
Smythe St E14 119 D6
Snakes La EN4,N14 3 C1
Snakes La E IG8 37 A4
Snakes La W IG8 37 B4
Snaresbrook Dr HA7 26 A6
Snaresbrook Hall 11 E18 55 A6
Snaresbrook Ho E18 54 D5
Snaresbrook Prim Sch E18 55 A5
Snaresbrook Rd E11 54 D5
Snaresbrook Sta E11 55 A4
Snarsgate St W10 90 C2
Sneath Ave NW11 47 B2
Snell's Pk N18 33 D4
Sneyd Rd NW2 68 C4
Snowberry Cl E11 76 B4
Snowbury Rd 6 SW6 135 D3
Snow Ct 6 HA0 65 D3
Snowden Ave UB10 82 D5
Snowden St EC2 95 C3 243 A5
Snowdon Cres UB3 105 A3
Snowdon Dr NW9 45 C3
Snowdon Rd TW6 149 A5
Snowdown Cl SE20 184 D2
Snowdrop Cl 2 TW12 173 C4
Snow Hill EC1 94 D2 241 C3
Snow Ho SE27 160 D1
Snowman Ho NW6 91 D6
Snowsfield Prim Sch SE1 117 C4 253 A2
Snowsfields SE1 117 B4 252 D2
Snowshill Rd E12 78 A3
Snowy Fielder Waye TW7 131 B3
Soames St SE15 139 D2
Soames Wlk KT3 177 C2
Soane Cl W5 109 D4
Soane Ct 8 NW1 71 C1
Soane Ho SE17 262 D1
Soane Mus* WC2 94 B1 240 C2
Soaphouse La TW8 132 A5
Soham Rd EN3 7 B6
Soho* W1 93 D1 239 C2
Soho Mills SM6 203 B1
Soho Parish CE Prim Sch W1 115 D6 249 C6
Soho Sq W1 93 D1 239 C2
Soho St W1 239 C2
Sojourner-Truth Cl 11 E8 74 B2
Solander Gdns 12 E1 118 C6
Stepney E1 118 B6
Solar Ct N3 29 D3
Soldene Ct N7 72 B2
Solebay St E1 97 A3
Solent Ct SW16 182 B1
Solent Ho 6 E1 97 A2
Solent Rd NW6 69 C3
Solent Rise E13 99 A4
Soley Mews WC1 234 A2
Solna Ave SW15 156 C6
Solna Rd N21 17 B4
Solomon Ave N9 34 A6
Solomon's Pas SE15 140 B1
Solon New Rd SW4 138 A1
Solon Rd SW2 138 A1
Solway Cl TW4 129 A2
Solway Ho 12 E1 96 D3
Solway Lo 4 IG8 37 A3
Solway Rd SE22 140 A1
Tottenham N22 32 D2
Somaford Gr EN4 14 B5
Somali Rd NW2 69 B3
Somborne Ho SW15 156 A4
Sombrook Ho SE11 261 A3
Somerby Rd IG11 79 B1
Somercoates Cl EN4 2 C2
Somer Ct SW6 265 A5
Somerfield Ho SE16 118 D1
Somerfield Rd N4 72 D6
Somerford Cl HA5 40 A5
Somerford Gr N16 73 D4
Tottenham N17 34 A3
Somerford Grove Est N16 73 D4
Somerford St E1 96 B3
Somerford Way SE16 119 A4
Somerhill Ave DA15 168 B4
Somerhill Rd DA16 146 B3
Somerleyton Rd SW9 138 C1
Somersby Est SE20 184 C3
Somersby Gdns IG4 56 B4
Somers Cl NW1 232 C4
Somers Cres W2 237 A1
Somerset Ave DA16 145 D1
Chessington KT9 213 D4
Wimbledon SW20 178 B1
Somerset Cl
New Malden KT3 199 C3
Tottenham N17 33 B1
Woodford IG8 37 A2
Somerset Ct Ealing W7 86 D1
2 Hampton TW12 173 C2
Somerset Gdns N6 49 A2
SE13 141 D3
Teddington TW11 174 C5
Thornton Heath SW16 204 B6
Tottenham N17 33 C3
Somerset Hall N17 33 C3
Somerset Ho* WC2 116 B6 250 D6
Wimbledon SW19 157 A1
Somerset Lo
9 Brentford TW8 131 D6
Putney SW15 134 B1
Somerset Rd E17 53 C3
N17 51 D6
NW4 46 C5
W4 111 B3
Brentford TW8 131 C6
Ealing W13 109 C5
Edmonton N18 33 D5
Harrow HA1 42 A4
Holdbrook EN3 7 C5
Kingston KT1 176 B1
New Barnet EN5 14 A6
Southall UB1 85 C2
Teddington TW11 174 C5
Wimbledon SW19 157 A1
Somerset Sq W14 113 B4 244 C1
Somerset Waye TW5 129 A5
Somersham Rd DA7 147 A3
Somers Pl SW2 160 B4
Somers Rd E17 53 B5
SW2 160 B5
Somers Town Est NW1 93 C5 232 B3
Somers Way WD23 8 A4
Somerton Ave TW9 132 D2
Somerton Rd NW2 69 A5
SE15 140 B1
Somertrees Ave SE12 165 B2
Somervell Rd HA2 63 C3
Somerville Ave SW13 134 C6
Somerville Ct SW16 181 D4
Somerville Ho 10 SW15 156 D5
Somerville Point SE16 119 B4
Somerville Rd
Dagenham RM6 58 C4
Penge SE20 184 D3
Sonderburg Rd 13 N7 72 B6
Sondes St SE17 139 B6
Sonia Ct N12 30 A6
Sonia Ct *continued*
Edgware HA8 26 B3
Sonia Gdns N12 30 A6
NW10 67 D4
Heston TW5 129 C5
Sonning Ct CR0 222 A6
Sonning Gdns TW12 173 A4
Sonning Ho 32 E2 95 D4
Sonning Rd CR0 206 A3
Soper Cl E4 35 B5
4 Forest Hill SE23 162 D2
Soper Mews EN3 7 C5
Sophia Cl N7 72 B2
Sophia Ho N15 51 D5
10 W6 112 C1
Sophia Rd E10 53 D1
E13 99 B2
Sophia Sq 14 SE16 119 A6
Sopwith 2 NW9 27 D2
Sopwith Ave KT9 214 A3
Sopwith Cl TW10 176 B5
Sopwith Rd TW5 128 C5
Sopwith Way SW11 268 C4
Kingston KT2 176 A2
Sorbus Ct EN2 4 D3
Sorenson Ct 2 E10 75 D6
Sorrel Cl SE28 124 A5
Sorrel Gdns E6 100 A2
Sorrel Ho TW3 130 A4
Sorrel La 16 E14 98 B1
Sorrell Cl SE14 141 A5
7 SW9 138 C3
Sorrento Rd SM1 217 D5
Sotheby Rd N5 73 A4
Sotheran Cl E8 96 A6
Sotheron Pl SW6 265 D3
Soudan Rd SW11 136 D4 267 C1
Souldern Rd 10 W14 112 D3
South Access Rd E17 53 A3
South Acre NW9 27 D1
Southacre Way HA5 22 C2
South Acton Sta W3, W4 111 A3
South Africa Rd W12 112 B6
Southall Ct UB1 107 B6
Southall Ent Ctr UB2 107 C4
Southall La TW5 106 B1
Southall Norwood Hospl UB2 107 B3
Southall Pl SE1 252 C1
Southall Sta UB1 107 B4
Southall & West London Coll UB1 107 A5
Southam Ho 9 W10 91 A3
Southampton Bldgs WC2 241 A3
Southampton Gdns CR4 204 A4
Southampton Pl WC1 240 B3
Southampton Rd NW5 70 D3
Stanwell TW19,TW6 148 B5
Southampton Row WC1 94 A2 240 B4
Southampton St WC2 250 B6
Southampton Way SE5 139 C5
Southam St W10 91 A3
South Audley St W1 115 A5 248 B4
South Ave NW11 47 D5
Chingford E4 20 A4
Richmond TW9 132 C3
Southall UB1 107 B6
Wallington SM5 219 A1
South Avenue Gdns UB1 107 B6
Southbank KT7 197 B2
South Bank KT6 198 A3
South Bank Bsns Ctr SW8 137 D6 269 D5
South Bank Lo 2 KT6 198 A3
South Bank Terr KT6 198 A3
South Bank Univ SW8 137 D4 269 D2
SE1 116 D3 261 D6
South Bermondsey Sta SE16 118 C1
South Birkbeck Rd E11 76 B5
South Black Lion La W6 112 A1
South Bldg SW1 259 B5
South Block 19 E1 118 C6
South Bolton Gdns SW10 255 D2
Southborough Cl KT6 197 D1
Southborough Ho SE17 263 B2
Southborough La BR1, BR2 210 B4
Southborough Prim Sch BR2 210 C4
Southborough Rd E9 96 D6
Bromley BR1,BR2 210 A5
Surbiton KT6 198 A1
Southborough Rd (The Lane) KT6 198 A1
Southborough Sch KT6 214 A5
Southbourne BR2 209 A2
Southbourne Ave NW9 27 B1
Southbourne Cl HA5 41 A2
Southbourne Cres NW4 47 A5
Southbourne Ct NW9 27 A1
Southbourne Gdns
SE12 165 B6
Ilford IG1 79 A3
Ruislip HA4 40 B1
Southbridge Pl CR0 221 A4
Southbridge Rd CR0 221 A4
Southbridge Way UB2 107 A4
Southbrook Mews SE12 164 D5
Southbrook Rd SE12 164 D5
Thornton Heath SW16 182 A2
South Building SE10 142 B5
Southbury NW8 229 B6
Southbury Ave EN1 6 A1
Southbury Prim Sch EN3 6 C1
Southbury Rd Enfield EN1 5 D1
Enfield EN1,EN3 6 B1
Southbury Sta EN3 6 B1
South Camden Com Sch NW1 93 D5 232 C3
South Carriage Dr SW1,SW7 114 D4 247 C2
South Church Ct E6 100 B5
Southchurch Rd E6 100 B5
South Cl DA6 146 D1
N6 49 B3
Barnet EN5 1 B2
Dagenham RM10 103 C6
Morden SM4 201 C3
Pinner HA5 22 D2
Pinner HA5 41 B2
Twickenham TW2 151 C1
West Drayton UB7 104 C3
South Colonnade E14 119 C5
Southcombe St W14 254 A4
South Common Rd UB8 60 A2
Southcote Ave
Feltham TW13 150 A2
Tolworth KT5 198 D2
Southcote Rd E17 53 A4
N19 71 C4
Croydon SE25 206 B3
Southcote Rise HA4 39 B2
Southcott Ho 31 E3 97 D4
W9 236 B5
South Cres E16 98 B3
WC1 239 C3
Southcroft Ave DA16 145 C2
West Wickham BR4 224 A6
Southcroft Rd BR6 227 C5
Streatham SW17 181 A4
South Cross Rd IG6 57 A4
South Croxted Rd SE21 183 B6
South Croydon Sta CR2 221 B3
South Ct 17 SW15 156 D5
Southdean Gdns SW19 157 B2
South Dene NW7 11 B1
Southdene Ct N11 15 C1
Southdown N7 72 A2
Southdown Ave W7 109 A3
Southdown Cres
Harrow HA2 42 A1
Ilford IG2 57 C4
Southdown Dr SW20 178 D3
Southdown Rd SW20 178 D2
South Dr Orpington BR6 227 C3
Ruislip HA4 39 C1
South Ealing Cemy W5 109 D2
South Ealing Rd W5 109 D3
South Ealing Sta W5 109 D3
South Eastern Ave N9 17 D1
South Eaton Pl SW1 115 A2 258 B4
South Eden Park Rd BR3 207 D4
South Edwardes Sq W8 255 A5
South End W8 113 D3 255 D6
Croydon CR0 221 A4
Southend Cl SE9 166 D5
South End Cl NW3 70 C4
Southend Cres SE9 166 D5
South End Gn NW3 70 C4
Southend La SE6 185 C6
Southend Rd E6 78 B1
South End Rd NW3 70 C4
Southend Rd
Beckenham BR3 185 C2
Woodford IG8 37 D1
Southend Road (North Circular Rd) E17,E18 36 C2
South End Row W8 113 D3 255 D6
Southern Ave
East Bedfont TW14 150 A3
South Norwood SE25 205 D6
Southerngate Way SE14 141 A5
Southern Gr E3 97 B3
Southernhay IG10 21 D6
Southern Perimeter Rd
Harlington TW14,TW6 14
Harlington TW19,TW6 14
Stanwell TW6 14
Southern Rd E13 9
N2 4
Southern Road Inf Sch E13 9
Southern Road Prim Sch E13 9
Southern Row W10 9
Southern St N1 23
Southern Way SE10 12
Romford RM7 5
Southerton Rd W6 11
South Esk Rd E7 7
Southey Ho SE17 26
Southey Rd N15 5
SW9 13
Merton SW19 17
Southey St SE20 18
Southfield EN5 1
Southfield Cl UB8 8
Southfield Cotts W7 10
Southfield Gdns TW1, TW2 17
Southfield Pk HA2 4
Southfield Prim Sch W4 11
Southfield Rd W4 11
Enfield EN3 1
St Paul's Cray BR7 21
Southfields Hendon NW4 4
Thames Ditton KT8 19
Southfields Ave TW15 17
Southfields Com Coll SW18 15
Southfields Ct SM3 21
Southfields Rd SW18 15
Southfields Sta SW18 1
Southfleet Rd BR6 22
South Gate Ave TW13 17
Southgate Cir 3 N14
Southgate Coll N14
Southgate Ct N1
Southgate Gr N1
Southgate Ho 7 E17 5
Southgate Rd N1 73 B1 23
Southgate Sch EN4
Southgate Sta N14
Southgate Way N2
South Gdns
Mitcham SW19 18
Wembley HA9
South Gipsy Rd DA16 14
South Glade DA5 16
South Gn NW9 2
South Gr E17
N15
N6 4
South Greenford Sta UB6
South Grove Ho N6
South Grove Prim Sch E17
South Hampstead High S
NW3
South Hampstead Jun S
NW3 7
South Hampstead Sta NW8 7
South Harringay Jun &
Schs N4 5
South Harrow Sta HA2 6
South Hill BR7 18
South Hill Ave HA1,HA2 6
South Hill Gr HA1 6
South Hill Pk NW3 7
South Hill Pk Gdns NW3
South Hill Rd BR2 20
Southholme Cl SE19 18
Southill La HA5
Southill Rd BR7 18
Southill St E14
South Island Pl SW9 13
South Kensington Sta SW7 114 B2 25
South Kenton Sta HA9
South La Kingston KT1 19
New Malden KT3 1
Southlake Prim Sch SE2 1
South Lambeth Pl SW8 2
South Lambeth Rd SW8 138 A5 2
Southland Rd SE18 14
Southlands Ave BR6 22
Southlands Coll SW15 1
Southlands Dr SW19 1
Southlands Gr BR1 2
Southlands Rd BR1, BR2 20
Southland Way TW7 1
South La W KT3 1
South Lo NW8 2
6 New Barnet EN5

South Lo *continued*
Twickenham TW2 152 A5
South Lodge Ave CR4, CR7,SW16 204 A5
South Lodge Cres EN2 3 D1
South Lodge Dr N14 15 D6
South London Montessori Sch SW11 267 A1
South London Tamil Sch CR0 205 A2
South Mall The N9 18 A1
South Mead NW9 27 D2
West Ewell KT19 215 D1
Southmead Prim Sch SW19 157 A3
Southmead Rd SW19 157 A3
South Merton Sta SW20 201 B6
South Molton La W1 93 B1 238 C1
South Molton Rd E16 99 A1
South Molton St W1 93 B1 238 C1
Southmont Rd KT10 212 C5
Southmoor Way E9 75 B3
South Mount N20 14 A2
South Norwood Ctry Pk* SE25 206 C5
South Norwood Hill SE19,SE25 183 D1
South Norwood Prim Sch SE25 206 A5
South Oak Rd SW16 182 B6
Southold Rise SE9 166 B1
Southolm St SW11 137 B4 268 D1
South Ordnance Rd EN3 7 C5
Southover BR1 187 A5
N12 29 C6
South Par W4 111 B2
Edgware HA8 26 C1
South Parade SW3 114 B1 256 D2
South Park Cres Catford SE6 164 D3
Ilford IG1 79 C5
South Park Ct 24 BR3 185 C3
South Park Dr Barking IG11 79 C4
Ilford IG3 79 C5
South Park Gr KT3 199 A5
South Park Hill Rd CR2 221 B4
South Park Mews SW6 135 D2
South Park Prim Sch IG3 79 C5
South Park Rd Ilford IG1 79 B5
Wimbledon SW19 179 D4
South Park Terr IG1 79 C5
South Park Villas IG3 79 C4
South Park Way HA4 62 C3
South Pl EC2 95 B2 242 D3
Enfield EN3 18 C6
Surbiton KT5 198 B2
South Pl Mews EC2 242 D3
Southport Rd SE18 123 B2
South Quay Plaza E14 119 D4
South Quay Sta E14 119 D4
South Rd W5 109 D2
Edgware HA8 26 D2
Edmonton N9 18 A3
Feltham TW13 172 D5
Forest Hill SE23 162 D2
Hampton TW12 173 B4
Mitcham SW19 180 B4
Southall UB1 107 B5
Twickenham TW2 152 B1
West Drayton UB7 104 C3
Heston TW5 128 D6
South Residence IG3 58 B4
Southridge Pl SW20 178 D3
South Rise W2 247 B6
South Rise Prim Sch SE18 123 B1
South Rise Way SE18 123 B2
South Row SE3 142 D3
South Ruislip Sta HA4 62 C3
Southsea Rd KT1 198 A5
South Sea St SE16 119 B3
Southside N7 71 D4
South Side W6 111 D3
Southside Comm SW19 178 D4
Southside Ind Est SW8 269 A2
Southside Quarter 4 SW11 136 D3
Southspring SE9 167 B4
South Sq NW11 47 D3
WC1 241 A3
South St BR1 187 A1
W1 115 A5 248 B4
Enfield EN3 18 D6
Isleworth TW7 131 A2
South Tenter St E1 95 D1 243 D1
South Terr N22 31 D1
South Terr *continued*
SW7 114 C2 257 A4
Surbiton KT6 198 A3
South Thames Coll SW18 157 D6
Putney SW15 156 D6
South Tottenham Sta N15 51 D4
South Vale Harrow HA1 64 C4
West Norwood SE19 183 C4
Southvale Rd SE3 142 C3
South View BR1 187 C1
Wimbledon SW19 178 D4
Southview Ave NW10 67 D3
Southview Cl SW17 181 A5
South View Cl DA5 169 B5
South View Cres IG2 56 D3
South View Ct
8 Forest Hill SE23 162 C3
South Norwood SE19 183 A3
Southview Dr E18 55 B6
Southview Gdns SM6 219 C1
South View Rd N8 50 A6
Southview Rd BR1 186 B6
South View Rd HA5 22 B4
South Villas NW1 71 D2
Southville SW8 137 D4 269 D1
Southville Cl East Bedfont TW14 149 C3
West Ewell KT19 215 B1
Southville Cres TW14 149 C3
Southville Jun Sch TW14 149 D3
Southville Rd East Bedfont TW14 149 C4
Thames Ditton KT7 197 B2
Southwark Bridge SE1,EC4 117 A6 252 B5
Southwark Bridge Office Village SE1 252 B3
Southwark Bridge Rd SE1 117 A5 252 B3
Southwark Cath* SE1 117 B5 252 C4
Southwark Coll SE1 116 D4 251 C2
SE15 140 B5
Southwark Coll (Blackfriars Ctr) SE1 251 C3
Southwark Coll (Camberwell Ctr) SE5 139 C5
Southwark Coll (Grange Ctr) SE1 263 B5
Southwark Coll (Surrey Docks Ctr) SE16 118 B3
Southwark Park Est 11 SE16 118 B2
Southwark Park Prim Sch SE16 118 B3
Southwark Park Rd SE16 118 A2 263 D4
Southwark Pl BR1 210 B6
Southwark St SE1 117 A5 252 A3
Southwater Cl 8 E14 97 B1
Beckenham BR3 185 D3
Southway N20 13 C2
NW11 47 D4
South Way N11 31 C4
N9 18 C2
Southway Hayes BR2 209 A2
Wallington SM6 219 C4
West Barnes SW20 200 D5
South Way Croydon CR0 223 A5
Harrow HA2 41 C5
Wembley HA9 66 C3
Southwell Ave UB5 63 C2
Southwell Gdns SW7 256 A3
Southwell Grove Rd E11 76 C6
Southwell Ho 13 N16 73 C3
8 SE16 118 B2
Southwell Rd SE5 139 A2
Harrow HA3 43 D3
Thornton Heath CR0 204 C3
South Western Rd TW1 153 B5
Southwest Rd E11 54 B1
South Wharf Rd W2 92 B1 236 D2
Southwick Mews W2 236 D2
Southwick Pl W2 237 A1
Southwick St W2 92 C1 237 A2
Southwick Yd W2 237 A1
South Wimbledon Sta SW19 179 D3
South Wlk Coney Hall BR4 224 C5
Hayes UB3 83 B2
Southwold Dr IG11 80 A3
Southwold Mans W9 91 C4
Southwold Prim Sch E5 74 B6
Southwold Rd DA5 169 D5
E5 74 C6
Southwood Ave N6 49 B2
Kingston KT2,KT3 177 A2
Southwood Cl BR1 210 B5
North Cheam KT4 200 D1
Southwood Ct EC1 234 C1
NW11 47 D4
Southwood Dr KT5 199 A1
South Woodford Sta E18 37 B1
Southwood Gdns Hinchley Wood KT10 213 A5
Ilford IG2 56 D5
Southwood Hall N6 49 A3
Southwood Ho SE9 166 D2
W11 244 A6
Southwood Hospl (Geriatric) N6 49 A2
Southwood Hts N6 49 B2
Southwood La N6 49 A2
Southwood Lawn Rd N6 49 B2
Southwood Mans N6 49 B3
Southwood Park N6 49 A2
Southwood Prim Sch RM9 81 A4
Southwood Rd SE9 166 D2
Woolwich SE28 124 B5
Southwood Smith Ho 4 E2 96 B4
Southwood Smith St N1 234 C5
South Worple Way SW14 133 B2
Southwyck Ho SW9 138 C1
South Yd EC1 242 C4
Sovereign Bsns Ctr EN3 7 B2
Sovereign Cl Ealing W5 87 C2
Ruislip HA4 39 C1
Stepney E1 118 B6
Sovereign Cres SE16 119 A6
Sovereign Ct BR2 210 B3
East Molesey KT8 195 B5
Harlington UB7 126 D5
3 Richmond TW9 132 B1
Stepney E1 118 B6
Sovereign Gr HA0 65 D5
Sovereign Ho 23 E1 96 B3
NW7 27 B6
SE18 122 B3
Ashford TW15 170 A6
3 Wimbledon SW19 179 A4
Sovereign Mews 6 E2 95 D5
Barnet EN4 2 D2
Sovereign Pk NW10 88 D3
Sovereign Pl HA1 42 D4
Sovereign Rd IG11 102 C4
Sowerby Cl SE9 166 B6
Space Waye TW14 150 B6
Spa Cl SE19 183 C2
Spa Ct 12 SE16 118 A3
Spafield St EC1 241 A6
Spa Hill CR7,SE19 183 B2
Spalding Cl HA8 27 C3
Spalding Ct HA8 26 B6
Spalding Ho SE4 163 A6
Spalding Rd NW4 46 C3
Streatham SW17 181 B5
Spanby Rd E3 97 C3
Spangate SE3 142 D2
Spaniards Cl NW11 48 B1
Spaniards End NW3 48 B1
Spaniards Rd NW3 70 A6
Spanish Pl W1 238 B2
Spanish Rd SW18 158 A6
Spa Rd SE16 117 D3 263 D5
Sparkbridge Rd HA1 42 C5
Sparke Terr 2 E16 98 D1
Sparkford Gdns N11 31 A5
Sparkford Ho SW11 266 D2
Sparks Cl W3 89 B1
Dagenham RM8 80 D6
Hampton TW12 173 A4
Sparrow Cl TW12 173 A4
Sparrow Dr BR5 211 B1
Sparrow Farm Com Jun Sch KT17 216 B4
Sparrow Farm Dr TW14 150 D4
Sparrow Farm Inf Sch TW14 150 C4
Sparrow Farm Jun Sch TW14 150 C4
Sparrow Farm Rd KT17,KT4 216 B4
Sparrow Gn RM10 81 D5
Sparrow's Farm L Ctr SE9 167 A4
Sparrows Herne WD23 8 A4
Sparrows La SE9 167 A3
Sparrows Way WD23 8 A4
Sparsholt Rd N19 50 B1
Barking IG11 101 C6
Sparta St SE10 142 A4
Spa Sch SE1 118 A2
Spa View 6 SW16 160 B1
Speakers' Corner* W1 114 D6 247 D6
Speaker's Ct 8 CR0 205 B1
Speakman Ho SE4 141 A2
Spearman St 8 SE18 144 C6
Spear Mews SW5 113 C2 255 B3
Spearpoint Gdns IG2 57 D5
Spears Rd N19 50 A1
Speart La TW5 129 A5
Spectrum Ho NW5 71 A4
Spedan Cl NW3 70 A5
Speechly Mews E8 73 D3
Speed Ho EC2 242 B4
Speedwell Ct 7 N12 29 D6
Speedwell Ho 9 N12 29 D6
Speedwell St 5 SE8 141 C5
Speedy Pl WC1 233 A1
Speer Rd KT7 196 D3
Speirs Cl KT3 199 D3
Spekehill SE9 166 B1
Speke Rd CR7 183 B1
Speldhurst Cl 2 BR2 208 D4
Speldhurst Rd E9 74 D1
W4 111 B3
Spellbrook Wlk N1 235 B6
Spelman Ho 14 E1 96 A2
Spelman St E1 96 A2
Spelthorne Coll TW15 170 B6
Spelthorne Cty Inf Sch TW15 171 B4
Spelthorne Gr TW16 171 D3
Spelthorne La TW15, TW17 171 A2
Spence Cl SE16 119 B4
Spencer Ave Bowes Park N13 32 B4
Hayes UB4 84 A2
Spencer Cl BR6 227 D6
N3 29 C1
Ealing NW10 88 B4
Woodford IG8 37 C5
Spencer Ct 5 BR6 227 A3
Wimbledon SW20 178 B2
Spencer Dr N2 48 A3
Spencer Gdns SW14 155 A6
Spencer Hill SW19 179 A3
Spencer Hill Rd SW19 179 A3
Spencer Ho NW3 70 B5
NW4 46 B4
31 SW8 137 D3
24 Putney SW19 156 D3
Wimbledon SW19 156 D1
Spencer Mews W6 264 A6
Spencer Park Ct SW18 158 B6
Spencer Pk SW18 158 B6
Spencer Pl 10 N1 72 D1
SW1 259 B5
Thornton Heath CR0 205 B2
Spencer Rd E6 99 D6
N11 31 B6
N8 50 B4
SW18 158 B6
W3 111 A5
Bromley BR1 186 D3
Carshalton CR4 203 A2
Chingford E17 36 A1
Chiswick W4 133 A5
East Molesey KT8 196 A4
Harrow HA3 24 C1
Hounslow TW3,TW5, TW7 130 A4
Ilford IG3 57 D1
Mitcham CR4 203 A6
South Croydon CR2 221 C3
Tottenham N17 34 A2
Twickenham TW2 152 C2
Wembley HA0 65 C6
Wimbledon SW20 178 B2
Spencer Rise NW5 71 B5
Spencer St EC1 94 D4 234 C1
Southall UB2 106 D4
Spencer Wlk 15 NW3 70 A4
Putney SW15 134 D1
Spenlow Ho 2 SE16 118 A3
Spenser Ct 5 TW10 175 D6
Spenser Gr N16 73 C4
Spenser Mews SE21 161 B3
Spenser Rd SE24 160 D6
Spenser St SW1 259 B6
Spens Ho WC1 240 C5
Spensley Wlk N16 73 B5
Speranza St SE18 123 D1
Sperling Rd N17 33 C1
Spert St E14 119 A6
Speyside N14 15 C5
Spey St E14 98 A2
Spezia Rd NW10 90 A5
Spice Ct 2 E1 118 A5
10 SW11 136 A2
Spice Quay Heights SE1 253 D3
Spicer Cl SE5,SW9 138 D3
Walton-on-T KT12 194 C3
Spicer Ct EN1 5 C2
Spices Yd CR0 221 A4
Spigurnell Rd N17 33 B2
Spikes Bridge Rd UB1 107 A6
Spilsby Cl NW9 27 C1
Spindle Cl SE18 122 A3
Spindle Ho 8 DA15 168 A1
Spindlewood Gdns CR0 221 C4
Spindrift Ave E14 119 D2
Spinel Cl SE18 123 D1
Spinnaker Cl IG11 102 B4
Spinnaker Ct 2 KT1 175 D2
Spinnaker Ho E14 119 C4
Spinnells Rd HA2 41 B1
Spinney Cl Beckenham BR3 207 D5
New Malden KT3 199 C4
Worcester Park KT4 215 D6
Yiewsley UB7 104 A6
Spinney Dr TW14 149 A4
Spinney Gdns Dagenham RM9 81 A3
Dulwich SE19 183 D5
Spinney Oak BR1 188 A1
Spinneys The BR1 188 B1
Spinney The DA14 191 A5
Barnes SW13 134 B6
Barnet EN5 1 D3
Cheam SM3 216 C4
Southgate N21 16 C4
Stanmore HA7 26 A6
Streatham SW16 159 D1
Sunbury TW16 172 A2
Wembley HA0 65 A5
Spire Ct 10 TW10 154 A5
Spire Ho W2 246 B6
Spires The EN5 1 A2
Spirit Quay E1 118 B5
Spital Sq E1 95 C2 243 B4
Spital St E1 96 A2
Spital Yd E1 243 B4
Spitfire Est The TW5 106 C1
Spitfire Rd SM6 220 B1
Spitfire Way TW5 106 C1
Splendour Wlk SE16 118 C1
Spode Ho SE11 261 A5
Spode Wlk NW3 69 D3
Spondon Rd N15 52 A5
Spoonbill Way UB4 84 D2
Spooner 8 NW9 27 D3
Spooner Ho TW5 129 C6
Spooner Wlk SM6 219 D3
Sporle Ct 6 SW11 136 B2
Sportsbank St SE6 164 A4
Spottons Gr N17 33 A2
Spout Hill CR0 223 C3
Spratt Hall Rd E11 55 A3
Spray St SE18 122 D2
Spreighton Rd KT8 195 D5
Sprewell SW15 157 A5
Spriggs Ho 14 N1 72 D1
Sprimont Pl SW3 114 D2 257 C2
Springall St 9 SE15 140 B5
Springalls Wharf 2 SE16 118 A4
Springbank N21 16 B5
Springbank Rd SE13 164 C5
Springbank Wlk NW1 71 D1
Springbourne Ct BR3 186 A2
Spring Bridge Rd W5 109 D6
Spring Cl Barnet EN5 12 D6
Dagenham RM8 58 D1
Springclose La SM3 217 A2
Spring Cnr TW13 149 D1
Spring Cott 10 W12 112 A4
Spring Cotts KT6 197 D4
Spring Court Rd EN2 4 C5
Springcroft Ave N2 48 D5
Spring Ct Ealing W7 108 B6
10 Wanstead E18 55 B6
Springdale Rd N16 73 B4
Spring Dr HA5 40 A3
Springett Ho 15 SW2 160 B6
Springfield E5 52 B1
Bushey WD23 8 B3
South Norwood SE25 206 A6
Springfield Ave N10 49 C6
Hampton TW12 173 D4
Merton SW20 201 B6
Springfield Cl N12 29 D5
Stanmore HA7 9 A1
Springfield Ct E5 52 B1
NW3 70 C1
7 W3 89 A1
2 Ilford IG1 78 D3
9 Kingston KT1 198 A6
Wallington SM6 219 B3
Springfield Dr IG2 57 A3
Springfield Gdns BR1 210 B5
E5 52 B1
NW9 45 B4
Ruislip HA4 40 B1
West Wickham BR4 223 D6
Woodford IG8 37 C3
Springfield Gr SE7 143 C6
Sunbury TW16 172 A2
Springfield Ho 1 SE5 139 C3
W3 111 A5
Springfield Hospl SW17 158 C1
Springfield La NW6 91 D6
Springfield Mount NW9 45 C4
Springfield Pl KT3 199 A5
Springfield Rd BR1 210 B5
DA16 146 B2
DA7 147 D1
E15 98 C4
E17 53 B3
E6 78 B1
N11 31 C5
N15 52 A5
NW8 92 A6 229 B5
Ashford TW15 170 B5
Chingford E4 20 C4
Ealing W7 108 C5
Harrow HA1 42 C3
Hayes UB4 106 C5
Kingston KT1 198 A6
Penge SE26 184 B5
South Norwood CR7 183 A2
6 Teddington TW11 175 A5
Twickenham TW2 151 C3
Wallington SM6 219 B3
Wimbledon SW19 179 B5
Springfield Rise SE26 162 B1
Springfields 9 EN5 13 D6
Springfield Wlk 3 BR6 211 B1
NW6 91 D6
Spring Gdns N5 73 A3
SW1 116 A5 250 A4
East Molesey KT8 196 A5
Wallington SM6 219 C3
Woodford IG8 37 C3
Spring Gr Brentford W4 132 C6
Hampton TW12 173 D2
Loughton IG10 21 D5
Mitcham CR4 181 A2
Spring Grove Cres TW3,TW5 130 A4
Spring Grove Prim Sch TW7 130 B3
Spring Grove Rd Hounslow TW3,TW5, TW7 130 A4
Richmond TW10 154 B6
Springhallow Sch W13 87 A1
Spring Hill E5 52 A2
Forest Hill SE26 184 C6
Springhill Cl SE5 139 B2
Spring Ho WC1 234 A1
Merton SW19 179 B2
Springhurst Cl CR0 223 B4
Spring La E5 52 B1
N10 49 A6
Croydon SE25 206 B3
Spring Lake HA7 25 B6
Spring Mews W1 237 D4
Spring Park Ave CR0 222 D6
Springpark Dr N4 51 A1
Beckenham BR3 208 A6
Spring Park Prim Sch CR0 223 C5
Spring Park Rd CR0 222 D6
Spring Pl N3 47 C6
NW5 71 B3
Springpond Rd RM9 81 A3
Spring Rd TW13 149 D1
Springrice Rd SE13 164 B5
Spring Shaw Rd BR5 190 A2
Spring St W2 92 B1 236 C1
Spring Terr TW10 154 A6
Spring Vale DA7 147 D1
Springvale Ave TW8 110 A1
Springvale Ct SE12 143 A1
Springvale Terr 5 W14 112 D3
Spring Villa Rd HA8 26 C3
Springwater WC1 240 C4
Springwater Cl SE18 144 C4
Springway HA1 42 B2
Springwell Ave NW10 89 D6
Springwell Cl SW16 182 B6
Springwell Ct TW5 128 D3
Springwell Jun & Inf Schs TW5 129 A5
Springwell Rd Heston TW5 128 D4
West Norwood SW16 182 C5
Spring Wlk E1 96 A2
Springwood Cres HA8 11 A2
Springwood Ct CR2 221 C4
Sprowston Mews E7 77 A3
Sprowston Rd E7 77 A3
Spruce Ct W5 110 A3
Sprucedale Gdns CR0 222 D4
Spruce Hills Rd E17 36 A1
Spruce Ho 15 SE16 118 D4
Spruce Pk BR2 208 D5
Sprules Rd SE4 141 A3
Spurfield KT8 195 D6
Spurgeon Ave SE19 183 B2
Spurgeon Rd SE19 183 B3
Spurgeon's Coll SE25 183 C1
Spurgeon St SE1 117 B3 262 C6
Spurling Rd SE22 139 D1
Dagenham RM9 81 B2
Spur Rd N15 51 B5

Spur Rd *continued*
SE1 116 C4 251 A2
Brentford TW7 131 B5
Edgware HA8 26 A6
Feltham TW14 128 B1
Wallend IG11 101 A4
Spurstowe Rd E8 74 B2
Spurstowe Terr E8 74 B3
Spurway Par 2 IG2 56 B4
Square Rigger Row 7
SW11 136 A2
Square The SW6 265 A1
W6 112 C1
Hayes UB11 105 B5
Ilford IG1 56 C2
12 Richmond TW10 153 D6
Wallington SM5 219 A3
Woodford IG8 37 A5
Squarey St SW17 158 A1
Squire Ct 2 CR0 205 C1
Squire Gdns NW8 229 C1
Squire's Almshouses 7
E17 53 D5
Squires Bridge Rd
KT17 192 B5
Squires Ct N3 30 A2
SW4 270 B1
Wimbledon SW19 179 C6
Squires Ho 3 SE18 144 D6
Squires La N3 30 A2
Squire's Mount NW3 70 B5
Squire's Rd TW17 192 C5
Squires The RM7 59 D3
Squires Wlk TW15 171 B3
Squires Wood Dr BR7 188 B3
Squirrel Cl TW4 128 C2
Squirrel Mews W13 109 A6
Squirrels Cl N12 30 A6
Hillingdon UB10 60 C1
Orpington BR6 211 C1
Squirrels Ct 4 KT4 215 D6
Squirrels Gn KT4 216 A6
Squirrel's La IG9 21 D1
Squirrels The SE13 142 B2
Bushey WD23 8 B5
Pinner HA5 41 B6
Squirrels Trad Est
UB3 105 D3
Squirries St E2 96 A4
Stable Cl UB5 85 C5
Stable Mews SE27 183 A5
Stables End BR6 227 A5
Stables The IG9 21 C4
Stables Way
SE11 116 C1 261 A2
Stable Way W10 90 C1
Stable Wlk N2 30 B2
Stable Yd Rd
SW1 115 C4 249 B2
Staburn Ct HA8 27 A1
Stacey Ave N18 34 C6
Stacey Cl E10 54 B4
Stacey St N7 72 C5
WC2 93 D1 239 D1
Stack Ho SW1 258 B3
Stackhouse St SW1 257 C6
Stacy Path 21 SE5 139 C5
Staddon Ct BR3 207 A5
Stadium Bsns Ctr HA9 66 D5
Stadium Rd SE7,SE18 144 B6
Stadium Ret Pk HA9 66 C5
Stadium St
SW10 136 A5 266 B3
Stadium Way HA9 66 C4
Staffa Rd E10 53 A1
Stafford Cl E17 53 B3
NW6 91 C4
Cheam SM3 217 A2
Southgate N14 15 C6
Stafford Cripps Ho
30 E2 96 C4
SW6 264 D5
Stafford Cross CR0 220 B3
Stafford Ct SW8 270 A2
W8 255 B6
Ealing W7 86 D1
Stafford Gdns CR0 220 B3
Stafford Ho SE1 263 D2
Stafford Mans SW11 267 C3
13 SW4 138 A1
13 W14 112 D3
Stafford Morris Ho 9
E15 98 C6
Stafford Pl
SW1 115 C3 259 A6
Richmond TW10 154 B4
Stafford Rd E3 97 B5
E7 77 D2
NW6 91 C4
Croydon CR0 220 C4
Harrow HA3 24 A3
Kingston KT3 199 A6
Ruislip HA4 61 D4
Sidcup DA14 189 C6
Wallington CR0,SM6 220 A3
Staffordshire St SE15 140 A4
Staffordshire St *continued*
SE15 140 B4
Stafford St W1 249 A4
Stafford Terr
W8 113 C3 255 A6
Stag Cl HA8 27 A1
Stagg Hill EN4 2 C6
Stag La Chigwell IG9 21 B2
Edgware HA8,NW9 45 A6
Roehampton SW15 155 D2
Stag Lane Fst & Mid Schs
HA8 26 C1
Stag Pl SW1 115 C3 259 A6
Stags Ct KT7 197 A2
Stagshaw Ho 17 SE22 139 C2
Stags Way TW7 130 D6
Stainbank Rd CR4 203 B6
Stainby Cl UB7 104 A3
Stainby Rd N15 51 D5
Stainer Ho SE9 143 C1
Stainer St SE1 252 D3
Staines Ave SM3 216 D6
Staines By-Pass
TW15 170 A4
Staines Rd
East Bedfont TW14 149 B4
Feltham TW14,TW3 150 C6
Ilford IG1 79 B4
Twickenham TW13,TW2 151 D1
Hounslow TW3 129 C1
Twickenham TW2 152 A1
Staines Rd E TW12,
TW16 172 C2
Staines Rd W TW15 171 B3
Staines Wlk DA14 190 C4
Stainford Cl TW15 171 B5
Stainforth Rd E17 53 C5
Ilford IG2 57 B2
Staining La EC2 242 B2
Stainmore Cl BR7 189 B2
Stainsbury St 26 E2 96 C5
Stainsby Pl E14 97 C1
Stainsby Rd E14 97 C1
Stainton Rd Enfield EN3 6 C4
Lewisham SE13 164 B4
Stalbridge Ho NW1 232 A3
Stalbridge St NW1 237 B4
Stalham St SE16 118 B3
Stambourne Ho SW8 270 B2
Stambourne Way
Penge SE19 183 D3
West Wickham BR4 224 A5
Stamford Bridge Stadium
(Chelsea FC)
SW6 135 D5 265 C4
Stamford Brook Ave
W6 111 D3
Stamford Brook Gdns 1
W6 111 D3
Stamford Brook Mans 2
W6 111 D2
Stamford Brook Rd
W6 111 D3
Stamford Brook Sta
W6 111 D2
Stamford Cl N15 52 A5
2 NW3 70 A5
Harrow HA3 24 C3
Southall UB1 107 C6
Stamford Ct W6 112 A2
Edgware HA8 26 B6
Stamford Dr BR2 208 D5
Stamford Gdns RM9 80 C1
Stamford Grove E 1
N16 52 A1
Stamford Grove W 4
N16 52 A1
Stamford Hill N16 51 D1
Stamford Hill Mans 1
N16 51 D1
Stamford Hill Prim Sch
N15 51 B3
Stamford Hill Sta N16 51 C2
Stamford Ho N15 52 A5
Stamford Hospl W6 112 A2
Stamford Lo 2 N16 51 D2
Stamford Mans 2 N16 52 A1
Stamford Rd E6 100 A6
N1 73 C2
N15 52 A4
Dagenham RM9 80 C1
Stamford St
SE1 116 C5 251 B4
Stamp Pl E2 95 D4
Stanard Cl N16 51 C2
Stanborough Cl TW12 173 B4
Stanborough Ho 4 E3 97 D3
Stanborough Pas E8 73 D2
Stanborough Rd TW3,
TW7 130 B2
Stanbridge Mans
SW15 134 C2
Stanbridge Pl N21 16 D2
Stanbridge Rd SW15 134 C2
Stanbrook Ct W1 249 A4
Stanbrook Rd SE2 124 B4
Stanburn Fst & Mid Schs
HA7 25 C3
Stanbury Ct 16 NW3 70 D2
Stanbury Rd SE15 140 B3
SE15 140 C3
Stancroft NW9 45 C4
Standale Gr HA4 39 A4
Standard Ind Est E16 122 B4
Standard Pl 14 EC2 95 C4
Standard Rd DA6 147 A1
NW10 89 B3
Belvedere DA17 125 C1
Enfield EN3 7 A6
Hounslow TW4 129 A2
Standen Rd SW18 157 C4
Standfield Gdns RM10 81 C2
Standfield Rd RM10 81 C3
Standish Ho SE9 143 B1
6 W6 112 A2
Standish Rd W6 112 A2
Standlake Point 1
SE23 162 D1
Stane Cl SW19 179 D3
Stanedge Ct SW16 182 A5
Stanesgate Ho 20
SE15 140 A5
Stanetto Ct 3 RM6 58 B2
Stane Way SE18 144 A5
Stanfield Ho NW8 236 D6
9 Northolt UB5 84 D5
Stanfield Rd 13 E3 97 A5
Stanford Cl
Hampton TW12 173 B4
Romford RM7 59 D3
Ruislip HA4 39 A3
Stanford Ct N11 31 A5
SW6 265 D1
W8 255 D5
Stanford Ho IG11 102 B5
Stanford Pl
SE1 117 C2 263 A3
Stanford Rd N11 30 D5
W8 113 D3 255 D6
Thornton Heath SW16 182 A1
Stanford St SW1 259 C3
Stanford Way SW16 181 D1
Stangate Cres WD6 11 C6
Stangate Gdns HA7 25 B6
Stangate Lo N21 16 B4
Stangate Mansi TW1 152 D1
Stanger Rd SE25 206 A5
Stanhope Ave N3 47 B6
Harrow HA3 24 B2
Hayes BR2 209 A1
Stanhope Cl 28 SE16 118 D4
Stanhope Ct N3 29 B1
Stanhope Gate W1 248 B4
Stanhope Gdns N4 51 A3
N6 49 C3
NW7 27 D5
SW7 114 A2 256 B4
Dagenham RM8 81 B5
Redbridge IG1 56 B1
Stanhope Gr BR3 207 B5
Stanhope Ho 5 N11 31 B6
N6 49 C3
SE8 141 B5
4 Putney SW15 156 C6
Stanhope Mews E
SW7 114 A2 256 B4
Stanhope Mews S
SW7 256 B3
Stanhope Mews W
SW7 114 A2 256 B4
Stanhope Park Rd UB6 86 A3
Stanhope Pl W2 237 C1
Stanhope Prim Sch
UB6 86 A3
Stanhope Rd DA7 147 A3
E17 53 D4
N12 30 A5
N6 49 C2
Barnet EN5 12 D5
Dagenham RM8 81 B5
Sidcup DA15 190 A6
Southall UB6 86 A2
South Croydon CR0 221 C5
Wallington SM5 219 A1
Stanhope Row W1 248 C3
Stanhope St
NW1 93 C4 232 A1
Stanhope Terr
W2 114 B6 246 D6
Stanier Cl SW5 254 D1
Stanlake Rd W12 112 C5
Stanlake Villas W12 112 C5
Stanley Ave
Barking IG11 101 D5
Beckenham BR2,BR3 208 A6
Dagenham RM8 59 B2
Greenford UB6 86 A6
Wembley HA0 66 A1
West Barnes KT3 200 A4
Stanley Bldgs NW1 233 A3
Stanley Cl SW8 270 C5
Wembley HA0 66 A1
Stanley Cres
W11 113 B6 244 C6
Stanleycroft Cl TW7 130 C4
Stanley Ct
Belmont SM2 217 D1
11 Ealing W5 87 C2
Stanley Ct *continued*
Wallington SM5 219 A1
Wimbledon SW19 179 C4
Stanley Gardens Rd
TW11 174 C5
Stanley Gdns NW2 68 C3
W11 244 C6
W3 111 C4
Mitcham CR4 181 A4
Wallington SM6 219 C2
Stanley Gr SW11 137 A3
Thornton Heath CR0 204 C3
Stanley Ho E11 54 C3
18 E14 97 C1
35 SW8 137 D3
Stanley Horstead Twr
E10 75 D6
Stanley Inf Sch TW2 174 C6
Stanley Jun Sch TW2 174 C6
Stanley Mans SW10 266 B6
Upper Tooting SW17 158 D2
Stanley Park Dr HA0 88 B6
Stanley Park High Sch
SM5 219 A2
Stanley Park Inf Sch
SM5 218 D1
Stanley Park Jun Sch
SM5 218 D1
Stanley Park Rd SM5,
SM6 219 A1
Stanley Rd BR6 211 D1
E10 53 D3
E12 78 A3
E15 98 B6
N10 31 B3
N11 31 D5
N15 50 D5
N2 48 B6
2 NW9 46 A2
W3 111 A3
Ashford TW15 170 A5
Belmont SM2 217 D1
Bromley BR2 209 C5
Chingford E4 20 B3
Edmonton N9 17 D2
Enfield EN1 5 C2
Harrow HA2 64 A6
Ilford IG1 79 B6
Isleworth TW3 130 A1
Mitcham CR4 181 A3
Morden SM4 201 C5
Mortlake SW14 132 D1
Northwood HA6 22 A2
Sidcup DA14 168 A1
Southall UB1 107 A6
Teddington TW11,TW2 174 C5
Thornton Heath CR0 204 C3
Twickenham TW2 152 B1
Wallington SM5 219 A1
Wembley HA9 66 B2
Wimbledon SW19 179 C4
Woodford E18 36 D2
Stanley St SE14,SE8 141 B5
Stanley Studios SW10 266 B6
Stanley Tech High Sch for
Boys SE25 205 D6
Stanley Terr 7 N19 72 A6
Stanmer St SW11 136 C3
Stanmore Coll HA7 25 C4
Stanmore Gdns
Richmond TW9 132 B2
Sutton SM1 218 A5
Stanmore Hill HA7 25 A6
Stanmore Ho 21 SW8 137 D3
Stanmore Lo HA7 25 B6
Stanmore Pl NW1 231 D6
Stanmore Rd E11 54 D1
N15 50 D5
Richmond TW9 132 B2
Stanmore St N1 94 B6 233 C6
Stanmore Sta HA7 25 D6
Stanmore Terr 3 BR3 185 C1
Stannard Cotts 23 E1 96 C3
Stannard Mews E8 74 A2
Stannard Rd E8 74 A2
Stannary Pl SE11 261 B1
Stannary St
SE11 116 C1 261 B1
Stannet Way SM6 219 C4
Stansbury Ho 3 W10 91 A4
Stansfeld Ho SE1 263 D3
Stansfeld Rd E6 99 D1
Stansfield Rd SW9 138 B2
Cranford TW4,TW5 128 B3
Stansgate Rd RM10 81 C5
Stanstead Cl BR2 208 D3
Stanstead Gr SE23 163 B3
Stanstead Ho E3 98 A3
Stanstead Manor SM1 217 C2
Stanstead Rd
Forest Hill SE23,SE6 163 A3
Wanstead E11 55 B4
Stansted Cres DA5 168 D3
Stansted Rd TW6 148 B5
Stanswood Gdns SE5 139 C5
Stanthorpe Cl SW16 182 A5
Stanthorpe Rd SW16 182 A5
Stanton Ave TW11 174 C4
Stanton Cl
Chessington KT19 214 D3
North Cheam KT4 200 D1
Stanton Ct 5 DA15 168 A1
N16 51 B2
N3 29 C2
Stanton Ho 8 SE10 142 A6
Stanton Rd
Barnes SW13 133 D3
Thornton Heath CR0 205 A2
Wimbledon SW20 178 D2
Stanton Sq SE26 185 B6
Stanton Way SE26 185 B6
Stanway Ct 23 N1 95 C5
Stanway Gdns HA8 27 A5
Acton W3 110 C5
Stanway St N1 95 C5
Stanwell Rd
Ashford TW15 170 A6
East Bedfont TW14,
TW19,TW6 148 D4
Stanwell TW15 148 A1
Ashford TW15 148 A1
Stanwick Rd
W14 113 B2 254 C3
Stanworth Ct TW5 129 C5
Stanworth St SE1 253 D1
Stanyhurst SE23 163 A3
Stapelhurst Ho 18 E5 74 B3
Stapenhill Rd HA0 65 B5
Staplefield Cl
Pinner HA5 23 A3
3 Streatham SW2 160 A3
Stapleford N17 33 C1
Stapleford Ave IG2 57 C4
Stapleford Cl
Chingford E4 20 A1
Kingston KT1 198 C6
Putney SW19 157 A4
Stapleford Rd HA0 65 D1
Stapleford Way IG11 102 B4
Staplehurst Ct SW11 158 D5
Staplehurst Rd SE13 164 C6
Sutton SM5 218 C1
Staple Inn WC2 241 A3
Staple Inn Bldgs WC2 241 A3
Staples Cl SE16 119 A5
Staples Corner Bsns Pk
NW2 46 B1
Staples Corner (East)
NW2 46 B1
Staples Corner (West)
NW2 46 B1
Staple St SE1 117 B4 252 D1
Stapleton Gdns CR0 220 C3
Stapleton Hall N4 50 B2
Stapleton Hall Rd N4 50 B2
Stapleton Ho 19 E2 96 B4
Stapleton Rd DA7 147 B6
Orpington BR6 227 D5
Upper Tooting SW17 159 A1
Stapley Rd DA17 125 C1
Staplyton Rd EN5 1 A2
Star Alley EC3 253 B6
Star and Garter Hill
TW10 154 A4
Starboard Way E14 119 C3
Starcross St
NW1 93 C4 232 B1
Star Ct UB10 83 A3
Starfield Rd W12 112 A4
Star & Garter Mans
SW15 134 D2
Star La E16 98 C3
Starliner Ct N7 72 C2
Starling Cl
Buckhurst Hill IG9 21 A3
Pinner HA5 40 C6
Starling Ho NW8 230 A4
Starling Wlk TW12 173 A5
Starmans Cl RM9 103 A6
Star Path UB5 85 C5
Star Pl E1 118 A6
Star Prim Sch E16 98 C3
Star Rd W14 113 B1 254 C1
Hillingdon UB10 83 A3
Hounslow TW7 130 B3
Star St W2 92 C1 237 A2
Starts Cl BR6 226 C5
Starts Hill Ave BR6 226 D4
Starts Hill Rd BR6 226 D4
Starveall Cl UB7 104 B3
Star Works NW10 90 A4
Star Yd WC2 94 C1 241 A2
State Farm Ave BR6 227 A4
Staten Gdns TW1 152 D3
Statham Gr N16 73 B5
Edmonton N18 33 C5
Statham Ho SW8 269 A2
Stathard Ho 18 E1 96 C3
Station App BR6 227 D6
BR7 188 A4
BR7 188 C1
DA16 146 A3
DA7 147 A3
E17 53 C4
E7 77 B4
N11 31 B5
N12 29 D6
Station App *continued*
NW10 89 D4
SE3 143 B2
SE9 166 B3
Ashford TW15 170 B6
5 Beckenham BR3 185 C2
Belmont SM2 217 A1
Fulham SW6 135 A2
Greenford UB6 64 B1
Hampton TW12 173 C2
Hayes BR2 209 A1
Hayes UB3 105 D3
Hinchley Wood KT10 212 D5
4 Kingston KT1,KT2 176 C2
New Barnet EN5 2 A1
6 New Malden KT4 200 A1
Penge SE26 185 B5
Pinner HA5 41 A6
Richmond TW9 132 C4
Ruislip HA4 39 D1
Ruislip HA4 62 B3
Shepperton TW17 193 A4
3 South Croydon CR0 221 B6
Streatham SW16 181 D5
Sunbury TW16 172 A2
1 Surbiton KT6 198 A3
Wanstead E11 55 A4
Wembley HA0 65 B2
2 Woodford E18 37 B1
Woodford IG9 37 D6
Worcester Park KT19 216 A3
Yiewsley UB7 104 A5
Station App Rd
SE1 116 C4 251 A2
Station Approach Rd
W4 133 A5
Station Ave 5 SW9 138 D2
Kingston KT3 199 C6
13 Richmond TW9 132 C4
West Ewell KT19 215 D1
Station Bldgs SW20 178 C1
Station Blgs W5 110 B5
Station Cl N3 29 C2
Hampton TW12 173 D2
Station Cres N15 51 B5
SE3 121 A1
Ashford TW15 170 A6
Wembley HA0 65 B2
Station Ct 1 E10 53 D2
5 SE15 140 C3
Stationers Hall Ct EC4 241 D1
Station Est
Beckenham BR3 206 D5
1 Woodford E18 37 B1
Station Estate Rd
TW14 150 B3
Station Gdns W4 133 A5
Station Hill BR2 225 A6
Station House Mews
N9 34 A6
Station Par 4 N14 15 D3
NW2 68 C2
Acton W3 88 C1
Ashford TW15 170 B6
Barking IG11 79 A1
Cockfosters EN4 3 A1
Dagenham RM10 81 C2
Ealing W5 110 B5
Edgware HA8 26 A3
Feltham TW14 150 B4
Harrow HA2 63 D4
Harrow HA3 25 A1
Richmond TW9 132 C4
Ruislip HA4 61 B6
4 Upper Tooting SW12 159 A3
2 Wanstead E11 55 A4
Woodford IG9 37 D6
Station Pas SE15 140 C4
Woodford E18 37 B1
Station Pl N4 72 C6
Station Rd BR1 187 A2
BR6 227 D6
DA7 147 A2
E10 76 A5
E12 78 A4
E17 53 A4
E7 77 A4
N11 31 B5
N17 52 A6
N19 71 C5
N3 29 C1
NW10 89 D5
NW4 46 A4
NW7 27 C4
SE13 142 A2
Ashford TW15 170 B6
Ashford TW16 172 A3
Barnes SW13 133 D3
Beckenham BR2 186 C1
Belvedere DA17 125 C3
Carshalton SM5 218 D4
Chessington KT9 214 A3
Chingford E4 20 B3
Claygate KT10 212 C3
Croydon CR0 205 A1
Dagenham RM6 58 D2
Ealing W5 88 B1
Ealing W7 108 C5
Edgware HA8 26 C4

Station Rd *continued*
Esher KT10 212 B6
Hampton TW12 173 D2
Harrow HA1 42 D4
Harrow HA1,HA2 41 D4
Hayes UB3 105 C2
Hounslow TW3 129 D1
Ilford IG1 78 D5
Ilford IG6 57 B6
Kingston KT2 176 C2
Merton SW19 180 A2
New Barnet EN5 13 D6
Penge SE20 184 C4
Shepperton TW17 193 A4
Sidcup DA14,DA15 168 A1
Southgate N21 16 D3
South Norwood SE25 205 D5
Teddington KT1 175 D2
Teddington TW11 175 A4
Thames Ditton KT7 196 D2
Twickenham TW1 152 D4
West Barnes KT3 200 B4
West Drayton UB7 104 A4
West Wickham BR4 208 A1
Wood Green N22 32 B1
Station Rd N DA17 125 D3
Station Rise SE27 160 D2
Station Sq BR5 211 A4
Station St E15 76 B1
E16 122 D5
Station Terr NW10 90 D5
SE5 139 A4
Station View UB6 86 B6
Station Way
Cheam SM2,SM3 217 A1
Woodford IG9 37 D6
Station Yd TW1 153 A4
Staunton Ho SE17 263 A3
Staunton Rd KT2 176 B3
Staunton St SE8 141 B6
Staveley NW1 232 A2
Staveley Cl E9 74 C3
N7 72 A4
SE15 140 C4
8 SE15 140 B4
Staveley Ct 4 E11 55 A4
Staveley Gdns W4 133 B4
Staveley Rd
Ashford TW15 171 B4
Chiswick W4 133 B5
Staverdale Lo W14 254 D6
Stavers Ho 18 E3 97 B5
Staverton Rd NW2 68 C1
Stave Yard Rd SE16 119 A5
Stavordale Rd N5 72 D4
Carshalton SM5 202 A2
Stayner's Rd E1 96 D3
Stayton Rd SM1 217 C5
Steadfast Rd KT1 175 D2
Steadman Ct EC1 242 B6
Steadman Ho 4 RM10 81 C5
Stead St SE17 117 B2 262 C3
Steam Farm La TW14 127 D1
Stean St E8 95 D6
Stebbing Ho 8 W11 112 D5
Stebbing Way IG11 102 A5
Stebondale St E14 120 A2
Stebon Prim Sch E14 97 C2
Stedham Pl WC1 240 A2
Stedman Cl UB10 60 C5
Steedman St
SE17 117 A2 262 A3
Steeds Rd N10 30 D2
Steele App IG11 102 B5
Steele Rd E11 76 C4
N17 51 C6
NW10 89 A5
W4 111 A3
Isleworth TW7 131 A1
Steele's Mews N NW3 70 D2
Steele's Mews S NW3 70 D2
Steele's Rd NW3 70 D2
Steele Wlk DA8 147 D5
Steel's La 23 E1 96 C1
Steen Way 7 SE22 161 C6
Steep Cl BR6 227 D2
Steep Hill
South Croydon CR0 221 C4
Streatham SW16 159 D1
Steeple Cl Fulham SW6 135 A3
Wimbledon SW19 179 A6
Steeple Ct 19 E1 96 B3
Steeplestone Cl N18 33 A5
Steeple Wlk N1 235 B6
Steerforth St SW18 158 A2
Steers Mead CR4 180 D2
Steers Way SE16 119 A4
Steetley Ct 14 SM2 218 A1
Steinman Ct TW7 130 D2
Stelfax Ho WC1 233 D2
Stella Rd SW17 180 D4
Stellar Ho 4 N17 33 D4
Stellman Cl E5 74 A5
Stembridge Rd SE20 184 B1
Sten Cl EN3 7 C6
Stephan Cl E8 96 A6
Stephen Cl BR6 227 D5
Stephen Ct 18 SW19 156 D3
Stephendale Rd SW6 136 A3
Stephen Fox Ho 7
W4 111 C1
Stephen Hawking Sch
E14 97 A1
Stephen Mews W1 239 C3
Stephen Pl SW4 137 C2
Stephen Saunders Ct
SW11 158 C6
Stephens Ct E16 98 D3
SE4 141 A2
Stephens Lo N12 14 A1
Stephenson Ct SM2 217 B1
Stephenson Ho
6 NW3 70 D3
2 NW5 71 B4
SE1 262 A6
SE2 124 D1
Stephenson Rd E17 53 A4
Ealing W7 86 D1
Twickenham TW4 151 C4
Stephenson St E16 98 C2
NW10 89 D4
Stephenson Way
NW1 93 C3 239 B6
Stephen's Rd E15 98 C6
Stephen St W1 239 C3
Stepney Cswy E1 96 D1
Stepney Day Hospl E1 96 C1
Stepney Gn E1 96 D2
Stepney Greencoat CE Prim Sch The E14 97 B1
Stepney Green Ct 3
E1 96 D2
Stepney Green Sch E1 96 D2
Stepney Green Sta E1 96 D3
Stepney High St E1 96 D2
Stepney Way E1 96 C2
Sterling Ave
Edgware HA8 26 B6
Upper Halliford TW17 193 C6
Sterling Cl NW10 68 A1
Sterling Gdns SE14 141 A6
Sterling Ho SE9 143 B1
Sterling Ind Est RM10 81 D4
Sterling Pl W5 110 A2
Sterling Rd EN2 5 B5
Sterling St SW7 257 B6
Sterling Way (North Circular Rd) N18 33 C5
Stern Cl IG11 102 C5
Sterndale Rd W14 112 D3
Sterne St W12 112 D4
Sternhall La SE15 140 A2
Sternhold Ave SW12,
SW2 159 D2
Sterry Cres RM10 81 C3
Sterry Dr
Thames Ditton KT7 196 C3
Worcester Park KT19 215 C4
Sterry Gdns RM10 81 C2
Sterry Rd Barking IG11 101 D6
Dagenham RM10 81 C3
Sterry St SE1 252 C1
Steucers La SE23 163 A3
Stevanne Ct 1 DA17 125 C1
Steve Biko Ct W10 90 D3
Steve Biko La SE6 185 C6
Steve Biko Rd N7 72 C5
Steve Biko Way TW3 129 C2
Stevedale Rd DA16 146 C3
Stevedore St 3 E1 118 B5
Stevenage Rd
Fulham SW6 134 D4
Wallend E6 78 C2
Stevens Ave E9 74 C2
Stevens Cl
Beckenham BR3 185 C4
Hampton TW12 173 B4
Pinner HA5 40 C4
Stevens Ct BR3 185 C4
Stevens Gn WD23 8 A3
Stevens Ho KT1 175 D1
Stevens' La KT10 213 A2
Stevenson Cl EN5 14 B5
Stevenson Cres SE16 118 B1
Stevenson Ho NW8 229 A6
1 SW11 136 D3
Wembley HA9 65 D6
Stevens Rd RM8 80 C5
Stevens St SE1 263 B6
Steventon Rd W12 111 D6
Stewards Holte Wlk 3
N11 31 B6
Steward St E1 95 C2 243 B4
Stewart Ave TW17 192 C5
Stewart Cl BR7 188 D6
NW9 45 A3
Hampton TW12 173 A4
Stewart Fleming Prim Sch
SE20 206 C6
Stewart Headlam Prim Sch
E1 96 B3
Stewart Ho SE1 263 A5
Stewart Quay UB3 105 C4
Stewart Rainbird Ho 1
E12 78 C3
Stewart Rd E15 76 B4
Stewartsby Cl N18 33 A5
Stewart's Gr
SW3 114 C1 257 A2
Stewart's Rd
SW8 137 C4 269 A2
Stewart St E14 120 A4
Stew La EC4 252 A6
Steyne Rd W3 110 D5
Steyning Gr SE9 188 B6
Steynings Way N12 29 C5
Steyning Way TW4 128 C1
Steynton Ave DA5 168 D2
Stickland Rd DA17 125 C2
Stickleton Cl UB6 85 D4
Stifford Ho E1 96 C2
Stilecroft Gdns HA0 65 B5
Stile Hall Gdns W4 110 C1
Stile Hall Par 6 W4 110 C1
Stileman Ho 4 E3 97 B2
Stile Path TW16 194 A5
Stiles Cl BR2 210 B3
Erith DA8 125 D1
Stillingfleet Rd SW13 134 A6
Stillington St
SW1 115 C2 259 B4
Stillness Jun & Inf Schs
SE23 163 A5
Stillness Rd SE23 163 B5
Stilwell Dr UB8 82 B3
Stilwell Rdbt UB8 104 D6
Stipularis Dr UB4 84 D3
Stirling Ave Pinner HA5 41 A2
Wallington SM6 220 A1
Stirling Cl SW16 181 C2
Stirling Cnr EN5,WD6 11 B5
Stirling Ct EC1 241 C6
WC2 240 C1
Ealing W13 109 B6
Stirling Gr TW3 130 A3
Stirling Ho 5 SE18 122 D1
Stirling Mans NW6 70 A2
Stirling Rd E13 99 B5
E17 53 A6
SW9 138 A3
W3 110 D3
Harrow HA3 42 D6
Hayes UB3 106 B6
Stanwell TW19,TW6 148 B5
Tottenham N17 34 A2
Tottenham N22 32 D2
Twickenham TW2 151 D4
Stirling Way
Borehamwood WD6 11 B6
Thornton Heath CR0 204 A2
Stiven Cres HA2 63 B5
Stoatley Ho 10 SW15 156 A3
Stockbeck NW1 232 B3
Stockbridge Ho EN2 4 D3
Stockbury Rd CR0 206 C3
Stockdale Rd RM8 81 B6
Stockdove Way UB6 86 D4
Stocker Gdns RM9 80 C1
Stock Exchange★
EC2 242 D1
Stockfield Rd
Claygate KT10 212 C3
Streatham SW16 160 B1
Stockholm Ho E1 118 A6
Stockholm Rd SE16 118 C1
Stockholm Way 9 E1 118 A5
Stockhurst Cl SW15 134 D3
Stockingswater La EN3 7 B2
Stockleigh Hall NW8 230 B4
Stockley Cl UB7 104 D4
Stockley Ctry Pk UB7 104 C6
Stockley Farm Rd
UB7 104 D3
Stockley Park Bsns Pk
UB11 105 A5
Stockley Rd UB7,UB8,
UB11 104 D4
Stock Orchard Cres N7 72 B3
Stock Orchard St N7 72 B3
Stockport Rd SW16 181 D2
Stocks Ct 5 E1 96 D3
Stocksfield Rd E17 54 A6
Stocks Pl 16 E14 119 B6
Hillingdon UB10 82 C6
Stock St E13 99 A5
Stockton Cl EN5 2 A1
Stockton Gdns NW7 11 C1
Tottenham N17 33 A3
Stockton Ho 16 E2 96 B4
Harrow HA2 41 C1
Stockton Rd
Edmonton N18 34 B4
Tottenham N17 33 A3
Stockwell Ave SW9 138 B2
Stockwell Cl BR1 187 B1
Stockwell Gdns
SW9 138 B4 270 C1
Stockwell Gn SW9 138 B3
Stockwell La SW9 138 B3
Stockwell Park Cres
SW9 138 B3
Stockwell Park Rd
SW9 138 B4 270 D1
Stockwell Park Sch
SW9 138 B4 270 C1
Stockwell Park Wlk
SW9 138 C2
Stockwell Prim Sch
SW9 138 B2
Stockwell St SE10 142 A6
Stockwell Sta SW4 138 A3
Stockwell Terr SW9 270 C1
Stodart Rd SE20 184 C2
Stoddart Ho SW8 270 D5
Stodmarsh Ho 28 SW9 138 C4
Stofield Gdns SE9 165 D1
Stoford Cl SW19 157 A4
Stokenchurch St
SW6 135 D4 265 C1
Stoke Newington Church St
N16 73 C6
Stoke Newington Comm
N16 73 D6
Stoke Newington High St
N16 73 D5
Stoke Newington Rd
N16 73 D4
Stoke Newington Sch
N16 73 B5
Stoke Newington Sta
N16 73 D6
Stoke Pl NW10 89 D4
Stoke Rd KT2 177 A3
Stokesby Rd KT9 214 B2
Stokes Ct N2 48 C5
Stokesley St W12 89 D1
Stokes Rd Croydon CR0 206 D3
Newham E6 100 A3
Stokley Ct N8 50 A5
Stoll Cl NW2 68 C5
Stoms Path SE6 185 C5
Stonard Rd
Dagenham RM8 80 B4
Palmers Green N13 16 C1
Stondon Pk SE23 163 A5
Stondon Wlk E6 100 A5
4 E6 99 D5
Stonebanks KT12 194 A2
Stone Bldgs
WC2 94 B2 240 D3
Stonebridge Ct 8
NW10 67 B1
Stonebridge Ctr The
N15 52 A4
Stonebridge Park HA9 66 D1
Stonebridge Park Sta
NW10 66 D1
Stonebridge Pk NW10 67 B1
Stonebridge Rd N15 51 D4
Stonebridge Sch The
NW10 89 B6
Stonebridge Sh Ctr 6
NW10 89 B6
Stonebridge Way HA9 66 D2
Stonechat Sq 6 E6 100 A2
Stone Cl SW4 137 C3
Dagenham RM8 81 B6
Yiewsley UB7 104 B5
Stonecot Cl SM3 201 A1
Stonecot Hill SM4 201 A1
Stone Cres TW14 149 D4
Stonecroft Way CR0 204 A2
Stonecutter St EC4 241 C2
Stonefield N4 72 B6
Stonefield Cl DA7 147 C2
Ruislip HA4 63 A3
Stonefield Mans N1 234 A5
Stonefield St
N1 94 C6 234 B6
Stonefield Way SE7 143 D5
Ruislip HA4 63 A3
Stone Gate 8 NW5 71 A2
Stone Gr HA8 26 B5
Stone Grove Ct HA8 26 B5
Stonegrove Gdns HA8 26 A5
Stonehall Ave IG1 56 A3
Stone Hall Rd N21 16 C4
Stoneham Rd N11 31 C5
Stonehaven BR3 185 D1
Stonehill Cl SW14 155 B6
Stonehill Ct E4 19 D4
Stonehill Rd W4 110 C1
Mortlake SW14 155 B6
Stonehills Ct SE21 161 C1
Stonehill's Mans 3
SW16 160 A2
Stonehill Woods Pk
DA14 169 D3
Stonehorse Rd EN3 18 C6
Stonehouse NW1 232 B5
Stonehouse Ct EC2 243 B2
Stonehouse Ho 27 W2 91 C2
Stone Lake Ind Pk
SE7 121 C2
Stone Lake Ret Pk
SE7 121 C2
Stoneleigh Ave
Enfield EN1 6 B4
North Cheam KT17,KT4 216 A5
Stoneleigh Broadway
KT17 216 A3
Stoneleigh Cres KT19 215 D3
Stoneleigh Ct
Redbridge IG5 56 A6
Stoneleigh Ct *continued*
4 Tottenham N17 33 D1
Stoneleigh Fst Sch
KT17 216 B4
Stoneleigh Lo 13 TW9 132 B4
Stoneleigh Park Ave
CR0 206 D3
Stoneleigh Park Rd
KT19,KT4 216 A3
Stoneleigh Pl W11 112 D6
Stoneleigh Rd
Carshalton SM5 202 C2
Redbridge IG5 56 B6
Tottenham N17 33 D1
Stoneleigh St W11 112 D6
Stoneleigh Sta KT19 216 A3
Stoneleigh Terr N19 71 B6
Stonell's Rd SW11 158 D6
Stonemasons Cl N15 51 B5
Stonenest St N4 50 B1
Stone Park Ave BR3 207 D5
Stone Pl KT4 216 A6
Stone Rd BR2 208 D4
Stones End St SE1 252 A1
Stonewall E6 100 C2
Stoneworth Ct SE25 206 A3
Stoney Alley SE18 144 C3
Stoneyard La E14 119 D6
Stoneycroft Cl SE12 164 D4
Stoney Deep TW11 175 A6
Stoneydown E17 53 A5
Stoneydown Ave E17 53 A5
Stoneydown Ho 2 E17 53 A5
Stoneydown Park Sch
E17 53 A5
Stoneyfields Gdns HA8 27 A6
Stoneyfields La HA8 27 A6
Stoney La E1 243 B2
Penge SE19 183 D4
Stoney St SE1 117 B5 252 C4
Stonhouse St SW4 137 D1
Stonor Rd
W14 113 B2 254 C3
Stonycroft Cl EN3 7 A3
Stopes St SE15 139 D5
Stopford Rd E13 99 A6
SE17 261 D1
Stopher Ho SE1 251 D1
Storace Ho 6 SW4 138 A1
Store Rd E16 122 C4
Storers Quay E14 120 B2
Store St E15 76 B3
WC1 93 D2 239 C4
Storey Ct NW8 229 C1
Storey Ho 12 E14 119 D6
Storey Prim Sch E16 122 D5
Storey Rd E17 53 B5
N6 48 D3
Storey's Gate
SW1 115 D4 249 D1
Storey St E16 122 C4
Stories Rd SE5 139 C2
Stork Rd E7 77 A2
Storksmead Rd HA8 27 C3
Storks Rd SE16 118 A3
Stormont House Sch
E5 74 B4
Stormont Rd N6 48 D2
SW11 137 A1
Stormont Way KT9 213 C3
Stormount Dr UB3 105 A4
Storrington WC1 233 B1
Storrington Rd CR0 205 D1
Story St N1 72 B1
Stothard Pl E1 243 B4
Stothard St 11 E1 96 C3
Stott Cl SW18 158 B5
Stoughton Ave SM3 217 A3
Stoughton Cl SE11 260 D3
Roehampton SW15 156 A3
Stour Ave UB2 107 C3
Stour Cl BR2 225 C4
Stourcliffe Cl W1 237 C2
Stourcliffe St W1 237 C1
Stourhead Cl 6 SW19 156 D4
Stourhead Gdns SW20 200 A6
Stour Rd E3 75 C1
Dagenham RM10 81 C6
Stourton Ave TW13 173 B6
Stowage SE8 141 D6
Stow Cres E17 35 A3
Stowe Cres HA4 39 A3
Stowe Gdns N9 17 D3
Stowe Ho 11 N16 73 C5
NW11 48 A3
Stowell Ho 2 N8 50 A5
Stowe Pl N15 51 C6
Stowe Rd W12 112 B4
Stowford Coll SM2 218 A1
Stowting Rd BR6 227 C4
Stox Mead HA3 24 B2
Stracey Rd E7 77 A4
NW10 89 B6
Strachan Pl SW19,
SW20 178 C4
Stradbroke Gr
Buckhurst Hill IG9 21 D3
Redbridge IG5 56 B6
Stradbroke Rd N5 73 A4
Stradbrook Cl HA2 63 B5
Stradella Rd SE24 161 A5
Straffan Lo 8 NW3 70 C2
Strafford Ho 9 SE8 119 B1
Strafford Rd Acton W3 111 A4
Barnet EN5 1 A2
Hounslow TW3 129 B2
Twickenham TW1 153 A4
Strafford St E14 119 C4
Strahan Rd E3 97 A4
Straightsmouth SE10 142 A5
Straight The UB2 107 A4
Strait Rd E6 122 B6
Straker's Rd SE15 140 B1
Strale Ho 17 N1 95 C6
Strand WC2 116 B6 250 C6
Strandfield Cl SE18 123 C1
Strand La WC2 250 D6
Strand-on-the-Green
W4 132 C6
Strand-on-the-Green Sch
W4 132 C6
Strand Pl N18 33 C6
Strang Ho N1 235 A5
Strangways Terr W14 254 C5
Stranraer Way N1 72 A1
1 Stanwell TW6 148 A5
Strasburg Rd
SW11 137 B4 268 C1
Stratfield Ho SE12 165 A2
Stratfield Park Cl N21 16 D4
Stratford Ave UB10 82 B5
Stratford Bus Sta E15 76 B1
Stratford Cir E15 76 B2
Stratford Cl IG11 80 A1
Stratford Ct KT3 199 B5
Stratford Ctr E15 76 B1
Stratford Gr SW15 134 D1
Stratford House Ave
BR1 210 A6
Stratford Office Village The
1 E15 76 C1
Stratford Pl W1 238 C1
Stratford Rd E13 99 A6
W8 113 C3 255 B5
Harlington TW6 149 A6
Hayes UB4 84 B3
Southall UB2 107 A2
Thornton Heath CR7 204 D6
Stratford Sta E15 76 B1
Stratford Studios W8 255 C5
Stratford Villas NW1 71 D1
Stratford Workshops
E15 98 B6
Strathan Cl SW18 157 A5
Strathaven Rd SE12 165 B5
Strathblaine Rd SW11 136 B1
Strathbrook Rd SW16 182 B3
Strathcona Rd HA9 65 D6
Strathdale SW16 182 B5
Strathdon Dr SW17 158 B1
Strathearn Ave
Harlington UB3 127 D5
Twickenham TW2 152 A3
Strathearn House W2 247 A6
Strathearn Pl
W2 114 C6 247 A6
Strathearn Rd
Sutton SM1 217 C3
Wimbledon SW19 179 C6
Stratheden Par SE3 143 A5
Stratheden Rd SE3 143 A5
Strathfield Gdns IG11 79 B2
Strathleven Rd SW2 160 A6
Strathmore Ct NW8 230 A2
Strathmore Gdns N3 29 D2
W8 245 B4
Edgware HA8 26 D1
Strathmore Rd
Teddington TW11,TW2 174 C6
Thornton Heath CR0 205 B2
Wimbledon SW19 157 C1
Strathmore Sch TW10 153 D2
Strathnairn St SE1 118 A2
Strathray Gdns NW3 70 C2
Strath Terr SW11 136 C1
Strathville Rd SW18 157 D2
Strathyre Ave SW16 204 C6
Stratton Ave EN2 5 B6
Stratton Cl DA7 147 A2
Edgware HA8 26 B4
Heston TW5 129 C4
Merton SW19 179 C1
Walton-on-T KT12 194 C1
Stratton Ct 4 N1 73 C1
10 Kingston KT6 198 A4
Strattondale St E14 120 A3
Stratton Dr IG11 79 D2
Stratton Gdns UB1 85 C1
Stratton Ho HA8 26 B6
Stratton Rd DA7 147 A2
Merton SW19 179 C1
Sunbury TW16 171 D1
Stratton St
W1 115 B5 248 D4
Strauss Rd W4 111 B4

Strawberry Hill Cl TW1 152 D1
Strawberry Hill Rd TW1 152 D1
Strawberry Hill Sta TW2 152 D1
Strawberry La SM5 219 A5
Strawberry Terr N10 30 D2
Strawberry Vale N2 30 B2
Twickenham TW1 153 A1
Strayfield Rd EN2 4 D6
Streakes Field Rd NW2 68 A6
Streamdale SE2 146 B6
Streamline Mews SE22 162 A3
Streamside Cl BR2 209 A5
Edmonton N9 17 D3
Stream Way DA17 147 C6
Streatfield Ave E6 100 B6
Streatfield Rd HA3,HA7 43 D6
Streatham Cl SW16 160 A2
Streatham & Clapham High Sch SW16 159 D1
Streatham Comm N SW16 182 B5
Streatham Common Sta SW16 181 D3
Streatham Comm S SW16 182 B4
Streatham Ct SW16 160 A1
Streatham High Rd SW16,SW2 182 A5
Streatham Hill SW2 160 A3
Streatham Hill & Clapham High Sch SW2 160 B3
Streatham Hill Sta SW2 160 A2
Streatham Pl SW2 160 A4
Streatham Rd CR4 181 A2
Streatham St WC1 240 A2
Streatham Sta SW16 181 D5
Streatham & Tooting Adult Inst SW16 160 B2
Streatham Vale SW16 181 D3
Streathbourne Rd SW17 159 A1
Streathem Wells Prim Sch SW2 160 C2
Streatleigh Par 4 SW16 160 A2
Streatley Pl NW3 70 B4
12 NW3 70 A4
Streatley Rd NW6 69 B1
Streeters La SM6 219 D5
Streetfield Mews SE3 143 A2
Streimer Rd E15 98 A5
Strelley Way W3 111 C6
Stretton Lo W13 109 B6
Stretton Mans 16 SE8 141 C6
Stretton Rd
Croydon CR0 205 C2
Richmond TW10 153 C2
Strickland Ct SE15 140 A2
Strickland Ho 26 E2 95 D4
Strickland Row SW18 158 B4
Strickland St SE8 141 C4
Strickland Way 4 BR6 227 D4
Stride Rd E13 98 D5
Strimon Cl N9 18 C2
Stringer Hos 18 N1 95 C6
Strode Cl N10 31 A3
Strode Ho 3 SW2 160 C3
Strode Rd E7 77 A4
NW10 68 A2
SW6 135 A5 264 A4
Tottenham N17 33 C1
Strome Ho NW6 91 D5
Strone Rd E7,E12 77 D2
Strone Way UB4 85 A3
Strongbow Cres SE9 166 B6
Strongbow Rd SE9 166 B6
Strongbridge Cl HA2 41 C1
Stronsa Rd W12 111 D4
Strood Ho SE1 252 D1
12 Penge SE20 184 C3
Stroud Cres SW15 156 A1
Stroudes Cl KT4 199 D2
Stroud Field UB5 63 A2
Stroud Gate HA2 63 D4
Stroud Green Gdns CR0 206 C2
Stroud Green JMI Sch N4 50 C1
Stroud Green Rd N4 50 C1
Stroud Green Way CR0 206 C3
Stroudley Ho SW8 269 B2
Stroudley Wlk E3 97 D4
Stroud Rd
Croydon SE25 206 A3
Wimbledon SW19 157 C1
Strouds Cl RM6 58 B4
Stroud Way TW15 171 A4
Strout's Pl 2 E2 95 D4
Struan Ho 11 E11 55 A4
Strudwick Ct SW4 270 B1
Strutton Ground SW1 115 D3 259 C5
Strype St E1 243 C3
Stuart Ave NW9 46 A2
W5 110 B4
Harrow HA2 63 B5
Hayes BR2 209 A1
Walton-on-T KT12 194 B1
Stuart Cl UB10 60 C2
Stuart Cres
Croydon CR0 223 B5
Hayes UB3 83 A1
Wood Green N22 32 B2
Stuart Ct Chingford E4 20 D2
2 Elstree WD6 9 D5
Stuart Evans Cl DA16 146 C2
Stuart Gr TW11 174 C5
Stuart Ho 1 E9 74 D1
5 SW4 138 A1
W14 254 A4
Stuart Lo SE25 183 C1
Stuart Mill Ho N1 233 C3
Stuart Pl CR4 180 D2
Stuart Rd DA16 146 B4
NW6 91 C4
SE15 140 C1
W3 111 A5
East Barnet EN4 14 D4
Harrow HA3 42 D6
Richmond TW10 153 B1
South Norwood CR7 205 A5
Wimbledon SW19 157 C1
Stubbs Cl NW9 45 A4
Stubbs Dr SE16 118 B1
Stubbs Ho 1 E2 96 D4
N4 50 B1
Stubbs Mews RM8 80 B4
Stubbs Point E13 99 B3
Stubbs Way SW19 180 B2
Stucley Pl 18 NW1 71 B1
Stucley Rd TW5,TW7 130 A5
Studdridge St SW6 135 C3
Studd St N1 94 D6 234 C6
Studholme Ct NW3 69 C4
Studholme St SE15 140 B5
Studio Pl SW1 247 D1
Studios Rd TW17 192 B6
Studios The 4 SW4 137 C1
SW8 269 D1
Studland SE17 262 C2
Studland Cl DA15 167 D1
Studland Ho E14 97 A1
Studland Rd Ealing W7 86 C1
Forest Hill SE26 184 D5
Kingston KT2 176 A4
Studland St W6 112 B2
Studley Ave E4 36 B3
Studley Cl E5 75 A3
Studley Ct DA14 190 B5
9 Poplar E14 120 B6
Redbridge IG4 55 D3
Studley Dr IG4 55 D3
Studley Grange Rd W7 108 D4
Studley Rd E7 77 B2
SW4 138 A3
Dagenham RM9 80 D1
Study Prep Sch The SW19 178 C5
Study Sch The KT3 199 C4
Stukeley Rd E7 77 B1
Stukeley St WC2 94 A1 240 B2
Stumps Hill La BR3 185 C4
Stunnell Ho 23 SE14 140 D6
Sturdee Ho 2 E2 96 A5
Sturdy Ho 28 E3 97 A5
Sturdy Rd SE15 140 B3
Sturge Ave E17 35 D1
Sturgeon Rd SE17 117 A1 262 A1
Sturges Field BR7 189 B4
Sturgess Ave NW4 46 B2
Sturge St SE1 117 A4 252 A2
Sturmer Way N7 72 B3
Sturminster Cl UB4 84 C1
Sturminster Ho SW8 270 D3
Sturrock Cl N15 51 B5
Sturry St E14 97 D1
Sturt St N1 235 B3
Stutfield St E1 96 A1
Stuttle Ho 9 E1 96 A3
Styles Gdns SW9 138 D2
Styles Ho SE1 251 C3
Styles Way BR3 208 A5
Sudbourne Prim Sch SW2 160 B6
Sudbourne Rd SW2 160 B6
Sudbrooke Rd SW12 159 A5
Sudbrook Gdns TW10 154 A1
Sudbrook La TW10 154 A2
Sudbury E6 100 C1
Sudbury Ave HA0 65 D4
Sudbury Court Dr HA1 65 A5
Sudbury Court Rd HA1 65 A5
Sudbury Cres BR1 187 A5
Wembley HA0 65 B3
Sudbury Croft HA0 64 D4
Sudbury Ct E5 75 A4
SW8 269 D2
Sudbury Gdns CR0 221 C4
Sudbury & Harrow Road Sta HA0 65 B3
Sudbury Heights Ave UB6 65 A3
Sudbury Hill HA1 64 C5
Sudbury Hill Cl HA0 64 D5
Sudbury Hill Harrow Sta HA1 64 C4
Sudbury Hill Sta HA1 64 C4
Sudbury Ho SW18 157 D6
Sudbury Jun & Inf Schs HA0 65 B4
Sudbury Rd IG11 79 D3
Sudbury Town Sta UB6 65 B2
Sudeley St N1 94 D5 234 D3
Sudlow Rd SW18 157 C6
Sudrey St SE1 252 A1
Suez Ave UB6 86 D5
Suez Rd EN3 7 A2
Suffield Ho SE17 261 D2
Suffield Rd 2 N15 51 D4
Chingford E4 35 D6
Penge SE20 184 C1
Suffolk Cl WD6 11 B6
Suffolk Ct Ilford IG3 57 C3
3 West Norwood SW16 182 C6
Suffolk Ho 11 Acton W3 88 C1
Penge SE20 184 C2
4 South Croydon CR0 221 B6
Suffolk La EC4 252 C6
Suffolk Park Rd E17 53 A5
Suffolk Pl SW1 249 D4
Suffolk Rd 4 E13 99 A4
N15 51 B3
NW10 67 C1
Barking IG11 79 B1
Barnes SW13 134 A5
Dagenham RM10 81 D3
Enfield EN3 18 B6
Harrow HA2 41 B4
Ilford IG3 57 C3
Sidcup DA14 190 C4
South Norwood SE25 205 D5
Worcester Park KT4 215 D6
Suffolks Prim Sch EN1 6 B3
Suffolk St E7 77 A4
SW1 115 D5 249 D4
Sugar House La E15 98 A5
Sugar Loaf Wlk 6 E2 96 C4
Sugden Rd SW11 137 A1
Long Ditton KT7 197 B1
Sugden Way IG11 101 D5
Sulby Ho SE4 141 A1
Sulgrave Gdns 11 W6 112 C4
Sulgrave Rd W6 112 C3
Sulina Rd SW2 160 A4
Sulivan Ct SW6 135 C3
Sulivan Ent Ctr SW6 135 C2
Sulivan Prim Sch SW6 135 C3
Sulivan Rd SW6 135 C2
Sulkin Ho 11 E2 96 D4
Sullivan Ave E16 99 D2
Sullivan Cl SW11 136 C2
East Molesey KT8 195 D6
Northolt UB4 84 C2
Sullivan Ct N16 51 D1
SW5 255 B4
4 Croydon CR0 206 A1
Sullivan Ho SE11 260 D3
SW1 268 D6
Isleworth TW2 152 B5
Sullivan Rd SE11 116 C2 261 B4
Sullivans Reach KT12 193 D2
Sullivan Way WD6 9 C5
Sultan Rd E11 55 B5
Sultan St SE5 139 A5
Penge BR3 184 D1
Sumal Ct E9 76 B6
Sumatra Rd NW6 69 C2
Sumburgh Rd SW12 159 A5
Summer Ave KT8 196 C4
Summercourt Rd E1 96 C1
Summerene Cl SW16 181 C3
Summerfield 6 BR1 187 B2
Summerfield Ave N12 30 C4
NW6 91 A5
Summerfield La KT6 213 D6
Summerfield Rd
Ealing W5 87 B3
Loughton IG10 21 D5
Summerfield St SE12 164 D4
Summer Gdns KT8 196 C4
Summer Gr WD6 9 D5
Summer Hill BR7 188 C1
Borehamwood WD6 10 C6
Summerhill Cl BR6 227 C5
Summerhill Gr EN1 17 C5
Summerhill Rd N15 51 B5
Summerhill Way CR4 181 A2
Summer Ho SE13 142 B1
Summerhouse Ave TW5 129 A4
Summerhouse Rd N16 73 C6
Summerland Gdns N10 49 B6
Summerland Grange N10 49 B6
Summerlands Ave W3 111 A6
Summerlands Lo BR6 226 C4
Summerlee Ave N2 48 D5
Summerlee Gdns N2 48 D5
Summerley St SW18 157 D2
Summer Rd
East Molesey KT8 196 B4
Thames Ditton KT7,KT8 196 D4
Summersby Rd N6 49 B3
Summers Cl
Belmont SM2 217 C1
Wembley HA9 44 D1
Summersell Ho SE27 183 B5
Summerside Prim Sch N12 30 B4
Summerskille Cl N9 18 B2
Summers La N12 30 B3
Summers Row N12 30 C4
Summers St EC1 241 A5
Summerstown SW17 180 A6
Summerton Way SE28 102 D1
Summer Trees TW16 172 B2
Summerville Gdns SM1 217 B2
Summerwood Rd TW1,TW7 152 D5
Summit Ave NW9 45 B4
Summit Bsns Pk The TW16 172 A3
Summit Cl N14 15 C2
NW9 45 B5
Edgware HA8 26 C3
Summit Ct NW2 69 A3
Summit Dr IG8 37 D1
Summit Est N16 52 A2
Summit Rd E17 53 D5
Northolt UB5 63 C1
Summit The TW16 172 A3
Summit Way N14 15 B2
South Norwood SE19 183 C3
Sumner Ave SE15 139 D4
Sumner Bldgs SE1 252 A4
Sumner Cl BR6 227 A4
Sumner Ct SW8 270 A2
Sumner Gdns CR0 204 C1
Sumner Ho 1 E3 97 D2
Sumner Pl SW7 114 B2 256 D3
Sumner Place Mews SW7 256 D3
Sumner Rd SE15 139 D5
Harrow HA1 42 A2
Thornton Heath CR0 204 D1
Sumner Rd S CR0 204 C1
Sumner St SE1 117 A5 252 A4
Sumpter Cl NW3 70 A2
Sun Alley 6 TW9 132 A1
Sunbeam Cres W10 90 C3
Sunbeam Rd NW10 89 B3
Sunbury Ave NW7 27 B6
Mortlake SW14 133 B1
Sunbury Cl KT12 194 A3
Sunbury Court Island TW16 194 D6
Sunbury Court Rd TW16 172 C1
Sunbury Cres TW13 171 D6
Sunbury Cross TW16 172 A3
Sunbury Cross Ctr 9 TW16 171 D3
Sunbury Ct 3 SE14 140 D6
2 Barnet EN5 1 A1
Sunbury TW16 172 D1
Sunbury Ct (Con Ctr) TW16 172 D1
Sunbury Gdns NW7 27 B5
Sunbury Ho 38 E2 95 D4
Sunbury Int Bsns Ctr TW16 171 C2
Sunbury La SW11 136 B4 266 D2
Walton-on-T KT12 194 A3
Sunbury Manor Sch TW16 171 D2
Sunbury Rd
Cheam SM3 217 A5
Feltham TW13 171 D6
Sunbury St SE18 122 B3
Sunbury Sta TW16 172 A2
Sunbury Way TW13 172 C5
Sunbury Workshops 39 E2 95 D4
Suncroft Pl SE26 162 C1
Sun Ct EC3 242 D1
Sunderland Ct
Dulwich SE22 162 A4
12 Stanwell TW19 148 A5
Sunderland Ho 26 W2 91 C2
Sunderland Mount SE23 162 D2
Sunderland Pt E16 123 A5
Sunderland Rd W5 109 D3
Forest Hill SE23 162 D2
Sunderland Terr W2 91 D1
Sunderland Way E12 77 D6
Sundew Ave W12 112 A6
Sundew Ct 9 HA0 88 A5
Sundial Ave SE25 205 D6
Sundial Ct KT5 214 D6
Sundorne Rd SE7 121 C1
Sundown Rd TW15 171 A5
Sundridge Ave DA16 145 B2
Bromley BR1,BR7 188 A3
Sundridge Ho 4 E9 74 D1
Sundridge Par BR1 187 B3
Sundridge Park Sta BR1 187 B3
Sundridge Rd CR0 206 A1
Sunfields Pl SE3 143 B5
Sun in the Sands SE3 143 B5
Sunken Rd CR0 222 C3
Sun La SE3 143 B5
Sunland Ave DA6 147 A1
Sunleigh Ct HA0 88 A6
Sunleigh Rd HA0 88 A6
Sunley Gdns UB6 87 A6
Sun Life Trad Est TW14 128 A2
Sunlight Cl SW19 180 A4
Sunlight Sq 29 E2 96 B4
Sunmead Rd TW16 194 A6
Sunna Gdns TW16 172 B1
Sunniholme Ct CR2 221 A3
Sunningdale N14 31 D5
Ealing W13 87 B2
Sunningdale Ave W3 111 C6
Barking IG11 79 B1
Feltham TW13 151 A2
Ruislip HA4 40 C1
Sunningdale Cl E6 100 B4
22 SE16 118 B1
Erith SE28 103 A1
Stanmore HA7 25 A3
3 Surbiton KT6 214 A6
Sunningdale Ct
13 Kingston KT2 176 C3
13 Southall UB1 86 A1
Sunningdale Gdns NW9 45 A4
W8 255 B5
Sunningdale Rd BR1,BR2 210 A4
Cheam SM1 217 B4
Sunningfields Cres NW4 28 B1
Sunningfields Rd NW4 46 B6
Sunninghill Ct 9 W3 111 A4
Sunninghill Gdns IG2 57 D4
Sunninghill Rd SE13 141 D3
Sunny Bank SE25 206 A6
Sunny Cres NW10 67 A1
Sunnycroft Rd
Hounslow TW3 129 D3
Southall UB1 85 C2
South Norwood SE25 206 A6
Sunnydale BR6 226 C6
Sunnydale Gdns NW7 27 C4
Sunnydale Rd SE12 165 B6
Sunnydene Ave
Chingford E4 36 B5
Ruislip HA4 62 A6
Sunnydene Gdns HA0 65 C2
Sunnydene St SE26 185 A6
Sunnyfield NW7 27 D6
Sunnyfields Prim Sch NW4 46 B6
Sunny Gardens Par NW4 28 B1
Sunny Gardens Rd NW4 46 C6
Sunny Hill NW4 46 B6
Sunnyhill Cl E5 75 A4
Sunny Hill Ct NW4 28 B1
Sunnyhill Prim Sch SW16 182 B6
Sunnyhill Rd SW16 182 A6
Sunnyhurst Cl SM1 217 C5
Sunnymead Ave CR4 203 D6
Sunnymead Ct W5 109 D6
Sunnymead Rd NW9 45 B2
Putney SW15 156 B6
Sunnymede Ave KT19 215 C1
Sunnymede Dr IG6 56 D5
Sunny Nook Gdns CR2 221 B2
Sunny Pl NW4 46 C5
Sunny Rd The EN3 6 D4
Sunnyside 3 NW2 69 B5
Walton-on-T KT12 194 C4
Wimbledon SW19 179 A4
Sunnyside Dr E4 20 A4
Sunnyside Ho 2 NW2 69 B5
Sunnyside Pl SW19 179 A4
Sunnyside Rd E10 53 C1
N19 49 D2
Ealing W5 109 D5
Ilford IG1 79 B5
Teddington TW11 174 B6
Sunnyside Rd E N9 18 A1
Sunnyside Rd N N9 18 A1
Sunnyside Rd S N9 18 A1
Sunny View NW9 45 B4
Sunny Way N12 30 C3
Sun Pas 8 SE16 118 A3
Sunray Ave BR2 210 B3
SE5,SE24 139 B1
Sunray Ave *continued*
Tolworth KT5 214 D6
Sun Rd W14 113 B1 254 C1
Sunrise Cl TW13 151 B1
Sunrise View NW7 27 D4
Sunset Ave Chingford E4 19 D3
Woodford IG8 36 D6
Sunset Ct 4 IG8 37 C3
Sunset Gdns SE25 183 D1
Sunset Rd SE28 124 A5
SE5 139 B1
Wimbledon SW19 178 B5
Sunset View EN5 1 A3
Sunshine Way CR4 180 D1
Sun St EC2 95 B2 242 D4
Sun St Pas EC2 95 C2 243 A3
Sunwell Cl SE15 140 B4
Superior Dr 4 BR6 227 D2
Surbiton Cres KT1,KT6 198 A5
Surbiton Ct KT6 197 D3
Surbiton Hall Cl KT1 198 A5
Surbiton High Sch KT1 198 A5
Surbiton High Sch Jun Sch for Girls KT1 198 A5
Surbiton Hill Pk KT5 198 C4
Surbiton Hill Rd KT6 198 A4
Surbiton Hospl KT6 198 A3
Surbiton Prep Sch KT6 198 A4
Surbiton Rd KT1 198 A5
Surbiton Sta KT6 198 A3
Surcot Ho 2 SW4 137 D3
Surlingham Cl SE28 124 D6
Surma Cl E1 96 A3
Surmans Cl RM9 102 C6
Surrendale Pl W9 91 C3
Surrey Canal Rd SE14, SE16,SE8 140 D6
Surrey Cres 1 W4 110 C1
Surrey Ct N3 47 A6
Surrey Gdns N4 51 A3
Surrey Gr SE17 263 A1
Carshalton SM1 218 B5
Surrey Ho 8 SE16 118 D5
Surrey La SW11 136 C4 267 B1
Surrey Lo SW20 178 C1
Surrey Mews SE27 183 C6
Surrey Mount SE23 162 B3
Surrey Quays Rd SE16 118 D4
Surrey Quays Sh Ctr SE16 118 D3
Surrey Quays Sta SE16 118 D2
Surrey Rd SE15 162 D6
Barking IG11 79 C1
Dagenham RM10 81 D3
Harrow HA1 42 A4
West Wickham BR4 207 D1
Surrey Row SE1 116 D4 251 D2
Surrey Sq SE17 117 C1 263 B2
Surrey Square Inf Sch SE17 117 C1 263 A2
Surrey Square Jun Sch SE17 117 C1 263 A2
Surrey St 4 E13 99 B4
WC2 116 B6 250 D6
Croydon CR0 221 A5
Surrey Terr SE17 263 B2
Surrey Water Rd SE16 118 D5
Surrey Wharf SE1 140 A6
Surridge Ct 15 SW9 138 A3
Surridge Gdns SE19 183 B4
Surr St N7 72 A3
Sury Basin KT2 176 A2
Susan Constant Ct 3 E14 120 B6
Susan Lawrence Ho 3 E12 78 C4
Susan Lawrence Prim Schs E14 97 D1
Susannah St E14 98 A1
Susan Rd SE3 143 B3
Susan Wood BR7 188 C2
Sussex Ave TW7 130 C2
Sussex Cl N19 72 A6
New Malden KT3 199 C5
Redbridge IG4 56 B4
4 Twickenham TW1 153 B5
Sussex Cres UB5 63 C2
Sussex Ct SE10 142 A6
W2 236 C1
4 Barnes SW13 133 D3
Mitcham CR4 204 A4
Sussex Gate N6 48 D4
Sussex Gdns N4 51 A4
N6 48 D4
W2 92 B1 236 D1
Chessington KT9 213 D2
Sussex Ho NW3 70 C2
Richmond TW9 132 B3
Sussex House Sch SW3 114 D2 257 C3
Sussex Lo W2 236 D1
Sussex Mans SW7 256 C3
WC2 250 B6

ussex Mews SE6 ...163 C3
ussex Mews E W2 ...236 D1
ussex Mews W W2 ...246 D6
ussex Pl NW1 .92 D3 237 C6
W2 ...92 B1 236 D1
22 W6 ...112 C1
New Malden KT3 ...199 C5
ussex Rd DA14 ...190 B5
DA8 ...147 D5
Barking E6 ...100 C6
Harrow HA1 ...42 A4
Mitcham CR4 ...204 A4
New Malden KT3 ...199 C5
Southall UB2 ...106 D3
South Croydon CR2 ...221 B2
Uxbridge UB10 ...61 A3
Wallington SM5 ...218 D2
2 West Wickham BR4 .207 D1
ussex Ring N12 ...29 C5
ussex Sq W2 114 B6 246 D6
ussex St E13 ...99 B4
SW1 ...258 D2
ussex Way N19 ...49 D1
N7,N19 ...72 A6
Cockfosters EN4 ...15 B6
utcliffe Cl NW11 ...47 D4
utcliffe Ho UB3 ...84 A1
utcliffe Rd SE18 ...145 C6
Bexley DA16 ...146 C3
utherland Ave BR5 ..211 D4
DA16 ...145 C1
W9 ...92 A3 236 A6
Ealing W13 ...87 B1
Hayes UB3 ...106 A2
Sunbury TW16 ...171 D1
utherland Cl EN5 ...1 A1
utherland Ct N16 ...73 B5
NW9 ...44 D4
2 W9 ...91 C3
utherland Dr SW19 ..180 B2
utherland Gdns
Mortlake SW14 ...133 C2
North Cheam KT4 ...200 B1
Sunbury TW16 ...171 D1
utherland Gr
Putney SW18,SW19 ...157 B4
Teddington TW11 ...174 C5
utherland Ho 9 NW6 .70 A2
8 SE18 ...144 B4
W8 ...255 C5
Ealing W13 ...109 A6
7 Putney SW15 ...156 C4
Richmond TW10 ...153 C2
utherland Pl W2 ...91 C1
utherland Point 1 E5 74 B4
utherland Rd E17 ...53 A6
E3 ...97 B5
Belvedere DA17 ...125 C3
Chiswick W4 ...133 C6
Ealing W13 ...87 A1
Edmonton N9 ...18 B3
Enfield EN3 ...18 D6
Southall UB1 ...85 B1
Thornton Heath CR0 ...204 C2
Tottenham N17 ...34 A2
utherland Row SW1 .258 D2
utherland Sq
SE17 ...117 A1 262 A1
utherland St
SW1 ...115 B1 258 D2
utherland Wlk SE17 .262 B1
utlej Rd SE7 ...143 C5
utterton St N7 ...72 B2
utton Arc SM1 ...217 D3
utton Cl
Beckenham BR3 ...185 D2
Pinner HA5 ...40 A4
utton Common Rd
Cheam SM3 ...201 C1
Sutton SM1,SM3 ...217 D6
utton Common Sta
SM1 ...217 D6
utton Courtenay Ho
SW17 ...180 B6
utton Court Rd E13 ...99 C4
Chiswick W4 ...133 A6
Hillingdon UB10 ...82 D6
Sutton SM1,SM2 ...218 A2
utton Cres EN5 ...12 D6
utton Ct 9 E5 ...74 B4
Chiswick W4 ...133 A6
Ealing W5 ...110 A5
East Molesey KT8 ...195 B4
Penge SE19 ...183 D3
Sutton SM2 ...218 A2
utton Dene TW3 ...129 D4
utton Est
SW3 ...114 C1 257 B2
utton Est The W10 ...90 C2
utton Gdns
Barking IG11 ...101 C5
Croydon CR0 ...205 D4
utton Gn IG11 ...101 C6
utton Gr SM1 ...218 B3
utton Gram Sch For Boys
SM1 ...218 A3
utton Hall Rd TW5 ...129 C5
utton High Sch SM1 .217 D2
utton Ho N21 ...16 B6

Sutton La TW3,TW4,
TW5 ...129 B3
Sutton La N W4 ...111 A1
Sutton La S W4 ...133 A6
Sutton Par NW4 ...46 C5
Sutton Park Rd SM1,
SM2 ...217 D2
Sutton Pl E9 ...74 C3
Sutton Rd E13 ...98 D3
E17 ...34 D2
N10 ...31 A2
Barking IG11 ...101 C6
Heston TW5 ...129 C4
Sutton Row W1 ...239 D2
Sutton Sq E9 ...74 C3
Hounslow TW5 ...129 B4
Sutton St E1 ...96 C1
Sutton Sta SM2 ...218 A2
Suttons Way EC1 ...242 B5
Sutton Way W10 ...90 C2
Hounslow TW5 ...129 B4
Sutton Wlk
SE1 ...116 B5 250 D3
Swaby Rd SW17,SW18 .158 A2
Swaffield Prim Sch
SW18 ...158 A4
Swaffield Rd SW18 ...158 A4
Swain Cl SW16 ...181 B4
Swain Rd CR7 ...205 A4
Swains Cl UB7 ...104 A4
Swain's La N6 ...71 B6
Swainson Ho N7 ...72 C4
Swainson Rd W3 ...111 D4
Swains Rd CR4,SW17,
SW19 ...180 D3
Swakeleys Dr UB10 ...60 C3
Swakeleys Rd UB10 ...60 C5
Swakeleys Rdbt UB8,
UB10 ...60 A4
Swakeleys Sch UB10 ...82 D5
Swaledale Cl N11 ...31 A4
Swallands Rd SE6 ...163 C1
Swallowbrook Bsns Ctr
UB4 ...106 D5
Swallow Cl SE14 ...140 D4
Bushey WD23 ...8 A3
Swallow Ct 1 SE12 ...165 A4
4 W9 ...91 C2
Chingford IG8 ...36 B3
Ilford IG2 ...56 D4
5 Ruislip HA4 ...40 C1
Swallow Dr NW10 ...67 B2
Northolt UB5 ...85 C5
Swallowfield NW1 ...231 D1
Swallowfield Rd SE7 ...121 B1
Swallowfield Way
UB3 ...105 B4
Swallow Gdns SW16 ...181 D5
Swallow Ho N8 ...50 B6
NW8 ...230 A4
Swallow Pk KT6 ...214 B5
Swallow Pl W1 ...238 D1
Swallows Ct 5 SE20 .184 D3
Swallow St E6 ...100 A2
W1 ...115 C6 249 B5
Swaminarayan Sch The
NW10 ...67 B2
Swanage Ct 5 N1 ...73 C1
Swanage Ho SW8 ...270 C3
Swanage Rd SW18 ...158 A5
Chingford E4 ...36 A3
Swanage Waye UB4 ...84 C1
Swan App E6 ...100 A2
Swanbourne SE17 ...262 A3
Swanbourne Ho NW8 .237 A6
Swanbridge Rd DA7 ...147 C4
Swan Cl E17 ...35 A3
Croydon CR0 ...205 C2
Feltham TW13 ...173 A6
Swan Ct E14 ...97 B1
N20 ...14 A2
SW3 ...257 B1
SW6 ...265 A3
Swan Ctr SW17 ...158 A1
Swandon Way SW18 ..135 D1
Swan Dr NW9 ...27 C1
Swanfield St E2 ...95 D4
Swan Ho N1 ...73 B1
Enfield EN3 ...18 C6
Swan La EC4 ..117 B6 252 D5
N20 ...14 A1
Loughton IG10 ...21 C4
Swan Lane Pier
EC4 ...117 B6 252 C5
Swanlea Sec Sch E1 ...96 B3
Swanley Ho SE17 ...263 B2
Swanley Rd DA16 ...146 C4
Swan Mead
SE1 ...117 C3 263 A5
Swan Mews SW9 ...138 B3
Swanmore Ct SW18 ...158 A5
Swann Ct 6 TW7 ...131 A2
Swanne Ho 12 SE10 ...142 A5
Swan Pas 4 E1 ...118 A6
Swan Pl SW13 ...133 D3
Swan Rd SE16 ...118 C4
SE18 ...121 D3
Feltham TW13 ...173 A6
Southall UB1 ...85 D1

Swan Rd *continued*
West Drayton UB7 ...104 A4
Swanscombe Ho
1 BR5 ...190 B1
11 W11 ...112 D5
Swanscombe Point 7
E16 ...98 D2
Swanscombe Rd W11 112 D5
5 W4 ...111 C1
Swansea Ct E16 ...122 D5
Swansea Rd Enfield EN3 ..6 C1
Harlington TW14,TW6 ..149 B5
Swansland Gdns E17 ...35 A2
Swansmere Sch KT12 .194 C1
Swan St SE1 ..117 A4 252 B1
Isleworth TW7 ...131 B2
Swan The BR4 ...224 A6
Swanton Gdns SW19 .156 D3
Swanton Rd DA8 ...147 D5
Swan Way EN3 ...6 D3
Swanwick Cl SW15 ...155 D4
Swan Wlk
SW3 ...136 D6 267 C6
Oatlands Park TW17 ...193 C2
Swan Yd N1 ...72 D2
Swaton Rd E3 ...97 C3
Swaylands Rd DA17 ...147 C6
Swaythling Cl N18 ...34 B6
Swaythling Ho 2
SW15 ...155 D5
Swedenborg Gdns E1 .118 B6
Sweden Gate SE16 ...119 A2
Swedish Sch The
SW13 ...133 D6
Sweeney Cres SE1 ...253 D1
Sweet Briar Gn N9 ...17 D1
Sweet Briar Gr N9 ...17 D1
Sweet Briar Wlk N18 ...33 D6
Sweetcroft La UB10 ...60 C1
Sweetmans Ave HA5 ...40 D6
Sweets Way N20 ...14 B2
Swell Ct E17 ...53 D3
Swetenham Wlk SE18 123 A1
Swete St E13 ...99 A5
Sweyn Pl SE3 ...143 A3
Swift Cl E17 ...35 A3
Harrow HA2 ...63 D6
Hayes UB3 ...83 D1
Swift Ct SM2 ...217 D1
Swift Ctr CR0 ...220 B1
Swift Ho 24 E1 ...96 C1
15 N16 ...73 C5
1 SW9 ...138 C5
8 Wanstead E18 ...55 B6
Swift Rd Feltham TW13 .173 A6
Southall UB2 ...107 B3
Swiftsden Way BR1 ...186 C4
Swift St SW6 ..135 B4 264 C2
Swinbrook Rd W10 ...91 A2
Swinburne Cres CR0 ..206 C3
Swinburne Ct 4 SE5 ..139 B1
Swinburne Ho 15 E2 ...96 C4
Swinburne Rd SW15 ...134 A1
Swinderby Rd HA0 ...66 A2
Swindon Cl IG3 ...57 C1
Swindon Rd TW6 ...149 A6
Swindon St W12 ...112 C5
Swinfield Cl TW13 ...173 A6
Swinford Gdns SW9 ...138 D2
Swingate La SE18 ...145 C5
Swingfield Ho 5 E9 ...96 C6
Swinley Ho NW1 ...231 D2
Swinnerton St E9 ...75 A3
Swinton Cl HA9 ...44 D1
Swinton Ho 17 E2 ...96 A4
Swinton Pl WC1 ...233 C2
Swinton St WC1 94 B4 233 C2
Swires Shaw BR2 ...225 D4
Swiss Cottage NW3 ...70 B1
Swiss Cottage Sch
NW8 ...92 B6 229 D6
Swiss Cottage Sta NW3 70 B1
Swiss Re Building★
EC2 ...243 B2
Swiss Terr 7 NW3 ...70 B1
Swithland Gdns SE9 ..188 C6
Swyncombe Ave W5 ..109 B2
Swynford Gdns 7 NW4 46 A5
Sybil Elgar Sch UB2 ..107 B3
Sybil Mews N4 ...50 D3
Sybil Phoenix Cl SE8 .118 D1
Sybil Thorndike Casson Ho
SW5 ...255 B1
Sybil Thorndike Ho 7
N1 ...73 A2
Sybourn Inf Sch Annexe
E10 ...53 A1
Sybourn Jun & Inf Schs
E17 ...53 B2
Sybourn St E17 ...53 B2
Sycamore Ave DA15 ...167 D5
N3 ...47 D6
W5 ...109 D3
Bow E3 ...97 B6
Hayes UB3 ...105 C6
Sycamore Cl E16 ...98 C3
W3 ...111 C5
2 HA8 ...27 A6
Carshalton SM5 ...218 D4

Sycamore Cl *continued*
Chislehurst SE9 ...166 A2
Edmonton N9 ...34 A6
Feltham TW13 ...150 A1
New Barnet EN4 ...14 B5
Northolt UB5 ...85 A6
South Croydon CR2 ...221 C3
Yiewsley UB7 ...104 B6
Sycamore Ct E7 ...77 A2
N19 ...71 D5
NW6 ...91 C6
SE12 ...164 D5
4 SE5 ...139 A4
Forest Hill SE26 ...184 C6
Hillingdon UB8 ...82 C3
Hounslow TW4 ...129 A1
Surbiton KT6 ...198 A2
10 West Norwood
SW16 ...182 C5
Sycamore Gdns N15 ...51 D5
W6,W12 ...112 B3
Mitcham CR4 ...180 B1
Sycamore Gr NW9 ...45 A2
SE6 ...164 A5
Kingston KT3 ...199 C6
Penge SE20 ...184 A2
Sycamore Hill N11 ...31 A4
Sycamore Ho 2 N16 ...73 B6
18 N2 ...30 B1
13 NW3 ...70 D2
17 SE16 ...118 D4
3 W6 ...112 B4
4 Buckhurst Hill IG9 ...21 D2
Penge SE20 ...184 D4
Sycamore Lo
7 Ashford TW16 ...171 D3
Putney SW15 ...134 B2
Sycamore Mews 4
SW4 ...137 C2
Sycamore Rd SW19,
SW20 ...178 C4
Sycamore St EC1 ...242 A5
Sycamore Way TW11 .175 C4
Sycamore Wlk 1 W10 .91 A3
Ilford IG6 ...57 A5
Sydenham Ave
Penge SE26 ...184 B5
Southgate N21 ...16 B6
Sydenham High Sch For
Girls SE26 ...184 B6
Sydenham Hill SE21,
SE22,SE23,SE26,SE19 .162 A1
Sydenham Hill Sta
SE21 ...161 D1
Sydenham Ho 16 KT6 .197 D2
Sydenham Ind Est
SE26 ...185 B5
Sydenham Park Mans 2
SE26 ...162 C1
Sydenham Park Rd
SE23,SE26 ...162 C1
Sydenham Pk SE26 ...162 C1
Sydenham Rd
Forest Hill SE26 ...184 D5
Forest Hill SE26 ...185 A6
Thornton Heath CR0 ...205 B2
Sydenham Rise SE23 .162 B2
Sydenham Sec Sch
SE26 ...162 B1
Sydenham Sta SE26 ..184 C6
Sydenham Station App
SE26 ...184 C6
Sydmons Ct SE23 ...162 C4
Sydner Mews N16 ...73 D4
Sydner Rd N16 ...73 D4
Sydney Cl SW3 ...256 D3
Sydney Cotts KT10 ...212 D2
Sydney Cres TW15 ...170 D4
Sydney Ct Hayes UB4 ...84 C3
Surbiton KT6 ...214 A6
Sydney Gr NW4 ...46 C4
Sydney Ho 4 W4 ...111 C2
Sydney Mews SW3 ...256 D3
Sydney Pl SW7 ...257 A3
Sydney Rd DA6 ...146 D1
N10 ...31 B3
N8 ...50 C5
SE2 ...124 D3
Ealing W13 ...109 A4
East Bedfont TW14 ...150 A3
Enfield EN2 ...5 B1
Richmond TW10,TW9 ...132 A1
Sidcup DA14 ...189 C6
Sutton SM1 ...217 C4
Teddington TW11 ...174 D5
Wanstead E11 ...55 B3
West Barnes SW20 ...178 D1
Woodford IG8 ...37 A6
Sydney Russell Sch The
RM9 ...80 D3
Sydney St
SW3 ...114 C1 257 A2
Sydney Terr KT10 ...212 D2
Sylva Ct 3 SW15 ...156 D4
Sylvana Cl UB10 ...82 B6
Sylvan Ave N3 ...29 C1
NW7 ...27 D4
Dagenham RM6 ...59 B3
Wood Green N22 ...32 C3

Sylvan Ct N12 ...29 D6
South Croydon CR2 ...221 A2
Sylvan Gdns KT6 ...197 D2
Sylvan Gr NW2 ...68 D4
SE15 ...140 B6
Sylvan Hill SE19 ...183 C2
Sylvan Ho N21 ...16 B6
Sylvan Rd E17 ...53 C4
E7 ...77 B2
Ilford IG1 ...79 A6
South Norwood SE19 ...183 D2
Wanstead E11 ...55 A4
Sylvan Way
Coney Hall BR4 ...224 C4
Dagenham RM8 ...80 B5
Sylvan Wlk BR1 ...210 B6
Sylverdale Rd CR0 ...220 D5
Sylvester Ave BR7 ...188 B4
Sylvester Ho 7 E8 ...74 B2
Sylvester Path 8 E8 ...74 B2
Sylvester Rd E17 ...53 B2
E8 ...74 B2
N2 ...30 B1
Wembley HA0 ...65 C3
Sylvestrus Cl KT1 ...176 C1
Sylvia Ave HA5 ...23 B4
Sylvia Cotts 3 SE8 ...141 C4
Sylvia Ct N1 ...235 C3
Wembley HA9 ...66 D1
Sylvia Gdns HA9 ...66 D1
Sylvia Pankhurst Ho
14 E2 ...96 D4
10 Dagenham RM10 ...81 C5
Sylvia Young Theatre Sch
NW1 ...237 B5
Symes Mews NW1 ...232 A4
Symington Ho SE1 ...262 C5
Symington Mews E9 ...74 D3
Symister Mews N1 ...95 C4
Symons St
SW3 ...114 D2 257 D3
Symphony Mews 16
W10 ...91 A4
Syon Gate Way
Brentford TW7,TW8 ...131 A5
Brentford TW8 ...131 B5
Syon Ho TW8 ...131 C2
Syon La
Brentford TW7,TW8 ...131 B5
Hounslow TW7 ...130 D6
Syon Lane Sta TW7 ...131 A5
Syon Lo 6 SE12 ...165 A4
Syon Park Cotts TW8 .131 C2
Syon Park Gdns TW7 .130 D5
Syringa Ho SE4 ...141 B2

T

Tabard Ct 3 E14 ...98 A1
Tabard Ho SE1 ...262 D6
Teddington KT1 ...175 C2
Tabard St SE1 .117 B3 262 C6
Tabernacle Ave 7 E13 .99 A3
Tabernacle St
EC2 ...95 B3 242 D6
Tableer Ave SW4 ...159 D6
Tabley Rd N7 ...72 A4
Tabor Ct 3 SM3 ...217 A2
Tabor Gdns SM2,SM3 .217 B1
Tabor Gr SW19 ...179 B3
Tabor Rd W6 ...112 B3
Tachbrook Est
SW1 ...115 D1 259 D1
Tachbrook Mews
SW1 ...259 A4
Tachbrook Rd
East Bedfont TW14 ...149 D4
Southall UB2 ...106 D2
Tachbrook St
SW1 ...115 C2 259 B3
Tack Mews SE4 ...141 C2
Tadbourne Ct 1 HA8 ...27 A3
Tadema Ho NW8 ...236 D5
Tadema Rd
SW10 ...136 A5 266 B3
Tadlow KT1 ...198 C6
Tadmor Cl TW16 ...193 D5
Tadmor St W12 ...112 D5
Tadworth Ave KT3 ...199 D4
Tadworth Ho SE1 ...251 C1
Tadworth Rd NW2 ...68 A6
Taeping St E14 ...119 D2
Taffy's How CR4 ...202 C6
Taft Way 44 E3 ...97 D4
Taggs Ho KT1 ...175 D1
Tailworth St 15 E1 ...96 A2
Tait 7 NW9 ...27 D3
Tait Ct 9 E3 ...97 B6
SW8 ...269 D2
Tait Ho 2 N19 ...71 C4
SE1 ...251 B3
Tait Rd CR0 ...205 C2
Tait Rd Ind Est CR0 ...205 C2
Takhar Mews SW11 ...136 C3
Talacre Rd NW5 ...71 A2
Talbot Ave N2 ...48 B6
Talbot Cl N15 ...51 D5
Talbot Cres NW4 ...46 A4

Talbot Ct EC3 ...252 D6
NW9 ...67 B5
Talbot Gdns IG3 ...80 A6
Talbot Grove Ho 9
W11 ...91 A1
Talbot Ho E14 ...97 D1
N7 ...72 C5
Talbot Pl SE3 ...142 C3
Talbot Rd E7 ...77 A4
N15 ...51 D5
N6 ...49 A3
SE22 ...139 C1
W11 ...91 B1
W2 ...91 C1
Ashford TW15 ...170 A5
Dagenham RM9 ...81 B1
Ealing W13 ...109 A5
Harrow HA3 ...24 D1
Isleworth TW1,TW7 ...131 A1
Southall UB2 ...107 A2
South Norwood CR7 ...205 B5
Twickenham TW2 ...152 D3
Wallend E6 ...100 C5
Wallington SM5 ...219 A3
Wembley HA0 ...65 D2
Wood Green N22 ...31 C2
Talbot Sq W2 ...92 B1 236 C1
Talbot Wlk NW10 ...67 C2
W11 ...91 A1
Talbot Yd SE1 ...252 C3
Talcott Path 12 SW2 ...160 C3
Talfourd Pl SE15 ...139 D4
Talfourd Rd SE15 ...139 D4
Talgarth Rd
W14 ...113 A1 254 B2
W6 ...112 D1
Talgarth Wlk NW9 ...45 C4
Talia Ho E14 ...120 A3
Talina Ctr SW6 ...266 A1
Talisman Cl 2 IG3 ...58 B1
Talisman Sq SE26 ...184 A6
Talisman Way HA9 ...66 B5
Tallack Cl HA3 ...24 C3
Tallack Rd E10 ...53 B1
Tall Elms Cl BR2 ...208 D4
Talleyrand Ho SE5 ...139 A3
Tallis Cl E16 ...99 B1
Tallis Gr SE7 ...143 B6
Tallis St EC4 ...251 B6
Tallis View NW10 ...67 B2
Tall Trees SW16 ...204 B6
Talma Gdns TW2 ...152 C4
Talmage Cl SE23 ...162 C4
Talman Gr HA7 ...25 D4
Talma Rd SW2 ...138 C1
Talmudical Coll N16 ...51 B2
Talmud Torah Sch N16 .51 D2
Talwin St E3 ...97 D4
Tamar Cl E3 ...97 B6
Tamar Ho SE11 ...261 B2
Tamarind Ct 8 W3 ...89 A1
Tamarind Ho 4 SE15 .140 A5
Tamarind Yd 5 E1 ...118 A5
Tamarisk Sq W12 ...111 D6
Tamar Sq IG8 ...37 B4
Tamar St SE7 ...122 A2
Tamar Way N17 ...52 A6
Tamesa Ho TW17 ...192 C2
Tamesis Gdns KT4 ...215 C6
Tamian Ind Est TW4 ...128 C1
Tamian Way TW4 ...128 C1
Tamworth N7 ...72 A2
Tamworth Ave IG8 ...36 C4
Tamworth La CR4 ...203 B6
Tamworth Manor High Sch
CR4 ...203 D6
Tamworth Pk CR4 ...203 B6
Tamworth Pl 3 CR0 ...221 A6
Tamworth Rd CR0 ...221 A6
Tamworth St
SW6 ...135 C6 265 A5
Tancred Rd N4 ...50 D3
Tandem Ctr SW19 ...180 B2
Tandridge Ct SM2 ...217 D2
Tandridge Dr BR5,BR6 .211 B1
Tandridge Pl 2 BR6 ...211 B1
Tanfield Ave NW2 ...67 D5
Tanfield Rd CR0 ...221 A4
Tangier Rd TW10 ...132 D2
Tangleberry Cl BR1 ...210 B5
Tangle Tree Cl N3 ...29 D1
Tanglewood Cl
Hillingdon UB10 ...82 C3
South Croydon CR0 ...222 C5
Stanmore HA7 ...8 C2
Tanglewood Way
TW13 ...150 B1
Tangley Gr SW15 ...155 D4
Tangley Park Rd
TW12 ...173 B4
Tanglyn Ave TW17 ...192 D4
Tangmere WC1 ...233 C1
Tottenham N17 ...33 B1
Tangmere Gdns UB5 ...84 C5
Tangmere Gr KT2 ...175 D5
Tangmere Way NW9 ...27 C1

Tanhurst Ho 27 SW2 ... 160 A4
Tankerton Rd KT6 ... 214 B6
Tankerton St WC1 ... 233 B1
Tankerton Terr CR0 ... 204 B3
Tankerville Rd SW16 ... 182 A3
Tankridge Rd NW2 ... 68 B6
Tanner Ho SE1 ... 253 B1
 1 Merton SW19 ... 180 A2
Tanner Point E13 ... 99 A6
Tanners Cl KT12 ... 194 B3
Tanners End La N18 ... 33 C5
Tanner's Hill SE8 ... 141 C4
Tanners La IG6 ... 57 A6
Tanner St SE1 ... 117 C4 253 B1
 Barking IG11 ... 79 A2
Tanners Yd 12 E2 ... 96 B5
Tannery Cl
 Beckenham BR3,CR0 ... 206 D4
 Dagenham RM10 ... 81 D5
Tannery Ho 20 E1 ... 96 A2
Tannington Terr N5 ... 72 C5
Tannsfeld Rd SE26 ... 184 D5
Tansley Cl N7 ... 71 D3
Tanswell St SE1 ... 251 A1
Tansy Cl E6 ... 100 C1
Tantallon Rd SW12 ... 159 A3
Tant Ave E16 ... 98 D1
Tantony Gr RM6 ... 58 D6
Tanworth Gdns HA5 ... 22 C1
Tan Yard La DA5 ... 169 C4
Tanza Rd NW3 ... 70 D4
Tapestry Cl SM2 ... 217 D1
Tapley Ho 11 SE1 ... 118 A4
Taplow NW3 ... 70 B1
Taplow Ct CR4 ... 202 C5
Taplow Ho 38 E2 ... 95 D4
Taplow Rd N13 ... 33 A6
Taplow St N1 ... 95 A5 235 B3
Tappesfield Rd SE15 ... 140 C2
Tapping Cl 5 KT2 ... 176 C3
Tapp St E1 ... 96 B3
Tapster St EN5 ... 1 B2
Tara Ct
 4 Beckenham BR3 ... 185 D1
 9 Buckhurst Hill IG9 ... 21 C2
Taranto Ho 11 E1 ... 96 D2
Tarbert Rd SE22 ... 161 C6
Tarbert Wlk E1 ... 118 C6
Target Cl TW14 ... 149 C5
Target Ho W13 ... 109 B5
Target Rdbt UB5 ... 85 B6
Tariff Rd N17 ... 34 A4
Tarleton Ct 2 N22 ... 32 C1
Tarleton Gdns SE23 ... 162 B3
Tarling Cl DA14 ... 168 B1
Tarling Ho 27 E1 ... 96 B1
Tarling Rd E16 ... 98 D1
 N2 ... 30 A1
Tarling St E1 ... 96 C1
Tarnbank EN2 ... 16 A6
Tarnbrook Ct SW1 ... 258 A3
Tarn St SE1 ... 117 A3 262 A5
Tarns The NW1 ... 232 A2
Tarnwood Pk SE9 ... 166 B3
Tarplett Ho 22 SE14 ... 140 D6
Tarquin Ho SE26 ... 184 A6
Tarragon Cl SE14 ... 141 A5
Tarragon Gr SE26 ... 184 D4
Tarranbrae NW6 ... 69 A1
Tarrant Ho E2 ... 96 C4
Tarrant Pl W1 ... 237 C3
Tarrantt Ho W14 ... 254 B5
Tarriff Cres SE8 ... 119 B2
Tarrington Cl SW16 ... 159 D1
Tartan Ho 8 E14 ... 98 A1
Tarver Rd
 SE17 ... 116 D1 261 D2
Tarves Way SE10 ... 141 D5
Tash Pl N11 ... 31 B5
Tasker Cl UB7 ... 127 A5
Tasker Ho 18 E14 ... 97 B2
 Barking IG11 ... 101 B5
Tasker Rd NW3 ... 70 D3
Tasman Ct 9 E14 ... 119 D2
 Ashford TW16 ... 171 C3
Tasman Ho 11 E1 ... 118 B5
Tasmania Terr N18 ... 33 A4
Tasman Rd SW9 ... 138 A2
Tasman Wlk E16 ... 99 D1
Tasso Rd W6 ... 135 A6 264 A6
Tasso Yd W6 ... 264 A5
Tatchbury Ho 3
 SW15 ... 155 D5
Tate Britain★
 SW1 ... 116 A2 260 A3
Tate Gdns WD23 ... 8 C4
Tate Ho 13 E2 ... 96 D5
Tate Modern★
 EC4 ... 116 D5 251 C3
Tate Rd Newham E16 ... 122 B5
 Sutton SM1 ... 217 C3
Tatham Pl NW8 ... 92 B5 229 D4
Tatnell Rd SE23 ... 163 A5
Tattersall Cl SE9 ... 166 A6
Tatton Cres E5,N16 ... 51 D2
Tatum Rd NW10 ... 67 B1
Tatum St SE17 ... 117 C2 262 D3
Tauheed Cl N4 ... 73 A6
Taunton Ave
 Hounslow TW3 ... 130 A3
 Wimbledon SW20 ... 178 B1
Taunton Cl SM3 ... 201 C1
Taunton Dr N2 ... 30 A1
 Enfield EN2 ... 4 C2
Taunton Ho W2 ... 236 A1
Taunton Mews NW1 ... 237 C5
Taunton Pl
 NW1 ... 92 D3 237 C6
Taunton Rd SE12 ... 164 D6
 Greenford UB6 ... 85 D6
Taunton Way HA7 ... 26 A1
Tavern Cl SM5 ... 202 C2
Taverner Ho N16 ... 73 B5
Taverners Cl W11 ... 244 A3
Taverners Ct HA9 ... 66 B6
Taverner Sq 4 N5 ... 73 A4
Taverners Way E4 ... 20 C3
Tavern La SW9 ... 138 C3
Tavistock Ave E17 ... 53 A6
 NW7 ... 28 D3
 Wembley UB6 ... 87 A5
Tavistock Cl N16 ... 73 C3
Tavistock Cres W11 ... 91 B2
 Mitcham CR4 ... 204 A5
Tavistock Ct WC1 ... 239 D6
 1 Croydon CR0 ... 205 B1
Tavistock Gdns IG3 ... 79 C4
Tavistock Gr CR0 ... 205 B2
Tavistock Ho 2 W11 ... 91 B2
Tavistock Mews 1
 W11 ... 91 B1
Tavistock Pl
 WC1 ... 94 A3 240 A6
 East Barnet N14 ... 15 B5
Tavistock Rd DA16 ... 146 C4
 E15 ... 76 D2
 E7 ... 76 D4
 N4,N15 ... 51 B3
 NW10 ... 89 D5
 W11 ... 91 B2
 4 Beckenham BR2 ... 208 D5
 Carshalton SM5 ... 202 B1
 Croydon CR0 ... 205 B1
 Edgware HA8 ... 26 C2
 Uxbridge UB10 ... 61 A3
 Wanstead E18 ... 55 A6
Tavistock Sq
 WC1 ... 93 D3 239 D6
Tavistock St
 WC2 ... 116 A6 250 B6
Tavistock Terr N19 ... 71 D5
Tavistock Twr SE16 ... 119 A3
Tavistock Wlk SM5 ... 202 B1
Taviton St WC1 ... 93 D3 239 C6
Tavy Bridge SE2 ... 124 C4
Tavy Cl SE11 ... 261 B2
Tawney Rd SE28 ... 124 B6
Tawny Cl Ealing W13 ... 109 B5
 Feltham TW13 ... 150 A1
Tawny Way SE16 ... 118 D2
Tayben Ave TW2 ... 152 C5
Taybridge Rd SW11 ... 137 A1
Tayburn Cl E14 ... 98 A1
Tayfield Cl UB10 ... 61 A5
Tay Ho 8 E3 ... 97 B5
Tayler Ct NW8 ... 229 C6
Taylor Ave TW9 ... 132 D3
Taylor Cl 3 BR6 ... 227 D4
 Hampton TW12 ... 174 A5
 Hounslow TW3 ... 130 A4
 Tottenham N17 ... 34 A3
Taylor Ct E15 ... 76 A3
 Ealing W13 ... 109 C5
 Penge SE20 ... 184 C1
Taylor Ho 10 SW2 ... 160 C3
Taylor Rd Mitcham CR4 ... 180 C3
 Wallington SM6 ... 219 B3
Taylor's Bldgs SE18 ... 122 D2
Taylors Cl DA14 ... 167 D1
Taylors Ct TW13 ... 150 A2
Taylor's Gn W3 ... 89 C1
Taylor's La NW10 ... 67 C1
 Barnet EN5 ... 1 B4
 Forest Hill SE26 ... 184 B6
Taylorsmead NW7 ... 28 A5
Taymount Grange 2
 SE23 ... 162 C2
Taymount Rise SE23 ... 162 C2
Tayport Cl N1 ... 72 A1
Tayside Ct 6 SE5 ... 139 B1
Tayside Dr HA8 ... 10 D2
Taywood Rd UB5 ... 85 B4
Teak Cl SE16 ... 119 A5
Tealby Ct N7 ... 72 B2
Teal Cl E16 ... 99 D2
Teal Ct NW10 ... 67 B2
 30 SE8 ... 141 B6
 Wallington SM6 ... 219 C3
Teale St E2 ... 96 A5
Tealing Dr KT19 ... 215 B4
Teal Pl SM1 ... 217 B3
Teasel Cl CR0 ... 206 D1
Teasel Way E15 ... 98 C4
Teather St 20 SE5 ... 139 C5
Tebbs Ho 14 SW2 ... 160 C4
Tebworth Rd N17 ... 33 D3
Teck Cl TW7 ... 131 A3
Tedder 5 NW9 ... 27 D3
Tedder Cl
 Chessington KT9 ... 213 C3
 Hillingdon UB10 ... 60 B1
Tedder Rd CR2 ... 222 D1
Teddington Memorial Hospl
 TW11 ... 174 C4
Teddington Park Rd
 TW11 ... 174 D6
Teddington Pk TW11 ... 174 D5
Teddington Sch TW11 ... 175 C4
Teddington Sta TW11 ... 175 A4
Ted Hennem Ho RM10 ... 81 D5
Ted Roberts Ho 24 E2 ... 96 B5
Tedworth Gdns SW3 ... 257 C1
Tedworth Sq
 SW3 ... 114 D1 257 C1
Tees Ave UB6 ... 86 D5
Tees Ct W7 ... 86 B1
Teesdale Ave TW7 ... 131 A4
Teesdale Cl E2 ... 96 B5
Teesdale Gdns
 Isleworth TW7 ... 131 A4
 South Norwood SE25 ... 183 C1
Teesdale Rd E11 ... 54 D2
Teesdale St E2 ... 96 B5
Teesdale Yd 33 E2 ... 96 B5
Teeswater Ct DA18 ... 124 D3
Tee The W3 ... 89 C1
Teevan Cl CR0 ... 206 A2
Teevan Rd CR0 ... 206 A2
Teignmouth Cl
 6 SW4 ... 137 D1
 Edgware HA8 ... 26 B1
Teignmouth Gdns UB6 ... 87 A4
Teignmouth Rd NW2 ... 68 D2
 Bexley DA16 ... 146 C3
Telcote Way HA4 ... 40 C2
Telegraph Hill NW3 ... 69 D5
Telegraph La KT10 ... 212 D3
Telegraph Mews IG3 ... 58 A1
Telegraph Pl E14 ... 119 D2
Telegraph Rd SW15 ... 156 C4
Telegraph St EC2 ... 242 C2
Telemann Sq SE3 ... 143 B2
Telfer Cl 4 W3 ... 111 A4
Telfer Ho EC1 ... 234 D1
 8 Dulwich SE21 ... 183 C6
Telferscot JMI Sch
 SW12 ... 159 D3
Telferscot Prim Sch
 SW12 ... 159 D3
Telferscot Rd SW12 ... 159 D3
Telford Ave SW12,SW2 ... 160 A3
Telford Avenue Mans 7
 SW2 ... 160 A3
Telford Cl E17 ... 53 A2
 Penge SE19 ... 183 D4
Telford Dr KT12 ... 194 C2
Telford Ho SE1 ... 262 A6
 8 W10 ... 91 A2
 2 Belvedere DA17 ... 125 C3
Telford Parade Mans 8
 SW2 ... 160 A3
Telford Rd 2 NW9 ... 46 A3
 W10 ... 91 A2
 Sidcup BR7,DA15 ... 167 B2
 Southall UB1 ... 85 D1
 Twickenham TW4 ... 151 C4
Telford Rd (North Circular
 Rd) N11 ... 31 C5
Telford Terr SW1 ... 269 A6
Telford Way W3 ... 89 C2
 Hayes UB4 ... 85 A2
Telham Rd E6 ... 100 C5
Tell Gr SE22 ... 139 D1
Tellson Ave SE18 ... 144 A4
Telscombe Cl BR6 ... 227 C6
Telscombe Ho SW11 ... 268 A1
Temair Ho 1 SE10 ... 142 A5
Temeraire St SE16 ... 118 C4
Temperley Rd SW12 ... 159 A4
Templar Ct RM7 ... 59 D5
Templar Dr SE28 ... 102 D1
Templar Ho 9 E5 ... 74 C6
 NW2 ... 69 B2
Templar Pl TW12 ... 173 C3
Templars Ave NW11 ... 47 B3
Templars Cres N3 ... 29 C1
Templars Dr HA3 ... 24 B4
Templars Ho E15 ... 75 D3
Templar St SE5 ... 138 D3
Temple Ave
 EC4 ... 116 C6 251 B6
 N20 ... 14 B4
 Croydon CR0 ... 223 B5
 Dagenham RM8 ... 59 C1
Temple Cl E11 ... 54 C2
 N3 ... 29 B1
 SE18 ... 123 A3
Templecombe Rd E9 ... 96 C6
Templecombe Way
 SM4 ... 201 A4
Templecroft TW15 ... 171 B4
Temple Ct SW8 ... 270 A3
Templedene BR2 ... 186 B1
Temple Dwellings 7
 E2 ... 96 B5
Temple Fortune Ct 9
 NW11 ... 47 B4
Temple Fortune Hill
 NW11 ... 47 C4
Temple Fortune Ho 3
 NW11 ... 47 B4
Temple Fortune La
 NW11 ... 47 C3
Temple Fortune Par 5
 NW11 ... 47 B4
Temple Gdns NW11 ... 47 B3
 Dagenham RM8 ... 80 D5
 Edmonton N21 ... 16 D2
Temple Gr NW11 ... 47 C3
 Enfield EN2 ... 4 D2
Temple Hall Ct 1 E4 ... 20 B2
Temple Ho 11 E17 ... 53 D6
 4 N7 ... 71 C5
 13 SW11 ... 136 C2
Templehof Ave NW2 ... 46 C2
Temple La EC4 ... 94 C1 241 B1
Temple Lo EN5 ... 14 B4
Templeman Rd W7 ... 86 D2
Templemead Cl W3 ... 89 C1
Temple Mead Cl HA7 ... 25 B4
Templemead Ho E9 ... 75 A4
Temple Mills La E10,
 E15 ... 76 A4
Temple Mills Rd E9 ... 75 C4
Templemore DA14 ... 190 B5
Temple Par EN5 ... 14 B4
Temple Pk UB8 ... 82 C4
Temple Pl
 WC2 ... 116 B6 250 D6
Temple Rd E6 ... 100 A6
 N8 ... 50 B5
 NW2 ... 68 C5
 W4 ... 111 A3
 W5 ... 109 D3
 Croydon CR0 ... 221 B4
 Isleworth TW3 ... 130 A1
 Richmond TW9 ... 132 B2
Temple Sheen SW14 ... 155 A6
Temple Sheen Rd
 SW14 ... 133 A1
Temple St E2 ... 96 B5
Temple Sta
 WC2 ... 116 C6 251 A6
Temple Terr N22 ... 32 C1
Templeton Ave E4 ... 35 D6
Templeton Cl 25 N16 ... 73 C3
 South Norwood SE19 ... 183 B2
Templeton Ct E10 ... 53 D1
Templeton Pl
 SW5 ... 113 C2 255 B3
Templeton Rd N4,N15 ... 51 B3
Temple Way SM1 ... 218 B5
Temple West Mews
 SE11 ... 261 C5
Templewood W13 ... 87 B2
Templewood Ave NW3 ... 69 D5
Templewood Gdns
 NW3 ... 69 D5
Templewood Point
 NW2 ... 69 B6
Tempsford Cl EN2 ... 5 A2
Tempsford Ct HA1 ... 42 D3
Temsford Cl HA2 ... 24 A1
Tenbury Cl E7 ... 77 D3
Tenbury Ct SW12 ... 159 D3
Tenby Ave HA3 ... 25 B1
Tenby Cl N15 ... 51 D5
 Dagenham RM6 ... 59 A3
Tenby Ct E17 ... 53 A4
Tenby Gdns UB5 ... 63 C2
Tenby Ho N7 ... 72 C4
 W2 ... 236 A1
 Hayes UB3 ... 105 A3
Tenby Rd DA16 ... 146 D4
 E17 ... 53 A4
 Dagenham RM6 ... 59 A3
 Edgware HA8 ... 26 B1
 Enfield EN3 ... 6 C1
Tench St E1 ... 118 B5
Tenda Rd SE16 ... 118 B2
Tendring Ho SW2 ... 160 C5
Tendring Way RM6 ... 58 C4
Tenham Ave SW2 ... 159 D2
Tenison Ct W1 ... 249 A6
Tenison Way SE1 ... 251 A3
Tenniel Cl W2 ... 245 D6
Tennison Ave WD6 ... 10 D6
Tennison Rd SE25 ... 205 D4
Tennis St SE1 ... 117 B4 252 C2
Tenniswood Rd EN1 ... 5 C4
Tennyson Ave E12 ... 78 A1
 NW9 ... 45 A6
 Twickenham TW1 ... 152 D3
 Wanstead E11 ... 55 A2
 West Barnes KT3 ... 200 B4
Tennyson Cl DA16 ... 145 D4
 Enfield EN3 ... 18 D6
 Feltham TW14 ... 150 A5
Tennyson Ct SW6 ... 265 D1
 3 Richmond TW10 ... 175 D6
Tennyson Ho SE17 ... 262 B2
 2 Erith DA17 ... 125 B1
Tennyson Rd E10 ... 75 D6
 E15 ... 76 C1
 E17 ... 53 B3
 NW6 ... 91 B6
 NW7 ... 28 A5
 Ashford TW15 ... 170 A5
 Ealing W7 ... 108 D6
 Hounslow TW3 ... 130 A3
 Penge SE20 ... 184 D3
 Wimbledon SW19 ... 180 A4
Tennyson St SW8 ... 137 B3
Tensing Ct TW19 ... 148 A3
Tensing Ho N1 ... 72 D2
Tensing Rd UB2 ... 107 C3
Tentelow La UB2 ... 107 D3
Tenterden Cl NW4 ... 46 D6
 SE9 ... 188 B6
Tenterden Dr NW4 ... 46 D6
Tenterden Gdns NW4 ... 46 D6
 Croydon CR0 ... 206 A2
Tenterden Gr NW4 ... 46 D6
Tenterden Ho SE17 ... 263 B2
Tenterden Rd
 Croydon CR0 ... 206 A2
 Dagenham RM8 ... 81 B6
 Tottenham N17 ... 33 D3
Tenterden St W1 ... 238 D1
Tenter Ground E1 ... 243 C3
Tent Peg La BR5 ... 211 A4
Tent St E1 ... 96 B3
Tenzing Ct 4 SE9 ... 166 A2
Terborah Way 6
 SE22 ... 161 C6
Terence Ct 6 DA17 ... 147 B6
Terence Messenger Twr
 E10 ... 75 D6
Teresa Mews E17 ... 53 C5
Teresa Wlk N10 ... 49 B4
Terling Cl E11 ... 76 D5
Terling Ho W10 ... 90 C2
Terling Rd RM8 ... 81 C6
Terling Wlk N1 ... 235 A6
Terminal Rdbt TW6 ... 149 A5
Terminus Pl SW1 ... 258 D5
Tern Ho 8 SE15 ... 139 D4
Terrace Ave NW10 ... 90 C4
Terrace Gdns SW13 ... 133 D3
Terrace La TW10 ... 154 A5
Terrace Rd E13 ... 99 B6
 E9 ... 74 C1
 Walton-on-T KT12 ... 194 B3
Terraces The 6 SW20 ... 178 D3
Terrace The EC4 ... 241 B1
 N2 ... 49 A5
 NW6 ... 91 C6
 9 SE8 ... 119 B2
 SW13,SW14 ... 133 C3
 Chingford E4 ... 20 C1
 1 Woodford IG8 ... 37 A4
Terrace Wlk RM9 ... 81 A3
Terrapin Ct SW17 ... 159 B1
Terrapin Rd SW17 ... 159 B1
Terrapins KT6 ... 197 D2
Terrick Rd N22 ... 32 A2
Terrick St W12 ... 90 B1
Terrilands HA5 ... 41 B6
Territorial Ho SE11 ... 261 B3
Terront Rd N15 ... 51 A5
Terry Ho SW2 ... 160 C3
Tersha St TW9 ... 132 B1
Tessa Sanderson Pl 6
 SW8 ... 137 B2
Tessa Sanderson Way
 UB6 ... 64 B3
Testerton Wlk 3 W11 ... 112 D6
Testwood Ct W7 ... 108 C6
Tetcott Rd
 SW10 ... 136 A5 266 A3
Tetherdown N10 ... 49 A6
Tetherdown Prim Sch
 N10 ... 49 A5
Tetty Way BR1,BR2 ... 187 A1
Teversham La
 SW8 ... 138 A4 270 B2
Teviot Cl DA16 ... 146 B4
Teviot St E14 ... 98 A2
Tewkesbury Ave
 Forest Hill SE23 ... 162 B4
 Pinner HA5 ... 41 A4
Tewkesbury Cl N15 ... 51 B3
Tewkesbury Gdns NW9 ... 44 D6
Tewkesbury Rd N15 ... 51 B3
 Carshalton SM5 ... 202 B1
 Ealing W13 ... 109 A6
Tewkesbury Terr N11 ... 31 D4
Tewson Rd SE18 ... 123 C1
Teyham Ct SW11 ... 158 D5
Teynham Ave EN1 ... 17 B5
Teynham Gn BR2 ... 209 A4
Teynham Ho SE9 ... 167 B5
Teynton Terr N17 ... 33 A2
Thackeray Ave N17 ... 34 A1
Thackeray Cl
 Harrow HA2 ... 41 C1
 Hayes UB8 ... 82 D1
 Isleworth TW7 ... 131 A3
 Wimbledon SW19 ... 178 D3
Thackeray Ct SW3 ... 257 C2
 W14 ... 254 A5
Thackeray Ct *continued*
 Ealing W5 ... 88 B
Thackeray Dr RM6 ... 58 B
Thackeray Ho WC1 ... 240 A
Thackeray Manor
 SM1 ... 218 A
Thackeray Mews E8 ... 74 A
Thackeray Rd E6 ... 99 D
 SW8 ... 137 B
Thackeray St W8 ... 255 D
Thackery Lo TW14 ... 149 B
Thackran Cl N2 ... 30 A
Thakeham Cl SE26 ... 184 B
Thalia Cl SE10 ... 142 B
Thame Rd SE16 ... 118 D
Thames Ave
 SW10 ... 136 A4 266 B
 Dagenham RM9,RM13 ... 103 D
 Wembley UB6 ... 86 D
Thames Bank SW14 ... 133 A
Thamesbank Pl SE28 ... 102 C
Thames Barrier Visitor
 Ctr★ SE18 ... 121 D
Thames Circ E14 ... 119 C
Thames Cl TW12 ... 173 D
Thames Cres W4 ... 133 C
Thames Ct 10 SE15 ... 139 D
 West Molesey KT8 ... 173 D
Thames Ditton Cty Fst Sch
 KT7 ... 196 D
Thames Ditton Island
 KT7 ... 197 A
Thames Ditton Jun Sch
 KT7 ... 196 D
Thames Ditton Sta
 KT7 ... 196 D
Thames Dr HA4 ... 39 A
Thames Eyot 7 TW1 ... 153 A
Thamesfield Ct TW17 ... 193 A
Thamesgate Cl TW10 ... 175 B
Thames Gateway Pk
 RM9 ... 103 B
Thames Haven KT6 ... 197 D
Thames Hts SE1 ... 253 C
Thameside TW11 ... 175 D
Thameside Ctr TW8 ... 132 B
Thameside Ind Est
 E16 ... 121 D
Thames Link Ho 7
 TW9 ... 132 A
Thames Mead KT12 ... 194 A
Thames Meadow
 East Molesey KT8 ... 195 C
 Lower Halliford KT12,
 TW17 ... 193 C
Thamesmead Sec Sch
 TW17 ... 193 B
Thamesmead Sh Ctr
 SE28 ... 124 A
Thamesmere Dr SE28 ... 124 A
Thames Pl SW15 ... 134 D
Thamespoint TW11 ... 175 D
Thames Quay E14 ... 119 D
 SW10 ... 266 B
Thames Rd E16 ... 121 D
 Barking IG11 ... 102 A
 Chiswick W4 ... 132 D
Thames Reach W6 ... 134 C
Thames Road Ind Est
 E16 ... 121 D
Thames Side
 Teddington KT1 ... 175 D
 Thames Ditton KT7 ... 197 B
Thames St SE10 ... 141 D
 Hampton TW12 ... 173 D
 Kingston KT1,KT2 ... 175 D
 Sunbury TW16 ... 194 B
 Walton-on-T KT12 ... 193 D
Thamesvale Cl TW3 ... 129 C
Thames Valley Univ
 W5 ... 109 D
Thames View Ho
 TW12 ... 194 A
Thames View Inf Sch
 IG11 ... 102 A
Thames View Jun Sch
 IG11 ... 101 D
Thames View Lodge
 IG11 ... 101 C
Thames Village W4 ... 133 A
Thames Wlk
 SW11 ... 136 C5 267 A
Thane Mans N7 ... 72 B
Thanescroft Gdns
 CR0 ... 221 C
Thanet Ct 14 W3 ... 88 C
Thanet Dr BR2 ... 225 D
Thanet Ho WC1 ... 233 A
 1 West Norwood SE27 ... 160 D
Thanet Lo NW2 ... 69 A
Thanet Pl CR0 ... 221 A
Thanet Rd DA5 ... 169 C
Thanet St WC1 ... 94 A4 233 A
Thane Villas N7 ... 72 B
Thane Works N7 ... 72 B
Thanington Ct DA15 ... 167 C
Thant Cl E10 ... 75 D
Tharp Rd SM6 ... 219 D
Thatcham Ct N20 ... 14 A

Thatcham Gdns N20 ...14 A4
Thatcher Cl UB7 ...104 A4
Thatchers Way TW7 ...152 B6
Thatches Gr RM6 ...59 A5
Thavie's Inn EC4 ...241 B2
Thaxted Ct N1 ...235 D3
Thaxted Ho SE16 ...118 C2
Dagenham RM10 ...81 D1
Thaxted Lo 3 E18 ...55 B6
Thaxted Pl 9 SW20 ...178 D2
Thaxted Rd SE9 ...167 A2
Buckhurst Hill IG9 ...21 D4
Thaxton Rd
W14 ...135 B6 264 D6
Thayers Farm Rd BR3 185 A2
Thayer St W1 ..93 A2 238 B2
Theatre Mus★ WC2 ..250 B6
Theatre Sq E15 ...76 B2
Theatre St SW11 ...136 D2
Theberton St
N1 ...94 D6 234 C6
Theed St SE1 .116 C5 251 B3
Thelbridge Ho 28 E3 ...97 D4
Thelma Gdns SE3 ...144 A4
Thelma Gr TW11 ...175 A4
Theobald Cres HA3 ...24 A2
Theobald Rd E17 ...53 C2
Croydon CR0 ...220 D6
Theobalds Av N12 ...30 A6
Theobalds Ct N4 ...73 A6
Theobalds Park Rd EN2 .4 D6
Theobald's Rd
WC1 ...94 B2 240 C4
Theobald St SE1 ...262 C5
Theodora Way HA5 ...39 D6
Theodore Ho 1 SW15 156 A6
Theodore Rd SE13 ...164 B5
Therapia La
Thornton Heath CR0 ...204 A2
Thornton Heath CR0 ...204 A3
Wallington CR0 ...203 D2
Therapia Lane Sta
CR0 ...204 A2
Therapia Rd SE22 ...162 C5
Theresa Rd W6 ...112 A2
Therfield Ct N4 ...73 A6
Thermopylae Gate
E14 ...119 D2
Theseus Ho 2 E14 ...98 B1
Theseus Wlk N1 ...234 D3
Thesiger Rd SE20 ...184 D3
Thessaly Ho SW8 ...269 A3
Thessaly Rd
SW8 ...137 C4 269 B2
Thesus Ho 2 E14 ...98 B1
Thetford Cl N13 ...32 D4
Thetford Ct
3 Dulwich SE21 ...162 B2
New Malden KT3 ...199 C4
Thetford Gdns RM9 ...103 A6
Thetford Ho SE1 ...263 C6
Thetford Rd
Ashford TW15 ...148 A1
Dagenham RM9 ...80 D1
New Malden KT3 ...199 C4
Thetis Terr TW9 ...132 C6
Theydon Gr IG8 ...37 C4
Theydon Rd E5 ...74 C6
Theydon St E17 ...53 B2
Thicket Cres SM1 ...218 A4
Thicket Gr
Dagenham RM9 ...80 C2
Penge SE20 ...184 A3
Thicket Rd Penge SE20 184 B3
Sutton SM1 ...218 A4
Thicket The UB7 ...82 A1
Third Ave E12 ...78 B3
3 E13 ...99 A4
E17 ...53 C4
W10 ...91 A4
W3 ...111 D5
Dagenham RM10 ...103 D5
Dagenham RM6 ...58 C3
Enfield EN1 ...17 D6
Hayes UB3 ...105 D5
Wembley HA9 ...65 D6
Third Cl KT8 ...196 A5
Third Cross Rd TW2 ...152 B2
Third Way HA9 ...66 D4
Thirleby Rd HA8 ...27 B2
SW1 ...115 C3 259 B5
Thirlestone Ct N10 ...31 A1
Thirlmere NW1 ...231 D2
Thirlmere Ave UB6 ...87 C4
Thirlmere Gdns HA9 ...43 D1
Thirlmere Ho 20 N16 ...73 B4
Isleworth TW1 ...152 D6
Thirlmere Rd N10 ...31 B2
Streatham SW16 ...181 D6
Thirlmere Rise BR1 ...186 D4
Thirsk Cl UB5 ...63 C2
Thirsk Rd SW11 ...137 A1
Mitcham CR4 ...181 A3
South Norwood SE25 ...205 B5
Thisilefield Cl DA5 ...168 D3
Thistlebrook SE2 ...124 C4
Thistlecroft Gdns HA7 .25 D1
Thistle Ct N17 ...52 B5
Thistledene KT7 ...196 C3
Thistledene Ave HA2 ...63 A5
Thistledown Ct SE25 ..205 C6
Thistle Gr SW7 ...256 B1
Thistle Ho 6 E14 ...98 A1
Thistlemead BR7 ...188 D1
Thistlewaite Rd E5 ...74 B5
Thistlewood Cl 3 N7 ..72 B6
Thistleworth Cl TW7 ..130 B5
Thistley Cl N12 ...30 C4
Thistly Ct SE8 ...141 D6
Thomas a' Beckett Cl
HA0 ...64 D4
Thomas Arnold Prim Sch
RM9 ...81 B1
Thomas Baines Rd
SW11 ...136 B2
Thomas Burt Ho 9 E2 .96 B4
Thomas Buxton Jun & Inf
Sch E1 ...96 A3
Thomas Cribb Mews
E6 ...100 B1
Thomas Ct E17 ...53 D4
Dagenham RM8 ...80 B3
Ealing W7 ...86 C1
Thomas Dean Rd SE26 185 B6
Thomas Dinwiddy Rd
SE12 ...165 B2
Thomas Doyle St SE1 .261 D6
Thomas Fairchild Comm
Sch N1 ...95 A5 235 B4
Thomas Gamuel Prim Sch
E17 ...53 C3
Thomas Hardy Ho N22 .32 B2
Thomas Hewlett Ho
HA1 ...64 C4
Thomas Ho 3 E9 ...74 C2
4 SW4 ...138 A1
Thomas Hollywood Ho 3
E2 ...96 C5
Thomas Jones Prim Sch
W11 ...91 A1
Thomas' La SE6 ...163 C4
Thomas More Ho EC2 242 A3
Thomas More Sq E1 ..118 A6
Thomas More St E1 ..118 A5
Thomas More Way N2 .48 A6
Thomas North Terr 3
E16 ...98 D2
Thomas Pl W8 ...255 C5
Thomas Pooley Ct
KT6 ...198 A2
Thomas Rd E14 ...97 C2
Thomas Road Ind Est
E14 ...97 C1
Thomas's London Day Schs
SW11 ...136 B4 266 D2
Thomas's Prep Sch
Clapham SW11 ...158 D6
Thomas St SE18 ...122 D2
Thomas Tallis Sch
SE3 ...143 B2
Thomas Wall Cl SM1 .217 D3
Thomas Watson Cottage
Homes The EN5 ...13 A6
Thompson Ave TW9 ..132 C2
Thompson Cl Ilford IG1 .79 A6
Morden SM3 ...201 C1
Thompson Ho SE14 ...140 D6
11 W10 ...91 A3
Thompson Rd SE22 ...161 D5
Dagenham RM9 ...81 B5
Hounslow TW3 ...129 D1
Uxbridge UB10 ...60 A1
Thompson's Ave 6
SE5 ...139 A5
Thomson Cres CR0 ...204 C1
Thomson Ho SE17 ...263 A3
SW1 ...259 D1
Southall UB1 ...107 A6
Thomson Rd HA3 ...42 C6
Thorburn Ho SW1 ...248 A1
Thorburn Sq SE1 ...118 A2
Thorburn Way SW19 ..180 B2
Thoresby Ho N16 ...73 B5
Thoresby St N1 .95 A4 235 B2
Thorkhill Gdns KT7 ...197 B1
Thorkhill Rd KT7 ...197 B2
Thornaby Gdns N18 ...34 B5
Thornaby Ho 15 E2 ...96 B4
Thorn Ave WD23 ...8 A3
Thornbill Ho 1 SE15 .140 A5
Thornbury 3 NW4 ...46 C5
Thornbury Ave TW7 ..130 B5
Thornbury Cl N16 ...73 C3
Thornbury Ct W11 ...245 A6
Croydon CR2 ...221 B3
Hounslow TW7 ...130 C5
Thornbury Ho N6 ...49 C1
Thornbury Rd SW2 ...160 A5
Hounslow TW7 ...130 B4
Thornbury Sq N6 ...49 C1
Thornby Rd E5 ...74 C5
Thorn Cl BR2 ...210 C3
Northolt UB5 ...85 B4
Thorncliffe Ct SW2 ...160 A5
Thorncliffe Rd SW2 ...160 A5
Southall UB2 ...107 B1
Thorncombe Rd SE22 .161 C6
Thorncroft Rd SM1 ..217 D4
Thorncroft St
SW8 ...138 A5 270 A3
Thorndale Ho N16 ...51 C1
Thorndean St SW18 ..158 A2
Thorndene Ave N11 ...15 A3
Thorndike Ave UB5 ...84 D6
Thorndike Cl
SW10 ...136 A5 266 A4
Thorndike Ho SW1 ...259 C2
Thorndike St
SW1 ...115 D2 259 C3
Thorndon Cl BR5 ...189 D1
Thorndon Gdns KT19 .215 C4
Thorndon Rd BR5 ...189 D1
Thorndyke Ct HA5 ...23 B3
Thorne Cl DA8 ...147 D6
E11 ...76 C4
E16 ...99 A1
Littleton TW15 ...171 A3
Thorne Ho 4 E14 ...120 A3
34 E2 ...96 C4
Thorneloe Gdns CR0,
CR9 ...220 D3
Thorne Pas 7 SW13 ..133 D3
Thorne Rd
SW8 ...138 A5 270 B3
Thorne's Cl BR3 ...208 A6
Thorness Ct SW18 ...158 A5
Thorne St SW13,SW14 .133 C2
Thornet Wood Rd
BR1 ...210 C6
Thornewill Ho 7 E1 ..118 C6
Thorney Cres
SW11 ...136 B5 266 D3
Thorneycroft Cl KT12 .194 C3
Thorneycroft Dr EN3 ...7 C6
Thorneycroft Ho 11
W4 ...111 C1
Thorney Ct W8 ...246 A1
Thorney Hedge Rd
W4 ...110 D2
Thorney St
SW1 ...116 A2 260 A4
Thornfield Ave NW7 ...29 A2
Thornfield Ct NW7 ...29 A2
Thornfield Ho 4 E14 .119 C6
Thornfield Par NW7 ...29 A3
Thornfield Rd W12 ..112 B4
Thornford Rd SE13 ...164 A6
Thorngate Rd W9 ...91 C3
Thorngrove Rd E13 ...99 B6
Thornham Gr E15 ...76 B3
Thorn Ham Ho SE1 ...262 D6
Thornham St SE10 ...141 D6
Thornhaugh St WC1 ..239 D5
Thornhill Ave SE18 ...145 C5
Surbiton KT6 ...214 A6
Thornhill Bridge Wharf
N1 ...233 C5
Thornhill Cres N1 ...72 B1
Thornhill Ct N8 ...49 D3
Thornhill Gdns E10 ...75 D6
Barking IG11 ...79 C1
Thornhill Gr N1 ...72 C1
Thornhill Ho N1 ...72 C1
12 W4 ...111 C1
Thornhill Prim Sch N1 .72 C1
Thornhill Rd E10 ...75 D6
N1 ...72 C1 234 A6
Ickenham UB10 ...60 C4
Surbiton KT6 ...214 B6
Thornton Heath CR0 ...205 A2
Thornhill Sq N1 ...72 B1
Thornhill Way TW17 ..192 C4
Thornicroft Ho 12
SW9 ...138 B3
Thornlaw Rd SE27 ...182 D6
Thornley Cl N17 ...34 A3
Thornley Dr HA2 ...63 D6
Thornley Pl 2 SE10 ..120 C1
Thornsbeach Rd SE6 .164 A2
Thornsett Pl SE20 ...184 B1
Thornsett Rd
Penge SE20 ...184 B1
Wandsworth SW18 ...157 D3
Thornsett Terr SE20 ...184 B1
Thornton Ave W4 ...111 C2
Streatham SW2 ...159 D3
Thornton Heath CR0 ...204 B3
West Drayton UB7 ...104 B3
Thornton Cl UB7 ...104 B3
Thornton Ct N7 ...72 A3
West Barnes SW20 ...200 D4
Thornton Dene BR3 ..185 C1
Thornton Gdns SW12 .159 D3
Thornton Gr HA5 ...23 C4
Thornton Heath Pond
CR7 ...204 C4
Thornton Heath Sta
CR7 ...205 A5
Thornton Hill SW19 ..179 A3
Thornton Ho SE17 ...263 A3
7 Wanstead E11 ...55 A3
Thornton Lo CR7 ...205 A6
Thornton Pl W1 ...237 D4
Thornton Rd BR1 ...187 A5
E11 ...76 B6
N18 ...18 C1
Barnet EN5 ...1 A2
Thornton Rd *continued*
Belvedere DA17 ...125 D2
Carshalton SM5 ...202 B1
Ilford IG1 ...78 D4
Mortlake SW14 ...133 B2
Streatham SW12,SW2 ..159 D3
Thornton Heath CR0,CR7 204 B3
Wimbledon SW19 ...178 D3
Thornton Rd E SW19 .178 D4
Thornton Row CR7 ...204 C4
Thornton St SW9 ...138 C3
Thornton Way NW11 ...47 D4
Thorntree Ct W5 ...88 A2
Thorntree Rd SE7 ...121 D1
Thorntree Sch SE7 ...121 B1
Thornville Gr CR4 ...180 B1
Thornville St SE8 ...141 C4
Thornwell Ct W7 ...108 C4
Thornwood Cl E18 ...37 B1
Thornwood Rd SE13 ..164 C6
Thornycroft Ct TW9 ..132 B3
Thorogood Gdns E15 ..76 C3
Thorold Ho SE1 ...252 A2
6 Streatham SW2 ...160 A4
Thorold Rd Ilford IG1 ...57 A1
Wood Green N22 ...32 A3
Thorparch Rd
SW8 ...137 D5 269 D3
Thorpebank Rd W12 ..112 A5
Thorpe Cl BR6 ...227 C6
W10 ...91 A1
Forest Hill SE26 ...184 D6
Thorpe Coombe Hospl
E17 ...54 A6
Thorpe Cres E17 ...35 B1
Thorpe Ct EN2 ...4 D2
Thorpedale Gdns IG6 ..56 D5
Thorpedale Rd N4 ...50 B1
Thorpe Hall W5 ...87 D2
Thorpe Hall Rd E17 ...36 A2
Thorpe Ho N1 ...233 D5
Thorpe Rd E6 ...100 B6
E7 ...76 D4
N15 ...51 C3
Barking IG11 ...79 B1
Chingford E17 ...36 A1
Kingston KT2 ...176 A3
Thorpewood Ave SE23,
SE26 ...162 B2
Thorpland Ave UB10 ...61 A5
Thorsden Way 2
SE19 ...183 C5
Thorverton Rd NW2 ...69 A5
Thoydon Rd E3 ...97 A5
Thrale Almhouses
SW16 ...182 A5
Thrale Rd SW16 ...181 C5
Thrale St SE1 ...252 B3
Thrasher Cl 20 E8 ...95 D6
Thrawl St E1 ...95 D2 243 D3
Thrayle Ho 2 SW9 ...138 B2
Threadgold Ho 8 N1 ...73 B2
Threadneedle St
EC2,EC3 ...95 B1 242 D1
Three Bridges Bsns Ctr
UB2 ...108 A4
Three Bridges Prim Sch
UB2 ...107 D3
Three Colts La E2 ...96 B3
Three Colt St E14 ...119 B6
Three Corners DA7 ...147 D3
Three Cups Yd WC1 ..240 D3
Three Kings Yd W1 ...248 C6
Three Meadows Mews
HA7 ...24 D2
Three Mill La E3 ...98 A4
Three Nun Ct EC2 ...242 B2
Three Oak La SE1 ...253 C2
Three Oaks Cl UB10 ...60 B5
Threshers Pl W11 ...244 A6
Thriffwood SE23,SE26 .162 D1
Thrigby Rd KT9 ...214 B2
Thring Ho 2 SW9 ...138 B3
Throckmorten Rd E16 .99 B1
Throgmorton Ave
EC2 ...95 B1 242 D2
Throgmorton St
EC2 ...95 B1 242 D2
Throwley Cl SE2 ...124 C3
Throwley Rd SM1 ...217 D3
Throwley Way SM1 ...217 D3
Thrupp Cl CR4 ...181 B1
Thrush Gn HA2 ...41 C5
Thrush St SE17 ...262 A2
Thunderer Rd RM9 ...103 B3
Thunder Rd RM9 ...103 B3
Thurbarn Rd SE6 ...185 D5
Thurland Ho 3 SE16 .118 B2
Thurland Rd SE16 ...118 A3
Thurlby Cl HA1 ...43 A3
Thurlby Croft NW4 ...46 C6
Thurlby Rd
Wembley HA0 ...65 D2
West Norwood SE27 ...182 C6
Thurleigh Ave SW12 ..159 A5
Thurleigh Ct SW12 ...159 A5
Thurleigh Rd SW12 ...159 A5
Thurleston Ave SM4 ..201 A4
Thurlestone Ave N12 ..30 D4
Thurlestone Ave *continued*
Ilford IG3 ...79 D4
Thurlestone Cl TW17 .193 A3
Thurlestone Ct 1 UB1 .85 D1
Thurlestone Par
TW17 ...193 A3
Thurlestone Rd SE27 .182 C6
Thurloe Cl SW7 ...257 A4
Thurloe Ct SW3 ...257 A3
Thurloe Pl
SW7 ...114 B2 256 D4
Thurloe Place Mews
SW7 ...256 D4
Thurloe Sq
SW7 ...114 C2 257 A4
Thurloe St
SW7 ...114 B2 256 D4
Thurlow Cl E4 ...35 D4
Thurlow Ct 6 E11 ...55 A4
Thurlow Gdns HA0 ...65 D3
Thurlow Hill SE21 ...161 A2
Thurlow Ho 17 SW16 .160 A1
Thurlow Park Rd SE21,
SE24 ...161 A2
Thurlow Rd NW3 ...70 B3
W7 ...109 A4
Thurlow St
SE17 ...117 C1 263 A1
Thurlow Terr NW5 ...71 A3
Thurlow Twrs SE27 ...160 C1
Thurlston Rd HA4 ...62 A5
Thurnby Ct TW2 ...152 C1
Thurnscoe NW1 ...232 A5
Thursland Rd DA14 ...191 A5
Thursley Cres CR0 ...224 B1
Thursley Gdns SW19 ..156 D2
Thursley Ho
3 Kingston KT2 ...176 D3
10 Streatham SW2 ...160 B4
Thursley Rd SE9 ...166 B1
Thurso Ho NW6 ...91 D5
Thurso St SW17 ...180 B6
Thurstan Rd SW20 ...178 B3
Thurston Ho 4 BR3 ...185 D4
Thurston Ind Est SE13 141 D2
Thurston Rd SE8,SE13 .141 D3
Southall UB1 ...85 B1
Thurtle Rd E2 ...95 D5
Thurza Ct TW7 ...130 D3
Thyer Cl BR6 ...227 A4
Thyra Gr N12 ...29 D4
Tibbatt's Rd E3 ...97 D3
Tibbenham Pl SE6 ...163 C2
Tibbenham Wlk E13 ...98 D5
Tibbets Cl SW19 ...156 D3
Tibbet's Corner SW19 156 D4
Tibbet's Ride SW19 ..156 D4
Tiber Gdns N1 ...233 B5
Ticehurst Cl BR5 ...190 A3
Ticehurst Rd SE23 ...163 A2
Tickford Cl SE2 ...124 C4
Tickford Ho NW8 ...230 A1
Tidal Basin Rd E16 ...120 D6
Tidbury Ct SW8 ...269 A3
Tidemill Prim Sch
SE8 ...141 C5
Tidenham Gdns CR0 ..221 C5
Tideside Ct SE18 ...122 A3
Tideswell 10 NW5 ...71 B4
Tideswell Rd
Croydon CR0 ...223 C5
Putney SW15 ...134 C1
Tideway Cl TW10 ...175 C6
Tideway Ct 9 SE16 ...118 D5
Tideway Ho E14 ...119 C4
Tideway Ind Est
SW8 ...137 C6 269 B5
Tideway Wharf SW13 .133 C3
Tideway Yd SW13 ...133 C3
Tidey St E3 ...97 C2
Tidford Rd DA16 ...145 D3
Tidworth Ho 13 SE22 .139 C2
Tidworth Rd E3 ...97 C3
Tiepigs La BR2,BR4 ...208 D1
Tierney Ct 4 CR0 ...221 D6
Tierney Rd SW2 ...160 A3
Tierney Terr SW2 ...160 A3
Tiffin Girls' Sch KT2 .176 A4
Tiffin Sch KT2 ...176 B1
Tiger Ho WC1 ...232 D1
Tiger La BR2 ...209 B5
Tiger Way E5 ...74 B4
Tigris Cl N9 ...18 C2
Tilbrook Rd SE3,SE9 ..143 C2
Tilbury Cl BR5 ...190 B1
13 SE15 ...139 D5
Tilbury Ho 4 SE14 ...140 D6
Tilbury Rd E10 ...54 A2
E6 ...100 B5
Tildesley Rd SW15 ...156 C5
Tile Farm Rd BR6 ...227 B5
Tilehurst NW1 ...231 D1
Tilehurst Point 2 SE2 124 C4
Tilehurst Rd
Cheam SM3 ...217 A3
Wandsworth SW17,
SW18 ...158 B3
Tile Kiln La N6 ...49 C1
Edmonton N13 ...33 A5
Tile Kiln La *continued*
Harefield UB9 ...38 D2
Tileyard Rd N7 ...72 A1
Tilford Ave CR0 ...224 A1
Tilford Gdns SW19 ...156 D3
Tilford Ho 8 SW2 ...160 B4
Tilia Rd E5 ...74 B4
Tilia Wlk 21 SW9 ...138 D1
Tilleard Ho 4 W10 ...91 A4
Tiller Ho 30 N1 ...95 C6
Tiller Rd E14 ...119 C3
Tillet Sq SE16 ...119 A4
Tillett Cl NW10 ...67 A2
Tillet Way 4 E2 ...96 A4
Tilley Rd TW14 ...150 A3
Tillingbourne Gdns N3 .47 B6
Tillingbourne Way N3 .47 B5
Tillingham Way N12 ...29 D6
Tilling Ho 1 SE15 ...140 B2
Tilling Rd NW2 ...46 C2
Tilling Way HA9 ...65 D6
Tillman Ho 8 SW2 ...160 B3
Tillman St E1 ...96 B1
Tillotson Ct SW8 ...269 D3
Tillotson Rd
Edmonton N9 ...17 D2
Harrow HA3 ...23 D3
Ilford IG1 ...56 C2
Tilney Ct EC1 ...242 B6
Kingston KT6 ...197 D4
Woodford IG9 ...21 A2
Tilney Dr IG9 ...21 A2
Tilney Gdns 12 N1 ...73 B2
Tilney Rd Chigwell IG9 ..21 B2
Dagenham RM9 ...81 B2
Southall UB2 ...106 C2
Tilney St W1 ...248 B4
Tilson Cl 2 SE15 ...139 C5
Tilson Gdns SW2,SW4 .160 A4
Tilson Ho SW2 ...160 A4
Tilson Rd N17 ...34 A2
Tilston Cl E11 ...76 D5
Tilton St SW6 ...264 B5
Tiltwood The W3 ...111 A6
Tilt Yard App SE9 ...166 B5
Timber Cl BR7 ...188 C1
Timbercroft KT19 ...215 C4
Timbercroft La SE18 ..145 C5
Timbercroft Prim Sch
SE18 ...145 C5
Timberdene NW4 ...28 D1
Timberland Cl 15
SE15 ...140 A5
Timberland Rd E1 ...96 B1
Timber Mill Way SW4 137 D2
Timber Pond Rd SE16 118 D4
Timber St EC1 ...242 A6
Timberwharf Rd N16 ..52 A3
Time Sq E8 ...73 D3
Times Sq SM1 ...217 D3
Timothy Cl 1 SW4 ...159 C6
Bexley DA6 ...169 A6
Timothy Ho DA18 ...125 A3
Timothy Rd E3 ...97 B2
Timsbury Wlk 5
SW15 ...156 A3
Tina Ct SW16 ...160 C1
Tindal St SW9 ...138 D4
Tinniswood Cl N5 ...72 C3
Tinsley Rd E1 ...96 C2
Tintagel Cres SE22 ...139 D1
Tintagel Ct EC1 ...241 C6
Tintagel Dr HA7 ...25 D6
Tintagel Ho SE20 ...184 A3
Tintern Ave NW9 ...44 D6
Tintern Cl
Putney SW15 ...157 A6
Wimbledon SW19 ...180 A4
Tintern Ct W13 ...109 A6
Tintern Gdns N14 ...16 A4
Tintern Ho NW1 ...231 D3
SW1 ...258 C3
Tintern Path NW9 ...45 C3
Tintern Rd
Carshalton SM5 ...202 B1
Tottenham N22 ...33 A2
Tintern St SW4 ...138 A1
Tintern Way HA2 ...41 D1
Tinto Rd E16 ...99 A3
Tinwell Mews WD6 ...11 B6
Tinworth St
SE11 ...116 A1 260 B2
Tippett Ct E6 ...100 B5
Tippetts Cl EN2 ...5 A4
Tipthorpe Rd SW11 ...137 A2
Tipton Dr CR0 ...221 C4
Tiptree 7 NW1 ...71 B1
Tiptree Cl E4 ...20 A1
Tiptree Cres IG5 ...56 C6
Tiptree Ct EN2 ...5 B1
Tiptree Dr EN2 ...5 B1
Tiptree Rd HA4 ...62 B4
Tirlemont Rd CR2 ...221 A1
Tirrell Rd CR0 ...205 A3
Tisbury Ct W1 ...249 C6
Tisbury Rd SW16 ...182 A1

Tisdall Pl SE17 117 B2 262 D3
Tissington Ct 4 SE16 118 D2
Titan Bsns Est 3 SE8 141 C5
Titan Ct TW8 110 B1
Titchborne Row W2 237 B1
Titchfield Rd
NW8 92 D6 230 C4
Carshalton SM5 202 B1
Enfield EN3 7 A6
Titchfield Wlk SM5 202 B2
Titchwell Rd SW18 158 B3
Tite St SW3 136 D6 267 C6
Tithe Barn Cl KT2 176 B2
Tithe Barn Way UB5 84 B5
Tithe Cl NW7 28 A2
Hayes UB4 83 D2
Walton-on-T KT12 194 B3
Tithe Ct NW4 28 A2
Tithe Farm Ave HA2 63 C5
Tithe Farm Cl HA2 63 C5
Tithe Wlk NW7 28 A2
Titian Ave WD23 8 C4
Titley Cl E4 35 C5
Titmus Cl UB8 83 A1
Titmuss Ave SE28 124 B6
Titmuss St W12 112 C4
Tivendale N8 50 A6
Tiverton Ave IG5 56 C6
Tiverton Dr SE9 167 A3
Tiverton Prim Sch N15 51 B3
Tiverton Rd N4,N15 51 B3
NW6,NW10 90 D6
Edgware HA8 26 B1
Edmonton N18 33 C5
Hounslow TW3 130 A3
Ruislip HA4 62 A5
Wembley HA0 88 A5
Tiverton St
SE1 117 A3 262 A6
Tiverton Way KT9 213 D3
Tivoli Ct SE16 119 B5
Tivoli Gdns 11 SE7 122 A2
Tivoli Rd N8 49 D4
Hounslow TW4 129 A1
West Norwood SE27 183 A5
Toad La TW4 129 B1
Tobago St E14 119 C4
Tobin Cl NW3 70 C1
Toby Ct N9 18 C4
Toby La E1 97 A3
Toby Way KT5,KT6 214 D6
Todber Ho W14 254 B5
Todd Ho 3 N2 30 B1
Todds Wlk N7 72 B6
Tokenhouse Yd EC2 242 C2
Tokyngton Ave HA9 66 C2
Toland Sq SW15 156 A6
Tolcairn Ct 2 DA17 125 C1
Tolcarne Dr HA5 40 B6
Tolchurch 2 W11 91 C1
Toley Ave HA3,HA9 44 A2
Tollbridge Cl W10 91 A3
Tollesbury Gdns IG6 57 B6
Tollet St E1 96 D3
Tollgate Dr
Dulwich SE21 161 C2
Hayes UB4 106 D6
Tollgate Ho 1 NW6 91 D5
Tollgate Prim Sch E13 99 C3
Croydon CR0 206 C3
Tollgate Rd E6 100 A2
Tollhouse Way N19 71 C6
Tollington Ct N4 72 B6
Tollington Pk N4 72 B6
Tollington Pl N4 72 B6
Tollington Rd N7 72 B4
Tollington Way N7 72 A5
Tolmers Sq
NW1 93 C3 239 B6
Tolpaide Ho SE11 261 A3
Tolpuddle Ave 2 E13 99 C6
Tolsford Rd E5 74 B3
Tolson Ho 2 TW7 131 A2
Tolson Rd TW7 131 A2
Tolverne Rd SW20 178 C2
Tolworth Cl KT6 198 D1
Tolworth Gdns RM6 58 D4
Tolworth Girls' Sch
KT6 214 B5
Tolworth Hospl KT6 214 C6
Tolworth Inf Sch KT6 198 B1
Tolworth Junc KT6 214 D6
Tolworth Jun Sch KT6 198 B1
Tolworth Par RM6 59 A4
Tolworth Park Rd KT6 214 B6
Tolworth Rd KT6 214 A6
Tolworth Rise N KT5 198 D1
Tolworth Rise S KT5 198 D1
Tolworth Sta KT5 214 D6
Tolworth Underpass
KT5,KT6 214 D6
Tomahawk Gdns 4
UB5 84 D4
Tom Coombs Cl SE9 144 A1
Tom Cribb Rd SE18,
SE28 123 B3
Tom Groves Cl E15 76 B3
Tom Hood Cl E15 76 B3
Tom Hood Sch E11 76 D5
Tom Jenkinson Rd 5
E16 121 A5
Tomkyns Ho SE11 261 A3
Tomline Ho SE1 252 A3
Tomlin's Gr E3 97 C4
Tomlinson Cl E2 95 D4
5 W4 110 D1
Tomlins Orch IG11 101 A6
Tomlin's Terr E14 97 A1
Tomlins Wlk 4 N7 72 B6
Tom Mann Cl IG11 101 C6
Tom Nolan Cl E15 98 C5
Tompion Ho EC1 241 D6
Tompion St EC1 234 D1
Tom Smith Cl SE10 142 C6
Tom Smith Ho 3 E17 54 A4
Tomson Ho SE1 263 C6
Tom Williams Ho
SW6 264 C5
Tonbridge Cres HA3 44 A5
Tonbridge Hos WC1 233 A1
Tonbridge Rd KT12,
KT8 195 B5
Tonbridge St
WC1 94 A4 233 A1
Toneborough 14 NW8 91 D6
Tonfield Rd SM3 201 B1
Tonge Cl BR3 207 C4
Tonsley Hill SW18 157 D6
Tonsley Pl SW18 157 D6
Tonsley Rd SW18 157 D6
Tonsley St SW18 157 D6
Tonstall Rd CR4 181 A1
Tooke Cl HA5 23 A2
Tookey Cl HA3 44 B2
Took's Ct EC4 241 A2
Tooley St SE1 117 C5 253 A3
Toorack Rd HA3 24 B1
Tooting Bec SW17 159 A1
Tooting Bec Gdns
SW16 181 D6
Tooting Bec Rd
Streatham SW16 181 C5
Upper Tooting, Furzedown
SW17 181 B6
Tooting Bec Sta SW17 159 A1
Tooting Broadway
SW17 180 D5
Tooting Broadway Sta
SW17 180 C5
Tooting Gr SW17 180 C5
Tooting High St SW17,
SW19 180 C5
Tooting Sta SW17 180 D4
Tootswood Rd BR2,
BR3 208 C5
Topaz Ho KT4 199 B1
Topaz Wlk NW2 46 D2
Topcliffe Dr BR6 227 B4
Topham Ho 8 SE10 142 A5
Topham Sq N17 33 A2
Topham St EC1 241 A6
Top House Rise E4 20 A4
Topiary Sq TW9 132 B2
Topley St SE9 143 D1
Topmast Point E14 119 C4
Top Pk BR3 208 C4
Topsfield Cl N8 49 D4
Topsfield Par N8 50 A3
Topsfield Rd N8 50 A4
Topsham Rd SW17 181 A6
Torbay Ct 13 NW1 71 B1
Torbay Mans NW6 91 B6
Torbay Rd NW6 69 B1
Harrow HA2 63 A6
Torbay St 15 NW1 71 B1
Torbitt Way IG2 57 D4
Torbridge Cl HA8 26 A3
Torbrook Cl DA5 169 A5
Torcross Dr SE23 162 C2
Torcross Rd HA4 62 C5
Tor Ct W8 245 B2
Torfell 5 E18 36 D1
Tor Gdns W8 113 C4 245 A2
Tor Ho N6 49 B3
Tormead Cl SM1 217 C2
Tormount Rd SE18 145 C6
Tornay Ho E9 74 C1
N1 233 C4
Toronto Ave E12 78 B4
Toronto Rd IG1 57 A1
Torquay Gdns IG4 55 D5
Torquay St W2 91 D2
Tor Rd DA16 146 C4
Torrens Ct SE5 139 B2
Torrens Rd E15 76 D2
SW2 160 B6
Torrens Sq E15 76 D2
Torrens St EC1 94 D5 234 C3
Torres Sq E14 119 C1
Torre Wlk SM5 202 C1
Torriano Ave NW5 71 D3
Torriano Cotts NW5 71 C3
Torriano Jun & Inf Schs
NW5 71 D3
Torridge Gdns SE15 140 C1
Torridge Rd CR7 204 D4
Torridon Ho NW6 91 D5
Torridon Inf Sch SE6 164 B2
Torridon Jun Sch SE6 164 B2
Torridon Rd SE13,SE6 164 B3
Torrington Ave N12 30 B5
Torrington Cl N12 30 B6
Claygate KT10 212 C2
Torrington Ct N12 30 B6
Forest Hill SE26 184 A5
Harrow HA2 63 D5
Torrington Dr HA2 63 D5
Torrington Gdns N11 31 C4
Wembley UB6 65 C1
Torrington Gr N12 30 C5
Torrington Pk N12 30 B6
Torrington Pl E1 118 A5
WC1 93 D2 239 C4
Torrington Rd
Claygate KT10 212 C2
Dagenham RM8 59 B1
Ruislip HA4 62 A5
Wanstead E18 55 A6
Wembley UB6 87 C6
Torrington Sq
WC1 93 D3 239 D5
Thornton Heath CR0 205 B2
Torrington Way SM4 201 C3
Torr Rd SE20 184 D3
Tortington Ho 1 SE15 140 B5
Torver Rd HA1 42 C5
Torver Way BR6 227 B5
Torwood Rd SW15 156 A6
Totham Lo SW20 178 B2
Tothill Ho SW1 259 D4
Tothill St SW1 115 D4 249 D1
Totland Ho SW18 157 D5
Totnes Rd DA16 146 C5
Totnes Villas N11 31 C5
Totnes Wlk N2 48 B5
Tottan Terr E1 96 D1
Tottenhall 5 NW1 71 A1
Tottenhall Inf Sch N13 32 C4
Tottenhall Rd N13 32 D4
Tottenham Court Rd
W1 93 C2 239 B4
Tottenham Court Road Sta
W1 93 D1 239 D2
Tottenham Gn E 2
N15 51 D5
Tottenham Gn E South Side
3 N15 51 D5
Tottenham Hale N15 52 A5
Tottenham Hale Ret Pk
N15 52 A5
Tottenham Hale Sta
N17 52 B6
Tottenham La N8 50 B4
Tottenham Mews W1 239 B4
Tottenham Rd N1 73 C2
Tottenham St
W1 93 C2 239 B4
Totterdown St SW17 180 D5
Totteridge Comm N20 12 C3
Totteridge Ho SW11 136 B3
Totteridge La N20 13 D3
Totteridge Rd EN3 6 D6
Totteridge Village N20 13 B3
Totteridge & Whetstone Sta
N20 14 A2
Totternhoe Cl HA3 43 C4
Totton Rd CR7 204 C6
Touchard Ho N1 235 D1
Toulmin St
SE1 117 A4 252 A1
Toulon St SE5 139 A5
Toulouse Ct 2 SE16 118 B1
Tournay Rd
SW6 135 B5 264 D4
Toussaint Wlk 18
SE16 118 A3
Tovil Cl SE20 184 B1
Tovy Ho 6 SE1 118 A1
Towcester Rd E3 98 A3
Tower 42★ EC2 243 A2
Tower Bldgs 22 E1 118 B5
Tower Br App E1,EC3 253 C5
Tower Bridge★
E1,EC3,SE1 117 D5 253 C4
Tower Bridge Bsns Complex
SE16 118 B3
Tower Bridge Bsns Sq
SE16 118 B2
Tower Bridge Piazza
SE1 253 C3
Tower Bridge Prim Sch
SE1 117 D4 253 C2
Tower Bridge Rd
SE1 117 C4 253 C3
Tower Bridge Sq SE1 253 C2
Tower Cl NW3 70 B3
Orpington BR6 227 D5
Penge SE20 184 B3
Tower Ct E5 51 D2
NW8 230 B4
WC2 240 A1
Tower Gardens Rd N17 33 B2
Towergate SE1 263 A4
Towergate Cl UB8 60 A3
Tower Gateway Sta
EC3 117 D6 253 C6
Tower Gdns KT10 213 A1
Tower Gr KT13 193 C1
Tower Hamlets Coll E1 96 C2
E1 96 D1
E14 119 D6
E14 97 D1
Tower Hamlets Rd E17 53 C6
E7 76 D3
Tower Hill
EC3 117 D6 253 C5
Tower Hill Sta
EC3 117 D6 253 C6
Tower Hill Terr EC3 253 B5
Tower La HA9 65 D5
Tower Mans SE1 263 C5
Tower Mews E17 53 C5
E5 75 A3
Tower Millennium Pier
EC3 117 C5 253 B4
Tower Mill Rd 1
SE15 139 C5
Tower Rd DA7 147 D1
NW10 68 A1
Orpington BR6 227 D5
Twickenham TW1,TW2 152 D1
Tower Rise TW9 132 A2
Tower Royal EC4 252 C6
Towers Ave UB10 83 A4
Towers Ct UB10 83 A4
Towers Pl TW10 154 A6
Towers Rd Pinner HA5 23 A2
Southall UB1 85 C3
Tower St WC2 240 A1
Towers The NW5 71 B5
1 Richmond TW9 132 B1
Tower Terr SE4 141 A1
Wood Green N22 32 B1
Tower The★
EC3 117 D6 253 C5
Tower View CR0 207 A2
Tower Wharf SE1 253 C2
Tower Wlk SE1 263 A4
Towfield Ct TW13 151 B2
Towfield Rd TW13 151 B2
Towncourt Cres BR5 211 B5
Towncourt La BR5 211 B2
Towncourt Path N4 51 A1
Townend Ct 6 BR1 186 D2
Towney Mead UB5 85 B5
Towney Mead Ct UB5 85 B5
Townfield Rd UB3 105 D5
Townfield Sq UB3 105 D6
Town Field Way TW7 131 A3
Town Hall Approach Rd
N15 51 D5
Townhall Ave 3 W4 111 B1
Town Hall Rd SW11 136 D2
Townholm Cres W7 108 D3
Town La TW19 148 A2
Townley Ct E15 76 D2
Townley Gram Sch for Girls
DA5 169 B6
Townley Rd DA6 169 B6
SE22 161 C6
Townley St
SE17 117 B1 262 C2
Townmead Bsns Ctr
SW6 136 A2
Town Meadow TW8 131 D5
Townmead Rd SW6 136 A3
Richmond TW9 132 D3
Town Quay IG11 100 D6
Town Quay Wharf
IG11 100 D6
Town Rd N9 18 B2
Townsend Ave N14 31 D6
Townsend Ho 12 SE1 118 A2
Townsend Ind Est
NW10 89 A5
Townsend La NW9 45 B3
Townsend Prim Sch
SE17 117 C2 263 A4
Townsend Rd N15 51 D4
Ashford TW15 170 A5
Southall UB1 107 A5
Townsend St
SE1,SE17 117 C2 263 A4
Townsend Way HA6 22 A3
Townsend Yd N6 49 B1
Townshend Cl DA14 190 C4
Townshend Ct NW8 230 B4
Townshend Est
NW8 92 C5 230 A4
Townshend Ho 19
SE18 122 B2
Townshend Rd
NW8 92 C6 230 A5
Chislehurst BR7 188 D5
Richmond TW9 132 B1
Townshend Terr TW9 132 B1
Towns Ho 4 SW4 137 D2
Townson Ave UB5 84 B5
Townson Way UB5 84 A5
Town The EN2 5 B2
Town Tree Rd TW15 170 C5
Towpath TW17 192 B1
Towpath Way CR0 205 D4
Towton Rd SE27 161 A2
Toxteth Ho N4 51 A2
Toynbec Cl BR7 188 D6
Toynbee Rd SW19,
SW20 179 A2
Toynbee St E1 95 D2 243 C3
Toyne Way N6 48 D3
Tracey Ave NW2 68 C3
Tracy Ct HA7 25 C3
Tracy Ho 12 E3 97 B4
Trade Cl N13 32 C6
Trader Rd E6 100 D1
Tradescant Ho 15 E9 74 C1
Tradescant Rd
SW8 138 A5 270 B3
Trade Twr 8 SW11 136 A2
Trade Winds Ct 1 E1 118 A5
Trading Estate Rd
NW10 89 A3
Traemore Ct SW16 160 C1
Trafalgar Ave SE15 139 D6
North Cheam KT4,SM3,
SM4 200 D1
Tottenham N17 33 C4
Trafalgar Bsns Ctr
IG11 101 D3
Trafalgar Cl 1 SE16 119 A2
Trafalgar Ct Barking E6 100 C6
Hounslow TW3 129 B2
West Barnes KT3 200 B6
Trafalgar Gdns E1 96 D2
W8 255 D6
Trafalgar Gr SE10 142 B6
Trafalgar Ho SE17 262 B2
Barking IG11 102 B4
Trafalgar Inf Sch TW2 152 B2
Trafalgar Jun Sch
TW2 152 B2
Trafalgar Mews E9 75 B2
Trafalgar Pl
Edmonton N18 34 A5
Wanstead E11 55 A5
Trafalgar Rd SE10 120 C1
Merton SW19 180 A3
Twickenham TW2 152 B2
Trafalgar Sq★
SW1 115 D5 249 D4
Trafalgar St
SE17 117 B1 262 D2
Trafalgar Terr HA1 42 C1
Trafalgar Trad Est EN3 7 A1
Trafalgar Way E14 120 A5
Croydon CR0 220 C6
Trafford Cl E15 75 D3
Trafford Ho N1 235 D4
Trafford Rd CR7 204 B4
Tragail SW15 157 A6
Traherne Lo 3 TW11 174 D5
Traitors Gate★
EC3 117 D5 253 C4
Tralee Ct 31 SE16 118 B1
Tramsheds The CR0,
CR4 203 D2
Tramway Ave E15 76 B1
N9 18 C4
Tramway Path CR4 202 C5
Trance Way W3 110 C3
Tranmere Ct 5 SM2 218 A1
Tranmere Ho 7 N7 72 C3
Tranmere Rd
Edmonton N9 17 D4
Twickenham TW2 151 D4
Wandsworth SW17,
SW18 158 A2
Tranquil Pass SE3 142 D3
Tranquil Vale SE3 142 C3
Transept St NW1 237 B3
Transmere Cl BR5 211 A3
Transmere Rd BR5 211 A3
Transom Cl SE16 119 A2
Transom Sq E14 119 D1
Transport Ave TW8 131 B6
Tranton Rd SE16 118 B3
Trappes Ho 2 SE16 118 B2
Traps La KT2,KT3 177 C2
Travel Clinic, Hospl for
Tropical Diseases
WC1 93 C3 239 B5
Travellers Way TW5 128 C3
Travers Cl E17 34 D2
Travers Ho 6 SE10 142 B6
Travers Rd N7 72 C5
Travis Ho SE10 142 A4
Treacy Cl WD23 8 A2
Treadgold Ho 7 W11 112 D6
Treadgold St W11 112 D6
Treadway St E2 96 B5
Treasury Buildings
SW1 250 A2
Treaty Ctr TW3 129 D2
Treaty St N1 94 B6 233 C5
Trebeck St W1 248 C3
Treborough Ho W1 238 A4
Trebovir Rd
SW5 113 C2 255 B3
Treby St E3 97 B3
Trecastle Way 3 N7 71 D4
Tredegar Rd E3 97 B5
N11 31 D3
Tredegar Sq E3 97 B
Tredegar Terr E3 97 B
Trederwen Rd E8 96 A
Tredown Rd SE26 184 C
Tredwell Cl BR2 210 A
Tredwell Rd SE27 182 D
Tree Cl TW10 153 D
Treen Ave SW13 133 D
Tree Rd E16 99 C
Trees The N16 51 B
Tree Tops 1 IG8 37 A
Treetops Cl SE2 125 A
Treetops Ct CR7 205 A
Treetops View IG10 21 D
Treeview Cl SE19 183 C
Treewall Gdns BR1 187 B
Trefgarne Rd RM10 81 C
Trefil Wlk N7 72 A
Trefoil Ho DA18 125 A
Trefoil Rd SW18 158 A
Trefusis Ct TW5 128 B
Tregaron Ave N8 50 A
Tregaron Gdns KT3 199 C
Tregarvon Rd SW11 137 A
Tregenna Ave HA2 63 C
Tregenna Cl 1 N14 15 C
Tregenna Ct HA2 63 C
Tregony Rd BR6 227 D
Trego Rd E9 75 C
Tregothnan Rd SW9 138 A
Tregunter Rd
SW10 114 A1 256 A
Treherne Ct SW9 138 D
Upper Tooting SW17 181 A
Trehern Rd 12 SW14 133 B
Trehurst St E5 75 A
Trelawney Est E9 74 C
Trelawney Ho SE1 252 A
Trelawn Rd E10 76 A
SW2 160 C
Trelawny Cl E17 53 D
Trellis Ho SW19 180 A
Trellis Sq 1 E3 97 B
Treloar Gdns SE19 183 B
Tremadoc Rd SW4 137 D
Tremaine Cl SE4 141 C
Tremaine Rd SE20 184 B
Trematon Ho SE11 261 B
Trematon Pl TW11 175 C
Tremlett Gr N19 71 C
Tremlett Mews N19 71 C
Trenance Gdns IG3 80 A
Trenchard Ave HA4 62 B
Trenchard Cl NW9 27 C
Stanmore HA7 25 B
Trenchard Ct SM4 201 C
Trenchard St SE10 120 B
Trenchold St
SW8 138 A6 270 A
Trend Ct W13 109 B
Trendell Ho 4 E14 97 C
Trenholme Cl SE20 184 B
Trenholme Rd SE20 184 B
Trenholme Terr SE20 184 B
Trenmar Gdns NW10 90 B
Trenmar Lo NW10 90 B
Trent Ave W5 109 C
Trent CE Prim Sch EN4 2 D
Trent Ct E11 55 A
Trent Ctry Pk EN4 3 A
Trent Gdns N14 15 B
Trentham Lo 8 EN1 17 C
Trentham St SW18 157 C
Trent Ho SE15 140 C
4 Kingston KT2 175 D
Trent Rd SW2 160 B
Buckhurst Hill IG9 21 B
Trent Way Hayes UB4 83 C
North Cheam KT4 216 C
Trentwood Side EN2 4 B
Treport St SW18 157 D
Tresco Cl BR1 186 C
Trescoe Gdns HA2 41 A
Tresco Gdns IG3 80 A
Tresco Ho SE11 261 A
Tresco Rd SE15 140 B
Tresham Cres
NW8 92 C3 237 A
Tresham Rd IG11 79 D
Tresham Wlk E9 74 C
Tresidder Ho 10 SW4 159 D
Tresilian Ave N21 16 B
Tressel Cl 20 N1 72 D
Tressillian Cres SE4 141 C
Tressillian Rd SE4 141 C
Trestis Cl UB4 84 C
Treswell Rd RM9 103 A
Tretawn Gdns NW7 11 C
Tretawn Pk NW7 27 C
Trevallyn Lo 1 KT2 176 C
Trevanion Rd W14 254 B
Treve Ave HA1 42 B
Trevelayan Rd SW17 180 D
Trevelyan Ave E12 78 B
Trevelyan Cres HA3 43 D
Trevelyan Ct KT3 199 D
Trevelyan Gdns NW10 90 C
Trevelyan Ho 16 E2 96 D
SE5 138 D

lyan Ho *continued*
vickenham TW1 153 C5
lyan Rd E15 76 D4
nna Ho 13 SE23 162 D1
ris St SE1 251 D3
rsh Ct 7 BR1 186 D2
rton St W10 90 D3
rton Twr W10 90 D2
s Cl N21 16 B6
s Ho E1 96 A3
le St SW15 156 B4
o Rd SE23 163 A2
hick Cl TW14 149 D3
hick Ho 3 NW5 71 B4
E16 118 B2
269 C2
hick St SE8 141 C6
ne Gdns HA5 41 A3
r Cl Harrow HA3 24 D3
s BR2 209 A2
orth TW7 152 D6
Barnet EN4 14 B5
olt UB5 84 C5
r Cres HA4 61 D4
r Gdns HA8 27 B2
olt UB5 84 C5
r Pl SW7 114 C4 247 B1
r Rd HA8 27 B2
s UB3 105 C4
bledon SW19 179 A3
lford IG8 37 A3
r Roberts Tutorial Coll 70 B1
r Sq SW7 114 C4 247 B1
r St SW7 114 C4 247 B1
se Ho SE11 260 D2
se Rd E17 36 B2
enna Dr KT9 213 D3
nce Rd SW20 178 C2
nt St SW18 158 A2
sbury Ho 2 SE2 124 D4
sbury Rd SE26 184 D5
dra Way UB4 84 D2
gle Ct E16 99 C2
gle Ctr UB1 108 B5
gle Est The SE11 261 A1
gle Ho SE1 253 C2
gle Pl SW4 137 D1
gle Rd 7 E8 96 B6
gle The E8 96 B6
241 D6
49 D2
ing IG11 79 A2
ston KT3 177 A1
ne Ct 16 NW9 46 A5
nt Gdns 6 UB5 84 D4
nt Ho 9 E14 98 A1
nt St SE16 118 D2
nt Way UB2 106 B3
te Ct SW12 158 D3
n Rd 138 B5 270 D4
y Rd SE23 162 D2
Ct IG1 57 C2
don NW1 232 B5
ner Ct TW7 130 D2
ner Wlk 11 TW8 132 A6
St SE8 141 B6
er Gdns N19 50 A1
er Rd N4,N19 50 A1
et EN5 12 C6
Ave Ealing W5 110 B5
hall UB1 85 B1
bley HA9 66 C2
Cl IG2 57 B4
Ct TW1 175 A6
dad Ho 17 E14 119 B6
dad St E14 119 B6
y Ave N2 48 B6
ld EN1 17 D5
y Church Rd
3 134 B6
y Church Sq 117 A3 262 B6
y Cl E11 76 C6
142 B1
W4 137 C1
slow TW4 129 A1
on Mark BR2 210 A1
y Cotts TW9 132 B2
y Cres SW17 159 A2
y Ct 2 N1 95 C6
119 A4
166 D5
240 C6
Chingford E4 20 A2
onton N18 33 D4
st Hill SE23 162 C1
hgate N21 16 D3
nton Heath SE25 205 C3
kenham TW2 152 C2
ty Gdns E16 98 D2
,SW9 138 B1
Wanstead E18 55 B6
ty Gn E1 96 C2
ty Gr 8 SE10 142 A4
ty Ho 5 E17 53 D6
262 B6
ty Homes 14 SW2 138 B1

Trinity Mews SE9 167 B5
Penge SE20 184 B2
Wandsworth SW18 157 C3
Trinity Par TW3 129 D2
Trinity Pl DA6 147 B1
EC3 253 C5
Trinity RC High Sch (Lower) IG8 37 A6
Trinity RC High Sch (Upper Sch) IG8 36 D6
Trinity RC High Sch (Upper) IG8 37 A6
Trinity Rd N2 48 B6
Ilford IG6 57 A6
Richmond TW9 132 B2
Southall UB1 107 A5
Wandsworth SW17, SW18 158 C4
Wimbledon SW19 179 C4
Wood Green N22 32 A3
Wood Green N22 32 B2
Trinity Rise SE24,SW2 160 D4
Trinity Sch
Croydon CR0 222 C6
Dagenham RM10 81 C4
Trinity Sq EC3 117 C6 253 B6
Trinity St 9 E16 99 A2
SE1 117 B3 262 C6
Enfield EN2 5 A3
Trinity St Mary's CE Prim Sch SW12 159 A3
Trinity Terr IG9 21 B4
Trinity Way E4 35 B4
W3 111 D6
Trio Pl SE1 117 A4 252 B1
Triscott Ho UB3 106 A5
Tristan Ct 41 SE8 141 B6
Tristan Sq SE3 142 C2
Tristram Cl E17 54 B6
Tristram Rd BR1 186 D6
Triton Ct EC2 242 D5
Triton Ho 2 E14 119 D2
Triton Sq NW1 239 A6
Tritton Ave CR0 220 A4
Tritton Ho N21 17 B5
Tritton Rd SE21,SE27 161 B1
Triumph Cl UB7 127 A4
Triumph Ho IG11 102 A4
Triumph Rd E6 100 B1
Triumph Trad Est N17 34 A4
Trocette Mans SE1 263 B6
Trojan Ct NW6 69 A1
9 Ealing W7 109 A5
Trojan Ind Est NW10 67 D2
Trojan Way CR0 220 B5
Troon Cl 34 SE16 118 B1
Erith SE28 102 D1
Troon Ho 11 E14 97 A1
Troon St E1 97 A1
Tropical Ct 2 W10 90 D4
Trosley Rd DA17 147 C6
Trossachs Rd SE22 161 C6
Trothy Rd SE1 118 A2
Trotman Ho SE14 140 C4
Trott Rd N10 31 A3
Trott St SW11 136 C4 267 A1
Trotwood Ho 3 SE16 118 B4
Troubridge Ct 12 W4 111 A1
Troughton Rd SE7 121 B1
Troutbeck NW1 231 D1
Troutbeck Rd SE14 141 A4
Trouville Rd SW4 159 C5
Trowbridge Rd E9 75 B2
Trower Ho 5 E9 75 A2
Trowlock Ave TW11 175 C4
Trowlock Island TW11 175 D4
Trowlock Way TW11 175 D4
Troy Ct 5 SE18 122 D2
W8 255 A6
Troyes Ho NW3 70 D3
Troy Rd SE19 183 B4
Troy Town SE15 140 A2
Troy Town Flats SE15 140 A2
Trubshaw Rd UB2 107 D3
Truesdale Rd E6 100 B1
Trulock Ct N17 34 A3
Trulock Rd N17 34 A3
Truman Cl 2 HA8 27 A3
Truman's Rd 24 N16 73 C3
Trumpers Way W7 108 D3
Trumpeters Inn TW9 153 C6
Trumpington Rd E7 76 D4
Trump St EC2 242 B1
Trundlers Way WD23 8 C3
Trundle St SE1 252 A2
Trundleys Rd SE8 141 A6
Trundley's Rd SE8 118 D1
Trundley's Terr SE8 118 D2
Truro Gdns IG1 56 A2
Truro Ho 25 W2 91 C2
Truro Rd E17 53 B5
Wood Green N22 32 B3
Truro St NW5 71 A2
Truro Way UB4 83 C4
Truslove Rd SE27 182 D5
Trussley Rd W6 112 C3
Trust Wlk SE21 160 D3
Tryfan Cl IG4 55 D4
Tryon Cres E9 96 C6

Tryon St SW3 114 D1 257 C2
Trystings Cl KT10 213 A2
Tuam Rd SE18 145 B6
Tubbenden Cl BR6 227 C5
Tubbenden Dr BR6 227 B4
Tubbenden Jun & Inf Schs BR6 227 B4
Tubbenden La BR6 227 C5
Tubbenden La S BR6 227 B3
Tubbs Rd NW10 89 D5
Tudor Ave
Hampton TW12 173 C3
North Cheam KT4 216 B4
Tudor Cl BR7 188 B2
N6 49 C2
NW3 70 C2
NW7 28 A4
NW9 67 A6
SW2 160 B5
Ashford TW15 170 A6
Cheam SM3 217 A2
Chessington KT9 214 A3
Hampton TW12 174 A5
Pinner HA5 40 A4
Wallington SM6 219 C1
Woodford IG8 37 B5
Tudor Cres EN2 5 A4
Tudor Ct E17 53 B2
N1 73 C2
5 SE16 118 D5
W5 110 C4
Feltham TW13 172 C6
Sidcup DA14 168 A1
4 Stanwell TW19 148 A5
Teddington TW11 174 D4
3 Ealing W13 87 C1
Tudor Ct N HA9 66 C3
Tudor Ct S HA9 66 C3
Tudor Dr Kingston KT2 176 A5
Walton-on-T KT12 194 D1
West Barnes SM4 201 A3
Tudor Ent Pk HA3 42 B6
Tudor Est NW10 88 D5
Tudor Gables NW7 27 D6
Tudor Gdns NW9 67 A6
Acton W3 88 C1
Harrow HA3 24 B1
Mortlake SW14 133 C2
Twickenham TW1 152 D3
West Wickham BR4 224 A5
Tudor Gr E9 74 C1
Tudor Ho 34 E9 74 C1
W14 112 D2
Tolworth KT6 198 C1
Tudor Mews 2 NW10 68 A2
Tudor Par SE9 144 A1
Dagenham RM6 58 D2
Tudor Pl SW19 180 C3
Tudor Prim Sch N3 30 A2
Southall UB1 107 A6
West Barnes SM4 200 D2
Tudor Rd E6 99 C6
E9 96 B6
N9 18 C4
Ashford TW15 171 B4
Barking IG11 101 D6
Barnet EN5 1 D2
Beckenham BR3 208 A6
Chingford E4 35 D4
Croydon SE25 206 B4
Hampton TW12 173 C3
Harrow HA3 24 B1
Hayes UB3 83 B1
Isleworth TW3 130 B1
Kingston KT2 176 C3
Penge SE19 183 D3
Pinner HA5 22 C1
Southall UB1 107 A6
Tudor Sq UB3 83 B2
Tudor St EC4 116 C6 251 B6
Tudors The 2 BR3 185 D1
Tudor Way BR5 211 B3
N14 15 D3
W3 110 C4
Hillingdon UB10 60 C2
Tudor Well Cl HA7 25 B5
Tudor Wlk DA5 169 A5
Tudway Rd SE3,SE9 143 C1
Tufnell Ct 12 E3 97 B6
Tufnell Park Mans 2 N7 72 A5
Tufnell Park Prim Sch N7 71 D4
Tufnell Park Rd N19,N7 71 D4
Tufnell Park Sta N19 71 C4
Tufton Ct SW1 260 A5
Tufton Gdns KT8 173 D1
Tufton Rd E4 35 C6
Tufton St SW1 116 A3 260 A5
Tugboat St SE28 123 C4
Tugela Rd CR0 205 B3
Tugela St SE6 163 B2
Tugmutton Cl BR6 226 D4
Tuke Sch SE15 140 B4
Tulip Cl 5 E6 100 B2
Croydon CR0 206 D1
Hampton TW12 173 B4
Southall UB2 108 A4
Tulip Gdns Chingford E4 20 B1

Tulip Gdns *continued*
Ilford IG1 78 D2
Tullis Ho 12 E9 74 C1
Tull St CR4 202 D2
Tulse Cl BR3 208 A6
Tulse Hill
Streatham SW2 160 D2
Streatham SW2,SE24 160 D4
Tulse Hill Sta SE27 160 D2
Tulse Ho SW2 160 C5
Tulsemere Rd SE21, SE27 161 A2
Tumbling Bay KT12 194 A3
Tummons Gdns SE25 183 C1
Tunbridge Ct 1 SE26 162 A1
Tunbridge Ho EC1 234 C2
Tuncombe Rd N18 33 C6
Tunis Rd W12 112 B5
Tunley Gn 16 E14 97 B2
Tunley Rd NW10 89 C6
Upper Tooting SW12, SW17 159 A2
Tunmarsh La E13 99 C4
Tunnan Leys E6 100 C1
Tunnel Avenue Trad Est SE10 120 B4
Tunnel Gdns N11 31 C3
Tunnel Link Rd TW6 148 C6
Tunnel Rd SE16 118 C4
Tunnel Rd E TW6 126 D4
Tunnel Rd W TW6 126 D4
Tunstall Cl BR6 227 C4
Tunstall Ct 14 TW9 132 B4
Tunstall Rd SW9 138 B1
Croydon CR0 205 C1
Tunstall Wlk 10 TW8 132 A6
Tunstock Way DA17 125 A3
Tunworth Cl NW9 45 A3
Tunworth Cres SW15 155 D5
Tupelo Rd E10 75 D6
Tupman Ho 21 SE16 118 A4
Turberville Ho 1 SW9 138 B2
Turene Cl SW18 136 A1
Turin Rd N9 18 C4
Turin St E2 96 A4
Turkey Oak Cl SE19 183 C2
Turkey St Enfield EN1 6 B6
Enfield EN3 6 B6
Turkey Street Sta EN3 6 C6
Turks Cl UB8 82 C4
Turk's Head Yd EC1 241 C4
Turks Row SW3 114 D1 257 D2
Turle Rd N4 72 B6
Thornton Heath SW16 182 A1
Turlewray Cl N4 50 B1
Turley Cl E15 98 C6
Turnagain La EC4 241 C2
Turnage Rd RM8 59 A1
Turnant Rd N17 33 A2
Turnberry Cl NW4 28 D1
24 SE16 118 B1
Turnberry Way BR6 211 B1
Turnbull Ho N1 234 D6
Turnbury Cl SE28 102 D1
Turnchapel Mews 1 SW4 137 B2
Turner Ave N15 51 C5
Mitcham CR4 180 D2
Twickenham TW2 152 A1
Turner Cl NW11 47 D3
7 SW9 138 D4
Hillingdon UB4 83 A4
Wembley HA0 65 D2
Turner Ct 19 SE16 118 C4
9 SE5 139 B1
Turner Dr NW11 47 D3
Turner Ho N4 50 B1
NW8 230 A4
SW1 259 D3
WC2 250 B5
6 Twickenham TW1 153 D5
Turner Lo 10 SW19 156 D3
Turner Pl SW11 158 C6
Turner Rd E17 54 A6
Edgware HA8 26 B1
New Malden KT3 199 B2
Turners Meadow Way BR3 185 B2
Turner's Rd E3 97 B2
Turner St E1 96 B2
E16 98 D1
Turners Way CR0 220 C6
Turneville Rd W14 135 B6 264 C6
Turney Rd SE21 161 B4
Turney Sch SE21 161 A4
Turnham Green Sta W4 111 C2
Turnham Green Terr W4 111 C2
Turnham Ho SE4 141 A1
Turnham Prim Sch SE4 141 A1
Turnham Rd SE4 141 A1
Turnmill Ho 8 SW2 160 C6
Turnmill St EC1 94 D2 241 C4
Turnour Ho 32 E1 96 B1
Turnpike Cl SE8 141 B5

Turnpike Ct DA6 146 D1
Turnpike Ho EC1 234 D1
Turnpike La N8 50 C6
Sutton SM1 218 A3
Uxbridge UB10 82 A5
Turnpike Lane Sta N15 50 D6
Turnpike Link CR0 221 C6
Turnpike Way TW7 131 A4
Turnpin La 2 SE10 142 A6
Turnstone Cl E13 99 A4
NW9 27 C1
Uxbridge UB10 60 D3
Turpentine La SW1 115 B1 258 D1
Turpin Cl EN3 7 C6
Turpington Cl BR2 210 A2
Turpington La BR2 210 A3
Turpin Ho SW11 268 C2
Turpin Rd TW14 149 D5
Turpin Way N19 49 D1
Wallington SM6 219 B1
Turquand St SE17 262 B3
Turret Gr SW4 137 C2
Turret Ho KT2 176 A4
Turton Ho 5 SE18 144 D6
Turton Rd HA0 66 A3
Turville Ho NW8 237 A6
Turville St E2 243 C6
Tuscan Ho 33 E2 96 C4
Tuscan Rd SE18 123 B1
Tuskar St SE10 120 C1
Tutorial Coll of West London UB1 107 B5
Tuttlebee La IG9 21 A2
Tuttle Ho SW1 259 D1
Tweedale Ct E15 76 A3
Tweed Ct W7 86 C1
Tweeddale Gr UB10 61 A5
Tweeddale Jun & Inf Schs SM5 202 B2
Tweeddale Rd SM5 202 B1
Tweed Ho E14 98 A3
Tweedmouth Rd E13 99 B5
Tweedy Cl EN1 17 D6
Tweedy Rd BR1 187 A2
Tweezer's Alley WC2 251 A6
Twelve Acre Ho 5 E12 78 C5
Twelvetrees Cres E3 98 A3
Twentyman Cl IG8 37 A5
Twickenham Bridge TW9 153 C6
Twickenham Cl CR0 220 B5
Twickenham Gdns
Greenford UB6 65 A3
Harrow HA3 24 C3
Twickenham Rd E11 76 B6
Isleworth TW1,TW7 131 A2
Richmond TW1,TW9 131 C1
Teddington TW11 175 A6
Twickenham TW13 151 B1
Twickenham Rugby Football Union Ground★ TW2 152 C5
Twickenham Sta TW1 153 A4
Twickenham Trad Ctr TW1 152 D5
Twig Folly Cl E2 96 D5
Twilley St SW18 157 D4
Twine Cl IG11 102 B4
Twine Ct E1 118 C6
Twineham Gn N12 29 C6
Twining Ave TW2 152 B1
Twinn Rd NW7 29 A4
Twisden Rd NW5 71 B4
Twiss Ho 6 SE18 122 D1
Twybridge Way NW10 67 A1
Twyford Abbey Rd NW10 88 B4
Twyford Ave N2 48 D6
Acton W3 110 C6
Twyford CE High Sch W3 110 D5
Twyford Cres W3 110 C5
Twyford Ct N10 49 A6
Acton W3 110 C6
6 Wembley HA0 88 A5
Twyford Ho 6 N15 51 C3
N5 72 D5
Twyford Par KT6 198 C1
Twyford Pl WC2 240 C2
Twyford Rd
Carshalton SM5 202 B1
Harrow HA2 41 D2
Ilford IG1 79 A3
Twyford St N1 94 B6 233 C6
Twynholm Mans SW6 264 A4
Tyas Rd E16 98 D3
Tybenham Rd SW19 201 C6
Tyberry Rd EN3 6 C2
Tyburn La HA1 42 D2
Tyburn Tree (site of)★ W2 247 C6
Tyburn Way W1 247 D6
Tye La BR6 227 A3
Tyer's Est SE1 253 A2
Tyers Gate SE1 117 C4 253 A1
Tyers Ho 1 SW16 181 C5
Tyers St SE11 116 B1 260 C2

Tyers Terr SE11 116 B1 260 D1
Tyeshurst Cl SE2 125 A1
Tylecroft Rd SW16 182 A1
Tylehurst Gdns IG1 79 A3
Tyler Cl E2 95 D5
Tyler Rd UB2 107 D3
Tylers Ct 4 E17 53 C5
5 Wembley HA0 88 A5
Tylers Gate HA3 44 A3
Tylers Path SM5 218 D4
Tyler St SE10 120 C1
Tylers Way WD23 8 C6
Tylney Ave SE19 183 D5
Tylney Ho 19 E1 96 B1
Tylney Rd BR1 187 D1
E7 77 C4
Tymperley Ct SW19 157 A3
Tynamara KT1 197 D5
Tynan Cl TW14 150 A3
Tyndale La N1 72 D1
Tyndale Mans N1 72 D1
Tyndale Terr 13 N1 72 D1
Tyndall Gdns E10 76 A6
Tyndall Rd DA16 145 D2
E10 76 A6
Tyne Ct W7 86 C1
Tynedale Ct E14 119 D1
Tyneham Cl 10 SW11 137 A2
Tyne Ho 8 KT2 175 D2
Tynemouth Cl E6 100 D1
Tynemouth Dr EN1 6 A5
Tynemouth Rd N15 51 D5
SE18 123 C1
Mitcham CR4 181 A3
Tynemouth St SW6 136 A3
Tynemouth Terr 8 N15 51 D5
Tyne St E1 243 D2
Tynsdale Rd NW10 67 C2
Tynte Ct E9 75 A3
Tynwald Ho 14 SE26 162 A1
Type St E2 96 D5
Tyrawley Rd SW6 265 C2
Tyrell Cl HA1 64 C4
Tyrell Ct SM5 218 D4
Tyrols Rd SE23 162 D3
Tyrone Rd E6 100 B4
Tyron Way DA14 189 D5
Tyrrell Ave DA16 168 B6
Tyrrell Ho SW1 269 B6
Catford BR3 185 D5
Tyrrell Rd SE22 140 A1
Tyrrell Sq CR4 180 C2
Tyrrel Way NW9 46 A2
Tyrwhitt Rd SE4 141 C2
Tysoe Ave EN3 7 B6
Tysoe St EC1 234 B1
Tyson Rd SE23 162 C4
Tyssen Rd N16 73 D5
Tyssen Sch N16 52 A1
Tyssen St E8 73 D2
N1 95 C5
Tytherton 30 E2 96 C5
Tytherton Rd N19 71 D5

U

Uamvar St E14 97 D2
Uckfield Gr CR4 181 A2
Uckfield Rd EN3 6 D6
Udall St SW1 259 B3
Udimore Ho W10 90 C2
Udney Park Rd TW11 175 A4
Uffington Rd NW10 90 B6
West Norwood SE27 182 C6
Ufford Cl HA3 23 D3
Ufford Rd HA3 23 D3
Ufford St SE1 116 C4 251 B2
Ufton Ct UB5 84 D4
Ufton Gr N1 73 B1
Ufton Rd N1 73 C1
Uhura Sq 19 N16 73 C5
Ujima Ct N19 50 A1
Streatham SW16 182 A6
Ujima Ho SW16 182 A6
Uk Cotts UB3 105 B4
Ullathorne Rd SW16 181 C6
Ulleswater Rd N14 16 B1
Ullin St E14 98 A2
Ullswater SW15 156 D5
Ullswater Cl
Bromley BR1 186 C3
Hayes UB4 83 C5
Kingston KT2,SW15 177 B6
Ullswater Cres SW15 177 B6
Ullswater Ct
2 Woodford E18 37 A1
Harrow HA2 41 C2
Ullswater Ho SE15 140 C6
Ullswater Rd
Barnes SW13 134 A5
West Norwood SE27, SW16 160 D2
Ulster Ct KT2 175 D4

Ulster Gdns N13 ... 33 A6
Ulster Pl NW1 ... 238 C5
Ulundi Rd SE3 ... 142 C6
Ulva Rd SW15 ... 134 D1
Ulverscroft Rd SE22 ... 162 A6
Ulverstone Rd SE27 ... 160 D2
Ulverston Rd E17 ... 36 B1
Ulysses Rd NW6 ... 69 B3
Umberston St E1 ... 96 B1
Umbria St SW15 ... 156 A5
Umfreville Rd N4 ... 50 D3
Una Ho 7 NW5 ... 71 B2
Under Cliff SE10 ... 142 A4
Undercliff Rd SE13 ... 141 D2
Underhill EN5 ... 13 C6
Underhill Ct EN5 ... 13 C6
Underhill Ho 7 E14 ... 97 C2
Underhill Jun & Inf Schs EN5 ... 13 A6
Underhill Pas NW1 ... 231 D6
Underhill Rd SE21, SE22 ... 162 B4
Underhill St NW1 ... 231 D5
Underne Ave N14 ... 15 B2
Undershaft EC3 95 C1 243 A1
Undershaw Rd BR1 ... 164 D1
Underwood CR0 ... 224 A3
Underwood Ct 3 E10 ... 53 D1
Underwood Ho W6 ... 112 B3
Underwood Rd E1 ... 96 A3
Chingford E4 ... 35 D5
Woodford IG8 ... 37 D3
Underwood Row N1 ... 235 B2
Underwood St N1 ... 95 A4 235 B2
Underwood The SE9 ... 166 B2
Undine Rd E14 ... 119 D2
Undine St SW17 ... 180 D5
Uneeda Dr UB6 ... 86 B6
Unicorn Bldg 14 E1 ... 118 D6
Unicorn Sch TW9 ... 132 B4
Unicorn Works N17 ... 34 C3
Union Cl E11 ... 76 B4
Union Ct SW4 ... 138 A3
45 W2 ... 91 C2
2 Richmond TW10 ... 154 A6
Union Dr E1 ... 97 A3
Union Gr SW8 ... 137 D3
Union Mews SW9 ... 138 A3
Union Rd BR2 ... 209 D4
N11 ... 31 D4
SW8 ... 137 D3
Northolt UB5 ... 85 C5
Thornton Heath CR0 ... 205 A2
Wembley HA0 ... 66 A2
Union Sq N1 ... 95 A6 235 B5
Union St E15 ... 98 B6
SE1 ... 117 A5 252 A3
Barnet EN5 ... 1 A2
Kingston KT1 ... 175 D1
Union Wlk E2 ... 95 C4
Union Yd W1 ... 238 D1
Unity Cl NW10 ... 68 A2
West Norwood SE19 ... 183 A5
Unity Mews NW1 ... 232 C4
Unity Rd EN3 ... 6 C6
Unity Way SE18 ... 121 D3
Univ College Hospl (Annexe) W1 ... 93 A2 238 B4
Univ Coll Jun Sch NW3 70 A4
Univ Coll London
W1 ... 93 C2 239 B4
WC1 ... 93 D3 239 C6
WC1 ... 94 A3 240 B6
University Cl NW7 ... 27 D3
University Coll Hospl WC1 ... 93 C3 239 B5
University Coll Sch NW3 ... 70 A3
University Gdns DA5 ... 169 B4
University Mans SW15 134 D2
University of North London (Tufnel Park Hall) N7 ... 71 C5
University Pl DA8 ... 147 D5
University Rd SW19 ... 180 B4
University St WC1 ... 93 C3 239 B5
University Way E16 ... 122 D6
Univ of East London
E15 ... 76 C2
E15 ... 98 B6
E6 ... 122 C6
Barking RM8 ... 80 A4
Univ of East London (Holbrook Ctr) E15 ... 98 D5
Univ of Greenwich Avery Hill Campus Mansion Site SE9 ... 167 A5
Univ of Greenwich Avery Hill Campus Southwood Site SE9 ... 167 B4
Univ of Greenwich Rachel Mcmillan Campus SE8 ... 141 C6
Univ of Greenwich Riverside Ho Annexe SE18 ... 122 C3
Univ of Greenwich The SW15 ... 156 A4
Univ of London WC1 ... 94 A4 233 A1
Univ of London (King's Coll Hall) SE5 ... 139 B2
Univ of London Observatory NW7 ... 27 D4
Univ of London (Queen Mary & Westfield Coll) E1 ... 97 A3
Univ of Westminster
NW1 ... 93 C3 239 A6
NW8 ... 92 C3 237 A5
W1 ... 93 A2 238 A4
W1 ... 93 B1 238 D2
Univ of Westminster (Harrow Campus) HA1 ... 43 A2
Unwin Ave TW14 ... 149 B6
Unwin Cl SE15 ... 140 A6
Unwin Rd SW7 114 B3 256 D6
Isleworth TW7 ... 130 C2
Upbrook Mews W2 ... 92 A1 236 B1
Upcerne Rd SW10 ... 136 A5 266 B3
Upchurch Cl SE20 ... 184 B3
Upcott Ho 33 E3 ... 97 D4
4 E9 ... 74 C1
Upcroft Ave HA8 ... 27 A6
Updale Rd DA14 ... 189 D6
Upfield CR0 ... 222 B5
Upfield Rd W7 ... 86 D2
Upgrove Manor Way 12 SE24 ... 160 C4
Uphall Prim Sch IG1 ... 78 D3
Uphall Rd IG1 ... 78 D3
Upham Park Rd W4 ... 111 C2
Uphill Dr NW7 ... 27 C5
NW9 ... 45 A4
Uphill Gr NW7 ... 27 C6
Uphill Rd NW7 ... 27 C6
Upland Ct SE23 ... 162 C2
Upland Inf Sch DA7 ... 147 B2
Upland Jun Sch DA7 ... 147 B2
Upland Rd DA7 ... 147 B2
8 E13 ... 99 A3
SE22 ... 162 A5
Croydon CR2 ... 221 B3
Sutton SM2 ... 218 B1
Uplands BR3 ... 185 C1
Uplands Ave E17 ... 34 D1
Uplands Bsns Pk E17 ... 52 D6
Uplands Cl SW14 ... 154 D6
Uplands Ct N21 ... 16 C4
Uplands Park Rd EN2 ... 4 C3
Uplands Rd N8 ... 50 B4
East Barnet EN4 ... 15 A3
Ilford RM6 ... 58 D6
Woodford IG8 ... 37 D3
Uplands The HA4 ... 40 A1
Uplands Way N21 ... 16 C6
Upnall Ho 16 SE15 ... 140 C6
Upney La IG11 ... 79 D1
Upney Sta IG11 ... 79 D1
Upnor Way SE17 ... 263 B2
Uppark Dr IG2 ... 57 A3
Upper Abbey Rd DA17 125 C2
Upper Addison Gdns W14 ... 113 A4 244 A2
Upper Belgrave St SW1 ... 115 A3 258 B6
Upper Berkeley St W1 ... 92 D1 237 D1
Upper Beulah Hill SE19 ... 183 C2
Upper Brighton Rd KT6 ... 198 A2
Upper Brockley Rd SE4 ... 141 B3
Upper Brook St W1 ... 115 A6 248 A6
Upper Butts TW8 ... 131 C6
Upper Caldy Wlk 14 N1 73 A2
Upper Cavendish Ave N3 ... 47 C6
Upper Cheyne Row SW3 ... 136 C6 267 A6
Upper Clapton Rd E5 ... 74 B6
Upper Clarendon Wlk 13 W11 ... 91 A1
Upper Dengie Wlk N1 235 A6
Upper Elmers End Rd BR3 ... 207 A4
Upper Farm Rd KT8 ... 195 B5
Upper Fosters NW4 ... 46 C5
Upper Gn E CR4 ... 203 A6
Upper Gn W CR4 ... 180 D1
Upper Gr SE25 ... 205 D5
Upper Grosvenor St W1 ... 115 A6 248 A5
Upper Grotto Rd TW1 152 D2
Upper Ground SE1 ... 116 C5 251 A4
Upper Grove Rd DA17 ... 147 B6
Upper Gulland Wlk 19 N1 ... 73 A2
Upper Halliford Rd TW17 ... 193 C6
Upper Halliford Sta TW16 ... 171 C1
Upper Ham Rd KT2, TW10 ... 175 D6
Upper Harley St NW1 ... 238 B5
Upper Hawkwell Wlk N1 ... 235 B6
Upper Holloway Sta N19 ... 71 D6
Upper Holly Hill Rd DA17 ... 125 D1
Upper James St W1 ... 249 B6
Upper John St W1 ... 249 B6
Upper Lodge Mews TW12 ... 174 A4
Upper Mall W6 ... 112 B1
Upper Marsh SE1 ... 116 B4 260 D6
Upper Montague St W1 ... 92 D2 237 C3
Upper Mulgrave Rd SM2 ... 217 A1
Upper North St E3,E14 ... 97 C2
Upper Park Rd BR1 ... 187 C2
N11 ... 31 C5
NW3 ... 70 D3
Belvedere DA17 ... 125 D2
Kingston KT2 ... 176 C4
Upper Phillimore Gdns W8 ... 113 C4 245 A1
Upper Pk IG10 ... 21 D6
Upper Rawreth Wlk N1 ... 235 B6
Upper Rd E13 ... 99 A4
N2 ... 30 C2
Wallington SM6 ... 219 D3
Upper Richmond Rd SW15 ... 134 C1
Upper Richmond Rd W TW10,SW14,SW15 ... 133 A1
Upper Selsdon Rd CR2 ... 221 D1
Upper Sheridan Rd DA17 ... 125 C2
Upper Shirley Rd CR0 222 D5
Upper Sq TW7 ... 131 A2
Upper St N1 ... 94 D6 234 C5
Upper St Martin's La WC2 ... 250 A6
Upper Sunbury Rd TW12 ... 173 C2
Upper Sutton La TW5 ... 129 C4
Upper Tachbrook St SW1 ... 259 B4
Upper Teddington Rd KT1,KT8 ... 175 C2
Upper Terr NW3 ... 70 A5
Upper Thames St EC4 ... 117 A6 252 B6
Upper Tollington Pk N4 ... 50 C1
Upperton Rd DA14 ... 189 D5
Upperton Rd E E13 ... 99 C4
Upperton Rd W E13 ... 99 C4
Upper Tooting Park Mans 1 SW17 ... 159 A2
Upper Tooting Pk SW17 ... 158 D2
Upper Tooting Rd SW17 ... 158 D1
Upper Town Rd UB6 ... 85 D3
Upper Tulse Hill SW2 ... 160 B3
Upper Vernon Rd SM1 218 B3
Upper Walthamstow Rd E17 ... 54 B6
Upper Wickham La DA16 ... 146 B4
Upper Wimpole St W1 ... 93 A2 238 B4
Upper Woburn Pl NW1,WC1 ... 93 D4 232 D1
Uppingham Ave HA7 ... 25 C1
Upsdell Ave N13 ... 32 C4
Upshire Ho E17 ... 35 B1
Upstall St SE5 ... 138 D4
Upton Ave E7 ... 77 A1
Upton Cl NW2 ... 69 A5
Sidcup DA5 ... 169 B5
Upton Cross E13 ... 99 A6
Upton Cross Prim Sch E13 ... 99 B6
Upton Ct Penge SE20 ... 184 C3
Southall UB1 ... 107 D5
4 Wimbledon SW19 ... 178 D3
Upton Day Hospl DA6 ... 147 A1
Upton Dene SM2 ... 217 D1
Upton Gdns HA3 ... 43 C3
Upton La E7 ... 77 A1
Upton Lodge Cl WD23 ... 8 A4
Upton Park Rd E7 ... 77 B1
Upton Park Sta E13 ... 99 C6
Upton Prim Sch DA5 ... 169 B6
Upton Rd SE18 ... 145 A6
Bexley DA6 ... 169 A6
Edmonton N18 ... 34 A5
Upton Rd *continued*
Hounslow TW3 ... 129 C2
South Norwood CR7 ... 183 B1
Upton Rd S DA5 ... 169 B5
Upton Villas 4 DA6 ... 147 A1
Upway N12 ... 30 C4
Upwood Rd SE12 ... 165 A5
Thornton Heath SW16 ... 182 A2
Urlwin St SE5 ... 139 A6
Urlwin Wlk SW9 ... 138 D4
Urmston Dr SW19 ... 157 A3
Urmston Ho 3 E14 ... 120 A2
Urquhart Ct BR3 ... 185 B3
Ursula Lo DA14 ... 190 B5
Ursula Mews N4 ... 51 A1
Ursula St SW11 ... 136 C4 267 A1
Ursuline High Sch SW20 ... 178 D2
Urswick Gdns RM9 ... 81 A1
Urswick Rd E5,E9 ... 74 C3
Dagenham RM9 ... 81 A1
Usborne Mews SW8 ... 270 D4
Usher Rd E3 ... 97 B5
Usk Rd SW11 ... 136 A1
Usk St E2 ... 96 D4
Utopia Village NW1 ... 71 A1 231 A6
Uvedale Rd
Dagenham RM10 ... 81 C5
Enfield EN2 ... 17 B6
Uverdale Rd SW10 ... 136 A5 266 B3
Uxbridge Coll
Hayes UB3 ... 106 A6
Uxbridge UB8 ... 60 A2
Uxbridge High Sch UB8 82 A5
Uxbridge Rd W12 ... 112 B5
Acton W3,W5 ... 110 C5
Ealing W13 ... 109 C6
Feltham TW13 ... 150 D2
Hampton TW12,TW13 ... 173 D5
Hayes UB4 ... 106 C6
Hillingdon UB10,UB4 ... 83 C2
Kingston KT1,KT6 ... 197 D4
Southall UB1,UB2,W5, W7 ... 108 B5
Stanmore HA7 ... 25 A5
Uxbridge Road (Harrow Weald) HA3 ... 24 B3
Uxbridge Road (Hatch End) HA5 ... 23 B3
Uxbridge St W8 ... 113 C5 245 A4
Uxendon Cres HA3,HA9 ... 44 A1
Uxendon Hill HA9 ... 44 B2
Uxendon Manor Prim Sch HA3 ... 44 A4

V

Vaine Ho 4 E9 ... 75 A2
Valance Ave E4 ... 20 D3
Valan Leas BR2 ... 208 C6
Vale Ave WD6 ... 10 D6
Vale Cl N2 ... 48 D6
W9 ... 92 A4 229 A1
Orpington BR6 ... 226 C4
Twickenham TW1 ... 153 A1
Vale Cres SW15 ... 177 C6
Vale Croft
Claygate KT10 ... 212 D1
Pinner HA5 ... 41 A4
Vale Ct W3 ... 111 D5
W9 ... 92 A4 229 A1
Barnet EN5 ... 1 D1
Wembley HA0 ... 65 C5
Vale Dr EN5 ... 13 C6
Vale End SE22 ... 139 D1
Vale Est The W3 ... 111 C5
Vale Farm Sports Ctr HA0 ... 65 B4
Vale Gr N4 ... 51 A2
W3 ... 111 B5
Vale La W3 ... 88 C2
Vale Lo SE23 ... 162 C2
Valence Ave RM8 ... 80 D6
Valence Cir RM8 ... 81 A5
Valence House Mus★ RM8 ... 81 A6
Valence Inf Sch RM8 ... 80 D6
Valence Jun Sch RM8 ... 80 D6
Valence Wood Rd RM8 ... 81 A5
Valencia Rd HA7 ... 25 C6
Valens Ho 1 SW2 ... 160 C3
Valentia Pl SW9 ... 138 C1
Valentine Ave DA5 ... 169 A3
Valentine Ct SE23 ... 162 D2
Valentine Ho 11 SW4 ... 159 C5
Valentine Pl SE1 ... 116 D4 251 C2
Valentine Rd E9 ... 74 D2
Harrow HA2 ... 64 A5
Valentine Row SE1 ... 251 C1
Valentines High Sch IG2 ... 56 C3
Valentines Rd IG1 ... 56 D1
Vale of Health NW3 ... 70 B5
Vale Rd BR1 ... 188 C1
E7 ... 77 B2
N4 ... 51 A2
Claygate KT10 ... 212 D1
Mitcham CR4 ... 203 D5
Sutton SM1 ... 217 D4
Worcester Park KT19, KT4 ... 215 D5
Vale Rd N KT6 ... 214 A6
Vale Rd S KT6 ... 214 A6
Valerian Way E15 ... 98 C4
Valerie Ct Belmont SM2 217 D1
Bushey WD23 ... 8 A4
Vale Rise NW11 ... 47 B1
Vale Row N5 ... 72 D5
Vale Royal N7 ... 72 A1
Valery Pl TW12 ... 173 C3
Vale Sch The N4 ... 51 B3
Valeswood Rd BR1 ... 186 D5
Vale Terr N4 ... 51 A3
Vale The N10 ... 31 A2
NW11 ... 69 A6
SW3 ... 136 B6 266 D6
W3 ... 111 C5
Ashford TW16 ... 172 A4
Croydon CR0 ... 222 D6
Feltham TW14 ... 150 B5
Heston TW5 ... 129 A6
Ruislip HA4 ... 62 C4
Southgate N14 ... 16 A4
Woodford IG8 ... 37 A3
Valetta Gr E13 ... 99 A5
Valetta Rd W3 ... 111 D4
Valette Ct N10 ... 49 B5
Valette Ho E9 ... 74 C2
Valette St E8 ... 74 B2
Valiant Cl 13 UB5 ... 84 D4
Valiant Ho 5 SE7 ... 121 C1
SW11 ... 266 D1
Valiant Way E6 ... 100 B2
Vallance Rd E1 ... 96 A3
N22 ... 31 C1
Vallentin Rd E17 ... 54 A5
Valley Ave N12 ... 30 B6
Valley (Charlton Athletic FC) The SE7 ... 121 C1
Valley Cl HA5 ... 22 B1
Valley Ct IG8 ... 37 B3
Valley Dr NW9 ... 44 D3
Valleyfield Rd SW16 ... 182 B5
Valley Fields Cres EN2 ... 4 C3
Valley Gdns
Mitcham SW19 ... 180 B3
Wembley HA0 ... 66 B1
Valley Gr SE7 ... 121 C1
Valley Ho E5 ... 52 C1
4 Edmonton N9 ... 18 A1
Valley L Ctr SE9 ... 167 A4
Valleylink Est EN3 ... 19 A5
Valley Mews TW1 ... 153 A2
Valley Pl KT6 ... 198 A3
Valley Prim Sch BR2 ... 186 D1
Valley Prospect 3 SE19 ... 183 C4
Valley Rd BR5 ... 190 B2
Beckenham BR2 ... 186 C1
Streatham SW16 ... 182 B6
Uxbridge UB10 ... 82 A5
Valleyside SE7 ... 121 D1
Valley Side E4 ... 19 C3
Valley Side Par E4 ... 19 C2
Valley View EN5 ... 13 A5
Valley Wlk CR0 ... 222 C6
Valliere Rd NW10 ... 90 A4
Valliers Wood Rd DA15 ... 167 C3
Vallis Way
Chessington KT9 ... 213 D4
Ealing W13 ... 87 A2
Valmar Rd SE5 ... 139 A4
Valmar Trad Est 7 SE5 ... 139 A4
Valnay St SW17 ... 180 D5
Valognes Ave E17 ... 35 A2
Valois Ho SE1 ... 263 C6
Valonia Gdns SW18 ... 157 B5
Vambery Rd SE18 ... 145 A6
Vanbern Ho NW5 ... 71 A2
Vanborough Ct 4 SM2 ... 218 A2
Vanbrough Cres UB5 ... 84 C6
Vanbrugh Cl 2 E16 ... 99 D2
Vanbrugh Ct SE11 ... 261 B3
Vanbrugh Dr KT12 ... 194 C3
Vanbrugh Fields SE3 ... 142 D5
Vanbrugh Hill SE10, SE3 ... 142 D6
Vanbrugh Ho 6 E9 ... 74 C1
Vanbrugh Mews KT12 194 C2
Vanbrugh Park Rd SE3 ... 142 D5
Vanbrugh Park Rd W SE3 ... 142 D5
Vanbrugh Pk SE3 ... 142 D5
Vanbrugh Rd W4 ... 111 B3
Vanbrugh Terr SE3 ... 142 D4
Vanburgh Cl BR6 ... 211 C1
Vanburgh Ho E1 ... 243 C4
Vancouver Rd
Edgware HA8 ...
Forest Hill SE23 ...
Hayes UB4 ...
Richmond TW10 ...
Vancover Ho 33 E1 ...
Vanderbilt Rd SW18 ...
Vanderbilt Villas 1 W12 ...
Vanderville Gdns N2 ...
Vandome Cl E16 ...
Vandon Ct SW1 ...
Vandon Pas SW1 ...
Vandon St SW1 ...
Van Dyck Ave KT3 ...
Vandyke Cl SW15 ...
Vandyke Cross SE9 ...
Vandy St EC2 ...
Vane Cl NW3 ...
Harrow HA3 ...
Vane Ho 18 N2 ...
Vanessa Cl DA17 ...
Vane St SW1 ...
Vanfame Ct KT3 ...
Vangaurd Way TW6 ...
Vange Ho W10 ...
Van Gogh Ct E14 ...
Vanguard Bldg 12 E14
Vanguard Cl E16 ...
Thornton Heath CR0 ...
Vanguard Ho
7 Merton SW19 ...
6 Stanwell TW19 ...
Vanguard St SE8 ...
Vanguard Trad Ctr E15
Vanguard Way SM6 ...
Vanneck Sq SW15 ...
Vanoc Gdns BR1 ...
Vansittart Rd E7 ...
Vansittart St 7 SE14
Vanston Pl SW6 ... 135 C5
Vantage Mews E14 ...
Vant Rd SW17 ...
Vantrey Ho SE11 ...
Varcoe Rd SE16 ...
Vardens Rd SW11 ...
Varden St E1 ...
Vardon Cl W3 ...
Vardon Ho SE10 ...
Varey Ho E1 ...
Varley Ho 5 NW6 ...
Varley Par NW9 ...
Varley Rd E16 ...
Varley Way CR4 ...
Varna Rd SW6 ... 135 B5
Hampton TW12 ...
Varndell St NW1 ... 93 C4
Varsity Dr TW1,TW7 ...
Varsity Row SW14 ...
Vartry Rd N15 ...
Vassal Ho E3 ...
Vassall Rd SW9 ...
Vat Ho SW8 ...
Vauban Est SE16 ...
Vauban St SE16 ... 117 D3
Vaudeville Ct N4 ...
Vaughan Almshouses TW15 ...
Vaughan Ave NW4 ...
W6 ...
Vaughan Est 3 E2 ...
Vaughan Fst & Mid Sch HA1 ...
Vaughan Gdns IG1 ...
Vaughan Ho SE1 ...
Vaughan Rd DA16 ...
E15 ...
SE5 ...
Harrow HA1 ...
Thames Ditton KT7 ...
Vaughan St SE16 ...
Vaughan Way E1 ...
Vaughan Williams Cl SE8 ...
Vauxhall Bridge Rd SW1 ... 115 C2
Vauxhall Cross SE1,SE8 ... 116 A1
Vauxhall Gdns CR2 ...
Vauxhall Gr SW8 ... 138 B6
Vauxhall Prim Sch SE11 ... 116 B1
Vauxhall St SE11 ... 116 B1
Vauxhall Sta SE11 ... 116 A1
Vauxhall Wlk SE11 ...
Vawdrey Cl E1 ...
Vaynor Ho N7 ...
Veals Mead CR4 ...
Vectis Ct SW18 ...
Vectis Gdns SW17 ...
Vectis Rd SW17 ...
Veda Rd SE13 ...
Vega Cres HA6 ...

d WD23 8 A4
Cl TW14 149 D4
e Way HA2 63 B5
Vay 1 SE22 161 C6
tt Ho W12 90 B1
Ho 17 E2 96 D5
Dr SM5 219 A5
es Cl RM10 81 D4
es St
92 B2 236 D4
rt Pl W6 112 A2
an Rd SE5 139 A3
Rd N4 50 D3
109 D4
Ct 14 SE5 139 A5
Manor SE27 182 C5
ad Ct DA17 125 C2
Rd SE26 184 C5
o N1 233 D5
t SW4 137 C1
r Ave HA7 25 B1
r Dr N20 13 D2
r Gdns IG11 79 C2
r Mans IG11 79 C2
r Rd SE14 140 D5
t SM2 217 D1
r Terr N15 52 A5
e Cl DA5 169 A4
e Ct 3 SE12 165 A4
St E14 98 A2
Rd SE18 122 B3
e N21 16 C6
1 W2 91 D1
nn Cl 5 E7 77 A4
l SW6 135 A4 264 B2
a Cl E16 98 D3
a Gdns W6 112 A1
t Ct 3 SE6 164 C4
t La SE6 164 C3
ne Ave CR0 222 D6
o 2 NW6 91 A5
Rd SE18,SE2 146 A6
SW13 134 A5
ank SW19 157 B3
r Dr TW16 194 A6
r Rd W14 254 B1
t W1 93 B1 238 C1
Cl W11 91 A1
Ct N9 18 D3
Ho 15 E3 97 B4
er Ct E14 120 B3
nt Cl EN2 4 D1
nt Ho E17 35 B1
nt Rd
SM1 217 D5
worth SW18 157 D5
lorwood SE19 183 C4
Ct 9 W3 111 A3
Gdns RM9 81 A4
Ho NW8 237 A6
rth TW3 130 A1
Rd SE16 118 B1
iam RM9 81 A4
St NW10 67 B5
Way SE16 118 B1
m Rd SE18 145 A6
Ave Ilford E12 78 B4
arnes SW20 178 D1
rd IG8 37 B3
Cl KT19 215 A2
Cres EN4 15 A5
Ct NW2 69 B5
W5 109 C6
ore HA7 25 B2
Dr HA7 25 A2
Ho NW9 45 D4
260 D1
House Sch
67 B3
Mews W14 254 B3
Pl WC1 240 B3
Rd E11 54 C1
76 C1
53 B4
97 B5
50 C6
n TW13 149 D2
IG3 57 D1
ke SW14 133 B2
SM1 218 B3
Rise WC1 233 D2
ord UB6 64 B3
Sq WC1 233 D2
St
113 A2 254 B3
Yd
113 B6 244 C6
Rd DA7 147 A3
Ct 10 SE14 140 D6
111 C1
Dr KT6 214 A6
Rd E7 77 A1
ca Gdns CR4,
181 C2
ca Ho SE4 141 B2
ca Rd SW17 159 B2
que Gdns IG6 57 A4
Rd SW12 159 B4
les Rd SE20 184 A3

Verulam Ave E17 53 B2
Verulam Ct NW9 46 A2
4 Southall UB1 86 A1
Verulam Ho 1 W6 112 C4
Verulam Rd UB6 85 C3
Verulam St EC1 94 C2 241 A4
Vervain Ho 2 SE15 140 A5
Verwood Dr EN4 2 D2
Verwood Ho SW8 270 D3
Verwood Lo 1 E14 120 B2
Verwood Rd HA2 24 A1
Veryan Ct 2 N8 49 D4
Vesage Ct EC1 241 B3
Vesey Path 15 E14 97 D1
Vespan Rd W12 112 A4
Vesta Rd SE4,SE14 141 A3
Vestris Rd SE23 162 D2
Vestry House (Mus)★
E17 53 D5
Vestry Mews 12 SE5 139 C4
Vestry Rd E17 53 D5
SE5 139 C4
Vestry St N1 95 B4 235 C2
Vevey St SE23,SE6 163 B2
Veysey Gdns RM10 81 C5
Viaduct Pl 28 E2 96 B4
Viaduct Rd N2 30 C1
Viaduct St E2 96 B4
Viaduct The Harrow HA2 64 A5
Woodford E18 37 B1
Vian St SE13 141 D2
Viant Ho 11 NW10 67 B1
Vibart Gdns SW2 160 B4
Vibart Wlk N1 233 B6
Vicarage Ave SE3 143 A5
Vicarage Cl
New Malden KT4 199 C1
Northolt UB5 63 B1
Ruislip HA4 39 B2
Vicarage Cres
SW11 136 B4 266 C1
Vicarage Ct N12 29 D5
W8 245 C2
Beckenham BR3 207 A6
East Bedfont TW14 149 A4
7 Putney SW15 156 A4
Vicarage Dr
Barking IG11 79 A1
Beckenham BR3 185 C2
Mortlake SW14 155 B6
Vicarage Farm Ct
TW5 129 B5
Vicarage Farm Rd
TW3,TW4,TW5 129 A4
Vicarage Fields KT12 194 C3
Vicarage Fields Sh Ctr The
IG11 79 A1
Vicarage Gate
W8 113 D5 245 C3
Vicarage Gdns W8 245 B3
Mitcham CR4 202 C6
Mortlake SW14 155 B6
Vicarage Gr SE5 139 B4
Vicarage Ho 1 KT1 176 B1
Vicarage La E15 76 D1
Ilford IG1 57 B1
Wallend E6 100 C4
Vicarage Pk SE18 123 A1
Vicarage Prim Sch E6 100 B4
Vicarage Rd DA5 169 D3
E10 53 D1
E15 76 D1
NW4 46 A3
SE18 123 A1
Ashford TW16 171 D4
Croydon CR0 220 C5
Dagenham RM10 81 D1
Kingston KT1,KT2 175 D1
Mortlake SW14 155 B6
Sutton SM1 217 D5
Teddington KT1,KT8 175 C2
Teddington TW11 175 A5
Tottenham N17 34 A2
Vicarage Way NW10 67 B5
Harrow HA2 41 C2
Vicarage Wlk
SW11 136 B4 266 D2
Vicars Bridge Cl HA0 88 A5
Vicar's Cl E15 99 A6
E9 96 C6
Enfield EN1 5 C3
Vicar's Green Prim Sch
HA0 87 C5
Vicars Hill SE13 141 D1
Vicar's Moor La N21 16 D4
Vicars Oak Rd SE19 183 C4
Vicar's Rd NW5 71 A3
Vicar's Wlk RM8 80 B5
Viceroy Cl N2 48 C6
Viceroy Ct NW8 230 B4
6 Croydon CR0 205 B1
Viceroy Lo 6 KT6 198 A4
Viceroy Par N2 48 C6
Viceroy Rd
SW8 138 A4 270 A2
Vic Johnson Ho 14 E3 97 B6
Vickers Cl SM6 220 B1
Vickers Ct 10 TW19 148 A5
Vickery Ct EC1 242 B6

Vickery Ho 12 SW4 138 A1
Victor Cazalet Ho N1 234 C6
Victor Gr HA0 66 A1
Victor Ho N20 14 D1
Victoria & Albert Mus★
SW7 114 B3 256 D5
Victoria Arc SW1 258 D5
Victoria Ave E6 99 D6
EC2 243 B3
N3 29 B2
Barnet EN4 2 B1
East Molesey KT8 195 D6
Hackbridge SM5,SM6 219 A5
Hillingdon UB10 60 D1
Hounslow TW3,TW4 151 C6
Surbiton KT6 197 D3
Wembley HA9 66 D2
Victoria Bglws DA14 191 B3
Victoria Bldgs 13 E8 96 B6
Victoria Bsns Ctr
DA16 146 B3
Victoria Cl Barnet EN4 2 B1
East Molesey KT8 195 C6
Harrow HA1 42 D3
Hayes UB3 83 B1
Victoria Coach Sta
SW1 115 B2 258 C3
Victoria Cotts N10 31 A1
3 E1 96 A2
Ilford IG6 57 A4
2 Richmond TW9 132 C4
Victoria Cres N15 51 C4
Merton SW19 179 B3
West Norwood SE19 183 C4
Victoria Ct 3 E1 118 A6
5 SW4 159 D5
W3 110 C4
Penge SE26 184 C4
1 Wanstead E18 55 B6
Wembley HA9 66 C2
Victoria Dock Rd E16 121 B6
Victoria Dr SW19 156 D3
Victoria Emb
WC2 116 C6 251 A5
Victoria Gdns
W11 113 C5 245 A4
Heston TW5 129 A4
Victoria Gr N12 30 B5
W8 114 A3 256 A6
Victoria Gr Mews W2 245 C5
Victoria Ho SW1 258 C2
6 SW4 159 D5
2 W12 112 A4
Edgware HA8 26 D4
Victoria Ind Est W3 89 C2
Victoria Jun Sch The
TW13 150 B3
Victoria La Barnet EN5 1 B1
Hayes UB3 105 B1
Victoria Lo 4 SW19 178 C3
Victoria Mans 8 N7 72 C3
NW10 68 B1
Victoria Mews NW6 91 C6
Wandsworth SW18 158 A3
Victorian Gr N16 73 C5
Victorian Rd N16 73 D5
Victoria Park Ct 11 E9 74 C1
Victoria Park Ind Ctr
E3 75 B1
Victoria Park Lofts E9 96 D6
Victoria Park Rd E9 74 D1
Victoria Park Sq E2 96 C4
Victoria Pas NW8 236 C6
Victoria Pl 18 TW10 153 D6
Victoria Point 10 E13 99 A5
Victoria Rd BR2 209 D4
BR7 188 C5
DA15 168 A1
E11 76 C4
E13 99 A5
N15 52 A5
N22 31 D2
N4 50 B1
NW10 89 C3
NW4 46 D5
NW6 91 B6
NW7 27 D5
W8 114 A3 256 A6
Barking IG11 78 D2
Barnet EN4 2 B1
Bexley DA6 147 C1
Buckhurst Hill IG9 21 D2
Chingford E17 36 A1
Chingford, Chingford Green
E4 20 C3
Dagenham RM10 81 D3
Ealing W5 87 B2
Edmonton N18 33 D6
Edmonton N9 17 D1
Feltham TW13 150 B3
Kingston KT1 176 B1
Mitcham CR4 180 D3
Mortlake SW14 133 B2
Ruislip HA4 62 B4
Southall UB2 107 B3
Surbiton KT6 197 D3
Sutton SM1 218 B3
Teddington TW11 175 A4
Twickenham TW1 153 B4

Victoria Rd *continued*
Wanstead E18 55 B6
Victoria Ret Pk HA4 62 D3
Victoria Rise SW4 137 B2
Victoria Sq SW1 258 D6
Victoria St E15 76 C1
SW1 115 C3 259 B5
Erith DA17 125 B1
Victoria Sta
SW1 115 B2 258 D4
Victoria Terr N4 50 C1
NW10 89 C3
Harrow HA1 42 C1
Victoria Villas TW9 132 B1
Victoria Way SE7 143 C6
Victoria Yd 31 E1 96 A1
Victor Mills Cotts BR8 191 C3
Victor Rd NW10 90 B4
Harrow HA2 42 A6
Penge SE20 184 D3
Teddington TW11 174 C6
Victors Dr TW12 173 A4
Victor Seymour Inf Sch
SM5 218 D4
Victors Way EN5 1 B2
Victor Villas N9 17 B1
Victory Ave SM4 202 A4
Victory Bsns Ctr The
TW7 130 D1
Victory Ct IG11 102 B4
Victory Day Sch
SW11 137 A4 268 A1
Victory Pl 6 E14 119 A6
SE17 117 B2 262 C4
West Norwood SE19 183 C4
Victory Prim Sch
SE17 117 A2 262 B4
Victory Rd
Merton SW19 180 A3
Wanstead E11 55 B5
Victory Road Mews 5
SW19 180 A3
Victory Way SE16 119 A4
Hounslow TW5 106 C1
Victory Wharf E14 119 A6
Victory Wlk SE8 141 C4
Video Ct N4 50 A2
Vidler Cl KT9 213 C2
Vienna Cl IG5 37 D1
View Cl N6 48 D2
Harrow HA1 42 B5
View Cres N8 49 D4
Viewfield Cl HA3 44 A2
Viewfield Rd DA5 168 C3
Wandsworth SW18 157 B5
Viewland Rd SE18 123 D1
View Point SE3 142 D2
View Rd N6 48 D3
Viewside Lo N6 49 C3
View The SE2 125 A1
Viga Rd N21 16 C5
Vigilant Cl SE26 184 A6
Vignoles Rd RM7 59 C2
Vigo St W1 115 C6 249 A5
Vi & John Rubens Ho
IG2 56 C3
Viking Cl 12 E3 97 A5
Viking Ct TW12 173 D2
Viking Fst & Mid Sch
UB5 84 D4
Viking Gdns E6 100 A3
Viking Ho 3 SE5 139 A3
3 SE7 122 A2
Viking Pl E10 53 B1
Viking Rd UB1 107 A6
Villacourt Rd SE18,SE2 146 A6
Village Arc The 2 E4 20 A3
Village Cl NW3 70 B3
Chingford E4 36 A5
Village Ct E17 53 D4
SE3 142 C2
Village Gate TW17 192 D4
Village Home The IG6 57 A6
Village Hts IG8 36 D5
Village Inf Sch RM10 81 C1
Village Mount 18 NW3 70 A4
Village Park Cl EN1 17 C5
Village Rd N3 29 A1
Enfield EN1 17 C6
Village Row SM2 217 C1
Village Sch The NW3 70 D2
Village The SE7 143 D6
SW11 136 D2
Village Way NW10 67 B4
SE21 161 B5
Ashford TW15 170 C6
Beckenham BR3 207 C6
Pinner HA5 41 B2
Village Way E HA2 41 C2
Villa Rd SW9 138 C2
Villas Rd SE18 123 A2
Villa St SE17 117 B1 262 D1
Villiers Ave
Kingston KT5 198 B5
Twickenham TW2 151 B3
Villiers Cl E10 75 C6
Kingston KT5 198 B5
Villiers Ct N20 14 A4
SW11 267 B2

Villiers High Sch UB1 107 B5
Villiers Ho W5 109 D6
Villiers Rd NW2 68 A2
Isleworth TW7 130 C3
Kingston KT1 198 B6
Penge BR3 184 D1
Southall UB1 107 B5
Villiers St WC2 250 B4
Vincam Cl TW2 151 C4
Vince Ct N1 235 D1
Vincent Ave KT5 215 A6
Vincent Cl BR2 209 B5
DA15 167 C3
Barnet EN5 1 D2
Harmondsworth UB7 126 C6
Vincent Ct N4 50 A1
NW4 46 D5
SW9 270 D1
W1 237 C2
Vincent Dr
Hillingdon UB10 82 B6
Upper Halliford TW17 193 C6
Vincent Gdns NW2 67 D5
Vincent Ho KT3 199 D5
Vincent Rd N15 51 A5
SE18 122 D2
W3 111 A3
Chingford E4 36 B4
Croydon CR0 205 C2
Dagenham RM9 81 A1
Hounslow TW4 128 D2
Hounslow TW7 130 B4
Kingston KT1 198 C6
Wembley HA0 66 B1
Wood Green N22 32 C1
Vincent Row TW12 174 A5
Vincents Cl SE16 119 A4
Vincents Path UB5 63 A2
Vincent Sq
SW1 115 D2 259 C4
Wood Green N22 32 C1
Vincent St E16 98 D2
SW1 115 D2 259 D4
Vincent Terr
N1 94 D5 234 D4
Vince St EC1 95 B4 235 D1
Vine Cl Surbiton KT5 198 B3
Sutton SM1 218 A5
West Drayton UB7 104 C2
Vine Cotts
3 Ealing W7 108 C5
Southall UB2 107 D2
Vine Ct E1 96 A2
Harrow HA3 44 A3
Vinegar St E1 118 B5
Vinegar Yd SE1 253 A2
Vine Gdns IG1 79 A3
Vine Gr UB10 60 C1
Vine Hill EC1 241 A5
Vine La SE1 117 C5 253 B3
Hillingdon UB10 82 B6
Uxbridge UB10 60 B1
Vine Lo N12 30 A4
Vine Pl Ealing W5 110 A5
Hounslow TW3 129 D1
Vine Rd BR6 227 D2
E15 76 D1
Barnes SW13 133 D2
East Molesey KT8 196 A5
Vineries Bank NW7 28 B5
Vineries Cl
Dagenham RM9 81 B2
Harmondsworth UB7 126 C6
Vineries The Enfield EN1 5 C2
Southgate N14 15 C5
Viners Cl KT12 194 C3
Vines Ave N3 29 D2
Vine Sq W14 254 D1
Vines Sch The SW11 137 A1
Vine St EC3 95 D1 243 C1
W1 249 B5
Vine St Bridge EC1 241 B5
Vinewood Ct E17 54 B4
Vineyard Ave NW7 29 A3
Vineyard Cl
Forest Hill SE6 163 C3
Kingston KT1 198 B6
Vineyard Gr N3 29 D2
Vineyard Hill Rd
SW19 179 C6
Vineyard Path SW14 133 B2
Vineyard Rd TW13 150 A1
Vineyard Row KT1,KT8 175 C2
Vineyard Sch The
TW10 154 A5
Vineyards The TW13 150 A1
Vineyard The TW10 154 A6
Vineyard Wlk EC1 241 A6
Viney Ct 9 SW4 159 D5
Vine Yd SE1 252 B2
Viney Rd SE13 141 D2
Vining St SW2,SW9 138 C1
Vinlake Ave UB10 60 C5
Vinson Ho N1 235 D3
Vinter Ct TW17 192 C4
Vintners Ct EC4 252 B6
Vintry Mews 3 E17 53 C5
Viola Ave SE2 124 B1
Feltham TW14 150 C5

Viola Ave *continued*
Stanwell TW19 148 A3
Viola Sq W12 111 D6
Violet Ave Enfield EN2 5 B5
Hillingdon UB8 82 B2
Violet Cl E16 98 C3
44 SE8 141 B6
Hackbridge SM6 203 A1
Violet Gdns CR0 220 D3
Violet Hill NW8 92 A5 229 A3
Violet Hill Ho NW8 229 A3
Violet La CR0 220 D3
Violet Rd E17 53 C3
E3 97 D3
Woodford E18 37 B1
Violet St E2 96 B3
Violet Terr UB8 82 C2
Violette Szabo Ho 4
SE27 183 B6
VIP Trad Est SE7 121 C2
Virgil Pl W1 237 C3
Virgil St SE1 116 B3 260 D6
Virginia Cl KT3 199 A5
Virginia Ct 7 SE16 118 D4
Virginia Ho 3 E14 120 A6
Teddington TW11 175 A5
Virginia Prim Sch E2 95 D4
Virginia Rd 19 E2 95 D4
South Norwood CR7 182 D2
Virginia St E1 118 A6
Virginia Wlk SW2 160 B5
Viscount Cl N11 31 B5
Viscount Ct 9 W11 91 C1
Viscount Dr E6 100 B2
Viscount Gr 3 UB5 84 D4
Viscount Point 7
SW19 179 C3
Viscount Rd TW19 148 A3
Viscount St EC1 242 A4
Viscount Way TW6 127 C1
Vista Ave EN3 6 D3
Vista Dr IG4 55 D4
Vista The SE9 165 D4
Vista Way HA3 44 A3
Vita Et Pax Sch N14 15 B6
Vittoria Ho N1 233 D5
Vittoria Prim Sch
N1 94 C5 234 A4
Viveash Cl UB3 105 D3
Vivian Ave NW4 46 B4
Wembley HA9 66 C2
Vivian Ct N12 29 D5
Vivian Gdns HA9 66 C3
Vivian Ho N4 51 B2
Vivian Mans 1 NW4 46 B4
Vivian Rd E3 97 A5
Vivian Sq SE15 140 B2
Vivian Way N2 48 B4
Vivien Cl KT9 214 A1
Vivienne Cl TW1 153 D5
Voce Rd SE18 145 B5
Voewood Cl KT3 199 D3
Vogans Mill SE1 253 D2
Vogler Ho 8 E1 118 C6
Vollasky Ho 5 E1 96 A2
Volta Cl N9 18 C1
Voltaire 2 SE5 139 D4
15 Richmond TW9 132 B4
Voltaire Ct 12 SW11 137 A3
Voltaire Rd SW4 137 D2
Voltaire Way UB3 105 C6
Volt Ave NW10 89 C4
Volta Way CR0 204 B1
Voluntary Pl E11 55 A3
Vorley Rd N19 71 C6
Voss Ct SW16 182 A4
Voss St E2 96 A4
Voyager Bsns Est 10
SE16 118 A3
Voyagers Cl IG11 102 C1
Voysey Cl N3 47 A6
Vulcan Cl E6 100 C1
Vulcan Gate EN2 4 C3
Vulcan Rd SE4 141 B3
Vulcan Sq E14 119 C2
Vulcan Terr SE4 141 B3
Vulcan Way N7 72 B2
Vyner Ct E5 74 A6
Vyner Rd W3 111 B6
Vyners Sch UB10 60 B4
Vyner St E2 96 B6
Vyners Way UB10 60 C3
Vyne The DA7 147 D2
Vyvyan Ho SE18 144 C4

W

Wadbrook St KT1 175 D1
Wadding St
SE17 117 B2 262 C3
Waddington Cl EN1 5 C1
Waddington Rd E15 76 B2
Waddington St E15 76 B2
Waddington Way
SE19 183 B2

Waddon Cl CR0 220 C5
Waddon Court Rd
CR0 220 C5
Waddon Inf Sch CR9 220 C3
Waddon Marsh Sta
CR0 220 C6
Waddon Marsh Way
CR0 204 B1
Waddon New Rd CR0 220 D6
Waddon Park Ave
CR0 220 C5
Waddon Rd CR0 220 D5
Waddon Sta CR0 220 C4
Waddon Way CR0,CR2,
CR9 220 D2
Wade Ct N10 31 B3
Wembley HA0 65 D5
Wade Ho 13 SE1 118 A4
1 Enfield EN1 17 C6
Wade's Gr N21 16 C4
Wade's Hill N21 16 C4
Wade's La TW11 175 A5
Wadeson St E2 96 B5
Wade's Pl E14 119 D6
Wadeville Ave RM6 59 B2
Wadeville Cl DA17 125 C1
Wadham Ave E17 35 D3
Wadham Cl TW17 193 A2
Wadham Gdns
NW3 70 C1 230 A6
Wadham Rd
Chingford, Highams Park
E17 35 D2
Putney SW15 135 A1
Wadhurst Cl SE20 184 B1
Wadhurst Ct E6 100 C5
Wadhurst Rd W4 111 B3
Wadley Rd E11 54 C2
Wadsworth Bsns Ctr
UB6 87 C5
Wadsworth Cl
Enfield EN3 18 D6
Wembley UB6 87 C5
Wadsworth Rd UB6 87 C5
Wager St E3 97 B3
Waggoners Rdbt TW5 128 B4
Waggon Mews N14 15 C3
Waghorn Rd E13 99 C6
Harrow HA3 43 D6
Waghorn St SE15 140 A2
Wagner St SE15 140 C5
Wagon Rd EN4,EN5 1 D6
Wagstaff Gdns RM9 80 C1
Wagtail Cl NW9 27 C1
Wagtail Wlk BR3 208 A4
Waights Ct KT2 176 A2
Waikato Lo IG9 21 C3
Wainford Cl SW19 156 D3
Wainwright Gr TW7 130 B1
Wainwright Ho 3 E1 118 C5
Waite Davies Rd SE12 164 D4
Waitelands Ho KT3 199 B5
Waite St SE15 139 D6
Waithman St EC4 241 C1
Wakefield Gdns
Redbridge IG1 56 A3
South Norwood SE19 183 C3
Wakefield Ho 6 SE15 140 A4
Dulwich SE22 162 B3
Wakefield Mews WC1 233 B1
Wakefield Rd N11 31 D5
N15 51 D4
19 Richmond TW10 153 D6
Wakefield St E6 100 A6
WC1 94 A4 233 B1
Edmonton N18 34 A5
Wakeford Cl SW4 159 C6
Wakehams Hill HA5 41 B6
Wakeham St 9 N1 73 B2
Wakehurst Rd SW11 158 D6
Wakeling Ho 8 SE27 160 D1
Wakeling Rd W7 86 D2
Wakeling St 18 E14 97 A1
Wakelin Ho 19 N1 72 D1
Forest Hill SE23 163 A4
Wakelin Rd E15 98 C5
Wakeman Ho HA8 26 A6
Wakeman Rd NW10 90 D4
Wakemans Hill Ave
NW9 45 B4
Wakering Rd IG11 79 A1
Wakerings The IG11 79 A2
Wakerly Cl 6 E6 100 B1
Wakley St EC1 94 D4 234 C2
Walberswick St SW8 270 B3
Walbrook EC4 252 C6
9 Wanstead E18 55 A6
Walbrook Ct 32 N1 95 C5
Walburgh St E1 96 B1
Walcorde Ave SE17 262 B3
Walcot Ct CR0 222 A6
Walcot Gdns SE11 261 A4
Walcot Ho 9 SE22 139 C2
Walcot Rd EN3 7 B3
Walcot Sq
SE11 116 C2 261 B4
Walcott St SW1 259 B4
Waldair Ct E16 122 D4
Waldeck Gr SE27 160 D1
Waldeck Rd N15 50 D6
Brentford W4 132 C6
Ealing W13 87 B1
Mortlake SW14 133 A2
Waldeck Terr SW14 133 A2
Waldegrave Ct
11 Barking IG11 101 B6
1 Teddington TW11 174 D5
Waldegrave Gdns
TW1 152 D1
Waldegrave Ho 5
SW15 156 C6
Waldegrave Pk TW1 174 D6
Waldegrave Rd BR1 210 B5
N8 50 C6
Dagenham RM8 80 C6
Ealing W5 110 B6
Penge SE19 183 D3
Teddington TW11 174 D6
Waldegrave Sch TW2 152 B1
Waldegrove CR0 221 D5
Waldemar Ave
Ealing W13 109 C5
Fulham SW6 135 A3
Waldemar Avenue Mans
SW6 264 A1
Waldemar Rd SW19 179 C5
Walden Ave BR7 188 B6
Edmonton N13 33 A6
Walden Cl DA17 125 B1
Walden Ct SW8 269 D2
Walden Gdns CR7,
SW16 204 B5
Walden Ho SW1 258 B3
8 SW11 137 A3
Barnet EN4 2 C1
Walden Rd BR7 188 B4
Tottenham N17 33 B2
Waldenshaw Rd SE23 162 C3
Walden St E1 96 B1
Walden Way NW7 28 D4
Waldo Cl SW4 159 C6
Waldo Ind Est BR1 209 D6
Waldo Pl SW19 180 C3
Waldo Rd BR1 209 D6
NW10 90 B4
Waldorf Cl CR2 220 D1
Waldram Cres SE23 162 C3
Waldram Park Rd
SE23 162 D3
Waldram Pl 6 SE23 162 C3
Waldrist Way DA18 125 B4
Waldron Gdns BR2 208 B6
Waldron Ho 17 SW2 160 B6
Waldronhyrst CR0,CR2 220 D4
Waldron Mews SW3 266 D6
Waldron Rd
Harrow HA1,HA2 42 C1
Wandsworth SW18 158 A1
Waldrons The CR0 221 A4
Waldron's Yd HA2 64 B6
Waldstock Rd SE28 124 A6
Waleran Cl HA7 24 D4
Walerand Rd SE13 142 A3
Waleran Flats SE1 263 A4
Wales Ave SM5 218 C3
Wales Cl SE15 140 B6
Wales Farm Rd W3 89 B2
Waleton Acres SM6 219 C2
Waley St 1 E1 97 A2
Walfield Ave N20 13 D4
Walford Ct SE1 263 B6
Walford Ho 4 E1 96 B1
Walford Rd N16 73 C4
Walfrey Gdns RM9 81 A1
Walham Ct 15 NW3 70 D2
Walham Gr
SW6 135 C5 265 A4
Walham Green Arc
SW6 265 B4
Walham Rise 1 SW19 179 A4
Walham Yd SW6 265 A4
Walkden Hall (Hall of
Residence) KT2 177 B6
Walkden Rd BR7 188 C5
Walker Cl N11 31 C6
SE18 123 A2
Ealing W7 108 C5
East Bedfont TW14 149 D4
Hampton TW12 173 B4
Walker Ho NW1 232 C3
Walker Mews SW2 160 C6
Walker Prim Sch N14 15 D2
Walkerscroft Mead
SE21 161 A3
Walker's Ct W1 249 C6
Walkers Lo 7 E14 120 A4
Walker's Pl SW15 135 A1
Walkinshaw Ct 14 N1 73 A1
Walks The N2 48 B6
Walk The
Ashford TW16 171 D3
Palmers Green N13 16 C1
Walkynscroft 1 SE15 140 B3
Wallace Cl SE28 124 D6
Upper Halliford TW17 193 B5
Wallace Cl *continued*
Uxbridge UB10 82 A5
Wallace Collection★
W1 238 A2
Wallace Cres SM5 218 D3
Wallace Ho N7 72 B2
Wallace Rd N1,N5 73 A2
Wallasey Cres UB10 60 C5
Wallbrook Bsns Ctr
TW4 128 B2
Wallbrook Ho N9 18 C2
Wallbutton Rd SE4 141 A3
Wallcote Ave NW2 46 D1
Wall Ct N4 50 B1
Walled Garden Cl BR3 207 D5
Walled Gdn The TW16 194 B6
Wall End Ct E6 100 C6
Wall End Rd E6 78 C1
Waller Dr HA6 22 A2
Waller Rd SE14 140 D3
Wallers Cl RM9 103 B6
Wallett Ct 9 NW1 71 C1
Wallflower St W12 111 D6
Wallgrave Rd SW5 255 C3
Wallingford Ave W10 90 D1
Wallington Cl HA4 39 A3
Wallington Ct 10 SM6 219 B2
Wallington Cty Gram Sch
SM6 219 B5
Wallington Green
SM6 219 B4
Wallington Rd IG3 57 D2
Wallington Sq 4 SM6 219 C2
Wallington Sta SM6 219 B2
Wallis Alley SE1 252 B2
Wallis Cl SW11 136 B2
Wallis Rd E9 75 C2
Southall UB1 85 D1
Wallorton Gdns SW14 133 B1
Wallside EC2 242 B3
Wall St N1 73 B2
Wallwood Rd E11 54 B2
Wallwood St E14 97 B2
Walmar Cl EN4 2 B4
Walmer Cl BR6 227 B4
Chingford E4 19 D2
Walmer Gdns W13 109 A4
Walmer Ho 8 W10 90 D1
11 Penge SE20 184 C3
Walmer Pl W1 237 C4
Walmer Rd W10 90 C1
W11 113 A6 244 A5
Walmer St NW1 237 C4
Walmer Terr SE18 123 B2
Walmgate Rd UB6 87 B6
Walmington Fold N12 29 C4
Walm La NW2 68 C2
Walmsley Ho 1 SW16 181 C6
Walnut Ave UB7 104 C3
Walnut Cl SE8 141 B6
Hayes UB3 105 C6
Ilford IG6 57 A5
Wallington SM5 218 D3
Walnut Ct 2 E17 54 A5
Walnut Gdns E15 76 C3
Walnut Gr EN1 17 B6
Walnut Mews SM2 218 A1
Walnut Rd E10 75 D6
Walnut Tree Ave CR4 202 C6
Walnut Tree Cl
Barnes SW13 133 D4
Chislehurst BR7 189 A2
Walnut Tree Cotts
SW19 179 A5
Walnut Tree Ho SW10 265 D6
Walnut Tree Rd SE10 120 C1
Brentford TW8 132 A6
Charlton TW17 171 A1
Dagenham RM8 81 A6
Heston TW5 129 B6
Walnut Tree Walk Prim Sch
SE11 116 C2 261 A4
Walnut Tree Wlk
SE11 116 C2 261 A4
Walnut Way
Buckhurst Hill IG9 21 D1
Ruislip HA4 62 C2
Walpole Ave TW9 132 B3
Walpole Cl W13 109 C4
Pinner HA5 23 C4
Walpole Cres 7
TW11 174 D5
Walpole Ct NW6 70 A1
7 W14 112 D3
Ealing W5 109 D5
Twickenham TW2 152 C2
Walpole Gdns W4 111 A1
Twickenham TW2 152 C1
Walpole Lo W13 109 C5
Walpole Mews NW8 229 C5
Walpole Pl 3 SE18 122 D2
6 Teddington TW11 174 D5
Walpole Rd BR2 209 D4
E17 53 A5
E6 77 C1
N17 51 A6
Mitcham SW19 180 B4
South Croydon CR0 221 B6
Surbiton KT6 198 A3
Walpole Rd *continued*
Teddington TW11 174 D5
Tottenham N17 33 A1
Twickenham TW2 152 C2
Woodford E18 36 D2
Walpole St
SW3 114 D1 257 D2
Walrond Ave HA9 66 A3
Walsham Cl N16 52 A1
SE28 124 D6
Walsham Ho SE14 140 D3
SE17 262 C2
Walsham Rd SE14 140 D3
Feltham TW14 150 B4
Walsingham NW8 229 D6
Walsingham Gdns
KT19 215 D3
Walsingham Ho E4 20 B4
Walsingham Lo SW13 134 A4
Walsingham Mans
SW6 265 D4
Walsingham Pk BR7 189 B1
Walsingham Pl SW4,
SW11 159 A5
Walsingham Rd BR5 190 B2
E5 74 A5
Ealing W13 109 A5
Enfield EN2 17 B6
Mitcham CR4 202 D4
Walsingham Wlk
DA17 147 C6
Walter Besant Ho 20
E1 96 D4
Walter Ct 3 W3 89 A1
Walter Green Ho SE15 140 C4
Walter Ho SW10 266 C4
Walter Hurford Par 4
E12 78 C4
Walter Northcott Ho 2
NW6 69 C3
Walter Savill Twr E17 53 C3
Walters Cl SE17 262 B3
Hayes UB3 105 D4
Walters Ho N1 234 D5
10 SE17 138 D6
3 SE5 139 C3
Walters Rd EN3 6 C1
Walter's Rd SE25 205 C5
Walter St E2 96 D4
2 Kingston KT2 176 A2
Walters Way SE23 162 D5
Walters Yd BR1 187 A1
Walter Terr E1 96 D1
Walterton Rd W9 91 C3
Walter Wlk HA8 27 A4
Waltham Ave NW9 44 C3
Hayes UB3 105 B3
Waltham Ct E17 36 A2
Waltham Dr HA8 44 C6
Waltham Forest Coll
E17 35 D1
Waltham Gdns EN3 6 C6
Waltham Green Ct
SW6 265 C3
Waltham Ho NW8 229 A6
10 SW9 138 B3
Waltham Park Way E17 35 C3
Waltham Pk E17 35 C2
Waltham Rd
Carshalton SM5 202 C1
Southall UB2 107 A3
Walthamstow Ave E4 35 C3
Walthamstow Ave (North
Circular Rd) E4 35 B4
Walthamstow Bsns Ctr
E17 36 A1
Walthamstow Central Sta
E17 53 C4
Walthamstow Queens Road
Sta E17 53 C4
Walthamstow Sch for Girls
E17 53 D5
Waltham Way E4 19 C2
Waltheof Ave N17 33 B2
Waltheof Gdns N17 33 B2
Walton Ave
Cheam SM3 217 B5
Harrow HA2 63 B4
New Malden KT3 199 D5
Wembley HA9 66 D5
Walton Bridge Rd
KT12,TW17 193 C2
Walton Cl E5 74 D5
NW2 68 B6
SW8 138 A5 270 B4
Harrow HA1 42 B5
Walton Croft HA1 64 C4
Walton Ct EN5 14 A6
Walton Dr NW10 67 B2
Harrow HA1 42 B5
Walton Gdns Acton W3 88 D2
Feltham TW13 171 D6
Wembley HA9 66 A6
Walton Gn CR0 224 A1
Walton Ho 10 E17 53 D6
E2 243 D6
N7 72 B5
SW18 157 C5
1 Edmonton N9 34 A6
Walton Ho *continued*
Kingston KT2 176 A3
Walton La
Oatlands Park KT13,
TW17 193 B1
Shepperton TW17 193 B2
Walton Pl SW3 257 C6
Walton Rd E13 99 C5
N15 51 D5
East Molesey KT8,KT12 195 C5
Harrow HA1 42 B5
Little Ilford E12 78 C4
Sidcup DA14 168 C1
Walton-on-T KT12&KT8 194 D4
Walton St
SW3 114 C3 257 B5
Enfield EN2 5 B4
Walton Way Acton W3 88 D2
Mitcham CR4 203 C5
Walt Whitman Cl 6
SE24 138 D1
Walworth Pl
SE17 117 A1 262 B1
Walworth Rd
SE17 117 A1 262 B2
Walworth Sch
SE17 117 C1 263 B1
Walwyn Ave BR1 209 D6
Wanborough Dr SW15 156 B3
Wanderer Dr IG11 102 C4
Wandle Bank
Mitcham SW19 180 B3
Wallington CR0 220 A5
Wandle Court Gdns
CR0 220 A5
Wandle Ct 4 W12 111 C4
Wallington CR0 220 A5
West Ewell KT19 215 A4
Wandle Ho NW8 237 A4
6 Catford BR1 186 B5
Wandsworth SW18 157 D4
Wandle Lo CR0 220 A5
Wandle Pk Sta CR0 220 C6
Wandle Prim Sch
SW18 157 D3
Wandle Rd
Croydon CR0 221 A5
Hackbridge SM6 219 B6
Morden SM4 202 B4
Upper Tooting SW17 158 C2
Wallington CR0 220 A5
Wandle Side
Hackbridge SM6 219 B5
Wallington CR0 220 B5
Wandle Tech Pk CR4 202 D2
Wandle Trad Est CR4 202 D2
Wandle Valley Sch
SM5 202 C2
Wandle Way
Mitcham CR4 202 D4
Wandsworth SW18 157 D3
Wandon Rd
SW6 135 D5 265 D3
Wandsworth Bridge Rd
SW6 135 D2 265 C1
Wandsworth Common Sta
SW12 158 D4
Wandsworth Common West
Side SW18 158 A6
Wandsworth Gyratory
SW18 157 D6
Wandsworth High St
SW18 157 D6
Wandsworth Plain
SW18 157 D6
Wandsworth Rd
SW8 138 A5 270 A3
Wandsworth Road Sta
SW4 137 C3
Wandsworth Town Sta
SW18 135 D1
Wangey Rd RM6 58 D2
Wangford Ho 13 SW9 138 D1
Wanless Rd SE24 139 A2
Wanley Rd SE5 139 B1
Wanlip Rd E13 99 B3
Wansbeck Ct EN2 4 D2
Wansbeck Rd E3,E9 75 B1
Wansdown Pl
SW6 135 D5 265 C4
Wansey St
SE17 117 A2 262 B3
Wansford Rd IG8 37 C2
Wanstead Church Sch
E11 55 A4
Wanstead Cl BR1 187 C1
Wanstead High Sch
E11 55 C3
Wanstead Hospl E11 55 B5
Wanstead La IG1 56 A3
Wanstead Park Ave
E12 77 D6
Wanstead Park Rd IG1 56 A1
Wanstead Park Sta E7 77 B4
Wanstead Pl E11 55 A4
Wanstead Rd BR1 187 C1
Wanstead Sta E11 55 B3
Wantage Rd SE12 164 D6
Wantz Rd RM10 81 D3
Wapping Dock St 19
E1
Wapping High St E1
Wapping La E1
Wapping Sta E1
Wapping Wall E1
Warbank La KT2
Warbeck Rd W12
Warberry Rd N22
Warboys App KT2
Warboys Cres E4
Warboys Rd KT2
Warburton Cl 6 N1
Stanmore HA3
Warburton Ct SE15
Ruislip HA4
Warburton Ho 5 E8
Warburton Rd 8 E8
Twickenham TW2
Warburton St 6 E8
Warburton Terr E17
Wardalls Ho 12 SE8
Ward Cl CR2
Ward Cotts TW19
Wardell Cl NW7
Wardell Ct N2
Wardell Ho 6 SE10
Warden Ave HA2
Warden Rd NW5
Wardens Field Cl 2
BR6
Wardens Gr SE1
Wardle St E9
Wardley Lo E11
Wardley St SW18
Wardlow 8 NW5
Wardo Ave
SW6 135 A4
Wardour Mews W1
Wardour St W1 93 D1
Ward Point SE11
Ward Rd E15
N19
Wardrobe Pl EC4
Wardrobe Terr EC4
Wardrobe The 3
TW9
Wards Rd IG2
Ware Ct Cheam SM1
Edgware HA8
Wareham Cl TW3
Wareham Ct 2 N1
Wareham Ho SW8
Waremead Rd IG2
Ware Point Dr SE28
Warfield Rd NW10
East Bedfont TW14
Hampton TW12
Warfield Yd 6 NW10
Wargrave Ave N15
Wargrave Ho 46 E2
Wargrave Rd HA2
Warham Rd N4
Croydon CR2
Harrow HA3
Warham St SE5
Waring Cl BR6
Waring Dr BR6
Waring Ho 10 E2
Waring Rd DA14
Waring St SE27
Warkworth Gdns TW7
Warkworth Rd N17
Warland Rd SE18
Warley Ave
Dagenham RM8
Hayes UB4
Warley Cl E10
Warley Ho N1
Warley Rd N9
Hayes UB4
Woodford IG8
Warley St E2
Warlingham Rd CR7
Warlock Rd W9
Warlow Cl EN3
Warlters Cl N7
Warlters Rd N7
Warltersville Mans N1
Warltersville Rd N4,N8
N19
War Memorial Homes
W4
Warming Cl E5
Warmington Rd SE24
Warmington St 3 E13
Warminster Gdns
SE25
Warminster Rd SE25
Warminster Sq SE25
Warminster Way CR4
Warmsworth NW1
Warncliffe Ho 3
SW15
Warndon St SE16
Warneford Rd HA3
Warneford St E9
Warne Pl 4 DA15
Warner Ave SM3

er Cl E15 76 C3
46 A2
oton TW12 173 B5
ngton UB3 127 B5
er Ct SM3 217 A6
er Ho 4 E9 74 D2
229 A2
141 D3
eckenham BR3 185 D4
er Pl E2 96 A4
er Rd E17 53 A5
49 D5
139 A4
ley BR1 186 D3
ers Cl IG8 37 A5
er St EC1 94 C3 241 A5
er Yd EC1 241 A5
ford Ho SW15 155 C5
ford Ind Est UB3 105 C4
ford Rd BR6 227 D3
ham WC1 233 C1
ham Court Rd
218 D1
ham Ho 6 SW2 160 B4
ham Rd N12 30 C5
le Mews W3 111 C4
le Way W3,W12 111 C4
en Ave E11 76 B5
ley BR1 186 C3
lake SW14,TW10 132 D1
igton BR6 227 D3
Croydon CR2 222 D1
en Cl DA6 169 C6
18 D4
s UB4 84 C2
bley HA9 65 D6
Norwood SE21 161 A4
KT10 212 A4
en Comp Sch RM6 59 B4
en Cres N9 17 D4
en Ct N1 234 A4
52 A6
eckenham BR3 185 C3
roydon CR0 205 C1
aling W5 87 C2
en Cutting KT2 177 B3
ender Prim Sch
39 D2
ender Rd N19 71 C4
ender Way HA4 40 A2
en Dr
nford UB6 86 A3
p HA4 40 D2
en Dr N KT5,KT6 198 D1
en Dr S KT5 199 A1
en Dr The E11 55 C2
en Fields HA7 25 C6
en Gdns E15 76 B3
en Hill IG10 21 C6
en Ho 21 E3 97 D4
en Jun Sch RM6 59 B4
en La SE18 122 D3
more HA7 9 A2
en Mews W1 239 A5
en Park Rd SM1,
218 C2
en Pk KT2 177 A4
en Pond Rd E4 20 D4
en Rd BR2 225 A6
169 C6
76 A5
67 D6
ord TW15 171 C3
ey WD23 8 B3
ford E4 20 A2
don CR0 205 D1
ham UB10 60 B4
IG6 57 B4
orth TW2 152 B5
ton KT2 177 A4
am SW19 180 C4
p DA14 168 C1
stead E11 55 C2
en Rise KT3 177 B2
en Road Prim Sch
227 D4
ens Shawe La HA8 10 D2
en St W1 93 C3 239 A5
en Street Sta
93 C3 239 B6
en Terr RM6 58 D5
en The E12 78 A4
s UB4 84 A1
n TW5 129 B5
ester Park KT19 215 B5
en Way NW7 29 A4
en Wlk 1 SE7 143 C6
en Wood Cl BR2 225 A6
ner Dr N9 18 A1
ner Gdns
137 A4 268 A1
ngton Cres
92 A3 236 A6
ngton Gdns W9 236 A5
ngton Pl E14 120 A5
ngton Rd
don CR0 220 D5
nham RM8 81 A6
w HA1 42 C4

Warrington Rd *continued*
21 Richmond TW10 153 D6
Warrington Sq RM8 80 D6
Warrior Sq E12 78 C4
Warsaw Cl HA4 62 B2
Warspite Ho 3 E14 119 D2
Warspite Rd SE18 122 A3
Warton Rd E15 98 A6
Warwall E6 100 D1
Warwick W14 113 B2 254 D3
Warwick Ave HA8 11 A1
W9 92 A3 236 A5
Harrow HA2 63 B4
Warwick Avenue Sta
W9 92 A3 236 A5
Warwick Chambers
W8 255 A6
Warwick Cl DA5 169 B4
Bushey WD23 8 C4
Hampton TW12 174 A3
New Barnet EN4 14 B6
Warwick Cres
W2 92 A2 236 A4
Hayes UB4 83 D3
Warwick Ct 3 E5 74 B6
N11 31 D4
5 N2 48 A6
NW2 69 A3
WC1 240 D3
1 Beckenham BR2 186 C1
Ealing W7 86 D1
Harrow HA1 42 C6
Merton SW19 179 C2
Northolt UB5 63 C3
Surbiton KT6 214 A6
Warwick Dene W5 110 A5
Warwick Dr SW15 134 B2
Warwick Gdns N4 51 A4
W14 113 B2 254 D4
Ilford IG1 56 D1
Thames Ditton KT7 196 D4
Thornton Heath CR7 204 C5
Warwick Gr E5 52 B1
Surbiton KT5 198 B2
Warwick Ho 10 E5 74 C6
N4 51 A1
11 SW9 138 C3
9 Acton W3 88 C1
6 Kingston KT2 176 A2
6 Putney SW15 156 C4
Warwick House St
SW1 249 D4
Warwick La
EC4 94 D1 241 D1
Warwick Lo
Cheam SM1 217 B4
Twickenham TW2 151 D1
Warwick Mans SW5 255 A4
Warwick Park Sch
SE15 139 D4
Warwick Pas EC4 241 D2
Warwick Pl W5 109 D4
W9 92 A2 236 A4
Warwick Pl N SW1 259 A3
Warwick Rd DA14 190 B5
E12 78 A3
E15 76 D2
E17 35 B1
N11 31 D4
W14,SW5 113 B2 254 D4
Ashford TW15 170 A5
Barnet EN5 1 D1
Bexley DA16 146 C2
Chingford E4 35 C5
Ealing W5 110 A5
Edmonton N18 33 D6
Enfield EN3 7 B6
Hounslow TW4 128 B2
Kingston KT3 199 A6
Penge SE20 206 B6
Southall UB2 107 B3
Sutton SM1 218 A3
Teddington KT1 175 C2
Thames Ditton KT7 196 D4
Thornton Heath CR7 204 C6
Twickenham TW2 152 C3
Wanstead E11 55 B4
Yiewsley UB7 104 A5
Warwick Row
SW1 115 B3 258 D6
Warwick Sch for Boys
E17 54 A5
Warwickshire Path
SE8 141 B5
Warwickshire Rd N16 73 C4
Warwick Sq EC4 241 D2
SW1 115 C1 259 A2
Warwick Sq Mews
SW1 259 A3
Warwick St
W1 115 C6 249 B6
Warwick Terr E17 54 B4
SE18 145 B6
Warwick Way
SW1 115 B2 258 D2
Warwick Yd EC1 242 B5
Wasdale NW1 231 D1
Washbrook Ho SW2 160 C5
Washington Ave E12 78 B4

Washington Cl 45 E3 97 D4
Washington Ct SW17 180 D4
Washington Ho E17 35 B1
SW1 247 C1
Washington Rd E6 77 C1
Barnes SW13 134 A5
Kingston KT1 176 C1
North Cheam KT4 200 B1
2 Woodford E18 36 D1
Wastdale Rd SE23 162 D3
Watchfield Ct 7 W4 111 A1
Watcombe Cotts TW9 132 C6
Watcombe Rd SE25 206 B4
Waterbank Rd SE6 186 A6
Waterbeach Rd RM9 80 C2
Water Brook La NW4 46 C4
Watercress Pl N1 73 C1
Waterdale Rd SE2 146 A6
Waterden Cres E9 75 C3
Waterden Rd E15 75 C2
Waterer Ho 7 SE6 186 A6
Waterer Rise SM6 219 D2
Waterfall Cl N14 15 C1
Waterfall Cotts SW19 180 B4
Waterfall Rd N11,N14 15 C1
Mitcham SW19 180 B4
Waterfall Terr SW17 180 C4
Waterfield Cl
Belvedere DA17 125 C3
Woolwich SE28 124 B5
Waterfield Gdns SE25 205 C4
Waterford Rd
SW6 135 D5 265 C3
Watergardens The
KT2 177 A4
Watergate EC4 251 C6
Watergate Ho 5 SE18 122 C2
Watergate Sch SE13 141 D1
Watergate St SE8 141 C6
Watergate Wlk WC2 250 B4
Water Gdns HA7 25 B4
Water Gdns The
W2 92 C1 237 B2
Waterglade Ctr The
W5 109 D6
Waterhall Ave E4 36 C6
Waterhall Cl E17 34 D2
Waterhead NW1 232 A2
Waterhedge Mews EN1 17 D6
Waterhouse Cl E16 99 D2
NW3 70 B3
W6 112 D1
Waterhouse Ct 5
TW11 174 D5
Wateridge Cl E14 119 C3
Wateringbury Cl BR5 190 B1
Water La E15 76 C2
SE14 140 C5
Edmonton N9 18 B4
Ilford IG3 79 D5
Richmond TW10,TW9 153 D6
Sidcup DA14 169 B2
Teddington KT1 175 D2
Twickenham TW1 153 A3
Water Lily Cl UB2 108 A4
Waterloo Bridge
SE1,WC2 116 B6 250 D5
Waterloo Cl E9 74 C3
East Bedfont TW14 149 D3
Waterloo East Sta
SE1 116 C5 251 B3
Waterloo Gdns E2 96 C5
Waterloo Int Sta
SE1 116 B4 250 D2
Waterloo Pier SE1 250 C2
Waterloo Pl
SW1 115 D5 249 C4
Waterloo Rd E10 53 C2
E6 77 C1
E7 76 D3
NW2 68 A6
SE1 116 C4 251 B2
Sutton SM1 218 B3
Waterloo Sta
SE1 116 C4 251 A2
Waterloo Terr N1 72 D1
Waterlow Ct NW11 47 D2
Waterlow Rd N19 49 C1
Waterman Bldg 4
E14 119 C4
Watermans Mews 1
W5 110 A6
Waterman St SW15 134 D2
Waterman Way E1 118 B5
Watermead TW14 149 C3
Watermead Ho E9 75 B3
Watermead La CR4 202 D2
Watermeadow La
SW6 136 A3
Watermead Rd SE6 186 A6
Watermeads High Sch
SM4 202 B3
Watermead Way N17 34 B1
Watermen's Sq 1
SE20 184 C3
Water Mews SE15 140 C1
Watermill Bsns Ctr EN3 7 B3
Watermill Cl TW10 153 C1
Watermill La N18 33 C5

Watermill Way
Feltham TW13 151 C2
Merton SW19 180 A2
Watermint Quay N16 52 A2
Water Rd HA0 88 B6
Watersedge KT19 215 A4
Water's Edge SW6 134 C4
Watersfield Way HA8 26 A3
Waters Gdns RM10 81 C3
Watership Down Ho
E11 54 D2
Waterside E17 52 C3
4 Beckenham BR3 185 C2
Waterside Cl E3 97 B6
28 SE16 118 A4
Barking IG11 80 A4
Northolt UB5 85 B4
Surbiton KT6 214 A6
Waterside Ct SE13 142 B1
Waterside Dr KT12 194 B4
Waterside Pl NW1 231 B6
Waterside Point SW11 267 B4
Waterside Rd UB2 107 C3
Waterside Sch SE18 123 B1
Waterside Trad Ctr
W7 108 C3
Waterside Way SW17 180 A5
Watersmeet Way
SE28 102 D1
Waterson St E2 95 D4
Waters Pl SW15 134 C3
Watersplash Cl KT1 198 A6
Watersplash La
Hayes UB3 106 A2
Southall TW5 106 B1
Watersplash Rd TW17 192 C5
Waters Rd Catford SE6 164 C1
Kingston KT1 176 D1
Waters Sq KT1 198 D6
Water St WC2 251 A6
Water Tower Cl UB8 60 A3
Water Tower Hill CR0 221 B4
Water Tower Ho W8 245 A3
Water Tower Pl N1 234 C5
Waterview Ho E14 97 A2
Waterworks Cnr E17 36 C1
Waterworks La E5 74 D6
Waterworks Rd SW2 160 B5
Watery La DA14 190 B4
Hayes UB3 105 B1
Merton SW19,SW20 179 B1
Northolt UB5 84 C5
Wates Way CR4 202 D3
Wateville Rd N17 33 A2
Watford Cl SW11 267 B2
Watford Rd E16 99 A2
Elstree WD6 9 C5
Harrow HA0,HA1 65 A5
Harrow HA1 43 A1
Northwood HA6 22 A4
Watford Way NW4 46 A5
Watford Way (Barnet
By-Pass) NW9 27 D3
Watkin Ho N16 51 D2
Watkin Rd HA9 66 D5
Watkinson Rd N7 72 B2
Watling Ave HA8 27 B2
Watling Ct EC4 242 B1
1 Elstree WD6 9 D5
Watling Gate NW9 45 C5
Watling Gdns NW2 69 A2
Watling Ho 10 SE18 144 C6
Watlings Cl CR0 207 A3
Watling St DA6,DA7 147 D1
EC4 95 A1 242 B1
4 SE15 139 C6
Watlington Gr SE26 185 A5
Watney Cotts SW14 133 A2
Watney Mkt E1 96 B1
Watney Rd SW14 133 A2
Watneys Rd CR4 203 D4
Watney St E1 96 B1
Watson Ave
Cheam SM3 217 A6
Wallend E6 78 C1
Watson Cl N16 73 B3
Mitcham SW19 180 C3
Watson Ho 3 SW2 160 A4
Watsons Lo 4 RM10 81 D2
Watson's Mews W1 237 B3
Watsons Rd N22 32 B2
Watson's St SE8 141 C5
Watson St E13 99 B5
Wattisfield Rd E5 74 C5
Watts Cl N15 51 C4
Watts Gr E3 97 D2
Watts Ho 6 W10 91 A2
Watt's La
Chislehurst BR7 189 A2
Teddington TW11 175 A5
Watts Point E13 99 A6
Watts Rd KT7 197 A2
Watts St E1 118 B5
SE15 139 D4
Wat Tyler Ho N8 50 A6
Wat Tyler Rd SE10 142 B4
Wauthier Cl N13 32 D5
Wavel Ct 7 E1 118 C5
7 Streatham SW16 160 A1

Wavell Dr DA15 167 C5
Wavell Ho N6 49 A3
Wavel Mews N8 49 D5
NW6 69 D1
Wavel Pl SE26 183 D6
Wavendon Ave W4 111 B1
Waveney Ave SE15 140 B1
Waveney Cl E1 118 A5
Waveney Ho SE15 140 B1
Waverley Ave E17 54 B6
E4 35 B6
Sutton SM1 217 D6
Tolworth KT5 199 A3
Twickenham TW2,TW4 151 C3
Wembley HA9 66 B3
Waverley Cl BR2 209 D4
East Molesey KT8 195 C4
Hayes UB3 105 B2
Woodford E18 37 C1
Waverley Cres SE18 123 B1
Waverley Ct 3 NW6 69 A1
W1 238 B4
Enfield EN2 5 A2
Waverley Gdns E6 100 A2
Barking IG11 101 C5
Ealing NW10 88 B5
Ilford IG6 57 B6
Northwood HA6 22 A2
Waverley Gr N3 47 A6
Waverley Ind Pk HA1 42 B6
Waverley Pl N4 50 D1
NW8 92 B5 229 C4
Waverley Rd E17 54 A6
N8 50 A2
SE18 123 B1
Croydon SE25 206 B6
Enfield EN2 4 D2
Harrow HA2 41 A1
Southall UB1 107 C6
Stoneleigh KT17,KT4 216 B3
Tottenham N17 34 B3
Woodford E18 37 C2
Waverley Sch EN3 6 C1
Waverley Sch (lower)
SE22 162 B6
Waverley Sch (Upper)
SE15 162 C6
Waverley Way SM2,
SM5 218 C2
Waverly Ct NW3 70 D2
Waverton Ho 2 E3 97 B6
Waverton Rd SW18 158 A4
Waverton St
W1 115 B5 248 C4
Wavertree Ct 9 SW2 160 A3
Wavertree Rd
Streatham SW2 160 B3
Woodford E18 37 A1
Waxham NW5 70 D3
Waxlow Cres UB1 85 C1
Waxlow Ho UB4 84 C2
Waxlow Rd NW10 89 B5
Waxwell Cl HA5 22 D1
Waxwell La HA5 22 D1
Wayborne Gr HA4 39 A3
Waye Ave TW5 128 A4
Wayfarer Rd UB5 85 A4
Wayfield Link SE9 167 B5
Wayford St SW11 136 C3
Wayland Ave E8 74 A3
Wayland Ho 13 SW9 138 C3
Waylands UB3 83 B2
Waylands Ct IG1 79 B4
Waylands Mead BR3 185 D2
Waylett Ho SE11 261 A1
Waylett Pl Wembley HA0 65 D4
West Norwood SE27 160 D1
Wayman Ct E8 74 B2
Wayne Cl BR6 227 D5
Waynflete Ave CR0 220 D5
Waynflete Sq 16 W10 112 D6
18 W10 90 D1
Waynflete St SW18 158 A2
Wayside NW11 47 A1
Mortlake SW14 155 A6
New Addington CR0 223 D2
Wayside Ave WD23 8 B5
Wayside Cl N14 15 C5
Wayside Commercial Est
IG11 102 A5
Wayside Ct
Isleworth TW7 130 C3
Twickenham TW1 153 C5
Wembley HA9 66 C5
Wayside Gdns RM10 81 C3
Wayside Gr BR7,SE9 188 B6
Wayside Mews IG2 56 C4
Weald Cl BR2 226 A6
16 SE16 118 B1
Weald Fst & Mid Schs
HA3 24 D3
Weald La HA3 24 B2
Weald Rd UB10 82 C5
Weald Rise HA3 24 D2
Weald Sq E5 74 B6
Wealdstone Rd SM3 217 B6
Weald The BR7 188 B4
Weald Way Hayes UB4 83 C4
Romford RM7 59 D3

Wealdwood Gdns HA5 23 D4
Weale Rd E4 20 B1
Weall Ct HA5 41 A5
Weardale Ct EN5 12 C6
Weardale Gdns EN2 5 B4
Weardale Ho N4 51 A2
Weardale Rd SE13 142 B1
Wearmouth Ho 1 E3 97 B2
Wear Pl 13 E2 96 B4
Wearside Rd SE13 141 D1
Weatherbury 6 W2 91 C1
Weatherbury Ho 3
N19 71 D5
Weatherill Ct SE25 206 B3
Weatherley Cl E3 97 B2
Weathersfield Ct SE9 166 B5
Weaver Cl E16 122 D6
South Croydon CR0 221 D4
Weaver Ct 2 E2 96 B3
Weaver Ho 13 E1 96 A3
Weavers Cl TW7 130 C1
Weavers Ho 4 E11 55 A3
Weaver's La
SE1 117 C5 253 B3
Weaver St E1 96 A3
Weavers Way NW1 232 C6
6 NW1 71 D1
Weaver Wlk SE27 182 D6
Webb Ct 6 SE28 124 B6
W3 110 D4
Webber Cl WD6 9 D5
Webber Ho 6 IG11 78 D1
Webber Row
SE1 116 D4 251 C1
Webber St
SE1 116 D4 251 C1
Webb Est E5 52 A2
Webb Gdns 1 E13 99 A3
Webb Ho SW8 269 D3
2 Dagenham RM10 81 C5
Feltham TW13 151 A1
Webb Pl NW10 89 D4
Webb Rd SE3 142 D6
Webbscroft Rd RM10 81 D4
Webb's Rd SW11 158 D6
Webbs Rd UB4 84 B4
Webb St SE1 117 C3 263 A5
Webheath 6 NW6 69 B1
Webster Gdns W5 109 D5
Webster Ho 16 N16 73 C3
Webster Rd E11 76 A5
SE16 118 A3
Weddell Ho 23 E1 96 D3
Wedderburn Rd NW3 70 B3
Barking IG11 101 C6
Wedgewood Ct DA5 169 B4
1 Beckenham BR2 208 D5
Wedgewood Ho SW1 259 A1
Wedgewood Mews
W1 239 D1
Wedgewood Wlk NW3 69 D3
Wedgwood Ho 17 E2 96 D4
SE11 261 A5
Wedgwood Way SE19 183 A3
Wedlake St W10 91 A3
Wedmore Gdns N19 71 D6
Wedmore Rd UB6 86 B4
Wedmore St N19 71 D5
Weech Rd NW6 69 C4
Weedington Rd NW5 71 A3
Weedon Ho W12 90 A1
Weekley Sq SW11 136 B2
Weeks Ho TW10 175 C6
Weigall Rd SE12,SE3 143 A1
Weighhouse St W1 238 B1
Weighton Rd
Harrow HA3 24 B2
Penge SE20 184 B1
Weihurst Ct SM1 218 C3
Weihurst Gdns SM1 218 B3
Weimar St SW15 135 A2
Weirdale Ave N20 14 D2
Weir Hall Ave N18 33 A4
Weir Hall Gdns N18 33 B5
Weir Hall Rd N18 33 B4
Weir Ho 8 SW12 159 C4
Weir Rd Sidcup DA5 169 D4
Streatham SW12 159 C4
Walton-on-T KT12 194 A3
Wimbledon SW18,SW19 157 D1
Weir's Pas NW1 232 D2
Weiss Rd SW15 134 D2
Welbeck Ave BR1 187 B6
DA15 168 A3
Hayes UB4 84 B3
Welbeck Cl N12 30 B5
New Malden KT3 199 D4
Stoneleigh KT17 216 A1
Welbeck Ct W14 254 C4
Hayes UB4 83 B3
Welbeck Mans 10 NW6 69 C3
Welbeck Rd E6 99 D4
Carshalton SM1,SM5 218 B6
East Barnet EN4 14 C5
Harrow HA2 41 D1
Carshalton SM5 202 C1

n Avenue Bsns Pk
.88 D3
n Ct N3 .29 C4
.89 B1
.91 B5
l UB2 .107 A3
n Dr TW17 .193 B3
n Eye Hospl The
.92 D2 237 C4
n Gdns W5 .110 C6
n Ho 1 W9 .91 B3
n International
t UB2 .106 B2
n La SW12 .159 A4
n Mews W9 .91 B3
n Par EN5 .13 D6
n Pl 13 SE16 .118 C4
n Rd E13 .99 C5
.54 A4
.48 D5
.89 A3
.138 C2
W5 .109 D6
n CR4,SW19 .180 C1
l UB2 .106 D2
SM1 .217 C3
Green N22 .32 B1
n Terr W6 .112 A1
n View UB3 .105 D4
nville Gdns IG2 .57 A2
n Way SE28 .123 C4
arnet EN5 .13 D5
n Wharf 2
.140 A6
well Inf Sch
.215 B3
rry Cir E14 .119 C5
rry Rd E14 .119 C3
rry Sta E14 .119 C6
eld 1 BR6 .227 A3
.69 C4
on IG10 .21 C6
eld Cl NW9 .45 A6
.266 A3
SM1 .217 B4
EN3 .7 A2
eld Ct 1 W10 .90 D4
on KT6 .197 D4
eld Dr HA3 .43 D5
eld Gdns HA3 .43 D5
eld Ho 6 SE16 .118 D2
eld La HA3 .43 D5
eld Pk HA5 .23 B3
eld Rd NW7 .11 C1
ham BR3 .185 B1
SM1 .217 B4
n CR0 .220 D6
ham RM9 .81 B4
W13 .109 A5
on KT6 .197 D4
n CR4 .180 D1
on-T KT12 .195 A2
elds SW13 .133 D2
elds Ave SW13 .133 C2
elds Gdns RM6 .58 C3
elds Rd W3 .88 D2
elds Sch SW13 .133 D2
ld St SE18 .121 D3
ld Way E1 .97 A3
HA4 .61 D5
nchley Sta N3 .29 D4
arden Pl W2 .237 B1
ate W5 .88 A4
te Bsns Ctr
.90 D3
) .91 A3
ate Ct 16 SW9 .138 C2
kenham BR3 .186 A2
am SE12 .165 A3
te Est TW14 .148 D3
te Rd
ham BR3 .186 A2
SE25 .206 B5
ate St E8 .96 B6
ate Terr
.135 D6 265 D6
dns
n SW19 .180 C4
E1 .118 B6
ade Ct HA3 .43 D4
SE10 .142 B4
ord IG8 .37 C5
reen Pl UB6 .86 B6
reen Prim Sch
.51 A5
reen Rd N15 .51 B5
ove La SE10 .142 A4
rove Prim Sch
.15 D4
alkin St
.115 A3 258 A6
allowes SE9 .166 A3
all Rd TW9 .132 D4
am Church Prim Sch
.98 D6
am La E15 .76 C1
ampstead Mews
.69 D2

West Hampstead Sta
NW6 .69 C2
West Hampstead
Thameslink Sta NW6 .69 C2
West Ham Sta E15 .98 C4
West Harding St EC4 .241 B2
West Harrow Sta HA1 .42 A3
West Hatch Manor HA4 39 D2
Westhay Gdns SW14 .154 D6
West Heath Ave NW11 .47 C1
West Heath Cl NW3 .69 C5
West Heath Ct NW11 .47 C1
West Heath Dr NW11 .47 C1
West Heath Gdns NW3 .69 C5
West Heath Rd NW3 .69 D5
SE2 .146 D6
West Hill N6 .49 A1
Harrow HA2 .64 C6
Putney SW15 .157 A5
South Croydon CR2 .221 C1
Wembley HA9 .44 B1
Westhill Ct W11 .244 D6
West Hill Ct N6 .71 A5
West Hill Hall HA2 .64 C6
Westhill Pk N6 .70 D6
N6 .71 A6
West Hill Prim Sch
SW18 .157 C6
West Hill Rd SW18 .157 B5
West Hill Way N20 .13 D3
West Ho Barking IG11 .78 D2
4 Penge SE20 .184 D3
9 Streatham SW12 .159 C4
Westholm NW11 .47 D5
Westholme BR6 .211 D2
Westholme Gdns HA4 .40 A1
Westhope Ho 13 E2 .96 A4
Westhorne Ave SE9,
SE12 .165 C5
Westhorpe Gdns NW4 .46 C6
Westhorpe Rd SW15 .134 C2
West House Cl SW19 .157 A3
Westhurst Dr BR7 .188 D5
West India Ave E14 .119 C5
West India Dock Rd
E14 .119 C6
West India Ho 1 E14 .119 C6
West India Quay Sta
E14 .119 C6
West Kensington Ct
W14 .254 C2
West Kensington Mans
W14 .254 C1
West Kensington Sta
W14 .113 B1 254 C2
West La SE16 .118 B4
Westlake 10 SE16 .118 C2
Westlake Cl Hayes UB4 .85 A3
Palmers Green N13 .16 C1
Westlake Rd HA9 .65 D6
Westland Cl TW19 .148 A5
Westland Ct 9 UB5 .84 D4
Westland Dr BR2,BR4 .224 D6
Westland Ho 1 E16 .122 C5
Westland Lo 1 BR1 .187 C1
Westland Pl N1 .235 C2
Westlands Cl UB3 .106 A2
Westlands Ct KT8 .196 C5
Westlands Terr 3
SW12 .159 C5
Westlea Rd W7 .109 A3
West Lea Sch N9 .17 C1
Westleigh Ave SW15 .156 C6
Westleigh Ct N12 .29 D4
12 Wanstead E11 .55 A4
Westleigh Dr BR1 .188 A2
Westleigh Gdns HA8 .26 C1
West Links HA0 .87 D4
Westlinton Cl NW7 .29 A4
West Lodge Ave W3 .110 C5
West Lodge Ct W3 .110 C5
West Lodge Fst & Mid Schs
HA5 .40 D5
West Lodge Sch DA15 168 A1
West London Shooting
Grounds UB5 .84 B5
West London Stad The
W12 .90 B2
Westly Ct NW2 .68 D2
Westmacott Dr TW14 .149 D3
Westmacott Ho NW8 .236 D5
West Mall W11 .245 B4
Westmark Point 13
SW15 .156 B3
Westmead SW15 .156 B5
West Mead Ruislip HA4 .62 C4
West Ewell KT19 .215 C2
Westmead Cnr SM5 .218 C4
Westmead Rd SM1 .218 B4
Westmeath Ho NW2 .68 A5
Westmere Dr NW7 .11 B1
West Mersea Cl 9
E16 .121 B5
West Mews SW1 .259 A3
West Middlesex Univ Hosp
TW7 .131 A3
Westmill Ct N4 .73 A6
Westminster Abbey*
SW1 .116 A3 260 A6

Westminster Abbey Choir
Sch SW1 .115 D3 259 D6
Westminster Ave CR7 .182 D1
Westminster Boating Base
SW1 .269 C6
Westminster Bridge
SE1,SW1 .116 A4 250 B1
Westminster Bridge Rd
SE1 .116 B4 250 C1
Westminster Cath*
SW1 .115 C3 259 A5
Westminster Cath Choir
Sch SW1 .115 C2 259 B4
Westminster Cath RC Prim
Sch SW1 .115 D1 259 D2
Westminster City Hall
SW1 .259 B6
Westminster City Sch
SW1 .259 B6
Westminster Cl
East Bedfont TW14 .150 A3
Teddington TW11 .175 A5
Westminster Coll of Bsns &
Computing HA9 .66 A3
Westminster Ct
22 SE16 .118 D5
5 SW18 .157 C6
South Norwood CR7 .183 A1
Wanstead E11 .55 B3
Westminster Dr N13 .32 A5
Westminster Gdns
SW1 .260 A4
Barking IG11 .101 C5
Chingford, Chingford Green
E4 .20 C3
Westminster Ind Est
E16 .121 D3
Westminster Kingsway Coll
SW11 .137 A4 268 B2
WC1 .94 B4 233 C1
Westminster Pier
SW1 .250 B1
Westminster Rd
Carshalton SM1,SM5 .218 B6
Ealing W7 .108 C5
Edmonton N9 .18 B3
Westminster Sch
SW1 .116 A3 260 A6
Westminster Sta
SW1 .116 A4 250 B1
Westmoat Cl BR3 .186 A3
Westmont Rd KT10 .212 C6
Westmoor Gdns EN3 .6 D3
Westmoor Rd EN3 .6 D3
Westmoor St SE7 .121 D3
Westmore Ct SW15 .157 A6
Westmoreland Ave
DA16 .145 C1
Westmoreland Ho
NW10 .90 A4
Westmoreland Pl
5 BR1 .209 A6
SW1 .258 D1
Ealing W5 .87 D2
Westmoreland Rd
BR2 .209 A5
HA3,NW9 .44 B5
SE17 .139 B6
Barnes SW13 .134 A4
Beckenham BR2,BR3 .208 D5
Westmoreland St W1 .238 B3
Westmoreland Terr
SW1 .115 B1 258 D1
Penge SE20 .184 B3
Westmorland Cl
3 Twickenham TW1 .153 B5
Wanstead E12 .77 D6
Westmorland Ct 12
KT6 .197 D2
Westmorland Dr SM2 .217 D1
Westmorland Rd BR2 .209 A5
E17 .53 C3
Harrow HA1 .41 D4
Westmorland Sq CR4 .204 A4
Westmorland Way
CR4 .203 D4
Westmount Ct W5 .88 B2
Westmount Rd SE9 .144 C1
West Norwood Sta
SE27 .160 D1
West Oak BR3 .186 B2
Westoe Rd N9 .18 B2
Weston Ave
East Molesey KT8 .195 B5
Thames Ditton KT10,KT7 196 C2
Westonbirt Ct 6 SE15 139 D6
Weston Ct N20 .14 A4
N4 .73 A5
3 Kingston KT1 .198 A6
Weston Dr HA7 .25 B2
Weston Ed Ctr The
SE5 .139 A3
West One Ho W1 .239 A3
Westone Mans 5 IG11 79 D1
Weston Gdns TW7 .130 C4
Weston Gn
Dagenham RM9 .81 B4
Thames Ditton KT7 .196 C1
Weston Gr 1 BR1 .186 D2

Weston Green Prep Sch
KT7 .196 C1
Weston Green Rd KT7 196 C2
Weston Ho 9 E9 .96 C6
4 NW6 .69 A1
Weston Park Cl KT7 .196 C1
Weston Park Prim Sch
N8 .50 B4
Weston Pk N8 .50 B3
Kingston KT1 .176 A1
Thames Ditton KT10,KT7 196 C1
Weston Rd W4 .111 A3
Bromley BR1 .186 D3
Dagenham RM9 .81 A4
Enfield EN2 .5 B3
Ruislip HA4 .61 D1
Thames Ditton KT7 .196 C1
Weston Rise N1,
WC1 .94 B4 233 D2
Weston St SE1 117 B4 252 D2
Weston Wlk 3 E8,E9 .74 B1
Westover Hill NW3 .69 C6
Westover Rd SW18 .158 A5
Westow Hill SE19 .183 D4
Westow St SE19 .183 C4
Westpark W5 .87 D1
West Park Ave TW9 .132 D4
West Park Cl
Heston TW5 .129 B6
Ilford RM6 .58 D4
West Park Rd
Richmond TW9 .132 C4
Southall UB2 .108 B5
West Parkside SE10 .121 A2
Greenwich SE10 .120 D3
West Pk SE9 .166 A3
West Pl SW19 .178 C5
West Point 2 SE1 .118 A1
Westpoint
Beckenham BR2 .208 B6
Putney SW15 .156 D5
Westpoint Trad Est W3 .88 D2
Westpole Ave EN4 .3 B1
Westport Ct UB4 .84 C3
Westport Rd E13 .99 B3
Westport St E1 .96 D1
West Poultry Ave EC1 .241 C3
West Quarters W12 .90 A1
West Quay Dr UB4 .85 A2
West Ramp TW6 .126 C4
West Rd E15 .98 D6
N2 .30 B2
SW3 .136 D6 267 D6
SW4 .159 D6
Dagenham RM6 .59 A3
Ealing W5 .88 A2
East Barnet EN4 .15 A3
East Bedfont TW14 .149 B4
Kingston KT2,KT3 .177 A2
Tottenham N17 .34 B4
West Drayton UB7 .104 B3
West Ridge Gdns UB6 .86 A5
West Row W10 .91 A3
Westrow SW15 .156 C5
Westrow Dr IG11 .80 A2
Westrow Gdns IG3 .79 D5
West Ruislip Elementary
Sch UB10 .61 A5
West Ruislip Sta HA4 .61 A6
West Sheen Vale TW9 .132 B1
Westside N2 .48 D6
NW4 .28 B1
West Side Comm
SW19 .178 C5
Westside Ct 1 W9 .91 C3
West Smithfield
EC1 .94 D2 241 D3
West Sq SE11 .116 D3 261 C5
West St BR1 .187 A1
DA7 .147 B2
E11 .76 C5
E17 .53 D4
26 E2 .96 B5
WC2 .93 D1 239 D1
Carshalton SM5 .218 D4
Croydon CR0 .221 A4
Harrow HA1 .42 C1
Sutton SM1 .217 D3
West Street La SM5 .218 D4
West Street Pl 1 CR0 221 A4
West Surrey Ests
TW15 .171 A2
West Sutton Sta SM1 .217 C4
West Temple Sheen
SW14 .154 D6
West Tenter St
E1 .95 D1 243 D1
West Terr DA15 .167 C3
West Thames Coll
TW7 .130 C4
West Thamesmead Bsns Pk
SE28 .123 D3
West Thornton Prim Sch
CR0 .204 B3
West Towers HA5 .40 D3
West Twyford Prim Sch
NW10 .88 C5
Westvale Mews W3 .111 C4
Westview W7 .86 C1

West View
Dagenham RM6 .58 C4
East Bedfont TW14 .149 A4
Westview Cl NW10 .67 D3
W10 .90 C1
Westview Cres N9 .17 C4
Westview Ct 3 WD6 .9 D5
Westview Dr IG8 .37 D1
West View Gdns WD6 .9 D5
Westville Rd W12 .112 A4
Thames Ditton KT7 .197 A2
Westward Rd E4 .35 B5
Westward Way HA3 .44 A3
West Warwick Pl SW1 259 A3
Westway W10,W12 .112 A6
West Way BR5 .211 B4
HA8 .27 A4
NW10 .67 B5
Westway SW20 .200 C5
West Way Croydon CR0 223 A5
Edmonton N18 .33 B6
Hounslow TW5 .129 B4
Pinner HA5 .40 D5
Ruislip HA4 .39 D1
Shepperton TW17 .193 B3
West Wickham BR4 .208 C3
Westway Cl SW20 .200 B6
Westway Cross Sh Pk
UB6 .86 C6
Westway Ct UB5 .85 C6
Westway (Elevated Rd)
W10 .91 B2
West Way Gdns CR0 .222 D6
Westway Lo 35 W2 .91 C2
Westways KT19 .215 D4
West Ways HA6 .22 A1
Westwell 4 NW5 .71 A2
Westwell Rd SW16 .182 A4
Westwell Road App
SW16 .182 A4
Westwick 7 KT1 .176 C1
Westwick Gdns W14 .112 D4
Cranford TW4,TW5 .128 B3
West Wickham Sta
BR3 .208 A2
West Wlk
East Barnet EN4 .15 A3
Hayes UB3 .106 A5
Westwood Ave
Harrow HA2 .63 D4
South Norwood SE19 .183 A2
Westwood Cl BR1 .209 D6
Esher KT10 .212 A5
Ruislip HA4 .38 D3
Westwood Ct
Enfield EN1 .17 C5
3 Forest Hill SE23 .162 C3
7 Wimbledon SW19 .179 B5
Westwood Gdns
SW13 .133 D2
Westwood Hill SE26 .184 B6
Westwood Ho 5 N4 .51 B2
W12 .112 C5
Westwood La DA16 .145 D1
Westwood Language
College for Girls
SE19 .183 B3
Westwood Pk SE23 .162 B4
Westwood Pl SE26 .184 A6
Westwood Prim Sch
DA16 .145 C1
Westwood Rd 12 E16 .121 B5
Barnes SW13 .133 D2
Ilford IG3 .58 A2
Westwood Sch WD23 .8 B2
West Woodside DA5 .169 A3
Westwood Tech Coll
DA16 .145 C1
Wetheral Ct SW17 .180 B6
Wetheral Dr HA7 .25 C1
Wetherby Cl UB5 .63 D2
Wetherby Ct SE25 .183 C1
Wetherby Gdns
SW5 .114 A2 256 A3
Wetherby Mans SW5 .255 C2
Wetherby Mews SW5 .255 D2
Wetherby Pl
SW7 .114 A2 256 B3
Wetherby Rd EN2 .5 A4
Wetherby Way KT9 .214 A1
Wetherden St E17 .53 B2
Wetherell Rd E9 .96 D6
Wetherill Rd N10 .31 A2
Wetland Centre The*
SW13 .134 B5
Wevco Wharf SE15 .140 B6
Wexford Ho 9 E1 .96 C2
Wexford Rd SW12 .158 D4
Weybourne St SW18 .158 A2
Weybridge Ct 19 SE16 118 B1
Weybridge Ho N4 .51 A2
Weybridge Point 11
SW11 .136 D3
Weybridge Rd CR7 .204 C5
Wey Ct KT19 .215 A4
Weydown Cl SW19 .157 A3
Weyhill Ho 27 SE5 .139 A3
Weyhill Rd 6 E1 .96 A1
Wey Ho NW8 .236 D5

Weylands Cl KT12 .195 B1
Weylond Rd RM8 .81 B5
Weyman Rd SE3 .143 C4
Weymarks The N17 .33 B4
Weymouth Ave NW7 .27 C5
W5 .109 C3
Weymouth Cl 1 E6 .100 D1
Weymouth Ct 5 E2 .95 D5
Belmont SM2 .217 C1
15 Streatham SW2 .160 B4
Weymouth Ho SW8 .270 C3
Bromley BR2 .186 D1
Weymouth Mews
W1 .93 B2 238 C4
Weymouth Rd UB4 .83 C4
Weymouth St
W1 .93 B2 238 C4
Weymouth Terr E2 .95 D5
Weymouth Wlk HA7 .25 A4
Whadcoat St N4 .72 C6
Whadden Ho 10 SE5 .139 C2
Whaddon Ho SW1 .247 D1
Whalebone Ave RM6 .59 B3
Whalebone Gr RM6 .59 B3
Whalebone La E15 .76 C1
Whalebone La N RM6 .59 A6
Whalebone La S RM6,
RM8 .59 B2
Whales Yd E15 .76 C1
Wharfdale Cl N11 .31 A4
Wharfdale Rd
N1 .94 A5 233 B4
Wharfedale Ct 5 E5 .74 D4
Wharfedale Gdns CR7,
SW16 .204 B6
Wharfedale St SW10 .255 C1
Wharf La TW1 .153 A3
Wharf Pl E2 .96 B6
Wharf Rd E15 .98 B6
N1 .95 A5 235 A3
NW1 .93 D6 232 D5
Enfield EN3 .19 A5
Wharfside HA0 .88 A6
Wharfside Rd E16 .98 C2
Wharf St E16 .98 C2
Wharncliffe Dr UB1 .108 B5
Wharncliffe Gdns
SE25 .183 C1
Wharncliffe Rd SE25 .183 C1
Wharton Cl NW10 .67 C2
Wharton Ho SE1 .263 C6
Wharton Rd BR1 .187 B2
Wharton St
WC1 .94 B4 233 D1
Whateley Rd SE22 .161 D6
Penge SE20 .184 D3
Whatley Ave SW20 .201 A6
Whatman Rd SE23 .162 D4
Wheatfields E6 .100 D1
Enfield EN3 .7 A3
Wheatfield Way KT1 .176 A1
Wheathill Ho SE20 .184 B1
Wheathill Rd SE20 .206 B6
Wheatland Ho 7
SE22 .139 C2
Wheatlands TW5 .129 C6
Wheatlands Rd SW17 .159 A1
Wheatley Cl NW4 .28 A1
Wheatley Gdns N9 .17 C2
Wheatley Ho NW5 .71 B4
3 Putney SW15 .156 A4
Wheatley Mans 8 IG11 80 A1
Wheatley Rd TW7 .130 D2
Wheatley's Ait TW16 .194 A4
Wheatley St W1 .238 B3
Wheatly Cres UB3 .106 A6
Wheat Sheaf Cl E14 .119 D2
Wheatsheaf Cl UB5 .63 A3
Wheatsheaf La SW6 .134 C5
SW8 .270 B4
Wheatsheaf Par 6
BR4 .207 D1
Wheatsheaf Terr SW6 264 D3
Wheatstone Cl SW19 .180 C2
Wheatstone Ho 7 W10 91 A2
Wheatstone Rd W10 .91 A2
Wheeler 2 NW9 .27 D3
Wheeler Ct 5 SW11 .136 B2
Wheeler Gdns N1 .233 B6
Wheelers Cross IG11 .101 B5
Wheelers Dr HA4 .39 A3
Wheeler's St SM1 .217 C5
Wheelock Cl DA8 .147 D5
Wheelwright St N7 .72 B1
Whelan Way SM6 .219 D5
Wheldon Ct SE1 .253 C2
Wheler Ho E1 .243 C5
Wheler St E1 .95 D3 243 C5
Whellock Rd W4 .111 C3
Whernside Cl SE28 .124 C6
Whetstone Cl N20 .14 B2
Whetstone Park
WC2 .94 B1 240 C2
Whetstone Rd SE3 .143 D4
Whewell Rd N19 .72 A6
Whichcote St SE1 .251 A3

Whidborne Bldgs WC1 233 A1
Whidborne Cl SE8 141 C3
Whidborne St WC1 233 B1
Whimbrel Cl SE28 124 C6
Whimbrel Way UB4 84 D2
Whinchat Rd SE18, SE28 123 B3
Whinfell Cl SW16 181 D5
Whinyates Rd SE9 144 A2
Whippendell Cl BR5 190 B2
Whippendell Way BR5 190 B1
Whippingham Ho 17 E3 97 B4
Whipps Cross E17 54 B4
Whipps Cross Ho E17 54 B4
Whipps Cross Hospl E10,E11 54 B3
Whipps Cross Rd E11 54 C3
Whiskin St EC1 94 D4 234 C1
Whisperwood Cl HA3 24 C3
Whistler Gdns HA8 26 B1
Whistler Mews 2 SE15 139 D5
Dagenham RM8 80 B3
Whistlers Ave SW11 136 B5 266 D3
Whistler St N5 72 D3
Whistler Twr SW10 266 A3
Whistler Wlk SW10 266 B4
Whiston Ho 18 N1 72 D1
Whiston Rd E2 96 A6
Whitakers Lo EN2 5 B4
Whitbread Cl N17 34 A2
Whitbread Ctr EC1 242 C5
Whitbread Rd SE4 141 B1
Whitburn Rd SE13 142 A1
Whitby Ave NW10 88 D4
Whitby Ct N7 72 A4
Whitby Gdns NW9 44 C6
Carshalton SM1,SM5 218 B6
Whitby Ho NW8 229 A5
Whitby Rd SE18 122 B2
Carshalton SM1,SM5 218 B6
Harrow HA2 64 A5
Ruislip HA4 62 C6
Whitby St E1 243 C6
Whitcher Cl SE14 141 A6
Whitcher Pl NW1 71 C2
Whitchurch Ave HA8 26 B3
Whitchurch Cl HA8 26 B4
Whitchurch Ct SW17 180 B6
Whitchurch Fst & Mid Schs HA7 25 D3
Whitchurch Gdns HA8 26 B4
Whitchurch Ho 16 W10 90 D1
Catford SE6 164 A1
Whitchurch La HA8 26 B3
Whitchurch Rd W11 112 D6
Whitcomb Ct W1 249 D5
Whitcombe Mews TW9 132 D4
Whitcomb St WC2 115 D6 249 D5
Whiteadder Way E14 119 D2
Whitear Wlk E15 76 B2
Whitebarn La RM10 103 C6
Whitebeam Ave BR2 210 C3
Whitebeam Cl SW9 270 D3
Whitebeam Ho 3 NW3 70 D2
White Bear Pl NW3 70 B4
White Bear Yd EC1 241 A5
White Bridge Ave CR4 202 B6
White Bridge Cl TW14 149 D5
White Butts Rd HA4 62 D5
Whitechapel High St E1 95 D1 243 D2
Whitechapel Rd E1 96 B2
Whitechapel Sta E1 96 B2
Whitechurch La 2 E1 96 A1
White City W10 90 C1
White City Cl W12 112 C6
White City Est 21 W12 112 B6
White City Rd W12 112 C6
White City Sta W12 112 C6
Whitecliff Ho SW18 157 D5
White Conduit St N1 234 B4
Whitecote Rd UB1 86 A1
White Craig Cl HA5 23 C5
Whitecroft Cl BR3 208 B5
Whitecroft Way BR3 208 B5
Whitecross Pl EC2 242 D4
Whitecross St EC1 95 A3 242 B5
White Cube art gallery* N1 95 C4
Whitefield Ave NW2 46 C1
Whitefield Cl SW15 157 A5
Whitefield Sch NW11 46 D2
Chingford E17 36 A1
Whitefoot La BR1 164 B1
Whitefoot Terr BR1 164 D1
Whitefriars Ave HA3 24 C1
Whitefriars Centre Coll HA3 42 C6
Whitefriars Ct N12 30 B5
Whitefriars Dr HA3 24 C1
Whitefriars Fst & Mid Sch HA3 24 C1
Whitefriars St EC4 94 C1 241 B1
Whitefriars Trad Est HA3 24 B1
White Gate Gdns HA3 24 D3
Whitegates 4 EN5 13 D6
White Gdns RM10 81 C2
Whitehall SW1 250 A2
Whitehall Cres KT9 213 D3
Whitehall Ct SW1 116 A5 250 B3
Whitehall Gdns SW1 250 A3
Acton W3 110 C5
Chingford, Chingford Green E4 20 C3
Chiswick W4 132 D6
Whitehall La IG9 21 A2
Whitehall Lo N10 49 A6
Woodford IG8 21 A1
Whitehall Mans 3 N19 49 C1
Whitehall Park Rd W4 132 D6
Whitehall Pk N19 49 C1
Whitehall Pl WC2,SW1 116 A5 250 A3
Wallington SM5 219 B4
Whitehall Prim Sch E4 20 C2
Whitehall Rd W7 109 A4
Bromley BR2 209 D5
Chingford E4 20 C2
Harrow HA1 42 C2
Thornton Heath CR7 204 C4
Woodford IG8 21 A1
Whitehall St N17 33 D3
White Hart Ct EC2 243 A3
White Hart La NW10 67 D2
Mortlake SW13 133 C2
White Hart Lane Sch N22 32 D3
White Hart Lane Sta N17 33 D3
White Hart Lane (Tottenham Hotspur FC) N17 34 A3
White Hart Rd SE18 123 C2
White Hart Rdbt UB5 84 D5
White Hart St EC4 241 D2
SE11 116 C1 261 B2
White Hart Terr N17 33 D3
White Hart Yd SE1 252 C3
Whitehaven Cl BR2 209 A5
Whitehaven St NW8 237 A5
Whitehead Cl
Edmonton N18 33 B5
Wandsworth SW18 158 A4
Whitehead Ct N10 31 A2
Whitehead Ho 8 SW15 156 D6
Whitehead's Gr SW3 114 C2 257 B3
White Heart Ave UB8 83 A2
Whiteheath Ave HA4 39 A2
Whiteheath Inf Sch HA4 39 A3
Whiteheath Jun Sch HA4 39 A2
White Heron Mews TW11 174 D4
White Ho N9 18 C2
2 SW11 136 B3
3 Streatham SW4 159 D4
Whitehorn Ho 6 E1 118 C5
White Horse Hill BR7, SE9 188 C6
White Horse La E1 96 D2
Whitehorse La SE25 205 C5
Whitehorse Manor Inf Sch CR7 205 B5
Whitehorse Manor Jun Sch CR7 205 B5
Whitehorse Mews SE1 261 C6
Whitehorse Rd E1 97 A2
White Horse Rd E1 97 A1
E6 100 B4
Whitehorse Rd CR0, CR7 205 B3
White Horse St W1 115 B5 248 D3
White Horse Yd EC2 242 C2
White Ho The N17 51 C6
NW1 238 D6
White House Ct N14 15 D2
1 Beckenham BR3 186 A2
White House Dr HA7 25 C6
Whitehouse Est E10 54 A3
White House La EN2 5 A4
Whitehouse Way N14 15 B1
White Kennett St E1 243 B2
Whitelands Coll, Roehampton, Univ of Surrey SW18 157 A4
Whitelands Ho SW3 257 D2
Whiteledges W13 87 C1
Whitelegg Rd E13 98 D5
Whiteley Ho 9 SW4 159 D4
Whiteley Rd SE19 183 B5
Whiteleys Ctr W2 91 D1
Whiteleys Ho TW13 151 C1
Whiteleys Par 5 UB10 82 D3
Whiteleys Way TW13 151 C1
White Lion Ct EC3 243 A1
White Lion Hill EC4 116 D6 251 D6
White Lion St N1 94 C5 234 B3
White Lion Yd W1 248 C6
White Lo 7 Ealing W5 87 C2
South Norwood SE19 182 D3
Whitelock Ho 21 E9 74 D2
White Lodge Cl N2 48 B3
Sutton SM2 218 A1
White Lodge The Royal Ballet Sch TW10 155 B3
Whitely Ct TW13 151 B1
Whiteness Ho 18 SW9 138 C4
White Oak Dr BR3 186 A1
White Oak Gdns DA15 167 D4
Whiteoak Ho SE19 183 A3
Whiteoaks La UB6 86 B5
White Orchards
Barnet N20 13 B3
Stanmore HA7 25 A5
White Post La E9 75 C2
White Post St SE14, SE15 140 C5
White Rd E15 76 C1
Whites Ave IG2 57 C3
Whites Dr BR2 208 D2
White's Grounds SE1 117 C4 253 B2
White's Grounds Est SE1 253 B2
White's Mdw BR1 210 C5
White's Row E1 95 D2 243 C3
White's Sq SW4 137 D1
White St UB2 106 D4
Whitestile Rd TW8 109 D1
Whitestone La NW3 70 A5
Whitestone Wlk NW3 70 A5
Whitethorn Ave UB7 104 B6
Whitethorn Gdns
Croydon CR0 222 B6
Enfield EN2 17 B6
Whitethorn Pl UB7 104 B5
Whitethorn St E3 97 C2
Whiteways NW4 46 D5
Whitewebbs Way BR5 189 D2
Whitfield Ct SW4 270 A1
3 Dulwich SE21 183 C6
Redbridge IG1 56 B2
Whitfield Gdns W1 239 B4
Whitfield Ho NW8 237 A5
Whitfield Pl W1 239 B5
Whitfield Rd DA7 147 B5
E6 77 C1
SE10,SE13 142 B4
Whitfield St W1 93 C2 239 B4
Whitford Gdns CR4 202 D6
Whitgift Ave CR2 221 A3
Whitgift Ct CR2 221 A3
Whitgift Ctr CR0 221 A6
Whitgift Ho SE11 260 C4
SW11 267 A2
Croydon CR2 221 A3
Whitgift Sch CR2 221 A3
Whitgift St SE11 116 B2 260 C4
Croydon CR0 221 A5
Whiting Ave IG11 78 D1
Whitings Hill Prim Sch EN5 12 C6
Whitings Rd EN5 12 C6
Whitings The IG2 57 C4
Whitings Way E6 100 C2
Whitington Ave EC3 243 A1
Whitland Rd SM5 202 B1
Whitley Cl TW19 148 A5
Whitley Ho SW1 269 B6
Whitley Rd N17 33 C1
Whitlock Dr SW19 157 A3
Whitman Ho 20 E2 96 C4
Whitman Rd E3 97 A3
Whitmead Cl CR2 221 C2
Whitmore Cl N11 31 B5
Whitmore Comm Sch N1 235 C6
Whitmore Gdns NW10 90 C5
Whitmore High Sch HA1,HA2 42 A1
Whitmore Ho 20 E1 95 C6
N11 30 D6
Whitmore Rd N1 95 C6
Beckenham BR3 207 B6
Harrow HA1 42 A2
Whitnell Ct 7 SW15 156 D6
Whitnell Way SW15 156 D6
Whitney Ave IG4 55 D5
Whitney Ho 6 SE22 139 C2
Whitney Rd E10 53 D2
Whitney Wlk DA14 191 A4
Whitstable Cl
Beckenham BR3 185 B2
Ruislip HA4 61 C6
Whitstable Ho 11 W10 90 D1
Whitstable Pl 9 CR0 221 A4
Whitsters Ho SE1 253 C2
Whittaker 3 NW9 27 D3
Whittaker Ave TW10, TW9 153 D6
Whittaker Ct SW4 270 B1
Whittaker Pl 24 TW10 153 D6
Whittaker Rd E6 77 D1
Cheam SM3 217 B5
Whittaker St SW1 258 A3
Whittaker Way 17 SE1 118 A2
Whittam Ho SE27 183 A5
Whitta Rd E12 77 D4
Whittell Gdns SE26 162 C1
Whitten Lo N12 30 C6
Whittingham 6 N17 34 B3
Whittingham Ct W4 133 C5
Whittingstall Mans SW6 264 D1
Whittingstall Rd SW6 135 B4 264 D1
Whittington Ave UB4 83 D2
Whittington Ct N2 48 D4
Penge SE20 184 B1
Whittington Hospl The N19 71 C6
Whittington Mews N12 30 A6
Whittington Rd N22 32 A3
Whittington Way HA5 41 A4
Whittle 4 NW9 27 D3
Whittlebury Cl SM5 218 D1
Whittlebury Ho N4 51 A2
Whittle Cl E17 53 A2
Southall UB1 85 D1
Whittle Rd Heston TW5 128 C5
Southall UB2 107 D4
Whittlesea Cl HA3 24 A3
Whittlesea Path HA3 24 A2
Whittlesea Rd HA3 24 A2
Whittlesea Sch HA3 24 A3
Whittlesey St SE1 116 C5 251 B3
Whitton NW3 70 D1
Whitton Ave E UB6 65 A2
Whitton Ave W UB5,UB6 64 B3
Whitton Cl UB6 65 B2
Whitton Dene
Isleworth TW3,TW7 152 B5
Isleworth TW3,TW7 152 B6
Whitton Dr UB6 65 A2
Whitton Manor Rd TW7 152 A5
Whitton Rd
Hounslow TW3 151 D6
Twickenham TW1 153 A4
Whitton Road Rdbt TW1 152 D5
Whitton Sch TW2 151 D2
Whitton Sta TW2 152 A4
Whitton Waye TW2, TW3 151 C5
Whitton Wlk E3 97 C4
Whitwell Ho 11 E5 74 B6
Whitwell Rd E13 99 A4
Whitworth Cres EN3 7 C6
Whitworth Ho SE1 262 B5
Whitworth Rd SE18 144 C5
South Norwood SE25 205 D5
Whitworth St SE10 120 C1
Whorlton Rd SE15 140 B2
Whychcote Point NW2 46 C2
Whymark Ave N22 50 D6
Whytecroft TW5 128 D5
Whyteville Ho E7 77 B2
Whyteville Rd E7 77 B2
Whytlaw Ho 11 E3 97 B2
Wickers Oake SE19 183 D6
Wicker St 2 E1 96 B1
Wicket Rd UB6 87 A4
Wickets The TW15 170 A6
Wicket The CR0 223 C3
Wickfield Ho 28 SE16 118 A4
Wickford Ho 4 E1 96 C3
Wickford St E1 96 C3
Wickford Way E17 52 D5
Wickham Ave
Cheam KT4,SM3 216 C3
Croydon CR0 207 A1
Wickham Chase BR4 208 C2
Wickham Cl E1 96 C2
Enfield EN3 6 C2
New Malden KT3 199 D4
Wickham Common Prim Sch BR4 225 A4
Wickham Court Rd BR4 224 A6
Wickham Cres BR4 224 A6
Wickham Ct DA16 145 C3
Wickham Gdns SE4 141 B2
Wickham Ho SW15 156 D5
Wickham La SE2,SE18 146 A6
Wickham Mews SE4 141 B3
Wickham Rd SE4 141 B2
Beckenham BR3 207 D6
Chingford E4 36 A3
Croydon CR0 207 B1
Harrow HA3 24 B1
Wickham St DA16 146 A4
SE11 116 B1 260 C2
Bexley DA16 145 C3
Wickham Way BR3 208 A4
Wick Ho 1 KT1 175 D2
Wick La E3 75 B1
E3 97 C6
Wickliffe Ave N3 29 A1
Wickliffe Gdns HA9 66 D6
Wicklow Ct SE26 184 C5
Wicklow Ho N16 51 D1
Wicklow St WC1 94 B4 233 C2
Wick Mews 1 E9 75 A2
Wick Rd E9 75 A2
Hackney E9 74 D2
Teddington TW11 175 C3
Wicks Cl SE12 187 D6
Wick Sq E9 75 B2
Wickstead Ho TW8 110 B1
Wicksteed Ho SE1 262 B5
Wickway Ct 7 SE15 139 D6
Wickwood St SE5 138 D3
Widdenham Rd N7 72 B4
Widdicombe Ave HA2 63 A6
Widdin St E15 76 C1
Widecombe Ct N2 48 B4
Widecombe Gdns IG4 56 A5
Widecombe Ho 33 SE5 139 A3
Widecombe Rd SE9 166 A1
Widecombe Way N2 48 B5
Widegate St E1 243 B3
Widenham Cl HA5 40 C4
Wide Way CR4 203 D6
Widewing Cl TW11 175 B3
Widford 8 NW1 71 B2
Widford Ho N1 234 C3
Widgeon Cl E16 99 B1
Widgeon Path SE28 123 B3
Widley Rd W9 91 C3
Widmer Ct TW5 129 A3
Widmore Lodge Rd BR1 187 D1
Widmore Rd BR1 187 C1
Hillingdon UB8 82 D3
Widnes Ho 6 N7 72 C3
Wieland Rd HA6 22 A3
Wigan Ho E5 52 B1
Wigeon Way UB4 84 D1
Wiggins La TW10 153 C2
Wiggins Mead NW9 27 D3
Wigginton Ave HA9 66 D2
Wightman Rd N4,N8 50 C4
Wighton Mews TW7 130 C3
Wigley Rd TW13 150 D3
Wigmore Ct 4 W13 109 A5
Wigmore Hall W1 238 C2
Wigmore Pl W1 93 B1 238 C2
Wigmore Rd SM5 202 C1
Wigmore St W1 93 A1 238 B2
Wigmore Wlk SM5 218 B6
Wigram Ct SW11 267 A2
Wigram Ho 6 E14 119 D6
Wigram Rd E11 55 C3
Wigram Sq E17 54 A6
Wigston Cl N18 33 C5
Wigston Rd E13 99 B3
Wigton Gdns HA7 26 A2
Wigton Pl SE11 261 B1
Wigton Rd E17 35 B2
Wilberforce Ct 2 SE28 124 C5
Edgware HA8 26 B6
Wilberforce Ho 4 SW11 136 B2
Wilberforce Prim Sch W10 91 A4
Wilberforce Rd N4 72 D6
N4,N5 73 A5
NW9 46 A3
Wilberforce Way SW19 178 D4
Wilbraham Ho SW8 270 A3
Wilbraham Pl SW1 258 A4
Wilbury Prim Sch N18 33 B5
Wilbury Way N18 33 B5
Wilby Mews W11 113 B5 244 D4
Wilcox Cl SW8 270 B4
Wilcox Gdns TW17 192 B6
Wilcox Ho 6 E3 97 B2
Wilcox Pl SW1 259 B5
Wilcox Rd SW8 138 A5 270 A4
Sutton SM1 217 D4
Teddington TW11 174 B6
Wildcroft Gdns HA8 25 D4
Wildcroft Manor SW15 156 C4
Wildcroft Rd SW15 156 C4
Wild Ct WC2 94 B1 240 C2
Wilde Cl E8 96 A6
Wilde Pl Edmonton N13 32 D4
Wandsworth SW18 158 B4
Wilder Cl HA4 40 B1
Wilde Rd DA8 147 D5
Wilderness Mews SW4 137 B1
Wilderness Rd BR7 188 D3
Wilderness The
East Molesey KT8 196 A4
Wilderness The contin
Hampton TW12
Wilderton Rd N16
Wildfell Rd SE6
Wild Goose Dr SE14
Wild Hatch NW11
Wilding Ho 17 E9
Wild March Ct EN3
Wild's Rents
SE1 117 C
Wild St WC2 94 B
Wildwood Cl SE12
Wildwood Gr NW3
Wildwood Rd NW11
Wildwood Rise NW11
Wildwood Terr NW3
Wilford Cl EN2
Wilford Ho 3 SE18
Wilford Rd CR0
Wilfred Fienburgh Ho
N7
Wilfred Owen Cl
SW19
Wilfred St
SW1 115 C
Wilfrid Gdns W3
Wilkes Rd 3 TW8
Wilkes St E1 95 D
Wilkie Ho SW1
Wilkins Cl Hayes UB3
Mitcham CR4
Wilkins Ho SW1
Wilkinson Cl UB10
Wilkinson Ct SW17
Wilkinson Ho N1
Isleworth TW7
Wilkinson Rd E16
Wilkinson St
SW8 138 B
Wilkinson Way W4
Wilkin St NW5
Wilks Gdns CR0
Wilks Pl N1
Willan Rd N17
Willan Wall E16
Willard St SW8
Willbury Ho 4 N7
Willcocks Cl KT9
Willcott Rd W3
Will Crooks Gdns SE9
Willenfield Rd NW10
Willenhall Ave EN5
Willenhall Ct EN5
Willenhall Dr UB3
Willenhall Rd SE18
Willersley Ave BR6
DA15
Willersley Cl DA15
Willesden Communit
The NW10
Willesden Green Sta
NW2
Willesden High Sch
NW10
Willesden Junction S
NW10
Willesden La NW2,NW
Willes Rd NW5
Willet Cl 3 UB5
Willett Cl BR5
Willett Ho 7 E13
SW9
Willett Pl CR7
Willett Rd CR7
Willett Way BR5,BR6
William Allen Ho HA8
William Atkinson Ho
N17
William Banfield Ho
SW6
William Barefoot Dr
SE9
William Bellamy Inf S
RM10
William Bellamy Jun
RM10
William Booth Meml
Training Coll SE5
William Booth Rd
SE20
William Brown Ct
SE27
William Byrd Sch UB3
William Carey Way
HA1
William Caslon Ho
E2
William Channing Ho
E2
William C Harvey Sch
N17
William Cl SE13
Finchley N2
Southall UB2
William Covell Cl EN2
William Ct 4 Ealing W
Ilford IG6
William Davies Prim
E7

n Davis Prim Sch 96 A3
Dromey Ct 69 B1
Dunbar Ho 91 B5
Dyce Mews 1 ....181 D6
Ellis Sch NW5 .71 A5
Ellis Way 16 ....118 A3
Evans Ho 9 ....118 D2
Ford CE Jun Sch 81 C1
Gdns SW15 ...156 B6
Guy Gdns 47 ....97 D4
Harvey Ho 1 ....157 A3
Ho NW2 ....68 C5
on N13 ....32 D4
Hunt Mans 134 C6
IV St 116 A6 250 A5
Margrie Cl 1 ....140 A3
Mews 114 D4 247 D1
Morley Cl E6 ..99 D6
Morris Acad 112 D1
Morris Cl E17 ..53 B6
Morris Ho 134 D6
Morris Mid Sch 203 D6
Morris Sch 35 A2
Morris Way 136 A3
Patten Prim Sch 73 D6
Pl 31 E3 ....97 B5
Rainbird Ho 8 ....33 D3
Rathbone Ho 3 ....96 B4
Rd 93 C4 232 A1
SM1 ....218 A3
edon SW19 ....179 A3
Rushbrooke Ho 4 ....118 A2
ns Ave E17 ....35 B2
Saville Ho 2 ....91 B5
n's Bldgs 1 E2 ..96 C3
ns Cl SW6 ....
ns Dr TW3 ....129 C1
ns Gr
on KT6 ....197 C3
Green N22 ....32 C2
ns Ho 9 E3 ....97 C4
....96 B6
eatham SW2 ....160 C3
ns La
n SM4 ....202 A4
ke SW14 ....133 A3
n Smith Ho 10 ....125 C3
nson Cl SE10 ..120 D1
nson Ct SE17 ..262 A1
nson Rd N4 ....50 D3
nson St N7 ....72 A4
nson Way NW7 ..29 A4
n Sq 15 SE16 ..119 A6
ns Rd UB2 ....107 A2
n's Rd W13 ....109 A5
n St E10 ....53 D3
....114 D4 247 D1
g IG11 ....79 A1
lton SM5 ....218 D5
ham N17 ....33 D3
ns Terr CR0 ....220 C2
n Torbitt Prim Sch 57 D4
n Tyndale Prim Sch 72 D1
n Winter Ct 29 ....160 C4
n Wood Ho 3 ....162 C1
eld Way NW11 ..47 C4
gale Cl IG8 ....37 C4
gdon Rd N22 ....32 D1
gham Cl 4 NW5 .71 C3
gham Terr NW5 ..71 C3
gham Way KT1 .176 C1
gton Ct E5 ....75 A5
gton Prep Sch 179 B5
gton Rd SW9 ..138 A2
Ave SM2 ....218 C2
Ho 7 E14 ....119 D6
ord E12 ....78 C5
Rd E15 ....98 D5
on Heath CR0 ....205 A2

Willis St E14 ....97 D1
Willows The CR0 ....223 A6
Will Miles Ct 6 SW19 180 A3
Willmore End SW19 ..179 D1
Willoughby Ave CR0 ..220 B4
Willoughby Gr N17 ....34 B3
Willoughby Hall Dyslexia Ctr NW3 ....70 B4
Willoughby Ho 34 E1 .118 B5
EC2 ....242 C3
Willoughby La N17 ....34 B3
Willoughby Mews N17 .34 B3
Willoughby Park Rd
N17 ....34 B3
Willoughby Rd N8 ....50 C5
NW3 ....70 B4
Kingston KT2 ....176 B2
Twickenham TW1 ....153 D6
Willoughby St WC1 ..240 A3
Willoughbys The
SW14 ....133 C1
Willoughby Way SE7 ..121 B2
Willow Ave DA15 ....168 A5
Barnes SW13 ....133 D3
Yiewsley UB7 ....104 B6
Willowbank SW6 ....135 A2
Willow Bank TW10 ....153 B1
Willowbank Rd SE15 ..139 D6
Willow Bridge Rd N1 ..73 A2
Willowbrook Rd
Southall UB2 ....107 C3
Stanwell TW19 ....148 A2
Willow Bsns Pk SE26 .162 C1
Willow Cl BR2 ....210 B4
Brentford TW8 ....131 C6
Buckhurst Hill IG9 ....21 D1
12 Catford SE6 ....164 D3
Sidcup DA5 ....169 B5
Willow Cotts
Carshalton CR4 ....202 D2
Feltham TW13 ....151 A1
Richmond TW9 ....132 C6
Willowcourt Ave HA3 ..43 B4
Willow Ct EC2 ....243 A6
N7 ....72 B3
SW9 ....138 C4
40 W2 ....91 C2
7 E11 ....76 C6
Ashford TW16 ....171 C3
Beckenham BR3 ....185 C2
Chiswick W4 ....133 C5
8 Dagenham RM8 ....58 D2
Edgware HA8 ....26 A6
Harrow HA3 ....24 D2
Ilford IG1 ....79 A3
Kingston KT3 ....198 D6
3 Streatham SW16 ....160 B1
Thornton Heath CR7 ....205 B4
Willow Ctr The CR4 ..202 D3
Willow Dean HA5 ....22 D1
Willowdene N6 ....48 D2
1 SE15 ....140 B4
5 SE15 ....140 B5
Willow Dene WD23 ....8 C4
Willowdene Cl TW2 ..152 A4
Willowdene Ct N20 ....14 A4
Willow Dene Sch
SE18 ....145 C4
Willow Dr EN5 ....1 A1
Willow End N20 ....13 C2
Northwood HA6 ....22 A4
Surbiton KT6 ....198 A1
Willow Farm La SW15 134 B2
Willowfields Cl SE18 ..123 C1
Willowfield Sec Sch
E17 ....52 D6
Willow Gdns
Heston TW5 ....129 C4
Ruislip HA4 ....61 D6
Willow Gn NW9 ....27 C2
Borehamwood WD6 ....11 B6
Willow Gr BR7 ....188 D4
E13 ....99 A5
Ruislip HA4 ....39 D1
Willow Hall NW3 ....70 B4
Willowhayne Dr KT12 .194 B2
Willowhayne Gdns
KT4 ....216 C4
Willow Ho 14 N2 ....30 B1
9 NW3 ....70 D2
W10 ....90 D3
Feltham TW14 ....150 B6
Willow La SE18 ....122 C2
Mitcham CR4 ....202 D3
Willow Lo
6 Ashford TW16 ....171 D3
Fulham SW6 ....134 D4
New Barnet EN5 ....14 A6
Putney SW15 ....134 B2
Willow Lodge 10 SW8 .137 B2
Willow Manor SM1 ....217 B4
Willowmead Cl W5 ....87 D2
Willowmere KT10 ....212 A4
Willow Mount CR0 ....221 C5
Willow Pl SW1 115 C2 259 B4
Willow Rd NW3 ....70 B4
W5 ....110 A4
Dagenham RM6 ....59 A3
Enfield EN1 ....5 C3

Willow Rd *continued*
New Malden KT3 ....199 A5
Wallington SM6 ....219 B1
Willows Ave SM4 ....201 D4
Willows Cl HA5 ....22 C1
Willows Sch The UB4 ..84 D3
Willow St EC2 ..95 C3 243 A6
Chingford E4 ....20 B4
Willows Terr NW10 ....89 D5
Willows The N20 ....14 A1
Beckenham BR3 ....185 C2
Claygate KT10 ....212 C2
Wallend E12 ....78 C1
Loughton IG10 ....21 D6
Willow Tree Cl E3 ....97 B6
Willowtree Cl UB10 ....61 A5
Willow Tree Cl
Hayes UB4 ....84 C3
Wandsworth SW18 ....157 D3
Willow Tree Ct DA14 ..189 D5
5 Wembley HA0 ....65 D3
Willow Tree La UB4 ....84 C3
Willow Tree Prim Sch
UB5 ....63 A2
Willowtree Way SW16 182 C2
Willow Tree Wlk BR1 ..187 B2
Willow Vale BR7 ....188 D4
W12 ....112 A5
Willow View SW19 ....180 B2
Willow Way N3 ....29 D3
9 W11 ....112 D6
Forest Hill SE26 ....162 C1
Sunbury TW16 ....194 A5
Twickenham TW2 ....151 D2
Wembley HA0 ....65 A5
West Ewell KT19 ....215 B2
Willow Wlk BR6 ....226 D5
E17 ....53 B4
N15 ....50 D5
12 N2 ....30 B1
SE1 ....117 D2 263 C4
Cheam SM1,SM3 ....217 B5
Southgate N21 ....16 B5
Willow Wood Cres
SE25 ....205 C3
Willrose Cres SE2 ....124 B1
Willsbridge Ct 1
SE15 ....139 D6
Wills Cres TW3 ....151 D5
Wills Gr NW7 ....28 B5
Willshaw St SE14 ....141 C4
Will Thorne Pav The
E16 ....100 A1
Wilman Gr E8 ....74 A1
Wilmar Cl UB4 ....83 B3
Wilmar Gdns BR4 ....207 D1
Wilmcote Ho W2 ....91 D2
Wilmer Cl TW10 ....176 B5
Wilmer Cres KT2,TW10 176 B5
Wilmer Gdns N1 ....95 C6
Wilmer Ho 5 E3 ....97 A5
Wilmer Lea Cl E15 ....76 B1
Wilmer Pl N16 ....73 D6
Wilmers Ct 5 NW10 ....89 B6
Wilmer Way N14 ....31 D5
Wilmington Ave W4 ..133 B5
Wilmington Ct SW16 .182 A3
Wilmington Gdns IG11 .79 C1
Wilmington Sq
WC1 ....94 C4 234 A1
Wilmington St WC1 ..234 A1
Wilmot Cl N2 ....30 A1
SE15 ....140 A5
Wilmot Pl NW1 ....71 C1
Ealing W7 ....108 C5
Wilmot Rd E10 ....75 D6
N17 ....51 B6
Wallington SM5 ....218 D3
Wilmot St E2 ....96 B3
Wilmount St SE18 ....122 D2
Wilna Rd SW18 ....158 A4
Wilnett Ct 4 RM6 ....58 B2
Wilnett Villas 5 RM6 ...58 B2
Wilsham St
W11 ....113 A5 244 A4
Wilshaw Ho 10 SE8 ....141 C5
Wilsmere Dr HA3 ....24 C3
Wilson Ave CR4 ....180 C2
Wilson Cl Croydon CR2 .221 B3
Wembley HA9 ....44 B2
Wilson Dr HA9 ....44 B2
Wilson Gdns HA1 ....42 A2
Wilson Gr SE16 ....118 B4
Wilson Ho NW6 ....70 A1
2 SE7 ....143 C6
39 SW8 ....137 D3
Wilson Rd E6 ....99 D4
SE5 ....139 C4
Chessington KT9 ....214 B2
Redbridge IG1 ....56 B2
Wilson's Ave 2 N17 ....33 D1
Wilson's Pl E14 ....97 B1
Wilson's Rd W6 ....112 D1
Wilson's Sch SM6 ....220 A2
Wilson St E17 ....54 A4
EC2 ....95 B2 242 D4
Southgate N21 ....16 C4
Wilstone Cl UB4 ....85 A3
Wiltern Ct NW2 ....69 A2

Wilthorne Gdns RM10 ..81 D1
Wilton Ave W4 ....111 C1
Wilton Cres
SW1 ....115 A4 248 A1
Merton SW19 ....179 B2
Wilton Ct 16 E1 ....96 B1
N10 ....31 A1
4 Richmond TW10 ....154 A6
7 Woodford IG8 ....37 A4
Wilton Est E8 ....74 A2
Wilton Gdns
East Molesey KT8 ....195 C6
Walton-on-T KT12 ....194 D1
Wilton Gr Merton SW19 179 B2
New Malden KT3 ....199 D3
Wilton Ho 8 SE22 ....139 C2
Wilton Mews
SW1 ....115 B3 258 B6
Wilton Par TW13 ....150 B2
Wilton Pl SW1 115 A4 248 A1
2 Beckenham BR3 ....208 A6
4 Harrow HA1 ....42 D3
Wilton Rd N10 ....31 A1
SE2 ....124 C2
SW1 ....115 C2 259 A4
Cockfosters EN4 ....2 D1
Hounslow TW4 ....128 D2
Mitcham SW19 ....180 C3
Wilton Row SW1 ....248 A1
Wilton Sq N1 ..95 B6 235 C6
Wilton St SW1 115 B3 258 C6
Wilton Terr SW1 ....258 A6
Wilton Villas N1 ....235 C5
Wilton Way E8 ....74 A2
Wilton Wlk TW13 ....150 B3
Wiltshire Cl NW7 ....27 D5
SW3 ....257 C3
Wiltshire Ct 2 N4 ....50 B1
Barking IG11 ....79 A2
Wiltshire Gdns N4 ....51 A3
Twickenham TW2 ....152 A3
Wiltshire La HA5 ....40 A5
Wiltshire Rd SW9 ....138 C2
Thornton Heath CR7 ....204 C6
Wiltshire Row
N1 ....95 B6 235 D5
Wilverley Cres KT3 ....199 C3
Wimbart Rd SW2 ....160 B4
Wimbledon Bridge
SW19 ....179 B4
Wimbledon Central
SW19 ....179 B4
Wimbledon Chase Prim Sch
SW20 ....179 A2
Wimbledon Chase Sta
SW20 ....179 A1
Wimbledon Cl 2
SW20 ....178 D3
Wimbledon Coll
SW19 ....178 D3
Wimbledon Common★
SW19 ....178 B6
Wimbledon Common Prep
Sch SW19 ....178 D3
Wimbledon High Sch
SW19 ....179 A4
Wimbledon Hill Rd
SW19 ....179 B4
Wimbledon House Sch
SW19 ....179 C2
Wimbledon Lawn Tennis
Mus★ SW19 ....157 A1
Wimbledon Park Ct
SW19 ....157 B3
Wimbledon Park First Sch
SW19 ....157 D2
Wimbledon Park Rd
SW18,SW19 ....157 B3
Wimbledon Park Side
SW19 ....156 D3
Wimbledon Park Sta
SW19 ....157 C1
Wimbledon Rd SW17 .180 A6
Wimbledon Sch of Art
SW19 ....179 A2
Wimbledon Sch of Art
Annexe SW19 ....179 C3
Wimbledon Sta SW19 .179 B4
Wimbledon Stadium
SW17 ....180 A6
Wimbledon Stadium Bsns
Ctr SW17 ....157 D1
Wimbledon Windmill Mus★
SW19 ....156 C1
Wimbolt St E2 ....96 A4
Wimborne 2 DA14 ....190 B6
Wimborne Ave
Hayes UB4 ....84 B1
Southall UB2 ....107 C2
Wimborne Cl SE12 ....164 D6
Buckhurst Hill IG9 ....21 C2
North Cheam KT4 ....200 C1
Wimborne Ct 1 UB5 ....63 C2
Wimborne Dr HA8,NW9 .44 C6
Pinner HA5 ....41 A2
Wimborne Gdns W13 ....87 B2
Wimborne Ho E16 ....120 D6
NW1 ....237 B5
SW8 ....270 D3

Wimborne Ho *continued*
Croydon CR0 ....206 C4
Upper Tooting SW12 ....159 C1
Wimborne Rd
Edmonton N9 ....18 A2
Tottenham N17 ....33 C1
Wimborne Way BR3 ..207 A5
Wimbourne Ct N1 ....235 C4
Mitcham SW19 ....180 B3
South Croydon CR2 ....221 C2
Wimbourne St
N1 ....95 B5 235 C4
Wimpole Cl
Bromley BR2 ....209 C5
1 Kingston KT1 ....176 C1
Wimpole Mews
W1 ....93 B2 238 C3
Wimpole St W1 93 B1 238 C2
Wimshurst Cl CR0 ....204 A1
Winans Wlk SW9 ....138 C3
Winant Ho 17 E14 ....119 D6
Wincanton Cres UB5 ....63 C3
Wincanton Gdns IG6 ....56 D6
Wincanton Rd SW18 ..157 B4
Winchcombe Rd SM5 .202 C1
Winchcomb Gdns SE9 143 D2
Winchelsea Ave DA7 ..147 B5
Winchelsea Cl SW15 ..156 D6
Winchelsea Ho 11
SE16 ....118 C4
Winchelsea Rd E7 ....77 A4
N17 ....51 C6
NW10 ....89 B6
Winchelsey Rise CR2 .221 D2
Winchendon Rd
Fulham SW6 ..135 B4 264 D2
Teddington TW11,TW12 .174 B6
Winchester Ave NW6 ..69 A1
NW9 ....44 C6
Heston TW5 ....129 B6
Winchester Cl SE17 ..261 D3
Beckenham BR2 ....208 D6
Enfield EN1 ....17 C6
Kingston KT2 ....176 D3
11 Newham E6 ....100 B1
Winchester Ct W8 ....245 C2
Belvedere DA17 ....125 C1
Winchester Dr HA5 ....40 D4
Winchester Ho 18 E3 ....97 B4
1 SE18 ....143 D5
SW3 ....266 D5
W2 ....236 A1
5 Barking IG11 ....80 A1
Winchester Pk BR2 ..208 D6
Winchester Pl 6 E8 ....73 D3
N6 ....49 B1
Winchester Rd N6 ....49 B1
NW3 ....70 B1
Beckenham BR2 ....208 D6
Bexley DA16 ....146 D3
Chingford E4 ....36 A3
Edmonton N9 ....18 A3
Harlington UB3 ....127 C5
Harrow HA3 ....44 A5
Ilford IG1 ....79 B5
Northwood HA6 ....40 A6
Twickenham TW1 ....153 B5
Twickenham TW13 ....151 B1
Walton-on-T KT12 ....194 A1
Winchester Sq SE1 ..252 C4
Winchester St
SW1 ....115 B1 258 D2
Acton W3 ....111 A4
Winchester Wlk SE1 ..252 C4
Winchet Wlk CR0 ....206 C3
Winchfield Cl HA3 ....43 C3
Winchfield Ho SW15 ..155 D5
Winchfield Rd SE26 ..185 A5
Winch Ho SW10 ....266 B4
Winchilsea Cres KT8 .174 A1
Winchilsea Ho NW8 ..229 D1
Winchmore Hill Rd
N14,N21 ....16 A4
Winchmore Hill Sta
N21 ....16 D4
Winchmore Sch N21 ...17 A2
Winchmore Villas N21 ..16 B4
Winchstone Cl TW17 .192 B5
Winckley Cl HA3 ....44 B4
Wincott St
SE11 ....116 C2 261 B3
Wincrofts Dr SE9 ....145 B1
Windall Cl SE20 ....184 A2
Windborough Rd SM5 219 A1
Windcott Ct HA3 ....43 C2
Windermere NW1 ....231 D2
12 Putney SW15 ....156 D5
Windermere Ave N3 ....47 C6
NW6 ....91 A6
Merton SW19 ....201 D6
Ruislip HA4 ....40 D2
Wembley HA9 ....43 C1
Windermere Cl BR6 ..226 D5
East Bedfont TW14 ....149 D3
Stanwell TW19 ....148 A2
Windermere Ct
Barnes SW13 ....133 D6
Barnet EN5 ....1 D1
Carshalton SM5 ....219 A5

Windermere Ct *continued*
Wembley HA9 ....43 C2
Windermere Gdns IG4 .56 A4
Windermere Gr HA9 ....43 C1
Windermere Hall HA8 ..26 B5
Windermere Ho E3 ....97 B3
Isleworth TW1 ....152 D6
Windermere Point 3
SE15 ....140 C5
Windermere Rd N10 ....31 B2
N19 ....71 C6
W5 ....109 C3
Croydon CR0 ....205 D1
Kingston SW15 ....177 C5
Mitcham SW16 ....181 D1
Southall UB1 ....85 B2
West Wickham BR4 ....224 C6
Windermere Way UB7 104 B5
Winders Rd SW11 ....136 C3
Windfield Cl SE26 ....184 D6
Windham Rd TW9 ....132 B2
Winding Way RM8 ....80 C5
Windlass Pl SE8 ....119 A2
Windlesham Gr SW19 156 D3
Windley Cl SE23 ....162 C2
Windmill WC1 ....240 C4
Windmill Alley 7 W4 .111 C2
Windmill Ave UB2 ....108 A4
Windmill Bridge Ho 1
CR0 ....205 C1
Windmill Bsns Ctr
UB2 ....108 A5
Windmill Bsns Village
TW16 ....171 C2
Windmill Cl NW2 ....69 A5
11 SE1 ....118 A2
3 SE13 ....142 A3
Ashford TW16 ....171 C3
Kingston KT6 ....197 C2
Windmill Ct NW2 ....69 A2
W5 ....109 C2
Windmill Dr BR2 ....225 C4
SW4 ....159 B6
Windmill Gdns EN2 ....4 C2
Windmill Gr CR0 ....205 A3
Windmill Hill NW3 ....70 A5
1 NW3 ....70 A4
Enfield EN2 ....5 A2
Ruislip HA4 ....39 D1
Windmill Ho SE1 ....251 B3
Windmill La E15 ....76 B2
Bushey WD23 ....8 C3
Edgware EN5 ....11 D5
Isleworth TW7,UB2,W7 .108 C2
Southall UB2 ....108 A4
Southall UB6 ....86 A2
Thames Ditton KT7 ....197 B2
Windmill Lo TW16 ....171 C2
Windmill Pas 10 W4 ....111 C2
Windmill Rd SW18 ....158 B5
W4 ....111 C2
Brentford TW8,W5 ....109 C1
Charlton TW16 ....171 C2
Edmonton N18 ....33 B6
Hampton TW12 ....174 A5
Mitcham CR4 ....203 C5
Roehampton SW19 ....156 B1
Thornton Heath CR0 ....205 A2
Windmill Rd W TW16 .171 C1
Windmill Rise KT2 ....176 D3
Windmill Row SE11 ..261 A1
Windmill St W1 93 D2 239 C3
Bushey WD23 ....8 C3
Windmill Terr TW17 ..193 C2
Windmill Trad Est
TW16 ....171 C2
Windmill Way HA4 ....39 D1
Windmill Wlk SE1 ....251 B2
Windmore Cl HA0 ....65 A3
Windrose Cl SE16 ....118 D4
Windrush KT3 ....199 A5
Windrush Cl SW11 ....136 B1
Chiswick W4 ....133 A5
Ickenham UB10 ....60 B4
Windrush Ho NW8 ....236 D4
Windrush La SE23 ....162 D1
Windrush Prim Sch
SE28 ....124 B5
Windrush Rd NW10 ....89 B6
Windsock Cl 1 SE16 .119 B2
Windsor Ave E17 ....35 A1
Cheam SM3 ....217 A5
East Molesey KT8 ....195 C6
Edgware HA8 ....10 D1
Hillingdon UB10 ....60 D1
Merton SW19 ....180 A2
New Malden KT3 ....199 A4
Windsor Cl N3 ....29 A1
Brentford TW8 ....131 B6
Chislehurst BR7 ....188 D5
Harrow HA2 ....63 C5
Pinner HA6 ....22 A1
West Norwood SE27 ....183 A6
Windsor Cres
Harrow HA2 ....63 C5
Wembley HA9 ....66 D5

Windsor Ct BR1 ... 210 A6
E17 ... 53 B6
N11 ... 30 D5
N14 ... 15 C4
NW11 ... 47 A3
NW3 ... 69 C4
20 SE16 ... 118 D5
SW11 ... 136 B3
4 SW18 ... 157 C6
SW3 ... 257 B2
2 SW4 ... 137 C1
W2 ... 245 C6
Bushey WD23 ... 8 A4
Fulham SW6 ... 135 A2
South Norwood SE19 ... 183 C2
Sunbury TW16 ... 172 A3
Windsor Ctr The SE27 ... 183 A6
Windsor Dr EN4 ... 14 D5
Windsor Gdns W9 ... 91 C3
Hayes UB3 ... 105 B3
Wallington CR0 ... 220 A5
Windsor Gr SE27 ... 183 A6
Windsor Ho 4 E2 ... 96 D4
N1 ... 235 B4
N4 ... 51 A1
NW1 ... 231 D2
NW2 ... 69 A2
2 NW4 ... 28 D1
4 W4 ... 111 A1
7 Northolt UB5 ... 63 C2
Windsor Mews
Catford SE6 ... 164 A3
Forest Hill SE23 ... 163 A3
Windsor Park Rd UB3 127 D5
Windsor Pk SW19 ... 180 A2
Windsor Pl SW1 ... 259 B4
Windsor Rd DA6 ... 147 A1
E10 ... 75 D6
E7 ... 77 C3
N3 ... 29 A1
N7 ... 72 A5
NW2 ... 68 B2
Ashford TW16 ... 172 A4
Barnet EN5 ... 12 D5
Chingford E4 ... 35 D6
Cranford TW4,TW5 ... 128 C3
Dagenham RM8 ... 81 A5
Ealing W5 ... 110 A6
Harrow HA3 ... 24 B2
Ilford IG1 ... 79 A4
Kingston KT2 ... 176 A3
Palmers Green N13 ... 16 C1
Richmond TW9 ... 132 B3
Southall UB2 ... 107 B3
South Norwood CR7 ... 182 D1
Teddington TW11 ... 174 B5
Tottenham N17 ... 34 A1
Wanstead E11 ... 77 A6
Worcester Park KT4 ... 216 A6
Windsor St N1 . 94 D6 234 D6
Windsor Terr
N1 ... 95 A4 235 B2
Windsor Way
W14 ... 113 A2 254 A4
Windsor Wharf E9 ... 75 B3
Windsor Wlk SE5 ... 139 B3
Walton-on-T KT12 ... 194 D1
Windspoint Dr SE15 ... 140 B6
Windus Rd N16 ... 51 D1
Windus Wlk N16 ... 51 D1
Windy Ridge BR1 ... 188 A2
Windy Ridge Cl SW19 178 D5
Wine Cl E1 ... 118 C6
Wine Office Ct EC4 ... 241 B2
Winery La KT1 ... 198 B6
Winey Cl KT9 ... 213 C1
Winfield Ho SW11 ... 136 B3
Winford Ct 15 SE15 ... 140 A4
Winford Ho E3 ... 75 B1
Winford Par 9 UB1 ... 85 D1
Winforton St SE10 ... 142 A4
Winfrith Rd SW18 ... 158 A3
Wingate Cres CR0 ... 204 A3
Wingate Ho 26 E3 ... 97 D4
8 N16 ... 73 B4
Wingate Rd W6 ... 112 B3
Ilford IG1 ... 78 D3
Sidcup DA14 ... 190 C4
Wingate Trad Est N17 ... 33 D3
Wingfield Ct 10 E14 ... 120 B6
Wingfield Ho 16 E2 ... 95 D4
NW6 ... 91 D5
Wingfield Mews SE15 . 140 A2
Wingfield Prim Sch
SE3 ... 143 B2
Wingfield Rd E15 ... 76 C4
E17 ... 53 D4
Kingston KT2 ... 176 C4
Wingfield St SE15 ... 140 A2
Wingfield Way HA4 ... 62 B2
Wingford Rd SW2 ... 160 A5
Wingham 3 NW5 ... 71 A2
Wingham Ho 3 SE26 . 184 B5
Wingmore Rd SE24 ... 139 A2
Wingrad Ho 14 E1 ... 96 C2
Wingrave SE17 ... 262 C3
Wingrave Rd W6 ... 134 C6
Wingreen 13 NW8 ... 91 D6
Wingrove Rd SE6 ... 164 C2
Wings Cl SM1 ... 217 C4
Winicotte Ho W2 ... 236 D4
Winifred Cl EN5 ... 11 D5
Winifrede Paul Ho 7
NW5 ... 71 B4
Winifred Pl N12 ... 30 A5
Winifred Rd
Dagenham RM8 ... 59 A1
Hampton TW12 ... 173 C6
Merton SW19 ... 179 C2
Winifred St E16 ... 122 B5
Winifred Terr EN1 ... 17 D4
Winkfield Rd E13 ... 99 B5
Wood Green N22 ... 32 C2
Winkley Ct N10 ... 49 B5
Harrow HA2 ... 63 C5
Winkley St 6 E2 ... 96 B5
Winkworth Cotts 13 E1 96 C3
Winlaton Rd BR1 ... 186 B6
Winmill Rd RM8 ... 81 B5
Winn Common Rd
SE18 ... 145 C6
Winnett St W1 ... 249 C6
Winningales Ct IG5 ... 56 A6
Winnings Wlk UB5 ... 63 A2
Winnington Cl N2 ... 48 B3
Winnington Ho
8 SE5 ... 139 A5
19 W10 ... 91 A3
Winnington Rd N2 ... 48 B3
Enfield EN3 ... 6 C6
Winnipeg Dr 3 BR6 ... 227 D2
Winnipeg Ho UB4 ... 84 B3
Winn Rd SE12 ... 165 B3
Winns Ave E17 ... 53 B6
Winns Mews N15 ... 51 C5
Winns Prim Sch E17 ... 35 B1
Winns Terr E17 ... 53 C6
Winsbeach E17 ... 36 B1
Winscombe Cres W5 ... 87 D3
Winscombe Ct W5 ... 87 D3
Winscombe St N19 ... 71 B6
Winscombe Way HA7 ... 25 A5
Winsford Rd SE6 ... 163 B1
Winsford Terr N18 ... 33 B5
Winsham Gr SW11 ... 159 A6
Winsham Ho NW1 ... 232 D2
Winslade Ho 4 E5 ... 74 B6
Winslade Rd SW2 ... 160 A6
Winslade Way SE6 ... 163 D4
Winsland Mews W2 ... 236 C2
Winsland St W2 92 B1 236 C2
Winsley St W1 ... 239 B2
Winslow SE17 ... 263 A1
Winslow Cl 2 NW10 ... 67 C5
Pinner HA5 ... 40 B3
Winslow Gr E4 ... 20 C2
Winslow Rd W6 ... 134 C6
Winslow Way TW13 ... 151 A1
Winsmoor Ct EN2 ... 4 D2
Winsor Prim Sch E6 ... 100 C1
Winsor Terr E6 ... 100 C2
Winstanley Rd SW11 ... 136 B2
Winston Ave NW9 ... 45 C2
Winston Cl Harrow HA3 . 24 D4
Romford RM7 ... 59 D5
Winston Ct 7 BR1 ... 187 B2
Harrow HA3 ... 23 D3
Winston Ho WC1 ... 239 D6
Winston Rd N16 ... 73 B4
Winston Way IG1 ... 79 A5
Winston Wlk W4 ... 111 B2
Winter Ave E6 ... 100 A6
Winterborne Ave BR6 . 227 B5
Winterbourne Ho
W11 ... 244 A5
Winterbourne Jun & Inf
Schs CR7 ... 204 C5
Winterbourne Rd
Dagenham RM8 ... 80 C6
Forest Hill SE6 ... 163 B3
Thornton Heath CR7 ... 204 C5
Winter Box Wlk TW10 154 B6
Winterbrook Rd SE24 . 161 A5
Winterburn Cl N11 ... 31 A4
Winterfold Cl SW19 ... 157 A2
Wintergreen Cl 7 E6 . 100 A2
Winterleys 7 NW6 ... 91 B5
Winter Lo 19 SE16 ... 118 A1
Winter's Ct E4 ... 19 D1
Winterslow Ho 20 SE5 139 A3
Winters Rd KT7 ... 197 B2
Winterstoke Gdns NW7 28 A5
Winterstoke Rd SE6 ... 163 B3
Winterton Ct KT1 ... 175 D2
Winterton Ho 15 E1 ... 96 C1
Winterton Pl SW10 ... 266 B6
Winterwell Rd SW2 ... 160 A6
Winthorpe Rd SW15 ... 135 A1
Winthrop Ho 10 W12 . 112 B6
Winthrop St E1 ... 96 B2
Winthrop Wlk HA9 ... 66 A5
Winton Ave N11 ... 31 C3
Winton Cl N9 ... 18 D4
Winton Ct 15 KT6 ... 197 D2
Winton Gdns HA8 ... 26 B3
Winton Prim Sch
N1 ... 94 B5 233 C3
Winton Rd BR6 ... 226 D4
Winton Way SW16 ... 182 C5
Wintour Ho HA9 ... 65 D6
Wirrall Ho 15 SE26 ... 162 A1
Wirral Wood Cl BR7 ... 188 C4
Wisbeach Rd CR0 ... 205 B4
Wisden Ho SW8 ... 270 D5
Wisdom Ct 5 TW7 ... 131 A2
Wisdons Cl RM7,RM9 ... 59 D1
Wise La NW7 ... 28 A4
Wiseman Ct 12 SE19 ... 183 C5
Wiseman Rd E10 ... 75 C6
Wise Rd E15 ... 98 B6
Wiseton Rd SW17 ... 158 D3
Wishart Rd SE3 ... 143 D3
Wishaw Wlk N13 ... 32 A4
Wisley Ho SW1 ... 259 C2
Wisley Rd SW11 ... 159 A6
St Paul's Cray BR5 ... 190 B3
Wistaria Cl BR6 ... 226 D6
Wisteria Cl NW7 ... 27 D4
Ilford IG1 ... 78 D3
Wisteria Rd SE13 ... 142 B1
Wistow Ho 14 E2 ... 96 A6
Witanhurst La N6 ... 49 A1
Witan St E2 ... 96 B4
Witchwood Ho 11
SW9 ... 138 C2
Witcombe Point 13
SE15 ... 140 A4
Witham Ct E10 ... 75 D5
Upper Tooting SW17 ... 158 D1
Witham Ho 35 SE5 ... 139 A3
Witham Rd
Dagenham RM10 ... 81 C3
Ealing W13 ... 109 B5
Hounslow TW7 ... 130 B4
Penge SE20 ... 206 C6
Witherby Cl CR0 ... 221 C4
Witherington Rd N5 ... 72 C3
Withers Cl KT9 ... 213 C2
Withers Mead NW9 ... 27 D2
Withers Pl EC1 ... 242 B6
Witherston Way SE9 ... 166 C1
Withington Rd N2 ... 30 C2
Withycombe Rd SW19 156 D4
Withy Ho 4 E1 ... 96 D3
Withy La HA4 ... 39 A4
Withy Mead E4 ... 20 B1
Witley Cres CR0 ... 224 A2
Witley Ct UB2 ... 107 B2
Witley Gdns UB2 ... 107 B2
Witley Ho 2 SW2 ... 160 B4
Witley Ind Est UB2 ... 107 B2
Witley Point 8 SW15 . 156 B3
Witley Rd N19 ... 71 C6
Witney Cl
Ickenham UB10 ... 60 B4
Pinner HA5 ... 23 B4
Witney Path SE23 ... 162 D1
Wittenham Way E4 ... 20 B1
Witten Ho KT3 ... 199 B1
Wittering Cl KT2 ... 175 D5
Wittering Ho 9 SW11 136 D3
Wittersham Rd BR1 ... 186 D5
Wittingham Com Prim Sch
E17 ... 35 A2
Witts Ho KT2 ... 198 B6
Wivenhoe Cl SE15 ... 140 B2
Wivenhoe Ct TW4 ... 129 B1
Wivenhoe Rd IG11 ... 102 B5
Wiverton Rd SE26 ... 184 C5
Wixom Ho SE9 ... 143 C1
Wix Prim Sch SW4 ... 137 B1
Wix Rd RM9 ... 102 D6
Wix's La SW4 ... 137 B1
Woburn W13 ... 87 B2
Woburn Cl SE28 ... 102 D1
Bushey WD23 ... 8 A5
Wimbledon SW19 ... 180 A4
Woburn Ct 32 SE16 ... 118 B1
1 DA6 ... 147 A1
Croydon CR0 ... 205 A1
Richmond TW9 ... 132 B2
4 Woodford E18 ... 37 A1
Woburn Pl WC1 94 A3 240 A5
Woburn Rd
Carshalton SM5 ... 202 C1
Croydon CR0 ... 205 A1
Woburn Sq
WC1 ... 93 D3 239 D5
Woburn Twr 14 UB5 ... 84 D4
Woburn Wlk WC1 ... 232 D1
Wodehouse Ave SE15 . 139 D4
Wodehouse Ct 10 W3 . 111 A3
Woffington Cl KT1,KT8 175 C2
Woking Cl SW15 ... 133 D1
Wolcot Ho NW1 ... 232 B3
Woldham Pl BR2 ... 209 C5
Woldham Rd BR2 ... 209 C5
Wolds Dr BR6 ... 226 C4
Wolfe Cl Hayes BR2 ... 209 A3
Hayes UB4 ... 84 B4
Wolfe Cres 34 SE16 ... 118 D4
SE7 ... 121 D1
Wolfe Ho 19 W12 ... 112 B6
Wolferton Rd E12 ... 78 B4
Wolf Fields Prim Sch
UB2 ... 107 B2
Wolfington Rd SE27 ... 182 D6
Wolfram Cl SE13 ... 164 C6
Wolfson Ct NW11 ... 47 A2
SE1 ... 253 D2
Wolfson Hillel Prim Sch
N14 ... 15 D5
Wolftencroft Cl SW11 . 136 B2
Wollaston Cl SE1 ... 262 A4
Wolmer Cl HA8 ... 26 D6
Wolmer Gdns HA8 ... 10 C1
Wolmer Rd HA8 ... 26 D6
Wolseley Ave SW18,
SW19 ... 157 C2
Wolseley Gdns W4 ... 132 D6
Wolseley Rd E7 ... 77 B1
N8 ... 49 D4
Acton W4 ... 111 A2
Carshalton CR4 ... 203 A2
Harrow HA3 ... 42 C6
Wood Green N22 ... 32 B2
Wolseley St
SE1 ... 117 D4 253 D1
Wolsey Ave E17 ... 53 B6
Wallend E6 ... 100 C4
Wolsey Cl
Isleworth TW3 ... 130 A1
Kingston KT2 ... 176 D2
Southall UB2 ... 108 A3
Wimbledon SW20 ... 178 B3
Worcester Park KT19,
KT4 ... 216 A4
Wolsey Cres SM4 ... 201 B2
Wolsey Ct NW6 ... 70 A1
SE9 ... 166 B5
Bromley BR1 ... 186 D3
Wolsey Dr
Kingston KT2 ... 176 A4
Walton-on-T KT12 ... 194 D1
Wolsey Gr HA8 ... 27 B3
Wolsey Ho 2 TW12 ... 173 D4
Wolsey Inf Sch CR0 ... 224 A1
Wolsey Jun Sch CR0 ... 224 A1
Wolsey Mews NW5 ... 71 C2
Orpington BR6 ... 227 D3
Wolsey Rd N1 ... 73 B3
Ashford TW15 ... 170 B6
Ashford TW16 ... 171 D4
East Molesey KT8 ... 196 B5
Enfield EN1 ... 6 B3
Hampton TW12 ... 174 A4
Wolsey St E1 ... 96 C2
Wolsey Way KT9 ... 214 C3
Wolstenholme HA7 ... 25 B5
Wolstonbury N12 ... 29 C5
Wolvercote Rd SE2 ... 124 D4
Wolverley St E2 ... 96 B4
Wolverton SE17 ... 263 A2
Wolverton Ave KT2 ... 176 C2
Wolverton Gdns W6 ... 112 D2
Ealing W5 ... 110 B6
Wolverton Mans W5 ... 110 B5
Wolverton Rd HA7 ... 25 B3
Wolverton Way N14 ... 15 C6
Wolves La N22 ... 32 C4
Womersley Rd N4,N8 ... 50 B3
Wonford Cl KT2,KT3 ... 177 C2
Wontner Cl 5 N1 ... 73 A1
Wontner Rd SW12,
SW17 ... 158 D2
Wooburn Cl UB8 ... 82 D3
Woodall Cl 24 E14 ... 119 D6
Chessington KT9 ... 213 D2
Woodall Ho TW7 ... 130 D2
Woodall Rd EN3 ... 18 D5
Woodbank Rd BR1 ... 164 D1
Woodbastwick Rd
SE26 ... 185 A5
Woodberry Ave
Edmonton N21 ... 16 D2
Harrow HA2 ... 42 A5
Woodberry Cl NW7 ... 28 D3
Ashford TW16 ... 172 A4
Woodberry Cres N10 ... 49 B6
Woodberry Down N4 ... 51 A2
Woodberry Down Com Prim
Sch N4 ... 51 A2
Woodberry Gdns N12 ... 30 A4
Woodberry Gr N12 ... 30 A4
N4 ... 51 A2
Woodberry Way N12 ... 30 A4
Chingford E4 ... 20 A4
Woodbine Cl TW2 ... 152 B2
Woodbine Gr Enfield EN2 . 5 B5
Penge SE20 ... 184 B3
Woodbine La KT4 ... 216 C5
Woodbine Pl E11 ... 55 A3
Woodbine Rd DA15 ... 167 C3
Woodbines Ave KT1 ... 197 D6
Woodbine Terr E9 ... 74 C2
Woodborough Rd
SW15 ... 134 B1
Woodbourne Ave
SW16 ... 159 D1
Woodbourne Cl SW16 160 A1
Woodbourne Dr KT10 212 D2
Woodbourne Gdns
SM6 ... 219 B1
Woodbridge Cl 10 N7 ... 72 B6
4 NW2 ... 68 A5
Woodbridge Ct N16 ... 73 B5
Woodbridge High Sch
IG8 ... 37 B3
Woodbridge Ho E11 ... 54 D1
Woodbridge Rd IG11 ... 79 D3
Woodbridge St
EC1 ... 94 D3 241 C6
Woodbrook Rd SE2 ... 146 B6
Woodbrook Sch BR3 ... 185 B2
Woodburn Cl NW4 ... 46 D4
Woodbury Cl
Croydon CR0 ... 221 D6
Wanstead E11 ... 55 B5
Woodbury Ct 1 W13 ... 87 B3
Woodbury Ho 4 SE26 162 B1
Woodbury Park Rd
W13 ... 87 B3
Woodbury Rd E17 ... 53 D5
Woodbury St SW17 ... 180 C5
Woodchester Sq W2 ... 91 D2
Woodchurch Cl DA14 . 167 B1
Woodchurch Dr BR1 ... 187 D3
Woodchurch Ho 15
SW9 ... 138 C4
Woodchurch Rd NW6 ... 69 D1
Wood Cl E2 ... 96 A3
NW9 ... 45 B2
Harrow HA1 ... 42 B2
Woodclyffe Dr BR7 ... 188 C1
Woodcock Ct HA3 ... 44 A2
Woodcock Dell Ave
HA3 ... 43 D2
Woodcock Hill HA3 ... 43 C3
Woodcock Ho 4 E14 ... 97 C2
Woodcocks E16 ... 99 D2
Woodcombe Cres
SE23 ... 162 C3
Woodcote Ave NW7 ... 28 C4
Thornton Heath CR7 ... 204 D5
Wallington SM6 ... 219 B1
Woodcote Cl Enfield N9 . 18 C5
Kingston KT2 ... 176 B5
Woodcote Dr BR6 ... 211 B2
Woodcote Ho 4 SE8 . 141 B6
Woodcote Mews
Loughton IG10 ... 21 D4
Wallington SM6 ... 219 B2
Woodcote Pl 1 SE27 . 182 D5
Woodcote Rd
Wallington SM6 ... 219 C1
Wanstead E11 ... 55 A2
Woodcott Ho 1 SW15 156 A4
Woodcroft SE9 ... 166 B1
South Croydon CR0 ... 221 C5
Southgate N21 ... 16 C3
Wembley UB6 ... 65 A2
Woodcroft Ave NW7 ... 27 C4
Stanmore HA7 ... 25 A2
Woodcroft Cres UB10 ... 82 D6
Woodcroft Jun & Inf Schs
HA8 ... 27 C3
Woodcroft Mews SE8 . 119 A2
Woodcroft Rd CR7 ... 204 D3
Wood Dene 6 SE15 ... 140 B4
Wood Dr BR7 ... 188 A4
Woodedge Cl E4 ... 20 D3
Woodend
South Norwood SE19 ... 183 A4
Sutton SM1 ... 218 A6
Thames Ditton KT10 ... 212 A6
Wood End UB3 ... 83 C1
Wood End Ave HA2 ... 64 A4
Wood End Cl UB5 ... 64 B3
Woodend Gdns EN2 ... 4 A1
Wood End Gdns UB5 ... 64 A3
Wood End Green Rd
UB3 ... 83 C1
Wood End Inf Sch UB5 . 64 B3
Wood End Jun Sch
UB6 ... 64 B3
Wood End La UB5 ... 63 D3
Wood End Park Jun & Inf
Sch UB3 ... 105 A6
Woodend Rd E17 ... 36 A1
Wood End Rd HA1,UB5 . 64 B4
Wood End Way UB5 ... 64 A3
Wooder Gdns E7 ... 77 A4
Wooderson Cl SE25 ... 205 C5
Woodfall Ave EN5 ... 13 B6
Woodfall Rd N4 ... 72 C6
Woodfall St SW3 ... 257 C1
Woodfarrs SE5 ... 139 B1
Wood Field NW3 ... 70 D3
Woodfield Ave NW9 ... 45 C5
Ealing W5 ... 87 C3
Streatham SW16 ... 159 D1
Wallington SM5 ... 219 A1
Wembley HA0 ... 65 C5
Woodfield Cl
1 Enfield EN1 ... 5 C1
South Norwood SE19 ... 183 A3
Woodfield Cres W5 ... 87 D3
Woodfield Ct SW16 ... 159 D1
Woodfield Ctr The
SW16 ... 159 D2
Woodfield Dr EN4 ... 15 A3
Woodfield Gdns KT3 ... 199 D4
Woodfield Gr SW16 ..
Woodfield Ho 6 E5 ..
11 Forest Hill SE23 ...
New Malden KT3 ...
Woodfield Pl W9 ...
Woodfield Rd W9 ...
Cranford TW4,TW5 ...
Ealing W5 ...
Hinchley Wood KT10,
KT7 ...
Woodfield Rise WD23
Woodfield Sch NW9 .
Woodfields Ct SM1 ..
Woodfield Way N11 ..
Woodford Ave IG2,IG4,
IG5,IG8 ...
Woodford Bridge Rd
IG4 ...
Woodford Cres HA5 ..
Woodford Cty High Sc
IG8 ...
Woodforde Ct UB3 ...
Woodford Green Prep
IG8 ...
Woodford Ho 13 SE18
5 Wanstead E18 ...
Woodford New Rd E17
Woodford E18 ...
Woodford Pl HA9 ...
Woodford Rd E7 ...
Wanstead E18 ...
Woodford Sta IG8 ...
Woodford Trad Est IG8
Woodgate Ave KT9 ..
Woodgate Cres HA6 ..
Woodgate Dr SW16 ..
Woodger Rd W12 ...
Woodget Cl E6 ...
Woodgrange Ave N12
Ealing W5 ...
Enfield EN1 ...
Harrow HA3 ...
Woodgrange Cl HA3 ..
Woodgrange Ct 1
BR2 ...
Woodgrange Gdns EN1
Woodgrange Inf Sch
E7 ...
Woodgrange Mans
HA3 ...
Woodgrange Park Sta
E12 ...
Woodgrange Rd E7 ...
Woodgrange Terr EN1
Wood Green Sta N22
Woodhall NW1 ...
Woodhall Ave
Dulwich SE21 ...
Pinner HA5 ...
Woodhall Dr
Dulwich SE21 ...
Pinner HA5 ...
Woodhall Gate HA5 ...
Woodhall Ho SW18 ...
Woodhall La WD19 ...
Woodhall Sch WD19 ..
Woodham Ct E11 ...
Woodham Rd SE6 ...
Woodhatch Cl 16 E6 ..
Woodhaven Gdns IG6 .
Woodhayes BR7 ...
Woodhayes Rd SW19,
SW20 ...
Woodhead Dr BR6 ...
Woodheyes Rd NW10 .
Woodhill SE7,SE18 ...
Woodhill Cres HA3 ...
Woodhill Prim Sch
SE18 ...
Wood Ho 6 NW6 ...
4 SW4 ...
Woodhouse Ave UB6 .
Woodhouse Cl
Hayes UB3 ...
Wembley UB6 ...
Woodhouse Eaves HA6
Woodhouse Gr E12 ...
Woodhouse Rd E11 ...
N12 ...
Woodhouse Sixth Form
N12 ...
Woodhurst Ave BR5 ..
Woodhurst Rd SE2 ...
W3 ...
Woodington Cl SE9 ...
Woodison St E3 ...
Woodknoll Dr BR7 ...
Wood La N6 ...
NW9 ...
W12 ...
Dagenham RM10 ...
Hounslow TW7 ...
Ruislip HA4 ...
Stanmore HA7 ...
Woodford IG8 ...
Woodland App UB6 ...
Woodland Cl NW9 ...
Uxbridge UB10 ...
West Ewell KT19 ... 2

land Cl continued
Norwood SE19 183 C4
ford IG8 21 B1
land Cres SE10 142 C6
16 118 D4
land Ct NW4 47 A4
n SM1 217 C2
anstead E11 55 A4
land Gdns E17 54 C5
49 B4
orth TW7 130 C2
land Gr SE10 120 C1
land Hill SE19 183 C4
land Rd N11 31 B5
ford E4 20 A3
SE19 183 D4
ton Heath CR7 204 C5
land Rise N10 49 B5
oley UB6 65 A2
lands N12 30 A4
47 A4
137 B1
nham BR3 185 D3
w HA2 41 C5
Barnes SW20 200 D5
lands Ave DA15 167 C3
30 A2
W3 110 D5
nham RM6 59 A2
ton KT3 177 B2
HA4 40 D2
ead E11 55 B1
ester Park KT4 216 A6
lands Cl BR1 188 B1
47 A4
ate KT10 212 D1
lands Ct NW10 90 D6
omley BR1 186 D2
ch SE22 162 B4
all UB1 107 C6
lands Dr
w HA7 24 D4
ury TW16 172 C1
lands Gr TW7 130 C3
lands Gt SW15 157 B6
lands Inf Sch IG1 79 B3
lands Jun Sch
79 B3
lands Par TW15 171 A4
lands Park Jun & Inf
N15 51 A4
lands Park Rd
51 A4
142 C6
lands Rd BR1 188 B1
147 A2
76 C6
54 A6
18 C3
s SW13 133 D2
d EN2 5 B4
w HA1 42 D4
IG1 79 A5
orth TW7 130 C3
all UB1 106 D5
on KT6 197 D2
lands St SE13 164 B4
land St 2 E8 73 D2
lands The N14 15 B3
73 A4
orth TW7 130 D3
ham SE13 164 B4
am CR4 203 A6
Norwood SE19 183 A3
nore HA7 25 B5
es Ditton KT10 212 A6
lands Way SW15 157 B6
land Terr SE7 122 A2
land Way BR5 211 A4
27 D4
124 D2
on CR0 207 A1
n SM4 201 B5
am CR4 181 A3
gate N21 16 C2
rth KT5 214 D6
Wickham BR4 224 A5
ford IG8 21 B1
land Wlk NW3 70 C3
10 120 C1
ington KT19 214 C2
lane High Sch
90 B1
lawn Cl SW15 157 B6
lawn Cres TW2 151 D2
lawn Dr TW13 150 D2
lawn Rd SW6 134 D4
lea Dr BR2 208 C4
lea Lo EN1 17 C5
lea Rd N16 73 C5
leigh
ngston KT5 198 B4
oodford E18 37 A2
leigh Ave N12 30 C4
leigh Ct N22 32 B2
leigh Gdns
160 A1
ley Cl SW17 180 D3
ley La SM1,SM5 218 C5

Woodlodge 4 SW19 179 B5
Wood Lodge Gdns
BR1 188 A3
Wood Lodge La BR4 224 A5
Woodman La E4 20 C6
Woodman Par 4 E16 122 C5
Woodmans Gr NW10 67 D3
Woodmans Mews W12 90 B2
Woodman St E16 122 C5
E16 122 D5
Woodmansterne Prim Sch
SW16 181 D2
Woodmansterne Rd
Mitcham SW16 181 D2
Sutton SM5 218 C1
Wood Mead N17 34 A4
Woodmere SE9 166 B3
Woodmere Ave CR0 206 D2
Woodmere Cl
10 SW11 137 A2
Croydon CR0 206 D2
Woodmere Ct N14 15 B4
Woodmere Gdns CR0 206 D2
Woodmere Way BR3 208 B4
Woodnook Rd SW16 181 B5
Woodpecker Cl
Bushey WD23 8 A3
Enfield N9 18 B5
Harrow HA3 24 D2
Woodpecker Mews
SE13 142 B1
Woodpecker Rd
6 SE14 141 A6
Woolwich SE28 124 C6
Wood Point 8 E16 99 A2
Woodquest Ave SE24 161 A6
Wood Rd TW17 192 C5
Wood Ride Barnet EN4 2 B4
Orpington BR5 211 C5
Woodridge Cl EN2 4 C4
Woodridge Prim Sch
N12 13 C1
Woodridings Ave HA5 23 B2
Woodridings Cl HA5 23 B3
Woodridings Ct N22 31 D2
Woodriffe Rd E11 54 B2
Wood Rise HA5 40 A4
Woodrow SE18 122 B2
Woodrow Ave UB4 83 D3
Woodrow Cl UB6 65 B1
Woodrow Ct 3 N17 34 B3
Woodruff Ho SW2 160 C5
Woodrush Cl 4 SE14 141 A5
Woodrush Way RM6 58 D5
Woodseer St
E1 95 D2 243 D4
Woodsford SE17 262 C1
Woodsford Sq
W14 113 A4 244 B2
Woodshire Rd RM10 81 D5
Woods Ho SW8 269 A2
Woodside N10 49 A6
NW11 47 C4
Buckhurst Hill IG9 21 C2
Palmers Green N13 16 C1
Walton-on-T KT12 194 A1
Wimbledon SW19 179 B5
Woodside Ave N12 30 A6
N6 48 D5
Chislehurst BR7 189 A5
Croydon SE25 206 B4
Thames Ditton KT10 196 C2
Wembley HA0 88 A6
Woodside Cl Ruislip HA4 39 B3
Stanmore HA7 25 B5
Tolworth KT5 199 A2
Wembley HA0 88 A6
Woodside Court Rd
CR0 206 A2
Woodside Cres DA15 167 C1
Woodside Ct 8 N12 29 D6
Ealing W5 110 A5
Enfield EN2 4 D4
Woodside End HA0 88 A6
Woodside Gdns
Chingford E4 35 D4
Tottenham N17 33 D1
Woodside Gn SE25 206 A3
Woodside Gr N12 14 A1
Woodside Grange Rd
N12 29 D6
Woodside Ho SW19 179 B4
Woodside Jun & Inf Sch
CR0 206 A2
Woodside Jun & Inf Schs
E17 54 A6
Woodside La DA5 168 D5
N12 14 A1
Woodside Park Ave
E17 54 B5
Woodside Park Rd N12 30 A6
Woodside Pk SE25 206 B3
Woodside Pl HA0 88 A6
Woodside Rd BR1 210 A4
E13 99 C3
Croydon SE25 206 B3
Kingston KT2 176 A3
Kingston KT3 177 C1
Northwood HA6 22 A3

Woodside Rd continued
Sidcup DA15 167 C1
Sutton SM1 218 A5
Woodford IG8 37 A6
Wood Green N22 32 C3
Woodside Sch DA17 125 D2
Woodside Sta SE25 206 B3
Woodside Way
Croydon CR0 206 C3
Streatham CR4 181 C2
Wood's Mews
W1 115 A6 248 A6
Woodsome Rd NW5 71 B5
Wood's Pl SE1 263 B5
Woodspring Rd SW19 157 A2
Wood's Rd SE15 140 B4
Wood St E16 121 B6
E17 54 B5
EC2 95 A1 242 B2
W4 111 C1
Barnet EN5 1 A1
Carshalton CR4 203 A2
Kingston KT1 175 D1
Kingston KT2 176 A2
Woodstar Ho 3 SE15 140 A5
Woodstead Gr HA8 26 A4
Woods The
Moor Park HA6 22 A5
Uxbridge UB10 60 D4
Woodstock Ave NW11 47 A2
W13 109 A3
Cheam SM3 201 B2
Isleworth TW7 153 A6
Southall UB1 85 B4
Woodstock Cl DA5 169 B3
Stanmore HA7 26 A1
Woodstock Cres N9 18 B5
Woodstock Ct SE11 260 D2
SE12 165 A5
Kingston KT2 176 D1
Woodstock Dr UB10 60 B4
Woodstock Gdns
Beckenham BR3 185 D3
Hayes UB4 83 D2
Ilford IG3 80 A6
Woodstock Gr W12 112 D4
Woodstock Ho 2 N5 73 A4
Hayes UB3 83 B2
Woodstock La N KT6 213 C6
Woodstock La S KT10,
KT6 213 C4
Woodstock Mews W1 238 B3
Woodstock Rd E7 77 C1
N4 50 C1
NW11 47 B1
W4 111 C3
Bushey WD23 8 D4
Chingford E17 36 B1
South Croydon CR0 221 B5
Wallington SM5,SM6 219 A3
Wembley HA0 66 B1
Woodstock Rise SM3 201 B2
Woodstock St W1 238 C1
Woodstock Terr E14 119 D6
Woodstock The SM3 201 B2
Woodstock Way CR4 181 C1
Woodstone Ave KT17,
KT4 216 A3
Wood Street Sta E17 54 B5
Woodsyre SE26 183 D6
Woodthorpe Rd
Ashford TW15 170 A6
Putney SW15 134 B1
Woodtree Cl NW4 28 C1
Wood Vale N10 49 C4
Dulwich SE22 162 B4
Woodvale Ave SE25 183 D1
Woodvale Ct BR1 187 B1
South Norwood SE25 205 D6
Woodvale Way NW11 68 D5
Woodvale Wlk SE27 183 A5
Woodview Ave E4 36 A6
Woodview Cl N4 50 D2
Kingston SW15 177 B6
Orpington BR6 227 A6
Woodville SE3 143 B4
Woodville Cl SE12 165 A6
Teddington TW11 175 A6
Woodville Ct 3 SE10 142 A4
Woodville Gdns NW11 46 D2
Ealing W5 88 A1
Ilford IG6 56 D5
Ruislip HA4 39 A2
Surbiton KT6 197 D2
Woodville Gr 2 DA16 146 A2
Woodville Ho SE1 263 C6
Woodville Rd E11 54 D1
E17 53 B5
N16 73 C3
NW11 47 A2
NW6 91 B5
Barnet EN5 1 D2
Ealing W5 87 D1
Morden SM4 201 C5
Richmond TW10 153 C1
South Norwood CR7 205 B6
Woodford E18 37 B1
Woodville St 16 SE7 122 A2
Woodville The W5 87 D1

Woodward Ave NW4 46 A4
Woodward Cl KT10 212 D2
Woodwarde Rd SE22 161 C5
Woodward Gdns
Dagenham RM9 80 C1
Harrow HA7 24 D3
Woodward Rd RM9 80 C1
Wood Way BR6 226 C6
Woodway Cres HA1 43 A3
Woodwell St SW18 158 A6
Wood Wharf SE10 142 A6
Woodyard Cl NW5 71 A3
Woodyard La SE21 161 C4
Woodyates Rd SE12 165 B4
Woolacombe Rd SE3 143 C3
Woolacombe Way
UB3 105 C2
Woolcombes Ct 4
SE16 118 D5
Woolden Ho 2 E4 20 C4
Wooler St
SE17 117 B1 262 D2
Woolf Cl SE28 124 B5
Woolf Ct 7 W3 111 A3
Woolf Mews WC1 240 A6
Woollaston Rd N4 50 D3
Woolley Ho SW9 138 D2
Woollon Ho 1 E1 96 C1
Woolmead Ave NW9 46 A2
Woolmer Gdns N18 34 A5
Woolmer Ho 2 E5 74 B6
Woolmer Rd N18 34 A5
Woolmore Prim Sch
E14 120 A6
Woolmore St E14 120 A6
Woolneigh St SW6 135 D3
Woolpack Ho 1 E9 74 C2
Wool Rd SW20 178 B4
Woolridge Way E9 74 C1
Woolstaplers Way
SE16 118 A2
Woolston Cl E17 34 D1
Woolstone Ho 7 E2 96 A6
Woolstone Rd SE23 163 A2
Woolven Ho SE3 142 D6
Woolwich Arsenal Sta
SE18 122 D2
Woolwich Church St
SE7,SE18 122 A3
Woolwich SE18 122 C3
Woolwich Comm
SE18 144 C6
Woolwich Dockyard Ind Est
SE18 122 A3
Woolwich Dockyard Sta
SE18 122 B2
Woolwich & Greenwich
Com Coll SE18 123 A2
Woolwich High St
SE18 122 C3
Woolwich Manorway
E16 122 D4
Woolwich Manor Way
E16 122 D5
E6 100 C1
Woolwich New Rd
SE18 122 D2
Woolwich Poly Sch for Boys
SE28 124 A5
Woolwich Rd DA7 147 C2
Belvedere DA17 125 C1
Erith SE2 125 B1
Greenwich SE7,SE10 121 C2
Wooster Gdns E14 98 B1
Wootton KT10 212 A4
Wootton Gr N3 29 C2
Wootton Ho SE9 167 B5
Wootton St
SE1 116 C5 251 B3
Worbeck Rd SE20 184 C1
Worcester Ave N17 34 A3
Worcester Cl NW2 68 B5
Croydon CR0 223 C6
Mitcham CR4 181 A1
Worcester Cres NW7 11 C1
Woodford IG8 37 C6
Worcester Ct N12 29 D5
40 W2 91 C2
Ashford TW15 170 D5
Ealing W7 86 D1
Harrow HA1 42 C6
Walton-on-T KT12 194 C1
Worcester Park KT4 215 C5
Worcester Dr W4 111 C4
Ashford TW15 170 D5
Worcester Gdns
SW11 158 D6
Northolt UB6 64 B2
Redbridge IG1 56 A2
Worcester Park KT4 215 C5
Worcester Ho SE11 261 A5
W2 236 A1
9 Putney SW15 156 C4
Worcester Mews 2
NW6 69 D2
Worcester Park Rd
KT4 215 B5
Worcester Park Sta
KT4 200 A1

Worcester Rd E17 34 D1
Belmont SM2 217 C1
Ilford E12 78 B4
11 Wimbledon SW19 179 B5
Worcesters Ave EN1 6 A5
Worcesters Prim Sch
EN1 5 D5
Wordsworth N8 50 C5
Wordsworth Ave E12 78 A1
E18 54 D6
Greenford UB6 86 B5
Wordsworth Ct HA1 42 B2
Wordsworth Dr KT4,
SM3 216 C4
Wordsworth Ho NW6 91 C4
15 SE18 144 C6
Wordsworth Par 1
N15 50 D5
Wordsworth Pl 11 NW5 70 D3
Wordsworth Rd DA16 145 C4
N16 73 C4
SE1 263 D3
Hampton TW12,TW13 173 B6
Penge SE20 184 D3
Wallington SM6 219 D2
Wordsworth Way UB7 104 B2
Wordsworth Wlk NW11 47 C5
Worfield St
SW11 136 C5 267 B3
Worgan St
SE11 116 B1 260 C2
SE16 118 D2
Working Men's Coll The
NW1 93 C5 232 A4
Worland Rd E15 76 C1
World Bsns Ctr TW6 127 A4
Worlds End La BR6 227 D1
World's End La EN2 4 B1
World's End Pas
SW10 266 C4
World's End Pl SW10 266 B4
Worley Ct NW2 68 D5
Worlidge St W6 112 C1
Worlingham Rd SE22 139 D1
Wormholt Park Prim Sch
W12 112 A6
Wormholt Rd W12 112 A5
Wormwood St EC2 243 A2
Wornington Rd W10 91 A2
Wornum Ho 3 NW6 91 A5
Woronzow Rd
NW8 92 C6 230 A5
Worple Ave
Isleworth TW7 153 A6
Wimbledon SW19 178 D3
Worple Cl HA2 41 B1
Worple Ct SW19 179 A4
Worple Prim Sch TW7 131 A1
Worple Rd
Isleworth TW7 131 A1
Wimbledon SW19,SW20 178 D2
Worple Road Mews
SW19 179 B4
Worple St SW14 133 B2
Worple Way Harrow HA2 41 B1
Richmond TW10 132 A1
Worship St EC2 95 C3 243 A5
Worslade Rd SW17 180 B6
Worsley Bridge Jun Sch
BR3 185 C3
Worsley Bridge Rd
BR3,SE6 185 C5
Worsley Ct N3 29 D4
Worsley Gr E5 74 A4
Worsley Ho 9 SE23 162 B2
Worsley Rd E11 76 C4
Worsopp Dr SW4 159 C6
Worth Cl BR6 227 C4
Worthfield Cl KT19 215 B1
Worth Gr SE17 262 C1
Worthing Cl 5 E15 98 C6
Worthing Rd TW5 129 B6
Worthington Cl CR4 203 B6
Worthington Ho EC1 234 B2
16 Streatham SW2 160 C4
Worthington Rd KT6 198 B1
Wortley Rd E6 77 D1
Thornton Heath CR0 204 C2
Worton Ct TW7 130 C1
Worton Gdns TW7 130 B3
Worton Hall Ind Est
TW7 130 C1
Worton Rd TW7 130 C2
Worton Way TW3,TW7 130 B3
Wotton Ct 8 E14 120 B6
Wotton Rd NW2 68 C5
18 SE8 141 B6
Wouldham Rd E16 98 D1
Wragby Rd E11 76 C5
Wrampling Pl N9 18 A3
Wrangthorne Wlk
CR0 220 C4
Wray Ave IG5 56 C6
Wrayburn Ho 25 SE16 118 A4
Wray Cres N4 72 B6
Wray Ct N4 72 B6
Wrayfield Rd SM3 216 D5
Wray Ho 11 SW2 160 A3
Wraysbury Cl TW4 151 A6

Wrays Way UB4 83 C3
Wrekin Rd SE18 145 A5
Wren Ave NW2 68 C4
Southall UB2 107 B2
Wren Cl E16 98 D1
N9 18 D3
Wren Cres WD23 8 A3
Wren Ct CR0 221 B4
Wren Gdns RM9 80 D3
Wren Ho 27 E3 97 A5
SW1 259 C1
4 Hampton TW12 173 D4
Wren Landing E14 119 C5
Wrenn Ho SW13 134 C6
Wren Path SE28 123 B4
Wren Rd SE5 139 B4
Dagenham RM9 80 D3
Sidcup DA14 168 C1
Wrens Ave TW15 171 A6
Wren's Park Ho E5 74 B6
Wren St WC1 94 B3 240 D6
Wrentham Ave NW10 90 D5
Wrenthorpe Rd BR1 186 C6
Wren View N6 49 C1
Wrenwood Way HA5 40 B5
Wrestlers Ct EC3 243 A2
Wrexham Rd E3 97 C5
Wricklemarsh Rd SE3 143 D4
Wrigglesworth St
SE14 140 D5
Wright Cl SE13 142 B1
Wright Gdns TW17 192 C4
Wright Ho SW15 156 B6
Wrighton Ct SM1 217 B2
Wright Rd TW5 128 C5
Wrights Cl RM10 81 D4
Wright's Gn SW4 137 D1
Wright's La
W8 113 D3 255 C6
Wrights Pl NW10 67 A2
Wright's Rd E3 97 B5
Wrights Rd SE25 205 C6
Wright's Row SM5 219 B4
Wrights Wlk SW14 133 B2
Writtle Ho 33 NW9 27 D1
Wrotham Ho SE1 262 D6
Beckenham BR3 185 B3
Wrotham Rd DA16 146 C4
11 NW1 71 C1
Barnet EN5 1 A3
Ealing W13 109 C5
Wrottesley Rd NW10 90 A5
SE18 145 A6
Wroughton Rd SW11 158 D5
Wroughton Terr NW4 46 B5
Wroxall Rd RM9 80 C2
Wroxham Gdns N11 31 D3
Wroxham Rd SE28 124 D6
Wroxton Rd SE15 140 C3
Wrythe Gn SM5 218 D5
Wrythe Green Rd SM5 218 D5
Wrythe La SM1,SM5,
SM4 218 C5
Wulfstan St W12 89 D1
Wyatt Cl SE16 119 B4
Bushey WD23 8 C4
Feltham TW13 150 D3
Hayes UB4 84 A2
Wyatt Ct HA0 66 A1
Wyatt Dr SW13 134 B5
Wyatt Ho NW8 236 D5
SE3 142 D3
Wyatt Park Mans 1
SW2 160 A2
Wyatt Park Rd SW2 160 B2
Wyatt Rd E7 77 A2
N5 73 A5
Wyatt's La E17 54 A6
Wybert St NW1 239 A6
Wyborne Ho NW10 67 A1
Wyborne Prim Sch
SE9 166 D3
Wyborne Way NW10 67 A1
Wyburn Ave EN5 1 B2
Wyche Gr CR2 221 A1
Wycherley Cl SE3 142 D5
Wycherley Cres EN5 13 D5
Wychwood Ave
Edgware HA8 25 D4
South Norwood CR7 205 A6
Wychwood Cl
Ashford TW16 172 A4
Edgware HA8 25 D4
Wychwood End N6 49 C2
Wychwood Gdns IG5 56 C5
Wychwood Ho N4 51 A2
Wychwood Way SE19 183 B4
Wyclif Ct EC1 234 C1
Wycliffe Cl DA16 145 D4
Wycliffe Ho 13 N16 73 C4
Wycliffe Rd SW19 179 D4
Wyclif St EC1 234 C1
Wycombe Ct SE3 143 A5
Wycombe Gdns NW11 69 C6
Wycombe Ho NW8 237 A6
Wycombe Pl SW18 158 A5

Wycombe Rd
Redbridge IG2 .56 B4
Tottenham N17 .34 A2
Wembley HA0 .88 C6
Wydell Cl SM4 .200 D3
Wydenhurst Rd CR0 .206 B2
Wydeville Manor Rd
SE12 .187 B6
Wye Cl BR6 .211 D2
Ashford TW15 .170 D6
Ruislip HA4 .39 A3
Wye Ct W13 .87 B2
Wyemead Cres E4 .20 C2
Wyersdale Ho N4 .51 A2
Wye St SW11 .136 B3
Wyevale Cl HA5 .40 A6
Wyfold Ho 10 SE2 .124 D4
Wyfold Rd
SW6 .135 A5 264 A3
Wyke Cl TW7 .130 D6
Wyke Gdns W7 .109 A3
Wykeham Ave RM9 .80 C2
Wykeham Cl UB7 .126 C6
Wykeham Ct NW4 .46 C4
Wykeham Gn RM9 .80 C2
Wykeham Hill HA9 .44 B1
Wykeham Ho SW19 .179 C2
Wykeham Prim Sch
NW9 .67 C5
Wykeham Rd NW4 .46 C4
Harrow HA3 .43 B5
Wykeham Rise N20 .13 A3
Wykehurst Ho SW17 .180 B5
Wyke Rd E3 .75 C1
Merton SW20 .178 C1
Wylchin Cl HA5 .39 D6
Wyldes Cl NW11 .48 A1
Wyldfield Gdns N9 .17 D2
Wyld Way HA9 .66 D2
Wyleu St SE23 .163 A4
Wylie Rd UB2 .107 C3
Wyllen Cl E1 .96 C3
Wylo Dr EN5 .12 A5
Wymering Mans 6 W9 91 C4
Wymering Rd W9 .91 C4
Wymondham Ct NW8 .229 D6
Wymond St SW15 .134 C2
Wynan Rd E14 .119 D1
Wynard Terr SE11 .260 D2
Wynash Gdns SM5 .218 C3
Wynaud Ct N22 .32 B4
Wynbourne Ct SE20 .184 B1
Wyncham Ave DA15 .167 C3
Wynchgate Harrow HA3 .24 C3
Southgate N14 .16 A4
Wyncroft Cl BR1 .210 B6
Wyndale Ave NW9 .44 C3
Wyndcliff Rd SE7 .143 B6
Wyndcroft Cl EN2 .4 D2
Wyndham Cl
Belmont SM2 .217 C1
Orpington BR6 .211 A1
Wyndham Cres N19 .71 C5
Hounslow TW4 .151 C5
Wyndham Ct W7 .109 A2
Wyndham Deedes Ho 27
E2 .96 A5
Wyndham Ho SW1 .258 A3
Wyndham Mews W1 .237 C3
Wyndham Pl W1 .237 C3
Wyndham Rd E6 .77 D1
SE5 .139 A5
W13 .109 B3
Barnet, London EN4 .14 D3
Kingston KT2 .176 B3
Wyndham St
W1 .92 D2 237 C4
Wyndham Yd W1 .237 C3
Wyneham Rd SE24 .161 B6
Wynell Rd SE23 .162 D1
Wynford Pl DA17 .147 C6
Wynford Rd N1 .94 B5 233 D4
Wynford Way SE9 .166 B1
Wynlie Gdns HA5 .22 B1
Wynn Bridge Cl IG8 .37 D2
Wynndale Rd E18 .37 B2
Wynne Ct 4 TW7 .131 A2
Wynne Ho SE14 .140 D4
Wynne Rd SW9 .138 C3
Wynn's Ave DA15 .168 A6
Wynnstay Gdns
W8 .113 C3 255 B6
Wynter Ho 20 SW9 .138 B3
Wynter St SW11 .136 A1
Wynton Gdns SE25 .205 D4
Wynton Pl W3 .88 D1
Wynyard Ho SE11 .260 D2
Wynyatt St EC1 .94 D4 234 C2
Wyre Gr Edgware HA8 .10 D1
Hayes UB3 .106 A2
Wyresdale Cres UB6 .86 D4
Wyteleaf Cl HA4 .39 A3
Wytham Ho NW8 .236 D5
Wythburn Ct W1 .237 C2
Wythburn Pl W1 .237 C2
Wythenshawe Rd RM10 81 C5
Wythens Wlk SE9 .166 D5
Wythes Cl BR1 .188 B1
Wythes Rd E16 .122 A5
Wythfield Rd SE9 .166 B5
Wyvenhoe Rd HA2 .64 A5
Wyvern Est The KT3 .200 A5
Wyvil Prim Sch
SW8 .138 A5 270 B4
Wyvil Rd SW8 .138 A5 270 A4
Wyvis St E14 .97 D2

X

Xavier Ho E17 .35 B1

Y

Yabsley St E14 .120 A5
Yaldam Ho SE1 .263 A3
Yalding Ho 20 E5 .74 B3
Yalding Rd SE16 .118 A2
Yale Cl TW4 .151 B6
Yale Ct NW6 .69 D3
Yarborough Rd SW19 .180 B2
Yardley Cl E4 .19 D6
Yardley Ct SM3 .216 D4
Yardley La E4 .19 D6
Yardley Prim Sch E4 .20 A5
Yardley St WC1 .234 A1
Yarmouth Cres N17 .52 B4
Yarmouth Pl W1 .248 C3
Yarnfield Sq 14 SE15 .140 A4
Yarnton Way DA17,
DA18 .125 B3
Yarrow Cres E6 .100 A2
Yarrow Ho 10 E14 .120 A3
W10 .90 C2
Yateley St SE18 .121 D3
Yatesbury Ct E5 .75 A3
Yates Ct NW2 .68 D2
Yates Ho 15 E2 .96 A4
Yatton Ho W10 .90 C2
Yeading Ave HA2 .41 A1
Yeading Ct UB4 .84 C3
Yeading Fork UB4 .84 C3
Yeading Gdns UB4 .84 B2
Yeading Ho UB4 .84 D2
Yeading Jun & Inf Schs
UB4 .84 C2
Yeading La Hayes UB4 .84 B2
Hayes, Northolt UB4,UB5 .84 C4
Yeadon Ho W10 .90 C2
Yeames Cl W13 .87 A1
Yearby Ho W10 .90 C3
Yeate St N1 .73 B1
Yeatman Rd N6 .48 D3
Yeats Cl NW10 .67 C2
Yeend Cl KT8 .195 C5
Yeldham Ho W6 .112 D1
Yeldham Rd W6 .112 D1
Yellowhammer Ct NW9 27 C1
Yelverton Lo TW1 .153 C4
Yelverton Rd SW11 .136 B3
Ye Market CR0 .221 B3
Yenston Cl SM4 .201 C3
Yeoman Cl E16 .122 D6
West Norwood SE27 .160 D1
Yeoman Ct TW5 .129 B5
Yeoman Ho SE1 .263 D2
Yeoman Rd UB5 .63 A1
Yeomans Acre HA4 .40 A3
Yeomans Mews TW7 .152 B6
Yeoman's Row
SW3 .114 C3 257 B5
Yeoman St SE8 .119 A2
Yeomans Way EN3 .6 C3
Yeoman's Yd E1 .253 D6
Yeo St E3 .97 D2
Yeovil Cl BR6 .227 C6
Yeovil Ho N7 .72 B6
W10 .90 C3
Yeovilton Pl KT2 .175 C5
Yerbury Prim Sch N19 .71 D5
Yerbury Rd N19 .71 D5
Yesodey Hatorah Sch
N16 .51 D2
Yester Dr BR7 .188 A3
Yester Pk BR7 .188 B4
Yester Rd BR7 .188 B3
Yew Ave UB7 .104 A6
Yew Cl IG9 .21 D2
Yewdale Cl BR1 .186 C4
Yewfield Rd NW10 .67 D2
Yew Gr NW2 .68 D4
Yew Ho SE14 .141 B3
Yews The TW15 .170 D6
Yew Tree Ave N2 .47 D6
Yew Tree Cl DA16 .146 A4
Yewtree Cl Harrow HA2 .41 D5
Wood Green N22 .31 C2
Yew Tree Cl
New Malden KT4 .199 C1
Southgate N21 .16 C4
Yew Tree Cotts KT10 .212 B6
Yew Tree Ct 4 NW11 .47 B4
Elstree WD6 .9 D5
8 Sutton SM2 .218 A1
Yew Tree Gdns RM6 .59 A4
Yew Tree Grange 2
W5 .109 C6
Yew Tree Ho KT4 .199 C1
Yew Tree Rd W12 .111 D6
Yewtree Rd BR3 .207 B6
Yew Tree Rd UB10 .82 B6
Yew Trees TW17 .192 B5
Yew Tree Wlk TW4 .151 B6
Yew Wlk HA1 .42 C1
Yiewsley Ct UB7 .104 A5
Yoakley Rd N16 .73 C6
Yoke Cl N7 .72 A2
Yolande Gdns SE9 .166 A6
Yonge Pk N4,N7 .72 C5
York Ave DA15 .167 D2
SE17 .262 B2
Ealing W7 .108 C5
Hayes UB3 .83 A1
Mortlake SW14 .155 A6
Stanmore HA7 .25 B1
York Bldgs
WC2 .116 A6 250 B5
York Bridge
NW1 .93 A3 238 A6
York Cl 17 SE5 .139 A3
Ealing W7 .108 C5
Morden SM4 .201 D5
Newham E6 .100 B1
York Ct Beckenham BR3 186 B2
Kingston KT2 .175 D4
Wallington SM6 .219 C3
York Gate NW1 .238 B5
Southgate N14 .16 A4
York Gr SE15 .140 C4
York Hill SE27,SW16 .160 D1
York Ho N1 .233 C3
N5 .72 C3
3 N7 .71 D2
1 NW4 .28 D1
SE1 .116 B3 260 D5
SW3 .257 D2
York Ho *continued*
W1 .237 C4
W3 .111 A6
W8 .245 C2
10 Acton W3 .88 C1
Chingford E4 .35 C6
Enfield EN2 .5 B4
Forest Hill SE26 .184 C5
1 Ilford IG1 .78 D6
4 Kingston KT2 .176 B3
Richmond TW10 .154 C6
Richmond TW9 .132 C4
South Norwood SE25 .205 C5
York House Pl
W8 .113 D4 245 C2
Yorkland Ave DA16 .145 D1
Yorkley Ho W10 .90 C3
York Mans 1 NW9 .46 A3
SW11 .268 B2
W1 .238 A4
York Mews NW5 .71 B3
Ilford IG1 .78 C5
York Par NW9 .46 A3
Brentford TW8 .109 D1
York Pl SW11 .136 B2
WC2 .250 B5
Ilford IG1 .78 C6
York Place Mans
NW1 .237 D4
York Rd E10 .76 A5
E17 .52 D4
E7 .77 A2
N11 .31 D4
SE1 .116 B4 250 D2
SW11,SW18 .136 B2
W3 .89 B1
W5 .109 C3
Belmont SM1,SM2 .217 C1
Brentford TW8 .109 D1
Chingford E4 .35 C5
Edmonton N18 .34 B5
Hounslow TW3 .129 D2
Ilford IG1 .78 C6
Kingston KT2 .176 B3
New Barnet EN5 .14 B6
Pinner HA6 .22 A1
4 Richmond TW10 .154 B6
Southgate N21 .17 B4
Teddington TW11 .174 C6
Thornton Heath CR0 .204 C2
Wimbledon SW19 .180 A4
York Rise BR6 .227 C6
NW5 .71 B5
York Road Bsns Ctr
SW11 .136 B3
Yorkshire Cl N16 .73 C5
Yorkshire Gdns N18 .34 B5
Yorkshire Grey SE9 .165 D6
Yorkshire Grey Yd
WC1 .240 C3
Yorkshire Rd E14 .97 A1
Mitcham CR4 .204 A5
York Sq 14 E14 .97 A1
York St W1 .92 D2 237 D4
Barking IG11 .101 A6
York St *continued*
Carshalton CR4 .2
Twickenham TW1 .1
York St Chambers W1 2
York Terr EN2 .
York Terr E
NW1 .93 A3 2
York Terr W
NW1 .93 A3 2
Yorkton St E2 .
York Way N1 .2
N1,N7,NW1 .
N20 .
Chessington KT9 .2
Twickenham TW13 .1
York Way Ct N1 .2
Youngmans Cl EN2 .
Young Rd E16 .
Young's Bldgs EC1 .2
Youngs Ct SW11 .2
Youngs Rd IG2 .
Young St W8 .113 D4 2
Yoxall Ho W10 .
Yoxley App IG2 .
Yoxley Dr IG2 .
Yukon Rd SW12 .1
Yuletide Cl NW10 .
Yunus Khan Cl E17 .

Z

Zampa Rd SE16 .1
Zander Ct E2 .
Zangwill Ho NW6 .
Zangwill Rd SE18,SE3 .1
Zealand Ave UB7 .1
Zealand Ho 11 SE5 .1
4 SE7 .1
Zealand Rd E3 .
Zennor Rd SW12 .1
Zenoria St SE22 .1
Zermatt Rd CR7 .2
Zetland Ho W8 .2
Zetland St E14 .
Zion Ho 6 E1 .
Zion Pl CR7 .2
Zion Rd CR7 .2
Zoar St SE1 .117 A5 2
Zodiac Ct CR0 .2
Zodiac Ho 3 E3 .
Zoffany St N19 .

List of numbered locations

atlas shows thousands more place names than
other London street atlas. In some busy areas it
possible to fit the name of every place.

re not all names will fit, some smaller places are
vn by a number. If you wish to find out the
e associated with a number, use this listing.

*places in this list are also listed normally in
ndex.*

34

A5 8 St James's Ct

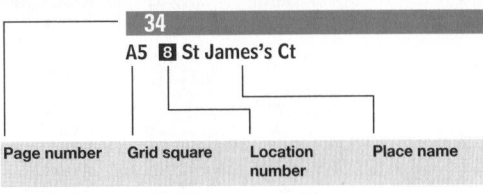

Page number | Grid square | Location number | Place name

Hertswood Ct
Sunbury Ct
Meriden Ho
Norfolk Ct
Morrison Ct
Kingshill Ct
Baronsmere Ct
Chartwell Ct

Braeburn Ct
Bramley Ct
Cox Ct
Golden Ct
Pippin Ct
Russet Ct
High Birch Ct
Joystone Ct
Mark Lo
Edgeworth Ct

Woodfield Cl
Fielders Cl

Watling Ct
Stuart Ct
Westview Ct
Potters Mews

3
Rowan Wlk
Ford Ho
Glenwood Ho
Whitegates
Lisa Lo
South Lo
Hockington Ct
Eysham Ct
Springfields
Bure Ct
Coleridge Ct
Chaucer Ct

4
Redrose Trad Ctr
Lancaster Road Ind Est
Feline Ct
Brookhill Ct
Littlegrove Ct
Desmond Ho

5
Tregenna Cl
Catherine Ct
Conisbee Ct
Ashmead
Dennis Par
Broadway The
Southgate Cir
Station Par
Bourneside
Bourneside Cres

7
Wade Ho
Newport Lo
Halcyon
Lerwick Ct
Anchor Ct
Grassmere Ct
Datchworth Ct
Trentham Lo
Austin Ct
Cedar Grange
Brookview Ct
Chestbrook Ct

13 Paddock Lo
14 Hamlet Ct
15 Haven Lo

18
A1 1 Plevna Ho
2 Lea Ho
3 Brook Ho
4 Valley Ho
5 Chiltern Ho
6 Blenheim Ho
7 Penn Ho
8 Romany Ho
9 Gilpin Ho
10 Anvil Ho
11 Well Ho
12 Passmore Ho
13 Durbin Ho
A2 1 Market Par
2 Beechwood Mews
3 Keats Par
4 Cedars Rd
5 Cross Keys Cl
6 Dorman Pl
7 Concourse The

20
1 Lea Ct
2 Park Ct
3 Conference Cl
4 Berrybank Cl
5 Russell Lo
6 Brunswick Lo
7 Kenilworth Ct
8 Trinity Ct
9 Kingsmead Lo
10 Fairlawns
A3 1 Knight Ct
2 Grant Ct
3 Chantry The
4 Bowyer Ct
5 Pineview Ct
6 Ellen Ct
7 Leaview Ct
8 Chelsea Ct
9 Bramley Ct
10 Garenne Ct
11 Kendal Ct
B2 1 Temple Hall Ct
2 Larkshall Bsns Ctr
3 Endlebury Ct
4 James Ct
5 Holmes Ct
B3 1 Maddox Ct
2 Village Arc The
3 Cambridge Rd
4 Crown Bldgs
5 Pentney Rd
6 Scholars Ho
7 Cranworth Cres
C4 1 Connaught Ct
2 Woolden Ho
3 Fairmead Ct
4 Lockhart Lo
5 Cavendish Ct
6 Oakwood Ct
7 Plains The
8 Hadleigh Ct
9 Forest Ho
10 Mathieson Ho

21
C2 1 Westbury Ct
2 Palmerston Ct
3 Ibrox Ct
4 Richard Burton Ct
5 Queens Ct
6 Gunnels Ct & Hastingwood Ct
7 Marlborough Ct
8 Avenue The
9 Tara Ct
D2 1 Regency Lo
2 Kings Ct
3 Beech Ct
4 Sycamore Ho

22
C1 1 Northcote
2 Edwin Ware Ct
3 Chalfont Wlk
4 Maple Ct
5 Montesole Ct

23
B3 1 St Cuthberts Gdns
2 Cherry Croft Gdns
3 Cornwall Cl
4 Dunsford Ct

25
C5 1 Belgrave Gdns
2 Heywood Ct
3 Norfolk Ho
4 Garden Ct
5 Chatsworth Ct
6 Chartridge Ct
7 Hardwick Cl
8 Cheltenham Ct
9 Cargrey Ho
10 Holbein Ho
11 Goodwood Cl
C6 1 Bickley Ct
2 Kelmscott Ct
3 Elstree Ho
4 Brompton Ct
5 Kenmare Ct

27
A1 1 Colesworth Ho
2 Crokesley Ho
3 Curtlington Ho
4 Clare Ho
5 Kedyngton Ho
A3 1 Tadbourne Ct
2 Truman Cl
3 Lords Ct
4 Hutton Row
5 Compton Cl
6 Botham Cl
7 Bradman Row
A6 1 Iris Wlk
2 Sycamore Cl
B5 1 Monarchs Ct
2 Kensington Ct
C2 1 Rufforth Ct
2 Riccal Ct
3 Lindholme Ct
4 Driffield Ct
5 Jack Ashley Ct
6 Folkingham La
7 Leander Ct
8 Daniel Ct
9 Nimrod
10 Nisbet
11 Pixton
12 Rapide
13 Ratier
D1 1 Gauntlet
2 Guilfoyle
3 Grebe
4 Gates
5 Galy
6 Folland
7 Firefly
8 Halifax
9 Debussy
10 Crosbie
11 Grant Ct
12 Ham Ct
13 Deal Ct
14 Ember Ct
15 Canterbury Ct
16 Beaumont Ct
17 Cirrus
18 Defiant
19 Dessouter
20 Douglas
21 Cobham
22 Clayton
23 Camm
24 Bradon
25 Boarhound
26 Bodmin
27 Bleriot
28 Blackburn
29 Audax
30 Anson
31 Albatross
32 Arran Ct
33 Mavis Ct
34 Goosander Ct
35 Platt Halls (a)
36 Writtle Ho
37 Platt Halls (b)
38 Platt Halls (c)
D2 1 Slatter
2 Sopwith
3 Saimet
4 Sassoon
5 Roe
6 Orde
7 Osprey
8 Prodger
9 Randall
10 Porte
11 Norris
12 Nardini
13 Noel
14 Nicolson
15 Napier
16 Nighthawk
17 Moorhouse
18 Moineau
19 Mitchell
20 Lysander
21 Lillywhite
22 Martynside
23 March
24 Kemp
25 Mercury
26 Merlin
27 Hudson
28 Hawker
29 Hawfinch
30 Heracles
31 Hector
D3 1 Wellington
2 Wheeler
3 Whittaker
4 Whittle
5 Tedder
6 Cranwell Ct
7 Tait
8 Spooner

28
D1 1 York Ho
2 Windsor Ho
3 Regency Cres
4 Normandy Ho
5 Allerton Ct

29
C2 1 Sherringham Ct
2 St Ronan's
3 Crescent Rise
4 Elm Ct
D6 1 Brookfield Ct
2 Magnolia Ct
3 Dunbar Ct
4 Haughmond
5 Nansen Village
6 Beechcroft Ct
7 Speedwell Ct
8 Woodside Ct
9 Speedwell Ho
10 Rebecca Ho
11 Ashbourne Ct
12 Forest Ct
13 Beecholme
14 Greville Lo
15 St Johnstone Ho

30
B1 1 New Trinity Rd
2 Garden Ho
3 Todd Ho
4 Sayers Ho
5 Mowbray Ho
6 Bouchier Ho
7 Cleveland Ho
8 Goodyear Ho
9 Lochleven Ho
10 Berwick Ho
11 Oak Ho
12 Willow Wlk
13 Craven Ho
14 Willow Ho
15 Vane Ho
16 Foskett Ho
17 Elmfield Ho
18 Sycamore Ho
19 Netherwood
D5 1 Halliwick Ct
2 Halliwick Court Par
3 Queen's Par
4 St John's Village
5 Hartland Ct
6 Kennard Mans
7 Bensley Cl

31
A3 1 Campe Ho
2 Betstyle Ho
3 Pymmes Brook Ho
4 Mosswell Ho
5 Hampden Ct
6 Crown Ct
B1 1 Cedar Ct
2 Carisbrook
3 St Ivian Ct
4 Barrington Ct
5 Essex Lo
B5 1 Caradoc Evans Cl
2 Roberts Ho
3 Lorne Ho
B6 1 Grovefield
2 Lapworth
3 Stewards Holte Wlk
4 Sarnes Ct
5 Stanhope Ho
6 Holmsdale Ho
C5 1 Barbara Martin Ho
2 Jerome Ct
3 Limes Cl
4 Arnos Grove Ct
5 Cedar Ct
6 Betspath Ho
7 Curtis Ho
8 Mason Ho
9 Danford Ho
10 New Southgate Ind Est
11 Palmer's Ct

32
A4 1 Brownlow Ct
2 Latham Ct
3 Fairlawns
4 Beaumaris
C1 1 Penwortham Ct
2 Tarleton Ct
3 Holmeswood Ct
4 Kwesi Johnson Ct
5 Sandlings The

33
D1 1 Honeysett Rd
2 Wilson's Ave
3 Palm Tree Ct
4 Stoneleigh Ct
5 Brook St
D3 1 Charles Ho
2 Moselle Ho
3 Ermine Ho
4 Kathleen Ferrier Ct
5 Concord Ho
6 Rees Ho
7 Nursery Ct
8 William Rainbird Ho
D4 1 Regan Ho
2 Isis Ho
3 Boundary Ct
4 Stellar Ho
5 Cooperage Cl

34
A5 1 Angel Pl
2 Cross St
3 Scott Ho
4 Beck Ho
5 Booker Rd
6 Bridport Ho
7 Cordwain Ho
8 St James's Ct
9 Highmead
A6 1 Walton Ho
2 Alma Ho
3 Brompton Ho
4 Field Ho
5 Bradwell Mews
6 Angel Corner Par
7 Paul Ct
8 Cuthbert Rd
9 Brockenhurst Mews
B3 1 Kenneth Robbins Ho
2 Charles Bradlaugh Ho
3 Woodrow Ct
4 Cheviot
5 Corbridge
6 Whittingham
7 Eastwood Cl
8 Alnwick
9 Bamburgh
10 Bellingham
11 Briaris Cl

36
B5 1 Hedgemoor Ct
2 Hewitt Ho
3 Castle Ho
4 Bailey Ct
5 Harcourt Ho
6 Gerboa Ct
D1 1 Chatham Rd
2 Washington Rd
3 Cherry Tree Ct
4 Grosvenor Lo
5 Torfell
D2 1 Hillboro Ct
2 Dorchester Ct

37
A1 1 Chiltons The
2 Ullswater Ct
3 Leigh Ct
4 Woburn Ct
A2 1 Lindal Ct
2 Hockley Ct
3 Woodleigh
4 Milne Ct
5 Cedar Ct
6 Elizabeth Ct
7 Silvermead
8 Laurel Mead Ct
9 Mitre Ct
10 Pevensey Ct
11 Lyndhurst Ct
A3 1 New Jubilee Ct
2 Chartwell Ct
3 Greenwood
4 Solway Lo
A4 1 Terrace The
2 Broomhill Ct
3 Clifton Ct
4 Fairstead Lo
5 Hadleigh Lo
6 Broadmead Ct
7 Wilton Ct
8 Fairfield Ct
9 Higham Ct
A6 1 Tree Tops
2 Cranfield Ct
B1 1 Station Est
2 Station App
3 James Ct
C3 1 Liston Way
2 Elizabeth Ct
3 Coopersale Cl
4 Sunset Ct
5 Lambourne Ct
C4 1 Hope Cl
2 Rex Par
3 Shalford
4 Rodings The

40
C1 1 Salisbury Ho
2 Rodwell Cl
3 Pretoria Ho
4 Ottawa Ho
5 Swallow Ct

42
D3 1 Nightingale Ct
2 St John's Ct
3 Gayton Ct
4 Wilton Pl
5 Murray Ct
6 Cymbeline Ct
7 Knowles Ct
8 Charville Ct
9 Lime Ct
10 Petherton Ct
12 Chalfont Ct
D4 1 Crystal Ctr The
2 Blue Point Ct
3 Ryan Ho
5 Bruce Ho
7 Ingram Ho
8 Arless Ho
9 Leaf Ho

46
A2 1 Milton Rd
2 Stanley Rd
A3 1 York Mans
2 Telford Rd
A5 1 Pilkington Ct
2 Cousins Ct
3 Seton Ct
4 Frensham Ct
5 Chatton Ct
6 Geraldine Ct
7 Swynford Gdns
8 Miller Ct
9 Roffey Ct
10 Peace Ct

11 Rambler Ct
12 Lion Ct
13 Wenlock Gdns
14 Dogrose Ct
15 Harry Ct
16 Tribune Ct
17 Bonville Gdns
18 Pearl Ct
B4 1 Vivian Mans
2 Parade Mans
3 Georgian Ct
4 Florence Mans
5 Park Mans
6 Cheyne Cl
7 Queens Par
8 Central Mans
C5 1 Courtney Ho
2 Golderton
3 Thornbury
4 Brampton La
5 Ashwood Ho
6 Longford Ct
7 Short St
D5 1 Midford Ho
2 Rockfield Ho
3 Lisselton Ho
4 Acrefield Ho

47

B2 1 Berkeley Ct
2 Exchange Mans
3 Beechcroft Ct
4 Nedahall Ct
B3 1 Charlton Lo
2 Clifton Gdns
B4 1 Hallswelle Par
2 Belmont Par
3 Temple Fortune Ho
4 Yew Tree Ct
5 Temple Fortune Par
6 Courtleigh
7 Arcade Ho
8 Queens Ct
9 Temple Fortune Ct
B5 1 Monkville Par
2 Ashbourne Par

48

A6 1 St Mary's Gn
2 Dunstan Cl
3 Paul Byrne Ho
4 Longfield Ct
5 Warwick Ct
6 Branksome Ct
7 Sherwood Hall

49

B6 1 Dorchester Ct
2 Old Chapel Pl
3 Athenaeum Pl
4 Risborough Cl
C1 1 Calvert Ct
2 Academy The
3 Whitehall Mans
4 Pauntley St
5 Archway Hts
6 Pauntley Ho
D1 1 Louise White Ho
2 Levison Way
3 Sanders Way
D2 1 Eleanor Rathbone Ho
2 Christopher Lo
3 Monkridge
4 Marbleford Ct
5 High London
6 Garton Ho
7 Hilltop Ho
8 Caroline Martyn Ho
9 Arthur Henderson Ho
10 Margaret Mcmillan Ho
11 Enid Stacy Ho
12 Mary McArthur Ho
13 Bruce Glasier Ho
14 John Wheatley Ho
15 Keir Hardie Ho
16 Monroe Ho
17 Iberia Ho
18 Lygoe Ho
19 Lambert Ho
20 Shelbourne Ho
21 Arkansas Ho
22 Lafitte Ho
23 Shreveport Ho
24 Packenham Ho
25 Orpheus Ho
26 Fayetville Ho
27 Bayon Ho
D4 1 Kelland Cl
2 Veryan Ct
3 Coulsdon Ct

50

A1 1 Beeches The
2 Lambton Ct
A2 1 Marie Lloyd Gdns
2 Jessie Blythe La
3 Leyden Mans
4 Brambledown
5 Lochbie
6 Edith Cavell Cl
A5 1 Mackenzie Ct
2 Stowell Ho
3 Campsbourne Ho
B1 1 Lawson Ct
2 Wiltshire Ct
3 Hutton Ct
D5 1 Wordsworth Par

51

A2 1 Finmere Ho
2 Keynsham Ho
3 Kilpeck Ho
4 Knaresborough Ho
5 Leighfield Ho
6 Lonsdale Ho
7 Groveley Ho
8 Wensleydale Ho
9 Badminton Ct
B2 1 Selwood Ho
2 Mendip Ho
3 Ennerdale Ho
4 Delamere Ho
5 Westwood Ho
6 Bernwood Ho
7 Allerdale Ho
8 Chattenden Ho
9 Farningham Ho
10 Oakend Ho
C1 1 Godstone Ct
2 Farnham Ct
3 Milford Ct
4 Cranleigh Ct
5 Haslemere Ct
6 Belmont Ct
7 Hockworth Ho
8 Garratt Ho
9 Fairburn Ho
C3 1 Oatfield Ho
2 Perry Ct
3 Henrietta Ho
4 Bournes Ho
5 Chisley Rd
6 Twyford Ho
7 Langford Cl
8 Hatchfield Ho
D1 1 Stamford Hill Mans
2 Montefiore Ct
3 Berwyn Ho
4 Clent Ho
5 Chiltern Ho
6 Laindon Ho
7 Pentland Ho
D2 1 Regent Ct
2 Stamford Lo
3 Holmwood Ct
D3 1 Sherboro Rd
2 Westcott Cl
3 Cadoxton Ave
4 Slater Ho
D4 1 Westerfield Rd
2 Suffield Rd
D5 1 Greenway Cl
2 Tottenham Gn E
3 Tottenham Gn E South Side
4 Deaconess Ct
5 Elliot Ct
6 Bushmead Cl
7 Beaufort Ho
8 Tynemouth Terr
D6 1 Holcombe Rd
2 Chaplin Rd
3 Reynardson's Ct
4 Protheroe Ho

52

A1 1 Stamford Grove E
2 Stamford Mans
3 Grove Mans
4 Stamford Grove W
B1 1 Hawkwood Mount
2 Holmbury View
3 High Hill Ferry
4 Leaside Ho
5 Courtlands
6 Ivy Ho
7 Shelford Ct

53

A4 1 Hammond Ct
2 St James Apartments
3 Grange The
A5 1 Bristol Park Rd
2 Stoneydown Ho
3 Callonfield
4 Hardyng Ho
C1 1 Wellington Mans
2 Clewer Ct
3 Cochrane Ct
C5 1 Westbury Ho
2 Hatherley Ho
3 Vintry Mews
4 Tylers Ct
5 Merchants Lo
6 Gillards Mews
7 Blacksmiths Ho
8 Central Par
D1 1 Fitzgerald Ct
2 Bechervaise Ct
3 Underwood Ct
D2 1 Station Ct
2 Howell Ct
3 Atkinson Ct
4 Russell Ct
5 St Luke Ct
6 St Matthews Ct
7 St Mark's Ct
8 St Elizabeth Ct
9 Emmanuel Ct
10 St Thomas Ct
11 Beaumont Ho
12 Shelley Ct
13 St Paul's Twr
14 Flack Ct
15 King Ct
16 Osborne Ct
17 Muriel Ct
18 All Saints Twr
19 St Josephs Ct
20 Mitchell Ct
21 Cornwell Ct
D5 1 Nash Ho
2 St Columbas Ho
3 Attlee Terr
4 Astins Ho
5 Lindens The
6 Kevan Ct
7 Squire's Almshouses
8 Berry Field Cl
9 Holmcroft Ho
10 Connaught Ct
D6 1 Hollingbury Ct
2 Mace Ho
3 Gaitskell Ho
4 Hancocke Ho
5 Trinity Ho
6 Fanshaw Ho
7 Hilltop
8 Batten Ho
9 Bradwell Ho
10 Walton Ho
11 Temple Ho
12 Gower Ho
13 Maple Ho
14 Poplars Ho
15 Cedars Ho
16 Kimm Ho
17 O'Grady Ho
18 Latham Ho
19 Powell Ct
20 Crosbie Ho

54

A2 1 Ayerst Ct
2 Dare Ct
3 St Edwards Ct
A4 1 Jane Sabina Colard's Almshouses
2 Ellen Miller Ho
3 Tom Smith Ho
A5 1 Northwood Twr
2 Walnut Ct
3 Albert Whicher Ho
4 Pelly Ct
5 Ravenswood Road Ind Est
6 Holland Ct
7 Emberson Ho
8 St Mark's Ho
9 Alfred Villas
A6 1 St David's Ct
2 Golden Par
3 Chestnuts Ct
4 Matthew Ct
5 Gilbert Ho
6 Manning Ho
7 Southgate Ho
8 Boyden Ho
9 Prospect Ho
10 Newton Ho

55

A3 1 Aldham Hall
2 Parkside Ct
3 Mapperley Cl
4 Weavers Ho
5 Cyns Ct
6 Reed Mans
7 Thornton Ho
8 Hardwick Ct
A4 1 Kingsley Grange
2 Station Par
3 Gwynne Ho
4 Staveley Ct
5 Devon Ho
6 Thurlow Ct
7 Hollies The
8 Little Holt
9 Dudley Ct
10 Woodland Ct
11 Struan Ho
12 Westleigh Ct
A5 1 Shernwood Ho
2 Orwell Lo
3 Hermitage Ct
4 Gowan Lea
5 Woodford Ho
6 Eagle Ct
7 Newbury Ct
8 Shelley Ct
9 Hardy Ct
10 Dickens Ct
11 Byron Ct
A6 1 Millbrook
2 Elmbrook
3 Grange The
4 Glenavon Lo
5 Glenwood Ct
6 Ferndown
7 Embassy Ct
8 Orestes Ct
9 Walbrook
10 Helmsley
11 Snaresbrook Hall
B4 1 Nightingale Ct
2 Chelston Ct
3 Grosvenor Ct
4 Louise Ct
5 St Davids Ct
6 Cedar Ct
7 Shrubbery The
B6 1 Victoria Ct
2 Kenwood Gdns
3 Thaxted Lo
4 Albert Rd
5 Albert Ho
6 Falcon Ct
7 Deborah Ct
8 Swift Ho
9 Pulteney Gdns
10 Spring Ct
11 Trinity Gdns

56

B4 1 High View Par
2 Spurway Par

57

A3 1 Catherine Ct
2 Lincoln Ct
3 Ivy Terr
4 Newbury Cotts

58

B1 1 Caledonian Cl
2 Talisman Cl
3 Norseman Cl
4 Frank Slater Ho
5 Brook's Mans
6 Brook's Par
B2 1 Mitre Ct
2 Coppins The
3 Stanetto Ct
4 Wilnett Ct
5 Wilnett Villas
D2 1 Pavement Mews
2 Chadview Ct
3 Granary Ct
4 Bedwell Ct
5 Chapel La
6 Faulkner Cl
7 Maple Ct
8 Willow Ct
9 Cedar Terr

63

C2 1 Wimborne Ct
2 Haydock Green Flats
3 Brighton Dr
4 Blaydon Ct
5 Fakenham Cl
6 Rutland Ho
7 Windsor Ho

65

D3 1 Oaklands Ct
2 Lowry Lo
3 Morritt Ho
4 Lancelot Par
5 Willow Tree Ct
6 Snow Ct

66

A2 1 Montrose Cres
2 Peggy Quirke Ct
3 Copland Mews
4 Coronet Par
5 Charlotte Ct
A3 1 Market Way
3 Lodge Ct
4 Central Sq
5 Manor Ct
6 Rupert Ave

67

A5 1 Curie Ho
2 Darwin Ho
6 Priestley Ho
7 Rutherford Ho
8 Fleming Ho
9 Lister Ho
10 Edison Ho
B1 1 Kingthorpe Terr
2 Scott Ho
3 Peary Ho
4 Shackleton Ho
5 Amundsen Ho
6 Brentfield Ho
7 Nansen Ho
8 Stonebridge Ct
9 Magellan Ct
10 Leadbetter Ct
11 Viant Ho
12 Jefferies Ho
13 Diamond St
C1 1 Beveridge Rd
C5 1 Hazelwood Ct
2 Winslow Cl

68

A2 1 Regency Mews
2 Tudor Mews
A5 1 Bourne Ho
2 Carton Ho
3 Woodbridge Cl
4 Mackenzie Ho
5 Banting Ho

69

A1 1 Fountain Ho
2 Kingston Ho
3 Waverley Ct
4 Weston Ho
5 Mapes Ho
6 Athelstan Gdns
7 Leff Ho
B1 1 Alma Birk Ho
2 Brooklands Ct
3 Brooklands Court Apartments
4 Cleveland Mans
5 Buckley Ct
6 Webheath
B5 1 Mortimer Cl
2 Sunnyside Ho
3 Sunnyside
4 Prospect Pl
C1 1 Linstead St
2 Embassy Ho
3 Acol Ct
4 Kings Wood Ct
5 Douglas Ct
6 King's Gdns
7 Carlton Mans
8 Smyrna Mans
9 New Priory Ct
10 Queensgate Pl
11 Brondesbury Mews
C2 1 Dene Mans
2 Sandwell Cres
3 Sandwell Mans
4 Hampstead West
5 Redcroft
C3 1 Orestes Mews
2 Walter Northcott Ho
3 Polperro Mans
4 Lyncroft Mans
5 Marlborough Mans
6 Alexandra Mans
7 Cumberland Mans
8 Cavendish Mans
9 Ambassador Ct
10 Welbeck Mans
11 Inglewood Mans
C5 1 Portman Hts
2 Hermitage Ct
3 Moreland Ct
4 Wendover Ct
D2 1 Beswick Mews
2 Worcester Mews
3 Minton Mews
4 Doulton Mews
5 Laurel Ho
6 Sandalwood Ho
7 Iroko Ho
8 Banyan Ho
10 Ebony Ho
11 Rosemont Mans

70

A1 1 Harrold Ho
2 Glover Ho
3 Byron Ct
4 Nalton Ho
A2 1 Petros Gdns
2 Heath Ct
3 Imperial Twrs
4 Fairhurst
5 St John's Ct
6 New College Ct
7 Chalford
8 Sutherland Ho
A4 1 Windmill Hill
2 Highgrove Point
3 Gainsborough Ho
4 Heath Mans
5 Pavilion Ct
6 Holly Berry La
7 New Campden Ct
8 Benham's Pl
9 Holly Bush Vale
10 Gardnor Mans
11 Mansfield Pl
12 Streatley Pl
13 New Ct
14 Bird In Hand Yd
15 Spencer Wlk
16 Wells Ct
17 Perrin's Ct
18 Village Mount
19 Prince Arthur Ct
20 Prince Arthur Mews
21 Monro Ho
22 Ellerdale Cl
23 Holly Bush Hill
24 Prospect Pl
A5 2 Stamford Cl
B1 1 New College Par
2 Northways Par
3 Noel Ho
4 Campden Ho
5 Centre Hts
6 Hickes Ho
7 Swiss Terr
8 Leitch Ho
9 Jevons Ho
10 Langhorne Ct
11 Park Lo
12 Avenue Lo
B2 1 Belsize Park Mews
2 Baynes Mews
3 McCrone Mews
B3 1 Belsize Court Garages
2 Roscommon Ho
3 Akenside Ct
C2 1 Banff Ho
2 Glenloch Ct
3 Havercourt
4 Holmfield Ct
5 Gilling Ct
6 Howitt Cl
7 Manor Mans
8 Straffan Lo
9 Romney Ct
10 Lancaster Stables
11 Eton Garages
D1 1 Hancock Nunn Ho
2 Higginson Ho
3 Duncan Ho
4 Mary Wharrie Ho
5 Rockstraw Ho
6 Cleaver Ho
7 Chamberlain St
8 Sharples Hall St
9 Primrose Mews
10 Rothwell St
11 St Georges Mews
D2 1 Alder Ho
2 Hornbeam
3 Whitebea
4 Aspen Ho
5 Rowan Ho
6 Beech Ho
7 Chestnut H
8 Oak Ho
9 Willow Ho
10 Sycamore
11 Maple Ho
12 Hazel Ho
13 Elaine Ct
14 Faircourt
15 Walham C
16 Stanbury C
17 Priory Mar
18 Wellington
19 Grange Th
D3 1 Cayford Ho
2 Du Maurie
3 Isokon Fla
4 Palgrave H
5 Garnett Ho
6 Stephenso
7 Park Dwel
8 Siddons H
9 Mall Studi
10 Park Hill W
11 Wordswort
12 Fraser Reg Ct
13 St Pancras Almshouse

71

A1 1 Bridge Ho
2 Hardingtor
3 Mead Cl
4 Rugmere
5 Tottenhall
6 Beauvale
7 Broomfield
A2 1 Silverbirch
2 Penshurst
3 Wingham
4 Westwell
5 Chislet
6 Burmarsh
7 Shipton Ho
8 Stone Gate
9 Leysdown
10 Headcorn
11 Lenham
12 Halstow
13 Fordcombe
14 Cannington
15 Langridge
16 Athlone Ho
17 Pentland H
18 Beckington
19 Hawkridge
20 Edington
B1 1 Ferdinand
2 Harmood H
3 Hawley Rd
4 Hawley Me
5 Leybourne
6 Barling
7 Tiptree
8 Havering
9 Candida Ct
10 Lorraine Ct
11 Donnington
12 Welford Ct
13 Torbay Ct
14 Bradfield C
15 Torbay St
16 Leybourne
17 Haven St
18 Stucley Pl
B2 1 Ashington
2 Priestley H
3 Leonard Da
4 Old Dairy M
5 Monmouth
6 Alpha Ct
7 Una Ho
8 Widford
9 Hey Bridge
10 Roxwell
B4 1 Denyer Ho
2 Stephenson
3 Trevithick H
4 Brunel Ho
5 Newcomen
6 Faraday Ho
7 Winifrede P Ho
8 Wardlow
9 Fletcher Ct
10 Tideswell
11 Grangemill
12 Hambrook
13 Calver
C1 1 Durdans Ho
2 Philia Ho
3 Bernard Sh Ct
4 Foster Ct

5 Bessemer Ct
6 Hogarth Ct
7 Rochester Ct
8 Soane Ct
9 Wallett Ct
10 Inwood Ct
11 Wrotham Rd
12 Caulfield Ct
13 Bruges Pl
14 Reachview Cl
15 Lawfords Wharf
C3 1 Eleanor Ho
2 Falkland Pl
3 Kensington Ho
4 Willingham Cl
5 Kenbrook Ho
6 Aborfield
7 Great Field
8 Appleford
9 Forties The
C4 1 Benson Ct
2 Tait Ho
3 Manorfield Cl
4 Greatfield Cl
5 Longley Ho
6 Lampson Ho
7 Davidson Ho
8 Palmer Ho
9 Lambourn Cl
10 Morris Ho
11 Owen Ho
C5 1 Hunter Ho
2 Fisher Ho
3 Lang Ho
4 Temple Ho
5 Palmer Ho
C6 1 Flowers Mews
2 Sandridge St
3 Bovingdon Cl
5 Laurel Cl
6 Forest Way
7 Larch Cl
8 Pine Cl
9 Alder Mews
10 Aspen Cl
D1 1 Hillier Ho
2 Gairloch Ho
3 Cobham Mews
4 Bergholt Mews
5 Blakeney Cl
6 Weavers Way
7 Allensbury Pl
D2 1 Rowstock
2 Carters Cl
3 York Ho
4 Hungerford Rd
5 Cliff Ct
6 Camelot Ho
D3 1 Blake Ho
2 Quelch Ho
3 Lee Ho
4 Willbury Ho
5 Howell Ho
6 Holmsbury Ho
7 Leith Ho
8 Betchworth Ho
9 Rushmore Ho
10 Dugdale Ho
11 Horsendon Ho
12 Colley Ho
13 Coombe Ho
14 Ivinghoe Ho
15 Buckhurst Ho
16 Saxonbury Ct
17 Charlton Ct
18 Apollo Studios
19 Barn Cl
20 Long Meadow
21 Landleys Field
22 Margaret Bondfield Ho
23 Haywood Lo
D4 1 Fairlie Ct
2 London Metropolitan Univ (Carleton Grange Hall)
3 Trecastle Way
4 Hilldrop Est
5 Hyndman Ho
6 Carpenter Ho
7 Graham Ho
D5 1 Melchester Ho
2 Norcombe Ho
3 Weatherbury Ho
4 Wessex Ho
5 Archway Bsns Ctr
D6 1 Bowerman Ct
2 Hargrave Mans
3 Church Garth
4 John King Ct

72

A3 1 Kimble Ho
2 Saxonbury Ct
3 Poynder Ct
4 Pangbourne Ho
5 Moulsford Ho
A4 1 Arcade The
2 Macready Pl
A5 1 Northview
2 Tufnell Park Mans
A6 1 Christie Ct
2 Ringmer Gdns
3 Kingsdown Rd
4 Cottenham Ho
5 St Paul's Ct
6 Rickthorne Rd
7 Stanley Terr
B1 1 Kerwick Cl
2 Rydston Cl
3 Skegness Ho
4 Frederica St
5 Ponder St
6 Kings Ct
7 Freeling St
B4 1 Buckmaster Ho
2 Loreburn Ho
3 Cairns Ho
4 Halsbury Ho
5 Chelmsford Ho
6 Cranworth Ho
B6 1 Berkeley Wlk
2 Lazar Wlk
3 Thistlewood Cl
4 Tomlins Wlk
5 Andover Ho
6 Barmouth Ho
7 Chard Ho
8 Methley Ho
9 Rainford Ho
10 Woodbridge Cl
11 Allerton Wlk
12 Falconer Wlk
13 Sonderburg Rd
C1 1 Mountfort Terr
2 Davey Lo
3 Carfree Cl
4 New College Mews
C3 1 Slaney Pl
2 Wells Yd
3 Milton Pl
4 Hartnoll Ho
5 St James School Flats
6 Widnes Ho
7 Tranmere Ho
8 Victoria Mans
9 Formby Ct
10 Mersey Ho
11 Birkenhead Ho
C6 1 Brookfield
2 Churnfield
D1 1 Islington Park Mews
2 Evelyn Denington Ct
3 Bassingbourn Ho
4 Cadmore Ho
5 Adstock Ho
6 Garston Ho
7 Flitton Ho
8 Datchworth Ho
9 Battishill St
10 Almeida St
11 Edward's Cotts
12 Hyde's Pl
13 Tyndale Terr
14 Spriggs Ho
15 Barratt Ho
16 Spencer Pl
17 Chadston Ho
18 Whiston Ho
19 Wakelin Ho
20 Tressel Cl
21 Canonbury Ct
22 Shillingford St
23 Halton Ho
D4 1 Chestnuts The
2 Bowen Ct
3 Peckett Sq

73

A1 1 Haslam Ho
2 Horsfield Ho
3 Astey's Row
4 Melville Pl
5 Wontner Cl
6 Hedingham Cl
7 Eric Fletcher Ct
8 Ashby Ho
9 Annette Cres
10 Bentham Ct
11 New Bentham Ct
12 Cardigan Wlk
13 Lindsey Mews
14 Walkinshaw Ct
15 Laundry La
A2 1 Crowline Wlk
2 Bardsey Wlk
3 Handa Wlk
4 Lismore Wlk
5 Sark Ho
6 Clephane Rd
7 Sybil Thorndike Ho
8 Guernsey Rd
9 Guernsey Ho
10 Herm Ho
11 Florence Nightingale Ho
12 Jersey Ho
13 Jethou Ho
14 Upper Caldy Wlk
15 Caldy Wlk
16 Alderney Ho
17 Marquess Rd S
18 Oronsay Rd
19 Upper Gulland Wlk
20 Gulland Wlk
21 Church Rd
A3 1 Pearfield Ho
2 Larchfield Ho
3 Beresford Terr
4 Pondfield Ho
5 Ashfield Ho
6 Elmfield Ho
A4 1 Fountain Mews
2 Woodstock Ho
3 Henson Ct
4 Taverner Sq
B2 1 John Kennedy Ct
2 John Kennedy Lo
3 Ball's Pond Pl
4 Haliday Wlk
7 Rona Wlk
8 Threadgold Ho
9 Wakeham St
10 Saffron Ct
11 Callaby Terr
12 Tilney Gdns
13 Westcliff Ho
14 Ilford Ho
15 Ongar Ho
16 Greenhills Terr
17 Romford Ho
B4 1 Ledo Ho
2 Salween Ho
3 Prome Ho
4 Arakan Ho
5 Rangoon Ho
6 Mandalay Ho
7 Karen Ho
8 Wingate Ho
9 Jubet Ho
10 Orde Ho
11 Chindit Ho
12 Mabel Thornton Ho
13 Crawshay Ho
14 Avon Ho
15 Connaught Mans
16 Jonson Ho
17 Herrick Ho
18 Donne Ho
19 Grasmere Ho
20 Thirlmere Ho
B6 1 Chestnut Cl
2 Sycamore Ho
3 Lordship Ho
4 Clissold Ho
5 Beech Ho
6 Laburnum Ho
7 Ormond Ho
C1 1 Dorchester Ct
2 Wareham Ct
3 Dorset Ct
4 Stratton Ct
5 Swanage Ct
6 Blandford Ct
7 Portland Ct
8 Oscar Faber Pl
9 Lancaster Cl
C2 1 Kingsland Gn
2 Kingsland Pas
3 Metropolitan Benefit Societies Almshs
4 Nimrod Pas
5 De Beauvoir Pl
6 Warburton Cl
7 Buckingham Mews
C3 1 Hewling Ho
2 Matthias Ho
3 Port Royal Pl
4 Cressington Cl
5 King Henry's Yd
6 Bronte Ho
7 Sewell Ho
8 Lydgate Ho
9 Patmore Ho
10 Congreve Ho
11 Elton St
12 Conrad Ho
13 Southwell Ho
14 Neptune Ho
15 Campion Ho
16 Webster Ho
17 Meredith Ho
18 Beckford Ho
19 Ashley Ct
20 Hayling Cl
21 Millard Cl
22 Lydford Cl
23 Salcombe Rd
24 Truman's Rd
25 Templeton Cl
26 John Campbell Rd
27 Gillett Pl
28 Bradbury St
C4 1 Londesborough Ho
2 Knebworth Ho
3 Knebworth Rd
4 Bransby Ct
5 Imperial Ave
6 Leonard Pl
7 Shakspeare Mews
8 Binyon Ho
9 Shelley Ho
10 Browning Ho
11 Burns Ho
12 Andrew Marvell Ho
13 Wycliffe Ho
14 Blake Ho
15 Marlowe Ho
16 Fletcher Ho
17 Chaucer Ct
C5 1 Gujarat Ho
2 Marton Rd
3 Painsthorpe Rd
4 Selkirk Ho
5 Defoe Ho
6 Edward Friend Ho
7 Sheridan Ho
8 Barrie Ho
9 Arnold Ho
10 Macaulay Ho
11 Stowe Ho
12 Carlyle Ho
13 Shaftesbury Ho
14 Lillian Cl
15 Swift Ho
16 Dryden Ho
17 Scott Ct
18 Kingsfield Ho
19 Uhura Sq
D1 1 Hilborough Rd
2 Shoreditch Ct
3 Evergreen Sq
D2 1 Prospect Ho
2 Woodland St
3 Crosby Wlk
4 Kirkland Wlk
5 Bowness Cl
6 Carlisle Wlk
7 Skelton Cl
8 Camerton Cl
9 Buttermere Wlk
10 Houghton Cl
11 Hayton Cl
D3 1 Miller's Terr
2 Chow Sq
3 Drysdale Flats
4 Gateway Mews
5 Birkbeck Mews
6 Winchester Pl
D4 1 Coronation Ave
2 Morris Blitz Ct
3 Shacklewell Ho
4 Alexandra Ct
D5 1 Lawrence's Bldgs
2 Cottage Wlk
3 Batley Pl
D6 1 Garnham St
2 Garnham Cl
3 Sanford La
4 Sandford Wlk
5 Abney Gdns
6 Fleet Wood

74

A1 1 Aldington Ct
2 Bayton Ct
3 Rochford Wlk
A3 1 Kingsdown Ho
2 Glendown Ho
3 Moredown Ho
4 Blakeney Cl
5 Beeston Cl
6 Benabo Ct
7 David Devine Ho
8 Kreedman Wlk
9 Hermitage Row
10 Grafton Ct
11 Lushington Terr
A5 1 Ravenscourt
2 Mellington Ct
3 Rendlesham Ho
4 Florence Ct
5 Burnaston Ho
A6 1 Cazenove Mans
2 Chedworth Ho
3 Aldergrove Ho
4 Abbotstone Ho
5 Briggeford Cl
6 Inglethorpe Ho
7 Ashdown Ho
B1 1 Fortescue Ave
2 Pemberton Pl
3 Weston Wlk
4 Bayford St Ind Ctr
5 Bayford St
6 Sidworth St
7 Helmsley St
B2 1 Bohemia Pl
2 Graham Mans
3 Marvin St
4 Boscobel Ho
5 Royal Oak Rd
6 Colonnades The
7 Sylvester Ho
8 Sylvester Path
9 Doctor Spurstowe Almshos
10 Great Eastern Bldgs
11 Sojourner-Truth Cl
B3 1 Birchington Ho
2 Bicknor Ho
3 Boxley Ho
4 Adisham Ho
5 Cranbrook Ho
6 Marden Ho
7 Broome Ho
8 Crandale Ho
9 Cheriton Ho
10 Ditton Ho
11 Langley Ho
12 Dymchurch Ho
13 Elham Ho
14 Bodney Mans
15 Pembury Pl
16 Downs Ct
17 Perrywood Ho
18 Stapelhurst Ho
19 Pegwell Ho
20 Yalding Ho
21 Northbourne Ho
22 Monkton Ho
23 Milsted Ho
24 Athlone Cl
25 Clarence Pl
26 Gould Terr
27 Quested Ct
28 Brett Pas
29 Marcon Ct
B4 1 Sutherland Point
2 Embley Point
3 Downs La
4 Gaviller Pl
5 Robert Owen Lo
6 Apprentice Way
7 Arrowe Ct
8 Gilwell Ct
9 Sutton Ct
10 Kinnoull Mans
11 Rowhill Mans
12 Sladen Pl
13 Mothers Sq The
14 Richborough Ho
15 Sandgate Ho
16 Sheppey Ho
B6 1 Wentwood Ho
2 Woolmer Ho
3 Warwick Ct
4 Winslade Ho
5 Moriss Ho
6 Woodfield Ho
7 Rossendale Ho
8 Ettrick Ho
9 Charnwood Ho
10 Boyne Ho
11 Whitwell Ho
12 Scardale Ho
13 Hendale Ho
14 Brampton Cl
15 Aveley Ct
16 Aldeburgh Cl
17 Dennington Cl
C1 1 Pitcairn Ho
2 Lyme Grove Ho
3 Shakespeare Ho
4 Upcott Ho
5 Loddiges Ho
6 Parkinson Ho
7 Sloane Ho
8 Vanbrugh Ho
9 Cambridge Pas
10 Lyttleton Ho
11 Victoria Park Ct
12 Tullis Ho
13 Fairchild Ho
14 Forsyth Ho
15 Tradescant Ho
16 Mason Ho
17 Capel Ho
18 Cordwainers Ct
19 Bridgeman Ho
20 St Thomas's Pl
21 Barclay Ho
22 Clayton Ho
23 Danby Ho
24 Sherard Ho
25 Catesby Ho
26 Petiver Cl
27 Leander Ct
28 Philip Turner Est
29 Grendon Ho
30 Shore Mews
31 Shore Bsns Ctr
32 Kendal Ho
33 Classic Mans
34 Tudor Ho
35 Park Ho
36 Alpine Gr
37 Clarendon Cl
C2 1 Woolpack Ho
2 Elvin Ho
3 Thomas Ho
4 Hockley Ho
5 Retreat Ho
6 Butfield Ho
7 Brooksbank Ho
8 Cresset Ho
9 Brooksbank St
10 Lennox Ho
11 Milborne Ho
12 Collent Ho
13 Middlesex Pl
14 Devonshire Hall
15 Brent Ho
C6 1 Haybridge Ho
2 Framlingham Cl
3 Halesworth Cl
4 Harleston Cl
5 Lowestoft Cl
6 Cecil Ho
7 Clapton Ho
8 Howard Ho
9 Templar Ho
10 Warwick Ho
11 Audley Ho
D1 1 Stuart Ho
2 Gascoyne Ho
3 Chelsfield Point
4 Sundridge Ho
5 Banbury Ho
D2 1 Musgrove Ho
2 Cheyney Ho
3 Haynes Ho
4 Warner Ho
5 Gilby Ho
6 Gadsden Ho
7 Risley Ho
8 Baycliffe Ho
9 Sheldon Ho
10 Offley Ho
11 Latimer Ho
12 Ribstone Ho
13 Salem Ho
14 Fieldwick Ho
15 Lever Ct
16 Matson Ho
17 Wilding Ho
18 Rennell Ho
19 Dycer Ho
20 Granard Ho
21 Whitelock Ho
22 Harrowgate Ho
23 Cass Ho
24 Lofts on the Park
D4 1 Cromford Path
2 Longford Ct
3 Overbury Ho
4 Heanor Ct
5 Wharfedale Ct
6 Ladybower Ct
7 Ilkeston Ct
8 Derby Ct
9 Rushmore Cres
10 Blackwell Cl

75

A2 1 Wick Mews
2 Wellday Ho
3 Selman Ho
4 Vaine Ho
5 Trower Ho
B2 3 Merriam Ave
D6 1 Hammond Ct
2 Sorenson Ct
3 Hinton Ct

76

B4 1 Mulberry Ct
2 Rosewood Ct
3 Gean Ct
4 Blackthorn Ct
5 Cypress Ct
C1 1 Stratford Office Village The
2 Mandrake Way
3 Brimstone Ho
C5 1 Acacia Bsns Ctr
2 Brook Ct
3 Doreen Capstan Ho
5 Peppermint Pl
6 Denmark St
7 Mills Ct
8 Paramount Ho
C6 1 Nansen Ct
2 Mallinson Ct
3 Barbara Ward Ct
4 Noel Baker Ct
5 Corigan Ct
6 Norman Ho
7 Willow Ct
8 Lime Ct

77

A4 1 Bronte Cl
2 Anna Neagle Cl
3 Brownlow Rd
4 Carrington Gdns
5 Vera Lynn Cl

78

C3 1 Stewart Rainbird Ho
2 Rede Ho
3 George Comberton Wlk
C4 1 Annie Taylor Ho
2 Richard Fell Ho
3 Susan Lawrence Ho
4 Walter Hurford Par
5 John Cornwell VC Ho
6 Alfred Prior Ho
7 Cardamom Ct
C5 1 Charlbury Ho
2 Willis Ho
3 Arthur Walls Ho
4 Blakesley Ho
5 Twelve Acre Ho
6 Beech Ct
7 Golding Ct
D1 1 Aveley Mans
2 Harlow Mans
3 Danbury Mans
4 Mayland Mans
5 Bowers Ho
6 Webber Ho
7 Paulson Ho
8 Collins Ho
9 Jack Cook Ho
D3 1 St Luke's Path
2 Springfield Ct
D5 1 Postway Mews
2 Oakfield Ho
3 Janice Mews
4 Kenneth Moor Rd
5 Clements Ct
6 Handforth Rd
7 Churchill Ct
8 Oakfield Lo
9 Langdale Ct
D6 1 York Ho
2 Opal Mews
3 Florentine Ho
4 Hainault Bridge Par

79

D1 1 Gibbards Cott
2 Edgefield Ct
3 Manor Ct
4 Lambourne Gdns
5 Westone Mans
6 Loveland Mans
7 Edward Mans
8 Clarke Mans
9 Dawson Gdns
10 Sebastian Ct

80

A1 1 Bristol Ho
2 Canterbury Ho
3 Durham Ho
4 Wells Ho
5 Winchester Ho
6 Rosalind Ct
7 Exeter Ho
8 Wheatley Mans
9 Greenwood Mans

10 Plymouth Ho
11 Graham Mans
12 Portia Ct

81

C5 1 Markham Ho
2 Webb Ho
3 Preston Ho
4 Steadman Ho
5 Hyndman Ho
6 Clynes Ho
7 Henderson Ho
8 Blatchford Ho
9 Rogers Ho
10 Sylvia Pankhurst Ho
11 Mary Macarthur Ho
12 Ellen Wilkinson Ho
D2 1 Picador Ho
2 Centurion Ho
3 Louis Ct
4 Watsons Lo
5 Carpenters Ct
6 Bell Ho
7 Rounders Ct
8 Oldmead Ho
9 Jervis Ct
10 Bartletts Ho
11 Royal Par
12 Richardson Gdns

82

D3 1 Marlborough Par
2 Blenheim Par
3 Lea Ct
4 Westbourne Par
5 Whiteleys Par
6 Hillingdon Par
7 New Broadway

84

C4 1 Dilston Cl
2 Wells Cl
3 Willet Cl
4 Merlin Cl
5 Glyndebourne Ct
6 Albury Ct
7 Osterley Ct
8 Hatfield Ct
9 Gayhurst Ct
D4 1 Caravelle Gdns
2 Forman Gr
3 Viscount Gr
4 Tomahawk Gdns
5 Martlet Gr
6 Trident Gdns
7 Latham Ct
8 Jupiter Ct
9 Westland Ct
10 Seasprite Cl
11 Convair Wlk
12 Mayfly Gdns
13 Valiant Cl
14 Woburn Twr
15 Brett Cl
16 Friars Cl
D5 1 Medlar Cl
2 Cranberry Cl
3 Lely Ho
4 Kneller Ho
5 Girtin Ho
6 Cotman Ho
7 Raeburn Ho
8 Gainsborough Twr
9 Stanfield Ho
10 Millais Ct
11 Hunt Ct
12 Poynter Ct
13 Hogarth Ho
14 Constable Ho
15 Bonnington Ct
16 Romney Ct
17 Landseer Ho

85

D1 1 Thurlestone Ct
2 Disley Ct
3 Burgess Ct
4 Selsdon Ct
5 Lytham Ct
6 Abbeydale Ct
7 Cromer Ct
8 Brunel Pl
9 Winford Par
10 Rutherford Twr

86

A1 1 Farnham Ct
2 Gleneagles Twr
3 Birkdale Ct
4 Verulam Ct
5 Hartsbourne Ct
6 Ferndown Ct
7 Deal Ct
8 St David's Ct
9 Portrush Ct
10 Alnmouth Ct
11 Panmure Ct
12 Peterhead Ct
13 Sunningdale Ct
D2 1 Denbigh Ct
2 Devon Ct
3 Dorset Ct
4 Glamorgan Ct
5 Gloucester Ct
6 Hereford Ct
7 Merioneth Ct
8 Oxford Ct
9 Monmouth Ct
10 Paddington Ct
11 Pembroke Ct
12 Chadwick Cl
13 Cotts Cl
D3 1 Berkshire Ct
2 Buckingham Ct
3 Cardigan Ct
4 Carmarthen Ct
5 Cornwall Ct
6 Merlin Ct
7 Osprey Ct
8 Pelham Pl
D5 1 Medway Par
2 Brabstone Ho
3 Cotswold Ct

87

B3 1 Woodbury Ct
2 Edward Ct
3 Park Lo
C1 1 Hurley Ct
2 Amherst Gdns
3 Tudor Ct
4 Hilton Ho
C2 1 Hutton Ct
2 Cain Ct
3 Langdale Ct
4 William Ct
5 Castlebar Ct
6 Warren Ct
7 White Lo
8 Queen's Ct
9 King's Ct
10 Cheriton Cl
11 Stanley Ct
12 Juniper Ct
C3 1 Holtoake Ct
2 Pitshanger Ct
3 Holtoake Ho

88

A4 1 Nelson Ho
2 Gordon Ho
3 Frobisher Ho
4 Wellington Ho
5 Fairfax Ho
A5 1 Carlyon Mans
2 Ainslie Ct
3 Millers Ct
4 Priory Ct
5 Tylers Ct
6 Twyford Ct
7 Rose Ct
8 Laurel Ct
9 Sundew Ct
10 Campion Ct
11 Foxglove Ct
C1 1 Buckingham Ho
2 Chester Ct
3 Devon Ct
4 Essex Ho
5 Fife Ct
6 Gloucester Ct
7 Hereford Ho
8 Inverness Ct
9 Warwick Ho
10 York Ho
11 Suffolk Ho
12 Perth Ho
13 Norfolk Ho
14 Thanet Ct
15 Rutland Ct
16 Oxford Ct

89

A1 1 Avon Ct
2 Bromley Lo
3 Walter Ct
4 Lynton Terr
5 Acton Ho
6 Fells Haugh
7 Springfield Ct
8 Tamarind Ct
9 Lynton Ct
B1 1 Rosebank Gdns
2 Rosebank
3 Edinburgh Ho
4 Western Ct
5 Kilronan
B6 1 Fitzsimmons Ct
2 Bernard Shaw Ho
3 Longlents Ho
4 Mordaunt Ho
5 Wilmers Ct
6 Stonebridge Sh Ctr
D5 1 New Crescent Yd
2 Harlesden Plaza
3 St Josephs Ct

90

D1 1 Kelfield Ct
2 Downing Ho
3 Crosfield Ct
4 Robinson Ho
5 Scampston Mews
6 Girton Villas
7 Ray Ho
8 Walmer Ho
9 Goodrich Ct
10 Arthur Ct
11 Whitstable Ho
12 Kingsnorth Ho
13 Bridge Cl
14 Prospect Ho
16 Whitchurch Ho
17 Blechynden Ho
18 Waynflete Sq
19 Bramley Ho
D4 1 Westfield Ct
2 Tropical Ct
3 Chamberlayne Mans
4 Quadrant The
5 Queens Park Ct
6 Warfield Yd
7 Cherrytree Ho

91

A1 1 Malton Mews
2 Lancaster Lo
3 Manning Ho
4 Galsworthy Ho
5 Hudson Ho
6 Cambourne Mews
7 Camelford Ct
8 Camelford Wlk
9 Talbot Grove Ho
10 Clarendon Wlk
11 Kingsdown Cl
12 Lower Clarendon Wlk
13 Upper Clarendon Wlk
A2 1 Murchison Ho
2 Macaulay Ho
3 Chesterton Ho
4 Chiltern Ho
5 Lionel Ho
6 Watts Ho
7 Wheatstone Ho
8 Telford Ho
9 Golborne Mews
10 Millwood St
11 St Columb's Ho
12 Norfolk Mews
A3 1 Sycamore Wlk
2 Westgate Bsns Ctr
3 Buspace Studios
4 Bosworth Ho
5 Golborne Gdns
6 Appleford Ho
7 Adair Twr
8 Gadsden Ho
9 Southam Ho
10 Norman Butler Ho
11 Thompson Ho
12 Wells Ho
13 Paul Ho
14 Olive Blythe Ho
15 Katherine Ho
16 Breakwell Ct
17 Pepler Ho
18 Edward Kennedy Ho
19 Winnington Ho
A4 2 Slomon Ho
3 Stansbury Ho
4 Tilleard Ho
6 Selby Ho
8 Mundy Ho
9 Macfarren Ho
10 Mounsey Ho
11 Courtville Ho
12 Croft Ho
13 Batten Ho
14 Bantock Ho
15 Banister Ho
16 Symphony Mews
17 Bliss Mews
A5 1 Lancefield Ct
2 Verdi Ho
3 Wornum Ho
B1 1 Tavistock Mews
2 Silvester Ho
3 Melchester
4 Clydesdale Ho
5 Pinehurst Ct
6 Colville Sq Mews
7 Denbigh Ho
8 Golden Cross Mews
B2 1 Blagrove Rd
2 Tavistock Ho
3 Leamington Ho
B3 1 Western Ho
2 Russell's Wharf
B4 1 Boyce Ho
2 Farnaby Ho
3 Danby Ho
4 Purday Ho
5 Naylor Ho
6 St Judes Ho
7 Leeve Ho
8 Longhurst Ho
9 Harrington Ct
10 Mulberry Ct
11 Quilter Ho
12 Romer Ho
13 Kilburn Ho
B5 1 Claremont Ct
2 William Saville Ho
3 Western Ct
4 Bond Ho
5 Crone Ct
6 Wood Ho
7 Winterleys
8 Carlton Ho
9 Fiona Ct
C1 1 Shottsford
2 Tolchurch
3 Casterbridge
4 Sandbourne
5 Anglebury
6 Weatherbury
7 Westbourne Gr Mews
8 Rosehart Mews
9 Viscount Ct
10 Hereford Mans
11 Hereford Mews
C2 1 Ascot Ho
2 Ashgrove Ct
3 Lockbridge Ct
4 Swallow Ct
5 Nightingale Lo
6 Hammond Lo
7 Penfield Lo
8 Harvey Lo
9 Hunter Lo
10 Barnard Lo
11 Falcon Lo
12 Johnson Lo
13 Livingstone Lo
14 Nuffield Lo
15 Finch Lo
16 Polesworth Ho
17 Oversley Ho
18 Derrycombe Ho
19 Buckshead Ho
20 Combe Ho
21 Culham Ho
22 Dainton Ho
23 Devonport Ho
24 Hanwell Ho
25 Truro Ho
26 Sunderland Ho
27 Stonehouse Ho
28 Riverford Ho
29 Portishead Ho
30 Mickleton Ho
31 Keyham Ho
32 Moulsford Ho
33 Shrewsbury Mews
34 St Stephen's Mews
35 Westway Lo
36 Langley Ho
37 Brindley Ho
38 Radway Ho
39 Astley Ho
40 Willow Ct
41 Larch Ct
42 Elm Ct
43 Beech Ct
44 Worcester Ct
45 Union Ct
46 Leicester Ct
47 Kennet Ct
48 Oxford Ct
49 Fazerley Ct
C3 1 Westside Ct
2 Sutherland Ct
3 Fleming Cl
4 Hermes Cl
C4 1 Masefield Ho
2 Austen Ho
3 Fielding Ho
4 Park Bsns Ctr
5 John Ratcliffe Ho
6 Wymering Mans
8 Pavilion Ct
9 Nelson Cl
C5 1 Wells Ct
2 Cambridge Ct
3 Durham Ct
C6 1 Ryde Ho
2 Glengall Pass
3 Leith Yd
4 Daynor Ho
5 Varley Ho
6 Sandby Ho
7 Colas Mews
8 Bishopsdale Ho
9 Lorton Ho
10 Marshwood Ho
11 Ribblesdale Ho
12 Holmesdale Ho
13 Kilburn Vale Est
14 Kilburn Bridge
D1 1 Vera Ct
2 Alexander Mews
3 Gurney Ho
4 Burdett Mews
5 Greville Lo
6 Hatherley Ct
7 Bridge Field Ho
8 Ralph Ct
9 Peters Ct
10 Riven Ct
11 Cervantes Ct
12 Bishops Ct
13 Newbury Ho
14 Marlow Ho
15 Lynton Ho
16 Pembroke Ho
17 Pickering Ho
D3 1 Ellwood Ct
D5 1 Tollgate Ho
2 Regents Plaza
3 Royal Langford
D6 1 Farndale Ho
2 Birchington Ct
3 Greville Mews
4 Goldsmith's Pl
5 Remsted Ho
6 Bradwell Ho
7 Cheshunt Ho
8 Haliwell Ho
9 Braddock Ho
10 Philip Ho
11 Hillsborough Ct
12 Sandbourne
13 Wingreen
14 Toneborough
15 Silverthorn
16 Kington Ho
17 Marrick Ho
18 Broadoak Ho
18 Boadoak Ho

95

C4 1 Pimlico Wlk
2 Aske Ho
3 Hathaway Ho
4 Haberdasher Pl
5 Fairchild Ho
6 Burtt Ho
7 Enfield Cloisters
8 McGregor Ct
9 Royal Oak Ct
10 Hoxton Mkt
11 Bath Pl
12 Chapel Ct
13 Chapel Pl
14 Standard Pl
16 Cleeve Ho
17 Printing House Yd
18 Perseverance Works
19 Crooked Billet Yd
20 Drysdale Ho
21 Castlefrank Ho
22 School App
23 Basing House Yd
24 Mail Coach Yd
C5 1 Bracer Ho
2 Scorton Ho
3 Fern Cl
4 Macbeth Ho
5 Oberon Ho
6 Buckland Ct
7 Crondall Ct
8 Osric Path
9 Caliban Twr
10 Celia Ho
11 Juliet Ho
12 Bacchus Wlk
13 Malcolm Ho
14 Homefield St
15 Crondall Pl
16 Blanca Ho
17 Miranda Ho
18 Falstaff Ho
19 Charmian Ho
20 Myrtle Wlk
21 Arden Ho
22 Sebastian Ho
23 Stanway Ct
24 Jerrold St
25 Rosalind Ho
26 Cordelia Ho
27 Monteagle Ct
28 John Parry Ct
29 James Anderson Ct
30 Ben Jonson Ct
31 Sara Lane Ct
32 Walbrook Ct
C6 1 Portelet Ct
2 Trinity Ct
3 Rozel Ct
4 St Helier Ct
5 Corbiere Ho
6 Kenning Ho
7 Higgins Ho
8 Cavell Ho
9 Girling Ho
10 Fulcher Ho
11 Francis Ho
12 Norris Ho
13 Kempton Ho
14 Nesham Ho
15 Crossbow Ho
16 Catherine Ho
17 Strale Ho
18 Horner Hos
19 Stringer Hos
20 Whitmore Ho
21 Nightingale Ho
22 Fletcher Ho
24 Arrow Ho
25 Archer Ho
26 Meriden Ho
27 Rover Ho
28 Bowyer Ho
29 Longbow Ho
30 Tiller Ho
31 Canalside Studios
32 Bishopgate
33 Holburn
34 Fenchurch
D4 1 Gorsuch Pl
2 Strout's Pl
3 Vaughan Est
4 George Loveless Ho
5 Baroness Rd
6 James Brine Ho
7 Arthur Wade Ho
8 Robert Owen Ho
9 Sivill Ho
10 Georgina Gdns
11 Old Market Sq
12 Cuff Point
13 Bakers Rents
14 Leopold Bldgs
15 Dunmore Point
16 Wingfield Ho
17 Gascoigne Pl
18 Mandela Ho
19 Virginia Rd
20 Briggs Ho
21 Packenham Ho
22 Gowan Ho
24 Chambord Ho
25 Ducal St
26 Strickland Ho
27 Alliston Ho
28 Gibraltar Wlk
29 Equity Sq
30 Shacklewell St
31 Rochelle St
32 Sonning Ho
33 Culham Ho
34 Hurley Ho
35 Palissy St
36 Taplow Ho
37 Chertsey Ho
38 Sunbury Ho
39 Sunbury Workshops
40 Datchett Ho
41 Hocker St
42 Coll Sharp Ct
43 Marlow Studio Workshops
44 Marlow Ho
45 Shiplake Ho
46 Wargrave Ho
47 Iffley Ho
D5 1 Queensbridge Ct
2 Godwin Ho
3 Kent Ct
4 Brunswick Ho
5 Weymouth Ct
6 Sovereign Mews
7 Dunloe Ct
8 Cremer Bsns Ctr
9 James Hammett Ho
10 Allgood St
11 Horatio St
12 Cadell Ho
13 Horatio Ho
14 Shipton Ho
D6 1 Hilborough Ct
2 Scriven Ct
3 Livermere Ct
4 Angrave Ct
5 Angrave Pas
6 Benfleet Ct
7 Belford Ho
8 Orme Ho
9 Clemson Ho
10 Longman Ho
11 Lowther Ho
12 Lovelace Ho
13 Harlowe Ho
14 Pamela Ho
15 Samuel Ho
16 Acton Ho
17 Loanda Cl
18 Phoenix Cl
19 Richardson Cl
20 Thrasher Cl
21 Mary Secole Cl
22 Canal Path
23 Pear Tree Cl
24 Hebden Ct
25 Charlton Ct
26 Laburnum Ct
27 Mansfield Ct
28 Garden Pl
29 Amber Wharf

96

A1 1 Manningtree St
2 Whitechurch La
3 Morrison Bldgs
4 Mountford St
5 Mulberry St
6 Weyhill Rd
7 Fordham St
8 Myrdle Ct
9 Buckle St
10 Plough St
12 Goodman's Stile
13 Mitali Pas
14 Basil Ho
15 Hogarth Ct
16 Ropewalk Gdns
17 Golding Terr
18 Delafield Ho
19 Drewett Ho
20 Harkness Ho
21 Batson Ho
22 Danvers Ho
23 Bicknell Ho
24 Everard Ho
25 Philchurch Pl
26 Hadfield Ho
27 Kindersley Ho
28 Langmore Ho
29 Halliday Ho
30 Berner Terr
31 Victoria Yd
A2 1 Arthur Deakin Ho
2 Albert Cotts
3 Victoria Cotts
4 Boden Ho
5 Vollasky Ho
6 Daplyn St
7 Hobsons Pl
8 Hanbury Ho
9 Links Yd
10 Casson Ho
11 Ramar Ho
12 Greatorex Ho
13 Chicksand Ho
14 Spelman Ho
15 Tailworth St
16 Monthorpe Rd
17 Bloomfield Ho
18 Davenant Ho
19 Pauline Ho
20 Tannery Ho
21 Green Dragon Yd
22 King's Arms Ct
23 Fieldgate Mans
24 Mosque Tower
A3 1 Bentworth Ct
2 Kerbela St
3 Fuller Cl
4 Kinsham Ho
5 Menotti St
6 Barwell Ho

7 Grimsby St
8 Eckersley St
9 Stuttle Ho
10 McGlashon Ho
11 Fleet Street Hill
12 Bratley St
13 Weaver Ho
14 John Pritchard Ho
1 Lygon Ho
2 Brabner Ho
3 Delta St
4 Tillet Way
5 Mullet Gdns
6 Elver Gdns
7 Cobden Ho
8 Lampern Sq
9 Jeremy Bentham Ho
10 Waring Ho
11 St James Ct
12 Hague St
13 Westhope Ho
14 Johnson Ho
15 Yates Ho
16 Simmons Ho
17 Swinton Ho
18 Eversley Ho
19 Rapley Ho
20 Dence Ho
21 Dickinson Ho
22 Hutton Ho
23 McKinnon Wood Ho
24 Satchwell Rd
25 Lorden Wlk
A5 1 London Terr
2 Sturdee Ho
3 Maude Ho
4 Haig Ho
5 Jellicoe Ho
6 Ropley St
7 Guinness Trust Bldgs
8 Ion Ct
9 Moye Cl
10 Morrel Ct
11 Courtauld Ho
12 Drummond Ho
13 Atkinson Ho
14 Gurney Ho
15 Halley Ho
16 Goldsmith's Sq
17 Ken Wilson Ho
18 Shahjalal Ho
19 Crofts Ho
20 April Ct
21 Sebright Ho
22 Beechwood Ho
23 Gillman Ho
24 Cheverell Ho
25 Besford Ho
26 Dinmont Ho
27 Wyndham Deedes Ho
28 Sheppard Ho
29 Mary James Ho
30 Hadrian Est
31 Blythendale Ho
32 George Vale Ho
33 Lion Mills
34 Pritchard Ho
A6 1 Broke Wlk
2 Rochemont Wlk
3 Marlborough Ave
4 Rivington Wlk
5 Magnin Cl
6 Gloucester Sq
7 Woolstone Ho
8 Marsworth Ho
9 Cheddington Ho
10 Linslade Ho
11 Cosgrove Ho
12 Blisworth Ho
13 Eleanor Ct
14 Wistow Ho
15 Muscott Ho
16 Boxmoor Ho
17 Linford Ho
18 Pendley Ho
19 North Church Ho
20 Debdale Ho
21 Broadway Market Mews
22 Welshpool Ho
23 Ada Ho
B1 1 Jacob Mans
2 Wicker St
3 Langdale St
4 Walford Ho
5 Welstead Ho
6 Peter Best Ho
7 Sly St
8 Barnett St
9 Kinder St
10 Richard St
11 Sarah Ho
12 Mellish Ho
13 Dickson Ho
14 Joscoyne Ho
15 Bridgen Ho
16 Wilton Ct
17 Silvester Ho
18 Greenwich Ct
19 Tylney Ho
20 Damien Ct
21 Siege Ho
22 Melwood Ho
23 Colstead Ho
24 Hungerford St
25 Burwell Cl
26 Chapman Ho
27 Tarling Ho
28 Sheridan St
29 Brinsley St
30 Dunch St
31 Luke Ho
32 Turnour Ho
33 Norton Ho
B3 1 Rochester Ct
2 Weaver Ct
3 Greenheath Bsns Ctr
4 Glass St
5 Herald St
6 Northesk Ho
7 Codrington Ho
8 Heathpool Ct
9 Mocatta Ho
10 Harvey Ho
11 Blackwood Ho
12 Rutherford Ho
13 Bullen Ho
14 Fremantle Ho
15 Pellew Ho
16 Ashington Ho
17 Dinnington Ho
18 Bartholomew Sq
19 Steeple Ct
20 Orion Ho
21 Fellbrigg St
22 Eagle Ho
23 Sovereign Ho
24 Redmill Ho
25 Berry Ho
26 Grindall Ho
27 Collingwood Ho
B4 1 Charles Dickens Ho
2 Adrian Bolt Ho
3 William Rathbone Ho
4 Southwood Smith Ho
5 Rushmead
6 William Channing Ho
7 John Cartwright Ho
8 Charles Darwin Ho
9 Thomas Burt Ho
10 John Fielden Ho
11 Gwilym Maries Ho
12 Joseph Priestley Ho
13 Wear Pl
14 John Nettleford Ho
15 Thornaby Ho
16 Stockton Ho
17 Barnard Ho
18 Gainford Ho
19 Stapleton Ho
20 James Middleton Ho
21 Kedleston Wlk
22 Queen Margaret Flats
23 Hollybush Ho
24 Horwood Ho
25 Norden Ho
26 Newcourt Ho
27 Seabright St
28 Viaduct Pl
29 Sunlight Sq
B5 1 Dinmont St
2 Marian St
3 Claredale Ho
4 Bradley Ho
5 Connett Ho
6 Winkley St
7 Temple Dwellings
8 Argos Ho
9 Helen Ho
10 Lysander Ho
11 Antenor Ho
12 Paris Ho
13 Nestor Ho
14 Hector Ho
15 Ajax Ho
16 Achilles Ho
17 Priam Ho
18 Peabody Est
19 Felix St
20 Cambridge Cres
21 Peterley Bsns Ctr
22 Beckwith Ho
23 Parminter Ind Est
24 Ted Roberts Ho
25 Cambridge Ct
26 West St
27 Millennium Pl
28 William Caslon Ho
29 Hugh Platt Ho
30 Mayfield Ho
31 Apollo Ho
32 Tanners Yd
33 Teesdale Yd
B6 1 Welshpool St
2 Broadway Ho
3 Regents Wharf
4 London Wharf
5 Warburton Ho
6 Warburton St
7 Triangle Rd
8 Warburton Rd
9 Williams Ho
10 Booth Cl
11 Albert Cl
12 King Edward Mans
13 Victoria Bldgs
C1 1 Woollon Ho
2 Dundalk Ho
3 Anne Goodman Ho
4 Newbold Cotts
5 Kerry Ho
6 Zion Ho
7 Longford Ho
8 Bromehead St
9 Athlone Ho
10 Jubilee Mans
11 Harriott Ho
12 Brayford Sq
13 Clearbrook Way
14 Rochelle Ct
15 Winterton Ho
16 Sheridan Ho
17 Brinsley Ho
18 Dean Ho
19 Foley Ho
20 Robert Sutton Ho
21 Montpelier Pl
22 Masters Lo
23 Steel's La
24 Swift Ho
25 Glastonbury Pl
C2 1 Fulneck
2 Gracehill
3 Ockbrook
4 Fairfield
5 Dunstan Hos
6 Cressy Ct
7 Cressy Hos
8 Callahan Cotts
9 Wexford Ho
10 Sandhurst Ho
11 Colverson Ho
12 Beckett Ho
13 Jarman Ho
14 Wingrad Ho
15 Armsby Ho
16 Miranda Cl
17 Drake Ho
18 Louise De Marillac Ho
19 Sambrook Ho
20 St Vincent De Paul Ho
21 Jean Pardies Ho
22 Clichy Ho
23 Le Moal Ho
24 Odette Duval Ho
25 Dagobert Ho
26 Charles Auffray Ho
27 Boisseau Ho
28 Paymal Ho
C3 1 William's Bldgs
2 Donegal Ho
3 Frederick Charrington Ho
4 Wickford Ho
5 Braintree Ho
6 Doveton Ho
7 Doveton St
8 Cephas Ho
9 Sceptre Ho
10 Bancroft Ho
11 Stothard St
12 Redclyf Ho
13 Winkworth Cotts
14 Ryder Ho
15 Hadleigh Ho
16 Hadleigh Cl
17 Amiel St
18 Stathard Ho
19 Barbanel Ho
20 Colebert Ho
21 Kenton Ho
22 Ibbott St
23 Stannard Cotts
24 Rennie Cotts
25 Rickman St
26 Rickman Ho
27 Pemell Cl
28 Pemell Ho
29 Leatherdale St
30 Gouldman Ho
31 Lamplighter Cl
32 Hamilton Lo
33 Cleveland Gr
34 Montgomery Lo
35 Bardsey Pl
36 Cromwell Lo
37 Colin Winter Ho
38 Allport Mews
C4 1 Mulberry Ho
2 Gretton Ho
3 Merceron Ho
4 Montfort Ho
5 Westbrook Ho
6 Sugar Loaf Wlk
7 Museum Ho
8 Burnham Est
9 Globe Terr
10 Moravian St
11 Shepton Hos
12 Mendip Hos
13 Academy Ct
14 Pepys Ho
15 Swinburne Ho
16 Moore Ho
17 Morris Ho
18 Burns Ho
19 Milton Ho
20 Whitman Ho
21 Shelley Ho
22 Keats Ho
23 Dawson Ho
24 Bradbeer Ho
25 Forber Ho
26 Hughes Ho
27 Silvester Ho
28 Rogers Est
29 Pavan Ct
30 Stafford Cripps Ho
31 Sidney Godley (VC) Ho
32 Butler Ho
33 Butler St
34 Thorne Ho
35 Bevin Ho
36 Tuscan Ho
C5 1 Evesham Ho
2 James Campbell Ho
3 Thomas Hollywood Ho
4 James Docherty Ho
5 Ebenezer Mussel Ho
6 Jameson Ct
7 Edinburgh Cl
8 Roger Dowley Ct
9 Sherbrooke Ho
10 Calcraft Ho
11 Burrard Ho
12 Dundas Ho
14 Barnes Ho
15 Paget Ho
17 Maitland Ho
18 Chesil Ct
19 Reynolds Ho
20 Cleland Ho
21 Goodrich Ho
22 Rosebery Ho
23 Sankey Ho
24 Cyprus Pl
25 Royston St
26 Stainsbury St
27 Hunslett St
28 Baildon
29 Brockweir
30 Tytherton
31 Malmesbury
32 Kingswood
33 Colville Ho
C6 1 Halkett Ho
4 Christ Church Sq
5 Swingfield Ho
6 Greenham Ho
7 Dinmore Ho
8 Anstey Ho
9 Weston Ho
10 Carbroke Ho
16 Bluebell Cl
17 Cherry Tree Cl
19 Georgian Ct
20 Park Cl
21 Regency Ct
22 Norris Ho
D1 1 Pattison Ho
2 St Thomas Ho
3 Arbour Ho
4 Bladen Ho
5 Antill Terr
6 Billing Ho
7 Dowson Ho
8 Lipton Rd
9 Chalkwell Ho
10 Corringham Ho
11 Ogilvie Ho
12 Edward Mann Cl
13 Lighterman Mews
D2 1 Roland Mews
2 Morecambe Cl
3 Stepney Green Ct
4 Milrood Ho
5 Panama Ho
6 Galway Ho
7 Caspian Ho
8 Darien Ho
9 Rigo Ho
10 Flores Ho
11 Taranto Ho
12 Aden Ho
13 Frances Grey Ho
14 Master's St
15 Diggon St
D3 1 Raynham Ho
2 Pat Shaw Ho
3 Colmar Cl
4 Withy Ho
5 Stocks Ct
6 Downey Ho
7 Bay Ct
8 Sligo Ho
9 Pegasus Ho
10 Barents Ho
11 Biscay Ho
12 Solway Ho
13 Bantry Ho
14 Aral Ho
15 Pacific Ho
16 Magellan Ho
17 Levant Ho
18 Adriatic Ho
19 Genoa Ho
20 Hawke Ho
21 Palliser Ho
22 Ionian Ho
23 Weddell Ho
D4 1 Stubbs Ho
2 Holman Ho
3 Clynes Ho
4 Windsor Ho
5 Gilbert Ho
6 Chater Ho
7 Ellen Wilkinson Ho
8 George Belt Ho
9 Ayrton Gould Ho
10 O'Brian Ho
11 Sulkin Ho
12 Jenkinson Ho
13 Bullards Pl
14 Sylvia Pankhurst Ho
15 Mary Macarthur Ho
16 Trevelyan Ho
17 Wedgwood Ho
18 Pemberton Ct
20 Walter Besant Ho
21 Barber Beaumont Ho
22 Brancaster Ho
23 Litcham Ho
D5 1 Kemp Ho
2 Piggott Ho
3 Mark Ho
4 Sidney Ho
5 Pomeroy Ho
6 Puteaux Ho
7 Doric Ho
8 Modling Ho
9 Longman Ho
10 Ames Ho
11 Alzette Ho
12 Offenbach Ho
13 Tate Ho
14 Norton Ho
15 St Gilles Ho
16 Harold Ho
17 Velletri Ho
18 Bridge Wharf
19 Gathorne St
20 Bow Brook The
22 Palmerston Ct
23 Peach Walk Mews
23 Lakeview
25 Caesar Ct

97

A1 1 Coltman Ho
2 Repton Ho
3 Causton Cotts
9 Darnley Ho
10 Mercer's Cotts
11 Troon Ho
12 Ratcliffe Ho
13 Wakeling St
14 York Sq
15 Anglia Ho
16 Cambria Ho
17 Caledonia Ho
18 Ratcliffe La
19 Bekesbourne St
20 John Scurr Ho
21 Regents Canal Ho
22 Basin App
23 Powlesland Ct
A2 1 Waley St
2 Edith Ramsay Ho
3 Andaman Ho
4 Atlantic Ho
5 Pevensey Ho
6 Solent Ho
7 Lorne Ho
8 Cromarty Ho
12 Greaves Cotts
13 Donaghue Cotts
14 Ames Cotts
A3 1 Formosa Ho
2 Galveston Ho
3 Arabian Ho
4 Greenland Ho
5 Coral Ho
6 Anson Ho
7 Lindop Ho
8 Moray Ho
9 Azov Ho
10 Sandalwood Cl
11 Broadford Ho
A5 1 Bunsen Ho
2 Bunsen St
3 Beatrice Webb Ho
4 Margaret Bondfield Ho
5 Wilmer Ho
6 Sandall Ho
7 Butley Ct
8 Josseline Ct
9 Dalton Ho
10 Brine Ho
11 Ford Cl
12 Viking Cl
13 Stanfield Rd
14 Ruth Ct
15 School Bell Cloisters
16 Schoolbell Mews
17 Medhurst Cl
18 Olga St
19 Conyer St
20 Diamond Ho
21 Daring Ho
22 Crane Ho
23 Exmoor Ho
24 Grenville Ho
25 Hyperion Ho
26 Sturdy Ho
27 Wren Ho
28 Ardent Ho
29 Senators Lo
30 Hooke Ho
31 Mohawk Ho
32 Ivanhoe Ho
33 Medway Mews
B1 1 Dora Ho
2 Flansham Ho
3 Gatwick Ho
4 Ashpark Ho
5 Newdigate Ho
6 Salmon St
6 Midhurst Ho
7 Redbourne Ho
8 Southwater Cl
9 Aithan Ho
10 Britley Ho
11 Cheadle Ho
12 Elland Ho
13 Butler Ho
14 Fitzroy Ho
15 Leybourne Ho
B2 1 Wearmouth Ho
2 Elmslie Point
3 Grindley Ho
4 Stileman Ho
5 Baythorne St
6 Wilcox Ho
8 Robeson St
9 Couzens Ho
10 Perley Ho
11 Whytlaw Ho
12 Printon Ho
13 Perkins Ho
14 Bowry Ho
15 Booker Cl
16 Tunley Gn
17 Callingham Cl
18 Tasker Ho
B4 1 Trellis Sq
2 Sheffield Sq
3 Howcroft Ho
4 Astra Ho
6 Byas Ho
7 George Lansbury Ho
8 Regal Pl
9 Coborn Mews
10 Cavendish Terr
11 Buttermere Ho
12 Tracy Ho
12 Hanover Pl
13 Coniston Ho
14 St Clair Ho
15 Verity Ho
16 Icarus Ho
17 Whippingham Ho
18 Winchester Ho
19 Hamilton Ho
20 Longthorne Ho
B5 1 Roman Square Mkt
2 John Bond Ho
3 McKenna Ho
4 Dennis Ho
5 McBride Ho
6 Libra Rd
7 Dave Adams Ho
8 Tay Ho
9 Sleat Ho
10 Ewart Pl
11 Brodick Ho
12 Lunan Ho
13 Mull Ho
14 Sinclairs Ho
15 Driftway Ho
16 Clayhall Ct
17 Berebinder Ho
18 Stavers Ho
19 Barford Ho
20 Partridge Ho
21 Gosford Ho
22 Gullane Ho
23 Cruden Ho
24 Anglo Rd
25 Dornoch Ho
26 Dunnet Ho
27 Enard Ho
28 Fraserburgh Ho
29 Forth Ho
30 Ordell Ct
31 William Pl
B6 1 Hampstead Wlk
2 Waverton Ho
3 Elton Ho
4 Locton Gn
5 Birtwhistle Ho
6 Clare Ho
7 Magpie Ho
8 Atkins Ct
9 Tait Ct
10 Ranwell Ho
11 Ranwell Cl
12 Tufnell Ct
13 Pulteney Cl
14 Vic Johnson Ho
C1 1 Landin Ho
2 Charlesworth Ho
3 Gurdon Ho
4 Trendell Ho
5 Menteath Ho
6 Minchin Ho
7 Donne Ho
8 Denison Ho
9 Anglesey Ho
10 Gough Wlk
11 Baring Ho
12 Hopkins Ho
13 Granville Ho
14 Gladstone Ho
15 Russell Ho
16 Pusey Ho
17 Overstone Ho
18 Stanley Ho
19 Old School Sq
C2 1 Bredel Ho
2 Linton Ho
3 Matthews Ho
4 Woodcock Ho
5 Limborough Ho
6 Maydwell Ho
7 Underhill Ho

97 C2
8 Meyrick Ho
9 Ambrose Ho
10 Carpenter Ho
11 Robinson Ho
12 Bramble Ho
13 Bilberry Ho
14 Bracken Ho
15 Berberis Ho
16 Busbridge Ho
17 Metropolitan Cl
18 Invicta Cl
19 Bellmaker Ct
C3 1 Fairmont Ho
2 Healy Ho
3 Zodiac Ho
4 Buick Ho
5 Consul Ho
6 Bentley Ho
7 Cresta Ho
8 Daimler Ho
9 Riley Ho
10 Jensen Ho
11 Lagonda Ho
12 Ireton St
13 Navenby Wlk
14 Burwell Wlk
15 Leadenham Ct
16 Sleaford Ho
C4 1 Jarret Ho
2 Marsalis Ho
3 Lovette Ho
4 Drapers Almhouses
5 Mallard Point
6 Creswick Wlk
7 Bevin Ho
8 Huggins Ho
9 Williams Ho
10 Harris Ho
11 Marina Ct
12 Electric Ho
13 Matching Ct
14 Wellington Bldgs
15 Grafton Ho
16 Columbia Ho
17 Berkeley Ho
D1 1 Colebrook Ho
2 Essex Ho
3 Salisbury Ho
4 Maidstone Ho
5 Osterley Ho
6 Norwich Ho
7 Clarissa Ho
8 Elgin Ho
9 Shaftesbury Lo
10 Shepherd Ho
11 Jeremiah St
12 Elizabeth Cl
13 Chilcot Cl
14 Fitzgerald Ho
15 Vesey Path
16 Ennis Ho
17 Kilmore Ho
D2 1 Sumner Ho
2 Irvine Ho
3 David Ho
4 Brushwood Ho
5 Limehouse Cut
6 Colmans Wharf
7 Foundary Ho
8 Radford Ho
D3 1 Broxbourne Ho
2 Roxford Ho
3 Biscott Ho
4 Stanborough Ho
5 Hillstone Ct
D4 1 Bradley Ho
2 Prioress Ho
3 Alton Ho
4 Foxley Ho
5 Munden Ho
6 Canterbury Ho
7 Corbin Ho
8 Barton Ho
9 Jolles Ho
10 Rudstone Ho
11 Baxter Ho
12 Baker Ho
13 Insley Ho
14 Hardwicke Ho
15 Glebe Terr
16 Priory St
17 Sadler Ho
18 Ballinger Point
19 Henshall Point
20 Dorrington Point
21 Warren Ho
22 Fairlie Ct
23 Regent Sq
24 Hackworth Point
25 Priestman Point
26 Wingate Ho
27 Nethercott Ho
28 Thelbridge Ho
29 Bowden Ho
30 Kerscott Ho
31 Southcott Ho
32 Birchdown Ho
33 Upcott Ho
34 Langmead Ho
35 Limscott Ho
36 Northleigh Ho
37 Huntshaw Ho
38 Chagford Ho
39 Ashcombe Ho
40 Shillingford Ho
41 Patrick Connolly Gdns
42 Lester Ct
43 Franklin St
44 Taft Way
45 Washington Cl
46 Elizabeth Ho
47 William Guy Gdns
48 Denbury Ho
49 Holsworthy Ho

98

A1 1 Langdon Ho
2 Balfron Twr
3 Tabard Ct
4 Delta Bldg
5 Kilbrennan Ho
6 Thistle Ho
7 Heather Ho
8 Tartan Ho
9 Trident Ho
A2 1 Mills Gr
3 Duncan Ct
B1 1 Lansbury Gdns
2 Thesus Ho
2 Theseus Ho
3 Adams Ho
4 Jones Ho
5 Sam March Ho
6 Arapiles Ho
7 Athenia Ho
8 Jervis Bay Ho
9 Helen Mackay Ho
10 Gaze Ho
11 Ritchie Ho
12 Circle Ho
13 Dunkeld Ho
14 Braithwaite Ho
15 Rosemary Dr
16 Sorrel La
17 East India Dock Road Tunnel
C6 1 Barnby Sq
2 Barnby St
3 Brassett Point
4 David Lee Point
5 Worthing Cl
6 Bexhill Wlk
7 Old Borrowfield
8 Elmgreen Cl
9 Stafford Morris Ho
10 Nina Mackay Cl
11 Lime Wlk
D1 1 Newton Point
2 Sparke Terr
3 Montesquieu Terr
4 Crawford Point
5 Rathbone Ho
6 George St
7 Emily St
8 Fendt Cl
9 Sabbarton St
D2 1 Radley Terr
2 Rathbone Mkt
3 Thomas North Terr
4 Bernard Cassidy St
5 Mary St
6 Hughes Terr
7 Swanscombe Point
8 Rawlinson Point
9 Kennedy Cox Ho
10 Cooper St
D6 1 Harris Cotts
2 Moorey Cl
3 Euro Bsns Ctr
4 Ladywell St
5 Caistor Ho
6 Redfern Ho

99

A2 1 Odeon Ct
2 Edward Ct
3 Newhaven La
4 Ravenscroft Cl
5 Douglas Rd
6 Ferrier Point
7 Harvey Point
8 Wood Point
9 Trinity St
10 Pattinson Point
11 Clinch Ct
12 Mint Bsns Pk
A3 1 Webb Gdns
2 Eric Shipman Terr
3 Warmington St
4 Jellicoe Rd
5 Frank St
6 Seaton Cl
7 Tabernacle Ave
8 Upland Rd
9 Clove St
10 Edward St
A4 1 Bob Anker Cl
2 Lea Ct
3 Third Ave
4 Suffolk Rd
A5 1 Lettsom Wlk
2 Ashburton Terr
3 Grasmere Rd
4 Dimsdale Wlk
5 Rawstone Wlk
6 Scott Ho
7 Willett Ho
8 James Cl
9 Cordwainers Wlk
10 Victoria Point
11 Settle Point
12 Middle Rd
A6 1 Royston Ct
B4 1 Barbers Alley
2 Grengate Lo
3 Augurs La
4 Surrey St
5 Dongola Rd W
6 Bemersyde Point
7 Rowntree Clifford Cl
C5 1 Wellby Ct
2 Bishop Wilfred Wood Ct
3 Castle Point
4 Moat Dr
C6 1 Queen's Mkt
2 Tolpuddle Ave
3 Crown Mews
4 Lilac Ct
5 Hamara Ghar
6 Greenleaf Rd
7 Massey Ct
8 Florence Rd
9 Sissulu Ct
10 Austin Ct
D2 1 Partridge Cl
2 Vanbrugh Cl
3 Meadowsweet Cl
4 St Michaels Cl
5 Long Mark Rd
6 Congreve Wlk
D5 1 Foxcombe Ct
2 Rochford Cl
3 Kylemore Cl
4 Stondon Wlk
5 Imperial Mews
6 Dominica Cl
D6 1 Oldegate Ho
2 Gaitskell Ho
3 Cabot Way

100

A1 1 Hadleigh Wlk
2 Hawksmoor Cl
3 Fraser Cl
4 Moncrieff Cl
5 Burlington Cl
6 Dundonald Cl
7 Oakley Cl
8 Ashwell Cl
A2 1 Orchid Cl
2 Bellflower Cl
3 Partridge Sq
4 Larkspur Cl
5 Lobelia Cl
6 Stonechat Sq
7 Wintergreen Cl
8 Garnet Wlk
9 Mavis Wlk
10 Beacons Cl
11 Abbess Cl
12 Elmley Cl
13 Chetwood Wlk
14 Selby Cl
15 Denny Cl
16 Woodhatch Cl
A6 1 Oakwood Ct
2 Harrow Rd
3 Ray Massey Way
4 Madge Gill Way
5 Pilgrims Way
B1 1 Bowers Wlk
2 Barton Cl
3 Clayton Cl
4 Dixon Cl
5 Gautrey Sq
6 Wakerly Cl
7 Canterbury Cl
8 Goose Sq
9 Coventry Cl
10 Butterfield Sq
11 Winchester Cl
B2 1 Fleetwood Ct
2 Lymington Cl
3 Holyhead Cl
4 Bondfield Rd
5 Tulip Cl
6 Ambrose Cl
7 Sage Cl
8 Lindwood Cl
D1 1 Weymouth Cl
2 Founder Cl
3 Admirals Ct

101

A6 1 Wellington St
2 St Ann's Rd
3 Bamber Ho
B6 1 Jarvis Cl
2 Mayflower Ho
3 Westbury Ct
4 Millicent Preston Ho
5 Louise Graham Ho
6 Grange Ho
7 Basing Ho
8 Barnes Ho
9 Lexham Ho
10 Ripple Ct
11 Waldegrave Ct
12 Howard Ct

104

A6 1 Milburn Dr
2 Cousins Cl
3 Leacroft Cl

108

C5 1 Marlow Ct
2 Andrews Ct
3 Vine Cotts
4 Benjamin Ct
5 Broadway Bldgs
D5 1 Silverdale Cl
2 Burdett Cl
3 Hopefield
4 Maunder Rd

109

A5 1 Glastonbury Ct
2 Evesham Ct
3 Lacock Ct
4 Wigmore Ct
5 Melrose Ct
6 Brownlow Rd
7 Chignell Pl
8 Shirley Ct
9 Trojan Ct
10 Hatfield Rd
C6 1 Abbey Lo
2 Yew Tree Grange
3 Abinger Ct

110

A1 1 Burford Ho
2 Hope Cl
3 Centaur Ct
4 Phoenix Ct
A6 1 Watermans Mews
2 Hills Mews
3 Grosvenor Ct
4 Elton Lo
5 Hambledon Ct
C1 1 Surrey Cres
2 Forbes Ho
3 Haining Cl
4 Melville Ct
5 London Stile
6 Stile Hall Par
7 Priory Lo
8 Kew Bridge Ct
9 Meadowcroft
10 St James Ct
11 Rivers Ho
C5 1 Grosvenor Par
2 Oakfield Ct
3 Hart Grove Ct
4 Grosvenor Ct
D1 1 Churchdale Ct
2 Cromwell Cl
3 Cambridge Rd S
4 Oxbridge Ct
5 Tomlinson Cl
6 Gunnersbury Mews
7 Grange The
8 Gunnersbury Cl
D4 1 Cheltenham Pl
2 Beaumaris Twr
3 Arundel Ho
4 Pevensey Ct
5 Jerome Twr
6 Anstey Ct
7 Bennett Ct
8 Gunnersbury Ct
D5 1 Lantry Ct
2 Rosemount Ct
3 Moreton Twr
4 Acton Central Ind Est
5 Rufford Twr
6 Narrow St
7 Mount Pl
8 Sidney Miller Ct
9 Mill Hill Terr
10 Mill Hill Gr

111

A1 1 Arlington Park Mans
2 Sandown Ho
3 Goodwood Ho
4 Windsor Ho
5 Lingfield Ho
6 Ascot Ho
7 Watchfield Ct
8 Belgrave Ct
9 Beverley Ct
10 Beaumont Ct
11 Harvard Rd
12 Troubridge Ct
A2 1 Chiswick Green Studios
2 Bell Ind Est
3 Fairlawn Ct
4 Dukes Gate
5 Dewsbury Ct
6 Chiswick Terr
A3 1 Blackmore Twr
2 Bollo Ct
3 Kipling Twr
4 Lawrence Ct
5 Maugham Ct
6 Reade Ct
7 Woolf Ct
8 Shaw Ct
9 Verne Ct
10 Wodehouse Ct
11 Greenock Rd
12 Garden Ct
13 Barons Gate
14 Cleveland Rd
15 Chapter Cl
15 Carver Cl
16 Beauchamp Cl
17 Holmes Ct
A4 1 Belgrave Cl
2 Buckland Wlk
3 Frampton Ct
4 Telfer Cl
5 Harlech Twr
6 Corfe Twr
7 Barwick Ho
8 Charles Hocking Ho
9 Sunninghill Ct
10 Salisbury St
11 Jameson Pl
A5 1 Rectory Rd
2 Derwentwater Mans
3 Market Pl
4 Hooper's Mews
5 Cromwell Pl
6 Locarno Rd
7 Edgecote Cl
8 Harleyford Manor
9 Coopers Ct
B1 1 Chatsworth Lo
2 Prospect Pl
3 Townhall Ave
4 Devonhurst Pl
5 Heathfield Ct
6 Horticultural Pl
7 Merlin Ho
8 Garth Rd
C1 1 Glebe Cl
2 Devonshire Mews
3 Binns Terr
4 Ingress St
5 Swanscombe Rd
6 Brackley Terr
7 Stephen Fox Ho
8 Manor Gdns
9 Coram Ho
10 Flaxman Ho
11 Thorneycroft Ho
12 Thornhill Ho
13 Kent Ho
14 Oldfield Ho
C2 1 Chestnut Ho
2 Bedford Ho
3 Bedford Cnr
4 Sydney Ho
5 Bedford Park Cnr
6 Priory Gdns
7 Windmill Alley
8 Castle Pl
9 Jonathan Ct
10 Windmill Pas
11 Chardin Rd
12 Gable Ho
C3 1 Fleet Ct
2 Ember Ct
3 Emlyn Gdns
4 Clone Ct
5 Brent Ct
6 Abbey Ct
7 Ormsby Lo
8 St Catherine's Ct
C4 1 Longford Ct
2 Mole Ct
3 Lea Ct
4 Wandle Ct
5 Beverley Ct
6 Roding Ct
7 Crane Ct
D1 1 Miller's Ct
2 British Grove Pas
3 British Grove S
4 Berestede Rd
5 North Eyot Gdns
D2 1 Flanders Mans
2 Stamford Brook Mans
3 Linkenholt Mans
4 Prebend Mans
5 Middlesex Ct
D3 1 Stamford Brook Gdns
2 Hauteville Court Gdns
3 Ranelagh Gdns

112

A2 1 Hamlet Ct
2 Derwent Ct
3 Westcroft Ct
4 Black Lion Mews
5 St Peter's Villas
6 Standish Ho
7 Chambon Pl
8 Court Mans
A4 2 Victoria Ho
3 Lycett Pl
4 Kylemore Ct
5 Alexandra Ct
6 Lytten Ct
7 Becklow Mews
8 Northcroft Ct
9 Bailey Ct
10 Spring Cott
11 Landor Wlk
12 Laurence Mews
13 Hadyn Park Ct
14 Askew Mans
B2 1 Albion Gdns
2 Flora Gdns
3 Lamington St
4 Felgate Mews
5 Galena Ho
6 Albion Mews
7 Albion Ct
8 King Street Cloisters
9 Dimes Pl
10 Clarence Ct
11 Hampshire Hog La
12 Marryat Ct
B4 1 Westbush Ct
2 Goldhawk Mews
3 Sycamore Ho
4 Shackleton Ct
5 Drake Ct
6 Scotts Ct
B6 1 Abercrombie Ho
2 Bathurst Ho
3 Brisbane Ho
4 Bentinck Ho
5 Ellenborough Ho
6 Lawrence Cl
7 Mackenzie Cl
8 Carteret Ho
9 Calvert Ho
10 Winthrop Ho
11 Auckland Ho
12 Blaxland Ho
13 Havelock Cl
14 Hargraves Ho
15 Hudson Cl
16 Phipps Ho
17 Lawson Ho
18 Hastings Ho
19 Wolfe Ho
20 Malabar Ct
21 White City Es
21 Commonwea Ave
22 Charnock Ho
23 Canning Ho
24 Cornwallis Ho
26 Champlain Ho
27 Grey Ho
28 Durban Ho
29 Baird Ho
30 Campbell Ho
31 Mitchell Ho
32 Denham Ho
33 Mackay Ho
34 Evans Ho
35 Daws Ho
36 Mandela Cl
C1 1 Bridge Avenue Mans
2 Bridgeview
3 College Ct
4 Beatrice Ho
5 Amelia Ho
6 Edith Ho
7 Joanna Ho
8 Mary Ho
9 Adela Ho
10 Sophia Ho
11 Henrietta Ho
12 Charlotte Ho
13 Alexandra Ho
14 Bath Pl
15 Elizabeth Ho
16 Margaret Ho
17 Peabody Est
18 Eleanor Ho
19 Isabella Ho
20 Caroline Ho
21 Chancellors Wharf
22 Sussex Pl
C2 1 Phoenix Lodge Mans
2 Samuel's Cl
3 Broadway Arc
4 Brook Ho
5 Hammersmith Broadway
C4 1 Verulam Ho
2 Grove Mans
3 Frobisher Ct
4 Library Mans
5 Pennard Mans
6 Lanark Mans
7 Kerrington Ct
8 Granville Mans
9 Romney Ct
10 Rayner Ct
11 Sulgrave Gdns
12 Bamborough Gdns
D3 1 Grosvenor Residences
2 Blythe Mews
3 Burnand Ho
4 Bradford Ho
5 Springvale Terr
6 Ceylon Rd
7 Walpole Ct
8 Bronte Ct
9 Boswell Ct
10 Souldern Rd
11 Brook Green Flats
12 Haarlem Rd
13 Stafford Mans
14 Lionel Mans
D4 1 Vanderbilt Villas
2 Bodington Ct
3 Kingham Cl
4 Clearwater Terr
5 Lorne Gdns
6 Cameret Ct
7 Bush Ct
8 Shepherds Ct
9 Rockley Ct
10 Grampians The
11 Charcroft Ct
12 Addison Park Mans
13 Sinclair Mans
D5 1 St Katherine's Wlk
2 Dorrit Ho
3 Pickwick Ho
4 Dombey Ho
5 Caranday Villas
6 Mortimer Ho
7 Nickleby Ho
8 Stebbing Ho
9 Boxmoor Ho
10 Poynter Ho
11 Swanscombe Ho
12 Darnley Terr

13 Norland Ho
14 Hume Ho
D6 1 Frinstead Ho
2 Hurstway Wlk
3 Testerton Wlk
4 Grenfell Wlk
5 Grenfell Twr
6 Barandon Wlk
7 Treadgold Ho
8 St Clements Ct
9 Willow Way
10 Florence Ho
11 Dora Ho
12 Carton Ho
13 Agnes Ho
14 Marley Ho
16 Waynflete Sq

118

A1 1 Alison Ct
2 West Point
3 Centre Point
4 East Point
5 Proctor Ho
6 Tovy Ho
7 Brettinghurst
8 Colechurch Ho
9 Harman Cl
10 Avondale Ho
11 Lanark Ho
12 George Elliston Ho
13 Eric Wilkins Ho
14 Archers Lo
15 Culloden Cl
16 Fallow Ct
17 Fern Wlk
18 Ivy Ct
19 Winter Lo
A2 1 Cadbury Way
2 Robert Bell Ho
3 Robert Jones Ho
4 William Rush-brooke Ho
5 Helen Taylor Ho
6 Peter Hills Ho
7 Charles Mackenzie Ho
8 Drappers Way
9 Abbey Gdns
10 Maria Cl
11 Windmill Cl
12 Townsend Ho
13 Mason Ho
14 Langdon Way
15 Hannah Mary Way
16 Kotree Way
17 Whittaker Way
A3 1 Rudge Ho
2 Spenlow Ho
3 Darnay Ho
4 Carton Ho
5 Giles Ho
6 Bowley Ho
7 Casby Ho
8 Sun Pas
9 Ness St
10 Voyager Bsns Est
11 Dockley Road Ind Est
12 Spa Ct
13 Discovery Bsns Pk
14 Priter Road Hostel
15 Salisbury Ct
16 William Ellis Way
17 John McKenna Wlk
18 Toussaint Wlk
19 Gillison Wlk
20 Bromfield Ct
21 Ben Smith Way
22 Major Rd
23 Old Jamaica Bsns Est
A4 1 Providence Twr
2 Springalls Wharf
3 St Saviours Ho
4 Providence Sq
5 Farthing Alley
6 Peter Butler Ho
7 Brownlow Ho
8 Fleming Ho
9 Dombey Ho
10 Copperfield Ho
11 Tapley Ho
12 Parkers Row
13 Wade Ho
14 Bardell Ho
15 Nickleby Ho
16 John Felton Rd
18 Pickwick Ho
19 Oliver Ho
20 Weller Ho
21 Tupman Ho
22 Haredale Ho
23 Havisham Ho
24 Micawber Ho
25 Wrayburn Ho
26 Dartle Ct
27 Burnaby Ct
28 Waterside Cl
29 Wickfield Ho
30 Fountain Ho
31 Fountain Green Sq
A5 1 Trade Winds Ct
2 Spice Ct
3 Leeward Ct
4 Bridgeport Pl
5 Tamarind Yd
6 Cope Yd
7 Nightingale Ho
8 St Anthony's Cl
9 Stockholm Way
10 Miah Terr
11 Seville Ho
12 Douthwaite Sq
13 Codling Cl
14 Hermitage Ct
15 Capital Wharf
16 Cinnabar Wharf East
17 Cinnabar Wharf Central
18 Cinnabar Wharf West
19 Halcyon Wharf
A6 1 Conant Mews
2 Hanson Ho
3 Victoria Ct
4 Swan Pas
5 Royal Mint Pl
6 Flank St
7 Ensign Ct
8 Sapphire Ct
9 George Ley-bourne Ho
10 Fletcher St
11 Wellclose St
12 Noble Ho
13 Hatton Ho
14 Shearsmith Ho
15 Breezer's Ct
16 Pennington Ct
17 Onedin Point
18 Liberty Pl
B1 1 Hockney Ct
2 Toulouse Ct
3 Lowry Ct
4 Barry Ho
5 Lewis Ct
6 Gainsborough Ct
7 Renoir Ct
8 Blake Ct
9 Raphael Ct
10 Rembrandt Ct
11 Constable Ct
12 Da Vinci Ct
13 Gaugin Ct
14 Michelangelo Ct
15 Monet Ct
16 Weald Cl
17 Jasmin Lo
18 Birchmere Lo
19 Weybridge Ct
20 Florence Ho
21 Gleneagles Cl
22 Sunningdale Cl
23 Muirfield Cl
24 Turnberry Cl
25 St Andrews Cl
26 Kingsdown Cl
27 St Davids Cl
28 Galway Cl
29 Edenbridge Cl
30 Birkdale Cl
31 Tralee Ct
32 Woburn Ct
33 Belfry Cl
34 Troon Cl
35 Holywell Cl
B2 1 Market Pl
2 Trappes Ho
3 Thurland Ho
4 Ramsfort Ho
5 Hambley Ho
6 Holford Ho
7 Pope Ho
8 Southwell Ho
9 Mortain Ho
10 Radcliffe Ho
11 Southwark Park Est
12 Galleywall Road Trad Est
13 Trevithick Ho
14 Barlow Ho
15 Donkin Ho
16 Landmann Ho
17 Fitzmaurice Ho
18 Dodd Ho
B3 1 Perryn Rd
2 Chalfont Ho
3 Prestwood Ho
4 Farmer Ho
5 Gataker Ho
6 Gataker St
7 Cornick Ho
8 Glebe Ho
9 Matson Ho
10 Hickling Ho
11 St Andrews Ho
B4 1 Butterfield Cl
2 Janeway Pl
3 Trotwood Ho
4 Cranbourn Ho
5 Cherry Garden Ho
6 Burton Ho
7 Morriss Ho
8 King Edward The Third Mews
9 Cathay St
10 Rotherhithe St
B5 1 China Ct
2 Wellington Terr
3 Stevedore St
4 Portland Sq
5 Reardon Ho
6 Lowder Ho
7 Meeting House Alley
8 Farthing Fields
9 Oswell Ho
10 Park Lo
11 Doughty Ct
12 Inglefield Sq
13 Chopin's Ct
14 Welsh Ho
15 Hilliard Ho
16 Clegg St
17 Tasman Ho
18 Ross Ho
19 Wapping Dock St
20 Bridewell Pl
21 New Tower Bldgs
22 Tower Bldgs
23 Chimney Ct
24 Jackman Ho
25 Fenner Ho
26 Franklin Ho
27 Frobisher Ho
28 Flinders Ho
29 Chancellor Ho
30 Beechey Ho
31 Reardon Path
32 Parry Ho
33 Vancouver Ho
34 Willoughby Ho
35 Sanctuary The
36 Dundee Ct
37 Pierhead Wharf
38 Scandrett St
39 St Johns Ct
B6 1 Newton Ho
2 Richard Neale Ho
3 Maddocks Ho
4 Cornwall St
5 Brockmer Ho
6 Dellow Ho
7 Bewley Ho
8 Artichoke Hill
C2 1 Damory Ho
2 Antony Ho
3 Roderick Ho
4 Pedworth Gdns
5 Beamish Ho
6 Gillam Ho
7 George Walter Ho
8 Richard Ho
9 Adron Ho
10 Westlake
11 McIntosh Ho
C3 1 Blick Ho
2 Neptune Ho
3 Scotia Ct
4 Murdoch Ho
5 Edmonton Ct
6 Niagara Ct
7 Columbia Point
8 Ritchie Ho
9 Wells Ho
10 Helen Peele Cotts
11 Orchard Ho
12 Dock Offices
13 Landale Ho
14 Courthope Ho
C4 1 Mayflower St
2 St Mary's Est
3 Rupack St
4 Frank Whymark Ho
5 Adams Gardens Est
6 Hatteraick St
7 Hythe Ho
8 Seaford Ho
9 Sandwich Ho
11 Winchelsea Ho
12 Kenning St
13 Western Pl
14 Ainsty St
15 Pine Ho
16 Beech Ho
17 Larch Ho
18 Seth St
19 Turner Ct
20 Risdon Ho
21 Risdon St
22 Aylton Est
23 Manitoba Ct
24 Calgary Ct
25 Irwell Est
26 City Bsns Ctr
27 St Olav's Sq
C5 1 John Rennie Wlk
2 Malay Ho
3 Wainwright Ho
4 Riverside Mans
5 Shackleton Ho
6 Whitehorn Ho
7 Wavel Ct
8 Prusom's Island
C6 1 Gosling Ho
2 Vogler Ho
3 Donovan Ho
4 Knowlden Ho
5 Chamberlain Ho
6 Moore Ho
7 Thornewill Ho
8 Fisher Ho
9 All Saints Ct
10 Coburg Dwellings
11 Lowood Ho
12 Solander Gdns
13 Chancery Bldgs
14 Ring Ho
15 Juniper St
16 Gordon Ho
17 West Block
18 North Block
19 South Block
D2 1 John Kennedy Ho
2 Brydale Ho
3 Balman Ho
4 Tissington Ct
5 Harbord Ho
6 Westfield Ho
7 Albert Starr Ho
8 John Brent Ho
9 William Evans Ho
10 Raven Ho
11 Egret Ho
12 Fulmar Ho
13 Dunlin Ho
14 Siskin Ho
15 Sheldrake Ho
16 Buchanan Ct
17 Burrage Ct
18 Biddenham Ho
19 Ayston Ho
20 Empingham Ho
21 Deanshanger Ho
22 Codicote Ho
D4 1 Schooner Cl
2 Dolphin Cl
3 Clipper Cl
4 Deauville Ct
5 Colette Ct
6 Coniston Ct
7 Virginia Ct
8 Derwent Ct
9 Grantham Ct
10 Serpentine Ct
11 Career Ct
12 Lacine Ct
13 Fairway Ct
14 Harold Ct
15 Spruce Ho
16 Cedar Ho
17 Sycamore Ho
18 Woodland Cres
19 Poplar Ho
20 Adelphi Ct
21 Basque Ct
22 Aberdale Ct
23 Quilting Ct
24 Chargrove Cl
25 Radley Ct
26 Greenacre Sq
27 Maple Leaf Sq
28 Stanhope Cl
29 Hawke Pl
30 Drake Cl
31 Brass Talley Alley
32 Monkton Ho
33 James Ho
34 Wolfe Cres
D5 1 Clarence Mews
2 Raleigh Ct
3 Katherine Cl
4 Woolcombes Ct
5 Tudor Ct
6 Quayside Ct
7 Princes River-side Rd
8 Surrey Ho
9 Tideway Ct
10 Edinburgh Ct
11 Falkirk Ct
12 Byelands Cl
13 Gwent Ct
14 Lavender Ho
15 Abbotshade Rd
16 Bellamy's Ct
17 Blenheim Ct
18 Sandringham Ct
19 Hampton Ct
20 Windsor Ct
21 Balmoral Ct
22 Westminster Ct
D6 1 Barnardo Gdns
2 Roslin Ho
3 Glamis Est
4 Peabody Est
5 East Block
6 Highway Trad Ctr The
7 Highway Bsns Pk The
8 Cranford Cotts
9 Ratcliffe Orch
10 Scotia Bldg
11 Mauretania Bldg
12 Compania Bldg
13 Sirius Bldg
14 Unicorn Bldg
15 Keepier Wharf

119

A2 1 Trafalgar Cl
2 Hornblower Cl
3 Cunard Wlk
4 Caronia Ct
5 Carinthia Ct
6 Freswick Ho
7 Graveley Ho
8 Husbourne Ho
9 Crofters Ct
10 Pomona Ho
11 Hazelwood Ho
12 Cannon Wharf Bsns Ctr
13 Bence Ho
14 Clement Ho
15 Pendennis Ho
16 Lighter Cl
17 Mast Ct
18 Rushcutters Ct
19 Boat Lifter Way
A6 1 St Georges Sq
2 Drake Ho
3 Osprey Ho
4 Fleet Ho
5 Gainsborough Ho
6 Victory Pl
7 Challenger Ho
8 Conrad Ho
9 Lock View Ct
10 Shoulder of Mutton Alley
11 Frederick Sq
12 Helena Sq
13 Elizabeth Sq
14 Sophia Sq
15 William Sq
16 Lamb Ct
17 Lockside
19 Ionian Bldg
20 Regents Gate Ho
B1 1 Gransden Ho
2 Daubeney Twr
3 North Ho
4 Rochfort Ho
5 Keppel Ho
6 Camden Ho
7 Sanderson Ho
8 Berkeley Ho
9 Strafford Ho
10 Richman Ho
11 Hurleston Ho
12 Grafton Ho
13 Fulcher Ho
14 Citrus Ho
B2 1 Windsock Cl
2 Linberry Wlk
3 Lanyard Ho
4 Golden Hind Pl
5 James Lind Ho
6 Harmon Ho
7 Pelican Ho
8 Bembridge Ho
9 Terrace The
10 George Beard Rd
11 Colonnade The
12 Pepys Ent Ctr
B6 1 Hamilton Ho
2 Imperial Ho
3 Oriana Ho
4 Queens Ct
5 Brightlingsea Pl
6 Faraday Ho
7 Ropemaker's Fields
8 Oast Ct
9 Mitre The
10 Bate St
11 Joseph Irwin Ho
12 Padstow Ho
13 Bethlehem Ho
14 Saunders Cl
15 Roche Ho
16 Stocks Pl
17 Trinidad Ho
18 Grenada Ho
19 Kings Ho
20 Dunbar Wharf
21 Limekiln Wharf
C1 3 Hudson Ct
4 Shackleton Ct
5 Perry Ct
6 Maritime Quay
C2 1 Olympian Ct
2 Aphrodite Ct
3 Mercury Ct
4 Poseidon Ct
5 Neptune Ct
6 Artemis Ct
7 Hera Ct
8 Ares Ct
9 Cyclops Mews
10 Magellan Pl
11 Britannia Rd
12 Deptford Ferry Rd
13 Ironmonger's Pl
14 Radnor Wlk
15 Ashdown Wlk
16 Rothsay Wlk
17 Dartmoor Wlk
18 Ringwood Gdns
19 Dockers Tanner Rd
20 Apollo Bldg
21 Nova Bldg
C3 1 St Hubert's Ho
2 John Tucker Ho
3 Clare Grant Ho
4 Gilbertson Ho
5 Bowsprit Point
6 Scoulding Ho
7 Cord Way
8 Cressall Ho
9 Alexander Ho
10 Kedge Ho
C4 3 Jefferson Bldg
4 Waterman Bldg
5 Pierpoint Bldg
6 Franklin Bldg
7 Bellamy Cl
8 Bosun Cl
11 Edison Bldg
12 Vanguard Bldg
C6 1 West India Ho
2 Birchfield Ho
3 Elderfield Ho
4 Thornfield Ho
5 Gorsefield Ho
6 Arborfield Ho
7 Colborne Ho
8 East India Bldgs
9 Compass Point
10 Salter St
11 Kelly Ct
12 Flynn Ct
13 Mary Jones Ho
14 Horizon Bldg
15 Berber Pl
D2 1 Brassey Ho
2 Triton Ho
3 Warspite Ho
4 Rodney Ho
5 Conway Ho
6 Exmouth Ho
7 Akbar Ho
8 Arethusa Ho
9 Tasman Ct
D6 1 Westcott Ho
2 Corry Ho
3 Malam Gdns
4 Devitt Ho
5 Leyland Ho
6 Wigram Ho
7 Willis Ho
8 Balsam Ho
9 Finch's Ct
10 Poplar Bath St
11 Lawless St
12 Storey Ho
13 Abbot Ho
14 Landon Wlk
15 Goodhope Ho
16 Goodfaith Ho
17 Winant Ho
18 Lubbock Ho
19 Goodwill Ho
20 Martindale Ho
21 Holmsdale Ho
22 Norwood Ho
23 Constant Ho
24 Woodall Cl

120

A2 1 Betty May Gray Ho
2 Castleton Ho
3 Urmston Ho
4 Salford Ho
5 Capstan Ho
6 Frigate Ho
7 Galleon Ho
8 Barons Lo
A3 1 Cardale St
2 Hickin St
3 John McDonald Ho
4 Thorne Ho
5 Skeggs Ho
6 St Bernard Ho
7 Kimberley Ho
8 Kingdon Ho
9 Lingard Ho
10 Yarrow Ho
11 Sandpiper Ct
12 Nightingale Ct
13 Robin Ct
14 Heron Ct
A4 1 Llandovery Ho
2 Rugless Ho
3 Ash Ho
4 Elm Ho
5 Cedar Ho
6 Castalia Sq
7 Walkers Lo
7 Antilles Bay
7 Alice Shepherd Ho
8 Oak Ho
9 Ballin Ct
10 Martin Ct
11 Grebe Ct
12 Kingfisher Ct
A6 1 Discovery Ho
2 Mountague Pl
3 Virginia Ho
4 Collins Ho
5 Lawless Ho
6 Carmichael Ho
7 Commodore Ho
8 Mermaid Ho
9 Bullivant St
10 Anderson Ho
11 Mackrow Wlk
12 Robin Hood Gdns
B2 1 Verwood Lo
2 Fawley Lo
3 Lyndhurst Lo
4 Blyth Cl
5 Farnworth Ho
6 Francis Cl
B6 2 Settlers Ct
3 Susan Constant Ct
4 Adventurers Ct
5 Bartholomew Ct
6 Atlantic Ct
7 Cape Henry Ct
8 Wotton Ct
9 Studley Ct
10 Wingfield Ct
C1 1 Bellot Gdns
2 Thornley Pl
3 King William La
4 Bolton Ho
5 Miles Ho
6 Mell St
7 Sam Manners Ho
8 Hatcliffe Almshouses
9 Woodland Wlk
10 Earlswood Cl
D1 1 Baldrey Ho
2 Christie Ho
3 Dyson Ho
4 Cliffe Ho
5 Moore Ho
6 Collins Ho
7 Lockyer Ho

8 Halley Ho
9 Kepler Ho

121

A1 1 Layfield Ho
2 Westerdale Rd
3 Mayston Mews
A5 1 Capulet Mews
2 Pepys Cres
3 De Quincey Mews
4 Hardy Ave
5 Tom Jenkinson Rd
6 Hanameel St
7 Kennacraig Cl
9 Gatcombe Rd
10 Badminton Mews
11 Holyrood Mews
12 Britannia Gate
13 Dalemain Mews
A6 1 Clements Ave
2 Martindale Ave
B1 1 Phipps Ho
2 Hartwell Ho
3 Nicholas Stacey Ho
4 Frank Burton Cl
B5 1 Beaulieu Ave
2 Charles Winchup Rd
3 Audley Dr
4 Julie Garfield Mews
4 Julia Garfield Mews
5 Rayleigh Rd
6 Pirie St
7 Rayleigh Rd
7 Hanameel St
8 Ramsgate Cl
9 West Mersea Cl
10 Hanameel St
10 Dunlop Point
11 Ramsgate Cl
12 Westwood Rd
C1 1 Ransom Rd
2 Linton Cl
3 Cedar Pl
4 Gooding Ho
5 Valiant Ho
6 Chaffey Ho
7 Benn Ho
8 Wellesley Cl
9 Gollogly Terr

122

A2 1 Harden Ct
2 Albion Ct
3 Viking Ho
4 Zealand Ho
5 Glenalvon Way
6 Parish Wharf
7 Elsinore Ho
8 Lelland Ho
9 Denmark Ho
10 Jutland Ho
11 Tivoli Gdns
12 Rance Ho
13 Peel Yates Ho
14 Rosebank Wlk
15 Paradise Pl
16 Woodville St
B2 1 Bowling Green Row
2 Sara Turnbull Ho
3 Brewhouse Rd
4 Red Barracks Rd
5 Marine Dr
7 Cambridge Ho
11 Hastings Ho
12 Cambridge Barracks Rd
13 Len Clifton Ho
14 Granby Ho
15 Milne Ho
16 Harding Ho
17 Rendlebury Ho
18 Rutland Ho
19 Townshend Ho
20 Mulgrave Ho
21 Murray Ho
22 Chatham Ho
23 Biddulph Ho
24 Carew Ho
25 Eleanor Wlk
C2 1 Preston Ho
2 Lindsay Ho
3 Fraser Ho
4 Pickering Ho
5 Watergate Ho
6 Grinling Ho
7 Glebe Ho
13 Slater Cl
14 Elliston Ho
15 Sir Martin Bowes Ho
16 Jim Bradley Cl
17 Bathway
18 Limavady Ho
C5 1 Westland Ho
2 Queensland Ho
3 Pier Par
4 Woodman Par
5 Shaw Ho
6 Glen Ho
7 Brocklebank Ho
D1 1 Branham Ho
2 Ford Ho
3 Wilford Ho
4 Parker Ho
5 Stirling Ho
6 Twiss Ho
7 Hewett Ho
D2 1 Beresford Sq
2 Central Ct
3 Walpole Pl
4 Anglesea Ave
5 Troy Ct
6 Ormsby Point
7 Haven Lo
8 Green Lawns
9 Eardley Point
10 Sandham Point
11 Bingham Point

123

A1 1 Glenmount Path
2 Claymill Ho
3 George Akass Ho
B1 1 Bert Reilly Ho
C1 1 Fox Hollow Cl
2 Goldsmid St

124

B5 1 Rowntree Path
2 Macaulay Way
3 Manning Ct
4 Chadwick Ct
5 Simon Ct
B6 1 Beveridge Ct
2 Hammond Way
3 Leonard Robbins Path
4 Lansbury Ct
5 Raymond Postgate Ct
6 Webb Ct
7 Curtis Way
8 Lytton Strachy Path
9 Keynes Ct
10 Marshall Path
11 Cross Ct
12 Octavia Way
13 Passfield Path
14 Mill Ct
15 Besant Ct
C4 1 Binsey Wlk
2 Tilehurst Point
3 Blewbury Ho
4 Coralline Wlk
5 Evenlode Ho
C5 1 Kingsley Ct
2 Wilberforce Ct
3 Shaftesbury Ct
4 Hazlitt Ct
5 Ricardo Path
6 Nassau Path
7 Malthus Path
8 Bright Ct
9 Cobden Ct
D4 1 Oakenholt Ho
2 Trewsbury Ho
3 Penton Ho
4 Osney Ho
5 Jacob Ho
6 Masham Ho
7 St Helens Rd
8 Clewer Ho
9 Maplin Ho
10 Wyfold Ho
11 Hibernia Point
12 Duxford Ho
13 Radley Ho

125

A3 1 Harlequin Ho
2 Dexter Ho
3 Argall Ho
4 Mangold Way
5 Lucerne Ct
6 Holstein Way
7 Abbotswood Cl
8 Plympton Cl
9 Benedict Cl
B1 1 Shakespeare Ho
2 Tennyson Ho
3 Dickens Ho
3 Chestnuts The
4 Scott Ho
5 Lansbury Ho
6 Shaw Ho
C1 1 Stevanne Ct
2 Tolcairn Ct
3 Chalfont Ct
4 Alonso Ct
5 Ariel Ct
6 Miranda Ho
7 Prospero Ho
8 Laurels The
9 Camden Ct
10 Newnham Lo
11 Court Lo
12 Flaxman Ct
13 Hertford Wlk
14 Riverview Ct
C3 1 Cressingham Ct
2 Telford Ho
3 Kelvin Ho
4 Faraday Ho
5 Jenner Ho
6 Keir Hardy Ho
7 Lennox Ho
8 Mary Macarthur Ho
9 Elizabeth Garrett Anderson Ho
10 William Smith Ho
11 Baden Powell Ho
12 Baird Ho
13 Boyle Ho

129

D1 1 Heathwood Ct
2 Aldermead
3 Northumberland Ct

130

C4 1 Osterley Lo
2 St Andrew's Cl
3 Parkfield
4 Fairways
5 Granwood Ct
6 Grovewood Ct

131

A2 1 Brewery Mews Bsns Ctr
2 Tolson Ho
3 Percy Gdns
4 Wynne Ct
5 Wisdom Ct
6 Swann Ct
7 Shrewsbury Wlk
8 King's Terr
9 Gistelword Ho
D5 1 Galba Ct
2 Servius Ct
3 Maurice Ct
4 Leo Ct
5 Otho Ct
6 Nero Ct
7 Romulus Ct
8 Pump Alley
D6 1 Brockshot Cl
2 Westbury Pl
4 Braemar Ct
5 Brook Ct
6 Clifden Ho
7 Cedar Ct
8 Cranbrook Ct
9 Somerset Lo
10 Alexandra Rd
11 Berkeley Ho

132

A1 1 St John's Gr
2 Michel's Row
3 Michelsdale Dr
4 Blue Anchor Alley
5 Clarence St
6 Sun Alley
7 Thames Link Ho
8 Benns Wlk
A6 1 Ferry Sq
3 Wilkes Rd
4 Albany Par
5 Charlton Ho
6 Albany Ho
7 Alma Ho
8 Griffin Ct
9 Cressage Ho
10 Tunstall Wlk
11 Trimmer Wlk
12 Running Horse Yd
13 Mission Sq
14 Distillery Wlk
B1 1 Towers The
2 Longs Ct
3 Sovereign Ct
4 Robinson Ct
5 Calvert Ct
6 Bedford Ct
7 Hickey's Almshouses
8 Church Estate Almshouses
9 Richmond International Bsns Ctr
10 Abercorn Mews
B4 1 Primrose Ho
2 Lawman Ct
3 Royston Ct
4 Garden Ct
5 Capel Lo
6 Devonshire Ct
7 Celia Ct
8 Rosslyn Ho
9 Branstone Ct
10 Lamerton Lo
11 Kew Lo
12 Dunraven Ho
13 Stoneleigh Lo
14 Tunstall Ct
15 Voltaire
C4 1 Clarendon Ct
2 Quintock Ho
3 Broome Ct
4 Lonsdale Mews
5 Elizabeth Cotts
6 Sandways
7 Victoria Cotts
8 North Ave
9 Grovewood
10 Hamilton Ho
11 Melvin Ct
12 Power Ho
13 Station Ave
14 Blake Mews
D1 1 Hershell Ct
2 Deanhill Ct
3 Park Sheen
4 Furness Lo
5 Merricks Ct

133

B2 1 Rann Ho
2 Craven Ho
3 John Dee Ho
4 Kindell Ho
5 Montgomery Ho
6 Avondale Ho
7 Addington Ct
8 Dovecote Gdns
9 Firmston Ho
10 Glendower Gdns
11 Chestnut Ave
12 Trehern Rd
13 Rock Ave
D3 1 Melrose Rd
2 Seaforth Lo
3 St John's Gr
4 Sussex Ct
5 Carmichael Ct
6 Hampshire Ct
7 Thorne Pas
9 Beverley Path

134

D1 1 Olivette St
2 Mascotte Rd
3 Glegg Pl
4 Crown Ct
5 Charlwood Terr
D6 1 Cobb's Hall
2 Dorset Mans
3 St Clements Mans
4 Bothwell St
5 Hawksmoor St

135

B3 1 Plato Pl
2 Mustow Pl
3 Laurel Bank Gdns
4 Ranelagh Mans
5 Churchfield Mans
6 Bear Croft Ho
7 Elysium Gate
8 Ethel Rankin Ct
9 Arthur Henderson Ho
10 William Banfield Ho
D3 1 Brightwells
2 Broughton Road App
3 Bulow Ct
4 Langford Rd
5 Elizabeth Barnes Ct
6 Snowbury Rd

136

A2 1 Molasses Ho
2 Molasses Row
3 Cinnamon Row
4 Calico Ho
5 Calico Row
6 Port Ho
7 Square Rigger Row
8 Trade Twr
9 Ivory Ho
10 Spice Ct
11 Sherwood Ct
12 Mendip Ct
13 Chalmers Ho
14 Coral Row
B1 1 Burke Ho
2 Fox Ho
3 Buxton Ho
4 Pitt Ho
5 Romsey Ho
6 Beverley Cl
7 Florence Ho
8 Linden Ct
9 Dorcas Ct
10 Johnson Ct
11 Agnes Ct
12 Hilltop Ct
13 Courtyard The
14 Old Laundry The
15 Oberstein Rd
16 Fineran Ct
17 Sangora Rd
18 Harvard Mans
B2 1 Benham Cl
2 Milner Ho
3 McManus Ho
4 Wilberforce Ho
5 Wheeler Ct
6 Sporle Ct
7 Holliday Sq
8 John Parker Sq
9 Carmichael Cl
10 Fenner Sq
11 Clark Lawrence Ct
12 Shaw Ct
13 Sendall Ct
14 Livingstone Rd
15 Farrant Ho
16 Jackson Ho
17 Darien Ho
18 Sheppard Ho
19 Ganley Ct
20 Arthur Newton Ho
21 Chesterton Ho
22 John Kirk Ho
23 Mantua St
24 Heaver Rd
B3 1 Archer Ho
2 White Ho
3 Powrie Ho
4 Morgan Ct
5 Fairchild Cl
6 Musjid Rd
C2 1 Kiloh Ct
2 Lanner Ho
3 Grifton Ho
4 Kestrel Ho
5 Kite Ho
6 Peregrine Ho
7 Hawk Ho
8 Inkster Ho
9 Harrier Ho
10 Eagle Hts
11 Kingfisher Ct
12 Lavender Terr
13 Temple Ho
14 Ridley Ho
15 Eden Ho
16 Hertford Ct
17 Nepaul Rd
C3 1 Meecham Ct
2 McKiernan Ct
3 Banbury St
4 Colestown St
5 Crombie Mews
6 Frere St
D3 1 Stevenson Ho
2 Ambrose Mews
3 Harling Ct
4 Southside Quarter
5 Latchmere St
6 Dovedale Cotts
7 Roydon Cl
8 Castlemaine
9 Wittering Ho
10 Berry Ho
11 Weybridge Point

137

A2 1 Shaftesbury Park Chambers
2 Selborne
3 Rush Hill Mews
4 Marmion Mews
5 Crosland Pl
6 Craven Mews
8 Basnett Rd
10 Woodmere Cl
10 Tyneham Cl
A3 1 Hopkinson Ho
2 Macdonald Ho
3 Rushlake Ho
4 Bishopstone Ho
5 Dresden Ho
6 Millgrove St
7 Farnhurst Ho
8 Walden Ho
9 Kennard St
10 Langhurst Ho
11 Kennard Ho
12 Voltaire Ct
13 Barloch Ho
B2 1 Turnchapel Mews
2 Redwood Mews
3 Phil Brown Pl
4 Bev Callender Cl
5 Keith Connor Cl
6 Tessa Sanderson Pl
7 Daley Thompson Way
8 Rashleigh Ct
9 Abberley Mews
10 Willow Lodge
11 Beaufoy Rd
B3 1 St Philip Sq
2 Montefiore St
3 Gambetta St
4 Scott Ct
5 Radcliffe Path
6 Moresby Wlk
C1 1 Polygon The
2 Windsor Ct
3 Trinity Cl
3 Hanscomb Mews
4 Studios The
5 Bourne Ho
C2 1 Clapham Manor Ct
2 Clarke Ho
3 Gables The
4 Sycamore Mews
5 Maritime Ho
7 Floris Pl
C3 1 Seymour Ho
2 Lucas Ho
3 Durrington Twr
4 Amesbury Twr
5 Fovant Ct
6 Allington Ct
7 Welford Ct
8 Ilsley Ct
D1 1 Kendoa Rd
2 Felmersham Cl
3 Abbeville Mews
4 Saxon Ho
5 Gifford Ho
6 Teignmouth Cl
7 Holwood Pl
8 Oaklands Pl
D2 1 Chelsham Ho
2 Lynde Ho
3 Greener Ho
4 Towns Ho
5 Hugh Morgan Ho
6 Roy Ridley Ho
7 Lendal Terr
8 Slievemore Cl
9 Cadmus Cl
D3 1 Haltone Ho
2 Surcot Ho
3 Kingsley Ho
4 Wood Ho
5 Dalemain Ho
6 Fallodon Ho
7 Dartington Ho
8 Esher Ho
9 Kneller Ho
10 Lostock Ho
11 Croxteth Ho
12 Donnington Ho
13 Farnley Ho
14 Hardwick Ho
15 Bradfield Ho
16 Brocket Ho
17 Colchester Ho
18 Clive Ho
19 Chessington Ho
20 Rushbrook Ho
21 Stanmore Ho
22 Newton Ho
23 Netherby Ho
24 Oakwell Ho
25 Rydal Ho
26 Rushton Ho
27 Harcourt Ho
28 Metcalfe Ho
29 Lydwell Ho
30 Raleigh Ho
31 Spencer Ho
32 Shipley Ho
33 Naylor Ho
34 Mordaunt Ho
35 Stanley Ho
36 Alderley Ho
37 Effingham Ho
38 Grant Ho
39 Wilson Ho
40 Fraser Ho

138

A1 1 Morris Ho
2 Gye Ho
3 Clowes Ho
4 Thomas Ho
5 Stuart Ho
6 Storace Ho
7 Bedford Ho
8 Ascot Ct
9 Ascot Par
10 Ashmere Ho
11 Ashmere Gr
12 Vickery Ho
13 Stafford Mans
14 Beresford Ho
A2 1 Callingham Ho
2 Russell Pickering Ho
4 Lopez Ho
5 Coachmaker Mews
A3 1 Barling Ct
2 Jeffrey's Ct
3 Brooks Ct
4 Dalmeny Ct
5 Fender Ct
6 Fishlock Ct
7 Bedser Ct
8 Gover Ct
9 Clarence Wlk
10 Barton Ct
11 Allom Ct
12 Garden Ho
13 Otha Ho
14 Hayward Ct
15 Surridge Ct
16 Knox Ct
17 Jephson Ct
18 Holmes Ct
19 McIntyre Ct
20 Richardson Ct
21 Cassell Ho
22 Packington Ho
23 Bain Ho
24 Enfield Ho
25 Fawcett Ho
26 Sidgwick Ho
27 Jowett Ho
28 Beckett Ho
29 Arden Ho
30 Pinter Ho
31 Barrington Ct
B1 1 Freemens Hos
2 Roger's Almshouses
3 Gresham Almshouses
4 Exbury Ho
5 Glasbury Ho
6 Dalbury Ho
7 Fosbury Ho
8 Chalbury Ho
9 Neilson-Terry Ct
10 Pavilion Mans
11 Daisy Dormer Ct
12 George Lashwood Ct
13 Marie Lloyd Ct
14 Trinity Homes
15 Lethaby Ho
16 Edmundsbury Ct Est
17 Regis Pl
18 Belvedere Pl
19 Alpha Ho
20 Beta Pl
21 Cedars Ho
B2 1 Turberville Ho
2 Thrayle Ho
3 Percheron Ct
4 Draymans Ct
B3 1 Maurice Ho
2 Thring Ho
3 Paton Ho
4 Huxley Ho
5 Morell Ho
6 Mary Ho
7 Beale Ho
8 Rosa Parks Ho
9 Birrell Ho
10 Waltham Ho
11 Burford Ho
12 Thornicroft Ho
13 Addington Ho
14 Goffton Ho
15 Redmayne Ho

16 Norton Ho
17 Aytoun Ct
18 Colwall Ho
19 Burrow Ho
20 Wynter Ho
21 Crowhurst Ho
22 Lidcote Gdns
23 Cumnor Cl
24 Park View Mews
1 Electric Mans
2 Electric La
3 Connaught Mans
4 Clifton Mans
5 Hereford Ho
6 Chaplin Ho
7 Brixton Oval
8 Lord David Pitt Ho
9 Marcus Garvey Way
10 Montgo Cl
11 Bob Marley Way
12 Leeson Rd
1 Buckmaster Cl
3 Albermarle Ho
4 Goodwood Mans
5 Angell Park Gdns
6 Fyfield Rd
7 Howard Ho
8 Harris Ho
9 Broadoak Ct
10 Burgate Ct
11 Witchwood Ho
12 Blacktree Mews
13 Chartham Ct
14 Chilham Ct
15 Northgate Ct
16 Westgate Ct
17 Dover Mans
3 1 Norval Gn
2 Hilda Terr
4 Church Gn
5 Lord Holland La
7 Sorrell Cl
8 Burton Rd
9 Holles Ho
10 Leys Ct
11 Warwick Ho
12 Fairfax Ho
13 Wayland Ho
14 Dudley Ho
15 Denchworth Ho
16 Fitzgerald Ho
17 Lambert Ho
18 Chute Ho
19 Bedwell Ho
20 Ferrey Mews
21 Serenaders Rd
C4 1 Hector Ct
2 Jason Ct
3 Creon Ct
4 Hermes Ct
5 Argos Ct
6 Cadmus Ct
7 Appollo Ct
8 Mercury Ct
9 County Ho
10 Seasalter Ho
11 Downbarton Ho
12 Garlinge Ho
13 Maria Ho
14 Alvanley Ho
15 Woodchurch Ho
16 Durlock Ho
17 Hallam Ho
18 Whiteness Ho
19 Bromstone Ho
20 Penelope Ho
21 Melbourne Sq
22 Cloisters The
23 Cliffsend Ho
24 Sacketts Ho
25 Hanway Ho
26 Brickworth Ho
27 Redlynch Ho
28 Stodmarsh Ho
29 Kingsgate Ho
30 Chardin Ho
31 Annesley Ho
32 Knowlton Ho
33 Russell Gr
34 Eamann Casey Ho
C5 1 Swift Ho
2 Listowel Cl
3 Deal Wlk
4 Plover Ho
5 Aigburth Mans
6 Glencoe Mans
7 Glenshaw Mans
8 Cleveland Mans
9 Leda Ct
10 Jupiter Ct
11 Juno Ct
12 Healy Ho
13 Ashton Ho
14 Ramsey Ho
15 Annesley Ho
16 Cowley Rd
C6 1 Sherwin Ho
3 Kilner Ho
4 Read Ho
5 Lohmann Ho
6 Hornby Ho
7 Abel Ho
8 Blythe Ho
9 Key Ho
10 Lockwood Ho
11 Alverstone Ho
12 Blades Ho
13 Rothesay Ct
D1 1 Mahatma Ganhi Ind Est
2 Dylan Rd
3 Bessemer Park Ind Est
4 Pablo Neruda Cl
5 Langston Hughes Cl
6 Walt Whitman Cl
7 James Joyes Wlk
8 Alice Walker Cl
9 Louise Bennett Cl
10 Chadacre Ho
11 Burwood Ho
12 Pyrford Ho
13 Wangford Ho
14 Ashford Ho
15 Kenwood Ho
16 Moyne Ho
17 Elveden Ho
19 Carrara Wlk
20 Broughton Dr
21 Tilia Wlk
21 Angela Davis Ind Est
D2 1 Mallams Mews
2 Amberley Ct
3 Harper Ho
4 Leicester Ho
5 Station Ave
6 Wellfit St
7 Loughborough Ct
8 Belinda Rd
9 Higgs Ind Est
D3 1 Langport Ho
2 Iveagh Ho
3 Newark Ho
4 Edgehill Ho
5 Hopton Ho
6 Ashby Ho
7 Nevil Ho
D4 1 Fairbairn Gn
2 Hammelton Gn
3 Foxley Sq
4 Silverburn Ho
5 Butler Ho
6 Dalkeith Ho
7 Turner Cl
8 Bathgate Ho
9 Black Roof Ho
D6 1 Faunce Ho
2 Garbett Ho
3 Harvard Ho
4 Doddington Pl
5 Kean Ho
6 Jephson Ho
7 Cornish Ho
8 Bateman Ho
9 Molesworth Ho
10 Walters Ho
11 Cruden Ho
12 Brawne Ho
13 Prescott Ho
14 Chalmer's Wlk
15 Copley Cl

139

A3 1 Bergen Ho
2 Oslo Ho
3 Viking Ho
4 Jutland Ho
5 Norvic Ho
6 Odin Ho
7 Baltic Ho
8 Nobel Ho
9 Mercia Ho
10 Kenbury Gdns
11 Zealand Ho
12 Elsinore Ho
13 Norse Ho
14 Denmark Mans
15 Dane Ho
16 Canterbury Cl
17 York Cl
18 Kenbury Mans
19 Parade Mans
20 Winterslow Ho
21 Lilford Ho
22 Cutcombe Mans
23 Bartholomew Ho
24 Guildford Ho
25 Boston Ho
26 Hereford Ho
27 Weyhill Ho
28 Lichfield Ho
29 Lansdown Ho
30 Honiton Ho
31 Pinner Ho
32 Baldock Ho
33 Widecombe Ho
34 Nottingham Ho
35 Witham Ho
36 Barnet Ho
37 Empress Mews
A4 1 Bertha Neubergh Ho
2 Mornington Mews
3 Badsworth Rd
4 Sycamore Ct
5 Elm Tree Ct
6 Samuel Lewis Trust Dwellings
7 Valmar Trad Est
8 Keswick Ho
9 Mitcham Ho
A5 1 Boundary Ho
2 Day Ho
3 Burgess Ho
4 Carlyle Ho
5 Myers Ho
6 Thompson's Ave
7 Palgrave Ho
8 Winnington Ho
9 Brantwood Ho
10 Lowell Ho
11 Jessie Duffett Ho
12 Otterburn Ho
13 Crossmount Ho
14 Venice Ct
15 Bowyer St
16 Livingstone Ho
17 Gothic Ct
18 Coniston Ho
19 Harlynwood
20 Carey Ct
21 Finley Ct
22 Grainger Ct
23 Hayes Ct
24 Moffat Ho
25 Marinel Ho
26 Hodister Cl
27 Arnot Ho
28 Lamb Ho
29 Kipling Ho
30 Keats Ho
31 Kenyon Ho
32 New Church Rd
33 Sir John Kirk Cl
B1 1 Shaftesbury Ct
2 Mayhew Ct
3 Morris Ct
4 Swinburne Ct
5 Perth Ct
6 Tayside Ct
7 Matlock Ct
8 Hunter Ct
9 Turner Ct
B3 1 Selborne Rd
2 Hascombe Terr
B4 1 Joiners Arms Yd
2 Butterfly Wlk
3 Cuthill Wlk
4 Colonades The
5 Artichoke Mews
6 Peabody Bldgs
7 Brighton Ho
8 Park Ho
9 Peabody Ct
10 Lomond Ho
11 Lamb Ho
12 Kimpton Ct
13 Belham Wlk
14 Datchelor Pl
15 Harvey Rd
B5 1 Masterman Ho
2 Milton Ho
3 Pope Ho
4 Chester Ct
5 Marvel Ho
6 Flecker Ho
7 Landor Ho
8 Evelina Mans
9 Habington Ho
10 Langland Ho
11 Drinkwater Ho
12 Procter Ho
13 Shirley Ho
14 Drayton Ho
15 Bridges Ho
16 Cunningham Ho
17 Hood Ho
18 Herrick Ho
19 Dekker Ho
20 Sansom St
20 Houseman Way
21 Coleby Path
22 Jago Wlk
B6 1 Queens Ho
2 Arnside Ho
3 Horsley St
4 St Peter's Ho
5 St Johns Ho
6 St Marks Ho
7 St Stephens Ho
8 St Matthew's Ho
9 Red Lion Cl
10 Boyson Rd
11 Bradenham
C2 1 Harfield Gdns
2 Karen Ct
3 Seavington Ho
4 Appleshaw Ho
5 Birdsall Ho
6 Whitney Ho
7 Wheatland Ho
8 Wilton Ho
9 Walcot Ho
10 Whadden Ho
11 Melbrook Ho
12 Ledbury Ho
13 Tidworth Ho
14 Riseholme Ho
15 Ringmer Ho
16 Petworth Ho
17 Stagshaw Ho
18 Ivybridge Ho
19 Inwood Ho
20 Gatcombe Ho
21 Gatebeck Ho
22 Felbridge Ho
23 Cowdray Ho
C3 1 Springfield Ho
2 Craston Ho
3 Walters Ho
4 Edgecombe Ho
5 Fowler Ho
6 Rignold Ho
7 Chatham Ho
C4 1 Barnwell Ho
2 Brunswick Villas
3 St Giles Twr
4 Bentley Ho
5 Dawson Ho
6 Dryden Ho
7 Mayward Ho
8 Longleigh Ho
9 Fairwall Ho
10 Bodeney Ho
11 Sandby Ho
12 Vestry Mews
13 Netley
14 Lakanal
15 Racine
C5 1 Tower Mill Rd
2 Tilson Cl
6 Dorton Cl
8 Granville Sq
10 Farnborough Way
13 Hordle Prom W
15 Samuel Jones Ind Est
16 Dibden Ho
17 Marchwood Cl
18 Pilgrims Cloisters
19 Beacon Ho
20 Teather St
21 Stacy Path
22 Rumball Ho
23 Ballow Cl
24 Rill Ho
C6 3 Pearse St
4 Watling St
5 Gandolfi st
7 Andoversford Ct
8 Downend Ct
D1 1 Dulwich Mews
2 St James's Cloisters
D4 1 Colbert
2 Voltaire
3 Finch Mews
4 Charles Coveney Rd
5 Crane St
6 Curlew Ho
7 Mallard Ho
8 Tern Ho
9 Crane Ho
10 Falcon Ho
11 Bryanston Ho
12 Basing Ct
13 Marcus Ho
14 Sheffield Ho
D5 2 Whistler Mews
1 Painswick Ct
2 Sharpness Ct
3 Hordle Prom N
4 Mattingly Way
5 Calypso Cres
6 Samuel St
7 Hordle Prom S
8 Cinnamon Cl
9 Savannah Cl
10 Thames Ct
11 Amstel Ct
12 Danube Ct
13 Tilbury Cl
14 Hordle Prom E
15 Indus Ct
16 Oakcourt
17 Palm Ct
18 Rowan Ct
19 Blackthorn Ct
20 Pear Ct
21 Lidgate Rd
D6 1 Willsbridge Ct
2 Cam Ct
3 Quedgeley Ct
4 Saul Ct
5 Quenington Ct
6 Westonbirt Ct
7 Wickway Ct

140

A3 1 William Margrie Cl
2 Choumert Sq
3 Parkstone Rd
4 Atwell Rd
A4 2 Angelina Ho
3 Jarvis Ho
4 Richland Ho
5 Honeywood Ho
6 Wakefield Ho
7 Primrose Ho
8 Hardcastle Ho
9 Dunstall Ho
10 Purdon Ho
11 Flamborough Ho
12 Lambrook Ho
13 Witcombe Point
14 Yarnfield Sq
15 Winford Ct
16 Portbury Cl
17 Robert Keen Cl
A5 1 Thornbill Ho
2 Vervain Ho
3 Woodstar Ho
4 Tamarind Ho
5 Hereford Retreat
6 Haymerle Ho
7 Furley Ho
8 Applegarth Ho
9 Freda Corbett Cl
10 Rudbeck Ho
11 Henslow Ho
12 Lindley Ho
13 Collinson Ho
14 Sister Mabel's Way
15 Timberland Cl
16 Hastings Cl
17 Neville Cl
18 Sidmouth Ho
19 Budleigh Ho
20 Stanesgate Ho
21 Braemore Ho
22 Ely Ho
A6 1 Bowles Rd
2 Western Wharf
3 Northfield Ho
4 Millbrook Ho
5 Denstone Ho
6 Deerhurst Ho
7 Caversham Ho
8 Battle Ho
9 Cardiff Ho
10 Bridgnorth Ho
11 Exeter Ho
12 Grantham Ho
13 Aylesbury Ho
14 Royston Ho
B2 1 Tilling Ho
2 Goodwin Ho
3 Citron Terr
4 Cheam St
B3 1 Walkynscroft
2 Ryegates
3 Hathorne Cl
4 Pilkington Rd
5 Russell Ct
6 Heaton Ho
7 Magdalene Cl
B4 1 Willowdene
2 Pinedene
3 Oakdene
4 Beechdene
5 Hollydene
6 Wood Dene
8 Staveley Cl
9 Carnicot Ho
10 Martock Ct
11 Kendrick Ct
B5 1 Tortington Ho
2 Credenhill Ho
3 Bromyard Ho
4 Hoyland Cl
5 Willowdene
6 Ashdene
7 Acorn Par
8 Carlton Gr
9 Springall St
10 Harry Lambourn Ho
C3 1 Honiton Gdns
2 Selden Ho
3 Hathway Ho
4 Hathway St
5 Station Ct
C5 1 Ambleside Point
2 Grasmere Point
3 Windermere Point
4 Roman Way
5 Laburnham Cl
7 Romney Cl
8 Hammersley Ho
9 Hutchinson Ho
10 Hammond Ho
11 Fir Tree Ho
12 Glastonbury Ct
13 Highbridge Ct
14 Filton Ct
15 Chiltern Ct
16 Cheviot Ct
C6 1 Penshurst Ho
2 Reculver Ho
3 Mereworth Ho
4 Camber Ho
5 Chilam Ho
6 Otford Ho
7 Olive Tree Ho
8 Aspen Ho
9 Lewis Silkin Ho
10 Richborough Ho
11 Dover Ho
12 Eynsford Ho
13 Horton Ho
14 Lamberhurst Ho
15 Canterbury Ind Pk
16 Upnall Ho
17 Sissinghurst Ho
18 Rochester Ho
19 Leybourne Ho
20 Lullingstone Ho
D1 1 Laxton Path
2 Barlings Ho
3 Bayfield Ho
4 Coston Wlk
5 Coverham Ho
6 Gateley Ho
7 Dereham Ho
8 Greenwood Ho
9 Hilton Ho
10 Goodall Ho
11 Horsley Ho
12 Jordan Ho
D5 1 Richard Anderson Ct
2 Palm Tree Ho
3 Edward Robinson Ho
4 Antony Ho
5 Gerrard Ho
6 Palmer Ho
7 Pankhurst Cl
D6 1 Harrisons Ct
2 Grantley Ho
3 Sunbury Ct
4 Tilbury Ho
5 Graham Ct
6 Connell Ct
7 St Clements Ct
8 Henderson Ct
9 Jemotts Ct
10 Verona Ct
11 Heywood Ho
12 Francis Ct
13 Hind Ho
14 Donne Ho
15 Carew Ct
16 Burbage Ho
17 Newland Ho
18 Dobson Ho
19 Dalton Ho
20 Greene Ct
21 Redrup Ho
22 Tarplett Ho
23 Stunnell Ho
24 Gasson Ho
25 Bryce Ho
26 Barnes Ho
27 Barkwith Ho
28 Bannister Ho
29 Apollo Ind Bsns Ctr

141

A5 1 Batavia Ho
2 Marlowe Bsns Ctr
3 Batavia Mews
4 Woodrush Cl
5 Alexandra St
6 Primrose Wlk
7 Vansittart St
8 Granville Ct
9 Cottesbrook St
A6 1 Portland Ct
2 Phoenix Ct
3 Rainbow Ct
4 Hawke Twr
6 Woodpecker Rd
B5 1 Austin Ho
2 Exeter Way
3 Crossleigh Ct
4 Mornington Pl
5 Maple Ho
B6 1 Chester Ho
2 Lynch Wlk
3 Arlington Ho
4 Woodcote Ho
5 Cornbury Ho
6 Prospect Pl
7 Akintaro Ho
8 Mulberry Ho
9 Laurel Ho
10 Linden Ho
11 Ashford Ho
12 Wardalls Ho
13 Magnolia Ho
14 Howard Ho
15 Larch Cl
16 Ibis Ct
17 Merganser Ct
18 Wotton Rd
19 Kingfisher Sq
20 Sanderling Ct
21 Dolphin Twr
22 Mermaid Twr
23 Scoter Ct
24 Shearwater Ct
25 Brambling Ct
26 Kittiwake Ct
28 Guillemot Ct
29 Marine Twr
30 Teal Ct
31 Lapwing Twr
34 Cormorant Ct
36 Shelduck Ct
39 Eider Ct
40 Pintail Ct
41 Tristan Ct
42 Skua Ct
43 Rosemary Ct
44 Violet Cl
45 Diana Cl
C4 1 Admiralty Cl
2 Harton Lo
3 Sylvia Cotts
4 Pitman Ho
5 Heston Ho
C5 1 Sandpiper Ct
2 Flamingo Ct
3 Titan Bsns Est
4 Rochdale Way
5 Speedwell St
6 Reginald Pl
7 Fletcher Path
8 Frankham Ho
9 Cremer Ho
10 Wilshaw Ho
11 Castell Ho
12 Holden Ho
13 Browne Ho
14 Lady Florence Ctyd
15 Covell Ct
C6 1 Dryfield Wlk
2 Blake Ho
3 Hawkins Ho
4 Grenville Ho
5 Langford Ho
6 Mandarin Ct
8 Bittern Ct
9 Lamerton St
10 Armada St
11 Armada Ct
12 Benbow Ho
13 Oxenham Ho
14 Caravel Mews
15 Hughes Ho
16 Stretton Mans
D5 1 Finch Ho
2 Jubilee The
3 Gordon Ho
4 Haddington Ct
5 Maitland Cl
6 Ashburnham Retreat

142
A3 1 Ellison Ho
2 Pitmaston Ho
3 Windmill Cl
4 Hertmitage The
5 Burnett Ho
6 Lacey Ho
A4 1 Penn Almshouse
2 Jarvis Ct
3 Woodville Ct
4 Darnell Ho
5 Renbold Ho
6 Lindsell St
7 Plumbridge St
8 Trinity Gr
9 Hollymount Cl
10 Cade Tyler Ho
11 Robertson Ho
A5 1 Temair Ho
2 Glaisher St
3 Prince of Orange La
4 Lombard Ho
5 St Marks Cl
6 Ada Kennedy Ct
7 Arlington Pl
8 Topham Ho
9 Darnell Ho
10 Hawks Mews
11 Royal Pl
12 Swanne Ho
13 Maribor
14 Serica Ct
15 Queen Elizabeth College
A6 1 Greenwich Mkt
2 Turnpin La
3 Durnford St
4 Sexton's Ho
5 Bardsley Ho
6 Wardell Ho
7 Clavell St
8 Stanton Ho
9 Macey Ho
10 Boreman Ho
B6 1 Frobisher Ct
2 Hardy Cotts
3 Palliser Ho
4 Bernard Angell Ho
5 Corvette Sq
6 Travers Ho
7 Reade Ho
8 Maze Hill Lo
D5 1 Westcombe Ct
2 Kleffens Ct
3 Ferndale Ct
4 Combe Mews
5 Mandeville Cl
6 Heathway
7 Pinelands Cl

143
A5 1 Mary Lawrenson Pl
2 Bradbury Ct
3 Dunstable Ct
A6 1 Nethercombe Ho
2 Holywell Cl
C6 1 Warren Wlk
2 Wilson Ho
3 Priory Ho
4 Mar Ho
5 Langhorne Ho
6 Games Ho
7 Erskine Ho
8 Ducie Ho
9 Downe Ho
10 Bayeux Ho
11 Elliscombe Mount
12 Harold Gibbons Ct
13 Mascalls Ct
14 Leila Parnell Pl
15 East Mascalls
16 Birch Tree Ho
17 Cherry Tree Ct
18 Elm Tree Ct
19 Cedar Ct
D5 1 Winchester Ho
2 Brentwood Ho
3 Shenfield Ho
4 Chesterford Ho

144
A4 1 Master Gunner's Pl
2 Nicholson Ho
3 Borgard Ho
4 Macleod Ho
5 Brome Ho
6 Ross Ho
7 Horne Ho
8 Pendlebury Gn
9 Dickson Ho
10 Roberts Ho
A5 1 Leyburn Ho
2 Greenwich Hts
3 Gardiner Ho
B4 1 Galton Ho
2 Florence Ho
3 Sidney Ho
4 Robertson Ho
5 Mennie Ho
6 Godwin Ho
7 Panbro Ho
8 Sutherland Ho
C6 1 Lawson Ho
2 Mabbett Ho
3 Petrie Ho
4 Memess Path
5 Ruegg Ho
6 Nile Path
7 Leslie Smith Sq
8 Spearman St
9 Siedle Ho
10 Watling Ho
11 O'Neill Path
12 Old Clem Sq
13 Jefferson Wlk
14 Millward Wlk
15 Wordsworth Ho
16 Fenwick Cl
D6 1 Acworth Ho
2 Griffiths Ho
3 Squires Ho
4 Cowen Ho
5 Turton Ho
6 Alford Ho
7 Boxshall Ho
8 Macallister Ho
9 Marvin Ho
10 Kelham Ho
11 Kimber Ho
12 Maxwell Ho
13 Woodford Ho
14 Penfold Ho

146
A2 1 Wellingfield Ct
2 Woodville Gr
3 Midwinter Cl
4 St Leonards Cl

147
A1 1 Woburn Ct
2 Arundel Ct
3 Longleat Villas
4 Upton Villas
B6 1 Bevercote Wlk
2 Boevey Path
3 Lullingstone Rd
4 Benjamin Ct
5 Charton Cl
6 Terence Ct
7 Renshaw Cl
8 Grove Rd
C1 1 Friswell Pl
2 Market Pl
3 Geddes Pl
4 Janet Ct
5 Broadway Sh Ctr
6 Mall The
7 Norwich Pl
8 Pincott Rd

148
A5 1 Stranraer Way
2 Deri Dene Cl
3 Lord Knyvetts Ct
4 Tudor Ct
5 Wessex Ct
6 Vanguard Ho
7 Shackleton Ct
8 Fleetwood Ct
9 Clifton Ct
10 Vickers Ct
11 Bristol Ct
12 Sunderland Ct

153
A3 1 Katharine Rd
2 Garfield Rd
4 Flood La
5 John Wesley Ct
6 King Street Par
7 Thames Eyot
A4 1 Perryn Ct
2 Ivybridge Cl
3 Brook Ho
4 Latham Cl
5 March Rd
6 Berkley Ct
7 Cole Court Lo
8 Cheltenham Ave
9 Railway App
A5 1 Greenways The
2 Cole Park View
B4 1 Melton Ct
2 Amyand Park Gdns
3 Crown Ct
4 Burrell Ho
5 Owen Ho
6 Brentford Ho
7 Leeson Ho
8 Westbourne Ho
9 Orleans Ct
10 Lebanon Ct
B5 1 Grove The
2 Cumberland Cl
3 Westmorland Cl
4 Sussex Cl
5 Norfolk Cl
6 Nicol Cl
7 Old Lodge Pl
8 Kelvin Ct
9 St Margaret's Ct
10 Park Cotts
11 St Margarets Bsns Ctr
12 Amyand Cotts
C5 1 Howmic Ct
2 Sefton Lo
3 Ravensbourne
4 Arlington Ct
5 Georgina Ct
6 Trevelyan Ho
7 Caradon Ct
8 Green Hedges
9 Old House Gdns
10 Queens Keep
11 Beresford Ct
12 Langham Ct
13 Poplar Ct
D5 1 Richmond Bridge Mans
2 Heatherdene Mans
3 Kenton Ct
4 Arosa Rd
5 Darling Ho
6 Turner Ho
7 Blanchard Ho
8 Ashe Ho
9 Bevan Ct
10 Lawley Ho
11 Leicester Ct
12 Roseleigh Cl
13 Beaulieu Cl
14 Richmond Mans
15 Mallard Ct
D6 1 Garrick Cl
2 Old Palace Yd
3 Wardrobe The
4 Maids of Honour Row
5 Hunters Ct
6 Queensberry Ho
7 Green The
8 Old Palace Terr
9 Paved Ct
10 Golden Ct
11 Brewers La
12 Square The
13 Lower George St
14 St James's Cotts
15 Church Wlk
16 Victoria Pl
17 Castle Yd
18 Lewis Rd
19 Wakefield Rd
20 Church Terr
21 Warrington Rd
22 Ormond Ave
23 St Helena Terr
24 Whittaker Pl
25 Heron Sq
26 Northumberland Pl
27 Church Ct
28 Holbrooke Pl

154
A5 1 Lancaster Cotts
2 Lancaster Mews
3 Bromwich Ho
4 Priors Lo
5 Richmond Hill Ct
6 Glenmore Ho
7 Hillbrow
8 Heathshot
9 Friars Stile Pl
10 Spire Ct
11 Ridgeway
12 Matthias Ct
A6 1 Lichfield Terr
2 Union Ct
3 Carrington Lo
4 Wilton Ct
5 Egerton Ct
6 Beverley Lo
7 Bishop Duppa's Almshouses
8 Regency Wlk
9 Clearwater Ho
10 Onslow Avenue Mans
11 Michels Almshouses
12 Albany Pas
13 Salcombe Villas
B5 1 Chester Cl
2 Evesham Ct
3 Queen's Ct
4 Russell Wlk
5 Charlotte Sq
6 Jones Wlk
7 Hilditch Ho
8 Isabella Ct
9 Damer Ho
10 Eliot Ho
11 Fitzherbert Ho
12 Reynolds Pl
13 Chisholm Rd
B6 1 Alberta Ct
2 Beatrice Rd
3 Lorne Rd
4 York Rd
5 Connaught Rd
6 Albany Terr
7 Kingswood Ct
8 Selwyn Ct
9 Broadhurst Cl

155
D5 1 Allenford Ho
2 Swaythling Ho
3 Tatchbury Ho
4 Penwood Ho
5 Bramley Ho
6 Shalden Ho
7 Dunbridge Ho
8 Denmead Ho
9 Charcot Ho
10 Portswood Pl
11 Brockbridge Ho
12 Hurstbourne Ho

156
A3 1 Farnborough Ho
2 Rushmere Ho
3 Horndean Cl
4 Highcross Way
5 Timsbury Wlk
6 Foxcombe Rd
7 Ryefield Path
8 Greatham Wlk
9 Gosport Ho
10 Stoatley Ho
11 Milland Ho
12 Clanfield Ho
13 Fareham Ho
14 Grayswood Point
A4 1 Woodcott Ho
2 Lyndhurst Ho
3 Wheatley Ho
4 Allbrook Ho
5 Bordon Wlk
6 Chilcombe Ho
7 Vicarage Ct
8 Shawford Ct
9 Eastleigh Wlk
10 Kings Ct
A6 1 Theodore Ho
2 Nicholas Ho
3 Bonner Ho
4 Downing Ho
5 Johsen Ho
6 Fairfax Ho
7 Devereux Ho
8 David Ho
9 Leigh Ho
10 Clipstone Ho
11 Mallet Ho
12 Arton Wilson Ho
B3 1 Ramsdean Ho
2 Purbrook Ho
3 Portsea Ho
4 Blendworth Point
5 Eashing Point
6 Hindhead Point
7 Hilsea Point
8 Witley Point
9 Buriton Ho
10 Grately Ho
11 Hascombe Ho
12 Dunhill Point
13 Westmark Point
14 Longmoor Point
15 Cadnam Point
C4 1 Cumberland Ho
2 Devonshire Ho
3 Cornwall Ho
4 Norfolk Ho
5 Leicester Ho
6 Warwick Ho
7 Sutherland Ho
8 Carmarthen Ho
9 Worcester Ho
10 Rutland Ho
C6 1 Inglis Ho
2 Ducie Ho
3 Warncliffe Ho
4 Stanhope Ho
5 Waldegrave Ho
6 Mildmay Ho
7 Mullens Ho
D3 1 Sandringham Cl
2 Eastwick Ct
3 Oatlands Ct
4 Banning Ho
5 Grantley Ho
6 Caryl Ho
7 Duncombe Ho
8 Chilworth Ct
9 Kent Lo
10 Turner Lo
11 Marlborough
12 Parkland Gdns
13 Lewesdon Cl
14 Pines Ct
15 Ashtead Ct
16 Mynterne Ct
17 Arden
18 Stephen Ct
19 Marsham Ct
20 Doradus Ct
21 Acorns The
22 Heritage Ho
23 Conifer Ct
24 Spencer Ho
25 Chartwell
26 Blenheim
27 Chivelston
28 Greenfield Ho
29 Oakman Ho
30 Radley Lo
31 Simon Lo
32 Admirals Ct
D4 1 Brett Ho
2 Brett House Cl
3 Sylva Ct
4 Ross Ct
5 Potterne Cl
6 Stourhead Cl
7 Fleur Gates
8 Greenwood
D5 1 Balmoral Cl
2 Glenalmond Ho
3 Selwyn Ho
4 Keble Ho
5 Bede Ho
6 Gonville Ho
7 Magdalene Ho
8 Armstrong Ho
9 Newnham Ho
10 Somerville Ho
11 Balliol Ho
12 Windermere
13 Little Combe Cl
14 Classinghall Ho
15 Chalford Ct
16 Garden Royal
17 South Ct
18 Anne Kerr Ct
19 Ewhurst
D6 1 Geneva Ct
2 Laurel Ct
3 Cambalt Ho
4 Langham Ct
5 Lower Pk
6 King's Keep
7 Whitnell Ct
8 Whitehead Ho
9 Halford Ho
10 Humphry Ho
11 Jellicoe Ho

157
A3 1 William Harvey Ho
2 Highview Ct
3 Cameron Ct
4 Galgate Cl
5 Green Ho The
6 King Charles Wlk
7 Florys Ct
8 Augustus Ct
9 Albert Ct
10 Hertford Lo
11 Mortimer Lo
12 Allenswood
13 Ambleside
A6 1 Claremont
2 Downside
3 Cavendish Cl
4 Ashcombe Ct
5 Carltons The
6 Draldo Ho
7 Millbrooke Ct
8 Coysh Ct
9 Keswick Hts
10 Lincoln Ho
11 Avon Ct
B6 1 Burlington Mews
2 Cumbria Ho
3 St Stephen's Gdns
4 Atlantic Ho
5 Burton Lo
6 Manfred Ct
7 Meadow Bank
8 Hooper Ho
C6 1 Pembridge Pl
2 Adelaide Rd
3 London Ct
4 Windsor Ct
5 Westminster Ct
6 Fullers Ho
7 Bridge Pk
8 Lambeth Ct
9 Milton Ct
10 Norfolk Mans
11 Francis Snary Lo
12 Bush Cotts
13 Downbury Mews
14 Newton's Yd
D6 1 Fairfield Ct
2 Blackmore Ho
3 Lancaster Mews
4 Cricketers Mews

159
A2 1 Upper Tooting Park Mans
2 Cecil Mans
3 Marius Mans
4 Boulevard The
5 Elmfield Mans
6 Holdernesse Rd
A3 1 Heslop Ct
2 St James's Terr
3 Boundaries Mans
4 Station Par
5 Old Dairy Mews
A4 1 Hollies Way
2 Endlesham Ct
A5 1 Rayne Ho
2 St Anthony's Ct
3 Earlsthorpe Mews
B3 1 Holbeach Mews
2 Hildreth Street Mews
3 Coalbrook Mans
4 Hub Buildings The
B4 1 Meyer Ho
2 Faraday Ho
3 Hales Ho
4 Frankland Ho
5 Graham Ho
6 Gibbs Ho
8 Anslie Wlk
9 Rokeby Ho
10 Caister Ho
11 Ivanhoe Ho
12 Catherine Baird Ct
13 Marmion Ho
14 Devonshire Ho
C4 1 Limerick Ct
2 Homewoods
3 Jewell Ho
4 Glanville Ho
5 Dan Bryant Ho
6 Olding Ho
7 Quennel Ho
8 Weir Ho
9 West Ho
10 Neville Ct
C5 1 Joseph Powell Cl
2 Cavendish Mans
3 Westlands Terr
4 Cubitt Ho
5 Hawkesworth Ho
6 Normanton Ho
7 Eastman Ho
8 Couchman Ho
9 Poynders Ct
10 Selby Ho
11 Valentine Ho
12 Gorham Ho
13 Deauville Mans
14 Deauville Ct
C6 1 Timothy Cl
2 Shaftsbury Mews
3 Brook Ho
4 Grover Ho
5 Westbrook Ho
6 Hewer Ho
7 Batten Ho
8 Mandeville
9 George Bea Lo
D3 1 Sinclair Ho
2 MacGregor
3 Ingle Ho
4 St Andrews Mews
D4 1 Riley Ho
2 Bennett Ho
3 White Ho
4 Rodgers Ho
5 Dumphreys
6 Homan Ho
7 Prendergast
8 Hutchins Ho
9 Whiteley Ho
10 Tresidder Ho
11 Primrose Ct
12 Angus Ho
13 Currie Ho
D5 1 Parrington H
2 Savill Ho
3 Blackwell Ho
4 Bruce Ho
5 Victoria Ct
6 Victoria Ho
7 Belvedere Ct
8 Ingram Lo
9 Viney Ct
10 Bloomsbury
11 Belgravia Ho
12 Barnsbury Ho

160
A1 1 De Montfort Par
2 Leigham Hall Par
3 Leigham Hall
4 Endsleigh Mar
5 John Kirk Ho
6 Raebarn Ct
7 Wavel Ct
8 Homeleigh Ct
9 Howland Ho
10 Beauclerk Ho
11 Bertrand Ho
12 Drew Ho
13 Dowes Ho
14 Dunton Ho
15 Raynald Ho
16 Sackville Ho
17 Thurlow Ho
18 Astoria Mans
A2 1 Wyatt Park Mans
2 Broadlands Mans
3 Stonehill's Mans
4 Streatleigh Par
5 Dorchester Ct
A3 1 Beaumont Ho
2 Christchurch Ho
3 Staplefield Cl
4 Chipstead Ho
5 Coulsdon Ho
6 Conway Ho
7 Telford Avenue Mans
8 Telford Parade Mans
9 Wavertree Ct
10 Hartswood Ho
11 Wray Ho
A4 1 Picton Ho
2 Rigg Ho
3 Watson Ho
4 MacArthur Ho
5 Sandon Ho
6 Thorold Ho
7 Pearce Ho
8 Mudie Ho
9 Miller Ho
10 Lycett Ho
11 Lafone Ho
12 Lucraft Ho
13 Freeman Ho
14 New Park Par
15 Argyll Ct
16 Dumbarton Ct
17 Kintyre Ct
18 Cotton Ho
19 Crossman Hos
20 Cameford Ct
21 Parsons Ho
22 Brindley Ho
23 Arkwright Ho
24 Perry Ho
25 Brunel Ho
26 New Park Ct
27 Tanhurst Ho
A6 1 King's Mews
2 Clapham Court Terr
3 Clapham Ct

4 Clapham Park Terr
5 Queenswood Ct
6 Oak Tree Ct
7 Park Lofts
1 1 Carisbrook Ct
2 Pembrook Lo
3 Willow Ct
4 Poplar Ct
5 Mountview
6 Spa View
3 1 Charlwood Ho
2 Earlswood Ho
3 Balcombe Ho
4 Claremont Cl
5 Holbrook Ho
6 Gwynne Ho
7 Kynaston Ho
8 Tillman Ho
9 Regent Lo
10 Hazelmere Ct
11 Dykes Ct
B4 1 Archbishop's Pl
2 Witley Ho
3 Outwood Ho
4 Dunsfold Ho
5 Deepdene Lo
6 Warnham Ho
7 Albury Lo
8 Tilford Ho
9 Elstead Ho
10 Thursley Ho
11 Brockham Ho
12 Capel Lo
13 Leith Ho
14 Fairview Ho
15 Weymouth Ct
16 Ascalon Ct
17 China Mews
18 Rush Common Mews
B6 1 Beatrice Ho
2 Florence Ho
3 Evelyn Ho
4 Diana Ho
5 Brixton Hill Ct
6 Austin Ho
7 Manor Ct
8 Camsey Ho
9 Romer Ho
10 Gale Ho
11 Byrne Ho
12 Farnfield Ho
13 Marchant Ho
14 Rainsford Ho
15 Springett Ho
16 Mannering Ho
17 Waldron Ho
C3 1 Valens Ho
2 Loveday Ho
3 Strode Ho
4 Ethelworth Ct
5 Harbin Ho
6 Brooks Ho
7 Godolphin Ho
8 Sheppard Ho
9 McCormick Ho
10 Taylor Ho
11 Saunders Ho
12 Talcott Path
13 Derrick Ho
14 Williams Ho
15 Baldwin Ho
16 Berkeley Ct
17 Churston Cl
18 Neil Wates Cres
19 Burnell Ho
20 Portland Ho
C4 1 Ellacombe Ho
2 Booth Ho
3 Hathersley Ho
4 Brereton Ho
5 Holdsworth Ho
6 Dearmer Ho
7 Cherry Cl
8 Greenleaf Cl
9 Longford Wlk
10 Scarlette Manor Wlk
11 Chandlers Way
12 Upgrove Manor Way
13 Ropers Wlk
14 Tebbs Ho
15 Bell Ho
16 Worthington Ho
17 Courier Ho
18 Mackie Rd
19 Hamers Ho
20 Kelyway Ho
21 Harriet Tubman Cl
22 Estoria Cl
23 Leckhampton Pl
24 Scotia Rd
25 Charles Haller St
26 Sidmouth Ho
27 Hunter Ct
28 Onslow Lo
29 William Winter Ct
30 Langthorne Lo
C5 1 Eccleston Ho
2 Scarsbrook Ho
3 Purser Ho
4 Rudhall Ho
5 Hardham Ho
6 Heywood Ho
7 Haworth Ho
8 Birch Ho
9 Lonsdell Ho
10 Lomley Ho
11 Laughton Ho
13 Bascome St
14 Dudley Mews
15 Herbert Mews
16 Blades Lo
17 Dick Shepherd Ct
18 Charman Ho
19 Morden Ho
20 Bishop Ct
21 Blackburn Ct
22 Leigh Ct
23 John Conway Ho
C6 1 Crownstone Ct
2 Brockwell Ct
3 Nevena Ct
4 St George's Residences
5 Hanover Mans
6 Fleet Ho
7 Langbourne Ho
8 Turnmill Ho
10 Cossar Mews
11 Carter Ho
D1 1 Thanet Ho
2 Chapman Ho
3 Beaufoy Ho
4 Easton Ho
5 Roberts Ho
6 Lloyd Ct
7 Kershaw Ho
8 Wakeling Ho
9 Edridge Ho
10 Jeston Ho
11 Lansdowne Wood Cl

161

B2 1 Coppedhall
2 Shackleton Ct
3 Bullfinch Ct
4 Gannet Ct
5 Fulmar Ct
6 Heron Ct
7 Petrel Ct
8 Falcon Ct
9 Eagle Ct
10 Dunnock Ct
11 Dunlin Ct
12 Cormorant Ct
C6 1 Velde Way
2 Delft Way
3 Arnhem Way
4 Isel Way
5 Kempis Way
6 Terborah Way
7 Steen Way
8 Deventer Cres
9 Nimegen Way
10 Hilversum Cres
11 St Barnabas Cl

162

A1 1 Tunbridge Ct
2 Harrogate Ct
3 Bath Ct
4 Leamington Ct
5 Porlock Ho
6 Cissbury Ho
7 Eddisbury Ho
8 Dundry Ho
9 Silbury Ho
10 Homildon Ho
11 Highgate Ho
12 Richmond Ho
13 Pendle Ho
14 Tynwald Ho
15 Wirrall Ho
16 Greyfriars
A6 1 Dorothy Charrington Ho
2 Keswick Ct
3 Kendall Ct
4 Halliwell Ct
B1 1 River Ho
2 Fordington Ho
3 Arbury Terr
4 Woodbury Ho
5 Gainsborough Mews
6 Forest Hill Ct
B2 1 Bromleigh Ct
2 Parfew Ct
3 Thetford Ct
4 Attleborough Ct
5 Dunton Ct
6 Frobisher Ct
7 Julian Taylor Path
8 Grizedale Terr
9 Worsley Ho
C1 1 Forest Lo
2 Sydenham Park Mans
3 William Wood Ho
C2 1 Fitzwilliam Hts
2 Taymount Grange
3 McLeod Ho
4 Featherstone Ave
5 Kingswear Ho
6 Salcombe Ho
C3 1 Harlech Ct
2 Angela Ct
3 Westwood Ct
4 New Belmont Ho
5 Pearcefield Ave
6 Waldram Pl
7 Horniman Grange
8 South View Ct
9 Heron Ct
10 Katherine Ct
D1 1 Standlake Point
2 Radcot Point
3 Newbridge Point
4 Northmoor
5 Kelmscott
6 Radnor Ct
7 Heathwood Point
8 Ashleigh Point
9 Deepdene Point
10 Rosemount Point
11 Woodfield Ho
12 Clairville Point
13 Trevenna Ho
14 Hyndewood
D2 4 Soper Cl

164

C4 1 Beaumont Terr
2 Littlebourne
3 Verdant Ct
D2 1 Kinross Ct
2 Montrose Ct
3 Rattray Ct
4 Rothesay Ct
D3 1 Edinburgh Ct
2 McMillan Ct
3 Rowallan Ct
4 Meridian Ct
5 Braemar Ct
6 Barrow Ct
7 Blair Ct
8 Darlington Ct
9 Hamilton Ct
10 Inverness Ct
11 Oak Cottage Cl
12 Willow Cl
13 Keswick Ct

165

A4 1 Swallow Ct
2 Honeysuckle Ct
3 Venture Ct
4 Cheriton Ct
5 Askham Lo
6 Syon Lo

166

A2 1 Portland Cres
2 Bourdillon Ct
3 Hillary Ct
4 Tenzing Ct
5 John Hunt Ct
6 Everest Ct
A6 1 Horsfield Gdns
2 Foxhole Rd
C5 1 Roper St
2 Arcade The
3 Elm Terr
4 Imber Ct
5 Ashcroft Ct
6 Fairlands Ct
7 Brecon Ct
8 Newlands Ct
9 Harvard Ct
10 Garden Ct
11 Chiltern Ct
12 Fairway Ct

167

A2 1 Mervyn Stockwood Ho
2 Michael Marshall Ho
3 Keith Sutton Ho

168

A1 1 Ham Shades Cl
2 Aspen Ho
3 Medlar Ho
4 Cornel Ho
5 Stanton Ct
6 Hornbeam Ho
7 Beech Ho
8 Spindle Ho
9 Moat Ct
10 Hunters Lo
11 Edam Ct
12 Monica James Ho
13 Oak Ho
14 Crescent Ct
B5 1 Rochester Cl
2 Cobham Cl
3 Shorne Cl
4 Warne Pl

169

C4 1 Close The
2 Parkhurst Gdns
3 Chichester Ct
4 Pound Green Ct

171

D3 1 Bishops Ct
2 Ash Lo
3 Lime Lo
4 Oak Lo
5 Elm Ct
6 Willow Lo
7 Sycamore Lo
8 Priscilla Ho
9 Sunbury Cross Ctr
10 Isobel Ho

173

A6 1 Gabriel Cl
2 Metcalfe Wlk
3 Dunmow Cl
4 Burgess Cl
5 Chamberlain Wlk
C2 1 Sherbourne Ct
2 Somerset Ct
3 Jubilee Ho
4 Rushbury Ct
5 Hemming Cl
6 Ryedale Ct
7 Norman Ct
C4 1 Begonia Pl
2 Snowdrop Cl
3 Hyacinth Cl
4 Cyclamen Cl
5 Jonquil Gdns
6 Gladioli Cl
7 Daffodil Pl
8 Partridge Rd
D4 1 Acorn Cl
2 Wolsey Ho
3 Lytton Ho
4 Wren Ho
5 Faraday Ho

174

C5 1 Knaggs Ho
2 Keeling Ho
3 Elizabeth Ct
4 Oakhurst Cl
D5 1 Waldegrave Ct
2 Gresham Ho
3 Traherne Lo
4 Fishers Ct
5 Waterhouse Ct
6 Walpole Pl
7 Walpole Cres
8 Alice Mews
9 Bychurch End

175

A5 1 Cherrywood Ct
2 Cambridge Ho
3 Gleneagles Ct
4 Christchurch Ave
5 Hales Ct
6 Springfield Rd
D2 1 Wick Ho
2 Spinnaker Ct
3 Osiers Ct
4 Trent Ho
5 Arun Ho
6 Medway Ho
7 Avon Ho
8 Tyne Ho
9 Clyde Ho
10 Mersey Ct
11 Severn Ct
12 John Williams Cl
D6 1 Byron Ct
2 Coleridge Ct
3 Tennyson Ct
4 Herrick Ct
5 Spenser Ct
6 Marlowe Ct
7 Brooke Ct
8 Gray Ct
9 Shelley Ct
10 Pope Ct
11 Dryden Ct

176

A1 1 Cleave's Almshos
2 Parade The
3 Drovers Ct
4 Gough Ho
5 Eden Wlk
6 Alderman Judge Mall
7 Lady Booth Rd
8 Caversham Ho
9 Littlefield Cl
10 Bentall Sh Ctr The
11 Adams Wlk
12 Kingfisher Sports Ctr The
13 Greencoat Ho
A2 1 Regents Ct
2 Walter St
3 Canbury 2000 Bsns Pk
4 Sigrist Sq
5 Ashway Ctr
6 Warwick Ho
B1 1 Vicarage Ho
2 Rayleigh Ct
3 School Pas
4 Chippenham
5 Camm Gdns
B2 1 Onslow Ho
2 Dowler Ct
B3 1 McDonald Ho
2 Elm Ho
3 Dale Ct
4 York Ho
5 Florence Ho
6 Florence Rd
7 Roupell Ho
8 Delft Ho
C1 1 Wimpole Cl
2 Burwell
3 Caldecote
4 Fordham
5 Connington
6 Chesterton Terr
7 Westwick
8 Eureka Rd
9 Fulbourn
10 Comberton
11 Madingley
12 Grantchester
13 Cambridge Grove Rd
14 Oakington
15 Harston
16 Graveley
17 Croxton
18 Brinkley
19 Impington
20 Shelford
21 Duxford
C2 1 Farthings The
2 Brae Ct
3 Princeton Mews
4 Station App
C3 1 Queen's Ct
2 St George's Rd
3 Park Road Ho
4 Dagmar Rd
5 Tapping Cl
6 Arthur Rd
7 Borough Rd
8 Belvedere Ct
9 Braywick Ct
10 Dean Ct
11 Rowan Ct
12 Richmond Ct
13 Sunningdale Ct
14 Hawker Ct
15 Cromwell Ct
16 Kings Ct
D2 1 Trevallyn Lo
2 Chichester Ho
3 Beechcroft
4 Cedars The
5 Liddlesdale Ho W
6 Liddlesdale Ho E
7 Deerhurst
8 Brockworth
9 Alderton
D3 1 Bramley Ho
2 Abinger Ho
3 Thursley Ho
4 Ridge Ho
5 Clone The
6 Mount Ct
7 Hillside Ct
8 Hill Ct
9 Royal Ct
10 Lakeside
11 High Ashton
D4 1 Godstone Ho
2 Hambledon Ho
3 Kingswood Ho
4 Leigh Ho
5 Milton Ho
6 Newdigate Ho
7 Farleigh Ho
8 Ockley Ho
9 Effingham Ho
10 Dunsfold Ho
11 Pirbright Ho
12 Clandon Ho
13 Ripley Ho

178

C3 1 Roskeen Ct
2 Chimneys Ct
3 Rosemary Cotts
4 Victoria Lo
D2 1 Beaufort Ho
2 Kinnear Ct
3 Ranmore Ct
4 Lantern Ct
5 Crescent Ho
D3 1 Kings View Ct
1 Kingsdown
2 Wimbledon Cl
3 Beryl Harding Ho
4 Upton Ct
5 Marian Lo
6 Terraces The
7 Lanherne Ho
8 Cumberland Cl
9 Thaxted Pl
10 Rathbone Ho
11 Princess Ct
12 Downs Ct
13 Ravenscar Lo
14 Haverley
15 Savona Cl
16 Beaumont Ct
17 Gordon Ct
D5 1 Lancaster Pl
2 Haygarth Pl
3 Allington Cl
4 Homefield Pl

179

A3 1 Mayfair Ct
2 Brunswick Ct
3 Pavilion Ct
A4 1 Walham Rise
2 Grosvenor Ct
3 Sovereign Ho
4 Holly Lo
5 Florence Ct
6 Linden Cotts
7 Sheep Walk Mews
B5 1 Lawns The
2 Prentice Ct
3 Catherine Ct
4 Woodlodge
5 Queen Alexandra's Ct
6 Lake Cl
7 Westwood Ct
8 Brambles The
9 Lismore
10 Rose Ct
11 Worcester Rd
C3 1 Ashbourne Terr
2 Sir Cyril Black Way
3 Downing Ho
4 Palmerston Gr
5 Gladstone Ct
6 Harefield Ct
7 Viscount Point
D2 1 Gilbert Cl
2 Becket Cl
3 Priory Cl
4 Hudson Ct
5 Ryder Ho
6 Eleanor Ho
7 Ramsey Ho
D3 1 Hamilton Road Mews
2 Dowman Cl

180

A2 1 Tanner Ho
2 May Ct
3 Marsh Ct
4 Lovell Ho
A3 1 Fiske Ct
2 Mellor Ct
3 Olive Rd
4 Allerton Ho
5 Victory Road Mews
6 Will Miles Ct
7 Vanguard Ho
8 Mychell Ho
9 Merton Pl
10 De Burgh Ho
11 Norfolk Ho
12 Hotham Road Mews
B1 1 Ripley Ct
2 Brooklands Ct
3 Horner La
C2 1 Linford Ct
2 Searle Ct
3 Gunnell Ct
C5 1 Robertson Ho
2 Dewar Ho
3 Jean Ho
4 Marion Ct
5 Gravenel Gdns
D1 1 Elms Cotts
2 Sibthorp Rd
3 Armfield Cotts

181

A1 1 Kennedy Cl
2 Pearce Cl
3 Mainwaring Ct
4 Coningsby Ct
5 Laburnum Ct
6 Beaumont Ct
7 Penfold Ct
8 Fitch Ct
A5 1 Osbourne Terr
2 Limetree Wlk
C5 1 Tyers Ho
2 Boothby Ho
3 Adams Ho
4 Burney Ho
5 Boswell Ho
6 Chesterfield Ho
7 Garrick Ho
8 Levett Ho
9 Shelburne Ho
10 Marchmont Ho
11 Ryland Ho
C6 1 Walmsley Ho
2 Chambers Ho
3 Fordyce Ho
4 Percy Ho
5 Langton Ho
6 Moorfields Ct
7 Hidaburn Ct
8 Salter Ho
D6 1 William Dyce Mews

182

C5 1 Belltrees Gr
2 Ash Ct
3 Alder Ct
4 Beech Ct
5 Acacia Ct
6 Blackthorn Ct
7 Cypress Ct
8 Hawthorn Ct
9 Hazel Ct
10 Sycamore Ct
11 Maple Ct
12 Laburnam Ct
13 Fern Lo
C6 1 James Boswell Cl
2 St Albans Ho
3 Suffolk Ct
4 Rockhampton Cl
5 Delphian Ct
D5 1 Woodcote Pl
2 Joe Hunte Ct
3 Cork Tree Ho
4 Lake Ho
5 Cedars Ho
6 Portobello Ho
7 Cooper Ho
8 Farnsworth Ho
9 Hook Ho
10 Crest The
11 Renshaw Ho
12 Ruscoe Ho
13 Sardeson Ho

183

A6 1 Moore Ho
2 Chaucer Ho
3 Bushell Ho
4 Bligh Ho
5 Hobbs Rd
6 Hogarth Ho
7 Goodbehere Ho
8 Astley Ho
9 Elder Gdns
10 Elderberry Gr
11 Pavement The
12 Dunkirk St
B6 1 Josef Perrin Ho
2 Jean Humbert Ho

183 B6
3 Charles Staunton Ho
4 Violette Szabo Ho
5 Lilian Rolfe Ho
6 Odette Ho
7 Robert Gerard Ho
8 St Bernards Cl
9 Champness Cl
10 Pennington Cl
11 Queenswood Ct
C4 1 Northwood Way
2 High Limes
3 Valley Prospect
4 Plane Tree Wlk
5 City Prospect
6 Bankside Way
7 Ridge Way
8 Rochdale
9 Barrington Wlk
10 Gatestone Ct
11 Childs La
12 Carberry Rd
13 Norwood Heights Sh Ctr
C5 1 Oakdene
2 Thorsden Way
3 Oakfield Gdns
4 Georgetown Cl
5 Bridgetown Cl
6 Mountbatten Cl
7 Brabourne Cl
8 Alexandra Wlk
9 Compton Ct
10 Battenberg Wlk
11 Burma Terr
12 Wiseman Ct
C6 1 Linley Ct
2 Mellor Ho
3 Whitfield Ct
4 Michaelson Ho
5 Holberry Ho
6 Hovenden Ho
7 Huntley Ho
8 Telfer Ho
9 Markham Ho
10 Oldham Ho
11 Parnall Ho
12 Pierson Ho
13 Roper Ho
14 Roundell Ho
15 Sawyer Ho
16 Ransford Ho
17 Carmichael Ho
18 Bonne Marche Terr Mews
D3 1 Hetley Gdns
2 Claybourne Mews
3 Highland Lo
4 Mason Ct
5 Kendall Ct
6 High View

184
A3 1 Hanover Ct
2 Brunswick Ct
3 New Church Ct
4 Regency Ct
7 Owen Wlk
8 Bargrove Cl
9 Beaver Cl
B2 1 Dorset Ho
2 Collingwood Cl
3 Chartwell Way
4 Essex Twr
5 Appletree Cl
6 Ditton Pl
7 Kelvin Ct
8 Readman Ct
9 Glen Ct
10 Kingsbridge Ho
11 Carlton Ct
12 Benhurst Ct
13 Carole Ho
14 Dover Ho
15 Bettswood Ct
B5 1 Ragwort Ct
2 Firs The
3 Wingham Ho
4 Seath Ho
5 Ripley Ho
6 Lathwood Ho
7 Hurst Ho
8 George Ho
9 Browne Ho
10 Beacon Ho
11 Bailey Ho
12 Agate Ho
C2 1 Challin St
2 Rutland Ho
3 Pine Cl
C3 1 Watermen's Sq
2 St John's Cotts
3 Gladstone Mews
6 Middlesex Ho
8 Bethesda Ct
9 Ospringe Cl
10 Goudhurst Ho
11 Walmer Ho
12 Strood Ho
13 Greatstone Ho
14 John Baird Ho
D3 1 Groombridge Ho
2 Provincial Terr
3 Smithers Ho
4 West Ho
5 Swallows Ct

185
A1 1 Clock House Ct
2 Blandford Ave
3 Old School Cl
4 Lynsted Ct
5 Florence Rd
A6 1 Paxton Ct
2 Kenton Ct
3 Grove Ct
4 Shirley Lo
B2 1 Ashton Ct
2 Coombe Ct
3 Fontaine Ct
4 Richfield Ct
5 Sheridan Way
C1 1 Christ Church Rd
2 Lea Rd
3 Stanmore Terr
C2 1 Erindale Ct
2 Bearsted Terr
3 Beck River Pk
4 Waterside
5 Station App
C3 1 Gardenia Ct
2 Brackendale Ct
3 Daniel Ct
4 Moliner Ct
5 Chartwell Lo
6 Randmore Ct
7 Dover Ho
8 Lucerne Ct
9 Malling Ho
10 Westerham Lo
11 Brasted Lo
12 Milton Ho
13 Bradsole Ho
14 Sandgate Ho
15 Adelaide Ct
16 Nettlestead Cl
17 Warren Ct
18 Alton Ct
19 Rockingham Ct
20 Camellia Ct
21 Sinclair Ct
22 Regents Ct
23 Minshull Pl
24 South Park Ct
D1 1 Parkside
2 Tudors The
3 Oakbrook
4 Tara Ct
5 Redlands The
6 Cambria
7 Hillworth
8 Kelsey Gate
9 Burrells
10 Lincoln Lo
11 Courtlands
12 Fairleas
13 Ashdown Cl
D2 1 Mayfair Ct
2 Clifton Ct
3 Fire Station Mews
D4 1 Warner Ho
2 Clifford Ho
3 Lloyd Ho
4 Thurston Ho
5 Byron Ho
6 Blake Ho
7 Keats Ho

186
A2 1 White House Ct
2 Hunters The
3 Sandringham Ct
4 Glenhurst
5 Copperfields
6 Westgate Ct
A6 1 Dedham Ho
2 Flatford Ho
3 Radley Ct
4 Langthorne Ct
5 Hoover Ho
6 Brunner Ho
7 Waterer Ho
8 Marriott Ho
9 Bourbon Ho
B5 1 Longford Ho
2 Ingrebourne Ho
3 Brent Ho
4 Darent Ho
5 Beverley Ho
6 Wandle Ho
7 Rythe Ho
8 Ember Ho
9 Crane Ho
10 Ravensbourne Ho
C1 1 Warwick Ct
2 Maplehurst
3 Mount Arlington
4 Arundel Ct
D2 1 Weston Gr
2 Gibbs Ho
3 Longfield
4 Hammelton Ct
5 Bracken Hill Cl
6 Townend Ct
7 Treversh Ct
8 Cameron Ho
9 Woodlands Ct
10 Blythwood Pk
11 Bromley Pk
D3 1 Homecoppice Ho
2 Kimberley Gate
3 Inglewood Ct
4 Mavery Ct
5 Glen Ct
6 Cawston Ct
7 Blendon Path

187
B2 1 Hansom Terr
2 Dainton Cl
3 St Timothy's Mews
4 Andringham Lo
5 Kendall Lo
6 Summerfield
7 Winston Ct
8 Laurels The
C1 1 Westland Lo
2 Dairsie Ct
3 Beechfield Cotts
4 Oasis The
5 Cromarty Ct
6 Silverstone Ct

188
A6 1 Beaconsfield Par
2 Cranley Par
3 Kimmeridge Gdns
4 King & Queen Cl
C1 1 Merewood Cl
2 Alpine Copse
C2 1 Ivybridge Ct
2 Greenbank Lo

190
A6 1 Minshaw Ct
2 Cyril Lo
3 Milton Lo
4 Glenwood Ct
5 Culverton Ct
6 Holmbury Manor
B1 1 Swanscombe Ho
2 Haverstock Ct
3 Arrandene Ho
4 Broomfield Ho
5 Headley Ho
6 Kenley Ho
7 Ladywell Ho
B6 1 Chudleigh
2 Wimborne
3 St John's Par
4 Holly Ct
5 Rectory Bsns Ctr

197
A2 1 Raleigh Ho
2 Leicester Ho
3 Gresham Ho
D2 1 Napier Ct
2 Darlington Ho
3 Charminster Ct
4 Mulberry Ct
5 Leander Ct
6 Clinton Ho
7 Hollingworth Ct
8 Gloucester Ct
9 Palmerston Ct
10 Redwood Ct
11 Hursley Ct
12 Westmorland Ct
13 Lawson Ct
14 Alexander Ct
15 Winton Ct
16 Sydenham Ho
17 Caroline Ct
18 Ellswood Ct
19 Masefield Ct

198
A1 1 Ash Tree Cl
2 Shrubbery The
3 Malvern Ct
4 Gate Ho
A3 1 Station App
2 South Bank Lo
3 Bramshott Ct
4 Pandora Ct
5 Wellington Ct
6 Glenbuck Ct
7 Leighton Ho
8 Oakhill Ct
9 Downs View Lo
10 Osborne Ct
A4 1 Effingham Lo
2 Maple Ho
3 Channon Ct
4 Falconhurst
5 Ferndown
6 Viceroy Lo
7 Frensham Ho
8 Kingsley Ho
9 Rannoch Ct
10 Stratton Ct
11 Moray Ho
12 Dulverton Ct
13 Westerham
14 Hill Ct
15 Assheton-Bennett Ho
16 Hatfield Ho
17 Oxford Ct
18 Pennington Lo
19 Austin Ho
20 Wentworth Ct
21 Priory The
22 Sheraton The
A5 1 Marquis Ct
2 Garrick Ho
A6 1 College Rdbt
2 Edinburgh Ct
3 Weston Ct
4 Grebe Terr
5 Heron Ct
6 Agar Ho
7 St James' Ct
8 Grove Ct
9 Springfield Ct
10 College Wlk
B3 1 Percy Ct
2 Holmwood
3 Middle Green Cl
B4 1 Woodleigh
2 Highcroft
3 Caernarvon Ct
4 Regency Ct
D1 1 Oakleigh Way
2 Chandler Ct

199
C2 1 Goodland Ho
2 Furzeland Ho
3 Oakcroft Ho
4 Meadcroft Ho
5 Newhouse
C4 1 Merryweather Ct
2 Roebuck Ct
3 Sable Ct
C5 1 Acacia Ho
2 Kingston Lo
3 Fairholme Ho
4 Marshall Ho
5 Norton Ho
6 Martin Ho

200
A1 1 Brookside Cres
2 Beverley Gdns
3 Purdey Ct
4 Avenue The
5 Briarwood Ct
6 Station App

202
D6 1 Fair Green Ct
2 Regal Ct
3 Lewes Ct
4 Esher Mews
5 Sibford Ct

205
B1 1 Tavistock Ct
2 Chartwell Cl
3 Speaker's Ct
4 Cumberland Ct
5 Viceroy Ct
6 Oriel Ct
7 Cherry Orchard Gdns
C1 1 Windmill Bridge Ho
2 Squire Ct
3 Houston Ct
4 St James's Lo
5 Kendal Ho
6 Warren Ct
7 Kendal Ct
D1 1 Hastings Pl
2 Grant Pl
3 Clive Ho
4 Havelock Ho
5 Bellmore Ct
6 Hereford Ct
7 Chequers Ct
8 Havelock Hall

206
A1 1 Farleycroft
2 Edgecumbe Ct
3 Wesson Ho
4 Sullivan Ct
5 Kenley Ho
6 Christopher Ct
7 Jayson Ct
D1 1 Cottongrass Cl
2 Oxlip Cl
3 Eyebright Cl

207
1 North Rd
2 Sussex Rd
3 Riverside Wlk
4 Christie Ho
5 Sherwood Ct
6 Wheatsheaf Par
D6 1 Linden Ct
2 Park Ct
3 Chilchester Ct
4 Iveagh Ct

208
A6 1 Overbury Ct
2 Wilton Pl
D1 1 Woodgrange Ct
2 Maycroft
3 Farnborough Cres
D4 1 Knowlton Gn
2 Speldhurst Cl
3 Bidborough Cl
4 Penshurst Wlk
D5 1 Wedgewood Ct
2 Birches The
3 Eccleshill
4 Tavistock Rd
5 Montpelier Ct

209
A5 1 Montague Terr
2 Chatsworth Ho
A6 1 Marina Cl
2 Cheveney Wlk
3 Bromley Manor Mans
4 Mall The
5 Westmoreland Pl

211
B1 1 Gleneagles Gn
2 Tandridge Pl
3 Springfield Wlk
4 Pinehurst Wlk
5 Cromer Pl
6 Oakmont Pl

214
A6 1 St Bernards Ho
2 Wentworth Ct
3 Sunningdale Cl
4 Arklow Mews
5 Edward Pinner Ct

215
D6 1 Kingsley Dr
2 Kingsley Ct
3 Mowat Ct
4 Squirrels Ct

216
A6 1 Lansdowne Copse
2 Lansdowne Ct

217
A2 1 Cheam Court Flats
2 Farnham Ct
3 Tabor Ct
C1 1 Lancaster Ct
2 Redclyffe Terr
3 Kenilworth Terr
4 Lincoln Terr
5 Garden Ct
6 Ashwood Pk
7 Lyndhurst Ct
8 Banbury Ct
9 Holly Ct
10 Castle Ho
11 Balmoral Ct
12 Hereford Ct
13 Lorac Ct
14 Camilla Ct
15 Midsummer Apmts
D1 1 Hadrian Ct
3 Magnolia Ct
4 Larchvale Ct
5 Alford Ct
6 Brockham Ct
7 Berrylands Ct
8 Camberley Ct
9 Dunsfold Ct
10 Courtlands
11 Leith Towers
12 Kingslee Ct

218
A1 1 Beauclere Ho
2 Melford Ct
3 Elmhurst Lo
4 Mansard Manor
5 Tranmere Ct
6 Beechcroft Lo
7 Savin Lo
8 Yew Tree Ct
9 Avondale Ct
10 Devonshire Ho
11 Hidcote Ho
12 Munstead Ct
13 Lodden Lo
14 Steetley Ct
15 Grampian Cl
A2 1 Grosvenor Ct
2 Forest Dene Ct
3 Cedar Ct
4 Vanborough Ct
A3 1 Goossens Cl
2 Cliffe Wlk
3 Marlins Cl
4 Clowser Cl
5 Montana Gdns

219
B2 1 Runnymede Ct
2 Dolphin Ct
3 Kings Ct
4 Cheyne Ct
5 Hendfield Ct
6 Ellerslie Ct
7 Embassy Ct
8 Chandler Ct
9 Hambledon Ct
10 Wallington Ct
11 Jasmine Ct
B4 1 Loraine Ho
2 Harcourt Lo
3 Coniston Ct
4 Alcester Ct
5 Friars Ct
6 Campbell Ho
7 Brodie Ho
8 Lesley Ct
9 Birch Ct
10 Airborne Ho
C2 1 Rossendon Ct
2 Mulberry Mews
3 Nairn Ct
4 Wallington Sq
5 Rosemount Towers
6 Connell Ho
7 Ashby Grange

221
A4 1 West Street Pl
2 Maple Ct
3 St Andrew's Rd
4 Albury Ct
5 Chestnut Ct
6 Elgin Ct
7 Beechfield Ct
8 Barham Ct
9 Whitstable Pl
10 Ledbury Pl
A5 1 Mann Cl
2 Halstead Cl
3 Fellmongers Yd
A6 1 Otterbourne Rd
2 Charrington Rd
3 Tamworth Pl
4 Priddy's Yd
5 Hospital of the Holy Trinity (Almshouses)
6 Bellhill
B4 1 Holmlea Ct
2 Garlands Ct
3 Coombe Ct
4 Deepdale Ct
5 Galloway Path
B6 1 Wellesley Court Rd
2 Norfolk Ho
3 Station App
4 Suffolk Ho
5 Cherry Orchard Gdns
6 Harrington Ct
D6 1 Cheyne Ct
2 Fourways
3 Princess Ct
4 Tierney Ct
5 Sinclair Ct
6 Guinness Ct
7 Mayfair Ct
8 Bishopscourt
9 Gloucester Lo
10 Beverley Hyrst
11 Melton Ct
12 Cecil Ct
13 Napier Ct

227
A3 1 Westfield
2 Farnborough Ct
3 Fern Hill Pl
4 Churchill Ct
5 Spencer Ct
6 Ladycroft Gdns
7 Crabbs Croft Cl
8 Clifton Cl
D2 1 Brittenden Cl
2 Wardens Field Cl
3 Winnipeg Dr
4 Superior Dr
5 Huron Cl
6 Manitoba Gdns
7 Lynne Cl
8 Flint Cl
9 Bakers Mews
D3 1 Osgood Gdns
2 Amberley Cl
3 Rawlings Cl
4 Beblets Cl
5 Fir Tree Cl
6 Raleigh Mews
7 King Henry Mews
D4 1 Healy Dr
2 Marsden Way
3 Taylor Cl
4 Strickland Way
5 Dryland Ave
6 Adcot Wlk
7 Lichlade Cl

Hospitals

Hospitals with accident and emergency departments are highlighted in green

A
- Acton Hospital W3 110 C4
- Ashford Hospital, Stanmore Road, Ashford, Middlesex TW15 3AA 148 A2 ☎ 01784 884488
- Athlone House (The Middlesex Hospital) N6 48 D1
- Atkinson Morley Hospital SW20 178 B3

B
- Barking Hospital IG11 79 D1
- Barnes Hospital SW14 133 C2
- Beckenham Hospital BR3 185 B1
- Bethlem Royal Hospital The BR3 207 C2
- Blackheath Hospital SE3 142 C2
- Bolingbroke Hospital The SW11 158 C6
- Bowden House Hospital (Private) HA1 64 C6
- British Home and Hospital for Incurables SW16 182 D5
- Bromley Hospital Cromwell Avenue, Bromley, Kent BR2 9AJ 209 B5 ☎ 020 8289 7000
- Brompton Hospital SW3 114 B1 256 D2
- BUPA Bushey Hospital WD2 8 D3

C
- Carshalton, War Memorial Hospital SM5 218 D2
- Cassel Hospital TW10 175 D6
- Castlewood Day Hospital SE18 144 C4
- Central Middlesex Hospital Acton Lane, Park Royal, London, NW10 7NS 89 A4 ☎ 020 8965 5733
- Central Public Health Laboratory NW9 45 C6
- Chadwell Heath Hospital RM6 58 B4
- Charing Cross Hospital Fulham Palace Road, London W6 8RF (A&E entrance off St Dunstan's Road) 112 D1 ☎ 020 8846 1234
- Charter Nightingale Hospital The NW1 92 C2 237 B4
- Chase Farm Hospital The Ridgeway, Enfield, Middlesex, EN2 8JL 4 C5 ☎ 020 8366 6600
- Chelsea Hospital for Women SW3 114 C1 257 A2
- Chelsea and Westminster Hospital 369 Fulham Road, London SW10 9NH 136 A6 266 B5 ☎ 020 8746 8000
- Chingford Hospital E4 20 A1
- Chiswick Maternity Hospital W4 111 D1
- Clayponds Hospital and Day Treatment Ctr TW8 110 A2
- Clementine Churchill Hospital The HA1 64 D5
- Colindale Hospital NW9 45 C6
- Connaught Day Hospital E11 54 C3
- Coppetts Wood Hospital N10 30 D2
- Cromwell Hospital SW5 113 D2 255 C4

D
- Devonshire Hospital W1 93 A2 238 B4
- Dulwich Hospital SE22 139 C1

E
- Ealing Hospital Uxbridge Road, Southall, Middlesex UB1 3HW 108 B4 ☎ 020 8574 2444
- East Ham Memorial Hospital E7 77 D1
- Eastman Dental Hospital WC1 94 B4 240 C6
- Edgware General Hospital HA8 26 D3
- Elizabeth Garrett Anderson and Obstetric Hospital WC1 93 C3 235 B5

F
- Farnborough Hospital BR6 226 C4
- Finchley Memorial Hospital N12 30 A3
- Fitzroy Nuffield Hospital W1 92 D1 237 C2

G
- Garden Hospital The NW4 46 C6
- Goldie Leigh Hospital SE2 146 C6
- Goodmayes Hospital IG3 58 A4
- Gordon Hospital The SW1 115 D2 259 C3
- Great Ormond St Hospital for Children WC1 94 B3 240 C5
- Greenwich District Hospital Vanbrugh Hill, Greenwich, London, SE10 9HE 120 D1 ☎ 020 8858 8141
- Grovelands Priory N14 16 A3
- Guy's Hospital SE1 117 B5 252 D2

H
- Hackney Hospital E9 75 A3
- Hamlet (Day) Hospital The TW9 132 A2
- Hammersmith Hospital Du Cane Road, London W12 0HS 90 B1 ☎ 020 8383 1111
- Harrow Hospital HA2 64 C6
- The Heart Hospital W1 93 B2 238 C3
- Hillingdon Hospital Pield Heath Road, Uxbridge, Middlesex UB8 3NN 82 B2 ☎ 01895 238282
- Homerton University Hospital Homerton Row, E9 6SR 74 D3 ☎ 020 8510 5555
- Hornsey Central Hospital N8 49 D4
- Hospital for Tropical Diseases WC1 232 C5
- Hospital of St John and St Elizabeth NW8 92 B5 229 C3

I
- Inverforth House Hospital NW3 70 A6

J
- Jewish Home and Hospital at Tottenham The N15 51 D5

K
- King George Hospital Barley Lane, Goodmayes, Ilford, Essex IG3 8YB 58 A4 ☎ 020 8983 8000
- King's College Hospital Denmark Hill, (A&E in Ruskin Wing) SE5 9RS 139 B3 ☎ 020 7737 4000
- Kings Oak Hospital (Private) The EN2 4 C5
- Kingsbury Hospital NW9 44 C5
- Kingston Hospital Galsworthy Road, Kingston-upon-Thames, Surrey KT2 7QB 176 D2 ☎ 020 8546 7711

L
- Langthorne Hospital E11 76 B5
- Lewisham Hospital High Street, Lewisham, London SE13 6JH 163 D6 ☎ 020 8333 3000
- Lister Hospital SW1 115 B1 258 C1
- London Bridge Hospital SE1 117 B5 252 D4
- London Chest Hospital E2 96 C5
- London Clinic NW1 93 A3 238 B5
- London Foot Hospital W1 93 C3 239 A5
- London Hospital (Mile End) The E2 96 D4
- London Hospital (St Clements) The E3 97 B4
- London Independent Hospital The E1 96 D2

M
- Maida Vale Psychiatric Hospital W9 92 A3 236 B6
- Manor House Hospital NW11 47 D1
- Marlborough Day Hospital NW8 92 A5 229 A4
- Maudsley Hospital The SE5 139 B3
- Mayday University Hospital Mayday Road, Thornton Heath CR7 7YE 204 D3 ☎ 020 8401 3000
- Memorial Hospital SE18 144 C3
- Middlesex Hospital W1 93 C2 239 B3
- Mildmay Mission Hospital E2 95 D4
- Molesey Hospital KT8 195 C4
- Moorfields Eye Hospital EC1 95 B4 235 C1
- Morland Road Day Hospital RM10 103 C6

N
- National Hospital for Neurology and Neurosurgery N2 48 C5
- National Hospital The WC1 94 A3 240 B5
- National Physical Laboratory TW11 174 C4
- Nelson Hospital SW20 179 B1
- New Cross Hospital SE14 140 C5
- New Victoria Hospital KT3 177 C2
- Newham General Hospital Glen Road, Plaistow, London E13 8SL 99 C3 ☎ 020 7476 4000
- Normansfield Hospital KT8 175 C3
- North London Nuffield Hospital EN2 4 C3
- North Middlesex Hospital Sterling Way, Edmonton, London, N18 1QX 33 C5 ☎ 020 8887 2000
- Northwick Park Hospital Watford Road, Harrow, Middlesex HA1 3UJ 43 A2 ☎ 020 8864 3232
- Northwood Pinner and District Cottage Hospital HA6 22 A2
- Norwood Hospital SE19 183 B4

O
- Orpington Hospital BR6 227 D4

P
- Paddington Com Hospital W9 91 C2
- Penny Sangam Day Hospital UB2 107 B3
- Plaistow Hospital E13 99 C5
- Portland Hospital for Women and Children The W1 93 B3 238 D5
- Princess Grace Hospital The W1 93 A3 238 A5
- Princess Louise Hospital W10 90 C2
- Priory Hospital The SW15 133 D1
- Putney Hospital SW15 134 C2

Q
- Queen Charlotte's Hospital W12 90 B1
- Queen Elizabeth Hospital for Children The E2 96 A5
- Queen Elizabeth Hospital SE18 144 A5
- Queen Mary's Hospital Frognal Avenue, Sidcup, Kent DA14 6LT 190 A4 ☎ 020 8302 2678
- Queen Mary's Hospital NW3 70 A5
- Queen Mary's University Hospital SW15 156 A5
- Queen's Hospital CR0 205 A3

R
- Roding Hospital IG4 55 D6
- Royal Brompton and Nat Heart Hospital The SW3 114 C1 257 A2
- Royal Ear Hospital WC1 93 C3 239 B5
- Royal Free Hospital Pond Street, London NW3 2QG 70 C3 ☎ 020 7794 0500
- Royal Hospital SW15 157 A5
- Royal London Homeopathic Hospital The WC1 94 A2 240 B4
- Royal London Hospital (Whitechapel) Whitechapel Road, London E1 1BB 96 B2 ☎ 020 7377 7000
- Royal Marsden Hospital SW3 114 B1 256 D2
- Royal Masonic Hospital W6 112 A2
- Royal National Orthopaedic Hospital HA7 9 C2, W1 93 B3 238 D5
- Royal Nat TN&E Hospital The W5 87 C2, WC1 94 B4 233 C2

S
- St Andrew's Hospital E3 97 D3
- St Ann's General Hospital N4,N15 51 A4
- St Anthony's Hospital KT4 200 D1
- St Bartholomew's Hospital EC1 94 D2 241 D3
- St Charles' Hospital W10 90 D2
- St Christopher's Hospice SE26 184 C5
- St George's Hospital Blackshaw Road, London SW17 180 B5 ☎ 020 8672 1255
- St Giles Hospital SE5 139 C4
- St Helier Hospital Wrythe Lane, Carshalton, Surrey SM5 1AA 202 A1 ☎ 020 8296 2000
- St Joseph's Hospice E9,E8 96 B6
- St Leonard's Hospital N1 95 C5
- St Luke's Hospital W1 93 C3 239 A5
- St Luke's Woodside Hospital N10 49 A5
- St Mark's Hospital EC1 94 D4 234 D2
- St Mark's Hospital HA1 43 A2
- St Mary's Cottage Hospital TW12 173 B2
- St Mary's Hospital Praed Street, Paddington W2 1NY 92 B1 236 D2 ☎ 020 7886 6666
- St Michael's Hospital EN2 5 B4
- St Pancras Hospital NW1 93 D6 232 C5
- St Thomas's Hospital Lambeth Palace Road, London SE1 7EH 116 B3 260 C6 ☎ 020 7928 9292
- St Vincent's Hospital HA5 39 D6
- Samaritan Hospital for Women NW1 237 C4
- Shirley Oaks Hospital CR0 206 C2
- Sloane Hospital BR3 186 B2
- South Western Hospital SW9 138 B2
- Southwood Hospital (Geriatric) N6 49 A2
- Springfield Hospital SW17 158 C1
- Stepney Day Hospital E1 96 C1
- Surbiton Hospital KT6 198 A3

T
- Teddington Memorial Hospital TW11 174 C4
- Thorpe Coombe Hospital E17 54 A6
- Tolworth Hospital KT6 214 C6
- Travel Clinic, Hospital for Tropical Diseases WC1 93 C3 239 B5

U
- University College Hospital A&E at Cecil Fleming House, Grafton Way, London, WC1E 3BG 93 C3 239 B5 ☎ 020 7387 9300
- Upton Day Hospital DA6 147 A1

W
- Wanstead Hospital E11 55 B5
- Wellington Hospital (North) NW8 92 B5 229 D3
- Wellington Hospital (South) NW8 92 B5 229 D3
- Wembley Hospital HA0 65 D2
- West Middlesex University Hospital Twickenham Road, Isleworth, Middlesex TW7 6AF 131 A3 ☎ 020 8560 2121
- Western Hospital The NW1 92 D2 237 C4
- Whipps Cross Hospital Whipps Cross Road, Leytonstone London E11 1NR 54 B3 ☎ 020 8539 5522
- Whittington Hospital Highgate Hill, London, N19 5NF 71 C6 ☎ 020 7272 3070
- Willesden Community Hospital The NW10 68 A1
- Winifred House Hospital EN5 11 D5

FITZROVIA
Screen on Baker St
PADDINGTON STREET
BAKER STREET
MARYLEBONE HIGH STREET
WEYMOUTH STREET
PORTLAND PLACE
GREAT PORTLAND STREET
NEW CAVENDISH STREET
HOWLAND ST
THAYER ST
LANGHAM PLACE
MORTIMER STREET
BERNERS ST
PLACE
Wigmore Hall
CAVENDISH SQUARE
CAVENDISH PLACE
REGENT ST
MANDEVILLE PL
PORTMAN SQUARE
WIGMORE STREET
JAMES ST
ORCHARD ST
PORTMAN ST
Niketown
Top Shop
BHS
H&M
John Lewis
House of Fraser
Debenhams
OXFORD STREET
Oxford Circus
Laura Ashley
Borders
Marks and Spencer
Palladium
Marks and Spencer
Selfridges
Bond Street
HMV
West One Shopping Centre
DAVIES STREET
Mothercare
NEW BOND STREET
REGENT STREET
Dickins & Jones
Liberty
Jaeger
Fenwick
Sotheby's
Hamleys
CONDUIT STREET
Burberry
Next
KNIGHTSBRIDGE
Curzon Minema
Knightsbridge
Harvey Nichols
BROMPTON ROAD
SLOANE STREET
Harrods
BRUTON ST
MAYFAIR
BERKELEY SQUARE
Asprey and Garrard
Cartier
Aquascutum
Austin Reed
Burlington Arcade
Waterstones
FITZMAURICE PL
BERKELEY ST
PICCADILLY
Hatchards
Fortnum and Mason
ST. JAMES'S STREET
PONT STREET
CURZON STREET
Curzon Mayfair
Green Park
Christie's
BROMPTON
General Trading Company
CLIVEDEN PL
GREEN PARK
SLOANE SQUARE
Royal Court
Peter Jones
Sloane Square
WH Smith
LOWER SLOANE

Cinemas, theatres shopping streets

Empire Cinema
Aldwych Theatre
Purcell Room Concert hall
Fortnum & Mason Shop
Shopping street
– up-market
– high street
– books
– electronics
– furniture
Habitat
Heals
Drill Hall
The Pier
Goodge Street
GOODGE ST
TOTTENHAM COURT ROAD
STREET
MONTAGUE PL
SQUARE
SOUTHAMPTON
BEDFORD SQUARE
BAYLEY ST
BLOOMSBURY ST
BLOOMSBURY WAY
Odeon Tottenham Ct. Rd.
HOLBORN
Dominion
NEW OXFORD ST
Virgin
Forbidden Planet
Shaftesbury
The Plaza
Tottenham Court Road
STREET
A. BORDE ST
Astoria
ST. GILES HIGH ST
HIGH
Books Etc
New London
DRURY LANE
GT. QUEEN
KINGSWAY
Peacock
WARDOUR STREET
CHARING CROSS ROAD
Foyles
Curzon Phoenix
Odeon Covent Garden
Phoenix
Soho
ENDELL STREET
Donmar Warehouse
Blackwell's
MONMOUTH ST
SOHO
Prince Edward
AVE
Cambridge
LONG ACRE
BOW ST
Fortune
ALDWYCH
Aldwych
STRAND
New Ambassadors
Palace
St Martin's
Covent Garden
Royal Opera House
Theatre Royal Drury Lane
Strand
Curzon Soho
SHAFTESBURY
Arts Theatre
UPPER ST. MARTIN'S LANE
Duchess
Stanford's
Queen's
Gielgud
Warner Village West End
Leicester Square
Lyceum
Apollo
Prince Charles
Albery
Lyric
The OTHER Cinema
UCI Empire
The Venue
Wyndham's
LANCASTER PL
Piccadilly
UGC Trocadero
Imax
Odeon Wardour St.
Odeon Leicester Square & Mezzanine
Vaudeville
Adelphi
Savoy
Piccadilly Circus
Trocadero
Duke of York's
Coliseum
Criterion
Prince of Wales
Odeon West End
ST. MARTIN'S LANE
Garrick
Tower Records
Lilywhites
REGENT STREET
Odeon Panton St
EMBANKMENT
WATERLOO BRIDGE
Odeon Haymarket
HAYMARKET
Comedy
Jermyn St
Mitsukoshi
Theatre Royal Haymarket
DUNCANNON ST
TRAFALGAR
Charing Cross
VICTORIA
UGC Haymarket
PALL MALL EAST
Her Majesty's
Charing Cross Players
Embankment
ST. JAMES'S
COCKSPUR ST
SQUARE
NORTHUMBERLAND AVENUE
Playhouse
Queen Elizabeth Hall and Purcell Room
Royal Festival Hall
Whitehall
PALL MALL
ICA
Royal National Theatre
National Film Theatre
STAMFORD
SOUTH BANK
BFI London Imax
Waterloo East
St. James's Park Lake
Waterloo
Waterloo International
YORK ROAD
WATERLOO
Young Vic
ST JAMES'S PARK
Old Vic

Hospital of St John and Elizabeth
13,46
82,113,187
274
London Zoo
Abercorn Place
ST JOHN'S WOOD
139,189
Circus Rd
WELLINGTON RD
PRINCE ALBERT ROAD
REGENT'S PARK
MAIDA VALE
Lord's Cricket Ground
Grove End Rd
13,82,113,274
Maida Vale
Hall Rd
46,187
London Mosque
Queen Mary's Gardens
Chester Rd
16,98,187,414
ST. JOHN'S WOOD RD
Outer Circle
Regent's Park Lake
Randolph Ave
Open Air Theatre
Sutherland Ave
PARK RD
Inner Circle
MAIDA VALE
6,16,46,98
187,414
Lisson Grove
13,82,113
139,189,274
Regent's Canal
Warwick Avenue
6,46,187
Clifton Gardens
Church St
Rossmore Rd
Madame Tussaud's
139,189
Planetarium
Blomfield Rd
Marylebone
Warwick Avenue
EDGWARE RD
Baker St
Grand Union Canal
Broadley St
205,453
ROAD
MARYLEBONE
2,18,27,30
74,205,453
National Heart Hospital
Marylebone High St
18
18
Edgware Road
18,27
GLOUCESTER PL
BAKER ST
Harrow Road
Edgware Road
Chapel St
Seymour Pl
PADDINGTON
New Cavendish
18
St Mary's Hospital
6,7,15,16,23
27,36,98,205
414,436,705
BISHOP'S BRIDGE RD
Eastbourne Terrace
Westbourne Terrace
Paddington
Praed St
SUSSEX GARDENS
2,13,30,74
82,113,139
189,274
Wallace Collection
George St
7,23,27,36
EDGWARE RD
Wigmore St
BAYSWATER
Connaught St
Seymour St
7,15,23,27,36
205,436,705
Marble Arch
OXFORD STREET
Davies St
Bond St
Craven Rd
70
Lancaster Gate
N Audley St
8
BAYSWATER ROAD
274
The Ring
2,6,7,10,12,15,16
23,30,36,73,74,82
94,98,137,148,159
274,390,414,436,705
Grosvenor St
12,70,94,148
Mount St
PARK LANE
South Audley St
KENSINGTON GARDENS
HYDE PARK
2,10,16,36,73
74,82,137,148
414,436,705
Curzon St
Serpentine Gallery
Kensington Palace
The Ring
The Serpentine
Apsley House and Wellington Museum
Hyde Park Corner
9,10,49
52,70
South Carriage Road
9,10,14
19,22,52,74
137,414,C1
KNIGHTSBRIDGE
2,8,9,10,14
16,19,22,36
38,52,73,74
82,137,148
414,436,705
GROSVENOR PL
KENSINGTON ROAD
Palace Gate
Queen's Gate
Royal Albert Hall
KNIGHTSBRIDGE
360
14,74,414,C1
Knightsbridge
SLOANE STREET
Science Museum
BROMPTON RD
BELGRAVIA
Exhibition Rd
70,360
49
705
Belgrave Place
Brompton Oratory
Natural History Museum
Victoria and Albert Museum
Pont St
BROMPTON
Gloucester Rd
70,74,360
CROMWELL RD
14,74
414,C1
19,22
137,C1
C1
KING'S RD
Sth Kensington

Central London buses

Scale
0
250 m
½ km
0
220 yds
¼ mile
King's Cross Thameslink
Crescent
Polygon Rd
Brill Pl
Midland Rd
46
214
King's Cross
390
17,91
259
30,73,205,
214,476
PENTONVILLE RD
C2
ALBANY STREET
HAMPSTEAD RD
EVERSHOLT ST
Ossulston St
British Library
St. Pancras
10,17,30,45,46
63,73,91,205
214,259,390,476
168
253
24,27,29
88,134
Stanhope St
Euston
ROAD
Judd St
63
19,38
341
AVE
Skinner Street
FARRINGDON ROAD
Royal College of Physicians
Euston Square
EUSTON
10,18,30,59,68
73,91,168,205
253,390,476
UPPER WOBURN PLACE
Tavistock Pl
GRAY'S INN RD
Calthorpe St
10,18,24,27
29,30,73,88
134,205,390
10,18,24,27,29
30,73,134,205,390
18,27,30,88
205,453,C2
University College Hospital
Warren Street
TOTTENHAM CT RD
Russell Square
Gt. Ormond Street Hospital
Guilford St
Doughty St
Dickens House
ROSEBERY
63
55,243
Park Cr
Great Portland Street
PORTLAND PL
Torrington Pl
GOWER ST
BLOOMSBURY
7,188
X68
RUSSELL SQUARE
59,68
91,168
Lamb's Conduit St
Queen's Sq
17,19,38,45,46
55,243,341
CLERKENWELL ROAD
Cleveland St
BT Tower
Gt Portland St
THEOBALDS RD
British Museum
7
Goodge Street
10,24,29
73,134,390
8,17,25
45,46,242
341,521
Street
Middlesex Hospital
1,8,25,59,68,91,98,168
171,188,242,243
521,X68
HOLBORN
BBC
Mortimer St
Newman St
Tottenham Court Road
NEW OXFORD ST
HIGH
Sir John Soane's Museum
Chancery Lane
3,6,7,8,10,12,13,15
23,25,55,73,88,94
98,113,137,139,159
176,189,390,453,C2
1,8,10,19,24
25,29,38,55
73,98,134
242,390
Holborn
Chancery La
OXFORD STREET
7,8,10,14,24,25
29,38,55,73,98
134,176,242,390
CHARING
Gt. Queen St
KINGSWAY
Old Curiosity Shop
4,11,15
23,26,76
172,341
OXFORD ST
Oxford Circus
Wardour St
SOHO
AVE
Drury Lane
Law Courts
FLEET S
8
London Transport Museum
ALDWYCH
Temple
Brook St
14,19,24
29,38
176
Long Acre
Covent Garden
1,4,6,9,11,13,15,23,26,59,68
76,77A,91,168,171,172
176,188,243,341,521,X68
New Bond St
Conduit St
REGENT ST
3,6,9,12,13
14,15,19,22
23,38,88,94
139,159,453
SHAFTESBURY
CROSS RD
Bow St
Temple
Leicester Square
Somerset House Art Centre
8
Berkeley Square
Old Bond St
Royal Academy
National Gallery
National Portrait Gallery
THE STRAND
WATERLOO BRIDGE
THAMES
HAYMARKET
REGENT ST
8
Piccadilly Circus
THE
MAYFAIR
Jermyn St
Trafalgar Square
Charing Cross
Embankment
EMBANKMENT
National Theatre
381,7
BFI London IMAX
PICCADILLY
St. James's St
NORTHUMBERLAND AVE
3,6,9,11,12,13
15,23,24,29
77A,88,91,139
159,176,453
Q. Elizabeth & Royal Festival Halls
STAMFORD STREET
Green Park
Pall Mall
VICTORIA
1,4,26,59,68,76,77
139,168,171,172,1
188,211,243,341,38
507,521,705,X68
ST JAMES'S
THE MALL
Hayward Gallery
BA London Eye
St. James's Palace
Downing Street
WHITEHALL
YORK RD
Green Park
Waterloo
WATERLOO RD
Cabinet War Rooms
London Aquarium
CONSTITUTION HILL
St. James's Pk
Westminster
Buckingham Palace
PARLIAMENT
WESTMINSTER
BRIDGE
12,53,76,77,148
159,211,341,381
507,453,705
Birdcage Walk
3,11,12,24,53
77A,88,148
159,211,453
SQUARE
Queen's Gallery
Lambeth North
ST. GEORGE RD
Buckingham Place
Petty France
New Scotland Yard
St. James's Park
Houses of Parliament
St. Thomas' Hospital
LAMBETH PALACE RD
12,53,59,76
148,159,344
360,453,705
88
Westminster Abbey
2,8,11,16,24,36,38,52
73,82,148,185,211,239
436,507,705,C1,C10
VICTORIA ST
MILLBANK
77
507
705
RIVER
C1
11,24,148,211
507,705
Great Smith St
Lambeth Palace
Westminster Cathedral
Rochester Row
11,211
239,C1
C10
3,77A,507
705,C10
3,77,344,507
705,C10
RD
LAMBETH
3,59
159,360
88,507,705,C10
LAMBETH
BRIDGE
Victoria
2,36,185,436
Horseferry Rd
Lambeth Walk

D
C
B
A
Chesham
Chalfont & Latimer
Amersham
Chorleywood
Rickmansworth
Watford
Croxley
Aylesbury
Denham
High Wycombe
Moor Park
Northwood
Northwood Hills
Pinner
North Harrow
Harrow-on-the-Hill
West Harrow
West Ruislip
Ruislip
Ruislip Manor
Hillingdon
Uxbridge
Ickenham
Eastcote
Ruislip Gardens
Rayners Lane
South Ruislip
South Harrow
Northolt Park
Northolt
Sudbury Hill Harrow
Sudbury Hill
Sudbury Town
Sudbury & Harrow Road
Greenford
Alperton
Perivale
South Greenford
Castle Bar Park
Drayton Green
Hanger Lane
Park Royal
North Ealing
Ealing Broadway
West Acton
North Acton
East Acton
Acton Main Line
West Ealing
Ealing Common
Hanwell
Southall
West Drayton
Iver
Slough
Hayes & Harlington
South Acton
Acton Central
Acton Town
South Ealing
Northfields
Boston Manor
Hounslow East
Osterley
Hounslow West
Hounslow Central
Heathrow Terminals 1,2,3
Hatton Cross
Heathrow Terminal 4
BAA Heathrow Express. Travelcards not valid.
Bus to Heathrow Airport
Feltham
Ashford
Staines Windsor
Shepperton
Sunbury
Hampton
Fulwell
Teddington
Hampton Wick
Whitton
Strawberry Hill
Hounslow
Twickenham
St. Margarets
Isleworth
Syon Lane
Brentford
Kew Bridge
Chiswick
Gunnersbury
Kew Gardens
Richmond
North Sheen
Mortlake
Barnes Bridge
Barnes
River Thames
Chiswick Park
Turnham Green
Stamford Brook
Ravenscourt Park
Hammersmith
Barons Court
West Kensington
Earl's Court
Kensington (Olympia)
Watford Junction
Carpenders Park
Hatch End
Headstone
Harrow & Wealdstone
Kenton
Northwick Park
Preston Road
Wembley Park
South Kenton
North Wembley
Wembley Stadium
Wembley Central
Stonebridge Park
Harlesden
Willesden Junction
Kensal Green
Queen's Park
Kensal Rise
Brondesbury Park
Brondesbury
Kilburn High Road
South Hampstead
Kilburn Park
Maida Vale
Warwick Avenue
Royal Oak
Westbourne Park
Ladbroke Grove
Latimer Road
White City
Shepherd's Bush
Goldhawk Road
Holland Park
Notting Hill Gate
Stanmore
Canons Park
Queensbury
Kingsbury
Neasden
Dollis Hill
Willesden Green
Kilburn
Edgware
Burnt Oak
Colindale
Hendon
Hendon Central
Brent Cross
Golders Green
Hampstead
Cricklewood
Luton
Radlett
Elstree & Borehamwood
Mill Hill Broadway
Mill Hill East
High B
Hampstead Heath
Gospel Oak
Kentish Town West
Finchley Road & Frognal
Belsize Park
West Hampstead
Chalk Farm
Camden Town
Finchley Road
Swiss Cottage
Mornington Crescent
St. John's Wood
Baker Street
Great Portland Street
Euston
Edgware Road
Marylebone
Paddington
Warren Street
Euston Square
Regent's Park
Goodge Street
Bayswater
Queensway
Marble Arch
Oxford Circus
Holborn
Lancaster Gate
Bond Street
Tottenham Court Road
Green Park
Covent Garden
Hyde Park Corner
Piccadilly Circus
Leicester Square
High Street Kensington
Knightsbridge
Gloucester Road
Charing Cross
Sloane Square
Victoria
Westminster
Embankment
South Kensington
St. James's Park
Pimlico
Waterloo
Southwark
Lambeth North
West Brompton
Fulham Broadway
Parsons Green
Putney Bridge
Battersea Park
Vauxhall
Queenstown Road Battersea
Wandsworth Road
Oval
Kennington
Clapham Junction
Clapham High Street
Clapham North
Stockwell
Loughborough Junction
Putney
East Putney
Wandsworth Town
Clapham Common
Brixton
Southfields
Earlsfield
Wandsworth Common
Clapham South
Balham
Wimbledon Park
Haydons Road
Tooting Bec
Herne Hill
Wimbledon
Dundonald Road
Tooting Broadway
Tulse Hill
Wimbledon Chase
Colliers Wood
Tooting
Streatham Hill
Raynes Park
Merton Park
South Wimbledon
New Maiden
Motspur Park
Norbiton
Kingston
Berrylands
Morden Road
Morden
Phipps Bridge
Belgrave Walk
Mitcham
South Merton
Morden South
Surbiton
Hampton Court
Thames Ditton
Malden Manor
Tolworth
Esher
Woking Guildford
Chessington North
Chessington South
Hinchley Wood
St. Helier
Sutton Common
Worcester Park
Mitcham Junction
Therapia Lane
Waddon Marsh
Wandle Park
Beddington Lane
Ampere Way
Hackbridge
West Sutton
Carshalton
Sutton
Carshalton Beeches
Wallington
Waddon
Cheam
Stoneleigh
Smitham
Woodmansterne
Reedham
Belmont
Banstead
Chipstead
Ewell West
Ewell East
Guildford
Epsom
Epsom Dorking
Epsom Downs
Tattenham Corner
1
2
3
4
5
6
Travelcard Zones
Explanation of Zones
Station outside the zones
Station in Zone D
Station in Zone C
Station in Zone B
Station in Zone A
Station in Zone 6 and Zone A
Station in Zone 6
Station in Zone 5
Tram stop in Zone 4 or 5 or 6
Station in Zone 4
Station or Tram stop in Zone 3
Station in both zones
Station in Zone 2
Station in both zones
Station in Zone 1
Equivalent Bus zones
The rail and bus zones vary at a few locations.
Details of bus zones are shown in Local Guides.

© Transport for London

Welwyn Garden City
Stevenage
Cheshunt
Stansted Airport Hertford East
Potters Bar
Cuffley
Theobalds Grove
Waltham Cross
Hadley Wood
Crews Hill
Turkey Street
Enfield Lock
Gordon Hill
Enfield Town
Epping
Debden
Theydon Bois
Loughton
Cockfosters
Enfield Chase
Bush Hill Park
Brimsdown
Chingford
New Barnet
Oakwood
Grange Park
Buckhurst Hill
Totteridge & Whetstone
Oakleigh Park
Southgate
Winchmore Hill
Southbury
Ponders End
Woodside Park
New Southgate
Arnos Grove
Palmers Green
Edmonton Green
Highams Park
West Finchley
Bounds Green
Silver Street
Angel Road
Roding Valley
Chigwell
Finchley Central
Bowes Park
White Hart Lane
Grange Hill
Shenfield Southend
East Finchley
Wood Green
Woodford
Brentwood
Alexandra Palace
Turnpike Lane
Bruce Grove
Northumberland Park
Wood Street
Hainault
Shoeburyness Basildon
Highgate
Hornsey
Harringay
Harringay Green Lanes
South Tottenham
South Woodford
Fairlop
Harold Wood
Archway
Barkingside
Crouch Hill
Gidea Park
Romford
West Horndon
Tufnell Park
Manor House
Seven Sisters
Tottenham Hale
Blackhorse Road
Snaresbrook
Newbury Park
Upminster
Upper Holloway
Walthamstow Central
Redbridge
Emerson Park
Ockendon
Stamford Hill
Walthamstow Queen's Road
Wanstead
Gants Hill
Chadwell Heath
Upminster Bridge
Tilbury
Kentish Town
Finsbury Park
Leytonstone
Arsenal
Stoke Newington
Leyton Midland Road
Hornchurch
St. James Street
Holloway Road
Elm Park
Camden Road
Caledonian Road
Rectory Road
Clapton
Leytonstone High Road
Drayton Park
Hackney Downs
Goodmayes
Dagenham East
Hackney Central
Homerton
Wanstead Park
Dagenham Heathway
Caledonian Road & Barnsbury
Highbury & Islington
Leyton
Seven Kings
Becontree
King's Cross St. Pancras
Canonbury
Dalston Kingsland
London Fields
Hackney Wick
Stratford
Ilford
Cambridge Heath
Maryland
Forest Gate
Manor Park
Angel
Bethnal Green
Essex Road
Woodgrange Park
Upney
Farringdon
Old Street
Pudding Mill Lane
Barbican
Liverpool Street
Bethnal Green
Mile End
West Ham
Plaistow
East Ham
Barking
Shoreditch
Bow Road
Bromley-by-Bow
Moorgate
Stepney Green
Bow Church
Upton Park
Devons Road
St. Paul's
Aldgate East
Whitechapel
All Saints
Bus to London City Airport
Canning Town
Dagenham Dock
Bank
Aldgate
Shadwell
Westferry
Blackwall
Cannon Street
Limehouse
Poplar
East India
Custom House for ExCeL
Mansion House
Monument
Tower Hill
Royal Victoria
Prince Regent
Rainham
Grays
Tower Gateway
Fenchurch Street
Wapping
West India Quay
Royal Albert
Beckton Park
Purfleet
River Thames
Gallions Reach
Rotherhithe
Canary Wharf
North Greenwich
Silvertown
Cyprus
Beckton
Bermondsey
Canada Water
Heron Quays
North Woolwich
South Quay
London Bridge
Surrey Quays
Crossharbour & London Arena
Mudchute
Island Gardens
Foot tunnel and ferry
Cutty Sark for Maritime Greenwich
Westcombe Park
Charlton
Woolwich Arsenal
Abbey Wood
Belvedere
Deptford
Greenwich
South Bermondsey
Maze Hill
Woolwich Dockyard
Plumstead
Erith
Queens Road Peckham
Deptford Bridge
Elverson Road
New Cross
Slade Green
New Cross Gate
St. Johns
Blackheath
Kidbrooke
Falconwood
Bexleyheath
Denmark Hill
Lewisham
Eltham
Welling
Barnehurst
Peckham Rye
Nunhead
Brockley
Hither Green
Honor Oak Park
Ladywell
East Dulwich
Crofton Park
Lee
New Eltham
Albany Park
Crayford
Gravesend Gillingham
Forest Hill
Catford
Catford Bridge
Mottingham
Sidcup
Bexley
Dartford
Sydenham
Bellingham
Grove Park
North Dulwich
Elmstead Woods
West Dulwich
Sydenham Hill
Lower Sydenham
Beckenham Hill
Penge East
Penge West
Kent House
Sundridge Park
Chislehurst
Medway Towns Maidstone Ashford
West Norwood
Gipsy Hill
Crystal Palace
Anerley
New Beckenham
Ravensbourne
Bromley North
Bickley
St. Mary Cray
Swanley
Shortlands
Bromley South
Streatham
Birkbeck
Avenue Road
Beckenham Road
Beckenham Junction
Orpington
Streatham Common
Petts Wood
Norbury
Chelsfield
Harrington Road
Clock House
Knockholt
Dunton Green
Norwood Junction
Elmers End
Sevenoaks
Thornton Heath
Arena
Woodside
Eden Park
West Croydon
Blackhorse Lane
West Wickham
Wellesley Road
Addiscombe
Hayes
Lebanon Road
Sandilands
Church Street
George Street
East Croydon
South Croydon
Lloyd Park
Coombe Lane
Addington Village
Gravel Hill
King Henry's Drive
Fieldway
New Addington
Purley Oaks
Sanderstead
Purley
Coulsdon South
Kenley
Riddlesdown
Merstham
Whyteleafe
Upper Warlingham
Gatwick Airport
Caterham
East Grinstead
1
2
3
4
5
6
A Travelcard or LT Card valid in Zone 4 or 5 or 6 (or combination of these Zones) is available on Tramlink services throughout the grey area. If travelling on Tramlink services outside the grey area a Travelcard or LT Card which includes Zone 3 availability must be held
Some stations and lines have restricted opening times.
London Travel Information
020 7222 1234 24 hours
The national rail routes shown on this map are a guide to weekday, off-peak services but do not guarantee direct trains between the stations shown.
National Rail Enquiries
08457 48 49 50 24 hours
(all calls charged at local rate)
Key to lines
Station
Interchange Station
Bakerloo
Central
Circle
District
East London
Peak hours and Sunday mornings
Hammersmith & City
Jubilee
Metropolitan
Northern
Piccadilly
Victoria
Waterloo & City
Docklands Light Railway
Tramlink
National Rail
Reg. user No. 03/3952

Places of interest

Central

West End

Admiralty Arch SW1 .... 249 D4
Apple Market WC2 .250 B6
Banqueting House SW1 .... 250 A3
Big Ben SW1 ...... 250 B1
British Library WC1 .... 93 D4 232 D2
British Museum WC1 .... 94 A2 240 A3
BT Tower W1 .... 93 C2 239 A4
Buckingham Palace SW1 ...... 115 C4 249 A1
Cabinet War Rooms SW1 ...... 115 D4 249 D2
Carnaby Street W1 .... 93 C1 239 A1
Cenotaph SW1 .... 250 A2
Changing of the Guard (site of) SW1 ..... 249 A1
Chinatown W1 .... 115 D6 249 D6
Clarence House SW1 ...... 115 C5 249 B3
Cleopatra's Needle WC2 ...... 116 B5 250 C5
Courtauld Galleries WC2 .... 250 C6
Covent Garden WC2 ...... 116 A6 250 B6
Dickens House Museum WC1 .... 94 B3 240 D5
Downing Street SW1 ...... 116 A4 250 A2
Eros W1 ... 115 D6 249 C5
Green Park SW1,W1 ... 115 B4 248 D2
Guards Museum SW1 ...... 115 C4 249 B1
Holocaust Memorial Garden W2 .... 114 D4 247 D2
Horse Guards Parade SW1 ...... 115 D5 249 D3
Houses of Parliament SW1 ...... 116 A3 260 B6
Hyde Park W2 .... 114 D5 247 C3
Leicester Square WC2 ...... 115 D6 249 D5
London's Transport Museum WC2 ..... 250 B6
Marble Arch W1 .... 114 D6 247 D6
Methodist Central Hall SW1 ...... 115 D4 249 D1
National Gallery W1 .... 115 D6 249 D5
National Portrait Gallery W1 .... 115 D6 249 D5
Nelson's Monument WC2 .... 250 A4
New Scotland Yard SW1 ...... 115 D3 259 C6
Parliament Square SW1 ...... 116 A4 250 A1
Pepsi Trocadero W1 .... 249 C5
Piccadilly Circus W1 .... 115 D6 249 C5
Queen Victoria Memorial SW1 ... 249 A2
Queen's Gallery SW1 ...... 115 B4 248 D1
Rotten Row SW1 ...... 114 D4 247 C2
Royal Academy of Arts W1 .... 115 C6 249 A5
Royal Mews SW1 ...... 115 B3 258 D6
Royal United Services Museum SW1 .... 250 A3
St James's Palace SW1 ...... 115 C5 249 B3
St James's Park SW1 .... 249 C2
Serpentine Gallery W2 .... 114 B4 246 D2
Soho W1 .... 93 D1 239 C2
Somerset House WC2 ...... 116 B6 250 D6
Speakers' Corner W1 .... 114 D6 247 D6
Tate Britain SW1 ...... 116 A2 260 A3
Theatre Museum WC2 .... 250 B6
Trafalgar Square SW1 ...... 115 D5 249 D4
Tyburn Tree (site of) W2 ...... 247 C6
Wallace Collection W1 .... 238 A2
Wellington Arch SW1 .... 248 B2
Wellington Museum (Apsley House) SW1 ...... 115 A4 248 B2
Westminster Abbey SW1 ...... 116 A3 260 A6
Westminster Cathedral SW1 ...... 115 C3 259 A5

City

Bank of England EC2 .... 242 C1
Barbican Arts and Conference Centre EC2 .95 A2 242 B4
Central Criminal Court (Old Bailey) EC4 .... 94 D1 241 D2
Custom House EC3 ...... 117 C6 253 A5
Dr Johnson's House EC4 .... 241 B1
Gray's Inn WC1 .... 94 B2 240 D4
Guildhall EC2 95 A1 242 B2
Inner Temple EC4 .. 251 A6
John Wesley's House & Museum EC1 .... 242 D6
Lincoln's Inn WC2 .... 94 B1 240 D2
Lloyd's Building EC3 .... 95 C1 243 A1
Mansion House EC4 .... 242 C1
Merchant Taylors Hall EC3 .... 242 D1
Middle Temple EC4 ...... 116 C6 251 A6
Monument, The EC3 .... 252 D6
Museum of London EC2 .... 95 A2 242 A3
Nat West Tower EC2 .... 243 A2
National Postal Museum EC1 .... 95 A1 242 A2
Petticoat Lane Market EC2 .... 95 D2 243 C3
Public Record Office Museum EC4,WC2 . 241 A2
Royal Exchange EC3 .... 242 D1
St Katharine Dock E1 .... 117 D5 253 D4
St Mary le Bow Church EC2 .... 242 B1
St Paul's Cathedral EC4 .... 95 A1 242 A1
Sir John Soane's Museum WC2 .... 94 B1 240 C2
Spitalfields Market E1 .... 95 D2 243 C4
Stock Exchange EC2 .... 242 D1
Tower Bridge E1,EC3,SE1 .117 D5 253 C4
Tower of London EC3 .... 117 D6 253 C5
Traitors Gate EC3 .... 117 D5 253 C4
Ye Olde Cheshire Cheese EC4 ...... 241 B2

Northern

Business Design Centre N1 .. 94 C6 234 B5
Camden Market NW1 .... 93 B6 231 D6
London Canal Museum N1 .... 94 A5 233 B4
London Central Mosque NW8 .... 92 C4 230 B1
London Zoo NW1 .... 93 A5 231 A4
Lord's Cricket Ground NW8 .... 92 B4 229 D2
Madame Tussaud's NW1 .... 93 A3 238 A5
Open Air Theatre, Regent's Park NW1 .... 231 A1
Planetarium NW1 .... 93 A3 238 A5
Primrose Hill NW1 .... 92 D6 230 C6
Queen Mary's Gardens NW1 .... 231 A1
Regent's Park NW1 .... 93 A4 231 A3
St George's Cathedral NW1 .... 231 D2
Sherlock Holmes Museum NW1 .... 92 D3 237 D5

Southern

Battersea Park SW11 ..... 137 A5 268 A3
Battersea Power Station SW8 ...... 137 B6 268 D6
Brompton Oratory SW7 ...... 114 C3 257 A5
Bear Gardens Museum SE1 .... 117 A5 252 A4
Bermondsey Market SE1 .... 117 C3 263 B8
Borough Market SE1 .... 252 C3
Design Museum SE1 .... 117 D4 253 D2
Florence Nightingale Museum SE1 ..... 250 D1
Gabriel's Wharf SE1 .... 251 A4
George Inn SE1 .. 252 C3
Globe Theatre SE1 . 252 A5
Hayward Gallery SE1 ...... 116 B5 250 D4
HMS Belfast SE1 ... 253 B4
Imperial War Museum SE1 .... 116 C3 261 B5
Lambeth Palace SE1 .... 116 B3 260 C5
London Aquarium SE1 .... 250 C1
London Dungeon SE1 .... 117 B5 252 D4
London Eye SE1 .... 116 B4 250 C2
London Peace Pagoda SW11 .... 267 D4
Millennium Bridge SE1,EC4 .... 252 A5
Museum of Garden History SE1 .... 260 C5
National Film Theatre SE1 .... 250 D4
National Theatre SE1 .... 116 B5 250 D4
Old County Hall SE1 .... 250 C2
Operating Theatre Museum and Herb Garret SE1 117 B5 252 D3
Oxo Tower SE1 ..... 251 B5
Royal Festival Hall SE1 .... 116 B5 250 D3
Saatchi Gallery SE1 250 C2
St George's RC Cathedral SE1 .... 116 C3 261 B6
Shakespeare's Globe Theatre (site of) SE1 .... 252 B4
Southwark Cathedral SE1 .... 117 B5 252 C4
Tate Modern SE1 .... 116 D6 251 D4
Vinopolis SE1 ...... 117 B5 252 C4

Western

Albert Memorial SW7 ...... 114 B4 246 C1
Carlyle's House SW3 .... 267 A5
Chelsea Barracks SW1 ...... 115 A1 258 B1
Chelsea Physic Garden SW1 ...... 115 A1 267 C6
Commonwealth Institute W8 ..... 113 C3 255 A6
Geological Museum SW7 ...... 114 B3 256 D5
Kensington Gardens W2 .... 114 A5 246 B3
Kensington Palace W8 .... 113 D5 245 D3
Leighton House W14 ...... 254 D6
Lindsey House SW10 ...... 266 D4
Little Venice W9 .... 92 A2 236 A4
London Toy and Model Museum W2 .... 114 A6 246 A6
National Army Museum SW3 ...... 136 D6 267 D6
Natural History Museum SW7 ...... 114 B3 256 C5
Ranelagh Gardens SW1 ...... 115 A1 258 B1
Royal Albert Hall SW7 ...... 114 B4 246 C1
Royal Hospital (Army Pensioners) SW1 ...... 115 A1 258 A1
Science Museum SW7 ...... 114 B3 256 C5
Victoria and Albert Museum SW7 ...... 114 B3 256 D5

East

Bethnal Green Museum of Childhood E2 ...... 96 C4
Canary Wharf E14 .119 D5
Docklands Museum E14 ..... 119 D6
Epping Forest IG10 .21 B6
Geffrye Museum E2 .95 D5
London Docklands Visitor Centre E14 120 A4
London Gas Museum E16 .... 98 B3
Museum of the Great Eastern Railway E16 ..... 122 C4
Queen Elizabeth's Hunting Lodge Museum E4 .20 D4
Ragged School Museum E3 .... 97 A2
Vestry House (Museum) E17 ..... 53 D5
Whitechapel Art Gallery E1 .... 95 D1

North

Alexandra Palace N22 .... 31 D1
Barnet Museum EN5 .1 A1
Battle of Britain Museum NW9 .... 27 D1
Bruce Castle Museum N17 .... 33 C2
Church Farm House Museum NW4 ...... 46 B6
Coppetts Centre N12 30 D3
Forty Hall EN2 .... 5 D6
Freud Museum NW3 70 A2
Grange Museum of Community History NW10 .... 67 D4
Hampstead Heath NW3 .... 70 B6
Harrow Museum and Heritage Centre HA2 .... 42 A6
Highgate Cemetery N19 .... 71 B6
Kensal Green Cemetery (All Souls) NW10 ... 90 C4
Kenwood House NW3 .... 48 C1
Old Court (Museum and Library) HA0 .... 65 C3
RAF Museum NW9 .. 28 A1
Ruislip Lido HA4,HA5 39 B5
Ruislip Lido Railway HA4 .... 39 B5
White Cube N1 .... 95 C4

South east

Blackheath SE3 ... 142 C4
Brockwell Park SE24 .... 160 D5
Cutty Sark SE10 .. 142 A6
Docklands Heritage Museum SE16 .... 119 B5
Dulwich Picture Gallery SE21 ...... 161 C4
Eltham Palace SE9 .166 A4
Flamsteed House SE10 .... 142 B5
Gipsy Moth IV SE10 142 A6
Greenwich Park SE10 .... 142 C5
Horniman Museum and Gardens SE23 ..... 162 B3
Livesey Museum SE15 .... 140 B6
Meridian Building SE10 14
Millennium Dome SE10 12
National Maritime Museum SE10 14
Old Royal Observatory Greenwich SE10 .. 14
Queen's House SE10 14
Rotunda Museum SE18 12
Scadbury Park Nature Reserve BR7 18
South Norwood Count Park SE25 20
Thames Barrier Visito Centre SE18 12
Well Hall Pleasaunce SE9 14

South west

Barnes Common SW13 13
Clapham Common SW4 13
Fulham Palace SW6 13
Hampton Court Palace KT8 19
Kingston Museum KT1 17
Wandsworth Museum SW15 13
Wetland Centre SW13 13
Wimbledon Common SW19 17
Wimbledon Lawn Tenr Museum SW19 ... 15
Wimbledon Windmill Museum SW19 ... 15

West

Chiswick House W4 13
Eel Pie Island TW1 15
Gunnersbury Park Museum W3 11
Ham House TW10 .. 15
Kew Bridge Steam Museum TW8 11
Kew Gardens (Royal Botanic Gardens) TW9 13
Kew Observatory TW9 13
Kew Palace TW9 ... 13
London Butterfly House TW8 13
Marble Hill TW1 ... 15
Museum of Richmond TW10 .. 15
Musical Museum TW8 13
Osterley Park TW7 .10
Pitshanger Manor Museum and Art Gallery W5 10
Portobello Road Market W10 9
Richmond Park TW10 15
Syon House TW8 .. 13
Walled Garden TW16 19